ISBN 978-0-282-39875-0
PIBN 10850371

THE WINSTON SIMPLIFIED DICTIONARY

INCLUDING ALL THE WORDS IN COMMON USE DEFINED SO THAT THEY CAN BE EASILY UNDERSTOOD

Edited by

WILLIAM D. LEWIS, A.M., Ped.D.
PRINCIPAL OF THE WILLIAM PENN HIGH SCHOOL
PHILADELPHIA

AND

EDGAR A. SINGER, Ph.D.
PROFESSOR OF HISTORY AND MODERN PHILOSOPHY
UNIVERSITY OF PENNSYLVANIA

Illustrated

THE JOHN C. WINSTON COMPANY
PHILADELPHIA CHICAGO

PREFACE.

The Winston Simplified Dictionary has been made to meet a distinct need felt by many teachers. It is obviously desirable that everyone should form the habit of consulting a dictionary. The dictionary habit will develop a more accurate understanding of the meaning of words, and a larger vocabulary. Young people are apt, however, to become discouraged in their efforts to use a dictionary if they do not find the desired information in a form they can readily understand and use.

Clear and Complete Definitions. One of the most important qualities of a dictionary should be that the definitions be clear and complete. Many dictionaries have been made by condensing larger ones. This plan is apt to result in definitions that are harder to understand than those of the larger dictionary. For example, a child who finds that contagion is "transmission of disease" will fail to get the idea unless he knows the meaning of *transmission.* If he looks at the next word, *contagious,* he finds that it is "communicable or spreading by contagion." If he is industrious enough to look up transmission, he finds that it is "the act of transmitting; state of being transmitted." He may look below to the verb *transmit* and find the key to his problem; or he may satisfy himself with a guess long before he has run the definition down by repeated references.

The Winston Simplified Dictionary makes every entry clear. At considerable expense of space it explains every word in such simple language that only a single reference will be needed. For example, even in closely related words like the noun *transmission* and the verb *transmit,* each word is complete in itself.

Wealth of Verbal Illustration. Thousands of words are much more easily understood from their context in sentences than from formal definitions. For this reason, the Winston Simplified Dictionary gives many more illustrative sentences and phrases than any other similar dictionary.

Pictorial Illustrations. In a similar way the meanings of many words can be immediately made clear by pictures. The illustrations in this dictionary are new pictures prepared for their teaching value in clarifying the meanings of words that need pictorial illumination.

Typography. The type used for each entry in the Winston Simplified Dictionary is large and clear, thereby quickly assisting the location of any word. It is the result of careful tests, the most modern facilities of the typemakers' art having been employed to produce the most legible page. The use of capitals has been limited to the proper nouns, names, etc. The seeker thus finds each word as it appears in general usage.

Pronunciation. The pronunciation of words is indicated by a phonetic respelling with diacritical markings. These diacritical marks will be easily understood. No attempt has been made to indicate obscure and difficult distinctions. The system is a simplified adaptation of those in most common use in school and college textbooks. As a further aid to obtain the quick pronunciation of each word, the Key to Pronunciation is given at the foot of each page.

Vocabulary. The selection of the vocabulary of the Winston Simplified Dictionary has been made with particular care. It includes not only all the words in ordinary use, but also the vocabularies of the science, history, civics, and current events that are so rapidly growing in both elementary and secondary schools. Particular attention has been given to the very considerable new vocabulary that has grown out of the World War.

Special Features. The Winston Simplified Dictionary includes several unusual features calculated to furnish essential information and to stimulate scholarly interest. Not only does it give the tables of weights and measures, abbreviations, prefixes, suffixes, etc., usually found in such volumes, but it also gives a most valuable chapter entitled "How Our Language Has Grown," which should be mastered by every English-speaking person. Another feature of unusual value is the Dictionary of Mythology which is particularly needed in clearing up allusions not only to the mythology of the Greeks and Romans but also to that of the Scandinavian and Teutonic races. In the Dictionary of Names and Places will be found listed the more important cities, countries, lakes, rivers, seas, and mountains of the world, as well as the outstanding characters in history. Men and women whose names stand for achievement in art, literature, science, politics, philanthropy and the varied branches of human activity are mentioned. These include the great figures of the past as well as those living to-day.

The World War stimulated interest in the places where the fighting was at its fiercest, and pains have been taken to include as many of these as space would permit. Here, too, will be found names of the fighting men who were most prominent in that great conflict.

The Glossary of Business Terms also is of great value in these days when the practical affairs of life are claiming larger and larger attention in schools.

A New Book on a New Plan. Winston's Simplified Dictionary is not a revision of an older work nor an abridgment of a larger dictionary. The experienced and efficient teachers who produced it have chosen a vocabulary with special reference to educational needs; they have expanded and illustrated the definitions so as to make them immediately intelligible; they have included the new words that are coming into our vocabulary in such profusion; they have introduced new features that have long been needed in a practical everyday dictionary for school and home, and have avoided the error of defining difficult words by repeating the words themselves, or by introducing other words equally difficult.

CONTENTS.

PUBLISHER'S STATEMENT.

In a very literal sense, The Winston Simplified Dictionary is a new and original work. The publishers feel that some account of the process by which it was made is due to the editors, compilers, and the large corps of assistants, who for more than three years worked diligently in its preparation.

The publishers placed in the hands of the editors as a basis for their work, a dictionary somewhat larger than the present volume, and very similar to the dictionaries in general use. This work was based on the foundation laid by Noah Webster and other lexicographers. As this dictionary (published by ourselves) had been recently revised and was in general use, it was thought that with comparatively little change it could be made to serve the purpose of the present work. It was then tested by the fundamental principle underlying the new work—THAT OF MAKING THE MEANING OF EVERY WORD SO CLEAR THAT A CHILD COULD NOT MISUNDERSTAND IT. This test revealed the essential weakness of all dictionaries made on any other principle.

The result of this experiment, made necessary an extraordinary amount of the most careful, original work. The first copy was revised by a capable editor; then the entire book was copied in long-hand. Several experienced scholars amplified, restated and illustrated the definitions in galley proof. New kinds of material were introduced; new methods of clarifying meanings were discovered, and with great labor and expense, the entire book was harmonized. The entire book was reset, and further refinements were insured by having every word revised by a corps of experts. *Over eight hundred new illustrations were made expressly for this book.*

The editors whose names appear on the title-page divided their responsibility. Besides exercising careful judgment on every question of method and form, one of them passed upon the simplicity and adequacy of the definitions and the correctness of the English, and the other upon the scientific and technical accuracy of all scientific statements.

From this description it is evident that The Winston Simplified Dictionary represents original work based upon careful scholarship, and wide pedagogical experience, such as has not been given to any elementary dictionary previously published. We believe that the editors and their assistants have done their work well, and are entitled to high praise for their accomplishment. This dictionary is offered to the schools of America and to the general public, in full confidence that it will be of immense value to all who use it.

THE JOHN C. WINSTON CO.

HOW OUR LANGUAGE HAS GROWN.

The study of a foreign language may have given you your first realization of the relationship between English and the other languages of the world. When you begin the study of a foreign speech, you are surprised to find how many words in the language you are studying are like English words. If you study Latin, you will meet *parens*, for instance, which by the simple change of the *s* to *t* becomes our English word *parent*. The word *rumor* is exactly like the English word. *November*, *transfero* (*transfer*), and a great many more are easily recognized by their resemblance to English words.

If you study French, you will have the same experience. In French you will find, for instance, *annoncer*, *to announce*, *consoler*, *to console*, and a large number of other words much like their English equivalents.

The English language, therefore, is closely related to several other languages. French and Anglo-Saxon are her parents; she is a granddaughter of Latin and a distant cousin of Greek. And, as is the case with the descendants of human families, English has some traits from all the languages which have helped to make her what she is.

The story of the birth and development of English is most interesting. Twelve or thirteen centuries ago England was not the busy, important island she is now, but was covered with forests and inhabited by the Britons, a people belonging to a race called the Celts. They used one of the forms of the Celtic language, for no *English* language was then in existence.

Over on the eastern coast of Europe, where your maps now show you Denmark and Holland and Germany, lived tribes of bold and cruel pirates called the Angles, the Saxons, and the Jutes. These peoples spoke a language somewhat like the present German language, or perhaps more like the Dutch spoken in Holland. These pirates, in their many-oared boats, made their way to the coast of Britain in search of food or of treasure. But once on the shores of the island, they found this land so much pleasanter than their own cold and stormy home on the other side of the North Sea that many of them decided to stay and make new homes for themselves in Britain.

And thus grew up in Britain the Anglo-Saxon tongue, a result of the mixture of the forms of German spoken by the two strongest invading tribes. The name of the country, too, was changed, and became Angleland or Engelond, taking the name of one of the pirate tribes. From this it is easy to see how the name became *England* and the language came to be called *English*.

Though at first Anglo-Saxon words seem entirely unfamiliar, a closer study will show you a number whose resemblance to English is easily recognizable. *Morgan tid* is easily converted into *morning tide*. *Godes* means *of God* or *God's*, for the apostrophe has come to take the place of the *e* in the Old English possessive. *Condel* becomes *candle* by only a slight change, and *beorht* merely shifts the position of *r* and changes *eo* to *ig* to become *bright*.

A rather hasty study shows how nearly related are English and Anglo-Saxon. But there is another interesting fact to be observed in this study. The life of these people was so simple that it was occupied chiefly with the simplest needs of existence—eating and drinking and keeping themselves alive in spite of many foes. It naturally followed that the words that have been inherited by modern English from the Anglo-Saxon tongue are for the most part simple words. These simple words are sometimes called "*homely* words," because they "come home" to people as the everyday words of everyday life. Such words are *home, light, fire, God.* In this list are also included most of our common prepositions and conjunctions, such as *to, from, over, and.*

A new element was brought into the language, however, by the introduction of Christianity in the sixth and seventh centuries. The Anglo-Saxons were heathens, worshiping many gods who, they believed, presided over the forces of nature. Thus there were Thor, the thunderer, famous for his strength, and Balder, the sun god, and Œstre (compare *Easter*), the goddess of spring. But in the year 597 there came from Rome a missionary of the Christian religion, named St. Augustine. Other missionaries followed him, who established the church in Britain and converted many of the people. The church services were read in Latin. And so there came into the language a number of Latin words, some of them having a Greek origin. These words, for the most part, have to do with religion and the church, as *bishop, priest, creed*, and similar words. Such words do not come to us directly from the Latin. As they were used by the Anglo-Saxons, they came to be slightly changed. The word *bishop* will show how such modifications came about. The Latin form was *episcopus* (compare the English word *episcopal*—pertaining to a bishop); under the influence of the Anglo-Saxon it became *biscop*, for the tendency of the simple, unlearned English was to shorten the long, ponderous Latin words, and to change a *p* into a *b;* our modern word is *bishop*, the *c* being changed to *h* for the sake of greater smoothness in pronunciation. Similar changes took place in many of the other Latin words which at this time enriched the language.

But the most important new element was yet to come. In 1066 a band of men from the continent of Europe, under the leadership of William of Normandy, known as William the Conqueror, landed in England. These people, known as Normans, or Norman French, came from a district in the northwestern part of France, called Normandy. As their name shows, the Normans were originally Northmen, from the shores of Denmark, Sweden, and Norway. During their piratical raids they had often landed on the coast of France, and being pleased with the fertile soil and the balmy climate, had at last forced the king of France to grant them some territory, and made permanent homes for themselves in the land.

But the Northmen had adopted the civilization and, in large part, the language of the French. This language was a form of the Latin language, for the Gauls, ancestors of the French, had been subjects of the Romans and had used their speech, adapting it to their own speech and needs. Thus the Norman French spoken by William of Normandy and his followers was a tongue founded on the Latin, or, as it is often called, a Romance language, because it was one of those languages based on the speech of the Romans.

Thus was brought into England an entirely new language family. And it had come to stay; for the Normans in a great battle conquered the Saxon king, Harold, and William became king of England. As the Normans were now the ruling race on the island, French became the language used in law courts, the language of literature, of the rich, and of the nobles. French was taught in the schools. It was used at the court of the king. It was the language of writing.

The Anglo-Saxons, however, who hated the Normans as their conquerors and despised the French language as the language of the conquerors, clung to their native tongue. Thus for a long time the two languages existed side by side—French, the language of the noble, rich, and educated; Saxon, the speech of the simple and the poor.

As time wore on, however, contempt on one hand and bitter hatred on the other gave way to a feeling of interest and friendship. The people ceased to be French and Anglo-Saxon, and became Englishmen, citizens of a common country. It thus became more and more necessary that all the people be able to communicate with each other; Normans used more Anglo-Saxon, Anglo-Saxons more French. The result was a new language, the slow growth of many years, the vocabulary of which was largely Anglo-Saxon, the grammar, largely French.

As we noticed that the words expressing simple, homely ideas are largely from Anglo-Saxon, so the language of learning and formal speech is from the French; for the Norman French were more highly civilized and educated than the Saxons. As the French had Latin as its foundation, a large Latin element came, in changed form, with the French into English. The following table will help to make this clear:

Anglo-Saxon Origin	*Latin-French Origin*	*Anglo-Saxon Origin*	*Latin-French Origin*
home	residence	king	sovereign
show	signify	horseman	cavalier
help	relieve	break	destroy
dear	precious	keep	maintain
hard	difficult	kind	gracious
hide	conceal	buy	purchase
freeze	congeal	feeling	sentiment

It is thus to Anglo-Saxon that we look back as the source of our familiar, everyday speech; to Latin, through French, as that tongue which has enriched and dignified our language with the terms of science, learning, and more formal speech.

The Norman French was the last great influence brought to bear upon the English language. Year by year, century by century, English has grown and changed. How different from present-day English, for instance, is the language of Shakespeare!

These changes come about in various ways. Sometimes words creep into the language from foreign tongues, as, for example, the French word *chic*, stylish, or the Latin expression *vice versa*, which have now become a real part of the English language. Often words drop out of use altogether or come gradually to have new meanings. Thus the old word *clept*, meaning named, and *an*, meaning if, are no longer used. The word *humorous* originally meant, not funny or causing laughter, but full of whims; *straight* meant at one time immediately, as Shakespeare writes, "I'll be with you *straight*." *Presently* formerly had the same meaning; when a man said, "I will come presently," he meant *immediately* and not *in a short time*, which is our modern meaning. Again, new conditions and new inventions call for new words. Thus *automobile* and *phonograph* and *airplane* and many, many more words came into the language as the things they name came into existence. Such words, too, as *mugwump*, *carpet-bagger*, *landslide* were originally political slang, but are now recognized parts of the English language. So also, any one can give numerous illustrations of new words that came into the language during the World War. Some such change in our speech is brought to pass almost every day.

Such, in outline, is the story of the growth of the English tongue—a growth which will never cease as long as English is spoken. For language is alive, a real being, growing, developing, changing, as man, as the race, grows, develops, changes, and bearing from year to year traces of the history of the race.

Making New Words

Now that you know something of the history of our language, you will be interested to learn how some of the separate words became a part of the

English language, and how some have been put together and built up from others.

Interesting stories are connected with many of our words. Have you ever wondered, for instance, why two slices of bread with meat or some other food between them is called a sandwich? In the eighteenth century an English nobleman, as he was sitting at table one day, quite by chance, or perhaps as an experiment, put a slice of meat between two slices of bread and ate it. What the nobles do their followers copy; thus others about the table tried the same experiment. The new dainty soon grew popular, and was named after the man who invented it, the Earl of Sandwich.

Another instance of a "story word" is the word *palace*, meaning the house where a king or a wealthy and important person lives. This was so named from the Palatium, one of the seven hills of Rome, where lived Augustus, the first great Roman Emperor.

Many more such story words might be mentioned; but there are other and more common ways in which words are adopted into the English language. As we shall see, one of the most common ways is by fitting together parts of words from other tongues, especially from Latin and from German. Most words of more than one syllable are formed of two or more distinct parts. The most important part, or foundation, of the word—the part that really gives the *thought* of the word—is called the *root* or the *stem*. For instance, in the word *marine*, the stem is *mar*, from the Latin word *mare* (pronounced mä-rā), meaning sea. Thus *marine* means pertaining to the sea; we have extended its meaning so that we say that marines are sailors of the sea, and marine trade means trade on the sea. The same stem appears in the words *maritime* and *mariner*. The stem of the word *dictate* is *dict*, meaning speak or say, a stem which we find also in such words as *predict*, to say before or foretell, *contradict*, to say against or oppose, and *dictionary*, that which says. The stem of the Latin word for foot is *ped*. So we have *ped* as a stem in *pedal*, *quadruped*, and *pedestrian*.

In many words there are two parts of equal importance, or two stems. Such a word is *phonograph*. *Phon* is a Greek stem meaning sound, found also in *telephone*, *megaphone*, and other words; *graph* is also a Greek stem meaning write. You will recognize it in such words as *telegraph*, *autograph*, and *paragraph*. A phonograph, then, in its literal meaning, is a contrivance that writes sounds.

The word *thermometer* is another two-stem word. *Thermo* is from a Greek word meaning heat, and *meter* is a common stem meaning measure. Thus a thermometer is an instrument that measures heat, as a thermostat is a device for keeping the temperature of a room always the same. For *thermo*, as we have seen, means heat and *stat* is from a Greek word meaning to stand still. Many more such words of two stems you will find from a study of an unabridged dictionary.

Words of one stem, however, are much more common than those of two or more. Most words have just one important part whose meaning is more or less changed by a less important syllable. If this syllable is put before a stem, it is called a *prefix;* if it is added after a stem, it is called a *suffix*.

A knowledge of prefixes and suffixes is a great help to a fuller understanding of English words. A prefix usually alters the meaning of the word itself, and the suffix changes the part of speech. Thus if to the word *take* we prefix *mis*, the meaning becomes to take wrongly, or to make an error; for *mis* means wrongly. If, however, we add to *mistake* the suffix *en*, the word is changed from a verb to an adjective, though the meaning of the word itself is not changed. Again, to prefix *trans* to the word *plant* adds to the original meaning the idea of removal from place to place, but to add to *transplant* the suffix *able* merely makes the word an adjective without changing the thought.

The following table will help you to see how words are built up from stems, prefixes, and suffixes. Notice that, though the literal meaning and the meaning in common use are by no means always the same, yet the literal meaning helps, decidedly, the understanding of the word. Notice also that the prefix frequently becomes changed in form for the sake of greater ease in pronunciation. Thus *ad*, meaning *to* or *for* or *against*, becomes *ac* when used with a stem whose first letter is *c*, as in the words *accept* (*ac*, to; *cept*, take = take to oneself) and *accede* (*ac*, to; *cede*, yield = yield to). When *ad* is placed before a stem beginning with *f*, the *d* becomes *f*. Such a change has taken place, for instance, in the word *affix* (*af*, to; *fix*, fasten = fasten to). Again *con* becomes *col* when used before a stem whose initial letter is *l*, as in the word *collect* (*col*; together; *lect*, to gather = gather together).

Word	Prefix	Stem	Suffix	Literal Meaning	Common Meaning
transport	*trans-* across	*-port* carry		to carry across	to remove, to carry
portable		*port-* carry	*-able* able to be	able to be carried	easily carried
action		*ac-* (g) do	*-tion* act of	act of doing	performance of a deed
reference	*re-* again or back	*fer-* carry	*-ence* that which	that which carries back	that which sends one elsewhere for information
expend	*ex-* out	*-pend* weigh out or pay		to pay out	to pay out
benefactor	*bene-* well	*fact-* do	*-or* one who	one who does well	one who confers a benefit

Some of the more common prefixes and suffixes derived from Latin, with their meanings, are included in the following lists:

Prefixes	Used in Words
a- or *ab-* = away, from	*ab*-duct, *ab*-stract, *ab*-sent, *ab*-normal
ad-, *ac-*, *af-* = to, at	*ad*-here, *ad*-just, *af*-fix, *ac*-cept
ante- = before	*ante*-date, *ante*-cedent
anti-, *ant-* = against (Greek)	*anti*-slavery, *anti*-septic, *ant*-agonist
auto- = self (Greek)	*auto*-mobile, *auto*-graph, *auto*-biography
bi- = two	*bi*-sect, *bi*-cycle, *bi*-ped
circum- = around	*circum*-ference, *circum*-stance
con-, *col-*, *com-*, *co-*, *cor-* = with or together	*con*-nect, *col*-lect, *co*-operate
de- = away from, from, down	*de*-tach, *de*-scend, *de*-pend

PREFIXES	USED IN WORDS
equi- = equal	*equi*-distant, *equi*-angular
ex-, *e-* or *ec-* = out, from	*ex*-cept, *ex*-clude, *ex*-pel
in-, *il-*, *im-*, *ir-*, *en-*, etc. = in, on, not	*in*-dorse, *in*-clude, *il*-legal
inter- = between	*inter*-pose, *inter*-cede
mon-, *mono-* = one, alone (Greek)	*mono*-tone, *mono*-logue
per- = through	*per*-ceive, *per*-mit
post- = after, behind	*post*-pone, *post*-script
pre- = before	*pre*-pare, *pre*-cede
pro- = before, for, forth, forward	*pro*-vide, *pro*-cession, *pro*-pose
re-, *red-* = back, again	*re*-gain, *re*-read, *re*-fresh
sub-, *suc-*, *suf-*, *sug-*, *sum-*, *sup-* = under	*sub*-ject, *suf*-fer, *sub*-mit
trans- = across	*trans*-fer, *trans*-pose, *trans*-port
un-, *uni-* = one	*uni*-form, *uni*-corn

SUFFIXES	USED IN WORDS
-able, *-ible* = capable of	cap-*able*, measur-*able*
-age = amount, state	mile-*age*, cour-*age*
-ance, *-ence* = relating to, condition of	appear-*ance*, independ-*ence*
-ar, *-ary* = relating to	muscul-*ar*, pulmon-*ary*
-ate = to act, to cause	anim-*ate*
-ation = action, condition	degener-*ation*, civiliz-*ation*, vari-*ation*
-ceous, *-cious* = like	falla-*cious*, gra-*cious*
-cy = quality, state	pira-*cy*, luna-*cy*
-fy = make	satis-*fy*, horri-*fy*
-ic, *-ical* = one who or that which	class-*ical*, geometr-*ic*
-icious = like unto	del-*icious*, mal-*icious*
-ion = action, being, condition	miss-*ion*, rebell-*ion*
-ions = full of	relig-*ions*, suspic-*ions*
-ise, *-ize* = to do, or make	critic-*ise*, bapt-*ize*
-ive = having the character, given to	talkat-*ive*, posit-*ive*
-ment = state	astonish-*ment*, banish-*ment*
-ous = full of, of the nature of	peril-*ous*, wondr-*ous*
-ty = condition or character	digni-*ty*, puri-*ty*

The Latin roots, prefixes, and suffixes, however, form by no means the whole of the English language. They have been spoken of first because they are the easiest to understand, as they are little changed, in form and meaning, from the original. The real strength of the language, the more familiar, simpler words, the words of common, everyday speech, are Teutonic in origin. They were brought into England by Teutonic tribes, the Angles and the Saxons, who settled there in the fifth century.

A study of the following list of Anglo-Saxon words will give some idea of the influence of the Teutonic element in the familiar speech of every Englishman and American.

bacan = bake	bake, baker
beatan = strike	beat, beater
beran = bear	bear, bearer, bearable
bindan = bind	bind, bound, bond, band
bitan = bite	bite, bitten, bit
bugan = bend	bow, bough
cat = cat	cat, kitten
ceap = bargain	cheap, chop

cleofan = split................cleave, cleft, cliff
cnawan = know................know, knew, knowledge
cunnan = know................cunning
daelan = divide................deal
dragan = to draw................draw, drag, dray
faran = go or travel................far, fare, farewell
fleogan = flee................flee, fled
hlaf = bread................loaf, lord (= bread-keeper, from *hlaf* + *weard*, a guard), lady (= bread-kneader, from *hlaf* + *digan*, to knead)
licgan = to lie................lie, lay
maegan = be able................may, might, mighty
raedan = read or guess................read, riddle
tredan = to walk................tread, trot
treow = good faith................true, truth
witan = know................wit, wot, witty

A comparison of these stems with the Latin stems mentioned above will show that the Anglo-Saxon stems have been far more changed in their conversion into English words than have the Latin. These changes, however, have come about for the very reason that the Anglo-Saxon is the oldest element of our language and has thus been much altered because of the passage of many centuries and the influence of other tongues brought later into England. Similar changes are seen in the Anglo-Saxon prefixes and suffixes.

Prefixes

an- or *a-* = on................*a*-bed, *a*-board
fore- = before................*fore*-bode, *fore*-cast
for- = thoroughly................*for*-give, *for*-get
gegen- or *gain-* = back or again................*gain*-say
mis- = wrong................*mis*-lead, *mis*-trust, *mis*-deed
un- = not................*un*-holy, *un*-do, *un*-bind
al- or *all-* = quite................*al*-one, *al*-most, *al*-mighty
in- = in................*in*-come, *in*-step, *in*-land
of- or *off-* = from................*off*-spring, *off*-shoot
over- = above or over................*over*-cast, *over*-throw
twi- = two................*twi*-light
under- = under................*under*-stand, *under*-bid

Suffixes

-craft = skill................handi-*craft*
-dom = power, office................king-*dom*, prince-*dom*
-en = diminutive................chick-*en* (from *cock*), kitt-*en* (from *cat*)
-er = one who or that which................bak-*er*, work-*er*
-hood = state or rank................boy-*hood*, man-*hood*
-ing (originally son of) = part of................farth-*ing* (fourth part)
-ung or *-ing* = verbal noun suffix................sing-*ing*
-kin, *-ling* = diminutives................lamb-*kin*, dar-*ling*
-loch or *-ledge* = gift, sport................know-*ledge*
-scipe or *-ship* = shape or form................king-*ship*, wor-*ship*
-stede or *-stead* = place................home-*stead*
-ed or *-en* = material................gold-*en*, wood-*en*, gild-*ed*
-feast or *-fast* = firm................stead-*fast*
-feald or *-fold* = denotes multiplication..mani-*fold*, two-*fold*
-isc or *-ish* = nature of................child-*ish*, fool-*ish*

Suffixes

-less = loose from	hope-*less*, power-*less*
-like or *-ly* = like	home-*ly*, love-*ly*, lady-*like*
-sum or *-some* = like	win-*some*
-ward = direction	back-*ward*
-ling or *-long* = direction	head-*long*
-wise = manner	like-*wise*

Another kind of words which come to us from the Anglo-Saxon is the group of "self-explaining" phrase compounds. Such words are *offhand, meanwhile, throughout, nobody, oftentimes, whenever*, and a number of others which will readily occur to you. For the Old English was rich in words formed by the union of two independent words.

From the word *land*, for instance, there were once sixty-three compounds. Most of these are no longer part of the language, though some remain, as *landlord* and *landmark*.

Though the Anglo-Saxon language forms, as has been shown, the basis of the English language, and the Latin has made a very large contribution, no small part of our vocabulary has been transferred bodily from other languages besides these two. Italy, Spain, India, Arabia, the West Indies, all have contributed their share. From Italy we have borrowed many terms pertaining to music and to the refinements of cultured life. Such words are *libretto, crescendo, balcony, cameo, intaglio, catacomb*. Spain has contributed many words naming commercial products, as *indigo, guava, vanilla, alligator*, as well as some others such as *matador* and *mosquito*. From Holland and Scandinavia come words pertaining to commerce and the sea, among which are *schooner, wagon, yacht, skipper, sloop*. India and Arabia with their products sent words naming them, such as *chintz, candy, orange, borax, divan, alcohol, amber, coffee, cotton*. Biblical literature brings us Hebrew terms, as *cherub, jubilee, amen, alleluia, ephod*.

America's contributions to the English language have come from the Mexicans, from the peoples of South America and the West Indies, and from the North American Indians. From Mexico come *chocolate, coyote, tomato;* from South America, *tapioca, guano, jaguar, quinine, alpaca;* from the West Indies, *hurricane, maize, potato*. The North American Indians have given us such terms as *moccasin, moose, raccoon, tobacco, squaw, papoose*—words which name things common in an Indian's daily life.

In this way has the whole world contributed and still is contributing to the language of the English-speaking peoples. What wonder, then, that the English tongue is full and rich and flexible? Its wealth of meaning, its beauty, its power, are the result of centuries of growth and of the gifts bestowed by East and West, by North and South. Such a heritage may well be the pride of every Englishman and every American.

SIMPLE RULES FOR SPELLING DERIVATIVE WORDS

1. Monosyllables, and polysyllables accented on the last syllable, ending in a single consonant preceded by a single vowel, double the final consonant before a suffix beginning with a vowel.

   plan { + ed = planned.
+ ing = plan'ning.

   oc-cur' { + ing = oc-cur'ring.
+ ence = oc-cur'rence.

2. Words ending in two or more consonants, words ending in a consonant preceded by two or more vowels, and polysyllables not accented on the last syllable, do not double the final consonant before a suffix beginning with a vowel.

   act + or = actor.
feud + al = feudal.
of'fer + ing = of'fer-ing.

3. Words ending in a double consonant usually drop the last consonant before a suffix.

   full + ness = fulness.
skill + ful = skilful.

Usage permits many such words to be spelled with either a single or a double consonant.

4. Words ending in silent *e* retain the *e* before a suffix beginning with a consonant, and drop the *e* before a suffix beginning with a vowel.

   state + ment = statement.
state + ing = stating.

EXCEPTIONS:

whole + ly = wholly.
acknowledge } + ment = { acknowledgment.
judge } + ment = { judgment.
due } + ly = { duly.
true } + ly = { truly.
awe + ful = awful.
argue + ment = argument.
dye + ing = dyeing.

Words ending in *ce* (as place) and *ge* (as courage) retain the *e* before *a* or *o*, so that *c* and *g* may have their soft sounds:

peace + able = peaceable.
courage + ous = courageous.

5. Words ending in *ie* drop *e* and change *i* to *y* before *ing*.

   die + ing = dying.

6. Words ending in *y*, if a consonant precedes *y*, change *y* to *i* before any suffix except one beginning with *i*; if a vowel precedes *y*, the *y* is unchanged.

   pity + ful = pitiful.
   pity + ing = pitying.
   buy + er = buyer.

7. The regular rule for formation of plurals of nouns is to add *s* to the singular. If the final letter of the singular will not unite with *s* (as *ch*, *sh*, *s*, *j*, *x*, *z*), add *es*.

   church, churches.
   fox, foxes.

8. Nouns ending in a consonant and *y* form the plural by changing *y* to *i* and adding *es*.

   daisy. daisies.

9. Nouns ending in a consonant followed by *o* form the plural by adding *es*.

   negro, negroes.

10. The formation of the third person singular present of verbs follows the rules for the plurals of nouns.

EXPLANATORY NOTES.

Varied Spellings. If two or more variations of the spelling of a single word exist, the rule followed is to let each appear in its proper alphabetical place in the list, with pronunciation, definition, etc., given as usual, followed by "Also," and the variant in heavy type. An exception is made to this rule when the position of the two variants is consecutive or practically so. In this case, the word given first, and defined, is that selected as preferable. For illustration, see *ægis* and *fusileer*.

Analogous Forms. In cases where two derivatives from the same root word are practically identical in meaning, the less common one has been given in heavy type, with "Also," and has not been listed elsewhere. See *accusatory*, *acceptability*. Cross references have occasionally been used, with "Also," in words almost identical in meaning. See *heather*.

Capitals. When the word listed is a proper noun or adjective, it appears in the vocabulary with a capital. If it has two forms, one common, one proper, the form given in the vocabulary is the original or more important form of the word, the other being repeated beneath, with the definition belonging to it. See *genesis*.

Hyphens. A light hyphen is used to mark division into syllables, except after an accented syllable; as, *e-lab'o-rate*. A heavy hyphen is used to separate the parts of a compound word; as, *fa'ther-in-law*.

Pronunciation. Pronunciation of every word in the vocabulary is given in parenthesis immediately after the word. If a word serves as more than one part of speech, and the second is pronounced differently from the first, the pronunciation of the second is inserted in parenthesis after the name of the part of speech. See *alternate*.

Grammatical Information. Principal parts of verbs are given in brackets after the name of the part of speech (*v.i.* or *v.t.*), if the verb is irregular or if they are desirable for other reasons. Similarly, irregular plurals of nouns and comparative and superlative degrees of adjectives are given in brackets.

Etymology. No attempt has been made to analyze sources of words, except when a word or phrase has been adopted bodily from a foreign language. In that case the name of the foreign language appears in brackets after the definition.

Derivatives. Certain derivative words which come directly from words listed in the vocabulary are given after the definition of the original word, with the part of speech of the derivative indicated. See *adorable*.

ABBREVIATIONS USED IN THIS BOOK.

adj.	Adjective.	It.	Italy, Italian.
A. D.	Anno Domini (Year of our Lord).	Jap.	Japan, Japanese
adv.	Adverb.	Lat.	Latin.
Am.	America, American.	*masc.*	Masculine.
Ant.	Antonym.	Meth.	Methodist.
Ar.	Arabic.	Mex.	Mexico.
A. S.	Anglo-Saxon.	mt.	Mountain.
Aus.	Austria, Austrian.	*n.*	Noun.
B. C.	Before Christ.	N.	North.
Bapt.	Baptist.	*naut.*	Nautical.
Bel.	Belgium, Belgian.	*neut.*	Neuter.
Br.	Britain, British.	N. Z.	New Zealand.
Can.	Canada, Canadian.	*obs.*	Obsolete.
Cath.	Catholic.	*p.adj.*	Participial adjective.
C.	Centigrade.	*pf'd.*	Preferred.
Co.	Company.	*pl.*	Plural.
co.	County.	Poet.	Poetic.
Colloq.	Colloquial.	Port.	Portugal, Portuguese.
com.	Commonly.	*p.p.*	Past participle.
comp.	Comparative.	*p.pr.*	Present participle.
Confed.	Confederate.	Pres.	President.
Cong.	Congregationalist.	*prep.*	Preposition.
C. S.	Christian Science.	*pres.*	Present.
Dept.	Department.	Presby.	Presbyterian.
E.	East.	*pron.*	Pronoun.
Egypt.	Egyptian.	prov.	Province.
Eng.	England, English.	*p.t.*	Past tense.
Epis.	Episcopal, Episcopalian.	Russ.	Russia, Russian.
etc.	Et cetera (and so forth).	S.	South.
F.	Fahrenheit.	Scot.	Scottish.
fem.	Feminine.	*sing.*	Singular.
Fr.	France, French.	Span.	Spanish.
G. Br.	Great Britain.	sq.	Following.
Gen.	General.	sq. m.	Square miles.
Ger.	German, Germany.	*superl.*	Superlative.
Gr.	Greece, Greek.	Switz.	Switzerland.
Hind.	Hindu.	*Syn.*	Synonym.
Hung.	Hungary, Hungarian.	Teut.	Teutonic.
i.e.	(Id est) that is.	Turk.	Turkey, Turkish.
interj.	Interjection.	Unit.	Unitarian.
Ir.	Ireland, Irish.	U. S.	United States.
		v.i.	Verb intransitive.
		v.t.	Verb transitive.
		W.	West.

See "Abbreviations Used in Writing and Printing," page 803.

A GUIDE TO PRONUNCIATION.

Key to the Signs Indicating Sound.

Accent.

The word *accent* is applied to the special emphasis which is placed upon certain syllables in words of more than one syllable. Sometimes a word has one accented syllable, which is indicated by a single mark [′] after the syllable. Sometimes a word has two accented syllables, a principal, or heavier, one and a secondary, or lighter, one. The principal accent is indicated by a single mark [′], and the secondary by a double mark [″].

Vowels.

ā, as in āte, pāle, fā′vor, is called *long a.* It occurs in accented syllables.

ā, as in fo′li-āge, sen′āte, often represents *long a in unaccented syllables.*

â, as in râre, pâr′ent, pre-pâre′, represents *a in accented syllables ending in r.*

ă, as in căt, găr′ret, is called *short a.* It occurs in accented syllables.

ă, as in lo′căl, ăf-fect′, often represents *short a in unaccented syllables* ending in a consonant.

ä, as in cälm, fär, cärt, is called *broad* or *Italian a.*

à, as in àsk, com-mànd′, is called *intermediate a.*

ȧ, as in bȧ-na′nȧ, pȧ-rade′, represents *intermediate a in unaccented syllables,* usually those not ending in a consonant. It is called *indeterminate a.*

ē, as in ē′ven, scēne, con-cēde′, is called *long e.* It occurs in accented syllables.

ē, as in ē-vent′, dē-scribe, crē-ate′, pro-pri′ē-ty, often represents *long e in unaccented syllables.*

ĕ, as in de-fĕct′, ĕx′tra, ĕdge, ĕf-fĕct′, ĕnd-ĕd, is called *short e.* It occurs in accented syllables and in unaccented first and last syllables.

ĕ, as in nov′ĕl, re′cĕnt, often represents *short e* in *unaccented syllables.*

ẽ, as in writ′ẽr, re-fẽr′, con′fẽr-ence, represents *unaccented e before r.*

ī, as in rīght, de-līght′, ī-de′a, is called *long i.* It occurs in accented and unaccented syllables.

ĭ, as in sĭn, be-gĭn, dĭs-sect′, is called *short i.* It occurs in accented and unaccented syllables.

ō, as in hōpe, cōld, ech′ō, is called *long o.* It occurs in accented and unaccented syllables.

ō, as in pō-ta′to, ō-bey′, often represents *long o in unaccented syllables.*

ô, as in côrd, ôr′der, a-dôrn′, clôth, is called *open* or *intermediate o.* It occurs in accented syllables ending in a consonant, often before *r.*

ŏ, as in cŏr′al, stŏp, ŏb-la′tion, is called *short o.* It occurs in accented and unaccented syllables.

ŏ, as in cŏm-pare, cor′ŏ-net, usually represents *short o in unaccented syllables.*

ū, as in cūre, ū′nit, hū′man, is called *long u.* It occurs in accented syllables.

ū, as in ū-nite, hū-mane′, cir′cū-late, represents *long u in unaccented syllables.*

û, as in bûrn, oc-cûr′, fûr, represents *accented u before a single r in the same syllable.*

ŭ, as in hŭr′ry, ŭp-set′, cŭt, is called *short u.* It occurs in accented and unaccented syllables.

ủ, as in fo′củs, sủp-port′, sủc-ceed, usually represents *short u in unaccented syllables.*

ü, as in me′nü, represents French *u* or German *u*-umlaut.

Sometimes a certain sound of one vowel is indicated by a special marking of another. Thus:

a, as in all, wa′ter, walk, is represented by **ô**.
a, as in what, was, is represented by **ŏ**.
e, as in re-fer′, herd, is represented by **û**.
e, as in there, where, is represented by **â**.
i, as in stir, irk′some, is represented by **û**.
i, as in e-lix′ir (unaccented), is represented by **ẽ**.
i, as in ma-chine, mo-bile′, is represented by **ē**.
o, as in move, do, to, is represented by **ōō**.
o, as in wom′an, wor′sted, is represented by **ŏŏ**.
o, as in come, hon′ey, is represented by **ŭ**.
o, as in word, worse, is represented by **û**.
u, as in true, sure, is represented by **ōō**.
u, as in pull, su′gar, is represented by **ŏŏ**.

Diphthongs.

ai, as in vain, **ay**, as in play, } have the sound of **ā**.
au, as in haul, **aw**, as in law, } have the sound of **ô**.
ai, as in aisle, **ay**, as in aye, } have the sound of **ī**.
au, as in laugh, has the sound of **ä**.
ea, as in steak, **ei**, as in veil, **ey**, as in they, } have the sound of **ā**.
ea, as in learn, has the sound of **û**.
ea, as in steam, **ee**, as in meet, **ei**, as in seize, **eo**, as in peo′ple, **ey**, as in key, } have the sound of **ē**.
ei, as in height, **ey**, as in eye, } have the sound of **ī**.
eu, as in feud, **ew**, as in new, } have the sound of **ū**.
eu, as in rheum, **ew**, as in threw, } have the sound of **ōō**.

ew, as in sew, has the sound of ō.
ie, as in yield, has the sound of ē.
ie, as in tie, has the sound of ī.

oa, as in foam,
oe, as in doe,
oo, as in door,
ow, as in blow,
} have the sound of ō.

oy, as in toy, has the sound of oi.
oo, as in boot, is marked o͞o, long.
oo, as in foot, is marked o͝o, short.
ou, as in soup. has the sound of o͞o.
ou, as in could, has the sound of o͝o.
ow, as in prowl, has the sound of ou.

Consonants.

Certain consonants are used to indicate other special consonant sounds. Thus:

ch, as in chase, is used to indicate {
tch, as in catch.
ti, as in question.
te, as in righteous.

f, as in feel, is used to indicate {
ph, as in physician.
gh, as in cough.

g, as in good (hard *g*), is used to indicate {
gu, as in guest.
gue, as in plague.
gh, as in ghastly.

gz is used to indicate x, as in ex-ist, ex-ample.
hw is used to indicate wh, as in when, where.

j, as in joy, is used to indicate {
g, as in gem (soft *g*).
gi, as in religion.
ge, as in pigeon.
di, as in soldier.
dge, as in judge.

k, as in kept, is used to indicate {
ch, as in chorus (hard *ch*).
c, as in cure (hard *c*).
ck, as in back.
qu, as in conquer.

kh is used to indicate the German ch, as in loch.
ks is used to indicate x, as in sex, extra.
kw is used to indicate qu, as in inquire.
n is used to indicate gn, as in design.
ṅ, as in bank, function, is used before hard *g* or *k*.
ṅ is used to indicate French nasal *n* or *m*, as in enfant.

ṅg, as in long, singer, {
is used when *g* is soft.
indicates gue, as in tongue.

r, as in red, is used to indicate rh, as in rheumatism.

s, as in seem (sharp *s*), is used to indicate { c, as in center (soft *c*). sc, as in science. ss, as in miss.

sh, as in show, is used to indicate { ch, as in machine. ce, as in ocean. ci, as in racial. sci, as in conscience. si, as in version. ss, as in issue. ti, as in motion.

t, as in try, is used to indicate { ed, as in stopped. th, as in thyme.

th is used to indicate th, as in thin, thick.

th is used to indicate th, as in soothe, they.

v, as in vain, is used to indicate f, as in of.

z, as in gaze, is used to indicate { s, as in rise (soft *s*). x, as in Xerxes.

zh is used to indicate { z, as in azure. zi, as in glazier. s, as in measure. si, as in provision. g, as in rouge.

THE WINSTON SIMPLIFIED DICTIONARY

A

A, a (ā or ȧ), *adj.* and *indef. art.* (contraction of *an*), one; any: used before words beginning with a consonant or the sound of *h*: *prep.* to; in; into; as, once *a* month; to go *a*-Maying.

Aar-on (âr'ŭn), *n.* in the Bible, the brother of Moses; the first high priest of the Hebrews.—Exodus iv, *sq.*

a-back (ȧ-băk'), *adv.* backward: said of sails when pressed back against the mast: used frequently with *taken* to mean disconcerted; as, he was taken *aback* when he was refused admittance.

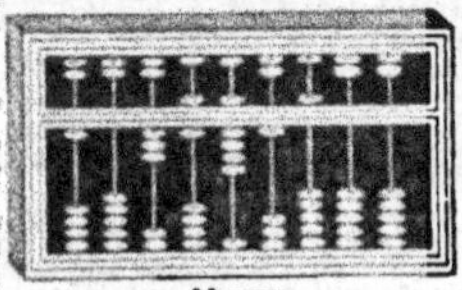

Abacus

ab-a-cus (ăb'ȧ-kŭs), *n.* a device for counting, consisting of beads or balls strung on wires or rods set in a frame; the top layer of a column or pillar.

a-baft (ȧ-băft'), *adv.* and *prep.* a nautical term: at, towards, or in the direction of the stern or back part of a ship; astern.

a-ban-don (ȧ-băn'dŭn), *v.t.* to give up entirely; as, the sailors were forced to *abandon* the sinking ship; to desert or forsake; to give up all claim to: *n.* freedom of manner; dash; careless ease.

Syn., v. leave, forsake, desert, renounce, relinquish, quit, forego, let go.
Ant. (see keep, cherish).

a-ban-doned (ȧ-băn'dŭnd), *p.adj.* forsaken, deserted, given up entirely; shameless; wicked.

a-ban-don-ment (ȧ-băn'dŭn-mĕnt), *n.* total desertion; absence of self-restraint or control.

a-base (ȧ-bās'), *v.t.* to humble or degrade; to take away self-pride; to cast down, as in rank or office; to dishonor.

a-bash (ȧ-băsh'), *v.t.* to put to shame; to disconcert; to humiliate.

Syn. bewilder, confuse, shame, embarrass.
Ant. (see embolden).

a-bate (ȧ-bāt'), *v.t.* to lessen; suppress: *v.i.* to decrease; moderate; subside; as, the storm *abates*.

Syn. decrease, diminish, lessen, moderate, reduce.
Ant. (see continue, increase).

a-bate-ment (ȧ-bāt'mĕnt), *n.* decrease; a lessening, as of grief or pain.

ab-a-tis (ăb'ȧ-tĭs; FR. ȧ"bȧ"tē'), *n.* a barricade or defense of felled trees with the branches pointing outward; in modern warfare, a barbed wire entanglement. Also, **abattis.**

a-bat-toir (ȧ"bȧ"twär'), *n.* a building in which animals are slaughtered and their meat prepared for use.

Ab-ba (ăb'ȧ), *n.* father; a title of a bishop, used in some far Eastern churches; a name for God found in the New Testament; as, "And he said, *Abba*, Father, all things are possible unto thee."—Mark xiv. 36.

ab-bé (ȧ"bā'), *n.* an abbot; a title of respect given to men who have studied theology. [FR.]

ab-bess (ăb'ĕs), *n.* the head of a convent or nunnery; the lady, or mother, superior.

ab-bey (ăb'ĭ), *n.* [*pl.* abbeys (-ĭz)], an institution where persons of either sex live apart from the world and devote themselves to a religious life; also, the building in which they live; monastery (for males); convent or nunnery (for females); the church of a monastery.

ab-bot (ăb'ŭt), *n.* the male superior, or head, of an abbey or monastery; literally, father.

ab-bre-vi-ate (ȧ-brē'vĭ-āt), *v.t.* to shorten, as by contraction of a word, as *Dec.* for *December*.

ab-bre-vi-a-tion (ȧ-brē"vĭ-ā'shŭn), *n.* the shortened or contracted form of a word or phrase, as *U. S. A.* for *United States of America*.

ab-di-cate (ăb'dĭ-kāt), *v.t.* to give up or withdraw from; as, the king was forced to *abdicate* his throne in favor of his cousin.

ab-di-ca-tion (ăb"dĭ-kā'shŭn), *n.* the act of giving up an office, power or authority, right or trust.

ab-do-men (ăb-dō'mĕn), *n.* the lower cavity of the body, containing the digestive organs.

ab-dom-i-nal (ăb-dŏm'ĭ-năl), *adj.* pertaining to the lower cavity of the body.

ab-duct (ăb-dŭkt'), *v.t.* to carry off by stealth or force; to kidnap.

ab-duc-tion (ăb-dŭk'shŭn), *n.* the act of carrying off wrongfully; kidnaping.

a-beam (ȧ-bēm′), *adv.* a nautical term: opposite the middle part of a ship's side, and in line with its main-beam; in a direction at right angles to the keel of a ship; as, we had the wind *abeam*.

a-bed (ȧ-bĕd′), *adv.* in bed; to bed; as, the sluggard is still *abed* when the sun is high.

A-bel (ā′bĕl), *n.* in the Bible, the son of Adam and Eve, slain by his brother Cain.—Genesis iv.

ab-er-ra-tion (ăb″ẽr-ā′shŭn), *n.* a wandering from the right way, especially from truth; error; mental disorder.—*adj.* **aberrant.**

a-bet (ȧ-bĕt′), *v.t.* [*p.t.* and *p.p.* abetted, *p.pr.* abetting], to encourage; to aid or assist in doing an act, usually of a criminal nature.—*n.* **abetter, abettor.**
Syn. aid, assist, countenance, sanction, support, uphold.
Ant. (see hinder, impede).

a-bey-ance (ȧ-bā′ăns), *n.* a holding or keeping back for a time; a holding over; temporary inactivity.

ab-hor (ăb-hôr′), *v.t.* [*p.t.* and *p.p.* abhorred, *p.pr.* abhorring], to shrink from with horror, dread, or disgust; to hate; to loathe.
Syn. despise, detest, dislike.
Ant. (see admire, approve).

ab-hor-rence (ăb-hŏr′ĕns), *n.* a feeling of strong hatred; loathing.

ab-hor-rent (ăb-hŏr′ĕnt), *adj.* hateful, repulsive; repugnant.

a-bide (ȧ-bīd′), *v.t.* [*p.t.* and *p.p.* abode, *p.pr.* abiding], to wait for; put up with; tolerate: *v.i.* to dwell, reside, remain; as, "Except these *abide* in the ship, ye cannot be saved."—Acts xxvii. 31.
Syn. dwell, lodge, remain, sojourn, stop, reside, live.
Ant. (see abandon, depart).

a-bid-ing (ȧ-bīd′ĭng), *p.adj.* remaining; staying; steadfast; as, an *abiding* faith; *abiding* purpose; *abiding* love.

a-bil-i-ty (ȧ-bĭl′ĭ-tĭ), *n.* power or capacity to do or act; mental gifts; skill; talent.

ab-ject (ăb′jĕkt), *adj.* cast down; ignoble; cringing; mean; low; hopeless; as, *abject* poverty.—*adv.* **abjectly.**—*n.* **abjectness.**

ab-jure (ăb-jŏŏr′), *v.t.* to renounce or give up upon oath; to recant; to disavow; withdraw formally from; as, to *abjure* allegiance to a king.

ab-la-tive (ăb′lȧ-tĭv), *n.* one of the cases of Latin nouns, expressing chiefly separation or removal.

a-blaze (ȧ-blāz′), *adj.* and *adv.* on fire; well alight; in a blaze; eager; in a state of excitement; ardent.

a-ble (ā′bl), *adj.* possessed of power, fitness, or means; as, he is not *able* to pay so much; competent; as, he is an *able* lawyer; vigorous, active, strong.—*adv.* **ably.**

a-ble-bod-ied (ā′bl-bŏd″ĭd), *adj.* physically strong and sound; capable or efficient for duty.

a-bloom (ȧ-blōōm′), *adj.* and *adv.* in blossom or in flower; blooming.

ab-lu-tion (ăb-lū′shŭn), *n.* a washing or cleansing of the body; any ceremonial washing done as a religious duty.

ab-ne-gate (ăb′nē-gāt), *v.t.* to refuse (anything) to oneself; to deny and reject; give up or surrender.

ab-ne-ga-tion (ăb-nē-gā′shŭn), *n.* self-sacrifice; denial; a giving up.

ab-nor-mal (ăb-nôr′măl), *adj.* irregular; deformed; unnatural; out of the common; not conforming to rule or type.—*adv.* **abnormally.**—*n.* **abnormality.**

a-board (ȧ-bōrd′), *adv.* on or within a ship or railroad train: used also in the command to enter a ship or train; as, "All *aboard!*"

a-bode (ȧ-bōd′), *n.* a place of continued residence; a dwelling; a habitation; a home; residence generally.

a-bol-ish (ȧ-bŏl′ĭsh), *v.t.* to do away with; put an end to; as, the Civil War *abolished* slavery.
Syn. destroy, end.
Ant. (see continue, renew).

ab-o-li-tion (ăb″ō-lĭsh′ŭn), *n.* the act of destroying or doing away with; extinction; the state of being done away with; the annulment or ending of decrees, rites, customs, etc.

ab-o-li-tion-ist (ăb″ō-lĭsh′ŭn-ĭst), *n.* one who is in favor of doing away with some law or custom; one of those who, during the Civil War, believed that negro slavery should be ended.

a-bom-i-na-ble (ȧ-bŏm′ĭ-nȧ-bl), *adj.* hateful; odious; offensive; unclean; vile.—*adv.* **abominably.**

a-bom-i-nate (ȧ-bŏm′ĭ-nāt), *v.t.* to regard with feelings of disgust or hatred; to abhor.

a-bom-i-na-tion (ȧ-bŏm″ĭ-nā′shŭn), *n.* excessive hatred of disgust; anything vile or hateful.
Syn. nuisance, annoyance, offense, shame.
Ant. (see blessing, delight).

ab-o-rig-i-nal (ăb″ō-rĭj′ĭ-năl), *adj.* original; first; existing from the beginning: *n.* one of the class of animals or plants which have originated or had their beginning in a certain place.

ab-o-rig-i-nes (ăb″ō-rĭj′ĭ-nēz), *n.pl.* the first or earliest inhabitants of a country; the native animals or plants of any part of the world.

a-bor-tion (ȧ-bôr′shŭn), *n.* a premature birth; any fruit which fails to mature; any failure to complete what has been begun.

a-bor-tive (ȧ-bôr′tĭv), *adj.* born too soon; imperfectly developed; failing; fruitless.

a-bound (ȧ-bound′), *v.i.* to have in plenty or abundance; to exist in great numbers or quantity: followed by *in* or *with*; as, the sea *abounds* with fish.

a-bout (ȧ-bout′), *adv.* around; on every side; nearly; near to; in a reversed position; half around; as, *about* face; intending; as, he was *about* to go; in rotation; as, turn *about* is fair play: *prep.* concerned in; somewhere near; all around; over; beside; relating to; as, the story was *about* animals.

a-bove (ȧ-bŭv′), *adv.* in a higher place; overhead; in heaven; before, especially in a book or writing; as, from what has been said *above: prep.* superior to; as, to be *above* doing a mean thing; beyond; in excess of; as, happiness *above* measure.

a-bove-board (ȧ-bŭv′bōrd″), *adj.* and *adv.* openly; without trickery.

ab-rade (ăb-rād′), *v.t.* to wear or rub away; to remove, as by friction; to corrode, as by acids.

A-bra-ham (ā′brȧ-hăm), *n.* in the Bible, the first great patriarch of the Hebrews: founder of the race: originally called *Abram*.—Genesis xi, *sq.*

ab-ra-sion (ăb-rā'zhŭn), *n.* a wearing or rubbing away, as of stones by running water, or coins by constant handling.

a-breast (ȧ-brĕst'), *adv.* side by side; in the line with; opposite to; at the same level.

a-bri (ȧ'brē'), *n.* an underground retreat, such as a cellar, dugout, etc., used as a place of refuge during bomb attacks by enemy airplanes. [Fr.]

a-bridge (ȧ-brĭj'), *v.t.* to shorten; condense; as, to *abridge* a dictionary.

a-bridg-ment (ȧ-brĭj'mĕnt), *n.* a shortened form of a book, etc.; a smaller reproduction.

a-broad (ȧ-brôd'), *adv.* widely; beyond the limits of house or country; out of doors; out of the country or to a foreign country.

ab-ro-gate (ăb'rō-gāt), *v.t.* to abolish, annul, or repeal by authority; to do away with.—*n.* **abrogation.**

ab-rupt (ăb-rŭpt'), *adj.* broken; ending suddenly; steep; as, an *abrupt* cliff; precipitous; rough; unceremonious or discourteous; unconnected; sudden.—*adv.* **abruptly.**—*n.* **abruptness.**

Ab-sa-lom (ăb'sȧ-lŏm), *n.* in the Bible, the favorite but rebellious son of David.—2 Samuel xviii.

ab-scess (ăb'sĕs), *n.* [*pl.* abscesses (-ĕz)], a collection of pus in the tissues of the body; a boil.

ab-scond (ăb-skŏnd'), *v.i.* to flee or retire in haste from one's residence or post of duty; quit the country in secret; to hide oneself; to disappear, often to avoid arrest.

Syn. run off, steal away.

ab-sence (ăb'sĕns), *n.* the state of being not present; the period of being away.

ab-sent (ăb-sĕnt'), *v.t.* to withdraw or keep (oneself) away from: *adj.* (ăb'sĕnt), not present; away; unoccupied.

Syn., adj inattentive, listless, dreamy; abstracted.

Ant. (see present).

ab-sen-tee (ăb'sĕn-tē'), *n.* one who is away or keeps away purposely from home or duty.

ab-sent-ly (ăb'sĕnt-lĭ), *adv.* in an abstracted manner; inattentively; forgetfully.

ab-sent-mind-ed (ăb'sĕnt-mīn'dĕd), *adj.* forgetful; inattentive; abstracted.

ab-so-lute (ăb'sō-lūt), *adj.* free as to condition; perfect; fixed; despotic; applied to a system of government in which the ruler is free to act unrestrained by any law; positive; unlimited.—*adv.* **absolutely.**—*n.* **absoluteness.**

Syn. supreme, arbitrary, unequalized.

ab-so-lu-tion (ăb'sō-lū'shŭn), *n.* the act of forgiving or freeing from the consequences of sin; the declaring an accused person innocent of a charge; forgiveness of sins in the sacrament of penance.

ab-solve (ăb-sŏlv'), *v.t.* to release or set free; clear of crime or guilt; to forgive.

Syn. pardon, release, clear, acquit.

Ant. (see condemn, bind).

ab-sorb (ăb-sôrb'), *v.t.* to drink in; suck or swallow up; as, a sponge *absorbs* water; to engross or engage wholly.

Syn. consume, swallow, take in, engross.

Ant. (see emit, dissipate).

ab-sorb-ent (ăb-sôr'bĕnt), *n.* anything which drinks, soaks, or takes in: *adj.* swallowing or taking in; as, *absorbent* cotton.

ab-sorb-ing (ăb-sôrb'ĭng), *p.adj.* taking or drinking in; engaging wholly, as the attention.

ab-sorp-tion (ăb-sôrp'shŭn), *n.* the process or act of taking in, imbibing, or swallowing up; the mental state of being entirely occupied with.

ab-stain (ăb-stān'), *v.i.* to do without; refrain; hold aloof; keep away from; as, to *abstain* from the use of tobacco.

ab-stain-er (ăb-stān'ẽr), *n.* one who voluntarily goes without; especially, one who gives up intoxicants; a teetotaler.

ab-ste-mi-ous (ăb-stē'mĭ-ŭs), *adj.* moderate and sparing in the use of food and drink; temperate.—*adv.* **abstemiously.**—*n.* **abstemiousness.**

ab-sti-nence (ăb'stĭ-nĕns), *n.* self-denial; partial or total giving up of food or drink.

Syn. moderation, sobriety, temperance.

Ant. (see excess, intemperance).

ab-stract (ăb'străkt), *n.* a summing up of the principal parts of a larger work: *v.t.* (ăb-străkt'), to take or draw away; separate; purloin or steal; to reduce to a summary; separate from and consider apart: *adj.* considered apart; as, *abstract* truth; ideal; expressing a quality apart from any subject; as, *abstract* words.

Syn., v. detach, remove, separate, withdraw, divert.

Ant. (see restore, complete).

ab-stract-ed (ăb-străkt'ĕd), *p.adj.* absent-minded; separated from other things.—*adv.* **abstractedly.**

ab-strac-tion (ăb-străk'shŭn), *n.* withdrawal, as of the mind from any object, or a quality from a thing of which it is a part; absence of mind; dishonest removal; theft; something unreal.

ab-stract-ly (ăb-străkt'lĭ), *adv.* separately; by itself.

ab-struse (ăb-stroos'), *adj.* obscure; hidden; hard to understand.—*adv.* **abstrusely.**—*n.* **abstruseness.**

ab-surd (ăb-sûrd'), *adj.* contrary to reason or sense; ridiculous; untrue.—*adv.* **absurdly.**—*n.* **absurdness.**

Syn. foolish, incorrect, monstrous, senseless, wild, nonsensical.

Ant. (see consistent, sensible).

ab-surd-i-ty (ăb-sûr'dĭ-tĭ), *n.* [*pl.* absurdities (-tĭz)], the state of being ridiculous; want of common sense; that which is contrary to reason or sense.

a-bun-dance (ȧ-bŭn'dăns), *n.* plenty; an overflowing quantity; profusion.

a-bun-dant (ȧ-bŭn'dănt), *adj.* ample; plentiful; sufficient.—*adv.* **abundantly.**

a-buse (ȧ-būs'), *n.* ill-treatment; insulting speech; the excessive, extreme, or improper use of anything; as, *abuse* of privileges; insult: *v.t.* (ȧ-būz'), to use improperly; treat rudely or wrongfully; to defile or violate; use violent or insulting language towards; upbraid.

Syn. v. revile, vilify, reproach, defame, slander, malign, traduce, ill-use.

Ant. (see praise).

a-bu-sive (ȧ-bū'sĭv), *adj.* wrongly used; ill-natured; using harsh words;

corrupt; as, an *abusive* use of power.—*adv.* **abusively.**—*n.* **abusiveness.**

a-but (*ă*-bŭt′), *v.t.* [*p.t.* and *p.p.* abutted, *p.pr.* abutting], to border upon; touch at one end; terminate or end: with *on, upon, against.*

a-but-ment (*ă*-bŭt′mĕnt), *n.* that which borders upon something else; the supporting structure at the end of an arch or bridge.

a-byss (*ă*-bĭs′), *n.* great depth of water or space; a bottomless gulf.

a-ca-cia (*ă*-kā′sh*ă*), *n.* the plant yielding gum arabic and other gums; a thorny yellow-flowering plant of the bean family.

ac-a-dem-ic (ăk″*ă*-dĕm′ĭk), *n.* a college student or member of a university: *adj.* scholarly; literary; theoretical not practical. Also, **academical.**

a-cad-e-my (*ă*-kăd′ē-mĭ), *n.* a private school or seminary for the teaching of the higher branches of education; a school for instruction in special subjects; an association or society of men famous in literature, science, and art; a building devoted to educational purposes.

A-ca-di-an (*ă*-kā′dĭ-*ă*n), *adj.* of or pertaining to Acadia or Nova Scotia: *n.* a native of Acadia.

a-can-thus (*ă*-kăn′thŭs), *n.* a plant of southern Europe characterized by prickly leaves. In Greek art the leaves are frequently used as models in decorating the tops of pillars, etc., especially the Corinthian pillar.

Acanthus

ac-cede (ăk-sēd′), *v.i.* to agree or yield; as, to *accede* to some request; to succeed, as to a throne.
Syn. assent, consent, acquiesce, comply with, coincide, concur, approve.
Ant. (see protest).

ac-cel-er-ate (ăk-sĕl′ẽr-āt), *v.t.* to hasten; to cause to move or advance faster; to quicken the speed of; to bring nearer in time.
Syn. hurry, expedite.
Ant. (see retard).

ac-cel-er-a-tion (ăk-sĕl-ẽr-ā′shŭn), *n.* the act of increasing speed; the state of being increased in speed.

ac-cel-er-a-tor (ăk-sĕl′ẽr-ā″tẽr), *n.* one who, or that which, increases speed; any method in photography to shorten the time of exposure; any mechanical attachment or device for increasing speed; as, the *accelerator* of an automobile.

ac-cent (ăk′sĕnt), *n.* the stress laid by the voice upon a particular syllable of a word, so as to render it more prominent than the rest; a mark or character used in writing and printing to show the proper pronunciation of a word; a peculiarity of utterance or expression distinguishing the language of different parts or districts of the same country or of a foreign country; the emphasis placed upon certain notes of a bar of music: *v.t.* (ăk-sĕnt′), to express the emphatic syllable in, or denote the vocal division of, a word by stress or modulation of the voice; to pronounce; mark the stressed syllable of a word by use of a sign; dwell upon or emphasize, as a passage of music.

ac-cen-tu-ate (ăk-sĕn′tū-āt), *v.t.* to emphasize in speaking or writing; to lay stress upon.—*n.* **accentuation.**

ac-cept (ăk-sĕpt′), *v.t.* to take or receive with approval, as a gift, or an office; to agree to, or acquiesce in; as, to *accept* an excuse; to recognize as true; to agree to pay; as, to *accept* a draft.
Syn. receive, take, admit.
Ant. (see refuse).

ac-cept-a-bil-i-ty (ăk-sĕp″t*ă*-bĭl′ĭ-tĭ), *n.* the quality of being welcome or agreeable. Also, **acceptableness.**

ac-cept-a-ble (ăk-sĕp′t*ă*-bl), *adj.* pleasing; welcome; agreeable; as, an *acceptable* gift.—*adv.* **acceptably.**

ac-cept-ance (ăk-sĕp′t*ă*ns), *n.* the act of taking what is offered; a receiving with approval; agreement to pay a note, or bill of exchange.

ac-cep-ta-tion (ăk″sĕp-tā′shŭn), *n.* an assent to an opinion or belief; the meaning in which a word or statement is generally understood.

ac-cept-er (ăk-sĕp′tẽr), *n.* in commerce, the person who receives a bill of exchange. Also, **acceptor.**

ac-cess (ăk′sĕs), *n.* admittance or approach to a person or place; means of approach or admission; as, the *access* to a building; addition or increase, as of land.

ac-ces-sa-ry (ăk-sĕs′*ă*-rĭ), *n.* one who, or that which, aids in an action; an accompaniment: *adj.* contributing. Also, **accessory.**—*adv.* **accessarily.**

ac-ces-si-bil-i-ty (ăk-sĕs″ĭ-bĭl′ĭ-tĭ), *n.* the condition of being easily reached.

ac-ces-si-ble (ăk-sĕs′ĭ-bl), *adj.* capable of being approached; easy to be reached; attainable.

ac-ces-sion (ăk-sĕsh′ŭn), *n.* a coming to, as by succession or by right; as, the *accession* of a prince to the throne; the acquirement of property by improvement, growth, or labor expended.

ac-ces-so-ry (ăk-sĕs′ō-rĭ), [*pl.* **accessories** (-rĭz)], *adj.* aiding a design or assisting a chief agent; contributory; additional; aiding in a crime: *n.* one who, or that which, aids the principal agent; one who, though not present, aids or abets in a crime either before or after its commission; an agent or accomplice. Also, **accessary.**
Syn., n. abetter, ally, confederate, helper.
Ant. (see hinderer, opponent).

ac-ci-dent (ăk′sĭ-dĕnt), *n.* an unexpected or unforeseen event, generally unfortunate.
Syn. incident, adventure, chance.
Ant. (see certainty, calculation).

ac-ci-den-tal (ăk″sĭ-dĕn′t*ă*l), *adj.* happening by chance or unexpectedly; casual; as, an *accidental* meeting; connected with, but not necessarily belonging to; nonessential; incidental: *n.* that which happens unexpectedly; a sign used in music to lower or raise the note before which it is placed.—*n.* **accidentalness.**

ac-ci-den-tal-ly (ăk″sĭ-dĕn′t*ă*l-ĭ), *adv.* in a casual manner; unexpectedly.

ac-claim (ă-klām′), *v.t.* to shout applause: *n.* a shout of joy or praise.

ac-cla-ma-tion (ăk″l*ă*-mā′shŭn), *n.* a shout of applause, or other demonstration of hearty approval: an outburst of joy, or praise; the adoption of a resolution by word of mouth.

ac-cli-mate (ă-klī′māt), *v.t.* to accustom to different or foreign conditions of temperature, moisture, etc.; to adapt to new conditions of temperature, moisture, etc. Also, **acclimatize.**

ac-cli-ma-tion (ăk″lĭ-mā′shŭn), *n.* the process of becoming used to new or different conditions of temperature, moisture, etc. Also, **acclimatization.**

ac-cli-ma-tize (ă-klī'mȧ-tīz), *v.t.* and *v.i.* to accustom, or become accustomed, to new or foreign conditions of temperature, moisture, etc.: said of plants or animals. Also, **acclimate.**

ac-cliv-i-ty (ă-klĭv'ĭ-tĭ), *n.* [*pl.* **acclivities** (-tĭz)], an ascent or upward slope of the earth, as the side of a hill.

ac-co-lade (ăk"ō-läd'; ăk"ō-lād'), *n.* the salutation used in conferring knighthood, formerly a kiss or embrace, now usually the tap on the shoulder with the flat blade of the sword: in France, when the croix de guerre or other award of honor is given, the *accolade* is a kiss on each cheek.

ac-com-mo-date (ă-kŏm'ō-dāt), *v.t.* to adapt or make fit or suitable; to adjust, settle; supply or furnish; do a favor to; to lend money for the convenience of a borrower.
Syn. serve, oblige, adapt, fit, suit.
Ant. (see disoblige, impede).

ac-com-mo-dat-ing (ă-kŏm'ō-dāt"-ĭng), *p.adj.* obliging; of a yielding disposition; adapting oneself to the desires of others.

ac-com-mo-da-tion (ă-kŏm"ō-dā'-shŭn), *n.* adaptation or adjustment; that which supplies a want or desire; lodging; a loan of money, as a favor: **accommodation paper,** notes, or bills of exchange, not actual sales.

ac-com-pa-ni-ment (ă-kŭm'pȧ-nĭ-mĕnt), *n.* that which goes with; something which is added to the principal thing by way of ornament, or for the sake of harmony; as, the violin and harp were a pleasing *accompaniment* to the voice of the singer.

ac-com-pa-ny (ă-kŭm'pȧ-nĭ), *v.t.* to go with; to escort; join in movement or action; in music, to supply the instrumental background for a voice, a chorus, or another instrument.—*n.* **accompanist.**

ac-com-plice (ă-kŏm'plĭs), *n.* an associate or companion in crime.
Syn. confederate, accessory, abettor, assistant, ally.
Ant. (see adversary).

ac-com-plish (ă-kŏm'plĭsh), *v.t.* to bring to pass; to complete; to finish.
Syn. effect, execute, achieve, perfect.

ac-com-plished (ă-kŏm'plĭsht), *p.adj.* completed; polished; finished; perfected; possessed of social qualifications.

ac-com-plish-ment (ă-kŏm'plĭsh-mĕnt), *n.* the completion of an act or undertaking; fulfillment; attainment; skill in some art.
Syn. qualification, acquirement.

ac-cord (ă-kôrd'), *v.t.* and *v.i.* to agree; give; grant; as, to *accord* due praise; to adjust or bring to agreement; to be in harmony; to agree in pitch and tone: *n.* agreement; unison; harmony.
Syn., *v.* grant, allow, admit.
Ant. (see deny).

ac-cord-ance (ă-kôr'dăns), *n.* agreement; harmony; as, his acts were in *accordance* with his belief.

ac-cord-ant (ă-kôr'dănt), *adj.* corresponding; of the same mind.

ac-cord-ing (ă-kôrd'ĭng), *p.adj.* agreeing; harmonizing: *adv.* in agreement with; accordingly; agreeably; as, he acted *according* to his belief.

ac-cord-ing-ly (ă-kôrd'ĭng-lĭ), *adv.* in agreement with; consequently; agreeably; as, he believed he was right and acted *accordingly.*

ac-cor-di-on (ă-kôr'dĭ-ŭn), *n.* a small keyed musical instrument which opens and shuts like a bellows, producing sound by the play of the wind upon free metallic reeds.

Accordion

ac-cost (ă-kŏst'), *v.t.* to speak to first; to salute; to greet; to address.

ac-count (ă-kount'), *v.t.* to reckon; compute; count: *v.i.* to assign or give an explanation: with *for*; take into consideration; relate: *n.* a reckoning; a financial statement or memorandum; a narrative; anything in the form of a statement, written or verbal; reason or consideration; profit; estimation; importance.
Syn. *n.* narrative, description, narration, recital, reckoning, bill, charge.

ac-count-a-bil-i-ty (ă-koun"tȧ-bĭl'ĭ-tĭ), *n.* responsibility for the carrying out of an obligation or trust. Also, **accountableness.**

ac-count-a-ble (ă-koun'tȧ-bl), *adj.* answerable; responsible; liable to be called to explain one's actions.—*adv.* **accountably.**
Syn. punishable, amenable.

ac-coun-tan-cy (ă-koun'tăn-sĭ), *n.* the art or practice of one skilled in the keeping of books.

ac-coun-tant (ă-koun'tănt), *n.* one skilled in the keeping or examination of books; an expert bookkeeper.

ac-cou-ter (ă-kōō'tẽr), *v.t.* to dress; equip; to array in military dress; to outfit a soldier. Also, **accoutre.**

ac-cou-ter-ments (ă-kōō'tẽr-mĕnts), *n.pl.* dress; military equipments or outfit. Also, **accoutrements.**

ac-cred-it (ă-krĕd'ĭt), *v.t.* to trust; to have confidence in; to authorize; stamp with authority; send with credentials, as an ambassador to a foreign country; to believe and accept as true.

ac-cre-tion (ă-krē'shŭn), *n.* increase by natural growth; as, the filling a channel by an *accretion* of shifting sand.

ac-crue (ă-krōō'), *v.i.* to grow; to increase; to come to, or happen naturally; to come or be added by increase, as interest on money lent.

ac-cu-mu-late (ă-kū'mū-lāt), *v.t.* to collect or bring together; amass; heap up: *v.i.* to increase in size, number, or quantity; to add to.

ac-cu-mu-la-tion (ă-kū'mū-lā'shŭn), *n.* an amassing; a collecting together; a heap.

ac-cu-mu-la-tive (ă-kū'mū-lā-tĭv), *adj.* tending to, or disposed to, collect or heap up; collective.

ac-cu-ra-cy (ăk'ū-rȧ-sĭ), *n.* the quality of being correct; exactness or precision.

ac-cu-rate (ăk'ū-rāt), *adj.* conforming to fact; free from error; precise.—*adv.* **accurately.**—*n.* **accurateness.**
Syn. correct, exact, truthful.
Ant. (see erroneous, careless).

ac-cursed (ă-kûrst; ă-kûr'sĕd), *p.adj.* doomed to destruction; blasted; ruined; detestable. Also, **accurst.**

ac-cu-sa-tion (ăk"ū-zā'shŭn), *n.* a charge of wrongdoing; a declaration of the commission of a crime or error.

ac-cu-sa-tive (ă-kū'zȧ-tĭv), *n.* the objective case, denoting the object of the verb or preposition.

ac-cu-sa-to-ry (ă-kū'zȧ-tō-rĭ), *adj.* pertaining to, or containing, a charge of wrongdoing. Also, **accusational.**

ac-cuse (ă-kūz), *v.t.* to charge with guilt or blame; to find fault with.

ac-cus-er (ă-kūz'ĕr), *n.* one who formally charges an offense against another.

ac-cus-tom (ă-kŭs'tŭm), *v.t.* to become familiar with by use; as, to *accustom* oneself to new conditions.

ac-cus-tomed (ă-kŭs'tŭmd), *p.adj.* frequent; usual; often practiced.

ace (ās), *n.* [*pl.* aces (-ĕz)], a unit; a card or die marked with a single spot; a very small quantity; an earned point, in tennis or similar games; an aviator who has brought down at least five enemy airplanes.

a-cer-bi-ty (ȧ-sûr'bĭ-tĭ), *n.* [*pl.* acerbities (-tĭz)], sourness, as of unripe fruit; sharpness; harshness or severity of temper or expression.

ac-et-an-i-lide (ăs"ĕt-ăn'ĭ-lid; -lĭd), *n.* a pungent white powder: one of the coal tar products, used as a medicine to prevent or reduce fever.

a-ce-tic ac-id (ȧ-sĕt'ĭk ăs'ĭd), a clear liquid, with a strong sour taste and peculiar sharp smell; the acid in vinegar.

a-cet-y-lene (ȧ-sĕt'ĭ-lēn), *n.* a colorless gas produced by mixing water with calcium carbide: the most brilliant illuminating gas known, used extensively for lighting purposes and in working iron and steel.

ache (āk), *n.* pain, more or less constant: *v.i.* to suffer, or be in pain, bodily or mental; as, my tooth *aches;* my heart *aches.*

a-chieve (ȧ-chēv'), *v.t.* to perform, carry out, accomplish; to gain or bring to a successful end by an effort: *v.i.* to bring about a desired result.

Syn. do, accomplish, effect, fulfil, execute, gain, win.

a-chieve-ment (ȧ-chēv'mĕnt), *n.* a successful action; a great or heroic deed; something accomplished or carried out by boldness or unusual ability.

A-chil-les (ȧ-kĭl'ēz), *n.* the greatest Greek hero of the Trojan War; hero of Homer's *Iliad.*

ach-ing (āk'ĭng), *p.adj.* enduring or causing pain; painful.—*adv.* **achingly.**

ach-ro-mat-ic (ăk"rō-măt'ĭk), *adj.* colorless: a term used in optical work to describe glass that transmits light without affecting its quality; as, the *achromatic* lens of a camera; in music, without accidentals or modulation.

ac-id (ăs'ĭd), *adj.* sour, and sharp or biting to the taste, as vinegar: *n.* a sour substance, usually liquid; that which combines with a base to form a salt.

a-cid-i-fy (ȧ-sĭd'ĭ-fī), *v.t.* and *v.i.* [*p.t.* and *p.p.* acidified, *p.pr.* acidifying], to make or become sour; to embitter.

a-cid-i-ty (ȧ-sĭd'ĭ-tĭ), *n.* sourness; tartness. Also, **acidness.**

ac-knowl-edge (ăk-nŏl'ĕj), *v.t.* [*p.t.* and *p.p.* acknowledged, *p.pr.* acknowledging], to admit or own to be true; to recognize; as, to *acknowledge* an acquaintance by bowing; to confess; to admit the receipt of; as, to *acknowledge* a letter.

Syn. avow, grant, allow, concede.
Ant. (see deny).

ac-knowl-edg-ment (ăk-nŏl'ĕj-mĕnt), *n.* the admission or recognition of a truth; confession; avowal; the expression of appreciation of a favor or benefit conferred; a receipt.

ac-me (ăk'mē), *n.* the top; the highest point; the crisis of a disease.

ac-o-lyte (ăk'ō-līt), *n.* an attendant; an assistant; the boy who waits upon or serves a priest at the altar during the Mass.

ac-o-nite (ăk'ō-nīt), *n.* a poisonous plant with blue or purple flowers, the monkshood being one of the family; a pain-soothing extract from the plant, especially used for fever or neuralgia.

a-corn (ā'kôrn; ā'kẽrn), *n.* the seed or fruit of the oak; a small nut with its base held in a natural woody cup.

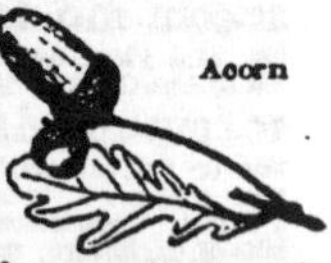
Acorn

a-cous-tic (ȧ-kōōs'tĭk; ȧ-kous'tĭk), *adj.* having to do with the sense of hearing; pertaining to the science of sound; as, we heard every word because of the unusual *acoustic* properties of the room. Also, **acoustical.**—*adv.* **acoustically.**

a-cous-tics (ȧ-kōōs'tĭks; ȧ-kous-tĭks), *n.* the science of sound; the study of the effects of sound upon the organs of hearing.

ac-quaint (ă-kwānt'), *v.t.* to notify; make familiar with; furnish information to; as, to *acquaint* oneself with facts.

Syn. enlighten, make aware, make known, communicate.

ac-quaint-ance (ă-kwān'tăns), *n.* personal knowledge of either persons or things; a person known to one, but with whom one is not very intimate. —*n.* **acquaintanceship.**

ac-quaint-ed (ă-kwān'tĕd), *p.adj.* having personal or mutual knowledge.

ac-qui-esce (ăk'wĭ-ĕs), *v.i.* to agree by not objecting; to quietly comply or submit; to assent by silence: followed usually by *in;* as, to *acquiesce* in a policy determined upon.—*adj.* **acquiescent.**—*adv.* **acquiescently.**

Syn. agree, accede, comply, consent.
Ant. (see protest).

ac-qui-es-cence (ăk"wĭ-ĕs'ĕns), *n.* the act of submitting; silent assent.

ac-quire (ă-kwīr'), *v.t.* to gain or obtain possession of, usually by one's own physical or mental exertions; as, to *acquire* a habit.

ac-quire-ment (ă-kwīr'mĕnt), *n.* the act of gaining, as knowledge, skill, etc.; attainment; that which is gained.

ac-qui-si-tion (ăk"wĭ-zĭsh'ŭn), *n.* the act of gaining possession; as, the *acquisition* of property; a material possession gained by any means.

ac-quit (ă-kwĭt'), *v.t.* [*p.t.* and *p.p.* acquitted, *p.pr.* acquitting], to release; set free; discharge, as a debt; to pro-

nounce not guilty; as, the prisoner was *acquitted*.
Syn. pardon, forgive, clear.
Ant. (see condemn, convict).

ac-quit-tal (ă-kwĭt'ăl), *n.* the act of setting free; the state of being set free; the judicial declaration of "not guilty."

ac-quit-tance (ă-kwĭt'ăns), *n.* a discharge or release from debt or other liability; a receipt in full, or a written statement freeing one from further payment.

a-cre (ā'kēr), *n.* the quantity of land containing 160 square rods, or 43,560 square feet; a field.

a-cre-age (ā'kēr-āj), *n.* the number of acres in a tract of land; the entire quantity of land in a tract.

ac-rid (ăk'rĭd), *adj.* sharp or bitter to the taste, as vinegar; pungent; irritating; stinging: *n.* an acrid or irritant poison.—*adv.* acridly.—*n.* acridness.

ac-ri-mo-ni-ous (ăk"rĭ-mō'nĭ-ŭs), *adj.* bitter; sarcastic; stinging: said of language or temper.—*adv.* acrimoniously.

ac-ri-mo-ny (ăk'rĭ-mō-nĭ), *n.* bitterness or severity of temper or speech. Also, acrimoniousness.
Syn. sharpness, tartness, sourness, harshness.
Ant. (see gentleness, courtesy).

ac-ro-bat (ăk'rō-băt), *n.* one who performs daring gymnastic feats, such as tumbling, vaulting, trapezing, etc.—*adj.* acrobatic.—*adv.* acrobatically.

a-crop-o-lis (ă-krŏp'ō-lĭs), *n.* [*pl.* acropolises (-ĕz); Gr. -leis (-līs)], the highest part or citadel of a Grecian city, usually the site of the original settlement; as, the most splendid production of Greek art, the Parthenon, is on the *acropolis* of Athens.

a-cross (ă-krŏs'), *adv.* and *prep.* from side to side; crosswise; from one side to another.

a-cros-tic (ă-krŏs'tĭk), *n.* a composition, usually in verse, in which one or more sets of letters, taken in order, form a motto, phrase, name, or word.

act (ăkt), *n.* a deed; that which is done; the process of doing; a decree, edict, or law; as, many *acts* were passed by the legislature; the judgment of a court; a formal writing; one of the principal divisions of a drama or play: *v.t.* to perform or play, as on the stage; personate; feign: *v.i.* to exert force or energy; to behave; to do; to perform on the stage.
Syn., n. action, achievement, exploit, feat, motion, work, effect.
Ant. (see suspension, cessation).

act-ing (ăk'tĭng), *p.adj.* operating; doing the duties of another, as those of an official; as, the *acting* chairman.

ac-tion (ăk'shŭn), *n.* the state of being in motion, as opposed to that of being at rest; the doing of something; the effect of one body or substance upon another: only when singular; something done; conduct; behavior: only when plural; a suit begun by one party against another in a court of law; the manner of a speaker, as his gestures, etc.; effective motion, as of machinery; a military or naval engagement.
Syn. deed, achievement, feat, exploit, accomplishment, battle, engagement, deportment.

ac-tion-a-ble (ăk'shŭn-ă-bl), *adj.* giving grounds for a lawsuit.

ac-tive (ăk'tĭv), *adj.* having or using the power or quality of motion or force; lively; busy; moving freely or quickly; in grammar, denoting the voice or form of the verb which represents the subject as a doer of something, and as exerting force on something.—*adv.* actively.
Syn. sprightly, alert, agile, nimble, brisk, quick, supple, prompt, vigilant, industrious.
Ant. (see lazy, passive).

ac-tiv-i-ty (ăk-tĭv'ĭ-tĭ), *n.* [*pl.* activities (-tĭz)], energy; quickness in doing; the quality of doing promptly; a mode of doing. Also, activeness.

ac-tor (ăk'tēr), *n.* a doer; one who takes the part of a character in a play; a theatrical or motion picture player.

ac-tress (ăk'trĕs), *n.* a woman who performs on the stage or before the camera.

ac-tu-al (ăk'tū-ăl), *adj.* existing in fact; real as opposed to merely possible; present.
Syn. positive, genuine, certain.
Ant. (see fictitious).

ac-tu-al-i-ty (ăk"tū-ăl'ĭ-tĭ), *n.* [*pl.* actualities (-tĭz)], reality; fact; that which is in full existence.

ac-tu-al-ly (ăk'tū-ăl-ĭ), *adv.* really; in truth; as a matter of fact; as, he *actually* came at last.

ac-tu-a-ry (ăk'tū-ā-rĭ), *n.* [*pl.* actuaries (-rĭz)], a registrar or clerk of a court; one who is skilled in computing life insurance, risks, premiums, etc.

ac-tu-ate (ăk'tū-āt), *v.t.* to move or incite to effort; as, men are *actuated* by various motives; to put into motion.

a-cu-men (ă-kū'mĕn), *n.* quickness of perception; penetration; discrimination; keenness of insight.
Syn. insight, keenness, sagacity, sharpness, cleverness.
Ant. (see bluntness, stupidity).

a-cute (ă-kūt), *adj.* sharp-pointed; mentally keen; clever; quick of perception; severe, as pain or symptoms attending a disease; high in pitch; shrill.—*adv.* acutely.
Syn. shrewd, intelligent, penetrating, piercing, keen.
Ant. (see blunt or dull).

a-cute-ness (ă-kūt'nĕs), *n.* the quality of being sharp or mentally alert.

ad-age (ăd'āj), *n.* an ancient proverb or pithy saying in current use; as, "a stitch in time saves nine."

a-da-gio (ă-dä'jō), *adj.* and *adv.* in music, slow; slowly; with grace: *n.* a piece of music in which the movement is slow.

Ad-am (ăd'ăm), *n.* in the Bible story of the creation, the first man.—Genesis ii.

ad-a-mant (ăd'ă-mănt), *n.* a real or imaginary stone of great hardness; any substance of extreme hardness, such as the diamond: *adj.* unyielding; hard.

ad-a-man-tine (ăd"ă-măn'tĭn), *adj.* made of a very hard substance; impenetrable.

Ad-am's ap-ple (ăd'ămz ăp'l), the lump or enlargement in front of the throat, most noticeable in males.

a-dapt (ă-dăpt'), *v.t.* to make suitable; to conform to; as, to *adapt* oneself to conditions; remodel or fit by alteration; as, to *adapt* a story for the stage.—*adj.* adaptable.
Syn. accommodate, suit, fit, conform.

a-dapt-a-bil-i-ty (ȧ-dăp″tȧ-bĭl′ĭ-tĭ), *n.* the quality of being able to conform to conditions.

ad-ap-ta-tion (ăd″ăp-tā′shŭn), *n.* the act of adjusting; the state of being adjusted or fitted; adjustment to circumstances.

add (ăd), *v.t.* to join; unite; sum up; increase; affix; to go on to say.
Syn. adjoin, annex, append, attach, extend.
Ant. (see deduct, reduce).

ad-den-dum (ă-dĕn′dŭm), *n.* [*pl.* addenda (-dȧ)], a thing to be joined to something; an appendix to a book.

ad-der (ăd′ẽr), *n.* a kind of snake; the popular name for the viper; a person or thing that sums up numbers.

ad-dict (ă-dĭkt′), *v.t.* to devote or give oneself up to: often in a bad sense; as, he is *addicted* to drink.

ad-di-tion (ă-dĭsh′ŭn), *n.* the act, process, or result of summing up numbers; the thing joined; the uniting of two or more numbers in one sum; a title placed after a name, denoting rank, as esquire; a dot placed at the side of a note to indicate the lengthening of the sound by one-half.
Syn. increase, accession, enlargement, extension, annex.
Ant. (see subtraction, separation).

ad-di-tion-al (ă-dĭsh′ŭn-ăl), *adj.* joined; extra; more.—*adv.* **additionally.**

ad-dle (ăd′l), *adj.* rotten: applied to eggs; muddled or confused: *v.t.* to make corrupt; to spoil: *v.i.* to become spoiled.

ad-dle-head-ed (ăd′l-hĕd′ĕd), *adj.* stupid; weak-brained; muddled. Also, **addle-pated.**

ad-dress (ă-drĕs′), *v.t.* to speak or write to; to direct, as a letter; consign or intrust to another; to pay court, as a lover; *n.* a speech delivered or written; manners and bearing; tact; cleverness; a person's place of residence.

ad-dress-ee (ă-drĕs″ē′), *n.* one to whom anything, as a letter or a package, is directed.

ad-dress-o-graph (ă-drĕs′ō-grȧf), *n.* a trade-mark name for a machine used to direct circulars, letters, etc.

ad-duce (ă-dūs′), *v.t.* to bring forward as a reason; to present, or offer proof or evidence in support of some statement; to cite; to quote.

ad-e-noid (ăd′ē-noid), *n.* a spongy growth in the passage leading from the nose to the throat, often causing difficulty in breathing: *adj.* in the form of a gland; of or relating to glands.

a-dept (ȧ-dĕpt′), *adj.* well skilled: *n.* one who is fully proficient or skilled in an art; an expert.—*n.* **adeptness.**

ad-e-qua-cy (ăd′ē-kwȧ-sĭ), *n.* sufficiency or suitability for a particular purpose.

ad-e-quate (ăd′ē-kwāt), *adj.* equal to requirement; sufficient enough.—*adv.* **adequately.**—*n.* **adequateness**
Syn. competent, suitable.
Ant. (see insufficient).

ad-here (ăd-hēr′), *v.i.* to stick fast as if glued; to become firmly attached.

ad-her-ence (ăd-hēr′ĕns), *n.* the act or state of holding fast to; unwavering attachment or devotion.

ad-her-ent (ăd-hēr′ĕnt), *adj.* sticking; clinging: *n.* one who holds fast to; a follower or supporter, as of a political party.

ad-he-sion (ăd-hē′zhŭn), *n.* the state or act of being stuck together, united, or attached; firmness in opinion; as, a man's *adhesion* to truth.
Syn. adherence, attachment, fidelity, devotion.
Ant. (see aloofness).

ad-he-sive (ăd-hē′sĭv), *adj.* holding fast; gummed for use; sticky; as, *adhesive* plaster.—*adv.* **adhesively.**—*n.* **adhesiveness.**

a-dieu (ȧ-dū′), *n.* [*pl.* adieus (ȧ-dūz′); adieux (ȧ-dū′)], a farewell; good wishes at parting: *interj.* good-by; farewell. [Fr.]

ad-ja-cen-cy (ă-jā′sĕn-sĭ), *n.* the state of being close to; nearness. Also, **adjacence.**

ad-ja-cent (ă-jā′sĕnt), *adj.* near; close; adjoining.
Syn. bordering, neighboring.
Ant. (see distant).

ad-jec-tive (ăj′ĕk-tĭv), *n.* a part of speech expressing quality or condition; a word used to qualify, limit, or define a noun.—*adv.* **adjectively.**

ad-join (ă-join′), *v.t.* to lie close together: *v.t.* to lie next to; as, the properties *adjoin.*

ad-join-ing (ă-join′ĭng), *p.adj.* being close to; joining to; as, *adjoining* houses.

ad-journ (ă-jûrn′), *v.t.* to put off to another day or time; as, they *adjourned* the meeting: *v.i.* to cease business for a time; as, the court *adjourned;* the legislature *adjourned.*
Syn. postpone, close, end, suspend.

ad-journ-ment (ă-jûrn′mĕnt), *n.* the act of putting off; the postponement of a meeting till another day, or time specified, or without day.

ad-judge (ă-jŭj′), *v.t.* to decide a dispute according to law; to award; to assign; to determine; bestow; to sentence; to condemn.

ad-judged (ă-jŭjd′), *p.adj.* determined by the court's decree or sentence.

ad-ju-di-cate (ă-jōō′dĭ-kāt), *v.t.* to hear, or try, and decide a case in court.—*n.* **adjudicator.**

ad-ju-di-ca-tion (ă-jōō″dĭ-kā′shŭn), *n.* the act of deciding legally, or by a court; a judicial decision.

ad-junct (ăj′ŭnkt), *n.* something added to another thing, but not a necessary part of it.
Syn. addition, appendage.

ad-junc-tive (ă-jŭnk′tĭv), *adj.* having the quality of joining or uniting.

ad-ju-ra-tion (ăj″ōō-rā′shŭn), *n.* the solemn charging on oath; the form of an oath.

ad-jure (ă-jōōr′), *v.t.* to command on oath under pain of a penalty; to charge solemnly; to entreat earnestly.

ad-just (ă-jŭst′), *v.t.* to fit, or make exact; to make similar; to make accurate; to settle or bring to a satisfactory state; as, to *adjust* accounts.—*adj.* **adjustable.**
Syn. set right, fit, put in order.

ad-just-er (ă-jŭs′tẽr), *n.* one who regulates, sets right, or makes to fit; one who settles the amount of claims in cases of losses by fire, as an insurance agent.

ad-just-ment (ă-jŭst′mĕnt), *n.* the act of regulating or setting right; settlement or arrangement.

ad-ju-tan-cy (ăj'o͞o-tăn-sĭ), *n.* the office of an army officer who assists a colonel or other high officer.

ad-ju-tant (ăj'o͞o-tănt), *n.* a helper; a regimental staff-officer who assists the commanding officer; a large stork, common in India.

Adjutant

ad-ju-tant gen-er-al (ăj'o͞o-tănt jĕn'ẽr-ăl), [*pl* adjutants general], the chief staff-officer of an army, through whom are received all orders, etc., issued by the commanding general.

ad-min-is-ter (ăd-mĭn'ĭs-tẽr), *v.t.* to manage as chief agent or minister, as a king, president, or judge; direct the application of the laws; dispense; as, to *administer* justice or relief; to cause to be taken, as medicine; to give, as an oath or a sacrament; to settle a deceased person's estate.

ad-min-is-tra-tion (ăd-mĭn"ĭs-trā'shŭn), *n.* official part of a government or the part which enforces or carries out the laws; the ministry or any body of men entrusted with executive powers; the act of managing, dispensing, or giving, as government, justice, medicine, a sacrament, or a deceased person's estate.

ad-min-is-tra-tive (ăd-mĭn'ĭs-trā-tĭv), *adj.* pertaining to the management of affairs or to government; executive.

ad-min-is-tra-tor (ăd-mĭn'ĭs-trā"tẽr), *n.* one who manages, directs, or governs affairs; one who settles the estate of a person dying without making a will.

ad-min-is-tra-trix (ăd-mĭn"ĭs-trā'trĭks), *n.* [*pl.* administratrices (-trā-trī'sēz)], a woman appointed by law to settle a deceased person's estate.

ad-mi-ra-ble (ăd'mĭ-rȧ-bl), *adj.* worthy of extreme approval; excellent.—*adv.* **admirably.**

Syn. striking, surprising, wonderful, astonishing.

Ant. (see detestable).

ad-mi-ral (ăd'mĭ-răl), *n.* the chief commander of a fleet; a naval officer of the highest rank.

ad-mi-ral-ty (ăd'mĭ-răl-tĭ), *n.* [*pl.* admiralties (-tĭz)], the department of the English government having authority over naval affairs; the building in which British naval affairs are transacted; the office of the chief commander of a fleet.

ad-mi-ra-tion (ăd"mĭ-rā'shŭn), *n.* wonder mingled with approval excited by beauty or excellence.

ad-mire (ăd-mīr'), *v.t.* to regard with strong approval or pleasure.—*n.* **admirer.**

ad-mis-si-ble (ăd-mĭs'ĭ-bl), *adj.* worthy of being allowed to enter; allowable.—*adv.* **admissibly.**

ad-mis-sion (ăd-mĭsh'ŭn), *n.* the power or permission to enter; admittance; acknowledgment that something is true; as, he made full *admission* of his guilt.

ad-mit (ăd-mĭt'), *v.t.* [*p.t.* and *p.p.* admitted, *p.pr.* admitting], to permit to enter; allow in argument; to receive.—*adj.* **admittable.**

Syn. allow, permit, suffer, tolerate.

Ant. (see deny).

ad-mit-tance (ăd-mĭt'ăns), *n.* the power or permission to enter; actual entrance. Also, **admission.**

ad-mix (ăd-mĭks'), *v.t.* to mix, or combine, with something else.

ad-mix-ture (ăd-mĭks'tŭr), *n.* that which is mixed; a compound made by mixing two or more ingredients.

ad-mon-ish (ăd-mŏn'ĭsh), *v.t.* to reprove gently; to warn; to instruct; to direct; to guide; to caution.

ad-mo-ni-tion (ăd"mō-nĭsh'ŭn), *n.* friendly reproof or warning.

ad-mon-i-to-ry (ăd-mŏn'ĭ-tō-rĭ), *adj.* giving reproof or warning.

a-do (ȧ-do͞o'), *n.* unnecessary bustle; fuss; haste; trouble; as, much *ado* about nothing.

a-do-be (ȧ-dō'bē), *n.* unburnt brick dried in the sun, used for building in Central America and Mexico.

ad-o-les-cence (ăd"ō-lĕs'ĕns), *n.* the period during which the human body attains its full growth and powers; youth.

ad-o-les-cent (ăd"ō-lĕs'ĕnt), *adj.* growing up; passing from childhood to manhood or womanhood; youthful.

a-dopt (ȧ-dŏpt'), *v.t.* to choose or take to be one's own, as a child, an opinion, or a course of action.—*p.adj.* **adopted.**—*n.* **adopter.**

a-dop-tion (ȧ-dŏp'shŭn), *n.* the act of taking as one's own; the act of accepting and putting into use; as, the *adoption* of reformed spelling.

a-dor-a-ble (ȧ-dōr'ȧ-bl), *adj.* worthy of worship or the utmost love.—*adv.* **adorably.**

ad-o-ra-tion (ăd'ō-rā'shŭn), *n.* the act of worship; profound reverence; the utmost love.

a-dore (ȧ-dōr'), *v.t.* to pay divine honors to; to honor highly; to love intensely; to admire greatly: *v.i.* to offer worship.—*p.adj.* **adoring.**—*n.* **adorer.**

a-dorn (ȧ-dôrn'), *v.t.* to beautify; to dignify; to ornament; to decorate; to bedeck.

a-dorn-ment (ȧ-dôrn'mĕnt), *n.* ornament; decoration.

a-drift (ȧ-drĭft'), *adj.* and *adv.* floating at random; at the mercy of the wind; drifting.

a-droit (ȧ-droit'), *adj.* skilful; expert; clever; cunning; ready in invention.—*adv.* **adroitly.**

a-droit-ness (ȧ-droit'nĕs), *n.* the quality of being skilful.

ad-u-la-tion (ăd"ū-lā'shŭn), *n.* excessive or unmerited praise; flattery.

ad-u-la-to-ry (ăd'ū-lȧ-tō-rĭ), *adj.* excessively flattering; praising extravagantly.

a-dult (ȧ-dŭlt'), *adj.* grown up to full age, size, and strength: *n.* a man or a woman.

a-dul-ter-ate (ȧ-dŭl'tẽr-āt), *v.t.* to corrupt, debase, or make impure by mixing in a foreign or poorer substance; as, to *adulterate* milk by pouring water into it.—*n.* **adulterator.**

a-dul-ter-a-tion (ȧ-dŭl"tẽr-ā'shŭn), *n.* the substitution or placing of something of an inferior quality in a mixture and passing it for the genuine article.

a-dul-ter-y (ȧ-dŭl'tẽr-ĭ), *n.* [*pl.* **adulteries** (-ĭz)], the act of breaking or violating the marriage vow; unchastity.

ad va-lo-rem (ăd vȧ-lō'rĕm), according to value: **ad valorem duty**, an import duty or charge on goods at a certain rate per cent based on their actual value at the port of shipment. [Lat.]

ad-vance (ăd-văns'), *v.t.* to go forward: *v.t.* to cause to go forward; to propose; as, to *advance* an opinion; to increase; as, to *advance* prices; to further; as, to *advance* a cause; to make a payment of beforehand: *n.* a moving forward; improvement; an addition to or rise in value; an approach, as toward acquaintance: usually in plural; a loan; payment beforehand: *adj.* being or occurring before; as, an *advance* sale of tickets; an *advance* agent.

ad-vance-ment (ăd-văns'mĕnt), *n.* furtherance; progress; promotion.

ad-van-tage (ăd-văn'tāj), *n.* a state of advance or forwardness; superior position; a benefit; anything that aids or assists; as, he had the *advantage* of a good education.

ad-van-ta-geous (ăd"văn-tā'jŭs), *adj.* beneficial; profitable; favorable.—*adv.* **advantageously.**

ad-vent (ăd'vĕnt), *n.* a coming or arrival; as, the *advent* of a visitor; the *advent* of winter.—**Advent**, the period of the year including the four Sundays before Christmas, which prepares for the coming of Jesus Christ.

Ad-vent-ism (ăd'vĕn-tĭzm), *n.* the doctrine that Christ is coming a second time to establish a personal kingdom on earth.

Ad-vent-ist (ăd'vĕn-tĭst), *n.* one who believes in the second coming of Christ.

ad-ven-ti-tious (ăd"vĕn-tĭsh'ŭs), *adj.* happening by chance; casual; accidental; produced out of normal and regular order.—*adv.* **adventitiously.**

ad-ven-ture (ăd-vĕn'tūr), *n.* a bold undertaking; a daring feat; the encountering of risks; a remarkable experience; the taking part in an uncertain enterprise.

ad-ven-tur-er (ăd-vĕn'tūr-ẽr), *n.* one who engages in new and dangerous enterprises; a soldier of fortune; one who seeks distinction by false show or pretense.

ad-ven-tur-ess (ăd-vĕn'tūr-ĕs), *n.* a woman who seeks distinction by false show or pretense.

ad-ven-tur-ous (ăd-vĕn'tūr-ŭs), *adj.* inclined to incur danger; full of risk; daring; requiring courage; venturesome. Also, **adventuresome.**—*adv.* **adventurously.**

ad-verb (ăd'vûrb), *n.* a word used to modify a verb, an adjective, or another adverb.

ad-ver-bi-al (ăd-vûr'bĭ-ăl), *adj.* modifying a verb, adjective, or adverb.—*adv.* **adverbially.**

ad-ver-sa-ry (ăd'vẽr-să-rĭ), *n.* [*pl.* **adversaries** (-ĭz)], an enemy; foe; opponent; antagonist.

ad-ver-sa-tive (ăd-vûr'sȧ-tĭv), *adj.* expressing opposition; as, an *adversative* conjunction is one that connects contrasting words or ideas.

ad-verse (ăd'vẽrs), *adj.* opposed to; opposite; unfavorable; contrary; hostile; unfortunate; as, *adverse* circumstances.—*adv.* **adversely.**

ad-ver-si-ty (ăd-vûr'sĭ-tĭ), *n.* the reverse or opposite of prosperity; misery; distress or unhappiness.

ad-vert (ăd-vûrt'), *v.i.* to turn one's attention to; to refer to incidentally; to allude to; as, to *advert* to what we were saying a while ago.

ad-vert-ence (ăd-vûr'tĕns), *n.* attention; notice; heed.

ad-vert-ent (ăd-vûr'tĕnt), *adj.* attentive; heedful.

ad-ver-tise (ăd'vẽr-tīz"; ăd"vẽr-tīz'), *v.t.* to give notice to; to turn the attention of others to; announce; inform; publish: *v.i.* to give notice, as in a newspaper, etc. Also, **advertize.**—*n.* **advertiser.**

ad-ver-tise-ment (ăd-vûr'tĭz-mĕnt; ăd"vẽr-tīz'mĕnt), *n.* a notice in a public print; an announcement; a bringing into public notice.

ad-vice (ăd-vīs'), *n.* an opinion given that is worthy to be followed; counsel; as, I have come to you for *advice* concerning my choice of a college; information given by letter; as, *advices* from Europe indicate a desire for peace.

ad-vis-a-bil-i-ty (ăd-vīz"ȧ-bĭl'ĭ-tĭ), *n.* the quality of being in accordance with good judgment; desirability. Also, **advisableness.**

ad-vis-a-ble (ăd-vīz'ȧ-bl), *adj.* proper to be done; in accordance with good judgment; prudent; expedient or suitable.—*adv.* **advisably.**

ad-vise (ăd-vīz'), *v.t.* to offer an opinion; to counsel; inform; to recommend as wise, prudent, etc., to suggest as a proper course of action.—*n.* **adviser.**

ad-vis-ed-ly (ăd-vīz'ĕd-lĭ), *adv.* with caution; purposely; not hastily.

ad-vise-ment (ăd-vīz'mĕnt), *n.* consideration; as, I will take the matter under *advisement.*

ad-vi-so-ry (ăd-vī'sō-rĭ), *adj.* having power to suggest or to counsel; as, an *advisory* committee.

ad-vo-ca-cy (ăd-vŏ'kȧ-sĭ), *n.* the act of pleading for, supporting, or recommending.

ad-vo-cate (ăd'vō-kāt), *n.* one called to the aid of another; one who pleads the cause of another in a court of law; a pleader in favor of any person or thing; as, an *advocate* of peace.

adz (ădz), *n.* a cutting tool, somewhat like an ax, having a curved blade at right angles to the handle, and used for dressing timber. Also, **adze.**

æ-dile (ē'dīl), *n.* Roman official who had charge of public and private buildings, public games, etc. Also, **edile.**

æ-gis (ē'jĭs), *n.* any influence or power which protects; originally, in Greek myth, the storm-cloud around the thunderbolt, the especial weapon of Zeus; in art, it is usually shown as a shield bordered with serpents, carried by Athena. Also, **egis.**

Æ-o-li-an (ē-ō'lĭ-ăn), *adj.* pertaining to the winds: from Æolus, the god of the winds: **æolian harp**, an instrument, the strings of which give out musical sounds when the wind blows through them. Also, **eolian.**

æ-on (ē'ŏn), *n.* a period of time too long to measure; an age. Also, **eon.**

a-ër-ate (ā'ẽr-āt), *v.t.* to charge with gas, as air or carbon dioxide; to expose to the action of air; to treat with oxygen, as the blood.

a-ër-at-ed bread (ā'ĕr-āt"ed brĕd), bread raised by charging the dough with gas, instead of using yeast or baking powder.

a-ë-ri-al (ā-ē'rĭ-ăl), *adj.* relating to the air; existing or happening in the air; airy; hence, high; lofty; as, *aërial* flight.

a-er-ie (ē'rĭ, or ā'ĕr-ĭ), *n.* an eagle's nest; a brood of eagles or hawks. Also, **aery, eyrie, eyry.**

a-ër-i-form (ā'ĕr-ĭ-fôrm), *adj.* having the form of air; gaseous.

a-ër-i-fy (ā'ĕr-ĭ-fī), *v.t.* [*p.t.* and *p.p.* aërified, *p.pr.* aërifying], to combine with air; to fill with air.

a-ër-o-drome (ā'ĕr-ō-drōm"), *n.* a building where flying machines are stored and tested; a ground or field used for airplane instruction and practice. Also, **airdrome.**

a-ër-o-foil (ā'ĕr-ō-foil), *n.* a thin winglike structure, flat or curved, designed to support bodies by its reaction on the air through which it moves.

a-ër-o-gram (ā'ĕr-ō-grăm), *n.* a wireless telegraph message.

a-ër-o-gun (ā'ĕr-ō-gŭn"), *n.* a gun for use against aëroplanes and airships.

a-ër-o-lite (ā'ĕr-ō-līt"), *n.* a meteorite or shooting star. Also, **aërolith.**

a-ër-ol-o-gy (ā"ĕr-ŏl'ō-jĭ), *n.* the science of the air; atmospheric laws and conditions.

a-ër-o-me-chan-ic (ā"ĕr-o-mē-kăn'-ĭk), *n.* one who is expertly trained in the care, adjustment, and repair of flying machines.—*adj.* **aëromechanical.**

a-ër-om-e-ter (ā"ĕr-ŏm'ē-tēr), *n.* an instrument for weighing the air.

a-ër-o-naut (ā'ĕr-ō-nôt), *n.* an aërial navigator; an aviator or balloonist.

a-ër-o-nau-tic (ā"ĕr-ō-nô'tĭk), *adj.* relating to the science or art of flying. Also, **aëronautical.**

a-ër-o-nau-tics (ā"ĕr-ō-nô'tĭks), *n.* aërial navigation; the science or art of traveling in the air.

a-ër-o-plane (ā'ĕr-ō-plān"), *n.* an aircraft or flying machine, kept aloft by the reaction of motor-propelled planes upon the air. Also, **airplane.**

a-ër-o-plan-ist (ā'ĕr-ō-plān"ĭst), *n.* the operator of an aëroplane.

a-ër-o-stat (ā'ĕr-ō-stăt), *n.* a balloon; a flying machine.

a-ër-o-stat-ics (ā"ĕr-ō-stăt'ĭks), *n.* the branch of science that deals with the properties of air and of gases not in motion, and with the balance between them: used in connection with the operation of gas balloons or lighter-than-air flying machines.

a-ër-o-sta-tion (ā"ĕr-ō-stā'shŭn), *n.* that part of the science of aërial navigation that deals with lighter-than-air flying machines, or aircraft unprovided with motive power.

æs-thet-ic (ĕs-thĕt'ĭk), *adj.* pertaining to beauty; appreciating the beautiful. Also, **esthetic.**—*adv.* **esthetically, æsthetically.**

æs-thet-ics (ĕs-thĕt'ĭks), *n.* the science or theory of the beautiful in nature or art. Also, **esthetics.**

a-far (*á*-fär), *adv.* at, to, or from a distance; as, the sound came from *afar*.

af-fa-bil-i-ty (ăf"*á*-bĭl'ĭ-tĭ), *n.* the quality of being friendly or courteous.

af-fa-ble (ăf'*á*-bl), *adj.* easy of approach; courteous in manner; kind.—*adv.* **affably.**—*n.* **affableness.**

af-fair (ă-fâr'), *n.* that which is done, or is to be done; business of any kind: often in plural.

af-fect (ă-fĕkt'), *v.t.* to produce an effect upon; as, heat *affects* the body; to influence; to be fond of; to frequent; to pretend.

af-fec-ta-tion (ăf"ĕk-tā'shŭn), *n.* the assuming of a manner which is not one's own; pretense; display.

af-fect-ed (ă-fĕk'tĕd), *p.adj.* acted upon or influenced; attacked, as by disease; not natural; as, *affected* manners.—*adv.* **affectedly.**

af-fect-ing (ă-fĕk'tĭng), *p.adj.* having power to excite the emotions; pathetic.—*adv.* **affectingly.**

af-fec-tion (ă-fĕk'shŭn), *n.* the state of having the feelings touched or excited; inclination; attachment; fondness; disease.

Syn. love, attraction, liking.

Ant. (see aversion).

af-fec-tion-ate (ă-fĕk'shŭn-āt), *adj.* having or expressing love; kind; fond.—*adv.* **affectionately.**

af-fi-ance (ă-fī'ăns), *n.* trust; faith; a marriage-contract: *v.t.* to betroth, or bind by promise of marriage.

af-fi-da-vit (ăf"ĭ-dā'vĭt), *n.* a sworn statement in writing.

af-fil-i-ate (ă-fĭl'ĭ-āt), *v.t.* to adopt; to receive into a family as a son or daughter; to receive into a society or club; to join; as, to *affiliate* oneself with a certain set of people: *v.i.* to be intimately connected or associated: followed by *with*; as, he *affiliated* with a number of learned societies. —*n.* **affiliation.**

af-fin-i-ty (ă-fĭn'ĭ-tĭ), *n.* [*pl.* affinities (-tĭz)], nearness of kin; relationship by marriage, in distinction to relationship by blood; a natural liking for a person; physical or chemical attraction; a relationship between species or groups depending on likeness of structure.

af-firm (ă-fûrm'), *v.t.* to assert strongly: *v.i.* to confirm, as a judgment, decree, or order, in court; to tell with confidence.

af-fir-ma-tion (ăf"ĕr-mā'shŭn), *n.* the act of asserting or declaring anything to be true; a solemn statement or declaration in court that he will tell the truth, by one opposed to taking an oath.

af-firm-a-tive (ă-fûr'mȧ-tĭv), *n.* that which declares; a statement which asserts that a fact is so: *adj.* positive; confident.

af-fix (ă-fĭks'), *v.t.* to attach; to fasten to: *n.* (ăf'ĭks), a letter or syllable added to the beginning or end of a word; a suffix or prefix.

af-flict (ă-flĭkt'), *v.t.* to cause prolonged pain to body or mind; to distress; to cast down; to trouble grievously.

af-flic-tion (ă-flĭk'shŭn), *n.* prolonged pain of body or mind; great trouble.

Syn. pain, calamity, misfortune, adversity, distress.

af-flu-ence (ăf'lōō-ĕns), *n.* an abundant supply, as of thoughts, words, riches; wealth.

af-flu-ent (ăf'lōō-ĕnt), *n.* a stream or river that flows into another: *adj.* having abundance; wealthy; flowing freely.—*adv.* **affluently.**

af-ford (ă-fōrd'), *v.t.* to supply; produce; yield; to be able to bear the expense of.

af-fray (ă-frā'), *n.* the fighting of two or more persons in a public place to the terror of others; a noisy quarrel.

af-fright (ă-frīt'), *v.t.* to frighten; terrify; alarm; confuse.

af-front (ă-frŭnt'), *v.t.* to confront; oppose face to face; insult designedly or intentionally.
Syn. annoy, displease, insult, irritate, offend, provoke.
Ant. (see please, conciliate).

af-ghan (ăf'găn), *n.* a crocheted or knitted soft wool blanket or carriage robe. —**Afghan,** a native of Afghanistan: *adj.* relating to Afghanistan.

a-field (*ȧ*-fēld'), *adv.* to, in, or on, the field; astray; out of the way.

a-fire (*ȧ*-fīr'), *adj.* and *adv.* on fire; as, a house *afire;* to set *afire.*

a-flame (*ȧ*-flām'), *adj.* and *adv.* on fire; ablaze; as, *aflame* with patriotism.

a-float (*ȧ*-flōt'), *adj.* and *adv.* borne on the water; on shipboard; in circulation; unfixed; adrift; moving.

a-foot (*ȧ*-fŏŏt'), *adv.* on foot; as, they traveled *afoot;* astir; stirring; about.

a-foul (*ȧ*-foul'), *adj.* and *adv.* in entanglement or collision; as, to fall *afoul* of an obstacle.

a-fraid (*ȧ*-frād'), *adj.* frightened; filled with fear.

af-reet (ăf'rēt; *ȧ*-frēt'), *n.* a powerful and evil spirit, demon, or monstrous giant, in Arabian legends. Also, **afrit.**

a-fresh (*ȧ*-frĕsh'), *adv.* again; anew; newly; over again.

Af-ri-can (ăf'rĭ-kăn), *n.* a native of Africa: *adj.* relating to Africa.

aft (ȧft), *adj.* and *adv.* a nautical term, meaning towards the stern or back part; as, the *aft* part of the ship; the sailor went *aft.*

aft-er (ȧf'tẽr), *adj.* next; subsequent; later; as, *after*-days; behind in place; as, the *after* part of a ship: *adv.* behind; subsequently in time or place: *prep.* in succession to; later in time; in imitation of; according to; next in rank or excellence; in pursuit of.

aft-er-clap (ȧf'tẽr-klăp"), *n.* something happening after an affair is supposed to be at an end.

aft-er-damp (ȧf'tẽr-dămp"), *n.* the suffocating gas found in coal mines after an explosion of fire-damp or marsh gas: called also *choke-damp.*

aft-er-glow (ȧf'tẽr-glō"), *n.* the reflection left in the western sky after sunset.

aft-er-math (ȧf'tẽr-măth), *n.* a second mowing in a season; that which follows any condition, circumstance, or emotion; as the *aftermath* of love.

aft-er-noon (ȧf"tẽr-nōōn'), *n.* the part of the day between noon and evening.

aft-er-thought (ȧf'tẽr-thôt"), *n.* reflection begun after an act is finished; an idea that comes too late.

aft-er-wards (ȧf'tẽr-wẽrdz), *adv.* at a later time; subsequently. Also, **afterward.**

a-gain (*ȧ*-gĕn'), *adv.* a second time; once more; in return; further; anew; on the other hand; besides; repeatedly; as, *again* and *again.*

a-gainst (*ȧ*-gĕnst'), *prep.* opposite to; in opposition to; contrary to one's inclinations or wishes.

a-gape (*ȧ*-găp'; *ȧ*-gāp'), *adj.* and *adv.* gaping; with the mouth wide open in a state of expectation, astonishment, or eager attention.

ag-ate (ăg'ăt), *n.* a precious stone, with colors in stripes, clouds, etc.; a boy's playing marble; a small size of type.

age (āj), *n.* a particular period of time in life or in history; the length of time already lived; time: *v.i.* and *v.t.* to grow old; to make old.

ag-ed (āj'ĕd; āj'd), *p.adj.* old; far on in years; having lived long.

a-gen-cy (ā'jĕn-sĭ), *n.* operation; action; the business of one acting for another; a place where business is done for another person or firm.

a-gent (ā'jĕnt), *n.* one who acts, especially for another; an active power or cause.
Syn. actor, doer, factor, operator, performer, instrument.
Ant. (see principal, chief).

ag-glom-er-ate (ă-glŏm'ẽr-āt), *v.t.* to gather into a cluster or heap; accumulate: *adj.* (ă-glŏm'ẽr-āt), gathered into a heap or cluster: *n.* a collection or heap of things of different kinds.

ag-glom-er-a-tion (ă-glŏm"ẽr-ā'shŭn), *n.* a confused collection or heap of things.

ag-glu-ti-nate (ă-glōō'tĭ-nāt), *v.t.* to unite, as by glue: *adj.* glued together; adhering.

ag-gran-dize (ăg'răn-dīz), *v.t.* to make greater in power, rank, or riches; enlarge; elevate; extend.

ag-gran-dize-ment (ă-grăn'dĭz-mĕnt), *n.* advancement; increase in power, honor, size.

ag-gra-vate (ăg'r*ȧ*-vāt), *v.t.* to add to a burden; to make heavier or worse; to increase; to trouble or annoy.—*n.* **aggravation.**

ag-gra-vat-ing (ăg'r*ȧ*-vāt"ĭng), *p.adj.* making worse or more annoying.—*adv.* **aggravatingly.**

ag-gre-gate (ăg'rē-gāt), *v.t.* to collect or bring together; to amount to; as, his debts *aggregated* fifty dollars; gather into a mass or body; accumulate: *n.* (ăg'rē-gāt), total; as, the *aggregate* of his debts; the entire number; mass; a mass formed by the union of similar particles: *adj.* formed into a mass or total; as, the *aggregate* amount.

ag-gre-ga-tion (ăg"rē-gā'shŭn), *n.* a collection gathered into one whole or mass.

ag-gres-sion (ă-grĕsh'ŭn), *n.* unprovoked attack or assault; an act of unfriendliness or offense, as an unlawful entering upon another's rights or territory.

ag-gres-sive (ă-grĕs'ĭv), *adj.* moving forward with vigor; unjustly attacking.—*adv.* **aggressively.**—*n.* **aggressiveness.**

ag-gres-sor (ă-grĕs'ẽr), *n.* one who attacks or injures another.

ag-grieve (ă-grēv'), *v.t.* to bear heavily upon; to oppress; to cause sorrow to; to afflict.

a-ghast (*ȧ*-gȧst'), *adj.* struck with sudden surprise, horror, or terror.

ag-ile (ăj'ĭl), *adj.* quick-moving; brisk; active; nimble: said of the mind as well as the body.

a-gil-i-ty (ȧ-jĭl'ĭ-tĭ), *n.* nimbleness; quickness; briskness.

ag-i-o (ăj'ĭ-ō; ā'jĭ-ō), *n.* [*pl.* agios (-ōz)], the premium on money or foreign bills of exchange; discount; loosely, money changing.

ag-i-tate (ăj'ĭ-tāt), *v.t.* to stir violently; discuss; excite; disturb; keep constantly before the public.

ag-i-ta-tion (ăj'ĭ-tā'shŭn), *n.* the act of exciting or arousing; excitement; open, active discussion; violent motion or emotion.

ag-i-ta-tor (ăj'ĭ-tā"tẽr), *n.* one who starts or keeps up a political or other excitement; an implement for stirring.

a-glow (ȧ-glō'), *adj.* and *adv.* in a glow; glowing; flushed with pleasure or excitement; as, her cheeks were all *aglow*.

ag-no-men (ăg-nō'mĕn), *n.* an additional expression or name applied to a person; as, Washington received the *agnomen*, Father of his Country.

ag-nos-tic (ăg-nŏs'tĭk), *n.* one who denies that man knows the final or ultimate nature of things; one who neither affirms nor denies the existence of God: *adj.* relating to those who deny all knowledge of God or to their teachings; expressing ignorance.

ag-nos-ti-cism (ăg-nŏs'tĭ-sĭzm), *n.* the belief or doctrine that God and the essential nature of things are unknowable or at least unknown.

a-go (ȧ-gō'), *adj.* gone; past; used always after the noun; as, a thousand years *ago*: *adv.* in past time; as, long *ago*.

a-gog (ȧ-gŏg'), *adj.* and *adv.* in a state of eager desire; highly excited by eagerness or curiosity; astir; alive with interest; as, the village was all *agog*.

ag-o-nize (ăg'ō-nīz), *v.i.* to suffer extreme pain; to make great effort of any kind: *v.t.* to cause to suffer greatly.

ag-o-niz-ing (ăg'ō-nīz'ĭng), *p.adj.* full of anguish; torturing.—*adv.* **agonizingly.**

ag-o-ny (ăg'ō-nĭ), *n.* [*pl.* agonies (-nĭz)], intense suffering; extreme mental or physical pain; death struggle.

a-gra-ri-an (ȧ-grā'rĭ-ăn), *adj.* relating to land, or to the right or manner f holding real estate; growing wild in the fields: *n.* one who is in favor of a redistribution of public lands.

a-gra-ri-an-ism (ȧ-grā'rĭ-ăn-ĭzm), *n.* the principle of a uniform or equal division of public land; agitation with respect to land or real estate holding.

a-gree (ȧ-grē'), *v.i.* to harmonize physically, mentally, or morally; to yield assent; consent; accede; to accord; to come to one opinion; to be similar; match; to be suitable; as, the same food does not *agree* with everybody; settle; arrange.

a-gree-a-bil-i-ty (ȧ-grē"ȧ-bĭl'ĭ-tĭ), *n.* the quality of giving pleasure; easiness of disposition. Also, **agreeableness.**

a-gree-a-ble (ȧ-grē'ȧ-bl), *adj.* pleasing to the mind or senses; comfortable; suitable.

Syn. pleasant, pleasing, charming.
Ant. (see disagreeable).

a-gree-a-bly (ȧ-grē'ȧ-blĭ), *adv.* suitably; pleasantly.

a-gree-ment (ȧ-grē'mĕnt), *n.* harmony of opinions or feelings; correspondence of one word with another in gender, number, case, or person; a compact; a contract; mutual understanding.

ag-ri-cul-tur-al (ăg"rĭ-kŭl'tūr-ăl), *adj.* pertaining to the cultivation of land.

ag-ri-cul-ture (ăg'rĭ-kŭl"tūr), *n.* the science and art of cultivating fields by use of the plow, etc.; tillage; farming.

ag-ri-cul-tur-ist (ăg"rĭ-kŭl'tūr-ĭst), *n.* one engaged in tillage; a farmer.

a-ground (ȧ-ground'), *adj.* and *adv.* on the ground; in the situation of a ship whose keel touches the bottom; stranded; opposite to *afloat;* hence, brought to a stop by lack of something.

a-gue (ā'gū), *n.* a malarial fever occurring at regular intervals and attended by chills, fever, and sweating; a chill, or state of shaking as with cold.

ah (ä), *interj.* an exclamation expressive of sudden emotion, as contempt, pity, triumph.

a-ha (ȧ-hä'), *interj.* an exclamation expressive of triumph, satisfaction, surprise, or contempt.

a-head (ȧ-hĕd'), *adv.* to or in the front; forward; onward.

a-hem (ȧ-hĕm'), *interj.* an utterance, clearing of the throat, or slight cough to attract attention.

a-hoy (ȧ-hoi'), *interj.* a term used in hailing a vessel; as, Ship *ahoy!*

aid (ād), *v.t.* to assist; support: *n.* help; assistance; a person or thing that helps.

aid-de-camp (ād'dē-kămp'; ăd'dē-kän'), *n.* [*pl.* aides-de-camp], an officer who assists a general; called also an *aide*. Also, **aide-de-camp.**

ai-grette (ā-grĕt'; ā'grĕt), *n.* the small white heron; a plume arranged in imitation of the feathers of the heron, worn on helmets and as an article of woman's headdress. Also, **aigret, egret.**

ail (āl), *v.t.* [*p.t.* and *p.p.* ailed, *p.pr.* ailing], to give or cause pain to; as, something *ails* the child: *v.i.* to feel pain; be afflicted with pain.

ai-le-ron (ā'lĕ-rŏn), *n.* a small hinged wing tip on an airplane, operated by the pilot, for preserving or destroying the horizontal balance of the machine.

ail-ment (āl'mĕnt), *n.* a slight disorder or disease of the body or mind; sickness; illness; indisposition.

aim (ām), *v.i.* [*p.t.* and *p.p.* aimed, *p.pr.* aiming], to endeavor; to point a weapon at something: *v.t.* to point or direct (a weapon) at so as to hit; to direct against; as, to *aim* a remark at any one: *n.* a purpose; an endeavor; target.

Syn., *n.* mark, object, design.

aim-less (ām'lĕs), *adj.* without definite intention; purposeless.—*adv.* **aimlessly.**—*n.* **aimlessness.**

air (âr), *v.t.* to expose to the air; dry thoroughly, as clothes; to display; bring into public notice; as, to *air* one's views: *n.* the fluid which we breathe; the atmosphere; external manner; behavior; in music, a melody: *pl.* affected manners.

air brake (âr' brāk), a railway brake operated by compressed air.

air cas-tle (âr' kȧs'l), a day dream; a reverie.

air cham-ber (âr' chām'bẽr), a compartment filled with air; as, the *air chamber* of a lifeboat.

air-craft (âr'kráft), *n.* [*pl.* aircraft], any form of craft or machine for flying or sailing through the air, as an airplane, balloon, etc.

air-drome (âr'drōm), *n.* an aviation field; a building where airplanes are stored. Also, **aërodrome.**

air gas (âr găs), an illuminating gas made from air charged with the vapor of petroleum, naphtha, etc.

air gun (âr gŭn), a gun from which the projectile is expelled by compressed air.

air hole (âr' hōl), a local region in the atmosphere having a downward movement and offering less than the usual support to a flying machine; a spot in the ice not frozen over.

air-ing (âr'ĭng), *n.* a walk, ride, or drive in the open air; exposure to the air or fire.

air line (âr līn), a straight line between two places; a bee line.

air-lock (âr'lŏk"), *n.* an air-tight antechamber for a submarine caisson; in the World War, the space between two damp blankets, placed at the opening of a dugout to make it gas proof.

air-plane (âr'plān"), *n.* an aircraft or flying machine kept aloft by the reaction of motor-propelled planes upon the air. Also, **aëroplane.**

air plant (âr plánt), a plant unconnected with the ground, which appears to live upon air; popular name for certain orchids.

air pump (âr pŭmp), a machine for exhausting, compressing, or transmitting air.

air-ship (âr'shĭp"), *n.* any large machine for navigating the air; most often, a machine supported by gas-filled bags and propelled through the air by mechanical power, as the dirigible or steerable balloon.

air-speed me-ter (âr'spēd" mē'tẽr), an instrument for measuring the speed of aircraft, or flying machines.

air-tight (âr'tīt"), *adj.* so thoroughly closed that no air can enter.

air-y (âr'ĭ), *adj.* exposed to, or composed of, air; breezy; unsubstantial; gay.—*adv.* **airily.**—*n.* **airiness.**

aisle (īl), *n.* a passageway leading to the seats in a church or other place of assembly; an aislelike space, as in a store or train.

a-jar (*à*-jär'), *adj.* and *adv.* slightly turned or opened, as a door; out of harmony; as, his nerves were *ajar.*

a-kim-bo (*à*-kĭm'bō), *adj.* and *adv.* with the hands on the hips and the elbows turned outwards.

a-kin (*à*-kĭn'), *adj.* and *adv.* of kin; related by blood; allied by nature, or having the same properties; as, envy and jealousy are *akin.*

al-a-bas-ter (ăl'*à*-bás"tẽr), *n.* a white, marblelike mineral, found, chiefly, near Florence, Italy.

à la carte (ä' lä kärt'), according to the card or bill of fare: used of a menu card with the price of each dish given. [Fr.]

a-lack (*à*-lăk'), *interj.* an exclamation expressive of blame, sorrow, or surprise.

a-lac-ri-ty (*à*-lăk'rĭ-tĭ), *n.* eager readiness; joyous activity; briskness; as, to move with *alacrity*

al-a-mode (ăl'*à*-mōd"; ä"lä-mōd'), *adv.* in the fashion: *adj.* fashionable; served in a special manner, as pie with ice cream, beef with vegetables, etc.: *n.* a thin, light, glossy black silk. Also, **à la mode.** [Fr.]

a-larm (*à*-lärm'), *v.t.* to arouse to a sense of danger; strike with fear of danger: *n.* a call to arms; a warning of danger; the fear of danger. Also, **alarum.**

a-larm-ing (*à*-lärm'ĭng), *p.adj.* exciting apprehension or fear; disturbing with sudden fear; filling with anxiety.

a-larm-ist (*à*-lärm-ĭst), *n.* one who excites fear by exaggerating bad news or foretelling calamities.

a-la-ry (ā'lȧ-rĭ; ăl'*à*-rĭ), *adj.* of or pertaining to wings; wing-shaped.

a-las (*à*-lás'), *interj.* an exclamation expressive of unhappiness.

alb (ălb), *n.* a church vestment of white linen worn over the cassock.

al-ba-tross (ăl'bȧ-trŏs), *n.* a sea-bird of the petrel family, inhabiting southern seas and the whole Pacific Ocean, but not the Northern Atlantic.

Albatross

al-be-it (ôl"bē'ĭt), *conj.* although; even though; notwithstanding.

al-bi-no (ăl-bī'nō), *n.* a person with white skin and hair and pinkish eyes; an animal or plant unusually white in color.

al-bum (ăl'bŭm), *n.* a blank book in which to insert autographs, photographs, stamps, etc.

al-bu-men (ăl-bū'mĕn), *n.* the white of an egg; a thick, sticky substance found in many animals or plants. Also, **albumin.**

al-bu-mi-nous (ăl-bū'mĭ-nŭs), *adj.* containing a form of nourishing matter like the white of an egg. Also, **albuminose.**

al-cal-de (ăl-kăl'dā), *n.* in Spain, the mayor or judge of a town.

al-che-mist (ăl'kē-mĭst), *n.* one who studied or practiced early chemistry.

al-che-my (ăl'kē-mĭ), *n.* the crude chemistry of the Middle Ages; the professed art of transmuting or changing the baser metals into gold.

al-co-hol (ăl'kō-hŏl), *n.* a colorless liquid formed by the fermentation of a watery sugar solution, usually prepared by the action of malt on starch; a powerful stimulant and antiseptic; diluted with water, an intoxicant: **wood alcohol,** a by-product of charcoal, extensively used commercially.—*adj.* **alcoholic.**

al-co-hol-ism (ăl'kō-hŏl-ĭzm), *n.* a diseased condition produced by the too great use of fermented or distilled liquors.

al-cove (ăl'kōv; ăl-kōv'), *n.* a recess in a room, as for a bed, bookcases, etc.; a retired spot.

al-der (ôl'dẽr), *n.* a class of shrubs growing in moist land and related to the birch.

al-der-man (ôl'dẽr-măn), *n.* [*pl.* aldermen (-mĕn)], in English and Irish municipalities, a magistrate next in rank to the mayor; in the United States, one with varied powers and duties, representing a city ward or district.

ale (āl), *n.* a light-colored beer made from malt.

a-lee (ȧ-lē'), *adj.* and *adv.* a nautical term: on the lee or sheltered side of the ship, the side away from the wind: opposite to *aweather*.

al-em (ăl'ĕm), *n.* the imperial standard of the Turkish Empire.

a-lert (ȧ-lûrt'), *adj.* on the watch; active; brisk; ready; vigilant: *n.* the lookout; a guarding against surprise; as, to be on the *alert*.—*adv.* **alertly.**

a-lert-ness (ȧ-lûrt'nĕs), *n.* the act or quality of being vigilant or watchful; activity.

Al-ex-an-drine (ăl'ĕg-zăn'drĭn), *n.* a verse of six feet of two syllables each, the accent falling on the second syllable of each foot.

al-fal-fa (ăl-făl'fȧ), *n.* a deep-rooted plant of European origin which grows from one to four feet in height and produces two to six crops a year. In the western part of the United States it is the staple hay and forage plant.

al-ge-bra (ăl'jē-brȧ), *n.* a branch of mathematics using letters and other symbols to represent quantities.

al-ge-bra-ic (ăl'jē-brā'ĭk), *adj.* occurring in, or dealing with, that branch of mathematics which uses letters and symbols to represent quantities. Also, **algebraical.**—*adv.* **algebraically.**

a-li-as (ā'lĭ-ăs), *n.* [*pl.* aliases (-ĕz)], an assumed name: *adv.* otherwise named.

al-i-bi (ăl'ĭ-bī), *n.* the plea of having been elsewhere at the time an offense was committed.

al-ien (āl'yĕn), *n.* a foreigner; a person living in a country other than his own without the rights of citizenship; a stranger: *adj.* foreign; strange; different.

al-ien-ate (āl'yĕn-āt), *v.t.* to estrange or turn away, as the affections; transfer to another, as property.

al-ien-a-tion (āl-yĕn-ā'shŭn), *n.* a withdrawing or an estrangement, as of feeling or the affections; transference; insanity.

a-lien-ist (āl'yĕn-ĭst), *n.* a doctor engaged in the study and treatment of mental diseases.

a-light (ȧ-līt'), *v.i.* to dismount; to descend and settle; to come upon accidentally: *adj.* and *adv.* in a flame.

a-lign (ȧ-līn'), *v.t.* to place in a straight line; to adjust to a line; to form in line, as troops. Also, **aline.**

a-lign-ment (ȧ-līn'mĕnt), *n.* act of arranging in a line or lines; the state of being so adjusted. Also, **alinement.**

a-like (ȧ-līk'), *adj.* resembling one another; similar: *adv.* in the same manner.

al-i-ment (ăl'ĭ-mĕnt), *n.* food; nutriment; hence, that which sustains or supports.—*adj.* **alimental.**

al-i-men-ta-ry (ăl'ĭ-mĕn'tȧ-rĭ), *adj.* pertaining to food; nutritious or nourishing.

al-i-men-ta-ry ca-nal (ăl'ĭ-mĕn'tȧ-rĭ kȧ-năl'), the great duct or tube which conveys food to the stomach and carries off unused matter.

al-i-mo-ny (ăl'ĭ-mō-nĭ), *n.* means of living; an allowance made by decree of court to a wife out of her husband's estate on separation or divorce, or pending an action for the same.

a-line (ȧ-līn'), *v.t.* to lay out or adjust by a line: *v.i.* to form or fall into a line. Also, **align.**

a-line-ment (ȧ-līn'mĕnt), *n.* the act of laying out or adjusting by a line; the ground-plan of a railway or road. Also, **alignment.**

a-live (ȧ-līv'), *adj.* having life; in a state of action; sprightly; attentive; sensitive; opposite to *dead*.

al-ka-li (ăl'kȧ-lī; ăl'kȧ-lĭ), *n.* [*pl.* alkalies: alkalis (-līz; -lĭz)], one of a class of substances, as soda or potash, having the common properties of being soluble in water and in alcohol, of combining with fats to form soap, and of changing the tint of many coloring matters; in chemistry, a base.

al-ka-line (ăl'kȧ-līn; ăl'kȧ-lĭn), *adj.* relating to, or having the properties of, an alkali.

all (ôl), *adj.* the whole quantity of, as substance, duration, extent, amount, or degree; the whole number of, collectively, as individuals, particulars, or parts; every, as *all* kinds; any: used after a preposition or verb; as, he was free from *all* thought of danger: *pron.* the whole; the whole quantity or amount; total; aggregate: *n.* a whole; an entirety; one's entire possessions; *adv.* wholly; entirely; completely.

Al-lah (ăl'ȧ; Ar. ăl-lä'), *n.* the Arabic name for God, in use among the Mohammedans.

al-lay (ȧ-lā'), *v.t.* to quiet or calm; to assuage; to appease; to pacify; to abate or lessen; to mitigate; as, to *allay* pain or grief.

al-le-ga-tion (ăl'ē-gā'shŭn), *n.* assertion; declaration; that which is asserted or offered as a plea, excuse, or justification; the statement, by a party to a suit, of that which he is prepared to prove.

al-lege (ă-lĕj'), *v.t.* to produce as argument, plea, or excuse; affirm; declare; assert.

al-le-giance (ă-lē'jăns), *n.* the tie or obligation of a citizen or subject to his sovereign or government; fidelity to a cause or person; devotion; the duty of loyalty.

al-le-gor-i-cal (ăl'ē-gŏr'ĭ-kăl), *adj.* figurative; describing by resemblance. Also, **allegoric.**

al-le-gor-i-cal-ly (ăl'ē-gŏr'ĭ-kăl-ĭ), *adv.* figuratively.

al-le-go-ry (ăl'ē-gō-rĭ), *n.* [*pl.* allegories (-rĭz)], a manner of treating a subject by the use of other terms or circumstances than the real ones; representation in a story of one thing under the image or likeness of another; a narrative in which the meaning of something is conveyed symbolically; as, *Pilgrim's Progress* is a great *allegory*.—*n.* **allegorist.**

al-le-lu-ia (ăl'ē-lōō'yȧ), *interj.* Praise ye the Lord! *n.* a song or cry of thanksgiving and joy. Also, **alleluiah, hallelujah, hallelujah.**

al-le-vi-ate (ă-lē'vĭ-āt), *v.t.* to lighten; lessen; make easier; mitigate.—*n.* **alleviation.**

al-ley (ăl'ĭ), *n.* [*pl.* alleys (-ĭz)], a passage; a narrow way in a city; a lane.

al-ley-way (ăl'ĭ-wā'), *n.* a short or narrow passageway.

all hail (ôl hāl), all health! a phrase of salutation or greeting.

All-hal-lows (ôl'hăl'ōz), *n.pl.* All Saints' Day, celebrated on the first of November, in honor of all the saints.

al-li-ance (ȧ-lī'ăns), *n.* relation or connection by birth or marriage; union between nations or parties.

Syn. confederacy, fusion, league, partnership, union, coalition, compact.

Ant. (see separation).

al-li-ga-tor (ăl'ĭ-gā"tẽr), *n.* the American crocodile.

Alligator

al-lit-er-a-tion (ȧ-lĭt"ẽr-ā'shŭn), *n.* the repetition of the same initial letter in closely succeeding words, or in words directly following each other; as, "apt *alliteration's* artful aid."

al-lit-er-a-tive (ȧ-lĭt'ẽr-ȧ-tĭv), *adj.* pertaining to, or characterized by, the repetition of words beginning with the same letter; as, the *alliterative* quality of Tennyson's verse is illustrated in, ". . . shocks, and the splintering spear."

al-lo-di-al (ȧ-lō'dĭ-ăl), *adj.* free of rent; not feudal: *n.* land thus held. Also, **alodial.**

al-lo-path (ăl'ō-păth), *n.* one who favors or practices a system of medicine which treats disease by inducing an action opposite to that of the disease treated. Also, **allopathist.**

al-lo-path-ic (ăl"ō-păth'ĭk), *adj.* relating to the system of medicine which treats disease by causing an action opposite to that of the disease treated.

al-lop-a-thy (ȧ-lŏp'ȧ-thĭ), *n.* a method of treating disease by inducing an action opposite to the disease it is sought to cure: distinguished from *homeopathy.*

al-lot (ȧ-lŏt'), *v.t.* [*p.t.* and *p.p.* allotted, *p.pr.* allotting], to distribute or divide, as by lot; apportion, as shares; assign or grant for a specific or definite purpose.

al-lot-ment (ȧ-lŏt'mĕnt), *n.* act of dividing fairly; that which is so divided; an allowance; especially, an allowance made to a soldier's family for their support during his absence for service in war.

al-low (ȧ-lou'), *v.t.* to grant; consent to, yield; admit; deduct; set apart; as, to *allow* so much for loss; permit; approve: *v.i.* to make concession or provision; followed by *for.*

al-low-a-ble (ȧ-lou'ȧ-bl), *adj.* permissible; lawful; praiseworthy; acceptable.—*adv.* **allowably.**

al-low-ance (ȧ-lou'ăns), *n.* admission; concession; a definite sum or quantity granted; as, an *allowance* of spending money; an *allowance* of food; sanction or approval: *v.t.* to limit to a fixed expenditure or consumption of money, food, etc.

al-loy (ȧ-loi'), *n.* any mixture of metals; a baser metal used in mixture with a finer one; an admixture of good with evil: *v.t.* to combine; to form a compound by the fusion or mixing of two or more metals; reduce in standard or quality by mixture; as to *alloy* gold or silver with copper; debase.

all-round (ôl'round"), *adj.* versatile, or many-sided; capable of doing many things; as, a good *all-round* workman.

All Souls' Day (ôl sōlz dā), the day, celebrated November second, by the Catholic Church, in honor of the dead.

all-spice (ôl'spīs"), *n.* the fruit or berry of the pimento, a tree of the West Indies: so named because it is supposed to combine the flavors of cinnamon, nutmeg, and cloves.

al-lude (ȧ-lūd'), *v.i.* to refer indirectly: with *to;* to hint at.

al-lure (ȧ-lūr'), *v.t.* to tempt by the offer of something good, real, or apparent; entice; attract.

al-lure-ment (ȧ-lūr'mĕnt), *n.* the act of attracting; temptation.

al-lur-ing (ȧ-lūr'ĭng), *p.adj.* tempting; enticing; fascinating.

al-lu-sion (ȧ-lū'zhŭn), *n.* a casual reference to, or slight mention of, something; a comparison or reference for illustration.

al-lu-sive (ȧ-lū'sĭv), *adj.* having reference to something not definitely or fully expressed.—*adv.* **allusively.**—*n.* **allusiveness.**

al-lu-vi-al (ȧ-lū'vĭ-ăl), *adj.* relating to, or composed of, clay, mud, or other material left by running water.

al-lu-vi-on (ȧ-lū'vĭ-ŏn), *n.* land added to a shore or river-bank by the action of the water.

al-lu-vi-um (ȧ-lū'vĭ-ŭm), *n.* [*pl.* alluvia (-ȧ)], a deposit of earth, sand, and clay (mud), or of layers of sand and clay, made by a river against its banks.

al-ly (ȧ-lī'), *v.t.* [*p.t.* and *p.p.* allied, *p.pr.* allying], to unite by marriage, treaty, league, or confederacy; bind or connect by friendship or resemblance: *n.* [*pl.* allies (ȧ-līz')], one united, related, or associated by these means; a confederate.

Al-ma Ma-ter (ăl'mȧ mā'tẽr), the college or institution in which one has been educated; literally, fostering mother. [Lat.]

al-ma-nac (ôl'mȧ-năk), *n.* a year-book, or calendar, giving the order of the days of the week and month, facts about the heavens, tide-tables, church festivals and fasts, and other varied information.

al-might-y (ôl-mīt'ĭ), *adj.* possessing all power; of unlimited might.—**The Almighty,** the omnipotent God.

al-mond (ä'mŭnd; ăl'mŭnd), *n.* the nut-like kernel of the fruit of a small tree somewhat like the peach; the tree itself; anything like the almond in shape.

al-mon-er (ăl'mŭn-ẽr), *n.* one who dispenses or distributes charity.

al-most (ôl'mōst), *adv.* nearly; very nearly; well-nigh; all but.

alms (ämz), *n.sing.* [used sometimes as *n.pl.*], charity; anything freely given to relieve the poor.

alms-house (ämz'hous"), *n.* a house endowed by private or public charity and devoted to the use of the poor.

al-oe (ăl'ō), *n.* [*pl.* aloes (-ōz)], the common name for a number of plants, natives of the warm climates of the Old World, and especially of the southern part of Africa.

al-oes (ăl'ōz), *n.pl.* a very bitter drug, made from the juice of the leaves of several kinds of aloe; the fragrant resin or wood of the wood-aloe: the usual meaning in the Bible.

a-loft (*ȧ*-lŏft'), *adv.* a nautical term: on high; far above the earth; at the masthead, or on the higher yards or rigging of a ship.

a-lone (*ȧ*-lōn'), *adj.* and *adv.* without or apart from another; solitary; single or singly; only; by itself.

a-long (*ȧ*-lŏng), *prep.* and *adv.* by the length; lengthwise; in a line parallel with the length; onward; as, let us walk *along*.

a-long-side (*ȧ*-lŏng'sīd'), *adv.* by the side; side by side.

a-loof (*ȧ*-lōōf'), *adv.* at a distance but within sight; purposely keeping apart; as, to stand *aloof*.

a-loof-ness (*ȧ*-lōōf'nĕs), *n.* the state of keeping away from; exclusiveness; as, *aloofness* of manner.

a-loud (*ȧ*-loud'), *adv.* with raised voice; loudly; with a great noise; audibly.

al-pac-a (ăl-păk'*ȧ*), *n.* a sheeplike animal native of the Andes of Chili and Peru; the cloth made from the long, soft, silky wool of this animal.

al-pen-horn (ăl'pen-hôrn"), *n.* a long and nearly straight horn used by the mountaineers of the Alps.

al-pen-stock (ăl'pĕn-stŏk"), *n.* a stout staff, furnished with an iron spike, used by mountain-climbers.

al-pha (ăl'f*ȧ*), *n.* the first letter of the Greek alphabet; hence, the first or beginning of anything.

al-pha-bet (ăl'f*ȧ*-bĕt), *n.* the letters of a language arranged in the usual order.

al-pha-bet-ic (ăl"f*ȧ*-bĕt'ĭk), *adj.* relating to the letters of a language in their proper order.

al-pha-bet-i-cal (ăl"fȧ-bĕt'ĭ-kăl), *adj.* arranged in the usual order of the letters of a language; as, an *alphabetical* list of names.—*adv.* **alphabetically.**

al-pha-bet-ize (ăl'f*ȧ*-bĕt-īz), *v.t.* to arrange in the usual order of the letters of a language.

al-read-y (ôl-rĕd'ĭ), *adv.* by or before a particular time; beforehand.

al-so (ôl'sō; ŏl'sō), *adv.* and *conj.* in like manner; likewise; further, or in addition; too; besides.

al-tar (ôl'tẽr), *n.* in the Christian Church, the Communion table; in ancient times and in heathen countries, a raised place of earth or stone, on which to offer sacrifice or burn incense to the gods.

Altar

al-ter (ôl'tẽr), *v.t.* to change in some respect; to vary somewhat: *v.i.* to become somewhat different.

al-ter-a-tion (ôl"tẽr-ā'shŭn), *n.* a change of form or state; the act of making the change.

al-ter-cate (ăl'tẽr-kāt; ôl'tẽr-kāt), *v.i.* to contend or dispute in words; wrangle; dispute with anger or heat.

al-ter-ca-tion (ăl"tẽr-kā'shŭn), *n.* a dispute; angry debate.

al-ter-nate (ăl'tẽr-nāt; ôl'tẽr-nāt), *v.t.* to cause to occur by turns: *v.i.* to take place by turns: followed by *with*: *adj.* (ăl-tûr'nāt; ăl'tẽr-nāt), taking place by turns; first one and then the other; in botany, following each other by turns on opposite side *n.s* of a stem: a substitute.

al-ter-na-tion (ăl"tẽr-nā'shŭn; ôl"tẽr-nā'shŭn), *n.* the taking turns or the following in succession, one after another; as, the *alternation* of day and night.

al-ter-na-tive (ăl-tûr'n*ȧ*-tĭv; ôl-tûr'n*ȧ*-tĭv), *adj.* giving the choice of two things, only one of which may be taken, done, etc.: *n.* something that must be done, taken, etc., instead of something else; a choice between two things.—*adv.* **alternatively.**

Syn., *n.* choice, option, preference, pick.

Ant. (see compulsion).

al-though (ôl-*th*ō'), *conj.* though; even if; notwithstanding. Also, **altho.**

al-tim-e-ter (ăl-tĭm'ē-tẽr), *n.* aneroid barometer graduated to show altitude instead of pressure: used on airplanes, etc.

al-ti-tude (ăl'tĭ-tūd), *n.* space extended upward; height; as, the *altitude* of a mountain; highest point or degree.

al-to (ăl'tō), *adj.* high: *n.* the part sung by the lowest female voice, between the tenor and soprano; the contralto; the tenor violin or viola.

al-to-geth-er (ôl"tōō-gĕ*th*'ẽr), *adv.* wholly; completely; entirely; without exception.

al-tru-ism (ăl'trōō-ĭzm), *n.* regard for the interests of others: opposite to *selfishness*.

al-tru-ist (ăl'trōō-ĭst), *n.* a person devoted to the welfare of others.

al-tru-is-tic (ăl-trōō-ĭs'tĭk), *adj.* mindful of the wants and interests of others.

al-um (ăl'ŭm), *n.* a white, transparent, saltlike substance largely used in medicine and industry: common alum is a double sulphate of aluminum and potassium.

a-lu-mi-na (*ȧ*-lū'mĭ-n*ȧ*), *n.* a compound from two parts aluminum and three parts oxygen: the most abundant of all the earths; the main part of all clays: largely used in dyeing and calico-printing.

a-lu-mi-num (*ȧ*-lū'mĭ-nŭm), *n.* a bluish-white metal noted for its lightness: the most plentiful of all metallic substances, but never found in a pure state. Also, **aluminium.**

a-lum-na (*ȧ*-lŭm'n*ȧ*), *n.* [*pl.* alumnæ (-nē)], a woman graduate of a school, college, or university.

a-lum-nus (*ȧ*-lŭm'nŭs), *n.* [*pl.* alumni (-nī)], a man graduate of a school, college, or university.

al-ways (ôl'wāz; ôl'wāz), *adv.* at all times; constantly; ever; continually.

a-lys-sum (*ȧ*-lĭs'ŭm), *n.* a plant bearing small, white, sweet-scented flowers: commonly called *sweet alyssum*.

a-main (*ȧ*-mān'), *adv.* with force or violence; suddenly; at full speed.

a-mal-gam (*ȧ*-măl'găm), *n.* any metallic mixture of which mercury is the chief ingredient; a mixture or compound of different things.

a-mal-ga-mate (*ȧ*-măl'g*ȧ*-māt), *v.t.* to alloy or mix mercury with another metal; mix to form a compound: *v.i.* to mix or combine so as to make uniform; as, one race *amalgamates* with another.

a-mal-ga-ma-tion (*ȧ*-măl"g*ȧ*-mā'shŭn), *n.* the act of mixing mercury with another metal; the separation of precious metals from the mother-rock by means of quicksilver; the blending or mixing of different elements or things; the union or consolidation of two or more companies or businesses into one concern.

a-man-u-en-sis (ȧ-măn″ū-ĕn′sĭs), *n.* [*pl.* amanuenses (-sēz)], one who writes at the dictation or direction of another; a secretary.

am-a-ranth (ăm′ȧ-rănth), *n.* an imaginary flower said by poets to be unfading; a plant; a color-mixture in which the chief ingredient is magenta, a dark red dye.

am-a-ran-thine (ăm″ȧ-răn′thĭn), *adj.* never-fading; undying; of a purplish color.

a-mass (ȧ-măs′), *v.t.* to collect into a heap; gather together in great quantity; to accumulate.
Syn. collect, gather, hoard, store up.
Ant. (see disperse).

am-a-teur (ăm″ȧ-tûr′; ăm′ȧ-tūr), *n.* one who practices any art, study, or pursuit for pleasure but not professionally for money.—*adj.* amateurish.

am-a-to-ry (ăm′ȧ-tō-rĭ), *adj.* relating to, or expressive of, love.

a-maze (ȧ-māz′), *v.t.* to bewilder with fear, surprise, or wonder; astonish; perplex.—*adv.* amazedly.

a-maze-ment (ȧ-māz′mĕnt), *n.* astonishment; perplexity or bewilderment arising from sudden surprise.
Syn. awe, wonder, surprise, confusion, admiration, bewilderment.
Ant. (see composure).

a-maz-ing (ȧ-māz′ĭng), *adj.* very wonderful, astonishing.—*adv.* amazingly.

A-ma-zon (ăm′ȧ-zŏn), *n.* one of a fabulous race of female warriors: amazon, an unusually tall, strong, or masculine woman.

am-bas-sa-dor (ăm-băs′ȧ-dẽr), *n.* a government agent of highest rank representing his country's interests at a foreign court; any representative or agent of another charged with a special mission. Also, embassador.—*adj.* ambassadorial.

am-bas-sa-dor ex-traor-di-na-ry (ăm-băs′ȧ-dẽr ĕks-trôr′dĭ-nā-rĭ), a minister or agent sent on a special mission by the government of one country to another.

am-bas-sa-dor plen-i-po-ten-ti-a-ry (ăm-băs′ȧ-dẽr plĕn″ĭ-pō-tĕn′shĭ-ā-rĭ), an agent sent by one country to another with full powers to make a treaty or agreement.

am-bas-sa-dress (ăm-băs′ȧ-drĕs), *n.* the wife of an ambassador; a woman charged with the performance of a special mission.

am-ber (ăm′bẽr), *n.* a yellowish resin or gummy substance found on the shores of the Baltic: *adj.* made of amber; yellowish in color.

am-ber-gris (ăm′bẽr-grēs), *n.* a fragrant waxy substance coming from the sperm-whale, usually found floating in tropical seas: used in perfumery.

am-bi-dex-trous (ăm″bĭ-dĕks′trŭs), *adj.* able to use both hands alike.

am-bi-gu-i-ty (ăm″bĭ-gū′ĭ-tĭ), *n.* [*pl.* ambiguities (-tĭz)], doubtfulness or uncertainty, especially of language. Also, ambiguousness.

am-big-u-ous (ăm-bĭg′ū-ŭs), *adj.* doubtful; having two or more possible meanings.—*adv.* ambiguously.

am-bi-tion (ăm-bĭsh′ŭn), *n.* an eager desire to obtain some object, as political power or literary fame.

am-bi-tious (ăm-bĭsh′ŭs), *adj.* eager for advancement; strongly desirous; as, *ambitious* of wealth; showy.—*adv.* ambitiously.

am-ble (ăm′bl), *v.i.* as applied to people, to go at an easy pace; to meander; as applied to horses, to go at a peculiar pace in which the animal moves by lifting the two feet on the same side together: *n.* a peculiar gait of a horse; any easy gait.

am-bro-si-a (ăm-brō′zhĭ-ȧ), *n.* anything exquisitely pleasing to taste or smell; in mythology, the food of the gods; ragweed.

am-bro-si-al (ăm-brō′zhĭ-ăl), *adj.* delicious; fragrant; sweet-smelling.

am-bro-type (ăm′brō-tīp), *n.* a photographic process by which the light parts of a photograph are produced in silver, the dark parts showing as a background through the clear glass.

am-bu-lance (ăm′bū-lăns), *n.* a cart or wagon for the conveyance of the sick and wounded to a hospital; a field hospital.

am-bu-la-to-ry (ăm′bū-lȧ-tō-rĭ), *adj.* having the power to walk about; movable; temporary: *n.* a place for walking; a covered way, such as a corridor.

am-bus-cade (ăm″bŭs-kād′), *n.* a place where troops lie hidden to attack the enemy unexpectedly; the act of hiding for such a purpose.

am-bush (ăm′bŏŏsh), *n.* a concealed station where troops lie hidden to attack the enemy unexpectedly; the act of lying concealed in order to make such an attack; *v.t.* to waylay; to station for the purpose of attacking by surprise.

a-meer (ȧ-mēr′), *n.* a prince; governor; the Mohammedan ruler of Afghanistan. Also, amir, emir.

a-mel-io-rate (ȧ-mēl′yō-rāt), *v.t.* to make better; *v.i.* to grow better; improve.

a-mel-io-ra-tion (ȧ-mēl″yō-rā′shŭn), *n.* improvement.

a-men (ā″mĕn′; ä″mĕn′), *adv.* verily; a word used at the end of a prayer meaning "so be it."

a-me-na-ble (ȧ-mē′nȧ-bl), *adj.* easy to lead; ready to accept advice; as, *amenable* to criticism; accountable; liable; as, *amenable* to the law.—*adv.* amenably.—*n.* amenability.

a-mend (ȧ-mĕnd′), *v.t.* to change for the better; improve; correct.
Syn. better, mend.
Ant. (see impair).

a-mend-a-to-ry (ȧ-mĕn′dȧ-tō-rĭ), *adj.* corrective; as, an *amendatory* or supplementary clause was added when the law was found defective.

a-mend-ment (ȧ-mĕnd′mĕnt), *n.* a change for the better; a freeing from faults; the alteration or change of a government bill; an addition to the United States Constitution or to a state constitution.

a-mends (ȧ-mĕndz′), *n.pl.* compensation or payment for loss or injury; as, to make *amends*.

a-men-i-ty (ȧ-mĕn′ĭ-tĭ), *n.* [*pl.* amenities (-tĭz)], pleasantness; geniality; civility.

a-merce (ȧ-mûrs′), *v.t.* to punish by a fine or by taking away any right or privilege.—*n.* amercement.

A-mer-i-can (*d*-mĕr'ĭ-kăn), *adj.* pertaining to, or situated in, America; pertaining to the United States; as, an *American* citizen: *n.* an inhabitant of America.

A-mer-i-can-ism (*d*-mĕr'ĭ-kăn-ĭzm), *n.* a phrase, word, trait, custom, or object, peculiar to, or originating in, the United States.

A-mer-i-can-ize (*d*-mĕr'ĭ-kăn-īz), *v.t.* to bring into agreement or accord with the manners and customs of the United States.—*n.* **Americanization.**

am-e-thyst (ăm'ē-thĭst), *n.* a violet-purple variety of quartz or rock-crystal; a precious stone.

am-e-thys-tine (ăm"ē-thĭs'tĭn), *adj.* containing, composed of, or colored like, amethyst.

Am-ex (ăm'ĕks), *n.* in the World War, an abbreviation for *American Expeditionary Forces*, the American army abroad.

a-mi-a-bil-i-ty (ā"mĭ-*d*-bĭl'ĭ-tĭ), *n.* excellence of disposition; lovableness.

a-mi-a-ble (ā'mĭ-*d*-bl), *adj.* friendly; lovable; kindly.—*adv.* **amiably.**

am-i-ca-ble (ăm'ĭ-k*d*-bl), *adj.* friendly; peaceable; as, an *amicable* agreement.—*adv.* **amicably.**

a-mid (*d*-mĭd), *prep.* in the middle of; among. Also, **amidst.**

a-mid-ships (*d*-mĭd'shĭps), *adv.* in the middle of a ship.

a-miss (*d*-mĭs'), *adj.* wrong; faulty: *adv.* wrongly; out of the way.

am-i-ty (ăm'ĭ-tĭ), *n.* friendly or peaceful relations; friendship.

am-mo-ni-a (ă-mō'nĭ-*d*), *n.* a clear, sharp, or pungent gas, readily soluble in water, used in medicine, for manufacturing ice, and in many other ways.

am-mu-ni-tion (ăm"ū-nĭsh'ŭn), *n.* formerly, military stores and the storehouse for them; now, the material used in the discharge of cannon, firearms, etc., such as powder, balls, shells, bombs, etc. Also, **munitions.**

am-nes-ty (ăm'nĕs-tĭ), *n.* a general pardon or conditional offer of pardon for offenses against a government; a pardon for political offenders.

a-mœ-ba (*d*-mē'b*d*), *n.* [*pl.* amœbas (-b*d*z) and amœbæ (-bē)], a tiny or microscopic animal found in fresh-water ponds: the simplest form of animal life. Also, **ameba.**

a-mong (*d*-mŭng'), *prep.* in the midst of; surrounded by; in the group with; so as to be shared by. Also, **amongst.**

am-or-ous (ăm'ō-rŭs), *adj.* fond of the opposite sex; loving.

a-mor-phous (*d*-mŏr'fŭs), *adj.* formless; irregularly shaped.

A-mos (ā'mŏs), *n.* a book of the Old Testament which contains the prophecies of Amos, the herdsman, concerning the punishment of Israel.

a-mount (*d*-mount'), *v.i.* to reach; to be equal to; as, his answer *amounted* almost to a threat: *n.* the total sum.

am-pere (ăm-pâr'), *n.* the unit of measurement of the strength of an electrical current.

Am-phib-i-a (ăm-fĭb'ĭ-*d*), *n.pl.* animals living both on land and in water, such as frogs and turtles; the fourth division of animals with backbones, midway between fishes and reptiles, which in their early state breathe by gills.

am-phib-i-an (ăm-fĭb'ĭ-ăn), *n.* an animal living both on land and in water: *adj.* relating to animals that live both on land and in water; amphibious.

am-phib-i-ous (ăm-fĭb'ĭ-ŭs), *adj.* having the power of living both on land and in water. Also, **amphibian.**

am-phi-the-a-ter (ăm"fĭ-thē'*d*-tĕr), *n.* an oval or circular building with rows of seats rising around a central space; commonly, the highest gallery in a theater or opera house.

Amphitheater (The Coliseum at Rome.)

am-ple (ăm'pl), *adj.* full, large; extensive; spacious; abundant; sufficient to meet all needs.

am-pli-fi-ca-tion (ăm"plĭ-fĭ-kā'shŭn), *n.* enlargement; extension; as, the *amplification* of a subject.

am-pli-fi-er (ăm'plĭ-fī"ĕr), *n.* one who, or that which, makes larger; a telephone device used for receiving and transmitting sound; it has the qualities of a very sensitive telephone transmitter.

am-pli-fy (ăm'plĭ-fī), *v.t.* [*p.t.* and *p.p.* amplified; *p.pr.* amplifying], to make larger or more full: *v.i.* to add to what has been said or written; to speak or write at great length.

Syn. develop, expand, extend, widen, enlarge.

Ant. (see abbreviate).

am-pli-tude (ăm'plĭ-tūd), *n.* the extension in space, especially breadth and width; largeness of mind; breadth of thought.

am-ply (ăm'plĭ), *adv.* liberally; abundantly; as, he is *amply* provided for.

am-pu-tate (ăm'pū-tāt), *v.t.* in surgery, to cut off a human limb or part of a limb; to prune, as branches of trees or vines.

am-pu-ta-tion (ăm"pū-tā'shŭn), *n.* the operation of cutting off a limb.

a-muck (*d*-mŭk'), *adv.* in a reckless or frenzied way: used in the phrase, to run *amuck.*

am-u-let (ăm'ū-lĕt), *n.* a charm worn to protect against disease or bad luck; a talisman.

a-muse (*d*-mūz'), *v.t.* to entertain; divert; as, to *amuse* children with toys.

a-muse-ment (*d*-mūz'mĕnt), *n.* that which diverts or entertains; a pastime.

an (ăn), *indef. art.* any; each: properly an *adj.*, used before nouns of the singular number only, and only before words having an initial vowel or silent *h*: it has a distributive force in such expressions as once *an* hour; a dime *an* ounce.

a-nab-a-sis (*d*-năb'*d*-sĭs), *n.* a military advance into a country.

an-ach-ro-nism (ăn-ăk'rō-nĭzm), *n.* an error in the order of time; a mistake in the date of an event; especially, the placing of something in a wrong time; as, Shakespeare places a clock in *Julius Cæsar,* although clocks had not yet been invented at the time when Cæsar lived.

an-a-con-da (ăn″ȧ-kŏn′dȧ), *n.* a very large South American snake which crushes its victims, usually birds and small animals; any large snake that kills its prey by squeezing it; a python or boa.

a-næ-mi-a (ȧ-nē′mĭ-ȧ), *n.* the condition of not having enough blood, or of having blood of poor quality. Also, **anemia.**

an-a-gram (ăn′ȧ-grăm), *n.* the changing of the order of the letters of a word or sentence so as to form a new word or sentence; a word obtained by reading the letters of another word backwards; as, *live* is an *anagram* of *evil.*

a-nal (ā′năl), *adj.* relating to the anus or end of the digestive tube or alimentary canal.

an-al-ges-ic (ăn″ăl-jĕs′ĭk), *adj.* pain-dulling; insensible to pain. *n.* **analgesia.**

a-nal-o-gous (ȧ-năl′ō-gŭs), *adj.* having some resemblance; similar; corresponding to something else.

a-nal-o-gy (ȧ-năl′ō-jĭ), *n.* [*pl.* analogies (-jĭz)], agreement or resemblance between things somewhat different; as, we say study enlightens the mind, thus making an *analogy* between study and light, the former being to the mind what the latter is to the eye.—*adj.* **analogical.**—*adv.* **analogically.**

Syn. likeness, similarity, relation, proportion, comparison.

Ant. (see unlikeness).

a-nal-y-sis (ȧ-năl′ĭ-sĭs), *n.* [*pl.* analyses (-sēz)], the division or separation of a thing into the parts that compose it; as, *analysis* of a plant; *analysis* of a chemical compound; *analysis* of a sentence; *analysis* of a mathematical problem; *analysis* of the contents of a book.

an-a-lyst (ăn′ȧ-lĭst), *n.* one who divides or separates things into the parts that compose them, especially in chemistry or mathematics.

an-a-lyt-ic (ăn″ȧ-lĭt′ĭk), *adj.* relating to, or separating into, component parts. Also, **analytical.**—*adv.* **analytically.**

an-a-lyze (ăn′ȧ-līz), *v.t.* to separate into component parts; to examine closely and critically. Also, **analyse.**—*n.* **analyzer.**

An-a-ni-as (ăn-ȧ-nī′ăs), *n.* in the Bible, a follower of the Apostles, who, with his wife, Sapphira, was struck dead for lying; hence, a liar.—Acts v.

an-a-pest (ăn′ȧ-pĕst), *n.* a poetic foot or measure consisting of three syllables, with the accent on the last; as, I am mon′ | arch of all′ | I survey′. Also, **anapæst.**—*adj.* **anapestic, anapæstic.**

a-nar-chic (ȧ-när′kĭk), *adj.* in a state of lawlessness or disorder; without rule or government; in confusion. Also, **anarchical.**

an-arch-ism (ăn′ȧr-kĭzm), *n.* lawlessness; confusion; anarchy; the doctrine that all government is an evil.

an-arch-ist (ăn′ȧr-kĭst), *n.* one who regards all government as evil and believes as a political ideal in living without any government; any person who stirs up violent revolt against established rule or custom.

an-arch-y (ăn′ȧr-kĭ), *n.* absence or lack of government; a lawless condition of society; disorder; confusion in general; the theory of individual liberty.

a-nath-e-ma (ȧ-năth′ē-mȧ), *n.* [*pl.* anathemas (-mȧz)], the solemn curse of the Church in excommunication; a prayer that calamity may fall upon a person; the thing or person so cursed.

an-a-tom-ic (ăn″ȧ-tŏm′ĭk), *adj.* relating to dissection, or to the parts or structure of the body. Also, **anatomical.**—*adv.* **anatomically.**

a-nat-o-mist (ȧ-năt′ō-mĭst), *n.* one having a complete knowledge, derived from dissection, of the structure of plants and animals.

a-nat-o-my (ȧ-năt′ō-mĭ), *n.* [*pl.* anatomies (-mĭz)], the science of the structure of plants or animals, but especially of the human body; the art or science of dissection; a descriptive account of the parts of an organic body.

an-ces-tor (ăn′sĕs-tẽr), *n.* a person from whom one is descended in direct line; a forefather; a progenitor.

an-ces-tral (ăn-sĕs′trăl), *adj.* pertaining to, or connected with, one's forefathers; derived from one's progenitors; lineal.

an-ces-try (ăn′sĕs-trĭ), *n.* the line of one's descent traced from a period more or less remote; the persons comprising such a line; lineage.

Anchor. *a,* stock; *b,* shank; *c, c,* arms; *d,* crown or throat; *e,* fluke; *f, g,* bills or peaks; *h,* eye; *o,* ring or shackle.

an-chor (ăṅ′kẽr), *n.* a heavy iron implement for securing a vessel to the ground under water; that on which dependence is placed for security or stability; a metallic clamp securing a tie-rod connecting opposite walls to prevent bulging: *v.t.* to secure a vessel by a heavy iron implement lowered into the water; grapple; hold fast.

an-chor-age (ăṅ′kẽr-āj), *n.* a suitable or customary place for the securing of vessels to the ground under water; the hold attained by an anchor; harbor-dues for mooring vessels in a port.

an-cho-ret (ăṅ′kō-rĕt), *n.* one who voluntarily leaves the world and lives alone, usually to devote his time to the study of religion or philosophy; a recluse; a hermit. Also, **anchorite.**

an-cho-vy (ăn-chō′vĭ; ăn′chō-vĭ), *n.* [*pl.* anchovies (-vĭz)], a very small herringlike fish found in the Mediterranean, noted for its peculiar flavor, and used for pickling and as a sauce.

an-cient (ān′shĕnt), *adj.* of or relating to the early history of the world; of past times or remote ages; of great age or antiquity: *n.* one who lived in times long ago; a standard bearer, or ensign: now obsolete.

and (ănd), *conj.* a word connecting a word, clause, or sentence with one of like kind and equal rank that precedes it.

and-i-rons (ănd′ī″ŭrnz), *n.pl.* the two metal supports for holding logs in a fireplace; fire-dogs.

an-ec-dot-al (ăn′ĕk-dōt″ăl), *adj.* relating to or consisting of short personal stories.

an-ec-dote (ăn′ĕk-dōt), *n.* a brief story of an entertaining character; a terse and pithy account of some incident, chiefly about a well-known person.

a-ne-mi-a (ȧ-nē′mĭ-ȧ), *n.* lack of blood in a living body. Also, **anæmia.**—*adj.* **anemic.**

an-e-mom-e-ter (ăn″ē-mŏm′ē-tẽr), *n.* a wind-gauge; an instrument which measures the speed, or force, of the wind.

Anemometer

a-nem-o-ne (ȧ-nĕm′ō-nē), *n.* [*pl.* **anemones** (-nēz)], the wind-flower or wood-anemone.

an-er-oid (ăn′ẽr-oid), *adj.* not containing a liquid, such as quicksilver; as, an *aneroid* battery; an aneroid barometer: **aneroid** barometer, an instrument in which atmospheric pressure is shown by the movements of the elastic top of a closed box from which the air has been partially exhausted, so that a pointer is moved, indicating on a scale the air-pressure: much used in measuring altitudes.

an-es-the-si-a (ăn″ĕs-thē′sĭ-ȧ; -zhĭ-ȧ), *n.* a loss of feeling due to the influence of drugs or disease. Also, **anaesthesia.**

an-es-thet-ic (ăn″ĕs-thĕt′ĭk), *adj.* relating to loss of the sense of feeling: *n.* a drug which produces insensibility. Also, **anaesthetic.**

a-new (ȧ-nū′), *adv.* afresh; over again; in a new manner or style.

an-gel (ān′jĕl), *n.* a messenger of God; one of an order of spiritual attendants supposed to form a connection between heaven and earth, as from God to mankind; a spirit of evil, as a fallen *angel;* an old English gold coin bearing an image of the archangel Michael.

an-gel-ic (ăn-jĕl′ĭk), *adj.* celestial; pure; beautiful; saintly. Also, **angelical.**

An-ge-lus (ăn′jē-lŭs), *n.* a prayer or devotion, said morning, noon, and night, in memory of the annunciation by the Angel Gabriel to the Virgin Mary of the incarnation of Christ; the church bell which is rung to announce the time of such devotions or prayers: commemorated in a famous picture by Millēt called *The Angelus.*

an-ger (ăṅ′gẽr), *n.* excessive emotion or passion aroused by a sense of injury or wrong; wrath: *v.t.* to provoke to resentment; excite to wrath; enrage.

Syn. fury, ire, passion, offense, temper, indignation.

Ant. (see forbearance, love).

an-gi-na (ăn′jĭ-nȧ; ăn-jī′nȧ), *n.* an inflamed condition of the throat, as in quinsy, mumps, etc.

an-gi-na pec-to-ris (ăn′jĭ-nȧ pĕk′tō-rĭs), a muscular spasm of the chest, very often accompanied by heart disease and often fatal. [LAT.]

an-gle (ăṅ′gl), *n.* the figure formed by two lines or surfaces meeting; a sharp or projecting corner; a corner; a nook: *v.t.* to fish with a hook and line: *v.i.* to fish for prey.

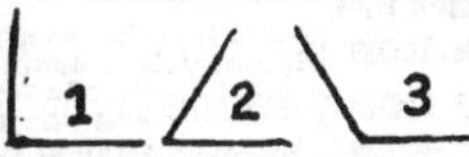

Angles. 1, right; 2, acute; 3 obtuse.

an-gler (ăṅ′glẽr), *n.* one who fishes with rod and line; the name of a fish that feeds on smaller fish: also called fishing-frog and sea-devil.

an-gle-worm (ăṅ′gl-wûrm″), *n.* an earthworm used as bait in fishing.

An-gli-can (ăṅ′glĭ-kăn), *adj.* English; relating to the Established Church of England and to churches in other countries in accord with it: *n.* a member of the Anglican Church or the Church of England.

An-gli-can-ism (ăṅ′glĭ-kăn-ĭzm), *n.* the principles and ritual or rites of the Church of England.

An-gli-cize (ăṅ′glĭ-sīz), *v.t.* to make English; to make to accord or agree with English manners and customs.

an-gling (ăṅ′glĭng), *n.* the art of fishing with rod and line.

An-glo-A-mer-i-can (ăṅ″glō-ȧ-mĕr′ĭ-kăn), *adj.* relating to England and the United States together, as to commerce or population: *n.* an American citizen of English descent.

An-glo-ma-ni-a (ăṅ″glō-mā′nĭ-ȧ), *n.* an excessive or undue respect for, or imitation of, that which is English or peculiar to England.

An-glo-pho-bi-a (ăṅ″glō-fō′bĭ-ȧ), *n.* an intense dislike or fear of England and everything English.

An-glo-Sax-on (ăṅ″glō-săk′sŭn), *adj.* relating to the Saxon settlers in England prior to the Conquest, or to their language: *n.* one of the Saxon settlers in England as apart from those on the Continent; the language of the Anglo-Saxons: *pl.* the English race.

An-go-ra (ăṅ-gō′rȧ), *n.* a town in Asia Minor giving the name to the cat and goat so called; a light cloth made from Angora goats' wool and used for coats and cloaks; a kind of knitting yarn.

an-gri-ly (ăṅ′grĭ-lĭ), *adv.* in an indignant or enraged manner.

an-gry (ăṅ′grĭ), *adj.* inflamed with passion; provoked; feeling resentment; wrathful; fierce; enraged.

an-guish (ăṅ′gwĭsh), *n.* intense pain or grief; acute suffering, bodily or mental; torture.

an-gu-lar (ăṅ′gū-lȧr), *adj.* having an outline in which lines meet or intersect; sharp, bent, or cornered; pointed, or full of points; ungraceful; moving awkwardly.—*adv.* **angularly.**—*n.* **angularity.**

an-il (ăn′ĭl), *n.* a West Indian plant from which indigo is made.

an-i-line (ăn′ĭ-lĭn; ăn′ĭ-lēn), *n.* a colorless oily compound which is the base or starting-point in the preparation of many rich dyes. Also, **anilin.**

an-i-mad-ver-sion (ăn″ĭ-măd-vûr′shŭn), *n.* censure; criticism; reproof.

an-i-mad-vert (ăn″ĭ-măd-vûrt′), *v.i.* to pass unfavorable comment upon; criticise; censure.

an-i-mal (ăn′ĭ-măl), *n.* a living creature possessing feeling and voluntary motion; a beast; an inferior being; a brute: *adj.* of or belonging to feeling and moving creatures; as, the *animal* kingdom; an *animal* instinct.

an-i-mal-cu-lar (ăn″ĭ-măl′kū-lȧr), *adj.* of or relating to any minute or microscopic creature.

an-i-mal-cule (ăn″ĭ-măl′kūl), *n.* one of a class of minute or nearly invisible creatures.

an-i-mal-ism (ăn″ĭ-măl-ĭzm), *n.* the state of being influenced by sensual instincts or appetites; the theory which regards mankind as mere beasts, or as dominated by brutish qualities and passions, and not by spiritual impulses.

an-i-mate (ăn'ĭ-māt), *v.t.* to impart life to; to inspire with energy or action; enliven; stimulate; rouse: *adj.* (ăn'ĭ-māt), endowed with natural life; full of spirit and vigor.—*p.adj.* animated.

an-i-ma-tion (ăn'ĭ-mā'shŭn), *n.* the act of giving life or spirit; the state of being enlivened; vivacity; exhilaration; eagerness; sprightliness.

an-i-mos-i-ty (ăn'ĭ-mŏs'ĭ-tĭ), *n.* [*pl.* animosities (-tĭz)], hostility; hatred; active enmity.

an-i-mus (ăn'ĭ-mŭs), *n.* mind; moving spirit, or purpose; hostile intention.

an-ise (ăn'ĭs), *n.* the common name for an Egyptian plant yielding the aromatic aniseed.

an-kle (ăŋ'kl), *n.* the joint or articulation connecting the foot with the leg.

an-klet (ăŋ'klĕt), *n.* an ornamental ring for the ankle; a fetter or shackle; a support for the ankle.

an-nal-ist (ăn'ăl-ĭst), *n.* a compiler of historical events as they occur year by year.

an-nals (ăn'ălz), *n.pl.* a description, history, or register issued from time to time, of events as they happen year by year; chronicles.

an-neal (ă-nēl'), *v.t.* to render soft and tough by heat; as, to *anneal* glass so that it will be less brittle; bake or fuse.

an-nex (ă-nĕks'), *v.t.* to add or attach at the end; to affix or connect; to unite, as a smaller thing to a greater; as, to *annex* a conquered province to a kingdom: *n.* something attached to something else; an auxiliary building.

an-nex-a-tion (ăn'ĕk-sā'shŭn), *n.* the act of adding or joining; as, the *annexation* of territory; that which is joined or added.

an-nex-a-tion-ist (ăn'ĕk-sā'shŭn-ĭst), *n.* one who believes in, or promotes, the addition of territory to his own country by joining to it the whole or part of another country.

an-ni-hi-late (ă-nī'hĭ-lāt), *v.t.* to reduce to nothing; wipe out of existence; destroy.

an-ni-hi-la-tion (ă-nī'hĭ-lā'shŭn), *n.* total destruction; nonexistence.

an-ni-ver-sa-ry (ăn'ĭ-vûr'sȧ-rĭ), *n.* [*pl.* anniversaries (-rĭz)], the return in each year of the date of an event; the annual commemoration of an event; a day for the annual celebration of an event.

an-no Do-mi-ni (ăn'ō dŏm'ĭ-nī), in the year of our Lord; in the year (specified) of the Christian era: commonly abbreviated A. D. [Lat.]

an-no-tate (ăn'ō-tāt), *v.t.* to mark or note by way of explanation or criticism, as a book.

an-no-ta-tion (ăn'ō-tā'shŭn), *n.* a note of explanation, comment, or criticism, made in connection with any text.

an-no-ta-tor (ăn'ō-tā'tĕr), *n.* one who writes remarks by way of comment or criticism upon the work or works of an author; a commentator.

an-nounce (ă-nouns'), *v.t.* to proclaim or make known, formally or in a public manner; to pronounce by judicial sentence; to publish; to proclaim.

an-nounce-ment (ă-nouns'mĕnt), *n.* the act of proclaiming or declaring; that which is set forth or made known; a proclamation; publication; notification.

an-noy (ă-noi'), *v.t.* [*p.t.* and *p.p.* annoyed; *p.pr.* annoying], to vex or trouble by repeated acts; tire or disturb by petty injury or opposition.

an-noy-ance (ă-noi'ăns), *n.* the act of causing vexation; a feeling of trouble or vexation; the thing or act which teases, bothers, or troubles.

an-noy-ing (ă-noi'ĭng), *adj.* vexing; teasing; irritating.

an-noy-ing-ly (ă-noi'ĭng-lĭ), *adv.* in a vexatious or troublesome manner.

an-nu-al (ăn'ū-ăl), *adj.* happening once in twelve months; yearly; of or pertaining to a year; completed in a year; lasting or living for only a year or season; as, an *annual* plant: *n.* a book or literary collection published once a year; anything that lasts but one year, as a plant.—*adv.* annually.

an-nu-i-tant (ă-nū'ĭ-tănt), *n.* one who is in receipt of, or is entitled to receive, a certain sum of money each year.

an-nu-i-ty (ă-nū'ĭ-tĭ), *n.* [*pl.* annuities (-tĭz)], a sum of money payable in periodical or yearly installments; a yearly income granted by another.

an-nul (ă-nŭl'), *v.t.* [*p.t.* and *p.p.* annulled, *p.pr.* annulling], to make void, abolish, or do away with, as a law, decree, or compact.

an-nul-ment (ă-nŭl'mĕnt), *n.* the act of destroying the force of; abolition.

an-nun-ci-ate (ă-nŭn'shĭ-āt), *v.t.* to make known officially or publicly; announce.

an-nun-ci-a-tion (ă-nŭn'sĭ-ā'shŭn; ă-nŭn'shĭ-ā'shŭn), *n.* the act of making known; proclamation.—**Annunciation**, the Catholic Church festival (Lady Day, March 25) celebrating the announcement to Mary, by the angel Gabriel, of the incarnation of Christ.—Luke i. 28–38.

an-nun-ci-a-tor (ă-nŭn'shĭ-ā'tĕr), *n.* a signaling device; an indicator used in hotels, elevators, etc. and connected with the bells and telephones to show where attendance is required.

an-o-dyne (ăn'ō-dīn), *adj.* assuaging or relieving pain: *n.* a drug which relieves pain; an opiate.

a-noint (ȧ-noint'), *v.t.* to pour oil upon; in a religious ceremony, to pour oil upon by way of consecration; consecrate.

a-nom-a-lous (ȧ-nŏm'ȧ-lŭs), *adj.* deviating or turning aside from the common order; abnormal; irregular.

a-nom-a-ly (ȧ-nŏm'ȧ-lĭ), *n.* a deviation or turning from the natural order; anything that deviates from the common rule.

a-non (ȧ-nŏn'), *adv.* soon; straightway; without delay; again.

a-non-y-mous (ȧ-nŏn'ĭ-mŭs), *adj.* without the author's name; nameless; as, an *anonymous* letter.

an-oth-er (ă-nŭth'ĕr), *adj.* and *pron.* one more; not the same; as, he has become *another* man; any other; any or some one else.

an-swer (ȧn'sĕr), *n.* a response or rejoinder; a reply to a charge; a solution, as of a mathematical problem: *v.t.* to speak or write in reply to a question, request, challenge, demand, letter, or anything said or written; respond to an act; as, to *answer* the bell; to be accountable for; as, he had to *answer* for his sins; to reply to a charge.

an-swer-a-ble (ăn'sẽr-ȧ-bl), *adj.* admitting of a satisfactory reply; liable to give an account; responsible.

ant (ănt), *n.* a small insect, usually social like the bees.

an-tag-o-nism (ăn-tăg'ō-nĭzm), *n.* the active opposition of two opponents or opposing forces; hostility.

an-tag-o-nist (ăn-tăg'ō-nĭst), *n.* a competitor; one who contends with another in combat or argument; an opponent.

an-tag-o-nis-tic (ăn-tăg"ō-nĭs'tĭk), *adj.* contending against; acting in opposition; opposed.

an-tag-o-nis-ti-cal-ly (ăn-tăg"ō-nĭs'-tĭ-kăl-ĭ), *adv.* in rivalry or opposition.

an-tag-o-nize (ăn-tăg'ō-nīz), *v.t.* to oppose; hinder; counteract; contend against; compete with: *v.i.* to act in opposition.

ant-arc-tic (ănt-ärk'tĭk), *adj.* opposite to the arctic, or north pole; relating to the south-polar regions; southern: **Antarctic Ocean**, the south-polar ocean.

ant-eat-er (ănt'ēt"ẽr), *n.* an animal which feeds upon ants.

an-te bel-lum (ăn'tē bĕl'ŭm), before the war; usually, before the American Civil War. [LAT.]

an-te-cede (ăn"tē-sēd'), *v.t.* to precede or go before in time or space.

an-te-ced-ence (ăn"tē-sēd'ĕns), *n.* the act or state of going before in time, place, rank, or order; precedence; priority. Also, **antecedency**.

an-te-ced-ent (ăn"tē-sēd'ĕnt), *n.* the noun to which a relative or other pronoun refers; as, Lincoln is the president who is most beloved by the common people: "president" is the *antecedent* of "who": *pl.* the previous events and influences in a person's life: *adj.* preceding.

an-te-cham-ber (ăn'tē-chăm"bẽr), *n.* an apartment leading into the principal room; an outer room where persons wait for an interview.

an-te-date (ăn'tē-dāt"), *v.t.* to give an earlier date to than the right one; as, to *antedate* a check; to occur at an earlier time; as, the Civil War *antedated* emancipation; Shakespeare *antedates* Milton: *n.* a date earlier than the actual date.

an-te-di-lu-vi-an (ăn"tē-dĭ-lū'vĭ-ăn), *adj.* of or relating to the time or period before the Flood; pertaining to very ancient times; antiquated: *n.* one who, or that which, lived before the Flood.

an-te-lope (ăn'tē-lōp), *n.* an animal belonging to the same family as the deer and the goat.

an-te-me-rid-i-an (ăn"tē-mē-rĭd'ĭ-ăn), *adj.* before noon; relating to the forenoon: regularly abbreviated or shortened to A. M.

an-te-na-tal (ăn"tē-nā'tăl), *adj.* occurring or existing before birth.

an-ten-na (ăn-tĕn'ȧ), *n.* [*pl.* antennæ (-ē)], one of the jointed horns or feelers upon the heads of insects; a framework of wires supported in the air for sending and receiving the electric waves of wireless telegraphy.

an-te-nup-tial (ăn"tē-nŭp'shăl), *adj.* preceding marriage; made before marriage; as, an *antenuptial* agreement about property.

an-te-pe-nult (ăn"tē-pē'nŭlt; ăn"tē-pē-nŭlt'), *n.* the last syllable but two of a word; the third syllable from the end. Also, **antepenultima**.

an-te-pe-nul-ti-mate (ăn"tē-pē-nŭl'-tĭ-măt), *adj.* relating to the last but two: *n.* that which is last but two.

an-te-ri-or (ăn-tē'rĭ-ẽr), *adj.* situated more to the front; former; earlier; preceding.

an-te-room (ăn'tē-rōōm"), *n.* a room before, or forming an entrance to, another; an antechamber.

an-them (ăn'thĕm), *n.* a composition from the Scriptures or liturgy set to sacred music; a song of praise or gladness.

an-ther (ăn'thẽr), *n.* the part of a flower containing the pollen.

an-thol-o-gy (ăn-thŏl'ō-jĭ), *n.* a collection of choice poems, epigrams, or other literary extracts by different authors.

an-thra-cite (ăn'thrȧ-sīt), *n.* a hard, mineral coal burning without smoke and giving intense heat.

an-thrax (ăn'thrăks), *n.* [*pl.* anthraces (-sēz)], a contagious disease of animals, especially of cattle and sheep; a burning ulcer or tumor, like a boil.

an-thro-poid (ăn'thrō-poid), *adj.* manlike: *n.* one of the higher apes resembling man.

an-thro-pol-o-gist (ăn"thrō-pŏl'ō-jĭst), *n.* one who studies the science and history of the human race.

an-thro-pol-o-gy (ăn"thrō-pŏl'ō-jĭ), *n.* the science of man or mankind; a systematic study of man as regards his origin, nature, original condition, etc.—*adj.* **anthropologic**, **anthropological**.

an-thro-po-met-ric (ăn"thrō-pō-mĕt'-rĭk), *adj.* relating to the measurement or proportions of the human body.

an-thro-po-mor-phic (ăn"thrō-pō-môr'fĭk), *adj.* manlike or resembling man. Also, **anthropomorphous**.

an-tic (ăn'tĭk), *n.* a funny trick or action: *v.i.* to perform odd actions; play tricks; cut capers: *adj.* odd or strange in form, dress, or gesture; fantastic; grotesque.

an-ti-air-craft (ăn'tĭ-âr'krȧft), *adj.* directed against airships; as, *anti-aircraft* guns; equipped to shoot against airships; as, *anti-aircraft* batteries.

An-ti-christ (ăn'tĭ-krīst), *n.* an opponent of Christ; especially, the great personal opponent expected by many to appear before the end of the world.—1 John ii. 22.

an-tic-i-pate (ăn-tĭs'ĭ-pāt), *v.t.* to look forward to; to expect; to foresee and do beforehand; to prevent: *v.i.* to treat of something before the proper time; to recur at shorter intervals than usual.—*adj.* **anticipatory**, **anticipative**.

Syn. apprehend, expect, hope, forecast, forestall.

an-tic-i-pa-tion (ăn-tĭs"ĭ-pā'shŭn), *n.* the act of taking beforehand; expectation; hope; foretaste; foresight.

an-ti-cli-max (ăn'tĭ-klī'măks), *n.* a ludicrous or ridiculous drop in thought and expression; an abrupt descent from the mention of more important to less important things: opposite to *climax*.

an-ti-cy-clone (ăn'tĭ-sī'klōn), *n.* an atmospheric condition in which the ordinary features of a cyclone are reversed, or when the winds, which are light, flow from instead of towards the center.

an-ti-dot-al (ăn'tĭ-dōt'ăl), *adj.* of the nature or quality of a remedy for poison.

an-ti-dote (ăn'tĭ-dōt), *n.* a medicine which counteracts the effects of poison or disease; that which annuls, counteracts, or tends to prevent evil; a remedy.

an-ti-fe-brile (ăn'tĭ-fē'bril), *adj.* tending to cure or prevent fever.

an-ti-ma-cas-sar (ăn'tĭ-mȧ-kăs'ȧr), *n.* a cover for the back or arms of a chair, a sofa, etc.; a tidy.

an-ti-mo-ny (ăn'tĭ-mō-nĭ), *n.* a white shining metallic element entering into various important alloys, as pewter, Babbitt metal, type metal, etc.; also used in certain medicines, as tartar emetic.

an-tin-o-my (ăn'tĭn'ō-mĭ), *n.* the opposition of one rule, law, or principle to another; any rule or law opposed to another.

an-tip-a-thy (ăn-tĭp'ȧ-thĭ), *n.* [*pl.* antipathies (-thĭz)], a strong aversion or dislike; loathing; disgust; the object of dislike: followed by *to*, *against*, *between*, or *for*.

Syn. aversion, distaste, hatred, hostility, repulsion.

Ant. (see attraction).

an-ti-phon (ăn'tĭ-fŏn), *n.* a musical response, as in a chant.

an-tiph-o-nal (ăn-tĭf'ō-năl), *adj.* relating to responsive singing: *n.* a book of anthems; a collection of musical responses, charts, or hymns.

an-tiph-o-ny (ăn-tĭf'ō-nĭ), *n.* [*pl.* antiphonies (-nĭz)], the alternate or responsive singing by a choir divided into two parts, each part rendering alternately verses of a hymn or anthem; a musical setting of sacred verses arranged for alternate singing.

an-tip-o-dal (ăn-tĭp'ō-dăl), *adj.* relating to the opposite sides of the globe; diametrically opposite.

an-ti-pode (ăn'tĭ-pōd), *n.* one who resides on the opposite side of the earth; that which is directly opposite to something else.

an-tip-o-des (ăn-tĭp'ō-dēz), *n.pl.* those who, residing at opposite sides of the globe, have their feet directly opposed to each other; the two portions of the earth's surface which are exactly opposite to each other; the direct opposite of a person or thing.

an-ti-py-rin (ăn'tĭ-pī'rĭn), *n.* a drug, obtained from coal-tar, used for the relief of neuralgia, nervous headaches, and fevers.

an-ti-qua-ri-an (ăn'tĭ-kwā'rĭ-ăn), *adj.* relating to ancient things or times: *n.* a student of ancient things.

an-ti-qua-ry (ăn'tĭ-kwā-rĭ), *n.* one who is attached to ancient things and is learned in their history; one who collects relics of former times for the purpose of study.

an-ti-quat-ed (ăn'tĭ-kwāt'ĕd), *p.adj.* grown old; old-fashioned; obsolete or out of use; ancient.

an-tique (ăn-tēk'), *adj.* of or pertaining to a former age; ancient: *n.* something of great age; a relic of ancient times.

Syn., *adj.* old-fashioned.

Ant. (see modern, new).

an-tiq-ui-ty (ăn-tĭk'wĭ-tĭ), *n.* [*pl.* antiquities (-tĭz)], great age; early ages; the people or races of ancient times; that which belonged to, or survives from, ancient times; a relic.

an-ti-sep-tic (ăn'tĭ-sĕp'tĭk), *adj.* destroying the germs of disease or decay: *n.* any substance which destroys disease germs or prevents their growth.

an-tith-e-sis (ăn-tĭth'ē-sĭs), *n.* [*pl.* antitheses (-sēz)], opposition; contrast; expression by contrast or opposition of words or ideas; a figure of speech that shows contrast; as, "To err is human; to forgive divine."—*adj.* antithetic, antithetical.

an-ti-tox-in (ăn'tĭ-tŏk'sĭn), *n.* a preventive of, or cure for, diphtheria and other contagious diseases.

an-ti-trade (ăn'tĭ-trād'), *n.* a tropical or southern wind blowing steadily in an opposite direction to the trade wind, which blows easterly toward the equator.

ant-ler (ănt'lēr), *n.* the entire horn, or any branch of the horn, of any member of the deer family.

an-to-nym (ăn'tō-nĭm), *n.* a word which is the opposite, in meaning, of another word in the same language: opposite to *synonym*.

a-nus (ā'nŭs), *n.* the posterior opening of the digestive tube or alimentary canal.

an-vil (ăn'vĭl), *n.* a block, usually of iron faced with steel, on which metals are hammered and shaped.

Anvil

anx-i-e-ty (ăng-zī'ē-tĭ), *n.* [*pl.* anxieties (-tĭz)], a condition of mental uneasiness arising from fear or solicitude.

Syn. concern, care, dread, fear, worry, trouble.

Ant. (see ease, calmness).

anx-ious (ănk'shŭs), *adj.* deeply concerned; greatly troubled; very solicitous or uneasy; desirous; as, *anxious* to please.—*adv.* anxiously.—*n.* anxiousness.

an-y (ĕn'ĭ), *adj.* one, indeterminately or indefinitely; some; one of an indefinite number, quantity, or degree: *pron.* one; anyone: (*pl.*) some: *adv.* to any extent; at all; in any degree: used with comparatives; as, *any* better.

an-y-bod-y (ĕn'ĭ-bŏd-ĭ), *n.* an ordinary person; any person; some one of importance; as, Is he *anybody*? Everybody who was *anybody* was there.

an-y-how (ĕn'ĭ-hou), *adv.* in any way or manner; in any case; at any rate.

an-y-thing (ĕn'ĭ-thĭng), *n.* a thing of any sort; something or other, no matter what; any object, state, act, event or fact, whatever.

an-y-way (ĕn'ĭ-wā), *adv.* in any manner; anyhow; no matter what happens; nevertheless. Also, anyways.

an-y-where (ĕn'ĭ-hwâr), *adv.* in or at any place; as, I cannot find it *anywhere*.

an-y-wise (ĕn'ĭ-wīz), *adv.* in any way or manner; anyhow; at all.

An-zac (ăn-zăc'), *n.* a name given in 1915 to the troops from the self-governing colonies of Australia and New Zealand in the British Empire: composed of the initial letters of Australia–New Zealand Army Corps.

a-or-ta (ā-ôr'tȧ), *n.* [*pl.* aortæ (-tē)], the chief artery which carries the blood from the heart to all parts of the body except the lungs.

a-pace (ȧ-pās'), *adv.* quickly; at a quick pace; speedily; rapidly.

A-pa-che (ȧ-pä'chā), *n.* one of a tribe of American Indians originally inhabiting what is now part of New Mexico, Arizona, and Mexico; a member of a gang of desperate criminals infesting the streets of Paris.

a-part (ȧ-pärt'), *adv.* separately; aside; asunder; so as to be separated for use.

a-part-ment (ȧ-pärt'mĕnt), *n.* a separate room or several connected rooms of a building; two or more rooms of a house set apart as a home: *pl.* any suite of rooms.

ap-a-thet-ic (ăp"ȧ-thĕt'ĭk), *adj.* without feeling or emotion; passionless; languid. Also, **apathetical.**—*adv.* **apathetically.**

ap-a-thy (ăp'ȧ-thĭ), *n.* [*pl.* apathies (-thĭz)], lack of feeling; want of passion or emotion; indifference.

Syn. composure, unconcern, sluggishness.
Ant. (see agitation, anxiety).

ape (āp), *n.* a tailless monkey resembling man in structure and organs, semierect, with very long arms: the family of the apes includes the gorilla, chimpanzee, orang-outang, etc.; a silly mimic; a fool: *v.t.* to mimic, as an ape.

a-peak (ȧ-pēk'), *adv.* a nautical term: in a nearly upright position; in an up and down direction.

a-pe-ri-ent (ȧ-pē'rĭ-ĕnt), *n.* a mild laxative medicine or food, like figs or prunes: *adj.* gently laxative; opening the bowels.

ap-er-ture (ăp'ẽr-tûr), *n.* an opening: a gap, hole, chasm, or passage; any direct inlet or outlet.

a-pex (ā'pĕks), *n.* [*pl.* apices (ăp'ĭ-sēz), and apexes (ā'pĕk-sēz)], the point, tip, or summit of anything.

a-pha-si-a (ȧ-fā'zhĭ-ȧ), *n.* loss of the power of speech, or the proper use of words, due to disease or injury of the brain.

a-phel-i-on (ȧ-fēl'yŭn; ȧ-fē'lĭ-ŏn), *n.* [*pl.* aphelia (-yȧ)], that point in the orbit or path of a planet or a comet which is farthest from the sun.

a-phid (ā'fĭd; ăf'ĭd), *n.* a plant louse; a small, wingless insect, parasitic on plants.

aph-o-rism (ăf'ō-rĭzm), *n.* a concise or brief statement of a rule or precept; a maxim.

Aph-ro-di-te (ăf"rō-dī'tē), *n.* the Greek goddess of love and beauty; Venus.—**aphrodite,** a richly colored butterfly.

a-pi-a-ry (ā'pĭ-ā-rĭ), *n.* [*pl.* apiaries (-rĭz)], a place where bees are kept; a bee-house; a collection of hives.

a-piece (ȧ-pēs'), *adv.* to or for each person or thing; each; severally.

ap-ish (āp'ĭsh), like an ape in manners; silly; affected; foppish; foolish; prone to servile imitation.

a-plomb (à"plôn'), *n.* self-possession; assurance; a perfect confidence in oneself. [Fr.]

a-poc-a-lypse (ȧ-pŏk'ȧ-lĭps), *n.* revelation; discovery; disclosure: **Apocalypse,** the last book of the New Testament, called the Revelation of St. John the Divine.—*adj.* **apocalyptic.**

a-poc-ry-pha (ȧ-pŏk'rĭ-fȧ), *n.pl.* used as a *sing.* with *pl.* apocryphas (-fȧz), a writing or statement of doubtful authorship: **Apocrypha,** certain writings appended or added to the Old Testament which are received by some Christians and rejected by others.

a-poc-ry-phal (ȧ-pŏk'rĭ-făl), *adj.* of doubtful authority; fictitious; false; of or relating to the doubtful writings formerly printed with the Bible.

ap-o-gee (ăp'ō-jē), *n.* that point in the orbit or path of a planet, especially of the moon, which is most distant from the earth; the highest or most distant point; the height; the climax; the culmination.

A-pol-lo (ȧ-pŏl'ō), *n.* the god of the sun, music, poetry, eloquence, medicine, and the fine arts; son of Jupiter and Leto. Also, **Helios.**

a-pol-o-get-ic (ȧ-pŏl"ō-jĕt'ĭk), *adj.* defending by words or argument; making defense or excuse. Also, **apologetical.**—*adv.* **apologetically.**

a-pol-o-gize (ȧ-pŏl'ō-jīz), *v.i.* to make an excuse; to express regret or make amends for anything said or done, on one's own behalf or that of another.

ap-o-logue (ăp'ō-lŏg), *n.* a fable or tale which teaches a useful lesson; a fictitious story containing a moral truth, such as Æsop's fables.

a-pol-o-gy (ȧ-pŏl'ō-jĭ), *n.* [*pl.* apologies (-jĭz)], a vindication or excuse; something spoken, written, or offered in defense; an explanation by way of amends; a temporary substitute; a makeshift.

Syn. acknowledgment, justification, plea.
Ant. (see censure).

ap-o-plec-tic (ăp"ō-plĕk'tĭk), *adj.* relating to, or of the nature of, the physical state caused by too high blood pressure; afflicted with loss of power through the breaking of a blood-vessel in the brain. Also, **apoplectical.**

ap-o-plex-y (ăp'ō-plĕk"sĭ), *n.* the sudden loss of consciousness and motion, resulting from a broken blood-vessel in the brain.

a-pos-ta-sy (ȧ-pŏs'tȧ-sĭ), *n.* [*pl.* apostasies (-sĭz)], the giving up of what one has professed or believed, as faith, principles, or party.

a-pos-tate (ȧ-pŏs'tāt), *n.* one who has forsaken his faith or party; one who abandons his profession after having been in holy orders; a renegade: *adj.* false; traitorous.

a-pos-tle (ȧ-pŏs'l), *n.* one charged with a high mission; one of the twelve persons specially selected by Christ to teach his gospel.—Luke vi. 13; the first missionary who plants the Christian faith in any region; one who labors with special success as a moral or social reformer.

A-pos-tles' Creed (ȧ-pŏs'lz krēd), an early summary of the Christian religion, in its present wording dating from about 500 A. D.

ap-os-tol-ic (ăp′ŏs-tŏl′ĭk), *adj.* of or relating to the twelve followers of Christ, chosen to preach his gospel, or to their age, doctrine, or practice; as, the *apostolic* age or the *apostolic* faith. Also, **apostolical.**

a-pos-tro-phe (*d*-pŏs′trŏ-fē), *n.* a breaking off in a speech to address directly a person or persons who may or may not be present; the sign ['], used to denote the omission from a word of one or more letters, or to denote the possessive case of nouns.

a-poth-e-ca-ry (*d*-pŏth′ē-kā-rĭ), *n.* [*pl.* apothecaries (-rĭz)], one who prepares and sells medicines and drugs for profit; a pharmacist.

a-poth-e-ca-ries' weight (*d*-pŏth′ē-kā-rĭz wāt), the weight used for dispensing drugs, and comprising the pound (12 oz.), the ounce (8 drachms), the drachm (3 scruples), the scruple (20 grains), and the grain.

ap-o-thegm (ăp′ō-thĕm), *n.* a short, pithy, instructive saying; a maxim. Also, **apophthegm.**

ap-o-the-o-sis (ăp′ō-thē′ō-sĭs; *d*-pŏth′ē-ō′sĭs), *n.* [*pl.* apotheoses (-sēz)], deification, or the bestowing of godlike qualities upon a person; excessive honor paid to a distinguished person; during the Roman Empire such divine honors were given deceased emperors and members of the royal family.

ap-o-the-o-size (ăp′ō-thē′ō-sīz), *v.t.* to exalt or elevate to the rank of a god; to deify; to glorify.

ap-pall (ă-pôl′), *v.t.* [*p.t.* and *p.p.* appalled, *p.pr.* appalling], to frighten, depress, or discourage by fear; to dismay; to terrify.

ap-pall-ing (ă-pôl′ĭng), *p.adj.* inspiring horror or dismay; frightful.

ap-pa-ra-tus (ăp′*d*-rā′tŭs), *n. sing.* and *pl.* an outfit of tools, utensils, or instruments adapted to, or necessary for, the accomplishment of any branch of work, or for the performance of an experiment or operation; a set of such appliances; machinery; mechanism.

ap-par-el (ă-păr′ĕl), *n.* clothing, dress, or garb: *v.t.* [*p.t.* and *p.p.* appareled, *p.pr.* appareling], to clothe; furnish or fit out.

ap-par-ent (ă-păr′ĕnt), *adj.* open to view; capable of being easily understood; evident.—*adv.* **apparently.**

Syn. likely, probable, seeming.
Ant. (see doubtful).

ap-pa-ri-tion (ăp′*d*-rĭsh′ŭn), *n.* a visible object; an appearance of something not real or tangible; a ghost or specter; the first appearance of a star after having been obscured or invisible.

ap-peal (ă-pēl′), *v.t.* to transfer or refer to a superior court or judge; as, to *appeal* a case: *v.i.* to refer to another person or tribunal; entreat, call for, or invoke aid, sympathy, or mercy: *n.* a call or invocation for aid or sympathy; the right of referring a judicial decision to a higher court; a summons to answer a charge; a call or reference to another for proof.—*p.adj.* **appealing.**—*adv.* **appealingly.**

ap-pear (ă-pēr′), *v.i.* to come or be in sight; to become visible; come before; as, to *appear* in court; to seem; as, he *appears* to be very ill; to come before the public.

ap-pear-ance (ă-pēr′ăns), *n.* the act of becoming visible; the object seen; an apparition; outward show; the act of coming before the public; the coming into, or the being present in, court; outward look, bearing, or aspect.

ap-pease (ă-pēz′), *v.t.* to quiet; to satisfy; to pacify; as, to *appease* anger.

ap-pel-lant (ă-pĕl′ănt), *n.* one who appeals to a higher court; one who appeals to a judge, or to any tribunal.

ap-pel-late (ă-pĕl′āt), *adj.* relating to appeals; as, an *appellate* court.

ap-pel-la-tion (ăp′ĕ-lā′shŭn), *n.* the name, title, or designation by which a person or thing is called or known; the act of appealing from a lower to a higher court.

ap-pend (ă-pĕnd′), *v.t.* to attach, hang, or suspend; add to; annex.

ap-pen-dage (ă-pĕn′dāj), *n.* something added or attached which is a proper part of a greater thing, such as an arm; something added as an adjunct or that is not a necessary part, such as a porch to a house.

Syn. accessory, adjunct, addition.
Ant. (see total).

ap-pen-di-ci-tis (ă-pĕn′dĭ-sī′tĭs), *n.* an inflammation or disease of the vermiform appendix, or small blind intestine.

ap-pen-dix (ă-pĕn′dĭks), *n.* [*pl.* appendixes (-dĭk-sĕz), appendices (-dĭ-sēz)], that which is added as supplemental; as, the *appendix* to a book; the vermiform appendix, a wormlike organ, ordinarily three or four inches in length, situated at the beginning of the intestine in man and some animals.

ap-per-cep-tion (ăp′ĕr-sĕp′shŭn), *n.* an act of voluntary attention; the act of the mind by which it becomes conscious of its ideas as its own.

ap-per-tain (ăp′ĕr-tān′), *v.i.* to belong to by right, nature, and custom; to pertain.

ap-pe-tite (ăp′ē-tīt), *n.* a physical craving for food; the desire to satisfy a want or inclination; a mental longing.

ap-pe-tiz-er (ăp′ē-tīz′ĕr), *n.* something that excites or whets the desire for anything; anything that gives a relish for food.—*adj.* **appetizing.**

ap-plaud (ă-plôd′), *v.t.* to express approval or approbation of by clapping of the hands; to commend: *v.i.* to clap the hands in praise or approval.

ap-plause (ă-plôz′), *n.* the expression of approval by clapping; approbation or praise expressed openly.

ap-ple (ăp′l), *n.* the round fleshy fruit of a well-known tree almost universally cultivated in temperate regions, of which there are many varieties; the tree itself.

ap-pli-ance (ă-plī′ăns), *n.* the act of putting into use; something used as a means to an end, as tools, machinery; as, the *appliances* of a trade; the *appliances* of war.

ap-pli-ca-bil-i-ty (ăp′lĭ-k*d*-bĭl′ĭ-tĭ), *n.* fitness for use; appropriateness; suitability.

ap-pli-ca-ble (ăp′lĭ-k*d*-bl), *adj.* fit; suitable; appropriate; as, that remark was not *applicable* to me.—*adv.* **applicably.**

ap-pli-cant (ăp′lĭ-kănt), *n.* one who asks or requests something; a candidate.

ap-pli-ca-tion (ăp′lĭ-kā′shŭn), *n.* the act of putting on; as, the pain was lessened by the *application* of heat; the thing put on; the practical demonstration of a principle; the act of requesting; a request; close attention.

ap-plied (ă-plīd'), *p.adj.* put on or to; employed or used; as, *applied* mechanics.

ap-pli-qué (ă"plē"kā'), *n.* any ornamentation in dress or upholstery cut from other patterns and laid on to a foundation of any material: *adj.* laid on. [Fr.]

ap-ply (ă-plī'), *v.t.* [*p.t.* and *p.p.* applied, *p.pr.* applying], to bring into contact with something; lay on; to put into practice; to devote to a particular purpose; to fix the mind upon: *v.i.* to ask; to petition; to request; to have some connection; as, their remarks do not *apply* to you.

ap-point (ă-point'), *v.t.* to name; to establish by decree; to assign; to designate for an office; to fix the time and order of; to furnish or equip: *v.i.* to decree; ordain; determine; nominate.

ap-point-ee (ă-poin"tē'), *n.* one who is chosen to fill an office or position of trust.

ap-point-ment (ă-point'mĕnt), *n.* the act of assigning to an office or trust; the position or office assigned or held; an engagement; an arrangement to meet by mutual agreement: *pl.* furniture or equipment.

ap-por-tion (ă-pōr'shŭn), *v.t.* to assign by some rule; distribute or set out in just proportions.

Syn. allot, assign, appoint, divide.

Ant. (see collect).

ap-por-tion-ment (ă-pōr'shŭn-mĕnt), *n.* the act of dividing into just shares.

ap-po-site (ăp'ō-zĭt), *adj.* appropriate; suitable; well adapted; fit.

ap-po-si-tion (ăp"ō-zĭsh'ŭn), *n.* the act of placing side by side; the setting of a word or phrase beside another without a connective, by way of explanation; as, St. Mark, the Evangelist.

ap-po-si-tive (ă-pŏz'ĭ-tĭv), *adj.* explanatory: *n.* a word or phrase set beside another to explain it.

ap-prais-al (ă-prāz'ăl), *n.* the act of valuing or putting a price upon; valuation.

ap-praise (ă-prāz'), *v.t.* to set a price upon; value; estimate the worth of.

ap-praise-ment (ă-prāz'mĕnt), *n.* the act of valuing; an authorized estimate or valuation.

ap-prais-er (ă-prāz'ẽr), *n.* a person licensed and sworn to estimate the value of goods or estate.

ap-pre-ci-a-ble (ă-prē'shĭ-ȧ-bl), *adj.* capable of being valued, perceived, or estimated; perceptible.

ap-pre-ci-ate (ă-prē'shĭ-āt), *v.t.* to value; estimate the worth of; esteem highly; to recognize worth and quality of; to prize; to be sensible of; to raise in value: *v.i.* to rise in price or value.

ap-pre-ci-a-tion (ă-prē"shĭ-ā'shŭn), *n.* the just valuation, or proper recognition of worth or merit; sympathetic understanding; a rise in value.

ap-pre-ci-a-tive (ă-prē'shĭ-ā-tĭv), *adj.* showing esteem or interest; as, an *appreciative* audience.

ap-pre-hend (ăp"rē-hĕnd'), *v.t.* to take or lay hold of; seize; arrest; take mental hold of; as, to *apprehend* the meaning of a statement; anticipate or expect, usually, with fear: *v.i.* to incline to believe; suppose; catch the idea or meaning; to look forward with fear.

ap-pre-hen-si-ble (ăp"rē-hĕn'sĭ-bl), *adj.* capable of being conceived; understandable.

ap-pre-hen-sion (ăp"rē-hĕn'shŭn), *n.* the act of seizure or of laying hold of; arrest; mental grasp; perception; anticipation of evil; fear or distrust of the future; anxiety.

ap-pre-hen-sive (ăp"rē-hĕn'sĭv), *adj.* quick to learn, or grasp; fearful of evil; anxious for the future; worried.—*adv.* **apprehensively.**—*n.* **apprehensiveness.**

ap-pren-tice (ă-prĕn'tĭs), *n.* one bound by agreement to serve another a certain number of years in order to learn a trade or craft; a novice, or one slightly versed in anything: *v.t.* to put under the care of a master for instruction in a trade or craft.

ap-pren-tice-ship (ă-prĕn'tĭs-shĭp), *n.* the term of service, or time served while learning a trade.

ap-prise (ă-prīz'), *v.t.* to give notice to by way of warning; to advise; to inform. Also, **apprize.**

ap-prize (ă-prīz'), *v.t.* to put a value upon; to appraise.

ap-proach (ă-prōch'), *v.i.* to draw or be near: *v.t.* to come near to in quality, character, or condition; to nearly equal; *n.* the act of drawing near; access; as, the *approach* to kings; passage or avenue; as, the *approaches* to the city were well guarded.—*adj.* **approachable.**

ap-pro-ba-tion (ăp"rō-bā'shŭn), *n.* the act of pronouncing good; commendation; sanction.

ap-pro-pri-ate (ă-prō'prĭ-āt), *v.t.* to take to oneself, in exclusion of others; claim or use, as by an exclusive or sole right; set apart or assign to a particular use; as, the government *appropriated* money for the building of good roads: *adj.* (ă-prō'-prĭ-āt), fit; apt; suitable; proper.—*adv.* **appropriately.**—*n.* **appropriateness.**

ap-pro-pri-a-tion (ă-prō"prĭ-ā'shŭn), *n.* the act of setting apart for a particular use or person; the act of taking to oneself; anything set apart for a special use or purpose.

ap-prov-al (ă-pro͞ov'ăl), *n.* approbation; sanction; ratification; consent.

ap-prove (ă-pro͞ov'), *v.t.* to test, or demonstrate; ratify; pronounce efficient or sufficient; be pleased or satisfied with; commend: *v.i.* to express satisfaction with: usually followed by *of.*—*p.adj.* **approving.**

ap-prov-ing-ly (ă-pro͞ov'ĭng-lĭ), *adv.* in a commendatory manner or one implying satisfaction.

ap-prox-i-mate (ă-prŏk'sĭ-māt), *v.t.* to come close to; to cause to approach: *v.i.* to approach closely; to be nearly equal: *adj.* (ă-prŏk'sĭ-māt), near in resemblance or position; almost equal; nearly correct.—*adv.* **approximately.**

ap-pur-te-nance (ă-pûr'tē-năns), *n.* that which belongs or relates to something else; an adjunct or appendage; that which belongs to an estate or property, as trees and shrubbery.

ap-pur-te-nant (ă-pûr'tē-nănt), *adj.* pertaining to a more important thing; accessory; incident.

a-pri-cot (ā'prĭ-kŏt; ăp'rĭ-kŏt), the fruit of a tree allied to both the plum and the peach.

A-pril (ā'prĭl), *n.* the fourth month of the year, containing thirty days.

A-pril fool (ā'prĭl fōōl), one who is imposed upon or deceived on April 1, or All Fools' Day.

a pri-o-ri (ā prī-ō'rī; ä-prē-ō'rē), from the former; characterizing an argument proceeding from cause to effect. [Lat.]

a-pron (ā'prŭn; ā'pûrn), *n.* an article made of cloth, leather, or other material, worn on the front of a person's clothes for protection or ornament; a leathern covering for use in an open carriage; anything like an apron in form or use.

a-pro-pos (ăp"rō-pō'), *adv.* to the purpose; to the point; seasonably; with reference to; as, *apropos* of that remark; by the way: *adj.* seasonable; happy. Also, **à propos.** [Fr.]

apse (ăps), *n.* [*pl.* apses (-ĕz)], a semicircular recess terminating the choir or sanctuary of a church.

apt (ăpt), *adj.* suitable; pertinent; appropriate; liable; inclined; prone; ready; expert; quick of comprehension.—*n.* **aptness.**

apt-i-tude (ăp'tĭ-tūd), *n.* capacity for anything; fitness; readiness in learning.

a-qua (ā'kwȧ), *n.* water: a term much used as *Aq.* in pharmacy to indicate the addition of water. [Lat.]

a-qua-ma-rine (ā"kwȧ-mȧ-rēn'), *n.* a transparent beryl, bluish-green in color, used as a gem.

aq-ua-relle (ăk"wȧ-rĕl'), *n.* a painting in water colors.

a-qua-ri-um (ȧ-kwā'rĭ-ŭm), *n.* [*pl.* aquaria (-ȧ), and aquariums (-ŭmz)], a tank or globe in which water plants and animals, such as fish, etc., are kept; a public building devoted to the showing of large collections of water plants and animals.

a-quat-ic (ȧ-kwăt'ĭk), *adj.* relating to water; growing or living in or upon water; performed in or upon water; as, *aquatic* sports: *n.* an animal or plant that lives in water: *pl.* water sports.

a-qua vi-tæ (ā'kwȧ vī'tē), brandy and other distilled spirits. [Lat., water of life.]

aq-ue-duct (ăk'wē-dŭkt), *n.* a conduit or artificial channel for conducting water from a distant source, such as the Catskill *aqueduct*, by means of which New York is supplied with water.

a-que-ous (ā'kwē-ŭs), *adj.* of the nature of, or abounding in, water; watery; formed in or by means of water.

aq-ui-line (ăk'wĭ-lĭn; -līn), *adj.* relating to, or resembling, an eagle; curved, as the beak of an eagle; hooked; prominent; as, an *aquiline* nose.

Ar-ab (ăr'ăb), *n.* a native of Arabia; a desert-dweller; a Bedouin, one of the Arabic races spread over the African and Syrian deserts: **arab,** a homeless street-urchin or outcast.

Arabesque

ar-a-besque (ăr"ȧ-bĕsk'), *n.* a kind of ornamentation in low relief consisting of the representation of plants, fruits, flowers, foliage, etc., fancifully combined or oddly grouped.

Ar-a-bic (ăr'ȧ-bĭk), *adj.* Arabian; pertaining to Arabia or the Arabs: *n.* the Semitic language used by the Arabs.

Ar-a-bic nu-mer-als (ăr'ȧ-bĭk nū'mĕr-ălz), the figures 0, 1, 2, 3, etc., of Hindu origin, used by the Arabs and introduced into Europe in the twelfth century.

ar-a-ble (ăr'ȧ-bl), *adj.* fit for the plow; suited to the purposes of cultivation; as, *arable* land.

ar-bi-ter (är'bĭ-tẽr), *n.* a person having the power to decide a dispute; an umpire or judge. Also, **arbitrator.**

ar-bit-ra-ment (är-bĭt'rȧ-mĕnt), *n.* the right or power of deciding; the decision of chosen judges or umpires; an award.

ar-bi-tra-ri-ly (är'bĭ-trā-rĭ-lĭ), *adv.* in a capricious or unreasonable manner; imperiously.

ar-bi-tra-ry (är'bĭ-trā-rĭ), *adj.* not fixed by rule or law; capricious; imperious; unreasonable; despotic.

ar-bi-trate (är'bĭ-trāt), *v.t.* and *v.i.* to act or decide as judge in a dispute; to settle a dispute as umpire; mediate.

ar-bi-tra-tion (är"bĭ-trā'shŭn), *n.* the settlement of a dispute by a group of persons chosen by those on each side; settlement of a question by mutual agreement; as, disputes between modern nations should be settled by *arbitration.*

ar-bi-tra-tor (är'bĭ-trā"tẽr), *n.* one chosen by the parties in a dispute to settle the difference between them; one who has power to decide. Also, **arbiter.**

ar-bor (är'bẽr), *n.* a bower formed by trees or vines trained over a latticework so as to make a leafy roof; a shaded nook or walk.

Ar-bor Day (är'bẽr dā), a day legally set apart in certain States for the planting of trees.

ar-bo-re-al (är-bō'rē-ăl), *adj.* like, or pertaining to, a tree or trees; attached to, or living among, trees.

ar-bo-res-cent (är"bō-rĕs'ĕnt), *adj.* treelike; branching like a tree.

ar-bo-re-tum (är"bō-rē'tŭm), *n.* [*pl.* arboretums (-tŭmz)], a place in which rare trees are cultivated and exhibited for scientific purposes.

ar-bo-ri-cul-ture (är"bō-rĭ-kŭl"tūr), *n.* the cultivation of trees or shrubs.

ar-bor vi-tæ (är"bŏr vī'tē), an evergreen tree extensively cultivated in gardens, etc. [Lat., tree of life.]

ar-bu-tus (är'bū-tŭs; är-bū'tŭs), *n.* a genus or class of evergreen trees, including the strawberry tree; a creeping plant with small fragrant flowers; the Mayflower.

arc (ärk), *n.* a curved line; any section of a curve forming part of a circle; the portion of a circle described by the sun or any heavenly body in its apparent passage through the heavens; a bow; an arch.

ar-cade (är-kād'), *n.* a row of arches supported by pillars; an arched gallery, or promenade, lined with shops or stores.

Arcade

Ar-ca-di-a (är-kā'dĭ-ȧ), *n.* a mountain district in ancient Greece inhabited by simple.

contented pastoral people; hence, any region or scene of simple pleasure or quiet happiness. Also, **Arcady**.—*adj.* **Arcadian**.

arch (ärch), *n.* a structure of brick or masonry, the wedge-shaped parts of which follow a curved line: usually forming the top of a door, window, or gateway; part of

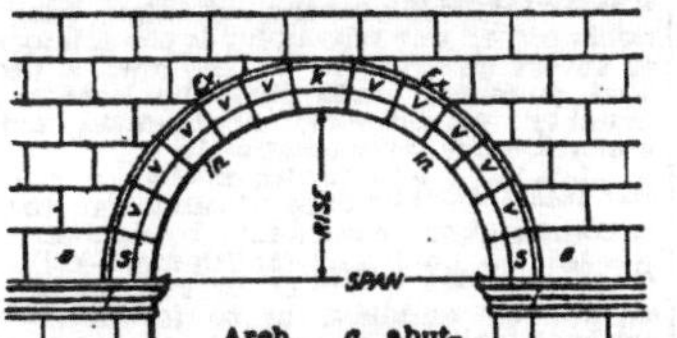

Arch. *a*, abutments; *v*, voussoirs, or arch stones; *s*, springers; *i*, impost; *In*, intrados; *p*, piers; *k*, keystone; *Ex*, extrados.

a curved line: *v.t.* to cover with a curved structure; to bend or curve: *v.i.* to form a bent or curved top or covering; curve: *adj.* chief; of the first rank: used as a prefix; as, *arch*bishop; cunning; crafty; shrewd; mischievous; roguish; sportive; coy.

ar-chæ-ol-o-gist (är'kē-ŏl'ō-jĭst), *n.* one versed in the study of ancient things; an antiquary. Also, **archeologist**.

ar-chæ-ol-o-gy (är'kē-ŏl'ō-jĭ), *n.* the science of antiquities; the study of prehistoric remains, or the relics of the early races of mankind. Also, **archeology**.—*adj.* **archæologic, archæological**.

ar-cha-ic (är-kā'ĭk), *adj.* relating to a remote period; old-fashioned; antiquated. Also, **archaical**.

ar-cha-ism (är'kā-ĭzm), *n.* an antiquated or old-fashioned word, expression, or idiom.

arch-an-gel (ärk'ān'jĕl), *n.* an angel of the highest order.

arch-bish-op (ärch'bĭsh'ŭp), *n.* the chief of the bishops of a church district or province in the Greek, Roman, and English churches.

arch-bish-op-ric (ärch'bĭsh'ŭp-rĭk), *n.* the office, district, or province of an archbishop; the province over which the archbishop has authority.

arch-dea-con (ärch'dē'kn), *n.* a church officer ranking next below a bishop.

arch-duch-ess (ärch'dŭch'ĕs), *n.* the wife of an archduke; a daughter of the imperial family of Austria.

arch-duch-y (ärch'dŭch'ĭ), *n.* [*pl.* archduchies (-ĭz)], the territory or rank of an archduke or archduchess.

arch-duke (ärch'dūk'), *n.* a prince of the imperial house of Austria.

arch-en-e-my (ärch'ĕn'ē-mĭ), *n.* a principal enemy; Satan.

arch-er (är'chẽr), *n.* a bowman; one skilled in the use of the bow and arrow.

arch-er-y (är'chẽr-ĭ), *n.* the art, practice, or skill of one who uses the bow and arrow.

ar-che-type (är'kē-tīp), *n.* the original pattern upon or after which a thing is made; a model; the original or fundamental type-structure from which a natural group of plants or animals have descended.

arch-fiend (ärch'fēnd'), *n.* the chief of demons; Satan.

Arch-ie (är'chĭ) *n.* in the World War, an anti-aircraft gun.

arch-ing (är'chĭng), *p.adj.* curving above something; as, the *arching* elms shaded the street.

ar-chi-pel-a-go (är'kĭ-pĕl'ȧ-gō), *n.* [*pl.* archipelagoes, -gos (-gōz)], any sea or body of water containing numerous islands; the island-group itself.

ar-chi-tect (är'kĭ-tĕkt), *n.* one versed in the art of building and its various styles; one who plans or designs buildings and superintends their construction; hence, one who plans, devises, or plots; a contriver; a designer; a maker.

ar-chi-tec-tur-al (är'kĭ-tĕk'tūr-ăl), *adj.* relating to the art of building; in harmony with the rules of the building art.—*adv.* **architecturally**.

ar-chi-tec-ture (är'kĭ-tĕk'tūr), *n.* the science or art of building, especially of fine or beautiful buildings; the method or style of building; construction; workmanship.

ar-chi-trave (är'kĭ-trāv), *n.* the lowest division of an entablature, or wall supported by columns; that part which rests immediately on the columns of a building or structure.

ar-chive (är'kīv), *n.* [*pl.* archives (-kīvz)], a record preserved as evidence: *pl.* the place where public or state records are kept; state or public documents, or records of historical value relating to a nation or to a family.

arch-ly (ärch'lĭ), *adv.* in a coy manner; roguishly; playfully.

arch-ness (ärch'nĕs), *n.* coyness; roguishness; playfulness.

ar-chon (är'kŏn), *n.* a chief magistrate of ancient Athens; one of the nine chief magistrates chosen to superintend civil and religious matters.

arch-way (ärch'wā), *n.* an opening or passage beneath a curved or vaulted roof.

arc light (ärk līt), a light produced by a current of electricity passing between two carbon points placed a short distance from each other, such as the lights used on city streets.

arc-tic (ärk'tĭk), *adj.* relating to the region of the north pole; polar; northern; frigid: *n.* in the United States, a warmly lined, waterproof overshoe.—**Arctic Ocean**, the north-polar ocean.

arc-tic cir-cle (ärk'tĭk sûr'kl), an imaginary circle parallel to the equator and distant 23° 28′ from the north pole.

ar-dent (är'dĕnt), *adj.* hot; burning; fiery; warm; glowing; passionate; eager; zealous; vehement.

ar-dent spir-its (är'dĕnt spĭr'ĭts), alcoholic liquids, such as brandy, whisky, etc.

ar-dor (är'dẽr), *n.* warmth of affection or passion; eager desire; zeal.

ar-du-ous (är'dū-ŭs), *adj.* steep; hard to climb; attended with great labor or exertion; difficult.—*adv.* **arduously**.

are (är), present tense plural number of the verb *to be*.

are (är), *n.* in the metric system, a measure of surface; 100 square meters, equal to 119.6 square yards.

a-re-a (ā'rē-ȧ), *n.* [*pl.* areas (-ȧz)], any surface having bounds, whether natural or artificial, as the floor of a hall, etc.; any defined extent of land-surface; the sunken space at the base of a building separating it from the street and affording light to the basement; extent; range; scope; region; tract; as, the settled *area* of the United States.

a-re-na (ȧ-rē'nȧ), *n.* [*pl.* arenas (-nȧz)], the central inclosed space (usually strewn with sand) of a Roman amphitheater, in which the gladiatorial combats took place; hence, a scene or field for combat or exertion of any kind; as, the western *arena* of the great European War.

Ar-e-op-a-gus (ăr"ē-ŏp'ȧ-gŭs), *n.* the tribunal, or highest court, of ancient Athens, so named from its situation on the hill of Ares (Mars); hence, any high court or tribunal.

ar-gent (är'jĕnt), *adj.* made of, or resembling, silver; silvery white; bright like silver.

A-res (ā'rēs), *n.* the Greek god of war: called by the Romans Mars.

Ar-go-naut (är'gō-nôt), *n.* one of the band of Greek heroes who sailed in the ship Argo to Colchis in quest of the golden fleece; one of the gold seekers who went to California in 1849.

ar-go-sy (är'gō-sĭ), *n.* [*pl.* argosies (-sĭz)], a large merchant vessel filled with costly goods.

ar-gue (är'gū), *v.i.* to show or offer reasons in support of, or in opposition to, a proposition, opinion, or measure; to reason, dispute, discuss; contend in debate: *v.t.* to debate or discuss; prove.

Syn. debate, dispute, reason upon.

ar-gu-ment (är'gū-mĕnt), *n.* a presentation of proofs of, or reasons for or against, something; a discussion, controversy, or debate; the subject of a discourse or writing; an abstract or summary of a book.

ar-gu-men-ta-tion (är"gū-mĕn-tā'-shŭn), *n.* the act of reasoning and disputing; discussion.

ar-gu-men-ta-tive (är"gū-mĕn'tȧ-tĭv), *adj.* consisting of, or exhibiting a process of, reasoning; given to discussion; showing reasons for; controversial.

Ar-gus (är'gŭs), *n.* a giant fabled to have a hundred eyes: **argus**, a watchful person.

ar-gus-eyed (är'gŭs-īd"), *adj.* watchful; vigilant; extremely observant; sharp-sighted.

a-ri-a (ä'rĭ-ȧ; ā'rĭ-ȧ), *n.* an air; a melody or tune for a single voice with accompaniment; an elaborate solo part in a cantata or oratorio, etc.

A-ri-an (ā'rĭ-ăn), *adj.* relating to the doctrines of Arius, who taught that Christ was the noblest of men, but that he was not divine.

ar-id (ăr'ĭd), *adj.* having little or no rainfall; dry; parched; barren

a-rid-i-ty (ȧ-rĭd'ĭ-tĭ), *n.* the state of being dry; barrenness; want of life or interest. Also, **aridness**.

a-right (ȧ-rīt), *adv.* correctly; in a proper way or form; without sin or error.

a-rise (ȧ-rīz'), *v.i.* [*p.t.* arose, *p.p.* arisen, *p.pr.* arising], to mount up or ascend; to come into view; to rise or get up; to spring up; to come into existence or action; to originate.

Syn. flow, spring, proceed, rise, issue.

ar-is-toc-ra-cy (ăr"ĭs-tŏk'rȧ-sĭ), *n.* [*pl.* aristocracies (-sĭz)], government by persons of the highest rank in a state; the nobility or chief persons in a state; those regarded as superior to the rest of their community in rank, wealth, or intellect.

a-ris-to-crat (ȧ-rĭs'tō-krăt), *n.* a personage of high rank or noble birth; one who upholds the aristocracy or favors government by the few; a person who possesses traits like the nobility; a haughty person.—*adj.* **aristocratic**, **aristocratical**.—*adv.* **aristocratically**.

a-rith-me-tic (ȧ-rĭth'mē-tĭk), *n.* the science of numbers; the art of computation or reckoning by figures.

ar-ith-met-i-cal (ăr"ĭth-mĕt'ĭ-kăl), *adj.* of or relating to the science of numbers, or to its rules.—*adv.* **arithmetically**.

a-rith-me-ti-cian (ȧ-rĭth"mē-tĭsh'ăn; ăr"ĭth-mē-tĭsh'ăn), *n.* one skilled in the science of numbers.

ark (ärk), *n.* a chest; the oblong box, kept in the Holy of Holies, containing the Covenant, or tables of the Law, in the Jewish Tabernacle, and later placed in the Temple of Solomon.—Exod. xxv., 1 Kings viii; the ship in which Noah and his family remained during the Deluge.—Gen. vi; hence, a place of safety or refuge.

arm (ärm), *n.* the limb of the human body which extends from the shoulder to the hand; the anterior or fore-limb of any animal having a backbone; any projecting or diverging organ or part of a main body or trunk, as the branch of a tree, the side-piece of a chair, an inlet of the sea; a weapon: *v.t.* to furnish or equip with weapons of offense or defense; fortify or provide against: *v.i.* to fit oneself with weapons, or take to oneself means of defense.

ar-ma-da (är-mā'dȧ), *n.* a fleet of armed vessels; a squadron: **Invincible Armada**, the Spanish fleet sent against England in 1588, by Philip II.

ar-ma-dil-lo (är"mȧ-dĭl'ō), *n.* [*pl.* armadillos (-ōz)], a four-footed animal found in South America and Texas having the body and head covered with an armor of small bony plates, like a coat of mail.

ar-ma-ment (är'mȧ-mĕnt), *n.* a body of forces prepared for war, either military or naval; the cannon and small arms of a fort or warship; the number and weight of guns of a war vessel; the equipment or act of equipping for defense or resistance.

ar-ma-ture (är'mȧ-tūr), *n.* armor; that which serves as a means of defense; iron bars or framework used to strengthen a building; in dynamo-electric machines, that part in which electric power is produced in a generator or consumed in a motor.

arm-chair (ärm'châr"), *n.* a chair furnished with supports for the elbows.

arm-ful (ärm'fo͝ol), *n.* as much as the arms can hold.

ar-mi-stice (är'mĭ-stĭs), *n.* a brief pause in war by agreement of the opposing forces; a truce.

Armlets

arm-let (ärm'lĕt), *n.* a small inlet of the sea; a

metal band for the arm used for ornament or for protection.

ar-mor (är′mẽr), *n.* defensive weapons; protective covering for the body in battle; the steel plating of a warship.

ar-mor-clad (är′mẽr-klăd), *adj.* iron- or steel-clad: *n.* a war vessel protected by steel plating.

ar-mor-er (är′mẽr-ẽr), *n.* formerly, a maker of weapons, shields, etc., or one who had charge of the military outfit of another; the keeper of the weapons of a troop or battleship.

ar-mo-ri-al (är-mō′rĭ-ăl), *adj.* relating to armor or to the arms or escutcheon of a family: *n.* a book or dictionary of heraldic devices with the names of persons entitled to use them.

ar-mor plate (är′mẽr plāt), the iron or steel plate with which a fort or ship is covered for protection against shell-fire.

ar-mor-y (är′mẽr-ĭ), *n.* [*pl.* armories (-rĭz)], a place for the storing of weapons; a place for the assembling of soldiers, usually containing a drill hall, offices, etc.; a manufactory of weapons, such as, pistols, rifles, etc.

Armor. 1, basinet; 2, jeweled orle around the basinet; 3, gorget, or gorgiere of plate; 4, 5, pauldrons; 6, rerebraces; 7, gauntlets; 8, dagger or misericorde hanging from military belt or cingulum, richly jeweled; 9, skirt; 10, tuilles or tuillets; 11, cuisses, 12, genouillères or knee-pieces; 13, jambes; 14, spur straps; 15, solerets; 16, sword, suspended by a transverse belt.

arm-pit (ärm′pĭt″), *n.* the hollow beneath the arm near the shoulder.

arms (ärmz), *n.pl.* weapons of offense or defense; the military service; as, a call to *arms;* war as a profession; heraldic bearings or devices; as, the *coat of arms* of the United States.

ar-my (är′mĭ), *n.* [*pl.* armies (-mĭz)], a body of men trained and equipped for war on land, and organized in regiments, brigades, or similar divisions under proper officers; a great number or multitude; an organized body of persons engaged in moral warfare; a host; an array; forces; troops.

ar-my worm (är′mĭ wûrm), the very destructive larva of a moth, so called because of the great numbers in which it marches across a country, stripping the land of all young grain and grasses.

ar-ni-ca (är′nĭ-kȧ), *n.* a medicinal plant or herb; the mountain tobacco: from the roots or flowers of this herb a valuable remedy for bruises is made.

a-ro-ma (ȧ-rō′mȧ), *n.* [*pl.* aromas (-mȧz)], the odor of plants or other substances, generally of an agreeable or spicy nature; perfume; fragrance.

ar-o-mat-ic (ăr″ō-măt′ĭk), *adj.* fragrant; spicy: *n.* a plant, herb, or drug yielding a fragrant smell, as ginger, cinnamon, etc. Also, **aromatical**.—*adv.* **aromatically**.

a-rose (ȧ-rōz′), past tense of the intransitive verb *arise.*

a-round (ȧ-round′), *adv.* in a circle; on every side; roundabout: *prep.* about; on all sides; encircling; encompassing.

a-rous-al (ȧ-rouz′ăl), *n.* the act of awakening; the state of being awakened.

a-rouse (ȧ-rouz′), *v.t.* to excite or stir to action; put in motion that which is at rest; awaken from sleep or a state of rest; stimulate; animate: *v.i.* to waken; become active.

a-row (ȧ-rō′), *adv.* in a line; in order; successively.

ar-peg-gio (är-pĕd′jō), *n.* the tones of a chord produced in rapid succession, as in playing a harp.

ar-que-bus (är′kwē-bŭs), *n.* a kind of gun in use before the musket. Also, **harquebus**.

ar-raign (ă-rān′), *v.t.* to call to account; to summon (a prisoner) into court to answer to a charge; censure or accuse publicly; impeach; indict; denounce.

ar-raign-ment (ă-rān′mĕnt), *n.* an accusation; an impeachment; denouncement.

ar-range (ă-rānj′), *v.t.* to put in proper order or sequence; classify; adjust or settle; adapt; group.

ar-range-ment (ă-rānj′mĕnt), *n.* the act of putting in proper form or order; that which is ordered or disposed; the method or style of disposition; preparation; settlement; classification; adjustment; adaptation.

ar-rant (ăr′ănt), *adj.* notorious; thorough or downright (in a bad sense); as, an *arrant* coward; shameless.

ar-ras (ăr′ăs), *n.* tapestry; hangings covering the walls of a room, usually made of rich figured material.

ar-ray (ă-rā′), *n.* order; the grouping or arrangement of a body of men when drawn up for battle; an orderly collection or series of things imposingly displayed; clothing, especially gay clothing; apparel: *v.t.* [*p.t.* and *p.p.* arrayed, *p.pr.* arraying], to place or dispose in order; to marshal; to deck or dress.

ar-rear (ă-rēr′), *n.* the state of being behindhand; that which is undone, outstanding, or unpaid; a debt which remains unpaid; as, *arrears* in rent or taxes: commonly in plural.

ar-rear-age (ă-rēr′āj), *n.* the state or condition of being behindhand; that which remains unpaid and overdue after a previous payment.

ar-rest (ă-rĕst′), *v.t.* to stop or stay; to check or hinder the action or motion of; to seize, take, or apprehend by legal authority; to seize and fix, as the eye or attention: *n.* the act of seizing; stoppage or a holding back by force or restraint; the state of being seized or detained by legal authority.

Syn. *n.* and *v.* capture, hold, detain, secure.
Ant. (see release).

ar-riv-al (ă-rīv′ăl), *n.* the act of coming to a place, or reaching a destination from a distance; attainment of any object; the person or thing coming, or that has come, to a place.

ar-rive (ă-rīv′), *v.i.* to come to or reach, as a destination; reach a point or stage; gain or compass an object; attain to a state or result: with *at.*

ar-ro-gance (ăr′ō-găns), *n.* a feeling of personal superiority; an exorbitant or undue claim to dignity, rank, or estimation; a lordly contempt of others.

ar-ro-gant (ăr′ō-gănt), *adj.* overestimating one's importance; overbearingly haughty.—*adv.* **arrogantly**.

ar-ro-gate (ăr'ō-gāt), *v.t.* legally, to lay claim to on behalf of another; to claim unduly or with presumptuous pride.

ar-ro-ga-tion (ăr'ō-gā'shŭn), *n.* the act of making unjust claims; the act of taking more than one is entitled to take.

ar-row (ăr'ō), *n.* a slender, pointed shaft, usually feathered and barbed, made to be shot from a bow; a figure used in maps, etc., to indicate direction.

ar-row-head (ăr'ō-hĕd), *n.* the head or barb of an arrow; an aquatic or water plant so named from its leaves.

ar-row-root (ăr'ō-rōōt'), *n.* a starch obtained from the root-stock of several kinds of West Indian plants, much used for food.

ar-se-nal (är'sē-năl), *n.* a building for the storage or manufacture of arms and military stores for land or naval service.

ar-se-nic (är'sē-nĭk), *n.* a deadly mineral poison used in medicine, rat poisons, dyes, etc.: called also *white arsenic.*

ar-son (är'sŭn), *n.* the malicious or intentional setting fire to and burning of any building.

art (ärt), *n.* the use of means to the accomplishment of some end; music, painting, sculpture, or literature, or the practice of one of them; practical skill; knack; cunning; *pl.* the branches of learning included in the ordinary course of academic study: *v. i.* second pers. pres. indic. sing. of the verb *be:* used only in solemn or poetic style.

Ar-te-mis (är'tē-mĭs), the Greek goddess of the moon and of the hunt: called by the Romans Diana.

ar-te-ri-al (är-tē'rĭ-ăl), *adj.* relating to, or contained in, the large blood-vessels.

ar-ter-y (är'tēr-ĭ), *n.* [*pl.* arteries (-ĭz)], one of a system of tubes or vessels which carry the blood from the heart to all parts of the body; any great channel: as an *artery* of trade.

ar-te-sian well (är-tē'zhăn wĕl), a deep well made by boring into the earth.

art-ful (ärt'fōōl), *adj.* cunning; crafty; unreal.—*adv.* **artfully.**—*n.* **artfulness.**

Syn. shy, tricky, insincere.
Ant. (see candid).

ar-ti-choke (är'tĭ-chōk), *n.* a tall plant, of the aster family, having a flower head that is used as food; the root of an American sunflower (Jerusalem artichoke) used as a substitute for potatoes.

ar-ti-cle (är'tĭ-kl), *n.* a distinct portion or member; a single clause, item, or particular, as in a formal agreement or treaty; a concise statement; a prose composition, complete in itself, in a newspaper, magazine, or work of reference; as, an *article* on peace; a material thing, as one of a class; as, an *article* of clothing; an item; any of the English words *a, an,* and *the* used before nouns and substantives to define or limit their application; also, their equivalents in other languages: *v.t.* to bind by written agreement, as an apprentice.

ar-tic-u-lar (är-tĭk'ū-lär), *adj.* relating to the joints or to a joint.

ar-tic-u-late (är-tĭk'ū-lāt), *v.i.* to join together; unite by a joint; to form words; utter in distinct syllables; speak as a human being: *v.t.* to utter distinct sounds; speak with distinctness: *adj.* (är-tĭk'ū-lāt), jointed; formed with joints; uttered with distinctness.—*adv.* **articulately.**

ar-tic-u-la-tion (är-tĭk'ū-lā'shŭn), *n.* the act of speaking distinctly; a distinct utterance; the act of joining; a joint or juncture between bones; the point of separation of organs or parts of a plant.

ar-ti-fice (är'tĭ-fĭs), *n.* a skilful contrivance; a crafty device; a ruse, wile, trick, or stratagem.

Syn. finesse, cunning, craft.
Ant. (see openness).

ar-tif-i-cer (är-tĭf'ĭ-sēr), *n.* a skilled or artistic worker; a mechanic; a maker or constructor; an inventor.

ar-ti-fi-cial (är-tĭ-fĭsh'ăl), *adj.* made or contrived by art; produced by human skill or labor; as, *artificial* heat; feigned; unreal; assumed; affected; not genuine or natural.—*adv.* **artificially.**

ar-ti-fi-ci-al-i-ty (är'tĭ-fĭsh'ĭ-ăl'ĭ-tĭ), *n.* the quality of being unreal or unnatural; that which is affected or unnatural. Also, **artificialness.**

ar-til-ler-y (är-tĭl'ēr-ĭ), *n.* mounted cannon; great guns; ordnance; the officers and men handling the mounted guns of an army.

ar-ti-san (är'tĭ-zăn), *n.* a trained workman; a mechanic; a handicraftsman. Also, **artizan.**

art-ist (är'tĭst), *n.* a person of especial skill, talent, or ability in painting, sculpture, music, or literature: especially applied to a painter or sculptor.

ar-tis-tic (är-tĭs'tĭk), *adj.* beautiful; conceived and executed with skill; as, an *artistic* ending to a play or book; displaying perfection of design or coloring; characterized by esthetic feeling or having an appreciation of beautiful things; as, an *artistic* temperament.

ar-tis-ti-cal-ly (är-tĭs'tĭ-kăl-ĭ), *adv.* in a manner agreeable to the rules and practice of art.

art-less (ärt'lĕs), *adj.* free from guile; honest; simple; natural; unaffected; sincere.—*adv.* **artlessly.**—*n.* **artlessness.**

Ar-yan (är'yăn; är'ĭ-ăn), *adj.* relating to the Aryans, or to their language: *n.* one of the race of mankind from which the white people of Europe and southern Asia have descended.

as (ăz), *adv.* equally; in like manner; for example; because; similar to: *conj.* while; when; because.

as-a-fet-i-da (ăs'ă-fĕt'ĭ-dā), *n.* a valuable drug with a persistent odor and a bitter taste made from the roots of certain Oriental plants of the celery family and especially useful in treating hysteria or in quieting the nerves. Also, **asafœtida, asafetida.**

as-bes-tos (ăs-bĕs'tŏs; ăz-bĕs'tŏs), *n.* a soft, fibrous, incombustible material used in fireproof curtains, clothing, roofing, etc. Also, **asbestus.**

as-cend (ă-sĕnd'), *v.i.* to take an upward direction; mount; go up; rise; to proceed from an inferior to a superior position; rise from a lower to a higher pitch or tone: *v.t.* to go or move upward upon; climb; go toward the source; as, to *ascend* a river.

as-cend-an-cy (ă-sĕn'dăn-sĭ), *n.* a governing or controlling power or influence; domination; sway. Also, **ascendency.**

as-cend-ant (ă-sĕn'dănt), *adj.* rising; superior; predominant; above the horizon: *n.* superiority; a commanding influence; predominance; an ancestor; opposite to *descendant.* Also, **ascendent.**

as-cen-sion (ă-sĕn'shŭn), *n.* the act of moving upward; a rising: **Ascension,** the ascent of Christ into heaven.

As-cen-sion Day (ă-sĕn'shŭn dā), the Thursday, forty days after Easter, on which is celebrated Christ's ascension into heaven.—Acts i.

as-cent (ă-sĕnt'), *n.* the act of rising; an upward movement; the act of climbing; the way or means of reaching a height; a hill or high place; an upward slope.

as-cer-tain (ăs'ĕr-tān'), *v.t.* to make certain; to find out; to determine definitely by test or examination.

as-cet-ic (ă-sĕt'ĭk), *adj.* severely self-denying; exceedingly rigid in the exercise of religious duties: *n.* one who gives up the things of the world and devotes himself to religious exercises; one who subjects himself to severe methods of living; a hermit; a recluse.—*adv.* **ascetically.**

as-cet-i-cism (ă-sĕt'ĭ-sĭzm), *n.* the condition or mode of life adopted by one who renounces world'y affairs; severe self-denial.

as-cribe (ăs-krīb'), *v.t.* to attribute, impute, or refer, as to a cause; to consider to belong to; to assign; set down; as, losses may often be *ascribed* to imprudence.—*adj.* **ascribable.**—*n.* **ascription.**

a-sep-tic (ȧ-sĕp'tĭk), *adj.* free from the germs of disease; surgically clean.

ash (ăsh), *n.* [*pl.* **ashes** (-ĕz)], a common timber and shade tree belonging to the olive family; the wood of the ash tree; hence, something made of the wood, as a staff or the shaft of a spear or lance; what remains of a body or substance that is burned: *pl.* the waste of burned coal; the remains of a human body.

a-shamed (ȧ-shāmd'), *p.adj.* affected or touched by contempt or disgrace; cast down or dejected by conscious guilt; abashed by a sense of indecorum or misbehavior; reluctant or hesitating through fear of reproach.

ash-en (ăsh'ĕn), *adj.* relating to the ash-tree; made of ash; of the pale grayish color of ashes; pale.

a-shore (ȧ-shōr), *adv.* on shore; to the shore; as, a ship driven *ashore* in a gale; on land.

Ash Wednes-day, (ăsh wĕnz'dā), the first day of Lent; so called because of the former custom of sprinkling ashes on the heads of penitents.

a-side (ȧ-sīd'), *adv.* on or to one side; out of a given direction; apart; away from: *n.* a speech or remark made in a lower tone than the rest of the conversation, and assumed to be heard only by the person for whom it is intended; something apart from the main issue.

as-i-nine (ăs'ĭ-nīn), *adj.* relating to the ass; having the nature or qualities of an ass; obstinate; stupid; silly; as, an *asinine* remark.

as-i-nin-i-ty (ăs'ĭ-nĭn'ĭ-tĭ), *n.* the quality of being like an ass; obstinate stupidity.

ask (ȧsk), *v.t.* to request; seek to obtain by words; petition or beg for; claim or demand; expect or require; as, what price do you *ask?* inquire respecting; as, to *ask* the way; question; invite: *v.i.* to make request; inquire after.

Syn. crave, beg, beseech, petition, request, solicit.

Ant. (see command).

a-skance (ȧ-skăns'), *adv.* sideways; awry; from the corner of the eye; disdainfully; distrustfully. Also, **askant.**

a-skew (ȧ-skū'), *adj.* and *adv.* awry; out of order or position; crooked.

a-slant (ȧ-slȧnt'), *adj.* and *adv.* not at right angles; sloping; oblique; obliquely: *prep.* across in a slanting position.

a-sleep (ȧ-slēp'), *adj.* and *adv.* in a state of slumber; dormant; unconscious; numbed.

a-slope (ȧ-slōp'), *adj.* and *adv.* in an inclined position; in a sloping direction; leaning.

asp (ăsp), *n.* a small poisonous snake of Egypt; the common viper, or adder, of Europe. Also, **aspic.**

Asp

as-par-a-gus (ăs-păr'ȧ-gŭs), *n.* a plant of the lily family having tender eatable shoots, used as a vegetable.

as-pect (ăs'pĕkt), *n.* visual or mental appearance; look; mien; air; outlook or prospect; appearance; view.

asp-en (ăs'pĕn; ȧs'pĕn), *n.* a kind of poplar tree whose leaves tremble in the slightest breeze: *adj.* relating to such a tree; quivering like a leaf of such a tree; tremulous; shaking.

as-per-i-ty (ăs-pĕr'ĭ-tĭ), *n.* [*pl.* **asperities** (-tĭz)], roughness of surface; unevenness; roughness or harshness of sound; sourness; bitterness of taste or temper; crabbedness; moroseness.

as-perse (ăs-pûrs'), *v.t.* to spread false reports against a person or his character; to slander; to besprinkle.

as-per-sion (ăs-pûr'shŭn), *n.* injury by false charges; a slanderous report; calumny; a sprinkling, as of dust or water.

as-phalt (ăs'fălt), *n.* a black bitumen; a mineral pitch used for paving, roofing, and cementing: *v.t.* to lay down or cover with bitumen. Also, **asphaltum.**

as-pho-del (ăs'fō-dĕl), *n.* the name of several plants of the lily family; the daffodil of the older English poets; in Greek mythology, the *asphodel* was the flower of the dead, its pale blossoms covering the meadows of Hades.

as-phyx-i-a (ăs-fĭk'sĭ-ȧ), *n.* a stopping of the pulse; the lifeless condition caused by the stopping of the breath, as in choking, drowning, etc.; suffocation. Also, **asphyxy.**

as-phyx-i-ate (ăs-fĭk'sĭ-āt), *v.t.* to suffocate; to cause death or its symptoms, by depriving of oxygen.

as-pic (ăs'pĭk), *n.* a poisonous asp, or Egyptian viper; a clear meat jelly containing fowl, game, fish, etc.; the spike lavender yielding a volatile oil.

as-pir-ant (ăs-pīr'ănt), *adj.* ambitious: *n.* one who seeks to attain, or is ambitious for, some high object or position; a candidate.

as-pi-rate (ăs'pĭ-rāt), *v.t.* to pronounce with a full breathing; to prefix or add the sound of the letter *h*: *n.* the sound of the letter *h*, as in *horse*: *adj.* (ăs'pĭ-răt), pronounced with the audible breath.

as-pi-ra-tion (ăs"pĭ-rā'shŭn), *n.* the act of breathing; a breath; the yearning desire for something higher or better than that already possessed; ambition.

as-pi-ra-to-ry (ăs-pīr'ȧ-tō-rĭ), *adj.* relating to breathing; suited to the inhaling of air.

as-pire (ăs-pīr'), *v.i.* to seek after or desire with longing; yearn for that which is better or nobler; rise or ascend; to soar.

as-pi-rin (ăs'pĭ-rĭn), *n.* a white powder or pellet used as a remedy for rheumatism, headache, colds, etc.

a-squint (ȧ-skwĭnt'), *adj.* and *adv.* to or out of the corner of the eye; askance; furtive; furtively.

ass (ăs), *n.* an animal of the horse family having longer ears and a shorter mane than the horse; a dull, stupid fellow.

as-sa-fet-i-da (ăs"ȧ-fĕt'ĭ-dȧ), *n.* a drug with a persistent odor and bitter taste made from the fetid gum resin of certain Oriental plants of the celery family. Also, **assafœtida, asafetida.**

as-sail (ă-sāl'), *v.t.* to fall upon or attack violently; to attack with argument or abuse.—*adj.* **assailable.**

as-sail-ant (ă-sāl'ănt), *adj.* assaulting; attacking: *n.* one who, or that which, attacks.

as-sas-sin (ă-săs'ĭn), *n.* one who kills, or attempts to kill, secretly as the agent of another or others, or for reward; a murderer.

as-sas-si-nate (ă-săs'ĭ-nāt), *v.t.* to kill by secret or treacherous means; slay suddenly or unawares; murder by sudden or treacherous violence.

as-sas-si-na-tion (ă-săs"ĭ-nā'shŭn), *n.* the act of slaying in secret, sometimes at the bidding of others or for reward; murder.

as-sault (ă-sôlt'), *n.* an attack with violence by physical means; an onslaught; an attack by military force; a violent attack by moral force, as by use of argument or hostile words; an attempt or threat to do bodily violence or injury to another; the charge of an attacking party on a fortified position: *v.t.* to attack violently; storm, as by armed force; attack by moral force; threaten or attempt by visible means bodily violence or injury to another; attack a fortified position by a sudden charge.

as-say (ă-sā'), *n.* the act or process of finding the quantity or proportion of any one or more metals in a metallic compound, ore, or alloy, especially the standard purity of gold or silver coin or bullion; the substance or metal to be tested; in the days of chivalry, a trial by danger; risk; adventure: *v.t.* [*p.t.* and *p.p.* assayed, *p.pr.* assaying], to subject to analysis; to find the quantity or proportion of one or more of the parts of a metal.

as-say-er (ă-sā'ẽr), *n.* one who analyzes metals; an officer of the Mint appointed to test the purity of bullion and coin.

as-sem-blage (ă-sĕm'blăj), *n.* the act of gathering together; the state of being collected in one place; a group or collection of persons or particular things; the fitting together of parts and of pieces, as of machinery; a congregation; an audience.

as-sem-ble (ă-sĕm'bl), *v.t.* to collect or gather together into one place or body; congregate; to fit the parts of machinery together: *v.i.* to meet or come together; convene.

as-sem-bly (ă-sĕm'blĭ), *n.* [*pl.* assemblies (-blĭz)], a collection or company of persons brought together in one place and for a common object, whether religious, educational, political, or social; a meeting; a congregation; a legislative body; a bugle call to bring troops together; the second beating of a drum before a march, upon which the soldiers strike their tents.

as-sem-bly-man (ă-sĕm'blĭ-măn), *n.* a member of a legislative, or lawmaking, body.

as-sent (ă-sĕnt'), *v.i.* to admit as true; to concede, to agree to; to consent: *n.* the act of agreeing to; consent; acquiescence; approval; concurrence.

as-sert (ă-sûrt'), *v.t.* to maintain; to declare positively, or with assurance; to affirm; to declare; to defend by words; as, to *assert* our rights and liberties.

as-ser-tion (ă-sûr'shŭn), *n.* the act of declaring positively; that which is affirmed; a positive declaration without attempt at proof; an unsupported statement.

as-ser-tive (ă-sûr'tĭv), *adj.* positive; confident in statement.

as-sess (ă-sĕs'), *v.t.* to fix or determine, as damages; to fix, rate, or set a certain charge upon, as a tax; as, the property was *assessed* too high; to estimate or value officially for the purpose of taxation.—*adj.* **assessable.**

as-sessed tax-es (ă-sĕst tăks'ĕz), taxes levied on income, houses, and other property.

as-sess-ment (ă-sĕs'mĕnt), *n.* the act of determining an amount to be paid; an official valuation of property, or income, for the purpose of taxation; the tax paid on property.

as-ses-sor (ă-sĕs'ẽr), *n.* one appointed to estimate the value of property for taxation.

as-sets (ăs'ĕts), *n.pl.* all the property of a person, firm, or estate which may be used to pay his or its debts; property which is usable for paying creditors; all that one owns; property in general: *sing.* any item of one's property.

as-sev-er-ate (ă-sĕv'ẽr-āt), *v.t.* to affirm or aver positively, or with solemnity.

as-sev-er-a-tion (ă-sĕv"ẽr-ā'shŭn), *n.* a solemn affirmation or declaration, as upon oath; an emphatic assertion.

as-si-du-i-ty (ăs"ĭ-dū'ĭ-tĭ), *n.* [*pl.* assiduities (-tĭz)], close application or unremitting attention to; diligence; perseverance; constancy: *pl.* studied and persevering efforts to please.

as-sid-u-ous (ă-sĭd'ū-ŭs), *adj.* constant in application; devoted; attentive; perseveringly diligent; unremitting; untiring.—*adv.* **assiduously.**

as-sign (ă-sīn'), *v.t.* to allot; to appoint; mark out; apportion; make over; fix; to set apart for a particular purpose; point out exactly; to transfer or make over to another, as for the benefit of creditors: *n.* one to whom property or interest is left or made over by will or deed; as, a deed to a man, his heirs, and *assigns*.

as-sig-na-tion (ăs"ĭg-nā'shŭn), *n.* an appointment for meeting; used chiefly in speaking of love affairs and now usually in a bad sense.

as-sign-ee (ăs″ĭ-nē′), *n.* one to whom anything is made over, either in trust or for his own use and enjoyment.

as-sign-ment (ă-sīn′mĕnt), *n.* a setting apart, allotment, or appointment to some particular person or use; transfer of title or interest; the deed of writing effecting such a transfer.

as-sign-or (ăs″ĭ-nôr′), *n.* one who transfers an interest; one who appoints or allots. Also, assigner.

as-sim-i-late (ă-sĭm′ĭ-lāt), *v.t.* to bring to likeness or agreement with something else; to absorb or take into itself, as nourishment: *v.i.* to become similar; harmonize.

as-sim-i-la-tion (ă-sĭm″ĭ-lā′shŭn), *n.* the act or process of bringing into agreement or harmony; the state of being absorbed, or of becoming a part of.

as-sist (ă-sĭst′), *v.t.* to act as a helper; to help; to aid; give support to; attend; relieve: *v.i.* to lend help or aid.

as-sis-tance (ă-sĭs′tăns), *n.* help; aid; succor; support.

as-sis-tant (ă-sĭs′tănt), *adj.* helping; lending aid; auxiliary: *n.* one who, or that which, helps; a helper; an auxiliary.

as-size (ă-sīz′), *n.* [*pl.* assizes (-ĕz)], a court or session of justice for the trial by jury of civil or criminal cases; the sessions held regularly in each county of England by judges of the Supreme Court: usually in plural: the time or place of holding the assize: usually in plural; in English History, an ordinance fixing the weight, measure, and price of articles of general use sold in market; as, the *assise* of bread and ale.

as-so-ci-ate (ă-sō′shĭ-āt), *n.* a companion; a confederate; an ally; one belonging to a society or institution: *adj.* joined in interest, object, or purpose; sharing office or employment, as a colleague or partner; connected by habit, function, or sympathy: (ă-sō′shĭ-āt), *v.t.* to unite; join with; connect; accompany, as a companion, friend, or confederate: *v.i.* to unite in company; to have fellowship; to unite in action.

as-so-ci-a-tion (ă-sō″sĭ-ā′shŭn; ă-sō″shĭ-ā′shŭn), *n.* the act of joining together or the state of fellowship; the union of persons in a society or club; a body of persons organized for a common object; a corporation; a connection of ideas; that which is mentally connected with a thing.

Syn. combination; company; partnership; society.

Ant. (see isolation).

as-so-nance (ăs′ō-năns), *n.* resemblance of sound; rhyme in which vowels correspond but consonants do not; as, *baby* and *lady*.

as-so-nant (ăs′ō-nănt), *adj.* having resemblance of sound.

as-sort (ă-sôrt′), *v.t.* to divide or separate into lots, classes, or kinds; to classify; arrange: *v.i.* to agree; to suit; be in accordance with.

as-sort-ment (ă-sôrt′mĕnt), *n.* the act of separating and arranging; a classified collection of articles or goods of a varied character; as, the box contains a choice *assortment* of candy.

as-suage (ă-swāj′), *v.t.* to soften or soothe; allay or lessen, as pain or grief; appease or pacify, as passion.

as-sume (ă-sūm′), *v.t.* to take to; take up or into; take upon oneself; appropriate; take for granted; take in appearance; pretend to possess: *v.i.* to be arrogant; to presume.—*p.adj.* assuming.

Syn. claim, arrogate, appropriate.

as-sump-tion (ă-sŭmp′shŭn), *n.* the act of taking to or upon oneself; the act of taking for granted; the thing supposed; the taking of a person to heaven; a verbal or unsealed contract; arrogance; supposition; a disposition to claim more than is one's due.

as-sur-ance (ă-shŏŏr′ăns), *n.* the act or state of being sure; certain expectation; a pledge; confidence; certain proof; clear evidence; self-possession; self-reliance; courage; impudence; a deed or other legal evidence of the conveyance of property; insurance.

as-sure (ă-shŏŏr′), *v.t.* to make sure or certain; to inspire confidence by declaration or promise; to secure to another; to free from uncertainty; to insure, as against loss by fire or death.

as-sured (ă-shŏŏrd′), *p.adj.* made certain; guaranteed; self-possessed; insured: *n.* a person in whose favor an insurance policy stands.

as-sur-ed-ly (ă-shŏŏr′ĕd-lĭ), *adv.* certainly; without doubt; with firmness.

as-sur-ed-ness (ă-shŏŏr′ĕd-nĕs), *n.* certainty; full confidence.

As-syr-i-a (ă-sĭr′ĭ-ă), an ancient country of Asia east of the river Tigris, long at the head of a powerful empire which included Babylonia, Palestine, and the neighboring countries.

As-syr-i-an (ă-sĭr′ĭ-ăn), *adj.* relating to Assyria, its people, or their language: *n.* a native of Assyria; the language of Assyria.

as-ter (ăs′tĕr), *n.* a variety of garden plant of the thistle family, with alternate leaves and ray-flowers which vary from white to lilac, blue, or purple, common in the United States; any plant of this class.

as-ter-isk (ăs-tĕr-ĭsk), *n.* the figure of a star [*] used in printing or writing as a reference mark, or to indicate letters or words omitted [* * *]: *v.t.* to mark with such a star.

a-stern (ȧ-stûrn′), *adj.* and *adv.* a nautical term: at or toward the back of a ship; behind a ship.

as-ter-oid (ăs′tĕr-oid), *n.* one of the many small planets whose orbits lie between Jupiter and Mars: *adj.* starlike; star-shaped.

asth-ma (ăz′mȧ; ăs′mȧ), *n.* a disease, attended by difficulty of breathing.

asth-mat-ic (ăz-măt′ĭk; ăs′măt′ĭk), *adj.* affected with difficulty in breathing: *n.* a person suffering from a disease attended by difficulty in breathing.

as-tig-mat-ic (ăs″tĭg-măt′ĭk), *adj.* relating to, affected with, or curing, a defect of the eyes because of which the rays of light do not focus properly.

as-tig-ma-tism (ȧ-stĭg′mȧ-tĭzm), *n.* a defect in the structure of the eye because of which the rays of light do not meet in a point on the retina but form a line; the same defect in a lens.

a-stir (ȧ-stûr′), *adj.* or *adv.* on the move; active; stirring.

as-ton-ish (ăs-tŏn′ĭsh), *v.t.* to strike with sudden wonder; to surprise; to amaze.

as-ton-ish-ing (ăs-tŏn′ĭsh-ĭng), *p.adj.* very wonderful; surprising.

as-ton-ish-ment (ăs-tŏn'ĭsh-mĕnt), *n.* the state of being surprised; amazement.

as-tound (ăs-tound'), *v.t.* to strike with amazement; shock; alarm; stun.—*p.adj.* **astounding.**—*adv.* **astoundingly.**

a-strad-dle (*ȧ*-străd'l), *adv.* with one leg on each side of something; astride.

as-tra-khan (ăs'trȧ-kăn), *n.* the skins of young lambs, the curly wool of which looks like fur, obtained from Astrakhan, a city in Russia; an imitation of this wool or fur.

as-tral (ăs'trăl), *adj.* relating to the stars; starry; star-shaped.

a-stray (*ȧ*-strā'), *adv.* out of the right way or proper place; wandering.

a-stride (*ȧ*-strīd'), *adv.* with the legs wide apart; astraddle.

as-trin-gen-cy (ăs-trĭn'jĕn-sĭ), *n.* the quality of being binding; harshness; severity.

as-trin-gent (ăs-trĭn'jĕnt), *adj.* binding; contracting: opposite to *laxative*: *n.* a substance or medicine that contracts the tissues and checks discharges.

as-tro-labe (ăs'trō-lāb), *n.* an instrument formerly used for measuring the height of the sun or stars: now, superseded or replaced by the sextant.

as-trol-o-ger (ăs-trŏl'ō-jẽr), *n.* one who claims to foretell events by means of the stars.

as-trol-o-gy (ăs-trŏl'ō-jĭ), *n.* astronomy in its earliest form; the art of predicting or foretelling events by the appearance of the heavens, or by reading the stars.

as-tron-o-mer (ăs-trŏn'ō-mẽr), *n.* one who studies or is versed in the science dealing with the stars, planets, and other heavenly bodies.

as-tro-nom-ic-al (ăs"trō-nŏm'ĭk-ăl), *adj.* relating to, or according to, the laws of the heavenly bodies. Also, **astronomic.**—*adv.* **astronomically.**

as-tro-nom-i-cal signs (ăs"trō-nŏm'-ĭ-kăl sīnz), the signs of the zodiac, or paths of the moon and principal planets.

as-tro-nom-i-cal year (ăs"trō-nŏm'-ĭ-kăl yẽr), a year the length of which is determined by observing the heavenly bodies.

as-tron-o-my (ăs-trŏn'ō-mĭ), *n.* the study of the heavenly bodies; the science which describes the heavenly bodies and their motions.

as-tute (ăs-tūt'), *adj.* shrewd; keen; cunning; crafty; subtle.—*adv.* **astutely.** *Syn.* acute, sharp, sagacious, skilled, wily. *Ant.* (see blind).

as-tute-ness (ăs-tūt'nĕs), *n.* cunning; shrewdness.

a-sun-der (*ȧ*-sŭn'dẽr), *adv.* apart; separately; into parts; in pieces.

a-sy-lum (*ȧ*-sī'lŭm), *n.* [*pl.* asylums (-lŭmz)], a place of refuge, retreat, or security; an institution for the care or relief of the aged, poor, or afflicted.

at (ăt), *prep.* simple presence or position in, on, nearby, or the like; as, *at* the center; *at* the top; *at* home; *at* hand, etc.; position, state, condition, etc.; as, *at* dinner; *at* play; *at* work, etc.; relative position, degree, price, time, etc.; as, *at* the beginning; *at* the fourth house from the corner; *at* ten years of age, etc.

at-a-vism (ăt'*ȧ*-vĭzm), *n.* a similarity or likeness to a distant ancestor or relative, such as the strong resemblance of a child to his great-grandfather, but not to his own father; the return of any disease from which an ancestor in remote generations has suffered.

at-a-vis-tic (ăt"*ȧ*-vĭs'tĭk), *adj.* of or relating to the resemblance to ancestors.

ate (āt), past tense of the transitive and intransitive verb **eat.**

a-te-lier (ȧ"tē-lyā'), *n.* a workshop; a studio; specifically, the studio of a painter or sculptor. [Fr.]

a-the-ism (ā'thē-ĭzm), *n.* disbelief in, or denial of, the existence of a God.

a-the-ist (ā'thē-ĭst), *n.* one who disbelieves or denies the existence of a God.

a-the-is-tic (ā"thē-ĭs'tĭk), *adj.* pertaining to, containing, or implying, disbelief in God. Also, **atheistical.**

A-the-na (*ȧ*-thē'nȧ), *n.* in Greek mythology, the goddess of wisdom and of war: called by the Romans Minerva.

ath-e-ne-um (ăth"ē-nē'ŭm), *n.* [*pl.* atheneums (-ŭmz) and athenea (-*ȧ*)], an institution or club devoted to the study of literature and art; a building used as a library or reading room. Also, **athenæum.**

a-thirst (*ȧ*-thûrst'), *adj.* thirsty; figuratively, having a keen desire; as, *athirst* for knowledge.

ath-lete (ăth'lēt), *n.* one trained to contend in feats of physical strength; one possessed of great physical power and endurance.

ath-let-ic (ăth-lĕt'ĭk), *adj.* relating to those trained for physical contests, or to their performances; strong; robust; vigorous; muscular.—*adv.* **athletically.**

ath-let-ics (ăth-lĕt'ĭks), *n.* any system of training by gymnastic exercises or outdoor sports; the system of rules and principles used in physical or bodily training, as running, rowing; gymnastic exercises collectively.—*n.* **athleticism.**

a-thwart (*ȧ*-thwôrt'), *adv.* across; from side to side; crosswise: *prep.* across the course or direction of, as of a ship; from side to side of.

a-tilt (*ȧ*-tĭlt'), *adj.* and *adv.* in the position or with the action of a person making a thrust; tilted.

At-lan-tic O-cean (ăt-lăn'tĭc ō'shăn), the ocean which separates Europe and Africa from America.—*adj.* **Atlantic.**

Atlas

at-las (ăt'lăs), *n.* [*pl.* atlases (-ĕz)], a collection of maps bound in a volume.—**Atlas,** in mythology, one of the Titans condemned to bear up the heavens or the earth.

at-las pow-der (ăt'lăs pou'dẽr), a powerful explosive used for blasting purposes, as in building railroads, removing tree stumps, etc.

at-mos-phere (ăt'mŏs-fēr), *n.* the air which surrounds the earth; the influence, mental and moral, exerted on a person by his environment or surroundings.

at-mos-pher-ic (ăt"mŏs-fĕr'ĭk), *adj.* relating to, resembling, consisting of, existing in, or dependent upon, the air. Also, **atmospherical.**

at-mos-pher-ic pres-sure (ăt′mŏs-fĕr′ĭk prĕsh′ūr), the pressure exerted in every direction upon a body by the air; equal to 14 2/3 pounds to the square inch.

a-toll (ȧ-tŏl′; ăt′ŏl), *n.* a coral island in the form of an outer ring of coral surrounding a basin or lagoon.

at-om (ăt′ŭm), *n.* the smallest part into which an element can be divided without losing its nature; a minute quantity; as, he has not an *atom* of sense.

a-tom-ic (ȧ-tŏm′ĭk), *adj.* consisting of matter in the smallest particles; extremely minute. Also, **atomical**.

at-om-ize (ăt′ŭm-īz), *v.t.* to reduce to very fine particles; to spray.

at-om-iz-er (ăt′ŭm-īz″ẽr), *n.* an instrument for changing a liquid to a fine spray in order to disinfect, cool, etc.

a-tone (ȧ-tōn), *v.i.* [*p.t.* and *p.p.* atoned, *p.pr.* atoning], to make reparation or amends, as for injury done or implied; give satisfaction for: *v.t.* to expiate.

a-tone-ment (ȧ-tōn′mĕnt), *n.* amends or satisfaction for wrong or injury; something done or suffered by way of reparation.

a-tri-um (ā′trĭ′ŭm), *n.* a square hall or court lighted from above, into which the other rooms of the house open: in ancient Greece, the main room of the house; the main part of the auricle of the heart.

a-tro-cious (ȧ-trō′shŭs), *adj.* wicked in the highest degree; extremely criminal or cruel; outrageous.—*adv.* **atrociously**.

a-troc-i-ty (ȧ-trŏs′ĭ-tĭ), *n.* [*pl.* atrocities (-tĭz)], enormous wickedness; extreme cruelty.

at-ro-phy (ăt′rō-fĭ), *n.* a wasting of the body, or any part of the body, due to the lack of food, or arising from lack of nourishment: *v.i.* [*p.t.* and *p.p.* atrophied, *p.pr.* atrophying], to waste away; to dwindle.

at-ro-pine (ăt′rō-pĭn), *n.* a very dangerous poison found in the deadly nightshade or belladonna. Also, **atropin**.

at-tach (ă-tăch′), *v.t.* to fasten, or fix, to or on; bind; connect with or appoint to; connect by ties of affection; to take, or seize, by legal authority: *v.i.* to adhere or belong to; as, no blame *attached* to him.

at-ta-ché (ȧ″tȧ″shā′), *n.* one who is attached to an embassy or legation in a foreign court, as an aide or assistant to the ambassador; an officer on the staff of a higher officer. [Fr.]

at-tach-ment (ă-tăch′mĕnt), *n.* adherence; fidelity; affection or regard; that which connects, or the thing which is connected; in law, a seizure of the person, goods, or estate by legal process.

at-tack (ă-tăk′), *v.t.* to assault; fall upon with force; assail with intent to overcome, or to damage, discredit, or bring into ridicule; begin to affect or act upon, as disease: *v.i.* to make an onset: *n.* the act of assailing in any sense of the word; specifically, a battle; a seizure by illness.

Syn., *v.* assail, assault, encounter.

Ant. (see defend).

at-tain (ă-tān′), *v.t.* to achieve; gain; accomplish: *v.i.* to reach; come, or arrive, at.

at-tain-a-ble (ȧ-tān′ȧ-bl), *adj.* that may be reached or gained.

at-tain-der (ă-tān′dẽr), *n.* the depriving of civil and legal rights of persons under sentence of death for treason or felony.

at-tain-ment (ă-tān′mĕnt), *n.* the act of arriving at or reaching as the result of exertion or effort; an acquirement.

at-taint (ă-tānt′), *v.t.* to taint; to corrupt; sully or stain by disgrace.

at-tar of ros-es (ăt′ár of rōz′ĕz), an essential or pure oil from the petals of the rose. Also, **atar**, **ottar**, **otto**.

at-tempt (ă-tĕmpt′), *v.t.* to make an effort to accomplish; try; endeavor or essay to perform; try to win; attack, or invade: *n.* a trial or endeavor; an effort to gain a point; an attack or assault.

at-tend (ă-tĕnd), *v.t.* [*p.t.* and *p.p.* attended, *p.pr.* attending], to wait upon; accompany or be present with; serve or look after in any capacity; be present at; accompany or follow: *v.i.* to pay heed or regard to; listen; care for.

at-tend-ance (ă-tĕn′dăns), *n.* the act of waiting on; presence; the persons in waiting.

at-tend-ant (ă-tĕn′dănt), *n.* one who accompanies in the service or train of another; one who is present; that which is consequent upon anything else: *adj.* accompanying or immediately following; as, intemperance, with all its *attendant* evils; being present; depending on or owing duty or service to.

at-ten-tion (ă-tĕn′shŭn), *n.* the act of applying the mind to anything; consideration or regard for any person or thing; a mark or act of civility or courtesy; care for the comfort of others; a military command to assume the attitude of motionless erectness and heed.

at-ten-tive (ă-tĕn′tĭv), *adj.* heedful; intent; mindful; regardful of the wishes of others.

at-ten-u-ate (ă-tĕn′ū-āt), *v.t.* to make thin or slender; thin out by dilution: *v.i.* to become thin, slender, or fine; lessen: *adj.* (ă-tĕn′ū-āt), thin; slender.

at-ten-u-a-tion (ă-tĕn″ū-ā′shŭn), *n.* the act or process of making slender, or of thinning out by dilution; the state of being slender.

at-test (ă-tĕst′), *v.t.* to bear witness to; to certify as being genuine or true, especially in an official sense; to give proof of; to manifest.

at-tes-ta-tion (ăt″ĕs-tā′shŭn), *n.* the act of certifying; testimony or evidence given on oath, or by official declaration; swearing in.

at-tic (ăt′ĭk), *n.* the room or space immediately beneath the roof of a house; a garret.

At-tic (ăt′ĭk), *adj.* relating to Attica, in Greece; classical; delicate.

at-tire (ă-tīr′), *n.* dress; clothes; habit; garb: *v.t.* to dress; clothe; array; adorn.

at-ti-tude (ăt′ĭ-tūd), *n.* bodily position or posture; the bearing assumed by a person which shows or indicates his feeling, opinions, or intuitions; pose.

at-tor-ney (ă-tûr′nĭ), *n.* [*pl.* attorneys (-nĭz)], a lawyer or legal representative; one legally qualified to act for another in the transaction of private business, or in the management, prosecution, or defense of actions at law.

at-tor-ney-gen-er-al (ă-tûr′nĭ-jĕn′ẽr-ăl), *n.* the

chief law officer appointed to act for a government; the chief law officer of a state.

at-tract (ă-trăkt'), *v.t.* to draw to, or towards; cause to approach; draw by moral influence; invite; allure.

at-trac-tion (ă-trăk'shŭn), *n.* the power or act of drawing to or towards; charm; that which charms.

at-trac-tive (ă-trăk'tĭv), *adj.* charming; alluring; inviting.

at-trib-ute (ă-trĭb'ūt), *v.t.* to ascribe; impute; assign: *n.* (ăt'rĭ-būt), trait; property; a characteristic.

at-tri-bu-tion (ăt"rĭ-bū'shŭn), *n.* the act of imputing a quality or characteristic to a person or thing; an ascribed quality or character; designation.

at-trib-u-tive (ă-trĭb'ū-tĭv), *n.* a word denoting a quality; a word joined to and describing a noun; an adjective or adjective phrase.

at-tri-tion (ă-trĭsh'ŭn), *n.* the act of wearing by rubbing; abrasion; the state of being worn; grief for sin arising only from fear of punishment.

at-tune (ă-tūn'), *v.t.* to put in tune; bring into accordance or harmony.

au-burn (ô'bûrn), *adj.* reddish-brown: said usually of the hair.

auc-tion (ôk'shŭn), *n.* a public sale of property or goods to the highest bidder; the property or effects so offered for sale: *v.t.* to sell to the highest bidder: **auction bridge**, a variety of the game of bridge whist.

auc-tion-eer (ôk"shŭn-ēr'), *n.* one licensed to sell property or goods by public sale: *v.t.* to sell to the highest bidder.

au-da-cious (ô-dā'shŭs), *adj.* bold; daring; spirited; insolent; impudent.—*adv.* audaciously.

au-dac-i-ty (ô-dăs'ĭ-tĭ), *n.* [*pl.* audacities (-tĭz)], boldness; daring; spirit; presumptuousness; impudence.
Syn. impertinence, hardihood.
Ant. (see meekness).

au-di-ble (ô-dĭ-bl), *adj.* loud enough to be heard.—*adv.* audibly.

au-di-ence (ô'dĭ-ĕns), *n.* an assembly of hearers; admittance to a hearing or formal interview with one of high position.

au-dit (ô'dĭt), *n.* official examination of claims or accounts; a regular settlement of accounts: *v.t.* to examine and adjust, as accounts or claims: *v.i.* to act as examiner of accounts.

au-di-tor (ô'dĭ-tēr), *n.* a hearer or listener; a person appointed to examine and verify accounts and claims.

au-di-to-ri-um (ô"dĭ-tō'rĭ-ŭm), *n.* [*pl.* auditoria (-ȧ), and auditoriums (-ŭmz)], the space in a theater or other public building assigned to the audience.

au-di-to-ry (ô'dĭ-tō-rĭ), *adj.* relating to hearing, or to the sense or organs of hearing: *n.* an audience; a place or space allotted to hearers; an auditorium.

au-ger (ô'gēr), *n.* a carpenter's tool for boring holes larger than those bored by a gimlet.

aught (ôt), *n.* anything; any part; in arithmetic, a cipher; hence, naught, nothing: *adv.* in any way; at all. Also, ought.

aug-ment (ôg-mĕnt'), *v.t.* to increase; to enlarge in size or extent: *v.i.* to grow larger; increase in strength.

au-gur (ô'gûr), *n.* in ancient times, one who officially foretold events by natural signs or omens, such as the flight of birds, thunder and lightning, etc.; one who professes to foretell events by omens; a soothsayer; a prophet: *v.i.* to infer from signs or omens: *v.t.* to predict, betoken or infer.
Syn. v. forebode, predict, prophesy, foretell.
Ant. (see assure).

au-gu-ry (ô'gū-rĭ), *n.* [*pl.* auguries (-rĭz)], the art or practice of foretelling events by reference to natural signs or omens; an omen; prediction.

au-gust (ô-gŭst'), *adj.* imposing; having grandeur and dignity; majestic; of a nature to inspire awe and reverence; of high rank; eminent; noble; solemn; awful.—**August**, *n.* the eighth month of the year, having thirty-one days: named by the Roman emperor, Augustus Cæsar, in his own honor.

aunt (ănt), *n.* the sister of one's father or mother; also, an uncle's wife.

au-ra (ô'rȧ), *n.* an imaginary influence, force, or matter issuing from the human body and surrounding it like an atmosphere.

au-re-ate (ô'rē-āt), *adj.* golden; gilded; splendid.

au-re-o-la (ô-rē'ō-lȧ), *n.* a halo, radiance, or bright cloud surrounding the figures of Christ, the Virgin, and the saints, as represented by the painters. Also, aureole.

au-ri-cle (ô'rĭ-kl), *n.* the outer ear; that part of the ear which projects from the head; one of the two chambers of the heart which receive the blood from the veins.

au-ric-u-lar (ô-rĭk'ū-lȧr), *adj.* relating to the ear or to the sense of hearing; privately addressed, as to the priest in the confessional; perceived by the ear; known by report; obtained by the ear; ear-shaped; belonging to the chambers of the heart.

au-rif-er-ous (ô-rĭf'ēr-ŭs), *adj.* gold-bearing; yielding or containing gold; as, *auriferous* quartz or strata.

au-ri-form (ô'rĭ-fôrm), *adj.* ear-shaped; having the form of the human ear; as, an *auriform* shell.

au-ro-ra (ô-rō'rȧ), *n.* [*pl.* auroras (-rȧz)], the rising light of the morning; the dawn or dayspring: **Aurora**, the Roman goddess of dawn.—*adj.* auroral.

au-ro-ra bo-re-a-lis (ô-rō'rȧ bō"rē-ā'lĭs), the brilliant radiance of the sky in far northern latitudes at night. [LAT.]

au-ro-ra aus-tra-lis (ô-rō'rȧ ôs-trā'lĭs), the radiant night lights of the southern polar sky. [LAT.]

aus-pice (ôs'pĭs), *n.* [*pl.* auspices (-ĕz)], an omen or sign drawn from birds; an omen or sign in general; as, an *auspice* of good fortune; protection; patronage; favoring influence: generally in plural.

aus-pi-cious (ôs-pĭsh'ŭs), *adj.* having promise of success or happiness; favorable; fortunate; prosperous.

aus-tere (ôs-tēr'), *adj.* unadorned; severe or strict; rigid in character or mode of living; severely simple; sour; harsh; rough to the taste.—*adv.* austerely.
Syn. rigid, rigorous, stern.
Ant. (see dissolute).

aus-ter-i-ty (ôs-tĕr'ĭ-tĭ), *n.* roughness or severity of manner or life; harsh discipline; stern simplicity.

au-then-tic (ô-thĕn'tĭk), *adj.* genuine; original; duly authorized; true; trustworthy. Also, authentical.

au-then-ti-cal-ly (ô-thĕn'tĭ-kăl-ĭ), *adv.* in a trustworthy manner; authoritatively; actually; really; with certainty.

au-then-ti-cate (ô-thĕn'tĭ-kāt), *v.t.* to establish as correct or genuine.

au-then-ti-ca-tion (ô-thĕn"tĭ-kā'shŭn), *n.* the act of showing the genuineness, truth, or credibility of anything; in law, the official verification of a written document.

au-then-tic-i-ty (ô"thĕn-tĭs'ĭ-tĭ), *n.* the quality of being true, correct, or genuine; the state of being entitled to acceptance.

au-thor (ô-thẽr), *n.* [*fem.* authoress], the beginner or prime mover of anything; an originator; a creator; one who composes or writes a book; one who makes a profession of writing; a composer.

au-thor-i-ta-tive (ô-thŏr'ĭ-tā-tĭv), *adj.* having the right to demand obedience; with the air of being duly empowered; dictatorial; positive; commanding; as, he acted in an *authoritative* manner.—*adv.* **authoritatively.**

au-thor-i-ty (ô-thŏr'ĭ-tĭ), *n.* [*pl.* authorities (-tĭz)], power or right to act or command; dominion; power derived from respect or reputation; influence; justification or support for statement or action; a person with, or given, power to act or command; a ruler; one to whom appeal or reference can be made: *pl.* the government or legal officials.

au-thor-i-za-tion (ô"thŏr-ĭ-zā'shŭn), *n.* the act of having legal power; sanction; warrant.

au-thor-ize (ô'thŏr-īz), *v.t.* to clothe with power; give a right to act or command; empower; legalize.

au-to- (ô'tō-), *prefix* meaning self; of oneself; of itself; as, *auto*mobile, moving of itself.

au-to-bi-o-graph-ic (ô"tō-bī"ō-grăf'-ĭk), *adj.* relating to a self-written life history. Also, **autobiographical.**—*adv.* **autobiographically.**

au-to-bi-og-ra-phy (ô"tō-bī-ŏg'rá-fĭ), *n.* [*pl.* autobiographies (-fĭz)], a biography, account, or character-sketch, of a person written by himself.

au-to-car (ô'tō-kär"), *n.* a carriage or wagon moved by motor power within itself; an automobile. Also, **autoboat, autobus, autocycle.**

au-toc-ra-cy (ô-tŏk'rá-sĭ), *n.* [*pl.* autocracies (-sĭz)], absolute supremacy; government by one invested with absolute and uncontrolled authority.

au-to-crat (ô'tō-krăt), *n.* an absolute prince or sovereign; a monarch who rules without restriction; one whose rule is undisputed in any company.

au-to-crat-ic (ô"tō-krăt'ĭk), *adj.* absolute; holding unlimited powers of government; despotic; dictatorial. Also, **autocratical.**—*adv.* **autocratically.**

au-to-graph (ô'tō-grăf), *adj.* written in one's own handwriting: *n.* a person's own handwriting or signature; a manuscript written by the author himself.

au-tog-ra-phy (ô-tŏg'rá-fĭ), *n.* the science or study of original signatures and original manuscripts; a way of making printed copies of writings or drawings.

au-to-in-tox-i-ca-tion (ô"tō-ĭn-tŏk"-sĭ-kā'shŭn), *n.* a form of poisoning, or the state of being poisoned from substances produced within one's own body.

au-to-mat-ic (ô"tō-măt'ĭk), *adj.* having the power of self-motion or self-action; done unconsciously or from force of habit: *n.* a pistol which can be rapidly discharged without raising the hammer. Also, **automatical.**—*adv.* **automatically.**

au-tom-a-ton (ô-tŏm'á-tŏn), *n.* [*pl.* automata (-tá) and automatons (-tŏnz)], that which has the power of movement without consciousness; a self-acting machine, especially one made to imitate living beings, as a mechanical doll.

au-to-mo-bile (ô"tō-mō'bĭl; ô"tō-mō-bēl'), *n.* a vehicle moved by a source of power within itself; a motor-car; an autocar.

au-to-mo-bil-ist (ô'tō-mō"bĭl-ĭst), *n.* one who uses and controls a motor-car; a chauffeur.

au-to-mo-tor (ô"tō-mō'tẽr), *n.* a self-acting machine.

au-ton-o-mist (ô-tŏn'ō-mĭst), *n.* a supporter of self-government.

au-ton-o-mous (ô-tŏn'ō-mŭs), *adj.* self-governing; independent in government.

au-ton-o-my (ô-tŏn'ō-mĭ), *n.* [*pl.* autonomies (-mĭz)], the power or right of self-government; the state of political independence.

au-to-sta-bil-i-ty (ô"tō-stá-bĭl'ĭ-tĭ), *n.* stability or steady poise secured in an airplane either by virtue of the shape and proportions of the planes or by self-operative mechanical devices.

au-top-sy (ô'tŏp-sĭ), *n.* a post-mortem examination, or the inspection of a dead body, to find out the cause of death.

au-to-truck (ô'tō-trŭk), *n.* a self-moving truck; a motor-truck.

au-to-type (ô'tō-tīp"), *n.* the name of a process for making permanent prints or copies of pictures; a picture made by this process; a copy; a reproduction in facsimile, or an exact copy.

au-tumn (ô'tŭm), *n.* the season between summer and winter, beginning about September 22, and ending about December 23: often called *fall*, as being the time of the falling of the leaves; a period of decline or decay; as, the *autumn* of life.

au-tum-nal (ô-tŭm'năl), *adj.* pertaining or peculiar to the fall; produced or gathered in the fall; relating to the period of life when middle age is past.

au-tum-nal e-qui-nox (ô-tŭm'năl ē'kwĭ-nŏks), the time of the sun's southward passage across the equator, about September 22.

aux-il-i-a-ry (ôg-zĭl'yá-rĭ), *adj.* helping; aiding; assisting: *n.* [*pl.* auxiliaries (-rĭz)], a helper; an assistant; a confederate or ally; aid of any kind; a verb which helps to form the moods and tenses of other verbs: *pl.* foreign troops in the service of a nation at war.

a-vail (á-vāl'), *v.i.* to be of use, value, or service; to give aid toward an end; to serve for a purpose; as, wealth does not *avail* on a desert island: *v.t.* to take advantage of, or profit by; as, I *availed* myself of his offer: *n.* use; means towards an end; advantage toward success.

a-vail-a-ble (á-vāl'á-bl), *adj.* usable; suitable for one's purpose; as, an *avail*'*ble* candidate.

av-a-lanche (ăv'ȧ-lănch), *n.* the sudden sliding of a mass of snow or ice down a mountain slope; a fall of rocks or earth from the heights of a mountain; anything that overwhelms by sudden and resistless force; as, an *avalanche* of woe.

av-a-rice (ăv'ȧ-rĭs), *n.* an insatiable desire for wealth; covetousness; cupidity; greediness.

av-a-ri-cious (ăv'ȧ-rĭsh'ŭs), *adj.* eager to possess and to keep riches; greedy for gain; grasping; rapacious; miserly.
Ant. (see generous).

a-vast (ȧ-văst'), *interj.* a nautical term: stop! cease! hold!

a-vaunt (ȧ-vônt'; ȧ-vänt'), *interj.* begone! depart! an expression of contempt or abhorrence.

quality; midway between extremes; ordinary; *n.* any estimate or general statement based on a comparison of a number of different cases; the general type; *v.t.* to find the average by arithmetic by dividing proportionally among a number; to reduce to a mean.

a-verse (ȧ-vûrs'), *adj.* unwilling; reluctant; having a repugnance or disinclination to; as, he was *averse* to entering the contest.—*n.* averseness.

a-ver-sion (ȧ-vûr'shŭn), *n.* opposition or repugnance of mind; antipathy; fixed dislike; the object or cause of dislike or repugnance.
Syn. hatred, antipathy.
Ant. (see affection).

a-vert (ȧ-vûrt'), *v.t.* to turn aside or away; turn or ward off; prevent.

Stages in Aviation. 1, Langley airplane (1896); 2, Wright biplane (1911); 3, Bleriot monoplane (1913); 4, Curtiss biplane (1915); 5, Caproni triplane (1918).

a-ve (ā'vē; ä'vā), *interj.* hail! farewell! *n.* a salutation: **Ave,** an Ave Maria ("Hail, Mary").

a-venge (ȧ-vĕnj'), *v.t.* to inflict injury or evil in return for: *v.i.* to execute vengeance; to require satisfaction for injury; as, time *avenges*.

av-e-nue (ăv'ē-nū), *n.* a way or means of approach to a place; a wide roadway or drive usually bordered by trees leading to a country house; a broad street; figuratively, means of access or attainment; as, hard work is the surest *avenue* to success.

a-ver (ȧ-vûr'), *v.t.* [*p.t.* and *p.p.* averred, *p.pr.* averring], to affirm positively; declare to be true.

av-er-age (ăv'ẽr-āj), *adj.* equal in amount to the sum of all the different quantities of the same kind added together and divided by the number of them; as, if a pound of sugar cost at various times 5, 6, 7, 8, 9 cents, the *average* price for the year would be 7 cents; of medium character or

A-ves-ta (ȧ-vĕs'tȧ), *n.* the bible or sacred scriptures of Persia, of which Zoroaster is the author; the Zend-Avesta.

a-vi-a-ry (ā'vĭ-ā-rĭ), *n.* [*pl.* aviaries (-ĭz)], a house, large cage, or inclosure for the keeping and rearing of birds.

a-vi-a-tion (ā'vĭ-ā'shŭn), *n.* the art of flying; the act of mechanical flight; the art or science of traveling by airplanes.

a-vi-a-tor (ā'vĭ-ā'tẽr), *n.* a flyer; the operator of a flying machine; the driver of an airplane.

a-vi-a-trix (ā'vĭ-ā'trĭks), *n.* a woman who drives an airplane. Also, aviatress.

a-vi-cul-ture (ā'vĭ-kŭl'tūr), *n.* the breeding and rearing of birds.

a-vid-i-ty (ȧ-vĭd'ĭ-tĭ), *n.* as applied to the senses, greediness; strong appetite; as applied to the mind, eagerness; as, to read with *avidity*; intenseness of desire; in chemistry, degree of affinity.

av-o-ca-tion (ăv-ō-kā′shŭn), *n.* a secondary or occasional occupation; work that is outside of one's regular business; a diversion or distraction.

a-void (ȧ-void′), *v.t.* to keep away from; to shun; to abstain from.

a-void-ance (ȧ-void′ăns), *n.* the act of shunning anything disagreeable or unwelcome.

av-oir-du-pois (ăv′ẽr-dŭ-poiz′), *n.* a system of weights in which one pound contains sixteen ounces: used for weighing all commodities except precious metals, gems, and drugs.

a-vouch (ȧ-vouch′), *v.t.* to affirm or acknowledge openly; to maintain; to declare positively; to vouch for or answer for; to guarantee; admit or confess.

a-vow (ȧ-vou′), *v.t.* to declare openly; acknowledge frankly; to admit and justify.—*adj.* avowed.—*adv.* avowedly.

Syn. aver, confess.

Ant. (see deny).

a-vow-al (ȧ-vou′ăl), *n.* an open declaration; a frank acknowledgment; a confession.

a-vun-cu-lar (ȧ-vŭn′kū-lẽr), *adj.* pertaining to or like an uncle.

a-wait (ȧ-wāt′), *v.t.* to wait for; to look for or expect; to be ready for.

a-wake (ȧ-wāk′), *v.t.* [*p.t.* and *p.p.* awoke, awaked, *p.pr.* awaking], to arouse from sleep, or from any state resembling sleep; put into action; to infuse new life into: *v.i.* to cease to sleep; to rouse oneself; to become alert: *adj.* not sleeping; roused from sleep or inactivity; in a state of vigilance or action.

a-wak-en-ing (ȧ-wāk′n-ĭn), *n.* the act of rousing from sleep; a revival: *adj.* rousing; exciting; stirring.

a-ward (ȧ-wôrd′), *v.t.* to assign by judicial sentence, or arbitration; as, he was *awarded* heavy damages; bestow in consideration of merit; as, they *aw rded* prizes in a contest; to determine or make an award: *n.* a prize; a judgment; a decision; a sentence; the decision of arbitrators on po nts submitted to them; the document containing such decision; that which is awarded or assigned, as a medal for merit, or a sum of money as damages, etc.

a-ware (ȧ-wâr′), *adj.* on guard watchful; conscious; vigilant.—*n.* awareness.

a-wash (ȧ-wŏsh′), *adj.* and *adv.* level, or just above the surface of the water so that the waves break over, as wreckage just appearing above the wa er; covered with water; kept wet; as, the decks were *awash*; tossed about by the waves.

a-way (ȧ-wā′), *adv.* absent; at a distance; out of existence; off; removed; remote; in another direction; cont nuously; as, he worked *away*: *interj.* begone! depart!

awe (ô), *n.* solemn fear; the feeling or emotion inspired by viewing something sublime; a sense of deep admiration and respect; reverence: *v.t.* to strike or inspire with feelings of solemn respect or fear; restrain by fear or respect.

Syn. *n.* dread, fear, reverence.

Ant. (see familiarity).

a-weath-er (ȧ-wĕth′ẽr), *adv.* toward the wind; opposite to *alee*.

awe-some (ô′sŭm), *adj.* appalling; causing terror; weird.

aw-ful (ô′fōōl), *adj.* inspiring or impressing with great fear or reverence; as, the *awful* majesty of God; of a dreadful or appalling nature; solemn.—*n.* awfulness.

aw-ful-ly (ô′fōōl-ĭ), *adv.* dreadfully; terribly; sublimely; majestically.

a-while (ȧ-hwīl′), *adv.* for a period of time: properly written as two words.

awk-ward (ôk′wẽrd), *adj.* wanting cleverness; unskilful; ungraceful or ungainly in shape, movement, or manners; clumsy.—*adv.* awkwardly.—*n.* awkwardness.

Syn. uncouth, boorish.

awl (ôl), *n.* a pointed tool for making small holes in leather, wood, etc.

Awl

awn-ing (ôn′ĭng), *n.* a movable, rooflike covering of canvas or other cloth stretched upon a frame and used over any place, or in front of a door or window as a shelter from wind or sun.

a-woke (ȧ-wōk′), *p.t.* of *awake*; as, he *awoke* with a start to his danger.

a-wry (ȧ-rī′), *adj.* and *adv.* turned or twisted toward one side; as, his face was *awry* with pain; not straight; crooked; as, her cap was *awry*; perverse or perversely.

ax (ăks), *n.* a tool, consisting of an iron head with a cutting edge of steel, attached to a handle, used for the hewing of timber and chopping of wood; also a weapon of defense. Also, axe.

ax-il (ăk′sĭl), *n.* the angle formed by the upper side of a leaf, branch, etc. with the stem or trunk to which it is attached.

ax-i-om (ăk′sĭ-ŭm), *n.* a self-evident truth; a proposition or statement generally believed to be true; one of the principles of an art or science.

Syn. adage, byword, maxim, proverb, saying, saw.

Ant. (see absurdity).

ax-i-o-mat-ic (ăk′sĭ-ō-măt′ĭk), *adj.* self-evident; proverbial; of the nature of a received principle. Also, axiomatical.—*adv.*, axiomatically.

ax-is (ăk′sĭs), *n.* [*pl.* axes (-sēz)], the motionless, straight line, real or imaginary, passing through a body, upon or around which such a body revolves, or is supposed to revolve; as, the earth turns on its *axis*; that on which any matter hinges or turns.

ax-le (ăk′sl), *n.* the cross-bar or spindle which supports a vehicle, and on which the wheels turn.

ax-le-tree (ăk′sl-trē), *n.* a bar connecting the opposite wheels of a carriage, on the rounded ends of which the wheels revolve.

aye (ā), *adv.* always; forever; continually. Also, ay.

aye (ī), *adv.* yes; yea; even so; indeed: *n.* [*pl.* ayes (-īz)], a vote in the affirmative; an expression of assent. Also, ay.

Ayr-shire (âr′shẽr; âr′shĭr), *n.* a fine breed of cattle, grown in, and named for, the county or shire of Ayr, Scotland.

a-za-le-a (ȧ-zā′lē-ȧ), *n.* [*pl.* azaleas (-ȧz)], a kind of plant, belonging to the shrub family, related to the rhododendron, and remarkable for its beautiful flowers.

Az-tec (ăz′tĕk), *n.* a member of the Indian tribe which founded the Mexican empire conquered by Cortez in 1519: *adj.* relating to the Aztec race or language.

az-ure (ăzh′ŭr), *adj.* like the clear blue of the sky; sky blue: *n.* the clear blue sky; the blue vault of heaven.

B

baa (bä), *v.i.* to bleat or cry, as a sheep: *n.* the bleating or cry of a sheep or lamb.

Ba-al (bā'ăl), *n.* the sun god, or supreme being worshiped especially by the Phœnicians before the time of Christ.

Ba-ba (bä'bä), *n.* father: an Eastern title of respect. [TURK.]

bab-ble (băb'l), *v.i.* to utter indistinct or imperfect sounds; to prattle; to talk childishly; to jabber; to murmur constantly: *v.t.* to utter indistinctly or imperfectly; to tell, as secrets; blab: *n.* unmeaning or foolish talk; a confused murmur.

Syn., *v.* and *n.* chatter; prattle.

bab-bler (băb'lẽr), *n.* one who talks idly or thoughtlessly, or who chatters heedlessly or mischievously.

babe (bāb), *n.* [*pl.* babes (bābz)], an infant or young child of either sex.

Ba-bel (bā'bĕl), *n.* the city and tower described in Genesis, where the confusion of languages took place; tumult; confusion; a place of confusion: often *babel*.

bab-i-rous-sa (băb″ĭ-rōō'sȧ), *n.* the wild hog of Eastern Asia. It has upturned hornlike tusks.

Babiroussa

ba-boon (bă-bōōn'), *n.* the popular name of the large apes or monkeys with doglike muzzles, of Africa and Arabia.

ba-by (bā'bĭ), *n.* [*pl.* babies (-bĭz)], a child in arms; an infant of either sex; a small child: **baby bond**, colloquially, a bond having a face value of $100.—*adj.* **babyish.**

Bab-y-lon (băb'ĭ-lŏn), *n.* the capital of the ancient empire of Babylonia in the Euphrates Valley, famed for its wealth, luxuriousness, and extravagance; hence, any rich but wicked city.

Bab-y-lo-ni-an (băb″ĭ-lō'nĭ-ăn), *adj.* relating to Babylon or Babylonia; luxurious; grand; magnificent. Also, **Babylonish.**

bac-ca-lau-re-ate (băk″ȧ-lô'rē-āt), *n.* the degree of bachelor, or first degree, given by universities and colleges: *adj.* relating to the degree of bachelor: **baccalaureate sermon**, a farewell sermon delivered to a graduating class.

bac-ca-rat (băk″ȧ-rä'), *n.* a French gambling game of cards of mere chance.

bac-cha-na-li-an (băk″ȧ-nā'lĭ-ăn), *adj.* pertaining to the Bacchanalia, a feast in honor of Bacchus, the god of wine; hence, pertaining to drunkenness and revelry. Also, **bacchanal.**

bac-chant (băk'ănt), *n.* [*fem.* bacchante], one devoted to the worship of Bacchus, the god of wine; hence, a drunken reveler. Also, **bacchanal.**

Bac-chus (băk'ŭs), *n.* the Roman god of wine; the Greek Dionysus.

bach-e-lor (băch'ĕ-lẽr), *n.* an unmarried man; one who has taken the first degree in any field of learning at a college or university.

bach-e-lor's-but-ton (băch'ĕ-lẽr's-bŭt'n), any of the flowering plants the blossoms of which resemble small balls or buttons, as the cornflower and ragged robin.

ba-cil-lus (bȧ-sĭl'ŭs), *n.* [*pl.* bacilli (-ī)], any of a genus, or kind of rod-shaped vegetable organisms, visible only under the microscope. Some are harmless; others cause disease. Especially in plural, any bacteria, commonly known as *bacteria*.

back (băk), *n.* the hinder part of the body of man, or of other animals, from the neck to the end of the backbone; the whole region of the spine; that which is opposed to the front; the rear or hinder part of anything; the part of a book where it is sewed in binding; the part of a knife, sword, etc., opposite to the cutting edge: *v.t.* to furnish with a back or backing; get upon the back of, or mount; second or support: usually with *up;* bet or wager on the successful outcome of; sign or indorse; to cause to move in a backward direction: *v.i.* to move or go backward: *adj.* lying or being behind, or in the rear, as to time, situation, or direction; in a backward direction; in arrears; overdue; no longer current; as, the *back* numbers of a magazine: *adv.* to or toward the rear; to or toward a former place, state, or condition; to or toward time past; in withdrawal; as, to take *back* hasty words; to keep concealed or in reserve; as, to keep *back* part of the truth; in return; as, to pay *back*.

back-bite (băk'bīt″), *v.t.* [*p.t.* backbit, *p.p.* backbit and backbitten, *p.pr.* backbiting], to slander or speak evil of (one who is not present): *v.i.* to find fault with or blame spitefully one who is absent.

back-bone (băk'bōn'), *n.* the spine; firmness; the courage to cling to and act upon principles of right.

back-er (băk'ẽr), *n.* one who aids or assists another; especially, one who bets in favor of a person, animal, or thing in a contest.

back-gam-mon (băk'găm-ŭn), *n.* a game of chance played by two persons upon a board made with four marked-off spaces called "tables." Each person plays with fifteen pieces whose moves he determines by throwing dice.

back-ground (băk'ground″), *n.* the distant portion of the landscape; the portion of a picture farthest away from the spectator, or lying between or above the chief figures; the whole of a surface upon which patterns or designs are executed; that which is dimly seen because it is far away; a place obscure or out of sight; that which is back of something and against which it can be looked at or viewed.

back-hand (băk'hănd″), *n.* handwriting which slopes upward to the left: *adj.* made with the back of the hand, or with the hand turned backward; as, a *backhand* stroke; indirect; insincere.—*adj.* **backhanded.**

back-ing (băk'ĭng), *n.* something placed behind to support or strengthen; aid or support given to a person or cause.

back-sheesh (băk'shēsh), *n.* an Oriental term for a present or gratuity. Also, **backshish, bakhsheesh, bakshish.**

back-side (băk'sīd'), *n.* the hind part of anything, or that which is opposed to the front; the hind part of an animal.

back-slide (băk'slīd'), *v.i.* [*p.t.* backslid, *p.p.* backslid, backslidden, *p.pr.* backsliding], to slip back; gradually to turn away or fall away from a religion once believed in.—*n.* **backslider.**

back-stays (băk'stāz'), *n.pl.* a nautical term: long ropes stretched from the masthead to the side of the ship, to assist in supporting the mast; any support devised to strengthen at the back.

back-ward (băk'wẽrd), *adj.* directed to the rear; moving or done in a way opposite to the normal way; reversed; reluctant; hesitating; retiring; bashful; behind in learning or progress; dull; as, a *backward* pupil; behindhand; late: *adv.* toward the rear; with the back coming first or foremost; as, to tumble over *backward*.—*adv.* **backwards, backwardly.**—*n.* **backwardness.**

back-wa-ter (băk'wô'tẽr), *n.* water held back by a dam or weir; the body of water thus held back; water thrown back by the turning of a water-wheel or the paddles of a steamer.

back-woods (băk'wŏŏdz'), *n.pl.* forests or partly cleared land on the outskirts of a newly settled country; a rough or thinly settled district far from any town or city.

ba-con (bā'kn), *n.* the salted and dried or smoked flesh of the hog, especially the back and sides.

bac-te-ri-a (băk-tē'rĭ-ȧ), *n.pl.* vegetable organisms which can be seen only under the microscope. Some cause decay; some cause fermentation; and many cause disease.

bac-te-ri-ol-o-gist (băk-tē'rĭ-ŏl'ō-jĭst), *n.* one who studies the germs causing disease.

bac-te-ri-ol-o-gy (băk-tē'rĭ-ŏl'ō-jĭ), *n.* the scientific study of bacteria, microbes, or disease germs.

bad (băd), *adj.* [*compar.* worse, *superl.* worst], evil; morally wicked; vicious; corrupting; hurtful; offensive; defective; legally worthless; severe; as, a *bad* cold; unfortunate: **in bad form,** not in good taste; not according to accepted social customs.—*adv.* **badly.**—*n.* **badness.**

Syn. Imperfect, inferior, wrong, sinful, immoral, detrimental, disagreeable.

Ant. (see good).

badge (băj), *n.* a distinctive mark, sign, or token to denote the occupation, association, or achievements of the person by whom it is worn; the mark or token of anything.

badg-er (băj'ẽr), *n.* a hairy, flesh-eating animal which burrows in the ground, like a mole: *v.t.* to annoy; to pester; to tease; to worry.

bad-i-nage (bȧ'dē'nōzh'; băd'ĭ-nāj), *n.* light or playful jesting or banter; good-humored pleasantry. [Fr.]

baf-fle (băf'l), *v.t.* to bring the efforts of to nothing by placing difficulties in the way; hence, to hinder, foil, or check.

Syn. balk, frustrate, counteract, checkmate.

Ant. (see promote).

baf-fling (băf'lĭng), *adj.* disconcerting; confusing; perplexing.

baf-fy (băf'ĭ), *n.* in the game of golf, a wooden club used to play lofting shots.

bag (băg), *n.* a sack; a pouch; a wallet; that which is contained in a bag; a sac or receptacle in animal bodies, containing a fluid or other substance; a certain quantity of grain, etc., purchased "by the bag": *v.t.* to inclose in a bag; secure or capture, as game: *v.i.* to bulge; hang down like a full bag.

bag-a-telle (băg'ȧ-tĕl'), *n.* a trifle; a game played with a billiard cue and nine balls on an oblong board containing nine holes; a short, light piece of piano music.

bag-gage (băg'āj), *n.* the tents, clothing, utensils, etc., of an army; the trunks, packages, etc., which a traveler requires; luggage; a worthless person, usually, a worthless woman; familiarly or jokingly, a playful, saucy, young woman; a flirt.

bag-ging (băg'ĭng), *n.* the act of putting into bags; coarse cloth or other material used for bags.

bag-gy (băg'ĭ), *adj.* having a loose or flabby appearance; swelled, loose, or puffed out like a bag.

bag-pipe (băg'pīp'), *n.* a shrill-toned Scottish musical instrument consisting of a leathern wind-bag from which air is forced by the performer's arm into pipes, one pipe (the *chanter*) giving the melody: commonly in plural.—*n.* **bagpiper.**

bail (bāl), *v.t.* to liberate or set free from arrest upon receipt of a guarantee (money or bond) that the person thus freed will return at a stated time; to empty of water by dipping or throwing it out; as, to *bail* a boat; to dip or scoop out, as water, with a pail or other utensil: *v.i.* to dip water from a boat, etc.: *n.* the person or persons who provide security for the release of a prisoner; the security tendered, or accepted; the scoop or pail used in dipping water out of a boat; in cricket, either of two crosspieces placed end to end on the wicket.

bail-iff (bāl'ĭf), *n.* a sheriff's officer or constable; an overseer or under-steward on an estate.

bail-i-wick (bāl'ĭ-wĭk), *n.* the district within which a sheriff or bailiff has legal power.

bail-ment (bāl'mĕnt), *n.* a delivery of goods in trust to another; the action of becoming surety for a prisoner or accused person.

bairn (bârn), *n.* a child; a son or daughter of any age. [Scot.]

bait (bāt), *n.* any substance used to entice or allure fish or other animals with a view to catching them; temptation; refreshment taken on a journey: *v.t.* to harass or provoke, as an animal, by the setting on of dogs for sport; to worry by biting or tearing; to torment; annoy persistently; to prepare, as a hook, trap, or snare, by covering with food; give food and drink to upon a journey; to feed (an animal): *v.i.* to take food or drink upon a journey; hence, to stop for rest.

baize (bāz), *n.* a coarse woolen stuff, with a long nap, for table covers, etc.

bake (bāk), *v.t.* to cook or prepare, as food, in an oven; to dry and harden by dry heat, as bricks: *v.i.* to do the work of baking; to become hard by heat.

bak-er (bāk'ẽr), *n.* one whose business it is to make and sell bread, biscuits, cakes, etc.

bak-er-y (bāk'ẽr-ĭ), *n.* [*pl.* bakeries (-ĭz)], a place where bread, cakes, pies, etc., are made and sold.

bak-ing (bāk'ing), *n.* the act or process of baking; the quantity of bread or pies, etc., made at the same time; a batch.

bal-ance (băl'ăns), *n.* a pair of scales for weighing; a steel-yard; the act of weighing or estimating mentally; equal poise of any opposing forces, especially mental poise; steadiness of mind; sanity; an equality between the totals of two sides of an account; the excess shown on either side; the sum or weight necessary to make two unequal sums or weights equal; poise; a movement in dancing; *v.t.* to weigh by means of a balance; weigh by means of the mind; hence, to compare, estimate, etc.; to set off, as one thing against another; to equal or make equal; to find out the difference between the debits and credits of, or to bring about an equality between; as, to *balance* an account: *v.i.* to be of equal weight, force, or amount; in dancing, to move to and fro.

Balance

bal-ance of pow-er (băl'ăns ŏv pou'ẽr), such a division of power among certain nations as guarantees the independence of each; the power of a small party to join with either of two larger ones and so gain a majority.

bal-ance of trade (băl'ăns ŏv trād), the difference between the actual value in money of the imports and exports of a country.

bal-ance sheet (băl'ăns shēt), a statement made to show the true condition of a business: a balance sheet should show the capital or assets, the liabilities or debts, and the profit and loss of the business.

bal-ance wheel (băl'ăns hwēl), a wheel in a watch which regulates its rate of motion.

bal-brig-gan (băl-brĭg'ăn), *n.* a knitted cotton fabric for either hosiery or underwear.

bal-co-ny (băl'kō-nĭ), *n.* [*pl.* balconies (-nĭz)], a platform or gallery built out from the wall of a building, and inclosed by a balustrade or railing.

bald (bôld), *adj.* destitute of hair; without the natural or usual covering of hair, feathers, fur, foliage, etc., to the head, summit, or top; unadorned; bare; without disguise; as, a *bald* statement; as applied to birds, having a white spot or patch on the head; as, the *bald* eagle.—*adv.* **baldly.**

bal-der-dash (bôl'dẽr-dăsh), *n.* nonsense; a foolish jumble of words; silly talk or writing; bombast; jargon.

bald-ness (bôld'nĕs), *n.* lack or loss of hair; bareness; as, *baldness* in style of writing.

bal-dric (bôl'drĭk), *n.* a broad belt, often richly decorated, worn around the waist, or over one shoulder and across the breast, usually to support a bugle or sword. Also, **baldrick.**

bale (bāl), *n.* a large bundle or package of goods; as, a *bale* of cotton: *v.t.* to make up into large bundles for storage or packing.

bale-ful (bāl'fŏŏl), *adj.* full of deadly intent; direful; woeful; destructive; wretched; miserable.

balk (bôk), *n.* a strip or ridge of land left unplowed; a thick, heavy piece of timber; a barrier or check; disappointment: *v.t.* to hinder; to thwart; to check or disappoint: *v.i.* to stop short or swerve. Also, **baulk.**—*adj.* **balky.**

ball (bôl), *n.* a social gathering of persons of both sexes for the purpose of dancing; a round body; any mass resembling a sphere; a round body used for play; a bullet; any roundish part of the body; a game played with a round body, which is pitched, kicked, or knocked; the globe or earth: *v.t.* to make into a round mass: *v.i.* to form or gather into a round mass.

bal-lad (băl'ăd), *n.* a short, popular, narrative poem, adapted or suitable for reciting or singing.

bal-last (băl'ăst), *n.* heavy material carried by a ship to balance or steady her; sand carried in the car of a balloon to steady it; gravel filling the space between the sleepers or ties of a railway; that which gives strength to the character: *v.t.* to place heavy material in or on in order to steady or balance; strengthen or give steadiness to.

ball bear-ing (bôl bâr'ing), a method of reducing friction by causing a shaft to rest upon or be surrounded by loose balls of metal partly contained in sockets and turning with the shaft.

bal-let (băl'ā"), *n.* an artistic dance; a complete pantomime or play in which a story is told, and actions, characters, and passions are shown by gestures, accompanied by music and dancing; the company of persons who perform the dance or the play.

bal-lis-tics (bă-lĭs'tĭks), *n.* that branch of gunnery which deals with the motion and impact of projectiles, with the forces involved.

bal-lo-net (băl"ō-nĕt'), *n.* a small balloon in a larger balloon for controlling the ascent or descent, and for maintaining pressure on the outer envelope to prevent its collapse. Also, **balloonet.**

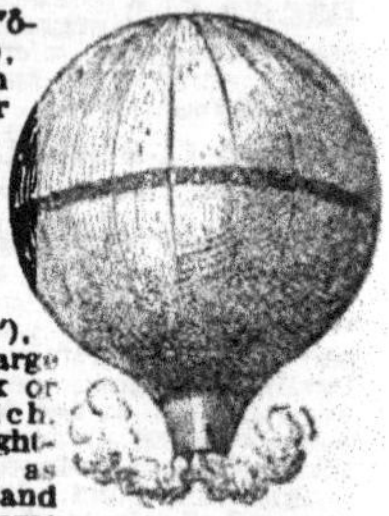

Fire Balloon

bal-loon (bă-lōōn'), *n.* a large bag of prepared silk or other material, which, when filled with a lighter-than-air gas such as hydrogen, ascends and floats in the atmosphere; a large, inflated ball: **fire balloon**, a hot-air balloon, inflated from fire attached beneath.

bal-loon-ist (bă-lōōn'ĭst), *n.* one who makes, or ascends in, a balloon; an aëronaut.

bal-lot (băl'ŭt), *n.* originally, a little ball used for secret voting; a ball, ticket, or paper by which a secret vote is registered or taken; the system of secret voting by the use of a printed form; election by secret vote; also, the total number of votes cast or recorded: *v.t.* and *v.i.* to vote or choose by using a printed form, or ticket.

balm (bäm), *n.* an oily, gummy substance coming from certain trees or shrubs, used for healing or soothing; balsam; anything which heals or soothes pain; a healing ointment.

balm-i-ness (bäm'ĭ-nĕs), *n.* the state or quality of being soothing or refreshingly fragrant.

balm of Gil-e-ad (bäm ŏv gĭl'ē-ăd), the name of various

kinds of fragrant resins, as that of the evergreen tree of Arabia; the balsam fir.

Bal-mo-ral (băl-mŏr′ăl), *n.* a striped woolen stuff, strong and durable; a laced walking shoe.

balm-y (bäm′ĭ), *adj.* soft; mild; soothing; spicy; fragrant; refreshing; as, the *balmy* air of spring.—*adv.* balmily.

bal-sam (bôl′săm), *n.* an oily, fragrant substance obtained from certain trees or shrubs, and used for medicine or in perfumery; balm; the name applied to several trees, shrubs, or plants yielding an oily, resinous substance; as, the *balsam* fir; anything soothing or healing.

bal-sam-ic (bôl-săm′ĭk), *adj.* having the qualities of, or yielding, a fragrant, oily, resinous substance; soft; soothing; healing.

bal-us-ter (băl′ŭs-tẽr), *n.* one of a set of small pillars that support the hand rail of a parapet or balustrade.

bal-us-trade (băl′ŭs-trăd), *n.* a row of small pillars, or balusters, topped by a protective rail.

Balustrade

bam-bi-no (băm-bē′nō), *n.* [*pl.* bambini (-nē)], a child or baby; a figure of the infant Christ wrapped in swaddling clothes. [IT.]

bam-boo (băm-bōō′), *n.* the name of certain tropical grasses having hard, thick-jointed stems, used for furniture, poles, canes, etc.

ban (băn), *n.* a public announcement or edict; a sentence of excommunication passed by the church; a curse; any authoritative prohibition: *pl.* public announcement given in a church of an intended marriage: *v.t.* [*p.t.* and *p.p.* banned, *p.pr.* banning], to curse; to call evil down upon; to place under a curse; to forbid the use of.

ban-al (băn′ăl; bā′năl), *adj.* commonplace; trivial; hackneyed; trite.

ba-nal-i-ty (bȧ-năl′ĭ-tĭ), *n.* a commonplace remark, idea, etc.

ba-na-na (bȧ-nä′nȧ; bȧ-năn′ȧ), *n.* a tropical plant which bears a fruit used as food; the fruit of the plant.

band (bănd), *n.* that which binds together; that which connects; that which embraces, supports, or restrains; a strap, tie, shackle, or fetter; collar; a driving belt; a company of persons united by a common object; a body of soldiers; a body of musicians performing on wood and brass wind-instruments: *v.t.* to unite in a troop, company, or confederacy; to mark with a band: *v.i.* to associate or unite together for some common purpose.

band-age (băn′dāj), *n.* a strip of cotton or other material used in dressing and binding up wounds, etc.; a band: *v.t.* to dress, cover, or bind with a strip of any soft material.

ban-dan-na (băn-dăn′ȧ), *n.* a large, bright colored, silk or cotton handkerchief, having a red or blue background with yellow or white dots or figures upon it. Also, **bandana**.

band-box (bănd′bŏks′), *n.* a light box of pasteboard, etc., for holding bonnets or hats.

ban-deau (băn-dō′), *n.* [*pl.* bandeaux (-dōz)], a narrow band or fillet, as of ribbon, worn above the forehead or around the hair.

band-ed (băn′dĕd; băn′dĭd), *p.adj.* allied, confederated; united; marked by stripes of different color or material.

ban-de-role (băn′dē-rōl), *n.* a little flag or streamer; a small flag carried at the head of a lance or mast.

ban-dit (băn′dĭt), *n.* [*pl.* bandits (-dĭts) and banditti (-dĭt′ĭ)], an outlaw; a brigand; a robber; a highwayman.

ban-do-leer (băn′dō-lēr′), *n.* a broad leather belt, worn over the shoulder and across the breast, for holding cartridges. Also, **bandolier**.

band saw (bănd sô), an endless steel saw running on pulleys; a belt-saw.

ban-dy (băn′dĭ), *v.t.* [*p.t.* and *p.p.* bandied, *p.pr.* bandying], to throw or knock to and fro, as a ball in play; to toss from one to another; give and take; to exchange; as, to *bandy* words: *v.i.* to contend; strive: *n.* a club bent at the end for striking a ball; a hockey-stick; a game played with such a club, commonly called hockey: *adj.* bent outward at the knees; as, *bandy*-legged.

bane (băn), *n.* a scourge; disease; poison; that which causes death, ruin, or destruction; hence, a deadly poison, vice, or sin; as, intemperance is the *bane* of society.

Syn. poison, ruin, injury, destruction, pest.

bane-ful (băn′fōōl), *adj.* poisonous; pernicious; deadly.—*adv.* banefully.

bang (băng), *n.* a heavy blow; a loud, sudden noise; front hair cut short and worn in a fringe over the forehead: *v.t.* to beat, as with a club or cudgel; to thump; to handle roughly; to produce a loud sound by or from; as, to *bang* the door; to cut straight across, as the hair over the forehead: *v.i.* to make a loud noise; to thump violently.

ban-gle (băṅ′gl), *n.* an ornamental ring worn upon the wrists and ankles in India and Africa; a ring-bracelet, generally with small ornaments hanging from it.

ban-ian tree (băn′yȧn trē), the Indian fig-tree, which spreads over a large area by sending down shoots from its branches: these take root and become new trunks. Also, **banyan**.

ban-ish (băn′ĭsh), *v.t.* to condemn to exile; expel from the country as a punishment; to drive away; to dispel from the mind.

Syn. eject, dismiss, evict, oust, dislodge.

ban-ish-ment (băn′ĭsh-mĕnt), *n.* the act of expelling or driving away; the state of being expelled; exile; expulsion.

ban-is-ter (băn′ĭs-tẽr), *n.* a baluster: *pl.* a balustrade of a staircase.

ban-jo (băn′jō), *n.* a stringed musical instrument somewhat like a guitar, having a long neck, and a body like a tambourine.—*n.* **banjoist**.

bank (băṅk), *n.* a place for the custody, loan, exchange, or issue of money; the office of a banking company; a heap, mound, or ridge of earth; a steep slope; an elevation or rising ground beneath the sea or at the mouth of a river, forming a shoal or shallow; as, the *Banks* of Newfoundland; the ground forming the sides of a river or stream; a bench for rowers; a row of oars: *v.t.* to put, as money, in a bank; to inclose, defend, or fortify with a bank; pile or heap up; to incline (an airplane) laterally, or make to revolve about the fore and aft axis: *v.i.* to have an account with a banker: **right bank**, to incline (an airplane) with the right wing down: **to bank a fire**, to cover with ashes and use other means to prevent it from burning too quickly and yet at the same time to prevent it from going out.

bank bill (bănk bĭl), a note issued by a bank, payable on demand, and current as money; a draft or bill of exchange of a bank payable on demand.

bank book (bănk bŏŏk), the pass book kept by a depositor, in which are entered credits and charges, and which serves as a receipt for deposits.

bank cred-it (bănk krĕd'ĭt), the amount a person, on giving proper security, is allowed to draw upon a bank.

bank dis-count (bănk dĭs'kount), an amount which equals the interest at a certain rate upon the principal of a note from the time of discounting until it becomes due.

bank-er (bănk'ẽr), *n.* one who engages in the business of lending, exchanging, issuing, or caring for money.

bank-ing (bănk'ĭng), *n.* the business of lending, exchanging, issuing, or caring for money.

bank note (bănk nōt), a promissory note issued by a legally authorized bank, payable on demand, and forming part of the money in circulation; a note payable at a bank.

bank-rupt (bănk'rŭpt), *n.* a person legally declared to be unable to pay his debts: *adj.* unable to meet one's obligations; insolvent: *v.t.* to exhaust the financial credit of; to impoverish; as, to *bankrupt* a corporation.

bank-rupt-cy (bănk'rŭpt-sĭ), *n.* [*pl.* bankruptcies (-sĭz)], the state of being legally insolvent, or unable to pay all debts; failure in business.

ban-ner (băn'ẽr), *n.* a piece of cloth or silk attached to a pole or staff, and usually worked with some device or motto; an ensign, standard, or flag of a country, state, or order.

ban-nock (băn'ŭk), *n.* a thick cake made of oatmeal, barley-meal, or pease-meal, and baked on an iron plate or griddle.

banns (bănz), *n.pl.* the due notice of a proposed marriage, given out, as in church. Also, **bans**.

ban-quet (băn'kwĕt), *n.* an elaborate or costly feast or sumptuous entertainment: *v.t.* and *v.i.* to feast.

ban-shee (băn'shē), *n.* a supernatural being, a woman, who, according to the belief of the poor of Ireland, and some parts of Scotland, attaches herself to a particular house, and foretells the death of any member of the family by appearing and uttering a weird, wild, mournful cry.

ban-tam (băn'tăm), *n.* a fowl of any of numerous small breeds; slang, a soldier under the standard army height of five feet, three inches.

ban-ter (băn'tẽr), *n.* good-natured pleasantry or teasing; colloquially, a challenge: *v.t.* to address good-humoredly; attack jestingly; make fun of: to trick meanly; impose upon; colloquially, to challenge.

Syn., n. chaff, mockery, ridicule, jeering, derision.

bant-ling (bănt'lĭng), *n.* a young child; a callow or inexperienced youth.

ban-yan (băn'yăn), *n.* an East Indian tree the branches of which send out aërial roots that grow down to the ground and form additional roots. Also, **banian**.

ban-zai (băn'zä'ē), *interj.* the Japanese hurrah: an expression meaning ten thousand years, used as a salutation to the Japanese ruler, and equivalent to "Long live the Emperor!"

Baobab

ba-o-bab (bā'ō-băb), *n.* an African tree with an enormously thick trunk. Also, **monkey bread**.

bap-tism (băp'tĭzm), *n.* the sacrament in which immersion or sprinkling with water symbolizes the washing away of sin, and which admits to membership in the Christian church; the act of sprinkling or immersing as a sacrament, or of being sprinkled or immersed; any experience by which one is cleansed spiritually, or any sanctifying ordeal; as, the adventurer here suffered his *baptism* of fire.

bap-tis-mal (băp-tĭz'măl), *adj.* relating to the sacrament of sprinkling or immersion.

Bap-tist (băp'tĭst), *n.* one of a Christian denomination, which bases its administration and government on the New Testament only, and believes that Christians should be immersed completely, or put under water in the baptismal ceremony, after a public declaration of faith has been made; the denomination described.

bap-tis-ter-y (băp'tĭs-tẽr-ĭ), *n.* [*pl.* baptisteries (-ĭz)], a building or portion of the church building in which the rite of baptism is performed. Also, **baptistry**.

bap-tize (băp-tīz'), *v.t.* to sprinkle or pour water on, or immerse in water, as a religious ceremony; to admit to the Christian church by applying water; to christen; to name.

bar (bär), *n.* a rigid piece of wood, metal, or other solid matter, long in proportion to its thickness; a quantity contained in such a shape; as, a *bar* of chocolate; a rail; a barrier; anything which impedes or obstructs; a bank of sand, gravel, etc., obstructing navigation at the entrance to a harbor or mouth of a river; the railing inclosing the space occupied by counsel in courts of law; the place in court where prisoners are stationed for trial, or sentence; the profession of a lawyer; any tribunal; the portion of a hotel, etc., where liquors are served; a band or stripe; in a bridle, the mouthpiece connecting the checks; one of the upright lines drawn through the staff of a piece of music, dividing it into equal measures of time; the space and notes inclosed by two such lines: *v.t.* [*p.t.* and *p.p.* barred, *p.pr.* barring], to fasten with a bar; to hinder; to obstruct; to exclude; to close; to prohibit; to mark with bars.

barb (bärb), *n.* that which resembles a beard at the mouth of animals; one of a race of horses noted for speed and endurance, brought by the Moors to Spain; the sharp point extending backward from the point of an arrow, fish-hook, etc., any sharp projection resembling such a point: *v.t.* to furnish with sharp points.

bar-ba-ri-an (bär-bā'rĭ-ăn), *n.* in history, a foreigner, usually in a belittling sense; a man in a rude state above that of the savage; a cruel, brutal man: *adj.* rude; uncivilized; inhuman.

bar-bar-ic (bär-băr'ĭk), *adj.* relating to, or like, uncivilized people; cruel; rude; roughly gorgeous; as, *barbaric* splendor; striking or picturesque; wildly magnificent; foreign.

bar-ba-rism (bär'bȧ-rĭzm), *n.* a word or expression not in good use; uncivilized state; rudeness of manners; ignorance of art and literature.

bar-bar-i-ty (bär-băr'ĭ-tĭ), *n.* [*pl.* barbarities (-tĭz)], brutal or inhuman conduct; an act of savage cruelty; as, the *barbarities* of war; lack of good taste in style or art.

bar-ba-rous (bär'bȧ-rŭs), *adj.* uncivilized; rude and ignorant; cruel; inhuman; wild; unpolished in speech; rude or harsh in sound.—*adv.* **barbarously.**

Syn. brutal, rude, uncouth.

bar-ba-rize (bär'bȧ-rīz), *v.t.* and *v.i.* to make or become rude or uncivilized.

bar-be-cue (bär'bē-kū), *n.* a frame on which all kinds of meat or fish are roasted or smoke-dried; the carcass of an ox, hog, etc., roasted whole; a social or political feast at which animals are roasted whole: *v.t.* to dress and roast whole, as a hog. Also, **barbacue.**

barbed (bärbd; bär'bĕd), *adj.* having a sharp point or points; as, *barbed* wire entanglements are placed before trenches: **barbed wire,** a twisted wire full of sharp points, or thornlike projections.

bar-ber (bär'bẽr), *n.* one whose business is to shave the beard and cut and dress the hair.

bar-ber-ry (bär'bĕr-ĭ), *n.* a shrub bearing bright red berries.

bar-bette (bär-bĕt'), *n.* the platform or breastwork of a fortification, from which cannon may be fired over a parapet; naval, an armored parapet protecting guns which are fired over the turret and not through portholes.

bar-bi-can (bär'bĭ-kăn), *n.* a tower or other outpost which defends the entrance to a castle or city.

bar-ca-role (bär'kȧ-rōl), *n.* a simple, popular song or melody sung by Venetian gondoliers; an imitation of such a song. Also, **barcarolle.**

bard (bärd), *n.* formerly, a poet and singer who composed and sang verses in honor of heroes and princes, generally to the accompaniment of a harp; a poet.

bare (bâr), *adj.* uncovered; naked; nude; having the head uncovered; unconcealed; simple; unadorned; unfurnished; plain; threadbare; empty; poor; scanty; mere: *v.t.* to uncover; to reveal; to expose. —*adv.* **barely.**—*n.* **bareness.**

bare-back (bâr-băk'), *adj.* and *adv.* on a horse without saddle or covering; as, a *bareback* rider; he was used to riding *bareback.*

bare-faced (bâr'fāst), *adj.* without concealment; undisguised; shameless; audacious; impudent.—*adv.* **barefacedly.**

bar-gain (bär'gĕn; -gĭn), *n.* an agreement or contract between two or more parties with reference to the sale or transfer of property; a compact or pledge mutually agreed upon; that which is acquired or sold at a low price; an advantageous purchase: *v.i.* to make a contract or agreement; to trade; to negotiate: *v.t.* to hand over for a consideration; barter; trade.

barge (bärj), *n.* a flat-bottomed vessel, of large carrying capacity, used in loading and unloading ships, and for carrying freight on rivers and canals; a pleasure boat; a large double-banked boat or a warship, used by a flag officer.—*n.* **bargeman.**

bar-i-tone (băr'ĭ-tōn), *n.* a male voice midway between a tenor and a bass and having some of the characteristics of each; a person having such a voice: *adj.* having a range of voice higher than bass and lower than tenor. Also, **barytone.**

bark (bärk), *n.* a three-masted vessel; any small boat or vessel; the covering of the trunk, branches, stems, etc., of trees and other plants; the sound or cry made by dogs, or a sound resembling it: *v.t.* to remove by stripping; to scrape the skin from; to tan by means of an infusion of bark: *v.i.* to utter a sharp, short sound like the noise made by a dog; to cough.

bar-ley (bär'lĭ), *n.* a grain, used as a food and in the manufacture of malt liquors; the plant which yields the grain.

bar-ley-corn (bär'lĭ-kôrn"), *n.* a grain of barley: **John Barleycorn,** the personification of strong drink.

barm (bärm), *n.* the foam rising upon beer or other malt liquors when fermenting, and used as leaven in bread making; yeast.

bar-maid (bär'mād"), *n.* a girl or woman who serves food and drink at the liquor counter of an inn or other place of refreshment.

Bar-me-cide (bär'mē-sīd), *adj.* imaginary; unreal; sham. In the *Arabian Nights* it is related of one of the Barmecides, a Persian family, that, having invited a beggar to dine with him, he served his guest only imaginary food.

barn (bärn), *n.* a covered building for the storage of grain or other farm produce: often used as a stable.

bar-na-cle (bär'nȧ-kl), *n.* a kind of wild goose of northern seas; a shellfish that clings or adheres to rocks and the bottom of ships.

bar-o-graph (băr'ō-grȧf), *n.* a self-registering device for recording the pressure of the atmosphere.

bar-o-gram (băr'ō-grăm), *n.* the record of a barograph.

ba-rom-e-ter (bȧ-rŏm'ē-tẽr), *n.* an instrument for measuring the weight or pressure of the atmosphere; used for showing or foretelling changes of weather, or to find heights, etc.

bar-o-met-ric (băr"ō-mĕt'rĭk), *adj.* relating to, made with, or shown by, a barometer, or instrument for measuring the weight and pressure of the atmosphere. Also, **barometrical.**

bar-on (băr'ŭn), *n.* in Great Britain and other countries, the title of a peer, or nobleman, of the lowest rank

bar-on-age (băr'ŭn-āj), *n.* formerly, the whole body of British peers; now, the body of peers of the lowest rank; the dignity or rank of a member of the lowest grade in the peerage.

bar-on-ess (băr'ŭn-ĕs), *n.* a baron's wife; a lady holding a baronial title in her own right.

bar-on-et (băr'ŭn-ĕt), *n.* an inherited title or degree of honor next below a baron and above a knight; the person holding this title.

bar-on-et-cy (băr'ŭn-ĕt-sĭ), *n.* the title and dignity of a baronet.

ba-ro-ni-al (bȧ-rō'nĭ-ăl), *adj.* relating to a baron, or peer of the lowest grade, or to a barony; as, a *baronial* castle.

bar-on-y (băr'ŭ-nĭ), *n.* [*pl.* baronies (-ĭz)], the rank of a baron, or peer of the lowest grade; the domain of a baron.

bar-o-scope (băr'ō-skōp), *n.* an instrument for showing changes in the pressure of the atmosphere without measuring its weight; a storm- or weather-glass.

ba-rouche (bȧ-rōōsh'), *n.* a roomy, four-wheeled carriage with a folding or falling top.

barque (bärk), *n.* a small three-masted vessel; any small boat. Also, **bark.**

bar-rack (băr'ȧk), *n.* a large structure or row of buildings for lodging soldiers and officers; a building or collection of huts within an inclosure in which a body of men are lodged: generally in plural.

bar-rage (bȧ'rŏzh'), *n.* a curtain of bursting shells fired by artillery so as to pass over the heads of advancing troops and fall in a line in front of them to protect them from attack. [Fr.]

bar-rel (băr'ĕl), *n.* a round, bulging cask or vessel, of greater length than breadth, and having flat ends or heads; the quantity which a barrel should contain; anything like a barrel in shape; the tube of a firearm; a drum or cylinder: *v.t.* [*p.t.* and *p.p.* barreled, *p.pr.* barreling], to put or pack in a barrel.

bar-rel or-gan (băr'ĕl ôr'găn), a portable organ turned by a crank.

bar-ren (băr'ĕn), *adj.* unproductive; unfruitful; sterile; lacking; profitless; empty: *n.* an unproductive tract of land.—*adv.* **barrenly.**—*n.* **barrenness.**

bar-ri-cade (băr'ĭ-kād'), *n.* a fort made in haste of such materials as are nearest to hand, and which will serve to obstruct the progress or attack of an enemy, or shield a besieged party; any bar or obstruction: *v.t.* to obstruct or stop up; fortify or inclose by a barrier.

bar-ri-er (băr'ĭ-ẽr), *n.* anything which hinders or obstructs; a bar or obstacle to progress, approach, or attack; an inclosing fence or boundary wall; a limit or boundary.

Syn. bar, hindrance, obstacle, obstruction, rampart, bulwark.

Ant. (see opening).

bar-ri-er reef (băr'ĭ-ẽr rēf), a reef of coral surrounding an island, or skirting the mainland, and inclosing an open channel or lake.

bar-ring (băr'ĭng), *p.pr.* obstructing; keeping out: *prep.* excepting; leaving out of account.

bar-ris-ter (băr'ĭs-tẽr), *n.* in England, a lawyer; in Scotland, an advocate; an attorney or counselor at law.

bar-row (băr'ō), *n.* a frame covered with boards, and fitted with handles at both ends, or with a wheel at one end and shafts at the other, and used for transporting goods by hand; a light hand-carriage carried by two men.

bar-ter (bär'tẽr), *v.i.* to traffic or trade by exchanging one commodity for another: *v.t.* to give in exchange.

bar-y-tone (băr'ĭ-tōn), *adj.* intermediate between bass and tenor, as a male voice or instrument: *n.* a person with such a voice; a voice having such a compass. Also, **baritone.**

bas-al (bās'ăl), *adj.* relating to or forming the base; fundamental; essential.

ba-salt (bȧ-sôlt'; băs'ôlt), *n.* a hard, greenish-black rock of volcanic origin.—*adj.* **basaltic.**

base (bās), *n.* the part of a thing on which it rests; a foundation or groundwork; that which combines with an acid to form a salt; a fortified line from which the operations of an army proceed; a starting place; in some games, a station or goal: *v.t.* to lay a foundation for; establish: *adj.* worthless; inferior; spurious or false; of mean spirit; morally abject or low; deep or grave in sound: commonly, *bass.*—*adv.* **basely.**

Syn., adj. vile, mean, dishonorable.

Ant. (see noble).

base-ball (bās'bôl'), *n.* the national game of the United States, played with bat and ball by nine players on a side, on a field with four stations known as bases, arranged in the shape of a diamond.

base-board (bās'bōrd"), *n.* a board forming the foundation or bottom of something; a wide molding at the bottom of the walls of a room.

base-born (bās'bôrn"), *adj.* of low or mean parentage; mean; plebeian; illegitimate.

base-less (bās'lĕs), *adj.* unfounded; groundless; untrue.

base-line (bās-līn), *n.* a measured line used in surveying and triangulation; a line traced in the rear of a gun.

base-man (bās'măn), *n.* [*pl.* basemen (-mĕn)], *n.* any one of the players who, in baseball, are stationed at the first, second, and third bases or stations, respectively.

base-ment (bās'mĕnt), *n.* the lowest part of a structure; the lowest story of a building.

base-ness (bās'nĕs), *n.* the state or quality of being mean or dishonorable; meanness; disgraceful conduct.

bash-ful (băsh'fōōl), *adj.* shy; easily embarrassed; modest to excess; retiring; diffident.—*adv.* **bashfully.**—*n.* **bashfulness.**

ba-sic (bās'ĭk), *adj.* fundamental; as, a *basic* principle; in chemistry, performing the office of a base in a salt.

ba-sil-i-ca (bȧ-sĭl'ĭ-kȧ), *n.* [*pl.* basilicas (-kȧz)], in ancient Rome, a public hall of simple oblong design used as a court of law; a church built on such a plan: for example, St. Peter's, in Rome.

bas-i-lisk (băz'ĭ-lĭsk; băs'ĭ-lĭsk), *n.* a fearful, imaginary creature, a kind of serpent, lizard, or dragon, whose breath and look were supposed to be fatal in their effect; the name of a lizard.

ba-sin (bā'sn), *n.* a round, wide vessel for holding water or other liquid; the quantity such a vessel will hold; a pond, or dock, or other reservoir for water; the land drained by a river and its tributaries.

ba-sis (bā'sis), *n.* [*pl.* bases (-sēz)], a base or foundation; the groundwork or first principle of anything; the chief ingredient.

bask (bȧsk), *v.i.* and *v.t.* to lie in warmth; as, to *bask* in the sun; to expose, or to be exposed to cheerful heat; be at ease and thriving under benign or kindly influences.

bas-ket (bȧs'kĕt), *n.* a vessel made of rushes, twigs, splints, reeds, or other flexible material, plaited or interwoven; the quantity or amount which such a vessel will hold.

bas-ket-ball (bȧs'kĕt-bôl), *n.* a popular game somewhat resembling football, usually played in a gymnasium with teams of five on a side, and with goals or *baskets* at each end; a spherical air-filled ball used in the game.

bas-ket-ry (bȧs'kĕt-rĭ), *n.* the art of making baskets.

bas-re-lief (bä'rē-lēf; bȧs'rē-lēf), *n.* low relief; in sculpture, a form of cutting in which the figures stand out very slightly from the background. Also, **bass-relief, basso-relievo, basso-rilievo.**

bass (bȧs), *n.* the name of various fishes of the perch family; the American lime-tree; matting made from its bark.

bass (bās), *adj.* low in tone; deep; grave: *n.* the lowest part in the harmony of a musical composition; the lowest male voice; one who sings the lowest male part. Also, **base.**

bass-bar (bās'bär''), *n.* a piece of wood placed lengthwise inside stringed instruments to resist the pressure of the bridge.

bass clef (bās klĕf), the character placed at the beginning of the lowest, or bass, staff.

bass horn (bās hôrn), a deep-toned wind instrument.

Bass Horn

bas-si-net (bȧs'ĭ-nĕt), *n.* a wicker basket with a hood at one end, used as a cradle for young children.

bas-soon (bă-sōōn'), *n.* a wind instrument of deep tones having a long curved mouthpiece, and a doubled wooden tube.

bass staff (bās stȧf), the parallel lines on which the notes of the lowest part of a piece of music are written.

bass vi-ol (bās vī'ŏl), a large stringed instrument of the violin class, used for playing the lowest part in music.

bast (bȧst), *n.* the tough inner fibrous bark of various trees, especially of the lime; rope or matting made from this bark.

bas-tard (bȧs'tẽrd), *n.* a child whose parents were not married; an animal of inferior quality or breed: *adj.* begotten and born out of lawful wedlock; not genuine; false.

baste (bāst), *v.t.* to beat with a stick; to drip or pour melted fat or butter on, while roasting; to sew slightly, or fasten temporarily with long stitches, as in dressmaking.

bas-tile (bȧs-tēl'; bȧs'tīl), *n.* a tower or fortification used for the defense of a fortified place:—**Bastile,** an old castle in Paris used as a state prison, destroyed by the people in 1789. Also, **bastille.**

bas-ti-na-do (bȧs''tĭ-nā'dō), *n.* an Oriental form of punishment, consisting of beating an offender upon the soles of his feet with a stick or rod: *v.t.* [*p.t.* and *p.p.* bastinadoed, *p.pr.* bastinadoing], to beat on the soles of the feet with a stick or cudgel; to flog. Also, **bastinade.**

bas-tion (bȧs'chŭn), *n.* an earthwork faced with brick or stone, projecting from the main body of a fort, commanding the outworks and grounds before it.

bat (băt), *n.* a heavy wooden stick or club; the wooden club used in baseball, cricket, and similar games; a batsman; a brickbat or part of a brick; a nocturnal flying creature which has a soft furry body, and wings formed by a skin stretched between the fingers, legs, and tail, and which feeds on insects: *v.t.* [*p.t.* and *p.p.* batted, *p.pr.* batting], to hit or strike: *v.i.* to use a club in baseball or cricket.

batch (băch), *n.* the quantity of bread baked at one time; a quantity of anything produced at one time; a group or collection of similar things.

ba-teau (bȧ-tō'), *n.* [*pl.* bateaux, batteaux (-tōz)], a light boat used on American rivers; a clumsy boat with a flat bottom. Also, **batteau.**

bath (bȧth), *n.* [*pl.* baths (bȧthz)], the act of washing or covering the body with water, or of exposing it to any other fluid or vapor; the state of being covered with a fluid, as sweat; a vessel holding water for bathing; a building or room fitted up for bathing purposes; a vessel containing a liquid for treatment of an object put into it; the water or other liquid used in bathing.

bathe (bāth), *v.t.* to put into water or other liquid; to wash; to lave; to wet; to overspread; put into or surround with anything, as vapor or light: *v.i.* to take a bath.—*n.* **bather.**

ba-thos (bā'thŏs), *n.* a ridiculous descent from the lofty to the commonplace in writing or speech.

ba-tiste (bȧ-tēst'), *n.* a fine cotton or linen muslin.

ba-ton (bȧ''tôn'; băt'ŭn), *n.* a staff used as a weapon, or as a badge of office; the stick used by the leader of a chorus or an orchestra with which to beat time.

bat-tal-ion (bă-tăl'yŭn), *n.* a body of foot-soldiers, usually forming about one-third of a regiment.

bat-ten (băt'n), *n.* a narrow strip of wood used for various purposes, such as fastening the edges of a piece of canvas to the deck of a ship; the slope of a wall: *v.t.* to fasten or form with strips of wood; to make fat by plenteous living; as, the sheep-raiser *battens* his flocks in rich pastures; fertilize or enrich: *v.i.* to grow or become fat; be prosperous at the expense of others.

bat-ter (băt'ẽr), *v.t.* to strike with heavy, repeated blows, so as to bruise, shatter, or destroy; injure: *v.i.* to make an attack by heavy blows: *n.* a thick, liquid mixture of several materials, as flour, eggs, etc., beaten together and used in cookery; the backward slope of a retaining wall.

bat-ter-ing-ram (băt'ẽr-ĭng-răm''), *n.* a military engine used in ancient days to beat down the walls of besieged places, and consisting of a large beam with a head of iron somewhat resembling the head of a ram.

bat-ter-y (băt'ẽr-ĭ), *n.* [*pl.* batteries (-ĭz)], the act of beating another; as, in law, assault and *battery*; a number of large guns with their accompaniment of officers, men, and equipments, for field operations; any raised work where guns are mounted and gunners protected; an apparatus for producing electricity.

bat-ting (băt'ĭng), *n.* wool or cotton prepared in sheets; the act of hitting or striking, as in a ball game.

bat-tle (băt'l), *n.* a fight or encounter between opposing forces; a combat; a contest or struggle for mastery: *v.i.* to contend in a fight; to struggle; as, to *battle* against difficulties.

Syn., *n.* action, combat, engagement.

bat-tle-dore (băt'l-dōr), *n.* a kind of light racket used for playing battledore and shuttlecock, a game in which a light ball is tossed back and forth between two players with rackets. Also, battledoor.

bat-tle-ment (băt'l-mĕnt), *n.* a wall for defense or a castle tower, consisting of alternate solid and open spaces; a parapet with open spaces.

bat-tle-plane (băt'l-plān), *n.* an airplane equipped with machine guns, etc.

bat-tle-ship (băt'l-shĭp'), *n.* a large, strongly armored ship carrying heavy guns.

bau-ble (bô'bl), *n.* a trifling piece of finery; anything showy or gay but without real value; as, Christmas trees are trimmed with many a pretty *bauble*; a child's plaything; the wand or staff carried by a court jester, or king's fool.

bawd-y (bôd'ĭ), *adj.* obscene; immoral; indecent; lewd.

bawl (bôl), *v.i.* to cry out with a loud, full, and sustained sound: *v.t.* to proclaim loudly; to shout: *n.* a loud prolonged cry.—*n.* bawler.

bay (bā), *n.* a curve or inlet in the shore of a sea or lake; the body of water between two capes or headlands; a recess or opening in walls; a place for storing coal; the fore part of a ship between decks; the laurel-tree, noble laurel, or sweet-bay; an honorary garland or crown, composed of woven laurel leaves, given as a prize to conquerors and successful poets; the deep-toned prolonged bark of a dog; state or position of anyone obliged to face an enemy or other pursuer when no escape is possible; as, to stand at *bay*; a horse of a red or reddish color approaching to chestnut: *v.i.* to bark with a deep sound, as hounds in the chase: *v.t.* to bark at; to pursue with barking: *adj.* red or reddish approaching to chestnut: applied to horses.

bay-ber-ry (bā'bĕr-ĭ), *n.* the laurel tree; the wax myrtle.

bay-o-net

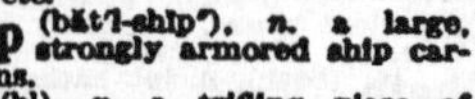

Bayonet

(bā'ō-nĕt), *n.* a short dagger-like instrument attached to the muzzle of a rifle: *v.t.* to stab or drive with a bayonet.

bay-ou (bī'ōō), *n.* [*pl.* bayous (-ōōz)], in the southern United States, the outlet of a lake, or one of the mouths of a river; a slow watercourse.

bay rum (bā rŭm), a fragrant liquid, prepared from the leaves of the bayberry and used for toilet purposes.

bay win-dow (bā wĭn'dō), the window or windows forming a bay, or recess, in a room, and extending outwards from the wall: usually of a many-sided shape.

ba-zaar (bȧ-zär'), *n.* in the East, a market-place or exchange; a hall or series of rooms with stalls for the sale of goods; a sale of fancy articles, usually in aid of some charity. Also, bazar.

be (bē), *v.i.* [*p.t.* was, *p.p.* been, *p.pr.* being], to exist; have existence in fact, physical or mental; to include or involve as a result; produce; become; last; mean; to happen; to concern; to belong.

beach (bēch), *n.* [*pl.* beaches (-ĕz)], the portion of the shore of the sea or of a lake which is washed by the waves, especially the sandy or pebbly part: *v.t.* to run or haul up, as a vessel or boat, upon the beach: *v.i.* to land on a beach; to strand.

beach comb-er (bēch kōm'ẽr), a long curling wave rolling in from the ocean; one who waits about wharves or along the shore on the lookout for wreckage or plunder.

bea-con (bē'kn), *n.* a signal of warning or guidance, on sea or land; formerly, a fire lighted on a hill or in a high tower to signal danger or assemble troops, etc.: *v.t.* to light up, as a beacon; furnish with beacons: *v.i.* to shine as a beacon.

bead (bēd), *n.* a little ball of any material, pierced through and intended to be strung with others and worn as an ornament, or to form a rosary, etc.; any small body shaped like a little globe; a drop or bubble; as, a *bead* of perspiration; a small knob of metal at the end of a gun-barrel used in taking aim; hence, *to draw a bead* is to take aim; a narrow, rounded molding or projecting band: *v.t.* to ornament with beading.

bead-ing (bēd'ĭng), *n.* bead ornaments; beads collectively; froth on liquors; a kind of openwork trimming through which ribbon or tape is run.

bea-dle (bē'dl), *n.* a messenger or crier of a court; a parish officer with various small duties connected with a church or vestry, etc.

bea-gle (bē'gl), *n.* a small hound, formerly used for hunting hares.

beak (bēk), *n.* the bill of a bird; the horny jaws of some animals; anything which is pointed or shaped like the bill of a bird; the metal-covered prow of an ancient ship intended to pierce the vessels of an enemy; the powerful projection of steel forming part of the bow of modern war vessels.—*adj.* beaked.

beak-er (bēk'ẽr), *n.* a large drinking cup or vessel with a wide mouth; an open-mouthed vessel with a projecting lip.

beam (bēm), *n.* a long piece of timber or iron used to support the rafters of a building; one of the principal crosswise horizontal timbers of a building or ship; the extreme breadth of a ship; the bar of a balance on which the scales are hung; the principal stem of a deer's horns which bears the antlers; a ray or the parallel rays of light given out from the sun or any other body which gives forth light: *v.t.* to send forth, as rays of light: *v.i.* to shine.

beam com-pass (bēm kŭm'pȧs), an instrument used for drawing large circles.

beam-ing (bēm'ĭng), *p.adj.* radiant; bright; cheerful; giving forth rays.—*adv.* beamingly.

bean (bēn), *n.* the smooth, kidney-shaped seed of many plants; the plant itself; the popular name of other vegetable seeds or fruits resembling true beans.

bear (bâr), *n.* a large, heavy wild animal which lives on flesh, and insects; the name of two groups of stars in the northern hemisphere called the Great Bear and the Little Bear; one who attempts to lower the value of stock in order to buy cheap: opposite to *bull;* a rude, uncouth, or brutal person: *v.t.* [*p.t.* bore, bare, *p.p.* borne, *p.pr.* bearing], to support or hold up; carry or convey; suffer or endure; be answerable for, as blame; possess, wear, or use; have in or on; contain; keep, especially in the mind; as, to *bear* no malice or hatred in my heart; admit or be capable of; as, his life will not *bear* examination; show or exhibit; bring forth or produce; as, the oak tree *bears* acorns: *v.i.* to be capable of supporting; be fruitful; to press, or weigh upon or against; tend; be related; take effect; be situated: when used passively *bear* (to produce) has as its *p.p. born;* as, an infant was *born.*

bear-a-ble (bâr′ȧ-bl), *adj.* capable of being borne or endured; tolerable.

bear bait-ing (bâr bāt′ing), the sport of setting dogs to fight with captive bears.

beard (bērd), *n.* the hair that grows on the human face, chiefly of male adults; anything which resembles this hairy growth; as, the *beard* of a goat; the bristle-like hairs on the heads of barley and other grains; any of various points or projections, as the point projecting backward on an arrow to prevent it from being easily drawn out of a wound, etc.: *v.t.* to take by the beard; oppose face to face; to defy; as, to *beard* the lion in his den.—*adj.* bearded.

beard-less (bērd′lĕs), *adj.* without a growth of hair on the face or anything resembling such growth; as, a *beardless* youth; *beardless* wheat; youthful. *n.*—beardlessness.

bear-er (bâr′ẽr), *n.* one who, or that which, carries or sustains; as, a *bearer* of dispatches; a tree or plant that yields a good crop of fruit; one who holds a check or other order for the payment of money.

bear gar-den (bâr gär′dn), a place where bears are kept for sport; hence, any scene or place of tumult or disorder.

bear-ing (bâr′ing), *n.* the act of enduring with patience; manner of carrying the head and body; as, I knew him by his *bearing;* behavior; meaning or significance; the act or power of producing; the part of a machine that supports the friction; the direction or point of the compass in which an object is seen; the position of one object with respect to another: usually in plural; as, it was so dark that it was impossible for us to get our *bearings;* an emblem or figure on a coat of arms: usually in plural.

bear-ish (bâr′ish), *adj.* rude; surly; as, *bearish* behavior.

beast (bēst), *n.* any four-footed animal, as distinguished from birds, insects, fishes, and man; a person rude, coarse, or filthy, or whose actions degrade him below the level of a reasonable being; a brute.

beast-ly (bēst′lĭ), *adj.* brutal; low; vile; beastlike; as, *beastly* habits.—*n.* beastliness.

beat (bēt), *v.t.* [*p.t.* beat, *p.p.* beaten, beat, *p.pr.* beating], to strike with repeated blows; thrash; knock; pound or break; flatten or spread by blows; in hunting, to range over in order to rouse and drive out game; as, to *beat* a thicket for a hare; dash or strike against, as water or wind; tread, as a path; overcome or vanquish; excel; be too difficult for; flutter, as wings: *v.i.* to strike repeatedly; throb; dash or fall with force or violence; to sound a signal or summons, as by a drum; to sail against the wind by tacking: *n.* a stroke which is made again and again; a throb; a footfall; a round or course which is frequently gone over; as, the policeman's *beat;* the rise or fall of the hand or foot marking the divisions of time.

beat-en (bēt′n), *p.adj.* worn by use, as by the tread of feet; conquered; exhausted; baffled.

beat-en-work (bēt′n-wûrk), *n.* metal shaped by being pounded on an anvil.

be-a-tif-ic (bē″ȧ-tĭf′ĭk), *adj.* having power to bless or render perfectly happy; blissful: **beatific vision**, the direct vision of God, regarded as the bliss of the angels and saints. Also, **beatifical.**

be-at-i-fi-ca-tion (bē-ăt″ĭ-fĭ-kā′shŭn), *n.* the act of blessing or the state of being blessed; in the Roman Catholic Church, the act of the Pope in declaring a dead person to have reached the rank of the blessed.

be-at-i-fy (bē-ăt′ĭ-fī), *v.t.* [*p.t.* and *p.p.* beatified, *p.pr.* beatifying], to make happy; bless with complete heavenly enjoyment; in the Roman Catholic Church, to declare by public decree that a dead person has attained the rank of "the blessed," giving him the right to public religious honor.—*n.* beatification.

beat-ing (bēt′ing), *n.* the act of striking; a flogging; a pulsing or throbbing; a defeat.

be-at-i-tude (bē-ăt′ĭ-tūd), *n.* bliss of the highest kind; blessedness; any one of the nine declarations made in the sermon on the Mount (Matt. v.) with regard to the blessedness of those who have certain virtues.

beau (bō), *n.* [*pl.* beaus or beaux (bōz)], a man who dresses himself strictly according to the fashion; a ladies' man or suitor; an escort; a lover.

beau i-de-al (bō′ ī-dē′ăl), an ideal of excellence; a faultless model.

beau monde (bō″ mônd′), the fashionable world. [Fr.]

beau-te-ous (bū′tē-ŭs), *adj.* beautiful.—*adv.* beauteously.—*n.* beauteousness.

beau-ti-ful (bū′tĭ-fo͝ol), *adj.* possessing qualities which charm and delight the senses; lovely.
Syn. fine, handsome, comely, exquisite.
Ant. (see homely, ugly).

beau-ti-ful-ly (bū′tĭ-fo͝ol-ĭ), *adv.* in a charming or attractive manner.

beau-ti-fy (bū′tĭ-fī), *v.t.* [*p.t.* and *p.p.* beautified, *p.pr.* beautifying], to make charming or delightful; to adorn.

beau-ty (bū′tĭ), *n.* [*pl.* beauties (-tĭz)], those qualities which are most pleasing to the eye or ear, or to the mind; a particular grace or charm; a charming, graceful woman.

beau-ty spot (bū′tĭ spŏt), a patch or spot placed on the face to increase or call attention to its charm.

bea-ver (bē′vẽr), *n.* an animal living partly on land and partly in water, having teeth formed for gnawing, and feet for both swimming and walking: noted for its skill in building dams across streams, and valuable for its fur; a gentleman's high hat: so called because formerly made of beaver skin, though now of silk; a heavy woolen cloth; the fur of the beaver.

bea-ver tree (bē′vẽr trē), the sweet-bay, common in the United States: so called because beavers eat its bark.

be-calm (bē-käm′), *v.t.* to make still: in nautical language, to keep (a ship) motionless because of a lack of wind.

be-cause (bē-kôz′), *adv.* by reason of; as, you are ill *because* of your own imprudence: *conj.* for the reason that; since; inasmuch as; as, you are punished *because* you do wrong.

be-chance (bē-chåns′), *v.t.* and *v.i.* to befall; to happen.

beck (bĕk), *n.* a little brook, or the valley through which it runs; a nod, or other gesture full of meaning; as, they come and go at your *beck* and call.

beck-et (bĕk′ĕt), *n.* a contrivance in ships to confine small spars or loose ropes, etc.

beck-on (bĕk′n), *v.i.* and *v.t.* to make a signal to another by a motion of the head or hand; call or signal by signs.

be-cloud (bē-kloud′), *v.t.* to darken; to obscure; to dim.

be-come (bē-kŭm′), *v.i.* [*p.t.* became, *p.p.* become, *p.pr.* becoming], to pass from one state to another; come or grow to be: *v.t.* to suit, or be suitable to; agree with; grace or adorn.

be-com-ing (bē-kŭm′ĭng), *p.adj.* fit; proper; appropriate; befitting; as, respect for old age is *becoming* in a young person.
Syn. decent, seemly, suitable.
Ant. (see unbecoming).

bed (bĕd), *n.* an article of furniture upon which one rests or sleeps; anything which serves as a resting-place, or in which something lies or is imbedded; a portion of a garden prepared and set apart for plants; the bottom of a river or any body of water; a layer of rock; either of the horizontal surfaces of a building stone: *v.t.* [*p.t.* and *p.p.* bedded, *p.pr.* bedding], to furnish with a bed; plant, as flowers; lay in a layer; lay flat, or in order: *v.i.* to go to bed.

be-dab-ble (bē-dăb′l), *v.t.* to sprinkle; to splash; to wet.

be-daub (bē-dôb′), *v.t.* to smear over with something oily or dirty; to soil; besmear.

be-daz-zle (bē-dăz′l), *v.t.* to dazzle; to bewilder; to confuse.

bed-bug (bĕd′bŭg″), *n.* a blood-sucking, flat-bodied insect, of vile odor, frequently found in furniture, etc., especially beds.

bed-ding (bĕd′ĭng), *n.* a bed and its covers, etc.; the materials of a bed, whether for man or beast; bed clothes.

be-deck (bē-dĕk′), *v.t.* to adorn; to decorate; to ornament; to garnish.

be-dew (bē-dū′), *v.t.* to moisten with, or as with, dew.

bed-fel-low (bĕd′fĕl-lō), *n.* one who shares another's bed; hence, (*pl.*) two people sharing the same experiences.

be-dim (bē-dĭm′), *v.t.* to darken; to cloud; to dim; as, tears *bedim* the eyes.

be-diz-en (bē-dĭz′n; bē-dī′zn), *v.t.* to deck or adorn with vulgar finery.

bed-lam (bĕd′lăm), *n.* a madhouse; an asylum or hospital for lunatics; hence, any scene of uproar and confusion.

Bed-ou-in (bĕd′ōō-ĭn; bĕd′ōō-ēn), *n.* a wandering Arab or tent-dweller of Arabia, Syria, and northern Africa.

be-drag-gle (bē-drăg′l), *v.t.* to make wet and dirty by dragging (as garments) in mud or rain.

bed-rid (bĕd′rĭd″), *adj.* confined to bed by age or sickness; bedfast. Also, **bedridden.**

bed-rock (bĕd′rŏk), *n.* a mining term: the solid rock underlying the superficial upper crust; solid bottom.

bed-stead (bĕd′stĕd), *n.* the framework supporting a bed.

bed-tick (bĕd′tĭk), *n.* a bag or case of strong linen or cotton for containing the feathers or other materials of a bed.

bee (bē), *n.* an insect which stores up the pollen of flowers for food, or which makes honey and wax; the honey-bee kept in hives for the sake of its honey and wax; an industrious person; a social meeting for work on behalf of a neighbor, a charitable object, or for some other purpose; as, a spelling *bee*, a quilting *bee*, or a husking *bee*.

bee-bread (bē′brĕd″), *n.* a brown bitter substance, consisting of the pollen of flowers, collected and stored by bees as food for their young.

beech (bēch), *n.* [*pl.* beeches (-ĕz)], a tree yielding a hard timber and edible triangular nuts.

beech-en (bēch′n), *adj.* pertaining to, or made of, the wood or bark of the beech.

bee eat-er (bē ēt″ẽr), a brightly colored bird of the Old World that feeds on bees.

beef (bēf), *n.* [*pl.* beeves (bēvz)], the flesh of an ox, bull, or cow, when killed for food; the name applied in a cattle country to an ox, cow, or bull when full grown.

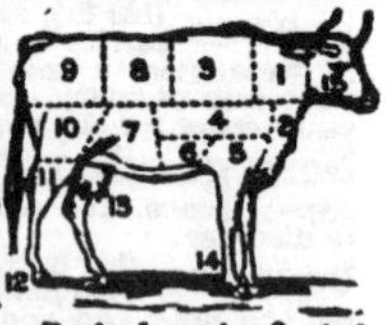

Beef. 1, neck; 2, shaking piece; 3, chine; 4, ribs; 5, clod, 6, brisket; 7, flank; 8, loin; 9, rump; 10, round, 11, leg; 12, foot; 13, udder; 14, shin; 15, cheek.

beef-eat-er (bēf′ēt″ẽr), *n.* one who eats beef; hence, a large, fleshy person; a popular name for one of the Yeomen of the Guard in England who attend the king on state occasions: also applied to the guards of the Tower of London.

beef-steak (bēf′stāk″), *n.* a slice of beef suitable for cooking by broiling or frying.

beef-y (bēf′ĭ), *adj.* fleshy; brawny; fat; dull.

bee-hive (bē′hīv″), *n.* a box or other covering for a swarm of bees, and serving for the storage of honey.

bee line (bē līn), the straight course pursued by a bee returning laden to the hive; hence, the most direct way from one point to another.

Be-el-ze-bub (bē-ĕl′zē-bŭb), *n.* in the Bible, the prince of demons or devils; hence, the devil himself.

bee moth (bē mŏth), a moth which lays its eggs in beehives, and whose young feed upon the wax.

been (bĭn; bēn), past participle of the verb *be*.

beer (bēr), *n.* a fermented liquor made from any grain from which flour may be made, but generally from barley which has been soaked and allowed to sprout, with hops or other substances added to give a bitter flavor; a fermented extract of the roots and other parts of various plants, as ginger, spruce, etc., such as ginger *beer*.

bees-wax (bēz'wăks"), *n.* the wax of which bees make their comb.

beet (bēt), *n.* a plant cultivated for its sweet, edible, fleshy root: used as a vegetable and also in making sugar.

bee-tle (bē'tl), *n.* any insect having four wings, the outer pair being hardened and serving as a horny covering to the inner pair; a heavy wooden mallet: *v.t.* to use a heavy wooden mallet on; to finish, as cotton, cloth, etc., by beating with a heavy wooden mallet: *v.i.* to be prominent; jut out; overhang, as a cliff: *adj.* overhanging; prominent; as, a *beetle* brow.

bee-tling (bē'tlĭng), *adj.* standing out; overhanging; as, *beetling* eyebrows; a *beetling* cliff.

be-fall (bē-fôl'), *v.t.* [*p.t.* befell, *p.p.* befallen, *p.pr.* befalling], to happen or occur to: *v.i.* come to pass.

be-fit (bē-fĭt'), *v.t.* [*p.t.* and *p.p.* befitted, *p.pr.* befitting], to be worthy of; suitable for.—*p.adj.* befitting.—*adv.* befittingly.

be-fog (bē-fŏg'), *v.t.* to envelop in a fog or mist; hence, to confuse.

be-fool (bē-fōōl'), *v.t.* to deceive; to lead astray; to delude.

be-fore (bē-fōr'), *prep.* in front of; coming first in space, time, or rank; in presence or sight of; earlier than: *adv.* in front; in advance; previously; formerly; already: *conj.* sooner than; rather than.

be-fore-hand (bē-fōr'hănd"), *adv.* in advance; before the time: *adj.* forehanded.

be-foul (bē-foul'), *v.t.* to soil; to dirty; to pollute; to foul.

be-friend (bē-frĕnd'), *v.t.* to act as a friend to; aid or shield; to assist; to favor; to benefit.

be-fud-dle (bē-fŭd'dl), *v.t.* to confuse; to becloud, as with liquor.

beg (bĕg), *v.t.* and *v.i.* [*p.t.* and *p.p.* begged, *p.pr.* begging], to ask in charity; ask for earnestly; beseech; entreat with humility; ask as a favor; to practice asking for alms: **I beg to**, in polite usage, to ask, request, desire; as, *I beg to* state.

Syn. implore, solicit, supplicate.
Ant. (see give).

be-gan (bē-găn'), past tense of the verb *begin*.

be-get (bē-gĕt'), *v.t.* [*p.t.* begot, begat, *p.p.* begotten, begot, *p.pr.* begetting], to be the father or sire of; produce; cause to exist; as, idleness *begets* discontent.

beg-gar (bĕg'ẽr), *n.* one who asks with humility; one who makes it his business to ask for alms; one who is reduced to extreme poverty: *v.t.* to take everything away from; to use up all the possibilities of; as, the horrors of a battlefield *beggar* description.

beg-gar-li-ness (bĕg'ẽr-lĭ-nĕs), *n.* extreme poverty; meanness.

beg-gar-ly (bĕg'ẽr-lĭ), *adj.* like, or in the condition of, one in great poverty; poor; mean; contemptible.

beg-gar-y (bĕg'ẽr-ĭ), *n.* the act or state of one who asks alms; extreme poverty.

be-gin (bē-gĭn'), *v.i.* [*p.t.* began, *p.p.* begun, *p.pr.* beginning], to come into existence; to arise; to take the first step or do the first act; to start: *v.t.* to cause to be; to commence.

be-gin-ner (bē-gĭn'ẽr), *n.* one who enters upon anything for the first time; a founder; an originator.

be-gin-ning (bē-gĭn'ĭng), *n.* the first cause; the first stage of anything; the source; the starting point.

be-gone (bē-gŏn'), *interj.* go away! depart! as, *begone* from my sight!

be-go-ni-a (bē-gō'nĭ-ȧ), a kind of plant cultivated for its ornamental leaves and showy flowers.

be-got (bē-gŏt'), past tense and past participle of the verb *beget*.

be-got-ten (bē-gŏt'n), past participle of the verb *beget*; as, wealth *begotten* of toil.

be-grime (bē-grīm'), *v.t.* to soil with dirt; as, smoke and dust *begrime* the workers.

be-grudge (bē-grŭj'), *v.t.* to grumble at; to envy the possessions of.

be-guile (bē-gīl'), *v.t.* to impose upon or deceive by a trick or a false statement; to ensnare; to cause to pass pleasantly, as the time; entertain.—*n.* beguilement.

be-gun (bē-gŭn'), past participle of the verb *begin*.

be-half (bē-häf'), *n.* advantage; favor; support; defense; stead; interest: preceded always by the prepositions *in*, *on*, or *upon*.

be-have (bē-hāv'), *v.t.* to conduct, carry, or manage: *v.i.* to act; conduct oneself in a proper manner.

be-hav-ior (bē-hāv'yẽr) *n.* conduct and manners whether good or bad; carriage; deportment; demeanor. Also, behaviour.

be-head (bē-hĕd'), *v.t.* to cut off the head of; to execute by cutting off the head.

be-held (bē-hĕld'), past tense and past participle of the verb *behold*.

be-hest (bē-hĕst'), *n.* a command; precept; as, to do his master's *behest*.

be-hind (bē-hīnd'), *prep.* at the back of; on the other side of; remaining after; inferior to: *adv.* at the back; in the rear; toward the back; out of sight; past in point of time; in arrears.

be-hind-hand (bē-hīnd'hănd"), *adj.* and *adv.* back in time or in progress; late; backward; in arrears in payment.

be-hold (bē-hōld'), *v.t.* [*p.t.* and *p.p.* beheld, *p.pr.* beholding], to fix the eyes upon; have in sight; look at; observe with care: *v.i.* to look; direct or fix the mind.—*n.* beholder.

be-hold-en (bē-hōl'dn), *p.adj.* indebted; obliged; bound in gratitude; as, the world is much *beholden* to its great inventors.

be-hoove (bē-hōōv'), *v.t.* to be necessary, or be fit; as, it will *behoove* you to mend your ways. Also, behove.

be-ing (bē'ĭng), *p.pr.* of *be*, continuing to exist: *n.* the state of existing; that which exists in any form; as, God, the Supreme *Being;* a person.

be-jew-el (bē-jū′ĕl; bē-jōō′ĕl), *v.t.* [*p.t.* and *p.p.* bejeweled, *p.pr.* bejeweling], to ornament or furnish with gems.

be-la-bor (bē-lā′bēr), *v.t.* to beat with hard blows; to thrash. Also, **belabour.**

be-lat-ed (bē-lāt′ĕd), *p.adj.* delayed; overtaken by darkness; benighted.

be-lay (bē-lā′), *v.t.* make fast, as to wind a rope around a pin, cleat, etc. so as to hold fast.

belch (bĕlch), *v.t.* to throw out with force or violence; as, factory chimneys *belch* forth black smoke: *v.i.* to force wind from the stomach: *n.* the act of forcing out wind from the stomach.

bel-dam (bĕl′dăm), *n.* an ugly old woman; a hag. Also, **beldame.**

be-lea-guer (bē-lē′gēr), *v.t.* to besiege; to surround with an army so as to make escape impossible.

bel-fry (bĕl′frĭ), *n.* a bell tower; that part of a steeple or tower in which a bell is hung: called also *bell-tower,* or *campanile.*

Belfry

Be-li-al (bē′lĭ-ăl; bēl′yăl), *n.* the ancient Hebrew name for an imaginary person representing evil; as, "Certain men, the children of *Belial,* are gone out from among you."—Deut. xiii. 13; the devil; any fiend; the spirit of evil or lawlessness.

be-lie (bē-lī′), *v.t.* to speak falsely about; to slander; to show to be false; to misrepresent.

be-lief (bē-lēf′), *n.* a state or habit of mind in which one accepts as true something stated, without personal knowledge; trust; the religious doctrines considered true by any body of people; as, the *belief* of the Mohammedans is founded on teachings of the Koran, their sacred book; creed.
Syn. credit, faith, confidence, conviction.
Ant. (see doubt).

be-liev-a-ble (bē-lēv′ȧ-bl), *adj.* capable or worthy of being accepted as truth; credible.

be-lieve (bē-lēv′), *v.t.* to accept as true, without personal knowledge; place confidence in; as, to *believe* the Bible; expect or hope; *v.i.* to have faith; be more or less sure of the truth of anything; to think or suppose: often with *in;* as, to *believe* in ghosts.

be-liev-er (bē-lēv′ẽr), *n.* one who accepts as truth something not actually seen; one who accepts a religious faith; a Christian.

be-lit-tle (bē-lĭt′l), *v.t.* to cause to appear small; to run down by speaking slightingly of; to depreciate.

bell (bĕl), *n.* a hollow metallic vessel, usually cup-shaped, and giving forth a clear, ringing sound when struck; anything in the form of a bell, as the corolla of a flower; *pl.* the divisions of daily time marked each half-hour by strokes on a bell, especially on shipboard: *v.t.* to put a bell on: as, to *bell* a cat.

bel-la-don-na (bĕl′ȧ-dŏn′ȧ), *n.* the deadly nightshade, a European poisonous plant with reddish bell-shaped flowers and shining black berries: used in medicine to relieve pain.

bell buoy (bĕl boi), a buoy bearing a bell, which is made to ring by the movement of the water, and thus warn mariners of rocks, or shoal water.

belle (bĕl), *n.* a fair lady; a handsome society woman; a reigning beauty; a very popular young lady; as, Mary was the *belle* of the ball.

belles-let-tres (bĕl′lĕt′r), *n.pl.* literature regarded as an art; polite or elegant literature, including poetry and fiction.

bell-flow-er (bĕl′flou″ẽr), *n.* a kind of plant whose flowers resemble little bells; in England, a daffodil; a variety of apple.

bel-li-cose (bĕl′ĭ-kōs), *adj.* inclined to fight; quarrelsome; warlike; pugnacious.

bel-lig-er-ence (bē-lĭj′ẽr-ĕns), *n.* the act or state of warfare. Also, **belligerency.**

bel-lig-er-ent (bē-lĭj′ẽr-ĕnt), *adj.* waging war; relating to war or warfare; warlike: *n.* a power which is carrying on war; as, the chief *belligerents* in the World War.

bell jar (bĕl jär), a bell-shaped glass vessel used by chemists.

bell-man (bĕl′măn), *n.* [*pl.* bellmen (-mĕn)], one who uses a bell to attract attention to a public announcement; a town crier; formerly, a night watchman whose duty was to call out the hours, the state of the weather, and other information as he passed.

bell met-al (bĕl mĕt′ăl), a variety of bronze; a mixture of copper and tin, of which bells are made.

Bel-lo-na (bē-lō′nȧ), *n.* the goddess of war; a high-spirited and vigorous woman.

bel-low (bĕl′ō), *v.i.* to utter a full, roaring sound, as a bull; bawl; roar, as the sea in a tempest, or as the wind when violent; as, the *bellowing* river: *v.t.* to utter with a loud, full voice; as, he *bellowed* out his orders. *n.* the roar of a bull; a loud, resounding outcry.

bel-lows (bĕl′ōz), *n. sing.* and *pl.* an instrument for producing a current of air, and used for various purposes, such as blowing fires, or filling the pipes of an organ.

bell-weth-er (bĕl′wĕth″ẽr), *n.* a sheep which wears a bell on his neck and leads the flock.

bel-ly (bĕl′ĭ), *n.* [*pl.* bellies (-ĭz)], that part of the human body which extends from the breast to the thighs, and contains the bowels; the abdomen; the corresponding part in the lower animals; the part of anything that swells out into a larger size; as, the *belly* of a flask: *v.t.* [*p.t.* and *p.p.* bellied, *p.pr.* bellying], to swell and extend; bulge out, as sails in the wind: *v.t.* to cause to swell out; as, the winds *belly* the sails.

bel-ly-band (bĕl′ĭ-bănd), *n.* a band fastened around the belly, as of a horse; a girth.

be-long (bē-lŏng′), *v.i.* to be the property (of); go along (with); be a part (of); be added (to), or connected (with); be the concern or business (of); to live in; be suitable (to); be the due (of); be native (to).

be-long-ing (bē-lŏng′ĭng), *n.* that which is one's own: generally in plural; property; possessions; goods; effects.

be-loved (bē-lŭv′ĕd or bē-lŭvd′) *p.adj.* regarded with great affection;

dear to the heart: *n.* one who is greatly loved.

be-low (bē-lō'), *prep.* under in place; beneath; not so high; lower (than) in rank or excellence; lower in value, price, etc.: *adv.* in a lower place; on the earth; in hell, or the regions of the dead; in a lower rank or grade; under.

Bel-shaz-zar (bĕl-shăz'ẽr), *n.* in the Bible, the last king of Babylon.—Daniel v.

belt (bĕlt), *n.* a girdle or band used around the waist; anything like a band, or anything which encircles, restrains, or supports as a band; a strip; a band; a badge showing knightly rank; one of the rings around the planet Jupiter; an endless band connecting two wheels, pulleys, or cylinders and passing motion from one to the other, such as the *belt* connecting the two wheels of a sewing machine: *v.t.* to encircle, as with a band or girdle; surround; to gird on, as a sword.

belt-ed (bĕlt'ĕd), *adj.* wearing a distinctive belt; as, a *belted* knight; marked or adorned with a band or circle; as, the *belted* kingfisher.

bel-ve-dere (bĕl'vē-dēr'; IT. bĕl'vā-dā'rā), *n.* literally, a beautiful view; an open structure raised upon the top of a house affording a wide view; a summerhouse built on a little hill so as to command a view.

be-mire (bē-mīr'), *v.t.* to soil by passing through mud; to fix in the mud.

be-moan (bē-mōn'), *v.t.* to lament; bewail; pity; to grieve for; as, to *bemoan* one's lot.

bench (bĕnch), *n.* [*pl.* benches (-ĕz)], a long seat; a strong table on which mechanics do their work; the seat where judges sit in court; the persons who sit as judges; the court.

bench war-rant (bĕnch wŏr'ănt), a legal paper, providing for the arrest of an offender, given out by a court or judge, as distinguished from a justice's warrant given out by a magistrate.

bend (bĕnd), *v.t.* to curve or make crooked; move or turn aside out of a straight line; direct to a certain point; cause to yield; fasten: *v.i.* to be or to become curved or crooked; be turned towards; bow or be submissive: *n.* a curve; a turn; a crook; as, the *bend* of a river.

Syn., *v.* deviate, incline, twist.

be-neath (bē-nēth'; bē-nēth'), *prep.* lower in place, with reference to something above; under the pressure of; lower in rank, dignity, or excellence than; unworthy of: *adv.* in a lower place; below.

ben-e-dict (bĕn'ē-dĭkt), *n.* a newly married man, especially one who has been long a bachelor: from *Benedick* in Shakespeare's *Much Ado about Nothing*.

ben-e-dic-tion (bĕn'ē-dĭk'shŭn), *n.* the act of blessing; a blessing or expression of kind wishes solemnly or affectionately called down upon one; the short blessing pronounced at the close of public worship.

ben-e-fac-tion (bĕn'ē-făk'shŭn), *n.* the act of conferring a benefit; a benefit conferred; a charitable gift.

ben-e-fac-tor (bĕn'ē-făk'tẽr), *n.* [*fem.* benefactress], literally, one who does good; one who does a favor or performs an act of kindness; a friendly helper or patron.

ben-e-fice (bĕn'ē-fĭs), *n.* originally, an estate in lands granted for life only, and held at the pleasure of the donor; the position of priest in some especial parish in the Church of England; a church in possession of a regular income; the income itself.

be-nef-i-cence (bē-nĕf'ĭ-sĕns), *n.* active goodness; a kind act, gift, or work.

be-nef-i-cent (bē-nĕf'ĭ-sĕnt), *adj.* doing or producing good; charitable; kindly.—*adv.* beneficently.

Syn. bountiful, generous, liberal.

Ant. (see covetous, miserly).

ben-e-fi-cial (bĕn'ē-fĭsh'ăl), *adj.* useful; helpful; profitable.—*adv.* beneficially.

ben-e-fi-ci-a-ry (bĕn'ē-fĭsh'ĭ-ā-rĭ), *n.* one who receives anything as a gift; one who receives a benefit or advantage, as the person who receives the proceeds of a will, or insurance policy; a priest who has been given a church living: *adj.* of the nature of a charity or donation; as, *beneficiary* gifts.

ben-e-fit (bĕn'ē-fĭt), *n.* an act of kindness; a favor conferred; whatever promotes the happiness and well-being of a person or thing, or adds to the value of property; a theatrical performance, the proceeds of which go to one of the actors, etc.: *v.t.* to do good to; be of service to: *v.i.* to gain advantage; make improvement.

Syn., *n.* favor, advantage, kindness, civility.

Ant. (see injury).

be-nev-o-lence (bē-nĕv'ō-lĕns), *n.* the will to do good; charitableness; good-will; an act of kindness; a royal tax formerly imposed upon the people under the name of a gift to the ruler.

Syn. beneficence, humanity, kindness, tenderness.

Ant. (see malevolence).

be-nev-o-lent (bē-nĕv'ō-lĕnt), *adj.* kindly; charitable; generous; ready to give to good objects.—*adv.* benevolently.

Ben-gal light (bĕn-gôl' līt), a firework: used also for signaling at sea because it gives a steady bright blue light. called also *blue light*.

be-night (bē-nīt'), *v.t.* to enshroud in darkness; overtake by night: usually in past participle: **benighted**, overtaken by darkness; ignorant; depraved.

be-nign (bē-nīn'), *adj.* of a kind or gentle disposition; favorable; healthful; as, a *benign* influence.—*adv.* benignly.

be-nig-nant (bē-nĭg'nănt), *adj.* kind; gracious; as, he showed a *benignant* interest in our small affairs; genial; helpful; gentle; salutary.—*n.* benignancy.

be-nig-ni-ty (bē-nĭg'nĭ-tĭ), *n.* [*pl.* benignities (-tĭz)], kindliness of nature; graciousness; gentleness; mildness; as, *benignity* of character.

ben-i-son (bĕn'ĭ-zn; bĕn'ĭ-sn), *n.* a blessing; a benediction.

Ben-ja-min (bĕn'jȧ-mĭn) *n.* in the Bible, the youngest son of Jacob.—Genesis xxxv. 18.

bent (bĕnt), *p.t.* and *p.p.* of *bend*: *adj.* curved; crooked; strongly inclined; determined: *n.* a turn; a leaning (mental or intellectual) toward something; as, a *bent* for music or art; disposition; a stiff or wiry grass.

be-numb (bē-nŭm'), *v.t.* to stupefy; to deprive of feeling; as, a foot *benumbed* by cold; to render inactive; to deaden.

ben-zene (bĕn'zēn; bĕn-zēn'), *n.* a liquid which evaporates quickly and is very easily set on fire, obtained commercially from coal tar, and used in gas, in the manufacture of dyes, etc.

ben-zine (bĕn'zĭn; bĕn'zēn), *n.* a liquid which evaporates quickly and is very easily set on fire, obtained from natural oil or petroleum, and used for cleaning, dyeing, painting, etc.

ben-zo-in (bĕn'zō-ĭn), *n.* the fragrant juice of a tree of Sumatra, etc., used chiefly in toilet preparations, perfumes, and incense. Also, benzoine.

ben-zol (bĕn'zŏl; bĕn'zōl), *n.* a liquid obtained from coal tar, and used in gas, in making dyes, etc. Also, benzole.

be-queath (bē-kwēth'), *v.t.* to give or leave by will; hand down; transmit by inheritance.—*n.* bequeathment.

be-quest (bē-kwĕst'), *n.* the act of leaving by will; something left by will; a legacy.

be-rate (bē-rāt'), *v.t.* to scold; to rail at; to chide harshly; to rate.

Ber-ber (bûr'bẽr), *n.* a member of a native North African race; any Moor or native of Barbary.

be-reave (bē-rēv'), *v.t.* [*p.t.* and *p.p.* bereaved, bereft, *p.pr.* bereaving], to deprive of; make destitute; strip; rob: with *of* before the thing taken away; as, "If I be *bereaved* of my children, I am *bereaved*."—Genesis xliii. 14.

be-reave-ment (bē-rēv'mĕnt), *n.* the act or state of being deprived of something valuable, etc.; the loss of a relative or friend by death; a grievous loss.

be-reft (bē-rĕft'), past tense and past participle of the verb *bereave*.

berg (bûrg), *n.* a large floating mass of ice; an iceberg; a high pointed rock projecting from the sea.

ber-ga-mot (bûr'gȧ-mŏt), *n.* a kind of lemon, the rind of which yields the oil of bergamot, much used in perfumery; a kind of pear; a variety of mint.

berm (bûrm), *n.* a horizontal ledge on a slope; in the World War, a narrow ledge cut along the walls of a trench to prevent earth from falling in.

ber-ry (bĕr'ĭ), *n.* [*pl.* berries (-ĭz)], any small pulpy fruit, as the strawberry, etc.; in botany, any simple fruit, as the currant, cranberry, etc.; the dry seed or kernel of certain plants, as the coffee berry: *v.i.* [*p.t.* and *p.p.* berried, *p.pr.* berrying], to bear, produce, or gather berries.

ber-serk (bûr'sûrk), *n.* a savage heathen warrior of old Scandinavia; one given to fits of wild violence. Also, berserker.

berth (bûrth), *n.* enough room at sea for a ship to throw an anchor in; a station which a ship occupies at port; a room in a vessel set apart for officers or seamen; a bunk or bed for a passenger on a ship or railway carriage; a situation or appointment: *v.t.* to give an anchorage to; to give space to lie in; to give a sleeping place to: *v.i.* to come to an anchoring place.

ber-tha (bûr'thȧ), *n.* a kind of cape or collar, often of lace, used as a trimming for a woman's dress.—big Bertha, in the World War, slang, a name given by the Allies to the large German guns: so called from the first name of the owner of the Krupp munition works at Essen, Germany.

ber-yl (bĕr'ĭl), *n.* a precious stone of varying colors, commonly green or greenish-blue; as, the aquamarine and the emerald are *beryls*.—*adj.* beryline.

be-seech (bē-sēch'), *v.t.* [*p.t.* and *p.p.* besought, *p.pr.* beseeching], to entreat; implore; beg eagerly for; to ask earnestly.—*p.adj.* beseeching.—*adv.* beseechingly.—*n.* beseechingness.

be-seem (bē-sēm'), *v.t.* and *v.i.* [*p.t.* and *p.p.* beseemed, *p.pr.* beseeming], be suitable or becoming to; to befit; to seem.

be-set (bē-sĕt'), *v.t.* [*p.t.* and *p.p.* beset, *p.pr.* besetting], to set with ornaments or prominent objects; as, a crown *beset* with gems; a sky *beset* with stars; to attack; to harass; to hem in; to surround; as, a spy is constantly *beset* with dangers; to press upon all sides.

be-set-ting (bē-sĕt'ĭng), *p.adj.* constantly waylaying; habitually attacking or coming upon; as, a *besetting* sin.

be-shrew (bē-shrōō'), *v.t.* to call down evil upon: a word used as a mild curse; as, "*Beshrew* your eyes!"—SHAKESPEARE.

be-side (bē-sīd'), *prep.* at or by the side of; near by; as, sit *beside* me.

be-sides (bē-sīdz'), *adv.* more than that; in addition; also; as well: *prep.* over and above; separate or distinct from; other than; except.

be-siege (bē-sēj'), *v.t.* to surround with armed forces, in order to compel to surrender; press upon all sides; to harass in any way.—*n.* besieger.

be-smear (bē-smēr'), *v.t.* to besmirch; to sully; to cover with any soft or sticky substance.

be-smirch (bē-smûrch'), *v.t.* to soil; discolor; dishonor; as, to *besmirch* a man's reputation.

be-som (bē'zŭm), *n.* a brush of twigs for sweeping; a broom.

be-sot (bē-sŏt'), *v.t.* [*p.t.* and *p.p.* besotted, *p.pr.* besotting], to make brutish, as with drink; to deaden; to stupefy; sometimes, to fill with blind or foolish admiration of.

be-sought (bē-sôt'), past tense and past participle of the verb *beseech*.

be-span-gle (bē-spăn'g'l), *v.t.* to adorn with spangles; dot or sprinkle with something that glitters.

be-spat-ter (bē-spăt'ẽr), *v.t.* to soil by splashing with a wet substance; spot with mud; injure by speaking evil of.

be-speak (bē-spēk'), *v.t.* [*p.t.* bespoke, *p.pr.* bespeaking], to ask for beforehand; to order or arrange in advance; to show, as by signs or marks; as, the relics left by the Aztec Indians *bespeak* a high degree of civilization.

best (bĕst), *adj.* [*superl.* of good], having the highest degree of goodness or excellence; of the first quality or standing; most desirable, suitable, advantageous, etc.; largest: *n.* the highest state of excellence; the greatest endeavor; all one can do or show: *adv.* [*superl.* of well], in the highest degree; with most advantage or success: *v.t.* to get the better of; to surpass.

be-stead (bē-stĕd'), *v.t.* to put in an undesirable situation or place: used now only in past participle; as, many are worse *bestead* than he. Also, bested.

bes-tial (bĕs'chȧl), *adj.* having the qualities of a beast; beastly; brutal; as, the Roman gladiatorial shows were *bestial* amusements.—*adv.* bestially.

bes-tial-i-ty (bĕs-chăl'ĭ-tĭ; bĕs'chĭ-ăl'ĭ-tĭ), *n.* the qualities or nature of a beast; conduct or mental condition unworthy of human nature.

be-stir (bē-stûr'), *v.t.* [*p.t.* and *p.p.* bestirred, *p.pr.* bestirring], to put into brisk or vigorous action; to move with life and vigor; as, to *bestir* oneself.

be-stow (bē-stō'), *v.t.* to lay up in store; deposit in safe keeping; use or apply; give or confer; as, to *bestow* a person in marriage; *bestow* gifts.

be-stow-al (bē-stō'ăl), *n.* the act of giving or conferring; that which is given. Also, **bestowment.**

be-strew (bē-strōō'), *v.t.* to strew or scatter over; to cover with things scattered; as, to *bestrew* flowers; *bestrew* a place with flowers. Also, **bestrow.**

be-stride (bē-strīd'), *v.t.* [*p.t.* bestrode and bestrid; *p.p.* bestridden, bestrid; *p.pr.* bestriding], to stand or sit on with one leg on each side; embrace with the legs, as a horse; to straddle; to pass over with one long step.

bet (bĕt), *n.* the act of wagering; that which is laid, staked, or pledged on any event or contest, the outcome of which is uncertain; the terms on which a wager is arranged: *v.t.* [*p.t.* and *p.p.* bet and betted, *p.pr.* betting], to stake or wager on the possibility of some future happening: *v.i.* to lay a wager.

be-take (bē-tāk'), *v.t.* [*p.t.* betook, *p.p.* betaken, *p.pr.* betaking], to resort (to); to remove or go (to); to take oneself (to); as, to *betake* oneself to a place of safety.

be-tel (bē'tl), *n.* a climbing kind of pepper, which grows in the East Indies, and the leaves of which, with the nutlike seed and a little lime, are chewed by the natives.

bête noire (bât' nwär'), literally, a black beast; something especially disliked; an aversion; a bugbear. [Fr.]

beth-el (bĕth'ĕl), *n.* a holy place; in England, a chapel in which people worship who are not members of the English Church; a seaman's chapel.

be-think (bē-thĭnk'), *v.t.* and *v.i.* [*p.t.* and *p.p.* bethought, *p.pr.* bethinking], to call to mind; to consider; to remind oneself; to remember; to recollect; to recall.

be-tide (bē-tīd'), *v.t.* to happen to; to befall; as, woe *betide* the wanderer: *v.i.* to come to pass.

be-times (bē-tīmz'), *adv.* in good season or time; before it is too late; early; soon; as, come *betimes* in the morning.

be-tok-en (bē-tō'kn), *v.t.* to give promise of; to show by signs; to serve as a sign or token of; as, a plentiful supply of nuts is said to *betoken* a cold winter.

be-took (bē-tŏŏk'), past tense of the verb *betake.*

be-tray (bē-trā'), *v.t.* [*p.t.* and *p.p.* betrayed, *p.pr.* betraying], to give over into the hands of an enemy by treachery; as, Judas *betrayed* his Master for thirty pieces of silver; to fail to be true to through fraud or unfaithfulness; as, to *betray* a trust; to disclose, as a secret or that which one is bound in honor not to make known; to deceive; to indicate or show; as, his manner *betrays* uneasiness.—*n.* **betrayal, betrayer.**

be-troth (bē-trōth'; bē-trôth'), *v.t.* to promise formally to give in marriage; to engage to marry.

be-troth-al (bē-trōth'ăl; bē-trôth'ăl), *n.* an engagement to marry; the state of being engaged; a promise of future marriage made between a man and a woman.

bet-ter (bĕt'ẽr), *adj.* [*compar.* of *good*], having good qualities in a greater degree than another; preferable or more suitable; improved in health; more perfect; larger; greater: *adv.* [*compar.* of *well*], in a superior or more excellent manner; more correctly or thoroughly; in a higher degree; more in extent: *v.t.* to improve; to increase the good qualities of; as, organized charities try to *better* the condition of the poor; to surpass; to outdo: *v.i.* to become more excellent: *n.* a superior: usually in plural; superiority, or advantage over: usually with *of.*

bet-ter (bĕt'ẽr), *n.* one who wagers or lays bets. Also, **bettor.**

bet-ter-ment (bĕt'ẽr-mĕnt), *n.* a making more suitable or excellent; an improvement; the improvement of lands or houses.

be-tween (bē-twēn'), *prep.* in the space or time which separates; as, the space *between* the eyes; the distance *between* Washington and Philadelphia; from one to another of; shared in common; with relation to both of; as, to choose *between* good and evil.

be-twixt (bē-twĭkst'), *prep.* and *adv.* between; in the space which separates.

bev-el (bĕv'ĕl), *v.t.* [*p.t.* and *p.p.* beveled, *p.pr.* beveling], to cut to an angle other than a right angle; to give a sloping edge to; as, to *bevel* the edge of a table: *v.i.* to slant or incline off to an oblique angle: *n.* the angle that one line or surface makes with another when they are not perpendicular to each other; an instrument consisting of two rules or arms, opening at any angle, used for drawing angles: *adj.* aslant; oblique.

Bevel

bev-er-age (bĕv'ẽr-ĭj), *n.* a drink of any description; liquor for drinking: especially applied to refreshing drinks.

bev-y (bĕv'ĭ), *n.* a company or assembly of persons, especially of girls or women; a flock of birds, especially quails or larks.

be-wail (bē-wāl'), *v.t.* to mourn or weep aloud for; to lament: *v.i.* to express grief or sorrow.

be-ware (bē-wâr'), *v.i.* to be on one's guard; to be wary or cautious: *v.t.* to look out for; be wary of.

be-wil-der (bē-wĭl'dẽr), *v.t.* to perplex or confuse; to puzzle; to mystify.

be-wil-der-ment (bē-wĭl'dẽr-mĕnt), *n.* the state of being greatly puzzled or perplexed; a tangled or confused network; as, a *bewilderment* of passages.

be-witch (bē-wĭch'), *v.t.* to cast a spell over; to enchant; to fascinate; to charm.

be-witch-ing (bē-wĭch'ĭng), *adj.* having power to fascinate; charming; enchanting.—*adv.* **bewitchingly.**—*n.* **bewitchment.**

bey (bā), *n.* a governor of a province or district in the Turkish dominions; a title of respect.

be-yond (bē-yŏnd'), *prep.* on the farther side of; before; as, history reaches back *beyond* the earliest written record; past; out of reach of; later than; above; in a degree or amount exceeding or surpassing; as, he succeeded *beyond* his highest hope: *adv.* at a distance farther away; yonder: *n.* the existence after death, or in the future.

be-zant (bĕz'ănt), *n.* a gold coin of Byzantium or Constantinople, in use in Europe from the 6th to the 16th century. Also, **byzant.**

bez-el (bĕz'ĕl), *n.* the slope at the edge of a cutting tool; the rim which surrounds and fastens a gem in its setting; the upper part of the gem which is above the setting; the groove in which the glass of a watch is fitted.

be-zique (bē-zēk'), *n.* a game played with cards from which the two and six spots have been taken.

bi- (bī-), a *prefix* meaning two; twice; doubly. Also, **bin-.**

bi-an-nu-al (bī-ăn'ū-ăl), *adj.* twice a year; semiannual.—*adv.* **biannually.**

bi-as (bī'ăs), *n.* [*pl.* biases (-ĕz)], an oblique or diagonal line, especially a cut across a fabric; hence, in dressmaking, a seam formed by uniting the edges of two pieces of cloth cut across the threads of the material; a leaning of the mind toward a particular thing, desire, or opinion; prejudice: *v.t.* [*p.t.* and *p.p.* biased, *p.pr.* biasing], to give a particular direction to; incline to one side; influence; prejudice;. as, the newspapers we read *bias* our opinions: *adv.* in a slanting manner.

bib (bĭb), *n.* a cloth placed under the chin, especially of a child, to protect the clothes.

bib-ber (bĭb'ĕr), *n.* a man who drinks frequently; a tippler.

bib-cock (bĭb'kŏk), *n.* a faucet having a turned down nozzle.

Bi-ble (bī'bl), *n.* the sacred writings of the Old and New Testaments, whether in the original tongue or translated; the Scriptures.

Bib-li-cal (bĭb'lĭ-kăl), *adj.* of or pertaining to the Bible; scriptural.—*adv.* **Biblically.**

bib-li-og-ra-pher (bĭb"lĭ-ŏg'rȧ-fĕr), *n.* one who writes about books, especially in regard to their authorship, date, editions, etc.

bib-li-og-ra-phy (bĭb"lĭ-ŏg'rȧ-fĭ), *n.* the science or description of books, their authors, material, style of printing, dates, editions, classification, history, etc.; a list of books relating to any given subject. Also, **bibliology.**

bib-li-o-ma-ni-a (bĭb"lĭ-ō-mā'nĭ-ȧ), *n.* a rage for collecting and possessing rare and curious books.

bib-li-o-ma-ni-ac (bĭb"lĭ-ō-mā'nĭ-ăk), *n.* one who has a craze for collecting and possessing rare books.

bib-li-o-phile (bĭb'lĭ-ō-fīl; -fĭl), *n.* a lover of books.

bib-u-lous (bĭb'ū-lŭs), *adj.* readily soaking up fluids; spongy; fond of drinking; given to tippling.

bi-cam-er-al (bī-kăm'ĕr-ăl), *adj.* two-chambered: relating to or consisting of two legislative chambers.

bi-car-bon-ate (bī-kär'bŏn-āt), *n.* a substance containing two parts of carbonic acid and one of some other substance.

bi-cen-te-na-ry (bī-sĕn'tē-nā-rĭ), *n.* the two hundredth anniversary of any event, or its celebration: *adj.* pertaining to a bicentenary.

bi-cen-ten-ni-al (bī"sĕn-tĕn'ĭ-ăl), *adj.* consisting of two hundred years: *n.* the two hundredth anniversary of an event, or its celebration.

bi-ceps (bī'sĕps), *n.* a muscle having two places of attachment to the bone; the large muscle of the front of the upper arm and thigh.

bi-chlo-ride (bī-klō'rīd; -rĭd), *n.* a compound of two or more parts of chlorine combined with another substance; as, *bichloride* of mercury. Also, **bichlorid.**

bick-er (bĭk'ĕr), *v.i.* to engage in petty quarreling; to wrangle; to move rapidly with a noise; to quiver; to flicker, as flame: *n.* an angry or petty dispute.

bi-corn (bī'kôrn), *adj.* having two horns; crescentlike. Also, **bicornus.**

bi-cus-pid (bī-kŭs'pĭd), *adj.* having two points: *n.* one of the double-pointed teeth forming the first pair of grinding teeth on each side of the jaw, above and below. Also, **bicuspidate.**

bi-cy-cle (bī'sĭ-kl), *n.* a light vehicle having two wheels one behind the other connected by a metal frame and supporting a saddle for the rider, the machine being sent forward by the feet by means of treadles attached to cranks or levers: *v.i.* to ride on such a vehicle.

bi-cy-cling (bī'sĭ-klĭng), *n.* the practice or art of riding a bicycle. (The abbreviation *cycling* is now in common use.) Also, **bicyclism.**

bi-cy-clist (bī'sĭ-klĭst), *n.* one who rides a bicycle; a cyclist.

bid (bĭd), *v.t.* [*p.t.* bade (băd) or bid, *p.p.* bidden, bid, *p.pr.* bidding], to make an offer of; to propose as a price; to offer for; to invite; as, "Go ye into the highways, and as many as ye shall find, *bid* to the marriage." —Matt. xiv; to offer or express by words; as, to *bid* a welcome; to command; to order or direct: *v.i.* to make an offer; to offer a price: *n.* an offer of a price; a price offered at auction.

bid-da-ble (bĭd'ȧ-bl), *adj.* obedient; docile; as, a *biddable* child.

bid-der (bĭd'ĕr), *n.* one who offers a price, as at a sale or auction.

bid-ding (bĭd'ĭng), *n.* an order; command; proclamation; the act of offering a price at auction.

bide (bīd), *v.i.* [*p.t.* and *p.p.* bode, bided, *p.pr.* biding], to live in; to reside; *v.t.* to endure; suffer; to wait for; as, I *bide* my time.

bi-den-tal (bī-dĕn'tăl), *adj.* having two teeth, or two toothlike projections. Also, **bidentate.**

bid-ing (bīd'ĭng), *n.* an awaiting; expectation; a place to live.

bi-en-ni-al (bī-ĕn'ĭ-ăl), *adj.* happening once in two years; as, a *biennial* convention; continuing or existing for two years, as plants: *n.* a plant which produces roots and leaves in the first year, and flowers, fruit, and seed in the second, after which it dies; an event which is held once in two years.—*adv.* **biennially.**

bier (bēr), *n.* a frame or carriage on which a corpse or the coffin containing it is placed or carried to the grave; a hearse; a tomb.

bi-fo-cal (bī-fō'kăl), *adj.* bringing together rays of light at two points: *n.* a lens which brings together rays of light at two points, as eyeglasses which may be used both for reading and long distance.

bi-fo-li-ate (bī-fō′lĭ-āt), *adj.* in botany, having two leaves.

bi-fur-cate (bī-fûr′kāt; bī′fûr-kāt), *v.t.* to divide in two directions: *adj.* (bī-fûr′kāt), divided into two branches; forked. Also, *adj.* **bifurcated.**

bi-fur-ca-tion (bī″fûr-kā′shŭn), *n.* a forking, or division into two branches.

big (bĭg), *adj.* [*compar.* bigger, *superl.* biggest], large, bulky; grown up; full of something important; full to overflowing; as, *big* with grief; teeming; as, *big* with promise; pompous; as, to feel *big*.—*n.* **bigness.**

big-a-mist (bĭg′ȧ-mĭst), *n.* one who has more than one husband or wife at one time.

big-a-my (bĭg′ȧ-mĭ), *n.* the crime of having two wives or husbands at one time.—*adj.* **bigamous.**

big-horn (bĭg′hôrn″), *n.* the wild sheep of the Rocky Mountains.

bight (bīt), *n.* a bend in a coast-line forming an open bay; a small bay between two headlands; a loop in a rope anywhere but at the ends.

big-ot (bĭg′ŭt), *n.* one who is unreasonably and blindly attached to a particular creed, church, or party; one who will not allow to others the enjoyment of opinions which differ from his own.

big-ot-ed (bĭg′ŭt-ĕd), *adj.* obstinately and bluntly attached to some creed, practice, or party; unwilling to allow to others opinions differing from one's own; illiberal.

big-ot-ry (bĭg′ŭt-rĭ), *n.* [*pl.* bigotries (-rĭz)], the state or condition of a narrow-minded person; blind and obstinate devotion to a particular creed, party, or opinion; intolerance.

big-wig (bĭg′wĭg″), *n.* an important person: originally, a slang phrase referring to the large wigs worn by judges and others in authority in Great Britain.

bi-jou (bē″zhōō′; bē′zhōō), *n.* [*pl.* bijoux (bē″zhōō′; bē′zhōōz)], a jewel; a trinket; any small and elegantly finished article. [Fr.]

bi-lat-er-al (bī-lăt′ẽr-ăl), *adj.* relating to, or having two sides; two-sided.

bil-bo (bĭl′bō), *n.* [*pl.* bilboes (-bōz)], a rapier or sword; *pl.* a long bar of iron with chains for the feet, and a hook at the end, formerly used to fasten the feet of prisoners.

bile (bīl), *n.* a yellow bitter fluid produced by the liver from blood; ill-humor; peevishness.

bilge (bĭlj), *n.* the bulging part of a cask; the broadest part of a ship's bottom, on which the vessel rests when aground: *v.i.* to spring a leak by a break in the bottom, or bilge, of a ship.

bilge wa-ter (bĭlj wô′tẽr), water which gathers in the bottom of a ship, usually very disagreeable in odor.

bi-lin-gual (bī-lĭn′gwăl), *adj.* written or expressed in two languages; using two languages.—*adv.* **bilingually.**

bil-ious (bĭl′yŭs), *adj.* suffering from an illness usually accompanied by indigestion, headache, and drowsiness, with a coated tongue, etc.; having the health out of order because the liver does not act properly; ill-tempered; peevish.—*adv.* **biliously.**—*n.* **biliousness.**

bi-lit-er-al (bī-lĭt′ẽr-ăl), *adj.* consisting of two letters: *n.* a word, root, or syllable consisting of two letters.

bilk (bĭlk), *v.t.* to deceive or defraud, as by failing to pay a debt or fulfil an engagement; to escape or steal away from (a person, place, or thing); to dodge.

bill (bĭl), *n.* an account for goods sold, services given, or work done; a paper binding the signer or signers to pay a definite sum at a certain date or on demand; a copy of a proposed law presented to a legislature; a printed advertisement; any written paper containing a statement of particulars; a written declaration of wrong or injury; the beak of a bird; a kind of hatchet with a blade hook-shaped toward the point, used in pruning, etc.; a battle-ax, attached to a long staff, formerly used by soldiers on foot; the end of the fluke or hook of an anchor: *v.t.* to advertise by bills or posters; to make a list of; as, to *bill* goods: *v.i.* to join bills; as, doves *bill* and coo; hence, to caress fondly.

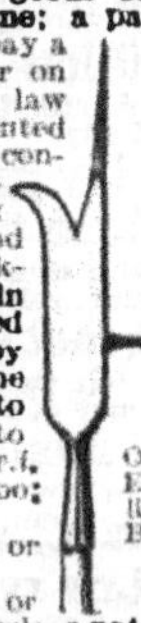

Old English Bill

billed (bĭld), *adj.* having a bill or beak; posted.

bil-let (bĭl′ĕt), *n.* a small stick or log of wood used for fuel; a note or short letter; a ticket directing a soldier to board and lodge at a certain house; a place where a soldier is lodged; in the World War, the village or camp to which a soldier is sent for rest and nonfighting work after his duty in the trenches: *v.t.* to quarter or lodge, as soldiers: *v.i.* to be quartered or lodged.

bil-let-doux (bĭl′ĕ-dōō′; Fr. bē″yĕ″dōō′), *n.* [*pl.* billets-doux (bĭl′ĕ-dōōz′; Fr. bē″yĕ″dōō′)], a love-letter: from *billet*, note, and *doux*, sweet. [Fr.]

bill-hook (bĭl′hŏŏk″), *n.* a small kind of hatchet with a hooked point.

bil-liards (bĭl′yẽrdz), *n.* a game played on an oblong, cloth-covered table, with ivory balls and a cue.

bil-lings-gate (bĭl′ĭngz-gāt″), *n.* coarse or profane language.

bil-lion (bĭl′yŭn), *n.* in the United States and France, one thousand millions (1,000,000,000): in England and Germany, a million millions (1,000,000,000,000).

bill of en-try (bĭl ŏv ĕn′trĭ), a written account of goods entered at the custom house whether imported or for export.

bill of ex-change (bĭl ŏv ĕks-chānj′), a written order from one person or house (the drawer) to another (the accepter) to pay to the person named a certain sum at a fixed time, in payment for value received.

bill of health (bĭl ŏv hĕlth), a certificate given to the master of a vessel, signed by a consul or other authority, making statement of the state of the health of a ship's company or passengers at the time of her leaving port.

bill of lad-ing (bĭl ŏv lād′ĭng), a paper issued by a common carrier, signed by the proper officials, acknowledging the receipt of goods to be shipped by land or water, and promising to deliver them safely to the person to whom they are addressed.

bill of mor-tal-i-ty (bĭl ŏv môr-tăl′ĭ-tĭ), an account of the number of deaths (also births) in a place within a given time.

bill of sale (bĭl ŏv sāl), a formal paper given by the seller of personal property to the buyer.

bil-lon (bĭl'ŭn), *n.* a mixture of gold and silver, with a large amount of copper or other base metal, used in making coins of low value.

bil-lot (bĭl'ŏt), *n.* uncoined gold or silver in the mass or bar.

bil-low (bĭl'ō), *n.* a great wave of the sea swelled by the wind: *v.i.* to rise and roll in large waves or surges.—*adj.* billowy.

bil-ly (bĭl'ĭ), *n.* a bludgeon or club; a policeman's club.

bi-me-tal-lic (bī-mĕ-tăl'ĭk), *adj.* of, relating to, or using, a double metal standard for a system of coins or currency; relating to two metals.

bi-met-al-lism (bī-mĕt'ăl-ĭzm), *n.* the adoption by law of two metals (as gold and silver) to be used in the money of a country at a fixed relative value.

bi-month-ly (bī-mŭnth'lĭ), *adj.* occurring once in two months; as, a *bimonthly* magazine.

bin (bĭn), *n.* an inclosed place used as a receptacle for any material; as, a coal *bin.*

bi-na-ry (bī'nȧ-rĭ), *adj.* consisting of two things or parts; as, water is a *binary* compound because it is composed of two substances, hydrogen and oxygen.

bind (bīnd), *v.t.* [*p.t.* and *p.p.* bound, *p.pr.* binding], to confine or make fast with a cord or band; confine or hold by physical force; unite by bonds of affection, loyalty, or duty; hold by any moral tie; hinder or restrain; protect or strengthen by a band, border, or cover; fasten together; cause to stick together; to oblige by a promise, law, duty, etc.; to fasten together in a cover, as a book: *v.i.* to tie up something; as, to reap and *bind;* to have the force of a duty or necessity; grow hard or stiff; to stick: *n.* anything which holds or ties; a twining stem; a stalk of hops; a musical sign or brace grouping notes together.

Syn., v. fasten, restrain, restrict, shackle.
Ant. (see free).

bind-er-y (bīn'dẽr-ĭ), *n.* a place where books are bound.

bind-ing (bīnd'ĭng), *n.* the act of making fast; a bandage; the cover of a book; something that secures the edges of cloth from fraying.

bind-weed (bīnd'wēd"), *n.* any plant of the genus *Convolvulus;* black bindweed, a species of bryony; rough bindweed, a species of smilax.

bine (bīn), *n.* the twining stem of a hop vine or other climbing plant.

bin-na-cle (bĭn'ȧ-kl), *n.* a wooden case or box on board a ship in which are kept the compass and lights.

bin-o-cle (bĭn'ō-kl), *n.* a field or opera glass with two eye-tubes for the use of both eyes at once.

bin-oc-u-lar (bĭn-ŏk'ū-lẽr, bī-nŏk'ū-lẽr), *adj.* adapted to the use of both eyes at the same time; as, *binocular* glasses: *n.* any glass fitted for use of both eyes at one time, as a field glass, an opera glass.

bi-no-mi-al (bī-nō'mĭ-ăl), *n.* an expression or quantity consisting of two terms connected by the sign plus [+] or minus [−], as b + 6: *adj.* consisting of two terms; having two names.

bi-o-graph (bī'ō-grȧf), *n.* a device for throwing moving pictures upon a screen.

bi-og-ra-pher (bī-ŏg'rȧ-fẽr), *n.* one who writes the history of a person's life.

bi-o-graph-ic (bī"ō-grăf'ĭk), *adj.* consisting of a life history. Also, biographical.—*adv.* biographically.

bi-og-ra-phy (bī-ŏg'rȧ-fĭ), *n.* [*pl.* biographies (-fĭz)], the written history of a person's life; such writings in general.

bi-o-log-i-cal (bī"ō-lŏj'ĭ-kăl), *adj.* relating to the science which treats of living forms. Also, biologic.

bi-ol-o-gist (bī-ŏl'ō-jĭst), *n.* one who studies, or is skilled in, the science of living forms.

bi-ol-o-gy (bī-ŏl'ō-jĭ), *n.* the science which deals with the origin and life-history of plants and animals.

bi-ped (bī'pĕd), *n.* an animal having two feet, as man: *adj.* having two feet.

bi-plane (bī'plān"), *n.* an airplane with two supporting surfaces or guiding boards, in typical forms, one above the other, as in the Wright machine.

birch (bûrch), *n.* [*pl.* birches (-ĕz)], a tree or shrub which has a smooth outer bark and close-grained wood which takes a high polish; a rod formed of birch twigs, used for punishment; a birch-bark canoe: *adj.* made of birch: *v.t.* to punish with a birch rod; flog; whip.

birch-en (bûr'chn), *adj.* relating to, or consisting of, birch.

bird (bûrd), *n.* a warm-blooded, feathered, egg-laying animal, with wings; any small bird shot by a gunner, as distinguished from a waterfowl: *v.i.* to shoot or catch birds.

bird fan-ci-er (bûrd făn'sĭ-ẽr), one who collects or rears rare and curious birds; one who sells caged birds.

bird-lime (bûrd'līm"), *n.* a sticky substance prepared from holly-bark, and used for catching small birds: *v.t.* to smear with birdlime.

bird of par-a-dise (bûrd ŏv păr'ȧ-dīs), a bird found in New Guinea and near-by islands, noted for its magnificent feathers.

bird's-eye (bûrdz'ī"), *adj.* seen from above, as by a flying bird: hence, general, not detailed; as, from the top of Washington Monument can be seen a *bird's-eye* view of Washington City; marked with spots resembling a bird's eyes; as, *bird's-eye* maple.

bi-reme (bī'rēm), *n.* an ancient boat or galley, having two banks of oars.

bi-ret-ta (bĭ-rĕt'ȧ), *n.* a square cap worn by priests, and other church officials or ministers. Also, beretta.

birth (bûrth), *n.* the act of coming into life; the fact of being born; the act of bringing forth; descent; as, Abraham Lincoln was a man of humble *birth;* origin; beginning.

birth-day (bûrth'dā"), *n.* the day on which one is born; the time of origin or beginnings; the anniversary of such a day or time.

birth-rate (bûrth'rāt"), *n.* the increase of population as shown by the percentage of births to the number of inhabitants in a district within a certain period.

birth-right (bûrth'rīt"), *n.* any right or privilege or possession to which a person is entitled by birth; the right of the first born.

bis-cuit (bĭs'kĭt), *n.* a kind of unraised bread, baked hard and dry, and

BIRDS OF NORTH AMERICA

1. Mocking bird. 2. Humming bird. 3. Catbird. 4. House wren. 5. Carolina cuckoo. 6. Cedar bird. 7. Baltimore oriole. 8. Chicken hawk (male). 9. Blue yellow-backed warbler. 10. Great-horned owl 11. Brown thrush. 12. Lady Gould finch. 13. Cardinal (male). 14. Wild turkey. 15. Kingfisher. 16. Peal's Egret heron. 17. Red-headed woodpecker.

shaped into flat cakes; crackers; pottery after the first baking and before it is glazed and burned.

bi-sect (bī-sĕkt'), *v.t.* to cut or divide into two equal parts.—*n.* **bisection.**

bi-sec-tor (bī-sĕk'tẽr), *n.* that which divides an object into two equal parts; a straight line which divides an angle into two equal parts.

bish-op (bĭsh'ŭp), *n.* one of the highest orders of an Episcopal Church, below an archbishop in rank, but above a priest; a spiritual overseer; the spiritual head or ruler of a diocese or church district; one of the pieces used in playing chess.

bish-op-ric (bĭsh'ŭp-rĭk), *n.* the office or dignity of a bishop; a diocese, or church district presided over by a bishop.

bisk (bĭsk), *n.* soup or broth composed of several kinds of meat or fish boiled together; a kind of ice cream into which crushed macaroons are stirred. Also, **bisque.**

bis-muth (bĭz'mŭth; bĭs'mŭth), *n.* a light, reddish-colored metallic element of brittle texture.

bi-son (bī'sŭn), *n.* an animal, somewhat like the ox, still found in Lithuania; a wild animal of America, inaccurately termed the buffalo, which has now almost disappeared.

bisque (bĭsk), *n.* an unglazed white porcelain, used for statuettes, etc.; soup or broth composed of several kinds of meat or fish boiled together; a kind of ice cream into which crushed macaroons are stirred. Also, **bisk.**

bit (bĭt), *p.t.* and *p.p.* of the verb *bite: n.* a tool for boring; the metal mouthpiece of a bridle; the part of a key which enters the lock and acts on the bolts and tumblers; the cutting blade of a plane; a small piece or fragment of anything; any small coin; anything that curbs or restrains; in southern and western United States, twelve and a half cents: *v.t.* [*p.t* and *p.p.* bitted, *p.pr.* bitting], to put a bridle upon; put a bit in the mouth of; check; restrain.

bitch (bĭch), *n.* the female of the dog, wolf, fox, etc.

bite (bīt), *v.t.* [*p.t.* bit, *p.p.* bitten, bit, *p.pr.* biting], to seize, grip, cut, or crush with the teeth; sting, as an insect; cause smarting pain to; cut; pinch, as with intense cold; blight or blast; take fast hold of; to eat into: *v.i.* to have the habit or exercise the power of biting; cause injury with the teeth; to sting or smart; take a bait; take a firm hold: *n.* the act of seizing with the teeth; a wound made by the teeth, or by a sting; a mouthful; a hold or grip.—*n.* **biter.**

bit-ing (bīt'ĭng), *adj.* sharp; cutting; sarcastic.—*adv.* **bitingly.**

bitt (bĭt), *n.* a post of wood or iron on ships to which cables, ropes, etc., are made fast: generally in plural: *v.t.* to put round the cable posts.

bit-ter (bĭt'ẽr), *adj.* having a sharp or harsh taste; sharp to the feeling; as, *bitter* cold; painful; grievous; as, *bitter* woe; severe; reproachful; sarcastic; as, *bitter* words; cruel; full of hatred; as, a *bitter* enemy: *n.* any substance that is sharp or harsh to the taste.—*adv.* **bitterly.**

Syn., *adj.* acid, acrid, keen, mournful, sharp, sour.

Ant. (see sweet).

bit-ter-cup (bĭt'ẽr-kŭp), *n.* a cup made of quassia wood, which imparts a bitter taste to liquids poured into it.

bit-tern (bĭt'ẽrn), *n.* a wading bird of the heron family; the brine remaining after the salt is extracted, from which Epsom salts is prepared.

bit-ter-ness (bĭt'ẽr-nĕs), *n.* a quality in things which causes a biting, disagreeable sensation on the tongue; sharpness; severity.

bit-ters (bĭt'ẽrz), *n.pl.* liquor in which herbs or roots are soaked.

bit-ter-sweet (bĭt'ẽr-swēt"), *n.* the woody nightshade, the roots and leaves of which when chewed produce first a bitter, then a sweet taste.

bi-tu-men (bĭ-tū'mĕn; bĭt'ū-mĕn), a name used for various substances found in the earth, which are easily set on fire and have a strong smell; mineral pitch.

bi-tu-mi-nous (bĭ-tū'nĭ-nŭs), *adj.* having the qualities of, or containing, bitumen; easily set on fire; as, *bituminous* or soft coal.

bi-valve (bī'vălv), *n.* a shellfish whose shell is composed of two parts or valves, connected by a ligament or hinge, and opened or closed by muscles, as the oyster or mussel: *adj.* having two valves or shells united by a soft hinge. Also, *adj.* **bivalved, bivalvular.**

biv-ou-ac (bĭv'wăk; bĭv'ōō-ăk), *n.* a camp of soldiers in the open air, without tents; hence, any open-air encampment; a kind of tent made of waterproof sheets: *v.i.* to encamp without tents in the open during the night.

bi-week-ly (bī'wēk'lĭ), *adj.* occurring or appearing every two weeks; as, a *biweekly* magazine; fortnightly; *n.* a periodical issued once in two weeks.—*adv.* **biweekly.**

bi-zarre (bĭ-zär'), *adj.* odd in manner or appearance; fanciful; grotesque.

blab (blăb), *v.t.* [*p.t.* and *p.p.* blabbed, *p.pr.* blabbing], to tell thoughtlessly: *v.i.* to talk unwisely; tell tales: *n.* one who lets out secrets, or tells tales. Also, *n.* **blabber.**

black (blăk), *adj.* entirely without light; of the darkest hue; opposed to white; wrapped in darkness; dismal; gloomy or forbidding; without moral light or goodness; evil; threatening; clouded with anger; sullen: *n.* the darkest color; the opposite of white; a black color or dye; a negro; mourning: *v.t.* to make black; blacken; apply blacking to.

black-a-moor (blăk'ȧ-mōōr), *n.* a negro, especially an African negro.

black art (blăk ärt), the magic practiced by witches and conjurers.

black-ball (blăk'bôl"), *v.t.* to reject or exclude, as a candidate, by, or as by, placing black balls in the ballot box.

black-ber-ry (blăk'bĕr-ĭ), *n.* the fruit of several kinds of prickly shrubs, of the genus *Rubus*, the British name for which is bramble. There are two American species.

black-bird (blăk'bûrd), *n.* an English song-bird, a kind of thrush, called also merle, ousel, or black thrush; a crowlike bird of North America; formerly, a name given to a kidnaped negro or Polynesian.

black-board (blăk'bōrd"), *n.* a large slate, or board painted black, to be written or drawn on with chalk.

black-cap (blăk'kăp"), *n.* the popular name of several black-crested birds; the cap worn by a judge when pronouncing sentence of death; the black raspberry.

black-en (blăk'n), *v.i.* to grow black or dark: *v.t.* to make black; to soil; to speak evil of, as of the character or reputation.

black flag (blăk flăg), the flag of a pirate, decorated with a skull and crossbones.

black fri-ar (blăk frī'ẽr), a monk of the Dominican order: so called from the black gown worn by members of the order.

black-guard (blăg'ärd), *n.* a man of low character who habitually uses foul or abusive language; a scoundrel: *adj.* vicious; low; vile; indecent; abusive: *v.t.* to speak contemptuously of, in vile and indecent language.

Black Hand (blăk hănd), a Sicilian secret society organized to force money from people by fearful threats.

black-ing (blăk'ĭng), *n.* a mixture for giving a shining black polish to boots.

black-jack (blăk'jăk"), *n.* a small bludgeon or club with a flexible handle, used as a weapon.

black lead (blăk lĕd), a mineral formed of carbon and iron and used as the "lead" in pencils; plumbago: *v.t.* to cover with black lead or plumbago.

black-leg (blăk'lĕg), *n.* a cheating gambler; a contemptuous term for a workman who is not a member of any trade union.

black let-ter (blăk lĕt'ẽr), the old English or Gothic letter used in the early manuscripts and the first printed books: *adj.* written or printed in such letters.

black list (blăk lĭst), a list of persons who are considered deserving of punishment, or whom it is desirable to exclude from business transactions: *v.t.* (blăk'lĭst"), to enroll as undesirable or as deserving of punishment.

black-mail (blăk'māl"), *n.* a tax anciently paid in money, corn, or cattle, in the north of England, and in Scotland, to the agents of robbers, to secure protection from theft; hence, the securing of money by frightening one into giving it up: *v.t.* to secure money or goods from by causing fear of any kind.

black-smith (blăk'smĭth"), *n.* a person who works in iron and makes iron utensils, horseshoes, etc.

black-snake (blăk'snāk"), *n.* any of several very dark serpents; a heavy whip made of braided cowhide. Also, **black snake**.

black-thorn (blăk'thôrn"), *n.* a shrub bearing large thorns and small black cherries, largely used for hedges; called also *sloe;* a stick cut from the stem of the sloe; a kind of hawthorn.

blad-der (blăd'ẽr), *n.* a thin elastic bag or sac in animals, in which a fluid is collected; any sac or blister, containing fluid or air.

blade (blād), *n.* the leaf of a grass; the young stalk or spire of a grass; the broad expanded part of a leaf; the cutting part of a knife or other instrument; the broad part of an oar; anything resembling the broad flat cutting part of a knife; a dashing, reckless, rollicking fellow: *v.t.* to put forth blades.—*adj.* **bladed.**

blain (blān), *n.* a blister; an inflamed sore or swelling.

blam-a-ble (blām'ȧ-bl), *adj.* deserving of blame or censure; faulty.—*adv.* **blamably.**—*n.* **blamableness.**

blame (blām), *n.* an expression of disapproval of something thought to be wrong; a fault; responsibility for anything wrong: *v.t.* to find fault with; reproach.—*adj.* **blameworthy.**

Syn., *v.* condemn, reprove, upbraid, censure.
Ant. (see praise).

blame-less (blām'lĕs), *adj.* free from fault or wrongdoing.—*adv.* **blamelessly.**—*n.* **blamelessness.**

blanch (blȧnch), *v.t.* to take the color out of and make white; as, celery growers *blanch* the celery stalks by burying them away from the light; to make white by removing the peel; as, to *blanch* almonds: *v.i.* become white; turn pale.

blanc-mange (blȧ-mänzh'), *n.* a white jellylike dessert composed of some gelatinous or starchy substance, such as cornstarch, combined with milk.

bland (blănd), *adj.* mild; soft-spoken: gentle; as, a *bland* smile.—*adv.* **blandly.**—*n.* **blandness.**

blan-dish-ment (blăn'dĭsh-mĕnt), *n.* a flattering expression or action; an artful caress; coaxing.

blank (blăṅk), *n.* any empty space; an unfilled space in a written or printed document; a lottery ticket which fails to draw a prize; disk of metal before it is stamped; the white spot in the center of a target: *adj.* free from writing or print; without result or interest; confused; empty; absolute; as, *blank* silence; without rhyme; as, *blank* verse.—*adv.* **blankly.**—*n.* **blankness.**

blan-ket (blăṅ'kĕt), *n.* a soft, loosely-woven, heavy cloth, usually of wool, used as a bed covering, as robes, or as a cover for a horse, etc.: *v.t.* to cover, as with a blanket; to take the wind out of the sails of (a vessel) by sailing to windward of (her).

blare (blâr), *n.* a harsh noise like the blast of a trumpet: *v.i.* to bellow; to give forth a loud brazen sound like a trumpet: *v.t.* to sound loudly; to trumpet forth.

blar-ney (blär'nĭ), *n.* soft, coaxing speech; flattery: *v.t.* [*p.t.* and *p.p.* blarneyed, *p.pr.* blarneying], to influence or deceive by soft, coaxing speeches; to humbug with flattery; to wheedle.

Blar-ney stone (blär'nĭ stōn), a stone in the wall of Blarney Castle, Ireland, upon kissing which a person is said to become a skilled flatterer.

bla-sé (blȧ"zā'), *adj.* wearied by too much pleasure so as to have lost the power of enjoyment. [Fr.]

blas-pheme (blȧs-fēm"), *v.t.* to speak irreverently of; to mock at (sacred things): *v.i.* to use profane or impious language.—*n.* **blasphemer.**

blas-phe-mous (blȧs'fē-mŭs), *adj.* uttering, containing, or showing mockery of sacred things; profane.—*adv.* **blasphemously.**

blas-phe-my (blȧs'fē-mĭ), *n.* [*pl.* blasphemies (-mĭz)], impious, profane, or mocking speech concerning God or sacred things; expressed contempt or hatred for the personality or authority of God; the claiming of equality with God; sacrilege.

blast (blȧst), *n.* a violent or sudden gust of wind; a forcible stream of air from an opening; as, a *blast* of heat comes from the opened furnace door; the sound produced by blowing a wind instrument; any sudden harmful influence, as a wind upon plants or animals; a blight; the explosion of gunpowder, dynamite, etc., in rending or removing rocks, or the charge so used: *v.t.* to injure; cause to fade or wither by some evil influence; to ruin or destroy; to break open or shatter by any explosive agent.

blast-ed (blȧst'ĕd), *adj.* blighted; withered; accursed; detestable.

blast-ing (blȧst'ing), *n.* a breaking open of stone, etc., by explosives; a blighting or withering.

bla-tant (blā'tănt), *adj.* bellowing; bawling; noisy; conspicuous; coarse; offensively obtrusive.—*adv.* **blatantly**.—*n.* **blatancy**.

blath-er (blăth'ẽr), *n.* foolish talk: *v.i.* and *v.t.* to talk foolishly.

blaze (blāz), *n.* a fire; a body of flame; intense direct light, as brilliant sunlight; a sudden bursting out; as a *blaze* of anger; brilliant display; as, a *blaze* of glory; splendor; a white spot on the face of a horse or other animal; a white mark cut on a tree, to serve as a guide: *v.t.* to mark, as trees, by removing a portion of the bark, so as to mark out a path or boundary; as, to *blaze* a trail; to publish widely: *v.i.* to flame; to burn up; to send forth a brilliant light; to be clearly and quickly seen.

blaz-er (blāz'ẽr), *n.* a bright colored striped jacket, originally worn at tennis, cricket, etc.

bla-zon (blā'zn), *n.* a coat of arms; a description of the figures on coats of arms, banners, etc.; showy display: *v.t.* to explain in proper terms the figures on coats of arms, banners, etc.; to adorn; display; as, a drunkard's face *blazons* his character; to proclaim boastingly.

bla-zon-ry (blā'zn-rĭ), *n.* figures on coats of arms; the art of describing and explaining coats of arms, heraldic shields, and armorial bearings.

bleach (blēch), *v.t.* to make white or whiter by a chemical process or by exposing to the sun's rays: *v.i.* to grow or become white.

bleach-ers (blēch'ẽrs), *n.* the low-priced, roofless space or seats for spectators at baseball and other games.

bleak (blēk), *adj.* exposed to wind and cold; desolate; unsheltered; cheerless; piercing; cold and cutting; as, a *bleak* wind.—*adv.* **bleakly**.—*n.* **bleakness**.

blear (blẽr), *adj.* sore or dim from a watery discharge: said of the eyes: *v.t.* to make sore or watery, as the eyes; to dim or obscure; hence, to deceive or hoodwink.

bleat (blēt), *n.* the cry of a sheep, goat, or calf: *v.i.* to cry as, or like, a sheep. Also, **blat**.

bleb (blĕb), *n.* a blister; a bubble; a bubble in a solid substance that has been fluid; as, a *bleb* in glass.

bleed (blēd), *v.i.* [*p.t.* and *p.p.* bled, *p.pr.* bleeding], to give forth or lose blood; to shed one's blood; to lose sap or juice; as, trees *bleed* if trimmed after the sap is up in the spring; to be filled with sympathy or pity; as, all hearts *bleed* for Belgium: *v.t.* to take blood from; to take money, etc., from.

blem-ish (blĕm'ish), *n.* any defect or deformity, physical or moral: *v.t.* to injure; to mar; to sully; to stain; to disfigure; to tarnish; to injure (reputation or character).

Syn., *n.* flaw, speck, spot, stain.
Ant. (see ornament).

blench (blĕnch), *v.i.* to start back; to shrink back or from; to give way; to quail; to blanch or turn white; grow pale: *v.t.* to make white or pale.

blend (blĕnd), *v.t.* to mix together, so that the things mixed cannot be separated or distinguished from each other: *v.i.* to mingle; to shade into each other: said of colors; *n.* a thorough mixture of colors, liquids, tobaccos, teas, etc.; a shading of one color, etc., into another.

bless (blĕs), *v.t.* [*p.t.* and *p.p.* blessed and blest, *p.pr.* blessing], to set apart for a holy purpose; to call down a blessing upon; to give happiness to; as, "O Lord, *bless* thy people"; to praise or extol.—*p.adj.* **blessed**.

bless-ed-ness (blĕs'ĕd-nĕs), *n.* felicity; bliss; happiness; heavenly joys; complete prosperity and contentment.

bless-ing (blĕs'ing), *n.* a wish of happiness or holiness for another; a benediction; that which causes prosperity; a divine benefit or gift; a mercy or boon; grateful worship.

blest (blĕst), past tense and past participle of the verb *bless*: *p.adj.* blessed.

blew (bloo͞), past tense of the transitive and intransitive verb *blow*.

blew-its (bloo͞'its), *n.* the purple mushroom used for food.

blight (blīt), *n.* a disease that causes plants to wither partly or wholly; smut; mildew; anything which serves to check, nip, or destroy: *v.t.* to affect with a withering disease, or baleful influence; to check, nip, destroy, or frustrate.—*n.* **blighter**.

Blight-y (blī'tĭ), *n.* an East Indian word meaning "over the seas"; in the World War, used by the British soldiers to signify home, or Britain; as, back to *Blighty* on a furlough. [SLANG.]

blimp (blĭmp), *n.* a small dirigible balloon, used to locate submarines. [SLANG.]

blind (blīnd), *adj.* without the sense of sight; sightless; unable or unwilling to understand, judge, or realize; heedless; unthinking; as, *blind* haste, *blind* admiration; hidden; closed at one end; as, a *blind* alley; without understanding: *n.* anything which serves to hinder or obstruct vision, or hinders the passage of light; a window-shade; a hinged shutter for windows; a blinker on a horse's bridle; something to mislead the eye or the understanding; as, photographs of wild animals in their natural homes may be taken if the camera is hidden behind a *blind* made of boughs and leaves; an ambush; a subterfuge: *v.t.* to deprive of sight; to make blind, mentally or morally; to hide; to dazzle; to conceal.—*adv.* **blindly**.

blind-er (blīn'dẽr), *n.* one who or that which prevents from seeing; a blinker on a horse's bridle.

blind fish (blīnd fĭsh), a very small fish without eyes, found in the waters of Mammoth Cave, Kentucky.

blind-fold (blīnd'fōld"), *adj.* having the eyes covered so as to be unable to see; having the understanding darkened; hence, reckless; heedless: *v.t.* to cover the eyes of, as with a bandage; to hinder from seeing.

blind man's buff (blīnd mănz bŭf), a game in which some one who is blindfolded must catch and name one of the other players.

blind-ness (blīnd'nĕs), *n.* want of sight; sightlessness; want of thought, wisdom, or understanding.

blind shell (blīnd shĕl), a shell which falls without exploding, or which contains no charge.

blind spot (blīnd spŏt), that point where the optic nerve enters the eye and which cannot be affected by light.

blind-worm (blīnd'wûrm"), *n.* a small, slender, limbless lizard with tiny eyes, so named from the popular but wrong belief that it cannot see.

blink (blĭnk), *v.i.* to see indistinctly, as with half-closed eyes; to wink with, or as with, the eye; twinkle; to get a glimpse; to glimmer: *v.t.* to evade or shut one's eyes to; to shirk; to ignore (what one is looking at); as, he *blinks* a question: *n.* a glimpse or glance; a gleam; a glimmer; a twinkle.

blink-er (blĭnk'ẽr), *n.* one who winks or evades; a leather flap placed one on each side of a horse's bridle to prevent him from seeing objects beside or behind him; *pl.* colored glasses to shield the eyes from too much light; hence, any obstruction to sight or understanding.

bliss (blĭs), *n.* the highest degree of happiness; blessedness; the perfect joy of heaven.

bliss-ful (blĭs'fo͞ol), *adj.* filled with gladness or joy; extremely happy.—*adv.* blissfully.—*n.* blissfulness.

blis-ter (blĭs'tẽr), *n.* a small, bladderlike cavity under the skin containing watery matter; any eruption resembling one made by such a cavity under the skin, as the *blister* raised by heat on painted surfaces; something put on the skin to produce an eruption: *v.t.* to cause such an eruption to come upon: *v.i.* to rise in, or become covered with, such an eruption.

blithe (blīth), *adj.* gay; joyous; glad; mirthful; cheery; happy.—*adv.* blithely.

blithe-some (blīth'sŭm), *adj.* cheery; gay; merry; joyous.

bliz-zard (blĭz'ẽrd), *n.* a furious hurricane of wind accompanied by fine driving snow, and intense cold.

bloat (blōt), *v.t.* to cure or dry (herrings) in smoke; to cause to swell; to distend or puff out, as with water or air; inflate; make vain: *v.i.* to become swollen; to become puffed out.

bloat-er (blōt'ẽr), *n.* a large herring, salted, smoked, and partially dried.

block (blŏk), *n.* any unshaped solid mass of matter, as of wood, stone, etc.; a piece of wood for supporting the neck of a person condemned to be beheaded; a piece of hard wood prepared for the tool of the engraver; a wooden mold for shaping hats; a grooved pulley or pulleys in a frame to which is attached a hook or ring by which it may be suspended; a row of buildings; a square or portion of a city inclosed by streets; that which closes the way or channel; an obstacle; a hindrance; quantity, section, or number of something dealt with as a unit; as, a *block* of seats in a theater; shares of stock bought or sold in the mass: *v.t.* to stop the passage of; to obstruct; stop up; to plan or sketch without working out any details; to secure or support by blocks; to mold or shape on a block; to stop (a train) by signal.

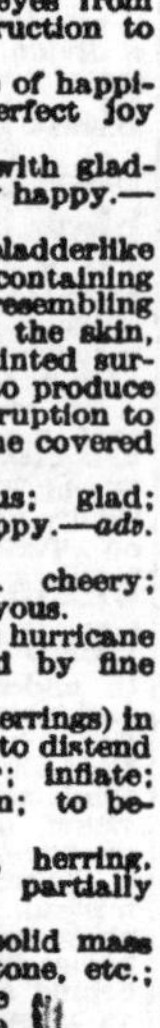

Block and Tackle

block-ade (blŏk-ād'), *n.* the shutting up of a place, as a port, by ships or troops of an enemy in order to prevent anything from coming in or going out: *v.t.* to surround and shut up; to block.

block-head (blŏk'hĕd"), *n.* a stupid fellow; a dolt.

block-house (blŏk'hous"), *n.* a military building or fortress built of heavy timber, furnished with loopholes for musketry, and having a projecting upper story.

block sys-tem (blŏk sĭs'tĕm), a system providing for the safe passage of railway trains, by which the line is divided into short sections. No train is allowed to leave a section until the next section is signaled clear.

blond (blŏnd), *adj.* of a fair color; light colored: *n.* a person of very fair complexion and light hair. Also, usually feminine, blonde.

blood (blŭd), *n.* the red fluid which circulates in the heart, arteries, and veins of an animal; sometimes, the juice of anything, especially if red; kinship; relationship; as, "God has made of one *blood* all nations of men for to dwell on earth."—Acts xvii. 26; descent; lineage; a line of royal ancestors; as, a prince of royal *blood;* a man of fire and spirit; a rake; as, a young *blood;* temper, accompanied by cold or hot; as, a murder in cold *blood;* slaughter or murder.

blood-ed (blŭd'ĕd), *adj.* of the best stock or breed.

blood heat (blŭd hēt), the normal temperature of the human blood in health which is 98.6° F.

blood-hound (blŭd'hound"), *n.* one of a breed of large dogs remarkable for their acute sense of smell, employed to track wounded game and escaped prisoners or criminals.

blood-i-ly (blŭd'ĭ-lĭ), *adv.* in a murderous manner; relentlessly; cruelly.

blood-i-ness (blŭd'ĭ-nĕs), *n.* the state of being bloody; a disposition to kill by savage methods.

blood-less (blŭd'lĕs), *adj.* without blood: used of a run-down physical condition; pale; spiritless; cold-hearted; unfeeling.

blood mon-ey (blŭd mŭn'ĭ), money obtained at the cost of another's life; as, Judas, when he betrayed Jesus, received thirty pieces of silver as *blood money;* the reward paid for discovery or capture of a murderer; money paid by the slayer to the next of kin of a slain person.

blood root (blŭd ro͞ot), a plant of the poppy family, having red roots and white sap, and bearing a white flower which blooms in early spring.

blood-shed (blŭd'shĕd"), *n.* slaughter; destruction of life.

blood-shot (blŭd'shŏt"), *adj.* red and inflamed: said of the eyes.

blood-stone (blŭd'stōn"), *n.* a dark green variety of quartz spotted with red jasper.

blood-suck-er (blŭd'sŭk"ẽr), *n.* an animal that sucks blood; especially, a leech; one who forces money from another; an extortioner.

blood-thirs-ty (blŭd'thûrs"tĭ), *adj.* murderous; eager to kill; cruel.

blood-y (blŭd'ĭ), *adj.* relating to, containing, or resembling blood; bloodstained; cruel; murderous; attended with slaughter.

bloom (blo͞om), *n.* a blossom; the flower of a plant; the state of having flowers; as, the tree is in *bloom;* a state or period of health and growth, promising higher perfection, or showing freshness and beauty; the delicate color or powdery coating upon certain fruits or leaves; as, the *bloom* on peaches, plums, grapes, etc.; a flush; a glow; a rough mass of iron from the melting furnace, intended to be drawn out under the hammer or rolled into bars: *v.i.* to produce blossoms; flower; show the freshness and beauty of youth; glow.

bloom-er (blōōm'ẽr), *n.* a costume for women introduced by a Mrs. Bloomer, of New York, in 1849–50, and consisting of loose trousers under a short dress: *pl.* loose wide trousers gathered below the knee, and worn, with or without an overskirt, by women in athletic sports.

bloom-er-y (blōōm'ẽr-ĭ), *n.* the first forge through which iron passes after it is melted from the ore; the forge in which iron is wrought into masses ready for the hammer.

bloom-ing (blōōm'ĭng), *p.adj.* blossoming; flowering; thriving in health, vigor, and beauty.

blos-som (blŏs'ŭm), *n.* the flower of a plant; the state of flowering: *v.i.* to put forth flowers; to flower; to flourish.

blot (blŏt), *n.* a spot or stain; a wiping out or erasure; a spot on the reputation; disgrace: *v.t.* [*p.t.* and *p.p.* blotted, *p.pr.* blotting], to spot or stain; to disfigure; to dishonor; to stain with disgrace; to cancel: usually with *out;* to destroy utterly; as, Sodom was utterly *blotted* out; to dry (ink) with absorbent, or blotting, paper; to darken or hide; as, a cloud *blots* out the moon: *v.i.* to make a blot or blots.

blotch (blŏch), *n.* a large irregular spot, as of ink; a clumsy daub; a coarse eruption; as, a *blotch* of pimples on the face: *v.t.* to mark or disfigure with irregular blots or spots.—*adj.* **blotchy.**

blot-ter (blŏt'ẽr), *n.* a sheet of paper intended to dry or suck up wet ink.

blot-ting pa-per (blŏt'ĭng pā'pẽr), paper specially prepared to dry or suck up wet ink.

blouse (blouz; blous), *n.* a light, loose overgarment originally worn by workmen as a protection from dust; a shirtwaist; a loosely-fitting waist worn by children.

blow (blō), *v.i.* [*p.t.* blew, *p.p.* blown, *p.pr.* blowing], to blossom; to flower; to move, as air, at different rates of speed and force; to pant; to breathe quickly; to sound by having air forced into, as a whistle; to spout water: *v.t.* to drive a current of air upon; to send forward or impel by a current of air; to cause to sound by forcing air through, as a whistle; to clear by forcing air through; form by forcing air into, as bubbles; put out of breath by fatigue; scatter or shatter by explosives: *n.* a flower; a blossom; a blast; a gale of wind; an egg laid by a fly; the spouting of a whale; a stroke with the hand or with a weapon; an act of enmity; a sudden shock or misfortune. —*adj.* **blowy.**

blow-er (blō'ẽr), *n.* a device for causing air to move in a current.

blow-fly (blō'flī), *n.* any kind of fly which lays its eggs on meat or in wounds.

blow-gun (blō'gŭn"), *n.* a long tube of cane or reed, used by South American Indians and the Dyaks of Borneo, to shoot arrows by the force of the breath.

blow-pipe (b...'pīp"), *n.* a tube through which a current of air or gas is driven upon a flame so as to bring all its heat upon a substance to melt it.

blowz-y (blouz'ĭ), *adj.* ruddy-faced; high-colored; coarse-complexioned, as by exposure to the weather; disordered by wind; as, *blowzy* hair. Also, **blowzed.**

blub-ber (blŭb'ẽr), *v.i.* to weep noisily and so as to disfigure the face: *v.t.* to disfigure (the face) with weeping; to utter sobbingly: *n.* the act of weeping noisily; the fat of whales and other sea animals, from which train oil is prepared; a jelly-fish.

blu-cher (blōō'chẽr; blōō'kẽr), *n.* a strong half-boot, so named from the Prussian general Blücher; also, a low or high shoe in which the tongue and toe are made of one piece of leather.

bludg-eon (blŭj'ŭn), *n.* a short heavy stick used as a weapon, one end of which is heavier than the other or is loaded with lead, etc.

blue (blōō), *adj.* of the color of the clear sky; azure; low-spirited; dismal: *n.* color of the clear sky; one of the three original or primary colors (blue, yellow, and red) from which the others are made; a dye or paint which colors blue; pale without glare; as, a *blue* flame: *pl.* low spirits; melancholy: *v.t.* to make, or dye, blue.

blue-bell (blōō'bĕl"), *n.* the wild hyacinth; the harebell of Scotland.

blue-ber-ry (blōō'bĕr-ĭ), *n.* [*pl.* berries (-ĭz)], a small berry, blue in color, suitable for eating; also, the shrub which bears this fruit.

blue-bird (blōō'bûrd"), *n.* a small American song bird of blue color.

blue blood (blōō blŭd), the blood of old and honorable families; a person of such a family.

blue-bot-tle (blōō'bŏt"l), *n.* the cornflower; a large fly with steel-blue body.

blue-jack-et (blōō'jăk"ĕt), *n.* a sailor; an enlisted man in the navy.

blue laws (blōō lôz), certain very strict laws enacted by the Puritans; hence, any severe laws, especially in regard to Sunday amusements.

blue pe-ter (blōō' pē"tẽr), a blue flag with a white square in the center, indicating that a ship is about to sail.

blue rib-bon (blōō rĭb"ŭn), usually, the highest award in a competition; a prized honor.

blue-stock-ing (blōō'stŏk"ĭng), a scholarly woman, so interested in books that she cares for little else.

blu-et (blōō'ĕt), *n.* a delicate, dainty plant with small, bluish flowers, found in the United States; called also *quaker-ladies.*

bluff (blŭf), *adj.* having a broad, flattened front; rising steeply or boldly; rough and hearty; surly; gruff: *n.* a high steep bank; a cliff or headland with a broad steep face; the act of putting on an air of confidence for the purpose of deceiving: *v.t.* to deceive by putting on a confident air in order to accomplish some purpose or escape some danger: *v.i.* to deceive an opponent by putting on an air of strength.—*n.* **bluffness.**

bluff-ly (blŭf'lĭ), *adv.* in a blunt, outspoken, or offhand manner.

blu-ing (blōō'ĭng), *n.* a bluish preparation, as of indigo, used in laundering; the act of giving a blue color to iron or steel. Also, **blueing.**

blun-der (blŭn'dẽr), *n.* a stupid mistake; a serious error: *v.i.* to make a bad mistake from stupidity, ignorance, etc.; err stupidly; to move or act clumsily.—*adj.* **blundering.**—*adv.* **blunderingly.**

blun-der-buss (blŭn'dẽr-bŭs), *n.* a kind of short gun or firearm, no longer in use; a stupid fellow.

blunt (blŭnt), *adj.* having a thick or rounded edge or point; not sharp; dull in understanding; stupid; abrupt in speech or manner; plain-spoken: *v.t.* to dull the edge or point of; to make weaker or less keen: *v.i.* to become dull; lose keenness.—*adv.* **bluntly.**—*n.* **bluntness.**

blur (blûr), *v.t.* [*p.t.* and *p.p.* blurred, *p.pr.* blurring], to make indistinct in outline; to dim by causing imperfect vision in; to stain; to blemish: *v.i.* to become indistinct in outline: *n.* a smudge; indistinctness; a moral stain; a dim confused appearance.

blurt (blûrt), *v.t.* to speak out suddenly and without thought; to utter unwisely: usually with *out;* as, to *blurt* out a secret.

blush (blŭsh), *v.i.* to redden or become rosy; to become red in the face, as from shame or confusion; to feel shame: with *for:* *n.* the red color that rises in the cheeks or face through shame, confusion, modesty, etc.; a red or reddish color; a rosy tint.

blus-ter (blŭs'tẽr), *v.i.* to be windy and boisterous, as the weather; to talk in a noisy, swaggering style; to bully; to use empty threats: *v.t.* to utter with noisy violence: with *forth* or *out:* *n.* the noise and violence of a storm, or of the wind in gusts; noisy talk; empty threats; swagger.

blus-ter-ous (blŭs'tẽr-ŭs), *adj.* noisy; rough; windy. Also, **blustery.**

bo-a (bō'*a*), *n.* [*pl.* boas (-*a*z)], any large snake which crushes its prey; a long fur or feather tippet or neckpiece.

bo-a con-stric-tor (bō'*a* kŏn-strĭk'tẽr), a serpent found in tropical America, remarkable for its length and its power of crushing its prey to death in its coils.

Boa Constrictor

boar (bōr), *n.* the male of swine; the wild hog.

board (bōrd), *n.* a piece of timber sawed thin, and much broader and longer than it is thick; a table for food; provision of meals, usually given for pay; entertainment, in the sense of food and shelter; a number of persons elected to the management of some public or private office or trust; a thin, usually folding, square on which a game is played; as, a checker*board;* paste*board;* one of the two stiff covers of a book; the side of a ship; as, over*board:* *pl.* the stage of a theater: **by the board,** away; as, her career had gone by the *board:* **on board,** on a ship or in a train: *v.t.* to cover with flat timbers; furnish with food, or food and lodging, in return for money; to cause to be lodged and fed, as a horse at a stable; go on (a ship) or enter (a train): *v.i.* to be supplied with meals, or obtain food and lodging, at a fixed charge.

board-er (bōr'dẽr), *n.* one who pays for lodging or food by the day or week at the table or house of another; one who gets upon a ship.

board foot (bōrd' fo͝ot'), a volume equal to that of a timber one foot by one foot by one inch, or 144 cubic inches: used in measuring lumber.

board-ing (bōrd'ĭng), *n.* light timber; a covering of light timber; the act of supplying, or state of being supplied with, food and lodging, for a stated sum; the act of going on a ship.

board meas-ure (bōrd' mĕzh'ūr), measurement of timber or lumber in board feet.

boast (bōst), *v.i.* to brag; to speak of oneself or belongings in loud and vain terms; to exult: *v.t.* to brag of: *n.* a proud, vainglorious speech; a cause or occasion of pride, vanity, or praiseworthy triumph; as, it is England's *boast* that the sun never sets on her possessions.

boast-er (bōs'tẽr), *n.* one given to loud, vain bragging.

boast-ful (bōst'fo͝ol), *adj.* given to bragging, or full of vanity.—*adv.* **boastfully.**—*n.* **boastfulness.**

boat (bōt), *n.* a small open vessel usually moved by oars or paddles but often by means of a sail; a ship; any vessel for navigating the water; an open dish resembling a ship in form: *v.i.* to go in a small open vessel; to row; to sail.

boat hook (bōt ho͝ok), a pole usually having a sharp point and a hook, used in holding a boat to a ship's side or to a wharf, or for pushing off.

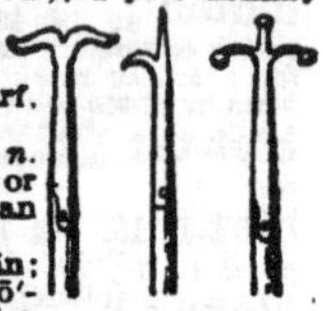

Boat Hooks

boat-ing (bōt'ĭng), *n.* act of sailing or rowing, particularly as an amusement.

boat-swain (bōt'swān; *naut.* bō'-sn), *n.* a petty officer of a ship who has charge of the rigging, anchors, cables, and cordage, and who calls the crew to their duty.

bob (bŏb), *v.t.* [*p.t.* and *p.p.* bobbed, *p.pr.* bobbing], to give a short jerking motion to; to cut short, as the hair: *v.i.* to have a short jerking motion; move or play to and fro, or up and down; to fish with a weight on the line: *n.* any small round object playing loosely at the end of a cord, chain, etc.; a pendant; the weight at the end of a pendulum, plumbline, fishing-line, etc.; a knot of worms or rags on a string, used in fishing for eels; a short jerking action or motion.

bob-bin (bŏb'ĭn), *n.* one of the pins or small cylinders of wood used to carry and steady the threads in pillow-lace making; a spool or reel with a head at one or both ends, used on machines to hold yarn or thread for spinning, weaving, or sewing; a cord or braid run through a casing.

bob-bi-net (bŏb'ĭ-nĕt'; bŏb'ĭ-nĕt), *n.* a machine-made cotton netting.

bob-o-link (bŏb'ō-lĭnk), *n.* an American song-bird: called also, in certain localities, *ricebird, reedbird.*

bob-sled (bŏb'slĕd), *n.* a sled made of two short sleds called bobs placed one behind the other, used for hauling lumber and, when smaller, for coasting; sometimes called a double-runner.

bob-tail (bŏb'tāl), *n.* a short tail or a tail cut short; colloquially, in "rag-tag and *bobtail*," used to mean the rabble, or lowest class of people.—*adj.* **bobtailed.**

bob-white (bŏb'hwīt), *n.* the common American quail or partridge.

boche (bôsh), *n.* [*pl.* boches (bôsh'ĕz)], in the World War, a soldier of the German army: from the French *caboche*, a hobnail with a hard, rough, square head. [SLANG.]

bode (bōd), *v.t.* and *v.i.* to portend; to foretell; to be a sign of: usually of ill; as, to *bode* misfortune or disaster.

bod-ice (bŏd'ĭs), *n.* the close-fitting waist or body of a woman's dress; a wide belt or girdle.

bod-ied (bŏd'ĭd), *adj.* possessing or having a body: usually found in compounds; as, able-*bodied* seamen were asked for.

bod-i-less (bŏd'ĭ-lĕs), *adj.* possessing no concrete form; not made up of matter.

bod-i-ly (bŏd'ĭ-lĭ), *adj.* pertaining to, or belonging to, the body; as, *bodily* sickness or harm: *adv.* in the form of the body; entirely; completely.

bod-ing (bōd'ĭng), *n.* an omen; a belief or feeling that harm or evil is approaching: *p.adj.* foreshadowing evil; ominous.—*adv.* **bodingly.**

bod-kin (bŏd'kĭn), *n.* a pointed instrument for piercing holes in embroidery; a blunt needle with a large eye for drawing tape, ribbon, etc. through a hem, eyelets, etc.; a long pin or stiletto to fasten up the hair.

bod-y (bŏd'ĭ), *n.* [*pl.* bodies (-ĭz)], the form and substance of an animal living or dead; the trunk or main portion of an animal or tree; the main or principal part of anything; as, the *body* of a letter is the part that carries the message; a person; a number of individuals united by some common tie or distinct purpose; a mass; as, a *body* of troops; a material thing; a certain thickness or weight; as, china silk is a material of very little *body*: *v.t.* [*p.t.* and *p.p.* bodied, *p.pr.* bodying], to furnish with a material form; to embody; to picture as if existing in material form: usually with *forth*; as, to *body* forth the form of things unseen.

Syn., *n.* carcass, clay, form, frame, trunk, corpse, system.

Ant. (see spirit).

bod-y-guard (bŏd'ĭ-gärd"), *n.* one who protects or defends the person; a group of soldiers or police officers assigned to protect the person of some ruler or official.

bod-y pol-i-tic (bŏd'ĭ pŏl'ĭ-tĭk), the people of a nation, state, or community regarded as a political unit; a number of people, considered collectively, living under an organized political government.

Boer (bōōr), *n.* a South African colonist or farmer of Dutch descent.

bog (bŏg), *n.* a tract of wet, spongy ground, composed of decayed and decaying vegetable matter; a quagmire; marsh; morass: *v.t.* and *v.i.* [*p.t.* and *p.p.* bogged, *p.pr.* bogging], to sink or submerge in a marsh or quagmire.

bo-gey (bō'gĭ), *n.* a hobgoblin; a specter; a bugbear; a four-wheeled truck used to partly support a locomotive; an estimated or arbitrary amount; in golf, an arbitrary score for each hole supposed to be made by Colonel Bogey, a mythical opponent against whom the players contend. Also, **bogie, bogy.**

bog-gle (bŏg'l), *v.i.* to hesitate; waver; act clumsily; bungle: *v.t.* to make a bungle of.

bog-gy (bŏg'ĭ), *adj.* full of wet, muddy places; marshy; swampy.

bo-gus (bō'gŭs), *adj.* counterfeit; not genuine; as, a quack is a name sometimes given to a *bogus* physician; sham.

bog-wood (bŏg'wŏŏd"), *n.* the wood of trees preserved in peat bogs, shiny black in color, and much used for ornament.

bo-gy (bō'gĭ), *n.* [*pl.* bogies (-gĭz)], *n.* a hobgoblin; a specter; a bugbear. Also, **bogie, bogey.**

Bo-he-mi-an (bō-hē'mĭ-ăn), *n.* a native of Bohemia; the language of Bohemia; a person interested in art, literature, etc. who disregards the conventional observances of social life, or shows a wild or roving disposition; a gipsy: *adj.* pertaining to Bohemia; unconventional; free and easy.—*n.* **Bohemianism.**

boil (boil), *v.i.* to bubble through the action of heat; in case of liquid, to become so hot that the liquid begins to turn into gas; be cooked in water; to seethe with an agitation like boiling; as, the swollen river *boiled* and swirled; be excited by passion and anger; as, his blood *boiled*: *v.t.* to heat to the boiling point; cause to bubble by heat; to cook in a boiling liquid: *n.* an inflamed, hard, festering, and painful tumor in the skin, with a central core, caused by bacterial infection.

boil-er (boil'ẽr), *n.* a strong metallic vessel, in which steam is produced for driving engines or for other purposes; a tank for storing hot water; a vessel in which a liquid is heated.

boil-ing (boil'ĭng), *adj.* heated to the point of seething or bubbling; swelling with heat: *n.* the act of bubbling and seething as a result of heat; the effect of subjecting to the action of hot liquid: **boiling point,** the temperature at which a liquid begins to change into gas.

bois-ter-ous (bois'tẽr-ŭs), *adj.* violent; rough; loud; stormy; noisy; rude; turbulent; tumultuous; uproarious.

bold (bōld), *adj.* courageous; fearless; venturesome; planned or carried out with courage and spirit; steep, abrupt, as a cliff; prominent; as, newspaper headlines are printed in *bold* type; in high relief; rude; presuming; overstepping limitations.

Syn. brave, daring, intrepid, undaunted, brazen, vigorous.

Ant. (see timid).

bold-face (bōld'fās"), *n.* a term used in printing to denote a particularly heavy and conspicuous type.

bold-ly (bōld'lĭ), *adv.* in a fearless manner; courageously; rudely; impudently; vigorously.

bold-ness (bōld'nĕs), *n.* courage; daring; dauntlessness; rudeness; forwardness.

bole (bōl), *n.* the trunk or stem of a tree; any of several kinds of easily crumbled clay.

bo-le-ro (bō-lā'rō), *n.* a lively Spanish dance; the music accompanying such a dance; a short jacket.

boll (bōl), *n.* the pod or seed-vessel of a plant, as of flax: *v.i.* to form into a seed-vessel; go to seed.

boll wee-vil (bōl′ wē′vl), a grayish beetle about a quarter of an inch long, which infests the cotton plant.

boll-worm (bōl′wûrm), *n.* the larva of a moth which devours the unripe pods of the cotton plant, and which also feeds on corn, tomatoes, beans, etc.

Bol-she-vi-ki (bŏl″shĕ-vē′kē), *n.pl.* (*sing.* *Bolshevik*), literally, the majority: a Russian party of extreme radicals, having as its aim the immediate realization of a socialist commonwealth: opposed to the *Mensheviki* or moderate socialists.

bol-she-vism (bŏl′shĕ-vizm), *n.* the theory of government of the Bolsheviki.

bol-ster (bōl′stẽr), *n.* a long pillow or cushion used to support the head; a pad to ease pressure; a cushioned or padded part of a saddle: *v.t.* to support with a pillow or cushion; prop; support: usually with *up.*

bolt (bōlt), *n.* a short, thick arrow with a blunt head; a stream of lightning, so called from its darting like an arrow; a stout pin or rod of iron or some other metal, usually with a permanent head at one end, used for holding objects together; a sliding catch for securing a door, gate, etc.; the portion of a lock shot or withdrawn by the key; a shackle; a sudden departure; a roll or certain length, as of cloth; in United States politics, a refusal to support a nomination made by one's party, or withdrawal from one's party: *adv.* directly; suddenly; straight, as *bolt* upright: *v.t.* expel with force; cause to spring forth; fasten or secure with a sliding catch; blurt out; swallow hurriedly or without chewing; in United States politics, to withdraw from (a party), or decline to support a (candidate); to sift or separate the coarser particles from; as, to *bolt* flour; hence, to examine with care; separate: *v.i.* to shoot forth or fall suddenly; to depart with suddenness; to start and run away; in United States politics, to refuse to support the policy or the nominee of a party: **thunderbolt,** *n.* the name given to a lightning flash that seems to strike the earth in an electric storm.

bo-lus (bō′lŭs), *n.* [*pl.* boluses (-ĕz)], a medicine in the form of a soft rounded mass, larger than an ordinary pill; hence, anything disagreeable which must be accepted.

bomb (bŏm; bŭm), *n.* a hollow iron ball or shell filled with an explosive material, fired from a short, heavy cannon called a mortar, and usually exploded by a tube filled with some substance easily burned and called a fuse; any shell similarly constructed and thrown by the hand or dropped from an airship: **aërial bomb,** a long steel cylinder filled with high explosive, dropped by airplanes: **incendiary bomb,** a shell that, when exploded, throws out a flaming liquid which sets fire to anything combustible within a large area: **bombing post,** a trench running from a front line trench to within a short distance of an enemy trench and used as a station for bomb-throwers.—*n.* **bomber.**

bom-bard (bŏm-bärd′; bŭm-bärd′), *v.t.* to attack with cannon; fire shot or shell at or into; to assail persistently with artillery.

bom-bar-dier (bŏm″bär-dēr′; bŭm″bär-dēr′), *n.* an artilleryman; a gunner.

bom-bard-ment (bŏm-bärd′mĕnt; bŭm-bärd′mĕnt), *n.* a continuous attack with shot and shell, rockets, etc.; the act or process of shelling a town or fort.

bom-bast (bŏm′băst; bŭm′băst), *n.* high-sounding words; high-sounding language or style without much meaning.

bom-bas-tic (bŏm-băs′tĭk), *adj.* swelled or puffed-up in manner or style. Also, **bombastical.**—*adv.* **bombastically.**

bomb-proof (bŏm′prōōf), *adj.* secure against damage, or resisting injury, from the explosive force of shells.

bomb-shell (bŏm′shĕl″), *n.* an explosive missile, or bomb; anything very sudden and surprising.

bo-na fi-de (bō′nȧ fī′dē), genuine; without deceit; in good faith. [Lat.]

bo-nan-za (bō-năn′zȧ), *n.* a rich vein of ore in a mine; hence, anything which brings wealth or good fortune.

bon-bon (bŏn′bŏn″), *n.* a sugarplum; a sugar candy; a sweetmeat.

bond (bŏnd), *n.* anything that fastens or confines; a manacle; a cause of union; a uniting influence; as, the *bond* of peace; an obligation; an agreement under seal by which a person promises that he and his heirs, etc. will do, or abstain from doing, a certain act; a promise to pay a certain sum on or before a definite date; a certificate, bearing interest, issued by a government or company, in return for money borrowed: *pl.* chains, fetters; imprisonment; captivity: *v.t.* to put (dutiable goods) into a warehouse, the duties remaining unpaid till the goods are taken out, but security being given for their payment; to place under a mortgage: *adj.* in a state of servitude or slavery; captive; as, "whether he be *bond* or free."

bond-age (bŏn′dȧj), *n.* the act of serving against one's will; slavery, whether physical or moral; imprisonment.
Syn. captivity, serfdom, thralldom.
Ant. (see freedom).

bond-ed (bŏn′dĕd), *adj.* held in bond, or under pledge, for payment of duties; secured by written agreement, as a debt: **bonded warehouse,** a place in which bonded goods are kept.

bonds-man (bŏndz′măn), *n.* a slave or serf; a bondman; one who makes himself responsible for another's payment of a debt, appearance for trial, etc.

bone (bōn), *n.* the hardened tissue forming the skeleton of the higher orders of animals; one of the parts or pieces of an animal skeleton; a stay of whalebone, steel, etc., for a corset: *pl.* pieces of bone or ivory held between the fingers and rattled together as an accompaniment to music: *v.t.* to remove the bones from; to stiffen with whalebone, as a dress: **bone dry,** very dry, as sun-dried bone: said of those states in which alcoholic liquors of every kind are prohibited by law to be made or sold or received from another state.

bone-set (bōn′sĕt″), *n.* a coarse herb of the aster family with white-rayed flower heads, much used by old-fashioned housewives to brew a bitter-tasting remedy or spring tonic known as boneset tea.

bon-fire (bŏn′fīr′), *n.* any large fire made in the open air to celebrate an event or to destroy rubbish or trash.

bon-ho-mie (bŏn″ō-mē′), *n.* good nature; a frank, pleasant, easy manner. Also, **bonhommie.** [Fr.]

bon-net (bŏn'ĕt), *n.* a soft woolen cap worn by men in Scotland; a woman's or child's outdoor head-covering, usually having strings, but having no brim; anything resembling such a head-covering in shape or use: *v.t.* to provide with a cap or other similar headgear.

bon-ny (bŏn'ĭ), *adj.* good-looking; pretty; cheerful; gay; blithe; comely. Also, **bonnie.**

bon-ny clab-ber (bŏn'ĭ klăb'ẽr), cottage cheese; milk that has thickened in souring.

bon ton (bôṅ' tôṅ'), the style of persons in high society; good breeding; fashionable society; height of fashion. [Fr.]

bo-nus (bō'nŭs), *n.* [*pl.* bonuses (-ĕz)], a sum given, or paid, over and above what is strictly due, or actually payable; an additional payment made to the shareholders in a company out of the profits; a sum paid in addition to regular pay or wages.

bon-y (bōn'ĭ), *adj.* like, or full of, bones; having prominent or conspicuous bones; thin and angular in figure.

boo (bōō), *interj.* an expression of dislike, aversion, or contempt; an exclamation made to frighten.

boo-by (bōō'bĭ), *n.* a dunce; a stupid fellow; in a game, the player ending with the lowest score.

boo-dle (bōō'dl), *n.* a political slang term meaning money paid for votes, or political influence; bribe money; graft.

boo-hoo (bōō'hōō'; bōō'hōō"), *n.* and *interj.* the noise or act of loud crying, weeping, or laughter: *v.i.* to cry loudly.

book (bŏŏk), *n.* a collection of sheets of paper and other material, blank, written, or printed, bound together in a volume; a composition of some length on a particular subject, printed and bound; a division, section, or part of a literary composition; a register or record; in card playing, a certain number of tricks held by one side; in horse-racing, a list of horses entered and the bets laid on them: **Book,** the Bible: *v.t.* to enter or register, as to *book* an order; to record.

book-bind-er (bŏŏk'bīn"dẽr), *n.* one whose business it is to fasten together or bind books.—*n.* **bookbinding.**

book-case (bŏŏk'kās"), *n.* a set of shelves for books.

book-ing of-fice (bŏŏk'ĭng ŏf'ĭs), in England, an office where tickets are sold for railway or steamship traveling, or for seats in a theater; a ticket office.

book-ish (bŏŏk'ĭsh), *adj.* fond of study; given to reading; better acquainted with books than with men; learned; pedantic; making a display of learning; as, *bookish* talk.—*n.* **bookishness.**

book-keep-er (bŏŏk'kēp"ẽr), *n.* one whose business it is to keep accounts; an accountant.

book-keep-ing (bŏŏk'kēp"ĭng), *n.* the art of recording accounts or business transactions in a regular and systematic manner.

book-let (bŏŏk'lĕt), *n.* a small volume, usually intended either for ornament or for advertising purposes.

book-mak-er (bŏŏk'māk"ẽr), *n.* one who writes or publishes books; a professional betting man.

book mus-lin (bŏŏk mŭz'lĭn), a fine kind of transparent cotton cloth, folded in book form.

book-worm (bŏŏk'wûrm"), *n.* one of various kinds of insects which live in and injure books; a person who is unusually devoted to reading and study.

boom (bōōm), *n.* a long pole or spar run out to extend the bottom of a sail; a strong chain, cable, or line of spars bound together, extended across a river or harbor to keep out an enemy's ships; a deep, hollow sound; a sudden demand for something on sale, accompanied by a rapid rise in price; as, the increased use of automobiles caused a *boom* in rubber and gasoline; a rapid growth in population: *v.i.* to make a deep, hollow sound; to grow rapidly in value, population, or popular esteem: *v.t.* to give forth with a hollow, resounding noise, usually with *out*; to cause to grow rapidly in value, population, or popular esteem.

boom-er-ang (bōōm'ẽr-ăng), *n.* a weapon used by the Australian natives, consisting of a piece of flat curved hard wood, which, when thrown by the hand in a certain manner, makes a number of curves, and finally returns to the thrower, striking the ground behind him; hence, any plot or action the result of which recoils upon the maker to his disadvantage.

boon (bōōn), *n.* a benefit; a gift; a privilege; a favor: *adj.* gay; kind; jovial; merry; convivial; as, a *boon* companion.

boor (bōōr), *n.* a peasant; a rustic; a rude, ill-mannered person.

boor-ish (bōōr'ĭsh), *adj.* clownish; awkward in manner; ignorant; ungainly; without culture.—*n.* **boorishness.**

boost (bōōst), *v.t.* to lift by pushing from behind: *n.* a push or shove that aids one to rise or advance.

boot (bōōt), *n.* a leather covering for the foot and the lower part of the leg; a compartment at the back of a coach, carriage, or automobile for holding baggage; that which is thrown in to persuade one to make a bargain, or to make an exchange equal; as, I will exchange my house for yours and give you one hundred dollars to *boot*; an old instrument of torture consisting of a kind of wooden rack or leather case so made as to squeeze the leg very tightly: *v.t.* to profit; to benefit; as, it *boots* me nothing; to put boots on; kick with the boot.

boot-black (bōōt'blăk"), *n.* one whose occupation is to polish shoes.

boo-tee (bōō-tē'), *n.* a little boot; a lady's, or child's, light boot or half-boot.

booth (bōōth), *n.* a covered stall or other temporary structure made of boards, canvas, etc., at a fair or polling place, etc.

boot-jack (bōōt'jăk"), *n.* an instrument for pulling off boots or shoes.

boot-less (bōōt'lĕs), *adv.* without avail; without advantage; useless; as, a *bootless* errand.

boots (bōōts), *n.* the servant in a hotel who cleans and polishes the shoes of the guests; a bootblack.

boot-tree (bōōt'trē"), *n.* a block to stretch boots or to keep them from losing their shape.

boo-ty (bōō'tĭ), *n.* [*pl.* booties (-tĭz)], food, guns, etc., taken from the enemy in war; plunder; that which is seized by violence and robbery; any rich spoil.

booze (bōōz), *v.i.* to drink to excess; to tipple: *n.* liquor; drink; a carouse; spree. Also, **boose.** [Colloq.]

bo-peep (bō-pēp'), *n.* a quick, playful peeping out and withdrawing in a child's game.

bo-rac-ic (bō-răs'ĭk), *adj.* pertaining to, or produced from, borax; boric: **boracic acid,** a colorless crystalline compound, largely used in solution as an eyewash and antiseptic.

bo-rat-ed (bō'rāt-ĕd), *adj.* mixed or filled with borax or boric acid; as, *borated* talcum powder.

bo-rax (bō'răks), *n.* a salt compounded of boracic acid and soda: used as an antiseptic, for cleaning metals, and in making glass, enamel, artificial gems, etc.

bor-der (bôr'dẽr), *n.* the outer part or edge of anything; a margin; boundary; rim; brink; frontier; verge; a narrow flower bed usually along a path: *v.t.* to make a decorative margin about: *v.i.* to touch at the edge or boundary: with *on* or *upon;* to approach.

bor-der-er (bôr'dẽr-ẽr), *n.* one who dwells on the edge of a district.

bor-der-land (bôr'dẽr-lănd), *n.* land forming a frontier; an uncertain or doubtful district; as, the *borderland* between right and wrong is often uncertain.

bore (bōr), *v.t.* [*p.t.* of *bear*], to pierce or drill a hole in; to form by piercing or drilling; to force (as a passage) with effort; to weary by tiresome repetition, or by dulness; to annoy; *v.i.* to make a hole; pierce; to push forward toward a certain point: *n.* a hole made by piercing or drilling; hence, the cavity or hollow of a gun; the inside diameter of a gun; hole; a stupid, uninteresting person; any person or thing that causes dull weariness; a tidal flood which breaks in the mouths of some rivers, and being hindered in its course by the narrowing channel, rises in a watery ridge and courses along with great force and noise.

bo-re-al (bō'rē-ăl), *adj.* northern; relating to the North, or to the north wind. Also, **borean.**

Bo-re-as (bō'rē-ăs), *n.* the north wind: one of the names by which the Greeks personified the four winds.

bore-dom (bōr'dŭm), *n.* dulness and weariness of spirit; state of being wearied by dulness.

bor-er (bōr'ẽr), *n.* one who, or that which, pierces or eats a hole, as certain worms, tools, etc.

bo-ric (bō'rĭk), *adj.* pertaining to, or produced from, borax. Also, **boracic.**

bo-ride (bō'rīd), *n.* a compound of boron with some metallic substance.

born (bôrn), *p.p.* of the verb *bear* when used passively: *p.adj.* brought forth or into being, as offspring; natural; made of a certain character by birth; ingrained; as, a *born* musician.

borne (bōrn), *p.p.* of the verb *bear*, carried; supported.

bo-ron (bō'rŏn), *n.* an element containing no metal, and found naturally only in combination, as in borax.

bor-ough (bŭr'ō), *n.* a town which has been organized into a self-governing body under a mayor, etc.

bor-row (bŏr'ō), *v.t.* to obtain the use of a thing, for a time, with the understanding that it is to be returned; to take; to copy; to adopt; as, almost all republics *borrow* their constitutions from the United States; in arithmetical subtraction, to take a number from the next higher denomination in order to add it to the next lower: *v.i.* to receive something with the intention of returning it.

bosh (bŏsh), *n.* absurd or empty talk; utter nonsense. [COLLOQ.]

bosk (bŏsk), *n.* a grove; a thicket; a small wood. Also, **bosket, bosquet.**

bosk-y (bŏs'kĭ), *adj.* woody; bushy; caused by a bosk; as, *bosky* shades.

bos-om (bo͝oz'ŭm), *n.* the breast of a human being; the part of a garment which covers the breast; the breast as the seat of the affections or passions, or as the center of emotions, or desires; the heart: hence, any deep, central place; as, the *bosom* of the lake: *adj.* intimate; beloved; as, a *bosom* friend; worn on the breast: *v.t.* to place or protect close to the heart; to keep tenderly; to conceal.

boss (bŏs), *n.* [*pl.* bosses (-ĕz)], an ornament of silver, ivory, or other material, which stands out on a flat surface; as, the *boss* ornamenting a shield; a knob; a raised ornament on a ceiling: *v.t.* to decorate with ornamental nails, knobs, or studs.

boss (bŏs), *n.* from the Dutch *baas*, meaning master; hence, a master-workman; a manager; a superintendent; colloquially [U. S.], a political dictator: *v.t.* to hold mastery over; to direct; to manage: *v.i.* to be master.—*adj.* **bossy.**

bo-tan-ic (bō-tăn'ĭk), *adj.* pertaining to botany, the science which treats of plant life. Also, **botanical.**—*adv.* **botanically.**

bot-a-nist (bŏt'á-nĭst), *n.* one who studies or is skilled in a knowledge of plants; one who is a specialist in botany.

bot-a-nize (bŏt'á-nīz), *v.i.* to seek after plants for the purpose of studying them; to go into the fields and woods for the sake of plant study.

bot-a-ny (bŏt'á-nĭ), *n.* the science which treats of plants.

botch (bŏch), *n.* a patch badly or clumsily put on; bungling work: *v.t.* to spoil; to disfigure; to mend or patch in a clumsy manner; to put together unskilfully: *v.t.* to do a poor piece of work.—*n.* **botcher.**

botch-y (bŏch'ĭ), *adj.* poorly or clumsily done; poorly repaired.

bot-fly (bŏt'flī"), *n.* a fly which, in one stage of its life, lives in horses and other animals.

both (bōth), *adj.* and *pron.* the one and the other; the two; *conj.* and *adv.* as well, equally, not only: with *and;* as, *both* the living and the dead; also; as, here were hate and love *both.*

both-er (bŏth'ẽr), *v.t.* to annoy; to tease; to worry; to give trouble to: *v.i.* to feel trouble or care; be troublesome: *n.* a source of worry; annoyance; vexation; perplexity; one that gives trouble.

both-er-a-tion (bŏth"ẽr-ā'shŭn), *n.* the act of annoying or worrying; the state of being vexed or perplexed.

both-er-some (bŏth'ẽr-sŭm), *adj.* troublesome; annoying; causing worry.

bots (bŏts), *n.pl.* the larva or first stage in the life of a kind of gadfly, which lives in horses, oxen, sheep, etc. Also, **botts.**

bot-tle (bŏt'l), *n.* a hollow vessel, usually with a narrow neck, and no handles, made of glass or earthenware, for holding liquids; the contents of such a vessel: *v.t.* to put into such vessels; to shut in or to hold back; as, to *bottle* up one's feelings.

bot-tom (bŏt'ŭm), *n.* the deepest part of anything; the base; foundation; root; the ground under any body of water; the seat of a chair; low land; power to endure; the part of a vessel below the waterline; hence, a ship: *adj.* lowest; undermost: *v.t.* to found or build upon; furnish with a foundation; to understand fully; to get to the root or base.—*adj.* **bottomless.**

bou-doir (bōō'dwär'), *n.* a small room, usually a lady's private sitting room.

bouffe (bōōf), *n.* light opera; comic opera; in Paris, Italian opera. [Fr.]

bough (bou), *n.* a limb or branch of a tree, especially a main branch.

bought (bôt), past tense and past participle of the verb *buy.*

bou-illon (bōō'yôn'; bōōl'yôn'), *n.* a kind of clear beef soup; a meat broth. [Fr.]

boul-der (bōl'dẽr), *n.* a large stone worn or rounded by running water; a large piece of rock which has been detached from its original bed. Also, **bowlder.**

bou-le-vard (bōō'lĕ-värd), *n.* a broad street usually bordered with trees.

bounce (bouns), *v.t.* to cause to move with an elastic motion; to cause to bound: *v.i.* to strike against anything so as to spring back again; to leap or spring suddenly: *n.* a sudden bound or spring; a heavy sudden thrust or thump; boasting.

bounc-er (boun'sẽr), *n.* one who, or that which, bounds or springs back; something unusually big.

bound (bound), *v.i.* to jump or spring suddenly or move in jumps, one after the other; to leap; *v.t.* to cause to spring back with elastic motion; to serve as a limit to; to inclose; geographically, to lie alongside of; as, Austria *bounds* Italy on the north; to name the countries or waters surrounding; as, to *bound* Italy: *p.t.* and *p.p.* of *bind*: *n.* a leap, spring, or jump; a light elastic step; a limit; extent; a country or body of water lying alongside another: *pl.* territory within certain limits: *adj.* tied; restrained; confined; intending to go; on the way; as, *bound* for France; inclosed in a cover, as a book; compelled; destined.

bound-a-ry (boun'dȧ-rĭ), *n.* [*pl.* boundaries (-rĭz)], that which marks the extent or limit of anything, especially of territory.

bound-less (bound'lĕs), *adj.* without a limit; unlimited; as, America has almost *boundless* wealth.

boun-te-ous (boun'tē-ŭs), *adj.* giving freely; liberal in gifts; very generous; plentiful.—*adv.* **bounteously.**

boun-ti-ful (boun'tĭ-fōōl), *adj.* liberal in bestowing gifts or favors; generous; plentiful.—*adv.* **bountifully.**

boun-ty (boun'tĭ), *n.* [*pl.* bounties (-tĭz)], generosity in giving gifts or favors; that which is freely given; sometimes, a prize offered by a government to persuade men to enlist in the army or navy, or to encourage some branch of industry.

bou-quet (bōō-kā'), *n.* a bunch of flowers; an aroma, as of wine; perfume.

bour-geois (bōōr'zhwä'), *n.* [*fem.* bourgeoise], a French citizen of the merchant class; a shopkeeper; one who, in France, is above the rank of peasant but below that of gentleman; in other countries, one of the middle class: *adj.* wanting in dignity; slightly vulgar; commonplace; as, *bourgeois* manners. [Fr.]

bour-geoi-sie (bōōr'zhwä'zē'), *n.* the French middle classes; the middle class connected with the trade of any country. [Fr.]

bour-geon (bûr'jŭn), *v.i.* to put forth buds: *n.* a bud; a shoot. Also, **burgeon.**

bourn (bōrn), *n.* a stream; a rivulet; a bound; a place toward which one is traveling; a goal; a limit; end.

bourse (bōōrs), *n.* a stock exchange for the transaction of business, especially the *Bourse* or Stock Exchange of Paris.

bout (bout), *n.* a going and returning, as in mowing, etc.; as much as is performed at one time; a trial; a round; a contest; as, a fencing *bout.*

bou-ton-nière (bōō'tô'nyâr'), *n.* a buttonhole bouquet. [Fr.]

bo-vine (bō'vīn; bō'vĭn), *adj.* oxlike; sluggish; patient; stolid; dull.

bow (bou), *v.t* to cause to bend or incline; bend, as the head or body, in token of respect, submission, etc.; to crush; to usher in or out; to express, as thanks, by bending the head or body: *v.i.* to bend the head in greeting; to bend the knee or head in respect, submission, etc.: *n.* a bending of the head or of the body, as a salute, or sign of reverence, respect, agreement, or of yielding to the authority or power of another; the forepart or prow of a vessel or an airship.

bow (bō), *n.* a weapon for shooting arrows; anything curved; as, a rain*bow*; an implement; as, a violin *bow*; a looped knot of ribbon or other material: *v.t.* to bend or curve like a bow: *v.i.* become bent or curved.

bow-el (bou'ĕl), *n.*, usually *pl.* the intestine of an animal; the interior part of anything; in the Bible, the center of tenderness or pity; as, *bowels* of mercy or compassion.

bow-er (bou'ẽr), *n.* shelter made of boughs or twining plants; an arbor; in poetry, a bedchamber or a lady's private apartment; a boudoir; an anchor carried at the bow of a ship; in the game of euchre, the knave of the trump suit (the right *bower*) and the knave of the suit of the same color as the trump suit (the left *bower*): the two highest cards after the joker.

bow-er-y (bou'ẽr-ĭ), *adj.* sheltered by trees or vines; like a bower, or arbor.—**Bowery,** *n.* a famous street in New York, full of cheap resorts, etc.: *adj.* cheap, tawdry, or vulgar; as, the *Bowery* boy, the queerest product of America in his day.

bow-ie knife (bō'ĭ nīf; bōō'ĭ nīf), a strong hunting knife; a sheath-knife, long and curved.

bowl (bōl), *n.* a circular hollow vessel for holding liquids; a large drinking cup, especially for wine; hence, convivial drinking; the hollow part of anything; as, the *bowl* of a spoon; a weighted ball of wood used in the games of bowls and skittles: *pl.* a game played with such balls; ninepins; tenpins: *v.i.* to play with bowls; in cricket, to serve the ball smoothly; roll a bowl or a cricket ball; to move rapidly and smoothly like a ball: *v.t.* to roll, as a bowl or ball; in cricket, to put out (a batsman) by bowling; to knock down; to prostrate; as, to *bowl* anyone over.—*n.* **bowler.**

bowl-der (bōl'dẽr), *n.* any detached and rounded or worn piece of rock. Also, **boulder.**

bow-leg (bō'lĕg), *n.* a crooked leg; a leg bowed or curved outward.—*adj.* **bowlegged.**

bow-line (bō'lĭn; bō'līn), *n.* a rope fastened near the middle of a square sail, to keep the ship nearer the wind; a knot; as, single, double, or running *bowline.*

bowl-ing (bōl'ĭng), *n.* the sport of playing at bowls; or the game itself: **bowling alley,** a place for playing bowls.

bow-man (bō'măn), *n.* [*pl.* bowmen (-mĕn)], an archer; (bou'măn), one who is rowing the foremost oar in a boat.

bow-sprit (bō'sprĭt; bou'sprĭt), *n.* a large spar running out from the forward end of a ship or other vessel.

bow-string (bō'strĭng"), *n.* the string of a bow; string used by the Turks for strangling criminals: *v.t.* [*p.t.* and *p.p.* bowstrung, *p.pr.* bowstringing], to strangle with a bowstring.

box (bŏks), *n.* [*pl.* boxes (-ĕz)], an evergreen shrub or small tree, yielding a hard, close-grained wood; a case or container with a bottom and sides, which has, or may have, a lid; the quantity such a case contains; the driver's seat on a carriage; a compartment in a theater or other public place; a place of shelter for a man on duty; as, a sentry *box;* a blow on the head with the fist, or on the ear with the open hand: *v.t.* to shut up in a box; to confine; to stow; to pack; to strike with the fist or hand: *v.i.* to fight with the fists; specifically, to spar with gloves.

box-er (bŏk'sẽr), *n.* a pugilist; one who fights with gloved fists; a box packer.—**Boxer,** a member of the Chinese society which in 1900 tried to rid China of all foreigners by massacre.

box-ing (bŏks'ĭng), *n.* the art of fighting with the fists, or sparring with boxing gloves; material used for making boxes.

box-wood (bŏks'wo͝od"), *n.* the hard, smooth wood of the box tree, used by engravers, etc.

boy (boi), *n.* a male child from birth to about sixteen years of age; a young lad; sometimes used familiarly, to refer to a man; a male servant, especially when, as in China, he is a slave or of an inferior race.

boy-cott (boi'kŏt), *v.t.* to exclude from all dealings or intercourse; to combine against (a person) so as to shut out from society, and prevent or hinder from carrying on business or a profession, as a means of punishment: *n.* a combination of persons to refuse to deal or associate with another; the act of so refusing.

boy-hood (boi'ho͝od), *n.* the state of being a boy; the time of being a boy.

boy-ish (boi'ĭsh), *adj.* pertaining to a boy or boyhood; childish; youthful; immature; young.

boy scout (boi skout), a member of an organization for training boys in character by nonmilitary methods, such as outdoor or camp life, civic service, etc.

brace (brās), *n.* that which holds anything tightly or supports it firmly; a prop; a bandage; a pair; as, a *brace* of pistols; a curve connecting two or more lines of print [{]; a curved instrument for holding and turning boring tools; a timber to strengthen the framework of a building: *pl.* the leathern bands clasping the cords at the side of a drum; shoulder-straps to support the trousers: *v.t.* to bind or tie closely; strengthen; furnish with supports; to stimulate: often with *up.*

brace-let (brās'lĕt), *n.* an ornamental band or ring for the wrist.

brac-er (brās'ẽr), *n.* that which supports; a tonic; a stimulant; a guard for the wrist.

bra-chi-um (brā'kĭ-ŭm), *n.* [*pl.* brachia (-ȧ)], the part of the arm from the shoulder to the elbow.—*adj.* **brachial.**

brac-ing (brās'ĭng), *p.adj.* giving strength or vigor; as, *bracing* air.

brack-en (brăk'n), *n.* any of various large ferns.

brack-et (brăk'ĕt), *n.* a supporting piece projecting from a wall; a single or jointed gas-pipe, burner, etc., projecting from a wall or pillar; one of two marks [ ], used to inclose a word or note, or to set something off from the rest of the text: *v.t.* to furnish with, or inclose within, brackets; connect by brackets; to couple together.

brack-ish (brăk'ĭsh), *adj.* salty; hence, distasteful; apt to make one sick.

brad (brăd), *n.* a small, slender nail, sometimes flat and having a projection on one side: *v.t.* [*p.t.* and *p.p.* bradded, *p.pr.* bradding], to nail or secure with brads.

brad-awl (brăd'ôl"), *n.* a straight awl having a chisel edge.

brae (brā; brē), *n.* a hillside; sloping ground. [Scot.]

brag (brăg), *v.t.* [*p.t.* and *p.p.* bragged, *p.pr.* bragging], to boast; to vaunt; speak boastingly of: *v.i.* to talk boastfully; to talk with swagger: *n.* boasting; a thing boasted of; one who boasts.—*n.* **bragger.**

brag-ga-do-ci-o (brăg"ȧ-dō'shĭ-ō), *n.* a boaster; a swaggerer; empty boasting; brag.

brag-gart (brăg'ȧrt), *n.* a boaster; a vain fellow: *adj.* boastful.

brah-ma (brä'mȧ; brā'mȧ), *n.* a useful variety of large domestic fowl.—**Brahma** (brä'mȧ), the first member of the trinity in Hindu religion; the Creator.

Brah-man (brä'măn), *n.* a Hindu of the highest, or the priestly, caste. Also, **Brahmin.**

Brah-man-ism (brä'măn-ĭzm), *n.* the religion or doctrines of the high caste Hindus. Also, **Brahminism.**

braid (brād), *v.t.* to weave, interlace, or intertwine; to plait; to trim or outline with braid: *n.* a plaited band; a narrow silk, wool, or cotton band used for trimming and binding clothing.

braille (brāl), *n.* a system of printing for the blind, invented by Louis Braille, in which points raised above the surface are used to represent letters, as ˙ a, .: c, . e, :: g, etc.; the symbols themselves.

brain (brān), *n.* the soft whitish mass of nerve tissue occupying the skull, forming the center of the nervous system; the seat of consciousness and will: hence, often in the plural, understanding; power of mind: *v.t.* to dash out the brains of; hence, to destroy.

brain-less (brān'lĕs), *adj.* without understanding; without wit.—*adv.* **brainlessly.**—*n.* **brainlessness.**

brain-pan (brān'păn"), the cranium; the part of the skull inclosing the brain.

brain-sick (brān'sĭk"), *adj.* disordered in the mind.—*n.* **brainsickness.**

brain-y (brān'ĭ), *adj.* possessed of understanding; acute; sharp-witted; powerful of mind.

braise (brāz), *v.t.* to stew or broil (as meat) in a covered vessel: *n.* meat thus cooked.

brake (brāk), *n.* an instrument or machine to separate the woody part of flax from the fiber; any long lever, as a pump handle; a baker's kneading trough; a sharp bit; a frame for holding unmanageable horses while shoeing; a kind of small wagon with high wheels; a heavy harrow for breaking clods of earth; a device for checking, by friction, the motion of a vehicle or machine, as a bicycle; a place overgrown with shrubs and brambles; the common fern: *v.t.* to crush in a brake; to stop by using a brake.

brake-man (brāk'măn), *n.* one who puts on the brakes or stops a railroad car, or acts as an assistant to the conductor. Also, **brakesman.**

brake shoe (brāk shōō), that part of a brake which presses against the wheel.

bram-ble (brăm'bl), *n.* the English blackberry; any prickly bush or shrub.—*adj.* **brambly.**

bran (brăn), *n.* the husks of wheat, rye, etc., separated from the flour by sifting or bolting.

branch (brănch), *n.* [*pl.* branches (-ĕz)], a shoot or limb from a main bough; any member or part of a body or system; a department; a division of a family descended from some particular ancestor; a section or subdivision: *adj.* turning aside from the trunk or main body; as, the Pennsylvania Railroad system includes many *branch* roads: *v.i.* to divide from the main body; to diverge: with *out*: *v.t.* to divide.

brand (brănd), *n.* a burning piece of wood; a mark burned with a hot iron, as upon cattle; any form of trademark; hence, any quality or any kind; a mark of disgrace: *v.t.* to mark with a hot iron, or by other means; hence, to mark as infamous.

brand-ed (brăn'dĕd), *p.adj.* marked with a brand; as, cattle are *branded* with the mark of their owner.

brand-ish (brăn'dĭsh), *v.t.* to move, wave, or shake, as a raised weapon; to flourish.

brand-new (brănd'nū'), *adj.* quite new. Also, **bran-new.**

bran-dy (brăn'dĭ), *n.* [*pl.* brandies (-dĭz)], an alcoholic liquor distilled from wine or the husks of grapes, or from other fruits.—*adj.* **brandied.**

brant (brănt), *n.* a small wild goose inhabiting the Northern Hemisphere.

bra-sier (brā'zhẽr), *n.* an open pan for burning charcoal; a person who works with brass. Also, **brazier.**

brass (brȧs), *n.* [*pl.* brasses (-ĕz)], an alloy made by mixing copper with zinc, or, sometimes, tin; a colloquial term meaning impudence: *pl.* instruments, vessels, ornaments, etc. made of a copper and zinc alloy, especially the brass wind instruments of a band.

bras-sard (brȧs'ärd), *n.* a badge worn on the arm as an insignia of rank, etc. Also, **brassart.**

bras-sie (brȧs'ĭ), *n.* in golf, a wooden club with a brass hole. Also, **brassy.**

bras-sière (brȧ'syâr'), *n.* an underwaist worn by women. [Fr.]

brass-y (brȧs'ĭ), *adj.* made of, or like, brass; impudent; brazen: *n.* a club used in the game of golf.—*adv.* **brassily.**

brat (brăt), *n.* a child: used contemptuously.

bra-va-do (brȧ-vä'dō; brȧ-vā'dō), *n.* bragging pretense of courage or indifference; boastful defiance.

brave (brāv), *adj.* bold; courageous; fearless; making a fine show; as, *brave* attire: *n.* an Indian warrior: *v.t.* to meet with courage; as, a soldier must *brave* dangers and hardships; to challenge.—*adv.* **bravely.**

Syn., adj. bold: *v.* dare, defy.
Ant. (see afraid).

brav-er-y (brāv'ẽr-ĭ), *n.* the quality of being fearless; gallantry; heroism; bright show.

Syn. courage, valor.
Ant. (see cowardice).

bra-vo (brä'vō), *interj.* well done! good! *n.* [*pl.* bravos, bravoes (-vōz)], a shout of applause; a hired assassin; a bandit.

brawl (brôl), *n.* a noisy quarrel: *v.i.* to quarrel or wrangle noisily; make a loud noise, as of water rushing over a rocky bed.

brawn (brôn), *n.* firm, strong muscles, especially of the arm or leg; muscular strength; boar's flesh, especially when prepared by boiling and pickling.

brawn-y (brôn'ĭ), *adj.* muscular; strong; as, the blacksmith has a *brawny* arm.—*n.* **brawniness.**

bray (brā), *n.* a loud, harsh cry or sound; as, the *bray* of a donkey; the *bray* of trumpets: *v.t.* [*p.t.* and *p.p.* brayed, *p.pr.* braying], to pound or beat fine or small; to utter in a loud, harsh way: *v.i.* to utter a loud, harsh cry, as the ass.

braze (brāz), *v.t.* to join with hard solder, especially with an alloy of zinc and copper; to make of, or ornament with, brass.

bra-zen (brā'zn), *adj.* made of brass; resembling brass; impudent; shameless.—*adv.* **brazenly.**—*n.* **brazenness.**

bra-zier (brā'zhẽr), *n.* an open pan for burning charcoal; also, a cast iron pot used as a dugout stove; one who works in brass. Also, **brasier.**

Bra-zil nut (brȧ-zĭl' nŭt), an edible nut, the seed of a South American tree.

breach (brēch), *n.* the act of making an opening or separation; the breaking of a law, a contract, or any other obligation; a gap; a rupture of friendly relations; a quarrel: *v.t.* to make an opening in.

bread (brĕd), *n.* dough made from the flour or meal of some kind of grain and baked; food in general; as, he works hard for his daily *bread*: *v.t.* to cover with bread crumbs before cooking.

bread-fruit (brĕd'frōōt''), *n.* the fruit of a tree native to the Pacific islands: when roasted, somewhat like bread.

bread-stuff (brĕd'stŭf''), *n.* any material, such as corn, flour, meal, from which bread is made.

breadth (brĕdth), *n.* the measure of any surface from side to side; freedom from narrowness; broad effect; liberality; a piece of fabric of uniform width; as, two *breadths* of cloth are needed for a skirt.

break (brāk), *v.t.* [*p.t.* broke, *p.p.* broken, *p.pr.* breaking], to separate into parts or pieces by a blow or strain; to force open; as, to *break* open a door; to interrupt or disconnect; as, to *break* silence; to *break* ranks; to fracture, as a bone; weaken or destroy; as, to *break* a fall; to *break* pride; to scatter: with *up;* as, to *break* up a party; to set aside or fail to obey, as a promise or a law; to degrade, as an officer to the ranks; to tell cautiously or to inform; as, to *break* bad news; tame or subdue, as a horse; to plow or dig up; as, to *break* ground: *v.i.* to separate into parts or pieces suddenly or violently; to begin or change suddenly; to fail, as in health, strength, credit, etc.; to burst; to burst forth violently, as a storm; to be scattered, as clouds; to cease to be friendly (with): *n.* an opening; an open place; an interruption; a first appearance or marked change; as, the *break* of day; a pause; a sudden fall in prices; as, a *break* in the stock market; an abrupt change in the musical quality of a tone; as, a *break* in a boy soprano's voice.

Syn. v. bruise, crush, pound.

Ant. (see bind).

break-age (brāk'āj), *n.* the act of breaking; state of being broken; allowance for things broken by accident.

break-down (brāk'doun"), *n.* a physical collapse; failure; downfall; a noisy, shuffling dance, sometimes accompanied by singing.

break-er (brāk'ẽr), *n.* one who, or that which, separates by force; a machine to crush coal, rocks, etc.; a wave dashing itself into foam upon the shore or against a rock: usually in plural.

break-fast (brĕk'fast), *n.* the first meal in the day: *v.t.* to provide with, or entertain at, the morning meal: *v.i.* to eat the morning meal.

break-neck (brāk'nĕk"), *adj.* dangerously fast; causing risk of life.

break-wa-ter (brāk'wô"tẽr), *n.* any structure built to exhaust the force of the waves, and protect shipping, as a seawall.

bream (brēm), *n.* a broad-shaped, freshwater European fish of the carp family: *v.t.* to clear, as a ship's bottom, of shells, seaweed, etc., by fire.

breast (brĕst), *n.* the fore part of the body between the neck and the abdomen; one of the glands in women, and some other mammals, for the secretion of milk; the front of anything; figuratively, the affections; the conscience: *v.t.* to present the front to; meet or oppose manfully or openly; as, to *breast* a storm of opposition.

breast-bone (brĕst'bōn"), *n.* a bone in the front part of the chest to which some of the ribs are joined.

breast-pin (brĕst'pĭn"), *n.* an ornamental pin worn on the front of a waist.

breast-plate (brĕst'plāt"), *n.* a portion of armor covering the front of the body; a square ornament worn by the Jewish high priest, bearing twelve precious stones engraved with the names of the twelve tribes of Israel.

breast-work (brĕst'wûrk"), *n.* a hastily constructed defensive wall or parapet of moderate height.

breath (brĕth), *n.* the air drawn in and forced out of the lungs; a single act of drawing in or forcing out air; as, to take a long *breath;* the power to use the lungs freely; as, to lose one's *breath;* life; a pause; an instant; air in gentle motion; a mere word; fragrance; as, the garden is sweet with the *breath* of flowers.

breathe (brēth), *v.i.* to draw air into the lungs and force it out again; to be alive; to rest from action; to exhale; as, perfume *breathes* from flowers; to blow softly: *v.t.* to draw into and force out of the lungs, as air; to give forth; as, the flower *breathes* perfume; to express; to whisper softly; as, to *breathe* a secret; to infuse; as, to *breathe* courage into.

breath-ing (brēth'ĭng), *n.* the act of drawing in air to the lungs and forcing it out again; air in gentle motion; a gentle influence; eager desire.

breath-less (brĕth'lĕs), *adj.* spent with action, or out of breath; without breath, or dead; holding the breath; as, *breathless* with fear; eager; excited; as, *breathless* attention.

breech (brēch), *n.* the hinder part of anything; the part of a cannon or other firearm behind the part which contains the powder: *v.t.* to put into breeches; to whip on the breech, or buttocks; to fasten (a cannon on shipboard) by a rope.

breech-es (brĭch'ĕz), *n.pl.* a garment worn by men, covering the legs from the knees to the hips; less properly, trousers or pantaloons.

breech-es buoy (brĭch'ĕz boi), a life-saving device consisting of short-legged canvas breeches attached below a cork ring, by which persons can be hauled along a rope from a wrecked vessel to the shore.

breech-ing (brĭch'ĭng; brēch'ĭng), *n.* the harness which passes round the hind part of a horse's body; in gunnery, on board a ship, a strong rope fastened to a cannon and to rings in the ship's side to prevent the gun from rolling.

breech-load-er (brēch'lōd"ẽr), *n.* a firearm loaded at the back instead of at the muzzle.—*adj.* **breech-loading.**

breed (brēd), *v.t.* [*p.t.* and *p.p.* bred, *p.pr.* breeding], to hatch; to produce or cause; to train; to rear: *v.i.* to bear young; to be fruitful; to come into being: *n.* a race or offspring from the same parents or stock; as, horses or cattle of good *breed;* a class or kind.—*n.* **breeder.**

breed-ing (brēd'ĭng), *n.* the process of producing, especially of producing young; the bringing up or training of the young; polite and courteous manners; good behavior; as, a person of good *breeding.*

breeze (brēz), *n.* a fresh soft wind; a moderately brisk wind not so strong as a gale; as, a stiff *breeze;* a slight excitement or disturbance; house sweepings; sifted ashes and cinders used in burning bricks; fine coal or coke; a gadfly or horsefly; a breeze-fly.

breez-y (brēz'ĭ), *adj.* airy; fresh; brisk; vivacious; as, a *breezy* manner.

breth-ren (brĕth'rĕn), *n.* plural of *brother:* used in solemn address and to the members of religious orders.

Bret-on (brĕt'ŭn; brĭt'ŭn), *n.* a native of Brittany, a district in northwestern France; the native language of Brittany: *adj.* relating to Brittany.

breve (brēv), *n.* in music, a note of time; a mark [˘] used to indicate a short vowel.

bre-vet (brē-vĕt'; brĕv'ĕt), *n.* an official note to an officer in the army giving him a higher nominal rank, but without change of duty or increase of pay; thus, a *brevet* major serves as captain and receives pay as such: *v.t.* [*p.t.* and *p.p.* brevetted, *p.pr.* brevetting], to confer brevet rank upon: *adj.* conferred by brevet.

bre-vi-a-ry (brē'vĭ-ā-rĭ), *n.* [*pl.* breviaries (-rĭz)], a book containing the daily service and prayers of the Roman Catholic Church.

brev-i-ty (brĕv'ĭ-tĭ), *n.* [*pl.* brevities (-tĭz)], shortness in speech, writing, or style; conciseness.

brew (brōō), *v.t.* to make liquors from malt or other materials; to plot; as, to *brew* mischief: *v.i.* to be in preparation; as, a storm is *brewing*: *n.* the process of making liquor from malt; a particular brand or make of malt liquor.—*n.* **brewer.**

brew-er-y (brōō'ēr-ĭ), *n.* the house and apparatus where beer or other liquors are made from malt, etc. Also, **brewhouse.**

brew-ing (brōō'ĭng), *n.* the making of beer and other malt liquors; all the liquor made at one time.

bri-ar (brī'ēr), *n.* any plant with a woody stem bearing thorns or prickles; as, the *briar* rose, the blackberry *briars.* Also, **brier.**

bri-ar root (brī'ēr rōōt), the root of the white heath, used in making tobacco pipes. Also, **brier root.**

bribe (brīb), *n.* a sum of money or other gift given or promised with the object of causing him who receives it to decide a cause or do some act against what he believes to be truth, justice, or uprightness; as, an ignorant Mexican will sell his vote for so small a *bribe* as a drink of liquor: *v.t.* to influence by a gift of money: *v.i.* to give or offer money in order to influence another.—*n.* **briber.**

brib-er-y (brīb'ēr-ĭ), *n.* [*pl.* briberies (-ĭz)], the act or practice of buying another's influence or action, or of corrupting another.

bric-à-brac (brĭk'ȧ-brăk"), *n.* rare or antique articles, as plate or china; knickknacks; ornaments which are pretty or odd; articles with no real value: sometimes used contemptuously.

brick (brĭk), *n.* an oblong block of clay dried in the sun or burned in a kiln: *adj.* made of, or resembling, brick: *v.t.* to lay or build with bricks; to place in brickwork; to surround, close, or wall in, with bricks.

brick-bat (brĭk'băt"), *n.* a piece or fragment of a brick, especially one used as a missile.

brick-kiln (brĭk'kĭl"), *n.* a furnace in which bricks are baked or burnt.

brick-lay-er (brĭk'lā-ēr), *n.* one whose occupation is the laying of bricks in buildings, walls, etc.—*n.* **bricklaying.**

bri-cole (brĭ-kōl'; brĭk'ŭl), *n.* harness worn by men for dragging guns or loads.

brid-al (brīd'ăl), *n.* a marriage: *adj.* pertaining to a bride or wedding; nuptial.

bride (brīd), *n.* a woman newly married, or about to be married.

bride-groom (brīd'grōōm"), *n.* a man newly married, or about to be married.

brides-maid (brīdz'măd"), *n.* a young unmarried woman who attends a bride at her wedding.

bride-well (brīd'wĕl), *n.* a house of correction for the confinement of disorderly persons.

bridge (brĭj), *n.* a structure of iron, stone, or wood, built across a river, road, valley, etc.; anything resembling a bridge in form or use, as the upper bony part of the nose, or the arch for the strings on a violin; a game of cards, first known as bridge-whist; the platform above the deck of a ship used as an observation station by the officer in charge: *v.t.* to build a bridge over; span; find a way of overcoming.

bridge-board (brĭj'bōrd"), *n.* a notched board into which the ends of the steps of wooden stairs are fastened. Also, **notch board.**

bridge-head (brĭj'hĕd"), *n.* a fortified position or group of military works intended to protect one or more bridges or the crossing of a river.

bridge train (brĭj' trān"), a portion of an army with its equipment that constructs temporary bridges by which to cross a river; a pontoon train.

bridg-ing (brĭj'ĭng), *n.* a piece of wood between two beams to keep them apart.

bri-dle (brī'dl), *n.* the headstall, bit, and reins by which a horse is managed; a restraint: *v.t.* to put a bit and reins on; to control; to guide: *v.i.* to hold the head up, or toss it, as a sign of pride, scorn, or anger.

bri-dle path (brī'dl pȧth), a path only wide enough for horsemen or pack animals to pass one at a time.

brief (brēf), *adj.* short; concise; condensed: *n.* a short statement of a case for the instruction of a lawyer: *v.t.* to shorten; to make a shortened statement of.—*adv.* **briefly.**—*n.* **briefness.**

brief-less (brēf'lĕs), *adj.* having no clients; as, a *briefless* lawyer.

bri-er (brī'ēr), *n.* a thorny plant or shrub; a brierwood pipe. Also, **briar.**

gade, and ranking next below a major general. Also, **brigadier general.**

brig-and (brĭg'ănd), *n.* a robber; a member of a gang of robbers, often living in mountainous districts; a highwayman.

brig-and-age (brĭg'ăn-dāj), *n.* the life and practices of a robber or outlaw; organized robbery; as, the Doones, a band of English outlaws, lived by *brigandage.*

brig-an-tine (brĭg'ăn-tēn; brĭg'ăn-tĭn), *n.* a small, two-masted square-rigged vessel differing from a brig in not carrying a square mainsail.

bright (brīt), *adj.* [*comp.* brighter, *superl.* brightest], showing light; brilliant; shining; sparkling; glorious; witty; clever; lively; fortunate; glowing.—*adv.* **brightly.**—*n.* **brightness.**

bright-en (brit'n), *v.i.* to grow clearer, lighter, or more radiant; as, the day *brightens*: *v.t.* to make light or shining; to make gay or cheerful; as, to *brighten* the neighborhood.

Bright's dis-ease (brits' dĭ-zēz'), any of several forms of kidney disease, marked by the persistent presence of albumen in the urine, and attended by disintegration and wasting of the organ: so named from Dr. Richard Bright, of London.

brill (bril), *n.* a European flat fish resembling the turbot.

brim (brim), *n.* the edge or margin of anything, as a fountain, the rim of a hat, etc.: *v.t.* [*p.t.* and *p.p.* brimmed, *p.pr.* brimming], to fill to the upper edge of: *v.i.* to be full to the very top or edge.

brim-ful (brim'fōōl"), *adj.* full to the edge; completely filled.

brim-stone (brim'stōn), *n.* sulphur: *adj.* made of sulphur; of the yellow color of sulphur.

brin-dled (brin'dld), *adj.* of a gray or dark yellow color, with spots or streaks; as, a *brindled* cat.

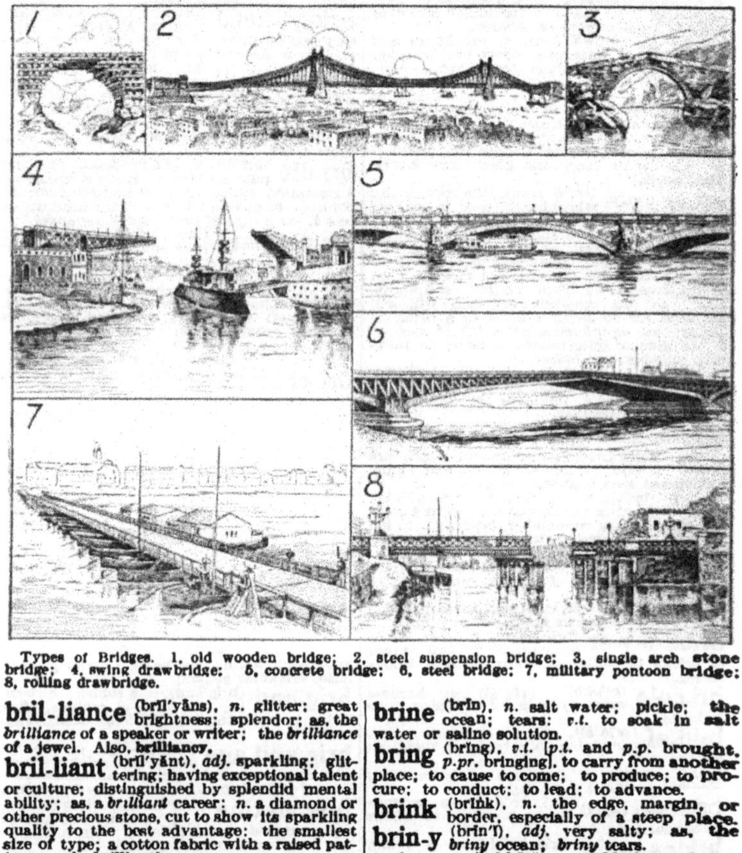

Types of Bridges. 1, old wooden bridge; 2, steel suspension bridge; 3, single arch stone bridge; 4, swing drawbridge; 5, concrete bridge; 6, steel bridge; 7, military pontoon bridge; 8, rolling drawbridge.

bril-liance (bril'yāns), *n.* glitter; great brightness; splendor; as, the *brilliance* of a speaker or writer; the *brilliance* of a jewel. Also, **brilliancy.**

bril-liant (bril'yānt), *adj.* sparkling; glittering; having exceptional talent or culture; distinguished by splendid mental ability; as, a *brilliant* career: *n.* a diamond or other precious stone, cut to show its sparkling quality to the best advantage; the smallest size of type; a cotton fabric with a raised pattern.—*adv.* **brilliantly.**

bril-lian-tine (bril'yān-tēn), *n.* a mixture for giving a smooth, shining appearance to the hair; a dress material of fine quality somewhat like alpaca.

brine (brin), *n.* salt water; pickle; the ocean; tears: *v.t.* to soak in salt water or saline solution.

bring (bring), *v.t.* [*p.t.* and *p.p.* brought, *p.pr.* bringing], to carry from another place; to cause to come; to produce; to procure; to conduct; to lead; to advance.

brink (brink), *n.* the edge, margin, or border, especially of a steep place.

brin-y (brin'ĭ), *adj.* very salty; as, the *briny* ocean; *briny* tears.

bri-quet (bri-kĕt'), *n.* a block or brick made of coal dust and used as fuel. Also, **briquette.**

bri-quet (bri-kā'), *n.* a steel (for striking a light); a tinder box. [FR.]

brisk (brisk), *adj.* lively; animated; active; swift; sparkling; nimble; burning freely; as, a *brisk* fire; rapid; quick: *v.t.* and *v.i.* to make or become lively, swift, etc.: generally with *up.*—*adv.* **briskly.**

brisk-ness (brisk'nĕs), *n.* the state of being lively, quick, etc.

bris-ket (bris'kĕt), *n.* that part of an animal's breast where the ribs join the breast-bone.

bris-tle (bris'l), *n.* a short, stiff, coarse hair, especially upon the back and sides of pigs; any stiff, sharp hair: *v.t.* to cause to stand up in a stiff, prickly way; to furnish with bristles, as a brush: *v.i.* to stand up in a stiff, prickly way; to be covered with, or full of, sharp points; as, the battle front *bristles* with bayonets; to become angry; as, to *bristle* up at an insulting remark.

bris-tly (bris'lĭ), *adj.* covered with stiff, sharp hair; rough.

bris-tol board (bris'tŭl bōrd), a thick, smooth, white cardboard.

bris-tol pa-per (bris'tŭl pā'pĕr), a kind of stout drawing paper.

brit (brit), *n.* the young of the herring and sprat; small animals upon which whales feed.

Bri-tan-ni-a (brĭ-tăn'ĭ-ȧ), *n.* the United Kingdom of Great Britain and Ireland; the female figure symbolizing it.

Bri-tan-ni-a met-al (brĭ-tăn'ĭ-ȧ mĕt'-ăl), a white metal mixture of tin, copper, antimony, and bismuth.

Brit-ish (brit'ĭsh), *adj.* of or relating to Great Britain or its inhabitants; relating to the ancient Britons.

Brit-on (brit'ŭn), *n.* a native of Great Britain.

brit-tle (brit'l), *adj.* easily broken; fragile; breakable; not tough.—*n.* **brittleness.**

broach (brōch), *n.* a spike; a skewer; any boring tool; a stonecutter's chisel: *v.t.* to tap or pierce, as a keg of wine; to begin a discussion about; as, it is difficult to *broach* an unpleasant subject.

broad (brôd), *adj.* [*comp.* broader, *superl.* broadest], wide; ample; vast; liberal; as, *broad* opinions; widely distributed; open; clear; unrestrained; evident; bold; as, a *broad* hint; indelicate.—*adv.* **broadly.**

broad ar-row (brôd ăr'ō), a mark by which the British government distinguishes its property.

broad-ax (brôd'ăks"), *n.* an ax for cutting timber; an ancient military weapon. Also, **broadaxe.**

broad-brim (brôd'brĭm), *n.* a hat like those worn by Friends, or Quakers; a name applied in jest to a Friend, or Quaker.

broad-cast (brôd'kăst"), *v.t.* to scatter or throw by hand in all directions, as seed: *adj.* scattered far and wide; widely suffused: *adv.* so as to scatter widely; as, to sow seeds *broadcast:* *n.* a casting or scattering of seed far and wide.

broad-cloth (brôd'klŏth), *n.* a fine woolen cloth with a smooth finished surface, usually of double width.

broad-en (brôd'n), *v.i.* to grow wide or wider: *v.t.* to make wider.

broad-piece (brôd-pēs), *n.* an old English coin broader than a guinea.

broad seal (brôd' sēl"), the public seal of a country, especially the great seal of England.

broad-side (brôd'sīd"), *n.* the entire side of a ship above the water-line; shots from all the cannon at once on one side of a warship; a sheet printed on one side only, and containing information of a popular character; a printed or verbal attack on some public person: *adv.* with the side turned or exposed.

broad-sword (brôd'sōrd"), *n.* a sword with a wide cutting blade.

Brob-ding-nag-i-an (brŏb"dĭng-năg'-ĭ-ăn), *adj.* resembling an inhabitant of the fabled country of Brobdingnag in Swift's *Gulliver's Travels;* hence, colossal; gigantic: *n.* a giant.

bro-cade (brō-kād'), *n.* a rich silken material woven with gold and silver threads, or ornamented with raised figures in silk or velvet, in designs of flowers, fruits, etc.: *v.t.* to decorate with a raised pattern.—*p.adj.* **brocaded.**

broc-a-tel (brŏk'ȧ-tĕl), *n.* a material made of silk and wool, silk and cotton, or pure wool with a silky surface; a colored marble obtained from Italy and Spain. Also, **brocatelle.**

broc-co-li (brŏk'kō-lĭ), *n.* a variety of the common cabbage closely resembling cauliflower.

bro-chure (brō-shŏŏr"), *n.* a booklet dealing with a subject of passing interest.

bro-gan (brō'găn), *n.* a coarse, heavy shoe laced or buckled over the instep.

brogue (brōg), *n.* a coarse, rough shoe; a pronunciation of English used in a certain section of a country, especially that common in Ireland.

broil (broil), *v.t.* to cook directly over a hot fire, as on a gridiron or a fork: *v.i.* to be exposed to great heat; to be heated by excitement: *n.* a noisy quarrel; as, a street *broil;* a brawl.

broil-er (broil'ĕr), *n.* a utensil for cooking food directly over the fire; a bird suitable to be so cooked; a person who quarrels noisily.

broke (brōk), past tense and past participle of the verb *break.*

bro-ken (brō'kn), *p.adj.* not entire; in pieces; rough; hilly; as, *broken* country; transgressed; as, a *broken* law; bankrupt; crushed; infirm; imperfect; interrupted; as, *broken* sleep; trained to obedience: used especially of a horse.

bro-ken-heart-ed (brō'kn-härt'ĕd), *adj.* overcome by grief and misery; not to be comforted.

bro-ker (brō'kĕr), *n.* a dealer in drafts, notes, money, stocks, etc.; one who acts as agent to transact business for another.

bro-ker-age (brō'kĕr-āj), *n.* the business of a broker; his fee or commission.

bro-mide (brō'mīd; brō'mĭd), *n.* a compound of bromine and some other drug; a drug with a soothing effect; a person who thinks and talks in platitudes; a platitude; a commonplace person or remark: **bromide of potassium,** a compound of bromine, used largely in medicine to relieve pain. Also, **bromid.**—*adj.* **bromidic.**

bro-mine (brō'mĭn; brō'mēn), *n.* a substance related to chlorine and iodine; a reddish-brown element with a disagreeable odor. Also, **bromin.**

bron-chi (brŏn'kī), *n. pl.* the two principal branches of the windpipe or trachea.—*sing.* **bronchus.**

bron-chi-a (brŏn'kĭ-ȧ), *n.pl.* the tiny tubes into which the windpipe divides in the lungs.

bron-chi-al (brŏn'kĭ-ăl), *adj.* of or pertaining to the small tubes in the lungs.

bron-chi-tis (brŏn-kī'tĭs), *n.* an inflammation of the mucous lining of the bronchial tubes, accompanied by coughing.

bron-cho (brŏn'kō), *n.* a small, hardy Indian pony or mustang, especially one that is unbroken or imperfectly broken. Also, **bronco.**

bron-chus (brŏn'kŭs), *n.* [*pl.* bronchi (-kī)], one of the two principal branches of the windpipe or trachea.

bronze (brŏnz), *n.* an alloy of copper and tin, to which other metallic substances, especially zinc, are sometimes added; a work of art cast or wrought in this alloy; a yellowish or reddish brown, the color of bronze: *adj.* made of, or resembling, bronze: *v.t.* to make of the color of bronze; tan by exposure to the sun; apply bronze color to.

bronze age (brŏnz āj), the age following the stone age, the ornaments and weapons of that period being made of bronze.

bronz-ine (brŏn'zĭn), *n.* a metal resembling bronze.

brooch (brōch; brōōch), *n.* an ornamental pin used for fastening the dress, etc.; a breastpin.

brood (brōōd), *n.* offspring; the young birds hatched at one time: *v.i.* to sit on eggs, as a hen; linger over sorrowfully: with *on* or *over*: *v.t.* to sit over, cover, and cherish; as, to *brood* eggs.

brook (brōōk), *n.* a small, natural stream of water: *v.t.* to bear; to tolerate; to put up with; as, I cannot *brook* your insolence.

brook-let (brōōk'lĕt), *n.* a little brook; a rill or rivulet.

broom (brōōm), *n.* a stiff brush used for sweeping floors, etc., originally made from twigs of the broom-plant; a shrub, bearing large yellow flowers.

broom-corn (brōōm'kôrn'), *n.* a species of sorghum, with a jointed stem, growing eight to ten feet high, used in making brooms.

broom-stick (brōōm'stĭk'), *n.* the handle of a broom.

broth (brŏth), *n.* a kind of thin soup made by cooking meat slowly in water, sometimes with vegetables.

broth-er (brŭth'ẽr), *n.* [*pl.* brothers (-ẽrz), and brethren (brĕth'rĕn)], a male who has the same father and mother as another; one closely united to another by a common interest; a member of a religious order; a fellow creature.

broth-er-hood (brŭth'ẽr-hōōd), *n.* the state or quality of being a brother; an association of men for any purpose; as, the various orders of monks are religious *brotherhoods*; a fraternity.

broth-er-in-law (brŭth'ẽr-ĭn-lô'), *n.* the brother of one's husband or wife; one's sister's husband.

Broth-er Jon-a-than (brŭth'ẽr jŏn'ȧ-thăn), a humorous imaginary character representing New England, or, more broadly, the United States.

broth-er-ly (brŭth'ẽr-lĭ), *adj.* becoming to, or like, a brother; as, *brotherly* love; affectionate; kind: *adv.* in a way suitable to a brother.—*n.* **brotherliness.**

brough-am (brōō'ŭm; brōōm; brō'ŭm), *n.* a close four-wheeled carriage for one or two horses.

Brougham

brought (brôt), *p.t.* and *p.p.* of the verb *bring.*

brow (brou), *n.* the forehead; the arch of hair over the eye; the edge of a steep place; the upper portion of a hill.

brow-beat (brou'bēt'), *v.t.* [*p.t.* browbeat, *p.p.* browbeaten, *p.pr.* browbeating], to depress or bear down with haughty, stern, or impudent looks or words.

brown (broun), *adj.* of a dusky or dark color: *n.* a dark color between black and red or yellow: *v.i.* to become brown: *v.t.* to make brown.

brown-ie (broun'ĭ), *n.* a good-natured elf supposed to haunt old farmhouses and perform certain services, such as churning, etc. [Scot.]

brown-stone (broun'stōn'), *n.* a dark kind of sandstone.

browse (brouz), *n.* the tender shoots or twigs of shrubs and trees fit for the food of cattle and other animals: *v.t.* to feed on; to pasture; to graze, as cattle, deer, etc.: *v.i.* to eat or nibble off twigs or buds; to graze.

bru-in (brōō'ĭn), *n.* a common name for the brown bear: so called in popular tales.

bruise (brōōz), *n.* an injury to the flesh of an animal, or to a plant or other body, caused by a blow, but causing no breaking of the skin, etc.: *v.t.* to injure, crush, or indent by a blow or pressure without cutting; to crush by beating or pounding: *v.i.* to fight with the fists; box.

bruis-er (brōōz'ẽr), *n.* a boxer; a pugilist; as, these men were mighty *bruisers* at close quarters; a machine for crushing grain, etc.

bruit (brōōt), *n.* report, rumor; fame: *v.t.* to report; spread abroad.

bru-nette (brōō-nĕt'), *n.* a girl or woman with a brown or dark complexion, usually with dark hair and eyes: *adj.* having such coloring. Also, **brunet.**

brunt (brŭnt), *n.* the heaviest part or utmost violence of a shock, strain, or attack; as, the President of the United States bears the *brunt* of responsibility in international affairs.

brush (brŭsh), *n.* an implement made of bristles, feathers, or other material fixed in a back or handle and used for cleaning, smoothing, applying paint, etc.; the bushy tail of a fox; a thicket of small trees; the small trees and shrubs of a wood; a slight battle; a skirmish; the act of cleaning or smoothing with a brush; thin metallic plates or wires bound together, to conduct a current to or from an electric motor, etc.: *v.t.* to sweep, cleanse, or rub with a brush; touch lightly in passing: *v.i.* to move with haste; to skim over with a light touch.—*adj.* **brushy.**

brush hook (brŭsh hōōk), a hook for cutting small trees and shrubs.

brush-wood (brŭsh'wōōd), *n.* rough, close bushes; a thicket; small wood, suitable for the fire.

brusk (brŭsk), *adj.* blunt: abrupt in manner. Also, **brusque.**

brusk-ness (brŭsk'nĕs), *n.* abruptness; blunt manner. Also, **brusqueness.**

Brus-sels car-pet (brŭs'ĕlz kär'pĕt), a strong kind of woolen carpet.

Brus-sels lace (brŭs'ĕlz lās), various kinds of costly lace, made originally at Brussels.

Brus-sels sprouts (brŭs'ĕlz sprouts), a vegetable consisting of small green heads, each a tiny cabbage, of two or three inches diameter.

bru-tal (broo'tăl), *adj.* savage; cruel; inhuman; unfeeling; rude; coarse. —*adv.* **brutally.**

bru-tal-i-ty (broo-tăl'ĭ-tĭ), *n.* pitiless cruelty; savageness; inhumanity; a savage act.

bru-tal-ize (broo'tăl-īz), *v.t.* to make cruel or inhuman; as, war tends to *brutalize* men.

brute (broot), *adj.* inhuman; without reason or intelligence; irrational; unthinking; soulless; rough; uncivilized: *n.* a beast; an inhuman person; as, a lazy, sensual *brute.*

brut-ish (broot'ĭsh), *adj.* savage; stupid; coarse.—*n.* **brutishness.**
Syn. base, sensual, sottish, vile, bestial.
Ant. (see refined).

bub-ble (bŭb'l), *n.* a small globe of water or other fluid filled with air or gas; a small body of air or gas rising to the surface of a liquid; anything unreal or fanciful, as an empty scheme to deceive people into investing their money without offering anything of value in exchange: *v.i.* to rise in bubbles; run with a gurgling sound.

buc-ca-neer (bŭk'ă-nēr'), *n.* a pirate; a sea robber; one of the pirates who, during the 17th century, made raids on the Spaniards in America.

bu-cen-taur (bū-sĕn'tôr), *n.* an imaginary monster, half man and half bull; the state barge of Venice used by the doges, or former rulers, in the annual ceremony of wedding the city to the Adriatic.

buck (bŭk), *n.* the male of the fallow deer, goat, rabbit, hare, etc.; a gay fellow; a male Indian or negro: *v.i.* to spring with a quick plunging leap: said of a horse: *v.t.* to throw by a quick plunging leap.

buck-board (bŭk'bōrd'), *n.* a light wagon in which the body and springs are replaced by a long, elastic board.

buck-et (bŭk'ĕt), *n.* a vessel for drawing or holding water, etc.; the scoop of a dredging machine or of a grain elevator.

buck-et shop (bŭk'ĕt shŏp), an office for gambling in stocks, grain, etc., in small amounts, by going through the forms of buying and selling with no actual purchases or sales.

buck-eye (bŭk'ī'), *n.* the American horse-chestnut tree; a native of Ohio, the Buckeye State.

buck-le (bŭk'l), *n.* a metal clasp consisting of a frame with movable tongue or catch, used for securing straps, bands, etc.; a bend, or kink, in metal, as in a saw blade: *v.t.* to fasten with a buckle; confine; join together: *v.i.* to prepare for action; to set to work with energy; as, to *buckle* down to hard work; to shrivel or bend under application of heat.

buck-ler (bŭk'lẽr), *n.* a kind of ancient shield, composed of wood or wicker, covered with skin or leather, strengthened with plates of brass or other metal, and worn on the left arm.

buck-ram (bŭk'răm), *n.* coarse cloth of linen, cotton, or hemp stiffened with glue: *adj.* made of, or resembling, such cloth; hence, stiff; precise.

buck-saw (bŭk'sô'), *n.* a saw set in a frame and worked with both hands.

buck-shot (bŭk'shŏt'), *n.* shot of large size: so called from its use in shooting deer.

buck-skin (bŭk'skĭn'), *n.* a soft grayish-yellow leather made from the skin of a deer or, usually, of a sheep; clothes made of such skin: *adj.* made of such skin.

buck-wheat (bŭk'hwēt'), *n.* a plant cultivated for its triangular seeds, which are ground into meal and used for food; the flour made from the seeds.

bu-col-ic (bū-kŏl'ĭk), *adj.* pastoral; rustic; relating to country affairs and to a shepherd's life and occupation: *n.* a poem which deals with such matters.

bud (bŭd), *n.* the early stage of a branch, leaf, or flower; a young girl in her first season in society: *v.t.* [*p.t.* and *p.p.* budded, *p.pr.* budding], to graft: *v.i.* to put forth or produce new shoots; begin to grow; to sprout; to be like a young flower in youth and freshness, as a *budding* virgin.

Bud-dha (bŏŏd'ȧ), *n.* Gautama Siddhartha, the founder of Buddhism, a religion of East Asia.

Bud-dhism (bŏŏd'ĭzm), *n.* a religion of Eastern Asia, named for its founder, which teaches self-denial, virtue, and wisdom.

Bud-dhist (bŏŏd'ĭst), *n.* one who accepts the doctrines of Buddhism: *adj.* pertaining to Buddha or Buddhism.

budge (bŭj), *v.i.* to move from one's position; to stir: *v.t.* to change the position of: *n.* lambskin dressed like fur and used for linings and edgings.

budg-et (bŭj'ĕt), *n.* a bag with its contents; hence, a quantity or store; as, a *budget* of news; the annual statement of the financial needs for the year to come of a nation or organization.

buff (bŭf), *n.* a thick leather prepared from the skin of the buffalo, ox, etc., dressed with oil; a pale or faded yellowish orange; the bare skin: *adj.* made of thick oiled leather; of a pale yellow color.

buf-fa-lo (bŭf'ȧ-lō), *n.* [*pl.* buffaloes (-lōz)], an animal of the ox family; a name given to various wild oxen, such as the North American bison, the East Indian water buffalo, and the South African Cape buffalo.

buff-er (bŭf'ẽr), *n.* any device which serves to deaden the shock caused by the striking together of two bodies; as, a *buffer* is placed at each end of a railway car to lessen the jar when two cars come together.

buf-fet (bŭf'ĕt), *n.* a blow with the hand; any blow: *v.t.* to strike with the hand or fist; to box; to beat; to struggle against; as, to *buffet* the waves: *v.i.* to fight with blows; to force one's way; as, to *buffet* with wind and waves.

buf-fet (bŏŏ-fā'), *n.* a sideboard with shelves for the display of china or silverware; a counter for refreshments. [Fr.]

buf-fo (bōōf'ō), *n.* the comic actor in an opera: *adj.* comic. [It.]

buf-foon (bŭ-fōōn'), *n.* one who amuses others by low jests, antics, odd gestures, etc., as a clown.

buf-foon-er-y (bŭ-fōōn'ẽr-ĭ), *n.* [*pl.* buffooneries (-ĭz)], the arts and practices of a clown or low comedian; vulgar tricks.

bug (bŭg), *n.* an insect, especially a beetle or other crawling insect.

bug-a-boo (bŭg'ȧ-bōō"), *n.* a fancied cause of fear; a fearful object.

bug-bear (bŭg'bâr"), *n.* a frightful object; an object of dislike or terror.

bug-gy (bŭg'ĭ), *n.* a light four-wheeled carriage: *adj.* infested with bugs.

bu-gle (bū'gl), *n.* a hunting horn; a military instrument of music; an oblong glass bead of various colors, but commonly black.

Key Bugle

bu-gler (bū'glẽr), *n.* one who plays or sounds signals on the bugle.

buhl (bōōl), *n.* cabinet work or furniture inlaid with tortoise shell, yellow and white metal, etc.

buhr-stone (bûr'stōn"), *n.* a rock used to make a grindstone. Also, burrstone.

build (bĭld), *v.t.* [*p.t.* and *p.p.* built, builded, *p.pr.* building], to construct; to erect, as a house; to form by art; to raise on a support or foundation; to establish: *v.i.* to construct a building; to depend, or rely: with *on* or *upon.*

build-ing (bĭld'ĭng), *p.pr.* of *build:* *n.* the act of constructing, raising, or establishing; a structure put up for use or convenience, as a house, a church, etc.

bulb (bŭlb), *n.* an onion-shaped root; a kind of leaf bud; any swelling, or rounded portion of a stem or tube; a small globe containing an electric light.

bulb-ous (bŭl'bŭs), *adj.* pertaining to, or resembling, a bulb.

bul-bul (bōōl'bōōl), *n.* the Persian nightingale.

Bul-ga-ri-an (bōōl-gā'rĭ-ăn; bŭl-gā'rĭ-ăn), *n.* a native of Bulgaria, one of the Balkan states.—*adj.* **Bulgarian.**

bulge (bŭlj), *n.* the bilge or widest part of a cask; a bending outwards; the part of a wall, a ship, etc. which swells out; a sudden rise in price, as a *bulge* in stocks: *v.i.* to jut out; to swell out: **to get the bulge on,** slang, to secure an advantage over.

bulk (bŭlk), *n.* size; complete dimensions; the main mass or body; the cargo of a ship when stowed; volume; a small protruding structure; a stall.

bulk-head (bŭlk'hĕd"), *n.* an upright partition in a vessel which separates one part of it from another; a structure built to stand the pressure of water or earth.

bulk-i-ness (bŭl'kĭ-nĕs), *n.* greatness in size and weight.

bulk-y (bŭl'kĭ), *adj.* massive; ponderous; of great size or weight.—*adv.* **bulkily.**

bull (bōōl), *n.* the male of the species of animals of which the cow is the female; the male of various large animals, as the whale, elephant, etc.; in the stock market, one who endeavors to raise the price of stock in order that he may sell dear: the opposite of a bear; an official letter or order sent out by the Pope; as, a papal *bull;* a ridiculous contradiction in language; slang, absurdly exaggerated statements or pretensions.

bull bait-ing (bōōl bāt'ĭng), the sport of attacking bulls with dogs: a favorite sport in Elizabethan England.

bull-dog (bōōl'dŏg"), *n.* a variety of dog of strong muscular build, and remarkable for its courage and fierceness: formerly used for baiting bulls: *adj.* having courage and the quality of holding to a thing: as, a *bulldog* firmness of disposition.

bull-doze (bōōl'dōz"), *v.t.* to bully; to frighten; to intimidate. [Colloq.]

bul-let (bōōl'ĕt), *n.* a small ball made of lead to be shot from a gun.

bul-le-tin (bōōl'ĕ-tĭn), *n.* an official report regarding some matter or event of public interest; a periodical publication: *v.t.* to publish or announce in a brief authorized statement.

bull-fight (bōōl'fīt"), *n.* a combat held in an arena for public amusement, between armed men and a bull; popular in Spanish-speaking lands.—*n.* **bullfighter.**

bull-finch (bōōl'fĭnch"), *n.* a common British song bird.

bull-frog (bōōl'frŏg"), *n.* a large North American species of frog abounding in marshy places, remarkable for its loud, bellowing croak.

bull-head (bōōl'hĕd"), *n.* a broad-headed scaleless fish; catfish.

bul-lion (bōōl'yŭn), *n.* uncoined gold or silver; foreign coin; a heavy twisted fringe covered with fine gold- or silver-wire, used for epaulets, etc.

Bull Moose (bōōl mōōs), a large male animal of the deer family, noted for its strength and endurance; a member of the Progressive political party formed in 1912 under the leadership of Theodore Roosevelt.

bull-ock (bōōl'ŭk), *n.* an ox or steer over four years old.

bull's-eye (bōōlz'ī"), *n.* any circular opening for light or air; among seamen, a small cloud with a reddish center, supposed to show that a hurricane is coming; a lantern with a convex or bulging lens; a round piece of thick glass in the deck, port, or skylight covering of a vessel to admit light; one of the plates of glass attached to a microscope; the center of a target; a shot that hits the center of a target.

bull-y (bōōl'ĭ), *n.* [*pl.* bullies (-ĭz)], one who rules over others by insolence or threats; an overbearing fellow: *v.t.* [*p.t.* and *p.p.* bullied, *p.pr.* bullying], to overrule with bluster and threats: *v.i.* to be rudely noisy and quarrelsome: *adj.* slang, fine; excellent: **bully beef,** slang, canned cornbeef issued as army food.

bul-rush (bōōl'rŭsh"), *n.* the popular name for rushlike plants growing in water or marshes.

bul-wark (bōōl'wẽrk), *n.* a mound of earth raised around a place as a defense against cannon-shot; a fortlike structure; a rampart; the boarding round the sides of a ship, above the level of the deck; any means of protection or defense.

bum (bŭm), *n.* a worthless loafer; an idle, dissolute fellow. Also, **bummer.** [Colloq.]

bum-ble-bee (bŭm'bl-bē"), *n.* a large hairy bee, so named from its humming noise. Also, **humblebee.**

bum-boat (bŭm'bōt'), *n.* a boat used in England to carry provisions, fruit, etc., for sale to vessels in port or lying off the shore.

bump (bŭmp), *n.* a shock from a blow; a swelling due to a knock or blow: *v.t.* to bring violently together; thump: *v.i.* to come in collision; to strike heavily.

bump-er (bŭm'pẽr), *n.* an overflowing cup, especially in drinking a toast: *adj.* overflowing; very large.

bump-kin (bŭmp'kĭn), *n.* an awkward, clumsy countryman.

bump-tious (bŭmp'shŭs), *adj.* self-conceited; forward; self-assertive.—*adv.* **bumptiously.**—*n.* **bumptiousness.**

bun (bŭn), *n.* a small light cake or slightly sweetened biscuit. Also, **bunn.**

bunch (bŭnch), *n.* a cluster; a collection of things of the same kind growing or fastened together: *v.i.* to stick out; to form a cluster; *v.t.* to form into a cluster; to gather into folds; group together.—*adj.* **bunchy.**—*n.* **bunchiness.**

bun-co (bŭṅ'kō), *n.* a swindling game or scheme: *v.t.* to swindle or cheat by trickery. Also, **bunko.**

bun-combe (bŭṅ'kŭm), *n.* speechmaking to gain public applause; idle or showy speech, especially if intended to secure votes, etc.; anything done for mere show. Also, **bunkum.** [Colloq.]

bun-dle (bŭn'dl), *n.* a number of things bound together; a roll or package; two reams of printing or brown paper: *v.t.* to tie or bind in a bundle or roll; to send, as a person, off in a hurry: with *off* or *out.*

bung (bŭng), *n.* a large cork for stopping the hole in a cask or barrel; the hole itself: *v.t.* to stop with such a cork; close or shut up: **bunghole,** the hole in a cask or barrel stopped with a bung.

bun-ga-low (bŭṅ'gȧ-lō), *n.* a one-story house, lightly built, and generally surrounded by a porch or veranda.

bun-gle (bŭṅ'gl), *v.i.* and *v.t.* to perform in a clumsy manner: *n.* a clumsy performance; a botch.—*n.* **bungler.**

bun-ion (bŭn'yŭn), *n.* a painful swelling on the foot, usually over the joint of the great toe. Also, **bunyon.**

bunk (bŭṅk), *n.* a shelf or recess used for a bed in a ship, sleeping car, etc.: *v.i.* to sleep in a bunk; to go to bed.

bunk-er (bŭṅk'ẽr), *n.* a large bin, especially one for coal on shipboard; any rough, hazardous ground on a golf links, especially an artificially built-up hazard.

bun-ko (bŭṅ'kō), *n.* a swindling game: *v.t.* to cheat or swindle. Also, **bunco.**

bunk-y (bŭṅk'ĭ), *n.* a berthmate; roommate; tentmate. Also, **bunkie.**

bun-ny (bŭn'ĭ), *n.* a squirrel or rabbit: a pet name.

Bun-sen burn-er (bŏŏn'sĕn bûrn'ẽr), a tube a few inches in length, with small air holes at the bottom, forming a mixture of air and gas which burns with a blue flame that gives intense heat.

bunt (bŭnt), *v.t.* and *v.i.* to butt with head or horns; to push as with horns: *n.* a push with, or as with, horns; the middle part of a square sail, or of a fishing net.

bun-ting (bŭn'tĭng), *n.* a bird related to the finches and the sparrows; a light, loosely woven woolen stuff used chiefly for making flags.

bunt-line (bŭnt'lĭn; bŭnt'līn), *n.* one of the ropes attached to a square sail to draw the sail up to the yard.

buoy (boi; bōō'ĭ; bwoi), *n.* a floating body moored to the bottom to show the position of rocks or shoals beneath the water, or to mark a channel; a device to support a person in the water to prevent drowning: usually called a life *buoy:* *v.t.* and *v.i.* to keep afloat in a fluid: usually with *up;* to mark with floats to indicate a channel; to support; to sustain; as, to *buoy* up one's hope.

buoy-an-cy (boi'ăn-sĭ; bōō'ĭ-ăn-sĭ), *n.* the property of floating on the surface of a liquid; power of a liquid to sustain a body floating in it; upward pressure of a liquid upon a body floating in it; lightness; gaiety of spirits.

buoy-ant (boi'ănt; bōō'ĭ-ănt), *adj.* able to float in a fluid; not easily depressed; light-hearted.

bur (bûr), *n.* the rough prickly seed-case of certain plants; the throaty pronunciation of the rough *r;* any humming sound. Also, **burr.**

bur-den (bûr'dn), *n.* that which is borne or carried; a load; something grievous, wearisome, or oppressive; a chorus or refrain; the bearing of loads or packs; as, a beast of *burden;* a topic of conversation or thought on which one dwells; the gist of a matter: *v.t.* to load; to lay a weight upon; to put too much upon; hence, to oppress. Also, **burthen.**

bur-den-some (bûr'dn-sŭm), *adj.* hard to bear; oppressive; weighty; troublesome. Also, **burthensome.**

bur-dock (bûr'dŏk), *n.* a large wayside weed with rough broad leaves.

bu-reau (bū'rō; bū-rō'), *n.* [*pl.* bureaus or bureaux (-rōz)], a chest of drawers for clothing; a desk or writing table furnished with drawers; an office; as, a *bureau* of information; a governmental department for the transaction of public business; as, the Secret Service *Bureau.*

bu-reau-cra-cy (bū-rō'krȧ-sĭ) *n.* [*pl.* bureaucracies (-sĭz)], government by bureaus, or departments, each under a head or chief; government by an official class; officials of the government spoken of collectively.

bu-rette (bū-rĕt'), *n.* a finely graduated glass tube, from which a small quantity of a solution can be drawn off at a time: used in chemical analysis.

Burette

bur-gess (bûr'jĕs), *n.* a citizen or freeman of a borough; in Pennsylvania, the chief administrative officer of a borough; in Connecticut, a member of the town council.

bur-glar (bûr'glẽr), *n.* one who breaks into a house at night to steal.

bur-gla-ry (bûr'glȧ-rĭ), *n.* the act or crime of breaking into a house at night to steal.

bur-go-mas-ter (bûr'gō-mȧs'-tẽr), *n.* the chief magistrate of a town in Holland, Flanders, or Germany.

Bur-gun-dy (bûr'gŭn-dĭ), *n.* a wine, red or white, made in Burgundy in France.

bur-i-al (bĕr'ĭ-ăl), *n.* the act of placing a body in the grave; interment.

bu-rin (bū'rĭn), *n.* an engraving tool of pointed steel.

burl (bûrl), *n.* a small knot or lump in thread or cloth; a knot on a tree: *v.t.* to pick knots, etc., from, as in finishing cloth.

bur-lap (bûr'lăp), *n.* a coarse fabric made of jute or hemp, used for bagging, curtains, etc. Also, **burlaps.**

bur-lesque (bûr-lĕsk'), *n.* a ridiculous, overdrawn representation; a travesty; a parody; a composition in which a trifling subject is treated as a subject of dignity or importance: *v.t.* and *v.i.* to ridicule or make ridiculous by caricatured representation: *adj.* tending to excite laughter by exaggerating the peculiarities or prominent features.

bur-ly (bûr'lĭ), *adj.* bulky; large; stout and muscular of body; corpulent. —*n.* **burliness.**

bur ma-ri-gold (bûr mă'rĭ-gōld), any of a certain kind of coarse herbs of the aster family.

Bur-mese (bûr'mēz'; bûr'mēs'), *n.* in both singular and plural, a native or natives of Burma; in the singular, the language of the Burmese.—*adj.* **Burmese.**

burn (bûrn), *v.t.* [*p.t.* burnt and burned, *p.pr.* burning], to destroy or injure by fire; to reduce to ashes; to scorch; to inflame or tan the skin; to affect with a burning feeling; in surgery, to apply heat or acid to for curative purposes: *v.i.* to be on fire; to suffer from, or be injured by, too much heat; to glow; to shine; to be inflamed with passion or desire; as, he *burns* to win fame: *n.* an injury to the flesh caused by fire; the result of too much heat.

Syn., *v.* blaze, brand, consume, cremate, scorch, singe.

Ant. (see cool).

burn (bûrn), *n.* a rivulet; a brook or small stream. [Scot.]

burn-er (bûr'nẽr), *n.* one who sets fire to anything; the part of a lamp, gas fixture, etc. from which the flame comes.

burn-ing glass (bûrn'ĭng glȧs), a flat glass, bulging on each side, used to set fire to something by bringing the direct rays of the sun to a point, or focus, on it.

burn-ing point (bûrn'ĭng point), the temperature at which a volatile oil will take fire from a light held close to its surface.

bur-nish (bûr'nĭsh), *v.t.* to polish by rubbing or friction; make smooth and shining; [as, we *burnish* brass: *n.* polish; brightness.

bur-noose (bûr-no͞os'; bûr'no͞os), *n.* a garment worn by Moors and Arabs, consisting of a cloak and a hood woven in one piece. Also, **burnous.**

burnt (bûrnt), *adj.* charred, destroyed, or affected by fire.

burr (bûr), *n.* the prickly seed-case of a plant; a thin ridge or roughness left by a tool in cutting or shaping metal; a whirring noise; the rough sound of *r:* *v.t.* to pronounce with this sound. Also, **bur.**

bur-ro (bo͝or'ō; bûr'ō), *n.* [*pl.* burros (-rōz)], the name used in the southwestern section of the United States for an ass or donkey.

bur-row (bûr'ō), *n.* a hole in the ground dug by a rabbit or other animal, as a refuge and home; a similar shelter: *v.i.* to dig; to work a way into or under something; *v.t.* to make burrows in, or build by burrowing.

burr-stone (bûr'stōn'), *n.* a rock used for millstones. Also, **buhrstone.**

bur-sar (bûr'sẽr), *n.* the treasurer of a college; a purser; a Scotch university student who receives an allowance for his support.

burst (bûrst), *v.i.* [*p.t.* and *p.p.* burst, *p.pr.* bursting], to break open by flying to pieces; to explode; to break suddenly into action, speech, or feeling; usually with *out, upon, into,* etc.; as, to *burst* into tears; appear or disappear suddenly; as, a scene *bursts* upon the view: *v.t.* to break by violence; to open suddenly: *n.* a violent or sudden breaking forth; as, a *burst* of applause; a sudden explosion; a rush; a spurt.

bur-y (bĕr'ĭ), *v.t.* [*p.t.* and *p.p.* buried, *p.pr.* burying], to place and cover in a grave or tomb, or in any final resting-place; hence, keep secret; hide; as, to *bury* one's past.

bur-y-ing (bĕr'ĭ-ĭng), *n.* an interment: *p.adj.* pertaining to burial; as, a *burying* ground or cemetery.

bus (bŭs), *n.* a colloquial form of omnibus, a public carriage or automobile.

bush (bo͝osh), *n.* a thick shrub; a forest region; wild, uncleared country; a lining or tube of hard metal inserted in a hole to reduce wear by friction.

bush-el (bo͝osh'ĕl), *n.* a dry measure containing four pecks or thirty-two quarts; a vessel of such a capacity: *v.t.* [U. S.], to mend or alter, as men's clothes.—*n.* **busheler.**

bush-ing (bo͝osh'ĭng), *n.* a metallic, detachable lining for a hole. Also, **bush.**

bush-man (bo͝osh'măn), *n.* [*pl.* bushmen (-mĕn)], an Australian woodsman.—**Bushman,** one of a tribe of men near the Cape of Good Hope, South Africa.

bush-rang-er (bo͝osh'rān'jẽr), *n.* one who leads the life of a plunderer, in the bush country, especially in Australia; originally, a criminal who escaped and lived a lawless life in the bush of Australia.

bush-whack-er (bo͝osh'hwăk'ẽr), *n.* a backwoodsman; in the Civil War, a Confederate guerrilla fighter; a tool for cutting brushwood.

bush-y (bo͝osh'ĭ), *adj.* thick and spreading like a bush; overgrown with shrubs.

busi-ness (bĭz'nĕs), *n.* employment; trade; profession; something necessary to be done; duty; mission; right of action; affair; matter; vocation; engagement: *adj.* pertaining to business; practical; as, a *business* man.

bus-kin (bŭs'kĭn), *n.* a covering for the foot reaching to the middle of the calf of the leg; a high shoe with a very thick sole worn by ancient tragic actors to increase their height.

buss (bŭs), *n.* a flying machine; as, the sky is stiff with *busses.*

bust (bŭst), *n.* the human chest or thorax; the part of the human body between the head and waist; a piece of sculpture representing the head, shoulders, and breast of a person.

bus-tard (bŭs'tẽrd), *n.* an Old World and Australian game bird related to the plovers and cranes.

bus-tle (bŭs'l), *n.* tumult; noisy activity; a pad or cushion formerly worn by women beneath the skirt, below the waist at the back: *v.i.* to be noisily busy; to move quickly; to make a fuss or stir.

Syn., *n.* stir, tumult, fuss.

bus-y (bĭz'ĭ), *adj.* earnestly, actively, or closely at work; characteristic of, or pertaining to, industry or diligence; as, the *busy* hum of the factory; bustling; full of employment; as, a *busy* day; meddlesome: *v.t.* and *v.i.* [*p.t.* and *p.p.* busied, *p.pr.* busying], to keep constantly engaged; to occupy. —*adv.* **busily.**

bus-y-bod-y (bĭz'ĭ-bŏd"ĭ), *n.* [*pl.* busybodies (-ĭz)], a person who continually concerns himself with the affairs of others; a person who meddles.

but (bŭt), *prep.* except; besides: *conj.* still; even if; however; yet; nevertheless; *adv.* only; no more than.

butch-er (bŏŏch'ẽr), *n.* one who kills animals to sell for food; sometimes, a cruel and bloody murderer: *v.t.* to kill (animals) for food; to murder in a horrible and cruel manner; to botch or mangle; to ruin.

butch-er bird (bŏŏch'ẽr bûrd), a name given to certain birds from their habit of hanging their prey upon thorns.

butch-er-y (bŏŏch'ẽr-ĭ), *n.* the business of killing cattle; horrible, cruel, and unnecessary murder.

but-ler (bŭt'lẽr), *n.* a manservant in a household who has charge of the dining-room, silver, wines, etc.; the chief servant in a large household.

butt (bŭt), *n.* a push or thrust delivered by the head of an animal; as, the *butt* of a goat; the thicker end of anything; a target; an embankment back of a target to stop bullets; that at which anything is aimed; therefore, one at whom jest or ridicule is directed; as, the *butt* of a joke; a large cask, chiefly for wine; a certain amount of wine in a cask, usually 126 gallons: *v.t.* to strike with the head; to join end to end.

butte (bŭt), *n.* a steep hill or ridge standing alone.

but-ter (bŭt'ẽr), *n.* the fat or oily substance obtained from cream or milk by churning: *v.t.* to spread or smear with this fat.

but-ter-cup (bŭt'ẽr-kŭp"), *n.* a plant bearing yellow cup-shaped flowers.

but-ter-fly (bŭt'ẽr-flī"), *n.* [*pl.* butterflies (-flīz)], a general name for an insect with four down-covered, brightly colored wings, which flies by day; a gay, showily dressed idler or trifler.

but-ter-ine (bŭt'ẽr-ēn"; bŭt'ẽr-ĭn), *n.* an artificial butter; oleomargarine.

but-ter-milk (bŭt'ẽr-mĭlk"), *n.* a thin, watery fluid separated from the cream in butter-making.

but-ter-nut (bŭt'ẽr-nŭt"), *n.* the North American white walnut or its fruit.

but-ter-y (bŭt'ẽr-ĭ), *n.* [*pl.* butteries (-ĭz)], a room or closet in which provisions, wines, etc., are kept; the butler's pantry: *adj.* like butter; containing or spread with butter.

but-tock (bŭt'ŭk), *n.* the rump or hinder part of a man or animal usually in plural; the part of a ship under the stern.

but-ton (bŭt'n), *n.* any small, rounded object used for fastening or securing a garment, or attached for ornament; a pivoted fastening for a door or window, etc.; the knob at the end of a fencing foil: *pl.* young mushrooms; a page boy: *v.t.* to fasten or furnish with buttons: *v.i.* to be capable of, or to admit of, being fastened by buttons; as, this dress *buttons* easily.

but-ton-hole (bŭt'n-hōl"), *n.* a hole in a garment for fastening a button: *v.t.* to hold in conversation against the will; to furnish with buttonholes; to edge (cloth) with buttonhole stitching.

but-ton stick (bŭt'n stĭk), a brass device ten inches long which slides over the buttons and protects the coat in cleaning.

but-ton-wood (bŭt'n-wŏŏd"), *n.* a name given to the large North American plane tree because of its small, round, rough, buttonlike fruit.

Buttress and Flying Buttress

but-tress (bŭt'rĕs), *n.* masonry or brickwork built on to an outside wall to afford support; a support; *v.t.* to support by a buttress; to prop.

bux-om (bŭk'sŭm), *adj.* cheerful; jolly; robust; plump and handsome; lively and vigorous.

buy (bī), *v.t.* [*p.t.* and *p.p.* bought, *p.pr.* buying], to obtain by paying an agreed price; to purchase; sometimes, to bribe.

buzz (bŭz), *n.* a constant humming noise, as of bees; a confused or blended murmur, as of many voices; a whispered report or rumor: *v.i.* to make a low humming sound; to speak with a low humming voice: *v.t.* to spread secretly.—*adv.* **buzzingly.**

buz-zard (bŭz'ẽrd), *n.* an American vulture; the name given to several other kinds of hawk.

buz-zer (bŭz'ẽr), *n* an electric instrument for signaling; an instrument making a buzzing sound, used instead of an electric bell.

by (bī), *prep.* next or near to; with; along, over; through; in, on, or at; past and beyond; after: *adv.* near, present, aside: **by and by**, after some time.

by-gone (bī'gŏn"), *adv.* past; gone by: *n.* something in the past.

by-law (bī'lô"), *n.* a private rule, usually of action, framed by a company; a secondary law; as, a society has a constitution and *by-laws*.

by-path (bī'påth"), *n.* [*pl.* bypaths (bī'påthz")], a side, private, indirect, or retired path or way.

by-stand-er (bī'stăn"dẽr), *n.* one looking on but not taking part in; a spectator; an onlooker.

by the bye (bī *th*ē bī), a phrase meaning by the way: the only way in which *bye*, as a noun, is now used.

by-way (bī'wā"), *n.* a private or secluded way.

by-word (bī'wûrd"), *n.* a proverb; nickname; sometimes, an object of laughing scorn.

By-zan-tine (bĭ-zăn'tĭn; bĭz'ăn-tĭn; bĭz'ăn-tīn), *adj.* of or belonging to Byzantium, now called Constantinople, the ancient capital of the Eastern Roman Empire.

C

Ca-a-ba (kä'ȧ-bȧ; kä'bȧ), *n.* the shrine of Mecca, the chief object of pilgrimage of Mohammedans: it contains a black stone said to be a ruby brought from heaven, and changed black by the sins of those who have touched it. Also, **Kaaba.**

cab (kăb), *n.* a public carriage with two or four wheels, drawn by one horse; the shelter for the driver of a locomotive.

ca-bal (kȧ-băl'), *n.* a secret combination of a few persons for carrying out some special plan, usually evil: *v.i.* [*p.t.* and *p.p.* caballed, *p.pr.* caballing], to unite in secret with others to effect some design.

cab-a-la (kăb'ȧ-lȧ), *n.* a secret system of the Jewish rabbis to find the hidden meaning of the first five books of the Bible. Also, **cabbala.**

cab-a-lism (kăb'ȧ-lĭzm), *n.* secret and mysterious doctrine.—*n.* **cabalist.**

cab-a-lis-tic (kăb'ȧ-lĭs'tĭk), *adj.* mysterious; suggesting the secret; occult. Also, **cabbalistic.**

ca-bal-le-ro (kä'băl-yā'rō), *n.* a Spanish knight or gentleman; a stately Spanish dance.

cab-a-ret (kăb'ȧ-rĕt; kȧ'bȧ'rĕ'), *n.* a restaurant in which guests are entertained at meals by dancing and vaudeville acts.

cab-bage (kăb'ĕj), *n.* a common vegetable of great food value, with a compact head of leaves; the terminal head of palm-trees.

cab-in (kăb'ĭn), *n.* a small hut, cottage, or room; a room in a ship for officers or passengers: *v.t.* to confine in a cabin.

cab-i-net (kăb'ĭ-nĕt), *n.* a small apartment; a private room; a piece of furniture to hold objects of art, curiosity, etc.; a committee of the heads of governmental departments; as, the President appoints his own *cabinet*: *adj.* secret; small; as, a *cabinet* organ; of or pertaining to the advisory council of the chief executive of a nation.

cab-i-net-mak-er (kăb'ĭ-nĕt-māk'ẽr), *n.* one whose business it is to make household furniture, etc.

ca-ble (kā'bl), *n.* a large strong rope or chain; a submarine telegraph line; a measure of distance used at sea equal to 100 to 140 fathoms: *v.t.* to fasten with a cable; to send by submarine telegraph.

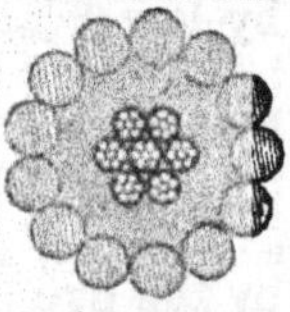

Section of a Submarine Cable

ca-ble-gram (kā'bl-grăm'), *n.* a message sent by submarine telegraph.

ca-boose (kȧ-bōōs'), *n.* the kitchen of a ship; the trainmen's car attached to a freight train.

ca-bré (kȧ'brā'), *n.* a flying attitude in which the angle of attack is greater than normal; that is, with tail down, down by the stern, or tail low. [Fr.]

cab-ri-o-let (kăb'rĭ-ō-lā'), *n.* a covered carriage with two or four wheels, drawn by one horse.

ca-ca-o (kȧ-kā'ō; kȧ-kä'ō), *n.* a small evergreen tree of tropical America and West Indies, from the seeds of which cocoa and chocolate are made.

cache (kăsh), *n.* a hiding-place for food or supplies: *v.t.* to hide or store away.

ca-chet (kȧ'shā'), *n.* a seal; hence, a stamp of individuality. [Fr.]

cach-in-na-tion (kăk'ĭ-nā'shŭn), *n.* loud or uncontrolled laughter.

cack-le (kăk'l), *n.* the cry of a hen or goose; chatter; idle talk: *v.i.* to cry like a hen or goose: especially applied to the cry made by a hen which has laid an egg; giggle; prattle.

cac-tus (kăk'tŭs), *n.* [*pl.* cacti (-tī), and cactuses (-ĕz)], a prickly fleshy plant with showy flowers.

cad (kăd), *n.* a vulgar, ill-bred fellow of mean principles.

ca-da-ver (kȧ-dă'vẽr), *n.* a dead body; a corpse being used for dissection.

ca-dav-er-ous (kȧ-dăv'ẽr-ŭs), *adj.* like a corpse; pale; ghastly.

cad-die (kăd'ĭ), *n.* a lad who carries the clubs for golf players. Also, **caddy.**

cad-dis (kăd'ĭs), *n.* a worm; the larva form of the caddis fly. Also, **caddice.**

cad-dis fly (kăd'ĭs flī), an insect whose larva, growing in water, and called *caddis worm*, lives in and drags about a silklike case.

cad-dish (kăd'ĭsh), *adj.* mean; unmanly; ill-bred.—*adv.* **caddishly.**—*n.* **caddishness.**

cad-dy (kăd'ĭ), *n.* [*pl.* caddies (-ĭz)], a small box for keeping tea.

ca-dence (kā'dĕns), *n.* the rise and fall of the voice in reading or speaking; rhythm; a musical run or trill; a uniform time and pace in marching.

ca-det (kȧ-dĕt'), *n.* a younger son; a student in a naval or military academy.

ca-det-ship (kȧ-dĕt'shĭp), *n.* the position, or rank, of a younger son, or of a young man in training for naval or military service; the commission of a youth in naval or military training.

cad-mi-um (kăd'mĭ-ŭm), *n.* a rare metallic element, white in color, malleable, and ductile.

ca-di (kä'dĭ; kā'dĭ), *n.* a Mohammedan judge: usually over a town or village.

ca-du-ce-us (kȧ-dū'sē-ŭs), *n.* the winged staff of Mercury, the messenger of the gods, entwined with serpents.

Caduceus

cæ-cum (sē'kŭm), *n.* [*pl.* cæca (-kȧ)], the beginning of the large intestine.

Cæ-sar (sē'zȧr), *n.* a Roman emperor: taken as a title by the first Roman emperor who was an adopted son of Julius Cæsar; any dictator or autocrat.

cæ-su-ra (sē-zū'rȧ; sē-sū'rȧ), *n.* a pause or division in a verse.—*adj.* **cæsural.**

ca-fé (kȧ'fā'), *n.* a coffee-house; a restaurant. [Fr.]

caf-e-te-ri-a (kăf'ĕ-tē'rĭ-ȧ), *n.* a quick lunch restaurant where the patrons serve themselves.

caf-fe-ine (kăf'ē-ĭn; kăf'ē-ēn), *n.* a bitter, stimulating substance obtained from coffee. Also, **caffein.**

caf-tan (kăf'tăn; kȧf-tän'), *n.* a girdled, long-sleeved gown worn in Eastern countries. Also, **kaftan.**

cage (kāj), *n.* a box or inclosure furnished with bars for confining birds, or other animals; a basket for raising and lowering men in a mine shaft; anything resembling a cage in form; the boxlike compartment or car of an elevator, in which passengers are carried: *v.t.* to confine in a boxlike compartment; to shut up.

ca-ique (kȧ'ēk'), *n.* a skiff or light rowing boat used on the Bosphorus.

Cain (kān), *n.* in the Bible, the son of Adam and brother of Abel, whom he killed; hence, a murderer.

cairn (kârn), *n.* a cone-shaped heap of stones erected as a monument, especially those in the British Isles, apparently the work of the early Britons.—*adj.* **cairned.**

cairn-gorm (kârn'gôrm'), *n.* a yellow or brown quartz or rock-crystal. Also, **Cairngorm stone.**

cais-son (kā'sŏn), *n.* an ammunition wagon or chest; in war, a box filled with explosives for firing a mine; a water-tight box or casing used for building structures in water; a structure for raising and floating sunken vessels.

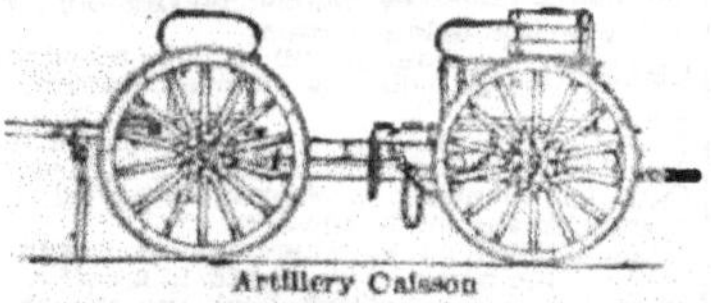

Artillery Caisson

cai-tiff (kā'tĭf), *n.* a mean villain; a cowardly wretch: *adj.* despicable; vile; cowardly.

ca-jole (kȧ-jōl'), *v.t.* and *v.i.* to coax or deceive by flattery; wheedle; cheat; as, the daughters of King Lear were able to *cajole* their father into giving up his throne.

ca-jol-er-y (kȧ-jōl'ēr-ĭ), *n.* the act of deceiving or wheedling by means of flattery; deceit.

cake (kāk), *n.* a small mass of dough, sweetened and baked; a compressed or solidified mass of any substance, especially if thin or flat: *v.t.* and *v.i.* to form into a hard mass; as, dry weather causes mud to *cake.*

cal-a-bash (kăl'ȧ-băsh), *n.* the hard-shelled fruit of a tree of tropical America; a vessel made from the dried shell.

Calabash

cal-a-boose (kăl'ȧ-bōōs'), *n.* a jail; a lockup.

ca-lam-i-tous (kȧ-lăm'ĭ-tŭs), *adj.* producing, or resulting from, disaster; as, *calamitous* floods often result from the overflowing of the Ohio River.—*adv.* **calamitously.**—*n.* **calamitousness.**

ca-lam-i-ty (kȧ-lăm'ĭ-tĭ), *n.* [*pl.* calamities (-tĭz)], any cause that produces evil, disaster, or extreme misfortune; distress; affliction.

Syn. mischance, mishap, catastrophe.
Ant. (see good-fortune).

cal-a-mus (kăl'ȧ-mŭs), *n.* [*pl.* calami (-mī)], a kind of palm producing the rattan canes; the sweet flag.

ca-lash (kȧ-lăsh'), *n.* a light carriage with low wheels and a folding removable top; a cover for the head formerly worn by women.

cal-ca-re-ous (kăl-kā'rē-ŭs), *adj.* of the nature of, or containing, lime; as, *calcareous* earth or stone.

cal-cif-er-ous (kăl-sĭf'ēr-ŭs), *adj.* bearing, containing, or producing, lime.

cal-ci-fy (kăl'sĭ-fī), *v.t.* [*p.t.* and *p.p.* calcified, *p.pr.* calcifying], to convert into lime: *v.i.* to become strong by conversion into lime.

cal-ci-mine (kăl'sĭ-mĭn; kăl'sĭ-mīn), *n.* white or tinted wash for walls or ceilings: *v.t.* to cover with such a wash.

cal-ci-na-tion (kăl'sĭ-nā'shŭn), *n.* the act or process of reducing to powder by heat: thus, lime is produced from chalk and certain shells by *calcination.*

cal-cine (kăl-sīn'; kăl'sĭn), *v.t.* to reduce (a substance) to powder by heat: *v.i.* to undergo the change to powder under the influence of heat.

cal-cite (kăl'sīt), *n.* calcium carbonate; natural lime, chalk, marble, etc.

cal-ci-um (kăl'sĭ-ŭm), *n.* a soft white metallic element occurring only in combination because of its strong chemical activity.

cal-cu-la-ble (kăl'kū-lȧ-bl), *adj.* capable of being determined or reckoned.—*adv.* **calculably.**

cal-cu-late (kăl'kū-lāt), *v.t.* to add, subtract, multiply, or divide any sum to find the result; to determine by any process of reasoning; estimate; as, no one can *calculate* the benefits of electricity to the world: *v.i.* to make a computation; to rely: with *on* or *upon.*

cal-cu-la-tion (kăl'kū-lā'shŭn), *n.* the use of numbers for arriving at a result; a result of reasoning or inference; estimate; opinion.

cal-cu-la-tive (kăl'kū-lā-tĭv), *adj.* of or pertaining to computation; inclined to compute or reckon.

cal-cu-la-tor (kăl'kū-lā'tēr), *n.* one who, or a machine that, computes or reckons.

cal-cu-lous (kăl'kū-lŭs), *adj.* stony; gritty; as, a *calculous* mass.

cal-cu-lus (kăl'kū-lŭs), *n.* [*pl.* calculi (-lī)], any branch of mathematics involving calculation, especially the differential calculus and the integral calculus; a hard substance sometimes formed in the kidneys or bladder.

cal-dron (kôl'drŭn), *n.* a large kettle or boiler. Also, **cauldron.**

cal-en-dar (kăl'ĕn-dēr), *n.* a register of the days, weeks, and months of the year, etc.; a register or list; a list of criminal cases arranged for trial; *v.t.* to register or place on a list.

cal-en-der (kăl'ĕn-dēr), *n.* a machine containing heated rollers for smoothing and glazing paper or cloth: *v.t.* to press in a smoothing machine, as paper or cloth.

calf (kăf), *n.* [*pl.* calves (kăvz)], a young cow; the young of certain sea animals, as the whale; leather made from the skin of a calf; a small island or iceberg near a larger one; the thick fleshy part of the lower part of the leg.

cal-i-ber (kăl'ĭ-bẽr), *n.* the diameter of a round body; especially, the diameter of the mouth of a gun or cannon; the diameter of a projectile or billet; sometimes, mental capacity: as, many positions are open to a man of large *caliber*. Also, **calibre.**

cal-i-brate (kăl'ĭ-brāt), *v.t.* to compare (an instrument or device) with a standard to determine accuracy or to produce a scale; as, to *calibrate* a thermometer.

cal-i-co (kăl'ĭ-kō), *n.* [*pl.* calicoes and calicos (-kōz)], white or printed cotton cloth.

cal-i-per (kăl'ĭ-pẽr), *n.* a compasslike device with bent legs, used in determining the inside or outside diameters of pipes, tubes, etc.: *v.t.* and *v.i.* to measure with such instruments. Also, **calliper.**

ca-liph (kā'lĭf; kăl'ĭf), *n.* among the Mohammedans, one having supreme dignity and power in all matters of religion and government. Also, **calif, kalif, khalif, khalifi.**

cal-is-then-ics (kăl"ĭs-thĕn'ĭks), *n.pl.* the art of promoting health by physical exercise; simple athletic gymnastics. Also, **callisthenics.**

calk (kôk), *v.t.* to drive oakum or hemp rope fiber into the seams of (a ship) to keep out water; to furnish with metal projections to prevent slipping: *n.* a piece of metal projecting from the shoe of a horse or an ox to prevent slipping. Also, **caulk.**

calk-er (kôk'ẽr), *n.* one who drives oakum into the seams of a ship to keep out water. Also, **caulker.**

call (kôl), *v.t.* to summon from, or invite to, any place; officially choose for an office; as, to *call* a minister; name; exhort; as, John the Baptist *called* men to repentance; utter in a loud voice; rouse from sleep; a contract requiring the delivery of some commodity, as stocks, cotton, or grain, at a stipulated price: opposite to *put*; *v.i.* speak in a loud voice; make a brief visit: *n.* a summons or invitation; a request or command; a short visit; the cry or note uttered by certain animals.—*n.* **caller.**

cal-la (kăl'ȧ), *n.* a well-known plant; the calla lily.

cal-lig-ra-phy (kă-lĭg'rȧ-fĭ), *n.* elegant or beautiful writing; handwriting. Also, **caligraphy.**—*adj.* **calligraphic.**

call-ing (kôl'ĭng), *n.* the act of summoning; a summons or invitation; a vocation; trade, or profession; a crying aloud.

Cal-li-o-pe (kă-lī'ō-pē), *n.* the muse of epic poetry and eloquence: **calliope,** an organ in which steam produces the notes.

cal-los-i-ty (kă-lŏs'ĭ-tĭ), *n.* the quality or state of being hardened; a thick or hardened place on skin or on outer covering like bark.

cal-lous (kăl'ŭs), *adj.* hardened, as the skin; unfeeling in mind or heart.—*adv.* **callously.**—*n.* **callousness.**

cal-low (kăl'ō), *adj.* unfledged; very young and inexperienced; as, a *callow* youth.—*n.* **callowness.**

cal-lus (kăl'ŭs), *n.* [*pl.* calli (-ī)], the hardening of the skin from pressure; bony matter which unites the ends of fractured bones; a thick, hard place on the skin.

calm (käm), *n.* stillness; serenity: *v.t.* to quiet; still; pacify: *v.i.* to become quiet: with *down*: *adj.* tranquil; still; undisturbed.—*adv.* **calmly.**—*n.* **calmness.**

Syn. collected, composed, placid, serene.
Ant. (see stormy, unsettled).

cal-o-mel (kăl'ō-mĕl), *n.* a preparation of mercury, used as a medicine to move the bowels.

ca-lor-ic (kȧ-lŏr'ĭk), *adj.* of or pertaining to heat.

cal-o-rie (kăl'ō-rĭ), *n.* the amount of heat required to raise the temperature of one gram of water one degree centigrade. Also, **calory.**

cal-o-rim-e-ter (kăl"ō-rĭm'ē-tẽr), *n.* a machine for measuring heat units, or calories.

ca-lotte (kȧ-lŏt'), *n.* a skull cap worn by Roman Catholic clergymen; the close-fitting crown of any headdress; as the *calotte* of a helmet; a dome, or caplike ceiling; a caplike covering for a spire.

cal-trop (kăl'trŏp), *n.* a small four-pronged instrument used to obstruct the advance of cavalry by piercing the feet of the horses; one of several kinds of plants with spiny heads, as the star thistle.

Calumet

cal-u-met (kăl'ū-mĕt), *n.* the tobacco pipe of the North American Indians, smoked as a symbol of peace or to confirm treaties.

ca-lum-ni-ate (kȧ-lŭm'nĭ-āt), *v.t.* to accuse falsely and with ill-will: *v.i.* to start evil reports for the purpose of injuring another's character.—*n.* **calumniation, calumniator.**

ca-lum-ni-ous (kȧ-lŭm'nĭ-ŭs), *adj.* slanderous; defamatory; injurious.—*adv.* **calumniously.**

cal-um-ny (kăl'ŭm-nĭ), *n.* [*pl.* calumnies (-nĭz)], a false accusation; a slander.

Cal-va-ry (kăl'vȧ-rĭ), *n.* the place where Jesus was crucified: in Roman Catholic countries, a representation of the crucifixion erected in the open air.

calve (käv), *v.i.* to bring forth the young of the cow; to give birth to a calf.

Cal-vin-ism (kăl'vĭn-ĭzm), *n.* the doctrines of John Calvin [1509-64], the French reformer, who taught that God predestines man, and elects those who are to be saved.

Cal-vin-ist (kăl'vĭn-ĭst), *n.* one who holds the doctrines of Calvin, the French reformer.—*adj.* **Calvinistic.**

ca-lyx (kā'lĭks; kăl'ĭks), *n.* [*pl.* calyxes (kā'lĭks-ĕz), calices (kăl'ĭ-sēz)], the circle of small leaves beneath the petals of a flower.

cam (kăm), *n.* a piece of machinery consisting of a rotating or sliding piece or projection for moving, or receiving motion from, a pin, roller, etc., moving against its edge.

cam-ber (kăm'bẽr), *n.* slight convexity of a part; the convexity of the surface of the deck of a ship.

cam-bi-um (kăm'bĭ-ŭm), *n.* the layer of growing tissue which lies between the young wood and the bark of trees and produces the new wood.

Cam-bri-an (kăm'brĭ-ăn), *adj.* pertaining to, or having reference to, one of the earliest geologic eras.

cam-bric (kām'brĭk), *n.* a very fine, thin, white linen: *adj.* pertaining to, or made of, linen.

cam-bric mus-lin (kām'brĭk mŭz'lĭn), a fine cotton imitation of cambric.

came (kām), past tense of the intransitive verb *come*

cam-el (kăm'ĕl), *n.* a large four-footed animal that chews the cud, of which there are two kinds: the Arabian camel or dromedary, with a single hump, and the Bactrian camel, with two humps.

Bactrian Camel

ca-mel-li-a (kȧ-mĕl'ĭ-ȧ; kȧ-mēl'yȧ), *n.* a hothouse shrub with evergreen leaves and either red or white flowers; the Japan rose.

ca-mel-o-pard (kȧ-mĕl'ō-pärd), *n.* the giraffe.

Cam-e-lot (kăm'ē-lŏt), *n.* the place where King Arthur, of ancient legend, had his palace and court.

cam-e-o (kăm'ē-ō), *n.* [*pl.* cameos (-ōz)], a precious stone or shell on which raised figures are engraved.

cam-er-a (kăm'ẽr-ȧ), *n.* [*pl.* cameras (-ȧz)], in photography, the apparatus by which images can be thrown on a plate sensitive to light.

ca-mi-on (kȧ"mĭ-ôṅ'), *n.* a motor-truck or motor-lorry: used in the World War. [Fr.]

cam-let (kăm'lĕt), *n.* an Eastern or Oriental fabric of great beauty; any imitation of it.

cam-o-mile (kăm'ō-mīl), *n.* a plant whose flowers have a bitter taste, and are largely used in medicine.

cam-ou-flage (kȧ"mōō"flȧzh'), *n.* in war, the art of disguising or deceiving by false appearances: the deception may take a variety of forms: shrubbery and painted landscapes are so employed that roads and gun-emplacements are invisible to air scouts; ships are so marked and their smokestacks so painted that the enemy range-finder is deceived as to the length of the boat, her rate of speed, which way she is headed, etc. [Fr.]

camp (kămp), *n.* the ground occupied by an army, with tents, huts, etc.; a place where tents are put up for shelter; as, a fishing *camp;* those persons in an encampment: *v.i.* to live temporarily in tents: often with *out.*

cam-paign (kăm-pān'), *n.* a series of military operations; the period during which an army carries on active operations in the field; a series of operations designed to produce a certain result; as, a political *campaign:* *v.i.* to serve in such a series of operations.—*n.* campaigner.

Campanile

cam-pa-ni-le (kăm"pä-nē'lā), *n.* [*pl.* campaniles (-lāz)], a bell tower detached from the body of a church.

cam-pan-u-late (kăm-păn'ū-lāt), *adj.* bell-shaped: applied especially to flowers.

cam-phor (kăm'fẽr), *n.* a whitish substance which wastes away on exposure to the air, obtained from various trees and plants of eastern Asia.

cam-phor tree (kăm'fẽr trē), a kind of laurel from which camphor is obtained.

cam-phor-ate (kăm'fẽr-āt), *v.t.* to saturate or treat with camphor.

camp meet-ing (kămp mēt'ĭng), an outdoor religious gathering.

camp stool (kămp stōōl), a folding stool or seat.

cam-pus (kăm'pŭs), *n.* the grounds of a college.

can (kăn), *v.i.* [*p.t.* could], to be able; to possess power physically, morally, or mentally: used as an auxiliary verb: *v.t.* [*p.t.* and *p.p.* canned, *p.pr.* canning], to put up in metal vessels for preservation: *n.* a metal vessel of small size, for holding liquids or preserving solids.

Ca-naan (kā'năn), *n.* in the Bible, the "Promised Land" of the Israelites; generally speaking, Palestine.—*adj.* Canaanitish.—*n.* Canaanite.

Ca-na-di-an (kȧ-nā'dĭ-ăn), *n.* a native of Canada: *adj.* pertaining to Canada.

ca-nal (kȧ-năl'), *n.* a man-made navigable waterway; a tube for the passage of fluids; as, the alimentary *canal* is the passage from the mouth through the intestines; a channel or groove.

ca-nal-ize (kȧ-năl'īz; kăn'ȧ-līz), *v.t.* to furnish with canals; to cause to resemble a canal.

ca-nard (kȧ-närd'), *n.* a ridiculous rumor sent abroad to deceive the people.

ca-na-ry (kȧ-nā'rĭ), *n.* a light wine; a pale or bright yellow color; a small singing bird with yellow plumage, a native of the Canary Islands: *adj.* bright yellow.

can-cel (kăn'sĕl), *v.t.* [*p.t.* and *p.p.* canceled, *p.pr.* canceling], to deface writing by drawing lines across it; to destroy; as, to *cancel* a stamp, to mark out; as, to *cancel* figures; to annul; in mathematics, to strike out, as in taking out a common factor from the numerator and denominator of a fraction, etc.

Syn. abolish, efface, nullify, repeal, revoke, erase.

Ant. (see confirm).

can-cel-la-tion (kăn"sĕ-lā'shŭn), *n.* the act of annulling or revoking; the act of destroying the force or legal authority of; in mathematics, the process of striking out figures.

Can-cer (kăn'sẽr), *n.* one of the twelve divisions, called Signs, through which the sun passes in its yearly course: this sign, represented by a crab, is the northernmost point of the sun's course; the sign of the summer solstice, or the time when the sun is farthest from the equator: cancer, a disease characterized by a tumor or growth very dangerous to life.—*adj.* cancerous.

Candelabrum

can-de-la-brum (kăn"dē-lā'brŭm), *n.* [*pl.* candelabra (-brȧ), candelabrums (-brŭmz)], a lampstand; an ornamented branched candlestick.

can-des-cence (kăn-dĕs'ĕns), *n.* a state of glowing caused by great heat.

can-did (kăn'dĭd), *adj.* honest; outspoken; sincere: applied to persons; fair; as, a *candid* view of a matter.—*adv.* candidly.—*n.* candidness.

Syn. artless, frank, truthful.
Ant. (see crafty).

can-di-da-cy (kăn'dĭ-dȧ-sĭ), *n.* the position or state of one who presents himself, or is put up by others, as a contestant for an office, etc. Also, candidature.

can-di-date (kăn'dĭ-dāt), *n.* one who offers himself, or is proposed by others, to fill some office; as, Henry Clay was twice a *candidate* for the presidency.

can-died (kăn'dĭd), *p.adj.* preserved with, or covered with, a hard coat of sugar; changed to sugar.

can-dle (kăn'dl), *n.* a slender rounded body of tallow, wax, or other fatty material, inclosing a wick of cotton, and used to furnish light; anything resembling a candle in form or purpose.

can-dle-light (kăn'dl-līt"), *n.* the light of a candle or candles; light produced by artificial means; twilight.

Can-dle-mas (kăn'dl-mȧs), *n.* February 2, the day of the feast of the Purification of the Virgin Mary.

can-dle pow-er (kăn'dl pou'ẽr), the lighting power of a standard candle taken as a measure to determine the power of any light.

can-dle-stick (kăn'dl-stĭk"), *n.* a device for holding, or a support for, a candle.

can-dor (kăn'dẽr), *n.* openness; frankness; as, *candor* of speech; fairness; as, to judge with *candor*.

can-dy (kăn'dĭ), *n.* a confection of sugar, combined with flavoring or coloring substances; any sweetmeat made of, or cooked with, sugar or molasses: *v.t.* [*p.t.* and *p.p.* candied, *p.pr.* candying], to make into or become sugar; to preserve in sugar: *v.i.* to become coated with sugar; to become sugar.

can-dy-tuft (kăn'dĭ-tŭft"), *n.* a plant bearing clustered or tufted flowers, originally from Candia.

cane (kān), *n.* the stem of certain palms, grasses, and other plants, as the bamboo, sugar cane, rattan, etc.; a walking-stick: *v.t.* to beat with a walking stick; furnish with parts made of grasses, rattan, bamboo, etc.; as, to *cane* chairs.

cane-brake (kān'brāk"), *n.* a dense thicket of palm growths or canes.

Ca-nic-u-la (kȧ-nĭk'ū-lȧ), *n.* in astronomy, the Dog Star.

ca-nine (kȧ-nīn'; kā'nīn), *adj.* pertaining to dogs; having the nature or qualities of a dog; doglike: pertaining to the sharp-pointed teeth next to the incisors: *n.* the sharp-pointed tooth next to the incisors, or one shaped like it.

ca-nine teeth (kȧ-nīn' tēth; kā'nīn tēth), two sharp-pointed teeth on each side of the upper and lower jaws of most animals. Also, canines.

can-is-ter (kăn'ĭs-tẽr), *n.* a metal box or case for tea, coffee, etc.; a shell containing shot, or scraps of iron, which explodes when fired from a gun.

can-ker (kăn'kẽr), *n.* anything which causes rot or decay, or destroys by gradual eating or wearing away; a gangrenous ulcer, particularly in the mouth; a popular name for certain small white sores in the mouth: *v.t.* infect with poisonous influence: *v.i.* to become diseased; be infected with disease.—*adj.* cankerous.

can-ker-worm (kăn'kẽr-wûrm"), *n.* a caterpillar destructive to trees or plants; something, as sorrow, evil, etc., that destroys one's happiness.

can-na (kăn'ȧ), *n.* any of certain tropical American plants with large leaves and flowers; the flower of any of these plants.

canned (kănd), *adj.* preserved in tin receptacles; as, *canned* meats, vegetables, fruits.

can-nel coal (kăn'ĕl kōl), a soft coal that burns with a clear bright flame.

can-ner-y (kăn'ẽr-ĭ), *n.* [*pl.* canneries (-rĭz)], an establishment for preserving meat, fish, etc., in cans.

can-ni-bal (kăn'ĭ-bȧl), *n.* a human being who eats human flesh; any animal that eats the flesh of its own kind: *adj.* pertaining to, or like, a human being who eats human flesh.

can-ni-bal-ism (kăn'ĭ-bȧl-ĭzm), *n.* the act or practice of human beings of eating human flesh, or of animals of eating others of like kind; barbarity.

can-non (kăn'ŭn), *n.* [*pl.* cannons (-ŭnz), or cannon (collectively)], a large gun; a piece of artillery.

can-non-ade (kăn"ŭn-ād'), *n.* the act of discharging artillery against a town, fort, etc.: *v.t.* to attack with artillery.

can-non ball (kăn'ŭn bôl'), the round projectile discharged by a cannon; any missile for cannon.

can-non bone (kăn'ŭn bōn), the bone from the hock joint to the fetlock found on hoofed animals.

can-non-eer (kăn"ŭn-ēr'), *n.* an artillery gunner; the member of the gun section who sights the gun on its object.

can-not (kăn'nŏt), (*can* and *not*), am, are, or is, unable.

can-ny (kăn'ĭ), *adj.* shrewd; knowing; as, the Scotch are a *canny* race; cautious; reasonable; quiet; easy; safe. Also, cannie.—*adv.* cannily.

ca-noe (kȧ-nōō'), *n.* [*pl.* canoes (-nōōz)], any light boat driven forward by paddles: *v.i.* [*p.t.* and *p.p.* canoed, *p.pr.* canoeing], to paddle or sail in a light boat.—*n.* canoeist.

can-on (kăn'ŭn), *n.* a law or rule in general, especially regarding religious doctrines; the books of the Holy Scriptures received as authoritative by the Christian Church: called the Sacred Canon; a catalog of saints acknowledged in the Roman Catholic Church: a person who performs divine service in a cathedral.

ca-ñon (kăn'yŭn), *n.* a narrow deep passage between hills or mountains. Also, canyon.

ca-non-i-cal (kȧ-nŏn'ĭ-kȧl), *adj.* pertaining to, or conforming to, laws or rules of the church; pertaining to the books of the Bible which are accepted as authoritative.—*adv.* canonically.

ca-non-i-cals (kȧ-nŏn'ĭ-kȧlz), *n.pl.* the dress or vestments prescribed by the rules of the church to be worn by a clergyman officiating at services.

can-on-ize (kăn'ŭn-īz), *v.t.* to declare a deceased person a saint and enter his name in the catalog of the saints.—*n.* canonization.

can-o-py (kăn′ō-pĭ), *n.* [*pl.* canopies (-pĭz)], a covering fixed above a bed, or hung over a throne; any similar covering, as the arch of the sky: *v.t.* [*p.t.* and *p.p.* canopied, *p.pr.* canopying], to cover with, or as with, an overhanging shelter; as, the elm that *canopies* thy dwelling.

can't (känt; kȧnt), the contraction of *cannot*. [Colloq.]

cant (kănt), *n.* a whining manner of speech; the speech assumed by beggars; the slang spoken by thieves, gipsies, beggars, etc.; the insincere words and phrases used by a certain party, sect, etc.; the use of certain phrases and forms of speech without sincerity, especially those of a religious character; or the insincere use of sacred words; a slope; an inclination: *v.t.* to give a tilt or slant to: *v.i.* to speak in a whining voice, or with an assumed or hypocritical tone; make whining pretensions to goodness; to lean: *adj.* of the nature of affectation; as, a *cant* phrase.

can-ta-le-ver (kăn′tȧ-lē′vẽr; kăn′tȧ-lĕ′vẽr), *n.* a bracket or block projecting from the wall of a house, to support a balcony, cornice, etc.; a form of bridge truss, usually supported on a pier, balanced or counterweighted and projecting towards a similar truss on the opposite side of the space bridged, with which it is connected directly or by a girder. Also, cantilever.

can-ta-loupe (kăn′tȧ-lōōp; kăn′tȧ-lōp), *n.* a melon of delicate flavor. Also, cantaleup.

can-tan-ker-ous (kăn-tăn′kẽr-ŭs), *adj.* ill-tempered; quarrelsome. [Colloq.]—*adv.* cantankerously.

can-ta-ta (kăn-tä′tȧ), *n.* a poem or story set to music.

can-teen (kăn-tēn′), *n.* a kind of shop in barracks or camp where provisions and supplies are sold; a vessel used by soldiers for carrying water or other liquid when on the march; a box containing mess utensils, etc., for officers when on foreign service.

can-ter (kăn′tẽr), *n.* an easy gallop: *v.t.* and *v.i.* to move, or to cause to move, in an easy gallop.

can-thar-i-des (kăn-thăr′ĭ-dēz), *n.pl.* in medicine, a preparation made from any of several kinds of beetles, dried and powdered: used for blistering.

cant hook (kănt hŏŏk), a movable iron hook at or near the end of a wooden handle or lever: used to handle or turn over logs, etc.

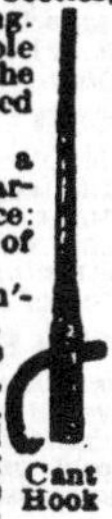

Cant Hook

can-ti-cle (kăn′tĭ-kl), *n.* a song; a passage of the Bible arranged for chanting in church service: Canticles, the Song of Songs, or Song of Solomon.

can-ti-le-ver (kăn′tĭ-lē′vẽr; kăn′tĭ-lĕv′ẽr), *n.* a bracket or block projecting from the wall of a house, to support a balcony, cornice, etc.; a form of bridge truss, usually supported on a pier, balanced or counterweighted and projecting towards a similar truss on the opposite side of the space bridged, with which it is connected directly or by a girder. Also, cantalever.

cant-ing (kănt′ĭng), *p.adj.* affectedly pious; whining; hypocritical.

can-tle (kăn′tl) *n.* the upwardly projecting rear part of a saddle.

can-to (kăn′tō), *n.* [*pl.* cantos (-tōz)], a division of a long poem, corresponding to a chapter of prose.

can-ton (kăn′tŏn; kăn-tŏn′), *n.* a district or division of a territory; one of the states of Switzerland: *v.t.* to distribute separate quarters to; as, to *canton* troops.

Can-ton flan-nel (kăn′tŏn flăn′ĕl), a strong cotton cloth with long fleecy nap.

can-ton-ment (kăn′tŏn-mĕnt; kăn-tōōn′mĕnt), *n.* the place assigned to troops for quarters.

can-vas (kăn′vȧs), *n.* a coarse heavy cloth of hemp or flax, used for tents, sails, etc., and also for painting; sails in general; sometimes, a painting: *adj.* made of this coarse hempen cloth.

can-vas-back (kăn′vȧs-băk′), *n.* a North American wild duck.

can-vass (kăn′vȧs), *n.* a close inspection or examination; discussion; a solicitation of votes, interest, orders, etc.: *v.t.* to examine; discuss thoroughly; as, to *canvass* a subject; ask for votes or opinions; to traverse (a district) for the purpose of securing votes, interest, orders, etc.; as, a book agent may *canvass* a town: *v.i.* to seek for orders, or solicit; as, he *canvassed* for subscriptions.

can-yon (kăn′yŭn), *n.* a deep, narrow gorge or ravine between mountains. Also, cañon.

caout-chouc (kōō′chŏŏk; kou′chŏŏk), *n.* the gum obtained from the juice of many tropical plants.

cap (kăp), *n.* a covering for the head, usually without a brim; anything resembling such a head-covering; a small copper or brass shell used in exploding gunpowder; the top or summit; a certain size of writing paper, usually 14 by 17 inches: *v.t.* [*p.t.* and *p.p.* capped, *p.pr.* capping], to put a cap on; cover with, or as with, a cap; cover the top end of; complete; crown; match or exceed; as, to *cap* the climax.

ca-pa-bil-i-ty (kā′pȧ-bĭl′ĭ-tĭ), *n.* the quality of being able to do; *pl.* mental attainments.

ca-pa-ble (kā′pȧ-bl), *adj.* having power, skill, or ability; as, *capable* of crime; *capable* of exertion; *capable* of improvement.—*adv.* capably.—*n.* capableness.

Syn. able, competent.
Ant. (see incompetent).

ca-pa-cious (kȧ-pā′shŭs), *adj.* roomy; having the power to hold much; as, a *capacious* trunk.—*adv.* capaciously.—*n.* capaciousness.

ca-pac-i-tate (kȧ-păs′ĭ-tāt), *v.t.* to enable; to make able; to make fit.

ca-pac-i-ty (kȧ-păs′ĭ-tĭ), *n.* [*pl.* capacities (-tĭz)], the power of receiving or containing; the power of containing a certain quantity exactly; the amount that can be contained; as, the *capacity* of the cask is four gallons; mental ability; as, suit the instruction to the *capacity* of the child; profession; position; as, Oliver Goldsmith once served in the *capacity* of a teacher.

cap-a-pie (kăp′ȧ-pē′), *adv.* from head to foot; as, a knight fought armed *cap-a-pie.*

ca-par-i-son (kȧ-păr′ĭ-sŭn), *n.* an ornamental covering for a horse; gay or rich clothing: *v.t.* to cover with rich clothing, as a horse; adorn with rich dress; as, kings were formerly *caparisoned* in velvet and ermine.

cape (kāp), *n.* a covering for the shoulders, worn separately or attached; a point of land projecting into the sea.

ca-per (kā'pẽr), *n.* a playful leap or spring; a skip; a prank; a plant, the flower-buds of which are pickled and used as a seasoning; the buds themselves: *v.i.* to skip; jump.

cap-il-lar-i-ty (kăp'ĭ-lăr'ĭ-tĭ), *n.* in physics, the action by which the surface of a liquid is raised or lowered where in contact with a solid: seen best in capillary tubes.

cap-il-la-ry (kăp'ĭ-lā-rĭ; kȧ-pĭl'ȧ-rĭ), *n.* a tube with a small bore: *pl.* one of the minute blood-vessels connecting the arteries with the veins: *adj.* resembling a hair; slender; pertaining to the minute tubes or vessels of the body.

cap-il-la-ry at-trac-tion (kăp'ĭ-lā-rĭ ă-trăk'-shŭn), the power possessed by porous bodies of drawing up a fluid; as, a blotter absorbs ink by *capillary attraction*.

cap-i-tal (kăp'ĭ-tăl), *n.* the chief city or town in a kingdom or state; a letter of the larger kind such as is used to begin sentences, proper nouns, etc.; the sum invested in any particular business; stock or resources of any kind, moral or physical; that part of wealth which is saved and is available for, or employed in, the production of more money; the head or top of a column or pillar: *adj.* punishable with death; as, treason and murder are *capital* crimes; first in importance; chief; principal; as, the *capital* points in a discussion; good; excellent; first-rate.

Capital

cap-i-tal-ism (kăp'ĭ-tăl-ĭzm), *n.* the possession of great wealth, especially by a few; the power of combined wealth.

cap-i-tal-ist (kăp'ĭ-tăl-ĭst), *n.* one who has wealth; especially a person of large wealth which may or may not be used in business.—*adj.* capitalistic.

cap-i-tal-i-za-tion (kăp'ĭ-tăl-ĭ-zā'-shŭn), *n.* the act of changing or converting into money for use in business; the amount of money resulting; the act of writing or printing with large, or capital, letters.

cap-i-tal-ize (kăp'ĭ-tăl-īz), *v.t.* to count up or have in possession the present value of in money, as a periodical payment; to convert into available money for use in business; also, to write or print with large, or capital, letters.

cap-i-tal-ly (kăp'ĭ-tăl-ĭ), *adv.* with loss of life; as, a murderer is *capitally* punished; in an excellent manner.

Cap-i-tol (kăp'ĭ-tŏl), *n.* originally, the temple of Jupiter at Rome, on the summit of the Capitoline Hill; now, the building occupied by the United States Congress at Washington; the house occupied by a State legislature.

Cap-i-to-line (kăp'ĭ-tō-līn), *adj.* indicating, or pertaining to, one of the seven hills of Rome: *n.* one of the seven hills of Rome

ca-pit-u-late (kȧ-pĭt'ū-lāt), *v.i.* to surrender to an enemy on conditions agreed upon; as, the Southern army *capitulated* to the Northern in 1865.

ca-pit-u-la-tion (kȧ-pĭt"ū-lā'shŭn), *n.* the act of surrendering; the written paper containing the terms of surrender; a summary.

ca-pit-u-lum (kȧ-pĭt'ū-lŭm), *n.* [*pl.* capitula (-lȧ)], a cluster of flowers attached directly at the base, as in the clover.

cap-lin (kăp'lĭn), *n.* a small fish of the smelt family, largely used as bait for cod.

ca-pon (kā'pŏn), *n.* a cock which has been castrated and fattened for the table.—*v.t.* caponize.

ca-pouch (kȧ-pōōsh'), *n.* a monk's hood or cowl; the hood of a cloak.

ca-price (kȧ-prēs'), *n.* a whim, freak, or fancy; as, children have many *caprices*.

ca-pri-cious (kȧ-prĭsh'ŭs), *adj.* unsteady; fickle; as, a *capricious* temper.—*adv.* capriciously.—*n.* capriciousness.

cap-ri-ole (kăp'rĭ-ōl), *n.* a leap of a horse made without advancing: *v.i.* to execute such a leap.

Cap-ri-corn (kăp'rĭ-kôrn), *n.* in astronomy, a southern constellation; the tenth sign of the zodiac, into which the sun enters about December 21. Also, Capricornus.

cap-ri-fi-ca-tion (kăp"rĭ-fĭ-kā'shŭn), *n.* an artificial method of pollinating the cultivated fig in order to make sure of its ripening.

cap-ri-fig (kăp'rĭ-fĭg), *n.* the wild fig, found in Asia Minor and in southern Europe.

cap-si-cum (kăp'sĭ-kŭm), *n.* any of several varieties of the nightshade plants bearing pungent berries; the dried and powdered fruit of these plants.

cap-size (kăp-sīz'), *v.i.* to be overturned; upset: *v.t.* to turn over or upset.

cap-stan (kăp'stăn), *n.* an upright drum or cylinder revolving upon an iron pivot and worked by bars or levers: used for winding a rope or raising heavy weights, especially the anchor of a ship.

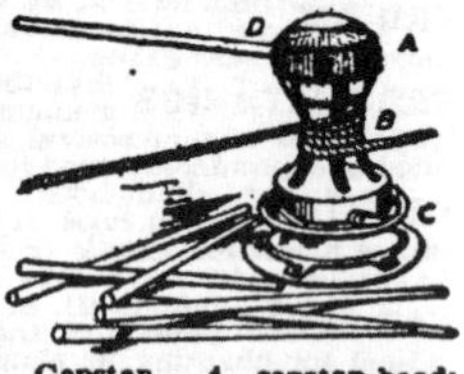

Capstan. *A*, capstan-head; *B*, barrel; *C*, pawl-rim and pawls; *D*, capstan-bar.

cap-stone (kăp'stōn"), *n.* the coping, or top course of the wall of a structure; the top of a wall.

cap-sule (kăp'sūl), *n.* a metallic seal or cover for a bottle; a small envelope of gelatin inclosing medicine; a seed-vessel or pod which opens when ripe; a small shallow vessel; a skinlike sac inclosing some part or organ of the body.—*adj.* capsular, capsulary, capsulated.

cap-tain (kăp'tĭn), *n.* one who has command of, or authority over, others; a chief; a commander; in the army, the commander of a company; in the navy, an officer commanding a ship of war; the master of a merchant vessel; the head of a team or side in athletic games, as football and baseball.

cap-tain-cy (kăp'tĭn-sĭ), *n.* the rank, post, or commission of one at the head of a company in the army, a ship of war in the navy, a merchant vessel, or an athletic team.

cap-tion (kăp'shŭn), *n.* the heading of a written or printed chapter, section, page, or article; the title of an illustration; the taking of a person under warrant of arrest; the introductory part of certain legal documents, as indictments, showing circumstances, authority, etc.

cap-tious (kăp'shŭs), *adj.* ready to catch at faults or take offense; as, a *captious* temper.—*adv.* **captiously.**—*n.* **captiousness.**

Syn. fretful, cross, peevish, petulant.
Ant. (see good-natured).

cap-ti-vate (kăp'tĭ-vāt), *v.t.* to enslave or hold captive by beauty or excellence; to charm or lure; to fascinate; as, a person may be *captivated* by the melody of a song or the beauty of a poem.

cap-ti-va-tion (kăp"tĭ-vā'shŭn), *n.* the act of charming; the state of being charmed.

cap-tive (kăp'tĭv), *adj.* made prisoner; held in bondage; fascinated: *n.* one who is taken prisoner, especially one so taken in war; one fascinated.

cap-tiv-i-ty (kăp'tĭv'ĭ-tĭ), *n.* the state of being held in bondage or confinement.

cap-tor (kăp'tŏr), *n.* one who captures, or takes any person or thing in such a way as to limit the freedom of the one captured.

cap-ture (kăp'tūr), *n.* the act of seizing or taking, as a prisoner or a prize; arrest; the thing taken: *v.t.* to take or seize by force, surprise, or trick; to make a prisoner or prize of.

Cap-u-chin (kăp'ū-chĭn; kăp"ū-shēn'), *n.* one of the monks of the order of St. Francis: named from the long pointed hood, or capouch, worn by the members; a woman's cloak and hood.

car (kär), *n.* a wheeled vehicle, especially one running on railroad tracks as part of a train; as, a baggage *car;* the basket suspended beneath a balloon to contain the balloonist; an automobile; the cage of an elevator; in poetry, a chariot of war or state.

ca-ra-ba-o (kä-rä-bä'ō), *n.* a water buffalo used as a draft animal in the Philippine Islands.

car-a-cole (kăr'ȧ-kōl), *n.* a half turn which a horseman makes, either to the right or left: *v.i.* to move in such a way; to wheel. Also, **caracol.**

ca-rafe (kȧ-răf'), *n.* a glass water-bottle for the table; a decanter.

car-a-mel (kăr'ȧ-mĕl), *n.* burnt sugar, used for coloring spirits, gravies, soups, etc.; a kind of sweetmeat.

car-at (kăr'ăt), *n.* the weight of 3.17 grains, used for weighing precious stones and pearls; a twenty-fourth part: a term used to express the fineness of gold used in jewelry; as, gold 22 *carats* fine contains 22 parts of pure gold and 2 of copper or silver. Also, **karat.**

car-a-van (kăr'ȧ-văn; kăr"ȧ-văn'), *n.* a company of travelers, merchants, or pilgrims, traveling together for safety, especially when passing through deserts or regions frequented by robbers; a large covered wagon or carriage for the conveyance of traveling exhibitions or passengers; a van.

car-a-van-sa-ry (kăr"ȧ-văn'sȧ-rĭ), *n.* [*pl.* caravansaries (-rĭz)], in the East, a kind of inn consisting of a large unfurnished building surrounding a spacious court, where caravans rest at night; a large hotel. Also, **caravanserai.**

car-a-vel (kăr'ȧ-vĕl), *n.* a small sixteenth century vessel, used by the Spaniards and Portuguese, with broad bows, narrow, high prow, three or four masts, and three-cornered sails. Also, **carvel.**

Columbus' Caravel

car-a-way (kăr'ȧ-wā), *n.* a plant of the celery family whose seeds are used for flavoring foods, and in medicine.

car-bide (kär'bīd; kär'bĭd), *n.* a compound of carbon with a metal.

car-bine (kär'bīn), *n.* a short rifle used chiefly by cavalry.

car-bo-hy-drate (kär"bō-hī'drāt), *n.* a compound of carbon, hydrogen, and oxygen.

car-bo-lat-ed (kär'bō-lāt'ĕd), *adj.* containing, or treated with, carbolic acid; as, *carbolated* vaseline.

car-bol-ic (kär-bŏl'ĭk), *adj.* pertaining to, or obtained from, coal-tar and oil: **carbolic acid,** an acid obtained from coal-tar: largely used as an antiseptic in surgery, and as a disinfectant: technically known as *phenol,* or *phenic* acid.

car-bo-lize (kär'bō-līz), *v.t.* to treat or mingle with carbolic acid.

car-bon (kär'bŏn), *n.* a nonmetallic element occurring in nature as the diamond and as graphite, and in coal, charcoal, coke, etc. and all organic substances; anything made of carbon, as the rod of an arc lamp.—*adj.* **carbonaceous.**

car-bon-ate (kär'bŏn-āt), *n.* a compound of carbonic acid with some other substance: *v.t.* to charge with carbonic acid.

car-bon di-ox-ide (kär'bŏn dī-ŏk'sīd), carbonic acid gas.

car-bon-ic (kär-bŏn'ĭk), *adj.* pertaining to, or obtained from, carbon: **carbonic acid,** a poisonous gas composed of carbon and oxygen; carbon dioxide.

car-bon-if-er-ous (kär"bŏn-ĭf'ĕr-ŭs), *adj.* containing or yielding carbon or coal; as, *carboniferous* layers of soil.

car-bon-ize (kär'bŏn-īz), *v.t.* to convert into carbon by the action of fire, or of an acid, or by any other means; to coat with carbon.—*n.* **carbonization.**

car-bo-run-dum (kär"bō-rŭn'dŭm), *n.* a compound of carbon with silicon: a very hard substance.

car-boy (kär'boi), *n.* a large glass bottle, protected by basket-work, used to contain or carry certain acids.

car-bun-cle (kär-bŭṅ'kl), *n.* a beautiful gem of a deep red color; an inflamed tumor or malignant boil.

car-bu-ret (kär'bū-rĕt), *v.t.* to charge or saturate with a volatile carbon compound.

car-bu-ret-or (kär'bû-rĕt'ĕr), *n.* an apparatus used to charge air with gas from gasoline for producing light or power; as, the *carburetor* supplies the fumes of gasoline, mixed with air, to the engine of an automobile. Also, **carbureter, carburettor.**

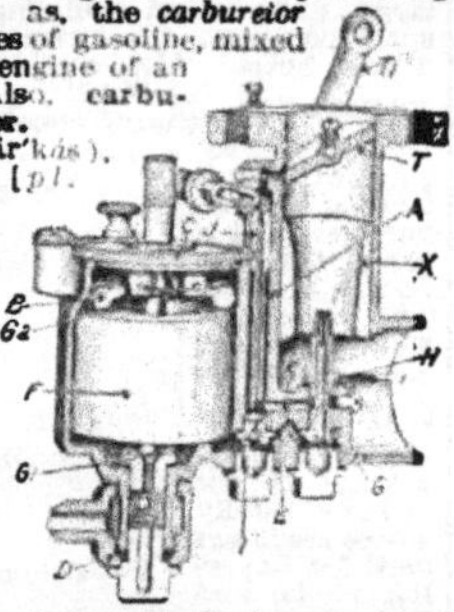

Automobile Carburetor. Gasoline enters the strainer *D*, rising to the float chamber through needle valve *G1*; as soon as the gasoline reaches the proper height, the float *F* rises and acting through the levers *B* and collar *G2*, closes the needle valve *G1*. Gasoline flows through three different channels to the motor according to the speed of the motor and the degree of opening of the throttle valve *T*. With the throttle wide open most of the gasoline flows through the channel *E* and main jet *G*; some flows through compensator *I* which is located at the bottom of a well open to the atmosphere through holes *A*, then through channel *K* to the cap jet *H* which surrounds the main jet *G*. Air enters through large opening at right and is mixed with the gasoline in Venturi tube *X* in constant proportion regardless of motor speed. For idling, or very slow motor speed, gasoline is drawn up idling tube *J*, mixed with air in the chamber at the top and the mixture enters at the edge of the butterfly valve *T* where there is strong suction.

car-cass (kär'kȧs), *n.* [*pl.* carcasses (-ĕz)], the dead body of an animal; in contempt, the corpse of a human being; hence, the decaying remains of a bulky thing; the framework or skeleton of a building, ship, etc.; in contempt, the living human body. Also, **carcase.**

card (kärd), *n.* a printed piece of pasteboard used for various social or business purposes; as, a post*card;* a calling *card;* such a piece printed, bearing certain devices or figures, used for playing games: *pl.* any game or games played with cards: *pl.* card playing; a short business advertisement in a newspaper; the dial of a mariner's compass; an implement for raising the nap on cloth; an instrument for combing the fibers of wool, flax, or cotton, to prepare the material for weaving or spinning: *v.t.* to comb, as wool, flax, etc., with, or as with, such an instrument.—*n.* **carder.**

card-a-mom (kär'dȧ-mŭm), *n.* the aromatic fruit of any of several Oriental plants of the ginger family; any of the plants. Also, **cardamon, cardamum.**

card-board (kärd'bōrd'), *n.* pasteboard of different qualities: used in making cards, etc.

car-di-ac (kär'dĭ-ăk), *adj.* pertaining to, or situated near, the heart; quickening the heart's action; pertaining to a certain part of the stomach: *n.* a medicine which increases the action of the heart and stomach.

car-di-gan (kär'dĭ-gǎn), *n.* a knitted woolen jacket or waistcoat. Also, **cardigan jacket.**

car-di-nal (kär'dĭ-nǎl), *adj.* chief; important; of a rich red color: necessary; as, justice is one of the *cardinal* virtues: *n.* a high official in the Roman Catholic Church, appointed by the Pope; a cardinal-bird; a rich red color.

car-di-nal-ate (kär'dĭ-nǎl-āt), *n.* the rank, dignity, or office of a cardinal. Also, **cardinalship.**

car-di-nal num-bers (kär'dĭ-nǎl nŭm'bẽrz), the numbers *one, two, three,* etc., in distinction from *first, second, third,* etc., the *ordinal* numbers.

car-di-nal points (kär'dĭ-nǎl points), north, east, south, west.

car-di-nal winds (kär'dĭ-nǎl windz), winds which blow directly from the north, south, east, and west.

card-ing (kärd'ing), *n.* the preparing of fibers for drawing or spinning; as, the *carding* of wool or flax.

care (kâr), *n.* concern; uneasiness of mind; anxiety; a burdensome responsibility; caution; charge or oversight; attention; watchfulness; an object of watchful attention and regard: *v.i.* to be anxious or solicitous; be concerned, troubled, or interested; to desire or wish; as, she did not *care* to go; to have a fondness: with *for.*

Syn., n. anxiety, concern, solicitude, heed.

Ant. (see heedlessness, negligence).

ca-reen (kȧ-rēn'), *v.t.* to turn (a ship) over on one side for the purpose of closing leaks, cleansing, or repairing: *v.i.* to incline on one side, as a ship under sail.

ca-reer (kȧ-rēr'), *n.* a run at full speed; general course of action, especially when remarkable; as, it is interesting to read of the *careers* of great men; an occupation, or calling: *v.i.* to move or run rapidly.

care-ful (kâr'fŏŏl), *adj.* done with care· formerly used to mean anxious; now, attentive; watchful; cautious; thoughtful.—*adv.* **carefully.**—*n.* **carefulness.**

care-less (kâr'lĕs), *adj.* neglectful; heedless; free from care.—*adv.* **carelessly.**—*n.* **carelessness.**

ca-ress (kȧ-rĕs'), *n.* any act expressing affection; an embrace: *v.t.* to treat with tokens of affection; fondle; bestow signs of affection upon.

Syn., v. kiss, embrace.

Ant. (see spurn, buffet).

car-et (kăr'ĕt; kā'rĕt), *n.* a mark [^] used in writing, or in correcting proofs, to indicate the place where something is omitted or is to be added.

care-worn (kâr'wōrn'), *adj.* showing the marks of anxiety; tired; harassed.

car-go (kär'gō), *n.* [*pl.* cargoes (-gōz)], the lading or freight of a ship; load.

car-i-bou (kăr'ĭ-bōō; kăr'ĭ-bōō'), *n.* the North American reindeer.

car-i-ca-ture (kăr'ĭ-kȧ-tūr), *n.* a picture or description of a person or thing, in which the defects or peculiarities are exaggerated so as to produce a laughable effect; as, every *caricature* of ex-President Roosevelt shows him with enormous teeth: *v.t.* to represent in a ridiculous or exaggerated style.—*n.* **caricaturist.**

Syn., n. mimicry, imitation, burlesque, exaggeration.

ca-ri-es (kā'rĭ-ēz), *n.* the ulceration and decay of a bone or tooth.—*adj.* **carious.**

cark-ing (kärk'ing), *p.adj.* causing vexation; wearing, as a trouble.

car-min-a-tive (kär-mĭn′ȧ-tĭv), *adj.* tending to relieve the stomach and bowels of gas; relieving colic: *n.* a remedy for colic or griping.

car-mine (kär′mĭn; kär′mīn), *n.* the coloring matter of cochineal, which has a rich crimson color; this color.

car-nage (kär′nāj), *n.* great slaughter; great destruction of life by violence; as, modern methods of war produce dreadful *carnage.*

car-nal (kär′năl), *adj.* pertaining to the body, its passions and its appetites; impure; not spiritual, but human; as, a *carnal* appetite.—*adv.* **carnally.**

car-na-tion (kär-nā′shŭn), *n.* a light rose-pink; flesh color; the parts of a picture in which flesh is represented; a pink.

car-nel-ian (kär-nēl′yăn), *n.* a reddish variety of chalcedony, light or dark red in color: used for jewelry and seals. Also, **cornelian.**

car-ni-val (kär′nĭ-văl), *n.* the season of rejoicing before Lent, observed in Roman Catholic countries; feasting or revelry.

car-niv-o-ra (kär-nĭv′ō-rȧ), *n.pl.* animals that feed on flesh.—*adj.* **carnivorous.**

car-ol (kăr′ŭl), *n.* a song of joy or praise; a lay: *v.t.* and *v.i.* [*p.t.* and *p.p.* caroled, *p.pr.* caroling], to sing in joy; warble.

car-om (kăr′ŭm), *v.i.* to move swiftly in a slanting line, as a billiard ball: *n.* the striking of a billiard ball against two others in succession.

ca-rot-id (kȧ-rŏt′ĭd), *n.* one of the two principal arteries, one on either side of the neck, which convey the blood to the head: *adj.* pertaining to the two great arteries of the neck.

ca-rous-al (kȧ-rouz′ăl), *n.* a carouse; revelry; a drinking match or bout.

ca-rouse (kȧ-rouz′), *n.* a feast or festival; a noisy drinking bout or revel: *v.i.* to drink heartily and with noisy jollity; to revel.—*n.* **carouser.**

car-ou-sel (kăr″ōō-zĕl′), *n.* a merry-go-round; a military pageant. Also, **carrousel.** [FR.]

carp (kärp), *v.i.* to find unreasonable fault: with *at*: *n.* a fresh-water fish, often bred in ponds.

car-pal (kär′păl), *adj.* pertaining to the wrist.

car-pel (kär′pĕl), *n.* a simple one-celled seed-vessel, or one of the parts of a compound pistil.

car-pen-ter (kär′pĕn-tẽr), *n.* one who works in timber and prepares the woodwork of houses, ships, etc.

car-pen-try (kär′pĕn-trĭ), *n.* the art of cutting, framing, and joining timber.

car-pet (kär′pĕt), *n.* a thick woven or felted fabric, with a pattern, used for covering floors or stairs; a soft covering upon which one may walk; as, a *carpet* of grass: *v.t.* to cover with a carpet.

car-pet-bag (kär′pĕt-băg), *n.* a traveling bag, originally made of carpetlike material.

car-pet-bag-ger (kär′pĕt-băg″ẽr), *n.* a political adventurer from the North in the Southern States after the Civil War: a term of contempt.

car-pet bee-tle (kär′pĕt bē′tl), a small beetle whose larvæ destroy carpets, etc. Also, **carpet bug.**

car-pet-ing (kär′pĕt-ĭng), *n.* cloth for carpets; carpets in general.

car-pet knight (kär′pĕt nīt), one upon whom the honor of knighthood or other distinction has been conferred for other than active service; a knight who has spent his time in luxury.

carp-ing (kärp-ĭng), *p.adj.* complaining; faultfinding; apt to catch at faults.

car-riage (kăr′ĭj), *n.* the act of conveying or transporting; cost of transporting; behavior; manner of bearing oneself; as, an erect *carriage* is necessary to correct breathing; a wheeled vehicle; a wheeled stand or support, as of a cannon.

car-ried (kăr′ĭd), past tense and past participle of *carry.*

car-ri-er (kăr′ĭ-ẽr), *n.* one who, or that which, transports or conveys; one whose business is to transport goods for hire; a frame for holding photographic plates or magic-lantern slides; a messenger; a basket, as of fruit; as, these peaches cost twenty cents per *carrier.*

car-ri-er pi-geon (kăr′ĭ-ẽr pĭj′ŭn), a variety of pigeon trained to carry letters, messages, etc., as during war.

car-ri-on (kăr′ĭ-ŭn), *n.* dead or decaying flesh; filth; garbage; as, the buzzard often feeds on *carrion: adj.* pertaining to, or feeding on, dead decaying flesh.

car-ron-ade (kăr″ŭ-nād′), *n.* a short cannon with large cavity for close shooting, formerly used in the navy.

car-rot (kăr′ŭt), *n.* a plant with a yellow, tapering root that is used for food; the root itself.

car-ry (kăr′ĭ), *v.t.* [*p.t.* and *p.p.* carried, *p.pr.* carrying], to convey from one point to another; bear; to gain possession of by force; as, to *carry* a fort; lead; transfer; as, to *carry* an amount from one page of a ledger to another; accomplish; gain possession of; extend or continue in time or space; with *up* or *back;* as, the book of Genesis *carries* us back to the creation; exhibit; as, his face always *carries* a smile; imply; have in charge or conduct; as, to *carry* on business; to bear (oneself); to secure the passage of, as a bill or motion; to sustain; to bear the burden of; as, the office *carries* a great responsibility with it: *v.i.* to reach a distant point; as, his voice *carries* well: **carry on,** in the World War, to keep on; to bear up under difficulties and continue; to resume.

Syn. lift, sustain, transport, bear, bring.

car-ry-all (kăr′ĭ-ôl″), *n.* a light covered carriage for family use.

cart (kärt), *n.* a vehicle for carrying heavy goods; a light delivery wagon used by tradesmen, etc.: *v.t.* to carry or convey in a cart.—*n.* **carter.**

cart-age (kär′tāj), *n.* the charge made for carrying by a cart; the act of carting.

carte blanche (kärt blänsh′), a blank paper; a signed sheet of paper given to another to be filled up as he pleases; hence, absolute freedom of action; as, he had *carte blanche* to spend as much as he chose. [FR.]

car-tel (kär′tĕl; kär-tĕl′), *n.* an agreement between hostile states regarding the exchange of prisoners; a challenge to single combat.

Car-tha-gin-i-an (kär″thȧ-jĭn′ĭ-ăn), *adj.* of or pertaining to the city of Carthage: *n.* a native of Carthage.

car-ti-lage (kär'tĭ-lāj), *n.* a smooth, solid, elastic animal tissue; gristle.

car-ti-lag-i-nous (kär"tĭ-lăj'ĭ-nŭs), *adj.* pertaining to, or in the form of, gristle, or cartilage; having a skeleton of gristle, as sharks.

car-ton (kär'tŏn), *n.* a pasteboard box; the pasteboard for making such boxes.

car-toon (kär-to͞on'), *n.* a picture dealing with a political or social subject in an amusing or offensive manner; a full-size sketch to serve as a design for a work to be copied from it in oil, tapestry, etc.—*n.* **cartoonist.**

car-tridge (kär'trĭj), *n.* a case of card-board, metal, or other material, containing the powder, or powder and ball, for a cannon, gun, etc.; a roll of protected films for a camera.

U. S. 30 Caliber Cartridge

carve (kärv), *v.t.* to form (a design or shape) by cutting; as, to *carve* a design in wood; to cut or grave out of stone, wood, or metal; cut into slices; as, to *carve* meat; to mark with lines or furrows; as, her face was *carved* with wrinkles; *v.i.* to make graven work or figures; to cut up meat, as at table. —*n.* **carver.**

car-vel (kär'vĕl), *n.* any of several kinds of small sailing vessels. Also, **caravel.**

carv-ing (kärv'ĭng), *n.* the act or art of one who sculptures or designs by cutting; the work so accomplished; ornamental sculpture.

car-y-at-id (kăr"ĭ-ăt'ĭd), *n.* a column in the form of a figure of a woman in long robes.

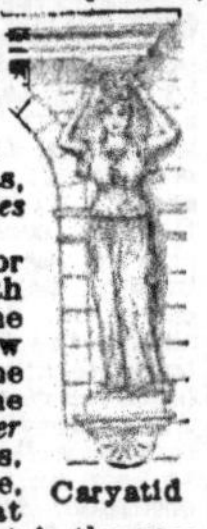

Caryatid

cas-cade (kăs-kād'), *n.* a small waterfall; as, there are several beautiful *cascades* in Ausable Chasm.

case (kās), *n.* a covering or container; also, a box with its contents; in carpentry, a frame or casing; in printing, a shallow tray for type, divided into the *upper case*, which contains the capital letters, etc., and the *lower case*, which contains small letters, figures, etc.; the peculiar state, conditions, or circumstances that surround a person; as, since that is the *case*, I shall let the matter drop; the matters involved in a question under discussion or investigation; as, a *case* for a detective; a certain form or instance of disease; a suit or action at law; one of the forms or inflections in the declension of a noun, pronoun, or adjective showing its relation to other words; as, the nominative *case*: *v.t.* to cover with, or inclose in, a case; as, to *case* anyone in armor; to *case* a wall with stone or a box with metal; to cover (an object of glass) with a layer of glass of another color fused on.

case-hard-en (kās'här"dn), *v.t.* to harden the surface of (as iron) by conversion into steel, while the interior keeps the toughness of iron.

ca-se-in (kā'sē-ĭn), *n.* the curd matter of milk, forming the main part of cheese.

case knife (kās nīf), a knife provided with a sheath; a table knife.

case-mate (kās'māt), *n.* a shell-proof vault or battery, having openings through which cannon may be pointed and discharged.

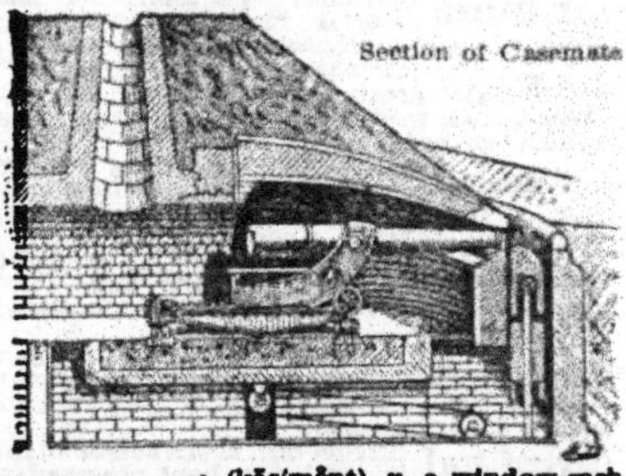

Section of Casemate

case-ment (kās'mĕnt), *n.* a window-sash made to open on hinges; loosely, any window.

cash (kăsh), *n.* money; ready money: *v.t.* to turn into, or exchange for, money; as, to *cash* a check.

cash-book (kăsh'bo͝ok"), *n.* a book in which an account is kept of money received or paid out.

ca-shew (kȧ-sho͞o'), *n.* a tropical American tree; its edible nut.

cash-ier (kăsh-ēr'), *n.* one who has charge of the money, and superintends the payments and receipts of a bank or other business: *v.t.* to dismiss in disgrace from a position of trust or from military service.

cash-mere (kăsh'mēr; kăsh"mēr'), *n.* a soft woolen fabric for shawls, etc., originally made in Cashmere, India, from the downy hair of the wild goat of Thibet and the Himalayas; also, a soft woolen dress fabric made in imitation of the real fabric.

cas-ing (kās'ĭng), *n.* the act of covering with, or placing in, a case; a covering; a framework; as, a window *casing.*

ca-si-no (kȧ-sē'nō), *n.* [*pl.* Eng. casinos (-nōz); It. casini (-nē)], a small country house; a public room or building used for social meetings, dancing, gaming, etc.; a game played with cards.

cask (kȧsk), *n.* a barrel-shaped vessel with flat heads and wooden staves, bound by iron hoops, for holding liquors; the quantity contained in such a vessel.

cas-ket (kȧs'kĕt), *n.* a small chest or box for jewels; a costly coffin.

casque (kȧsk), *n.* in former times, a piece of armor to cover the head; hence, a helmet.

cas-sa-va (kȧ-sä'vȧ), *n.* a plant of tropical America and Africa, cultivated for its roots, which yield a starch; also, the starch, from which tapioca is made.

cas-se-role (kăs'ĕ rōl; kăs'ĕ-rōl'), *n.* a covered earthenware baking dish, often with a metal stand or container; a saucepan; a baked dish consisting of vegetables or meat contained in a surrounding layer of rice, mashed potato, etc.

cas-sia (kăsh'ȧ; kăsh'ĭ-ȧ), *n.* a cheap grade of cinnamon; a kind of plant from the leaves of which the drug senna is obtained.

cas-si-mere (kăs'ĭ-mēr), *n.* a thin woolen cloth used for men's garments. Also, **casimere, kerseymere.**

cas-sock (kăs'ŭk), *n.* a long, close-fitting garment worn by clergymen, choristers, etc., under the surplice.

cas-so-wa-ry (kăs'ŏ-wâ-rĭ), *n.* [*pl.* cassowaries (-rĭz)], a large bird resembling the ostrich, inhabiting Australia and the Papuan Islands.

Cassowary

cast (kȧst), *v.t.* [*p.t.* and *p.p.* cast, *p.pr.* casting], to throw; hurl; to project; shed; as, the snake *casts* its skin; direct or turn; as, *cast* the eyes; throw violently; as, to *cast* a prisoner into jail; calculate, as, *cast* up a bill; form into a certain shape; assign (as parts in a play) to various actors: *v.i.* to throw the line in angling; receive form or shape in a mold: *n.* the act of throwing a line, shaping a mold, etc.; the distance to which a thing may be thrown; motion or turn: said of the eye; the form or shape; manner; appearance; as, a *cast* of countenance; a tinge; as, a *cast* of green; the company of actors to whom the parts of a play are assigned; an impression or mold.

cas-ta-nets (kăs'tȧ-nĕts; kăs"tȧ-nĕts'), *n.pl.* small spoon-shaped shells of hard wood or ivory, fastened loosely at the top, a pair of which is fastened to each thumb and shaken with the fingers to beat time to dances and music.

Castanets

cast-a-way (kȧst'ȧ-wā"), *n.* a person or vessel wrecked on a barren coast; as, Robinson Crusoe was a *castaway;* an outcast; one who has lost the favor of God: *adj.* shipwrecked; rejected.

caste (kȧst), *n.* one of the hereditary divisions of society into which Hindus are restricted by Brahman religious law; the custom of this division; any similar division of society.

cas-tel-lat-ed (kăs'tĕ-lāt"ĕd), *adj.* furnished with turrets and battlements; like a castle.

cast-er (kȧs'tẽr), *n.* one who, or that which, throws, molds, calculates, etc.; a cruet or small vessel for holding salt, pepper, vinegar, etc., at table; a small roller on a swivel fastened under a piece of furniture, etc. Also, **castor.**

cas-ti-gate (kăs'tĭ-gāt), *v.t.* to correct; chastise; punish; subject to severe criticism.—*n.* **castigator.**

cas-ti-ga-tion (kăs"tĭ-gā'shŭn), *n.* the act of correcting; a whipping; severe punishment.

Cas-tile soap (kăs-tēl' sōp), a superior kind of soap, originally made at Castile, Spain.

Cas-til-ian (kăs-tĭl'yăn), *adj.* of or pertaining to Castile: *n.* a native of Castile; pure Spanish.

cast-ing (kȧst'ĭng), *n.* the act or process of forming from melted metal any article according to a given design; the process of taking impressions of statues, medals, etc.

cast-ing vote (kȧst'ĭng vōt), the deciding vote of a chairman when the votes are equal.

cast i-ron (kȧst ī'ŭrn), iron melted and run into molds: **cast-iron,** *adj.* made of melted or cast iron; very hard.

cas-tle (kȧs''l), *n.* a house fortified for defense against an enemy; a fortress; a strong and imposing mansion of a noble and wealthy person; one of the pieces at chess: called also *rook:* *v.t.* to inclose in, or as in, a fortified place.

cas-tor (kȧs'tẽr), *n.*, a cruet for vinegar, oil, etc., at table; a small roller on a swivel fastened under a piece of furniture, etc.: also, **caster:** a heavy, all-wool fabric for overcoats; a hat, especially of beaver fur; an odorous secretion of beavers: used in perfumery.

cas-tor oil (kȧs'tẽr oil), an oil from the castor bean, used as a medicine.

cas-trate (kăs'trāt), *v.t.* to deprive of virile power; to remove from the male the semen-producing glands.—*n.* **castration.**

cas-u-al (kăzh'ŭ-ăl; kăz'ŭ-ăl), *adj.* happening by chance; accidental; as, a *casual* meeting; coming without regularity; as, *casual* expenses.—*adv.* **casually.**

cas-u-al-ty (kăzh'ŭ-ăl-tĭ), *n.* [*pl.* casualties (-tĭz)], an accident, especially, if resulting in bodily injury or death; as, the railroads are responsible for many *casualties:* *pl.* in military and naval usage, losses in general, caused by death, wounds, desertion, or discharge.

cas-u-ist (kăzh'ŭ-ĭst; kăz'ŭ-ĭst), *n.* one who studies questions of right or wrong in conduct.—*adj.* **casuistic, casuistical.**—*adv.* **casuistically.**

cas-u-ist-ry (kăzh'ŭ-ĭs-trĭ; kăz'ŭ-ĭs-trĭ), *n.* science dealing with questions of right or wrong in conduct; false reasoning as to morals; hairsplitting distinctions in these connections.

cat (kăt), *n.* a flesh-eating animal; especially, the familiar household pet; a stoutly-built vessel, with a narrow stern, projecting quarters, and a deep waist.

cat-a-clysm (kăt'ȧ-klĭzm), *n.* a deluge; flood; a violent or sudden change of the earth's surface, such as an earthquake; hence, an upheaval, social or political, such as a great war.

cat-a-comb (kăt'ȧ-kōm), *n.* an underground burial place with niches hollowed out for the dead: commonly in plural; as, the *catacombs* of Rome.

cat-a-falque (kăt'ȧ-fălk), *n.* a temporary structure erected, usually in a church, to support the coffin of a famous person during the funeral.

cat-a-lep-sy (kăt'ȧ-lĕp"sĭ), *n.* a sudden suspension of motion and feeling, in which the patient is speechless, senseless, and motionless. Also, **catalepsis.**—*adj.* **cataleptic.**

cat-a-log (kăt'ȧ-lŏg), *n.* an arranged list; or register of; *v.t.* to enter in, or make, a list or register of; to put in a list. Also, **catalogue.** —*n.* **cataloger, cataloguer.**

ca-tal-pa (kȧ-tăl'pȧ), *n.* a tree of the trumpet-flower family.

cat-a-ma-ran (kăt"ȧ-mȧ-răn'), *n.* a kind of float or raft made of logs or pieces of wood lashed together and propelled by paddles or sails; any vessel with twin hulls; a flat-bottomed boat.

cat-a-mount (kăt'ȧ-mount), *n.* the wild cat; the puma, cougar, or mountain lion.

Catapult

cat-a-pult (kăt'ȧ-pŭlt), *n.* an ancient military engine for hurling darts and stones; sometimes a forked stick with an elastic band by which stones, dried peas, etc. are thrown: *v.t.* to throw from, or as from, such an engine.

cat-a-ract (kăt'ȧ-răkt), *n.* a large waterfall; a furious rush or downpour of water; a disease of the eye in which the vision becomes impaired or is lost.

ca-tarrh (kȧ-tär'), *n.* an affection of any mucous membrane, especially of the nose or air passages; cold in the head.

ca-tarrh-al (kȧ-tär'ăl), *adj.* pertaining to, or produced by, catarrh; as, a *catarrhal* condition of the throat; of the nature of catarrh.

ca-tas-tro-phe (kȧ-tăs'trō-fē), *n.* a great calamity or disaster; the outcome of a plot: applied to a play.
Syn. calamity, disaster, mischance, mishap.
Ant. (see blessing).

Ca-taw-ba (kȧ-tô'bȧ), *n.* a light red variety of American grape; a light wine made from this grape.

cat-bird (kăt'bûrd"), *n.* the mocking-thrush: so named from its cry of alarm.

cat-boat (kăt'bōt"), *n.* a small boat with one sail on a mast near the bow.

cat-call (kăt'kôl"), *n.* a sound, like the cry of a cat, made in theaters to express disapproval; a squeaking instrument used for the same purpose: *v.t.* and *v.i.* to deride or to express disapproval by such calls.

catch (kăch), *v.t.* [*p.t.* and *p.p.* caught, *p.pr.* catching], to seize or grasp; lay hold of suddenly; take captive; to please or charm; to take, by contagion, infection, or sympathy, as a disease; attack; communicate to, as a fire; come upon unexpectedly; detect; to comprehend; as, to *catch* the idea; come up to; reach in time, as a train: *n.* the act of seizing or grasping; that which is taken; as, a good *catch* of fish; a song the parts of which are taken up by different voices; a scrap of song.—*n.* **catcher.**

catch-all (kăch'ôl"), *n.* a receptacle for holding a great variety of things.

catch-ing (kăch'ĭng), *p.adj.* contagious; infectious: said of diseases; captivating; fascinating.

catch-pen-ny (kăch'pĕn"ĭ), *n.* [*pl.* catchpennies (-ĭz)], an article of little value made attractively to effect a quick sale: *adj.* cheap; showy; made to sell to the unwary.

catch-up (kăch'ŭp), *n.* a sauce made from mushrooms, tomatoes, walnuts, etc. Also, **catsup, ketchup.**

catch-word (kăch'wûrd"), *n.* a word or phrase that takes the popular fancy; a cue.

catch-y (kăch'ĭ), *adj.* attractive; quick to win popular approval; as, a *catchy* tune; captivating.

cat-e-chet-i-cal (kăt"ē-kĕt'ĭ-kăl), *adj.* consisting of questions and answers; as, the *catechetical* method of teaching.

cat-e-chise (kăt'ē-kīz), *v.t.* to instruct by means of questions and answers, and by offering explanations; especially, to instruct in the Christian religion; ask questions or examine. Also, **catechize.**—*n.* **catechist.**

cat-e-chism (kăt'ē-kĭzm), *n.* a small book of instruction in the form of question and answer, especially in the principles of the Christian religion.

cat-e-gor-i-cal (kăt"ē-gŏr'ĭ-kăl), *adj.* of or pertaining to, or in the form of, a general classification of things; absolute; unconditional; positive; as, a *categorical* answer.—*adv.* **categorically.**

cat-e-go-ry (kăt'ē-gō-rĭ), *n.* [*pl.* categories (-rĭz)], a class in any general classification; any comprehensive class; one of the classes into which the objects of knowledge or thought can be divided, such as time, place, passion, etc.

cat-e-na-ry (căt'ē-nā-rĭ), *n.* in mathematics, a certain curve formed by a flexible cord suspended by its ends: *adj.* indicating such a curve.

ca-ter (kā'tẽr), *v.i.* to supply food: as, it is hard to *cater* to the uncertain appetite of an invalid; to supply what is desired or needed: with *to* or *for*.—*n.* **caterer.**

cat-er-pil-lar (kăt'ẽr-pĭl"ẽr), *n.* the hairy wormlike stage in the life of a butterfly or winged insect; in the World War, a powerful traction engine used for hauling heavy guns.

cat-er-waul (kăt'ẽr-wôl), *v.i.* to cry, as cats at night; hence, to utter harsh, unpleasant sounds.

cat-fish (kăt'fĭsh"), *n.* an American fish of several species, differing much in size.

cat-gut (kăt'gŭt"), *n.* a kind of cord made from the intestines of animals, usually sheep, and used as strings for musical instruments and for some other purposes.

ca-thar-tic (kȧ-thär'tĭk), *adj.* cleansing the bowels; purgative: *n.* a medicine to cause movement of the bowels.

ca-the-dral (kȧ-thē'drăl), *n.* the chief church of a diocese or church district under the special charge of the bishop: *adj.* pertaining to such a church or the diocese of which it is the center.

cath-ode (kăth'ōd), *n.* the terminal by which an electric current leaves the substance through which it passes, known as the negative pole: opposite to *anode*: **cathode rays**, a stream of rays produced when an electrical discharge is passed through a gas at low pressure: when these rays strike on the surface of a solid, they produce Röntgen rays, popularly called *X-rays*. Also, **kathode.**

cath-o-lic (kăth'ō-lĭk), *adj.* universal; general; including all; as, a person who likes to read all kinds of books has a *catholic* taste in literature; liberal; large-hearted; including all mankind.—**Catholic**, pertaining to the Church of Rome: *n.* a member of the Catholic Church, especially of the Roman Catholic Church.

Ca-thol-i-cism (kȧ-thŏl'ĭ-sĭzm), *n.* the belief of, or adherence to, the Catholic Church, or faith, especially to that of the Roman Catholic Church. Also, **Catholicity.**

cath-o-lic-i-ty (kăth"ō-lĭs'ĭ-tĭ), *n.* the quality of being universal or large-minded; liberality.

Ca-thol-i-cize (kȧ-thŏl'ĭ-sīz), *v.t.* to convert to Roman Catholicism: *v.i.* to become Catholic or Roman Catholic.

cat-kin (kăt'kĭn), *n.* the hanging blossoms of the willow, birch, etc.

cat-nip (kăt'nĭp"), *n.* a common plant of the mint family. Also, **catmint.**

cat-o'-nine-tails (kăt"ō-nīn'tālz"), *n.* a whip with nine lashes of knotted cord, formerly used for punishment in the English army and navy: an implement used for flogging.

cat's-paw (kăts'pô), *n.* a dupe; a person who is deceived into doing something to advance the interests of another: from the fable of the monkey, who used the cat's paw to get the roasted chestnuts from the fire.

cat-sup (kăt'sŭp), *n.* a sauce made of tomatoes, mushrooms, walnuts, etc. Also, **catchup, ketchup.**

cat-tail (kăt'tāl'), *n.* a tall plant which grows in marshes.

cat-tle (kăt'l), *n.* live stock, especially oxen, bulls, and cows.

Cau-ca-si-an (kô-kā'shăn; kô-kăsh'ăn), *adj.* of or pertaining to the Caucasus, a range of mountains between the Black and the Caspian Seas; more commonly, of or relating to the division of mankind including the chief races of Europe, North Africa, and southwestern Asia: *n.* a member of the Caucasian, or white, race; a native of the Caucasus.

cau-cus (kô'kŭs), *n.* a meeting of the leaders or members of a political party, to decide upon a policy to be submitted to a convention or larger meeting.

cau-dal (kô'dăl), *adj.* pertaining to a tail; as, the *caudal* fin of a fish is the fin which forms the tail.

caught (kôt), *p.t.* and *p.p.* of *catch;* as, fish are *caught* in a net; a moth is *caught* by a flame; he *caught* the idea.

caul (kôl), *n.* a membrane, such as the great omentum; the fold of the peritoneum which passes from the stomach to the large intestines; the enveloping membrane sometimes covering the head of a child at birth; a net, especially one covering the hair.

caul-dron (kôl'drŭn), *n.* a large kettle or boiler. Also, **caldron.**

cau-li-flow-er (kô'lĭ-flou"ẽr), *n.* a garden variety of cabbage with an edible flowering head; the flowering head.

caulk (kôk), *v.t.* to make tight by filling (crevices of) with soft material; as, to *caulk* the seams of a ship. Also, **calk.**

caus-al (kôz'ăl), *adj.* relating to, involving, or expressing a reason, agency, or ground; as, *hence* and *because* are *causal* words; a *causal* fact or event.

cau-sal-i-ty (kô-zăl'ĭ-tĭ), *n.* the relation of cause and effect; the action or agency that brings a thing about.

cau-sa-tion (kô-zā'shŭn), *n.* the act of bringing about or producing; also, the act or agency producing an effect.

caus-a-tive (kôz'ȧ-tĭv), *adj.* effective as an agency or cause; expressing causation.

cause (kôz), *n.* that which produces or contributes to a result; in law, ground for action; motive; reason; a movement; as, the suffrage *cause;* a side or party; as, the *cause* of right; a suit or action in court: *v.t.* to produce; to bring about.—*adj.* **causeless.**

cause-way (kôz'wā), *n.* a pathway raised, as over wet ground, and paved with stone; a highway.

caus-tic (kôs'tĭk), *adj.* burning; hot; having the power of gradually eating away by chemical action; sarcastic; as, a *caustic* remark: *n.* a substance which burns.—*adv.* **caustically.**—*n.* **causticity.**

cau-ter-ize (kô'tẽr-īz), *v.t.* to burn or sear with a hot iron, or with some other caustic substance.—*n.* **cauterization.**

cau-ter-y (kô'tẽr-ĭ), *n.* a burning or searing, as with a hot iron or other caustic substance; the instrument or substance used to cauterize.

cau-tion (kô'shŭn), *n.* a warning against evil; an act or word that conveys a warning; heedfulness; prudence in regard to danger; watchfulness: *v.t.* to warn of danger; notify of danger.

cau-tious (kô'shŭs), *adj.* exercising discretion; careful; heedful; prudent.—*adv.* **cautiously.**—*n.* **cautiousness.**

cav-al-cade (kăv'ăl-kād), *n.* a train or procession of persons, usually on horseback.

cav-a-lier (kăv"ȧ-lēr'), *n.* an armed horseman; especially, a knight or gentleman soldier; a gay military man; a beau or attendant upon a lady: *adj.* gay; sprightly; careless; haughty; as, a *cavalier* refusal: **Cavalier,** *n.* a partisan of Charles I in his struggle with the Parliament in the seventeenth century: *adj.* of or pertaining to the adherents of Charles I.—*adv.* **cavalierly.**

cav-al-ry (kăv'ăl-rĭ), *n.* horse soldiers; as, in present-day warfare, the *cavalry* is less frequently in action than formerly.—*n.* **cavalryman.**

cave (kāv), *n.* a hollow place in the earth; a large natural hole or a den; a falling away or receding: *v.t.* to hollow out: *v.i.* to fall in or down; give way: often with *in.*

cave man (kāv măn), a man of the prehistoric, or stone, age, who lived in a cave.

cav-ern (kăv'ẽrn), *n.* a large natural hollow under ground; a den; cave.

cav-ern-ous (kăv'ẽr-nŭs), *adj.* hollow like a cavern; filled with small holes.—*adv.* **cavernously.**

cav-i-ar (kăv'ĭ-är'), *n.* the roes, or eggs, of certain large fish, especially the sturgeon, salted and dried. Also, **caviare.**

cav-il (kăv'ĭl), *v.i.* [*p.t.* and *p.p.* caviled, *p.pr.* caviling], to find fault or offer objection without good reason; to raise foolishly critical or frivolous objections: followed by *at;* as, a generous man will not *cavil* at the little faults of his neighbors: *n.* a petty or frivolous objection.—*n.* **caviler.**

cav-i-ty (kăv'ĭ-tĭ), *n.* [*pl.* cavities (-tĭz)], a hollow place or part.

ca-vort (kȧ-vôrt'), *v.i.* to prance about, as a horse; as, at the sound of the trumpet the horse began to *cavort* madly. [SLANG.]

caw (kô), *v.i.* to cry like a crow, rook, or raven: *n.* the cry of the crow.

cay-enne (kā-ĕn'; kī-ĕn'), *n.* a kind of pepper made from the seeds and fruit of certain plants: called also *red pepper.*

cease (sēs), *v.i.* to come to an end; stop; followed by *from* before a noun: *v.t.* discontinue; end.

Syn. terminate, leave off, stop, desist, refrain.

cease-less (sēs'lĕs), *adj.* without end; without stop; incessant.—*adv.* **ceaselessly.**—*n.* **ceaselessness.**

ce-cro-pi-a moth (sē-krō'pĭ-ȧ môth), a large silkworm moth.

ce-dar (sē'dẽr), *n.* the name of several evergreen trees, having wood of great durability and fragrance: *adj.* pertaining to, or made of, cedar.

ce-darn (sē'dẽrn), *n.* of or pertaining to or made of cedar.

cede (sēd), *v.t.* to give up or surrender; as, the people must *cede* to the government some of their natural rights.

ce-dil-la (sē-dĭl'ȧ), *n.* a mark placed under c [ç] to indicate the sound of *s*, as in the French word *leçon*.

ceil (sēl), *v.t.* to overlay or cover the inner surface of a roof; furnish with a ceiling.

ceil-ing (sēl'ĭng), *n.* the inner roof of an apartment, usually made of laths and plaster; the altitude to which an airplane can ascend.

cel-an-dine (sĕl'ăn-dīn), *n.* a perennial herb of the poppy family, with small yellow flowers and poisonous juice.

cel-e-brant (sĕl'ē-brănt), *n.* one who performs a religious rite, especially the priest in offering Mass or celebrating the Communion.

cel-e-brate (sĕl'ē-brāt), *v.t.* to praise, or honor; to offer up the sacrifice of the Mass; commemorate; as, to *celebrate* the Fourth of July.
Syn. observe, keep, solemnize.
Ant. (see disregard).

cel-e-bra-ted (sĕl'ē-brāt"ĕd), *adj.* renowned; illustrious; distinguished; famous.

cel-e-bra-tion (sĕl"ē-brā'shŭn), *n.* the act of commemorating or honoring; an observance or ceremony in honor of anything.

ce-leb-ri-ty (sē-lĕb'rĭ-tĭ), *n.* [*pl.* celebrities (-tĭz)], fame; distinction; a renowned or famous person; as, Alexander Graham Bell attained *celebrity* through the invention of the telephone; he became a *celebrity*.

ce-ler-i-ty (sē-lĕr'ĭ-tĭ), *n.* rapidity; swiftness; speed.

cel-er-y (sĕl'ĕr-ĭ), *n.* a plant cultivated for use as a salad and vegetable.

ce-les-tial (sē-lĕs'chăl), *adj.* of or pertaining to the sky or heavens; as, the sun, the moon, and the stars are *celestial* bodies; heavenly; supremely excellent; of or pertaining to the Chinese dynasty: *n.* an inhabitant of heaven: **Celestial**, a native of China.—*adv.* **celestially**.

cel-i-ba-cy (sĕl'ĭ-bȧ-sĭ; sē-lĭb'ȧ-sĭ), *n.* the state of being unmarried; also, single life, especially that of a bachelor, or one bound by vows to an unmarried life.

cel-i-bate (sĕl'ĭ-bāt), *n.* an unmarried person: *adj.* single; unmarried.

cell (sĕl), *n.* a small room in a monastery, convent, or prison; a small or mean place of residence; a small cavity or hole; a tiny mass of living matter forming one of the units of every living body.

cel-lar (sĕl'ĕr), *n.* a vault or room under ground for storing provisions, wine, fuel, etc.

cel-lar-age (sĕl'ĕr-āj), *n.* cellars; the space occupied by cellars; charge for storage in cellars.

cel-lo (chĕl'ō), *n.* [*pl.* cellos (-ōz), celli (-ē)], a contraction for violoncello, a stringed musical instrument of the same form as the violin, but larger, and having deep, soft tones. Also, **'cello**.—*n.* **cellist, 'cellist**.

cel-lu-lar (sĕl'ū-lȧr), *adj.* pertaining to, or consisting of, or marked by having, cells.

cel-lu-loid (sĕl'ū-loid), *n.* a compound of camphor and gun-cotton, resembling ivory, but frequently colored.

cel-lu-lose (sĕl'ū-lōs), *n.* the substance resembling and allied to starch, which forms the main part of plant tissue, linen, paper, etc.

Celt (sĕlt), *n.* a member of the Celtic family of mankind, which includes the ancient Gauls and Britons, the Gaelic Scotch, the Irish, the Bretons, and the Welsh. Also, **Kelt**.—*adj.* **Celtic, Keltic**.

Celt-ic (sĕl'tĭk), *adj.* of or pertaining to the Celts or their language.

ce-ment (sē-mĕnt'; sĕm'ĕnt), *n.* any substance which makes two bodies stick together; mortar; the bony layer which forms the outer substance of a tooth: *v.t.* (sē-mĕnt'), to unite with a sticky substance: unite firmly.—*n.* **cementation**.

cem-e-ter-y (sĕm'ē-tĕr-ĭ), *n.* [*pl.* cemeteries (-ĭz)], a public burial ground; graveyard.

cen-o-bite (sĕn'ō-bīt; sē'nō-bīt), *n.* a member of a religious community; a monk.

Ce-no-zo-ic (sē'nō-zō'ĭk; sĕn'ō-zō'ĭk), *adj.* pertaining to the latest geological era, which includes the Tertiary and Quaternary periods: *n.* the latest geological era; the age of mammals.

cen-o-taph (sĕn'ō-tȧf), *n.* an empty tomb, or a monument erected in honor of a person buried elsewhere.

cen-ser (sĕn'sĕr), *n.* a covered cup-shaped vessel pierced with holes, in which incense is burned.

cen-sor (sĕn'sŏr; sĕn'sĕr), *n.* originally, one of two magistrates of ancient Rome who imposed taxes and regulated the manners and morals of a community; now, an official appointed to examine books, manuscripts, plays, motion pictures, letters, telegrams, etc., before publication, performance, or use, to ascertain that there is nothing immoral or offensive in them; hence, in general, one who blames or finds fault; a critic; in time of war, an official who examines all printed matter, mail, newspaper cablegrams or telegrams, etc., in which information of value to the enemy might be written.

cen-so-ri-ous (sĕn-sō'rĭ-ŭs), *adj.* inclined to find fault or condemn; faultfinding, critical.—*adv.* **censoriously**.—*n.* **censoriousness**.

cen-sor-ship (sĕn'sŏr-shĭp; sĕn'sĕr-shĭp), *n.* the office or position of an official whose duty it is to examine printed matter before publication in order to cut out objectionable matter, or, in war, information that could be used by the enemy.

cen-sur-a-ble (sĕn'shŭr-ȧ-bl), *adj.* deserving of, or subject to, blame; blameworthy; culpable.

cen-sure (sĕn'shŭr), *n.* blame; reproof; the act of finding fault; as, Benedict Arnold won the eternal *censure* of the world: *v.t.* to find fault with or condemn; as, do not *censure* what you do not understand: *v.i.* to find fault.
Syn. v. criticize.
Ant. (see praise).

cen-sus (sĕn'sŭs), *n.* an official count of the people of a country, with details of sex, age, etc., taken in the United States and some other countries every ten years.

cent (sĕnt), *n.* the hundredth part of a dollar, or a coin of this value: a hundred: used only in the phrase *per cent*.

cen-taur (sĕn'tŏr), *n.* an imaginary being, half man and half horse.

cen-te-na-ri-an (sĕn"tē-nā'rĭ-ăn), *n.* a person a hundred years old or over.

cen-te-na-ry (sĕn'tē-nā-rĭ), *n.* [*pl.* centenaries (-rĭz)], a period of a hundred years; the celebration of the hundredth anniversary of an event; as, the *centenary* of the signing of the Declaration of Independence was celebrated by a great World's Fair in Philadelphia.

cen-ten-ni-al (sĕn-tĕn'ĭ-ăl), *adj.* consisting of, or enduring, a hundred years; taking place once in a hundred years: *n.* the celebration of a hundredth anniversary.

cen-ter (sĕn'tẽr), *n.* that point of a circle or sphere, which is equally distant from every point of the circumference; the middle point of anything; the part or place around which things are collected; as, the *center* of a rebellion; the *center* of trouble; the *center* of a town; certain members of a lawmaking body who hold moderate views and occupy a place between those of extreme opinions; troops in a line between the wings: *v.t.* to place on or at the middle point; collect to a point; as, to *center* one's attention: *v.i.* to be in the center; as, his interests *center* in his children; to converge in the middle. Also, centre.

Syn., *n.* middle, midst.

Ant. (see circumference).

cen-ter-board (sĕn'tẽr-bōrd"), *n.* a pivoted keel that may be raised or lowered at pleasure: extensively used by racing boats. Also, centreboard.

cen-ter of grav-i-ty (sĕn'tẽr ŏv grăv'ĭ-tĭ), the point about which all the parts of a body balance each other, so that when that point is supported, the whole body is supported.

cen-ti-grade (sĕn'tĭ-grād), *adj.* graduated or divided into a hundred parts called degrees; pertaining especially to the centigrade thermometer, on which the distance between the freezing point and boiling point of water is divided into one hundred equal degrees.

cen-ti-gram (sĕn'tĭ-grăm), *n.* a weight equal to the hundredth part of a gram, or .15432 grain, troy. Also, centigramme.

cen-ti-li-ter (sĕn'tĭ-lē"tẽr), *n.* a measure of volume equal to the hundredth part of a liter, or .06102 cubic inch.

cen-time (säṅ-tēm'; sän'tēm), *n.* a small French coin equal to the hundredth part of a franc, or about one-fifth of a cent.

cen-ti-me-ter (sĕn'tĭ-mē"tẽr), *n.* a measure of length equal to the hundredth part of a meter, or .3937 inch.

cen-ti-pede (sĕn'tĭ-pēd), *n.* one of several varieties of small animals having many feet attached to a many-jointed flat body.

cen-tral (sĕn'trăl), *adj.* relating to, or situated in, the middle; chief; leading.—*adv.* centrally.

cen-tral-i-za-tion (sĕn"trăl-ĭ-zā'shŭn), *n.* the act or process of bringing to one chief or middle point; the act of bringing all local government under one principal government; as, the Constitution of the United States provides for a *centralization* of power in the national government.

cen-tral-ize (sĕn'trăl-īz), *v.t.* to draw or bring to one chief or middle point; bring under one control or system.

cen-tric (sĕn'trĭk), *adj.* placed in the middle; central. Also, centrical.

cen-trif-u-gal (sĕn-trĭf'ū-găl), *adj.* tending or causing to fly off from the center; passing outward from a central point; as, it is *centrifugal* movement that separates the cream from the milk in a separator.

cen-trip-e-tal (sĕn-trĭp'ē-tăl), *adj.* tending or causing to approach the center; as, the *centripetal* motion of a whirlpool or whirlwind.

cen-tu-ri-on (sĕn-tū'rĭ-ŭn), *n.* the captain of a hundred Roman soldiers.

cen-tu-ry (sĕn'tū-rĭ; sĕn'chŏŏ-rĭ), *n.* [*pl.* centuries (-rĭz)], a hundred; a hundred years, especially of the Christian era; a subdivision of the Roman people for taxation, voting, etc.; a subdivision of the Roman army.

cen-tu-ry plant (sĕn'tū-rĭ plănt), an American plant, so named because of the mistaken belief that it blooms only once in a hundred years.

cen-tu-ry run (sĕn'tū-rĭ rŭn), a hundred mile run on a bicycle, or other vehicle.

ce-phal-ic (sē-făl'ĭk), *adj.* of, pertaining to, or located near, the head.

ceph-a-lo-pod (sĕf'ȧ-lō-pŏd), *n.* any of the highest class of mollusks, including cuttlefish, etc.

ce-ram-ic (sē-răm'ĭk), *adj.* of or pertaining to pottery; as, the Greeks excelled in the *ceramic* arts: ceramics, *n.* the art of making things of baked clay; work executed wholly or partly in clay and baked. Also, keramic, keramics.

ce-rate (sē'rāt), *n.* a mixture of oil, lard, wax, etc., used as a plaster upon the skin.

cere (sēr), *v.t.* to cover or close with wax or cerecloth; to embalm.

ce-re-al (sē'rē-ăl), *adj.* pertaining to, or producing, wheat or eatable grain: *n.* eatable grain.

cer-e-bel-lum (sĕr"ē-bĕl'ŭm), *n.* a lobe of the brain; the little brain; the back part of the brain.—*adj.* cerebellar.

cer-e-bral hem-i-sphere (sĕr'ē-brăl hĕm'ĭ-sfēr), one of the two halves of the cerebrum, or larger part of the brain.

cer-e-brum (sĕr'ē-brŭm), *n.* [*pl.* cerebrums (-brŭmz)], the superior and larger part of the brain: the seat of the mind and will.

cere-cloth (sēr'klōth"), *n.* a cloth soaked with wax or some gummy substance, in which embalmed bodies are wrapped.

cere-ment (sēr'mĕnt), *n.*, a gravecloth or shroud; *pl.* grave-clothes.

cer-e-mo-ni-al (sĕr"ē-mō'nĭ-ăl), *adj.* relating to, or performed with, rites or formalities: *n.* ritual; rite; the proper order for a rite or function; as, the *ceremonial* of a coronation or of a church service.—*adv.* ceremonially.

cer-e-mo-ni-ous (sĕr"ē-mō'nĭ-ŭs), *adj.* characterized by formality; formal; observant of the prescribed form for any occasion; precise.—*adv.* ceremoniously.—*n.* ceremoniousness.

cer-e-mo-ny (sĕr'ē-mō-nĭ), *n.* [*pl.* ceremonies (-nĭz)], a sacred rite or observance; as, the marriage *ceremony*; a prescribed rite or formality; as, the inaugural *ceremony*; behavior regulated by the laws of strict etiquette.

ce-rise (sē-rēz'), *adj.* bright red; cherry-colored: *n.* the color of a bright red cherry.

cer-tain (sûr'tĭn), *adj.* sure; beyond a doubt; destined; fixed or stated; dependable; indefinite, but presumably known to the speaker; as, a *certain* city.
Syn. secure, sure, decided.
Ant. (see doubtful).

cer-tain-ly (sûr'tĭn-lĭ), *adv.* with assurance; surely; undoubtedly.

cer-tain-ty (sûr'tĭn-tĭ), *n.* [*pl.* certainties (-tĭz)], a thoroughly established fact; the state or fact of being sure, fixed, or definite.

cer-tif-i-cate (sûr-tĭf'ĭ-kāt), *n.* a written testimony to the truth of any fact; as, a *certificate* of marriage or baptism; a testimonial as to character or ability: **certificate of deposit**, the formal written statement from a bank of the amount a person has on deposit: *v.t.* (sûr-tĭf'ĭ-kāt), to give a proof or testimony of by means of a written statement.

cer-ti-fi-ca-tion (sûr'tĭ-fĭ-kā'shŭn), *n.* the act of testifying by means of a written statement, or of assuming the responsibility, as of a bank check; a written statement given as proof or testimony of facts, character, etc.

cer-ti-fy (sûr'tĭ-fī), *v.t.* [*p.t.* and *p.p.* certified, *p.pr.* certifying], to testify to or make known in writing; assure, as to guarantee the payment of a check by writing across its face "good," or the like, followed by the signature of the cashier of the bank on which the check is drawn.

cer-ti-tude (sûr'tĭ-tūd), *adj.* assurance; freedom from doubt; as, no one can say with *certitude* that the planet Mars is not inhabited.

ce-ru-le-an (sē-rōō'lē-ăn), *n.* and *adj.* azure; sky-colored.

ce-ru-men (sē-rōō'mĕn), *n.* earwax; as, the hardening of the *cerumen* may occasion deafness.

ce-ruse (sē'rōōs; sē-rōōs'), *n.* white-lead: used as a paint; a preparation made from it to beautify the skin.

cer-vi-cal (sûr'vĭ-kăl), *adj.* of or pertaining to the neck; as, the *cervical* vertebræ are those bones of the spine which are in the neck.

ces-sa-tion (sĕ-sā'shŭn), *n.* the act of ceasing; a pause.
Syn. intermission, rest, stop.
Ant. (see continuance).

ces-sion (sĕsh'ŭn), *n.* a giving up to another, as of territory, property, or rights; as, by the *cession* of the Philippine Islands to the United States, in 1898, Spain lost her only foothold in the East.

cess-pool (sĕs'pōōl'), *n.* a deep hole in the ground, or the well of a drain for the reception of sewage.

ces-tus (sĕs'tŭs), *n.* [*pl.* cestus (sĕs'tŭs)], a kind of glove used by ancient boxers, frequently loaded with lead or iron, and secured by leathern thongs to the hands and arms.

ce-su-ra (sē-zū'rȧ; sē-sū'rȧ), *n.* a break or pause in a line of poetry. Also, **cæsura**.

chafe (chāf), *v.t.* to make warm by friction; to wear away or make sore by rubbing; to anger; annoy; fret; irritate: *v.i.* to rub; move, as one body on or against another, causing friction; to be vexed.

chaff (chȧf), *n.* the husk of grain, especially when separated by threshing, etc.; straw or hay cut fine for cattle; anything worthless; good-natured raillery: *v.i.* and *v.t.* to tease; to make game of.

chaf-fer (chăf'ẽr), *n.* the act of bargaining: *v.i.* to haggle or dispute about a purchase.

chaf-finch (chăf'ĭnch; chȧf'ĭnch), *n.* a bird so named from its feeding on grain.

chaff-weed (chȧf'wēd'), *n.* a plant with short, dry, chafflike leaves: called also *false pimpernel*.

chaff-y (chȧf'ĭ), *adj.* resembling or full of chaff; light or worthless; inclined to tease.

chaf-ing-dish (chāf'ĭng-dĭsh), *n.* a small portable vessel supplied with an alcohol lamp, or some other means of cooking food or keeping it hot.

cha-grin (shȧ-grĭn'; Eng. shȧ-grēn'), *n.* vexation due to disappointment, or mortification: *v.t.* to excite vexation in; to mortify.
Syn., *n.* confusion, dismay, humiliation, shame, vexation.
Ant. (see delight).

chain (chān), *n.* a series of links or rings joined together; a measure of 100 links or 66 feet, used in surveying land; a connected series or succession; as, a *chain* of events: *pl.* fetters; shackles; bondage: *v.t.* to fasten, secure, or connect with a chain: fetter; restrain.

chain gang (chān găng), a gang of convicts working together in chains.

chain pump (chān pŭmp), a pump that raises water by means of buckets or disks which are attached to an endless chain passing through a tube.

chain mail (chān māl), easily bent armor made of metal links woven together.

chain stitch (chān stĭtch), a fancy stitch resembling a chain; a loop-stitch made by a sewing machine.

chair (châr), *n.* a movable seat with a back, for one person; a professorship; as, Longfellow once occupied the *chair* of modern languages and literature at Harvard College; the presiding officer of an assembly.

chair-man (châr'măn), *n.* [*pl.* chairmen (-mĕn)], the president of an assembly, meeting, public company, etc.—*n.* **chairmanship**.

chaise (shāz), *n.* a light two-wheeled carriage.

chal-ced-o-ny (kăl-sĕd'ō-nĭ; kăl'sē-dō-nĭ), *n.* [*pl.* chalcedonies (-nĭz)], a variety of quartz, partially transparent and commonly pale blue or gray, with a waxy luster.

chal-cid (kăl'sĭd), *n.* any of a large group of insects, mostly parasitic.

chal-co-py-rite (kăl'kō-pī'rīt), *n.* a yellow sulphide of copper and brass: called also *copper pyrites*.

Chal-de-an (kăl-dē'ăn), *adj.* pertaining to ancient Chaldea or Babylonia; pertaining to astrology or magic: *n.* one of the people of Chaldea; a soothsayer; the language of the Chaldeans.

chal-dron (chôl'drŭn), *n.* an old English measure for coal, coke, etc.

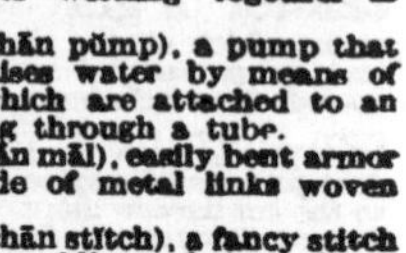
Swiss Chalet

cha-let (shȧ-lā'), *n.* a Swiss cottage or herdsman's dwelling; a small country house built in the Swiss style.

chal-ice (chăl'ĭs), *n.* a cup; especially, a cup used in the Communion service.

chalk (chôk), *n.* a soft limestone rock; especially, prepared crayons for drawing; a score in a game: *v.t.* to mark, or rub, or whiten, with crayon or chalk.—*adj.* **chalky.**—*n.* **chalkiness.**

Chalice

chal-lenge (chăl'ĕnj), *n.* an invitation to a contest; especially, a summons to fight; the demand of a countersign by a soldier on sentry duty: *v.t.* to summon to a contest; invite to a duel; take exception to; as, to *challenge* the truth of a statement; to demand the countersign from.—*n.* **challenger.**

chal-lis (shăl'ĭ; chăl'ĭs), *n.* a light-weight cotton or all-wool cloth. Also, **challie.**

cham-ber (chām'bẽr), *n.* an apartment; especially, a bedroom; a private room; a political or commercial body; a cavity; that part of a gun, etc., which contains the charge: *pl.* a suite of rooms.

cham-bered (chām'bẽrd), *p.adj.* having compartments; having chambers.

cham-ber-lain (chām'bẽr-lĭn), *n.* an officer who has charge of the private apartments of a ruler or nobleman; a male servant who has charge of a suite of rooms.

cham-ber-maid (chām'bẽr-mād), *n.* a woman having charge of bed-chambers, making the beds, etc.

cham-bray (shăm'brā), *n.* a plain-colored gingham dress fabric with a linen finish.

cha-me-le-on (kȧ-mē'lē-ŭn), *n.* a lizardlike reptile that is able to change its color.

cham-ois (shăm'ĭ), *n.* an antelope found on high European peaks; commonly, a soft leather.

Chamois

champ (chămp), *v.t.* and *v.i.* to bite with the teeth repeatedly and impatiently.

cham-pagne (shăm-pān'), *n.* a light, sparkling, amber-colored wine.

cham-paign (shăm-pān'), *n.* flat, open country; a clear, level landscape.

cham-pi-on (chăm'pĭ-ŭn), *n.* one who defends the cause of another, by combat or other means; a hero; valiant warrior; a successful competitor against all rivals: *v.t.* to defend or support; as, William L. Garrison *championed* the cause of anti-slavery.—*n.* **championship.**

chance (chȧns), *n.* an unforeseen event; an accident; a possibility; opportunity; risk: *v.i.* to happen; occur without design or expectation: *v.t.* to risk: with *it.*

Syn. fate, fortune, opening.
Ant. (see design).

chan-cel (chȧn'sĕl), *n.* that part of a church where the altar stands.

chan-cel-lor (chȧn'sĕl-ẽr), *n.* a judge of a court of equity; the president of a university; the president of the German Federal Council.—*n.* **chancellorship.**

chan-cer-y (chȧn'sẽr-ĭ), *n.* a court of equity or justice.

chan-de-lier (shăn'dĕ-lēr'), *n.* a hanging frame with branches for lights.

chan-dler (chȧn'dlẽr), *n.* a maker or seller of candles; a general name for a dealer or merchant, the particular meaning being shown by a prefix; as, tallow-*chandler;* a dealer in groceries and small wares.

change (chānj), *v.t.* to alter; exchange or give an equivalent for; to make different; convert: *v.i.* to undergo alteration; pass from one place to another; to put on different clothes; colloquially, to get out of one vehicle and into another; as, to *change* cars: *n.* a passing from one state or form to another; small coin; balance returned after subtraction of amount paid; a place where men meet to do business; any variation.

Syn., v. barter, exchange, substitute: *n.* substitute, alteration.
Ant. (see continue).

change-a-ble (chān'jȧ-bl), *adj.* capable of going from one thing to another or one mood to another; fickle; taking now one form or color and now another.—*adv.* **changeably.**—*n.* **changeability, changeableness.**

Syn. inconstant, mutable.
Ant. (see unchangeable).

change-less (chānj'lĕs), *adj.* free from alteration or substitution; immutable; monotonous.—*adv.* **changelessly.**—*n.* **changelessness.**

change-ling (chānj'lĭng), *n.* an unattractive child left in place of a beautiful one.

chan-nel (chăn'ĕl), *n.* the bed of a stream; the deepest part of a strait, bay, harbor, etc.; a long groove or furrow; a way by which anything may be carried; as, a *channel* of communication must be kept open between an army and its base of supplies: *v.t.* to cut or wear grooves or furrows in.

chant (chȧnt), *v.t.* to sing; intone: *v.i.* to make melody with the voice: *n.* a solemn or monotonous song.—*n.* **chanter.**

chant-ey (shȧn'tĭ; chȧn'tĭ), *n.* [*pl.* chanteys (-tĭz)], a song sailors sing while at work.

chan-ti-cleer (chăn'tĭ-klēr), *n.* a cock: so called from the loudness or clearness of his crow.

cha-os (kā'ŏs), *n.* confusion; a confused mixture; a state of disorder.

cha-ot-ic (kā-ŏt'ĭk), *adj.* in wild confusion; disordered; as, *chaotic* ideas.

chap (chăp), *v.t.* [*p.t.* and *p.p.* chapped, *p.pr.* chapping], to cause to crack or become rough; as, extreme cold may *chap* the skin: *v.i.* to crack or become rough; as, the skin may *chap* in cold weather: *n.*, colloquially, a fellow; as, a good-natured *chap.*

chap (chăp; chŏp), *n.* one of the jaws or its fleshy covering: usually in plural.

chap-ar-ral (chăp'ȧ-răl'), *n.* a dense thicket of dwarf oak or shrubs or cactus.

cha-peau (shȧ'pō'), *n.* [*pl.* chapeaux (-pōz)], a hat or head covering; the cocked hat worn by general officers. [Fr.]

chap-el (chăp'ĕl), *n.* a place of public worship, not so large or important as a church; a place of worship in a palace, institution, etc.

chap-er-on (shăp'ēr-ōn), *n.* a married or older woman who accompanies young unmarried women in public: *v.t.* to escort: as, the matron *chaperoned* a party of young girls.

chap-fal-len (chŏp'fôl"n; chăp'fôl"n), *adj.* dejected; crestfallen.

chap-lain (chăp'lĭn), *n.* a clergyman who performs service in the army, navy, a public institution, or a royal or private household.—*n.* **chaplaincy, chaplainship.**

chap-let (chăp'lĕt), *n.* a wreath or garland for the head; a rosary or part of a rosary.

chap-ter (chăp'tēr), *n.* a division of a book; a meeting of certain societies or orders; a body of those who hold such a meeting.

char (chär), *v.t.* [*p.t.* and *p.p.* charred, *p.pr.* charring], to burn partially, or to blacken by burning.

char-ac-ter (kăr'ăk-tēr), *n.* a letter, sign, or figure; reputation; nature; as, a woman of noble *character;* moral force; admirable qualities; quality; rank; distinctive qualities or traits; a certificate as to conduct or ability; a personage in a play.

char-ac-ter-is-tic (kăr"ăk-tēr-ĭs'tĭk), *adj.* typical; pertaining to, or displaying, the moral nature of; as, it was *characteristic* of Lincoln, that he would never defend a man whom he believed to be in the wrong: *n.* a distinguishing mark or quality.—*adv.* **characteristically.**

char-ac-ter-i-za-tion (kăr"ăk-tēr-ĭ-zā'shŭn), *n.* the act of describing by the peculiar or essential traits or marks: as, Shakespeare's *characterization* of King Richard III is not entirely true to history.

char-ac-ter-ize (kăr'ăk-tēr-īz), *v.t.* to describe by peculiar or essential qualities; to mark or distinguish; as, the Angora cat is *characterized* by long silky hair.

cha-rade (shā-räd'), *n.* an acted riddle based on a word with several significant parts, each of which, as well as the word, is to be guessed from the scenic or other representations.

char-coal (chär'kōl"), *n.* wood partially burnt in such a way as to be good for fuel.

charge (chärj), *v.t.* to rush on or attack; load, as a gun; to command; instruct; accuse; to demand as a price; to place something on record as due from, or as a debt of: *v.i.* to make an attack: *n.* an onset; quantity with which a firearm or apparatus is loaded; an office or obligation; an order or command; authoritative instruction or direction; price.

charge-a-ble (chär'jȧ-bl), *adj.* subject to tax; as, wine is *chargeable* with a heavy duty; capable of being charged.

char-gé d'af-faires (shär"zhā' dȧ"fâr'), [*pl.* chargés (shär"zhā')], a government official who acts for an ambassador in his absence, or at a court at which no ambassador is received.

charg-er (chär'jēr), *n.* a spirited horse; a large dish.

char-i-ot (chăr'ĭ-ŏt), *n.* an ancient two-wheeled car for war, state processions, racing, etc.—*n.* **charioteer.**

Roman Chariot

char-i-ta-ble (chăr'ĭ-tȧ-bl), *adj.* kind and liberal; as, a *charitable* woman; pertaining to charity; as, a *charitable* institution.—*adv.* **charitably.**—*n.* **charitableness.**

char-i-ty (chăr'ĭ-tĭ), *n.* [*pl.* charities (-tĭz)], the disposition to think well of others; alms; universal love and good will to the poor or suffering; an institution for the poor founded by a gift.

char-lotte russe (shär'lŏt rōōs'), whipped cream or custard inclosed in sponge cake.

charm (chärm), *n.* a spell or enchantment; that which causes admiration; as, the beauty of the flowers is the chief *charm* of California; a trinket; as, a watch *charm:* *v.t.* to influence by magic; give exquisite delight to: *v.i.* to work by magic powers.

Syn., *v.* captivate, enchant, enrapture, allure.

charm-ing (chärm'ĭng), *adj.* attractive; with power to cause admiration or give delight; fascinating; pleasing.—*adv.* **charmingly.**

char-nel (chär'nĕl), *adj.* containing flesh or dead bodies; as, foul *charnel* dungeons were said to lie beneath many old castles.

chart (chärt), *n.* a map of any part of the sea, river, etc., for the use of mariners; the map of a ship's course; a sheet giving information in tabular form; as, a nurse's *chart:* *v.t.* to map out.

char-ter (chär'tēr), *n.* an official paper bestowing certain rights and privileges; as, King James gave William Penn a *charter* to the province of Pennsylvania; a written order from the authorities of a society to establish another chapter, lodge, or branch: *v.t.* to grant a charter to; colloquially, to hire for one's own use.

char-wom-an (chär'wŏŏm"ăn; chär'-wŏŏm"ăn), *n.* [*pl.* charwomen (-wĭm'ĕn)], a woman hired by the day to do domestic work or cleaning work in corridors, offices, etc.

char-y (châr'ĭ; chā'rĭ), *adj.* careful; cautious; reserved; shy; frugal or sparing; as, a poor man must be *chary* in the use of his money.—*adv.* **charily.**—*n.* **chariness.**

chase (chās), *v.t.* to pursue; especially, to hunt; drive away; to decorate a metal surface by embossing, engraving, etc.; to cut, as the thread of a screw: *v.i.* to follow in pursuit: *n.* eager pursuit; hunting, especially of wild beasts; that which is hunted; an iron frame into which pages or columns of type are locked for printing; the part of a cannon in front of the supports.

chasm (kăzm), *n.* a deep opening in the earth; a cleft; a gap; a void.

chas-sis (shȧ'sē), *n.* the frame, machinery, and wheels of an automobile; the main framework of an airplane. [Fr.]

chaste (chāst), *adj.* virtuous; modest; morally pure; also, refined, as art.—*adv.* **chastely.**—*n.* **chasteness.**

chas-ten (chās'n), *v.t.* to punish for the purpose of making better; subdue; as, God *chastens* his people.

chas-tise (chăs-tīz′), *v.t.* to correct by punishment; as, the parent *chastises* the child.

chas-tise-ment (chăs′tĭz-mĕnt), *n.* punishment; discipline.

chas-ti-ty (chăs′tĭ-tĭ), *n.* moral purity; as, *chastity* is a Christian virtue.
Syn. purity, continence, virtue.

chat (chăt), *v.i.* [*p.t.* and *p.p.* chatted, *p.pr.* chatting], to talk in an easy familiar manner: *n.* familiar or informal speech; gossip.

châ-teau (shä′tō′), *n.* [*pl.* châteaux (-tōz)], a castle; a manor house or country seat. [Fr.]

chat-e-laine (shăt′ē-lān; Fr. shä″tĕ-lĕn′), *n.* a clasp to which is attached a chain for keys, trinkets, etc., worn at the waist by ladies; mistress of a château.

chat-tel (chăt′l), *n.* personal property not including houses or land: usually in plural.

chat-ter (chăt′ĕr), *v.i.* to utter sounds rapidly; rattle the teeth, as in shivering or from fright; talk idly or carelessly: *v.t.* to utter rapidly, idly, or indistinctly: *n.* sounds like those of the magpie, etc.; idle, rapid talk.

chat-ter-box (chăt′ĕr-bŏks), *n.* an incessant talker, especially a child. [Colloq.]

chat-ty (chăt′ĭ), *adj.* talkative in an easy, familiar way; gossipy.—*n.* chattiness.

chauf-feur (shō″fûr′; shō′fĕr), *n.* an operator of an automobile. [Fr.]

Chau-tau-qua (shȧ-tô′kwȧ), *n.* a system of education by summer mission schools and lectures, as at Chautauqua, N. Y.; home reading circles and correspondence.

Chau-vin-ism (shō″văn′ĭsm), *n.* narrow-minded braggart patriotism.—*n.* Chauvinist.

cheap (chēp), *adj.* purchasable at a low price; common; mean; of little value: *adv.* at a low price.—*adv.* cheaply.—*n.* cheapness.

cheap-en (chēp′n), *v.t.* to lessen or bring down in price: *v.i.* to become low in price.

cheat (chēt), *n.* a fraud or deception; one who defrauds another, as out of money: *v.t.* to deceive or defraud: *v.i.* to act as a trickster or deceiver.—*n.* cheater.

check (chĕk), *n.* a restraint; a reproof; a pass; ticket, or token; cloth woven in squares of alternate patterns; an order or draft on a bank for money; in chess, a word signifying an attack on the king; a setback; a mark signifying that something has been examined or verified: *v.t.* to restrain; stop; reprove; to examine by comparison, or mark as having been examined or verified; in chess, to put (a king) in danger; to mark in small squares: *v.i.* to pause, halt.

check-er (chĕk′ĕr), *n.* one of the squares of a pattern marked in squares; piece with which to play checkers: *pl.* game played on a checkerboard: *v.t.* to mark with small squares; to mark with many and irregular changes, as those caused by trouble, etc.

check-er-ber-ry (chĕk′ĕr-bĕr″ĭ), *n.* [*pl.* checkerberries (-ĭz)], the spicy red fruit of the American wintergreen; also, the plant.

check-er-board (chĕk′ĕr-bōrd″), *n.* a board on which the game of checkers is played.

check-mate (chĕk′māt), *n.* the winning move at chess; hence, a complete defeat from which there is no escape: *v.t.* in chess, to make impossible the escape of (the opponent's king); defeat utterly; as, to *checkmate* a plan.

check-rein (chĕk′rān″), *n.* a short rein attached to the saddle of a harness to keep a horse from lowering its head.

cheek (chēk), *n.* the side of the face beneath either eye; among mechanics, one of two corresponding sides; as, the *cheeks* of a lathe; slang, brazen impudence; bold assurance.—*adj.* cheeky.

cheep (chēp), *n.* a peep or squeak; a shrill noise, as that of a young chicken, or a mouse: *v.i.* to make such a noise.—*n.* cheeper.

cheer (chēr), *n.* temper or state of mind; especially, a state of gladness or joy; that which is furnished for entertainment; a shout of applause; sometimes, luck: *v.t.* to gladden; encourage; applaud; to greet, especially with shouts of welcome.

cheer-ful (chēr′fōōl), *adj.* full of, or causing, good spirits; as, a *cheerful* face; a *cheerful* dawn.—*adv.* cheerfully.—*n.* cheerfulness.
Syn. gay, merry, sprightly, enlivening.
Ant. (see mournful).

cheer-less (chēr′lĕs), *adj.* gloomy; joyless; dismal.—*adv.* cheerlessly.—*n.* cheerlessness.

cheer-y (chēr′ĭ), *adj.* cheerful; gay; as, a *cheery* voice; a *cheery* room.—*adv.* cheerily.—*n.* cheeriness.

cheese (chēz), *n.* a food consisting of the curd of milk.

cheese-cloth (chēz′klôth″), *n.* a thin, loosely woven cloth like that in which cheese is wrapped after pressing.

cheese-par-ing (chēz′pâr″ĭng), *adj.* miserly; as, *cheeseparing* methods in business.

chees-y (chēz′ĭ), *adj.* containing, like, or appearing like, cheese.

chee-tah (chē′tȧ), *n.* an animal of the cat family, of Persia, India, etc., as, the leopard. Also, chetah.

chef (shĕf), *n.* a chief or head cook, especially a French cook.

chef-d'œu-vre (shĕ′dû′vr), *n.* [*pl.* chefs-d'œu-vre (shĕ″-dû′vr)], a masterpiece. [Fr.]

chem-i-cal (kĕm′ĭ-kăl), *adj.* pertaining to chemistry; produced or used in operations where compounds are formed or separated.—*n.* a substance produced or used in a chemical process.—*adv.* chemically.

che-mise (shē-mēz′), *n.* a woman's short and loose undergarment.

chem-ist (kĕm′ĭst), *n.* one skilled in chemicals or chemistry; [Eng.], a dealer in drugs and medicines.

chem-is-try (kĕm′ĭs-trĭ), *n.* the science which treats of the nature and composition of substances, and the laws which govern their relations.

che-nille (shē-nēl′), *n.* silk or worsted cord.

cheque (chĕk), *n.* an order or draft on a bank. Also, check.

cher-ish (chĕr′ĭsh), *v.t.* to hold dear; as, America *cherishes* the memory of her martyred presidents; keep affectionately in the mind; treat with tenderness.—*n.* cherisher.

Cher-o-kee (chĕr″ō-kē′), *n.* one of a tribe of American Indians, originally inhabiting what is now northern Georgia, North Carolina, etc.: now in Oklahoma.

che-root (shē-ro͞ot'; chē-ro͞ot'), *n.* a kind of cigar, originally made in the Philippine Islands, having square ends.

cher-ry (chĕr'ĭ), *n.* [*pl.* cherries (-ĭz)], the fruit of a tree of the plum family; the tree itself: *adj.* of the color of the ripe fruit of this tree; ruddy.

cher-ub (chĕr'ŭb), *n.* [*pl.* cherubs (-ŭbz) or cherubim (chĕr'ū-bĭm; chĕr'o͞o-bĭm)], an angel; [*pl.* cherubs], a beautiful child.

che-ru-bic (chē-ro͞o'bĭk), *adj.* of or pertaining to cherubs; angelic; as, the *cherubic* face of a little child.

chess (chĕs), *n.* a game played by two persons with sixteen pieces each, on a checkered board divided into sixty-four squares.

Chessboard with Chessmen in Place

chest (chĕst), *n.* a large box; sometimes, the quantity such a box contains; a treasury or place for keeping a fund; the fund itself; the breast or thorax; a tight container for gas, etc.

chest-nut (chĕs'nŭt), *n.* the edible nut or seed of a forest tree, which grows in a prickly burr; the tree itself; its light coarse-grained timber; a reddish-brown color; a horse of such color; slang, an old or stale joke: *adj.* reddish-brown: **horse-chestnut,** a shade tree bearing a nut larger and somewhat similar to a chestnut, formerly used as feed for horses.

che-val glass (shē-văl' glȧs), a framed mirror large enough to reflect the full-length figure.

chev-a-lier (shĕv'ȧ-lēr'), *n.* a knight; in France, a member of an order of merit; often, a gallant young man.

Chev-i-ot (chĕv'ĭ-ŭt), *n.* a sheep bred on the Cheviot Hills between England and Scotland: **cheviot,** a rough cloth made from the wool of this sheep; a cotton fabric.

Chevron

chev-ron (shĕv'rŭn), *n.* a design on a coat of arms representing two rafters of a house meeting at the top; the badge on the coat sleeve of a military officer to show rank.

chew (cho͞o), *v.t.* to crush and grind with the teeth: *v.i.* to bite repeatedly: *n.* act of masticating, or chewing; that which can be chewed, as a cud or quid.

che-wink (chē-wĭnk'), *n.* a North American bird of the sparrow family: so called from its note.

Chey-enne (shī-ĕn'), *n.* one of a tribe of American Indians, originally inhabiting the region of the Upper Arkansas River in Colorado, and Wyoming: now in Oklahoma.

chic (shēk), *n.* Parisian elegance in dress: *adj.* stylish. [Colloq. Fr.]

chi-can-e-ry (shĭ-kān'ĕr-ĭ), *n.* [*pl.* chicaneries (-ĭz)], trickery; shrewd or sharp dealing or practice.

chick (chĭk), *n.* the young of a bird, especially of the common hen; hence, a child.

chick-a-dee (chĭk'ȧ-dē"), *n.* a bird; the American black-cap titmouse.

chick-a-ree (chĭk'ȧ-rē"), *n.* the American red squirrel: so called from its cry.

chick-en (chĭk'ĕn), *n.* the young of a fowl, especially of the domestic fowl; a young child or an inexperienced person.

chick-en-heart-ed (chĭk'ĕn-härt'ĕd), *adj.* timid.

chick-en pox (chĭk'ĕn pŏks), a mild disease of children.

chick-weed (chĭk'wēd"), *n.* a common wild plant with white blossoms.

chic-o-ry (chĭk'ō-rĭ), *n.* a plant with bright blue flowers and a tapering root, which, when roasted and ground, is used to mix with coffee.

chide (chīd), *v.t.* [*p.t.* chid, chided; *p.p.* chid, chided, chidden; *p.pr.* chiding], to find fault with; scold.

Syn. blame, rebuke, censure, reprimand.

chief (chēf), *n.* a commander or leader or principal person; also, the principal or most important part: *adj.* principal; leading; main.

Syn., *n.* chieftain, head, leader.
Ant. (see subordinate).

chief-ly (chēf'lĭ), *adv.* principally; for the most part; generally.

chief-tain (chēf'tĭn), *n.* a captain, leader, or commander; especially, the head of a class or tribe.—*n.* **chieftaincy, chieftainship.**

chif-fon (shĭf'ŏn; Fr. shē"fôn'), *n.* a kind of thin gauze fabric.

chif-fo-nier (shĭf"ŏ-nēr'), *n.* a piece of furniture fitted with drawers and shelves. Also, **chiffonnier.**

chi-gnon (shē"nyôn'; shēn'yŏn), *n.* a roll of natural or artificial hair worn by women over a pad at the back of the head. [Fr.]

chig-oe (chĭg'ō), *n.* a kind of flea found in the sandy regions of the West Indies and South America; the female burrows beneath the human skin; in southern United States, a mite with similar habits. Also, **chigre, jigger.**

chil-blain (chĭl'blān"), *n.* a sore or inflammation caused by frost or cold, usually affecting the feet or hands.

child (chīld), *n.* [*pl.* children (chĭl'drĕn)], a son or daughter; a baby; a very young person; sometimes, a descendant.

child-birth (chīld'bûrth"), *n.* the act or time of bringing forth a child.

child-hood (child'hŏŏd), *n.* the period from infancy to young manhood or womanhood.

child-ish (child'ish), *adj.* like a child; also, weak; foolish; as, a *childish* impulse in an adult.—*adv.* **childishly.** —*n.* **childishness.**

child-less (child'lĕs), *adj.* having no child; without a family.—*n.* **childlessness.**

child-like (child'lik"), *adj.* like, or belonging to, a child; suitable in, or becoming to, a child; characteristic of a child.

Chil-e-an (chil'ē-ăn), *adj.* of or pertaining to Chile: *n.* a native of Chile.

chil-i (chil'ĭ), *n.* [*pl.* chilies (-iz)], the red pepper. Also, **chile, chilli.**

chill (chil), *n.* a sudden coldness accompanied by shaking; the absence of heat in a substance: *adj.* having the sensation of cold; depressing; discourteous; as, a *chill* greeting: *v.t.* to make cold; as, snow *chills* the air; deject; depress: *v.i.* to become or feel cold.

chime (chim), *n.* the musical harmony or sound produced by striking a set of bells with hammers; a set of bells tuned to the musical scale and struck with hammers: *v.i.* to sound in harmony; to be in harmony or to agree: *v.t.* to cause to sound in harmony; to play tunefully upon, as bells.

chi-me-ra (ki-mē'rȧ; ki-mē'rȧ), *n.* an impossible fancy; as, the belief in a fountain of youth was a *chimera;* in mythology, a fearful monster which breathed forth fire. Also, **chimaera.**

chi-mer-i-cal (ki-mĕr'ĭ-kăl; ki-mĕr'ĭ-kăl), *adj.* merely imaginary; fantastic; given to impossible or impracticable schemes.

chim-ney (chim'nĭ), *n.* [*pl.* chimneys (-niz)], the passage through which smoke or heated air, etc., escapes; a glass tube for a lamp.

Chimpanzee

chim-pan-zee (chim-păn'zē; chim"păn-zē'), *n.* a large Central American ape related to the gorilla, but smaller and less fierce.

chin (chin), *n.* the part of the face below the under lip; as, the *chin* often shows character.

chi-na (chī'nȧ), *n.* a fine kind of porcelain: *adj.* of, or made of, china.

Chi-na-man (chī'nȧ-măn), *n.* [*pl.* Chinamen (-mĕn)], a native of China; a Chinese.

chi-na-ware (chī'nȧ-wâr"), *n.* porcelain ware; dishes in general.

chinch (chinch), *n.* an insect that destroys corn crops; the bedbug.

Chinchilla

chin-chil-la (chin-chil'ȧ), *n.* a small South American animal with a soft fine gray fur; the fur of this animal; a heavy woolen cloth with short, wavy nap.

chine (chin), *n.* the backbone or spine of an animal; a piece of the backbone of an animal with adjoining parts, cut for cooking.

Chi-nese (chi-nēs'; chi-nēz'), *adj.* of or pertaining to China: *n.* a native or natives of China; the language of the Chinese.

chink (chink), *n.* a small lengthwise crack or opening; a sharp metallic or jingling sound: *v.i.* and *v.t.* to make, or to cause to make, a sharp metallic sound; jingle.

chin-qua-pin (chin'kȧ-pin), *n.* a shrub or small tree, related to the chestnut, or its sweet edible nut: called also the *dwarf chestnut.* Also, **chinkapin.**

chintz (chints), *n.* cotton cloth, printed in various colors. Also, **chints.**

chip (chip), *v.t.* [*p.t.* and *p.p.* chipped, *p.pr.* chipping], to cut or break small pieces from: *v.i.* to break off in small bits: *n.* a small piece of stone, wood, etc., cut or broken off; a disk used in games as a counter.

chip-munk (chip'munk), *n.* a small squirrel-like animal of reddish-brown color, commonly striped; a ground squirrel or hackee.

Chip-pe-wa (chip'ē-wä), *n.* one of a tribe of American Indians, originally inhabiting the region around Lake Superior.

chi-rog-ra-phy (ki-rŏg'rȧ-fĭ), *n.* the art of writing.

chi-rop-o-dist (ki-rŏp'ō-dist), *n.* one who treats diseases of the feet and hands.—*n.* **chiropody.**

chi-ro-prac-tic (ki'rō-prăk'tik), *n.* a system of treatment of certain bodily disorders by means of rubbing or manipulating the body, especially the spine.

chirp (chûrp), *n.* a short cheerful note, as that of a bird: *v.i.* to utter such a note: *v.t.* to utter with such a note.

chir-rup (chir'ŭp), *v.i.* to chirp repeatedly; of persons, to make a sound like a chirp: *v.t.* to utter with a chirp: *n.* act or sound of chirping repeatedly.

chis-el (chiz'ĕl), *n.* an edged instrument of iron or steel for cutting wood, stone, or metal: *v.t.* [*p.t.* and *p.p.* chiseled, *p.pr.* chiseling], to cut, pare, gouge, or engrave with such a tool.

chit (chit), *n.* a child; a pert, forward girl or young woman.

chit-chat (chit'chăt), *n.* familiar talk of little importance; gossip.

chi-tine (ki'tin), *n.* the hard outer coat of insects; shellfish. Also, **chitin.**

chiv-al-ric (shiv'ăl-rik), *adj.* knightly; gallant; of courteous and kindly spirit.

chiv-al-rous (shiv'ăl-rŭs), *adj.* pertaining to chivalry; warlike; gallant; courteous; as, a gentleman is expected to be *chivalrous* to a lady.—*adv.* **chivalrously.**

chiv-al-ry (shiv'ăl-rĭ), *n.* the system of knighthood in the Middle Ages; the qualifications of a knight, as bravery, nobleness, courtesy, respect for womanly dignity, chastity, etc.

chive (chiv), *n.* a perennial herb allied to the onion: usually in plural.

chlo-ral (klō'răl), *n.* a strong sleep-producing drug which paralyzes the heart if taken in large doses.

chlo-rate (klō'rāt), *n.* a salt of chloric acid.

chlo-ric (klō'rik), *adj.* pertaining to, or obtained from, chlorine.

chlo-ride (klō'rīd; klō'rĭd), *n.* a compound of chlorine with another substance. Also, **chlorid.**

chlo-ride of lime (chlō'rĭd ŏv līm), a grayish-white powder, much used in bleaching and as a disinfectant.

chlo-rine (klō'rĭn; klō'rēn), *n.* a greenish-yellow, heavy, highly poisonous gas, used commercially as a bleaching agent: largely used in gas attacks in the World War.

chlo-ro-form (klō'rō-fôrm), *n.* a liquid used to make one unconscious of pain: *v.t.* to give chloroform to.

chlo-ro-phyl (klō'rō-fĭl), *n.* the green coloring matter of plants. Also, **chlorophyll.**

chock (chŏk), *n.* a block or wedge to fill in a space so as to prevent motion; on a ship, a type of casting or wooden part for ropes to run through: *v.t.* to furnish, wedge, or make fast, with a chock: *adv.* as tight as possible.

Chock

chock-full (chŏk'fo͝ol"), *adj.* full to capacity; full as possible. Also, **choke-full, chuck-full.**

choc-o-late (chŏk'ō-lāt), *n.* a paste of the roasted kernels of the cacao-nut, used in making the drink so called: *adj.* having the color of, or made of, chocolate.

Choc-taw (chŏk'tô), *n.* one of a tribe of American Indians, originally inhabiting the region between the Mobile and Mississippi Rivers in Alabama and Mississippi: now in Oklahoma.

choice (chois), *n.* the act of choosing; the right of choosing; the thing or person chosen; the best or preferable part; a number large enough to choose from: *adj.* select; carefully chosen; careful of: with *of;* uncommon.—*adv.* **choicely.**—*n.* **choiceness.**

choir (kwīr), *n.* a band of singers in a church; the place where they sing.

choke (chōk), *v.t.* to stop the breath of by closing the windpipe; to stifle, strangle, or suffocate; block up: *v.i.* to become suffocated; to become clogged: *n.* the act or sound of strangling, etc.

choke-cher-ry (chōk'chĕr"ĭ), *n.* a North American wild cherry; its fruit.

choke damp (chōk dămp), a poisonous gas, sometimes produced in wells, mines, and other pits.

chok-y (chōk'ĭ), *adj.* stifling; tending to strangle or choke, as through strong feeling. Also, **chokey.**

chol-er (kŏl'ẽr), *n.* anger; as, he was a man whose *choler* was quickly aroused.

chol-er-a (kŏl'ẽr-*á*), *n.* a disease accompanied by violent vomiting: **cholera infantum,** a disease of infants, accompanied by vomiting and diarrhea: **cholera morbus,** an acute disease characterized by violent vomiting, cramps, purging, and prostration.

chol-er-ic (kŏl'ẽr-ĭk), *adj.* high-tempered; as, "Go show your slaves how *choleric* you are."

choose (cho͞oz), *v.t.* [*p.t.* chose, *p.p.* chosen, *p pr.* choosing], to select; colloquially, to wish; to be pleased: *v.i.* to make a choice.—*n.* **chooser.**

Syn. elect, select, cull, pick.

Ant. (see refuse).

chop (chŏp), *v.t.* [*p.t.* and *p.p.* chopped, *p.pr.* chopping], to cut with repeated blows; to cut into very small pieces: *v.i.* to make a quick stroke, as with an ax; to shift or change direction suddenly, as the wind: *n.* a piece chopped off; especially, a small piece of meat; a jaw: usually in the plural: *pl.* the mouth cavity; the fleshy parts about the mouth.—*n.* **chopper.**

chop-fal-len (chŏp'fôl"n), *adj.* dejected. Also, **chapfallen.**

chop-py (chŏp'ĭ), *adj.* full of short, rough waves: said of the sea; changeable: said of the wind.

chop-sticks (chŏp'stĭks"), *n.pl.* two small sticks used by the Chinese in taking food.

chop su-ey (chŏp so͞o'ĭ), a Chinese dish of stewed chicken or pork, vegetables, and seeds.

cho-ral (kō'răl), *adj.* of or pertaining to a choir; chanted or sung by a choir; as, a *choral* service.

chord (kôrd), *n.* the string of a musical instrument; musical notes in harmony; a straight line joining the ends of a portion of the circumference of a circle: *v.i.* in music, to be in harmony; *v.t.* to provide with musical chords; to tune.

cho-re-a (kō-rē'*á*), *n.* a twitching nervous disease; St. Vitus's dance.

cho-ric (kō'rĭk; kŏr'ĭk), *adj.* of or pertaining to a chorus.

chores (chōrz), *n.pl.* in the United States and provincial England, small or odd jobs; the daily light work of a farm or household.

chor-is-ter (kŏr'ĭs-tẽr), *n.* a member of a choir, especially a male singer; [U. S.], a leader of a choir or of congregational singing.

chor-tle (chôr'tl), *v.i.* and *v.t.* to laugh in a chuckling, snorting fashion: the word was coined by Lewis Carroll, the author of *Alice in Wonderland,* and is used humorously.

cho-rus (kō'rŭs), *n.* a number singing together; that part of a musical composition in which the company all sing together; a piece of music arranged in parts; a refrain recurring at the end of each verse of a song; a band of singers and dancers in a Greek play.

chose (chōz), past tense of the verb *choose.*

cho-sen (chō'zn), *p.adj.* selected; picked out; as, a *chosen* few; a *chosen* band; a *chosen* people.

chow (chou), *n.* a breed of dogs in northern China, similar to a small Eskimo dog: slang, food: **Chow,** slang, a Chinaman.

chow-chow (chou'chou"), *n.* an East Indian mixed pickle.

chow-der (chou'dẽr), *n.* a dish of fresh fish; clams stewed together with pork, biscuits, etc.

chrism (krĭzm), *n.* oil blessed by the priest and used in baptism, confirmation, etc.

chris-ten (krĭs'n), *v.t.* to baptize; also, to give a Christian name to.

Chris-ten-dom (krĭs'n-dŭm), *n.* countries whose people are Christians; Christians collectively.

Chris-tian (krĭs'chăn), *n.* a believer in the religion of Christ: *adj.* possessing the religion of Christ.

Chris-ti-an-i-ty (krĭs"chĭ-ăn'ĭ-tĭ; krĭs-chăn'ĭ-tĭ), *n.* the religion taught by Christ.

Chris-tian-i-za-tion (krĭs"chăn-ĭ-zā'-shŭn), *n.* the act of converting to Christianity.

Chris-tian-ize (kris'chăn-īz), *v.t.* to convert to Christianity.

Chris-tian Sci-ence (kris'chăn sī'-ĕns), a system of religious belief which claims that sickness is a diseased belief shown in the body, and that all ills can be cured by correcting this belief.

Christ-mas (kris'măs), *n.* the festival (Dec. 25) which celebrates the birth of Christ.

chro-mat-ic (krō-măt'ĭk), *adj.* pertaining to colors; as, a *chromatic* chart; indicating a special kind of music including half tones, one after the other; as, a *chromatic* scale: *n.* a note affected by an accidental sharp or flat; *pl.* that branch of the science of light and vision which treats of colors.—*adv.* **chromatically.**

Chromatic Scale, Ascending and Descending

chro-mi-um (krō'mĭ-ŭm), *n.* a metallic element of a grayish-white color. Also, **chrome.**

chro-mo (krō'mō), *n.* [*pl.* chromos (-mōz)], a picture produced by printing in colors.

chron-ic (krŏn'ĭk), *adj.* continuing for a long time; returning again and again: said of a disease.

chron-i-cle (krŏn'ĭ-kl), *n.* a record of events; as, a diary is a *chronicle* of the daily events of one's life. *v.t.* to write

as, history *chronicles* the great events in the life of na-

ed.

Chronograph

chron-o-graph (krŏn'ō-grăf), *n.* an instrument for marking very short intervals of time, or for recording graphically the time or duration of an occurrence.

chron-o-log-i-cal (krŏn'ō-lŏj'ĭ-kăl), *adj.* pertaining to, or containing an account of, past events in the order of time; as, in your history text-book, the events are arranged in *chronological* order. —*adv.* **chronologically.**

chro-nol-o-gist (krō-nŏl'ō-jĭst), *n.* a person who attempts to discover the true dates of past events and to arrange them in their proper order. Also, **chronologer.**

chro-nol-o-gy (krō-nŏl'ō-jĭ), *n.* [*pl.* chronologies (-jĭz)], the science that treats of events and arranges their dates in proper order.

chro-nom-e-ter (krō-nŏm'ē-tẽr), *n.* an instrument for measuring time with extreme accuracy; an accurate watch or timepiece.

chrys-a-lis (kris'ă-lĭs), *n.* the last stage through which an insect, or a butterfly, passes before it is completely developed and emerges from its case or shell.

chrys-an-the-mum (krĭs-ăn'thē-mŭm), *n.* a plant allied to the aster family, having large, showy flowers; a flower of this plant.

chrys-o-lite (kris'ō-līt), *n.* a green-colored mineral, when transparent, sometimes used as a gem.

chub (chŭb), *n.* a fresh-water fish of several varieties; a plump person.

chub-by (chŭb'ĭ), *adj.* plump; fat and round; as, a *chubby* little boy.—*n.* **chubbiness.**

chuck (chŭk), *v.t.* to pat in a playful manner: *n.* a light blow under the chin; a contrivance for holding a tool in a lathe; the part of a beef extending from the neck to the shoulder-blade.

Drill Chuck

chuck-le (chŭk'l), *n.* a quiet, suppressed laugh: *v.i.* to laugh in such a manner.

chum (chŭm), *n.* one who lodges in the same apartment; an old or intimate friend: *v.i.* [*p.t.* and *p.p.* chummed, *p.pr.* chumming], to occupy the same room.—*adj.* **chummy.** [Colloq.]

chump (chŭmp), *n.* a short, thick, heavy piece of wood; slang, a stupid or awkward person.

chunk (chŭnk), *n.* a short, thick piece; as, a *chunk* of ice. [Colloq.]

chunk-y (chŭnk'ĭ), *adj.* short and thick; as, a *chunky* boy or girl. [Colloq.]

church (chûrch), *n.* a building set apart for divine worship; the entire body of Christians: **Church,** a particular body of Christians; as, the Presbyterian *Church.*

church-man (chûrch'măn), *n.* a member of the English Established Church; an adherent of an established church.

church-war-den (chûrch'wôr'dn), *n.* in the Church of England, or Protestant Episcopal Church, one of two officers chosen at Easter in every parish to attend to the business affairs of the church, and to act as the legal agents of the parish.

church-yard (chûrch'yärd'), *n.* the ground around a church, especially when used for burial.

churl (chûrl), *n.* formerly, a rustic or countryman; now, a surly, ill-bred person; a miser.

churl-ish (chûr'lĭsh), *adj.* ill-bred; miserly; hard to manage; stubborn.—*adv.* **churlishly.**—*n.* **churlishness.**

churn (chûrn), *n.* a vessel in which milk or cream is made into butter: *v.t.* to make (butter) by violently stirring cream; to stir by violent motion: *v.i.* to stir cream in making butter.

chute (shōōt), *n.* a slanting trough for sending articles down; as, a coal *chute;* a river-fall over which timber is floated.

chyle (kīl), *n.* a milklike fluid separated from digested matter in the stomach, absorbed by the lacteal vessels, and made a part of the blood.

chyme (kīm), *n.* the pulpy mass of partly digested food before the separation of the chlye.

ci-ca-da (sĭ-kā'dȧ), *n.* [*pl.* cicadas (-dȧz)], a class of insects having the power of making a shrill sound, commonly and incorrectly called locusts.

ci-ca-trix (sĭ-kā'trĭks; sĭk'ȧ-trĭks), *n.* [*pl.* cicatrices (sĭk"ȧ-trī'sēz)], the scar remaining after a wound has healed.

Cid (sĭd), *n.* a chief or commander; especially, the hero, Ruy Diaz, the Christian champion against the Moors; the name of a Spanish poem.

ci-der (sī'dēr), *n.* the juice of apples squeezed out and fermented.

ci-gar (sĭ-gär'), *n.* a small roll of tobacco-leaf used for smoking.

cig-a-rette (sĭg"ȧ-rĕt'), *n.* a small roll made of finely cut tobacco for smoking, usually rolled in thin paper.

cil-i-a (sĭl'ĭ-ȧ), *n.pl.* the hair of the eyelids; hairlike processes, as of a cell, or of certain plants.

cil-i-at-ed (sĭl'ĭ-āt"ĕd), *adj.* covered with cilia, or fine hair.

Cim-me-ri-an (sĭ-mē'rĭ-ăn), *adj.* belonging to the Cimmerii, an imaginary people mentioned by Homer as living in constant darkness; hence, intensely dark, gloomy; as, blind people spend their lives in *Cimmerian* darkness.

cinch (sĭnch), *n.* a saddle girth firmly fastened in place by loop and knots; a sure grip or hold; slang, a sure or easy thing.

Cin-cho-na (sĭn-kō'nȧ), *n.* a South American tree from the bark of which quinine is extracted: **cinchona,** the bark of the Cinchona tree.

cinc-ture (sĭnk'tūr), *n.* a belt or girdle worn round the waist; a raised or carved ring at the bottom and top of a pillar.

cin-der (sĭn'dēr), *n.* a thoroughly charred piece of wood or other combustible substance; slag from a metal furnace; an ember: *pl.*, colloquially, ashes.—*adj.* **cindery.**

cin-e-ma (sĭn'ē-mȧ), *n.* a motion picture camera.

cin-e-mat-o-graph (sĭn"ē-măt'ō-grȧf), *n.* an apparatus to show pictures of objects in seeming motion. Also, **kinematograph.**

cin-er-a-ry (sĭn'ēr-ā-rĭ), *adj.* pertaining to, or containing, ashes: applied to urns containing the ashes of human bodies.

cin-na-bar (sĭn'ȧ-bär), *n.* a compound of sulphur with mercury.

cin-na-mon (sĭn'ȧ-mŭn), *n.* the inner bark of an East Indian tree from which a spice is made.

cinque-foil (sĭnk'foil"), *n.* a plant of the rose family, called from its shape, five fingers; an ornament resembling five leaves.

ci-pher (sī'fēr), *n.* the symbol *0*; zero; naught; hence, a person or thing without value or power; a secret manner of writing, or the key to it; a code; as, cablegrams are sent in *cipher:* *v.i.* to work arithmetical examples with figures; to write with a private alphabet or other secret characters. Also, **cypher.**

Cir-ce-an (sûr-sē'ăn), *adj.* pertaining to Circe, the enchantress or witch; hence, bewitching and degrading.

cir-cle (sûr'kl), *n.* a round body; a plane surface bounded by a single curved line called its circumference, every part of which is equally distant from a point within it, called the center; the closed plane curve bounding such a surface; a number of persons or things united by a common bond; as, Goldsmith had a large *circle* of warm friends; something round, as a group of seats in a theater: *v.t.* to move around; to revolve: *v.t.* to surround.

cir-clet (sûr'klĕt), *n.* a small circle; especially, an ornament, as a ring or bracelet.

cir-cuit (sûr'kĭt), *n.* the act of going round anything; the arrangement by which an electrical current is kept up between the two poles of a battery or machine; the path of the electric current; circumference; compass; a route over which one passes regularly at intervals; a district, within certain boundaries, as that assigned to a judge.

cir-cu-i-tous (sēr-kū'ĭ-tŭs), *adj.* roundabout; as, they went home by a *circuitous* route; indirect.—*adv.* **circuitously.**

cir-cu-lar (sûr'kū-lȧr), *adj.* round like a circle; of or pertaining to a circle; roundabout; published for distribution to the public or to certain groups of persons; as, a *circular* letter: *n.* a printed or written letter or notice.—*adv.* **circularly.**

cir-cu-late (sûr'kū-lāt), *v.t.* to cause to pass from point to point or from one person to another: *v.i.* to move around and return to the same point; to pass from hand to hand.

cir-cu-la-tion (sûr"kū-lā'shŭn), *n.* the act of moving around, or passing or sending from place to place; also, the extent to which a thing is distributed or sent; as, the magazine has a large *circulation;* the movement of the blood through the vessels of the body; current coin, notes, or bills.

cir-cu-la-to-ry (sûr'kū-lȧ-tō-rĭ), *adj.* pertaining to circulation; circulating; roundabout.

cir-cum-am-bi-ent (sûr"kŭm-ăm'bĭ-ĕnt), *adj.* inclosing; surrounding.

cir-cum-am-bu-late (sûr"kŭm-ăm'-bū-lāt), *v.t.* and *v.i.* to walk about or around.

cir-cum-fer-ence (sēr-kŭm'fēr-ĕns), *n.* the line that bounds a circle or any curved plane figure; the distance around a circular body; circuit.

cir-cum-flex (sûr'kŭm-flĕks), *n.* a mark [~ ⌒ ^] over a vowel or syllable to denote accent or contraction: *adj.* marked with such an accent; curved or winding; bent, or bending round.

cir-cum-lo-cu-tion (sûr"kŭm-lō-kū'-shŭn), *n.* the use of many words where but few are necessary; a roundabout way of speaking; as, "to pass away" is a common *circumlocution* for "to die."

Syn. diffuseness, verbiage, wordiness, redundance.

Ant. (see brevity).

cir-cum-nav-i-gate (sûr"kŭm-năv'ĭ-gāt), *v.t.* to sail around; usually, to sail around the globe.—*n.* **circumnavigator, circumnavigation.**

cir-cum-po-lar (sûr"kŭm-pō'lȧr), *adj.* near or surrounding the north or the south pole; as, the *circumpolar* stars revolve around the pole without setting.

cir-cum-scribe (sûr"kŭm-skrīb'), *v.t.* to inclose within certain lines or boundaries; hence, to restrict; as, the power of the President of the United States is *circumscribed* by the law of the land; in geometry, to surround with a figure which touches at every possible point; as, to *circumscribe* a triangle with a circle; to *circumscribe* a circle with a polygon.—*n.* **circumscription.**

cir-cum-spect (sûr'kŭm-spĕkt), *adj.* cautious; prudent; watchful on all sides.—*adv.* **circumspectly.**—*n.* **circumspectness.**

cir-cum-spec-tion (sûr"kŭm-spĕk'shŭn), *n.* caution; watchfulness on every side; prudence.

cir-cum-stance (sûr'kŭm-stăns), *n.* something relative to a fact; an event, detail, or incident; as, an interesting *circumstance* in his life: *pl.* state of affairs surrounding any incident, fact, or condition; the general conditions surrounding one and determining one's way of living: *v.t.* to place under limiting conditions.
Syn. fact, incident.

cir-cum-stan-tial (sûr"kŭm-stăn'shăl), *adj.* consisting in, pertaining to, or dependent on, circumstances; presumptive; as, *circumstantial* evidence; incidental; accidental; detailed.—*adv.* **circumstantially.**—*n.* **circumstantiality.**

cir-cum-stan-ti-ate (sûr"kŭm-stăn'shĭ-āt), *v.t.* to show to be true in every particular.

cir-cum-val-la-tion (sûr"kŭm-vă-lā'shŭn), *n.* the act of throwing up walls or fortifications round a place.

cir-cum-vent (sûr"kŭm-vĕnt'), *v.t.* to gain an advantage over by deception; as, an army often *circumvents* the enemy and gains an advantage.

cir-cum-ven-tion (sûr"kŭm-vĕn'shŭn), *n.* the act of gaining an advantage by deceiving; a trick by which some advantage is to be gained.

cir-cus (sûr'kŭs), *n.* [*pl.* circuses (-ĕz)], a large level space for feats of horsemanship and feats of skill, with seats for the spectators arranged in rows, one above the other; also, the performance in such a space, and the performers of the feats.

cir-rus (sĭr'ŭs), *n.* a form of cloud spreading in wisps.

cis-tern (sĭs'tẽrn), *n.* a natural or man-made pit or hole for storing water.

cit-a-del (sĭt'ȧ-dĕl), *n.* a fortress; a castle; as, the British *citadel* on the Rock of Gibraltar commands the Strait of Gibraltar.

ci-ta-tion (sī-tā'shŭn), *n.* a summons to appear at a court of justice; act of quoting, or passage quoted, as from a book, for proof or argument; mention; especially, in the World War, honorable mention in the dispatches for bravery or distinguished merit.

cite (sīt), *v.t.* to summon to appear in court; quote; as, a minister *cites* as his text a passage from the Bible.

cith-ar-a (sĭth'ȧ-rȧ), *n.* the ancient Greek lyre, triangular in shape, with from seven to eleven strings.

Cithara

cit-i-zen (sĭt'ĭ-zĕn), *n.* a native of a town or city; a member of a state or nation who enjoys political rights and privileges, and gives in return his allegiance to the government: in a general sense, a permanent resident of a city or country; as, the *citizens* of New York.

cit-i-zen-ship (sĭt'ĭ-zĕn-shĭp"), *n.* the status or standing of a person who owes allegiance to the government in return for his political rights and privileges.

cit-rate (sĭt'rāt), *n.* a salt derived from citric acid.

cit-ric ac-id (sĭt'rĭk ăs'ĭd), an acid obtained from lemons and oranges.

cit-ron (sĭt'rŭn), *n.* the fruit of the citron tree: like the lemon, but larger and not so acid; a variety of melon.

Cit-rus (sĭt'rŭs), *n.* a genus of tree which includes the orange, lemon, lime, citron, grapefruit, etc.—*adj.* **citrous.**

cit-y (sĭt'ĭ), *n.* [*pl.* cities (-ĭz)], a large and important town; in the United States, a municipality having local self-government.

Civet

civ-et (sĭv'ĕt), *n.* a thick substance, of a yellowish color and a musklike odor, secreted by certain cats: used in perfumes; any of various catlike meat-eating animals. Also, **civet cat.**

civ-ic (sĭv'ĭk,) *adj.* pertaining to a city or citizenship; as, the founding of the city was celebrated by a great *civic* parade.—*adv.* **civically.**

civ-il (sĭv'ĭl), *adj.* pertaining to the affairs of a city or government; taking place in, or pertaining to, affairs within a nation; as, *civil* war; of or pertaining to citizens; not military or ecclesiastical; polite; often, barely polite; observing social etiquette, but with no warmth or cordiality.—*adv.* **civilly.**

ci-vil-ian (sĭ-vĭl'yăn), *n.* a citizen engaged in civil affairs.

ci-vil-i-ty (sĭ-vĭl'ĭ-tĭ), *n.* [*pl.* civilities (-tĭz)], good breeding; courtesy.

civ-i-li-za-tion (sĭv"ĭ-lĭ-zā'shŭn), *n.* a state marked by advancement, enlightenment, and progress in general; state of being refined in manners and improved in arts and letters; culture; refinement.

civ-i-lize (sĭv'ĭ-līz), *v.t.* to reclaim from a savage state; instruct in the arts and refinements of civilized life.

civ-il serv-ice (sĭv'ĭl sûr'vĭs), the paid service of the government not naval or military.

clab-ber (klăb'ẽr), *v.t.* to curdle, as milk: *n.* milk which has become thick and sour.

clack (klăk), *v.i.* to make a sudden, sharp sound; chatter rapidly and continuously: *n.* a sudden, sharp sound; continual prattle.—*n.* **clacker.**

clad (klăd), past tense and past participle of the verb *clothe;* as, gentle spring in sunshine *clad.*

claim (klām), *v.t.* to demand as a right, or by authority; to assert to be true: *v.i.* to be entitled to anything; to make a claim or assertion: *n.* a demand of a right; the asserting of a fact; the assertion of a right or title to anything; also, the thing demanded; especially, a piece of land which a miner marks out in accordance with mining law.—*adj.* **claimable.**—*n.* **claimer.**

claim-ant (klām'ănt), *n.* one who demands anything as his right.

clair-voy-ance (klâr-voi'ăns), *n.* the power claimed by some persons of seeing objects others cannot see, as, the power of reading minds.

clair-voy-ant (klâr-voi'ănt), *n.* [*fem.* clairvoyante], one who professes to have the power of clairvoyance, or the ability to see things hidden from others.—*adv.* **clairvoyantly.**

clam (klăm), *n.* an eatable shellfish of several varieties.

clam-ber (klăm'bẽr), *v.t.* and *v.i.* to ascend or climb with difficulty.

clam-my (klăm'ĭ), *adj.* soft and sticky and cold and moist.—*adv.* **clammily.**—*n.* **clamminess.**

clam-or (klăm'ẽr), *n.* a loud and continued noise, made especially with the voice: *v.t.* to shout with a loud voice: *v.i.* to make noisy demands. Also, **clamour.**

clam-or-ous (klăm'ẽr-ŭs), *adj.* noisy; as, a *clamorous* mob.—*adv.* **clamorously.**—*n.* **clamorousness.**

clamp (klămp), *n.* anything that fastens or binds; a piece of wood, metal, etc., used to bring two things together: *v.t.* to fasten or bind with such a device.

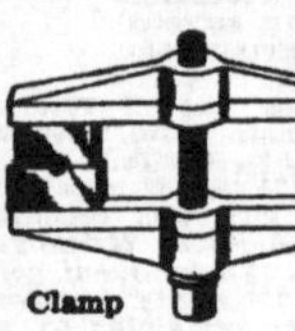

Clamp

clan (klăn), *n.* a tribe or association of families united under one chieftain, having one common parent and the same surname; a set or clique: used contemptuously.

clan-des-tine (klăn-dĕs'tĭn), *adj.* secret; private; as, the early Christians held *clandestine* meetings in caves.—*adv.* **clandestinely.**

clang (klăng), *n.* a loud, sharp, ringing metallic sound: *v.t.* to cause to resound with a sharp metallic sound: *v.i.* to give out a sharp metallic sound.

clan-gor (klăng'ẽr), *n.* a loud metallic sound; a clamorous noise; a sharp clang: *v.i.* to ring repeatedly and noisily.—*adj.* **clangorous.**—*adv.* **clangorously.**

clank (klănk), *n.* a sharp, hard metallic sound: *v.t.* and *v.i.* to rattle and sound, as chains.

clan-nish (klăn'ĭsh), *adj.* pertaining to a clan, family, or tribe; clinging, or inclined to cling, together; closely adherent; prejudiced; narrow.—*adv.* **clannishly.**—*n.* **clannishness.**

clap (klăp), *v.t.* [*p.t.* and *p.p.* clapped, *p.pr.* clapping], to strike (the hands) together with a quick, sharp noise; to applaud by striking the hands together; to put on, place, etc., quickly and suddenly; strike or slap suddenly: *v.i.* to show approval by striking the hands together; come together with a quick, sharp noise: *n.* a loud noise made by a sudden collision; applause expressed by striking the hands together: a blow delivered with suddenness.

clap-board (klăp'bōrd; klăb'ôrd; klăb'ẽrd), *n.* a long thin narrow board used for the outside covering of wooden houses.

clap-per (klăp'ẽr), *n.* one who, or that which, claps; the tongue of a bell; the clack of a mill-hopper; a door knocker.

clap-trap (klăp'trăp"), *n.* any device, expression, trick, language, or show, intended to gain applause or attention.

claque (klăk), *n.* an organized body of men paid to applaud or to express disapproval at theaters; hence, interested admirers.

clar-et (klăr'ĕt), *n.* the English name for the red wines of France; hence, any wine of a dark-red color: *adj.* purplish red.

clar-i-fy (klăr'ĭ-fī), *v.t.* [*p.t.* and *p.p.* clarified, *p.pr.* clarifying], to make clear or bright; to make understandable: *v.i.* to become bright.—*n.* **clarification, clarifier.**

clar-i-net (klăr'ĭ-nĕt), *n.* a musical wind instrument. Also, **clarionet.**

Clarinet

clar-i-on (klăr'ĭ-ŭn), *n.* a small trumpet; *adj.* sounding like this small trumpet.

clar-i-ty (klăr'ĭ-tĭ), *n.* clearness; as, he was remarkable for the *clarity* and precision of his English.

cla-ro (klä'rō), *adj.* mild and light in color: said of cigars. [SPAN.]

clash (klăsh), *v.i.* to make a loud harsh noise; to be in opposition; disagree; as, their opinions *clash*: *v.t.* to strike violently together: *n.* the noise so produced; opposition; contradiction.

clasp (klȧsp), *v.t.* to shut or fasten together with, or as with, a hook or fastener; to embrace; to hold firmly: *n.* a hook to hold anything close; a close embrace.—*n.* **clasper.**

clasp knife (klȧsp' nīf"), a knife the blades of which fold into the handle.

class (klȧs), *n.* a rank or order of persons having like interests, or of things which are similar; a number of students of the same rank or status; a group of animals or plants; a number of objects, events, etc., having characteristics in common.

Syn. degree, order, rank.

clas-sic (klăs'ĭk), *n.* any book or work of art that is, or may properly be regarded as, a standard; particularly, any Greek or Roman piece of literature or work of art; any author whose productions are of such excellence that they are regarded as standards: *adj.* of or pertaining to the highest class or rank in literature or art; conforming to the highest standard; pertaining to, or like, the Greek or Roman authors; pure, refined; clear-cut; modeled after, or like, the highest forms of ancient art or literature. Also, *adj.* **classical.**—*adv.* **classically.**

clas-si-cism (klăs'ĭ-sĭzm), *n.* agreement or adherence to classical style; the principles and idiom of the classic style; classical scholarship.—*n.* **classicist.**

clas-si-fi-ca-tion (klăs"ĭ-fĭ-kā'shŭn), *n.* act of forming in groups, or dividing into sets or sorts, according to some system or method.

clas-si-fy (klăs'ĭ-fī), *v.t.* [*p.t.* and *p.p.* classified, *p.pr.* classifying], to arrange in groups according to some method or standard; put in order; systematize.—*adj.* **classifiable.**

class-mate (klȧs'māt"), *n.* one belonging to the same class as another, as at school or at a university.

clat-ter (klăt'ẽr), *v.i.* to make a rattling sound; talk idly and noisily: *v.t.* to cause to make a rattling sound:

n. a continuous or confused noise; a rattling noise; idle gossip.

clause (klôz), *n.* a separate part of a written composition or document; in grammar, a division of a sentence containing a subject and predicate of its own.

clav-i-chord (klăv'ĭ-kôrd), *n.* a musical stringed instrument, invented in the Middle Ages. Also, **clarichord.**

clav-i-cle (klăv'ĭ-kl), *n.* a bone which connects the breast bone and the shoulder blade; the collar bone.—*adj.* **clavicular.**

cla-vi-er (klā'vĭ-ẽr; klā-vēr'), *n.* the keyboard of an organ, piano, or any stringed musical instrument.

claw (klô), *n.* a sharp hooked horny nail in the foot of an animal, as the cat; the whole foot of a bird; anything like a claw; the narrow part at the base of a leaf or footstalk of a petal: *v.t.* and *v.i.* to tear or scratch with, or as if with, claws.

clay (klā), *n.* soft, plastic earth; anything easily molded; the bodily or earthly nature of man: *adj.* made of, or like, clay.—*adj.* **clayey.**

clay-more (klā'mōr'), *n.* a two-handed, broadsword used by the Scotch Highlanders.

Claymore

clay stone (klā stōn), a calcareous mass formed in a bed of clay; a variety of rock containing clay.

clean (klēn), *adj.* free from dirt; unadulterated; free from imperfections; shapely; free from awkward bungling; completely cleared of some obstruction; morally or religiously pure: *adv.* wholly; without qualification or limitation: *v.t.* to remove dirt.—*n.* **cleanness.**

clean-cut (klēn'kŭt'), *adj.* well-shaped; definite;precise. Also, **clear-cut.**

clean-er (klēn'ẽr), *n.* a person or thing that removes dirt, stains, etc.

clean-ly (klĕn'lĭ), *adj.* neat; pure: *adv.* neatly; entirely.—*n.* **cleanliness.**

cleanse (klĕnz), *v.t.* to make free from dirt; to free from moral impurity or guilt.—*n.* **cleanser.**

clear (klēr), *adj.* bright; pure; undimmed; easily understood; unobstructed; audible, or capable of being heard: *v.t.* to make bright; render evident; free from obstructions; prove or declare innocent; to free from legal detention, as imported goods: *v.i.* to leave a port; become bright: *adv.* distinctly; completely.—*adv.* **clearly.**—*n.* **clearness.**

Syn., *adj.* bright, lucid, vivid.
Ant. (see opaque).

clear-cut (klēr'kŭt'), *adj.* having a sharp, clearly defined outline; clean-cut; concise.

clear-ance (klēr'ăns), *n.* the act of clearing; removal of obstruction; a legal certificate permitting a vessel to leave port.

clear-ing (klēr'ĭng), *n.* the act of removing obstructions from, etc.; the act of freeing; land cleared of trees and underbrush.

clear-ing-house (klēr'ĭng-hous'), *n.* an office to which banks send their representatives every day to exchange drafts and checks.

clear-starch (klēr'stärch'), *v.t.* to stiffen or dress with starch.

cleat (klēt), *n.* a thin piece of iron fastened under a shoe to preserve the sole and prevent slipping; a piece of wood or iron on ships to keep the ropes from slipping; a strip of wood nailed across a board to give strength, hold in position, etc.

Cleat

cleav-age (klēv'ăj), *n.* the act of splitting; the property of some minerals and rocks of being divided into layers.

cleave (klēv), *v.i.* [*p.t.* clave, cleaved, *p.p.* cleaved, *p.pr.* cleaving], to stick; to adhere; be attached strongly: *v.t.* [*p.t.* cleft, clove, *p.p.* cleft, cloven, cleaved, *p.pr.* cleaving], cut open; to divide by force: *v.i.* to split.—*adj.* **cleavable.**

cleav-er (klēv'ẽr), *n.* a butcher's heavy hatchet; a tool for splitting timber.

Cleaver

cleek (klēk), *n.* in golf, an iron-headed club of considerable driving power, sometimes used for putting.

clef (klĕf), *n.* a figure at the beginning of each staff in music to show the pitch of all the notes on one particular line or space.

cleft (klĕft), *n.* a crack; a crevice; as, the water trickled from a *cleft* in the rock.

clem-a-tis (klĕm'ȧ-tĭs), *n.* a hardy climbing plant of the crowfoot family with purple and white flowers.

clem-en-cy (klĕm'ĕn-sĭ), *n.* [*pl.* clemencies (-sĭz)], compassion; mercy; leniency; mildness or softness, when applied to the weather.

clem-ent (klĕm'ĕnt), *adj.* compassionate; forgiving; gentle; kind.

clench (klĕnch), *v.t.* to set closely together, as the teeth; to clinch; to grip: *n.* a thing that grips; an argument that cannot be answered; a clinch.—*n.* **clencher.**

clep-to-ma-ni-a (klĕp'tō-mā'nĭ-ȧ), *n.* an uncontrollable desire to steal. Also, **kleptomania.**—*n.* **cleptomaniac, kleptomaniac.**

clere-sto-ry (klēre'stō-rĭ), *n.* the highest story of a church, above the aisle-roofs, etc., having windows; a similar elevated part in the roof of other buildings. Also, **clearstory.**

cler-gy (klûr'jĭ), *n.* a body of men appointed for the service of the church.

cler-gy-man (klûr'jĭ-măn), *n.* [*pl.* clergymen (-mĕn)], a minister or preacher.

cler-i-cal (klĕr'ĭ-kăl), *adj.* pertaining to the clergy; pertaining to a clerk, writer, or copyist.—*adv.* **clerically.**

clerk (klûrk), *n.* one engaged in an office to conduct correspondence, keep books, or transact business generally; an assistant salesman in a store or shop; a scholar: *v.i.* to act as clerk or salesman.

clev-er (klĕv'ẽr), *adj.* skilful; mentally quick; expert.—*adv.* **cleverly.**—*n.* **cleverness.**

Syn. adroit, expert, skilful.
Ant. (see stupid).

clev-is (klĕv'ĭs), *n.* a U-shaped draft-iron at the end of the tongue of a plow, wagon, etc.

clew (klōō), *n.* a ball of thread, yarn, etc.; a thread that guides, as out of a labyrinth; a guide or key to the solution of a problem, plot, or mystery; a lower corner of a square sail; the after lower corner of a fore-and-aft sail; a loop at the corner of a sail: *v.t.* to haul (a sail) up, as for furling.

click (klĭk), *n.* a slight sharp sound; a catch for holding a bolt: *v.t.* and *v.i.* to make, or cause to make, a short, sharp noise.

cli-ent (klī'ĕnt), *n.* one who consults or employs a lawyer; one who seeks advice of an expert of any kind, such as an architect or a banker.

cli-en-tele (klī"ĕn-tĕl'; klē"ăn-tĕl'), *n.* the body of those who seek a person for professional advice; followers; clients collectively.

cliff (klĭf), *n.* a high steep rock or bank; a precipice.

cli-mate (klī'mȧt), *n.* the atmospheric and weather conditions of a place, especially as regards temperature, moisture, etc.

cli-mat-ic (klī-măt'ĭk), *adj.* pertaining to weather conditions.

cli-max (klī'măks), *n.* the highest point or the summit.

climb (klīm), *v.t.* and *v.i.* to mount or ascend, as by the hands and feet; ascend with difficulty; ascend by twining; *n.* act of mounting; ascent mounted.—*n.* **climber.**

clime (klīm), *n.* a country; region; as, in every *clime.* [Poet.]

clinch (klĭnch), *v.t.* to rivet; to fasten; to nail; double up tightly, as the fingers; to hold fast; to render unanswerable, as an argument: *n.* anything that holds both ways; a mode of fastening large ropes; an unanswerable argument. Also, **clench.**—*n.* **clincher.**

cling (klĭng), *v.i.* [*p.t.* and *p.p.* clung, *p.pr.* clinging], to adhere closely; to stick; hold fast by embracing or entwining.

clin-ic (klĭn'ĭk), *n.* a medical lecture on the nature and treatment of diseases, given in the presence of patients and students.—*adj.* **clinical.**—*adv.* **clinically.**

clink (klĭnk), *v.t.* to strike so as to make a slight sharp sound; to ring or jingle; *v.i.* to make a short sharp noise: *n.* a slight sharp vibrating noise.

Clinometer

clink-er (klĭnk'ẽr), *n.* a mass of burned coal formed into a hard stony substance; slag.

cli-nom-e-ter (klī-nŏm'ē-tẽr), *n.* an instrument for determining angular inclination, as of a gun, the deck of a ship, the dip of rock strata, the slope of a hillside, etc.

clip (klĭp), *v.t.* [*p.t.* and *p.p.* clipped, *p.pr.* clipping], to cut with shears or scissors; cut off; to cut short; as, to *clip* one's words: *n.* the wool of a season's shearing; a spring holder for holding papers; colloquially, a slight blow with the hand; a rapid gait.

Clipper

clip-per (klĭp'ẽr), *n.* one who, or that which, cuts off or snips; an instrument for cutting the hair; a clear-cut or well-shaped sailing vessel with a great spread of canvas.

clip-ping (klĭp'ĭng), *n.* the act of cutting or snipping off; that which is cut off or out of something; as, a newspaper *clipping.*

clique (klēk), *n.* a group of persons united for some common purpose; a coterie; a ring.—*adj.* **cliquish.**

cloak (klōk), *n.* a sleeveless, loose outer garment; hence, a pretext; disguise: *v.t.* to cover with, or as with, a cloak; cover up or conceal.

clock (klŏk), *n.* a machine to measure and indicate time by means of hands moving over a dial-plate; a woven or embroidered ornament on the ankle of a stocking.—*adj.* **clocked.**

clock-wise (klŏk'wīz"), *adj.* and *adv.* in the same direction as the motion of the hands of a clock.

clock-work (klŏk'wûrk"), *n.* the machinery of a clock; any mechanism resembling it.

clod (klŏd), *n.* a lump of earth, turf, or clay; a bait used in eel-fishing; a stupid, awkward fellow.

clod-hop-per (klŏd'hŏp"ẽr), *n.* a rustic; a clown; a boor; an awkward, rough, or rude person.

clog (klŏg), *v.t.* [*p.t.* and *p.p.* clogged, *p.pr.* clogging], to obstruct; embarrass: *v.i.* to become choked up: *n.* a load or weight; a hindrance; a kind of wooden shoe; a dance by one wearing such shoes.

clois-ter (klois'tẽr), *n.* an inclosure; a place of religious retirement; a monastery or nunnery; an arched way or covered walk inside the walls of a church building or college: *v.t.* to confine in, or as in, a convent or place of retirement; seclude from the world.

clois-tral (klois'trăl), *adj.* pertaining to, or confined in, a cloister; retired; secluded.

close (klōz), *v.t.* to shut; to shut up, as an opening by filling; to join, as an electric circuit; bring together; end: *v.i.* to come together; shut in; terminate or make an ending: followed by *with;* grapple with an opponent; to agree: *n.* an inclosed space; the grounds of a cathedral or abbey; an alley; end; cessation: *adj.* (klōs), having no outlet; confined; without ventilation; shut fast; narrow; secretive; stingy; near, as in time, etc.; intimate; having its parts near each other; compact; fitting snugly; open only to a certain few; restricted by law, as a game season; pronounced with the lips near together; as, a *close* vowel; oppressive; minute; precise: *adv.* near; tightly; narrowly; stingily. —*adv.* **closely.**—*n.* **closeness.**

closed shop (klōzd shŏp), a shop that is closed to workmen who are not members of a union.

close-fist-ed (klōs'fĭs"tĕd), *adj.* stingy; not inclined to part with money; miserly.—*n.* **closefistedness.**

close-mouthed (klōs-mouthd), *adj.* uncommunicative; reticent.

close-hauled (klōs'hôld"), *adj.* sailing as near the wind as possible.

clos-et (klŏz'ĕt), *n.* a small room for privacy or retirement; a place for storing valuable things, or clothing, utensils, provisions, etc.; a water-closet: *adj.* private; secluded: *v.t.* to receive in a private room for a personal interview.

clo-sure (klō'zhūr), *n.* the act of shutting up; that which incloses; the end; the proceeding by which a debate may be stopped by the vote of the majority: *v.t.* to end (a debate) by closure. Also, **cloture.**

clot (klŏt), *v.i.* [*p.t.* and *p.p.* clotted, *p.pr.* clotting], to coagulate, or thicken: applied to fluids: *v.t.* to make, form into, or cover with, lumps of coagulated matter: *n.* a hard or thick mass of coagulated matter.—*adj.* **clotty, clotted.**

cloth (klŏth), *n.* [*pl.* cloths (klŏthz)], a woven fabric of wool, hair, or other material; a table covering; the usual dress of any profession, especially the clerical.

clothe (klōth), *v.t.* to dress; to put raiment on; cover with, or as with, a garment.

clothes (klōthz), *n.pl.* covering for the body; raiment; garments collectively; coverings for beds.

clothes-press (klōthz'prĕs"), *n.* a chest or wardrobe for holding garments or wearing-apparel.

cloth-ier (klōth'yẽr), *n.* one who makes or sells garments; a dealer in ready-made garments.

cloth-ing (klōth'ĭng), *n.* clothes; dress; garments in general.

cloud (kloud), *n.* a mass of visible vapor floating in the air; a volume of smoke or dust; a dimmed appearance or spot, as in marble; anything threatening in aspect, or casting suspicion on one; a light woolen shawl: *v.t.* to overspread with, or as with, a mist or cloud; render gloomy; blacken or sully: *v.i.* to grow cloudy.

cloud-burst (kloud'bûrst"), *n.* a heavy downpour of rain over a very small area.

cloud-less (kloud'lĕs), *adj.* clear; bright; unshadowed; not overcast.

cloud-y (kloud'ĭ), *adj.* pertaining to a cloud or clouds; overcast; threatening (rain); vague; obscure; not clear; as, a *cloudy* liquid.—*adv.* **cloudily.**—*n.* **cloudiness.**

clout (klout), *n.* a piece of cloth or leather for patching; a cloth for any mean use; a rag; an arrow that has hit the target; colloquially, a blow on the head with the hand: *v.t.* to patch or mend coarsely; colloquially, to strike with the hand.

clove (klōv), *p.t.* of the verb *cleave*: *n.* a spice from the dried flower bud of a tropical tree of the myrtle family.

clo-ven (klō'vn), *p.adj.* divided into two parts; split; as, a *cloven* foot.

clo-ven-foot-ed (klō'vn-fo͝ot"ĕd), *adj.* having the foot deeply cleft, as the ox; having the foot divided into two or more parts; devilish; the cloven hoof or foot is an indication of devilishness, because the devil is often represented as having cloven hoofs.

clo-ver (klō'vẽr), *n.* a fragrant kind of grass, the leaves of which are divided into three leaflets, and the flowers collected into heads.

clown (kloun), *n.* a man of coarse manners; a boor; an ill-bred fellow; a professional jester, or one who amuses others by tricks, antics, etc.

clown-ish (kloun'ĭsh), *adj.* like a clown; rude; coarse; awkward.—*adv.* **clownishly.**—*n.* **clownishness.**

cloy (kloi), *v.t.* [*p.t.* and *p.p.* cloyed, *p.pr.* cloying], to fill too full; to gorge; surfeit.

club (klŭb), *n.* a heavy stick; one of the suits of playing cards; a number of persons associated for a common purpose or mutual benefit: *v.t.* [*p.t.* and *p.p.* clubbed, *p.pr.* clubbing], to beat with a cudgel; to give to a common expense: *v.i.* to combine for a common purpose; as, to *club* together to buy a football; to form a club.

club-foot (klŭb'fo͝ot"), *n.* a deformed foot; clumpfoot.—*adj.* **club-footed.**

cluck (klŭk), *v.i.* to cry or call like a hen to her chickens: *n.* a hen's call.

clue (klo͞o), *n.* anything that helps to solve a difficulty; a hint; a clew; a suggestion.

clump (klŭmp), *n.* a cluster or group of trees, etc.; a thick sole: *v.t.* to arrange in a cluster or group: *v.i.* to tread heavily.

clum-sy (klŭm'zĭ), *adj.* awkward; heavy; unskilful; ill-made; lacking ease or grace; as, a *clumsy* boy; a *clumsy* action.—*adv.* **clumsily.**—*n.* **clumsiness.**

clung (klŭng), *p.t.* of the verb *cling*; as, he *clung* to his old friends; the perfume *clung* to the gloves; the vine *clung* to the wall.

clus-ter (klŭs'tẽr), *n.* a number of things, such as fruits, of the same kind growing or collected together; a bunch; as, a great *cluster* of ripe grapes: *v.i.* to grow or gather in bunches: *v.t.* to gather or collect into bunches.

clutch (klŭch), *v.t.* to grasp, seize, or grip strongly; as, to *clutch* a dagger: *v.i.* to snatch or seize: with *at*: *n.* a grasp; a hand, or claw in the act of seizure: often used in the plural; as, keep out of his *clutches*; a device for gripping or holding; a device for coupling; as, an automobile *clutch*.

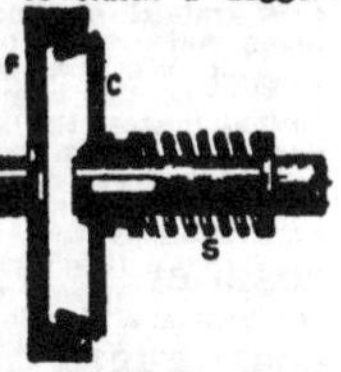

Automobile Cone Clutch. *F*, flywheel; *C*, leather-faced clutch; *S*, spring.

clut-ter (klŭt'ẽr), *n.* disorder; litter; confusion: *v.t.* to heap up in disorder and confusion; crowd together in disorder; disarrange.

coach (kōch), *n.* a large covered four-wheeled public or private carriage; colloquially, a tutor who especially prepares another for an examination or an athletic contest; a passenger car: *v.t.* colloquially, to instruct or train for an examination or contest.

coach-man (kōch'măn), *n.* [*pl.* coachmen (-mĕn)], one whose business it is to drive a coach or carriage.

co-act (kō-ăkt'), *v.i.* to act or work together: *v.t.* to force together; compel or restrain.—*adj.* **coactive.**

co-ac-tion (kō-ăk'shŭn), *n.* action together; compulsion; forced restraint.

co-ad-ju-tor (kō"ă-jo͞o'tẽr), *n.* an official helper or assistant.

co-ag-u-late (kō-ăg'ū-lāt), *v.t.* and *v.i.* to clot or curdle; to thicken.

co-ag-u-la-tion (kō-ăg"ū-lā'shŭn), *n.* the act of curdling or clotting; the change from a fluid to a thickened curdlike state.

co-ag-u-la-tive (kō-ăg'ū-lā-tĭv), *adj.* tending to produce curdling or clotting; having the property of curdling or clotting.

co-ag-u-lum (kō-ăg'ū-lŭm), *n.* [*pl.* coagula (-lȧ)], a clot of blood; a curdled mass.

coal (kōl), *n.* a black, or brownish-black, hard, combustible mineral, formed of the vegetation of prehistoric times, taken from the earth and used as fuel: *v.t.* to furnish with coal: *v.i.* to take in coal.

co-a-lesce (kō″ȧ-lĕs′), *v.i.* to grow together; combine; unite; fuse.

co-a-les-cence (kō″ȧ-lĕs′ĕns), *n.* the act or process of uniting.—*adj.* **coalescent.**

coal gas (kōl găs), gas produced by burning coal: used for heating and lighting.

co-a-li-tion (kō″ȧ-lish′ŭn), *n.* union in a body or mass; a combination of persons; an alliance of nations.

coal oil (kōl oil), petroleum; especially, kerosene.

coal tar (kōl tär), a thick dark liquid which is taken from soft coal, and from which many rich dye colors are obtained.

coam-ings (kōm′ingz), *n.pl.* the raised wood or iron borders of the hatches of a vessel.

coarse (kōrs), *adj.* of poor or inferior quality or appearance; large in texture or size; not refined; indelicate; gross.—*adv.* **coarsely.**—*n.* **coarseness.**
Syn. rude, rough, unpolished.
Ant. (see fine).

coars-en (kōr′sn), *v.t.* and *v.i.* to make large or rough (that which was close-grained or fine); to turn or become harsh, rude, rough, or unrefined.

coast (kōst), *n.* the margin or boundary of the land next the sea; in the United States, the act of sliding on a sled down a hill or an incline: *v.i.* to sail near or along the shore; descend an incline on a sled, or on a bicycle without working the pedals: *v.t.* to sail close to or near to.—*adj.* **coastal.**

coast-er (kōs′tẽr), *n.* a home-trading vessel; one who slides on a sled or glides on a bicycle.

coast guard (kōst gärd), a man who patrols the seacoast to save passengers on vessels in distress.

coast-ing trade (kōst′ing trād), the trade between ports of the same country.

coat (kōt), *n.* an outer garment covering the upper part of the body; an outside covering, as fur, etc.; a thin layer: *v.t.* to cover or spread over.—*n.* **coating.**

coat-ee (kōt″tē′), *n.* a close-fitting coat with short tails.

coat of arms (kōt ŏv ärmz), a light garment worn over the armor of English knights in the fifteenth and sixteenth centuries, and often bearing the heraldic signs of the wearer's rank or family; a shield bearing such device or imprint; an insignia, or sign used to represent a city, state, or nation; as, the *coat of arms* of the United States.

coat of mail (kōt ŏv māl), chain-mail; an ancient iron garment worn by soldiers.

coax (kōks), *v.t.* to wheedle; cajole; flatter; control in a gentle way: *v.i.* to use gentle persuasion or flattery.—*n.* **coaxer.**

cob (kŏb), *n.* the top; the head; the spike of Indian corn; a strong thick-set pony; a kind of breakwater: **corncob**, the spike or axis around which the kernels of Indian corn are set.

co-balt (kō′bôlt), *n.* a steel-gray metallic element, similar to nickel.

cob-ble (kŏb′l), *n.* a pebble; a round medium-sized stone; clumsy work: *v.t.* to mend or patch up coarsely; repair, as shoes: *v.i.* to work at the business of mending shoes.

cob-bler (kŏb′lẽr), *n.* one who mends boots and shoes; a clumsy workman; a cooling summer drink of iced wine, etc.; as, sherry *cobbler.*

cob-ble-stone (kŏb′l-stōn″), *n.* a rounded stone used for paving.

co-bra (kō′brȧ), *n.* a venomous snake, found in Asia, especially in India, where there is a particularly poisonous variety.

cob-web (kŏb′wĕb″), *n.* a spider's web; hence, a net or snare: *adj.* made of, or like, a cobweb; flimsy; entangling.

co-ca (kō′kȧ), *n.* the dried leaf of a small South American shrub, which yields cocaine, a powerful tonic.

co-ca-ine (kō′kȧ-in; kō′kȧ-ēn; kō-kān′), *n.* a powerful drug extracted from coca leaves: used as a local anesthetic. Also, **cocain.**

coc-cyx (kŏk′siks), *n.* [*pl.* coccyges (-sī-jēz)], the lower end of the spinal column.

coch-i-neal (kŏch′ĭ-nēl), *n.* a scarlet dye obtained from the dried body of an insect.

coch-le-a (kŏk′lē-ȧ), *n.* [*pl.* cochleæ (-lē-ē)], the spiral-shaped space of the inner ear.

cock (kŏk), *n.* the male of birds; a male chicken; a vane in the shape of a cock; a leader or chief; a turn-valve for releasing the flow of a liquid or gas; the hammer of a firearm; a small cone-shaped pile, especially of hay; the act of sticking or turning up jauntily, as a hat or an eye; the tilt given to a hat or eye so turned: *v.t.* to turn up or set (the hat or head) jauntily on one side; to stack up in conical piles; to raise the hammer of (a gun), in order to fire; as, to *cock* a pistol.

cock-ade (kŏk-ād′), *n.* a badge of ribbon or a rosette worn on the hat.

cock-a-too (kŏk′ȧ-tōō′), *n.* a crested bird of the parrot family.

cock-a-trice (kŏk′ȧ-trīs; kŏk′ȧ-trĭs), *n.* a fairy serpent said to have been hatched in a cock's egg, and able to kill by a glance of its eye.

cock-boat (kŏk′bōt″), *n.* a small row-boat; a tender.

cock-chaf-er (kŏk′chāf″ẽr), *n.* a kind of beetle destructive to vegetation; a May-bug.

cock-crow (kŏk′krō″), *n.* early morning, when the cock first crows. Also, **cockcrowing.**

cock-er (kŏk′ẽr), *n.* a small spaniel, or dog, used in hunting; a cock-fighter.

cock-er-el (kŏk′ẽr-ĕl), *n.* a young domestic cock less than a year old.

cock-eyed (kŏk′īd″), *adj.* having squinting eyes; cross-eyed.

cock-le (kŏk′l), *n.* an eatable shellfish with two heart-shaped wrinkled shells; the plant corncockle or darnell; a kiln for drying hops; a weed that grows among grain; a pucker or wrinkle: *v.t.* and *v.i.* to pucker or wrinkle: **cockleshell**, *n.* one of the shells of a cockle, scallop, etc.; a cockboat.

cock-loft (kŏk′lŏft″), *n.* a loft or attic under a roof.

cock-ney (kŏk′nĭ), *n.* a Londoner; the name given to one born within sound of the bells of Bow Church, Cheapside; an uneducated Londoner.

cock-pit (kŏk'pĭt"), *n.* an inclosed space for cockfighting; in small vessels, a space aft lower than the deck; in an airplane, the well in the body where the pilot's seat is placed.

cock-roach (kŏk'rōch"), *n.* a black beetle found in kitchens, pantries, etc.

cocks-comb (kŏks'kōm"), *n.* the comb or crest of a cock; a garden plant of the amaranth family; a red edge on a jester's cap; the cap; a coxcomb.

cock-sure (kŏk'shōōr"; kŏk"shōōr'), *adj.* certain; absolutely certain or sure. [COLLOQ.]

cock-swain (kŏk'swān; *naut.* kŏk'sn), *n.* the steersman of a ship's boat, a racing shell, etc. Also, **coxswain.**

cock-tail (kŏk'tāl"), *n.* a drink made of spirits, with bitters, sugar, and flavoring.

co-co (kō'kō), *n.* a palm which produces the coconut. Also, **cocoa, coco palm.**

co-coa (kō'kō), *n.* the ground seeds of the cacao or chocolate tree; the drinks made from it.

co-co-nut (kō'kō-nŭt), *n.* the fruit of the coco palm, a white meaty substance within a hard shell which also contains a milky liquid. Also, **cocoanut.**

co-coon (kŏ-kōōn'), *n.* the silky case which covers the eggs of many spinning insects until they are hatched.

cod (kŏd), *n.* the husk or pod of a seed; a large edible fish found in the northern seas, and especially on the banks of Newfoundland.

cod-dle (kŏd''l), *v.t.* to humor or pamper; treat tenderly; to stew gently.

code (kōd), *n.* a body of laws or regulations arranged in a certain order; a system of signals; a system of symbols used for brevity and secrecy.

cod-fish (kŏd'fĭsh"), *n.* the cod or the flesh of this fish served as food.

co-dex (kō'dĕks), *n.* [*pl.* codices (kŏd'ĭ-sēz; kō'dĭ-sēz)], a code; a volume of laws or statutes; a manuscript in the general form of a book, especially of the sacred Scriptures.

codg-er (kŏj'ẽr), *n.* a miser; an odd or testy old man.

cod-i-cil (kŏd'ĭ-sĭl), *n.* an addition; a supplement to a will.

co-di-fy (kō'dĭ-fī; kŏd'ĭ-fī), *v.t.* [*p.t.* and *p.p.* codified, *p.pr.* codifying], to reduce to a system, as laws; to make uniform; to arrange or systematize.—*n.* **codification.**

cod-ling (kŏd'lĭng), *n.* a young cod; a kind of stewing apple.

co-ed-u-ca-tion (kō-ĕd"ū-kā'shŭn), *n.* the education of both sexes in the same school.

co-ef-fi-cient (kō"ĕ-fĭsh'ĕnt), *adj.* coöperating: *n.* any agent that coöperates or works with another agent; any sign or group of signs placed before another or others as a multiplier; as, in 3 y the *coefficient* is 3.

co-e-qual (kō-ē'kwăl), *adj.* of the same value or importance: *n.* one of the same value or importance as another.

co-erce (kō-ûrs'), *v.t.* to restrain or constrain by force, especially legally or morally; compel.

co-er-cion (kō-ûr'shŭn), *n.* the act of constraining forcibly; compulsion.

co-er-cive (kō-ûr'sĭv), *adj.* serving or designed to compel; as, the drafting of men into the army is a *coercive* measure of the government.

co-e-val (kō-ē'văl), *adj.* of the same age or period: usually with the idea of long duration.

co-ex-ist (kō"ĕg-zĭst'), *v.i.* to exist together in time or place.—*adj.* **coexistent.**—*n.* **coexistence.**

co-ex-tend (kō"ĕks-tĕnd'), *v.t.* and *v.i.* to reach, or cause to reach, the same limits through the same space, time, etc., as another.

co-ex-ten-sive (kō"ĕks-tĕn'sĭv), *adj.* having the same limits; occupying the same measure of space.

cof-fee (kŏf'ĭ), *n.* the seeds of a plant which, when roasted and ground, are used to make a well-known drink: the drink; the plant: **coffeehouse,** a house where coffee and other refreshments are sold.

cof-fer (kŏf'ẽr), *n.* a casket, chest, or trunk for the storage of valuables; a kind of caisson or floating dock: *pl.* a treasury.

cof-fer-dam (kŏf'ẽr-dăm"), *n.* a watertight inclosure built in the water and pumped dry, to protect workmen.

cof-fin (kŏf'ĭn), *n.* a case or chest for the dead; the hollow part of a horse's hoof: *v.t.* to inclose in a chest or coffin: **coffin bone,** the foot bone of a horse's foot, inclosed within the hoof.

cog (kŏg), *n.* the tooth of a gear-wheel; a toothed cam, a projection on a beam to be received in a notch on another to join the two together: *v.t.* [*p.t.* and *p.p.* cogged, *p.pr.* cogging], to furnish with gear-teeth, cams, etc.

co-gent (kō'jĕnt), *adj.* having great force; convincing; as, a *cogent* reason.—*adv.* **cogently.**—*n.* **cogency.**

cog-i-tate (kŏj'ĭ-tāt), *v.i.* to think earnestly; to reflect: *v.t.* to devise or plan.—*adj.* **cogitative.**—*n.* **cogitation.**

co-gnac (kō'nyăk), *n.* a French brandy; any fine grape brandy.

cog-nate (kŏg'nāt), *adj.* related by blood; of the same stock, nature, or quality; related in origin; as, *cognate* languages: *n.* a person or thing that is akin to another by blood, derivation, etc.

cog-ni-tion (kŏg-nĭsh'ŭn), *n.* knowledge; the power or faculty of knowing.

cog-ni-za-ble (kŏg'nĭ-zȧ-bl; kŏn'ĭ-zȧ-bl), *adj.* capable of being known or perceived.

cog-ni-zance (kŏg'nĭ-zăns; kŏn'ĭ-zăns), *n.* judicial knowledge or notice; perception.

cog-ni-zant (kŏg'nĭ-zănt; kŏn'ĭ-zănt), *adj.* having knowledge (of anything); aware.

cog-no-men (kŏg-nō'mĕn), *n.* [*pl.* cognomens (-mĕnz)], a surname.

cog-wheel (kŏg'hwēl"), *n.* a wheel with teeth notched in its rim.

co-hab-it (kō-hăb'ĭt), *v.i.* to live together as husband and wife.—*n.* **cohabitation.**

co-heir (kō-âr'), *n.* [*fem.* coheiress], a person who inherits jointly with someone else.

co-here (kō-hēr'), *v.i.* to stick or cleave together; be united.

co-her-ence (kō-hēr'ĕns), *n.* the state or quality of being united; a sticking or cleaving together; connection; consistency. Also, **coherency.**

co-her-ent (kō-hēr'ĕnt), *adj.* sticking together; connected; as, a *coherent* argument.—*adv.* **coherently.**

co-her-er (kō-hēr'ēr), *n.* a device for detecting the signals used in wireless telegraphy.

co-he-sion (kō-hē'zhŭn), *n.* the force that unites particles of the same material; coherence; the act of uniting or sticking together.

co-he-sive (kō-hē'sĭv), *n.* causing to adhere, unite, or stick together; as, the *cohesive* force which holds a political party together.—*adv.* **cohesively.**—*n.* **cohesiveness.**

co-hort (kō'hôrt), *n.* a body of ancient Roman soldiers, the tenth part of a legion.

coif-fure (kwä'für'; kcif'ūr), *n.* a head-dress; manner of arranging the hair. [Fr.]

coign (koin), *n.* a projecting stone or angle; a corner: **coign of vantage,** an advantageous position.

coil (koil), *n.* a rope gathered into a ring; anything like it; a spiral; a series of connected pipes in windings, layers, etc.; a continuous spiral of conducting material: *v.t.* to gather or wind into a circular heap: *v.i.* to wind.

coin (koin), *n.* a piece of metal legally stamped and authorized to be used as money; coined money collectively; a corner or angle: *v.t.* to make (coins) by stamping pieces of metal; invent.

coin-age (koin'āj), *n.* the process of making pieces of money; the money made; the system of metal money used in a country; the cost of making metal money or the charge for making it; an invention.

co-in-cide (kō'ĭn-sīd'), *v.i.* to correspond exactly; occur at the same time.

co-in-ci-dence (kō-ĭn'sĭ-dĕns), *n.* a happening at the same time; accidental agreement; the act of concurring.

co-in-ci-dent (kō-ĭn'sĭ-dĕnt), *adj.* exactly corresponding; taking place at the same time; agreeing.

coin-er (koin'ēr), *n.* one who stamps coins; especially, one who makes counterfeit money.

coir (koir), *n.* the fiber of coconut husk, prepared for use in making cables, cordage, matting, etc.

co-i-tion (kō-ĭsh'ŭn), *n.* a coming together; sexual intercourse.

coke (kōk), *n.* partly burned coal, or what remains of coal after the gases have been taken from it by heating it in ovens: *v.t.* and *v.i.* to change into coke, etc.

col-an-der (kŭl'ăn-dēr), *n.* a metal strainer; a vessel with little holes in the bottom.

col-chi-cum (kŏl'kĭ-kŭm; kŏl'chĭ-kŭm), *n.* the meadow-saffron, the seeds and bulbs of which are used in medicine.

cold (kōld), *adj.* without heat or warmth; frigid; without passion or zeal; indifferent; insensible: *n.* the opposite of heat; the sensation produced by the loss of heat; disordered condition of the body, usually catarrhal, following exposure or infection; low temperature.—*adv.* **coldly.**—*n.* **coldness.**

Syn., *adj.* cool, frigid, wintry, unfeeling, stoical.

Ant. (see warm).

cold-blood-ed (kōld'blŭd'ĕd), *adj.* having blood below 90° Fahr. in temperature, as some fishes, reptiles, etc.; unfeeling; unsympathetic; as, *cold-blooded* advice.

cold sore (kōld sōr), a fever blister; an eruption about the mouth, usually appearing during a cold or fever.

cole (kōl), *n.* any one of the many cabbage plants, as cabbage, cauliflower, etc.

cole-slaw (kōl'slô'), *n.* a salad made of cabbage cut fine. Also, **cold-slaw.**

cole-wort (kōl'wûrt'), *n.* the garden cabbage before it forms into heads; a plant of the cabbage kind.

col-ic (kŏl'ĭk), *n.* a sharp, frequent pain in the abdomen and bowels: *adj.* pertaining to, or affecting, the bowels.—*adj.* **colicky.**

Col-i-se-um (kŏl'ĭ-sē'ŭm), *n.* the great amphitheater in Rome built in the first century A. D., a part of which is still standing. Also, **Colosseum.**

col-lab-o-rate (kō-lăb'ō-rāt), *v.i.* to work with another, to coöperate with others, especially in literary or scientific work.—*n.* **collaboration, collaborator.**

col-lapse (kō-lăps'), *n.* a falling in or together; sudden and complete failure; general prostration; as, the man's *collapse* was caused by overwork: *v.i.* to fall in or together; shrink up; break down.—*adj.* **collapsible.**

col-lar (kŏl'ẽr), *n.* something worn about the neck, for use, restraint, or ornament; a round ring or flange: **collar bone,** the clavicle: *v.t.* to seize by the collar; put a collar on.

col-lar-ette (kŏl'ẽr-ĕt'), *n.* a small collar of lace, etc.

col-late (kō-lāt'), *v.t.* to compare (one thing with another of the same kind), as manuscripts or text of books; as, to *collate* all the writings of an author; to examine, as the gathered sheets of a book, before binding.—*n.* **collator.**

col-lat-er-al (kō-lăt'ēr-ăl), *adj.* side by side; parallel; confirming or supporting, as testimony; incidental; subordinate; protected by additional security, as a loan; descended from the same stock, but in a different line: *n.* security additional to one's obligation.—*adv.* **collaterally.**

col-la-tion (kō-lā'shŭn), *n.* comparison, or the act of bringing together for comparison, as books, etc.; a light meal.

col-league (kŏl'ēg), *n.* an associate in the same office, employment, or profession: not used of partners in business.

col-lect (kŏl'ĕkt), *n.* a short prayer, often of but one sentence, asking for one blessing.

col-lect (kō-lĕkt'), *v.t.* to gather together; assemble; demand and obtain payment of: *v.i.* to meet together; accumulate.—*n.* **collector.**

col-lect-ed (kō-lĕk'tĕd), *adj.* self-possessed; brought together.—*adv.* **collectedly.**—*n.* **collectedness.**

col-lec-tion (kō-lĕk'shŭn), *n.* the act of gathering together; a mass; a crowd; an assemblage of works of art, or natural objects; as, there are many fine *collections* of art in America; a contribution to a special object.

col-lec-tive (kō-lĕk'tĭv), *adj.* united; accumulative; as, the *collective* claims of the miners; derived from a group, or characteristic of a group; common; in grammar, naming a number of objects as a group; as, army is a *collective* noun.—*adv.* **collectively.**

col-lege (kŏl'ĕj), *n.* a society of men possessing certain powers and rights, and engaged in some common pursuit, especially literary studies; an educational institution in which advanced courses are given.

col-le-gi-an (kŏ-lē'jĭ-ăn), *n.* a member of a college; a college student.

col-le-gi-ate (kŏ-lē'jĭ-āt), *adj.* of or pertaining to a college.

col-lide (kŏ-līd'), *v.i.* to strike together with force; as, the ships *collided;* to come into conflict; clash.

col-lie (kŏl'ĭ), *n.* a Scotch sheep-dog of much intelligence, with a shaggy coat.

col-lier (kŏl'yẽr), *n.* a coal-digger; a vessel in the coal trade.

col-lier-y (kŏl'yẽr-ĭ), *n.* [*pl.* collieries (-ĭz)], a coal mine and its surrounding buildings.

col-li-sion (kŏ-lĭzh'ŭn), *n.* the striking of two bodies violently together; concussion; as, many were injured in the *collision;* clash; opposition.

Syn. contact, conflict, impact, encounter, meeting.

Ant. (see concord).

col-lo-di-on (kŏ-lō'dĭ-ŭn), *n.* a substance made by dissolving guncotton in ether; used to form films for wounds, photography, etc.

col-lo-qui-al (kŏ-lō'kwĭ-ăl), *adj.* used in ordinary conversation; belonging to everyday speech; informal.—*adv.* **colloquially.**

col-lo-qui-al-ism (kŏ-lō'kwĭ-ăl-ĭzm), *n.* a familiar, informal, not literary, form of speech.

col-lo-quy (kŏl'ō-kwĭ), *n.* [*pl.* colloquies (-kwĭz)], a conversation; a dialog.

col-lude (kŏ-lūd'), *v.i.* to conspire; to work with others secretly, with evil intent.

col-lu-sion (kŏ-lū'zhŭn), *n.* secret agreement for an unlawful or evil purpose; as, persons may be in *collusion* to defraud another.—*adj.* **collusive.**—*adv.* **collusively.**

co-logne (kŏ-lōn'), *n.* a perfume made of alcohol and fragrant oils. Also, **cologne water.**

co-lon (kō'lŏn), *n.* a mark of punctuation [:]; the largest of the intestines.

colo-nel (kûr'nĕl), *n.* the chief officer of a regiment.—*n.* **colonelcy.**

co-lo-ni-al (kŏ-lō'nĭ-ăl), *adj.* pertaining to a colony, or settlement of people subject to a mother country; as, *colonial* rights or customs.—*n.* **colonialism.**

col-o-nist (kŏl'ō-nĭst), *n.* a member of a colony, or settlement of people subject to a mother country; a settler.

col-o-nize (kŏl'ō-nīz), *v.t.* to settle or form a colony in; as, England *colonized* Australia; to bring together in a colony: *v.i.* to unite in a colony.—*n.* **colonization.**

col-on-nade (kŏl'ŏ-nād'), *n.* a row of columns.

col-o-ny (kŏl'ō-nĭ), *n.* [*pl.* colonies (-nĭz)], a body of people who leave their native country and settle in another land, but remain subject to the mother country; the country thus settled; a group of people living close together; as, a *colony* of writers; a number of animals or plants living or growing together.

col-or (kŭl'ẽr), *n.* the hue or appearance that a body presents to the eye; a pigment or paint; complexion; redness: *pl.* a military or naval flag: *v.t.* to impart a color to; tint; dye. Also, **colour.**

Syn., *v.* dye, stain, tinge.

col-or-a-ble (kŭl'ẽr-ȧ-bl), *adj.* capable of being colored; having a false appearance of right; deceptive; plausible. Also, **colourable.**

col-or-blind (kŭl'ẽr-blīnd'), *adj.* unable to distinguish colors. Also, **colour-blind.**—*n.* **color-blindness, colour-blindness.**

col-o-ra-do (kŏl'ō-rä'dō), *adj.* of medium strength and color: said of cigars. [SPAN.]

Col-o-ra-do bee-tle (kŏl'ō-rä'dō bē'tl), a yellowish beetle, having its back marked with ten black stripes, which destroys potato crops.

col-ored (kŭl'ẽrd), *adj.* having color; belonging to a dark-skinned race: applied to negroes or those of negro blood; exaggerated; heightened in interest by the addition of details. Also, **coloured.**

col-or-ing (kŭl'ẽr-ĭng), *n.* the act or art of giving a color to, as in painting; the color so applied; false or specious appearance. Also, **colouring.**

col-or-ist (kŭl'ẽr-ĭst), *n.* an artist whose works are notable for beauty of color. Also, **colourist.**

col-or-less (kŭl'ẽr-lĕs), *adj.* having no color; uninteresting; impartial; marked by no outstanding qualities. Also, **colourless.**—*adv.* **colorlessly, colourlessly.**—*n.* **colorlessness, colourlessness.**

co-los-sal (kŏ-lŏs'ăl), *adj.* huge; like a colossus; gigantic; immense.—*adv.* **colossally.**

Col-os-se-um (kŏl'ŏ-sē'ŭm), *n.* the amphitheater in ancient Rome built about 80 A. D., the greater part of which is still standing. Also, **Coliseum.**

Co-los-si-ans (kŏ-lŏsh'ĭ-ănz: kŏ-lŏsh'ănz), *n.pl.* a book of the New Testament, containing the Epistle, or letter, of the apostle Paul to the Christians at Colossæ.

co-los-sus (kŏ-lŏs'ŭs), *n.* [*pl.* colossi (-sī)], a statue of great size; as, the *Colossus* of Rhodes was a statue of Apollo; any very great person or object.

col-por-tage (kŏl'pôr"tĭj: kŏl"pôr-täzh'), *n.* the system of distributing Bibles and other religious books by travelers who sell or give away the books.

col-por-teur (kŏl'pôr"tẽr; kŏl"pôr"tûr'), *n.* a person employed to sell or give away Bibles.

colt (kōlt), *n.* a young male horse; one who resembles a colt, especially in youth and inexperience.

col-ter (kōl'tẽr), *n.* a cutter or blade on a plow to cut the sod.

colt-ish (kōl'tĭsh), *adj.* like, or pertaining to, a colt; frisky.—*adv.* **coltishly.**—*n.* **coltishness.**

colts-foot (kōlts'fŏŏt"), *n.* an herb used as a medicine.

Co-lum-bi-an (kŏ-lŭm'bĭ-ăn), *adj.* of or pertaining to the United States or to Columbus, the discoverer of America.

col-um-bine (kŏl'ŭm-bīn; kŏl'ŭm-bĭn), *adj.* pertaining to, or like, a dove or pigeon: *n.* a plant, of the crowfoot family, with flowers of five petals.

col-umn (kŏl'ŭm), *n.* a round pillar to support or adorn a building; a division of the page of a book, etc.; a formation of a body of troops or ships; anything suggestive of a column or shaft; as, a *column* of figures; the spinal *column*.

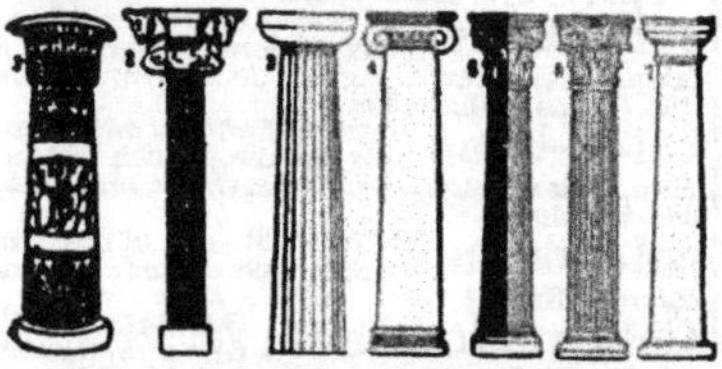

Columns. 1, Egyptian; 2, Assyrian; 3, Doric; 4, Ionic; 5, Corinthian; 6, Composite; 7, Tuscan.

co-lum-nar (kŏ-lŭm'nȧr), *adj.* having the form or shape of a column or shaft; formed in columns.

co-ma (kō'mȧ), *n.* prolonged unconsciousness; as, he was in a state of *coma* for three days; insensibility; stupor: [*pl.* comæ (-mē)], the cloudy, hairlike envelope surrounding the nucleus, or center, of a comet.

Co-man-che (kō-măn'chē), *n.* one of a fierce predatory tribe of American Indians, originally living in what is now northern Texas.

com-a-tose (kŏm'ȧ-tōs; kō'mȧ-tōs), *adj.* torpid; lethargic; morbidly drowsy; affected by coma.

comb (kōm), *n.* a toothed instrument to separate, adjust, or confine, the hair; the crest of a cock; the crest of a wave or hill; a honeycomb; a currycomb; an instrument for carding wool: *v.t.* to dress (the hair) with a toothed instrument; to cleanse, as with a comb; to search through: *v.i.* to roll over and break into foam: said of the crest of a wave.—*n.* **comber.**

com-bat (kŏm'băt), *v.t.* to fight; to contend; struggle: *v.t.* to oppose; resist: *n.* a struggle; fight.

com-bat-ant (kŏm'băt-ănt), *n.* one who fights: *adj.* disposed to fight; bearing arms.

com-ba-tive (kŏm'bȧ-tĭv; kŏm-băt'ĭv), *adj.* pugnacious; showing a disposition to fight or oppose; as, the fox terrier has a *combative* disposition.—*adv.* **combatively.**—*n.* **combativeness.**

com-bi-na-tion (kŏm"bĭ-nā'shŭn), *n.* the state of being united; as, a *combination* of ideas; the union of bodies or qualities; an association of persons for a common object; a suit of underwear.

Syn. conspiracy, plot.

com-bine (kŏm-bīn'), *v.t.* to unite or join; link closely together: *v.i.* to unite; agree; as, two political parties will *combine* to defeat a third party: *n.* (often, kŏm'bīn), colloquially, a secret joining together of persons generally for unlawful purposes.

com-bus-ti-ble (kŏm-bŭs'tĭ-bl), *adj.* capable of taking fire and burning; as, wood and coal are *combustible:* *n.* any substance which may be burned.—*n.* **combustibleness, combustibility.**

com-bus-tion (kŏm-bŭs'chŭn), *n.* the act of burning; the state of being burnt; the union of an inflammable substance with oxygen, etc., producing light and heat.

come (kŭm), *v.i.* [*p.t.* came, *p.p.* come, *p.pr.* coming], to move towards; draw near; reach; become visible; arrive; be present; to issue from or forth from, as a source; become; occur as a result; resemble or approach in kind or quality; happen.

co-me-di-an (kō-mē'dĭ-ăn), *n.* [*fem.* comédienne (kō-mā"dyĕn')], a comic actor or player; a writer of comedy.

com-e-dy (kŏm'ē-dĭ), *n.* [*pl.* comedies (-dĭz)], a humorous play or drama full of lively entertainment, and usually ending happily.

come-ly (kŭm'lĭ), *adj.* graceful; handsome; as, a *comely* person; suitable; proper; as, *comely* behavior.—*n.* **comeliness.**

co-mes-ti-ble (kō-mĕs'tĭ-bl), *n.* an eatable: *adj.* edible; pertaining to food.

com-et (kŏm'ĕt), *n.* a blazing star, often having a long blazing train or tail.

com-fit (kŭm'fĭt), *n.* a dried fruit preserved in sugar; a sweetmeat.

com-fort (kŭm'fẽrt), *v.t.* to console; to cheer; strengthen: *n.* a state of quiet enjoyment; consolation; encouragement; a quilted bedcover.

com-fort-a-ble (kŭm'fẽrt-ȧ-bl), *adj.* being at ease; enjoying contentment or freedom from care: *n.* a padded quilt for beds.—*adv.* **comfortably.**

Syn. agreeable, snug, satisfied, at ease.

Ant. (see cheerless).

com-fort-er (kŭm'fẽr-tẽr), *n.* one who consoles or aids; a long woolen scarf.

com-fort-less (kŭm'fẽrt-lĕs), *adj.* having none of the cheer or consolation of ease; cheerless; miserable; forlorn.

com-ic (kŏm'ĭk), *adj.* pertaining to, or like, comedy; exciting mirth; droll; funny; comical.

com-i-cal (kŏm'ĭ-kăl), *adj.* relating to comedy; comic; witty; droll; colloquially, odd; queer.—*adv.* **comically.**—*n.* **comicality.**

com-ing (kŭm'ĭng), *n.* an arrival: *adj.* expected; future; as, *coming* events.

com-i-ty (kŏm'ĭ-tĭ), *n.* civility; politeness; acts of courtesy between nations.

com-ma (kŏm'ȧ), *n.* a punctuation mark [,] indicating a slight separation in ideas or construction.

com-mand (kŏ-mȧnd'), *v.t.* to order or charge with authority; control; exercise supreme authority over; lead; to overlook, as from a height; to exact; to be able to obtain: *v.i.* to act as a leader; to rule: *n.* authority; an order or mandate; a dominating situation; a naval or military force under the command of a certain officer.

Syn., n. injunction, order, precept: *v.* order, bid, enjoin.

com-man-dant (kŏm"ȧn-dănt'), *n.* an officer in command of a fortified place or a body of troops.

com-man-deer (kŏm"ȧn-dēr'), *v.t.* to compel to military service; to take forcibly for military purposes.

com-mand-er (kŏ-mȧn'dẽr), *n.* one who is a leader; a military chief or leader; a naval officer next below a captain.

com-mand-ing (kŏ-mȧnd′ĭng), *p.adj.* impressive; authoritative; qualified to take charge.

com-mand-ment (kŏ-mȧnd′mĕnt), *n.* a mandate or order; a precept; a law; especially, any one of the Ten Commandments, or Decalog.

com-mem-o-rate (kŏ-mĕm′ō-rāt), *v.t.* to call to remembrance by a solemn act; celebrate with honor.

com-mem-o-ra-tion (kŏ-mĕm″ō-rā′shŭn), *n.* the act of calling to remembrance; a memorial.

com-mem-o-ra-tive (kŏ-mĕm′ō-rȧ-tĭv), *adj.* preserving, or intended to preserve, the memory of; as, a *commemorative* tablet.

com-mence (kŏ-mĕns′), *v.i.* to come into existence; begin: *v.t.* to enter upon; perform the first act of.

com-mence-ment (kŏ-mĕns′mĕnt), *n.* beginning; origin; the occasion when degrees or diplomas are conferred at schools and colleges.

com-mend (kŏ-mĕnd′), *v.t.* to recommend as worthy of notice; praise; intrust; to give the regards of.—*adj.* **commendable.**—*adv.* **commendably.**

com-men-da-tion (kŏm″ĕn-dā′shŭn), *n.* the act of praising or intrusting; approval.

com-mend-a-to-ry (kŏ-mĕn′dȧ-tō-rĭ), *adj.* serving to intrust or give in care of; containing praise.

com-men-su-ra-ble (kŏ-mĕn′shōō-rȧ-bl), *adj.* having, or reducible to, a common measure; as, a yard and a foot are *commensurable*; proportionate.—*adv.* **commensurably.**—*n.* **commensurability.**

com-men-su-rate (kŏ-mĕn′shōō-rāt), *adj.* reducible to a common measure; equal; adequate; corresponding in amount; as, our fortunes are often not *commensurate* with our desires: *v.t.* to reduce to a common measure; to make proportionate. — *adv.* **commensurately.** — *n.* **commensuration.**

com-ment (kŏm′ĕnt), *n.* a spoken or written remark; especially, a written note by way of explanation, illustration, or criticism: *v.i.* (kŏm′ĕnt; kŏ-mĕnt′), to write notes of explanations or criticism upon the text of an author; make observations.

com-men-ta-ry (kŏm′ĕn-tā-rĭ), *n.* [*pl.* commentaries (-rĭz)], an explanation; a series of explanatory notes; as, a *commentary* on the Bible.

com-men-ta-tor (kŏm″ĕn-tā′tẽr), *n.* one who writes notes to explain a writing, book, etc.

com-merce (kŏm′ẽrs), *n.* interchange of merchandise on a large scale between nations or individuals; intercourse.

com-mer-cial (kŏ-mûr′shăl), *adj.* pertaining to trade or business; mercantile.—*adv.* **commercially.**

com-mer-cial-ism (kŏ-mûr′shăl-ĭzm), *n.* business principles, habits, methods, or spirit; a business practice or expression.

com-mer-cial pa-per (kŏ-mûr′shăl pā′pẽr), notes, bills of exchange, trade acceptances, or other evidences of debt, which may be, used as security for a loan from a bank.

com-min-gle (kŏ-mĭn′gl), *v.t.* and *v.i.* to mix; blend.

com-mis-er-ate (kŏ-mĭz′ẽr-āt), *v.t.* to feel pity for; sympathize with in distress.—*adj.* **commiserative.**

com-mis-er-a-tion (kŏ-mĭz″ẽr-ā′shŭn), *n.* pity; condolence.

com-mis-sa-ri-at (kŏm″ĭ-sā′rĭ-ăt), *n.* the department of an army that furnishes provisions and other supplies.

com-mis-sa-ry (kŏm′ĭ-sā-rĭ), *n.* [*pl.* commissaries (-rĭz)], one to whom some charge is committed by a superior; a delegate; an official in the food department of an army.

com-mis-sion (kŏ-mĭsh′ŭn), *n.* the entrusting of business to anyone; the act of doing or committing; a trust; a charge; the warrant by which anything is done; one or more persons appointed to perform certain specified duties; brokerage or allowance; a document conferring military or naval rank or authority; a body of persons empowered to act under public authority; as, this city is governed by a *commission*: *v.t.* to empower; to send with authority; to confer military or naval rank or authority.

com-mis-sion-aire (kŏ-mĭsh″ŭn-âr′; Fr. kō-mē″syō-nâr′), *n.* one who buys or sells another's goods on commission, or percentage; a commission merchant or agent; in Europe, the hotel attendant who meets trains and boats to secure patrons. [Fr.]

com-mis-sion-er (kŏ-mĭsh′ŭn-ẽr), *n.* a person holding authority under a commission, or warrant; an officer in charge of some department of the public service; as, the *Commissioner* of Pensions at Washington; one of a body governing a political unit, as a city, county, or township, under public authority.

com-mit (kŏ-mĭt′), *v.t.* [*p.t.* and *p.p.* committed, *p.pr.* committing], to give in charge or trust; surrender; learn by heart; send for trial, or to prison; as, the prisoner was *committed* to prison; to do; to devote or bind oneself: with *to.*

com-mit-ment (kŏ-mĭt′mĕnt), *n.* the act of sending, charging, learning by rote, consigning, etc.; usually, the sending of a person to prison. Also, **committal.**

com-mit-tee (kŏ-mĭt′ē), *n.* one or more persons appointed to consider or manage any matter.

com-mode (kŏ-mōd′), *n.* a bureau or chest of drawers; a covered washstand containing basin, wastepipe, or other conveniences; a night chair or stool.

com-mo-di-ous (kŏ-mō′dĭ-ŭs), *adj.* useful; convenient; roomy; affording ample accommodation; as, a large family needs a *commodious* house.—*adv.* **commodiously.**—*n.* **commodiousness.**

com-mod-i-ty (kŏ-mŏd′ĭ-tĭ), *n.* [*pl.* commodities (-tĭz)], that which is useful; an article of commerce: *pl.* in commerce, anything movable that is bought and sold, except animals; goods; merchandise.

com-mo-dore (kŏm′ō-dōr″), *n.* in the United States, a retired naval officer ranking between a captain and a rear admiral; in Great Britain, the commander of a squadron.

com-mon (kŏm′ŭn), *adj.* belonging equally to more than one; as, *common* to the human race; public; usual; frequent; inferior; of low birth or origin; in grammar, applied to both masculine and feminine gender, or to any individual of a class; as, a *common* noun: *n.* a tract of open public land.—*n.* **commonness.**

Syn., adj. mean, ordinary, vulgar.
Ant. (see uncommon, extraordinary).

com-mon-al-ty (kŏm′ŭn-ăl-tĭ), *n.* the common people.

com-mon-er (kŏm′ŭn-ẽr), *n.* one of the common people; a person of low rank; a member of the British House of Commons.

com-mon law (kŏm′ŭn lô), the unwritten law, or the law of custom or usage not in the written statutes of a country.

com-mon-ly (kŏm′ŭn-lĭ), *adv.* usually; ordinarily; to a usual degree.

com-mon-place (kŏm′ŭn-plās″), *n.* an ordinary topic or remark; anything ordinary: *adj.* uninteresting; common; neither new nor striking; dull.

com-mons (kŏm′ŭnz), *n.pl.* the mass of the people; rations or fare in common: **Commons,** the House of Commons, or lower house of Parliament in Great Britain and Canada.

com-mon sense (kŏm′ŭn sĕns), good judgment in ordinary affairs; sound, practical judgment.

com-mon-weal (kŏm′ŭn-wēl′), *n.* general welfare; the public good; as, all laws should be made for the *commonweal.* Also, **common weal.**

com-mon-wealth (kŏm′ŭn-wĕlth″), *n.* the public; the whole body of people in a state; a state.

com-mo-tion (kŏ-mō′shŭn), *n.* violent agitation; as, a *commotion* of the waves; disorder; tumult.

com-mu-nal (kŏm′ū-năl; kŏ-mū′năl), *adj.* pertaining to ownership in common; public.—*adj.* **communalistic.**

com-mu-nal-ism (kŏm′ū-năl-ĭzm), *n.* the theory that each community or township should be self-governed and the state a combination of such communities; self-government on the widest possible scale.

com-mune (kŏ-mūn′), *v.i.* to converse together; take counsel; partake of the Eucharist, or Holy Communion.

com-mune (kŏm′ūn), *n.* the smallest political division in France; a local, self-governing community.

com-mu-ni-ca-ble (kŏ-mū′nĭ-kȧ-bl), *adj.* capable of being made known, imparted, or conveyed; as, a *communicable* disease.

com-mu-ni-cant (kŏ-mū′nĭ-kănt), *n.* a partaker, especially of the Eucharist, or Lord's Supper; one who imparts or makes known.

com-mu-ni-cate (kŏ-mū′nĭ-kāt), *v.t.* to impart; reveal; to make known; to tell: *v.i.* to share; partake of the Eucharist, or Lord's Supper; to be, or get, in connection; to hold intercourse.—*n.* **communicator.**

com-mu-ni-ca-tion (kŏ-mū″nĭ-kā′shŭn), *n.* the act of making oneself understood; an expression of thoughts or opinions; as, the *communication* of ideas; means of passing from one place to another; news; intercourse.

com-mu-ni-ca-tive (kŏ-mū′nĭ-kā-tĭv), *adj.* unreserved; talkative.—*n.* **communicativeness.**

com-mun-ion (kŏ-mūn′yŭn), *n.* intercourse; fellowship; common possession; a religious body: **Communion,** the sacrament of the Lord's Supper or the partaking of it.

com-mu-ni-qué (kŏ-mū″nĭ-kā′), *n.* an official report of news or intelligence published in time of war.

com-mu-nism (kŏm′ū-nĭzm), *n.* the doctrine of having property in common; a system of social organization demanding the abolition of private property, and community control of means of production, etc.

com-mu-nist (kŏm′ū-nĭst), *n.* one who believes in communism, or the theory that each community or township should be self-governed, and the state a combination of such communities; a believer in communal control of property, etc.; a member of the Commune of Paris (1871).

com-mu-nis-tic (kŏm-ū-nĭs′tĭk), *adj.* pertaining to communism, or the theory that each township or community should be self-governed, and the state a combination of such communities; as, *communistic* theories pertaining to communal control.

com-mu-ni-ty (kŏ-mū′nĭ-tĭ), *n.* [*pl.* communities (-tĭz)], a body of persons having common rights, interests, and privileges; a body of people living in the same locality; as, Philadelphia is made up of a group of small *communities;* joint participation, sharing, or ownership; a corporation; society generally.

com-mut-a-ble (kŏ-mūt′ȧ-bl), *adj.* capable of being exchanged or interchanged.

com-mu-ta-tion (kŏm″ū-tā′shŭn), *n.* the acceptance or exchange of a less thing for a greater; the putting of something less severe in place of something severe; as, the *commutation* of sentence of death to life imprisonment; in electrical usage, the change from alternating current to direct current, or the reverse, by means of a device called the commutator.

com-mu-ta-tion tick-et (kŏm″ū-tā′shŭn tĭk′ĕt), a transportation ticket issued at a reduced rate for a certain time.

com-mu-ta-tor (kŏm′ū-tā″tẽr), *n.* a device for changing alternating electrical current to direct current, or direct current to alternating current: generally used on a generator or motor.

com-mute (kŏ-mūt′), *v.t.* to exchange; substitute; in electrical usage, to alter a current; reduce the severity of; as, the governor was asked to *commute* the prisoner's sentence: *v.i.* to pay in gross, at a reduced rate, as railroad fare.

com-mut-er (kŏ-mūt′ẽr), *n.* one who changes; one who uses a railroad ticket issued at a reduced rate.

com-pact (kŏm′păkt), *n.* an agreement, as between persons or states; as, the men formed a business *compact;* a plot or conspiracy: *v.t.* (kŏm-păkt′), to press or pack closely; make solid; render close or dense: *adj.* closely or firmly united; knit or pressed together; as, a *compact* mass.—*adv.* **compactly.**—*n.* **compactness.**

com-pan-ion (kŏm-păn′yŭn), *n.* a comrade; an associate or partner: *v.t.* to accompany; attend: **companionway,** the stairway leading from the deck to the cabin of a ship.—*adj.* **companionable.**—*n.* **companionableness.**

com-pan-ion-ship (kŏm-păn′yŭn-shĭp), *n.* fellowship; association.

com-pa-ny (kŭm'pȧ-nĭ), *n.* [*pl.* companies (-nĭz)], a group of people; a body of persons associated together; society; associates; as, a man is known by the *company* he keeps; a body of actors; guest, or guests; fellowship; a firm; a ship's crew; a section of a regiment commanded by a captain.
Syn. assemblage, crowd, gathering, group, host, throng.
Ant. (see loneliness).

com-pa-ra-ble (kŏm'pȧ-rȧ-bl), *adj.* capable of being likened to someone or something; capable of being declared similar or dissimilar to someone or something; worthy of being so likened.—*adv.* comparably.

com-par-a-tive (kŏm-păr'ȧ-tĭv), *adj.* estimated by, or resulting from, comparison; relative; in grammar, naming the second degree in the inflection of adjectives and adverbs: *n.* in grammar, the second degree in the inflection of an adjective or adverb.—*adv.* comparatively.

com-pare (kŏm-pâr'), *v.t.* to make one thing the measure of another; to examine in order to discover likeness and unlikeness; in grammar, to name over in order, as, *much, more, most,* the degrees in the inflection of adjectives and adverbs: *v.i.* to be like or equal; to be worthy of, or suitable for, comparison.

com-par-i-son (kŏm-păr'ĭ-sŭn), *n.* the act of perceiving likenesses or differences; an illustration or simile; the study of things to discover likenesses and differences; relative resemblance; in grammar, the inflection of adjectives and adverbs which shows a difference in degree.

com-part-ment (kŏm-pärt'mĕnt), *n.* one of the parts into which an inclosed space is divided; a division made by a partition; a separate section, as of a carriage; a panel.

com-pass (kŭm'pȧs), *v.t.* to encircle; walk around; to accomplish; attain; besiege: *n.* a circle; a circumference; extent; moderate bounds; an instrument used on ships for finding the directions, north, south, east, and west: *pl.* an instrument for dividing and drawing circles; in music, range of tones possible to a given voice or instrument.

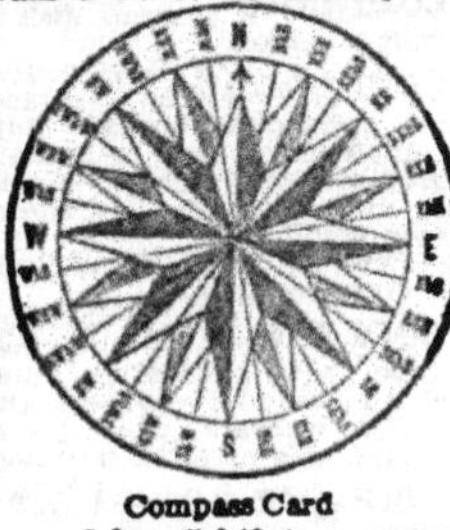
Compass Card

com-pas-sion (kŏm-păsh'ŭn), *n.* sorrow for the sufferings of others.
Syn. sympathy, pity.
Ant. (see cruelty, severity).

com-pas-sion-ate (kŏm-păsh'ŭn-āt), *adj.* sympathetic; merciful.—*adv.* compassionately.

com-pat-i-bil-i-ty (kŏm-păt'ĭ-bĭl'ĭ-tĭ), *n.* the quality of being able to exist together in harmony; congeniality; as, *compatibility* of temper is necessary for friendship.

com-pat-i-ble (kŏm-păt'ĭ-bl), *adj.* harmonious; agreeable; as, friendship can exist only between those who have *compatible* tastes.—*adv.* compatibly.

com-pa-tri-ot (kŏm-pā'trĭ-ŭt), *n.* a citizen or fellow countryman.

com-peer (kŏm-pēr'), *n.* an equal in rank; a companion or associate.

com-pel (kŏm-pĕl'), *v.t.* [*p.t.* and *p.p.* compelled, *p.pr.* compelling], to urge irresistibly; to oblige; to force; as, circumstances *compel* us to reduce expenses.
Syn. force, oblige, necessitate.
Ant. (see coax, lead).

com-pend (kŏm'pĕnd), *n.* an abridgment; a brief summary; a compendium.

com-pen-di-ous (kŏm-pĕn'dĭ-ŭs), *adj.* containing the substance in condensed form; summarized; abridged; compact.—*adv.* compendiously.—*n.* compendiousness.

com-pen-di-um (kŏm-pĕn'dĭ-ŭm), *n.* an abridgment; a summary; a condensed account of a book or subject; as, a *compendium* of science.

com-pen-sate (kŏm'pĕn-sāt), *v.t.* to make a fit return for; to recompense; make amends for: *v.i.* to make amends.—*adj.* compensatory.—*n.* compensator.

com-pen-sa-tion (kŏm'pĕn-sā'shŭn), *n.* recompense or payment; whatever makes good any lack or loss; as, the man received *compensation* for his injuries; a set-off; payment; amends; something given in return for a service or for something of value.
Syn. remuneration, requital, reward.

com-pete (kŏm-pēt'), *v.i.* to enter into rivalry with another; to contend; as, to *compete* for a prize.

com-pe-tence (kŏm'pē-tĕns), *n.* the state of being able or capable; ability; as, no one doubts his *competence* for the task; moderate fortune; sufficiency; as, an army pension provides a *competence* for a retired soldier. Also, competency.

com-pe-tent (kŏm'pē-tĕnt), *adj.* fit; able; suitable; qualified.—*adv.* competently.

com-pe-ti-tion (kŏm'pē-tĭsh'ŭn), *n.* the act of trying to gain something sought by another at the same time; rivalry; as, *competition* in business or in sports.

com-pet-i-tive (kŏm-pĕt'ĭ-tĭv), *adj.* pertaining to, or based on, the contention of two or more for the same object; pertaining to rivalry; as, the *competitive* system produces the best results.

com-pet-i-tor (kŏm-pĕt'ĭ-tẽr), *n.* one who contends with others for the same object; a rival.

com-pi-la-tion (kŏm'pĭ-lā'shŭn), *n.* a collection; the act of bringing together, as a book made from other books or papers; the thing so made from material gathered from books and papers.

com-pile (kŏm-pīl'), *v.t.* to put together in fresh form; as, to *compile* a new book from several old ones.—*n.* compiler.

com-pla-cence (kŏm-plā'sĕns), *n.* inward satisfaction; self-satisfaction. Also complacency.

com-pla-cent (kŏm-plā'sĕnt), *adj.* showing satisfaction; pleased with oneself.—*adv* complacently.

com-plain (kŏm-plān'), *v.i.* to express grief, pain, resentment, or discontent; as, to *complain* and grumble is the habit of discontented men; to make a formal accusation.—*n.* complainer.
Syn. lament, murmur, repine.
Ant. (see rejoice).

com-plain-ant (kŏm-plān'ănt), *n.* one who grumbles; a plaintiff, or petitioner.

com-plaint (kŏm-plānt'), *n:* in law, a formal charge against a party; an expression of grief or pain; ailment.

com-plai-sance (kŏm'plā-zăns"; kŏm-plā'zăns), *n.* courtesy; disposition to please.

com-plai-sant (kŏm'plā-zănt"; *adj.* courteous; obliging; compliant.—*adv.* **complaisantly.**

com-ple-ment (kŏm'plē-mĕnt), *n.* full number or quantity; as, the regiment had its *complement* of men; a complete set; something that completes that which was not complete; the angle or arc by which a given angle or arc falls short of 90 degrees; the color that, when combined with a given color, produces white: *v.t.* to complete (an incomplete amount or number); to supply a lack in.

com-ple-men-ta-ry (kŏm"plē-mĕn'tȧ-rĭ), *adj.* forming, or of the nature of, a complement, or completing part; as, *complementary* colors; additional: **complementary angles**, two angles which together make a right angle, or 90 degrees. Also, **complemental.**

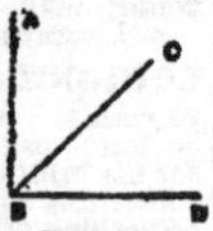

Complementary Angles, *ABC, CBD.*

com-plete (kŏm-plēt'), *adj.* lacking nothing; entire; perfect; full; as, in *complete* armor; absolute; finished: *v.t.* to make whole or perfect; fulfil; finish.—*adv.* **completely.**—*n.* **completeness.**

com-ple-tion (kŏm-plē'shŭn), *n.* act of making, or state of being, whole or perfect; accomplishment; fulfilment.

com-plex (kŏm'plĕks), *adj.* composed of various parts; involved; intricate; not simple; as, a *complex* machine.

com-plex-ion (kŏm-plĕk'shŭn), *n.* the color of the skin, especially of the face; aspect; general appearance.

com-plex-i-ty (kŏm-plĕk'sĭ-tĭ), *n.* the state of being intricate or involved: opposite to *simplicity*

com-pli-a-ble (kŏm-plī'ȧ-bl), *adj.* capable of yielding; compliant.

com-pli-ance (kŏm-plī'ăns), *n.* act or state of yielding or consenting; submission; as, in *compliance* with our desires. Also, **compliancy.**

com-pli-ant (kŏm-plī'ănt), *adj.* disposed to consent; yielding.—*adv.* **compliantly.**

com-pli-cate (kŏm'plĭ-kāt), *v.t.* to make confused or hard to understand; involve; *adj.* (kŏm'plĭ-kăt), difficult; complex.

com-pli-ca-tion (kŏm'plĭ-kā'shŭn), *n.* the act of confusing or making hard to understand; the state of being hard to understand; difficulty; intricacy

com-plic-i-ty (kŏm-plĭs'ĭ-tĭ), *n.* partnership, as in wrongdoing.

com-pli-ment (kŏm'plĭ-mĕnt), *n.* a formal act or expression of courtesy; an expression of approval or admiration; delicate flattery; as, a *compliment* is not always sincere praise: *v.t.* to flatter, congratulate; praise.

com-pli-men-ta-ry (kŏm"plĭ-mĕn'tȧ-rĭ), *adj.* conveying approval, admiration, or commendation; expressive of regard or preference; as, *complimentary* language.

com-ply (kŏm-plī'), *v.i.* [*p.t.* and *p.p.* complied, *p.pr.* complying], to yield assent; agree; consent.
Syn. accede, conform, submit.
Ant. (see refuse).

com-po-nent (kŏm-pō'nĕnt), *adj.* forming a part; composing; constituent; as, the *component* parts of a machine: *n.* a necessary portion or part of any substance or thing.

com-port (kŏm-pōrt'), *v.t.* to conduct or behave: used with the reflexive; as, to *comport* oneself in a dignified manner: *v.i.* to agree, accord, or suit.

com-pose (kŏm-pōz'), *v.t.* to form by combination; to write, as an author; to make up; to calm; adjust; arrange in proper order; to set (type); put together: *v.i.* to engage in composition, as of musical or literary work.—*n.* **composer.**

com-posed (kŏm-pōzd'), *adj.* tranquil; calm; serene; quiet.—*adv.* **composedly.**—*n.* **composedness.**

com-pos-ite (kŏm-pŏz'ĭt; kŏm'pŏ-zĭt), *adj.* made up of distinct parts; as, a *composite* photograph; compound: *n.* a composition; a combination; a compound.—*adv.* **compositely.**

com-po-si-tion (kŏm"pō-zĭsh'ŭn), *n.* the union of different things or principles to make a whole; the act or art of writing a literary or musical work; the work written; a piece written for practice in the use of language; make-up, as of a picture; the setting up of type; a mass formed by mingling various materials; an agreement, as to settle a dispute; compromise.

com-pos-i-tor (kŏm-pŏz'ĭ-tẽr), *n.* one who sets type.

com-post (kŏm'pōst), *n.* a mixture of various substances for fertilizing the ground; a mixture used for plastering.

com-po-sure (kŏm-pō'zhûr), *n.* tranquillity; serenity.

com-pote (kŏm'pōt), *n.* a stewed fruit; a small dish in which stewed fruit is served.

com-pound (kŏm-pound'), *v.t.* to mix or combine together; as, to *compound* drugs: *adj.* (kŏm'pound), composed of two or more elements or ingredients or words: *n.* a combination of two or more elements, ingredients, or parts.—*n.* **compounder.**
Syn., adj. complex, combined.
Ant. (see simple).

com-pre-hend (kŏm"prē-hĕnd'), *v.t.* to include or comprise; grasp with the mind; conceive; to understand; as, to *comprehend* an idea.
Syn. embrace, grasp, perceive.
Ant. (see exclude, mistake).

com-pre-hen-si-ble (kŏm"prē-hĕn'sĭ-bl), *adj.* intelligible; understandable.—*n.* **comprehensibility.**

com-pre-hen-sion (kŏm"prē-hĕn'shŭn), *n.* the act of understanding or including; understanding: the power of grasping with the mind.

com-pre-hen-sive (kŏm"prē-hĕn'sĭv), *adj.* including much; full; complete; as, a *comprehensive* account of the war.—*adv.* **comprehensively.**—*n.* **comprehensiveness.**

com-press (kŏm-prĕs'), *v.t.* to press together; condense: *n.* (kŏm'prĕs), a soft pad used in surgery to maintain pressure.

com-press-i-ble (kŏm-prĕs'ĭ-bl), *adj.* condensable; capable of being forced into a small space.—*n.* **compressibility.**

com-pres-sion (kŏm-prĕsh′ŭn), *n.* the act of making compact or of pressing together; condensation.

com-pres-sive (kŏm-prĕs′ĭv), *adj.* tending to, or having the power to, press together or make more compact.

com-prise (kŏm-prīz′), *v.t.* to comprehend; contain; include; as, the British Empire *comprises* many colonies. Also, **comprize.**
Syn. contain, embrace.

com-pro-mise (kŏm′prō-mīz), *n.* the settlement of any dispute by which both parties concede or give up part of what was first demanded; as, the strike was settled by a *compromise;* exposure to scandal, suspicion, risk, etc.; *v.t.* to settle by adjustment or mutual agreement; to endanger the interests of, by exposure to risk, gossip, etc.; *v.i.* to make a settlement by adjustment or concession.

comp-trol-ler (kŏn-trōl′ẽr), *n.* a public officer who oversees and verifies the accounts of officials under him. Also, **controller.**

com-pul-sion (kŏm-pŭl′shŭn), *n.* the act of coercing, or the state of being coerced; force; constraint.

com-pul-so-ry (kŏm-pŭl′sō-rĭ), *adj.* exercising force or restraint; obligatory; enforced.—*adv.* **compulsorily.**

com-punc-tion (kŏm-pŭnk′shŭn), *n.* regret; remorse; uneasiness of the conscience.

com-pu-ta-tion (kŏm″pū-tā′shŭn), *n.* the act of reckoning or figuring; an estimate so arrived at.

com-pute (kŏm-pūt′), *v.t.* to figure; number; reckon; to calculate; as, to *compute* the distance of the moon from the earth.—*n.* **computer.**

com-rade (kŏm′răd; kŏm′răd), *n.* an intimate friend; a companion or mate.—*n.* **comradeship.**

con (kŏn), *v.t.* [*p.t.* and *p.p.* conned, *p.pr.* conning], to study carefully; to commit to memory; to direct (a helmsman) how to steer: *adv.* on the negative side: the opposite of *pro:* *n.* the person who votes on the opposing side; one of the arguments against.

con-cat-e-nate (kŏn-kăt′ē-nāt), *v.t.* to link together; connect, as in a series.

con-cat-e-na-tion (kŏn-kăt″ē-nā′shŭn), *n.* a series of things united like links; as, a *concatenation* of events.

con-cave (kŏn′kāv), *adj.* hollow and curved, as the interior of a sphere or circle.

Concave Lens

con-cave lens (kŏn′kāv lĕnz), a lens one or both sides of which are slightly hollow and curved.

con-cav-i-ty (kŏn-kăv′ĭ-tĭ), *n.* [*pl.* concavities (-tĭz)], hollowness; the state of being concave, or hollow and curved; the inner surface of a rounded hollow body.

con-ceal (kŏn-sēl′), *v.t.* to hide; keep secret.—*adj.* **concealable.**
Syn. secrete, cover, disguise.
Ant. (see uncover).

con-ceal-ment (kŏn-sēl′mĕnt), *n.* the act of hiding or keeping secret; a place of hiding; shelter.

con-cede (kŏn-sēd′), *v.t.* to yield; admit; to grant as a right; as, the government *conceded* the right of the negro to vote.

con-ceit (kŏn-sēt′), *n.* an idea; an overestimate of one's own abilities or powers; vanity; a quaint fancy.

con-ceit-ed (kŏn-sēt′ĕd), *adj.* having too good an opinion of oneself; excessively vain.—*adv.* **conceitedly.**

con-ceiv-a-ble (kŏn-sēv′á-bl), *adj.* imaginable; thinkable; capable of being imagined.—*adv.* **conceivably.**

con-ceive (kŏn-sēv′), *v.t.* to become pregnant with (an embryo); to imagine; understand; to take into the mind; *v.i.* to think; to become pregnant.
Syn. comprehend.

con-cen-trate (kŏn′sĕn-trāt), *v.t.* and *v.i.* to bring or approach to one point or common center; increase in strength; condense; fix, as the attention; mass, as troops at a given point.

con-cen-tra-tion (kŏn″sĕn-trā′shŭn), *n.* the act of placing together or the state of being placed together; close attention; condensation; the collecting of the different parts of an army at one place; **concentration camp**, a place where troops are assembled.

con-cen-tric (kŏn-sĕn′trĭk), *adj.* having a common center; as, *concentric* circles were made in the water. Also, **concentrical.**—*adv.* **concentrically.**

con-cept (kŏn′sĕpt), *n.* an idea, notion, thought, or mental impression.

con-cep-tion (kŏn-sĕp′shŭn), *n.* the act or power of understanding; an idea or notion; the act of becoming pregnant.

con-cern (kŏn-sûrn′), *v.t.* to relate or belong to; interest or engage; make uneasy: *n.* that which belongs or relates to one; business; affair; interest; anxiety; a business firm; colloquially, a contrivance.

con-cern-ing (kŏn-sûrn′ĭng), *prep.* relating to; regarding.

con-cert (kŏn-sûrt′), *v.t.* and *v.i.* to contrive or devise together; adjust or arrange mutually: *n.* (kŏn′sẽrt), a musical entertainment; harmony, or mutual agreement.

Concertina

con-cert-ed (kŏn-sûr′tĕd), *adj.* mutually planned or agreed upon; as, *concerted* action; arranged in parts.

con-cer-ti-na (kŏn″sẽr-tē′nȧ), *n.* a musical instrument, of polygonal shape, with an extendible bellows.

Conch

con-ces-sion (kŏn-sĕsh′ŭn), *n.* the act of granting or yielding; as, a *concession* of land or *concession* of a point in an argument; the thing conceded; land, privileges, etc., granted by a government to a company, etc., for some special purpose.

con-ces-sion-aire (kŏn-sĕsh″ŭn-âr′), *n.* a person holding a concession or privilege.

conch (kŏnk), *n.* a large, spiral sea shell; the shell of a mollusk.

con-cha (kŏn'kȧ), *n.* [*pl.* conchæ (-kē)], the outer ear; the dome of an apse; the recess or projecting portion of some church buildings.

con-chol-o-gy (kŏn-kŏl'ō-jĭ), *n.* that part of zoölogy which treats of mollusks and their shells.

con-cierge (kôn"syĕrzh'), *n.* in France, a doorkeeper or janitor. [Fr.]

con-cil-i-ate (kŏn-sĭl'ĭ-āt), *v.t.* to reconcile; win or gain the affections of; to appease; as, William Penn wisely tried to *conciliate* the Indians.—*n.* **conciliator.**

con-cil-i-a-tion (kŏn-sĭl"ĭ-ā'shŭn), *n.* act of appeasing or gaining the good will of; act of winning by pacifying measures.

con-cil-i-a-to-ry (kŏn-sĭl'ĭ-ȧ-tō-rĭ), *adj.* tending to pacify; showing a spirit that is willing to come half way; desirous of pacifying.

con-cise (kŏn-sīs'), *adj.* condensed; terse; brief; putting much in few words.—*adv.* **concisely.**—*n.* **conciseness.**

con-clave (kŏn'klāv), *n.* a private meeting, as of cardinals for the election of a Pope; the rooms in which such meetings are held.

con-clude (kŏn-klōōd'), *v.t.* to come to a decision about; determine; settle; bring about as a result; to end; as, to *conclude* an argument: *v.i.* to draw an inference; to come to an end; as, he *concludes* wisely; the meeting *concluded* with his speech.

con-clu-sion (kŏn-klōō'zhŭn), *n.* a final determination; result; inference; judgment; the closing part, as of a discussion; end; as, at the *conclusion* of the Civil War slavery was abolished.

con-clu-sive (kŏn-klōō'sĭv), *adj.* decisive; final; as, a *conclusive* answer.—*adv.* **conclusively.**—*n.* **conclusiveness.**

con-coct (kŏn-kŏkt'), *v.t.* to prepare, as food, by mixing various things together; to form; make up; plot; as, the men tried to *concoct* a plot to destroy the government.

con-coc-tion (kŏn-kŏk'shŭn), *n.* the act of preparing or mixing; a plan or plot; a mixture of various articles of food.

con-com-i-tant (kŏn-kŏm'ĭ-tănt), *n.* that which accompanies or is combined with something else; an attendant; as, culture and refinement are not always *concomitants* of wealth: *adj.* attendant; accompanying; combined with; as, *concomitant* circumstances.—*adv.* **concomitantly.**

con-cord (kŏn'kôrd; kŏn'kôrd), *n.* harmony; union; agreement; in grammar, the agreement of words, as in gender, person, number, and case.

con-cord-ance (kŏn-kôr'dăns), *n.* agreement; a dictionary of words or passages, with references to the places where they occur; especially, an index of the Bible.

con-cord-ant (kŏn-kôr'dănt), *adj.* agreeing; harmonious.—*adv.* **concordantly.**

con-course (kŏn'kōrs; kŏn'kôrs), *n.* a meeting together; as, a *concourse* of waters; an assembly or crowd; as, a great *concourse* of persons attended the convention; a place, usually not inclosed, where crowds assemble.

con-crete (kŏn'krēt; kŏn-krēt'), *adj.* formed into a mass by mixing; pertaining to actual events or things; not abstract or general; specific in application: *n.* a compact or solid mass of lime, sand, gravel, etc., used for making bridges and buildings, especially the foundations: *v.t.* and *v.i.* to form or unite in a mass; cover with concrete.—*adv.* **concretely.**—*n.* **concreteness.**

con-cre-tion (kŏn-krē'shŭn), *n.* the act or process of forming into a solid mass; the act of covering something with concrete; a hardened mass.

con-cu-bine (kŏn'kū-bīn), *n.* a woman who lives with a man outside the bonds of wedlock.

con-cur (kŏn-kûr'), *v.i.* [*p.t.* and *p.p.* concurred, *p.pr.* concurring], to agree or unite in action or opinion; coincide; as, their opinions *concurred.*

con-cur-rence (kŏn-kûr'ĕns), *n.* the act of agreeing; agreement; consent; coincidence.

con-cur-rent (kŏn-kûr'ĕnt), *adj.* acting in union or conjunction; joint and equal in authority; meeting at one point; happening at the same time; existing at the same time; coöperating.—*adv.* **concurrently.**

con-cus-sion (kŏn-kŭsh'ŭn), *n.* a shaking; the shock caused by two bodies coming violently together; injury by a fall; as, *concussion* of the brain.

con-demn (kŏn-dĕm'), *v.t.* to pronounce or judge guilty; blame; censure; declare to be forfeited or taken for public use; as, to *condemn* land; to pronounce to be unfit for use; as, to *condemn* a prison.—*adj.* **condemnatory.**—*n.* **condemner.**

Syn. disapprove, doom.

Ant. (see justify, exonerate).

con-dem-na-tion (kŏn"dĕm-nā'shŭn), *n.* the act of pronouncing guilty, or wrong, or of declaring unfit or forfeited, etc.; the state of being pronounced guilty, wrong, or unfit or forfeited; as, he cannot escape *condemnation.*

con-den-sa-ble (kŏn-dĕn'sȧ-bl), *adj.* capable of compression or reduction in size; capable of being made more dense; as, vapor is *condensable.*

con-den-sa-tion (kŏn"dĕn-sā'shŭn), *n.* reduction in size; compression; the act of making dense or denser; the change from vapor to liquid form; as, the *condensation* of clouds results in rain.

con-dense (kŏn-dĕns'), *v.t.* to compress; make close or thick; to make dense or denser; to concentrate: *v.i.* to grow dense.

con-dens-er (kŏn-dĕns'ẽr), *n.* one who, or that which, makes dense, concentrates, or compresses; a machine for reducing gases or vapors to a liquid or solid form; a device for storing electricity; a lens for concentrating or bringing together rays of light.

con-de-scend (kŏn"dē-sĕnd'), *v.i.* to stoop; descend; deign; to come voluntarily to the plane of inferiors.—*adv.* **condescendingly.**

con-de-scen-sion (kŏn"dē-sĕn'shŭn), *n.* the act of stooping to the level of inferiors; voluntary humiliation or manifestation of courtesy to an inferior.

con-di-ment (kŏn'dĭ-mĕnt), *n.* a seasoning such as pepper, salt, and spices.

con-di-tion (kŏn-dĭsh'ŭn), *n.* state; rank; qualification; an essential provision to the doing of something; circumstances; terms of a contract: *v.t.* to contract or stipulate; to limit; to subject to examination, as a student.

con-di-tion-al (kŏn-dĭsh'ŭn-ăl), *adj.* of or pertaining to certain stipulations or provisions; not absolute; depending on certain stipulated circumstances.

con-di-tion-al-ly (kŏn-dĭsh'ŭn-ăl-ĭ), *adv.* with certain limitations; not absolutely; under certain stipulated circumstances or provisions.

con-di-tioned (kŏn-dĭsh'ŭnd), *adj.* subject to certain stipulations and provisions; required, as a student, to complete certain subjects before full admission to college, or promotion to a higher class.

con-dole (kŏn-dōl'), *v.i.* to express sympathy for another: with *with*.

con-do-lence (kŏn-dō'lĕns), *n.* sympathy; as, a message of *condolence*.

con-done (kŏn-dōn'), *v.t.* to pardon or overlook, as a fault.—*n.* **condonation**.

con-dor (kŏn'dŏr), *n.* a very large American vulture found in the highest Andes.

con-duce (kŏn-dūs'), *v.i.* to lead or tend to; contribute.

con-du-cive (kŏn-dū'sĭv), *adj.* leading or tending to; as, temperance is *conducive* to happiness.—*n.* **conduciveness**.

con-duct (kŏn-dŭkt'), *v.t.* to guide; direct; manage; behave; to be a medium or channel for: *n.* (kŏn'dŭkt), personal behavior or practice; management.

Syn., *v.* lead, govern, regulate; *n.* guidance, escort, deportment.

con-duct-i-bil-i-ty (kŏn-dŭk"tĭ-bĭl'ĭ-tĭ), *n.* the capability of being carried or transmitted; as, the *conductibility* of electricity or of heat.

con-duct-i-ble (kŏn-dŭk'tĭ-bl), *adj.* capable of being transmitted.

con-duc-tion (kŏn-dŭk'shŭn), *n.* transmission by a conductor; the act of leading; guidance.

con-duc-tive (kŏn-dŭk'tĭv), *adj.* having the quality or power of transmitting, as heat, etc.; as, *conductive* bodies such as metals.

con-duc-tiv-i-ty (kŏn"dŭk-tĭv'ĭ-tĭ), *n.* the quality or power of transmitting, as heat, electricity, etc.

con-duc-tor (kŏn-dŭk'tẽr), *n.* one who, or that which, leads or directs; a leader or guide; one who has charge of a car or train; a substance which readily transmits certain forces; as, water is a good *conductor* of sound.

con-duit (kŏn'dĭt), *n.* a canal or pipe for carrying water, etc.; a trough, tube, or subway for electric wires and cables.

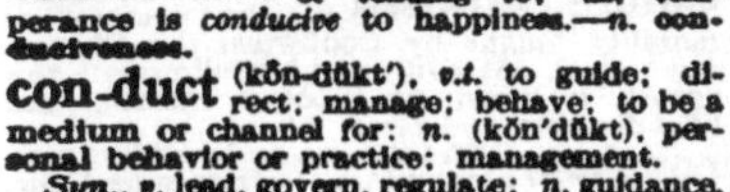

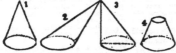

Cones. 1, right circular cone; 2, oblique cone; 3, right cone; 4, truncated cone.

cone (kōn), *n.* a solid body which tapers equally to a point from a circular base; anything of similar shape; the fruit of the fir, pine, etc.; in geometry, a surface generated by the movement of an indefinite line, one point of which is fixed.

co-ney (kō'nĭ; kŭn'ĭ), *n.* a rabbit. Also, **cony**.

con-fab-u-late (kŏn-făb'ū-lāt), *v.i.* to gossip or chat familiarly.—*n.* **confabulation**. [Colloq.]

con-fec-tion (kŏn-fĕk'shŭn), *n.* anything preserved with sugar; candy; a sweetmeat.

con-fec-tion-er (kŏn-fĕk'shŭn-ẽr), *n.* one who prepares and sells candy, sweetmeats, etc.

con-fec-tion-er-y (kŏn-fĕk'shŭn-ẽr-ĭ), *n.* [*pl.* confectioneries (-ĭz)], candies, ice-cream, cakes, preserves, etc.

con-fed-er-a-cy (kŏn-fĕd'ẽr-ȧ-sĭ), *n.* [*pl.* confederacies (-sĭz)], persons, states, or nations united for mutual support or joint action of any kind; alliance; sometimes, unlawful combination: **Confederacy**, the Confederate States of America.

con-fed-er-ate (kŏn-fĕd'ẽr-āt), *v.i.* to unite in a league: *adj.* (kŏn-fĕd'ẽr-āt), united by a league or agreement: *n.* a member of a league or union; an ally; an accomplice.

con-fed-er-a-tion (kŏn-fĕd"ẽr-ā'shŭn), *n.* the act of joining together or forming a league; an alliance; a union of states previously independent.

con-fer (kŏn-fûr'), *v.t.* [*p.t.* and *p.p.* conferred, *p.pr.* conferring], to give or bestow; as, to *confer* an honor or a medal on a person: *v.i.* to consult together; converse: with *with*; as, the President *confers* with his cabinet.—*n.* **conferee**.

con-fer-ence (kŏn'fẽr-ĕns), *n.* the act of consulting together formally; an appointed meeting for discussing some topic or business; a religious convention; as, the annual *conference* of ministers.

con-fer-va (kŏn-fûr'vȧ), *n.* [*pl.* confervæ (-vē)], a kind of green, freshwater algæ, or any other similar threadlike plant.

con-fess (kŏn-fĕs'), *v.t.* to admit or acknowledge; avow; grant; profess; hear a confession from: said of a priest: *v.i.* disclose the state of one's conscience to a priest and receive absolution; of a priest, to hear a confession; to make an acknowledgment: with *to*.

Syn. admit, concede, prove, grant, acknowledge, certify.

Ant. (see deny).

con-fess-ed-ly (kŏn-fĕs'ĕd-lĭ), *adv.* admittedly; through acknowledgment; avowedly.

con-fes-sion (kŏn-fĕsh'ŭn), *n.* act of acknowledging or admitting; the act of making known one's sins to a priest; a profession of belief; anything disclosed or acknowledged.

con-fes-sion-al (kŏn-fĕsh'ŭn-ăl), *n.* the closed place where a priest hears confessions.

con-fes-sor (kŏn-fĕs'ẽr), *n.* one who admits or acknowledges a wrong; one who expresses belief in a certain form of religion; a priest who hears confessions.

con-fet-ti (kŏn-fĕt'tē), *n.pl.* of *confetto*, bonbons or sweetmeats; plaster or paper imitations of bonbons, etc., often thrown at carnivals, weddings, etc.

con-fi-dant (kŏn"fĭ-dănt'), *n.* [*fem.* confidante], an intimate friend.

con-fide (kŏn-fīd'), *v.i.* to have trust or faith (in): as, the king *confides* in

his ministers: *v.t.* to put into another's trust or keeping; to entrust: with *to;* to tell as a secret.

con-fi-dence (kŏn'fĭ-dĕns), *n.* belief; reliance; trust; boldness; security; something told in private conversation; a secret.

con-fi-dent (kŏn'fĭ-dĕnt), *adj.* full of trust or certainty; positive; sure; bold; dogmatic.—*adv.* **confidently.**

con-fi-den-tial (kŏn"fĭ-dĕn'shăl), *adj.* spoken or written as a secret; as, *confidential* correspondence; intimate; trustworthy; as, a *confidential* secretary.—*adv.* **confidentially.**

con-fid-ing (kŏn-fīd'ĭng), *adj.* trustful; full of simple faith.—*adv.* **confidingly.**

con-fig-u-ra-tion (kŏn-fĭg"ū-rā'shŭn), *n.* the figure or contour; structural arrangement.

con-fine (kŏn'fīn), *n.* a boundary, border, or limit; a frontier: usually plural; as, to keep within the *confines* of the country: *v.t.* (kŏn-fīn'), to restrict within limits; imprison; as, he was *confined* to prison; to keep in the house or in bed on account of sickness.

con-fine-ment (kŏn-fīn'mĕnt), *n.* the act of restricting or imprisoning; the state of being restricted; a woman's illness at the time of childbirth.

con-firm (kŏn-fûrm'), *v.t.* to strengthen; ratify; as, our fears were *confirmed* by the report; administer the rite of confirmation, or of reception to full membership in a church.

Syn. corroborate, approve, sustain.
Ant. (see contradict).

con-fir-ma-tion (kŏn"fĕr-mā'shŭn), *n.* the act of verifying, ratifying, making sure, etc.; evidence; admission to full communion after baptism.

con-firm-a-to-ry (kŏn-fûr'mȧ-tō-rĭ), *adj.* serving to verify or prove true; corroborative. Also, **confirmative.**

con-firmed (kŏn-fûrmd'), *p.adj.* admitted to full church privileges; habitual; settled, as a habit or mannerism.

con-fis-cate (kŏn'fĭs-kāt; kŏn-fĭs'kāt), *v.t.* to seize as forfeited or as belonging to the state or public treasury; as, the traitor's land was *confiscated;* to claim and take for public use.—*adj.* **confiscatory.**—*n.* **confiscator.**

con-fis-ca-tion (kŏn"fĭs-kā'shŭn), *n.* the act of taking private property for public use; appropriation.

con-fla-gra-tion (kŏn"flȧ-grā'shŭn), *n.* a great fire; as, there was a terrible *conflagration* in Chicago in 1871.

con-flict (kŏn-flĭkt'), *v.i.* to strike together in collision, or clash; contend; fight; to disagree; as, opinions that *conflict:* *n.* (kŏn'flĭkt), a fight or struggle for the mastery; a battle; as, the *conflict* lasted three years; a violent collision; antagonism, as of ideas.

Syn., n. combat, contest, contention, struggle.
Ant. (see peace, quiet).

con-flict-ing (kŏn-flĭk'tĭng), *adj.* opposing.

con-flu-ence (kŏn'flōō-ĕns), *n.* a flowing together of streams; place where they meet; a flocking together, as of people.—*adj.* **confluent.**

con-form (kŏn-fôrm'), *v.t.* to make like; bring into harmony; as, a foreigner must *conform* his behavior to our customs: usually with *to:* *v.i.* to be in harmony; comply: with *to* or *with.*—*n.* **conformer.**

con-form-a-ble (kŏn-fôr'mȧ-bl), *adj.* like; corresponding in form; consistent; suitable; as, our actions should always be *conformable* with our ideals; compliant; submissive.—*adv.* **conformably.**

con-for-ma-tion (kŏn"fôr-mā'shŭn), *n.* form; structure; arrangement; shape; as, the *conformation* of the earth's surface.

con-form-ist (kŏn-fôr'mĭst), *n.* a member of the Established Church of England.

con-form-i-ty (kŏn-fôr'mĭ-tĭ), *n.* likeness; harmony; compliance with established forms; resemblance; agreement or correspondence in manner, character, etc.: usually followed by *to.*

con-found (kŏn-found'), *v.t.* perplex; bewilder; throw into disorder; confuse; put to shame; abash.

con-frère (kôn"frâr'), *n.* an associate; a fellow member; as, the professors in a college are *confrères.* [Fr.]

con-front (kŏn-frŭnt'), *v.t.* to put face to face: with *with;* as, to *confront* a prisoner with evidence; face defiantly; oppose.

Con-fu-cian-ism (kŏn-fū'shăn-ĭzm), *n.* the system of morality taught by Confucius, the Chinese sage (B. C. 551–478), and his followers: this system is based on ancestor worship and filial devotion and piety.

con-fuse (kŏn-fūz'), *v.t.* to bewilder; perplex; mingle; mix; render indistinct; to mistake for another.—*adv.* **confusedly.**

con-fu-sion (kŏn-fū'zhŭn), *n.* the act of perplexing, embarrassing, etc.; the state of being abashed or embarrassed; perplexity; loss of self-possession; disorder; tumult.

con-fute (kŏn-fūt'), *v.t.* to prove to be false or untrue; convict of error; as, he was unable to *confute* the argument.—*n.* **confutation.**

Syn. disprove, refute, oppugn.
Ant. (see approve).

con-gé (kôn"zhā'), *n.* a bow or formal act of taking leave; dismissal; as, the ambassador received his *congé.* [Fr.]

con-geal (kŏn-jēl'), *v.t.* to change from a liquid to a solid state, as by cold; as, when cold *congeals* water, ice is formed: *v.i.* to harden by cold; grow stiff, as by coagulation, etc.—*adj.* **congealable.**

con-ge-ni-al (kŏn-jēn'yăl), *adj.* kindred; pleasant and sympathetic; as, *congenial* tastes; having the same tastes; agreeable; naturally suited to one.—*adv.* **congenially.**

con-ge-ni-al-i-ty (kŏn-jē"nĭ-ăl'ĭ-tĭ; kŏn-jēn-yăl'ĭ-tĭ), *n.* the state or quality of being agreeable or of sharing the same tastes; agreeableness; as, the *congeniality* of artists.

con-gen-i-tal (kŏn-jĕn'ĭ-tăl), *adj.* existing, or produced, at birth.—*adv.* **congenitally.**

con-ger (kŏŋ'gĕr), *n.* a large marine, or sea, eel. Also, **conger eel.**

con-gest (kŏn-jĕst'), *v.t.* to cause the blood vessels of (an organ or part of the body) to become too full; to make overfull or overcrowded; as, to *congest* traffic: *v.i.* to become too full of blood: said of an organ or part of the body; to gather into a mass.

con-gest-ed (kŏn-jĕst'ĕd), *p.adj.* unduly crowded; as, the *congested* streets of a city; containing too much blood.

con-ges-tion (kŏn-jĕs'chŭn), *n.* an overcrowded condition; overfullness of the blood vessels; as, *congestion* of the lungs.

con-glom-er-ate (kŏn-glŏm'ẽr-āt), *v.t.* to gather into a ball or round mass: *adj.* (kŏn-glŏm'ẽr-āt), collected, clustered, or massed together: *n.* a mass of varied materials; a rock composed of pebbles, etc., cemented together.

con-glom-er-a-tion (kŏn-glŏm"ẽr-ā'shŭn), *n.* the act of gathering into a mass; a mixed collection.

con-grat-u-late (kŏn-grăt'ū-lāt), *v.t.* to rejoice with, or express sympathetic pleasure to, on account of some happy event: with *on* or *upon*.

con-grat-u-la-tion (kŏn-grăt"ū-lā'shŭn), *n.* the act of expressing sympathetic pleasure.

con-grat-u-la-to-ry (kŏn-grăt'ū-lȧ-tō-rĭ), *adj.* expressing happiness or sympathetic pleasure.

con-gre-gate (kŏn'grē-gāt), *v.t.* and *v.i.* to collect into a crowd, mass, etc.; to assemble; gather together.

con-gre-ga-tion (kŏn"grē-gā'shŭn), *n.* an assembly, especially of persons for religious worship.

con-gre-ga-tion-al (kŏn"grē-gā'shŭn-ăl), *adj.* pertaining to a congregation; as, *congregational* singing: **Congregational**, pertaining, or belonging, to Congregationalism or Congregationalists.

con-gre-ga-tion-al-ism (kŏn"grē-gā'shŭn-ăl-ĭzm), *n.* a form of church government in which each congregation governs itself: **Congregationalism**, the faith and policy of the denomination founded upon the principle that each congregation is supreme within its own limits.

Con-gre-ga-tion-al-ist (kŏn"grē-gā'shŭn-ăl-ĭst), *n.* one who belongs to the Congregational Church.

con-gress (kŏn'grĕs), *n.* a conference; an assembly of ambassadors, etc., for the settlement of international affairs: **Congress**, the national legislature of the United States; as, *Congress* holds its sessions at Washington, D. C.

Con-gres-sion-al (kŏn-grĕsh'ŭn-ăl), *adj.* pertaining to Congress.

Con-gress-man (kŏn'grĕs-măn), *n.* a member of Congress, especially of the House of Representatives.

con-gru-i-ty (kŏn-grōō'ĭ-tĭ), *n.* agreement; consistency; fitness; appropriateness; an instance of agreement or appropriateness.

con-gru-ous (kŏn'grōō-ŭs), *adj.* marked by agreement; appropriate; accordant.—*adv.* **congruously.**

con-ic (kŏn'ĭk), *adj.* pertaining to, or shaped like, a cone, or solid body which tapers equally to a point from a circular base. Also, **conical.**—*adv.* **conically.**

co-ni-fer (kō'nĭ-fẽr), *n.* a tree of the pine or yew family.

co-nif-er-ous (kō-nĭf'ẽr-ŭs), *adj.* bearing cones; as, the pine and fir are *coniferous* trees; pertaining to a tree of the pine or yew family.

con-jec-tur-al (kŏn-jĕk'tūr-ăl), *adj.* doubtful; implying a guess; as, a *conjectural* opinion.—*adv.* **conjecturally.**

con-jec-ture (kŏn-jĕk'tūr), *n.* a probable inference; a guess: *v.t.* to imagine; surmise; as, we can only *conjecture* what the future holds: *v.i.* to form opinions by surmise; to guess.

con-join (kŏn-join'), *v.t.* to join together; connect or associate: *v.i.* to unite.

con-joint (kŏn-joint'), *adj.* united; coöperating; as, *conjoint* action in an enterprise.—*adv.* **conjointly.**

con-ju-gal (kŏn'jōō-găl), *adj.* of or pertaining to marriage.—*adv.* **conjugally.**

con-ju-gate (kŏn'jōō-gāt), *v.t.* to name over the different forms of (a verb), as I love, you love, he loves, etc., covering their various changes according to voice, mood, tense, number, and person: *adj.* (kŏn'jōō-gāt), combined in pairs; of words, similar in meaning and origin.

con-ju-ga-tion (kŏn"jōō-gā'shŭn), *n.* the act of naming the different forms of a verb according to their inflectional changes; the inflection of a verb; union.

con-junct (kŏn-jŭnkt'), *adj.* joined together; conjoined; as, *conjunct* degrees in music.—*adv.* **conjunctly.**

con-junc-tion (kŏn-jŭnk'shŭn), *n.* union; association; connection; the apparent meeting of two or more stars or planets; as, the *conjunction* of the moon with the sun; a word used to connect sentences or words.

con-junc-ti-va (kŏn"jŭnk-tī'vȧ), *n.* the mucous membrane lining the eyelids and covering the eyeball.

con-junc-tive (kŏn-jŭnk'tĭv), *adj.* connective; uniting; closely connected.—*adv.* **conjunctively.**

con-junc-ti-vi-tis (kŏn-jŭnk"tĭ-vī'tĭs), *n.* inflammation of the mucous membrane covering the eyeball and lining the eyelids.

con-junc-ture (kŏn-jŭnk'tūr), *n.* a combination of many circumstances or causes; a critical time; as, at this *conjuncture* the citizens were asked to be strictly neutral.

con-ju-ra-tion (kŏn"jōō-rā'shŭn), *n.* the act of calling forth or sending away by magic; the practice of magic; a seeking for magical aid.

con-jure (kŏn-jōōr'), *v.t.* to appeal to solemnly; to implore; to call on in a sacred name: *v.t.* (kŭn'jẽr), to command or summon (a devil, evil spirit, etc.), by an invocation or spell; to influence by, or as if by, magic: *v.i.* to practice the arts of a conjurer or magician.

con-jur-er (kŭn'jẽr-ẽr), *n.* one who produces illusions by magic or sleight of hand; a juggler; as, the *conjurers* of India perform wonders. Also, **conjuror.**

con-nate (kŏn'āt; kŏ-nāt'), *adj.* inborn; existing together; cognate.

con-nect (kŏ-nĕkt'), *v.t.* to bind or fasten together; unite; associate with: *v.i.* to join; to be associated.

con-nect-ed (kŏ-nĕk'tĕd), *adj.* marked by coherence; linked together.—*adv.* **connectedly.**

con-nec-tion (kŏ-nĕk'shŭn), *n.* the state of being joined or united; relationship; the act of joining or uniting; continuity of words or ideas; a bond; relation by marriage or blood; surroundings;

acquaintance; denomination; one's customers, etc. Also, connexion.

con-nect-ive (kŏ-nĕk'tĭv), *adj.* fitted for the work of joining; as, tendons and ligaments of the body are *connective* tissues: *n.* that which joins, as, in grammar, a conjunction.

con-ning tow-er (kŏn'ĭng tou'ĕr), the low shot-proof pilothouse of an armored vessel; on submarines, a low tower on the deck which serves as a post of observation: it has a hinged top which may be lifted to permit men to enter or leave the boat.

con-niv-ance (kŏ-nīv'ăns), *n.* the act of secretly aiding; silent or secret assent, as to wrongdoing; a pretense of ignorance of a fault or crime; as, the *connivance* of the officer with the two men made their escape possible.

con-nive (kŏ-nīv'), *v.i.* to close the eyes upon a fault; to pretend ignorance; to aid secretly; as, to *connive* at the breaking of a law.

con-nois-seur (kŏn"ĭ-sûr'; kŏn"ĭ-sûr'), *n.* a critical and competent judge; as, a *connoisseur* of art.

con-no-ta-tion (kŏn"ō-tā'shŭn), *n.* inference; definition; that which is suggested in addition to the primary meaning; as, the *connotation* of the word rainbow includes the seven primary colors.

con-note (kŏ-nōt'), *v.t.* to signify; to mean in addition to; to imply as an attribute; as, the word man *connotes* life, action, form, etc.—*adj.* **connotative.**

con-nu-bi-al (kŏ-nū'bĭ-ăl), *adj.* of or pertaining to marriage.—*adv.* **connubially.**

con-quer (kŏṅ'kẽr), *v.t.* to gain by conquest; overcome; subdue; as, Cæsar *conquered* Gaul: *v.i.* to be victorious.—*adj.* **conquerable.**—*n.* **conqueror.**

Syn. surmount, vanquish.
Ant. (see defeat).

con-quer-or (kŏṅ'kẽr-ẽr), *n.* a victor; as, Napoleon was a great *conqueror.*

con-quest (kŏṅ'kwĕst), *n.* the act of subduing; subjugation; victory; that which is overpowered.

con-san-guin-i-ty (kŏn"săṅ-gwĭn'ĭ-tĭ), *n.* blood relationship.—*adj.* **consanguineous.**

con-science (kŏn'shĕns), *n.* one's inmost private thoughts; the moral sense or consciousness within oneself which determines right and wrong; as, thus *conscience* doth make cowards of us all.

con-sci-en-tious (kŏn"shĭ-ĕn'shŭs), *adj.* influenced or regulated by conscience; scrupulous; as, a good and *conscientious* man.—*adv.* **conscientiously.**—*n.* **conscientiousness.**

con-scious (kŏn'shŭs), *adj.* aware of one's own thoughts and actions or of something outside of oneself; embarrassed; self-conscious.—*adv.* **consciously.**

Syn. advised, aware, sensible, assured.
Ant. (see ignorant).

con-scious-ness (kŏn'shŭs-nĕs), *n.* the knowledge of that which passes in one's own mind; as, our *consciousness* of right is a protection.

con-script (kŏn-skrĭpt'), *v.t.* to compel to enter the army or navy; as, men were *conscripted* for army service during the Civil War: *adj.* (kŏn'skrĭpt), registered; enrolled in the army: *n.* one thus enrolled.

con-scrip-tion (kŏn-skrĭp'shŭn), *n.* the act of compelling a person to perform military or naval service; the draft system.

con-se-crate (kŏn'sē-krāt), *v.t.* to set apart as sacred; dedicate to the service of God; set apart to a sacred office; hallow; devote: *adj.* set apart as sacred; made sacred.

con-se-cra-tion (kŏn"sē-krā'shŭn), *n.* the act of hallowing or sanctifying; the state of being hallowed or sanctified; a setting apart or devoting to a sacred use or office.

con-sec-u-tive (kŏn-sĕk'ū-tĭv), *adj.* successive; without interruption.—*adv.* **consecutively.**—*n.* **consecutiveness.**

con-sen-sus (kŏn-sĕn'sŭs), *n.* general agreement; as, the *consensus* of opinion.

con-sent (kŏn-sĕnt'), *n.* a yielding of the mind or will; agreement: *v.i.* to comply; yield; accede; concur.

con-se-quence (kŏn'sē-kwĕns), *n.* that which naturally follows a cause; inference; result; importance; significance.

Syn. effect, event, issue.
Ant. (see cause).

con-se-quent (kŏn'sē-kwĕnt), *adj.* following as a result or natural effect; as, war and the *consequent* poverty: *n.* a result or effect; in mathematics, the second term of a ratio.—*adv.* **consequently.**

con-se-quen-tial (kŏn"sē-kwĕn'shăl), *adj.* following as the effect; self-important.—*adv.* **consequentially.**

con-ser-va-tion (kŏn"sẽr-vā'shŭn), *n.* the act of preserving from decay, loss, or injury; as, America should be interested in the *conservation* of her forests.

con-serv-a-tism (kŏn-sûr'vȧ-tĭzm), *n.* the tendency to adhere to existing conditions, institutions, laws, etc.; the disposition that is opposed to change or progress; the practice of the principle of adhering to present conditions, etc.

con-serv-a-tive (kŏn-sûr'vȧ-tĭv), *adj.* having the tendency or power to preserve or keep, as salt; naturally opposed to change: *n.* that which preserves; one opposed to hasty changes in the political, religious, or civil institutions of the country; as, the *conservative* is seldom progressive: **Conservative,** *adj.* naming, or pertaining to, an English political party which is opposed to radical reform measures or changes in church and state, for which it believes the time is not ripe: *n.* a member of the party referred to.

con-serv-a-to-ry (kŏn-sûr'vȧ-tō-rĭ), *adj.* tending to preserve: *n.* a greenhouse; a public place of instruction, especially for music.

con-serve (kŏn-sûrv'), *v.t.* to preserve from injury or destruction; as, to *conserve* the peace of society; to preserve with sugar: *n.* (kŏn'sûrv), preserved or candied fruit: *pl.* preserves.

con-sid-er (kŏn-sĭd'ẽr), *v.t.* to fix the mind upon; treat with thoughtfulness; look upon; contemplate: *v.i.* to deliberate; reflect.

Syn. ponder, weigh, ruminate.

con-sid-er-a-ble (kŏn-sĭd'ẽr-ȧ-bl), *adj.* worthy of notice; important; valuable; worthy of regard by reason of size, quantity, etc.—*adv.* **considerably.**

con-sid-er-ate (kŏn-sĭd'ẽr-ăt), *adj.* having regard for others; prudent; thoughtful; careful.—*adv.* **considerately.**

con-sid-er-a-tion (kŏn-sĭd'ẽr-ā'shŭn), *n.* the act of taking thought or reflecting; claim to notice; importance; mature thought; as, to take into *consideration* the result of an act; regard for others; thoughtfulness; as, to have *consideration* for others.

con-sid-er-ing (kŏn-sĭd'ẽr-ĭng), *prep.* taking into account; allowing for.

con-sign (kŏn-sīn'), *v.t.* to deliver in a formal manner to another; yield in trust; to send to another to be sold, cared for, etc., as merchandise.

con-sign-ee (kŏn'sī-nē'; kŏn'sĭ-nē'), *n.* the person to whom goods are sent; an agent or factor.

con-sign-ment (kŏn-sīn'mĕnt), *n.* the act of delivering formally or of sending goods; the thing consigned or sent; as, he received a large *consignment* of goods; the writing by which anything is delivered formally or shipped.

con-sign-or (kŏn-sīn'ẽr; kŏn'sī-nôr'), *n.* the person who sends goods to another. Also, **consigner.**

con-sist (kŏn-sĭst'), *v.i.* to be made; to be composed: followed by *of*; to have as its foundation or nature: followed by *in*.

con-sist-en-cy (kŏn-sĭs'tĕn-sĭ), *n.* degree of density or firmness; as, the *consistency* of a liquid; harmony; agreement; especially, the agreement between a person's deeds and his statements of what he is going to do, or between his conduct at one time and another. Also, **consistence.**

con-sist-ent (kŏn-sĭs'tĕnt), *adj.* solid; not fluid; not self-contradictory; standing together or in agreement; as, his deeds were *consistent* with his belief.—*adv.* **consistently.**

Syn. constant, compatible.
Ant. (see inconsistent).

con-sis-to-ry (kŏn-sĭs'tō-rĭ; kŏn'sĭs-tō-rĭ), *n.* the governing body of a church; also, the place where such a body meets.

con-sols (kŏn-sŏlz'), *n.pl.* the principal government security of Great Britain.

con-sol-a-ble (kŏn-sōl'ȧ-bl), *adj.* capable of being soothed or cheered in time of distress; comforted or relieved mentally.

con-so-la-tion (kŏn'sō-lā'shŭn), *n.* the act of giving or state of receiving sympathy; a means of relieving distress; comfort for mental or physical distress; solace.

con-sol-a-to-ry (kŏn-sŏl'ȧ-tō-rĭ), *adj.* soothing; tending to relieve or comfort.

con-sole (kŏn-sōl'), *v.t.* to give comfort to; cheer in sorrow; to solace.

con-sole (kŏn'sōl), *n.* in architecture, a corbel; a bracketlike support or ornament. [Fr.]

con-sol-i-date (kŏn-sŏl'ĭ-dāt), *v.t.* to make solid; harden; condense; to unite: *v.i.* to become solid or united.—*n.* **consolidator.**

con-sol-i-da-tion (kŏn-sŏl'ĭ-dā'shŭn), *n.* the act of making solid or bringing together into one; the state of having been made solid or united; combination.

con-som-mé (kôn'sô'mā'), *n.* a strong clear soup. [Fr.]

con-so-nance (kŏn'sō-năns), *n.* agreement of sounds; harmony; concord; as, *consonance* of musical tones. Also, **consonancy.**

con-so-nant (kŏn'sō-nănt), *adj.* harmonious; accordant: *n.* a sound which cannot be easily uttered except when combined with a vowel; a letter representing such a sound.—*adv.* **consonantly.**

con-sort (kŏn'sôrt), *n.* a companion; a partner; a husband or wife; a ship accompanying another: *v.t.* and *v.i.* (kŏn-sôrt'), to associate; keep company; with *with*.

con-spic-u-ous (kŏn-spĭk'ū-ŭs), *adj.* mentally or physically visible; manifest; distinguished; striking; obvious.—*adv.* **conspicuously.**—*n.* **conspicuousness.**

con-spir-a-cy (kŏn-spĭr'ȧ-sĭ), *n.* [*pl.* conspiracies (-sĭz)], a plot; a combination of two or more persons engaged together for an unlawful or evil purpose.

con-spir-a-tor (kŏn-spĭr'ȧ-tẽr), *n.* one who plots.

con-spire (kŏn-spīr'), *v.i.* to plan together to commit a crime; combine for an unlawful purpose; to plan; agree to work to one end.—*n.* **conspirer.**

con-sta-ble (kŭn'stȧ-bl), *n.* a high court officer of the Middle Ages; a peace officer.

con-stab-u-la-ry (kŏn-stăb'ū-lā-rĭ), *adj.* pertaining to constables, or peace officers: *n.* constables collectively; as, the State *constabulary.*

con-stan-cy (kŏn'stăn-sĭ), *n.* firmness; stability; fidelity.

Syn. steadiness, consistency.
Ant. (see fickleness).

con-stant (kŏn'stănt), *adj.* continuous; faithful; firm; steadfast; true; unchanging; invariable under given conditions; regular: *n.* that which is not subject to change, as gravity; a quality whose value is always the same.

con-stant-ly (kŏn'stănt-lĭ), *adv.* in a faithful or regular manner; continually; invariably; uniformly.

con-stel-la-tion (kŏn'stĕ-lā'shŭn), *n.* a group or cluster of fixed stars, having a special name; an assemblage of brilliant and distinguished persons.

con-ster-na-tion (kŏn'stẽr-nā'shŭn), *n.* great terror, wonder, or surprise; perturbation.

con-sti-pa-tion (kŏn'stĭ-pā'shŭn), *n.* inaction of the bowels.

con-stit-u-en-cy (kŏn-stĭt'ū-ĕn-sĭ), *n.* [*pl.* constituencies (-sĭz)], the body of electors voting for a member of Congress, or other officer.

con-stit-u-ent (kŏn-stĭt'ū-ĕnt), *adj.* forming a necessary part; component; as, oxygen and hydrogen are the *constituent* parts of water: *n.* an essential or necessary part; a voter; one who is represented by another.

con-sti-tute (kŏn'stĭ-tūt), *v.t.* to compose or make up; appoint; elect; enact; establish.

con-sti-tu-tion (kŏn'stĭ-tū'shŭn), *n.* the act of establishing; the thing established; bodily strength; mental or physical temperament; the system of fundamental laws of nation, state, or society; as, the *Constitution* of the United States.

con-sti-tu-tion-al (kŏn″stĭ-tū′shŭn-ăl), *adj.* inherent in the make-up of a person or thing; fundamental; in accordance with the fundamental law of a state or society: *n.* colloquially, a walk taken for the benefit of the health.—*adv.* **constitutionally.**

con-sti-tu-tion-al-i-ty (kŏn″stĭ-tū″-shŭn-ăl′ĭ-tĭ), *n.* the quality or state of being in accordance with the fundamental law of some state or society.

con-strain (kŏn-strān′), *v.t.* to hold down or keep back by force; as, the handcuffs *constrained* his action; restrain; to urge, drive, or compel; as, his conscience *constrains* him to do right.

con-strained (kŏn-strānd), *p.adj.* characterized by unnaturalness or repression; compelled.—*adv.* **constrainedly.**

con-straint (kŏn-strānt′), *n.* compulsion; force; necessity; repression; lack of naturalness.

con-strict (kŏn-strĭkt′), *v.t.* to bind; cramp; contract.

con-stric-tion (kŏn-strĭk′shŭn), *n.* compression; contraction.

con-stric-tive (kŏn-strĭk′tĭv), *adj.* of or pertaining to compression or contraction produced by binding.

con-stric-tor (kŏn-strĭk′tẽr), *n.* that which binds or squeezes; a serpent that crushes its prey.

con-struct (kŏn-strŭkt′), *v.t.* to build; form; put together; compose.—*n.* **constructor.**

con-struc-tion (kŏn-strŭk′shŭn), *n.* the act of building; that which is built; an edifice; interpretation; arrangement and grammatical relationship of words in a sentence.

con-struc-tive (kŏn-strŭk′tĭv), *adj.* having the character of upbuilding; having the power to form or frame; tending toward the positive and affirmative; tending to help rather than to hinder or depress; as, *constructive* work; *constructive* criticism.—*adv.* **constructively.**

con-strue (kŏn′strōō; kŏn-strōō′), *v.t.* to analyze or take apart (a sentence) so as to show the word-relationship and make plain the meaning; translate; interpret; as, to *construe* Greek or Latin.

con-sul (kŏn′sŭl), *n.* an officer commissioned by a government to reside in a foreign port or city, to promote the interests of his country's trade, and protect its subjects; the chief magistrate of the Roman Republic, and of the French Republic (1799–1804).—*n.* **consulship.**

con-sul gen-er-al (kŏn′sŭl jĕn′ẽr-ăl), a chief consul; as, the *consul general* has charge of all the consuls of his government in a foreign country.

con-su-lar (kŏn′sū-lár), *adj.* pertaining to a consul; as, *consular* duties; *consular* service.

con-su-late (kŏn′sū-lāt), *n.* the office and residence of a consul; the term of office of a consul.

con-sult (kŏn-sŭlt′), *v.t.* to ask advice of; to have regard to: *v.i.* to take counsel together.—*n.* **consulter.**

con-sul-ta-tion (kŏn″sŭl-tā′shŭn), *n.* the act of conferring; a conference or deliberation on some special matter; a meeting of experts for conference; as, a *consultation* of physicians.

con-sume (kŏn-sūm′), *v.t.* to destroy; waste; spend: *v.i.* waste away; be exhausted.—*n.* **consumer.**

con-sum-mate (kŏn′sŭ-māt), *v.t.* to complete; to finish: *adj.* (kŏn-sŭm′āt), perfect.—*adv.* **consummately.**

con-sum-ma-tion (kŏn″sŭ-mā′shŭn), *n.* conclusion; accomplishment; as, the *consummation* of a wish; completion.

con-sump-tion (kŏn-sŭmp′shŭn), *n.* the act of using up; as, the *consumption* of sugar in the United States is enormous; the state or process of being used up; a gradual wasting away; pulmonary tuberculosis; as, the modern cure for *consumption* is fresh air.

con-sump-tive (kŏn-sŭmp′tĭv), *adj.* pertaining to, or inclined to, or afflicted with, pulmonary tuberculosis: *n.* one afflicted with pulmonary tuberculosis.

con-tact (kŏn′tăkt), *n.* a coming together of two things; a touching; close union; the joining-point of two conductors through which an electric current passes; in an airplane, the closing of the ignition switch, controlling the engine of the machine.

con-ta-gion (kŏn-tā′jŭn), *n.* the giving of disease to another by direct or indirect contact; an agency, as virus, used to transmit disease; the communication of emotions, manners, etc., to others.

con-ta-gious (kŏn-tā′jŭs), *adj.* transmitted by contact; as, diseases are *contagious.*—*adv.* **contagiously.**—*n.* **contagiousness.**

con-tain (kŏn-tān′), *v.t.* to hold, as a vessel; keep within bounds; inclose; to hold or be equivalent to; to restrain or hold back: used with the reflexive pronoun; as, she could scarcely *contain herself;* to be a multiple of, or to be exactly divisible by.—*n.* **container.**

con-tam-i-nate (kŏn-tăm′ĭ-nāt), *v.t.* to pollute or make impure.

Syn. corrupt, defile, taint.

con-tam-i-na-tion (kŏn-tăm″ĭ-nā′-shŭn), *n.* the act of making impure; taint; as, it is very necessary to keep drinking water from *contamination.*

con-temn (kŏn-tĕm′), *v.t.* to scorn; to look upon or treat with contempt.

con-tem-plate (kŏn′tĕm-plāt), *v.t.* to look at or consider with continued attention; meditate on; to look forward to; intend; *v.i.* to meditate.

con-tem-pla-tion (kŏn-tĕm-plā′shŭn), *n.* the act of looking at or thinking over carefully; meditation; expectation; intention.

con-tem-pla-tive (kŏn-tĕm′plá-tĭv), *adj.* thoughtful; as, a *contemplative* state of mind.—*adv.* **contemplatively.**

con-tem-po-ra-ne-ous (kŏn-tĕm″pō-rā′nē-ŭs), *adj.* living, occurring, or existing at the same time.—*adv.* **contemporaneously.**

con-tem-po-ra-ry (kŏn-tĕm′pō-rā-rĭ), *adj.* existing or occurring at the same time: *n.* one living at the same time as another; as, Thackeray and Dickens were *contemporaries.*

con-tempt (kŏn-tĕmpt′), *n.* disdain; scorn; as, *contempt* is the keenest rebuke for drunkenness: disobedience to the orders, etc., of a court; disgrace; shame.

con-tempt-i-ble (kŏn-tĕmp'tĭ-bl), *adj.* meriting scorn.—*adv.* **contemptibly.**—*n.* **contemptibleness.**
Syn. despicable, paltry, pitiful, vile, mean.
Ant. (see noble).

con-temp-tu-ous (kŏn-tĕmp'tū-ŭs), *adj.* disdainful; scornful.—*adv.* **contemptuously.**—*n.* **contemptuousness.**

con-tend (kŏn-tĕnd'), *v.i.* to strive in opposition; vie; as, to *contend* for the prize; dispute or debate: *v.t.* to maintain or assert.—*n.* **contender.**
Syn. contest, struggle, combat.

con-tent (kŏn-tĕnt'), *adj.* satisfied; willing: *v.t.* to satisfy; gratify; appease: *n.* the state of being satisfied; mental satisfaction; (kŏn'tĕnt; kŏn-tĕnt'), that which is contained; that which is discussed, covered, or treated in a book, etc.; extent; size: usually in plural.

con-tent-ed (kŏn-tĕn'tĕd), *p.adj.* gratified; satisfied; as, to be *contented* is true happiness.—*adv.* **contentedly.** —*n.* **contentedness.**

con-ten-tion (kŏn-tĕn'shŭn), *n.* contest; debate; quarrel; strife.

con-ten-tious (kŏn-tĕn'shŭs), *adj.* causing disputes or strife; quarrelsome; as, a *contentious* spirit and unruly tongue.—*adv.* **contentiously.**—*n.* **contentiousness.**

con-tent-ment (kŏn-tĕnt'mĕnt), *n.* satisfaction; content.

con-ter-mi-nous (kŏn-tûr'mĭ-nŭs), *adj.* contained within the same limits; having the same bounds. Also, **conterminal.**

con-test (kŏn-tĕst'), *v.t.* to dispute; as, to *contest* an election; oppose; litigate: *v.i.* to strive; contend; vie: *n.* (kŏn'tĕst), a struggle for superiority; dispute.

con-test-ant (kŏn-tĕs'tănt), *n.* one who disputes, opposes, or questions, especially an election, or a will.—*adj.* **contestable.**—*adv.* **contestably.**

con-text (kŏn'tĕkst), *n.* the part of a discourse which precedes, follows, or is closely connected with any special sentence or word, and which determines its meaning.—*adj.* **contextual.**

con-ti-gu-i-ty (kŏn"tĭ-gū'ĭ-tĭ), *n.* contact; a continuous mass or series; nearness.

con-tig-u-ous (kŏn-tĭg'ū-ŭs), *adj.* touching; adjoining; near to; as, the suburbs are *contiguous* to the city.—*adv.* **contiguously.**—*n.* **contiguousness.**

con-ti-nence (kŏn'tĭ-nĕns), *n.* self-control, especially in regard to passions and desires. Also, **continency.**

con-ti-nent (kŏn'tĭ-nĕnt), *adj.* temperate; exercising self-control, especially over passions and desires: *n.* a large division of land; as, the *continent* of North America; mainland: **Continent**, the mainland of Europe, as distinguished from any of the various outlying islands, especially the British Isles.—*adv.* **continently.**

con-ti-nen-tal (kŏn"tĭ-nĕn'tăl), *adj.* pertaining to a continent: **Continental**, of or pertaining to the mainland of Europe; in American history, of or pertaining to the colonies at the time of the Revolution: *n.* a soldier of the Continental army.

con-tin-gen-cy (kŏn-tĭn'jĕn-sĭ), *n.* [*pl.* contingencies (-sĭz)], a chance or possible occurrence. Also, **contingence.**

con-tin-gent (kŏn-tĭn'jĕnt), *adj.* possible; accidental; conditional; as, a *contingent* liability: *n.* a possibility; a quota of troops.

con-tin-u-al (kŏn-tĭn'ū-ăl), *adj.* proceeding without interruption; incessant; constant.—*adv.* **continually.**
Syn. continuous, perpetual.
Ant. (see intermittent).

con-tin-u-ance (kŏn-tĭn'ū-ăns), *n.* permanence; uninterrupted succession; duration.

con-tin-u-a-tion (kŏn-tĭn"ū-ā'shŭn), *n.* the act of carrying on, or the state of being carried on, without, or after, interruption; that which carries on or resumes; as, a *continuation* of a story.

con-tin-ue (kŏn-tĭn'ū), *v.t.* to carry on without interruption; persist in; as, *continue* thy loving kindness: extend or prolong; postpone or keep undecided; as, to *continue* a law case: *v.i.* to remain; abide; endure; persevere.

con-ti-nu-i-ty (kŏn"tĭ-nū'ĭ-tĭ), [*pl.* continuities (-tĭz)], uninterrupted succession or connection.

con-tin-u-ous (kŏn-tĭn'ū-ŭs), *adj.* connected; uninterrupted.—*adv.* **continuously.**

con-tort (kŏn-tôrt'), *v.t.* to bend or twist out of shape.

con-tor-tion (kŏn-tôr'shŭn), *n.* unnatural twisting or writhing; a bending out of shape.

con-tor-tion-ist (kŏn-tôr'shŭn-ĭst), *n.* an acrobat who distorts his body into unnatural positions; as, a *contortionist* must train his muscles.

con-tour (kŏn'tōōr"; kŏn"tōōr'), *n.* an outline; profile; as, the *contour* of the face or of the land: **contour line**, a line connecting points on a land surface which have the same elevation.

con-tra-band (kŏn'trȧ-bănd), *adj.* forbidden to be brought in: *n.* smuggled goods; as, arms and munitions are *contraband* in time of war: **contraband of war**, certain materials used in warfare which a neutral nation is forbidden, by international law, to supply the nations at war, except at the risk of seizure and condemnation.

con-tract (kŏn-trăkt'), *v.t.* to draw closer together; shorten; condense; wrinkle; to become affected with; acquire; to establish by formal agreement; betroth: *v.i.* to shrink; bargain or agree to do something; make a promise of marriage: *n.* (kŏn'trăkt), a written agreement; as, the merchant made many *contracts* for cotton goods.

con-tract-ed (kŏn-trăk'tĕd), *p.adj.* drawn together; shortened; narrow; mean; not extensive.—*adv.* **contractedly.** —*n.* **contractedness.**

con-tract-i-ble (kŏn-trăk'tĭ-bl), *adj.* capable of being shortened or drawn together.

con-trac-tile (kŏn-trăk'tĭl), *adj.* tending to, or capable of, shortening or drawing together.—*n.* **contractility.**

con-trac-tion (kŏn-trăk'shŭn), *n.* the act of drawing together; shrinkage; decrease; act of acquiring; the shortening of a word, or two words, by the cutting out of a letter or letters, as *can't* for *cannot*.

con-trac-tor (kŏn-trăk'tēr), *n.* one of the parties to a written agreement; one who undertakes to supply or construct for a stated sum.

con-tra-dict (kŏn"trȧ-dĭkt'), *v.t.* to assert the opposite of; to deny: *v.i.* to oppose in words; gainsay.
Syn. gainsay.
Ant. (see confirm).

con-tra-dic-tion (kŏn"trȧ-dĭk'shŭn), *n.* the act of saying the opposite; denial.

con-tra-dic-to-ry (kŏn"trȧ-dĭk'tō-rĭ), *adj.* opposite; denying; given to opposition.—*adv.* contradictorily.—*n.* contradictoriness.

con-tra-dis-tinc-tion (kŏn"trȧ-dĭs-tĭnk'shŭn), *n.* distinction by contrast.

con-tral-to (kŏn-träl'tō; kŏn-trăl'tō), *n.* a voice in quality and range between soprano and tenor; the lowest female voice.

con-tra-ri-e-ty (kŏn"trȧ-rī'ĕ-tĭ), *n.* the state or quality of being contradictory, opposed, or perverse; an inconsistency.

con-tra-ri-wise (kŏn'trȧ-rĭ-wīz"; kŏn'-trā-rĭ-wīz"), *adv.* conversely; in the opposite way.

con-tra-ry (kŏn'trā-rĭ), *adj.* opposed; contradictory; conflicting; opposite in direction; perverse; wayward: *n.* a thing of qualities opposite or contradictory to those of some other thing; the opposite of some assertion or declaration.—*adv.* contrarily.—*n.* contrariness.

con-trast (kŏn-trȧst'), *v.t.* to place in such a way as to show differences; to compare in order to show unlikeness; to state the difference between: *v.i.* to be very different, as shown by comparison: *n.* (kŏn'trȧst), opposition or difference of qualities shown by comparison; the thing or quality opposed to another.

con-tra-vene (kŏn"trȧ-vēn'), *v.t.* to obstruct; act contrary to; defeat; violate.

con-tra-ven-tion (kŏn"trȧ-vĕn'shŭn), *n.* opposition; violation; as, the act was in *contravention* of the treaty.

con-trib-ute (kŏn-trĭb'ūt), *v.t.* to give to some common stock; to give in common with others; furnish as a share: *v.i.* to lend one's aid for the accomplishment of a common purpose; to give something to a cause.—*n.* contributor.

con-tri-bu-tion (kŏn"trĭ-bū'shŭn), *n.* the act of giving or sharing for a common purpose; a subscription; tax; a writing furnished to a newspaper or magazine.

con-trib-u-tive (kŏn-trĭb'ū-tĭv), *adj.* tending, in common with other factors, to produce a result; giving; lending aid.—*adv.* contributively.

con-trib-u-tory (kŏn-trĭb'ū-tō-rĭ), *adj.* giving or lending aid; of the nature of a contribution; tending, in common with other factors, to produce a result.

con-trite (kŏn'trīt), *adj.* humble; penitent; as, a *contrite* sinner.—*adv.* contritely.—*n.* contriteness.

con-tri-tion (kŏn-trĭsh'ŭn), *n.* sorrow for sin.

con-triv-ance (kŏn-trīv'ăns), *n.* a device; apparatus; scheme.

con-trive (kŏn-trīv'), *v.t.* to devise; invent; plan: *v.i.* scheme; as, he *contrived* to win his point.—*n.* contriver.

con-trol (kŏn-trōl'), *n.* a check; restraint; superintendence; authority; the apparatus regulating the movement of an airplane: *v.t.* [*p.t.* and *p.p.* controlled, *p.pr.* controlling], to restrain; govern; regulate.

con-trol-la-ble (kŏn-trōl'ȧ-bl), *adj.* subject to control; capable of being restrained.—*adv.* controllably.

con-trol-ler (kŏn-trōl'ẽr), *n.* one who, or that which, governs; a public officer who oversees and verifies the accounts of officials under him. Also, in the latter sense, comptroller.

con-tro-ver-sial (kŏn"trō-vûr'shăl), *adj.* pertaining to, or like, a dispute; contentious.—*adv.* controversially.—*n.* controversialist.

con-tro-ver-sy (kŏn'trō-vûr'sĭ), *n.* [*pl.* controversies (-sĭz)], debate; discussion; dispute; quarrel; as, there was a great *controversy* over the discovery of the North Pole.

con-tro-vert (kŏn"trō-vûrt'), *v.t.* to dispute; to contend against; refute; disprove.—*n.* controverter.

con-tro-ver-ti-ble (kŏn"trō-vûr'tĭ-bl), *adj.* capable of being disputed or disproved.—*adv.* controvertibly.

con-tu-ma-cious (kŏn"tū-mā'shŭs), *adj.* obstinate; stubborn; scorning authority.—*adv.* contumaciously.—*n.* contumaciousness.

con-tu-ma-cy (kŏn'tū-mȧ-sĭ), *n.* [*pl.* contumacies (-sĭz)], obstinate or stubborn opposition to lawful authority.

con-tu-me-li-ous (kŏn"tū-mē'lĭ-ŭs), *adj.* showing haughty contempt or scorn; exhibiting insolence or rudeness.—*adv.* contumeliously.

con-tu-me-ly (kŏn'tū-mē-lĭ), *n.* [*pl.* contumelies (-lĭz)], haughty and scornful rudeness; scornful and insolent abuse; as, the traitor could not escape the *contumely* of his countrymen.

con-tuse (kŏn-tūz'), *v.t.* to bruise; injure by a blow.—*n.* contusion.

co-nun-drum (kō-nŭn'drŭm), *n.* a riddle or puzzle; anything that puzzles.

con-va-lesce (kŏn"vȧ-lĕs'), *v.i.* to recover strength and health after illness; as, he will *convalesce* rapidly.

con-va-les-cence (kŏn"vȧ-lĕs'ĕns), *n.* gradual recovery after illness; the period of such recovery.

con-va-les-cent (kŏn"vȧ-lĕs'ĕnt), *adj.* recovering health; of or pertaining to the recovery from illness or the period of recovery: *n.* one in a convalescent state.

con-vec-tion (kŏn-vĕk'shŭn), *n.* a carrying or transmitting; especially, the transmitting of heat through a liquid or gas by means of currents.

con-vene (kŏn-vēn'), *v.i.* to meet together; as, Congress *convenes* in December: *v.t.* cause to assemble.

con-ven-ience (kŏn-vēn'yĕns), *n.* fitness; freedom from discomfort; suitableness; ease; accommodation; that which adds to comfort or makes work easier; as, the fireless cooker is a great *convenience*. Also, conveniency.

con-ven-ient (kŏn-vēn'yĕnt), *adj.* suitable; appropriate; affording accommodation; handy; saving work or trouble.—*adv.* conveniently.

con-vent (kŏn'vĕnt), *n.* an association of persons devoted to a religious life; nunnery; monastery.

con-ven-ti-cle (kŏn-vĕn'tĭ-kl), *n.* a meeting or an assembly for worship, especially a private or illegal one.

con-ven-tion (kŏn-vĕn′shŭn), *n.* a meeting; a social, commercial, or political assembly, met for some definite object; as, the annual *conventions* of bankers, or railroad men; a diplomatic agreement; something established by general consent or opinion; hence, a fixed custom or usage.

con-ven-tion-al (kŏn-vĕn′shŭn-al), *adj.* formal; sanctioned by, or growing out of, custom or tradition; based on accepted models or artistic rules; in art, following fixed rules in design, technique, etc.—*adv.* **conventionally.**

con-ven-tion-al-ism (kŏn-vĕn′shŭn-ăl-ĭzm), *n.* regard for that which is formal or artificial in conduct, art, etc.; a formality; a customary practice or usage.

con-ven-tion-al-i-ty (kŏn-vĕn″shŭn-ăl′ĭ-tĭ), *n.* [*pl.* conventionalities (-tĭz)], adherence to formal or set rules or precedents; artificiality.

con-ven-tion-al-ize (kŏn-vĕn′shŭn-ăl-īz), *v.t.* to make to conform to custom, usage, or rule, as conduct, art, etc.

con-ven-tu-al (kŏn-vĕn′tū-ăl), *adj.* pertaining to, or characteristic of, a convent.

con-verge (kŏn-vûrj′), *v.i.* to tend to meet at one point: *v.t.* to cause to meet at one point.

con-ver-gence (kŏn-vûr′jĕns), *n.* the act or quality of tending towards one point; a coming together at one point. Also, **convergency.**

con-ver-gent (kŏn-vûr′jĕnt), *adj.* tending to one point; gradually approaching each other; approaching a limit.

con-ver-sant (kŏn′vẽr-sănt), *adj.* acquainted or familiar with: with *with;* as, he was *conversant* with the rules.

con-ver-sa-tion (kŏn″vẽr-sā′shŭn), *n.* informal or familiar talk.
Syn. chat, talk, parley.

con-ver-sa-tion-al (kŏn″vẽr-sā′shŭn-ăl), *adj.* given to chatty talk; ready to talk; pertaining to familiar spoken interchange of ideas.—*adv.* **conversationally.**—*n.* **conversationalist.**

con-verse (kŏn-vûrs′), *v.i.* to interchange thoughts; talk familiarly: *adj.* (kŏn′vûrs), reversed in order or relation; opposite: *n.* the opposite of something else; as, the *converse* of the theory is true; familiar talk.—*adv.* **conversely.**

con-ver-sion (kŏn-vûr′shŭn), *n.* change from one state, or from one religion, to another; as, after his *conversion* he was a better man; the act of changing from one thing to another; the state of being changed.

con-vert (kŏn-vûrt′), *v.t.* to transform; to change from one religion or course to another; cause to undergo a moral change; as, the Christian missionaries try to *convert* the heathen; to exchange or give for an equivalent: *n.* (kŏn′vûrt), one who changes from one belief to another; one who has undergone a moral change.
Syn., *n.* disciple.

con-vert-er (kŏn-vûr′tẽr), *n.* one who, or that which, changes; a vessel in which materials are changed from one condition to another; as, in certain processes, pig iron is changed to steel in a *converter;* in electrical usage, a device for changing alternating current to direct current, or the reverse; a device to change the frequency of alternating current: commonly called a *frequency changer.*

con-vert-i-ble (kŏn-vûr′tĭ-bl), *adj.* capable of being changed into; interchangeable; as, iron is *convertible* into steel.—*adv.* **convertibly.**—*n.* **convertibility.**

con-vex (kŏn′vĕks), *adj.* curved on the surface; bulging: opposite to *concave;* as, a *convex* mirror: *n.* a convex body: **convex lens,** a magnifying glass, curved out on one or both sides.—*adv.* **convexly.**

Convex Lens

con-vex-i-ty (kŏn-vĕk′sĭ-tĭ), *n.* roundness; the bulging surface of anything.

con-vey (kŏn-vā′), *v.t.* [*p.t.* and *p.p.* conveyed, *p.pr.* conveying], to carry or transport; as, *convey* the wheat to market; transmit; impart; communicate; transfer to another, as the title to property.—*n.* **conveyer, conveyor.**
Syn. carry, cede, grant.
Ant. (see keep).

con-vey-ance (kŏn-vā′ăns), *n.* transport; the act or means of transmitting, communicating, etc.; a vehicle, as an automobile; the change of property from one owner to another.

con-vey-anc-er (kŏn-vā′ăn-sẽr), *n.* one whose business is to draw up deeds, etc., transferring property.

con-vey-anc-ing (kŏn-vā′ăn-sĭng), *n.* the business of drawing deeds, leases, etc., and of investigating titles to property.

con-vict (kŏn-vĭkt′), *v.t.* to prove or pronounce guilty of a crime charged: *n.* (kŏn′vĭkt), a criminal sentenced to prison; one serving his time in prison.

con-vic-tion (kŏn-vĭk′shŭn), *n.* the act of finding guilty; the state of being found guilty; strong belief; as, a *conviction* of what is right.

con-vince (kŏn-vĭns′), *v.t.* to satisfy by evidence or argument; persuade; cause to believe.—*adv.* **convincingly.**

con-viv-i-al (kŏn-vĭv′ĭ-ăl), *adj.* festive; jovial; gay.—*adv.* **convivially.**

con-viv-i-al-i-ty (kŏn-vĭv″ĭ-ăl′ĭ-tĭ), *n.* mirth and good humor that attend a feast; good fellowship.

con-vo-ca-tion (kŏn″vō-kā′shŭn), *n.* the act of calling together an assembly, especially of bishops and clergy, or heads of universities; a meeting of ministers.

con-voke (kŏn-vōk′), *v.t.* to call or summon together; convene; as, Parliament was *convoked* in June.

con-vo-lute (kŏn′vō-lūt), *adj.* rolled inward from one side; rolled together, one part on another.—*adj.* **convoluted.**

con-vo-lu-tion (kŏn-vō-lū′shŭn), *n.* a coiling or winding together, as of a thing folded or rolled upon itself; a coil.

con-vol-vu-lus (kŏn-vŏl′vū-lŭs), *n.* a trumpet-shaped flower like the morning glory.

con-voy (kŏn-voi′), *v.t.* [*p.t.* and *p.p.* convoyed, *p.pr.* convoying], to accompany on the way, for protection, by sea or land; as, the fleet was *convoyed* into the harbor: *n.* (kŏn′voi), a protecting force accompanying ships, goods, persons, etc.; an escort; the act of escorting or the state of being escorted; as, the ambassador had a safe *convoy* home.

con-vulse (kŏn-vŭls'), *v.t.* to agitate violently; shake; affect with spasms.

con-vul-sion (kŏn-vŭl'shŭn), *n.* an agitation; tumult; a violent and unnatural shortening of the muscles; a spasm; a fit; a violent disturbance of the earth, such as an earthquake.

con-vul-sive (kŏn-vŭl'sĭv), *adj.* producing abnormal muscular contractions; spasmodic; of the nature of a spasm or fit.—*adv.* **convulsively.**—*n.* **convulsiveness.**

co-ny (kō'nĭ), *n.* [*pl.* conies (-nĭz)] a rabbit. Also, **coney.**

coo (ko͞o), *v.i.* [*p.t.* and *p.p.* cooed, *p.pr.* cooing], to cry like a dove or pigeon; to act or converse in a loving manner: *n.* the sound uttered by doves and pigeons.—*n.* **cooer.**

cook (ko͝ok), *v.t.* to prepare for eating by boiling, baking, or roasting: *v.i.* to act as a cook: *n.* one who prepares food for the table.

cook-er (ko͝ok'ẽr), *n.* a special apparatus or vessel for preparing food for the table: **fireless cooker**, a device by means of which foods which have been thoroughly heated or partially cooked on the stove are kept hot long enough to complete the cooking process.

cook-er-y (ko͝ok'ẽr-ĭ), *n.* [*pl.* cookeries (-ĭz)], the art or practice of preparing food for the table.

cook-y (ko͝ok'ĭ), *n.* [*pl.* cookies (-ĭz)], a small flat sweet cake. Also, **cookie.**

cool (ko͞ol), *adj.* [*compar.* cooler, *superl.* coolest], slightly or moderately cold; calm; deliberate; not admitting heat; as, a *cool* suit of clothes; chilling; lacking in cordiality; as, a *cool* reception; impudent; colloquially, not exaggerated or overstated; as, he made a *cool* thousand: *v.t.* to make slightly cold; to chill: *v.i.* to become slightly cold.—*adv.* **coolly.**

Syn., *adj.* cold, frigid.
Ant. (see hot).

cool-er (ko͞ol'ẽr), *n.* that which makes or keeps things slightly cold, or cold enough to preserve them, as food in hot weather; as, an ice *cooler.*

coo-lie (ko͞o'lĭ), *n.* a Chinese or East Indian contract laborer: the coolie may be a porter, a house servant, a chair carrier, or one who does other menial work. Also, **cooly.**

cool-ness (ko͞ol'nĕs), *n.* the state of being slightly cold; calmness; lack of cordiality; as, *coolness* of weather; *coolness* in time of danger; *coolness* of manner.

coon (ko͞on), *n.* short for raccoon; slang, a negro.

coop (ko͞op), *n.* a cage; pen: *v.t.* to confine in, or as in, a cage; inclose.

coop-er (ko͞op'ẽr; ko͝op'ẽr), *n.* a maker of barrels, casks, etc.

coop-er-age (ko͞op'ẽr-āj), *n.* the business or workshop of a maker of barrels, casks, etc.; price for such work.

co-ŏp-er-ate (kō-ŏp'ẽr-āt), *v.i.* to act or work jointly; work together to produce the same effect; as, the Red Cross *coöperates* with the army.

co-ŏp-er-a-tion (kō-ŏp"ẽr-ā'shŭn), *n.* the act of working jointly together; concurrence.

co-ŏp-er-a-tive (kō-ŏp'ẽr-ā-tĭv), *adj.* working together for certain ends; as, *coöperative* stores have been successful.—*adv.* **coöperatively.**

co-ŏr-di-nate (kō-ôr'dĭ-nāt), *v.t.* to place in the same order or class; to put in harmony; adjust: *v.i.* to be of the same order, etc.; harmonize: *adj.* (kō-ôr'dĭ-nāt), of the same rank or order; as, *coördinate* clauses: *n.* in mathematics, any of certain lines or angles by which position is determined; one who, or that which, is of the same rank, order, etc.—*adv.* **coördinately.**

co-ŏr-di-na-tion (kō-ôr"dĭ-nā'shŭn), *n.* state of working together or acting in harmony.

co-ŏr-di-na-tive (kō-ôr'dĭ-nā-tĭv), *adj.* adjusted; equal in rank or importance; making equal in rank; as, a *coördinative* conjunction.

coot (ko͞ot), *n.* any of certain birds of the rail family, resembling ducks.

coo-tie (ko͞o'tĭ), *n.* [*pl.* cooties (-tĭz)], in the World War, the name given to the lice that infested the clothing of the men in trenches and billets. [SLANG.]

cop (kŏp), *n.* the top or head of a thing; the tuft on the head of a bird; a roll of thread on the spindle of a spinning wheel; in golf, the top or face of a bunker; slang, a policeman.

co-pal (kō'păl), *n.* a hard clear resin used in making varnishes.

co-part-ner-ship (kō-pärt'nẽr-shĭp), *n.* the state of being associated with others in business; a partnership.—*n.* **copartner.**

cope (kōp), *n.* a large semicircular cloak or mantle worn by bishops and priests over the surplice: *v.i.* to strive or contend with: with *with;* as, we must be prepared to *cope* with our enemy.

co-peck (kō'pĕk), *n.* a Russian coin worth from one-half to three-fourths of a cent. Also, **kopeck, kopek.**

Co-per-ni-can (kō-pûr'nĭ-kăn), *adj.* pertaining to Copernicus, who conceived the sun to be the center of the solar system.

cope-stone (kōp'stōn"), *n.* the top stone of a wall; one of the stones of a coping.

cop-i-er (kŏp'ĭ-ẽr), *n.* one who makes a reproduction from an original; an imitator.

cop-ing (kōp'ĭng), *n.* the top masonry of a wall, often sloping so as to shed water.

co-pi-ous (kō'pĭ-ŭs), *adj.* plenteous; profuse in words; ample; abundant; as, *copious* supplies.—*adv.* **copiously.**—*n.* **copiousness.**

cop-per (kŏp'ẽr), *n.* a common, reddish metallic element, easily worked, and an excellent conductor of heat and electricity; something made of this metal, as the cent.—*adj.* **coppery.**

cop-per-as (kŏp'ẽr-ăs), *n.* a green chemical used in dyeing.

cop-per-head (kŏp'ẽr-hĕd"), *n.* a poisonous American snake: **Copperhead**, a Northerner whose sympathies lay with the South during the Civil War.

cop-per-plate (kŏp'ẽr-plāt"), *n.* a polished copper plate on which something is engraved for printing; as, paper money is engraved on a *copperplate*; engraving or printing done on such a plate: *adj.* pertaining to the art of engraving on such a plate.

cop-pice (kŏp'ĭs), *n.* a wood of small trees or bushes; a copse.

cop-ra (kŏp′rȧ), *n.* the dried kernel of the coconut; dried coconut meat.

copse (kŏps), *n.* a grove or thicket of small trees or bushes.

Cop-tic (kŏp′tĭk), *adj.* of or pertaining to the Copts, a native Egyptian race descended from the ancient Egyptians. *n.* the language of the Copts.

cop-u-la (kŏp′ū-lȧ), *n.* [*pl.* copulas (-lȧz)], a word which joins the subject and predicate in a sentence, as the word *is* in the sentence, the man *is* walking.

cop-u-late (kŏp′ū-lāt), *v.i.* to unite, especially in sexual intercourse. —*n.* **copulation.**

cop-u-la-tive (kŏp′ū-lā-tĭv), *adj.* uniting; as, a *copulative* conjunction; serving to connect; as, a *copulative* verb.

cop-y (kŏp′ĭ), *n.* [*pl.* copies (-ĭz)], an imitation; a duplicate; a writing exercise; a pattern given for imitation; manuscript to be set up in type: *v.t.* to transcribe; reproduce; as, many artists *copy* the works of the great masters: *v.i.* to imitate.

cop-y-ist (kŏp′ĭ-ĭst), *n.* one who makes reproductions from originals; one who imitates.

cop-y-right (kŏp′ĭ-rīt″), *n.* the exclusive right to reproduce, publish, sell, etc., a literary or artistic work for a certain number of years: *v.t.* to secure the exclusive right to publish, sell, etc., any literary or artistic work.

co-quet (kō-kĕt′), *v.i.* [*p.t.* and *p.p.* coquetted, *p.pr.* coquetting], to flirt; seek to attract attention or admiration; trifle.

co-quet-ry (kō′kĕt-rĭ), *n.* [*pl.* coquetries (-rĭz)], the act of seeking men's admiration; flirtation; trifling in love.

co-quette (kō-kĕt′), *n.* a vain woman who seeks to gain men's attention and admiration; a flirt.—*adj.* **coquettish.** —*adv.* **coquettishly.**—*n.* **coquettishness.**

co-qui-na (kō-kē′nȧ), *n.* a soft rock, found in the southern part of the United States, composed of the broken pieces of sea shells: used as building material.

cor-a-cle (kŏr′ȧ-kl), *n.* a boat made of basketwork covered with leather or oilcloth.

cor-al (kŏr′ăl), *n.* the hard skeleton of certain sea animals: *adj.* made of coral; having a red color, like coral.

cor-al-line (kŏr′ă-lĭn), *adj.* pinkish-red, like coral; pertaining to, or composed of, coral.

cor-bel (kôr′bĕl), *n.* a piece of stone, wood, or iron, projecting from the side of a wall, often ornamented with odd-looking figures: used for support; a sculptured basket of flowers, fruit, etc.

cord (kôrd), *n.* a twisted string; a measure of wood equal to 128 cu. ft.; a tendon or nerve; a small rope: *v.t.* to fasten or connect with string or rope; to pile up, as wood, in piles 8 ft. by 4 ft. by 4 ft.

cord-age (kôr′dāj) *n.* a quantity of strings or ropes; ropes and rigging collectively; the number of cords, as of wood, on any given piece of land.

cor-date (kôr′dāt), *adj.* shaped like a heart: a botanical term, used of leaves.

cor-dial (kôr′jăl; kôrd′yăl), *adj.* tending to revive, as a medicine; hearty; sincere; cheering; as, a *cordial* manner: *n.* a medicine or drink that revives or cheers; a sweet aromatic alcoholic beverage.—*adv.* **cordially.**

cor-dial-i-ty (kôr-jăl′ĭ-tĭ; kôr″dĭ-ăl′ĭ-tĭ), *n.* sincere, sympathetic geniality; sincerity; heartiness; as, the stranger was greeted with *cordiality.*

cor-dil-le-ra (kôr″dĭl-yā′rȧ; kôr-dĭl′ĕr-ȧ), *n.* a mountain range or system; the main system of mountain ranges of a continent.

cord-ing (kôr′dĭng), *n.* the ribbed surface of a corded fabric, like corduroy.

cor-dite (kôr′dīt), *n.* a form of smokeless gunpowder of high explosive power, made in the form of cords.

cor-don (kôr′dŏn), *n.* a ribbon worn as the badge of an order; a line of men or ships stationed as sentinels; as, the prisoners were surrounded by a *cordon* of soldiers; a line of soldiers.

cor-do-van (kôr′dō-văn), *n.* a Spanish leather, made of goatskin, or split horsehide tanned and dressed. Also, **cordwain.**

cor-du-roy (kôr′dū-roi″; kôr′dū-roi′), *n.* a stout ribbed or corded cotton cloth which has a velvety surface; colloquially, *pl.* trousers, or a suit, made of this material: *adj.* made of logs laid side by side transversely; as, it is rough traveling over a *corduroy* road.

core (kōr), *n.* the heart or innermost part of anything, especially of fruit; the substance or essential point, as of a subject; a solid form, placed in a mold, which, when metal is poured about it, shapes the interior of a hollow casting: *v.t.* to remove the center, or core, from, as an apple; to mold or cast on a central shaping form.—*n.* **corer.**

co-re-op-sis (kō″rē-ŏp′sĭs; kŏr″ē-ŏp′sĭs), *n.* any of several varieties of plants of the aster family.

co-re-spond-ent (kō″rē-spŏn′dĕnt), *n.* a joint respondent; the person named as the guilty party in a divorce suit.

co-ri-an-der (kō″rĭ-ăn′dẽr), *n.* a plant of the parsley family, bearing aromatic seeds.

Co-rin-thi-an (kō-rĭn′thĭ-ăn), *adj.* of or pertaining to Corinth, a celebrated city of ancient Greece, noted for its luxury; pertaining to the Corinthian order of architecture: **Corinthians,** *n.pl.* two books of the New Testament, containing the Epistles, or letters, of the apostle Paul to the Christians at Corinth.

Co-rin-thi-an or-der (kō-rĭn′thĭ-ăn ôr′dẽr), the lightest and most highly decorated of the classic orders of architecture, with a bell-shaped capital, and ornamented with a certain kind of leaves.

cork (kôrk), *n.* the outer layer of the bark of the cork tree; a kind of oak; a stopper for a bottle; anything made of cork or serving the purpose of a cork: *v.t.* to stop with a cork, as a bottle; hence, to hold back or restrain: with *up*: *adj.* made of cork.—*adj.* **corky.**

cork-screw (kôrk′skrōō″), *n.* an instrument for drawing the corks from bottles: usually made of a spirally twisted piece of strong wire, with a sharpened point and a transverse handle: *adj.* shaped like a corkscrew.

corm (kôrm), *n.* a bulblike fleshy stem, short, and of solid texture, as in the crocus.

cor-mo-rant (kôr′mō-rănt), *n.* a diving bird that feeds on fish.

corn (kôrn), *n.* grain, as wheat, barley, etc.; maize, or Indian corn; in the

United States, maize; in Britain, wheat; in Scotland, oats are called corn: *v.t.* to preserve in salt; season in brine; as, to *corn* beef.

corn (kôrn), *n.* a horny outgrowth on the toe, or foot, due to friction or pressure.

corn-cob (kôrn'kŏb"), *n.* the spike or woody axis inside an ear of Indian corn, on which the corn is set.

corn cock-le (kôrn kŏk'l), a tall weed of the pink family, bearing bright red flowers.

cor-ne-a (kôr'nē-ȧ), *n.* the clear part of the coat of the eyeball which covers the iris and pupil and admits light to the interior.

corned (kôrnd), *adj.* preserved or pickled in brine or salt; as, *corned* beef.

cor-nel (kôr'nĕl), *n.* one of various shrubs or low trees; a plant of the dogwood family.

cor-nel-ian (kôr-nēl'yăn), *n.* a reddish kind of chalcedony, light or dark red in color: used for jewelry and seals. Also, **carnelian.**

cor-ner (kôr'nẽr), *n.* an angle; as, the *corner* of the room; the point where two lines, sides, or edges meet; a nook; a secluded place: a remote point; as, the *corners* of the earth: *v.t.* to drive or force into some position of difficulty from which there is no escape: **corner the market,** to buy up stock or property, so as to obtain exclusive control or possession of it; a term used in the Stock Exchange; as, a *corner* on wheat. —*adv.* **cornerwise.**

cor-ner stone (kôr'nẽr stōn), a stone at the corner of a building uniting two walls; as, the laying of the *corner stone* of an important public building.

Cornet

cor-net (kôr'nĕt; kôr-nĕt'), *n.* a small musical wind-instrument; a kind of trumpet; a troop of cavalry.—*n.* **cornetist.**

corn-flow-er (kôrn'flou"ẽr), *n.* a plant found in cornfields, especially the bachelor's button, or bluebottle, of the aster family, having flowery heads of different colors.

cor-nice (kôr'nĭs), *n.* the highest part or border of a wall or column.

Cornice

Cor-nish (kôr'nĭsh), *adj.* pertaining to Cornwall, England, or its language: *n.* the language formerly spoken in Cornwall.

corn-stalk (kôrn'stôk"), a stalk of maize, or Indian corn.

corn-starch (kôrn'stärch"), *n.* a flour made from Indian corn: used for puddings, etc.

cor-nu-co-pi-a (kôr"nū-kō'pĭ-ȧ), *n.* [*pl.* cornucopiæ (-ē) or cornucopias (-ȧz)], in ancient art, the horn of plenty full of fruit and flowers; a horn-shaped paper holder, usually filled with nuts and candy.

co-rol-la (kō-rŏl'ȧ), *n.* the inner envelope of a flower composed of two or more petals.

cor-ol-la-ry (kŏr'ō-lā-rĭ), *n.* in mathematics a fact discovered in proving some other fact; an inference.

co-ro-na (kō-rō'nȧ), *n.* [*pl.* coronæ (-nē)], a crown; as, in ancient Rome, a hero was rewarded for his bravery by a *corona* of oak leaves or gold; the flat projecting part of a cornice; a halo surrounding heavenly bodies; anything like a crown, as the pappus or tuft of the dandelion.—*adj.* **coronal.**

cor-o-na-tion (kŏr"ō-nā'shŭn), *n.* the act or ceremony of crowning a king or queen; as, the *coronation* of a king is a religious ceremony.

cor-o-ner (kŏr'ō-nẽr), *n.* an officer who finds out the causes of sudden or accidental death.

cor-o-net (kŏr'ō-nĕt), *n.* a wreath for the head; a crown denoting various degrees of rank below that of the sovereign.

cor-po-ral (kôr'pō-răl), *n.* the lowest non-commissioned officer in the army: *adj.* pertaining to the body; as, *corporal* punishment: **corporal's guard,** a detachment of several men under arms.—*adv.* **corporally.**

cor-po-rate (kôr'pō-rāt), *adj.* united in a body or community by law; as, Congress is a *corporate* body elected to make laws for the United States.—*adv.* **corporately.**

cor-po-ra-tion (kôr"pō-rā'shŭn), *n.* a group of persons who have legal power to act for a large number of other persons; as, a railroad company is a *corporation.*

cor-po-re-al (kôr-pō'rē-ăl), *adj.* having a material body; physical. —*adv.* **corporeally.**

corps (kōr), *n.* [*pl.* corps (kōrz)], a body of troops; a body of persons associated in a common work; as, an army *corps* is a large number of soldiers; the hospital *corps* takes care of the wounded.

corpse (kôrps), *n.* a dead body, usually a human body.

cor-pu-lence (kôr'pū-lĕns), *n.* bulkiness or largeness of body; great fatness. Also, **corpulency.**

cor-pu-lent (kôr'pū-lĕnt), *adj.* bulky; fat; having a large, fleshy body; as, a *corpulent* man.

Cor-pus Chris-ti (kôr'pŭs krĭs'tĭ), a Roman Catholic festival (the first Thursday after Trinity Sunday), in honor of the Eucharist, or sacrament of the Lord's Supper. [LAT.]

cor-pus-cle (kôr'pŭs-l), *n.* a minute particle of matter; a cell; as, a red or white *corpuscle* in the blood.—*adj.* **corpuscular.**

cor-ral (kō-răl'; SPAN. kō-räl'), *n.* a pen for horses or cattle; an inclosure or wide circle of wagons formed for protection in crossing the plains; a strong stockade for capturing wild elephants: *v.t.* [*p.t.* and *p.p.* corralled, *p.pr.* corralling], to drive into, or secure in, a pen or inclosure; to take possession of, or capture; to corner; as, it is exciting sport to *corral* elephants.

cor-rect (kŏ-rĕkt'), *v.t.* to set straight; to make right; punish for faults; amend: *adj.* exact; accurate; free from error; measuring up or meeting a standard of morals, taste, manners, etc.—*adv.* **correctly.**—*n.* **correctness.**

Syn., *v.* rectify, reform.

cor-rec-tion (kŏ-rĕk'shŭn), *n.* the act of pointing out mistakes; the act of changing something wrong and making it right; that which is put in the place of something wrong; reproof.

cor-rec-tive (kŏ-rĕk'tĭv), *adj.* having the power to make right: *n.* that which amends or makes right; an antidote.—*adv.* **correctively.**

cor-rect-or (kŏ-rĕk'tẽr), *n.* one that sets things right.

cor-re-late (kŏr'ē-lāt), *v.i.* to be related by connection, parallelism, etc.: *v.t.* to put or bring into some relation of connection, etc.; to connect by exhibiting a mutual relation.

cor-re-la-tion (kŏr'ē-lā'shŭn), *n.* reciprocal or mutual relation; similarity: the act of bringing into relation through connection, similarity, etc.; as, the *correlation* between matter and energy.

cor-rel-a-tive (kŏ-rĕl'ȧ-tĭv), *adj.* having mutual relation; as, in the sentence, either John or James did it, *either* and *or* are *correlative* terms: *n.* one of two persons or things that are mutually related.—*adv.* **correlatively.**

cor-re-spond (kŏr'ē-spŏnd'), *v.i.* to agree; to match; as, the hat should *correspond* with the dress; suit; agree; as, his words and acts do not *correspond*; to write letters; as, he will *correspond* with his teacher.

cor-re-spond-ence (kŏr'ē-spŏn'dĕns), *n.* communication by letters; as, their *correspondence* extended over a period of many years; agreement; similarity.

cor-re-spond-ent (kŏr'ē-spŏn'dĕnt), *adj.* agreeing with; similar: *n.* one with whom we exchange letters; one who writes for a newspaper or magazine; as, he was in Europe as the war *correspondent* of a newspaper.

cor-re-spond-ing (kŏr'ē-spŏnd'ĭng), *p.adj.* agreeing; matching; holding communication by means of letters.—*adv.* **correspondingly.**

cor-ri-dor (kŏr'ĭ-dôr), *n.* a hallway; an open passage in a building.

cor-ri-gi-ble (kŏr'ĭ-jĭ-bl), *adj.* capable of being corrected or reformed; submissive under correction.

cor-rob-o-rate (kŏ-rŏb'ō-rāt), *v.t.* to confirm; to make certain; as, he was asked to *corroborate* the news of the wreck; strengthen; establish; verify.—*n.* **corroboration.**

cor-rob-o-ra-tive (kŏ-rŏb'ō-rȧ-tĭv), *adj.* tending to prove, strengthen, verify, or make sure; confirmatory. Also, **corroboratory, corroborating.**—*adv.* **corroboratively.**

cor-rode (kŏ-rōd'), *v.t.* to eat away gradually, as by chemical action; consume; disintegrate; rust; as, water will *corrode* iron.

cor-ro-sion (kŏ-rō'zhŭn), *n.* the act of eating or gnawing away; a condition produced by the gradual eating or wearing away of some substance; as, a tin roof is painted to prevent *corrosion* or rust.

cor-ro-sive (kŏ-rō'sĭv), *adj.* having the power of gradually eating away, as by chemical action: *n.* that which eats away or destroys tissue, as an acid: **corrosive sublimate**, mercuric chloride, a white crystalline poisonous compound.—*adv.* **corrosively.**

cor-ru-gate (kŏr'ŏŏ-gāt), *v.t.* to draw or shape into wrinkles or folds, or alternate ridges and grooves; as, time will *corrugate*, or wrinkle, the face: **corrugated iron**, sheet iron pressed into parallel ridges and grooves.

cor-ru-ga-tion (kŏr'ŏŏ-gā'shŭn), *n.* the act of shaping into folds, or parallel ridges and grooves; a fold or wrinkle.

cor-rupt (kŏ-rŭpt'), *v.t.* to injure; spoil; make impure; bribe; to debase; to pervert: *v.i.* to rot; to become bad: *adj.* depraved; putrid; spoiled; abounding in errors; open to bribery.—*adv.* **corruptly.**

cor-rupt-i-ble (kŏ-rŭp'tĭ-bl), *adj.* capable of being changed for the worse; subject to decay; capable of being bribed.—*n.* **corruptibleness, corruptibility.**

cor-rup-tion (kŏ-rŭp'shŭn), *n.* the act of changing for the worse: applied to loss of purity or honor, or to physical destruction by means of decay; the state of being changed for the worse; decay; putrid matter; impurity; depravity.

cor-sage (kôr'sāj; kôr'sȧzh'), *n.* the bodice or waist of a woman's dress. [Fr.]

cor-sair (kôr'sâr), *n.* one who sails on the seas in search of booty; a pirate; a pirate's armed vessel.

corse (kôrs), *n.* a dead body: used in poetry for *corpse.*

corse-let (kôrs'lĕt), *n.* in former times, the complete armor for the body of a soldier; sometimes, just the breastplate. Also, **corslet.**

cor-set (kôr'sĕt), *n.* a close-fitting bodice, worn to support or give shape to the figure; stays: *v.t.* to inclose in stays.

Cor-si-can (kôr'sĭ-kăn), *adj.* pertaining to the island of Corsica or its people.

cor-tège (kôr'tĕzh), *n.* a train of attendants; retinue; procession; as, the Spanish king was followed by a *cortège* of nobles and soldiers. [Fr.]

Cor-tes (kôr-tĕz), *n.pl.* the governing body, or parliament, of Spain and Portugal.

cor-tex (kôr'tĕks), *n.* the bark or rind; the outer layer of gray matter of the brain.

co-run-dum (kō-rŭn'dŭm), *n.* an extremely hard mineral used for polishing: it has several colored varieties used as gems, such as the sapphire, the Oriental ruby, etc.: its granular variety is emery.

cor-us-cate (kŏr'ŭs-kāt), *v.i.* to sparkle; flash; gleam, like lightning or fireflies.

cor-us-ca-tion (kŏr'ŭs-kā'shŭn), *n.* a sudden flash or play of light; as, the *coruscation* of the lightning dazzled the eyes.

cor-vette (kôr-vĕt'), *n.* a wooden ship of war. Also, **corvet.**

co-se-cant (kō-sē'kănt), *n.* one of the trigonometric functions; in a right-angled triangle, the ratio of the hypotenuse to the side opposite an acute angle.

co-sey (kō'zĭ), *adj.* snug; comfortable; settled contentedly. Also, **cosy, cozy.** —*adv.* **cosily.**

co-sine (kō'sīn), *n.* one of the trigonometric functions; in a right-angled triangle, the ratio of the side adjacent to an acute angle, to the hypotenuse.

cos-met-ic (kŏz-mĕt'ĭk), *n.* a grease, paint, or wash used to make the face or hair beautiful: *adj.* beautifying.

cos-mic (kŏz'mĭk), *adj.* pertaining to the universe and the laws which govern it; hence, orderly, as opposed to *chaotic*; in astronomy, rising or setting with the sun, as a star. Also, **cosmical.**

cos-mism (kŏz'mĭzm), *n.* a theory of the universe or cosmos.

cos-mog-o-ny (kŏz-mŏg'ō-nĭ), *n.* a theory or an account of the world's origin and growth.

cos-mo-pol-i-tan (kŏz'mō-pŏl'ĭ-tăn), *n.* a citizen of the world; as, a man who travels all over the world is a *cosmopolitan;* one free from local prejudices: *adj.* at home in any part of the world; of plants, distributed all over the world; free from local prejudices.

cos-mop-o-lite (kŏz-mŏp'ō-līt), *adj.* world-wide: *n.* one at home in all parts of the world; a cosmopolitan.

cos-mos (kŏz'mŏs), *n.* order, harmony; the system of law and order in the universe: opposite to *chaos.*

Cos-sack (kŏs'ăk), *n.* one of a warlike tribe of southern Russia, skilled as horsemen.

cos-set (kŏs'ĕt), *n.* a pet lamb; a pet of any kind: *v.t.* to fondle; pet.

cost (kŏst; kôst), *v.t.* to require in exchange for; to be the price of; as, the diamond *cost* a great deal of money; to cause to bear or suffer; as, the attempt *cost* him much trouble; to require to be expended for: *n.* charge, expense, labor; as, the labor was done at great *cost: pl.* the expenses of a lawsuit.—*adj.* **costly.**—*n.* **costliness.**

cos-tal (kŏs'tăl), *adj.* pertaining to, or situated near, a rib or ribs.

cos-ter-mon-ger (kŏs'tẽr-mŭn'gẽr), *n.* a peddler of fruit, vegetables, fish, etc.

cos-tive (kŏs'tĭv), *adj.* constipated, or likely to cause constipation.

cos-tume (kŏs'tūm), *n.* dress in general; style of dress; a walking or tailor-made dress for a woman; the dress of a given time, period, class, etc.: *v.t.* (kŏs-tūm'), to dress in, or provide with, appropriate garments; as, to *costume* the actors in a play.—*n.* **costumer.**

co-sy (kō'zĭ), *adj.* comfortably settled; contented; snug. Also, **cosey, cozy.**—*adv.* **cosily.**

cot (kŏt), *n.* a cottage; a hut; a cover, as for a hurt finger; small bed, usually made of canvas.

co-tan-gent (kō-tăn'jĕnt), *n.* one of the trigonometric functions; in a right-angled triangle, the ratio between the side adjacent and the side opposite to an acute angle.

cote (kōt), *n.* a hut; a sheepfold; as, the sheep are penned in the *cote* at night.

co-tem-po-ra-ry (kō-tĕm'pō-rā-rĭ), *n.* one living at the same time as another.

co-te-rie (kō'tē-rĭ), *n.* an association or set of persons who meet for social or other intercourse; a clique; as, a musical club is a *coterie* of musicians.

co-til-lion (kō-tĭl'yŭn), *n.* a brisk, lively dance for eight or more persons, in which favors are given to the dancers: called also the *german;* music for such a dance. Also, **cotillon.**

cot-tage (kŏt'āj), *n.* a small dwelling; any house at a summer resort.—*n.* **cottager.**

cot-ter (kŏt'ẽr), *n.* one who dwells in a cottage; one who lives rent free on a common. Also, **cottar, cottier.**

cot-ton (kŏt'n), *n.* a white, soft, downy substance, resembling wool and inclosing the seeds of the cotton-plant; the annual crop of that substance; thread or cloth made of cotton; as, a spool of *cotton* contains 200 yards: *adj.* pertaining to, or made of, cotton: *v.i.* colloquially, to fit or go well together; be very intimate: often with *with.*—*adj.* **cottony.**

cot-ton bat-ting (kŏt'n băt'ĭng), cotton prepared in rolls for quilting, padding, etc.

cot-ton gin (kŏt'n jĭn), a machine for separating the seeds from cotton: invented by Eli Whitney in 1792.

cot-ton-tail (kŏt'n-tāl'), *n.* the common American rabbit.

cot-ton-wood (kŏt'n-wŏŏd'), *n.* any of several American species of poplar, having fluffy, cottony tuft about the seeds.

cot-y-le-don (kŏt'ĭ-lē'dŭn), *n.* the seed leaf of a plant; the first leaf.—*adj.* **cotyledonal, cotyledonous.**

couch (kouch), *v.t.* to lay upon a bed or other resting-place; to put into words; as, to *couch* a letter in strong words; to lower, as a lance or spear for attack; to remove, as a cataract from the eye: *v.i.* to lie down; stoop; to hide: *n.* a bed; sofa; any place for resting.

couch-ant (kouch'ănt), *adj.* in heraldry, crouching or lying down: as, the *couchant* lion.

cough (kôf), *v.i.* to expel air from the lungs by a violent effort: *v.t.* to expel from the lungs: followed by *up: n.* an effort of the lungs, attended with noise, to expel irritating or foreign matter; a disease which makes one cough.

could (kŏŏd), past tense of the verb *can:* used as an auxiliary.

cou-lomb (kōō-lŏm'), *n.* the practical unit for measuring quantity of electric current.

coun-cil (koun'sĭl), *n.* an assembly of persons met in consultation, or to give advice; a municipal body; as, the common *council* is a body of men elected to govern a city.

coun-cil-man (koun'sĭl-măn), *n.* [*pl.* councilmen (-mĕn)], a member of the council, or governing body, of a borough, town, or city.

coun-cil-or (koun'sĭ-lẽr), *n.* a member of a common council.

coun-sel (koun'sĕl), *n.* interchange of opinion; advice; consultation; as, a family *counsel* was called to discuss the will; opinion or purpose as the result of consultation; a barrister or lawyer: *v.t.* [*p.t.* and *p.p.* counseled, *p.pr.* counseling], to give advice to; advise.

coun-se-lor (koun'sĕ-lẽr), *n.* one who gives advice, especially legal advice; a lawyer.

count (kount), *n.* a title of nobility in France, Spain, and Italy.

count (kount), *v.t.* to number, as one, two, three, etc.; to sum up; enumerate; esteem; as, he *counts* himself rich: *v.i.* to tell off articles or numbers; rely: with *on* or *upon;* to be of value; in law, to plead: with *on;* to mark time: *n.* the act of numbering or reckoning; the total ascertained; a separate and distinct charge in a law case; rhythm.

coun-te-nance (koun'tē-năns), *n.* the face; the expression; appearance; support: *v.t.* to support; encourage; favor; as, the nations cannot *countenance* the breaking of solemn treaties.

coun-ter (koun'tẽr), *n.* one who, or that which, reckons or serves to keep an account; as, a *counter* of metal or wood is used in many games to keep the score; a shop table; as, the *counter* in a store; a blow given in trying to ward off a blow; the leather that strengthens the heel of a shoe: *v.i.* in boxing, to give a return blow while trying to escape a blow: *adv.* contrary; adverse; in an opposite direction; in the wrong way; as, to go *counter* to advice: *prefix*, contrary; opposite; as, *counter*-evidence, evidence opposing other evidence; *counter*-balance, to weigh or act against with equal force.

coun-ter-act (koun'tẽr-ăkt'), *v.t.* to act in opposition to so as to defeat or hinder; neutralize; to bring to nothing.—*adj.* **counteractive.**—*n.* **counteraction.**

coun-ter-bal-ance (koun'tẽr-băl'ăns), *n.* equal weight or power; a force equal to another: *v.t.* to oppose by an equal power; as, the general called for more troops to *counterbalance* those of the enemy.

coun-ter-claim (koun'tẽr-klām), *n.* an opposing claim or demand.

coun-ter-feit (koun'tẽr-fĭt), *v.t.* to copy for a dishonest purpose; to imitate with intent to deceive or defraud; as, to *counterfeit* money; forge: *v.i.* to carry on deception: *adj.* feigned; spurious; forged: *n.* an imitation made with intent to deceive; a forgery.—*n.* **counterfeiter.**

coun-ter-feit-ing (koun'tẽr-fĭt'ĭng), *n.* the crime of making false coins or bank notes.

coun-ter-ir-ri-tant (koun'tẽr-ĭr'ĭ-tănt), *n.* a medicine to excite irritation in one place with the purpose of relieving irritation in another.

coun-ter-mand (koun'tẽr-månd'), *v.t.* to change (an order or command): contradict the orders of; to revoke (an order): *n.* a contrary order or command; as, the general's message was a *countermand* of the order to march forward.

coun-ter-march (koun'tẽr-märch'), *v.t.* and *v.i.* to march back; as, after the drill the men were ordered to *countermarch* to the armory: *n.* a return march or change of front; a reversal.

coun-ter-mine (koun'tẽr-mīn'), *n.* in military usage, an underground passageway made to intercept and destroy similar works of the enemy; hence, any means by which an opponent's plans are defeated: *v.t.* and *v.i.* to excavate a passageway in order to meet and destroy (similar works of the enemy); hence, to defeat or baffle by secret means.

coun-ter-of-fen-sive (koun'tẽr-ŏ-fĕn'sĭv), *n.* aggressive methods or operation against an enemy who has previously adopted similar tactics.

coun-ter-pane (koun'tẽr-pān'), *n.* a bedspread, especially when woven of cotton and having raised figures.

coun-ter-part (koun'tẽr-pärt'), *n.* a duplicate; a person exactly like some one else; as, each twin was the *counterpart* of the other.

coun-ter-point (koun'tẽr-point'), *n.* in music, the science of harmony; a melody, in itself melodious, added to another melody as an accompaniment.

coun-ter-poise (koun'tẽr-poiz'), *n.* a counterbalance; an equal opposing force or power: *v.t.* to weigh (one thing) against another.

coun-ter-sign (koun'tẽr-sīn'), *v.t.* to confirm by signing a document already signed by another: *n.* an additional signature to a document to make it of value; a private word or phrase; a signal, given to soldiers on guard; a military watchword; as, no one can enter the fort without knowing the *countersign*.

coun-ter-sink (koun'tẽr-sĭnk'), *v.t.* to drill (a conelike depression) to receive a screw or bolt; to drive or sink (a screw or bolt) into such a depression, so that the head is level with the surface.

coun-tess (koun'tĕs), *n.* the wife or widow of an earl or count.

count-ing (koun'tĭng), *p.adj.* reckoning; adding up.

count-ing-house (koun'tĭng-hous'), *n.* the room in a place of business where accounts are kept and bookkeeping is done. Also, **countingroom.**

count-less (kount'lĕs), *adj.* incapable of being reckoned up or counted: innumerable.

coun-tri-fied (kŭn'trĭ-fīd), *adj.* having rustic manners or aspect as opposed to city ideas and manners.

coun-try (kŭn'trĭ), *n.* [*pl.* countries (-trĭz)], a tract of land; region; rural parts; as, "God made the *country* and man made the town"; one's native land; as, we are all ready to defend our *country*: *adj.* rural, rustic, unpolished.

coun-try-dance (kŭn'trĭ-dăns'), *n.* a dance in which some of the couples dance between opposite lines made by others.

coun-try-man (kŭn'trĭ-măn), *n.* [*pl.* countrymen (-mĕn), *fem.* countrywoman], one who lives in the rural regions; one who lives in the same country as another.

coun-try-side (kŭn'trĭ-sīd'), *n.* a section of the country, or the people living there.

coun-ty (koun'tĭ), *n.* [*pl.* counties (-tĭz)], a definite district of a country separated from the rest for political purposes; its inhabitants: *adj.* pertaining to, or referring to, such a district.

coup (kōō), *n.* a stroke or blow; hence, figuratively, a master stroke of stratagem, coming with sudden force. [Fr.]

cou-pé (kōō'-pā'), *n.* the front compartment of a French stage-coach or of a European first-class railway carriage; a close four-wheeled carriage. [Fr.]

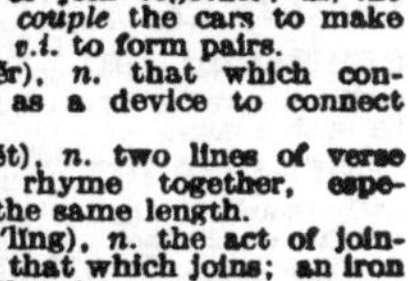

Coupé

cou-ple (kŭp'l), *n.* two of the same kind connected together; a pair; a brace; man and wife; a betrothed man and woman; partners at a dance: *v.t.* to link or join together; as, the brakeman has to *couple* the cars to make up a train; unite: *v.i.* to form pairs.

cou-pler (kŭp'lẽr), *n.* that which connects, as a device to connect cars.

cou-plet (kŭp'lĕt), *n.* two lines of verse which rhyme together, especially two lines of the same length.

cou-pling (kŭp'lĭng), *n.* the act of joining; that which joins; an iron link uniting two railroad cars.

cou-pon (kōō'pŏn), *n.* part of a printed ticket which can be detached or pulled off, such as a ticket for the theater, proving the holder's right to his seat; a certificate having a section which is intended to be cut off and presented for the payment of dividends when due.

cour-age (kûr'āj), *n.* bravery; boldness; fearlessness; valor.

cou-ra-geous (kŭ-rā'jŭs), *adj.* brave; bold; fearless.—*adv.* **courageously.**—*n.* **courageousness.**

cou-ri-er (kōō'rĭ-ẽr; kōōr'ĭ-ẽr), *n.* an express messenger; a traveling attendant who makes arrangements at hotels, buys railroad tickets, and looks after all the details of traveling; a government messenger.

course (kōrs), *n.* a race; a path or track; progress; career; direction or line of motion; the portion of a meal served at one time; conduct; behavior; the direction in which a ship is steered; a series of acts arranged in order or at stated periods; as, a *course* of nursing or a *course* of lectures: *v.t.* to pursue with dogs; to cause to run; to run through or over: *v.i.* to move swiftly; pursue game with dogs.

cours-er (kōr'sẽr), *n.* a swift and spirited horse; a war horse: used mostly in poetry; as, Merlin rode on a great gray *courser*.

cours-ing (kōrs'ĭng), *p.pr.* of *course*, running through or over; as, the blood *coursing* through the veins: *n.* the sport of hunting hares or rabbits with greyhounds.

court (kōrt), *n.* an inclosed space, or a space for playing games; a small paved place surrounded by houses; a royal palace; a prince or king with his retinue and ministers considered as a political body; a hall of justice; the place where prisoners are tried; as, the prisoner was brought into *court;* the judges engaged there; the judge hearing a case; as, the *court* sustained the objection; the session of a judicial assembly; address; flattery: *v.t.* to pay attention to, as a lover; woo; flatter; solicit: *v.i.* to make love.

cour-te-ous (kûr'tē-ŭs; kōrt'yŭs), *adj.* courtly; affable; polite.—*adv.* **courteously.**—*n.* **courteousness.**

cour-te-sy (kûr'tē-sĭ; kōr'tē-sĭ), *n.* [*pl.* courtesies (-sĭz)], politeness combined with kindness; an act of civility and respect; favor.

courte-sy (kûrt'sĭ), *n.* a gesture of greeting or respect made by women by bending the knees, dropping the body gracefully and then rapidly raising it: *v.i.* to make such a gesture. Also, **curtsey, curtsy.**

court-house (kōrt'hous"), *n.* a public building where justice is administered by those legally qualified.

court-ier (kōrt'yẽr), *n.* one who attends the court of a prince; one who solicits favor; a flatterer.

court-ly (kōrt'lĭ), *adj.* refined; elegant: said of manners.—*n.* **courtliness.**

court-mar-tial (kōrt"mär'shăl), *n.* [*pl.* courts-martial], a military or naval court of justice: *v.t.* to try by such a court.

court-plas-ter (kōrt'plȧs"tẽr), *n.* a kind of sticking plaster, originally used by ladies at court as beauty patches on the face.

court-ship (kōrt'shĭp), *n.* the act of wooing.

court-yard (kōrt'yärd"), *n.* an inclosed space adjoining a house.

cous-in (kŭz'n), *n.* the son or daughter of an uncle or aunt; a distant relative.—*adj.* **cousinly.**

cove (kōv), *n.* a small sheltered inlet or creek; a retired nook; a hollow molding.

cov-e-nant (kŭv'ē-nănt), *n.* a written agreement; deed; bargain; a solemn agreement of fellowship and faith between members of a church: *v.i.* to enter into a formal agreement; bind oneself by contract.

cov-e-nant-er (kŭv'ē-năn-tẽr), *n.* one who enters into an agreement.

Cov-en-try (kŭv-ĕn-trĭ), *n.* a town in Warwickshire, England: **to send to Coventry,** to banish or exclude from social intercourse.

cov-er (kŭv'ẽr), *v.t.* to put something over; to conceal; to overspread, as the top of anything; to sit upon or incubate, as a hen her eggs; to overrun; extend thickly over an area; to include or be sufficient for; to pass over, as a space or distance; shelter; clothe: *v.i.* put on a hat or headdress: *n.* that which is laid on something else; a protection; as, he went under the *cover* of an escort of soldiers; a shelter; a covert; thicket, etc., concealing game; the table equipment at a meal, especially for one person.

cov-er-ing (kŭv'ẽr-ĭng), *n.* that which is laid around anything or protects; dress.

cov-er-let (kŭv'ẽr-lĕt), *n.* a bed quilt, especially an outer quilt.

cov-ert (kŭv'ẽrt), *adj.* concealed; covered; disguised; secret; in law, under the authority or protection of her husband: said of a married woman: *n.* a place that protects or shelters; a thicket; shelter for game.

cov-er-ture (kŭv'ẽr-tûr), *n.* a cover; shelter; the legal status or standing of a married woman.

cov-et (kŭv'ĕt), *v.t.* to desire earnestly; to wish, wrongly and eagerly, for (what belongs to another): *v.i.* to have an extreme or unlawful desire for something.

cov-et-ous (kŭv'ē-tŭs), *adj.* very desirous, especially of that which belongs to another; eager, especially for money.—*adv.* **covetously.**—*n.* **covetousness.**

cov-ey (kŭv'ĭ), *n.* a hatch or brood of birds, especially partridges.

cow (kou), *n.* [*pl.* cows (kouz); poetic, kine, (kīn)], the mature female of the ox family of animals domesticated and kept for its milk; the female of various other animals, such as the whale, elephant: *v.t.* to depress with fear; as, to *cow* the spirit by harsh treatment.

cow-ard (kou'ẽrd), *n.* one without courage; a craven; a dastard; a timid person: *adj.* lacking courage; timid; unduly fearful.

cow-ard-ice (kou'ẽr-dĭs), *n.* want of courage; dishonorable fear.
Syn. timidity.
Ant. (see courage).

cow-ard-ly (kou'ẽrd-lĭ), *adj.* timid; dastardly; base; befitting a coward; mean.—*n.* **cowardliness.**

cow-bird (kou'bûrd"), *n.* an American blackbird: so called because often found with cattle.

cowboy (kou'boi"), *n.* a boy who looks after cows; a mounted employee of a stockman or ranchman who looks after the cattle while they graze.

cow-catch-er (kou'kăch'ẽr), *n.* a wedge-shaped iron frame on the front of a locomotive for removing anything that obstructs the train, such as cows on the track.

cow-er (kou'ẽr), *v.i.* to crouch or sink down through fear; tremble: as, many persons *cower* in terror at a flash of lightning.

cow-herd (kou'hûrd"), *n.* one who tends cattle at pasture.

cow-hide (kou'hīd"), *n.* the tanned and dressed skins of cows; a stout flexible whip made of rawhide: *adj.* made of cowhide leather: *v.t.* to whip with a cowhide.

cowl (koul), *n.* a monk's hood; a revolving cover for a chimney pot: *v.t.* to cover or conceal with, or as with, a cowl. —*adj.* **cowled.**

cow-lick (kou'lĭk"), *n.* a tuft of hair turned up or awry on the forehead.

co-work-er (kō"wûr'kẽr), *n.* one who works with another; a fellow worker.

cow-pea (kou'pē"), *n.* a certain plant of the bean family; its edible seed.

cow-pox (kou'pŏks"), *n.* an acute contagious disease of cows, which, when communicated to man, as by vaccination, prevents smallpox.

cow-rie (kou'rĭ), *n.* a kind of shell used as money in Africa and parts of Asia. Also, **cowry.**

cow-slip (kou'slĭp"), *n.* a common name for the primrose.

cox-comb (kŏks'kōm"), *n.* something resembling a cock's comb, formerly worn by licensed jesters; a vain, conceited fellow; a fop.

cox-swain (kŏk'swān; *naut.* kŏk'sn), *n.* the steersman of a boat, especially in a race. Also, **cockswain.**

coy (koi), *adj.* modest; bashful; demure; shy; as, a *coy* little girl.—*adv.* **coyly.** —*n.* **coyness.**

coy-o-te (kī-ō'tē; kī'ōt), *n.* the prairie wolf of North America.

coz-en (kŭz'n), *v.t.* and *v.i.* to cheat in a petty way; deceive; swindle; as, the dishonest man tried to *cozen* his neighbor.

co-zy (kō'zĭ), *adj.* warm and comfortable; snug: *n.* a woolen cover to keep a teapot warm.—*adv.* **cozily.**—*n.* **coziness.** Also, **cosy, cosey.**

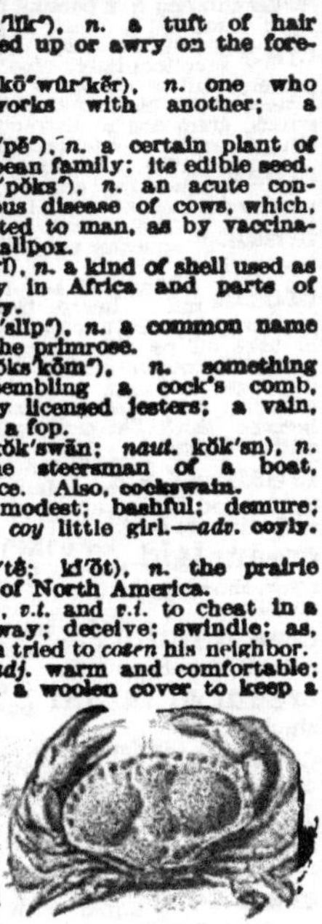

Crab

crab (krăb), *n.* a short-tailed, hard-shelled animal that lives under water; a crab apple; a name of various mechanical devices or machines; colloquially, a sour, cranky person: **Crab,** a sign (Cancer) in the Zodiac.

crab-bed (krăb'ĕd), *adj.* cross; morose; peevish; hard to understand; cramped, as writing.—*adv.* **crabbedly.**—*n.* **crabbedness.**

crack (krăk), *n.* a chink or fissure; a narrow fracture; a sharp sound; as, the *crack* of a whip; colloquially, a sharp blow; a mental or moral defect; an altered tone of voice: *v.t.* to burst, break, or sever; cause to make a sharp snap; tell spiritedly, as a joke; to craze; colloquially, to praise; as, to *crack* up a good cook; injure; open, as a bottle: *v.i* to make a sharp, snapping sound; to split or break: *adj.* colloquially, of superior excellence; as, a *crack* regiment.

crack-brained (krăk'brānd"), *adj.* crazy; weak-minded; queer.

cracked (krăkt), *adj.* having a fracture; split; blemished; ground coarsely; as, *cracked* wheat; imperfect; broken; insane; slang, out of money.

crack-er (krăk'ẽr), *n.* a hard biscuit; a firework; in the southern United States, one of the lower class of rural white people.

crack-le (krăk'l), *v.i.* to make a slight, sharp, explosive noise, frequently repeated; as, the leaves *crackle* underfoot; to crack slightly and repeatedly: *v.t.* to cover, as china, with a delicate network of minute cracks; to break with slight, rapid crushing: *n.* a noise made by frequent and slight cracks and reports, the appearance of the surface glaze on glass or porcelain that has cracked in all directions.

crack-ling (krăk'lĭng), *n.* the giving out of small abrupt reports in quick succession; as, the cheerful *crackling* of a log fire.

crack-nel (krăk'nĕl), *n.* a hard biscuit in some fancy shape.

cracks-man (krăks'măn), *n.* [*pl.* cracks-men (-mĕn)], a burglar. [SLANG.]

cra-dle (krā'dl), *n.* a baby's crib or little bed, often on rockers; infancy; birthplace or origin; as, the *cradle* of liberty; a case for a broken limb; a device for rescuing shipwrecked persons; a frame of timbers placed under a ship for launching it; a steel tool used in engraving; a gold-washing machine; as, in gold-mining, a *cradle* is used to separate the gold from the gravel; a frame of wood, with long teeth, fastened to a scythe, used in harvesting grain; a frame on a wagon, for keeping hay or grain from the wheels: *v.t.* to rock or place in a cradle; nurse or train in infancy; as, *cradled* in luxury; wash in a miner's cradle; mow with a cradle scythe; as, to *cradle* oats.

craft (krȧft), *n.* ability; skill; a trade; cunning; fraud; a small trading vessel; vessels, collectively; manual art; those working at any trade, collectively; guild.

crafts-man (krȧfts'măn), *n.* [*pl.* crafts-men (-mĕn)], a skilled workman; a member of a particular trade.

craft-y (krȧf'tĭ), *adj.* cunning; artful; wily; deceitful.—*adv.* **craftily.**—*n.* **craftiness.**

crag (krăg), *n.* a steep, rugged rock that stands out prominently.

crag-gy (krăg'ĭ), *adj.* rough; rugged; full of broken rocks.

crake (krāk), *n.* a small railbird with a harsh cry.

cram (krăm), *v.t.* [*p.t.* and *p.p.* crammed, *p.pr.* cramming], to stuff; fill to overflowing; colloquially, to put hastily through a course of study, as in preparation for an examination: *v.i.* colloquially, to study hard for an examination; to eat greedily.

cramp (krămp), *n.* a piece of iron bent at the ends, with a tightening screw at one end to hold blocks of wood, stone, etc.; a sharp pain: *v.t.* to affect with muscular spasms; confine; secure with a cramp.

cran-ber-ry (krăn'bĕr-ĭ), *n.* [*pl.* cranberries (-ĭz)], the marsh whortleberry, with red acid berries.

crane (krān), *n.* a large wading bird with very long legs and neck, and a long straight bill: a machine for raising heavy weights; as, the traveling *crane*: *v.t.* and *v.i.* to stretch or bend (the neck) like a crane.

Portable Crane

cra-ni-al (krā'nĭ-ăl), *adj.* of or pertaining to the skull.

cra-ni-ol-o-gy (krā"nĭ-ŏl'ō-jĭ), *n.* the scientific study of skulls and their characteristics.

cra-ni-um (krā'nĭ-ŭm), *n.* [*pl.* craniums (-ŭmz) and crania (-ȧ)], the skull, especially the part inclosing the brain.

crank (krăṅk), *n.* a device for causing an axis or shaft to move; an iron brace; a twist or turn; a fanciful form of speech; whim; fancy; colloquially, a person who has too many whims and fancies, or an impracticable person: *adj.* liable to lurch or upset; opposite to *stiff*; hence, shaky.

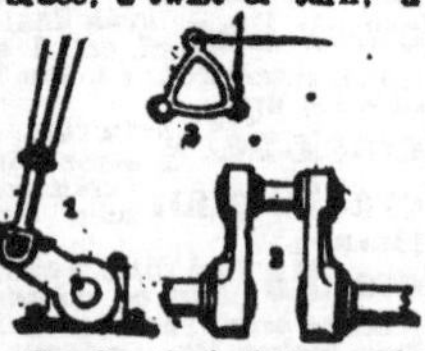

Cranks. 1, single throw; 2, double throw; 3, bell crank.

crank shaft (krăṅk shȧft), a shaft driven by a crank. Also, crankshaft.

crank-y (krăṅk'ĭ), *adj.* full of whims or irritability; liable to be upset; in a shaky or loose condition.—*adv.* crankily.—*n.* crankiness.

cran-nied (krăn'ĭd), *adj.* full of chinks; as, the flower grew in the *crannied* wall.

cran-ny (krăn'ĭ), *n.* [*pl.* crannies (-ĭz)], a crack or chink.

crape (krāp), *n.* a thin black gauze made of raw silk and gummed; as, *crape* is a sign of mourning; a thin, crimped fabric, sometimes silk, sometimes cotton.

crash (krăsh), *v.t.* to dash in pieces noisily; to clash together with violence: *v.i.* to break in pieces with a noise; to make a loud, clattering noise: *n.* a loud, sudden, confused noise; as, the china fell with a *crash;* a coarse, heavy linen fabric.

crass (krăs), *adj.* gross; dense; stupid; as, the mistake was due to *crass* igno ance.—*adv.* crassly.—*n.* crassness.

crate (krāt), *n.* a wickerwork basket for shipping china, glassware, etc.; a case made of wooden slats, used for shipping goods: *v.t.* to pack in a case or basket.

cra-ter (krā'tẽr), *n.* the cup-shaped cavity of a volcano; an ancient goblet; the pit formed by an explosion.

cra-vat (krȧ-văt'), *n.* a necktie or neckcloth usually worn by men.

crave (krāv), *v.t.* to ask for with humility; beg earnestly; long for eagerly: *v.i.* to desire greatly.

cra-ven (krā'vn), *adj.* cowardly; base: *n.* a coward.

crav-ing (krāv'ĭng), *n.* a strong desire or appetite; a yearning.

craw (krô), *n.* a bird's first stomach or crop.

craw-fish (krô'fĭsh), *n.* the common name of a fresh-water lobster-like animal; the spiny lobster. Also, crayfish.

crawl (krôl), *v.i.* to move slowly and with difficulty by drawing the body along the ground; to have the feeling as of live things upon the body; to creep: *n.* the act of creeping or making one's way with difficulty; a pen on the sea-coast for fish, turtles, etc.

cray-on (krā'ŏn), *n.* a kind of chalk; a drawing done with such chalk: *adj.* drawn with chalk: *v.t.* to sketch out, as with a piece of chalk.

craze (krāz), *v.i.* to become demented or insane; open in slight cracks: said of pottery: *v.t.* to produce cracks, as in pottery; render insane: *n.* a passing fashion or infatuation; a mania; a crack in pottery glaze.

cra-zy (krā'zĭ), *adj.* insane; unsound; colloquially, foolishly eager; of pottery, full of cracks or flaws: crazy bone, a place at the back of the elbow, which, when struck, gives one a distracting, nervous, tingling sensation.—*adv.* crazily.—*n.* craziness.

creak (krēk), *v.i.* to make a sharp, harsh, squeaking sound: *v.t.* to cause to make such a sound: *n.* a harsh, grating sound.

creak-y (krēk'ĭ), *adj.* apt to make harsh, squeaky noises; as, *creaky* floors; *creaky* shoes.

cream (krēm), *n.* the rich, oily part of milk; hence, the choicest part of anything; a soft cosmetic: *v.t.* to skim or take off by skimming; remove the best part of; in cooking, to beat together, as shortening, sugar, and eggs, until they form a smooth mixture: *v.i.* to become covered with cream; become thick like cream; to froth; to grow stiff or formal.

cream-er-y (krēm'ẽr-ĭ), *n.* [*pl.* creameries (-ĭz)], a place where butter and cheese are made, or where cream and milk are sold.

cream-laid (krēm'lād"), *adj.* denoting a paper of a creamy-white color, showing the lines of the mold impressed on it.

cream nut (krēm nŭt), the Brazil nut; the triangular-shaped seed of a South American tree.

cream of tar-tar (krēm ŏv tär'tȧr), purified tartar or argol.

cream-y (krēm'ĭ), *adj.* containing, or like, cream; smooth; luscious.

crease (krēs), *n.* a mark made by folding or doubling anything; a line drawn to define the limits of bowler and batsman: *v.t.* to make a wrinkle or mark in: *v.i.* to become wrinkled.

cre-a-sote (krē'ȧ-sōt), *n.* a heavy oily liquid with a smoky smell, obtained from wood-tar: used as an antiseptic. Also, creosote.

cre-ate (krē-āt'), *v.t.* to cause to come into existence; form out of nothing; invest with a new rank, office, or function; to originate.

cre-a-tion (krē-ā'shŭn), *n.* the act of making, forming, or originating; the thing made, formed, or originated; the universe.

cre-a-tive (krē-ā'tĭv), *adj.* constructive; productive; as, a *creative* mind; *creative* power.

cre-a-tor (krē-ā'tẽr), *n.* one who makes, brings into existence, or originates: Creator, the Supreme Being; God.

crea-ture (krē'tūr), *n.* a created living being; one dependent on the influence of another.

cre-dence (krē'dĕns), *n.* belief; credit; trust; as, it was difficult to give *credence* to the report.

cre-den-tial (krē-dĕn'shăl), *n.pl.* letters or certificates given to a person to show he has a right to confidence or to the exercise of authority.

cred-i-bil-i-ty (krĕd'ĭ-bĭl'ĭ-tĭ), *n.* the quality of being credible, or believable; trustworthiness, as of records.

cred-i-ble (krĕd'ĭ-bl), *adj.* believable; not impossible or absurd; as, a *credible* story.—*adv.* **credibly.**

cred-it (krĕd'ĭt), *v.t.* to believe; trust; have confidence in; enter on the credit side of an account; to ascribe: *n.* belief; honor; trust placed in one; that which adds to one's reputation; sale on trust; time allowed for payment of goods sold; financial standing; value received: opposite to *debit.*

cred-it-a-ble (krĕd'ĭt-*ȧ*-bl), *adj.* praiseworthy; deserving esteem.—*adv.* **creditably.**

cred-it-or (krĕd'ĭ-tẽr), *n.* one to whom another is indebted for money or goods: opposite to *debtor.*

cre-do (krē'dō), *n.* [*pl.* credos (-dōz)], a creed; in particular, the Apostles' Creed, in church service; the musical setting for it. [Lat.]

cre-du-li-ty (krē-dū'lĭ-tĭ), *n.* ready belief; especially, an inclination to believe on insufficient evidence.

cred-u-lous (krĕd'ū-lŭs), *adj.* apt to believe on slight evidence; easily imposed upon.—*adv.* **credulously.**

creed (krēd), *n.* a brief, authoritative statement of religious belief; belief in any matter.

creek (krēk), *n.* a small bay or cove; a small stream, between a brook and a river in size.—**Creek,** one of a tribe of American Indians, originally inhabiting the region between the Mobile and Savannah Rivers, in Alabama and Georgia: now in Oklahoma.

creel (krēl), *n.* a wicker fishing basket; a wickerwork cage: *v.t.* to put in a wicker basket; catch.

creep (krēp), *v.i.* [*p.t.* and *p.p.* crept, *p.pr.* creeping], to move slowly along the ground, as a worm or reptile; crawl; to have the feeling as of touching crawling things; grow along the ground, as a plant; move secretly or stealthily; fawn: *n.* the act of crawling along the ground; the sensation of being covered with crawling things: often colloquially in plural.

creep-er (krēp'ẽr), *n.* one who, or that which, moves slowly, close to or touching the ground; a plant which clings by rootlets or tendrils to some support; as, the English ivy is an evergreen *creeper;* the name of certain birds; a wingless insect.

creep-y (krēp'ĭ), *adj.* shivering; chilled with fear; as, a *creepy* feeling.—*n.* **creepiness.**

creese (krēs), *n.* a short dagger with a waved blade used by Malayans. Also, **cris.**

cre-mate (krē-māt'), *v.t.* to reduce to ashes by heat, especially dead bodies.—*n.* **cremator.**

cre-ma-tion (krē-mā'shŭn), *n.* the act of burning to ashes, especially a corpse.

crem-a-to-ry (krĕm'*ȧ*-tō-rĭ; krē'm*ȧ*-tō-rĭ), *adj.* pertaining to cremation: *n.* [*pl.* crematories (-rĭz)], a furnace or an establishment for burning dead bodies. Also, **crematorium.**

Cre-mo-na (krē-mō'n*ȧ*), *n.* a violin of unmatched excellence, formerly made at Cremona, Italy.

cren-el-lat-ed (krĕn'ĕl-āt"ĕd), *adj.* decorated with indented moldings or scalloped with notches.

Cre-ole (krē'ōl), *n.* a native of Spanish America or the West Indies, descended from European (originally Spanish) ancestors: *adj.* pertaining to a Creole. Also, **creole.**

cre-o-sol (krē'ō-sōl), *n.* an oily liquid resembling phenol or carbolic acid.

cre-o-sote (krē'ō-sōt), *n.* a heavy oily liquid with a smoky smell, obtained from wood-tar: used as an antiseptic: *v.t.* to fill or saturate with this liquid. Also, **creasote.**

crêpe (krāp), *n.* a soft silk fabric, closely woven and wavy in appearance; crêpe de Chine; crape. [Fr.]

crep-i-tate (krĕp'ĭ'tāt), *v.i.* to crackle; to make a succession of snapping sounds.—*n.* **crepitation.**

crept (krĕpt), past tense and past participle of the intransitive verb *creep.*

cre-scen-do (krē-shĕn'dō; krē-sĕn'dō), *n.* a gradual increase in force of a musical sound; as, the music ended with a loud *crescendo: adj.* slowly growing in force or loudness.

cres-cent (krĕs'ĕnt), *adj.* growing; shaped like the new moon: *n.* an increasing or new moon; a figure like a new moon; the national emblem of Turkey.

Crescent

cress (krĕs), *n.* any of numerous small green plants growing near a stream, such as watercress; the plants have a biting taste, and are used for salads.

cres-set (krĕs'ĕt), *n.* a vessel for holding burning oil, etc., for lighting.

crest (krĕst), *n.* a plume of feathers on the head of a bird; a helmet; the ridge of a wave; the summit of a hill, or ridge; a heraldic device, usually worn above the shield: *v.t.* to furnish with, or serve as, a crest; to crown: *v.i.* to take the form of a crest or ridge.

crest-fal-len (krĕst'fôl"n), *adj.* dejected; disappointed; dispirited; cast down.

cre-ta-ceous (krē-tā'shŭs), *adj.* containing, or like, chalk; chalky.

Cre-tan (krē'tăn), *adj.* of or pertaining to Crete, an island in the eastern Mediterranean: *n.* an inhabitant of Crete.

cre-tonne (krē-tŏn'; krē'tŏn), *n.* an unglazed cotton fabric printed on one side and used for covering chairs, etc.

cre-vasse (krĕ-văs'), *n.* a deep crack or fissure in glacier ice; a breach in a levee or embankment of a river.

crev-ice (krĕv'ĭs), *n.* a crack; fissure; as, a *crevice* in a wall; a *crevice* in rocks.

crew (krōō), *n.* any band or company of armed men; a ship or boat's company; as, the captain and the sailors form the *crew* of a ship; a group or gang doing the same work; as, a train *crew.*

crew-el (krōō'ĕl), *n.* loosely twisted worsted yarn used in fancy work.

crib (krĭb), *n.* a rack or manger; a stall for horses or cattle; a child's bed; a small cottage; a petty theft; especially, in school slang, an illegitimate aid, as a key or a translation, used by a student: *v.t.* [*p.t.* and *p.p.* cribbed, *p.pr.* cribbing], to confine; steal: *v.i.* in school slang, to make notes for dishonest use in an examination, or otherwise improperly to use keys or translations.

crib-bage (krĭb'āj), *n.* a card game played by two or more persons: **cribbage board**, a board with holes and pegs, used in the game of cribbage for scoring.

crick (krĭk), *n.* a painful stiffness of the muscles of the neck or back.

crick-et (krĭk'ĕt), *n.* a famous English game played with wickets, bats, and a ball, by eleven players on each side; a chirping insect; a low stool.

cri-er (krī'ẽr), *n.* one who cries or proclaims an announcement.

crime (krīm), *n.* the breaking of the law; an offense against morality or the public welfare; wrongdoing; as, stealing is a *crime*.
Syn. sin, vice, misdemeanor.
Ant. (see virtue).

crim-i-nal (krĭm'ĭ-năl), *n.* one guilty of an offense against the law: *adj.* pertaining to, or guilty of, a grave offense against the law.—*adv.* **criminally.**
Syn., *n.* convict, culprit, felon, malefactor.

crim-i-nal-i-ty (krĭm'ĭ-năl'ĭ-tĭ), *n.* the fact of being guilty of a serious offense against the law; guilt.

crim-i-nate (krĭm'ĭ-nāt), *v.t.* to accuse or declare guilty of crime; involve in a crime.—*n.* **crimination.**

crim-i-nol-o-gy (krĭm'ĭ-nŏl'ō-jĭ), *n.* the science of investigating and studying crime and criminals.

crimp (krĭmp), *v.t.* to bend or twist; to cause to pucker or wrinkle; to curl; as, to *crimp* the hair; decoy for enlistment: *n.* the act of curling or twisting; formerly, one who entrapped men for the English navy or army, or the merchant service.—*n.* **crimper.**

crimp-y (krĭm'pĭ), *adj.* having a wrinkled or plaited appearance; frizzly.

crim-ple (krĭm'pl), *n.* a wrinkle; rumple: *v.t.* to cause to wrinkle.

crim-son (krĭm'zn), *n.* a deep red color somewhat like purple: *adj.* deep-red; bloody: *v.t.* to dye with this color: *v.i.* to blush.

cringe (krĭnj), *v.i.* to bend or crouch from fear or with servility: *n.* a servile bow.

crin-gle (krĭn'gl), *n.* an eye, loop, or ring, in a sail, or on the side of a rope.

crin-kle (krĭn'kl), *n.* a wrinkle; bend: *v.t.* to wrinkle: *v.i.* to become corrugated or crimped; to rustle.—*adj.* **crinkly.**

crin-o-line (krĭn'ō-lĭn), *n.* a hoop-skirt; a stiff fabric for stiffening a garment.

crip-ple (krĭp'l), *n.* one who is lame or maimed: *v.t.* to deprive of the use of a limb; disable.

crip-pling (krĭp'lĭng), *n.* spars or timber used to support the sides of a building.

cris (krēs), *n.* a short dagger with a waved blade used by Malayans. Also, **creese.**

cri-sis (krī'sĭs), *n.* [*pl.* crises (-sēz)], a turning point; as, a *crisis* in history; a critical turn in the course of a disease; emergency; time of danger or difficulty.

crisp (krĭsp), *adj.* wavy; curled; brittle; cheerful; terse; sparkling: *v.t.* to curl; ripple; to make brittle: *v.i.* to form into little curls along an edge; to become brittle.—*adv.* **crisply.**—*n.* **crispness.**

cris-pin (krĭs'pĭn), *n.* a shoemaker: in allusion to St. Crispin, the patron saint of shoemakers: October 25 is St. Crispin's Day.

criss-cross (krĭs'krŏs'), *adj.* crossing in different directions, as lines: *adv.* in such a way as to cross something else: *n.* tit-tat-to, a child's game played on crossed lines.

cri-te-ri-on (krī-tē'rĭ-ŭn), *n.* [*pl.* criteria (-ȧ)], a standard, law, or rule by which a correct judgment can be formed; measure; test.

crit-ic (krĭt'ĭk), *n.* one skilled in judging things; as, a musical *critic*; one who judges harshly.

crit-i-cal (krĭt'ĭ-kăl), *adj.* inclined to find fault; as, a *critical* person always finds something wrong; nicely exact; skilled in careful judgment, particularly of literary works, etc.; pertaining to the turning point of a disease; decisive; crucial.—*adv.* **critically.**

crit-i-cism (krĭt'ĭ-sĭzm), *n.* the art of judging and defining the merits of a literary or artistic work; as, the author finds honest *criticism* very helpful; censure.

crit-i-cize (krĭt'ĭ-sīz), *v.t.* to examine or judge as a critic; censure; as, to *criticise* others is a bad habit: *v.i.* to review; to act as a judge. Also, **criticise.**

cri-tique (krĭ-tēk'), *n.* a careful analysis of a literary or artistic production; criticism; review.

croak (krōk), *v.i.* to make a sound like a raven, etc.; grumble: *n.* the low, hoarse sound of the raven or frog.—*n.* **croaker.**

Cro-a-tian (krō-ā'shăn), *adj.* of or pertaining to Croatia, a province of Hungary: *n.* a native of Croatia; the Croatian language. Also, **Croat.**

cro-chet (krō-shā'), *n.* a kind of knitting with a hooked needle, in cotton, wool, etc.: *v.t.* to knit with a hooked needle.

crock (krŏk), *n.* soot, as the soot or smut on a kettle; coloring matter which rubs off from cloth; an earthenware pot or vessel: *v.t.* to blacken with soot; smudge; to give off coloring matter to something else.

crock-er-y (krŏk'ẽr-ĭ), *n.* earthenware of any kind, especially kitchen jars, bowls, etc.

crock-et (krŏk'ĕt), *n.* an ornament or a pointed decoration in ancient architecture on the angles of spires, gables, and canopies; one of the ends of a stag's horns.

Crocodile

croc-o-dile (krŏk'ō-dīl), *n.* a large, lizard-like reptile, with hard square scales on its back and tail.—*adj.* **crocodilian.**

cro-cus (krō'kŭs), *n.* the earliest spring flower, yellow and white in color, from one class of which saffron is obtained; a polishing powder.

croft (krŏft), *n.* a small field near a house; in Scotland, a very small farm.—*n.* **crofter.**

Croix de Guerre (krwä dē gâr), the French war cross, given only for acts of great bravery under fire.

crom-lech (krŏm'lĕk), *n.* an ancient monument of rough stones with one huge flat stone resting across the others.

crone (krōn), *n.* a withered old woman; as, a toothless, wrinkled *crone.*

cro-ny (krō'nĭ), *n.* [*pl.* cronies (-nĭz)], a familiar friend; a chum.

crook (krŏŏk), *n.* a bend; as, a *crook* in the river; a shepherd's hooked staff; a bishop's staff; colloquially, a dishonest person; a swindler: *v.t.* to bend: *v.i.* to curve; to grow crooked.

crook-ed (krŏŏk'ĕd), *adj.* bent; curved; not upright in conduct; dishonest.—*adv.* crookedly.—*n.* crookedness.

crook-neck (krŏŏk'nĕk"), *n.* either of two kinds of squash with curved necks.

croon (krōōn), *v.i.* to utter a hollow continued moan; sing in a soft, plaintive tone: *v.t.* to sing or hum softly: *n.* the sound made by singing softly and plaintively.

crop (krŏp), *n.* the produce of the ground, as corn; harvest; anything likened to the harvest; as, a *crop* of ice; a bird's craw; a stout hunting whip; hair cut close or short: *v.t.* [*p.t.* and *p.p.* cropped, cropt, *p.pr.* cropping], to cut off the top or ends of; reap; mow; to clip the hair of: *v.i.* to appear unexpectedly; to sprout; as, in all gardens the weeds *crop* out.

crop-per (krŏp'ẽr), *n.* one who raises farm crops on shares; a pigeon with a large crop; a pouter; slang, a fall headlong, as from a horse; as, the hunter came a *cropper.*

cro-quet (krō-kā'), *n.* a lawn game played with mallets, balls, and arches.

cro-quette (krō-kĕt'), *n.* a ball of minced meat, fish, or fowl, seasoned, and fried brown.

cro-sier (krō'zhẽr), *n.* the staff of a bishop or abbot, the symbol of his office as a shepherd of God's flock. Also, crozier.

cross (krôs), *n.* a gibbet of wood formed of an upright and a cross piece, used in the punishment of crucifixion: now, the emblem of the Christian faith; a device like a cross; a mark made on a document by those who cannot write; a trial of patience; suffering for Christ's sake: *v.t.* to put, or draw, across; cancel; pass; oppose; obstruct; make the sign of the cross upon: *v.i.* to be athwart; be inconsistent: *adj.* not parallel; fretful; ill-humored; peevish; perverse; as, the *cross* child.—*adv.* crossly.—*n.* crossness.

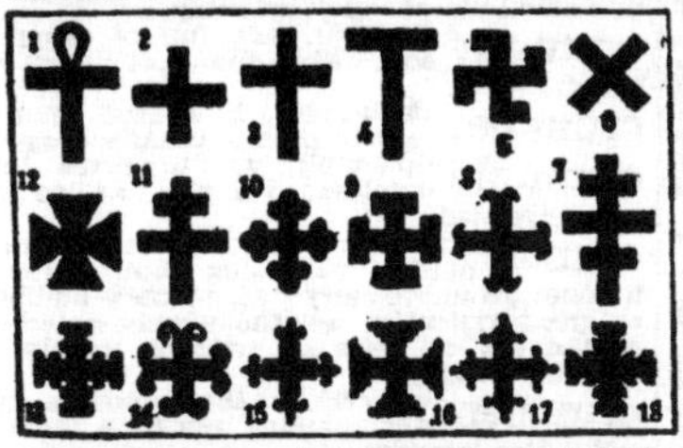

Forms of Crosses. 1, Ansate; 2, Greek; 3, Latin; 4, Tau; 5, Fylfot, Gammadian or Swastika; 6, St. Andrew's; 7, Papal; 8, Anchor; 9, Potent or Jerusalem; 10, Crosslet; 11, Lorraine; 12, Maltese; 13, Indented; 14, Hooped; 15, Flory or fleur de lis; 16, Stepped; 17, Knobbed; 18, Branched.

cross-bar (krôs'bär"), *n.* a bar or line going crosswise or transversely.

cross-bill (krôs'bĭl"), *n.* any of several kinds of finches having mandibles whose points cross each other when the beak is closed.

cross-bones (krôs'bōnz"), *n.pl.* a representation of two bones crossing each other, and usually topped by a skull: a symbol of death.

cross-bow (krôs'bō"), *n.* a shooting weapon, having a bow across the stock.

cross-breed (krôs'brēd"), *n.* the offspring of two animals or plants of different species or races; a hybrid.

cross-bun (krôs'bŭn"), *n.* a bun or small cake marked with a cross, usually eaten on Good Friday.

crosse (krôs), *n.* the racket or bat used in the game of lacrosse; the game itself.

cross-ex-am-i-na-tion (krôs'ĕg-zăm"ĭ-nā'-shŭn), *n.* the questioning of a witness by the opposing counsel; as, the *cross-examination* of a witness is intended to bring out facts which were omitted on his first examination.

cross-grained (krôs'grānd"), *adj.* with an irregular grain or fiber; contrary in temper; as, a *cross-grained* old man.

cross-ing (krôs'ĭng), *n.* a patch across; intersection, as of two streets; opposition.

cross-pol-li-na-tion (krôs'pŏl"ĭ-nā'-shŭn), *n.* the depositing of pollen, the fertilizing substance, from one flower on the stigma of another, as by insects or wind.—*v.t.* cross-pollinate.

cross-pur-pose (krôs'pûr"pŭs), *n.* a contrary or conflicting purpose: more commonly used in the plural; as, they worked at *cross-purposes,* and accomplished nothing: *pl.* a game of questions and answers.

cross-ques-tion (krôs'kwĕs"chŭn), *v.t.* to cross-examine; to question again and again; as, the police were asked to *cross-question* the prisoner.

cross ref-er-ence (krôs'rĕf'ẽr-ĕns), a reference or specific direction from one part of a book or passage to another.

cross-road (krôs'rōd"), *n.* a road that crosses from a main road to another; the place where roads intersect: usually in plural.

cross-tie (krôs'tī), *n.* a log of wood under rails on a railroad, called a railroad sleeper.

cross-trees (krôs'trēz"), *n.pl.* short pieces of timber at the upper ends of the lower and top masts, to support the rigging.

cross-way (krôs'wā"), *n.* one of two or more roads that cross each other; the place of intersection; a road that crosses from a main road to another.—*n.* crossroad.

cross-wise (krôs'wīz"), *adv.* across; in the shape of a cross; as, the church was built *crosswise.*

crotch (krŏch), *n.* a hook or fork; a separation into two branches; as, a *crotch* of a tree.—*adj.* crotched.

crotch-et (krŏch'ĕt), *n.* a quarter-note in music; a bracket; a whim or fancy.—*adj.* crotchety.

cro-ton bug (krō'tŭn bŭg), a small, active, winged cockroach.

cro-ton oil (krō'tŭn oil), a vegetable oil taken from the seeds of the croton plant of tropical countries.

crouch (krouch), *v.i.* to stoop low; cringe; as, to *crouch* behind a wall; to *crouch* in fear.

croup (krōōp), *n.* the portion of a horse's back behind the saddle; a child's disease of the throat which causes coughing and choking; inflammation of the trachea and larynx or windpipe, with a hoarse cough and difficult breathing.—*adj.* **croupy, croupous.**

crou-pi-er (krōō'pĭ-ẽr; krōō'pẽr), *n.* one who collects or pays out the money lost or won at a gaming table.

crow (krō), *v.i.* [*p.t.* and *p.p.* crowed, crew, *p.pr.* crowing], to make a shrill sound like a cock; boast in triumph; utter a cry of pleasure: *n.* the cry of a cock; a general name for black birds: **Crow**, one of a tribe of American Indians, originally inhabiting the region of the Yellowstone River.

crow-bar (krō'bär"), *n.* a long, straight iron lever, flattened at one end.

crowd (kroud), *n.* a number of persons or things collected closely together; as, a large *crowd* at the ball game; the populace, or common people: *v.t.* to press closely together; fill to excess; as, to *crowd* too many people on a boat: *v.i.* to press in numbers.

crow-foot (krō'fŏŏt"), *n.* [*pl.* crowfoots (-fŏŏts)], the buttercup.

crown (kroun), *n.* the ornament a king wears on his head as a sign of his position; sovereignty; the sovereign: with *the*; the top; as, the *crown* of the head; an English silver coin worth five shillings, or $1.20 in United States money; the corona of a flower; something like a crown; as, the *crown* of a hill or tooth; a size of printing paper (15 x 20 in.): *v.t.* to invest with a crown; adorn or dignify; complete; reward.

British Royal Crown

crown glass (kroun glȧs), the finest window glass.

crown-land (kroun'lănd"), *n.* the land belonging to the sovereign; in certain countries, as Bohemia, an administrative division.

crown prince (kroun' prĭns'), the heir apparent to a throne.

crown prin-cess (kroun' prĭn'sĕs), the wife of a crown prince.

crow's-foot (krōz'fŏŏt"), *n.* [*pl.* crow's-feet (-fēt)], one of the wrinkles due to age, at the outer corners of the eyes.

crow's nest (krōz nĕst), a lookout or watch-tower on the maintopmast crosstrees of a vessel.

cru-cial (krōō'shăl), *adj.* having the form of a cross; intersecting; severe; searching; as, the opportunity to steal was a *crucial* test of his honesty.—*adv.* **crucially.**

Crucible

cru-ci-ble (krōō'sĭ-bl), *n.* a melting pot; as, a *crucible* is used for melting metals.

cru-ci-fix (krōō'sĭ-fĭks), *n.* [*pl.* crucifixes (-ĕz)], a cross with the sculptured figure of Christ.

cru-ci-fix-ion (krōō"sĭ-fĭk'shŭn), *n.* the act of crucifying, especially the nailing of Christ upon the cross; as, *crucifixion* was an ancient form of punishment for highway robbers; great mental trial, or suffering.

cru-ci-form (krōō'sĭ-fôrm), *adj.* cross-shaped; as, a *cruciform* church.

cru-ci-fy (krōō'sĭ-fī), *v.t.* [*p.t.* and *p.p.* crucified, *p.pr.* crucifying], to put to death by nailing the hands and feet to a cross; to torture; destroy the power of; subdue.

crude (krōōd), *adj.* being in a raw, unprepared state; in a natural state; as, all metals are *crude* when taken out of the earth; unripe; raw; immature; uncultured; as, *crude* manners; wanting in grace or taste; harsh in color.—*adv.* **crudely.**—*n.* **crudeness.**

cru-di-ty (krōō'dĭ-tĭ), *n.* [*pl.* crudities (-tĭz)], the state or condition of being without maturity, culture, or taste; an instance of this lack.

cru-el (krōō'ĕl), *adj.* disposed to give pain to others; merciless; hard-hearted; fierce; painful; unrelenting.—*adv.* **cruelly.**
Syn. barbarous, brutal, inhuman, savage.
Ant. (see kind).

cru-el-ty (krōō'ĕl-tĭ), *n.* [*pl.* cruelties (-tĭz)], inhumanity; savageness; a savage or inhuman deed.

cru-et (krōō'ĕt), *n.* a small glass vial, especially for vinegar, etc., for the dining table.

cruise (krōōz), *n.* an earthen pot or dish; a small vessel for holding liquids. Also, **cruse.**

cruise (krōōz), *v.i.* to sail to and fro: *n.* a voyage from place to place; as, the millionaire took a long *cruise* in his yacht.

cruis-er (krōōz'ẽr), *n.* one that sails to and fro; a man-of-war inferior in armor and armament to a battleship.

crul-ler (krŭl'ẽr), *n.* a ring-shaped cake, fried brown.

crumb (krŭm), *n.* the soft inner part of bread; a fragment of bread; a little piece: *v.t.* to break into little pieces.

crum-ble (krŭm'bl), *v.t.* to break into crumbs; cause to fall into pieces: *v.i.* to disappear gradually; to fall into small pieces.—*adj.* **crumbly.**

crum-my (krŭm'ĭ), *adj.* full of crumbs; soft, like the soft part of bread.

crum-pet (krŭm'pĕt), *n.* a kind of teacake or muffin, usually toasted.

crum-ple (krŭm'pl), *v.t.* to press into wrinkles; rumple: *v.i.* to become rumpled.

crunch (krŭnch), *v.t.* to crush or grind noisily; as, a dog likes to *crunch* a bone; grind violently: *v.i.* to chew audibly; to grind violently; as, the wheels *crunched*: *n.* the act or noise of grinding noisily or chewing audibly.

crup-per (krŭp'ẽr), *n.* the looped leather band passing under a horse's tail. Also, **crouper.**

cru-sade (krōō-sād'), *n.* a military expedition under the banner of the cross engaged in by one of the Christian powers to recover the Holy Land; as, the first real *crusade* resulted in the capture of

Jerusalem; vigorous concerted action for the defense of some cause, or the advancement of some idea; as, the *crusade* against slavery: *v.i.* to engage in a crusade.—*n.* **crusader.**

cruse (krōōs; krōōz), *n.* an earthen pot or dish; a small vessel for holding liquids, as oil, water, etc.

crush (krŭsh), *v.t.* to press between two opposite bodies; squeeze; break by pressure; as, to *crush* a chair by sitting on it; to *crush* a mineral; bruise; as, to *crush* a limb; ruin; quell; conquer; as, to be *crushed* by despair: *v.i.* to be pressed out of shape or into smaller compass; as, the dresses have *crushed:* *n.* a violent compression or collision; a crowd; colloquially, a social gathering.—*n.* **crusher.**

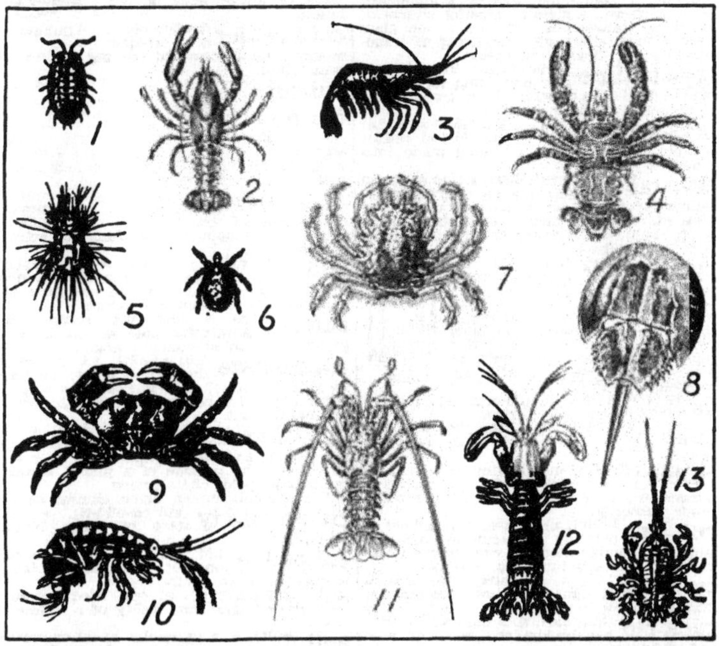

Crustacea and Arachnida. 1, wood louse; 2, crayfish; 3, prawn; 4, plated lobster; 5, cheese mite; 6, harvest bug; 7, spider crab; 8, king crab; 9, land crab; 10, fresh-water shrimp; 11, spiny lobster; 12, mantis shrimp or squilla; 13, porcelain crab.

crust (krŭst), *n.* a hard outside coating or rind; the exterior solid part of the earth's surface; a shell or hard covering: *v.t.* to cover over with a hard covering: *v.i.* to become covered with a hard covering; as, the pond was *crusted* with ice.

Crus-ta-ce-a (krŭs-tā'shē-ȧ), *n.pl.* a class of animals having a crust-like shell, including crabs, lobsters, etc.—*n.* and *adj.* **crustacean.**

crust-y (krŭs'tĭ), *adj.* like a crust; rough in manner; cross; surly; snappish; as, the old sea captain had a *crusty* manner. —*adv.* **crustily.**—*n.* **crustiness.**

crutch (krŭch), *n.* a staff with a crosspiece to fit under the arm, used as a support for cripples; any mechanical device like such a support; the forked rest on a woman's saddle.

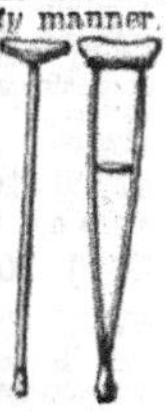

Crutches

cry (krī), *v.i.* [*p.t.* and *p.p.* cried, *p.pr.* crying], to call aloud; to complain loudly; exclaim vehemently; require redress; shed tears: *v.t.* to utter loudly and publicly in giving notice; as, to *cry* the hour of the night; to affect or cause by weeping: *n.* loud or passionate utterance, especially of weeping or lamentation; as, a *cry* of joy, fear, anger, pain, etc.; the *cry* of the wolf; an exclamation of wonder or triumph; outcry; clamor; demand; as, the *cry* for liberty; acclamation; proclamation; as, the peddler's *cry;* common report; the characteristic call of an animal; a fit of weeping; a battle cry; a party catch-word or phrase.

cry-ing (krī'ing), *p.adj.* specially demanding notice; notorious; urgent; as, it is a *crying* shame.

crypt (kript), *n.* an underground cell or vault, usually under a church: sometimes used as a chapel or shrine; as, the *crypt* under a cathedral contains tombs and monuments.

cryp-tic (krip'tik), *adj.* hidden; secret; as, there are strange *cryptic* signs on the Egyptian tombs.

cryp-to-gam (krip'tō-găm), *n.* a plant having no true flower or seed

cryp-to-gram (krip'tō-grăm), *n.* a writing, or a system of writing, in cipher; as, a government uses a *cryptogram* or secret code.

crys-tal (kris'tăl), *n.* transparent quartz; a body formed by a solidifying element or compound, having symmetrical plane surfaces; a glass of superior clearness; anything transparent and clear; the glass over a watch-dial: *adj.* consisting of transparent glass; clear; transparent.

crys-tal-line (kris'tăl-in; kris'tăl-in), *adj.* pertaining to, or having the form of, a crystal; clear; transparent; composed of grains or particles.

crys-tal-li-za-tion (kris"tăl-ĭ-zā'shŭn; kris"tăl-ĭ-zā'shŭn), *n.* the act of forming or being made into a definite shape.

crys-tal-lize (kris'tăl-iz), *v.t.* to cause to form grains or become crystalline; give fixed shape to: *v.i.* to be converted into grains; assume a definite shape.

cub (kŭb), *n.* the young of certain animals, as the fox and bear.

cub-by-hole (kŭb'ĭ-hōl), *n.* a pigeon-hole; a closet; [a small inclosed space.

Cube

cube (kūb), *n.* a regular solid body with six equal square sides or faces; the product obtained by multiplying the square of a quantity by the quantity itself, as 5 × 5 × 5 = 125, the cube of 5: *v.t.* to raise to the third power.

cu-beb (kū'bĕb), *n.* the small spicy berry of a kind of pepper.

cube root (kūb rōōt), the first power of a cube; as, 5 is the *cube root* of 125.

cu-bic (kū'bik), *adj.* having the form or properties of a cube; having three dimensions; as, a *cubic* yard. Also, **cubical.** —*adv.* **cubically.**

cub-ism (kūb'ĭzm), *n.* a modern school of painting and sculpture working largely in combinations of straight lines and angles to express volume.—*n.* **cubist.**

cu-bit (kū'bit), *n.* an ancient measure of about eighteen inches; the forearm from the elbow to the wrist.

cuck-old (kŭk'ŭld), *n.* a man whose wife has broken the marriage vow of faithfulness.

cuck-oo (kōōk'ōō), *n.* a bird with dark feathers and curved bill that lays its eggs in the nests of other birds for them to hatch: so named from the sound of its note.

cu-cum-ber (kū'kŭm-bēr), *n.* a creeping plant, the fruit of which is used as a salad or pickle.

cud (kŭd), *n.* food brought from the first stomach of an animal back into the mouth; as, the cow chews its *cud.*

cud-dle (kŭd'l), *v.t.* to embrace closely: *v.i.* to lie close or snug: *n.* a close embrace.

cudg-el (kŭj'ĕl), *n.* a short thick stick: *v.t.* [*p.t.* and *p.p.* cudgeled, *p.pr.* cudgeling], to beat with a thick club.

cue (kū), *n.* the tail or end of a thing; a queue, or hanging braid of hair on the back of the head; as, the Chinese wears his hair in a *cue;* a hint; the last word of an actor's speech, as indicating the time for the next speaker; the part one has to play; the tapering rod used in billiards.

cuff (kŭf), *n.* a blow; slap; as, he gave the dog a *cuff* on the head; the ornamental fold on the sleeve of a garment at the wrist: *v.t.* to strike with the hand; slap.

Cuirass

cui-rass (kwē-răs'), *n.* a piece of armor covering the body from the neck to the waist; a breast-plate, or armor worn on the breast.

cui-ras-sier (kwē-rā-sēr"), *n.* a soldier mounted on a horse and wearing a cuirass, or breastplate.

cui-sine (kwē-zēn'), *n.* the kitchen of a hotel; style or quality of cooking.

cul-de-sac (kōō"d-săk'; kōōl"dē-săk'), *n.* [*pl.* culs-de-sac (kōō"d-săk'; kōōlz"dē-săk')], a blind alley; a passage open only at one end; a position in which an army finds itself when hemmed in with no exit but in front.

cu-li-na-ry (kū'li-nā-rĭ), *adj.* pertaining to the kitchen, or to the art or process of cooking; as, the *culinary* secrets are taught in the domestic science course.

cull (kŭl), *v.t.* to pick out; select; gather; as, to *cull* the flowers from a garden: *n.* something picked or sorted out from the rest: usually of an inferior nature.

culm (kŭlm), *n.* coal dust; refuse coal; an anthracite coal of an inferior grade; the jointed stem of a grass.

cul-mi-nate (kŭl'mi-nāt), *v.i.* to reach the highest point; to come to a final result; as, Napoleon was a great general, but his career *culminated* in defeat and banishment.

cul-mi-na-tion (kŭl"mi-nā'shŭn), *n.* the attainment of the highest point; as, the *culmination* of a man's ambition; the passage of a planet through the highest point of its course.

Syn. summit, crown, acme, climax, zenith.

cul-pa-bil-i-ty (kŭl"pȧ-bĭl'ĭ-tĭ), *n.* the state of being blameworthy.

cul-pa-ble (kŭl'pȧ-bl), *adj.* deserving censure; criminal; blameworthy.—*adv.* **culpably.**

cul-prit (kŭl'prit), *n.* one tried before a judge; one guilty of a crime or fault.

cult (kŭlt), *n.* a particular ritual or system of worship; a subject of special study; devoted or extravagant homage or adoration.

cul-ti-vate (kŭl'tĭ-vāt), *v.t.* to till; as, to *cultivate* the ground; improve by care, labor, or study; to cherish, as a friendship; to foster or promote the growth of, as plants or bacteria; to devote oneself to, as literature; to seek the society of.

cul-ti-va-tion (kŭl"tĭ-vā'shŭn), *n.* the act of tilling; the state of being tilled; tillage; culture; the cherishing, as of friendship; devotion to, as literature; the breeding, as of bacteria.

cul-ti-va-tor (kŭl'tĭ-vā"tēr), *n.* one who, or that which, tills the ground, etc.; a farmer; an agricultural or farm tool.

cul-tur-al (kŭl'tūr-ăl), *adj.* pertaining to tillage; pertaining to those means by which an advanced state of civilization is reached; pertaining to the production of bacteria, etc., for medical use; broadly educational; as, there are *cultural* advantages in a city.

cul-ture (kŭl'tūr), *n.* the training or refining of the mental or moral powers; the enlightenment which results from mental and moral training; as, *culture* or civilization includes education, manners, and morals; refinement; tillage; care given to the growth and development of animals and plants; the breeding of bacteria for scientific use; the product of such breeding.—*adj.* **cultured.**

cul-ver-in (kŭl'vẽr-ĭn), *n.* a long cannon of the sixteenth century with serpent-shaped handles.

cul-vert (kŭl'vẽrt), *n.* a drain or waterway of masonry or brickwork under a road.

cum-ber (kŭm'bẽr), *v.t.* to burden or obstruct; as, the ground was *cumbered* with rocks; to hinder; embarrass; oppress; perplex.

cum-ber-some (kŭm'bẽr-sŭm), *adj.* burdensome; unwieldy; as, a *cumbersome* machine.

cum-brous (kŭm'brŭs), *adj.* troublesome; heavy; obstructing.

cum-in (kŭm'ĭn), *n.* a dwarf plant of the parsley family; its aromatic seeds, used in parts of the East as a condiment. Also, **cummin.**

cu-mu-late (kū'mū-lāt), *v.t.* to add to by heaping together; to increase by additions.

cu-mu-la-tion (kū"mū-lā'shŭn), *n.* the act of heaping up; a gathered mass or heap.

cu-mu-la-tive (kū'mū-lā-tĭv), *adj.* adding to, or gradually increasing, the number or amount of; made up of portions gathered one after another; subject to addition in this way; as, *cumulative* dividends.

cu-mu-lo-stra-tus (kū"mū-lō-strā'tŭs), *n.* a cloud form or shape combining the characteristics of cumulus and stratus, or of masses and layers.

cu-mu-lus (kū'mū-lŭs), *n.* [*pl.* cumuli (-lī)], a cloud having the appearance of round woolly masses.

Cuneiform Writing

cu-ne-i-form (kū-nē'ĭ-fôrm), *adj.* having the form of a wedge: said of the wedge-shaped characters of the Assyrian and ancient Persian inscriptions.

cun-ner (kŭn'ẽr), *n.* any of several small sea fishes that can be used for food.

cun-ning (kŭn'ĭng), *adj.* skilful; done with skill or ingenuity; crafty; sly; as, the fox is a *cunning* animal; designing; subtle; colloquially, pretty, attractive, or interesting: *n.* deceit; craftiness.—*adv.* **cunningly.**

cup (kŭp), *n.* a small drinking vessel; something shaped like a cup; a chalice or goblet; a piece of plate offered as a prize; a vessel for drawing blood; a portion of suffering to be endured: used figuratively; in golf, a small hole in the course: *v.t.* [*p.t.* and *p.p.* cupped, *p.pr.* cupping], to bleed by means of a cupping glass: *v.i.* to strike or indent the ground with a golf-club when striking the ball.

cup-board (kŭb'ẽrd), *n.* a closet fitted with shelves for holding cups, plates, etc.

cup-ful (kŭp'fŏŏl), *n.* [*pl.* cupfuls (-fŏŏlz)], as much as a cup will contain; in cookery, a half pint.

Cu-pid (kū'pĭd), *n.* in Roman mythology, the god of love: called Eros by the Greeks.

cu-pid-i-ty (kū-pĭd'ĭ-tĭ), *n.* covetousness; greed; as, the sight of the money aroused the *cupidity* of the miser; eager desire; longing.

cu-po-la (kū'pō-lȧ), *n.* [*pl.* cupolas (-lȧz)], a spherelike, cup-shaped roof; a revolving shot-proof turret or tower.

cup-ping (kŭp'ĭng), *n.* the process of drawing blood with a cupping glass: **cupping glass,** a glass cup, from which the air has been partly exhausted by heat, used to draw blood by creating a vacuum at the point applied.

cur (kûr), *n.* a mongrel or inferior dog; contemptuously, a surly, ill-bred person.

cur-a-ble (kūr'ȧ-bl), *adj.* capable of being healed or cured; as, the patient has a *curable* disease.—*n.* **curability.**

cu-ra-çao (kū'rȧ-sō'; kōō"rȧ-sō'), *n.* a cordial flavored with the dried peel of bitter oranges.

cu-ra-cy (kū'rȧ-sĭ), *n.* the duties, office, or district of a curate.

cu-rate (kū'rāt), *n.* a clergyman or an assistant minister: the *curate* is a priest of the lowest degree in the Church of England.

cur-a-tive (kūr'ȧ-tĭv), *adj.* pertaining or referring to the cure of diseases; promoting cure; as, sick people go to Hot Springs for the *curative* waters: *n.* that which cures or serves to cure.

cu-ra-tor (kū-rā'tẽr), *n.* the superintendent of a museum, art gallery, etc.

curb (kûrb), *v.t.* to restrain; keep in subjection; as, it is difficult to *curb* an unruly tongue; furnish with a check rein, as a horse, or an inclosing border, as a sidewalk; to furnish with anything suggestive of a curb in purpose: *n.* that which checks, restrains, or subdues; a part of a horse's bridle; an inclosing border of stone, as along a roadway or street; in New York City, the street as a market for securities not listed in the stock exchange. Also, **kerb.**

curb-ing (kûrb'ĭng), *n.* curbstones collectively; material for curbstones. Also, **kerbing.**

curb-stone (kûrb'stōn"), *n.* the stone-edge of a street or sidewalk. Also, **kerbstone.**

curd (kûrd), *n.* the coagulated or thickened part of milk; as, cheese is formed of *curd*: *v.t.* to cause to curdle: *v.i.* to curdle.

cur-dle (kûr'dl), *v.t.* to thicken into curd: *v.i.* to coagulate.

cure (kūr), *n.* the act, or art, of healing; a remedy; as, quinine is a *cure* for colds; spiritual charge; the office of a parish priest or curate: *v.t.* to heal; restore to health; as, the doctor was called to *cure* the disease; set free from; preserve by salting.

cu-ré (kū"rā'), *n.* in France, a Roman Catholic parish priest. [Fr.]

cure-all (kūr′ôl″), *n.* a remedy for all diseases, evils, or ills; a panacea.

cur-few (kûr′fū), *n.* formerly, the ringing of a bell at a fixed hour in the evening as a warning that fires and lights were to be put out; the time of ringing; the bell itself.

cu-ri-o (kū′rĭ-ō), *n.* [*pl.* curios (-ōz)], a rare piece of bric-à-brac; a curiosity.

cu-ri-os-i-ty (kū″rĭ-ŏs′ĭ-tĭ), *n.* [*pl.* curiosities (-tĭz)], eager desire to get knowledge; inquisitiveness; something strange or rare.

cu-ri-ous (kū′rĭ-ŭs), *adj.* anxious to know; inquisitive; scrutinizing; queer; extraordinary; rare. — *adv.* curiously. — *n.* curiousness.

curl (kûrl), *n.* a small ring or ringlet of hair; an undulation or bend; a disease in fruit trees and potatoes: *v.t.* to twist into ringlets; crisp; coil; raise in undulations or waves; curve: *v.i.* to contract or bend into ringlets; move in spirals or undulations; become coiled; play at the game of curling.

curl-er (kûrl′ẽr), *n.* one who, or that which, coils, or twists in spirals; as, a hair-*curler;* one who plays at the game of curling.

cur-lew (kûr′lū), *n.* a wading bird of the snipe family.

curl-ing (kûr′lĭng), *n.* a popular Scottish game played on the ice with smooth, flat, cheese-shaped stones, fitted with handles.

curl-y (kûr′lĭ), *adj.* having curls; wavy; as, *curly* hair; a *curly* little dog.

cur-mudg-eon (kûr-mŭj′ŭn), *n.* a grasping, churlish fellow; a miser; a niggard.

cur-rant (kûr′ănt), *n.* a small seedless raisin; a common garden shrub and its berry.

cur-ren-cy (kûr′ĕn-sĭ), *n.* a continual passing from hand to hand; circulation, as of bank notes; uninterrupted course; that which is used for money, as notes and coin: the *currency* of the United States includes paper money and gold, silver, and copper coins.

cur-rent (kûr′ĕnt), *adj.* widely circulated; passing from hand to hand; now passing, as time; as, the *current* year; generally accepted; common; as, the *current* opinion: *n.* a flow or passing: said of fluids; body of air or water flowing in a certain direction; as, the boat moved down the river with the *current;* a movement of electricity, or the rate of such movement.—*adv.* currently.

cur-ric-u-lum (kŭ-rĭk′ū-lŭm), *n.* [*pl.* curriculums (-lŭmz); curricula (-lȧ)], a course; a prescribed regular course of study in a university, school, etc.; as, the school *curriculum* includes cooking and sewing.

cur-ri-er (kŭr′ĭ-ẽr), *n.* one who dresses and colors leather.

cur-ry (kŭr′ĭ), *v.t.* [*p.t.* and *p.p.* curried, *p.pr.* currying], to dress after tanning: said of leather; beat; to rub down and clean; as, to *curry* a horse; to seek to gain favor by flattery: *n.* [*pl.* curries (-ĭz)], a highly spiced East Indian sauce; a stew of rice, fowl, etc., flavored with this condiment.

cur-ry-comb (kŭr′ĭ-kōm″), *n.* a metallic comb, used in cleaning horses.

curse (kûrs), *n.* an oath; a prayer for injury to come to some one; that which brings or causes evil or trouble: *v.t.* to wish evil upon; to call on a divine power to send evil upon; to torment; to bring evil upon: *v.i.* to swear.

curs-ed (kûr′sĕd), *p.adj.* under a curse; hateful; detestable.

cur-sive (kûr′sĭv), *adj.* flowing: said of writing in which the letters are joined and the angles often rounded: *n.* a letter used in such writing, or manuscript written in such characters.

cur-so-ry (kûr′sō-rĭ), *adj.* hasty, superficial, careless; as, he gave the book a *cursory* reading.—*adv.* cursorily.—*n.* cursoriness.

Syn. desultory, hasty.
Ant. (see thorough).

curst (kûrst), past participle of the verb *curse.* Also, cursed.

curt (kûrt), *adj.* abrupt; short; as, the child gave a *curt* answer.—*adv.* curtly.—*n.* curtness.

cur-tail (kûr-tāl′), *v.t.* to cut short; reduce; as, to *curtail* expenses.

cur-tail-ment (kûr-tāl′mĕnt), *n.* the act of reducing or shortening.

cur-tain (kûr′tĭn; kûr′tn), *n.* a hanging screen which can be drawn up or aside; as, a window *curtain;* the stage *curtain* in a theater; in a fort, the part of the rampart and parapet between two bastions or gates: *v.t.* to inclose in, or as with, screens or curtains: curtain fire, a wall of dropping shells from massed artillery.

curt-sy (kûrt′sĭ), *n.* [*pl.* curtsies (-sĭz)], a bow; a salutation made by bending the knees and gracefully drooping the body; *v.i.* [*p.t.* and *p.p.* curtsied, *p.pr.* curtsying], to salute by making such a gesture. Also, courtesy, curtsey.

cur-va-ture (kûr′vȧ-tūr), *n.* a bending; as, *curvature* of the spine; the measure of the bending of a line or surface.

curve (kûrv), *n.* a bending without angles; a draftsman's instrument for forming such bendings: *v.t.* to cause to bend; as, to *curve* a line: *v.i* to bend; as, the line *curves* to the right: *adj.* bent without angles.

cur-vet (kûr′vĕt; kûr-vĕt′), *n.* a particular leap of a horse; a frisk or bound: *v.i.* (kûr-vĕt′; kûr′vĕt), to leap, as a horse; frisk or bound: *v.t.* to cause to leap or bound.

cur-vi-lin-e-ar (kûr″vĭ-lĭn′ē-ȧr), *adj.* made up of curved lines; bounded by curved lines.

curv-ing (kûr′vĭng), *n.* a bending; as, the many *curvings* of the road made driving dangerous.

cur-vom-e-ter (kûr-vŏm′ē-tẽr), *n.* an instrument for measuring the length of curves.

cush-ion (kŏŏsh′ŭn), *n.* a pillow or soft pad to sit, lie, or rest upon; a pillow used in lace-making; the elastic rim of a billiard table: *v.t.* to seat upon a soft pad; furnish with a soft pad; as, to *cushion* a chair: *v.t.* make the cue ball strike against the rim of a billiard table.

cusp (kŭsp), *n.* a pointed end; the horn of a crescent; as, the *cusp* of the crescent moon; a sharp point; a spear-shaped ornament.

Curvometer

cus-pid (kŭs'pĭd), *n.* a pointed tooth; a canine or dog tooth.

cus-pi-date (kŭs'pĭ-dāt), *adj.* furnished with a sharp, spearlike point.

cus-pi-dor (kŭs'pĭ-dôr; kŭs'pĭ-dôr), *n.* a spittoon.

cus-tard (kŭs'tẽrd), *n.* a mixture of eggs and milk, etc., baked or boiled.

cus-to-di-an (kŭs-tō'dĭ-ăn), *n.* a keeper; one who has the care of anything; as, the *custodian* of a museum.

cus-to-dy (kŭs'tō-dĭ), *n.* guardianship; care; as, the welfare of a city should be in the *custody* of upright men; restraint of liberty; imprisonment; as, the *custody* of a prisoner; charge; as, the jewels were in his *custody*.

cus-tom (kŭs'tŭm), *n.* a usual course of action; a frequent repetition of the same act; established or recognized usage; as, it is the *custom* to exchange gifts at Christmas; business support; unwritten law: *pl.* duties on imported or, less frequently, exported goods: *adj.* made to order; as, *custom* shoes; *custom* clothes; doing only work that is ordered; as, a *custom* tailor.
Syn., *n.* fashion, manner, practice.

cus-tom-a-ry (kŭs'tŭm-ā-rĭ), *adj.* habitual; conventional; common; usual.—*adv.* customarily.—*n.* customariness.

cus-tom-er (kŭs'tŭm-ẽr), *n.* a purchaser; one who regularly buys from a store or tradesman.

cus-tom-house (kŭs'tŭm-hous"), *n.* a building where duties or taxes are paid on exported or imported goods, and vessels are entered and cleared.

cut (kŭt), *v.t.* [*p.t.* and *p.p.* cut, *p.pr.* cutting], to cleave or separate with a sharp instrument; as, to *cut* meat; make an incision in; divide; trim; excavate; intersect; diminish; colloquially, to pass deliberately without recognition; wound deeply; as, to *cut* a friend by unkind words; divide (a pack of cards) at random; in tennis, to strike (a ball) so as to send it at right angles to the batsman; colloquially, to absent oneself from; as, to *cut* a class: *v.i.* to make an incision; do the work of a sharp instrument; as, the knife *cuts* well; to make a short cut by going across: followed by *across*; as, we *cut* across the field: *n.* an incision or wound made by a sharp instrument; gash; a sharp stroke; a slight; a trench, channel, groove, etc., made by digging; a slice; a straight, short passage; as, a short *cut* to a place; a block on which an engraving is made; the fashion of a garment; shape; colloquially, the deliberate ignoring of an acquaintance; the division of a pack of cards; a particular stroke in cricket and lawn tennis; one of several pieces, as of cardboard or straw, used in drawing lots; a reduction in price: *adj.* divided or separated; gashed; having the surface ornamented or fashioned: not wrought or hand-made.

cu-ta-ne-ous (kū-tā'nē-ŭs), *adj.* pertaining to the skin; as, a *cutaneous*, or skin, disease.

cut-a-way (kŭt'ȧ-wā"), *adj.* cut back from the waist: *n.* a coat, the skirts of which slope from the waist.

cute (kūt), *adj.* sharp; sly; as, a *cute* trick; clever; attractive because of beauty or daintiness; as, a *cute* child.—*adv.* cutely.—*n.* cuteness.

cut glass (kŭt glȧs), flint glass cut into facets or figures.

cu-ti-cle (kū'tĭ-kl), *n.* the outer layer of skin called the epidermis; the thin bark of a plant.

cut-lass (kŭt'lȧs), *n.* a short, heavy, curved sword used by sailors.

cut-ler (kŭt'lẽr), *n.* one who makes or sells knives or other cutting tools.

cut-ler-y (kŭt'lẽr-ĭ), *n.* edged or cutting tools collectively.

cut-let (kŭt'lĕt), *n.* a slice of meat, cut from the ribs or leg, for broiling or frying; as, veal *cutlet*.

cut-off (kŭt'ôf), *n.* that which shortens, as a short or straight road; a new, shorter channel cut by a river across a bend; a device for stopping steam from entering the cylinder of an engine; the act of thus shutting off steam, or the point at which it is effected.

cut-out (kŭt'out"), *n.* a switchlike contrivance to cut off an electric light from the circuit; a circuit breaker; a device by which an internal-combustion engine exhausts directly into the air, instead of, as regularly, through a muffler.

cut-purse (kŭt'pûrs), *n.* one who cuts purses to steal their contents; hence, a pickpocket; a robber.

cut-ter (kŭt'ẽr), *n.* one who cuts out and shapes garments; a light sleigh for two persons; a small fast-sailing vessel; a man-of-war's boat.

Cutter

cut-throat (kŭt'thrōt"), *n.* a murderous villain; a ruffian.

cut-ting (kŭt'ĭng), *p.adj.* dividing by an edged instrument; deeply wounding the feelings; sarcastic; piercing; chilling; sharp; as, a *cutting* remark. *n.* a piece cut off or from; a slip; as, August is the month to make a *cutting* from geraniums; an incision or cutting.

cut-tle (kŭt'l), *n.* the cuttle-fish, a fish with ten arms, suckers, two large eyes, and an ink-bag containing a dark fluid.

cut-worm (kŭt'wûrm"), *n.* a destructive caterpillar which feeds on cabbage, corn, etc.

cy-a-nide (sī'ȧ-nīd), *n.* a compound of cyanic acid with an element or radical, especially potassium-cyanide.

cy-an-o-gen (sī-ăn'ō-jĕn), *n.* a colorless poisonous gas burning with a purple flame, with the odor of peach blossoms.

cy-an-o-type (sī-ăn'ō-tīp), *n.* a photographic process in which the picture is taken in Prussian blue.

cyc-la-men (sĭk'lȧ-mĕn), *n.* any of various plants of the primrose family.

cy-cle (sī'kl), *n.* a period of time, or order of events, which repeats itself regularly; a revolution of a certain period of time; an imaginary circle in the heavens; the stories and traditions surrounding some famous event or hero; as, the story of the Knights of the Round Table is called the Arthurian *cycle*: an age or long period; a bicycle or tricycle: *v.i.* [*p.t.* and *p.p.* cycled, *p.pr.* cycling], to occur or recur, at regular intervals; to ride a bicycle or tricycle.—*n.* cycler, cyclist.

cy-cle-car (sī'kl-kär'), *n.* a very light, small vehicle driven by a motor.

cyc-lic (sĭk'lĭk; sī'klĭk), *adj.* pertaining to, or moving in, a cycle; belonging to the literary cycle of Greek poets who wrote on the Trojan War and its heroes. Also, **cyclical.**

cy-cling (sī'klĭng), *p.adj.* bicycling; riding on a bicycle.

cy-cloid (sī'kloid), *n.* a geometrical curve traced out by any point of a circle rolling along a straight line until it has completed a revolution.—*adj.* **cycloidal.**

cy-clom-e-ter (sī-klŏm'ē-tẽr), *n.* an instrument for measuring the distance traveled on a wheel.

cy-clone (sī'klōn), *n.* a violent storm in which the wind whirls inward towards a center; a tornado or any destructive storm.—*adj.* **cyclonic.**

cy-clo-no-scope (sī-klō'nō-skōp'), *n.* an instrument for recording the motions of atmospheric currents which produce cyclones.

cy-clo-pe-di-a (sī'klō-pē'dĭ-*d*), *n.* an encyclopedia; a book containing brief information upon all subjects alphabetically arranged. Also, **cyclopædia, encyclopedia, encyclopædia.**—*adj.* **cyclopedic, cyclopædic.**

Cy-clo-pe-an (sī'klō-pē'ăn), *adj.* pertaining to the Cyclops, a race of giants; hence, huge and rough; terrific; vast; massive.

cy-clo-ra-ma (sī'klō-rä'm*d*), *n.* a series of moving pictures extended circularly so as to appear natural to the spectator standing in the center.

cyg-net (sĭg'nĕt), *n.* a young swan, a large and graceful aquatic bird.

cyl-in-der (sĭl'ĭn-dẽr), *n.* the surface generated by a straight line moving parallel to itself; a long round body; a roller; a chamber in which force is exerted on the piston of a steam engine; the barrel of a pump; a round roller for printing; a roller-shaped stone with cuneiform or wedge-shaped inscriptions.

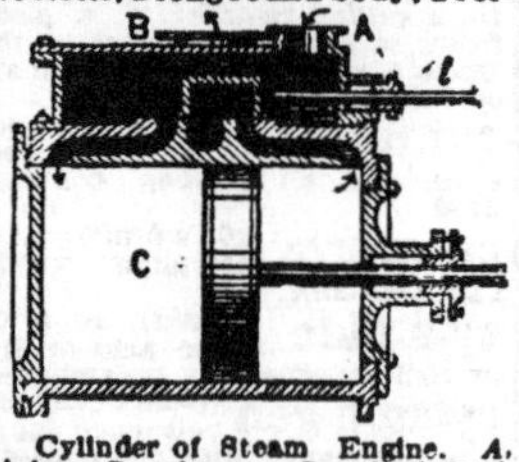

Cylinder of Steam Engine. *A*, inlet; *B*, exhaust; *C*, cylinder; *t*, steam valve; *T*, valve.

cy-lin-dric (sĭ-lĭn'drĭk), *adj.* having the form, or properties, of a cylinder. Also, **cylindrical.**

cy-mar (sĭ-mär'), *n.* a literary term indicating a loose garment or chemise worn by women.

cym-bal (sĭm'băl), *n.* a musical instrument, formed of two metal plates to be struck together: usually plural.

Cymbals

cyme (sīm), *n.* a certain kind of flowering plant, in which the primary, as well as the secondary, axis terminates in a flower; hence, any flat or convex flower-formation, as the forget-me-not.—*adj.* **cymose.**

Cym-ric (kĭm'rĭk), *adj.* of or pertaining to the Welsh race or their speech, or to peoples speaking a language allied to theirs: *n.* the Welsh language or allied languages.

Cyn-ic (sĭn'ĭk), *n.* one of a sect of ancient Greek philosophers who taught that virtue, the basis of which was self-control and individual independence, was the only good: later, this term came to signify, in a general sense, contempt for the opinions of others: **cynic**, one whose opinion it is that self-interest is the sole motive behind the actions of human beings; a sarcastic, surly person.

cyn-i-cal (sĭn'ĭ-kăl), *adj.* surly; sarcastic; as, a sneering, *cynical* remark; given to sneering at purity of thought or high motives.—*adv.* **cynically.**

Cyn-i-cism (sĭn'ĭ-sĭzm), *n.* the philosophy of the Greek Cynics: **cynicism**, the quality of mind that expresses itself in surliness, sarcasm, and lack of faith in disinterested motives.

cy-no-sure (sī'nō-shōōr; sĭn'ō-shōōr), *n.* an object of general attraction; anything that attracts attention; as, the *cynosure* of all eyes.

cy-pher (sī'fẽr), *n.* the character 0, meaning zero; a secret method of writing and the key to it; something of no value: *v.t.* to work out by means of arithmetic; to write with a private alphabet or other secret characters. Also, **cipher.**

cy-press (sī'prĕs), *n.* a cone-bearing evergreen tree, the emblem of mourning: *adj.* pertaining to, or made of, the wood of this tree.

cyst (sĭst), *n.* a sac, or pouch, in animal bodies containing diseased matter; any membranous receptacle; as, the urinary *cyst.*

cyst-ic (sĭs'tĭk), *adj.* pertaining to, or contained in, a cyst, or sac of diseased matter.

czar (zär), *n.* an emperor or absolute monarch; a supreme lord: **Czar**, the title of a Russian emperor: a form of **Cæsar.** Also, **tsar, Tsar.**

czar-e-vitch (zär'ē-vĭch), *n.* the eldest son of a czar. Also, **czarewitch, tsarevitch, Cæsarewitch.**

cza-rev-na (zä-rĕv'n*d*), *n.* the wife of a czarevitch. Also, **tsarevna.**

cza-ri-na (zä-rē'n*d*), *n.* an empress of Russia; the wife of a czar. Also, **tsarina.**

Czech (chĕk), *n.* a member of the most westerly branch of the Slavonic family, including Bohemians, Moravians, and Slovaks; the language of these peoples.

Czecho-Slav (chĕk'ō-släv; -släv), *n.* a member of the Czech branch of the Slavonic race including Bohemians, Moravians, and Slovaks; a Czech; the language of the Czechs.

Czecho-Slovak (chĕk'ō-slō-văk'; -slō'văk), *adj.* referring to the Czechs and Slovaks or their language; referring to the people of Bohemia, Moravia, and Northwestern Hungary, or to their language: *n.* a member of that race or people.

D

dab (dăb), *v.t.* [*p.t.* and *p.p.* dabbed, *p.pr.* dabbing], to strike or touch lightly; to smear; as, to *dab* paint on a canvas: *n.* a small soft lump; a gentle blow; a quick, sharp stroke; the flounder, a salt water fish; colloquially, an expert.

dab-bing (dăb'ĭng), *n.* the process of indenting the surface of a stone by a pick-shaped tool.

dab-ble (dăb'l), *v.t.* to wet by dipping slightly and often; moisten; spatter: *v.i.* to paddle with the hands in water; do anything in a careless manner; as, to *dabble* in art.—*n.* **dabbler.**

dab-ster (dăb'stẽr), *n.* one who is skilled; an expert; as, he is a *dabster* at tennis. [Colloq.]

dachs-hund (däks'hŏŏnt"), *n.* the German badger-dog, a hound with a long body and very short, crooked legs.

dac-tyl (dăk'tĭl), *n.* a metrical foot, consisting of one long or accented, and two short or unaccented, syllables.—*adj.* **dactylic.**

dad (dăd), *n.* a father: a name used by children and rustics. Also, **daddy.**

dad-dy long-legs (dăd'ĭ lŏng'lĕgz"), a name for various kinds of crane fly; also, a kind of spider with many long legs.

da-do (dā'dō; dä'dō), *n.* [*pl.* dadoes (-dōz)], an ornamental border around the lower part of the wall of a room, etc.: *v.t.* to ornament with such a border.

daf-fo-dil (dăf'ō-dĭl), *n.* a kind of narcissus with large yellow single or double flowers.

daft (dȧft), *adj.* weak-minded; simple; silly; as, he is *daft* on that subject.

dag-ger (dăg'ẽr), *n.* a short weapon for stabbing; a reference mark in printing [†].

da-go (dā'gō), *n.* [*pl.* dagos (-gōz)], a nickname for a dark-skinned person, especially of Spanish, Portuguese, or Italian descent; a sailor's name for a person speaking Portuguese or Spanish. [Slang.]

da-guerre-o-type (dȧ-gĕr'ō-tīp), *n.* an early kind of photograph; the process preceding photography.

Dahabiyeh

da-ha-biy-eh (dä-hä-bē'ĕ), *n.* a passenger boat used on the Nile, having a sharp bow and broad stern, and one or two masts with lateen sails. Also, **dahabieh.**

dahl-ia (däl'yȧ; often, dāl'yȧ or dăl'yȧ), *n.* [*pl.* dahlias (-yȧz)], a tuberous-rooted plant of the aster family.

dai-ly (dā'lĭ), *n.* [*pl.* dailies (-lĭz)], a newspaper published each week day: *adj.* occurring or recurring each successive day; diurnal; as, we have *daily* need of food: *adv.* on every day; day by day; as, they bring supplies *daily.*

dain-ty (dān'tĭ), *n.* [*pl.* dainties (-tĭz)], something choice or delicious; as, white grapes are considered a *dainty*: *adj.* delicious; elegant; delicate; as, a *dainty* piece of China; sensitive; choice; fastidious; charming.—*adv.* **daintily.**—*n.* **daintiness.**

dai-ry (dā'rĭ; dâr'ĭ), *n.* [*pl.* dairies (-rĭz)], a place where milk is kept and converted into butter and cheese; a shop where milk, butter, and cheese are sold.

dai-ry-ing (dā'rĭ-ĭng), *n.* the business or occupation of producing milk, butter, and cheese.

da-is (dā'ĭs; dās), *n.* a raised platform for the chief seats in a hall.

dai-sy (dā'zĭ), *n.* [*pl.* daisies (-zĭz)], a wild field flower of the aster family, with a yellow center and white petals, or a brown center and yellow petals.

Da-ko-ta (dȧ-kō'tȧ), *n.* one of a tribe of American Indians, originally inhabiting the region of the Upper Mississippi River.

dale (dāl), *n.* a valley; glen; as, they went up hill and down *dale.*

dalles (dălz), *n.* a rapid, especially one in a rocky gorge.

dal-li-ance (dăl'ĭ-ăns), *n.* the act of trifling, loitering, or playing.

dal-ly (dăl'ĭ), *v.i.* [*p.t.* and *p.p.* dallied, *p.pr.* dallying], to trifle; to waste time; loiter; as, to *dally* on the road.

dal-ton-ism (dôl'tŭn-ĭzm), *n.* colorblindness: so called from John Dalton, who first described it.

dam (dăm), *n.* a bank or wall across a watercourse; any man-made contrivance to stop the flow of water or gas; a female parent of mammals; a sheet of rubber used by a dentist: *v.t.* [*p.t.* and *p.p.* dammed, *p.pr.* damming], to confine, or raise the level of, by a dam; restrain: usually with *in* or *up;* as, to *dam* up the stream.

dam-age (dăm'āj), *n.* injury or harm; as, the flood caused great *damage;* harm wilfully done to a person's character, person, or estate; as, the story did great *damage* to the man's character: *pl.* money recovered for injury or loss suffered: *v.t.* to injure; harm; impair.

dam-a-scene (dăm"ȧ-sēn'; dăm'ȧ-sēn), *v.t.* to decorate, in manufacturing iron and steel, with etching or inlaid designs, as was done at Damascus: *adj.* of or pertaining to damask or damascening. **Damascene,** of or pertaining to Damascus. Also, *v.* **damaskeen.**

Da-mas-cus steel (dȧ-măs'kŭs stēl), a flexible steel first made at Damascus, used for sword blades.

dam-ask (dăm'ȧsk), *n.* silk or linen material woven with elaborate patterns; a fine twilled linen with patterns made by threads woven in opposite directions; Damascus steel or work; a deep pink color: *adj.* pertaining to, or made of, damask.

dam-ask rose (dăm'ȧsk rōz), a large, deep pink, fragrant rose, native of Damascus.

dame (dām), *n.* a lady; also, a title formerly used instead of Mistress or Madam; a school mistress; a matron; an elderly woman.

damn (dăm), *v.t.* to sentence to punishment or death; to doom to eternal punishment; to invoke a curse upon; to condemn as bad or as a failure; as, "to *damn* with faint praise": *v.i.* to swear; to curse: *n.* a curse.

dam-na-ble (dăm'nȧ-bl), *adj.* deserving to be condemned or eternally punished; detestable.—*adv.* **damnably.**

dam-na-tion (dăm-nā'shŭn), *n.* eternal punishment; condemnation; a sin deserving condemnation.

damned (dămd), *p.adj.* condemned to eternal punishment; condemned as bad or as a failure; cursed.

dam-oi-selle (dăm"ĭ-zĕl'), *n.* a young unmarried woman; a maiden. Also, **damsel, damosel, damozel, demoiselle.**

damp (dămp), *n.* moisture; fog: *adj.* moist; foggy; humid: *v.t.* to moisten; discourage; depress; as, the bad news was enough to *damp* our joy.—*adv.* **damply.** —*n.* **dampness.**

damp-en (dăm'pn), *v.t.* to make moist or wet; to depress or discourage.

damp-er (dăm'pẽr), *n.* something which depresses or discourages; a movable plate to regulate the draft in a stove; a device to check the vibrations of a musical instrument; as, the *damper* in a piano is made of wood covered with felt.

dam-sel (dăm'zĕl), *n.* a maiden; a young unmarried woman. Also, **damoiselle, damosel, damozel, demoiselle.**

dam-son (dăm'zn), *n.* a small, oval, purple plum; also, the tree that bears this fruit.

dance (dȧns), *v.i.* to move the body and feet rhythmically to music; perform the figures of a dance; move nimbly or merrily: *v.t.* to give a dancing motion to; as, to *dance* the baby up and down; perform; as, to *dance* a jig: *n.* a regulated movement of the feet to a rhythmical musical accompaniment; as, the one-step is a modern *dance;* a dancing party, less formal than a ball; one round of dancing at such a party.

dan-de-li-on (dăn'dē-lī"ŭn), *n.* a common weed of the chicory family with yellow flowers.

dan-der (dăn'dẽr), *n.* temper; anger; as, to have one's *dander* up.

dan-dle (dăn'dl), *v.t.* to move up and down in affectionate play; fondle; as, to *dandle* a baby.

dan-druff (dăn'drŭf), *n.* dried skin on the scalp or head which comes off in small scales or pieces.

dan-dy (dăn'dĭ), *n.* [*pl.* dandies (-dĭz)], a fop; a man who gives a great deal of attention to dress; as, Beau Brummel was the *dandy* of his time: *adj.* slang, excellent or very fine.—*adj.* **dandyish.**

dan-dy-ism (dăn'dĭ-ĭzm), *n.* foppishness; as, Beau Brummel was the most noted representative of the *dandyism* of the early part of the 19th century.

Dane (dān), *n.* a native or inhabitant of Denmark: **great Dane,** a very large dog.

dan-ger (dān'jẽr), *n.* peril; exposure to loss, injury, or death; a case of such exposure.
Syn. hazard, risk, harm.
Ant. (see safety).

dan-ger-ous (dān'jẽr-ŭs), *adj.* unsafe; involving, or beset with danger; ready to do harm or injury, perilous; hazardous; as, it is *dangerous* to play with strange dogs.—*adv.* **dangerously.**—*n.* **dangerousness.**

dan-gle (dăn'gl), *v.i.* to hang or swing loosely; to hang about or depend on anyone; follow: *v.t.* to cause to swing loosely.—*n.* **dangler.**

Dan-iel (dăn'yĕl), *n.* a book of the Old Testament narrating the story of the Hebrew prophet of that name, captive at Babylon, and containing his prophecies.

Dan-ish (dān'ĭsh), *adj.* pertaining to Denmark or its people: *n.* the language of Denmark.

dank (dăṅk), *adj.* humid; damp; moist; wet; as, *dank* hair; *dank* weeds; a cold, *dank* cave.

dan-seuse (dän"sûz'), *n.* a professional female dancer; a ballet-dancer: **premiere danseuse,** the leading female dancer in a ballet. [Fr.]

dap-per (dăp'ẽr), *adj.* small and active; trim and neat in appearance.

dap-ple (dăp''l), *adj.* spotted; as, a *dapple*-gray horse.

dare (dâr), *v.i.* [*p.t.* dared, durst, *p.p.* dared, *p.pr.* daring], to have courage; to be bold enough to do something; venture: *v.t.* to venture to do; to defy; challenge: *n.* a taunting defiance.

dare-dev-il (dâr'dĕv"l), *adj.* characteristic of a reckless man: *n.* a reckless fellow.

dar-ing (dâr'ĭng), *n.* bravery; boldness: *adj.* fearless; bold; venturesome; rash.

dark (därk), *adj.* without light; not reflecting light; wholly black or gray; of a brunette complexion; as, the Indian has a *dark* skin; gloomy; as, a *dark* mood; mysterious; as, a *dark* saying; ignorant; as, the mind of the savage is *dark;* dastardly; as a dark deed; *n.* absence of light; a place where there is little light; nightfall; state of being secret; often, underhand secrecy; as, to work in the *dark;* ignorance; as, I am in the *dark* on the subject.
Syn., adj. dismal, opaque, dim.
Ant. (see light).

dark-en (där'kn), *v.t.* to make dark; to shut out the light; to obscure; to make gloomy; as, the misfortunes of war *darken* many homes: *v.i.* to become dark.

dark-en-ing (där'kn-ĭng), *n.* the act of growing, or making, dark; twilight; gloaming.

dark-ling (därk'lĭng), *adj.* dimly seen: *adv.* in the dark. [Poet.]

dark-ly (därk'lĭ), *adv.* dimly; imperfectly; faintly; not clearly; mysteriously.

dark-ness (därk'nĕs), *n.* absence of light, partial or total; obscurity; gloom; physical obscurity of vision; blindness; mental or moral blindness; as, the *darkness* of ignorance; wickedness.

dark-some (därk'sŭm), *adj.* gloomy; without light; mysterious.

dark-y (där'kĭ), *n.* [*pl.* darkies (-kĭz)], a negro. Also, **darkey.** [Colloq.]

dar-ling (där'lĭng), *n.* one dearly loved; a favorite; pet: *adj.* tenderly loved; very dear.

darn (därn), *v.t.* to mend (a rent) by filling in with yarn or thread by means of a needle; colloquially, to damn: a mild form of profanity: *n.* a patch made by filling in a hole with interlaced stitches.

dar-nel (där'nĕl), *n.* a common grass or weed in grain fields.

dart (därt), *n.* a small lance or spear; the arrow of a blowgun; anything that wounds sharply; a swift, sudden movement: *v.t.* to throw; as, the invaders *dart* their spears: *v.i.* to move swiftly; start suddenly and go quickly; as, the fish *dart* through the water.

Dar-win-i-an (där-win'ĭ-ăn), *adj.* relating to Charles Darwin, the naturalist, or to his theories: *n.* an evolutionist, or believer in the theory that new kinds of plants and animals develop by natural selection and the survival of the fittest.

Dar-win-ism (där'wĭn-ĭzm), *n.* the theory of evolution by natural selection taught by Darwin.

dash (dăsh), *v.t.* to throw violently or hastily; break by collision; hurl; shatter; splash; ruin; as, to *dash* one's hopes; to perform hastily, as writing or sketching; depress; confuse: *v.i.* to rush with violence; strike on a surface with a violent noisy motion: *n.* a collision; a slight addition; a vulgar display; as, to cut a *dash* with fine clothes; a mark [—] in writing or printing; something that causes discouragement; the striking of water in noisy motion; as, the *dash* of the waves; a sudden rush; a short, very quick race.

dash-board (dăsh'bōrd'), *n.* a screen on the front of a carriage or wagon to protect from mud; a splashboard.

da-sheen (dă-shēn'), *n.* a root vegetable, similar to the potato in its food characteristics, adapted for cultivation in rich, moist soils: grown extensively in the West Indies and recently introduced into the Southern States.

dash-er (dăsh'ẽr), *n.* the part of a churn which is moved up and down to make milk into butter.

dash-ing (dăsh'ĭng), *p.adj.* spirited; bold; as, a *dashing* soldier; showy; gay.

das-tard (dăs'tẽrd), *n.* a coward: *adj.* meanly shrinking from danger; cowardly.—*n.* **dastardliness.**

das-tard-ly (dăs'tẽrd-lĭ), *adv.* cowardly; slyly base or wicked.

da-ta (dā'tȧ), *n.pl.* of *datum*, a collection of facts; as, he collected the necessary *data* for his report to the committee.

date (dāt), *n.* the time of an event or transaction; as, July 4 is the *date* on which we celebrate our independence; duration; a statement which names the time of issuing of a writing, book, document, etc.; the present time: used in *out of date* and *up to date;* colloquially, an engagement for a fixed time; the edible fruit of the date palm: *v.t.* to mark with a definite time; to find the definite time of: *v.i.* to bear the statement of a time; reckon to have existed from a given time.

date palm (dāt päm), a tree with feathery leaves, and long trunk, native to northern Africa, and yielding a great quantity of fruit.

da-tive (dā'tĭv), *adj.* denoting the case of a noun or pronoun which expresses the indirect object: usually indicated in English by *to* or *for* with the objective case; for example, in the sentence, she gave him good advice, *him* is in the *dative* case: *n.* the dative case; as, *him* in the preceding sentence is the *dative.*

da-tum (dā'tŭm), *n.* [*pl.* data (-tȧ)], something assumed, known, or granted for the basis of an argument or inference: usually in plural; a certain level assumed, from which heights and depths are measured.

daub (dôb), *v.t.* to cover or smear with mud, plaster, etc.; paint coarsely or unskilfully: *n.* a coarse or rude painting; a smear; a cheap kind of mortar.

daub-ing (dôb'ĭng), *n.* bad painting; the application of rough mortar to a wall to imitate stone.

daugh-ter (dô'tẽr), *n.* the female offspring of human parents; a female descendant; as, Helen of Troy was a *daughter* of the gods; a woman of a certain country; as, a *daughter* of France; anything called feminine looked at in relation to its origin; as, charity is the *daughter* of civilization.—*adj.* **daughterly.**

daugh-ter-in-law (dô'tẽr-ĭn-lô), *n.* [*pl.* daughters-in-law], a son's wife.

daunt (dänt; dônt), *v.t.* to frighten; to discourage; to dishearten.

daunt-less (dänt'lĕs), *adj.* fearless; undiscouraged; as, the *dauntless* captain brought his ship safely through the storm.—*adv.* **dauntlessly.**—*n.* **dauntlessness.**

dau-phin (dô'fĭn), *n.* the title of the eldest son of the king of France from 1349 to 1830.

dav-en-port (dăv'ĕn-pōrt), *n.* a kind of small writing desk or table; also, a long low sofa: sometimes made to convert into a bed.

Da-vid (dā'vĭd), *n.* in the Bible, the youngest son of Jesse of Bethlehem, second king of Israel, and writer of many songs contained in the Old Testament book of Psalms.

dav-it (dăv'ĭt; dā'vĭt), *n.* one of a pair of f-shaped pieces of iron on the side of a vessel, for suspending or lowering a boat.

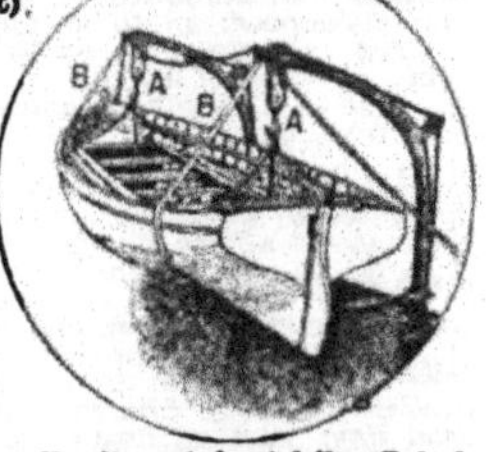

Davits. *A*, boat falls; *B*, lashings to prevent sway.

da-vy (dā'vĭ), *n.* [*pl.* davies (-vĭz)], a miner's safety lamp surrounded by fine gauze wire, invented by Sir Humphry Davy as a protection against explosions of fire damp: abbreviated from full name, *Davy lamp.*

daw (dô), *n.* a bird of the crow family; a jackdaw.

daw-dle (dô'dl), *v.i.* to waste time in a trifling manner; loiter.—*n.* **dawdler.**

dawn (dôn), *v.i.* to begin to grow light; glimmer; break, as the day: *n.* the first appearance of light in the morning; as, the cock crows at *dawn* before the sun rises; beginning or unfolding.

dawn-ing (dôn'ĭng), *n.* daybreak; beginning or unfolding.

day (dā), *n.* the period of light between sunrise and sunset; daylight; sunshine; the period of twenty-four hours, reckoning from midnight to midnight (the civil day), or from noon to noon (the astronomical day); in the East, a distance that can be traveled in twenty-four hours; a specified time or period; as, the *day* of chivalry; the number of hours allowed by law or custom for work; as, printers work an eight-hour *day*.

day-book (dā'bōōk'), *n.* a book in which business accounts of the day are kept.

day-break (dā'brāk'), *n.* the dawn; as, at *daybreak* the birds began their song.

day-dream (dā'drēm'), *n.* a visionary fancy: *v.i.* to dream idly; as, he *daydreams* and builds castles in the air.

day la-bor-er (dā lā'bẽr-ẽr), a workman, usually unskilled, who is paid by the day.

day let-ter (dā lĕt'ẽr), a telegram sent at a special rate in consideration of messages at regular rates having precedence in time of sending.

day-light (dā'līt'), *n.* light given by the sun; time between sunrise and sunset.

days of grace (dāz ŏv grās), the usual time (three days) allowed for the payment of a note after it becomes due.

day-spring (dā'spring'), *n.* the dawn; the beginning of the day.

day-star (dā'stär'), *n.* the first star of morning; an emblem of hope; the sun. [Poet.]

day-time (dā'tīm'), *n.* the hours during which the sun gives light.

daze (dāz), *v.t.* to confuse; to stupefy; to dazzle: *n.* the state of being confused; as, he was in a *daze* after the blow.

daz-zle (dăz'l), *v.t.* to confuse by a glare of light, or by splendor; to bewilder; as, the jewels of the rich *dazzle* the eyes of the poor: *v.i.* to be confused by excess of light; as, my eyes *dazzle* in the strong light: *n.* excess of light.

de- (dē-), a *prefix* meaning down, away, from, etc.

dea-con (dē'kn), *n.* an inferior or subordinate church officer; a man appointed to assist the minister and manage the material affairs of a church.

dea-con-ess (dē'kn-ĕs), *n.* a woman who acts as deacon; a woman trained for church work and set apart for it.

dead (dĕd), *adj.* having ceased to live; without life; inanimate; resembling death; inactive; disused; complete; as, a *dead* loss; sure as death; as, a *dead* shot; out of the game or play: *n.* one or many dead persons: used after *the*; the point or degree of greatest lifelessness; as, the *dead* of night: *adv.* absolutely; exactly; as, he was *dead* wrong.

dead-beat (dĕd'bēt'), *adj.* thoroughly exhausted: *n.* a movement with no recoil; colloquially, one who lives by shifts or tricks.

dead cen-ter (dĕd sĕn'tẽr), that position of a crank in which the crank axle, crank pin, and the connecting rod are all in a straight line.

dead-en (dĕd'n), *v.t.* to lessen the sharpness, intensity, or vigor of; as, the medicine was given to *deaden* the pain; retard; blunt; render nonconductive; make tasteless or stale; deprive of gloss or brilliancy; kill (trees) by girdling.

dead-eye (dĕd'ī'), *n.* a round, flat block of wood bound with an iron band and pierced with three holes to receive lanyards or ropes: formerly used in firing old-style cannon on shipboard; now used for setting up rigging.

dead-head (dĕd'hĕd'), *n.* colloquially, a person who has a free pass on railways or to places of amusement, etc.; a wooden buoy.

dead let-ter (dĕd lĕt'ẽr), an unclaimed letter, the owner of which cannot be found; that which has lost its authority; as, the old whipping post has become a *dead letter*.

dead-lights (dĕd'līts'), *n.pl.* strong, wooden shutters placed over cabin windows in stormy weather.

dead-load (dĕd'lōd), *n.* a constant motionless weight or pressure.

dead-lock (dĕd'lŏk), *n.* a lock worked on one side by a handle and on the other by a key; complete standstill; point when two opposing forces equal each other in strength, so that neither can go ahead.

dead-ly (dĕd'lĭ), *adj.* causing death; destructive; fatal; as, Asiatic cholera is a *deadly* disease; relentless: *adv.* relentlessly.—*n.* **deadliness.**

Syn., *adj.* fatal, mortal.

dead-march (dĕd'märch), *n.* a piece of solemn music, often played at a military funeral.

dead-ness (dĕd'nĕs), *n.* absence of life; inactivity.

dead reck-on-ing (dĕd'rĕk'n-ing), the method of finding a ship's place at sea by the log and the compass courses.

dead rise (dĕd rīs), in steel shipbuilding the slope of the bottom upwards from the keel.

dead set (dĕd sĕt), the fixed position of a dog in pointing game; colloquially, a determined effort or attack: *adj.* determined to do something.

dead wa-ter (dĕd wô'tẽr), the water that closes in under the stern of a ship; eddy-water.

dead weight (dĕd wāt), heaviness of, or like that of, a lifeless body; the weight of the vehicle plus that of the load to be carried; freight charged for by weight instead of by bulk; the heaviest part of a ship's cargo.

dead wind (dĕd wĭnd), a wind blowing directly opposite to a ship's course.

deaf (dĕf), *adj.* unable to hear; unwilling to hear or pay regard to.

deaf-en (dĕf'n), *v.t.* to make unable to hear; to drown out, as a sound; to make sound proof.

deaf-en-ing (dĕf'n-ing), *p.adj.* making sound proof; making unable to hear; so loud as to drown out other sounds; as, a *deafening* noise: *n.* material used in a floor or wall to deaden sound.

deaf-mute (dĕf'mūt'), *n.* one deaf and dumb; one who is dumb from lack of hearing.

deaf-ness (dĕf'nĕs), *n.* the condition of being without hearing.

deal (dēl), *n.* a division; a part; a portion; a division of cards to the players; colloquially, a bargain or a secret agreement; as, a *deal* between politicians;

the wood of the fir or pine tree cut into boards or planks: *v.t.* [*p.t.* and *p.p.* dealt; *p.pr.* dealing], to distribute, apportion, or divide; throw about; scatter: *v.i.* to conduct business; as, they *deal* directly with the farmers; make a private arrangement.

deal-er (dēl'ẽr), *n.* one who does business with others; a trader; one who buys and sells goods; one who distributes cards in a game.

deal-ing (dēl'ĭng), *n.* conduct towards others; as, fair *dealing* means honesty: *pl.* business relations; traffic.

dealt (dĕlt), past tense and past participle of the verb *deal*.

dean (dēn), *n.* the head of a group of clergy in cathedral and collegiate churches; the member of a college faculty who supervises, or looks after, the students; the administrative officer of a college or university next below the president; the oldest member, by reason of service, in a body of men of a certain profession: a term of courtesy.

dean-er-y (dēn'ẽr-ĭ), *n.* [*pl.* deaneries (-ĭz)], the position, extent of authority, or residence of a dean.

dear (dēr), *adj.* expensive; costly; as, meat has become very *dear;* beloved; highly esteemed; precious: *n.* a darling; favorite: *adv.* at a high price or rate; as, his carelessness cost him *dear: interj.* expressing surprise, pity, or emotion.—*n.* **dearness.**

Syn., adj. precious, expensive.

Ant. (see despised, cheap).

dear-ly (dēr'lĭ), *adv.* with great affection; at a high price or rate; as, he paid *dearly* for his pleasures.

dearth (dûrth), *n.* want; scarcity; famine; as, the war has caused a *dearth* of good dyes.

death (dĕth), *n.* cessation of life or feeling; the state of having ceased to live; total loss; decay; something as terrible as death; slaughter; bloodshed.

Syn. departure, decease, demise.

Ant. (see life).

death-bed (dĕth'bĕd''), *n.* the bed of a person's last sickness; last hours of life.

death bell (dĕth bĕl), a bell tolled to announce a death.

death-blow (dĕth'blō''), *n.* something which causes death; a shock from which one cannot recover.

death-less (dĕth'lĕs), *adj.* immortal; never dying; as, *deathless* fame.

death-ly (dĕth'lĭ), *adj.* mortal; fatal: *adv.* fatally, or as if fatally.

death point (dĕth point), the degree of heat or cold which destroys animal life.

death rate (dĕth rāt), the percentage or number of deaths, usually reckoned at per thousand, among the people of a country or city for a certain period.

death's-head (dĕths'hĕd''), *n.* a skull or likeness of a skull, meaning death.

death war-rant (dĕth wŏr'ănt), a paper giving power to carry out a sentence of death; something which ends happiness.

death-watch (dĕth'wŏch''), *n.* a watch or guard beside a dying person; a guard set over a criminal prior to his execution.

de-ba-cle (dē-bä'kl; dē-băk'l), *n.* a stampede; a disorderly flight in battle; the breaking up of ice on a river; a violent flood, carrying with it débris or rubbish in great masses; as, the Ohio River *debacle* caused great suffering.

de-bar (dē-bär'), *v.t.* [*p.t.* and *p.p.* debarred, *p.pr.* debarring], to shut out; exclude; hinder from approach, enjoyment, or action: with *from;* as, the railroad gates *debar* people from crossing the tracks.

de-bark (dē-bärk'), *v.i.* to disembark; to go ashore from a vessel.

de-bar-ka-tion (dē''bär-kā'shŭn), *n.* the act of going ashore from a vessel; as, the *debarkation* of the troops from the ships.

de-base (dē-bās'), *v.t.* to reduce from a higher to a lower state; to lower in character, virtue, purity, or quality; as, to *debase* a gold coin by boring a hole in it.

de-base-ment (dē-bās'mĕnt), *n.* act of lowering in value or character; a condition of being lowered in value, quality, or character.

de-bat-a-ble (dē-bāt'*ȧ*-bl), *adj.* disputable; admitting of question or debate; as, the cause of the war was a *debatable* question.

de-bate (dē-bāt'), *n.* contention in words; argument; discussion; a formal presentation of arguments on both sides of a question, by several speakers, before an audience: *v.t.* discuss by presenting arguments for and against; dispute; meditate upon: *v.i.* to argue or discuss a point; reflect.

de-bat-er (dē-bāt'ẽr), *n.* a person who takes part in an argument, usually of a formal nature.

de-bauch (dē-bôch'), *v.t.* to corrupt in morals or principles; pollute; vitiate: *n.* excess in eating and drinking; a carouse.—*adj.* **debauched.**

deb-au-chee (dĕb''ō-shē'), *n.* a dissipated person; a drunkard. [Fr.]

de-bauch-er-y (dē-bôch'ẽr-ĭ), *n.* [*pl.* debaucheries (-ĭz)], intemperance; drunkenness; gluttony; seduction from virtue; corruption of fidelity.

de-ben-ture (dē-bĕn'tūr), *n.* a written acknowledgment of a debt.

de-bil-i-tant (dē-bĭl'ĭ-tănt), *adj.* weakening: *n.* a remedy to lessen excitement.

de-bil-i-tate (dē-bĭl'ĭ-tāt), *v.t.* to weaken; to enfeeble; to enervate.—*p.adj.* **debilitated.**

de-bil-i-ta-tion (dē-bĭl''ĭ-tā'shŭn), *n.* act of weakening; state of weakness.

de-bil-i-ty (dē-bĭl'ĭ-tĭ), *n.* [*pl.* debilities (-tĭz)], weakness; languor; feebleness.

deb-it (dĕb'ĭt), *n.* entry in an account of money due another: opposite to *credit: adj.* relating to debts: *v.t.* to charge with debt.

deb-o-nair (dĕb''ō-nâr'), *adj.* gay and light-hearted; of gentle manners or breeding; elegant; as, the Frenchman had *debonair* manners. Also, **debonaire, debonnaire.**

de-bouch (dē-bōōsh'), *v.i.* to march out of a confined spot, as a wood, into open ground; to emerge or come out; as, the regiment was ordered to *debouch* into the open plain.

dé-bou-ché (dā''bōō''shā'), *n.* an opening; a market for goods; an opening in military works for troops. [Fr.]

dé-bris (dā″brē′), *n.* fragments; rubbish; loose pieces of rock at the base of a mountain; as, a landslide brings down tons of *débris.* [Fr.]

debt (dĕt), *n.* that which is due from one person to another; obligation; as, an unpaid bill is a *debt;* sin; as, "Forgive us our *debts.*"

debt-or (dĕt′ẽr), *n.* one who owes something to another; one who is under obligation to another.

dé-but (dā″bü′; dā-bü′), *n.* a first appearance in society, or before the public; as, a singer's *début.*

dé-bu-tant (dā″bü″täṅ′; dĕb″ū-tänt′), *n.* [*fem.* débutante], one who makes a début, or first appearance in society, or in public.

dec-ade (dĕk′ād), *n.* a group of ten; ten consecutive years; as, the census is taken every *decade.* Also, **decad.**

de-ca-dence (dē-kā′dĕns; dĕk′ȧ-dĕns), *n.* decay; decline. Also, **decadency.**

de-ca-dent (dē-kā′dĕnt; dĕk′ȧ-dĕnt), *adj.* decaying or falling into ruin: *n.* one that has declined or decayed.

dec-a-gon (dĕk′ȧ-gŏn), *n.* a plane figure having ten sides and ten angles.

de-cag-o-nal (dē-kăg′ō-năl), *adj.* pertaining to a decagon, or figure with ten angles and ten sides.

dec-a-gram (dĕk′ȧ-grăm), *n.* a metric weight of ten grams, or 0.3527 oz. Also, **decagramme.**

dec-a-he-dron (dĕk″ȧ-hē′drŏn), *n.* [*pl.* decahedra (-drȧ)], a solid figure having ten equal sides.—*adj.* **decahedral.**

dec-a-li-ter (dĕk′ȧ-lī′tẽr), *n.* a metric measure of capacity containing ten liters, or 2.64 gals. Also, **decalitre.**

Dec-a-log (dĕk′ȧ-lŏg), *n.* the Ten Commandments; the moral law. Also, **Decalogue.**

dec-a-me-ter (dĕk′ȧ-mē″tẽr), *n.* a metric measure of length of ten meters, or 32.808 feet. Also, **decametre.**

de-camp (dē-kămp′), *v.i.* to break up camp; to run away; to depart suddenly or secretly.

de-cant (dē-kănt′), *v.t.* to pour off gently, as from one vessel to another.—*n.* **decantation.**

de-cant-er (dē-kăn′tẽr), *n.* an ornamental glass bottle for holding wines, liquors, etc.

de-cap-i-tate (dē-kăp′ĭ-tāt), *v.t.* to cut off the head of.

de-cap-i-ta-tion (dē-kăp″ĭ-tā′shŭn), *n.* beheading.

de-car-bon-ize (dē-kär′bŏn-īz), *v.t.* to deprive of carbon. Also, **decarbonate.**

dec-are (dĕk′âr″; dĕk-âr′), *n.* a metric measure of surface containing ten ares, or 0.2471 acre.

dec-a-stere (dĕk′ȧ-stēr), *n.* a metric measure of capacity containing ten cubic meters, or 13.08 cu. yd.

dec-ath-lon (dĕk-ăth′lŏn), *n.* an athletic contest in which each contestant takes part in ten different events.

de-cay (dē-kā′), *v.i.* [*p.t.* and *p.p.* decayed, *p.pr.* decaying], to rot; decline or fail; *n.* decline; gradual failure in mind or body; ruin; rottenness; corruption.
Syn., *n.* consumption, impairment.
Ant. (see growth).

de-cease (dē-sēs′), *v.i.* to die: *n.* death; as, the *decease* of a great man.—*p.adj.* **deceased.**

de-ce-dent (dē-sē′dĕnt), *n.* in law, a deceased person.

de-ceit (dē-sēt′), *n.* fraud; cheat; deception; falsehood; double dealing; a trick.
Syn. imposition, trick, delusion, guile, treachery, sham.
Ant. (see truthfulness).

de-ceit-ful (dē-sēt′fo͝ol), *adj.* full of fraud and trickery; insincere; false; as, *deceitful* conduct.—*adv.* **deceitfully.**—*n.* **deceitfulness.**

de-ceiv-a-ble (dē-sēv′ȧ-bl), *adj.* capable of being, or liable to be, tricked, or cheated.

de-ceive (dē-sēv′), *v.t.* to cheat; to mislead or cause to err; delude; impose upon; disappoint.—*n.* **deceiver.**
Syn. overreach, gull, dupe, cheat.

De-cem-ber (dē-sĕm′bẽr), *n.* the twelfth and last month of the year.

de-cem-vir (dē-sĕm′vẽr), *n.* [*pl.* decemviri (-vĭ-rī)], one of ten Roman magistrates, especially one of those who possessed absolute authority in ancient Rome (451–449 B. C.), and wrote the laws known as the Twelve Tables.

de-cem-vi-rate (dē-sĕm′vĭ-rāt), *n.* a body of ten men in authority; their office, or term of office.

de-cen-cy (dē′sĕn-sĭ), *n.* [*pl.* decencies (-sĭz)], propriety; modesty; the state of being respectable.

de-cen-ni-al (dē-sĕn′ĭ-ăl), *adj.* consisting of ten years; occurring every ten years: an anniversary observed every tenth year.

de-cent (dē′sĕnt), *adj.* becoming; suitable; respectable; modest; as, *decent* clothes; passable.—*adv.* **decently.**—*n.* **decentness.**

de-cep-tion (dē-sĕp′shŭn), *n.* the act of tricking or cheating; the state of being cheated or misled; fraud; a delusion.

de-cep-tive (dē-sĕp′tĭv), *adj.* tending to trick, cheat, or mislead; as, *deceptive* appearances.—*adv.* **deceptively.**—*n.* **deceptiveness.**

de-cide (dē-sīd′), *v.t.* to settle; to determine; to bring to an issue or conclusion; resolve: *v.i.* to give a judgment or decision; arbitrate.
Syn. determine, settle, adjudicate, terminate, resolve.

de-cid-ed (dē-sīd′ĕd), *p.adj.* free from doubt; determined; unquestionable; resolute.—*n.* **decidedness.**

de-cid-ed-ly (dē-sīd′ĕd-lĭ), *adv.* positively; certainly; without doubt.

de-cid-u-ous (dē-sĭd′ū-ŭs), *adj.* losing foliage or leaves every year; not evergreen; as, the maple is a *deciduous* tree.

dec-i-gram (dĕs′ĭ-grăm), *n.* a metric measure of weight equal to one-tenth of a gram, or 1.5432 grains. Also, **decigramme.**

dec-i-li-ter (dĕs′ĭ-lē″ter), *n.* a metric measure of capacity equal to one-tenth of a liter, or 3.38 fluid ounces. Also, **decilitre.**

de-cil-lion (dē-sĭl′yŭn), *n.* in France and the United States, a unit followed by thirty-three ciphers; in England, a unit followed by sixty ciphers.

dec-i-mal (dĕs'ĭ-măl), *adj.* pertaining to, or based upon, the number ten: *n.* a decimal fraction.—*adv.* **decimally.**

dec-i-mal-ly (dĕs'ĭ-măl-ĭ), *adv.* by decimals, or by tens or tenths.

dec-i-mal place (dĕs'ĭ-măl plās), the place of a figure after the decimal point.

dec-i-mal point (dĕs'ĭ-măl point), a dot separating a decimal fraction from a whole number, also indicating, when standing alone, its fractional character.

dec-i-mal sys-tem (dĕs'ĭ-măl sĭs'tĕm), a system of reckoning or measuring by ten, or powers of ten.

dec-i-mate (dĕs'ĭ-māt), *v.t.* to take the tenth of; put to death, or punish, every tenth man; as, to *decimate* the ranks of an army; destroy a large part.

dec-i-ma-tion (dĕs"ĭ-mā'shŭn), *n.* destruction on a large scale.

dec-i-me-ter (dĕs'ĭ-mē"tẽr), *n.* a metric measure of length equal to one-tenth of a meter, or 3.937 inches. Also, **decimetre.**

de-ci-pher (dē-sī'fẽr), *v.t.* to translate from secret or unknown characters into known terms; discover or make out the meaning of, as something puzzling or hardly legible; interpret.—*adj.* **decipherable.**

Syn. read, spell, interpret.

de-ci-sion (dē-sĭzh'ŭn), *n.* the act of reaching a fixed opinion; the quality of being fixed and firm; determination; judgment; settlement; as, the *decision* of a court or of a case.

Syn. conclusion, resolution; firmness.

Ant. (see vacillation).

de-ci-sive (dē-sī'sĭv), *adj.* final; conclusive; as, a *decisive* victory; prompt; positive; determined.—*adv.* **decisively.**—*n.* **decisiveness.**

dec-i-stere (dĕs'ĭ-stâr), *n.* a metric measure of capacity equal to one cubic meter.

deck (dĕk), *n.* a platform serving as a floor for a section of ship, and as a covering for the space below; the floor of an airplane; a pack of playing cards: *v.t.* to put finery or ornaments on; adorn.

deck-le-edged (dĕk'l-ĕjd'), *adj.* having the edges rough and uncut: said of books.

de-claim (dē-klām'), *v.t.* to utter in rhetorical style; speak as an exercise in elocution: *v.i.* to harangue; to speak oratorically in public; to recite a selection as an exercise; as, the boy was asked to *declaim.*—*n.* **declaimer.**

dec-la-ma-tion (dĕk"lȧ-mā'shŭn), *n.* speech delivered in public; act of reciting; a selection recited from memory; harangue.

Syn. oratory, elocution, effusion, debate.

de-clam-a-to-ry (dē-klăm'ȧ-tō-rĭ), *adj.* pertaining to, or characterized by, rhetorical speech; noisy in style; appealing to the passions.

dec-la-ra-tion (dĕk"lȧ-rā'shŭn), *n.* the act of announcing or proclaiming; that which is announced; an assertion; publication; a statement reduced to writing.

Syn. avowal, manifestation, statement, profession.

de-clar-a-tive (dē-klăr'ȧ-tĭv), *adj.* making a statement; as, a *declarative* sentence; explanatory.

de-clar-a-to-ry (dē-klăr'ȧ-tō-rĭ), *adj.* affirmative; as, a *declaratory* statement.

de-clare (dē-klâr), *v.t.* to make known; tell openly or publicly; proclaim formally; publish; make a solemn affirmation of before witnesses; make a full statement of, as to goods, etc.: *v.i.* to make a statement; avow: with *for* or *against.*

de-clen-sion (dē-klĕn'shŭn), *n.* a sloping down; a falling off or away; in grammar, the inflection of nouns, pronouns, and adjectives.

de-clin-a-ble (dē-klīn'ȧ-bl), *adj.* capable of being declined, or inflected; as, pronouns and adjectives are *declinable.*

dec-li-na-tion (dĕk"lĭ-nā'shŭn), *n.* the act or state of bending, or moving, downwards; dipping, as the *declination* of a magnetic needle; a slant from some definite direction; decline; decay; the distance of a heavenly body north or south of the equator; nonacceptance.

de-cline (dē-klīn'), *v.i.* to bend or lean downwards; droop; draw to a close; become weak; move from the right path: *v.t.* to refuse; as, to *decline* an invitation; bend downwards; depress; inflect, as a noun or pronoun: *n.* a lessening; decay; a growing worse; the closing part of something; a wasting away with disease.

de-clin-o-graph (dē-klī'nō-grȧf), *n.* a self-acting instrument for recording: used in astronomy.

dec-li-nom-e-ter (dĕk"lĭ-nŏm'ē-tẽr), *n.* an instrument used for measuring the dip of the magnetic needle.

de-cliv-i-tous (dē-klĭv'ĭ-tŭs), *adj.* moderately steep; sloping downward; as, a *declivitous* path.

de-cliv-i-ty (dē-klĭv'ĭ-tĭ), *n.* [*pl.* declivities (-tĭz)], a gradual descent; deviation or change from a horizontal line; downward slope.

de-coct (dē-kŏkt'), *v.t.* to obtain the flavor, essence, or medicinal qualities of, by boiling.

de-coc-tion (dē-kŏk'shŭn), *n.* an extract obtained by boiling or digesting in hot water.

dé-col-le-té (dā"kŏl"-tā'), *adj.* [*fem.* décolletée], cut low in the neck so as to expose the neck and shoulders; as, a *décolleté* dress; wearing a low-necked dress. [Fr.]

de-com-pos-a-ble (dē"kŏm-pōz'ȧ-bl), *adj.* capable of being separated into parts.

de-com-pose (dē"kŏm-pōz'), *v.t.* to separate into elementary parts; cause to decay or rot: *v.i.* to become separated into parts; to rot.

de-com-po-si-tion (dē-kŏm"pō-zĭsh'ŭn), *n.* the act of separating into elementary parts; as, *decomposition* of water produces oxygen and hydrogen; analysis; disintegration; state of decay.

dec-o-rate (dĕk'ō-rāt), *v.t.* to ornament; as, *decorate* a stage for an entertainment; adorn, or beautify; confer a badge of honor upon; grace.

dec-o-ra-tion (dĕk"ō-rā'shŭn), *n.* the art of adorning; an ornament; a badge of honor.

Dec-o-ra-tion Day (dĕk'ō-rā'shŭn dā), the day (May 30) on which the graves of those who fell in the Civil War (1861–65) are decorated: called also *Memorial Day.*

dec-o-ra-tive (dĕk'ô-rā-tĭv), *adj.* tending to adorn; ornamental.—*adv.* **decoratively.**—*n.* **decorativeness.**

dec-o-ra-tor (dĕk"ô-rā'tẽr), *n.* one who adorns or beautifies; a person whose business it is to do ornamental painting, etc., in houses; as, an interior *decorator*.

de-co-rous (dē-kō'rŭs; dĕk'ô-rŭs), *adj.* marked by propriety; decent; fit; proper; polite; as, *decorous* behavior.—*adv.* **decorously.**—*n.* **decorousness.**

de-co-rum (dē-kō'rŭm), *n.* propriety and becomingness of words, dress, and conduct; suitableness, as for occasion; seemliness; dignity.

de-coy (dē-koi'), *n.* a deceptive trick or snare; a lure; a piece of inclosed water into which wild fowl are induced to enter; the figure of a bird used to attract live birds within gunshot: *v.t.* [*p.t.* and *p.p.* decoyed, *p.pr.* decoying], to lead or allure into danger by a trick; entice: *v.i.* to be allured by means of a trick.

de-coy duck (dē-koi' dŭk), a tame, or imitation, duck used to allure wild fowl; hence, a person who entraps others.

de-crease (dē-krēs'), *v.i.* to grow less; diminish; dwindle; as, his income steadily *decreased;* abate; as, the storm *decreased* in violence: *v.t.* to cause to grow less; as, to *decrease* the length of the working day; reduce gradually in size or extent: *n.* gradual lessening or decay; the amount or degree of lessening; the wane of the moon.

Syn., *v.* diminish, dwindle, lessen, decline, retrench, curtail, reduce.

Ant. (see grow, growth).

de-cree (dē-krē'), *n.* an ordinance, law, or edict; a judicial decision; the award of an umpire or arbitrator; *v.t.* to determine by a law, decision, etc.; ordain; assign: *v.i.* to make a law, decision, etc.; determine.

de-crep-it (dē-krĕp'ĭt), *adj.* feeble from age, or infirmity; wasted; worn out; as, a *decrepit* man.

de-crep-i-tude (dē-krĕp'ĭ-tūd), *n.* the state of being infirm from old age.

de-cres-cent (dē-krĕs'ĕnt), *adj.* growing less; as, in its last quarter the moon is *decrescent*.

de-cri-al (dē-krī'ăl), *n.* a crying down; a clamorous censure; outspoken blame.

de-cri-er (dē-krī'ẽr), *n.* one who blames or censures; as, Lincoln stood firm in spite of the attacks of his *decriers*.

de-cry (dē-krī'), *v.t.* [*p.t.* and *p.p.* decried, *p.pr.* decrying], to blame noisily; cry down; censure; disparage.

ded-i-cate (dĕd'ĭ-kāt), *v.t.* to set apart by a solemn act or religious ceremony; as, to *dedicate* a church; devote or set apart to some work or duty; as, to *dedicate* ourselves to peace; inscribe, as a literary work.—*n.* **dedicator.**

Syn. devote, consecrate, offer, set, apportion.

ded-i-ca-tion (dĕd"ĭ-kā'shŭn), *n.* the act of devoting to a religious purpose; as, the *dedication* of a church; an inscription or address expressing gratitude or respect for a patron or friend, prefixed to a literary or artistic work.—*adj.* **dedicatory.**

de-duce (dē-dūs'), *v.t.* to draw; to gather by reasoning; infer: with *from* or *out of;* derive.—*adj.* **deducible.**

de-duct (dē-dŭkt'), *v.t.* to take away; as, *deduct* a dollar from the bill.

de-duc-tion (dē-dŭk'shŭn), *n.* the act or process of taking away; subtraction; as, some stores make a *deduction* for cash payment; the drawing of conclusions from what is accepted.

de-duc-tive (dē-dŭk'tĭv), *adj.* tending to take away; drawing a conclusion from what is accepted; as, *deductive* reasoning.—*adv.* **deductively.**

deed (dēd), *n.* that which is done; an act; a great achievement; a written paper for the transfer of land: *v.t.* to convey by deed.

Syn., *n.* act, action, commission, instrument, document.

deem (dēm), *v.t.* to think; regard; believe; as, I *deem* it wise to prevent fire; *v.i.* to have, or be of, an opinion; judge.

Syn. estimate, consider, suppose, conceive.

deem-ster (dēm'stẽr), *n.* a judge or umpire; the title of either of the two chief judges of the Isle of Man. Also, **dempster.**

deep (dēp), *adj.* extending far below the surface; as, a *deep* well; extending far back; as, a *deep* lot; penetrating; sagacious; profound; difficult to understand; as, philosophy is a *deep* subject; absorbed; grave in tone, or low in pitch; intense; heavy; as, a *deep* sleep; strongly colored: *n.* that which extends far downward; a great body of water; an abyss; the culmination; as, the *deep* of night; the interval between two marks on a sounding line.—*n.* **deepness.**

Syn., *adj.* subterranean, submerged, designing, abstruse, learned.

Ant. (see shallow).

deep-en (dēp'n), *v.t.* to extend farther downward or backward; make darker; make more profound, etc.: *v.i.* to extend farther down; become more difficult; become darker.

deep-laid (dēp'lād), *adj.* well-concerted: carefully concealed; as, a *deep-laid* plot.

deep-sea (dēp'sē"), *adj.* pertaining to the open sea, or deeper parts of the ocean.

deer (dēr), *n. sing.* and *pl.* wild, horned, ruminating, or cud chewing, animals: their horns are called antlers and their flesh venison.

deer-hound (dēr'hound"), *n.* a dog used in hunting deer; a staghound.

deer lick (dēr lĭk), a spot of salt ground which deer like to nibble or lick.

deer-stalk-ing (dēr'stôk"ĭng), *n.* the hunting of deer by stealing upon them unawares.

de-face (dē-fās'), *v.t.* to mar or destroy the surface of; disfigure; impair the clearness of; injure; spoil; as, chalk marks *deface* the wall of the house.

Syn. mar, disfigure, impair, efface.

Ant. (see beautify).

de-face-ment (dē-fās'mĕnt), *n.* the act of marring the appearance of; the condition of being spoiled in appearance; injury.

de fac-to (dē făk'tō), actually existing in fact; as, a *de facto* government: distinguished from *de jure*. [LAT.]

de-fal-cate (dē-făl'kāt), *v.i.* to embezzle, or use for one's own purposes, money held in trust.—*n.* **defalcator.**

de-fal-ca-tion (dē"făl-kā'shŭn), *n.* a loss of funds through dishonesty; embezzlement, or dishonest use of trust funds; as, the bank lost money by the *defalcation* of the cashier; decrease.

def-a-ma-tion (dĕf'ȧ-mā'shŭn), *n.* slander; a malicious injuring of the good name or reputation of another; libel; as, to accuse an honest man of stealing is a *defamation* of his character.

de-fam-a-to-ry (dē-făm'ȧ-tō-rĭ), *adj.* slanderous; as, to spread *defamatory* reports.

de-fame (dē-fām'), *v.t.* to injure or destroy the good reputation of; speak of falsely and maliciously.—*n.* **defamer.**

de-fault (dē-fôlt'), *n.* neglect; failure in a contract; failure to appear at a time and place required: **in default of,** in case of failure of: *v.t.* to make a failure in, as a payment, an appearance in court, etc.; to neglect: *v.i.* to fail to account for trust funds; to fail to pay a debt; to fail to appear in court, etc.

Syn., *n.* lapse, forfeit, omission, absence, want, failure.

de-fault-er (dē-fôlt'ẽr), *n.* one who makes a failure in payment or performance; one who fails to make a proper accounting of money or property intrusted to his charge.

de-feat (dē-fēt'), *v.t.* to overthrow or vanquish; as, to *defeat* an enemy; bring to naught; frustrate; as, to *defeat* a purpose; *n.* act of preventing or bringing to naught; overthrow; the state of being conquered.

de-feat-ist (dē-fēt'ĭst), *n.* one who desires, or works for, the defeat of his country in war, in the hope that ultimate good may result.

de-fect (dē-fĕkt'), *n.* moral or physical imperfection; fault; error; lack of something necessary to complete; want.

Syn. imperfection, flaw, blemish.

de-fec-tion (dē-fĕk'shŭn), *n.* a falling away from duty or allegiance; desertion.

de-fec-tive (dē-fĕk'tĭv), *adj.* having a blemish or flaw of any kind; incomplete; faulty; wanting some of the usual grammatical forms.—*adv.* **defectively.** —*n.* **defectiveness.**

de-fend (dē-fĕnd'), *v.t.* to guard or protect from harm or violence; as, the navy *defends* our seacoast; maintain or uphold, as one's legal rights, by force of argument or evidence; contest, as a suit.—*n.* **defender.**

Syn. guard, protect, justify.

de-fend-ant (dē-fĕn'dănt), *n.* a person who is sued in a court of law: *adj.* making or interposing an excuse.

de-fense (dē-fĕns'), *n.* the act or state of guarding or being guarded; protection; a plea or answer in court to a charge or a suit. Also, **defence.**—*adj.* **defenseless.**

Syn. excuse, bulwark, rampart.

de-fen-si-ble (dē-fĕn'sĭ-bl), *adj.* capable of being protected.

de-fen-sive (dē-fĕn'sĭv), *adj.* serving to guard or protect; carried on for protection; as, *defensive* warfare.—*adv.* **defensively.**

de-fer (dē-fûr'), *v.t.* [*p.t.* and *p.p.* deferred, *p.pr.* deferring], to put off to a future time; delay; leave undone: *v.i.* to yield; to give in: followed by *to;* as, to *defer* to the judgment of an older person.

Syn. postpone, prorogue, adjourn.

Ant. (see impel, expedite).

def-er-ence (dĕf'ẽr-ĕns), *n.* a yielding to the opinions or wishes of another; regard; submission; respect.

def-er-en-tial (dĕf'ẽr-ĕn'shăl), *adj.* expressing regard for the wishes of another; respectful.—*adv.* **deferentially.**

de-fer-ment (dē-fûr'mĕnt), *n.* the act of postponement; delay.

de-fi-ance (dē-fī'ăns), *n.* contemptuous disregard; a challenge; refusal to obey.

de-fi-ant (dē-fī'ănt), *adj.* full of, or expressing, resistance or opposition.—*adv.* **defiantly.**

de-fi-cien-cy (dē-fĭsh'ĕn-sĭ), *n.* [*pl.* deficiencies (-sĭz)], the state of being incomplete; incompleteness; insufficiency; scarcity; failure.

de-fi-cient (dē-fĭsh'ĕnt), *adj.* wanting; incomplete; defective.

Syn. short, inadequate, scanty.

def-i-cit (dĕf'ĭ-sĭt), *n.* a shortage, especially of money.

de-fi-er (dē-fī'ẽr), *n.* one who refuses to obey; as, a *defier* of the law.

de-file (dē-fīl'), *v.t.* to make foul or impure; tarnish; corrupt: *v.i.* to march off in a line: *n.* a long, narrow mountain pass; a marching in file.—*n.* **defiler.**

Syn., *v.* pollute, corrupt, sully.

de-file-ment (dē-fīl'mĕnt), *n.* corruption; pollution; uncleanness.

de-fin-a-ble (dē-fīn'ȧ-bl), *adj.* capable o having its meaning clearly stated.

de-fine (dē-fīn'), *v.t.* to state the exact meaning of; to explain; to fix the limits of.—*n.* **definer.**

Syn. fix, settle, limit.

def-i-nite (dĕf'ĭ-nĭt), *adj.* precise; exact; having fixed or distinct limits; certain; pointing out.—*adv.* **definitely.**—*n.* **definiteness.**

def-i-ni-tion (dĕf'ĭ-nĭsh'ŭn), *n.* a brief explanation of the exact meaning of a term, phrase, etc.; a concise or clear statement.

de-fin-i-tive (dē-fĭn'ĭ-tĭv), *adj.* positive; final; determining; conclusive: *n.* in grammar, a word used to limit the meaning of a noun.—*adv.* **definitively.**—*n.* **definitiveness.**

de-flect (dē-flĕkt'), *v.t.* to bend from a straight line: *v.i.* to swerve; bend or turn aside.

de-flec-tion (dē-flĕk'shŭn), *n.* a bending or turning aside; the movement from one side to the other in sighting a field gun to bring the gun to bear on its object, as distinguished from elevation.

de-flec-tive (dē-flĕk'tĭv), *adj.* tending to bend or turn aside.

de-flec-tor (dē-flĕk'tẽr), *n.* a plate or cone in a furnace or lamp to bring flames or gases into close contact, and thus increase the fire.

de-flow-er (dē-flou'ẽr), *v.t.* to deprive of flowers or bloom; to rob of beauty or grace; to ravish; to spoil.

de-fo-li-ate (dē-fō'lĭ-āt), *v.t.* to strip or deprive of leaves: *adj.* deprived of leaves.—*n.* **defoliation.**

de-for-est (dē-fŏr'ĕst), *v.t.* to clear of trees; cut down; clear away, or destroy, the trees of.—*n.* **deforestation.**

de-form (dē-fôrm'), *v.t.* to render ugly or unshapely; disfigure; mar; deface.—*p.adj.* **deformed.**—*n.* **deformation.**

de-form-i-ty (dē-fôr'mĭ-tĭ), *n.* [*pl.* deformities (-tĭz)], that which disfigures or spoils the shape of; state of being misshapen; want of beauty or harmony.

de-fraud (dē-frôd'), *v.t.* to cheat; to deceive; withhold wrongfully from.—*n.* **defrauder.**

de-fray (dē-frā'), *v.t.* [*p.t.* and *p.p.* defrayed, *p.pr.* defraying], to pay; settle; as, to *defray* the expenses of a journey.
Syn. liquidate, discharge.

de-fray-al (dē-frā'ăl), *n.* the act of paying, as expenses. Also, **defrayment.**

deft (dĕft), *adj.* skilful; dexterous; handy; clever; as, the *deft* fingers of our grandmothers.—*adv.* **deftly.**—*n.* **deftness.**

de-funct (dē-fŭnkt'), *adj.* dead; extinct: *n.* a dead person; usually, one lately deceased; the dead collectively.

de-fy (dē-fī'), *v.t.* [*p.t.* and *p.p.* defied, *p.pr.* defying], to challenge or provoke to strife; to dare; to act in contempt of; resist openly; as, to *defy* the law; resist successfully; baffle.

de-gen-er-a-cy (dē-jĕn'ẽr-ȧ-sĭ), *n.* the state of being degraded or of growing worse than formerly; lowness of morals.

de-gen-er-ate (dē-jĕn'ẽr-āt), *v.i.* to be or grow worse; to decline; to become inferior in goodness or quality; deteriorate: *adj.* (dē-jĕn'ẽr-āt), of a low grade of morals; deteriorated; as, *degenerate* times; degraded; as, *degenerate* offspring: *n.* a person or organism that has become worse than its kind; a person of low morals.—*adv.* **degenerately.**

de-gen-er-a-tion (dē-jĕn"ẽr-ā'shŭn), *n.* the act, state, or process of growing worse; degeneracy; decline.

deg-lu-ti-tion (dĕg"lōō-tĭsh'ŭn), *n.* the act, process, or power of swallowing.

deg-ra-da-tion (dĕg"rȧ-dā'shŭn), *n.* the act of lowering, or of being lowered, in rank, morals, etc.; disgrace.

de-grade (dē-grād'), *v.t.* to reduce in grade or rank; deprive of honors, office, or dignity; as, to *degrade* a soldier to a lower rank; lower physically or morally; tone down; lessen; wear away.

de-gree (dē-grē'), *n.* a step or grade; rank or station in life; a stage in progress; a remove in relationship; academical rank conferred by an institution; as, a doctor's *degree;* one of three grades in the comparison of an adjective or adverb; a relative amount, extent, quality, etc.; the 360th part of the circumference of a circle; sixty geographical miles; a unit for measuring heat, cold, etc.
Syn., grade, extent, measure.

de-i-fi-ca-tion (dē"ĭ-fĭ-kā'shŭn), *n.* the act of making a god of, or worshiping as a god.

de-i-fy (dē'ĭ-fī), *v.t.* [*p.t.* and *p.p.* deified, *p.pr.* deifying], to praise or worship as a god; as, the Druids *deified* the oak tree; idolize.

deign (dān), *v.i.* to condescend; vouchsafe; as, he did not *deign* to listen to our request: *v.t.* to grant; to condescend to give; as, he would *deign* us no reply.

de-ism (dē'ĭzm), *n.* a belief in God founded on reason, rather than on revelation.

de-ist (dē'ĭst), *n.* one whose belief in God is founded on reason, rather than on revelation.

de-is-tic (dē-ĭs'tĭk), *adj.* pertaining to a reasoned belief in a personal God. Also, **deistical.**

de-i-ty (dē'ĭ-tĭ), *n.* [*pl.* deities (-tĭz)], a god, goddess, or person worshiped as a divine being; the character, nature, or attributes of God: **the Deity,** God; Jehovah; the Godhead.

de-ject (dē-jĕkt'), *v.t.* to depress the spirits of; dishearten; sadden.

de-ject-ed (dē-jĕk'tĕd), *p.adj.* cast down; depressed; low-spirited.—*adv.* **dejectedly.**

de-jec-tion (dē-jĕk'shŭn), *n.* lowness of spirits; melancholy; depression. Also, **dejectedness.**

de ju-re (dē jōō'rē), by right or lawful title; as, a government *de jure.* [LAT.]

de-laine (dē-lān'), *n.* a light fabric made of wool, or of wool and cotton.

Del-a-ware (dĕl'ȧ-wâr), *n.* one of a tribe of American Indians, originally inhabiting the region of the Delaware River.

de-lay (dē-lā'), *v.t.* [*p.t.* and *p.p.* delayed, *p.pr.* delaying], to put off; to postpone; make late; hinder for a time: *v.i.* to act or proceed slowly: *n.* postponement; detention; as, the *delay* was caused by a storm; procrastination.—*n.* **delayer.**

de-le (dē'lē), *v.t.* to take out (a letter, etc.) in proof reading: *n.* a mark [₰] indicating that a letter, etc., is to be deleted, or taken out.

de-lec-ta-ble (dē-lĕk'tȧ-bl), *adj.* pleasing; delightful; as, ice-cream is *delectable* on a hot day.—*adv.* **delectably.**—*n.* **delectableness.**

de-lec-ta-tion (dē"lĕk-tā'shŭn), *n.* delight; pleasure.

del-e-gate (dĕl'ē-gāt), *n.* one sent to represent, and act for, others; as, the *delegates* to a convention; representative: *v.t.* (dĕl'ē-gāt), to send as an agent with authority to act; intrust; commit; as, the people *delegate* power to Congress.
Syn., *n.* agent, deputy, substitute.

del-e-ga-tion (dĕl"ē-gā'shŭn), *n.* a sending away; the act of authorizing a person or body of persons to act for others; the body of persons chosen to act; as, each State sends a *delegation* to the Republican convention.

de-lete (dē-lēt'), *v.t.* to blot out; erase; as, the printer is expected to *delete* all mistakes before printing a book.

del-e-te-ri-ous (dĕl"ē-tē'rĭ-ŭs), *adj.* harmful, morally or physically; poisonous; as, some drugs have a *deleterious* effect on the body.—*adv.* **deleteriously.**—*n.* **deleteriousness.**

delft-ware (dĕlft'wâr"), *n.* a kind of glazed earthenware, made first at Delft, in Holland. Also, **delft, delf.**

de-lib-er-ate (dē-lĭb'ẽr-āt), *v.t.* to reflect on; to think upon or consider; weigh in the mind; as, he *deliberated* the matter before deciding; ponder: *v.i.* to take counsel with oneself or others; as, the men elected to make laws are expected to *deliberate* before passing a law: *adj.* (dē-lĭb'ẽr-āt), circumspect; slow in determining or in action; well-considered; watchful; cautious; prudent; wary.—*adv.* **deliberately.**—*n.* **deliberator.**
Syn., *v.* consider, meditate, consult, ponder, debate.

de-lib-er-a-tion (dē-lĭb"ẽr-ā'shŭn), *n.* calm and careful consideration; slowness in action. Also, **deliberateness.**

de-lib-er-a-tive (dē-lĭb′ẽr-ȧ-tĭv), *adj.* of or pertaining to discussion; having the form of debate; existing for legislative discussion; characterized by careful consideration.

del-i-ca-cy (dĕl′ĭ-kȧ-sĭ), *n.* [*pl.* delicacies (-sĭz)], the state or quality of being agreeable to the taste or other senses; a luxury; grace; sensitiveness; refinement; sensibility; consideration for the feelings of others; sensitiveness to disease.

Syn. nicety, daintiness, refinement, tact, softness, modesty.

Ant. (see boorishness, indelicacy).

del-i-cate (dĕl′ĭ-kāt), *adj.* pleasing to the taste; as, a *delicate* flavor; tender; refined; as, *delicate* attentions; physically frail; as a *delicate* child; sensitive.—*adv.* **delicately.**

del-i-ca-tes-sen (dĕl″ĭ-kȧ-tĕs′ĕn), *n.pl.* prepared foods, as cooked meats, preserves, and relishes; table delicacies. [GER.]

de-li-cious (dē-lĭsh′ŭs), *adj.* highly pleasing to the senses, taste, or mind; exquisite.—*adv.* **deliciously.**—*n.* **deliciousness.**

Syn. sweet, palatable.

Ant. (see nauseous).

de-light (dē-līt′), *v.t.* to gratify or please greatly; charm: *v.i.* be highly gratified or pleased: with *in*: *n.* an extreme degree of pleasure; high satisfaction; joy.

Syn., n. enjoyment, pleasure, happiness, transport, ecstasy, gladness, rapture, bliss.

Ant. (see annoyance).

de-light-ed (dē-līt′ĕd), *p.adj.* greatly pleased; gratified; charmed.

de-light-ful (dē-līt′fōōl), *adj.* affording enjoyment; pleasing; charming.—*adv.* **delightfully.**—*n.* **delightfulness.**

de-lim-it (dē-lĭm′ĭt), *v.t.* to mark out or fix the limits of, as territory; bound.

de-lin-e-ate (dē-lĭn′ē-āt), *v.t.* to mark out with lines; sketch; draw; describe minutely and accurately in words.

de-lin-e-a-tion (dē-lĭn″ē-ā′shŭn), *n.* the act or art of picturing or describing; a sketch, description, etc.

de-lin-e-a-tor (dē-lĭn′ē-ā″tẽr), *n.* one who pictures or describes.

de-lin-quen-cy (dē-lĭn′kwĕn-sĭ), *n.* [*pl.* delinquencies (-sĭz)], neglect of, or failure in, duty; a misdeed; fault.

de-lin-quent (dē-lĭn′kwĕnt), *adj.* falling short of duty: *n.* one who neglects, or fails to perform, a duty; an offender.

del-i-quesce (dĕl″ĭ-kwĕs′), *v.i.* to dissolve gradually and become liquid by taking in moisture from the air, as certain salts.—*adj.* **deliquescent.**—*n.* **deliquescence.**

de-lir-i-ous (dē-lĭr′ĭ-ŭs), *adj.* light-headed; insane; raving because of fever; frantic with delight; as, the gift of a pony makes a child *delirious* with joy.—*adv.* **deliriously.**

de-lir-i-um (dē-lĭr′ĭ-ŭm), *n.* a temporary mental disorder, often caused by fever, and marked by wandering speech and fancies; excitement; wild enthusiasm; as, a *delirium* of joy.

de-lir-i-um tre-mens (dē-lĭr′ĭ-ŭm trē′mĕnz), a disease of the brain caused by drinking intoxicating liquors to excess.

de-liv-er (dē-lĭv′ẽr), *v.t.* to set free; save; yield possession or control of; carry and hand to an owner; send forth vigorously; discharge; communicate; utter; as, to *deliver* a speech.

Syn. liberate, free, rescue, pronounce, give, hand over.

de-liv-er-ance (dē-lĭv′ẽr-ăns), *n.* the act of setting free; rescue; release; a public utterance.

de-liv-er-y (dē-lĭv′ẽr-ĭ), *n.* [*pl.* deliveries (-ĭz)], the act of releasing; a setting free; a surrender; transfer; manner of speaking; as, the orator had a splendid *delivery;* a distribution of letters, etc.; the act or manner of throwing a ball.

dell (dĕl), *n.* a small valley; a ravine; a retired glen.

de-lous-er (dē-louz′ẽr), *n.* an apparatus for disinfecting clothing to destroy body lice.

Del-phic (dĕl′fĭk), *adj.* pertaining to Delphi, or to the famous sanctuary of Apollo with its priestess, or the games celebrated there in honor of Apollo. Also, **Delphian.**

Del-sarte (dĕl-särt′), *n.* a system of physical exercise first taught by F. Delsarte, a Frenchman.

del-ta (dĕl′tȧ), *n.* [*pl.* deltas (-tȧz)], a deposit of sand or soil, shaped like the Greek letter delta, formed at the mouth of a river; as, the Nile River forms a *delta;* any triangular surface.

de-lude (dē-lūd′), *v.t.* to cheat; beguile; deceive; as, to *delude* oneself with false hopes.

del-uge (dĕl′ūj), *n.* an inundation or flood; a great overflowing of the land by water, especially that of the time of Noah (Genesis vii); a sudden and resistless calamity: *v.t.* to overwhelm; to overflow.

de-lu-sion (dē-lū′zhŭn), *n.* the act of leading astray; deceit; false idea; state of being deceived; as, he was under the *delusion* that all men were honest.

Syn. error, illusion, fallacy, hallucination.

Ant. (see fact, reality).

de-lu-sive (dē-lū′sĭv), *adj.* tending to mislead or deceive; deceptive. Also, **delusory.**—*adv.* **delusively.**—*n.* **delusiveness.**

de luxe (dē lŭks), made unusually fine or elegant; as, an edition *de luxe* of Shakespeare's plays. [FR.]

delve (dĕlv), *v.t.* to dig; fathom; penetrate: *v.i.* to work with a spade; to make laborious search for information; as, the scientist *delves* into the secrets of nature.

de-mag-net-ize (dē-măg′nĕt-īz), *v.t.* to deprive of magnetic properties.

dem-a-gog (dĕm′ȧ-gŏg), *n.* a popular orator; leader of the rabble; an insincere political leader. Also, **demagogue.**

dem-a-gog-ic (dĕm″ȧ-gŏj′ĭk), *adj.* like a demagog, or an insincere leader. Also, **demagogical.**

dem-a-gog-ism (dĕm′ȧ-gŏg-ĭzm), *n.* the principles or practice of a demagog, or an insincere leader of the people.

de-mand (dē-mȧnd′), *v.t.* to claim; to exact; to question; summon; require: *v.i.* to inquire by authority: *n.* authoritative claim; an imperative request; the state of being sought after; as, coal is in great *demand.*

de-mar-ca-tion (dē″mär-kā′shŭn), *n.* the act of defining, or marking, the bounds of; a line of separation; as, the fence is the *demarcation* of the property.

de-mean (dē-mēn′), *v.t.* to behave; to conduct; as, to *demean* oneself in a proper manner; to humble, lower, or degrade; as, to be rude is to *demean* oneself.

de-mean-or (dē-mēn′ẽr), *n.* behavior; deportment; bearing. Also, **demeanour.**

de-ment-ed (dē-mĕn′tĕd), *p.adj.* insane; mad; deprived of reason.

de-men-ti-a (dē-mĕn′shĭ-ȧ), *n.* unsoundness of mind; insanity.

de-mer-it (dē-mĕr′ĭt), *n.* action which deserves blame; ill desert; a mark for bad conduct.

de-mesne (dē-mān′; dē-mēn′), *n.* possession of land as one's own; landed estate attached to a manor: *adj.* pertaining to a landed estate. Also, **demain.**

dem-i- (dĕm′ĭ-), half: a prefix used in composition; as, *demi*-quaver, a note equal in length to half a quaver.

dem-i-god (dĕm′ĭ-gŏd″), *n.* an inferior god; one whose nature is partly divine; a hero.

dem-i-john (dĕm′ĭ-jŏn), *n.* a large glass bottle with a small neck and large body, usually incased in wickerwork and used for holding liquors.

de-mise (dē-mīz′), *n.* death, especially of a royal personage; the conveyance or transfer of an estate by will or lease: *v.t.* to give or grant by will: *v.i.* to bequeath property by will.

de-mo-bil-ize (dē-mō′bĭ-līz; dē-mŏb′ĭ-līz), *v.t.* to disband or dismiss troops that have been mobilized, or called to arms; change from a war footing to a peace footing.

de-moc-ra-cy (dē-mŏk′rȧ-sĭ), *n.* [*pl.* democracies (-sĭz)], government by the people; republic; as, the United States is a *democracy;* practical or social equality opposed to aristocracy; as, the world must be safe for *democracy:* **Democracy,** the Democratic party or its principles.

dem-o-crat (dĕm′ō-krăt), *n.* one who believes in and upholds the principles of popular government or social equality: **Democrat,** a member of the Democratic party.

dem-o-crat-ic (dĕm″ō-krăt′ĭk), *adj.* pertaining to democracy, or government by the people; believing in, or tending to, social equality: **Democratic party,** one of the two greater parties in the United States, so named in 1828.—*adv.* **democratically.**

dem-oi-selle (dĕm″ĭ-zĕl′), *n.* an unmarried woman. [Fr.]

de-mol-ish (dē-mŏl′ĭsh), *v.t.* to throw down; reduce to ruins; destroy; annihilate.—*n.* **demolisher.**
Syn. raze, ruin, overthrow.
Ant. (see build, repair).

dem-o-li-tion (dĕm″ō-lĭsh′ŭn), *n.* the act or process of tearing down or destroying; destruction.

de-mon (dē′mŏn), *n.* an evil spirit; devil; in mythology, a being midway between the gods and men; a guardian spirit or genius; a very wicked person.

de-mon-e-tize (dē-mŏn′ē-tīz), *v.t.* to deprive of value, as money; withdraw from use, as money; as, the government will *demonetise* old torn paper money.—*n.* **demonetization.**

de-mo-ni-ac (dē-mō′nĭ-ăk), *n.* one possessed of an evil spirit; a lunatic or insane person: *adj.* possessed by, or like, an evil spirit; devilish; frantic; insane. Also, *adj.* **demoniacal.**—*adv.* **demoniacally.**

de-mon-ism (dē′mŏn-ĭzm), *n.* belief in evil spirits or devils; the nature of an evil spirit.

de-mon-ol-a-try (dē-mŏn-ŏl′ȧ-trĭ), *n.* the worship of devils or evil spirits.

de-mon-ol-o-gy (dē-mŏn-ŏl′ō-jĭ) *n.* the study of devils or evil spirits.

de-mon-stra-ble (dē-mŏn′strȧ-bl), *adj.* capable of being shown or proved.—*adv.* **demonstrably.**

dem-on-strate (dĕm′ŏn-strāt; dē-mŏn′-strāt), *v.t.* to prove beyond the possibility of a doubt; teach by examples; prove; as, the pupil learns to *demonstrate* arithmetic problems.
Syn. prove, show, exhibit, illustrate.

dem-on-stra-tion (dĕm″ŏn-strā′shŭn), *n.* the act of showing or proving; a proof beyond the possibility of a doubt; manifestation; outward expression of feeling; a public exhibition of sympathy with some political or social movement; as, a party *demonstration;* the exhibition and description of examples in art and science teaching, especially anatomy; a show of military force.
Syn. certainty, evidence, proof, deduction.

de-mon-stra-tive (dē-mŏn′strȧ-tĭv), *adj.* having the power of showing or proving; serving to point out, as a *demonstrative* pronoun; conclusive; showing the feelings openly and strongly: *n.* a pronoun which itself defines or indicates that to which it refers; as, *this, that, these, those.*—*adv.* **demonstratively.**—*n.* **demonstrativeness.**

dem-on-stra-tor (dĕm′ŏn-strā″tẽr), *n.* one who proves, points out, or shows; a teacher of practical anatomy, or physical science.

de-mor-al-ize (dē-mŏr′ăl-īz), *v.t.* to corrupt; deprive of spirit or energy; throw into confusion; disorganise; confuse.—*n.* **demoralization.**

de-mount-a-ble (dē-moun′tȧ-bl), *adj.* that can be easily taken apart; as, a *demountable* rim on an automobile.

demp-ster (dĕmp′stẽr), *n.* a judge in the Isle of Man. Also, **deemster.**

de-mur (dē-mûr′), *v.i.* [*p.t.* and *p.p.* demurred, *p.pr.* demurring], to hesitate; raise objections: *n.* an objection or exception.

de-mure (dē-mūr′), *adj.* grave; sober; modest; as, a *demure* manner.—*adv.* **demurely.**—*n.* **demureness.**

de-mur-rage (dē-mûr′āj), *n.* the holding of a vessel in port, or of a railroad car, beyond the time allowed for loading, unloading, etc.; the money paid by the freighter for such delay.

de-mur-rer (dē-mûr′ẽr), *n.* one who hesitates or objects; an objection on a point of law.

den (dĕn), *n.* cavern; the cave of a wild beast; lair; any cozy and private room, as for studying.

de-na-tion-al-ize (dē-năsh′ŭn-ăl-īz), *v.t.* to deprive of national rights or character; render local.

de-nat-u-ral-ize (dē-năt′ū-răl-īz), *v.t.* to make unnatural: to deprive of the rights and duties of a citizen or subject.

de-na-tured (dē-nā′tūrd), *adj.* changed in nature or character; made unfit for its ordinary use by addition of other materials; as, *denatured* alcohol.

de-ni-al (dē-nī'ăl), *n.* refusal to grant, believe, or admit; contradiction; noncompliance.

den-im (dĕn'ĭm), *n.* a coarse cotton material used for hangings, floor coverings, etc.

den-i-zen (dĕn'ĭ-zĕn), *n.* an inhabitant; citizen; an alien, or foreigner, who has received papers admitting him to the rights of citizenship: *v.t.* to admit to the rights of citizenship; to populate with citizens.

de-nom-i-nate (dē-nŏm'ĭ-nāt), *v.t.* to designate, or give a name to; call; name: *adj.* having a specific name; concrete; as, five cents is a *denominate* number.

de-nom-i-na-tion (dē-nŏm'ĭ-nā'shŭn), *n.* the act of designating or naming; a sect, class, or division; a name for a certain class or unit in a series; as, we have coins of many *denominations*.

de-nom-i-na-tion-al (dē-nŏm"ĭ-nā'-shŭn-ăl), *adj.* pertaining to, or carried on by, a class or sect. —*adv.* **denominationally.**—*n.* **denominationalism.**

de-nom-i-na-tive (dē-nŏm'ĭ-nā-tĭv), *adj.* giving a name: *n.* a word derived from a noun or adjective; as, a *denominative* verb.

de-nom-i-na-tor (dē-nŏm'ĭ-nā"tẽr), *n.* one who, or that which, gives a name to; the expression of a fraction which, when placed below the line, gives the name or value to the unit.

de-no-ta-tion (dē"nō-tā'shŭn), *n.* a plain marking out; a clear sign; an indication; a name.

de-note (dē-nōt'), *v.t.* to signify or identify; mark out plainly; indicate; betoken.

dé-noue-ment (dā-nōō'mäṅ; dā"nōō'-mäṅ'), *n.* the unraveling or solving of the plot of a story or play; the solving of a mystery. [Fr.]

de-nounce (dē-nouns'), *v.t.* to threaten or accuse publicly; censure; to condemn.

dense (dĕns), *adj.* thick; as, a *dense* fog; compact; as, a *dense* crowd; intense; stupid.—*adv.* **densely.**—*n.* **denseness.**

den-si-ty (dĕn'sĭ-tĭ), *n.* closeness or compactness, as of matter; depth, as of shade; proportion of mass to bulk.

dent (dĕnt), *n.* small hollow; a slight depression caused by a blow or pressure; the tooth of a wheel; a cog; tooth of a comb or metallic brush: *v.t.* to make a small hollow in.

den-tal (dĕn'tăl), *adj.* pertaining to the teeth; pronounced by the aid of the teeth: *n.* a letter pronounced by the aid of the teeth.

den-tate (dĕn'tāt), *adj.* toothed; as, *dentate* leaves. Also, **dentated.**

den-ti-form (dĕn'tĭ-fôrm), *adj.* having the shape of a tooth.

den-ti-frice (dĕn'tĭ-frĭs), *n.* a powder, liquid, or paste used for cleaning the teeth.

den-til (dĕn'tĭl), *n.* one of the small square blocks or projections in cornices of roofs. Also, **dentel.**

den-tine (dĕn'tĭn), *n.* the hard, dense tissue which forms the body of a tooth.

den-tist (dĕn'tĭst), *n.* one who practices dental surgery, as filling and extracting teeth.

den-tist-ry (dĕn'tĭst-rĭ), *n.* the art of a dentist; dental surgery.

den-ti-tion (dĕn-tĭsh'ŭn), *n.* the process or period of cutting the teeth; arrangement of the teeth.

den-u-da-tion (dĕn"ū-dā'shŭn; dē"nū-dā'shŭn), *n.* the act of stripping or making bare.

de-nude (dē-nūd'), *v.t.* to make bare or naked; as, to *denude* one of clothing; lay bare (rocks) by the wearing action of water.

de-nun-ci-a-tion (dē-nŭn"sĭ-ā'shŭn; dē-nŭn"shĭ-ā'shŭn), *n.* the act of accusing publicly; a threat; menace.

de-nun-ci-a-tor (dē-nŭn'sĭ-ā"tẽr; dē-nŭn'shĭ-ā"tẽr), *n.* one who accuses publicly.

de-nun-ci-a-to-ry (dē-nŭn'shĭ-*ȧ*-tō-rĭ; dē-nŭn'sĭ-*ȧ*-tō-rĭ), *adj.* relating to, or containing, an accusation or threat. Also, **denunciative.**

de-ny (dē-nī'), *v.t.* to refuse to believe or admit; contradict; to withhold.

Syn. gainsay, dispute, oppose, contest.

de-o-dor-ant (dē-ō'dẽr-ănt), *n.* something which takes away odor; a disinfectant.

de-o-dor-ize (dē-ō'dẽr-īz), *v.t.* to disinfect or deprive of odor.

de-part (dē-pärt'), *v.i.* to go or move away; leave; die; desist; deviate.

Syn. quit, decamp, retire, withdraw, vanish.

Ant. (see remain).

de-part-ment (dē-pärt'mĕnt), *n.* a distinct division; a separate room or office for business; a branch of business, study, or science; a division of government; as, the *Department* of Agriculture; a province.

de-part-men-tal (dē"pärt-mĕn'tăl), *adj.* pertaining to a branch or division; governed by departments.

de-par-ture (dē-pär'tūr), *n.* the act of leaving; a going away; a changing from an old to a new plan or method; death.

de-pend (dē-pĕnd'), *v.i.* to rely for support; trust; be conditioned; with *on* or *upon;* hang down.

de-pend-ant (dē-pĕn'dănt), *n.* one who relies on another for support. Also, **dependent.**

de-pend-ence (dē-pĕn'dĕns), *n.* the state of being supported or influenced by, or subject to, another; connection; reliance; trust; as, the *dependence* of a child on its father; that on which one relies; state of hanging down.

de-pend-en-cy (dē-pĕn'dĕn-sĭ), *n.* [*pl.* dependencies (-sĭz)], a country under control of another country.

de-pend-ent (dē-pĕn'dĕnt), *adj.* hanging down; relying on someone or something else for support; conditional; subordinate: *n.* one who relies on another for support; something which hangs down. Also, *n.* **dependant.**

de-pict (dē-pĭkt'), *v.t.* to paint or portray; describe or show vividly; as, the writer was able to *depict* a wonderful scene.

de-plete (dē-plēt'), *v.t.* to empty; to unload; to exhaust.

de-ple-tion (dē-plē'shŭn), *n.* the act of emptying; exhaustion; as, the *depletion* of energy by overwork; bloodletting.

de-plor-a-ble (dē-plōr'*ȧ*-bl), *adj.* sad; calamitous; grievous; as, a *deplorable* accident.—*adv.* **deplorably.**

de-plore (dē-plōr'), *v.t.* to lament; grieve for; as, to *deplore* the loss of a friend; *deplore* wrongdoing.

de-ploy (dē-ploi'), *v.t.* and *v.i.* [*p.t.* and *p.p.* deployed, *p.pr.* deploying], to spread out in line of battle; extend the front line, as troops: *n.* a movement by which a body of troops is spread out in front.—*n.* **deployment.**

de-po-nent (dē-pō'nĕnt), *adj.* having a passive form and an active meaning: used of a Latin verb: *n.* a witness who makes a statement, usually in writing.

de-pop-u-late (dē-pŏp'ū-lāt), *v.t.* to deprive of inhabitants or people.—*n.* **depopulation.**

de-port (dē-pōrt'), *v.t.* to carry from one country to another; banish; behave (oneself).

de-por-ta-tion (dē"pōr-tā'shŭn), *n.* act of carrying, or state of being carried, into another country; the sending back to his own country of an alien seeking entrance into another; forcible removal of people from a conquered country.

de-port-ment (dē-pōrt'mĕnt), *n.* conduct; behavior; demeanor.

de-pose (dē-pōz'), *v.t.* to remove from a throne, or other high station; deprive of office; bear witness to: *v.i.* testify on oath.

de-pos-it (dē-pŏz'ĭt), *v.t.* to put or set down; place; put in a bank; intrust to another for security: *n.* something committed to the care of another; a pledge; money kept in a bank; something set or laid down.

de-pos-i-ta-ry (dē-pŏz'ĭ-tā-rĭ), *n.* one with whom something is intrusted; a guardian; place where something is put for safe-keeping. Also, **depository.**

dep-o-si-tion (dĕp"ō-zĭsh'ŭn; dē"pō-zĭsh'ŭn), *n.* the act of putting down, placing in trust, etc.; removing from a throne or office; testimony under oath.

de-pos-i-tor (dē-pŏz'ĭ-tẽr), *n.* one who puts down, or places in trust; one who puts money in a bank.

de-pos-i-to-ry (dē-pŏz'ĭ-tō-rĭ), *n.* [*pl.* depositories (-rĭz)], the place where, or person with whom, anything is put for safe-keeping, as a bank. Also, **depositary.**

de-pot (dē'pō; dā'pō; dĕp'ō), *n.* a warehouse; a building for military stores, etc.; the headquarters of a regiment; a railway station.

de-prave (dē-prāv'), *v.t.* to make bad or corrupt: applied to morals.

de-praved (dē-prāvd'), *p.adj.* morally debased; corrupt; made bad or worse.

de-prav-i-ty (dē-prăv'ĭ-tĭ), *n.* the state of being immoral or corrupt; wickedness.

dep-re-cate (dĕp'rē-kāt), *v.t.* to disapprove strongly of; express regret for; as, the store manager *deprecates* the rudeness of the salesman to a customer.—*adv.* **deprecatingly.**

dep-re-ca-tion (dĕp"rē-kā'shŭn), *n.* the act of disapproving.

dep-re-ca-to-ry (dĕp'rē-kȧ-tō-rĭ), *adj.* apologetic; serving as a protest against something; disapproving.

de-pre-ci-ate (dē-prē'shĭ-āt), *v.t.* to lower the value or rate of; speak slightingly of: *v.i.* to fall in value; as, the property will *depreciate* in value if it is not kept in repair.—*adj.* **depreciative.**

de-pre-ci-a-tion (dē-prē"shĭ-ā'shŭn), *n.* the act of lessening the value or worth of; a fall in value.

dep-re-date (dĕp'rē-dāt), *v.t.* to pillage; rob; lay waste; prey upon.

dep-re-da-tion (dĕp"rē-dā'shŭn), *n.* robbery; pillage; a destroying, or laying waste.

dep-re-da-tor (dĕp'rē-dā'tẽr), *n.* a plunderer or robber; a destroyer.

de-press (dē-prĕs'), *v.t.* to press or thrust down; sadden; dispirit; as, the horrors of war *depress* us all; lower or cheapen; make dull, as trade.

de-pressed (dē-prĕst'), *p.adj.* cast down in spirits; lowered in position; flattened from above.

de-pres-sion (dē-prĕsh'ŭn), *n.* the act of making lower; the sinking or falling in of a surface; low spirits; dulness of trade; as, the *depression* of business caused a panic.

de-pres-sor (dē-prĕs'ẽr), *n.* one who, or that which, makes lower; a muscle that draws down an organ or part.

dep-ri-va-tion (dĕp"rĭ-vā'shŭn), *n.* the act of taking away; loss.

de-prive (dē-prīv'), *v.t.* to take from; dispossess; debar; depose, as from office: with *of.*

Syn. strip, bereave, despoil, rob.

depth (dĕpth), *n.* distance below the surface; profoundness; extent of penetration; richness of tone or color; that which is deep; as, the ocean *depths;* in an airplane, the perpendicular distance from the chord to the farthest point of a curved surface: **depth bomb,** in the World War, an effective contrivance arranged to explode at a certain depth under water, and thus destroy a submarine boat, if in the vicinity. Also, **depth charge.**

dep-u-ta-tion (dĕp"ū-tā'shŭn), *n.* the act of appointing, or giving power to, an agent; the persons so appointed to act; as, a *deputation* visited the governor.

de-pute (dē-pūt'), *v.t.* to appoint as an agent or deputy; send with authority to act on behalf of the principal.

Syn. commission, charge, intrust, delegate, authorize, accredit.

dep-u-tize (dĕp'ū-tīz), *v.t.* to appoint as a deputy or agent.

dep-u-ty (dĕp'ū-tĭ), *n.* [*pl.* deputies (-tĭz)], one appointed to act for another; an agent; a delegate.

de-rail (dē-rāl'), *v.i.* to run off the rails: *v.t.* to cause to leave the rails; as, an open switch will *derail* a train.—*n.* **derailment.**

de-range (dē-rānj'), *v.t.* to disorder; confuse; disturb; to make insane.—*p.adj.* **deranged.**

de-range-ment (dē-rānj'mĕnt), *n.* the act of putting out of order; insanity.

der-by (dûr'bĭ; Eng. där'bĭ), *n.* [*pl.* derbies (-bĭz)], a kind of stiff felt hat, with a dome-shaped crown and curved brim: **Derby,** a race, founded 1780, for three-year-old horses, run annually at Epsom, England.

der-e-lict (dĕr'ĕ-lĭkt), *adj.* abandoned; adrift; unfaithful: *n.* anything left, forsaken, or cast away intentionally, as at sea; as, the wrecked ship became a *derelict*; a social outcast: *pl.* abandoned goods of ships found at sea.

der-e-lic-tion (dĕr″ē-lĭk′shŭn), *n.* neglect; omission, as of obligation or duty; abandonment.

de-ride (dē-rīd′), *v.t.* to mock; laugh at: *v.i.* to indulge in mockery, scorn, or ridicule.—*n.* **derider.**

de-rid-ing-ly (dē-rīd′ĭng-lĭ), *adv.* with mockery or scorn.

de-ris-i-ble (dē-rĭz′ĭ-bl), *adj.* open to scorn or ridicule.

de-ri-sion (dē-rĭzh′ŭn), *n.* the act of mocking; ridicule; scorn; contempt.

Syn. contumely, disrespect.

de-ri-sive (dē-rī′sĭv), *adj.* expressing ridicule or scorn.—*adv.* **derisively.**

de-riv-a-ble (dē-rīv′ȧ-bl), *adj.* capable of being obtained from a source; deducible.

der-i-va-tion (dĕr″ĭ-vā′shŭn), *n.* the act of obtaining, or the condition of being obtained, from a definite source; the process of tracing a word from its original source; as, the *derivation* of many words from the Latin; evolution; deduction; the source from which something is drawn.

Syn. origin, source, beginning, cause, etymology, root.

de-riv-a-tive (dē-rĭv′ȧ-tĭv), *adj.* obtained or taken from another; obtained from some other by a process of deduction; secondary: *n.* a word formed from another; a modification.

de-rive (dē-rīv′), *v.t.* to draw from an original source; obtain by transmission or descent; trace (a word) to its original root or stem; deduce; infer.

der-ma (dûr′mȧ), *n.* the true skin; also, skin in general.

der-mal (dûr′măl), *adj.* pertaining to, or consisting of, skin. Also, **dermic.**

der-ma-tol-o-gy (dûr″mȧ-tŏl′ō-jĭ), *n.* the science which treats of the skin and its diseases.

der-mic (dûr′mĭk), *adj.* of or pertaining to the skin. Also, **dermal.**

der-o-gate (dĕr′ō-gāt), *v.t.* to detract from; lessen the value, etc. of: *v.i.* take away; detract: with *from.*

der-o-ga-tion (dĕr″ō-gā′shŭn), *n.* the act of lessening in value; detraction; depreciation.

de-rog-a-to-ry (dē-rŏg′ȧ-tō-rĭ), *adj.* tending to degrade; belittling; disparaging.

der-rick (dĕr′ĭk), *n.* a framework with ropes and pulleys for lifting heavy weights.

der-rin-ger (dĕr′ĭn-jẽr), *n.* a pocket pistol with a short barrel of very large caliber.

der-vish (dûr′vĭsh), *n.* a Mohammedan monk who professes extreme poverty, chastity, and humility.

des-cant (dĕs′kănt), *n.* a song in parts; a discourse or series of remarks on one theme: *v.i.* (dĕs-kănt′), to comment freely; talk at length; to sing in parts.

de-scend (dē-sĕnd′), *v.i.* to go or come down from a higher to a lower position; to come or fall violently or in force; as, the army was ordered to *descend* upon the town; be derived; fall in order of inheritance, or from one generation to another: *v.t.* to go down or along.

de-scend-ant (dē-sĕn′dănt), *n.* one who is descended from a special ancestor; offspring; as, a *descendant* of the early Pilgrims: *adj.* coming down; falling; coming from a source. Also, *adj.* **descendent.**

de-scent (dē-sĕnt′), *n.* change from a higher to a lower place; a sudden hostile invasion or attack; as, the *descent* of the enemy upon the coast; a coming from a common ancestor; birth; a passage from a higher to a lower pitch.

de-scrib-a-ble (dē-skrīb′ȧ-bl), *adj.* capable of being pictured in words.

de-scribe (dē-skrīb′), *v.t.* to give an account of; to represent by words or drawing; set forth; to make a picture of in words.—*n.* **describer.**

Syn. portray, illustrate, define, picture.

de-scrip-tion (dē-skrĭp′shŭn), *n.* the act of giving an account of in words or writing; a picture in words; a class; sort; kind.

de-scrip-tive (dē-skrĭp′tĭv), *adj.* tending to, or serving to, picture in words.—*adv.* **descriptively.**

de-scry (dē-skrī′), *v.t.* to discover with the eye, especially in the distance or through obscurity; to discern; perceive; detect.

des-e-crate (dĕs′ē-krāt), *v.t.* to change from a sacred to a secular or worldly use; profane; as, to *desecrate* a holy place.

Syn. misuse, abuse, pollute.

des-e-cra-tion (dĕs″ē-krā′shŭn), *n.* act of profanation; sacrilege; as, the *desecration* of a shrine.

de-sert (dē-zûrt′), *v.t.* to forsake; abandon: *v.i.* to run from duty: *n.* a deserved reward or punishment; merit.

des-ert (dĕz′ẽrt), *n.* a wilderness; waste; a solitude: *adj.* pertaining to a desert.

de-ser-tion (dē-zûr′shŭn), *n.* the act of forsaking; a leaving one's post; state of being forsaken.

de-serve (dē-zûrv′), *v.t.* to earn by service; be worthy of; to merit: *v.i.* to be worthy or deserving: usually with *well* or *ill.*—*n.* **deserver.**

Syn. merit, earn, justify, win.

de-serv-ed-ly (dē-zûr′vĕd-lĭ), *adv.* justly; according to merit; as, he was *deservedly* punished.

des-ha-bille (dĕz″ȧ-bēl′), *n.* a loose, careless garment; a state of being partly or carelessly dressed. Also, **dishabille.** [Fr.]

des-ic-cate (dĕs′ĭ-kāt), *v.t.* to dry thoroughly; dry up; preserve by taking the moisture from: *v.i.* to become dry.

des-ic-ca-tion (dĕs″ĭ-kā′shŭn), *n.* the act of drying.

des-ic-ca-tor (dĕs′ĭ-kā″tẽr), *n.* an apparatus for drying foods and other substances.

de-sid-er-a-tum (dē-sĭd″ẽr-ā′tŭm), *n.* [*pl.* desiderata (-tȧ)], anything desired; a want or desire generally felt and recognized.

de-sign (dē-zīn′), *v.t.* to draw, mark, or plan out; project; intend; set apart mentally; as, to *design* a thing for a purpose: *v.i.* to make decorative plans or execute original work: *n.* an outline, plan, or drawing; project; intention.

Syn., n. delineation, sketch, drawing, contrivance, artfulness.

des-ig-nate (dĕs′ĭg-nāt; dĕz′ĭg-nāt), *v.t.* to indicate by marks, lines, or a description, the limits of; point out; distinguish; name.—*adj.* **designative.**

des-ig-na-tion (dĕs″ĭg-nā′shŭn; dĕz″ĭg-nā′shŭn), *n.* the act of naming or pointing out; a distinctive mark or title; appointment.

de-sign-ed-ly (dē-zīn′ĕd-lĭ), *adv.* intentionally; purposely; by plan.

de-sign-er (dē-zīn′ẽr), *n.* one who makes plans or original sketches for decoration, etc.

de-sign-ing (dē-zīn′ĭng), *adj.* scheming; artful; cunning; wily: *n.* the act or art of making sketches; the act of plotting.

de-sir-a-bil-i-ty (dē-zīr″ȧ-bĭl′ĭ-tĭ), *n.* the state or quality of being pleasing or acceptable.

de-sir-a-ble (dē-zīr′ȧ-bl), *adj.* pleasing; agreeable.—*adv.* **desirably.**

Syn. expedient, advisable, valuable, acceptable, proper, judicious, beneficial, profitable, good.

de-sire (dē-zīr′), *v.t.* to wish earnestly for; crave; to express a wish for; ask: *n.* a longing for the possession of some object; an earnest wish; a petition or prayer; the object longed for.

Syn. n. longing, affection, craving.

de-sir-ous (dē-zīr′ŭs), *adj.* full of a wish or longing; solicitous; anxious; as, he was *desirous* to please others.

de-sist (dē-zĭst′), *v.i.* to cease from action; stop; forbear; often followed by *from*.

Syn. discontinue, quit, abstain.

Ant. (see continue, persevere).

desk (dĕsk), *n.* a frame or table for reading or writing upon; a pulpit.

des-o-late (dĕs′ō-lāt), *v.t.* to lay waste; deprive of inhabitants; overwhelm with sorrow; forsake: *adj.* (dĕs′ō-lāt), deprived of inhabitants; solitary; laid waste; abandoned; miserable.—*adv.* **desolately.**—*n.* **desolateness.**

Syn., adj. bereaved, forlorn, forsaken, deserted, wild, waste, bare, bleak, lonely.

Ant. (see pleasant, happy).

des-o-la-tion (dĕs″ō-lā′shŭn), *n.* the act of laying waste; the state of being laid waste or abandoned; a solitude; ruin; destruction; affliction; misery.

de-spair (dē-spâr′), *v.i.* to abandon all hope, or expectation; become hopeless: *n.* loss of hope or confidence; hopelessness; that which causes loss of hope or which is looked upon as hopeless.—*p.adj.* **despairing.**—*adv.* **despairingly.**

des-patch (dē-spăch′), *v.t.* to send off quickly; put to death; finish quickly: *n.* speedy performance; celerity; promptness; a quick message, as a telegram; a government document sent to a minister abroad. Also, **dispatch.**

des-patch-er (dē-spăch′ẽr), *n.* one who sends something off promptly or at the right time; as, a train *despatcher*. Also, **dispatcher.**

des-per-a-do (dĕs″pẽr-ā′dō), *n.* [*pl.* desperadoes or desperados (-dōz)], a bold and reckless criminal.

des-per-ate (dĕs′pẽr-āt), *adj.* reckless from rage or despair; furious; frantic; beyond hope or cure.—*adv.* **desperately.**—*n.* **desperateness.**

des-per-a-tion (dĕs″pẽr-ā′shŭn), *n.* state of being without hope, and frantic; the recklessness of despair.

des-pi-ca-ble (dĕs′pĭ-kȧ-bl), *adj.* contemptible; mean; fit to be looked down on.—*adv.* **despicably.**

de-spise (dē-spīz′), *v.t.* to look down upon with scorn or contempt; disdain.

de-spite (dē-spīt′), *n.* extreme contempt; malicious anger; scorn; hatred. *prep.* notwithstanding.

de-spite-ful (dē-spīt′fŏŏl), *adj.* malicious; insulting; malignant.—*adv.* **despitefully.**—*n.* **despitefulness.**

de-spoil (dē-spoil′), *v.t.* to rob; deprive of belongings; pillage.

de-spond (dē-spŏnd′), *v.i.* to be cast down in spirits; give way to melancholy.

de-spond-en-cy (dē-spŏn′dĕn-sĭ), *n.* absence of hope or courage; deep mental depression. Also, **despondence.**

de-spond-ent (dē-spŏn′dĕnt), *adj.* without hope; deeply depressed.—*adv.* **despondently.**

des-pot (dĕs′pŏt), *n.* an absolute ruler; tyrant; as, Nero was a *despot*.

des-pot-ic (dĕs-pŏt′ĭk), *adj.* absolute in power; autocratic; irresponsible; arbitrary; tyrannical. Also, **despotical.**—*adv.* **despotically.**

des-pot-ism (dĕs′pŏt-ĭzm), *n.* absolute power or government; tyranny.

des-sert (dē-zûrt′), *n.* a course of fruits, nuts, or sweets, served last at dinner.

des-ti-na-tion (dĕs″tĭ-nā′shŭn), *n.* purposed end or object; ultimate or final design; goal; stated end of a journey.

des-tine (dĕs′tĭn), *v.t.* to appoint to any purpose or end; settle the future use of; decree the future of; foreordained.

des-ti-ny (dĕs′tĭ-nĭ), *n.* [*pl.* destinies (-nĭz)], fate; inevitable or unavoidable necessity; lot; fortune.

Syn. decree, doom, end.

des-ti-tute (dĕs′tĭ-tūt), *adj.* without means; penniless; being wholly without (something needed); lacking.

des-ti-tu-tion (dĕs″tĭ-tū′shŭn), *n.* extreme poverty; want; lack.

de-stroy (dē-stroi′), *v.t.* [*p.t.* and *p.p.* destroyed, *p.pr.* destroying], to pull down; overturn; lay waste; render desolate; kill; put an end to.

de-stroy-er (dē-stroi′ẽr), *n.* one who spoils or puts an end to; a war vessel of the torpedo-boat class.

de-struct-i-bil-i-ty (dē-strŭk″tĭ-bĭl′ĭ-tĭ), *n.* ability to be spoiled or put an end to.

de-struct-i-ble (dē-strŭk′tĭ-bl), *adj.* that may be spoiled, put an end to, or laid waste.

de-struc-tion (dē-strŭk′shŭn), *n.* the act or process of spoiling or putting an end to; overthrow; ruin; death.

de-struc-tive (dē-strŭk′tĭv), *adj.* deadly; tending to, or causing, desolation; ruinous; hurtful; as, a *destructive* epidemic, or a *destructive* fire.—*adv.* **destructively.**

Syn. detrimental, noxious, injurious, baneful.

Ant. (see creative).

de-struc-tive-ness (dē-strŭk′tĭv-nĕs), *n.* the quality of being ruinous; an inclination to destroy.

des-ue-tude (dĕs'wē-tūd), *n.* disuse of custom, practice, or fashion.
Syn. discontinuance, cessation.
Ant. (see maintenance).

des-ul-to-ry (dĕs'ŭl-tō-rĭ), *adj.* passing from one thing to another without order or method; aimless; erratic. *adv.* **desultorily**.—*n.* **desultoriness**.
Syn. rambling, discursive, loose, unmethodical, superficial, unsettled, fitful.
Ant. (see thorough).

de-tach (dē-tăch'), *v.t.* to separate; to disconnect; detail for a special purpose; send away from.—*adj.* **detachable**.

de-tach-ment (dē-tăch'mĕnt), *n.* the act of separating; the thing separated; a body of troops, or certain ships, separated from the main body and sent on special service.

de-tail (dē-tāl'), *v.t.* to relate minutely; enumerate; tell off for a given duty; to give particulars of: *n.* (dē-tāl'; dē'tāl), an item; a particular or minute account; a small detachment (of troops), for special service: *pl.* minute parts of a picture, statue, etc.

de-tain (dē-tān'), *v.t.* to hold back; restrain from departure; delay; keep in custody; as, the magistrate ordered the prisoner to be *detained*.

de-tain-er (dē-tān'ĕr), *n.* one who holds back; a writ for holding a person in custody or under arrest.

de-tect (dē-tĕkt'), *v.t.* to discover; (something obscure); bring to light; expose; find out.

de-tect-a-ble (dē-tĕk'tȧ-bl), *adj.* that may be found out. Also, **detectible**.

de-tec-tion (dē-tĕk'shŭn), *n.* the act of finding out, or its result; discovery.

de-tec-tive (dē-tĕk'tĭv), *n.* a person who investigates crimes and mysteries: *adj.* employed, or skilled, in exposing or finding out; pertaining to detectives, or detection.

de-tec-tor (dē-tĕk'tĕr), *n.* one who, or that which, finds out; a discoverer; a device for detecting.

de-ten-tion (dē-tĕn'shŭn), *n.* the act of keeping back or withholding; confinement; restraint; delay.

de-ter (dē-tûr'), *v.t.* [*p.t.* and *p.p.* deterred, *p.pr.* deterring], to discourage, or hinder, by fear; restrain; dishearten.

de-ter-gent (dē-tûr'jĕnt), *n.* a cleansing substance, used for wounds, etc.: *adj.* having cleansing qualities; purging.

de-te-ri-o-rate (dē-tē'rĭ-ō-rāt), *v.t.* to reduce to a lower quality or value: impair: *v.i.* to grow worse.

de-te-ri-o-ra-tion (dē-tē"rĭ-ō-rā'shŭn), *n.* act of growing worse; degeneracy.

de-ter-mi-na-ble (dē-tûr'mĭ-nȧ-bl), *adj.* capable of being decided or settled; that may be found out.

de-ter-mi-nant (dē-tûr'mĭ-nănt), *adj.* causing decision; *n.* that which serves to settle, decide, or establish.

de-ter-mi-nate (dē-tûr'mĭ-nāt), *adj.* having definite or fixed limits; clearly defined; specific.—*adv.* **determinately**.—*n.* **determinateness**.

de-ter-mi-na-tion (dē-tûr"mĭ-nā'shŭn), *n.* the act of deciding; the state of being firm in decisions; purpose; resolution.

de-ter-mi-na-tive (dē-tûr'mĭ-nȧ-tĭv), *adj.* determining, limiting, or defining: *n.* that which indicates the quality or character of something else.

de-ter-mine (dē-tûr'mĭn), *v.i.* to reach a decision: *v.t.* to fix or settle the bounds of; put an end to; restrict; decide; resolve; find out.

de-ter-mined (dē-tûr'mĭnd), *p.adj.* resolute; decided; fixed.—*adv.* **determinedly**.

de-ter-rent (dē-tĕr'ĕnt; dē-tûr'ĕnt), *adj.* serving, or tending, to prevent or hinder: *n.* that which prevents; as, the fear of punishment is a *deterrent* from crime.

de-test (dē-tĕst'), *v.t.* to hate intensely; abhor.

de-test-a-ble (dē-tĕs'tȧ-bl), *adj.* worthy to be hated or loathed; hateful.—*adv.* **detestably**.—*n.* **detestableness**.

de-tes-ta-tion (dē"tĕs-tā'shŭn; dĕt"ĕs-tā'shŭn), *n.* extreme dislike or abhorrence; loathing.

de-throne (dē-thrōn'), *v.t.* to remove from a throne; deprive of authority or power.—*n.* **dethronement**.

det-o-nate (dĕt'ō-nāt; dē'tō-nāt), *v.t.* to cause to explode with a loud and sudden report, as a cannon firecracker: *v.i.* to explode loudly and suddenly.

det-o-na-tion (dĕt"ō-nā'shŭn), *n.* a sudden explosion with a loud report; as, the *detonation* was terrific when the powder mills blew up.

det-o-na-tor (dĕt'ō-nā"tĕr), *n.* a substance that explodes a percussion cap; a device in a bomb that, when ignited by a fuse, explodes the charge.

de-tour (dē-tōōr'), *n.* a roundabout way; as, he made a *detour* to avoid going through the woods.

de-tract (dē-trăkt'), *v.t.* to draw or take away, especially so as to lessen value: *v.i.* to take away a part, especially of reputation or credit; with *from*.

de-trac-tion (dē-trăk'shŭn), *n.* depreciation; defamation; slander.

de-trac-tor (dē-trăk'tĕr), *n.* one who takes away; a muscle that draws away some part.

de-train (dē-trān'), *v.t.* to remove from a train, as troops: *v.i.* alight from a train.

det-ri-ment (dĕt'rĭ-mĕnt), *n.* that which injures, reduces in value, or causes damage; injury; damage.
Syn. loss, harm, disadvantage.

det-ri-men-tal (dĕt"rĭ-mĕn'tăl), *adj.* injurious.—*adv.* **detrimentally**.

de-tri-tus (dē-trī'tŭs), *n.* accumulations arising from fragments of rocks broken off or worn away; débris; waste.

de trop (dē trō), too much; out of place; not wanted: said of a person whose presence is not desired. [Fr.]

deuce (dūs), *n.* a card or dice with two spots; a term used in scoring at lawn tennis, meaning forty all; an expletive meaning the devil!

deuce-ace (dūs'ās), *n.* the one and two thrown at dice.

Deu-ter-on-o-my (dū"tĕr-ŏn'ō-mĭ), *n.* the fifth book of the Old Testament, in which the law of Moses is repeated a second time.

de-vap-o-ra-tion (dē-văp"ō-rā'shŭn), *n.* the change of vapor into water.

dev-as-tate (dĕv'ăs-tāt), *v.t.* to lay waste; as, a forest fire will *devastate* many acres of timber land; desolate; ravage; plunder.

dev-as-ta-tion (dĕv'ăs-tā'shŭn), *n.* the act of devastating, or laying waste; desolation; waste; destruction; as, a cyclone causes *devastation*.

dev-as-ta-tor (dĕv'ăs-tā'tēr), *n.* one who devastates, or lays waste.

de-vel-op (dē-vĕl'ŏp), *v.t.* to unfold gradually; make known in detail; complete; cause to grow; treat (a photographic plate or film) with chemicals so as to bring out the picture: *v.i.* to advance from one stage to another; become gradually apparent.
Syn. unfold, amplify, expand, enlarge.

de-vel-op-ment (dē-vĕl'ŏp-mĕnt), *n.* the act of unfolding; growth; expansion.

de-vel-op-ment-al (dē-vĕl'ŏp-mĕn'-tăl), *adj.* pertaining to growth or expansion.

de-vi-ate (dē'vĭ-āt), *v.i.* to turn aside; diverge; wander: *v.t.* to change the direction or position of.

de-vi-a-tion (dē'vĭ-ā'shŭn), *n.* the act of turning aside; digression; error.

de-vi-a-tor (dē'vĭ-ā'tēr), *n.* one who turns aside.

de-vice (dē-vīs'), *n.* a scheme; invention; trick; stratagem; a fanciful design or pattern; a heraldic emblem.
Syn. artifice, expedient.

dev-il (dĕv''l), *n.* the evil spirit, Satan; a fallen angel; a false god or demon; an excessively wicked person; an expletive; a printer's helper; a machine for dividing rags or cotton in paper-making, and one for making wood-screws.

dev-il-fish (dĕv''l-fĭsh'), *n.* a large, ugly kind of octopus.

dev-il-ish (dĕv''l-ĭsh), *adj.* diabolical; extremely wicked; infernal: *adv.* colloquially, excessively.—*adv.* **devilishly.**

dev-il-kin (dĕv''l-kĭn), *n.* a little devil; an imp; as, the pranks of mischievous elves and gnomes and other *devilkins* are related in many old folk-tales.

dev-il-ment (dĕv''l-mĕnt), *n.* roguishness; mischief, often without evil intent.

dev-il-ry (dĕv''l-rĭ), *n.* wanton mischief; diabolical wickedness.

de-vi-ous (dē'vĭ-ŭs), *adj.* indirect; rambling; circuitous or roundabout; straying from the way of right and duty.—*adv.* **deviously.**—*n.* **deviousness.**

de-vis-a-ble (dē-vīz'ȧ-bl), *adj.* capable of being imagined; that may be given by will.

de-vise (dē-vīz'), *v.t.* to image; scheme; contrive; concoct; bequeath or give by will: *n.* a gift of real property by will; a will.

dev-i-see (dĕv''ĭ-zē'), *n.* the person to whom a bequest or gift by will has been made.

de-vis-er (dē-vīz'ēr), *n.* one who imagines or invents; a contriver.

de-vis-or (dē-vī'zôr; dē-vī'zŏr), *n.* one who bequeaths or gives by will.

de-vi-tal-ize (dē-vī'tăl-īz), *v.t.* to deprive of vital, or life, power; destroy vitality; make lifeless.

de-void (dē-void'), *adj.* entirely without; lacking; destitute: with *of*: as, to be *devoid* of sense, sympathy, patience.
Syn. void, wanting, destitute, unendowed, unprovided.

de-voir (dē-vwär'; dē-vwôr'), *n.* a service or duty owed; an act of courtesy or respect: usually in plural. [Fr.]

de-volve (dē-vŏlv'), *v.t.* to hand on or down; to pass or transfer from one to another; transmit; as, to *devolve* a duty upon another: *v.i.* to be handed down or over; to be transferred or transmitted; as, the duty *devolved* upon him.

de-vote (dē-vōt'), *v.t.* to dedicate or consecrate; to doom; give up wholly to; apply (oneself, etc.) to some object.

de-vot-ed (dē-vōt'ĕd), *p.adj.* wholly given up to; attached; dedicated; doomed.—*adv.* **devotedly.**—*n.* **devotedness.**

dev-o-tee (dĕv''ō-tē'), *n.* one entirely given up to a special interest; one zealous in religion; an enthusiast.

de-vo-tion (dē-vō'shŭn), *n.* the act of dedicating or consecrating; the state of being dedicated; strong affection; ardent love; as, the *devotion* of a mother to her child; religious worship; piety; prayer: usually in plural.

de-vo-tion-al (dē-vō'shŭn-ăl), *adj.* devout; expressing piety or worship; as, the meeting was opened with a brief *devotional* service.—*adv.* **devotionally.**

de-vour (dē-vour'), *v.t.* to swallow greedily or ravenously; consume or destroy rapidly; annihilate; as, to *devour* food or news; flames *devour* a building.

de-vout (dē-vout'), *adj.* devoted to religious thoughts and exercises; heartfelt.—*adv.* **devoutly.**

dew (dū), *n.* moisture from the atmosphere deposited in small drops; that which falls lightly and in a refreshing manner.

dew-claw (dū'klô'), *n.* the little claw behind a dog's foot; the false hoof of a deer.

dew-i-ness (dū'ĭ-nĕs), *n.* state of being moist with dew.

dew-lap (dū'lăp'), *n.* the loose skin that hangs from the neck of an ox or cow.

dew-y (dū'ĭ), *adj.* moist with dew; looking as if covered with dew.

dex-ter (dĕks'tēr), *adj.* right; opposite to *left*; as, the *dexter* hand.

dex-ter-i-ty (dĕks-tĕr'ĭ-tĭ), *n.* skill with the hands; physical skill; mental or physical adroitness; cleverness.
Syn. aptitude, expertness, readiness, skill.

dex-ter-ous (dĕks'tēr-ŭs), *adj.* skilful with the hands; possessing physical skill; quick, mentally or physically; adroit; clever; as, the game was won by a *dexterous* kick of the ball. Also, **dextrous.**—*adv.* **dexterously, dextrously.**

dex-tral (dĕks'trăl), *adj.* pertaining to the right side or hand.

dex-trin (dĕks'trĭn), *n.* a white gummy substance found in plant sap, etc., used as gum. Also, **dextrine.**

dex-trose (dĕks'trōs), *n.* a white crystalline variety of sugar found in sweet fruits, as the grape, cherry, etc., and in diabetic urine.

dey (dā), *n.* the former title of the governor of Algiers and of the chief of the Janissaries.

di-a-be-tes (dī'ȧ-bē'tēz), *n.* a disease of the kidneys.

di-a-bet-ic (dī'ȧ-bĕt'ĭk; dī'ȧ-bē'tĭk), *adj.* pertaining to diabetes, or a kidney disease.

di-a-bol-ic (dī'ȧ-bŏl'ĭk), *adj.* devilish; outrageously wicked; impious. Also, **diabolical.**—*adv.* **diabolically.**

di-ab-o-lism (dī-ăb'ō-lĭzm), *n.* the actions of, or possession by, the devil.

di-a-cous-tics (dī"*ȧ*-kōōs'tĭks; dī"*ȧ*-kous'tĭks), *n.pl.* the science of sounds, as affected by passing through different mediums; diaphonics.

di-a-crit-i-cal (dī"*ȧ*-krĭt'ĭ-kăl), *adj.* serving to separate or distinguish, as a point or sign applied to a letter to distinguish it in form or sound: **diacritical mark**, a mark used to distinguish particular sounds of letters and to indicate their true pronunciation; as, ă, ŏ.

di-a-dem (dī'*ȧ*-dĕm), *n.* a crown; tiara; as, the *diadem* is the symbol of royalty.

di-ær-e-sis (dī-ĕr'ē-sĭs; Br. dī-ĕ'rē-sĭs), *n.* a mark [¨] over the second of two similar vowels, separating them in pronunciation, as in coöperate; the division of a diphthong into two vowels, as in aëroplane. Also, **dieresis**.

di-ag-nose (dī"ăg-nōs'), *v.t.* to ascertain, as a disease, by its general symptoms; as, the doctor was asked to *diagnose* the case.

di-ag-no-sis (dī"ăg-nō'sĭs), *n.* [*pl.* diagnoses (-sēz)], the recognition of a disease by its symptoms; explanation based on an examination of facts.

di-ag-nos-tic (dī"ăg-nŏs'tĭk), *adj.* characteristic: *n.* a symptom of a disease.

Diagonal

di-ag-o-nal (dī-ăg'ō-năl), *adj.* extending from one angle to another: *n.* a straight oblique line dividing a rectangular figure into equal parts.—*adv.* **diagonally**.

di-a-gram (dī'*ȧ*-grăm), *n.* a geometrical figure; a mechanical plan; an outline, drawing, or figure; as, the circular of a hotel sometimes contains a *diagram* of the rooms: *v.t.* to illustrate by, or put in the form of, an outline or drawing.

di-a-gram-mat-ic (dī"*ȧ*-gr*ȧ*-măt'ĭk), *adj.* pertaining to, or shown by, an outline or drawing. Also, **diagrammatical**.—*adv.* **diagrammatically**.

di-a-graph (dī'*ȧ*-grăf), *n.* an instrument for drawing figures or objects mechanically.

di-al (dī'ăl), *n.* a flat surface on which a metal finger casts a shadow in such a way as to show the time by the sun; the face of a timepiece; any plate on which an index finger marks revolutions, pressure, etc.; an insulated fixed wheel used in telegraphy: *v.t.* to measure or indicate by a dial; survey with a miner's compass.

di-a-lect (dī'*ȧ*-lĕkt), *n.* the peculiar manner in which a language is spoken in a province or district of a country; idiom.

di-a-lec-tic (dī"*ȧ*-lĕk'tĭk), *adj.* pertaining to the art of debate; pertaining to a peculiar style of speech. Also, **dialectical**.

di-a-lec-tics (dī"*ȧ*-lĕk'tĭks), *n.pl.* the art of debating.

di-a-lec-ti-cian (dī"*ȧ*-lĕk-tĭsh'ăn), *n.* a logician, or one skilled in debate.

di-al-ing (dī'ăl-ĭng), *n.* the art of making dials. Also, **dialling**.

di-a-log (dī'*ȧ*-lŏg), *n.* a conversation between two or more persons; a literary composition in which persons are represented as reasoning on, or discussing, a subject. Also, **dialogue**.

di-a-mag-net-ism (dī'*ȧ*-măg-nĕt-ĭzm), *n.* the property possessed by certain bodies when under the influence of magnetism, and freely suspended, of taking a position at right angles to the magnetic meridian.—*adj.* **diamagnetic**.

di-am-e-ter (dī-ăm'ē-tĕr), *n.* a straight line through the center of a figure, dividing it in half; as, the *diameter* of the earth is 7,926 miles; the distance through the lower part of the shaft of a column.

di-a-met-ri-cal (dī"*ȧ*-mĕt'rĭ-kăl), *adj.* pertaining to a diameter; directly opposite.—*adv.* **diametrically**.

di-a-mond (dī'*ȧ*-mŭnd), *n.* a brilliant white precious stone; crystallized carbon, hardest of known substances; a plane figure, with four equal straight lines, and two acute and two obtuse angles; a playing card with one or more lozenge-shaped figures; a glass cutter's tool; the smallest kind of type generally used: *adj.* resembling a diamond: **diamond drill**, a rod or tube furnished at the end with diamonds for boring a very hard rock.

Di-an-a (dī-ăn'*ȧ*; Lat. dī-ā'n*ȧ*), *n.* in Roman mythology, goddess of the moon and of the hunt: identified with the Greek Artemis.

di-a-pa-son (dī"*ȧ*-pā'zŏn), *n.* the entire compass of a voice or instrument; a recognized musical standard of pitch; the foundation stops of an organ.

di-a-per (dī'*ȧ*-pĕr), *n.* linen cloth woven in geometric patterns; a napkin; surface decoration of one or more simple figures repeated: *v.t.* to variegate or embroider; work in a geometric pattern.

di-aph-a-nous (dī-ăf'*ȧ*-nŭs), *adj.* gauzy; transparent; as, a *diaphanous* dress.

di-a-phragm (dī'*ȧ*-frăm), *n.* the muscular partition which divides the chest from the abdomen; any elastic substance that separates or divides.

di-a-rist (dī'*ȧ*-rĭst), *n.* one who keeps a record of daily events.

di-ar-rhe-a (dī"*ȧ*-rē'*ȧ*), *n.* a looseness of the bowels. Also, **diarrhœa**.

di-a-ry (dī'*ȧ*-rĭ), *n.* [*pl.* diaries (-rĭz)], a record of daily events; a book for daily memoranda.

di-a-stase (dī'*ȧ*-stās), *n.* a soluble white compound which acts as a ferment, formed in germinating grain and animal fluids, and having the property of converting starch into dextrine and sugar.

di-as-to-le (dī-ăs'tō-lē), *n.* the rhythmical expansion and dilatation of the heart and arteries in beating: opposed to the systole, or contraction; the lengthening of a syllable naturally short.

di-a-ton-ic (dī"*ȧ*-tŏn'ĭk), *adj.* designating the regular tones of a key or scale in music.

di-a-tribe (dī'*ȧ*-trīb), *n.* an abusive speech or discourse; a strain of violent abuse; bitter criticism.

dib-ble (dĭb'l), *n.* a gardening tool for making holes in the earth: *v.t.* to plant with a dibble: *v.i.* to dip bait gently into the water.

dice (dīs), *n.pl.* [*sing.* die], small cubes marked on the sides with one to six spots: used in games of chance: *v.i.* to play with dice: *v.t.* to decorate with woven patterns to resemble cubes; cut into cubes.

di-chro-mism (dī'krō-mizm), *n.* color-blindness; inability to see more than two of the three primary colors.

dic-ing (dīs'ing), *n.* gaming with dice; stamped leather ornamented with squares.

dick-er (dĭk'ẽr), *v.i.* to barter or trade on a small scale; as, to *dicker* with salesmen to reduce the price of something.

dick-y (dĭk'ĭ), *n.* [*pl.* dickies (-ĭz)], a small separate shirt front; a seat at the back of a coach; a child's bib or pinafore; a high shirt collar.

dic-ta-graph (dĭk'tȧ-grȧf), *n.* a trade name for a kind of telephone attached to a phonograph, which records what is said in the room where it is placed: much used by detectives. Also, **dictograph.**

dic-ta-phone (dĭk'tȧ-fōn), *n.* a trade name for an instrument like a phonograph, used for dictating to a stenographer.

dic-tate (dĭk'tāt), *v.t.* to declare with authority; express orally so that another may take down in writing; as, the business man *dictates* a letter to his stenographer: *v.i.* to speak with final authority; prescribe: *n.* an injunction; command; a controlling principle.

Syn., v. prompt, suggest, enjoin, order, command.

dic-ta-tion (dĭk-tā'shŭn), *n.* the act of speaking words to be written down; the words so spoken; authoritative utterance; rulership or control.

dic-ta-tor (dĭk-tā'tẽr), *n.* one who dictates; one invested with absolute powers of government; an ancient Roman magistrate with supreme authority, appointed in times of emergency.

dic-ta-to-ri-al (dĭk"tȧ-tō'rĭ-ăl), *adj.* pertaining to one who gives positive commands; overbearing; imperious. —*adv.* **dictatorially.**

Syn. imperative, domineering, arbitrary, tyrannical.

Ant. (see **submissive**).

dic-tion (dĭk'shŭn), *n.* manner of speaking or expression; choice of words; as, the *diction* of Robert Louis Stevenson; style.

dic-tion-a-ry (dĭk'shŭn-ā-rĭ), *n.* [*pl.* dictionaries (-rĭz)], a book explaining the words of a language arranged alphabetically; a lexicon; vocabulary; word-book.

dic-tum (dĭk'tŭm), *n.* [*pl.* dicta (-tȧ)], a positive opinion; a dogmatic or authoritative assertion; aphorism.

did (dĭd), past tense of the transitive and intransitive verb *do.*

di-dac-tic (dī-dăk'tĭk), *adj.* teaching; instructing; explanatory. Also, **didactical.**—*adv.* **didactically.**

di-dac-tics (dī-dăk'tĭks), *n.pl.* the art of teaching.

did-dle (dĭd'l), *v.t.* to overreach or cheat: *v.i.* to totter like a child; trifle. [Colloq.]

di-do (dī'dō), *n.* a caper; an extravagant action; antic. [Colloq.]

die (dī), *v.i.* [*p.t.* and *p.p.* died, *p.pr.* dying], to cease to live; expire; perish; wither; become extinct gradually; faint: *v.t.* to mold, stamp, or cut (a design) in metal: *n.* a small cube (*pl.* dice); a stamp used for coining money, medals, etc.; a tool used in cutting the threads of screws or bolts, etc.; a kind of knife used by envelope makers, and in shoe factories.

Syn., v.i. expire, depart, perish, decline, languish, wane, sink, decay.

Threading Die

di-er-e-sis (dī-ĕr'ē-sĭs), *n.* a sign [¨] placed over the second of two separate vowels to show that each has a separate sound in pronunciation, as aërated; a division in a line or verse; cell-division. Also, **diæresis.**

Die-sel en-gine (dē'zĕl ĕn'jĭn), an internal combustion oil engine of high efficiency, invented by Rudolph Diesel in 1893, which operates at a very high compression pressure: used in marine construction and on German railroads.

di-e-sis (dī'ē-sĭs), *n.* the double dagger [‡], used in printing as a reference mark; the difference between a greater and less semitone or halftone in music.

di-et (dī'ĕt), *n.* solid or liquid food; manner of living, with special reference to food; a prescribed course of food, intended as a health measure; a national or lawmaking assembly.

Syn. food, victuals, nourishment, nutriment, sustenance, fare.

di-et-a-ry (dī'ĕt-ā-rĭ), *adj.* pertaining to the rules of proper food; as, the food for patients in a hospital is prepared in a *dietary* kitchen: *n.* a certain fixed allowance of food; system of regulating food.

di-e-tet-ic (dī"ē-tĕt'ĭk), *adj.* regulating food or diet. Also, **dietetical.**

di-e-tet-ics (dī"ē-tĕt'ĭks), *n.pl.* that branch of hygiene which relates to healthful foods.

di-et-ing (dī'ĕt-ĭng), *n.* the act of eating according to a strict rule.

dif-fer (dĭf'ẽr), *v.i.* to be unlike; be distinguished from, or have unlike properties or qualities; disagree; contend; dispute.

dif-fer-ence (dĭf'ẽr-ĕns), *n.* the act or state of being unlike; distinction; controversy; quarrel: *v.t.* to distinguish between; discriminate; subtract from.

Syn., n. separation, disagreement, dissent, estrangement, variety.

dif-fer-ent (dĭf'ẽr-ĕnt), *adj.* unlike; distinct.—*adv.* **differently.**

Syn. various, manifold, diverse.

Ant. (see **similar**).

dif-fer-en-ti-a (dĭf"ẽr-ĕn'shĭ-ȧ), *n.* [*pl.* differentiæ (-ē)], that which distinguishes one species from another of the same group.

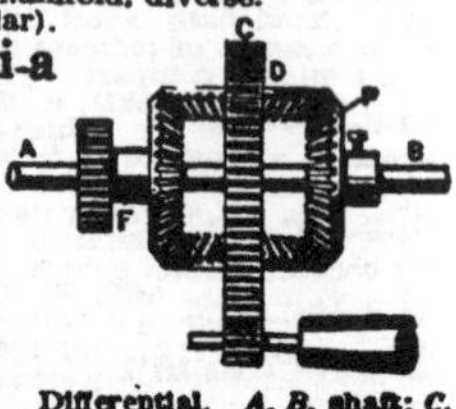

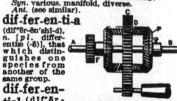

Differential. *A, B,* shaft; *C,* main driving gear; *D,* differential gear carried by main gear; *F,* driven gear; *P,* fixed gear.

dif-fer-en-tial (dĭf"ẽr-ĕn'shăl), *adj.* indicating unlikeness; having inequality; as, a *differential* gear on a motor car which allows one rear wheel to turn faster than the other; pertaining to, or involving, an infinitesimal difference: *n.* an infinitesimal difference between two values of a quantity; a decrease of rates, charged by a railroad: **differential calculus**, a branch of higher mathematics.

dif-fer-en-tial du-ties (dĭf″ẽr-ĕn′shăl dū′tĭz), duties imposed unequally on similar produce from foreign countries.

dif-fer-en-tial-ly (dĭf″ẽr-ĕn′shăl-ĭ), *adv.* in a manner which has, or allows for, inequalities.

dif-fer-en-ti-ate (dĭf″ẽr-ĕn′shĭ-āt), *v.t.* to observe or state an unlikeness between; specialize in structure or functions of; to make (a person or thing) unlike another: *v.i.* to acquire a distinctive and separate character; recognize difference.

dif-fer-en-ti-a-tion (dĭf″ẽr-ĕn″shĭ-ā′shŭn), *n.* the act of separating or classifying; specialization; a seeing of unlikenesses between two persons or things.

dif-fi-cult (dĭf′ĭ-kŭlt), *adj.* not easy; hard; perplexing; not easily managed; as, a man of genius often has a *difficult* temper.

Syn. intricate, involved, obscure, unmanageable.

Ant. (see easy).

dif-fi-cul-ty (dĭf′ĭ-kŭl-tĭ), *n.* [*pl.* difficulties (-tĭz)], state of being hard or perplexing; something hard to do; scruple; objection; hindrance: *pl.* complication of affairs; embarrassment; perplexity.

dif-fi-dence (dĭf′ĭ-dĕns), *n.* lack of self-reliance; modest reserve; shyness.

dif-fi-dent (dĭf′ĭ-dĕnt), *adj.* lacking self-reliance; shy; modest.

dif-frac-tion (dĭ-frăk′shŭn), *n.* the turning aside of a ray of light when passing the edge of a body that will not admit light; the change suffered by such a ray.

dif-fuse (dĭ-fūz′), *v.t.* to pour out and spread all around; scatter; circulate: *adj.* (dĭ-fūs′), widely spread; wordy; as, a *diffuse* style of writing.—*adv.* **diffusely.** —*n.* **diffuseness.**

Syn., adj. discursive, prolix, copious.

dif-fus-i-bil-i-ty (dĭ-fūz″ĭ-bĭl′ĭ-tĭ), *n.* the capability of being poured out or spread.

dif-fus-i-ble (dĭ-fūz′ĭ-bl), *adj.* capable of being poured out or spread.

dif-fu-sion (dĭ-fū′zhŭn), *n.* the act of pouring out or spreading; a spreading abroad; as, the *diffusion* of light or knowledge.

dif-fu-sive (dĭ-fū′sĭv), *adj.* capable of pouring out; spreading every way; widely reaching.

dig (dĭg), *v.t.* [*p.t.* and *p.p.* dug, or digged, *p.pr.* digging], to work with a spade; cast up earth; colloquially, to study hard; as, a student will *dig* in his books just before an examination: *v.t.* to loosen or break up (ground) with a spade; to bring up from under ground; as, to *dig* potatoes; thrust or force in: with *into:* *n.* a poke or thrust; colloquially, a plodding student.—**dig in,** to make a hole or trench for protection against enemy fire.

di-gest (dī′jĕst), *n.* a classification; as, a *digest* of laws; a classified arrangement of written or printed material; as, a literary *digest:* *v.t.* (dĭ-jĕst′), to arrange methodically under proper heads or titles; classify; think over and arrange in the mind; dissolve in the stomach; soften and prepare by heat: *v.i.* to be dissolved in the stomach; to be prepared by heat.

di-gest-er (dĭ-jĕst′ẽr), *n.* a machine for extracting the essence of a substance by heat.

di-gest-i-bil-i-ty (dĭ-jĕs″tĭ-bĭl′ĭ-tĭ), *n.* capability of being dissolved by the stomach.

di-gest-i-ble (dĭ-jĕs′tĭ-bl), *adj.* capable of being dissolved by the stomach; as, the white of egg is given to invalids because it is *digestible.*

di-ges-tion (dĭ-jĕs′chŭn), *n.* the act of digesting; the conversion of food by the action of the gastric juices into forms that can be used by the body; mental or physical assimilation; as, the *digestion* of food in the stomach and the *digestion* of ideas in the mind.

di-ges-tive (dĭ-jĕs′tĭv), *adj.* pertaining to the absorption of food by the body; as, the *digestive* organs.

dig-ger (dĭg′ẽr), *n.* one who works with a spade; an implement for turning up the soil: **Digger,** a name of a class of California Indians who live chiefly on roots.

dig-ging (dĭg′ĭng), *n.* the act of excavating, or throwing up earth with a spade: *pl.* a locality where mining operations, especially for gold, are carried on.

dig-it (dĭj′ĭt), *n.* a finger or toe; a measure (¾ inch); one-twelfth of the diameter of the sun or moon; any one of the Arabic numerals.

dig-it-al (dĭj′ĭ-tăl), *adj.* pertaining to a digit, or finger or toe.

dig-i-ta-lis (dĭj″ĭ-tā′lĭs), *n.* a plant used for medicine; the foxglove.

dig-i-tate (dĭj′ĭ-tāt), *adj.* finger shaped; as, *digitate* leaves.

dig-ni-fied (dĭg′nĭ-fīd), *adj.* lofty in manner; noble; stately.

dig-ni-fy (dĭg′nĭ-fī), *v.t.* [*p.t.* and *p.p.* dignified, *p.pr.* dignifying], to exalt; confer honor upon; elevate.

Syn. aggrandize, invest, exalt, advance, promote, honor.

Ant. (see degrade).

dig-ni-ta-ry (dĭg′nĭ-tā-rĭ), *n.* [*pl.* dignitaries (-rĭz)], one who holds a position of dignity or honor; a high church official; as, an archbishop is a *dignitary.*

dig-ni-ty (dĭg′nĭ-tĭ), *n.* [*pl.* dignities (-tĭz)], elevation of rank; degree of excellence; moral worth; qualities suited to inspire or command respect and reverence; stateliness of manner.

di-graph (dī′grăf), *n.* combination of two sounds or letters to represent one simple sound, as *ea* in *read.* Also, **digram.**

di-gress (dĭ-grĕs′; dī-grĕs′), *v.i.* to turn aside; deviate from the main subject or line of argument; wander; as, a question about the war caused the teacher to *digress.*

di-gres-sion (dĭ-grĕsh′ŭn), *n.* the act of turning aside; the angular distance of the planets Mercury and Venus from the sun.

di-gres-sive (dĭ-grĕs′ĭv), *adj.* tending to turn aside or wander.—*adv.* **digressively.**

di-he-dral (dī-hē′drăl), *adj.* having two plane faces or sides; in a kite or airplane, having wings which make an angle with each other; in flying machines, referring to wings inclined at an upward angle to each other.

dike (dīk), *n.* a ditch; an embankment thrown up as a protection against the sea, or floods; as, the *dike* has been a great protection to Holland: *v.t.* to surround, protect, or inclose with an embankment; drain by ditching. Also, **dyke.**

di-lap-i-date (dĭ-lăp'ĭ-dāt), *v.t.* to bring into partial ruin by neglect or misuse: *v.i.* to become ruined; to fall into decay.

di-lap-i-dat-ed (dĭ-lăp'ĭ-dāt-ĕd), *adj.* fallen into decay; neglected; ruined.

di-lap-i-da-tion (dĭ-lăp"ĭ-dā'shŭn), *n.* a state of partial ruin, especially through neglect or misuse; as, the old mill is in a state of *dilapidation.*

di-lat-a-ble (dĭ-lāt'ȧ-bl), *adj.* capable of being enlarged; expansible.

dil-a-ta-tion (dĭl"ȧ-tā'shŭn; dĭ"lȧ-tā'-shŭn), *n.* expansion; extension; as, a bright light caused the *dilatation* of the pupil of the eye. Also, **dilation.**

di-late (dĭ-lāt'; dī-lāt'), *v.t.* to enlarge or widen in all directions; distend: *v.i.* to be extended or enlarged; speak fully and copiously; as, the explorer was glad to *dilate* on his experiences.—*n.* **dilation.**

Syn. stretch, widen, expand, swell, enlarge.

di-la-tor (dĭ-lā'tẽr), *n.* one who, or that which, widens or enlarges; a muscle that extends the parts on which it acts.

dil-a-to-ry (dĭl'ȧ-tō-rĭ), *adj.* causing, or tending to cause, delay; slow; inactive.—*adv.* **dilatorily.**—*n.* **dilatoriness.**

Syn. tardy, procrastinating, behindhand, lagging, dawdling.

Ant. (see prompt).

di-lem-ma (dĭ-lĕm'ȧ; dī-lĕm'ȧ), *n.* an awkward situation; a difficult position or choice.

dil-et-tan-te (dĭl"ĕ-tăn'tē; It. dē"lĕt-tän'tā), *n.* [*pl.* It. dilettanti (-tē); Eng. dilettantes (-tēz)], one who pursues the fine arts, literature, or science, only for amusement; an amateur: opposite to *connoisseur.*

dil-et-tant-ism (dĭl"ĕ-tănt'ĭzm), *n.* the characteristics of those who amuse themselves with the fine arts; amateurish pursuit of art, literature, etc.: used in a disparaging sense.

dil-i-gence (dĭl'ĭ-jĕns), *n.* careful attention; carefulness; industry; (dē"lē"zhäns'), a French stagecoach.

Syn. care, heed, attention.

Ant. (see negligence).

dil-i-gent (dĭl'ĭ-jĕnt), *adj.* showing or acting with industry; persevering; painstaking.—*adv.* **diligently.**

dill (dĭl), *n.* an herb belonging to the parsley family, with an aromatic or fragrant fruit.

dil-ly-dal-ly (dĭl'ĭ-dăl"ĭ), *v.i.* [*p.t.* and *p.p.* dillydallied, *p.pr.* dillydallying], to loiter; trifle.

di-lute (dĭ-lūt'; dī-lūt'), *v.t.* to thin or weaken by mixing with another fluid, especially water: *v.i.* to become thinner.—*adj.* **diluted.**

di-lu-tion (dĭ-lū'shŭn), *n.* the act of mixing with water, or weakening; a weak liquid.

di-lu-vi-al (dĭ-lū'vĭ-ăl), *adj.* pertaining to, produced by, or resulting from, a deluge or flood, especially the Deluge. Also, **diluvian.**

dim (dĭm), *adj.* [*comp.* dimmer; *superl.* dimmest], somewhat dark; hazy; obscure; faint; tarnished; ill-defined: *v.t.* [*p.t.* and *p.p.* dimmed, *p.pr.* dimming], to render obscure or less distinct; cloud; tarnish; dull: *v.i.* to become indistinct; fade.

dime (dīm), *n.* a silver coin equal to one-tenth of a dollar, or ten cents: *adj.* of the value of ten cents: **dime novel,** a cheap, exciting storybook.

di-men-sion (dĭ-mĕn'shŭn), *n.* measure, as length, breadth, thickness: *pl.* size or extent of a body in these measurements; also, *pl.* size; importance; as, a task of great *dimensions.*

di-men-sion-al (dĭ-mĕn'shŭn-ăl), *adj.* pertaining to size or extent; having length, breadth, etc.; as, a two-*dimensional* figure.

di-me-tal-lic (dī"mē-tăl'ĭk), *adj.* having two atoms of a metallic element; as, a *dimetallic* salt.

di-min-ish (dĭ-mĭn'ĭsh), *v.t.* to make less; reduce in bulk or amount; weaken; impair; detract from; reduce in authority, or rank; degrade: *v.i.* to lessen; dwindle.

Syn. reduce, contract, curtail.

Ant. (see increase).

di-min-u-en-do (dĭ-mĭn"ū-ĕn'dō), *adj.* gradually growing softer in sound: a musical term. [It.]

dim-i-nu-tion (dĭm"ĭ-nū'shŭn), *n.* the act of making less; reduction; lessening.

di-min-u-tive (dĭ-mĭn'ū-tĭv), *adj.* below the average size; little; contracted; narrow: *n.* a word formed from another to express the sense of littleness; as, Kitty is the *diminutive* of Katherine.—*adv.* **diminutively.**—*n.* **diminutiveness.**

dim-i-ty (dĭm'ĭ-tĭ), *n.* [*pl.* dimities (-tĭz)], a cotton material with fine corded stripes.

dim-ly (dĭm'lĭ), *adv.* in a faint, obscure, or dull manner.

dim-mer (dĭm'ẽr), *n.* a choke coil in an electric lighting system, used to regulate the current: often used on automobiles to reduce the power of the headlights.

dim-ness (dĭm'nĕs), *n.* darkness; obscurity; dulness; faintness.

dim-ple (dĭm'pl), *n.* a small dent or hollow in the cheek or chin; an indentation: *v.i.* to form dimples; sink in slight depressions: *v.t.* to mark with dimples.

din (dĭn), *n.* a continued and violent noise: *v.t.* [*p.t.* and *p.p.* dinned, *p.pr.* dinning], to utter with insistent and confusing noise; as, he *dinned* his complaint into our ears: *v.i.* to make a clamor.

dine (dīn), *v.i.* to take dinner; as, to *dine* at seven o'clock: *v.t.* to give or provide a dinner for; feed.

din-er (dīn'ẽr), *n.* a person who is having dinner; colloquially, a railroad car where meals are served.

ding (dĭng), *v.i.* to sound, as a bell, with a continuous monotonous tone: *v.t.* to impress by noisy repetition. [Colloq.]

ding-dong (dĭng'dŏng"), *n.* the sound of bells; a monotonous repetition of a word, phrase, etc.

din-ghy (dĭn'gĭ), *n.* the smallest boat of a man-of-war; an East Indian ferryboat; a small boat of various kinds. Also, **dinghey, dingy.**

din-gi-ly (dĭn'jĭ-lĭ), *adv.* in a dark or grimy manner; dully.

din-gle (dĭn'gl), *n.* a narrow hollow between hills; the inclosed weather-porch of a house.

din-gle-dan-gle (dĭn′gl-dăn″gl), *adv.* so as to swing backwards and forwards; so as to hang loosely.

din-go (dĭn′gō), *n.* the wild fox-like dog of Australia.

din-gy (dĭn′jĭ), *adj.* dark-colored; dirty; as, the houses look *dingy* in a smoky city; discolored; faded.

din-ing car (dīn′ĭng kär), a railroad car in which meals are served.

din-ing room (dīn′ĭng rōōm), a room in which meals are served.

Dingo

din-ner (dĭn′ẽr), *n.* the chief meal of the day; a dinner party.

di-no-saur (dī′nō-sôr), *n.* a large reptile of prehistoric times.

di-no-the-ri-um (dī″nō-thē′rĭ-ŭm), *n.* a large elephantlike animal of prehistoric times.

dint (dĭnt), *n.* dent; a mark left by a blow or pressure; force or power: with *of*; as, the trunk was closed by *dint* of much effort: *v.t.* to make a mark on or in.

di-oc-e-san (dī-ŏs′ē-săn; dī″ō-sē′săn), *adj.* of or pertaining to a diocese or church district controlled by a bishop: *n.* a bishop.

di-o-cese (dī′ō-sēs; dī′ō-sĕs), *n.* [*pl.* dioceses (-sē-sĕz)], the district in which a bishop has authority, called the bishop's see; a bishopric.

di-op-tric (dī-ŏp′trĭk), *adj.* assisting vision by means of the refraction of light: used of lenses. Also, **dioptrical**.

di-ox-ide (dī-ŏk′sīd; dī-ŏk′sĭd), *n.* a compound of two atoms of oxygen and one atom of a metal. Also, **dioxid**.

dip (dĭp), *v.t.* [*p.t.* and *p.p.* dipped, dipt, *p.pr.* dipping], to plunge; put quickly into liquid and take out again; to scoop up with a ladle; baptize by putting under water; lower and raise quickly: *v.i.* to immerse oneself; enter slightly into anything; incline downwards; sink: *n.* the act of putting into water temporarily; as, to take a *dip* in the ocean; a downward slope; in aviation, a quick descent followed by an ascent.

di-phos-gene (dī-fŏs′jēn), *n.* in the World War, a poisonous gas used in shells with deadly effect.

diph-the-ri-a (dĭf-thē′rĭ-ȧ), *n.* a contagious disease of the throat.—*adj.* **diphtheritic**.

diph-thong (dĭf′thŏng), *n.* the union of two vowel sounds pronounced in one syllable; as, *ou* in *out*, *oi* in *oil*.—*adj.* **diphthongal**.

di-plo-ma (dĭ-plō′mȧ), *n.* a writing conferring some honor or degree; a paper showing the completion of a course of study; as, the student receives a *diploma* on graduating from school.

di-plo-ma-cy (dĭ-plō′mȧ-sĭ), *n.* [*pl.* diplomacies (-sĭz)], the art of conducting negotiations or dealings between two states or nations; skill in conducting negotiations; tact; skill in social matters: **dollar diplomacy**, diplomatic negotiations governed solely by considerations of monetary advantage.

dip-lo-mat (dĭp′lō-măt), *n.* a person skilled in carrying on dealings between two nations; one employed in such dealings; a tactful person.

dip-lo-mat-ic (dĭp″lō-măt′ĭk), *adj.* pertaining to the management of affairs between two nations; as, an ambassador is appointed to look after *diplomatic* business; characterized by special tact in the management of affairs.—*adv.* **diplomatically**.

di-plo-ma-tist (dĭ-plō′mȧ-tĭst), *n.* one who is skilled in the art of managing affairs between nations; a tactful person.

dip-per (dĭp′ẽr), *n.* one who, or that which, dips, especially a cup or ladle for water, etc.; a water-fowl; the group of seven stars, in the northern sky, arranged like a ladle.

dip-so-ma-ni-a (dĭp″sō-mā′nĭ-ȧ), *n.* an unnatural and uncontrollable craving for alcoholic drinks.

dip-so-ma-ni-ac (dĭp″sō-mā′nĭ-ăk), *n.* one who suffers from an uncontrollable desire for strong drink: *adj.* pertaining to dipsomania.

dire (dīr), *adj.* dreadful; mournful; as, the *dire* news of an explosion.

di-rect (dĭ-rĕkt′), *adj.* straight; open; plain; straightforward; as, a *direct* manner of speaking: *v.t.* to aim or drive in a straight line; guide or show: *v.i.* to act as a guide.

di-rec-tion (dĭ-rĕk′shŭn), *n.* act of guiding or showing; aim; line of motion; address, as of a letter, etc.

Syn. aim, course, tendency, way.

di-rect-ly (dĭ-rĕkt′lĭ), *adv.* in a straight line; immediately; soon; as, I will come *directly*; openly.

di-rect-ness (dĭ-rĕkt′nĕs), *n.* the quality of being straight or to the point; straightforwardness; freedom from ambiguity, or doubt.

di-rect-or (dĭ-rĕk′tẽr), *n.* one who guides or shows; one appointed to transact the affairs of a company; a spiritual guide or adviser.

di-rect-or-ate (dĭ-rĕk′tō-rāt), *n.* the office of a guide, manager, or adviser; a group of persons managing the affairs of an organized body.

di-rec-to-ry (dĭ-rĕk′tō-rĭ), *n.* a book of names and addresses; a collection of rules; a board of managers, of a company, etc.: *adj.* containing rules; guiding; commanding.

dire-ful (dīr′fōōl), *adj.* dreadful; dismal; as, the *direful* news of the destruction of the ship with all on board appalled the world.—*adv.* **direfully**.

dirge (dûrj), *n.* a funeral hymn; a song or tune expressing mourning.

dir-i-gi-ble (dĭr′ĭ-jĭ-bl), *adj.* that may be guided or steered; as, a *dirigible* balloon: *n.* a cigar-shaped balloon driven by motors and provided with a car for passengers; as, the Zeppelin *dirigibles* of Germany.

dirk (dûrk), *n.* a dagger; especially, a dagger without a guard, used by the Scotch Highlanders.

dirt (dûrt), *n.* mud; filth; as, the streets are full of *dirt*; dust; garden earth.

dirt-i-ly (dûr′tĭ-lĭ), *adv.* filthily; meanly; contemptibly; despicably.

dirt-i-ness (dûr′tĭ-nĕs), *n.* the state or quality of being soiled.

dirt-y (dûr′tĭ), *adj.* unclean; impure; soiled; disgusting; muddy; sleety; rainy; despicable; contemptible: *v.t.* [*p.t.*

and *p.p.* dirtied, *p.pr.* dirtying], to soil; sully; tarnish.

dis- (dĭs-), a *prefix* meaning apart, away from, with the idea of separation, privation, or denial.

dis-a-bil-i-ty (dĭs″ȧ-bĭl′ĭ-tĭ), *n.* [*pl.* disabilities (-tĭz)], want of power; state of being without ability.
Syn. incapacity, inability.

dis-a-ble (dĭs-ā′bl), *v.t.* to deprive of power; make unable; disqualify; impoverish or make poor; incapacitate or render unable.—*adj.* disabled.

dis-a-buse (dĭs″ȧ-būz′), *v.t.* to undeceive; set free from mistake; as, to *disabuse* oneself or some one else of a wrong idea.

dis-ad-van-tage (dĭs″ăd-văn′tāj), *n.* a hindrance; a cause of loss or injury; an unfavorable position; loss; detriment; as, the country without an army is at a *disadvantage* when war is declared.

dis-ad-van-ta-geous (dĭs-ăd″văn-tā′jŭs), *adj.* unfavorable; likely to cause loss, injury, or failure.—*adv.* disadvantageously.

dis-af-fect (dĭs″ă-fĕkt′), *v.t.* to fill with discontent; alienate or take the affections from; disturb the functions of.

dis-af-fect-ed (dĭs″ă-fĕkt′ĕd), *adj.* discontented; no longer friendly; out of sympathy.

dis-af-fec-tion (dĭs″ă-fĕk′shŭn), *n.* disloyalty; ill will; hostility.

dis-a-gree (dĭs″ȧ-grē′), *v.i.* to differ in opinion; to be unlike or unsuited; be unfavorable or unsuitable.

dis-a-gree-a-ble (dĭs″ȧ-grē′ȧ-bl), *adj.* unpleasant; offensive.—*adv.* disagreeably.—*n.* disagreeableness.

dis-a-gree-ment (dĭs″ȧ-grē′mĕnt), *n.* difference of opinion; act or state of disagreeing; a quarrel.

dis-al-low (dĭs″ă-lou′), *v.t.* to refuse to permit; disapprove; reject.

dis-ap-pear (dĭs″ă-pēr′), *v.i.* to pass from sight; vanish; to become invisible.

dis-ap-pear-ance (dĭs″ă-pēr′ăns), *n.* removal from sight.

dis-ap-point (dĭs″ă-point′), *v.t.* to fail to gratify; to defeat of hope; frustrate; fail to keep an appointment with.

dis-ap-point-ed (dĭs″ă-point′ĕd), *p.adj.* defeated of hope or expectation.

dis-ap-point-ment (dĭs″ă-point′mĕnt), *n.* defeat or failure of expectation; state of depression caused by failure; that which causes failure of expectation.

dis-ap-pro-ba-tion (dĭs-ăp″rō-bā′shŭn), *n.* the act or state of failing to approve, or of thinking that something is wrong; blame; unfavorable judgment.

dis-ap-prov-al (dĭs″ă-prōōv′ăl), *n.* unfavorable opinion; failure to approve; blame.

dis-ap-prove (dĭs″ă-prōōv′), *v.t.* to condemn; refuse assent to; censure: *v.i.* to express unfavorable judgment.—*adv.* disapprovingly.

dis-arm (dĭs-ärm′), *v.t.* to deprive of weapons; reduce to a peace footing; render harmless; subdue.

dis-ar-ma-ment (dĭs-är′mȧ-mĕnt), *n.* the act of depriving of weapons; reduction to a peace footing.

dis-ar-range (dĭs″ă-rānj′), *v.t.* to put out of order; disturb; confuse.

dis-ar-ray (dĭs″ă-rā′), *v.t.* [*p.t.* and *p.p.* disarrayed, *p.pr.* disarraying], to undress; to overthrow; to throw into disorder; rout: *n.* disordered or insufficient dress; confusion.

dis-as-ter (dĭz-ȧs′tēr), *n.* a calamity; misfortune; a serious accident.

dis-as-trous (dĭz-ȧs′trŭs), *adj.* unlucky; unfortunate; calamitous; attended with evil results.—*adv.* disastrously.

dis-a-vow (dĭs″ȧ-vou′), *v.t.* to deny; disclaim; disown.

dis-a-vow-al (dĭs″ȧ-vou′ăl), *n.* denial; rejection; as, he made a complete *disavowal* of responsibility for his brother's acts.

dis-band (dĭs-bănd′), *v.t.* to dismiss from military service; break up, as a society; scatter: *v.i.* to be dispersed or broken up.—*n.* disbandment.

dis-bar (dĭs-bär′), *v.t.* [*p.t.* and *p.p.* disbarred, *p.pr.* disbarring], to deprive (a lawyer) of the right to appear in court as an attorney.

dis-be-lief (dĭs″bē-lēf′), *n.* the act or state of refusing to believe; refusal of trust.

dis-be-lieve (dĭs″bē-lēv′), *v.t.* and *v.i.* to refuse to believe; to distrust.

dis-bur-den (dĭs-bûr′dn), *v.t.* to remove a burden from; relieve of anything annoying or oppressive: *v.i.* to ease one's mind.

dis-burse (dĭs-bûrs′), *v.t.* to expend; to pay out; as, the treasurer of a company *disburses* the money.

dis-burse-ment (dĭs-bûrs′mĕnt), *n.* money expended or paid out.

disc (dĭsk), *n.* a flat, circular plate; anything resembling such a plate. Also, disk.

dis-card (dĭs-kärd′), *v.t.* to cast off as useless; dismiss from service; reject as useless; throw away: *v.i.* in card-playing, to throw out cards not required.

dis-cern (dĭ-zûrn′), *v.t.* to discover; to see; to distinguish mentally, or with the eye; detect: *v.i.* to make distinction.
Syn. descry, observe, recognize, see, discriminate, perceive.

dis-cern-i-ble (dĭ-zûr′nĭ-bl), *adj.* perceptible; capable of being seen.—*adv.* discernibly.

dis-cern-ment (dĭ-zûrn′mĕnt), *n.* clearness in judgment; penetration; insight; discrimination.

dis-charge (dĭs-chärj′), *v.t.* to unload; disembark; send away; send out, or emit; free from any burden; free from restraint or custody; let fly, as an arrow; fire, as a gun; explode; perform (a trust or duty): *v.i.* to get rid of any burden: *n.* the act of unloading, or that which is unloaded; performance (of duty): the getting rid of a burden; an explosion; a firing off (of a gun); a sending away; dismissal; liberation.

dis-ci-ple (dĭ-sī′pl), *n.* a pupil; especially one who believes the teaching of another; a scholar; a follower; a student.

dis-ci-plin-a-ble (dĭs′ĭ-plĭn-ȧ-bl), *adj.* capable of instruction; liable to punishment for disobeying.

dis-ci-plin-a-ri-an (dis'ĭ-plĭn-ā'rĭ-ăn), *n.* one who believes in, or enforces, strict rules: *adj.* pertaining to strict training.

dis-ci-plin-a-ry (dĭs'ĭ-plĭn-ā-rĭ), *adj.* pertaining to strict training or correction.

dis-ci-pline (dĭs'ĭ-plĭn), *n.* mental or moral training; education; subjection to control; military regulation; as, under strict *discipline*: *v.t.* to train to obedience or efficiency; regulate; punish.

Syn., *n.* order, strictness, training, coercion, punishment.

Ant. (see confusion, demoralization).

dis-claim (dĭs-klām'), *v.t.* to disown; repudiate; deny any connection with.

dis-claim-er (dĭs-klām'ẽr), *n.* disavowal; denial.

dis-close (dĭs-klōz'), *v.t.* to uncover; reveal; divulge; bring to light.

dis-clo-sure (dĭs-klō'zhūr), *n.* the act of revealing anything secret; discovery; uncovering.

dis-coid (dĭs'koid), *adj.* disk-shaped, or round and flat: *n.* a disk-shaped object.

dis-col-or (dĭs-kŭl'ẽr), *v.t.* to change from the natural color; give a false complexion to; stain. Also, **discolour.** —*n.* **discoloration.**

dis-com-fit (dĭs-kŭm'fĭt), *v.t.* to defeat; rout; balk; frustrate; thwart.

dis-com-fi-ture (dĭs-kŭm'fĭ-tūr), *n.* defeat; disappointment; embarrassment.

dis-com-fort (dĭs-kŭm'fẽrt), *n.* want of ease; state of being uncomfortable; distress; as, the *discomfort* of traveling in hot weather: *v.t.* to disturb; to make uncomfortable.

dis-com-mode (dĭs-kŏ-mōd'), *v.t.* to disturb; annoy; cause inconvenience to.

dis-com-pose (dĭs-kŏm-pōz'), *v.t.* disarrange; vex; ruffle.

dis-com-pos-ure (dĭs'kŏm-pō'zhūr), *n.* agitation; unrest.

dis-con-cert (dĭs'kŏn-sẽrt'), *v.t.* to disturb the composure or self-possession of; confuse; frustrate; embarrass.

dis-con-nect (dĭs'kŏ-nĕkt'), *v.t.* to disunite; unfasten; dissociate; separate.—*n.* **disconnection.**

dis-con-nect-ed (dĭs'kŏ-nĕkt'ĕd), *p.adj.* disjointed; separate; broken; interrupted.—*adv.* **disconnectedly.**

dis-con-so-late (dĭs-kŏn'sō-lāt), *adj.* hopeless; sad; as, to be *disconsolate* over the loss of a friend; cheerless; saddening.—*adv.* **disconsolately.**

dis-con-tent (dĭs'kŏn-tĕnt'), *n.* dissatisfaction; displeasure; uneasiness: *v.t.* to displease; dissatisfy.

dis-con-tent-ed (dĭs'kŏn-tĕnt'ĕd), *p.adj.* not pleased with what one has; dissatisfied.—*adv.* **discontentedly.**

dis-con-tent-ment (dĭs'kŏn-tĕnt'mĕnt), *n.* state of being displeased or dissatisfied.

dis-con-tin-u-ance (dĭs'kŏn-tĭn'ū-ăns), *n.* a stopping; a breaking off.

dis-con-tin-ue (dĭs'kŏn-tĭn'ū), *v.t.* to stop; to cease doing; to put an end to; to give up; as, to *discontinue* taking a magazine.—*n.* **discontinuation.**

dis-cord (dĭs'kôrd), *n.* disagreement; a confused noise; lack of harmony; strife; uproar.—*n.* **discordance.**

dis-cord-ant (dĭs-kôr'dănt), *adj.* inharmonious; jarring; full of noise and strife; as, the *discordant* street noises.

dis-count (dĭs'kount), *n.* a sum deducted or allowed for prompt payment of an account; a deduction made according to the current rate of interest: *v.t.* to deduct a sum from for prompt payment; advance money on, deducting a certain rate per cent; make a deduction from; anticipate; allow for exaggeration in, as a story.

dis-coun-te-nance (dĭs-koun'tē-năns), *v.t.* to disapprove of; to make ashamed.

dis-cour-age (dĭs-kŭr'āj), *v.t.* to depress; to deprive or lessen the courage of; dishearten; deter.

dis-cour-age-ment (dĭs-kŭr'āj-mĕnt), *n.* the act of depriving of confidence; that which destroys courage; state of being without courage.

dis-course (dĭs-kōrs'), *n.* speech or language; conversation; sermon: *v. i.* to talk or converse: *v. t.* to utter, as to *discourse* wisdom.

dis-cour-te-ous (dĭs-kŭr'tē-ŭs), *adj.* impolite; rude; wanting in civility.—*adv.* **discourteously.**

dis-cour-te-sy (dĭs-kŭr'tē-sĭ), *n.* rudeness; impoliteness; an unmannerly act.

dis-cov-er (dĭs-kŭv'ẽr), *v.t.* to bring to light; reveal; find (something previously unknown).—*adj.* **discoverable.**—*n.* **discoverer.**

Syn. make known, invent, contrive, expose, reveal.

dis-cov-er-y (dĭs-kŭv'ẽr-ĭ), *n.* [*pl.* discoveries (-ĭz)], a bringing to light, or making known, especially for the first time; disclosure.

dis-cred-it (dĭs-krĕd'ĭt), *n.* lack of belief; distrust; lack of reputation; dishonor: *v.t.* to refuse to believe; to dishonor; to take away reputation from.—*adj.* **discreditable.**—*adv.* **discreditably.**

dis-creet (dĭs-krēt'), *adj.* careful; prudent; as, a *discreet* answer; *discreet* behavior.—*adv.* **discreetly.**

Syn. cautious, wary, judicious.

dis-crep-an-cy (dĭs-krĕp'ăn-sĭ), *n.* inconsistency; disagreement; as, the man's accounts and the bank balance showed a *discrepancy*.

Syn. difference, variance.

Ant. (see agreement).

dis-crete (dĭs-krēt'; dĭs'krēt), *adj.* separate from others; distinct; not continuous; composed of distinct parts.

dis-cre-tion (dĭs-krĕsh'ŭn), *n.* prudence; judgment; caution; skill.

dis-crim-i-nate (dĭs-krĭm'ĭ-nāt), *v.t.* to distinguish; to observe or mark the differences between; select: *v.i.* to make a difference or distinction.

dis-crim-i-na-tion (dĭs-krĭm'ĭ-nā'shŭn), *n.* power of distinguishing; faculty of exact judgment between two things or persons.

Syn. acuteness, discernment, judgment, caution.

dis-crim-i-na-tive (dĭs-krĭm'ĭ-nā-tĭv), *adj.* showing exact judgment; penetrating; acute; discriminating.

dis-cur-sive (dĭs-kŭr'sĭv), *adj.* passing from one thing to another; digressive; rambling.

dis-cur-sive-ly (dĭs-kûr'sĭv-lĭ), *adv.* in a lengthy or rambling manner.

dis-cur-sive-ness (dĭs-kûr'sĭv-nĕs), *n.* tendency to digress or ramble in talk; as, *discursiveness* of thought; *discursiveness* in a speech.

Discus Thrower

dis-cus (dĭs'kŭs), *n.* a heavy, circular piece of metal or stone thrown in ancient and modern athletic contests.

dis-cuss (dĭs-kŭs'), *v.t.* to debate; agitate; reason upon; argue; colloquially, to try the taste of, as food.

dis-cus-sion (dĭs-kŭsh'ŭn), *n.* argument; debate; consideration of a question.

dis-dain (dĭs-dān'), *v.t.* to scorn; to despise; look upon with contempt or scorn: *n.* contempt; haughty or indignant scorn.

dis-dain-ful (dĭs-dān'fool), *adj.* contemptuous; scornful; as, a *disdainful* look or reply.—*adv.* **disdainfully.**

dis-ease (dĭ-zēz'), *n.* disorder of mind or body; malady; illness: *v.t.* to cause disease in; derange.

Syn. complaint, ailment, sickness.

dis-em-bark (dĭs"ĕm-bärk'), *v.t.* and *v.i.* to remove from, or go ashore from, a vessel.—*n.* **disembarkation.**

dis-em-bar-rass (dĭs"ĕm-băr'ăs), *v.t.* to free from hindrances or entanglements.

dis-em-bod-y (dĭs"ĕm-bŏd'ĭ), *v.t.* to strip the body or physical existence from.

dis-em-bow-el (dĭs"ĕm-bou'ĕl), *v.t.* [*p.t.* and *p.p.* disemboweled, *p.pr.* disemboweling], to deprive of bowels; wound in the abdomen, so that the bowels protrude.

dis-en-chant (dĭs"ĕn-chănt'), *v.t.* to set free from charm, fascination, or delusion.

dis-en-chant-ment (dĭs"ĕn-chănt'mĕnt), *n.* state of being set free from charm or delusion.

dis-en-cum-ber (dĭs"ĕn-kŭm'bĕr), *v.t.* to free from encumbrance or claim; remove a hindrance from; unburden.

dis-en-gage (dĭs"ĕn-gāj'), *v.t.* to release from; disentangle; extricate; clear.—*n.* **disengagement.**

dis-en-tan-gle (dĭs"ĕn-tăn'gl), *v.t.* to set free from entanglement or embarrassing connection; clear; extricate; disengage.

dis-fa-vor (dĭs-fā'vẽr), *n.* want of regard or esteem; state of not being well regarded: *v.t.* to disapprove of. Also, **disfavour.**

dis-fig-ure (dĭs-fĭg'ūr), *v.t.* to mar; to injure the shape, form, or beauty of; deform.—*n.* **disfigurement.**

dis-fran-chise (dĭs-frăn'chīz; dĭs-frăn'chĭz), *v.t.* to deprive of a political right, as suffrage, or the right to vote.

dis-gorge (dĭs-gôrj'), *v.t.* to give up; as, plunder; to force out of the mouth or stomach with violence: *v.i.* surrender what has been unlawfully obtained; vomit.

dis-grace (dĭs-grās'), *n.* ignominy; shame; dishonor: *v.t.* to bring shame, reproach, or dishonor upon; dismiss with dishonor.

Syn., n. disrepute, odium, reproach.

dis-grace-ful (dĭs-grās'fool), *adj.* characterized by or occasioning dishonor; shameful.—*adv.* **disgracefully.**

dis-guise (dĭs-gīz'), *v.t.* to conceal or change the appearance of, as by an unusual dress; to counterfeit; to conceal or cover by a pretense: *n.* a dress designed to conceal the identity of the wearer; counterfeit appearance; false pretense; cloak; mask.

dis-gust (dĭs-gŭst'), *n.* dislike; strong aversion: *v.t.* to cause distaste or loathing in; offend the taste or moral sense of.—*p.adj.* **disgusting.**—*adv.* **disgustingly.**

Syn., n. distaste, loathing, abomination, abhorrence.

dish (dĭsh), *n.* a deep or shallow hollow vessel with a rimmed edge, used for serving food; food served in a dish: *v.t.* to put into a dish for serving at table: often with *up*.

dis-ha-bille (dĭs"ȧ-bēl'; dĭs"ȧ-bĭl'), *n.* undress or careless attire. Also, **deshabille.** [Fr.]

dis-heart-en (dĭs-här'tn), *v.t.* to discourage.

di-shev-el (dĭ-shĕv'ĕl), *v.t.* [*p.t.* and *p.p.* disheveled, *p.pr.* disheveling], to disorder (the hair) or cause to hang negligently or loosely; to throw into disorder.

dis-hon-est (dĭs-ŏn'ĕst), *adj.* lacking in uprightness or fairness; inclined to cheat or deceive; false.—*adv.* **dishonestly.**

dis-hon-es-ty (dĭs-ŏn'ĕs-tĭ), *n.* deceit; fraud; unfairness; lack of truth and uprightness.

dis-hon-or (dĭs-ŏn'ẽr), *v.t.* to disgrace; bring shame upon the character of; refuse, or fail, to pay (a bill or note when due and presented): *n.* disgrace; ignominy; shame; a dishonest act. Also, **dishonour.**

dis-hon-or-a-ble (dĭs-ŏn'ẽr-ȧ-bl), *adj.* discreditable; shameful; ignominious. Also, **dishonourable.**—*adv.* **dishonorably, dishonourably.**

dis-il-lu-sion (dĭs"ĭ-lū'zhŭn), *v.t.* to set free from a mistaken idea or wrong impression.

dis-in-cli-na-tion (dĭs-ĭn"klĭ-nā'shŭn), *n.* unwillingness; dislike.

dis-in-cline (dĭs"ĭn-klīn'), *v.t.* to make unwilling: *v.i.* to be unwilling.

dis-in-fect (dĭs"ĭn-fĕkt'), *v.t.* to cleanse from infection; to purify.—*n.* **disinfection, disinfector.**

dis-in-fect-ant (dĭs"ĭn-fĕk'tănt), *n.* a substance used to cleanse or purify.

dis-in-gen-u-ous (dĭs-ĭn-jĕn'ū-ŭs), *adj.* not frank or candid; deceitful.—*adv.* **disingenuously.**—*n.* **disingenuousness.**

dis-in-her-it (dĭs"ĭn-hĕr'ĭt), *v.t.* to refuse to leave property to, as an heir.—*n.* **disinheritance.**

dis-in-te-grate (dĭs-ĭn'tē-grāt), *v.t.* to break up: *v.i.* separate.

dis-in-te-gra-tion (dĭs-ĭn"tē-grā'shŭn), *n.* the act of disintegrating, or breaking up; wearing down of rocks; separation.

dis-in-ter-est-ed (dĭs-ĭn'tẽr-ĕs-tĕd), *adj.* not considering oneself; without a selfish motive.

dis-junc-tive (dis-jŭnk'tiv), *adj.* serving or tending to disjoin or separate: *n.* a conjunction which connects grammatically two words or clauses disjoined in meaning; as, *although, either, or, neither, nor,* etc.

disk (disk), *n.* a flat circular plate, or anything resembling it: **disk grinder,** a machine with disk-shaped wheels for sharpening tools. Also, **disc.**

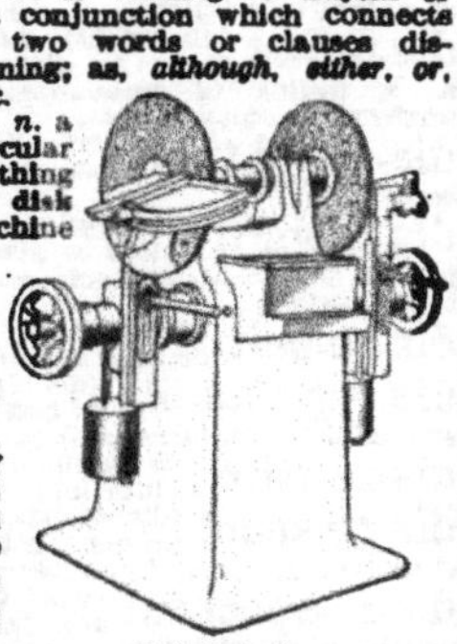

Disk Grinder

dis-like (dis-līk'), *n.* a strong feeling of aversion: *v.t.* to regard with aversion; be displeased with.

dis-lo-cate (dis'lō-kāt), *v.t.* to put out of joint: displace; interrupt the continuation of.

dis-lo-ca-tion (dis'lō-kā'shŭn), *n.* the act of displacing or disjoining; a joint put out of its socket; a displacement of rocks in layers.

dis-lodge (dis-lŏj'), *v.t.* to remove; drive from a hiding place or chosen station.

dis-loy-al (dis-loi'ăl), *adj.* false to one's government or one's friends; faithless; disobedient.—*n.* **disloyalty.**

dis-mal (diz'măl), *adj.* gloomy; depressing; as, *dismal* weather; dark; horrid; sorrowful.—*adv.* **dismally.**

dis-man-tle (dis-măn'tl), *v.t.* to strip or deprive of furniture, equipment, or means of defense; as, to *dismantle* a house is to take out all the furniture; demolish.

dis-mast (dis-măst'), *v.t.* to deprive of a mast; as, the ship was caught in a gale and *dismasted.*

dis-may (dis-mā'), *v.t.* [*p.t.* and *p.p.* dismayed, *p.pr.* dismaying], to terrify; dispirit; discourage: *n.* loss of courage through fear; a condition of terror.

Syn., v. frighten, scare, daunt, appall, dishearten.

Ant. (see encourage).

dis-mem-ber (dis-mĕm'bẽr), *v.t.* to cut or tear limb from limb; sever into parts and distribute; dislocate; sever; divide.—*n.* **dismemberment.**

dis-miss (dis-mis'), *v.t.* to send away; permit to depart; discharge from office or employment; to put away; as, to *dismiss* idle fears.

Syn. discard, banish.

Ant. (see retain).

dis-miss-al (dis-mis'ăl), *n.* the act of sending away; removal from office. Also, **dismission.**

dis-mount (dis-mount'), *v.i.* to get off a horse, bicycle, etc.: *v.t.* to remove from a carriage: said of artillery; to put off from a horse.

dis-o-be-di-ence (dis'ō-bē'di-ĕns), *n.* refusal or neglect to obey an order or command.

dis-o-be-di-ent (dis'ō-bē'di-ĕnt), *adj.* refusing or neglecting to obey.—*adv.* **disobediently.**

dis-o-bey (dis'ō-bā'), *v.t.* to fail to comply with; refuse to carry out the orders of.

dis-o-blige (dis-ō-blīj'), *v.t.* to refuse to accommodate.—*p.adj.* **disobliging.**—*adv.* **disobligingly.**

dis-or-der (dis-ôr'dẽr), *n.* want of order or arrangement; lack of system; irregularity; breach of public order; confusion; as, the earthquake caused great *disorder* in California; riot; mental or physical disease: *v.t.* to throw into confusion; disarrange.

dis-or-dered (dis-ôr'dẽrd), *p.adj.* irregular; loose; unruly; disreputable; upset; disarranged.

dis-or-der-ly (dis-ôr'dẽr-li), *adj.* confused; turbulent; unruly.—*n.* **disorderliness.**

dis-or-gan-ize (dis-ôr'găn-īz), *v.t.* to destroy the regularity of; to throw into confusion.—*n.* **disorganization.**

dis-own (dis-ōn'), *v.t.* to deny; reject; refuse to claim as one's own; as, to *disown* one's country; his family *disowned* him.

dis-par-age (dis-păr'āj), *v.t.* to treat with contempt; criticize unjustly; belittle; speak slightingly of.—*adv.* **disparagingly.**

dis-par-age-ment (dis-păr'āj-mĕnt), *n.* the act of speaking slightingly of; depreciation; reproach; disgrace: often with *to.*

dis-par-i-ty (dis-păr'i-ti), *n.* [*pl.* disparities (-tiz)], inequality; difference; disproportion.

dis-pas-sion-ate (dis-păsh'ŭn-āt), *adj.* free from passion; cool; calm; unprejudiced; impartial.—*adv.* **dispassionately.**

dis-patch (dis-păch'), *v.t.* to send off; finish quickly: *n.* speedy performance. Also, **despatch.**

dis-patch-er (dis-păch'ẽr), *n.* one who sends something off promptly, or at the right time; as a train *dispatcher.* Also, **despatcher.**

dis-pel (dis-pĕl'), *v.t.* [*p.t.* and *p.p.* dispelled, *p.pr.* dispelling], to drive away by, or as by, scattering; disperse; dissipate.

Syn. scatter, dispose of.

Ant. (see collect).

dis-pen-sa-ble (dis-pĕn'sȧ-bl), *adj.* capable of being administered; capable of being done without.

dis-pen-sa-ry (dis-pĕn'sȧ-ri), *n.* [*pl.* dispensaries (-riz)], a place where medicines are kept and made up; a charitable institution for providing the poor with medical advice and medicines.

dis-pen-sa-tion (dis'pĕn-sā'shŭn), *n.* the act of giving out in portions; distribution; that which is appointed or bestowed by a higher power; the suspending of a rule or law in some particular case; a license granted from the Pope, or by a bishop.

dis-pense (dis-pĕns'), *v.t.* to deal out in portions; as, to *dispense* food; distribute; carry out; enforce; as, to *dispense* justice: *v.i.* to give up or do without; as, to *dispense* with the doctor; to give special license.—*n.* **dispenser.**

dis-perse (dis-pûrs'), *v.t.* to scatter; spread; cause to vanish; as, the hot sun will *disperse* the mist: *v.i.* to separate; go to different parts; vanish out of sight; as, the crowd *dispersed.*

dis-per-sion (dĭs-pûr'shŭn), *n.* the act of scattering or spreading; the separation of light into different colored rays in passing through a prism.

dis-per-sive (dĭs-pûr'sĭv), *adj.* tending to scatter; as, the *dispersive* power that separates colors to form a spectrum.

dis-pir-it (dĭs-pĭr'ĭt), *v.t.* to depress the spirits of; dishearten; render cheerless; discourage.

dis-place (dĭs-plās'), *v.t.* to put out of place; disorder; depose from office or dignity; as, to *displace* a dishonest official.
Syn. derange, remove, disturb, confuse.
Ant. (see adjust).

dis-place-ment (dĭs-plās'mĕnt), *n.* the act of putting out of place; substitution; apparent change of position; the weight of water displaced by a solid body immersed in it; as, the *displacement* of a ship.

dis-play (dĭs-plā'), *v.t.* [*p.t.* and *p.p.* displayed, *p.pr.* displaying], to spread out; unfold; exhibit; show mentally or physically: *v.i.* to make a show of something: *n.* an exhibit; a parade or show; as, the fashion *display* at the opera.
Syn., v. show, expose, indicate.
Ant. (see hide).

dis-please (dĭs-plēz'), *v.t.* to vex; annoy; offend; to arouse a dislike.

dis-pleas-ure (dĭs-plĕzh'ŭr), *n.* annoyance; vexation; distaste.

dis-port (dĭs-pōrt'), *v.t.* to amuse or divert: with *self;* as, to *disport* oneself in the ocean; to display gaily: *v.i.* to play.

dis-pos-al (dĭs-pōz'ăl), *n.* arrangement; order; control; right of giving or bestowing.

dis-pose (dĭs-pōz'), *v.t.* to place; arrange; order; distribute; adapt; incline.
Syn. give, bestow.

dis-po-si-tion (dĭs"pō-zĭsh'ŭn), *n.* the act of placing or arranging; order; method; arrangement; inclination; tendency; temper or frame of mind; as, she has a cheerful *disposition.*

dis-pos-sess (dĭs"pō-zĕs'), *v.t.* to remove from ownership, especially of land; eject.—*n.* **dispossession.**

dis-proof (dĭs-prōōf'), *n.* a showing that a statement is not true or not reasonable.

dis-pro-por-tion (dĭs"prō-pōr'shŭn), *n.* want of symmetry; lack of proper or suitable relation in form, size, importance, etc.—*adj.* **disproportionate.**

dis-prove (dĭs-prōōv'), *v.t.* to show to be untrue or unreasonable.

dis-pu-ta-ble (dĭs'pū-tȧ-bl), *adj.* liable to be called in question or contested.

dis-pu-tant (dĭs'pū-tănt), *adj.* given to arguing; engaged in controversy: *n.* an arguer or reasoner.

dis-pu-ta-tion (dĭs"pū-tā'shŭn), *n.* a debate; verbal controversy; an altercation.

dis-pu-ta-tious (dĭs"pū-tā'shŭs), *adj.* contentious; inclined to argue.

dis-pute (dĭs-pūt'), *v.i.* to debate; argue; quarrel: *v.t.* contend for by words or actions; express doubt of; controvert; contest: *n.* a contest in words; a quarrel.
Syn., v. argue, question, impugn.
Ant. (see assent).

dis-qual-i-fy (dĭs-kwŏl'ĭ-fī), *v.t.* to make unfit; to disable; to deprive of a right or privilege.—*n.* **disqualification.**

dis-qui-et (dĭs-kwī'ĕt), *v.t.* to make uneasy; to disturb; to worry: *n.* a feeling of uneasiness; disturbance; anxiety.—*n.* **disquietude.**

dis-qui-si-tion (dĭs"kwĭ-zĭsh'ŭn), *n.* a discussion; an elaborate essay.

dis-re-gard (dĭs"rē-gärd'), *v.t.* to fail to notice or give consideration to; to slight; to neglect: *n.* lack of attention; neglect.

dis-re-pair (dĭs"rē-pâr'), *n.* state of needing repair; dilapidation.

dis-rep-u-ta-ble (dĭs-rĕp'ū-tȧ-bl), *adj.* of bad character; low; shameful.—*adv.* **disreputably.**

dis-re-pute (dĭs"rē-pūt'), *n.* lack of good reputation; bad character.

dis-re-spect (dĭs"rē-spĕkt'), *n.* lack of proper courtesy toward elders or superiors; impoliteness.

dis-re-spect-ful (dĭs"rē-spĕkt'fōōl), *adj.* failing in proper courtesy, especially to elders or superiors.—*adv.* **disrespectfully.**

dis-rupt (dĭs-rŭpt'), *v.t.* and *v.i.* to break apart; to separate with violence.

dis-rup-tion (dĭs-rŭp'shŭn), *n.* act of rending or tearing apart; forcible separation; breach.

dis-rup-tive (dĭs-rŭp'tĭv), *adj.* causing a breach or violent separation.

diss (dĭs), a reedlike grass of Algeria, used for making hats, paper, etc.

dis-sat-is-fac-tion (dĭs-săt"ĭs-făk'shŭn), *n.* state of discontent; lack of satisfaction; absence of pleasure in that which one has.

dis-sat-is-fy (dĭs-săt'ĭs-fī), *v.t.* to cause displeasure by lack of something; to fail to content.

dis-sect (dĭ-sĕkt'), *v.t.* to cut in pieces and examine minutely.

dis-sec-tion (dĭ-sĕk'shŭn), *n.* the act of dissecting, or cutting in pieces for critical examination; anatomy.

dis-sec-tor (dĭ-sĕk'tẽr), *n.* an anatomist, or one who dissects bodies.

dis-sem-ble (dĭ-sĕm'bl), *v.t.* to hide under a false appearance; to disguise; as, to *dissemble* one's real intentions: *v.i.* to act the hypocrite; as, they *dissemble* and fawn in their efforts to gain favor.—*n.* **dissembler.**

dis-sem-bling (dĭ-sĕm'blĭng), *n.* disguise or concealment.

dis-sem-i-nate (dĭ-sĕm'ĭ-nāt), *v.t.* to scatter abroad, like seed; propagate; diffuse.—*n.* **dissemination.**

dis-sem-i-na-tor (dĭ-sĕm'ĭ-nā"tẽr), *n.* one who, or that which, scatters.

dis-sen-sion (dĭ-sĕn'shŭn), *n.* contention; strife; disagreement; as, *dissension* between political parties; quarrel.

dis-sent (dĭ-sĕnt'), *v.i.* to disagree in opinion: with *from:* *n.* difference of opinion; refusal to acknowledge or conform to an established church.
Syn., v. disagree, differ, vary.
Ant. (see assent).

dis-sent-er (dĭ-sĕnt'ẽr), *n.* one who differs in opinion, especially one who separates from the established church.

dis-sent-ing (dĭ-sĕnt'ĭng), *p.adj.* relating to, or characterized by, disagreement; separating from an established church, especially that of England.

dis-ser-ta-tion (dĭs'ẽr-tā'shŭn), *n.* a formal discourse; treatise.

dis-sev-er (dĭ-sĕv'ẽr), *v.t.* to cut in two; disjoin; divide; separate.

dis-si-dence (dĭs'ĭ-dĕns), *n.* discord; disagreement; difference in opinion.

dis-si-dent (dĭs'ĭ-dĕnt), *adj.* not agreeing or conforming: *n.* one who disagrees or dissents.

dis-sim-i-lar (dĭ-sĭm'ĭ-lẽr), *adj.* unlike; different; as, *dissimilar* tastes.—*adv.* **dissimilarly.**—*n.* **dissimilarity.**

dis-sim-u-late (dĭ-sĭm'ū-lāt), *v.i.* and *v.t.* to dissemble; feign; disguise; pretend.—*adj.* **dissimulative.**

dis-sim-u-la-tion (dĭ-sĭm"ū-lā'shŭn), *n.* hypocrisy; false pretense; false appearance.

dis-si-pate (dĭs'ĭ-pāt), *v.t.* to scatter completely; drive in different directions; squander; as, to *dissipate* a fortune: *v.i.* to spend one's energies intemperately.

dis-si-pat-ed (dĭs'ĭ-pāt"ĕd), *p.adj.* scattered; dispersed; intemperate.

dis-si-pa-tion (dĭs"ĭ-pā'shŭn), *n.* the act or state of being scattered or wasted; mental distraction; excess; intemperate living.

dis-so-ci-ate (dĭ-sō'shĭ-āt), *v.t.* to separate; disconnect.

dis-sol-u-bil-i-ty (dĭs"ō-lū-bĭl'ĭ-tĭ; dĭ-sŏl"ū-bĭl'ĭ-tĭ), *n.* the capacity of being absorbed into a liquid; as, the *dissolubility* of salt in water.

dis-sol-u-ble (dĭs'ō-lū-bl; dĭ-sŏl'ū-bl), *adj.* capable of being dissolved or absorbed into a liquid.

dis-so-lute (dĭs'ō-lūt), *adj.* loose; vicious; given to vice or dissipation.—*adv.* **dissolutely.**—*n.* **dissoluteness.**

dis-so-lu-tion (dĭs"ō-lū'shŭn), *n.* the act of dissolving or converting into a liquid; separation of the soul from the body; death; disorganization.

dis-solv-a-ble (dĭ-zŏl'vȧ-bl), *adj.* capable of being absorbed into a liquid.

dis-solve (dĭ-zŏlv'), *v.t.* to liquefy; melt; terminate; separate into elements; annul; break up: *v.i.* to become a liquid; waste away; separate.

dis-so-nance (dĭs'ō-năns), *n.* discord; a disagreeable mingling of sounds.

dis-so-nant (dĭs'ō-nănt), *adj.* harsh in sound; discordant; unharmonious.—*adv.* **dissonantly.**

dis-suade (dĭ-swād'), *v.t.* to advise or counsel against;, divert by argument or persuasion.

dis-sua-sion (dĭ-swā'zhŭn), *n.* the act of counseling against; advice or persuasion against a purpose or action.

dis-sua-sive (dĭ-swā'sĭv), *adj.* tending to advise against a purpose or action: *n.* an argument employed to persuade against a purpose or action.

dis-syl-la-ble (dĭ-sĭl'ȧ-bl), *n.* a word of two syllables.

dis-taff (dĭs'tȧf), *n.* [*pl.* distaffs (-tȧfs)]. the staff from which flax is drawn in spinning.

dis-tance (dĭs'tăns), *n.* the length of the straight line between two objects or points; as, the *distance* from New York to Philadelphia is ninety miles; remoteness of time, rank, relationship, or place; interval between two notes; reserve of manner: *v.t.* to place remotely; leave behind in a race.

dis-tant (dĭs'tănt), *adj.* remote; reserved; not cordial, but repelling in manner.—*adv.* **distantly.**

dis-taste (dĭs-tāst'), *n.* dislike of drink or food; aversion; disinclination; repugnance.

dis-taste-ful (dĭs-tāst'fo͝ol), *adj.* unpleasant to the taste; disagreeable; displeasing to the feelings.—*adv.* **distastefully.**—*n.* **distastefulness.**

dis-tem-per (dĭs-tĕm'pẽr), *v.t.* to disorder or disease; compound (colors) for use in painting: *n.* a disease, especially of animals; a method of painting; mural or wall decoration.

dis-tend (dĭs-tĕnd'), *v.t.* to stretch out in all directions; expand: *v.i.* to swell.

dis-ten-tion (dĭs-tĕn'shŭn), *n.* a swelling out or expansion.

dis-tich (dĭs'tĭk), *n.* a couplet, or two lines. of verse that make complete sense.

dis-til (dĭs-tĭl'), *v.i.* [*p.t.* and *p.p.* distilled, *p.pr.* distilling], to fall in drops; flow gently; trickle forth; *v.t.* to let fall in drops; to obtain by heating, evaporating, and then condensing; as, to *distil* water. Also, **distill.**—*n.* **distiller.**

dis-til-late (dĭs-tĭl'āt; dĭs'tĭ-lāt), *n.* the product obtained from a substance by heating, evaporating, and then condensing.

dis-til-la-tion (dĭs"tĭ-lā'shŭn), *n.* the process of heating and evaporating to produce pure spirit; the substance so obtained.

dis-till-er-y (dĭs-tĭl'ẽr-ĭ), *n.* a place where liquids, especially alcoholic liquors, are produced by heating, evaporating, and then condensing.

dis-tinct (dĭs-tĭnkt'), *adj.* separate; different; clear; plain.—*n.* **distinctness.**

Syn. obvious, evident, unconfused.

Ant. (see obscure, indistinct).

dis-tinc-tion (dĭs-tĭnk'shŭn), *n.* difference; separateness; state of deserving special honor; eminence; superiority; fame; as, Lincoln has the *distinction* of having given the slaves freedom.

dis-tinc-tive (dĭs-tĭnk'tĭv), *adj.* marking a difference or separation; characteristic; discriminating; plain.

dis-tinct-ly (dĭs tĭnkt'lĭ), *adv.* clearly; plainly.

dis-tin-gué (dēs-tăn'gā), *adj.* distinguished. [Fr.]

dis-tin-guish (dĭs-tĭn'gwĭsh), *v.t.* to separate from others by some mark of honor or preference; designate by special characteristics; discriminate; see clearly; make known: *v.i.* to make a distinction: with *between.*

dis-tin-guished (dĭs-tĭn'gwĭsht), *p.adj.* eminent; celebrated; conspicuous; noted.

Syn. famous, glorious, far-famed, noted. illustrious.

Ant. (see obscure, unknown)

dis-tort (dĭs-tôrt'), *v.t.* to twist or turn from the natural shape or figure; twist; turn from the true meaning; misrepresent; as, to *distort* the truth.

dis-tor-tion (dĭs-tôr'shŭn), *n.* the act of twisting out of shape; perversion; a deformity.

dis-tract (dis-träkt'), *v.t.* to perplex; divert (attention); harass; confuse the mind of; bewilder; derange.

dis-trac-tion (dis-träk'shŭn), *n.* state of having the attention diverted; that which diverts attention; perplexity; embarrassment; mental confusion or distress; insanity.

dis-trac-tive (dis-träk'tiv), *adj.* causing confusion or perplexity.

dis-train (dis-trān'), *v.t.* to take as security for a debt; as, to *distrain* household furniture for rent: *v.i.* to levy a distress, or seizure of goods.

dis-traint (dis-trānt'), *n.* the act of distraining, or holding for debt.

dis-trait (dēs"trā'), *adj.* absent-minded; wandering; distracted. [Fr.]

dis-traught (dis-trôt'), *adj.* bewildered or harassed; distracted.

dis-tress (dis-trĕs'), *v.t.* to inflict pain or suffering upon; grieve; harass; perplex; in law, to seize for debt: *n.* physical or mental anguish; the act of distraining or seizing and holding for debt; goods taken in distraint.—*adj.* **distressful.**

dis-trib-ute (dis-trĭb'ūt), *v.t.* to deal out or divide; allot; as, they have collected newspapers and magazines to *distribute* to the soldiers; arrange according to classification; dispose of separately; separate and return (as printers' types) to their respective cases.—*n.* **distributor.**

Syn. share, dispense, deal.

Ant. (see collect).

dis-tri-bu-tion (dis-trĭ-bū'shŭn), *n.* the act or manner of dealing out or dividing; apportionment; arrangement; classification.

dis-trib-u-tive (dis-trĭb'ū-tĭv), *adj.* apportioning or dealing out; as, *distributive* classes: *n.* in grammar, denoting groups of persons or things acting individually, as *any, all, both, each, either, neither*.

dis-trict (dis'trĭkt), *n.* province; territory; circuit; region or tract of country.

dis-trust (dis-trŭst'), *n.* want of confidence, faith, or reliance; suspicion; discredit: *v.t.* to have no confidence or faith in; doubt; suspect.

dis-trust-ful (dis-trŭst'fo͝ol), *adj.* suspicious; lacking confidence.—*adv.* **distrustfully.**

dis-turb (dis-tûrb'), *v.t.* to trouble; vex; throw into confusion; agitate; displace.—*n.* **disturber.**

Syn. derange, rouse, interrupt, confuse, trouble, annoy, vex, worry.

Ant. (see pacify, quiet).

dis-turb-ance (dis-tûr'băns), *n.* the interruption of a settled state; uproar; confusion; mental agitation.

di-sul-phate (dī-sŭl'fāt), *n.* a sulphate containing one atom of hydrogen, replaceable by a basic element.

di-sul-phide (dī-sŭl'fīd; dī-sŭl'fĭd), *n.* a chemical salt of sulphur and another element.

dis-un-ion (dis-ūn'yŭn), *n.* separation; a breaking apart; a division.

dis-u-nite (dis"ū-nīt'), *v.t.* and *v.i.* to divide; separate; fall, or make to fall, apart.

dis-use (dis-ūs'), *n.* a ceasing to use; neglect: *v.t.* (dis-ūz'), to cease to use.

ditch (dĭch), *n.* a trench cut in the earth; a moat: *v.i.* to make a ditch: *v.t.* to surround with a ditch; run into a ditch.

dit-to (dĭt'ō), *n.* the same thing; that which has been said; a duplicate: *adv.* as before; likewise.

dit-ty (dĭt'ĭ), *n.* [*pl.* ditties (-ĭz)], a little song; lay.

dit-ty box (dĭt'ĭ bŏks), a tin box with a lock, in which sailors keep their personal possessions, such as shaving gear, etc.

di-ur-nal (dī-ûr'năl), *adj.* pertaining to a day; daily; performed in twenty-four hours; active during the daytime.

di-ur-nal-ly (dī-ûr'năl-ĭ), *adv.* daily; by day.

di-va (dē'vȧ), *n.* a prima donna; an opera singer. [It.]

di-van (dĭ-văn'; dī'văn), *n.* a court of justice; a council of state in Turkey; as, sixty old men formed his *divan*; a council hall; a smoking room; café; couch.

dive (dīv), *v.i.* to plunge headforemost into water; enter deeply into any subject or question: *n.* a plunge headforemost into water; as, to take a high *dive* requires nerve.—*n.* **diver.**

di-verge (dĭ-vûrj'), *v.i.* to spread out from one point: opposite to *converge*; to differ.

di-ver-gence (dĭ-vûr'jĕns), *n.* a moving away from each other along different lines; a separation; a tending apart. Also, **divergency.**

di-ver-gent (dĭ-vûr'jĕnt), *adj.* tending to move apart or separate; different.

di-vers (dī'vĕrz), *adj.* various; sundry; several.

di-verse (dĭ-vûrs'; dī'vĕrs), *adj.* essentially different; dissimilar; varied; unlike.—*adv.* **diversely.**

di-ver-si-fi-ca-tion (dĭ-vûr"sĭ-fĭ-kā'shŭn), *n.* act of making, or state of being, varied; variation; variety.

di-ver-si-fy (dĭ-vûr'sĭ-fī), *v.t.* [*p.t.* and *p.p.* diversified, *p.pr.* diversifying], to make different from another; give variety to; discriminate.

di-ver-sion (dĭ-vûr'shŭn), *n.* variation; alteration; pastime; the act of turning the attention of an enemy from the real point of attack.

di-ver-si-ty (dĭ-vûr'sĭ-tĭ), *n.* difference; variety.

di-vert (dĭ-vûrt'), *v.t.* to turn aside from any direction or course; draw away from; entertain; amuse; as, to *divert* the mind of a crying child by a story.

di-vest (dĭ-vĕst'), *v.t.* to strip or deprive of anything; despoil; make bare.

di-vide (dĭ-vīd'), *v.t.* to cut into two or more parts; separate; keep apart; distribute: *v.i.* to separate; cleave; diverge; to separate in voting: *n.* a watershed; as, the Rocky Mountain watershed is called the great *divide*.

Syn., v. distribute, deal out, sever, sunder.

div-i-dend (dĭv'ĭ-dĕnd), *n.* a share of the profits of a public company or business; interest payable on money invested in the public funds; a number or quantity to be divided.

di-vid-ers (dĭ-vīd'ẽrz), *n. pl.* an instrument used in mechanical drawing, for dividing lines, etc.

Dividers

div-i-na-tion (dĭv'ĭ-nā'shŭn), *n.* the act of foreseeing or foretelling; the pretended art of foreseeing future events; as, *divination* by a fortune teller.

di-vine (dĭ-vīn'), *adj.* partaking of the nature of God; as, the *divine* love of God; godlike; sacred; holy; pertaining to theology: *n.* a theologian; clergyman: *v.t.* to guess or foresee; know by intuition; presage: *v.i.* to conjecture; guess.
Syn., *adj.* godlike, holy, heavenly, sacred.

div-ing (dīv'ĭng), *n.* the act of plunging into water: *p.adj.* connected with, or used in, diving.

div-ing bell (dīv'ĭng bĕl), a hollow chamber supplied with air, in which men may work under water without danger. Also, submarine diving bell.

di-vin-ing rod (dĭ-vīn'ĭng rŏd), a forked rod or branch, as of witch-hazel, which, when held loosely in the hand, is said to be drawn downward towards places under which water or minerals are situated.

di-vin-i-ty (dĭ-vĭn'ĭ-tĭ), *n.* [*pl.* divinities (-tĭz)], the state or quality of being godlike; Godhead; a pagan or heathen deity; theology.

di-vis-i-bil-i-ty (dĭ-vĭz'ĭ-bĭl'ĭ-tĭ), *n.* capability of being separated into parts.

di-vis-i-ble (dĭ-vĭz'ĭ-bl), *adj.* capable of being separated into parts; capable of division without a remainder.

di-vi-sion (dĭ-vĭzh'ŭn), *n.* the act or state of being separated into parts; a partition; section; discord; difference; as, when members of a church disagree about anything it causes *division;* the separating of the members of a lawmaking or municipal assembly in order to take a vote; two or more army brigades under the command of a general officer; the process of finding how many times one number or quantity is contained in another.—*adj.* divisional.

di-vi-sor (dĭ-vī'zẽr), *n.* the number by which another (the dividend) is divided.

di-vorce (dĭ-vōrs'), *n.* legal dissolution of the marriage contract; disunion: *v.t.* to dissolve the marriage contract between; release from close union.—*n.* divorcement.

div-ot (dĭv'ŏt), *n.* in golf, a piece of turf cut from the sod by a stroke.

di-vulge (dĭ-vŭlj'), *v.t.* to make known, as something previously kept secret; disclose.

Dix-ie (dĭk'sĭ), *n.* the Southern States of the United States; a favorite Southern song.—dixie, in the World War, an iron pot with two handles, used for cooking in the trenches.

diz-en (dĭz'n; dī'zn), *v.t.* to deck out; dress; bedizen; as, to *dizen* oneself with jewels.

diz-zi-ness (dĭz'ĭ-nĕs), *n.* giddiness; as, to whirl about rapidly will cause *dizziness.*

diz-zy (dĭz'ĭ), *adj.* giddy; causing giddiness; as, a *dizzy* height.—*adv.* dizzily.

do (dōō), *v.t.* [*p.t.* did, *p.p.* done, *p.pr.* doing], to perform; achieve; cause to bring about; make ready for some object or purpose; colloquially, to cheat or swindle: *v.i.* to act or behave; succeed; fare as to health; be enough.
Syn. effect, make, perform, accomplish, finish, transact.

do (dō), *n.* the first of the syllables used in the musical scale; the tone C.

do-cile (dŏs'ĭl; dō'sīl), *adj.* easy to teach; tractable; easily managed; as, a gentle, *docile* pony.—*adv.* docilely.
Syn. teachable, compliant, tame.
Ant. (see stubborn).

do-cil-i-ty (dō-sĭl'ĭ-tĭ), *n.* the quality of being gentle or easily managed.

dock (dŏk), *n.* a place for building and keeping ships; the place where a prisoner stands in a court to be tried; a coarse weed with broad leaves; the solid part of the tail of a horse: *v.t.* to cut off or curtail; deduct from; diminish; bring to a pier, and moor, as a ship.

dock-age (dŏk'āj), *n.* reduction; provision or accommodation for the docking of vessels; money paid for the use of a dock.

dock-et (dŏk'ĕt), *v.t.* to mark the contents or titles of papers on the back of them; indorse: *n.* a directed label or ticket tied on goods; a summary of a larger writing; a digest; a formal program for the proceedings of an assembly.

dock-yard (dŏk'yärd'), *n.* a place where ships are built and naval stores are kept.

doc-tor (dŏk'tẽr), *n.* one holding the highest degree conferred by a university; a learned man; a medical practitioner: *v.t.* colloquially, to treat medically; slang, tamper with or give a false appearance to: *v.i.* colloquially, to practice medicine or undergo medical treatment.

doc-tor-ate (dŏk'tẽr-āt), *n.* the degree of doctor.

doc-tri-naire (dŏk'trĭ-nâr'), *n.* one who theorizes on political or other matters, disregarding practical considerations: *adj.* visionary. [Fr.]

doc-tri-nal (dŏk'trĭ-năl), *adj.* pertaining to, or containing, a teaching or dogma.—*adv.* doctrinally.

doc-trine (dŏk'trĭn), *n.* that which is taught; the principles, belief, or dogma of any church, sect, or party; as, the *doctrines* of Christianity.
Syn. tenet, creed, dogma.

doc-u-ment (dŏk'ū-mĕnt), *n.* a record; a paper that gives information or evidence.

doc-u-men-ta-ry (dŏk'ū-mĕn'tă-rĭ), *adj.* pertaining to, derived from, or consisting of, official papers or records.

do-dec-a-gon (dō-dĕk'ă-gŏn), *n.* a figure with twelve sides and twelve angles.

do-dec-a-he-dron (dō'dĕk-ă-hē'drŏn), *n.* a solid with twelve faces.

dodge (dŏj), *v.i.* to start aside and shift about; evade; avoid; practice tricky devices: *v.t.* to escape from by starting aside: *n.* the act of dodging; a trick.

dodg-er (dŏj'ẽr), *n.* a small handbill or poster; an Indian-meal cake; a tricky fellow.

do-do (dō'dō), *n.* [*pl.* dodos (-dōz)], a large extinct bird with a short neck, a large hooked bill, short wings and legs.

doe (dō), *n.* the female of a buck or fallow deer, or of an antelope, rabbit, or hare.

does (dŭz), third person singular present of the verb *do.*

doe-skin (dō'skĭn'), *n.* the skin of a doe, or female deer; a fine woolen cloth with a smooth finish.

doff (dŏf), *v.t.* to take or put off, as clothes; remove (the hat) in saluting.

dog (dŏg), *n.* an intelligent and affectionate domestic animal of the wolf kind; name of various mechanical contrivances; a worthless fellow: *v.t.* [*p.t.* and *p.p.* dogged, *p.pr.* dogging], to follow like a hound; as, he *dogged* their steps.—*adj.* **doggish.**

Lathe Dog

dog-cart (dŏg'kärt"), *n.* a light cart with two wheels, and two seats set back to back.

dog days (dŏg dāz), a period in July and August when the Dog Star, or Sirius, rises and sets with the sun: usually the hottest part of the summer.

doge (dōj), *n.* the title of the chief magistrates of the ancient republics of Venice and Genoa.

dog-fish (dŏg'fĭsh"), *n.* a kind of small shark very destructive to fish.

dog-ged (dŏg'ĕd), *adj.* stubborn; persistent.—*adv.* **doggedly.**

dog-ger (dŏg'ẽr), *n.* a two-masted vessel with a broad beam: used in the cod and herring fisheries by the Dutch in the North Sea.

dog-ger-el (dŏg'ẽr-ĕl), *n.* a kind of verse devoid of sense or rhythm: *adj.* weak and absurd in construction: said of verse or poetry.

dog-ma (dŏg'mȧ), *n.* [*pl.* dogmas (-mȧz) or dogmata (-mȧ-tȧ)], an established principle, tenet, or doctrine; a doctrine stated in a formal manner and received by the church as authoritative.—*n.* **dogmatist.**

dog-mat-ic (dŏg-măt'ĭk), *adj.* pertaining to, or of the nature of, established doctrine; positive; authoritative: *n.pl.* doctrinal theology. Also, **dogmatical.**

Syn. arrogant, imperious, dictatorial.

dog-mat-i-cal-ly (dŏg-măt'ĭ-kăl-ĭ), *adv.* in a positive or doctrinal manner.

dog-ma-tism (dŏg'mȧ-tĭzm), *n.* positive assertion of opinion; sometimes, unwarranted positiveness.

dog-ma-tize (dŏg'mȧ-tīz), *v.i.* to make dogmatic assertions; utter positive assertions without adducing proof: *v.t.* to treat dogmatically.

dog rob-ber (dŏg rŏb'ẽr), a soldier who works for an officer. [SLANG.]

dog's-ear (dŏgz'ēr"), *n.* the corner of a page in a book turned down: *v.t.* to turn down the corner of (a leaf in a book).

dog-trot (dŏg'trŏt"), *n.* a slow run, like that of a dog.

dog-watch (dŏg'wŏch"), *n.* one of two watches on board ship of two hours each, between four and eight p. m.

dog-wood (dŏg'wŏŏd"), *n.* a wild tree bearing in spring a white or pink blossom.

doi-ly (doi'lĭ), *n.* [*pl.* doilies (-lĭz)], a small mat or napkin used on the table.

do-ings (dōō'ĭngz), *n.pl.* things done; acts; conduct; as, the day's *doings.*

dol-drums (dŏl'drŭmz), *n.pl.* a sailor's term for the tropical zones of calms and variable winds; dulness; depression of spirits; the dumps.

dole (dōl), *n.* that which is dealt out sparingly; a charitable gift of money or food; alms: *v.t.* to deal out sparingly.

dole-ful (dōl'fŏŏl), *adj.* sorrowful; dismal; full of grief.—*n.* **dolefulness.**

Syn. dolorous, woebegone, rueful, piteous, grievous, gloomy.

Ant. (see joyous, glad, gay, merry).

dole-ful-ly (dōl'fŏŏl-ĭ), *adv.* sorrowfully; dismally; ruefully.

doll (dŏl), *n.* a girl's puppet or toy baby; a childish-featured girl or woman.

dol-lar (dŏl'ẽr), *n.* a silver coin used in the United States and Canada equal to one hundred cents; a bank note, treasury note, etc., of the legal value of one hundred cents; a large silver coin of various other countries.

doll-y (dŏl'ĭ), *n.* [*pl.* dollies (-ĭz)], a little doll; a block used in pile driving; a machine for washing clothes; a contrivance for washing ore in mining.

Doll-y Var-den (dŏl'ĭ vär'dĕn), a woman's dress of light, bright-figured muslin, worn over a plain bright-colored petticoat; a large hat for women, with one side bent down and trimmed with numerous flowers.

dol-man (dŏl'măn), *n.* a long outer garment with sleeves, worn by the Turks; a hussar's uniform jacket; a woman's sleeveless mantle.

dol-men (dŏl'mĕn), *n.* a monument for a tomb, consisting of a large unhewn stone resting on two or more others.

do-lor (dō'lẽr), *n.* sorrow; pain; grief; lamentation; anguish.

dol-or-ous (dŏl'ẽr-ŭs), *adj.* sorrowful; full of grief; sad.—*adv.* **dolorously.**

dol-phin (dŏl'fĭn), *n.* the name of various small-toothed fish, such as porpoises.

Dolphin

dolt (dōlt), *n.* a heavy stupid fellow; a dunce; blockhead.

Dom (dŏm), *n.* a title of respect applied to gentlemen in Portugal and Brazil; in Portugal, a title of the king and royal family.

do-main (dō-mān'), *n.* lordship; authority; empire; landed property; range; scope.

dome (dōm), *n.* a large cupola; as, the *dome* of the Capitol at Washington.

do-mes-tic (dō-mĕs'tĭk), *adj.* pertaining to the house or household affairs; private; home-made; tame; pertaining to one's own country in distinction to foreign countries: *n.* a household servant: *pl.* articles of home manufacture, especially cotton-cloths; as, the use of *domestics* increases when foreign goods are not imported.

do-mes-tic e-con-o-my (dō-mĕs'tĭk ē-kŏn'ō-mĭ), the art of managing household affairs in the best and thriftiest manner.

do-mes-ti-cate (dō-mĕs'tĭ-kāt), *v.t.* to make suitable for a household; familiarize with home life; tame; as, it is possible to *domesticate* some wild animals: *v.i.* to become domestic; to settle oneself at home.—*n.* **domestication.**

do-mes-tic-i-ty (dō"mĕs-tĭs'ĭ-tĭ), *n.* [*pl.* domesticities (-tĭz)], the state of being suited to home life; home-loving character.

dom-i-cile (dŏm'ĭ-sĭl), *n.* a permanent residence or place of abode;

home: *v.t.* to establish in a fixed residence; as, many aliens or foreigners are *domiciled* in the United States.

dom-i-cil-i-a-ry (dŏm′ĭ-sĭl′ĭ-ā-rĭ), *adj.* of or pertaining to the residence of a person or family.

dom-i-nant (dŏm′ĭ-nănt), *adj.* exercising chief authority or control; ruling; predominant; ascending: *n.* the fifth tone of an ascending musical scale.—*n.* **dominance.**

dom-i-nate (dŏm′ĭ-nāt), *v.t.* to govern or control; rule; as, the rock of Gibraltar *dominates* the straits; predominate over: *v.i.* to have or exercise control.

dom-i-na-tion (dŏm′ĭ-nā′shŭn), *n.* the act of controlling; absolute authority; power.

dom-i-neer (dŏm′ĭ-nēr′), *v.i.* to exercise authority arrogantly or tyrannically; bluster; swagger.

dom-i-neer-ing (dŏm′ĭ-nēr′ĭng), *p.adj.* masterful; tyrannical; overbearing.

do-min-i-cal (dō-mĭn′ĭ-kăl), *adj.* pertaining to Christ as Lord, or to Sunday: *n.* a dominical letter.

do-min-i-cal let-ter (dō-mĭn′ĭ-kăl lĕt′ẽr), one of the letters (A B C D E F G) used in the calendar of the Prayer Book to denote Sunday throughout the year, and to determine the date of Easter Day.

Do-min-i-can (dō-mĭn′ĭ-kăn), *adj.* pertaining to a religious order named after St. Dominic: *n.* a friar of that order.

dom-i-nie (dŏm′ĭ-nĭ; dō′mĭ-nĭ), *n.* a clergyman or minister, especially of the Dutch Reformed Church; a schoolmaster. Also, in first sense, **domine.**

do-min-ion (dō-mĭn′yŭn), *n.* supreme authority or control; sovereignty; rule; independent right or possession; a territory or country subject to the control of one government.

dom-i-no (dŏm′ĭ-nō), *n.* [*pl.* **dominos** (-nōz)], a large loose silk cape or cloak with large sleeves and a hood, used as a masquerade garment; a dotted piece of bone or wood used for a game: *pl.* a game played with oblong dotted pieces of bone or wood.

don (dŏn), *v.t.* [*p.t.* and *p.p.* donned, *p.pr.* donning], to put on; assume: *n.* a great person; in England, a university fellow or a head of a college: **Don** [*fem.* **Doña**], a Spanish title of rank.

do-nate (dō′nāt), *v.t.* to give, especially to some religious or charitable object.—*adj.* **donative.**—*n.* **donator.**

do-na-tion (dō-nā′shŭn), *n.* a charitable gift; benefaction; present.

done (dŭn), *p.p.* of *do: p.adj.* completed; published officially; cooked sufficiently; thoroughly fatigued; cheated.

don-go-la (dŏŋ′gō-lȧ), *n.* a goatskin or sheepskin tanned to resemble kid.

don-jon (dŭn′jŭn; dŏn′jŏn), *n.* the principal tower or keep of an ancient castle, containing the prison. Also, **dungeon.**

don-key (dŏŋ′kĭ), *n.* [*pl.* donkeys (-kĭz)], an ass; a stupid or obstinate fellow.

don-na (dŏn′ȧ; IT. dōn′nä), *n.* a lady; madam; mistress: **Donna,** the title of a lady in Italy.

don-nish (dŏn′ĭsh), *adj.* pertaining to, or like, a distinguished gentleman; pedantic; formal.

do-nor (dō′nôr), *n.* a giver; one who makes a donation or present, especially a large public or charitable gift.

don't (dōnt), colloquial contraction of *do not:* not to be used for *does not*

doom (dōōm), *n.* judgment; sentence; destiny which cannot be changed; as, the judge pronounced the murderer's *doom;* fate; ruin; the Day of Judgment. *v.t.* to pronounce condemnation upon; sentence to punishment; pronounce as a penalty.
Syn., *n.* verdict, condemnation, lot.

dooms-day (dōōmz′dā′), *n.* the day of final and universal judgment.

door (dōr), *n.* the gate or entrance of a house; a movable barrier, sliding or swinging on hinges, which opens and closes to allow or prevent entrance to a house, room, etc.; portal; means of entrance.

door-keep-er (dōr′kēp′ẽr), *n.* one who guards an entrance.

door-way (dōr′wā′), *n.* the opening through which a door gives entrance.

dope (dōp), *n.* a thick liquid, as food; a grease for making machinery run easier; a drug that produces unconsciousness; colloquially, advance information, especially concerning speed or condition of race horses.

Do-ri-an (dō′rĭ-ăn), *adj.* pertaining to, or characteristic of, Doris, a small district of ancient Greece; after the style of the Dorians, especially in art and verse; simple; direct: *n.* a member of the Doric or Dorian race, one of the four great divisions of the ancient Greeks.

Dor-ic (dŏr′ĭk), *adj.* Dorian; of the simplest form of Greek architecture: *n.* the broad hard dialect or language of the Dorians; also, an unrefined, broad, or rustic dialect of English.

Dor-ic or-der (dŏr′ĭk ôr′dẽr), the oldest and simplest of the three orders of Greek architecture.

dor-king (dôr′kĭng), *n.* one of a breed of domestic fowls, characterized by five toes on each foot.

dor-mant (dôr′mănt), *adj.* sleeping; quiet; in temporary inaction.—*n.* **dormancy.**

dor-mer (dôr′mẽr), *n.* a gable window built upright in a sloping roof.

dor-mi-to-ry (dôr′mĭ-tō-rĭ), *n.* [*pl.* dormitories (-rĭz)], a sleeping room, usually containing several beds; a building containing many such rooms.

dor-mouse (dôr′mous′), *n.* [*pl.* dormice (-mīs)], a small European squirrel-like animal.

dor-my (dôr′mĭ), *adj.* in golf, being as many holes ahead of your opponent as there are holes to play.

dor-sal (dôr′săl), *adj.* pertaining to, or situated near, the back.

do-ry (dō′rĭ), *n.* [*pl.* dories (-rĭz)], a popular name for a golden-colored fish, known in England as the John-dory; the wall-eyed pike-perch; a small flat-bottomed boat with a sharp prow.

Dory

dose (dōs), *n.* the quantity of medicine to be taken at one time; anything sickening: *v.t.* to give medicine to; to give anything objectionable or unpleasant to.

dost (dŭst), second person singular present of the verb *do*.

dot (dŏt), *n.* a small point or speck; a dowry: *v.t.* [*p.t.* and *p.p.* dotted, *p.pr.* dotting], to mark with spots or specks.

dot-age (dōt'āj), *n.* childishness of old age; foolish or excessive affection.

do-tard (dō'tẽrd), *n.* one whose mind is impaired by age; one who is foolishly affectionate: *adj.* imbecile; senile; silly.

dote (dōt), *v.i.* to show the weakness of age; give excessive love: with *on* or *upon*.—*adv.* **dotingly**.

dot-ter-el (dŏt'ẽr-ĕl), *n.* a small bird of Europe and Asia, formerly common in England.

dou-ble (dŭb'l), *adj.* twofold; being in pairs; being twice as much; deceitful; insincere; folded over: *n.* twice the quantity; a duplicate; trick; a turning back to escape pursuit; a fold or plait: *v.t.* to make double; duplicate; repeat; fold; sail round or by: *v.i.* to become twice the quantity; return on one's track; march at double-quick time: *adv.* twice over.

dou-ble dag-ger (dŭb'l dăg'ẽr), a mark to guide a reader to a note [‡].

dou-ble-deal-ing (dŭb'l-dēl'ĭng), *n.* dishonesty; the acting of two parts at once.—*n.* **double-dealer**.

dou-ble-en-ten-dre (dōō'bl-äṅ"täṅ'-dr), *n.* a word or phrase with two meanings, one of which is usually improper. [Fr.]

dou-ble-faced (dŭb'l-fāst"), *adj.* playing two parts; hypocritical.

dou-ble-ness (dŭb'l-nĕs), *n.* the state of being twofold; duplicity; insincerity.

dou-ble-quick (dŭb'l-kwĭk"), *adj.* marching so fast as to be almost running: *n.* such a step or march.

dou-blet (dŭb'lĕt), *n.* a duplicate; one of a pair; a close-fitting garment for men, worn in western Europe from the 15th to the 17th century.

dou-bloon (dŭb-lōōn'), *n.* a Spanish gold coin, no longer issued, formerly worth about $16, later $5.

dou-bly (dŭb'lĭ), *adv.* in twice the quantity or degree; in a double or twofold manner; deceitfully.

doubt (dout), *v.i.* to waver in opinion; hesitate; be in suspense: *v.t.* to suspect; distrust; question: *n.* uncertainty of mind; suspense; scruple; perplexity; apprehension; as, he was full of grave *doubt* as to the outcome of the affair; fear; disbelief.
Syn., *n.* hesitation, scruple, suspicion.
Ant. (see certainty).

doubt-ful (dout'fōōl), *adj.* of uncertain issue; questionable; hazardous; insecure; dubious.—*adv.* **doubtfully**.

doubt-less (dout'lĕs), *adv.* assuredly; certainly; unquestionably; without doubt.—*adv.* **doubtlessly**.

douche (dōōsh), *n.* a jet or current of water directed upon some part of the body to benefit it.

dough (dō), *n.* a soft mixture of flour and other ingredients ready for baking.

dough-boy (dō'boi"), *n.* in the United States army, an infantry soldier. [Slang.]

dough-nut (dō'nŭt"), *n.* a small cake made with yeast and fried in deep fat.

dough-ty (dou'tĭ), *adj.* able; brave; strong; as, old romances are filled with the brave deeds of *doughty* knights.—*adv.* **doughtily**.—*n.* **doughtiness**.

dough-y (dō'ĭ), *adj.* soft like dough; flabby and pale; as, a *doughy* complexion.

douse (dous), *v.t.* to plunge suddenly into a liquid; drench; slang, extinguish or put out; as, *douse* the light; strike; slacken or lower suddenly, as sails: *v.i.* to fall suddenly into water. Also, **dowse**.

dove (dŭv), *n.* a pigeon; a term of endearment; one gentle and pure.

dove-cote (dŭv'kōt"), *n.* a small house or box raised above the ground, with compartments for doves. Also, **dovecot**.

dove-tail (dŭv'tāl"), *n.* in carpentry, an interlocking joint resembling a dove's tail spread out: *v.t.* to join by such a joint; to fit closely and exactly.

dow-a-ger (dou'ȧ-jẽr), *n.* the widow of a king, prince, or person of rank; a widow who has inherited property.

dow-di-ly (dou'dĭ-lĭ), *adv.* in a shabby or untidy manner; carelessly.

dow-dy (dou'dĭ), *n.* [*pl.* dowdies (-dĭz)], a slatternly or untidy woman who wears finery: *adj.* slovenly or ill-dressed; shabby.

dow-el (dou'ĕl), *n.* a pin to connect two pieces of wood by being sunk in the edges of each; a piece of wood driven into a wall to secure something else: *v.t.* to fasten by dowels.

dow-er (dou'ẽr), *n.* that part of a husband's property which his widow enjoys during her life: *v.t.* to furnish with a dower or dowry; to endow.

dow-las (dou'lȧs), *n.* a kind of coarse linen cloth made in the north of England and Scotland, now nearly replaced by calico.

down (doun), *n.* soft feathers, hair, or wool; the soft fibers of plants: *pl.* a tract of bare, hilly land used for pasturing sheep; banks or small, rounded hills of sand: *adv.* from a higher to a lower degree or position; at the lowest point; on the ground; below the horizon; opposite to *up*; from earlier to later times; in hand, or on the counter; as, to pay *down* for goods; on paper, or in a book: *adj.* dejected; downcast: *prep.* along a descent; from a higher place to a lower; along the course or current of.

down-cast (doun'kȧst"), *adj.* directed downwards; sad: *n.* the ventilating shaft of a mine.

down-fall (doun'fôl"), *n.* a falling downwards; sudden fall from rank or reputation; ruin.—*adj.* **downfallen**.

down grade (doun' grād"), a downward movement or incline; a descent; as, the train is on the *down grade*: opposite to *up grade*; reverse of fortune; the approach to failure: usually in a financial sense.

down-heart-ed (doun'härt"ĕd), *adj.* depressed; discouraged; sad.—*adv.* **downheartedly**.—*n.* **downheartedness**.

down-right (doun"rīt'; doun'rīt"), *adj.* thorough; out-and-out; straight to the point; blunt: *adv.* perpendicularly; completely; thoroughly.

down-trod-den (doun'trŏd"n), *adj.* oppressed; tyrannized over; held under by a stronger power.

down-ward (doun'wẽrd), *adj.* tending to the ground; moving from a higher to a lower place, grade, or direction; descending: *adv.* from a higher to a lower condition, state, or place; from the source. Also, *adv.* **downwards.**

down-y (doun'ĭ), *adj.* covered with, or made of, soft feathers, hair, or wool; soft; restful; cunning; artful.

dow-ry (dou'rĭ), *n.* [*pl.* dowries (-rĭz)], the property a woman brings to a husband at marriage; gift or possession.

dox-ol-o-gy (dŏk-sŏl'ō-jĭ), *n.* [*pl.* doxologies (-jĭz)], a short hymn of praise to God, used at the opening or close of religious services.

doze (dōz), *v.i.* to sleep lightly or fitfully: *n.* a light sleep, or nap.

doz-en (dŭz'n), *n.* twelve things of a kind, taken together.

doz-y (dōz'ĭ), *adj.* sleepy; drowsy; sluggish; as, the *dozy* or drowsy hum of bees.

drab (drăb), *n.* a kind of thick dull brown or yellowish-gray woolen cloth; a tint of such a color: *adj.* of a dull brown or gray color.

drab-ble (drăb'l), *v.t.* to make wet or dirty by dragging through mud or water: *v.i.* to fish with a long line and rod.

drach-ma (drăk'md), *n.* [*pl.* drachmæ (-mē), drachmas (-mdz)], a Greek silver coin worth 19.3 cents.

draff (drăf), *n.* waste matter from malt breweries; hog's-wash.

draft (drăft), *n.* a sketch or outline; bill of exchange; an order for money; the plan of recruiting soldiers by conscription, or forced selection, rather than by voluntary enlistment; a contingent of new soldiers; the act of drawing a load by beasts; the quantity of fish caught at one draw of the net; the depth of water a vessel draws or to which she sinks; a current of air; a drink: *v.t.* to sketch out; select for military service by drawing numbers; as, England was obliged to *draft* married men into service. Also, **draught.**—*adj.* **drafty.**

drag (drăg), *v.t.* [*p.t.* and *p.p.* dragged, *p.pr.* dragging], to pull or draw along by force; draw along slowly or heavily; haul; tug; search by drawing a net or trawl; along the bottom of (the water): *v.i.* to trail along the ground; to move heavily; to lag behind: *n.* the act of drawing along the ground; a net drawn along the bottom of the water to raise sunken bodies; a coach drawn by four horses; a sledge for heavy loads.

Drag

drag-gle (drăg'l), *v.t.* to wet or soil by drawing in the mud or along the ground: *v.i.* to be drawn along the ground so as to become dirty or wet.

drag-o-man (drăg'ō-măn), *n.* [*pl.* dragomans (-mănz)], in the East, one who explains the meaning of things; a guide, or agent for travelers.

drag-on (drăg'ŭn) *n.* a very large, imaginary animal represented in fables or stories as a winged serpent or lizard; a fierce person: *adj.* fierce; destructive.

drag-o-nade (drăg"ō-nād'), *n.* any form of punishment inflicted by soldiers; as, the punishment of the French Protestants by the soldiery under Louis XIV was called a *dragonade.* Also, **dragonnade, dragoonade.**

drag-on fly (drăg'ŭn flī), an insect with a long, slender body, large eyes, and four narrow, finely veined wings.

drag-on's blood (drăg'ŭnz blŭd), the red juice and gum of several South American and East Indian or tropical trees.

dra-goon (drd-gōōn'), *n.* formerly, a soldier trained to serve either mounted or on foot; now a cavalryman, or mounted soldier, heavily equipped.

drain (drān), *v.t.* to draw off gradually; empty: *v.i.* to become dry: *n.* a channel or pipe for useless water; a sewer; the act of drawing off completely.

drain-age (drān'āj), *n.* the manner in which the waters of a country pass off by its streams; a system of pipes or sewers for removing waste water from towns.

drake (drāk), *n.* the male of any kind of duck.

dram (drăm), *n.* one-eighth of an ounce troy, and one-sixteenth of an ounce avoirdupois; a small quantity of spirituous liquor. Also, **drachm.**

dra-ma (drä'md), *n.* a prose or poetical composition telling a story of human life by means of the speech and action of the characters: usually intended to be acted on a stage; that branch of literary art concerned with the making of stage plays; real life so exciting as to seem like a play.

dra-mat-ic (drd-măt'ĭk), *adj.* pertaining to, or like, the drama; as, *dramatic* art; a *dramatic* situation; full of intense human interest. Also, **dramatical.**—*adv.* **dramatically.**

dra-ma-tis per-so-næ (drăm'd-tĭs pẽr-sō'nē), the characters or persons in a play or drama. [LAT.]

dram-a-tist (drăm'd-tĭst), *n.* a writer of plays; as, Shakespeare is the world's greatest *dramatist.*

dram-a-tize (drăm'd-tīz), *v.t.* to compose or write in the form of a play.—*n.* **dramatization.**

drank (drănk), past tense and past participle of the verb *drink.*

drape (drāp), *v.t.* to cover with cloth; arrange in folds; as, to *drape* curtains.

dra-per (drā'pẽr), *n.* a dealer in woolen or cotton cloth, etc.

dra-per-ied (drā'pẽr-ĭd), *adj.* furnished or covered with hangings of any kind: used especially of the human figure in sculpture and in painting.

dra-per-y (drā'pẽr-ĭ), *n.* [*pl.* draperies (-ĭz)], cloths or fabrics used for garments or hangings; hence, hangings, curtains, or loose garments such as are often represented in sculpture or painting.

dras-tic (drăs'tĭk), *adj.* acting rapidly and violently; as, a *drastic* remedy; powerful; vigorous.

draught (drăft), *n.* the act of drawing; that which is drawn: *v.t.* to draw. Also, **draft.**

draughts (drăfts), *n.* the game of checkers: so called in Great Britain.

draw (drô), *v.t.* [*p.t.* drew, *p.p.* drawn, *p.pr.* drawing], to pull along or haul; suck in; pull out; force out; to extend in length; stretch; disembowel; as, to *draw* a fowl; take or bring out, as water; a number in a lottery, etc.; to represent on paper with a pen or pencil; to describe; as, to *draw* a character; to write in legal form; require to float in; as, the vessel *draws* twenty feet of water; inhale; as, to *draw* a sigh; attract or allure; induce; receive; leave undecided; as, to *draw* a game: *v.i.* act as an inducement; shrink; take, pull, or force something out; move; as, to *draw* near; to be pulled; to practice the art of making pictures with a pen or pencil; to write a formal demand for money, supplies, etc.; as, you may *draw* on the bank for the amount; to allow a current of air to pass; as, the chimney *draws* well: *n.* the act of drawing; a lot or chance drawn; a game left undecided.

Syn., *v.* pull, haul, drag, attract, inhale, sketch, describe.

draw-back (drô'băk"), *n.* loss of advantage; a discouragement; hindrance; money paid back, especially money paid by a government, to a dealer exporting goods, equal to the customs duty paid on the same goods when imported.

draw-bridge (drô'brĭj"), *n.* a bridge which may be wholly or partially lifted up, let down, or drawn aside.

draw-ee (drô'ē), *n.* one on whom an order, bill of exchange, or a draft is drawn, with the expectation that he will pay the amount.

draw-er (drô'ẽr), *n.* one who draws; a draftsman; a sliding boxlike arrangement for holding clothes, papers, etc.; one who issues a bill of exchange, or an order for the payment of money: *pl.* an undergarment for the lower part of the body and legs.

draw-ing (drô'ĭng), *n.* a representation or picture on a plane surface of the appearance of objects; a sketch; a distribution of tickets in a lottery.

draw-ing-room (drô'ĭng-rōōm), *n.* a room for the reception or admission of company; literally, the room to which guests retire after dinner; a reception of company, or the company assembled, in such a room.

drawl (drôl), *v.t.* to utter in a slow, lazy tone: *n.* a slow, lazy manner of speaking.

drawn (drôn), *p.adj.* left undecided; as, it was a *drawn* game because the score was even; having the bowels removed; as, a *drawn* fowl; contracted; shrunk.

dray (drā), *n.* a low, stoutly-built cart used for hauling heavy loads.

dread (drĕd), *v.t.* to fear greatly; to look forward to or anticipate with shrinking or fear: *v.i.* to be in great fear: *n.* imaginative terror; fear mingled with respect and affection; as, a *dread* of the judgment of God: *adj.* awful; solemn.

Syn., *n.* horror, terror, alarm, dismay.
Ant. (see boldness, assurance).

dread-ful (drĕd'fōōl), *adj.* fearful; terrible; full of fear or awe; arousing fear or awe; as, a *dreadful* disaster.
Syn. frightful, shocking, awful, horrible.

dread-naught (drĕd'nôt"), *n.* a fearless person; a thick woolen cloth to exclude storm and cold; a battleship of 18,000 tons burden or over. Also, **dreadnought.**

dream (drēm), *n.* a train of thoughts or images passing through the mind during sleep; something seen in the imagination; a state of abstraction or reverie; an idle fancy; as, a *dream* of greatness; a wild scheme: *v.t.* [*p.t.* and *p.p.* dreamt, *p.pr.* dreaming], to see or imagine in sleep; to see in the imagination, as possible future events: *v.i.* to have a train of ideas in sleep; to imagine possible or impossible future events; to indulge in idle fancies.—*n.* **dreamer.**

dream-land (drēm'lănd"), *n.* the lovely, imaginary country seen in the imagination, waking or sleeping.

dream-like (drēm'līk"), *adj.* unreal; like something seen in a vision.

dream-y (drēm'ĭ), *adj.* pertaining to, or full of, dreams; imaginative; fanciful; not awake to realities; not clear, or indistinct; unreal.—*adv.* **dreamily.**—*n.* **dreaminess.**

drear (drēr), *adj.* dismal or gloomy to the eye or ear; sorrowful; as, a *drear* old age.

drear-y (drēr'ĭ), *adj.* cheerless; gloomy; as, a *dreary* day; a *dreary* scene. —*adv.* **drearily.**—*n.* **dreariness.**

dredge (drĕj), *n.* a drag or instrument for sweeping the bottom of a river to bring up something; a box with perforated lid, or a lid full of holes, used to sift or sprinkle with: called also *dredger*: *v.t.* to clean out and deepen by a dredge; as, *dredge* a deeper passage in a river; gather with a dredge; sprinkle with flour, etc. from a dredge.

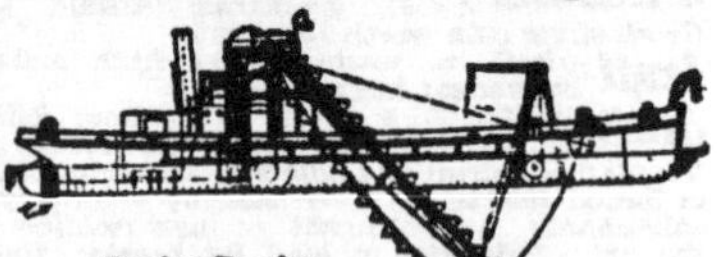

Bucket Dredge

dredg-er (drĕj'ẽr), *n.* a box with a lid containing holes, used in cooking to sprinkle flour, sugar, etc. Also, **dredge.**

dregs (drĕgz), *n.pl.* the matter which goes to the bottom of liquor; lees; worthless matter.

Drei-bund (drī'bōōnt"), *n.* a triple alliance or union, especially that (1882) between Germany, Austria-Hungary, and Italy for defending each other.

drench (drĕnch), *v.t.* to wet thoroughly; soak; forcibly give a dose to; as, to *drench* a horse: *n.* a large drink, often one forced down the throat; a dose of medicine for a horse or ox.

Dres-den (drĕz'dĕn), *n.* a fine porcelain made near Dresden, in Saxony, Germany.

dress (drĕs), *n.* covering for the body; clothing; elegant or fashionable attire; a woman's or a child's gown; outside finish or ornament: *v.t.* [*p.t.* and *p.p.* dressed or drest, *p.pr.* dressing], to cover with, or as with, clothing; adorn; deck out; prepare or make ready; arrange; to prepare for the table; curry or rub down; adjust to a straight line, as soldiers; prune or trim; to treat, as a wound, with medicines, bandages, etc.: *v.i.* to put on clothes; to form a line.

Syn., *n.* clothing, attire, apparel, garments, costume, garb, livery.

dress-er (drĕs'ẽr), *n.* one who regulates or adjusts clothing; a surgeon's assistant; a set of shelves or open cupboard for plates, etc.; a combination of mirror and bureau.

dress-ing (drĕs'ĭng), *p.pr.* of *dress*: *n.* the act of putting on clothes;

material used in stiffening fabrics; the smoothing of the surface of stone; sauce or stuffing used for preparing a dish; as, a mayonnaise *dressing;* a beating; a reprimand; medicines, bandages, etc., applied to a wound; the preparation of mineral ores for the furnace.

dress-ing gown (drĕs′ing goun), a light, easy, loose gown worn while dressing.

dress-mak-er (drĕs′māk′ẽr), *n.* a maker of women's costumes.

dress-y (drĕs′ĭ), *adj.* fond of clothes, especially showy or elaborate ones; stylish.

drew (dro͞o), past tense of the transitive and intransitive verb *draw.*

drib-ble (drĭb′l), *v.i.* to fall in small drops; trickle: *v.t.* to let fall in drops; give out or deal in small portions; in football, to give a slight kick or shove to: *n.* a drizzling shower; a trickling out in small drops.

drib-let (drĭb′lĕt), *n.* a small piece, part, or sum; as, he gave the money to them in *driblets.* Also, **dribblet.**

dried (drīd), *p.t.* and *p.p.* of *dry: p.adj.* made dry; withered.

dri-er (drī′ẽr), *n.* one who, or that which, dries; a substance added to paint, etc., causing it to dry quickly; an apparatus for removing moisture.

drift (drĭft), *n.* the direction in which anything is driven; a force which drives anything ahead; act or state of being driven; tendency or aim of an act, remark, etc.; overbearing influence; a collection of floating matter heaped up by the sea or wind; as, a *drift* of snow; the horizontal or crosswise passage of a mine; a collection of loose earth, rocks, etc., transported from a distance by ice; the direction of a current: *v.t.* to drive along or heap up; as, the winds *drift* dry leaves into piles: *v.i.* to be carried along by a current, or by circumstances; gather together in heaps.

Syn., n. purpose, meaning, scope, aim, tendency, direction.

drift-age (drĭft′āj), *n.* that which is driven along by a current of air or water; a turning aside from a ship's course caused by wind or sea currents.

drift-er (drĭft′ẽr), *n.* a type of naval vessel used to look for and remove submarine mines.

drift-wood (drĭft′wo͝od′), *n.* floating wood cast ashore by the sea.

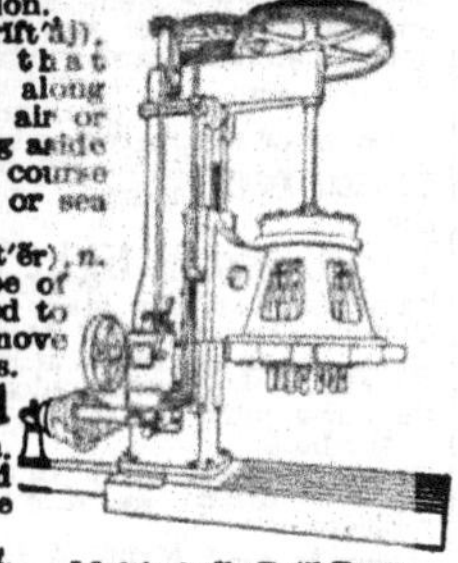

Multispindle Drill Press

drill (drĭl), *v.t.* to pierce with a boring tool; bore; instruct thoroughly; train; sow in lines or rows: *v.i.* to engage in military exercises: *n.* a tool for boring or making holes in a hard substance; a machine for sowing seeds in rows; military exercise; thorough instruction, especially by means of frequent repetition: **drill press,** a drilling machine for working in metal.

Oil Tube Drill

drill-ing (drĭl′ĭng), *n.* the act of using an instrument or tool for making holes in hard substances; a heavy, firm twilled cloth.

drink (drĭnk), *v.t.* [*p.t.* drank, *p.p.* drunk, *p.pr.* drinking], to swallow a liquid; to take alcoholic liquors habitually: *v.t.* to swallow; to suck in; to receive through the senses; as, the eye *drinks* in the beauty of the scene: *n.* any liquid swallowed to quench thirst; as much liquor as can be taken at once; strong or intoxicating liquor.—*adj.* **drinkable.**—*n.* **drinker, drinking.**

drip (drĭp), *v.i.* [*p.t.* and *p.p.* dripped, *p.pr.* dripping], to fall in drops; as, the rain *drips* from the trees: *v.t.* to let fall in drops: *n.* that which falls in drops; a projecting cornice to throw off rain.

drip-ping (drĭp′ĭng), *p.pr.* of *drip: n.* the act of falling in drops; that which falls in drops; the fat from roasted meat.

drip-ping pan (drĭp′ĭng păn), a pan to receive the fat which falls in drops from roasting meat.

drive (drīv), *v.t.* [*p.t.* drove, *p.p.* driven, *p.pr.* driving], to urge forward by force; propel; give motion to; control the motion of, as horses attached to a carriage, a motor car, etc.; hence, to carry in a vehicle; to carry through; as, to *drive* a bargain; to put into a certain state; as, to *drive* one crazy; to overtask; as, to *drive* slaves: *v.i.* to press or be moved forward with violence; travel in a carriage or motor car; aim a blow: with *at:* *n.* the act of driving or sending forward; a strong blow; a road prepared for vehicles; a trip in a carriage or motor car; an annual gathering of cattle for branding; a forward blow given to a ball at cricket or tennis; in military use, a violent attempt to break a line of defense by throwing an army against it.

Syn., v. compel, impel, ride, repulse, push.

driv-el (drĭv′l), *v.i.* to let saliva drip from the mouth; be weak or foolish; talk or act like a fool: *n.* saliva flowing from the mouth; foolish talk.

driv-en (drĭv′n), past participle of the verb *drive.*

driv-er (drīv′ẽr), *n.* one who forces something into motion; one who directs the motions of persons or things, as a chauffeur, a coachman, an overseer, etc.; in golf, a wooden-headed club, with full length shaft, somewhat supple, for driving the ball the greatest distances; a part of a machine which imparts motion to another part.

drive-way (drīv′wā′), *n.* a road, usually private, for the use of animals and vehicles.

driv-ing wheel (drīv′ĭng hwēl), a wheel that passes on motion in a machine, or moves a train of wheels.

driz-zle (drĭz′l), *v.i.* to rain slightly or in misty drops: *n.* fine misty rain.

driz-zly (drĭz′lĭ), *adj.* shedding fine rain; as, a *drizzly* sky or day.

droit (drwä), *n.* a legal right of ownership; right; justice. [Fr.]

droll (drōl), *adj.* ridiculous; queer; amusing; as, a *droll* manner; a *droll* remark.

Syn. funny, laughable, comic, whimsical, amusing.

Ant. (see solemn).

droll-er-y (drōl′ẽr-ĭ), *n.* [*pl.* drolleries (-ĭz)], jesting; humor; as, the company greatly enjoyed his *drollery;* oddity.

drom-e-da-ry (drŭm'ē-dā-rĭ), *n.* [*pl.* dromedaries (-rĭz)], the Arabian, or one-humped, camel, noted for its speed.

Dromedary

drone (drōn), *v.i.* to utter a monotonous tone or sound; live in idleness: *v.t.* to read or speak in a monotonous tone: *n.* a dull, monotonous tone; as, the *drone* of bees or of a wheel in motion; one of the pipes of a bagpipe; the male of the honeybee, which produces no honey; a lazy fellow.—*adj.* dronish.

droop (drōōp), *v.i.* to sink or hang down; to grow weak and faint or spiritless; bend down gradually: *v.t.* cause to hang down: *n.* the act of hanging down or growing weak.

drop (drŏp), *v.i.* [*p.t.* and *p.p.* dropped, dropt, *p.pr.* dropping], to fall in small round masses of fluid; sink to a lower position; become lower in sound; as, her voice *dropped;* fall in death; visit informally: with *in;* to move easily over the water; as, the ship *drops* down to sea; to be left behind; as, the tired soldier *dropped* out of ranks: *v.t.* to let fall; to let fall in small globules; to have done with; hence, to leave or place; as, to *drop* a kiss; utter in an indirect or cautious manner; send off (a hasty note); to lower, as the eyes: *n.* a small round mass of moisture; something that hangs like a drop; a small quantity of liquid; a falling trapdoor; the painted curtain of a thea r: *pl.* any liquid medicine given in small doses.—*n.* dropper.

drop shut-ter (drŏp shŭt'ẽr), a device in a camera, operated by a spring, for taking photographs instantly.

drop-si-cal (drŏp'sĭ-kăl), *adj.* affected with dropsy.

drop-sy (drŏp'sĭ), *n.* an unnatural collection of watery, or serous, fluid in any cavity of the body or its tissues.

dross (drŏs), *n.* the scum or refuse of melted metal; any worthless matter.

drought (drout), *n.* continued absence of rain or moisture; dryness. Also, drouth.

drove (drōv), *p.t.* of *drive;* *n.* a collection of cattle or sheep driven in a body; a crowd.

dro-ver (drō'vẽr), *n.* one who drives cattle, etc., to market; a buyer of cattle for sale elsewhere.

drown (droun), *v.i.* to perish by suffocation in water; *v.t.* to suffocate in water; overwhelm; flood.

Syn. swamp, submerge, engulf.

drowse (drouz), *v.i.* to be heavy with sleepiness; be half-asleep: *n.* a light sleep.

drow-si-ness (drou'zĭ-nĕs), *n.* sleepiness; sluggishness; lethargy.

drow-sy (drou'zĭ), *adj.* sleepy; sluggish; as, a *drowsy* feeling; a *drowsy* day.—*adv.* drowsily.

drub (drŭb), *v.t.* [*p.t.* and *p.p.* drubbed, *p.pr.* drubbing], to beat vigorously: *n.* a thump.

drudge (drŭj), *v.i.* to labor hard at mean or disagreeable tasks; slave: *n.* one employed in slavish work who works hard for small pay.

drudg-er-y (drŭj'ẽr-ĭ), *n.* hard, disagreeable work; mean, slavish labor.

drug (drŭg), *n.* a substance used in medicine; an unsalable article: *v.t.* [*p.t.* and *p.p.* drugged, *p.pr.* drugging], to mix drugs with; as, to *drug* wine; render stupid by a substance which deadens feeling.

drug-get (drŭg'ĕt), *n.* a coarse woolen fabric, usually used for floor covering.

drug-gist (drŭg'ĭst), *n.* a dealer in medicines and the substances used in them.

dru-id (drōō'ĭd), *n.* a priest of the ancient religion of Britain, Gaul, and Germany.—*adj.* druidic, druidical.

drum (drŭm), *n.* a musical instrument consisting of a hollow cylinder with vellum or dried skins stretched across the ends, and beaten with sticks; the membrane or skin of the inner ear; a drum-shaped box for figs; a cylinder or revolving shaft: *v.t.* [*p.t.* and *p.p.* drummed, *p.pr.* drumming], to beat a drum; beat rapidly with the fingers; to make a noise like that of a beaten drum; *v.t.* to play (a tune) on the drum; drum; to gather together, as customers: with *up;* to expel in disgrace, with drumbeat, as from camp; with *out;* to din, or repeat constantly; as, to *drum* a complaint into one's ears.

Drums. 1, side drum; 2, snare drum; 3, long drum; 4, bass drum.

drum-head (drŭm'hĕd"), *n.* the parchment or skin stretched over one end of a drum; the top of a capstan or upright windlass used on shipboard.

drum ma-jor (drŭm mā'jẽr), the leader of an army band or drum corps, or of any marching band.

drum-mer (drŭm'ẽr), *n.* one who plays a drum; a commercial traveler.

Drum-mond light (drŭm'ŭnd līt), the calcium or limelight used on the stage and invented by Captain Drummond of England.

drum-stick (drŭm'stĭk"), *n.* the stick with which a drum is beaten; the outer joint of a fowl's leg from the knee to the heel.

drunk (drŭnk), *p.p.* of *drink: adj.* intoxicated; as, they were *drunk* with pleasure.

drunk-ard (drŭnk'ẽrd), *n.* one frequently intoxicated; one given over to the use of strong liquors; a sot.

drunk-en (drŭnk'n), *p.adj.* overcome by strong drink; frequently intoxicated.—*adv.* drunkenly.—*n.* drunkenness.

dry (drī), *adj.* [*comp.* drier, *superl.* driest], free from moisture or wetness; not yielding juices; without interest; unintentionally humorous or quaint; without sweetness or fruity flavor; thirsty; solid, as opposed to liquid; as, *dry* measure: *v.t.* to free from moisture or juice; stop the flow of;

parch: *v.i.* to lose or be deprived of moisture.—*n.* dryness.

Syn., *adj.* arid, parched, dull, tedious, uninteresting, meager.

Ant. (see moist, interesting, succulent).

dry-ad (drī'ăd), *n.* a nymph, or imaginary maiden of the woods.

dry goods (drī gŏŏdz), textile, or woven fabrics, such as cloth, lace, ribbon, etc.

dry-ly (drī'lĭ), *adv.* without moisture; in an uninteresting manner; coldly; sarcastically. Also, **drily.**

dry-salt (drī'sôlt"), *v.t.* to cure by salting and drying, as meat.

dry-shod (drī'shŏd"), *adj.* without wetting the feet; as, the Israelites were led *dry-shod* across the Red Sea.

du-al (dū'ăl), *adj.* expressing or composed of the number two; as, Austria-Hungary is a *dual* monarchy: *n.* the form of the noun or verb meaning two persons or things.

du-al-ism (dū'ăl-ĭzm), *n.* a twofold division; the doctrine of two independent and separate natures in man, the spiritual and the bodily; the theory that there are two independent eternal principles, one evil and the other good, as God and the devil.

du-al-ist (dū'ăl-ĭst), *n.* one who holds any of the theories of philosophy based on a twofold division.

du-al-is-tic (dū"ăl-ĭs'tĭk), *adj.* twofold; characterized by, or pertaining to, a belief in a twofold system.

du-al-i-ty (dū-ăl'ĭ-tĭ), *n.* the state or quality of being twofold; division into two.

dub (dŭb), *v.t.* [*p.t.* and *p.p.* dubbed, *p.pr.* dubbing], to bestow knighthood on by striking the shoulder with a sword; confer any rank, dignity, character, or name upon; rub, dress, or smooth; as, to *dub* a stick of timber smooth: *n.* slang, an awkward or stupid person.

du-bi-ous (dū'bĭ-ŭs), *adj.* doubtful; as, a *dubious* reply; of questionable character; as, a *dubious* transaction.—*adv.* **dubiously.**—*n.* **dubiousness, dubiety.**

du-cal (dū'kăl), *adj.* pertaining to a duke; as, a *ducal* crown.

duc-at (dŭk'ăt), *n.* formerly, a gold or silver European coin varying in value from about 83 cents to \$2.25: *pl.* money in general; cash at command.

duch-ess (dŭch'ĕs), *n.* the wife or widow of a duke; a woman sovereign of a duchy.

duch-y (dŭch'ĭ), *n.* [*pl.* duchies (-ĭz)], the territory or dominions of a duke.

duck (dŭk), *n.* a common swimming bird with short neck and legs and flat bill; the female of this bird, as distinguished from the male, or drake; a strong linen or cotton material: *pl.* colloquially, sailors' trousers or light clothes worn in hot climates: *v.t.* to plunge the head under water and then withdraw it quickly; bob the head: *v.i.* to dip or plunge under water; throw into water; wet thoroughly.

duck-board (dŭk'bōrd), *n.* in the World War, a plank laid along the bottom of a muddy trench to give solid footing.

duck-ing (dŭk'ĭng), *p.pr.* of *duck*: *n.* the act of plunging under water; a thorough wetting; the sport of shooting wild ducks.

duck-ing stool (dŭk'ĭng stōōl), a stool in which female scolds were formerly tied and plunged under water as a punishment.

duck-ling (dŭk'lĭng), *n.* a young duck; as, there was once an ugly *duckling* that became a swan.

duck-pins (dŭk'pĭns), *n.pl.* a game resembling tenpins, but played with shorter pins and smaller balls.

duck-weed (dŭk'wēd"), *n.* a common fresh-water plant.

duct (dŭkt), *n.* a passage, tube, or canal by which a fluid or other substance is carried.

duc-tile (dŭk'tĭl), *adj.* capable of being drawn out into threads or strands, as wire; easily led; yielding to persuasion or instruction; as, the mind of a small child is usually *ductile.*

duc-til-i-ty (dŭk-tĭl'ĭ-tĭ), *n.* capability of being drawn into threads or wire; capability of being influenced or taught.

dud (dŭd), *n.* an article of clothing; in the World War, a shell or bomb which has failed to explode because of a defective fuse: *pl.* colloquially, clothes in general, especially when old and shabby.

dude (dūd), *n.* a kind of dandy, characterized by over-fashionable manners, dress, etc. [Colloq.]

dudg-eon (dŭj'ŭn), *n.* sullen anger; ill will; as, he went away in high *dudgeon.*

dud-ism (dūd'ĭzm), *n.* the foolish pretensions or social peculiarities of dudes. Also, **dudeism.**

due (dū), *adj.* owed or owing; payable; suitable to a case; resulting from; proper: *adv.* exactly; directly; as, the ship sailed *due* west: *n.* that which belongs or may be claimed as a right; that which is owed or required; a custom, toll, tribute, or fee: *pl.* an amount of money payable at stated intervals for membership in a club, etc.: **due bill,** a written acknowledgment of a debt.

Syn., *adj.* owing to, attributable to, just, fair, proper, right.

du-el (dū'ĕl), *n.* a battle, usually planned beforehand, between two persons with deadly weapons: *v.i.* to fight in such a combat.

du-el-ing (dū'ĕl-ĭng), *n.* the fighting a duel. Also, **duelling.**

du-en-na (dū-ĕn'ȧ; dū-ĕn'yȧ), *n.* an elderly Spanish or Portuguese lady who acts as a guardian to a younger one; a governess. Also, **dueña.** [Sp.]

du-et (dū'ĕt), *n.* a musical composition to be sung or played by two performers. Also, **duetto.**

duff (dŭf), *n.* pudding of flour, etc., boiled in a bag; decayed vegetable matter in forest ground.

duf-fel (dŭf'ĕl), *n.* a woolen fabric; a heavy kersey cloth; outfit; supplies.

duff-er (dŭf'ẽr), *n.* in England, a peddler of feminine articles of dress, flash jewelry, etc.; a dull, stupid, inefficient person. [Slang.]

dug (dŭg), *p.t.* and *p.p.* of *dig*: *n.* a nipple (of an animal).

dug-out (dŭg'out"), *n.* a canoe hollowed out from a log; a rough kind of shelter dug in the side of a hill or bank; in the World War, a shelter dug in the back wall of a trench, where front line troops may rest.

duke (dūk), *n.* one of the highest order of English nobility, ranking next below an archbishop and the royal princes; prince or high noble in European countries.

duke-dom (dūk'dŭm), *n.* a duchy or the title of a duke; a duke's province.

dul-cet (dŭl'sĕt), *adj.* sweet or pleasant to the ear; as, *dulcet* tones.

dul-ci-an-a (dŭl'sĭ-ăn'ȧ), *n.* a soft-toned organ stop.

dul-ci-mer (dŭl'sĭ-mẽr), *n.* a musical instrument with wire strings which are struck with light hammers.

dull (dŭl), *adj.* slow of understanding or action; stupid; without sensibility; not bright or clear to the eye; blunt; not brisk or active; wearisome; cloudy: *v.t.* to take away the sharpness of; make stupid or heavy; tarnish: *v.i.* to become stupid; become dull or blunt; lose brightness.—*adv.* **dully.**

Syn., adj. depressing, gloomy, sad, dismal, commonplace.

Ant. (see bright).

dull-ard (dŭl'ẽrd), *n.* a stupid person; blockhead: *adj.* stupid.

dul-ness (dŭl'nĕs), *n.* the state or quality of being slow or stupid; bluntness; lack of brightness. Also, **dullness.**

du-ly (dū'lĭ), *adv.* in a fit and becoming manner; fitly; regularly.

Du-ma (do͞o'mä), *n.* the national legislature or lawmaking body of Russia, created by the czar in 1905 and discontinued at the revolution of 1917.

dumb (dŭm), *adj.* unable or unwilling to speak; silent.—*adv.* **dumbly.**—*n.* **dumbness.**

dumb-bell (dŭm'-bĕl"), *n.* one of a pair of heavy weights used for muscular exercise.

Dumb-bell

dumb show (dŭm shō), gesture without speech; as, the actors in motion pictures must tell most of the story in *dumb show.*

dumb-wait-er (dŭm wāt'ẽr), *n.* a small elevator with shelves on which dishes are moved from one floor to another.

dum-dum bul-let (dŭm'dŭm bo͝ol'ĕt), a partly steel-cased bullet, the soft core of which spreads when it strikes, adding much to the injury of the wound.

dum-found (dŭm"found'), *v.t.* to amaze; to make dumb with surprise or fear. Also, **dumbfound, dumfounder, dumbfounder.**

dum-my (dŭm'ĭ), *n.* [*pl.* dummies (-ĭz)], one who is mute or silent; a sham or make-believe; an exposed hand at whist played by the opposite player when three persons are playing: *adj.* imitation; noiseless; apparently acting for oneself, but really for another, as, a *dummy* director in a company.

dump (dŭmp), *n.* a thud or heavy sound; anything short, thick, and heavy; a place of deposit for rubbish; a pit for the storage of ammunition or military supplies: *pl.* low spirits: *v.t.* to throw down and empty, especially abruptly; unload from a cart.

dump-ling (dŭmp'lĭng), *n.* a pudding of paste or dough, often inclosing fruit or meat.

dump-y (dŭm'pĭ), *adj.* short and thick; discontented; sulky.

dun (dŭn), *adj.* of a dull brown color: *n.* a person who presses persistently for payment of a debt; a request for payment; a fortified height; earthwork; mound: *v.t.* [*p.t.* and *p.p.* dunned, *p.pr.* dunning], to urge, especially for a debt; cure, as codfish, after salting, by laying in a pile in a dark place, covered with salt grass, etc., to impart a dark color.

dunce (dŭns), *n.* a dull, ignorant person; a backward student.

Syn. simpleton, fool, idiot.

Ant. (see sage).

dun-der-head (dŭn'dẽr-hĕd"), *n.* a dunce; a numskull; a blockhead.

dune (dūn), *n.* a heap of drifted sand piled up on the seashore by the action of the wind.

dung (dŭng), *n.* the waste material cast off through the bowels of animals; anything filthy or rotten: *v.t.* to manure, as with dung.

dun-geon (dŭn'jŭn), *n.* the principal defended part of an ancient castle; a dark underground cell; a prison. Also, **donjon.**

dung-hill (dŭng'hĭl"), *n.* a heap of manure: *adj.* vile, ignoble.

Dun-ker (dŭn'kẽr), *n.* one of a sect of German-American Baptists, properly termed Brethren. Also, **Dunkard.**

dun-nage (dŭn'āj), *n.* loose wood, fagots, etc., stowed in the hold of a vessel to protect the cargo from injury; personal baggage: used by sailors.

dun-nish (dŭn'ĭsh), *adj.* inclined to a dull brown color.

dunn-ite (dŭn'īt), *n.* a powerful explosive, of American invention.

du-o-dec-i-mal (dū"ō-dĕs'ĭ-măl), *adj.* consisting of, or counting by, twelves or any power of twelve: *n.* a twelfth power of anything: *pl.* a system of computing by twelves the number of square feet and inches in a rectangular area.

du-o-dec-i-mo (dū"ō-dĕs'ĭ-mō), *n.* a sheet folded into twelve leaves [12mo]: said of a book.

du-o-de-num (dū"ō-dē'nŭm), *n.* [*pl.* duodena (-nȧ)], the first portion of the small intestine.

du-o-tone (dū'ō-tōn), *n.* and *adj.* a process of photo-engraving in which two plates are made from the same negative and one printed over the other, giving a two-tone effect in the picture.

dup-a-ble (dūp'ȧ-bl), *adj.* capable of being easily deceived; gullible.

dupe (dūp), *n.* one who is, or can be, easily tricked; a person who believes everything that he is told: *v.t.* to deceive by trickery; cheat.

du-plex (dū'plĕks), *adj.* double; compound; having two parts that work at the same time, as a machine with two cutters, a device for sending two telegraph messages over one wire at the same time, etc.: *v.t.* to arrange a telegraphic system so that two messages can be sent in opposite directions at one time.

du-pli-cate (dū'plĭ-kāt), *v.t.* to make double; make a copy or copies of: *adj.* (dū'plĭ-kāt), corresponding exactly with another; twofold; double; growing in pairs; in cards, playing the same hands twice; as, *duplicate* whist: *n.* facsimile; counterpart; an exact copy.

Syn., n. copy, likeness, imitation.

du-pli-ca-tion (dū"plĭ-kā'shŭn), *n.* the act of making double or making a copy or copies of; a fold; multiplication by two.

du-plic-i-ty (dū-plĭs'ĭ-tĭ), *n.* deceitfulness; double-dealing.

du-ra-bil-i-ty (dū'rȧ-bĭl'ĭ-tĭ), *n.* state or quality of lasting or of wearing well; as, serge is much used in making clothing because of its *durability*.

du-ra-ble (dū'rȧ-bl), *adj.* not perishing; permanent; lasting.—*adv.* **durably.**—*n.* **durableness.**
Syn. abiding, continuing.
Ant. (see ephemeral, perishable).

du-ra ma-ter (dū'rȧ mā'tẽr), the tough covering of the brain and spinal cord. Also, **dura.**

dur-ance (dūr'ăns), *n.* imprisonment; confinement.

du-ra-tion (dū-rā'shŭn), *n.* continuance in time; as, the *duration* of the Civil War was about four years; permanency.

dur-bar (dûr'bär), *n.* a prince's court; audience chamber; state reception in India: **Durbar,** the coronation of the king of Great Britain and Ireland as Emperor of India.

du-ress (dū'rĕs; dū-rĕs'), *n.* restraint of personal liberty by fear or physical force; the compelling a person to do some act; as, the man had committed the act under *duress* and therefore escaped severe punishment; imprisonment.

dur-ing (dūr'ĭng), *prep.* in the time of; at some period of.

durst (dûrst), past tense of the transitive and intransitive verb *dare.*

dusk (dŭsk), *adj.* tending to darkness; shadowy: *n.* approaching darkness, as in late twilight.

dusk-y (dŭs'kĭ), *adj.* partially dark; tending to blackness; as, a *dusky* complexion.—*adv.* **duskily.**—*n.* **duskiness.**

dust (dŭst), *n.* fine dry particles of matter; a cloud or film of such fine particles; any fine powder; the particles into which a decaying body falls; pollen; a low condition: *v.t.* to brush away dust from; cover with powder; as, to *dust* a cake with sugar.

dust-er (dŭs'tẽr), *n.* cloth or bunch of feathers or the like for dusting; a light overgarment to protect clothing from the dust; a box, etc., having holes in the lid for sifting.

dust-y (dŭs'tĭ), *adj.* [*comp.* dustier, *superl.* dustiest], covered with dust.

Dutch (dŭch), *adj.* pertaining to, or like, the people of Holland, or their language: *n.* the language of Holland: **the Dutch,** the people of Holland.

du-te-ous (dū'tē-ŭs), *adj.* fulfilling service owed; obedient; showing respect.—*adv.* **duteously.**—*n.* **duteousness.**

du-ti-a-ble (dū'tĭ-ȧ-bl), *adj.* subject to payment of custom; as, when travelers return to America from abroad their baggage is searched for *dutiable* articles.

du-ti-ful (dū'tĭ-fŏŏl), *adj.* respectful; obedient to parents or superiors.—*adv.* **dutifully.**—*n.* **dutifulness.**

du-ty (dū'tĭ), *n.* [*pl.* duties (-tĭz)], service owed; conduct owing to parents or superiors; action required in a certain position; that which one is morally bound to do; tax levied by the government on certain articles.

dwarf (dwôrf), *n.* a human being, animal, or plant much below the average height: *adj.* of smaller size or height than the average: *v.t.* to hinder from growing to the natural size: *v.i.* to become stunted; grow smaller.—*adj.* **dwarfish.**

dwell (dwĕl), *v.i.* [*p.t.* and *p.p.* dwelt, *p.pr.* dwelling], to reside for a length of time; have a fixed place to live in; continue; linger.—*n.* **dweller.**
Syn. stay, abide, sojourn, tarry.

dwell-ing (dwĕl'ĭng), *n.* a house or place to live in; residence.

dwin-dle (dwĭn'dl), *v.i.* to become gradually less; diminish; to grow smaller.
Syn. pine, waste, fall off.
Ant. (see grow).

dye (dī), *v.t.* [*p.t.* and *p.p.* dyed, *p.pr.* dyeing], to stain or color: *v.i.* to follow the trade of a dyer: *n.* a coloring liquid or stain.

dy-ing (dī'ĭng), *p.adj.* passing away from life; decaying physically; drawing to a close: *n.* the act of giving up life.

dyke (dīk), *n.* a bank of earth built as a barrier. Also, **dike.**

dy-nam-ic (dī-năm'ĭk), *adj.* pertaining to power or physical energy; pertaining to forces producing motion. Also, **dynamical.**

dy-nam-ics (dī-năm'ĭks), *n.pl.* that branch of mechanics which treats of the effects of force in producing motion.

dy-na-mite (dī'nȧ-mīt; dĭn'ȧ-mīt), *n.* a highly explosive compound of nitroglycerine mixed with sawdust or similar material: *v.t.* to destroy by dynamite.

Alternating Current Dynamo

dy-na-mo (dī'nȧ-mō), *n.* a machine for producing electric current.

dy-na-mom-e-ter (dī'nȧ-mŏm'ē-tẽr; dĭn'ȧ-mŏm'ē-tẽr), *n.* an apparatus for measuring force or power, etc.

dy-nas-tic (dī-năs'tĭk; dĭn-ăs'tĭk), *adj.* pertaining to a line of sovereigns of a particular family.

dy-nas-ty (dī'năs-tĭ; dĭn'ăs-tĭ), *n.* [*pl.* dynasties (-tĭz)], a line or succession of sovereigns of a particular family; the length of time during which a certain family reigns.

dyne (dīn), *n.* a unit used in the measurement of force; the force which, acting upon a mass of one gram for one second, produces a speed of one centimeter per second.

dys-en-ter-y (dĭs'ĕn-tẽr-ĭ), *n.* a disease of the bowels, characterized by a severe inflammation of the mucous membrane of the large intestine, attended with fever.—*adj.* **dysenteric.**

dys-pep-si-a (dĭs-pĕp'sĭ-ȧ; dĭs-pĕp'shȧ), *n.* a very common ailment, affecting digestion, generally chronic; indigestion.

dys-pep-tic (dĭs-pĕp'tĭk), *adj.* pertaining to, causing, or afflicted with, indigestion: *n.* a person having chronic indigestion.

E

each (ēch), *pron.* and *adj.* every one of a number considered separately; as, *each* (*pron.*) or, *each* man (*adj.*) is expected to do his duty.

ea-ger (ē'gẽr), *adj.* impetuous; earnest; enthusiastic; keenly desirous.—*adv.* **eagerly.**—*n.* **eagerness.**
Syn. ardent, fervent, impatient, spirited.
Ant. (see diffident).

ea-gle (ē'gl), *n.* a bird of prey of the falcon family, noted for its strength, size, and keenness of vision; the ten dollar gold piece of the United States; the military standard of ancient Rome.

ea-glet (ē'glĕt), *n.* a young eagle; as, the *eaglets* of some species do not grow their full plumage until the third or fourth year.

ear (ēr), *n.* the entire organ of hearing; the outer part of that organ; the sense of hearing, or delicate perception of sounds; as, he has an *ear* for music; attention; that part of a cereal plant containing the flowers and seeds; as, an *ear* of corn.

ear-drum (ēr'drŭm"), *n.* a thin membrane, like the head of a drum, that closes the cavity of the middle ear.

eared (ērd), *adj.* having ears of a given type; as, a long-*eared* or short-*eared* animal.

ear-ing (ēr'ĭng), *n.* a small rope for fastening the upper corner of a sail to a wooden bar; the formation of ears, as in wheat.

earl (ûrl), *n.* a British nobleman next in rank below a marquis.

earl-dom (ûrl'dŭm), *n.* the dignity, possessions, or authority of an earl.

ear-ly (ûr'lĭ), *adj.* [*comp.* earlier, *superl.* earliest], being near the beginning; before the usual time; in good time: *adv.* at or near the beginning; soon; seasonably.

ear-mark (ēr'märk"), *n.* a mark by which a person or thing may be known.

earn (ûrn), *v.t.* to gain a just pay for one's labor, service, etc.; to merit.
Syn. acquire, win, gain, achieve.

earn-est (ûr'nĕst), *adj.* serious in speech or action; zealous; eager; ardent; hearty; *n.* a portion of something given or done in advance as a pledge; as, the warmth of spring is an *earnest* of the heat of summer.—*adv.* **earnestly.**—*n.* **earnestness.**
Syn., adj. serious, solemn, warm.
Ant. (see trifling).

earn-ings (ûr'nĭngz), *n.pl.* money or other compensation received for services; wages; reward.

ear-ring (ēr'rĭng"), *n.* an ornament for the ear: usually of gold or precious stones.

earth (ûrth), *n.* the globe or planet on which we live; the solid materials which compose the globe; ground; soil; a region or land; worldly things or interests; the inhabitants of the globe; as, the whole *earth* rejoiced.

earth-en (ûr'thn), *adj.* made of earth or clay; as, an *earthen* jar.

earth-en-ware (ûr'thn-wâr"), *n.* vessels or other objects made of burnt or baked clay, or a similar substance.

earth-ly (ûrth'lĭ), *adj.* pertaining to this world; as, *earthly* joys; pertaining to the present life; material.—*n.* **earthliness.**

earth-quake (ûrth'kwāk"), *n.* a shaking or trembling of the ground produced by explosions or slidings beneath the surface.

earth-work (ûrth'wûrk"), *n.* a cutting or embankment made by removing or filling in with soil; a fortification made of clay, sand, gravel, etc.

earth-worm (ûrth'wûrm"), *n.* a common name for worms that live in damp ground.

earth-y (ûr'thĭ), *adj.* pertaining to, composed of, or resembling, the soil; unrefined; coarse.—*n.* **earthiness.**

ear-wig (ēr'wĭg"), *n.* a well-known insect with a pair of curved forceps at its tail, supposed to creep into the ear; a common name for any small centipede.

ease (ēz), *n.* freedom from pain, disturbance, labor, or stiffness; as, *ease* of manner; quiet; repose: *v.t.* to free from pain, anxiety, trouble, or tension; give rest or relief to; as, to *ease* a horse of his load.
Syn., v. calm, alleviate, pacify, rid.
Ant. (see annoy, worry).

ea-sel (ē'zĕl), *n.* a frame or tripod for holding a canvas, blackboard, picture, etc.

east (ēst), *n.* that part of the heavens where the sun is seen to rise; one of the four points of the compass; the part of the earth lying toward the sunrise: *adj.* coming from the direction of the sunrise; lying on the right hand when one faces the north: *adv.* in the direction of the sunrise: **East,** the Orient or far East, as the countries of Asia; eastern part of the United States.

Easel

East-er (ēs'tẽr), *n.* a festival of the Christian Church to commemorate the resurrection of Jesus Christ: *adj.* pertaining to that festival.

east-er-ly (ēs'tẽr-lĭ), *adj.* and *adv.* situated, or moving towards, the sunrise: in the direction of the sunrise.

east-ern (ēs'tẽrn), *adj.* situated towards, or lying in, the part of the earth towards the sunrise.—*n.* **easterner.**

East-ern Church (ēs'tẽrn chûrch), the Orthodox, Oriental, or Greek Church.

East-ern Em-pire (ēs'tẽrn ĕm'pīr), that part of the later Roman Empire which had its capital at Byzantium (Constantinople).

East-ern Ques-tion (ēs'tẽrn kwĕs'chŭn), the term applied to the difficult problems arising out of the possession by the Turks of the southeast part of Europe, and of their relations to Russia and adjoining states.

east-ward (ēst'wẽrd), *adv.* toward or in the direction of the sunrise. Also, **eastwards.**

eas-y (ēz'ĭ), *adj.* [*comp.* easier, *superl.* easiest], comfortable; not difficult; not burdensome; as, an *easy* task; moderate; not exacting.—*adv.* **easily.**—*n.* **easiness.**

eat (ēt), *v.t.* [*p.t.* ate, *p.p.* eaten, *p.pr.* eating], to chew and swallow, as food; devour; consume; corrode; waste or wear away; as, rust *eats* away the surface: *v.i.* to take food; to become corroded.—*n.* **eater.**

eat-a-ble (ēt'ȧ-bl), *adj.* good for food; fit to be swallowed; edible.

eau (ō), *n.* [*pl.* eaux (ōz)], water, especially as applied to perfumes, cordials, etc.; as, *eau* de cologne. [Fr.]

eaves (ēvz), *n.pl.* the lower edges of the roof which overhang a building.

eaves-drop (ēvz'drop''), *v.i.* [*p.t.* and *p.p.* eavesdropped, *p.pr.* eavesdropping], to listen secretly to the private conversation of others.

ebb (ĕb), *n.* the flowing back of the tide; ebb-tide; decline: *v.i.* to flow back or return, as the tide to the sea; decline; recede or go back.

eb-on (ĕb'ŭn), *adj.* made of, or like, ebony; very black.

eb-on-ite (ĕb'ŭn-īt), *n.* a hard black rubber, used for buttons, combs, etc.

eb-on-ize (ĕb'ŭn-īz), *v.t.* to make black by staining.

eb-o-ny (ĕb'ŭn-ĭ), *n.* [*pl.* ebonies (-ĭz)], a hard, heavy, durable, black-colored wood: *adj.* made of, or like, that wood; very black.

e-bul-lient (ē-bŭl'yĕnt), *adj.* in a bubbling or boiling state.

eb-ul-li-tion (ĕb''ŭ-lĭsh'ŭn), *n.* the act of boiling; bubbling; a sudden outburst of feeling; violent agitation.

ec-cen-tric (ĕk-sĕn'trĭk), *adj.* not in the center; peculiar in manner or character; as, an *eccentric* person; erratic; irregular; not having the same center: *n.* a circle or sphere not having the same center as another circle; as, the drive-wheel of an engine works on an *eccentric*.

Syn., adj. irregular, singular, odd, abnormal, wayward, peculiar, strange.

Ant. (see regular, ordinary).

ec-cen-tric-i-ty (ĕk''sĕn-trĭs'ĭ-tĭ), *n.* [*pl.* eccentricities (-tĭz)], a peculiarity of manner or character; oddity.

Ec-cle-si-as-tes (ĕ-klē''zĭ-ăs'tēz), *n.* a book of wisdom in the Old Testament.

ec-cle-si-as-tic (ĕ-klē'zĭ-ăs'tĭk), *adj.* pertaining to the church: *n.* a person in holy orders; a clergyman.

ec-cle-si-as-ti-cal (ĕ-klē''zĭ-ăs'tĭ-kăl), *adj.* pertaining to the church and its organization or government.—*adv.* **ecclesiastically.**

ec-cle-si-as-ti-cism (ĕ-klē''zĭ-ăs'tĭ-sĭzm), *n.* strong attachment to the forms, usages, organization, and privileges of the church.

ech-e-lon (ĕsh'ĕ-lŏn), *n.* the arrangement of a body of troops in the form of steps; an arrangement of the vessels of a fleet in V form: *v.t.* to form in such an arrangement.

ech-o (ĕk'ō), *n.* [*pl.* echoes (-ōz)], the repetition of a sound caused by the reflection of sound waves; the repeating of the word or opinions of others; one who copies his opinions and words from others: *v.i.* [*p.t.* and *p.p.* echoed; *p.pr.* echoing], to give back or repeat a sound: *v.t.* to repeat the sound of; as, the mocking-bird *echoes* nearly all other birds; repeat closely (the words, etc., of others).

é-clair (ā''klâr'), *n.* a small oblong cake containing flavored cream, etc., covered with sugar or chocolate. [Fr.]

é-clat (ā''klä'), *n.* renown; striking effect; splendor. [Fr.]

ec-lec-tic (ĕk-lĕk'tĭk), *adj.* selecting; choosing from various sources or systems; made up of choice, selected material.

e-clipse (ē-klĭps'), *n.* the total or partial darkening of the light of the sun, moon, or other heavenly body caused by its entering the shadow of another body; an overshadowing; temporary failure: *v.t.* to darken or conceal, as one body by another; surpass.

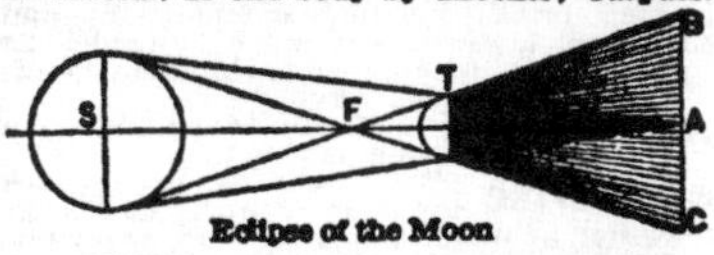

Eclipse of the Moon

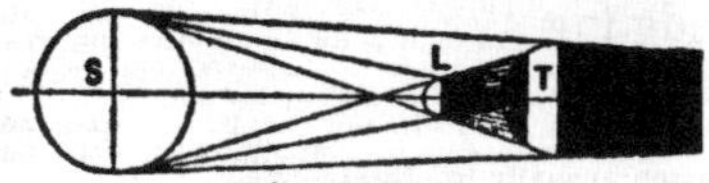

Eclipse of the Sun

S, sun; *T*, earth; *L*, moon; *F*, focus; *A, B, C*, shadow of the earth.

e-clip-tic (ē-klĭp'tĭk), *n.* the great circle which is the apparent path of the sun, or real path of the earth in the heavens during a year: *adj.* pertaining to the darkening of a heavenly body.

ec-logue (ĕk'lŏg), *n.* a poem about the country or about rural life; as, the *Eclogues* of Virgil.

e-co-nom-ic (ē''kō-nŏm'ĭk), *adj.* frugal; pertaining to the science of economics. Also, **economical.**—*adv.* **economically.**

e-co-nom-ics (ē''kō-nŏm'ĭks), *n.* the science that treats of the production and use of wealth; political economy.

e-con-o-mist (ē-kŏn'ō-mĭst), *n.* one who is careful in the use of time, labor, or money; a student of the theory of the production and use of wealth.

e-con-o-mize (ē-kŏn'ō-mīz), *v.t.* to manage with care or frugality; to treat savingly or sparingly: *v.i.* to be careful in outlay; to avoid waste and extravagance; as, to *economize* in housekeeping.

e-con-o-my (ē-kŏn'ō-mĭ), *n.* [*pl.* economies (-mĭz)], the regulation and management of means and resources; freedom from waste in the use of anything; thrift.

é-cru (ā'kroo; ĕk'roo), *adj.* unbleached; having the pale brown color of raw silk, or of undyed linen. [Fr.]

ec-sta-sy (ĕk'stȧ-sĭ), *n.* [*pl.* ecstasies (-sĭz)], the state of being beside oneself; excessive joy; a kind of trance.

ec-stat-ic (ĕk-stăt'ĭk), *adj.* overpowering; rapturous; entrancing. Also, **ecstatical.**—*adv.* **ecstatically.**

ec-u-men-i-cal (ĕk''ū-mĕn'ĭ-kăl), *adj.* general; universal; pertaining to the Christian church throughout the world; said of certain councils of the church. Also, **ecumenic.**

ec-ze-ma (ĕk'zē-mȧ), *n.* a disease of the skin usually attended by intense itching.

Ed-da (ĕd'ȧ), *n.* a collection of the ancient poems of Iceland.

ed-dy (ĕd'ĭ), *n.* [*pl.* eddies (-ĭz)], a current of air or water running opposite to the main current, thus causing a circular motion; a small whirlpool: *v.i.* to move with a circular motion; whirl.

e-del-weiss (ā'dĕl-vīs), *n.* a small, white, woolly plant and flower of the aster family, native to the Alps.

E-den (ē'dn), *n.* the garden in which Adam and Eve were placed; any very delightful region or abode; paradise.

edge (ĕj), *n.* the thin, sharp, or cutting part of a knife or tool; extreme border; brink; margin; keenness: *v.t.* and *v.i.* to put a border on; move forward little by little; as, to *edge* one's way through a crowd.

Syn., *n.* rim, brim, verge.

edge tool (ĕj tōōl), any sharp tool, as a hatchet or chisel.

edge-wise (ĕj'wīz), *adv.* on, by, or with the edge; with the edge towards; as if by the edge. Also, **edgeways.**

edg-ing (ĕj'ĭng), *p.pr.* of the verb *edge*: *n.* that which forms a border; narrow lace or embroidery for a garment; the operation of shaping or ornamenting anything.

ed-i-ble (ĕd'ĭ-bl), *adj.* fit to be eaten as food: *n.* something fit to be eaten: usually in plural.

e-dict (ē'dĭkt), *n.* a public announcement or order issued by a ruler and having the force of a law.

ed-i-fi-ca-tion (ĕd'ĭ-fĭ-kā'shŭn), *n.* a building up or improving of the mind, in a moral or religious sense; instruction; education.

ed-i-fice (ĕd'ĭ-fĭs), *n.* a structure; a building of large size.

ed-i-fy (ĕd'ĭ-fī), *v.t.* [*p.t.* and *p.p.* edified, *p.pr.* edifying], to instruct and improve, especially in faith or morals.

ed-it (ĕd'ĭt), *v.t.* to revise and prepare for publication; to direct, select, and adapt for publication.

e-di-tion (ē-dĭsh'ŭn), *n.* the published form of a literary work; the number of copies of a book, magazine, or newspaper published at one time.

ed-i-tor (ĕd'ĭ-tẽr), *n.* one who superintends, revises, or prepares a literary work for publication; one who conducts a newspaper, magazine, etc.

ed-i-to-ri-al (ĕd'ĭ-tō'rĭ-ăl), *adj.* pertaining to an editor, or his duties: *n.* a leading article in a paper giving an opinion on some subject.—*adv.* **editorially.**

ed-u-cate (ĕd'ū-kāt), *v.t.* to impart knowledge to; increase the mental or moral power of; instruct; train; teach.

ed-u-ca-tion (ĕd"ū-kā'shŭn), *n.* the systematic training of the mental or moral powers; the knowledge and ability gained through a systematic course of training.

Syn. culture, information, learning, study, instruction.

Ant. (see ignorance).

ed-u-ca-tor (ĕd'ū-kā"tẽr), *n.* one who knows the art, theory, and methods of education; one who urges the promotion and extension of education; a teacher or tutor.

e-duce (ē-dūs'), *v.t.* to draw out; as, from a study of horses he *educed* a method of teaching them tricks; bring to light.

e-duc-tion (ē-dŭk'shŭn), *n.* an inference or conclusion.

eel (ēl), *n.* a slimy, snakelike fish; as, as slippery as an *eel*.

eel-pout (ēl'pout"), *n.* a fish with a long, narrow, tapering body; the burbot of the cod family.

e'en (ēn), *adv.* a short form of *even*: *n.* a short form of *evening*.

e'er (âr; ār), *adv.* a short form of *ever*; as, the sweetest song that *e'er* I heard.

ee-rie (ē'rĭ), *adj.* lonely; weird; gloomy; mysterious. Also, **eery.**

ef-face (ĕ-fās'), *v.t.* to erase; remove; destroy; blot out; wipe out; cancel.

ef-face-ment (ĕ-fās'mĕnt), *n.* the act of blotting out; the state of being blotted out or erased.

ef-fect (ĕ-fĕkt'), *v.t.* to produce as a cause, consequence, or result; accomplish; bring about; as, to *effect* a change in another's plans: *n.* result; purpose; impression: *pl.* goods; personal estate.

Syn., *n.* consequence, result, issue, event, operation.

ef-fec-tive (ĕ-fĕk'tĭv), *adj.* having the power to produce a result; efficient; powerful; producing an impression of beauty or a feeling of admiration; as, an *effective* picture; impressive; striking: *n.* a soldier fit for duty.—*adv.* **effectively.**—*n.* **effectiveness.**

ef-fec-tu-al (ĕ-fĕk'tū-ăl), *adj.* producing or having result.—*adv.* **effectually.**

ef-fem-i-na-cy (ĕ-fĕm'ĭ-nȧ-sĭ), *n.* a term of reproach applied to a man of weak character; want of manliness; womanishness.

ef-fem-i-nate (ĕ-fĕm'ĭ-nāt), *v.t.* to make womanish or delicate; unman: *v.i.* become womanish: *adj.* (ĕ-fĕm'ĭ-nāt), having the qualities or characteristics of a woman; delicate or unmanly.

ef-fer-ent (ĕf'ẽr-ĕnt), *adj.* conveying or discharging outwards; as, an *efferent* nerve, or as a river flowing from and bearing away the waters of a lake.

ef-fer-vesce (ĕf"ẽr-vĕs'), *v.i.* to bubble up; to hiss; to work, as new wine; to be lively or gay.

ef-fer-ves-cence (ĕf"ẽr-vĕs'ĕns), *n.* the state or condition of bubbling; uncontrollable excitement; a display of feeling.

ef-fer-ves-cent (ĕf"ẽr-vĕs'ĕnt), *adj.* gently bubbling and hissing from the giving off of gas; gay.

ef-fete (ĕ-fēt'), *adj.* worn out, as a result of age; barren; exhausted; useless.

ef-fi-ca-cious (ĕf"ĭ-kā'shŭs), *adj.* producing, or capable of producing, a desired effect.—*adv.* **efficaciously.**—*n.* **efficaciousness.**

ef-fi-ca-cy (ĕf'ĭ-kȧ-sĭ), *n.* power to produce results or effects; ability; efficiency; energy; agency.

ef-fi-cien-cy (ĕ-fĭsh'ĕn-sĭ), *n.* effectual agency or power; the state of being competent or of having the power of producing desired effects or results.

ef-fi-cient (ĕ-fĭsh'ĕnt), *adj.* producing or causing desired effects or results; powerful; ready; competent; as, an *efficient* teacher.—*adv.* **efficiently.**

Syn. capable, fitted.

ef-fi-gy (ĕf'ĭ-jĭ), *n.* [*pl.* effigies (-jĭz)], an image; a likeness or figure in sculpture, painting, or on coins, etc.

ef-flo-resce (ĕf"lō-rĕs'), *v.i.* to blossom; become covered with a whitish crust or fine white crystals, as by evaporation, etc.

ef-flo-res-cence (ĕf"lō-rĕs'ĕns), *n.* the time or state of flowering; the production of flowers; redness of

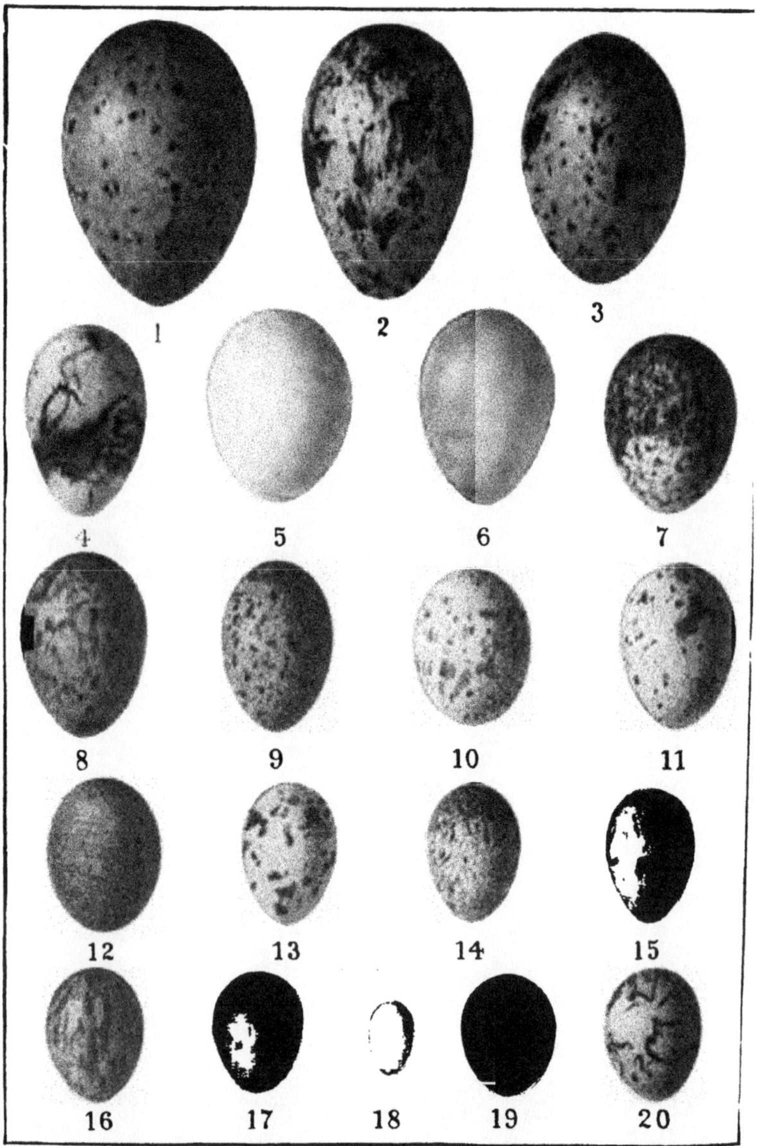

EGGS OF NORTH AMERICAN BIRDS

1. Northern raven. 2. American raven. 3. American crow. 4. Great-tailed grackle. 5. Belted kingfisher 6. Pileated woodpecker. 7. Nighthawk. 8. American magpie. 9. Blue jay. 10. Whip-poor-will. 11 Meadowlark. 12. Black-billed cuckoo. 13 Kingbird. 14. Cowbird. 15 Baltimore oriole. 16. Crested flycatcher. 17. Skylark. 18. Ruby-throated hummingbird. 19. Bobolink. 20. Red-winged blackbird.

the skin; the formation of fine white crystals on the surface of certain substances through chemical action.

ef-flo-res-cent (ĕf′lō-rĕs′ĕnt), *adj.* blossoming or flowering.

ef-flu-ence (ĕf′lōō-ĕns), *n.* an issuing or flowing out.

ef-flu-ent (ĕf′lōō-ĕnt), *adj.* flowing or issuing forth: *n.* a stream which flows out of another or forms the outlet of a lake.

ef-flu-vi-al (ĕ-flōō′vĭ-ăl), *adj.* pertaining to the invisible vapor that comes from decaying matter.

ef-flu-vi-um (ĕ-flōō′vĭ-ŭm), *n.* [*pl.* effluvia (-*ȧ*)], an invisible vapor or disagreeable odor arising from decaying matter.

ef-fort (ĕf′ort; ĕf′ĕrt), *n.* severe exertion, physical or mental; struggle; attempt.

ef-front-er-y (ĕ-frŭn′tĕr-ĭ), *n.* impudence; boldness; shamelessness.

ef-ful-gence (ĕ-fŭl′jĕns), *n.* a great luster, brightness, or splendor.

ef-ful-gent (ĕ-fŭl′jĕnt), *adj.* pouring forth light; radiant.

ef-fu-sion (ĕ-fū′zhŭn), *n.* the act of pouring out, or shedding forth; an outpouring of thought or sentiment; the escape of a fluid from the vessel inclosing it.

ef-fu-sive (ĕ-fū′sĭv), *adj.* pouring forth freely; gushing; expressing exaggerated feeling.—*adv.* **effusively.**—*n.* **effusiveness.**

eft (ĕft), *n.* a newt, or small lizard of the salamander family.

egg (ĕg), *n.* the oval or roundish body laid by birds and certain other animals, from which their young are produced; something shaped like an egg; the germ or first principle of anything: *v.t.* to urge on or incite.

egg-nog (ĕg′nŏg′), *n.* a nourishing drink made of eggs, milk, and sugar, beaten up light and flavored with wine, etc.

egg-plant (ĕg′plănt′), *n.* a cultivated herb, with large egg-shaped edible fruit, used as a vegetable.

e-gis (ē′jĭs), *n.* in Greek mythology, the storm-cloud around the thunderbolt of Zeus; in art, a shield bordered with serpents carried by Athena. Also, **ægis.**

eg-lan-tine (ĕg′lăn-tīn), *n.* the wild rose or sweetbrier.

e-go (ē′gō; ĕg′ō), *n.* self; personality; as, the *ego* is oneself; the non-*ego*, all that is not oneself.

e-go-ism (ē′gō-ĭzm; ĕg′ō-ĭzm), *n.* the habit of regarding self as the center of everything; selfishness; conceit or vanity.

e-go-ist (ē′gō-ĭst), *n.* one who thinks always of self; a selfish person.—*adj.* **egoistic, egoistical.**

e-go-tism (ē′gō-tĭzm), *n.* the habit of talking or writing too much about oneself; vanity.
Syn. conceit, self-confidence.
Ant. (see modesty).

e-go-tist (ē′gō-tĭst), *n.* one who is full of vanity and talks much of himself, his experiences, and his views.

e-go-tis-tic (ē′gō-tĭs′tĭk), *adj.* characterized by thought of self. Also, **egotistical.**—*adv.* **egotistically.**

e-gre-gious (ē-grē′jŭs), *adj.* unusual; extraordinary; extreme: usually in a bad sense.—*adv.* **egregiously.**

e-gress (ē′grĕs), *n.* exit or departure, as from a building; a means or place of exit.

e-gret (ē′grĕt; ĕg′rĕt), *n.* a kind of heron or wading bird with long neck and legs; a heron's plume, or the aigrette of commerce; the feathery down of seeds. Also, **aigret, aigrette.**

E-gyp-tian (ē-jĭp′shăn), *adj.* of or pertaining to Egypt or its people: *n.* a native of Egypt; the language of the ancient Egyptians.

E-gyp-tol-o-gy (ē′jĭp-tŏl′ō-jĭ), *n.* the science or study of Egyptian relics and writings.

eh (ā; ĕ), *interj.* what: an exclamation of doubt or inquiry.

ei-der (ī′dẽr), *n.* a large salt-water duck, valued for its downy feathers.

ei-der-down (ī′dẽr-doun′), *n.* the soft breast feathers of the eider duck, used in pillows, coverlets, etc.

Elder Duck

eight (āt), *adj.* one more than seven: *n.* the number consisting of seven plus one; a sign representing eight units, as 8 or viii.

eight-een (ā′tēn′; ā′tēn′), *adj.* twice nine; eight plus ten: *n.* the number consisting of seventeen and one; a sign representing eighteen units, as 18 or xviii.

eight-een-mo (ā′tēn′mō), *n.* a book whose sheets are folded into eighteen leaves. Also, **18mo, octodecimo.**

eight-eenth (ā′tēnth′; ā′tēnth′), *adj.* next in order after seventeenth: *n.* the ordinal of eighteen; one of eighteen equal parts into which a thing may be divided.

eighth (ātth), *adj.* next in order after seventh: *n.* the ordinal of eight; one of eight equal parts into which anything may be divided; in music, a note of one-eighth the value of a whole note.

eight-y (ā′tĭ), *adj.* eight times ten; fourscore: *n.* the number consisting of the sum of eight tens; a sign representing eighty units, as 80 or lxxx.

ei-ther (ē′*th*ẽr; ī′*th*ẽr), *adj.* one or the other of two: *pron.* one of two: *conj.* the correlative of *or;* in one of two cases.

e-jac-u-late (ē-jăk′ū-lāt), *v.t.* to speak out suddenly; as, to *ejaculate* a wish or a prayer: *v.i.* to utter brief exclamations.

e-jac-u-la-tion (ē-jăk′ū-lā′shŭn), *n.* the act of speaking suddenly and briefly; an exclamation.

e-jac-u-la-to-ry (ē-jăk′ū-lȧ-tō-rĭ), *adj.* spoken suddenly or sharply.

e-ject (ē-jĕkt′), *v.t.* to cast forth; dismiss from office; evict or turn out; as, to *eject* a tenant.

e-jec-tion (ē-jĕk′shŭn), *n.* a driving forth; expulsion; dismissal.

e-ject-ment (ē-jĕkt′mĕnt), *n.* the act of casting out; a legal action for the recovery of lands, etc.

eke (ēk), *v.t.* to extend or lengthen; make barely enough; as, to *eke* out a living: with *out.*

e-lab-o-rate (ē-lăb′ō-rāt), *v.t.* to produce with labor; to work out with great care; improve or refine with

or labor: *adj.* (ĕ-lăb′ō-rāt), highly
l; complicated.—*adv.* **elaborately.**—*n.*
ɩteness.

ɔ-o-ra-tion (ĕ-lăb″ō-rā′shŭn), *n.* quality of being
, out with care; a high state of polish or
ion; as, *elaboration* in style; *elaboration*
s; a varied development on a single

ɩ (ā′läɴ′), *n.* dash; ardor; enthusiasm;
ɩ as, the soldiers went into the battle
eat *élan.* [Fr.]

ɩd (ē′lănd), *n.* a large antelope or goat-like animal with twisted horns.

ɔse (ĕ-lăps′), *v.i.* to slip or glide away; as, a long time has *elapsed* since then.

ɩ-tic (ĕ-lăs′tĭk), *adj.* springing back; having the power of returning to
ginal form; rebounding; springy; capa-
extension: *n.* an elastic woven cloth
n part of India rubber.—*adv.* **elastically.**

ɩ-tic-i-ty (ĕ-lăs-tĭs′ĭ-tĭ), *n.* the quality of being springy; power
ing back after being stretched; ability
ɔver from depression or gloom.

ɩ-tic tis-sue (ĕ-lăs′tĭk tĭsh′ū), elastic light-yellow tissue
ligaments, or tissues, of the vertebræ,
ɩal column.

ːe (ĕ-lāt′), *v.t.* to raise the spirits of; cause to feel happy; excite; puff up.

·tion (ē-lā′shŭn), *n.* a happy state of mind; joyful excitement.

ɔw (ĕl′bō), *n.* the joint or bend of the arm; a pipe connection bent or
l like a human elbow: *v.t.* to thrust on
de: *v.i.* to jut or project into an angle;
or curve abruptly, as a stream; push
way rudely; as, to *elbow* through a crowd.

er (ĕl′dĕr), *adj.* older; prior in time, origin, or appointment: *n.* one older
, rank, or station; a member of the Jew-
ɩnhedrim or supreme court of ancient
ɩlem: in certain Protestant churches, a
ɩing officer, or minister; a shrub or tree
ɩ spongy pith and purple berries.

er-ber-ry (ĕl′dĕr-bĕr″ĭ), *n.* the fruit of the common elder tree.

er-ly (ĕl′dĕr-lĭ), *adj.* somewhat old; as, an *elderly* man.

est (ĕl′dĕst), *adj.* oldest; first-born; as, the *eldest* son.

ɔo-ra-do (ĕl dō-rä′dō), an imaginary country in South America,
rich in gold and precious stones; any
or business full of money-making oppor-
ɔs.

ct (ĕ-lĕkt′), *v.t.* to choose for any office or use; choose by ballot; select
ɩ number: *adj.* chosen for office but not
ɩ charge; as, the president *elect;* taken
ference: *n.* those chosen to eternal life
vine sovereignty.

c-tion (ĕ-lĕk′shŭn), *n.* the act of choosing a person for some
or position by show of hands, or ballot;
lection by divine sovereignty of certain
duals to eternal life.

c-tion-eer (ĕ-lĕk″shŭn-ēr′), *v.i.* to canvas for votes; to
y or use means for influencing the choice
official by vote.

c-tive (ĕ-lĕk′tĭv), *adj.* appointed or governed by choice; using the
of choice: *n.* one of several courses
l by a school or college among which a
it may choose.

c-tor (ĕ-lĕk′tĕr), *n.* one lawfully able to vote: a member of the
l States electoral college, or body of men chosen every four years to vote for a president; one of the German princes who formerly held the power of choosing the emperor.—*adj.* **electoral.**

e-lec-to-ral col-lege (ĕ-lĕk′tō-răl kŏl′ĕj), a body of citizens elected by the voters of every State to choose a president of the United States.

e-lec-to-rate (ĕ-lĕk′tō-rāt), *n.* the whole body of persons entitled to vote; the dignity or territory of a prince of the old German empire.

e-lec-tric (ĕ-lĕk′trĭk), *adj.* relating to, containing, generated by, or produced by, electricity: electric eel, a fish found in Brazil having an eel-like body, and the power of giving an electric shock. Also, **electrical.**—*adv.* **electrically.**

Electric Eel

e-lec-tri-cian (ĕ-lĕk-trĭsh′ăn), *n.* one who is skilled in the science of electricity; an inventor or maker of electrical appliances.

e-lec-tric-i-ty (ĕ-lĕk-trĭs′ĭ-tĭ), *n.* an invisible force, or substance, producing light, heat, and other physical effects; the science of the laws of this force, or substance.

e-lec-tri-fi-ca-tion (ĕ-lĕk″trĭ-fĭ-kā′shŭn), *n.* the act of charging with electricity; the state of being so charged.

e-lec-tri-fy (ĕ-lĕk′trĭ-fī), *v.t.* [*p.t.* and *p.p.* electrified, *p.pr.* electrifying]. to charge with, or act upon, by electricity; pass an electric current through; to fit for using electric power, as a railway; to thrill.

e-lec-tro- (ĕ-lĕk′trō-), a *prefix* denoting the use of, or pertaining to, electricity as the motive power, or operating agent: used in many words, the meaning of which is self-evident; as, *electro*-engrave, *electro*gild, etc.

e-lec-tro-cul-ture (ĕ-lĕk″trō - kŭl′tūr), *n.* the process of hastening the growth of crops by means of electricity.

e-lec-tro-cute (ĕ-lĕk′trō-kūt), *v.t.* to put to death by an electric current, as a criminal.

e-lec-tro-cu-tion (ĕ-lĕk″trō-kū′shŭn), *n.* the act of putting to death by means of an electric current.

e-lec-trode (ĕ-lĕk′trōd), *n.* either end or pole of an electric battery, dynamo, or any source of electricity.

e-lec-tro-dy-nam-ics (ĕ-lĕk″trō-dī-năm′ĭks; ĕ-lĕk″trō-dĭ-năm′ĭks), *n.* the science or study of electric currents and their action on one another.

e-lec-tro-dy-na-mom-e-ter (ĕ-lĕk″trō-dī″nȧ-mŏm′ē-tĕr), *n.* an instrument for measuring the strength of an electric current.

e-lec-tro-graph (ĕ-lĕk′trō-grȧf), *n.* a machine for preparing copper cylinders used in printing fabrics and wall papers.

e-lec-trog-ra-phy (ĕ-lĕk″trŏg′rȧ-fĭ), *n.* the art of copying fine engravings on copper or steel by means of an electrocopper deposit.

e-lec-tro-ki-net-ics (ē-lĕk'trō-kĭ-nĕt'-ĭks), *n.* the science or study of electric currents, or electricity in motion: opposite to *electrostatics*.

e-lec-tro-lier (ē-lĕk"trō-lēr'), *n.* a metal bracket or fixture for supporting electric lamps.

e-lec-trol-y-sis (ē-lĕk-trŏl'ĭ-sĭs), *n.* the separation of a chemical compound into its several parts by electricity.

Electro-magnet

e-lec-tro-mag-net (ē-lĕk'trō-măg'nĕt), *n.* a core of soft iron magnetized by electricity passing through a coil of wire around it.

e-lec-tro-mo-tive (ē-lĕk"trō-mō'tĭv), *adj.* producing an electric current; pertaining to an electric current or electricity.

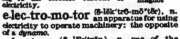

e-lec-tro-mo-tor (ē-lĕk'trō-mō"tẽr), *n.* an apparatus for using electricity to operate machinery: the opposite of a *dynamo*.

e-lec-tron (ē-lĕk'trŏn), *n.* one of the components of atoms; the smallest known component of matter; an electrical unit.

e-lec-tro-plate (ē-lĕk'trō-plāt"), *v.t.* to cover with metal by means of an electric current: *n.* an article thus coated: generally applied to silver plate.

e-lec-tro-scope (ē-lĕk'trō-skōp), *n.* an instrument for finding the presence of electricity.

e-lec-tro-type (ē-lĕk'trō-tīp), *n.* a metal copy of any plate or cut for printing, made by covering a wax mold of the original with copper by the action of electricity.

el-ee-mos-y-na-ry (ĕl"ē-mŏs'ĭ-nā-rĭ), *adj.* pertaining to alms; devoted to charitable purposes; dependent upon charity: *n.* one who lives on alms.

el-e-gance (ĕl'ē-găns), *n.* [*pl.* elegances (-găn-sĕz)], beauty resulting from perfect propriety; studied refinement.

el-e-gant (ĕl'ē-gănt), *adj.* luxurious; fastidious; tasteful; free from coarseness: often suggesting that the person or thing to which it is applied has a somewhat studied or artificial beauty.—*adv.* elegantly.

el-e-gi-ac (ē-lē'jĭ-ăk; ĕl"ē-jī'ăk), *adj.* plaintive; mournful: *n.* a song expressing sorrow; a funeral song.

el-e-gy (ĕl'ē-jĭ), *n.* [*pl.* elegies (-jĭz)], a mournful song or poem; dirge.

el-e-ment (ĕl'ē-mĕnt), *n.* a first or main principle; one of the main parts of the physical world, as fire, water, air, etc.; natural environment, or life with which one is familiar; as, he is out of his *element*; ingredient; in chemistry, a substance which cannot be separated into other substances: *pl.* the letters or sounds of the alphabet; the first steps in any branch of knowledge or art; the sacramental bread and wine.

el-e-men-tal (ĕl"ē-mĕn'tăl), *adj.* relating to, or characteristic of, the natural world; having to do with first principles; forming a necessary part of something; fundamental; simple.—*adv.* elementally.

el-e-men-ta-ry (ĕl"ē-mĕn'tȧ-rĭ), *adj.* pertaining to first principles; introductory; as, an *elementary* education.

African Elephant

el-e-phant (ĕl'ē-fănt), *n.* a large animal with a flexible trunk and large tusks: the largest of existing land animals.

el-e-phan-ti-a-sis (ĕl"ē-făn-tī'ȧ-sĭs), *n.* a disease resembling leprosy.

el-e-phan-tine (ĕl"ē-făn'tĭn; ĕl"ē-făn'-tīn), *adj.* unduly large; huge; unwieldy; clumsy; resembling an elephant.

el-e-vate (ĕl'ē-vāt), *v.t.* to raise from a lower to a higher position; ennoble; animate; inspire; raise by training or education.—*adj.* elevated.

el-e-va-tion (ĕl"ē-vā'shŭn), *n.* the act of raising; the state of being raised; a sketch plan of the front or principal side of a building; the height of a heavenly body above the earth.

el-e-va-tor (ĕl'ē-vā"tẽr), *n.* that which raises up or exalts; a hoisting machine or lift; a cage moving up and down in a shaft, to carry people or goods from one level to another; a warehouse for the storage of grain; a hinged wing or plane of an airplane, etc., for controlling its position in the air.

e-lev-en (ē-lĕv'n), *adj.* ten plus one: *n.* the sum of ten plus one; a sign representing eleven units, as 11 or xi; a team in cricket or football.

e-lev-enth (ē-lĕv'nth), *adj.* next after tenth: *n.* the ordinal of eleven; one of eleven equal parts into which a thing may be divided.

elf (ĕlf), *n.* [*pl.* elves (ĕlvz)], a tiny, mischievous sprite supposed to haunt hills and wild places; a dwarf; fairy; goblin.

elf child (ĕlf chīld), a child believed to have been left by the fairies in the place of one stolen by them; a changeling.

elf-in (ĕl'fĭn), *n.* a child of fairyland; a sportive child: *adj.* pertaining to sprites or goblins.

elf fire (ĕlf fīr), the will-o'-the-wisp: often supposed to be caused by the elves.

elf-ish (ĕl'fĭsh), *adj.* resembling, or caused by, a sprite or goblin; impish; mischievous.—*adv.* elfishly.

elf-lock (ĕlf'lŏk"), *n.* a knot of hair twisted in an intricate manner, as if by fairies; disheveled or unusually tangled hair.

e-lic-it (ē-lĭs'ĭt), *v.t.* to draw out; as, to *elicit* a reply.

e-lide (ē-līd'), *v.t.* to slur over, or cut off, as a final vowel.

el-i-gi-bil-i-ty (ĕl"ĭ-jĭ-bĭl'ĭ-tĭ), *n.* the quality of being worthy to be chosen; suitableness.

el-i-gi-ble (ĕl'ĭ-jĭ-bl), *adj.* capable of being, or fit to be, chosen; desirable; as, an *eligible* tenant; legally qualified for election or appointment.—*adv.* eligibly.

E-li-jah (ē-lī'jȧ), *n.* in the Bible, one of the greatest of the Hebrew prophets, told of in the books of First and Second Kings.

e-lim-i-nate (ē-lĭm'ĭ-nāt), *v.t.* to leave out of consideration, or to cast aside; to remove (an unknown quantity).—*n.* **elimination.**

Syn. expel, eject, oust, dislodge, banish.

E-li-sha (ē-lī'shȧ), *n.* in the Bible, a great Hebrew prophet, disciple and successor of Elijah, told of in the books of First and Second Kings.

e-li-sion (ē-lĭzh'ŭn), *n.* the cutting off of a vowel or syllable for the sake of euphony, as I'll for I will.

é-lite (ā'lēt'), *n.* the best part; the choicest part, as of society, a profession, an army, etc. [Fr.]

e-lix-ir (ē-lĭk'sẽr), *n.* a tincture, essence, or cordial; an imaginary liquid for prolonging life indefinitely, or for changing baser metals, such as iron, into gold.

Elk

E-liz-a-be-than (ē-lĭz'ȧ-bē'thăn; ē-lĭz'ȧ-bĕth'ăn), *adj.* pertaining to the times of Queen Elizabeth, or the latter half of the 16th century.

elk (ĕlk), *n.* a very large deer of North America and northern Europe; the moose-deer; the largest member of the deer family.

ell (ĕl), *n.* an addition to or wing of a house, giving it the shape of the letter L; a right-angle joint of pipe; a measure formerly used in measuring cloth, in England about forty-five inches.

el-lipse (ē-lĭps'), *n.* a curve that is longer than it is wide; one of the conic sections, or curves formed by cutting a cone.

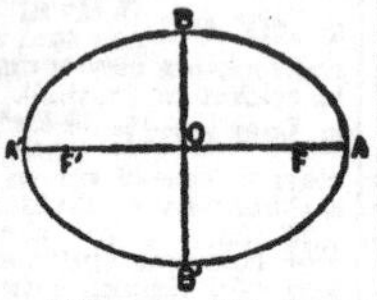

Ellipse. *A'A*, long axis; *B'B*, short axis; *F'F*, foci; *O*, center.

el-lip-sis (ē-lĭp'sĭs), *n.* the omission of a word or words needed in the grammatical structure of a sentence, the sense of which is nevertheless clear without the omitted word or words.

To Draw an Ellipse. *A*, *B*, fixed points; *C*, moving point; *A*, *B*, *C*, string.

el-lip-tic (ē-lĭp'tĭk), *adj.* relating to, or formed like, an ellipse; having a part omitted; defective. Also, **elliptical.**

elm (ĕlm), *n.* a shade tree whose hard timber is valuable for many purposes.

el-o-cu-tion (ĕl'ō-kū'shŭn), *n.* the art which teaches the proper use of voice and gesture in public speaking.

el-o-cu-tion-a-ry (ĕl'ō-kū'shŭn-ā-rĭ), *adj.* pertaining to the art of public speaking.

el-o-cu-tion-ist (ĕl'ō-kū'shŭn-ĭst), *n.* one skilled in, or a teacher of, the art of public speaking.

El-o-him (ĕl'ō-hĭm), *n.* one of the Old Testament names of God.

e-lon-gate (ē-lôn'gāt; ē'lôn-gāt), *v.t.* to stretch out; extend; lengthen.

e-lon-ga-tion (ē'lôn-gā'shŭn), *n.* extension; a lengthening.

e-lope (ē-lōp') *v.i.* to escape privately; to run away with a lover.

e-lope-ment (ē-lōp'mĕnt), *n.* the act of running away or escaping, especially with a lover.

el-o-quence (ĕl'ō-kwĕns), *n.* the art of speaking with ease and elegance; the power of exciting emotion, sympathy, or interest in any way.

Syn. oratory, rhetoric, declamation.

el-o-quent (ĕl'ō-kwĕnt), *adj.* having the power of expressing strong emotion in vivid and appropriate speech; as, he was an *eloquent* preacher.—*adv.* **eloquently.**

else (ĕls), *adv.* besides; otherwise; differently: *adj.* and *pron.* other; as, somebody *else*.

else-where (ĕls'hwâr"), *adv.* in another place; as, he is not here; you must look *elsewhere* for him.

e-lu-ci-date (ē-lū'sĭ-dāt), *v.t.* to make clear; explain; illustrate; as, an experiment may *elucidate* a theory.

e-lude (ē-lūd'), *v.t.* to avoid by deceit or cleverness; baffle; shun.

Syn. evade, avoid, escape.

e-lu-sion (ē-lū'zhŭn), *n.* act of escaping or avoiding; evasion.

e-lu-sive (ē-lū'sĭv), *adj.* deceptive; hard to grasp; slippery.—*adv.* **elusively.**

e-lu-so-ry (ē-lū'sō-rĭ), *adj.* likely to escape one's notice; evasive; deceptive.

e-lu-tion (ē-lū'shŭn), *n.* the removal or separation of impurities by washing, as in sugar refining.

elves (ĕlvz), *n.* plural of *elf;* as, the old folk tales tell of both friendly and mischievous *elves*.

E-ly-sian (ē-lĭzh'ăn; ē-lĭz'ĭ-ăn), *adj.* pertaining to paradise; full of the highest enjoyment, bliss, or happiness.

E-ly-si-um (ē-lĭz'ĭ-ŭm; ē-lĭzh'ĭ-ŭm), *n.* the Greek paradise or abode of the blessed after death: called the *Elysian Fields.*

em (ĕm), *n.* in printing, the square of any size of type, serving as a unit of measurement.

e-ma-ci-ate (ē-mā'shĭ-āt), *v.t.* to cause to lose flesh so as to become very thin: *adj.* (ē-mā'shĭ-āt), very thin or lean.—*n.* **emaciation.**

em-a-nate (ĕm'ȧ-nāt), *v.i.* to flow out, issue or proceed, as from a source; as, light *emanates* from the sun.

em-a-na-tion (ĕm'ȧ-nā'shŭn), *n.* a flowing forth; that which flows forth from a source; as, perfume is an *emanation* from the flower.

e-man-ci-pate (ē-măn'sĭ-pāt), *v.t.* to release from slavery or bondage; set free.—*n.* **emancipator.**

e-man-ci-pa-tion (ē-măn'sĭ-pā'shŭn), *n.* act of setting free; liberation; release; freedom.

e-mas-cu-late (ē-măs'kū-lāt), *v.t.* to weaken: *adj.* (ē-măs'kū-lāt), deprived of vigor.

em-balm (ĕm-bäm'), *v.t.* to preserve from decay by balsams or fragrant spices; keep from putrefaction or decay by antiseptics or preservatives.—*n.* **embalmer.**

em-bank (ĕm-băṅk'), *v.t.* to inclose with, or protect by, a ridge of earth.

em-bank-ment (ĕm-băṅk'mĕnt), *n.* a ridge of earth, stones, etc., for protection or defense.

em-bar-go (ĕm-bär'gō), *n.* a government act restraining vessels from leaving or entering a port, or stopping transportation by railway; any hindrance or restraint on commerce by law.

em-bark (ĕm-bärk'), *v.t.* to put on board ship; venture or invest, as money: *v.i.* to go on board a vessel; engage in any affair; as, to *embark* in a business.—*n.* **embarkation.**

em-bar-rass (ĕm-băr'ăs), *v.t.* to hinder; perplex; disturb by money difficulties; as, lack of funds will *embarrass* the traveler; distress; confuse; mortify.
Syn. entangle, trouble.
Ant. (see assist).

em-bar-rass-ment (ĕm-băr'ăs-mĕnt), *n.* confusion of mind; financial difficulties; mortification.

em-bas-sa-dor (ĕm-băs'ȧ-dēr), *n.* an envoy or minister representing a country at the capital of another. Also, **ambassador.**

em-bas-sy (ĕm'bȧ-sĭ), *n.* [*pl.* embassies (-sĭz)], the public function, mission, or official residence of an ambassador; a legation.

em-bat-tled (ĕm-băt'ld), *p.adj.* furnished with battlements, or walls for defense; drawn up in fighting array.

em-bed (ĕm-bĕd'), *v.t.* to lay in, or as in, a bed; set in surrounding matter; as, to *embed* a thing in clay. Also, **imbed.**

em-bel-lish (ĕm-bĕl'ĭsh), *v.t.* to make beautiful or elegant; set off by ornamentation.
Syn. adorn, decorate, bedeck.
Ant. (see disfigure).

em-ber (ĕm'bēr), *n.* a small live coal smoldering in ashes.

em-ber days (ĕm'bēr dāz), days in each of the four seasons of the year set apart by the Catholic churches for prayer and fasting.

em-bez-zle (ĕm-bĕz'l), *v.t.* to steal something entrusted to one's care.—*n.* **embezzler.**

em-bez-zle-ment (ĕm-bĕz'l-mĕnt), *n.* the dishonest appropriation of property entrusted to one's care.

em-bit-ter (ĕm-bĭt'ēr), *v.t.* to make unhappy; exasperate, or annoy exceedingly. Also, **imbitter.**

em-bla-zon (ĕm-blā'zn), *v.t.* to adorn with heraldic figures, such as the symbols on a coat of arms; blazon; decorate; celebrate the praises of; to display brilliantly.

em-bla-zon-ry (ĕm-blā'zn-rĭ), *n.* [*pl.* emblazonries (-rĭz)], heraldic decoration, as on coats of arms; bright figures on flags, etc.

em-blem (ĕm'blĕm), *n.* a symbolical figure or design; a visible sign of an idea; as, a white robe is an *emblem* of purity; the flag is the *emblem* of the nation.
Syn. sign, figure, image, symbol.

em-blem-at-ic (ĕm"blĕm-ăt'ĭk), *adj.* symbolic or symbolical. Also, **emblematical.**—*adv.* **emblematically.**

em-bod-i-ment (ĕm-bŏd'ĭ-mĕnt), *n.* the act of uniting as a whole; a concentrating into one body; a summing up in, or putting into, bodily form; as, she is the *embodiment* of virtue.

em-bod-y (ĕm-bŏd'ĭ), *v.t.* [*p.t.* and *p.p.* embodied, *p.pr.* embodying], to give bodily form to; to express in a concrete form; as, to *embody* thought in words; to collect into a united whole; as, to *embody* troops. Also, **imbody.**

em-bold-en (ĕm-bōl'dn), *v.t.* to make brave; to encourage.
Syn. inspirit, animate, cheer, urge, impel, stimulate.
Ant. (see discourage).

em-boss (ĕm-bŏs'), *v.t.* to ornament with raised work; raise in relief from the surface.

em-boss-ing (ĕm-bŏs'ĭng), *n.* the art of producing raised figures or designs in relief on surfaces, as on the cover of a book.

em-bow-er (ĕm-bou'ēr), *v.t.* to cover with, or as with, a roof of flowers, vines, etc.; as, a cottage *embowered* with roses: *v.i.* to rest, as under a roof of flowers. Also, **imbower.**

em-brace (ĕm-brās'), *v.t.* to hold in the arms, or press to the bosom with affection; hug; cling to; receive with willingness; include; inclose: *v.i.* to join in an embrace: *n.* the act of embracing; a clasping in the arms; a hug.

Embrasure. *A*, merlons; *B*, genouillère; *C*, cheeks.

em-bra-sure (ĕm-brā'zhŭr), *n.* an opening in a wall or fort from which to fire guns; a window or door having its sides slanted on the inside.

em-bro-cate (ĕm'brō-kāt), *v.t.* to moisten and rub (an injured or bruised part of the body) with liquid substance or liniment.—*n.* **embrocation.**

em-broid-er (ĕm-broid'ēr), *v.t.* to decorate or make beautiful with needlework.

em-broid-er-y (ĕm-broid'ēr-ĭ), *n.* [*pl.* embroideries (-ĭz)], ornamental work of gold, silver, silk, etc., done with the needle.

em-broil (ĕm-broil'), *v.t.* to disturb; confuse; involve in contention; mix up; entangle.—*n.* **embroilment.**

em-bry-o (ĕm'brĭ-ō), *n.* [*pl.* embryos (-ōz)], a germ; a rudiment; the first or undeveloped state of anything.

em-bry-ol-o-gy (ĕm"brĭ-ŏl'ō-jĭ), *n.* that part of biology which deals with undeveloped organisms.

em-bry-on-ic (ĕm"brĭ-ŏn'ĭk), *adj.* crude; not fully developed; rudimentary.

e-men-da-tion (ē"mĕn-dā'shŭn; ĕm"ĕn-dā'shŭn), *n.* the alteration or correction of a text, so as to give an improved reading.

e-men-da-tor (ē'mĕn-dā"tēr; ĕm'ĕn-dā"-tēr), *n.* one who corrects or improves the text of a work.

em-er-ald (ĕm'ēr-ăld), *n.* a precious stone of a rich, deep green color; a size of printer's type: *adj.* of a color like that of the emerald.

e-merge (ē-mûrj'), *v.i.* to rise up or come forth from anything which conceals; become apparent or visible; as, the sun *emerges* from behind a cloud.

e-mer-gen-cy (ē-mûr'jĕn-sĭ), *n.* [*pl.* emergencies (-sĭz)], a sudden or unexpected happening; pressing necessity; crisis: *adj.* pertaining to, or used in, a crisis requiring rapid action; as, an *emergency* brake.

e-mer-i-tus (ē-mĕr'ĭ-tŭs), *adj.* retired from service with honor: said of a college professor or clergyman.

e-mer-sion (ē-mûr'shŭn), *n.* the act of coming forth or rising out of;

the reappearance of a heavenly body after an eclipse.

em-er-y (ĕm'ẽr-ĭ), *n.* a very hard mineral substance, used when powdered for grinding or polishing.

e-met-ic (ē-mĕt'ĭk), *adj.* inducing vomiting: *n.* a medicine that induces vomiting.

e-meu (ē'mū), *n.* a large Australian ostrichlike bird. Also, **emu.**

em-i-grant (ĕm'ĭ-grănt), *n.* one who leaves his own country to settle in another: *adj.* moving from one country to another; pertaining to, or used by, people leaving their own country.

em-i-grate (ĕm'ĭ-grāt), *v.i.* to leave one's country to settle in another.

em-i-nence (ĕm'ĭ-nĕns), *n.* that which is lofty; elevation; height; exalted rank, station, celebrity, or repute; as, to attain *eminence* in a profession: **Eminence,** a title given to cardinals. Also, **eminency.**

em-i-nent (ĕm'ĭ-nĕnt), *adj.* high in office, rank, or reputation; distinguished; exalted.—*adv.* **eminently.**

Syn. conspicuous, noted, prominent, renowned, famous, glorious, illustrious.

Ant. (see obscure, unknown).

e-mir (ē-mēr'; ē'mẽr), *n.* a prince; a title of dignity given in Arabia, Turkey, and other Mohammedan countries to a prince or chieftain. Also, **ameer, amir.**

em-is-sa-ry (ĕm'ĭ-sā-rĭ), *n.* [*pl.* emissaries (-rĭz)] a person or agent sent on a mission, especially of a secret nature.

e-mis-sion (ē-mĭsh'ŭn), *n.* the act of sending out; a throwing out; as, the *emission* of heat from a fire; *emission* of smoke from chimneys; the amount issued at one time; as, an *emission* of bank notes.

e-mis-sive (ē-mĭs'ĭv), *adj.* sending out; throwing out.

e-mit (ē-mĭt'), *v.t.* [*p.t.* and *p.p.* emitted, *p.pr.* emitting], to send or give forth; to throw out; issue, and send into circulation, as bank notes.

Syn. exhale, discharge, vent.

e-mol-lient (ē-mŏl'yĕnt; ē-mŏl'ĭ-ĕnt), *adj.* softening; lubricating: *n.* a medicine that has a softening effect on living tissues.

e-mol-u-ment (ē-mŏl'ū-mĕnt), *n.* profit, wages; salary; income; gain.

e-mo-tion (ē-mō'shŭn), *n.* mental agitation; intense feelings of love, hate, joy, awe, grief, etc.

Syn. feeling, passion, sensation.

e-mo-tion-al (ē-mō'shŭn-ăl), *adj.* excitable; easily moved or agitated; tending to stir the feelings.—*adv.* **emotionally.**—*n.* **emotionalism.**

em-pen-nage (ĕm'pĕ-nŏzh'), *n.* a stabilizing tail to an airplane or dirigible balloon. [FR.]

em-per-or (ĕm'pẽr-ẽr), *n.* the sovereign or supreme ruler of an empire.

em-pha-sis (ĕm'fá-sĭs), *n.* a particular stress of the voice on a word or words in reading or speaking; special force of language or thought.

em-pha-size (ĕm'fá-sīz), *v.t.* to pronounce clearly and positively; to declare forcibly; to stress.

em-phat-ic (ĕm-făt'ĭk), *adj.* expressive; earnest; striking; marked by stress of voice.—*adv.* **emphatically.**

em-pire (ĕm'pīr), *n.* the region ruled over by an emperor or sovereign: supreme power or dominion; imperial rule or sovereignty; sway; control.

em-pir-ic (ĕm-pĭr'ĭk), *n.* one whose methods are purely experimental: *adj.* given to or guided by experience; experimental; practiced from mere experience without accurate knowledge, especially in medicine. Also, **empirical.**—*adv.* **empirically.**

em-pir-i-cism (ĕm-pĭr'ĭ-sĭzm), *n.* knowledge based on observation or practical experience; the practice of medicine without the usual medical training or experience; quackery.

em-place-ment (ĕm-plās'mĕnt), *n.* the position of guns within a fortification; a position built to hold a machine gun in trench warfare.

em-ploy (ĕm-ploi'), *v.t.* [*p.t.* and *p.p.* employed, *p.pr.* employing], to give occupation to; keep busy; exercise; make use of; apply or devote to an object; as, to *employ* one's time in reading: *n.* occupation.

Syn., v. occupy, busy, engross.

em-ploy-ee (ĕm-ploi-ē'), *n.* one who works for another. Also, **employé.**

em-ploy-er (ĕm-ploi'ẽr), *n.* a person engaging or keeping others in service.

em-ploy-ment (ĕm-ploi'mĕnt), *n.* business; occupation.

Syn. avocation, engagement, trade.

em-po-ri-um (ĕm-pō'rĭ-ŭm), *n.* a commercial center or place of trade; a large shop or store.

em-pow-er (ĕm-pou'ẽr), *v.t.* to give authority to; authorize, as by law; to impart force to; enable.

em-press (ĕm'prĕs), *n.* a woman who rules over an empire; the consort or widow of an emperor.

emp-ti-ness (ĕmp'tĭ-nĕs), *n.* the state of being without contents; want of knowledge or sense.

emp-ty (ĕmp'tĭ), *adj.* [*comp.* emptier, *superl.* emptiest], containing nothing; vague; unsatisfactory; as, *empty* dreams; destitute of, or lacking in, force, knowledge, or sense; as, *empty* words; fasting; hungry; vacant: *v.t.* [*p.t.* and *p.p.* emptied, *p.pr.* emptying], to deprive of the contents; pour out; discharge; make vacant: *v.i.* to become empty; discharge itself.—*adv.* **emptily.**

em-py-re-an (ĕm'pĭ-rē'ăn), *adj.* pertaining to the highest and purest region of heaven, or the region of pure fire; ethereal. Also, **empyreal.**

Emu

e-mu (ē'mū), *n.* a large Australian ostrichlike bird. Also, **emeu.**

em-u-late (ĕm'ū-lāt), *v.t.* to strive to equal or excel; as, to *emulate* the conduct of another; vie with; rival.—*adj.* **emulative.**

em-u-la-tion (ĕm'ū-lā'shŭn), *n.* rivalry; competition; effort to excel another.

em-u-lous (ĕm'ū-lŭs), *adj.* desirous to excel; rivaling; competitive.

e-mul-sion (ē-mŭl'shŭn), *n.* a liquid mixture in which a fatty substance is suspended in minute globules, as, an *emulsion* of cod-liver oil; a mixture used in the preparation of dry photographic plates.—*v.t.* **emulsify.**

en-a-ble (ĕn-ā'bl), *v.t.* to make capable; furnish with adequate or sufficient means or power; empower.

en-act (ĕn-ăkt′), *v.t.* to decree; make into law; act the part of.

en-act-ing clause (ĕn-ăkt′ĭng klôz), the first clause in a bill, usually beginning *be it enacted:* a common means of defeating a bill is to vote to strike out the *enacting clause*, which, if successful, carries all the rest with it.

en-act-ment (ĕn-ăkt′mĕnt), *n.* a statute or law; the passing of a bill into law.

en-am-el (ĕn-ăm′ĕl), *n.* a hard, glassy substance used in coating the surface of metals or porcelain, and afterwards fired; anything covered with such a coat; the dense white outer substance of the teeth: *v.t.* [*p.t.* and *p.p.* enameled, *p.pr.* enameling], to lay on, cover, or decorate with enamel; adorn with various hues: *v.i.* to practice the art of enameling.

en-am-or (ĕn-ăm′ẽr), *v.t.* to inflame with love; to captivate; to charm. Also, **enamour.**

en-camp (ĕn-kămp′), *v.i.* to settle in temporary quarters consisting of tents or huts; as, a company of soldiers *encamped* in the field: *v.t.* to put into temporary quarters; as, to *encamp* an army.

en-camp-ment (ĕn-kămp′mĕnt), *n.* a temporary resting place for an army or company of travelers.

en-chain (ĕn-chān′), *v.t.* to bind with fetters, etc.; to hold tightly; to captivate.

en-chant (ĕn-chȧnt′), *v.t.* to charm or subdue, as by spells or sorcery; bewitch; fill with delight.

en-chant-er (ĕn-chȧnt′ẽr), *n.* [*fem.* enchantress], one who uses magic, sorcery, or witchcraft; one who charms.

en-chant-ing (ĕn-chȧnt′ĭng), *p.adj.* charming; bewitching; delightful.—*adv.* **enchantingly.**

en-chant-ment (ĕn-chȧnt′mĕnt), *n.* the use or practice of magic, sorcery, charms, etc.; the state of being enchanted or charmed; rapture.

en-cir-cle (ĕn-sûr′kl), *v.t.* to surround; enclasp; embrace.

en-close (ĕn-klōz′), *v.t.* to insert within; to surround with a barrier.—*n.* **enclosure.** Also, **inclose, inclosure.**

en-co-mi-um (ĕn-kō′mĭ-ŭm), *n.* [*pl.* encomiums (-ŭmz)], formal praise; eulogy.

en-com-pass (ĕn-kŭm′pȧs), *v.t.* to surround; encircle; gird; beset.—*n.* **encompassment.**

en-core (äṅ′kōr′; äṅ′kōr′), *adv.* once more; again: *n.* a repetition in response to a call by an audience: *v.t.* to call for a repetition of (any part of a performance). [Fr.]

en-coun-ter (ĕn-koun′tẽr), *v.t.* to come upon suddenly; meet face to face: *v.i.* to come into collision with someone or something; meet someone in combat: *n.* a sudden or accidental meeting; conflict.

Syn., *n.* attack, assault, onset, engagement, battle, action.

en-cour-age (ĕn-kûr′āj), *v.t.* to give courage to; inspire with courage; stimulate.

Syn. countenance, sanction, support, cherish, inspirit.

en-cour-age-ment (ĕn-kûr′āj-mĕnt), *n.* the act of inspiring with confidence; that which incites to action or perseverance; an incentive or inducement.

en-cour-ag-ing (ĕn-kûr′āj-ĭng), *p.adj.* giving hope; urging to bravery.—*adv.* **encouragingly.**

en-croach (ĕn-krōch′), *v.i.* to invade another's rights by stealth; infringe upon or restrict another's right; enter, intrude, or trespass upon the property of some other person: usually with *on* or *upon*.

en-croach-ment (ĕn-krōch′mĕnt), *n.* intrusion; infringement; trespass.

en-crust (ĕn-krŭst′), *v.t.* to cover with a hard coat. Also, **incrust.**

en-cum-ber (ĕn-kŭm′bẽr), *v.t.* to impede or hinder; retard; clog; obstruct; load with debt; as, to *encumber* an estate with mortgages. Also, **incumber.**

en-cum-brance (ĕn-kŭm′brăns), *n.* that which burdens; a lien or liability attached to real property. Also, **incumbrance.**

en-cyc-li-cal (ĕn-sĭk′lĭ-kăl; ĕn-sī′klĭ-kăl), *adj.* sent to all members of a class or community; intended for general circulation: *n.* a circular letter sent by the Pope to the bishops, treating of topics of general church interest. Also, **encyclic.**

en-cy-clo-pe-di-a (ĕn-sī′klō-pē′dĭ-ȧ), *n.* the circle of the arts and sciences; a descriptive dictionary of the arts, sciences, and literature; a summary of the whole field of knowledge. Also, **encyclopædia, cyclopedia, cyclopædia.**

en-cy-clo-pe-dist (ĕn-sī′klō-pē′dĭst), *n.* a compiler of an encyclopedia; one whose studies embrace all branches of knowledge. Also, **encyclopædist.**

end (ĕnd), *n.* the extreme limit or terminal point of anything; purpose in view; design; death; final state; conclusion; issue: *v.t.* to bring to a completion; finish; terminate; destroy: *v.i.* to come to a completion; die.

Syn., *n.* aim, object, purpose, result, conclusion, upshot, close, termination.

en-dan-ger (ĕn-dān′jẽr), *v.t.* to bring into peril; hazard; to expose to loss or injury.

en-dear (ĕn-dēr′), *v.t.* to make beloved; attach to oneself.

en-dear-ment (ĕn-dēr′mĕnt), *n.* an act or utterance that expresses affection; a caress.

en-deav-or (ĕn-dĕv′ẽr), *v.i.* to strive for the attainment of some object; attempt: *n.* an effort or attempt; mental or physical effort towards the attainment of some object. Also, **endeavour.**

Syn., *v.i.* try, essay, strive, aim.

en-dem-ic (ĕn-dĕm′ĭk), *adj.* peculiar to a nation, people, or locality: chiefly applied to diseases.

end-ing (ĕn′dĭng), *n.* result; conclusion; termination.

en-dive (ĕn′dīv; ĕn′dĭv), *n.* an herb of the chicory family whose leaves are used as a salad.

Endive

end-less (ĕnd′lĕs), *adj.* enduring forever; having no termination; continuous because the ends are united.—*adv.* **endlessly.**

en-dorse (ĕn-dôrs′), *v.t.* to authorize; to write on the back of: said of a check or note. Also, **indorse.**

en-dow (ĕn-dou′), *v.t.* to bestow a permanent fund or source of income upon; as, to *endow* a college; equip or furnish with some gift; as, to be *endowed* with beauty, strength, or power.

en-dow-ment (ĕn-dou'mĕnt), *n.* property or a sum of money settled upon an institution or devoted permanently to any cause; the act of making such a settlement; any talent or gift that a person possesses by nature; as, an *endowment* of beauty: *pl.* natural gifts.

en-due (ĕn-dū'), *v.t.* to clothe; invest; assume; furnish with some moral or spiritual gift. Also, **indue.**

en-dur-a-ble (ĕn-dūr'ȧ-bl), *adj.* bearable; tolerable.—*adv.* **endurably.**

en-dur-ance (ĕn-dūr'ăns), *n.* the power of suffering without giving way; continuance; fortitude.

en-dure (ĕn-dūr'), *v.t.* to support without breaking or yielding; put up with; bear with patience: *v.i.* to remain firm, as under suffering; to suffer without giving up.

en-dur-ing (ĕn-dūr'ĭng), *p.adj.* permanent; lasting; long-suffering.

end-ways (ĕnd'wāz"), *adv.* on end; with the end forward or uppermost; lengthwise. Also, **endwise.**

en-e-ma (ĕn'ē-mȧ; ē-nē'mȧ), *n.* [*pl.* enemas (-mȧs)], a liquid injected into the rectum; an internal bath.

en-e-my (ĕn'ē-mĭ), *n.* [*pl.* enemies (-mĭz)], one hostile to another; foe; antagonist; a hostile army.
Syn. adversary, opponent.
Ant. (see friend).

en-er-get-ic (ĕn"ẽr-jĕt'ĭk), *adj.* vigorous in action; forcible; full of life; active.—*adv.* **energetically.**
Syn. industrious, effectual, powerful.
Ant. (see lazy).

en-er-gy (ĕn'ẽr-jĭ), *n.* [*pl.* energies (-jĭz)], capacity for work; power; force; vigor; spirit; animation.—*v.* **energize.**

en-er-vate (ĕn'ẽr-vāt; ē-nûr'vāt), *v.t.* to deprive of nerve, force, or vigor; render effeminate or feeble; debilitate or weaken.—*n.* **enervation.**

en fa-mille (äṅ" fȧ"mē'yē), with one's family; at home; in domestic fashion; informally. [Fr.]

en-fee-ble (ĕn-fē'bl), *v.t.* to weaken; to destroy the force of.

en-fi-lade (ĕn"fĭ-lād'), *n.* the situation of a place or a body of men liable to be raked with shot; a firing along a trench, a line of troops, etc.; a galling fire; *v.t.* to pierce or rake with shot in a straight line.

en-fold (ĕn-fōld'), *v.t.* to cover with folds; to wrap up; inclose; embrace. Also, **infold.**

en-force (ĕn-fōrs'), *v.t.* to urge with energy; to execute with vigor; to compel; to make clear or intelligible.

en-fran-chise (ĕn-frăn'chĭz; ĕn-frăn'-chĭz), *v.t.* to admit to the right of voting in public elections; to liberate or set free; make free of a state, city, or corporation.—*n.* **enfranchisement.**

en-gage (ĕn-gāj'), *v.t.* to pledge or bind by oath or contract; to betroth; to win; as, his smile *engages* every one to him; in machinery, to come into gear with; make liable for a debt; secure for aid or employment; as, to *engage* a workman; encounter in battle; occupy the time or attention of; as, to *engage* one in conversation: *v.i.* to promise or assume an obligation; occupy oneself; as, to *engage* in business; enter a conflict.

en-gaged (ĕn-gājd'), *p.adj.* busy or occupied; affianced or betrothed.

en-gage-ment (ĕn-gāj'mĕnt), *n.* betrothal; occupation; an appointment; in machinery, the state of being in gear; a battle between armies or fleets.

en-gag-ing (ĕn-gāj'ĭng), *p.adj.* winning; pleasing; as, an *engaging* manner.

en-gen-der (ĕn-jĕn'dẽr), *v.t.* to produce; cause; excite: *v.i.* to come into existence.

en-gine (ĕn'jĭn), *n.* anything used to effect a purpose; a machine by which power is applied for the performance of work; an apparatus for converting physical force, as heat, into mechanical power; a skilful mechanical contrivance.

en-gi-neer (ĕn"jĭ-nēr'), *n.* one who is skilled in the principles or practice of any branch of mechanical science; one who has charge of and manages an engine or locomotive; one of an army corps which builds bridges, roads, etc., for military use; one who carries through a scheme or undertaking: *v.t.* to plan, lay out, or direct; plan and execute the construction of (a road, canal, etc).

en-gi-neer-ing (ĕn"jĭ-nēr'ĭng), *n.* the science and art of constructing and using machinery, or of designing and constructing public works; skilful or tactful management.

Eng-lish (ĭṅ'glĭsh), *adj.* belonging to, characteristic of, or pertaining to, the language or the people of England, or those descended from them: *n.* the people of England or the language spoken by them, a size of printer's type.—*n.* **Englishman.**

en-grail-ment (ĕn-grāl'mĕnt), *n.* a ring of dots around the edge of a coin or medal.

en-grave (ĕn-grāv'), *v.t.* to cut or carve in sunken patterns; as, to *engrave* words on a monument; impress deeply or indelibly; imprint.—*n.* **engraver.**

en-grav-ing (ĕn-grāv'ĭng), *n.* the act, process, or art of producing designs, etc., cut in, or in relief on, metal, stone, or hard wood; a design or inscription so cut; an impression from an engraved plate; as, the *engraving* on visiting cards.

en-gross (ĕn-grōs'), *v.t.* to monopolize; to occupy wholly; as, business *engrosses* his attention; write in a large distinct round hand, as a public document; to make larger.
Syn. absorb, occupy, engage.

en-gulf (ĕn-gŭlf'), *v.t.* to swallow up in, or as in, a deep hollow or whirlpool. Also, **ingulf.**
Syn. absorb, drown, submerge, bury.

en-hance (ĕn-hȧns'), *v.t.* to increase or advance, as in attractiveness or value; to heighten.—*n.* **enhancement.**

en-har-mon-ic (ĕn-här-mŏn'ĭk), *adj.* proceeding by smaller intervals than a semitone. Also, **enharmonical.**—*adv.* **enharmonically.**

en-har-mon-ic scale (ĕn-här-mŏn'ĭk skāl), a musical scale having more than twelve tones to the octave.

e-nig-ma (ē-nĭg'mȧ), *n.* a riddle; anything that puzzles or baffles.

e-nig-mat-ic (ē"nĭg-măt'ĭk), *adj.* obscure or puzzling. Also, **enigmatical.**—*adv.* **enigmatically.**

en-join (ĕn-join'), *v.t.* to direct with authority or urgency; enforce; prohibit or restrain by judicial order.
Syn. order, ordain, appoint, prescribe.

en-joy (ĕn-joi'), *v.t.* to feel or perceive with pleasure; have the use or possession of.—*adj.* **enjoyable.**—*adv.* **enjoyably.**

en-joy-ment (ĕn-joi'mĕnt), *n.* pleasure; gratification; possession.

en-kin-dle (ĕn-kĭn'dl), *v.t.* to set on fire; to kindle; to rouse; to excite.

en-large (ĕn-lärj'), *v.t.* to increase in quantity; extend in limits or dimensions; extend to more purposes or uses: *v.i.* to become larger; as, a plant *enlarges* with growth.
Syn. increase, extend, augment, broaden, swell.
Ant. (see diminish).

en-large-ment (ĕn-lärj'mĕnt), *n.* increase in size; growth or development; a photograph reproduced in increased size.

en-light-en (ĕn-līt'n), *v.t.* furnish with increased knowledge; elevate morally or spiritually.—*n.* **enlightenment.**
Syn. illumine, instruct, inform.
Ant. (see befog, becloud).

en-list (ĕn-lĭst'), *v.t.* to enroll, as for military service; register; gain over, or employ in some cause: *v.i.* to engage oneself for military service.—*n.* **enlistment.**

en-liv-en (ĕn-līv'n), *v.t.* to make vigorous, active, or cheerful; to exhilarate; to inspirit.
Syn. cheer, animate, inspire.
Ant. (see sadden, quiet).

en masse (äṅ' mȧs'), collectively; altogether. [Fr.]

en-mi-ty (ĕn'mĭ-tĭ), *n.* [*pl.* enmities (-tĭz)], animosity; hatred; hostility; ill-will.
Syn. maliciousness, unfriendliness.
Ant. (see friendship).

en-no-ble (ĕ-nō'bl; ĕn-nō'bl), *v.t.* to dignify; exalt; make famous or illustrious; to raise to the nobility.

en-nui (äṅ'nwē'), *n.* languor of mind; a wearied state of mind due to lack of interest; boredom; listlessness. [Fr.]

e-nor-mi-ty (ē-nôr'mĭ-tĭ), *n.* [*pl.* enormities (-tĭz)], something outrageous or extremely immoderate; an atrocity; a grave offense.

e-nor-mous (ē-nôr'mŭs), *adj.* excessive; very great; immense; huge; greatly exceeding the normal size, number, etc.—*adv.* **enormously.**

e-nough (ē-nŭf'), *adj.* sufficient: *n.* a sufficiency: *adv.* so as to be sufficient; very: *interj.* stop.
Syn., n. plenty, abundance.
Ant. (see want).

en-quire (ĕn-kwīr'), *v.t.* and *v.i.* to ask or ask about; to examine into. Also, **inquire.**—*n.* **inquirer, enquirer, inquiry, enquiry.**

en-rage (ĕn-rāj'), *v.t.* to make intensely angry; to provoke to fury; exasperate.

en-rail (ĕn-rāl'), *v.t.* to place (a car) upon rails: opposite to *derail.*

en rap-port (äṅ' rȧ'pôr'), in sympathy with. [Fr.]

en-rapt (ĕn-răpt'), *adj.* filled with joy; enraptured; fascinated.

en-rap-ture (ĕn-răp'tūr), *v.t.* to transport or carry away with delight; please intensely; charm.
Syn. enchant, fascinate, captivate, bewitch.
Ant. (see repel).

en-rich (ĕn-rĭch'), *v.t.* to increase the wealth of; to make fertile; to improve; to adorn.

en-roll (ĕn-rōl'), *v.t.* to insert or write down in a register; enlist; record.—*n.* **enrollment.** Also, **enrol, enrolment.**

en route (äṅ' rōōt'), on the way or road. [Fr.]

en-san-guine (ĕn-săṅ'gwĭn), *v.t.* to smear or cover with blood.

en-sconce (ĕn-skŏns'), *v.t.* to fix securely or comfortably; to settle.

en-sem-ble (äṅ'säṅ'bl), *n.* the general appearance or effect; all the parts of a thing together. [Fr.]

en-shrine (ĕn-shrīn'), *v.t.* to place on an altar or in a holy place; keep sacred.

en-shroud (ĕn-shroud'), *v.t.* to cover with, or as with, a shroud; to conceal from observation; as, to *enshroud* one's purpose with mystery.

en-sign (ĕn'sīn), *n.* a flag; badge; (ĕn'sĭn), the lowest rank of commissioned officer in the navy.

en-si-lage (ĕn'sĭ-lāj), *n.* fodder or vegetable produce stored in the green state in a silo.

en-slave (ĕn-slāv'), *v.t.* to bring into bondage; enthrall or deprive of moral liberty or power; as, to be *enslaved* by drink.—*n.* **enslavement.**

en-snare (ĕn-snâr'), *v.t.* to take in, or as in, a trap; take by craft; allure. Also, **insnare.**

en-sue (ĕn-sū'), *v.i.* to follow as a consequence; succeed; come after.

en-tab-la-ture (ĕn-tăb'lȧ-tūr), *n.* the parts of a wall resting on the top of a pillar or column, as the cornice, etc.

en-tail (ĕn-tāl'), *n.* an estate that may be left only to a particular heir or heirs; the act of so restricting the leaving of property: *v.t.* to leave, as money, land, or other property, to a succession of heirs, so that no one of them can give or will it away; to necessitate; induce.

en-tan-gle (ĕn-tăṅ'gl), *v.t.* to involve; ensnare; perplex; bewilder.

en-tan-gle-ment (ĕn-tăṅ'gl-mĕnt), *n.* in the World War, barbed wire strung on steel posts driven in the ground outside a trench for a depth of some ten to forty yards, to make it harder to reach the trenches.

en-tente (äṅ'täṅt'), *n.* an agreement or understanding; as, the *Triple Entente,* the compact between England, France, and Russia in 1907–08. [Fr.]

en-ter (ĕn'tẽr), *v.t.* to go or come into; begin; penetrate; set down in writing; as, the clerk *entered* the account in the journal; join or become a member of; to go into or begin, as a business, etc.; place on the records of a court: *v.i.* to go or come in.

en-ter-ic (ĕn-tĕr'ĭk), *adj.* pertaining to, or situated near, the intestines.

en-ter-prise (ĕn'tẽr-prīz), *n.* an undertaking of importance or risk; boldness; energy and invention.
Syn. undertaking, endeavor, venture, effort.

en-ter-pris-ing (ĕn'tẽr-prīz'ĭng), *adj.* ambitious; adventurous; energetic; progressive.

en-ter-tain (ĕn'tẽr-tān'), *v.t.* to receive and treat hospitably; amuse; keep in the mind; to harbor, as a grudge; take into consideration; as, to *entertain* a proposition: *v.i.* to receive guests hospitably.

en-ter-tain-ing (ĕn'tẽr-tān'ĭng), *p.adj.* amusing; diverting.—*adv.* **entertainingly.**

en-ter-tain-ment (ĕn'tẽr-tān'mĕnt), *n.* hospitality at

table; a feast or banquet; a diverting or amusing performance; amusement.

en-thrall (ĕn-thrôl'), *v.t.* to enslave; bring or hold under some overmastering influence. Also, **enthral.**

en-throne (ĕn-thrōn'), *v.t.* to place on a seat of power; invest or endow with royal power and authority.

en-thu-si-asm (ĕn-thū'zĭ-ăzm), *n.* intense eagerness; ardor of mind; fervent zeal; intense interest, feeling, or emotion.
Syn. devotion, zeal, ardor.
Ant. (see lukewarmness).

en-thu-si-ast (ĕn-thū'zĭ-ăst), *n.* one who is filled with zeal; one who deems himself inspired; a visionary.

en-thu-si-as-tic (ĕn-thū'zĭ-ăs'tĭk), *adj.* ardent; zealous.—*adv.* **enthusiastically.**

en-tice (ĕn-tīs'), *v.t.* to attract or allure; tempt.—*adv.* **enticingly.**—*n.* **enticement.**

en-tire (ĕn-tīr'), *adj.* complete in all parts; whole; undivided or unbroken; consisting of one piece: *n.* the whole.

en-tire-ly (ĕn-tīr'lĭ), *adv.* fully; completely; wholly.

en-tire-ty (ĕn-tīr'tĭ), *n.* completeness; the whole; a complete thing.

en-ti-tle (ĕn-tī'tl), *v.t.* to give a name to; to dignify by a name or designation; to give a right to.

en-ti-ty (ĕn'tĭ-tĭ), *n.* [*pl.* entities (-tĭz)], being; anything that exists, or is supposed to exist.

en-tomb (ĕn-tōōm'), *v.t.* to place in, or as in, a grave; to bury; inter.

en-tomb-ment (ĕn-tōōm'mĕnt), *n.* the act of placing in a grave; burial.

en-to-mol-o-gy (ĕn'tō-mŏl'ō-jĭ), *n.* that branch of zoölogy which treats of insects and their habits.—*n.* **entomologist.**

en-tou-rage (äN'tōō'räzh'), *n.* associates; surroundings; retinue of attendants. [Fr.]

en-trails (ĕn'trālz), *n.pl.* the internal parts of animal bodies.

en-train (ĕn-trān'), *v.t.* and *v.i.* to dispatch or go (as troops) by train.

en-trance (ĕn'trăns), *n.* the act of going in; a door, passage, etc., through which one enters a place; permission to come in, etc.; the entry of a ship, or goods, at the custom house of a port: *v.t.* (ĕn-trăns'), to put into a state of ecstasy or excessive joy; delight; to throw into a trance, or unnatural sleep.—*adv.* **entrancingly.**

en-trap (ĕn-trăp'), *v.t.* to catch; entangle; inveigle; ensnare.

en-treat (ĕn-trēt'), *v.t.* to solicit or ask earnestly; beseech.

en-treat-y (ĕn-trēt'ĭ), *n.* [*pl.* entreaties (-ĭz)], an earnest petition or request; prayer.

en-trée (äN'trā'), *n.* entrance; admission; the act of entering; a dish served between the chief courses. [Fr.]

en-trench (ĕn-trĕnch'), *v.t.* to surround or defend with ditches, earthworks, etc.: *v.i.* to encroach. Also, **intrench.**

en-trench-ment (ĕn-trĕnch'mĕnt), *n.* a breastwork; a system of ditches, earthworks, etc., forming a battle line; any defense or protection; encroachment. Also, **intrenchment.**

en-tre nous (äN'tr nōō), between ourselves; confidentially. [Fr.]

en-trust (ĕn-trŭst'), *v.t.* to place in charge. Also, **intrust.**

en-try (ĕn'trĭ), *n.* [*pl.* entries (-trĭz)], a place for going in; a passage; the act of writing an item in a list or record; the item written in; the act of taking rightful possession of land by entering or setting foot on it; the act of reporting the arrival of a ship in port.

en-twine (ĕn-twīn'), *v.t.* to wind around; twist together.

e-nu-mer-ate (ē-nū'mĕr-āt), *v.t.* to reckon on or name singly; count; go over in detail.

e-nu-mer-a-tion (ē-nū'mĕr-ā'shŭn), *n.* the act of counting; a catalog; list.

e-nun-ci-ate (ē-nŭn'shĭ-āt; ē-nŭn'sĭ-āt), *v.t.* to declare or proclaim; utter; express; speak; pronounce.

e-nun-ci-a-tion (ē-nŭn'sĭ-ā'shŭn; ē-nŭn'shĭ-ā'shŭn), *n.* manner of uttering vocal sounds; articulation; a definite statement.

en-vel-op (ĕn-vĕl'ŭp), *v.t.* to surround with, or as with, a wrapper; to hide; to cover.

en-vel-ope (ĕn'vĕ-lōp; äN'vĕ-lōp), *n.* a paper wrapper, usually gummed, for safe conveyance of a letter by post, etc.; covering; wrapper. Also, **envelop.**

en-vel-op-ment (ĕn-vĕl'ŭp-mĕnt), *n.* the act of surrounding or covering; a wrapper; anything that surrounds or conceals.

en-ven-om (ĕn-vĕn'ŭm), *v.t.* to infuse poison into; to make poisonous; to embitter.

en-vi-a-ble (ĕn'vĭ-ȧ-bl), *adj.* exciting longing; capable of awakening the desire to possess.—*adv.* **enviably.**

en-vi-ous (ĕn'vĭ-ŭs), *adj.* feeling, or characterized by, a desire to possess something; jealously desirous of what is another's.—*adv.* **enviously.**

en-vi-ron (ĕn-vī'rŭn), *v.t.* to surround or inclose; encompass; hem in: *n.pl.* places near a town or city; suburbs.

en-vi-ron-ment (ĕn-vī'rŭn-mĕnt), *n.* the surroundings of one's life; conditions which influence character; as, a wholesome *environment.*

en-voy (ĕn'voi), *n.* a government agent, second in rank to an ambassador; one sent on a special mission, usually abroad.

en-vy (ĕn'vĭ), *v.t.* [*p.t.* and *p.p.* envied, *p.pr.* envying], to grudge; to wish for (what is another's); feel displeasure at (the excellence or prosperity of another); to covet: *v.i.* to feel or exhibit covetousness: *n.* ill-will or displeasure felt because of the excellence or good fortune of another.

E-o-cene (ē'ō-sēn), *adj.* pertaining to the earliest part of the Tertiary geological period, before the development of modern species: *n.* the earliest part of the Tertiary period, following immediately after the Mesozoic era.

E-o-li-an (ē-ō'lĭ-ăn), *adj.* pertaining to the winds: from Æolus, the god of the winds: **eolian harp,** a stringed instrument acted upon by a current of air. Also, **Æolian.**

e-o-lith-ic (ē'ō-lĭth'ĭk), *adj.* pertaining to the earliest part of the stone age.

e-on (ē'ŏn), *n.* a long period of time; age; era; a cycle. Also, **æon.**

E-o-zo-ic (ē'ō-zō'ĭk), *adj.* pertaining to the rocks of the oldest geological era.

ep-au-let (ĕp'ō-lĕt), *n.* a shoulder piece; an ornamental badge worn on the shoulder by naval and military officers. Also, epaulette.

e-phem-er-a (ē-fĕm′ẽr-ȧ), *n.* [*pl.* ephemeras (-rȧz)], that which exists but for a day; a May-fly.

e-phem-er-al (ē-fĕm′ẽr-ăl), *adj.* existing only for a day; short-lived.

E-phe-sians (ē-fē′zhănz), *n.pl.* a book of the New Testament, containing the Epistle or letter of the apostle Paul to the church at Ephesus.

eph-od (ĕf′ŏd), *n.* a priestly vestment or garment worn by the Jewish high priest of ancient times.

eph-or (ĕf′ŏr), *n.* [*pl.* ephori (ĕ-rī), ephors (-ŏrz)], one of the five Spartan magistrates.

ep-ic (ĕp′ĭk), *adj.* grand; noble; heroic; narrative: said of a poem: *n.* a long narrative poem of some heroic deed or event written in a lofty style.

ep-i-cure (ĕp′ĭ-kūr), *n.* a person of luxurious tastes and habits; one who is fond of good living; one devoted to the pursuit of pleasure.

ep-i-cu-re-an (ĕp′ĭ-kū-rē′ăn), *adj.* pertaining to the philosophy of Epicurus; devoted to the pleasures of the table: *n.* one who loves luxury: **Epicurean**, a follower of Epicurus.

ep-i-cy-cle (ĕp′ĭ-sī′kl), *n.* a small circle whose center is on the circumference of a greater circle.

ep-i-dem-ic (ĕp′ĭ-dĕm′ĭk), *adj.* attacking many at the same time: said of a disease: *n.* a general attack of a disease throughout a locality; a widespread occurrence of anything.

ep-i-der-mis (ĕp′ĭ-dûr′mĭs), *n.* the cuticle or outer skin of the body; the outer coating or bark of a plant.

ep-i-gas-tric (ĕp′ĭ-găs′trĭk), *adj.* pertaining to the walls of the abdomen.

ep-i-glot-tis (ĕp′ĭ-glŏt′ĭs), *n.* the leaf-shaped lid of cartilage which covers the larynx or upper part of the windpipe during the act of swallowing.

ep-i-gram (ĕp′ĭ-grăm), *n.* a verse or short poem with a witty point; a short phrase expressing a shrewd or witty thought.

ep-i-gram-mat-ic (ĕp″ĭ-gră-măt′ĭk), *adj.* witty; pointed. Also, **epigrammatical**. — *adv.* **epigrammatically**.

ep-i-graph (ĕp′ĭ-grăf), *n.* an inscription on a building, monument, etc.; a motto or quotation at the beginning of a book or chapter.

ep-i-lep-sy (ĕp′ĭ-lĕp″sĭ), *n.* a chronic nervous disease attended by loss of consciousness and convulsions.

ep-i-lep-tic (ĕp′ĭ-lĕp′tĭk), *adj.* pertaining to, or affected with, epilepsy: *n.* one affected with epilepsy.

ep-i-log (ĕp′ĭ-lŏg), *n.* a poem or speech at the end of a play. Also, **epilogue**.

E-piph-a-ny (ē-pĭf′ȧ-nĭ), *n.* a church festival (Jan. 6) to commemorate the visit of the three wise men to Bethlehem when Christ was born.

e-pis-co-pa-cy (ē-pĭs′kō-pȧ-sĭ), *n.* church government by bishops.

e-pis-co-pal (ē-pĭs′kō-păl), *adj.* pertaining to bishops; having government vested in a bishop.—*adv.* **episcopally**.

E-pis-co-pa-li-an (ē-pĭs″kō-pā′lĭ-ăn), *adj.* pertaining to the Protestant Episcopal Church: *n.* a member or supporter of that church.—*n.* **Episcopalianism**.

e-pis-co-pate (ē-pĭs′kō-pāt), *n.* the position and authority of a bishop; bishopric.

ep-i-sode (ĕp′ĭ-sōd), *n.* an incident or action standing by itself but more or less connected with a series of events; as, an *episode* of the war.—*adj.* **episodic, episodical**.

e-pis-tle (ē-pĭs′l), *n.* a formal letter; a written communication: **Epistle**, one of the letters written by the apostles, and recorded in the New Testament.

e-pis-to-la-ry (ē-pĭs′tō-lā-rĭ), *adj.* pertaining to letters; as, a graceful *epistolary* style.

ep-i-taph (ĕp′ĭ-tăf), *n.* an inscription or writing on a tomb or monument, in memory of the dead.

ep-i-tha-la-mi-um (ĕp″ĭ-thȧ-lā′mĭ-ŭm), *n.* a song or poem in celebration of a marriage.

ep-i-thet (ĕp′ĭ-thĕt), *n.* an adjective or phrase denoting some real quality of the person or thing described; as, a *miserly* man.

e-pit-o-me (ē-pĭt′ō-mē), *n.* a brief statement of the contents of a literary work; a summary or summing up; an abridgment; synopsis.

e-pit-o-mize (ē-pĭt′ō-mīz), *v.t.* to make a brief outline of; to abridge; condense.

ep-i-zo-an (ĕp″ĭ-zō′ăn), *n.* [*pl.* epizoa (-ȧ)], an animal which lives on the outside of another animal, as fleas or lice.

ep-och (ĕp′ŏk; ē′pŏk), *n.* a point of time, marked by events of great importance, from which succeeding years are reckoned; as, the Civil War marks an important *epoch* in American history; a period of years filled with unusual events; era; date.

ep-ode (ĕp′ōd), *n.* the last part of an ode or poem; a burden or refrain in music.

Ep-som salt (ĕp′sŭm sôlt), a white substance used in medicine, dyeing, finishing cotton goods, etc.

e-qua-bil-i-ty (ē″kwȧ-bĭl′ĭ-tĭ; ĕk″wȧ-bĭl′ĭ-tĭ), *n.* evenness; steadiness; as, *equability* of temper.

e-qua-ble (ē′kwȧ-bl; ĕk′wȧ-bl), *adj.* uniform; steady; even; proportionate.—*adv.* **equably**.

e-qual (ē′kwăl), *adj.* of the same extent or magnitude; uniform; adequate; of the same rank, degree, or value; just; equable: *n.* one of the same age, rank, office, talents, etc.: *v.t.* [*p.t.* and *p.p.* equaled, *p.pr.* equaling], to have the same size, rank, value, etc., with; return a full equivalent for; to fulfil the requirements of.

e-qual-i-ty (ē-kwŏl′ĭ-tĭ), *n.* [*pl.* equalities (-tĭz)], the state of being the same in size, rank, value, etc.; uniformity; evenness.

e-qual-ize (ē′kwăl-īz), *v.t.* to make the same in size, rank, value, etc.; render uniform.—*n.* **equalization**.

e-qual-i-zer (ē′kwăl-īz″ẽr), *n.* a sliding panel which stabilizes an airplane laterally.

e-qual-ly (ē′kwăl-ĭ), *adv.* in the same degree; uniformly; in evenly divided parts or shares.

e-qua-nim-i-ty (ē″kwȧ-nĭm′ĭ-tĭ), *n.* evenness of temper or mind; calmness.

e-quate (ē-kwāt'), *v.t.* to reduce to an average; to put into the form of an equation; to make equal.

e-qua-tion (ē-kwā'shŭn; ē-kwā'zhŭn), *n.* in mathematics, a proposition expressing the equality of two quantities, the sign = being placed between them; a representation of a chemical reaction expressed by symbols.

e-qua-tor (ē-kwā'tẽr), *n.* the imaginary circle which passes round the middle of the earth and divides it into two hemispheres or parts; a similar line dividing the sphere of the sky in two.—*adj.* **equatorial.** —*adv.* **equatorially.**

eq-uer-ry (ĕk'wẽr-ĭ; ē-kwĕr'ĭ), *n.* [*pl.* equerries (-ĭz)], an officer in the house of a prince or nobleman, who attends him in public, and has charge of his horses.

e-ques-tri-an (ē-kwĕs'trĭ-ăn), *adj.* pertaining to horses or horsemanship; performing with horses: *n.* one skilled in horsemanship.

e-ques-tri-enne (ē-kwĕs"trĭ-ĕn'), *n.* a skilful horsewoman.

e-qui-an-gu-lar (ē"kwĭ-ăn'gū-lẽr), *adj.* having equal angles.

e-qui-dis-tant (ē"kwĭ-dĭs'tănt), *adj.* situated equally far from a certain point or from each other.

e-qui-lat-er-al (ē"kwĭ-lăt'ẽr-ăl), *adj.* having all the sides equal. *n.* a figure with equal sides: **equilateral triangle**, a figure having three equal sides and three equal angles.—*adv.* **equilaterally.**

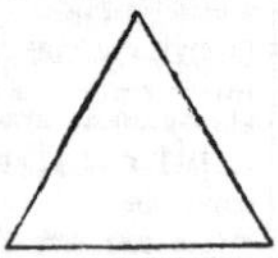

Equilateral Triangle

e-qui-lib-ri-um (ē"kwĭ-lĭb'rĭ-ŭm), *n.* equality of weight, power, force, etc.; equipoise or balance between opposing forces, actions, etc.

e-quine (ē'kwīn), *adj.* of, pertaining to, or like, a horse.

e-qui-noc-tial (ē"kwĭ-nŏk'shăl), *adj.* pertaining to the equinox, or to the time of equal day or night: *n.* the equator of the sky; a storm at the season of equal day and night.—*adv.* **equinoctially.**

e-qui-nox (ē'kwĭ-nŏks), *n.* the time when the sun crosses the equator of the sky, making the days and nights of equal length: about March 21 and September 22.

e-quip (ē-kwĭp'), *v.t.* [*p.t.* and *p.p.* equipped, *p.pr.* equipping], to furnish or fit out for any service or undertaking; as, to *equip* an army for the field; prepare or qualify; as, to *equip* a boy with knowledge; to dress; as, *equip* yourself for a walk.

eq-ui-page (ĕk'wĭ-pāj), *n.* the arms and outfit of an army, vessel, traveler, etc.; the carriage, horses, and liveried servants of a person of rank; a carriage of state.

e-quip-ment (ē-kwĭp'mĕnt), *n.* all the necessary supplies for any particular service, such as those needed in fitting out offices, stores, armies, a fleet, a railway, a person, etc.; the act of fitting out with supplies.

e-qui-poise (ē'kwĭ-poiz), *n.* equilibrium or balance; equality of weight.

e-qui-pon-der-ant (ē"kwĭ-pŏn'dẽr-ănt), *adj.* of the same weight.

eq-ui-ta-ble (ĕk'wĭ-tȧ-bl), *adj.* impartial; just; fair.—*adv.* **equitably.** —*n.* **equitableness.**

eq-ui-ty (ĕk'wĭ-tĭ), *n.* [*pl.* equities (-tĭz)], justice; just regard to right or claim; impartiality; the administration of law according to its spirit and not according to the letter.

e-quiv-a-lence (ē-kwĭv'ȧ-lĕns), *n.* equality of value or power. Also, **equivalency.**

e-quiv-a-lent (ē-kwĭv'ȧ-lĕnt), *adj.* equal in value or power; the same in significance or effect: *n.* a thing of the same value, weight, power, effect, etc.

e-quiv-o-cal (ē-kwĭv'ō-kăl), *adj.* of a doubtful or double meaning; open to suspicion or doubt; uncertain. —*adv.* **equivocally.**

Syn. dubious, doubtful, indefinite, obscure.

e-quiv-o-cate (ē-kwĭv'ō-kāt), *v.i.* to use words of double meaning; prevaricate, or evade the truth.

e-ra (ē'rȧ), *n.* the point of time from which a series of years is reckoned; a period of time starting from a given point; as, the Christian *era* dates from the birth of Christ; period; epoch.

e-rad-i-ca-ble (ē-răd'ĭ-kȧ-bl), *adj.* that can be rooted out or destroyed.

e-rad-i-cate (ē-răd'ĭ-kāt), *v.t.* to destroy thoroughly; exterminate; erase; wipe out.—*n.* **eradication.**

Syn. extirpate.

e-rase (ē-rās'), *v.t.* to rub or scrape out; blot or cross out; to efface.—*n.* **erasure.**

e-ras-er (ē-rās'ẽr), *n.* a knife or piece of rubber for scraping or rubbing out written marks; that which rubs out, as chalk marks.

ere (âr), *conj.* before; as, "the joys that came *ere* I was old"; sooner than; as, I will fight *ere* I will submit to tyranny: *prep.* before; as, I will return *ere* midnight.

Er-e-bus (ĕr'ē-bŭs), *n.* in Greek mythology, a place of utter darkness through which the dead pass to Hades.

e-rect (ē-rĕkt'), *v.t.* to construct; build; raise; establish: *adj.* upright; firmly uplifted; bold or unshaken.—*adv.* **erectly.**—*n.* **erectness.**

e-rec-tile (ē-rĕk'tĭl), *adj.* capable of being raised upright.

e-rec-tion (ē-rĕk'shŭn), *n.* the act of raising a structure, such as a wall or building; the structure raised; the state of being constructed.

e-rec-tive (ē-rĕk'tĭv), *adj.* tending or serving to raise or build up.

e-rec-tor (ē-rĕk'tẽr), *n.* one who, or that which, raises upright; a builder; a founder.

ere-long (âr'lŏng'), *adv.* before long; soon; shortly.

er-e-mite (ĕr'ē-mīt), *n.* a hermit; one dwelling alone in a desert to devote himself to religious thought.

er-go (ûr'gō), *conj.* and *adv.* therefore; consequently; hence. [LAT.]

er-got (ûr'gŏt), *n.* a black hornlike growth upon wheat, rye, etc.; a drug.

Er-in (ē'rĭn; ĕr'ĭn), *n.* a name often given to Ireland.

er-i-nite (ĕr'ĭ-nīt), *n.* a rich emerald-green metal containing copper.

er-mine (ûr'mĭn), *n.* a weasel-like animal, much valued for its fur, which becomes white in winter, except at the tip of the tail, where it remains black; the emblem, dignity, or office of a judge, whose state robe in European countries is lined with *ermine* as an emblem of purity.

ern (ûrn), *n.* in Scotland, a sea eagle: also applied to other eagles. Also, **erne.**

e-rode (ē-rōd'), *v.t.* to eat or wear away; to corrode; to wear away, as rocks by running water.

e-ro-sion (ē-rō'zhŭn), *n.* the act of wearing away; gradual destruction or eating away; commonly used of the action of water on rock or soil; the wearing away of the rifling of a gun, by heat and high pressure.

e-ro-sive (ē-rō'sĭv), *adj.* gnawing or wearing away; corrosive.

e-rot-ic (ē-rŏt'ĭk; ĕr-ŏt'ĭk), *adj.* pertaining to, or caused by, passionate love; amorous; *n.* a love poem or composition.

err (ûr), *v.i.* to commit a sin; make a mistake; to go astray morally; to be mistaken; to blunder.

er-rand (ĕr'ănd), *n.* a trip made to attend to some special business or to carry a message; the object for which the trip is made; a commission.

er-rant (ĕr'ănt), *adj.* roving, wandering, as in search of adventure; as, a knight *errant:* wayward; as, *errant* fancy; *errant* thoughts.

er-rant-ry (ĕr'ănt-rĭ), *n.* a roving in character, condition, or deed, such as a roving in search of knightly adventure; hence, knight-*errantry*.

er-rat-ic (ē-răt'ĭk), *adj.* having no fixed course; wandering; irregular; eccentric; queer; as, *erratic* behavior.—*adv.* **erratically.**

er-ra-tum (ē-rā'tŭm), *n.* [*pl.* **errata** (-tȧ)], a mistake in printing or writing.

er-ro-ne-ous (ē-rō'nē-ŭs), *adj.* incorrect; mistaken; wrong.—*adv.* **erroneously.**

er-ror (ĕr'ẽr), *n.* false belief; mistake; blunder; an inaccuracy.

Erse (ûrs), *adj.* pertaining to the Celts of Ireland or Scotland, or to their language; Gaelic: *n.* the Gaelic language.

er-u-dite (ĕr'ōō-dīt), *adj.* learned; scholarly.—*adv.* **eruditely.**

er-u-di-tion (ĕr'ōō-dĭsh'ŭn), *n.* knowledge obtained by the study of books; learning in literature, history, and arts as distinct from learning in the sciences.

e-rupt (ē-rŭpt'), *v.t.* and *v.i.* to burst forth, or cause to burst forth.

e-rup-tion (ē-rŭp'shŭn), *n.* act of bursting out or forth; that which bursts forth, as lava from a volcano; outbreak; violent commotion; a rash on the skin.

e-rup-tive (ē-rŭp'tĭv), *adj.* breaking out violently; bursting forth.

er-y-sip-e-las (ĕr'ĭ-sĭp'ē-lăs), *n.* an infectious disease of the skin, accompanied with fever and inflammation.

es-ca-drille (ĕs-kȧ-drĭl'; ĕs'kȧ'drē'yĕ), *n.* a squadron or fleet of airships; as, the Lafayette *escadrille.* [Fr.]

es-ca-lade (ĕs'kȧ-lād'), *n.* a scaling or climbing the walls of a fortified place by means of scaling-ladders: *v.t.* to storm by means of scaling-ladders.

es-ca-la-tor (ĕs'kȧ-lā'tẽr), *n.* a moving stairway.

es-cal-op (ĕs-kŏl'ŭp; ĕs-kăl'ŭp), *n.* a mollusk, or shellfish, having a ribbed shell with a wavy edge; a curved point in a wavy edge of lace, etc.; *v.t.* to prepare with bread crumbs, and bake; to shape in curved points, as the edge of lace, embroidery, etc. Also, **scallop, escallop.**

es-ca-pade (ĕs'kȧ-pād), *n.* a foolish or reckless adventure; misdeed; prank.

es-cape (ĕs-kāp'), *v.t.* to flee from; get out of the way of; to come safely out of; to avoid; to be unaffected by; as, he *escaped* contagion from the disease: *v.i.* to get out of danger; to flow out; as, gas *escapes* from a leak; to slip away; as, to *escape* from memory: *n.* a getting away from danger; flight; deliverance.

es-cape-ment (ĕs-kāp'mĕnt), *n.* a mechanical device for securing regularity of movement: used in clocks, watches, and motors.

Clock Escapement

es-carp (ĕs-kärp'), *v.t.* to give a steep slope to: *n.* the side of a ditch forming a steep slope next the rampart.

es-carp-ment (ĕs-kärp'mĕnt), *n.* a cliff; a slope; a steep side of a hill; a steep slope, almost vertical, around a fortress.

esch-a-lot (ĕsh'ȧ-lŏt'), *n.* a kind of small onion. Also, **shallot.**

es-cheat (ĕs-chēt), *v.t.* to take possession of (property to which there are no heirs): *v.i.* to revert or go back to the crown, the lord of the manor, or the state, because there are no legal heirs: *n.* land or tenements which fall to the crown, or lord of the manor, or, in the United States, to the state, by forfeiture or failure of heirs.

es-chew (ĕs-chōō'), *v.t.* to shun; avoid; as, to *eschew* bad company.

es-cort (ĕs'kôrt), *n.* a body of armed men acting as a guard; protection on a journey; a person who accompanies someone, usually a lady, to afford the protection of his presence: *v.t.* (ĕs-kôrt'), to accompany or go with.

es-cri-toire (ĕs'krĭ-twär'), *n.* a writing desk, or secretary. [Fr.]

es-cu-lent (ĕs'kū-lĕnt), *adj.* eatable; fit for food.

es-cutch-eon (ĕs-kŭch'ŭn), *n.* a shield on which the heraldic arms, or coat of arms, of a family are shown.

Es-ki-mo (ĕs'kĭ-mō), *n.* one of a race of people inhabiting Labrador, Greenland, Alaska, and other parts of arctic America. Also, **Esquimau.**

e-soph-a-gus (ē-sŏf'ȧ-gŭs), *n.* the gullet, or canal through which food and drink pass to the stomach. Also, **oesophagus.**

es-o-ter-ic (ĕs'ō-tĕr'ĭk), *adj.* pertaining to doctrines or beliefs taught only to a select circle of followers; secret; confidential; profound; opposite to *exoteric.*

es-pe-cial (ĕs-pĕsh'ăl), *adj.* particular; chief; special; exceptional among others of the same kind.—*adv.* **especially.**

Es-pe-ran-to (ĕs'pē-rän'tō), *n.* an artificial language designed for use throughout the world, thus enabling all peoples to converse with each other.

es-pi-al (ĕs-pī'ăl), *n.* the action of a spy; secret watching; discovery.

es-pi-o-nage (ĕs'pĭ-ō-nāj; ĕs-pī'ō-nāj), *n.* the secret watching of the acts or speech of another; the employment of spies or secret agents: especially in time of war.

es-pla-nade (ĕs'plȧ-nād'), *n.* an open space or road, especially by the seaside, for public use in walking or driving; a lawn.

es-pous-al (ĕs-pouz'ăl), *n.* the promising or giving in marriage; sometimes, the ceremony of marriage; the taking up of a cause with a view to supporting and defending it.

es-pouse (ĕs-pouz'), *v.t.* to promise, engage, or give in marriage; wed; adopt; advocate or defend.

es-prit de corps (ĕs"prē' dē kōr'), a spirit of common devotion, honor, and interest, binding together men of the same profession, society, etc.; comradeship. [Fr.]

es-py (ĕs-pī'), *v.t.* [*p.t.* and *p.p.* espied, *p.pr.* espying], to see at a distance; discover (something intended to be hid); to see unexpectedly.

Es-qui-mau (ĕs'kĭ-mō), *n.* [*pl.* **Esquimaux** (-mō; mōz)], one of a race of people living in the arctic regions of North America. Also, **Eskimo.**

es-quire (ĕs-kwīr'), *n.* originally, the armor-bearer or attendant on a knight; a title next below that of a knight: **Esquire,** a title given to lawyers and justices of the peace, and often used (after the name) instead of *Mr.* in the address of a letter: abbreviated *Esq.*

es-say (ĕs'ā), *n.* a literary composition on some special subject; an attempt; experiment: *v.t.* (ĕ-sā'), [*p.t.* and *p.p.* essayed, *p.pr.* essaying], to try or attempt.

es-say-ist (ĕs'ā-ĭst), *n.* one who writes in prose, on various subjects.

es-sence (ĕs'ĕns), *n.* the concentrated extract of any substance; as, *essence* of peppermint; perfume; that which is the real character of a thing; the true substance of anything.

es-sen-tial (ĕ-sĕn'shăl), *adj.* most important; necessary to the existence of a thing; indispensable; pure: *n.* that which is necessary to the existence of a thing; the basic principle; as, the *essentials* of education.—*adv.* **essentially.**

es-tab-lish (ĕs-tăb'lĭsh), *v.t.* to fix firmly; settle; prove legally; strengthen; restore; found.

es-tab-lish-ment (ĕs-tăb'lĭsh-mĕnt), *n.* the act of placing on a sure basis; settlement; a place of residence or business; a business, institution, or household.

es-tam-i-net (ăs"tăm"ĭ-nā') *n.* a French café or coffee-house, where smoking is permitted and wines and other drinks are sold. [Fr.]

es-tate (ĕs-tāt'), *n.* condition of life; rank, position, or quality; the title or interest one has in lands or tenements; property in general; any one of the different orders or classes of men in a country; any one of the political classes represented in a legislative assembly or lawmaking body, as the commons and the lords in the English parliament.

es-teem (ĕs-tēm'), *v.t.* to value highly; to respect; prize; consider: *n.* a favorable opinion; estimation; respect; reverence.

Syn., n. and *v.* regard, favor.

Ant. (see contempt).

Es-ther (ĕs'tẽr), *n.* one of the books of the Old Testament; the story of the Jewess, Esther, who delivered her people from the Persians.

es-thet-ic (ĕs-thĕt'ĭk), *adj.* having a love of the beautiful; pertaining to, or appreciative of, the fine arts. Also, **aesthetic.**—*adv.* **esthetically.**

es-thet-ics (ĕs-thĕt'ĭks), *n.pl.* the science of the beautiful in nature or art. Also, **aesthetics.**

es-ti-ma-ble (ĕs'tĭ-mȧ-bl), *adj.* worthy of respect, regard, or honor; deserving of esteem; calculable; as, *estimable* damage.—*adv.* **estimably.**

es-ti-mate (ĕs'tĭ-māt), *v.t.* to compute; determine the value of: *n.* (ĕs'tĭ-mȧt), the computed or reckoned cost or value of anything; as, the builder made an *estimate* of the cost of the house; appraisement.

Syn., v. appraise, appreciate, value, compute, rate.

es-ti-ma-tion (ĕs"tĭ-mā'shŭn), *n.* calculation; appraisement; honor, respect, or esteem; favorable opinion.

es-trade (ĕs-trăd'; ĕs-trăd'), *n.* a slightly raised platform.

es-trange (ĕs-trānj'), *v.t.* to alienate the affections of; turn from kindness to indifference; keep at a distance.—*n.* **estrangement.**

es-tray (ĕs-trā'), *n.* a domestic animal that has strayed from its owner; one wandering and unclaimed.

es-tu-a-ry (ĕs'tū-ā-rĭ), *n.* [*pl.* **estuaries** (-rĭz)], the wide mouth of a river where tide and current meet; a narrow inlet from the sea; a firth.

et-a-mine (ĕt'ȧ-mēn), *n.* a light woolen fabric resembling a fine quality of bunting.

et cet-er-a (ĕt sĕt'ẽr-ȧ), and others of the same kind; and so forth: abbreviated *etc.* Also, **et cetera.**

etch (ĕch), *v.t.* to engrave by biting out with an acid a design previously drawn with an etching-needle upon a copperplate.—*n.* **etching.**

e-ter-nal (ē-tûr'năl), *adj.* without beginning or end; everlasting; perpetual; incessant: **the Eternal,** God.—*adv.* **eternally.**

Syn. endless, unceasing, interminable.

Ant. (see finite).

e-ter-ni-ty (ē-tûr'nĭ-tĭ), *n.* [*pl.* **eternities** (-tĭz)], indefinite time; time that seems endless; life after death.

e-ther (ē'thẽr), *n.* the upper purer air; a liquid anesthetic, the vapor of which when inhaled produces unconsciousness and insensibility to pain; the medium through which the rays of light and heat are transmitted.

e-the-re-al (ē-thē'rē-ăl), *adj.* airy; light: exquisite; heavenly; spiritual.—*adv.* **ethereally.**

e-ther-ize (ē'thẽr-īz), *v.t.* to make unconscious, or insensible, with the anesthetic ether.—*n.* **etherization.**

eth-i-cal (ĕth'ĭ-kăl), *adj.* pertaining to right and wrong conduct; moral.—*adv.* **ethically.**

eth-ics (ĕth'ĭks), *n.pl.* the science that treats of right conduct; morals.

E-thi-o-pi-an (ē"thĭ-ō'pĭ-ăn), *adj.* pertaining to the ancient country of Ethiopia in Africa: *n.* a native of Ethiopia; an African; a negro.

eth-nic (ĕth'nĭk), *adj.* pertaining to, peculiar to, or indicating, races or peoples. Also, **ethnical.**—*adv.* **ethnically.**

eth-nog-ra-phy (ĕth-nŏg'rȧ-fĭ), *n.* the scientific description of the different races and peoples of mankind.

eth-nol-o-gy (ĕth-nŏl'ō-jĭ), *n.* the science that treats of races of men, their characteristics, etc.—*adj.* **ethnological.** —*n.* **ethnologist.**

et-i-quette (ĕt'ĭ-kĕt), *n.* rules of conduct observed in polite society or in official intercourse; the forms of polite behavior demanded by good breeding.

et-na (ĕt'nȧ), *n.* an apparatus in which a small quantity of liquid may be heated by means of a spirit lamp.

é-tude (ā'tūd'), *n.* a study; in music, an exercise affording practice on some particular point of technique.

et-y-mo-log-i-cal (ĕt"ĭ-mō-lŏj'ĭ-kăl), *adj.* pertaining to the study of words.—*adv.* **etymologically.**

et-y-mol-o-gist (ĕt"ĭ-mŏl'ō-jĭst), *n.* one who studies, teaches, or writes the history of words.

et-y-mol-o-gy (ĕt"ĭ-mŏl'ō-jĭ), *n.* [*pl.* etymologies (-jĭz)], a study of the origin of words; the account of such origin; that part of grammar which treats of the parts of speech and their inflections.

eu-ca-lyp-tus (ū"kȧ-lĭp'tŭs), *n.* [*pl.* eucalypti (-tī)], any of the various trees of the evergreen myrtle family, many species of which furnish gum and a valuable medicine: commonly called the *gum tree.*

Eu-cha-rist (ū'kȧ-rĭst), *n.* the Holy Communion; the sacrament of the Lord's Supper; the consecrated elements, bread and wine, used in that sacrament.

eu-cha-ris-tic (ū"kȧ-rĭs'tĭk), *adj.* pertaining to the Eucharist, or Holy Communion; expressing thanksgiving. Also, **eucharistical.**

eu-chre (ū'kẽr), *n.* a game of cards: *v.t.* to prevent (an opponent) in the game from scoring; hence, slang, to outwit.

eu-gen-ics (ū-jĕn'ĭks), *n.pl.* the science of improving the human race through better heredity.

eu-lo-gist (ū'lō-jĭst), *n.* one who praises highly or excessively.

eu-lo-gis-tic (ū"lō-jĭs'tĭk), *adj.* laudatory; containing high or excessive praise.

eu-lo-gize (ū'lō-jīz), *v.t.* to praise highly; to commend.

eu-lo-gy (ū'lō-jĭ), *n.* [*pl.* eulogies (-jĭz)], high praise, either written or spoken, of the life or character of a person, usually deceased. Also, **eulogium.**

eu-nuch (ū'nŭk), *n.* a man who has been deprived of virile power; a chamberlain or an attendant in a harem.

eu-pep-tic (ū-pĕp'tĭk), *adj.* assisting toward good digestion.

eu-phe-mism (ū'fē-mĭzm), *n.* the use of a mild or pleasing expression in place of one that is plainer or more accurate but which might be offensive or embarrassing; the expression so used.

eu-phe-mis-tic (ū"fē-mĭs'tĭk), *adj.* softened or mild in expression.

eu-pho-ni-ous (ū-fō'nĭ-ŭs), *adj.* pleasing or sweet in sound or tone; sounding well. Also, **euphonic, euphonical.**

eu-pho-ni-um (ū-fō'nĭ-ŭm), *n.* a brass musical instrument, bass in tone.

eu-pho-ny (ū'fō-nĭ), *n.* [*pl.* euphonies (-nĭz)], pleasantness of sound or pronunciation; sweetness of sound.

eu-phu-ism (ū'fū-ĭzm), *n.* an affected or high-flown style in writing or speaking.—*adj.* **euphuistic.**

eu-re-ka (ū-rē'kȧ), *interj.* "I have found it": an exclamation of triumph over a discovery or supposed discovery.

Eu-ro-pe-an (ū"rō-pē'ăn), *adj.* belonging or pertaining to Europe: *n.* a native of Europe.

Eu-sta-chi-an tube (ū-stā'kĭ-ăn tūb), the tube between the ear and the pharynx.

e-vac-u-ate (ē-văk'ū-āt), *v.t.* to make void or empty; abandon possession of, or withdraw from; vacate; as, the enemy *evacuated* the fort.

e-vac-u-a-tion (ē-văk"ū-ā'shŭn), *n.* the act of withdrawing; the act of voiding; that which is voided.

e-vade (ē-vād'), *v.t.* to elude cleverly, or by some trick; slip away from; as, to *evade* pursuers; baffle or foil.

ev-a-nes-cent (ĕv"ȧ-nĕs'ĕnt), *adj.* disappearing gradually from sight; vanishing; fleeting; as, the joys of life are *evanescent.*—*n.* **evanescence.**

e-van-gel (ē-văn'jĕl), *n.* good news, especially that of the gospel.

e-van-gel-i-cal (ē"văn-jĕl'ĭ-kăl), *adj.* relating to the gospel, or the four Gospels; maintaining the principal doctrines of the Protestant faith; spiritually minded: *n.* one who holds orthodox Protestant doctrines.—*adv.* **evangelically.**

e-van-gel-ism (ē-văn'jĕl-ĭzm), *n.* earnest effort for the spread of the gospel of Christ.—*adj.* **evangelistic.**

e-van-gel-ist (ē-văn'jĕl-ĭst), *n.* one of the four writers of the Gospels; an itinerant or traveling preacher.

e-van-gel-ize (ē-văn'jĕl-īz), *v.t.* to teach the gospel to; to convert to Christianity.

e-vap-o-rate (ē-văp'ō-rāt), *v.i.* to disperse or pass off in vapor; pass away without effect: *v.t.* to convert into vapor; as, heat *evaporates* water; to dry by removing moisture from, as fruit; concentrate, as milk.

e-vap-o-ra-tion (ē-văp"ō-rā'shŭn), *n.* the changing or conversion of a fluid into vapor or steam; the act or result of removing moisture, as from fruit, milk, etc.

e-va-sion (ē-vā'zhŭn), *n.* the act of eluding or getting out of the way; an artful escape; an excuse; subterfuge.

e-va-sive (ē-vā'sĭv), *adj.* tending or seeking to evade; as, an *evasive* reply; not readily understood; elusive; sly.—*adv.* **evasively.**—*n.* **evasiveness.**

eve (ēv), *n.* the fast or vigil before a church festival, or saint's day; the period immediately before some important event; as, the *eve* of departure; evening; the close of day.

Eve (ēv), *n.* in the Bible, the first created woman, wife of Adam.

e-ven (ē'vn), *adj.* level; uniform; smooth; parallel; divisible by two without a remainder; equal; balanced; calm; whole: *n.* poetically, evening: *v.t.* to be equal in any way; to be quits: *v.t.* to level or make even; to make equal: *adv.* verily; precisely; just; quite; as much as.—*adv.* **evenly.**

Syn., adj. level, plain, smooth.
Ant. (see uneven).

eve-ning (ēv'nĭng), *n.* the close of the day and beginning of the night; the latter part of life: *adj.* pertaining to the later part of the day; as, *evening* meal.

e-ven-ness (ē'vn-nĕs), *n.* smoothness; uniformity; regularity; equality of surface; as, the *evenness* of the ground; calmness.

e-vent (ē-vĕnt'), *n.* an occurrence; incident; the result or outcome of an action; any single item in a program of sports or games.

Syn. accident, adventure.

e-vent-ful (ē-vĕnt'fool), *adj.* full of incidents or happenings; momentous.—*adv.* **eventfully.**

e-ven-tide (ē'vn-tīd), *n.* evening; as, the dusk of *eventide.*

e-ven-tu-al (ē-vĕn'tū-ăl), *adj.* happening as a result; ultimate; final.

e-ven-tu-al-i-ty (ē-vĕn"tū-ăl'ĭ-tĭ), *n.* [*pl.* eventualities (-tĭz)], a possible occurrence or happening.

e-ven-tu-al-ly (ē-vĕn'tū-ăl-ĭ; ē-vĕn'-chōō-ăl-ĭ), *adv.* ultimately; finally.

e-ven-tu-ate (ē-vĕn'tū-āt), *v.i.* to happen; terminate; result.

ev-er (ĕv'ẽr), *adv.* at any time; as, I do not know that I shall *ever* go; always; as, the poor are *ever* with us; without end; in any degree; as, study as hard as *ever* you can.

ev-er-glade (ĕv'ẽr-glād), *n.* a low, swampy tract of land, with patches of tall grass.

ev-er-green (ĕv'ẽr-grēn"), *n.* a tree or plant which retains its leaves throughout the year: *adj.* always green or fresh.

ev-er-last-ing (ĕv"ẽr-lăs'tĭng), *adj.* perpetual; endless; eternal: *n.* a plant whose flowers retain their color when dried; eternity: **the Everlasting,** God, the Eternal.

ev-er-more (ĕv"ẽr-mōr'), *adv.* eternally; always; forever.

ev-er-y (ĕv'ẽr-ĭ; ĕv'rĭ), *adj.* and *adj. pron.* all taken one at a time; each; as, *every* man will do his duty; all possible; as, they were shown *every* kindness.

ev-er-y-bod-y (ĕv'ẽr-ĭ-bŏd"ĭ; ĕv'rĭ-bŏd"-ĭ), *n.* all persons, taken one at a time.

ev-er-y-day (ĕv'ẽr-ĭ-dā"; ĕv'rĭ-dā"), *adj.* coming on each day; usual; commonplace; as, *everyday* matters.

ev-er-y-thing (ĕv'ẽr-ĭ-thĭng"; ĕv'rĭ-thĭng"), *n.* all things; all that is concerned in a given matter.

ev-er-y-where (ĕv'ẽr-ĭ-hwâr"; ĕv'rĭ-hwâr"), *adv.* in all places or parts; thoroughly.

e-vict (ē-vĭkt'), *v.t.* to put out, expel, or dispossess by legal process; as, to *evict* a tenant who refuses to pay rent; remove by force.

e-vic-tion (ē-vĭk'shŭn), *n.* the act of putting out by force.

ev-i-dence (ĕv'ĭ-dĕns), *n.* proof; testimony: *v.t.* to prove; make evident or plain.

ev-i-dent (ĕv'ĭ-dĕnt), *adj.* clear to the vision or understanding; manifest; plain; obvious.—*adv.* **evidently.**

e-vil (ē'vl), *adj.* morally bad; wicked; sinful; hurtful; disastrous; of ill repute; worthless: *adv.* badly; harmfully: *n.* conduct showing harmful intention or purpose; something that injures; sin.—*adv.* **evilly.**

Syn., n. harm, misfortune, affliction.

Ant. (see good).

e-vil eye (ē'vl ī), an influence for injury, supposed to be exerted by certain persons who cast a hurtful glance at anyone.

e-vince (ē-vĭns'), *v.t.* to manifest or make evident; demonstrate; show clearly.

e-vin-ci-ble (ē-vĭn'sĭ-bl), *adj.* capable of proof or demonstration.

e-vis-cer-ate (ē-vĭs'ẽr-āt), *v.t.* to disembowel or remove the bowels from; to deprive of vital parts.

e-voke (ē-vōk'), *v.t.* to call forth; as, to *evoke* an answer.

ev-o-lu-tion (ĕv"ō-lū'shŭn), *n.* the act of unfolding or developing; growth; as, the *evolution* of a moth from a caterpillar; the *evolution* of the plot of a story; the thing developed or evolved; the movements of troops in marching or on the battlefield; the extraction of roots of any arithmetical or algebraic power; the gradual development of forms of life from the lowest stage; the theory concerning the gradual development of forms of life upward from the lowest stage.—*adj.* **evolutional, evolutionary.**—*n.* **evolutionist.**

e-volve (ē-vŏlv'), *v.t.* to develop; unfold; expand; work out: *v.i.* to become developed or unfolded.

ewe (ū), *n.* a female sheep, or the female of animals like the sheep.

ew-er (ū'ẽr), *n.* a large water jug with a wide mouth, especially used for the toilet.

ex-ac-er-bate (ĕg-zăs'ẽr-bāt), *v.t.* to make more sharp, virulent, or bitter; to irritate; aggravate.—*n.* **exacerbation.**

ex-act (ĕg-zăkt'), *adj.* correct or accurate; precise; methodical; strict; particular: *v.t.* require or claim; compel to be paid; insist upon; to extort.

Syn., adj. nice, punctual, precise.

Ant. (see inexact).

ex-act-ing (ĕg-zăkt'ĭng), *p.adj.* making unreasonable demands; severe; arduous.

ex-ac-tion (ĕg-zăk'shŭn), *n.* the act of rigidly demanding; something demanded in excess of what is due.

ex-act-i-tude (ĕg-zăk'tĭ-tūd), *n.* the quality of being precise or accurate.

ex-act-ly (ĕg-zăkt'lĭ), *adv.* accurately; precisely; strictly.

ex-act-ness (ĕg-zăkt'nĕs), *n.* accuracy; precision.

ex-ag-ger-ate (ĕg-zăj'ẽr-āt), *v.t.* to enlarge beyond truth or reason; to heighten by overstatement; color highly.

ex-ag-ger-at-ed (ĕg-zăj'ẽr-ā-tĕd), *p.adj.* enlarged or extended beyond truth or reason; overstated.

ex-ag-ger-a-tion (ĕg-zăj"ẽr-ā'shŭn), *n.* extravagant or untruthful representation; overstatement.

ex-alt (ĕg-zôlt'), *v.t.* to elevate in rank, station, or dignity; raise on high; glorify or extol.

Syn. ennoble, dignify, raise.

Ant. (see humble).

ex-al-ta-tion (ĕg"zôl-tā'shŭn), *n.* the act or state of being mentally or spiritually uplifted; a state of great dignity; a feeling of elation or pride.

ex-am-i-na-tion (ĕg-zăm"ĭ-nā'shŭn), *n.* the act of inquiring into carefully; a careful inquiry or inspection; a test of knowledge or fitness; a questioning, as of a witness.

ex-am-ine (ĕg-zăm'ĭn), *v.t.* to scrutinize or investigate carefully; search or inquire into; to question, as a witness; test orally or by papers the knowledge, qualifications, etc., of, as a candidate for a degree or office; analyze; test.—*n.* **examiner.**

ex-am-ple (ĕg-zăm'pl; ĕg-zȧm'pl), *n.* a pattern; a model or copy;

an illustration of a rule or precept; a parallel case; sample; specimen; a warning; a problem to be solved, as in arithmetic.

Syn. standard, type, instance.

ex-as-per-ate (ĕg-zăs'pĕr-āt), *v.t.* to irritate exceedingly; enrage greatly; embitter; intensify.

ex-as-per-a-tion (ĕg-zăs"pĕr-ā'shŭn), *n.* extreme irritation.

ex-ca-vate (ĕks'kȧ-vāt), *v.t.* to dig or hollow out; scoop or cut into; to bring to light by digging; as, to *excavate* the ruins of ancient cities.

ex-ca-va-tion (ĕks"kȧ-vā'shŭn), *n.* a hollow cavity or hole formed by cutting or digging out earth.

ex-ca-va-tor (ĕks'kȧ-vā"tĕr), *n.* a digging machine; a person who digs, often in search of ancient relics, etc.

ex-ceed (ĕk-sēd'), *v.t.* to go beyond the limit or measure of; surpass; excel: *v.i.* to be greater; go beyond bounds.

ex-ceed-ing (ĕk-sēd'ĭng), *p.adj.* very great; surpassing; extraordinary.

ex-ceed-ing-ly (ĕk-sēd'ĭng-lĭ), *adv.* extremely; surpassingly.

ex-cel (ĕk-sĕl'), *v.t.* [*p.t.* and *p.p.* excelled, *p.pr.* excelling], to possess good qualities in a great degree; to surpass others: *v.t.* to surpass; to outdo in comparison; to be superior to; exceed.

ex-cel-lence (ĕk'sĕ-lĕns), *n.* superior merit, goodness, or virtue.

ex-cel-len-cy (ĕk'sĕ-lĕn-sĭ), *n.* [*pl.* excellencies (-sĭz)], superior merit: **Excellency**, a title of honor of various high officials, as an ambassador, governor, etc.

ex-cel-lent (ĕk'sĕ-lĕnt), *adj.* of great value, merit, or virtue; highly useful or desirable; marked for goodness or ability.—*adv.* **excellently.**

ex-cel-si-or (ĕk-sĕl'sĭ-ôr), *adj.* yet higher; ever upward: the motto of New York State: *n.* a packing material made of long, fine wood shavings.

ex-cept (ĕk-sĕpt'), *v.t.* to omit or leave out; exclude: *v.i.* to object: *prep.* omitting; leaving out: *conj.* unless.

ex-cept-ing (ĕk-sĕp'tĭng), *prep.* and *conj.* excluding; except.

ex-cep-tion (ĕk-sĕp'shŭn), *n.* the act of omitting; omission; exclusion; that which is not included; objection; offense taken: with *to;* as, to take *exception* to what was said; a formal objection to a decision of a court during a trial.

ex-cep-tion-a-ble (ĕk-sĕp'shŭn-ȧ-bl), *adj.* objectionable; uncommon; liable to omission.

ex-cep-tion-al (ĕk-sĕp'shŭn-ăl), *adj.* unusual; uncommon; rare; extraordinary.—*adv.* **exceptionally.**

ex-cerpt (ĕk-sûrpt'), *v.t.* to take out or select from, as a passage from a book; quote: *n.* a selection or extract from a book or writing.

ex-cess (ĕk-sĕs'), *n.* an undue amount; the amount by which one thing is more than another; surplus; superfluity or overabundance; intemperance; an added charge to a railway passenger in addition to the regular fare, as for cash payment.

Syn. waste, dissipation, lavishness.

Ant. (see economy).

ex-cess-ive (ĕk-sĕs'ĭv), *adj.* extreme; unreasonable; extravagant.—*adv.* **excessively.**

ex-change (ĕks-chānj'), *v.t.* to give in return for something; to barter: *v.i.* to give one thing for another: *n.* the act of giving one thing for another; barter; reciprocity, or the act of giving and receiving; as, an *exchange* of visits; *exchange* of ideas; the act of resigning one thing for another; as, the *exchange* of country life for city life; a place where special business accounts are settled; as, a stock *exchange* (often *'change*); a central office; as, a hotel *exchange.*—*adj.* **exchangeable.**

ex-cheq-uer (ĕks-chĕk'ĕr), *n.* a treasury; cash or funds; formerly, an English court of law, now merged into the Queen's Bench division of the High Court of Justice.

ex-cise (ĕk-sīz'), *v.t.* to levy a duty or tax upon; to cut off: *n.* a tax or duty levied on the manufacture, sale, or consumption of articles or things within the country, such as tobacco or spirituous liquors.

ex-ci-sion (ĕk-sĭzh'ŭn), *n.* the act of cutting out, or off; the state of being cut off; destruction; ruin; amputation.

ex-cit-a-bil-i-ty (ĕk-sīt"ȧ-bĭl'ĭ-tĭ), *n.* [*pl.* excitabilities (-tĭz)], the state or quality of being easily stirred up; sensitiveness to irritation.

ex-cit-a-ble (ĕk-sīt'ȧ-bl), *adj.* easily roused or stirred up; irritable.—*n.* **excitableness.**

ex-cit-ant (ĕk-sīt'ănt), *n.* a stimulant: *adj.* having a tendency to arouse; stimulating to the nerves.

ex-ci-ta-tion (ĕk"sĭ-tā'shŭn), *n.* the act of arousing; the state produced by stirring up or rousing.

ex-cite (ĕk-sīt'), *v.t.* to animate; rouse; to encourage; put into motion or action; stimulate.

Syn. awaken, provoke, stir up.

Ant. (see lull).

ex-cit-ed (ĕk-sīt'ĕd), *p.adj.* aroused; provoked.—*adv.* **excitedly.**

ex-cit-ing (ĕk-sīt'ĭng), *p.adj.* stirring; lively; as, an *exciting* adventure.

ex-cite-ment (ĕk-sīt'mĕnt), *n.* condition of being stirred up; commotion; sensation; stimulation; warmth of temper.

ex-claim (ĕks-klām'), *v.i.* and *v.t.* to cry out abruptly and passionately.

ex-cla-ma-tion (ĕks"klȧ-mā'shŭn), *n.* an abrupt or sudden outcry; an expression of surprise, pain, etc.; a mark [!] in writing or printing to denote emotion, surprise, etc.

ex-clam-a-to-ry (ĕks-klăm'ȧ-tō-rĭ), *adj.* containing, expressing, or using, exclamation.

ex-clave (ĕks'klāv), *n.* a small part of a country lying within the territory of another power.

ex-clude (ĕks-klōōd'), *v.t.* to shut out; hinder from entrance or admission; prohibit; debar; except.

ex-clu-sion (ĕks-klōō-zhŭn), *n.* the act of shutting out; the state of being debarred; omission.

ex-clu-sive (ĕks-klōō'sĭv), *adj.* not liberal; open to or enjoyed only by a privileged number; as, the *exclusive* use of a thing; limiting social relations; as, an *exclusive* assembly; not taking into account.—*adv.* **exclusively.**

ex-com-mu-ni-cate (ĕks"kŏ-mū'nĭ-kāt), *v.t.* to punish by cutting off from the membership and communion of the church; to expel from membership in any association or club.—*n.* **excommunication.**

ex-co-ri-ate (ěks-kō'rĭ-āt), *v.t.* to strip off the skin of; to flay.—*n.* excoriation.

ex-cre-ment (ěks'krē-měnt), *n.* matter discharged from the body of an animal after digestion.—*adj.* excremental.

ex-cres-cence (ěks-krěs'ěns), *n.* an unnatural or disfiguring outgrowth, as a wart.

ex-cres-cent (ěks-krěs'ěnt), *adj.* pertaining to an unnatural growth; superfluous.

ex-cre-ta (ěks-krē'tȧ), *n.pl.* useless matter eliminated or expelled from the body.

ex-crete (ěks-krēt'), *v.t.* to throw (off waste matter) from the body: *n.* (ěks'krēt), that which is thrown off.

ex-cre-tion (ěks-krē'shŭn), *n.* the throwing off or ejection of waste matter from the body, as through the pores; that which is thrown off.—*adj.* excretory.

ex-cru-ci-ate (ěks-krōō'shĭ-āt), *v.t.* to inflict severe pains upon; torture; torment.

ex-cru-ci-at-ing (ěks-krōō'shĭ-ā-tĭng), *adj.* agonizing; as, *excruciating* pain.

ex-cru-ci-a-tion (ěks-krōō"shĭ-ā'shŭn), *n.* agony, torture.

ex-cul-pate (ěks-kŭl'pāt; ěks'kŭl-pāt), *v.t.* to clear from the imputation or charge of a fault; free from blame.

ex-cul-pa-to-ry (ěks-kŭl'pȧ-tō-rĭ), *adj.* freeing from blame; excusing.

ex-cur-sion (ěks-kûr'shŭn; ěks-kûr'zhŭn), *n.* a pleasure trip; a short or rapid tour.

Syn. jaunt, ramble, tour, trip.

ex-cur-sive (ěks-kûr'sĭv), *adj.* rambling, wandering; disconnected.

ex-cus-a-ble (ěks-kūz'ȧ-bl), *adj.* worthy of being freed from blame; pardonable; as, *excusable* delay.—*adv.* excusably.

ex-cuse (ěks-kūz'), *v.t.* to pardon; to free from blame, obligation, or duty; to make an apology for; to justify: *n.* (ěks-kūs'), a plea offered to justify some fault or neglect of duty; an apology; a pretext or pretended reason.

ex-e-cra-ble (ěk'sē-krȧ-bl), *adj.* accursed; outrageous; abominable.—*adv.* execrably.

ex-e-crate (ěk'sē-krāt), *v.t.* to curse; detest; abhor; abominate.

ex-e-cra-tion (ěk"sē-krā'shŭn), *n.* the act of cursing; utter detestation expressed; a curse.

ex-e-cute (ěk'sē-kūt), *v.t.* to carry into effect; as, to *execute* a purpose or plan; pursue to the end; make valid or legal by signing or sealing; as, to *execute* a deed or lease; to put to death under sentence of the law; to perform, as a musical selection: *v.i.* to perform any act or office; to play a piece of music; as, to *execute* with skill.

ex-e-cu-tion (ěk"sē-kū'shŭn), *n.* performance; the act or manner of carrying anything into effect; completion; a legal warrant or order; the act of making a legal paper valid or good; capital punishment, or punishment by death; destruction; effective work or operation; as, every shot did good *execution*.

ex-e-cu-tion-er (ěk"sē-kū'shŭn-ẽr), *n.* one who puts to death condemned criminals; a hangman; a headsman.

ex-ec-u-tive (ĕg-zěk'ū-tĭv; ěk-sěk'ū-tĭv), *adj.* pertaining to the governing body; administrative; active; efficient in carrying out plans: *n.* an official, or body, charged with carrying the laws into effect; as, the President of the United States is the chief *executive;* the administrative branch of a government.

ex-ec-u-tor (ĕg-zěk'ū-tẽr; ěk'sē-kū"tẽr), *n.* a person appointed to see that the terms of a will are duly carried out.

ex-ec-u-trix (ĕg-zěk'ū-trĭks), *n.* [*pl.* executrices (-trī'sēz); executrixes (-trĭk'sěz)], a woman appointed to administer a will.

ex-e-ge-sis (ěk"sē-jē'sĭs), *n.* explanation or interpretation of a text or passage, especially of the Bible.

ex-e-get-ic (ěk"sē-jět'ĭk), *adj.* expository or explanatory; interpretative: *n.pl.* the science of explaining the Bible.

ex-em-plar (ĕg-zěm'plȧr), *n.* something to be copied, or something serving as a model; an example or pattern.

ex-em-pla-ry (ĕg'zěm-plȧ-rĭ; ĕg-zěm'plȧ-rĭ), *adj.* serving as a copy or model; commendable; as, the boy's conduct was *exemplary;* worthy of imitation.—*adv.* exemplarily.

ex-em-pli-fi-ca-tion (ĕg-zěm"plĭ-fĭ-kā'shŭn), *n.* the showing or making plain by example; illustration.

ex-em-pli-fy (ĕg-zěm'plĭ-fī), *v.t.* [*p.t.* and *p.p.* exemplified, *p.pr.* exemplifying], to show by example; to illustrate.

ex-empt (ĕg-zěmpt'), *v.t.* to free from a duty or obligation; release; as, to *exempt* clergymen from military service: *adj.* free from a duty to which others are subject: with *from:* *n.* a person thus set free: one who is privileged.

ex-emp-tion (ĕg-zěmp'shŭn), *n.* act of releasing, or state of being released, from some duty or obligation: privilege.

ex-e-qua-tur (ěk"sē-kwā'tŭr), *n.* an official warrant or permission given to a consul or commercial agent authorizing him to use his authority in the place where he is stationed. [LAT.]

ex-er-cise (ěk'sẽr-sīz), *v.t.* to train by use; exert; practice; employ actively; make anxious: *v.i.* to undergo training: *n.* bodily exertion; activity for the sake of mental or physical development; labor; practice; a lesson or example for practice; the ceremony ending a course in school: usually in plural; as, graduating *exercises.*

ex-ert (ĕg-zûrt'), *v.t.* to put forth, as force or ability; use with an effort.

ex-er-tion (ĕg-zûr'shŭn), *n.* the active use of any power; effort.

ex-e-unt (ěk'sē-ŭnt), they go out: a word used in plays to denote that the actors retire from the stage: *pl.* of *exit.* [LAT.]

ex-ha-la-tion (ěks"hȧ-lā'shŭn; ěk"sȧ-lā'shŭn), *n.* a breathing or a giving out; as, the *exhalation* of vapor from a swamp, or of perfume from a flower; that which is breathed or given out.

ex-hale (ěks-hāl'; ĕgz-hāl'), *v.t.* to breathe forth; emit or send out; cause to evaporate: *v.i.* to rise in vapor; to breathe out.

ex-haust (ĕg-zôst'), *v.t.* to empty by drawing off the contents; drain; weaken; wear out by exertion; discuss or treat thoroughly; as, to *exhaust* a topic of conversation: *n.* that which is drawn off, as steam from an engine.

ex-haust-i-ble (ĕg-zôs'tĭ-bl), *adj.* capable of being emptied or worn out.—*n.* **exhaustibility.**

ex-haus-tion (ĕg-zôs'chŭn), *n.* the act of draining; the state or process of being drained; utter weariness or fatigue.

ex-haus-tive (ĕg-zôs'tĭv), *adj.* complete; thorough; as, an *exhaustive* treatment of a subject.—*adv.* **exhaustively.**

ex-hib-it (ĕg-zĭb'ĭt), *v.t.* to present to view; display; show; manifest publicly; present formally or officially: *n.* an object or collection of objects offered for public view; as, an *exhibit* of paintings.

ex-hi-bi-tion (ĕk'sĭ-bĭsh'ŭn), *n.* the act of displaying for inspection; the thing or things displayed; a public show or demonstration.

ex-hil-a-rant (ĕg-zĭl'á-rănt), *adj.* causing joy or pleasure; making lively; enlivening: *n.* that which enlivens.

ex-hil-a-rate (ĕg-zĭl'á-rāt), *v.t.* to make joyous, merry, or cheerful; to enliven; gladden.—*n.* **exhilaration.**

ex-hort (ĕg-zôrt; ĕgz-hôrt'), *v.t.* and *v.i.* to incite or urge, by appeal or argument, to good deeds; to caution; to give good advice.—*n.* **exhorter.**

ex-hor-ta-tion (ĕk'sôr-tā'shŭn), *n.* an effort to arouse or incite to that which is good; earnest appeal or advice.—*adj.* **exhortative, exhortatory.**

ex-hume (ĕks-hūm'), *v.t.* to disinter or dig up something that has been buried.—*n.* **exhumation.**

ex-i-geant (ĕgz'ē'zhäṅ'), *adj.* exacting; urgent. Also, **exigeante.** [Fr.]

ex-i-gen-cy (ĕk'sĭ-jĕn-sĭ), *n.* [*pl.* exigencies (-sĭz)], a time or case that needs immediate attention; pressing necessity or demand; urgency; emergency.—Also, **exigence.**

ex-i-gent (ĕk'sĭ-jĕnt), *adj.* urgent; pressing; demanding immediate attention or assistance.

ex-ig-u-ous (ĕg-zĭg'ū-ŭs; ĕk-sĭg'ū-ŭs), *adj.* scanty; slender; slim.

ex-ile (ĕk'sīl), *v.t.* to banish from one's native country: *n.* the state of being thus banished; the condition of living away from one's home or friends; a person sent away or expelled from his country.

ex-ist (ĕg-zĭst'), *v.i.* to have actual being; to live.

ex-ist-ence (ĕg-zĭs'tĕns), *n.* the state of being; life; duration; reality; an actuality.

ex-ist-ent (ĕg-zĭs'tĕnt), *adj.* having possession of vital being or conscious life.

ex-it (ĕk'sĭt), *n.* the act of going out; egress; a passage out; the departure of an actor from the stage.

ex li-bris (ĕks lī'brĭs), from the books (of): an inscription used in a book, with the owner's name; an exhibition of the books from the libraries of certain collectors. [Lat.]

ex-o-dus (ĕk'sō-dŭs), *n.* a going out; departure from a place: **Exodus,** the departure of the Israelites from Egypt: with *the;* the second book of the Bible.

ex of-fi-ci-o (ĕks·ō-fĭsh'ĭ-ō), by virtue or right of office and without other special authority. [Lat.]

ex-on-er-ate (ĕg-zŏn'ēr-āt), *v.t.* to free from the imputation or charge of a fault; acquit; justify; relieve from a duty, etc.—*n.* **exoneration.**

ex-or-a-ble (ĕk'sō-rá-bl), *adj.* capable of being persuaded.

ex-or-bi-tance (ĕg-zôr'bĭ-tăns), *n.* a going beyond due limits; excess. Also, **exorbitancy.**

ex-or-bi-tant (ĕg-zôr'bĭ-tănt), *adj.* excessive; as, an *exorbitant* amount was charged.—*adv.* **exorbitantly.**

ex-or-cise (ĕk'sôr-sīz), *v.t.* to expel (an evil spirit) by prayers or magical words; to deliver from evil spirits. Also, **exorcize.**—*n.* **exorcist.**

ex-or-cism (ĕk'sôr-sĭzm), *n.* the act of expelling evil spirits.

ex-or-di-um (ĕg-zôr'dĭ-ŭm), *n.* the opening part of a speech or composition.

ex-o-ter-ic (ĕk'sō-tĕr'ĭk), *adj.* external; suitable for the general public; popular; opposite to *esoteric.*

ex-ot-ic (ĕg-zŏt'ĭk), *adj.* foreign; strange; belonging, as a plant, to another part of the world: *n.* anything not native to a place.

ex-pand (ĕks-pănd'), *v.t.* to spread or stretch out; unfold; dilate; extend; as, to *expand* the chest: *v.i.* to increase in size.

ex-panse (ĕks-păns'), *n.* wide extent; uninterrupted stretch or area; as, an *expanse* of ocean or of sky; extent.

ex-pan-si-ble (ĕks-păn'sĭ-bl), *adj.* capable of being spread, extended, dilated, or diffused.

ex-pan-sion (ĕks-păn'shŭn), *n.* the act of spreading out; the state of being stretched out; increase in size or extent; enlargement.

ex-pan-sive (ĕks-păn'sĭv), *adj.* capable of being spread or stretched out; widely extended; large.—*adv.* **expansively.**

ex parte (ĕks pär'tē), one-sided; as, an *ex parte* statement: a law term. [Lat.]

ex-pa-ti-ate (ĕks-pā'shĭ-āt), *v.i.* to enlarge in statement or language; to use many words in discussion; talk freely and at length.—*n.* **expatiation.**

ex-pa-tri-ate (ĕks-pā'trĭ-āt), *v.t.* to drive from one's native country: *n.* (ĕx-pā'trĭ-āt), one who has given up or has been driven from his native country; an exile.

ex-pa-tri-a-tion (ĕx-pā'trĭ-ā'shŭn), *n.* exile; banishment.

ex-pect (ĕks-pĕkt'), *v.t.* to wait for; look for, in thought, as likely to happen; to look for with confidence; to count upon as to occur.

ex-pect-an-cy (ĕks-pĕk'tăn-sĭ), *n.* the act or state of waiting for, or looking forward to, something. Also, **expectance.**

ex-pect-ant (ĕks-pĕk'tănt), *adj.* looking forward with confidence; prospective.—*adv.* **expectantly.**

ex-pec-ta-tion (ĕks'pĕk-tā'shŭn), *n.* the act of looking forward to; anticipation; prospect of future advancement.

ex-pec-to-rant (ĕks-pĕk'tō-rănt), *n.* a medicine that promotes expectoration, or spitting.

ex-pec-to-rate (ĕks-pĕk'tō-rāt), *v.t.* to eject or throw off from the lungs by coughing, etc.; to spit.

ex-pec-to-ra-tion (ĕks-pĕk'tō-rā'shŭn), *n.* the act of spitting; the mucous matter expectorated or ejected.

ex-pe-di-en-cy (ĕks-pē'dĭ-ĕn-sĭ), *n.* [*pl.* expediencies (-sĭz)], suitableness; fitness for a special purpose; propriety; advisability. Also, **expedience.**

ex-pe-di-ent (ĕks-pē'dĭ-ĕnt), *adj.* fit; convenient; suitable for a special purpose; advisable; proper: *n.* that which aids as a means to an end; device.

ex-pe-dite (ĕks'pē-dīt), *v.t.* to hasten; quicken; as, to *expedite* work.

ex-pe-di-tion (ĕks"pē-dĭsh'ŭn), *n.* haste; dispatch; promptness; a march, voyage, etc., by an army or a group of persons for some particular purpose; the body of persons engaged in the enterprise.

ex-pe-di-tion-a-ry (ĕks"pē-dĭsh'ŭn-ā-rĭ), *adj.* pertaining to, or forming, a journey for a particular purpose; as, the American *Expeditionary* Forces.

ex-pe-di-tious (ĕks"pē-dĭsh'ŭs), *adj.* effective; speedy; as, *expeditious* work.—*adv.* **expeditiously.**—*n.* **expeditiousness.**

ex-pel (ĕks-pĕl'), *v.t.* [*p.t.* and *p.p.* expelled, *p.pr.* expelling], to drive away; force out; send away by authority.

ex-pend (ĕks-pĕnd'), *v.t.* to lay out; pay out; spend; as, to *expend* strength, time, money.

ex-pend-i-ture (ĕks-pĕn'dĭ-tŭr), *n.* a laying out, as of money, time, labor, etc.; disbursement.

ex-pense (ĕks-pĕns'), *n.* the paying out of money; drain on resources; detriment or injury; as, he did it at the *expense* of his health or his reputation; cost.

ex-pen-sive (ĕks-pĕn'sĭv), *adj.* costly.—*adv.* **expensively.**—*n.* **expensiveness.**

ex-pe-ri-ence (ĕks-pē'rĭ-ĕns), *n.* personal trial and practice; knowledge gained by trial and practice; something lived through: *v.t.* to come to know by personal trial or feeling.—*adj.* **experiential.**

ex-pe-ri-enced (ĕks-pē'rĭ-ĕnst), *p.adj.* skilled as a result of practice.

ex-per-i-ment (ĕks-pĕr'ĭ-mĕnt), *n.* a trial or operation to discover something previously unknown; a test by which something is confirmed or proved: *v.i.* to make trials or tests to find out something, confirm something, etc.

ex-per-i-men-tal (ĕks-pĕr"ĭ-mĕn'tăl), *adj.* pertaining to, or founded on, trial; guided, or learned, by experience.—*adv.* **experimentally.**

ex-pert (ĕks-pûrt'), *adj.* skilful; adroit; dexterous: *n.* (ĕks'pûrt), one who is skilled or thoroughly informed in any particular kind of knowledge or art; an experienced person; a specialist.—*adv.* **expertly.**—*n.* **expertness.**

ex-pi-ate (ĕks'pĭ-āt), *v.t.* to atone or make satisfaction for; as, to *expiate* a fault.—*n.* **expiation.**

ex-pi-a-tion (ĕks"pĭ-ā'shŭn), *n.* the act of making satisfaction for an offense; atonement.

ex-pi-a-to-ry (ĕks'pĭ-ȧ-tō-rĭ), *adj.* having the power or nature of atonement; atoning.

ex-pi-ra-tion (ĕks"pĭ-rā'shŭn), *n.* termination; end; as, the *expiration* of a year; act of breathing out, as air from the lungs.

ex-pire (ĕk-spīr'), *v.t.* to breathe out from the lungs: *v.i.* to die; to come to an end; as, a leave of absence *expires.*—*adj.* **expiratory.**

ex-plain (ĕks-plān'), *v.t.* to make intelligible or clear; expound or interpret; to illustrate; elucidate.

ex-pla-na-tion (ĕks"plȧ-nā'shŭn), *n.* the act of making clear; interpretation; a mutual clearing up of a misunderstanding.

ex-plan-a-to-ry (ĕks-plăn'ȧ-tō-rĭ), *adj.* serving to make clear; as, an *explanatory* clause.

ex-ple-tive (ĕks'plē-tĭv), *n.* a word not necessary for the sense, inserted in a sentence for ornament or to fill up a verse; hence, an oath: *adj.* filling up; added or inserted for emphasis, etc.

ex-pli-ca-ble (ĕks'plĭ-kȧ-bl), *adj.* that may be explained.

ex-plic-it (ĕks-plĭs'ĭt), *adj.* plain; definite; as, *explicit* instructions.—*adv.* **explicitly.**—*n.* **explicitness.**

ex-plode (ĕks-plōd'), *v.i.* to burst forth with sudden noise and violence; collapse: *v.t.* to cause to burst from a solid to a gaseous state; refute or disprove; as, to *explode* an idea or argument; do away with; as, to *explode* a custom; demolish.

ex-ploit (ĕks-ploit'), *v.t.* to make use of for one's own profit; put to use selfishly: *n.* a remarkable deed or heroic act.

ex-ploi-ta-tion (ĕks"ploi-tā'shŭn), *n.* the act of making use of or getting the value out of; the improvement of lands, working of mines, etc.; selfish use or employment, regardless of right; as, the *exploitation* of the laborer by the capitalist.

ex-plo-ra-tion (ĕks"plō-rā'shŭn), *n.* the discovery and investigation of an unknown country; careful investigation or search, especially geographical research; an examination.

ex-plore (ĕks-plōr'), *v.t.* to search or examine thoroughly; travel in or over (a country) to discover its characteristic features, etc.—*n.* **explorer.**

ex-plo-sion (ĕks-plō'zhŭn), *n.* the act of bursting from a solid to a gaseous state; a sudden bursting with a loud report; a sudden and violent outbreak.

ex-plo-sive (ĕks-plō'sĭv), *adj.* likely to burst forth loudly and violently, or to cause to do so; pronounced with a slight voiced expulsion of the breath, as the consonants *p, b, t,* etc.: *n.* any substance that causes a loud and violent bursting forth, as gunpowder; a consonant pronounced with a slight voiced expulsion of the breath.

ex-po-nent (ĕks-pō'nĕnt), *n.* a figure that shows how often a quantity is to be multiplied by itself, as, a³; one who explains or interprets the principles of something; as, the *exponent* of a principle.

ex-port (ĕks-pōrt'; ĕks'pōrt), *v.t.* to send or carry out of a country, as merchandise: *v.i.* to send goods to a foreign country: *n.* (ĕks'pōrt), any goods sold and sent to a foreign country.—*n.* **exportation.**

ex-pose (ĕks-pōz'), *v.t.* to lay open; uncover; reveal; put forward for sale; leave to the action of any force or circumstance; disclose; place in peril; lay open to censure or ridicule.

ex-po-sé (ĕks"pō"zā'), *n.* a formal recital of the facts of a case; an undesired or undesirable exposure. [Fr.]

ex-po-si-tion (ĕks"pō-zĭsh'ŭn), *n.* an explanation or interpretation; an exhibition; as, the San Francisco *Exposition* of 1915.

ex-pos-i-tor (ĕks-pŏz'ĭ-tẽr), *n.* one who expounds or interprets.

ex-pos-i-to-ry (ĕks-pŏz'ĭ-tō-rĭ), *adj.* serving to explain. Also, **expositive.**

ex post fac-to (ĕks pōst făk'tō), after the deed is done; judging a former state of facts from a later point of view; as, the *ex post facto* working of a law which makes an act punishable in a manner in which it was not punishable when committed. [LAT.]

ex-pos-tu-late (ĕks-pŏs'tū-lāt), *v.i.* to reason earnestly or remonstrate: followed by *with, on,* or *upon.*

ex-pos-tu-la-tion (ĕks-pŏs"tū-lā'shŭn), *n.* earnest pleading; kindly protest; remonstrance.

ex-po-sure (ĕks-pō'zhūr), *n.* the act of revealing, as a crime; the state of being open or subject to attack; as, *exposure* to the weather or to contagion; situation; as, a southern *exposure;* aspect.

ex-pound (ĕks-pound'), *v.t.* to set forth, explain, or interpret; make clear.

ex-press (ĕks-prĕs'), *v.t.* to make known in any way, especially by language; utter; show; represent; squeeze out; to send by quick and direct conveyance: *adj.* plainly stated; exact; not implied; specially prepared; pertaining to quick or direct conveyance; denoting a company whose business it is to transport goods; as, an *express* company: *n.* a person or vehicle that carries letters or small packages rapidly; a fast railway train stopping only at principal stations; a message or dispatch; a regular and systematic method of conveyance for passengers, mails, goods of small bulk, etc.
Syn., *v.* declare, signify, utter, tell.

ex-press-age (ĕks-prĕs'āj), *n.* the charge made for carrying packages by express; the business of carrying packages by express.

ex-press-i-ble (ĕks-prĕs'ĭ-bl), *adj.* capable of being made known, shown, or uttered; suitable to be sent by express.

ex-press-ion (ĕks-prĕsh'ŭn), *n.* the act or power of representing anything; a saying; mode of speech; change of the countenance; as, a peculiar *expression;* modulation of the voice; manner of speaking.

ex-pres-sive (ĕks-prĕs'ĭv), *adj.* full of significance or importance; forcible.—*adv.* **expressively.**—*n.* **expressiveness.**

ex-press-ly (ĕks-prĕs'lĭ), *adv.* plainly; specially; in a pointed manner; in direct terms.

ex-pul-sion (ĕks-pŭl'shŭn), *n.* a driving away by force; banishment; as, the *expulsion* of a student from college.

ex-pul-sive (ĕks-pŭl'sĭv), *adj.* serving to cast out or drive away.

ex-punge (ĕks-pŭnj'), *v.t.* to blot or rub out; erase; efface.

ex-pur-gate (ĕks'pŭr-gāt; ĕks-pŭr'gāt), *v.t.* to remove (whatever is offensive to good taste or morality): said of books.—*n.* **expurgation.**

ex-qui-site (ĕks'kwĭ-zĭt), *adj.* refined; delicate; nice; accurate; choice; excellent; highly finished; very intensely or sensitively felt; extreme: *n.* a person overrefined in dress; a dandy.—*adv.* **exquisitely.**—*n.* **exquisiteness.**

ex-tant (ĕks'tănt), *adj.* in existence; not destroyed or lost; as, old prints or writings that are still *extant.*

ex-tem-po-ra-ne-ous (ĕks-tĕm"pō-rā'nē-ŭs), *adj.* without previous notes or study; as, an *extemporaneous* speech; offhand; sudden. Also, **extemporary.**

ex-tem-po-re (ĕks-tĕm'pō-rē), *adv.* without study or meditation; as, to speak *extempore.*

ex-tem-po-rize (ĕks-tĕm'pō-rīz), *v.t.* to compose on the spur of the moment: *v.i.* to discourse, etc., without notes or previous study; to improvise.

ex-tend (ĕks-tĕnd'), *v.t.* to stretch out; enlarge; continue: *v.i.* to reach to any distance; be prolonged.

ex-ten-si-ble (ĕks-tĕn'sĭ-bl), *adj.* capable of being enlarged. Also, **extensile.**

ex-ten-sion (ĕks-tĕn'shŭn), *n.* the act of reaching or stretching out; the state of being lengthened; enlargement; an addition or annex.

ex-ten-sive (ĕks-tĕn'sĭv), *adj.* wide; comprehensive; far-reaching; as, *extensive* business interests; an *extensive* view.—*adv.* **extensively.**—*n.* **extensiveness.**

ex-ten-sor (ĕks-tĕn'sŏr), *n.* a muscle that serves to straighten any part of the body, as an arm or finger.

ex-tent (ĕks-tĕnt'), *n.* the space or degree to which a thing is enlarged; size; compass; reach; bulk; limit.

ex-ten-u-ate (ĕks-tĕn'ū-āt), *v.t.* to offer excuses for; as, he sought to *extenuate* his fault; to make less blamable.—*n.* **extenuation.**

ex-te-ri-or (ĕks-tē'rĭ-ĕr), *adj.* outward; external: *n.* that which is outside; outer surface: **exterior angle,** an angle formed by the side of a polygon and the adjacent side, produced; one of the four outside angles formed by a transversal cutting two parallels.

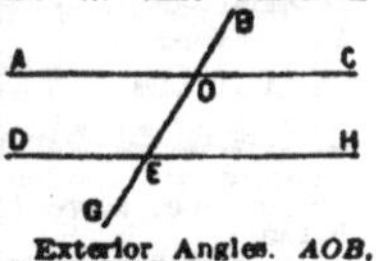

Exterior Angles. *AOB, BOC, DEG, GEH.*

ex-ter-mi-nate (ĕks-tûr'mĭ-nāt), *v.t.* to destroy utterly; annihilate; root out.—*n.* **exterminator.**

ex-ter-mi-na-tion (ĕks-tûr"mĭ-nā'shŭn), *n.* a destroying wholly; complete destruction.

ex-ter-nal (ĕks-tûr'năl), *adj.* outside; exterior; foreign; superficial: *n.* an outward part; an outward form, rite, or ceremony.—*adv.* **externally.**

ex-tinct (ĕks-tĭnkt'), *adj.* quenched; put out; worn out; inactive; as, an *extinct* volcano; nonexistent.

ex-tinc-tion (ĕks-tĭnk'shŭn), *n.* the act of putting out; state of being put out; a destroying or putting an end to; complete destruction.

ex-tin-guish (ĕks-tĭn'gwĭsh), *v.t.* to put out, as a light; to smother; put under a cloud; make unnoticed.—*adj.* **extinguishable.**—*n.* **extinguishment.**

ex-tin-guish-er (ĕks-tĭn'gwĭsh-ĕr), *n.* one who, or that which, puts out; a hollow cone for putting out a light.

ex-tir-pate (ĕks'tĕr-pāt; ĕks-tûr'pāt), *v.t.* to root out; destroy; exterminate.

ex-tir-pa-tion (ĕks-tĕr-pā'shŭn), *n.* a rooting out; complete destruction.

ex-tir-pa-tor (ĕks'tĕr-pā'tĕr), *n.* one who, or that which, roots out; a destroyer.

ex-tol (ĕks-tōl'; ĕks-tŏl'), *v.t.* [*p.t.* and *p.p.* extolled, *p.pr.* extolling], to praise highly; magnify; laud; celebrate.

ex-tort (ĕks-tôrt'), *v.t.* to obtain by threats, violence, or injustice; as, to *extort* money from the poor.

ex-tor-tion (ĕks-tôr'shŭn), *n.* the act of obtaining by force or threat; oppressive or unjust exaction, as of excessive price or interest.

ex-tor-tion-ate (ĕks-tôr'shŭn-āt), *adj.* oppressive; excessive; unjust; as, *extortionate* prices, taxes, or demands.—*adv.* **extortionately.**

ex-tor-tion-er (ĕks-tôr'shŭn-ẽr), *n.* one who demands more than is just and obtains by unjust means. Also, **extortionist.**

ex-tra (ĕks'trȧ), *n.* something in addition to what is usual; a copy of a newspaper issued in addition to the regular edition; *adj.* over and above what is ordinary; additional; unusually good: **extra-**, a *prefix* meaning over and above; beyond; besides; found in numerous words; as, *extra*-official, *extra*-parochial, *extra*-judicial, *extra*-mural, etc.

ex-tract (ĕks-trăkt'), *v.t.* to draw or obtain from a substance by some process; as, to *extract* perfume from flowers; to draw or pull out; as, to *extract* a tooth; to get by effort; as, to *extract* money from a miser; *extract* joy from life; to select; as, to *extract* a passage from a book; *n.* (ĕks'trăkt), an essential drawn out by heat or some chemical process; a quotation.—*adj.* **extractable.**

ex-trac-tion (ĕks-trăk'shŭn), *n.* the act of taking out; lineage; birth, or descent.

ex-trac-tor (ĕks-trăk'tẽr), *n.* one who, or that which, takes out.

ex-tra-di-ta-ble (ĕks"trȧ-dī'tȧ-bl), *adj.* liable or subject to surrender to another authority; making liable to such surrender; as, an *extraditable* offense.

ex-tra-dite (ĕks'trȧ-dīt), *v.t.* to surrender (a person) to another government under the terms of a treaty of extradition or special agreement.

ex-tra-di-tion (ĕks"trȧ-dĭsh'ŭn), *n.* the surrender by the government of one state or nation to another of a person guilty of a crime, in accordance with the terms of a treaty or agreement between the two states or nations.

ex-tra-ne-ous (ĕks-trā'nē-ŭs), external, foreign; not essential.—*adv.* **extraneously.**

ex-traor-di-na-ry (ĕks-trôr'dĭ-nā-rĭ; ĕks"trȧ-ôr'dĭ-nā-rĭ), *adj.* beyond or out of the usual course; uncommon; unusual; remarkable; rare; eminent; special.—*adv.* **extraordinarily.**

ex-trav-a-gance (ĕks-trăv'ȧ-găns), *n.* excess in anything, especially in spending money; waste; profusion. Also, **extravagancy.**

ex-trav-a-gant (ĕks-trăv'ȧ-gănt), *adj.* exceeding reasonable limits; wasteful; prodigal; irregular; needlessly lavish in spending money; visionary.

Syn. lavish, profuse, heedless.

Ant. (see parsimonious).

ex-trav-a-gan-za (ĕks-trav"ȧ-găn'zȧ), *n.* something out of rule; a stage burlesque; an irregular piece of music; a wild flight of language or feeling.

ex-treme (ĕks-trēm'), *adj.* of the highest degree; last; utmost; furthest; final; most severe or strict; *n.* the utmost degree of anything; extremity: excess; end: *pl.* points at the greatest distance from each other.—*adv.* **extremely.**

ex-trem-ist (ĕks-trĕm'ĭst), *n.* a supporter of very new and surprising, or very severe, views or measures.

ex-trem-i-ty (ĕks-trĕm'ĭ-tĭ), *n.* [*pl.* extremities (-tĭz)], the utmost point or degree; remotest part; utmost violence, vigor, or necessity; end: *pl.* the limbs of the body.

ex-tri-cate (ĕks'trĭ-kāt), *v.t.* to free from difficulties, complications, or perplexity; disembarrass; disentangle.—*adj.* **extricable.**—*n.* **extrication.**

ex-trin-sic (ĕks-trĭn'sĭk), *adj.* external; not belonging or necessary to a thing; foreign.

ex-trude (ĕks-trōōd'), *v.t.* to thrust or push out; to expel.

ex-u-ber-ance (ĕgz-ū'bẽr-ăns), *n.* superabundance; an overflowing supply; luxuriance. Also, **exuberancy.**

ex-u-ber-ant (ĕgz-ū'bẽr-ănt), *adj.* copious; abundant; overflowing.—*adv.* **exuberantly.**

ex-ude (ĕks-ūd'; ĕgz-ūd'), *v.t.* to discharge gradually through pores: *v.i.* to flow out slowly.—*n.* **exudation.**

ex-ult (ĕg-zŭlt'), *v.i.* to rejoice exceedingly; to triumph; be glad above measure.

ex-ul-tant (ĕg-zŭl'tănt), *adj.* rejoicing triumphantly.—*adv.* **exultantly.**

ex-ul-ta-tion (ĕg-zŭl-tā'shŭn), *n.* high spirits over success of any kind; triumphant joy.

eye (ī), *n.* the organ of sight; the eyeball; sight; observation; view; a small perforation or hole; as, the *eye* of a needle; bud; that which resembles an eye: *v.t.* [*p.t.* and *p.p.* eyed, *p.pr.* eying], to watch closely; keep in view; scrutinize.—*adj.* **eyeless.**

eye-ball (ī'bôl"), *n.* the globe or ball of the eye.

eye-brow (ī'brou"), *n.* the hairy arch above the eyes.

eye-glass (ī'glȧs"), *n.* a lens for the eyes; a monocle; the glass of a telescope or microscope nearest the eye.

eye-lash (ī'lăsh"), *n.* the fringe of hair that lines the eyelid.

eye-let (ī'lĕt), *n.* a small hole to receive a lace or cord; a ring of metal to strengthen such a hole.

eye-lid (ī'lĭd"), *n.* the movable skin which covers over and closes the eye.

eye-serv-ant (ī'sûr"vănt), *n.* one who does his duty only when watched.—*n.* **eyeservice.**

eye-sight (ī'sīt"), *n.* ability to see; range of vision; view.

eye-sore (ī'sōr"), *n.* anything that offends or is disagreeable to the sight.

eye-tooth (ī'tōōth"), *n.* [*pl.* eyeteeth (-tēth)], one of the upper canine front teeth in the human jaw.

eye-wit-ness (ī'wĭt"nĕs; ī"wĭt'nĕs), *n.* one who has seen an act; one who testifies to what he has seen.

ey-rie (ā'rĭ; ē'rĭ), *n.* the nest of a bird of prey, as an eagle or a hawk. Also, **eyry, aery, aerie.**

E-ze-ki-el (ē-zē'kĭ-ĕl; ē-zēk'yĕl), *n.* an Old Testament book, containing the preaching of the prophet Ezekiel.

Ez-ra (ĕz'rȧ), *n.* a book of the Old Testament, containing an account of the return of the Jews from the captivity in Babylon, and the life and teachings of Ezra the scribe.

F

fa (fä), *n.* the fourth note in the sol-fa musical notation = F.

Fa-bi-an (fā'bĭ-ăn), *adj.* practicing a policy of delay, as in the case of Fabius and Hannibal.

fa-ble (fā'bl), *n.* a fictitious tale; an untruth; a story intended to teach a useful or moral truth, in which, usually, animals talk and act like human beings: *v.i.* to write or tell stories of one's own invention; to lie: *v.t.* to pretend; to tell of falsely.

fab-ric (făb'rĭk), *n.* cloth woven from cotton, woolen, linen, or silk thread; any woven goods; the structure of anything.

fab-ri-cate (făb'rĭ-kāt), *v.t.* to construct; form by manufacture or art; to invent, as an untrue tale: **fabricated ship,** a standardized ship constructed with interchangeable parts.—*n.* **fabricator, fabrication.**

fab-u-list (făb'ū-lĭst), *n.* one who makes up or invents stories, usually moral tales.

fab-u-lous (făb'ū-lŭs), *adj.* not true or real; mythical.—*adv.* **fabulously.**

fa-çade (fȧ-säd'), *n.* front of a building; especially, the main front.

face (fās), *n.* the countenance; dial of a clock, etc.; front; visage; surface; appearance; outward aspect; confidence; personal influence; an expressive grimace; value, excluding discount or interest: said of a note, etc., as *face*-value: *v.t.* [*p.t.* and *p.p.* faced, *p.pr.* facing], to meet in front; oppose with boldness or confidence; stand opposite to; cover with an additional surface: *v.i.* to turn the body, as after the command "right face."

Syn., *n.* visage, countenance.

face card (fās kärd), a playing card; the king, queen, or jack of any suit.

faced (fāst), *p.adj.* having a face; dressed, as stone; furnished with a covering, as of metal or cloth.

fac-et (făs'ĕt), *n.* a small surface or face; one of the minute planes into which the surface of a diamond is cut: *v.t.* to cut or work small faces upon; as, to *facet* a diamond.

fa-ce-tious (fȧ-sē'shŭs), *adj.* humorous; jocular.—*adv.* **facetiously.**—*n.* **facetiousness.**

Syn., *adj.* pleasant, jocose, laughable.
Ant. (see serious).

fa-cial (fā'shăl), *adj.* pertaining to the face; as, *facial* expression.

fac-ile (făs'ĭl), *adj.* not hard to do; easily done; ready or quick in performing or doing; fluent.

fa-cil-i-tate (fȧ-sĭl'ĭ-tāt), *v.t.* to make easy or less difficult; lessen the labor of.

fa-cil-i-ty (fȧ-sĭl'ĭ-tĭ), *n.* [*pl.* facilities (-tĭz)], freedom from difficulty; dexterity; ease; pliancy; ready compliance: *pl.* the means by which any act may be more easily done.

fac-ing (fās'ĭng), *p.pr.* of *face*: *n.* a covering in front for ornamental or other purposes; *pl.* military movements in drill in turning to the right, left, etc.; the collars, cuffs, etc., of different color from the coat on a military uniform.

fac-sim-i-le (făk-sĭm'ĭ-lē), *n.* an exact reproduction, copy, or likeness of an original.

fact (făkt), *n.* anything that is done; that which certainly exists; reality; event; truth.

fac-tion (făk'shŭn), *n.* a group of persons in a state, political party, etc., who are working for a special end or aim; a party in disloyal opposition; dissension.—*adj.* **factional.**

fac-tious (făk'shŭs), *adj.* given to or characterized by a tendency to oppose; quarrelsome; turbulent.

fac-ti-tious (făk-tĭsh'ŭs), *adj.* artificial; sham; not natural.—*adv.* **factitiously.**—*n.* **factitiousness.**

fac-tor (făk'tẽr), *n.* an agent; one who transacts business for another; one of two or more quantities (multiplier and multiplicand) which, multiplied together, give a product; any circumstance, etc., which produces a result: *v.t.* resolve into mathematical factors.

Syn., *n.* agent, steward.

fac-tor-age (făk'tẽr-āj), *n.* a factor's commission; conduct of business by a factor.

fac-to-ry (făk'tō-rĭ), *n.* [*pl.* factories (-rĭz)], a place where goods are made; a manufactory; a trading station.

fac-to-tum (făk-tō'tŭm), *n.* a person employed for, or in charge of, all kinds of work; as, he was general *factotum* on the farm.

fac-ul-ty (făk'ŭl-tĭ), *n.* [*pl.* faculties (-tĭz)], any mental or physical power; mental ability; skill obtained by practice; ability; ease; readiness; the members collectively of any one of the learned professions, especially the medical; the masters and professors in a university, college, or school.

fad (făd), *n.* a pet idea or hobby; a passing fashion; as, Futurism in painting is probably a passing *fad*.

fad-dist (făd'ĭst), *n.* one who takes up every new idea; as, the king was charged with being a *faddist*.

fade (fād), *v.i.* to lose color or distinctness; wither; droop; die away.

fad-ing (fād'ĭng), *n.* decay; loss of color: *p.adj.* losing color; as, the *fading* sunset.

fæ-cal (fē'kăl), *adj.* pertaining to excrement, dregs, or sediment. Also, **fecal.**

fæ-ces (fē'sēz), *n.pl.* dregs; excrement; sediment. Also, **feces.**

fag (făg), *v.i.* [*p.t.* and *p.p.* fagged, *p.pr.* fagging], to work hard; grow weary; drudge for another: *v.t.* to tire out or exhaust; to compel to drudge for another: *n.* one who drudges for another, as a schoolboy for one in a higher class; fatigue or weariness; drudgery; slang, a cigarette.

fag-end (făg'ĕnd'), *n.* the latter or meaner part of anything; the frayed end of a piece of cloth, rope, etc.

fag-ot (făg'ŭt), *n.* a bundle of sticks bound together; a bundle of fish laid up for drying; a bundle of scrap- or wrought-iron or steel to be worked over: *v.t.* to form into fagots. Also, **faggot.**

Fah-ren-heit (fä'rĕn-hīt), *n.* the name of a thermometer scale, having 32 degrees as its freezing point, and 212 degrees as the boiling point of water.

fail (fāl), *v.i.* to fall short; be deficient; waste away; decline; turn out badly; become bankrupt: *v.t.* to be wanting, or insufficient for; forsake: *n.* failure; omission.
Syn., *v.* droop, fall, lose.
Ant. (see accomplish).

fail-ing (fāl'ĭng), *p.pr.* of *fail:* *n.* a fault; weakness; imperfection; the act of becoming bankrupt.

faille (fāl, or fä'yĕ), *n.* a soft silk used for dresses or bonnet, trimmings, etc., having a light grain, without gloss. [Fr.]

fail-ure (fāl'ūr), *n.* the act of falling short, wasting away, or turning out badly; omission; neglect or nonperformance; want of success; decay, or defect from decay; as, the *failure* of eyesight; the act of becoming bankrupt.

fain (fān), *adv.* willingly; gladly; as, I would *fain* do your pleasure: *adj.* glad; willing; constrained; as, she was *fain* to keep silence.

faint (fānt), *v.i.* to become feeble; lose consciousness; swoon; lose courage: *adj.* feeble; languid; depressed; spiritless; not bright or vivid in color; not loud or clear: *n.* a sudden loss of consciousness.

faint-ness (fānt'nĕs), *n.* languor; inactivity; loss of strength.

fair (fâr), *adj.* beautiful; pleasing to the eye or mind; free from any dark hue; blonde; spotless; not cloudy; fine; favorable; prosperous; just; equitable; legible; as, she made a *fair* copy; of good reputation; reasonable; passably good: *n.* the female sex: with *the;* a market held at particular times; a sale of useful and fancy goods, etc., for charity: *adv.* distinctly; openly; honestly; politely; favorably.

fair green (fâr grēn), in golf, the short cut grass between the tees and the putting greens.

fair-ly (fâr'lĭ), *adv.* honorably; openly; as, the game was *fairly* won.

fair-ness (fâr'nĕs), *n.* the quality of being just; lightness of coloring; beauty; equity or justice; clearness; candor.

fair-spo-ken (fâr'spō"kĕn), *adj.* uttered pleasantly; courteous; employing polite speech.

fair-way (fâr'wā"), *n.* the part of a road or river where the natural channel is; in golf, short cut grass between the tee and the green.

fair-y (fâr'ĭ), *n.* [*pl.* fairies (-ĭz)], an imaginary being of graceful and tiny human form, supposed to interfere in human affairs for good or evil; an elf; fay; sprite; brownie: *adj.* pertaining to, or like, fairies.

fair-y-land (fâr'ĭ-lănd"), *n.* the supposed abode of fairies; an enchanting and pleasant place.

fair-y ring (fâr'ĭ ring), a small circle of grass greener than the turf surrounding it, caused by an underground fungus or quick-growing plant, but said to be caused by fairies in their dances.

faith (fāth), *n.* belief; trust in the honesty and truth of another; trust in God; fidelity; honesty; a system of religion.
Syn. creed, doctrine.
Ant. (see unbelief, infidelity).

faith-ful (fāth'fŏŏl), *adj.* true to a promise or to a friend; trustworthy; truthful; honest; loyal.—*adv.* **faithfully.**—*n.* **faithfulness.**
Syn. true, constant.
Ant. (see faithless).

faith-less (fāth'lĕs), *adj.* untrustworthy; not truthful; disloyal; dishonest; false to promises; unbelieving.—*adv.* **faithlessly.**—*n.* **faithlessness.**

fake (fāk), *v.t.* to fold or coil, as a rope; to cover up imperfections; cheat or deceive; steal: *n.* a coil or turn of a rope; a cheat or dodge; hoax; a swindler or trickster.

faked (fākt), *p.adj.* imperfectly made; intended to cheat with.

fak-er (fāk'ẽr), *n.* one who deceives; a swindler; a street vendor.

fa-kir (fȧ-kēr'; fā'kẽr), *n.* a Mohammedan beggar or traveling wonder-worker.

Fakir

fal-chion (fôl'chŭn; fôl'shŭn), *n.* a short, slightly curved sword, with a broad blade.

fal-con (fô'kn; fôl'kn), *n.* a bird with a hooked beak, trained for hunting.

fal-con-er (fô'kn-ẽr), *n.* one who trains hawks for hunting or who hunts with hawks.

fal-con-ry (fô'kn-rĭ), *n.* the art of training hawks to pursue other birds.

fall (fôl), *v.i.* [*p.t.* fell, *p.p.* fallen, *p.pr.* falling], to drop from a higher to a lower place; drop from an erect position; descend; sink; flow into; perish; be degraded or disgraced; as, he will *fall* from his high position; befall or happen; as, night *falls;* become the property of; as, the estate *falls* to him: *adj.* pertaining to the autumn: *n.* the act of dropping from a higher to a lower place; distance through which anything drops; overthrow; ruin; death; waterfall; cataract; decrease in value; autumn.
Syn., *v.* drop, droop, sink, tumble.
Ant. (see rise).

fal-la-cious (fă-lā'shŭs), *adj.* deceptive; misleading; as, *fallacious* reasons or reasoning.—*adv.* **fallaciously.**

fal-la-cy (făl'ȧ-sĭ), *n.* [*pl.* fallacies (-sĭz)], a deceptive or false appearance; mistake; an unsound method of reasoning.

fall-en (fôl'n), *p.adj.* dropped; degraded; dead; lessened; decreased; disgraced; overthrown; prostrate.

fal-li-bil-i-ty (făl'ĭ-bĭl'ĭ-tĭ), *n.* the state of being likely to be wrong; liability to err.

fal-li-ble (făl'ĭ-bl), *adj.* liable to be deceived; liable to err, or fail; liable to be wrong; as, man's judgment is *fallible.*

fal-low (făl'ō), *v.t.* to keep untilled: *adj.* plowed but not sown for the season; untilled; neglected; of a pale yellow or reddish-yellow color: *n.* land plowed but left unseeded.

fal-low deer (făl'ō dēr), a kind of deer of yellowish-brown color, with branched and recurved horns.

false (fôls), *adj.* untrue; dishonest; disloyal; counterfeit; not well founded; unreliable; made for temporary use; in music, not in harmony.—*adv.* **falsely.**

false-hood (fôls'hŏŏd), *n.* an untruth; lie; misstatement with intention to deceive.

false keel (fôls kēl), the timber below the main keel of a vessel.

false-ness (fôls'nĕs), *n.* deceitfulness; inaccuracy; the state of being dishonest, untrue, or faithless.

fal-set-to (fôl-sĕt'ō), *n.* a tone higher than the natural voice; a false or artificial voice.

false work (fôls wûrk), something built as an aid to the completion of another construction; as, the *false work* of a bridge.

fal-si-fi-ca-tion (fôl"sĭ-fĭ-kā'shŭn), *n.* the act or process of proving (a statement, etc.) to be false; a counterfeit; a lie.

fal-si-fy (fôl'sĭ-fī), *v.t.* [*p.t.* and *p.p.* falsified, *p.pr.* falsifying], to make, or prove to be, untrue; as, to *falsify* a statement; to counterfeit; forge: *v.i.* to lie.—*n.* **falsifier.**

fal-si-ty (fôl'sĭ-tĭ), *n.* [*pl.* falsities (-tĭz)], the quality of being untrue; an untruth.

Fal-staff-i-an (fôl-stăf'ĭ-ăn), *adj.* like Falstaff, the fat knight in Shakespeare's *Henry IV* and *Merry Wives of Windsor;* hence, boasting, coarsely jovial, etc.

fal-ter (fôl'tẽr), *v.t.* to utter in a weak trembling manner: *v.i.* to show moral or physical hesitancy; waver; tremble; fail in utterance; stammer; as, his speech *falters.*

fame (fām), *n.* public report; rumor; celebrity; renown.

famed (fāmd), *p.adj.* renowned; celebrated; of high repute.

fa-mil-iar (fȧ-mĭl'yȧr), *adj.* well acquainted, or intimate, with; domestic; affable; easy; unconstrained; unceremonious: *n.* a familiar spirit; an intimate; a demon or evil spirit.—*adv.* **familiarly.**

fa-mil-i-ar-i-ty (fȧ-mĭl'ĭ-ăr'ĭ-tĭ; fȧ-mĭl"-yăr'ĭ-tĭ), *n.* [*pl.* familiarities (-tĭz)], intimacy; ease of conversation; freedom from ceremony or conventionality; liberty or freedom.

fa-mil-iar-ize (fȧ-mĭl'yȧr-īz), *v.t.* to make well acquainted; as, he *familiarized* himself with every quarter of the city.

fam-i-ly (făm'ĭ-lĭ), *n.* [*pl.* families (-lĭz)], a household; children as distinguished from the parent; a body of persons descended from a common ancestor; tribe; race; genealogy; class; a group of animals larger than a genus or class, but less than an order; in botany, an order.

fam-ine (făm'ĭn), *n.* scarcity of food; extreme dearth resulting in starvation.

fam-ish (făm'ĭsh), *v.t.* and *v.i.* to starve; as, the people *famished* while the nobles dwelt in luxury.

Electric Fan

fa-mous (fā'mŭs), *adj.* renowned; conspicuous; noted.—*adv.* **famously.**
Syn. celebrated, illustrious.

fan (făn), *v.t.* [*p.t.* and *p.p.* fanned, *p.pr.* fanning], to agitate or move, as the air, with, or as with, a fan; ventilate; winnow, or separate, as chaff from grain: *n.* an article with a thin, flat surface and a handle, intended for cooling the face by stirring the air; an instrument for exciting a current of air; anything like a fan in shape; colloquially, a baseball enthusiast; a fanatic on any form of sport, especially baseball.

fa-nat-ic (fȧ-năt'ĭk), *n.* one who is wildly extravagant in his views, especially on religious subjects: *adj.* characterized by wild enthusiasm; visionary. Also, **fanatical.**

fa-nat-i-cal-ly (fȧ-năt'ĭ-kăl-ĭ), *adv.* in an overenthusiastic or extravagant manner.

fa-nat-i-cism (fȧ-năt'ĭ-sĭzm), *n.* extravagant or frenzied zeal; wild enthusiasm.

fan-cied (făn'sĭd), *p.adj.* imaginary; existing merely in the mind.

fan-ci-er (făn'sĭ-ẽr), *n.* one who breeds or sells animals and birds.

fan-ci-ful (făn'sĭ-fŏŏl), *adj.* led by imagination; unreal; odd; whimsical; wild.—*adv.* **fancifully.**

fan-cy (făn'sĭ), *v.t.* [*p.t.* and *p.p.* fancied, *p.pr.* fancying], to imagine; take a liking to; be pleased with: *v.i.* to imagine something without proof or grounds for so doing; suppose: *adj.* ornamental; not plain; based on imagination; elegant; above actual worth; as, a *fancy* price: *n.* idea; imagination; notion; liking; caprice; pet pursuit.

fan-dan-go (făn-dăn'gō), *n.* a lively Spanish dance; a lively ball.

fane (fān), *n.* a temple; church; as, the Parthenon was a *fane* sacred to the goddess Athena.

fan-fare (făn'fâr"), *n.* a flourish of trumpets; noisy, ostentatious, or showy parade.

fan-fa-ron-ade (făn"fȧ-rŏn-ād'), *n.* blustering talk or swagger: *v.i.* to make a noisy parade.

fang (făng), *n.* the lower part of a tooth set in the socket; the poison-tooth of a serpent; a tusk, claw, talon, or pointed tooth.

fan-tail (făn'tāl"), *n.* a kind of pigeon having many tail feathers which spread out like a fan.

fan-tan (făn'tăn"), *n.* a Chinese gambling game played with coins or similar small objects.

fan-ta-si-a (făn"tȧ-zē'ȧ; făn-tā'zĭ-ȧ), *n.* a fanciful musical composition not restricted by the usual laws of form or time.

fan-tas-tic (făn-tăs'tĭk), *adj.* odd; whimsical; unreal; grotesque; imaginary. Also, **fantastical.**—*adv.* **fantastically.**

fan-ta-sy (făn'tȧ-sĭ), *n.* a grotesque idea; a whimsical fancy; a mental caprice; imagination; fancy. Also, **phantasy.**

far (fär), *adj.* [*comp.* farther, further, *superl.* farthest, furthest], remote; distant; extending widely or at length; contrary to design or purpose: *adv.* remotely; very much; to a certain point or degree; to a great distance; widely.—*n.* **farness.**

far-a-way (fär'ȧ-wā"), *adj.* dreamy; distant; absent-minded; abstracted; as, a *far-away* look.

farce (färs), *n.* a short comedy in which qualities and actions are much exaggerated; ridiculous or empty parade.

far-ci-cal (fär'sĭ-kăl), *adj.* pertaining to, or of the nature of, a ridiculous comedy; ludicrous; unreal.—*adv.* **farcically.**

fare (fâr), *v.i.* to be in any state, either good or ill; be entertained with food; live; succeed; *n.* the sum paid for a journey by rail, etc.; a person conveyed for hire in a vehicle; provisions of a table; entertainment; the quantity of fish taken in a fishing vessel.

fare-well (fâr″wĕl′; sometimes fâr′wel″), *interj.* may you fare well or prosper; good-by: *adj.* noting or accompanying a parting: *n.* an adieu.

far-fetched (fär′fĕcht″; fär″fĕcht′), *adj.* unnatural; forced; as, a *far-fetched* story.

fa-ri-na (fȧ-rī′nȧ; fȧ-rē′nȧ), *n.* starch; flour or meal obtained by grinding the seeds of cereals, nuts, etc.

far-i-na-ceous (făr″ĭ-nā′shŭs), *adj.* consisting of, made from, or producing, grain; like meal.

farm (färm), *n.* a portion of cultivated land under one ownership, with the buildings, etc., belonging to it: *v.t.* to cultivate (land) at a fixed rental; lease or let: *v.i.* to carry on the operation of cultivating land.

farm-er (fär′mẽr), *n.* one who cultivates a portion of land; an agriculturist; one who collects revenues, taxes, etc., for a certain commission or rate.

farm-house (färm′hous″), *n.* a dwelling house on a farm.

farm-ing (färm′ĭng), *p.adj.* pertaining to, or engaged in, agriculture: *n.* the leasing out or collection of taxes, revenues, etc., for a certain commission or rate per cent; the act of engaging in agriculture.

far-o (fâr′ō; fā′rō), *n.* a game of chance played with cards: so called from the picture of Pharaoh, which formerly was printed on one of the cards.

far-ra-go (fă-rā′gō), *n.* a medley; hotchpotch; as, the tale he told was a *farrago* of nonsense.

far-ri-er (făr′ĭ-ẽr), *n.* one who shoes horses; a noncommissioned cavalry officer in charge of the horses.

far-ri-er-y (făr′ĭ-ẽr-ĭ), *n.* the art or business of a horseshoer; the shop of a horseshoer.

far-row (făr′ō), *v.t.* to give birth to: said of pigs: *n.* a litter of pigs.

far-see-ing (fär′sē″ĭng), *p.adj.* seeing far; having foresight.

far-sight-ed (fär′sīt″ĕd), *adj.* able to look ahead; of keen judgment; able to see best at a distance from the object looked at.

far-ther (fär′thẽr), *adj.* comparative of *far;* more distant or remote; additional: *adv.* more remotely; moreover.

far-ther-most (fär′thẽr-mōst), *adj.* most distant; most remote.

far-thest (fär′thĕst), *adj.* superlative of *far;* most distant, most remote; longest: *adv.* to or at the greatest distance.

far-thing (fär′thĭng), *n.* an English piece of money equal to one-fourth of a penny.

far-thin-gale (fär′thĭn-gāl), *n.* a kind of hoop-skirt formed of circles of whalebone, worn by women of the 16th and 17th centuries. Also, **farthingdale.**

fas-ces (făs′ēz), *n.pl.* a bundle of rods containing an ax, carried before the magistrates of ancient Rome as a symbol of authority.

Fasces

fas-ci-nate (făs′ĭ-nāt), *v.t.* to influence, as if by enchantment; charm; allure; captivate; as, the subject *fascinates* him: *v.i.* to exercise a captivating power.—*adv.* **fascinatingly.**—*n.* **fascinator.**

fas-ci-na-tion (făs″ĭ-nā′shŭn), *n.* the act of bewitching; the state of being bewitched; any invisible influence that overpowers the mind or will; bewitchment; charm.

fas-cine (fă-sēn′), *n.* a bundle of sticks or fagots bound together and used for fortifying ditches, building earthworks, etc.

fash-ion (făsh′ŭn), *n.* the shape or form of anything; custom or usage, especially in dress; the following of the rules of good society; method; general practice: *v.t.* to mold, shape, or form.

fash-ion-a-ble (făsh′ŭn-ȧ-bl), *adj.* according to the prevailing mode; made in accordance with the style of the day; observant of the rules of polite society and its usages; well-bred.—*adv.* **fashionably.**—*n.* **fashionableness.**

fash-ion-er (făsh′ŭn-ẽr), *n.* one who forms, shapes, fits, or molds.

fast (fȧst), *v.i.* to abstain from food, either from necessity, or as a religious rite: *n.* the doing without food as a religious duty: *adj.* quick; speedy in motion; in advance of the standard: said of a timepiece; firm; immovable; close; faithful; gay: *adv.* rapidly, firmly.

Syn., adj. rapid, fleet, speedy.
Ant. (see slow).

fast day (fȧst dā), a day set apart by civil or church authority for religious fasting.

fast-en (fȧs′n), *v.t.* to fix securely; make firm; bolt or bar: *v.i.* to seize or take hold of something: generally with *on.*

fas-ten-ing (fȧs′n-ĭng), *p.pr.* of *fasten:* *n.* the act of making secure; a bolt or clasp.

fas-tid-i-ous (făs-tĭd′ĭ-ŭs), *adj.* hard or difficult to please; over-nice.—*adv.* **fastidiously.**—*n.* **fastidiousness.**

fast-ing (fȧst′ĭng), *p.pr.* of *fast:* *n.* a doing without food, especially as a religious duty.

fast-ness (fȧst′nĕs), *n.* the state or quality of being secure; a fortress or natural stronghold.

fat (făt), *adj.* [*comp.* fatter, *superl.* fattest], corpulent; fleshy; greasy; unusually extended: said of printers' type; broad; sluggish; stupid; dull; prosperous; profitable; fertile: *n.* a solid, oily, yellow or white substance forming part of the tissue of animals; the best or richest of anything: *v.t.* [*p.t.* and *p.p.* fatted, *p.pr.* fatting], to fatten; cause to gain flesh: *v.i.* to become fat.

fa-tal (fā′tăl), *adj.* causing death or destruction; as, a *fatal* accident; mortal; involving life and death; having important consequences.—*adv.* **fatally.**

fa-tal-ism (fā′tăl-ĭzm), *n.* the doctrine that all things are predetermined by fate and therefore happen regardless of one's efforts.

fa-tal-ist (fā′tăl-ĭst), *n.* a believer in the doctrine that all things are determined in advance of their happening.—*adj.* **fatalistic.**

fa-tal-i-ty (fȧ-tăl′ĭ-tĭ), *n.* [*pl.* **fatalities** (-tĭz)], predetermined order or series of events; destiny; a calamity; an event involving life and death.

Fa-ta Mor-ga-na (fä′tä môr-gä′nä), a medieval fairy; the mirage sometimes seen near the straits of Messina: **fata morgana**, figuratively, a fantastic conception. [IT.]

fate (fāt), *n.* destiny; inevitable or unavoidable necessity; death or destruction; predestined lot: **the Fates,** the three classic goddesses, Clotho, Lachesis, and Atropos, who were supposed to preside over the destinies of mankind.

fat-ed (fāt'ed), *p.adj.* decreed by fate; destined; doomed.

fate-ful (fāt'fo͝ol), *adj.* possessing fatal power or the power to kill; fatal.—*adv.* **fatefully.**

fa-ther (fä'*th*ẽr), *n.* a male parent or ancestor; one who stands in the relation of a father; an originator or founder; the official title of a dignitary, priest, or confessor of the Roman Catholic Church; the senior member of any class, profession, or body; a religious writer of the Early Christian Church: *v.t.* to adopt as a son or daughter; to assume authorship of or accept responsibility for; as, to *father* a bill in Congress: **Father,** the Creator; God.

fa-ther-hood (fä'*th*ẽr-ho͝od), *n.* paternity or parenthood; as, the *fatherhood* of God.

fa-ther-in-law (fä'*th*ẽr-in-lô'), *n.* the father of one's husband or wife.

fa-ther-land (fä'*th*ẽr-lănd'), *n.* one's native country.

fa-ther-less (fä'*th*ẽr-lĕs), *adj.* without a living father.

fa-ther-ly (fä'*th*ẽr-lĭ), *adj.* pertaining to a father; kind and affectionate, like a father.

fath-om (făth'ŭm), *n.* a measure of length equal to six feet: used of the depth of water: *v.t.* to measure by sounding; to sound; to get to the bottom of; to find the depth of.—*adj.* **fathomable.**

fath-om-less (făth'ŭm-lĕs), *adj.* so deep that it cannot be sounded; not possible to understand; as, a *fathomless* mystery.

fa-tigue (fȧ-tēg'), *n.* weariness; toil; bodily or mental exhaustion: *v.t.* to weary with bodily or mental effort; tire; harass.

fa-tigue du-ty (fȧ-tēg' dū'tĭ), the labor a soldier performs apart from the practice of arms.

fat-ling (făt'lĭng), *n.* a young animal fattened for slaughter.

fat-ness (făt'nĕs), *n.* the quality or state of being stout; corpulency; fertility.

fat-ten (făt'n), *v.t.* to make fat, plump, or stout; feed for the table; make fertile or abundant.

fat-ty (făt'ĭ), *adj.* consisting or having the qualities of fat; greasy; oily.

fa-tu-i-ty (fȧ-tū'ĭ-tĭ), *n.* weakness of intellect; foolishness; silliness.

fat-u-ous (făt'ū-ŭs), *adj.* weak in intellect; silly; obstinately foolish; idiotic.—*adv.* **fatuously.**—*n.* **fatuousness.**

fau-bourg (fō'bo͞or'; fō'bo͞org), *n.* a suburb; as, the *Faubourg* St. Germain is a delightful section of Paris. [Fr.]

fau-cet (fô'sĕt), *n.* a device fixed in a pipe to control the flow of liquid from it.

faugh (fô), *interj.* an exclamation of disgust or abhorrence.

fault (fôlt), *n.* a slight crime or offense; blemish; defect in character; omission; the loss of scent in hunting: said of a hound; an accidental leak in an electric circuit; an improper service in lawn tennis.

fault-find-er (fôlt'fīnd'ẽr), *n.* a person who is always criticizing the acts of others; a mechanical device for locating faults in an electric circuit.

fault-less (fôlt'lĕs), *adj.* without imperfection or blemish; blameless.—*adv.* **faultlessly.**—*n.* **faultlessness.**

fault-y (fôl'tĭ), *adj.* imperfect; defective; marked by faults of conduct.—*adv.* **faultily.**—*n.* **faultiness.**

faun (fôn), *n.* a classic woodland deity or god: represented in human form, but with pointed ears, small horns, and a tail.

Faun

fau-na (fô'nȧ), *n.* [*pl.* faunæ (-nē), faunas (-nȧz)], the animals belonging to any particular region, or period of history.

faux pas (fō' pä'), an error or slip, especially in respect of good manners or morality. [Fr.]

fa-vor (fā'vẽr), *n.* kindness; support; patronage; good will; partiality; bias; a love token; a bunch of ribbons worn on some special occasion: *v.t.* to regard with good will; befriend; resemble in features; spare. Also, **favour.**

fa-vor-a-ble (fā'vẽr-ȧ-bl), *adj.* convenient; advantageous; friendly; partial. Also, **favourable.**—*adv.* **favorably, favourably.**

fa-vored (fā'vẽrd), *p.adj.* treated with partiality; having a special aspect; as, hard-*favored.* Also, **favoured.**

fa-vor-ite (fā'vẽr-ĭt), *n.* one who, or that which, is particularly esteemed; one regarded with undue preference; a person or animal considered to have the best chance of winning in a contest: *adj.* preferred; esteemed. Also, **favourite.**

fa-vor-it-ism (fā'vẽr-ĭt-ĭzm), *n.* the disposition or tendency to treat one person or class well in preference to others possessing equal claims; partiality. Also, **favouritism.**

Fawn

fawn (fôn), *n.* a young deer: *v.i.* to flatter someone meanly: with *on* or *upon;* to show affection by leaping upon, cringing, or licking the hand of a person: said of a dog.

fawn-ing (fôn'ĭng), *p.pr.* of *fawn:* *n.* coarse or cringing flattery.

fay (fā), *n.* an elf; fairy: *v.t.* to fit (two pieces of wood) flush together: *v.i.* to fit closely: used only in shipbuilding.

faze (fāz), *v.t.* to worry; annoy; frighten; disturb; produce an effect on. [Colloq.] Also, **fease, feeze.**

fe-al-ty (fē'ăl-tĭ), *n.* fidelity to one's lord; the duty of an English tenant to his superior or landlord; loyalty; faithfulness.

fear (fēr), *n.* expectation of evil or danger; dread; anxiety; solicitude; reverence: *v.t.* to regard with apprehension; dread: *v.i.* to be in dread; feel anxiety.

Syn., *n.* timidity, timorousness.

Ant. (see bravery).

fear-ful (fēr'fo͝ol), *adj.* affected with dread or anxiety; timorous;

apprehensive; inspiring dread.—*adv.* **fearfully.**—*n.* **fearfulness.**

fear-less (fēr'lĕs), *adj.* without fear; bold; courageous; as, *fearless* explorers have discovered the North Pole.—*adv.* **fearlessly.**—*n.* **fearlessness.**

fear-some (fēr'sŭm), *adj.* dreadful; terrible; as, it is a *fearsome* thing to be alone on the wide sea.

fea-si-bil-i-ty (fē'zĭ-bĭl'ĭ-tĭ), *n.* practicability; capability of being done.

fea-si-ble (fē'zĭ-bl), *adj.* practicable; capable of being carried out; as, the plan that you suggest is not *feasible.*—*adv.* **feasibly.**—*n.* **feasibleness.**

feast (fēst), *n.* a costly repast, especially in commemoration of some event, etc.; a festival, especially of the church; anything affording pleasure to the taste or mind: *v.t.* to entertain sumptuously; delight: *v.i.* to eat of a feast; enjoy oneself.

feat (fēt), *n.* a notable achievement, deed, or performance.

feath-er (fĕth'ĕr), *n.* part of the outer covering of a bird; a plume; the water thrown up by the turn of an oar blade; kind or class; something like a feather, as, in mechanism, a wedge, fin, or flange: *v.t.* to ornament with feathers; cover with, or as with, feathers; turn the blade of (an oar) horizontally when leaving the water: *v.i.* to become covered with feathers.

feath-er-edged (fĕth'ĕr-ĕjd"), *adj.* thin at the edges, as a board; ornamented on the edge with loops or knots of braid or ribbon.

feath-er-weight (fĕth'ĕr-wāt"), *n.* in a handicap, the least weight that can be put on a race horse; any very light weight; a person of very light weight; one of slight ability or importance.

feath-er-y (fĕth'ĕr-ĭ), *adj.* covered with, or like, feathers; very light.

fea-ture (fē'tūr), *n.* any part of the face, such as the eyes, nose, chin, etc.; principal part; outline; characteristic; as, the principal *feature* of the book; appearance: *v.t.* to picture; to give prominence to.

fea-tured (fē'tūrd), *p.adj.* having a particular cast or shape of face; as, a sharp-*featured* man.

fea-ture-less (fē'tūr-lĕs), *adj.* having no marked characteristic or feature; possessing no outstanding characteristic.

feaze (fēz), *v.t.* to disturb; disconcert. [COLLOQ.] Also, **faze, feeze.**

feb-ri-fuge (fĕb'rĭ-fūj), *n.* a medicine that lessens or dispels fever.

fe-brile (fē'brĭl; fĕb'rĭl), *adj.* pertaining to, accompanied by, or indicating fever.

Feb-ru-a-ry (fĕb'rōō-ā-rĭ), *n.* the second month of the year.

fe-cal (fē'kăl), *adj.* relating to excrement, dregs, or sediment. Also, **faecal.**

fe-ces (fē'sēz), *n.pl.* dregs; excrement; sediment. Also, **faeces.**

fec-und (fĕk'ŭnd; fē'kŭnd), *adj.* fruitful; as, the *fecund* earth; prolific.

fe-cun-di-ty (fē-kŭn'dĭ-tĭ), *n.* fruitfulness; fertility of invention or power of creating; germination.

fed (fĕd), past tense and past participle of the verb *feed.*

fed-er-al (fĕd'ĕr-ăl), *adj.* pertaining to, constituting, or founded upon, a league or treaty; consisting of a union or compact between states, especially those of the United States and Switzerland; pertaining to the government of such a union; as, the *federal* constitution; supporting the Union in the American Civil War, 1861-65; as, the *federal* army: *n.* a supporter of federalism, or a union of states.—**Federal Reserve Bank,** an institution centralizing and coördinating the banking system of the United States, with branches in many cities.

fed-er-al-ism (fĕd'ĕr-ăl-ĭzm), *n.* the doctrine of a union of states; the support and development of the central government of the United States.

fed-er-al-ist (fĕd'ĕr-ăl-ĭst), *n.* a member of the party, after the American Revolution, which favored the union of states, under a central government; a supporter of the Union in the Civil War.

fed-er-al-ize (fĕd'ĕr-ăl-īz), *v.t.* to bring together in a political union: *v.i.* to unite in a league under a central government. Also, **federate.**

fed-er-ate (fĕd'ĕr-āt), *adj.* united: *v.i.* (fĕd'ĕr-āt), to combine into a league or union.

fed-er-a-tion (fĕd"ĕr-ā'shŭn), *n.* a league or union with a central government.—*adj.* **federative.**

fee (fē), *n.* payment for service rendered, especially professional service; as, the doctor's *fee;* an inherited estate; land held from a superior: *v.t.* to pay or give a fee to.

fee-ble (fē'bl), *adj.* weak; wanting in physical strength or mental power; infirm.—*adv.* **feebly.**—*n.* **feebleness.**

fee-ble-mind-ed (fē'bl-mīn"dĕd), *adj.* mentally weak; not capable of average or normal mental development; lacking in resolution.

feed (fēd), *v.t.* [*p.t.* and *p.p.* fed, *p.pr.* feeding], to give food to; nourish; to give as food; as, to *feed* oats to horses; supply with necessaries; furnish with materials; as, to *feed* a machine: *v.i.* to eat; subsist: with *on* or *upon;* to graze or pasture: *n.* a certain quantity of food given to animals at one time; fodder; pasture.

feed bag (fēd băg), a bag containing feed, fastened to the nose of an animal.

feed-er (fēd'ĕr), *n.* one who, or that which, feeds; one who fattens cattle; that which nourishes or supplies the needs of or increases the importance or value of; a branch canal or railway; an electric wire supplying a current to a main conductor.

feed-ing (fēd'ĭng), *p.pr.* of *feed:* *n.* the act of eating; pasture; as, he attended to the *feeding* of his flocks.

feed pipe (fēd pīp), a pipe which supplies water to the boiler of a steam engine.

feed pump (fēd pŭmp), a force pump which supplies water to the boiler of a steam engine.

feel (fēl), *v.t.* to perceive by the touch; be conscious of; understand; be influenced or moved by; as, he *felt* the necessity of it; experience, as pleasure or pain; examine by touching or handling: *v.i.* to seem to the touch; as, it *feels* rough; have the passions moved; to grope: *n.* the sense which perceives by touch; touch; sensation.

feel-er (fēl'ĕr), *n.* one who, or that which, feels; that part of an animal which serves as an organ of touch, as the antennae of insects, etc.; something put forth as a means of gaining information not directly obtainable.

feel-ing (fēl'ĭng), *p.adj.* easily affected; sympathetic; of great sensibility;

n. sense of touch; physical or mental sensation; perception; tenderness; sensitiveness; as, I hurt her *feelings*.—*adv.* **feelingly.**
Syn., *n.* sensibility, susceptibility.
Ant. (see insensibility).

fee sim-ple (fē sĭm'pl), an estate in land or tenements held by a person in his own right, without restrictions.

feet (fēt), *n.* plural of *foot;* as, he is six *feet* tall.

feeze (fēz), *v.t.* to disconcert; disturb; frighten. [Colloq.] Also, **faze, feaze, feese.**

feign (fān), *v.t.* to pretend; invent; as, to *feign* illness; *feign* friendship.

feigned (fānd), *adj.* pretended; counterfeited; invented; as, a *feigned* excuse.

feint (fānt), *n.* a pretense; mock attack, as in boxing or fencing.

feld-spar (fĕld'spär"), *n.* one of a common group of closely related crystalline minerals. Also, **felspar.**

fe-lic-i-tate (fē-lĭs'ĭ-tāt), *v.t.* to congratulate.—*n.* **felicitation.**

fe-lic-i-tous (fē-lĭs'ĭ-tŭs), *adj.* characterized by or causing bliss or happiness; delightful; neat; as, a *felicitous* compliment.—*adv.* **felicitously.**

fe-lic-i-ty (fē-lĭs'ĭ-tĭ), *n.* [*pl.* **felicities** (-tĭz)], a condition of supreme happiness; blissfulness; prosperity; appropriateness; a neat or well-chosen expression.

fe-line (fē'lĭn), *adj.* pertaining to, or like, a cat; stealthy; treacherous.

fell (fĕl), *p.t.* of *fall:* *v.t.* to hew, cut, or knock, down; cause to fall: as, to *fell* a tree; turn down (a seam) in a certain way and sew: *adj.* cruel; savage; barbarous; hideous; powerful: *n.* the skin of an animal; a hem laid level with the material; a rocky or barren hill; small pieces of ore.

fel-lah (fĕl'ȧ), *n.* [*pl.* **fellahs** (-āz), **fellaheen** (-hēn)], in Egypt and Syria, a peasant or laboring man.

fel-loe (fĕl'ō), *n.* a curved piece of wood forming the rim of a wheel. Also, **felly.**

fel-low (fĕl'ō), *n.* a companion or associate; one of the same kind; one of a pair; an individual; one held in slight esteem; a member of a society; a graduate member of a college who holds a fellowship; the trustee of a college: *adj.* associated or joined with; as, *fellow* members.

fel-low feel-ing (fĕl'ō fēl'ĭng), a likeness of spirit; sympathy.

fel-low-ship (fĕl'ō-shĭp), *n.* association; communion; intimacy; society; joint interest or feeling; a college endowment for the support of a graduate student.

fel-ly (fĕl'ĭ), *n.* [*pl.* **fellies** (-ĭz)], one of the curved pieces of wood which form the rim of a wheel; the rim. Also, **felloe.**

fel-on (fĕl'ŭn), *n.* one guilty of serious crime; a wicked person; a painful inflammation of a finger or toe: *adj.* malignant; traitorous.

fe-lo-ni-ous (fē-lō'nĭ-ŭs), *adj.* done with the intention of committing crime; malignant.

fel-o-ny (fĕl'ō-nĭ), *n.* [*pl.* **felonies** (-nĭz)], a serious crime, as treason, murder, robbery, etc., punishable by death or imprisonment.

fel-spar (fĕl'spär"), *n.* one of a common group of closely related crystalline minerals. Also, **feldspar.**

felt (fĕlt), *p.t.* of *feel:* *n.* an unwoven fabric made of wool, or wool and hair, forced together by pressure or heat.

felt-ing (fĕlt'ĭng), *n.* the material of which felt is made; the process of making felt.

fe-male (fē'māl), *n.* a human being or animal of the sex which bears young; woman; the plant or flower which bears the pistil and receives the pollen of the male flower: *adj.* pertaining to that sex which produces young; feminine; womanly; having pistils without stamens.

fem-i-nine (fĕm'ĭ-nĭn), *adj.* pertaining to, or like, women; delicate; tender; sensitive; wanting in manly traits; effeminate; in grammar, the gender to which females belong.

fem-i-nin-i-ty (fĕm"ĭ-nĭn'ĭ-tĭ), *n.* the state or quality of being like a woman; womankind.

femme de cham-bre (fȧm dē shäN'-br), a lady's maid; chambermaid. [Fr.]

fem-o-ral (fĕm'ō-răl), *adj.* relating to the thigh; as, the *femoral* artery.

fe-mur (fē'mŭr), *n.* the long bone that forms the skeleton of the thigh; the thigh.

Femur

fen (fĕn), *n.* low, flat, marsh land, covered with grass, etc.; a kind of mold or moss causing disease in hops.—*adj.* **fenny.**

fence (fĕns), *v.t.* to guard or protect; defend; to inclose or surround with a fence; fortify: *v.i.* to practice the art of fencing; *n.* the art of fencing; defense; guard; a boundary consisting of posts, wire, etc., inclosure; skill in debate.

fen-ci-ble (fĕn'sĭ-bl), *adj.* capable of defense, or being defended: *n.* a soldier enlisted for home service.

fenc-ing (fĕn'sĭng), *p.pr.* of *fence:* *n.* the art of skilfully using a foil or sword for attack or defense; materials used for making a fence; a collection of fences; guard; skilful debate.

fend (fĕnd), *v.t.* to ward off; protect with a fender: *v.i.* to provide; as, he must *fend* for himself.

fend-er (fĕn'dẽr), *n.* a cushion of rope, or piece of wood hung over the side of a vessel to prevent injury by contact with a landing-stage or wharf, etc.; a metal guard in front of a fireplace to prevent the hot coal from falling upon the floor; a device attached to the front of a street car, automobile, or locomotive, to prevent injury to people.

Fe-ni-an (fē'nĭ-ăn), *n.* a member of an Irish secret society, whose purpose is home rule for Ireland; one of a legendary band of Irish heroes.

fen-nel (fĕn'ĕl), *n.* a fragrant plant of the parsley family, with yellow flowers.

feod (fūd), *n.* land held in return for service to a feudal lord. Also, **feoff, fief, feud.**

fer-ment (fûr'mĕnt), *n.* that which causes chemical change or fermentation; a gentle boiling or swelling in a liquid; internal commotion; tumult: *v.t.* (fẽr-mĕnt'), to produce chemical change or fermentation in; excite: *v.i.* to be in a state of fermentation; effervesce or bubble; be excited.

fer-men-ta-tion (fûr"mĕn-tā'shŭn), *n.* a chemical change accompanied by effervescence, or bubbling up; working, as of yeast in liquor; excitement; agitation.

fern (fûrn), *n.* a flowerless plant with broad and feathery fronds or leaves.

fern-er-y (fûr'nẽr-ĭ), *n.* [*pl.* ferneries (-ĭz)], a place where ferns are cultivated.

fern-y (fûr'nĭ), *adj.* fernlike or abounding in ferns; as, a *ferny* woods.

fe-ro-cious (fē-rō'shŭs), *adj.* savage; fierce; cruel.—*adv.* **ferociously.**
Syn. wild, barbarous, cruel.
Ant. (see mild).

fe-roc-i-ty (fē-rŏs'ĭ-tĭ), *n.* [*pl.* ferocities (-tĭz)], savageness or cruelty of disposition; inhuman cruelty.

fer-rate (fĕr'āt), *n.* a salt of ferric acid.

fer-ret (fĕr'ĕt), *n.* a kind of weasel, used to hunt rats and rabbits from their holes; a kind of binding; an iron rod for making the rings at the mouths of bottles, or trying melted glass: *v.t.* to search perseveringly for or discover by cunning methods: with *out:* as, to *ferret* out a secret.

fer-ret-er (fĕr'ĕt-ẽr), *n.* one who hunts or searches out, as a secret.

fer-ri-age (fĕr'ĭ-āj), *n.* money paid for conveyance in a boat across a river.

fer-ric (fĕr'ĭk), *adj.* pertaining to, containing, or extracted from, iron: **ferric acid,** an acid composed of three parts of oxygen and one of iron. Also, **ferrous.**

fer-ro-type (fĕr'ō-tīp), *n.* a photograph taken upon a prepared iron plate.

fer-rous (fĕr'ŭs), *adj.* of, pertaining to, or obtained from, iron: **ferrous oxide,** a compound of iron and oxygen. Also, **ferric.**

fer-rule (fĕr'ōōl; fĕr'ĭl), *n.* a metal ring or cap placed at the end of a stick, etc., to strengthen it; as, the *ferrule* of an umbrella.

fer-ry (fĕr'ĭ), *n.* [*pl.* ferries (-ĭz)], a passage across a river, etc.; a boat to carry passengers across a river; the place where such a boat lands its passengers: *v.t.* [*p.t.* and *p.p.* ferried, *p.pr.* ferrying], to convey across a river, etc., in a boat: *v.i.* to go across water, as in a boat.

Ferryboat

fer-tile (fûr'tĭl), *adj.* producing abundantly; fruitful; reproductive; rich in resources or invention.
Syn. prolific, plenteous, productive.
Ant. (see sterile).

fer-til-i-ty (fẽr-tĭl'ĭ-tĭ), *n.* the state or quality of being fruitful; abundance; fecundity or fruitfulness; richness of resources or invention.

fer-ti-li-za-tion (fûr"tĭ-lĭ-zā'shŭn), *n.* the act or process of making fruitful; enrichment.

fer-ti-lize (fûr'tĭ-līz), *v.t.* to make or render fruitful; as, to *fertilize* the soil.

fer-ti-liz-er (fûr'tĭ-līz"ẽr), *n.* any material used as a manure for the land.

fer-ule (fĕr'ōōl; fĕr'ĭl), *n.* a rod or flat stick used in punishment: *v.t.* to chastise or punish with such a stick.

fer-ven-cy (fûr'vĕn-sĭ), *n.* earnestness; ardor; as, the *fervency* of an address; *fervency* of prayer.

fer-vent (fûr'vĕnt), *adj.* zealous; earnest; vehement; very hot. Also, **fervid.** —*adv.* **fervently.**

fer-vid (fûr'vĭd), *adj.* burning; ardent; fiery; intense; eager; vehement. Also, **fervent.**—*adv.* **fervidly.**

fer-vor (fûr'vẽr), *n.* intensity of feeling; zeal; warmth; as, the *fervor* of affection; patriotic *fervor.*

fes-tal (fĕs'tăl), *adj.* pertaining to a feast or holiday; joyous; festive; hilarious; happy.—*adv.* **festally.**

fes-ter (fĕs'tẽr), *v.t.* to cause to ulcerate or rankle: *v.i.* to become ulcerated or sore; generate pus; rankle; rot: *n.* a sore; act of ulcerating or rankling.

fes-ti-val (fĕs'tĭ-văl), *n.* a joyful celebration in commemoration of some event, religious or civil; an entertainment on behalf of some charity; a special kind of entertainment occurring at regular periods; as, the Bach music *festival.*

fes-tive (fĕs'tĭv), *adj.* pertaining to a feast; gay; joyous; merry.—*adv.* **festively.**

fes-tiv-i-ty (fĕs-tĭv'ĭ-tĭ), *n.* [*pl.* festivities (-tĭz)], social gaiety at an entertainment or feast; merrymaking; joyfulness; a celebration.

fes-toon (fĕs-tōōn'), *n.* a wreath or garland hung between two points; an architectural ornament of such form: *v.t.* to decorate with, or form into, such garlands.

fe-tal (fē'tăl), *adj.* of or pertaining to the unborn young of an animal. Also, **foetal.**

fetch (fĕch), *v.t.* to go after and bring; obtain as its price; call for and accompany; heave; as, to *fetch* a sigh; colloquially, fascinate: *v.i.* to move and turn; nautically, to hold a course: *n.* a wraith, apparition, or ghost of a living person: **fetch-light,** the appearance at night of a light resembling a candle, supposed to portend death.

fête (fāt; Fr. fāt), *n.* a festival or holiday; a birthday celebration; the celebration of the day of the saint whose name one bears: *v.t.* to entertain or honor with festivities. [Fr.]

fête cham-pê-tre (fāt shäṅ"pâ'tr), a country or open-air festival. [Fr.]

fet-id (fĕt'ĭd; fē'tĭd), *adj.* giving forth an offensive smell; stinking.

fe-tish (fē'tĭsh; fĕt'ĭsh), *n.* any material object, as a stone, weapon, feather, etc., supposed by the negroes of Western Africa to contain a spirit, and to give to its possessor power over such a deity; hence, any object of unreasoning devotion; an image or idol. Also, **fetich.**

Fetishes

fe-tish-ism (fē'tĭsh-ĭzm), *n.* the worship of, or belief in, fetishes, or the worship of spirits supposed to exist in material things such as stones; unreasoning or superstitious devotion. Also, **fetichism.**

fet-lock (fĕt′lŏk), *n.* a tuft of hair growing behind the lowest part of a horse's leg; the pastern or lowest joint.

fet-locked (fĕt′lŏkt), *p.adj.* having fetlocks; secured or fastened by the fetlocks.

fet-ter (fĕt′ẽr), *n.* a chain or shackle for the feet; a restraint; hindrance: *v.t.* to place in bonds; chain; bind; hinder; restrain.
Syn., n. bondage, custody.

fet-tle (fĕt′l), *v.t.* to put in order; cover or line; fasten: *v.i.* to repair; work with activity; clean up: *n.* good condition or repair; fuss.

fe-tus (fē′tŭs), *n.* the unborn young of an animal in the later stage of development. Also, **fœtus.**

feud (fūd), *n.* a long-established quarrel between clans or families; quarrel; enmity; hatred; land held from a lord on condition of rendering him service. Also, **feod, feoff, fief.**

feu-dal (fū′dăl), *adj.* pertaining to, or founded upon, a method of land-holding used in Europe in the Middle Ages, by which land was granted on condition of service rendered.—*adv.* **feudally.**

feu-dal-ism (fū′dăl-ĭzm), *n.* the feudal system, or the system of land-holding on condition of military or other service, used in Europe during the Middle Ages.

feu-dal-ize (fū′dăl-īz), *v.t.* to make conform to feudalism; as, the Norman French *feudalized* England.

feu-da-to-ry (fū′dȧ-tō-rĭ), *n.* [*pl.* feudatories (-rĭz)], one holding land in return for service rendered to its owner; a vassal: *adj.* pertaining to, or held by, right of service rendered by a vassal to a lord. Also, **feudary.**

fe-ver (fē′vẽr), *n.* any disease characterized by marked increase of heat of the skin, quickened pulse, great weakness, thirst, etc.; a temperature of the human body exceeding 98.6 degrees Fahrenheit; a condition of extreme nervous excitement: *v.t.* to put into a fever.

fe-ver-few (fē′vẽr-fū), *n.* a perennial plant of the aster family, bearing small white flowers.

fe-ver-ish (fē′vẽr-ĭsh), *adj.* affected with, indicating, or resembling fever.—*adv.* **feverishly.**—*n.* **feverishness.**

few (fū), *adj.* [*comp.* fewer, *superl.* fewest], not many; small in number; limited.

few-ness (fū′nĕs), *n.* smallness of number.

fez (fĕz), *n.* a brimless, close fitting, felt hat, usually red, with a black tassel: worn by Turks, Egyptians, etc.

Fez

fi-an-cé (fē″äN-sā′), *n.* [*fem.* fiancée], one who is betrothed or engaged to be married. [Fr.]

fi-as-co (fē-äs′kō), *n.* a complete or ludicrous failure, as of some enterprise of which high hopes were entertained; as, the entertainment given by the musician was a *fiasco;* a flask or bottle.

fi-at (fī′ăt), *n.* a command that something be done; an order of a court authorizing certain proceedings, as in bankruptcy.

fib (fĭb), *n.* a falsehood; white lie; a harmless or humorous untruth: *v.i.* [*p.t.* and *p.p.* fibbed, *p.pr.* fibbing], to tell small untruths; as, to *fib* out of it.

fib-ber (fĭb′ẽr), *n.* one who tells falsehoods or white lies; as, he was a confirmed *fibber.* Also, **fibster.**

fi-ber (fī′bẽr), *n.* a slender threadlike substance, or filament; as, woody *fiber;* raw material which can be separated into threads for making up textile or woven fabrics; as, the *fiber* of hemp. Also, **fibre.**

fi-bril (fī′brĭl), *n.* a very small fiber making up the substance of certain muscles; as, the retina of the eye is composed of *fibrils.*

fi-brin (fī′brĭn), *n.* a white substance formed when the blood is clotted; the part of flesh which appears like fine filaments or fibers.—*adj.* **fibrinous.**

fi-brous (fī′brŭs), *adj.* composed of, or of the nature or form of, fine filaments or threadlike substance. Also, **fibroid.**

fib-ster (fĭb′stẽr), *n.* a liar in a small way. Also, **fibber.**

fib-u-la (fĭb′ū-lȧ), *n.* [*pl.* fibulæ (-lē)], the outer and smaller of the two bones which form the lower leg.

fich-u (fĭsh′ōō; Fr. fē″shü′), *n.* a light three-cornered cape, usually made of muslin or lace, worn on the neck, or over the neck and shoulders. [Fr.]

fick-le (fĭk′l), *adj.* deceitful; inconstant; changeable; not to be depended on.—*n.* **fickleness.**

fic-tile (fĭk′tĭl), *adj.* readily molded; plastic; used of pottery.

fic-tion (fĭk′shŭn), *n.* the act of feigning or inventing; that which is imagined, feigned, or invented; a literary production of the imagination in prose form, as a novel, romance, etc.—*adj.* **fictional.**
Syn. falsehood, fabrication, fable.
Ant. (see fact).

fic-tion-ist (fĭk′shŭn-ĭst), *n.* a writer of stories; a novelist.

fic-ti-tious (fĭk-tĭsh′ŭs), *adj.* pertaining to, or of the nature of, invented stories; false; unreal.—*adv.* **fictitiously.**—*n.* **fictitiousness.**

fid (fĭd), *n.* an iron or wooden bar to support the topmast of a vessel; a large tapering wooden pin for opening the strands of a rope: *v.t.* to put into place and secure by such a bar or pin. Also, **fidd.**

fid-dle (fĭd′l), *n.* a violin; a frame used on board ship to prevent articles from rolling off the table in stormy weather: *v.i.* to play the violin: *v.t.* to play on a violin; as, to *fiddle* a tune; to trifle; as, to *fiddle* time away.

fid-dle-de-dee (fĭd″l-dē-dē′), *interj.* nonsense! *n.* a piece of nonsense.

fid-dle-fad-dle (fĭd′l-făd″l), *n.* nonsense; trifling conversation: *v.i.* to talk nonsense; fuss about trifles: *adj.* fussy about trifles. [Colloq.]

fid-dler (fĭd′lẽr), *n.* a violinist; a name of a common sand-piper; also, the name of a kind of crab and of beetle.

fid-dle-stick (fĭd′l-stĭk″), *n.* a bow for playing upon the violin: **fiddlesticks!** *interj.* nonsense!

fid-dling (fĭd′lĭng), *n.* the act of playing the violin: *p.adj.* trifling.

fi-del-i-ty (fī-dĕl′ĭ-tĭ), *n.* [*pl.* fidelities (-tĭz)], integrity; faithfulness; honesty; loyalty; reliability.

fidg-et (fĭj′ĕt), *n.* one who is fidgety: *pl.* nervous restlessness: *v.i.* to make uneasy; worry: *v.i.* to move about uneasily or restlessly.

fidg-et-i-ness (fĭj'ĕt-ĭ-nĕs), *n.* the state of being uneasy or restless.

fidg-et-y (fĭj'ĕt-ĭ), *adj.* restless; impatient; uneasy; nervous.

fi-du-ci-a-ry (fĭ-dū'shĭ-ā-rĭ), *n.* [*pl.* fiduciaries (-rĭz)], a trustee: *adj.* pertaining to, or of the nature of, a trust; confident; unwavering.

fie (fī), *interj.* for shame! as, out upon you! *fie* upon you! Also, **fy, fye.**

fief (fēf), *n.* an estate or manor held under a feudal superior. Also, **feod, feoff, feud.**

field (fēld), *n.* a piece of land inclosed for tillage or pasture; open country; a region yielding some natural product; site of a battle; sphere of action; a wide expanse; space within which telescopic or microscopic objects are viewed; outdoor work; in heraldry, the surface of the shield; the ground upon which a game is played: *v.t.* to catch or stop and return to the wicket-keeper, as a ball at cricket, etc.: *v.i.* to act as a fielder in baseball or cricket.

field ar-til-ler-y (fēld är-tĭl'ĕr-ĭ), artillery so mounted as to be easily handled in active service.

field book (fēld bŏŏk), a surveyor's notebook.

field day (fēld dā), a military review; a day of unusual excitement or display; a day devoted to outdoor scientific research; a day on which a series of athletic contests takes place.

field-er (fēl'dĕr), *n.* a baseball player stationed in left, right, or center field.

field-fare (fēld'fâr''), *n.* a small thrush, native to Europe.

field glass (fēld glȧs), a small portable telescope; a spyglass.

field hos-pi-tal (fēld hŏs'pĭ-tăl), a movable hospital of the army medical service, or of the Red Cross, immediately back of the lines in modern warfare; the hospital nearest to the scene of battle.

field mar-shal (fēld mär'shăl), a general officer of the highest rank in some armies.

field mouse (fēld mous), any of the kinds of wild mice that live in fields and meadows.

field of-fi-cer (fēld ŏf'ĭ-sĕr), a major, lieutenant colonel, or colonel of any army.

field-piece (fēld'pēs''), *n.* a small cannon used in artillery batteries on the battlefield.

Fieldpiece

field sports (fēld spōrts), outdoor diversions, especially hunting, shooting, etc.

field-work (fēld'wûrk''), *n.* outdoor operations or observations.

fiend (fēnd), *n.* an evil spirit; a demon; one who is intensely malicious.

fiend-ish (fēnd'ĭsh), *adj.* savage; wicked; malicious; cruel.—*adv.* **fiendishly.**—*n.* **fiendishness.**

fierce (fērs), *adj.* savage; violent; merciless; ferocious; unrestrained.—*adv.* **fiercely.**—*n.* **fierceness.**

fi-er-i-ness (fī'ĕr-ĭ-nĕs), *n.* a heated or inflamed condition; inflamed color; heat of temper.

fi-er-y (fī'ĕr-ĭ; fīr'ĭ), *adj.* [*comp.* fierier, *superl.* fieriest], like, pertaining to, or consisting of, fire; passionate; easily roused; fervent; ardent; heated or inflamed.—*adv.* **fierily.**

fife (fīf), *n.* a shrill-toned musical instrument of the flute class: *v.t.* and *v.i.* to play on, or play, such an instrument.

fif-er (fīf'ĕr), *n.* one who plays on the fife; as, the *fifer's* lively air.

fif-teen (fĭf'tēn''; fĭf''tēn'), *adj.* consisting of five and ten; a cardinal or principal numeral: *n.* the number made up of ten and five, or fourteen and one; the sign representing it, as 15 or xv; one point scored at lawn tennis.

fif-teenth (fĭf'tēnth''; fĭf''tēnth'), *adj.* next in order after fourteenth: *n.* a fifteenth part.

fifth (fĭfth), *adj.* next in order after fourth: *n.* one of five equal parts; in music, an interval of three tones and a semitone; the dominant.—*adv.* **fifthly.**

fif-ti-eth (fĭf'tĭ-ĕth), *adj.* next in order after forty-ninth: *n.* one of fifty equal parts.

fif-ty (fĭf'tĭ), *adj.* consisting of five times ten: *n.* [*pl.* fifties (-tĭz)], the number which amounts to five times ten, or forty-nine and one; the sign representing it, as 50 or l.

fig (fĭg), *n.* a small fruit tree with large leaves, known from the earliest times; the pear-shaped fruit of that tree; a snap of the fingers in token of contempt; as, I don't care a *fig;* anything insignificant or worthless.

fight (fīt), *v.i.* [*p.t.* and *p.p.* fought, *p.pr.* fighting], to contend in battle or in arms; to try to destroy or overcome an enemy or opponent; make war; offer resistance: *v.t.* to war against; strive for the mastery of; maneuver or manage in battle, as ships: *n.* a combat; battle or engagement; contest; a quarrel in which physical force is used.

fight-er (fīt'ĕr), *n.* one who strives to overcome resistance, usually by force; a combatant.

fight-ing (fīt'ĭng), *p.adj.* pertaining to conflict; qualified or trained to carry on conflict; skilled in warfare: *n.* combat.

fig-ment (fĭg'mĕnt), *n.* an invention; fiction; as, the whole story was a *figment* of the imagination.

fig-ur-a-tive (fĭg'ūr-ȧ-tĭv), *adj.* representing by figures, resemblances, or types; ornate; flowery; as, a description highly *figurative;* symbolical; unreal.—*adv.* **figuratively.**

fig-ure (fĭg'ūr), *n.* the outline or shape of a person or object; appearance; an image or statue; drawn or painted representation of a person; idea; pattern; type; sign or character denoting a number; a movement in a dance; musical phrase, or repeated theme; value or cost; as, the goods were sold at a high *figure;* a space bounded on all sides by lines or planes; a special or peculiar use of words; as, a *figure* of speech: *v.t.* to form into any determinate shape; show by resemblance; represent; symbolize; adorn or cover with a pattern; calculate or compute; *v.i.* to be conspicuous; colloquially, to cipher; calculate.

Syn., n. allegory, emblem, metaphor.

fig-ured (fĭg'ūrd), *p.adj.* covered or adorned with a design or pattern; symbolized; pictured; in music, adorned with elaborate phrases.

fig-ure-head (fĭg'ūr-hĕd'), *n.* a carved image of a human or other shape placed at the prow of a ship; a person who is important in name but who has no real authority.

fig-ur-ing (fĭg'ūr-ĭng), *p.pr.* of *figure*: *n.* computation; calculation; the act of making figures.

fig-wort (fĭg'wûrt'), *n.* a coarse herb, with small flowers, possessing medicinal value.

fil-a-ment (fĭl'ȧ-mĕnt), *n.* a fine thread, or threadlike fiber.

fil-a-men-ta-ry (fĭl'ȧ-mĕn'tȧ-rĭ), *adj.* consisting of, or like, a small fiber or thread.

fil-bert (fĭl'bẽrt), *n.* the edible nut of the cultivated hazel.

filch (fĭlch), *v.t.* to pilfer or steal in a small way; rob.

file (fīl), *n.* a wire, etc., on which papers are strung for safe-keeping or reference; a bundle of papers fastened together and endorsed with the date, contents, etc., of each; a case or cabinet in which papers may be arranged in an orderly way; a line of soldiers ranged one behind the other; a tool of hard steel with small grooves on the surface, used for cutting and smoothing: *v.t.* to cut or smooth with such a tool; to arrange and put away (papers, etc.) in orderly fashion, for reference; place among the records of a court or house of legislature: *v.i.* to march in a line.

fil-ial (fĭl'yȧl; fĭl'ĭ-ȧl), *adj.* pertaining to or befitting a son or daughter; due to a father; as, *filial* obedience.

fil-ial-ly (fĭl'yȧl-ĭ; fĭl'ĭ-ȧl-ĭ), *adv.* in a manner befitting a son or daughter.

fil-i-bus-ter (fĭl'ĭ-bŭs'tẽr), *n.* a freebooter or pirate; a lawless military adventurer who invades a foreign country in aid of revolution; a member of a lawmaking body who delays its action: *v.i.* to act as a pirate; to delay legislation or lawmaking by irregular methods, as by wilfully prolonging a debate, etc.

fil-i-gree (fĭl'ĭ-grē), *n.* ornamental work, resembling lace, in gold or silver wire; something delicate or ornamental, but not lasting: *adj.* made of, or like, filigree.

fil-i-greed (fĭl'ĭ-grēd), *p.adj.* ornamented with, or as with, filigree.

fil-ing (fīl'ĭng), *p.pr.* of *file*: *n.* the act of using a file: *pl.* fine fragments rubbed off by the action of a file, or grooved steel tool.

Fil-i-pi-no (fĭl'ĭ-pē'nō), *n.* a native of the Philippine Islands.

fill (fĭl), *v.t.* to make full; satisfy; crowd; occupy; to perform, as duties, in the place of someone: *v.i.* to become full; pour a glass or vessel full: *n.* as much as produces complete satisfaction; a full supply.

fill-er (fĭl'ẽr), *n.* one who, or that which, makes full; a funnel, usually a small glass tube, for filling bottles, etc.; material for stopping up holes or pores in wood before painting it; the body of a cigar; a pad of paper to be inserted in a notebook.

fil-let (fĭl'ĕt), *n.* a narrow band of metal, linen, silk, etc., worn around the forehead, for holding the hair; the fleshy part of the thigh: said of meat; a boneless lump of meat or fish served flat or rolled together and tied; a raised rim, narrow ornament, or molding; a plain line or band; the loins of a horse: *v.t.* to bind with a narrow band; ornament with a rim or molding; make into fillets, as veal, etc.

fill-ing (fĭl'ĭng), *p.adj.* serving to occupy the whole space; satiating or satisfying: *n.* something that serves to fill up a vacant space; the woof in weaving.

fil-lip (fĭl'ĭp), *n.* a sudden sharp jerk or stroke with the finger; an incitement; as, that acted as a *fillip* to my spirits: *v.t.* to strike with the nail of the finger by a sudden movement; urge.

fil-li-peen (fĭl'ĭ-pēn'), *n.* a game; the gift offered as a forfeit in this game. Also, **philopena.**

fil-ly (fĭl'ĭ), *n.* [*pl.* fillies (-ĭz)], a young mare; a female colt; a lively girl.

film (fĭlm), *n.* a thin skin or filament; a thin layer of some substance to receive a photographic impression: *v.t.* to cover with a thin skin or layer: *v.i.* to become covered with a thin skin or layer.

film-y (fĭl'mĭ), *adj.* resembling or having the nature of a film; gauzy.—*n.* **filminess.**

fil-ter (fĭl'tẽr), *n.* an apparatus for clearing or purifying liquids by straining; a strainer: *v.t.* to purify, as a liquid.

filth (fĭlth), *n.* foul matter; dirt; anything that makes physically or morally impure; nastiness.

filth-y (fĭl'thĭ), *adj.* [*comp.* filthier, *superl.* filthiest], foul; dirty; unclean morally or physically; low; contemptible.—*adv.* **filthily.**—*n.* **filthiness.**

fil-trate (fĭl'trāt), *n.* a liquid which has been strained and purified: *v.t.* to purify, as a liquid.—*n.* **filtration.**

fil-tra-tion plant (fĭl-trā'shŭn plănt), a place where the water for a city or locality is purified and made fit to drink.

fin (fĭn), *n.* a winglike extension from the body of a fish that helps to move, balance, or steer it in the water; a small plane or wing on an airplane, to promote stability or steadiness; as, vertical or upright tail *fins*, horizontal tail *fins*, etc.

fi-nal (fī'nȧl), *adj.* pertaining to the end; ultimate; finishing; decisive; as, a *final* judgment or decree: *n.* that which is last, or makes an end; the deciding heat of an athletic contest.

fi-na-le (fē-nä'lā), *n.* the last passage in a musical composition; the last act, etc., of a scene or performance; termination; close; end.

fi-nal-i-ty (fī-năl'ĭ-tĭ), *n.* completeness; the state of being fully settled; a decisive act or arrangement.

fi-nal-ly (fī'nȧl-ĭ), *adv.* lastly; completely; at last; as, the business was *finally* settled.

fi-nance (fĭ-năns'; fī-năns'), *n.* the science of the profitable management of money; the public revenue or income of a government, state, society, or individual: usually in plural: *v.t.* to manage, as the financial arrangement of; to raise money for some special object.

fi-nan-cial (fĭ-năn'shȧl), *adj.* pertaining to money; as *financial* prosperity; *financial* distress.—*adv.* **financially.**
Syn. fiscal, monetary, pecuniary.

fin-an-cier (fĭn'ăn-sēr'), *n.* one who is skilled in banking, or who conducts private or public monetary affairs.

fin-back (fĭn'băk'), *n.* a kind of whale: called also *finner* and *razorback.*

finch (finch), *n.* the common name for various small birds, as the chaffinch, canary, etc.

find (find), *v.t.* [*p.t.* and *p.p.* found, *p.pr.* finding], to discover; obtain by searching; learn by experiment; meet by accident; regain, as something lost; supply: *n.* the discovery of something valuable.
Syn., *v.* descry, discover, espy.
Ant. (see lose, overlook).

find-er (fin'dẽr), *n.* one who, or that which, discovers; an extra lens on a camera to show the position of the picture to be taken; a small telescope attached to a larger one to locate some particular star, etc., to be examined by the larger instrument.

fin de siè-cle (făṅ' dē syĕ'kl), at the end of the century; hence, up to date. [Fr.]

find-ing (find'ĭng), *p.pr.* of *find*: *n.* discovery; the verdict of a jury, or court: *pl.* the tools, etc., which a workman himself supplies.

fine (fin), *n.* money paid as a penalty; forfeiture: *v.t.* to impose, as a money penalty, upon someone; purify; refine; clarify: *adj.* slender; thin; keen; pure; refined; subtle; delicate; elegant; of small diameter; very handsome; noble; showy; admirable; splendid; beautiful in thought or language; free from clouds or rain; artful.—*adv.* finely.
Syn., *adj.* nice, clear, dainty, smooth.
Ant. (see coarse).

fine-cut (fin-kŭt), *adj.* delicately cut or chiseled; cut in small pieces, as tobacco.

fine-draw (fin'drô″), *v.t.* to sew up neatly, as a rent, so that it does not show; draw out to extreme fineness, as wire.

fine-drawn (fin'drôn″), *adj.* spun very fine; far-fetched; as, a *fine-drawn* distinction.

fine-ness (fin'nĕs), *n.* the proportion of pure metal contained in an alloy; freedom from foreign matter; purity; as, the *fineness* of liquor; slenderness; perfection.

fin-er-y (fin'ẽr-ĭ), *n.* [*pl.* fineries (-ĭz)], personal adornment, as showy clothes, etc.; outward show.

fi-nesse (fĭ-nĕs'), *n.* artifice or trick; skill; dexterity; in the game of whist, an endeavor to take a trick with a lower card than that held by an opponent, while holding a higher card.

fin-ger (fiṅ'gẽr), *n.* one of the five divisions of the hand; one of the four digits of the hand, as distinguished from a thumb; a finger's breadth or length; an eighth of a yard; any mechanical contrivance resembling a finger; as, the pointer of a clock, or watch; a part of a glove into which a finger is inserted: *v.t.* to handle, or perform, with the fingers; meddle with; steal: *v.i.* to use the fingers skilfully in performing upon a musical instrument or upon a typewriter.

fin-gered (fiṅ'gẽrd), *p.adj.* having fingers; played with the fingers; marked to show how the fingers are to be used.

fin-ger-er (fiṅ'gẽr-ẽr), *n.* one who fingers; a pilferer or one who does petty thieving.

fin-ger-ing (fiṅ'gẽr-ĭng), *p.pr.* of *finger*: *n.* the act of touching with the fingers; the manner of using the fingers on a musical instrument; fine work done by the fingers.

fin-ger-ling (fiṅ'gẽr-lĭng), *n.* a young trout no bigger than a man's finger.

fin-ger stall (fiṅ'gẽr stôl), a covering for an injured finger.

fin-i-cal (fin'ĭ-kăl), *adj.* fastidious; over-particular; as, *finical* tastes; a *finical* bachelor.—*adv.* finically.

fin-ick-ing (fin'ĭ-kĭng), *adj.* fussy or affectedly precise in trifles, as in dress, manners, etc. Also, finikin, finicky.

fin-ing (fin'ĭng), *n.* the act or process of purifying or refining; clarification or clearing.

fi-nis (fī'nĭs), *n.* the end: a word formerly placed at the end of a book. [Lat.]

fin-ish (fin'ĭsh), *v.t.* to bring to an end; complete; conclude; make perfect; polish; colloquially, kill or render powerless: *v.i.* to come to an end; expire: *n.* completion; the final touches given to a work.

fin-ished (fin'ĭsht), *p.adj.* complete; perfect; as, a *finished* poem; of superior excellence or quality; carefully elaborated.

fi-nite (fī'nīt), *adj.* having limits; as, the *finite* mind of man: *n.* that which is limited: with *the*.—*adv.* finitely.—*n.* finiteness.

fin keel (fin kēl), a downward projection shaped like the fin of a fish, attached to the keel of a yacht.

Finn (fin), *n.* a native of Finland.—*adj.* Finnish and Finnic.

fin-nan had-die (fĭn'ăn hăd'ĭ), a smoked haddock. [Scot.]

finned (find), *adj.* having fins or winglike extensions for swimming, as a fish.

fin-ny (fin'ĭ), *adj.* having fins; resembling, or abounding in, fish.

fiord (fyōrd), *n.* a long narrow inlet or arm of the sea between high rocks or banks. Also, fjord.

fir (fûr), *n.* the name of various cone-bearing evergreen trees, prized for resin and timber.

fire (fīr), *n.* heat and light developed by combustion or burning; the result of burning of bodies; a burning; conflagration, flame; discharge of firearms; light; intensity of feeling; ardor; spirit; severe trial or affliction: *v.t.* to set on fire; inflame; kindle; bake, as porcelain; to cause to explode; to discharge, as a gun; excite violently; irritate; illuminate: *v.i.* to become ignited; be inflamed; discharge, as firearms.
Syn., *n.* glow, heat, warmth.

fire-arms (fīr'ärmz″), *n.pl.* rifles, cannon, revolvers, etc.; as, the colonists carried their *firearms* to church.

fire-ball (fīr'bôl″), *n.* a ball filled with explosives; a ball of fire, as the sun; meteor.

fire bal-loon (fīr bă-lōōn'), a balloon filled with hot air; a balloon sent up with fireworks, which explode at a certain height.

fire box (fīr' bŏks″), in a steam boiler, the place for the fire.

fire-brand (fīr'brănd″), *n.* a piece of burning wood; an incendiary, or one who fires buildings; one who inflames the passions of others.

fire clay (fīr klā), a kind of clay capable of resisting intense heat.

fire-crack-er (fīr'krăk″ẽr), *n.* a small paper cylinder filled with gunpowder, used to make a noise in times of celebration.

fire damp (fīr dămp), a gas formed in coal mines, which explodes when mixed with air and ignited.

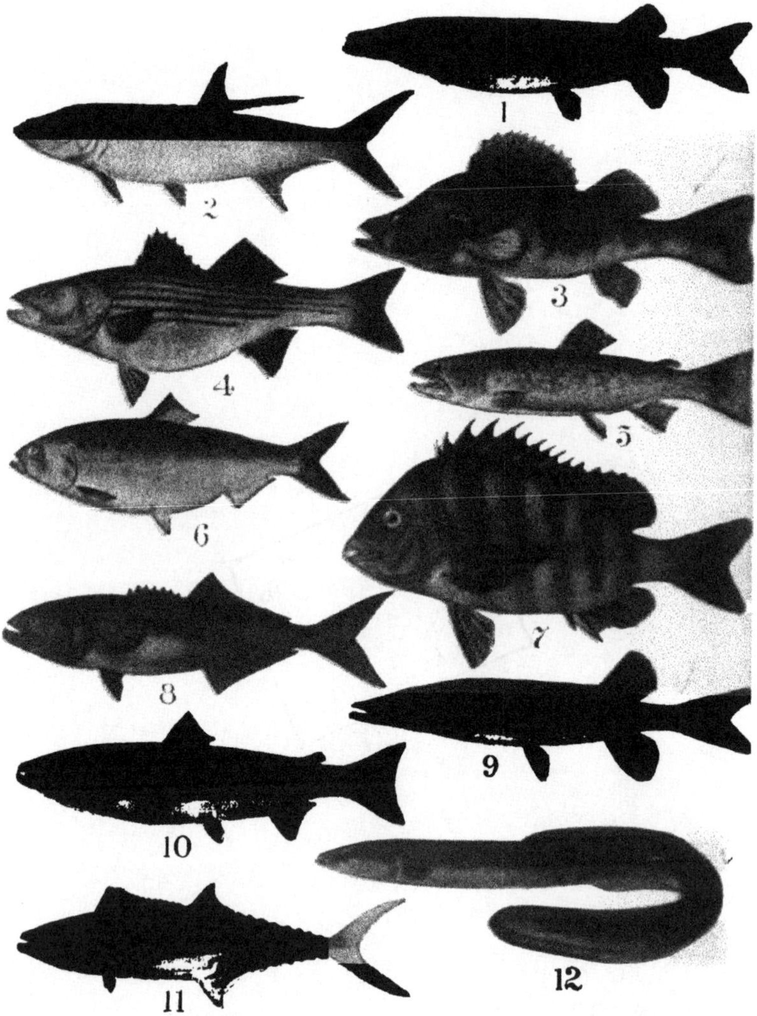

 AMERICAN FRESH AND SALT WATER FISH

1. Muskalonge. 2. Tarpon. 3. Yellow perch. 4 Striped bass. 5. Brook trout. 6. Shad. 7. Sheepshead. 8. Blue fish. 9. Pickerel. 10. Land-locked salmon. 11. Spanish mackerel 12. Common eel.

fire-dog (fīr'dôg″), *n.* an andiron or support for wood in a fireplace.

fire en-gine (fīr ĕn'jĭn), a hand or steam engine for throwing water through hose to put out a fire.

fire es-cape (fīr ĕs-kāp'), a kind of ladder, stairway, or other device for rescuing persons from the upper parts of a burning building.

fire-fly (fīr'flī″), *n.* a winged insect which emits light at night when flying.

fire i-rons (fīr ī'ŭrnz), the shovel, poker, and tongs.

fire-man (fīr'măn), *n.* [*pl.* firemen (-mĕn)], one trained to put out fires; a stoker, or one who tends fires.

fire-place (fīr'plās″), *n.* the open recess under a chimney in which a fire may be built.

fire-proof (fīr'pro͞of″), *adj.* made of such material as will resist fire; relatively speaking, not capable of being burned: *v.t.* to make proof against fire.

fire ship (fīr shĭp), a ship filled with explosives, set fire to and floated among the vessels of an enemy.

fire-side (fīr'sīd″), *n.* the hearth; hence, domestic life and comfort.

fire trap (fīr trăp), a building from which it is difficult or impossible to escape in case of fire.

fire wa-ter (fīr wô'tẽr), ardent spirits: the American Indian's name for strong drink.

fire-weed (fīr'wēd″), *n.* a hardy weed usually found in recently burned clearings.

fire-wood (fīr'wo͝od″), *n.* wood suitable for fuel; wood fit to use for fuel.

fire-works (fīr'wûrks″), *n.pl.* devices made from a great variety of materials, which, when set on fire, produce figures in fire or a brilliant display of light often variously colored.

fire wor-ship (fīr wûr'shĭp), the worship of fire as a deity or god.

fir-ing (fīr'ĭng), *n.* the act of discharging firearms; the application of intense heat, as in baking, etc.; fuel.

fir-kin (fûr'kĭn), *n.* a small wooden vessel for holding butter, lard, etc.; a measure of capacity equal to one fourth of a barrel; nine gallons.

firm (fûrm), *adj.* hard; compact; solid; closely compressed; unyielding; not easily moved; rigorous; staunch; as, a firm friend; unfaltering; steadfast: *n.* the title or style under which a business house transacts its business; a partnership or association of two or more persons for doing business.—*adv.* firmly.

Syn., *adj.* constant, fixed, stable.

Ant. (see weak).

firm-ness (fûrm'nĕs), *n.* the state of being unyielding; stability; steadfastness; resolution.

fir-ma-ment (fûr'mȧ-mĕnt), *n.* the sky; the arch of the heavens.

fir-man (fûr'măn; fẽr-män'), *n.* a special degree, edict, or license of an Oriental ruler, as of the Turkish Sultan; a passport; permit; a license.

first (fûrst), *adj.* the ordinal of one; foremost in place, rank, dignity, time, excellence, etc.; earliest; most important; chief: *adv.* before all others in order, place, rank, time, etc.; sooner: *n.* the beginning.

Syn., *adj.* foremost, chief, earliest.

Ant. (see last).

first-class (fûrst'klȧs″), *adj.* of the highest excellence, rank, or quality.

First day (fûrst dā), the name given to Sunday by the Society of Friends.

first fruits (fûrst fro͞ots), the first gatherings of the produce of the season; the first profits of any office or undertaking.

first-hand (fûrst'hănd″), *adj.* obtained direct from the producer or grower.

first-ling (fûrst'lĭng), *n.* the first-born; first produced.

first-ly (fûrst'lĭ), *adv.* in the first place: occasionally used for the adverb *first*.

first mate (fûrst māt), in the merchant service, the officer next in rank to the captain.

first-rate (fûrst'rāt″), *adj.* of the highest excellence; having the highest quality or character: *n.* a warship of the first class: *adv.* excellently: used colloquially.

firth (fûrth), *n.* the mouth of a tidal river; an arm of the sea. Also, **frith.** [SCOT.]

fis-cal (fĭs'kăl), *adj.* pertaining to the public treasury or revenue; financial: *n.* a treasurer; an attorney-general.

fish (fĭsh), *n.* [*pl.* fish, fishes (-ĕz)], a scaly animal living in water, breathing through gills instead of lungs; the flesh of fish used as food; a machine for hoisting an anchor; a piece of wood fastened to another to strengthen it: *pl.* one of the signs (Pisces) of the zodiac: *v.t.* to search in quest of fish; catch (fish); seek for and bring to light; draw up: *v.i.* to try to catch fish; seek to gain or obtain something by trickery or indirect methods.

fish beam (fĭsh bēm), a beam of timber bulging downwards.

fish-block (fĭsh'blŏk″), *n.* a hoisting-block for raising an anchor to the gunwale of a ship.

fish-er (fĭsh'ẽr), *n.* one who fishes; an animal of the weasel family.

fish-er-man (fĭsh'ẽr-măn), *n.* one whose work is to catch fish; a fishing smack or ship for catching fish.

fish-er-y (fĭsh'ẽr-ĭ), *n.* [*pl.* fisheries (-ĭz)], the business of catching fish; a fishing ground; the right to fish at a particular time or ground.

fish-gig (fĭsh'gĭg″), *n.* a sharp forklike instrument for spearing fish. Also, **fizgig.**

fish glue (fĭsh glo͞o), glue chiefly made from certain kinds of sturgeon; isinglass or gelatin dissolved in alcohol.

fish hawk (fĭsh hôk), the osprey or bald buzzard.

fish-hook (fĭsh'ho͝ok″), *n.* a hook for catching fish.

Fishhooks

fish-ing (fĭsh'ĭng), *n.* the art, sport, or business of taking fish; a fishing ground; the operation of raising an anchor up to the gunwale of a vessel.

fish joint (fĭsh joint), a pair of iron plates for fastening the ends of two railroad rails together.

fish-mon-ger (fĭsh'mŭn″gẽr), *n.* one who sells fish.

fish weir (fĭsh wēr), a dam for stopping or preserving fish.

fish-wife (fish'wif"), *n.* a woman who retails fish. Also, **fishwoman.**

fish-y (fish'ĭ), *adj.* pertaining to, consisting of, abounding in, or like, fish; dull; vacant; colloquially, incredible or extravagant, as a story.—*n.* **fishiness.**

fis-sure (fish'ūr), *n.* a cleft or crack; a narrow opening; furrow: *v.t.* to break or crack: *v.i.* to cleave; separate in cracks.

fist (fĭst), *n.* the hand when closed or clenched: *v.t.* to grip or strike with the clenched hand.

fis-tic (fĭs'tĭk), *adj.* pertaining to pugilism or boxing; as, a *fistic* encounter.

fist-i-cuffs (fĭs'tĭ-kŭfs"), *n.* a combat with the fists; boxing.

fis-tu-la (fĭs'tū-lȧ), *n.* a reed; a pipe; a wind-instrument of music; an abnormal opening into one of the passages of the body, often accompanied by an ulcer.

fit (fĭt), *v.t.* [*p.t.* and *p.p.* fitted, *p.pr.* fitting], to make suitable; adapt; accommodate to anything; qualify; adjust; equip: *v.i.* to be adapted to one; as, the coat *fits;* to be proper or suitable: *n.* adaptation of one thing to another; suitability: *adj.* [*comp.* fitter, *superl.* fittest], convenient; suitable; prepared; qualified.

Syn., v. accommodate, adapt, adjust, suit.

fit (fĭt), *n.* a sudden attack of disease attended with convulsions, and often with loss of consciousness; a brief attack of pain or illness; caprice.

fitch (fĭch), *n.* the European polecat; the fur of the polecat. Also, **fitchet.**

fit-ful (fĭt'fŏŏl), *adj.* capricious; spasmodic, or occurring by fits and starts; changeable; as, a *fitful* mood.—*adv.* **fitfully.**

fit-ly (fĭt'lĭ), *adv.* suitably; properly; in a right manner or time.

fit-ness (fĭt'nĕs), *n.* the state or quality of being suitable; as, he soon showed his *fitness* for the work.

fit-ter (fĭt'ẽr), *n.* one who adjusts pipes, or puts the parts of a machine together; one who puts on and shapes an article of dress.

fit-ting (fĭt'ĭng), *p.adj.* suitable; appropriate: *n.pl.* the necessary fixtures, etc., of a house or shop.

fitz (fĭts), *n.* a Norman French surname meaning the son of.

five (fīv), *adj.* consisting of four and one; a cardinal numeral: *n.* the sum of four and one; the sign representing it, as 5 or V: *pl.* a game resembling tennis.

five-fold (fīv'fōld), *adj.* five times as much or as great; multiplied by five.

fix (fĭks), *v.t.* to make fast, secure, or stable; set or place permanently; adjust; colloquially, to put to rights or repair; hold firmly; as, to *fix* the attention of an audience: *v.i.* to become solid or firm; become stable: *n.* colloquially, an awkward situation; a dilemma.

Syn., v. determine, establish, settle.

fix-a-tive (fĭk'sȧ-tĭv), *n.* something that serves to set color, as a mordant: used on charcoal drawings to prevent rubbing.

fixed (fĭkst), *p.adj.* firm; lasting; settled; permanent; stable; established; resolute.

fix-ed-ly (fĭk'sĕd-lĭ), *adv.* steadily; firmly; as, to gaze *fixedly*.

fix-ed-ness (fĭk'sĕd-nĕs), *n.* the state of being firm; steadfastness.

fixed star (fĭxst stär), a star which remains in the same position in the heavens.

fix-ing (fĭks'ĭng), *n.* the act of making firm, or rendering permanent; the act of adjusting or amending: *pl.* colloquially, ornaments, outfit, apparatus, etc.

fix-i-ty (fĭk'sĭ-tĭ), *n.* stability; permanence; a state of being fastened.

fix-ture (fĭks'tūr), *n.* that which is firmly fastened; an article of furniture attached to a house and regarded as part of it; one who is expected to remain permanently in his position.

fizz (fĭz), *n.* a hissing noise; an effervescent or bubbling liquid, as sparkling champagne: *v.i.* to make a hissing noise. Also, **fizzle.**

fiz-zle (fĭz'l), *v.i.* to make a hissing noise; colloquially, to fail ridiculously: *n.* colloquially, a state of restlessness; worry; a humiliating failure.

fjord (fyôrd), *n.* an arm of the sea, long and narrow, with high rocky banks. Also, **fiord.**

flab-ber-gast (flăb'ẽr-găst), *v.t.* to confound; astonish. [COLLOQ.]

flab-bi-ly (flăb'ĭ-lĭ), *adv.* in a limp manner; languidly; feebly.

flab-bi-ness (flăb'ĭ-nĕs), *n.* the state or quality of being limp and weak, or of lacking muscle.

flab-by (flăb'ĭ), *adj.* easily shaking or yielding to the touch; lacking muscle; mentally or physically feeble.

flac-cid (flăk'sĭd), *adj.* flabby; weak; limber; lacking firmness.

flac-cid-i-ty (flăk-sĭd'ĭ-tĭ), *n.* the state of being weak and without muscle.

flag (flăg), *n.* a piece of cloth or bunting on which usually some device is wrought, used as a standard, ensign, signal, etc.; a plant of the Iris family; a flagstone or paving stone: *v.t.* signal with a flag; pave with flagstones: *v.i.* [*p.t.* and *p.p.* flagged, *p.pr.* flagging], to become weary; lose vigor; hang down: **flag of truce,** a white flag indicating that a conference is desired.

flag-el-lant (flăj'ĕ-lănt; flȧ-jĕl'ănt), *adj.* using a whip or scourge: *n.* one who scourges himself as a religious duty.

flag-el-late (flăj'ĕ-lāt), *v.t.* to whip: *adj.* like a whiplash.

flag-el-la-tion (flăj'ĕ-lā'shŭn), *n.* a scourging; a whipping; a beating.

flag-eo-let 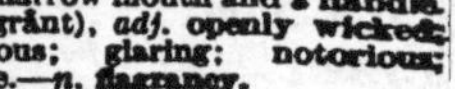

Flageolet

(flăj'ō-lĕt'; flăj'ō-lĕt), *n.* a musical instrument of the flute class.

flag-ging (flăg'ĭng), *p.adj.* weary; losing force: *n.* a pavement of flagstones, or large flat stones.

fla-gi-tious (flȧ-jĭsh'ŭs), *adj.* atrocious; wicked; highly criminal.—*adv.* **flagitiously.**—*n.* **flagitiousness.**

flag of-fi-cer (flăg ŏf'ĭ-sẽr), an officer commanding a fleet or squadron, as an admiral.

flag-on (flăg'ŭn), *n.* a large drinking vessel with a narrow mouth and a handle.

fla-grant (flā'grănt), *adj.* openly wicked; heinous; glaring; notorious; as, a *flagrant* crime.—*n.* **flagrancy.**

flag-ship (flăg'shĭp"), *n.* the ship that carries the commander and flies his flag. leads a fleet, carries the commander and flies his flag.

flag-staff (flăg'stăf"), *n.* [*pl.* flagstaffs (-stăfs) or staves (-stāvz)], a pole or staff on which a flag is hoisted.

flag-stone (flăg'stōn"), *n.* a large flat paving stone, used especially for sidewalks.

flail (flāl), *n.* a wooden instrument for threshing wheat, etc., by hand.

flake (flāk), *n.* a small film of anything loosely held together, as snow; a thin scaly piece of anything; a carnation with a single color in stripes on a white ground: *v.t.* and *v.i.* to form into flakes; scale or peel off.—*adj.* **flaky.**

Flail

flam-beau (flăm'bō), *n.* [*pl.* flambeaux (-bōz)], a flaming or lighted torch; a large ornamental candlestick. [Fr.]

flam-boy-ant (flăm-boi'ănt), *adj.* showy; especially as wanting in good taste; characterized by flamelike or waving curves, as the tracery of certain windows of Gothic architecture.

flame (flām), *n.* a burning gas or vapor; ardor of temper or passion; glow of imagination; excitement; a sweetheart: *v.t.* to heat; excite: *v.i.* to burst into flame; blaze.
Syn., *n.* and *v.* flare, flash, glare.

fla-men (flā'mĕn), *n.* one of fifteen priests in ancient Rome devoted to the service of a special deity or god.

flam-ing (flām'ĭng), *p.adj.* giving forth flames; blazing; causing excitement; violent.

fla-min-go (flȧ-mĭn'gō), *n.* a long-legged, web-footed, red-colored bird.

Flamingo

flange (flănj), *n.* a raised or projecting rim for preventing a wheel from slipping, such as the rims on tires of railroad-car wheels to keep them on the rails: *v.t.* to attach a rim to.

flank (flănk), *n.* the fleshy part of an animal between the ribs and hip; the side of an army, regiment, or building; that part of a fortification constructed to defend another: *v.t.* to attack or turn the flank or side of (an army); guard on the flank; to border or touch: *adj.* pertaining to, or cut from, the flank.

flank-er (flănk'ẽr), *n.* one of a body of troops thrown out to protect a line of march; a projecting fortification to protect the flank of an assailing body.

flan-nel (flăn'ĕl), *n.* a soft, loosely-woven cloth, usually made of wool.

flan-nel-et (flăn'ĕl-ĕt'), *n.* a soft cotton material resembling flannel.

flap (flăp), *n.* anything broad and flat hanging loosely, and fastened on one side; the motion or noise of anything broad and flat; a slap; the tail of a coat: *v.t.* [*p.t.* and *p.p.* flapped, *p.pr.* flapping], to strike with, or as with, a flap; let fall; wave backwards and forwards rapidly and with a loose motion: *v.i.* to move, as wings, with noise.

flap-jack (flăp'jăk'), *n.* a pancake or griddle cake: so called because of the way in which it is turned on the griddles.

flap-per (flăp'ẽr), *n.* one who, or that which, waves loosely to and fro; a young bird when first trying its wings; hence, colloquially, a young girl in her teens.

flare (flâr), *n.* a large, unsteady, glaring light; a spreading outward or upward; a signal: *v.i.* to burn with a broad, unsteady light; to spread outward or upward.

flare-back (flâr'băk'), *n.* a reverse outburst of flame from a furnace; a sharp change of method or policy.

flash (flăsh), *n.* a sudden, quick, fleeting blaze or light; as, a *flash* of lightning, or of a gun; sudden outburst, as of merriment, wit, or passion; a short, transient, or temporary state; an instant: *v.t.* to cause to act, burst, or appear suddenly; as, to *flash* a light; to *flash* a look: *v.i.* to shine with a sudden, quick, fleeting blaze or light; act, or burst forth, suddenly; gleam; splash: *adj.* pertaining to thieves or their language; cheap and gaudy; sham; showy.

flash light (flăsh līt), a sudden brilliant light for taking photographs; a light that comes and goes in flashes, as a signal; a small electric lamp to carry in the hand.

flash-i-ly (flăsh'ĭ-lĭ), *adv.* in a gaudy or showy manner; as, to be *flashily* dressed.

flash-i-ness (flăsh'ĭ-nĕs), *n.* gaudiness or showiness; great display.

flash-ing (flăsh'ĭng), *n.* a name for various operations in glassmaking: *pl.* pieces of lead or other metal used to keep roofs, etc., watertight: *adj.* emitting bursts of light.

flash-ing point (flăsh'ĭng point), the temperature below the burning point, at which a volatile liquid gives off vapor in sufficient quantity to ignite momentarily.

flash-y (flăsh'ĭ), *adj.* brilliant, but empty; gaudy; showy, but cheap in appearance.

flask (flȧsk), *n.* a small bottle; a vessel, usually metal or leather, for holding powder, shot, liquor, etc.

Flask

flat (flăt), *adj.* level; even; smooth; horizontal; insipid; as, a *flat* taste; positive; downright; low: said of prices; dull: said of sales; without interest; wanting prominence: said of figures in painting; sounded below the true pitch: *n.* a level or extended plain; a shallow; shoal; story or floor of a house; the broad or plane part of a thing, as of a sword or blade; surface without relief or prominence; a musical sign which lowers the succeeding note half a tone; the tone so lowered: *adv.* in a level or prostrate position; exactly: used of amounts, etc.; as, he ran the race in three minutes *flat*.—*adv.* **flatly.**

flat-fish (flăt'fĭsh'), *n.* any of a group of fishes, like the halibut, flounder, etc., that swim on one side.

flat-iron (flăt'ī'ẽrn), *n.* an iron with a polished surface on its under side, used for pressing or smoothing cloth.

flat-ness (flăt'nĕs), *n.* the state of being level; evenness; dulness; lack of flavor.

flat-ten (flăt'n), *v.t.* to make level or even; beat down; depress; make dull, insipid, or tasteless; lower in tone; *v.i.* to become even or level; become insipid.

flat-ter (flăt'ẽr), *v.t.* to gain over or please by complimentary speech, usually insincere; soothe; persuade; praise too highly; raise false hopes or expectations: *v.i.* to give false praise.

flat-ter-ing (flăt'ẽr-ĭng), *p.adj.* pleasing to pride or vanity; partial.—*adv.* **flatteringly.**

flat-ter-y (flăt'ẽr-ĭ), *n.* [*pl.* flatteries (-ĭz)], insincere complimentary speech; false praise.

flat-ting (flăt'ĭng), *n.* the act or process of making level or smooth; the process of rolling metal into sheets; the sounding of a note below the true pitch; a method of house painting by which the paint appears lusterless or dull.

flat-u-lence (flăt'ū-lĕns), *n.* wind in the stomach, caused by gases formed within it; emptiness; conceit. Also, **flatulency.**

flat-u-lent (flăt'ū-lĕnt), *adj.* affected with, or tending to, produce gas in the stomach and intestines; pretentious; conceited.

fla-tus (flā'tŭs), *n.* gas formed in the intestines, stomach, etc.

flat-ways (flăt'wāz"), *adv.* with the flat side downwards. Also, **flatwise.**

flaunt (flănt; flônt), *v.t.* to display with unnecessary show: *v.i.* to make a gaudy display in dress; to behave in a forward manner.

fla-vor (flā'vẽr), *n.* odor; fragrance; a particular smell or taste: *v.t.* to impart a special taste or smell to. Also, **flavour.**

fla-vor-ing (flā'vẽr-ĭng), *n.* an essence or extract for giving special taste or smell to food, etc. Also, **flavouring.**

flaw (flô), *n.* a blemish; a weak spot; crack: *v.t.* to make a flaw in; crack.—*adj.* **flawless.**

flax (flăks), *n.* a slender plant with blue flowers, from the fiber of which linen is made; the fiber of the plant ready to be spun.

flax-en (flăk'sn), *adj.* resembling or made of flax; of pale yellow color.

flax-seed (flăks'sēd"), *n.* the seed of the flax, much used in medicine, and from which linseed oil is obtained.

flay (flā), *v.t.* [*p.t.* and *p.p.* flayed, *p.pr.* flaying], to strip off; skin; torture.

flea (flē), *n.* a small blood-sucking insect, without wings, but with the power to leap.

flea-bane (flē'bān"), *n.* a plant of the aster family, supposed to be useful for driving away fleas.

flea-bite (flē'bīt"), *n.* the bite of a flea; the red spot it causes; a trifling wound or trouble; a very small quantity.

fleck (flĕk), *n.* a streak or spot: *v.t.* to streak or spot; variegate.

flec-tion (flĕk'shŭn), *n.* a bending; a grammatical variation; a turning; a curved or bent part; a turning, as of the eye; cast. Also, **flexion.**

fled (flĕd), past tense and past participle of the verb *flee.*

fledge (flĕj), *v.i.* to acquire the full plumage or feathers necessary for flight: *v.t.* to furnish with feathers ready for flight: usually in passive; as, the birds were *fledged.*

fledg-ling (flĕj'lĭng), *n.* a young bird just feathered and able to fly. Also, **fledgeling.**

flee (flē), *v.i.* [*p.t.* and *p.p.* fled, *p.pr.* fleeing], to run away from; avoid: *v.t.* to hasten away from danger; disappear.

fleece (flēs), *n.* the woolly coat of a sheep; the whole wool shorn from a sheep at one time: *v.t.* to shear (a sheep) of the wool; strip; plunder by injustice or fraud.

fleec-y (flēs'ĭ), *adj.* resembling a sheep's coat of wool; white and fluffy; as, *fleecy* clouds; *fleecy* cloth.

fleer (flēr), *n.* mockery or contempt expressed in words or gesture: *v.i.* to mock or sneer; grin contemptuously.

fleet (flēt), *adj.* swift; rapid; nimble: *n.* a company of warships or merchant vessels: *v.i.* to fly swiftly; hasten.—*adv.* **fleetly.**—*n.* **fleetness.**

fleet-ing (flēt'ĭng), *p.adj.* passing quickly; as, time is *fleeting.*

Flem-ing (flĕm'ĭng), *n.* a Belgian who speaks Flemish; especially a Belgian of Flanders.

Flem-ish (flĕm'ĭsh), *adj.* pertaining to the Flemings or to Flanders: *n.* the language of northern Belgium.

flesh (flĕsh), *n.* that part of an animal body beneath the skin, composed of soft muscular tissue; animal food; pulp of fruit, etc.; the body: opposite to *soul;* human nature or race; present life; kindred: *v.t.* to satiate or glut; feed dogs with meat so as to urge them to further exertion in hunting; colloquially, to put on weight: with *up.*

flesh-ly (flĕsh'lĭ), *adj.* pertaining to the body; corporeal; human; carnal: *adv.* carnally.—*n.* **fleshliness.**

flesh-pot (flĕsh'pŏt"), *n.* a vessel in which flesh is boiled or cooked; hence, plenty; luxury.

flesh-y (flĕsh'ĭ), *adj.* [*comp.* fleshier, *superl.* fleshiest], full of flesh; plump; corpulent; fat.—*n.* **fleshiness.**

Fletch-er-ism (flĕch'ẽr-ĭzm), *n.* a system of diet in which the food is thoroughly masticated or chewed: named after Horace Fletcher, its advocate.

fleur-de-lis (flûr"dē-lē'), *n.* [*pl.* fleurs-de-lis], the royal bearing or emblem of France; the name for various kinds of iris. [FR.]

Fleur-de-lis

flew (flōō), past tense of the transitive and intransitive verb *fly.*

flex (flĕks), *v.t.* to bend, or curve, as an arm or leg.

flex-i-bil-i-ty (flĕk"sĭ-bĭl'ĭ-tĭ), *n.* the state or quality of being pliant, or easily bent. Also, **flexibleness.**

flex-i-ble (flĕk'sĭ-bl), *adj.* easily bent; pliant; yielding to persuasion. Also, **flexile.**

Syn. pliable, supple.
Ant. (see inflexible).

flex-i-bly (flĕks'ĭ-blĭ), *adv.* in a pliable manner; plastically; compliantly; not stiffly.

flex-ion (flĕk'shŭn), *n.* the act or process of bending; a curve; grammatical variation of a word; inflection. Also, **flection.**

flex-or (flĕk'sôr), *n.* a muscle that acts in bending the joints: opposite to *extensor.*

flex-ure (flĕk'shûr; flĕks'ūr), *n.* the act of bending; the part bent; a curve or fold; joint.

flick (flĭk), *n.* a light, quick stroke, as with a whip; *v.t.* to whip lightly.

flick-er (flĭk'ẽr), *v.i.* to move with an unsteady and quick motion; flutter with the wings; *n.* an unsteady light or movement; the golden-winged woodpecker of North America.

flick-er-ing (flĭk'ẽr-ĭng), *n.* the state of burning or moving unsteadily: *p.adj.* wavering.—*adv.* **flickeringly.**

fli-er (flī'ẽr), *n.* one who flies or flees; a fugitive; an aviator; that part of a machine that regulates the motion: *pl.* a straight flight of steps. Also, **flyer.**

āte, senāte, râre, căt, locăl, fär, ȧsk, pȧrade; scēne, ēvent, ĕdge, novĕl, refẽr; rīght, sĭn; cōld, ōbey, côrd, stŏp, cŏmpare; ūnit, ūnite, bûrn, cŭt, focŭs, menü;

flight (flīt), *n.* the act, process, manner, or power of flying; hasty departure; birds flying together, or produced in the same season; a soaring forth; the ascent of an airplane; distance traveled by an airplane; the distance traveled by a projectile; a shower or volley; a series of steps.

flight-i-ly (flīt'ĭ-lĭ), *adv.* in a wild, imaginative manner; capriciously.

flight-i-ness (flīt'ĭ-nĕs), *n.* the state of being overfanciful; capriciousness; light-headedness.

flight-y (flīt'ĭ), *adj.* changeful; capricious; extravagant in fancy; giddy; wild; mildly insane.

flim-si-ness (flĭm'zĭ-nĕs), *n.* the state or quality of being unsubstantial or weak.

flim-sy (flĭm'zĭ), *n.* [*pl.* **flimsies** (-zĭz)], a thin paper; transfer paper, from which several copies may be made: *adj.* thin; weak; ineffective.—*adv.* **flimsily.**—*n.* **flimsiness.**

flinch (flĭnch), *v.i.* to shrink or draw back, as from pain, danger, etc.: *n.* the act of drawing back from pain.

flind-er (flĭn'dẽr), *n.* a splinter; fragment; as, the cyclone blew the house to *flinders.*

fling (flĭng), *v.t.* [*p.t.* and *p.p.* flung, *p.pr.* flinging], to throw or hurl; drive by violence; scatter; cast to the ground: *v.i.* to flounce; throw out the legs violently: *n.* the act of throwing or casting; a sneer or gibe; kick or leap; unrestrained pleasure; dash; a Highland dance.

flint (flĭnt), *n.* a very hard kind of quartz or rock which strikes fire with steel; anything hard like flint.

flint-lock (flĭnt'lŏk'), *n.* an old form of gun in which the powder was ignited or set on fire by a spark from a stroke of flint on steel.

Flintlock. 1, hammer with flint; 2, steel and powder pan.

flint-y (flĭn'tĭ), *adj.* composed of, or like, flint; hard; obdurate; cruel; as, a *flinty* heart.

flip (flĭp), *n.* a liquor composed of beer, spirit, sugar, etc.; a short quick stroke; a flick: *v.t.* to jerk with the fingers; strike with a short quick blow.

flip-pan-cy (flĭp'ăn-sĭ), *n.* pertness; thoughtless talk; as, the *flippancy* of her remarks displeased everybody.

flip-pant (flĭp'ănt), *adj.* lively and fluent in speech; talkative; impertinent; disrespectful; characterized by thoughtless speech, or pertness; trifling.—*adv.* **flippantly.**

flip-per (flĭp'ẽr), *n.* a broad fin, arm, or paddle used in swimming, as that of the whale, seal, or turtle.

flirt (flûrt), *v.t.* to move to and fro with a short rapid action; throw with a quick elastic motion: *v.i.* make love from mere amusement; coquet; *n.* a coquette; one who coquets; a sudden jerk or toss.

flir-ta-tion (flẽr-tā'shŭn), *n.* the act of pretending to make love; coquetry; pretense of affection.

flir-ta-tious (flẽr-tā'shŭs), *adj.* inclined to be coquettish.

flit (flĭt), *v.t.* [*p.t.* and *p.p.* flitted, *p.pr.* flitting], to remove (a thing) from one house to another [Scot.]: *v.i.* to pass lightly and swiftly along; fly away; skim; migrate.

flitch (flĭch), *n.* the side of a hog salted and cured; as, a *flitch* of bacon.

flit-ter-mouse (flĭt'ẽr-mous'), *n.* a bat; as, with darkness come the owl and *flittermouse.*

flit-ting (flĭt'ĭng), *p.pr.* of *flit:* *n.* the act of flying or moving lightly and swiftly; a removal.

float (flōt), *v.t.* to cause to rest or be moved on the surface of a liquid; convey without effort or will; smooth or level (plaster) with a suitable tool; to start, as a business, by providing the money needed: *v.i.* to be buoyed or held up on the surface of a liquid or gaseous fluid; move lightly or glide without apparent effort; drift about: *n.* anything that rests on the surface of a liquid or buoys up something; a raft; the cork or quill used in angling; a plasterer's tool, for spreading and smoothing; the water gauge of a steam-boiler.

float-er (flōt'ẽr), *n.* one who, or that which, floats; a voter not belonging to any particular party; one whose vote may be bought, or one who moves from place to place so as to repeat his vote.

float-ing (flōt'ĭng), *p.adj.* swimming or held up on the surface of a liquid; free to move about; circulating; not fixed or settled; ready for use.

flock (flŏk), *n.* a company or collection of sheep, birds, etc.; a congregation; crowd; a lock of wool; fiberlike material used for stuffing upholstery or cushions, etc.: *v.i.* to come together in a crowd; assemble.
Syn., *n.* brood, covey, bevy.

floe (flō), *n.* a large flat mass of floating ice, or a collection of such masses of ice; as, the vessel was caught in the *floe.*

flog (flŏg), *v.t.* [*p.t.* and *p.p.* flogged, *p.pr.* flogging], to whip; chastise or punish; to lash (the water) with the line in angling.

flog-ging (flŏg'ĭng), *p.pr.* of *flog:* *n.* a whipping; the act of beating with a whip or rod.

flood (flŭd), *n.* a great flow of water; inundation; high tide; the sea; an abundant supply or outpouring of anything: **the Flood,** the Deluge described in Genesis vii: *v.t.* to deluge; inundate; overflow.

flood-gate (flŭd'gāt'), *n.* a gate in a waterway, which when opened allows the water to escape when at a certain height.

flood tide (flŭd tīd), the rising tide: opposite to *ebb tide.*

floor (flōr), *n.* the bottom surface of a room or house on which one treads; story of a house; a level suite or set of rooms; any smooth or level area; pavement; the part of a legislative or lawmaking chamber occupied by the members; as, the *floor* of the Senate at Washington: *v.t.* to cover with a floor; strike down; hence, put to silence.

floor-ing (flōr'ĭng), *n.* materials for floors; floors collectively; pavement.

floor-walk-er (flōr'wôk'ẽr), *n.* in the United States, an overseer in the aisles of a large department store.

flop (flŏp), *v.t.* [*p.t.* and *p.p.* flopped, *p.pr.* flopping], to strike or drop heavily or with a jerk: *v.i.* to plump down; to wave back and forth, or to rise and fall, loosely and flatly: *n.* the sound caused by a soft flat body coming suddenly in contact with the ground: *adv.* suddenly. [Colloq.]

flo-ra (flō'rȧ), *n.* the native plants of a particular region, district, or period of the earth's history; a description of such plants.

flo-ral (flō'răl), *adj.* pertaining to, resembling, or consisting of, flowers; as, a *floral* wreath.

Flor-en-tine (flŏr'ĕn-tēn; flŏr'ĕn-tīn), *adj.* pertaining or belonging to Florence, Italy: *n.* an inhabitant of Florence.

flo-res-cent (flō-rĕs'ĕnt), *adj.* breaking into bloom; blossoming.

flo-ret (flō'rĕt), *n.* a little flower; one of the small flowers that make up the head of a composite flower such as the daisy, etc.

flo-ri-cul-tur-al (flō'rĭ-kŭl'tūr-ăl), *adj.* pertaining to floriculture, or the growing of flowers.

flo-ri-cul-ture (flō'rĭ-kŭl'tūr; flŏr'ĭ-kŭl'-tūr), *n.* the culture of flowers.

flo-ri-cul-tur-ist (flō'rĭ-kŭl'tūr-ĭst), *n.* one who is skilled in floriculture, or the culture of flowers.

flor-id (flŏr'ĭd), *adj.* bright in color; flushed; brilliant with decorations; profusely embellished or elaborately decorated.—*adv.* **floridly.**

flor-in (flŏr'ĭn), *n.* a European silver coin, ranging in value in different countries from forty to fifty cents.

flo-rist (flō'rĭst; flŏr'ĭst), *n.* one who cultivates flowers for pleasure, or sells them for profit.

floss (flŏs), *n.* waste silk fibers; the soft, downy, silken substance in the husks of certain plants.

floss silk (flŏs sĭlk), an inferior untwisted soft silk, chiefly used in embroidery.

floss-y (flŏs'ĭ), *adj.* pertaining to, or like, soft, untwisted silk; downy; light.

flot-age (flōt'āj), *n.* things that rest on the surface of a liquid, as driftwood; the ability of anything to float.

flo-ta-tion (flō-tā'shŭn), *n.* the act or state of resting on the surface of a liquid. Also, **flotage.**

flo-til-la (flō-tĭl'ȧ), *n.* a fleet of small vessels; as, a *flotilla* of destroyers was on the lookout for torpedo boats.

flot-sam (flŏt'săm), *n.* goods lost in shipwreck, and found floating upon the sea. Also, **flotson.**

flounce (flouns), *n.* a narrow piece of cloth sewed to the skirt of a dress or petticoat, with the lower border loose and spreading; a deep ruffle; a sudden jerk or movement of the body, showing impatience: *v.t.* to furnish or trim with deep ruffles: *v.i.* to throw the limbs and body about.

flounc-ing (floun'sĭng), *p.pr.* of *flounce: n.* material for skirt ruffles.

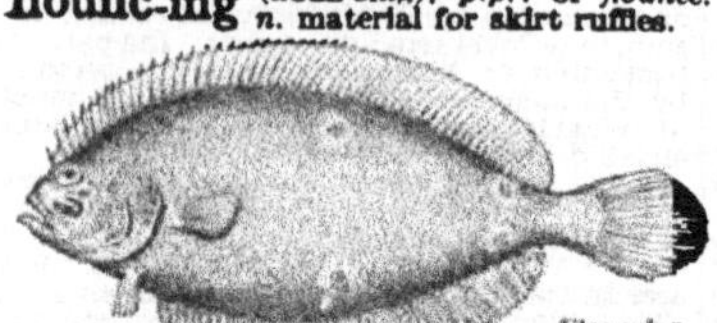

Flounder

floun-der (floun'dẽr), *v.i.* to struggle, roll, or proceed with difficulty, as an animal in the mire: *n.* a flat sea-fish; a shoemaker's tool.

flour (flour), *n.* the fine meal of ground wheat or other grain; a fine soft powder: *v.t.* to sprinkle flour upon.—*adj.* **floury.**

flour-ish (flŭr'ĭsh), *v.i.* to prosper or thrive; be vigorous; be copious or flowery in language; make ornamental lines with a pen; boast or brag: *v.t.* swing about or brandish: *n.* a figure formed by lines or strokes fancifully drawn; decoration; a musical passage intended only for display; ostentatious or showy parade; a waving about, as of a sword.

Syn., v. prosper, thrive.
Ant. (see decay).

flour-ish-ing (flŭr'ĭsh-ĭng), *p.adj.* prosperous; thriving; vigorous; as, the business is in a *flourishing* condition.

flout (flout), *v.t.* to insult; treat contemptuously; jeer: *v.i.* to scoff; sneer: *n.* an insult; contemptuous remarks.—*adv.* **floutingly.**

flow (flō), *v.i.* to run or spread, as water; circulate; glide; rise, as the tide; melt; issue forth: *v.t.* to overflow or inundate: *n.* a current or stream; the rise of the tide.

flow-er (flou'ẽr), *n.* that part of a plant which contains the reproductive organs; a blossom; the best, or choicest, part of anything; the prime; an ornamental expression: *v.i.* to put forth blossoms: *v.t.* to ornament or cover with blossoms or their representation.

Flower. 1, corolla; 2, calyx; 3, stamen; 4, pistil; 5, flower cup; 6, male flower; 7, flower of the melon family; 8, hermaphrodite linden flower; *co*, corolla; *ca*, calyx; *e*, stamens; *p*, pistil; *o*, ovary.

flow-er-et (flou'ẽr-ĕt), *n.* a little flower; a floret. Also, **flowret.**

flow-er-pot (flou'ẽr-pŏt'), *n.* a vessel containing earth in which to grow plants and flowers.

flow-er-y (flou'ẽr-ĭ), *adj.* abounding in, or adorned with, flowers; highly figurative or elaborate; as, *flowery* language.

flow-ing (flō'ĭng), *p.adj.* moving or pouring forth, as a stream; copious; fluent; hanging loosely or swaying.

flown (flōn), past participle of the transitive and intransitive verb *fly.*

fluc-tu-ate (flŭk'tū-āt), *v.i.* to roll to and fro, as a wave; rise and fall, as the stock market; be undecided or wavering.—*n.* **fluctuation.**

flue (floo), *n.* a pipe or passage to convey away smoke, hot air, etc.; soft downy matter; fluff.

ꟾ0. NORTH AMERICAN WILD FLOWERS
…phin. 3. Fringed gentian. 4. Day lily. 5. Smooth rose. 6. Lady's slipper. 7. March … the pulpit. 9. Phlox.

flu-en-cy (flōō'ĕn-sĭ), *n.* the quality of being eloquent; readiness and smoothness of speech; the quality of moving freely.

flu-ent (flōō'ĕnt), *adj.* possessing readiness and ease of speech; voluble; eloquent; moving freely; changeable.—*adv.* **fluently.**

Syn. flowing, glib, lively, unembarrassed, ready.

fluff (flŭf), *n.* light down or fur nap; a flash; puff; *v.t.* to spread out, as feathers.

fluff-i-ness (flŭf'ĭ-nĕs), *n.* the quality of being downy or feathery.

fluff-y (flŭf'ĭ), *adj.* consisting of, or covered with, light down; downy; feathery.

flu-id (flōō'ĭd), *adj.* capable of flowing; liquid or gaseous: *n.* a substance which flows.

Syn., n. gas, liquid.

flu-id-i-ty (flōō-ĭd'ĭ-tĭ), *n.* the state or quality of being liquid or gaseous; ability to flow.

fluke (flōōk), *n.* the broad part of an anchor which is fixed into the ground; a flounder; a disease in sheep; a kind of potato; one of the two lobes or ends of a whale's tail; a lucky chance stroke in billiards: *v.i.* to score by a lucky stroke; use the flukes in swimming: said of a whale.

flume (flōōm), *n.* a channel for carrying water; a gap through which a torrent passes.

flum-mer-y (flŭm'ẽr-ĭ), *n.* [*pl.* flummeries (-ĭz)], a custard or blancmange; nonsense.

flung (flŭng), past tense and past participle of the verb *fling.*

flunk (flŭnk), *n.* a complete failure: *v.i.* to fail completely; retire through fear. [SLANG.]

flunk-y (flŭnk'ĭ), *n.* [*pl.* flunkies (-ĭz)], a liveried servant; used contemptuously; a toady; snob. Also, **flunkey.**

flunk-y-ism (flŭnk'ĭ-ĭzm), *n.* the characteristics of a servant in uniform or of a toady. Also, **flunkeyism.**

flu-o-res-cence (flōō'ō-rĕs'ĕns), *n.* the quality existing in certain transparent or clear bodies of giving off under the action of light a color differing from their own; the property possessed by certain substances of becoming luminous or bright when exposed to X-rays or other forms of light.—*v.i.* **fluoresce.**—*adj.* **fluorescent.**

flu-or-ic (flōō-ŏr'ĭk), *adj.* pertaining to, or obtained from, fluorine, a pale greenish-yellow gas.

flu-or-ine (flōō'ŏr-ĭn; flōō'ŏr-ēn), *n.* a nonmetallic gaseous element, similar to chlorine.

flu-or-o-scope (flōō-ŏr'ō-skōp), *n.* a device for use in making X-ray examinations on a prepared screen.

flur-ry (flŭr'ĭ), *v.t.* [*p.t.* and *p.p.* flurried, *p.pr.* flurrying], to agitate, confuse, or bewilder: *n.* a sudden commotion or excitement; hurry; a sudden gust; as, a *flurry* of snowflakes.

flush (flŭsh), *v.t.* to cause to blush; excite; clean out with a rush of water; drive from cover: said of game birds: *v.i.* to blush; glow; to operate a mine where the continuous water supply is not sufficient, by damming up the water and releasing it at intervals in floods; to fill underground spaces, as in mines, with matter swept along by water, which after the space has been drained, settles and forms a solid mass: *n.* a sudden rush of water; flow of blood to the face; sudden excitement or impulse; a flock of game birds put to sudden flight; abundance; bloom; growth; a hand of cards all of the same suit; a bog or morass: *adj.* level with the surface; quite full; abundant; plentifully supplied with money; vigorous: *adv.* so as to be level.

flush deck (flŭsh dĕk), a deck level from stem to stern.

flus-ter (flŭs'tẽr), *v.t.* to confuse or agitate; hurry: *n.* agitation or confusion; excitement.

flute (flōōt), *n.* a musical wind instrument furnished with finger-holes and keys; a long channel or groove cut in the shaft of a column; a similar groove formed for decoration in wood, cloth, etc.: *v.t.* to sound a flute; form parallel grooves or channels in; to decorate (wood, cloth, etc.) with grooves; as, to *flute* a ruffle.

Flute

flut-ed (flōōt'ĕd), *p.adj.* having parallel grooves; having the tone or quality of a flute.

flut-ing (flōōt'ĭng), *p.pr.* of *flute: n.* a channel or groove; work decorated with grooves; as, the *fluting* of a woman's ruffle; a flute-shaped crimp or wrinkle; the act of sounding a flute.

flut-ist (flōōt'ĭst), *n.* a performer on the flute; a flute player.

flut-ter (flŭt'ẽr), *v.i.* to move or flap the wings rapidly; move rapidly and irregularly; be in agitation or uncertainty: *v.t.* to cause to move rapidly and irregularly; to throw into confusion: *n.* a quick and irregular motion; vibration; state of excitement or anxiety.

flut-ter wheel (flŭt'ẽr hwēl), a water wheel of moderate size placed at the bottom of a chute or trough, connected with a chute.

flut-y (flōōt'ĭ), *adj.* flutelike in tone; as, a *fluty* voice.

flu-vi-al (flōō'vĭ-ăl), *adj.* pertaining to, growing or living in, or caused by, rivers. Also, **fluviatile.**

flux (flŭks), *n.* any flow or issue of matter; flow of the tide: *v.t.* to melt or fuse.

flux-ion (flŭk'shŭn), *n.* the act of flowing or melting; matter that flows; *pl.* in mathematics, the analysis of very small quantities.

fly (flī), *v.i.* [*p.t.* flew, *p.p.* flown, *p.pr.* flying], to move through, or rise in, the air with wings; pass swiftly; to go quickly through the air as from some driving source; to float in the air, as a flag; move rapidly; run away; part with violence; as, the bottle *flew* into a thousand pieces; to flutter; *v.t.* to avoid or shun; cause to fly or float in the air: *n.* [*pl.* flies (flīz)], a two-winged insect of many kinds, including the common house fly; a hook dressed in imitation of a fly, used in fishing; the outer canvas of a double tent; a lap on a garment to cover a fastening; a disease in turnips; a hackney carriage: *pl.* space over a stage with apparatus for handling scenery, etc.

fly-a-way (flī'ȧ-wā"), *adj.* flighty; not level-headed; not restrained.

fly-blow (flī'blō"), *n.* the egg or larva of a fly: *v.t.* and *v.i.* [*p.p.* flyblown, *p.pr.* flyblowing], to lay eggs in meat, etc., and spoil it.

fly-er (flī'ẽr), *n.* one who, or that which, flies. Also, **flier.**

fly-ing (flī'ĭng), *p.adj.* adapted for flight; floating; waving; brief, or hurried; as, he paid a *flying* visit.

fly-ing but-tress (flī'ing bŭt'rĕs), an arched brace for strengthening and supporting a part of a building.

fly-ing fish (flī'ing fĭsh), a fish with long fins that is able to remain in the air for a short time.

fly-ing jib (flī'ing jĭb), a sail beyond the jib or foremost sail of a ship.

fly-leaf (flī'lēf"), *n.* a blank leaf at the beginning or end of a book.

fly-speck (flī'spĕk"), *n.* the dot or spot made by the excrement of a house fly; hence, any insignificant speck: *v.t.* to soil with flyspecks.

fly-wheel (flī'hwēl"), *n.* a heavy wheel in a machine to regulate its motion.

foal (fōl), *n.* the young of a horse, ass, or camel: *v.i.* to bring forth young: said of a mare, etc.

foam (fōm), *n.* the white substance formed on a liquid by violent shaking or fermentation; froth: *v.t.* to cause to foam: *v.i.* to gather foam; be enraged or greatly angered; froth.—*adj.* **foamy.**

fob (fŏb), *n.* a small pocket, especially for a watch; a short watch chain or ribbon.

fo-cal (fō'kăl), *adj.* pertaining to, or placed at, a focus or central point.

fo-cal dis-tance (fō'kăl dĭs'tăns), the distance between the center of a lens or mirror and the point where the rays converge or meet.

fo-cus (fō'kŭs), *n.* [*pl.* focuses (-ĕz), foci (-sī)], the point where a system of rays of light or heat meet after being reflected or refracted; any central point: *v.t.* [*p.t.* and *p.p.* focused, *p.pr.* focusing], to bring to a focus or center. Also, **focalize.**

fod-der (fŏd'ĕr), *n.* food for horses, cattle, or sheep; a weight for lead equal to twenty-one hundredweight: *v.t.* to feed with fodder.

foe (fō), *n.* a personal enemy; ill-wisher; an enemy in war.

foe-man (fō'măn), *n.* [*pl.* foemen (-mĕn)], an adversary or enemy in war.

fœ-tus (fē'tŭs), *n.* the unborn young of animals in the later stage of development. Also, **fetus.**—*adj.* **fœtal, fetal.**

fog (fŏg), *n.* condensed watery vapor near the surface of the sea or land; bewilderment; a cloud or haze obscuring a photographic plate: *v.i.* [*p.t.* and *p.p.* fogged, *p.pr.* fogging], to become clouded: *v.t.* to cover with mist; to puzzle.

fog bank (fŏg băṅk), a dense mass of fog at sea, appearing like land in the distance.

fog-gi-ly (fŏg'ĭ-lĭ), *adv.* in a cloudy manner; dimly; indistinctly.

fog-gi-ness (fŏg'ĭ-nĕs), *n.* the state of being cloudy; obscurity; bewilderment.

fog-gy (fŏg'ĭ), *adj.* abounding in, or filled with, mist and vapor; bewildered; obscure.

fog-horn (fŏg'hôrn"), *n.* a siren or horn sounded as a warning in a fog at sea or on the coast.

fo-gy (fō'gĭ), *n.* [*pl.* fogies (-gĭz)], a person of old-fashioned or eccentric habits and ideas. [COLLOQ.] Also, **fogey, fogie.**

foi-ble (foi'bl), *n.* a failing or defect in character; the weakest part of the blade in a sword.

foil (foil), *v.t.* to baffle or frustrate; defeat: *n.* a long thin fencing weapon with a button on the end; the trail of hunted game; a thin plate, or sheet of metal; a contrast to set something off to advantage; a small arc in the tracery of a Gothic window, etc.

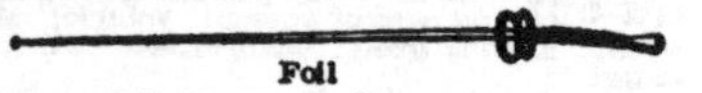

Foil

foist (foist), *v.t.* to insert wrongfully or surreptitiously; pass or palm off as genuine: with *in, into, upon.*

Fok-ker (fŏk'ĕr), *n.* an early type of German monoplane.

fold (fōld), *v.t.* to lay, as one part over another; inclose; wrap up; shut up in a pen or fold: *n.* a part bent or doubled over another; a plait; a pen for sheep; flock of sheep; the church.

fold-er (fōl'dĕr), *n.* one who, or that which, folds; a circular, map, or timetable; a name for various instruments or contrivances for folding.

fol-de-rol (fŏl'dē-rŏl"), *n.* mere nonsense; an idle fancy or conceit; a silly trifle. Also, **falderal.**

fold-ing doors (fōld'ing dōrz), a pair of doors hung on opposite side-posts and meeting in the middle.

fo-li-a-ceous (fō'lĭ-ā'shŭs), *adj.* resembling, shaped like, or having, leaves.

fo-li-age (fō'lĭ-āj), *n.* leaves collectively; the artistic representation of leaves, flowers, etc., as in architectural decoration.

fo-li-ate (fō'lĭ-āt), *adj.* leafy; in the shape of a leaf; beaten into a leaf, as metal.

fo-li-at-ed (fō'lĭ-āt"ĕd), *p.adj.* beaten, formed into, or covered with, thin plates; decorated with leaflike ornamentation.

fo-li-a-tion (fō'lĭ-ā'shŭn), *n.* the act of leafing; the act or process of beating a metal into thin plates; the number of the leaves of a book.

fo-li-o (fō'lĭ-ō; fōl'yō), *n.* a book of the largest size formed by folding a sheet of paper once; a page of manuscript or printed matter; the right and left hand pages of a ledger, etc.; in legal documents, seventy-two words of manuscript; in Congressional reports, one hundred words; a case for music, etc.: *adj.* consisting of a sheet of paper folded once: *v.t.* to page.

folk (fōk), *n.* people in general; a kindred tribe, race, or nation: *pl.*, colloquially, one's relatives.

folk dance (fōk dăns), a dance characteristic of some special race, usually of the peasants of that race.

folk-lore (fōk'lōr"), *n.* popular traditions, customs, beliefs, etc.

folk song (fōk sŏng), a popular song or ballad, illustrative of the common life of the people.

folk speech (fōk spēch), the language or dialect of uneducated people.

folk tale (fōk tāl), a story or legend handed down in a certain race from its ancestors, and characteristic of that race.

fol-li-cle (fŏl'ĭ-kl), *n.* a seed vessel; a very small tube or cavity; a simple gland.

fol-low (fŏl'ō), *v.t.* to go or come after; pursue; succeed in order; accompany; attend; support the opinions or cause of; imitate or conform to; watch or attend to

closely; to practice; as, to *follow* a profession: *v.i.* to go or come after another; result: *n.* a particular stroke in billiards or croquet.
Syn., *v.* succeed, ensue, imitate, copy, pursue.

fol-low-er (fŏl′ō-ẽr), *n.* one who goes after another; a disciple, attendant, or dependent; one of the same sect or party.
Syn. partisan, disciple, adherent, retainer, pursuer, successor.

fol-low-ing (fŏl′ō-ĭng), *p.adj.* succeeding: *n.* vocation or calling; disciples or adherents collectively.

fol-low through (fŏl′ō thrōō), a following stroke in golf, tennis, or other games by which distance and direction are given to the ball.

fol-ly (fŏl′ĭ), *n.* [*pl.* follies (-ĭz)], want of understanding; foolishness; unbecoming conduct; criminal weakness; sin.
Syn. silliness, foolishness, imbecility.
Ant. (see wisdom).

fo-ment (fō-mĕnt′), *v.t.* to bathe with warm or medicated liquids; excite; stir up or instigate.

fo-men-ta-tion (fō″mĕn-tā′shŭn), *n.* the act of applying warm or medicated liquids to a diseased part; the liquids so applied; encouragement.

fo-men-ter (fō-mĕnt′ẽr), *n.* one who instigates or causes trouble.

fond (fŏnd), *adj.* affectionate; loving; ardently attached or devoted; cherished; partial to; foolishly indulgent.—*adv.* **fondly.**
Syn. enamored, attached.
Ant. (see unfriendly).

fon-dle (fŏn′dl), *v.t.* to caress; treat with tenderness; handle tenderly; as, to *fondle* a pet.

fond-ling (fŏnd′lĭng), *n.* one who, or that which, is caressed or handled tenderly.

fond-ness (fŏnd′nĕs), *n.* tender, doting affection; relish.

font (fŏnt), *n.* a vessel to hold the water used in baptizing; a complete assortment of one size and style of type.

Baptismal Font

food (fōōd), *n.* nutriment; material for eating; that which nourishes or keeps active; as, *food* for thought.

fool (fōōl), *n.* a person lacking in reason or intelligence; idiot; in old times, a court jester; one who acts in an unwise manner; a victim or butt: *v.t.* to make a butt of; treat with contempt; disappoint; deceive.

fool-er-y (fōōl′ẽr-ĭ), *n.* [*pl.* fooleries (-ĭz)], habitual folly; absurd conduct or action.

fool-har-di-ness (fōōl′här″dĭ-nĕs), *n.* courage without sense or judgment.

fool-har-dy (fōōl′här″dĭ), *adj.* unwisely bold; daringly rash; regardless of consequences or results.
Syn. venturesome, incautious, hasty, adventurous.
Ant. (see cautious).

fool-ing (fōōl′ĭng), *n.* senseless speech or conduct; banter; nonsense.

fool-ish (fōōl′ĭsh), *adj.* acting without reason or judgment; weak-minded; silly; ridiculous; trifling; contemptible.
Syn. simple, brainless, absurd, ridiculous, nonsensical.
Ant. (see wise, discreet).

fool-ish-ly (fōōl′ĭsh-lĭ), *adv.* in a senseless manner; unwisely; indiscreetly.

fool-ish-ness (fōōl′ĭsh-nĕs), *n.* folly; an unwise act; the quality of being unwise.

fool-proof (fōōl′prōōf″), *adj.* designed to prevent thoughtless persons from harming themselves; as, this gun has not only the usual safety catch but another *foolproof* device as well.

fools-cap (fōōlz′kăp″), *n.* a size of paper about seventeen inches by fourteen inches: originally water-marked with the cap and bells formerly worn by professional jesters.

foot (fŏŏt), *n.* [*pl.* feet (fēt)], that part of the leg on which an animal walks or stands; the lower part, base, foundation, or end of anything; that part of a boot or stocking which receives the foot; a measure equal to twelve inches; unmounted soldiers; a certain number of syllables constituting part of a verse: *v.t.* to add a foot to, as a stocking; add figures in a column, and place the total at the bottom; colloquially, to pay; as, to *foot* the bill.

foot-ball (fŏŏt′bôl″), *n.* a favorite college game, in which two opposing teams try to pass a ball by carrying or kicking, through or beyond opposite goals; a large ball of inflated rubber cased in leather used in this game.

foot-board (fŏŏt′bōrd″), *n.* a board across the lower end of a bedstead; a board used to support the feet.

foot-ed (fŏŏt′ĕd), *adj.* having feet; having so many, or such, feet; as, four-*footed*, web-*footed*.

foot-fall (fŏŏt′fôl″), *n.* a footstep; the sound of a footstep.

foot-hill (fŏŏt′hĭl″), *n.* a low hill at the bottom of a mountain range.

foot-hold (fŏŏt′hōld″), *n.* secure position; a place where one may stand firmly.

foot-ing (fŏŏt′ĭng), *n.* ground or support for the feet; tread; act of moving on foot, as in dancing or walking; a firm or assured position; state or condition.

foot-lights (fŏŏt′līts″), *n.* a row of lights at the front of a theater stage, and on a level with it.

foot-man (fŏŏt′măn), *n.* [*pl.* footmen (-mĕn)], a servant in uniform who attends a carriage, waits on table, etc.

foot-note (fŏŏt′nōt″), *n.* an explanatory or illustrative statement placed at the bottom of a page.

foot-pad (fŏŏt′păd″), *n.* a highwayman who robs on foot; as, bright lights are a protection against *footpads*.

foot-path (fŏŏt′pàth″), *n.* a path for the use of people who are walking.

foot pound (fŏŏt pound), the unit of energy equal to the work required to raise one pound through a space of one foot.

foot-print (fŏŏt′prĭnt″), *n.* the mark made by a foot.

foot sol-dier (fŏŏt sōl′jẽr), a soldier who serves on foot; an infantryman.

foot-sore (fŏŏt′sōr″), *adj.* having sore feet, as from walking.

foot-stalk (fŏŏt′stôk″), *n.* the stem of a leaf; the lower part of a mill spindle.

foot-step (fo͝ot'stĕp"), *n.* a footfall; the action of the foot in stepping; the sound of a step; the imprint or mark of a foot.

foot-stool (fo͝ot'sto͞ol"), *n.* a stool to rest the feet on; a downtrodden person.

fop (fŏp), *n.* a man who is devoted to dress; a dandy; a foolish or silly person.
Syn. dude, beau, coxcomb, puppy, jackanapes.

fop-per-y (fŏp'ẽr-ĭ), *n.* [*pl.* fopperies (-ĭz)], dandyism; folly; foolery; absurdity.

fop-pish (fŏp'ĭsh), *adj.* like a dandy in dress and manners.

for (fôr), *prep.* in place of; on account of; for the sake of; notwithstanding; to the number or amount of: *conj.* because; since.

for-age (fŏr'ĭj), *n.* food for horses and cattle; a search for food or provisions for an army: *v.i.* to wander about in search of provisions or food: *v.t.* to supply with provisions; to strip of provisions, as a country in wartime.

for-as-much (fôr"ăz-mŭch'), *conj.* seeing or considering that; as, *forasmuch* as the time is short.

for-ay (fŏr'ā), *n.* in border warfare, a raid: *v.t.* to plunder or ravage.

for-bade (fŏr-băd'), past tense of the verb *forbid.*

for-bear (fŏr-bâr'), *v.t.* [*p.t.* forbore, *p.p.* forborne, *p.pr.* forbearing], to abstain from; excuse; spare: *v.i.* to restrain oneself; be patient.
Syn. abstain, refrain, withhold.

for-bear (fôr-bâr'; fôr'bâr), *n.* an ancestor. Also, **forebear.**

for-bear-ance (fŏr-bâr'ăns), *n.* patience; indulgence; self-command.

for-bid (fŏr-bĭd'), *v.t.* [*p.t.* forbade, *p.p.* forbidden, forbid, *p.pr.* forbidding], to prohibit; command not to do; oppose.

for-bid-ding (fŏr-bĭd'ĭng), *p.adj.* repellent; disagreeable; repulsive; as, a *forbidding* manner.

force (fōrs), *n.* active power; vigor; strength; energy; violence; power to persuade or convince; meaning; troops; armament; a trained or organized body; unlawful violence to property or person; any cause that produces motion, or a change of motion, in a body: *v.t.* to compel; overpower by strength; impel; push; press; strain; cause to grow or ripen by artificial or false means; as, to *force* plants to grow by artificial heat.
Syn., n. vigor, dint, might, energy, power, army, host.
Ant. (see weakness).

forced (fōrst), *p.adj.* compulsory; strained; as, a *forced* march; affected; as, a *forced* smile.

force-ful (fōrs'fo͝ol), *adj.* having vigor; strong; powerful; as, a *forceful* speech.—*adv.* **forcefully.**

force-meat (fōrs'mēt"), *n.* meat finely chopped and highly seasoned, served alone or used as a stuffing.

for-ceps (fôr'sĕps), *n.* pincers or pliers for seizing and extracting anything.

for-ci-ble (fōr'sĭ-bl), *adj.* characterized by mental or physical power; vigorous; violent.—*adv.* **forcibly.**

ford (fōrd), *n.* a shallow part of a stream, etc., which can be crossed on foot by men or animals: *v.t.* to wade through, or pass over without swimming.

fore (fōr), a *prefix* meaning before; in front: *n.* the forward part: *adj.* at or near the forward part: *interj.* a cry used by golfers as a signal to persons ahead to get out of the way.—**fore and aft,** the entire length of a ship.

fore-arm (fōr'ärm"), *n.* the arm between the wrist and elbow: *v.t.* (fōr-ärm'), to prepare for attack or resistance before the time of need.

fore-bear (fōr'bâr"; fōr'bâr'), *n.* an ancestor. Also, **forbear.**

fore-bode (fōr-bōd'), *v.t.* to presage or foretell, especially evil; to foresee: *v.t.* to foretell (evil).

fore-bod-ing (fōr-bōd'ĭng), *n.* a feeling that evil is coming upon one; a presentiment of evil; a portent.

fore-cast (fōr'kȧst"), *n.* foresight; prediction of the weather: *v.t.* (fōr-kȧst'), to plan or calculate beforehand; foresee; predict.
Syn., n. forethought, premeditation.

fore-cas-tle (fōr'kăs-l; *naut.* fōk'sl), *n.* the part of a vessel forward of the foremast where the seamen eat and sleep.

fore-close (fōr-klōz'), *v.t.* to cut off from the right of further chance to redeem a property: said of a mortgage.—*n.* **foreclosure.**

fore-doom (fōr-do͞om'), *v.t.* to doom beforehand; to destine to calamity beforehand.

fore-father (fōr'fä"thẽr), *n.* a male ancestor; as, America was settled by our *forefathers.*

fore-fin-ger (fōr'fĭn"gẽr), *n.* the finger next to the thumb; the index finger.

fore-foot (fōr'fo͝ot"), *n.* one of the front feet of a four-footed animal.

fore-front (fōr'frŭnt"), *n.* the place farthest front; the foremost place; as, the *forefront* of the battle.

fore-gath-er (fōr-găth'ẽr), *v.i.* to assemble; to associate: followed by *with.* Also, **forgather.**

fore-go (fōr-gō'), *v.t.* [*p.t.* forewent, *p.p.* foregone, *p.pr.* foregoing], to renounce or refrain from; go without; deny oneself; give up. Also, **forgo.**
Syn. quit, relinquish, waive.

fore-gone (fōr-gŏn'), *p.adj.* previous; that has gone before; determined in advance; as, a *foregone* conclusion; unavoidable.

fore-ground (fōr'ground"), *n.* that part of a landscape, picture, or scene nearest to the spectator.

fore-hand (fōr'hănd"), *adj.* in tennis, a direct stroke, holding the racket with the front of the hand toward the ball.

fore-hand-ed (fōr'hănd"ĕd), *adj.* done in good season or beforehand; thrifty in management; done with a view toward the future.

fore-head (fŏr'ĕd), *n.* that part of the face between the eyes and the hair; brow.

for-eign (fŏr'ĭn), *adj.* belonging to, or connected with, another nation or country; alien.

for-eign-er (fŏr'ĭn-ẽr), *n.* a citizen of a foreign country; an immigrant not admitted to citizenship.

fore-know (fōr-nō'), *v.t.* to know in advance; as, we cannot *foreknow* the future.

fore-land (fōr'lănd), *n.* a point of land projecting into the sea; headland.

fore-lock (fōr'lŏk"), *n.* a lock of hair growing on the forehead; a linchpin or bolt.

fore-man (fōr'măn), *n.* [*pl.* foremen (-mĕn)], the spokesman of a jury; an overseer.

fore-mast (fōr'màst), *n.* the mast nearest the bow or front of a vessel.

fore-most (fōr'mōst), *adj.* chief; first; as, the *foremost* man in the community; a matter of *foremost* interest.

fore-noon (fōr"nōōn'), *n.* that part of the day before twelve o'clock, midday; the early part of the day.

fo-ren-sic (fō-rĕn'sĭk), *adj.* pertaining to, or used in, courts of justice or public debate; as, a *forensic* term; suitable for argument.

fore-or-dain (fōr"ôr-dān'), *v.t.* to appoint beforehand; to predestine; to decree beforehand.—*n.* **foreordination.**

fore-run (fōr-rŭn'), *v.t.* [*p.t.* foreran, *p.p.* forerun, *p.pr.* forerunning], to go before; precede; announce.

fore-run-ner (fōr-rŭn'ẽr), *n.* a messenger sent before; herald; something that precedes a person or event.
Syn. harbinger, omen.

fore-sail (fōr'sāl"; *naut.* fōr'sl or fō'sl), *n.* a large square sail, the principal one on the foremast.

fore-see (fōr-sē'), *v.t.* to have knowledge of beforehand; to see beforehand.

fore-shad-ow (fōr-shăd'ō), *v.t.* to suggest beforehand; to show beforehand by an indistinct representation or figure.

fore-shore (fōr'shōr"), *n.* that part of a beach or shore between the high and low water marks.

fore-short-en (fōr-shôr'tn), *v.t.* in drawing or painting, to shorten or make objects smaller so that they will appear in the picture as they look when viewed obliquely, or so that objects in the background will appear smaller than those in the foreground; to give perspective to.

fore-sight (fōr'sīt"), *n.* the power of seeing in advance; heedful thought for the future.

for-est (fŏr'ĕst), *n.* a large extent of ground covered with trees; woodland; an uncultivated tract of land, more or less covered with trees and undergrowth: *adj.* pertaining to woodland; rustic; sylvan: *v.t.* to cover with trees or woods.

fore-stall (fōr-stôl'), *v.t.* to get ahead of; to hinder; prevent; anticipate or expect; buy up in advance.

fore-stay (fōr'stā"), *n.* a strong rope reaching from the foremast-head to the bow of a vessel to strengthen the foremast.

for-est-er (fŏr'ĕs-tẽr), *n.* one skilled in knowledge of trees and timber; an officer who has charge of a forest; an inhabitant of a forest or wild region.

for-est-ry (fŏr'ĕst-rĭ), *n.* the art of cultivating trees in woodland or managing timber.

fore-taste (fōr-tāst'), *v.t.* to enjoy before possessing: *n.* (fōr'tāst"), a brief experience beforehand.

fore-tell (fōr-tĕl'), *v.t.* to predict or prophesy; to tell beforehand.

fore-thought (fōr'thôt"), *n.* a planning-out beforehand; care taken beforehand so that affairs will shape themselves as desired.

fore-to-ken (fōr'tō"kn), *n.* an omen: *v.t.* (fōr-tō'kn), to be a sign coming before; to be an omen of; as, the violence of the storm *foretokened* disaster to the ships.

fore-top (fōr'tŏp"), *n.* the platform at the head of a foremast.

fore-top-mast (fōr"tŏp'màst), *n.* the section of a mast above the foremast.

for-ev-er (fŏr-ĕv'ẽr), *adv.* at all times; through eternity; perpetually.
Syn. endlessly, interminably, eternally, always, unceasingly.

for-ev-er-more (fŏr-ĕv'ẽr-mōr), *adv.* an emphatic word for forever.

fore-warn (fōr-wôrn'), *v.t.* to advise or warn beforehand; as, to *forewarn* a person of danger.

fore-word (fōr'wûrd"), *n.* a preface; introduction to a book.

for-feit (fôr'fĭt), *n.* a fine or penalty: *v.t.* to lose, as a position, right, or advantage, by neglect: *adj.* alienated or lost.

for-fei-ture (fôr'fĭ-tūr), *n.* the act of losing possession; that which is yielded; penalty.

for-fend (fôr-fĕnd'), *v.t.* to ward off; as, Heaven *forfend* such a disaster.

for-gath-er (fôr-găth'ẽr), *v.t.* to assemble, to come together. Also, **foregather.**

for-gave (fŏr-gāv'), past tense of the verb *forgive*.

forge (fōrj; fôrj), *v.t.* to fashion (a piece of metal) by heating and hammering; form into shape; invent; counterfeit, with intent to defraud; impel forward: *v.i.* to be guilty of counterfeiting with intent to defraud; go slowly or with difficulty: *n.* an open fire in which a blacksmith heats irons by forced draft, and fashions the metal while hot; a place where metal is heated and shaped; smithy; workshop.
Syn., *v.* coin, invent, frame, feign, counterfeit.

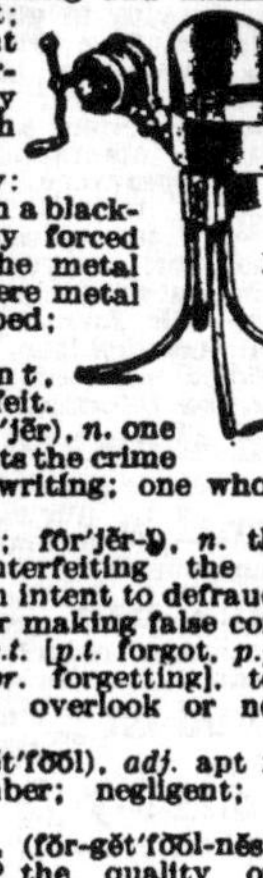

Forge

forg-er (fōr'jẽr; fôr'jẽr), *n.* one who commits the crime of counterfeiting handwriting; one who heats and shapes metal.

for-ger-y (fōr'jẽr-ĭ; fôr'jẽr-ĭ), *n.* the act of counterfeiting the handwriting of another with intent to defraud; the act of counterfeiting or making false coin.

for-get (fŏr-gĕt'), *v.t.* [*p.t.* forgot, *p.p.* forgotten, *p.pr.* forgetting], to lose the remembrance of; overlook or neglect; slight.

for-get-ful (fŏr-gĕt'fōōl), *adj.* apt not to remember; negligent; heedless.—*adv.* **forgetfully.**

for-get-ful-ness (fŏr-gĕt'fōōl-nĕs), *n.* the quality of not remembering; loss of remembrance; neglect.

for-get-me-not (fŏr-gĕt'mē-nŏt"), *n.* a small plant with small bright sky-blue flowers.

forg-ing (fōr'jĭng), *n.* metal shaped by hammering; as, the steel *forgings* in a bridge.

for-giv-a-ble (fŏr-gĭv'á-bl), *adj.* that may be pardoned.

for-give (fŏr-gĭv′), *v.t.* [*p.t.* forgave, *p.p.* forgiven, *p.pr.* forgiving], to pardon; remit, as a sin, offense, debt, etc.: *v.i.* to display clemency or leniency.
Syn. pardon, remit, absolve, acquit, excuse, except.

for-give-ness (fŏr-gĭv′nĕs), *n.* pardon; remission; as, *forgiveness* of sin.

for-go (fŏr-gō′), *v.t.* to give up; to deny oneself; to renounce; to abstain from. Also, **forego.**—*n.* **forgoer.**

for-got-ten (fŏr-gŏt′n), past participle of the verb *forget.*

fork (fôrk), *n.* an instrument with two or more prongs intended for picking up or holding something; anything resembling, or branching like, a fork; the angular opening or place of division caused by the meeting of two roads or rivers: *v.t.* to raise, throw, or dig with a pronged tool: *v.i.* to branch off.

forked (fôrkt, or fôrk′ĕd), *adj.* having prongs; opening into two or more parts; zigzag, as lightning.

for-lorn (fŏr-lôrn′), *adj.* abandoned; deserted; destitute; miserable; bereft; hopeless.
Syn. forsaken, desolate, lone.

for-lorn hope (fŏr-lôrn′ hōp), a body of men detached for some service of great danger; a hopeless enterprise or undertaking.

form (fôrm), *n.* the external or outward appearance or shape of anything; image; likeness; orderly arrangement; beauty; symmetry; determinate shape or structure; established practice, or ritual; a mold or pattern; a long bench without a back; a class; state of high condition or fitness; as, he was playing in good *form;* types, plates, etc., locked in a frame ready for printing: *v.t.* to give shape to; create; mold to a particular pattern; conceive or imagine; constitute; devise; adjust: *v.i.* to take shape.
Syn., *n.* observance, rite, figure, shape, fashion, appearance, semblance.

for-mal (fôr′măl), *adj.* according to custom or established rules; precise; ceremonious; conventional; essential; having the outward shape without the inward reality.—*adv.* **formally.**
Syn. ceremonious, precise, exact, stiff, methodical, affected.
Ant. (see information, natural).

form-al-de-hyde (fôr-măl′dē-hīd), *n.* a gas used largely as a disinfectant or purifier and as an antiseptic.

for-mal-in (fôr′mȧ-lĭn), *n.* a solution of formaldehyde, used for preserving animals, etc. Also, **formol.**

for-mal-ism (fôr′măl-ĭzm), *n.* exact observance of outward rites and customs, especially in religious duties; stiffness of manners or behavior.

for-mal-ist (fôr′măl-ĭst), *n.* one who observes strictly established customs.

for-mal-i-ty (fôr-măl′ĭ-tĭ), *n.* [*pl.* formalities (-tĭz)], strict adherence to external customs; ceremony; method or mode.

for-mal-ize (fôr′măl-īz), *v.t.* to give shape to; to make stiff, precise, or ceremonious.

for-ma-tion (fôr-mā′shŭn), *n.* the act of molding or shaping; that which is shaped; structure; figure; production; a group of strata or rock of nearly the same age having certain common characteristics.

form-a-tive (fôr′mȧ-tĭv), *adj.* giving shape to; tending to mold; plastic or pliable: *n.* a word made by adding a prefix or suffix.

for-mer (fôr′mẽr), *adj.* preceding in time or place; previously mentioned. *n.* (fôrm′ẽr), one who shapes or molds; a maker.
Syn., *adj.* antecedent, previous, prior, foregoing.

for-mer-ly (fôr′mẽr-lĭ), *adv.* anciently; some time ago; as, modes of travel were *formerly* less convenient than they are to-day.

for-mi-da-ble (fôr′mĭ-dȧ-bl), *adj.* exciting dread; fearful; powerful.—*adv.* **formidably.**

form-less (fôrm′lĕs), *adj.* without definite shape; lacking regularity of outline.—*n.* **formlessness.**

for-mol (fôr′mŏl), *n.* a solution of formaldehyde. Also, **formalin.**

for-mu-la (fôr′mū-lȧ), *n.* [*pl.* formulas (-lȧz), formulæ (-lē)], a prescribed rule or model; a group of symbols expressing the composition or contents of a chemical compound; an orderly statement of faith or doctrine; a prescription; a recipe; the expression of a rule by algebraic symbols.

for-mu-late (fôr′mū-lāt), *v.t.* to put into the terms of, or reduce to, a rule or recipe; fix or state, in definite terms. *n.* **formulation.**

for-ni-ca-tion (fôr′nĭ-kā′shŭn), *n.* unlawful sexual intercourse.

for-sake (fŏr-sāk′), *v.t.* [*p.t.* forsook, *p.p.* forsaken, *p.pr.* forsaking], to leave; desert; abandon; depart from.

for-sooth (fŏr-sōōth′), *adv.* verily; in truth; usually ironical; as, a gallant gentleman, *forsooth!*

for-swear (fôr-swâr′), *v.i.* [*p.t.* forswore, *p.p.* forsworn, *p.pr.* forswearing], to take an oath falsely: *v.t.* to deny on oath; renounce earnestly.

fort (fōrt), *n.* an inclosed fortified place: castle; fortress.

for-ta-lice (fôr′tȧ-lĭs), *n.* a small fort or fortified place.

forte (fōrt), *n.* one's strong point, or special talent; as, his *forte* was music.

for-te (fôr′tā), *adj.* and *adv.* loud: a term found in music. [It.]

forth (fōrth), *adv.* onward in time, place, or order; forward; abroad; away.

forth-com-ing (fōrth′kŭm′ĭng; fōrth′-kŭm′ĭng), *adj.* ready or about to appear: *n.* a coming forth.

forth-right (fōrth′rīt′; fōrth′rīt′), *adv.* straightforward; at once.

forth-with (fōrth′wĭth′; fōrth′wĭth′), *adv.* immediately; directly; as, he *forthwith* obeyed the command.

for-ti-eth (fôr′tĭ-ĕth), *adj.* next in order after thirty-ninth: *n.* one of forty equal parts.

for-ti-fi-ca-tion (fôr′tĭ-fĭ-kā′shŭn), *n.* the art or science of building or strengthening defenses; a military work erected for defense; a strengthening.
Syn. fort, citadel, stronghold.

for-ti-fi-er (fôr′tĭ-fī′ẽr), *n.* one who, or that which, fortifies or makes strong.

for-ti-fy (fôr′tĭ-fī), *v.t.* [*p.t.* and *p.p.* fortified, *p.pr.* fortifying], to strengthen by military works; make strong; encourage or confirm: *v.i.* to erect works of defense.

for-tis-si-mo (fôr-tĭs′ĭ-mō), *adj.* and *adv.* very loud: a term used in music. [It.]

for-ti-tude (fôr'tĭ-tūd), *n.* mental strength to endure suffering or adversity with courage.
Syn. endurance, resolution, fearlessness, dauntlessness.
Ant. (see weakness).

fort-night (fôrt'nĭt; fôrt'nīt), *n.* a period of two weeks.

fort-night-ly (fôrt'nīt-lĭ), *adv.* once every fourteen days: *adj.* coming or issued every fortnight; as, the *Fortnightly Review.*

for-tress (fôr'trĕs), *n.* a large permanent fortified place for defense or security; castle; fort.

for-tu-i-tous (fôr-tū'ĭ-tŭs), *adj.* happening by chance; accidental; casual.—*adv.* **fortuitously.**

for-tu-i-ty (fôr-tū'ĭ-tĭ), *n.* [*pl.* fortuities (-tĭz)], an accidental occurrence; chance.

for-tu-nate (fôr'tū-nāt), *adj.* happening by good fortune; lucky; successful.
Syn. happy, prosperous.
Ant. (see unfortunate).

for-tu-nate-ly (fôr'tū-nāt-lĭ), *adv.* luckily; happily; so as to bring success or prosperity.

for-tune (fôr'tūn), *n.* the good or ill that happens to mankind; chance; fate; estate; wealth; possessions; future destiny; as, to tell one's *fortune.*
Syn. luck, property, possession, riches.
Ant. (see loss, misfortune).

for-tune hunt-er (fôr'tūn hŭn'tẽr), one who seeks to marry an heiress or wealthy woman.

for-ty (fôr'tĭ), *adj.* one more than thirty-nine: *n.* the sum of ten and thirty; the sign representing it, as 40 or xl.

fo-rum (fō'rŭm), *n.* [*pl.* fora (-rȧ), forums (-rŭmz)], the public place of meeting in ancient Rome where the law courts, public offices, etc., were situated; hence, a place of public resort, or court of law; a gathering for public discussion.

for-ward (fôr'wẽrd), *adv.* onward; in advance; toward the forepart: *adj.* situated near the front; early in season or preparation; ready; prompt; presumptuous; unreserved; not overmodest; eager; earnest; impertinent: *interj.* on! *v.t.* to help forward; quicken or hasten; improve; transmit.

for-ward-ness (fôr'wẽrd-nĕs), *n.* the state or quality of being in advance; readiness; impertinence; pertness.

for-ward-er (fôr'wẽrd-ẽr), *n.* one who promotes or helps along; a merchant who transmits goods; in bookbinding, the workman who puts the book into its cover and passes it on to the finisher.

for-wards (fôr'wẽrdz), *adv.* forward; in the direction of the front or forepart. Also, **forward.**

fos-sil (fŏs'ĭl), *n.* any organic body, as an animal or plant, which by burial in the earth has become petrified or changed to stone; a person antiquated or old-fashioned in his ideas: *adj.* pertaining to, of the nature of, or converted into, a fossil; dug from the earth.

fos-sil-if-er-ous (fŏs'ĭl-ĭf'ẽr-ŭs), *adj.* containing fossils, or bodies changed into stone.

fos-sil-ize (fŏs'ĭl-īz), *v.t.* and *v.i.* to petrify or turn to stone; to render, or to become, antiquated or old-fashioned.

fos-ter (fŏs'tẽr), *v.t.* to nourish; nurse; rear up; sustain or support; cherish.
Syn. tend, harbor, nurture.
Ant. (see neglect).

fos-ter child (fŏs'tẽr chīld), a child nursed or reared by one who is not its parent.

fought (fôt), past tense and past participle of the verb *fight.*

foul (foul), *adj.* offensive, morally or physically; dirty; impure; filthy; hateful; loathsome; disgraceful; unfair; cloudy and stormy; contrary, as a wind; thick with weeds, etc.; entangled, as an anchor: *n.* an unfair play in football or other games; a wilful collision; in baseball, a ball struck by the batter which first strikes the ground outside of the base lines: *v.t.* to make dirty; sully or defile; come into collision with: *v.i.* to become dirty; in baseball, to strike a foul ball.—*adv.* **foully.**
Syn., adj. impure, nasty, unclean.
Ant. (see pure, clean).

fou-lard (fōō-lärd'; fōō'lär'), *n.* a light silk, or silk-cotton washable dress fabric; a silk handkerchief for wear round the neck or head. [Fr.]

foul-ness (foul'nĕs), *n.* the state or quality of being unclean.

found (found), past tense and past participle of the verb *find:* *v.t.* to lay the basis of; build; fix firmly; establish; originate; form by melting a metal and pouring it into a mold; cast.

foun-da-tion (foun-dā'shŭn), *n.* the basis or lowest part of a structure; groundwork; the principles or origin of anything; an endowment or gift of money to support an institution; the first stitches in knitting or crochet.

found-er (foun'dẽr), *n.* one who starts, lays the basis of, or originates; builder; one who casts metal: *v.t.* to sink by filling with water; disable or make lame: said of a horse: *v.i.* to fill and sink; go lame.

found-ing (found'ĭng), *n.* the method of making articles of cast iron, brass, etc., by melting and pouring into a mold; the establishment of an institution, etc.

found-ling (found'lĭng), *n.* a child found after having been deserted by its parents, who are unknown.

foun-dry (foun'drĭ), *n.* [*pl.* foundries (-drĭz)], the place where metal casting is carried on; as, an iron *foundry.*

fount (fount), *n.* a spring of water; original source; as, the *fount* of every blessing.

foun-tain (foun'tĭn), *n.* a natural or artificial spring of water; the head or source of a river; a jet or spout of water; the first cause or origin.

foun-tain-head (foun'tĭn-hĕd), *n.* the spring from which a stream flows; the first source.

foun-tain pen (foun'tĭn pĕn), a pen having a space in the holder for a supply of ink.

four (fōr), *adj.* consisting of one more than three; a cardinal numeral: *n.* the sum of three and one; the sign representing it, as 4 or iv; a four-oared boat, or its crew.

four-fold (fōr'fōld"), *n.* a quantity four times as much: *adj.* consisting or made up of four: *adv.* four times.

four-in-hand (fōr'ĭn-hănd"), *n.* a coach drawn by four horses and driven by one person; a necktie, worn tied in a knot so as to leave the ends hanging down: *adj.* and *adv.* with a team of four horses.

four-neau (fōōr'nō'), *n.* the chamber of a mine in which the powder is placed. [Fr.]

four-ra-gère (fōō'rä'zhâr'), *n.* a decoration granted to an entire body of troops for distinguished bravery in action, consisting of a braided cord of a designated color, to be worn about the left shoulder seam of the coat by every man of the unit so decorated. [Fr.]

four-some (fōr'sŭm), *n.* in golf, a match in which two play on each side.

four-square (fōr'skwâr'), *adj.* and *adv.* having four equal sides; upright and honest; in a square form.

four-teen (fōr'tēn"; fōr"tēn'), *adj.* consisting of four more than ten: *n.* the sum of thirteen and one; the sign representing it, as 14 or xiv.

four-teenth (fōr'tēnth"; fōr"tēnth'), *adj.* fourth in order after tenth: *n.* one of fourteen equal parts.

fourth (fōrth), *adj.* next in order after third: *n.* one of four equal parts; a musical interval or space of two tones and one semitone: **Fourth,** the fourth day of July; Independence Day.

fourth-ly (fōrth'lĭ), *adv.* in the fourth place; as, *fourthly,* I shall prove to you, etc.

fowl (foul), *n.* a bird, especially, the common rooster or hen; poultry; birds collectively: *v.i.* to catch or kill wild birds for sport or food.

fowl-er (foul'ẽr), *n.* one who catches or kills wild birds for sport or food.

fowl-ing (foul'ĭng), *n.* the act or practice of catching or shooting wild birds.

fowl-ing piece (foul'ĭng pēs), a light gun used for bird shooting and ordinary sport.

fox (fŏks), *n.* a small animal of the dog kind noted for its cunning; hence, a sly, cunning person: *v.t.* to make sour, or turn reddish; repair: said of boots; watch slyly: *v.i.* to turn sour or become reddish; act as a spy.

fox brush (fŏks brŭsh), the tail of a fox; as, the *fox brush* is the trophy of the chase.

foxed (fŏkst), *p.adj.* stained, as timber, or spotted, as prints, books, etc., with a reddish discoloration or stain; repaired

fox-glove (fŏks'glŭv), *n.* any of various plants of the figwort family, the most common having purple flowers, and leaves which are used in medicine.

fox grape (fŏks grāp), any one of several kinds of American grapes.

fox-hound (fŏks'hound"), *n.* one of a breed of dogs used for fox-hunting.

fox-i-ness (fŏk'sĭ-nĕs), *n.* sly cunning, or shrewdness; the state of being decayed, or sour.

fox-ing (fŏk'sĭng), *n.* a piece of leather used in mending the upper of a shoe.

fox-tail (fŏks'tāl"), *n.* the name of various kinds of grass; the tail or brush of a fox.

fox trot (fŏks trŏt), a modern dance in four-four time, including walking steps, two-step, etc.

fox-y (fŏk'sĭ), *adj.* pertaining to, or like, a fox; cunning; crafty; reddish-brown; soured; discolored or stained.

foy-er (foi'ẽr; fwȧ"yā'), *n.* the lobby or entrance hall of a theater, hotel, etc.; in France, a hearth or home. [Fr.]

fra-cas (frā'kȧs; Fr. frȧ"kä'), *n.* a noisy quarrel; as, the boys engaged in a general *fracas.*

frac-tion (frăk'shŭn), *n.* a part broken off; act of breaking; the state of being broken; a part of a unit, as ¾.

frac-tion-al (frăk'shŭn-ăl), *adj.* pertaining to, or constituting, a fraction; very small.

frac-tious (frăk'shŭs), *adj.* unruly; cross; peevish; rebellious; as, a *fractious* child.—*n.* **fractiousness.**

Syn. touchy, testy, peevish, fretful.
Ant. (see tractable).

frac-ture (frăk'tūr), *n.* a part broken; a break caused by violence; separation; the direction in which a mineral breaks so as to show its texture: *v.t.* and *v.i.* to break or crack, as a bone, etc.

frag-ile (frăj'ĭl), *adj.* easily broken; weak; delicate; as, *fragile* china.

Syn. brittle, frail, feeble.
Ant. (see strong).

fra-gil-i-ty (frȧ-jĭl'ĭ-tĭ), *n.* the state of being delicate or easily broken.

frag-ment (frăg'mĕnt), *n.* a part broken off from a whole; an imperfect part.

frag-men-ta-ry (frăg'mĕn-tā-rĭ), *adj.* pertaining to, or composed of, broken parts; disconnected. Also, **fragmental.**

fra-grance (frā'grăns), *n.* the state or quality of being sweet-smelling. Also, **fragrancy.**

fra-grant (frā'grănt), *adj.* sweet-smelling; as, a *fragrant* flower.—*adv.* **fragrantly.**

frail (frāl), *adj.* fragile or easily broken; brittle; weak, physically or morally; infirm: *n.* a basket made of rushes.

frail-ty (frāl'tĭ), *n.* [*pl.* frailties (-tĭz)], weakness; physical, mental, or moral; liability to be deceived or misled; a failing; a sin due to lack of control or moral weakness.

frame (frām), *n.* something constructed or made of parts fitted and joined together; that on which anything is held or stretched; as, a quilting *frame;* any contrivance for inclosing, admitting, or supporting something; as, a window *frame;* shape; temper; state; as, of the mind: *v.t.* to fit (one thing) into another; shape or form; adjust or regulate; invent; adapt.

Syn., v. construct, coin, forge, mold, feign, make.

fram-er (frām'ẽr), *n.* one who fits or shapes; a contriver; as, the *framers* of a tariff bill.

frame-work (frām'wûrk"), *n.* that which incloses or supports anything; the basis for a more complete structure.

franc (frănk), *n.* a French coin, the unit of monetary value equal to 19.3 cents.

fran-chise (frăn'chīz; frăn'chĭz), *n.* liberty; freedom; the constitutional right of suffrage, or right to vote; a particular privilege or right granted by a sovereign or by a legislative or lawmaking body to an individual, or to a business company; the district or jurisdiction to which a particular privilege extends.

Syn. right, exemption, immunity, privilege, freedom, suffrage.

Fran-cis-can (frăn-sĭs'kăn), *adj.* pertaining to the Order of St. Francis: *n.* a friar or monk of that order.

franc-ti-reur (frăñ'tē'rûr'), *n.* a soldier belonging to a detached corps of troops; a sharpshooter. [Fr.]

fran-gi-bil-i-ty (frăn′jĭ-bĭl′ĭ-tĭ), *n.* the state or quality of being frangible, or breakable.

fran-gi-ble (frăn′jĭ-bl), *adj.* easily broken; as, *frangible* bones.

frank (frăṅk), *adj.* open or ingenuous; candid; outspoken; unreserved: *n.* a signature that exempts or releases mail-matter from payment of postage; a letter privileged to go post-free: *v.t.* to send or have conveyed (as a letter) free of charge.
Syn., adj. artless, sincere, free, easy, familiar.
Ant. (see tricky, insincere).

frank-in-cense (frăṅk′ĭn-sĕns), *n.* a fragrant or sweet-smelling resin burnt as incense.

frank-lin (frăṅk′lĭn), *n.* in England, very early, a free tenant who held his land in his own right and not from a feudal lord; later, a well-to-do landowner.

frank-ly (frăṅk′lĭ), *adv.* candidly; openly; without concealment.

frank-ness (frăṅk′nĕs), *n.* candor; openness; as, he spoke with great *frankness.*

fran-tic (frăn′tĭk), *adj.* violently mad or distracted; wild and disorderly.—*adv.* **frantically.**
Syn. furious, raving, frenzied.
Ant. (quiet, subdued).

frap-pé (frȧ′pā′), *adj.* chilled with ice: *n.* a water ice. [Fr.]

fra-ter-nal (frȧ-tûr′năl), *adj.* pertaining to, becoming, or like, brothers.—*adv.* **fraternally.**

frat-er-nize (frăt′ēr-nīz), *v.i.* to associate or hold fellowship as brothers.

fra-ter-ni-ty (frȧ-tûr′nĭ-tĭ), *n.* [*pl.* fraternities (-tĭz)], brotherly relationship; a body of men banded together by a common bond of interest; men of the same profession or class; a college secret society.

frat-ri-cide (frăt′rĭ-sīd; frā′trĭ-sīd), *n.* the crime of killing a brother; one who kills a brother.

fraud (frôd), *n.* deceit; artifice; trick; cheat; a humbug.
Syn. deception, duplicity, guile, imposition.
Ant. (see honesty).

fraud-u-lence (frôd′ū-lĕns), *n.* deceitfulness; trickery; unfairness. Also, **fraudulency.**

fraud-u-lent (frôd′ū-lĕnt), *adj.* characterized by, founded on, or obtained by, unfair methods.—*adv.* **fraudulently.**

fraught (frôt), *p.adj.* laden; charged; as, the expedition was *fraught* with danger.

fray (frā), *n.* a riot; quarrel: *v.t.* and *v.i.* to chafe or wear away; to become unwoven: said of any fabric.

fray-ing (frā′ĭng), *p.pr.* of *fray: n.* the act of wearing away by friction or rubbing.

fraz-zle (frăz′l), *v.t.* to fray or tatter, as cloth: *n.* frayed ends; state of being frayed. [Colloq.]

freak (frēk), *n.* sudden or capricious change of mind, or whim; a prank; an abnormal animal or plant: *v.t.* to spot or streak.
Syn., n. fancy, humor, vagary, whim, caprice.
Ant. (see purpose, resolution).

freak-ish (frēk′ĭsh), *adj.* full of whims or pranks; odd; abnormal.—*adv.* **freakishly.**—*n.* **freakishness.**

freck-le (frĕk′l), *n.* a brownish spot in the skin: *v.t.* to mark with freckles: *v.i.* to become freckled.

free (frē), *adj.* [*comp.* freer, *superl.* freest], without restraint; at liberty; permitted; liberal; generous; open; guiltless; independent; familiar; without cost; not arbitrary or despotic; spirited; not attached or fixed; invested with, or having, the right to vote, etc.: *v.t.* to set at liberty; emancipate; rid or exempt; clear: often with *of: adv.* gratuitously; without restraint.—*adv.* **freely.**
Syn., adj. generous, bounteous, frank, artless, candid, familiar, unconfined, unreserved, exempt, easy, careless.
Ant. (see slavish, confined).

free-board (frē′bōrd″), *n.* that part of the side of a ship between the upper edge, or gunwale, and the water line.

free-boot-er (frē′bo͞ot″ēr), *n.* one who roves about for plunder or pillage; buccaneer or pirate.

freed-man (frēd′măn), *n.* [*pl.* freedmen (-mĕn)], a slave who has been legally emancipated, or set free.

free-dom (frē′dŭm), *n.* the state of being free; liberty; independence; ease in performance; particular privilege; absence of conventionality; undue familiarity.
Syn. unrestraint, license, franchise, exemption, privilege.
Ant. (see slavery).

free-hand (frē′hănd″), *adj.* drawn by the hand without the aid of instruments.

free-hand-ed (frē′hăn″dĕd), *adj.* generous, liberal; as, he was *free-handed* with his money.

free-hold (frē′hōld″), *n.* the holding of land for life, or so that it is given to one's heirs; also, the land itself.

free lance (frē lȧns), in the Middle Ages, one of a class of soldiers who sold their services to fight for the highest bidder; one who acts, speaks, or writes irrespective or regardless of any party.

free-man (frē′măn), *n.* [*pl.* freemen (-mĕn)], one who enjoys liberty or who is not subject to the will of another.

Free-ma-son (frē′mā″sn), *n.* a member of a secret society, consisting formerly of skilled craftsmen; now, a social company professing principles of brotherly love, charity, and mutual aid.

Free-ma-son-ry (frē′mā″sn-rĭ), *n.* the system, rites, etc., of the Freemasons: **freemasonry,** natural sympathy and interest in general.

free port (frē pōrt), a port where no duties are levied on merchandise.

Free-soil (frē′soil″), *adj.* opposed to the extension of slavery: said of the party formed at Boston, in 1848, to restrict slavery.

free-stone (frē′stōn″), *n.* a sandstone suitable for working or cutting without splitting; a kind of peach.

free-think-er (frē′thĭṅk″ēr), *n.* one who forms his opinions independently of others.

free trade (frē trād), trade with other countries free from tariffs or customs duties.

free-will (frē′wĭl″), *adj.* voluntary; holding the doctrine or belief that man is free to exercise his will for good or evil.

freeze (frēz), *v.t.* [*p.t.* froze, *p.p.* frozen, *p.pr.* freezing], to congeal or harden with cold; kill by cold: *v.i.* to be congealed or hardened with cold; be at or below the temperature of 32° Fahrenheit.

freez-ing point (frēz'ĭng point), the temperature at which a liquid begins to freeze: for water, 32° Fahrenheit, 0° centigrade.

freight (frāt), *n.* the goods with which a vessel, car, etc., is loaded; cargo; method of transporting bulky goods by common carriers, often slowly, as distinguished from express; the sum paid or charged for hauling goods: *adj.* used for hauling goods: *v.t.* to load with goods for hauling; hire or charter.

freight-age (frāt'āj), *n.* charge for freight; cargo; lading; as, the ship was lost, but its human *freightage* was saved.

freight car (frāt kär), a railway car for carrying freight; a box or platform car.

freight-er (frāt'ẽr), *n.* one who loads a ship or car; shipper; a vessel for carrying a cargo, but no passengers.

French (frĕnch), *adj.* pertaining to France, its people, or language: *n.* the people of France; the language of France.

French-i-fy (frĕn'chĭ-fī), *v.* [*p.t.* and *p.p.* frenchified, *p.pr.* frenchifying], to make French in manners, characteristics, or customs.

French leave (frĕnch lēv), departure without ceremony or notice; a hasty or secret departure.

fren-zied (frĕn'zĭd), *p.adj.* affected with madness; delirious; maddened; frantic.

fren-zy (frĕn'zĭ), *n.* [*pl.* frenzies (-zĭz)], violent agitation; temporary madness; fury: *v.t.* [*p.t.* and *p.p.* frenzied, *p.pr.* frenzying], to throw into a fury; render mad.

fre-quen-cy (frē'kwĕn-sĭ), *n.* the repeated occurrence of a thing at short intervals or periods. Also, **frequence.**

fre-quent (frē'kwĕnt), *adj.* occurring often; habitual: *v.t.* (frē-kwĕnt'), to resort to, or visit often.—*n.* **frequenter.**

Syn., *adj.* usual, general.
Ant. (see rare).

fre-quent-ly (frē'kwĕnt-lĭ), *adv.* often; repeatedly.

fres-co (frĕs'kō), *n.* [*pl.* frescos, frescoes (-kōz)], a method of wall painting in water colors on fresh plaster; a picture made on plaster: *v.t.* to decorate or paint in fresco.

fresh (frĕsh), *adj.* new; recent; unfaded; uninjured by time; in good condition; not forgotten; healthy; strong and active; not wearied; lively; brisk; pure and cool; refreshing; not salt; pert; inexperienced: *n.* a spring; freshet; the union of fresh and salt water in a river.

fresh-en (frĕsh'n), *v.t.* to make like new; render less salt; revive; slacken (a rope) to relieve the part exposed to friction: *v.i.* to become vigorous or strong; grow fresh; lose saltness.

fresh-et (frĕsh'ĕt), *n.* a flood caused by melting snow or heavy rain.

fresh-man (frĕsh'măn), *n.* [*pl.* freshmen (-mĕn)], a college or high school student in his first year.

fresh-water (frĕsh'wô"tẽr), *adj.* pertaining to, living in, found in, or formed in, water that is not salt; accustomed to river navigation or the coasting trade.

fret (frĕt), *v.t.* [*p.t.* and *p.p.* fretted, *p.pr.* fretting], to wear away by friction or by rubbing; injure by rubbing; agitate; vex; irritate; make rough on the surface; ornament with raised or interlaced work: *v.i.* to be worn away by friction or corrosion; be agitated or irritated; utter peevish complaints: *n.* the act or process of fretting; an ornament formed by small bands or fillets crossing each other at right angles; perforated or interlaced ornamental work; an agitation or bubbling on the surface of a liquid; chafing or irritation; a small ridge or bar on the keyboard of certain stringed instruments, such as the guitar.

Syn., *v.* gall, chafe, vex.

fret-ful (frĕt'fōōl), *adj.* peevish; irritable.—*adv.* **fretfully.**—*n.* **fretfulness.**

fret saw (frĕt sô), a long, thin, narrow saw with fine teeth: used in cutting scrolls, etc.

fret-work (frĕt'wûrk"), *n.* carved, raised, or open ornamental work.

Fretwork

fri-a-bil-i-ty (frī"ȧ-bĭl'ĭ-tĭ), *n.* the state or quality of being easily crumbled. Also, **friableness.**

fri-a-ble (frī'ȧ-bl), *adj.* readily crumbled or reduced to powder.

fri-ar (frī'ẽr), *n.* a brother, or member of certain religious orders in the Roman Catholic Church.

fri-ar-y (frī'ẽr-ĭ), *n.* an institution or brotherhood of friars.

frib-ble (frĭb'l), *n.* an insignificant or trifling action; a trifler: *v.t.* to treat in a trifling way: *v.i.* to act in a frivolous way; to totter: *adj.* of little value; frivolous; contemptible.

fric-as-see (frĭk"ȧ-sē'), *n.* a dish of chicken, rabbit, or other meat cut into small pieces, stewed and fried with gravy or sauce: *v.t.* to make into, or dress like, a fricassee.

fric-tion (frĭk'shŭn), *n.* the act of rubbing; resistance caused by rubbing; the act of rubbing to increase the circulation of the blood; irritation or disagreement caused by difference of opinion.

Fri-day (frī'dā), *n.* the sixth day of the week: named from Freya or Freyja, the Scandinavian goddess of love.

fried (frīd), past tense and past participle of the verb *fry*.

friend (frĕnd), *n.* one attached to another by affection, regard, or esteem; an intimate acquaintance; a supporter or favorer of a cause, etc.; an ally; a salutation or greeting: **Friend**, a member of the Society of Friends, or Quakers.

friend-less (frĕnd'lĕs), *adj.* without friends; unloved; uncared-for.—*n.* **friendlessness.**

friend-li-ness (frĕnd'lĭ-nĕs), *n.* the state or quality of being amicable, cordial, genial, etc.

friend-ly (frĕnd'lĭ), *adj.* pertaining to a friend; having the qualities of a friend; ready to become acquainted; not hostile; amicable; affable; genial; convenient; favorable; as, a *friendly* breeze: *adv.* amicably.

Syn. amicable, social, sociable.
Ant. (see distant, cool.)

friend-ship (frĕnd'shĭp), *n.* intimacy united with affection or esteem; mutual attachment; good will.

frieze (frēz), *n.* the part of an entablature, or wall supported by columns, below the cornice and above the architrave: usually ornamented with sculpture, etc.; an ornamental band around a wall, just below the ceiling; a coarse woolen cloth with a rough shaggy nap on one side.

Friese

frig-ate (frĭg'ăt), *n.* formerly, a warship with an upper deck, carrying from twenty-four to fifty guns.

frig-ate bird (frĭg'ăt bûrd), a swift sea bird found near land in the warmer seas.

fright (frīt), *n.* a sudden and violent fear; alarm; a person whose dress or appearance is ridiculous; anything shocking.

fright-en (frīt'n), *v.t.* to terrify; to alarm suddenly; as, it is a bad practice to *frighten* little children.

fright-ful (frīt'fo͝ol), *adj.* terrible; dreadful; alarming; shocking; grotesque.—*adv.* **frightfully.**—*n.* **frightfulness.**

Syn. fearful, dire, direful, terrific, awful, horrible, horrid.

frig-id (frĭj'ĭd), *adj.* without warmth; wintry; cold in temperament; stiff; formal; dull.—*adv.* **frigidly.**

fri-gid-i-ty (frĭ-jĭd'ĭ-tĭ), *n.* the state of being without warmth; coldness.

frill (frĭl), *n.* a pleated or crimped edging of fine linen on a garment, as a shirt front, etc.; ruffle; *pl.* colloquially, affectation of manner; ornamentation of dress, etc.: *v.i.* to ruffle or shiver the feathers with cold: said of a hawk; *v.t.* to make into a ruffle.

fringe (frĭnj), *n.* an ornamental border of hanging cords, etc.; any border or edging like a fringe: *v.t.* to border with, or as with, a fringe.

frip-per-y (frĭp'ẽr-ĭ), *n.* old clothes or furniture; tawdry finery; the place where old clothes are sold; trade in second-hand clothes: *adj.* trumpery; contemptible.

frisk (frĭsk), *v.i.* to gambol or dance in frolic: *n.* a gambol, dance, or frolic.

frisk-i-ness (frĭs'kĭ-nĕs), *n.* the state or quality of being frolicsome or lively.

frisk-y (frĭs'kĭ), *adj.* lively in action; sprightly; gay; frolicsome.

frith (frĭth), *n.* an inlet of the sea at the mouth of a river; a kind of weir or dam for capturing fish. Also, **firth.** [SCOT.]

frit-ter (frĭt'ẽr), *v.t.* to waste by degrees; cut up, as meat, into small pieces for frying: *n.* a small fried cake made of batter with meat or fruit in it; as, an apple *fritter*.

Fritz (frĭts), *n.* in the World War, a contemptuous term for a German soldier. [SLANG.]

fri-vol-i-ty (frĭ-vŏl'ĭ-tĭ), *n.* [*pl.* frivolities (-tĭz)], a trifling act, thought, or thing; lightness of thought, speech, or act.

friv-o-lous (frĭv'ō-lŭs), *adj.* trifling; trivial; petty; silly; of little importance.—*adv.* **frivolously.**

friz (frĭz), *v.t.* to curl or crisp; form into little hard burrs: said of the nap of cloth: *n.* that which is curled, as hair. Also, **frizz.**

friz-zle (frĭz'l), *v.t.* to cook on hot coals; curl or friz: *n.* a crisped or curled lock of hair.

fro (frō), *adv.* away from; backward or back; opposite to *toward;* as, the trees swayed to and *fro*.

frock (frŏk), *n.* a loose upper garment worn by children and women; dress; a monk's habit; a coarse overgarment worn by laborers, etc.; a coat worn by soldiers off duty.

frock coat (frŏk kōt), a close-fitting, straight-bodied coat for men, with wide skirts of the same length before and behind.

frog (frŏg), *n.* a small tailless animal that moves by leaping, usually found in damp or watery places; a tender horny substance growing in the middle of the sole of a horse's foot; a spindle-shaped button which fits into a loop, used for fastening military cloaks, ladies' mantles, etc.; a plate used on a railroad to guide the wheels where one track crosses another.

Frogs

frol-ic (frŏl'ĭk), *n.* a scene of merrymaking or gaiety; a sportive outburst; wild prank: *adj.* sportive; merry or gay: *v.i.* to indulge in tricks of mirth and levity or frivolity; play wild pranks.

frol-ic-some (frŏl'ĭk-sŭm), *adj.* full of sport or gaiety; as, a *frolicsome* mood; a *frolicsome* child.

from (frŏm), *prep.* out of; away; since; noting source or beginning, distance, absence, and departure.

frond (frŏnd), *n.* the union of a leaf and a branch; the leaf of a fern, palm, or seaweed.

front (frŭnt), *n.* the forehead; the fore part or foremost of anything; position directly before something; van; the most prominent part; impudence; a false shirt-bosom: *adj.* situated at the front: *v.t.* to stand, or be situated, opposite to: *v.i.* to have the front turned in a particular direction.

front-age (frŭn'tāj), *n.* the fore part of a building; the extent along a street or road of a building or of land; the space lying between a building and roadway.

fron-tal (frŭn'tăl), *adj.* pertaining to the front or forehead: *n.* something worn on the forehead; a drapery before a church altar; a small pediment or ornament over a window or door.

fron-tier (frŏn'tẽr; frŭn'tẽr; frŏn-tẽr'), *n.* the boundary or limit of a country; the most remote settled part of a country, facing an unexplored region: *adj.* pertaining to, or situated near, the boundary of a country.

fron-tiers-man (frŏn'tẽrz-măn), *n.* an inhabitant of the border section of a country, or of a newly settled region; a pioneer.

fron-tis-piece (frŭn'tĭs-pēs; frŏn'tĭs-pēs), *n.* an illustration facing the front page or title-page of a book.

front-let (frŭnt'lĕt), *n.* a fillet or band worn on the forehead; especially, a Jewish phylactery; the margin of the head of a bird behind the bill.

frost (frôst), *n.* minute frozen particles of moisture; the temperature of the atmosphere which causes the freezing of water; slang, an undertaking ending in failure: *v.t.* to cover with, or as with, hoarfrost; injure by frost; sharpen (horses' shoes) in cold weather; to cover (a cake) with icing.

frost-ed (frôs'tĕd), *p.adj.* covered with frost; injured by severe cold, or frostbitten; covered with icing, as a cake; having a dull or nontransparent finish, as glass.

frost-i-ly (frôs'tĭ-lĭ), *adv.* in an icy manner, or with severe coldness; as, she greeted them *frostily*.

frost-i-ness (frôs'tĭ-nĕs), *n.* the state or quality of being sharp and cold; as, a *frostiness* in the air gave promise of winter.

frost-ing (frôs'tĭng), *n.* a preparation of fine sugar and white of egg for covering cakes; rough powdered glass used in decorative work.

cold; wanting in warmth of feeling or sympathy.

fruc-ti-fy (frŭk'tĭ-fī), *v.t.* [*p.t.* and *p.p.* fructified, *p.pr.* fructifying], to make productive; fertilize: *v.i.* to bear fruit.

fru-gal (frōō'găl), *adj.* thrifty; economical; not extravagant.

Syn. provident, saving.

Ant. (see wasteful, extravagant).

fru-gal-i-ty (frōō-găl'ĭ-tĭ), *n.* thrift; economy; as, they owed their wealth to their *frugality*.

fru-gal-ly (frōō'găl-ĭ), *adv.* with economy; as, to live *frugally* is to live wisely.

fruit (frōōt), *n.* the product of a tree or plant containing the seed; product; result or profit; offspring: *v.i.* to produce fruit.

fruit-age (frōōt'āj), *n.* collective product of trees and plants; as, that year was remarkable for its rich *fruitage*; results of action.

fruit-er-er (frōōt'ĕr-ĕr), *n.* one who deals in fruits of all kinds.

fruit-ful (frōōt'fōōl), *adj.* yielding fruit; productive; fertile; abundant.

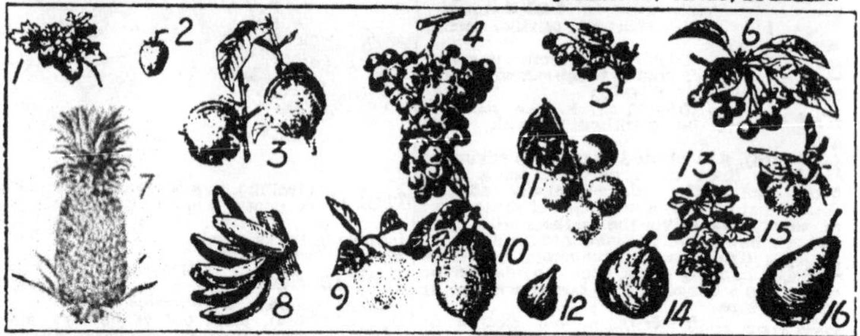

Fruit. 1, gooseberries; 2, strawberry; 3, peaches; 4, grapes; 5, raspberries; 6, cherries; 7, pineapple; 8, bananas; 9, orange; 10, lemon; 11, prunes; 12, fig; 13, currants; 14, seckel pear; 15, mandarin orange; 16, Bartlett pear.

frost-y (frôs'tĭ), *adj.* [*comp.* frostier, *superl.* frostiest], producing or accompanied with frost; frozen; hoary; cold or distant in manner.

froth (frôth), *n.* the mass of bubbles formed on the surface of a liquid by agitation, or fermentation; foam; superficial or shallow knowledge: *v.t.* to cause to foam; give vent to: *v.i.* to foam.

froth-i-ness (frôth'ĭ-nĕs), *n.* the state or quality of bubbling and foaming; shallowness; silly talkativeness.

froth-y (frôth'ĭ), *adj.* [*comp.* frothier, *superl.* frothiest], full of, or composed of, foam or bubbles; empty; frivolous or shallow; unsubstantial.

fro-ward (frō'wĕrd), *adj.* wilful; disobedient; peevish; wayward; as, a *froward* heart; a *froward* child.—*adv.* frowardly.—*n.* frowardness.

frown (froun), *n.* a scowl; stern look; look of dislike: *v.i.* to contract the brows as a result of displeasure, etc.; scowl; lower: *v.t.* to rebuke by a stern look; to suppress by scowling.

frow-zy (frou'zĭ), *adj.* dirty; untidy; slovenly. Also, **frouzy**.—*adv.* **frowzily**.—*n.* **frowziness**.

fro-zen (frō'zn), *p.adj.* congealed or hardened, benumbed, or killed with

fruit-ful-ly (frōōt'fōōl-ĭ), *adv.* abundantly; as, the land yielded *fruitfully*.

fruit-ful-ness (frōōt'fōōl-nĕs), *n.* the quality of being productive or fertile.

fru-i-tion (frōō-ĭsh'ŭn), *n.* the bearing of fruit; realization; as, the *fruition* of hopes.

fruit-y (frōōt'ĭ), *adj.* full-flavored; rich; resembling fruit.

frump (frŭmp), *n.* a dowdyish, quarrelsome, or vulgar woman. [Colloq.]

frus-trate (frŭs'trāt), *v.t.* to defeat or disappoint; thwart or oppose; bring to nothing.—*n.* **frustration**.

Syn. prevent, hinder, balk.

frus-tum (frŭs'tŭm), *n.* [*pl.* frustums (-tŭmz), frusta (-tȧ)], remainder of a pyramid or cone when the top is cut off.

fry (frī), *v.t.* [*p.t.* and *p.p.* fried, *p.pr.* frying], to cook with fat in a pan over a fire: *v.i.* to be cooked with fat in a pan; be subjected to intense heat: *n.* a dish of things fried; a swarm of young fish.

fuch-si-a (fū'shĭ-ȧ; fū'shȧ), *n.* a garden plant with beautiful flowers, usually red or pink.

fud-dle (fŭd'l), *v.t.* to stupefy or deaden with drink; intoxicate: *v.i.* to become intoxicated or drunk. [Colloq.]

fudge (fŭj), *n.* a made-up story; humbug; a kind of candy: *interj.* nonsense! *v.t.* to make or do in a bungling, careless manner: *v.i.* to contrive something by imperfect or improvised means.

fu-el (fū′ĕl), *n.* material for supplying a fire; anything that serves to inflame or sustain passion or excitement.

fu-gi-tive (fū′jĭ-tĭv), *adj.* unstable; fleeting; as, a *fugitive* idea; not permanent; fleeing from danger, pursuit, or duty; as, a *fugitive* slave: *n.* one who thus flees; a runaway or deserter; as, a *fugitive* from justice.

fugue (fūg), *n.* a musical composition in which the parts repeat at intervals the same subject or theme.

fu-guist (fū′gĭst), *n.* a composer or performer of fugues or special musical compositions.

ful-crum (fŭl′krŭm), *n.* [*pl.* fulcra (-krȧ), fulcrums (-krŭmz)], the support on which a lever rests.

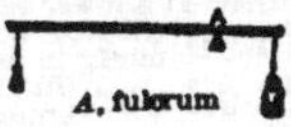
A, fulcrum

ful-fil (fŏŏl-fĭl′), *v.t.* to complete or accomplish; execute; perform or carry out (that which is promised, foretold, or expected). Also, fulfill.
Syn. accomplish, effect, complete.

ful-fil-ment (fŏŏl-fĭl′mĕnt), *n.* accomplishment; completion; execution. Also, fulfillment.

full (fŏŏl), *adj.* filled; having no empty space; well supplied; stored; saturated; satiated; copious; rounded out; plump; expressing much; clear; distinct; sonorous; having the whole disk illuminated; as, a *full* moon: *n.* the highest state, extent, or measure: *v.i.* to pucker: *v.t.* to scour and thicken, as cloth, in a mill; to give fulness to: *adv.* completely; quite: used in composition to express full extent or degree; as, *full-armed*, *full-fledged*, etc.

full back (fŏŏl băk), in football, the player furthest from the goal of the opposing side.

full dress (fŏŏl drĕs), dress required for formal or ceremonial occasions; as, *full dress* uniform.

full-er (fŏŏl′ẽr), *n.* one who thickens cloth by moistening, heating, and pressing; a half-round hammer used by blacksmiths.

full-er's earth (fŏŏl′ẽrz ûrth), a soft clay used for thickening cloth and for the removal of grease.

full-y (fŏŏl′ĭ), *adv.* completely; abundantly; as, they were *fully* equipped for their journey.
Syn. perfectly, thoroughly.

ful-mi-nate (fŭl′mĭ-nāt), *v.t.* to cause to explode; send out or utter, as a threat or denunciation: *v.i.* to make a loud sudden noise; detonate or explode: *n.* an explosive compound: fulminating powder, a mixture which upon being struck explodes with a loud noise.

ful-ness (fŏŏl′nĕs), *n.* completeness, abundance, plenty; the breadth of a garment. Also, fullness.

ful-some (fŭl′sŭm), *adj.* offensive from excess of flattery; gross; displeasing; disagreeable.—*adv.* fulsomely.—*n.* fulsomeness.
Syn. coarse, sickening, rank.
Ant. (see moderate).

fum-ble (fŭm′bl), *v.i.* to grope or feel about; in search; as, the boy began to *fumble* in his pockets: *v.t.* to handle or manage awkwardly, as the ball, in various games.

fume (fūm), *n.* vapor or gas: *v.i.* to send forth smoke; to complain angrily.

fu-mi-gate (fū′mĭ-gāt), *v.t.* smoke; perfume; disinfect or purify by the action of smoke or vapor.

fun (fŭn), *n.* pleasure; mirth; drollery; sport; amusement; play.

func-tion (fŭnk′shŭn), *n.* the act or performance of any duty, office, or business; faculty; power; the office of any organ, animal or vegetable; public or official ceremony; a quantity so connected with another quantity, that if any change is made in the one there will be a corresponding change in the other: *v.i.* to perform the duty or office for which a person or thing is intended.

func-tion-al (fŭnk′shŭn-ăl), *adj.* performing a duty; official.

func-tion-a-ry (fŭnk′shŭn-ā-rĭ), *n.* [*pl.* functionaries (-rĭz)], one who holds an office, or fills a responsible position; an official.

fund (fŭnd), *n.* stock or capital; money set apart for carrying out some permanent or temporary object; a stock in reserve: *pl.* a permanent debt due by the government on which interest is paid; money: *v.t.* to place in or turn into, a fund.

fun-da-men-tal (fŭn″dȧ-mĕn′tăl), *adj.* serving as a foundation or basis; essential; primary; as, who can give the *fundamental* reasons for the World War? *n.* a primary or necessary principle; basis; the musical note on which a chord is formed: fundamental bass, that part in musical harmony which contains the foundation notes or tones or chords.—*adv.* fundamentally.

fund-ed (fŭnd′ed), *p.adj.* existing in the form of bonds bearing regular interest; invested in the public funds.

fund-ed debt (fŭnd′ĕd dĕt), that part of a public debt which has been put in the form of bonds bearing regular interest.

fund-ing (fŭnd′ĭng), *n.* the act or process of turning money lent to the government into a permanent fund bearing a fixed rate of interest; investment in government stocks or funds.

fu-ner-al (fū′nẽr-ăl), *n.* the ceremony of burying a dead human body and the procession of mourners accompanying it: *adj.* pertaining to, or fit for, a funeral.

fu-ne-re-al (fū-nē′rē-ăl), *adj.* suitable for a burial; mournful; sad.—*adv.* funereally.

fun-gi-cide (fŭn′jĭ-sīd), *n.* anything that kills mushrooms, toadstools, molds, mildews, rusts, puff-balls, etc.

fun-gous (fŭn′gŭs), *adj.* growing up suddenly, as a toadstool does; of the nature of a fungus.

fun-gus (fŭn′gŭs), *n.* [*pl.* fungi (fŭn′jī), funguses (fŭn′gŭs-ĕz)], a plant growing up suddenly and not lasting, as a mushroom, toadstool, etc.; a spongy growth.

funk (fŭnk), *n.* a bad smell or odor; cowardice; fright: *v.i.* to be in a state of cowardly fear; to kick backwards; to back out in a cowardly manner.

fun-nel (fŭn′ĕl), *n.* a wide-mouthed vessel shaped like a cone and used for pouring liquids into small openings; the chimney of a steamship or steam engine; a smokestack.

fun-neled (fŭn′ĕld), *adj.* having or looking like a smokestack.

fun-ny (fŭn'ĭ), *adj.* [*comp.* funnier, *superl.* funniest], comical; droll; causing laughter; colloquially, strange, odd, or queer —*adv.* **funnily.**

fun-ny bone (fŭn'ĭ bōn), the lower part of the elbow.

fur (fûr), *n.* the soft hair of certain animals, growing thickly upon the skin; a light coating on the tongue; the lime coating on the inside of a boiler: *pl.* the dressed skins of fur-bearing animals, used for clothing; *adj.* lined or trimmed with fur or made of fur: *v.t.* [*p.t.* furred, *p.pr.* furring], to cover, line, or trim with fur; cover with lime.—*adj.* **furred.**

fur-be-low (fûr'bē-lō), *n.* a ruffle, flounce, or similar trimming used on women's clothing.

fur-bish (fûr'bĭsh), *v.t.* to make bright by rubbing or polishing.

fur-fur (fûr'fûr), *n.* dandruff, or scales of skin that resemble bran.

fu-ri-ous (fū'rĭ-ŭs), *adj.* very angry; mad; overcome with passion.—*adv.* **furiously.**—*n.* **furiousness.**
Syn. violent, boisterous, vehement, fierce.
Ant. (see calm).

furl (fûrl), *v.t.* to roll up and fasten to something, as a sail, flag, etc.

fur-long (fûr'lŏng), *n.* one-eighth of a mile; forty rods; two hundred twenty yards.

fur-lough (fûr'lō), *n.* leave of absence; as, the soldier came home on a *furlough:* *v.t.* to give leave of absence to.

fur-nace (fûr'nās), *n.* an inclosed structure where coal, wood, and other things are burned to make heat.

fur-nish (fûr'nĭsh), *v.t.* to fit out or to fit up with what is needed.

fur-nish-ings (fûr'nĭsh-ĭngz), *n.pl.* the necessary fittings of a house, etc.

fur-ni-ture (fûr'nĭ-tûr), *n.* the necessary fittings of a house, a ship, or a trade; outfit.

fu-ror (fū'rôr), *n.* a great outburst of excitement or enthusiasm; commotion. Also, **furore.**

fur-ri-er (fûr'ĭ-ẽr), *n.* one who prepares or sells furs; fur-dresser.

fur-row (fûr'ō), *n.* a trench made in the ground by a plow; a groove; wrinkle: *v.t.* to plow; make grooves or wrinkles in.

fur-ry (fûr'ĭ), *adj.* covered with, or made of, fur; as, the mole has a remarkably soft *furry* coat.

fur-ther (fûr'*th*ẽr), *adj.* more distant; additional: *adv.* to a greater distance or degree; moreover; also: *v.* to promote; help forward.

fur-ther-ance (fûr'*th*ẽr-āns), *n.* advancement; as, I will do all I can toward the *furtherance* of the plan.

fur-ther-more (fûr'*th*ẽr-mōr"), *adv.* moreover; besides; in addition to.

fur-ther-most (fûr'*th*ẽr-mōst"), *adj.* most distant; as, the *furthermost* points from the equator.

fur-thest (fûr'*th*ĕst), *adj.* most distant in time or degree: *adv.* at, or to, the greatest distance.

fur-tive (fûr'tĭv), *adj.* sly; secret; stealthy; as, *furtive* glances or actions.—*adv.* **furtively.**—*n.* **furtiveness.**

fu-ry (fū'rĭ), *n.* [*pl.* furies (-rĭz)], violent or very great temper; rage; madness.

furze (fûrz), *n.* a hardy spiny shrub, belonging to the bean family.—*adj.* **furzy.**

fuse (fūz), *v.t.* to melt by heat; make liquid: *v.i.* to become melted by heat; blend, as if melted: *n.* a small tube filled with a material easily set on fire, or a cord saturated with such material, used for exploding gunpowder, etc. Also, **fuze.**

fu-see (fū-zē'), *n.* a kind of match, used for setting fire to tobacco; a grooved cone in a watch, etc., around which the chain is wound. Also, **fuzee.**

fu-sel-age (fū'sē-lāj") *n.* the body or framework of an airplane in which the driver is seated and which contains the power plant, fuel, etc. [Fr.]

fu-sel oil (fū'zĕl oil), an oily poisonous liquid obtained from grape, potato, or corn spirits.

fu-si-ble (fū'zĭ-bl), *adj.* capable of being melted; as, some metals are *fusible* at a lower temperature than are others.

fu-sil (fū'zĭl), *n.* the flintlock musket formerly in use.

fu-sil-eer (fū"zĭ-lēr'), *n.* formerly, a soldier armed with a fusil, or flintlock musket: *pl.* the name of several British regiments. Also, **fusilier.**

fu-sil-lade (fū"zĭ-lād'), *n.* the discharge of a large number of firearms at the same time: *v.t.* to shoot down or shoot at with firearms all discharged at the same time.

fu-sion (fū'zhŭn), *n.* the act of melting together; as, the *fusion* of metals; the union or blending together of things; as, a *fusion* of parties.

fuss (fŭs), *n.* unnecessary or disturbing activity, especially in small matters; disorderly bustling about; confusion; stir: *v.i.* to worry; to be busy doing nothing.

fuss-y (fŭs'ĭ), *adj.* worrying, or taking great trouble, about small matters; fidgety; fretful.—*n.* **fussiness.**

fus-tian (fŭs'chăn), *n.* a kind of coarse twilled cotton cloth, as corduroy, velveteen, etc.; high-sounding speech; bombast: *adj.* made of fustian; bombastic.

fus-tic (fŭs'tĭk), *n.* a West India tree used for yellow dye.

fu-tile (fū'tĭl; Br. fū'tīl), *adj.* vain; useless; of no importance; worthless.—*adv.* **futilely.**
Syn. trifling, trivial, frivolous.
Ant. (see effective).

fu-til-i-ty (fū-tĭl'ĭ-tĭ), *n.* the quality of being useless; as, he soon saw the *futility* of trying to make them understand.

fu-ture (fū'tûr), *adj.* that will be hereafter: *n.* time yet to come; tense in grammar denoting time yet to come; a commodity, etc., sold or bought for future delivery.

Fu-tur-ism (fū'tûr-ĭzm), *n.* a movement in art, literature, and music, originating in Italy in 1910, and aiming at originality unhampered by tradition.

fu-tur-ist (fū'tûr-ĭst), *n.* one whose main interests are in what is to come; an artist in the field of painting, literature, or music whose ideas and practice are extremely radical; a follower of Futurism; one who believes that certain Biblical prophecies are yet to be fulfilled.

fu-tu-ri-ty (fū-tū'rĭ-tĭ), *n.* [*pl.* futurities (-tĭz)], time to come; future events.

fuzz (fŭz), *n.* fine minute particles of down, wool, etc.: *v.i.* to fly off in small pieces.

fuzz-y (fŭz'ĭ), *adj.* covered with, or like, fuzz or down.—*n.* **fuzziness.**

G

gab (găb), *n.* idle chatter; talkativeness: *v.t.* [*p.t.* and *p.p.* gabbed, *p.pr.* gabbing], to say falsely: *v.i.* to talk idly. [Colloq.]

gab-ar-dine (găb″ẽr-dēn′; găb′ẽr-dēn″), *n.* a kind of coat or cloak for rainy weather. Also, **gaberdine.**

gab-ble (găb′l), *v.t.* to say rapidly and senselessly: *v.i.* to talk disconnectedly, or without real meaning or sense; to make a clatter of meaningless sounds, as a bird or animal: *n.* rapid, meaningless talk.

ga-bi-on (gā′bĭ-ŭn), *n.* a large wicker basket filled with earth: used for purposes of military defense.

ga-ble (gā′bl), *n.* the triangular end of a building; as, many old houses were built with the *gable* toward the street; the entire end wall of a building; a gablelike construction in a building: **gable end,** the wall of a building on the end having a gable.

Gable

ga-ble roof (gā′bl rōōf), a roof having a vertical triangular portion or gable, at each end.

Ga-bri-el (gā′brĭ-ĕl), *n.* in the Bible, an angel sent as a herald of good tidings or comfort to man.

gad (găd), *n.* the act of going about without an object in view; as, she is always on the *gad;* a goad; an iron or steel pointed mining tool: *v.i.* [*p.t.* and *p.p.* gadded, *p.pr.* gadding], to go about without purpose; climb, as a creeping plant; ramble.

gad-a-bout (găd′*á*-bout), *n.* one who wanders continually with no apparent object in view.

gad-der (găd′ẽr), *n.* one who wanders about constantly without purpose.

gad-fly (găd′flī″), *n.* [*pl.* gadflies (-flīz)], an insect that stings cattle.

Gael (gāl), *n.* a Scottish Highlander; an Irish Celt.

Gael-ic (gāl′ĭk), *adj.* pertaining to the Celtic people of the Scottish Highlands and of Ireland, or to their language: *n.* the language of the Gaels.

gaff (găf), *n.* a large hook for landing salmon, etc.; a piece of wood upon which to extend the upper edge of a fore-and-aft sail: *v.t.* to seize or land a fish with a large hook.

gaf-fer (găf′ẽr), *n.* a respectable and good old man, especially a countryman: masculine of *gammer.*

gaff-top-sail (găf″tŏp′săl; *naut.* găf″-tŏp′sl), *n.* a light sail set above a gaff.

gag (găg), *n.* something placed in the mouth to hinder speech; words added by an actor in a play: *v.t.* [*p.t.* and *p.p.* gagged, *p.pr.* gagging], to stop the mouth; silence by physical force or by law: *v.i.* to strain, as in the effort to vomit.

gage (gāj), *n.* a standard of measure; the number of feet a vessel sinks in water; the position of one ship in relation to another and the wind; a measuring rod; the distance between the rails of a railway line; a promise or agreement; a security; a kind of plum; a challenge to fight; a glove, cap, or the like thrown on the ground as a challenge to fight: *v.t.* to measure; to find out, as the contents of any certain receptacle. Also, **gauge.**

gai-e-ty (gā′ĕ-tĭ), *n.* [*pl.* gaieties (-tĭz)], the state or quality of being merry; pleasure; glee; jollity. Also, **gayety.**

gai-ly (gā′lĭ), *adv.* merrily; finely; showily; as, to sing *gaily;* to dress *gaily.* Also, **gayly.**

gain (gān), *n.* advantage; profit: opposite to *loss:* *v.t.* to obtain, as profit or advantage; earn; win; arrive at: *v.i.* to improve or make progress; increase; advance: with *on* or *upon.*

Syn., n. benefit, winnings, earnings.

Ant. (see loss).

gain-ful (gān′fōōl), *adj.* yielding profit; advantageous.

gain-say (gān″sā′; gān′sā″), *v.t.* [*p.t.* and *p.p.* gainsaid, *p.pr.* gainsaying], to contradict; speak against; oppose; to deny.

gait (gāt), *n.* a manner of walking; as, a rapid *gait;* an awkward *gait.*

gait-er (gā′tẽr), *n.* a covering of cloth for the ankle, fitting over the top of the boot; a shoe with a cloth top.

ga-la (gā′l*á*), *n.* a show; finery; great display: **gala day,** a day of fun and pleasure; a holiday.

Gal-a-had (găl′*á*-hăd), *n.* a knight of Arthur's Round Table, who was successful in his quest for the Holy Grail; hence, any noble and chivalrous young man.

gal-a-te-a (găl″*á*-tē′*á*), *n.* a heavy cotton fabric, often striped.

Ga-la-tian (g*á*-lā′shăn), *n.* a native of Galatia, in Asia Minor; *pl.* in the Bible, the Epistle addressed to the Galatians

gal-ax-y (găl′ăk-sĭ), *n.* a gathering of splendid persons or things; as, a *galaxy* of beautiful women.—**Galaxy,** the Milky Way; as, the *Galaxy* consists of innumerable stars too small to be seen by the naked eye.

gale (gāl), *n.* a strong wind, less violent than a tempest; a quarrel; noisy merriment.

ga-le-na (g*á*-lē′n*á*), *n.* lead ore; as, most of the lead used in the arts is obtained from *galena.*

gal-i-pot (găl′ĭ-pŏt), *n.* a white juice which comes out of pine trees; an impure turpentine.

gall (gôl), *n.* the bile, especially that of the ox, which is used in making water-color paints and medicine; anything very bitter; a sore on the skin from chafing; a swelling on plants, caused by certain insects; evil feeling: *v.t.* to break or injure by rubbing, as the skin; render sore by friction; wear away; vex; fret; harass; weary: *v.i.* to fret; to become sore or worn by chafing.

gal-lant (găl′ănt), *adj.* brave; high-spirited; chivalrous; as, Sir Galahad was a *gallant* knight; (g*á*-lănt′), showing courtesy and respect to women: *n.* (g*á*-lănt′, găl′ănt), a person of sprightly and gay manners; a beau; a man who is attentive to women; as, the young *gallant* had excellent manners: *v.t.* (g*á*-lănt′), to pay court to; accompany; escort.—*adv.* **gallantly.**

Syn., adj. bold, courageous, gay, fine, showy, intrepid, heroic.

gal-lant-ry (găl′ănt-rĭ), *n.* [*pl.* gallantries (-rĭz)], bravery; heroic courage; polite and respectful attention to women.

gal-le-on (găl'ē-ŭn), *n.* a large Spanish three-decked vessel, once used as a warship, or as a merchantman for trading to South America.

Galleon

gal-ler-ied (găl'ĕr-ĭd), *adj.* fitted up with balconies; as, *galleried* churches, theaters, etc.

gal-ler-y (găl'ĕr-ĭ), *n.* [*pl.* galleries (-ĭz)], a long narrow hall, or place for walking; the upper seats of a theater, church, assembly room, etc.; the occupants of such parts of a building; a building, or room, used for the exhibition of works of art, etc.; a covered passage in a work for defense or for communication; a balcony.

gal-let (găl'ĕt), *n.* a small piece of stone chipped off by a wagon: *v.t.* to fill masonry joints with stone.—*n.* **galleting.** Also, **garret.**

gal-ley (găl'ĭ), *n.* [*pl.* galleys (-ĭz)], a low, flat, one-decked vessel moved by oars, and sometimes by sails; an open boat used by British men-of-war, river police and customs officers, and for pleasure; the cook house of a ship; in printing, a narrow oblong tray for holding set-up type.

gal-ley slave (găl'ĭ slāv), a slave compelled to row a galley; a convict condemned to such labor.

gall-fly (gôl'flī), *n.* an insect that deposits its eggs on plants, causing swelling.

Gal-lic (găl'ĭk), *adj.* pertaining to ancient Gaul, or modern France.

gal-lic ac-id (găl'ĭk ăs'ĭd), an acid found in gallnuts, tea, etc.

Gal-li-can (găl'ĭ-kăn), *adj.* pertaining to Gaul, or France, or to the Roman Catholic Church in France.

Gal-li-cism (găl'ĭ-sĭzm), *n.* a French manner of speech used in another language.

gal-li-na-ceous (găl'ĭ-nā'shŭs), *adj.* like, or pertaining to, domestic fowls; of that class of fowls which includes barnyard fowls, turkeys, guinea fowl, grouse, pheasants, etc.

gall-ing (gôl'ĭng), *p.adj.* chafing; irritating; as, the *galling* tyranny of the conquerors.
Syn. vexing, annoying.
Ant. (see soothing).

gal-li-pot (găl'ĭ-pŏt), *n.* a smooth, glass-like earthenware jar, used largely by druggists to hold medicines.

gal-li-um (găl'ĭ-ŭm), *n.* a hard, white element something like aluminum, found in some zinc ores.

gal-li-vant (găl'ĭ-vănt'), *v.i.* to play the beau; to wait upon the ladies; also, to roam about for pleasure without any real plan.

gall-nut (gôl'nŭt'), *n.* a round growth produced on the oak tree by the puncturing of the leaf buds by an insect, the gall-beetle: used, for the tannin contained in it, in making ink, dye, etc.

gal-lon (găl'ŭn), *n.* unit of liquid measure equal to four quarts, or of dry measure equal to one-eighth of a bushel.

gal-loon (gă-lōōn'), *n.* a cotton, silk, worsted, or gold lace trimming used for hats, shoes, uniforms, etc.

gal-lop (găl'ŭp), *n.* the rapid forward springing movement of a horse; the act of riding at this gait: *v.i.* to run with leaps, like a horse; ride a horse moving with a rapid forward spring; hasten: *v.t.* to cause to move with a rapid springing gait.

gal-lop-ing (găl'ŭp-ĭng), *p.adj.* going by springing leaps; moving very quickly.

gal-lows (găl'ōz; găl'ŭs), *n.* a wooden structure consisting of two uprights with a crossbar on the top, used for hanging criminals; anything resembling such a framework.

gall-stone (gôl'stōn'), *n.* a lump of solid matter formed in the gall bladder or biliary duct.

gal-op (găl'ŭp; găl'ō), *n.* a lively dance; the music for it. [Fr.]

ga-lore (gȧ-lōr') *adj.* very many; abundant; as, pretty girls *galore:* *adv.* in great plenty.

ga-losh (gȧ-lŏsh'), *n.* an overshoe of India rubber; a legging or gaiter. Also, **golosh, goloshe, galoche.**

gal-van-ic (găl-văn'ĭk), *adj.* producing electrical currents; spasmodic.

gal-van-ism (găl'vȧ-nĭzm), *n.* that branch of electric science which treats of currents arising from the chemical action of certain bodies placed in contact, or of an acid on a metal.

gal-van-ize (găl'vȧ-nīz), *v.t.* to cover with gold, silver, zinc, etc., by means of electricity; to excite, as by an electric shock.

gal-va-nom-e-ter (găl'vȧ-nŏm'ē-tẽr), *n.* an instrument for measuring the presence, extent, and direction of an electric current.

Galvanometer

gal-va-nom-e-try (găl'vȧ-nŏm'ē-trĭ), *n.* the art, science, or process of measuring currents of electricity.

gam-bit (găm'bĭt), *n.* an opening in chess in which a pawn, or piece, is sacrificed to obtain a favorable position for the action of the more important pieces.

gam-ble (găm'bl), *v.i.* to play for money or a prize; risk money on an event or a possible happening: *v.t.* to squander by playing for stakes: often with *away*.

gam-bler (găm'blẽr), *n.* one who plays for stakes or hazards money on the outcome of an event; especially, one who does so as a business.

gam-bling (găm'blĭng), *n.* the act of wagering or playing for stakes.

gam-boge (găm-bōj'; găm-bōōj'), *n.* a reddish-yellow gum resin which is found in the Orient, or eastern part of the Old World, and used as coloring matter or medicine.

gam-bol (găm'bŏl), *n.* a dancing or skipping about for joy or sport; frolic: *v.i.* to skip and dance about in play or frolic.

gam-brel (găm'brĕl), *n.* the joint of the hind leg of a horse; a bent stick, resembling a horse's leg, used by butchers; a roof with an obtuse angle in its slope.

gam-brel roof (găm'brĕl rōōf), a curb roof in which the slope is broken by an obtuse angle.

game (găm), *n.* a sport or amusement; fun; frolic; a single match at play; the advantage required in order to win; as, it's your *game*; wild animals pursued and killed by shooting or hunting; any object of pursuit: *pl.* athletic contests: *v.i.* to play at any sport or diversion; play for a stake or prize: *adj.* pertaining to animals or birds hunted or taken for sport; ready; plucky.
Syn., *n.* play, pastime.

game-cock (găm'kŏk"), *n.* a cock bred and trained for fighting.

game fowl (găm foul), one of a breed of fancy poultry, of a quarrelsome disposition, kept for fighting.

game-keep-er (găm'kēp'ẽr), *n.* one in charge of wild animals or birds that are to be hunted.

game-some (găm'sŭm), *adj.* merry; gay; playful; ready to play.

game-ster (găm'stẽr), *n.* one who habitually plays for stakes or wagers on the outcome of an event.

gam-in (găm'ĭn), *n.* a neglected, untrained, and too forward street child; a street Arab.

gam-ing (găm'ĭng), *n.* the act of playing games for stakes; gambling.

gam-mer (găm'ẽr), *n.* old woman; grandmother; especially an old countrywoman: feminine of *gaffer*.

gam-mon (găm'ŭn), *n.* the thigh of a hog salted and smoked; colloquially, nonsense: *v.t.* to impose upon with improbable stories; hoax; defeat at the game of backgammon; cure, as meat, by salting and smoking; attach or fix (a bowsprit) to a ship: *interj.* nonsense!

gam-ut (găm'ŭt), *n.* the lines and spaces upon which musical notes are written or printed; hence, entire range or extent.

gam-y (găm'ĭ), *adj.* plucky; ready; spirited; having the flavor of game.

gan-der (găn'dẽr), *n.* a male goose; as, in the old saying: "What is sauce for the goose is sauce for the *gander*."

gang (găng), *n.* a number of persons banded together for a particular purpose; a group of laborers under one foreman; as, my father has charge of one *gang* of men; a number of a ship's company selected for special duty; squad.

gan-gli-on (găn'glĭ-ŏn), *n.* [*pl.* ganglia (-ȧ), ganglions (-ŏnz)], a nerve center; a sort of swelling or unnatural growth under the skin.

gang-plank (găng'plănk), *n.* a movable platform by which to enter or leave a ship.

gan-grene (găn'grēn), *n.* the first state of mortification, or decay of some part of a living body: *v.t.* to cause to mortify: *v.i.* to become mortified or decayed. —*adj.* **gangrenous.**

gang-way (găng'wā"), *n.* a narrow platform of crosswise planks used as a temporary passageway, or as a bridge between a wharf and a ship; a passage into or out of any place; a passageway between two rows of seats; that part of a ship's side, within or without, by which persons enter or depart; the waist of a vessel or clear way by the side of the bulwarks; the main level of a mine.

gan-net (găn'ĕt), *n.* the solan goose; one of several kinds of sea birds.

gant-let (gȧnt'lĕt; gănt'lĕt), *n.* a mailed glove, or one with a long wrist-extension; a former military punishment. Also, **gauntlet.**

gaol (jāl), *n.* a place where persons awaiting trial or found guilty of minor offenses are confined; a prison. Also, **jail.**—*n.* **gaoler, jailer.**

gap (găp), *n.* an opening; cleft; passage; breach; a pass in a mountain ridge; in flying machines, the vertical distance between two surfaces, especially in a biplane.
Syn. chasm, hollow, cavity, crevice, rift.

gape (gāp; găp; gȧp), *v.i.* to open the mouth wide, as from drowsiness, wonder, etc.; yawn; open: *n.* the act of opening the mouth and staring; a yawn; the opening between the jaws of birds or of fishes: *pl.* a disease of poultry.

gar (gär), *n.* a long slender fish with a spearlike snout.

gar-age (gȧ'rŏzh'; gär'āj), *n.* a place in which automobiles or airships are kept for shelter or repair; a hangar.

garb (gärb), *n.* a dress; outside clothing; costume; fashion; as, he wore the *garb* of a gentleman: *v.t.* to clothe.

gar-bage (gär'bāj), *n.* offal; refuse; waste animal or vegetable matter from a kitchen; rubbish.

gar-ble (gär'bl), *v.t.* to cleanse by sifting; select such parts of as are wanted or may serve some particular purpose; to mutilate; to do, to make, or to say, in the wrong way; as, to *garble* a quotation; to *garble* an account.

gar-çon (gȧr'sôn'), *n.* a boy; a serving-man; a waiter. [FR.]

gar-den (gär'dn), *n.* a piece of ground set apart for the cultivation of flowers, fruit, vegetables, etc.; a place specially delightful, rich, or fruitful: *v.t.* and *v.i.* to cultivate, as a garden.

gar-den-ing (gär'dn-ĭng), *n.* the art or work of laying out and cultivating plots of ground.

gar-gle (gär'gl), *n.* a medicinal liquid for washing the throat: *v.t.* to wash, as the throat, with a medicinal liquid, not swallowed, but kept in the throat by breathing out: *v.i.* to use a wash for the throat.

gar-goyle (gär'goil), *n.* in Gothic architecture, a projecting stone waterspout, often in the form of a grotesquely shaped man or animal.

gar-i-bal-di (gär"ĭ-băl'dĭ), *n.* a loose blouse-shaped shirt, usually red: named for the Italian patriot, Garibaldi.

gar-ish (gâr'ĭsh), *adj.* gaudy; dazzling; showy; attracting attention; as, she wore *garish* jewelry.

gar-land (gär'lănd), *n.* a wreath made of flowers, branches, feathers, and sometimes of precious stones, to be worn on the head like a crown; as, the victor's *garland*; a collection of choice pieces of prose or poetry; a kind of food-bag used by sailors; in heraldry, a wreath of laurel, or oak-leaves and acorns: *v.t.* to deck or adorn with a wreath or chaplet.

gar-lic (gär'lĭk), *n.* a plant of the lily family, with a strong biting taste and unpleasant smell.

gar-ment (gär'mĕnt), *n.* any article of clothing: *pl.* clothing taken together as an outfit.

gar-ner (gär'nẽr), *n.* a granary; a building or place where grain is stored for safe-keeping: *v.t.* to gather for safe-keeping; to store as in a granary; gather up.

gar-net (gär'nĕt), *n.* a precious or semi-precious stone of various colors, oftenest deep red; a deep red color.

gar-nish (gär'nĭsh), *n.* an ornament or decoration; something laid round a dish as a decoration: *v.t.* to adorn; to make beautiful; decorate with something laid around a dish.
Syn., v. beautify, trim.

gar-nish-ee (gär'nĭsh-ē'), *n.* the person in whose hands the property of another is attached pending the satisfaction of the claims of a third party: *v.t.* to attach property by law to pay a debt.

gar-ret (găr'ĕt), *n.* the uppermost room of a house; an attic.

gar-ri-son (găr'ĭ-sn), *n.* a body of troops stationed in a fort or fortified place: *v.t.* to furnish (a fortified place) with troops.

gar-rote (gā-rōt'; gā-rŏt'), *n.* an instrument for strangling a criminal: used in Spain; strangulation: *v.t.* to execute by strangling; seize by the throat so as to render helpless.

gar-ru-li-ty (gā-rōō'lĭ-tĭ), *n.* talkativeness; as, the *garrulity* of old age.

gar-ru-lous (găr'ōō-lŭs), *adj.* talking much, especially about things that are trivial.

gar-ter (gär'tẽr), *n.* a band by which a stocking is held up on the leg: **the Garter,** the badge of the Order of the Garter, the highest order of British knighthood: *v.t.* to bind or fasten with a band called a garter; invest with the Order of the Garter.

gar-ter snake (gär'tẽr snāk), a small, harmless, yellow-striped snake, common in America.

gas (găs), *n.* [*pl.* gases (-ĕz)], elastic, airlike fluid; a thin, airlike mixture that is obtained from minerals and which is used to give light and heat; an airlike mixture of chemicals, poisonous to inhale; colloquially, gasoline: *v.t.* [*p.t.* and *p.p.* gassed, *p.pr.* gassing], to cause to inhale poisonous gas: a method of warfare introduced by the Germans in the World War.

gas bomb (găs bŏm), a shell used in trench warfare: it contains poison gas which is set free when the shell is burst by its charge of high explosive.

gas-con-ade (găs'kŏn-ād'), *n.* boastful, blustering, or bragging talk; as, the *gasconade* of the young soldier.

gas en-gine (găs ĕn'jĭn), an internal combustion engine; that is, an engine in which power is generated by the explosion of gas or oil in the engine cylinder.

Gas Engine

gas-e-ous (găs'ē-ŭs), *adj.* having the nature or form of gas.

gash (găsh), *n.*, a deep or gaping cut or wound: *v.t.* to cut deeply.

gas-i-fy (găs'ĭ-fī), *v.t.* [*p.t.* and *p.p.* gasified, *p.pr.* gasifying], to turn into gas by heat or by chemical action.

gas-ket (găs'kĕt), *n.* a flat plaited cord by which the sails are furled or tied to the yard; hemp, etc., used for packing the piston of a steam engine, etc.; a thin piece of rubber, metal, etc., placed between two flat surfaces to make a water-tight joint.

gas man-tle (găs' măn'tl), a tubelike structure consisting of oxides of certain rare metals, which, when placed over a Bunsen gas flame, is heated to incandescence, thus giving out light.

gas mask (găs măsk), a covering for the face to prevent the inhaling of poison gas. Also, **gas helmet.**

gas-o-line (găs'ō-lēn; găs'ō-lĭn), *n.* a liquid easily set on fire, used for heating, cooking, cleaning, etc., and for running engines of automobiles, etc. Also, **gasolene.**

gas-om-e-ter (găs-ŏm'ē-tẽr), *n.* a round hollow reservoir for storing gas, open at the bottom and closed at the top; something used for measuring gases.

Gasometer

gas-o-scope (găs'ō-skōp), *n.* an instrument for detecting the presence of inflammable gas from a gas leak in a coal mine or a house.

gasp (gȧsp), *n.* a quick painful effort to catch the breath: *v.i.* to catch the breath with difficulty: *v.t.* to breathe out in quick, painful breaths: with *away.*

gas-sy (găs'ĭ), *adj.* filled with gas; like gas; inflated.

gas-tric (găs'trĭk), *adj.* pertaining to the stomach; as, *gastric* fluid; *gastric* fever.

gas-tric juice (găs'trĭk jōōs), a thin watery liquid contained in a certain set of glands in the lining of the stomach: the greatest help to digestion.

gas-tri-tis (găs-trī'tĭs), *n.* inflammation of the stomach, especially of the mucous membrane which lines it.

gas-tron-o-my (găs-trŏn'ō-mĭ), *n.* the art of good eating, or of the preparation of food.—*adj.* **gastronomic, gastronomical.**

gate (gāt), *n.* an opening to allow entrance or passage; a frame or door which opens or closes such an entrance; a stately entrance to a city, castle, etc.; a valve or door to stop or permit a flow of water.

gate-way (gāt'wā'), *n.* an entrance fitted with a frame or door; approach.

gath-er (găth'ẽr), *v.t.* to assemble or bring together; collect; bring into one place; pick up; glean; pluck; accumulate; pucker or plait; infer: *v.i.* to congregate; generate pus; increase; ripen: *n.* a plait or pucker in cloth, made by drawing thread through the folds.
Syn., v. pick, cull, assemble, muster, infer.
Ant. (see scatter).

gath-er-ing (găth'ẽr-ĭng), *n.* the act of assembling or bringing together; an assemblage; a charitable contribution or gift; an abscess or sore filled with pus.

Gat-ling gun (găt'lĭng gŭn), a cannon with many small barrels, which are discharged very rapidly by turning a handle.

gaud (gôd), *n.* a piece of worthless finery; ornament.

gaud-y (gôd'ĭ), *adj.* [*comp.* gaudier, *superl.* gaudiest], showy; vulgarly gay or fine.—*adv.* **gaudily.**—*n.* **gaudiness.**
Syn., *adj.* flashy, tawdry, glittering.

gauge (gāj), *n.* a measure; a promise; a challenge; the depth of a ship in the water; its position in relation to another ship: *v.t.* to measure. Also, **gage.**

gaug-er (gāj'ẽr), *n.* an officer whose business it is to find out how much certain casks hold.

Gaul (gôl), *n.* an inhabitant of ancient Gaul or France.

gaunt (gänt), *adj.* pinched and lean; weak; as, the people were hollow-eyed and *gaunt* from hunger.—*n.* **gauntness.**
Syn. emaciated, scraggy, skinny, spare.

gaunt-let (gänt'lĕt; gônt'lĕt), *n.* a military or naval punishment, formerly practiced, by which the culprit was compelled to run between two lines of soldiers or sailors, who beat him with rods, ropes, etc.; also practiced by the Indians; a mailed glove, or one with a long wrist-extension. Also, **gantlet.**

gauze (gôz), *n.* a very thin, light, transparent silk or cotton fabric; light openwork material resembling this fabric.

gauz-y (gôz'ĭ), *adj.* thin and semitransparent.—*n.* **gauziness.**

gave (gāv), past tense of the irregular verb *give.*

gav-el (găv'ĕl), *n.* a small mallet used by a presiding officer; a small unbound sheaf or bundle of grain.

ga-votte (gȧ-vŏt'; găv'ŏt), *n.* a lively, but dignified, dance of the minuet class; a dance-tune in common time. [FR.]

gawk (gôk), *n.* a simpleton; a booby: *v.i.* to stare stupidly.

gawk-y (gôk'ĭ), *adj.* awkward; clumsy; ungainly.—*n.* **gawkiness.**

gay (gā), *adj.* lively; merry; full of glee; cheerful; sportive; given to pleasure; jolly; happy.—*adv.* **gaily, gayly.**—*n.* **gaiety, gayety.**
Syn. lively, jolly, sprightly, blithe.
Ant. (see solemn).

gaze (gāz), *v.i.* to look earnestly, or eagerly: *n.* a fixed look.—*n.* **gazer.**

Gazelles

ga-zelle (gȧ-zĕl'), *n.* a small, swift-footed antelope, with large, soft, black eyes.

ga-zette (gȧ-zĕt'), *n.* English government biweekly newspaper containing official announcements; a newspaper: *v.t.* to publish in a list.

gaz-et-teer (găz'ĕ-tēr'), *n.* a dictionary of geographical names; an official writer or publisher of news.

gear (gēr), *n.* clothing; garments; ornaments; apparatus; tackle; harness; dress; a toothed wheel; adjustment of parts to each other; as, out of *gear:* *v.t.* to put cogs or teeth on; harness; dress.

gear-ing (gēr'ĭng), *n.* a train or series of toothed wheels for transmitting motion; ropes and tackle.

gear wheel (gēr hwēl), a cogwheel or wheel with cogs: **bevel gear,** a wheel having inclined teeth.

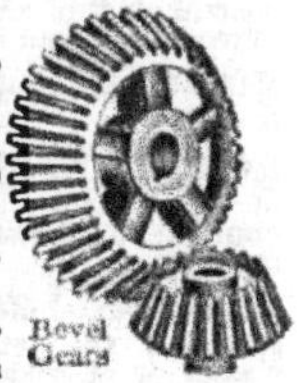
Bevel Gears

gee (jē), *v.t.* to turn to the off side or from the driver, who in England walks on the right-hand side of his cattle, in the United States on the left-hand side: opposite to *haw,* which means to turn toward the driver: *interj.* turn away!

geese (gēs), *n.* plural of the common noun *goose.*

gei-sha (gā'shȧ), *n.* in Japan, a singing and dancing girl.

gel-a-tin (jĕl'ȧ-tĭn), *n.* a substance found in bones, hoofs, connective tissue, etc., from which it is extracted by boiling; animal jelly. Also, **gelatine.**—*adj.* **gelatinous.**

gem (jĕm), *n.* a precious stone; leaf bud; any perfect or rare object; jewel: *v.t.* [*p.t.* and *p.p.* gemmed, *p.pr.* gemming], to adorn with, or as with, gems.

gem-i-nate (jĕm'ĭ-nāt), *adj.* twin; growing in pairs; as, *geminate* leaves: *v.t.* and *v.i.* to double; to become double.

gem-i-na-tion (jĕm'ĭ-nā'shŭn), *n.* repetition; a doubling, as of a consonant after a vowel.

Gem-i-ni (jĕm'ĭ-nī), *n.pl.* one of the clusters of stars in the heavens, in which are the two bright stars, Castor and Pollux; the Twins: a sign of the zodiac.

gem-ma-tion (jĕm-ā'shŭn), *n.* the period of bud opening; the arrangement of buds on a stalk or of leaves in the bud.

gen-darme (zhäṅ'därm'; jĕn'därm'), *n.* [*pl.* gendarmes (-därm; därmz)], in France and Belgium, an armed policeman. [FR.]

gen-darm-er-ie (jĕn-där'mẽr-ĭ; zhäṅ'-där'mẽ-rē'), *n.* a body of gendarmes or police. [FR.]

gen-der (jĕn'dẽr), *n.* the grammatical distinction of sex, expressed by a suffix, a prefix, or by a different word.

ge-ne-a-log-i-cal (jĕn'ē-ȧ-lŏj'ĭ-kăl; jē'nē-ȧ-lŏj'ĭ-kăl), *adj.* pertaining to pedigree; giving or tracing order of descent.—*adv.* **genealogically.**

ge-ne-al-o-gist (jĕn'ē-ăl'ō-jĭst; jē'nē-ăl'ō-jĭst), *n.* one skilled in tracing pedigrees or descent of persons or families.

ge-ne-al-o-gy (jĕn'ē-ăl'ō-jĭ; jē'nē-ăl'ō-jĭ), *n.* [*pl.* genealogies (-jĭz)], family pedigree; lineage; the science that treats of tracing pedigrees or descent of persons or families.

gen-e-ra (jĕn'ẽr-ȧ), *n.* plural of *genus;* as, the cat and dog belong to different *genera.*

gen-er-al (jĕn'ẽr-ăl), *n.* the whole; the chief part; the populace; the commander of an army division or brigade; the chief of a religious order; the roll of a drum to summon troops: *adj.* relating to a whole genus, kind, class, order, or race; not special or particular; pertaining to the majority; not restricted; usual; ordinary; common; extensive but not universal; indefinite; taken as a whole; senior or highest; as, Postmaster-*General.*
Syn., *adj.* usual, universal, customary.
Ant. (see rare).

gen-er-al of-fi-cer (jĕn'ĕr-ăl ŏf'ĭ-sẽr), a member of the general staff of an army, commanding a body of troops not less than a brigade.

gen-er-al-is-si-mo (jĕn"ĕr-ăl-ĭs'ĭ-mō), *n.* a commander-in-chief.

gen-er-al-i-ty (jĕn"ĕr-ăl'ĭ-tĭ), *n.* [*pl.* generalities (-tĭz)], the state of not being limited or particularized: opposite to *specific;* the greatest part; bulk; majority.

gen-er-al-i-za-tion (jĕn"ĕr-ăl-ĭ-zā'shŭn; jĕn"ĕr-ăl-ī-zā'-shŭn), *n.* the act or result of reducing to classes or of making statements opposed to the particular; an induction; sweeping inference or conclusion, not drawn from details.

gen-er-al-ize (jĕn"ĕr-ăl-īz), *v.t.* to reduce to, or arrange in, a class or classes; to make large in scope or meaning; to discover (a general rule) from particular instances: *v.i.* to draw broad, general conclusions.

gen-er-al-ly (jĕn'ĕr-ăl-ĭ), *adv.* commonly; in the main; without exact limitation.

gen-er-al or-ders (jĕn'ĕr-ăl ôr'dẽrz), commands issued by the superior officers in army units: general orders include standing instructions, detailed instructions, and reports of courts martial.

gen-er-al-ship (jĕn'ĕr-ăl-shĭp), *n.* the office, rank, or military skill of a chief or an army commander; skilful tactics or leadership; as, the *generalship* of Marshal Foch.

gen-er-ate (jĕn'ĕr-āt), *v.t.* to produce, as offspring; to cause; originate; trace out or form by motion.
Syn. form, make, beget.

gen-er-a-tion (jĕn"ĕr-ā'shŭn), *n.* the act or process of producing; a single succession in natural descent; people of the same period; as, your mother belongs to my *generation;* progeny.
Syn. race, breed, stock, kind, age, era.

gen-er-a-tive (jĕn'ĕr-ā-tĭv), *adj.* having the power to produce.

gen-er-a-tor (jĕn'ĕr-ā"tẽr), *n.* one who, or that which, causes or produces; an apparatus by which steam, electricity, or gas is produced; in music, the principal sound or sounds by which others are produced.

ge-ner-ic (jē-nĕr'ĭk), *adj.* pertaining to things of the same kind or class; opposite to *specific;* comprehensive. Also, **generical.**—*adv.* **generically.**

gen-er-os-i-ty (jĕn"ĕr-ŏs'ĭ-tĭ), *n.* [*pl.* generosities (-tĭz)], the quality of being liberal; liberality; magnanimity; as, *generosity* is seen in an estimation of other men's virtues.

gen-er-ous (jĕn'ĕr-ŭs), *adj.* characterized by liberality; munificent; bountiful; high-minded; honorable; strong; stimulating.—*adv.* **generously.**
Syn. beneficent, noble, liberal.
Ant. (see niggardly).

gen-e-sis (jĕn'ē-sĭs), *n.* the act or process of producing or originating; beginning: **Genesis,** the first book of the Old Testament: so called by the Greek translators, because it tells of the creation of the world and the human race.

gen-et (jĕn'ĕt; jē-nĕt'), *n.* an animal related to the civet or cat family, valued for its fur; the fur of a cat made to resemble genet. Also, **genette.**

gen-et (jĕn'ĕt; jē-nĕt'), *n.* a small Spanish horse. Also, **jennet.**

gen-et-ic (jē-nĕt'ĭk), *adj.* pertaining to generation or origin.

ge-ni-al (jē'nĭ-ăl; jēn'yăl), *adj.* kindly and sympathetic in disposition; cordial; contributing to cheerfulness and life; agreeably warm and cheerful.
Syn. hearty, festive, joyous.
Ant. (see distant, cold).

ge-ni-al-i-ty (jē"nĭ-ăl'ĭ-tĭ; jēn-yăl'ĭ-tĭ), *n.* the quality of being kindly; cheerfulness; sympathetic warmth of disposition and manners.

ge-ni-al-ly (jē'nĭ-ăl-ĭ; jēn'yăl-ĭ), *adv.* in a cordial manner; gaily; cheerfully.

ge-nie (jē'nĭ), *n.* in Mohammedan mythology, a good or bad spirit that could take the form of an animal, giant, etc.; as, the *genie* of the lamp, in the story of *Aladdin's Lamp.* Also, **jinnee.**

ge-ni-i (jē'nĭ-ī), *n.* plural of *genius* or *genie.* Also, when the plural of *genie,* **jinn.**

gen-i-tive (jĕn'ĭ-tĭv), *n.* a grammatical case, denoting origin, possession, or relation: it is the same as the possessive case in English.

gen-ius (jĕn'yŭs; jē'nĭ-ŭs), *n.* [*pl.* **geniuses**], bent of mind or disposition; remarkable ability or natural fitness for some special pursuit, etc.; character or necessary principle; embodiment; a person possessed of high mental powers or faculties: **genii** (-nĭ-ī), *pl.* a good or evil spirit supposed to preside over the destinies of men.
Syn. intellect, invention, talent, taste, nature, character, adept.

Gen-o-ese (jĕn"ō-ēz'; jĕn"ō-ēs'), *adj.* pertaining to the people of Genoa, Italy.

gen-re (zhäN'r), *n.* a style of painting or sculpture representing everyday life and manners. [Fr.]

gens (jĕns), *n.* [*pl.* gentes (jĕn'tēz)], a clan or family connection, including several families of the same stock, who had a common name and certain common religious rites or ceremonies; among the ancient Romans, a clan, house, or subdivision of a tribe. [Lat.]

gen-teel (jĕn-tēl'), *adj.* graceful or elegant in manners or dress; polite; well-bred —*adv.* **genteelly.**
Syn. refined, polished.
Ant. (see boorish).

gen-tian (jĕn'shăn), *n.* a bitter herb some kinds of which have tonic roots; a variety of this herb which has beautiful, fringed, blue flowers.

Gen-tile (jĕn'tīl), *n.* one who is not a Jew: *adj.* pertaining to non-Jewish people.

gen-til-i-ty (jĕn-tĭl'ĭ-tĭ), *n.* [*pl.* gentilities (-tĭz)], high or gentle birth; good breeding; social rank and refinement.

gen-tle (jĕn'tl), *adj.* mild and refined in manner and disposition; kindly; moderate in action; peaceful; docile; easy; well-born or descended: *n.* the larva or young of the flesh fly; a trained falcon or hawk.
Syn., adj. placid, mild, bland, tame.
Ant. (see rough, uncouth).

gen-tle-folk (jĕn'tl-fōk"), *n.* persons of good family or breeding.

gen-tle-man (jĕn'tl-măn), *n.* [*pl.* gentlemen (-mĕn)], one who is entitled to bear a coat of arms; a well-bred and honorable man; a person of independent income: *pl.* a term of politeness, used in addressing an assembly.

gen-tle-man-ly (jĕn'tl-măn-lĭ), *adj.* polite in manner; well-trained socially.

gen-tle-ness (jĕn'tl-nĕs), *n.* softness of manners; mildness; docility.

gen-tle-wom-an (jĕn'tl-wŏŏm"ăn), *n.* [*pl.* gentlewomen (-wĭm'ĕn)], a woman of good birth and breeding; a lady.

gen-tly (jĕn'tlĭ), *adv.* in a mild manner; mildly; softly; gradually.

gen-try (jĕn'trĭ), *n.* people of education and breeding; in England, the upper class of society.

gen-u-flec-tion (jĕn"ū-flĕk'shŭn), *n.* the bending of the knee, especially in worship. Also, **genuflexion.**

gen-u-ine (jĕn'ū-ĭn), *adj.* real; unadulterated; pertaining to, or derived from, the original or true stock; not hypocritical; open.—*adv.* **genuinely.**
Syn. true, unaffected, sincere.
Ant. (see false).

ge-nus (jē'nŭs), *n.* [*pl.* genera (jĕn'ĕr-*d*)], a broad, general class having under it several groups with certain common characteristics; as, in the animal kingdom the lion, leopard, tiger, cat, and panther are species of the catkind, or *genus;* in the vegetable kingdom all the species of oak form a certain *genus;* in logic, a class made up of two or more species, or lower classes.

ge-o-cen-tric (jē"ō-sĕn'trĭk), *adj.* pertaining to the center of the earth; having the earth as the center; viewed from the earth as a center.

ge-od-e-sy (jē-ŏd'ē-sĭ), *n.* the science of measuring large portions of the earth's surface; the determination of the earth's figure and size.

ge-o-det-ic (jē"ō-dĕt'ĭk), *adj.* pertaining to, determined by, or carried out by, geodesy, or the art of measuring large sections of the earth's surface. Also, **geodetical.**

ge-o-det-ic line (jē"ō-dĕt'ĭk līn), the shortest line between any two points on the earth's surface.

ge-og-ra-pher (jē-ŏg'rȧ-fĕr), *n.* one who is versed in, or a writer on, the science of the earth and its life.

ge-o-graph-i-cal (jē"ō-grăf'ĭ-kăl), *adj.* pertaining to the science of the earth and its life.—*adv.* **geographically.**

ge-og-ra-phy (jē-ŏg'rȧ-fĭ), *n.* [*pl.* geographies (-fĭz)], the science that describes the surface of the earth, and its division into continents, kingdoms, etc.

ge-o-log-i-cal (jē"ō-lŏj'ĭ-kăl), *adj.* pertaining to the science of the formation of the earth.—*adv.* **geologically.**

ge-ol-o-gist (jē-ŏl'ō-jĭst), *n.* one who knows the science of the formation of the earth.

ge-ol-o-gize (jē-ŏl'ō-jīz), *v.i.* to study the formation of the earth; to investigate the structure of the earth.

ge-ol-o-gy (jē-ŏl'ō-jĭ), *n.* the science that investigates the structure of the earth, the successive physical changes it has undergone, and the causes which have produced such changes in the crust of the globe.

ge-o-met-ric (jē"ō-mĕt'rĭk), *adj.* pertaining to, or done by, geometry, or the study of lines, angles, surfaces, etc.—*adv.* **geometrically.**

ge-om-e-tri-cian (jē-ŏm"ē-trĭsh'ăn), *n.* one who is skilled in that branch of mathematics called geometry.

ge-om-e-try (jē-ŏm'ē-trĭ), *n.* [*pl.* geometries (-trĭz)], that branch of mathematics that treats of the measurements of lines, angles, surfaces, and solids, with their various relations; a text-book on these subjects.

ge-ra-ni-um (jē-rā'nĭ-ŭm), *n.* a plant cultivated for its handsome scarlet or white flowers.

ger-fal-con (jûr'fô"kn; jûr'fôl"kn), *n.* a large northern falcon or hawk. Also, **gyrfalcon.**

germ (jûrm), *n.* the first principle of an organism; that from which anything springs; origin; first principle; any bacterial organism, especially one which may cause disease.

Ger-man (jûr'măn), *n.* one of the people of Germany; the language of the Germans; *adj.* pertaining to Germany, its people, or language.

ger-man (jûr'măn), *adj.* of the same stock or parentage; germane: *n.* a kind of round dance with many figures.

ger-mane (jĕr-mān'; jûr'măn), *adj.* related; akin; relevant; appropriate; fitting.

Ger-man-ic (jĕr-măn'ĭk), *adj.* pertaining to Germany; Teutonic.

Ger-man-ism (jûr'măn-ĭzm), *n.* a German custom, manner of speech, or characteristic; love of German institutions.

ger-ma-ni-um (jĕr-mā'nĭ-ŭm), *n.* one of the metallic elements; a brittle, silver-white metal discovered in 1885 in a silver ore at Freiberg.

Ger-man sil-ver (jûr'măn sĭl'vĕr), a white alloy of zinc, nickel, and copper.

ger-mi-cide (jûr'mĭ-sīd), *n.* something used to destroy disease germs.

ger-mi-cul-ture (jûr'mĭ-kŭl"tŭr), *n.* the artificial cultivation of bacteria or germs for scientific study.

ger-mi-nal (jûr'mĭ-năl), *adj.* pertaining to a germ or seed bud.

ger-mi-nant (jûr'mĭ-nănt), *adj.* sprouting; gradually developing; sending forth buds.

ger-mi-nate (jûr'mĭ-nāt), *v.i.* to sprout or bud; begin to grow or develop into a higher form.

ger-mi-na-tion (jûr"mĭ-nā'shŭn), *n.* the beginning of growth in a seed, bud, or germ.

germ-ule (jûr'mūl), *n.* a small germ; a germ beginning to develop.

ger-ry-man-der (gĕr"ĭ-măn'dĕr), *v.t.* to divide, as a state, voting district, etc., so as to give an unfair advantage to a particular political party; misrepresent; garble.

ger-und (jĕr'ŭnd), *n.* a verbal noun; as, his *earning* a salary depended upon his ability.

ger-un-dive (jĕ-rŭn'dĭv), *n.* in Latin, the future passive participle; as, *amandus*, to be loved: *adj.* pertaining to, or having the nature of the gerund.

ges-tic-u-late (jĕs-tĭk'ū-lāt), *v.i.* to make motions, as in speaking or attracting attention.

ges-tic-u-la-tion (jĕs-tĭk"ū-lā'shŭn), *n.* the act of making motions; a gesture.

ges-ture (jĕs'tûr), *n.* a movement of the face, body, or limbs, to express an idea, emotion, etc.
Syn. attitude, action, posture.

get (gĕt), *v.t.* [*p.t.* got, *p.p.* got, gotten, *p.pr.* getting], to obtain; procure; win; gain; acquire; receive; deserve; realize; learn; prevail upon: *v.i.* to arrive at; become; find time, opportunity, etc.; depart quickly; procreate.
Syn. earn, attain.

get-ter (gĕt'ĕr), *n.* one who gains, obtains, or acquires; as, a money-*getter*.

gew-gaw (gū'gô), *n.* a showy trifle; useless ornament; toy.

gey-ser (gī'sĕr; gī'zĕr), *n.* a boiling spring which frequently throws forth jets of water, mud, etc.

ghast-ly (gȧst'lĭ), *adj.* deathlike; pale; haggard; horrible; as, his face had a *ghastly* look.—*n.* **ghastliness.**
Syn. pallid, wan, hideous, grim, shocking.

ghee (gē), *n.* an oil made from butter; a solid white oil obtained from a tree of India.

gher-kin (gûr'kĭn), *n.* a small cucumber used for pickling. Also, **gerkin.**

ghet-to (gĕt'ō), *n.* [*pl.* ghettos (-ōz), ghetti (-tē)], the Jews' quarter in a city.

ghost (gōst), *n.* the spirit of a dead person; apparition; the soul; breath of life; shadow; a false image due to some defect in a lens.—*adj.* **ghostly.**
Syn. specter, sprite, phantom.

ghoul (gōōl), *n.* an imaginary evil being who robs graves and feeds on the flesh of the dead.—*adj.* **ghoulish.**

gi-ant (jī'ănt), *n.* a man of great bulk or stature; one possessed of great physical or mental power; in mythology, one of a race of beings of immense size who fought the gods: *adj.* like a person of great stature; huge.

gi-ant pow-der (jī'ănt pou'dĕr), a comparatively safe high explosive, made of nitroglycerin.

giaour (jour), *n.* the name applied by Mohammedans to those who do not believe in their religion, especially Christians.

gib (gĭb), *n.* the arm of a crane or machine for lifting heavy weights, such as engines, etc.; a piece in a machine to hold other parts together.

gib-ber (jĭb'ĕr; gĭb'ĕr), *v.i.* and *v.t.* to speak rapidly and indistinctly; chatter.

gib-ber-ish (gĭb'ĕr-ĭsh), *n.* rapid, disconnected talk: *adj.* unmeaning.

gib-bet (jĭb'ĕt), *n.* a gallows: *v.t.* to hang on a gibbet or gallows; expose to public scorn or ridicule.

gib-bon (gĭb'ŭn), *n.* an ape of southeastern Asia; the smallest and lowest of the manlike apes.

gib-bous (gĭb'ŭs), *adj.* excessively prominent; irregularly rounded; between full and half-full: said of the moon. Also, **gibbose.**

gibe (jīb), *n.* a scoff; taunt; sneering or sarcastic expression: *v.t.* to sneer at; taunt: *v.i.* to use taunts; cast reproaches; sneer; scoff. Also, **jibe.**
Syn., v. flout, jeer, mock, deride.

gib-let (jĭb'lĕt), *n.* the heart, liver, gizzard, etc., of poultry: usually in the plural.

gid (gĭd), *n.* a disease of sheep, often called the staggers.

gid-dy (gĭd'ĭ), *adj.* [*comp.* giddier, *superl.* giddiest], having a confused, whirling sensation in the head; light-headed; dizzy; frivolous; fickle.—*adv.* **giddily.**—*n.* **giddiness.**
Syn. unsteady, flighty, thoughtless.
Ant. (see steady).

gift (gĭft), *n.* something given or bestowed; present; donation; offering; benefaction; natural talent.
Syn. grant, alms, gratuity, boon, faculty, talent.
Ant. (see purchase).

gift-ed (gĭft'ĕd), *adj.* talented; having innate or inborn ability.

gig (gĭg), *n.* a light two-wheeled open carriage drawn by one horse; a machine for raising nap on cloth; a long ship's boat, rowed by alternate oars, and usually reserved for the commanding officer; a racing boat; a whirligig; a fishgig: *v.t.* [*p.t.* and *p.p.* gigged, *p.pr.* gigging], to fish with a fishgig.

gi-gan-tic (jī-găn'tĭk), *adj.* huge; colossal; immense; tremendous; of extraordinary size.—*adv.* **gigantically.**
Syn. enormous, prodigious.
Ant. (see diminutive).

gig-gle (gĭg'l), *n.* a nervous, silly laugh: *v.i.* to laugh in a nervous, foolish, tittering manner.—*n.* **giggler.**

gild (gĭld), *v.t.* [*p.t.* and *p.p.* gilded, gilt, *p.pr.* gilding], to overlay or wash with gold; give a fair outward appearance to; illuminate; to make attractive; to adorn; to brighten: *n.* a fraternity; an association. Also, *n.* **guild.**

gild-ing (gĭld'ĭng), *n.* the art or process of overlaying or covering with gold; gold leaf, powder, etc., applied to a surface; a light covering designed to give a fair outward appearance.

gill (gĭl), *n.* the breathing organ of water animals, especially fishes; the fleshy flap that hangs below the beak of a fowl; a deep, narrow glen through which a small stream flows: *pl.* the gill-shaped plates forming the under surface of a mushroom.

gill (jĭl), *n.* a liquid measure of one fourth of a pint; ground ivy. Also, **jill.**

gil-ly-flow-er (jĭl'ĭ-flou"ĕr), *n.* one of various plants of the mustard family, as the wall-flower, stock, etc. Also, **gilliflower.**

gilt (gĭlt), *adj.* covered with, or yellow like, gold: *n.* gilding; grand show.

gim-bal (gĭm'băl), *n.* one of two brass rings moving within each other at right angles: used for suspending a mariner's compass, chronometer, etc., so that it will stay level.

gim-crack (jĭm'crak"), *n.* a pretty, useless thing; toy: *adj.* showy, but of no value.

gim-let (gĭm'lĕt), *n.* a small boring tool with a pointed screw at the end: *v.t.* to make a hole in with such a tool.

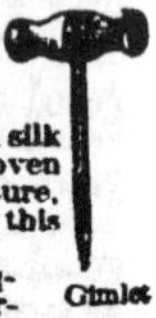
Gimlet

gimp (gĭmp), *n.* a kind of laced silk twist or trimming interwoven with wire or cord: used for furniture, dresses, etc.: *v.t.* to border with this trimming.

gin (jĭn), *n.* a fragrant alcoholic liquor flavored with juniper berries; a trap or snare; a machine for clearing cotton fibers from the seeds; a portable hoisting machine; a pile-driving machine: *v.t.* [*p.t.* and *p.p.* ginned, *p.pr.* ginning], to catch in a trap; to clear (cotton) of seeds by a machine.

gin-ger (jĭn'jĕr), *n.* the scraped and dried root of a hot and spicy East and

West Indian plant which is much used in cookery and in medicine; colloquially, courage, vim, or snap.—*adj.* **gingery.**

gin-ger beer (jĭn'jẽr bēr), a bubbling drink, or mild beer made from ginger, yeast, cream of tartar, and sugar.

gin-ger-bread (jĭn'jẽr-brĕd'), *n.* a dark-colored cake made of flour, ginger, molasses, sugar, etc.: cheap, flimsy ornamentation, especially on a house.

gin-ger-ly (jĭn'jẽr-lĭ), *adv.* cautiously; daintily; timidly.

gin-ger-snap (jĭn'jẽr-snăp"), *n.* a small, thin, brittle cooky flavored with ginger.

ging-ham (gĭng'ăm), *n.* a cotton dress-cloth dyed in the yarn before weaving: an umbrella.

gin-seng (jĭn'sĕng), *n.* an herb with a fragrant root much valued in China.

Gip-sy (jĭp'sĭ), *n.* [*pl.* Gipsies (-sĭz)], one of a wandering, dark-skinned, and dark-eyed race, of Eastern, probably Hindu, origin; the language of the Gipsies: called also *Romany:* **gipsy,** a person of dark complexion. Also, **Gypsy.**

gip-sy moth (jĭp'sĭ mŏth), an insect in New England, highly destructive to foliage.

gi-raffe (jĭ-răf'), *n.* an African animal with very long legs and neck.

Giraffes

gird (gûrd), *v.t.* [*p.t.* and *p.p.* **gird-ed, girt,** *p.pr.* **gird-ing**], to surround with a flexible band; bind; encircle; make ready.

gird-er (gûr'dẽr), *n.* the main beam in a floor; as, the *girders* in the building are of steel.

gir-dle (gûr'dl), *n.* a belt for the waist; anything that surrounds like a belt: *v.t.* to bind with, or as with, a belt; inclose; to kill or injure, as a tree, by making a cut in the bark around the trunk.

girl (gûrl), *n.* a female child; young unmarried woman.

girl-ish (gûrl'ĭsh), *adj.* like or befitting a young woman; as, *girlish* dress.—*adv.* **girlishly.**—*n.* **girlishness.**

girt (gûrt), *p.adj.* held so tight by two cables as not to swing to wind or tide.

girth (gûrth), *n.* the band by which the saddle is kept secured on a horse; the circumference of a tree, animal, etc.; anything that binds or encircles.

gist (jĭst), *n.* the substance of a matter; main point; object.

give (gĭv), *v.t.* [*p.t.* gave, *p.p.* given, *p.pr.* giving], to bestow; confer without price or reward; grant; yield; as, to *give* up a claim; deliver; as, to *give* a lecture; to pay; as, I *gave* three dollars for the book; to present; to utter; as, to *give* a cry; to produce; as, to *give* pain; to impart; as, to *give* an idea; *v.i.* to present gifts; to bestow charity; yield to pressure; as, the lock began to *give*; surrender; as, to *give* in: *n.* elasticity.

giv-en (gĭv'n), *p.adj.* inclined; addicted: usually with *to;* as, *given* to lying; stated; prearranged.

giz-zard (gĭz'ẽrd), *n.* the second stomach of fowl in which the food is crushed and ground.

gla-cé (glȧ'sā'), *adj.* iced or cooled; having a glossy surface; as, *glacé* nuts: *n.* a thin shiny silk. [FR.]

gla-cial (glā'shăl), *adj.* pertaining to, consisting of, or caused by, ice.

gla-cier (glā'shẽr; glăs'ĭ-ẽr), *n.* a vast collection of ice and snow which is formed among lofty mountains and moves slowly down the slopes and through the valleys until it melts or breaks off into icebergs.

gla-cis (glā'sĭs; glȧ'sēs'), *n.* a sloping bank of earth directly in front of a fort and designed for its defense; a protective slope on a warship to throw off hostile shot.

A, glacis; *F*, fosse.

glad (glăd), *adj.* [*comp.* gladder, *superl.* gladdest], joyous; gay; pleased; cheerful; satisfied.—*adv.* **gladly.**—*n.* **gladness.**

Syn. joyful, gladsome, cheering.

Ant. (see sad).

glad-den (glăd'n), *v.t.* to make happy: *v.i.* to rejoice; to become happy.

glade (glād), *n.* an open space or passage in a wood or forest.

glad-i-a-tor (glăd'ĭ-ā'tẽr), *n.* in ancient Rome, a professional swordsman who fought in the arena with other men or with animals.—*adj.* **gladiatorial.**

Gladiators

glad-some (glăd'sŭm), *adj.* joyous; gay; pleased; cheerful.

Glad-stone (glăd'stŭn), *n.* a four-wheeled pleasure carriage carrying two passengers; a long narrow traveling bag with a wide mouth.

glaive (glāv), *n.* a sharp-edged weapon in former use, often having a curved blade with the edge on the outside. Also, **glave.**

Glaive

glam-or (glăm'ẽr), *n.* a charm on the eyes making objects appear different from what they really are; fascination; witchery. Also, **glamour.**

glance (glȧns), *n.* a sudden shoot of light; quick passing look of the eye; a quick momentary view; a lustrous ore: *v.i.* to shoot a sudden ray; view with a quick movement of the eye; allude in passing; to strike slantingly and fly off; as, the blow *glanced* off his shield: *v.t.* to shoot suddenly or slantingly; to strike slantingly in passing.

gland (glănd), *n.* a bodily organ by which secretion is carried on; small secreting organ for sap in plants.

glan-ders (glăn'dẽrz), *n.pl.* a contagious disease in horses, marked by fever, swelling of the glands of the lower jaw, and a discharge of mucus from the nose.

glan-du-lar (glăn'dū-lȧr), *adj.* pertaining to, resembling, or having, secreting organs.

glan-dule (glăn'dūl), *n.* a small gland or secreting organ.

glare (glâr), *n.* a bright dazzling light; overpowering luster; a fierce piercing look; [U.S.] a smooth shining surface, as of ice: *v.i.* to shine with a dazzling, overpowering light; look with fierce piercing eyes; be excessively gaudy in dress or ornamentation.

glar-ing (glâr'ĭng), *p.adj.* sending forth, throwing out, or reflecting, a dazzling light; gaudy.

glass (glȧs), *n.* a hard, brittle, transparent substance, white or colored, made by melting together sand or silica with lime, potash, soda, or lead oxide, and is used for window-panes, mirrors, lamp or light globes, dishes, lenses, and many articles of ornament; an instrument or vessel made of glass; a drinking glass, or the quantity contained in it; a mirror; lens; a telescope, or barometer: *adj.* pertaining to, or made of, glass: *v.t.* to mirror, or reflect in a mirror; glaze.

glass-ful (glȧs'fo͝ol), *n.* [*pl.* glassfuls (-fo͝olz)], the amount that a tumbler or goblet will hold; the contents of a tumbler or goblet.

glass-wort (glȧs'wûrt), *n.* a common sea plant, with a juicy, brittle stem.

glass-y (glȧs'ĭ), *adj.* like glass, in smoothness, transparency, etc.; staring without expression: said of the eye or look. —*adv.* **glassily.**—*n.* **glassiness.**

glau-co-ma (glô-kō'mȧ), *n.* a disease of the eye marked by hardening of the eyeball, and resulting in dimness of vision and, finally, in blindness.

glau-cous (glô'kŭs), *adj.* sea-green; green with a bluish-gray tinge; covered with bloom of a bluish-white color.

glave (glāv), *n.* a sharp-edged weapon in former use, often having a curved blade with the edge on the outside. Also, **glaive.**

glaze (glāz), *v.t.* to furnish with glass; overlay with a smooth or transparent substance like glass: *v.i.* to become smooth, hard, and glossy on the surface; to become staring and expressionless, as the eyes: *n.* the glassy coating on potter's ware.

gla-zier (glā'zhẽr; glā'zĭ-ẽr), *n.* one whose trade is to set glass in windows, etc.

glaz-ing (glāz'ĭng), *n.* a coating of glass or smooth, transparent substance; the act of setting glass, or applying a coat of glass or smooth, transparent substance; window-panes; semitransparent colors passed thinly over other colors to tone down their effect.

gleam (glēm), *n.* a stream or shoot of light; brightness: *v.i.* to emit brightness; send out rays of light.
Syn., glimmer, glance, glitter, shine, flash.

glean (glēn), *v.t.* to gather, as grain that the reapers have left; collect little by little, or piece by piece; infer: *v.i.* to gather grain left by reapers; to collect a little at a time.

glean-ing (glēn'ĭng), *n.* the act of collecting after reapers; that which is collected laboriously from various sources.

glebe (glēb), *n.* ground or soil; land belonging to a parish church or assigned to a minister as part of his salary; in mining, a piece of land containing ore.

glee (glē), *n.* gaiety; mirth; entertainment; a musical composition for voices in harmony.
Syn. merriment, joviality, joy, hilarity.
Ant. (see sorrow).

glee-ful (glē'fo͝ol), *adj.* merry, joyous, gay; as, *gleeful* children just let loose from school.—*adv.* **gleefully.**

glen (glĕn), *n.* a narrow valley; a quiet or secluded hollow between hills.

glib (glĭb), *adj.* voluble; flippant; fluent: as, a *glib* talker; a *glib* tongue.—*adv.* **glibly.**—*n.* **glibness.**

glide (glīd), *n.* the act of moving along smoothly; in music, a slur; the movement of an airplane without any motor: *v.i.* to flow, or move along smoothly or noiselessly; in music, to slur; to move in an airplane under the influence of gravity only.
Syn., *v.* slip, slide, run.

glid-er (glīd'ẽr), *n.* one who, or that which, slides along smoothly; a form of aircraft similar to an airplane but without any motor.

glim (glĭm), *n.* a glance; a glimpse; a light or candle. [SLANG.]

glim-mer (glĭm'ẽr), *n.* a faint unsteady light: *v.i.* to shine faintly and unsteadily.
Syn., gleam, flicker, glitter.

glimpse (glĭmps), *n.* a weak, faint light; transient or temporary view; slight trace: *v.t.* to catch a momentary view of: *v.i.* to glance; appear for the moment.

glint (glĭnt), *n.* a gleam of light; sly glance: *v.i.* to gleam or flash out.

glis-ten (glĭs'n), *v.i.* to sparkle with light; shine; gleam: *n.* a glitter.

glis-ter (glĭs'tẽr), *v.i.* to glitter; be bright: *n.* a sparkle; luster.

glit-ter (glĭt'ẽr), *v.i.* to sparkle with light; gleam; be showy or attractive: *n.* brilliancy; specious or apparent luster.
Syn. gleam, shine, glisten.

gloam-ing (glōm'ĭng), *n.* twilight: *adj.* pertaining to twilight.

gloat (glōt), *v.i.* to stare or gaze earnestly, usually with lustful or cruel greed or satisfaction: often with *over.*

globe (glōb), *n.* a spherical body: ball; a sphere on which are represented the divisions of the earth, etc. (terrestrial *globe*), or the heavenly bodies (celestial *globe*): the globe, the earth.

globe-fish (glōb'fĭsh"), *n.* a fish that can suck in water or air and distend the body until it looks like a ball.

globe-flow-er (glōb'flou"ẽr), *n.* a plant of the crowfoot family with globelike flowers.

globe-trot-ter (glōb'trŏt"ẽr), *n.* an extensive traveler, or one who travels a great deal and to many places.

glo-bin (glō'bĭn), *n.* one of the parts that go to make up red blood corpuscles or cells.

glo-bose (glō'bōs"; glō"bōs'), *adj.* spherical in shape. Also, **globous.**

glob-u-lar (glŏb'ū-lȧr), *adj.* spherical in shape. Also, **globulous.**

glob-ule (glŏb'ūl), *n.* a little spherical body; a small pill.

glom-er-ate (glŏm'ẽr-āt), *adj.* gathered into a roundish head or mass; conglomerate.

gloom (glōōm), *n.* a partial darkness; obscurity; melancholy; depression; sadness; sullenness: *v.i.* to be or become cloudy or partially dark; present a dismal aspect: *v.t.* to make dark; deject or sadden.
Syn., n. cloud, dimness, dulness.
Ant. (see light, brightness, joy).

gloom-y (glōōm'ĭ), *adj.* [*comp.* gloomier, *superl.* gloomiest], overspread with, or wrapped in, darkness; dismal; melancholy; dispirited; cheerless; morose.—*adv.* **gloomily.**—*n.* **gloominess.**
Syn. lowering, lurid, dim, dusky.
Ant. (see bright, clear).

glo-ri-a (glō'rĭ-ȧ), *n.* praise; a doxology; especially, the *Gloria in Excelsis*, Glory be to God on high, and the *Gloria Patri*, Glory be to the Father; a musical setting of these.

glo-ri-fi-ca-tion (glō″rĭ-fĭ-kā'shŭn), *n.* the act of rendering homage to; exaltation to honor and dignity.

glo-ri-fy (glō'rĭ-fī), *v.t.* [*p.t.* and *p.p.* glorified, *p.pr.* glorifying], to raise in honor and dignity; magnify and honor in worship; adore; beautify.
Syn. magnify, celebrate, exalt.

glo-ri-ous (glō'rĭ-ŭs), *adj.* full of honor; illustrious; celebrated; magnificent; exal ed; excellent; splendid; inspiring admiration.
Syn. famous, renowned, distinguished, noble.
Ant. (see infamous).

glo-ry (glō'rĭ), *n.* [*pl.* glories (-rĭz)], splendor; magnificence; brightness; praise ascribed in adoration; distinction; renown; honor; the divine perfection or presence; the blessedness and enjoyment of heaven; in art, a circle of rays surrounding the head of a saint: *v.i.* [*p.t.* and *p.p.* gloried, *p.pr.* glorying], to rejoice or exult: with *in*.
Syn., n. fame, splendor, grandeur.
Ant. (see infamy).

gloss (glôs), *n.* luster from a polished surface; insincere show; an explanation or comment on some difficulty or obscurity in the text of a book; a plausible, insincere representation: *v.t.* to explain by notes or comments; cover up or hide by plausible insincere representation; varnish; make smooth and lustrous: *v.i.* to make comments on a text; to explain.

glos-sa-ry (glŏs'ȧ-rĭ), *n.* [*pl.* glossaries (-rĭz)], a collection of notes explaining a text; a dictionary of obsolete, difficult, uncommon, or technical words occurring in a certain book or in the works of a certain author.

glos-sy (glôs'ĭ), *adj.* [*comp.* glossier, *superl.* glossiest], having a shining smooth surface; smooth and plausible.—*adv.* **glossily.**—*n.* **glossiness.**

glot-tis (glŏt'ĭs), *n.* the small elastic oblong opening at the top of the windpipe.—*adj.* **glottal.**

glove (glŭv), *n.* a covering for the hand with a separate covering for each finger: *pl.* boxing gloves: *v.t.* to cover with, or as with, a glove.

glov-er (glŭv'ẽr), *n.* a maker or seller of gloves; as, Shakespeare's father was a *glover*.

glow (glō), *v.i.* to shine with intense heat; radiate heat and light; be incandescent or brilliant; be red or flushed; be animated or inspired with passion, love, zeal, etc.: *n.* intense or shining heat; incandescence; redness, or brightness of color; passion; ardor.

glow-er (glou'ẽr), *v.i.* to stare with a threatening or angry countenance; frown.

glow-worm (glō'wûrm″), *n.* a beetle, the wingless female of which gives forth a shining green light at night.

gloze (glōz), *v.t.* to gloss over; make light of; as, to *gloze* sin; *gloze* a mistake.

glu-cose (glōō'kōs), *n.* the form of sugar existing in many animal and vegetable organisms: produced for commercial use by the action of sulphuric acid on starch.

glue (glōō), *n.* a sticky substance made by boiling to a jelly the skins, hoofs, etc., of animals: *v.t.* to unite or join with glue.—*adj.* **gluey.**

glum (glŭm), *adj.* gloomy; moody; sullen; frowning; as, a *glum* expression.—*adv.* **glumly.**—*n.* **glumness.**

glume (glōōm), *n.* the husk or chaffy scales of corn or grasses.

glut (glŭt), *n.* an excess or superabundance: *v.t.* [*p.t.* and *p.p.* glutted, *p.pr.* glutting], to fill to repletion; oversupply.
Syn., v. gorge, stuff, cram.

glu-ten (glōō'tĕn), *n.* a sticky substance, the most nutritious part of wheat and other grains, not apparent until the flour is mixed with water, as in dough.

glu-ti-nous (glōō'tĭ-nŭs), *adj.* sticky; gluey; adhesive; covered with sticky matter.

glu-ti-tion (glōō-tĭsh'ŭn), *n.* the act of swallowing.

glut-ton (glŭt'n), *n.* one who eats to excess; a small, flesh-eating animal, akin to the mink and marten; the wolverine.

glut-ton-ize (glŭt'n-īz), *v.i.* to overeat; to eat to excess.

glut-ton-ous (glŭt'n-ŭs), *adj.* eating to excess; given to over-eating.—*adv.* **gluttonously.**

glut-ton-y (glŭt'n-ĭ), *n.* [*pl.* gluttonies (-ĭz)], the act or habit of eating to excess.

glyc-er-in (glĭs'ẽr-ĭn), *n.* a sweet, colorless, sticky liquid obtained from oils, fat, etc.: used extensively in various manufactures and in medicine. Also, **glycerine.**

gnarl (närl), *n.* a knot on the trunk or branch of a tree.

gnarled (närld), *adj.* full of knots; distorted; as, an old, *gnarled* oak.

gnash (năsh), *v.t.* to strike together, as the teeth: *v.i.* to grind the teeth in anger or in pain.

gnat (năt), *n.* a small stinging or biting winged insect of several kinds, like the mosquito.

gnaw (nô), *v.t.* to bite off, or eat away, by degrees; corrode; bite in agony, rage, or despair; fret: *v.i.* to exercise the teeth in biting repeatedly; act as if constantly biting.

gnaw-ing (nô'ĭng), *n.* a feeling of constant craving in the stomach; a fretting pain in the stomach.

gneiss (nīs), *n.* a crystallized rock composed of quartz, mica, and feldspar.

gnome (nōm), *n.* an imaginary guardian of the treasures of the inner parts of the earth; a dwarf; a person of strange appearance.—**gnome motor,** a leading type of air-cooled motor for airplanes.

gnom-ic (nōm'ĭk), *adj.* dealing in or containing pithy or instructive sayings; didactic. Also, **gnomical.**

Gnos-ti-cism (nŏs'tĭ-sĭzm), *n.* an ancient system of philosophy, intermediate between Christianity and paganism, according to which all created things were outflowings from the divine life.

gnu (nōō), *n.* a cud-chewing animal with a mane, a flowing tail, and curved horns, inhabiting Africa.

Gnu

go (gō), *v.i.* [*p.t.* went, *p.p.* gone, *p.pr.* going], to depart; proceed; move on; pass from one state or place to another; succeed; move by mechanism; be in harmony; as, red and yellow do not *go* well together; to continue to be; as, to *go* in rags; to resort or repair; as, *go* to him for advice; to extend; as, the road *goes* west: *v.t.* colloquially, to bear or afford; as, I can't *go* the price; to become responsible for; as, to *go* bail; to bet or wager; as, I'll *go* you a box of candy: *n.* colloquially, the fashion; energy; an agreement.

goad (gōd), *n.* a pointed stick to urge on cattle; any necessity that causes one to act; as, hunger was the *goad* that made him work: *v.t.* to urge on with, or as with, a spur; incite: *v.i.* to act as a spur or incentive.

goal (gōl), *n.* the winning post at a race or at football; the end aimed at; the final purpose; the desire or ambition.

goat (gōt), *n.* a small four-legged animal that is raised for its milk, flesh, and hair.

goat-ee (gō"tē'), *n.* a beard, like that of a goat, on the chin or lower lip of a man.

gob-ble (gŏb'l), *v.t.* to swallow hastily or greedily: *v.i.* to eat greedily; to utter a cry like a turkey: *n.* the noise of a turkey; a quick straight stroke in putting at golf.

gob-bler (gŏb'lẽr), *n.* a male turkey; a greedy eater; a glutton.

gob-e-lin (gŏb'ē-lĭn), *n.* a superior kind of French tapestry.

go-be-tween (gō'bē-twēn"), *n.* an intermediary; an agent; a broker: generally uncomplimentary.

gob-let (gŏb'lĕt), *n.* a drinking vessel with a stem and without a handle.

gob-lin (gŏb'lĭn), *n.* an evil, mischievous spirit; gnome; fairy.

go-by (gō'bĭ), *n.* [*pl.* gobies (-bĭz)], a fish having fins with sharp, stiff spines.

go-by (gō'bī"), *n.* avoidance; a thrusting away; intentional neglect; as, the mayor has given some of his workers the *go-by*; evasion.

go-cart (gō'kärt), *n.* a contrivance for teaching children to walk; a child's carriage; a light village cart.

God (gŏd), *n.* the Supreme Deity, and Creator or Upholder of the Universe; a being infinite, eternal, unchangeable, all-wise, and all-good.

Syn. Creator, Lord, Almighty, Jehovah, Providence.

god (gŏd), *n.* a supernatural being conceived of as possessing divine powers or attributes; an idol; a person or thing deified or honored to excess; an intelligence controlling the forces of good and evil.

god-child (gŏd'chīld"), *n.* one for whom a person becomes sponsor at baptism.

god-dess (gŏd'ĕs), *n.* a female deity; a woman of superior charms or excellence.

god-fa-ther (gŏd'fä"thẽr), *n.* a man who acts as sponsor for a child at baptism: *v.t.* to act as godfather to.

God-head (gŏd'hĕd), *n.* the divine essence, nature, and attributes, the Supreme Deity.

god-less (gŏd'lĕs), *adj.* without religion; wicked.—*n.* **godlessness.**

god-like (gŏd'līk), *adj.* like, or suitable for, a god or God; divine; noblest possible.—*n.* **godlikeness.**

god-li-ness (gŏd'lĭ-nĕs), *n.* piety; devotion; careful observance of the laws of God.

god-ly (gŏd'lĭ), *adj.* devout; pious; obedient to the commands of God.

Syn. righteous, holy, religious.

god-moth-er (gŏd'mŭth"ẽr), *n.* a woman who acts as sponsor for a child at baptism.

god-par-ent (gŏd'pâr"ĕnt), *n.* the godmother or godfather who acts as sponsor for a child at baptism.

God's a-cre (gŏdz ā'kẽr), a churchyard; a burying ground.

god-send (gŏd'sĕnd"), *n.* unexpected assistance or help; something sent by God; an unexpected piece of good fortune.

god-ship (gŏd'shĭp), *n.* deity; the character or rank of a god.

god-son (gŏd'sŭn"), *n.* a male child for whom one has stood sponsor at baptism.

God-speed (gŏd'spēd"), *n.* success; a wish for a prosperous journey; as, I wish you *Godspeed.*

gof-fer (gŏf'ẽr), *v.t.* to form flutes in; crimp; as, to *goffer* a flounce.

gof-fer-ing (gŏf'ẽr-ĭng), *n.* fluting for frills, etc.; indented ornamentation on the edge of a book.

gog-gle (gŏg'l), *v.i.* to strain or roll the eyes: *adj.* staring; prominent: *n.* a strained or affected rolling of the eyes: *pl.* a particular kind of spectacles for protecting the eyes from dust, excessive light, poison gas, etc.—*adj.* **goggle-eyed.**

go-ing (gō'ĭng), *p.pr.* of *go*: *n.* departure, motion, etc.; state of roads: *pl.* conduct or habit of life.

goi-ter (goi'tẽr), *n.* a swelling of the glands in the front and side of the neck.

Gol-con-da (gŏl-kŏn'dȧ), *n.* a mine of wealth; as, California was a veritable *Golconda* to the adventurers of 1849.

gold (gōld), *n.* a precious metallic element of a bright yellow color when pure, very heavy, soft, malleable, and ductile, admirably fitted and almost universally used for coinage and jewelry; money; wealth; precious or pure quality.

gold-beat-er (gōld'bēt"ẽr), *n.* one who beats gold into thin leaves for gilding or covering articles with gold.

gold dust (gōld dŭst), fine particles of gold, such as are obtained in washing sand or gravel.

gold-en (gōl'dn), *adj.* formed of, consisting of, or like, gold; shining; bright like gold; most valuable; excellent.

gold-en age (gōl'dn āj), the imaginary time of perfect human happiness and innocency; the period of greatest glory in the history, literature, etc., of any country; as, the *golden age* of literature.

gold-en pheas-ant (gōl'dn fĕz'ănt), a handsome Chinese pheasant.

gold-en-rod (gōl'dn-rŏd"), *n.* a tall autumn plant of the aster family with heads of small yellow flowers.

gold-en rule (gōl'dn rōōl), the principle of treating others as we would wish them to treat us.—Matt. vii. 12.

gold fields (gōld fēldz), deposits of gold that can be mined.

gold-finch (gōld'fĭnch"), *n.* a beautiful singing bird with yellow-streaked wings and a red throat.

gold-fish (gōld'fĭsh"), *n.* an orange-colored fresh-water fish of the carp family.

gold leaf (gōld lēf), sheets of gold beaten very thin, used in gilding, etc.

gold mine (gōld mīn), a place where gold is or may be mined; anything yielding great wealth.

gold-smith (gōld'smĭth), *n.* a worker in gold, or dealer in gold plate.

gold-y-locks (gōl'dĭ-lŏks), *n.* a common name for various plants with yellow flowers, such as the buttercup. Also, **goldilocks.**

Golf. 1. ball; 2. mashie; 3. driver.

golf (gŏlf; gŏf), *n.* a game played with a small hard ball and club-headed sticks, the object being to drive the ball into a series of small holes with the fewest possible strokes: *v.i.* to play the game of golf; as, is he going to *golf* to-day?

Gol-go-tha (gŏl'gō-thȧ), *n.* the place where Jesus was crucified.

go-losh (gō-lŏsh'), *n.* an overshoe. Also, **goloshe, galosh, galoche.**

gon-do-la (gŏn'dō-lȧ), *n.* a long narrow Venetian pleasure boat moved by one oar; a flat-bottomed boat or railway car used for carrying coal, produce, etc.; an elongated car attached to the under side of a dirigible balloon.

Gondola

gon-do-lier (gŏn'dō-lēr'), *n.* the rower of a gondola or pleasure boat used on the canals of Venice.

gone (gŏn), *p.p.* of *go: p.adj.* ruined; lost; faint or weak: carried away.

gone-ness (gŏn'nĕs), *n.* a state of weakness, faintness, or exhaustion.

gon-fa-lon (gŏn'fȧ-lŏn), *n.* a standard or ensign, usually with streamers; a name given to any flag which hangs from a crosspiece or frame instead of from the staff or the mast itself.

gong (gŏng), *n.* a tambourine-shaped musical instrument of bronze, which is struck by a padded stick; a kind of bell.

good (gōōd), *adj.* [*comp.* better, *superl.* best], having excellent qualities; proper, fit, or adapted to any particular work or use; as, she is a *good* student; fish are *good* for food; pious; moral; kind; favorable; beneficial; as, *good* counsel; cheerful; as, *good* spirits; gracious and pleasing; as, *good* manners; undamaged; as, the dress was old, but still *good;* honest or genuine; as, *good* coin; complete; as, he made a *good* job; of high rank; as, in *good* society: *n.* excellence, that which is right, not wrong; prosperity; benefit: *pl.* household furniture; fabric; merchandise; as, my *goods* came yesterday: *interj.* an expression of assent or pleasure; as, *good!* I am glad of it.

Syn., adj. virtuous, righteous, upright, just.
Ant. (see wicked, bad).

good-by (gōōd"bī'), *n.* a farewell: *interj.* adieu; farewell; a contraction of "God be with you." Also, **good-bye.**

Good Fri-day (gōōd frī'dā), the Friday before Easter, kept as the anniversary of Christ's death.

good hu-mor (gōōd hū'mẽr; ū'mẽr), a cheery mood; a kindly temper.—*adj.* **good-humored.**

good-ly (gōōd'lĭ), *adj.* [*comp.* goodlier, *superl.* goodliest], good-looking; noble; desirable; pleasant.—*n.* **goodliness.**

good na-ture (gōōd nā'tūr), unruffled, amiable, kindly disposition.—*adj.* **good-natured.**—*adv.* **good-naturedly.**

good-ness (gōōd'nĕs), *n.* the state or quality of being good; benevolence; excellence.

goods and chat-tels (gōōdz ănd chăt'lz), personal property, such as clothing, furniture, etc.; also money, capital, live stock, etc.

good tem-per (gōōd tĕm'pẽr), a disposition or spirit not easily provoked or irritated; habitual good nature.—*adj.* **good-tempered.**—*adv.* **good-temperedly.**

good-wife (gōōd'wīf"), *n.* [*pl.* goodwives (-wīvz)], the mistress of a house.

good will (gōōd wĭl), benevolence; kindly feeling; the value a business has in trade and custom over and above stock-in-trade.

good-y (gōōd'ĭ), *adj.* affectedly or weakly pious; namby-pamby: *n.* (*pl.* goodies), a person insincerely or weakly pious; a kind of candy or sweetmeat.

goose (gōōs), *n.* [*pl.* geese (gēs)], any web-footed bird larger than a duck but smaller than a swan; a tailor's smoothing iron; a silly person.

goose-ber-ry (gōōz'bĕr-ĭ; gōōs'bĕr-ĭ), *n.* [*pl.* gooseberries (-ĭz)], a green berry similar to the currant, but larger; the bush that bears it: *adj.* made of gooseberries.

goose-neck (gōōs'nĕk), *n.* anything curved like the neck of a goose, as a bar of iron for various purposes; a bent iron connecting a mast with a spar.

goose step (gōōs stĕp), a stiff manner of marching used by the German army, in which the legs are alternately lifted and held straight out.

goose-wing (gōōs'wĭng"), *n.* a kind of sail; the lower corner of a foresail or square mainsail when the body of the sail is furled.

go-pher (gō'fẽr), *n.* a North American burrowing, ratlike animal; a ground squirrel of the prairies; a burrowing land tortoise, common in the pine barrens of the southern United States; the indigo snake, a bright-colored, nonpoisonous snake common in the southern United States; the wood of which Noah's ark was made.

Gor-di-an (gôr'dĭ-ăn), *adj.* relating to Gordius, an ancient king, or to the hard knot tied by him; as, the *Gordian* knot: **gordian**, intricate or difficult.

gore (gōr), *n.* thick or clotted blood; as, the sword dripping *gore;* a three-cornered piece sewn into a dress, sail, etc.; a narrow or three-cornered piece of land: *v.t.* to pierce, as with a horn; as, the stag was *gored* to death; furnish with three-cornered pieces cut with slanting edges: said of a garment, etc.

gorge (gôrj), *n.* the throat; gullet; that which is swallowed; a filling or choking of a channel by an obstruction; as, an ice *gorge* in a river; a narrow passage between mountains or hills: *v.t.* to swallow greedily or in large mouthfuls; satiate: *v.i.* to eat greedily.

gor-geous (gôr'jŭs), *adj.* glittering in various colors; splendid; showy; inclined to magnificence.—*adv.* **gorgeously.**—*n.* **gorgeousness.**

Syn. superb, grand, splendid.

Ant. (see plain, simple).

gor-get (gôr'jĕt), *n.* a protective piece of armor for the throat or neck; a crescent-shaped breastplate.

Gor-gon (gôr'gŏn), *n.* one of three sisters in Greek mythology whose appearance was so terrible that anyone who beheld them was turned to stone: **gorgon**, an ugly or terrible woman.

go-ril-la (gō-rĭl'ȧ), *n.* an African manlike ape some five feet in height with a massive body and powerful limbs; the largest ape known.

gor-mand (gôr'mănd), *n.* a greedy or ravenous eater; a glutton; an expert in table delicacies; a gourmet. Also, **gourmand.**

gor-mand-ize (gôr'măn-dīz), *v.i.* to eat greedily or ravenously.

gorse (gôrs), *n.* an evergreen shrub with yellow flowers: called also *furze.*

gor-y (gōr'ĭ), *adj.* covered or stained with blood; as, *gory* locks.

gos-hawk (gŏs'hôk'), *n.* a large, short-winged hawk or falcon.

general doctrines of the New Testament; something received as absolutely true; any doctrine earnestly advocated by its supporters: **Gospel**, the history of the life and doctrines of Jesus Christ, contained in the four books, Matthew, Mark, Luke, and John; one of these books; a selection from these in the church service: *adj.* relating to, or in accordance with, the gospel.

gos-sa-mer (gŏs'ȧ-mẽr), *n.* a very fine spider's web which floats in the air; a very thin, soft, filmy, strong gauze; an outer garment made of waterproof material: *adj.* very thin; flimsy; gauzy.

gos-sip (gŏs'ĭp), *n.* familiar or idle talk; scandal; one who habitually talks of other people and their affairs: *v.i.* to tell idle tales about others; tattle; chat.—*adj.* **gossipy.**

gos-soon (gŏ-sōōn'), *n.* a young attendant or servant; in Ireland, a boy.

got (gŏt), past tense and past participle of the irregular verb *get.*

Goth (gŏth), *n.* one of an ancient Teutonic tribe that overran the Roman Empire (third and fourth centuries A. D.); a savage person, especially one who lacks artistic taste.

Goth-a (gō'tä), *n.* a very large and very speedy type of military biplane developed by Germany in the World War.

Goth-ic (gŏth'ĭk), *adj.* pertaining to the Goths or their language; pertaining to a style of architecture with high and pointed arches, steep roofs, and windows large in proportion to the wall space: *n.* the language of the Goths; the pointed style of architecture; a variety of type.

Gouges. 1, military; 2, surgeon's; 3, carpenter's; 4, cheese.

gouge (gouj; gōōj), *n.* a rounded hollow chisel for cutting grooves or holes: *v.t.* to scoop out with a gouge.

gourd (gōrd; gōōrd), *n.* fleshy, three-celled, many-seeded fruit, such as the melon, pumpkin, cucumber, etc.; especially, a nonedible variety of such fruit whose dried shell serves for bottles, cups, dippers, etc.; a vessel or dipper made from such a fruit; the plant bearing the fruit.

gour-met (gōōr'mā'), *n.* an epicure; one who is a good judge of things to eat and drink. [Fr.]

gout (gout), *n.* a constitutional disease, marked by painful swelling and inflammation of the joints or lower limbs, especially of the great toe.

gout-y (gout'ĭ), *adj.* pertaining to, or affected with, gout or a disease of the joints.—*n.* **goutiness.**

gov-ern (gŭv'ẽrn), *v.t.* to control by authority; regulate; direct; manage; steer; restrain; require to be in a particular grammatical mood, case, etc.; as, a preposition *governs* a noun in the objective case: *v.i.* to exercise authority; administer or execute the law.

Syn. rule, command.

gov-ern-a-ble (gŭv'ẽrn-ȧ-bl), *adj.* capable of being controlled: amenable to authority or restraint.

gov-ern-ance (gŭv'ẽr-năns), *n.* rule; control; arrangement; exercise of authority.

gov-ern-ess (gŭv'ẽrn-ĕs), *n.* a woman who teaches children and young people, especially in their own home.

gov-ern-ing (gŭv'ẽrn-ĭng), *p.adj.* exercising control; prevalent; ruling.

gov-ern-ment (gŭv'ẽrn-mĕnt), *n.* the act of administering or ruling; administration of public affairs; as, righteous *government;* established state or legal authority; self-control; relation between two words by which one determines the case or mood of another.

Syn. rule, state, control, sway.

gov-ern-men-tal (gŭv'ẽrn-mĕn'tăl), *adj.* pertaining to, made by, connected with, or proceeding from, government.

gov-ern-or (gŭv′ẽrn-ẽr), *n.* the chief executive of a state; one who is clothed with great legal authority; chief ruler; a mechanical device for regulating the speed of an engine.—*n.* **governorship.**

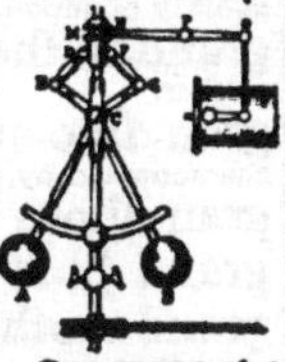

Governor of a steam engine. *A,B,* weights; *C, D, E, F, G,* bell crank levers and connecting rods to sliding sleeve *M*; *N,O,* lever pivoted at *P,* which operates valve in steam pipe.

gowk (gōk; gouk), *n.* a simpleton; a gawk; a cuckoo.

gown (goun), *n.* a woman's outer garment, or dress; a long loose robe worn by university and college students and by members of the learned professions; a long loose outer covering or wrapper, as a dressing gown, etc.

gowned (gound), *adj.* attired; clad; as, a beautifully *gowned* woman.

gowns-man (gounz′măn), *n.* one who wears a gown professionally; a student.

grab (grăb), *v.t.* and *v.i.* [*p.t.* and *p.p.* grabbed, *p.pr.* grabbing], to seize suddenly and forcibly; snatch: *n.* a sudden and forcible seizure or grasp.

grace (grās), *n.* excellence of character; attractiveness or charm, natural or acquired; elegance of action or language; beauty of form or movement; disposition to benefit or serve another; kindness; the unmerited favor and love of God towards man; spiritual excellence; virtue; a brief prayer before or after meals; a respectful title of address applied to an archbishop or duke; charm of behavior; indulgence or privilege; in music, an ornamental note or passage; *v.t.* to adorn or decorate; honor; dignify; favor.

grace-ful (grās′fo͝ol), *adj.* displaying beauty in form or action; easy and elegant in manners or demeanor; as, she is *graceful* in her bearing.—*adv.* **gracefully.**

Syn. becoming, comely, beautiful, elegant.
Ant. (see awkward).

grace-less (grās′lĕs), *adj.* lacking in good qualities; depraved; ill-mannered; awkward.

grace note (grās nōt), in music, an ornamental note; a note, usually one degree above or below the principal note.

gra-cious (grā′shŭs), *adj.* showing or bestowing goodness, kindness, or mercy; affable; polite; as, she is so very *gracious* that to know her is to love her.—*adv.* **graciously.**

Syn. merciful, kindly, beneficent.

gra-cious-ness (grā′shŭs-nĕs), *n.* affability; courteous bearing; charm of manner.

grack-le (grăk′l), *n.* a songbird of the family of the European starling and the American blackbird.

gra-date (grā′dāt), *v.t.* arrange parts in a whole, as colors in painting, etc., so that they harmonize; to bring to a certain strength of concentration; as, to *gradate* a saline, or salt, solution.

gra-da-tion (gră-dā′shŭn), *n.* a regular advance or progress, step by step; regular arrangement in order of rank, size, color, etc.; a gradual blending of one tint into another; series; order.

grade (grād), *n.* a step or degree in rank, dignity, quality, order, etc.; one of the successive parts of the course in a United States elementary school; the rise or descent of a road, etc.: *v.t.* to level and prepare, as a road or railway roadbed; arrange in regular series: *v.i.* to take rank: **grade crossing,** a crossing of two roads, on the same level, especially of a railroad track and a street or roadway.

gra-di-ent (grā′dĭ-ĕnt), *n.* the incline of a railway or road: *adj.* advancing by steps; fitted for walking; ascending or descending at a certain rate.

grad-u-al (grăd′ū-ăl), *adj.* proceeding by degrees; step by step; regular and slow; as, he shows a *gradual* improvement: *n.* in a church service, a response sung after the Epistle; an ancient book of anthems or Scripture sentences chanted by the choir during Mass.—*adv.* **gradually.**

Syn., adj. deliberate, progressive.
Ant. (see sudden).

grad-u-ate (grăd′ū-āt), *n.* one on whom a degree or a diploma has been conferred; as, he is a *graduate* of Harvard University: *v.t.* (grăd′ū-āt), to mark with degrees; to arrange according to degrees of quality, color, heat, etc.; to confer a degree or diploma upon; as, he was *graduated* at Columbia: *v.i.* to take or receive a college degree or a diploma; change by degrees: *adj.* having been given a degree; pertaining to those upon whom degrees have been conferred; as, a *graduate* student.

grad-u-a-tion (grăd″ū-ā′shŭn), *n.* the conferring or reception of a college degree or the diploma of a school; regular progression; a marking into degrees or parts.

grad-u-a-tor (grăd′ū-ā″tẽr), *n.* an instrument for dividing lines into equal minute parts; an electro-magnet for making and breaking gradually a telegraphic circuit.

graft (grȧft), *n.* a small shoot of a tree inserted into another tree; hence, something mixed with a foreign stock; colloquially, an unlawful or irregular acceptance of money, particularly from the government of a city or state; a bribe: *v.t.* to insert as a shoot in another tree; join so as to receive support from another thing; in surgery, to transplant (tissue): *v.i.* to practice grafting; colloquially, to accept bribe money: **grafting knife,** a knife adapted for cutting twigs or vines for grafting.—*n.* **grafter.**

Grafting Knives

Gra-ham flour (grā′ăm flour), whole or unbolted wheat flour.

grail (grāl), *n.* a dish or chalice; especially, the Holy Grail, the cup used by Christ at the Last Supper, said in some legends of the Middle Ages to have been preserved by Joseph of Arimathea, and taken to England, where it disappeared. Also, **graal.**

grain (grān), *n.* any very small hard seed or kernel; a single seed of corn; the fruit of certain grasses which furnish the chief food of man, as corn, wheat, rye, oats, etc., or the plants themselves; the smallest particle or amount; a unit of weight equal to 1/20 of a scruple or 1/24 pennyweight; the arrangement of particles in a body; as, the *grain* of any kind of wood; texture; *pl.* the refuse or dregs of malted barley: *v.t.* to form into small particles; to paint in imitation of the grain of wood.

grain-er (grān'ẽr), *n.* one who imitates the grain or texture of wood; the tool or brush used in doing this work.

grain-ing (grān'ing), *n.* painting in imitation of the grain or texture of wood; a process in dyeing; the pebbling of paper or leather in bookbinding.

gram (grăm), *n.* a weight; the unit of mass in the metric system, 15.43 grains troy. Also, **gramme.**

gra-mer-cy (grȧ-mûr'sĭ), *interj.* great thanks; as, "*Gramercy* for your aid," said the knight.

gram-i-niv-o-rous (grăm'ĭ-nĭv'ō-rŭs), *adj.* feeding on grasses.

gram-ma-log (grăm'ȧ-lŏg), *n.* in shorthand, a sign representing a single word, as *t* for *it*. Also, **grammalogue.**

gram-mar (grăm'ẽr), *n.* the science that treats of the principles that govern the words of a language in their relation to each other; the art of speaking or writing a language according to these principles; a book on this science.

gram-ma-ri-an (grȧ-mā'rĭ-ăn), *n.* one who knows, writes on, or teaches, the science of language.

gram-mar school (grăm'ẽr skōōl), in the United States, a graded school between the primary and the high school; in England, a school in which the classics, etc., are taught.

gram-mat-i-cal (grȧ-măt'ĭ-kăl), *adj.* pertaining to, or in agreement with, grammar, or its rules.—*adv.* **grammatically.**

gramme (grăm), *n.* the unit of weight in the metric system, 15.43 grains troy. Also, **gram.**

gram-o-phone (grăm'ō-fōn), *n.* an instrument for recording and reproducing speech.

Gramophone

gram-pus (grăm'pŭs), *n.* a sea animal akin to the whale, but smaller; a corpulent or stout person.

gran-a-ry (grăn'ȧ-rĭ), *n.* [*pl.* **granaries** (-rĭz)], a storehouse for grain; a country where grain is the chief product.

grand (grănd), *adj.* high in dignity or power; illustrious; chief; great; magnificent; splendid; sublime; noble; impressive; having wealth and high social position; conceived or expressed in dignified language; in the second degree of parentage or descent, as *grandfather*: *n.* a grand piano.

Syn., *adj.* majestic, stately, dignified, lofty, exalted, gorgeous, superb.

Ant. (see mean, shabby).

gran-dam (grăn'dăm), *n.* a grandmother; an old woman. Also, **grandame.**

grand-child (grănd'chīld"), *n.* the child of one's son or daughter.

grand-daugh-ter (grănd'dô"tẽr), *n.* the daughter of one's son or daughter.

grand duke (grănd dūk), a duke ruling over a country or state; in Russia, a son of the czar.

gran-dee (grăn-dē'), *n.* a Spanish nobleman of the highest rank.

gran-deur (grăn'dûr), *n.* greatness; vastness; sublimity; splendor of appearance; social distinction and display; elevation of thought, sentiment, or demeanor; nobility of action.

grand-fa-ther (grănd'fä"thẽr), *n.* the father of one's father or mother.

gran-dil-o-quent (grăn-dĭl'ō-kwĕnt), *adj.* speaking in, or characterized by, a lofty or pompous style.

gran-di-ose (grăn'dĭ-ōs), *adj.* impressive in reality or pretense.

grand ju-ry (grănd jōō'rĭ), a jury which tries grave offenses.

grand-moth-er (grănd'mŭth"ẽr), *n.* the mother of one's father or mother.

grand op-er-a (grănd ŏp'ẽr-ȧ), an elaborate and dignified musical drama.

grand-par-ent (grănd'pâr"ĕnt), *n.* the parent of one's parent.

grand-sire (grănd'sīr"), *n.* a grandfather; male ancestor.

grand-son (grănd'sŭn"), *n.* the son of one's son or daughter.

grand stand (grănd stănd), the principal range of seats at any outdoor entertainment, usually built in tiers.

grange (grānj), *n.* a farm with its buildings, etc.: **Grange**, a national association of farmers; a local lodge of the order.—*n.* **granger.**

gra-nif-er-ous (grȧ-nĭf'ẽr-ŭs), *adj.* bearing grain, or seeds like grain.

gran-ite (grăn'ĭt), *n.* a hard, crystalline rock, gray or red in color, composed of quartz, feldspar, and mica.

gran-ite ware (grăn'ĭt wâr), a kind of enameled iron ware.

gra-niv-o-rous (grȧ-nĭv'ō-rŭs), *adj.* eating grain or seeds.

gran-ny (grăn'ĭ), *n.* abbreviation of *grandmother*; an old woman.

grant (grȧnt), *v.t.* to give or confer, especially in response to a request; admit as true (what has not been proved); concede; transfer the title of: *n.* the act of conferring; a gift; an allowance; the thing conveyed; a transfer of property; an admission or concession.

Syn., *v.* bestow, impart, yield, cede, allow, invest.

grant-ee (grȧn-tē'), *n.* the person to whom property is transferred by law.

grant-or (grȧn'tôr; grȧn-tôr'), *n.* one who transfers property by law.

gran-u-lar (grăn'ū-lȧr), *adj.* composed of, or like, grains or granules.

gran-u-late (grăn'ū-lāt), *v.t.* to form into grains or small masses; roughen the surface of; *v.i.* to become grainlike or form into crystals; as, honey *granulates* into sugar.—*adj.* **granulated.**

gran-u-la-tion (grăn"ū-lā'shŭn), *n.* the state of being formed or collected into grains; the act of forming into grains; one of the grains so formed, or something like it; in surgery, the process of healing by which small, red, grainlike protuberances form on the surface of wounds or ulcers.

gran-ule (grăn'ūl), *n.* a small grain or particle; as, a *granule* of sugar.

gran-u-lose (grăn'ū-lōs"), *n.* the part of starch grains in plants capable of being formed into sugar.

grape (grāp), *n.* the smooth, round, edible fruit of the grapevine, used for making wine and raisins.

grape-fruit (grāp'frōōt"), *n.* a citrous fruit grown in the tropics, having an acid pulp, and a bitter-tasting rind.

grap-er-y (grāp'ẽr-ĭ), *n.* [*pl.* graperies (-ĭz)], a building or inclosure used for the cultivation of grapes.

grape-shot (grāp'shŏt"), *n.* a cluster of small shot arranged so as to scatter when fired.

grape-vine (grāp'vīn"), *n.* a well-known climbing plant, bearing smooth, round, edible fruit in clusters.

graph-ic (grăf'ĭk), *adj.* pertaining to the art of writing or delineating; vividly described; well delineated; lifelike. Also, **graphical**.—*adv.* **graphically**.
Syn. forcible, telling, picturesque, vivid, pictorial.

graph-ite (grăf'īt), *n.* a kind of carbon used for lead pencils, etc.

graph-o-phone (grăf'ō-fōn), *n.* an instrument for reproducing sound; a phonograph.

grap-nel (grăp'nĕl), *n.* a kind of small anchor usually with flukes or arrowlike arms; heavy tongs used for lifting stone, ice, etc.

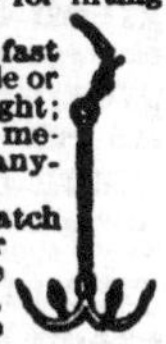
Grapple

grap-ple (grăp'l), *v.t.* to lay fast hold of: *v.i.* to struggle or contend in a close fight: *n.* a close fight; a close hold, as in wrestling; a mechanical device for taking hold of anything.

grasp (grȧsp), *v.t.* to seize or catch at; hold by clasping or contracting; as, *grasp* the rope quickly; to take hold of mentally, or understand: *v.i.* to endeavor to seize: with *at;* as, a drowning man *grasps* at a straw: *n.* a seizure of the hand; power of seizure; hold; mental capacity; as, his *grasp* of things is quick for one so young.
Syn., *v.* catch, seize, gripe, clasp.

grasp-ing (grȧsp'ĭng), *p.adj.* avaricious; greedy of gain; close; miserly; as, he is *grasping* and selfish.

grass (grȧs), *n.* herbage having hollow, jointed stalks, narrow leaves called blades, and seeds similar to those of grain; pasture: *v.t.* to cover with turf; bleach, by exposure on grass; pasture or graze.

grass-hop-per (grȧs'hŏp"ẽr), *n.* a small nimble insect of the locust kind.

grass-y (grȧs'ĭ), *adj.* covered with, or like, grass.—*n.* **grassiness**.

grate (grāt), *n.* a framework of iron bars to hold fuel; a set of bars, as in a window: *v.t.* to rub or wear away by the friction or rubbing of a rough body; produce (a sound) by the friction of rough or hard surfaces; grind down; furnish with iron bars: *v.i.* to make a harsh noise by rubbing roughly; produce mental irritation; as, her manner *grates* on me.

grate-ful (grāt'fŏŏl), *adj.* thankful; pleasurable; as, the cold air was *grateful* after the discomfort of the overheated room.—*adv.* **gratefully**.—*n.* **gratefulness**.
Syn. agreeable, pleasing.
Ant. (see harsh).

grat-er (grāt'ẽr), *n.* one who, or that which, grates; a rasping or grating implement; as, a nutmeg *grater*.

grat-i-fi-ca-tion (grăt"ĭ-fĭ-kā'shŭn), *n.* the act of pleasing; satisfaction; pleasure; reward or recompense.
Syn. enjoyment, pleasure, delight.
Ant. (see disappointment).

grat-i-fy (grăt'ĭ-fī), *v.t.* [*p.t.* and *p.p.* gratified, *p.pr.* gratifying], to afford pleasure to; indulge; delight; humor.

grat-ing (grāt'ĭng), *n.* an open framework or lattice of bars; an arrangement of parallel wires in an optical instrument: *p.adj.* harsh, irritating.

gra-tis (grā'tĭs), *adv.* without charge; out of favor or kindness; as, he gave me these flowers *gratis*. [LAT.]

grat-i-tude (grăt'ĭ-tūd), *n.* the state of being thankful; appreciation of favors received; thankfulness; kindness awakened by a favor received.

gra-tu-i-tous (grȧ-tū'ĭ-tŭs), *adj.* freely bestowed; voluntary; without cause or provocation; granted without merit or claim.—*adv.* **gratuitously**.

gra-tu-i-ty (grȧ-tū'ĭ-tĭ), *n.* [*pl.* gratuities (-tĭz)], a donation or present; free gift.

gra-va-men (grȧ-vā'mĕn), *n.* a legal term meaning cause of complaint or action.

grave (grāv), *adj.* serious; solemn; thoughtful; sedate; important; a common accent, or its sign [ˋ]; plain; slow in movement; in music, very deep in pitch: *n.* an excavation or hole in the earth for the reception of a dead body; place of burial; place of great slaughter or mortality: *v.t.* to shape or carve by cutting with a chisel; engrave.—*adv.* **gravely**.—*n.* **graveness**.
Syn., *adj.* sober, pressing, heavy: *n.* tomb.
Ant. (see giddy).

grav-el (grăv'ĕl), *n.* fragments of rock coarser than sand and frequently mixed with it; a disease caused by solid matter in the bladder and kidneys: *v.t.* to cover with fragments of rock; run aground on a beach: said of a vessel; embarrass; lame, as a horse, by a stone under the shoe.—*adj.* **gravelly**.

gra-ven (grā'vn), *p.adj.* cut; carved: **graven image**, an idol.

grav-er (grāv'ẽr), *n.* a cutting tool used by engravers and sculptors; an engraver or carver in stone.

grave-stone (grāv'stōn"), *n.* a stone, usually bearing an inscription, placed to mark a grave; a tombstone.

grave-yard (grāv'yärd"), *n.* a burial place; a cemetery.

grav-ing (grāv'ĭng), *n.* the act of engraving or incising; the clearing of the bottom of a ship.

grav-i-tate (grăv'ĭ-tāt), *v.i.* to be acted upon or attracted by a force which draws all bodies in the universe toward each other; be naturally attracted; as, office-seekers *gravitate* towards those in authority.

grav-i-ta-tion (grăv"ĭ-tā'shŭn), *n.* the force which draws all bodies in the universe toward each other.

grav-i-ty (grăv'ĭ-tĭ), *n.* that force which tends to move all bodies towards the center of the earth; weight; importance; seriousness; solemnity; weight of guilt; in music, lowness of a tone or note.

gra-vy (grā'vĭ), *n.* [*pl.* gravies (-vĭz)], the fatty juice from roasting flesh made into a dressing for food when it is served.

gray (grā), *n.* and *adj.* white mixed with black; the color of hair whitened by age. Also, **grey**.—*n.* **grayness**, **greyness**.

gray-beard (grā'bērd"), *n.* an old man. Also, **greybeard**.

gray-hound (grā'hound"), *n.* a slender, swift dog with keen sight. Also, **greyhound**.

gray-ling (grā'lĭng), *n.* a fresh-water fish of the salmon family. Also, **greyling**.

graze (grāz), *v.t.* to furnish pasture for; touch or rub lightly: *v.i.* to eat grass; move along while eating grass; to rub something in passing: *n.* a slight rub or touch; a rubbed or scratched place on a surface.

gra-zier (grā'zhẽr), *n.* one who pastures or breeds cattle for market.

grease (grēs), *n.* soft animal fat; oily matter: *v.t.* (grēz; grēs), to smear or rub with fat; cause to move easily by applying an oily substance.

greas-er (grēz'ẽr), *n.* one who, or that which, oils, or lubricates; slang, a Mexican, or Mexican creole.

greas-y (grēz'ĭ; grēs'ĭ), *adj.* [*comp.* greasier, *superl.* greasiest], resembling, smeared, or spotted with, fat; oily.—*adv.* **greasily**.—*n.* **greas'ness**.

great (grāt), *adj.* large; chief; principal; weighty; marvelous; eminent; illustrious; high in rank or position; sublime; noble; accomplished; long continued; magnanimous; high-minded; showing a step of relationship by blood; as, *great*-grandfather: *n.* noble, or influential, people: with *the*.—*adv.* **greatly**.—*n.* **greatness**.

Syn., adj. big, huge, majestic, vast, grand, august.

great-aunt (grāt'änt''), *n.* the sister of one's grandparent.

Great Bear (grāt bâr), a well-known group of stars in the north: called also *Ursa Major*, and the *Dipper*.

great-coat (grāt'kōt''), *n.* a heavy overcoat or topcoat.

great Dane (grāt dān), one of a breed of very large, savage, short-haired dogs.

great-est (grā'tĕst), *adj.* superlative of *great*: **greatest common divisor**, the greatest factor common to two or more numbers.

great-grand-child (grāt''grănd'chīld''), *n.* the child of one's grandchild.

great-grand-daugh-ter (grāt''grănd'-dô'tẽr), *n.* the daughter of one's grandchild.

great-grand-fa-ther (grāt''grănd'fä''thẽr), *n.* the father of one's grandparent.

great-grand-moth-er (grāt''grănd'-mŭth''ẽr), *n.* the mother of one's grandparent.

great-grand-son (grāt''grănd'sŭn''), *n.* the son of one's grandchild.

great-un-cle (grāt'ŭn''kl), *n.* the brother of one's grandparent.

Great Spir-it (grāt spĭr'ĭt), the title applied to the Supreme Being by the American Indians.

Great White Way (grāt hwīt wā), the theater section of Broadway, New York City, so called from the brightness of its lights at night.

greaves (grēvz), *n.pl.* armor to protect the legs from the ankle to the knee; the sediment or dregs of melted tallow.

Gre-cian (grē'shăn), *adj.* pertaining to Greece; *n.* a native of Greece; a Greek scholar.

greed (grēd), *n.* avarice; excessive hunger for something; an unnatural desire or longing; as, a *greed* for gain.

greed-y (grēd'ĭ), *adj.* [*comp.* greedier, *superl.* greediest], voracious; gluttonous; eagerly desirous; covetous.—*adv.* **greedily**.—*n.* **greediness**.

Greek (grēk), *adj.* pertaining to, or like, Greece or the Greeks: *n.* a native of Greece; the language of ancient and modern Greece: **Greek Church**, the Eastern Church; the National Church of Russia, Roumania, Serbia, and Bulgaria.

green (grēn), *n.* the color of growing grass or plants; a color between, or composed of, blue and yellow; a grassplot or common; a golf course, especially the closely-cut square of grass around any one of the holes: *pl.* fresh or evergreen foliage cut for decoration; as, Christmas *greens*: spinach or similar vegetables: *v.t.* to make of the color of plants and grass: *v.i.* to become the color of plants and grass: *adj.* having the color of growing grass or plants; of a color between, or composed of, blue and yellow; fresh; flourishing; unripe; not salted; immature; inexperienced; raw.—*adv.* **greenly**.—*n.* **greenness**.

green-back (grēn'băk''), *n.* any United States legal tender bank note or paper money with a green back.

green-er-y (grēn'ẽr-ĭ), *n.* verdure; a verdant clump or mass of plants; a place where green things are grown.

green-gro-cer (grēn'grō''sẽr), *n.* a retailer of fresh vegetables and fruit.—*n.* **greengrocery**.

green-finch (grēn'fĭnch''), *n.* a very common bird of Europe having olive-green and yellow feathers; the Texas sparrow.

green-horn (grēn'hôrn''), *n.* a simpleton; an inexperienced person.

green-house (grēn'hous''), *n.* a conservatory or glasshouse for the protection or cultivation of tender flowers and plants.

green-ing (grēn'ĭng), *n* the act of turning green or becoming green; any of a variety of green-skinned apples.

green-ish (grēn'ĭsh), *adj.* somewhat green; inexperienced.

green-room (grēn'rōōm''), *n.* the actors' retiring room in a theater.

green-sward (grēn'swôrd), *n.* turf well covered with grass.

green-wood (grēn'wŏŏd''), *n.* a forest in full leaf.

greet (grēt), *v.t.* to salute in kindness or respect; congratulate: *v.i.* to exchange salutations.

greet-ing (grēt'ĭng), *n.* salutation; welcome; compliment.

gre-ga-ri-ous (grē-gā'rĭ-ŭs), *adj.* associating or going together in herds.—*adv.* **gregariously**.

Gre-go-ri-an cal-en-dar (grē-gō'rĭ-ăn kăl'ĕn-dẽr), the reformed calendar introduced in 1582, by Pope Gregory XIII.

Gre-go-ri-an chant (grē-gō'rĭ-ăn chänt), a system of choral music, introduced by Pope Gregory the Great; plain song.

gre-nade (grē-nād'), *n.* an explosive shell fired by a fuse and usually thrown by hand; a flask or bottle containing chemicals to be thrown and burst, for putting out fires: **rifle grenade**, an explosive shell so made that it can be attached to the barrel of a rifle and carried by the bullet to the place desired.

gren-a-dier (grĕn''ȧ-dēr'), *n.* originally, a foot soldier of England who threw grenades; now, a member of a special regiment or corps.

gren-a-dine (grĕn'ȧ-dēn), *n.* a dress fabric of thin gauzy silk or wool; a dyestuff; a dish composed of veal and poultry, larded.

gres-so-ri-al (grĕ-sō'rĭ-ăl), *adj.* adapted for walking, as the feet of a barnyard fowl.

Gret-na Green (grĕt'nȧ grēn), a village in Scotland just across the English border, where English runaway couples went to be married.

grew (grōō), past tense of the irregular verb *grow*.

grew-some (grōō'sŭm), *adj.* inspiring horror; frightful; repulsive. Also, **gruesome.**

grey (grā), *adj.* white with a mixture of black; the color of hair whitened by age; hoary; mature: *n.* the color of white mixed with black; a grey horse. Also, **gray.**—*n.* **grayness, greyness.**

grey-beard (grā'bērd"), *n.* an old man; as, Rip Van Winkle went away a young man and returned a *greybeard.* Also, **graybeard.**

grey-hound (grā'hound"), *n.* a slender, swift dog with keen sight. Also, **grayhound.**

grid (grĭd), *n.* a grating of parallel bars; a gridiron.

grid-dle (grĭd''l), *n.* a shallow pan or plate used for cooking hot cakes.

grid-dle-cake (grĭd''l-kāk"), *n.* a thin batter cake, baked on a griddle.

gride (grīd), *v.t.* to grind harshly; to jar; grate: *v.i.* to make a grinding sound; to grate.

grid-i-ron (grĭd'ī"ŭrn), *n.* a grated iron utensil for broiling meat or fish; a football field.

grief (grēf), *n.* sorrow on account of present or past trouble; that which causes sorrow or sadness; affliction.
Syn. sorrow, trial, woe, tribulation.
Ant. (see joy).

griev-ance (grēv'ăns), *n.* a sense of wrong or oppression; just or supposed ground of complaint; an injustice; cause of annoyance.

grieve (grēv), *v.t.* to cause to experience grief; afflict mentally: *v.i.* to be in sorrow; lament.
Syn. mourn, sorrow, hurt, pain, wound, bewail.
Ant. (see rejoice).

Griffin

griev-ous (grēv'ŭs), *adj.* causing sadness or sorrow; hard to be borne; painful; oppressive; pitiable; harmful; vexatious.—*adv.* **grievously.**—*n.* **grievousness.**

grif-fin (grĭf'ĭn), *n.* a fabled animal with the body and legs of a lion, the wings and beak of an eagle, and with listening ears; a careful watcher. Also, **griffon, gryphon.**

grig (grĭg), *n.* a grasshopper; cricket; a mountebank; slang, money.

grill (grĭl), *n* a gridiron; a room in a hotel or restaurant, where food, especially broiled food, is cooked to order and promptly served; broiled meat: *v.t.* to broil: as, I am going to *grill* this meat; to torment: *v.i.* to be broiled; as, the fish *grilled* over the fire.

grille (grĭl), *n.* a grating, especially one which is made of wrought iron.

grim (grĭm), *adj.* [*comp.* grimmer, *superl.* grimmest], of a forbidding aspect; stern and surly; hideous; frightful; cruel; unyielding.—*adv.* **grimly.**—*n.* **grimness.**

gri-mace (grĭ-mās'), *n.* a twisting of the countenance; smirk: *v.i.* to distort the countenance; to make faces.

grime (grīm), *n.* foul matter; dirt deeply ingrained, or rubbed in: *v.t.* to make dirty or grimy.

grim-y (grīm'ĭ), *adj.* much soiled; covered with dirt.—*n.* **griminess.**

grin (grĭn), *n.* the act of showing the teeth in laughter, scorn, pain, etc.; a broad smile: *v.i.* [*p.t.* and *p.p.* grinned, *p.pr.* grinning], to show the teeth in laughter, scorn, or pain: *v.t.* to express by smiling in such a way as to show the teeth; as, he *grinned* his pleasure.

grind (grīnd), *v.t.* [*p.t.* and *p.p.* ground, *p.pr.* grinding], to make into powder by friction; sharpen or smooth by friction; as, to *grind* a knife; grate or rub together; oppress; harass; turn the crank of, as a hand-organ, etc.; *v.i.* to sharpen or polish something, or to make something into powder, by friction; be grated or rubbed together; college slang, to study hard: *n.* the act of sharpening, polishing, or making into powder; a grating or rubbing together; the turning of a crank; hard study for an examination; laborious and tedious work; wearisome routine; as, the daily *grind;* college slang, a student who studies laboriously.

grind-er (grīn'dẽr), *n.* one who, or that which, sharpens or makes into powder; a molar tooth; one who coaches pupils for an examination.

grind-stone (grīnd'stōn"), *n.* a flat, circular stone turning on an axle: used for sharpening tools, etc.

grin-go (grĭn'gō), *n.* [*pl.* gringos (-gōz)], a term of contempt applied by Mexicans and South Americans to foreigners, particularly to Americans.

grip (grĭp), *n.* a grasp with the hand; a holding fast; that by which anything is held firmly; a particular mode of grasping the hand, as among Freemasons; grasping power; colloquially, in the United States, a valise; a disease like a bad cold with a fever; influenza; la grippe: *v.t.* [*p.t.* and *p.p.* gripped, *p.pr.* gripping], to grasp, or seize: *v.i.* to take fast hold.—*n.* **gripper.**

gripe (grīp), *n.* a clasping with the hand or arms; a squeeze; pressure; pinching distress: *pl.* colic: *v.t.* to hold with closed fingers; grasp; hold tightly; to pain the bowels of; seize; clutch; oppress; pinch.

grippe (grĭp), *n.* influenza or epidemic catarrh; a feverish cold. Also, **grip, la grippe.**

gris-ly (grĭz'lĭ), *adj.* terrible; savage-looking; hideous; somewhat gray. Also, **grizzly.**—*n.* **grisliness.**

grist (grĭst), *n.* grain for grinding; ground corn; provision or supply.

gris-tle (grĭs''l), *n.* cartilage; clear, elastic tissue.—*adj.* **gristly.**

grist-mill (grist'mil), *n.* a mill for grinding grain.

grit (grit), *n.* rough, hard particles, as sand, etc.; a hard, coarse-grained sandstone; the coarse part of meal; firmness of character; courage: *pl.* oats hulled and coarsely ground; *v.i.* to give forth a grating sound: *v.t.* to grind; to grate; as, to *grit* the teeth.—*adj.* **gritty.**—*n.* **grittiness.**

griz-zle (griz'l), *n.* a mixture of white and black; a gray color: *v.t.* and *v.i.* to turn gray.—*adj.* **grizzled.**

griz-zly (griz'li), *n.* [*pl.* grizzlies (-liz)], the grizzly bear, a large, fierce bear of North America: *adj.* somewhat gray.

groan (grōn), *n.* a low, deep sound uttered in pain or sorrow; a deep, rumbling sound expressive of disapprobation or ridicule; as, his speech was received with *groans* from the audience; a low, dismal sound, as of the wind: *v.i.* to utter a deep sound of pain or sorrow; to creak; as, the door *groaned* on its hinges; lament; as, the very winds seem to *groan*: *v.t.* to express by low, moaning sounds; as, he *groaned* out his wish.

groat (grôt; grŏt), *n.* formerly, a silver coin current in England, value four pence, or eight cents in United States coin; a trifling sum: *pl.* hulled oats.

gro-cer (grō'sẽr), *n.* one who sells foodstuffs, such as tea, coffee, flour, sugar, etc.

gro-cer-y (grō'sẽr-i), *n.* [*pl.* groceries (-iz)], tea, coffee, sugar, spices, etc.: usually *pl.*: [U. S.], a grocer's shop.

grog (grŏg), *n.* a mixture of spirits and water; spirituous liquor.

grog-gy (grŏg'i), *adj.* tipsy; moving with an unsteady gait; staggering as if dazed.—*n.* **grogginess.** [Colloq.]

groin (groin), *n.* the depressed part of the human body between the thigh and the belly; the angular or sharp curve made by the intersection of two arches: *v.t.* to build or form into such intersections, as arches.

grom-met (grŏm'ĕt), *n.* a ring formed of a strand of rope laid round; an eyelet of metal; a cannon-wad made of rope, and rammed between the powder and the ball.

groom (grōōm), *n.* a man or boy who has charge of horses; a man recently married or about to be married; the title of several officers of a royal household: *v.t.* to feed and take care of, as a horse; curry and brush.

grooms-man (grōōmz'măn), *n.* one who attends a bridegroom; best man.

groove (grōōv), *n.* a channel or furrow, especially as cut by a tool; as, the plate sits in the *groove* on the rack; settled habit or routine: *v.t.* to form or cut a furrow in; as, *groove* that cement so that the water will run off.

grope (grōp), *v.i.* to feel one's way with the hands, as in the dark; seek blindly: *v.t.* to search out, as in the dark, by feeling with the hands.

gros-beak (grōs'bēk"), *n.* a kind of warbling bird with a large stout beak, related to the finch family.

gros-grain (grō'grān"), *adj.* having a heavy cord, as silk: *n.* a stout double-corded silk with little luster.

gross (grōs), *adj.* bulky; thick; coarse; rude; indelicate; flagrant; as, *gross* errors; dull; heavy; corpulent; dense; whole: total: opposite to *net*: *n.* twelve dozen; main body; mass; entire amount: often with *in* or *in the*; as, in the *gross*: **gross ton,** 2,240 pounds.—*adv.* **grossly.**—*n.* **grossness.**

Syn., *adj.* outrageous, unseemly, shameful, rough.

Ant. (see **delicate**).

gro-tesque (grō-tĕsk'), *n.* whimsical ornamentation, figures, or scenery; the incongruous or uncouth in art: *adj.* fantastically or oddly formed; extravagant; whimsical; ridiculous.—*adv.* **grotesquely.**—*n.* **grotesqueness.**

grot-to (grŏt'ō), *n.* [*pl.* grottos, grottoes (-tōz)], a natural or artificial cave or cavern in the earth.

grot-to-work (grŏt'ō-wûrk"), *n.* ornamental rockwork in imitation of a grotto or cave.

grouch (grouch), *n.* a fit of crossness or ill temper; one who indulges in fits of ill temper.—*adj.* **grouchy.**—*n.* **grouchiness.** [Slang.]

ground (ground), *p.t.* and *p.p.* of *grind*: *n.* the earth or soil; surface of a floor or pavement; land; territory; country; estate: usually in plural; foundation; cause or reason; origin; original principle; a fundamental or preparatory part in various arts; plain song: *pl.* dregs or sediment: *v.t.* to place or set on or in the earth; teach the first principles to; base; cover with paint or plaster: *v.i.* to run on to land: said of vessels: *adj.* fundamental.

ground floor (ground flōr), that floor of a building which is built on or slightly above the ground.

ground hog (ground hŏg), the woodchuck, a burrowing animal akin to the beaver, rat, etc.

ground-less (ground'lĕs), *adj.* without foundation; without reason; as, *groundless* fears.

ground-ling (ground'lĭng), *n.* one who, or that which, lives on the earth or ground; a land animal; a fish that keeps at the bottom of the water; one of the audience on the main floor of an early theater.

ground plan (ground plăn), a plan of the ground floor of any building; any first or preliminary plan.

ground-sel (ground'sĕl), *n.* a plant of the aster family, having yellow flowers; a timber used in a foundation; a doorsill.

ground swell (ground swĕl), a broad, deep, heavy, rolling sea, caused by a distant storm or earthquake.

ground-work (ground'wûrk"), *n.* foundation; basis; the essential or necessary part.

group (grōōp), *n.* a small crowd or assemblage; a cluster; as, a *group* of houses; a collection of figures or objects forming an artistic whole; a division of organisms with certain characteristics; the chief division of a geological system: *v.t.* to form into a collection or class.

Syn., *n.* assembly, cluster, clump, order, class.

grouse (grous), *n.* a game bird akin to the domestic fowl; partridge; pheasant; prairie hen: *v.i.* in World War slang, to grumble or complain in a good-natured way.

grout (grout), *n.* thin mortar or cement mixed with gravel, used for foundations and joints of masonry; a fine plaster for ceilings; coarse meal: *v.t.* to surround or fill in with such cement, as the joints between stones.

grout-y (grout'i), *adj.* cross; sulky; as, a *grouty* disposition.

grove (grōv), *n.* a small wood; a group of trees without undergrowth.

grov-el (grŏv'l), *v.i.* to lie prone; move with the body flat on the ground; be mean or debased.—*n.* **groveler.**
Syn. crawl, cringe, fawn, sneak.

grow (grō), *v.t.* [*p.t.* grew, *p.p.* grown, *p.pr.* growing], to cultivate: *v.i.* to increase in size by natural organic development; be produced by vegetation; enlarge; flourish; thrive; become; advance.—*n.* **grower.**
Syn. vegetate, expand.
Ant. (see decay, diminution).

growl (groul), *n.* a deep angry snarl or murmur; a murmuring complaint: *v.i.* and *v.t.* to snarl or murmur like a dog; grumble.—*n.* **growler.**

grown (grōn), past participle of the irregular verb *grow.*

growth (grōth), *n.* the progressive increase of animal or vegetable bodies; advancement; increase; progress; result; effect.

grub (grŭb), *v.t.* [*p.t.* and *p.p.* grubbed, *p.pr.* grubbing], to dig up; root out of the ground: *v.i.* to dig up something; drudge or toil; perform dirty work: *n.* the larva or egg of a beetle, moth, or other insect; slang, food; a slovenly or dirty person; a drudge.

grub-ber (grŭb'ẽr), *n.* one who, or that which, digs; especially a machine or tool that works like an ax in digging up roots, etc.

grudge (grŭj), *n.* secret malice or ill will; as, to hold a *grudge;* dislike, offense, or quarrel of long standing: *v.t.* to envy the ownership of; to grant with reluctance; to covet; to desire to get back again; to begrudge.—*adv.* **grudgingly.**
Syn., n. malice, rancor, spite, pique, hatred, aversion.

gru-el (grōō'ĕl), *n.* a light semiliquid food made of oatmeal, etc., for invalids: used also as a breakfast food.

grue-some (grōō'sŭm), *adj.* horrible of aspect; inspiring gloom or horror; ugly; frightful. Also, **grewsome.**—*adv.* **gruesomely, grewsomely.**—*n.* **gruesomeness, grewsomeness.**

gruff (grŭf), *adj.* rough or surly in voice or manner; harsh; hoarse.—*adv.* **gruffly.** —*n.* **gruffness.**
Syn. rugged, blunt, rude, bearish.
Ant. (see pleasant).

grum-ble (grŭm'bl), *n.* a surly speech; a complaint: *v.i.* and *v.t.* to murmur discontentedly; growl; rumble; find fault. —*n.* **grumbler.**

grump-y (grŭm'pĭ), *adj.* surly; cross; low-spirited; dissatisfied.—*adv.* **grumpily.**—*n.* **grumpiness.**

grunt (grŭnt), *n.* the guttural noise of a hog; an American sea fish good for food: *v.i.* to make a noise like a hog.—*n.* **grunter.**

gua-no (gwä'nō), *n.* a substance found abundantly in South America and Africa and on coasts of islands where there are many sea fowls: used as a fertilizer.

guar-an-tee (găr"ăn-tē'), *n.* a promise made by a third person to secure the fulfilment of an agreement or the payment of a debt, etc., by another; one who becomes surety for the performance of another's promises; property pledged as security for the performance of promises: *v.t.* to undertake that another shall perform a certain stipulation or agreement; warrant; be responsible for. Also, **guaranty.**

guar-an-tor (găr'ăn-tôr"), *n.* one who becomes surety for the performance of obligations of another.

guar-an-ty (găr'ăn-tĭ), *n.* [*pl.* **guaranties** (-tĭz)], a legal guarantee; an undertaking to answer for the payment of some debt, or the performance of some obligation, by another; surety: *v.t.* to warrant; be responsible for. Also, **guarantee.**

guard (gärd), *v.t.* to watch over or protect; preserve by caution; shield or defend: *v.i.* to watch; be cautious: with *against:* *n.* security or defense against injury or attack; a state of watchfulness or caution; attention; a position of defense in fencing; any contrivance or device for security; a man or body of men employed for defense or control; in England, an official in charge of a train; conductor.

guard-ed (gärd'ĕd), *p.adj.* defended; careful; cautious; circumspect.—*adv.* **guardedly.**

guard-house (gärd'hous"), *n.* a military jail; a house occupied by guards.

guard-i-an (gär'dĭ-ăn), *n.* one who has the care of the person or property of another; a warden: *adj.* protecting.—*n.* **guardianship.**

guard-room (gärd'rōōm), *n.* the room occupied by the guard during its term on duty; a place of imprisonment.

guard ship (gärd ship), a warship stationed at a port or harbor for its protection.

guards-man (gärdz'măn), *n.* [*pl.* **guardsmen** (-mĕn)], a man employed for defense or watching; an officer or soldier of any military body termed *Guards.*

gua-va (gwä'vȧ), *n.* a tree of South America yielding a pear-shaped fruit, from which a jelly is made.

gu-ber-na-to-ri-al (gū"bẽr-nȧ-tō'rĭ-ăl), *adj.* pertaining to a governor or to his office.

gud-geon (gŭj'ŭn), *n.* a small European fresh-water fish easily caught, and often used for food and bait; a person who is easily imposed upon; a simpleton; an iron pin or shaft on which a wheel revolves.

guer-don (gûr'dŭn), *n.* a reward given for deeds of courage or high merit.

Guern-sey (gûrn'zĭ), *adj.* denoting a breed of dairy cattle from the island of Guernsey.—**guernsey,** a close-fitting knitted woolen shirt.

guer-ril-la (gĕ-rĭl'ȧ), *n.* one of an irregular force engaged in harassing an enemy in small bands; petty warfare: *adj.* pertaining to, or consisting of, bandits or men engaged in irregular warfare; carrying on irregular warfare.

guess (gĕs), *n.* a hasty or chance conclusion; an opinion formed without sufficient or real evidence; the act of forming such an opinion: *v.t.* to hit upon, or judge of, at random; colloquially, believe or think: *v.i.* to form an opinion without sound reason for it.

guess-work (gĕs'wûrk"), *n.* random opinion, formed without sufficient reason; work performed by a random method.

guest (gĕst), *n.* one who is entertained at the house or table of another; a visitor.

guf-faw (gŭ-fô'), *n.* a rude or loud burst of laughter.

guid-ance (gīd'ăns), *n.* direction; leading; supervision.

guide (gīd), *n.* one who leads or directs; conductor; director; a soldier or other person who obtains information for an army; that by which one directs his course; a guidebook: *v.t.* to lead or direct; influence; regulate; govern by counsel.—*adj.* guidable.

guide-board (gīd'bōrd"), *n.* a board usually placed where roads meet or cross, with directions for travelers; a guidepost.

guide-book (gīd'bŏŏk"), *n.* a book of directions and information for travelers and tourists.

guide-post (gīd'pōst"), *n.* a post which bears a board containing directions for travelers.

guide rope (gīd rōp), a rope hung from a balloon so as to trail for about half its length: used to preserve a uniform altitude.

gui-don (gī'dŭn), *n.* a small flag serving as standard for a single company of troops.

guild (gĭld), *n.* a fraternity; corporation; association. Also, gild.

guild-er (gĭl'dẽr), *n.* the Dutch florin or silver coin, value about 40.2 cents: called also *gulden.*

guild-hall (gĭld'hôl"), *n.* the meeting place of a guild or association.

guile (gīl), *n.* deceit; cunning; duplicity; fraud.—*adj.* guileful.—*adv.* guilefully.

guile-less (gīl'lĕs), *adj.* free from guile; artless; innocent; frank.—*adv.* guilelessly.—*n.* guilelessness.

guil-lo-tine (gĭl'ō-tēn), *n.* an apparatus for beheading a criminal by means of a heavy knife sliding in two upright grooves; a paper-cutting machine: *v.t.* (gĭl"lō-tēn'), to behead with a machine.

guilt (gĭlt), *n.* the state of one who has sinned, or who is liable to a penalty for crime.—*adj.* guiltless.

guilt-y (gĭl'tĭ), *adj.* [*comp.* guiltier, *superl.* guiltiest], justly chargeable with, or responsible for, a crime; wicked; criminal; not innocent; as, a *guilty* look, a *guilty* act, a *guilty* feeling.—*adv.* guiltily.—*n.* guiltiness.
Syn. culpable, sinful.
Ant. (see innocent).

guin-ea (gĭn'ĭ), *n.* a gold coin, formerly current in England, value twenty-one shillings or about five dollars; a guinea fowl.

guin-ea fowl (gĭn'ĭ foul), [*fem.* guinea hen], a grayish-blue bird with white spots, originally from Guinea.

guin-ea pig (gĭn'ĭ pĭg), a small tame South American animal, usually white with spots of orange and black.

guise (gīz), *n.* external appearance; dress; manner; garb.

gui-tar (gĭ-tär'), *n.* a six-stringed instrument, of the lute class, played with the fingers.

Guitar

gulch (gŭlch), *n.* in the western United States, a narrow rocky valley; a gully.

gulf (gŭlf), *n.* an arm of the sea extending into the land, larger in size than a bay; a deep place in the earth; an abyss; whirlpool; an impassable chasm.

Gulf Stream (gŭlf strēm), an important warm ocean current flowing out from the Gulf of Mexico and northward along the American coast.

gulf-weed (gŭlf'wēd"), *n.* a floating seaweed, with round air vessels, found in the South Atlantic.

gull (gŭl), *n.* a web-footed sea fowl with long wings; one who is easily cheated: *v.t.* to cheat; deceive; impose upon; outwit; as, to *gull* a woman of her jewels.

gul-let (gŭl'ĕt), *n.* the throat; esophagus, or tube by which food and drink are carried from the mouth to the stomach.

gul-li-ble (gŭl'ĭ-bl), *adj.* capable of being easily deceived.—*n.* gullibility.

gul-ly (gŭl'ĭ), *n.* [*pl.* gullies (-ĭz)], a channel worn by water; narrow ravine.

gulp (gŭlp), *v.t.* to swallow eagerly or in large drafts: *n.* the act of swallowing in large drafts; a large swallow.

gum (gŭm), *n.* the soft fleshy part of the jaws by which the teeth are surrounded; a semitransparent sticky vegetable substance that comes out of certain trees and shrubs and hardens on the surface; as, *gum* arabic; mucilage; India rubber; in the United States, a preparation of some cohesive substance used for chewing: *pl.* locally, in the United States, overshoes: *v.t.* [*p.t.* and *p.p.* gummed, *p.pr.* gumming], to smear or close with mucilage: *v.i.* to become stiff or sticky.

gum ar-a-bic (gŭm ăr'ȧ-bĭk), a gum obtained from various kinds of trees and shrubs; mucilage.

gum-bo (gŭm'bō), *n.* a soup made from the pods of the okra, a southern plant of the mallow family; also, the okra plant or its pods; prairie mud.

gum-drop (gŭm'drŏp"), *n.* a candy made of vegetable gum or gelatin.

gum-my (gŭm'ĭ), *adj.* like gum; covered or filled with a sticky substance; sticky.—*n.* gumminess.

gump-tion (gŭmp'shŭn), *n.* colloquially, quickness of perception; common sense; in the fine arts, the art of preparing colors.

gun (gŭn), *n.* a weapon for discharging shot by the force of an explosive: *v.i.* to shoot with such a weapon.

gun-boat (gŭn'bōt"), *n.* a warship of light draft, next in size to a cruiser, carrying several heavy guns.

gun-cot-ton (gŭn'kŏt"n), *n.* a highly explosive substance formed by the action of nitric and sulphuric acid upon cotton, or some other vegetable fiber.

gun fire (gŭn fīr), the firing of a gun; the hour at which the morning and evening gun is fired.

gun-lock (gŭn'lŏk"), *n.* the mechanism of a gun by which, in some firearms, the charge is exploded.

gun met-al (gŭn mĕt'ăl), a mixture of copper and tin.

gun-nel (gŭn'ĕl), *n.* the upper edge of the side of a ship or vessel. Also, gunwale.

gun-ner (gŭn'ẽr), *n.* one who works a gun; an artilleryman; an officer in the navy who has charge of the ordnance or military supplies.

gun-ner-y (gŭn'ẽr-ĭ), *n.* the science of artillery, or the making and using of weapons of warfare.

gun-ning (gŭn'ĭng), *n.* the shooting of game, especially small game, with a gun.

gun-ny (gŭn'ĭ), *n.* [*pl.* gunnies (-ĭz)], a coarse sackcloth of jute or hemp.

gun pit (gŭn pĭt), an excavation for artillery to conceal it from enemy observation and fire.

gun plat-form (gŭn plăt'fôrm), a strong flooring for a cannon in action.

gun-pow-der (gŭn'pou"dẽr), *n.* an explosive substance composed of sulphur, niter, and charcoal; a fine kind of green tea.

gun-shot (gŭn'shŏt"), *n.* the range of a gun: *adj.* made by a gun; as, a *gunshot* wound.

gun-smith (gŭn'smĭth"), *n.* an armorer; one whose business it is to repair firearms.

Gun-ter's chain (gŭn'tẽrz chān), a surveyor's chain used in measuring land, 66 ft. long, and divided in 100 links of 7.92 in. each.

Gun-ter's scale (gŭn'tẽrz skāl), a large plane scale, with various lines of numbers engraved upon it, by means of which surveyors' and navigators' calculations are determined.

gun-wale (gŭn'ĕl), *n.* the upper edge of the side of a ship or vessel. Also, **gunnel**.

gur-gle (gûr'gl), *n.* a broken, bubbling noise: *v.i.* to flow or run with a murmuring, bubbling sound.

gush (gŭsh), *n.* a sudden and violent flow of a liquid from an inclosed space; outburst; colloquially, a very great display of sentiment: *v.i.* to issue with violence and rapidity; flow abundantly; colloquially, to display affection and enthusiasm in a silly, demonstrative manner.

gush-er (gŭsh'ẽr), *n.* one who makes a display of sentiment; that which pours forth violently; an oil well that discharges its contents without the aid of machinery.

gus-set (gŭs'ĕt), *n.* a small three-cornered piece of cloth inserted in a garment to strengthen or enlarge a part.

gust (gŭst), *n.* a sudden and violent windstorm, often accompanied with rain or snow; a violent outburst of passion.

gus-ta-to-ry (gŭs'tȧ-tō-rĭ), *adj.* pertaining to the sense of taste.

gus-to (gŭs'tō), *n.* zest; relish; fancy; as, to play with great *gusto*.

gust-y (gŭs'tĭ), *adj.* characterized by sudden blasts of wind; windy; stormy.—*adv.* **gustily**.

gut (gŭt), *n.* the intestinal canal; an intestine; catgut; a narrow channel or strait: *v.t.* [*p.t.* and *p.p.* gutted, *p.pr.* gutting], to extract the entrails of; to plunder, or empty entirely; destroy the inside of.

gut-ta-per-cha (gŭt"ȧ-pûr'chȧ), *n.* a substance similar to rubber, made of the thickened juice of a tree of the Malay Archipelago; the tree which gives the juice.

gut-ter (gŭt'ẽr), *n.* a channel for carrying away water: *v.t.* to cut into small channels; furnish with narrow channels for carrying off water: *v.i.* to divide into channels.

gut-ter-ing (gŭt'ẽr-ĭng), *n.* a making into hollows; the act of falling in drops; material for making narrow channels to carry off water.

gut-tur-al (gŭt'ûr-ăl), *adj.* pertaining to, or formed in, the throat: *n.* a letter sounded from the throat; as, *g* is a *guttural*.—*adv.* **gutturally**.

guy (gī), *n.* a rope, chain, etc., to swing and keep steady a heavy body; colloquially, a person of queer looks or dress: *v.t.* to steady or guide with a rope or chain; colloquially, to ridicule.

guz-zle (gŭz'l), *v.t.* and *v.i.* to drink greedily and to excess.—*n.* **guzzler**.

gym-na-si-um (jĭm-nā'zĭ-ŭm), *n.* [*pl.* gymnasia (-ȧ)], a building where athletic exercises are practiced; in Europe, especially in Germany, a secondary or preparatory school; in ancient Greece, a place for athletic exercises, provided with baths, etc.; also, in connection with it, apartments in which learned discussions were carried on.

gym-nast (jĭm'năst), *n.* one who practices, or is expert in, physical exercises.

gym-nas-tics (jĭm-năs'tĭks), *n.pl.* athletic exercises; the art of developing the physical powers by athletic exercises.—*adj.* **gymnastic**.

gyn-e-col-o-gy (jĭn"ē-kŏl'ō-jĭ; jī"nē-kŏl'ō-jĭ), *n.* that branch of medical science which treats of the diseases of women. Also, **gynæcology**.

gyp-sum (jĭp'sŭm), *n.* sulphate of lime, used for plaster of Paris.

Gyroscope

Gyp-sy (jĭp'sĭ), *n.* one of a race of wanderers; the language of Gipsies: called also *Romany*. Also, **Gipsy**.

gy-ral (jī'răl), *adj.* rotary; moving in a whirling path or way.

gy-rate (jī'rāt), *v.i.* to move round a central point; rotate; wheel.—*n.* **gyration**.

gy-ra-to-ry (jī'rȧ-tō-rĭ), *adj.* moving in a circle; revolving; whirling.

gy-ro-scope (jī'rō-skōp), *n.* an instrument consisting of a heavy-rimmed flywheel mounted in a ring so as to move freely in one or more directions, be acted upon by varying forces, and thus demonstrate the laws of rotary bodies, etc.

gy-ro-scope rail-way (jī"rō-skōp rāl'wā'), a single-rail railway upon which each car, called a *gyro-car*, is kept erect by the rotary force of two gyroscopes in rapid opposite motion.

gyve (jīv), *n.* a chain for the legs; a shackle: *v.t.* to fetter; to chain; to shackle.

H

ha (hä), *interj.* an expression of wonder, joy, hesitation, etc.: *v.i.* to express wonder, etc.; hesitate; as, to hem and *ha*.

Ha-bak-kuk (hȧ-băk′ŭk), *n.* a book of the Old Testament; the Hebrew prophet whose prayers are recorded in the book.

ha-be-as cor-pus (hā′bē-ăs kôr′pŭs), you may have the body; a writ or order to produce a prisoner at a stated time to determine the justice of his detention. [LAT.]

hab-er-dash-er (hăb′ẽr-dăsh′ẽr), *n.* a dealer in small wares, as ribbons, lace, tapes, needles, etc.; in the United States, usually one who deals in men's furnishings.

hab-er-dash-er-y (hăb′ẽr-dăsh′ẽr-ĭ), *n.* the wares sold by a dealer in small wares; men's furnishings; a shop where such goods are sold.

hab-er-geon (hăb′ẽr-jŭn; hȧ-bûr′jŭn), *n.* a coat of metal covering the neck and breast.

ha-bil-i-ment (hȧ-bĭl′ĭ-mĕnt), *n.* an article of clothing; a garment: *pl.* dress, in general.

hab-it (hăb′ĭt), *n.* the ordinary course of conduct; general condition or tendency; disposition; established custom; dress; a woman's riding dress; the distinctive dress worn by members of a religious order: *v.t.* to dress; furnish with a garb.
Syn. n. custom, practice.

hab-it-a-ble (hăb′ĭt-ȧ-bl), *adj.* fit to live in comfortably.

hab-i-tant (hăb′ĭ-tănt), *n.* a dweller; permanent resident; a farmer of French descent, in Canada and Louisiana.

hab-i-tat (hăb′ĭ-tăt), *n.* the natural locality of animals, plants, etc., in their wild state; geographical range.

hab-i-ta-tion (hăb′ĭ-tā′shŭn), *n.* residence or place of abode; occupancy.

hab-it-ed (hăb′ĭt-ĕd), *p.adj.* wearing a garb or dress; as, the Carmelite nuns are *habited* in white.

ha-bit-u-al (hȧ-bĭt′ū-ăl), *adj.* formed or acquired by use; customary; of long standing; as, he is an *habitual* coffee drinker.

ha-bit-u-al-ly (hȧ-bĭt′ū-ăl-ĭ), *adv.* by custom; as, she *habitually* makes calls on Sunday.

ha-bit-u-ate (hȧ-bĭt′ū-āt), *v.t.* to make familiar by use or custom; familiarize.

hab-i-tude (hăb′ĭ-tūd), *n.* customary manner or mode; familiarity; as, one who mingles with good company will acquire the *habitude* of correct speech.

ha-bit-u-é (hȧ-bĭt′ū-ā′; FR. ȧ′bē′tü-ā′), *n.* one who frequently visits a place, as a saloon or place of amusement.

ha-cien-da (ä-thē-ĕn′dä; hä′sĭ-ĕn′dȧ), *n.* in Spanish-America, a large plantation or ranch on which the owner resides; an isolated farm; an establishment for raising stock, farm produce, etc.

hack (hăk), *v.t.* to cut irregularly and into small pieces; injure by cutting; notch; kick (the shins of another), at football; let out for hire: *n.* a notch; hollow irregular cut; a horse, or a carriage, let out for hire; a kick on the shins at football; a literary drudge; a drying frame for fish; a place where bricks are dried; a feeding rack.

hack-ee (hăk′ē), *n.* the chipmunk or ground squirrel. Also, **hacky**.

hack-ing (hăk′ĭng), *adj.* cutting irregularly; irritating and wearing: said of a cough; as, the child has a *hacking* cough: *n.* the stacking of bricks for drying; a particular method of massage; a process in gem cutting.

hack-le (hăk′l), *v.t.* to dress or comb, as flax or hemp; tear into pieces; mangle in cutting: *n.* an implement with sharp spikes for cleansing flax or hemp; a long narrow feather in the neck of a cock, used for making artificial flies for angling; a feather fly for angling. Also, **hatchel, heckle**.

hack-ney (hăk′nĭ), *v.t.* [*p.t.* and *p.p.* hackneyed, *p.pr.* hackneying], to wear out by constant use; make commonplace: *adj.* let out for hire; common or trite: *n.* a coach, or a horse, kept for hire; a nag.

hack-ney coach (hăk′nĭ kōch), a licensed carriage.

hack-neyed (hăk′nĭd), *p.adj.* worn out; commonplace.

had (hăd), *p.t.* of *have*. Also used as auxiliary in the past perfect tense.

had-dock (hăd′ŭk), *n.* a sea fish of the cod family found in the North Atlantic.

Ha-des (hā′dēz), *n.* the abode and state of the dead; the invisible world; in Greek mythology, the god of the underworld; the place of departed spirits.—*adj.* **Hadean**.

hæ-mo-glo-bin (hē′mō-glō′bĭn), *n.* the normal coloring matter of the red blood. Also, **hemoglobin**.

hæm-or-rhage (hĕm′ō-rāj), *n.* any discharge of blood from the blood vessels. Also, **hemorrhage**.

hæm-or-rhoids (hĕm′ō-roidz), *n.pl.* a painful swelling; piles. Also, **hemorrhoids**.

haft (hȧft), *n.* a handle of a tool or knife: *v.t.* to furnish with a handle.

hag (hăg), *n.* a witch; an ugly old woman; an eel-like fish that eats other fish.

Hag-ga-i (hăg′ā-ī), *n.* a Hebrew prophet who lived about 500 B. C.; the book of the Old Testament in which his words are recorded.

hag-gard (hăg′ȧrd), *adj.* worn and anxious in appearance; lean and hollow-eyed.

hag-gis (hăg′ĭs), *n.* a Scotch dish made of chopped and highly seasoned mutton.

hag-gle (hăg′l), *v.t.* to cut roughly or hack; to cut into small pieces; to notch or cut in a rough way: *v.i.* to dispute about trifles; to higgle: *n.* the act or process of hacking; a dispute about a trifle.

ha-ha (hä-hä′), *n.* a hedge, fence, or wall which does not obstruct the view; a sunken fence.

hail (hāl), *n.* frozen raindrops; a call or salutation: *v.i.* to pour down hail: *v.t.* to pour down or out like hail; to call; to come: with *from*; as, the ship *hails* from England; I *hail* from the west; call to or salute: *interj.* an exclamation of respectful and friendly greeting; as, *Hail*, my friend, I am glad to see you.

Syn. *v.* accost, address, greet, welcome.

hail-stone (hāl′stōn″), *n.* a pellet of ice from the clouds.

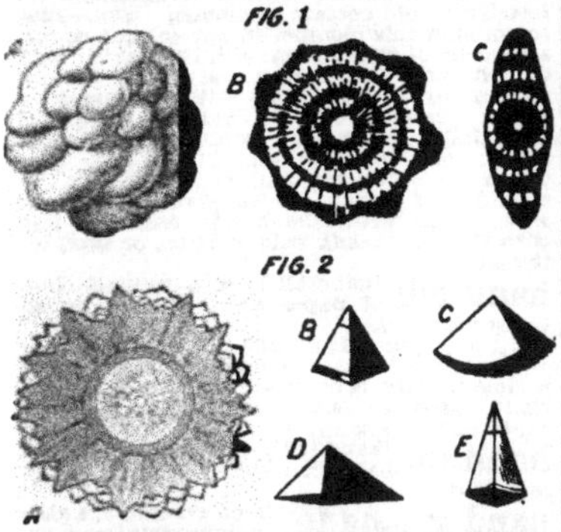

Forms of Hailstones. Fig. 1, *A*, large hailstone weighing 300 grains; *B*, *C*, sections of hailstones. Fig. 2, *A*, section of hailstone with pyramids on surface; *B*, *C*, *D*, *E*, fragments of same.

hair (hâr), *n.* one of the small filaments growing out of the skin of any animal; the mass of such threadlike growth; minute fibers on the surface of plants.—*adj.* **hairy.**

hair-breadth (hâr′brĕdth″), *n.* a very short distance: *adj.* very narrow. Also, **hair's breadth.**

hair-cloth (hâr′klŏth″), *n.* goods made of camel's hair or horsehair; used to cover furniture, etc.

hair-pin (hâr′pĭn″), *n.* a pin of wire or bone, with two points, used to fasten the hair.

hair-split-ting (hâr′splĭt″ĭng), *adj.* making trivial or very small distinctions, in reasoning or statement.

hair-spring (hâr′spring″), *n.* a very fine spring to regulate the balance wheel of a watch.

hair trig-ger (hâr trĭg′ẽr), a trigger of a gun so adjusted that very slight pressure discharges the weapon.

hake (hāk), *n.* an eatable sea fish like the cod, valued for its food and its oil.

hal-berd (hăl′bẽrd), *n.* an ancient weapon consisting of a long staff to which an ax with a broad, sharp blade and a spearlike point was fastened. Also, **halbert.**

hal-berd-ier (hăl″bẽr-dēr′), *n.* a foot soldier armed with a spear-like ax.

hal-cy-on (hăl′sĭ-ŭn), *adj.* pertaining to the kingfisher family of birds; peaceful; happy; calm: *n.* the kingfisher: so called because of the fable that its hatching season was in calm weather.

Halberdier

hale (hāl), *adj.* sound in body; healthy; hearty: *v.t.* to drag or draw by violence.

half (häf), *n.* [*pl.* halves (hävz)], one of two equal parts; a school term; in football, a half back: *adv.* equally; partly: *adj.* consisting of a half; partial; incomplete.

half back (häf băk), in football, a player occupying a position on the right or left side of the field, between the quarter back and full back.

half blood (häf blŭd), one whose parents are of different races; relationship between persons who have only one parent in common.

half-breed (häf′brēd″), *n.* a person of mixed blood; as, an Indian *half-breed.*

half broth-er (häf brŭth′ẽr), a brother by one parent only.

half-caste (häf′kȧst″), *n.* a person of an East Indian parent on one side and of a European on the other.

half crown (häf kroun), a silver coin, valued at two shillings and six pence, or 60 cents. [Eng.]

half-heart-ed (häf′härt″ĕd), *adj.* lacking in interest; not enthusiastic.

half-mast (häf′mȧst″), *n.* position of a flag midway of the staff, as an indication of death or distress.

half-moon (häf′mōōn″), *n.* the moon when half its disk gives light.

half-pen-ny (hā′pĕn-ĭ; häf′pĕn″ĭ), *n.* an English coin equivalent to one cent in United States money.

half sis-ter (häf sĭs′tẽr), a sister by one parent only.

half-tone (häf′tōn″), *n.* a photographic process of making plates for illustration; a picture made by this process.

half-wit-ted (häf′wĭt″ĕd), *adj.* mentally lacking.

hal-i-but (hăl′ĭ-bŭt; hŏl′ĭ-bŭt), *n.* a large eatable flat fish, often weighing more than three hundred pounds; an important food fish. Also, **holibut.**

hal-i-dom (hăl′ĭ-dŭm), *n.* holiness; a holy relic; something sacred; a holy place.

hall (hôl), *n.* a large building or room for the transaction of public business, entertainments, etc.; a court of justice; the passageway into a house; a college dining room; the dinner served there; a college in an English university; at Oxford, an unendowed college; in early times, the main living room of a castle; a vestibule, entrance room, etc., in a modern home.

hal-le-lu-jah (hăl″ē-lōō′yȧ), *n.* (Hebrew, Praise ye Jehovah), an exclamation or song of praise to God; a musical composition having as its theme similar words of praise: *adj.* singing, or containing, such praises. Also, **alleluia, alleluiah, halleluiah.**

hal-liard (hăl′yẽrd), *n.* a rope for hoisting a flag or sail. Also, **halyard.**

hall-mark (hôl′märk″), *n.* the official mark of the Goldsmiths' Company and other English assay offices, attesting the quality of the gold and silver articles on which it is impressed; hence, a mark or proof of genuineness or purity.

hal-loo (hă-lōō′), *interj.* and *n.* an exclamation to call attention to or cheer one; a shout to attract attention, or to cheer or urge on: *v.t.* to shout out; incite or cheer on, as dogs: *v.i.* to cry out loudly. Also, **halloa, hallo, hello, hollos, hullo.**

hal-low (hăl'ō), *v.t.* to consecrate; to make holy; to set apart for holy or religious use; devote to sacred purposes; revere.

Hal-low-e'en (hăl"ō-ēn'), *n.* the eve of All Saints or All Hallows, October 31. Also, **Hallowe'en.**

hal-lu-ci-na-tion (hă-lū"sĭ-nā'shŭn), *n.* belief in something imaginary; a delusion; something apparent, but not real, as the visions seen in a delirium.

ha-lo (hā'lō), *n.* a ring or circle of light around the sun or moon, caused by refraction; a glory; the bright ring represented in pictures as surrounding the heads of saints and other holy persons.

halt (hôlt), *n.* the act of limping; a stop in marching or in progress: *adj.* crippled or lame: *v.i.* to limp; to come to a stop; to stand still; to hesitate; to stop in marching: *v.t.* to cause to stop.

hal-ter (hôl'tẽr), *n.* one who limps; one who stops in marching; a rope for hanging criminals; a rope for leading or holding a horse: *v.t.* to put on, or secure with, a rope of this kind.

halve (häv), *v.t.* to divide into two equal parts, as an apple; fasten together, as timbers.

halves (hävz), *n.* plural of *half;* as, two *halves* make a whole.

hal-yard (hăl'yẽrd), *n.* a rope or tackle for hoisting a sail, flag, etc. Also, **halliard.**

ham (hăm), *n.* the hinder part of the thigh; a thigh of an animal, especially a pig, salted and smoked; a house; village: in place names of Anglo-Saxon origin, as Totten*ham*.

Ham-burg (hăm'bûrg), *n.* a rich kind of black grape; a breed of black domestic fowl; a kind of machine-made embroidery.

hame (hām), *n.* one of the curved bars on the collar to which the traces of a horse's harness are fastened.

ham-let (hăm'lĕt), *n.* a small village; as, a peaceful *hamlet* in the hills.

ham-mer (hăm'ẽr), *n.* an instrument with a handle and iron head, used for driving nails, beating metals, etc.; anything resembling this tool in its action or shape: *v.t.* to pound or beat with a heavy implement; to drive, as a nail, into place by pounding; to work out in the mind: *v.i.* to work hard.

ham-mer-cloth (hăm'ẽr-klŏth), *n.* the cloth which covers a coach box; canopy.

ham-mock (hăm'ŭk), *n.* a swinging bed, usually of network or canvas.

Hammock

ham-per (hăm'pẽr), *n.* a large wickerwork basket for carrying food, etc.; the rigging of a ship: *v.t.* to put into or inclose in a large basket; embarrass; perplex; impede.

ham-shack-le (hăm'shăk"l), *v.t.* to fasten the head of an animal to one of its forelegs by a rope or strap; as, to *hamshackle* a horse.

ham-string (hăm'strĭng"), *v.t.* [*p.t.* and *p.p.* hamstrung, *p.pr.* hamstringing], to lame (a horse) by cutting the muscles or tendons of the hinder part of the thigh: *n.pl.* the strong muscles or sinews at the back of the knee.

hand (hănd), *n.* the divided and lower part of the human arm connected with the wrist; a similar member terminating the fore-limb of certain animals; something resembling this member in appearance or use; a measure of four inches; ability or skill; right or left side; possession; style of writing; an employee who labors with his hands; a sailor; cards held; a game; pledge of betrothal; nearness; control; authority; agency of; index of any kind; turn of a player to serve the ball at tennis, etc.; a shoulder of pork: *v.t.* to give or transmit with, or as with, the hand; assist or lead with the hand: *adj.* belonging to, or used by, the hand.

hand-bill (hănd'bĭl"), *n.* a printed sheet of paper displayed for advertising purposes.

hand-cuff (hănd'kŭf"), *n.* a manacle or fetter confining the wrists; a ring usually connected with another by a chain, used to fasten the wrists together: *v.t.* to put fetters on.

hand-ful (hănd'fo͝ol), *n.* as much as a hand can hold; all that can be managed.

hand gre-nade (hănd grē-nād'), a glass bottle containing chemicals for putting out a fire; an explosive shell to be thrown by the hand in battle.

hand-i-cap (hăn'dĭ-kăp), *n.* an extra weight or distance imposed on a superior contestant in a race; a hindrance; as, the young man's inability to speak well was a distinct *handicap:* *v.t.* to hinder or retard; as, his inability to speak well *handicapped* him.

hand-i-craft (hăn'dĭ-krȧft), *n.* the work or skill of a craftsman or mechanic; manual skill, or labor.

hand-i-ly (hăn'dĭ-lĭ), *adv.* in a deft manner; skilfully; as, he used his tool *handily.*

hand-i-ness (hăn'dĭ-nĕs), *n.* the state or quality of being skilful.

hand-i-work (hăn'dĭ-wûrk"), *n.* work done or produced by manual effort; anything done personally; as, are these conditions I find the result of your own *handiwork?*

hand-ker-chief (hăn'kẽr-chĭf), *n.* a piece of cloth, usually square, for wiping the face, nose, etc.; a silk or cotton square for the neck.

han-dle (hăn'dl), *n.* that part of a tool, vessel, etc., grasped by the hand; an instrument to gain an end: *v.t.* to touch or feel with the hand; manage; manipulate; discourse on; act toward or treat; buy, sell, or invest in: *v.i.* to use the hands.

hand-maid (hănd'mād"), *n.* a female servant or attendant. Also, **handmaiden.**

hand or-gan (hănd ôr'găn), a sort of large music box, arranged to be wheeled through the streets, from which music is produced by the turning of a crank.

hand screw (hănd skro͞o), a device for lifting heavy articles; a clamp used by carpenters.

hand-sel (hănd'sĕl; hăn'sĕl), *n.* a pledge given to make good a contract; anything that is used, given, or delivered for the first time; a gift, especially at the

āte, senāte, râre, căt, locȧl, fär, ȧsk, pȧrade; scēne, ēvent, ĕdge, novĕl, refẽr; rīght, sĭn; cōld, ōbey, côrd, stŏp, cŏmpare; ūnit, ūnite, bûrn, cŭt, focŭs, menü;

time of the New Year, to children, servants, etc., on *Handsel* Monday: *v.t.* to give a pledge to; use or do for the first time. Also, **hansel**.

hand-some (hăn'sŭm), *adj.* pleasing to look upon; well formed; elegantly dressed; graceful; liberal; generous; ample.—*adv.* **handsomely**.—*n.* **handsomeness**.

hand-spike (hănd'spīk"), *n.* a wooden lever for moving heavy weights, heaving, etc.

hand-writ-ing (hănd'rīt-ĭng), *n.* the style of penmanship peculiar to a person.

hand-y (hăn'dĭ), *adj.* [*comp.* handier, *superl.* handiest], dexterous; skilful; convenient; close beside; manageable.

hang (hăng), *v.t.* [*p.t.* and *p.p.* hung, hanged, *p.pr.* hanging], to suspend, to fasten to something so as to be movable; suspend by the neck; cause to droop; display; show aloft; attach or fasten; furnish with ornaments or drapery suspended or fastened to the walls, etc.; catch fast: *v.i.* to be suspended; bend forward; be dependent upon; dangle; cling; be in a deadlock: *n.* manner in which something hangs; method of hanging; manner of doing or using; general tendency; slope.

han-gar (hăn'gär"), *n.* a shed for storing airplanes or vehicles.

hang-dog (hăng'dŏg), *adj.* of degraded, ashamed, or sneaking appearance.

hang-er (hăng'ẽr), *n.* one who, or that which, hangs; that by which something is hung, or suspended; a kind of cutlass, or short curved sword.

hang-ing (hăng'ĭng), *p.adj.* suspended or dangling; suggesting or involving death as a criminal: *n.* the act of putting to death by hanging: *pl.* drapery for a room.

hang-man (hăng'măn), *n.* [*pl.* hangmen (-mĕn)], a public officer who executes convicted criminals.

hang-nail (hăng'nāl"), *n.* a small piece of skin growing from the root of a finger nail.

hank (hănk), *n.* two or more skeins of thread, silk, wool, etc., fastened together; one of the wooden rings to which a fore-and-aft sail is bent; a withy or rope for fastening a gate: *v.t.* to form into hanks.

hank-er (hăn'kẽr), *v.i.* to desire eagerly: with *after;* crave; as, to *hanker* after pleasure.

han-ky-pan-ky (hăn'kĭ-păn'kĭ), *n.* jugglery; the chatter of fak·rs to divert attention from their tricks: *adj.* tricky; cheating.

Han-se-at-ic (hăn'sē-ăt'ĭk), *adj.* pertaining to the Hanse towns, or free German cities, on the Baltic and North Seas: used of the league formed by these towns to protect their trade.

han-som (hăn'sŭm), *n.* a two-wheeled cab: named after its inventor.

hap (hăp), *v.t.* [*p.t.* and *p.p.* happed, *p.pr.* happing], to happen; befall casually; *v.t.* [Scot.], cover or wrap: *n.* chance; a casual event; [Scot.], a cloak or wrapper.

hap-haz-ard (hăp'hăz"ẽrd), *n.* chance; accident; random: *adv.* by chance: *adj.* accidental.

hap-less (hăp'lĕs), *adj.* unfortunate; unlucky; unhappy; as, a *hapless* fate; the *hapless* Juliet.

hap-ly (hăp'lĭ), *adv.* by chance, luck, or accident; perhaps; perchance.

hap-pen (hăp'n), *v.i.* to come by chance; occur; take place; come to pass.

hap-pi-ly (hăp'ĭ-lĭ), *adv.* successfully; by good fortune; luckily; in a contented manner or state.

hap-pi-ness (hăp'ĭ-nĕs), *n.* the state of being satisfied or glad; good fortune; good luck; prosperity; contentment.

Syn. joyfulness, bliss, felicity.

Ant. (see unhappiness).

hap-py (hăp'ĭ), *adj.* [*comp.* happier, *superl.* happiest], enjoying pleasure or good; successful; prosperous; lucky; living in concord; satisfied; favored by luck or fortune; enjoying peace of any kind.

ha-ra-ki-ri (hä'rä-kē'rē), *n.* formerly, in Japan, a method of suicide by ripping open the bowels, permitted to nobles and military officers so as to escape the indignity of a public execution or official disgrace. Also, **harikari**.

ha-rangue (hȧ-răng'), *n.* a public address or speech or oration, especially without preparation; a noisy or pompous speech; ranting: *v.i.* to deliver a loud, ranting speech: *v.t.* to address by a noisy speech.

har-ass (hăr'ăs), *v.t.* to annoy or vex; fatigue or weary with labor or importunity; to tire out and annoy (an enemy) by incessant petty attacks; to worry; tease; disturb; torment; as, the merchant is *harassed* by many cares.

har-ass-er (hăr'ăs-ẽr), *n.* one who, or that which, vexes or plagues.

har-ass-ing (hăr'ăs-ĭng), *p.adj.* fatiguing; annoying; as, he fled from the *harassing* details of business.

har-ass-ment (hăr'ăs-mĕnt), *n.* the act of annoying; the state of being worried; worry; anxiety.

har-bin-ger (hăr'bĭn-jẽr), *n.* a messenger; forerunner; as, the bluebird is the *harbinger* of spring: *v.t.* to announce; foretell; usher in.

har-bor (hăr'bẽr), *n.* a port or haven for ships; any place of refuge or safety; formerly, an inn or lodging: *v.t.* to shelter or protect; cherish; indulge; as, to *harbor* resentment. Also, **harbour**.

Syn. n. haven, port, refuge.

har-bor-age (hăr'bẽr-āj), *n.* a port or anchorage for ships; shelter.

hard (härd), *adj.* compact and solid; firm; not easy to be pierced or broken; as, *hard* wood; unyielding; difficult of accomplishment; as, *hard* to understand; laborious; fatiguing; cruel; oppressive; severe; keen; austere; inflexible; unfeeling; exacting; not easily complied with; rough; coarse; not prosperous; uttered gutturally; stiff or formal: *adv.* forcibly; laboriously; diligently; tempestuously; closely; near; roughly; to the utmost extent; so as to become firm and unyielding; with vexation, trouble, or sorrow: *n.* a roadway of solid material by the sea; a pier or landing place: *pl.* the refuse of flax or wool; alum and salt mixed together, used for giving a white color to bread.

Syn. adj. firm, solid, arduous, difficult.

Ant. (see easy, soft).

hard-en (här'dn), *v.t.* to make firm or solid; confirm in impudence or wickedness; toughen; accustom: *v.i.* to become firm or solid; to become impudent or indifferent.—*adj.* **hardened**.

hard-i-hood (här'dĭ-ho͝od), *n.* impudence; boldness; physical endurance; bravery; pluck; resolution.

har-di-ly (här'dĭ-lĭ), *adv.* with endurance; boldly; stoutly; resolutely.

har-di-ness (här'dĭ-nĕs), *n.* capacity for endurance; ability to survive wintry weather.

hard la-bor (härd lā'bẽr), work imposed as an additional punishment to a term of imprisonment.

hard-ly (härd'lĭ), *adv.* with difficulty; scarcely; vigorously; severely; coarsely; unfavorably.

hard-ness (härd'nĕs), *n.* the quality of being firm and unyielding, literally or figuratively; as, *hardness* of rock; *hardness* of heart.

hard-pan (härd'păn"), *n.* in mining, a bed or layer of gravel or sand; a solid foundation.

hard-ship (härd'shĭp), *n.* oppression; severe labor or want; injustice.

hard-tack (härd'tăk"), *n.* a large solid cracker or biscuit baked for army and navy use.

hard-ware (härd'wâr"), *n.* manufactured articles of metal, as cutlery, kitchen utensils, chains, hatchets, etc.

hard wood (härd wŏŏd), the wood from broad-leaved trees; any dense, heavy wood.

har-dy (här'dĭ), *adj.* robust; capable of bearing hardship; bold; able to survive wintry weather: used of plants: *n.* a blacksmith's chisel with a square shank to fit into an anvil: sometimes called a *fuller*.

har-dy hole (här'dĭ hōl), a square hole in an anvil into which a hardy or chisel may be set.

hare (hâr), *n.* a small animal with long ears and a short tail, larger than a rabbit, characterized by its great timidity.

hare-bell (hâr'bĕl"), *n.* a small, slender, branching plant, having blue bell-shaped flowers.

hare-brained (hâr'brānd"), *adj.* wild; giddy; heedless; as, a *harebrained* girl.

hare-foot (hâr'fŏŏt"), *n.* a long narrow foot; a fast runner.

hare-hound (hâr'hound"), *n.* a small breed of dogs, used for hunting hares or rabbits.

hare-lip (hâr'lĭp"), *n.* a deformity of the upper lip, which is divided in the middle.

ha-rem (hā'rĕm), *n.* the apartments of the women and children in a Mohammedan house; the wives of a Mohammedan. Also, **hareem, haram.**

hare's-foot (hârz'fŏŏt"), *n.* a kind of fern; a kind of clover with soft silky heads; the foot of a hare or rabbit used by actors in making up.

hare's-tail (hârz'tāl"), *n.* a kind of cotton-grass related to, or like, the bulrushes.

har-i-cot (här'ĭ-kō; hăr'ĭ-kŏt), *n.* a kind of stew of meat and vegetables; the kidney bean.

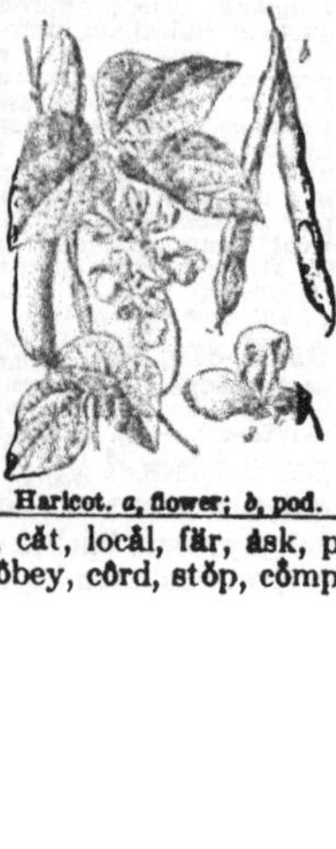

Haricot. *a*, flower; *b*, pod.

hark (härk), *v.i.* to listen: oftenest used in exclamation; as, *Hark!* listen.

hark-en (härk'n), *v.t.* to hear by listening; to attend or give heed to: *v.i.* to listen, or heed what is said; as, *harken* to me. Also, **hearken.**

Har-le-quin (här'lē-kwĭn; här'lē-kĭn), *n.* the performer in a pantomime who wears party-colored, spangled garments: **harlequin,** *n.* a buffoon: *adj.* fantastic or full of trickery; party-colored: *v.i.* to make fun by playing tricks.

har-lot (här'lŏt), *n.* a woman of bad character or ill-repute.

harm (härm), *n.* injury; damage; moral evil or wrongdoing: *v.t.* to inflict hurt, damage, or injury upon.

Syn. *n.* hurt, wrong, infliction.

Ant. (see benefit).

harm-ful (härm'fŏŏl), *adj.* hurtful; injurious; mischievous.—*adv.* **harmfully.**—*n.* **harmfulness.**

harm-less (härm'lĕs), *adj.* free from damage; not injurious; as, a *harmless* drug; innocent; without hurt; as, to escape *harmless.*

har-mon-ic (här-mŏn'ĭk), *adj.* pertaining to, or producing, a right concord of sound; musical; concordant; pleasing to the ear. Also, **harmonical.**—*adv.* **harmonically.**

har-mon-i-ca (här-mŏn'ĭ-kȧ), *n.* a musical instrument, the tones of which are produced by friction from a number of musical glasses filled to various heights with water; a mouth organ; an oblong musical instrument consisting of a number of glass slips which are struck by a mallet. Also, **harmonicon.**

har-mon-ics (här-mŏn'ĭks), *n.pl.* the science of musical sounds.

har-mo-ni-ous (här-mō'nĭ-ŭs), *adj.* concordant; musical; symmetrical; adapted to each other; agreeing in action and feeling; living in friendship.—*adv.* **harmoniously.**

har-mo-nist (här'mō-nĭst), *n.* one who is expert in musical science; one who explains the harmony of the Scriptures, especially of the Gospels.

Harmonium

har-mo-ni-um (här-mō'nĭ-ŭm), *n.* a reed organ, or small organ for church music.

har-mo-nize (här'mō-nīz), *v.t.* to render in accord; cause to agree; reconcile; *v.i.* to agree; be in peace and friendship; correspond.

har-mo-ny (här'mō-nĭ), *n.* [*pl.* harmonies (-nĭz)], the quality of being pleasing to the ear, as in singing or speaking; concord; just adaptation of parts to one another, so as to form a connected whole; accord in feeling, sentiment, etc.; as, I never saw more perfect *harmony* in any home; a literary work showing the agreement between parallel or similar histories or passages.

Syn. accord, unison, agreement, union.

Ant. (see discord).

har-ness (här'nĕs), *n.* the working gear of a horse; the dress and armor of a knight; any arrangement, as of straps, etc., for performing some mechanical operation: *v.t.* to put harness upon; equip, as a knight.

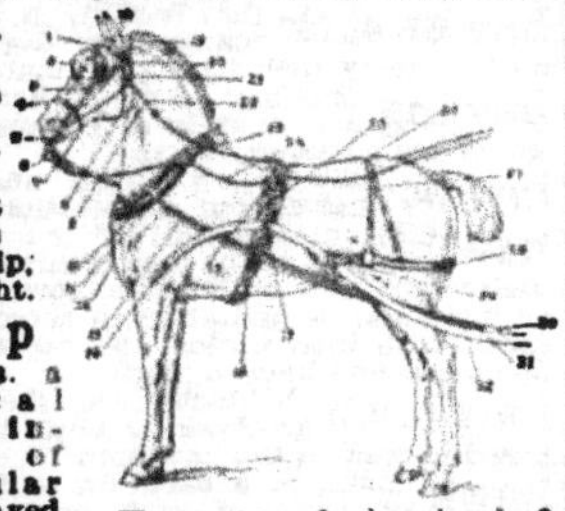

Harness. 1, browband; 2, blinders; 3, cheek piece; 4, noseband; 5, bit; 6, curb; 7, curb strap; 8, throatlatch; 9, checkrein; 10, collar; 11, collar pad; 12, martingale; 13, trace; 14, shaft; 15, saddle; 16, girth; 17, shaft ring; 18, bridle; 19, headstall; 20, cockade; 21, cheek ring; 22, checkrein buckle; 23, hames; 24, rein; 25, girth; 26, hip strap; 27, fork; 28, breeching; 29, breeching strap; 30, trace buckle; 31, shaft; 32, trace.

harp (härp), *n.* a musical stringed instrument of triangular shape, played with the fingers: *v.i.* to play on such an instrument; dwell unduly, tediously, or persistently on some particular subject: with *on* or *upon*.

harp-ing (här'pĭng), *p.pr.* of *harp*: *n.* the act of playing upon a harp: *pl.* the breadth of a ship at the bow.

har-poon (här-pōōn'), *n.* a long spear having a line attached to the staff, for striking and killing whales: *v.t.* to strike with a harpoon.

Harpoon

harp-si-chord (härp'sĭ-kôrd), *n.* a stringed instrument with a keyboard, in general use before the advent of the piano.

Har-py (här'pĭ), *n.* [*pl.* harpies (-pĭz)], in classical mythology, one of three grasping and filthy winged monsters with a woman's face, and the body and claws of a vulture: harpy, an extortioner; a large crested American eagle.

har-que-bus (här'kwē-bŭs), *n.* a kind of gun in use before the musket. Also, arquebus.

har-ri-er (hăr'ĭ-ẽr), *n.* a variety of dog used for hunting hares; a kind of hawk.

har-row (hăr'ō), *n.* an agricultural or farming instrument having sharp iron or wooden teeth, for breaking up clods and casting earth upon sown land: *v.t.* to break up, tear, or draw over with a sharp-toothed instrument; lacerate or torment; vex.

har-ry (hăr'ĭ), *v.t.* [*p.t.* and *p.p.* harried, *p.pr.* harrying], to plunder, lay waste; annoy or vex; tease; harass.

harsh (härsh), *adj.* discordant; jarring; rough to the ear, taste, or touch; austere.—*adv.* harshly.—*n.* harshness.
Syn. rough, rigorous, severe, gruff, morose.
Ant. (see gentle).

hart (härt), *n.* the male of the red deer; as, "The *hart* panteth after the water brooks."—Psalm xlii. 1.

harte-beest (härt'bēst'; här'tē-bēst'), *n.* a large African antelope or goat. Also, hartbeest, hartebeest.

harts-horn (härts'hôrn'), *n.* a preparation of ammonia and sweet oil: so called because ammonia was formerly distilled from the horns of a deer.

hart's-tongue (härts'tŭng'), *n.* a British fern, also found in Florida.

har-um-scar-um (hâr'ŭm-skâr'ŭm), *adj.* wild; thoughtless; rash; giddy; reckless; untidy; as, a *harum-scarum* girl. [Colloq.]

har-vest (här'vĕst), *n.* the season of reaping and gathering in grain and fruits; a crop of grain or fruit; the result of effort: *v.t.* to gather in, as corn; reap.—*n.* harvester.

har-vest home (här'vĕst hōm), an autumn festival; a church service of thanksgiving held during the season of the ingathering of crops.

har-vest moon (här'vĕst mōōn), the full moon which occurs about September 23.

har-vest mouse (här'vĕst mous), a small field mouse which builds its nest in stalks of corn.

has (hăz), third person singular present of the verb *have*.

hash (hăsh), *n.* a dish of meat cut and cooked with vegetables; a mixture: *v.t.* to chop small and mix.

hash-ish (hăsh'ēsh; hȧ-shēsh'), *n.* an Oriental intoxicant made from Indian hemp. Also, hasheesh.

hasp (hȧsp), *n.* a clasp folded over a staple and secured with a padlock: *v.t.* to shut or secure with a clasp and padlock.

has-sock (hăs'ŭk), *n.* a padded mat or cushion for kneeling upon in church, etc.; a tuft of coarse grass.

hast (hăst), second person singular present of the verb *have*.

haste (hāst), *n.* quickness of movement; celerity; speed; swiftness: *v.i.* and *v.t.* to hurry.

has-ten (hās'n), *v.t.* to cause to hurry; urge forward: *v.i.* to move with speed; be quick.
Syn. accelerate, dispatch, expedite, speed.
Ant. (see delay).

hast-i-ly (hās'tĭ-lĭ), *adv.* in a hurried manner; quickly; testily; peevishly.

hast-y (hās'tĭ), *adj.* [*comp.* hastier, *superl.* hastiest], precipitate; quick; speedy; eager; vehement; rash; testy; peevish; irritable.—*n.* hastiness.
Syn. fast.
Ant. (see deliberate).

hast-y pud-ding (hās'tĭ pŏŏd'ĭng), a pudding made by stirring Indian meal into boiling water; mush; in England, a batter of flour similarly prepared.

hat (hăt), *n.* a covering for the head, with a crown and brim; a cardinal's rank and dignity.

hat-band (hăt'bănd'), *n.* a band worn around the hat; a black cloth band worn as a token of mourning.

hatch (hăch), *v.t.* to produce (young) from eggs; plot or contrive; shade by narrow lines; close with, or as with, a half-door: *n.* the number of young produced from eggs at a sitting; a narrow line in engraving, or drawing; a door with an opening over it; a half-door: *pl.* doors or openings by which a descent is made from one deck of a ship to another; hatchways.

hatch-el (hăch'ĕl), *v.t.* to dress or comb, as flax or hemp; to tease or vex:

n. a comb for dressing flax or hemp. Also, **hackle, heckle.**

hatch-er-y (hăch'ẽr-ĭ), *n.* a place where eggs are artificially hatched, especially those of fish.

hatch-et (hăch'ĕt), *n.* a small ax with a short handle used with one hand.

hatch-ing (hăch'ĭng), *n.* a kind of drawing or engraving with narrow parallel or crossed lines.

hatch-ment (hăch'mĕnt), *n.* a sort of panel upon which the coat of arms of a deceased person is temporarily placed in front of his house, on a tomb, in a church, etc.

hatch-way (hăch'wā'), *n.* an opening in the deck of a vessel for passage below; a hatch.

hate (hāt), *v.t.* to dislike intensely; abhor; detest: *n.* detestation; thorough dislike.

hate-ful (hāt'fo͝ol), *adj.* causing or showing deep dislike, or abhorrence; as, a *hateful* spirit; a *hateful* foe.—*adv.* **hatefully.**—*n.* **hatefulness.**
Syn. odious, detestable.
Ant. (see lovable).

ha-tred (hā'trĕd), *n.* bitter aversion; continued hostility of feeling; detestation.
Syn. enmity, ill will, rancor.
Ant. (see friendship).

hat-ted (hăt'ĕd), *adj.* wearing a head-covering with crown and brim.

hat-ter (hăt'ẽr), *n.* a manufacturer of, or a dealer in, headgear.

hau-berk (hô'bẽrk), *n.* a coat of armor formed of steel rings, reaching below the knees.

haugh-ti-ly (hô'tĭ-lĭ), *adv.* in a proud manner; disdainfully.

haugh-ty (hô'tĭ), *adj.* [*comp.* haughtier, *superl.* haughtiest], proud and disdainful; overbearing; contemptuous.—*n.* **haughtiness.**
Syn. arrogant, proud.

haul (hôl), *v.t.* to pull or draw with force; transport by drawing: *v.i.* to change the course of a ship; shift: said of the wind: *n.* a strong pull; draft of a net; quantity of fish caught at one time; distance over which anything is drawn.

haul-er (hôl'ẽr), *n.* one who, or that which, pulls forcibly; a device for catching fish.

haunch (hänch; hônch), *n.* the hip; the hind part; of meats, the leg and loin taken together; a joint of deer meat or mutton; shoulder of an arch.

haunt (hänt; hônt), *n.* a place of accustomed resort: *v.t.* to visit frequently or habitually; trouble with frequent visits, as an apparition.

haut-boy (hō'boi), *n.* a wind instrument of the reed class and similar in shape to a clarinet. Also, **oboe.**

hau-teur (hō-tûr'), *n.* a haughty bearing or spirit; disdainful pride; arrogance.

Ha-van-a (hȧ-văn'ȧ), *n.* a cigar made of Cuban tobacco.

have (hăv), *v.t.* [*p.t.* and *p.p.* had, *p.pr.* having], to possess; take; hold or bear; enjoy; desire; be obliged; bring forth; cheat; obtain the advantage of.
Syn. hold, occupy, possess, own.

have-lock (hăv'lŏk), *n.* a white cover for a military cap, with a long rear flap as a protection from strong sunshine.

ha-ven (hā'vn), *n.* a sheltered anchorage for ships; harbor; place of shelter and safety.

hav-er-sack (hăv'ẽr-săk), *n.* a strong coarse linen bag in which soldiers carry their food when marching.

hav-ing (hăv'ĭng), *p.pr.* of *have*: *n.* the act or state of possession; that which one possesses; goods.

hav-oc (hăv'ŏk), *n.* wide and general destruction; devastation; waste.

haw (hô), *n.* the fruit of the hawthorn, or shrub of the rose family; a growth under the third eyelid of a horse; a hedge or inclosure; a hesitation in speech: *v.i.* to speak with interruption and hesitation; as, don't *haw* and hum so much.

haw-finch (hô'fĭnch'), *n.* the common grosbeak or finch bird: supposed to feed on the hawthorn.

hawk (hôk), *n.* a name for various kinds of birds of prey related to the buzzards, falcons, and kites; a forcible effort to clear the throat of phlegm; a square board, with a short handle, for holding mortar: *v.t.* to cry, or carry about, for sale: *v.i.* to make a forcible effort to cough up phlegm; to fly trained hawks at birds on the wing.

hawk-bill (hôk'bĭl'), *n.* a sea turtle that furnishes tortoise shell: so named from its curved upper jaw.

hawk-er (hôk'ẽr), *n.* one who cries and sells goods in the streets; peddler; one who breeds and trains hawks.

hawk-eyed (hôk'īd'), *adj.* sharp-sighted like a hawk; as, the *hawk-eyed* foreman kept strict watch over his men.

hawk moth (hôk mŏth), a large moth whose flight somewhat resembles that of a hawk.

hawk-weed (hôk'wēd'), *n.* a plant of the aster family with yellow flowers.

hawse (hôz; hôs), *n.* that part of a ship's bows where the cable holes are situated.

hawse hole (hôz hōl), one of the two holes under a ship's bow through which the cable passes when the vessel is moored.

haw-ser (hô'zẽr; hô'sẽr), *n.* a thick rope or cable used in towing or for securing a vessel.

haw-thorn (hô'thôrn), *n.* a prickly shrub or tree of the rose family.

hay (hā), *n.* grass, clover, etc., cut and dried for fodder.

hay-cock (hā'kŏk'), *n.* a cone-shaped pile of hay heaped up in the field.

hay fe-ver (hā fē'vẽr), a catarrh, accompanied by itching, sneezing, slight fever, and pains in the head, usually appearing in late summer.

hay-mow (hā'mou'), *n.* a mass of hay laid up in a barn; the place in which the hay is stored.

haz-ard (hăz'ȧrd), *n.* chance; accident; risk; danger; a dice game; a stroke at billiards which puts the ball in the pocket; in golf, a bunker, water, a ditch or other obstruction: *v.t.* to run the risk of; chance; put in peril.
Syn. *n.* and *v.* risk, venture.

haz-ard-ous (hăz'ȧr-dŭs), *adj.* risky; perilous; dangerous; as, a *hazardous* trip.

haze (hāz), *n.* a slight fog or mist; dimness of sight or knowledge: *v.i.* to be foggy or misty: *v.t.* pursue or harass by overwork or unpleasant tasks; play practical jokes upon, especially of a severe kind.

ha-zel (hā'zl), *n.* a shrub or tree bearing an oval-shaped nut; the nut borne by this tree; filbert.

haz-i-ness (hāz'ĭ-nĕs), *n.* mistiness; state of being confused; as, *haziness* of thought.

ha-zy (hā'zĭ), *adj.* misty; obscure; not clear; as, a *hazy* landscape; a *hazy* idea.—*adv.* **hazily.**

he (hē), *pron.* [*pl.* they (*th*ā)], the masculine pronoun of the third person: *n.* a male.

head (hĕd), *n.* the uppermost part of the body of an animal containing the face, brain, etc.; chief or principal part of anything; an individual: often used as a plural; as, a hundred *head* of cattle; leader or commander; place of honor or authority; top; fore part; the understanding or intellect; principal topic; a division; origin or source; pitch; crisis or height; latent or reserve force; froth on liquor: *adj.* principal or chief; acting against the front; as, a *head* wind: *v.t.* to lead or direct; take the first place in; get in front of; direct the course of; oppose; strain: *v.i.* to move forward; come to a climax.

head-ache (hĕd'āk"), *n.* severe or burning pain in the head.

head-dress (hĕd'drĕs"), *n.* a covering or ornament for the head.

head-ed (hĕd'ĕd), *adj.* in respect of understanding or intellect, or of the shape of the skull: much used in composition; as, clear-*headed*, flat-*headed*, etc.; formed into a compact center, as cabbage.

head-er (hĕd'ẽr), *n.* a plunge or fall foremost; one who puts heads on, as in pin making; a machine, etc., for making or removing heads; a brick or stone with its short face in front.

head-first (hĕd'fûrst'), *adv.* in thoughtless haste; without stopping; plunging forward. Also, **headforemost.**

head-gear (hĕd'gēr"), *n.* anything worn upon the head.

head-ing (hĕd'ĭng), *n.* a title; material from which heads of casks or barrels are made; the strip on the edge of embroidery, by which it may be sewed to a garment; the entrance to a mine.

head-land (hĕd'lănd), *n.* a promontory; a cape; as, they lighted a fire on the *headland* as a signal to the ship.

head-light (hĕd'līt"), *n.* a bright lamp or globe at the front of a locomotive, automobile, etc.

head-line (hĕd'līn"), *n.* a line of type at the top of a page, chapter, column of a newspaper, etc.: *pl.* the ropes at the top of a sail by which it is secured to the yard or long spar of a ship.

head-long (hĕd'lŏng"), *adv.* headforemost; rashly; precipitously: *adj.* rash; precipitate; violent; thoughtless.

head-piece (hĕd'pēs), *n.* a covering or armor for the head; the head; mental ability.

head-quar-ters (hĕd'kwôr'tẽrz), *n.pl.* the office or residence of a chief officer or official; a center of authority.

heads-man (hĕdz'măn), *n.* a public executioner who beheads those condemned to die. Also, **headman.**

head-stone (hĕd'stōn"), *n.* the corner piece in a foundation; as, the *headstone* of the corner; a marker for a grave; a tombstone.

head-strong (hĕd'strŏng), *adj.* ungovernable; self-willed; stubborn; unruly.

head-way (hĕd'wā"), *n.* forward motion of a vessel, etc.; momentum; progress or success of any kind; time between two railroad trains.

head-y (hĕd'ĭ), *adj.* precipitate; intoxicating; wilful; rash; ungovernable.

heal (hēl), *v.t.* to restore to health; cure; make sound; reconcile: *v.i.* to become well or sound.

heal-ing (hēl'ĭng), *p.adj.* tending to cure; soothing; as, *healing* effect of a medicine: *n.* cure.

health (hĕlth), *n.* freedom from bodily pain or disease; vigor of mind; moral purity; righteousness; healing power; a toast or pledge.

health-ful (hĕlth'fŏŏl), *adj.* promoting bodily welfare; wholesome; favorable.—*adv.* **healthfully.**—*n.* **healthfulness.**

health-i-ness (hĕl'thĭ-nĕs), *n.* the state of being free from disease.

health-y (hĕl'thĭ), *adj.* [*comp.* healthier, *superl.* healthiest], in a sound or wholesome condition; as, a *healthy* mind in a *healthy* body is the greatest blessing of mankind; enjoying or contributing to bodily welfare.—*adv.* **healthily.**
Syn. vigorous, salutary, wholesome.
Ant. (see unhealthy).

heap (hēp), *n.* a pile or collection of things thrown together; a quantity; accumulation; crowd: *v.t.* to form into a pile or mass; pile up; aggregate.
Syn. v. accumulate, amass, pile.

hear (hēr), *v.t.* [*p.t.* and *p.p.* heard, *p.pr.* hearing], to perceive by the ear; attend or listen to; give heed to; obey; accede to the wishes of; attend in an official manner: *v.i.* to have the sense of hearing; be told of.

hear-ing (hēr'ĭng), *n.* the sense by which sound is perceived; audience; judicial or official investigation.

heark-en (här'kn), *v.i.* to listen, to heed; as, "*Hearken* diligently unto me."—Isaiah lv. 2. Also, **hark, harken.**

hear-say (hēr'sā"), *n.* rumor or report: *adj.* secondhand; as, *hearsay* evidence is not accepted in a court of law.

hearse (hûrs), *n.* a vehicle for carrying dead bodies to the grave.

heart (härt), *n.* the organ in animals which causes the blood to circulate through the arteries, etc.; the vital, inner, or chief part of anything; the often assumed seat of the affections and passions; emotion; tenderness; affection; courage; will; spirit; energy; power; resolution; secret thoughts; conscience; one of a suit of cards marked with one or more red hearts; a kind of cherry: *pl.* a card game.

heart-ache (härt'āk"), *n.* sorrow; mental pang; grief; distress.

heart-bro-ken (härt'brō"kn), *adj.* deeply grieved; inconsolable; in despair.

heart-burn (härt'bûrn"), *n.* a burning in the stomach due to acidity.

heart-ed (härt'ĕd), *adj.* in respect of the feelings or qualities of character: used in compounds; as, good-*hearted*, chicken-*hearted*, etc.

heart-en (här'tn), *v.t.* to give courage to; inspirit; to animate or inspire.

heart-felt (härt'fĕlt"), *adj.* earnest; sincere; with deep emotion.

hearth (härth), *n.* that part of a room where the fire is made; hence, the family circle; as, they gathered round the *hearth* on wintry evenings.

hearth-stone (härth'stōn"), *n.* the stone forming a fireside.

heart-i-ly (här'tĭ-lĭ), *adv.* cordially; energetically; willingly; eagerly.

heart-i-ness (här'tĭ-nĕs), *n.* cordiality; vigor; as, the *heartiness* of a greeting; *heartiness* of appetite.

heart-less (härt'lĕs), *adj.* without feeling; cruel.

hearts-ease (härtz'ēz"), *n.* the pansy and some other species of violet.

heart-y (här'tĭ), *adj.* [*comp.* heartier, *superl.* heartiest], cordial; as, they gave us a *hearty* welcome; sincere; open; warm; strong; as, he is hale and *hearty;* vigorous; good-natured; kind; healthy; keen in appetite; abundant; as, I ate a *hearty* meal.

heat (hēt), *n.* a physical form of energy, due to vibration, or motion, of the molecules, or minute particles, of which a body is composed; the sensation produced by a hot body; high temperature; opposite to *cold;* as, the *heat* of summer; the state of being hot; effervescence or bubbling; agitation of sudden or violent passion; ardor; vehemence; redness or flush of the face; a course at a race; hot weather: *v.t.* to make hot; warm; excite with passion or desire; make feverish; animate: *v.i.* to become hot or warm.

heat-er (hēt'ẽr), *n.* one who, or that which, gives warmth; a stove, furnace, or other appliance used to make a place warm, as a house, store, building, etc.

heath (hēth), *n.* a small evergreen flowering shrub growing on level land; heather; a tract of waste or level land, especially with this evergreen shrub growing upon it.

hea-then (hē'*th*n), *n.* one who is ignorant of the true God; a pagan; idolater; a rude, irreligious, uncultured person.

hea-then-dom (hē'*th*n-dŭm), *n.* the state or condition of being a pagan; that part of the world inhabited by pagans.

hea-then-ish (hē'*th*n-ĭsh), *adj.* pertaining to, or like, a pagan; rude; ignorant, or uncultured; irreligious.

hea-then-ism (hē'*th*n-ĭzm), *n.* ignorance of the true God; paganism; idolatry.

hea-then-ize (hē'*th*n-īz), *v.t.* to make like a pagan or irreligious person.

heath-er (hĕ*th*'ẽr), *n.* a small evergreen plant, often with rose-colored flowers. Also, **heath.**—*adv.* **heathery.**

heave (hēv), *v.t.* to hoist or lift up; force from the breast, as a sigh; cause to swell; throw: *v.i.* to be lifted up; swell; rise and fall alternately; struggle or toil; pant; vomit: *n.* an effort or exertion upwards; lift; the act of throwing; swell or rising; haul; struggle, effort to vomit.

heav-en (hĕv'n), *n.* the abode of God and the blessed; the firmament, or sky; a state or condition of bliss; a sublime and exalted condition; any place of supreme happiness or great comfort; as, this place is a veritable *heaven* upon earth.

heav-en-li-ness (hĕv'n-lĭ-nĕs), *n.* supreme excellence; as, the *heavenliness* of great music.

heav-en-ly (hĕv'n-lĭ), *adj.* pertaining to, or like, heaven; celestial; divine; supremely excellent.

heav-er (hĕv'ẽr), *n.* one who, or that which, lifts; especially, one who loads or unloads goods, coal, etc.

heaves (hēvz), *n.* a disease of horses recognized by their difficult breathing, wheezing, a peculiar cough, etc.

heav-i-ness (hĕv'ĭ-nĕs), *n.* the quality of being weighty; dejection; grief; sadness.

heav-y (hĕv'ĭ), *adj.* [*comp.* heavier, *superl.* heaviest], large in extent, quality, or effects; as, we had a *heavy* fall of snow; the store has a *heavy* trade; ponderous; weighty; oppressive; grievous; laborious; obstructive; depressed; dull; dense; powerful; loud; indigestible; as, that cake was *heavy;* clayey.—*adv.* **heavily.**

Syn. burdensome, ponderous, weighty.

heav-y-weight (hĕv'ĭ-wāt"), *n.* a very powerful wrestler or boxer; one whose moral force or business ability, etc., gives him great influence.

heb-dom-a-dal (hĕb-dŏm'*ȧ*-dăl), *adj.* composed of seven days; of weekly occurrence.

He-bra-ic (hē-brā'ĭk), *adj.* pertaining to the Hebrews, the Jewish language, or literature.

He-bra-ism (hē'brā-ĭzm), *n.* a Hebrew phrase or custom; a characteristic of the Hebrews.

He-bra-ist (hē'brā-ĭst) *n.* one who is learned in the Hebrew language and literature.

He-brew (hē'brōō), *adj.* pertaining to the Hebrews; Jewish: *n.* the Hebrew language; a Jew: *pl.* a book of the New Testament, the Epistle to the Hebrews.

Hec-a-te (hĕk'*ȧ*-tē), *n.* an ancient Grecian goddess supposed to have threefold power over heaven, earth, and the underworld; the goddess of magic and witchcraft.

hec-a-tomb (hĕk'*ȧ*-tōm; hĕk'*ȧ*-tōōm), *n.* a sacrifice of a hundred oxen; any large sacrifice or slaughter.

heck-le (hĕk'l), *n.* an instrument for cleaning flax; a hackle or hatchel: *v.t.* to comb or dress, as flax or hemp; to hackle or hatchel; to question severely or annoy with questions; as, the audience *heckled* the speaker.

hec-tare (hĕk'târ), *n.* in the metric system, a land measure equal to 100 ares or 10,000 square meters, or 2.471 acres. Also, **hektare.**

hec-tic (hĕk'tĭk), *adj.* constitutional; slow, but of long continuance; pertaining to the fever that accompanies tuberculosis; feverish: *n.* a fever accompanying tuberculosis, characterized by a bright pink spot or flush on the cheeks.

hec-to-gram (hĕk'tō-grăm), *n.* in the metric system, a weight equal to 100 grams, or 3.527 ounces avoirdupois. Also, **hectogramme, hektogramme.**

hec-to-graph (hĕk'tō-grăf), *n.* an apparatus for multiplying copies of a letter or drawing, etc.

hec-to-li-ter (hĕk'tō-lē"tẽr), *n.* in the metric system, a liquid measure equal to 100 liters, or 26.42 gallons; one-tenth of a cubic meter. Also, **hectolitre, hektoliter, hektolitre.**

hec-to-me-ter (hĕk'tō-mē"tẽr), *n.* in the metric system, a measure of length equal to 100 meters, or 328 feet 1 inch. Also, **hectometre, hektometer, hektometre.**

hec-tor (hĕk'tẽr), *v.t.* to bully; to threaten; to tease; to irritate or provoke: *v.i.* to bluster.

hec-to-stere (hĕk'tō-stēr), *n.* in the metric system, a cubic measure equal to 100 cubic meters, or 3531.44 cubic feet. Also, **hektostere.**

hedge (hĕj), *n.* a fence of bushes or shrubs: *v.t.* to inclose with a border of bushes or shrubs; encircle; invest: *v.i.* to bet on both sides, so that the possibility of loss will be diminished; evade; skulk: *adj.* mean; contemptible; of the lowest class.

hedge-hog (hĕj'hŏg"), *n.* a small insect-eating animal covered on the back with spines or prickles.

hedge-row (hĕj'rō), *n.* a line of small trees or shrubs planted as a fence, or for ornament.

heed (hēd), *v.t.* to regard with care; take notice of; mind; attend; regard: *v.i.* to give attention: *n.* careful attention; regard; caution.

heed-ful (hēd'fŏŏl), *adj.* cautious; attentive; as, she is *heedful* of my welfare.—*adv.* **heedfully.**

heed-less (hēd'lĕs), *adj.* careless; inattentive; neglectful; as, that boy is very *heedless.*

heel (hēl), *n.* the hinder part of the foot; the hinder part of a boot, shoe, or stocking; anything shaped like a heel: *v.t.* to furnish with a heel: *v.i.* to lean on one side, as a ship.

heel-er (hēl'ẽr), *n.* one who follows close after, as a political hanger-on; one who heels shoes; a fast runner.

heel-ing (hēl'ĭng), *n.* the degree of inclination of a vessel from the perpendicular.

heel-tap (hēl'tăp"), *n.* leather for a shoe-heel; liquor left in a glass after drinking.

heft (hĕft), *n.* a handle; an effort; weight; the greater part or bulk: *v.t.* to try the weight of, by lifting or holding in the hand.

he-gem-o-ny (hē-jĕm'ō-nĭ), *n.* leadership; powerful influence: usually said of the influence of one government over another.

heg-i-ra (hĕj'ĭ-rȧ; hē-jī'rȧ), *n.* the flight of Mohammed from Mecca to Medina, September 13, 662 A. D.; a flight. Also, **hejira.**

heif-er (hĕf'ẽr), *n.* a young cow; as, the god Jupiter changed Io into a *heifer.*

heigh-ho (hī'hō"), *interj.* an expression of languor or uneasiness, surprise or joy.

height (hīt), *n.* altitude; elevation; highest state or degree; an eminence or hill; summit; stature; as, what is your *height?*

height-en (hīt'n), *v.t.* to raise; lift; elevate; intensify; set off; increase; aggravate; improve.

hei-nous (hā'nŭs), *adj.* hateful; extremely wicked; as, a *heinous* crime; flagrant; giving great offense.—*adv.* **heinously.**

heir (âr), *n.* one who succeeds another in the possession of property, title, office, mental gifts, etc.

heir ap-par-ent (âr ă-păr'ĕnt), an heir whose right to inherit property cannot be annulled if he outlives his ancestor.

heir-ess (âr'ĕs), *n.* a woman or girl who inherits property; as, she was the *heiress* of all her father's wealth.

heir-loom (âr'lōōm"), *n.* any movable or personal property, which by its connection with an estate descends to posterity.

heir pre-sump-tive (âr prē-zŭmp'-tĭv), one who will succeed as heir if his right is not barred by the birth of one nearer in succession than himself.

held (hĕld), past tense and past participle of the verb *hold.*

he-li-cop-ter (hē"lĭ-kŏp'tẽr), *n.* a flying machine held up by its propeller or by rotating planes.

he-li-o-cen-tric (hē"lĭ-ō-sĕn'trĭk), *adj.* having the sun as a center. Also, **heliocentrical.**

he-li-o-chrome (hē'lĭ-ō-krōm"), *n.* a photograph in natural colors.

he-li-o-graph (hē'lĭ-ō-grȧf"), *n.* an apparatus for signaling by reflecting the sun's rays; used chiefly in military operations.

he-li-om-e-ter (hē"lĭ-ŏm'ē-tẽr), *n.* an instrument for measuring small angles in the heavens.

he-li-o-scope (hē'lĭ-ō-skōp"), *n.* a telescope for observing the sun.

he-li-o-stat (hē'lĭ-ō-stăt"), *n.* an instrument for signaling by means of a mirror moved by clockwork.

he-li-o-trope (hē'lĭ-ō-trōp), *n.* a plant whose flowers follow the course of the sun; a green-colored variety of quartz with small red spots; bloodstone; the color of the flowers of heliotrope, bluish-pink.

he-li-o-type (hē'lĭ-ō-tīp"), *n.* an impression from a photograph taken on a gelatin plate hardened with alum.

he-li-um (hē'lĭ-ŭm), *n.* an element first observed in the spectrum of the sun, but recently discovered on the earth and some of its characteristics learned; a gaseous element found in the atmospheres of the sun and earth and in some rare minerals; a product yielded by one of the gases from radium, which it resembles.

hell (hĕl), *n.* the place of the dead or of departed souls (more correctly *Hades*); the grave; the place of punishment for the wicked after death; hence, any place or condition of extreme misery or evil; a gambling house.

hel-le-bore (hĕl'ē-bōr), *n.* any herb of the crowfoot family; the powdered root of the plant, used for medicinal purposes; the Christmas rose.

Hel-len-ic (hĕ-lĕn'ĭk; hĕ-lē'nĭk), *adj.* pertaining to, or characteristic of, the ancient Greeks, or Grecian art and literature.

Hel-len-ism (hĕl'ĕn-ĭzm), *n.* a Greek manner of speech; Grecian culture and the love of the beautiful in art.

Hel-len-ist (hĕl'ĕn-ĭst), *n.* a Jew who spoke Greek; one learned in Greek.

Hel-len-ize (hĕl'ĕn-īz), *v.t.* to cause to conform to Greek standards or usages.

hel-lo (hĕ-lō"), *interj.* and *n.* a cry to attract attention; a salutation: *v.i.* to call out. Also, **hollos, holla, hallos, halloo, hullo.**

helm (hĕlm), *n.* the apparatus for steering a ship; tiller; the place of its direction and government: poetically, a helmet: *v.t.* to guide or conduct.

hel-met (hĕl'mĕt), *n.* metal or leather armor for the head; the hooded upper lip of a flower.

Trench Helmet

helms-man (hĕlmz'-măn), *n.* the person who steers a ship or boat.

Hel-ot (hĕl'ŏt; hē'lŏt), *n.* a slave in ancient Sparta; slave or serf.

help (hĕlp), *v.t.* to give assistance to; aid; support; sustain; succor; relieve; avoid; prevent; distribute food to at table; remedy; cure: *v.i.* to lend aid; be available or useful: *n.* assistance; aid; support; succor; relief; that which forwards or promotes; a portion of food served at a meal; a hired servant.
Syn. v. assist, rescue.
Ant. (see hinder).

help-ful (hĕlp'fŏŏl), *adj.* giving aid; beneficial; useful.—*adv.* **helpfully.**

help-less (hĕlp'lĕs), *adj.* unable to do for oneself; feeble; dependent; beyond remedy.—*adv.* **helplessly.**—*n.* **helplessness.**

help-mate (hĕlp'māt"), *n.* an assistant; partner; companion, especially a wife. Also, **helpmeet.**

hel-ter-skel-ter (hĕl'tĕr-skĕl'tĕr), *adj.* and *adv.* in hurry and confusion; without definite purpose; as, away they run, pell-mell, *helter-skelter,* slapdash.

helve (hĕlv), *n.* the handle of an ax, hatchet, etc.; the handle of a forge hammer.

hem (hĕm), *n.* the edge of a cloth or garment doubled and sewed; sound used as an expression of hesitation, doubt, etc.; a little cough, better expressed by *hm:* *v.t.* [*p.t.* and *p.p.* hemmed, *p.pr.* hemming], to double and sew the edge of (a cloth or garment); to shut in; surround: *v.i.* utter the sudden sound, *hem.*

hem-a-tite (hĕm'ȧ-tīt; hē'mȧ-tīt), *n.* one of the most important of iron ores, so called because of its red color when powdered. Also, **hæmatite.**

hem-i- (hĕm'ĭ-), a *prefix* meaning half; as, *hemisphere,* a half sphere or globe.

hem-i-sphere (hĕm'ĭ-sfēr), *n.* a half sphere or globe; as, the northern or southern *hemisphere.*

hem-lock (hĕm'lŏk), *n.* a wild poisonous plant of the parsley family: **hemlock spruce,** an evergreen tree of the pine family; the lumber made from this tree.

hem-mer (hĕm'ĕr), *n.* one who, or that which, hems; an attachment to a sewing machine for hemming.

he-mo-glo-bin (hē'mō-glō'bĭn), *n.* the normal coloring matter of the red blood. Also, **hæmoglobin.**

hem-or-rhage (hĕm'ō-rāj), *n.* bleeding from the lungs, arteries, veins, etc.; any flow of blood from blood vessels. Also, **hæmorrhage.**

hem-or-rhoids (hĕm'ō-roidz), *n.pl.* bleeding piles. Also, **hæmorrhoids.**

hemp (hĕmp), *n.* a plant of the nettle family, the tough fiber of which is used for cordage and various kinds of coarse linen; in Asia, a drug and intoxicant, hashish, is obtained from this plant.

hem-stitch (hĕm'stĭch), *n.* a particular kind of ornamental stitching.

hen (hĕn), *n.* the female of a bird, especially the domestic fowl.

hen-bane (hĕn'bān"), *n.* a poisonous, coarse, hairy, wild herb of the nightshade family, deadly to fowls.

hence (hĕns), *adv.* from this place, source, or time; as, a week *hence* I shall go away; in consequence of this; for this reason; as, *hence* you may have the new hat: *interj.* away! begone!

hence-forth (hĕns"fōrth'; hĕns'fōrth"), *adv.* from this time.

hench-man (hĕnch'măn), *n.* [*pl.* henchmen (-mĕn)], formerly, a male attendant or servant; a follower; groom; one who serves in a political campaign under another because he expects reward in money, office, etc.

hen-pecked (hĕn'pĕkt"), *adj.* governed by one's wife; domineered over.

hen-ry (hĕn'rĭ), *n.* a term of measurement used in the science of electricity.

he-pat-ic (hē-păt'ĭk), *adj.* pertaining to the liver; as, *hepatic* disease.

he-pat-i-ca (hē-păt'ĭ-kȧ), *n.* a pretty wild spring flower.

He-pat-i-cæ (hē-păt'ĭ-sē), *n.* a subclass of plants, the liverworts.

hep-ta- (hĕp'tȧ-), a *prefix* meaning seven. Also, **hept.**

hep-ta-chord (hĕp'tȧ-kôrd), *n.* a series of seven notes; a seven-stringed musical instrument.

hep-ta-gon (hĕp'tȧ-gŏn), *n.* a plane figure having seven sides and seven angles.

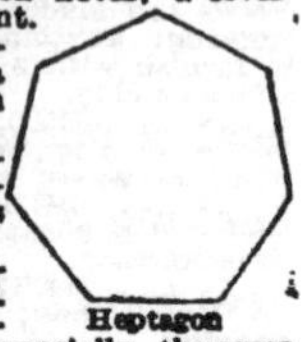
Heptagon

hep-tag-o-nal (hĕp-tăg'ō-năl), *adj.* having seven sides and seven angles.

hep-tarch-y (hĕp'tär-kĭ), *n.* [*pl.* heptarchies (-kĭz)], a government by seven rulers; especially, the seven Anglo-Saxon kingdoms established in England in the ninth century.

her (hûr), *pron.* the objective and possessive case of *she.*

her-ald (hĕr'ăld), *n.* formerly, an official who proclaimed peace and war, bore messages from a sovereign to a commander, superintended coronations and other public ceremonial functions, etc.; an official whose duty it is to grant, record, and blazon arms, trace pedigrees, etc.; a forerunner; harbinger; as, the lark is the *herald* of the morn; any messenger: *v.t.* to introduce; proclaim; usher in.

he-ral-dic (hē-răl'dĭk), *adj.* pertaining to those who design coats of arms; pertaining to the science of making coats of arms. Also, **heraldical.**—*adv.* **heraldically.**

her-ald-ry (hĕr'ăld-rĭ), *n.* the science that treats of armorial bearings or coats of arms, and of determining pedigrees, etc.

herb (ûrb; hûrb), *n.* a plant with a soft and juicy stem that, after flowering, withers away.

her-ba-ceous (hĕr-bā'shŭs), *adj.* pertaining to, or of the nature of, or feeding upon, herbs, grasses, or certain small plants.

herb-age (ûr'bāj; hûr'bāj), *n.* grass; pasturage; the right of pasture on the lands of another.

herb-al (hûr'bål), *adj.* pertaining to herbs or grasses: *n.* a book descriptive of plants.

her-ba-ri-um (hẽr-bā'rĭ-ŭm), *n.* [*pl.* herbaria (-*d*), herbariums (-ŭmz)], a collection of dried plants for purposes of study; a building where such a collection is kept.

her-bif-er-ous (hẽr-bĭf'ẽr-ŭs), *adj.* producing grasses and various small plants, called herbs.

Her-biv-o-ra (hẽr-bĭv'ō-rd), *n.pl.* animals that feed on grasses, small plants, or vegetables.

her-biv-o-rous (hẽr-bĭv'ō-rŭs), *adj.* feeding on small plants and vegetable matter.

her-cu-le-an (hẽr-kū'lē-ăn), *adj.* of exceeding strength and power; huge; vast; very difficult; as, his *herculean* task: **Herculean**, pertaining to Hercules, the hero of Grecian mythology, possessed of superhuman strength.

Her-cu-les (hûr'kū-lēz), *n.* a famous Greek hero, son of Zeus (Jupiter) and Alcmene.

herd (hûrd), *n.* a collection of beasts or cattle feeding or driven together; crowd; a keeper of cattle: *v.i.* to unite or associate, as beasts; crowd together.

herds-man (hûrdz'măn), *n.* one who keeps or tends a large number of beasts or cattle.

here (hẽr), *adv.* in, or to, this place: opposite to *there;* as, I live *here;* at this point; as, *here* is a good place to pause in the address; in the present life or state; on this occasion.

here-aft-er (hẽr-ăf'tẽr), *adv.* after this; at a later time: *n.* the life of the future; the life after death.

here-by (hẽr-bī'), *adv.* by virtue of this; as, you are *hereby* given the right to proceed; formerly, very near; as, he lives *hereby.*

he-red-i-ta-ble (hē-rĕd'ĭ-tȧ-bl), *adj.* that may be handed down from parent to child; that may be left to someone by will; that may be received from another through death. Also, **heritable.** —*adv.* **hereditably.**

he-red-i-ta-ry (hē-rĕd'ĭ-tā-rĭ), *adj.* passing from an ancestor to a descendant; transmitted from parent to child.

he-red-i-ty (hē-rĕd'ĭ-tĭ), *n.* the transmission of physical or mental characteristics or qualities from parent to child; the tendency of an organism to reproduce the characteristics of ancestors.

here-in (hẽr-ĭn'), *adv.* in this; as, you will find *herein* the information that you requested.

here-of (hẽr-ŏv'; hẽr-ŏf'), *adv.* of this; from this; about this; as, we will speak further *hereof.*

here-on (hẽr-ŏn'), *adv.* on this; hereupon; as, *hereon* he produced his proofs.

her-e-sy (hĕr'ē-sĭ), *n.* [*pl.* heresies (-sĭz)], an opinion or doctrine in opposition to views or opinions commonly accepted as true, as in religion, politics, literature, philosophy, etc.: used especially when the opposing doctrine leads to division.

her-e-tic (hĕr'ē-tĭk), *n.* one who holds or maintains opinions contrary to customary views or prevailing religion.

Syn. sectary, sectarian, schismatic.

he-ret-i-cal (hē-rĕt'ĭ-kăl), *adj.* pertaining to, or having the character of, doctrine contrary to accepted views; subversive of, or contrary to, orthodox or common belief.

here-to (hẽr-tōō'), *adv.* to this; as, the notes added *hereto* will make the matter clearer.

here-to-fore (hẽr'tōō-fōr'), *adv.* previously; hitherto; up to this time; in time past.

here-u-pon (hẽr'ū-pŏn'), *adv.* on this; hereon; as, the meeting *hereupon* adjourned.

here-with (hẽr-with'), *adv.* with this; as, I send *herewith* my check.

her-it-a-ble (hĕr'ĭt-ȧ-bl), *adj.* that may be handed down by will or received from another through death. Also, **hereditable.**

her-i-tage (hĕr'ĭ-tāj), *n.* an estate that passes from an ancestor to a descendant; a birthright; the people of God.

her-maph-ro-dite (hẽr-măf'rō-dīt), *n.* a plant or animal which combines the qualities of both sexes.—*adj.* **hermaphrodite.**

her-met-ic (hẽr-mĕt'ĭk), *adj.* perfectly closed and air-tight. Also, **hermetical.**—*adv.* **hermetically.**

her-mit (hûr'mĭt), *n.* one who retires from society and lives alone; a recluse.

her-mit-age (hûr'mĭ-tāj), *n.* the abode of a recluse, or one who lives alone; a variety of red and white French wine.

her-mit-i-cal (hûr-mĭt'ĭ-kăl), *adj.* pertaining to, or suited for, a hermit, or one who lives alone; solitary.

hern (hûrn), *n.* the heron, or wading bird with long neck and legs and soft feathers. Also, **hernshaw.**

her-ni-a (hûr'nĭ-*d*), *n.* a protrusion, or sticking out, of some part of the intestine, or of some other internal organ; rupture.

he-ro (hē'rō), *n.* [*pl.* heroes (-rōz)], a man of distinguished courage, moral or physical; as, every man is a *hero* to some one; the chief character in a play, novel, poem, etc.

he-ro-ic (hē-rō'ĭk), *adj.* having distinguished courage; brave; noble; fearless; producing men of great courage and noble deeds; larger than life; venturesome; drastic; as, we must use *heroic* measures. Also, **heroical.**—*adv.* **heroically.**

he-ro-ic age (hē-rō'ĭk āj), the age when the legendary great men of the Greeks and Romans, called the children of the gods, are supposed to have lived.

he-ro-ics (hē-rō'ĭks), *n.pl.* extravagant or boastful language.

he-ro-ic verse (hē-rō'ĭk vûrs), a kind of verse particularly suited to lofty or heroic subjects; in English, the iambic pentameter couplet or blank verse consisting of five iambic feet, each composed of an unaccented syllable followed by an accented one; as, The cur'few tolls' the knell' of part'ing day'.

her-o-ine (hĕr'ō-ĭn), *n.* a woman of distinguished courage, moral, or physical; the leading female character in a play, novel, etc.

Heron

her-o-ism (hĕr'ō-ĭzm), *n.* high and noble courage; fortitude; fearlessness.

her-on (hĕr'ŭn), *n.* a wading bird with a long neck and long legs.

her-on-ry (hĕr′ŭn-rĭ), *n.* a place where herons congregate and breed.

her-ring (hĕr′ĭng), *n.* a small sea fish that lives in shallow water: valuable for food.

her-ring-bone (hĕr′ĭng-bōn″), *n.* a kind of cross-stitch: *v.t.* and *v.i.* to work in such a stitch.

herse (hûrs), *n.* a portcullis, or kind of gate, in the form of a harrow set with spikes and hung above a gateway so that it may be quickly lowered to stop the advance of the enemy.

her-self (hẽr-sĕlf′), *pron.* an emphasized or reflexive form of *her*; one's individuality; as, she does not act like *herself*.

hes-i-tate (hĕz′ĭ-tāt), *v.i.* to be in suspense or uncertainty; pause; vacillate; stammer.
Syn. falter, stutter.

hes-i-ta-tion (hĕz″ĭ-tā′shŭn), *n.* a pause due to uncertainty; doubt; a stopping to consider; indecision; a faltering in speech; a halting movement in a dance. Also, **hesitancy**.

Hes-per (hĕs′pẽr), *n.* the evening star, especially Venus. Also, **Hesperus**.

Hes-pe-ri-an (hĕs-pē′rĭ-ăn), *adj.* western; in or of Hesperia, the name given by Greek poets to western lands.

Hes-per-i-des (hĕs-pĕr′ĭ-dēz), *n.pl.* in Grecian mythology, the four daughters of Nox (Night) and granddaughters of Hesperus, who guarded the golden apples given by Gaia to Hera on her marriage with Zeus (Jupiter); the garden containing the golden apples protected by an enchanted dragon.

Hes-per-us (hĕs′pẽr-ŭs), *n.* the evening star. Also, **Hesper**.

Hes-sian (hĕsh′ăn), *n.* one of the mercenary soldiers employed by Great Britain in the American Revolution; hence, a dishonest politician or any other person who can be bought off: *pl.* top-boots with tassels in front: *adj.* relating to Hesse in Germany or its inhabitants.

Hes-sian fly (hĕsh′ăn flī), a small fly, the larvæ or young of which are often destructive to wheat crops.

het-er-o-dox (hĕt′ẽr-ō-dŏks), *adj.* contrary to, or differing from, an accepted doctrine or standard of faith, etc.; heretical: opposite to *orthodox*, or common belief.

het-er-o-dox-y (hĕt′ẽr-ō-dŏk″sĭ), *n.* [*pl.* heterodoxies (-sĭz)], an unorthodox or uncommon doctrine or opinion; heresy.

het-er-o-ge-ne-i-ty (hĕt″ẽr-ō-jē-nē′ĭ-tĭ), *n.* difference in kind; dissimilarity.

het-er-o-ge-ne-ous (hĕt″ẽr-ō-jē′nē-ŭs), *adj.* opposite or dissimilar in character, quality, structure, etc.; not homogeneous.

het-man (hĕt′măn), *n.* a general or headman of the Cossacks.

hew (hū), *v.t.* [*p.t.* hewed, *p.p.* hewn, hewed, *p.pr.* hewing], to cut or shape, as with an ax or other sharp instrument; hack; chop; form laboriously.

hex-a- (hĕk′să-), a *prefix* meaning **six**; as, *hexachord*, a six-stringed musical instrument. Also, **hex**.

hex-a-gon (hĕk′să-gŏn), *n.* a plane figure having six angles and six sides.

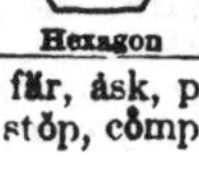

Hexagon

hex-ag-o-nal (hĕk-săg′ō-năl), *adj.* six-sided; as, *hexagonal crystals*.

hex-a-he-dron (hĕk″să-hē′drŏn), *n.* [*pl.* hexahedra (-dră)], a solid bounded by six plane faces; a cube.

hex-am-e-ter (hĕk-săm′ē-tẽr), *n.* a poetic line consisting of six feet; as, This′ is the | for′est pri | me′val. The | mur′muring | pines′ and the | hem′locks′.

hey (hā), *interj.* an exclamation to express surprise, attract attention, etc.

hey-day (hā′dā″), *interj.* an exclamation of surprise, joy, welcome, etc.: *n.* the time of greatest vigor and ardor; as, the *heyday* of youth.

hi-a-tus (hī-ā′tŭs), *n.* a break; vacancy; gap; a step lacking in a chain of proof; a space where something is wanting.

hi-ber-nal (hī-bẽr′năl), *adj.* wintry; as, the *hibernal* sleep of the toad.

hi-ber-nate (hī′bẽr-nāt), *v.i.* to pass the winter in a state of torpor or sleep, as do certain animals; to winter.

hi-bis-cus (hĭ-bĭs′kŭs), *n.* a kind of plant, often a shrub or small tree with large, showy flowers: some species are raised in India for their fiber, which is used for hemp.

hic-cup (hĭk′ŭp), *n.* a short convulsive cough: *v.i.* to utter a short convulsive cough. Also, **hiccough**.

hic ja-cet (hĭk jā′sĕt), a Latin inscription used on tombstones, meaning "here lies."

hick-o-ry (hĭk′ō-rĭ), *n.* [*pl.* hickories (-rĭz)], an American nut-bearing tree.

hid (hĭd), *p.adj.* concealed; not known: secret. Also, **hidden**.

hi-dal-go (hĭ-dăl′gō), *n.* in Spain, a nobleman of the lowest rank.

hide (hīd), *v.t.* [*p.t.* hid, *p.p.* hidden, *p.pr.* hiding], to conceal; to put out of view; to remove from danger; to shelter; secrete; not to confess; disguise: *v.i.* to lie concealed; to keep oneself out of view; to be withdrawn from view: *n.* an animal's skin, raw or dressed; formerly, a measure of land.
Syn. *v.* bury, screen, mask.
Ant. (see disclose).

hide-bound (hīd′bound″), *adj.* having the skin close or tight, prejudiced; bigoted.

hid-e-ous (hĭd′ē-ŭs), *adj.* offensive to the sight, ear, or taste; shocking; dreadful; horrible.—*adv.* **hideously**.—*n.* **hideousness**.
Syn. grim, ghastly, grisly.
Ant. (see beautiful).

hid-ing (hīd′ĭng), *p.pr.* of *hide*: *n.* concealment; the act of withholding from view or knowledge.

hie (hī), *v.t.* [*p.t.* and *p.p.* hied, *p.pr.* hieing], to cause to hasten; urge: *v.i.* to hasten; hurry: as, *hie* thee hence.

hi-er-arch (hī′ẽr-ärk), *n.* the chief ruler of a religious body; the leader of an angelic host; in ancient Greece, an officer who had charge of offerings given in fulfilment of a religious vow.—*adj.* **hierarchic, hierarchical**.

hi-er-arch-y (hī′ẽr-är″kĭ), *n.* [*pl.* hierarchies (-kĭz)], the clergy of a church in higher and lower ranks; priesthood; rank of holy beings, as angels; in biology, a series of systematic groups.

hi-e-rat-ic (hī'ēr-ăt'ĭk), *adj.* pertaining to priests; sacred; consecrated to sacred uses. Also, **hieratical.**

hi-er-o-glyph (hī'ēr-ō-glĭf"), *n.* a sacred character or symbol. Also, **hieroglyphic.**

hi-er-o-glyph-ic (hī"ēr-ō-glĭf'ĭk), *n.* a sacred character or symbol: *pl.* the picture writings of the ancient Egyptians, etc.: *adj.* belonging to hieroglyphics; emblematic.

Hieroglyphics

hig-gle (hĭg'l), *v.i.* to carry provisions about for sale; chaffer; dispute about trifles.

hig-gle-dy-pig-gle-dy (hĭg'l-dĭ-pĭg'l-dĭ), *adj.* in confusion; topsy-turvy: *adv.* in a confused manner; mixedly.

high (hī), *adj.* elevated in place; lofty; exalted in degree or quality; chief; head; honorable; noble; of large amount or quantity; strong; powerful; intense; tempestuous; full or complete; near to the wind; tainted; shrill; acute: *adv.* to a great altitude; eminently; luxuriously.
Syn. adj. lofty, tall, exalted.
Ant. (see deep).

High-Church (hī'chûrch), *adj.* attaching great importance to the authority of the Episcopal Church, its sacraments and priesthood; full of ceremony; extremely ritualistic.

high-col-ored (hī-kŭl'ērd), *adj.* having a strong, deep, or glaring color; flushed; vivid; exaggerated; pronounced.

high-est (hī'ĕst), *adj.* most high: *n.* a synonym for heaven; as, glory in the *highest.*

high-fa-lu-tin (hī"fȧ-lū'tĭn), *adj.* pompous; high-sounding; bombastic: *n.* bombastic speech.

high-flown (hī'flōn"), *adj.* elevated; proud; extravagant; inflated.

high-hand-ed (hī'hăn"dĕd), *adj.* violent; arbitrary; oppressive; overbearing.

high-land (hī'lănd), *n.* elevated or mountainous land: **Highlands,** the mountainous districts of Scotland; the mountains bordering the Hudson River, etc.

high-land-er (hī'lăn-dēr), *n.* a mountaineer: **Highlander,** a native of the Scotch Highlands.

high life (hī lĭf), fashionable society; its manner of living.

high-lows (hī'lōz"), *n.pl.* laced shoes reaching to the ankle.

high-ly (hī'lĭ), *adv.* in a lofty manner; in a great degree; with favorable esteem or opinion; proudly; arrogantly.

High Mass (hī mȧs), a Mass, usually at the high altar, at which a deacon and a subdeacon assist the priest.

high-ness (hī'nĕs), *n.* the state or quality of being lofty: **Highness,** a title of honor applied, with a possessive pronoun, to persons of princely rank; as, His Royal *Highness*

high priest (hī' prēst"), a chief priest, especially the principal priest of the Jewish hierarchy or council.

high-road (hī'rōd"), *n.* a chief road; a much traveled or main road; an easy course or method. Also, **highway.**

high seas (hī sēz), the open sea, beyond the limits of waters belonging to certain nations.

high-strung (hī'strŭng"), *adj.* extremely sensitive; easily excited; having nerves quickly affected; spirited.

hight (hīt), called or named; *p.p.* of a verb not now in use: a form found only in poetry.

high-toned (hī'tōnd"), *adj.* pitched in the upper range of musical or vocal sounds; high-principled; fashionable; honorable.

high-wa-ter (hī'wô'tēr), *adj.* pertaining to high tide, or its height or time.

high-way (hī'wā"), *n.* a public road; a course or path. Also, **highroad.**

high-way-man (hī'wā"măn), *n.* [*pl.* highwaymen (-mĕn)], one who robs on the public road.

high wine (hī wīn), an intoxicant containing a large amount of alcohol.

hike (hīk), *v.i.* to tramp; to take a long walk; to march: *n.* a long walk or march. [Colloq.]

hi-la-ri-ous (hĭ-lā'rĭ-ŭs; hī-lā'rĭ-ŭs), *adj.* merry; exhilarated; noisy; mirthful.—*adv.* **hilariously.**

hi-lar-i-ty (hĭ-lăr'ĭ-tĭ), *n.* [*pl.* hilarities (-tĭz)], noisy merriment; exhilaration; jollity.

hill (hĭl), *n.* an elevation less than a mountain; a small mound or heap: *v.t.* to draw earth about (plants) in mounds, as potatoes.

hill-ock (hĭl'ŭk), *n.* a small hill or elevation; a mound; as, the cart jolted over one *hillock* after another.

hill-y (hĭl'ĭ), *adj.* abounding with, or characterized by, hills; rugged; not level.—*n.* **hilliness.**

hilt (hĭlt), *n.* a handle, especially of a sword; as, the *hilt* of Arthur's sword was rich with jewels.

him (hĭm), *pron.* the objective case of *he;* as, they brought *him* home in triumph.

him-self (hĭm-sĕlf'), *pron.* a reflexive form of *him;* one's individuality; as, he came to *himself.*

hind (hīnd), *n.* the female of the stag or red deer; a farm servant; peasant: *adj.* backward; in the rear.

hind-er (hīn'dēr), *adj.* pertaining to, or constituting, the back or rear of anything; as, she was in the *hinder* part of the boat.

hin-der (hĭn'dēr), *v.t.* to obstruct or impede: *v.i.* to impose obstructions or impediments.

hind-er-most (hīn'dēr-mōst), *adj.* farthest in the rear; as, he was *hindermost* in the race. Also, **hindmost.**

hind-most (hīnd'mōst), *adj.* farthest from the front; in the extreme rear; last. Also, **hindermost.**

hin-drance (hĭn'drăns), *n.* obstruction; anything that is in the way; as, stooping is a *hindrance* to deep breathing.

Hin-du (hĭn'dōō; hĭn-dōō'), *n.* a native of Hindustan belonging to the Aryan race; Brahman: *adj.* pertaining to the Hindus or to Hinduism. Also, **Hindoo.**

Hin-du-ism (hĭn'dōō-ĭzm), *n.* the religion of the Hindus. Also, **Hindooism.**

Hin-du-sta-ni (hĭn"dōō-stä'nē), *n.* the official and common language of India; Urdu. Also, **Hindoostanee.**

hinge (hĭnj), *n.* the joints or hooks on which a door, gate, lid, etc., turn or swing; the joint of an oyster or similar shell;

that on which anything depends or turns: *v.t.* to furnish with a hinge: *v.i.* to turn or depend as on a hinge; as, my future *hinges* upon the decision of one person.

hint (hint), *v.t.* to suggest; mention casually: *n.* a suggestion; distant allusion.
Syn. v. refer, intimate, insinuate.

hip (hip), *n.* the upper fleshy part of the thigh; the thigh joint; haunch; the first joint of an insect's leg; the rafter at the junction of two sloping roofs; the fruit of the brier or dog-rose; melancholy: *interj.* a huzzah: *v.t.* [*p.t.* and *p.p.* hipped, *p.pr.* hipping], to sprain or fracture the thigh joint of; build with two sloping roofs joining at the top; throw by a certain hold in wrestling.

hip-po-drome (hip'ō-drōm), *n.* an ancient Greek race course for games and chariots; a circus.

hip-po-griff (hip'ō-grif), *n.* an imaginary winged monster, half horse, half griffin. Also, hippogryph.

hip-po-pot-a-mus (hip"ō-pŏt'á-mŭs), *n.* [*pl.* hippopotami (-mī), -muses (-ĕz)], a large water animal of Africa; the river horse.

hire (hīr), *v.t.* to engage for temporary service at a certain price; bribe; let or lease: *n.* recompense or consideration paid for the use of anything; wages; bribe.

hire-ling (hīr'lĭng), *n.* one who serves for wages: *adj.* mercenary.

hir-sute (hûr'sūt; hẽr-sūt'), *adj.* hairy; shaggy; as, the *hirsute* covering of animals; a *hirsute* growth on the face.

his (hĭz), *pron.* the possessive case of *he;* as, *his* merit is great; the credit is *his.*

His-pan-ic (hĭs-păn'ĭk), *adj.* pertaining to Hispania or Spain.

hiss (hĭs), *n.* a noise, made by forcing the breath between the tongue and upper teeth, and resembling that of a serpent or goose: *v.i.* to utter such a sound, especially as expressing disapprobation or contempt; as, they *hissed* at what he said: *v.t.* to condemn or express contempt for by such a sound; as, you are kindly asked not to applaud or *hiss* these pictures.

hist (hĭst), *interj.* silence! hark! as, *hist!* What was that sound?

his-tol-o-gy (hĭs-tŏl'ō-jĭ), *n.* the science of animal tissues.

his-to-ri-an (hĭs-tō'rĭ-ăn), *n.* a writer about, or student of, the events of the past.

his-tor-ic (hĭs-tŏr'ĭk), *adj.* pertaining to, contained in, or celebrated in, history; relating to the past. Also, historical. —*adv.* historically.

his-to-ri-og-ra-pher (hĭs-tō"rĭ-ŏg'rá-fẽr), *n.* a writer especially appointed to study and write of past events, usually in a particular country.

his-to-ry (hĭs'tō-rĭ), *n.* [*pl.* histories (-rĭz)], an account of past facts and events affecting one or more nations, etc., arranged in the order of their occurrence; the branch of knowledge that studies and explains such facts.
Syn. annals, story, record.
Ant. (see fable, legend).

his-tri-on-ic (hĭs"trĭ-ŏn'ĭk), *adj.* pertaining to actors or the stage; theatrical. Also, histrionical.—*adv.* histrionically.

his-tri-on-ics (hĭs"trĭ-ŏn'ĭks), *n.pl.* the art of theatrical representation.

hit (hĭt), *v.t.* [*p.t.* and *p.p.* hit, *p.pr.* hitting], to strike; give a blow to; touch (the mark); attain to; suit: *v.i.* to clash or collide; succeed: *n.* a stroke or blow; a lucky event; appropriate remark; as, his answer was a clever *hit.*

hitch (hĭch), *n.* a catch; that which acts like a catch; impediment; a pulling or jerking upwards: *v.i.* to become entangled or caught; move by jerks; strike the feet together, as horses: *v.t.* to fasten or tie; pull up with a jerk.

hitch-ing (hĭch'ĭng), *p.pr.* of *hitch:* *n.* a fastening in harness; as, the *hitching* of the horse was soon done.

hith-er (hĭth'ẽr), *adv.* to this place: *adj.* on the side nearest to the speaker.

hi-ther-to (hĭth'ẽr-tōō"; hĭth"ẽr-tōō'), *adv.* to this time; till now.

hive (hīv), *n.* a box or house for bees; a swarm of bees living in such a box; a busy group or society: *v.t.* to gather or put into a hive; harbor.

hives (hīvz), *n.pl.* nettle rash and similar diseases of the skin; croup.

ho (hō), *interj.* stop! hold! also, a cry of delight, surprise, etc., or, when repeated, of mockery; halloo! attend!

hoar (hōr), *adj.* white; gray with age; as, his locks were *hoar;* ancient.

hoard (hōrd), *n.* a store or treasure laid up secretly; a collection of things: *v.i.* to lay up money; to store goods; as, he *hoards* because it gives him pleasure: *v.t.* to collect and lay up; to store secretly; to accumulate; as, he *hoards* his money for others.

hoard-ing (hōrd'ĭng), *p.pr.* of *hoard:* *n.* the act of storing up; a fence of rough boards inclosing a building site.

hoar-frost (hōr'frŏst"), *n.* white particles of frozen dew or moisture.

hoar-hound (hōr'hound"), *n.* a plant which has a bitter taste, and is a weak tonic, used as a remedy for colds, coughs, etc. Also, horehound.

hoarse (hōrs), *adj.* rough and harsh in sound, as the voice when affected by a cold.

hoarse-ly (hōrs'lĭ), *adv.* in a rough, harsh voice; as, he shouted *hoarsely.*

hoarse-ness (hōrs'nĕs), *n.* the state of being rough or harsh in voice; huskiness.

hoa-ry (hōr'ĭ), *adj.* white or gray, as hair from age; aged; ancient.

hoax (hōks), *n.* a sportive deceptive trick; practical joke: *v.t.* to take in, or delude, by a trick.

hob (hŏb), *n.* the flat part of a grate on which things are placed to be kept warm; a sprite or fairy.

hob-ble (hŏb''l), *v.i.* to walk with a limp or awkward step: *v.t.* embarrass; perplex; shackle: *n.* limping or awkward step.

hob-ble-de-hoy (hŏb''l-dē-hoi'), *n.* a lad between boyhood and manhood; an inexperienced, awkward youth.

hob-ble skirt (hŏb''l skûrt), a woman's dress made tight below the knees.

hob-by (hŏb'ĭ), *n.* [*pl.* hobbies (-ĭz)], a favorite pursuit or object; an ambling nag; a kind of falcon or hawk.

hob-by-horse (hŏb'ĭ-hôrs"), *n.* a stick with a horse's head, across which children sit; a wooden rocking-horse; a character in old morris dances.

hob-gob-lin (hŏb'gŏb'lĭn), *n.* a goblin, sprite, or elf, especially one of frightful appearance; hence, an alarming apparition.

hob-nail (hŏb'nāl"), *n.* a short thick nail with a large head, used for protecting the soles of heavy boots.

hob-nob (hŏb'nob"), *v.i.* to drink or talk familiarly (with); associate intimately together; as, some neighbors spend much of their time *hobnobbing*.

ho-bo (hō'bō), *n.* an idle, shiftless, traveling workman; a tramp.

hock (hŏk), *n.* the joint between the knee and the shank of some quadrupeds, corresponding to the ankle in man; the back part of the human knee-joint; any white Rhine wine: *v.t.* slang, to pawn.

hock-ey (hŏk'ĭ), *n.* an outdoor game played with a ball or disk and with clubs curved at one end.

ho-cus (hō'kŭs), *v.t.* [*p.t.* and *p.p.* hocused, *p.pr.* hocusing], to cheat or trick; to stupefy or render insensible by means of drugged liquor in order to cheat or rob; *n.* a person who tricks or juggles; drugged liquor.

ho-cus-po-cus (hō'kŭs-pō'kŭs), *n.* a juggler's trick; a juggler; a cheat; nonsense; as, what you are telling is *hocus-pocus*.

hod (hŏd), *n.* a wooden trough, fastened to a long handle, for carrying mortar or bricks; a coal scuttle; a male ferret or weasel.

hod-car-ri-er (hŏd'kăr'ĭ-ẽr), *n.* a laborer who carries mortar and bricks. Also, **hodman.**

hodge-podge (hŏj'pŏj"), *n.* a mixed mass of ingredients, as in a *hodgepodge* pudding; a mixture; a medley. Also, **hotchpotch.**

hod-man (hŏd'măn), *n.* a bricklayer's laborer. Also, **hodcarrier.**

hoe (hō), *n.* a farmer's tool for cutting weeds, etc.: *v.t.* to cut, or till, with this tool; clear from weeds.

hoe-cake (hō'kāk), *n.* a kind of thin corn meal bread.

hog (hŏg), *n.* a swine; a kind of rough broom used for scrubbing a ship's bottom under water; a grasping, gluttonous person: *v.t.* [*p.t.* and *p.p.* hogged, *p.pr.* hogging], to scrub (a ship's bottom) under water; to cut (a horse's hair) short; to take more than a fair share of: *v.i.* to droop at both ends: said of a ship.

hog-gish (hŏg'ĭsh), *adj.* gluttonous; filthy; coarsely selfish.

hogs-head (hŏgz'hĕd), *n.* a measure of capacity equal to 52½ imperial gallons or 63 wine gallons; a large barrel or cask holding from 100 to 140 gallons.

Hoh-en-zol-lern (hō'ĕn-tsŏl'ẽrn), *n.* the family name of the house from which came the kings of Prussia after 1701 and the emperors of Germany after 1871.

hoi-den (hoi'dn), *n.* a rude rustic or country girl; romp: *adj.* inelegant; rustic; ill-mannered: *v.i.* to romp roughly or indelicately. Also, **hoyden.**

hoist (hoist), *v.t.* to lift or raise with tackle; heave: *n.* an apparatus for lifting goods from a lower to a higher floor, etc.; a lift.

hoi-ty-toi-ty (hoi'tĭ-toi'tĭ), *interj.* an exclamation of surprise, rebuke, etc.

ho-key-po-key (hō'kĭ-pō'kĭ), *n.* a cheap kind of ice cream sold in the streets. Also, **hoky-poky.** [COLLOQ.]

hold (hōld), *v.t.* [*p.t.* held, *p.p.* held, holden, *p.pr.* holding], to grasp and keep in the hand; clutch; retain; keep; possess; as, he *holds* office; connect; judge or consider; as, *hold* him a model of culture; entertain; contain; celebrate; use; maintain, as an opinion; as, I *hold* that he is correct; to call and conduct, as a meeting: *v.i.* to cling; adhere; stand good; as, this rule always *holds* good; continue; proceed; restrain oneself; refrain; maintain an opinion: *n.* the act of grasping or keeping; a grasp or clutch; an embrace; support; a fortified place; that part of a vessel where the cargo is stored.—*n.* **holder.**

Syn. v. detain, keep, retain.

hold-back (hōld'băk"), *n.* a check; hindrance; restraint; that part of the harness used in backing a carriage.

hold-fast (hōld'fąst"), *n.* a hook or support; something used to secure and keep in place something else, as a flat-headed nail, a catch, a clamp, etc.

hold-ing (hōld'ĭng), *n.* property owned; right of possession; a farm or other estate rented from another; that which secures, binds, or influences.

hole (hōl), *n.* an opening in or through something; a cavity; hollow place; pit; perforation; the burrow of an animal; a mean habitation; a difficulty or dilemma; in golf, a cavity in the putting green into which is sunk a metal cup; the distance between such points; the points scored.

hol-i-day (hŏl'ĭ-dā), *n.* a day of gaiety and joy in celebration of some event, etc.; a day of freedom from labor: *adj.* pertaining to a festival; joyous; gay. Also, **holy day, holyday.**

ho-li-ness (hō'lĭ-nĕs), *n.* the state or quality of being free from sin; moral and spiritual purity; sacredness: **Holiness**, a title of the Pope.

Syn. sanctity, piety, sacredness.

Ant. (see impiety).

hol-land (hŏl'ănd), *n.* fine unbleached linen, glazed or unglazed, used for window shades, children's garments, etc.: *pl.* a kind of gin.

hol-loa (hŏl'ō; hō-lō'), *v.i.* to shout to one at a distance: *n.* a shout: *interj.* a cry to attract attention. Also, **halloo, hallos, hello, holla, hollo, hullo.**

hol-low (hŏl'ō), *n.* a cavity; pit; groove; space between hills or elevations: *v.t.* to make hollow: *adj.* having an empty space within: opposite to *solid;* sunken; superficial; unreal; insincere; deep or low: used of sound: *adv.* colloquially, completely; thoroughly: sometimes with *all.*

hol-low-ness (hŏl'ō-nĕs), *n.* the state of being empty or sunken; insincerity; deepness (of sound).

hol-low ware (hŏl'ō wâr), cast-iron kitchen utensils, earthenware, etc.

hol-ly (hŏl'ĭ), *n.* a shrub or tree with glossy, prickly leaves and red berries, much used at Christmas time.

hol-ly-hock (hŏl'ĭ-hŏk), *n.* a tall plant of the mallow family with large flowers.

holm (hōm), *n.* an evergreen oak; low flat land by the side of a river; a small river island.

hol-o-caust (hŏl'ō-kôst), *n.* a sacrifice wholly consumed by fire; complete or total destruction, as by fire, of many human beings.

hol-ster (hōl'stẽr), *n.* a leather pistol case usually carried at the belt, or often at the front of a saddle.

holt (hōlt), *n.* a wooded hill; a group of trees.

ho-ly (hō'lĭ), *adj.* [*comp.* holier, *superl.* holiest], pure; morally and spiritually perfect; sinless; preëminently good; pious; sacred; consecrated.—*adv.* **holily.**
Syn. devout, religious.

ho-ly-day (hō'lĭ-dā''), *n.* a festival: generally used of religious celebrations. Also, **holy day, holiday.**

ho-ly Joe (hō'lĭ jō), an army chaplain. [SLANG.]

Ho-ly Land (hō'lĭ lănd), Palestine, the ancient home of the Jews, and the birthplace of Christianity.

ho-ly-stone (hō'lĭ-stōn), *n.* a large flat stone used for scouring the ship's decks: *v.t.* to scrub (a deck) with this stone.

hom-age (hŏm'āj), *n.* respect paid by external action; deference; reverence; honor; respect; in feudal times, the ceremony by which a tenant or vassal promised fealty and service to his landlord.

home (hōm), *n.* one's abode or residence; dwelling place of a man and his family; fatherland; locality where a plant or animal abounds; a benevolent or charitable institution: *adj.* pertaining to one's abode or country; domestic; to the point designed; as, a *home* thrust; near; effective: *adv.* to or at home; to the uttermost; closely.

home-li-ness (hōm'lĭ-nĕs), *n.* the state of being plain-featured; rudeness; lack of beauty.

home-ly (hōm'lĭ), *adj.* plain-featured; as, a *homely* man; uncultured; rude; benevolent, kindly, or homelike.
Syn. plain, ugly, coarse.

home-made (hōm'mād''), *adj.* of household or domestic manufacture; as, *homemade* bread.

ho-me-o-path-ic (hō''mē-ō-păth'ĭk), *adj.* of or pertaining to homeopathy, a system of treating disease; opposite to *allopathic;* extremely small in quantity. Also, **homœopathic.**

ho-me-op-a-thist (hō''mē-ŏp'ȧ-thĭst), *n.* one who practices or believes in homeopathy, or the giving of medicine in very small doses. Also, **homœopathist.**

ho-me-op-a-thy (hō''mē-ŏp'ȧ-thĭ), *n.* the medical system introduced by Hahnemann (1755–1843) which seeks to cure disease by giving, in minute quantities, medicines which produce in the patient symptoms similar to those that the same medicine would produce in a healthy person. Also, **homœopathy.**

Ho-mer-ic (hō-mĕr'ĭk), *adj.* pertaining to the time and works of the poet Homer.

home rule (hōm rōōl), local self-government; especially, that form of government for Ireland.

home-sick (hōm'sĭk''), *adj.* longing for home.—*n.* **homesickness.**

home-spun (hōm'spŭn''), *n.* cloth woven at home or made of yarn spun there; an unpolished rustic or countrified person: *adj.* of domestic make; plain and homely.

home-stead (hōm'stĕd), *n.* a dwelling house with the adjoining land; original abode.

home-ward (hōm'wẽrd), *adj.* and *adv.* towards home.

hom-i-cid-al (hŏm'ĭ-sīd''ăl), *adj.* pertaining to, or tending to, the killing of a human being; murderous.

hom-i-cide (hŏm'ĭ-sīd), *n.* the of a human being; one kills another.

hom-i-let-ic (hŏm''ĭ-lĕt'ĭk), *adj.* pert ing to the compositio sermons; like a sermon. Also, **homiletic**

hom-i-let-ics (hŏm''ĭ-lĕt'ĭks), *n.pl.* branch of rhetoric w treats of sermons and their composition.

hom-i-ly (hŏm'ĭ-lĭ), *n.* [*pl.* homilies (-lĭz)]. religious discourse or sermon.

hom-ing (hōm'ĭng), *adj.* returning to the place from which one started: said of carrier pigeons.

hom-i-ny (hŏm'ĭ-nĭ), *n.* Indian corn soaked so as to remove the hull, and then coarsely ground.

ho-mo- (hō'mō-), a *prefix* meaning like, same, similar; as, *homocercal*, lobed alike, as the tail of a mackerel.

ho-mœ-op-a-thy (hō''mē-ŏp'ȧ-thĭ), *n.* the medical system of Hahnemann, by which "like cures like." Also, **homeopathy.**—*n.* **homeopathist.**—*adj.* **homeopathic.**

ho-mo-ge-ne-i-ty (hō''mō-jē-nē'ĭ-tĭ), *n.* likeness; similarity; identity.

ho-mo-ge-ne-ous (hō''mō-jē'nē-ŭs; hŏm''ō-jē'nē-ŭs), *adj.* uniform; of the same kind or nature; composed of similar parts or elements.

ho-mol-o-gous (hō-mŏl'ō-gŭs), *adj.* identical; exactly alike in structure, position, etc.

ho-mol-o-gy (hō-mŏl'ō-jĭ), *n.* likeness of structure, as the relation between the leg and arm.

hom-o-nym (hŏm'ō-nĭm; hō'mō-nĭm), *n.* a word like another in sound, but differing in meaning, as *pair, pare, pear; to, too, two.*

hom-o-phone (hŏm'ō-fōn; hō'mō-fōn), *n.* a letter representing the same sound as another; a word having the same sound as another.

ho-moph-o-nous (hō-mŏf'ō-nŭs), *adj.* alike in sound, but differing in meaning; as, these are *homophonous* words, *so, sow,* and *sew.*

hone (hōn), *n.* a kind of fine whetstone for sharpening razors, etc.: *v.t.* to sharpen on such a whetstone.

hon-est (ŏn'ĕst), *adj.* upright; just; sincere; honorable; fair; righteous; chaste; frank or open.—*adv.* **honestly.**
Syn. trustworthy, candid, correct.

hon-es-ty (ŏn'ĕs-tĭ), *n.* the quality of being free from deceit; fairness and truth; chastity; uprightness.
Syn. integrity, probity.
Ant. (see dishonesty).

hon-ey (hŭn'ĭ), *n.* a sweet, sticky, syrupy substance collected by bees from flowers; sweetness; darling or sweet one: *v.t.* to talk to in an endearing or flattering manner; *adj.* very sweet.

hon-ey-bee (hŭn'ĭ-bē''), *n.* the common hive bee; as, the *honeybee* gathers honey from every flower.

hon-ey-comb (hŭn'ĭ-kōm''), *n.* the structure of waxen six-sided cells made by bees for their home and storehouse; any structure or substance full of holes; as, *honeycombs* or flaws in guns, caused by exploded powder: *v.t.* to fill with holes, etc., so as to leave only thin partitions.

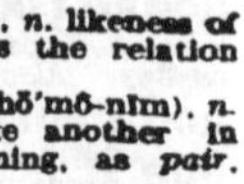

Honeycomb

hon-ey-dew (hŭn'ĭ-dū"), *n.* a sweet, sugary substance that comes out of the leaves of trees and other plants in small drops, like dew; a sweet substance secreted by certain kinds of insects, especially plant lice; a variety of tobacco; a variety of melon.

hon-ey lo-cust (hŭn'ĭ lō'kŭst), a large American tree of the bean family.

hon-ey-moon (hŭn'ĭ-mōōn"), *n.* the first month after marriage: so called from an ancient custom of drinking a beverage made of honey for a month after a wedding.

hon-ey-suck-le (hŭn'ĭ-sŭk"l), *n.* a climbing plant with fragrant flowers.

hon-or (ŏn'ẽr), *n.* respectful regard; high esteem; worship; reputation; exalted rank; fame; uprightness; scorn of meanness, deceit, or unfairness; self-respect; chastity; an outward mark of high esteem; a title used in addressing certain officials; one of the four highest trump cards in whist: *pl.* distinguished standing in school or college; as, he graduated with *honors*: *v.t.* to treat with respect, deference, or civility; revere or worship; bestow marks of esteem upon: followed by *with*; dignify; acknowledge; accept and pay when due; as, the bank will *honor* my check. Also, **honour**.

Syn. n. respect, reverence, esteem.

Ant. (see dishonor).

hon-or-a-ble (ŏn'ẽr-ȧ-bl), *adj.* worthy of, or conferring, esteem; distinguished in rank; high-minded; illustrious; upright; a title of distinction. Also, **honourable**.—*n.* **honorableness, honourableness.**

hon-or-a-bly (ŏn'ẽr-ȧ-blĭ), *adv.* with respect or esteem; fairly and uprightly. Also, **honourably.**

hon-o-ra-ri-um (ŏn"ō-rā'rĭ-ŭm), *n.* a fee paid to a professional man.

hon-or-a-ry (ŏn'ẽr-ā-rĭ), *adj.* done or conferred as a sign of high esteem: as, an *honorary* degree.

hood (hŏŏd), *n.* a soft wrapper or covering for the head; a head-covering attached to a monk's or woman's cloak; something resembling such a head-covering; a folding cover for a carriage; an ornamental fold hanging down the back denoting a university degree; a cowl: *v.t.* to cover or furnish with, or as with, a hood.

hood-lum (hŏŏd'lŭm), *n.* originally a California rough or bully; a rowdy. [Colloq.]

hoo-doo (hōō'dōō), *n.* a person or thing that causes ill luck: *v.t.* to bring ill luck upon. [Colloq.]

hood-wink (hŏŏd'wĭnk), *v.t.* to deceive; blindfold; as, he *hoodwinked* everybody with his tale of misfortune.

hoof (hōōf), *n.* [*pl.* hoofs], the horny substance covering the feet of certain animals, as horses, etc.; an animal with hoofs.

hook (hŏŏk), *n.* a curved piece of metal, bone, etc., to hold or catch something, as a fish-*hook*; a trap; an instrument for lopping or cutting, as a sickle; a cape or headland: *v.t.* to catch with, or as with, a hook; to gore or attack with the horns: said of a horned animal: *v.i.* to bend in the shape of a hook; become fastened to anything with a hook: with *on*; in golf, to drive widely to the left.

hook-ah (hŏŏk'ȧ), *n.* a pipe with a long tube, easily bent, which draws the smoke through a vase containing water. Also, **hooka.**

hooked (hŏŏkt; hŏŏk'ĕd), *p.adj.* curved like a hook; as, a *hooked* nose; a *hooked* stick.

hook-er (hŏŏk'ẽr), *n.* a fishing smack; a small Dutch vessel; any clumsy, ill-fitted, old craft.

hook-worm (hŏŏk'wûrm"), *n.* a blood-sucking parasitic worm, which invades the human intestines and causes great debility; a disease, causing one to be weak, tired, languid, etc.

hoop (hōōp), *n.* a circular metal or wooden band to hold together the staves of a cask, etc.; the band of a finger ring; a kind of crinoline or stiff cloth used to expand a woman's dress; a large circular ring of metal or wood used by children at play; anything curved like such a ring: *v.t.* to bind or secure with a curved band; encircle.

Hoo-sier (hōō'zhẽr), *n.* a citizen of the State of Indiana: a nickname.

hoot (hōōt), *n.* a contemptuous shout; the cry of an owl: *v.t.* to jeer or drive with contemptuous shouts: *v.i.* to utter a sharp cry.

hop (hŏp), *v.t.* [*p.t.* and *p.p.* hopped, *p.pr.* hopping], to leap over; add, or fill with, the bitter flowers of the hop vine; as, to *hop* beer: *v.i.* to proceed by short leaps on one leg; skip with both legs; limp; to pick hops: *n.* a jump on one leg; a dance; a plant, the ripened cones or flowers of which are used in brewing to impart a bitter taste to malt liquors: *pl.* the fruit of this plant which is used in making yeast: *adj.* pertaining to this plant.

hope (hōp), *n.* the desire of good accompanied by expectation; anticipation; confidence; the object of desire: *v.t.* to expect with confidence or desire: *v.i.* to cherish a desire for good; trust confidently.

Syn. n. expectation, trust.

Ant. (see fear, distrust).

hope-ful (hōp'fŏŏl), *adj.* full of confident expectation; as, he was *hopeful* that the war would soon end; promising success; as, *hopeful* prospects.—*n.* **hopefulness.**

hope-ful-ly (hōp'fŏŏl-ĭ), *adv.* with pleasant anticipation; with confidence; as, he continued on his way *hopefully*.

hope-less (hōp'lĕs), *adj.* without expectation of good; despairing; as, *hopeless* grief.—*adv.* **hopelessly.**—*n.* **hopelessness.**

hop-lite (hŏp'līt), *n.* an ancient Greek heavy armed foot soldier.

hop-per (hŏp'ẽr), *n.* one who, or that which, makes short leaps or skips; a name for various leaping insects; a wooden trough or funnel through which grain passes into a mill; mechanism in a piano for lifting the hammer; a seed-basket used in sowing grain; a hop picker; the basin of a water-closet.

hop-ple (hŏp'l), *n.* a fetter: *v.t.* to shackle or fetter; as, they *hoppled* the horses and turned them loose.

hop-scotch (hŏp'skŏch"), *n.* a child's game, in which a flat stone is driven by the foot while the player hops.

horde (hōrd), *n.* a wandering tribe or clan dwelling in tents or wagons; a vast multitude: *v.i.* to live or act together in large groups.

hore-hound (hōr'hound"), *n.* a plant that is used as a remedy for colds and coughs. Also, **hoarhound.**

ho-ri-zon (hō-rī'zŭn; hō-rī'zn), *n.* the circular line where the sky and earth or sea appear to meet; hence, the limit of one's mental vision.

hor-i-zon-tal (hŏr'ĭ-zŏn'tăl), *adj.* parallel to, or situated near, the line where earth meets sky; level: opposite to *vertical.*
Syn. flat, level, plain, even.
Ant. (see inclined).

hor-i-zon-tal-ly (hŏr"ĭ-zŏn'tăl-ĭ), *adv.* in a direction at right angles.

horn (hôrn), *n.* a hard and usually pointed projection, growing upon the head of certain animals, especially cattle, goats, deer, etc.; the material of which animals' horns are composed; a thickened form of tissue; a musical wind instrument; one of the extremities or ends of the moon when in crescent form.

horn-beak (hôrn'bēk"), *n.* the garfish, a fish with a snout like a spear.

horn-beam (hôrn'bēm"), *n.* a small tree of hard tough white wood: used for cogwheels, etc.

horn-bill (hôrn'bĭl"), *n.* a bird with a large horn-crested bill, something like the kingfishers.

horn-blende (hôrn'blĕnd"), *n.* a widely distributed dark-green or black-colored mineral composed chiefly of silica, magnesia, and lime.

horned (hôrnd; hôr-nĕd), *adj.* having horns; as, *horned* cattle; horn-shaped.

hor-net (hôr'nĕt), *n.* a kind of wasp which inflicts a severe sting; hence, a waspish, disagreeable person.

horn-pipe (hôrn'pīp"), *n.* a lively dance, especially by sailors; music for this dance; a musical wind instrument once much used in Wales.

horn-y (hôr'nĭ), *adj.* hard like horn; made of horn.

hor-ny-hand-ed (hôr'nĭ-hănd'ed), *adj.* having the hands hardened by labor.

hor-o-loge (hŏr'ō-lōj; hŏr'ō-lŏj), *n.* a timepiece of any kind, as a clock, watch, dial, etc.

ho-rol-o-gy (hō-rŏl'ō-jĭ), *n.* science or art of measuring time, or of making timepieces.

hor-o-scope (hŏr'ō-skōp), *n.* a representation of the heavens at any time, especially at one's birth, from which astrologers profess to foretell the future.

hor-ri-ble (hŏr'ĭ-bl), *adj.* terrible; dreadful; shocking; hideous.

hor-ri-ble-ness (hŏr'ĭ-bl-nĕs), *n.* the state of being terrible or dreadful; as, we all realize the *horribleness* of war.

hor-ri-bly (hŏr'ĭ-blĭ), *adv.* terribly; dreadfully; as, the workmen were *horribly* torn by the explosion.

hor-rid (hŏr'ĭd), *adj.* dreadful; terrible; hideous; most obnoxious; gloomy.

hor-rif-ic (hŏ-rĭf'ĭk), *adj.* causing dread or horror; as, the *horrific* fury of the storm.

hor-ri-fy (hŏr'ĭ-fī), *v.t.* [*p.t.* and *p.p.* horrified], to fill or strike with great fear, dread, terror, repugnance.

hor-ror (hŏr'ẽr), *n.* excessive fear accompanied with shuddering; extreme dread; great disgust; that which fills with dread or terror; as, the *horror* of a great crime: *pl.* extreme dread or depression.

horse (hôrs), *n.* a solid-hoofed quadruped used for riding or drawing burdens; a male of the species; cavalry; a framework or machine for the support of anything; a foot-rope to support the foot of a sailor under a yard or the bowsprit: *v.t.* to mount on, or furnish with, a horse; carry on horseback; place astride: *v.i.* to get on horseback: *adj.* coarse or large of its kind.

horse-chest-nut (hôrs"chĕs'nŭt), *n.* a kind of tree with large, nutlike seeds growing in burrs like chestnuts; the seed of this tree.

horse-fly (hôrs'flī"), *n.* a large fly that stings animals; a gadfly.

horse-hair (hôrs'hâr"), *n.* the hair of the mane or tail of a horse.

horse-man (hôrs'măn), *n.* a rider upon a horse; a cavalryman.—*n.* horsemanship.

horse-play (hôrs'plā"), *n.* coarse, rough, noisy fun.

horse pow-er (hôrs' pou"ẽr), a theoretical unit of work, equal to 33,000 pounds raised one foot in one minute. Also, horsepower.

horse-rad-ish (hôrs'răd"ĭsh), *n.* a plant of the cabbage family whose root is used as a relish or appetizer.

horse-shoe (hôrs'shōō"), *n.* a U-shaped metal shoe to protect the hoof of a horse; a small round or oval fortification; anything U-shaped; the king crab.

horse-weed (hôrs'wēd"), *n.* the fleabane, or common weed; horse cane.

horse-whip (hôrs'hwĭp"), *n.* a long leather whip with a lash.

hors-y (hôr'sĭ), *adj.* pertaining to horses; interested in horses. Also, horsey.

hor-ta-tive (hôr'tȧ-tĭv), *adj.* tending to rouse, encourage, or urge on; giving earnest advice. Also, hortatory.

hor-ti-cul-tur-al (hôr"tĭ-kŭl'tūr-ăl), *adj.* pertaining to the art of cultivating gardens or orchards.

hor-ti-cul-ture (hôr'tĭ-kŭl'tūr), *n.* the art of cultivating gardens or orchards.

hor-ti-cul-tur-ist (hôr"tĭ-kŭl'tūr-ĭst), *n.* one who is skilled in horticulture, or the science of growing fruits, vegetables, and plants.

ho-san-na (hō-zăn'ȧ), *n.* an exclamation of praise and glory to God.

hose (hōz), *n.* [*pl.* hose], coverings for the legs; stockings; rubberlike tubing for carrying water, etc., from a faucet, hydrant, or fire engine.

Ho-se-a (hō-zē'ȧ), *n.* a Hebrew prophet of the eighth century B. C.; the book of the Old Testament that contains his teachings.

ho-sier (hō'zhẽr), *n.* one who deals in stockings and other kinds of knit goods.

ho-sier-y (hō'zhẽr-ĭ), *n.* stockings, underclothing, etc.; a manufactory for such goods.

hos-pi-ta-ble (hŏs'pĭ-tȧ-bl), *adj.* receiving and entertaining friends or strangers; kind and generous to guests and strangers; as, the Southern people are very *hospitable.*—*adv.* hospitably.

hos-pi-tal (hŏs'pĭ-tăl), *n.* an institution for the medical treatment and care of the sick.

hos-pi-tal-i-ty (hŏs"pĭ-tăl'ĭ-tĭ), *n.* [*pl.* hospitalities (-tĭz)], the practice of entertaining friends and strangers with kindness and liberality.

host (hōst), *n.* a crowd; multitude; army; one who entertains another in public or private; a landlord of a hotel or inn; an animal or plant organism on which another lives.—**Host**, the consecrated bread or wafer of the Eucharist, in the Greek, Roman Catholic, and Lutheran Churches.

hos-tage (hŏs'tāj), *n.* a person who remains in the hands of another as a pledge for the fulfilment of certain conditions; a pledge.

hos-tel (hŏs'tĕl), *n.* formerly, an inn or hotel; as, the Tabard Inn was a famous *hostel*.

hos-tel-ry (hŏs'tĕl-rĭ), *n.* an inn or lodging-house; as, the Wayside Inn was a quaint old *hostelry*.

host-ess (hōs'tĕs), *n.* a woman who receives and entertains guests either in a home or of an inn: **hostess house**, in the World War, an establishment of the Young Women's Christian Association at camps and cantonments for extending aid and hospitality to women visitors.

hos-tile (hŏs'tĭl; hŏs'tĭl), *adj.* showing ill will or animosity; adverse; unfriendly; repugnant: *n.* an enemy; especially, an American Indian in enmity with the whites. —*adv.* **hostilely**.

hos-til-i-ty (hŏs-tĭl'ĭ-tĭ), *n.* [*pl.* hostilities (-tĭz)], the state of being opposed; antagonism; enmity; animosity; as, his *hostility* made all my efforts useless. *pl.* acts of warfare.

hos-tler (hŏs'lẽr; ŏs'lẽr), *n.* one who takes care of horses at an inn or stable; one who takes charge of a railroad locomotive after a trip. Also, **ostler**.

hot (hŏt), *adj.* [*comp.* hotter, *superl.* hottest], having much heat; burning; fiery; passionate; lustful; ardent; furious; pungent; acrid; unendurable; near to the object sought for.

hot-bed (hŏt'bĕd"), *n.* a bed of earth covered with glass and made artificially warm to force the growth of plants; hence, any place or condition that promotes rapid growth or great activity.

hotch-potch (hŏch'pŏch"), *n.* a mixture of various ingredients; a thick broth of meat and vegetables. Also, **hodgepodge**.

ho-tel (hō-tĕl'), *n.* a house for entertaining travelers or strangers; a superior inn or lodging house; the official residence of a French commanding general.

hot-foot (hŏt'fŏŏt"), *adv.* in great haste; as, he set off *hotfoot* in pursuit of the escaped prisoner.

hot-head-ed (hŏt"hĕd'ĕd), *adj.* hasty; impetuous, of fiery temper.

hot-house (hŏt'hous"), *n.* a glass house heated for raising tender plants; a drying room.

hot-spur (hŏt'spûr"), *n.* a rash, hasty, or hot-headed man: *adj.* hot-headed.

Hot-ten-tot (hŏt'n-tŏt), *n.* one of a savage South African race in Cape Colony; the language spoken by the Hottentots, characterized by a peculiar click.

hou-dah (hou'dȧ), *n.* a covered seat on the back of an elephant or camel. Also, **howdah**.

hough (hŏk), *n.* the joint between knee and shank of quadrupeds. Also, **hock**.

hound (hound), *n.* a kind of domestic dog, with large, drooping ears, which hunts squirrels, rabbits, foxes, etc.; a despicable, mean fellow: *v.t.* to chase with, or as with, hunting dogs; incite; set upon; nag.

hour (our), *n.* the 1/24 part of a day; 60 minutes; particular time: *pl.* life; in the Roman Catholic Church, prayers repeated at stated times; the book containing prayers.—*adj.* and *adv.* **hourly**.

hour-glass (our'glȧs"), *n.* a device for measuring time by running sand through a narrow neck of a glass vessel.

Hourglass

hou-ri (hŏŏ'rĭ; hou'rĭ), *n.* [*pl.* houris (-rĭz)], one of the dark-eyed nymphs or maidens of the Mohammedan paradise.

house (hous), *n.* a building for residence; place of abode; household manner of living; family or race, especially if of high rank; one of the divisions of a lawmaking or church-governing body; a quorum of the members of such a body, or enough to transact business; with qualifying term, a building for assembly, business, etc.; an audience; a business firm; in astrology, the station of a planet in the heavens, or the twelfth part of the heavens; a square on a chessboard; a workhouse: *v.t.* (houz), to place in a dwelling; shelter or lodge; make secure before a storm: *v.i.* hide; to take shelter.

house boat (hous bōt), a covered vessel fitted up as a river residence.

house-break-er (hous'brāk"ẽr), *n.* one who forcibly enters a dwelling with intent to steal; a burglar.

house-hold (hous'hōld"), *n.* a family living together: *adj.* domestic; pertaining to a family or home.—*n.* **householder**.

house-keep-ing (hous'kēp"ĭng), *n.* the management of domestic affairs.—*n.* **housekeeper**.

house-wife (hous'wīf"), *n.* the mistress of a home; one who manages domestic affairs; a small case for sewing materials, particularly in the army: pronounced *hus'ĭf*.—*adj.* **housewifely**.

hous-ing (houz'ĭng), *n.* act of giving shelter to; that which gives shelter; as, the *housing* of the workmen in the city; a saddle cloth: *pl.* ornamental trappings of a horse: *adj.* designating a form of periscope on a submarine.

hov-el (hŏv'ĕl), *n.* a poor cottage, hut, or cabin: *v.t.* to shelter in a hut or cabin.

hov-er (hŭv'ẽr), *v.i.* to flutter over or about; stand in suspense or expectation; move about in a neighborhood.

how (hou), *adv.* in what manner; to what degree or extent; for what reason.

how-be-it (hou-bē'ĭt), *adv.* nevertheless; although; however; yet.

how-dah (hou'dȧ), *n.* a protected seat for riding on an elephant or camel. Also, **houdah**.

Howdah

how-ev-er (hou"ĕv'ẽr), *adv.* in whatever manner or degree; at all events; in any case: *conj.* notwithstanding; yet.

how-itz-er (hou'ĭt-sẽr), *n.* a short light cannon used for throwing shells.

howl (houl), *n.* the prolonged cry of a dog or wolf; the cry of one in pain or distress: *v.i.* to cry like a dog or wolf; utter a prolonged cry of pain or distress; roar, like the wind: cry down by clamor: *v.t.* to utter in a loud wailing tone.

howl-er (houl'ẽr), *n.* one who wails or cries loudly; a South American monkey which climbs trees and wails at night.

howl-ing (houl'ĭng), *p.adj.* crying loudly; dreary; dismal; extreme.

how-so-ev-er (hou"sō-ĕv'ẽr), *adv.* in what manner soever; although; in whatever degree or extent.

hoy (hoi), *n.* a heavy one-masted coasting vessel: *interj.* ho!

hoy-den (hoi'dn), *n.* a rude, romping girl: *adj.* rough; ill-mannered. Also, **hoiden.**

Hoyle (hoil), *n.* a book of rules for card games, originally edited by Edmund Hoyle of England: **according to Hoyle,** adhering strictly to the rules in any game.

hub (hŭb), *n.* the central part of a wheel; the peg at which quoits are thrown; a kind of steel punch used in coining, etc.; a hilt; a jutting obstruction.

hub-bub (hŭb'ub), *n.* uproar; a loud noise of many voices; tumult.

huck-a-back (hŭk'ȧ-băk), *n.* a rough kind of linen or cotton cloth, used for toweling.

huck-le-ber-ry (hŭk'l-bĕr"ĭ), *n.* [*pl.* huckleberries (-ĭz)], a small black or dark blue berry that grows on bushes and is good to eat raw or cooked; the whortleberry; the blueberry.

huck-ster (hŭk'stẽr), *n.* a peddler or hawker; one who retails small articles; a mean tricky fellow.

hud-dle (hŭd'l), *v.t.* to crowd together in a disorderly manner; collect closely; place or perform in haste or disorder: *v.i.* to come in a crowd or haste: with *on, up, over:* *n.* confusion; crowd.

hue (hū), *n.* color; tint; a shouting; clamor; as, to raise the *hue* and cry.

hue and cry (hū ănd krī), in law, the common process of pursuing a felon, criminal, or wrongdoer; an official gazette in England advertising deserters from the army.

huff (hŭf), *n.* fit of petulance or ill humor; sudden offense taken: *v.t.* to puff or blow up; treat with insolence; bully; remove (a piece at checkers), when one's opponent fails to take with it.—*adj.* **huffy.**

hug (hŭg), *n.* a close embrace; a particular grip in wrestling: *v.t.* [*p.t.* and *p.p.* hugged, *p.pr.* hugging], to embrace closely; fondle; hold fast; keep close to.

huge (hūj), *adj.* vast; very large; immense; as, a *huge* crowd.

huge-ly (hūj'lĭ), *adv.* immensely; exceedingly; as, I like it *hugely.*

huge-ness (hūj'nĕs), *n.* vastness; very large bulk; as, the *hugeness* of a rock or an undertaking.

hug-ger-mug-ger (hŭg'ẽr-mŭg"ẽr), *adj.* secret; confused: *n.* confusion.

Hu-gue-not (hū'gē-nŏt), *n.* a name applied to French Protestants of the 16th and 17th centuries.

hulk (hŭlk), *n.* the body of a ship, especially if old or unseaworthy: *pl.* old mastless ships formerly used as convict prisons: with *the.*

hulk-ing (hŭlk'ĭng), *adj.* unwieldy; bulky; as, a *hulking* fellow.

hull (hŭl), *n.* outer covering, especially of grain or nuts; the pod, ... or frame of a vessel: *v.t.* to peel off the husk of or pierce (the hull of a vessel) with a shell: *v.i.* to drift to and fro upon ... like a ship without sails.

hul-la-ba-loo (hŭl"ȧ-bȧ-lōō'), *n.* uproar; noisy contention; tumult.

hul-lo (hŭ-lō'), *v., n.,* and *interj.* an informal salutation. Also, **halloo, hello, hollo,** etc.

hum (hŭm), *n.* the noise of bees and other insects in flight: *v.i.* [*p.t.* and *p.p.* hummed, *p.pr.* humming], to make such a noise; to be in energetic motion or action; as, he made things *hum:* *v.t.* to sing in a low undertone: *interj.* a sound with a pause implying hesitation or consideration.

hu-man (hū'măn), *adj.* pertaining to, or characteristic of, man or mankind; having the qualities of a man; not divine.

hu-mane (hū-mān'), *adj.* having the feelings proper to man; benevolent; kind; compassionate; elevating; gentle; sympathizing.

Syn. merciful, pitying, tender.
Ant. (see cruel).

hu-mane-ly (hū-mān'lĭ), *adv.* in a kind manner; benevolently; compassionately.

hu-mane-ness (hū-mān'nĕs), *n.* the quality of being kind and gentle; benevolence.

hu-man-ism (hū'măn-ĭzm), *n.* the state of belonging to mankind; interest in mankind; the study of the classics.

hu-man-ist (hū'măn-ĭst), *n.* a student of the classics; one versed in the knowledge of man's nature.

hu-man-is-tic (hū"măn-ĭs'tĭk), *adj.* pertaining to, or characteristic of, the classics; pertaining to mankind.

hu-man-i-ta-ri-an (hū-măn"ĭ-tā'rĭ-ăn), *n.* a philanthropist, or charitably inclined person; one who believes that the duty of man consists of acting rightly to others: *adj.* philanthropic.

hu-man-i-ty (hū-măn'ĭ-tĭ), *n.* [*pl.* humanities (-tĭz)], mankind; the state or quality of belonging to mankind; philanthropy, or charity towards others; kindness; benevolence: *pl.* classical learning and literature.

hu-man-ize (hū'măn-īz), *v.t.* to render like mankind; soften; to refine or civilize.

hu-man-kind (hū'măn-kīnd), *n.* the race of men.

hu-man-ly (hū'măn-lĭ), *adv.* after the manner of men; as, he was *humanly* kind.

hum-ble (hŭm'bl), *adj.* having a low estimate of oneself; modest; meek; submissive; lowly; mean; obscure; unassuming; as, they lived in a *humble* cottage by the sea: *v.t.* to make submissive; subdue; bring low; mortify; humiliate.

Syn. *v.* degrade, depress.
Ant. (see haughty).

hum-ble-bee (hŭm'bl-bē"), *n.* a kind of large bee. Also, **bumblebee.**

hum-ble pie (hŭm'bl pī), a pie made of the entrails of a deer, intended for the servants' table; hence, to eat *humble pie* is to make apologies, humiliate oneself, or withdraw one's words.

... (hŭm'bŭg"), *n.* a fraud or ... tion under fair

tenses; sham; a plausible deceiver; a spirit of trickery or deception.

hum-bug-ger-y (hŭm'bŭg'ẽr-ĭ), *n.* [*pl.* humbuggeries(-ĭz)], imposition or fraud.

hum-drum (hŭm'drŭm"), *adj.* dull; monotonous; commonplace; as, a *humdrum* life.

hu-mer-us (hū'mẽr-ŭs), *n.* [*pl.* humeri (-ī)], the bone of the arm from the shoulder to the elbow.

hu-mid (hū'mĭd), *adj.* damp; moist; somewhat wet or watery; as, *humid* air or atmosphere.

hu-mid-i-ty (hū-mĭd'ĭ-tĭ), *n.* dampness; moisture: said especially of the air or atmosphere; as, the *humidity* was very high to-day.

hu-mil-i-ate (hū-mĭl'ĭ-āt), *v.t.* to humble; abase; put to shame.

hu-mil-i-a-tion (hū-mĭl'ĭ-ā'shŭn), *n.* the act of putting to shame; the state of being put to shame; mortification; abasement.

hu-mil-i-ty (hū-mĭl'ĭ-tĭ), *n.* [*pl.* humilities (-tĭz)], the state or quality of being lowly in mind; modesty; self-abasement.

hum-ming bird (hŭm'ĭng bûrd), a very small bird noted for its bright colors, and for its habit of hovering about flowers, and moving its wings so rapidly as to make a buzzing, humming noise.

hum-mock (hŭm'ŭk), *n.* a large mass of floating ice; a hillock or mound.

hu-mor (hū'mẽr; ū'mẽr), *n.* wit; merriment; the tendency to look at things from the mirthful side; caprice; proud conceit; temper; as, good or bad *humor;* petulance; peevishness; moisture of the body and eye; disease: *v.t.* to indulge; yield to a particular desire of.

Syn. n. mood, temper.

hu-mor-ist (hū'mẽr-ĭst), *n.* one who indulges his own mood; a droll person; one whose writing or conversation is characterized by a spirit of fun.

hu-mor-ous (hū'mẽr-ŭs), *adj.* full of, or characterized by, mirth and fun; as, Mark Twain was a *humorous* writer; comical; diverting; witty; pleasant; merry.

hu-mor-some (hū'mẽr-sŭm), *adj.* full of moods; laughable; capricious; witty.

hump (hŭmp), *n.* a protuberance or bulging, especially that on the back of a camel, or that formed by a crooked back in man: *v.t.* to vex or annoy; slang, to exert (oneself).

hump-back (hŭmp'băk"), *n.* one with a deformed back; a crooked back. Also, **hunchback.**

humph (hŭmf), *interj.* an exclamation of doubt or dissatisfaction.

Hump-ty Dump-ty (hŭmp'tĭ dŭmp'tĭ), the hero of a nursery rime; a character in pantomime, or silent plays: **humpty-dumpty**, *adj.* characterized by short limbs and a round body.

hu-mus (hū'mŭs), *n.* vegetable mold; that part of soil formed by the decay of animal and vegetable matter which makes the earth rich.

Hun (hŭn), *n.* one of a warlike, wandering people of northern Asia, who, in the 5th century, overran and laid waste Europe; a name applied during the World War to the Germans, and later to their allies, because of their barbarities; any destructive person.

hunch (hŭnch), *n.* a hump; lump; a thrust with the fist or elbow.

hunch-back (hŭnch'băk"), *n.* a person with a crooked back. Also, **humpback.**

hun-dred (hŭn'drĕd), *adj.* ten times ten: *n.* the number of ten times ten; the symbol [C. or 100] denoting it; a division of an English county; the name given to a township in the State of Delaware.

hun-dredth (hŭn'drĕdth), *adj.* the ordinal of one hundred: *n.* one of a hundred equal parts.

hun-dred-weight (hŭn'drĕd-wāt"), *n.* the 1/20 part of a ton, or 100 pounds avoirdupois.

hung (hŭng), past tense and past participle of the verb *hang.*

Hun-ga-ri-an (hŭn-gā'rĭ-ăn), *adj.* pertaining to Hungary or its people: *n.* a native of Hungary.

hun-ger (hŭn'gẽr), *n.* keenness of appetite; pain or uneasiness caused by want of food; strong desire: *v.i.* to feel the desire for food; to have a longing or earnest desire.

hun-gry (hŭn'grĭ), *adj.* [*comp.* hungrier, *superl.* hungriest], having a keen appetite; feeling pain or uneasiness for want of food; emaciated or thin; eagerly desirous; unfertile: said of land.—*adv.* **hungrily.**

hunk (hŭnk), *n.* a lump or large piece; as, a *hunk* of bread or meat.

hunks (hŭnks), *n.* a niggardly or mean fellow; a covetous man; miser.

hunt (hŭnt), *v.t.* to pursue or chase, as game or wild animals; follow closely; search after: *v.i.* to follow the chase: *n.* pursuit of game or wild animals; pack of hounds; an association of huntsmen; district over which hounds pursue game; a search; as, a *hunt* for a house.

Syn., v. seek, chase, track.

hunt-er (hŭn'tẽr), *n.* one who pursues game; a horse or hound trained for pursuing game; a watch with a metal cover.

hunt-ing (hŭnt'ĭng), *p.pr.* of *hunt:* *n.* the act or practice of one who searches or pursues; pursuit; search.

hunt-ing box (hŭnt'ĭng bŏks), a temporary residence while following the chase.

hunt-ing watch (hŭnt'ĭng wŏch), a watch having its face protected with a metal cover.

hunt-ress (hŭn'trĕs), *n.* a woman who follows the chase; as, the goddess Diana was a *huntress.*

hunts-man (hŭnts'măn), *n.* [*pl.* huntsmen (-mĕn)], one who pursues game; one who manages a pack of hounds.

Hurdle

hur-dle (hûr'dl), *n.* a movable fence of interwoven twigs, branches, or steel; a fence or barrier to be leaped over in steeplechasing or in racing; a rude frame on which criminals were formerly dragged to execution: *v.t.* to cover or inclose with a fence or barrier to be leaped over in racing.

hur-dy-gur-dy (hûr'dĭ-gûr'dĭ), *n.* a musical instrument played by turning a crank; especially, a mechanical piano mounted on wheels and played on the street.

hurl (hûrl), *v.t.* to throw with violence; drive forcibly; utter with vehemence: *n.* the act of throwing.

hur-ly-bur-ly (hûr'lĭ-bûr'lĭ), *n.* tumult; great commotion; confusion.

hur-rah (hŏŏ-rä'; hû-rä'), *interj.* a shout of joy, triumph, applause, etc.: *v.i.* to utter such a shout in applause, etc. Also, **hurra, huzzah.**

hur-ri-cane (hûr'ĭ-kān), *n.* a gale of extreme violence, characterized by fitful changes of the wind; a violent storm; as, the *hurricane* struck us violently.

hur-ri-cane deck (hûr'ĭ-kān dĕk), the bridge-deck, or topmost deck, of a steamship.

hur-ried (hûr'ĭd), *p.adj.* exhibiting, or characterized by, haste; hasty; done in haste; going or working at speed; as, he always lived a *hurried* life.

hur-ry (hûr'ĭ), *v.t.* [*p.t.* and *p.p.* hurried, *p.pr.* hurrying], to impel to greater speed; hasten on: *v.i.* to act or move with haste: *n.* haste; urgency; precipitation; confusion; a coaling stage for loading vessels.

hur-ry-scur-ry (hûr'ĭ-skûr'ĭ), *n.* confused bustle: *adv.* in disorderly haste.

hurt (hûrt), *v.t.* [*p.t.* and *p.p.* hurt, *p.pr.* hurting], to cause or inflict pain in; wound; grieve; injure; impair or damage: *v.i.* to feel pain: *n.* a wound; injury; damage or loss.

hurt-ful (hûrt'fŏŏl), *adj.* injurious; harmful; as, *hurtful* exercise.
Syn. noxious, pernicious.
Ant. (see beneficial).

hurt-ful-ly (hûrt'fŏŏl-ĭ), *adv.* harmfully; injuriously.

hur-tle (hûr'tl), *v.t.* to move violently; impel forcibly: *v.i.* to clash; dash in collision.

hur-tle-ber-ry (hûr'tl-bĕr'ĭ), *n.* a kind of blueberry; a huckleberry. Also, **whortleberry.**

hus-band (hŭz'bănd), *n.* a married man; the correlative of *wife: v.t.* to manage or use with economy; as, she will *husband* her money.

hus-band-man (hŭz'bănd-măn), *n.* [*pl.* husbandmen (-mĕn)], a tiller of the soil; farmer.

hus-band-ry (hŭz'bănd-rĭ), *n.* agriculture; farming; frugality.
Syn. cultivation, tillage.

hush (hŭsh), *interj.* be still! silence! *n.* quietness; silence: *v.t.* to make silent; soothe.

husk (hŭsk), *n.* the dry outer covering of certain fruits or seeds: *v.t.* to remove hulls from; as, shall I *husk* this corn?

husk-i-ly (hŭs'kĭ-lĭ), *adv.* hoarsely; as, he spoke *huskily.*

husk-i-ness (hŭs'kĭ-nĕs), *n.* the state of being hoarse.

husk-ing bee (hŭs'kĭng bē), a social gathering to assist in hulling corn.

husk-y (hŭs'kĭ), *adj.* [*comp.* huskier, *superl.* huskiest], consisting of, or like, husks, or dry hulls; worthless; rough or hoarse: said of the voice; colloquially, powerful: *n.* an American Indian sledge dog; a well-developed, energetic man.

hus-sar (hŏŏ-zär'), *n.* a light-armed cavalry soldier in European armies.

hus-tings (hŭs'tĭngz), *n.pl.* a court held in the Guildhall before the Lord Mayor, Recorder, and sheriffs of London; formerly, the stand from which Parliamentary candidates, when nominated, addressed the electors; now, a place where campaign speeches are made.

hus-tle (hŭs'l), *v.t.* to push roughly; jostle; mob; shake together in confusion: *v.i.* exhibit energy and alacrity; to hurry. [COLLOQ.]

hut (hŭt), *n.* a small house or cabin; a temporary building for lodging troops.

Forms of Huts

hutch (hŭch), *n.* a bin, box, or chest in which things may be stored; as, a grain *hutch;* a coop or pen in which animals may be kept; as, a rabbit *hutch;* a mining trough for washing ore: *v.t.* to store; to wash (ore) in a trough.

huz-zah (hŭ-zä'; hŏŏ-zä'), *v., n.,* and *interj.* expressive of joy or applause. Also, **huzza, hurrah.**

hy-a-cinth (hī'*ȧ*-sĭnth), *n.* a well-known plant of the lily family with stalks of bell-shaped flowers; also, one of its bulbs or flowers; a kind of mineral used as a jewel.

hy-a-cin-thine (hī'*ȧ*-sĭn'thĭn), *adj.* pertaining to the hyacinth; like Hyacinthus, the handsome youth who, according to Greek myth, was accidentally killed by Apollo and transformed into the hyacinth; hence, handsome; beautiful.

Hy-a-des (hī'*ȧ*-dēz), *n.pl.* the five stars in the face of the constellation Taurus, supposed by the ancients to bring rain when they rose with the sun. Also, **Hyads.**

hy-æ-na (hī-ē'n*ȧ*), *n.* a bristly-maned, wolflike, flesh-eating animal. Also, **hyena.**

hy-brid (hī'brĭd), *n.* a mongrel; an animal or plant produced from the mixture of two distinct classes or varieties; a compound word, the elements of which are derived from different languages.

hy-dra (hī'dr*ȧ*), *n.* any evil which, when grappled with, appears to become greater; a kind of fresh-water plants which multiply on division: **Hydra,** in classical mythology, the water serpent with nine heads (slain by Hercules), each of which on being cut off became two.

hy-dran-ge-a (hī-drăn'jē-*ȧ*), *n.* a plant with large heads of showy flowers of many colors.

hy-drant (hī'drănt), *n.* a pipe with a valve and spout through which water may be drawn from the mains of water works; a water plug.

hy-drate (hī'drāt), *n.* a chemical compound containing a definite quantity of water: *v.t.* to combine with water to form this compound.

hy-drau-lic (hī-drô'lĭk), *adj.* pertaining to fluids in motion: *n.pl.* the science of liquids in motion, and the application of the forces which influence the motions of water for practical purposes, as raising water, etc.

hy-dro-air-plane (hī'drō-âr'plān), *n.* a flying machine, or aëroplane, so adapted that it can rise from, or alight upon, the surface of water. Also, **hydro-aëroplane.**

hy-dro-car-bon (hī'drō-kär'bŏn), *n.* one of a large class of compounds containing carbon and hydrogen, as acetylene, gasoline, etc.

hy-dro-chlo-rate (hī″drō-klō′rāt), *n.* a salt of hydrochloric or muriatic acid.

hy-dro-chlo-ric (hī″drō-klō′rĭk), *adj.* pertaining to, or composed of, hydrogen and chlorine: **hydrochloric acid,** a colorless, corrosive, gaseous compound of equal parts of hydrogen and chlorine, exceedingly soluble in water: in solution, often called *muriatic acid.*

hy-dro-cy-an-ic (hī″drō-sī-ăn′ĭk), *adj.* composed of hydrogen and cyanogen: **hydrocyanic acid,** an unstable, volatile, and extremely poisonous liquid.

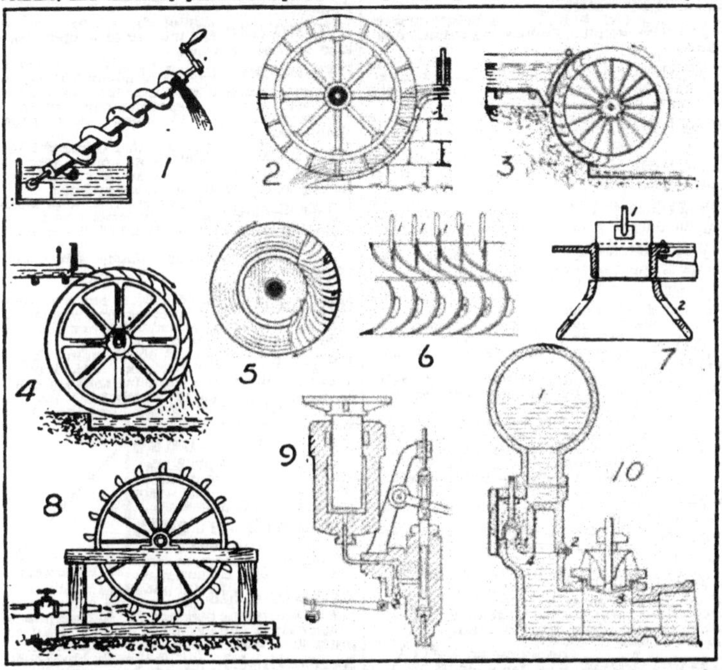

Hydraulic Devices. 1, Archimedes' screw; 2, breast water wheel; 3, undershot water wheel; 4, overshot water wheel; 5, inward flow turbine wheel; 6, guide blades and buckets of impulse turbine; 7, guide blade chamber and wheel of turbine in section; 8, Pelton wheel; 9, handpower hydraulic press; 10, hydraulic ram.

hy-dro-dy-nam-ic (hī″drō-dī-năm′ĭk), *adj.* pertaining to, or derived from, the pressure of water: *n.pl.* the science that treats of water pressure.

hy-dro-gen (hī′drō-jĕn), *n.* a colorless, gaseous, inflammable substance, which becomes liquid under great pressure, and is the lightest element yet known, much lighter than air; when combined with oxygen it produces water. Hydrogen is the standard unit for the estimation of atomic weights and volumes

hy-drog-ra-phy (hī-drŏg′rȧ-fĭ), *n.* the art of measuring and mapping the water surface of the earth, as oceans, lakes, coast-lines, etc., with information as to their depth, tide, beds, etc.

hy-drom-e-ter (hī-drŏm′ē-tẽr), *n.* an instrument for determining the specific gravity, strength, etc., of fluids.

hy-dro-path-ic (hī″drō-păth′ĭk), *adj.* pertaining to the treatment which cures disease by water pressure: *n.* an establishment where patients reside while under water treatment.

hy-dro-pho-bi-a (hī″drō-fō′bĭ-ȧ), *n.* a disease caused by the bite of a mad dog, due to the poisonous liquid from the saliva of the dog, and accompanied by convulsions and unnatural dread of water.

hy-dro-phone (hī′drō-fōn), *n.* an instrument for the detection of submerged sounds, both as to their direction and approximate distance.

hy-dro-plane (hī′drō-plān), *n.* a motor boat with sloping bottom which rises to the surface when driven at high speed; an airplane attachment to a boat which serves to lift it partly out of the water; a gliding boat; the diving rudder of a submarine boat.

hy-dro-stat (hī'drō-stăt), *n.* an apparatus for the prevention of boiler explosions; an electrical contrivance for indicating the leakage or overflow of water.

hy-dro-stat-ics (hī"drō-stăt'ĭks), *n.pl.* that branch of physics that treats of the pressure and equilibrium of fluids at rest: **hydrostatic,** *adj.* pertaining to this branch of physics.

hy-dro-ther-a-py (hī"drō-thĕr'ȧ-pĭ), *n.* treatment of disease by water; water cure.

hy-dro-ther-mal (hī"drō-thûr'măl), *adj.* pertaining to the action of hot water.

hy-e-na (hī-ē'nȧ), *n.* a bristly-maned, wolflike, flesh-eating animal. Also, **hyæna.**

hy-ge-ian (hī-jē'ăn), *adj.* pertaining to health or its preservation: **Hygeian,** pertaining to Hygeia, the goddess of health, daughter of Esculapius.

hy-gi-ene (hī'jĭ-ēn; hī'jēn), *n.* the science of health, its preservation, and the laws of sanitation.

hy-gi-en-ic (hī"jĭ-ĕn'ĭk), *adj.* pertaining to health or the science of health; healthful; sanitary.

hy-grom-e-ter (hī-grŏm'ē-tẽr), *n.* an instrument for measuring the degree of moisture in the atmosphere.

hy-grom-e-try (hī-grŏm'ē-trĭ), *n.* that branch of physics that treats of the moisture of the atmosphere.

hy-gro-scope (hī'grō-skōp), *n.* an instrument which shows whether there is more or less moisture in the atmosphere, without telling its amount.

hy-men (hī'mĕn), *n.* marriage: from Hymen, the fabled Grecian god of marriage.

hy-me-ne-al (hī"mē-nē'ăl), *adj.* pertaining to marriage; nuptial: *n.* a marriage song.

hymn (hĭm), *n.* a sacred song expressive of praise or adoration: *v.t.* to sing praises to; adore or praise by singing.

hym-nal (hĭm'năl), *n.* a collection of sacred songs for public worship.

hym-nol-o-gy (hĭm-nŏl'ō-jĭ), *n.* the study of sacred songs, their origin, use, etc.

hy-per- (hī'pẽr-), a *prefix* meaning over, beyond, excess, and, in chemistry, highest.

hy-per-bo-la (hī-pûr'bō-lȧ), *n.* a curve formed by the section of a cone when the cutting plane makes a greater angle with the base than is made by the surface of the cone.

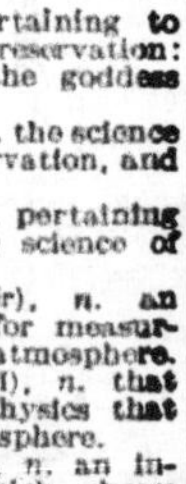

Hyperbola

hy-per-bo-le (hī-pûr'bō-lē), *n.* a figure of speech which expresses more than the truth; exaggeration.

hy-per-bol-ic (hī"pẽr-bŏl'ĭk), *adj.* in literature, pertaining to, or containing, overstatements or untruths; exaggerated; in mathematics, belonging to, or of the nature of, a hyperbola. Also, **hyperbolical.**

hy-per-bo-re-an (hī"pẽr-bō'rē-ăn), *adj.* arctic; very cold; frigid.

hy-per-crit-i-cal (hī"pẽr-krĭt'ĭ-kăl), *adj.* oversevere in comment or judgment; too quick to find fault; difficult to please; excessively nice or exact.

hy-per-me-tro-pi-a (hī"pẽr-mē-trō'pĭ-ȧ), *n.* farsightedness: the opposite of *myopia,* or nearsightedness.

hy-phen (hī'fĕn), *n.* a mark [-] to join words or to separate syllables: *v.t.* to join with, or separate by, such a mark.

hy-phen-a-ted (hī-fĕn-ā'tĕd), *adj.* connected by a hyphen.

hyp-no-sis (hĭp-nō'sĭs), *n.* a trance; an artificial sleep.

hyp-not-ic (hĭp-nŏt'ĭk), *adj.* pertaining to, or producing, artificial sleep: *n.* a person who can be put into a trancelike sleep.

hyp-no-tism (hĭp'nō-tĭzm), *n.* a method of causing a trancelike sleep.

hyp-no-tize (hĭp'nō-tīz), *v.t.* to cause to fall into, or to subject to, a kind of sleep or trance.

hyp-o-chon-dri-a (hĭp'ō-kŏn'drĭ-ȧ; hī"pō-kŏn'drĭ-ȧ), *n.* a disease attended with extreme melancholy, and with anxiety respecting one's state of health; melancholy; the blues. Also, **hypochondriasis.**

hyp-o-chon-dri-ac (hĭp"ō-kŏn'drĭ-ăk), *n.* one who is affected with extreme melancholy: *adj.* pertaining to, or affected with, melancholy.

hy-poc-ri-sy (hĭ-pŏk'rĭ-sĭ), *n.* a pretending to be what one is not; a putting on of an appearance of virtue which is not possessed.

Syn. cant, pretense, sham, affectation, deception.

Ant. (see truth).

hyp-o-crite (hĭp'ō-krĭt), *n.* one who practices pretense or deception to gain his own ends: a dissimulator or deceiver.

Syn. dissembler, impostor, cheat.

hy-po-der-mic (hī"pō-dûr'mĭk; hĭp"ō-dûr'mĭk), *adj.* inserted under the skin: *n.* a medicine thus injected.

hy-po-gas-tric (hī"pō-găs'trĭk), *adj.* pertaining to the lower part of the abdomen or belly.

hy-pot-e-nuse (hī-pŏt'ē-nūs; hī-pŏt'ē-nūs), *n.* the side of a right-angled triangle opposite the right angle. Also, **hypothenuse.**

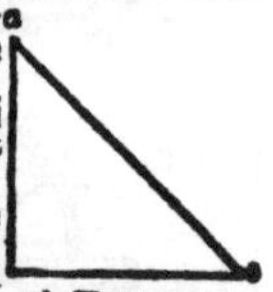

ab, Hypotenuse

hy-poth-e-cate (hī-pŏth'ē-kāt; hĭ-pŏth'ē-kāt), *v.t.* to give (property) as security for a debt; to mortgage.

hy-poth-e-sis (hī-pŏth'ē-sĭs; hĭ-pŏth'ē-sĭs), *n.* [*pl.* hypotheses (-sēz)], something assumed for the purpose of argument; a theory which may or may not prove to be true; supposition; conjecture.

hy-po-thet-ic (hī"pō-thĕt'ĭk; hĭp"ō-thĕt'ĭk), *adj.* based on supposition, or on something assumed; conjectural. Also, **hypothetical.**—*adv.* **hypothetically.**

hys-sop (hĭs'ŭp), *n.* a fragrant plant with blue flowers; an unidentified plant mentioned in the Bible.

hys-te-ri-a (hĭs-tē'rĭ-ȧ), *n.* a nervous affection of women, characterized by choking sensations, spasms of laughter or weeping, and frequently by the imitating of other diseases.

hys-ter-i-cal (hĭs-tĕr'ĭ-kăl), *adj.* pertaining to, or affected by, a nervous disease marked by laughing and crying; violently emotional.—*adv.* **hysterically.**

hys-ter-ics (hĭs-tĕr'ĭks), *n.pl.* a fit of nervous laughing and crying.

I

I (ī), *pron.* [*pl.* we (wē)], *nom. sing.* of the pronoun of the first person; the word by which the speaker or writer denotes himself.

i-am-bic (ī-ăm'bĭk), *adj.* having a verse form in which each foot consists of a short (unaccented) syllable followed by a long (accented) syllable: *n.* a metrical foot having a short syllable followed by a long one; a satirical poem in verse composed of such metrical feet.

i-am-bus (ī-ăm'bŭs), *n.* a metrical foot consisting of two syllables, of which the first is short and the second is long [⏑ —]; a word of two syllables, accented on the second syllable, as *ignore'*.

i-bex (ī'bĕks), *n.* a class of wild goats, having very large recurved horns, the best known species of which is the Alpine steinbok or bouquetin.

i-bis (ī'bĭs), *n.* a kind of large wading bird, having a long, curved beak, of which the most notable species is the sacred Ibis of the ancient Egyptians.

ice (īs), *n.* frozen water; any substance resembling ice, as menthol *ice;* a frozen confection, such as water *ice:* *v.t.* to change into a frozen state; freeze; preserve by freezing; cover with melted sugar; frost.

ice age (īs āj), the glacial epoch, or period: as, during the *ice age* the ice in North America was 1,500 feet deep at the margin of the ocean.

ice-berg (īs'bûrg"), *n.* a large mass of ice detached from a glacier, and floating in the sea.

ice boat (īs bōt), a strong steamboat used to break a channel through a frozen river, lake, etc.; a boat mounted on runners and propelled by sails on a frozen surface.

Ice Boat

iced (īst), *p.adj.* covered with ice or made cold with ice; as, *iced* tea; covered with icing; as, *iced* cake.

ice field (īs fēld), a very large sheet of floating ice.

ice floe (īs flō), a sheet of floating ice smaller than an ice field.

ice pack (īs păk), a field of broken and drifting ice, consisting of great masses packed together.

ich-neu-mon (ĭk-nū'mŏn), *n.* a weasel-like animal found in Asia, Africa, and Spain, which feeds on mice, rats, snakes, and birds, and is sometimes domesticated.

ich-neu-mon fly (ĭk-nū'mŏn flī), any of a large group of insects that deposit their eggs in or upon other insects which their larvæ, or young, will feed upon.

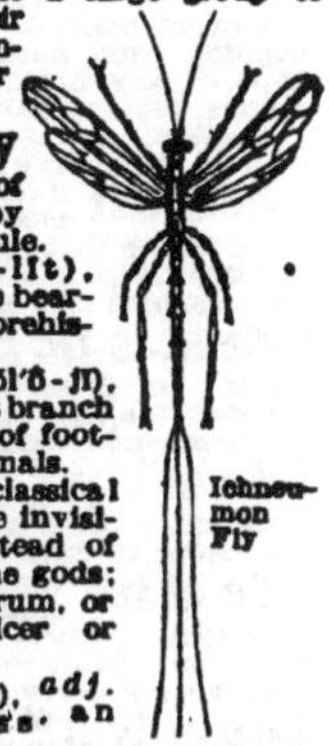
Ichneumon Fly

ich-nog-ra-phy (ĭk-nŏg'rȧ-fĭ), *n.* the art of drawing or tracing by means of compass and rule.

ich-no-lite (ĭk'nō-līt), *n.* a stone bearing the footprint of a prehistoric animal.

ich-nol-o-gy (ĭk-nŏl'ō-jĭ), *n.* that branch of science which treats of footprints of prehistoric animals.

i-chor (ī'kôr), *n.* in classical mythology, the invisible fluid which ran, instead of blood, in the veins of the gods; a thin, watery, acrid serum, or discharge, from an ulcer or wound.

ich-thy-ic (ĭk'thĭ-ĭk), *adj.* fishlike; as, an *ichthyic* vertebrate.

ich-thy-og-ra-phy (ĭk"thĭ-og'rȧ-fĭ), *n.* a treatise on fish.

ich-thy-o-lite (ĭk'thĭ-ō-līt), a fossil, or impression in stone, of an ancient fish.

ich-thy-ol-o-gy (ĭk"thĭ-ŏl'ō-jĭ), *n.* that branch of zoölogy which treats of fishes, their structure, classification, etc.; a natural history of fishes.

ich-thy-o-sis (ĭk-thĭ-ō'sĭs), *n.* a disease in which the skin is thick, rough, and scaly: called also *fishskin.*

i-ci-cle (ī'sĭ-kl), *n.* ice formed by the freezing of dripping water from the eaves of houses, etc.

i-ci-ly (ī'sĭ-lĭ), *adv.* in a frigid manner; coldly; as, she *icily* refused to be introduced.

i-ci-ness (ī'sĭ-nĕs), *n.* the state of being icy; coldness; as, the *iciness* of the streets made walking dangerous; *iciness* of manner.

ic-ing (īs'ĭng), *n.* frosting; a coating or covering on cake, made of sugar, milk, white of egg, etc.

i-con (ī'kŏn), *n.* [*pl.* icons (ī'kŏnz), icones (ī'kō-nēz)], in the Greek Church, a sacred image or picture. Also, **eikon, ikon.**

i-con-o-clast (ī-kŏn'ō-klăst), *n.* an image breaker; one who attacks superstitions or shams.

i-co-sa-he-dron (ī"kō-sȧ-hē'drŏn), *n.* a solid bounded by twenty plane faces.

ic-tus (ĭk'tŭs), *n.* a blow or stroke; in prosody and music, rhythmical or metrical accent or stress placed upon the accented syllable of a word.

i-cy (ī'sĭ), *adj.* [*comp.* icier, *superl.* iciest], pertaining to, resembling, or abounding in, ice; cold; chilling; indifferent.

i-de-a (ī-dē'ȧ), *n.* a mental image or picture; a conception of what ought to be; an abstract principle; opinion; belief; plan; a general notion; an impression.

Syn. thought, imagination, fancy.

i-de-al (ī-dē'ăl), *adj.* existing in imagination only; visionary; impractical; conforming to a standard of perfection; perfect: *n.* a mental conception or an individual regarded as the standard of perfection.

i-de-al-ism (ī-dē'ăl-ĭzm), *n.* in art, the stress put upon the value of the imagination as compared with the exact copying from nature to attain the highest type of any object; tendency to imagine things better than they are; the seeking of perfection; the doctrine that all our knowledge of objects is a knowledge of ideas.

i-de-al-ist (ī-dē'ăl-ĭst), *n.* one who pursues perfection; one who holds the doctrine that all our knowledge of objects is a knowledge of ideas; a visionary; one who sees the best side of people and things.

i-de-al-is-tic (ī-dē"ăl-ĭs'tĭk), *adj.* pertaining to a perfect type; pertaining to those who seek perfection or to the doctrine that makes everything to consist of ideas.—*adv.* **idealistically.**

i-de-al-i-ty (ī"dē-ăl'ĭ-tĭ), *n.* the quality of being unreal; the state of conforming with a standard of perfection; the power to form standards of excellence.

i-de-al-ize (ī-dē'ăl-īz), *v.t.* to make perfect; embody in a perfect form; represent (natural objects) so as to show their best characteristics only: *v.i.* to form standards of perfections.

i-de-al-ly (ī-dē'ăl-ĭ), *adv.* according to a standard of excellence; as, *ideally* perfect beauty; mentally.

i-den-ti-cal (ī-dĕn'tĭ-kăl), *adj.* expressing sameness; not different; differing in no essential or necessary point.

i-den-ti-cal-ly (ī-dĕn'tĭ-kăl-ĭ), *adv.* in the same or in a similar manner.

i-den-ti-fi-a-ble (ī-dĕn"tĭ-fī'ȧ-bl), *adj.* that may be proved to be the same.

i-den-ti-fy (ī-dĕn'tĭ-fī), *v.t.* [*p.t.* and *p.p.* identified, *p.pr.* identifying], to make, prove to be, or consider as, the same.

i-den-ti-ty (ī-dĕn'tĭ-tĭ), *n.* essential or practical sameness; likeness; individuality; as, the witness established the *identity* of the prisoner.

i-de-o-graph (ī'dē-ō-grăf"), *n.* a symbol or figure, not naming but suggesting the idea of an object; a word sign. Also, **ideogram.**

i-de-o-graph-ic (ī"dē-ō-grăf'ĭk), *adj.* representing ideas by symbols independently of sounds; as, 6 represents not the word "six" but the *idea* of the number itself. Also, **ideographical.**

i-de-og-ra-phy (ī"dē-ŏg'rȧ-fĭ), *n.* the direct representation of ideas by symbols, as sometimes is done in shorthand writing, etc.

ides (īdz), *n.pl.* in the ancient Roman calendar, the 15th of March, May, July, October, and the 13th of the other months.

id est (ĭd ĕst), that is: usually written *i. e.;* as, the engine has great momentum, *i. e.,* moving force. [Lat.]

id-i-o-cy (ĭd'ĭ-ō-sĭ), *n.* mental weakness; extreme lack of intelligence, usually due to incomplete development of the brain.

Syn. folly, imbecility, stupidity, senselessness.

Ant. (see intelligence).

id-i-o-graph (ĭd'ĭ-ō-grăf), *n.* a private mark or trade-mark.

id-i-om (ĭd'ĭ-ŭm), *n.* a mode of expression peculiar to a language; as, he spoke an unfamiliar *idiom;* the distinctive characteristics of a language; an expression whose grammatical relationships are peculiar to itself; an expression whose meaning as a whole cannot be obtained by joining together the meanings of its separate parts: for instance, "how do you do?" is an *idiom* whose meaning as a whole merely conveys greeting, but whose separate parts convey meanings very different from that of the expression as a whole.

id-i-o-mat-ic (ĭd"ĭ-ō-măt'ĭk), *adj.* peculiar to a language; given to, or marked by, the use of expressions characteristic of a language. Also, **idiomatical.**—*adv.* **idiomatically.**

id-i-o-syn-cra-sy (ĭd"ĭ-ō-sĭn'krȧ-sĭ), *n.* [*pl.* idiosyncrasies (-sĭz)], peculiarity of temperament; a characteristic peculiar to an individual born of that individual's own particular bent.

id-i-ot (ĭd'ĭ-ŏt), *n.* one of weak mind; a foolish person; dunce.

id-i-ot-ic (ĭd"ĭ-ŏt'ĭk), *adj.* pertaining to, or like, a weak-minded person, a simpleton, or an imbecile; foolish. Also, **idiotical.** —*adv.* **idiotically.**

i-dle (ī'dl), *adj.* empty; unoccupied; unemployed; unused; useless; vain; of no importance; futile; lazy: *v.i.* to be inactive or without employment: *v.t.* to spend, or waste (time): usually with *away.*

Syn., adj. indolent, lazy.

Ant. (see industrious).

i-dle-ness (ī'dl-nĕs), *n.* the state of being inactive; indolence; slothfulness; laziness.

i-dler (ī'dlĕr), *n.* one who wastes time in doing nothing; a lazy person.

i-dly (ī'dlĭ), *adv.* in an unoccupied or aimless manner; as, they wandered *idly* through the fields.

i-dol (ī'dŏl), *n.* an image of a divinity or a god employed as an object of worship; a person or thing greatly loved or adored.

Idol

i-dol-a-ter (ī-dŏl'ȧ-tĕr), *n.* an idol worshiper; one who pays divine honors to images, etc.; one who loves a person or thing to excess.

i-dol-a-tress (ī-dŏl'ȧ-trĕs), *n.* a female worshiper of idols.

i-dol-a-trous (ī-dŏl'ȧ-trŭs), *adj.* pertaining to, or practicing, the worshiping of images; marked by undue reverence or affection.

i-dol-a-try (ī-dŏl'ȧ-trĭ), *n.* [*pl.* idolatries (-trĭz)], the paying of divine honors to images, or any created object; very great admiration, veneration, or love for any person or thing.

i-dol-ize (ī'dŏl-īz), *v.t.* to make an object of worship of; love or admire to excess.

i-dyl (ī'dĭl), *n.* a short, pastoral poem; an episode forming a suitable subject for an idyl; sometimes, a descriptive or narrative poem of greater length; a description of simple, rural, pastoral scenes. Also, **idyll.**

i-dyl-ist (ī'dĭl-ĭst), *n.* a pastoral poet; a painter of pastoral scenes.

i-dyl-lic (ī-dĭl'ĭk), *adj.* pertaining to, or of the nature of, a short, pastoral poem, or an episode which is a fit subject for such a poem; pastoral.

if (ĭf), *conj.* on the condition; as, *if* I let you have the book, you must read it carefully; supposing that; as, *if* I do go to New York, what is the best train to take? whether; as, he asked *if* he might go; although; as, *if* the answer is correct, the work is not neatly done.

ig-ne-ous (ĭg'nē-ŭs), *adj.* pertaining to, consisting of, or resembling, fire; produced by fire.

ig-nes-cent (ĭg-nĕs'ĕnt), *adj.* sending out sparks when struck with steel; scintillating.

ig-nis fat-u-us (ĭg'nĭs făt'ū-ŭs), a strange light seen to flit above the ground in marshy places, etc.; a misleading influence: popularly known as Will-o'-the-wisp, Jack-o'-Lantern, Corpse-candle. [LAT.]

ig-nite (ĭg-nīt'), *v.t.* to set on fire; to heat strongly; subject to the action of intense heat: *v.i.* to take fire; glow with heat.

ig-nit-er (ĭg-nīt'ẽr), *n.* one who, or that which, kindles; a time exploder for setting on fire the powder of a torpedo.

ig-nit-i-ble (ĭg-nīt'ĭ-bl), *adj.* capable of being set on fire; easily kindled.

ig-ni-tion (ĭg-nĭsh'ŭn), *n.* the act of setting on fire or kindling; the state of being set on fire; the means of producing fire; the mechanism for exploding the charge in a gas engine.

ig-no-ble (ĭg-nō'bl), *adj.* of low birth or station; of mean character or quality; of little value; degraded; vile; dishonorable.

ig-no-ble-ness (ĭg-nō'bl-nĕs), *n.* the state or quality of being humble, base, or mean.

ig-no-bly (ĭg-nō'blĭ), *adv.* in a low or mean manner; basely.

ig-no-min-i-ous (ĭg"nō-mĭn'ĭ-ŭs), *adj.* marked with dishonor or public disgrace; as, to sell a vote is *ignominious;* shameful; deserving disgrace; despicable; as, his conduct is *ignominious.*
Syn. scandalous, infamous.
Ant. (see honorable).

ig-no-min-y (ĭg'nō-mĭn-ĭ), *n.* [*pl.* ignominies (-ĭz)], loss of one's good name; public disgrace or dishonor; cause or source of disgrace.
Syn. shame, disgrace, infamy, reproach.

ig-no-ra-mus (ĭg"nō-rā'mŭs), *n.* one without knowledge; especially, such a one who pretends to knowledge; a dunce.

ig-no-rance (ĭg'nō-răns), *n.* the state of being uneducated, or uninformed; want of knowledge.

ig-no-rant (ĭg'nō-rănt), *adj.* destitute of or without knowledge; uninstructed.
Syn. unlearned, illiterate, uninformed, uneducated.
Ant. (see educated).

ig-nore (ĭg-nōr'), *v.t.* to treat as unknown; disregard wilfully; fail to recognize; refuse to notice; throw out as false or unsupported by sufficient evidence.

i-gua-na (ĭ-gwä'nȧ), *n.* a large lizard found in South and Central America. There are several species, the largest attaining a length of five or six feet.

Tuberculated Iguana

il-e-um (ĭl'ē-ŭm), *n.* the lower part of the small intestine.

i-lex (ī'lĕks), *n.* holly; a class of evergreen trees and shrubs represented by the holly.

il-i-ac (ĭl'ĭ-ăk), *adj.* pertaining to the ilium, or upper bone of the pelvis.

Il-i-ad (ĭl'ĭ-ăd), *n.* a Greek epic poem in twenty-four books, written by Homer.

il-i-um (ĭl'ĭ-ŭm), *n.* the dorsal or upper bone of the pelvis.

ilk (ĭlk), *adj.* same: now rarely used except in the phrase: **of that ilk,** of the same family, name, or estate.

ill (ĭl), *adj.* [*comp.* worse, *superl.* worst], bad or evil; contrary to good; causing or attended by evil or suffering; in a bad or disordered state physically or morally; sick; diseased; unfriendly; not proper; unskilful; vicious: *n.* misfortune; disease; anything that prevents what is good; something morally bad; mischief: *adv.* not well; not easily.
Syn., adj. sick, indisposed, unwell.
Ant. (see good, well).

ill-bred (ĭl'brĕd"), *adj.* uncivil; rude; badly brought up; impolite.

il-le-gal (ĭ-lē'găl), *adj.* contrary to law; unlawful; illicit.—*adv.* **illegally.**

il-leg-i-ble (ĭ-lĕj'ĭ-bl), *adj.* badly written; as, this manuscript is *illegible;* defaced; not to be read easily.

il-le-git-i-mate (ĭl"ē-jĭt'ĭ-māt), *adj.* born out of wedlock; unlawful; illegal; illogical; unsound; contrary to good usage; not genuine.—*adv.* **illegitimately.** —*n.* **illegitimacy.**

ill-fa-vored (ĭl'fā'vẽrd), *adj.* ugly; offensive; unpleasant. Also, **ill-favoured.**

il-li-ber-al (ĭ-lĭb'ẽr-ăl), *adj.* not generous; not broad-minded; bigoted; mean.—*adv.* **illiberally.**—*n.* **illiberality.**

il-lic-it (ĭ-lĭs'ĭt), *adj.* not authorized or allowed; unlicensed; illegal; unlawful.

il-lim-it-a-ble (ĭ-lĭm'ĭt-ȧ-bl), *adj.* immeasurable; vast; infinite.—*adv.* **illimitably.**—*n.* **illimitableness.**

il-lit-er-a-cy (ĭ-lĭt'ẽr-ȧ-sĭ), *n.* ignorance of letters; want of learning; ignorance; inability to read or write; as, the *illiteracy* of the people is surprising.

il-lit-er-ate (ĭ-lĭt'ẽr-āt), *adj.* unable to read or write; unlearned; ignorant of letters or books; unrefined.

ill-na-tured (ĭl'nā'tūrd), *adj.* having a bad temper; spiteful; surly; cross.

ill-ness (ĭl'nĕs), *n.* the condition of being sick or evil; disease; sickness.

il-log-i-cal (ĭ-lŏj'ĭ-kǎl), *adj.* contrary to sound reasoning, or to the rules of logic.

il-lu-mi-nant (ĭ-lū'mĭ-nǎnt), *n.* anything which gives or produces light.

il-lu-mi-nate (ĭ-lū'mĭ-nāt), *v.t.* to give light to; as, they will *illuminate* the park with arc lights; decorate with lights, in token of rejoicing; as, we *illuminate* the Christmas tree with colored electric lights; enlighten; throw light upon; make plain; adorn, as a manuscript, with small designs in colors and gold: *v.i.* to display lights as a sign of rejoicing; as, the city has decided to *illuminate* during the convention.

il-lu-mi-na-tion (ĭ-lū"mĭ-nā'shŭn), *n.* supply of light; the act of giving light to, or state of being lighted; especially, the decoration of houses or cities with lights; the art of adorning books or manuscripts; a design in a work so adorned; intellectual light; inspiration.

il-lu-mi-na-tor (ĭ-lū'mĭ-nā"tẽr), *n.* one who, or that which, gives light; one who adorns books, manuscripts, etc.; a condenser or reflector.

il-lu-mine (ĭ-lū'mĭn), *v.t.* to light; as, the moon *illumines* the night: *v.i.* to be lighted.

il-lu-sion (ĭ-lū'zhŭn), *n.* deceptive appearance; false show; hallucination; tulle; delicate lace for veils.
Syn. fallacy, deception, phantasm.

il-lu-sion-ist (ĭ-lū'zhŭn-ĭst), *n.* one subject to false impressions; a sleight-of-hand performer.

il-lu-sive (ĭ-lū'sĭv), *adj.* deceiving by false impressions; deceptive; illusory.—*adv.* **illusively.**—*n.* **illusiveness.**

il-lu-so-ry (ĭ-lū'sō-rĭ), *adj.* causing deception; deceptive; fallacious.
Syn. imaginary, chimerical, visionary.
Ant. (see real).

il-lus-trate (ĭ-lŭs'trāt; ĭl'ŭs-trāt), *v.t.* to make clear or intelligible; as, I think that I can *illustrate* the subject so that you will be able to understand each sentence; explain by examples; to make plain by means of pictures, etc.; as, I wish you to *illustrate* this book.

il-lus-trat-ed (ĭ-lŭs'trā-tĕd; ĭl'ŭs-trāt-ĕd), *p.adj.* having pictures or sketches to adorn or explain the text.

il-lus-tra-tion (ĭl"ŭs-trā'shŭn), *n.* the act of making clear or adorning by pictures; the state of being explained or adorned by pictures; that which makes clear, as a comparison or example; a picture designed to make the text plain or clear.

il-lus-tra-tive (ĭ-lŭs'trā-tĭv; ĭl'ŭs-trā-tĭv), *adj.* tending to explain or make clear.—*adv.* **illustratively.**

il-lus-tra-tor (ĭ-lŭs'trā-tẽr; ĭl'ŭs-trā-tẽr), *n.* one who makes plain by example; one who draws pictures, as for magazines; a cartoonist.

il-lus-tri-ous (ĭ-lŭs'trĭ-ŭs), *adj.* distinguished by greatness; renowned; glorious; famous; honored; as, Colonel Roosevelt was one of the most *illustrious* persons of his day.
Syn. celebrated, eminent.
Ant. (see obscure).

im-age (ĭm'āj), *n.* an imitation of any person or thing; a statue; bust; an idol; a counterpart; likeness; as, "God created man in his own *image*"; a mental picture, conception, or idea; as, it is easy to form an *image* of the scene you describe; an extended metaphor; reflection of an object formed by rays of light; as, how I love to watch the *images* in the water: *v.t.* to form, or reflect, a likeness of; represent to the mental vision; imagine.
Syn., n. representation, effigy.

im-age-ry (ĭm'āj-rĭ), *n.* [*pl.* **imageries** (-rĭz)], the work of one whose business it is to make figures or likenesses of objects or persons; figures or imitations of objects taken collectively; figures of speech by way of decoration in discourse; forms o the fancy; work of the memory or the imagination.

im-ag-i-na-ble (ĭ-măj'ĭ-nȧ-bl), *adj.* capable of being pictured in the imagination or conceived; as, she has the prettiest home *imaginable.*—*adv.* **imaginably.**

im-ag-i-na-ry (ĭ-măj'ĭ-nā-rĭ), *adj.* existing only in the fancy; as, *imaginary* ills hurt as badly as real ones; unreal; idealistic; as, his trip was only *imaginary*, but he enjoyed it greatly.
Syn. ideal, fanciful, illusory.
Ant. (see real).

im-ag-i-na-tion (ĭ-măj"ĭ-nā'shŭn), *n.* the picture-forming power of the mind; the ability to create thoughts, ideas, or fancies; especially, the higher forms of this power exercised in art and poetry, usually termed the creative power; any product of this mind-power; a conception or idea; fanciful opinion; fancy; invention.

im-ag-i-na-tive (ĭ-măj'ĭ-nā-tĭv), *adj.* proceeding from, exhibiting, or endowed with, the picture-forming faculty of the mind; as, she is the most *imaginative* person I ever knew; inventive; fanciful.—*adv.* **imaginatively.**

im-ag-i-na-tive-ness (ĭ-măj'ĭ-nā-tĭv-nĕs), *n.* the quality of being fanciful or inventive.

im-ag-ine (ĭ-măj'ĭn), *v.t.* to form a mental picture of; as, I shall describe the place and see if you can *imagine* the scene; produce by the picture-forming quality of the mind; conceive; as, can you *imagine* any one's taking that risk? conjecture; think; scheme; suppose: *v.i.* to form a mental picture; fancy; as, the place is just as pretty as you *imagine;* surmise.

im-be-cile (ĭm'bē-sĭl; Br. ĭm'bē-sēl, ĭm"-bē-sēl'), *adj.* without strength, especially of mind; feeble-minded; idiotic: *n.* one of feeble mind.

im-be-cil-i-ty (ĭm"bē-sĭl'ĭ-tĭ), *n.* [*pl.* **imbecilities** (-tĭz)], mental weakness; inability; incapacity, or lack of power to do; foolishness; idiocy.
Syn. silliness, senility, dotage.

im-bed (ĭm-bĕd'), *v.t.* to inclose in surrounding matter; to sink or lay as in a bed. Also, **embed.**

im-bibe (ĭm-bīb'), *v.t.* to drink in; absorb, as if by drinking; receive or absorb into the mind: *v.i.* to drink; absorb moisture.—*n.* **imbiber.**

im-bod-y (ĭm-bŏd'ĭ), *v.t.* and *v.i.* to make definite and easily grasped or comprehended; as, to *imbody* ideas in words: to cause to become a body or part of a body; as, to *imbody* these suggestions in the text. Also, **embody.**

im-bri-cate (ĭm'brĭ-kāt), *adj.* with the edges lapped over each other, as scales or shingles, in regular order. Also, **imbricated.**

im-bri-ca-tion (im′brĭ-kā′shŭn), *n.* an overlapping of edges, as in scales or shingles.

im-bro-glio (im-brōl′yō), *n.* an intricate and perplexing state of affairs; misunderstanding; entanglement; strife; perplexity; complicated plot.

im-brue (im-brōō′), *v.t.* to wet or moisten; soak; drench, especially in blood.

im-bue (im-bū′), *v.t.* to cause to absorb; to saturate; tinge deeply; dye; to tincture deeply, as the mind with certain principles; as, I was quite *imbued* with his ideas.

im-i-ta-ble (im′ĭ-tȧ-bl), *adj.* capable of being copied or patterned after.

im-i-tate (im′ĭ-tāt), *v.t.* to duplicate in form, color, qualities, conduct, and the like; use as a model or pattern; to take example by; as, the boy *imitates* his father's every act and word; to copy; to appear to be like; to resemble in externals.
Syn. ape, mimic, mock.

im-i-ta-tion (im′ĭ-tā′shŭn), *n.* the act of following as a pattern or example, or of striving to copy; that which is made to resemble something: *adj.* made as a copy of an object of superior worth; not genuine.

im-i-ta-tive (im′ĭ-tā-tĭv), *adj.* inclined to copy an original; formed after a model.—*adv.* **imitatively.**

im-i-ta-tor (im′ĭ-tā″tẽr), *n.* one who copies; as, an *imitator* rarely possesses any originality.

im-mac-u-late (ĭ-măk′ū-lāt), *adj.* without blemish; unspotted; undefiled; pure.—*adv.* **immaculately.**
Syn. spotless, unsullied, stainless.

im-ma-nent (im′ȧ-nĕnt), *adj.* remaining within; indwelling; as, an *immanent* power of the mind.—*n.* **immanence.**

im-ma-te-ri-al (im″ȧ-tē′rĭ-ăl), *adj.* not consisting of matter; spiritual; disembodied; unimportant.—*adv.* **immaterially.**

im-ma-ture (im″ȧ-tūr′), *adj.* not ripe; not fully grown or developed; not finished or perfected; crude.

im-meas-ur-a-bil-i-ty (ĭ-mĕzh″ŭr-ȧ-bĭl′ĭ-tĭ; im-mĕzh″ŭr-ȧ-bĭl′ĭ-tĭ), *n.* the quality of being of indefinite extent or degree; as, the mind of man cannot grasp the *immeasurability* of eternity.

im-meas-ur-a-ble (ĭ-mĕzh′ŭr-ȧ-bl; im-mĕzh′ŭr-ȧ-bl), *adj.* not able to be reckoned in terms of length, breadth, etc.; immense; limitless; vast. Also, **immensurable.**

im-meas-ur-a-bly (ĭ-mĕzh′ŭr-ȧ-blĭ; im-mĕzh′ŭr-ȧ-blĭ), *adv.* to an indefinite extent or degree; as, the civilization of the twentieth century is *immeasurably* in advance of that of the fourteenth and fifteenth.

im-me-di-ate (ĭ-mē′dĭ-āt), *adj.* directly related; next; direct; acting without any agency, object, or time coming between; as, these are only the *immediate* causes of the war; there are others more deep-seated and remote; near at hand.—*n.* **immediateness, immediacy.**
Syn. pressing, next, proximate.

im-me-di-ate-ly (ĭ-mē′dĭ-āt-lĭ), *adv.* directly; instantly; at once.
Syn. forthwith, presently, straightway.

im-me-mor-i-al (im′ē-mō′rĭ-ăl), *adj.* extending beyond the reach of memory, record, or tradition; as, *immemorial* usage or custom.

im-mense (ĭ-mĕns′), *adj.* immeasurable; boundless; vast; very great or large: *n.* infinite space.—*adv.* **immensely.**
Syn., adj. enormous, huge, monstrous.

im-men-si-ty (ĭ-mĕn′sĭ-tĭ), *n.* [*pl.* immensities (-tĭz)], the character of being very large; boundless; immeasurableness; infinite space; vastness in extent or size.

im-men-sur-a-ble (ĭ-mĕn′shōō-rȧ-bl), *adj.* immense; limitless; incapable of having size, dimensions, etc. given, on account of vastness. Also, **immeasurable.**—*n.* **immensurability.**

im-merge (ĭ-mûrj′), *v.t.* to plunge into or under anything, especially a fluid; immerse: *v.i.* to disappear by entering into anything else; as, the moon *immerges* into the shadow of the earth.

im-merse (ĭ-mûrs′), *v.t.* to plunge into or under anything, especially a fluid; sink; dip; plunge into and be absorbed in, as an occupation; baptize by plunging into water.
Syn. immerge, submerge.

im-mersed (ĭ-mûrst′), *p.adj.* deeply plunged into anything, especially a fluid; deeply occupied, interested, or involved; growing wholly under water: said of a plant.

im-mer-sion (ĭ-mûr′shŭn), *n.* the act of plunging or dipping into a fluid; the state of being plunged or dipped into a fluid; baptism by dipping the whole person into water.

im-mi-grant (im′ĭ-grănt), *adj.* passing or coming into, as a new place of residence: *n.* one who comes into a country to settle.

im-mi-grate (im′ĭ-grāt), *v.i.* to come into a new place of residence; especially, to come into a country to settle.—*n.* **immigration.**

im-mi-nence (im′ĭ-nĕns), *n.* the condition of being about to happen immediately; as, in all ages there have been persons who have preached the *imminence* of the end of the world; nearness; threatening evil or danger.

im-mi-nent (im′ĭ-nĕnt), *adj.* threatening or about to fall or occur immediately: said especially of misfortune or peril; as, to the ancient Romans, a falling star meant some *imminent* calamity.
Syn. impending, threatening.
Ant. (see unexpected).

im-mo-bile (ĭ-mō′bĭl), *adj.* not movable; not to be affected by the emotions; motionless.

im-mo-bil-i-ty (im′ō-bĭl′ĭ-tĭ), *n.* fixedness in place or state; motionlessness; as, the American Indian was noted for the *immobility* of his face under suffering or pain.

im-mod-er-ate (ĭ-mŏd′ẽr-āt), *adj.* extreme; not confined to customary or just or reasonable limits; extravagant; intemperate.—*adv.* **immoderately.**—*n.* **immoderation.**

im-mod-est (ĭ-mŏd′ĕst), *adj.* forward; boasting; wanting in the restraint required by decency; indelicate; impure in word or deed.—*adv.* **immodestly.**

im-mod-es-ty (ĭ-mŏd′ĕs-tĭ), *n.* want of modesty, delicacy, or proper reserve; proud boasting; impurity.

im-mo-late (im′ō-lāt), *v.t.* to kill as a sacrifice; as, Abraham was about to *immolate* his son, Isaac; offer in sacrifice; make a sacrifice of; as, it is often necessary to *immolate* ambition on the altar of duty.—*n.* **immolation.**

im-mor-al (ĭ-mŏr'ăl), *adj.* contrary to the law of right and wrong; wicked; vicious; loose in acts or words; dishonest; unprincipled.—*adv.* **immorally.**

im-mo-ral-i-ty (ĭm"ŏ-răl'ĭ-tĭ), *n.* vice; wickedness; an evil act or practice.

im-mor-tal (ĭ-môr'tăl), *adj.* never-dying; imperishable; ever-living: *n.* one who never dies; one whose fame is undying or lasting: *pl.* the gods of Greek and Roman mythology.

im-mor-tal-i-ty (ĭm"ôr-tăl'ĭ-tĭ), *n.* exemption from death; unending existence.

im-mor-tal-ize (ĭ-môr'tăl-īz), *v.t.* to give unending life to; bestow lasting fame upon; as, Shakespeare's plays *immortalise* his name.

im-mor-tal-ly (ĭ-môr'tăl-ĭ), *adv.* eternally; undyingly; as, the name of Lincoln is *immortally* enshrined in the history of America.

im-mor-telle (ĭm"ôr-tĕl'), *n.* [*pl.* immortelles (-tĕlz)], a plant whose flowers may be dried without losing their form or color; a wreath made of such flowers.

im-mov-a-bil-i-ty (ĭ-mōōv"ȧ-bĭl'ĭ-tĭ), *n.* fixedness; steadfastness.

im-mov-a-ble (ĭ-mōōv'ȧ-bl), *adj.* incapable of being moved; fixed; steadfast; unchanging; unfeeling: *n.pl.* land, or things fixed to, or belonging to, land, as trees or buildings.—*adv.* **immovably.**

im-mune (ĭ-mūn'), *adj.* exempt; privileged; protected against a disease; as, vaccination usually makes one *immune* from smallpox: *n.* one who is not liable to take any particular disease by reason of having had it.

im-mu-ni-ty (ĭ-mū'nĭ-tĭ), *n.* [*pl.* immunities (-tĭz)], freedom from any duty, office, or tax; freedom from natural or usual duty, etc.; special privilege: usually in plural; the state of freedom from any particular disease because of protection against it.
Syn. privilege, prerogative, exemption.

im-mure (ĭ-mūr'), *v.t.* to inclose within walls; shut up in prison; confine.

im-mu-ta-bil-i-ty (ĭ-mū"tȧ-bĭl'ĭ-tĭ), *n.* unchangeableness.

im-mu-ta-ble (ĭ-mū'tȧ-bl), *adj.* unchangeable; unalterable; permanent.—*adv.* **immutably.**

imp (ĭmp), *n.* a young, little, or inferior devil; a hobgoblin; a pert or mischievous child.

im-pact (ĭm'păkt), *n.* a collision; a striking together of two objects; as, the *impact* of the two cars jarred the passengers from their seats.

im-pac-tion-ize (ĭm-păk'shŭn-īz), *v.t.* to store or pack closely together, as airplanes.

im-pair (ĭm-pâr'), *v.t.* to make worse; lessen in quantity, excellence, value, or strength; weaken; harm; as, the use of alcoholic drinks *impairs* the health.
Syn. injure, diminish, decrease.

im-pair-ment (ĭm-pâr'mĕnt), *n.* a lessening in value, excellence, or strength; injury.

im-pale (ĭm-pāl'), *v.t.* to pierce through with anything sharp; as, to *impale* an insect on a pin; put to death by thrusting through with a sharp stake fixed upright; surround with, or as with, pales or stakes.—*n.* **impalement.**

im-pal-pa-ble (ĭm-păl'pȧ-bl), *adj.* not perceivable by touch; as, the air is full of *impalpable* particles of dust; not consisting of matter; not capable of being felt.

im-pan-el (ĭm-păn'ĕl), *v.t.* to enter the names of (jurors) on a piece of parchment called a *panel;* summon to serve on a jury; draw from the list and swear in persons to form a jury; enroll.

im-part (ĭm-pärt'), *v.t.* to bestow a share or portion of; give; to communicate knowledge of; make known: *v.i.* to give a share.
Syn. reveal, divulge, disclose, bestow.

im-par-tial (ĭm-pär'shăl), *adj.* not favoring one more than another; fair; just; as, a judge must be absolutely *impartial* in his decisions.—*adv.* **impartially.**

im-par-ti-al-i-ty (ĭm-pär"shĭ-ăl'ĭ-tĭ; ĭm"pär-shăl'ĭ-tĭ), *n.* freedom from favoritism; fairness.

im-pass-a-ble (ĭm-pȧs'ȧ-bl), *adj.* not to be gone through or by; not admitting transit; as, the way was blocked by an *impassable* barrier.—*adv.* **impassably.**

im-pass-i-ble (ĭm-păs'ĭ-bl), *adj.* incapable of suffering from outside causes; free from harm or pain; not to be moved to passion, sympathy, or any sign of emotion; as, he met every trial with *impassible* courage.

im-pas-sioned (ĭm-păsh'ŭnd), *p.adj.* moved to strong feeling; excited; showing warmth of feeling; as, an *impassioned* appeal.
Syn. glowing, burning, fiery, vehement, intense.

im-pas-sive (ĭm-păs'ĭv), *adj.* not feeling or not showing pain, suffering, feeling, or emotion; calm.—*adv.* **impassively.**—*n.* **impassivity.**

im-pa-tience (ĭm-pā'shĕns), *n.* the state of being restless, irritable, or unwilling to wait.

im-pa-tient (ĭm-pā'shĕnt), *adj.* restless because of pain, delay, opposition, control, or circumstances; intolerant; showing or expressing restlessness, irritability, or intolerance; eager.—*adv.* **impatiently.**
Syn. peevish, fretful, hasty, choleric.

im-peach (ĭm-pēch'), *v.t.* to call in question; accuse of official misconduct before a court; challenge the truth or value of; as, to *impeach* the testimony of a witness or a document.
Syn. charge, arraign, censure.

im-peach-a-ble (ĭm-pēch'ȧ-bl), *adj.* guilty of such misconduct as makes a public officer liable to trial in court, or of making statements, especially on the witness stand, that can be challenged or called into question.

im-peach-ment (ĭm-pēch'mĕnt), *n.* the calling to trial of a public officer for wrongdoing in office; a discrediting of testimony or the like.

im-pec-ca-bil-i-ty (ĭm-pĕk"ȧ-bĭl'ĭ-tĭ), *n.* freedom from sin, error, or wrongdoing.

im-pec-ca-ble (ĭm-pĕk'ȧ-bl), *adj.* not liable to sin; faultless; as, God is *impeccable.*

im-pe-cu-ni-os-i-ty (ĭm'pē-kū"nĭ-ŏs'ĭ-tĭ), *n.* want of money; poverty.

im-pe-cu-ni-ous (ĭm′pē-kū′nĭ-ŭs), *adj.* without money; poor.

im-pede (ĭm-pēd′), *v.t.* to obstruct; hinder; make slower; prevent; as, snow and cold *impede* the advance of the army.

im-ped-i-ment (ĭm-pĕd′ĭ-mĕnt), *n.* that which hinders or obstructs progress or activity; obstruction; obstacle.
Syn. hindrance, barrier.
Ant. (see aid).

im-ped-i-men-ta (ĭm-pĕd′ĭ-mĕn′tȧ), *n.pl.* things which hinder progress; baggage; especially, military baggage; military supplies. [LAT.]

im-pel (ĭm-pĕl′), *v.t.* [*p.t.* and *p.p.* impelled, *p.pr.* impelling], to drive or urge forward or on; to force or influence to any kind of motion or action; as, fear and self-reproach *impel* him to confess.
Syn. animate, induce, incite, instigate, embolden.
Ant. (see retard).

im-pend (ĭm-pĕnd′), *v.i.* to hang over; be ready to fall; be at hand; threaten immediately.

im-pend-ing (ĭm-pĕnd′ĭng), *p.adj.* overhanging; suspended so as to threaten; close at hand; as, *impending* ruin or disaster.
Syn. imminent, threatening.

im-pen-e-tra-bil-i-ty (ĭm-pĕn′ē-trȧ-bĭl′ĭ-tĭ), *n.* incapability of being pierced or entered; that property of matter according to which no two bodies can occupy the same space at the same time.

im-pen-e-tra-ble (ĭm-pĕn′ē-trȧ-bl), *adj.* not to be entered or pierced; not admitting entrance; not capable of being understood or comprehended; as, an *impenetrable* mystery; not touched by reason, sympathy, etc.; as, an *impenetrable* heart; having the property of matter according to which no two bodies can occupy the same space at the same time; as, the *impenetrable* armor of a battleship.

im-pen-i-tence (ĭm-pĕn′ĭ-tĕns), *n.* hardness of heart; stubborn wickedness; failure to repent for wrong done. Also, **impenitency**.

im-pen-i-tent (ĭm-pĕn′ĭ-tĕnt), *adj.* not sorry for sin; finally neglecting the duty of repentance: *n.* one who finally neglects the duty of repentance; a hardened sinner.

im-per-a-tive (ĭm-pĕr′ȧ-tĭv), *adj.* expressing command; not to be avoided; as, an *imperative* necessity; in grammar, expressing command, entreaty, or exhortation; as, the *imperative* mood: *n.* something, as an act or word, that gives or expresses a command; the imperative mood. —*adv.* **imperatively**.
Syn., *adj.* commanding, urgent, despotic, authoritative.

im-per-cep-ti-bil-i-ty (ĭm′pĕr-sĕp′tĭ-bĭl′ĭ-tĭ), *n.* the incapability of being taken in by the senses or realized by the mind.

im-per-cep-ti-ble (ĭm′pĕr-sĕp′tĭ-bl), *adj.* not capable of being perceived by the senses, or realized by the mind; extremely small or brief; as, after an almost *imperceptible* pause, he spoke. —*adv.* **imperceptibly**.

im-per-fect (ĭm-pûr′fĕkt), *adj.* wanting in completeness, correctness, or excellence; wanting in some organ necessary to usual activity; incomplete; indicating that tense in grammar which expresses past action as uncompleted or continuous at the time denoted: *n.* in grammar, the form of the verb denoting incomplete action. —*adv.* **imperfectly**.

im-per-fec-tion (ĭm′pĕr-fĕk′shŭn), *n.* incompleteness; faultiness; a defect or blemish, physical, mental, or moral; failing.
Syn. fault, vice, weakness.

im-pe-ri-al (ĭm-pē′rĭ-ăl), *adj.* pertaining to an empire or emperor; fit or suitable for one who practices supreme authority; of superior size or excellence; supreme; sovereign: *n.* the top of a coach or carriage; an article of unusual excellence; a tuft of hair left unshaven on the lower lip and chin.

im-pe-ri-al-ism (ĭm-pē′rĭ-ăl-ĭzm), *n.* the power or government of an emperor; the policy of the extension of the control or dominion of a nation, either by gaining new territory or by a close union of more or less loosely connected parts.

im-pe-ri-al-ist (ĭm-pē′rĭ-ăl-ĭst), *n.* one who favors or upholds the policy of extending the control or dominion of a nation; the follower of an emperor.

im-pe-ri-al-is-tic (ĭm-pē′rĭ-ăl-ĭs′tĭk), *adj.* pertaining to, or favoring, the policy of extending the control or dominion of a nation.

im-per-il (ĭm-pĕr′ĭl), *v.t.* to put in danger or jeopardy; endanger; as, to *imperil* safety; *imperil* health.
Syn. hazard, risk.

im-pe-ri-ous (ĭm-pē′rĭ-ŭs), *adj.* commanding; overbearing; urgent; imperative. —*adv.* **imperiously**.
Syn. commanding, authoritative, lordly.

im-per-ish-a-ble (ĭm-pĕr′ĭsh-ȧ-bl), *adj.* indestructible; not subject to decay; permanently enduring; as, *imperishable* fame. —*adv.* **imperishably**.

im-per-me-a-bil-i-ty (ĭm-pûr′mē-ȧ-bĭl′ĭ-tĭ), *n.* the property of a substance by virtue of which it does not permit fluids, etc., to pass through its pores; incapability of being pervaded or passed through.

im-per-me-a-ble (ĭm-pûr′mē-ȧ-bl), *adj.* not permitting passage, as of a fluid through a substance; as, rubber is *impermeable* to water.

im-per-son-al (ĭm-pûr′sŭn-ăl), *adj.* not belonging or referring to a particular person; not existing as a separate person; as, most of us believe in an *impersonal* power called luck; in grammar, referring to a verb whose subject is never a person; as, it snows; it seems: **impersonal verb**, a verb used without a subject, or (in English) with only the pronoun *it*. —*adv.* **impersonally**.

im-per-son-ate (ĭm-pûr′sŭn-āt), *v.t.* to give to something the qualities of a person; to represent a person or character, especially on the stage.

im-per-son-a-tor (ĭm-pûr′sŭn-ā′tĕr), *n.* one who represents characters; an actor.

im-per-ti-nence (ĭm-pûr′tĭ-nĕns), *n.* that which has no relation to the matter in hand, as in speech or manners; a thing of no value; a trifle; lack of due respect for others in manners or speech; rudeness.

im-per-ti-nent (ĭm-pûr′tĭ-nĕnt), *adj.* of no relation to the matter in hand; not to the point; rude; uncivil.

or offensive in behavior; guilty of rude or unbecoming manners or speech.—*adv.* impertinently.

Syn. intrusive, meddling, rude, saucy.

im-per-turb-a-bil-i-ty (ĭm-pẽr-tûr′-bȧ-bĭl′ĭ-tĭ), *n.* the quality of being self-contained or calm.

im-per-turb-a-ble (ĭm″pẽr-tûr′bȧ-bl), *adj.* not easily disturbed, agitated, or embarrassed; self-contained; calm; as, the child regarded the stranger with an *imperturbable* stare.—*adv.* imperturbably.

im-per-vi-ous (ĭm-pûr′vĭ-ŭs), *adj.* impenetrable; not permitting passage, as of a fluid, through a substance.—*adv.* imperviously.

im-pet-u-os-i-ty (ĭm-pĕt″ū-ŏs′ĭ-tĭ), *n.* violence; force; the quality which leads to action without thought; impulsiveness.

im-pet-u-ous (ĭm-pĕt′ū-ŭs), *adj.* rushing with force and violence; as, an *impetuous* current; passionate in feeling; acting with sudden energy; hasty and rash in action and speech.—*adv.* impetuously.

Syn. violent, boisterous, furious, vehement, impulsive.

Ant. (see calm).

im-pe-tus (ĭm′pē-tŭs), *n.* the force which any moving body possesses by reason of its motion and weight; momentum; impulse; stimulus.

im-pi-e-ty (ĭm-pī′ĕ-tĭ), *n.* [*pl.* impieties (-tĭz)], want of reverence; disregard of the Supreme Being; ungodliness; an act of irreverence or wickedness; as, an act of downright *impiety*.

im-pinge (ĭm-pĭnj′), *v.i.* to strike or dash; clash; come in collision: with *on*, *upon*, and *against*; as, sound waves *impinge* on the eardrum, setting in motion a series of three tiny bones.

im-pi-ous (ĭm′pĭ-ŭs), *adj.* irreligious; wicked; profane; as, the third commandment warns us against *impious* language.

Syn. godless.

Ant. (see reverent).

imp-ish (ĭm′pĭsh), *adj.* having the character of a mischievous child or spirit; as, *impish* behavior.

im-pla-ca-bil-i-ty (ĭm-plā″kȧ-bĭl′ĭ-tĭ), *n.* a state of enmity which cannot be softened, or anger which cannot be lessened. Also, implacableness.

im-pla-ca-ble (ĭm-plā′kȧ-bl), *adj.* not to be pacified or appeased; constant in anger or enmity; relentless; as, an Indian is a loyal friend or an *implacable* enemy.—*adv.* implacably.

im-plant (ĭm-plȧnt′), *v.t.* to set in deeply; cause to take root; to give a firm foothold to; as, to *implant* a teaching in the mind.

im-ple-ment (ĭm′plē-mĕnt), *n.* that which supplies a want, or is a necessity to an end; especially, an instrument, tool, or utensil; as, a pickax is an *implement* for loosening the soil.

im-pli-cate (ĭm′plĭ-kāt), *v.t.* to fold or twist together; involve; entangle; bring into connection with; as, the evidence *implicates* many in the plot.

Syn. embarrass, compromise.

im-pli-ca-tion (ĭm″plĭ-kā′shŭn), *n.* entanglement; a meaning not expressed but understood; as, since he did not say anything of the matter, the *implication* is that he knows nothing about it.

im-plic-it (ĭm-plĭs′ĭt), *adj.* to be understood, though not expressed; as, *implicit* sympathy; trusting in the word or authority of another; blind; unreserved; as, *implicit* confidence.

im-plore (ĭm-plōr′), *v.t.* to entreat (a person, or for a thing) earnestly and humbly; to beg; pray; supplicate: *v.i.* to beg; supplicate.

im-plor-ing (ĭm-plōr′ĭng), *p.adj.* humbly begging; as, an *imploring* look.

im-ply (ĭm-plī′), *v.t.* [*p.t.* and *p.p.* implied, *p.pr.* implying], to mean something without directly saying so; to carry a certain meaning, plainly to be understood, though not directly expressed; as, your words *imply* distrust of him; express indirectly.

Syn. involve, compromise, infold, import, denote, signify.

im-po-lite (ĭm″pō-līt′), *adj.* wanting in good manners; boorish; coarse; rough; discourteous.—*adv.* impolitely.

im-po-lite-ness (ĭm″pō-līt′nĕs), *n.* discourteousness; roughness; rudeness; incivility.

im-pol-i-tic (ĭm-pŏl′ĭ-tĭk), *adj.* unwise; indiscreet.

im-pon-der-a-bil-i-ty (ĭm-pŏn″dẽr-ȧ-bĭl′ĭ-tĭ), *n.* the quality of being incapable of being weighed.

im-pon-der-a-ble (ĭm-pŏn′dẽr-ȧ-bl), *adj.* not capable of being weighed; without (sensible) weight.

im-port (ĭm-pōrt′), *v.t.* to bring goods or wares into a country from abroad for commercial purposes; bring in from without; to mean; betoken; be of interest or consequence to; concern: *v.i.* to be of consequence: *n.* (ĭm′pōrt), merchandise brought into a country from abroad: usually in plural; meaning; significance; consequence.

im-por-tance (ĭm-pôr′tȧns), *n.* the quality of being significant, weighty, or momentous; consequence; pompousness.

Syn. significance, avail, gravity, moment.

im-por-tant (ĭm-pôr′tȧnt), *adj.* of much consequence; bearing weight or consequence; of high standing; pompous.

im-por-ta-tion (ĭm″pōr-tā′shŭn), *n.* the act or practice of bringing merchandise into a country from abroad; that which is brought in; that which is recently introduced; as, the word chauffeur was an *importation* from France.

im-port-er (ĭm-pōr′tẽr), *n.* one who brings in goods from foreign countries for commercial purposes.

im-por-tu-nate (ĭm-pôr′tū-nāt), *adj.* persistent; unreasonable or troublesome in begging or asking; not to be repulsed; urgent.—*adv.* importunately.

im-por-tune (ĭm″pôr-tūn′; ĭm-pôr′tūn), *v.t.* to annoy with continual petitions or demands: *v.i.* to beg persistently or urgently.

im-por-tu-ni-ty (ĭm-pôr-tū′nĭ-tĭ), *n.* [*pl.* importunities (-tĭz)], persistent demand; ceaseless asking or begging; urgency.

im-pose (ĭm-pōz′), *v.t.* to place upon; as, to *impose* the hands in confirmation or ordination; lay upon, as a burden, punishment, or charge; as, Great Britain angered the American colonies by the taxes which she continued to *impose*; to pass off deceivingly; to intrude; as, to *impose* one's company on others; in printing, to arrange in order and lock up in a kind of box for printing: said of forms, pages, etc. *v.i.* to place a burden upon; to take too much for granted or too much liberty with: with *upon;* as, to *impose* upon good nature.

im-pos-ing (ĭm-pōz'ĭng), *p.adj.* commanding; stately; grand; impressive; as, the Carnegie Library in New York is an *imposing* building: *n.* in printing, the arrangement of pages or columns into forms.

Syn., adj. striking, majestic, august, noble.
Ant. (see insignificant).

im-po-si-tion (ĭm'pō-zĭsh'ŭn), *n.* a laying upon, especially of hands, in ordination or confirmation; that which is ordered, levied, or commanded; an extra exercise required of a student as a punishment; a trick, fraud, or deception; an excessive or uncalled-for requirement or burden; the arrangement of type into forms for printing.

im-pos-si-bil-i-ty (ĭm-pŏs'ĭ-bĭl'ĭ-tĭ), *n.* the utter incapability of being done; that which cannot exist or be done.

im-pos-si-ble (ĭm-pŏs'ĭ-bl), *adj.* not capable of occurring; not capable of being done; hopeless.

im-post (ĭm'pōst), *n.* a tax, tribute, or duty; especially, a customs-duty levied by government on goods brought into a country; the top member of a pillar on which the arch rests.

im-pos-tor (ĭm-pŏs'tẽr), *n.* one who deceives others by an assumed character or false pretensions.

im-pos-ture (ĭm-pŏs'tūr), *n.* deception, especially that which is practiced under an assumed character or by false pretensions.

im-po-tence (ĭm'pō-tĕns), *n.* the state of being weak in body or mind; feebleness; as, *impotence* is often the result of old age; lack of means to accomplish a purpose. Also, **impotency**.

Syn. weakness, incapacity, infirmity, frailty.
Ant. (see power).

im-po-tent (ĭm'pō-tĕnt), *adj.* wanting in physical, mental, or moral power; weak; without vigor.

Syn. feeble, helpless, infirm.
Ant. (see strong).

im-pound (ĭm-pound'), *v.t.* to shut up in a pen, as stray cattle; confine; hold in the keeping of a court.

im-pov-er-ish (ĭm-pŏv'ẽr-ĭsh), *v.t.* to make poor; reduce to destitution; as, wars *impoverish* many people; to use up the strength, richness, or fertility of, as land.

im-pov-er-ish-ment (ĭm-pŏv'ẽr-ĭsh-mĕnt), *n.* the act of making poor; the state of being reduced in circumstances; extreme penury.

im-prac-ti-ca-bil-i-ty (ĭm-prăk"tĭ-kȧ-bĭl'ĭ-tĭ), *n.* the incapability of being accomplished or done; the quality of not being easily dealt with; unmanageability.

im-prac-ti-ca-ble (ĭm-prăk'tĭ-kȧ-bl), *adj.* not to be effected by the means employed, or at command; not easily dealt with; unmanageable; impossible.—*adv.* **impracticably**.

im-pre-cate (ĭm'prē-kāt), *v.t.* to call down, especially an evil or curse, upon; to curse; to wish evil to.

im-pre-ca-tion (ĭm"prē-kā'shŭn), *n.* a curse; the act of calling down evil upon

im-preg-na-bil-i-ty (ĭm-prĕg"nȧ-bĭl'ĭ-tĭ), *n.* the quality of being unconquerable.

im-preg-na-ble (ĭm-prĕg'nȧ-bl), *adj.* not to be captured, as a fortress; not to be overcome, as virtue.—*adv.* **impregnably**.

im-pre-sa-ri-o (ĭm"prā-sä'rē-ō), *n.* the manager of an opera or concert company; one who engages singers and brings them before the public. [It.]

im-press (ĭm-prĕs'), *v.t.* to mark, stamp, or print by putting force upon; to affect with force, or stamp deeply on, the mind; to imprint; as, to *impress* footsteps on wet sand; compel to enter the public service, as soldiers or sailors; formerly, to seize, by force, for British naval service; seize for the public service, as money or provisions: *n.* (ĭm'prĕs), a mark made by bearing down upon; an image or figure; a mark of distinction; characteristic; stamp; as, the poem bears the *impress* of a great thinker; an image fixed in the mind.

im-press-i-ble (ĭm-prĕs'ĭ-bl), *adj.* capable of being mentally affected; sensitive; as, poetry appeals to *impressible* natures.

im-pres-sion (ĭm-prĕsh'ŭn), *n.* the mark made by a stamp or mold; as the *impression* on a coin; style or character formed by outside force or influence; the mark or stamp which is the result of outside force or influence; an image in the mind caused by something outside it; the immediate effect produced upon the mind by a sensation, passion, or emotion; an indistinct or vague notion, remembrance, or belief; as, the speech gave the audience the *impression* that the speaker was not interested in his subject; a copy taken by pressure from type; number of copies printed at once; edition.

im-pres-sion-a-bil-i-ty (ĭm-prĕsh"ŭn-ȧ-bĭl'ĭ-tĭ), *n.* the quality of being open to influence or external force.

im-pres-sion-a-ble (ĭm-prĕsh'ŭn-ȧ-bl), *adj.* capable of receiving effects from without or of being influenced by surroundings; as, an artist has usually a very *impressionable* nature.

im-pres-sion-is-tic (ĭm-prĕsh"ŭn-ĭs'tĭk), *adj.* pertaining to, or characterized by, the doctrine that natural objects should be painted, or described in literature, so as to convey only their general effect, not their minor details; as, *impressionistic* art.

im-pres-sive (ĭm-prĕs'ĭv), *adj.* capable of making or creating an effect on the feelings.—*adv.* **impressively**.—*n.* **impressiveness**.

Syn. stirring, exciting, affecting, moving.

im-print (ĭm-prĭnt'), *v.t.* to mark by pressure; to stamp, as letters and words on paper, by means of inked types; impress deeply, as on the mind or memory: *n.* (ĭm'prĭnt), an impression, impress, or mark left by something; the publisher's or printer's name, usually with time and place of issue, on the title-page or at the end of a book or other publication.

im-pris-on (ĭm-prĭz'n), *v.t.* to put into a jail; detain in custody; restrain or confine in any way; incarcerate.

Syn. immure, confine.
Ant. (see liberate).

im-pris-on-ment (ĭm-prĭz'n-mĕnt), *n.* state of being shut in, or as in, jail; confinement; restraint; the act of shutting one up in confinement.

Syn. captivity, durance.

im-prob-a-bil-i-ty (ĭm-prŏb″ā-bĭl′ĭ-tĭ), *n.* [*pl.* improbabilities (-tĭz)], unlikelihood; an event not likely to happen.

im-prob-a-ble (ĭm-prŏb′ā-bl), *adj.* unlikely; not to be expected.—*adv.* **improbably.**

im-promp-tu (ĭm-prŏmp′tū), *adv.* without preparation; offhand; as, the minister spoke *impromptu:* *adj.* thrown off on the spur of the moment; as, an *impromptu* address: *n.* a speech or an effort made without preparation.

im-prop-er (ĭm-prŏp′ẽr), *adj.* not well adapted or suited to the purpose; not according to usage; wrong; unseemly; unbecoming; indecent; in mathematics, indicating a fraction in which the numerator is greater than the denominator.—*adv.* **improperly.**

im-pro-pri-e-ty (ĭm″prō-prī′ē-tĭ), *n.* [*pl.* improprieties (-tĭz)], the quality of being unsuitable or inappropriate; unsuitableness; that which is not in accordance with usage, custom, decency, or correctness in act, expression, etc.

im-prov-a-ble (ĭm-prōōv′ā-bl), *adj.* capable of being bettered, or made more valuable.

im-prove (ĭm-prōōv′), *v.t.* to make better; use to advantage; intensify: *v.i.* to grow better; to make better: with *on* or *upon*.

Syn. amend, reform, rectify, use, employ.

Ant. (see deteriorate).

im-prove-ment (ĭm-prōōv′mĕnt), *n.* advancement of anything from one condition to a better; profitable use of anything; that by which the value of anything, especially property, is increased: *pl.* betterments; as, new paint and paper are *improvements* in a house.

im-prov-i-dence (ĭm-prŏv′ĭ-dĕns), *n.* want of foresight or thrift; as, poverty is often the result of *improvidence*.

im-prov-i-dent (ĭm-prŏv′ĭ-dĕnt), *adj.* lacking foresight or thrift; wanting care to provide for the future; careless; as, the five foolish virgins in the old parable were *improvident.*—*adv.* **improvidently.**

Syn. incautious, prodigal, wasteful, reckless, rash.

Ant. (see thrifty).

im-prov-i-sa-tion (ĭm-prŏv″ĭ-sā′shŭn; ĭm-prŏv″ĭ-zā′shŭn), *n.* the act of composing poetry or music without preparation; an impromptu.

im-pro-vise (ĭm″prō-vīz′), *v.t.* to compose without preparation or forethought, especially verse or music; bring about on a sudden, or without previous preparation; make up on the spur of the moment, or for a special occasion: *v.i.* to compose without previous thought; do a thing in an offhand way.

im-pru-dence (ĭm-prōō′dĕns), *n.* want of discretion; carelessness of consequences; inattention to one's interests; want of caution.

im-pru-dent (ĭm-prōō′dĕnt), *adj.* wanting caution or discretion; not attentive to consequences or one's interest; indiscreet; unwise; as, it is *imprudent* to go in a canoe if one cannot swim.

im-pu-dence (ĭm′pū-dĕns), *n.* want of modesty; shamelessness; rudeness; forwardness; sauciness.

Syn. assurance, impertinence, confidence, insolence.

im-pu-dent (ĭm′pū-dĕnt), *adj.* shameless; offensively forward; disrespectful.

Syn. saucy, brazen, bold, impertinent, insolent, immodest.

im-pugn (ĭm-pūn′), *v.t.* to attack by arguments; contradict; to attack as false.

im-pulse (ĭm′pŭls), *n.* force communicated suddenly; the result of a force that urges forward; a mental force directly urging to action; a sudden determination not arising from careful thought; as, she spoke on the *impulse* of the moment.

Syn. incentive, incitement, motive, instigation.

im-pul-sion (ĭm-pŭl′shŭn), *n.* the act of driving forward; the state of being driven forward; that which drives forward; the sudden agency of a body in motion on another body; the mental force that drives to action.

im-pul-sive (ĭm-pŭl′sĭv), *adj.* having the power of urging forward; influenced by, or resulting from, a force that urges forward; passionate; hasty; as, an *impulsive* action; acting by sudden and momentary feeling; not continuous: said of forces.—*adv.* **impulsively.**

Syn. rash, forcible, violent.

Ant. (see deliberate).

im-pul-sive-ness (ĭm-pŭl′sĭv-nĕs), *n.* the quality of being apt to act without thought; that characteristic that allows a person to act upon a quickly passing mental feeling rather than upon reflection.

im-pu-ni-ty (ĭm-pū′nĭ-tĭ), *n.* freedom from punishment, injury, or loss; as, one cannot long break the laws of health with *impunity*.

im-pure (ĭm-pūr′), *adj.* mixed with foreign or outside substance; as, sugar mixed with sand is *impure* sugar; not virtuous in thought, word, or deed; as, *impure* stories: unclean; dirty; not accurate: said of a language or style.—*adv.* **impurely.**

im-pure-ness (ĭm-pūr′nĕs), *n.* the quality of being unclean, unwholesome, or unchaste; that which makes unclean or unwholesome, as foul matter, action, language, etc.

im-pu-ri-ty (ĭm-pū′rĭ-tĭ), *n.* [*pl.* impurities (-tĭz)], uncleanness; a physical or moral blemish; that which makes unclean.

im-put-a-ble (ĭm-pūt′ā-bl), *adj.* capable of being charged; resulting from; as, suicide is frequently *imputable* to insanity.

im-pu-ta-tion (ĭm″pū-tā′shŭn), *n.* the act of charging; anything charged, especially in the way of discredit; blame; reproach.

Syn. censure, charge, accusation.

im-pute (ĭm-pūt′), *v.t.* to set to the account of; to charge, attribute, or ascribe, especially a fault; attribute (sin or righteousness) as received from another.

in (ĭn), *prep.* shows physical surrounding: as, clothed *in* purple; lost *in* the night; denotes being surrounded by activities, interests, etc.; as, *in* business; *in* trouble; *in* work up to his ears; signifies within a state or condition; as, still *in* death; *in* wintertime; indicates wholes; as, he was the most prominent man *in* town; means within; as, he lies now *in* his tomb; means into; as, go *in* the house: *adv.* indicates direction; as, he went *in;* nearness, or "at home"; as, my master is *in;* position in general in relation to surroundings, etc.

in-a-bil-i-ty (in-ȧ-bĭl'ĭ-tĭ), *n.* the state or condition of not having the power to do; lack of power; incapacity.

in-ac-ces-si-ble (in'ăk-sĕs'ĭ-bl), *adj.* not easy to get to or into; not approachable; not obtainable.—*n.* **inaccessibility.**

in-ac-cu-ra-cy (in-ăk'ū-rȧ-sĭ), *n.* the quality of being inexact; the fact of incorrectness; a mistake.

in-ac-cu-rate (in-ăk'ū-rāt), *adj.* incorrect; not exact; containing errors.

in-ac-tion (in-ăk'shŭn), *n.* lack of motion; the state of doing nothing; idleness.

in-ac-tive (in-ăk'tĭv), *adj.* having no power to move; not inclined to move; sluggish; idle.—*adv.* **inactively.** —*n.* **inactivity.**

in-ad-e-quate (in-ăd'ē-kwāt), *adj.* not equal to some demand or requirement; not sufficient.—*adv.* **inadequately.**—*n.* **inadequacy.**

in-ad-mis-si-ble (in-ăd-mĭs'ĭ-bl), *adj.* not worthy or privileged to enter; not to be granted or conceded as true; not allowable.—*adv.* **inadmissibly.**

in-ad-vert-ence (in'ăd-vûr'tĕns), *n.* want of attention; oversight; mistake. Also, **inadvertency.**

in-ad-vert-ent (in'ăd-vûr'tĕnt), *adj.* inattentive; heedless; careless; unconscious; as, an *inadvertent* slight.—*adv.* **inadvertently.**

in-al-ien-a-bil-i-ty (in-āl'yĕn-ȧ-bĭl'ĭ-tĭ), *n.* the incapability of being transferred; the incapability of estrangement.

in-al-ien-a-ble (in-āl'yĕn-ȧ-bl), *adj.* incapable of being surrendered, or transferred to another; as, in the United States, freedom of speech is one of man's *inalienable* rights; incapable of being withdrawn or estranged: said of the affections.—*adv.* **inalienably.**

in-am-o-ra-ta (in-ăm'ō-rä'tȧ), *n.* a woman with whom one is in love; sweetheart; mistress. [IT.]

in-ane (in-ān'), *adj.* empty; void; senseless; silly; pointless; as, *inane* remarks.

in-an-i-mate (in-ăn'ĭ-māt), *adj.* without life; dead; spiritless; lifeless.—*adv.* **inanimately.**

in-a-ni-tion (in'ȧ-nĭsh'ŭn), *n.* emptiness; exhaustion from lack of nourishment.

in-an-i-ty (in-ăn'ĭ-tĭ), *n.* [*pl.* **inanities** (-tĭz)], emptiness; senselessness; frivolity; *pl.* vanities.

in-ap-pli-ca-ble (in-ăp'lĭ-kȧ-bl), *adj.* not suitable or fit for some certain purpose or case; not bearing upon the case in hand.

in-ap-pre-ci-a-ble (in'ă-prē'shĭ-ȧ-bl), *adj.* not to be realized or measured; of no consequence; as, one thousandth of an inch is an *inappreciable* distance.—*adv.* **inappreciably.**

in-ap-pro-pri-ate (in-ă-prō'prĭ-āte), *adj.* not suitable for a particular occasion or in a particular person; not fit; not proper.—*adv.* **inappropriately.**—*n.* **inappropriateness.**

in-apt (in-ăpt'), *adj.* not suitable; not ready; unfit.—*adv.* **inaptly.**

in-apt-i-tude (in-ăp'tĭ-tūd), *n.* want of fitness; want of readiness; want of adaptation.

in-arch (in-ärch'), *v.t.* to graft by uniting two branches, etc., while both are growing on their own roots.

in-ar-tic-u-late (in'är-tĭk'ū-lāt), *adj.* not uttered in the form of words, as the sounds uttered by animals; incapable of speech; as, he was *inarticulate* with rage; not jointed or valved.—*adv.* **inarticulately.**

in-ar-tic-u-late-ness (in'är-tĭk'ū-lāt-nĕs), *n.* indistinctness of utterance; speechlessness.

in-ar-tis-tic (in-är-tĭs'tĭk), *adj.* not showing taste; not graceful; not skillful. Also, **inartistical.**—*adv.* **inartistically.**

in-as-much (in'ăz-mŭch'), *adv.* in a like degree; seeing that; with *as;* because; as, "*Inasmuch* as ye have done it unto one of the least of these my brethren, ye have done it unto me."—Matt. xxv. 40.

in-at-ten-tion (in-ȧ-tĕn'shŭn), *n.* heedlessness; the state of not putting one's mind on a duty; lack of regard.

in-at-ten-tive (in-ȧ-tĕn'tĭv), *adj.* paying no heed to; negligent; heedless.—*adv.* **inattentively.**

in-au-di-ble (in-ô'dĭ-bl), *adj.* incapable of being heard; not actually heard.—*adv.* **inaudibly.**

in-au-gu-ral (in-ô'gū-răl), *adj.* pertaining to the ceremonies accompanying the dedication of a public building; the formal installation of a person in an office, etc.: *n.* an address made on such an occasion as the dedication of a public building, the installation of a person in an office, etc.; as, the President's *inaugural.*

in-au-gu-rate (in-ô'gū-rāt), *v.t.* to admit or introduce into office with appropriate ceremonies; invest with office in a formal manner; consecrate; make a formal beginning of; as, to *inaugurate* a custom; begin, as a new policy; celebrate the first public use of by some opening ceremony; dedicate, as a public building.—*n.* **inauguration.**

in-aus-pi-cious (in'ôs-pĭsh'ŭs), *adj.* unfortunate; unlucky; unfavorable; as, superstitious people consider thirteen an *inauspicious* number.—*adv.* **inauspiciously.**

in-born (in'bôrn'), *adj.* implanted by nature; native.

in-bred (in'brĕd'), *adj.* born with one; natural; as, man has an *inbred* love of freedom.

in-breed (in-brēd'), *v.t.* to produce or develop within; to cause animals closely related to produce young.

In-ca (ĭn'kȧ), *n.* the Peruvian emperor, or a member of the royal race in Peru previous to the Spanish conquest; the savage Peruvian race.

in-cal-cu-la-ble (in-kăl'kū-lȧ-bl), *adj.* beyond reckoning; beyond estimate; very great; as, the *incalculable* benefits of civilization.—*adv.* **incalculably.**

in-ca-les-cent (in'kȧ-lĕs'ĕnt), *adj.* increasing in heat; growing warm.

in-can-des-cence (in'kăn-dĕs'ĕns), *n.* white heat; glowing due to heat, as an electric lamp. Also, **incandescency.**

in-can-des-cent (in'kăn-dĕs'ĕnt), *adj.* glowing; white with heat; hence, brilliant, shining, clear.

in-can-des-cent lamp (ĭn″kăn-dĕs′-ĕnt lămp), a lamp in which the light is produced by a thin strip of material heated to a white heat, or incandescence, by an electric current.

in-can-ta-tion (ĭn″kăn-tā′shŭn), *n.* a magical charm said or sung; enchantment; as, the Indian medicine men tried to cure diseases by *incantation*.

in-ca-pa-ble (ĭn-kā′pȧ-bl), *adj.* not having the power to do; inefficient; not able to receive or be influenced by; wanting sufficient ability.—*adv.* **incapably.**—*n.* **incapability.**

in-ca-pac-i-tate (ĭn″kȧ-păs′ĭ-tāt), *v.t.* to deprive of ability or natural power; render powerless or unfit; disable; as, old age *incapacitates* one for hard labor

in-ca-pac-i-ty (ĭn″kȧ-păs′ĭ-tĭ), *n.* lack of power, physical or mental; disability from any cause.

in-car-cer-ate (ĭn-kär′sẽr-āt), *v.t.* to imprison; confine: *adj.* imprisoned.

in-car-cer-a-tion (ĭn-kär″sẽr-ā′shŭn), *n.* imprisonment; confinement.

in-car-cer-a-tor (ĭn-kär′sẽr-ā″tẽr), *n.* one who imprisons.

in-car-na-dine (ĭn-kär′nȧ-dĭn), *v.t.* to dye red or flesh-color: *adj.* flesh-colored; pale red.

in-car-nate (ĭn-kär′nāt), *v.t.* to clothe with flesh; embody in flesh: *p.adj.* embodied in flesh; personified.

in-car-na-tion (ĭn″kär-nā′shŭn), *n.* the act of clothing with or of assuming flesh; embodiment in human form; an actual form representing a principle, ideal, etc.; the taking upon himself of human nature by the Son of God.

in-case (ĭn-kās′), *v.t.* to inclose in a box or solid covering; to surround with anything. Also, **encase.**—*n.* **incasement.**

in-cau-tious (ĭn-kô′shŭs), *adj.* wanting in care; heedless; careless; indifferent; unwary.

in-cen-di-a-rism (ĭn-sĕn′dĭ-ȧ-rĭzm), *n.* the act of one who, for evil purpose, burns property.

in-cen-di-a-ry (ĭn-sĕn′dĭ-ā-rĭ), *adj.* pertaining to the malicious burning of property; tending to excite passion or violence; as, an *incendiary* speech: *n.* one guilty of burning, for wicked mischief, the house or buildings of another; one who excites passion or violence.

in-cense (ĭn-sĕns′), *v.t.* to enkindle or excite, as a passion; inflame with anger; provoke; irritate: (ĭn′sĕns), to perfume with incense: *n.* any material which gives off perfume when burned, especially olibanum, the frankincense of the Jews, and also of the ancient Greeks and Romans; any pleasant odor, as of flowers; sometimes odor of spices and gums burned in religious rites or ceremonies.

in-cen-tive (ĭn-sĕn′tĭv), *adj.* arousing to action; encouraging: *n.* that which arouses to action; encouragement; motive; as, real interest in a subject is an *incentive* to study.

in-cep-tion (ĭn-sĕp′shŭn), *n.* beginning; first stage; as, the movement was successful from its *inception*.

in-cep-tive (ĭn-sĕp′tĭv), *adj.* beginning; relating to a beginning: *n.* a word or phrase that indicates the beginning of an action: used in grammar.

in-cer-ti-tude (ĭn-sûr′tĭ-tūd), *n.* doubtfulness; lack of decision.

in-ces-sant (ĭn-sĕs′ănt), *adj.* unceasing; ceaseless; continuous; as, the *incessant* dropping of water will wear a hollow in the hardest stone.

in-cest (ĭn′sĕst), *n.* sexual relations between persons related within the degrees of marriage forbidden by law.—*adj.* **incestuous.**

inch (ĭnch), *n.* one-twelfth of a foot; a small quantity or degree: *v.t.* to drive by small degrees; deal out sparingly: *v.i.* move slowly.

in-cho-ate (ĭn′kō-āt), *adj.* just begun; elementary; incomplete; as, according to some theories the world was at first an *inchoate* mass of matter.—*adv.* **inchoately.**

in-cho-a-tive (ĭn-kō′ȧ-tĭv), *adj.* expressing or pertaining to a beginning: *n.* a word which expresses the beginning of an action.

in-ci-dence (ĭn′sĭ-dĕns), *n.* the direction in which a ray of light or heat falls upon a surface.

in-ci-dent (ĭn′sĭ-dĕnt), *adj.* falling upon, as a ray of light on a reflecting surface; apt to occur; having to do with; occurring accidentally; depending on; as, the duties *incident* to his profession: *n.* occurrence; that which happens; chance happening; episode; event; accident.

in-ci-den-tal (ĭn″sĭ-dĕn′tăl), *adj.* casual; liable to happen unexpectedly; happening as a chance feature of something else; as, *incidental* expenses: *n.* something casual or subordinate: *pl.* minor expenses.—*adv.* **incidentally.**

in-cin-er-ate (ĭn-sĭn′ẽr-āt), *v.t.* to burn to ashes; as, to *incinerate* garbage.

in-cin-er-a-tion (ĭn-sĭn″ẽr-ā′shŭn), *n.* the act of burning to ashes.

in-cin-er-a-tor (ĭn-sĭn′ẽr-ā″tẽr), *n.* a furnace or oven for burning substances to ashes.

in-cip-i-ence (ĭn-sĭp′ĭ-ĕns), *n.* beginning; commencement. Also, **incipiency.**

in-cip-i-ent (ĭn-sĭp′ĭ-ĕnt), *adj.* beginning to be or to appear; as, the *incipient* stage of a disease.

in-cise (ĭn-sīz′), *v.t.* to cut in; to engrave; to carve in intaglio.

in-ci-sion (ĭn-sĭzh′ŭn), *n.* a cut made with a sharp instrument.

in-ci-sive (ĭn-sī′sĭv), *adj.* having the quality of cutting into; sharp; sarcastic; biting.—*adv.* **incisively.**—*n.* **incisiveness.**

in-ci-sor (ĭn-sī′zẽr; ĭn-sī′sẽr), *n.* a cutting tooth; especially, a tooth in front of the canines.

in-ci-so-ri-al (ĭn-sī-sō′rĭ-ăl), *adj.* pertaining to, or having the character of, an incisor tooth.

in-ci-so-ry (ĭn-sī′sō-rĭ), *adj.* having the power of cutting.

in-ci-ta-tion (ĭn″sī-tā′shŭn), *n.* the act of urging or spurring on: incentive.

in-cite (ĭn-sīt′), *v.t.* to move to action; stir up; spur on; encourage.

Syn. instigate, excite, provoke, stimulate, urge, impel.

in-cite-ment (ĭn-sīt′mĕnt), *n.* that which goads or spurs on; a spurring on; incentive; impulse; encouragement; as, praise is often an *incitement* to further effort.

in-ci-vil-i-ty (ĭn′sĭ-vĭl′ĭ-tĭ), *n.* [*pl.* incivilities (-tĭz)], lack of courtesy; impoliteness; any uncivil act.

in-clem-en-cy (ĭn-klĕm′ĕn-sĭ), *n.* [*pl.* inclemencies (-sĭz)], severity; storminess; adversity.

in-clem-ent (ĭn-klĕm′ĕnt), *adj.* harsh; severe; stormy; as, *inclement* weather.

in-clin-a-ble (ĭn-klīn′ȧ-bl), *adj.* disposed favorably; as, *inclinable* to pity; capable of sloping.

in-cli-na-tion (ĭn′klĭ-nā′shŭn), *n.* a leaning; a turning aside from normal direction or position; a nod; as, a courteous *inclination* of the head; tendency of the mind; disposition; a bent; as, a natural *inclination* toward business.

Syn. bias, affection, attachment, wish, liking, desire.

Ant. (see aversion).

in-cline (ĭn-klīn′), *v.i.* to turn from the normal direction or position; lean; bow; have a mental bent or tendency; be disposed: *v.t.* to cause to lean; direct; bow; give a tendency to; turn; dispose: *n.* a slope; a sloping surface.

Syn., *v.* slant, tend, bend, bias.

in-clined (ĭn-klīnd′), *p.adj.* having a tendency; sloping; disposed; bent into a bulging curve.

in-clined plane (ĭn-klīnd′ plān), a sloping surface.

in-cli-nom-e-ter (ĭn′klĭ-nŏm′ē-tẽr), *n.* an instrument used on aircraft or flying machines for measuring the angle or dip of such machines during their flight.

in-close (ĭn-klōz′), *v.t.* to shut in; surround; put into an envelope; separate from by a fence.

Syn. fence in, cover, wrap.

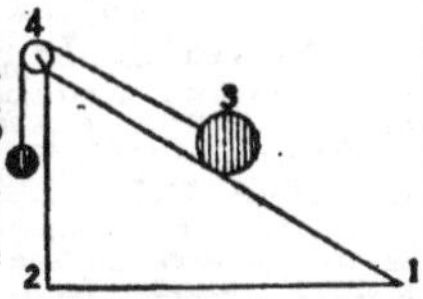

Inclined Plane. 1-2, base; 3, large weight; 4, pulley or roller.

in-clo-sure (ĭn-klō′zhŭr), *n.* the act of shutting in, or state of being shut in; that which is surrounded; that which surrounds, as a fence; something included with a letter in an envelope, as a bill, check, etc.

in-clude (ĭn-kl͞ood′), *v.t.* to inclose; hold, as in an inclosure; shut up within something; to contain as part of the whole.

in-clud-ed (ĭn-kl͞ood′ĕd), *p.adj.* inclosed; contained; comprehended.

in-clu-sion (ĭn-kl͞oo′zhŭn), *n.* the act of inclosing; the state of being inclosed or contained; that which is inclosed or contained.

in-clu-sive (ĭn-kl͞oo′sĭv), *adj.* inclosing; containing; taking in extremes; as, from Monday to Saturday *inclusive*: that is, taking in both Monday and Saturday. —*adv.* **inclusively.**

in-cog-ni-to (ĭn-kŏg′nĭ-tō), *adj.* unknown or disguised: *adv.* in disguise; under an assumed name; as, rulers sometimes like to travel *incognito*: *n.* [*fem.* incognita], a great personage who travels under an assumed title; the assuming of a character or title to avoid recognition; state of being unrecognized.

in-co-her-ence (ĭn′kō-hēr′ĕns), *n.* looseness; want of connection; as, the essay is marked by *incoherence* of thought.

in-co-her-ent (ĭn′kō-hēr′ĕnt), *adj.* without the quality of being held together; without connection; as, the speech of one who raves in a fever is *incoherent.*

in-co-he-sion (ĭn′kō-hē′zhŭn), *n.* want of the power of sticking together.

in-com-bus-ti-ble (ĭn′kŏm-bŭs′tĭ-bl), *adj.* that cannot be consumed by fire: *n.* an unburnable substance.

in-come (ĭn′kŭm), *n.* the gain which proceeds from labor, business, property, or capital; yearly receipts of a person or business company: **income tax**, a tax laid upon the yearly receipts or profits of an individual or corporation.

in-com-ing (ĭn′kŭm′ĭng), *p.adj.* coming in; accumulating, as profits: *n.* the act of coming in; that which comes in; as, the *incoming* administration.—*n.* **incomer.**

in-com-men-su-ra-ble (ĭn′kŏ-mĕn′sh͞oo-rȧ-bl), *adj.* having no common measure; having no common divisor except one: *n.* one of two (or more) quantities that have no common measure.—*n.* **incommensurability.**

in-com-men-su-rate (ĭn′kŏ-mĕn′sh͞oo-rāt), *adj.* having no common measure; not sufficient in measure; not great enough; as, his strength is *incommensurate* to the demands upon it.—*adv.* **incommensurately.**

in-com-mode (ĭn′kŏ-mōd′), *v.t.* to give inconvenience or trouble to; disturb.

Syn. annoy, plague, molest, inconvenience.

Ant. (see accommodate).

in-com-mo-di-ous (ĭn′kŏ-mō′dĭ-ŭs), *adj.* not giving ease or advantage, as *incommodious* apartments; troublesome; inconvenient.

in-com-mu-ni-ca-ble (ĭn′kŏ-mū′nĭ-kȧ-bl), *adj.* incapable of being given or told; as, health is an *incommunicable* blessing.

in-com-mu-ni-ca-tive (ĭn′kŏ-mū′nĭ-kā-tĭv), *adj.* not given to free speaking; reserved.

in-com-pa-ra-ble (ĭn-kŏm′pȧ-rȧ-bl), *adj.* not admitting of a statement of likeness and differences; unequaled; peerless.—*adv.* **incomparably.**

in-com-pat-i-bil-i-ty (ĭn′kŏm-păt′ĭ-bĭl′ĭ-tĭ), *n.* state of being unable to live together in comfort, harmony, or peace. Also, **incompatibleness.**

in-com-pat-i-ble (ĭn′kŏm-păt′ĭ-bl), *adj.* incapable of living or acting together in harmony; as, health and filth are *incompatible*: *n.pl.* persons or things disagreeing with each other.—*adv.* **incompatibly.**

in-com-pe-tence (ĭn-kŏm′pē-tĕns), *n.* inability, physical, mental, or moral; insufficiency. Also, **incompetency.**

in-com-pe-tent (ĭn-kŏm′pē-tĕnt), *adj.* wanting ability; wanting fitness; inadmissible; as, a man who has any defect of body is considered *incompetent* to serve as a soldier.

Syn. incapable, unable, insufficient.

Ant. (see competent).

in-com-plete (ĭn′kŏm-plēt′), *adj.* not fully finished or developed; as, an *incomplete* story; not having all its parts; imperfect; as, *incomplete* information.

in-com-plete-ly (in″kŏm-plēt′lĭ), *adv.* imperfectly; with lack of some part.

in-com-plete-ness (in″kŏm-plēt′nĕs), *n.* lack of perfection. Also, **incompletion.**

in-com-pre-hen-si-ble (in-kŏm″prē-hĕn′sĭ-bl), *adj.* not to be understood or grasped by the mind; as, the vastness of the universe is *incomprehensible* to man.—*adv.* **incomprehensibly.**—*n.* **incomprehensibility.**

in-com-press-i-ble (in″kŏm-prĕs′ĭ-bl), *adj.* incapable of being reduced by pressure; resisting pressure.

in-con-ceiv-a-bil-i-ty (in″kŏn-sēv″ȧ-bĭl′ĭ-tĭ), *n.* incapability of being grasped or imagined by the mind.

in-con-ceiv-a-ble (in″kŏn-sēv′ȧ-bl), *adj.* incapable of being grasped by the mind or imagined; unbelievable.—*adv.* **inconceivably.**

in-con-clu-sive (in″kŏn-klōō′sĭv), *adj.* leading to no definite result in evidence or argument; inconvincing; reaching no definite result in action; ineffective.—*adv.* **inconclusively.**

in-con-den-si-ble (in″kŏn-dĕn′sĭ-bl), *adj.* incapable of being made more compact, or of being reduced to liquid form.

in-con-gru-i-ty (in″kŏn-grōō′ĭ-tĭ), *n.* [*pl.* incongruities (-tĭz)], want of fitness; unsuitableness of one thing to another; as, one was struck by the *incongruity* of the huge building in the shabby little street.

in-con-gru-ous (in-kŏn′grōō-ŭs), *adj.* disagreeing; unsuited to one another; inappropriate; as, mirth would be *incongruous* at a funeral.
Syn. conflicting, inconsistent.
Ant. (see suitable).

in-con-se-quence (in-kŏn′sē-kwĕns), *n.* the quality of being illogical; unimportance.

in-con-se-quent (in-kŏn′sē-kwĕnt), *adj.* not reasonable; out of proper relation; having nothing to do with the subject in hand; as, an *inconsequent* answer.

in-con-se-quen-tial (in-kŏn″sē-kwĕn′shăl), *adj.* unrelated with the thing in hand; not logical; unimportant.

in-con-sid-er-a-ble (in″kŏn-sĭd′ĕr-ȧ-bl), *adj.* not deserving consideration; unimportant.—*adv.* **inconsiderably.**

in-con-sid-er-ate (in″kŏn-sĭd′ĕr-ăt), *adj.* not heeding the wishes, thoughts, or feelings of others; thoughtless of others.—*adv.* **inconsiderately.**

in-con-sis-ten-cy (in″kŏn-sĭs′tĕn-sĭ), *n.* [*pl.* inconsistencies (-sĭz)], want of agreement; as, there are *inconsistencies* between his words and his actions; incongruity; the quality of being changeable; contradiction of self-asserted principles or beliefs.

in-con-sis-tent (in″kŏn-sĭs′tĕnt), *adj.* lacking agreement; lacking uniformity; self-contradicting; as, the conduct of many Christians is *inconsistent* with their profession.

in-con-sol-a-ble (in″kŏn-sōl′ȧ-bl), *adj.* not to be comforted; disconsolate.—*adv.* **inconsolably.**

in-con-spic-u-ous (in″kŏn-spĭk′ū-ŭs), *adj.* not easily perceived; so small as to escape notice; hardly to be seen; not attracting attention; as, *inconspicuous* dress shows good taste.—*adv.* **inconspicuously.**

in-con-stan-cy (in-kŏn′stăn-sĭ), *n.* changeableness; fickleness; instability of temper.

in-con-stant (in-kŏn′stănt), *adj.* subject to change; unstable; variable; fickle.—*adv.* **inconstantly.**

in-con-test-a-ble (in″kŏn-tĕs′tȧ-bl), *adj.* not admitting of question or dispute.—*adv.* **incontestably.**

in-con-ti-nence (in-kŏn′tĭ-nĕns), *n.* lack of restraint, especially in indulging the passions. Also, **incontinency.**

in-con-ti-nent (in-kŏn′tĭ-nĕnt), *adj.* unrestrained; impure: *n.* an unchaste or immoral person.—*adv.* **incontinently.**

in-con-tro-vert-i-bil-i-ty (in-kŏn″trō-vûr″tĭ-bĭl′ĭ-tĭ), *n.* the state or quality of being beyond dispute or discussion.

in-con-tro-vert-i-ble (in-kŏn″trō-vûr′tĭ-bl), *adj.* not admitting of debate; indisputable.—*adv.* **incontrovertibly.**

in-con-ven-ience (in″kŏn-vēn′yĕns), *n.* want of comfort; unfitness; troublesomeness; disadvantage; discomfort: *v.t.* to put to trouble; annoy; molest.

in-con-ven-ient (in″kŏn-vēn′yĕnt), *adj.* disadvantageous; unfit; giving trouble or annoyance; uncomfortable.—*adv.* **inconveniently.**

in-con-vert-i-bil-i-ty (in″kŏn-vûr″tĭ-bĭl′ĭ-tĭ), *n.* the quality of being incapable of being changed into or for something else.

in-con-vert-i-ble (in″kŏn-vûr′tĭ-bl), *adj.* incapable of being changed into, or exchanged for, something else; as, Confederate bank notes were *inconvertible* into gold.—*adv.* **inconvertibly.**

in-cor-po-rate (in-kôr′pō-rāt), *v.t.* to combine into one body; give a body to; embody; unite; put in; as, to *incorporate* an idea in a written composition; blend; form into a company recognized by law: *v.i.* to unite with another body so as to form a part of it; be mixed or blended with: *adj.* (in-kôr′pō-rāt), closely united; united in one body.

in-cor-po-ra-tion (in-kôr″pō-rā′shŭn), *n.* combination; mixture; formation of a united body; a body of persons authorized by law to conduct a business under certain conditions.

in-cor-po-ra-tor (in-kôr′pō-rā″tẽr), *n.* one who embodies or unites; an original member of a society existing as one united body.

in-cor-po-re-al (in″kôr-pō′rē-ăl), *adj.* not made of matter.—*adv.* **incorporeally.**

in-cor-rect (in″kŏ-rĕkt′), *adj.* not according to model or rule; faulty; not according to fact; inaccurate; not in accordance with morality or good manners; improper.—*adv.* **incorrectly.**

in-cor-ri-gi-ble (in-kŏr′ĭ-jĭ-bl), *adj.* bad beyond correction or amendment; as, *incorrigible* boys are sent to reform schools.—*adv.* **incorrigibly.**—*n.* **incorrigibility.**

in-cor-ri-gi-ble-ness (in-kŏr′ĭ-jĭ-bl-nĕs), *n.* the quality of being bad beyond correction.

in-cor-rod-i-ble (in″kō-rŏ′dĭ-bl), *adj.* incapable of being gradually worn away, as by rust.

in-cor-rupt (in″kō-rŭpt′), *adj.* free from physical or moral spot; unharmed; upright; especially, above the influence of bribery; honest.

in-cor-rupt-i-bil-i-ty (in″kō-rŭp″tĭ-bĭl′ĭ-tĭ), *n.* incapability of being influenced by bribes, etc.; freedom from moral spot.

in-cor-rupt-i-ble (in″kō-rŭp′tĭ-bl), *adj.* incapable of physical corruption, or decay; not liable to moral contamination; especially, incapable of being bribed.—*adv.* **incorruptibly.**

in-cor-rup-tion (in″kō-rŭp′shŭn), *n.* freedom from possibility of decay; freedom from moral stain.

in-crease (in-krēs′), *v.i.* to become greater in any respect; multiply; grow: *v.t.* to make greater in any respect; enlarge: *n.* (in′krēs), a growing larger; that which is added to the original stock; growth; produce; profit; issue; offspring; the period of waxing: said of the moon.

Syn., *v.* extend, dilate, expand, raise, enhance, aggravate, magnify, grow.

Ant. (see decrease).

in-cred-i-bil-i-ty (in-krĕd″ĭ-bĭl′ĭ-tĭ), *n.* the quality of being hard to believe. Also, **incredibleness.**

in-cred-i-ble (in-krĕd′ĭ-bl), *adj.* surpassing belief; hard to believe; unimaginable.—*adv.* **incredibly.**

in-cre-du-li-ty (in″krē-dū′lĭ-tĭ), *n.* the quality of being unbelieving; disbelief; as, the beggar's story was met with *incredulity.*

in-cred-u-lous (in-krĕd′ū-lŭs), *adj.* indicating lack of belief; unbelieving; as, an *incredulous* expression on the face.

in-cre-ment (in′krē-mĕnt), *n.* increase; augmentation; produce.

in-cres-cent (in-krĕs′ĕnt), *p.adj.* increasing; as, the *increscent* moon; *increscent* strength.

in-crim-i-nate (in-krĭm′ĭ-nāt), *v.t.* to charge with a crime; accuse.

in-crust (in-krŭst′), *v.t.* to cover with, or as with, a crust; coat; overlay; to inlay, as mosaic, so as to form a decorative covering. Also, **encrust.**

in-crus-ta-tion (in″krŭs-tā′shŭn), *n.* a crust; covering; an incrusted or inlaid object or substance; a covering or inlaying of marble, mosaic, etc., attached to masonry.

in-cu-bate (in′kū-bāt), *v.t.* to sit upon (eggs) to hatch them; to keep (as eggs, etc.) under conditions of warmth favorable for hatching: *v.i.* to brood.

in-cu-ba-tion (in″kū-bā′shŭn), *n.* the act of hatching by any means.

in-cu-ba-tor (in′kū-bā″tẽr), *n.* one who, or that which, hatches; especially, an apparatus for hatching eggs artificially.

in-cu-bus (in′kū-bŭs), *n.* [*pl.* incubuses (-ĕz), incubi (-bī)], the nightmare; in the superstition of the Middle Ages, a demon believed to cause nightmare and the birth of deformed children; a heavy weight or burden. [LAT.]

in-cul-cate (in-kŭl′kāt; in′kŭl-kāt), *v.t.* to impress upon the mind by frequent warning or direction; as, to *inculcate* principles of honesty, etc.

in-cul-ca-tor (in-kŭl′kā-tẽr), *n.* one who teaches or impresses upon the mind by frequent warnings; as, his mother was the *inculcator* of his love of truth.

in-cum-ben-cy (in-kŭm′bĕn-sĭ), *n.* [*pl.* incumbencies (-sĭz)], the act or state of holding an office; full possession and exercise of any office; as, the governor accomplished many things during his *incumbency* of office.

in-cum-bent (in-kŭm′bĕnt), *adj.* lying upon; imposed as a duty; obligatory; demanded of; as, it is *incumbent* upon every good citizen to respect the rights of others: *n.* the holder of an office; a clergyman in possession of a parish.

in-cur (in-kûr′), *v.t.* [*p.t.* and *p.p.* incurred, *p.pr.* incurring], to become liable to, by one's own action; to bring upon oneself; as, every man *incurs* some measure of dislike; contract, as a debt.

in-cur-a-bil-i-ty (in-kūr″ȧ-bĭl′ĭ-tĭ), *n.* the state of being beyond the power of skill or medicine to heal.

in-cur-a-ble (in-kūr′ȧ-bl), *adj.* incapable of being healed; beyond the power of skill or medicine: *n.* a person diseased beyond the possibility of being restored to health.—*adv.* **incurably.**

in-cur-sion (in-kûr′shŭn), *n.* an inroad; raid; invasion; as, the enemy made an *incursion* into the country.

in-debt-ed (in-dĕt′ĕd), *p.adj.* owing someone money; being under obligation.—*n.* **indebtedness.**

in-de-cen-cy (in-dē′sĕn-sĭ), *n.* [*pl.* indecencies (-sĭz)], want of delicacy, refinement, modesty, or good manners; that which is grossly vulgar or impure; a word or act offensive to modesty.

in-de-cent (in-dē′sĕnt), *adj.* improper in language, behavior, etc.; immodest; indelicate; unfit to be heard or looked upon.

in-de-ci-sion (in″dē-sĭzh′ŭn), *n.* a wavering of the mind; hesitation; irresolution.

in-de-ci-sive (in″dē-sī′sĭv), *adj.* not bringing to a sure end; inconclusive; as, an *indecisive* battle.—*adv.* **indecisively.**

in-de-clin-a-ble (in″dē-klīn′ȧ-bl), *adj.* that cannot be varied by inflection: *n.* a word that cannot be inflected.

in-de-co-rous (in″dē-kō′rŭs; in-dĕk′ō-rŭs), *adj.* unsuitable or improper; unbecoming; against any accepted rule of conduct; as, it is *indecorous* to make fun of the aged and feeble.

in-de-co-rum (in″dē-kō′rŭm), *n.* violation of propriety or rules of conduct; breach of etiquette or civility.

in-deed (in-dēd′), *adv.* in fact; in truth; as, I was *indeed* surprised.

in-de-fat-i-ga-bil-i-ty (in″dē-făt″ĭ-gȧ-bĭl′ĭ-tĭ), *n.* the quality of being untiring.

in-de-fat-i-ga-ble (in″dē-făt′ĭ-gȧ-bl), *adj.* not to be wearied out; not yielding to fatigue; unceasing in labor or effort.—*adv.* **indefatigably.**

in-de-fea-si-bil-i-ty (in″dē-fē″zĭ-bĭl′ĭ-tĭ), *n.* the quality of not being able to be annulled or made void.

in-de-fea-si-ble (in″dē-fē′zĭ-bl), *adj.* not to be annulled or made void, as a title.—*adv.* **indefeasibly.**

in-de-fen-si-ble (ĭn″dē̆-fĕn′sĭ-bl), *adj.* that cannot be maintained or justified; as, an *indefensible* criminal act.—*adv.* **indefensibly.**—*n.* **indefensibility.**

in-de-fin-a-ble (ĭn″dē̆-fīn′ȧ-bl), *adj.* incapable of being described exactly; unexplainable; as, an *indefinable* charm.—*adv.* **indefinably.**

in-def-i-nite (ĭn-dĕf′ĭ-nĭt), *adj.* not exact; vague; uncertain; having no particular limit; large beyond the understanding of man, though not absolutely infinite; too numerous or variable to be easily counted; as, an *indefinite* number of grains of sand.—*adv.* **indefinitely.**

Syn. unsettled, loose, lax.

Ant. (see definite).

in-del-i-bil-i-ty (ĭn-dĕl″ĭ-bĭl′ĭ-tĭ), *n.* the quality of being incapable of being rubbed or blotted out.

in-del-i-ble (ĭn-dĕl′ĭ-bl), *adj.* not to be blotted out, effaced, or rubbed out; as, *indelible* ink.—*adv.* **indelibly.**

in-del-i-ca-cy (ĭn-dĕl′ĭ-kȧ-sĭ), *n.* [*pl.* indelicacies (-sĭz)], want of refinement; that which is offensive to modesty or refined taste.

in-del-i-cate (ĭn-dĕl′ĭ-kāt), *adj.* offensive to modesty; coarse; indecent.—*adv.* **indelicately.**

in-dem-ni-fi-ca-tion (ĭn-dĕm″nĭ-fĭ-kā′shŭn), *n.* the act of securing against loss; repayment for loss; an allowance to officers or soldiers for losses in actual service.

in-dem-ni-fy (ĭn-dĕm′nĭ-fī), *v.t.* [*p.t.* and *p.p.* indemnified, *p.pr.* indemnifying], to secure or insure against loss or damage; repay; as, fire insurance companies *indemnify* loss of property by fire.

in-dem-ni-ty (ĭn-dĕm′nĭ-tĭ), *n.* [*pl.* indemnities (-tĭz)], security against loss, damage, or punishment; repayment for loss; as, if the citizens of one nation injure the property of another, the former must pay *indemnity.*

in-dent (ĭn-dĕnt′), *v.t.* to make a depression in; cut into points like teeth; in printing or writing, to begin a line with a blank space; notch; bind out to service by a written agreement, as an apprentice: *n.* a notch in the border; a formal agreement.

in-den-ta-tion (ĭn-dĕn-tā′shŭn), *n.* a small hollow or depression, as from a blow; a binding out to service; a dent or dint; a space left in a margin.

in-dent-ed (ĭn-dĕnt′ĕd), *p.adj.* notched on the edge or border like a row of teeth; zigzag; having a space left in the margin; held by an agreement, as an apprentice.

in-den-ture (ĭn-dĕn′tûr), *n.* a written agreement, formerly in duplicate, with the edges notched so as to correspond: *v.t.* to bind by a written agreement, as an apprentice or assistant.

in-de-pend-ence (ĭn″dē̆-pĕn′dĕns), *n.* freedom from support or government by others; a sum of money sufficient for one's needs; self-reliance. Also, **independency.**

In-de-pend-ence Day (ĭn″dē̆-pĕn′-dĕns dā), July 4, the anniversary of the American Declaration of Independence, observed in the United States as a national holiday.

in-de-pend-ent (ĭn″dē̆-pĕn′dĕnt), *adj.* not relying on, supported by, or governed by, another; having enough to live on; free; not easily influenced; uncontrolled by others: *n.* one who supports measures or men without connection with any organized party.

in-de-scrib-a-ble (ĭn″dē̆-skrīb′ȧ-bl), *adj.* incapable of being expressed or portrayed; beyond the power of being expressed or portrayed.—*adv.* **indescribably.**

in-de-struct-i-bil-i-ty (ĭn″dē̆-strŭk″-tĭ-bĭl′ĭ-tĭ), *n.* incapability of being broken up, demolished, or ruined.

in-de-struct-i-ble (ĭn″dē̆-strŭk′tĭ-bl), *adj.* not to be broken up, ruined, or demolished; beyond ruin or demolition.—*adv.* **indestructibly.**

in-de-ter-min-a-ble (ĭn″dē̆-tûr′mĭn-ȧ-bl), *adj.* impossible to be known or defined definitely.

in-de-ter-mi-nate (ĭn″dē̆-tûr′mĭ-nāt), *adj.* not settled or fixed; indefinite; vague; not leading to a definite result; not exact; as, an *indeterminate* sentence for crime; in mathematics, having an indefinite number of values or solutions.—*adv.* **indeterminately.**

in-de-ter-min-a-tion (ĭn″dē̆-tûr″mĭ-nā′shŭn), *n.* an unsettled, indecisive state of mind; lack of decision.

in-dex (ĭn′dĕks), *n.* [*pl.* indexes (ĭn′dĕk-sĕs), indices (ĭn′dĭ-sēz)], that which points out or indicates; an alphabetical table of the contents of a book; the figure or letter which shows the number of times a quantity is to be multiplied together, as 3^4 means $3 \times 3 \times 3 \times 3$: *v.t.* to provide with an alphabetical table of references.

in-dex fin-ger (ĭn′dĕks fĭŋ′gẽr), the forefinger: so called because used in pointing.

In-di-a-man (ĭn′dĭ-ȧ-măn), *n.* [*pl.* Indiamen (-mĕn)], a large vessel formerly employed in the India trade.

In-di-an (ĭn′dĭ-ăn), *adj.* pertaining to the Indies, to the West Indies, or to the American Indians; made of maize or Indian corn: *n.* an East Indian, West Indian, or Anglo-Indian; one of the first inhabitants of America, or a Red Indian: **Indian Ocean,** the ocean lying between Asia, Africa, and Australia.

In-di-an club (ĭn′dĭ-ăn klŭb), a bottle-shaped club, swung by the hands in gymnastic exercises.

Indian Club

In-di-an corn (ĭn′dĭ-ăn kôrn), an American cereal plant: known also as *maize.*

In-di-an file (ĭn′dĭ-ăn fīl), single file, the usual method of traveling among Indians.

In-di-an red (ĭn′dĭ-ăn rĕd), a dark purplish-red earth originally imported from the Persian Gulf.

In-di-an sum-mer (ĭn′dĭ-ăn sŭm′ẽr), summer-like weather, with calm, and absence of rain, occurring in late autumn.

In-di-an yel-low (ĭn′dĭ-ăn yĕl′ō), a bright yellow color.

In-di-a rub-ber (ĭn′dĭ-ȧ rŭb′ẽr, or often ĭn″dĭ-ȧ-rŭb′ẽr), a tough elastic substance from the milky juice of certain tropical plants; an article made from this substance.

in-di-can (ĭn′dĭ-kăn), *n.* a substance obtained from the various indigo-producing plants, breaking up, by the action of acids, into sugar, indigo blue, and indigo red.

in-di-cant (In'dI-kănt), *adj.* serving to point out: *n.* that which points out.

in-di-cate (In'dI-kāt), *v.t.* to point out; show; mark; suggest; hint; make known; as, signposts *indicate* which way to go.

Syn. betoken, signify, denote.

in-di-ca-tion (In'dI-kā'shŭn), *n.* the act of showing or pointing out; that which has meaning; information; token; evidence; sign; symptom; as, the expression of the face is often an *indication* of character.

in-dic-a-tive (In-dIk'ȧ-tIv), *adj.* pointing out; as, cold hands are *indicative* of poor circulation of the blood; bringing to notice; naming that mood of the verb which affirms: *n.* the indicative mood.—*adv.* **indicatively.**

in-di-ca-tor (In'dI-kā'tẽr), *n.* one who, or that which, points out; the part of an instrument by which an effect is pointed out; as, the hands of a watch are *indicators* of the time.

in-di-ca-to-ry (In'dI-kȧ-tō-rI), *adj.* serving to point out; having meaning; as, sore throat, headache, and rash are symptoms *indicatory* of scarlet fever.

in-dict (In-dīt'), *v.t.* to charge with a crime in due form of law; as, he was *indicted* before the grand jury.

in-dict-a-ble (In-dīt'ȧ-bl), *adj.* liable to be charged with a crime in due form of law; liable to be charged with an offense; punishable.

in-dict-er (In-dīt'ẽr), *n.* one who charges with a crime. Also, **indictor.**

in-dict-ment (In-dīt'mĕnt), *n.* a written accusation against a prisoner presented by a grand jury to a court; an accusation.

in-dif-fer-ence (In-dIf'ẽr-ĕns), *n.* the state of being unconcerned; impartiality; absence of choice or interest; unconcernedness; unimportance.

Syn. apathy, carelessness, listlessness, insensibility.

Ant. (see assiduity, application).

in-dif-fer-ent (In-dIf'ẽr-ĕnt), *adj.* unconcerned; unimportant; mediocre; regardless.—*adv.* **indifferently.**

in-di-gence (In'dI-jĕns), *n.* the state of being destitute or very poor; poverty; want; as, *indigence* causes much suffering in the city slums. Also, **indigency.**

Syn. neediness, penury, destitution, privation.

Ant. (see affluence).

in-dig-e-nous (In-dIj'ē-nŭs), *adj.* born or produced in a country; not imported; native; as, cotton is *indigenous* to America.

in-di-gent (In'dI-jĕnt), *adj.* destitute; needy; as, an *indigent* widow.

in-di-gest-ed (In'dI-jĕs'tĕd), *adj.* unconverted into a form that can be assimilated into the system as food; not softened by heat; not sufficiently considered; mixed-up; confused.

in-di-gest-i-bil-i-ty (In'dI-jĕs'tI-bIl'I-tI), *n.* the quality of being incapable of being assimilated by the system as food; the incapability of being taken in mentally.

in-di-gest-i-ble (In'dI-jĕs'tI-bl), *adj.* not easily assimilated, or taken in, physically or mentally.—*adv.* **indigestibly.**

in-di-ges-tion (In'dI-jĕs'chŭn), *n.* difficulty in converting, or inability to convert, food into such a form as can be assimilated by the system.

in-dig-nant (In-dIg'nănt), *adj.* affected with anger or wrath because of unfair treatment; inflamed with mingled anger and scorn.

in-dig-na-tion (In'dIg-nā'shŭn), *n.* anger at what is unworthy, unjust, dishono able, or base; anger mingled with contempt or disgust.

Syn. wrath, ire, resentment.

in-dig-ni-ty (In-dIg'nI-tI), *n.* [*pl.* indignities (-tIz)], an action intended to lower the standing or self-respect of another; insult.

Syn. affront, outrage, reproach, ignominy.

Ant. (see honor).

in-di-go (In'dI-gō), *n.* a blue dyestuff obtained from the indigo plant, and by chemical methods; a deep violet blue.

in-di-rect (In'dI-rĕkt'), *adj.* not straight or in a line; as, an *indirect* road; resulting, in a roundabout manner, from a cause; not reaching the end aimed at by the most straightforward method; not straightforward or fair.—*adv.* **indirectly.**

in-di-rec-tion (In'dI-rek'shŭn), *n.* means or methods not straightforward; unfairness.

in-dis-cern-i-ble (In'dI-zûr'nI-bl), *adj.* incapable of being seen or perceived.

in-dis-creet (In'dIs-krēt'), *adj.* imprudent; unwise; as, it is *indiscreet* to risk all one has in a single venture.

in-dis-cre-tion (In'dIs-krĕsh'ŭn), *n.* rashness; imprudence; an unwise act.

in-dis-crim-i-nate (In'dIs-krIm'I-nāt), *adj.* not choosing carefully; undistinguishing; promiscuous; as, *indiscriminate* reading is unwise.—*adv.* **indiscriminately.**—*n.* **indiscrimination.**

Syn. indistinct, chance, confused.

Ant. (see select, chosen).

in-dis-crim-i-na-tive (In'dIs-krIm'I-nȧ-tIv), *adj.* making no distinction; promiscuously.

in-dis-pen-sa-ble (In'dIs-pĕn'sȧ-bl), *adj.* that cannot be done without; absolutely necessary.

Syn. essential, requisite.

Ant (see unnecessary).

in-dis-posed (In'dIs-pōzd'), *adj.* slightly ill in health; disinclined; unfit.

in-dis-po-si-tion (In-dIs'pō-zIsh'ŭn), *n.* slight illness; disinclination.

in-dis-pu-ta-ble (In-dIs'pū-tȧ-bl), *adj.* too evident to admit of debate or question; unquestionable; beyond question.—*adv.* **indisputably.**—*n.* **indisputability.**

Syn. undeniable, undoubted, incontestable, sure, infallible.

in-dis-so-lu-ble (In-dIs'ō-lū-bl; In'dI-sŏl'ū-bl), *adj.* not capable of being reduced to a liquid; as, fat is *indissoluble* in water; forever binding; as, an *indissoluble* agreement.—*adv.* **indissolubly.** —*n.* **indissolubility.**

in-dis-tinct (In'dIs-tIṅct'), *adj.* not distinguishable easily by the senses or the mind; faint; undefined; indefinite; confused.—*adv.* **indistinctly.**

in-dis-tin-guish-a-ble (ĭn″dĭs-tĭn′-gwĭsh-*ȧ*-bl), *adj.* incapable of being made out or discerned as separate and distinct; as, twins are often almost *indistinguishable*.—*adv.* **indistinguishably.**

in-dite (ĭn-dīt′), *v.t.* to compose; write; as, to *indite* a letter or an epistle.

in-di-vid-u-al (ĭn″dĭ-vĭd′ū-ăl), *adj.* existing as a single and distinct thing or personality; pertaining to, or characteristic of, a single person or thing; of a peculiar or striking character; as, an *individual* style of speaking: *n.* a single person, animal, or thing.—*adv.* **individually.**

in-di-vid-u-al-ism (ĭn″dĭ-vĭd′ū-ăl-ĭzm), *n.* the quality of being distinct or peculiar in character; a social system in which each person works for himself alone; the theory of government which disapproves the interference of the state in the affairs of the separate persons concerned.

in-di-vid-u-al-ist (ĭn″dĭ-vĭd′ū-ăl-ĭst), *n.* one who thinks or acts independently; one who believes in the system of government which disapproves of the interference of the state in the affairs of the separate persons concerned.—*adj.* **individualistic.**

in-di-vid-u-al-i-ty (ĭn″dĭ-vĭd″ū-ăl′ĭ-tĭ), *n.* the condition of being separate and distinct; separate or distinct existence; distinctive character.

in-di-vid-u-al-ize (ĭn″dĭ-vĭd′ū-ăl-īz), *v.t.* to make distinct in character; as, George Eliot and Thomas Hardy strikingly *individualize* the characters in their novels; note particularly.

in-di-vis-i-bil-i-ty (ĭn″dĭ-vĭz″ĭ-bĭl′ĭ-tĭ), *n.* the property of being incapable of being divided.

in-di-vis-i-ble (ĭn″dĭ-vĭz′ĭ-bl), *adj.* not separable into parts; not to be divided without a remainder; as, 10 is *indivisible* by 4.—*adv.* **indivisibly.**

in-doc-ile (ĭn-dŏs′ĭl), *adj.* unteachable; not easily governed or trained.

in-do-cil-i-ty (ĭn″dō-sĭl′ĭ-tĭ), *n.* the quality of being hard to teach or train.

in-doc-tri-nate (ĭn-dŏk′trĭ-nāt), *v.t.* to instruct in learning, principles, or doctrines.

In-do-Eu-ro-pe-an (ĭn″dō-ū″rō-pē′-ăn), *adj.* indicating, or pertaining to, the language family to which belong the languages of India, some other parts of Asia, and the chief countries of Europe; Aryan.

in-do-lence (ĭn′dō-lĕns), *n.* love of ease; objection to labor; laziness.

in-do-lent (ĭn′dō-lĕnt), *adj.* indulging in ease; causing little or hardly any pain; used in the science of medicine; avoiding labor; lazy.—*adv.* **indolently.**

in-dom-i-ta-ble (ĭn-dŏm′ĭ-t*ȧ*-bl), *adj.* untamable; irrepressible; not to be conquered; as, he has an *indomitable* will.—*adv.* **indomitably.**

in-dorse (ĭn-dôrs′), *v.t.* to write (the name), on the back of, as a check, etc.; approve. Also, **endorse.**
Syn. ratify, confirm, superscribe.

in-dor-see (ĭn″dôr-sē′), *n.* a person to whom a check, etc., is assigned, or made payable.

in-dorse-ment (ĭn-dôrs′mĕnt), *n.* the act of writing on the back of a check, etc.; that which is so written; approval.

in-dors-er (ĭn-dôr′sẽr), *n.* one who signs over a check, approves or recommends. Also, **indorsor.**

in-du-bi-ta-ble (ĭn-dū′bĭ-t*ȧ*-bl), *adj.* too evident to be doubted: unquestionable.—*adv.* **indubitably.**

in-duce (ĭn-dūs′), *v.t.* to lead on; to influence; prevail upon; bring on; effect; cause; as, no one can *induce* him to change his mind; produce by magnetic or electric action.

in-duced (ĭn-dūst′), *p.adj.* caused by induction, or the effect produced by nearness to an electrified or magnetized body; prevailed upon; brought on by.

in-duce-ment (ĭn-dūs′mĕnt), *n.* that which causes action, etc.; as, a reward is an *inducement* to the finder of a lost article to return it to its owner; motive; incentive; reason.

in-duc-i-ble (ĭn-dūs′ĭ-bl), *p.adj.* capable of being brought on, caused, or inferred.

in-duct (ĭn-dŭkt′), *v.t.* to introduce; install into an office; put into possession of a church.

in-duc-tion (ĭn-dŭk′shŭn), *n.* the introduction of a person into an office; the introduction of a clergyman into a charge; the process of discovering and proving general propositions from particular cases; as, the conclusion that the earth is round was arrived at by *induction* from the observation of such facts as the curve of the horizon, etc.; the conclusion so reached; electrical or magnetic influence produced by nearness to an electrified or magnetized body.
Syn. deduction, inference.

in-duc-tive (ĭn-dŭk′tĭv), *adj.* proceeding by the process of leading from one thing to another; producing an electrical or magnetic effect by nearness to a magnetized or electrified field; reasoning from discovered facts; reaching conclusions through experiment.—*adv.* **inductively.**

in-duc-tive sci-ence (ĭn-dŭk′tĭv sī′ĕns), any branch of science which allows and uses the method of experiment.

in-duc-tiv-i-ty (ĭn″dŭk-tĭv′ĭ-tĭ), *n.* power of giving off electricity or magnetism without touching the object electrified or magnetized.

in-duc-tor (ĭn-dŭk′tẽr), *n.* one who leads on, or discovers by experiment; that part of an electric apparatus which produces electricity or magnetism without touching the part or object electrified or magnetized.

in-due (ĭn-dū′), *v.t.* to clothe; put on, as clothes; furnish; supply; give to or endow; as, alcoholic liquors may *indue* one with a certain false strength for a while. Also, **endue.**

in-dulge (ĭn-dŭlj′), *v.t.* to be kind or give way to; humor; give free course to: *v.i.* to gratify oneself.
Syn. foster, cherish, fondle.
Ant. (see deny).

in-dul-gence (ĭn-dŭl′jĕns), *n.* freedom from restraint or control; permission; license; gratification; excess; as *indulgence* in laziness, etc.

in-dul-gent (ĭn-dŭl′jĕnt), *adj.* yielding to the humor, wishes, etc., of another; as, an *indulgent* parent makes a spoiled child; showing favor; kind.—*adv.* **indulgently.**

in-du-rate (ĭn′dū-rāt), *v.i.* to grow hard: *v.t.* to make hard; as, heat *indurates* clay; make unfeeling: *adj.* (ĭn'-dû-rāt), hardened.

in-dus-tri-al (ĭn-dŭs'trĭ-ăl), *adj.* pertaining to productive work; devoted to training for systematic labor; as, *industrial* courses are given in many schools; engaged in or constituting systematic labor; derived from, or engaged in, manufacturing on a big scale.—*adv.* **industrially.**

in-dus-tri-al-ism (ĭn-dŭs'trĭ-ăl-ĭzm), *n.* a state of society founded upon productive or business pursuits, as contrasted, for example, with militarism.

in-dus-tri-ous (ĭn-dŭs'trĭ-ŭs), *adj.* characterized by diligence or application; hard-working.
Syn. active, busy, diligent.
Ant. (see lazy).

in-dus-try (ĭn'dŭs-trĭ), *n.* [*pl.* industries (-trĭz)], steady attention to business or labor; productive labor; a particular branch of work or trade; as, the sugar *industry* is the chief dependence of the West Indies.

in-dwell (ĭn-dwĕl'), *v.t.* and *v.i.* to abide in or within; to inhabit.

in-e-bri-ate (ĭn-ē'brĭ-āt), *v.t.* to make drunk; intoxicate: *n.* (ĭn-ē'brĭ-āt), an habitual drunkard: *adj.* drunken; intoxicated.

in-e-bri-a-tion (ĭn-ē"brĭ-ā'shŭn), *n.* intoxication; drunkenness.

in-e-bri-e-ty (ĭn"ē-brī'ē-tĭ), *n.* intoxication; habitual drunkenness.

in-ef-fa-ble (ĭn-ĕf'ȧ-bl), *adj.* unspeakable; inexpressible; too sacred for utterance.—*adv.* **ineffably.**—*n.* **ineffableness.**

in-ef-face-a-ble (ĭn"ĕ-fās'ȧ-bl), *adj.* incapable of being blotted out or rubbed out.—*adv.* **ineffaceably.**

in-ef-fec-tive (ĭn"ĕ-fĕk'tĭv), *adj.* not producing the desired result; as, the company's efforts to end the strike were *ineffective.*—*adv.* **ineffectively.**

in-ef-fec-tu-al (ĭn"ĕ-fĕk'tû-ăl), *adj.* not producing the desired result; unavailing.—*adv.* **ineffectually.**
Syn. vain, useless, fruitless.
Ant. (see effective).

in-ef-fi-ca-cious (ĭn-ĕf"ĭ-kā'shŭs), *adj.* not powerful enough to produce the intended or desired result.—*adv.* **inefficaciously.**

in-ef-fi-ca-cy (ĭn-ĕf'ĭ-kȧ-sĭ), *n.* want of power to bring about the desired result; fruitlessness; as, the *inefficacy* of popular patent medicines to cure disease.

in-ef-fi-cien-cy (ĭn"ĕ-fĭsh'ĕn-sĭ), *n.* lack of power or skill to do well the task required.

in-ef-fi-cient (ĭn"ĕ-fĭsh'ĕnt), *adj.* not producing or not capable of producing the desired result; incapable.—*adv.* **inefficiently.**

in-e-las-tic (ĭn"ē-lăs'tĭk), *adj.* wanting the power to stretch and contract again, as rubber; as, disuse of the muscles causes them to become *inelastic.*—*adv.* **inelastically.**

in-el-e-gance (ĭn-ĕl'ē-găns), *n.* want of any quality required by good taste; want of refinement. Also, **inelegancy.**

in-el-e-gant (ĭn-ĕl'ē-gănt), *adj.* offensive to good taste; as, slang, to say the least of it, is *inelegant.*—*adv.* **inelegantly.**

in-el-i-gi-bil-i-ty (ĭn-ĕl"ĭ-jĭ-bĭl'ĭ-tĭ), *n.* the quality of being unsuitable or unfit.

in-el-i-gi-ble (ĭn-ĕl'ĭ-jĭ-bl), *adj.* unworthy of choice; unsuitable; legally unfitted for choice or election; as, a foreign born citizen of the United States is *ineligible* to the presidency.—*adv.* **ineligibly.**

in-ept (ĭn-ĕpt'), *adj.* not fit or suitable; not consistent with reason; absurd.—*adv.* **ineptly.**—*n.* **ineptitude.**

in-e-qual-i-ty (ĭn"ē-kwŏl'ĭ-tĭ), *n.* [*pl.* inequalities (-tĭz)], difference, especially of rank or station; unevenness; as, *inequality* of size, or of age; changeableness; insufficiency.
Syn. disparity, disproportion, dissimilarity.
Ant. (see equality).

in-eq-ui-ta-ble (ĭn-ĕk'wĭ-tȧ-bl), *adj.* not according to fairness or justice; unjust.—*adv.* **inequitably.**

in-eq-ui-ty (ĭn-ĕk'wĭ-tĭ) *n.* lack of fairness or justice; injustice.

in-e-rad-i-ca-ble (ĭn"ē-răd'ĭ-kȧ-bl), *adj.* incapable of being torn or rooted out.

in-ert (ĭn-ûrt'), *adj.* having no power of motion or action; as, Orpheus was said to make stones and other *inert* objects move in response to the music of his lute; lifeless; sluggish.

in-er-ti-a (ĭn-ûr'shĭ-ȧ), *n.* lack of activity; sluggishness; that property by virtue of which matter tends to remain at rest, if resting, or to move uniformly in a straight line, if moving.

in-es-ti-ma-ble (ĭn-ĕs'tĭ-mȧ-bl), *adj.* not to be measured; beyond measure or price; incalculable; invaluable.—*adv.* **inestimably.**

in-ev-i-ta-bil-i-ty (ĭn-ĕv"ĭ-tȧ-bĭl'ĭ-tĭ), *n.* impossibility of being avoided. Also, **inevitableness.**

in-ev-i-ta-ble (ĭn-ĕv'ĭ-tȧ-bl), *adj.* not to be evaded; unavoidable; as, death is *inevitable* for all men.—*adv.* **inevitably.**
Syn. certain, unescapable.

in-ex-act (ĭn"ĕg-zăkt'), *adj.* not precise, correct, accurate, or punctual.—*adv.* **inexactly.**—*n.* **inexactness.**

in-ex-cus-a-ble (ĭn"ĕks-kūz'ȧ-bl), *adj.* not admitting of pardon or apology; unpardonable.—*adv.* **inexcusably.**

in-ex-haust-i-ble (ĭn"ĕg-zôs'tĭ-bl), *adj.* not to be used up; as, the natural resources of the United States seem almost *inexhaustible;* unfailing; unwearied.—*adv.* **inexhaustibly.**—*n.* **inexhaustibility.**

in-ex-o-ra-bil-i-ty (ĭn-ĕk"sō-rȧ-bĭl'ĭ-tĭ), *n.* incapability of being moved by prayers. Also, **inexorableness.**

in-ex-o-ra-ble (ĭn-ĕk'sō-rȧ-bl), *adj.* not to be moved by prayers; unyielding; unrelenting; as, an *inexorable* ruler.—*adv.* **inexorably.**

in-ex-pe-di-en-cy (ĭn"ĕks-pē'dĭ-ĕn-sĭ), *n.* unsuitableness; inadvisability. Also, **inexpedience.**

in-ex-pe-di-ent (ĭn"ĕks-pē'dĭ-ĕnt), *adj.* unsuitable to circumstances; inadvisable; as, it is *inexpedient* to expose one's life needlessly to risks.

in-ex-pen-sive (ĭn"ĕks-pĕn'sĭv), *adj.* cheap; costing little; as, *inexpensive* clothes; *inexpensive* pleasures.

in-ex-pe-ri-ence (ĭn"ĕks-pē'rĭ-ĕns), *n.* want of actual enjoyment, suffering, or other personal contact with the different sides of life; or of the knowledge that comes from actual contact with life's fulness; lack of practice or skill of any particular kind.

in-ex-pe-ri-enced (in″ĕks-pē′rĭ-ĕnst), *adj.* lacking the personal knowledge that comes from actual living; unpracticed; unskilled; as, *inexperienced* workers are worth less money to their employers than those who are experienced.

in-ex-pert (in″ĕks-pûrt′), *adj.* unskilled; lacking the knowledge or skill gained from practice.—*adv.* **inexpertly.**

in-ex-pi-a-ble (in-ĕks′pĭ-ȧ-bl), *adj.* that cannot be atoned for; as, an *inexpiable* crime.

in-ex-pli-ca-ble (in-ĕks′plĭ-kȧ-bl), *adj.* not to be explained, made plain, or understood; not to be interpreted or accounted for; as, the growth of the simplest flower is an *inexplicable* mystery.—*adv.* **inexplicably.**—*n.* **inexplicability.**

in-ex-plo-sive (in″ĕks-plō′sĭv), *adj.* not liable to burst or expand violently.

in-ex-press-i-ble (in″ĕks-prĕs′ĭ-bl), *adj.* incapable of being uttered or described.—*adv.* **inexpressibly.**

in-ex-pres-sive (in″ĕks-prĕs′ĭv), *adj.* lacking distinct meaning; dull; as, an *inexpressive* face.—*adv.* **inexpressively.**

in-ex-ten-si-bil-i-ty (in″ĕks-tĕn″sĭ-bĭl′ĭ-tĭ), *n.* the quality of not stretching.

in-ex-ten-si-ble (in″ĕks-tĕn′sĭ-bl), *adj.* that cannot be stretched.—*adv.* **inextensibly.**

in-ex-tin-guish-a-ble (in″ĕks-tĭn′-gwĭsh-ȧ-bl), *adj.* unquenchable; as, *inextinguishable* flame.—*adv.* **inextinguishably.**

in-ex-tri-ca-ble (in-ĕks′trĭ-kȧ-bl), *adj.* incapable of being untied; incapable of being disentangled; as, an *inextricable* knot; hopelessly difficult or obscure.—*adv.* **inextricably.**

in-fal-li-bil-i-ty (in-făl″ĭ-bĭl′ĭ-tĭ), *n.* incapability of making mistakes.

in-fal-li-ble (in-făl′ĭ-bl), *adj.* incapable of erring; unfailing; as, the predictions of the weather bureau are not *infallible*.—*adv.* **infallibly.**

in-fa-mous (in′fȧ-mŭs), *adj.* having a very bad reputation; odious; scandalous; as, Benedict Arnold was an *infamous* traitor.
Syn. shameful, ignominious, disgraceful.
Ant. (see honorable).

in-fa-mous-ly (in′fȧ-mŭs-lĭ), *adv.* shamefully, wickedly; as, some of the negro slaves in the United States were *infamously* treated.

in-fa-my (in′fȧ-mĭ), *n.* public disgrace; baseness or vileness.

in-fan-cy (in′făn-sĭ), *n.* the state of being a babe in arms; early childhood; the first stage of anything; in law, the period of life from birth to the age of twenty-one.

in-fant (in′fănt), *n.* a young child; popularly, a child under two years; in law, a person who has not attained the age of twenty-one: *adj.* pertaining to the earliest stages of childhood, or to the legal period of minority; immature.

in-fan-ta (in-făn′tȧ), *n.* any daughter of the royal family of either Portugal or Spain; used also as a title.

in-fan-te (in-făn′tā), *n.* any son of the royal family of either Portugal or Spain, except the eldest; used also as a title.

in-fan-ti-cide (in-făn′tĭ-sīd), *n.* the murder of a newborn child; one who kills a newborn child.

in-fan-tile (in′făn-tīl; in′făn-tĭl), *adj.* pertaining to babies or the period of babyhood; childish. Also, **infantine.**

in-fan-try (in′făn-trĭ), *n.* a body of soldiers armed and equipped for service on foot.

in-fat-u-ate (in-făt′ū-āt), *v.t.* to lead into folly; to cause in one an extravagant admiration or affection.

in-fat-u-a-tion (in-făt″ū-ā′shŭn), *n.* extravagant folly; that which inspires with foolish and extravagant passion, admiration, or affection; as, an *infatuation* for gambling.

in-fect (in-fĕkt′), *v.t.* to give some (especially bad) quality to; taint, or harm, especially with disease, physical or moral; to inspire with a feeling; as, his gloominess *infected* everybody there.

in-fec-tion (in-fĕk′shŭn), *n.* the act of communicating disease or taint; that which communicates disease or corrupts; taint; communication of disease from the sick to the healthy; a disease that may be communicated.

in-fec-tious (in-fĕk′shŭs), *adj.* that may be given to others by communication; as, measles is an *infectious* disease; sympathetic; carrying the power to affect with a disease; as, the clothing a sick person has worn may be *infectious*.

in-fe-cun-di-ty (in″fē-kŭn′dĭ-tĭ), *n.* barrenness; unfruitfulness.

in-fe-lic-i-tous (in″fē-lĭs′ĭ-tŭs), *adj.* unfortunate; unhappy; inappropriate; ill-timed; as, an *infelicitous* remark.

in-fe-lic-i-ty (in″fē-lĭs′ĭ-tĭ), *n.* [*pl.* infelicities (-tĭz)], misfortune; unhappiness; inappropriateness; an unfortunate or ill-timed act or expression.

in-fer (in-fûr′), *v.t.* [*p.t.* and *p.p.* inferred, *p.pr.* inferring], to arrive at (a conclusion, etc.), by reasoning; as, from the study of Indian relics we *infer* that some tribes had no little civilization; accept as a fact or consequence; to lead to as a consequence; imply; to contain or include as a matter of course; as, your haste *infers* your eagerness; to make clear without direct statement: *v.i.* to conclude.

in-fer-a-ble (in-fûr′ȧ-bl), *adj.* capable of being arrived at by reasoning or deduction.

in-fer-ence (in′fĕr-ĕns), *n.* conclusion; that which is contained or included or understood as a matter of course, as, from their silence the *inference* is that all is well.
Syn. corollary, consequence.

in-fer-en-tial (in″fĕr-ĕn′shăl), *adj.* having the nature of a conclusion arrived at by reasoning from certain known facts or admissions.—*adv.* **inferentially.**

in-fe-ri-or (in-fē′rĭ-ĕr), *adj.* lower in place, rank, or quality; secondary, between the earth and the sun; as, *inferior* planets: *n.* one who ranks below another.

in-fe-ri-or-i-ty (in-fē″rĭ-ŏr′ĭ-tĭ), *n.* lower state or quality; as, *inferiority* of rank; mental *inferiority*.

in-fer-nal (in-fûr′năl), *adj.* pertaining to the regions of the dead; belonging to or resembling hell; hellish; fiendish; outrageous.—*adv.* **infernally.**

in-fer-nal ma-chine (in-fûr′năl mȧ-shēn′), an

apparatus designed to explode and destroy life or property.

in-fer-no (in-fûr'nō), *n.* [*pl.* infernos (-nōz)], a place or position of torment; hell, or a place resembling it.

in-fer-tile (in-fûr'til), *adj.* lacking fruitfulness; barren.

in-fer-til-i-ty (in″fẽr-til'ĭ-tĭ), *n.* unproductiveness; unfruitfulness; as, the *infertility* of the soil.

in-fest (in-fĕst'), *v.t.* to attack; haunt; overrun; to attack or annoy constantly and in numbers; as, moths *infest* woolen materials.—*n.* **infestation.**

Syn. annoy, plague, harass.

in-fi-del (in'fĭ-dĕl), *adj.* casting aside all religion; refusing to believe a religion asserted to be divinely revealed, especially the Christian religion; as, an *infidel* pamphlet, showing unbelief in creed or doctrine: *n.* one who rejects Christianity as a divine revelation; formerly, a Mohammedan, Jew, or heathen.

in-fi-del-i-ty (in″fĭ-dĕl'ĭ-tĭ), *n.* [*pl.* infidelities (-tĭz)], disbelief in some religion, especially in Christianity; the act of breaking a trust; unfaithfulness in marriage.

in-field (in'fēld″), *n.* in baseball, the space within the base line, thirty yards by thirty yards, called "the diamond."

in-fil-trate (in-fĭl'trāt), *v.t.* and *v.i.* to cause a liquid or gas to pass through pores or very small openings.

in-fil-tra-tion (in″fĭl-trā'shŭn), *n.* the act of causing a liquid to pass through pores or very small openings.

in-fi-nite (in'fĭ-nĭt), *adj.* perfect; unlimited; immeasurable: *n.* in mathematics, a limit that can be approached but never reached; an indefinite magnitude: **the Infinite,** God; the Absolute Being.

in-fi-nite-ly (in'fĭ-nĭt-lĭ), *adv.* beyond any measurable degree; vastly.

in-fi-nite-ness (in'fĭ-nĭt-nĕs), *n.* state of being limitless or boundless; immensity.

in-fin-i-tes-i-mal (in″fĭn-ĭ-tĕs'ĭ-măl), *adj.* immeasurably small; as, the weight of an insect's wing would be *infinitesimal;* very minute.

in-fin-i-tes-i-mal-ly (in″fĭn-ĭ-tĕs'ĭ-măl-ĭ), *adv.* in indefinitely small quantities.

in-fin-i-tive (in-fĭn'ĭ-tĭv), *adj.* without limitation of person or number: applied to that verb form which simply expresses the general sense of the verb: *n.* the infinitive verb form; as, *to sing.*

in-fin-i-ty (in-fĭn'ĭ-tĭ), *n.* [*pl.* infinities (-tĭz)], the state of being immeasurable; unlimited extent of time, space, or quantity; absolute perfection; an indefinitely great quantity: in mathematics, a limit that can be approached but never reached. Also, **infinitude.**

in-firm (in-fûrm'), *adj.* feeble in body or health; weak-minded; insecure; weakened; irresolute; uncertain.

Syn. weak, feeble, enfeebled.

Ant. (see robust).

in-fir-ma-ry (in-fûr'mȧ-rĭ), *n.* [*pl.* infirmaries (-rĭz)], a hospital for the sick and injured.

in-fir-mi-ty (in-fûr'mĭ-tĭ), *n.* [*pl.* infirmities (-tĭz)], the state of being weak or sick; weakness of body or of mind; illness; failing.

in-fix (in-fĭks'), *v.t.* to fasten in; implant; insert.

in-flame (in-flām'), *v.t.* to set on fire; fire with passion; excite; provoke; irritate; put into a state of redness, swelling, and pain; as, weeping *inflames* the eyes: *v.i.* to become inflamed.

Syn. anger, enrage, chafe, incense, aggravate, exasperate.

Ant. (see allay, soothe).

in-flamed (in-flāmd'), *p.adj.* heated; as, *inflamed* with anger; exasperated.

in-flam-ma-bil-i-ty (in-flăm″ȧ-bĭl'ĭ-tĭ), *n.* the quality or state of being easily set on fire.

in-flam-ma-ble (in-flăm'ȧ-bl), *adj.* easily set on fire; as, gasoline is an *inflammable* substance; easily excited; excitable; as, an *inflammable* temper. —*adv.* **inflammably.**

in-flam-ma-tion (in″flă-mā'shŭn), *n.* an unnatural condition of any part of the body shown by pain, redness, heat, and swelling.

in-flam-ma-to-ry (in-flăm'ȧ-tō-rĭ), *adj.* tending to excite passion, tumult, or rebellion; tending to produce, accompanied by, or showing, a condition of redness, swelling, etc.

in-flat-a-ble (in-flāt'ȧ-bl), *adj.* capable of being swelled out with air or gas.

in-flate (in-flāt'), *v.t.* to swell out with air or gas, as a balloon; puff up; make proud; expand or raise, as prices.

in-fla-tion-ist (in-flā'shŭn-ĭst), *n.* one in favor of the use of more paper money.

in-fla-tor (in-flāt'ẽr), *n.* a mechanical device for swelling (something) up with air or gas.

in-fla-tus (in-flā'tŭs), *n.* inspiration; as, the divine *inflatus* of the poet.

in-flect (in-flĕkt'), *v.t.* to bend; turn from a direct line; vary the form of (a noun, verb, or adjective) so as to show changes in the person, number, case, etc.: *v.i.* to undergo grammatical change of ending.

in-flect-ed (in-flĕk'tĕd), *p.adj.* bent or turned from a direct line or course; having changes in the form of words so as to show changes in meaning; as, the personal pronouns in English are all *inflected;* bent or turned inward or downward.

in-flec-tion (in-flĕk'shŭn), *n.* a bend or bending; rise and fall in the voice; as, the soft *inflection* of her voice showed her sympathy; variation of nouns, verbs, etc., by declension and conjugation. Also, **inflexion.**

in-flec-tion-al (in-flĕk'shŭn-ăl), *adj.* in grammar, showing changes in form to denote changes in meaning; as, *s* and *'s* are the chief *inflectional* endings of English nouns. Also, **inflexional.**

in-flect-ive (in-flĕk'tĭv), *adj.* capable of bending; possessing the various forms that show changes in the meanings of words according to their use; as, *inflective* languages.

in-flex-i-bil-i-ty (in-flĕk″sĭ-bĭl'ĭ-tĭ), *n.* incapability of being bent; stiffness; obstinacy.

in-flex-i-ble (in-flĕk'sĭ-bl), *adj.* not to be bent; rigid; stiff; not to be moved by prayers; not to be varied or changed; unalterable; as, an *inflexible* determination.—*adv.* **inflexibly.**

in-flex-i-ble-ness (in-flĕk'sĭ-bl-nĕs), *n.* the quality of being rigid; incapability of being bent or changed.

in-flict (ĭn-flĭkt′), *v.t.* to cause by, or as if by, striking; cause to be suffered; impose as a punishment.—*n.* **infliction.**

in-flo-res-cence (ĭn″flō-rĕs′ĕns), *n.* the general arrangement of flowers in any species or class of plant; a group of flowers growing upon a common main stem.

in-flu-ence (ĭn′flōō-ĕns), *n.* energy or power tending to produce effects by indirect or invisible means; as, a great leader must have real *influence* over men; power arising from wealth or station; as, political positions are often obtained through the *influence* of some one already in power; that which exerts power over some one or something: *v.t.* to have unseen power over, physically or mentally; to modify or change.

Syn., v.t. bias, sway, prejudice, prepossess: *n.* credit, favor, reputation, character, weight, authority.

in-flu-en-tial (ĭn″flōō-ĕn′shăl), *adj.* having or exerting power or sway; as, an *influential* citizen.

in-flu-en-tial-ly (ĭn″flōō-ĕn′shăl-ĭ), *adv.* in such a way as to affect or change; powerfully.

in-flu-en-za (ĭn-flōō-ĕn′zȧ), *n.* catarrh accompanied by fever, pains, and nervous prostration.

in-flux (ĭn′flŭks″), *n.* an inflow; inpouring; the addition or incoming of anything that may be likened to a stream; as, the discovery of gold in Alaska led to a great *influx* of adventurers; the point at which a stream flows into another or into the sea.

in-form (ĭn-fôrm′), *v.t.* to animate; mold; instruct; to give knowledge of; to tell: *v.i.* to give information.

in-for-mal (ĭn-fôr′măl), *adj.* not according to custom or rule; irregular; unceremonious.—*adv.* **informally.**

in-for-mal-i-ty (ĭn″fôr-măl′ĭ-tĭ), *n.* [*pl.* informalities (-tĭz)], want of regular, customary, or legal form; lack of ceremony.

in-form-ant (ĭn-fôr′mănt), *n.* one who gives news or knowledge of something.

in-for-ma-tion (ĭn″fôr-mā′shŭn), *n.* knowledge given; a lawsuit brought on behalf of the government; a declaration made before a magistrate to cause him to issue a summons or warrant.

in-form-er (ĭn-fôr′mẽr), *n.* one who informs a magistrate of a breaking of the law, or sues for a penalty under some law; a telltale.

in-frac-tion (ĭn-frăk′shŭn), *n.* the act of breaking, especially a law.

in-fre-quence (ĭn-frē′kwĕns), *n.* the state or fact of happening very seldom; rareness. Also, **infrequency.**

in-fre-quent (ĭn-frē′kwĕnt), *adj.* seldom occurring; as, *infrequent* visits; *infrequent* rains.—*adv.* **infrequently.**

in-fringe (ĭn-frĭnj′), *v.t.* to disregard, or break, as a law; to neglect to obey: *v.i.* to encroach or trespass: followed by *on* or *upon;* as, to *infringe* upon a patent.

Syn. invade, intrude, contravene, break, transgress, violate.

in-fringe-ment (ĭn-frĭnj′mĕnt), *n.* violation, or failure to observe, as of a law, patent, trade-mark, etc.; as, ignorance of a law is no excuse for its *infringement.*

in-fu-ri-ate (ĭn-fū′rĭ-āt), *v.t.* to enrage; madden; as, to *infuriate* a mob.—*n.* **infuriation.**

in-fuse (ĭn-fūz′), *v.t.* to introduce, as by pouring; to fill.

in-fu-si-ble (ĭn-fū′zĭ-bl), *adj.* incapable of being melted or liquefied.

in-fu-sion (ĭn-fū′zhŭn), *n.* a pouring in, or something poured in or mingled; the act of imparting or teaching gradually, as of good principles; a liquid extract obtained by soaking a vegetable substance in hot or cold water without boiling; as, tea is an *infusion* of tea leaves.

in-gath-er-ing (ĭn′găth″ẽr-ĭng), *n.* the act of bringing in, especially of a harvest.

in-gen-ious (ĭn-jēn′yŭs), *adj.* having inventive skill; clever; as, the penny-in-the-slot machine is an *ingenious* device for catching people's pennies.—*adv.* **ingeniously.**

in-gé-nue (ăn″zhā″nü′), *n.* a frank and innocent girl or young woman; an actress who acts such a character in a play. [Fr.]

in-ge-nu-i-ty (ĭn″jē-nū′ĭ-tĭ), *n.* cleverness in contriving or inventing; skill.

in-gen-u-ous (ĭn-jĕn′ū-ŭs), *adj.* frank; open; innocent; sincere, candid; as, an *ingenuous* child.—*adv.* **ingenuously.**

Syn., adj. generous, plain.

Ant. (see crafty).

in-gle (ĭn′gl), *n.* a fire or fireplace; a blaze; as, sit thee by the *ingle.*

in-gle-nook (ĭn′gl-nŏŏk″), *n.* the chimney corner; the fireside.

in-glo-ri-ous (ĭn-glō′rĭ-ŭs), *adj.* without fame; disgraceful; shameful; as, an *inglorious* defeat.

in-got (ĭn′gŏt; ĭn′gŏt), *n.* a mass of metal cast into some convenient shape; as, *ingots* of gold are in bars; of tin, in blocks.

in-grain (ĭn′grān″; ĭn-grān′), *v.t.* to dye in the fiber or before manufacture; dye with any deep, lasting color; saturate or fix in deeply; as, *ingrained* vice: *adj.* (ĭn′grān), dyed prior to being manufactured; thoroughly wrought or worked in; deep-seated: *n.* a carpet made of cotton and wool.

in-grate (ĭn′grāt), *adj.* not thankful: *n.* one who is not thankful.

in-gra-ti-ate (ĭn-grā′shĭ-āt), *v.t.* to bring by flattery, etc. (oneself) into the favor of another; as, he knew how to *ingratiate* himself with all about him; secure favorable reception for: with *into.*

in-grat-i-tude (ĭn-grăt′ĭ-tūd), *n.* absence of thankfulness; insensibility to kindness.

in-gre-di-ent (ĭn-grē′dĭ-ĕnt), *n.* a part of a compound or mixture; as, sugar is an *ingredient* of cake; an element.

in-gress (ĭn′grĕs), *n.* entrance; access; the place of entrance; liberty of access.

in-gulf (ĭn-gŭlf′), *v.t.* to swallow up in; bury; overwhelm. Also, **engulf.**

in-hab-it (ĭn-hăb′ĭt), *v.t.* to dwell in; occupy as a dwelling place.

in-hab-it-a-ble (ĭn-hăb′ĭt-ȧ-bl), *adj.* fit to be lived in; as, in a very short time they made the old house *inhabitable.* Also, **habitable.**

in-hab-it-ance (ĭn-hăb′ĭ-tăns), *n.* occupancy; residence. Also, **inhabitancy.**

in-hab-it-ant (ĭn-hăb′ĭ-tănt), *n.* one who, or that which, occupies; a permanent resident.

in-hab-i-ta-tion (ĭn-hăb′ĭ-tā′shŭn), *n.* the act of living in; continued residence.

in-hab-it-ed (ĭn-hăb′ĭ-tĕd), *adj.* peopled; lived in; occupied.

in-ha-lant (ĭn-hāl′ănt), *n.* an apparatus for drawing something into the lungs: that which is drawn into the lungs.

in-ha-la-tion (ĭn″hȧ-lā′shŭn), *n.* the act of drawing into the lungs; as, the *inhalation* of a sufficient quantity of ether produces unconsciousness.

in-hale (ĭn-hāl′), *v.t.* to draw into the lungs; as, *inhale* deeply all the pure air you can.

in-har-mo-ni-ous (ĭn″hār-mō′nĭ-ŭs), *adj.* unmusical; disagreeing; as, *inharmonious* sounds or colors.—*adv.* **inharmoniously.**

in-here (ĭn-hēr′), *v.i.* to be fixed or to exist in something else; be a part of.

in-her-ence (ĭn-hēr′ĕns), *n.* the state of existing inseparably in something else. Also, **inherency.**

in-her-ent (ĭn-hēr′ĕnt), *adj.* existing inseparably in something else; essential; inborn; as, fear of death is *inherent* in human nature.—*adv.* **inherently.**

in-her-it (ĭn-hĕr′ĭt), *v.t.* to possess from an ancestor by right of succession; receive by nature from one's ancestors; to receive by birth: *v.i.* to come into possession of property as the heir.—*adj.* **inheritable.**

in-her-it-ance (ĭn-hĕr′ĭ-tăns), *n.* the act of coming into a property handed down by ancestors or others; that which is received from an ancestor or other person; a possession or blessing, especially one bestowed.

in-her-i-tor (ĭn-hĕr′ĭ-tẽr), *n.* one who receives property or possessions from his ancestors or others; an heir.

in-hib-it (ĭn-hĭb′ĭt), *v.t.* to restrain; prevent; as, lockjaw *inhibits* the opening of the mouth; forbid; to prevent.—*n.* **inhibition.**

in-hos-pi-ta-ble (ĭn-hŏs′pĭ-tȧ-bl), *adj.* not welcoming strangers or guests; affording no shelter; barren; cheerless; as, the Pilgrims landed on the *inhospitable* New England coast.—*adv.* **inhospitably.**

in-hos-pi-tal-i-ty (ĭn-hŏs″pĭ-tăl′ĭ-tĭ), *n.* the want of cordiality or desire to welcome strangers or guests; the lack of facilities for shelter or food: used of desert wastes.

in-hu-man (ĭn-hū′măn), *adj.* cruel; unfeeling; without kindly qualities.—*adv.* **inhumanly.**

Syn. brutal, savage, barbarous, ruthless, merciless, ferocious.

Ant. (see humane).

in-hu-man-i-ty (ĭn″hū-măn′ĭ-tĭ), *n.* [*pl.* inhumanities (-tĭz)], the quality of being unfeeling or unkind; cruelty.

in-im-i-cal (ĭn-ĭm′ĭ-kăl), *adj.* hostile; acting against; as, weariness of body is *inimical* to hard brain work.—*adv.* **inimically.**

in-im-i-ta-ble (ĭn-ĭm′ĭ-tȧ-bl), *adj.* matchless; as, Shakespeare's *A Midsummer Night's Dream* is an *inimitable* fairy play.—*adv.* **inimitably.**

in-iq-ui-tous (ĭn-ĭk′wĭ-tŭs), *adj.* wicked; unjust; as, the buying and selling of slaves was an *iniquitous* practice.—*adv.* **iniquitously.**

in-iq-ui-ty (ĭn-ĭk′wĭ-tĭ), *n.* [*pl.* iniquities (-tĭz)], wickedness; injustice; unrighteousness; crime; evil.

Syn. wrong, grievance.

in-i-tial (ĭn-ĭsh′ăl), *adj.* placed at the beginning; beginning: *n.* a letter placed at the beginning of a word, etc.; *pl.* the first letters of a person's name placed separately: *v.t.* to mark with an initial.—*adv.* **initially.**

in-i-ti-ate (ĭn-ĭsh′ĭ-āt), *v.t.* to instruct in the first principles of anything; set on foot; bring in; to introduce; as, to *initiate* a series of reforms; to introduce into a club, secret society, etc., by special teachings and ceremonies: *adj.* (ĭn-ĭsh′ĭ-āt), introduced into a society; instructed: *n.* one who has been introduced into a society, etc.

in-i-ti-a-tion (ĭn-ĭsh′ĭ-ā′shŭn), *n.* the act of introducing into a club, society, business, literature, etc.; the rites, ceremonies, etc., with which one is made a member of a society, order, etc.

in-i-ti-a-tive (ĭn-ĭsh′ĭ-ā-tĭv), *adj.* introductory: *n.* an introductory or first step; power of commencing, especially applied to the introduction of laws; the starting-power energy required to begin or dare new undertakings.

in-i-ti-a-tor (ĭn-ĭsh′ĭ-ā″tẽr), *n.* one who introduces or begins.

in-i-ti-a-to-ry (ĭn-ĭsh′ĭ-ȧ-tō-rĭ), *adj.* introductory; as, the *initiatory* steps in an undertaking.

in-ject (ĭn-jĕkt′), *v.t.* to throw or cast in; introduce, as a liquid, by mechanical means; as, the doctor *injects* morphine under the skin to quiet the sufferer's pain.

in-jec-tion (ĭn-jĕk′shŭn), *n.* a forcing in; an enema; that which is forced in.

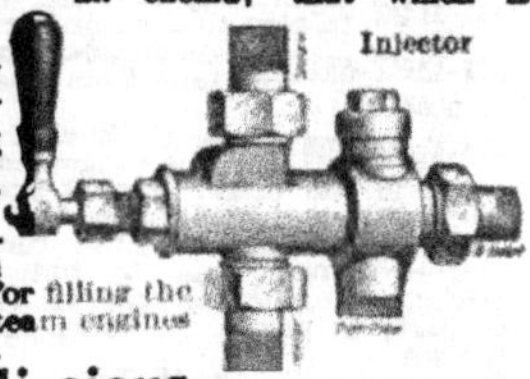

Injector

in-ject-or (ĭn-jĕk′tẽr), *n.* one who, or that which, forces in: used, especially, of an apparatus for filling the boilers of steam engines with water.

in-ju-di-cious (ĭn″jōō-dĭsh′ŭs), *adj.* indiscreet; unwise; as, *injudicious* advice; an *injudicious* remark.

in-junc-tion (ĭn-jŭnk′shŭn), *n.* the act of enjoining or commanding; that which is enjoined or commanded; command, order, or precept; a legal paper to restrain certain proceedings.

in-jure (ĭn′jŏŏr), *v.t.* to hurt; harm; damage, physically or morally.

Syn. wrong, spoil, mar, sully.

Ant. (see benefit).

in-ju-ri-ous (ĭn-jōō′rĭ-ŭs), *adj.* hurtful, physically or morally; unjust; harmful.—*adv.* **injuriously.**

Syn. baneful, noxious, damaging.

Ant. (see beneficial).

in-ju-ry (ĭn′jōō-rĭ), *n.* [*pl.* injuries (-rĭz)], that which causes harm morally or physically; loss; damage.

in-jus-tice (ĭn-jŭs′tĭs), *n.* the quality of being unfair; disregard of another's rights; injury; wrong.

Syn. iniquity, grievance.

Ant. (see right).

ink (ĭnk), *n.* a fluid material used for writing, printing, etc.: *v.t.* to spread ink upon; color or blacken with such a fluid.

ink-i-ness (ĭnk'ĭ-nĕs), *n.* the state of being covered with ink; blackness; as, the *inkiness* of the night.

ink-ling (ĭnk'lĭng), *n.* a slight knowledge; hint; as, I had an *inkling* of the truth.

ink-y (ĭnk'ĭ), *adj.* consisting of, or like, ink; discolored with ink; black.

in-laid (ĭn-lād'; ĭn'lād), *adj.* set into a flat surface in order to ornament it; so ornamented.

in-land (ĭn'lănd), *adj.* pertaining to, or situated in, the interior of a country; far from the sea; not foreign: *adv.* towards the interior or inside: *n.* the interior of a country.

in-lay (ĭn-lā'), *v.t.* [*p.t.* and *p.p.* inlaid, *p.pr.* inlaying], to ornament (a surface), by setting in pieces of ivory, wood, metal, etc.: *n.* (ĭn'lā"), materials for ornamenting by setting pieces of ivory, etc., into a surface.

in-let (ĭn-lĕt'), *v.t.* [*p.t.* and *p.p.* inlet, *p.pr.* inletting], to inlay; insert: *n.* (ĭn'lĕt), an entrance; a small bay or creek.

in-mate (ĭn'māt), *n.* one who dwells with others in a house; as, an *inmate* of a prison.

in-most (ĭn'mōst), *adj.* deepest within; as, the *inmost* wish of my heart. Also, **innermost.**

inn (ĭn), *n.* a house for the reception and entertainment of travelers; tavern; hotel; hostelry.

in-nate (ĭn'nāt; ĭn-nāt'), *adj.* inborn; native; natural; as, *innate* grace; *innate* courtesy.

in-ner (ĭn'ẽr), *adj.* internal; interior; pertaining to the mind or soul.

in-ner-most (ĭn'ẽr-mōst), *adj.* most distant from the outer part; inmost.

in-ner-va-tion (ĭn"ẽr-vā'shŭn), *n.* the arrangement of nerve fibers in the body; special activity in any part of the nervous system.

in-ning (ĭn'ĭng), *n.* the turn of a side or player to bat, in baseball, cricket, etc.; hence, the turn of a person or party in power: *pl.* lands reclaimed from the sea.

in-no-cence (ĭn'ō-sĕns), *n.* freedom from guilt; purity; simplicity of heart; harmlessness; simplicity bordering on silliness. Also, **innocency.**

in-no-cent (ĭn'ō-sĕnt), *adj.* free from guilt or wrongdoing; blameless; pure in heart and life; foolishly ignorant; without evil effect; as, an *innocent* joke; devoid; as, *innocent* of humor; harmless; as, an *innocent* medicine: *n.* one who is free from, or unacquainted with, sin; a simpleton. —*adv.* **innocently.**

Syn., *adj.* guiltless, sinless, inoffensive, innoxious.

Ant. (see guilty).

in-noc-u-ous (ĭ-nŏk'ū-ŭs), *adj.* harmless; safe; innocent; as, an *innocuous* dose.—*adv.* **innocuously.**

in-no-vate (ĭn'ō-vāt), *v.i.* to make changes in something already established; introduce new things.

in-no-va-tion (ĭn"ō-vā'shŭn), *n.* the introduction of something new; a change or novelty; as, the wide use of electricity has brought about many *innovations* in the home.

in-no-va-tor (ĭn'ō-vā"tẽr), *n.* one who introduces or seeks to introduce new things.

in-nox-ious (ĭn-nŏk'shŭs), *adj.* not hurtful; harmless; innocuous.

in-nu-en-do (ĭn"ū-ĕn'dō), *n.* [*pl.* innuendos, -does (-dōz)], an indirect reference, usually suggesting something bad, to a person or thing not named.

in-nu-mer-a-ble (ĭ-nū'mẽr-ȧ-bl), *adj.* that cannot be counted; countless; as, *innumerable* stars.—*adv.* **innumerably.**—*n.* **innumerability.**

in-nu-tri-tious (ĭn"ū-trĭsh'ŭs; ĭn"nū-trĭsh'ŭs), *adj.* not affording nourishment.

in-oc-u-late (ĭn-ŏk'ū-lāt), *v.t.* to communicate a disease to, in a mild form, by the insertion of infectious matter or germs into the system, in order to make the person so treated free from future attacks; in botany, to graft on by the insertion of buds; to inculcate (harmful ideas).

in-oc-u-la-tion (ĭn-ŏk"ū-lā'shŭn), *n.* the practice or art of inserting virus into the system for the purpose of producing a mild form of disease in order to ward off future attacks; the inculcation (of harmful ideas).

in-oc-u-la-tor (ĭn-ŏk'ū-lā"tẽr), *n.* one who communicates, especially a disease.

in-o-dor-ous (ĭn-ō'dẽr-ŭs), *adj.* free from smell or scent.

in-of-fen-sive (ĭn"ō-fĕn'sĭv), *adj.* harmless; free from disagreeable or disgusting qualities.—*adv.* **inoffensively.**

in-op-er-a-tive (ĭn-ŏp'ẽr-ā-tĭv), *adj.* not active; not capable of acting; producing no result.

in-op-por-tune (ĭn-ŏp"ŏr-tūn'), *adj.* not ready; not fit; untimely; unseasonable.—*adv.* **inopportunely.**

in-or-di-nate (ĭn-ôr'dĭ-nāt), *adj.* immoderate; excessive; unrestrained; as, *inordinate* love of eating or drinking.

Syn. intemperate, disorderly.

Ant. (see moderate).

in-or-di-nate-ly (ĭn-ôr'dĭ-nāt-lĭ), *adv.* immoderately; as, *inordinately* fond.

in-or-gan-ic (ĭn"ôr-găn'ĭk), *adj.* without organs; not produced by living organisms; as, rocks are *inorganic* substances: **inorganic chemistry**, that branch of chemistry which does not treat of carbon compounds. Also, **inorganical.**—*adv.* **inorganically.**

in-quest (ĭn'kwĕst), *n.* an official inquiry with the aid of a jury into the cause of a sudden death; inquiry; the body of men making such an inquiry.

in-qui-e-tude (ĭn-kwī'ē-tūd), *n.* a state of uneasiness or restlessness: *pl.* disturbing thoughts.

in-quire (ĭn-kwīr'), *v.t.* to seek for or after by questions; make examination into: with *for*, *into*, *after*, *about*. Also, **enquire.** —*n.* **inquirer, enquirer.**

in-quir-ing (ĭn-kwīr'ĭng), *p.adj.* given to asking questions or making investigations; inquisitive.—*adv.* **inquiringly.**

in-quir-y (ĭn-kwīr'ĭ), *n.* [*pl.* inquiries (-ĭz)], the act of asking about; search by question; investigation; question; research. Also, **enquiry.**

Syn. examination, scrutiny, query, interrogation.

in-qui-si-tion (ĭn″kwĭ-zĭsh′ŭn), *n.* inquiry; examination; an official inquiry in criminal matters.

in-quis-i-tive (ĭn-kwĭz′ĭ-tĭv), *adj.* given to asking questions; prying; curious.
Syn. peeping, peering.

in-quis-i-tor (ĭn-kwĭz′ĭ-tẽr), *n.* one who makes examinations or investigates.

in-quis-i-to-ri-al (ĭn-kwĭz″ĭ-tō′rĭ-ăl), *adj.* pertaining to an investigator or to his office; making searching or unpleasant inquiry.

in-road (ĭn′rōd), *n.* an invasion of an enemy, especially a sudden invasion; forcible entrance.

in-rush (ĭn′rŭsh), *n.* an influx; a sudden invasion; as, an *inrush* of waters.

in-sane (ĭn-sān′), *adj.* mentally disordered; mad; very unreasonable; very foolish; lunatic; crazy.
Syn. deranged, delirious.

in-san-i-ta-ry (ĭn-săn′ĭ-tā-rĭ), *adj.* not in accordance with the requirements for preserving health; not pertaining to health.

in-san-i-ty (ĭn-săn′ĭ-tĭ), *n.* disorder of mind or intellect; lunacy; madness; extravagant folly.
Syn. frenzy, delirium.
Ant. (see sanity).

in-sa-ti-a-bil-i-ty (ĭn-sā″shĭ-ȧ-bĭl′ĭ-tĭ; ĭn-sā″shȧ-bĭl′ĭ-tĭ), *n.* the quality of being unable to be gratified fully or satisfied.

in-sa-ti-a-ble (ĭn-sā′shĭ-ȧ-bl; ĭn-sā′shȧ-bl), *adj.* beyond gratification; immoderate; not to be satisfied; as, an *insatiable* appetite; an *insatiable* ambition. —*adv.* **insatiably.**

in-scribe (ĭn-skrīb′), *v.t.* to write or engrave upon; hence, to stamp deeply, as on the memory; to assign or address formally; as, to *inscribe* a poem to a friend; draw one figure within another, as a square within a circle.

in-scrip-tion (ĭn-skrĭp′shŭn), *n.* the act of printing or engraving for publication; the act of formally addressing a book to a person; that which is written, printed, or engraved for preservation, or to be read by the public; as, an *inscription* on a monument; an address or a formal dedication, as of a book to a person; the name, address, etc., on the envelope of a letter.

in-scru-ta-bil-i-ty (ĭn-skrōō″tȧ-bĭl′ĭ-tĭ), *n.* the quality of being incapable of being understood.

in-scru-ta-ble (ĭn-skrōō′tȧ-bl), *adj.* not to be penetrated by inquiry or reason; not to be understood; as, the *inscrutable* ways of God.—*adv.* **inscrutably.**

in-sect (ĭn′sĕkt), *n.* one of a numerous class of animals, the Insecta, having no skeletons, including bugs, bees, flies, etc.; figuratively, a despicable person.

in-sec-ti-cide (ĭn-sĕk′tĭ-sīd), *n.* a powder for killing bugs, flies, etc.

in-sec-tiv-o-rous (ĭn″sĕk-tĭv′ō-rŭs), *adj.* feeding on bugs, flies, etc.; as, many birds are *insectivorous*.

in-se-cure (ĭn″sē-kūr′), *adj.* not firm; unsafe; not shielded or certainly protected from danger; not assured of safety.—*adv.* **insecurely.**

in-se-cur-i-ty (ĭn″sē-kūr′ĭ-tĭ), *n.* lack or want of safety; the state of being unprotected from danger; lack of soundness or firmness.

in-sen-sate (ĭn-sĕn′sāt), *adj.* without feeling; soulless; mad; brutish; as, *insensate* ambition.

in-sen-si-bil-i-ty (ĭn-sĕn″sĭ-bĭl′ĭ-tĭ), *n.* the quality or state of being incapable of feeling.

in-sen-si-ble (ĭn-sĕn′sĭ-bl), *adj.* incapable of feeling; lacking the power to feel; by slow degrees; gradual; imperceptible.—*adv.* **insensibly.**

in-sep-a-ra-ble (ĭn-sĕp′ȧ-rȧ-bl), *adj.* incapable of being divided or parted.—*adv.* **inseparably.**—*n.* **inseparability.**

in-sert (ĭn-sûrt′), *v.t.* to place in or among; introduce into: *n.* (ĭn′sûrt), that which is put in; inset.

in-ser-tion (ĭn-sûr′shŭn), *n.* the act of putting in; that which is put in, as lace or embroidery in a garment, words in writing, etc.

in-set (ĭn′sĕt), *n.* a leaf or leaves inserted in a newspaper, magazine, etc.: *v.t.* (ĭn-sĕt′), to put in; implant.

in-shore (ĭn′shōr″; ĭn″shōr′), *adv.* near or towards the coast or bank; as, *inshore* fishing.

in-side (ĭn′sīd″), *adj.* interior; being within: *adv.* (ĭn″sīd′; ĭn′sīd″), within; in less time or space: *n.* that which is within; inner part; contents: *prep.* on the inner side of; within.

in-sid-er (ĭn″sīd′ẽr), *n.* one who is so situated as to be able to get reliable information; one who is close to the inner workings of something: opposite to *outsider*

in-sid-i-ous (ĭn-sĭd′ĭ-ŭs), *adj.* treacherous; deceitful; operating secretly; as, tuberculosis is an *insidious* disease.—*adv.* **insidiously.**

in-sight (ĭn′sīt″), *n.* penetration; mental vision; as, poetic *insight*; a man of remarkable *insight*.

in-sig-ni-a (ĭn-sĭg′nĭ-ȧ), *n.pl.* badges of honor or office; as, the crown and scepter were the ancient *insignia* of the power of a king.

in-sig-nif-i-cance (ĭn″sĭg-nĭf′ĭ-kăns), *n.* unimportance. Also, **insignificancy.**

in-sig-nif-i-cant (ĭn″sĭg-nĭf′ĭ-kănt), *adj.* without importance, force, influence, or meaning; trifling; mean; small.—*adv.* **insignificantly.**

in-sin-cere (ĭn″sĭn-sēr′), *adj.* deceptive; false; not to be trusted; hypocritical.—*adv.* **insincerely.**—*n.* **insincerity.**

in-sin-u-ate (ĭn-sĭn′ū-āt), *v.t.* to push, work, or introduce by slow, gentle, or artful means, as into the confidence or affections of; suggest or hint indirectly; as, do you mean to *insinuate* that I have not told the truth? introduce as by a winding motion; worm in: *v.i* work oneself into the confidence or affection of another.
Syn. hint, intimate, suggest, infuse, introduce.

in-sin-u-at-ing (ĭn-sĭn′ū-āt″ĭng), *p.adj.* gently gaining favor; slyly hinting; indirectly hinting.

in-sin-u-a-tion (ĭn-sĭn″ū-ā′shŭn), *n.* an indirect or sly hint; as, he slandered them more by *insinuations* than by direct statements.

in-sip-id (ĭn-sĭp′ĭd), *adj.* without flavor; tasteless; uninteresting; as, *insipid* conversation.—*adv.* **insipidly.**
Syn., *adj.* dull, flat, mawkish, inanimate, lifeless.
Ant. (see bright, sparkling).

in-si-pid-i-ty (ĭn″sĭ-pĭd′ĭ-tĭ), *n.* the quality of being tasteless or dull.

in-sist (ĭn-sĭst′), *v.i.* to urge or press a wish or command: with *on* or *upon;* to take a stand and refuse to give way; to persist.

in-sist-ence (ĭn-sĭs′tĕns), *n.* the act of persisting or holding fast to something; urgency. Also, **insistency.**

in-sist-ent (ĭn-sĭs′tĕnt), *adj.* urgent; compelling attention.—*adv.* **insistently.**

in-snare (ĭn-snâr′), *v.t.* to catch in, or as in, a trap or noose. Also, **ensnare.**

in-so-bri-e-ty (ĭn″sō-brī′ĕ-tĭ), *n.* intemperance; drunkenness.

in-so-lence (ĭn′sō-lĕns), *n.* contemptuous or haughty language or manner; offensive impertinence; insulting behavior; impudence.

in-so-lent (ĭn′sō-lĕnt), *adj.* haughty or contemptuously offensive to others; insulting; very rude.—*adv.* **insolently.**

Syn., adj. saucy, pert, impertinent, abusive.

in-sol-u-bil-i-ty (ĭn-sŏl″ū-bĭl′ĭ-tĭ), *n.* incapability of being dissolved; inability to be explained.

in-sol-u-ble (ĭn-sŏl′ū-bl), *adj.* that cannot be dissolved; as, fat is *insoluble* in water; not to be explained; as, an *insoluble* mystery.

in-sol-ven-cy (ĭn-sŏl′vĕn-sĭ), *n.* [*pl.* insolvencies (-sĭz)], the state of being unable to pay all debts.

in-sol-vent (ĭn-sŏl′vĕnt), *adj.* unable to pay all debts; bankrupt: *n.* one who cannot pay all his debts; a bankrupt.

in-som-ni-a (ĭn-sŏm′nĭ-ȧ), *n.* sleeplessness; as, *insomnia* is often caused by overwork.

in-so-much (ĭn″sō-mŭch′), *adv.* in such manner; to such a degree: usually followed by *that* or *as.*

in-spect (ĭn-spĕkt′), *v.t.* to examine closely and carefully, so as to find possible errors, etc.; as, men are sent out by the government to *inspect* all farms where milk is sold; to investigate.

in-spec-tion (ĭn-spĕk′shŭn), *n.* careful or critical examination.

in-spec-tor (ĭn-spĕk′tẽr), *n.* one who examines or oversees; an official who superintends some matter of public interest; a police officer ranking next below a superintendent.

in-spi-ra-tion (ĭn″spĭ-rā′shŭn), *n.* the act of drawing air into the lungs; the influence which causes creation in art, literature, music, etc.; influence gained from association with great minds, scenery, etc.; the supernatural influence of the Holy Spirit on sacred writers and teachers; as, John is believed to have written the Revelation under divine *inspiration.*

in-spire (ĭn-spīr′), *v.t.* to draw (air) into the lungs; breathe into; fill with ideas; to have a superior or supernatural influence upon; to pour into the mind or spirit; as, to *inspire* a person with a hatred of wrong: *v.i.* to draw air into the lungs.

Syn. animate, cheer, inhale.

in-spired (ĭn-spīrd′), *p.adj.* affected by a supernatural influence; as, the Bible is believed to have come from *inspired* sources; breathed in; presented or suggested to the mind by some one else; as, an *inspired* speech.

in-spir-it (ĭn-spĭr′ĭt), *v.t.* to give life or vitality to; exhilarate; cheer. —*adv.* **inspiritingly.**

in-sta-bil-i-ty (ĭn″stȧ-bĭl′ĭ-tĭ), *n.* want of firmness; inconstancy; fickleness.

Syn. mutability, mutableness, wavering.
Ant. (see stability, firmness).

in-stall (ĭn-stôl′), *v.t.* to place in an office or rank; to put into condition for use; as, to *install* an electric lighting system; to place.

in-stal-la-tion (ĭn″stô-lā′shŭn), *n.* the act of placing in an office or rank; introduction of machinery for use; as, business methods have been greatly changed by the *installation* of the telephone in almost every office and factory.

in-stal-ment (ĭn-stôl′mĕnt), *n.* the act of establishing; a part of a sum of money to be paid part by part at stated times; as, the third *instalment* on the piano is due to-morrow; one of a number of parts of anything produced part at a time; as, the first *instalment* of a new serial story is published in this month's magazine. Also, **installment.**

in-stance (ĭn′stăns), *v.t.* to refer to, or offer as an example: *n.* something offered as an illustration or example; suggestion, request; as, the work was begun at the *instance* of the publishers.

in-stant (ĭn′stănt), *adj.* urgent; immediate; passing; of the present month; as, the tenth *instant: n.* a particular moment of time.

in-stan-ta-ne-ous (ĭn″stăn-tā′nē-ŭs), *adj.* acting or occurring in a moment.

in-stan-ter (ĭn-stăn′tẽr), *adv.* immediately; without delay; as, I will go *instanter.* [Lat.]

in-stant-ly (ĭn′stănt-lĭ), *adv.* at once; without delay; as, when his father spoke to him, he obeyed *instantly: conj.* as soon as.

in-state (ĭn-stāt′), *v.t.* to put in office or rank; install; as, he *instated* himself in the favor of those in power.

in-stead (ĭn-stĕd′), *adv.* in room or place: followed by *of.*

in-step (ĭn′stĕp), *n.* the arched fore part of the upper side of the human foot; part of the hind leg of a horse.

in-sti-gate (ĭn′stĭ-gāt), *v.t.* to provoke or urge on (in a bad sense): as, to *instigate* one to murder.

Syn. persuade, animate, incite, urge, stimulate, encourage.

in-sti-ga-tion (ĭn″stĭ-gā′shŭn), *n.* an urging forward; an incitement: chiefly to bad actions.

in-sti-ga-tor (ĭn′stĭ-gā″tẽr), *n.* one who urges another on, usually to evil.

in-stil (ĭn-stĭl′), *v.t.* [*p.t.* and *p.p.* instilled, *p.pr.* instilling], to introduce gradually, as if by drops; as, to *instil* the principles of honor and self-reliance; pour in by drops. Also, **instill.**

Syn. implant, inculcate, infuse.

in-stil-la-tion (ĭn″stĭ-lā′shŭn), *n.* act of pouring in drop by drop; the act of infusing gradually. Also, **instilment, instillment.**

in-stinct (ĭn-stĭṅkt′), *adj.* charged or filled with; as, creatures *instinct* with life: *n.* (ĭn′stĭṅkt), natural impulse in animals; involuntary urging to any action; a natural tendency; as, an *instinct* for direction.

in-stinc-tive (ĭn-stĭnk'tĭv), *adj.* acting or prompted by natural impulse; as, self-protection is *instinctive* in all creatures; innate.—*adv.* **instinctively.**

in-sti-tute (ĭn'stĭ-tūt), *v.t.* to establish; set up; fix; originate; set in operation; as, to *institute* a new custom: *n.* established law; a maxim or principle; scientific or literary society; a building devoted to the work of advancing science, learning, etc.

in-sti-tu-tion (ĭn"stĭ-tū'shŭn), *n.* the act of establishing; that which is established; an organized body or society for promoting a particular object; the building where such a society meets; an establishment, especially one of public character; as, an almshouse is a charitable *institution.*

in-sti-tu-tion-al (ĭn"stĭ-tū'shŭn-ăl), *adj.* pertaining to an establishment; pertaining to a national law or custom; established.

in-sti-tu-tor (ĭn'stĭ-tū"tẽr), *n.* a founder of a system or society; as, Benjamin Franklin was the *institutor* of the library system of Philadelphia; an enactor of laws or rules; an instructor of youth.

in-struct (ĭn-strŭkt'), *v.t.* to teach; educate; furnish with orders or directions.

Syn. inform, teach, initiate.

in-struc-tion (ĭn-strŭk'shŭn), *n.* the act of teaching; that which teaches or directs: *pl.* orders or directions; knowledge imparted.

in-struc-tion-al (ĭn-strŭk'shŭn-ăl), *adj.* pertaining to orders, directions, or teaching.

in-struc-tive (ĭn-strŭk'tĭv), *adj.* tending to inform; giving knowledge.

in-struc-tor (ĭn-strŭk'tẽr), *n.* [*fem.* instructress], one who gives knowledge or informs; a teacher; as, an *instructor* of youth has a great work to perform.

in-stru-ment (ĭn'strōō-mĕnt), *n.* that by which anything is accomplished; a tool; a mechanical contrivance for producing musical sounds; agent; a writing containing the terms of a contract, as a deed.

in-stru-men-tal (ĭn"strōō-mĕn'tăl), *adj.* pertaining to, or done by, an instrument; helping to bring about some end; helpful; as, mountain air is sometimes *instrumental* in restoring health.—*adv.* **instrumentally.**

Syn., adj. conducive, assistant, helping.

in-stru-men-tal-i-ty (ĭn"strōō-mĕn-tăl'ĭ-tĭ), *n.* [*pl.* instrumentalities (-tĭz)], an agency; means.

in-stru-men-ta-tion (ĭn"strōō-mĕn-tā'shŭn), *n.* the arrangement of music for a combination of instruments; music thus arranged; use or method of using an instrument.

in-sub-or-di-nate (ĭn"sŭb-ôr'dĭ-nāt), *adj.* not submitting to authority; disobedient; mutinous.—*adv.* **insubordinately.**

in-sub-or-di-na-tion (ĭn"sŭb-ôr"dĭ-nā'shŭn), *n.* disobedience to authority.

in-sub-stan-tial (ĭn"sŭb-stăn'shăl), *adj.* not having solidity; frail; unreal.—*adv.* **insubstantially.**

in-suf-fer-a-ble (ĭn-sŭf'ẽr-ȧ-bl), *adj.* not to be borne; as, *insufferable* conduct.—*adv.* **insufferably.**

in-suf-fi-cient (ĭn"sŭ-fĭsh'ĕnt), *adj.* scanty; incompetent; not filling some certain requirement.—*adv.* **insufficiently.**—*n.* **insufficiency.**

in-su-lar (ĭn'sū-lẽr), *adj.* pertaining to an island or to the inhabitants of an island, their customs, etc.; standing alone; narrow (mentally).

in-su-lar-i-ty (ĭn"sū-lăr'ĭ-tĭ), *n.* the state of being isolated or of standing alone; narrowness of opinions, etc.

in-su-late (ĭn'sū-lāt), *v.t.* to place alone, or in a separate situation; separate by a material that will not conduct electricity, etc., from other bodies that do conduct electricity, heat, sound, etc.

in-su-la-tion (ĭn"sū-lā'shŭn), *n.* the act of separating by materials that will not conduct heat, electricity, sound, etc., from those that do; the state of being so separated.

in-su-la-tor (ĭn'sū-lā"tẽr), *n.* one who, or that which, isolates; that which acts as a nonconductor of heat, electricity, sound, etc.; a material that does not carry electricity, heat, or sound.

in-sult (ĭn'sŭlt), *n.* an affront or indignity; gross abuse in word or action: *v.t.* (ĭn-sŭlt'), to treat with gross contempt, or abuse, by word or act.

Syn., v. outrage, mock.

Ant. (see honor).

in-sult-ing (ĭn-sŭlt'ĭng), *adj.* containing offense or affront.

in-su-per-a-ble (ĭn-sū'pẽr-ȧ-bl), *adj.* not to be overcome; as, *insuperable* difficulties.—*adv.* **insuperably.**—*n.* **insuperability.**

in-sup-port-a-ble (ĭn"sŭ-pōr'tȧ-bl), *adj.* not capable of being endured; insufferable.—*adv.* **insupportably.**

in-sur-a-ble (ĭn-shōōr'ȧ-bl), *adj.* capable of being insured against loss, damage, etc.; proper to be insured; as, real estate and personal property are both *insurable.*

in-sur-ance (ĭn-shōōr'ăns), *n.* the act or system of securing against loss or damage; a contract whereby in consideration of a certain payment called premium, one party agrees to guarantee or indemnify another against certain risks such as fire, death, accident, etc., by the payment of money; the sum paid in settlement of such a contract.

in-sure (ĭn-shōōr'), *v.t.* to make a formal agreement on certain conditions to secure against loss or damage by fire, death, accident, etc.; make sure or secure: *v.i.* to undertake or contract to give security against loss by fire, death, accident, etc.; to underwrite.

in-sured (ĭn-shōōrd'), *n.* one that is secured against loss by fire, etc.

in-sur-er (ĭn-shōōr'ẽr), *n.* one who secures others against loss by fire, etc.

in-sur-gence (ĭn-sûr'jĕns), *n.* a revolt; an uprising against authority; rebellion.

in-sur-gent (ĭn-sûr'jĕnt), *adj.* rising against authority: *n.* a rebel.

in-sur-mount-a-ble (ĭn"sûr-moun'tȧ-bl), *adj.* incapable of being risen above or conquered.—*adv.* **insurmountably.**—*n.* **insurmountability.**

in-sur-rec-tion (ĭn"sŭ-rĕk'shŭn), *n.* active or open rebellion against authority; revolt.

in-sur-rec-tion-a-ry (ĭn"sŭ-rĕk'shŭn-ā-rĭ), *adj.* per

taining to, or engaged in, active or open rebellion; as, *insurrectionary* ideas.

in-sur-rec-tion-ist (ĭn″sŭ-rĕk′shŭn-ĭst), *n.* one who rebels against authority.

in-sus-cep-ti-ble (ĭn″sŭ-sĕp′tĭ-bl), *adj.* not easy to influence or impress.—*n.* **insusceptibility.**

in-tact (ĭn-tăkt′), *adj.* entire; uninjured; untouched; as, an express company guarantees that articles in its care will be delivered *intact.*

in-tag-lio (ĭn-tăl′yō; IT. ēn-tăl′yō), *n.* [*pl.* intagli, -glios (-yē, -yōz)], a gem or stone having a design cut in the surface; the art of making intaglios. [IT.]

in-tag-lio print-ing (ĭn-tăl′yō print′-ĭng), printing from an engraved metal plate.

in-take (ĭn′tăk″), *n.* a thing taken in; a taking in; the place where a fluid flows into a conduit, etc.

in-tan-gi-ble (ĭn-tăn′jĭ-bl), *adj.* incapable of being touched; vague; not easily expressed; as, the beauty of a poem is *intangible.*—*adv.* **intangibly.**—*n.* **intangibility.**

in-te-ger (ĭn′tē-jẽr), *n.* the whole; a whole number; as, 1, 2, 3, etc.

in-te-gral (ĭn′tē-grăl), *adj.* constituting a whole; complete; belonging to a whole number; necessary as a part: *n.* the whole made up of parts.

in-te-grant (ĭn′tē-grănt), *adj.* making part of a whole; necessary to constitute an entire thing.

in-te-grate (ĭn′tē-grāt), *v.t.* to bring together the parts of; give the sum total of.—*n.* **integration.**

in-teg-ri-ty (ĭn-tĕg′rĭ-tĭ), *n.* uprightness; virtue; honesty; soundness; uninjured or unbroken state of anything.

Syn. probity, entirety, completeness, purity.
Ant. (see dishonesty).

in-teg-u-ment (ĭn-tĕg′ū-mĕnt), *n.* an external covering or skin, as the human skin.

in-tel-lect (ĭn′tĕ-lĕkt), *n.* the mind or understanding; superior intelligence; knowledge gained.

Syn. sense, brains, mind, ability, talent, genius.
Ant. (see body).

in-tel-lec-tu-al (ĭn″tĕ-lĕk′tū-ăl), *adj.* pertaining to, or understood by, the mind; mental; endowed or gifted with the power of understanding; exercising the mind; as, *intellectual* pursuits.—*adv.* **intellectually.**

Syn. ideal, metaphysical.
Ant. (see brutal).

in-tel-lec-tu-al-ism (ĭn″tĕ-lĕk′tū-ăl-ĭsm), *n.* mental power or quality; the doctrine that all knowledge comes from pure reason.

in-tel-lec-tu-al-i-ty (ĭn″tĕ-lĕk″tū-ăl′ĭ-tĭ), *n.* the quality or state of being scholarly or endowed with a high degree of mentality.

in-tel-li-gence (ĭn-tĕl′ĭ-jĕns), *n.* power of mind; as, the dog has a great deal of *intelligence;* understanding; mind; knowledge gained; notification; news.

in-tel-li-gent (ĭn-tĕl′ĭ-jĕnt), *adj.* possessing power of mind or understanding; showing knowledge; clever; discerning.

in-tel-li-gi-ble (ĭn-tĕl′ĭ-jĭ-bl), *adj.* capable of being understood; clear; as, an *intelligible* explanation.—*adv.* **intelligibly.**

Syn. obvious, plain, distinct.
Ant. (see abstruse).

in-tem-per-ance (ĭn-tĕm′pẽr-ăns), *n.* want of moderation or self-restraint; excess, especially in the use of alcoholic liquors.

in-tem-per-ate (ĭn-tĕm′pẽr-ăt), *adj.* characterized by want of moderation or self-restraint; excessive; fond of alcoholic liquors.—*adv.* **intemperately.**

Syn., adj. immoderate, drunken, inordinate.
Ant. (see temperate).

in-tend (ĭn-tĕnd′), *v.t.* to purpose; as, we *intend* to win the war; propose; mean.

in-tend-an-cy (ĭn-tĕn′dăn-sĭ), *n.* the office or employment of one in charge of some public business.

in-tend-ant (ĭn-tĕn′dănt), *n.* a superintendent; as, an *intendant* of a hospital.

in-tend-ed (ĭn-tĕn′dĕd), *adj.* purposed; as, the *intended* meaning of a remark.

in-tense (ĭn-tĕns′), *adj.* extreme in degree; excessive; strained; forced; ardent; eager.—*adv.* **intensely.**

Syn., adj. earnest, glowing, fervid.

in-ten-si-fy (ĭn-tĕn′sĭ-fī), *v.t.* [*p.t.* and *p.p.* intensified, *p.pr.* intensifying], to make greater in degree; heighten; strengthen.

in-ten-sion (ĭn-tĕn′shŭn), *n.* determination; increase of energy.

in-ten-si-ty (ĭn-tĕn′sĭ-tĭ), *n.* [*pl.* intensities (-tĭz)], the state or quality of being extreme; extreme strength, force, or energy; as, *intensity* of heat; degree or amount; as, the spot of light in the window seemed to increase the *intensity* of the surrounding darkness.

in-ten-sive (ĭn-tĕn′sĭv), *adj.* serving to heighten; giving force or emphasis to.—*adv.* **intensively.**

in-tent (ĭn-tĕnt′), *adj.* having the mind strained or closely fixed on a subject; anxiously diligent; constantly giving attention to: with *on:* *n.* purpose; aim; meaning.—*adv.* **intently.**—*n.* **intentness.**

Syn., n. design, intention, drift, view, purport.

in-ten-tion (ĭn-tĕn′shŭn), *n.* purpose; design; aim; as, his *intention* was good.

in-ten-tion-al (ĭn-tĕn′shŭn-ăl), *adj.* done on purpose; done by design; as, an *intentional* wrong.

in-ter (ĭn-tûr′), *v.t.* [*p.t.* and *p.p.* interred, *p.pr.* interring], to bury.

in-ter-act (ĭn″tẽr-ăkt′), *v.i.* to exert influence upon each other; to have effect upon each other.

in-ter-ac-tion (ĭn″tẽr-ăk′shŭn), *n.* effect on one thing by another; mutual effect.

in-ter-breed (ĭn″tẽr-brēd′), *v.i.* and *v.t.* to propagate by crossing different varieties, kinds, or stocks.

in-ter-ca-la-ry (ĭn-tûr′kȧ-lā-rĭ), *adj.* inserted in the calendar, as February 29 in leap year; interpolated.

in-ter-ca-late (ĭn-tûr′kȧ-lāt), *v.t.* to insert, as a day, in the calendar; to interpolate.—*n.* **intercalation.**

in-ter-cede (ĭn″tẽr-sēd′), *v.i.* to mediate as a friend between persons who are unfriendly; plead for another.

in-ter-cel-lu-lar (ĭn″tẽr-sĕl′ū-lȧr), *adj.* lying between cells.

in-ter-cept (ĭn″tẽr-sĕpt′), *v.t.* to stop and seize in the way; cut off; to come in the way of; as, hedges and ditches *intercept* the passage of the army.

in-ter-ces-sion (ĭn″tẽr-sĕsh′ŭn), *n.* the act of trying to restore friendship between two who are separated by disagreement; the act of pleading for another.

in-ter-ces-sor (ĭn″tẽr-sĕs′ẽr), *n.* one who tries to restore friendly relations between two who are parted by differences; one who pleads for another.

in-ter-change (ĭn″tẽr-chānj′), *v.t.* to put one thing in the place of another; to vary: *n.* (ĭn′tẽr-chānj″), the exchange of two things, one for the other; alternate sequence or variation.

in-ter-change-a-ble (ĭn″tẽr-chānj′-ȧ-bl), *adj.* capable of being put in place of each other; capable of being exchanged.—*adv.* **interchangeably.**—*n.* **interchangeability.**

in-ter-col-le-gi-ate (ĭn″tẽr-kŏ-lē′jĭ-āt), *adj.* carried on, as games, between colleges; existing, as leagues, between colleges.

in-ter-com-mu-ni-cate (ĭn″tẽr-kŏ-mū′nĭ-kāt), *v.t.* and *v.i.* to impart or convey mutually.—*n.* **intercommunication.**

in-ter-cos-tal (ĭn″tẽr-kŏs′tăl), *adj.* between the ribs; as, *intercostal* rheumatism or neuralgia: *n.* a muscle thus situated.

in-ter-course (ĭn′tẽr-kōrs), *n.* connection, correspondence, or communication between individuals, nations, etc.; exchange; familiarity; fellowship.

Syn. commerce, connection, intimacy, acquaintance.

in-ter-de-pend-ence (ĭn″tẽr-dē-pĕn′-dĕnce), *n.* the state of being mutually reliant; a state of confidence, trust, and reliance, interchanged by two or more people, nations, etc.—*adj.* **interdependent.**

in-ter-dict (ĭn″tẽr-dĭkt′), *v.t.* to restrain or forbid; cut off from the spiritual services of the church: *n.* (ĭn′tẽr-dĭkt), an order that restrains or prohibits.

Syn., v. prohibit, inhibit, debar.

Ant. (see allow).

in-ter-est (ĭn′tẽr-ĕst), *v.t.* to engage the attention; awaken curiosity, care, etc., in; cause to take a share in; as, to *interest* oneself in politics: *n.* advantage; influence; as, he used his *interest* with the president to secure a position for his brother; personal concern; benefit; as, it will be to your *interest* to be present at the meeting; profit; sum paid for the use of money; share; as, an *interest* in a factory.

in-ter-est-ed (ĭn′tẽr-ĕs-tĕd), *p.adj.* having the feelings or emotions excited or held; concerned; having a share or a responsibility in.

in-ter-est-ing (ĭn′tẽr-ĕst-ĭng), *p.adj.* engaging the attention or curiosity; exciting the feelings or emotions.

in-ter-fere (ĭn″tẽr-fēr′), *v.i.* to enter into or meddle in the affairs of others; oppose; come into collision; injure the fetlock by striking it with the opposite hoof: ordinarily said of a horse.

in-ter-fer-ence (ĭn″tẽr-fēr′ĕns), *n.* the act of opposing or clashing with; the act of meddling in other people's affairs.

in-ter-fuse (ĭn″tẽr-fūz′), *v.t.* to cause to flow together; cause to blend; intermix.

in-ter-im (ĭn′tẽr-ĭm), *n.* intervening time or period; as, in the *interim* between the battle of Bunker Hill and the raising of the Bunker Hill monument, many important events had taken place.

in-te-ri-or (ĭn-tē′rĭ-ẽr), *adj.* inner; internal; far from the coast or frontier: *n.* the inside; the inland; home department of a government.—*adv.* **interiorly.**

in-ter-ject (ĭn″tẽr-jĕkt′), *v.t.* and *v.i.* to put in; to insert; to thrust in.

in-ter-jec-tion (ĭn″tẽr-jĕk′shŭn), *n.* an exclamation; a word thrown in without grammatical connection to express sudden emotion, feeling, etc.

in-ter-lace (ĭn″tẽr-lās′), *v.t.* and *v.i.* to join or unite by weaving or lacing together; to intermingle.

in-ter-lard (ĭn″tẽr-lärd′), *v.t.* to mix; to vary by mingling with; as, to *interlard* a serious discussion with jests.

in-ter-leave (ĭn″tẽr-lēv′), *v.t.* to insert a leaf in; as, to *interleave* a book with blank leaves or illustrations.

in-ter-line (ĭn″tẽr-lĭn′), *v.t.* to write in, or insert between the lines of; to put into a garment an extra lining beneath the ordinary one.

in-ter-lin-e-ar (ĭn″tẽr-lĭn′ē-ȧr), *adj.* written or printed between other lines, as a translation.

in-ter-lock (ĭn″tẽr-lŏk′), *v.t.* and *v.i.* to fasten together by linking or engaging with one another.

in-ter-loc-u-to-ry (ĭn″tẽr-lŏk′ū-tō-rĭ), *adj.* conversational; not final; in law, made or done during the process of an action.—*n.* **interlocutor.**

in-ter-lope (ĭn″tẽr-lōp′), *v.i.* to meddle; to intrude where one is not wanted.

in-ter-lop-er (ĭn′tẽr-lōp″ẽr), *n.* an intruder; as, he was an *interloper* in the family party and was very unwelcome.

in-ter-lude (ĭn′tẽr-lūd), *n.* short entertainment given between acts of a play, etc.; a short passage of music played between the stanzas of a hymn, acts of an opera, etc.

in-ter-mar-riage (ĭn″tẽr-măr′ĭj), *n.* a joining in wedlock as between two families.

in-ter-mar-ry (ĭn″tẽr-măr′ĭ), *v.t.* and *v.i.* to relate or become related by uniting in wedlock: said of families, etc.

in-ter-med-dle (ĭn″tẽr-mĕd′l), *v.i.* to interfere in other people's affairs.—*n.* **intermeddler.**

in-ter-me-di-a-ry (ĭn″tẽr-mē′dĭ-ā-rĭ), *adj.* coming between; as, there is an *intermediary* time of four months after a President of the United States is elected before he takes office: *n.* an agent; go-between; means.

in-ter-me-di-ate (ĭn″tẽr-mē′dĭ-āt), *adj.* existing or lying in the middle; coming between: *n.* that which lies between; a go-between.

in-ter-me-di-a-tion (ĭn″tẽr-mē″dĭ-ā′-shŭn), *n.* the act of coming between or of playing the part of a go-between.

in-ter-ment (ĭn-tûr′mĕnt), *n.* burial; as, *interment* in Westminster Abbey is a great honor.

in-ter-mez-zo (ĭn-tĕr-mĕd'zō), *n.* an interlude; as, the two parts of the opera are connected by a beautiful *intermezzo.* [IT.]

in-ter-mi-na-ble (ĭn-tûr'mĭ-nȧ-bl), *adj.* endless; boundless; immeasurable.—*adv.* **interminably.**

in-ter-min-gle (ĭn"tĕr-mĭn'gl), *v.t.* and *v.i.* to join together; to mix together.

in-ter-mis-sion (ĭn"tĕr-mĭsh'ŭn), *n.* interruption; pause; short break.

in-ter-mit (ĭn"tĕr-mĭt'), *v.t.* [*p.t.* and *p.p.* intermitted, *p.pr.* intermitting], to cause to cease for a time; interrupt.

in-ter-mit-tent (ĭn"tĕr-mĭt'ĕnt), *adj.* coming and going at intervals; as, *intermittent* sounds made by a hammer struck on a nail.—*adv.* **intermittently.**

in-ter-mix-ture (ĭn"tĕr-mĭks'tûr), *n.* a mingling together; a quantity or mass of ingredients mingled together.

in-tern (ĭn-tûrn'), *v.t.* to confine within a town or fortress, or in the interior of a country; place under arrest.

in-ter-nal (ĭn-tûr'năl), *adj.* belonging to the center; interior; inward; not foreign; domestic.

in-ter-nal-com-bus-tion (ĭn-tĕr'-năl-kŏm-bŭs'chŭn), *n.* the process by which power is generated in an engine by the explosion of fuel, such as gasoline, in the engine cylinder.

in-ter-nal-ly (ĭn-tûr'năl-ĭ), *adv.* inwardly; as, besides being at war with another nation, the country was *internally* in a state of rebellion.

in-ter-na-tion-al (ĭn"tĕr-năsh'ŭn-ăl), *adj.* pertaining to two or more nations; as, the new republic in America had *international* difficulties with England and France.—*adv.* **internationally.**

in-ter-ne-cine (ĭn"tĕr-nē'sĭn; ĭn"tĕr-nē'-sīn), *adj.* deadly; destructive of each other; as, *internecine* strife.

in-ter-pel-late (ĭn"tĕr-pĕl'āt), *v.t.* to question formally, as an officer, in explanation of his conduct.

in-ter-pen-e-trate (ĭn"tĕr-pĕn'ē-trāt), *v.t.* to pass into all parts of each other; form a union.—*n.* **interpenetration.**

in-ter-play (ĭn'tĕr-plā"), *n.* mutual action; action or influence exerted between or among; interaction.

in-ter-plead-er (ĭn"tĕr-plēd'ĕr), *n.* in law, the discussion of a clause to determine ownership of property.

in-ter-po-late (ĭn-tûr'pō-lāt), *v.t.* to insert in a book or writing new or foreign matter; to insert between other things or parts; to interrupt.

in-ter-po-la-tor (ĭn-tûr'pō-lā"tĕr), *n.* one who inserts new matter in a book or writing.

in-ter-po-la-tion (ĭn-tĕr"pō-lā'shŭn), *n.* that which is inserted; the act of inserting.

in-ter-pose (ĭn"tĕr-pōz'), *v.t.* to place between; thrust in: *v.i.* mediate; interrupt; come between.

Syn. arbitrate, interfere, meddle.

in-ter-po-si-tion (ĭn"tĕr-pō-zĭsh'ŭn), *n.* the act of coming between, interrupting, or mediating; that which is thrust in or interjected.

in-ter-pret (ĭn-tûr'prĕt), *v.t.* to explain the meaning of; as, to *interpret* a foreign language; to *interpret* a passage from Shakespeare.

Syn. elucidate, unfold, decipher.

in-ter-pre-ta-tion (ĭn-tûr"prē-tā'shŭn), *n.* the act of explaining the meaning of; explanation; translation.

in-ter-pre-ta-tive (ĭn-tûr'prē-tā-tĭv), *adj.* explanatory; intended or serving to explain or translate.

in-ter-pre-ter (ĭn-tûr'prĕt-ĕr), *n.* one who explains, or translates orally; especially, one who explains the principles of religion or law.

in-ter-reg-num (ĭn"tĕr-rĕg'nŭm), *n.* the period between two reigns, governments, or ministries; a break in a continuous event or series.

in-ter-re-lat-ed (ĭn"tĕr-rē-lāt'ĕd), *p.adj.* having a connection between each other or among one another.

in-ter-ro-gate (ĭn-tĕr'ō-gāt), *v.t.* to question: *v.i.* to ask questions.

in-ter-ro-ga-tion (ĭn-tĕr"ō-gā'shŭn), *n.* the act of asking questions; a question; inquiry; a mark [?] denoting a question.

in-ter-rog-a-tive (ĭn"tĕ-rŏg'ȧ-tĭv), *adj.* denoting or containing a question or inquiry: *n.* a word used in asking a question.—*adv.* **interrogatively.**

in-ter-ro-ga-tor (ĭn-tĕr'ō-gā"tĕr), *n.* one who asks questions.

in-ter-rog-a-to-ry (ĭn"tĕ-rŏg'ȧ-tō-rĭ), *adj.* containing or expressing a question.

in-ter-rupt (ĭn"tĕ-rŭpt'), *v.t.* to stop or hinder by breaking in upon; break into something which is continuous; as, a huge rock *interrupts* the course of the stream at one point; cause to be delayed; end suddenly.

in-ter-rupt-ed (ĭn"tĕ-rŭp'tĕd), *p.adj.* not continuing unbrokenly; broken.

in-ter-rup-tion (ĭn"tĕ-rŭp'shŭn), *n.* the act of breaking in upon; hindrance; something which blocks the way; sudden ceasing.

in-ter-sect (ĭn"tĕr-sĕkt'), *v.t.* to cut or divide; as, one street *intersects* another at a corner: *v.i.* to cross each other.

in-ter-sec-tion (ĭn"tĕr-sĕk'shŭn), *n.* the act of dividing by cutting across; place of crossing; the point or line in which two lines or two surfaces cut each other; as, the *intersection* of two faces of a cube makes an edge.

in-ter-sperse (ĭn"tĕr-spûrs'), *v.t.* to distribute widely; scatter objects upon; as, to *intersperse* a lawn with bushes.

in-ter-sper-sion (ĭn"tĕr-spûr'shŭn), *n.* the act of placing or scattering here and there among other things.

in-ter-state (ĭn'tĕr-stāt"), *adj.* existing between different states; including different states; as, the *Interstate* Fair Corporation; *interstate* commerce.

in-ter-stel-lar (ĭn"tĕr-stĕl'ȧr), *adj.* pertaining to, or situated in, space between the stars.

in-ter-stice (ĭn-tûr'stĭs), *n.* a narrow space between things closely set; as, the *interstices* of a window screen must be small enough to allow no insect to crawl through.

in-ter-twine (ĭn"tĕr-twīn'), *v.t.* and *v.i.* to twist with one another; wind or coil together.

in-ter-ur-ban (in″tẽr-ûr′băn), *adj.* lying between or running between cities or towns; between cities or towns.

in-ter-val (in′tẽr-văl), *n.* time or space between; the distance between soldiers in the ranks, between companies, etc.; the distance between two musical sounds.

in-ter-vene (in″tẽr-vēn′), *v.i.* to come or be situated between; as, a very short time should *intervene* between the sending of a letter and its receipt; interfere.

in-ter-ven-tion (in″tẽr-vĕn′shŭn), *n.* the act of coming between for any purpose; as, peace was brought about by the *intervention* of the United States; interference.

in-ter-view (in′tẽr-vū), *v.t.* tŏ visit, as a notable personage, in order to obtain facts about him or his opinions: *n.* a personal conference or meeting; the published account of a conversation with, or questioning by, a newspaper reporter.—*n.* **interviewer.**

in-ter-weave (in″tẽr-wēv′), *v.t.* and *v.i.* to twine together; to twist together; intermingle.

in-tes-ta-cy (in-tĕs′tȧ-sĭ), *n.* the state of dying without a will.

in-tes-tate (in-tĕs′tāt), *adj.* not having made a will; as, to die *intestate*: *n.* one who dies without having made a will.

in-tes-ti-nal (in-tĕs′tĭ-năl), *adj.* pertaining to, or found in, the bowels.—*adv.* **intestinally.**

in-tes-tine (in-tĕs′tĭn), *adj.* internal; not foreign; as, an *intestine* war: *n.pl.* the bowels.

in-ti-ma-cy (in′tĭ-mȧ-sĭ), *n.* [*pl.* intimacies (-sĭz)], close or confidential friendship.

in-ti-mate (in′tĭ-māt), *adj.* close in friendship; well acquainted; familiar; confidential: *v.t.* (in′tĭ-māt), to suggest indirectly; make known: *n.* a close friend.

Syn., *v.* hint, suggest, insinuate, express, signify, impart, tell.

in-ti-mate-ly (in′tĭ-māt-lĭ), *adv.* in a confidential manner.

in-ti-ma-tion (in″tĭ-mā′shŭn), *n.* an indirect suggestion or hint; announcement.

in-tim-i-date (in-tĭm′ĭ-dāt), *v.t.* to make afraid; to frighten, especially by threats.

Syn. dishearten, alarm, frighten, scare, appeal, daunt.

Ant. (see encourage).

in-tim-i-da-tion (in-tim″ĭ-dā′shŭn), *n.* the act of frightening by threats; the state of being frightened by threats.

in-to (in′tōō), *prep.* to the inside of; denoting passage inwards; as, he came *into* the room; she poured the tea *into* the cup.

in-tol-er-a-ble (in-tŏl′ẽr-ȧ-bl), *adj.* unbearable; as, the heat of the tropics is sometimes almost *intolerable.* —*adv.* **intolerably.**

Syn. insupportable, unendurable.

in-tol-er-ance (in-tŏl′ẽr-ăns), *n.* refusal to allow to others the enjoyment of their own opinions or practices; as, religious *intolerance* has caused many wars in Europe; inability to bear or endure.

in-tol-er-ant (in-tŏl′ẽr-ănt), *adj.* not allowing difference of opinion, especially in religious matters; unable to bear or e^n^du^r^e; with *of.*

in-to-nate (in tō-nāt), *v.t.* to recite in a musical manner, as in reading the church service; to recite musically.

in-to-na-tion (in″tō-nā′shŭn), *n.* the act or manner of sounding musical notes; rise and fall of the voice; act of chanting; as, the *intonation* of a prayer.

in-tone (in-tōn′), *v.t.* to recite in a single tone; to chant; as, to *intone* a church service.

in-tox-i-cant (in-tŏk′sĭ-kănt), *n.* that which makes drunk, as alcohol; anything which excites; as, to him success was an *intoxicant.*

in-tox-i-cate (in-tŏk′sĭ-kāt), *v.t.* to make drunk by alcoholic liquors; excite exceedingly; as, pleasure *intoxicates.*

in-tox-i-ca-tion (in-tŏk″sĭ-kā′shŭn), *n.* the act of making drunk; the state of being drunk; extreme excitement.

in-trac-ta-bil-i-ty (in-trăk″tȧ-bĭl′ĭ-tĭ), *n.* the quality or state of being unmanageable.

in-trac-ta-ble (in-trăk′tȧ-bl), *adj.* unmanageable; as, in former times an *intractable* pupil was punished by severe whipping.—*adv.* **intractably.**

in-trac-tile (in-trăk′tĭl), *adj.* incapable of being drawn out or extended; as, iron is an *intractile* metal.

in-tra-mu-ral (in″trȧ-mū′răl), *adj.* entirely within a city; as, an *intramural* railway.

in-tran-si-tive (in-trăn′sĭ-tĭv), *adj.* not carrying action over to a receiver; expressing action not received: said of certain verbs.—*adv.* **intransitively.**

in-trench (in-trĕnch′), *v.t.* to surround with a ditch; to make hollow: *v.i.* to enter upon; to take possession of: usually followed by *of* or *upon;* as, to *intrench* upon the rights of others.

in-trench-ment (in-trĕnch′mĕnt), *n.* a long, narrow ditch in the earth; in the military sense, a defensive work consisting of ditches with a protecting wall of earth thrown up before them.

in-trep-id (in-trĕp′ĭd), *adj.* bold; fearless; brave; daring.—*adv.* **intrepidly.**

Syn., *adj.* dauntless, courageous, valorous, heroic, gallant, chivalrous.

Ant. (see cowardly, faint-hearted).

in-tre-pid-i-ty (in″trē-pĭd′ĭ-tĭ), *n.* fearlessness; valor; boldness.

in-tri-ca-cy (in′trĭ-kȧ-sĭ), *n.* [*pl.* intricacies (-sĭz)], the quality of being entangled or complicated.

in-tri-cate (in′trĭ-kāt), *adj.* entangled, perplexed, complicated; as, an *intricate* plot in a play or story.—*adv.* **intricately.**

in-trigue (in-trēg′), *v.i.* to carry on a secret plot; engage in secret love affairs: *v.t.* colloquially, to interest keenly: *n.* (in-trēg′; in′trēg), a secret plot; secret love affair.

Syn., *n.* plot, conspiracy, artifice, ruse.

in-trin-sic (in-trĭn′sĭk), *adj.* pertaining to the very nature of a thing; as, we often value for their associations things whose *intrinsic* worth is small; real.—*adv.* **intrinsically.**

Syn. true, native, natural, essential.

Ant. (see extrinsic).

in-tro-duce (in″trō-dūs′), *v.t.* to conduct or bring in; bring into use or notice; bring into acquaintance; to put into something else.

in-tro-duc-tion (ĭn″trō-dŭk′shŭn), *n* the act of bringing into use; presentation; a preface.

in-tro-duc-to-ry (ĭn″trō-dŭk′tō-rĭ), *adj.* serving to bring in; preliminary. Also, **introductive.**

in-tro-it (ĭn-trō′ĭt). *n.* a part of the Mass in the Roman Catholic Church; a part of the service of the Anglican Church.

in-tro-spect (ĭn″trō-spĕkt′), *v.t.* to look into or within; examine the interior of.

in-tro-spec-tion (ĭn″trō-spĕk′shŭn), *n.* the act or process of examining one's own thoughts or feelings; as, too much *introspection* is bad for one.

in-tro-spec-tive (ĭn″trō-spĕk′tĭv), *adj:* inclined to look inward and search one's own thoughts and feelings.—*adv.* **introspectively.**

in-trude (ĭn-trōōd′), *v.i.* to come in without invitation or welcome: *v.t.* to thrust or force in.

in-tru-sion (ĭn-trōō′zhŭn), *n.* the act of entering without invitation or welcome.

in-tru-sive (ĭn-trōō′sĭv), *adj.* inclined or apt to thrust or force oneself in where one is not wanted or has no right; forward.—*adv.* **intrusively.**

in-trust (ĭn-trŭst′), *v.t.* to give into faithful keeping; confide; place in charge.

in-tu-i-tion (ĭn″tū-ĭsh′ŭn), *n.* knowledge or feeling which comes of itself without reasoning or a process of thought; insight; as, the child's *intuition* told him that the man could be trusted.

in-tu-i-tion-al (ĭn″tū-ĭsh′ŭn-ăl), *adj.* pertaining to instinctive knowledge or insight.

in-tu-i-tive (ĭn-tū′ĭ-tĭv), *adj.* known or felt immediately by the mind without reasoning; as, children seem to have *intuitive* power of recognizing real child lovers.—*adv.* **intuitively.**

in-un-date (ĭn′ŭn-dāt; ĭn-ŭn′dāt), *v.t.* to fill to overflowing; flood; as, the overflowing of the Nile *inundates* the fertile fields of Egypt.

in-un-da-tion (ĭn″ŭn-dā′shŭn), *n.* overflow; flood; as, the *inundation* of Egypt by the Nile.

in-ure (ĭn-ūr′), *v.t.* to accustom; toughen; as, an outdoor life will *inure* one to varying weather conditions.

in-vade (ĭn-vād′), *v.t.* to enter (a country) with a hostile army; to enter upon; take possession of.

in-val-id (ĭn-văl′ĭd), *adj.* of no force or authority: *n.* (ĭn′vȧ-lĭd), one who is weak or infirm in health; a disabled soldier or sailor: *v.t.* to register, enroll, send home, or to a hospital, as an invalid; affect with disease.

in-val-i-date (ĭn-văl′ĭ-dāt), *v.t.* to weaken or destroy the force or authority of; as, the will most recently made *invalidates* all others formerly made.

Syn. quash, cancel, overthrow, vacate, nullify, annul.

in-va-lid-i-ty (ĭn″vȧ-lĭd′ĭ-tĭ), *n.* want of legal force or argument.

in-val-u-a-ble (ĭn-văl′ū-ȧ-bl), *adj.* priceless; as, his services were *invaluable* to his employer.

in-va-ri-a-ble (ĭn-vā′rĭ-ȧ-bl), *adj.* constant; uniform; unchanging; as, his *invariable* custom was to walk to his office.—*adv.* **invariably.**—*n.* **invariability.**

in-va-sion (ĭn-vā′zhŭn), *n.* the act of entering a country with a hostile army; entrance forced by an enemy's army; encroachment.

Syn. irruption, inroad, aggression, raid, fray.

in-vec-tive (ĭn-vĕk′tĭv), *n.* violent blame, sarcasm, or abuse; as, the newspapers hurled *invectives* at the retiring cabinet officer: *adj.* abusive.

Syn., n. reproach, railing, sarcasm.

in-veigh (ĭn-vā′), *v.i.* to speak violently and bitterly against persons or things; utter blame or reproach; as, a Congressman may *inveigh* against a bill which has been proposed.

in-vei-gle (ĭn-vē′gl), *v.t.* to persuade, especially to something evil; to entrap; to draw on by flattery, etc.; as, in the old rime, the spider *inveigles* the fly into his web.

in-vent (ĭn-vĕnt′), *v.t.* to find out by study or inquiry; to produce for the first time; to think out; devise or contrive; originate.

Syn. frame, discover, design.

in-ven-tion (ĭn-vĕn′shŭn), *n.* the act of originating; the thing originated; discovery; the quality by which one creates or produces anything for the first time; that which is made up.

in-ven-tive (ĭn-vĕn′tĭv), *adj.* able to make new things or discoveries; quick at contriving; ready in thinking out ways to accomplish an end.—*adv.* **inventively.**

in-ven-tive-ness (ĭn-vĕn′tĭv-nĕs), *n.* skill; ingenuity; mental resourcefulness; as, American *inventiveness* has given the world its greatest inventions.

in-ven-tor (ĭn-vĕn′tẽr), *n.* one who contrives, discovers, or originates; as, Edison is America's greatest *inventor*.

in-ven-to-ry (ĭn′vĕn-tō-rĭ), *n.* [*pl.* inventories (-rĭz)], a catalog or list of goods, furniture, etc.; as, a merchant takes an *inventory* of his stock once a year; account: *v.t.* to draw up a list or catalog of goods.

in-verse (ĭn′vûrs; ĭn-vûrs′), *adj.* opposite in tendency, direction, or effect; turned upside down; as, subtraction is the *inverse* operation of addition.

in-verse-ly (ĭn-vûrs′lĭ), *adv.* in an opposite order.

in-ver-sion (ĭn-vûr′shŭn), *n.* the act of turning in the opposite direction, etc.; the state of being turned upside down; change of order or position.

in-vert (ĭn-vûrt′), *v.t.* to turn upside down, inside out, or in an opposite direction.

in-ver-te-brate (ĭn-vûr′tē-brāt), *n.* an animal without a backbone: *adj.* having no backbone; having no force of character; weak.

in-vert-ed (ĭn-vûr′tĕd), *adj.* turned in an opposite direction or turned upside down.

in-vest (ĭn-vĕst′), *v.t.* to place or lay out, as money at interest; clothe, as with office, authority, or dignity; surround; as, the armies *invest* the city: *v.i.* to put money into; as, to *invest* in oil stock.

in-ves-ti-gate (ĭn-vĕs′tĭ-gāt), *v.t.* to find out by careful inquiry; search; examine; as, to *investigate* the cause of a disaster.

in-ves-ti-ga-tion (in-vĕs′tĭ-gā′shŭn), *n.* the act of finding out by careful inquiry; inquiry; search.
Syn. examination, scrutiny.

in-ves-ti-ga-tor (in-vĕs′tĭ-gā′tẽr), *n.* one who finds out by careful search.

in-ves-ti-ture (in-vĕs′tĭ-tûr), *n.* the act or right of giving legal possession.

in-vest-ment (in-vĕst′mĕnt), *n.* the act of laying out money for the sake of profit; money so placed; the act of besieging or blockading.

in-ves-tor (in-vĕs′tẽr), *n.* one who puts out money for profit; as, many women are *investors* in railroad stock.

in-vet-er-a-cy (in-vĕt′ẽr-*a*-sĭ), *n.* the state of being firmly established as a habit.

in-vet-er-ate (in-vĕt′ẽr-āt) *adj.* deep-rooted; habitual; as, an *inveterate* cigarette smoker.
Syn. confirmed, chronic, malignant.

in-vid-i-ous (in-vĭd′ĭ-ŭs), *adj.* likely to provoke ill will or envy; as, *invidious* preferences or partiality; unpleasant.—*adv.* **invidiously.**
Syn., adj. envious, hateful, odious, malignant.

in-vig-or-ate (in-vĭg′ŏr-āt), *v.t.* to give vitality to; strengthen; as, sea air is likely to *invigorate* the weak.—*n.* **invigoration.**
Syn., v. brace, harden, nerve.
Ant. (see enervate).

in-vin-ci-bil-i-ty (in-vĭn′sĭ-bĭl′ĭ-tĭ), *n.* the quality of being unconquerable.

in-vin-ci-ble (in-vĭn′sĭ-bl), *adj.* unconquerable; as, Job showed *invincible* patience.—*adv.* **invincibly.**

in-vi-o-la-bil-i-ty (in-vī′ō-l*a*-bĭl′ĭ-tĭ), *n.* incapability of being profaned or broken.

in-vi-o-la-ble (in-vī′ō-l*a*-bl), *adj.* that cannot be profaned or injured; unbroken; as, an *inviolable* promise or command.—*adv.* **inviolably.**

in-vi-o-late (in-vī′ō-lāt), *adj.* uninjured; unbroken; pure.—*adv.* **inviolately.**

in-vis-i-bil-i-ty (in-vĭz′ĭ-bĭl′ĭ-tĭ), *n.* the state or quality of being unseen; incapability of being seen.

in-vis-i-ble (in-vĭz′ĭ-bl), *adj.* that cannot be seen; as, during the day the stars are *invisible*.—*adv.* **invisibly.**
Syn., adj. unseen, imperceptible, impalpable, unperceivable.

in-vi-ta-tion (in′vĭ-tā′shŭn), *n.* the act of requesting the presence of, begging, or attracting; polite request; the words or document by which one is asked to come to a place.

in-vite (in-vīt′), *v.t.* to ask, beg, or summon; request the presence of; persuade; attract; as, the title of the book *invites* the reader's interest.
Syn. call, solicit.

in-vit-ing (in-vīt′ĭng), *p.adj.* tempting; attractive; as, an *inviting* meal.—*adv.* **invitingly.**

in-vo-cate (in′vō-kāt), *v.t.* to address in prayer. Also, **invoke.**

in-vo-ca-tion (in′vō-kā′shŭn), *n.* the act or form of addressing in prayer, or calling for the help of some superior being; as, the *invocation* of God's help in time of sickness.

in-voice (in′vois), *n.* a document announcing the sending of goods, with their prices, quantity, etc.: *v.t.* to state in such a paper.

in-voke (in-vōk′), *v.t.* to address in prayer or supplication; as, to *invoke* a blessing; ask solemnly or earnestly (aid or protection).
Syn. invocate, appeal, refer, implore, beseech.

in-vo-lu-cre (in′vō-lū′kẽr), *n.* a rosette of leaves, often resembling a calyx, surrounding the main stem of a plant, and supporting a flower cluster or fruit.

in-vol-un-ta-ri-ly (in-vŏl′ŭn-tā-rĭ-lĭ), *adv.* not willingly; not from choice; not intentionally; as, if something strikes at one's face, one *involuntarily* closes the eyes.

in-vol-un-ta-ry (in-vŏl′ŭn-tā-rĭ), *adj.* without will or choice.

in-vo-lute (in′vō-lūt), *adj.* folded or rolled inwards, as certain leaves and flowers; coiled spirally: *n.* a particular kind of curve turned inward at the margin.

in-vo-lu-tion (in′vō-lū′shŭn), *n.* the act of infolding; complication; return of an organ or tissue to its normal size after having been stretched or swelled out; the process of raising an arithmetical or algebraical quantity to a given power; as, $3^4 = 81$: read, three to the fourth power equals eighty-one.

in-volve (in-vŏlv′), *v.t.* to complicate; entangle; surround; to draw into; as, to *involve* one in a quarrel; produce as a consequence; multiply a quantity by itself any given number of times.
Syn. implicate, compromise, envelop, surround.

in-vul-ner-a-bil-i-ty (in-vŭl′nẽr-*a*-bĭl′ĭ-tĭ), *n.* the quality of being incapable of being wounded.

in-vul-ner-a-ble (in-vŭl′nẽr-*a*-bl), *adj.* that cannot be wounded or injured; as, the Greek hero, Achilles, was *invulnerable* everywhere except in the heel; without any weak point.—*adv.* **invulnerably.**

in-ward (in′wẽrd), *adj.* situated within; as, to throw the light *inward*, from without; in the mind: *adv.* towards the center or interior; as, to bend *inward*. Also, **inwards.**

in-ward-ly (in′wẽrd-lĭ), *adv.* internally; especially, in the mind or feelings; secretly.

in-ward-ness (in′wẽrd-nĕs), *n.* the real nature of a thing; the quality of being internal; earnestness; as, the true *inwardness* of a plan.

in-wrought (in-rôt′; in′rôt′), *p.adj.* worked in; adorned with figures or patterns.

i-o-dide (ī′ō-dīd), *n.* a compound of iodine with another element. Also, **iodid.**

i-o-dine (ī′ō-dīn; ī′-ōdĭn), *n.* a non-metallic element occurring in nature always in combination as iodides, and giving off a rich violet vapor when heated: largely used in medicine, in making dyes, etc. Also, **iodin.**

i-o-do-form (ī-ō′dō-fôrm; ī-ŏd′ō-fôrm), *n.* a crystalline antiseptic compound, with a penetrating odor.

i-on (ī′ŏn), *n.* one of the electrified particles into which a gas, or a substance in solution, is broken up under the action of electricity.

I-o-ni-an (ī-ō′nĭ-ăn), *adj.* pertaining to Ionia, the western coast of Asia Minor, or its inhabitants. Also, **Ionic.**

I-on-ic or-der (ī-ŏn′ĭk ôr′dẽr), an order of classic architecture, characterized by the volute, or ram's-horn scroll, of its capital, or ornamental top.

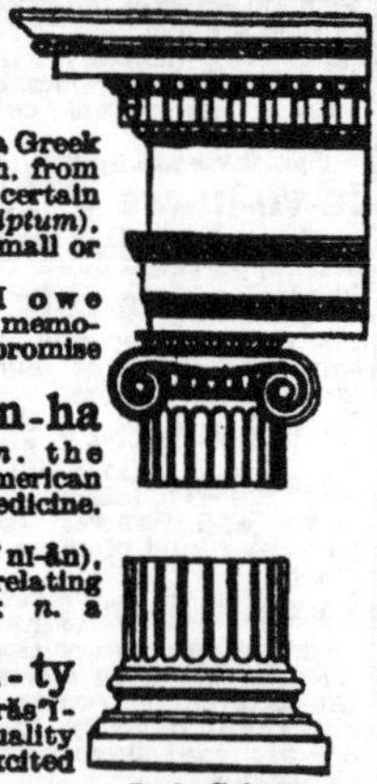

Ionic Column

i-o-ta (ī-ō′tȧ), *n.* a Greek letter which, from its being used under certain vowels (*iota subscriptum*), denotes anything small or insignificant.

I O U (ī ō ū), I owe you; a memorandum of a debt; promise to pay.

ip-e-cac-u-an-ha (ĭp″ē-kăk″ū-ăn′ȧ), *n.* the root of a South American plant: used in medicine. Also, **ipecac.**

I-ra-ni-an (ī-rā′nĭ-ăn), *adj.* relating to Persia or Iran: *n.* a modern Persian.

i-ras-ci-bil-i-ty (ī-răs″ĭ-bĭl′ĭ-tĭ; ĭ-răs″ĭ-bĭl′ĭ-tĭ), *n.* the quality of being easily excited to anger.

i-ras-ci-ble (ī-răs′ĭ-bl; ĭ-răs′ĭ-bl), *adj.* easily excited to anger; hot-headed.—*adv.* **irascibly.**

i-rate (ī-rāt′; ī′rāt), *adj.* angry; enraged; as, an *irate* old gentleman.—*adv.* **irately.**

ire (īr), *n.* anger; wrath; strong resentment; as, his *ire* was quickly aroused.—*adj.* **ireful.**

ir-i-des-cence (ĭr″ĭ-dĕs′ĕns), *n.* the coming and going of colors like those of the rainbow.

ir-i-des-cent (ĭr″ĭ-dĕs′ĕnt), *adj.* having changing colors like those of the rainbow.—*adv.* **iridescently.**

i-rid-i-um (ī-rĭd′ĭ-ŭm), *n.* a rare element somewhat like platinum, one of the heaviest known metals.

i-ris (ī′rĭs), *n.* [*pl.* **irises** (-ĕs; -ĭz), **irides** (ĭr′ĭ-dēz; ī′rĭ-dēz)], the pupil of the eye; the rainbow; a spring flower; commonly called *flag.*

i-ri-scope (ī′rĭ-skōp), *n.* an apparatus for showing the colors of the rainbow.

I-rish (ī′rĭsh), *adj.* pertaining to Ireland, its inhabitants, or language.

I-rish-ism (ī′rĭsh-ĭzm), *n.* an Irish peculiarity of speech; Irish character or traits.

irk (ûrk), *v.t.* to weary; as, the dull details of the business *irk* him.

irk-some (ûrk′sŭm), *adj.* tedious; wearisome; as, tasks may be *irksome.*
Syn. tiresome, annoying.
Ant. (see pleasant).

i-ron (ī′ûrn), *n.* a metallic element; the most common and useful of the metals; an instrument made of iron, especially one to smooth clothes by heat; anything especially hard; in golf, a club made of iron, with the head laid back to raise the ball: *pl.* chains or fetters for a prisoner: *adj.* pertaining to, resembling, or made of, iron: *v.t.* to smooth with an iron; furnish with iron; chain.

i-ron age (ī′ûrn āj), the latest prehistoric age, characterized by the use of iron for weapons, etc.; the last of the four ages of classic mythology.

i-ron-clad (ī′ûrn-klăd″), *n.* a warship protected wholly or partially with iron or steel plates: *adj.* covered or protected with iron armor.

i-ron-i-cal (ī-rŏn′ĭ-kăl), *adj.* expressing one thing and meaning another.

i-ron-i-cal-ly (ī-rŏn′ĭ-kăl-ĭ), *adv.* in a sarcastic manner; in a manner which expresses one thing and means another; as, he was speaking *ironically.*

i-ron-side (ī′ûrn-sīd″), *n.* a man of strength; a warship protected by steel plates: **Ironsides,** Cromwell's cavalry.

i-ron-ware (ī′ûrn-wâr″), *n.* hardware; articles made of iron.

i-ron-wood (ī′ûrn-wŏŏd″), *n.* a name for the timber of trees of unusual hardness.

i-ron-work (ī′ûrn-wûrk″), *n.* work in iron; a place where iron is smelted and articles are made from it.

i-ro-ny (ī′rō-nĭ), *n.* sarcasm; a mode of speech meaning the opposite of what is said; as, "to cry like a baby—that's a fine way for a man to act," said he with keen *irony.*
Syn. satire, ridicule, raillery.

Ir-o-quois (ĭr″ō-kwoi′), *n.* a member of the powerful Indian confederacy of that name formerly inhabiting Central New York; an Indian tribe: called also *the Five Nations.*

ir-ra-di-ant (ĭ-rā′dĭ-ănt), *adj.* giving forth rays of light; as, *irradiant* stars.—*n.* **irradiance.**

ir-ra-di-ate (ĭ-rā′dĭ-āt), *v.t.* to shed light upon; illuminate; brighten: *v.i.* emit rays of light.—*n.* **irradiation.**

ir-ra-tion-al (ĭ-răsh′ŭn-ăl), *adj.* lacking reasoning powers; contrary to reason; absurd.—*adv.* **irrationally.**

ir-re-claim-a-ble (ĭr″ē-klām′ȧ-bl), *adj.* incapable of being recovered, reformed, or restored.—*adv.* **irreclaimably.**

ir-rec-on-cil-a-ble (ĭ-rĕk″ŭn-sīl′ȧ-bl), *adj.* not adjustable, as differences or quarrels; not in agreement, as actions and beliefs: *n.* one that is not able to adjust himself to conditions; as, an *irreconcilable* opponent; one who is discontented.—*adv.* **irreconcilably.**

ir-re-cov-er-a-ble (ĭr″ē-kŭv′ẽr-ȧ-bl), *adj.* not capable of being regained.—*adv.* **irrecoverably.**

ir-re-deem-a-ble (ĭr″ē-dēm′ȧ-bl), *adj.* incapable of being bought back; not exchangeable for gold or silver: said of paper money; hopeless.—*adv.* **irredeemably.**

Ir-re-den-tist (ĭr″ē-dĕn′tĭst), *n.* one of a party which favors incorporating into Italy neighboring regions, known as *Italia irredenta,* or Italy unredeemed, largely Italian in population.

ir-re-du-ci-ble (ĭr″ē-dū′sĭ-bl), *adj.* incapable of being lessened or curtailed; in arithmetic, not capable of being changed in denomination or form without a change in value; not capable of being subdued or conquered.—*adv.* **irreducibly.**

ir-ref-ra-ga-ble (ĭ-rĕf″rȧ-gȧ-bl), *adj.* unanswerable.—*adv.* **irrefragably.**

ir-re-fut-a-ble (ĭr″ē-fūt′ȧ-bl; ĭ-rĕf″ū-tȧ-bl), *adj.* incapable of being proved false or incorrect, as an argument; unanswerable.—*adv.* **irrefutably.**

ir-reg-u-lar (ĭ-rĕg′ū-lẽr), *adj.* not straight; not symmetrical; not according to established method, standards, customs, or law; abnormal; not methodical. —*adv.* **irregularly.**—*n.* **irregularity.**

ir-rel-e-vant (ĭ-rĕl′ē-vănt), *adj.* not bearing upon the case; unrelated to the matter under discussion.—*adv.* **irrelevantly.**—*n.* **irrelevance, irrelevancy.**

ir-re-li-gious (ĭr″ē-lĭj′ŭs), *adj.* wanting religion; not godly; wicked. —*adv.* **irreligiously.**

ir-re-me-di-a-ble (ĭr″ē-mē′dĭ-ȧ-bl), *adj.* not capable of being relieved; incurable.—*adv.* **irremediably.**

ir-rep-a-ra-ble (ĭ-rĕp′ȧ-rȧ-bl), *adj.* not capable of being repaired or restored; not capable of being retrieved or made good.—*adv.* **irreparably.**

ir-re-press-i-ble (ĭr″ē-prĕs′ĭ-bl), *adj.* incapable of being subdued, curbed, or checked.—*adv.* **irrepressibly.**

ir-re-proach-a-ble (ĭr″ē-prōch′ȧ-bl), *adj.* incapable of being condemned or blamed; blameless.—*adv.* **irreproachably.**

ir-re-sist-i-ble (ĭr″ē-zĭs′tĭ-bl), *adj.* incapable of being withstood; not to be opposed; overpowering.—*adv.* **irresistibly.**

ir-res-o-lute (ĭ-rĕz′ō-lūt), *adj.* undecided; wavering; not determined. —*adv.* **irresolutely.**—*n.* **irresolution.**

ir-re-spec-tive (ĭr″ē-spĕk′tĭv), *adj.* regardless: with *of;* as, all male citizens of the United States may vote, *irrespective* of race or color.—*adv.* **irrespectively.**

ir-re-spon-si-ble (ĭr″ē-spŏn′sĭ-bl), *adj.* not accountable; free from care; not trustworthy.—*adv.* **irresponsibly.**—*n.* **irresponsibility.**

ir-re-triev-a-ble (ĭr″ē-trēv′ȧ-bl), *adj.* not recoverable; not to be made good.—*adv.* **irretrievably.**

ir-rev-er-ence (ĭ-rĕv′ẽr-ĕns), *n.* want of respect; lack of veneration; a disrespectful act or speech.

ir-rev-er-ent (ĭ-rĕv′ẽr-ĕnt), *adj.* disrespectful; showing a want of veneration.—*adv.* **irreverently.**

ir-re-vers-i-ble (ĭr″ē-vûr′sĭ-bl), *adj.* incapable of being turned back or around.—*adv.* **irreversibly.**

ir-rev-o-ca-ble (ĭ-rĕv′ō-kȧ-bl), *adj.* incapable of being recalled; unalterable.—*adv.* **irrevocably.**

ir-ri-gate (ĭr′ĭ-gāt), *v.t.* to moisten, as land, by causing water to flow over it by canals, etc.

ir-ri-ga-tion (ĭr-ĭ-gā′shŭn), *n.* the supplying of water to land by means of canals, etc.

ir-ri-ta-ble (ĭr′ĭ-tȧ-bl), *adj.* easily provoked to anger; easily caused to perform some physical function.—*n.* **irritability, irritableness.**

Syn. excitable, irascible, susceptible, sensitive.

Ant. (see calm).

ir-ri-ta-bly (ĭr′ĭ-tȧ-blĭ), *adv.* with vexation; petulantly.

ir-ri-tant (ĭr′ĭ-tănt), *adj.* causing redness or inflammation: *n.* anything which causes redness or inflammation; as, rough clothing is an *irritant* to the skin.

ir-ri-tate (ĭr′ĭ-tāt), *v.t.* to provoke or make angry; cause heat and redness in; as, to read in a poor light *irritates* the eyes.

Syn. aggravate, worry, embitter, madden, exasperate.

ir-ri-ta-tion (ĭr″ĭ-tā′shŭn), *n.* the act of exasperating; the state of being provoked or vexed; exasperation; vexation; impatience; the causing of muscular action by something outside the muscles; oversensitiveness of an organ or part of the body; heat and redness caused in an organ, etc.—*adj.* **irritative.**

ir-rup-tion (ĭ-rŭp′shŭn), *n.* a bursting or rushing in; sudden rushing in.

ir-rup-tive (ĭ-rŭp′tĭv), *adj.* tending to rush in upon; rushing in upon.

is (ĭz), third person singular present indicative of the verb *be.*

I-saac (ī′zȧk), *n.* in the Bible, a Hebrew patriarch; the son of Abraham and Sarah.

I-sa-iah (ī-zā′yȧ; ī-zī′ȧ), *n.* in the Bible, the greatest of the Hebrew prophets; a book of the Old Testament.

Is-car-i-ot (ĭs-kăr′ĭ-ŏt), *n.* the surname of Judas, who betrayed Christ into the hands of the Jews.

Ish-ma-el (ĭsh′mā-ĕl), *n.* in the Bible, a son of Abraham and Hagar; one socially ostracized.

Ish-ma-el-ite (ĭsh′mā-ĕl-īt), *n.* a descendant of Ishmael, a son of Abraham and Hagar; hence, a social outcast.—*adj.* **Ishmaelitish.**

i-sin-glass (ī′zĭn-glȧs), *n.* a white semitransparent substance or gelatin prepared from the air-bladders of the sturgeon, cod, etc.; a sheet of mica.

Is-lam (ĭs′lȧm; ĭz′lȧm; ĭs-läm′), *n.* the Mohammedan religion; the whole body of Mohammedans and the countries where the religion of Mohammed is professed.

is-land (ī′lănd), *n.* a tract of land surrounded by water; anything resembling such a tract of land.

is-land-er (ī′lăn-dẽr), *n.* an inhabitant or a native of an island.

isle (īl), *n.* an island; as, Shakespeare calls England "this sceptered *isle,*" and Byron sings of "the *isles* of Greece." [POET.]

is-let (ī′lĕt), *n.* a small island; as, many *islets* compose the Lesser Antilles.

ism (ĭzm), *n.* a system or theory; as, he was constantly talking about one *ism* or another.

i-so-bar (ī′sō-băr), *n.* a line which connects places on the earth's surface having the same atmospheric pressure at the sea level.

i-so-bar-ic (ī″sō-băr′ĭk), *adj.* of equal atmospheric pressure; pertaining to, or showing, lines denoting equal atmospheric pressure at sea level; as, an *isobaric* chart. Also, **isobarometric.**

i-so-chro-mat-ic (ī″sō-krō-măt′ĭk), *adj.* having the same color: a term used in the study of light and vision.

i-so-dy-nam-ic (ī″sō-dī-năm′ĭk), *adj.* having equal force: *n.* a line on the surface of the earth at all points of which the earth's magnetism is of equal intensity.

i-so-late (ī′sō-lāt; ĭs′ō-lāt), *v.t.* to place alone; to insulate; place in a situation apart from others; as, it is necessary to *isolate* people suffering from contagious diseases.

i-so-la-tion (ī″sō-lā′shŭn; ĭs″ō-lā′shŭn), *n.* the state of being placed apart or alone; detachment; as, *isolation* from one's family.

i-so-met-ric (ī″sō-mĕt′rĭk), *adj.* having equality of measure, as in the axial lines of a crystal.

i-so-met-ric pro-jec-tion (ī″sō-mĕt′-rĭk prō-jĕk′shŭn), a kind of drawing designed to show proportions without regard to the principle of perspective.

i-sos-ce-les (ī-sŏs′ē-lēz), *adj.* having two equal sides; as, an *isosceles* triangle.

i-so-therm (ī′sō-thûrm), *n.* an imaginary line connecting those places on the earth's surface which have the same average annual or seasonable temperature.

i-so-ther-mal (ī″sō-thûr′măl), *adj.* having uniform temperatures; pertaining to, or showing, lines indicating places which have the same temperature at the same time; as, an *isothermal* chart.

i-so-trop-ic (ī″sō-trŏp′ĭc), *adj.* having the same physical properties in every direction.

Is-ra-el (ĭz′râ-ĕl), *n.* in the Bible, the Hebrew patriarch Jacob; the descendants of Jacob; the Jews; as, the children of *Israel;* the northern kingdom after the division of the Jews; those who returned from the Babylonian captivity.

Is-ra-el-ite (ĭz′râ-ĕl-īt), *n.* a descendant of Israel or Jacob; a Hebrew; a Jew.

Is-ra-el-it-ish (ĭz′râ-ĕl-īt″ĭsh), *adj.* pertaining to the Israelites; Jewish. Also, **Israelitic.**

is-su-ance (ĭsh′ū-ăns), *n.* the act of sending or giving out; a sending forth; as, the *issuance* of an edict; issue.

is-sue (ĭsh′ū), *n.* the act of passing or flowing out; as, the *issue* of the passengers through the door of the car; that which flows or passes out; discharge; as, the *issue* of blood or pus from a wound; publication; as, the *issue* of a book; the entire number or amount sent out at one time or during a particular period; as, the January *issue* of a magazine; a government *issue* of bank notes; offspring; descendants; produce of the earth; profits of land, etc.; important points in pleading or debate; result; as, the *issue* of an investigation; an outcome; a running sore: *v.t.* to send out; publish; put into circulation; as, to *issue* a magazine: *v.i.* to come or pass out; arise, as from a source; as, the stream *issues* from a hill; flow; proceed; be descended.

Syn., *v.* emerge, rise, spring, emanate: *n.* end, upshot, effect, result.

isth-mi-an (ĭs′mĭ-ăn), *adj.* pertaining to a neck of land which connects two larger bodies of land: **Isthmian,** *n.* one who lives on, or who was born on, an isthmus.

isth-mus (ĭs′mŭs), *n.* a neck of land connecting two larger parts, or a peninsula, to the mainland.

it (ĭt), *pron.* the neuter pronoun of the third person singular.

I-tal-ian (ĭ-tăl′yăn), *adj.* pertaining to Italy, its people, or language: *n.* a native of Italy.

i-tal-ic (ĭ-tăl′ĭk), *adj.* denoting a slender, sloping kind of type (*italic*): used for emphasis, etc.: *n.pl.* italic type.

i-tal-i-cize (ĭ-tăl′ĭ-sīz), *v.t.* to write or print in italics; emphasize. Also, **italicise.**

itch (ĭch), *n.* a skin disease causing great irritation; a constant and teasing desire for something: *v.i.* to feel a particular uneasiness in the skin, causing a desire to scratch the part affected; have a constant and teasing desire for.

itch-y (ĭch′ĭ), *adj.* having the skin disease which causes constant irritation; pertaining to this disease; resembling this disease; feeling the persistent desire to scratch an irritated part of the skin.—*n.* **itchiness.**

i-tem (ī′tĕm), *n.* a separate article, entry, or particular; a sum entered in an account; a newspaper paragraph.

i-tem-ize (ī′tĕm-īz), *v.t.* to state by separate articles or entries; give particulars of; as, to *itemize* an account. —*n.* **itemization.**

it-er-ate (ĭt′ĕr-āt), *v.t.* to utter a second time; repeat; as, to *iterate* a threat or command.

it-er-a-tion (ĭt″ĕr-ā′shŭn), *n.* repetition; a second performance.

it-er-a-tive (ĭt′ĕr-ā-tĭv), *adj.* repeating; doing again; as, the *iterative* "Whoo, whoo, whoo" of the owl kept me awake.

i-tin-er-a-cy (ī-tĭn′ĕr-ā-sĭ), *n.* the practice of passing from place to place; the state of traveling about.

i-tin-er-an-cy (ī-tĭn′ĕr-ăn-sĭ), *n.* a passing from place to place, especially in the discharge of some official duty, as by a judge, a preacher, etc.

i-tin-er-ant (ī-tĭn′ĕr-ănt), *adj.* passing from place to place; as, an *itinerant* preacher: *n.* one who passes from place to place.

i-tin-er-a-ry (ī-tĭn′ĕr-ā-rĭ), *adj.* pertaining to, or done on, a journey; traveling from place to place: *n.* a traveler's guide or route-book; a rough sketch of the country through which troops are to pass; a diary of a journey; plan of an extended excursion.

i-tin-er-ate (ī-tĭn′ĕr-āt), *v.i.* to travel from place to place for, usually, some definite purpose, as preaching, giving lectures, etc.

its (ĭts), *pron.* the possessive case of the pronoun *it;* pertaining to a thing.

it's (ĭts), a contraction of the two words *it is.*

it-self (ĭt-sĕlf′), *pron.* the emphatic or reflexive form of *it;* as, he cared only for the work *itself,* and not for praise or money.

I've (īv), a colloquial contraction of the two words *I have.*

i-vied (ī′vĭd), *adj.* covered with, or overgrown with, ivy; as, *ivied* walls.

i-vo-ry (ī′vō-rĭ), *n.* the hard, bony, white substance which forms the tusks of the elephant, walrus, etc.: *adj.* made of, or like, ivory.

i-vo-ry nut (ī′vō-rĭ nŭt), the seed of a certain American palm, which, when dry, is hard, and, when polished, looks like ivory: used for buttons, etc.

i-vo-ry palm (ī′vō-rĭ päm), the palm from which are obtained the ivory nuts used as an imitation of ivory in making buttons.

i-vo-ry-type (ī″vō-rĭ-tīp′), *n.* a particular kind of photographic picture with an ivorylike surface.

i-vy (ī′vĭ), *n.* a clinging evergreen plant: frequently seen on the walls of churches and houses.

iz-ard (ĭz′ărd), *n.* the wild goat of the Pyrenees Mountains between France and Spain.

iz-zard (ĭz′ărd), *n.* an old name for the letter Z; as, from a to *izzard.*

J

jab (jăb), *v.t.* and *v.i.* to thrust or poke suddenly with something pointed: *n.* a sharp thrust. [Colloq.]

jab-ber (jăb'ẽr), *v.i.* to talk rapidly and indistinctly; chatter; as, the monkeys *jabber* in the trees.—*n.* **jabberer.**

ja-bot (zhȧ"bō'), *n.* a lace frill on a woman's waist; formerly, a ruffle on a shirt bosom. [Fr.]

ja-cinth (jā'sĭnth; jăs'ĭnth), *n.* hyacinth; the name of a gem almost pure orange in color.

jack (jăk), *n.* a fish: called also a *pike;* in bowls, a small ball serving as a mark to be aimed at; the male of some animals; a leather cup or jug; timber cut short of its usual length; a small flag used as a signal, bearing the same device as the union jack; the knave of cards, a leathern coat of armor; a name applied to various kinds of levers or mechanical labor-saving devices; as, a *jack*-screw, roasting-*jack*, etc.: *v.t.* to lift with a jack.

Jack

jack-al (jăk'ôl), *n.* a doglike, flesh-eating animal which hunts in packs; one who does base work for another: from the incorrect supposition that the *jackal* hunts prey for the lion.

jack-a-napes (jăk'*ȧ*-nāps"), *n.* a conceited or impertinent fellow.

jack-ass (jăk'ăs"), *n.* the male ass; donkey; a blockhead: used with contempt.

jack boots (jăk bōōtz), large boots reaching above the knee.

jack-daw (jăk'dô"), *n.* a glossy kind of crow which is often tamed and may be taught to imitate the human voice.

jack-et (jăk'ĕt), *n.* a short tailless coat; an outer covering put on like a coat, but not used as clothing; as, a cork *jacket* used as a life preserver; an outer covering of various kinds; a covering to prevent heat from being given off: *v.t.* to clothe with a short coat; to beat; thrash.

jack-in-the-pul-pit (jăk'ĭn-*th*ĕ-pŏŏl'-pĭt), *n.* a wild flower of the orchid family, green in color.

jack-knife (jăk'nīf"), *n.* a large pocket knife with two or more blades.

jack-o'-lan-tern (jăk'ō-lăn"tẽrn), *n.* a hollow pumpkin cut to resemble a human face, having a light inside it; a lantern similarly made, of cardboard, etc.

jack rab-bit (jăk răb'ĭt), a large hare with long legs and long ears.

jack-stays (jăk'stāz"), *n.pl.* ropes stretched along the yard of a ship to fasten the sails to.

jack-stones (jăk'stōnz"), *n.pl.* a game played by picking up pebbles or metal pieces; the pieces used in the game.

jack-straws (jăk'strôz"), *n.pl.* a game, in which light strips of wood are picked up with a hook; the strips of wood used in the game.

Ja-cob (jā'kŭb), *n.* in the Bible, a Hebrew patriarch, son of Isaac and Rebekah: afterwards called Israel; father of the twelve patriarchs.—Genesis xxv-l.

Jac-o-bin (jăk'ō-bĭn), *n.* one of a club of very extreme democrats during the French Revolution of 1789; hence, a violent extremist.—*adj.* **Jacobinic.**

Jac-o-bite (jăk'ō-bīt), *n.* in English history, a follower of James II or his family.

jac-o-net (jăk'ō-nĕt), *n.* a fine soft white cotton material somewhat like cambric; nainsook. Also, **jaconet.**

jade (jād), *n.* a tired or worn-out horse; a vicious woman; a young woman: used contemptuously or humorously; an opaque semiprecious stone of dark green color: *v.t.* to tire by long continued labor; harass.

Syn., *v.* weary, tire, worry.

jag (jăg), *n.* a notch; sharp projecting point: *v.t.* [*p.t.* and *p.p.* jagged, *p.pr.* jagging], to cut into notches or teeth.

jag-ged (jăg'ĕd), *p.adj.* notched; irregular on the edge; cut or torn in points.

jag-uar (jăg'wär; jȧ-gwär'), *n.* a fierce animal of South America, resembling the leopard; the American tiger.

Jaguar

ja-had (jȧ-hăd'), *n.* a Mohammedan holy war against the common enemies of Islam. Also, **jihad.**

jail (jāl), *n.* a prison; especially, a place where persons guilty of minor offenses are confined. Also, **gaol.**

jail-er (jāl'ẽr), *n.* a person in charge of a jail. Also, **jailor, gaoler.**

jam (jăm), *n.* a thick, sweet, fruit preserve; a squeeze; block; crush: *v.t.* [*p.t.* and *p.p.* jammed, *p.pr.* jamming], to squeeze or crush; press in tightly; block up by crowding.

jamb (jăm), *n.* one of the upright sides of a doorway, window-opening, or fireplace.

James (jāmz), *n.* in the Bible, the son of Zebedee, brother of John, one of the twelve apostles.—Matt. iv. 21; the son of Alpheus, one of the twelve apostles.—Matt. x. 3; a book in the New Testament, the Epistle of James.

jan-gle (jăn'gl), *v.i.* to quarrel or wrangle; sound out of tune; as, the bells *jangle* on the ragman's cart: *n.* a discordant sound; coarse quarrel; chatter.

Syn., *v.* conflict, disagree.

jan-i-tor (jăn'ĭ-tẽr), *n.* a doorkeeper; caretaker of a building; porter.

Jan-i-za-ry (jăn'ĭ-zȧ-rĭ), *n.* [*pl.* Janizaries (-rĭz)], a Turkish soldier: formerly, one of a body of infantry who acted as guard to the Sultan and were famous for their fierce fighting: often spelled with a small letter. Also, **Janissary.**

Jan-u-a-ry (jăn′ū-ā-rĭ), *n.* the first month of the year in the modern calendar.

ja-pan (jȧ-păn′), *n.* work varnished with a peculiar kind of shellac called lacquer, after the Japanese style of ornamentation; a kind of varnish: *v.t.* [*p.t.* and *p.p.* japanned, *p.pr.* japanning], to cover or varnish with lacquer; make black and glossy.

Jap-a-nese (jăp′ȧ-nēz′), *adj.* pertaining to Japan, its inhabitants, or language: *n.* a native of Japan; the language of Japan.

Jap-a-nesque (jăp′ȧ-nĕsk′), *adj.* resembling the Japanese style of art.

ja-pon-i-ca (jȧ-pŏn′ĭ-kȧ), *n.* the camellia, a plant with roselike, white or red flowers; the Japanese quince.

jar (jär), *n.* a deep, broad-mouthed vessel of earthenware or glass; a shake produced by a sudden shock; jolt; harsh sound; conflict of opinion or interest: *v.t.* [*p.t.* and *p.p.* jarred, *p.pr.* jarring], to cause to shake by a sudden shock; jolt: *v.i.* to interfere or clash; give out a harsh sound; to have a disagreeable effect.

jar-di-nière (zhär′dē′nyâr′), *n.* an ornamental flower stand or holder of porcelain or metal.

jar-gon (jär′gŏn), *n.* confused talk not to be understood; a mixture of two or more languages; the peculiar expressions of a party, sect, etc.

jas-mine (jăs′mĭn), *n.* a shrub with fragrant flowers. Also, **jasmin, jessamine.**

jas-per (jăs′pẽr), *n.* a many-shaded opaque kind of quartz, usually red, brown, or yellow: when polished, it is made into a variety of ornamental articles.

jaun-dice (jän′dĭs; jôn′dĭs), *n.* a disease characterized by yellowness of the eyeballs, skin, etc., caused by disorder of the bile; hence, a mental condition in which everything appears doleful, disagreeable, etc.—*adj.* **jaundiced.**

jaunt (jänt; jônt), *n.* a short excursion or ramble: *v.i.* to roam or ramble; take a short excursion or trip.

jaunt-ing car (jänt′ĭng kär), an Irish vehicle with seats on which the passengers sit sidewise, back to back.

jaun-ty (jän′tĭ; jôn′tĭ), *adj.* airy; gay; showy; stylish; as, he has a *jaunty* air.—*adv.* **jauntily.**

jave-lin (jăv′lĭn; jăv′ĕ-lĭn), *n.* a light spear intended to be thrown by the hand.

jaw (jô), *n.* either of the bones of the mouth in which the teeth are placed; mouth; maw.

jay (jā), *n.* a chattering bird akin to the magpie, with bright handsome feathers.

jeal-ous (jĕl′ŭs), *adj.* full of, or characterized by, envy or suspicious fear; unwilling to have a rival, or fearful of a rival, in affection; anxiously suspicious or watchful.—*adv.* **jealously.**

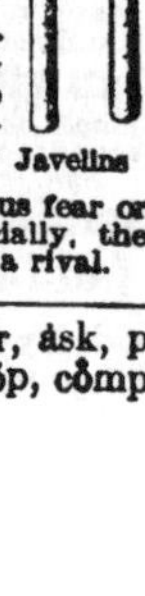

Javelins

jeal-ous-y (jĕl′ŭs-ĭ), *n.* suspicious fear or watchfulness; especially, the fear of having one's place taken by a rival.
Syn. suspicion, envy.

jean (jēn; jān), *n.* a kind of twilled cotton cloth: *pl.* a garment of this cloth; as, overalls, or blue *jeans.*

jears (jērs), *n.pl.* ropes and pulleys for moving the lower yards of a ship. Also, **jeers.**

jeer (jēr), *v.i.* to sneer at; make loud fun of; ridicule: *v.t.* to speak in a sneering or sarcastic manner: *n.* a sneer; coarse ridicule: *pl.* ropes and pulleys by which the lower yards of a vessel are raised or lowered.

Je-ho-vah (jē-hō′vȧ), *n.* a Hebrew word for the Supreme Being, thought by the Jews to be too sacred to be spoken; in the Christian use, Lord; God.

je-hu (jē′hū), *n.* one fond of driving, especially fast driving: a humorous term derived from the story of Jehu.—2 Kings ix.

je-june (jē-jōōn′), *adj.* empty; dry; without interest; as, a *jejune* tale.

je-ju-num (jē-jōō′nŭm), *n.* [*pl.* **jejuna** (-nȧ)], the middle division of the small intestine.

jel-ly (jĕl′ĭ), *n.* [*pl.* **jellies** (-ĭz)], the stiffened juice of fruit, meat, etc., after boiling; any semitransparent soft gluey substance: *v.i.* [*p.t.* and *p.p.* jellied, *p.pr.* jellying], to turn to, or become, jelly, or the consistency of jelly.

jel-ly-fish (jĕl′ĭ-fĭsh′), *n.* a small sea creature without bones and with a jellylike body.

jen-net (jĕn′ĕt), *n.* a small Spanish horse; as, old romances tell us of damsels who rode abroad on their *jennets.* Also, **genet.**

jen-ny (jĕn′ĭ), *n.* a machine for spinning; a name often used to denote a female bird; as, *jenny* jay, etc.; a female donkey.

jeop-ard (jĕp′ȧrd), *v.t.* to expose to loss or injury; risk; as, who would *jeopard* his life for nothing? Also, **jeopardize.**
Syn. peril, endanger, risk.

jeop-ard-y (jĕp′ȧr-dĭ), *n.* risk; peril; hazard; danger; as, "Why stand we in *jeopardy* every hour?"—1 Cor. xv. 30.

jer-bo-a (jẽr-bō′ȧ), *n.* a mouselike animal, having long hind legs, adapted for jumping: **Egyptian jerboa,** a burrowing animal, active at night, remarkable for its quick flying leaps.

Egyptian Jerboa

je-reed (jĕ-rēd′), *n.* a javelin or blunt kind of spear used in Turkey and Persia in mock battles; a game played with jereeds. Also, **jerrid.**

jer-e-mi-ad (jĕr′ē-mī′ăd), *n.* lamentation; a tale of sorrow, disappointment, or complaint: so called in allusion to the Book of Lamentations of Jeremiah.

Jer-e-mi-ah (jĕr′ē-mī′ȧ), *n.* a book of the Old Testament, containing the preachings and prophecies of the Hebrew prophet Jeremiah. Also, **Jeremias.**

jerk (jûrk), *v.t.* to give a sudden pull, twist, or push to; throw with a sudden quick movement; cut into long strips and dry in the sun, as beef: *n.* a sudden quick pull, twist, push, or motion; jerked beef.

jer-kin (jûr'kin), *n.* a short coat or jacket; close waistcoat; as, formerly a *jerkin* was made of buff leather.

jerk-y (jûr'kĭ), *adj.* moving with quick starts and frequent stops.—*adv.* **jerkily.**

Jer-sey (jûr'zĭ), *adj.* pertaining to the isle of Jersey, or to its breed of cattle; of or pertaining to New Jersey: *n.* a close-fitting thick woolen upper garment; fine yarn wool.

jess (jĕs), *n.* a leathern strap fastened to the leg of a hawk and provided with a ring to which is attached the leash or line wrapped around the falconer's hand.

Jes-u-it's bark (jĕz'ū-ĭts bärk), cinchona, a tree growing in the region of the Andes and yielding quinine, etc.

Je-sus (jē'zŭs), *n.* in the Bible, the Son of Mary; the founder of the Christian religion.—Matt. i. 21.

jet (jĕt), *n.* a stream of liquid suddenly thrown out; as, the whale spouts a *jet* of water; a sudden rushing forth, as of gas, etc.; a spout or nozzle through which a flow of gas, etc., is regulated; an opaque, very black mineral, akin to coal, which may be highly polished; tube for running molten metal into a mold: *v.t.* [*p.t.* and *p.p.* jetted,

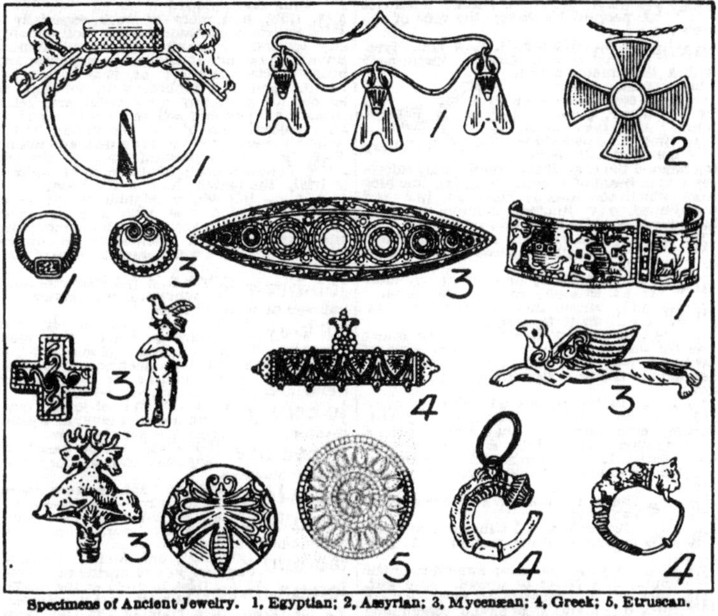

Specimens of Ancient Jewelry. 1, Egyptian; 2, Assyrian; 3, Mycenæan; 4, Greek; 5, Etruscan.

jes-sa-mine (jĕs'ȧ-mĭn), *n.* a shrub with fragrant flowers. Also, **jasmine, jasmin.**

jest (jĕst), *n.* a joke; fun; something or somebody laughed at: *v.i.* to joke; make merriment; make game of anything.
Syn. sport, divert, amuse.

jest-er (jĕs'tẽr), *n.* one who makes jokes; a court fool.

Jes-u-it (jĕz'ū-ĭt), *n.* a member of the Roman Catholic Society of Jesus, founded by Ignatius Loyola, 1534.

Jes-u-it-ic (jĕz'ū-ĭt'ĭk), *adj.* pertaining to, or resembling, the Jesuits, their principles, or practices: **jesuitic**, cunning; deceitful; crafty. Also, **Jesuitical, jesuitical.**

Jes-u-it-ism (jĕz'ū-ĭt-ĭzm), *n.* the principles, system, or practices of the Jesuits; secret diplomacy. Also, **Jesuitry.**

p.pr. jetting], to spurt out: *v.i.* to shoot or spout out; jut out.

jet-sam (jĕt'săm), *n.* that part of a ship's cargo which is thrown into the sea to lighten the vessel in case of peril; usually, such goods when washed ashore. Also, **jettison.**

jet-ti-son (jĕt'ĭ-sŭn), *n.* the act of throwing goods overboard to lighten a vessel in danger of being lost or wrecked; the goods so thrown overboard; jetsam: *v.t.* to throw overboard to lighten a vessel.

jet-ty (jĕt'ĭ), *n.* [*pl.* jetties (-ĭz)], a structure extending into the water, used as a pier, or wall, to protect a harbor or to direct currents; projection of a building: *v.i.* [*p.t.* and *p.p.* jettied, *p.pr.* jetting], to jut out or project: *adj.* made of, or like, jet.

Jew (jū; jōō), *n.* [*fem.* Jewess], an Israelite; Hebrew; as, Shylock is perhaps the most famous *Jew* in literature.

jew-el (jū'ĕl; jōō'ĕl), *n.* a valuable ornament; gem; precious stone; anything of great value or dear to one: *v.t.* to adorn with, or as with, gems; furnish with gems.

jew-el-er (jū'ĕl-ẽr; jōō'ĕl-ẽr), *n.* one who makes or deals in valuable ornaments, gems, etc. Also, **jeweller.**

jew-el-ry (jū'ĕl-rĭ; jōō'ĕl-rĭ), *n.* precious stones, ornaments of gold and silver, etc., taken collectively; the art or trade of a jeweler. Also, **jewellery.**

Jew-ish (jū'ĭsh; jōō'ĭsh), *adj.* pertaining to, or like, the Jews, their language, customs, etc.

Jew-ry (jū'rĭ; jōō'rĭ), *n.* Judea; a district peopled by Jews; the race of the Hebrews.

jew's-harp (jūz'härp"), *n.* a small lyre-shaped musical instrument with a thin metal tongue which, when placed between the teeth and struck by the finger, gives forth tones. Also, **jews'-harp.**

Jew's Harp

jib (jĭb), *n.* a large three-cornered sail projecting beyond the edge of the vessel; the projecting arm or beam of a crane or lifting machine from which the load is hung: *v.i.* [*p.t.* and *p.p.* jibbed, *p.pr.* jibbing], to move restlessly backwards or sideways: said of a horse.

jib boom (jĭb bōōm), a spar on which the jib, or three-cornered sail, of a vessel is set.

jibe (jīb), *n.* a scoff; taunt: *v.t.* to sneer at: *v.i.* to scoff; sneer. Also, **gibe.**

jif-fy (jĭf'ĭ), *n.* an instant; moment; as, I will do it in a *jiffy.*

jig (jĭg), *n.* a quick lively dance, or music for such a dance; a particular kind of fishhook: *v.i.* [*p.t.* and *p.p.* jigged, *p.pr.* jigging], to dance a jig: *v.t.* to jerk up and down.

jig-ger (jĭg'ẽr), *n.* one who jigs; a name for various mechanical contrivances, especially one that works with a jerky motion; a golf club; a small insect, or mite, found in the southern United States, which burrows under the skin: properly spelled *chigoe.*

jig-gle (jĭg'l), *v.t.* and *v.i.* to move slightly and jerkily.

jig-jog (jĭg'jŏg"), *n.* a jolting motion: *adj.* having a jolting motion: *adv.* joltingly.

jill (jĭl), *n.* a young woman; sweetheart; the female of a ferret or weasel. Also, **gill.**

jilt (jĭlt), *n.* a coquette or flirt: *v.t.* to discard (a lover) after having encouraged him: *v.i.* to play the jilt; practice deception in love.

jim-my (jĭm'ĭ), *n.* a short crowbar used by burglars.

Jim-son weed (jĭm'sn wēd), a tall, coarse, poisonous weed, with white, trumpet-shaped flowers.

jin-gle (jĭn'gl), *n.* a sharp tinkling metallic sound; a little bell or rattle; meaningless rime; a covered two-wheeled Irish car: *v.i.* to give a tinkling sound: *v.t.* to cause to give a tinkling sound; as, the sleigh bells *jingle.*

jin-go (jĭn'gō), *n.* [*pl.* jingoes (-gōz)], one of a political party who, at the time of the Russo-Turkish War of 1877-78, wished Great Britain to go to war with Russia: named from a popular song of the day; hence, one who favors or supports a warlike policy in foreign affairs; one who boasts noisily of the prowess of his country: by **jingo**, a mild oath.

jin-go-ism (jĭn'gō-ĭzm), *n.* the military spirit of the man who boasts of what he thinks his country can do in war.

jin-ni (jĭn'ĭ), *n.* [*pl.* jinn (jĭn)], a spirit subject to magic control, which often appears in Oriental tales. Also, **jinnee, genie.**

jin-rik-i-sha (jĭn-rĭk'ĭ-shä), *n.* a small Japanese two-wheeled carriage, drawn by one or more men. Also, **jinriksha.**

jit-ney (jĭt'nĭ), *n.* a passenger automobile; a five-cent fare for a motor ride.

jo (jō), *n.* [*pl.* joes (jōz)], a sweetheart of either sex. [Scot.]

job (jŏb), *n.* a piece of work, especially of an odd or occasional kind; colloquially, any scheme for making money or securing private advantage at the public expense; any event or circumstance; as, it is a bad *job* *v.t.* [*p.t.* and *p.p.* jobbed, *p.pr.* jobbing], to let out for hire; buy up (goods) and retail (them): *v.i.* buy and sell, as a stockbroker; do an occasional piece of work for wages; let out or hire horses; work for one's own advantage.

Job (jōb), *n.* a poetical book of the Old Testament, teaching lessons of patience in trial; the patient hero of the book.

job-ber (jŏb'ẽr), *n.* a middleman; especially, one who acts as agent between a stockbroker and the public; one who transacts public business for his own private interests; one who does odd pieces of work for hire.

job-ber-y (jŏb'ẽr-ĭ), *n.* [*pl.* jobberies (-ĭz)], low scheming for private advantage or political ends.

jock-ey (jŏk'ĭ), *n.* [*pl.* jockeys (-ĭz)], one who rides a horse in a race; groom; a dealer in horses; cheat: *v.t.* [*p.t.* and *p.p.* jockeyed, *p.pr.* jockeying], to cheat or deceive; jostle against and hinder by riding unfairly: *v.i.* to cheat, be tricky.

jo-cose (jō-kōs'), *adj.* full of jokes; sportive; humorous; merry; as, a *jocose* manner; *jocose* remark.—*adv.* **jocosely.**

jo-cos-i-ty (jō-kŏs'ĭ-tĭ), *n.* the quality of being humorous, gay, or merry. Also, **jocoseness.**

joc-u-lar (jŏk'ū-lȧr), *adj.* making jokes; done in joke.—*adv.* **jocularly.**

joc-u-lar-i-ty (jŏk"ū-lăr'ĭ-tĭ), *n.* merriment; quality of being humorous or inclined to joke.

joc-und (jŏk'ŭnd), *adj.* jovial; sportive; gay; as, *jocund* spring or dances.

jo-cun-di-ty (jō-kŭn'dĭ-tĭ), *n.* the quality of being merry; sportiveness.

Jo-el (jō'ĕl), *n.* a book of the Old Testament, recording the preachings of the Hebrew prophet Joel.

jog (jŏg), *v.t.* [*p.t.* and *p.p.* jogged, *p.pr.* jogging], to push or shake slightly, usually with the elbow or hand, by way of reminder; to call the attention to: *v.i.* to travel along with a slow trotting motion: *n.* a slight push or shake; slow trot.

jog-gle (jŏg'l), *v.t.* to shake slightly; nudge: *v.i.* to totter: *n.* a sudden shake or push.

John (jŏn), *n.* in the Bible, a son of Zebedee, one of the twelve apostles; the fourth Gospel, prepared by the apostle John; three other short books in the New Testament, containing Epistles, or letters, written by the apostle John, who was the author, also, of the book of Revelation; a preacher of repentance who preceded Jesus, called John the Baptist.—Matt. iii.

John Bull (jŏn bŏŏl), the English people personified, or a typical Englishman. [Colloq.]

john-ny-cake (jŏn'ĭ-kāk"), *n.* a flat Indian corn meal cake, mixed with milk or water, quickly prepared at an ordinary fire.

join (join), *v.t.* to unite; connect; to make act, hold, appear, etc., together as one; add or annex; become connected with; as, to *join* a club; to unite in marriage: *v.i.* be in contact; become associated or united; to come together as one: *n.* a joint or union.

join-der (join'dẽr), *n.* in law, the joining of two or more causes of action.

join-er (join'ẽr), *n.* one who, or that which, fastens together; especially, a skilled workman who finishes the woodwork for houses, etc.

join-er-y (join'ẽr-ĭ), *n.* skilled work in wood; the art of finishing and covering rough lumber.

joint (joint), *n.* the place where two or more things join; the point where two bones of the body are joined so as to allow motion; the part included between two joints or two knots; as, a *joint* in a grass stem; hinge; an opening which divides rock masses into blocks; a large piece of meat cut for roasting; slang, a place for low amusements: *adj.* produced by the action of two or more; united in or sharing: *v.t.* to form with, or unite by, joints; cut or divide into joints, as meat: **joint-stock company**, a company consisting of a number of persons doing business for gain, the shares owned by any member being transferable without the consent of the others. —*adv.* **jointly.**

join-ture (join'tūr), *n.* land or houses settled on a woman in consideration of her marriage, to be enjoyed by her after the death of her husband: *v.t.* to settle property upon (a wife).

joist (joist), *n.* a horizontal timber to which the boards of a floor or laths of a ceiling are fastened: *v.t.* to furnish with joists.

joke (jōk), *n.* something said or done to cause mirth; jest; sport: *v.i.* to jest: *v.t.* to make fun of.

jok-er (jōk'ẽr), *n.* a jester; an extra card used in certain card games.

jol-li-fi-ca-tion (jŏl"ĭ-fĭ-kā'shŭn), *n.* merrymaking; festivity.

jol-li-ty (jŏl'ĭ-tĭ), *n.* the state of being merry, gay, or sportive.

jol-ly (jŏl'ĭ), *adj.* [*comp.* jollier, *superl.* jolliest], full of life and mirth; gay; causing mirth; companionable: *v.t.* [*p.t.* and *p.p.* jollied, *p.pr.* jollying], slang, to make good-humored fun of.

jol-ly-boat (jŏl'ĭ-bōt"), *n.* a ship's small boat, used for general or rough work.

jolt (jōlt), *v.t.* to shake by sudden jerks: *v.i.* to have a jerky motion: *n.* a sudden jerk.

Jo-nah (jō'nȧ), *n.* a book of the Old Testament which tells the story of a lesser Hebrew prophet, Jonah, who, fleeing on a ship in disobedience to God, was thrown overboard as being the cause of a perilous storm, and was swallowed by a whale; hence, any person who brings ill luck.

Jon-a-than (jŏn'ȧ-thăn), *n.* in the Bible, the son of King Saul and close friend of David.—1 Samuel xviii-xx; 2 Samuel i. 26.

jon-quil (jŏn'kwĭl; jŭn'kwĭl), *n.* a plant of the narcissus family with yellow or white fragrant flowers. Also, **jonquille.**

jo-rum (jō'rŭm), *n.* a large drinking bowl, or that which it contains. [Colloq.]

Jo-seph (jō'zĕf), *n.* in the Bible, a Hebrew patriarch, the son of Jacob.—Genesis xxxvii-l; the husband of Mary, mother of Jesus.—Matt. i. 18–25; the rich man of Arimathea who buried Jesus.—Matt. xxvii. 57–60.

Josh-u-a (jŏsh'ū-ȧ), *n.* a book of the Old Testament, giving the history of the conquest of Canaan and the settlement of the Israelites in the promised land; the successor of Moses, who led the Israelites into Canaan, and whose name is given to the book.

joss (jŏs), *n.* a Chinese household divinity or idol: **joss house**, a Chinese temple: **joss stick**, Chinese incense stick.

jos-tle (jŏs'l), *v.t.* to push against; to run against and shake; to elbow.

jot (jŏt), *v.t.* [*p.t.* and *p.p.* jotted, *p.pr.* jotting], to make a memorandum of: with *down:* *n.* a tittle or very small particle; as, one *jot* or one tittle shall in no wise pass from the law.—Matt. v. 18.

jounce (jouns), *v.t.* and *v.i.* to shake up and down; to jolt: *n.* a jolt.

jour-nal (jûr'năl), *n.* a record of news or events; a daily newspaper or other periodical; diary; a book in which particular transactions are entered from the daybook; a ship's logbook.

jour-nal-ism (jûr'năl-ĭzm), *n.* the collection and publication at stated times of current news; the influence exercised by such literature; the profession of publishing, editing, or writing for, newspapers.

jour-nal-ist (jûr'năl-ĭst), *n.* an editor of, or contributor to, a newspaper; one who keeps a daily record of events.

jour-nal-is-tic (jûr"năl-ĭs'tĭk), *adj.* relating to newspapers, their makers, or the profession of making them.

jour-ney (jûr'nĭ), *n.* passage from one place to another; amount or time of travel; a day's work or travel: *v.i.* to travel from one place to another.
Syn. travel, tour, passage.

jour-ney-man (jûr'nĭ-măn), *n.* [*pl.* journeymen (-mĕn)], a mechanic who has served his apprenticeship or learned a trade and works, especially by the day, for another.

joust (jŭst; jōōst), *n.* a combat with lances between two knights on horseback; especially, a mock combat in the lists, or inclosed field, as part of a tournament or display; as, the *jousts* at King Arthur's court: *v.t.* to engage in such a combat. Also, **just.**

Jove (jōv), *n.* in Roman mythology, Jupiter, the greatest of the gods.

jo-vi-al (jō'vĭ-ăl), *adj.* jolly; merry; as, he was always a *jovial* comrade. —*adv.* **jovially.**—*n.* **joviality.**

jowl (jōl), *n.* the jaw or cheek; as, a man with a heavy *jowl;* head of a fish, cooked.

joy (joi), *n.* gaiety; gladness: *v.i.* to rejoice or be glad; as, to *joy* in happiness.
Syn., *n.* pleasure, mirth, delight.
Ant. (see grief).

joy-ful (joi'fŏŏl), *adj.* full of gladness; as, schooldays are the *joyful* days.—*adv.* **joyfully.**—*n.* **joyfulness.**

joy-less (joi'lĕs), *adj.* without gladness; gloomy; despairing.—*adv.* **joylessly.**—*n.* **joylessness.**

joy-ous (joi'ŭs), *adj.* glad; causing happiness; full of delight.—*adv.* **joyously.**—*n.* **joyousness.**

joy stick (joi stĭk), the lever in an airplane which corresponds to the steering wheel of an automobile.

ju-bi-lant (jōō'bĭ-lănt), *adj.* uttering songs of triumph; shouting with joy; exultingly glad.—*adv.* **jubilantly.**

ju-bi-late (jōō'bĭ-lāt), *v.i.* to utter triumphant rejoicing: *n.* (jū"bĭ-lä'tē; yōō"bē-lä'tā), the 100th Psalm: from its opening word in the Latin version; hence, a hymn of rejoicing.

ju-bi-la-tion (jōō"bĭ-lā'shŭn), *n.* a shouting for joy; expression of triumph.

ju-bi-lee (jōō'bĭ-lē), *n.* a Jewish festival celebrated every fiftieth year, to commemorate the deliverance of the Israelites from Egyptian bondage; the fiftieth anniversary of any event; a year of special indulgence granted by the Pope every twenty-fifth year.

Ju-da-ic (jōō'dā'ĭk), *adj.* pertaining to the Jews. Also, **Judaical.**

Ju-da-ize (jōō'dā-īz), *v.i.* to be converted to the ceremonies and doctrines of the Jews: *v.t.* to convert to Judaism.

Ju-da-ism (jōō'dā-ĭzm), *n.* the religious ceremonies and doctrines of the Jews.

Ju-das (jōō'dȧs), *n.* in the Bible, the disciple who betrayed Jesus; hence, one who betrays another under pretense of friendship.

Jude (jōōd), *n.* a book of the New Testament, containing the Epistle, or letter, written by Jude to the Christian believers.

Ju-de-an (jōō-dē'ăn), *adj.* pertaining to Judea, the land of Judah, one of the sons of Jacob. Also, **Judaean.**

judge (jŭj), *n.* the presiding official in a court of law, having authority to hear and decide civil and criminal causes; a person appointed to decide in a trial of skill, speed, etc., between two or more persons; one who has skill, knowledge, or experience to decide on the quality or value of anything; as, a *judge* of poetry; one of the chief rulers of the Israelites from the death of Joshua to the kingship of Saul: **Judges,** a book of the Old Testament, giving the history of the Jews during the time of the judges, from Joshua to Samuel: *v.t.* to examine and pass sentence upon; hold an opinion upon; consider; come to a conclusion concerning; to decide with authority; as, to *judge* a case: *v.i.* to form an opinion or decision after careful consideration; hear and determine a case and pass sentence.

Syn., *n.* justice, referee, arbitrator.

Judge Ad-vo-cate (jŭj ăd'vō-kāt), an officer of the government in the trial by court martial of an officer or soldier.

judg-ment (jŭj'mĕnt), *n.* the act of deciding or passing sentence; the decision of a court; mental power of deciding correctly by the comparison of facts and ideas; intelligence; criticism; opinion; punishment inflicted by God: **the Judgment,** the final trial of mankind by God.

Syn. discernment, discrimination, understanding.

ju-di-ca-ture (jōō'dĭ-kȧ-tŭr), *n.* a court of justice; power of doing justice by legal trial and judgment.

ju-di-cial (jōō-dĭsh'ăl), *adj.* pertaining to the administration of justice or to a judge; proceeding from, or inflicted by, a court of justice; impartial.—*adv.* **judicially.**

ju-di-ci-a-ry (jōō-dĭsh'ĭ-ā-rĭ), *n.* judges collectively; that branch of a government concerned with the carrying out of civil and criminal law: *adj.* pertaining to courts of justice; judicial.

ju-di-cious (jōō-dĭsh'ŭs), *adj.* prudent; wise; done with good judgment or discretion; as, a *judicious* choice.

jug (jŭg), *n.* an earthenware or metal vessel with a handle, used to carry liquids; slang, a prison or jail: *v.t.* to put into, or cook in, a jug; slang, to commit to jail.

Jug-ger-naut (jŭg'ĕr-nôt), *n.* the chief Hindu idol, under whose car wheels worshipers were supposed to sacrifice themselves; a custom or belief demanding victims; an object of blind devotion. Also, **Jagannath.**

jug-gle (jŭg'l), *v.t.* to cheat by tricks. to perform tricks with: *v.i.* to perform tricks by sleight of hand; to conjure: *n.* a trick by sleight of hand; imposture.

jug-gler (jŭg'lĕr), *n.* a conjurer; one who is skilled in sleight of hand tricks.

jug-gler-y (jŭg'lĕr-ĭ), *n.* [*pl.* **juggleries** (-ĭz)], magic, trickery; sleight of hand; deception.

Ju-go-Slav (yū'gō-slăv), *n.* one of the southern Slavs or Serbs, a race which includes the Serbo-Croatians, Bulgarians, and Slovenes.

ju-gu-lar (jōō'gū-lȧr), *adj.* pertaining to the neck or throat; connected with the large (jugular) vein, which returns the blood from the head: *n.* a jugular vein.

juice (jōōs), *n.* the fluid contents of plant or animal structures, consisting of water in which is dissolved sugar or other substances; slang, electric current.

juic-y (jōōs'ĭ), *adj.* full of fluid; as, *juicy* fruit; full of interest or scandal; as, a *juicy* bit of gossip.—*n.* **juiciness.**

ju-jube (jōō'jōōb), *n.* a kind of lozenge or small tablet flavored with, or in imitation of, the jujube fruit; the eatable fruit of a shrub or tree of the Mediterranean

ju-jut-su (jōō'jōōt"sōō), *n.* the Japanese art of wrestling, which opposes knowledge and skill to animal strength. Also, **jiujutsu.**

ju-lep (jōō'lĕp), *n.* a drink composed of brandy or whisky sweetened and flavored; a mixture of sugar and water in which medicine is given.

Jul-ian (jōōl'yăn), *adj.* pertaining to Julius Cæsar, or to the calendar as adjusted by Julius Cæsar, 46 B. C.: replaced by the Gregorian year (New Style) in England. 1752.

ju-lienne (zhü"lyĕn'; jōō"lĭ-ĕn'), *n.* a clear meat soup, with chopped vegetables, especially carrots; a method of frying potatoes after cutting them into long narrow strips.

Ju-ly (jōō-lī'), *n.* the seventh month of the year, so named from Julius Cæsar

jum-ble (jŭm'bl), *n.* a confused mass, mixture, or collection; disorder; a kind of thin cake: *v.t.* to mix in a confused mass; throw together without order: *v.i.* to mix or unite confusedly.

jum-bo (jŭm'bō), *n.* a huge person or animal: from the name (Jumbo) of the largest elephant ever in captivity.

jump (jŭmp), *n.* a spring or bound; the space jumped; a slipping of masses of rock in a mine: *v.t.* to cause to spring or bound; leap over; to take possession of (a mining claim) during the absence of the owner: *v.i.* to spring upward or forward.

jump-er (jŭm'pẽr), *n.* one who, or that which, jumps; a name applied to certain religious sects who practice dancing under religious excitement; a hooded fur jacket, worn in Arctic regions; a sort of blouse or loose jacket worn by workmen over their ordinary dress to protect it; a decorative, sleeveless, or short-sleeved, low-necked waist, worn by women and children.

junc-tion (jŭnk'shŭn), *n.* the act of being joined; union; a point or place of union; as, the *junction* of two rivers.

junc-ture (jŭnk'tůr), *n.* the point or line at which two bodies are joined; joint; particular or critical occasion.

June (jōōn), *n.* the sixth month of the year; as, there are thirty days in *June*.

jun-gle (jŭn'gl), *n.* a close, tropical thicket of forest trees, brushwood, tall grasses, etc.

jun-ior (jōōn'yẽr), *adj.* younger; of lower standing; as, the *junior* partner in a firm; belonging to youth: *n.* the younger of two; one of lower standing; in American colleges and high schools, a student in the next to the last year.

ju-ni-per (jōō'nĭ-pẽr), *n.* an evergreen shrub, the berries of which are used in flavoring gin.

junk (jŭnk), *n.* short pieces of old cable, rope, etc., used for making mats, oakum, etc.; hard salt ship beef; a Chinese flat-bottomed vessel with a square bow and high stern, having the mast in one piece; old metal, paper, glass, etc.

Junk-er (yŏŏng'kẽr), *n.* a member of the aristocratic party in Prussia, which came into power in 1862.

Junk-er-ism (yŏŏng'kẽr-ĭzm), *n.* the political and social theories of the aristocratic party in Prussia.

jun-ket (jŭn'kĕt), *n.* a preparation of curdled milk and cream; a kind of sweetmeat; excursion; picnic: *v.i.* to take part in an excursion or picnic.

Ju-no (jōō'nō), *n.* in Roman mythology, the goddess of marriage and childbirth, wife of Jupiter, god of the heavens; identified with the Greek Hera.

jun-ta (jŭn'tȧ), *n.* an assembly or council for making laws; as, the Cuban *junta*.

jun-to (jŭn'tō), *n.* [*pl.* juntos (-tōz)], a number of men secretly combined for some purpose, especially a political one.

Ju-pi-ter (jōō'pĭ-tẽr), *n.* in Roman mythology, the god of the heavens: identified with the Greek Zeno; the largest planet, and, except Venus, the brightest.

ju-rid-i-cal (jōō-rĭd'ĭ-kăl), *adj.* pertaining to law or to the proceedings of law courts: as, *juridical* days are days on which the courts are open.

ju-ris-dic-tion (jōō'rĭs-dĭk'shŭn), *n.* legal authority; extent of power; as, the *jurisdiction* of a court or state; the district over which any authority extends.

ju-ris-pru-dence (jōō'rĭs-prōō'dĕns), *n.* the science of law; system of laws of a country.

ju-rist (jōō'rĭst), *n.* one skilled in the science of law; as, Blackstone was a great English *jurist*.

ju-ror (jōō'rẽr), *n.* a juryman; one who serves on a jury.

ju-ry (jōō'rĭ), *n.* a body of men, usually twelve, selected according to law, and sworn to inquire into, or decide on, the evidence in a case of law before them; a committee of experts selected to award prizes, to adjudge the value of land, etc.

ju-ry-man (jōō'rĭ-măn), *n.* a juror; one who serves on a jury.

ju-ry mast (jōō'rĭ măst), a temporary mast in place of one that has been broken or carried away.

just (jŭst), *adj.* according to divine or human laws; upright; giving to every man his due; faithful; exact; regular; fair: *adv.* exactly; barely; nearly; almost; perfectly.—*adv.* **justly.**—*n.* **justness.**

just (jŭst), *v.i.* to tilt with lances on horseback: *n.pl.* a tournament. Also, **joust.**

jus-tice (jŭs'tĭs), *n.* the quality of being fair; uprightness in dealing with others; absolute fairness; a judge or magistrate.

Syn. equity, right.
Ant. (see injustice).

jus-ti-ci-a-ry (jŭs-tĭsh'ĭ-â-rĭ), *n.* [*pl.* justiciaries (-rĭz)], a judge: *adj.* pertaining to law or the work of the courts. Also, **justiciar.**

jus-ti-fi-a-ble (jŭs'tĭ-fī'ȧ-bl), *adj.* capable of being shown to be right; excusable; as, the killing of a man in self-defense is considered by law to be *justifiable*.—*adv.* **justifiably.**—*n.* **justifiableness.**

jus-ti-fi-ca-tion (jŭs'tĭ-fĭ-kā'shŭn), *n.* the act of showing a thing to be right; acceptable excuse; defense; as, there is no *justification* for his disobedience.—*adj.* **justificatory.**

jus-ti-fy (jŭs'tĭ-fī), *v.t.* [*p.t.* and *p.p.* justified, *p.pr.* justifying], to show or prove to be right; as, to *justify* the ways of God to men; pardon; pronounce free from blame; *v.i.* in printing, to make even by spacing properly, as lines, or type.

jut (jŭt), *v.i.* [*p.t.* and *p.p.* jutted, *p.pr.* jutting], to project beyond the main body; as, a rock *juts* out from a mountain side.

jute (jōōt), *n.* the fiber of an East Indian plant used for ropes, bagging, mats, etc.—**Jute,** a member of a Low German tribe living in Jutland, some of whom, with the Angles and Saxons, invaded, and settled in, Britain.

ju-ve-nes-cence (jōō'vē-nĕs'ĕns), *n.* a growing young again.

ju-ve-nes-cent (jōō'vē-nĕs'ĕnt), *adj.* becoming young again.

ju-ve-nile (jōō'vē-nĭl; jōō'vē-nīl), *adj.* youthful; characteristic of, or suitable to, youth; as, *juvenile* books: *n.* a young person; a book for children.

ju-ve-nil-i-ty (jōō'vē-nĭl'ĭ-tĭ), *n.* youthfulness; youth.

jux-ta-po-si-tion (jŭks'tȧ-pō-zĭsh'ŭn), *n.* a placing close together; state of being close together.

K

Ka-a-ba (kä'ȧ-bȧ; kä'bȧ), *n.* the shrine at Mecca towards which all Mohammedans turn when praying. Also, **Caaba.**

Ka-fir (kä'fẽr), *n.* a member of one of the negroid tribes of South Africa; their language; one of a non-Mohammedan race of Northern Afghanistan; an infidel, or one who is not a Mohammedan. Also, **Kaffir, Kaffre.**

kaf-tan (käf'tȧn; käf-tän'), *n.* a kind of long gown worn in Oriental countries. Also, **caftan.**

kai-ser (kī'zẽr), *n.* emperor; the title of the emperors of Germany and Austria: **kaiserism,** autocratic despotism.

ka-ki (kä'kē"), *n.* the Chinese or Japanese date plum, bearing a fruit about the size of a small apple.

kale (kāl), *n.* any kind of cabbage with open curled leaves. Also, **kail.**

ka-lei-do-scope (kȧ-lī'dō-skōp), *n.* an instrument containing small bits of colored glass, which, by an arrangement of mirrors, are caused to appear in a variety of beautiful patterns.

ka-lei-do-scop-ic (kȧ-lī"dō-skŏp'ĭk), *adj.* constantly moving and changing; changingly beautiful; as, a *kaleidoscopic* pattern.

kal-en-dar (kăl'ĕn-dȧr), *n.* a system of dividing time into years, months, etc., so as to fix dates; a table or set of tables, showing the divisions of a given year, with the days of the week on which dates fall. Also, **calendar.**

ka-lif (kā'lĭf; kăl'ĭf), *n.* in Mohammedan countries, one who has civil and religious authority. Also, **caliph.**

ka-me-rad (kä-mĕ-răt'), *n.* comrade: the expression used by a German soldier in surrendering. [Ger.]

ka-mis (kȧ-mēs'), *n.* a long, loose shirt with sleeves, worn by Mohammedans. Also, **camise.**

Kan-a-ka (kăn'ȧ-kȧ; kȧ-năk'ȧ), *n.* a Hawaiian Islander; a South Sea Islander. Also, **Kanacka.**

kan-ga-roo (kăn"gȧ-rōō'), *n.* an animal peculiar to Australia, having short fore legs, and long, powerful hind legs with which it leaps.

Kangaroo

ka-o-lin (kā'ō-lĭn; kä'ō-lĭn), *n.* a very pure white clay used to form the paste from which porcelain is made. Also, **kaoline.**

ka-ra-kul (kä"rȧ-kōōl'), *n.* a fine grade of astrakhan. Also, **caracul.**

kar-at (kăr'ăt), *n.* a unit of weight for precious stones: a term used to express the fineness of gold used in jewelry. Also, **carat.**

ka-ty-did (kā'tĭ-dĭd"), *n.* a large, green, tree insect which makes a shrill sound similar to the words "Katy did."

kay-ak (kī'ăk), *n.* a hunting canoe made of sealskin, used in arctic America. Also, **kaiak, kajak, kyack.**

kedge (kĕj), *n.* a small anchor used in light work: *v.t.* to move (a vessel, raft, etc.) by carrying a small anchor out in a boat, dropping it overboard, and hauling the vessel up to it.

keel (kēl), *n.* the chief and lowest timber or steel plate of a vessel, extending from stem to stern and supporting the whole frame; hence, a ship; in an airship, the lowest and central part of the body of the machine, which helps to keep the balance; a broad, flat vessel used on the Maine coast: *v.t.* to furnish with a keel: *v.i.* to turn up the keel; turn over.

keel-haul (kēl'hôl"), *v.t.* to drag under water beneath the bottom of a ship from one side to the other: formerly, a naval punishment; to rebuke sternly.

keel-son (kĕl'sŭn), *n.* a beam or timber laid on the middle of the floor timbers over the keel of a vessel to strengthen it. Also, **kelson.**

keen (kēn), *adj.* sharp; eager; as, *keen* interest; piercing; bitter; as, *keen* wind; acute; as, *keen* eyesight: *n.* in Ireland, a shrill bitter wail: *v.i.* to wail loudly.—*adv.* **keenly.** —*n.* **keenness.**

keep (kēp), *v.t.* [*p.t.* and *p.p.* **kept,** *p.pr.* keeping], to have the care of; guard; preserve; support; perform or observe; as, to *keep* a rule; maintain; as, to *keep* a servant; fulfil; as, to *keep* a promise; supply with the necessaries of life; detain; confine; hold back; as, to *keep* a secret: *v.i.* to remain in any state or condition; as, she *keeps* cheerful; stay: *n.* means or provision by which one is kept; the stronghold or donjon of an ancient castle.

Syn., v. preserve, save.

Ant. (see abandon).

keep-er (kēp'ẽr), *n.* one who guards, maintains, takes care of, etc.; as, the *keeper* in a prison.

keep-ing (kēp'ĭng), *n.* care; custody; charge; means of life; the condition of being fitting or becoming; as, gay music is not in *keeping* with sorrow.

keep-sake (kēp'săk"), *n.* something kept, or given to be kept, for the sake of the giver.

keg (kĕg), *n.* a small, strong barrel, usually containing from five to ten gallons.

kelp (kĕlp), *n.* the ashes of seaweeds, from which iodine is obtained; a large brown seaweed.

kel-pie (kĕl'pĭ), *n.* an evil water sprite, elf, or spirit, supposed to take the form of a horse, and believed to warn people who are to be drowned. Also, **kelpy.**

Kelt (kĕlt), *n.* a member of one of the primitive races of central and western Europe, from which are descended the Bretons, Welsh, Irish, and Gaelic Scotch; a member of one of these modern races; a person who speaks a Celtic language, or one derived from the early Celts. Also, **Celt.**—*adj* **Celtic, Keltic.**

ken (kĕn), *n.* view; knowledge: *v.t.* and *v.i.* [*p.t.* and *p.p.* kenned, *p.pr.* kenning], to know; understand. [Scot.]

ken-nel (kĕn'ĕl), *n.* a house for a dog or dogs; a place where dogs are bred and reared; hiding place of a fox; street gutter; vile lodging: *v.t.* to confine in a kennel: *v.i.* to live in a kennel.

ke-no (kē'nō), *n.* a game of chance played with numbered balls and cards.

ke-ram-ic (kē-răm'ĭk), *adj.* made of, or belonging to, pottery: *n.pl.* the art of making pottery. Also, **ceramic.**

kerb (kûrb), *n.* a restraint; the rein attached to a horse's bit; a border of stones, etc., at the edge of a sidewalk: *v.t.* to restrain; to make a stone edge to, as a sidewalk. Also, **curb.**

ker-chief (kûr'chĭf), *n.* a square of cloth worn by women on the head or about the neck.

ker-mes (kûr'mēz), *n.* the dried bodies of certain insects, furnishing a scarlet dye; a Mediterranean oak on which the kermes insect lives.

ker-mess (kûr'mĕs), *n.* a festival or fair; originally, a church festival. Also, **kirmess.**

kern (kûrn), *n.* the overhanging part of a type; formerly, an Irish foot soldier; in Scotland, the last sheaf of the harvest.

ker-nel (kûr'nĕl), *n.* a grain or seed; the eatable substance of a nut or fruit stone; the part of anything which is most full of meaning; as, the *kernel* of an argument.

Kestrel

ker-o-sene (kĕr'ō-sēn'), *n.* a refined oil used extensively for burning in lamps.

Ker-ry (kĕr'ĭ), *n.* an Irish breed of cattle Kerry.

ker-sey (kûr'zĭ), *n.* a coarse woolen cloth of light weight.

ker-sey-mere (kûr'zĭ-mēr), *n.* a light-weight woolen cloth used for men's garments. Also, **cassimere.**

kes-trel (kĕs'trĕl), *n.* a common European falcon, of small size and reddish color.

ketch (kĕch), *n.* a stoutly-built, two-masted, sailing vessel; in England, a hangman.

ketch-up (kĕch'ŭp), *n.* a sauce prepared from tomatoes, mushrooms, etc. Also, **catsup, catchup.**

ket-tle (kĕt'l), *n.* a metal vessel for boiling liquids; a teakettle; a tin pail.

ket-tle-drum (kĕt'l-drŭm"), *n.* a drum made of a hollow hemisphere of copper or brass with parchment stretched over the opening; afternoon tea party.

Kettledrum

key (kē), *n.* a metal instrument for turning a lock; an instrument by which something is turned, secured, or operated upon; that which allows or hinders entrance; as, Liège was the *key* to Belgium; solution; as, the *key* to a riddle; an exact translation; a low, small island; as, the Florida *keys;* a system of musical tones based on their relation to a note, called a keynote, from which the system is named; as, the *key* of G major; general pitch or tone of voice; as, men naturally speak in a lower *key* than women; a small lever, as in a piano, typewriter, etc., by which the instrument is made to act: *v.t.* to regulate the tone of.

Ward-lock Key and Keyhole. *A*, main ward or bridge; *B*, stem or body; *C*, pin; *D*, collar; *E*, bit or web; *F*, bow; *G*, eye; *H*, slot.

key-board (kē'bōrd"), *n.* the row of keys on a piano; the manual of an organ; the bank of keys of a typewriter, etc.

key-hole (kē'hōl"), *n.* a small opening in which a key is inserted to turn a lock.

key-note (kē'nōt"), *n.* the basal note in a system of musical notes; ruling principle.

key-stone (kē'stōn"), *n.* the central or wedge-shaped stone at the center of the crown of an arch.

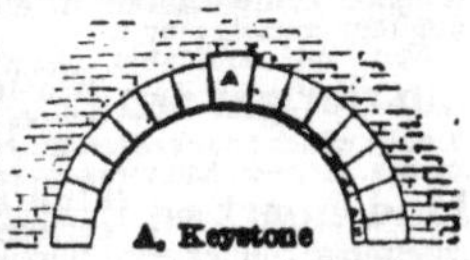

A, Keystone

kha-ki (kä'kē), *n.* a light drab-colored cloth, much used for uniforms; collectively, uniforms of this cloth; as, the boys in *khaki:* *adj.* of the color of dust.

khan (kän; kăn), *n.* an Asiatic prince, chief, or governor; in the Orient, an inn for the accommodation of travelers.

khe-dive (kĕ-dēv'), *n.* the official title of the ruler of Egypt.

kick (kĭk), *n.* a blow with the foot; a spring backward: *v.t.* to strike with the foot: *v.i.* resist; spring back.

kick-shaw (kĭk'shô"), *n.* something fanciful or out of the way; a delicacy.

kid (kĭd), *n.* the young of the goat; this animal's soft skin used for gloves, etc.; a small wooden tub; slang, a child: *adj.* made of kid: *v.t.* [*p.t.* and *p.p.* kidded, *p.pr.* kidding], to furnish or cover with kid; slang, humbug.

kid-nap (kĭd'năp"), *v.t.* [*p.t.* and *p.p.* kidnaped, *p.pr.* kidnaping], to steal, carry away, or disappear with: used of a human being, especially of a child.—*n.* **kidnaper.**

kid-ney (kĭd'nĭ), *n.* [*pl.* **kidneys** (-nĭz)], one of two oblong flattened organs which separate the urine from the blood; anything resembling a kidney; sort or kind; disposition.

kill (kĭl), *v.t.* to take life from; destroy; slay: *n.* a creek or channel; as, Cats*kill;* Schuyl*kill;* in fox-hunting, the death; as, to be in at the *kill.*—*n.* **killer.**

Syn., *v.* assassinate, murder, slay.

kiln (kĭl; kĭln), *n.* a furnace, oven, or pile for burning, drying, or hardening; as, bricks are dried in a *kiln.*

kil-o-gram (kĭl'ō-grăm), *n.* a thousand grams, equal to 2.2046 pounds. Also, **kilogramme.**

kil-o-li-ter (kĭl'ō-lē"tĕr), *n.* a thousand liters, equal to one cubic meter, or 264.18 gallons. Also, **kilolitre.**

kil-o-me-ter (kĭl'ō-mē'tẽr), *n.* a thousand meters, 3,280.8 feet, or 0.62137 mile. Also, **kilometre.**—*adj.* **kilometric, kilometrical.**

kil-o-watt (kĭl'ō-wŏt'), *n.* a unit for measuring the power of an electric current, equal to one thousand watts.

kilt (kĭlt), *n.* a short plaited petticoat worn by men of the Scottish Highlands; a skirt similarly made: *v.t.* to form into broad, flat plaits; tuck up: *v.i.* to move swiftly.

kil-ter (kĭl'tẽr), *n.* proper order; good condition; as, out of *kilter.* Also, **kelter.** [COLLOQ.]

ki-mo-no (kĭ-mō'nō; JAP. kĭm'ō-nō), *n.* the loose outer robe of the Japanese; a similar robe worn as a dressing gown by women of western nations.

kin (kĭn), *n.* relationship; relatives; as, one's nearest *kin;* a Chinese lute: *adj.* of the same ancestry; hence, of the same kind or nature; related.

kind (kīnd), *adj.* indulgent; gracious; inclined to do good to others; affectionate; sympathetic: *n.* class or species; quality; variety; sort.

Syn., adj. amicable, charitable, friendly.

kin-der-gar-ten (kĭn'dẽr-gär'tĕn), *n.* a school for young children in which they are taught by object lessons, games, etc.—*n.* **kindergartner.**

kind-heart-ed (kīnd'här'tĕd), *adj.* generous; sympathetic; charitable; full of good impulses.

kin-dle (kĭn'dl), *v.t.* to set fire to; inflame: *v.i.* to catch fire; to become excited.—*n.* **kindler.**

kind-li-ness (kīnd'lĭ-nĕs), *n.* the quality of being gracious and sympathetic; as, *kindliness* of disposition.

kind-ly (kīnd'lĭ), *adj.* sympathetic; gracious; benevolent: *adv.* in a gracious manner.

kind-ness (kīnd'nĕs), *n.* the state or quality of being ready to do good to others: a helpful or gracious act.

kin-dred (kĭn'drĕd), *adj.* of like nature or character; related by blood or marriage: *n.* relationship by birth or marriage; persons so related.

ki-ne-ma-col-or (kĭ-nē'må-kŭl'ẽr), *n.* the process of making and showing motion pictures in colors, based upon the three-color process of photography.

ki-net-ic (kĭ-nĕt'ĭk; kī-nĕt'ĭk), *adj.* pertaining to, or imparting, motion; active; as, *kinetic* energy: *n.pl.* the science which treats of the action of forces in causing or influencing motion.

ki-ne-to-graph (kĭ-nē'tō-gráf; kī-nē'tō-gráf), *n.* an apparatus for taking photographs of moving objects and afterwards reproducing them on a screen, as if in actual motion.—*adj.* **kinetographic.**—*n.* **kinetographer.**

ki-ne-to-phone (kĭ-nē'tō-fōn; kī-nē'tō-fōn), *n.* an instrument which combines sight and sound in motion pictures. Also, **phonocinematograph.**

ki-ne-to-scope (kĭ-nē'tō-skōp; kī-nē'tō-skōp), *n.* a machine for projecting motion pictures on a screen.

king (kĭng), *n.* a male sovereign or ruler; in chess, cards, etc., a piece or card representing a king; one who is specially distinguished in his class or kind; as, a *king* of men; the *king* of beasts.—**Kings,** two historical books in the Old Testament, recording the reigns of Jewish kings.

king-dom (kĭng'dŭm), *n.* the territory ruled by a king or queen; royal authority; sphere of influence; one of the classes into which all natural objects are divided; as, the animal, mineral, and vegetable *kingdoms.*

king-fish-er (kĭng'fĭsh'ẽr), *n.* a fish-eating bird with bright blue and green, or slate-blue and white feathers.

Kingfisher

king-ly (kĭng'lĭ), *adj.* pertaining to, or worthy of, a monarch.

king-ship (kĭng'shĭp), *n.* the state or position of a monarch.

king truss (kĭng' trŭs), a braced structure supporting a roof, with a vertical member called a king-post.

king wood (kĭng wo͝od), a hard violet-tinted wood imported from Brazil: used in fine cabinet work.

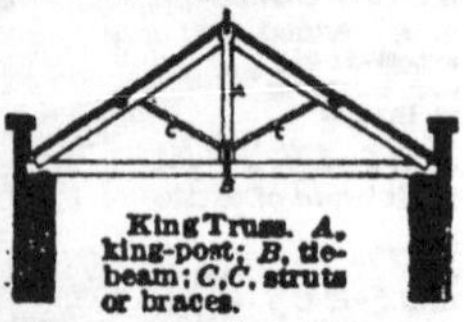

King Truss. *A,* king-post; *B,* tie-beam; *C,C,* struts or braces.

kink (kĭnk), *n.* a sudden twisted bend in a rope, wire, or thread; whim: *v.i.* and *v.t.* to form twists or loops.—*adj.* **kinky.**

kins-folk (kĭnz'fōk'), *n.* relatives; as, his *kinsfolk* came to his aid.

kin-ship (kĭn'shĭp), *n.* the state of being related; relationship.

kins-man (kĭnz'măn), *n.* [*fem.* **kinswoman**], one related by blood or marriage; a relative.

ki-osk (kē-ŏsk'), *n.* an Oriental open pavilion; a building of similar construction used as a news stand, etc.

kip (kĭp), *n.* the untanned skin of a calf or small cattle; leather made from such a skin.

kip-per (kĭp'ẽr), *n.* a salmon after having laid its eggs; a salmon, herring, etc., cut open, salted, and smoke-dried: *v.t.* to salt and preserve, as a salmon.

kirk (kûrk), *n.* a church: the **Kirk,** the established church of Scotland. [SCOT.]

kir-tle (kûr'tl), *n.* an upper garment; petticoat: *v.t.* to array in a kirtle; as, *kirtled* to the knees.

kis-met (kĭs'mĕt), *n.* fate; destiny; as, there is no escape from *kismet.*

kiss (kĭs), *n.* a salute or caress with the lips; a slight touch: *v.t.* to salute with the lips; touch slightly: *v.i.* to salute each other with the lips.

kit (kĭt), *n.* a small wooden tub; a small violin; traveling necessaries, outfit, etc.; a large bottle; a soldier's outfit for field service, carried upon his person; a bag or box in which a traveling or other outfit is packed.

kitch-en (kĭch'ĕn), *n.* a room or apartment set apart for cooking; the cooking department: *adj.* pertaining to the kitchen.

kitch-en-er (kich'ĕn-ẽr), *n.* a worker in, or head of, a kitchen; in England, a cooking range with ovens and all modern conveniences.

kitch-en-ette (kich'ĕn-ĕt'), *n.* a small kitchen.

kitch-en po-lice (kich'en pō-lēs), soldiers detailed for service in preparing food, etc.: soldiers are often assigned to *kitchen police* duty in punishment for petty offenses.

kite (kīt), *n.* a bird of prey, of the hawk family; a light frame of wood covered with paper or linen, for flying in the air; a light lofty sail: **kite balloon**, a captive balloon used for observation purposes.

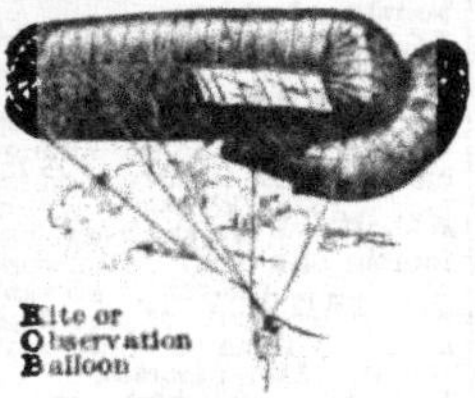

Kite or Observation Balloon

kith (kĭth), *n.* acquaintance, friends, neighbors: used only in the expression, *kith* and kin.

kit-ten (kĭt'n), *n.* a young cat; the young of any animal of the cat family; as, a tiger *kitten*.—*adj.* **kittenish.**

ki-wi (kē'wē), *n.* a flightless New Zealand bird, having loose plumage, and long bill with nostrils near the tip: the kiwis are nocturnal and feed mostly on earthworms; in army slang, a member of the flying corps who does not fly.

klep-to-ma-ni-a (klĕp'tō-mā'nĭ-ȧ), *n.* a form of insanity showing itself in an irresistible impulse to steal.

klep-to-ma-ni-ac (klĕp'tō-mā'nĭ-ăk), *n.* one who is under the influence of an insane and irresistible impulse to steal.

klip-spring-er (klĭp'spring'ẽr), *n.* a small African antelope, noted for its coarse hair and remarkable power of leaping up and down.

Klipspringer

knack (năk), *n.* quickness and cleverness in performance; as, she could never acquire the *knack* of using a needle.

knap-sack (năp'săk'), *n.* a leather or cloth traveling case carried on the back, used especially by soldiers: the modern soldier uses a blanket roll for the same purpose.

knap-weed (năp'wēd), *n.* a common European weed, naturalized in the United States in meadows and pastures, with heads of purple flowers: sometimes called *hill weed*.

knave (nāv), *n.* a dishonest or deceitful person; formerly, a servant or man of humble birth; a playing card with the figure of a soldier or servant.

knav-er-y (nāv'ẽr-ĭ), *n.* [*pl.* knaveries (-ĭz)], dishonesty; fraud; deceit.

knav-ish (nāv'ĭsh), *adj.* dishonest; mischievous; as, a *knavish* trick.—*adv.* **knavishly.**—*n.* **knavishness.**

knead (nēd), *v.t.* to work into a mass by pressing, usually with the hands, as dough; operate upon in massage.

knee (nē), *n.* the joint between the lower leg and the thigh; anything like a knee.

knee breech-es (nē brĭch'ĕz), breeches reaching just below the knee.

knee-cap (nē'kăp'), *n.* a flattened, triangular, movable bone on the fore part of the knee joint: called the *patella*. Also, **kneepan.**

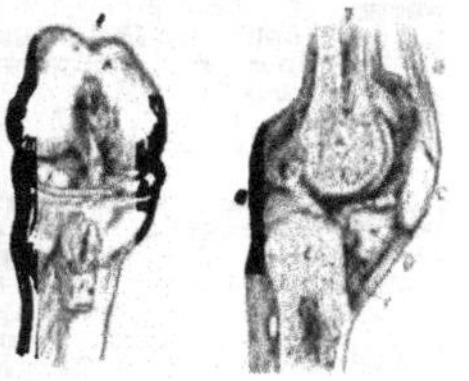

Human Knee Joint. 1. Right knee from the front showing ligaments: *A*, lower end of femur; *B*, anterior crucial ligament; *C*, posterior crucial ligament; *D*, interior semilunar cartilage; *E*, external cartilage; *F*, part of the ligament of the patella turned down; *G*, synovial bursa laid open beneath the ligature of the patella. 2. Longitudinal section of the left knee: *A*, lower end of femur; *B*, tendon of extensor muscles of leg; *C*, patella; *D*, ligament of patella; *E*, head of tibia; *F*, anterior crucial ligament; *G*, posterior ligament; *H*, mass of fat projecting into the cavity of the joint below the patella; *I*, bursa.

kneel (nēl), *v.i.* [*p.t.* and *p.p.* knelt, *p.pr.* kneeling], to bend or fall upon the knees.

knell (nĕl), *n.* the sound of a bell when struck, especially a funeral bell; a sign of coming evil: *v.i.* and *v.t.* to sound or toll, as a funeral bell.

Knick-er-bock-er (nĭk'ẽr-bŏk'ẽr), *n.* a member of an old New York family; especially, persons descended from the original Dutch settlers.—**knickerbockers**, *pl.* wide breeches gathered in below the knee.

knick-knack (nĭk'năk'), *n.* a little ornamental trifle; a toy.

knife (nīf), *n.* [*pl.* knives (nīvz)], a cutting instrument with a sharp-edged steel blade set in a handle; a sharp-edged blade in a machine: *v.t.* to stab with a knife.

knight (nīt), *n.* one who holds rank next below a baronet, giving him the title *Sir;* in the Middle Ages, one of high birth, who, after serving as an esquire, was admitted by certain ceremonies to military rank; a champion; lover; one of the pieces in chess: *v.t.* to confer the honor of knighthood upon.

knight-er-rant (nīt'ẽr'ănt), *n.* [*pl.* knights-errant], in the Middle Ages, a knight who went in search of adventure, to show his boldness and power, chivalry, etc.

knight-er-rant-ry (nīt'ẽr'ănt-rĭ), *n.* the practices or customs of wandering knights.

knight-hood (nīt'hŏŏd), *n.* the character, rank, or dignity of a knight; chivalry.

knight-ly (nīt'lĭ), *adj.* like a knight, or chivalrous; brave, gentle, and courteous.

Knight Tem-plar (nīt tĕm'plẽr), [*pl.* Knights Templars], a member of a high order of Freemasonry, supposed to have descended from the Templars of the Crusades.

knit (nĭt), *v.t.* [*p.t.* and *p.p.* knitted, *p.pr.* knitting], to tie, unite, or draw together; form, as a fabric, by weaving thread on needles: *v.i.* to weave thread or yarn in loops on needles; to join together; as, the broken limb *knitted* well.

knit-ting (nĭt'ĭng), *n.* the work of a knitter; the netted fabric thus woven.

knob (nŏb), *n.* the rounded handle of a door, etc.; round swelling, mass, or lump; a rounded hill.

knob-by (nŏb'ĭ), *adj.* full of humps or knolls; hilly; as a *knobby* field or landscape.

knock (nŏk), *n.* a blow or stroke with something hard or heavy; rap: *v.t.* to give a blow to; to strike with something hard or heavy; slang, to criticize harshly: *v.i.* to drive or strike against something.

knock-er (nŏk'ẽr), *n.* one who knocks; a loose handle attached to a door, to be used as a hammer by persons wishing to enter.

knock-kneed (nŏk'nēd"), *adj.* having the legs bent inward at the knees; hence, lame, weak.

knoll (nōl), *n.* a rounded hillock; hilltop; the tolling of a bell: *v.t.* to toll.

knop (nŏp), *n.* an architectural ornament of clustered leaves and flowers; a knob or button; a flower bud.

knot (nŏt), *n.* an interweaving or tying of thread or cord, etc.; anything resembling a knot; entanglement; difficulty; a hard part in a piece of wood; part of a tree where the branches shoot out; a nautical mile or 2,025 yards; bond of union; group; the red-breasted sandpiper: *v.t.* [*p.t.* and *p.p.* knotted, *p.pr.* knotting], to tie in a knot; unite firmly or closely: *v.i.* form knots or joints; make knots for fringe.

knot-ting (nŏt'ĭng), *n.* a kind of lace work; a paint of red lead, etc., for protecting metal.

knot-ty (nŏt'ĭ), *adj.* [*comp.* knottier, *superl.* knottiest], full of knots; rugged; difficult; as, a *knotty* problem.

knout (nout; nōōt), *n.* a leathern whip formerly used for punishing criminals or serfs in Russia: *v.t.* to punish with the knout.

know (nō), *v.t.* [*p.t.* knew, *p.p.* known, *p.pr.* knowing], to perceive with the mind; understand clearly; be aware of; to see as distinct from others; recognize; be acquainted with: *v.i.* to be informed.

know-ing (nō'ĭng), *p.adj.* having knowledge; intelligent; shrewd; cunning; as, a *knowing* look.—*adv.* **knowingly.**

knowl-edge (nŏl'ĕj), *n.* clear perception of a truth or fact; learning; skill from practice; acquaintance; information.
Syn. learning, science.
Ant. (see ignorance).

Know-Noth-ing (nō-nŭth'ĭng), *n.* a political party in the United States, in 1853 and a few years following, which claimed that none but native Americans should hold office.

knuck-le (nŭk'l), *n.* the joint of the fingers; the knee joint of a calf or pig: *v.i.* to bend the fingers; yield or submit: with *down* or *under*.

knurl (nûrl), *n.* a hard knot, or anything swelled or pushed beyond the surface, as in a tree trunk, stone, etc. Also, **knur.**—*adj.* **knurly.**

ko-a (kō'ä), *n.* a Hawaiian tree yielding a valuable timber used for building and cabinetwork.

ko-bold (kō'bŏld), *n.* in old folk tales, a brownie or gnome.

ko-dak (kō'dăk), *n.* a hand camera for taking snapshot photographs: *v.t.* to take a snapshot picture of; to describe minutely, or with photographic accuracy.—*n.* **kodaker, kodakry.**

Koh-i-noor (kō'hĭ-nōōr"; kō'ĭ-nōōr"), *n.* a famous large diamond, one of the British crown jewels.

ko-la (kō'lȧ), *n.* the nut of an African tree, bitter and containing caffeine: used for chewing, like tobacco, and in making a drink.

ko-peck (kō'pĕk), *n.* a Russian coin worth from one-half to three-fourths of a cent. Also, **copeck, kopek.**

Ko-ran (kō-rän'; kō'răn), *n.* the sacred book of the Mohammedans, believed by them to be the revelations of Allah (God). Also, **Alcoran.**

ko-sher (kō'shẽr), *adj.* bright; lawful; clean, according to Jewish law: used of food, especially meat slaughtered according to the Jewish law.

ko-to (kō'tō), *n.* a Japanese musical instrument, somewhat like the zither.

ko-tow (kō-tou'), *n.* a Chinese form of greeting from an inferior to a superior by touching the ground with the forehead: *v.i.* to salute by such an act. Also, **kowtow.**

kraal (kräl), *n.* a South African village consisting of a group of huts surrounded by a defense of stakes driven into the ground; a single hut; a sheepfold, or cattle-pen.

krem-lin (krĕm'lĭn), *n.* a Russian citadel or fortress, especially that of Moscow; a large inclosure which contains palaces, churches, etc.

kreut-zer (kroit'sẽr), *n.* an Austrian copper coin equal to one-half of a cent; formerly, a German coin worth two-thirds of a cent.

kris (krĭs), *n.* a short Malay sword or dagger. Also, **creese.**

Kris Krin-gle (krĭs krĭn'gl), the good spirit of Christmas; Santa Claus; St. Nicholas. [Ger.]

kro-ne (krō'nĕ), *n.* [*pl.* kronen (-nĕn)], a coin (crown) used in Germanic and Scandinavian countries and equal to twenty-seven cents.

Krupp gun (krōōp gŭn), a breech-loading cannon made at the Krupp works at Essen in Germany.

Ku-Klux (kū'klŭks"), *n.* the Ku-Klux Klan, a secret society in the southern United States after the Civil War, whose object was to frighten the negroes who were trying to control the whites, politically and socially. Also, **Kuklux.**

kul-tur (kōōl-tōōr'), *n.* advancement in all fields of education, civilization, etc.: used especially of the state-controlled German system of education and scientific advance which led to the German desire for world power. [Ger.]

ku-miss (kōō'mĭs), *n.* a fermented liquor made from milk. Also, **kumyss.**

Kurd (kōōrd), *n.* a member of a dark, fierce race of Kurdistan. Also, **Curd, Koord.**—*adj.* **Kurdish.**

ky-ack (kī'ăk), *n.* a hunting canoe made of sealskin, used in arctic America. Also, **kaiak, kajak, kayak.**

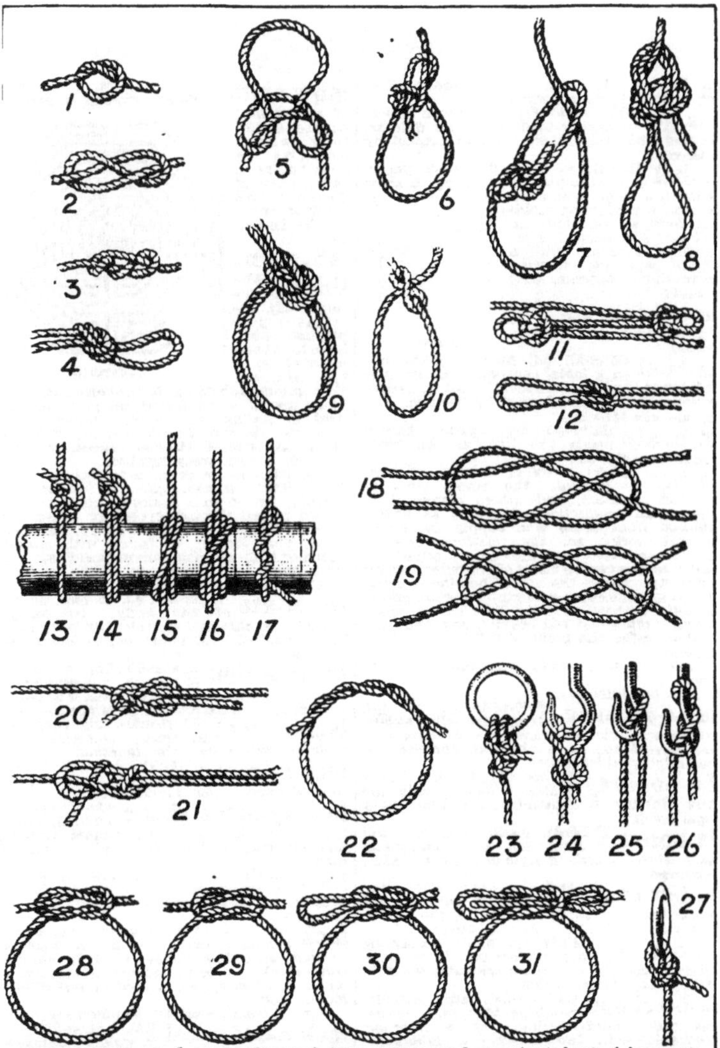

Important Knots. 1, overhand knot; 2, figure eight knot; 3, stevedore's knot; 4, loop knot; 5, harness hitch; 6, bowline (knot); 7, running bowline; 8, bowline with a bight; 9, bowline on a bight; 10, slide knot; 11, sheepshank; 12, slip or running knot; 13, half hitch; 14, rolling hitch; 15, clove hitch; 16, magnus hitch; 17, timber hitch; 18, 19, single and double carrick bend; 20, weaver's knot; 21, double sheet bend; 22, surgeon's knot; 23, fisherman's bend or anchor knot; 24, cat's-paw; 25, 26, single and double Blackwall hitch; 27, studding-sail tack bend; 28, reef, square or flat knot; 29, granny knot; 30, 31, single and double bowknot.

L

la (lä), *n.* the sixth note of the musical scale of C major, which is A.

laa-ger (lä'gēr; lô'gēr), *n.* in South Africa, a hastily made camp for defense, formed with wagons, etc.: *v.t.* to protect by a laager.

la-bel (lā'bĕl), *n.* a small slip of paper, etc., attached to anything to show where it is to go, who owns it, etc.; a projecting molding over an opening: *v.t.* [*p.t.* and *p.p.* labeled, *p.pr.* labeling], to mark with a slip of paper, etc., showing ownership, contents, etc.; classify.

Label

la-bel-lum (lȧ-bĕl'-ŭm), *n.* the lip, or lower petal, of an orchid.

la-bi-al (lā'bĭ-ăl), *adj.* formed by the lips; as, a *labial* consonant; of or pertaining to the lips; as, a *labial* vein: *n.* a letter representing a sound formed by the lips, as *b, p, m.*—*adv.* **labially.**

la-bi-ate (lā'bĭ-āt), *adj.* lipped; having petals like lips, as the snapdragon, catnip, etc.

la-bor (lā'bēr), *n.* toil or exertion, physical or mental; the whole class of workers, artisans, and others employed in the actual production of wealth as distinguished from those who supply money or mental work; as, the relations between capital and *labor* are difficult to adjust; a task; as, the twelve *labors* of Hercules; effort; difficulty; pain; the act of bearing a child: *v.i.* to use muscular strength or mental effort; to toil; be hard-pressed; take pains; move slowly; pitch and roll heavily, as a ship in a storm; suffer the pains of childbirth. Also, **labour.**

Syn., *n.* toil, work, exertion, drudgery, pains.

Ant. (see idleness).

lab-o-ra-to-ry (lăb'ō-rȧ-tō-rĭ), *n.* [*pl.* laboratories (-rĭz)], a place where scientific experiments and operations are carried on; as, a physical, chemical, or bacteriological *laboratory.*

La-bor Day (lā'bēr dā), in the United States, a day, usually the first Monday in September, set apart as a legal holiday.

la-bored (lā'bērd), *p.adj.* done with toil or care; not easy; elaborate; as, a *labored* speech or style of writing. Also, **laboured.**

la-bor-er (lā'bēr-ēr), *n.* one who toils; one who does for hire physical work that requires little skill; as, the *laborer* is worthy of his hire. Also, **labourer.**

la-bor-ing (lā'bēr-ĭng), *p.adj.* pertaining to, or performing, labor; as, a *laboring* woman; struggling against great difficulties; as, a *laboring* ship.

la-bo-ri-ous (lȧ-bō'rĭ-ŭs), *adj.* difficult; requiring toil; as, a *laborious* task; hard-working; as, a *laborious* mechanic.—*adv.* **laboriously.**—*n.* **laboriousness.**

la-bur-num (lȧ-bûr'nŭm), *n.* a European ornamental tree with yellow flowers.

lab-y-rinth (lăb'ĭ-rĭnth), *n.* a series of passages winding in and out of each other; a maze; a difficulty which cannot be solved; as, a *labyrinth* of doubt; the winding tubes of the inner ear.

Labyrinth

lab-y-rin-thine (lăb-ĭ-rĭn'-thĭn), *adj.* intricate; perplexing. Also, **labyrinthian, labyrinthic.**

lac (lăk), *n.* a gummy substance formed on certain trees by an insect: when melted, called *shellac,* and used in sealing wax, dyes, varnishes, and lacquers; the sap of various trees; in British India, the sum of 100,000 rupees, or about $50,000; a very great number.

lace (lās), *n.* an ornamental fabric of fine linen, cotton, gold, or silver, etc., threads, woven in a delicate, open pattern; a cord passed through eyelets or other holes in order to bind or fasten: *v.t.* [*p.t.* and *p.p.* laced, *p.pr.* lacing], to fasten with a cord; adorn or trim, as with narrow braid, etc.; as, cloth *laced* with silver; to weave or twine together; to beat or lash.

lac-er-ate (lăs'ēr-āt), *v.t.* to tear, as part of the body; to mangle, wound; as, shrapnel *lacerates* the body horribly; to afflict with pain; as, to *lacerate* the feelings.

lac-er-a-tion (lăs"ēr-ā'shŭn), *n.* the act of tearing; a jagged rent or wound; as, a *laceration* of the flesh is sewed up with catgut; a harrowing, as of the feelings.

lach-ry-mal (lăk'rĭ-măl), *adj.* pertaining to tears; secreting tears; as, *lachrymal* glands. Also, **lacrimal, lacrymal.**

lach-ry-mose (lăk'rĭ-mōs), *adj.* tearful; sad; as, a *lachrymose* tone of voice. Also, **lacrimose.**

lach-ry-mose shells (lăk'rĭ-mōs shĕlz), projectiles filled with gas which causes smarting and watering of the eyes: called also *tear shells.*

lac-ing (lās'ĭng), *p.pr.* of *lace: n.* a cord, string, braid, etc., passed through eyelets to fasten something, or used for trimming.

lack (lăk), *v.t.* to be without; as, to *lack* common sense; to be in want of; to need; as, to *lack* money: *v.i.* to be wanting; come short; as, to be *lacking* in wisdom: *n.* want, deficiency; as, a *lack* of self-respect; *lack* of food.

Syn., *n.* need, scarcity, insufficiency.

lack-a-dai-si-cal (lăk"ȧ-dā'zĭ-kăl), *adj.* languidly sentimental; listless.—*adv.* **lackadaisically.**

lack-er (lăk'ēr), *n.* a varnish made by dissolving shellac in alcohol: *v.t.* to cover with a shellac; varnish. Also, **lacquer.**

lack-ey (lăk'ĭ), *n.* an attendant of low rank; a footman; a person who follows and flatters another supposedly of higher rank: *v.t.* and *v.i.* to serve or attend as a servant. Also, **lacquey.**

la-con-ic (lȧ-kŏn'ĭk), *adj.* expressing much in few words; as, Benjamin Franklin was the author of many famous *laconic* sayings. Also, **laconical.**—*adv.* **laconically.**

lac-quer (lăk'ẽr), *n.* a varnish consisting of shellac dissolved in alcohol, and colored; Oriental varnish; Chinese or Japanese woodwork finished with a hard, polished varnish, and inlaid with gold, ivory, pearl, etc.; a composition for preserving cannon, carriages, etc: *v.t.* to cover with a varnish. Also, **lacker.**

lac-quey (lăk-ĭ), *n.* an attendant of low rank; a footman; a servile follower: *v.t.* and *v.i.* to serve or act as a servant. Also, **lackey.**

lac-ri-mal (lăk'rĭ-măl), *adj.* pertaining to tears; secreting tears; as, *lacrimal* glands. Also, **lachrymal, lacrymal.**

lac-ri-mose (lăk'rĭ-mōs), *adj.* tearful; sad; as, a *lacrimose* tone of voice. Also, **lachrymose.**

la-crosse (lȧ-krŏs'), *n.* a Canadian game like football, but played with a netted bat, or crosse.

Lacrosse Stick

lac-ta-rine (lăk'tȧ-rĭn), *n.* a preparation of casein, or milk curds: used extensively in calico printing.

lac-ta-tion (lăk-tā'shŭn), *n.* the production of milk from the body; the act or period of suckling.

lac-te-al (lăk'tē-ăl), *adj.* pertaining to, or like, milk; conveying the fluid called chyle, or lymph, which contains fats from digested food; as, *lacteal* ducts: *n.pl.* the ducts which convey chyle, or fat-containing lymph, from the intestines to the thorax.

lac-tic (lăk'tĭk), *adj.* pertaining to, or derived from, milk; as, *lactic* acid.

lac-tom-e-ter (lăk-tŏm'ē-tẽr), *n.* an instrument for measuring the richness of milk.

lac-tose (lăk'tōs), *n.* a sugar contained in milk: called also *milk sugar.*

la-cu-na (lȧ-kū'nȧ), *n.* [*pl.* lacunæ (-nē), lacunas (-nȧz)], a space from which something has been omitted, as in a manuscript; a small pit or hollow, such as those in the substance of bone.

lad (lăd), *n.* a boy or youth; a stripling; comrade or mate.

lad-der (lăd'ẽr), *n.* a framework consisting of two parallel side pieces connected by bars, etc., forming steps at suitable distances; any means by which one climbs or ascends; as, young ambition's *ladder.*

Scaling Ladder

lad-die (lăd'ĭ), *n.* a lad; sometimes, a boy sweetheart. Also, **laddy.** [Scot.]

lade (lād), *v.t.* [*p.t.* laded, *p.p.* laded, laden, *p.pr.* lading], to load; to put a burden on or in; throw out or in with a scoop or dipper; as, to *lade* water out of a tub.

lad-ing (lād'ĭng), *n.* the act of loading; freight; cargo; as, a bill of *lading;* burden.

la-dle (lā'dl), *n.* a deep spoon or dipper for dipping out liquids: *v.t.* to take up with a dipper.

la-dy (lā'dĭ), *n.* [*pl.* ladies (-dĭz)], a well-bred woman; a woman of good family or of high position in society; a sweetheart: **Lady,** the title of the wife of a knight, baronet, earl, etc.; the daughter of a duke, marquis, or earl; the Virgin Mary: with *Our.*

la-dy-bird (lā'dĭ-bûrd'), *n.* a red or orange-colored insect marked with black spots; a ladybug.

la-dy-bug (lā'dĭ-bŭg), *n.* a red beetle marked with black spots; a ladybird.

la-dy-like (lā'dĭ-līk'), *adj.* befitting a gentlewoman; courteous; well-bred.

la-dy-ship (lā'dĭ-shĭp), *n.* a term of address for a titled woman in England.

la-dy's-slip-per (lā'dĭz-slĭp'ẽr), *n.* a flower of the orchid family that looks somewhat like a slipper. Also, **lady-slipper.**

lag (lăg), *v.i.* [*p.t.* and *p.p.* lagged, *p.pr.* lagging], to move slowly; loiter; stay behind: *n.* a falling behind in movement.—*n.* **lagger.**

la-ger beer (lä'gẽr bẽr), a German brewed liquor laid up, or stored, for some months before use. Also, **lager.**

lag-gard (lăg'ȧrd), *n.* a person who acts more slowly than he should; loiterer; as, a *laggard* in love: *adj.* backward; slow.—*adv.* **laggardly.**

lag-ging (lăg'ĭng), *n.* slow motion; the act of holding back; strips of wood or planks used to support an arch during construction, or the roof of a mine.

la-goon (lȧ-gōōn'), *n.* a shallow lake formed at the mouth of a river or near the sea.

la-ic (lā'ĭk), *adj.* pertaining to those who are not clergymen or members of some particular profession: *n.* a layman.

laid (lād), *p.t.* and *p.p.* of *lay: adj.* marked with fine parallel ribbed lines: said of paper.

lain (lān), past participle of the intransitive verb *lie.*

lair (lâr), *n.* the den or resting place of a wild beast; as, the lion makes his *lair* in the jungle.

laird (lârd), *n.* a lord; the master of a landed estate. [Scot.]

lais-sez faire (lĕ-sā' fâr'), a term indicating a policy of letting every individual do as he pleases in social and economic matters, without regulation by the government. [Fr.]

la-i-ty (lā'ĭ-tĭ), *n.* the people, as distinguished from the clergy; all those who are outside any given profession.

lake (lāk), *n.* a large body of water surrounded by land; a purplish-red coloring matter.

lakh (lăk), *n.* in British India, the sum of 100,000 rupees, equal to $50,000; a very great number. Also, **lac.**

la-ma (lä'mȧ), *n.* in Tibet, a priest, monk, or nun of one branch (Lamaism) of the Buddhist faith.

lamb (lăm), *n.* the young of a sheep; the flesh of the young sheep; one who is gentle or innocent: *v.i.* to bring forth lambs.

lam-bent (lăm'bĕnt), *adj.* playing over the surface; flickering; touching lightly; as, a *lambent* flame; softly bright; as, the *lambent* light of stars.—*adv.* **lambently.**—*n.* **lambence, lambency.**

lamb-kin (lăm'kĭn), *n.* a little lamb; a child that is tenderly cherished.

lam-bre-quin (lăm'brē-kĭn; lăm'bĕr-kĭn), *n.* a drapery, hanging from the upper part of a window or doorway, from the edge of a shelf, etc.

lamb-skin (lăm'skĭn"), *n.* the skin of a lamb dressed with the fleece on and frequently colored; leather made from the skin of a lamb.

lame (lām), *adj.* crippled or disabled in the limbs; not sound or effective; as, a *lame* excuse: *v.t.* to cripple or disable.—*adv.* **lamely.**—*n.* **lameness.**

la-ment (lȧ-mĕnt'), *v.t.* to mourn for; as, to *lament* the loss of a friend: *v.i.* to express sorrow: *n.* an expression of sorrow.
Syn., *v.* mourn, grieve, weep.
Ant. (see rejoice).

lam-en-ta-ble (lăm'ĕn-tȧ-bl), *adj.* mournful; pitiable; as, a *lamentable* condition, occurrence, cry.—*adv.* **lamentably.**

lam-en-ta-tion (lăm"ĕn-tā'shŭn), *n.* grief expressed aloud; outcry: **Lamentations,** a book of the Old Testament.

la-ment-ed (lȧ-mĕn'tĕd), *p.adj.* mourned for as dead; regretted.

lam-i-na (lăm'ĭ-nȧ), *n.* [*pl.* laminæ (-nē)], a thin plate or scale; a coat or layer lying over another, as in minerals or bone; the blade of a leaf or petal.—*adj.* **laminar, laminary.**

lam-i-nate (lăm'ĭ-nāt), *adj.* composed of, or arranged in, thin coats, scales, or layers: *v.t.* and *v.i.* (lăm'ĭ-nāt), to roll, press, or divide into thin sheets, as metal.

lam-i-na-tion (lăm"ĭ-nā'shŭn), *n.* division into thin plates or sheets, as of rock; a structure so divided.

lamp (lămp), *n.* a vessel in which oil, etc., may be passed through a wick and ignited so as to produce light; any device for producing artificial light; as, an electric *lamp.*

Ancient Lamps

lamp-black (lămp'blăk"), *n.* fine soot obtained from the smoke of substances containing carbon, as from the smoke of an oil lamp; used as coloring matter: *v.t.* to apply such soot to.

lam-poon (lăm-pōōn'), *n.* an article, essay, etc., written to hold a person up to ridicule and contempt; as, Lincoln was the subject of many a disgraceful *lampoon:* *v.t.* to abuse or ridicule in a written article.

lam-prey (lăm'prĭ), *n.* an eel-like fish of which one kind is valued as food.

lance (lȧns), *n.* a long shaft of wood with a spear head: *v.t.* to pierce with a lance; cut open with a lancet, or surgeon's knife.—**lance corporal,** an assistant to a corporal; a private soldier acting as corporal.—**lance sergeant,** an acting sergeant. Also, **launce.**

lanc-er (lȧn'sẽr), *n.* a cavalry soldier armed with a long spear: *pl.* a kind of square dance arranged for four couples.

lan-cet (lȧn'sĕt), *n.* a surgeon's knife; a window with a sharply pointed arch.

lance-wood (lȧns'wŏŏd"), *n.* a tough elastic wood used in coach building, etc.

land (lănd), *n.* the solid portion of the surface of the globe; a country or district; ground or soil, with reference to its use; as, farm-*land;* real estate: *v.t.* to set on shore; as, to *land* passengers from a ship; capture and bring to shore; as, to *land* a fish; win; as, to *land* a prize; put down after carrying; as, the train *landed* him at his destination: *v.i.* to come or go on shore; to arrive at a dock, as a vessel; disembark; get down from, out of, or off from.

lan-dau (lăn'dô; lăn'dou), *n.* a four-wheeled covered carriage with a top that can be let down or thrown back.

lan-dau-let (lăn"dô-lĕt'), *n.* a motor car with a double top, folding hood, and two seats; a small landau.

land-ed (lăn'dĕd), *adj.* possessing, or consisting of, real estate; as, a *landed* proprietor; a *landed* estate.

land-grab-ber (lănd'grăb"ẽr), *n.* one who obtains public land by fraud; in Ireland, one who buys or occupies land from which another has been expelled.

land-hold-er (lănd'hōl"dẽr), *n.* an owner or holder of property in the form of land.

land-ing (lăn'dĭng), *n.* act of coming ashore; a place for going on shore or for alighting from a carriage, etc.; a platform at the end of a flight of steps.

land-la-dy (lănd'lā"dĭ), *n.* [*pl.* landladies (-dĭz)], a woman who lets houses, etc., to tenants; the mistress of a boarding house or inn.

land-locked (lănd'lŏkt"), *adj.* nearly surrounded by land; as, a *landlocked* bay; confined to fresh water by some barrier; as, *landlocked* fish.

land-lord (lănd'lôrd"), *n.* one who owns buildings or lands which he rents to others; the keeper of a hotel or inn.

land-lub-ber (lănd'lŭb"ẽr), *n.* a sailor's term for one who has not been to sea; hence, anyone who is awkward on shipboard.

land-mark (lănd'märk"), *n.* an object that marks the boundary of a tract of land; a familiar object that serves as a guide to a locality; any fact or event that helps to recall other facts and events.

land-own-er (lănd'ōn"ẽr), *n.* a person who possesses property in land.

land-poor (lănd'pōōr"), *adj.* possessing property in real estate but having little or no income with which to maintain it and pay taxes on it.

land-scape (lănd'skāp), *n.* the general appearance of a country as seen from one point of view; a picture representing a scene from nature, other than the sea.

land-slide (lănd'slīd"), *n.* the slipping of a mass of earth, etc., down a steep slope; the earth that slips down. Also, **landslip.**

lands-man (lăndz'măn), *n.* a person who lives on land: opposite to *seaman.*

Lands-thing (lȧns'tĭng"), *n.* the Upper House of the Danish Parliament or Rigsdag.

Land-sturm (lȧnt'stŏŏrm"), *n.* the last reserve of the German army, called out only in time of war. [Ger.]

Land-tag (länt'täk"), *n.* the Parliament of Prussia. [Ger.]

land-ward (lănd'wẽrd), *adj.* facing toward the shore: *adv.* toward the shore. Also, **landwards.**

Land-wehr (länt'vār"), *n.* the reserve forces of the German army. [Ger.]

lane (lān), *n.* a narrow path, as between hedges, walls, etc.; a narrow street; any narrow way or track.

lan-guage (lăn'gwāj), *n.* human speech, spoken or written; the speech of one nation or race as distinguished from that of another; as, the French *language;* style or expression peculiar to an individual, or to something written or spoken; as, the *language* of an address.
Syn. dialect, idiom, speech, tongue.

lan-guid (lăn'gwĭd), *adj.* wanting energy; weak; drooping.—*adv.* **languidly.** —*n.* **languidness.**

lan-guish (lăn'gwĭsh), *v.i.* to become weak or spiritless; pine away; as, to *languish* in sorrow; look with tenderness or wistfulness.

lan-guish-ing (lăn'gwĭsh-ĭng), *p.adj.* drooping; pining; sentimentally tender; as, *languishing* looks.—*adv.* **languishingly.**

lan-guor (lăn'gẽr; lăn'gwẽr), *n.* weariness of body or mind caused by exhaustion; feebleness; dreamy indolence. —*adj.* **languorous.**

lank (lănk), *adj.* lean; slender; shrunken; as, a man with a tall, *lank* figure.

lank-y (lănk'ĭ), *adj.* tall and thin; loosely hung; as, the *lanky* form of Ichabod Crane.—*n.* **lankiness.**

lan-o-lin (lăn'ō-lĭn), *n.* fat or grease from sheep's wool, purified and made into a healing ointment. Also, **lanoline.**

lan-tern (lăn'tẽrn), *n.* a transparent case for holding or carrying a light, and protecting it from the wind; the light-room of a lighthouse; a small tower on the roof of a building to admit light and air.

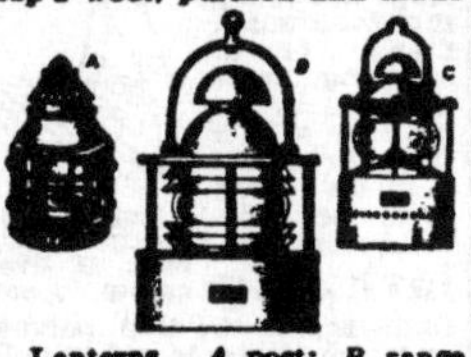

Lanterns. *A*, post; *B*, range light; *C*, riding light.

lan-tern-jawed (lăn'tẽrn-jôd), *adj.* having a long thin face.

lan-yard (lăn'yẽrd), *n.* a piece of rope, cord, etc., for fastening the tackle of a ship; a strong cord attached to the trigger of a field gun and pulled to fire the gun. Also, **laniard.**

lap (lăp), *n.* the loose part of a garment which may be doubled over; the part of the body from the waist to the knees of a person when seated; the clothing that covers that part of the body; the part of a thing that lies over the edge of another thing; the distance which one thing lies over another; one length of a course, especially one which has to be passed over more than once in a race; the act of licking up or washing against: *v.t.* [*p.t.* and *p.p.* lapped, *p.pr.* lapping], to lay or fold over; as, to *lap* one shingle over another; to wash or ripple against; as, the water *laps* the shore; lick up; as, a dog *laps* water: *v.i.* to lie partially over something else.

lap dog (lăp dôg), a small pet dog that may be held in the lap.

la-pel (lȧ-pĕl'), *n.* the part of a garment which is folded back; especially, the fold at each side of the front of a coat.

lap-i-da-ry (lăp'ĭ-dā-rĭ), *n.* [*pl.* lapidaries (-rĭz)], a skilled workman who cuts and sets precious stones; a dealer in, or collector of, gems.

la-pis la-zu-li (lā'pĭs lăz'ū-lī), a stone of a rich blue color; the azure blue of the stone. [Lat.]

Lapp (lăp), *n.* a Laplander; the language of Lapland.

lap-pet (lăp'ĕt), *n.* a little loose flap on a headdress or garment; a flap of flesh, as on the head of a bird; a wattle.

lapse (lăps), *v.i.* to glide or slip slowly away; as, to *lapse* into unconsciousness; his interest *lapsed;* to fall into ruin by degrees; as, buildings *lapse* into ruin; commit a fault or fail in duty; as, to *lapse* from good behavior; slide or fall anew into sin; pass to another owner by neglect or death: *n.* a gliding or passing away slowly; as, the *lapse* of time; slight fault or mistake; the ending of a claim, right, etc., through failure to assert or exercise it.—*p.adj.* **lapsed.**

lap-wing (lăp'wĭng"), *n.* a ploverlike bird of the Old World.

lar-board (lär'bōrd; lär'bẽrd), *n.* the term used formerly for the port or left-hand side of a ship.

lar-ce-ny (lär'sē-nĭ), *n.* the carrying away of another's property with the intention of defrauding the owner; theft.

larch (lärch), *n.* a tree of the pine family which has needlelike leaves and bears cones.

lard (lärd), *n.* the fat of swine melted down and solidified by cooling: *v.t.* to cover with fat; insert strips of bacon in before roasting; to enrich; hence, to decorate; as, to *lard* a speech with compliments.

lard-er (lär'dẽr), *n.* a pantry; household provisions.

la-res (lā'rēz), *n.pl.* the household gods of the Roman people.

large (lärj), *adj.* great in size; bulky; wide; extensive; comprehensive; broad in understanding or sympathy; as, a *large* mind: at **large,** in full; as, to discuss a subject *at large;* free; as, the thief is *at large;* for a whole state, district, etc.; as, a Congressman *at large.*—*adv.* **largely.**—*n.* **largeness.**
Syn. big, broad, huge, ample.
Ant. (see small).

lar-gess (lär'jĕs), *n.* a generous gift or bounty; as, the king scattered *largess* as he rode along. Also, **largesse.**

lar-go (lär'gō), *adj.* and *adv.* in music, slow, slowly: *n.* a musical composition of slow and dignified movement. [It.]

lar-i-at (lăr'ĭ-ăt), *n.* a rope or lasso, usually with a running noose, used for catching cattle, etc.

lark (lärk), *n.* a noted song-bird, not found in America; especially, the skylark; any of several similar American birds, as the meadow lark; colloquially, an amusing adventure.

lark-spur (lärk'spûr), *n.* any plant of the crowfoot family with showy blue flowers.

lar-va (lär'vȧ), *n.* [*pl.* larvæ (-vē)], an insect in the first stage of its life after leaving the egg; thus, the *larva* of the moth is a worm or caterpillar; the early form of any animal which changes in form as it develops, as the tadpole.

lar-val (lär'văl), *adj.* pertaining to a larva, or insect that has just left its shell.

la-ryn-ge-al (lȧ-rĭn'jē-ăl; lăr"ĭn-jē'ăl), *adj.* pertaining to, or situated near, the larynx, or upper windpipe.

lar-yn-gi-tis (lăr"ĭn-jī'tĭs), *n.* inflammation of the membrane of the larynx, or upper part of the throat.

lar-ynx (lăr'ĭnks), *n.* the upper part of the trachea, or windpipe; the special organ of the voice.

las-car (lăs'kȧr; lăs-kär'), *n.* an East Indian native sailor, army servant, or artillery soldier.

las-civ-i-ous (lă-sĭv'ĭ-ŭs), *adj.* lustful; wanton; exciting lust.—*adv.* **lasciviously.**—*n.* **lasciviousness.**

Syn. loose, unchaste, impure.
Ant. (see chaste).

lash (lăsh), *v.t.* to strike or scourge with a whip; whip; blame very severely; as, to *lash* vice; fasten or bind with a cord or rope; as, the sailors *lashed* him to the mast; to beat violently to and fro; as, the wind *lashed* the sails: *v.i.* to apply the whip; flog; to rush, pour, or beat: *n.* the thong of a whip; a stroke with a whip or anything used like a whip; sarcasm; one of the little hairs on the edge of an eyelid.

lash-ing (lăsh'ĭng), *n.* a cord, rope, etc., to secure or bind anything; a whipping; sharp reproof; as, a tongue *lashing.*

lass (lăs), *n.* a young woman; girl; a sweetheart: said usually of a Scotch girl or a country girl. Also, **lassie.**

las-si-tude (lăs'ĭ-tūd), *n.* bodily or mental weariness; lack of energy; as, very hot weather produces *lassitude.*

las-so (lăs'ō), *n.* a rope, usually of hide, with a running noose, used for catching wild horses and cattle: *v.t.* to catch with a noosed rope.

last (làst), *adj.* coming after all others in time, place, or order; lowest; utmost; least likely: *adv.* after all others; on the final time or occasion; at the end; finally: *v.i.* to remain in existence or operation; endure: *n.* a wooden tool for shaping boots and shoes; the end.

Syn., adj. final, latest, ultimate.
Ant. (see first).

last-ing (làst'ĭng), *p.adj.* wearing well; permanent: *n.* a fabric used for the uppers of women's shoes, for covering buttons, etc.—*adv.* **lastingly.**

last-ly (làst'lĭ), *adv.* finally; in conclusion; at the end.

latch (lăch), *n.* a catch for a door or gate, often not requiring a key: *v.t.* to secure or fasten with a catch.

Latch

latch-et (lăch'ĕt), *n.* a shoestring; a strip of leather that fastens a sandal.

late (lāt), *adj.* [*comp.* later, *superl.* latest], coming after the usual time; tardy; long delayed; as, a *late* spring; far on toward the end or close; as, a *late* hour of the day; recent; as, a *late* occurrence; formerly in office; as, the *late* secretary of state; recently dead; as, the *late* Mr. Brown: *adv.* after delay; as, to arrive *late;* after the usual time; as, to get up *late;* recently; of late, recently; as, I have not seen you *of late.*—*n.* **lateness.**

la-teen sail (lȧ-tēn' sāl), a three-cornered sail attached to a low mast: used in the Mediterranean.

Lateen Sails

late-ly (lāt'lĭ), *adv.* not long ago; as, I heard the news *lately;* they have *lately* come to town.

la-ten-cy (lā'tĕn-sĭ), *n.* the state of being concealed or invisible.

la-tent (lā'tĕnt), *adj.* concealed; invisible; present, but not active; as, disease germs often lie *latent* in the body for a long time before the disease develops.—*adv.* **latently.**

lat-er-al (lăt'ẽr-ăl), *adj.* pertaining to, proceeding from, or acting upon, the side; as, *lateral* buds are those along the sides of a branch or twig.—*adv.* **laterally.**

lath (làth), *n.* a thin, narrow strip of wood used for making framework to be covered with plaster in building.—*n.* **lather.**

lathe (lā*th*), *n.* a machine by which articles of wood, metal, etc., are held and turned while being shaped and polished by a tool.

Engine Lathe. *A*, bed; *B*, headstock; *C*, tailstock; *D*, tool rest; *E*, live center; *F*, dead center; *G*, cone driving pulley.

lath-er (lă*th*'ẽr), *n.* froth made by moistened soap; foam from sweating, as of a horse: *v.t.* to cover with froth or foam: *v.i.* to form foam or suds.—*adj.* **lathery.**

lath-ing (làth-ĭng), *n.* the thin, narrow strips of wood on which plaster is laid in building.

Lat-in (lăt'ĭn), *adj.* pertaining to, written or expressed in, the language of ancient Rome; pertaining to Latium, ancient Rome, its inhabitants or language, or to the races and languages derived from Rome; Roman: *n.* an ancient Roman; the language of ancient Rome and its literature.—**Latin Quarter,** a section of Paris, south of the Seine, populated largely by students.

Lat-in cross (lăt'ĭn krŏs), a cross having the lowest limb longer than the two sides and top.

Lat-in-ism (lăt'ĭn-ĭzm), *n.* an expression belonging peculiarly to the Latin language.

Lat-in-ize (lăt'ĭn-īz), *v.t.* to give Latin endings, or characteristics, to; translate into Latin.

lat-i-tude (lăt'ĭ-tūd), *n.* distance on the earth's surface as measured by degrees north or south from the equator; breadth; extent; freedom from rules.

lat-i-tu-di-nal (lăt"ĭ-tū'dĭ-năl), *adj.* relating to, or in the direction of, latitude, or distance in degrees north or south from the equator.

lat-i-tu-di-na-ri-an (lăt″ĭ-tū″dĭ-nā′rĭ-ăn), *adj.* wide in range or scope; not attached strictly to any particular belief or opinion, especially in religious matters; allowing others their own beliefs; as, *latitudinarian* ministers: *n.* one who holds views wide in range or scope or who cares little about forms of creed, worship, or church government.

la-trine (lȧ-trēn′), *n.* a privy for the use of soldiers.

lat-ter (lăt′ẽr), *adj.* being the second of two things already mentioned; recent; modern.—*adv.* **latterly.**

lat-tice (lăt′ĭs), *n.* crossed or interlaced openwork of metal or wood; hence, any door, window, gate, etc., made of such work: *v.t.* to furnish or cross with openwork of metal or wood: **latticework,** work made by crossing or interlacing strips or bars of materials such as wood or metal.

laud (lôd), *v.t.* to praise highly: *n.* praise; worship or hymn of praise.

laud-a-ble (lôd′ȧ-bl), *adj.* worthy of praise; as, a *laudable* effort.—*adv.* **laudably.**—*n.* **laudableness, laudability.**

lau-da-num (lô′dȧ-nŭm), *n.* a preparation of opium.

lau-da-tion (lô-dā′shŭn), *n.* high praise; extolment.

laud-a-to-ry (lôd′ȧ-tō-rĭ), *adj.* expressing praise; eulogizing.

laugh (läf), *n.* a convulsive sound caused by merriment; an expression, made only by man, of mirth, ridicule, etc.: *v.i.* to express merriment, etc., by such a sound; appear gay, pleasant, etc.; jeer: with *at:* *v.t.* to express or utter with laughter; to move or affect by merriment or ridicule; as, they *laughed* her out of her ill-temper.—*n.* **laugher.**

laugh-a-ble (läf′ȧ-bl), *adj.* funny; mirth-provoking; causing amusement; ridiculous.—*adv.* **laughably.**

laugh-ing gas (läf′ĭng găs), nitrous oxide gas, used as a light anesthetic, by dentists especially.

laugh-ing-stock (läf′ĭng-stŏk″), *n.* an object of ridicule.

laugh-ter (läf′tẽr), *n.* convulsive sounds and movements caused by merriment.

launch (länch; lônch), *v.t.* to move or cause to slide into the water, as a vessel; send forth; hurl; dart: *v.i.* to put to sea; plunge; enter on a new career: *n.* the sliding of a ship from the ways into the water; the largest boat of a man-of-war; a large, open pleasure boat, usually moved by steam, gas, or electricity.

laun-der (län′dẽr; lôn′dẽr), *v.t.* to wash and iron.

laun-dress (län′drĕs; lôn′drĕs), *n.* a washerwoman.

laun-dry (län′drĭ; lôn′drĭ), *n.* [*pl.* laundries (-drĭz)], an establishment or place where clothes are washed and ironed; colloquially, articles sent to be washed.

lau-re-ate (lô′rē-āt), *adj.* decked or crowned with laurel; hence, worthy of honor: *n.* one crowned with laurel: **poet laureate,** a title given by the English monarch to a poet whose duty is to compose poems for national occasions.—*n.* **laureateship.**

lau-rel (lô′rĕl; lŏr′ĕl), *n.* an evergreen shrub of southern Europe, called sweet bay, bay tree, etc.: used as a symbol of fame and honor; any of several shrubs resembling the bay, especially the flowering mountain laurel of the northern United States; a crown or wreath of bay given as a prize or an honor; hence, honor; distinction.—*adj.* **laureled.**

la-va (lä′vȧ), *n.* melted rock such as that which is thrown from a volcano.

la-val-lière (lȧ″văl″yâr′; lä″vȧ-lēr′), *n.* a lady's flat, round, or oval pendant, worn on a necklace, or chain around the neck. [Fr.]

lav-a-to-ry (lăv′ȧ-tō-rĭ), *n.* [*pl.* lavatories (-rĭz)], a place for washing the hands and face: found in more or less public places, such as hotels and railroad stations; a retiring room.

lave (lāv), *v.t.* and *v.i.* [*p.t.* and *p.p.* laved, *p.pr.* laving], to bathe or wash; to flow or wash gently against.

lav-en-der (lăv′ĕn-dẽr), *n.* a fragrant plant of the mint family; the perfume obtained from the plant; the pale lilac color of its flowers.

lav-ish (lăv′ĭsh), *adj.* liberal; extravagant: *v.t.* to expend or bestow liberally; squander; waste.—*adv.* **lavishly.**—*n.* **lavishness.**

law (lô), *n.* a rule of action established by authority or custom; the whole body of such binding rules or customs; as, he was careless of social *law;* act or enactment of a legislative, or lawmaking, body; judicial process; legal science; as, he studied *law;* the legal profession; as, he chose *law* as his career; the moral code, given by Moses and later lawgivers; a rule of science or art; a scientific statement of the action and relation of things in nature, etc., observed to be always the same under given conditions; as, the *law* of gravitation; an established principle.
Syn. code, edict, statute, decree.

law-ful (lô′fo͝ol), *adj.* according to established rule or custom; just; as, *lawful* acts; rightful; as, *lawful* ownership of property.—*adv.* **lawfully.**—*n.* **lawfulness.**
Syn. legal, legitimate.
Ant. (see illegal).

law-giv-er (lô′gĭv″ẽr), *n.* one who declares, or enacts a law, as Moses, Solon, etc.

law-less (lô′lĕs), *adj.* not obedient to, or controlled by, authority; not according to established rule or custom; ungoverned; unruly.—*adv.* **lawlessly.**—*n.* **lawlessness.**

law-mak-er (lô′māk″ẽr), *n.* one who, or a member of the body which, enacts a law.

lawn (lôn), *n.* a plot of grass kept closely mown; fine, thin cambric or muslin.

lawn ten-nis (lôn tĕn′ĭs), an outdoor game played with rackets, balls, and a net.

law-suit (lô′sūt″), *n.* an action in a court, etc., for the settlement of a claim or right.

law-yer (lô′yẽr), *n.* one skilled in knowledge of law; one who conducts lawsuits for others in the law courts.

lax (lăks), *adj.* not firm, tense, or rigid; loose; vague; weak; as, *lax* principles; *lax* discipline.—*adv.* **laxly.**—*n.* **laxness.**

lax-a-tive (lăk′sȧ-tĭv), *adj.* loosening; causing the bowels to move, as a medicine: *n.* a medicine which causes the bowels to move.

lax-i-ty (lăk′sĭ-tĭ), *n.* the state or quality of being loose, vague, or weak.

lay (lā), past tense of the intransitive verb *lie:* *v.t.* [*p.t.* and *p.p.* laid, *p.pr.* laying], to put or place; spread over; cause to lie; settle; calm; bring forth and drop, as an egg; wager; deposit; set or form secretly; as, to *lay* a trap or plot; impose, as a burden; as, to *lay* a task on someone: *v.i.* to produce eggs: *adj.* relating to the people, as distinguished from the clergy, or members of other professions; as, *lay* delegates to a church convention, not of a given profession; as, the *lay* mind understands little of the cause of disease: *n.* a simple song or poem.

lay-er (lā'ẽr), *n.* one that lays; a stratum, row, or bed; one thickness; as, a *layer* of earth; a *layer* of bricks; a runner of a plant fastened down and covered with earth.

lay-ette (lā-yĕt'), *n.* a complete outfit for a newborn child; a three-sided tray used to carry powder or explosives. [Fr.]

lay fig-ure (lā fĭg'ūr), a jointed model upon which to hang drapery; one who weakly follows the will of others; a person in a position of authority who exerts no real power or influence.

lay-man (lā'măn), *n.* [*pl.* laymen (-mĕn)], one of the people, as distinguished from a clergyman; a person not belonging to a given profession; as, a *layman's* opinion of a painting differs from that of an artist.

la-zar (lā'zẽr), *n.* a person, especially a beggar, who has a horrible disease; a leper.

laz-a-ret-to (lăz'ȧ-rĕt'ō), *n.* a hospital for persons suffering with infectious or dangerous diseases, as smallpox; a ship's storeroom. Also, **lazaret.**

Laz-a-rus (lăz'ȧ-rŭs), *n.* in the Bible, the brother of Mary and Martha.—John xi; also, in the parable, the beggar who lay at the rich man's door.—Luke xvi.

la-zi-ness (lā'zĭ-nĕs), *n.* indolence; sluggishness; dislike for work.

la-zy (lā'zĭ), *adj.* [*comp.* lazier, *superl.* laziest], not inclined to action or work; idle; indolent.—*adv.* **lazily.**

lea (lē), *n.* a meadow; a grassy field or pasture land.

leach (lēch), *n.* the material, as wood ashes, through which water passes in making lye; the solution obtained; the vessel in which lye is made: *v.t.* to pass water through (ashes) to form lye; to wash by draining water through: often with *out:* *v.i.* to come from by draining; as, lye *leaches* from the ashes.

lead (lĕd), *n.* a soft, heavy, bluish-gray metal; a weight attached to a rope for sounding depths at sea; a thin strip of metal for separating lines of type in printing; a stick of graphite or black carbon used in pencils: *adj.* consisting, wholly or partially, of lead: *v.t.* to cover, fit, or join with lead; in printing, to place thin metal strips between the lines of.

lead (lēd), *v.t.* [*p.t.* and *p.p.* led, *p.pr.* leading], to conduct by the hand; as, to *lead* a little child; show the way to; guide or conduct by advice or counsel; to have the direction or control of; as, to *lead* an army; to go ahead of; to be first among; as, to *lead* one's class; induce; spend; as, to *lead* an unhappy life; to begin a game by playing (a certain card): *v.i.* to take the first place; act as a guide, director, manager, etc.; to take a course; as, the path *leads* through the woods; to conduct; as, the broad way *leads* to destruction; play the first card or domino: *n.* guidance; first place or position; in games, the right to play first or the play made; the principal actor in a play, or the part he plays.

lead-bath (lĕd'bȧth), *n.* a furnace in which the powdered ores of gold or silver are brought in mechanical contact with melted lead: an alloy is thus formed from which the precious metals are afterwards extracted by various processes.

Lead-bath

lead-ed (lĕd'ĕd), *p. adj.* separated by strips of metal; as, *leaded* glass windows are made of small pieces of glass separated by strips of lead; set in or covered with lead.

lead-en (lĕd'n), *adj.* made of, or colored like, lead; heavy; sluggish; dull.

lead-er (lēd'ẽr), *n.* one who guides, directs, or conducts; one who occupies, or is fitted to occupy, the first or chief place; the chief editorial article of a newspaper; a tough, elastic band of tissue uniting a muscle to some other part: called also a *tendon;* the foremost horse when several are used to draw a vehicle; a pipe to carry off rainwater from the roof of a house. —*n.* **leadership.**

lead piece (lēd pēs), the first gun in position among the guns of a battery.

lead team (lēd tēm), the first pair of the six horses harnessed to a field gun, the left-hand horse being ridden by the artilleryman known as the lead driver.

leaf (lēf), *n.* [*pl.* leaves (lēvz)], one of the thin flat parts of a plant borne by the stem; a thinly beaten sheet; as, gold *leaf* used in gilding domes, etc.; something thin and flat, as a single sheet of a book with a page on each side, a part of a folding table top, one-half of a folding door, etc.

leaf-age (lēf'āj), *n.* leaves collectively; foliage.

leaf-let (lēf'lĕt), *n.* a small foliage leaf; a printed sheet or circular.

leaf-y (lēf'ĭ), *adj.* [*comp.* leafier, *superl.* leafiest], full of foliage.

league (lēg), *n.* an agreement between two or more persons, nations, or parties for the accomplishment of some purpose for their common good; a measure of three geographical miles: *v.t.* and *v.i.* to combine for mutual interests.

lea-guer (lē'gẽr), *n.* formerly, a siege or continued attack; a besieging camp; a member of a confederacy, or body of persons united for mutual interests: *v.t.* to besiege.

leak (lēk), *n.* a hole or crack which lets anything, especially a fluid, in or out, contrary to intention: *v.i.* to let anything, especially a fluid, in or out through a hole or crack, when not intended; to become gradually, often unintentionally, public.

leak-age (lēk'āj), *n.* the passing in or out of anything through a hole or crack; the quantity that passes in or out; allowance for such loss.

leak-y (lēk'ĭ), *adj.* allowing water or other fluid to pass in or out through holes or cracks; not able to keep a secret.

 AMERICAN TREE LEAVES, FLOWERS AND FRUITS

1. Black oak. 2. White ash. 3. White oak. 4. White elm. 5 Cucumber tree. 6. Yellow poplar. 7. Sycamore or Buttonwood. 8. Sugar maple. 9. Red cedar 10. Sweet or Red gum.

leal (lēl), *adj.* true-hearted; loyal; faithful. [Scot.]

lean (lēn), *v.i.* [*p.t.* and *p.p.* leaned, leant, *p.pr.* leaning], to slant from an upright position; to bend over for support; as, to *lean* on a cane; to rely; as, to *lean* on one's friends for advice; to tend; as, his opinion *leaned* toward the popular side: *v.t.* to cause to slant; rest: *adj.* thin; as, a *lean* person or animal; free from fat; as, *lean* meat; not productive; as, *lean* years; a *lean* harvest.—*n.* **leanness.**
Syn., adj. meager, spare.
Ant. (see fat).

lean-to (lēn′tōō″), *n.* a building whose rafters rest on another building, as a shed built against a house.

leap (lēp), *v.i.* [*p.t.* and *p.p.* leaped, leapt, *p.pr.* leaping], to pass over by a bound or jump; as, to *leap* a ditch; to cause to jump or spring over; as, to *leap* a horse over a hedge: *v.i.* to jump or spring off the ground or from a high place; as, to *leap* from a wall; to vault; to bound or move suddenly; as, my heart *leaps* up: *n.* the act of passing over with a bound; a jump; a spring; the space passed over in jumping.—*n.* **leaper.**

leap-frog (lēp′frŏg″), *n.* a boy's game, in which one player stoops and another jumps over him.

leap year (lēp yēr), a year of 366 days, when February has twenty-nine days; every year that is divisible by four, except those that are divisible by 100 and not by 400, such as 1800.

learn (lûrn), *v.t.* [*p.t.* and *p.p.* learned, learnt, *p.pr.* learning], to gain knowledge of; fix in the mind; as, to *learn* a lesson: *v.i.* to gain or receive knowledge or skill; as, to *learn* quickly.—*n.* **learner.**

learn-ed (lûr′nĕd), *p.adj.* having much knowledge; skilled; as, a *learned* professor or lawyer.—*adv.* **learnedly.**
Syn. trained, scholarly.
Ant. (see ignorant).

learn-ing (lûr′nĭng), *n.* knowledge of literature, languages, science, etc.; knowledge or skill gained by study or instruction.

lease (lēs), *n.* a written contract for the renting of land or buildings for a certain period of time; the time for which a property is rented: *v.t.* to grant possession for a certain time by a written contract; as, an owner *leases* a house to a tenant; take possession of by contract; as, a tenant *leases* a house from the owner.

lease-hold (lēs′hōld″), *n.* the holding of property by contract for a certain time: property so held.—*n.* **leaseholder.**

leash (lēsh), *n.* a thong of leather or a long cord by which a hawk or hound is held: three of one kind; as, a *leash* of dogs; "a *leash* of kings"; a band by which anything is held: *v.t.* to tie or hold with a thong or cord.

least (lēst), *adj.* superlative of *little;* smallest in degree, size, value, importance, etc.: *adv.* in the lowest or smallest degree.

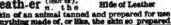

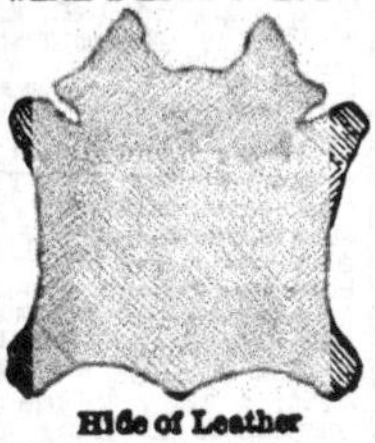
Hide of Leather

leath-er (lĕth′ẽr), *n.* the skin of an animal tanned and prepared for use; anything made of, or like, the skin so prepared.

leath-er-et (lĕth′ẽr-ĕt), *n.* an imitation leather made of paper. Also, **leatherette.**

leath-ern (lĕth′ẽrn), *adj.* made of, or like, leather.

leave (lēv), *n.* permission granted; departure; farewell; a short vacation given to a soldier on active service: *v.t.* [*p.t.* and *p.p.* left, *p.pr.* leaving], to allow to remain; as, they will *leave* him behind; to depart from; forsake; give up; bequeath; cease from; as, to *leave* work; refer for decision; as, *leave* it to me; *v.i.* to depart; go away.
Syn., n. liberty, permission, license; *v.* quit, relinquish.
Ant. (see prohibition).

leav-en (lĕv′n), *v.t.* to produce fermentation in; to make light, as dough; to touch with something which tends to spoil; to mix; as, to *leaven* correction with a little praise: *n.* a ferment mixed with a substance to render it light, as yeast with dough; any influence that, working silently and strongly, causes changes in things or opinions.

leav-ings (lēv′ĭngz), *n.pl.* what is left over; discarded remains.

lec-tern (lĕk′tẽrn), *n.* the reading desk of a church.

lec-ture (lĕk′tūr), *n.* a formal talk on any subject; a lengthy reproof: *v.i.* to deliver a formal talk: *v.t.* to rebuke formally.—*n.* **lecturer.**

ledge (lĕj), *n.* a shelf; ridge; layer; edge; as, a *ledge* of rock; the *ledge* of a window.

ledg-er (lĕj′ẽr), *n.* the principal account book of a business house.

lee (lē), *n.* the side or quarter towards which the wind blows; calm or sheltered side.

leech (lēch), *n.* a worm furnished with a sucker, used in medicine for sucking blood; formerly, the name for a physician; one who gets all he can out of another: *v.t.* to bleed with leeches.

leek (lēk), *n.* a plant of the lily family having a flavor like the onion, but stronger.

leer (lēr), *n.* a sly, sidelong look of malice, triumph, or evil desire: *v.i.* to look slyly or with a sidelong look.

lees (lēz), *n.pl.* the foreign matter (dregs) of liquor that has settled in the bottom of a cask or other holder.

lee-ward (lē′wẽrd; *naut.* lū′ẽrd), *adj.* being in the direction towards which the wind blows: *n.* the lee side, or the direction toward which the wind blows: *adv.* toward the lee side.

lee-way (lē′wā″), *n.* the sideways drift of a vessel in the direction towards which the wind blows; room for action.

left (lĕft), *p.t.* and *p.p.* of the verb *leave:* *adj.* pertaining to the weaker, less active side of the human body: opposite to *right;* placed to the left: *n.* that which is on the left side; the most liberal party in a European parliament: so called because often seated on the left of the chair.

left-hand-ed (lĕft′hăn″dĕd), *adj.* using the left hand with greater strength or skill than the right; awkward.

leg (lĕg), *n.* one of the limbs by which men and animals walk, especially, in man, that part of the lower limb between the knee and the ankle; anything resembling this limb, especially if used as a support; as, the *leg* of a chair; a covering for a lower limb.

leg-a-cy (lĕg′ȧ-sĭ), *n.* [*pl.* legacies (-sĭz)], a gift by will of money or property; anything that has come down from an ancestor; as, a *legacy* of family pride.

le-gal (lē'găl), *adj.* pertaining to law; permitted or authorized by law: **legal tender**, currency or coin which a government has declared shall be received in payment of debts; a forward offer of money in payment of a debt.—*adv.* **legally.**

le-gal-i-ty (lē-găl'ĭ-tĭ), *n.* conformity to law; lawfulness.

le-gal-ize (lē'găl-īz), *v.t.* to make lawful; as, to *legalise* the sale of intoxicating liquors.

leg-ate (lĕg'āt), *n.* a representative or agent of the Pope; an ambassador, delegate, or messenger; envoy.

leg-a-tee (lĕg"ȧ-tē'), *n.* a person to whom money or property is left by will.

le-ga-tion (lē-gā'shŭn), *n.* the authorizing of one person to act for another; an embassy; an ambassador and his associates; the official dwelling place of an ambassador.

le-ga-to (lā-gä'tō), *adj.* and *adv.* in music, moving smoothly without breaks between notes. [It.]

leg-end (lĕj'ĕnd; lē'jĕnd), *n.* a romantic or nonhistorical story handed down from the past; myth; fable; an inscription, as on a coin, under a picture, etc.

leg-end-a-ry (lĕj'ĕn-dā-rĭ), *adj.* told of in story, fable, or myth; as, Romulus was the *legendary* founder of Rome.

leg-er (lĕj'ĕr), *adj.* light and fine, as a line: **leger lines**, lines added above or below the musical staff.

leg-er-de-main (lĕj"ĕr-dē-măn'), *n.* sleight of hand; magic.

legged (lĕgd; or lĕg'ĕd), *adj.* having legs: used in combinations; as, a two-*legged* animal.

leg-gings (lĕg'ĭngz), *n.pl.* long gaiters used as protection from cold or wet. Also, **leggins.**

leg-horn (lĕg'hôrn), *n.* a kind of fine Italian straw braid, or a hat made of it; a breed of domestic fowls.

leg-i-bil-i-ty (lĕj"ĭ-bĭl'ĭ-tĭ), *n.* the quality of being easily read.

leg-i-ble (lĕj'ĭ-bl), *adj.* capable of being read; clear; distinct; apparent; as, vertical handwriting is *legible.*—*adv.* **legibly.** —*n.* **legibleness.**

le-gion (lē'jŭn), *n.* a division of the ancient Roman army; an army; a great number.

le-gion-a-ry (lē'jŭn-ā-rĭ), *adj.* belonging to, or consisting of, legions; too great to be numbered: *n.* a soldier of a Roman legion.

leg-is-late (lĕj'ĭs-lāt), *v.i.* to make or enact a law or laws; as, Congress *legislates* for our country: *v.t.* to bring about by the passage of law.

leg-is-la-tion (lĕj"ĭs-lā'shŭn), *n.* the act of making a law or laws; the laws so made.

leg-is-la-tive (lĕj'ĭs-lā-tĭv), *adj.* pertaining to, or enacted by, law; having the power to make laws.

leg-is-la-tor (lĕj'ĭs-lā"tĕr), *n.* a lawgiver; a member of a lawmaking body.

leg-is-la-ture (lĕj'ĭs-lā"tūr), *n.* that body in a state which has the power of enacting and repealing laws.

le-git-i-ma-cy (lē-jĭt'ĭ-mȧ-sĭ), *n.* the state or condition of being allowed by law; lawfulness of birth.

le-git-i-mate (lē-jĭt'ĭ-māt), *adj.* lawful; born of wedded parents; real; correct; reasonable; as, illness is a *legitimate* reason for absence from school: *v.t.* (lē-jĭt'ĭ-māt), to make or declare to be lawful or regular.—*adv.* **legitimately.**

le-git-i-mist (lē-jĭt'ĭ-mĭst), *n.* a supporter of the established government, especially of a hereditary monarchy.

leg-ume (lĕg'ūm; lē-gūm'), *n.* the seed or fruit of certain plants, as the bean, pea, etc.; a two-valved seed vessel having its seeds attached to one side only, as a peapod.—*adj.* **leguminous.**

lei-sure (lē'zhŭr; lĕzh'ŭr), *n.* spare time: *adj.* free from business; unoccupied; as, *leisure* hours.

lei-sured (lē'zhŭrd), *adj.* having much spare time; as, the *leisured* class of people.

lei-sure-ly (lē'zhŭr-lĭ), *adj.* not hasty; slow; deliberate: *adv.* not hastily; deliberately.—*n.* **leisureliness.**

lem-on (lĕm'ŭn), *n.* a well-known acid fruit of the orange family; the light-yellow color of the fruit: *adj.* flavored with, or colored like, a lemon.

lem-on-ade (lĕm"ŭn-ād'), *n.* a drink of sweetened water flavored with lemon juice.

le-mur (lē'mŭr), *n.* a small animal related to the monkey family.

lend (lĕnd), *v.t.* [*p.t.* and *p.p.* lent, *p.pr.* lending], to grant to another for use for a time; to afford; as, to *lend* aid; to devote; as, to *lend* oneself to a scheme: *v.i.* to make a loan.—*n.* **lender.**

length (lĕngth), *n.* the measure of anything from end to end; extent (of space or time); as, the *length* of a war; a given space taken as a measure; as, two *lengths* of cloth in a skirt; reach; forty-two lines of an actor's part: **at length**, in full; finally.

length-en (lĕng'thn), *v.t.* to make long or longer: *v.i.* to grow longer; as, daylight begins to *lengthen* in December.

length-wise (lĕngth'wīz"), *adv.* in the direction from end to end. Also, **lengthways.**

length-y (lĕng'thĭ), *adj.* long and tiresome; as, a *lengthy* speech.—*adv.* **lengthily.**—*n.* **lengthiness.**

le-ni-en-cy (lē'nĭ-ĕn-sĭ; lēn'yĕn-sĭ), *n.* forbearance; mildness; mercifulness. Also, **lenience.**

le-ni-ent (lē'nĭ-ĕnt; lēn'yĕnt), *adj.* indulgent; mild; merciful; as, a *lenient* judge.—*adv.* **leniently.**

len-i-tive (lĕn'ĭ-tĭv), *adj.* soothing; allaying pain or suffering: *n.* anything that allays pain or soothes passion.

len-i-ty (lĕn'ĭ-tĭ), *n.* mildness of temper or disposition; gentleness of treatment; forbearance.

lens (lĕnz), *n.* a piece of glass or other transparent substance, with one or two curved surfaces, fitted for changing the direction of rays of light; a body in the eyes of animals whose purpose is to bring the rays of light to a point on the sensitive membrane within the eye; the crystalline humor of the eye.

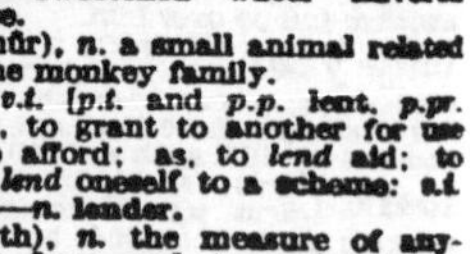

Lenses. *A*, plano-concave; *B*, double concave; *C*, plano-convex; *D*, double convex; *E*, meniscus; *F*, concavo-convex.

Lent (lĕnt), *n.* a fast of forty days (excluding Sundays) observed by some churches as a preparation for Easter, and a time of repentance for sin.—*adj.* **Lenten.**

len-tic-u-lar (lĕn-tĭk'ū-lår), *adj.* bulging out, or convex, on both sides; as, a magnifying glass is *lenticular* in form.

len-til (lĕn'tĭl), *n.* a plant of the same nature as the pea, bean, etc., whose seeds are used for food, or are ground into meal: *pl.* the seeds of the plant used for food.

Le-o (lē'ō), *n.* a group of stars called the Lion; one of the signs of the zodiac.

le-o-nine (lē'ō-nīn), *adj.* like a lion; powerful; kingly.

leop-ard (lĕp'ẽrd), *n.* a large catlike beast of prey, with a beautiful spotted skin of yellow and black.

lep-er (lĕp'ẽr), *n.* one suffering from an infectious disease marked by ulcers and white scaly scabs.

lep-ro-sy (lĕp'rō-sĭ), *n.* [*pl.* leprosies (-sĭz)], a contagious, usually fatal, skin disease marked by ulcers and white scaly scabs.

lep-rous (lĕp'rŭs), *adj.* having leprosy, a contagious disease marked by ulcers and white scaly scabs; covered with white scales; unclean.

lese maj-es-ty (lēz măj'ĕs-tĭ), a crime against the sovereign or ruling power; treason; as, in many European countries, any criticism of the ruler is considered *lese majesty.* Also, **lese majesty.**

le-sion (lē'zhŭn), *n.* injury; change in a function or organism caused by disease.

less (lĕs), *adj.* comparative of *little;* not so much; smaller; made smaller by taking away; as, ten *less* seven: *adv.* in a smaller or lower degree: *n.* a smaller quantity: a *suffix* meaning without; as, soul*less*, worth*less*, etc.

les-see (lĕs-ē'), *n.* a person to whom property is rented for a certain time, upon certain conditions.

less-en (lĕs'n), *v.t.* to make smaller; reduce; to disparage: *v.i.* to grow smaller; to shrink; to become less important.

less-er (lĕs'ẽr), *adj.* smaller; inferior; as, the *lesser* evil; the *lesser* value.

les-son (lĕs'n), *n.* that which a pupil learns, or repeats, or does for a teacher; instruction or lecture given at one time; an exercise; that which is learned or taught by experience, observation, etc.; a portion of scripture read at a church service; as, "Here endeth the first *lesson*."

les-sor (lĕs'ôr; lĕs-ôr'), *n.* the grantor of a lease; one who lets property to another for a certain time, upon certain conditions.

lest (lĕst), *conj.* that . . . not; for fear that; as, "Take heed *lest* ye fall"; that; as, I was in dread *lest* they should arrive too late: used without *not* after expressions indicating fear, anxiety, etc.

let (lĕt), *v.t.* [*p.t.* and *p.p.* let, *p.pr.* letting], to permit; grant to a tenant; lease; give out on contract: *v.i.* to be hired or leased; as, the house *lets* for fifty dollars a month; allow to be done: *n.* an obstacle: common only in the phrase, "without *let* or hindrance": otherwise obsolete.

le-thal (lē'thăl), *adj.* deadly; fatal; pertaining to death.

le-thar-gic (lē-thär'jĭk), *adj.* sluggish; dull; unnaturally drowsy.

leth-ar-gy (lĕth'ȧr-jĭ), *n.* unhealthy drowsiness; unnatural prolonged slumber; listlessness; as, the first symptom of certain diseases is extreme *lethargy;* state of inaction or indifference; as, war often awakes a nation from *lethargy.*

Le-the (lē'thē), *n.* in classic mythology, the underworld stream of forgetfulness, whose waters, when drunk, produced loss of memory of life on earth; hence, forgetfulness.

le-the-an (lē-thē'ăn), *adj.* having the power of the fabled waters of Lethe, which caused forgetfulness of the past; causing forgetfulness.

let-ter (lĕt'ẽr), *n.* a mark or character used to represent a sound; written or printed communication; a printing type; word for word meaning; as, the Hebrews kept the *letter* of the law; a document certifying certain privileges, authority, etc.; as, a *letter* of credit: *pl.* knowledge; learning; literature; as, great men of *letters: v.t.* to impress or write letters upon.

let-tered (lĕt'ẽrd), *adj.* learned; marked with letters.

let-ter-gram (lĕt'ẽr-grăm), *n.* a night telegram at reduced rates.

let-ter-head (lĕt'ẽr-hĕd"), *n.* a printed or engraved heading at the top of a sheet of writing paper.

let-ter-ing (lĕt'ẽr-ĭng), *n.* the act or process of marking with letters; the inscription, etc., made by marking; as, the *lettering* on a tombstone.

let-ters pat-ent (lĕt'ẽrz păt'ĕnt, or pā'-tĕnt), an official paper under seal of the government, giving a person authority or permission to do some act or enjoy some privilege.

let-tuce (lĕt'ĭs), *n.* a garden plant the leaves of which are used as a salad.

Le-vant (lē-vănt'), *n.* the near East; the Orient; the countries near the eastern Mediterranean.—*adj.* **Levantine.**

le-va-tor (lē-vā'tôr), *n.* a muscle that serves to raise an organ or some part.

lev-ee (lĕ-vē'; lĕv'ē), *n.* a morning reception held by a sovereign or personage of high rank: properly, one attended by gentlemen only; in the United States, any general reception, especially one at the White House; a river embankment built to prevent overflow: *v.t.* to embank.

lev-el (lĕv'ĕl), *n.* a horizontal surface or line; surface without inequalities; equality of height; as, this position is on a *level* with that; a horizontal plane which represents the height of a certain position above the sea; position reckoned in terms of height; as, at this *level* the air is rare; she reached a higher social *level;* standard; an instrument used in surveying; section of a canal from one lock to another: *adj.* even; horizontal; smooth; steady; equal to something else in importance: *adv.* in a horizontal direction: *v.t.* [*p.t.* and *p.p.* leveled, *p.pr.* leveling], to make even; free from inequalities; bring to the same plane; point in taking aim.—*n.* **levelness.**

lev-el-er (lĕv'ĕl-ẽr), *n.* that which, or one who, makes even or equal; one who would destroy distinctions of rank and society; a scraping instrument used in grading. Also, **leveller.**

le-ver (lē'vẽr; lĕv'ẽr), *n.* a bar of metal, etc., turning on a support (fulcrum) and raising a weight.

le-ver-age (lē'vẽr-āj; lĕv'ẽr-āj), *n.* the mechanical power gained by using a lever; lever action.

le-vi-a-than (lē-vī'ȧ-thăn), *n.* a large animal of the sea mentioned in several places in the Bible (Job xli. 1–8; Ps. civ. 2), but no longer known; an thing huge, as a whale, etc.: also often applied to very large ships.

lev-i-ta-tion (lĕv'ĭ-tā'shŭn), *n.* lightness; the state of being lighter than the surrounding water, air, etc.

Le-vite (lē'vīt), *n.* in Jewish history, one of the tribe of Levi, from which the priests were taken, and whose members helped in the care of the temple.—*adj.* **Levitical.**

Le-vit-i-cus (lē-vĭt'ĭ-kŭs), *n.* the third book of the Old Testament, containing the laws for the priests and Levites.

lev-i-ty (lĕv'ĭ-tĭ), *n.* lightness of disposition, conduct, etc.; trifling gaiety; as, *levity* is out of place when talking of sacred things; lightness of weight.

lev-y (lĕv'ĭ), *v.t.* [*p.t.* and *p.p.* levied, *p.pr.* levying], to raise or collect by compulsion, as an army or a tax: *v.i.* to seize in order to collect money; as, to *levy* on household goods for unpaid rent: *n.* the act of collecting or raising by compulsion, as money or men; the amount or number raised.

lev-y war (lĕv'ĭ wôr), to make war or begin hostilities.

lewd (lūd), *adj.* sensual; impure; as, *lewd* conversation.—*adv.* **lewdly.**—*n.* **lewdness.**

lex-i-cog-ra-pher (lĕk"sĭ-kŏg'rȧ-fẽr), *n.* the editor or compiler of a dictionary, or lexicon.

lex-i-cog-ra-phy (lĕk"sĭ-kŏg'rȧ-fĭ), *n.* the art or occupation of editing or compiling dictionaries, or lexicons.

lex-i-con (lĕk'sĭ-kŏn), *n.* a dictionary; a word book.

li-a-bil-i-ty (lī"ȧ-bĭl'ĭ-tĭ), *n.* [*pl.* liabilities (-tĭz)], the state of being exposed to or responsible for; as, *liability* to accident; *liability* for damages; that for which one is responsible: *pl.* debts.

li-a-ble (lī'ȧ-bl), *adj.* exposed to damage, danger, expense, etc.; as, *liable* to misfortune; answerable; responsible.

li-ai-son (lē"ā"zôṅ'), *n.* a bond or relationship; an improper intimacy between a man and a woman; a connection or communication established between two or more military units: **liaison officer,** a joint officer of two coöperating military units: **liaison patrol,** a small detachment of soldiers operating in territory jointly occupied by two military units. [Fr.]

li-ar (lī'ẽr), *n.* one who habitually tells untruths; one who intentionally tells that which is false.

li-ba-tion (lī-bā'shŭn), *n.* the act of pouring wine or other liquid on the ground as a sacrifice to a god; the liquid so poured out; as, the ancient Greeks poured a *libation* to their gods.

li-bel (lī'bĕl), *n.* any false or unjust writing, print, publication, or picture calculated to injure the reputation or character of anyone and bring him into public contempt: *v.t.* [*p.t.* and *p.p.* libeled, *p.pr.* libeling], to publish a false, injurious statement against; injure the character of.—*n.* **libeler, libeller; libelant, libellant; libelist, libellist; libelee, libellee.**

li-bel-ous (lī'bĕl-ŭs), *adj.* containing, or of the nature of, anything that defames; as, a *libelous* report. Also, **libellous.**—*adv.* **libelously, libellously.**

lib-er-al (lĭb'ẽr-ăl), *adj.* generous; plentiful; free from narrowness in ideas or doctrines: *n.* one who believes in extension of freedom in political, social, religious, and other institutions: **Liberal,** a member of the Liberal party of England.

lib-er-al arts (lĭb'ẽr-ăl ärts), the branches of academic learning leading to a degree of bachelor of arts, such as literature, history, science, language, etc.

lib-er-al-ism (lĭb'ẽr-ăl-ĭzm), *n.* the principles in politics or religion of one who believes in extension of freedom.

lib-er-al-i-ty (lĭb"ẽr-ăl'ĭ-tĭ), *n.* [*pl.* liberalities (-tĭz)], the quality of being free and generous; mental breadth.

lib-er-ate (lĭb'ẽr-āt), *v.t.* to set free from restraint or bondage; as, to *liberate* the slaves; to free from confinement; as, to *liberate* the waters of a stream that has been dammed.—*n.* **liberator.**

lib-er-a-tion (lĭb'ẽr-ā'shŭn), *n.* the act of setting free; state of being set free.

lib-er-tine (lĭb'ẽr-tĭn), *n.* one who does not restrain his evil impulses, appetites, and desires: *adj.* unrestrained morally or socially; loose in morals.—*n.* **libertinism.**

lib-er-ty (lĭb'ẽr-tĭ), *n.* [*pl.* liberties (-tĭz)], freedom; special privilege or permission; ungranted or undue freedom; as, to take a *liberty*.

Syn. independence, license.

Ant. (see captivity, constraint).

Lib-er-ty Bond (lĭb'ẽr-tĭ bŏnd), a United States government bond, issued during the World War, as security for repayment of money lent to the government for war expenses.

Lib-er-ty Loan (lĭb'ẽr-tĭ lōn), one of a series of several loans made by the people of the United States to the government during the World War, and secured by government bonds.

Lib-er-ty Mo-tor (lĭb'ẽr-tĭ mō'tẽr), a type of twelve cylinder gasoline motor, perfected during the World War, capable of great speed, and adopted for use, for the sake of uniformity, in all United States airplanes.

li-bra-ri-an (lī-brā'rĭ-ăn), *n.* one who has charge of a large collection of books.

li-bra-ry (lī'brā-rĭ), *n.* [*pl.* libraries (-rĭz)], an arranged collection of books: the building where such a collection is kept.

li-bret-tist (lĭ-brĕt'ĭst), *n.* the writer of a libretto, or book containing the words of an opera, etc.

li-bret-to (lĭ-brĕt'ō), *n.* a book containing the words of an opera, oratorio, etc.; the text itself.

lice (līs), *n.* plural of *louse;* as, there are numerous species of *lice*.

li-cense (lī'sĕns), *n.* authority to act at discretion; permission; leave; unrestrained liberty; legal permission to do something; as, no one can operate an automobile without a *license;* permitted variation from a rule; as, poetic *license:* *v.t.* grant permission by law. Also, **licence.**

li-cen-ti-ate (lī-sĕn'shĭ-āt), *n.* one given authority to preach or to practice a profession.

li-cen-tious (lī-sĕn′shŭs), *adj.* unrestrained morally; impure.

li-chen (lī′kĕn), *n.* one of an order of air-nourished plants or fungi growing on stones, etc.; a kind of skin eruption.—*adj.* **lichenous.**

lich gate (lĭch gāt), the roofed gate of a churchyard, under which a dead body is carried to the grave. Also, **lych gate.**

lick (lĭk), *v.t.* to pass the tongue over; caress with the tongue; lap up; to pass over like a tongue, as flames; colloquially, to whip, or to conquer in fight: *n.* the act of passing the tongue over; a quick or careless stroke; a small quantity; a place where salt is found on the surface of the earth and where wild animals come to lick it.

lic-o-rice (lĭk′ō-rĭs), *n.* a plant of the bean family; the dried root of this plant, or the juice extracted from it. Also, **liquorice.**

lic-tor (lĭk′tŏr), *n.* a Roman official who attended the chief magistrates and bore the badge of authority, a bundle of rods, having among them an ax with the blade projecting.

lid (lĭd), *n.* a movable cover closing an opening, as of a box; top; the cover of the eye.

lie (lī), *v.i.* [*p.t.* lay, *p.p.* lain, *p.pr.* lying], to rest in a reclining position; to take such a position; rest or remain; be situated or placed: *v.i.* [*p.t.* and *p.p.* lied, *p.pr.* lying], to speak a falsehood; represent falsely: *n.* a falsehood; in golf, the slant of a club held ready to strike; the situation of the ball to be played on.

lief (lēf), *adv.* willingly; as, I had as *lief* go as stay.

liege (lēj), *adj.* having the right to devotion and service; sovereign; as, he reverenced his *liege* lady; bound to give service and devotion: *n.* one bound to give service and devotion; a sovereign; a lord and master.—*n.* **liegeman.**

li-en (lē′ĕn; lēn), *n.* a legal claim upon property; security for payment.

lieu (lū), *n.* place; stead: used in the phrase *in lieu of.*

lieu-ten-an-cy (lū-tĕn′ăn-sĭ), *n.* the rank or authority of a lieutenant.

lieu-ten-ant (lū-tĕn′ănt; Br. lĕf-tĕn′ănt), *n.* an officer ranking next below a captain in the army and a lieutenant commander in the navy; one who acts for a superior in his absence: **lieutenant colonel,** an army officer next in rank above a major, and below a colonel: **lieutenant general,** an army officer next in rank above a major general, and below a general.

life (līf), *n.* the state of being alive; living existence; vitality; as, to bring to *life* that which appears to be dead; union of soul and body; a living person; as, but one *life* was saved from the wreck; living beings collectively; as, human *life;* animal *life;* period between birth and death; as, all the years of a man's *life;* manner of living; as, a *life* of pleasure; a biography; as, the *life* of Tennyson; animation; vivacity; as, to be full of *life;* to put *life* into an undertaking; the moving spirit; as, he was the *life* of the household.

life-blood (līf′blŭd″), *n.* the life-giving fluid in the veins; any source or spring of vital strength.

life-boat (līf′bōt″), *n.* a strong buoyant boat used in rescuing persons at sea.

life buoy (līf boi; līf bōōi), a float, often a buoyant ring, to keep persons from sinking in the water.

life guard (līf gärd), a body of troops defending the person of a high officer or dignitary.

life-less (līf′lĕs), *adj.* without vitality; dead; wanting in energy; listless; dull.—*adv.* **lifelessly.**—*n.* **lifelessness.**

life-like (līf′līk″), *adj.* like a living being; realistic; as, a *lifelike* portrait.

life-long (līf′lŏng″), *adj.* enduring or remaining throughout life.

life pre-serv-er (līf prē-zûrv′ẽr), a device for holding the body up from sinking in the water; a club or cane with a heavy metal head, used as a weapon.

Life Preserver

life-time (līf′tīm″), *n.* the length of time that life lasts.

lift (lĭft), *v.t.* to raise to a higher point; place in a higher position; to exalt; support in the air; colloquially, steal: *v.i.* to exert strength in raising; to rise: *n.* the act of raising to a higher point; high position; as, the proud *lift* of her head; aid; help; assistance; as, to give anyone a *lift* in carrying a load; a machine for carrying up or down; an elevator.

lig-a-ment (lĭg′ȧ-mĕnt), *n.* a strong elastic tissue connecting the ends of movable bones, or holding in place an organ of the body; a bond or tie.

lig-a-ture (lĭg′ȧ-tūr), *n.* a narrow bandage; in printing, a double character, or two or more letters united, as *æ;* a curve or line connecting musical notes, or the notes so connected: *v.t.* to bind with a narrow band.

light (līt), *n.* the condition of illumination upon which sight depends; opposite to *darkness;* as, the *light* of day; that which illuminates, as the sun, a candle, etc.; the brightness so given out; appearance from a special point of view; as, your explanation puts the matter in a new *light;* clear mental vision or that which gives it; as, to throw *light* on a problem; a window, or a pane of glass in a window; as, the hail beat against the window and broke three *lights: adj.* clear; bright; not dark; blond; not heavy or burdensome; delicate; not massive; gay; trifling; unimportant; nimble; short in weight; well raised, as bread; graceful; undignified; dizzy: *v.t.* [*p.t.* and *p.p.* lighted, lit, *p.pr.* lighting], to set fire to; cause to shine and give forth brightness; furnish with, or guide by, a light: *v.i.* to take fire; to begin to give forth brightness: usually followed by *up;* as, her face *lighted* up; to come down, fall, or settle, or to find by chance: with *on* or *upon.*

light ar-til-ler-y (līt är-tĭl′ẽr-ĭ), cannon accompanying troops in field operations.

light-en (līt′n), *v.t.* to make clear or bright; to illumine; make less heavy; to cheer; as, kind words *lighten* the heart: *v.i.* to brighten; shine out; flash, as in an electric storm; to become less heavy.

light-er (līt′ẽr), *n.* a large open barge used in loading and unloading vessels.

light-er-age (līt′ẽr-āj), *n.* the unloading of a cargo by large open barges; charge made for such work.

light-fin-gered (līt'fĭn"gẽrd), *adj.* deft and clever in picking pockets; thievish.

light-head-ed (līt'hĕd"ĕd), *adj.* dizzy; delirious, as with fever; thoughtless; heedless.

light-heart-ed (līt'härt"ĕd), *adj.* free from care; gay; cheerful.—*adv.* **light-heartedly.**—*n.* **light-heartedness.**

light-house (līt'hous"), *n.* a tower or other structure furnished with a brilliant light at the top to show points of danger to ships at sea.

Steel Lighthouse

light-ly (līt'lĭ), *adv.* with little force or weight; as, to walk *lightly;* in small degree or amount; as, to reward *lightly;* without heed; indifferently; as, to treat a matter *lightly;* gaily; cheerfully; as, to bear trouble *lightly;* swiftly; nimbly.

light-ness (līt'nĕs), *n.* state or degree of being illuminated; state or quality of being not heavy; hence, buoyancy; fickleness; nimbleness; grace.

light-ning (līt'nĭng), *n.* a sudden flash of electricity in the air, usually accompanied by thunder; a brightening or illumination; as, the *lightning* of the setting sun.

light-ning rod (līt'nĭng rŏd), a metal rod fastened on a building to protect it from lightning by catching the electric discharge and conducting it into the earth.

light-ship (līt'shĭp"), *n.* a vessel with a light moored at a dangerous place to warn sailors.

light-some (līt'sŭm), *adj.* cheerful; lively; nimble.

light-weight (līt'wāt"), *n.* one that weighs less than the average: *adj.* weighing less than the average; hence, of little account.

lig-ne-ous (lĭg'nē-ŭs), *adj.* composed of, or like, wood; woody.

lig-nite (lĭg'nīt), *n.* an imperfect kind of coal formed from wood.

lig-num-vi-tæ (lĭg'nŭm-vī'tē), *n.* the very heavy hard wood of certain South American, West Indian, and Australian trees.

like (līk), *adj.* similar; resembling; equal or nearly equal; in a mood or condition for; as, I feel *like* reading; it looks *like* rain: *adv.* and *prep.* to the same extent, or in the same manner, as; likely: only in such expressions as *like* enough: *n.* that which is equal or similar to another; a copy: *pl.* the things one prefers; fancies; as, our *likes* and dislikes: *v.t.* to have a taste for; enjoy: *v.i.* to choose: *suffix,* indicating resemblance. —*adj.* **likable, likeable.**

like-li-hood (līk'lĭ-hŏŏd), *n.* probability; as, there is little *likelihood* that it will happen.

like-ly (līk'lĭ), *adj.* [*comp.* likelier, *superl.* likeliest], credible; probable; as, a *likely* story; suitable; as, *likely* behavior; being such as to make probable; as, that is *likely* to happen: *adv.* probably.

lik-en (līk'n), *v.t.* to compare; as, "I will *liken* him unto a wise man."—Matt. vii. 24.

like-ness (līk'nĕs), *n.* resemblance; similarity; a portrait.

like-wise (līk-wīz), *adv.* and *conj.* in a similar manner; also; moreover; too.

lik-ing (līk'ĭng), *n.* fondness; inclination; desire.

li-lac (lī'lăk), *n.* a shrub with fragrant white or pale pinkish-purple flowers; the pale purple color of the lilac.

Lil-li-pu-tian (lĭl"ĭ-pū'shăn), *adj.* very small; like the tiny people of Lilliput, a country described in Swift's *Gulliver's Travels:* *n.* one of the tiny people of Lilliput; any extremely small person; a dwarf. Also, **Liliputian.**

lilt (lĭlt), *n.* a light or lively tune; a merry song; rhythmic movement; as, the *lilt* of verse: *v.t.* and *v.i.* to sing lightly or gaily; as, to *lilt* a song; to *lilt* and play.

lil-y (lĭl'ĭ), *n.* a plant with bulblike roots and handsome flowers: *adj.* lily-white.

limb (lĭm), *n.* a jointed part extending from an animal body, as a leg, an arm, or a wing; the branch of a tree; an edge or border; as, the *limb* of a planet's disk; colloquially, a roguish child: *v.t.* to cut or tear the legs and arms from.

Limber

lim-ber (lĭm'bẽr), *n.* the fore part of a gun carriage: *v.t.* to attach the fore part to (a gun carriage): make easy to bend: *adj.* easily bent; limp.—*n.* **limberness.**

lim-bo (lĭm'bō), *n.* a region between heaven and hell; a place for worthless things.

lime (līm), *n.* a kind of white earth obtained by the action of heat upon limestone, hard to melt, and having power to eat away any substance it touches: called also *quicklime;* a tree of the orange kind yielding a juicy, acid fruit; the linden tree; *v.t.* to apply quicklime to: birdlime, a sticky substance smeared on twigs to catch small birds.

lime-kiln (līm'kĭl"; līm'kĭln"), *n.* a furnace in which limestone is burned to yield lime.

lime-light (līm'līt"), *n.* a brilliant, incandescent light produced by the action of a very hot flame upon lime; the brilliantly lighted portion of a stage; a prominent position before the public; as, certain natures enjoy being always in the *limelight.*

Lim-er-ick (lĭm'ẽr-ĭk), *n.* a nonsense poem of five lines, of which lines one, two, and five form one rime and lines three and four another.

lime-stone (līm'stōn"), *n.* a rock containing carbonate of lime.

lim-it (lĭm'ĭt), *n.* a border or boundary; utmost extent; that which confines, ends, or checks: *v.t.* to confine within bounds; restrict.

lim-i-ta-tion (lĭm"ĭ-tā'shŭn), *n.* that which bounds, binds, or holds back; restriction; point beyond which one cannot progress.

lim-it-ed (lĭm'ĭt-ĕd), *p.adj.* restricted; controlled in action by constitutional provisions: said of a government; as, a *limited* monarchy: *n.* a fast express train with special accommodation for first-class passengers, and usually charging an extra fare.

lim-it-less (lĭm'ĭt-lĕs), *adj.* having no bounds; unconfined; as, *limitless* space.

limn (lĭm), *v.t.* to paint or draw; illuminate, as books and manuscripts.

li-mou-sine (lē"mōō-zēn'), *n.* the body of a large closed automobile.

limp (lĭmp), *n.* a halt in walking: *v.i.* to walk with a halt: *adj.* lacking stiffness, firmness, or strength.—*adv.* **limply.**—*n.* **limpness.**

lim-pet (lĭm'pĕt), *n.* a shellfish with a cone-shaped shell, found sticking to rocks or timbers.

lim-pid (lĭm'pĭd), *adj.* transparent; sparklingly clear; as, a *limpid* stream.—*adv.* **limpidly.**—*n.* **limpidness.**

linch-pin (lĭnch'pĭn"), *n.* a piece of iron, etc., which goes through the end of an axle and keeps the wheel in its place.

lin-den (lĭn'dĕn), *n.* a tree with heart-shaped leaves, and small clusters of cream-colored flowers: found in both Europe and America.

line (līn), *n.* a mark on paper, etc., having length but not breadth or thickness; a slender string or cord; a cord used for fishing; a row; as, a *line* of trees; a boundary; as, we crossed the *line* into Canada; an imaginary circle on the globe; as, a *line* of latitude; plan or method; as, follow this *line* of attack; a course of action; an industry or profession; as, he was an expert in his own *line;* a mark in the hand or face; a row of printed or written letters or words; a verse of poetry; particular class of goods; descent; as, a *line* of kings; vehicles, cars, trains, ships, etc., making up a system of transportation; in war, a row of defended positions; as, a trench in the front *line;* a row of soldiers marching abreast; a wire in a telegraph or telephone system: *pl.* the words of a part in a play: *v.t.* to draw lines upon; place along side by side; as, to *line* up soldiers; cover on the inside; as, to *line* a coat; strengthen by inner fortifications: *v.i.* to form a row; as, the men *line* up for inspection; **line officer,** a commissioned officer below the rank of a major.

lin-e-age (lĭn'ē-āj), *n.* descent from a common ancestor; family; as, a lady of high *lineage.*

lin-e-al (lĭn'ē-ăl), *adj.* composed of lines; in direct descent from an ancestor; as, the *lineal* descendants of the signers of the Declaration of Independence.—*adv.* **lineally.**

lin-e-a-ment (lĭn'ē-*ȧ*-mĕnt), *n.* feature, especially of the face; outline: usually in plural.

lin-e-ar (lĭn'ē-*ȧ*r), *adj.* pertaining to, or composed of, lines; having a straight direction; very narrow.

line-man (līn'măn), *n.* a man who repairs electric wires; one who carries tape, a line, or chain in surveying.

lin-en (lĭn'ĕn), *n.* a cloth made of flax; articles made of this cloth; underclothing: *adj.* made of, or like, linen.

lin-er (līn'ẽr), *n.* a steamship belonging to a regular line of vessels; one who makes inside coverings.

lin-ger (lĭṅ'gẽr), *v.i.* to delay; loiter; remain long in any state.

lin-ge-rie (lăṅ"zh-rē'), *n.* underclothing; linen articles of dress collectively. [Fr.]

lin-go (lĭṅ'gō), *n.* language; dialect: used generally in a humorous or contemptuous sense.

lin-gual (lĭṅ'gwăl), *adj.* pertaining to, or formed by, the tongue: *n.* a letter or sound formed by the tongue, as *l, r, th,* etc.

lin-guist (lĭṅ'gwĭst), *n.* one skilled in languages.

lin-guis-tic (lĭṅ-gwĭs'tĭk), *adj.* belonging to the study and comparison of languages.

lin-guis-tics (lĭṅ-gwĭs'tĭks), *n.pl.* the science of languages, or the study of their origins, growth, likenesses, and differences.

lin-i-ment (lĭn'ĭ-mĕnt), *n.* a liquid medical preparation for rubbing into the skin.

lin-ing (līn'ĭng), *n.* an inside covering; contents; as, the best *lining* for a purse is money.

link (lĭṅk), *n.* a single ring or division of a chain; single part of a connected series; as, a *link* in a chain of evidence; a surveyor's land measure, 7.92 inches; connection; torch made of pitch and tow, or coarse flax: *pl.* flat sandy soil; golfing grounds: *v.t.* to connect by, or as by, a link: *v.i.* to be connected.

lin-net (lĭn'ĕt), *n.* a small singing bird common in England.

li-no-le-um (lĭ-nō'lē-ŭm), *n.* a floor covering composed of ground cork, linseed oil, and chloride of sulphur, commonly used in kitchens, bathrooms, etc.

lin-o-type (lĭn'ō-tīp"; līn'ō-tīp"), *n.* a typesetting machine, operated by keys similar to those of a typewriter, which casts each line of type in one piece: hence the name; the slug, or line of type cast by such a machine.

lin-seed (lĭn'sēd"), *n.* the seed of flax, from which linseed oil is produced.

lin-sey-wool-sey (lĭn'zĭ-wōōl'zĭ), *n.* a cloth of mixed linen and wool. Also, **linsey.**

lint (lĭnt), *n.* the soft down obtained by scraping linen and used for dressing wounds; also, fluff from yarns or fabrics.

lin-tel (lĭn'tĕl), *n.* the horizontal top piece of a door or window.

li-on (lī'ŭn), *n.* [*fem.* lioness], a large powerful flesh-eating mammal of the cat family, found in the deserts of Africa and southern Asia; a person who possesses great courage; one who is noted and is sought by society: *adj.* (in composition), noble; majestic; courageous; as, *lion*-hearted.

li-on-ize (lī'ŭn-īz), *v.t.* to treat as a celebrity; to pay very great attention to socially; as, Americans delight to *lionize* great men.

lip (lĭp), *n.* one of the two fleshy borders of the mouth; the flaring or folding edge of anything hollow: *v.t.* [*p.t.* and *p.p.* lipped, *p.pr.* lipping], to touch with the lips; kiss: *adj.* spoken but not felt; insincere; as, *lip* service.

liq-ue-fac-tion (lĭk"wē-făk'shŭn), *n.* the process of making a solid into a fluid; state of being melted.

liq-ue-fy (lĭk'wē-fī), *v.t.* to melt or make fluid; as, extreme heat will *liquefy* iron: *v.i.* to become fluid.

li-queur (lē'kûr'; lĭ'kûr'), *n.* a light alcoholic drink sweetened and variously flavored.

liq-uid (lĭk'wĭd), *adj.* clear; smooth in sound; as, a *liquid* melody; not solid; freely flowing: *n.* a substance that flows freely; one of the consonants *l, m, n, r.*

liq-ui-date (lĭk'wĭ-dāt), *v.t.* to pay off, as a debt; arrange, as the affairs of a bankrupt.

liq-ui-da-tion (lĭk′wĭ-dā′shŭn), *n.* the act of paying off; the settlement of the affairs of a bankrupt's estate.

liq-uid fire (lĭk′wĭd fīr), in the World War, a highly inflammable liquid, such as gasoline, ejected from an apparatus usually carried on the back of the operator, and ignited so as to form a stream of fire.

liq-uor (lĭk′ẽr), *n.* an alcoholic drink: any substance that pours freely.

liq-uor-ice (lĭk′ō-rĭs), *n.* an herb of the bean family; the root of the plant or the juice extracted from it. Also, **licorice.**

li-ra (lē′rȧ), *n.* [*pl.* lire (lē′rā)], an Italian coin, worth nineteen cents; a Turkish coin equal to $4.40.

lisle (līl), *n.* a fine hard twisted cotton thread or fabric woven from it.

lisp (lĭsp), *v.i.* to pronounce *s* and *z* nearly like *th;* to speak imperfectly or with hesitation: *v.t.* to utter imperfectly or affectedly; to express in a childlike manner; to utter timidly or secretly: *n.* the imperfect utterance of *s* and *z.*

lis-som (lĭs′ŭm), *n.* limber; nimble; agile; swift and light in motion. Also, **lissome.**—*n.* **lissomeness.**

list (lĭst), *n.* a catalog, roll, or register; the edge or selvage of cloth; strip of cloth; a leaning or bending to one side: said of a ship; small square molding: *pl.* formerly, an inclosure where a tournament was held: *v.t.* to catalog, register, or enroll; cover with strips of cloth; sew together; listen to: *v.i.* to tilt over to one side; to enlist; choose; as, the wind bloweth where it *listeth;* hearken.

lis-ten (lĭs′n), *v.i.* to attend to closely, so as to hear; hearken; obey.—*n.* **listener.**

Syn. attend, hark, heed.
Ant. (see ignore).

lis-ten-ing post (lĭs′n-ĭng pōst), in the World War, a position occupied at night by one or two soldiers detailed to try to hear some indication of the movements of the enemy: **listening patrol,** the soldiers occupying a listening post.

list-less (lĭst′lĕs), *adj.* indifferent; languid; spiritless.—*adv.* **listlessly.** — *n.* **listlessness.**

lit (lĭt), past tense and past participle of the verb *light.* Also, **lighted.**

lit-a-ny (lĭt′ȧ-nĭ), *n.* a solemn form of prayer or supplication in which the clergyman leads and congregation responds.

li-ter (lē′tẽr), *n.* in the metric system, a measure equal to 61.026 cubic inches, or 1.0567 quarts. Also, **litre.**

lit-er-a-cy (lĭt′ẽr-ȧ-sĭ), *n.* the state of being able to read and write.

lit-er-al (lĭt′ẽr-ăl), *adj.* consisting of, or expressed by, letters; following the given words; exact; as, a *literal* translation; precise; as, the *literal* truth; matter-of-fact.—*adv.* **literally.**—*n.* **literalness.**

lit-er-a-ry (lĭt′ẽr-ā-rĭ), *adj.* pertaining to, or appropriate to, literature or men of letters; having a knowledge of, or engaged in, literature.

lit-er-ate (lĭt′ẽr-āt), *adj.* having a knowledge of letters or literature; able to read and write: *n.* a learned or educated person: opposite to *illiterate.*

lit-e-ra-ti (lĭt′ē-rä′tī), *n.pl.* men of letters. [Lat.]

lit-e-ra-tim (lĭt′ē-rā′tĭm), *adv.* literally or exactly; letter for letter. [Lat.]

lit-er-a-ture (lĭt′ẽr-ȧ-tūr), *n.* the written or printed productions of a country or period, especially those that are notable for beauty or force of style; the work of authors; the body of writing upon a given subject; printed matter issued for a special purpose; as, campaign *literature.*

lithe (līth), *adj.* bending easily; willowy; limber; nimble; supple; as, the cat has a *lithe* body.—*n.* **litheness.**

lithe-some (līth′sŭm), *adj.* nimble; limber; lissom.—*n.* **lithesomeness.**

lith-i-a (lĭth′ĭ-ȧ), *n.* a white crystalline substance obtained by burning lithium in oxygen, etc.

lith-i-um (lĭth′ĭ-ŭm), *n.* a silver-white metallic substance, the lightest metal known.

lith-o-graph (lĭth′ō-grȧf), *n.* a picture, etc., usually in colors, printed from a drawing on stone, or zinc: *v.t.* to draw, or engrave on stone, or zinc, and transfer to paper.—*n.* **lithographer.**

lith-o-graph-ic (lĭth′ō-grăf′ĭk), *adj.* pertaining to the art of printing pictures, or stationery, in colors or otherwise, etc., from stone, or zinc. Also, **lithographical.**—*adv.* **lithographically.**

li-thog-ra-phy (lĭ-thŏg′rȧ-fĭ), *n.* the art of making a design, usually in colors, on stone, or zinc, so that it may be transferred to paper.

lit-i-gant (lĭt′ĭ-gănt), *n.* one engaged in a lawsuit: *adj.* engaged in a lawsuit or inclined to resort to the law to settle claims, etc.

lit-i-gate (lĭt′ĭ-gāt), *v.t.* to make the subject of a lawsuit; to bring to a court of law for settlement; as, to *litigate* a dispute about boundaries of land: *v.i.* to engage in a lawsuit.

lit-i-ga-tion (lĭt′ĭ-gā′shŭn), *n.* the act or process of carrying on a lawsuit; a suit at law.

li-ti-gious (lĭ-tĭj′ŭs), *adj.* given to engaging in lawsuits; quarrelsome.

lit-mus (lĭt′mŭs), *n.* a purple dye, obtained from certain very small plants called lichens: used to dye chemical testing paper, which turns red in an acid and blue in an alkali.

lit-ter (lĭt′ẽr), *n.* straw, hay, etc., used for horses' bedding; a framework with a bed, for carrying a person who is lying down; state of confusion or untidiness; number of young produced at one birth, as pigs, etc.: *v.t.* to supply with straw, etc., for bedding; cover with straw; scatter about carelessly: *v.i.* to bring forth young.

lit-te-ra-teur (lē″tȧ″rȧ″tûr′), *n.* a scholarly man; a man of letters. [Fr.]

lit-tle (lĭt′l), *adj.* [*comp.* less, *superl.* least], small in size, quantity, dignity, or importance; brief in time; insignificant; young; mean: *adv.* in a small degree; not much: *n.* that which is small in size, quantity, etc.—*n.* **littleness.**

Syn., adj. diminutive, small.
Ant. (see great).

lit-to-ral (lĭt′ō-răl), *adj.* pertaining to, near, or living on, the shore; situated between high- and low-water mark: *n.* country lying near the shore of a sea, lake, etc.

li-tur-gic-al (lĭ-tûr′jĭk-ăl), *adj.* of or pertaining to a set form of divine service: as, a *liturgical* form of worship. Also, **liturgic.**

lit-ur-gy (lĭt'ûr-jĭ), *n.* [*pl.* liturgies (-jĭz)], the set form or service for public worship.

liv-a-ble (lĭv'à-bl), *adj.* endurable; fit or agreeable to live in or with. Also, **liveable.**

live (lĭv), *v.i.* to exist or have life; pass or enjoy life; as, to *live* happily; reside or dwell; as, to *live* in a house; to *live* in the woods; to get support or to subsist; as, to *live* on meat; to *live* within one's means; to continue to have life; as, to *live* to be old; to survive or endure: *v.t.* to pass or spend; as, to *live* a happy life: **to live down,** to recover from, or cause to be forgotten by later conduct; as, to *live down* disgrace: *adj.* (līv), having life; effective; burning; as, a *live* coal; full of activity or interest; as, a *live* topic.

live-li-hood (līv'lĭ-hŏŏd), *n.* means of existence; regular support.
Syn. living, maintenance, subsistence, support.

live-long (lĭv'lŏng''), *adj.* long in passing; tedious; whole; entire; as, they toiled the *livelong* day.

live-ly (līv'lĭ), *adj.* active; brisk; full of spirit; as, a *lively* disposition; vivid; as, a *lively* fancy; forcible; as, a *lively* impression.—*n.* **liveliness.**
Syn. merry, sportive, sprightly, vivacious.
Ant. (see slow, languid).

live oak (līv ōk), one of several species of American oak valuable as timber and for shipbuilding.

liv-er (lĭv'ẽr), *n.* one who exists, dwells, or spends time in some especial way; an organ of the body which produces bile and causes important changes in certain food substances in the blood.

liv-er-ied (lĭv'ẽr-ĭd), *adj.* clothed in the peculiar dress used by any group of persons, especially by servants.

liv-er-wort (lĭv'ẽr-wûrt), *n.* a mosslike plant; hepatica.

liv-er-y (lĭv'ẽr-ĭ), *n.* [*pl.* liveries (-ĭz)], a particular costume worn by servants or by any other special group of persons; the keeping and feeding of horses for a certain sum of money or the hiring out of horses and vehicles; a stable where horses are boarded or hired out.

liv-er-y-man (lĭv'ẽr-ĭ-măn), *n.* the keeper of a stable where horses and vehicles are boarded or hired out.

liv-er-y sta-ble (lĭv'ẽr-ĭ stā'bl), a stable where horses are kept and let out for hire.

liv-id (lĭv'ĭd), *adj.* black and blue; discolored as by a blow; as, a *livid* scar; ashy pale.

liv-ing (lĭv'ĭng), *p.adj.* having life; flowing, as a spring; vigorous; active; producing life, action, or strength: *n.* livelihood; in England, a church appointment or office; mode of life.

liz-ard (lĭz'ẽrd), *n.* a reptile having a scaly body, and four well-developed limbs, each with five toes.

Lizard

lla-ma (lä'mȧ), *n.* a South American animal somewhat like a camel, but smaller and without a hump. Also, **lama.**

lla-nos (lä'nōz; Span. lyä'nōs), *n.pl.* the broad level grassy plains of South America.

lo (lō), *interj.* behold! see! look! as, *lo!* he comes.

loach (lōch), *n.* a small European fresh-water fish of the carp family.

load (lōd), *v.t.* to put on as much as can be carried; to freight; to burden; weigh down; embarrass; to give to in great abundance; as, to *load* one with attentions; to put powder, etc., into, as a gun: *n.* a burden; mass or weight usually carried at once; as, a *load* of coal; cargo; something which hinders free or swift movement; a mental burden; as, a *load* of care or suffering; the powder, etc., with which a gun is charged.—*n.* **loader.**
Syn. burden, clog, encumbrance.

load-ed (lōd'ĕd), *p.adj.* laden; weighted, especially with lead; as, *loaded* dice.

load-star (lōd'stär''), *n.* a star that leads or guides; especially, the polestar, called the North Star; hence, anything which strongly influences or draws attention. Also, **lodestar.**

load-stone (lōd'stōn''), *n.* magnetic oxide of iron; a magnet. Also, **lodestone.**

loaf (lōf), *v.i.* to idle away time: *n.* [*pl.* loaves (lōvz)], a shaped mass of bread or cake; a shaped lump, as of sugar.

loaf-er (lōf'ẽr), *n.* an idler; hence, one who has the bad habits of street loungers.

loam (lōm), *n.* a rich soil composed of decayed vegetable matter, clay, and sand: *v.t.* to cover with such soil.—*adj.* **loamy.**

loan (lōn), *n.* a sum of money lent for a period, repayable with interest; something granted for temporary use: *v.t.* and *v.i.* to lend.

loath (lōth), *adj.* unwilling; reluctant; as, I was *loath* to go. Also, **loth.**

loathe (lō*th*), *v.t.* to regard with extreme dislike or disgust; detest.

loath-ing (lō*th*'ĭng), *n.* disgust; nausea; aversion; abhorrence.

loath-some (lō*th*'sŭm), *adj.* causing disgust and a feeling of sickness; as, smallpox is a *loathsome* disease; detestable.—*adv.* **loathsomely.**—*n.* **loathsomeness.**

loaves (lōvz), *n.* plural of *loaf;* as, five *loaves* of bread.

lo-bate (lō'bāt), *adj.* having rounded divisions or parts, as a leaf.

lob-by (lŏb'ĭ), *n.* [*pl.* lobbies (-ĭz)], a small hall or waiting room; passage opening into an apartment; that part of the hall where a lawmaking body meets to which the public have access; the persons who try to influence the votes of members of a lawmaking body: *v.t.* [*p.t.* and *p.p.* lobbied, *p.pr.* lobbying], to try to get the votes of members of a legislature or lawmaking body for a particular measure.

lob-by-ist (lŏb'ĭ-ĭst), *n.* a person, not a member, who tries to influence the votes of members of a legislative or lawmaking body.

lobe (lōb), *n.* any rounded projection or part; as, the *lobe* of the ear; the *lobes* of the brain.—*adj.* **lobed.**

lo-be-li-a (lō-bē'lĭ-ȧ; lō-bēl'yȧ), *n.* any of a certain kind of plants with beautiful red, blue, or white flowers, including the Indian tobacco plant, etc.

lob-ster (lŏb'stẽr), *n.* a large shellfish used as food.

lo-cal (lō'kăl), *adj.* pertaining to place; used in, or relating to, a particular place; as, *local* elections: *n.* in the United States, a newspaper paragraph of local interest; a train running between small towns.

lo-cale (lō"kăl'), *n.* place, as affected by surrounding conditions; locality. [Fr.]

lo-cal-ism (lō'kăl-ĭzm), *n.* a word, expression, or custom used in a particular region or district.

lo-cal-i-ty (lō-kăl'ĭ-tĭ), *n.* [*pl.* localities (-tĭz)], restriction or limitation to a definite place; a geographical region or position; a vicinity.

lo-cal-ize (lō'kăl-īz), *v.t.* to limit to a particular place; as, quarantine attempts to *localize* contagious diseases.—*n.* **localization.**

lo-cal op-tion (lō'kăl ŏp'shŭn), the right or duty of the people of a district to determine by vote whether the sale of alcoholic drinks shall be allowed within the district.

lo-cate (lō'kāt), *v.t.* to place in a particular spot; establish; mark out and determine the position of: *v.i.* colloquially, to settle.

lo-ca-tion (lō-kā'shŭn), *n.* exact position or place; plot of ground marked out by boundaries.

loch (lŏkh), *n.* a lake; a bay or arm of the sea. Also, **lough.** [Scot.]

lock (lŏk), *n.* a mechanical device furnished with a spring and bolt for fastening a door, etc., by means of a key; anything that fastens; an inclosure between gates in a canal, river, etc., used in raising or lowering boats as they pass from level to level; a mechanism for firing a gun; a hug in wrestling; a tuft of hair or wool; ringlet: *v.t.* to fasten or secure with a lock; shut up; confine: *v.i.* to become fast by a lock; entwine.

Syn., *n.* bar, bolt, hook, fastening.

lock-er (lŏk'ẽr), *n.* a drawer, cupboard, compartment, or chest secured by a lock; especially, a cupboard for individual use.

lock-et (lŏk'ĕt), *n.* a small gold or silver ornament, so made as to open and shut, attached to a necklace or chain.

lock-jaw (lŏk'jô"), *n.* a disease by which the lower jaw is drawn up and becomes fixed or locked; tetanus.

lock-out (lŏk'out"), *n.* the shutting out of workmen from a factory by an employer to compel them to accept his terms.

lock-smith (lŏk'smĭth"), *n.* a maker or repairer of locks.

lock-step (lŏk'stĕp"), *n.* the strict marching-step of men in close file.

lock-up (lŏk'ŭp"), *n.* a temporary prison for persons under arrest; a jail.

lo-co (lō'kō), *n.* a name for various poisonous American plants which cause disease to animals that eat them; also, the disease so caused: *v.t.* to poison with this weed; as, cattle are *locoed;* to make crazy.

lo-co-mo-bile (lō"cō-mō'bĭl), *adj.* having power to move from place to place.

lo-co-mo-tion (lō"kō-mō'shŭn), *n.* the act of moving or ability to move from place to place.

lo-co-mo-tive (lō"kō-mō'tĭv), *adj.* having the power of moving from place to place; moving from one place to another; pertaining to a machine that moves about under its own power: *n.* a steam engine or electric motor for drawing railway cars.

lo-co-mo-tor (lō"kō-mō'tẽr), *adj.* pertaining to motion from place to place.

lo-co-mo-tor a-tax-i-a (lō"kō-mō'tẽr ă-tăk'sĭ-ȧ), a disease of the nervous system, affecting especially the patient's control of the legs.

lo-cust (lō'kŭst), *n.* a destructive winged insect resembling the grasshopper, which travels from place to place; a tree of the bean family.

lo-cu-tion (lō-kū'shŭn), *n.* a particular form of speech; phrase; idiom.

lode (lōd), *n.* any deposit of metallic ore (gold, etc.) found within definite boundaries that separate it from the rocks; the fissure that is filled with the ore.

lode-star (lōd'stär"), *n.* a guiding star; the polestar. Also, **loadstar.**

lode-stone (lōd'stōn"), *n.* magnetic oxide of iron; a magnet. Also, **loadstone.**

lodge (lŏj), *v.t.* [*p.t.* and *p.p.* lodged, *p.pr.* lodging], to furnish with a temporary dwelling; deposit; settle; place; as, to *lodge* information against; to *lodge* authority in: *v.i.* to live in for a time; to live in a hired room or rooms in another's house; be deposited or fixed; as, seeds blown about by the wind often *lodge* in strange places: *n.* a small house in a park; gatekeeper's cottage; wild beast's den; hut or wigwam of an American Indian; place where members of an association meet, especially Freemasons; the members themselves.

lodg-er (lŏj'ẽr), *n.* one who resides in a hired room or apartment in a house occupied by others.

lodg-ing (lŏj'ĭng), *n.* a place where one is living only for a time: *pl.* a room or rooms hired in the house of another.

lodg-ment (lŏj'mĕnt), *n.* the act of giving shelter to, settling, or depositing; the state of being housed, settled, or deposited; a place for being settled in; as, the idea found *lodgment* in his brain; a collection of material deposited; occupation of a military position. Also, **lodgement.**

loft (lôft), *n.* a room directly beneath a roof; a floor or gallery raised above the main floor; as, an organ-*loft* in a church; a hay-*loft* in a barn; an upper floor in a warehouse.

loft-y (lôf'tĭ), *adj.* [*comp.* loftier, *superl.* loftiest], very high; proud; stately; sublime; as, *lofty* sentiments.—*adv.* **loftily.**—*n.* **loftiness.**

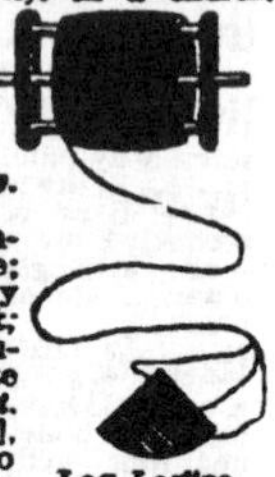

Log, Logline, and Logreel.

log (lŏg), *n.* a piece of timber in its natural state; the record of a ship's daily progress: called also *logbook;* a heavy dull fellow; an instrument for measuring the rate of progress of a ship: *v.t.* [*p.t.* and *p.p.* logged, *p.pr.* logging], to enter in a logbook: *v.i.* to hew down and get out trees: **logline,** the cord to which a ship's log is attached: **logreel,** a reel upon which a logline is wound.

log-a-rithm (lŏg'ȧ-rĭthm), *n.* the number of times a number (called the base) must be multiplied by itself to produce a given number; thus, since $4^3 = 64$, 3 is the *logarithm* of 64 to the base 4..

log-book (lŏg'book"), *n.* a ship's diary, or journal, recording the progress of a vessel, daily occurrences, etc.

log-ger-head (lŏg'ẽr-hĕd"), *n.* a blockhead; numskull; a kind of sea turtle: **to be at loggerheads,** to dispute or quarrel.

log-gia (lŏj'ȧ; lō'jī-ȧ), *n.* a covered gallery or portico; an open balcony in a theater. [It.]

log-ging (lŏg'ĭng), *n.* the business of cutting down timber.

log-ic (lŏj'ĭk), *n.* the science of correct reasoning; the power to think correctly.

log-i-cal (lŏj'ĭ-kăl), *adj.* pertaining to, or used in, the science of reasoning; according to the rules of correct reasoning; as, to reach a *logical* conclusion; reasonable; to be expected according to the laws of correct reasoning; as, sorrow and suffering are *logical* results of war.—*adv.* **logically.**

lo-gi-cian (lō-jĭsh'ăn), *n.* one skilled in the science of correct reasoning.

lo-gis-tics (lō-jĭs'tĭks), *n.* the branch of military science dealing with the transport and supply of armies; the use of the four fundamental operations in arithmetic.

log-o-graph (lŏg'ō-grȧf), *n.* a written word; an instrument for registering spoken words.

log-o-type (lŏg'ō-tīp), *n.* a type containing two or more letters, as *ff.*

log-roll-ing (lŏg'rōl"ĭng), *n.* the act of rolling logs from the place where they were cut down to the stream which floats them to the sawmill or the market; a combining to assist another with the expectation of receiving assistance in return, especially in political schemes.

log-wood (lŏg'wŏŏd"), *n.* the wood of a Central American tree used in dyestuffs to produce a deep-red color.

loin (loin), *n.* the lower part of the side of the body of an animal or man, between the lowest rib and the hip bone: usually in plural.

loi-ter (loi'tẽr), *v.t.* to spend idly: with *away,* in reference to time; as, to *loiter* away the afternoon; *v.i.* to spend time idly; delay; linger on the way; saunter.—*n.* **loiterer.**

loll (lŏl), *v.i.* to lounge at ease; to hang out loosely, as the tongue: *v.t.* to permit to hang out loosely, as the tongue.

lol-li-pop (lŏl'ĭ-pŏp), *n.* a kind of taffy, often a lump on a stick: *pl.* bonbons.

lone (lōn), *adj.* solitary; retired; by oneself; unmarried or widowed.

lone-li-ness (lōn'lĭ-nĕs), *n.* the state of being without companions, or solitary; seclusion; solitude; low spirits due to lack of companionship.

lone-ly (lōn'lĭ), *adj.* [*comp.* lonelier, *superl.* loneliest], deserted; solitary; without a companion; not often visited; depressed because alone; lonesome.

lone-some (lōn'sŭm), *adj.* shut off from society; depressed because of solitude; drearily solitary; secluded.—*adv.* **lonesomely.**—*n.* **lonesomeness.**

long (lông), *adj.* not short; covering a great distance from end to end; extended in time; having a definite measure in space or time; as, a yard *long;* drawn out or continued to a great extent; slow; tedious; lingering; far-reaching; holding for a rise; as, *long* of the market: *adv.* to a great length or period; at a time far distant; for a length of time: *v.i.* to desire something eagerly: with *for* or *after.*

long-boat (lông'bōt"), *n.* the largest and strongest small boat of a merchant ship.

long-bow (lông'bō"), *n.* a long powerful bow formerly used by English archers.

long-cloth (lông'klŏth), *n.* a superior cotton fabric.

lon-gev-i-ty (lŏn-jĕv'ĭ-tĭ), *n.* length of life; life prolonged to an unusually old age.

long-hand (lông'hănd"), *n.* ordinary handwriting, as distinguished from shorthand.

long-head-ed (lông'hĕd"ĕd), *adj.* far-seeing; shrewd; clever.

long-ing (lông'ĭng), *n.* an earnest desire; craving.

lon-gi-tude (lŏn'jĭ-tūd), *n.* distance east and west on the earth's surface measured from a meridian or definite place, and counted in degrees.

lon-gi-tu-di-nal (lŏn"jĭ-tū'dĭ-năl), *adj.* pertaining to longitude or to length.—*adv.* **longitudinally.**

long-lived (lông'līvd"), *adj.* of long continuance; living to great age.

long-shore-man (lông'shōr"măn), *n.* a wharf laborer, especially one who loads and unloads ships.

long-sight-ed (lông'sīt"ĕd), *adj.* far-seeing; sagacious.

long-stand-ing (lông'stănd"ĭng), *adj.* having lasted for a long time.

long-suf-fer-ing (lông'sŭf"ẽr-ĭng), *adj.* patient under injury or offense: *n.* patience under injury.

long-wind-ed (lông'wĭn"dĕd), *adj.* speaking or writing at too great length; as, a *long-winded* speech or speaker.

long-wise (lông'wīz"), *adv.* in the direction from end to end. Also, **longways.**

loo (lōō), *n.* a game of cards somewhat like whist, played with three or five cards.

look (lŏŏk), *v.i.* to direct the eye to anything, in order to view it; direct the mind or attention; as, to *look* into a matter; front or face; as, my windows *look* out on a beautiful garden; watch; as, to *look* for news; appear; as, she *looks* happy; to have a certain expression of face; to depend or turn; as, citizens *look* to the state for protection: *v.t.* to show by an expression of face; as, he *looked* his contempt; turn the eyes upon; as, he *looked* the boy up and down; to influence by looking; as, to *look* down opposition: *n.* the act of looking; appearance; expression of face; *interj.* see!

Syn., *v.* appear, seem.

look-ing-glass (lŏŏk'ĭng-glȧs"), *n.* a mirror; that which reflects.

look-out (lŏŏk'out"), *n.* the act of watching for someone to come or something to happen; a place for watching; a person engaged in watching.

loom (lōōm), *n.* a frame or machine for weaving cloth; an oar handle: *v.i.* to rise gradually and appear very large; as, difficulties *loom* up before him.

loon (lōōn), *n.* a fish-eating, diving bird of the North; a dull or stupid person; a dunce.

loop (lōōp), *n.* a folding or doubling of string, rope, etc.; a ring or eye through which a cord may be run; a noose; a ring-shaped figure, road, etc.: *v.t.* to form into, furnish with, or secure with, loops: *v.i.* to make a loop.

loop-hole (lōōp'hōl"), *n.* a narrow opening for observation or defense; means of barely avoiding something.

loop-line (lōōp'līn"), *n.* a railway line running out of and rejoining the main line.

loose (lōōs), *adj.* [*comp.* looser, *superl.* loosest], not fast; unbound; not fixed; not tight; not crowded together; vague; unconnected; not close or compact in substance or texture; not careful in principles or morals: *v.t.* [*p.t.* and *p.p.* loosed, *p.pr.* loosing], to set free; unbind; disengage; relax.—*adv.* **loosely.**—*n.* **looseness.**

loos-en (lōōs'n), *v.t.* to free from tightness or restraint: *v.i.* to become less tight or firm.

loot (lōōt), *v.t.* and *v.i.* to rob or plunder, especially a captured city: *n.* booty thus taken.

lop (lŏp), *v.t.* [*p.t.* and *p.p.* lopped, *p.pr.* lopping], to cut off, as branches from a tree; to cut branches, etc., from; trim; to permit to hang down; as, a horse *lops* his ears: *v.i.* to hang down, as the long ears of a dog: *n.* a hanging down; that part of a tree which is cut off.

lope (lōp), *n.* a slow, easy, swinging gait, as of a horse: *v.i.* [*p.t.* and *p.p.* loped, *p.pr.* loping], to move with such a gait.

lop-sid-ed (lŏp'sīd"ĕd), *n.* heavier on one side than the other; not symmetrical.

lo-qua-cious (lō-kwā'shŭs), *adj.* talkative; chattering.—*adv.* **loquaciously.**—*n.* **loquaciousness.**

lo-quac-i-ty (lō-kwăs'ĭ-tĭ), *n.* talkativeness; loquaciousness.

lord (lôrd), *n.* a ruler or governor; master; one who has supreme power; the owner of a manor; a baron in the British nobility; the son of a duke or marquis; eldest son of an earl; **Lord,** a title of honor given to British noblemen and to certain officials; as, the *Lord* Mayor; **the Lord,** God; Jehovah; Jesus Christ: *v.i.* to rule with absolute power: with *over* or *it.*

lord-ling (lôrd'lĭng), *n.* a little or insignificant person of high rank.

lord-ly (lôrd'lĭ), *adj.* suited to, or like, one of high rank; noble; proud; haughty.—*n.* **lordliness.**

lord-ship (lôrd'shĭp), *n.* the state, quality, or territory under the power of a lord; title or term of address for noblemen and judges: preceded by *his* or *your.*

Lord's Sup-per (lôrdz sŭp'ẽr), the sacrament held in memory of the last supper partaken of by Jesus before his crucifixion: called also *Communion* and *Eucharist.*

lore (lōr), *n.* learning; instruction; space between the eye and bill of a bird.

lor-gnette (lôr"nyĕt'), *n.* a long-handled opera glass; a pair of eyeglasses fixed to a long handle into which they shut.

lorn (lôrn), *adj.* forsaken; forlorn; desolate; lone.

lor-ry (lŏr'ĭ; lŭr'ĭ), *n.* [*pl.* lorries (-ĭz)], a long four-wheeled wagon without sides; a miner's handcart; in military use, a large, low autotruck for carrying men and supplies. Also, **lorrie.**

lose (lōōz), *v.t.* [*p.t.* and *p.p.* lost, *p.pr.* losing], to be deprived of; cease to have in possession; mislay; to wander from; as, to *lose* one's way; waste; miss; as, to *lose* an opportunity; fail to keep; as, to *lose* one's health; fail to win; as, to *lose* a battle: *v.i.* to fail of success; yield; be defeated.

Syn. forfeit.
Ant. (see gain).

loss (lôs), *n.* privation; injury; ruin; the state of having no longer; failure to keep or obtain; as, *loss* of wealth; defeat; as, *loss* of a battle; that which one ceases to have, through accident or misfortune; excess of outgo over income in a business; waste: *pl.* number of soldiers killed, wounded, or captured in battle.

lost (lôst), *p.adj.* missing; given up; not won; destroyed; perplexed; wasted.

lot (lŏt), *n.* fortune; fate; as, the *lot* of man; portion or parcel, especially a plot of land; a share; method of deciding questions by drawing numbers, blocks, dice, etc.; as, to choose by *lot;* one of the objects so drawn; colloquially, a great quantity: *v.t.* to separate into lots; assign.

loth (lōth), *adj.* reluctant; unwilling. Also, **loath.**

Lo-tha-ri-o (lō-thā'rĭ-ō), *n.* a gay deceiver, especially a deceiver of women; so called from a character in Rowe's *The Fair Penitent.*

lo-tion (lō'shŭn), *n.* a medicated fluid for bathing the skin or an injured or diseased part.

lot-ter-y (lŏt'ẽr-ĭ), *n.* [*pl.* lotteries (-ĭz)], a distribution of prizes by chance; selling of chances.

lot-to (lŏt'ō), *n.* a parlor game played with twenty-four cards and wooden disks numbered 1 to 100.

lo-tus (lō'tŭs), *n.* a plant of the water lily family, especially the sacred lotus of the ancient Nile; a name for various trees and shrubs, the fruit of which was fabled to cause forgetfulness of care and create a state of dreamy indolence. Also, **lotos.**

lo-tus-eat-er (lō'tŭs-ēt"ẽr), *n.* one who idles away his time in forgetful dreaming. Also, **lotos-eater.**

loud (loud), *adj.* high- or full-sounding; noisy; colloquially, showy in dress or manner; vivid, as *loud* color; striking or emphatic in sound.—*adv.* **loudly.**—*n.* **loudness.**

Syn. clamorous, high-sounding.
Ant. (see low, quiet).

lough (lŏk), *n.* a lake; a bay or arm of the sea. Also, **loch.** [Scot.]

lounge (lounj), *v.i.* [*p.t.* and *p.p.* lounged, *p.pr.* lounging], to saunter about in a lazy manner; loll; live lazily: *v.t.* to waste in laziness: followed by *away:* *n.* the act of lolling; lazy motion or gait; a low-backed couch; a comfortable and informal parlor or waiting room in a hotel, club, etc.

loung-er (loun'jẽr), *n.* an idler; one who stands or strolls about lazily.

louse (lous), *n.* [*pl.* lice (līs)], a small, flat, wingless insect living and feeding on the bodies of animals or men.

lous-y (louz'ĭ), *adj.* infested with lice; mean; foul.

lout (lout), *n.* an awkward fellow; a clown; a bumpkin.—*adj.* **loutish.**

lov-a-ble (lŭv'á-bl), *adj.* worthy of love; winning; amiable.—*adv.* **lovably.**—*n.* **lovableness.**

love (lŭv), *n.* a strong feeling of affection; fond and tender attachment; passionate devotion to one of the opposite sex; courtship; parental care; state of feeling kindly toward others and of desiring the welfare of all; as, in *love* and charity for all men; a sweetheart; the term used for zero in scoring at tennis: *v.t.* to regard with strong affection; feel devotion towards; delight in: *v.i.* to be in love; have strong affection.

love ap-ple (lŭv ăp'l), an old name for the tomato.

love bird (lŭv bûrd), a small bird of the parrot family which shows great affection for its mate.

love feast (lŭv fēst), a religious feast celebrated among certain denominations as a sign of brotherly love.

love-less (lŭv'lĕs), *adj.* having no affection; incapable of causing affection in others.

love-lock (lŭv'lŏk"), *n.* a conspicuous lock of hair.

love-lorn (lŭv'lôrn"), *adj.* deserted by one's love.

love-ly (lŭv'lĭ), *adj.* [*comp.* lovelier, *superl.* loveliest], causing affection or admiration; amiable; beautiful; inviting; delightful.—*n.* **loveliness.**

lov-er (lŭv'ẽr), *n.* one who loves; one deeply attached; a man who is in love: *pl.* a couple in love with each other.

love-sick (lŭv'sĭk"), *adj.* overcome with passionate affection; languishing; as, a *lovesick* swain.

lov-ing (lŭv'ĭng), *p.adj.* devoted; affectionate.—*adv.* **lovingly.**

lov-ing cup (lŭv'ĭng kŭp), a large ornamental drinking cup, having two or more handles.

low (lō), *adj.* not high; depressed; shallow; not noisy; subdued; near the horizon; as, the sun is *low* in the west; cheap; moderate; feeble or weak; below the recognized standard; vulgar; abject; in music, not high in pitch: *adv.* not on high; deeply; softly; quietly; at a small price; in humbleness, poverty, or disgrace: *n.* the moo or soft bellow of cattle: *v.i.* to bellow softly or moo like cattle.
Syn., *adj.* abject, mean.
Ant. (see noble).

Low Church (lō chûrch), pertaining to the section of the English or Protestant Episcopal Church which is opposed to an extreme use of ritual, form, and ceremony.

low-er (lō'ẽr), *v.t.* to lessen or bring down; reduce in price or value; weaken; humble; change to a less high pitch: *v.i.* to become less high; sink; fall: (lou'ẽr), to appear dark, gloomy, or threatening.

low-er-case (lō'ẽr-kās), *n.* that part of a printer's case which contains the small printing types; small (not capital) letters: *adj.* denoting small letters in distinction to capitals.

low-er-ing (lou'ẽr-ĭng), *p.adj.* overcast with clouds; threatening a storm; gloomy.—*adv.* **loweringly.**

low-er-most (lō'ẽr-mōst), *adj.* lowest: opposite to *uppermost.*

low-ing (lō'ĭng), *n.* the mooing or soft bellowing of cattle: *adj.* mooing.

low-land (lō'lănd), *adj.* pertaining to a low or level country: *n.* a low level country: often in plural.

low-lived (lō'lĭvd"), *adj.* vulgar; ill-bred; base in character and habits.

low-ly (lō'lĭ), *adj.* [*comp.* lowlier, *superl.* lowliest], low in rank or size; humble; modest: *adv.* modestly.—*n.* **lowliness.**

Low Mass (lō măs), Mass said without music and by one priest.

low-necked (lō'nĕkt"), *adj.* cut low at the top, as a dress.

low-spir-it-ed (lō'spĭr'ĭt-ĕd), *adj.* depressed; sad; downhearted.

loy-al (loi'ăl), *adj.* faithful, especially to one's ruler or country; true to friend, promise, or duty.—*adv.* **loyally.**

loy-al-ist (loi'ăl-ĭst), *n.* one who supports the authority of his ruler or country.

loy-al-ty (loi'ăl-tĭ), *n.* faithfulness to country, friend, promise, duty; constancy; devotion.

loz-enge (lŏz'ĕnj), *n.* a diamond-shaped figure with four equal sides; especially, a diamond-shaped figure used in designs on coats of arms, etc.; a sweetmeat; a cough drop.

lub-ber (lŭb ẽr), *n.* an awkward, clumsy fellow; a raw sailor.—*adj.* and *adv.* **lubberly.**

lu-bri-cant (lū'brĭ-kănt), *n.* a substance for making anything smooth, slippery, or easily bent.

lu-bri-cate (lū'brĭ-kāt), *v.t.* to make smooth or slippery, or easy to bend; as, to *lubricate* machinery with oil; certain liniments *lubricate* the joints.—*n.* **lubrication.**

lu-bri-ca-tor (lū'brĭ-kā"tẽr), *n.* one who, or that which, makes slippery or smooth; especially, a device for oiling machinery.

lu-bric-i-ty (lū-brĭs'ĭ-tĭ), *n.* smoothness; freedom from friction; uncertainty, as of fortune; impurity of thought, word, or action.

lu-cent (lū'sĕnt), *adj.* shining; bright; resplendent.

lu-cern (lū-sûrn'), *n.* alfalfa. Also, **lucerne.**

lu-cid (lū'sĭd), *adj.* clear; readily understood; as, a *lucid* explanation; mentally sound or sane; as, a *lucid* interval; shining; transparent; as, a *lucid* stream of water.—*adv.* **lucidly.**—*n.* **lucidness.**

lu-cid-i-ty (lū-sĭd'ĭ-tĭ), *n.* the state of being clear; as, *lucidity* of thought.

lu-ci-fer (lū'sĭ-fẽr), *n.* a match so prepared as to be lighted by striking: **Lucifer,** Venus, as the morning star; Satan.

luck (lŭk), *n.* an event happening by chance or accident; fortune, either good or bad; success.

luck-less (lŭk'lĕs), *adj.* unlucky; unfortunate; unfavorable.—*adv.* **locklessly.**—*n.* **lucklessness.**

luck-y (lŭk'ĭ), *adj.* [*comp.* luckier, *superl.* luckiest], having good fortune; successful; fortunate; of good omen.—*adv.* **luckily.**—*n.* **luckiness.**

lu-cra-tive (lū'krȧ-tĭv), *adj.* profitable; wealth producing; as he is engaged in a *lucrative* business.—*adv.* **lucratively.**—*n.* **lucrativeness.**

lu-cre (lū'kẽr; lōō'kẽr), *n.* money, as greedily sought; mean gain.

lu-cu-brate (lū'kū-brāt), *v.i.* to work by artificial light; hence, to study or write laboriously; reason closely.

lu-cu-bra-tion (lū'kū-brā'shŭn), *n.* close and earnest study; a literary composition produced as the result of long and toilsome study.

lu-di-crous (lū'dĭ-krŭs), *adj.* causing mirth; comical; droll.—*adv.* **ludicrously.**—*n.* **ludicrousness.**

luff (lŭf), *n.* the weather gauge; that part of a ship towards the wind; the act of sailing close to the wind: *v.i.* to steer nearer to the wind.

lug (lŭg), *v.t.* [*p.t.* and *p.p.* lugged, *p.pr.* lugging], to pull or draw along: *v.i.* to drag; move heavily; pull with difficulty: *n.* the act or effort of pulling or dragging along; the ear; that which projects like an ear, as the *lugs* of a kettle; a lugsail.

lug-gage (lŭg'āj), *n.* baggage: the usual word in Great Britain.

lug-ger (lŭg'ẽr), *n.* a small vessel with two or three masts and with four-sided sails fastened to spars hung obliquely to the masts.

lug-sail (lŭg'sāl"), *n.* a four-sided sail held out by a long spar, called a yard, that is, in an oblique position toward the mast.

1, Dipping Lugsail; 2, Standing Lugsail; 3, Split Lugsail.

lu-gu-bri-ous (lū-gū'brĭ-ŭs), *adj.* mournful; as, the skull and crossbones are *lugubrious* emblems of death; doleful; as, a *lugubrious* tone of voice.—*adv.* **lugubriously.**—*n.* **lugubriousness.**

lug-worm (lŭg'wûrm"), *n.* a sand worm. Also, **lugbait.**

Luke (lūk), *n.* the third book of the New Testament, containing the Gospel as told by the Evangelist St. Luke, a physician, companion of the apostle Paul.

luke-warm (lūk'wôrm"), *adj.* moderately warm; tepid; as, *lukewarm* tea; indifferent; as, *lukewarm* interest.

lull (lŭl), *v.t.* to soothe to sleep; quiet: *v.i.* to become calm: *n.* the state of being less noisy or violent; a calm lasting for a short time; as, a *lull* in the storm.

lull-a-by (lŭl'ȧ-bī"), *n.* [*pl.* lullabies (-bīz)], a cradle-song.

lum-ba-go (lŭm-bā'gō), *n.* rheumatism of the muscles of the lower part of the back.

lum-bar (lŭm'bȧr), *adj.* pertaining to the lower part of the back; as, the *lumbar* vertebræ.

lum-ber (lŭm'bẽr), *n.* rubbish; forest timber sawed for market: *v.t.* to fill with rubbish; heap together in disorder: *v.i.* to cut down timber and prepare it for market; to move or roll heavily along.

lum-ber-er (lŭm'bẽr-ẽr), *n.* one who cuts forest timber and shapes it for market.

lum-ber-man (lŭm'bẽr-măn), *n.* one who is engaged in the trade of cutting or dealing in forest timber; a foreman of a body of men engaged in cutting timber.

lu-mi-na-ry (lū'mĭ-nā-rĭ), *n.* [*pl.* luminaries (-rĭz)], a body giving forth light, especially a heavenly body; as, the sun is the greatest *luminary* of the heavens; one who enlightens or instructs.

lu-mi-nif-er-ous (lū"mĭ-nĭf'ẽr-ŭs), *adj.* giving forth or carrying light; as, the light of the sun is brought to us through the *luminiferous* ether.

lu-mi-nos-i-ty (lū-mĭ-nŏs'ĭ-tĭ), *n.* the quality of being bright or shining; luminousness.

lu-mi-nous (lū'mĭ-nŭs), *adj.* giving forth or spreading light; as, the stars are *luminous* bodies; bright; clear; easily understood; very intelligent.—*adv.* **luminously.**—*n.* **luminousness.**

lump (lŭmp), *n.* a small shapeless mass; a swelling: *v.t.* to unite in a body or mass; as, to *lump* expenses; to speak of collectively: *v.i.* to form into a mass; as, cornstarch will *lump* if it is cooked too fast.

lump-fish (lŭmp'fĭsh"), *n.* a thick fish with horny spines.

lump-ish (lŭmp'ĭsh), *adj.* gross; heavy; stupid.—*adv.* **lumpishly.**—*n.* **lumpishness.**

lump-y (lŭm'pĭ), *adj.* full of lumps; as, *lumpy* bread; choppy; rough; as, a *lumpy* sea.

lu-na-cy (lū'nȧ-sĭ), *n.* [*pl.* lunacies (-sĭz)], mental unsoundness.

Syn. derangement, craziness, insanity, mania, madness.

Ant. (see sanity).

lu-nar (lū'nȧr), *adj.* pertaining to, measured by, or influenced by, the moon.

lu-nar caus-tic (lū'nȧr kôs'tĭk), silver nitrate prepared for use in cauterizing, or burning the skin.

lu-nar month (lū'nȧr mŭnth), the period from one new moon to the next, or twenty-nine and one-half days.

lu-nate (lū'nāt), *adj.* crescent-shaped; as, a *lunate* leaf.

lu-na-tic (lū'nȧ-tĭk), *adj.* affected with, or characteristic of, insanity; crazy; as, *lunatic* notions: *n.* one who is insane.

lunch (lŭnch), *n.* a light meal between breakfast and dinner; luncheon: *v.i.* to eat a light meal.

lu-nette (lū-nĕt'), *n.* anything shaped like a half-moon, as in fortification, etc.; a flattened watchglass.

lung (lŭng), *n.* one of two organs of breathing in air-breathing higher animals.

lunge (lŭnj), *n.* a sudden thrust or pass with the sword; sudden lurch: *v.i.* to make a sudden thrust or pass.

lung-wort (lŭng'wûrt"), *n.* a European plant with white blotches suggestive of disease spots, once thought helpful as a remedy for disease of the lungs; a small colorless plant growing on trees and rocks.

lu-nu-la (lū'nū-lȧ), *n.* [*pl.* lunulæ (-lē)], the white crescent-shaped part of the finger nail near the root.

āte, senāte, râre, căt, locȧl, fär, ȧsk, pȧrade; scēne, ēvent, ĕdge, novẽl, refẽr; rīght, sĭn; cōld, ōbey, côrd, stŏp, cȯmpare; ūnit, ūnite, bûrn, cŭt, focŭs, menü;

lu-pine (lū'pīn), *adj.* like a wolf; eager to devour; pertaining to dogs and wolves: *n.* a plant of the bean family having an edible seed.

lurch (lûrch), *n.* a sudden roll to one side, as of a ship; a swaying, staggering motion; a difficult or forlorn position; as, to be left in the *lurch;* a losing position in cribbage: *v.i.* to roll or stagger suddenly to one side.

lurch-er (lûrch'ẽr), *n.* one who lies in wait; one who steals game, as deer, etc.; a dog noted for power of scent and silence in hunting.

lure (lūr), *v.t.* to draw by anything that promises profit or pleasure: *n.* anything used as a means of drawing by promising profit or pleasure; as, thousands of foreigners have answered the *lure* of the freedom offered them by America; bait; a device, resembling a bird, used by a falconer to recall the hawk; a long curved trumpet still used in Scandinavia.

lu-rid (lū'rĭd), *adj.* grayish-orange; wan; ghastly; pale; gloomy.—*adv.* **luridly.** —*n.* **luridness.**

lurk (lûrk), *v.i.* to lie in wait; lie concealed or unnoticed.

lus-cious (lŭsh'ŭs), *adj.* excessively sweet; delightful to the taste or sense. —*adv.* **lusciously.**—*n.* **lusciousness.**

lush (lŭsh), *adj.* full of juice; rich in growth or vegetation; as, *lush* meadows.

lust (lŭst), *n.* strong desire to possess and enjoy, usually in a bad sense; as, a *lust* for gold; sinful and impure desire; *v.i.* to desire something strongly; have impure desires: with *after.*

lus-ter (lŭs'tẽr), *n.* brightness; splendor; brilliancy of reflected light; fame; a chandelier ornamented with cut glass pendants; a dress-cloth with a sheen; the quality and brilliancy of light reflected from the surface of minerals; an old-fashioned kind of pottery, having a metallic finish, the making of which is a lost art. Also, **lustre.**

lust-ful (lŭst'fŏŏl), *adj.* having sinful and impure desires.—*adv.* **lustfully.**

lus-tral (lŭs'trăl), *adj.* pertaining to, or used in, purification; as, *lustral* water.

lus-tra-tion (lŭs-trā'shŭn), *n.* a ceremony of purification.

lus-tre (lŭs-tẽr), *n.* brightness; splendor; brilliancy of reflected light; fame. Also, **luster.**

lus-trous (lŭs'trŭs), *adj.* having a sheen or brightness.

lus-trum (lŭs'trŭm), *n.* a purification; the ceremonies of purification in ancient Rome every five years; a period of five years.

lust-y (lŭs'tĭ), *adj.* [*comp.* lustier, *superl.* lustiest], robust; vigorous; healthy; as, a *lusty* infant. —*adv.* **lustily.**—*n.* **lustiness.**

lute (lūt), *n.* a stringed musical instrument of the guitar family; a composition of clay, etc., used for making the joints of vessels air-tight, or protecting them from the action of fire: *v.t.* to play on the lute; to close up the cracks of with a composition of clay, etc.: *v.i.* to play the lute.

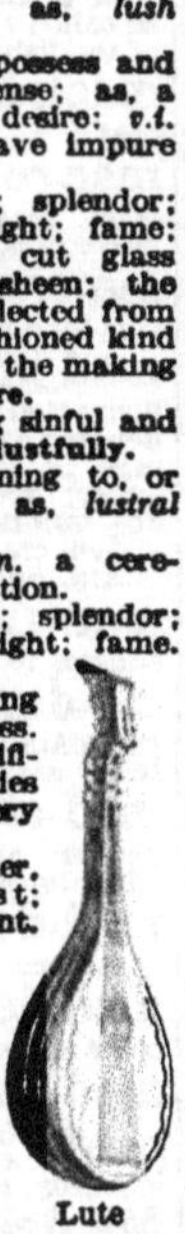

Lute

Lu-ther-an (lū'thẽr-ăn), *adj.* relating to Luther, the German reformer, or to the Lutheran Church and its doctrines: *n.* a member of the Lutheran Church.

lux (lŭks), *n.* [*pl.* luces (lū'sēz)], the unit of measure of the lighting power of electricity.

lux-u-ri-ance (lŭks-ū'rĭ-ăns; lŭg-zhŏŏ'-rĭ-ăns), *n.* rank, vigorous growth. Also, **luxuriancy.**

lux-u-ri-ant (lŭks-ū'rĭ-ănt; lŭg-zhŏŏ'rĭ-ănt), *adj.* rank and vigorous in growth; as, the morning-glory is a vine of *luxuriant* growth; hence, sometimes, existing too freely or plentifully; superabundant; superfluous.—*adv.* **luxuriantly.**

Syn. exuberant.

Ant. (see sparse).

lux-u-ri-ate (lŭks-ū'rĭ-āt; lŭg-zhŏŏ'rĭ-āt), *v.i.* to grow abundantly; live extravagantly; enjoy oneself unrestrainedly; as, to *luxuriate* in ease and plenty.

lux-u-ri-ous (lŭks-ū'rĭ-ŭs; lŭg-zhŏŏ'rĭ-ŭs), *adj.* pertaining to extravagant ease and plenty; indulging in, or administering to, extravagant ease.—*adv.* **luxuriously.**—*n.* **luxuriousness.**

lux-u-ry (lŭk'shŏŏ-rĭ), *n.* [*pl.* luxuries (-rĭz)], extravagant indulgence in the pleasures of the senses, dress, etc.; a dainty; anything which gives enjoyment but is not a necessity; as, the possession of a piano is a *luxury.*

ly-ce-um (lī-sē'ŭm), *n.* [*pl.* lyceums, lycea (-ŭmz, -ă)], a literary seminary; an academy; a literary association; an intermediate classical school: **Lyceum,** originally, the grove at Athens where Aristotle taught.

lyd-dite (lĭd'īt), *n.* a powerful explosive, consisting chiefly of picric acid, used as a shell explosive.

lye (lī), *n.* a strong caustic substance obtained especially by pouring water on wood ashes, used in making soap, etc.

ly-ing (lī'ĭng), *p.adj.* telling frequent falsehoods; as, a *lying* tongue; being in a reclining position: *n.* untruthfulness.

ly-ing to (lī'ĭng tōō), state of a vessel in which the sails act against one another and keep the ship nearly at rest.

lymph (lĭmf), *n.* a transparent, colorless fluid in animal bodies.

lym-phat-ic (lĭm-făt'ĭk), *adj.* pertaining to, carrying, or containing, a colorless fluid called lymph; sluggish: *n.pl.* the tiny tubes which carry lymph.

lynch (lĭnch), *v.t.* to inflict punishment upon, especially death by hanging, without legal trial.

lynch law (lĭnch lô), punishment by private individuals without the usual legal formalities, especially such action at the hands of a mob.

lynx (lĭnks), *n.* a fierce catlike animal, well known for its keenness of sight.

lyre (līr), *n.* a musical instrument of the harp kind; used by the ancients to accompany the voice.

lyre bird (līr bûrd), an Australian bird having a tail shaped like a lyre.

lyr-ic (lĭr'ĭk), *adj.* pertaining to, or adapted to singing to, a harplike musical instrument called a lyre: *n.* a poem expressing emotion.

lyr-i-cal (lĭr-ĭ-kăl), *adj.* suited to be sung; appropriate for song; expressive of a poet's feeling.—*adv.* **lyrically.**

lyr-ist (lĭr'ĭst; līr'ĭst), *n.* a player on the harplike musical instrument called a lyre; a composer of poems that express the feeling of the poet.

M

ma (mä), *n.* contraction of *mamma:* a childish, often vulgar, form.

ma'am (mäm; mäm), *n.* colloquially, contraction of *madam:* usually in direct address of inferiors to superiors.

Mac- (mäk-), a *prefix* in names of Scotch or Irish origin meaning *son:* often written, *Mc* or *M'*. [Scot. or Ir.]

mac-ad-am (mäk-ăd'ăm), *n.* a pavement of crushed stone; crushed stone used for such a pavement.

mac-ad-am-ize (măk-ăd'ăm-īz), *v.t.* to build or finish (a road) by covering it with a compact layer of small broken stone, so as to form a smooth, hard, rounded surface.—*n.* macadamization.

mac-a-ro-ni (măk"a-rō'nĭ), *n.* a food consisting of long, thin tubes made of a paste composed chiefly of fine wheat flour; a dandy or dude of the eighteenth century.

mac-a-ron-ic (măk"ȧ-rŏn'ĭk), *adj.* denoting a kind of writing in which words from several languages are used with humorous effect; as, *macaronic* verses; hence, confused; mixed.

mac-a-roon (măk'ȧ-rōōn'), *n.* a small cake made of flour, eggs, almonds, and sugar.

ma-caw (mȧ-kô'), *n.* a large and gaily colored parrot with a strong, hooked bill.

mace (mās), *n.* a large and heavy staff usually topped by a crown; a staff carried by or before an official as a symbol of authority; a person who bears such a staff; a medieval war club; a heavy billiard cue; a kind of aromatic spice consisting of the dried covering of the nutmeg.

mac-er-ate (măs'ẽr-āt), *v.t.* to soften or separate the parts of by soaking in a fluid; to cause to grow thin and weak.—*n.* maceration.

ma-che-te (mä-chā'tā), *n.* a large heavy knife used in Cuba and South America for cutting sugar cane, brush, etc.

Mach-i-a-vel-li-an (măk"ĭ-ȧ-vĕl'ĭ-ăn; măk"ĭ-ȧ-vĕl'yăn), *adj.* pertaining to Machiavelli, the Florentine statesman, or to his principles of political deceit; hence, crafty; double-dealing.—*n.* Machiavellianism.

ma-chic-o-la-tion (mȧ-chĭk"ō-lā'shŭn; măch"ĭ-cō-lā'shŭn), *n.* an opening in a parapet through which missiles can be shot or dropped on an enemy; a parapet with such openings.

mach-i-nate (măk'ĭ-nāt), *v.t.* and *v.i.* to plan; to contrive; to plot: usually with evil intent.

mach-i-na-tion (măk"ĭ-nā'shŭn), *n.* a hostile plot; a scheme to do evil; an artful design or plot; as, wars are often due to the *machinations* of deceitful politicians.

ma-chine (mȧ-shēn'), *n.* any contrivance to produce, increase, and regulate the power of motion so as to do work; an engine; a light carriage or vehicle; an automobile; one who acts without purpose or at the bidding of another; a body of persons acting together for a common purpose; a political organization which controls the policies and activities of a party.

ma-chine gun (mȧ-shēn' gŭn), a small, portable cannon capable of firing continuously: usually operated by mechanism.

Browning Machine Gun

ma-chin-er-y (mȧ-shēn'ẽr-ĭ), *n.* engines and other appliances collectively, or the parts of them; any means or combination by which something is kept in action or the result desired is obtained.

ma-chin-ist (mȧ-shēn'ĭst), *n.* one who makes or repairs engines and other appliances or is skilled in their design and principles; one who works about, or attends to, an engine or other mechanical appliances.

mack-er-el (măk'ẽr-ĕl), *n.* an edible fish, from twelve to eighteen inches in length, found in schools in the North Atlantic: **mackerel sky**, a sky covered with a mass of small white flecks of cloud: so called from its resemblance to the marking of the fish, and thought to be a sign of storm.

mack-in-tosh (măk'ĭn-tŏsh), *n.* an India rubber waterproof overcoat.

mac-ro-cosm (măk'rō-kŏzm), *n.* the universe; the world at large, exterior to man: used in contrast to *microcosm*, or man.

ma-cron (mā'krŏn; măk'rŏn), *n.* a mark [-] over a vowel to show that it is long in quantity, as in cāme.

mad (măd), *adj.* [*comp.* madder, *superl.* maddest], mentally disordered or distracted; insane; blindly or unreasonably devoted (to a person or thing); furious with rage or terror; colloquially, inflamed with anger; greatly excited; as, *mad* with joy.—*adv.* madly.—*n.* madness.

Syn. crazy, delirious, rabid, violent, frantic.
Ant. (see sane, rational).

mad-am (măd'ăm), *n.* a complimentary title, or form of courteous address to a lady.

ma-dame (mȧ'dȧm'; mȧ-dȧm'; often, măd'ăm), *n.* [*pl.* mesdames (mā'dȧm')], the French title for a married lady: abbreviated, *Mme.* [Fr.]

mad-cap (măd'kăp"), *n.* a wild, thoughtless person; a rattle-brained person: *adj.* given to wild follies; recklessly adventurous.

mad-den (măd'n), *v.t.* to craze or make furious: *v.i.* to become crazed or furious.

mad-der (măd'ẽr), *n.* a plant from the root of which a red dye and color are extracted.

mad-ding (măd'ĭng), *adj.* raging; furious; wild; raving.

made (mād), *p.t.* and *p.p.* of *make:* *adj.* artificially produced or formed; colloquially, assured of success.

Ma-dei-ra (mȧ-dē'rȧ; mȧ-dā'rȧ), *n.* wine made on the island of Madeira.

ma-de-moi-selle (măd"mwȧ"zĕl'; măd"ē-mō-zĕl';

colloquially, mȧm'zĕl'), *n.* [*pl.* **mesdemoiselles** (mād'mwȧ'zĕl')], a title of courtesy given in France to an unmarried lady: abbreviated, *Mlle.* [FR.]

made-up (mād'ŭp"), *adj.* not true; invented; artificial.

mad-man (măd'măn), *n.* an insane man: a lunatic; one whose mind is disordered or deranged.

Ma-don-na (mȧ-dŏn'ȧ), *n.* [*pl.* madonnas (-nȧz)], a picture of the Virgin Mary, usually with the Infant Christ; the Italian name for the Virgin Mary.

ma-dras (mȧ-drȧs'), *n.* a fabric of fine cotton, usually figured or corded.

mad-ri-gal (măd'rĭ-găl), *n.* a light, lyric love-song; a pastoral poem; a part song unaccompanied by music.

ma-du-ro (mä-dōō'rō), *adj.* of full strength and color: said of cigars. [SPAN.]

Mael-strom (māl'strŏm), *n.* a celebrated whirlpool on the Norwegian coast: **maelstrom**, any destructive or widespread and harmful influence; as, the *maelstrom* of war.

mæ-nad (mē'năd), *n.* [*pl.* mænads (-nădz)], a nymph or bacchante attendant upon Dionysius, the Greek god of wine; any frantic or frenzied woman.

maf-fi-a (măf'fē-ȧ), *n.* a Sicilian and Italian secret society, given to acts of lawlessness and violence. Also, **mafia**.

mag-a-zine (măg"ȧ-zēn'), *n.* a warehouse; a place for storing military supplies, as ammunition, etc.; the cartridge chamber of a gun; a literary or scientific publication, containing various articles, stories, etc., and issued at stated times.

mag-da-len (măg'dȧ-lĕn), *n.* a woman reformed from an evil and sinful life: from Mary Magdalene, said to be the repentant sinner forgiven by Christ. —Luke vii, *sq.* Also, **magdalene, Magdalene.**

ma-gen-ta (mȧ-jĕn'tȧ), *n.* a red dye; also, the peculiar shade of purplish-red produced by the dye.

mag-got (măg'ŏt), *n.* the larva of an insect, such as the house fly, in its wormlike stage of development; such a worm living in decaying flesh, food, etc.; a grub; whim.—*adj.* **maggoty.**

Ma-gi (mā'jī), *n.pl.* among the ancient Persians, the priestly and learned class; the wise men of the East.

mag-ic (măj'ĭk), *n.* the pretended art of working by power over the hidden forces of nature or by the assistance of supernatural beings; sorcery; witchcraft; enchantment; any hidden or secret power; as, the *magic* of beauty: *adj.* pertaining to, produced by, or exercising more than, human power; enchanted.—*adj.* **magical.**—*adv.* **magically.**

ma-gi-cian (mȧ-jĭsh'ăn), *n.* one skilled in the pretended art of putting into action the power of spirits; a conjurer; a sorcerer.

mag-ic lan-tern (măj'ĭk lăn'tērn), an optical instrument for throwing on a screen, in a darkened room, illuminated pictures enlarged by an arrangement of lenses.

mag-is-te-ri-al (măj"ĭs-tē'rĭ-ăl), *adj.* pertaining to, or suitable to, a master or magistrate; commanding; having an air of authority; as, a *magisterial* air or tone.—*adv.* **magisterially.**—*n.* **magisterialness.**

Syn. august, dignified, majestic, pompous, stately.

mag-is-tra-cy (măj'ĭs-trȧ-sĭ), *n.* [*pl.* magistracies (-sĭz)], the office or dignity of a civil officer with public authority, or of a justice of the peace; civil officers, such as justices of the peace, collectively.

mag-is-tral (măj'ĭs-trăl), *adj.* like a schoolmaster or magistrate; imperious; chief: *n.* the line from which the positions of the various units of a fortification are determined.

mag-is-trate (măj'ĭs-trāt), *n.* a civil officer who has public authority; a local justice; as, a justice of the peace is a *magistrate*.

Mag-na Char-ta (măg'nȧ kär'tȧ), the Great Charter, forming the basis of English civil liberty, granted by King John of England to the Barons, 1215. [LAT.]

mag-na-nim-i-ty (măg"nȧ-nĭm'ĭ-tĭ), *n.* greatness of mind or soul; nobility; as, to forgive an enemy is an act of *magnanimity*.

mag-nan-i-mous (măg-năn'ĭ-mŭs), *adj.* great of mind; elevated in soul or feeling; generous; courageous; heroic; as, to be *magnanimous* is indeed to be great.—*adv.* **magnanimously.**

mag-nate (măg'nāt), *n.* a person of rank or distinction; a person of influence.

mag-ne-si-a (măg-nē'zhĭ-ȧ; măg-nē'zhȧ; măg-nē'shĭ-ȧ; măg-nē'shȧ), *n.* a white, tasteless, earthy powder, used as a medicine.

mag-ne-si-um (măg-nē'zhĭ-ŭm; măg-nē'shĭ-ŭm), *n.* a silver-white metallic substance that burns with a brilliant light: much used in photography.

mag-net (măg'nĕt), *n.* the loadstone; a variety of ore having the property of attracting iron; a steel bar having the power to attract iron artificially given to it; a person or thing that attracts.

mag-net-ic (măg-nĕt'ĭk), *adj.* pertaining to, exhibiting, or produced by, the magnet, or its power of attraction; hence, having the power to attract; as, a *magnetic* personality; pertaining to animal power of attraction, or mesmerism: **magnetic needle**, a slim bar of steel, charged with the forces of attraction, which, swinging in a compass, indicates the earth's force of attraction, and hence, approximately, the north and south line.—*adv.* **magnetically.**

mag-net-ics (măg-nĕt'ĭks), *n.pl.* the science of magnetic attraction and repulsion.

mag-net-ism (măg'nĕt-ĭzm), *n.* that property possessed by various bodies, as iron or steel, of attracting or repelling each other according to certain physical laws; the force to which this attraction is due; the science that treats of the laws of physical attraction and repulsion; personal attraction; mesmerism.

mag-net-ite (măg'nĕt-īt), *n.* an iron oxide, strongly attracted by the magnet: called *loadstone* when it has the power of attraction for iron.

mag-net-ize (măg'nĕt-īz), *v.t.* to give force of attraction to; to make a magnet of; to attract by personal influence; to mesmerize.—*adj.* **magnetizable.**

mag-net-i-za-tion (măg"nĕt-ĭ-zā'shŭn), *n.* the extent or degree to which a body possesses the force of attraction; a giving of the force of attraction to.

mag-ne-to (măg-nē'tō; măg'nĕt-ō), *n.* a dynamo which generates the current for the ignition in certain internal-combustion engines, and which receives its driving force from the engine itself.

High Tension Magneto

mag-ne-to-e-lec-tric (măg'nĕt-ō-ē-lĕk'-trĭk; măg-nē'tō-ē-lĕk'trĭk), *adj.* characterized by, or pertaining to, electricity developed by magnets. Also, **magneto-electrical.**

Mag-nif-i-cat (măg-nĭf'ĭ-kăt), *n.* the song of thanksgiving of the Virgin Mary.—Luke i. 46–55.

mag-nif-i-cence (măg-nĭf'ĭ-sĕns), *n.* grandeur of appearance; splendor; pomp.

mag-nif-i-cent (măg-nĭf'ĭ-sĕnt), *adj.* grand in appearance; splendid; pompous; sublime; as applied to ideas, noble.—*adv.* **magnificently.**

mag-ni-fi-er (măg'nĭ-fī-ĕr), *n.* one who, or that which, makes, or makes to appear, greater or larger.

mag-ni-fy (măg'nĭ-fī), *v.t.* [*p.t.* and *p.p.* magnified, *p.pr.* magnifying], to make great or greater; to make the size of appear greater; to exaggerate; as, to *magnify* one's importance: *v.i.* to make greater the apparent size of an object by a lens.—*n.* **magnification.**

mag-nil-o-quent (măg-nĭl'ō-kwĕnt), *adj.* pompous in style or speech; bombastic.—*adv.* **magniloquently.** —*n.* **magniloquence.**

mag-ni-tude (măg'nĭ-tūd), *n.* comparative size or bulk; extent of dimensions (length, breadth, and thickness); importance; grandeur; in astronomy, the degree of brightness of a star.

mag-no-li-a (măg-nō'lĭ-ȧ), *n.* an ornamental tree, having aromatic bark and large fragrant flowers.

mag-pie (măg'pī), *n.* a chattering bird of the jay family; a chatterer.

mag-uey (măg'wā; SPAN. mä-gā'ē), *n.* the century plant, a species of agave, or American aloe.

Mag-yar (mŏd'yŏr), *n.* one of the ruling race in Hungary; the language of that race: *adj.* relating to that race or to its language.

ma-ha-ra-ja (mȧ-hä-rä'jȧ), *n.* a great prince among the Hindus. Also, **maharajah.**

Mah-dist (mä'dĭst), *n.* among the Mohammedans, a follower of the Mahdi, or claimant for the position of last leader of the faithful.

mahl-stick (mäl'stĭk"; môl'stĭk"), *n.* a stick used by painters as a rest for the hand while painting. Also, **maulstick.**

ma-hog-a-ny (mȧ-hŏg'ȧ-nĭ), *n.* a tree of tropical America yielding a dark, reddish-brown, hard wood, used for furniture; also, the wood.

Ma-hom-et-an (mȧ-hŏm'ĕt-ăn), *n.* a follower of Mahomet, or Mohammed, the founder of the religion that accepts Mohammed as the only prophet of God: *adj.* of or pertaining to Mohammed, or to the religion founded by him. Also, **Mahomedan, Mohammedan.**

ma-hout (mȧ-hout'), *n.* an East Indian name for an elephant driver or keeper.

maid (mād), *n.* an unmarried girl or woman; a virgin; a female servant: **maid of honor,** a noble lady, unmarried, who attends a queen; the bride's chief attendant at the wedding ceremony.

maid-en (mād'n), *n.* an unmarried girl or woman; a virgin: *adj.* pertaining to, or like, a virgin; pure; innocent; unsoiled; unused; untried: as, a *maiden* sword; a *maiden* knight; earliest or first: as, a *maiden* trip.

maid-en-hair (mād'n-hâr"), *n.* a beautiful, delicate fern found in damp woods. Also, **maidenhair fern.**

maid-en-hood (mād'n-hŏŏd), *n.* the state of being a young unmarried girl.

maid-en-ly (mād'n-lĭ), *adj.* like, or suitable to, a young girl; modest; gentle: *adv.* in a manner suitable to, or becoming, a young girl.—*n.* **maidenliness.**

maid-serv-ant (mād'sûr"vănt), *n.* a woman servant.

mail (māl), *n.* defensive body armor of steel, net, or platework; the government system for conveying letters, etc.; the bag or bags for carrying letters, etc., from one post office to another; letters, etc., carried by post: *v.t.* to clothe with, or as with, armor; to post, or send by post.

mail-a-ble (māl'ȧ-bl), *adj.* capable of being sent by post; lawful to post.

mailed (māld), *adj.* clad in, or covered by, armor; posted.

maim (mām), *v.t.* to deprive of the use of a limb; cripple or disfigure: *n.* an injury to the body by crippling or disfiguring. Also, *n.* **mayhem.**

main (mān), *adj.* chief; principal; sheer, as, by *main* strength; leading; direct; nautically, connected with the mainmast: *n.* the ocean; strength: now used only in the expression *with might and main;* the essential point; a principal conduit or pipe; as, a water *main:* **in the main,** for the most part.

main-land (mān'lănd), *n.* a continent; a broad expanse of land, generally, principal land as opposed to *island.*

main-ly (mān'lĭ), *adv.* principally; chiefly; for the most part; as, he is *mainly* a thinker.

main-mast (mān'măst), *n.* the principal mast of a vessel.

main-sail (mān'sāl"), *n.* the principal sail on the mainmast of a vessel.

main-sheet (mān'shēt"), *n.* one of the ropes by which the mainsail is extended and fastened.

main-spring (mān'sprĭng"), *n.* the principal spring, or driving spring, in a mechanism, as a watch; chief motive or reason; as, a sense of duty was the *mainspring* of all his actions.

main-stay (mān'stā"), *n.* the large, strong ropes extending from the foot of the foremast to the platform about the head of the mainmast; hence, principal dependence; chief support; as, the son is the *mainstay* of the household.

main-tain (mān-tān'; mĕn-tān'), *v.t.* to support or bear the expense of; sustain; to keep possession of; affirm and defend by argument; continue in or with; to keep up.

main-te-nance (mān'tē-nāns), *n.* the act of supporting, defending, etc.; means of support; defense; support; continuance; means of sustenance.

main-top (mān'tŏp″), *n.* a platform at the top of the mainmast: **main-top-mast**, the mast above the mainmast: **main-topgallant**, the mast, sail, or yard above the main-topmast.

maize (māz), *n.* Indian corn; field corn; the plant producing the grain.

ma-jes-tic (mȧ-jĕs'tĭk), *adj.* having great dignity of person or appearance; stately; noble; sublime; regal.—Also, **majestical**.—*adv.* **majestically**.

maj-es-ty (măj'ĕs-tĭ), *n.* [*pl.* majesties (-tĭz)], sovereignty; grandeur; nobility; sublimity: **Majesty**, a title given to a sovereign ruler; as, Your *Majesty*.

ma-jol-i-ca (mȧ-jŏl'ĭ-kȧ; mȧ-yŏl'ĭ-kȧ), *n.* a fine soft-enameled kind of pottery, decorated in colors.

ma-jor (mā'jẽr), *adj.* greater in number, extent, dignity, or quality; as, the *major* part of a man's day must be used for work; Isaiah was one of the *major* prophets; in music, a half tone higher than the minor: *n.* a military officer next in rank above a captain.

ma-jor-do-mo (mā″jẽr-dō'mō), *n.* the steward of a great household.

ma-jor gen-er-al (mā'jẽr jĕn'ẽr-ăl), a military officer next in rank below a lieutenant general.

ma-jor-i-ty (mȧ-jŏr'ĭ-tĭ), *n.* [*pl.* majorities (-tĭz)], the state of being greater; the greater of two numbers looked upon as parts of a whole; the difference between this greater number and the smaller; more than half of a total; the full legal age of twenty-one years; as, he has reached his *majority;* rank, etc., of a major.

make (māk), *v.t.* [*p.t.* and *p.p.* made, *p.pr.* making], to create; fashion; compose; frame; produce or bring about, prepare for use; obtain for oneself, as friends; to form, as plans; to compute to be; as, I *make* the amount fifty dollars; to amount to; as, three feet *make* a yard; to get; as, to *make* a fortune; raise to rank or dignity; as, his venture will *make* or break him; score; as, we *made* ten points in the game; arrive at, near, or in sight of; as, to *make* port; become; as, a good son *makes* a good husband; cause to be or become; as, to *make* him president; to cause to act in a certain manner; as, to *make* a child obey: *v.i.* to tend or move; as, he *made* toward the goal; have effect; as, the power that *makes* for righteousness; to put something into a specified condition; as, to *make* ready for a journey; to act in a specified manner; as, to *make* merry: *n.* shape; construction; build.

make-be-lieve (māk'bē-lēv″), *n.* a pretense; a child's game of pretending that something fancied is real: *adj.* pretended; fictitious; false.

mak-er (māk'ẽr), *n.* one that fashions, composes, or produces; one who signs a promissory note: **Maker**, the Creator.

make-shift (māk'shĭft″), *n.* that which can be used for a time in want of something better: *adj.* capable of being used for a time; serving as a temporary tool, convenience, etc.

make-up (māk'ŭp″), *n.* the way in which the parts of anything are put together; dress, paint, powder, etc., for a part on the stage; artificial preparation; arrangement of type, articles, headlines, etc., in newspapers or printed matter.

Mal-a-chi (măl'ȧ-kī), *n.* the name of a book of the Old Testament believed to have been written by the Hebrew prophet Malachi.

mal-a-chite (măl'ȧ-kīt), *n.* green carbonate of copper; a form of copper ore.

mal-ad-min-is-ter (măl″ăd-mĭn'ĭs-tẽr), *v.t.* to manage or conduct badly.—*n.* **maladministration**.

mal-a-droit (măl″ȧ-droit'), *adj.* unskilful; awkward; clumsy.—*adv.* **maladroitly**.—*n.* **maladroitness**.

mal-a-dy (măl'ȧ-dĭ), *n.* [*pl.* maladies (-dĭz)], a disease, especially a deep-seated or lingering disorder, mental or physical.

Mal-a-ga (măl'ȧ-gȧ), *n.* a variety of wine; a sweet, white, firm-fleshed grape.

Mal-a-gas-y (măl″ȧ-găs'ĭ), *n. sing.* and *pl.* a native of Madagascar; the language of Madagascar.

ma-laise (mȧ'lāz'; măl'āz), *n.* a vague feeling of uneasiness, often coming before an attack of illness. [FR.]

mal-a-pert (măl'ȧ-pẽrt), *adj.* pert; saucy; bold; impudent: *n.* a bold, saucy person.

mal-a-prop-ism (măl'ȧ-prŏp-ĭzm), *n.* a ridiculous misuse of fine words: from Mrs. Malaprop, in Sheridan's *The Rivals*.

mal-a-pro-pos (măl-ăp″rō-pō'), *adj.* out of place; coming at the wrong time; not appropriate: *adv.* inappropriately.

ma-lar (mā'lȧr), *adj.* pertaining to the cheek or cheek bone.

ma-la-ri-a (mȧ-lā'rĭ-ȧ), *n.* harmful vapors from marshy land, supposed to produce fevers, etc.; disease produced by the bite of certain mosquitoes which carry the germs; chills and fever; ague.

ma-la-ri-al (mȧ-lā'rĭ-ăl), *adj.* pertaining to, producing, or having, chills and fever; as, swamps are *malarial* regions. Also, **malarious**.

Ma-lay (mȧ-lā'; mā'lā), *n.* one of the race of brown men dominant in southeastern Asia and the islands off that coast; the language of these people: *adj.* of or pertaining to the brown race or their region.

Ma-lay-an (mȧ-lā'ăn), *adj.* of or pertaining to the Malay peoples, their region, or their language. Also, **Malaysian**.

mal-con-tent (măl'kŏn-tĕnt″), *adj.* discontented, especially with established authority: *n.* one who is discontented with the established order of things.

male (māl), *adj.* pertaining to the sex that fathers young; not female; masculine; in machinery, fitting into a corresponding hollow piece: *n.* a human being of the sex that fathers young; an animal or plant of such sex.

mal-e-dic-tion (măl″ē-dĭk'shŭn), *n.* a proclaiming of evil against anyone; curse; act of speaking evil; state of being slandered.
Syn. anathema, imprecation.
Ant. (see benediction).

mal-e-fac-tor (măl″ē-făk'tẽr), *n.* an evildoer; a criminal.—*n.* **malefaction**.

ma-lev-o-lence (mȧ-lĕv'ō-lĕns), *n.* spitefulness; ill will; intent to do injury to others.

ma-lev-o-lent (mȧ-lĕv'ō-lĕnt), *adj.* malicious; spiteful; wishing evil; disposed to injure others.

mal-fea-sance (măl-fē'zăns), *n.* an illegal act; an evil deed; wrongdoing by a public official.

mal-for-ma-tion (măl'fôr-mā'shŭn), *n.* faulty or abnormal structure of any body or part of the body; as, a clubfoot is a *malformation.*

mal-ice (măl'ĭs), *n.* evil intention to injure others; deliberate mischief; spite; in law, state of mind shown by intention to perform an unlawful act or deed.
Syn. rancor, ill-feeling, grudge, animosity, ill will.
Ant. (see benignity).

ma-li-cious (mȧ-lĭsh'ŭs), *adj.* bearing ill will or spite; influenced by hatred or spite; indulging in deliberate mischief; as, a *malicious* person; arising from ill-will; as, a *malicious* act.—*adv.* **maliciously.**—*n.* **maliciousness.**

ma-lign (mȧ-līn'), *v.t.* to speak evil of with spite or ill will; slander; as, to *malign* the character of another: *adj.* hurtful; tending to injure; baleful; evil; as, *malign* influences.—*adv.* **malignly.**

ma-lig-nan-cy (mȧ-lĭg'năn-sĭ), *n.* the state of being disposed to do harm; in medicine, the virulence of a disease which threatens to produce death.

ma-lig-nant (mȧ-lĭg'nănt), *adj.* malicious; having extreme, active enmity toward any one; intending or bringing about evil; of disease, tending to produce death; virulent.—*adv.* **malignantly.**

ma-lign-er (mȧ-līn'ẽr), *n.* one who speaks evil of another.

ma-lig-ni-ty (mȧ-lĭg'nĭ-tĭ), *n.* [*pl.* malignities (-tĭz)], the state of being disposed to do evil to others; malice; deadly quality; as, the *malignity* of cancer.

ma-lin-ger (mȧ-lĭṅ'gẽr), *v.t.* to pretend illness in order to escape duty, especially military duty.—*n.* **malingerer.**

mal-i-son (măl'ĭ-zn; măl'ĭ-sn), *n.* a curse; a malediction.

mall (môl), *n.* a large heavy wooden mallet; a public walk shaded by trees.

mal-lard (măl'ẽrd), *n.* the male of the common wild duck; any wild duck.

mal-le-a-bil-i-ty (măl'ē-ȧ-bĭl'ĭ-tĭ), *n.* the capability of being extended by hammering or rolling.

mal-le-a-ble (măl'ē-ȧ-bl), *adj.* capable of being extended by hammering or rolling; as, gold is the most *malleable* of all metals.

mal-let (măl'ĕt), *n.* a short-handled hammer used for driving a tool; the long-handled implement, hammer-like at one end, used to drive the balls in the game of croquet; the stick used in polo.

Mallet

mal-le-us (măl'ē-ŭs), *n.* one of the three small bones in the ear: called also the *hammer.*

mal-low (măl'ō), *n.* a plant having pink, purple, white, or yellow cup-shaped flowers.

malm-sey (mäm'zĭ), *n.* a rich variety of grape; a strong, full-flavored sweet wine: called also *malvoisie.*

mal-nu-tri-tion (măl'nū-trĭsh'ŭn), *n.* faulty use of food in the body; insufficient nourishment, either on account of actual lack of food or faulty digestive processes.

mal-o-dor-ous (măl-ō'dẽr-ŭs), *adj.* ill-smelling; having a disagreeable smell; objectionable.—*adv.* **malodorously.**

mal-prac-tice (măl-prăk'tĭs), *n.* the treatment of a case by a surgeon or physician in a manner contrary to accepted rules and with harmful results to the patient; the conduct of any profession in an illegal or wrong way.

malt (môlt), *n.* barley or other grain soaked in water, fermented, and dried for brewing: *v.i.* to ferment, or change into malt: said of grain: *v.t.* to make into or with malt, or fermented grain: *adj.* made with such fermented grain; as, beer and ale are *malt* liquors.—*adj.* **malty.**

Mal-tese (môl-tēz'; môl-tēs'), *adj.* relating to Malta, an island in the Mediterranean, or to its inhabitants: **Maltese cat,** a kind of tame cat with soft gray fur; **Maltese cross,** a cross with four arms of equal length, widening at the ends: *n. sing.* and *pl.* a native of Malta; the people of Malta or their language.

mal-treat (măl-trēt'), *v.t.* to treat ill or roughly; to treat unkindly.—*n.* **maltreatment.**

mam-ma (mȧ-mä'; mä'mȧ), *n.* a familiar name for mother. Also, **mama.**

mam-ma (măm'ȧ), *n.* [*pl.* mammæ (-ē)], a glandular organ secreting milk, found in all animals that suckle their young.

mam-mal (măm'ăl), *n.* one of the highest class of animals which feed their young with milk from the breast.

Mam-ma-li-a (mă-mā'lĭ-ȧ), *n.pl.* the highest class of animals which feed their young with milk from the breast.

mam-ma-li-an (mă-mā'lĭ-ăn), *adj.* belonging to the Mammalia, or those animals which feed their young with milk from the breast; pertaining to, or characteristic of, such animals.

mam-ma-ry (măm'ȧ-rĭ), *adj.* of or pertaining to the breasts, or mammæ.

mam-mon (măm'ŭn), *n.* wealth; worldly gain; greed or riches; from Mammon, the Syrian god of riches.

Mammoth

mam-moth (măm'ŏth), *n.* a kind of huge elephant no longer in existence. *adj.* gigantic; immense.

mam-my (măm'ĭ), *n.* a child's name for mother; in the South, a negro woman who cares for children.

man (măn), *n.* [*pl.* men (mĕn)], a human being; an adult male of the human species; mankind; with *a,* any one, in an indefinite sense; male servant; one possessed of manly qualities in a high degree; a husband: used only in *man and wife;* one of the pieces in chess, checkers, or similar games; a ship: used only in composition; as, *man-of-war*: *v.t.* [*p.t.* and *p.p.* manned, *p.pr.* manning], to furnish with men; guard: **to a man,** none being excepted.

man-a-cle (măn'ȧ-kl), *n.* a handcuff; a fetter: usually used in plural: *v.t.* to place handcuffs upon; put into chains.

man-age (măn'āj), *v.t.* to conduct or carry on; govern; make obedient or controllable; keep in a desired mood; to bring about by ingenious devices; contrive: *v.i.* to conduct or direct affairs; to make use of means in a thrifty fashion.
Syn. contrive, control, direct.

man-age-a-ble (măn'āj-ȧ-bl), *adj.* easy to be conducted or controlled; obedient; controllable; subject to guidance.—*adv.* **manageably.**—*n.* **manageableness.**

man-age-ment (măn'āj-mĕnt), *n.* the act or art of conducting or controlling; administration; control; skill in direction; those collectively who are responsible for the direction of an enterprise or business; the act of carrying on.
Syn. superintendence, conduct, care, charge.

man-a-ger (măn'ȧ-jẽr), *n.* one who directs or conducts anything; a person who conducts business or household affairs with skill and economy.—*adj.* **managerial.**

Man-chu (măn-chōō'), *n.* one of the natives of Manchuria, in China; the language of the Manchus: *adj.* pertaining to Manchuria or its inhabitants. Also, **Manchurian.**

man-da-mus (măn-dā'mŭs), *n.* a written paper given out by a superior court directing the person or inferior court to whom it is addressed to perform some public duty or act.

man-da-rin (măn'dȧ-rĭn), *n.* in China, an official of one of nine classes, which are distinguished by a particular kind of button worn on the cap; a variety of orange: **Mandarin**, the Chinese dialect in use by the official classes; loosely, the chief Chinese dialect.

man-date (măn'dāt), *n.* an order; command; an official charge or injunction.

man-da-to-ry (măn'dȧ-tō-rĭ), *adj.* containing or pertaining to an official command; expressing a command; carrying obligation: *n.* an attorney or agent who acts for another; a nation or state chosen to govern or administer a colony, or certain territory. Also, **manda'ary.**

man-di-ble (măn'dĭ-bl), *n.* the under jaw; in birds, either jaw.

man-do-lin (măn'dō-lĭn), *n.* a musical instrument which has a pear-shaped sound-box, a neck with frets, and a set of metal strings arranged like those of a violin.

man-drake (măn'drāk), *n.* a plant of the nightshade family with a very large forked root and a white or purple flower; the May apple.

man-drel (măn'drĕl), *n.* the part of a lathe on which the work to be turned is placed; the revolving axle of a circular saw. Also, **mandril.**

man-drill (măn'drĭl), *n.* the blue-faced baboon of Africa.

mane (mān), *n.* the long hair on the upper side or about the neck of certain animals, as the horse and the lion; a line of stubble left by mowers.—*adj.* **maned.**

ma-nège (mȧ'nĕzh'), *n.* a riding academy; a school where horsemanship is taught; the art of training, riding, or driving horses. Also, **manege.**

ma-nes (mā'nēz), *n.pl.* among the ancient Romans, the spirits of the dead and the gods of the lower regions.

ma-neu-ver (mȧ-nōō'vẽr; mȧ-nū'vẽr), *n.* swift and skilful management or operation in military or naval affairs; an artful device or proceeding; a stratagem; skilful management: *v.i.* to perform certain movements with troops or war vessels; manage with art and skill: *v.t.* to cause to make certain movements, as troops or vessels; to handle skilfully; to manage with dexterity; to make, move, or put into certain positions, by skilful management. Also, **manoeuvre.**

man-ful (măn'fŏŏl), *adj.* courageous; bravely determined.—*adv.* **manfully.**—*n.* **manfulness.**

man-ga-nese (măn'gȧ-nēs'; măn'gȧ-nēz'), *n.* a hard, brittle, metallic substance, of a grayish color slightly tinged with red: used in alloy in gun making, etc.

mange (mānj), *n.* a contagious skin disease of dogs, cattle, etc.

man-ger (mān'jẽr), *n.* a feeding trough for horses or cattle.

man-gle (măn'gl), *n.* a machine for smoothing cloth, especially damp linen, by the pressure of revolving rollers: *v.t.* to smooth (cloth) by the use of such a machine; to cut to pieces; to mutilate by cutting; to hack; to spoil in the doing; to injure in the performing; to make a botch of.

man-go (măn'gō), *n.* [*pl.* mangoes (-gōz)], a well-known tropical fruit of oblong shape, yellowish color, thick rind, and juicy pulp; the tree bearing the fruit.

man-grove (măn'grōv), *n.* an East and West Indian tree yielding a bark used in tanning, and having branches which take root and cause the tree to spread in a thick mass.

man-gy (mān'jĭ), *adj.* suffering or afflicted with a contagious skin disease, as dogs and cattle.—*n.* **manginess.**

man-hole (măn'hōl'), *n.* an opening by which a workman may enter a tank, sewer, etc.

man-hood (măn'hŏŏd), *n.* courage; manliness; the state of being a man; man's estate; men collectively; as, the *manhood* of the United States will rise against oppression; the manly qualities, taken collectively.

ma-ni-a (mā'nĭ-ȧ), *n.* violent insanity; intense excitement; excessive or unreasonable desire or enthusiasm; as, some people have a *mania* for collecting.
Syn. madness, lunacy.

ma-ni-ac (mā'nĭ-ăk), *adj.* affected with insanity; raving; frantic: *n.* a madman. Also, *adj.* **maniacal.**—*adv.* **maniacally.**

man-i-cure (măn'ĭ-kūr), *n.* the care of the hands, nails, etc.; one whose business it is to care for the hands and nails: *v.t.* and *v.i.* to care for (the hands and nails); to care for the hands and nails of.—*n.* **manicurist.**

man-i-fest (măn'ĭ-fĕst), *adj.* clear; plain; apparent to the sight or understanding: *v.t.* to make clear; place beyond doubt of understanding; to prove; to show the list of, as a cargo: *n.* the list of a cargo to be shown to the customhouse officials; an invoice.—*adv.* **manifestly.**
Syn., *adj.* evident, open, visible, unmistakable, overt, obvious, patent.
Ant. (see hidden).

man-i-fes-ta-tion (măn″ĭ-fĕs-tā′shŭn), *n.* a public display, either for showing feeling or gaining attention; a revealing or a disclosure; the act of making plain.

man-i-fes-to (măn″ĭ-fĕs′tō), *n.* [*pl.* manifestoes (-tōz)], a public declaration on the part of an official concerning political measures or intentions.

man-i-fold (măn′ĭ-fōld), *adj.* various in kind or quality; numerous; comprehensive: *v.t.* make many copies of by means of a duplicating machine: *n.* a copy made by a duplicating machine.—*adv.* **manifoldly.**—*n.* **manifoldness.**

Syn., adj. several, sundry, divers.

man-i-kin (măn′ĭ-kĭn), *n.* a dwarf; a little man; a model of the human body for study of the organs. Also, **mannikin, manakin.**

ma-nil-a (mȧ-nĭl′ȧ), *n.* a kind of cigar manufactured at Manila in the Philippine Islands; a hemp used for ropes, paper, etc., made from the fibers of a Philippine tree related to the banana. Also, **manilla.**

man-i-oc (măn′ĭ-ŏk; mā′nĭ-ŏk), *n.* a tropical plant from the roots of which tapioca and starch are made.

ma-nip-u-late (mȧ-nĭp′ū-lāt), *v.t.* to operate or work skilfully by means of the hands; to] treat; to influence artfully; control the action of, by skilful management; to falsify, as books, in bookkeeping: *v.i.* to use the hands, especially in scientific operations or mechanical processes.

ma-nip-u-la-tion (mȧ-nĭp″ū-lā′shŭn), *n.* the act or process of operating or working skilfully with the hands; falsification, of accounts, etc.; skilful management.—*n.* **manipulator.**

ma-nip-u-la-tive (mȧ-nĭp′ū-lā-tĭv), *adj.* pertaining to, or performed by, skilful use of the hands; managing skilfully.

man-i-tou (măn′ĭ-tōō), *n.* the Great Spirit of the North American Indians. Also, **manito, manitu.**

man-kind (măn″kīnd′), *n.* the human race; (măn′kīnd″), men, distinguished from women.

man-like (măn′līk″), *adj.* like, or suitable to, a man; manly.

man-li-ness (măn′lĭ-nĕs), *n.* the state or quality of being manly; courage; the upstanding, courageous qualities of a true man.

man-ly (măn′lĭ), *adj.* having the qualities of a man; manlike; courageous; noble; dignified; resolute: *adv.* like a man.

Syn., adj. masculine, vigorous, frank, brave, heroic.

Ant. (see effeminate).

man-na (măn′ȧ), *n.* a name given by the Israelites to the food miraculously supplied in the wilderness.—Ex. xvi. 15; spiritual nourishment; the sweet juice from certain kinds of ash of southern Europe.

man-ner (măn′ẽr), *n.* method; mode of action; habit; a way of acting; custom; sort; kind; species; aspect; style; fashion: *pl.* morals; behavior; rules of conduct; social observances; politeness.

Syn. way, air, look, appearance.

man-ner-ism (măn′ẽr-ĭzm), *n.* a peculiarity of style, action, or bearing, especially if strained or affected.

man-ner-less (măn′ẽr-lĕs), *adj.* without politeness; lacking in respect; impolite.

man-ner-ly (măn′ẽr-lĭ), *adj.* polite; respectful: *adv.* politely; respectfully.—*n.* **mannerliness.**

man-ni-kin (măn′ĭ-kĭn), *n.* a little man; a dwarf; a model of the human body for study of the organs. Also, **manikin, manakin.**

man-nish (măn′ĭsh), *adj.* masculine; characteristic of a man.—*adv.* **mannishly.**—*n.* **mannishness.**

ma-nœu-vre (mȧ-nōō′vẽr; mȧ-nū′vẽr), *n.* swift and skilful management; artful device; stratagem: *v.t.* to handle skilfully; to manage with dexterity: *v.i.* manage with art and skill; scheme. Also, **maneuver.**

man-of-war (măn″ŏv-wôr′), *n.* [*pl.* men-of-war], a large ship of war; an armed vessel belonging to a navy of recognized status.

man-or (măn′ẽr), *n.* the district over which a lord of the Middle Ages held authority; the land belonging to a lord, or so much as he formerly reserved for his own use; a tract of land occupied by tenants who pay rent to the owner: **manor house,** the dwelling house of the owner of the manor.

ma-no-ri-al (mȧ-nō′rĭ-ăl), *adj.* belonging to a manor, or district over which a lord exercised authority.

man-sard roof (măn′särd rōōf), a roof which has on all sides two slopes, the lower being steeper than the upper.

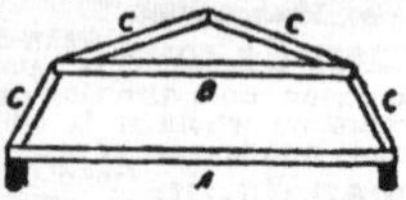

Mansard Roof. *A,* tie-beam; *B,* collar beam; *C,C,* rafters.

manse (măns), *n.* the home of a Presbyterian minister in Scotland; a parsonage.

man-serv-ant (măn′sûr″vănt), *n.* a male servant.

man-sion (măn′shŭn), *n.* a large dwelling house; a stately residence.

man-slaugh-ter (măn′slô″tẽr), *n.* the unlawful killing of a human being, but without malice or forethought.

man-teau (măn′tō; măn″tō′), *n.* [*pl.* manteaus (-tōz), manteaux (-tō′)], a cloak or mantle worn by women. Also, **mantua.**

man-tel (măn′tl), *n.* a narrow ornamental shelf above a fireplace. Also, **mantelpiece.**

man-tel-et (măn′tl-ĕt), *n.* a bullet-proof shelter, formerly movable, to protect besiegers, gunners, etc.; a short cloak or cape.

man-til-la (măn-tĭl′ȧ), *n.* a lady's light cloak or hood, worn in Mexico, Spain, etc.

man-tis (măn′tĭs), *n.* [*pl.* mantes (-tēz)], an insect allied to the grasshopper, noted for taking a position with its front legs folded as if praying.

man-tle (măn′tl), *n.* a loose cloak or cape: the outside fold of the skin of the body of the clam and other shellfish; a conelike network of material that will not burn, but which fits like a cap over a flame and gives light by glowing at high temperature: *v.t.* to cover with, or as with, a cloak; conceal: *v.i.* to become covered; to become suffused with blood; to froth.

man-tu-a (măn′tū-ȧ), *n.* a woman's loose gown or cloak, especially one having an open front. Also, **manteau.**

man-tu-a-mak-er (măn'tū-ȧ-māk'ẽr), *n.* one whose trade is the making of women's garments.

man-u-al (măn'ū-ăl), *adj.* pertaining to, or done by, the hands: *n.* a small book; a handbook; in military usage, an exercise in the handling of a weapon, done in a prescribed way; the keyboard of an organ or harmonium: **manual of arms**, an exercise in the systematic use of a weapon, done in a prescribed way.—*adv.* **manually.**

man-u-fac-to-ry (măn"ū-făk'tō-rĭ), *n.* [*pl.* manufactories (-rĭz)], a place where goods are made from raw materials; a factory.

man-u-fac-ture (măn"ū-făk'tūr; măn"-ū-făk'chŏŏr), *v.t.* to make from raw materials; produce artificially: *v.i.* to be occupied in the making of goods from raw materials: *n.* the changing of raw materials into articles for use; the thing made from the raw material.—*n.* **manufacturer.**

man-u-mis-sion (măn"ū-mĭsh'ŭn), *n.* the act of freeing from slavery.

man-u-mit (măn'ū-mĭt), *v.t.* [*p.t.* and *p.p.* manumitted, *p.pr.* manumitting], to set free from slavery.

ma-nure (mȧ-nūr'), *n.* any fertilizing substance used for enriching the soil: *v.t.* to enrich with fertilizing substances.

man-u-script (măn'ū-skrĭpt), *adj.* written by hand: *n.* [abbreviated MS., *pl.* MSS.], a book or paper written by hand; especially, an author's copy of his work, in handwriting or in typewriting; writing, as opposed to printing.

Manx (măṅks), *adj.* relating to the Isle of Man, to its people, or to the old language of the island: *n. sing.* and *pl.* the Manx language; the Manx people: **Manxman**, a native of the Isle of Man.

man-y (mĕn'ĭ), *adj.* [*comp.* more, *superl.* most], numerous; consisting of a great number: *n.* a great number; multitude; people.

Ma-o-ri (mä'ō-rĭ; mou'rĭ), *adj.* relating to the Maoris, or natives of New Zealand, or to their language: *n.* the natives of New Zealand, or their language.

map (măp), *n.* a representation on a flat surface of the earth or some portion of it; a chart of the heavens: *v.t.* [*p.t.* and *p.p.* mapped, *p.pr.* mapping], to picture or lay down in a chart; describe clearly; sketch or plan.

ma-ple (mā'pl), *n.* a well-known tree of many varieties, valued as a shade tree, for its wood, and, in some species, for its sap which is used for making sugar and syrup.

mar (mär), *v.t.* [*p.t.* and *p.p.* marred, *p.pr.* marring], to disfigure; injure; damage.

Syn. spoil, ruin.

Ant. (see improve).

mar-a-bou (măr'ȧ-bōō), *n.* a stork of an African species whose soft wing or tail feathers are used for dress trimming and for apparel. Also, **marabout.**

mar-a-schi-no (măr"ȧ-skē'nō), *n.* a delicate alcoholic cordial distilled from cherries.

ma-ras-mus (mȧ-răz'mŭs), *n.* a gradual wasting away of the body: usually, a disease of small children.

Mar-a-thon (măr'ȧ-thŏn), *n.* a long-distance foot race: so called from the runner who carried to Athens the news of the victory of Marathon.

ma-raud (mȧ-rôd'), *v.i.* to plunder; to rove in search of plunder; as, wild beasts *maraud* at night.—*n.* **marauder.**

mar-ble (mär'bl), *n.* a hard limestone of various colors capable of taking a fine polish; anything like such stone; a single piece of such stone; a small stone or glass ball used as a child's plaything: *pl.* the game played with these balls; a collection of sculpture in marble: *adj.* made of, or like, marble; cold; hard; unfeeling: *v.t.* to stain or vein like marble.

march (märch), *n.* a regular measured step or walk, especially of soldiers; the distance passed over in walking in such a manner from one place to another; steady onward movement; as, the *march* of the years; a musical composition to be played as troops march; frontier; borderland: *v.t.* to cause to move in a regular measured walk, as troops: *v.i.* to move with regular steps, or in military form.—**March**, the third month of the year.

Syn., *v.* tramp, tread, walk, step.

mar-chion-ess (mär'shŭn-ĕs), *n.* the wife or widow of a marquis; a lady of the rank of a marquis.

mar-co-ni-gram (mär-kō'nĭ-grăm), *n.* a message sent or received by Marconi's system of wireless telegraphy.

mar-co-ni-graph (mär-kō'nĭ-grăf), *n.* the apparatus used to send a message in Marconi wireless telegraphy.

Mar-di gras (mär'dĭ grä), Shrove Tuesday; the Tuesday before Ash Wednesday; the last day before Lent, celebrated in some cities, as Rome, Paris, New Orleans, with great merriment.

mare (mâr), *n.* the female of the horse, and similar animals.

mare's-nest (mârz'nĕst"), *n.* some discovery which at first seems to be wonderful but which proves to be a cheat.

mar-ga-rine (mär'gȧ-rēn; mär'gȧ-rĭn), *n.* artificial butter; oleomargarine, a butter substitute made from animal or vegetable fats.

mar-gin (mär'jĭn), *n.* border; the unprinted edge of a page; a limit; reserved amount, as of money, time, or space; as, he allowed a *margin* of an hour to catch the train; money, stock certificates, etc., given to a broker to secure him from loss in advancing funds for an investment; as, to buy on a *margin*: *v.t.* to furnish with an edge or border; enter upon the edge of a page.

Syn., *n.* edge, rim, brink, verge.

mar-gin-al (mär'jĭn-ăl), *adj.* pertaining to, or placed on, the edge or border.

mar-gra-vi-ate (mär-grā'vĭ-āt), *n.* the district presided over by a margrave, or German marquis.

mar-grave (mär'grāv), *n.* [*fem.* margravine], English form of markgraf, a German title of nobility equivalent to marquis.

mar-gue-rite (mär'gē-rēt; mär"gē-rēt'), *n.* the oxeye daisy; the garden daisy.

mar-i-gold (măr'ĭ-gōld), *n.* a plant of the aster family with showy yellow flowers; also, the flower.

ma-rine (mȧ-rēn'), *adj.* pertaining to, living in, or formed by, the sea; as, *marine* plants and animals; naval; relating to commerce at sea; near the sea; used at sea: *n.* a soldier who serves on a warship;

the navy of a nation; naval affairs; collective shipping of a country; a picture of a sea scene.

mar-i-ner (măr'ĭ-nẽr), *n.* a sailor or seaman.

mar-i-o-nette (măr'ĭ-ō-nĕt), *n.* an image in human form moved by strings or by the hand, as in a puppet show.

mar-i-tal (măr'ĭ-tăl), *adj.* of or pertaining to marriage.

mar-i-time (măr'ĭ-tīm; măr'ĭ-tĭm), *adj.* pertaining to, connected with, or bordering upon, the sea; relating to sea trade; as, the *maritime* power of England.

mar-jo-ram (mär'jō-răm), *n.* a fragrant mint used to flavor cookery.

mark (märk), *n.* a trait; a sign by which anything is known; a symptom; an indication; impression, as a line, stain, scratch, written word, etc.; a proof; target; a character made by one who cannot write his name; a proper bound or limit; as, he brought his business up to the *mark;* distinction; as, a man of *mark;* a German coin worth 24½ cents: *v.t.* to make a line, scratch, character, etc. on; notify by, or as by, a sign; point out from others; to notice; to single out, as by a sign; to indicate by a sign; to observe: *v.i.* to pay careful attention; take note.—**Mark**, the second book of the New Testament, containing the Gospel according to Mark, the Evangelist, who worked with the apostle Paul in spreading the gospel.

marked (märkt), *adj.* distinct; noticeable; conspicuous.—*adv.* **markedly.**

mark-er (mär'kẽr), *n.* one who, or that which, keeps record, or serves as a sign; a counter in card playing; one who keeps the score in a game, as in billiards; something that keeps a place in a book.

mar-ket (mär'kĕt), *n.* a public or private place for the sale or purchase of provisions; a region or country where anything can be sold; as, American manufactures find a ready *market;* state of trade as shown by rate or price; as, a dull *market:* *v.i.* to deal in a public place where provisions are exposed for sale; buy or sell goods or provisions: *v.t.* to offer for sale, or to sell, in a public place; to find a purchaser for.—*n.* **marketer.**

mar-ket-a-ble (mär'kĕt-ȧ-bl), *adj.* fit or suitable to be offered for sale; in demand; current in markets; as, *marketable* prices.

marks-man (märks'măn), *n.* [*pl.* marksmen (-mĕn)], one skilled in shooting.—*n.* **marksmanship.**

marl (märl), *n.* earth containing calcium mingled with clay and carbonate of lime, used as a manure: *v.t.* to fertilize with lime; to wind with marlines, or small cords.

mar-line (mär'lĭn), *n.* a two-stranded cord used for winding around ropes, etc.

mar-line-spike (mär'lĭn-spīk"), *n.* a pointed piece of iron used for opening the strands of a rope in splicing, or uniting two ropes by interweaving the strands. Also, **marlin spike.**

mar-ma-lade (mär'mȧ-lād), *n.* a preserve made of oranges or other fruit.

mar-mite (mär"mēt'), *n.* in the World War, a huge tin in which food was carried to the soldiers in the trenches: *adj.* pertaining to such a tin.

mar-mo-re-al (mär-mō'rē-ăl), *adj.* pertaining to, like, or made of, marble. Also, **marmorean.**

mar-mo-set (mär'mō-zĕt"), *n.* a small South American monkey.

mar-mot (mär'mŏt), *n.* a small, coarse-furred animal akin to the rat, squirrel, etc.

ma-roon (mȧ-rōōn'), *n.* formerly, a runaway slave in the West Indies; a dark brown color with a deep reddish tinge; one who is left alone or abandoned on an island or lonely coast: *v.t.* to place and leave alone on a desert island: *adj.* of a brownish-crimson color.

mar-plot (mär'plŏt"), *n.* one who spoils some plan by officious interference.

marque (märk), *n.* a license granted by a state to a private vessel to attack and capture the ships of another nation: no longer used except in the expression *letters of marque*, the official papers giving authority to private owners to make seizures.

mar-quee (mär-kē'), *n.* a large field tent such as is used by an officer of high rank, commonly used for outdoor entertainments.

mar-quet-ry (mär'kĕt-rĭ), *n.* inlaid work, as in furniture.

mar-quis (mär'kwĭs), *n.* [*fem.* marchioness, marquise], a nobleman ranking next below a duke. Also, **marquess.**

mar-riage (măr'ĭj), *n.* the act of legally uniting a man and woman in wedlock; the wedding ceremony; the state of being wedded; the relation existing between husband and wife.—*adj.* **marriageable.**

Syn. wedding, nuptials, matrimony, wedlock.

mar-ried (măr'ĭd), *p.adj.* united in wedlock; wedded; pertaining to matrimony.

mar-row (măr'ō), *n.* the oily tissue which fills the open canals of bones; the real meaning or significance of anything; **vegetable marrow**, a kind of squash.—*adj.* **marrowy.**

mar-row-bone (măr'ō-bōn"), *n.* a bone containing an edible substance, especially in sufficient quantity to be used in cookery.

mar-row-fat (măr'ō-făt"), *n.* a late, large variety of pea.

mar-ry (măr'ĭ), *v.t.* [*p.t.* and *p.p.* married, *p.pr.* marrying], to unite as husband and wife; to dispose of in wedlock; to bring together in close union; wed: *v.i.* to enter into the state of wedlock: *interj.* an exclamation of surprise or affirmation.

Mars (märz), *n.* the Roman god of war; one of the planets, notable for the redness of its light.

Mar-se-illaise (mär"sĕ-lāz'; mär"sā'-yāz'), *adj.* pertaining to Marseilles, a city in France, or to its people. *n.* national anthem of the Republic of France: composed by Rouget de l'Isle, 1792. Also, **Marseillais.**

mar-seilles (mär-sālz'), *n.* a double cotton fabric, sometimes ribbed or striped.

marsh (märsh), *n.* a swampy tract of land; a fen; a morass.

mar-shal (mär'shăl), *n.* an official of high rank who superintends and regulates ceremonies; an official of lower rank than a herald, but having similar duties; in the French army, the highest military officer: called also *field marshal;* one who arranges and regulates order, rank, etc., in a public ceremony; as, she was *marshal* of her class at commencement; one who has certain police duties; a sheriff: *v.t.* to arrange or dispose in order; to guide; usher.

marsh-mal-low (märsh'măl'ō), *n.* an herb of the mallow family; a confection made from the root of this herb.

marsh-y (mär'shĭ), *adj.* swampy; growing in swamps or fens; like a swamp or fen.—*n.* **marshiness.**

mar-su-pi-al (mär-sū'pĭ-ăl), *adj.* pertaining to the Marsupialia, a class of animals that carry their young in a marsupium, or pouch: *n.* one of the Marsupialia, as the opossum and kangaroo.

mart (märt), *n.* a place of public purchase and sale; a market. *v.t.* and *v.i.* to market.

mar-ten (mär'tĕn), *n.* a small animal of the weasel family; also, the fur of the animal: called also *sable.*

Marten

Mar-tha (mär'thȧ), *n.* in the Bible, the sister of Lazarus and Mary, and friend of Jesus.—Luke x; John xi.

mar-tial (mär'shăl), *adj.* pertaining to, or suited to, war or warriors; military; as, *martial* music stirs the blood.—*adv.* **martially.**

Syn. warlike, soldierly.

mar-tial law (mär'shăl lô), a set of laws enforced by the military power and used in governing citizens in time of war, insurrection, etc.; as, a conquered city or country is usually put under *martial law* until a permanent government can be established.

Mar-tian (mär'shăn), *n.* an inhabitant of Mars: *adj.* of or pertaining to the planet Mars, or to Mars, the god of war.

mar-tin (mär'tĭn), *n.* a kind of small swallow. Also, **martlet.**

mar-ti-net (mär'tĭ-nĕt'; mär'tĭ-nĕt'), *n.* one who requires strict obedience in all details and enforces such requirements sternly; an unusually strict disciplinarian: used, ordinarily, in an unfavorable sense.

mar-tin-gale (mär'tĭn-gāl; mär'tĭn-găl), *n.* a broad strap passing from the noseband to the girth of a horse, between its fore legs, to keep its head down; a rope or chain used to hold certain sails in place.

mar-tyr (mär'tẽr), *n.* one who dies for a faith, cause, or principle; one who suffers keenly, especially for a cause or principle: *v.t.* to put to death for loyalty to some belief, especially Christianity; persecute; torture; destroy.

mar-tyr-dom (mär'tẽr-dŭm), *n.* death or sufferings for the sake of a faith, cause, or principle; as, the *martyrdom* of the early Christians.

mar-tyr-ol-o-gy (mär'tẽr-ŏl'ō-jĭ), *n.* a register or history of martyrs, or those who have suffered and died for a faith or a cause.

mar-vel (mär'vĕl), *n.* a wonder; that which causes wonder; something extraordinary and astonishing: *v.i.* to be struck with astonishment; to wonder.

mar-vel-ous (mär'vĕl-ŭs), *adj.* causing wonder; scarcely to be believed; incredible. Also, **marvellous.**—*adv.* **marvelously.**—*n.* **marvelousness.**

Syn. wonderful, amazing, miraculous, strange.

Ma-ry (mā'rĭ), *n.* in the Bible, the mother of Jesus: called also *the Virgin Mary*; Mary of Bethany, the sister of Lazarus and Martha, and a friend of Jesus.—Luke x; John xi; Mary of Magdala, or Mary Magdalene, healed by Jesus of seven devils.—Luke viii. 2; John xx.

mas-cot (măs'kŏt), *n.* a person or thing that is supposed to bring good luck; as, a little yellow dog was the *mascot* of the baseball team.

mas-cu-line (măs'kū-lĭn), *adj.* pertaining to, having the qualities of, or suitable for, a man; manly; powerful; virile; coarse; mannish: said of a woman; in grammar, designating the gender of words that denote males, and of other words classed with them.

Syn. male, manful.

Ant. (see feminine, female).

mas-cu-lin-i-ty (măs-kū-lĭn'ĭ-tĭ), *n.* the quality or state of being manlike.

mash (măsh), *n.* a soft or pulpy mass; a warm mixture of bran and water for horses or other animals; bruised malt, or meal, soaked in hot water for making beer, etc.: *v.t.* to mix with hot water (as malt) in brewing; change into a soft pulpy state; to crush.—*n.* **masher.**

mash-ie (măsh'ĭ), *n.* an iron golf club similar in shape and use to the niblick.

mask (mȧsk), *n.* a full or partial cover for the face in order to disguise or protect it; as, a gas-*mask*; that which disguises or conceals; a pretense; as, under the *mask* of friendliness he hid his evil plans; an old form of play, in which the actors wore a mask, or face covering, or the composition for such a play; a masquerade: *v.t.* to conceal with, or as with, a mask; cover or hold in check, as troops about to launch a surprise attack: *v.i.* to take part in a masquerade; be disguised. Also, **masque.**

masked (mȧskt), *adj.* wearing or using a cover over the face; concealed; disguised; hidden.

mask-er (mȧs'kẽr), *n.* one who wears a disguise, or cover over the face, as at a masquerade.

ma-son (mā'sn), *n.* a builder in stone or brick.—**Mason,** a member of the society of Freemasons.

Ma-son and Dix-on's Line, (mā'sn ănd dĭk'sŭnz līn), the southern boundary of Pennsylvania: so called from two English surveyors who ran it.

Ma-son-ic (mȧ-sŏn'ĭk), *adj.* relating to Freemasons or to their society; pertaining to their craft or mysteries.

ma-son-ry (mā'sn-rĭ), *n.* the art or occupation of a builder in stone; materials used by builders in stone.—**Masonry,** Freemasonry: the institutions and practices of an ancient and secret association or fraternity.

masque (mȧsk), *n.* a masquerade; a short play, originally acted as entertainment at a great castle, etc. Also, **mask.**

mas-quer-ade (mȧs'kẽr-ād'), *n.* a ball or festive gathering where masks are worn; an acting or living under false pretenses; a disguise: *v.t.* to cover with a mask or disguise: *v.i.* to take part in a ball where the persons present are disguised; to take the part or character of another for amusement or deceit; to show falsely.

Mass (màs), *n.* the celebration of the Holy Communion in the Roman Catholic Church; a musical setting for certain parts of such a celebration; **mass**, the measure of the quantity of matter in a body; a large quantity; lump; body of things collectively: *pl.* common people: with *the:* *v.t.* and *v.i.* to collect into a lump or body.

mas-sa-cre (măs'ȧ-kēr), *n.* the killing of many people with violence and cruelty; wholesale slaughter or murder of people who cannot offer resistance: *v.t.* to slaughter in such a manner.

mas-sage (mȧ-säzh'), *n.* a method of medical treatment by rubbing or kneading the body: *v.t.* to treat by rubbing and kneading.

mas-seur (mȧ"sûr'), *n.* [*fem.* masseuse], one who performs the operation of massage, a method of treating the body, for purposes of health, by rubbing and kneading with the hands. [Fr.]

mas-si-cot (măs'ĭ-kŏt), *n.* yellow compound of oxygen and lead used as a paint, etc.

mas-sif (mȧ'sēf'), *n.* high ground; a plateau; a group of hills; the high ground around a higher central point; as, the *massif* of Mont Blanc. [Fr.]

mas-sive (màs'ĭv), *adj.* weighty; heavy; bulky; of large size; imperfectly and irregularly formed: used in speaking of minerals.—*adv.* **massively.**—*n.* **massiveness.**

Syn. ponderous, solid, substantial.
Ant. (see flimsy).

mass meet-ing (màs mēt'ĭng), a general assembly of people for the discussion of some question of public interest.

mass-y (màs'ĭ), *adj.* weighty; heavy; bulky; ponderous.

mast (màst), *n.* a long round piece of timber or iron tube, raised upright on the keel, through the decks, of a vessel to support the sails; any upright pole; the fruit of the oak, beech, etc., especially when used as food for swine.

mas-ter (màs'tēr), *n.* one who rules or commands people or things; director; employer; owner; head of a household, college, school, etc.; an expert; winner in a contest; a great artist; a skilled workman; commander of a merchant vessel: *adj.* exercising control; chief; skilled: *v.t.* to subdue or overcome; conquer; as, to *master* a task; to excel in: **Master,** a person holding an advanced university degree; a title used before the names of boys; a legal title.

mas-ter-ful (màs'tēr-fo͝ol), *adj.* showing power or control; inclined to be domineering.—*adv.* **masterfully.**

mas-ter key (màs'tēr kē), a key that will open several locks differing from each other.

mas-ter-ly (màs'tēr-lĭ), *adj.* characteristic of a chief or expert: *adv.* in the manner of, or with the skill of, a chief or expert.—*n.* **masterliness.**

mas-ter-piece (màs'tēr-pēs"), *n.* a thing which surpasses in excellence everything else done by the maker; anything made with wonderful skill; an extraordinary production.

mas-ter-ship (màs'tēr-shĭp), *n.* dignity of a chief; control; dominion; mastery; expert skill.

mas-ter-y (màs'tēr-ĭ), *n.* dominion; superiority or triumph in war or competition; display of skill.

Syn. rule, sway, ascendancy, supremacy.

mast-head (màst'hĕd"), *n.* the top of a mast: *v.t.* to send to the mast top as a punishment on shipboard.

mas-ti-cate (măs'tĭ-kāt), *v.t.* to grind with the teeth; chew.—*n.* **masticator.**

mas-ti-ca-tion (măs"tĭ-kā'shŭn), *n.* the act of grinding with the teeth; a chewing; as, *mastication* of food.

mas-tiff (màs'tĭf), *n.* a breed of large, powerful dogs, valued chiefly as watchdogs.

mas-to-don (măs'tō-dŏn), *n.* a variety of large animal, somewhat like the elephant, but no longer in existence.

Upper: mastodon restored. Lower: left, tooth; right, skull.

mas-toid (màs'toid), *adj.* breastlike; in animal bodies, denoting a projection of the bone of the skull behind the ear: *n.* the mastoid bone, a projection of the skull behind the ear.

mas-toi-di-tis (măs"toi-dī'tĭs), *n.* a disease caused by an abscess formed inside the mastoid bone and next the brain.

mat (măt), *n.* a flat piece of coarse woven fabric, made of straw, grass, etc., and used for a floor covering, for wiping mud from the feet, etc.; an ornamental article on which to place things at table; anything thickly overgrown or entangled, as weeds; a dull finish on a gilded or painted surface; the tool used to produce this effect; a border or edge serving as a margin for a picture: *v.t.* [*p.t.* and *p.p.* matted, *p.pr.* matting], to mass, knot, or twist together; to produce a dull surface upon: *v.i.* to become knotted or tangled.

mat-a-dor (măt'ȧ-dōr; măt'ȧ-dôr), *n.* the man chosen to kill the bull in a bullfight; one of the three principal cards in the games of omber and quadrille. Also, **matadore.**

match (măch), *n.* anything that is easily set on fire, especially a short slender piece of wood or other material tipped with a mixture by means of which fire is procured; anything which agrees with, or is exactly like, another thing; an equal; game or contest; marriage; one to be gained in marriage: *v.t.* to equal successfully; to set against; as, he *matched* his ability against mine; to get a counterpart of, or the equal of: *v.i.* to agree with, or be like, each other.

match-less (măch'lĕs), *adj.* not capable of being equaled; unequaled; peerless.

match-lock (măch'lŏk"), *n.* an old kind of musket.

match-mak-er (măch'māk"ēr), *n.* one who seeks to arrange marriages for others; one who makes matches for burning.

match-mak-ing (măch'māk"ĭng), *n.* the planning of marriages;

the scheming to bring them about: *adj.* busy trying to bring marriages about.

match play (măch plā), in golf, a competition in which the score is counted by the number of holes won.

mate (māt), *n.* a companion or associate; an equal; the male or female of a pair of animals for breeding; a ship's officer ranking below the captain: *v.t.* to match; to equal; marry; of animals, to pair: *v.i.* to be coupled or united.

ma-té (mä'tā), *n.* a tea made of the dried leaves of Brazilian holly: much used in South America. [SPAN.]

ma-ter (mā'tẽr), *n.* one of the two membranes (*dura mater, pia mater*) covering the brain. [LAT.]

ma-te-ri-al (mȧ-tē'rĭ-ăl), *adj.* consisting of matter or substance; not spiritual; pertaining to bodily wants; as, the *material* needs of the poor; important; as, it is not *material* to me what you do; of consequence: *n.* the substance of which anything is made.—*n.* **materiality.**

Syn., adj. bodily, physical, temporal, momentous, significant.

Ant. (see spiritual).

ma-te-ri-al-ism (mȧ-tē'rĭ-ăl-ĭzm), *n.* the doctrine that all the facts of life are the result of the action, etc., of substance or matter; the tendency to give too much importance to body or matter, and too little to spiritual and intellectual life.

ma-te-ri-al-ist (mȧ-tē'rĭ-ăl-ĭst), *n.* one who holds the doctrine that the universe consists of substance without spirit; one who is absorbed in bodily things to the exclusion of spiritual interests. —*adj.* **materialistic.**

ma-te-ri-al-ize (mȧ-tē'rĭ-ăl-īz), *v.t.* to make capable of being seen, heard, or felt; to express through outward objects; as, to *materialize* ambition; to give bodily form to: *v.i.* to become a fact; to come into actual being.—*n.* **materialization.**

ma-te-ri-al-ly (mȧ-tē'rĭ-ăl-ĭ), *adv.* with respect to body or substance; importantly; actually; to a great degree; as, our ideas of education *materially* change as time goes on.

ma-te-ri-a med-i-ca (mȧ-tē'rĭ-ȧ mĕd'ĭ-kȧ), a name for the various substances used in medicine; the science of remedies. [LAT.]

ma-ter-nal (mȧ-tûr'năl), *adj.* motherly; derived from a mother; peculiar to motherhood; coming through the relationship of one's mother.—*adv.* **maternally.**

ma-ter-ni-ty (mȧ-tûr'nĭ-tĭ), *n.* the character or relationship of a mother; the state of being a mother.

math-e-mat-i-cal (măth'ē-măt'ĭ-kăl), *adj.* pertaining to, or performed by, mathematics, or the science of quantities; exact; precise; accurate.—*adv.* **mathematically.**

math-e-ma-ti-cian (măth'ē-mȧ-tĭsh'ăn), *n.* one who is skilled in mathematics, or the science of quantities.

math-e-mat-ics (măth'ē-măt'ĭks), *n.* the science that treats of quantities and magnitudes, by the use of symbols, and the measuring, relations, and properties of such quantities and magnitudes.

mat-in (măt'ĭn), *adj.* pertaining to the morning or to morning prayer: *n.pl.* morning prayer.

mat-i-née (măt'ĭ-nā'), *n.* a reception or musicale held in the daytime; especially, a dramatic performance held in the afternoon.

mat-ing (māt-ĭng), *n.* a matching; a pairing: *adj.* suitable for pairing; as, the *mating* time.

mat-ri-cide (măt'rĭ-sīd; mā'trĭ-sīd), *n.* the murder of a mother by her son or daughter; one who murders one's mother.

ma-tric-u-late (mȧ-trĭk'ū-lāt), *v.t.* to admit to the membership of a college or university by entering one's name in a register: *v.i.* to be admitted as a member or student of a college, etc.

ma-tric-u-la-tion (mȧ-trĭk'ū-lā'shŭn), *n.* the act of registering and being admitted as a student in a college, etc.

mat-ri-mo-ni-al (măt'rĭ-mō'nĭ-ăl), *adj.* pertaining to marriage; nuptial.—*adv.* **matrimonially.**

mat-ri-mo-ny (măt'rĭ-mō-nĭ), *n.* marriage; wedlock; the marriage relation or state.

ma-trix (mā'trĭks), *n.* [*pl.* matrices (măt'-rĭ-sēz)], the womb; that which gives form, origin, or foundation to anything inclosed or embedded in it; a die or mold, as for the face of type, for linotype, or for a monotype typesetting machine; the rock in which a fossil or mineral is embedded; the five colors (black, white, blue, red, yellow) from which all others are formed in dyeing.

Linotype Matrix

ma-tron (mā'trŭn), *n.* a married woman, especially one who has borne children; a wife or a widow; the woman who superintends a hospital or other institution.—*adj.* **matronal.**

ma-tron-ly (mā'trŭn-lĭ), *adj.* like a married woman; elderly; sedate; as, elderly women wear *matronly* clothes: *adv.* like a married woman; sedately.

mat-ro-nym-ic (măt'rō-nĭm'ĭk), *n.* a man's or woman's name taken from that of a mother: *adj.* pertaining to a name so obtained.

mat-ted (măt'ĕd), *adj.* covered with a mat or mats; closely tangled together, as hair.

mat-ter (măt'ẽr), *n.* that which occupies space, and can be perceived by the senses; body; substance; as, the subject *matter* of a book; a thing of importance; business; as, the *matter* needs prompt attention; event; indefinite amount; ground; cause of difficulty; as, what is the *matter*? pus; set-up type for a printer: *v.i.* be of importance; as, it does *matter;* signify; to form pus.

mat-ter-of-fact (măt'ẽr-ŏv-făkt), *adj.* sticking to real things; literal; not imaginative nor dreamy; commonplace.

Mat-thew (măth'ū), *n.* the first book of the New Testament, containing the gospel as said to be written by Matthew, one of the twelve apostles.

mat-ting (măt'ĭng), *n.* a kind of carpeting made of woven straw, etc.

mat-tock (măt'ŭk), *n.* a pickax having one of its ends flat.

mat-tress (măt'rĕs), *n.* a quilted hair- or straw-stuffed bed; a spring bed; a mat made of trees or shrubs.

ma-ture (mȧ-tūr'), *v.t.* to become ripe; *v.t.* to bring or hasten to full growth: *adj.* [*comp.* maturer, *superl.* maturest], ripe; full-grown; completely developed; perfected; ready for use.—*adv.* **maturely.**

ma-tu-ri-ty (mȧ-tū'rĭ-tĭ), *n.* the state or quality of being full-grown; ripeness; full-development; as, the higher animals reach *maturity* much more slowly than the lower animals; a coming due: said of a note.

ma-tu-ti-nal (mȧ-tū'tĭ-năl; măt'ū-tī'năl), *adj.* pertaining to the morning; early.

maud-lin (môd'lĭn), *adj.* easily moved to tears; weakly and foolishly sentimental; drunkenly silly.

mau-ger (mô'gẽr), *prep.* in spite of; as, *mauger* all my pride. Also, **maugre.**

maul (môl), *n.* a large wooden hammer: *v.t.* to wound or bruise in a rough manner. Also, *n.* **mall.**

maul-stick (môl'stĭk'), *n.* a stick used by painters as a rest for the hand while painting. Also, **mahlstick.**

maun-der (môn'dẽr; män'dẽr), *v.t.* to utter without meaning or connection: *v.i.* to talk foolishly; to speak indistinctly; murmur or grumble.

Maun-dy Thurs-day (môn'dĭ thûrz'dā), the day before Good Friday; Thursday before Easter.

mau-ser (mou'zẽr), *n.* a repeating rifle, a shot from which carries a long distance.

mau-so-le-um (mô'sō-lē'ŭm), *n.* a stately tomb or monument: named from that of Mausolus, King of Caria, erected by his widow Artemesia; as, Grant's tomb is a handsome *mausoleum.*

mauve (mōv), *n.* a soft lilac or purple color.

ma-vis (mā'vĭs), *n.* the European song thrush.

maw (mô), *n.* the stomach, or the mouth and throat, of an animal; in birds, the craw; that which swallows up something greedily.

mawk-ish (môk'ĭsh), *adj.* apt to cause loathing; maudlin; foolishly sentimental; as, *mawkish* love stories.

max-il-la (măk-sĭl'ȧ), *n.* [*pl.* maxillæ (-ē)], the upper jawbone; one of the mouth parts of insects, shellfish, etc.

max-il-la-ry (măk'sĭ-lā-rĭ), *adj.* pertaining to, or situated near, the jaw, or one of the jawbones.

max-im (măk'sĭm), *n.* an established principle or truth; a proverb; a well-known saying; as, the old *maxim*, "Waste not, want not," is full of truth.
Syn. adage, saying, byword, saw.

Max-im gun (măk'sĭm gŭn), a machine gun named after its inventor, Hiram S. Maxim.

max-im-ite (măk'sĭm-īt), *n.* a high explosive, used as a bursting charge for armor-piercing projectiles: named for its inventor, Hudson Maxim.

max-i-mum (măk'sĭ-mŭm), *n.* the greatest number, quantity, or degree possible; as, a *maximum* of good result: opposite to *minimum: adj.* greatest in quantity or highest in degree that can be or has been reached or attained; highest allowed by law; as, the *maximum* price for wheat.

may (mā), *v. aux.* [*p.t.* might (mīt)], to be able; be allowed; to express earnest desire; as, *may* you never repent this act; to be, under the circumstances, possible; as, the illness *may* cause his death; to chance, or happen by chance.—**May**, the fifth month of the year.

May ap-ple (mā ăp'l), an American plant of the barberry family or its edible fruit: called also *mandrake.*

may-be (mā'bē), *adv.* it may happen that; perhaps.

May Day (mā dā), the first day of May: often celebrated by outdoor festivities.

May-fair (mā'fâr'), *n.* the section of London where the aristocracy lives; hence, the best London society.

May-flow-er (mā'flou'ẽr), *n.* in the United States, the trailing arbutus; in England, any of several plants flowering in May.

may-hem (mā'hĕm), *n.* the offense of disabling a person by injuring any of his members. Also, **maim.**

may-ing (mā'ĭng), *n.* the celebration of May Day by gathering flowers or by festivities.

may-on-naise (mā'ō-nāz'; mȧ'yō'-nāz'), *n.* a sauce or salad dressing of the raw yolk of eggs and olive oil. [Fr.]

may-or (mā'ẽr; mâr), *n.* [*fem.* mayoress], the chief magistrate of a city or borough.

may-or-al-ty (mā'ẽr-ăl-tĭ), *n.* the office, or term of office, of a mayor, or chief magistrate of a city; as, a candidate for the *mayoralty.*

May-pole (mā'pōl'), *n.* a pole decorated with flowers and ribbons around which May Day celebrations are held.

May-tide (mā'tīd'), *n.* the month of May. Also, **Maytime.**

may-weed (mā'wēd'), *n.* a pungent plant of the aster family with white and yellow daisylike flowers.

maze (māz), *n.* bewilderment; perplexity; confusion of mind; a confusing tangle; a network, as of passages.

ma-zur-ka (mȧ-zûr'kȧ; mȧ-zōōr'kȧ), *n.* a lively Polish dance; music set to such a dance. Also, **mazourka.**

ma-zy (mā'zĭ), *adj.* hard to unravel or to trace out; bewildering; winding.—*adv.* **mazily.**—*n.* **maziness.**

me (mē), *pron.* the objective case of *I*, the pronoun of the first person.

mead (mēd), *n.* a fermented liquor of honey, water, and spices; in poetry, a meadow.

mead-ow (mĕd'ō), *n.* a tract of rich pasture land; land from which hay is obtained; low grass land by the banks of streams.—*adj.* **meadowy.**

mead-ow lark (mĕd'ō lärk), an American bird with a yellow breast marked with black.

mea-ger (mē'gẽr), *adj.* thin; scanty; barren; lean; gaunt. Also, **meagre.**—*adv.* **meagerly.**—*n.* **meagerness.**
Syn. poor, lank, dry, uninteresting.
Ant. (see rich).

meal (mēl), *n.* grain coarsely ground; the portion of food taken at one time to satisfy the appetite; food prepared for use upon the table at one time; the act or time of eating.

meal-time (mēl'tīm'), *n.* the hour fixed for a meal.

meal-y (mēl'ĭ), *adj.* consisting of, sprinkled with, or like, coarsely ground grain; dry and soft; as, *mealy* potatoes.

meal-y-mouthed (mēl'ĭ-mouthd'), *adj.* using soft words; unwilling to tell the truth in plain words.

mean (mēn), *n.* the middle point, quantity, value, or degree; average; moderation: *pl.* secondary agency; instrument; as, he used every lawful *means* to find out; *pl.* resources; property; as, a man of large *means*: *v.t.* [*p.t.* and *p.p.* meant, *p.pr.* meaning], to have in the mind or intention; to purpose; as, I *mean* to go; signify; as, the French word poilu *means* hairy; denote; as, the word poilu *meant* a French soldier: *v.i.* to have an intention: *adj.* [*comp.* meaner, *superl.* meanest], wanting in dignity or honor; vulgar; ordinary; inferior; without importance; humble; stingy; middle; average; not too much or too little.

Syn., *adj.* niggardly, abject, vile, ignoble, degraded, contemptible, despicable: *v.* design, intend, contemplate, indicate.

me-an-der (mē-ăn'dẽr), *v.t.* to wind or flow round: *v.i.* to have a winding course, as a river; wander listlessly or without purpose: *n.* a winding, as of a stream: usually in plural.

mean-ing (mēn'ĭng), *p.adj.* intending; full of significance; as, a *meaning* glance: *n.* object; aim; intention; sense.—*adj.* **meaningless.**—*adv.* **meaningly.**

Syn. *n.* signification, import, acceptation, purport.

mean-ly (mēn'lĭ), *adv.* ignobly; contemptibly; poorly; shabbily.

mean-ness (mēn'nĕs), *n.* littleness or baseness of character; a base or contemptible deed; the state of being without qualities that gain respect.

meant (mĕnt), past tense and past participle of the verb *mean.*

mean-time (mēn'tīm"), *adv.* in the time between; at the same time. Also, **meanwhile.**

mea-sles (mē'zlz), *n.* [*pl.* in form, but used as *sing.*], an easily spread disease, especially of children, marked by fever and small red spots on the skin; a disease of swine and cattle.—*adj.* **measly.**

meas-ur-a-ble (mĕzh'ṻr-ȧ-bl), *adj.* capable of being estimated or computed; limited; moderate.

meas-ur-a-bly (mĕzh'ṻr-ȧ-blĭ), *adv.* in a limited degree; moderately; appreciably.

meas-ure (mĕzh'ṻr), *n.* the standard by which the volume or extent of anything is compared; as, the light given by a candle is the *measure* by which the power of other light is calculated; size or quantity, determined by the rule or standard; hence, standard of judgment, criticism, etc.; extent, or length, breadth, and thickness of a thing; proportion; a divisor leaving no remainder; as, five is a common *measure* of ten and fifteen; an instrument or vessel for finding length, quantity, etc.; as, a yard or a quart *measure*; a system of fixing quantities; as, dry *measure*, etc.; musical time; meter in poetry; a law or a legislative bill; method or step; as, to take *measures* to accomplish a purpose: *pl.* layers of rock or soil or deposits of minerals: *v.t.* to find out the extent, size, or volume of; mark out; confine within a limit; give out by a rule; as, to *measure* out rations; estimate; determine by rule or standard; regulate; as, to *measure* one's words or conduct: *v.i.* to take dimensions; extend or be of a given length; as, the room *measures* fifteen feet.

meas-ured (mĕzh'ṻrd), *adj.* determined by a standard; regular; as, soldiers march with *measured* tread; steady; resulting from thought; as, *measured* words.

meas-ure-less (mĕzh'ṻr-lĕs), *adj.* unlimited; vast; immense; of a size too large to be found out.

meas-ure-ment (mĕzh'ṻr-mĕnt), *n.* the act of finding the size, quantity, amount, etc., by some standard; size or quantity determined by such standard; size; area.

Meat Chopper

meat (mēt), *n.* animal flesh used as food; food in general; victuals: **meat chopper**, a kitchen utensil for rapidly cutting meat and vegetables into small pieces.

meat-y (mēt-ĭ), *adj.* full of substance; resembling meat; nourishing; hence, pithy.

me-chan-ic (mē-kăn'ĭk), *n.* a skilled workman, especially one who understands the construction and use of machinery; one who works as if he were a machine: *pl.* the science of the laws of matter and motion, especially the science of machinery: *adj.* of or pertaining to a workman, especially one with knowledge of machinery; involving skill with the hands; pertaining to machinery; as, the *mechanic* arts.

me-chan-i-cal (mē-kăn'ĭ-kăl), *adj.* pertaining to the laws of matter and motion; pertaining to, or produced by, machines or machinery; as, *mechanical* toys; done without thought, as from force of habit; as, a *mechanical* smile or gesture.—*adv.* **mechanically.**—*n.* **mechanicalness.**

me-chan-i-cal pow-ers (mē-kăn'ĭ-kăl pou'ẽrz), instruments which convert a smaller force acting through a greater space into a greater force acting through a lesser space, as the lever, inclined plane, wheel and axle, screw, pulley, and wedge.

mech-a-ni-cian (mĕk"ȧ-nĭsh'ăn), *n.* one skilled in the laws of matter and motion, or in the construction of machinery; a machinist.

me-chan-ic's lien (mē-kăn'ĭks lēn), a legal claim upon property for labor or material.

mech-a-nism (mĕk'ȧ-nĭzm), *n.* the relation of the working parts of an engine, etc.; construction of the works; as, the *mechanism* of a watch is most delicate; operation of the parts.

Mech-lin (mĕk'lĭn), *n.* a beautiful and very delicate kind of lace, made at Mechlin, Belgium.

med-al (mĕd'ăl), *n.* a coin-shaped piece of metal marked with a design or with words to commemorate some event, distinguished person, etc.; such a metal disk given as a reward.

Medallion

med-al-ist (mĕd'ăl-ĭst), *n.* one who designs or makes medals; the winner of a medal. Also, **medallist.**

me-dal-lion (mē-dăl'yŭn), *n.* a large antique medal; a round or oval tablet with figures formed so as to stand out from a flat background; a design (round, square, etc.) on the title-page or cover of a book; a lace ornament sewed into a garment.

med-al play (mĕd'ăl plā), in golf, a competition in which the score is counted by the total number of strokes made.

med-dle (mĕd'l), *v.i.* to interfere with what does not concern one.—*n.* **meddler.**

med-dle-some (mĕd'l-sŭm), *adj.* apt to interfere in the affairs of others.—*adv.* **meddlesomely.**—*n.* **meddlesomeness.**
Syn. officious, interfering.
Ant. (see unobtrusive).

me-di-æ-val (mē"dĭ-ē'văl; mĕd"ĭ-ē'-văl), *adj.* of, pertaining to, or characteristic of, the Middle Ages (eighth to fifteenth centuries A. D.). Also, **medieval.**

me-di-al (mē'dĭ-ăl), *adj.* pertaining to the middle; average; ordinary.

me-di-an (mē'dĭ-ăn), *adj.* pertaining to, or connected with, the middle of anything; as, the *median* vein of a leaf.

me-di-ate (mē'dĭ-āt), *v.i.* to interpose as a mutual friend between those who are openly disagreeing, so as to bring about friendly relations; to act as the means by which a settlement is brought about: *v.t.* to bring about by interposing between enemies or opponents; as, to *mediate* a peace: *adj.* (mē'dĭ-āt), not direct; acting by or through an agency.

me-di-a-tion (mē"dĭ-ā'shŭn), *n.* the act of trying to bring about friendly relations; reconciliation; intercession.

me-di-a-tor (mē'dĭ-ā"tẽr), *n.* one who tries to bring about friendly relations between those (persons, nations, etc.), who are openly disagreeing; as, the *mediator* between Japan and Russia.

me-di-a-to-ry (mē'dĭ-ȧ-tō-rĭ), *adj.* pertaining to, or having the nature of, a peacemaker or peacemaking. Also, **mediatorial.**

med-i-ca-ble (mĕd'ĭ-kȧ-bl), *adj.* curable; in a condition to be helped by medicine.

med-i-cal (mĕd'ĭ-kăl), *adj.* having a curative effect; pertaining to, or connected with, the science or art of medicine, or the treatment of disease: **medical corps,** the branch of an army which is in charge of the sick and wounded.—*adv.* **medically.**

me-dic-a-ment (mē-dĭk'ȧ-mĕnt), *n.* anything used for healing diseases or wounds; anything that heals.

med-i-cate (mĕd'ĭ-kāt), *v.t.* to treat with any curative or healing substance; to saturate or fill with any such substance; as, to *medicate* cotton; to cure.—*n.* **medication.**

me-dic-i-nal (mē-dĭs'ĭ-năl), *adj.* having the properties of, or used in, any curative or healing substance; as, *medicinal* springs.—*adv.* **medicinally.**

med-i-cine (mĕd'ĭ-sĭn), *n.* the science which relates to the prevention, treatment, and cure of disease; a substance or preparation for the cure of disease: **medicine chest,** a box or cabinet filled with the most necessary remedies, and a few of the most useful instruments.

med-i-cine man (mĕd'ĭ-sĭn măn), among certain tribes, as the North American Indians, one who professes to drive away evil spirits or disease by magical arts.

me-di-e-val (mē"dĭ-ē'văl; mĕd"ĭ-ē'văl), *adj.* pertaining to, or characteristic of, the Middle Ages (eighth to fifteenth centuries A. D.). Also, **mediæval.**

me-di-o-cre (mē'dĭ-ō"kẽr), *adj.* of medium excellence; ordinary; of a medium quality.

me-di-oc-ri-ty (mē"dĭ-ŏk'rĭ-tĭ), *n.* the quality of being ordinary or commonplace.

med-i-tate (mĕd'ĭ-tāt), *v.i.* to muse or think deeply; think: *v.t.* to think upon; design; purpose; plan.

med-i-ta-tion (mĕd"ĭ-tā'shŭn), *n.* the act of thinking long and deeply; close, deep, and long-continued thought.

med-i-ta-tive (mĕd'ĭ-tā-tĭv), *adj.* devoted to, or disposed to, long and deep thought.—*adv.* **meditatively.**—*n.* **meditativeness.**

me-di-um (mē'dĭ-ŭm), *n.* [*pl.* **media** (-ȧ), **mediums** (-ŭmz)], the mean; that which comes between or in the middle; agency; as, the newspaper is a great advertising *medium;* space or substance in which bodies exist or move; as, water is the only *medium* in which fish can live; a size of paper twenty-four by nineteen inches; a person through whom messages from the spirit world are delivered to earth; the liquid with which dry paints are mixed in preparing them for use; anything used to produce a picture, as charcoal, etc.: *adj.* having a middle position; halfway between two things, states, etc.
Syn., n. organ, channel, instrument, means.

med-lar (mĕd'lȧr), *n.* a small European tree of the apple family, with an eatable fruit; also, the fruit.

med-ley (mĕd'lĭ), *n.* mixture or confused mass; in music, a composition made up of passages selected from different songs or pieces, arranged as a continuous whole.
Syn. variety, diversity.

me-dul-la (mē-dŭl'ȧ), *n.* the marrow of bones; pith of plants: **medulla oblongata,** the lowest part of the brain, where the spinal cord joins it.

med-ul-la-ry (mĕd'ū-lā-rĭ; mē-dŭl'ȧ-rĭ), *adj.* pertaining to, or consisting of, marrow, or medulla.

me-du-sa (mē-dū'sȧ), *n.* the sea nettle or jellyfish.—**Medusa,** in classical mythology, one of the three Gorgons, whose fine hair was changed into snakes, and whose glance changed into stone all who looked on her.

meed (mēd), *n.* reward; recompense; that which is given in consideration of merit or on account of desert.

meek (mēk), *adj.* [*comp.* meeker, *superl.* meekest], gentle; yielding; mild of temper; humble; patient.—*adv.* **meekly.**—*n.* **meekness.**
Syn. unassuming, forbearing.
Ant. (see proud).

meer-schaum (mēr'shôm; mēr'shŭm), *n.* a claylike substance from which pipe bowls are made; a pipe of this material.

meet (mēt), *v.t.* [*p.t.* and *p.p.* met, *p.pr.* meeting], to come up to from a different direction; to come face to face with; to come into collision with; to be introduced to; to fight with; fall in with; undergo; as, the ship *met* disaster; to be perceived by; as, a sad sight *met* their gaze; satisfy; as, to *meet* a demand; come upon: *v.i.* to come together in one place; to come into touch with each other, as in introduction, opposition, etc.; to gather together; be united: *n.* a gathering of huntsmen, athletes, etc.; the place of coming together: *adj.* fit; suitable; appropriate; as, food *meet* for a king.—*adv.* meetly.

meet-ing (mēt'ĭng), *n.* a coming together of persons or things; an assembly; a gathering for a religious service; junction.

meg-a-lo-ma-ni-a (mĕg"ȧ-lō-mā'nĭ-ȧ), *n.* a craze or passion for greatness.

meg-a-phone (mĕg'ȧ-fōn), *n.* a contrivance, usually a very large funnel, enabling the voice to be carried for a long distance.

meg-a-the-ri-um (mĕg"ȧ-thē'rĭ-ŭm), *n.* a very large animal living ages ago, the bones of which have been discovered in South America.

me-grim (mē'grĭm), *n.* a nervous headache: *pl.* depression or low spirits.

mel-an-cho-li-a (mĕl"ăn-kō'lĭ-ȧ), *n.* a form of insanity marked by great depression of spirits; a case of this disease.

mel-an-chol-ic (mĕl"ăn-kŏl'ĭk), *adj.* affected with depression of spirits; downcast; sad; dejected.—*adv.* melancholically.

mel-an-chol-y (mĕl'ăn-kŏl-ĭ), *n.* despondence; dejection; depression of spirits: *adj.* depressed in spirits; dejected; mournful.

Syn., *adj.* dispirited, dreamy, sad.
Ant. (see jolly).

mé-lange (mā"lŏnzh'), *n.* a confused mixture; medley. [Fr.]

mel-a-nite (mĕl'ȧ-nīt), *n.* a black variety of garnet.

mê-lée (mā"lā'), *n.* a hand-to-hand conflict; scuffle; a rough fight in which many take part. [Fr.]

mel-i-nite (mĕl'ĭ-nīt), *n.* a powerful explosive.

mel-io-rate (mēl'yō-rāt), *v.t.* to improve or make better; to make more bearable: *v.i.* to grow better; improve.

mel-io-ra-tion (mēl"yō-rā'shŭn), *n.* improvement; act of making better; state of being made better.

mel-lif-lu-ence (mĕ-lĭf'lōō-ĕns), *n.* the quality of being smooth, sweet, and honeylike.

mel-lif-lu-ous (mĕ-lĭf'lōō-ŭs), *adj.* flowing with, or as with, honey; smooth and sweet; honeyed. Also, mellifluent.—*adv.* mellifluously.

mel-low (mĕl'ō), *adj.* fully ripe; not hard, harsh, or stiff; delicate; colloquially, half tipsy; made sweet or gentle by age or maturity: *v.i.* to become ripe, gentle, etc.: *v.t.* to make ripe, gentle, etc.; —*n.* mellowness.

Syn., *adj.* ripe, mature, soft.
Ant. (see immature).

me-lo-de-on (mē-lō'dē-ŭn), *n.* a small reed organ worked by treadles.

me-lo-di-ous (mē-lō'dĭ-ŭs), *adj.* full of, or produced by a sweet succession of sounds; musical.—*adv.* melodiously.—*n.* melodiousness.

Syn. tuneful, dulcet, sweet.
Ant. (see discordant).

mel-o-dist (mĕl'ō-dĭst), *n.* a composer or singer of tuneful music.

mel-o-dra-ma (mĕl"ō-drä'mȧ; mĕl'ō-drä"mȧ), *n.* a play in which are highly sensational or romantic incidents, with a happy conclusion.

mel-o-dra-mat-ic (mĕl"ō-drȧ-măt'ĭk), *adj.* pertaining to, or of the nature of, romantic or sensational plays; highly sensational.—*adv.* melodramatically.

mel-o-dy (mĕl'ō-dĭ), *n.* [*pl.* melodies (-dĭz)], the arrangement of different musical sounds for a single voice or part; tune or air; an agreeable succession of single tones, making a pleasing musical composition.—*adj.* melodic.—*v.* melodize.

mel-on (mĕl'ŭn), *n.* a plant of the cucumber family, with its eatable fruit; muskmelon; watermelon.

melt (mĕlt), *v.t.* and *v.i.* to change from a solid to a liquid state; dissolve; blend; soften to love and tenderness.

mem-ber (mĕm'bẽr), *n.* a limb or organ; a necessary part of anything; one of an association or community; a part of a whole.

mem-ber-ship (mĕm'bẽr-shĭp), *n.* the state of being one of an association or community; a collective body of persons belonging to an organization; as, the *membership* of the United States Senate.

mem-brane (mĕm'brān), *n.* a thin fold or layer of animal or vegetable tissue, forming the covering of some part or organ.

mem-bra-nous (mĕm'brȧ-nŭs), *adj.* pertaining to, consisting of, or like, a membrane, or layer of tissue covering some part or organ.

me-men-to (mē-mĕn'tō), *n.* [*pl.* mementoes (-tōz)], a souvenir; memorial.

mem-oir (mĕm'wŏr), *n.* the written account of a person's life; a record of what has been found out about a subject: *pl.* a history written from personal experience and knowledge; transactions or journal of a learned or scientific society.

mem-o-ra-bil-i-a (mĕm"ō-rȧ-bĭl'ĭ-ȧ), *n.pl.* things worthy of remembrance or record; the record of such things. [Lat.]

mem-o-ra-ble (mĕm'ō-rȧ-bl), *adj.* worthy of remembrance; remarkable; notable.—*adv.* memorably.

Syn. signal, marked.

mem-o-ran-dum (mĕm"ō-răn'dŭm), *n.* [*pl.* memoranda (-dȧ)], a note to assist one to remember; brief record of something to be remembered; a brief outline to help to remember.

me-mo-ri-al (mē-mō'rĭ-ăl), *adj.* in remembrance; commemorative; sacred to the memory of a deceased person, or of some event: *n.* an informal diplomatic paper; a written statement of facts addressed to a government, a public body, etc.; a thing intended to keep in mind an event, a place, or a person, as a monument: Memorial Day, in the United States, the thirtieth of May, appointed by law for observing the memory of those who died for the Union in the Civil War.

Syn., *n.* monument, memento.

me-mo-ri-al-ize (mē-mō'rĭ-ăl-īz), *v.t.* to request something from (the government, etc.), by sending a written statement of facts; to commemorate.

mem-o-rize (mĕm'ō-rīz), *v.t.* to keep in remembrance; to learn by heart.

mem-o-ry (mĕm'ō-rĭ), *n.* [*pl.* memories (-rĭz)], that faculty of the mind by which it keeps the knowledge of occurrences, facts, thoughts, etc., which are a part of the past, and recalls them; a particular

experience remembered; as, he was lost in *memories* of his youth; the range of time within which past happenings are remembered; as, within the *memory* of the oldest inhabitant; the subject of remembrance; as, his youthful ideals were but *memories* to him.
Syn. remembrance, recollection.

men-ace (mĕn'ās), *n.* a threat; something which threatens: *v.t.* to express the intention of inflicting evil upon; to threaten: *v.i.* to act in a threatening fashion or manner.—*adv.* **menacingly.**

mé-nage (mā'nȯzh'), *n.* a household; household management. [FR.]

me-nag-e-rie (mē-năj'ēr-ĭ; mē-năzh'ēr-ĭ), *n.* a place where wild animals are kept; a collection of wild animals for exhibition.

mend (mĕnd), *v.t.* to repair (that which is broken or worn); make good or better; reform; increase: *v.i.* to grow better; improve.—*n.* **mender.**
Syn. amend, correct, better, ameliorate, rectify.

men-da-cious (mĕn-dā'shŭs), *adj.* given to falsehood; lying; false.

men-dac-i-ty (mĕn-dăs'ĭ-tĭ), *n.* [*pl.* mendacities (-tĭz)], falsehood; habitual lying; the state of being given to falsehood.

men-di-can-cy (mĕn'dĭ-kăn-sĭ), *n.* the state of being a beggar; the act of begging; as, a person is liable to arrest for *mendicancy*. Also, **mendicity.**

men-di-cant (mĕn'dĭ-kănt), *n.* a beggar; a begging friar: *adj.* practicing begging; as, the *mendicant* friars of the Middle Ages were monks who begged for themselves and for the church; reduced to beggary.

me-ni-al (mē'nĭ-ăl; mēn'yăl), *n.* a domestic servant; one who performs servile or slavelike work: *adj.* pertaining to servants in a household; suitable for servants; mean; slavish.—*adv.* **menially.**

men-i-lite (mĕn'ĭ-līt), *n.* a variety of opal.

men-in-gi-tis (mĕn"ĭn-jī'tĭs), *n.* a disease in which the membranes inclosing the brain and the spinal cord become inflamed.

Men-she-vi-ki (mĕn'shĕ-vē"kē), *n.pl.* [*sing.* Menshevik], a Russian political party representing the moderate wing of the Socialists: opposite to the *Bolsheviki*, or radical wing.

men-su-ra-ble (mĕn'shŏŏ-rȧ-bl), *adj.* measurable.

men-su-ra-tion (mĕn"shŏŏ-rā'shŭn), *n.* the act or process of taking the measure or dimensions of anything; that branch of mathematics concerned with finding the length of lines, areas of surfaces, and volumes of solids.

men-tal (mĕn'tăl), *adj.* pertaining to the mind; intellectual.—*adv.* **mentally.**

men-tal-i-ty (mĕn-tăl'ĭ-tĭ), *n.* quality or amount of mental power; intellectual ability.

men-thol (mĕn'thōl; mĕn'thŏl), *n.* a substance with a mintlike, pungent odor: called also *mint camphor*: used to dull pain, especially in neuralgia, etc.

men-tion (mĕn'shŭn), *n.* a brief notice; light or chance remark; hint: *v.t.* to speak briefly of; notice lightly or by chance; name; refer to.
Syn. v. tell, communicate, impart, divulge, reveal, disclose.

men-tion-a-ble (mĕn'shŭn-ȧ-bl), *adj.* fit to be spoken of.

men-tor (mĕn'tŏr), *n.* a wise and faithful adviser: from Mentor, the friend and tutor of Ulysses.

me-nu (mĕn'ū), *n.* a bill of fare; a list of the dishes served at a meal; also, the dishes served. [FR.]

Meph-is-to-phe-li-an (mĕf"ĭs-tō-fē'lĭ-ăn; mĕf"ĭs-tō-fēl'yăn), *adj.* pertaining to, or like, Mephistopheles, the devil; hence, scoffing; relentless; possessed of devilish qualities.

mer-can-tile (mûr'kăn-tĭl; mûr'kăn-tīl), *adj.* having to do with, or engaged in, trade; pertaining to, or characteristic of, merchants.

mer-ce-na-ry (mûr'sē-nā-rĭ), *n.* [*pl.* mercenaries (-rĭz)], a soldier hired into foreign service; one who serves for pay: *adj.* serving for pay or reward; eager to gain money; caring only for self-interest; desirous only of gains.

mer-cer (mûr'sēr), *n.* a dealer in woven fabrics of silk, wool, etc.

mer-cer-ize (mûr'sēr-īz), *v.t.* to treat (cotton fiber or other material) in such a way as to strengthen, and to make more receptive of dyes; also, sometimes, to give a silken sheen to.

mer-chan-dise (mûr'chăn-dīz), *n.* goods, wares, or articles, bought and sold.

mer-chant (mûr'chănt), *n.* one who carries on trade on a large scale, especially with foreign countries; a shopkeeper: *adj.* pertaining to, or employed in, trade; mercantile.—*adj.* **merchantable.**

mer-chant-man (mûr'chănt-măn), *n.* [*pl.* merchantmen (-mĕn)], a trading vessel.

mer-chant ma-rine (mûr'chănt mȧ-rēn'), that part of the shipping of a country that is engaged in trade.

mer-ci-ful (mûr'sĭ-fŏŏl), *adj.* full of, or exercising, leniency or compassion; tender-hearted; full of pity.—*adv.* **mercifully.**—*n.* **mercifulness.**
Syn. lenient, clement, tender, gracious, kind.
Ant. (see cruel).

mer-ci-less (mûr'sĭ-lĕs), *adj.* without pity; unfeeling; cruel.—*adv.* **mercilessly.**—*n.* **mercilessness.**
Syn. hard-hearted, pitiless, remorseless, unrelenting.
Ant. (see kind).

mer-cu-ri-al (mẽr-kū'rĭ-ăl), *adj.* active; fickle; light-hearted; as, *mercurial* youth; pertaining to, made of, or caused by, mercury, or quicksilver.

mer-cu-ry (mûr'kū-rĭ), *n.* quicksilver; a heavy, liquid, metallic substance, used in thermometers and for other scientific purposes: **mercury arc**, an electric arc sent through mercury vapor in a vacuum tube. —**Mercury**, the planet nearest to the sun: in Roman mythology, the god of gain and the messenger of the gods: the same as Hermes in the Greek mythology.

mer-cy (mûr'sĭ), *n.* [*pl.* mercies (-sĭz)], willingness to forgive, spare, or pity; forbearance; pity; kindness; mildness.

mere (mēr), *adj.* [*superl.* merest], such and no more; simple; as, the *mere* mention of such a thing frightened him: *n.* formerly, a lake or pool.

mere-ly (mēr'lĭ), *adv.* simply; purely; only; not otherwise than.

mer-e-tri-cious (mĕr'ē-trĭsh'ŭs), *adj.* attracting by false show; tawdry; deceitfully alluring.

merge (mûrj), *v.t.* to absorb or swallow up: *v.i.* to be swallowed up or lost in something else.

merg-er (mûr'jẽr), *n.* the legal combination of two estates; the placing of two or more business corporations under the control of a single body.

me-rid-i-an (mē-rĭd'ĭ-ăn), *adj.* pertaining to midday: *n.* highest point reached by a heavenly body; highest point, as of success, prosperity, and the like; an imaginary circle around the earth in a north and south direction, passing through the poles.—*adj.* **meridional.**

me-ringue (mē-răng'), *n.* an icing made of eggs, sugar, and cream, and used on puddings, pies, etc., or baked into small cakes. [Fr.]

me-ri-no (mē-rē'nō), *n.* [*pl.* merinos (-nōz)], a breed of sheep with fine wool; the wool of such sheep; cloth or yarn made from this wool: *adj.* pertaining to, or made of, the wool of the merino sheep.

mer-it (mĕr'ĭt), *n.* excellence; worth; the quality or state of deserving; as, treat him according to his *merit;* deserved reward: *pl.* essential circumstances; as, it was hard to discover the real *merits* of the case: *v.t.* to earn; be entitled to; be deserving of.

mer-i-to-ri-ous (mĕr'ĭ-tō'rĭ-ŭs), *adj.* having worth or excellence; deserving of reward or praise.

merl (mûrl), *n.* the European blackbird. Also, **merle.**

mer-lon (mûr'lŏn), *n.* one of the solid intervals between two openings in a battlement.

mer-maid (mûr'mād), *n.* a creature, said in fable and fairy tale to live in the sea, having the body of a woman and the tail of a fish.

mer-man (mûr'măn), *n.* the male of the mermaid.

mer-ri-ment (mĕr'ĭ-mĕnt), *n.* mirth; fun; frolic; gaiety.
Syn. joviality, hilarity.
Ant. (see sorrow).

mer-ry (mĕr'ĭ), *adj.* [*comp.* merrier, *superl.* merriest], full of mirth and good humor; gay; jolly; pleasant.—*adv.* **merrily.**—*n.* **merriness.**
Syn. cheerful, mirthful, joyous, sprightly, jovial, blithe, sportive.
Ant. (see sad).

mer-ry-an-drew (mĕr'ĭ-ăn'drōō), *n.* one whose business is to make sport for others; a clown.

mer-ry-go-round (mĕr'ĭ-gō-round"), *n.* an amusement consisting of a revolving circular frame fitted with wooden horses or seats, on which persons ride.

mer-ry-mak-ing (mĕr'ĭ-māk"ĭng), *n.* festivity: *adj.* festive; gay.—*n.* **merrymaker.**

mer-ry-thought (mĕr'ĭ-thôt"), *n.* the wishbone of a fowl.

me-sa (mā'sä), *n.* a table-land or plateau with steep or sloping sides. [Span.]

mé-sal-liance (mā"zȧl"yäns'), *n.* a marriage with one of lower social position. Also, **misalliance.** [Fr.]

mes-dames (mā"dȧm'), *n.pl.* of *madam* and *madame.* [Fr.]

me-seems (mē-sēmz'), *v. impersonal,* it appears to me. [Poet.]

mesh (mĕsh), *n.* one of the openings of a net; as, a veil of coarse or fine *mesh;* network; in machinery, the engagement of gear teeth: *v.t.* and *v.i.* to catch or entangle in, or as in, the openings of a net; in machinery, to engage: said of gear teeth.

mes-mer-ic (mĕz-mĕr'ĭk), *adj.* pertaining to, or produced by, the control that one person may exercise over the entire nervous system of another; hence, strongly attractive; fascinating.

mes-mer-ism (mĕz'mẽr-ĭzm), *n.* the art of causing in another an unnatural state of the nervous system resembling sleep, in which the thoughts and actions of the patient are controlled by the will of the operator; personal magnetism; hypnotism.

mes-mer-ist (mĕz'mẽr-ĭst), *n.* one who practices the art of controlling the thoughts, acts, will, etc., of others by causing in them an unnatural state of the nervous system. Also, **mesmeriser.**

mes-mer-ize (mĕz'mẽr-īz), *v.t.* to cause an unnatural nervous condition in that puts the will of (the patient) under the complete control of another; hence, to influence strongly; to charm; to hypnotize.

mes-o-sperm (mĕs'ō-spûrm), *n.* the second membrane or skin of a seed.

Mes-o-zo-ic (mĕs"ō-zō'ĭk), *adj.* pertaining to the Secondary Age in the history of the development of the earth, or the era of reptiles.

mes-quite (mĕs-kēt'; mĕs'kēt), *n.* a shrub found in the southwestern United States and Mexico, having fragrant flowers and sugary pods. [Span.]

mess (mĕs), *n.* a number of persons who sit down to table together, especially soldiers or sailors; the army and navy name for any meal; colloquially, enough of some kind of food for one meal; as, he caught a *mess* of fish; a state of dirt or confusion; a muddle; a botch: *v.i.* to eat together; to putter; to make a muddle: *v.t.* to furnish with food; to soil; colloquially, to muddle; as, he *messed* the job: **mess kit,** in the World War, a soldier's canvas bag containing simple cooking utensils for use in the trenches: **mess orderly,** a soldier appointed to carry the army meals from the cookhouse: **mess tin,** a tin cooking pot for use by the soldiers in the trenches.

mes-sage (mĕs'āj), *n.* a communication, written or sent by word of mouth, from one person to another.

mes-sen-ger (mĕs'ĕn-jẽr), *n.* one who carries word from one person or place to another; an office worker who does errands or carries communications; a herald or bringer of news.

Mes-si-ah (mē-sī'ȧ), *n.* Christ, the Anointed One; the expected king and deliverer of the Hebrews. Also, **Messias.**—*adj.* **Messianic.**

mes-sieurs (mĕs'yẽrz; mā"syû'), *n.pl.* of *monsieur;* Sirs; sometimes *pl.* of *Mister;* abbreviated *Messrs.* [Fr.]

mess-mate (mĕs'māt"), *n.* a person, especially a fellow soldier or sailor, with whom one is associated at meals; hence, a friend or companion.

mess-y (mĕs'ĭ), *adj.* disorderly; soiled; botched.—*n.* **messiness.**

met (mĕt), past tense and past participle of the verb *meet.*

me-tab-o-lism (mē-tăb'ō-lĭzm), *n.* the process by which living cells or tissues are continually worn out by use and built up again by food.—*adj.* **metabolic.**

met-al (mĕt'ăl), *n.* a heavy, lustrous substance, capable of being drawn into a fine thread and beaten or hammered into thin plates, of being melted by heat, and of carrying electricity; material; substance; hence, spirit; temper; molten glass: *pl.* colloquially, the rails of a railroad: *v.t.* to cover with metal, such as gold, silver, iron, copper, etc.

me-tal-lic (mē-tăl'ĭk), *adj.* pertaining to, consisting of, or like, gold, silver, iron, copper, etc.

me-tal-lic ox-ide (mē-tăl'ĭk ŏk'sīd), a compound of metal with oxygen.

met-al-lif-er-ous (mĕt"ăl-ĭf'ēr-ŭs), *adj.* yielding metal or metallic ores, such as gold, silver, iron, copper, lead, etc.

met-al-lur-gic (mĕt"ăl-ûr'jĭk), *adj.* pertaining to the science of metals, such as gold, silver, iron, copper, lead, etc. Also, **metallurgical.**

met-al-lur-gist (mĕt'ăl-ûr"jĭst), *n.* one who is skilled in the science of metals, as gold, silver, iron, copper, lead, etc.

met-al-lur-gy (mĕt'ăl-ûr"jĭ), *n.* the art or science of preparing metals, such as gold, silver, iron, copper, lead, etc., for use by separating them from the materials in which they are found in the mines.

met-a-mor-phism (mĕt"ȧ-môr'fĭzm), *n.* the process by which any kind of rocks under pressure, heat, chemical action, etc., have changed from their original constitution, as limestone to marble. —*adj.* **metamorphic.**

met-a-mor-phose (mĕt"ȧ-môr'fōz; mĕt"ȧ-môr'fōs), *v.t.* to change into a different form.

met-a-mor-pho-sis (mĕt"ȧ-môr'fō-sĭs), *n.* change of form, shape, or structure; transformation, as of a chrysalis into a butterfly.

met-a-phor (mĕt'ȧ-fŏr), *n.* a figure of speech by which one thing is spoken of as something else to which it has some likeness; as, the ship *plows* the sea; we *rake* our brains.

met-a-phor-i-cal (mĕt"ȧ-fŏr'ĭ-kăl), *adj.* pertaining to, or containing, a figure of speech in which one thing is spoken of as if it were something else; figurative; as, *metaphorical* expressions. Also, **metaphoric.**—*adv.* **metaphorically.**

met-a-phys-i-cal (mĕt"ȧ-fĭz'ĭ-kăl), *adj.* pertaining to, or according to the rules of, abstract philosophy; abstruse; beyond the material world.—*adv.* **metaphysically.**

met-a-phy-si-cian (mĕt"ȧ-fĭ-zĭsh'ăn), *n.* one who is skilled in abstruse knowledge or philosophical mysteries.

met-a-phys-ics (mĕt"ȧ-fĭz'ĭks), *n.* that branch of knowledge which deals with the nature, character, and causes of being, the existence of God, etc.; the study of those things which relate to the mental as distinguished from the physical; philosophy.

mete (mēt), *v.t.* to give out by measure; allot.

me-temp-sy-cho-sis (mē-tĕmp"sĭ-kō'sĭs), *n.* passage of the soul after death into the body of another man or lower animal: believed in by the ancient Egyptians and other Eastern peoples; transmigration of souls.

me-te-or (mē'tē-ŏr), *n.* a falling or shooting star; hence, anything that dazzles or excites wonder for the moment.

me-te-or-ic (mē"tē-ŏr'ĭk), *adj.* pertaining to, formed of, or like, a falling or shooting star; flashing; rousing a passing wonder.

me-te-or-ite (mē'tē-ŏr-īt"), *n.* a stone or metallic body which has fallen upon the earth from outer space.

me-te-or-o-log-i-cal (mē"tē-ŏr-ō-lŏj'ĭ-kăl), *adj.* pertaining to the science of the atmosphere and its various changes of temperature, moisture, etc. Also, **meteorologic.**

me-te-or-ol-o-gist (mē"tē-ŏr-ŏl'ō-jĭst), *n.* one who is skilled in the science of the atmosphere.

me-te-or-ol-o-gy (mē"tē-ŏr-ŏl'ō-jĭ), *n.* the science of the atmosphere and its various changes of heat, moisture, etc., its winds, storms, etc.

me-ter (mē'tēr), *n.* an instrument for measuring and recording the quantity measured; as, a gas *meter*, etc.; the unit of length in the metric system, equal to 39.37 inches; a regular arrangement of syllables in verse; rhythm; poetical measure; in music, that part of musical structure which depends on the time values: **common meter**, four lines forming a stanza of a hymn, of which the first and third each have four iambic feet or eight syllables, the second and fourth, three iambic feet or six syllables: **long meter**, in a hymn, lines of four iambic feet or eight syllables, four lines usually forming a stanza: **short meter**, four lines forming a stanza of a hymn, of which the first, second and fourth each have three iambic feet or six syllables, the third four iambic feet or eight syllables: sometimes doubled to make eight lines. Also, **metre.**

me-theg-lin (mē-thĕg'lĭn), *n.* an old-fashioned fermented drink, made of honey and water.

me-thinks (mē-thĭnks'), *v. impersonal* [*p.t.* methought], it appears or seems to me. [POET.]

meth-od (mĕth'ŭd), *n.* regular arrangement of things; system; order; classification; way; plan or scheme.

Syn. manner, mode, process, order, rule.

me-thod-i-cal (mē-thŏd'ĭ-kăl), *adj.* arranged with regard to order; devoted to order; systematic. Also, **methodic.**—*adv.* **methodically.**

Meth-od-ism (mĕth'ŭd-ĭzm), *n.* the doctrines and worship of the Methodists, a religious denomination founded by John Wesley in 1729.

Meth-od-ist (mĕth'ŭd-ĭst), *n.* one of a religious denomination founded by John Wesley: *adj.* pertaining to this sect.

meth-od-ize (mĕth'ŭd-īz), *v.t.* to set in order; to make systematic.

Me-thu-se-lah (mē-thū'sē-lȧ), *n.* in the Bible, the longest lived of the patriarchs, 969 years old.—Genesis v. 27.

meth-yl (mĕth'ĭl), *n.* a compound of hydrogen and carbon, which forms the important part of methyl alcohol, or wood spirit.

me-tic-u-lous (mē-tĭk'ū-lŭs), *adj.* too careful of small details; very particular.—*adv.* **meticulously.**—*n.* **meticulousness.**

me-ton-y-my (mē-tŏn'ĭ-mĭ), *n.* a figure of speech in which a word is used in place of another which it suggests by association; as, the name of a part for that of the whole; as, he employs two hundred *hands;* the container for the thing contained; as, the *kettle* boils, etc.

me-tre (mē'tẽr), *n.* a regular arrangement of syllables in verse; rhythm; poetical measure; unit of length in the metric system equivalent to 39.37 inches; in music, that part of musical structure which depends upon time values. Also, **meter.**

met-ric (mĕt'rĭk), *adj.* pertaining to measurement, measure, or rhythm; or to the metric system: **metric system,** the French system of weights and measures, by which things are measured or counted by tens or fractions of tens. Also, **metrical.**—*adv.* **metrically.**

met-ro-graph (mĕt'rō-grȧf), *n.* an apparatus for measuring and recording the distance run by a locomotive, and the number and time of stoppages at stations, etc.

met-ro-nome (mĕt'rō-nōm), *n.* an instrument which beats musical time by means of a short pendulum.

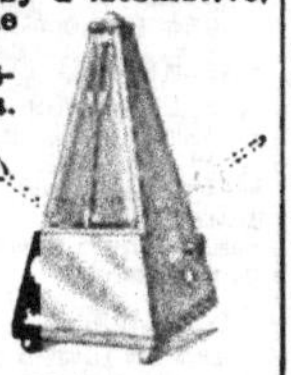
Metronome

me-trop-o-lis (mē-trŏp'ō-lĭs), *n.* the chief city or capital of a kingdom, country, or state; as, New York City is the *metropolis* of the United States; a principal center; as, London is the *metropolis* of the world.

met-ro-pol-i-tan (mĕt'rō-pŏl'ĭ-tăn), *adj.* pertaining to the chief city or capital of a kingdom, country, or state: *n.* the presiding bishop of a country or province; an archbishop.

met-tle (mĕt'l), *n.* ardor or spirit, especially as regards honor, etc.; disposition; courage.

met-tle-some (mĕt'l-sŭm), *adj.* high-spirited; fiery. Also, **mettled.**

mew (mū), *n.* the cry of a cat or an imitation of it; spelled also *miaow;* a seagull; a cage for hawks; a hiding place: *pl.* the royal stables in London; a range of stables about an open place: *v.t.* to inclose or confine, as in a cage: *v.i.* to cry like a cat; miaow.

Mex-i-can (mĕk'sĭ-kăn), *adj.* pertaining to Mexico or its people: *n.* a native of Mexico; the language of Mexico.

mez-za-nine (mĕz'ȧ-nĭn; mĕz'ȧ-nēn), *n.* a low story in a building between two higher ones.

mez-zo (mĕd'zō), *adj.* in music, middle, middling; not extreme. [It.]

mez-zo-so-pra-no (mĕd'zō-sō-prä'nō), *n.* a voice of rich quality between soprano and contralto; a person with such a voice.

mez-zo-tint (mĕd'zō-tĭnt; mĕz'ō-tĭnt), *n.* a variety of copper engraving. Also, **mezzotinto.**

mi (mē), *n.* in music, the third tone of the diatonic scale, or E in the scale of C.

mi-aow (mĭ-ou'), *n.* the cry of a cat: *v.i.* to cry like a cat. Also, **mew.**

mi-as-ma (mī ăz'mȧ), *n.* infectious germs or disease-producing matter in the air; air made poisonous by germs or material liable to cause disease; malaria.—*adj.* **miasmal, miasmatic.**

mi-ca (mī'kȧ), *n.* a mineral easily separated into thin, transparent plates which are used in lanterns, stove doors, etc., and popularly called isinglass.—*adj.* **micaceous.**

Mi-cah (mī'kȧ), *n.* a book of the Old Testament, containing the prophecies of Micah, a Hebrew prophet who lived about 757–700 B. C.

mice (mīs), *n.pl.* [*sing.* mouse], small animals with teeth formed for gnawing, that infest houses, granaries, etc.

mi-crobe (mī'krōb), *n.* an organism so tiny as to be seen only under the microscope: found in the blood of animals, especially those suffering from disease; a germ, usually of disease.—*adj.* **microbic, microbial.**

mi-cro-cosm (mī'krō-kŏzm), *n.* a little world; a world in miniature; hence, man, as opposed to the great universe about him: opposite to *macrocosm.*—*adj.* **microcosmic.**

mi-cro-graph (mī'krō-grȧf), *n.* an instrument for producing very tiny engraving or writing.

mi-crom-e-ter (mī-krŏm'ē-tẽr), *n.* an instrument for measuring very small distances or the apparent diameters of objects far away, as the stars: used in connection with a microscope or telescope: **micrometer caliper,** a gauge, or caliper, having a micrometer screw, for making accurate measurements.

Micrometer Caliper for fine measurements

mi-cro-ör-gan-ism (mī'krō-ôr'găn-ĭzm), *n.* a very tiny organism; a term for microbe.

mi-cro-phone (mī'krō-fōn), *n.* an instrument for making feeble sounds louder, as the transmitter of a telephone.

mi-cro-pho-tog-ra-phy (mī'krō-fō-tŏg'rȧ-fĭ), *n.* the art of making an exceedingly small photograph of an object, etc.

mi-cro-scope (mī'krō-skōp), *n.* an optical instrument for making very tiny objects appear larger, so that they may be seen and studied; a magnifying glass.

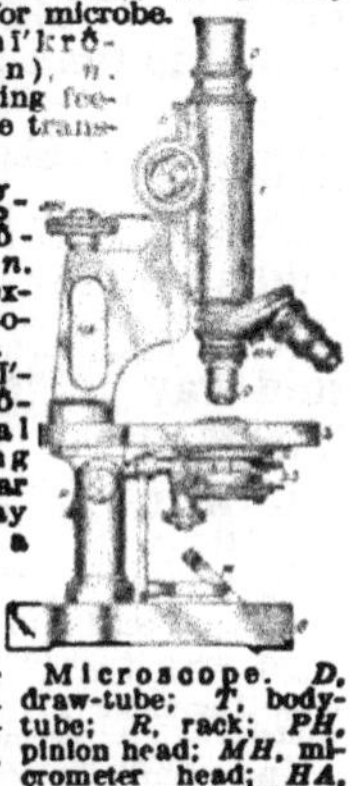
Microscope. *D,* draw-tube; *T,* body-tube; *R,* rack; *PH,* pinion head; *MH,* micrometer head; *HA,* handle arm; *RN,* revolving nosepiece; *O,* objective; *S,* stage; *SS,* substage; *P,* inclination pillar; *I,* inclination joint; *M,* mirror; *B,* base.

mi-cro-scop-ic (mī'krō-skŏp'ĭk), *adj.* pertaining to, seen, or discovered by, a magnifying glass; very small. Also, **microscopical.**—*adv.* **microscopically.**

mi-cros-co-pist (mī-krŏs'kō-pĭst; mī'krō-skō'pĭst), *n.* one skilled in the use of a microscope, or the study of objects through the microscope.

mi-cros-co-py (mī-krŏs'kō-pĭ), *n.* the use of the microscope; study by means of a microscope.

mid (mĭd), *adj.* middle; as, flying in *mid* air: *prep.* amid; among.

mid-day (mĭd'dā"), *n.* the middle hours of the day; noon.

mid-dle (mĭd'l), *n.* the point equally distant from two given points or extremes; central part: *adj.* equally distant from the extremes; halfway between two given points; mean; medial.

Mid-dle Ag-es (mĭd'l āj'ĕz), the period between the fifth and fifteenth centuries A. D.

mid-dle-aged (mĭd'l-ājd"), *adj.* neither young nor old: said of a person from about thirty to about sixty years old.

mid-dle-man (mĭd'l-măn), *n.* [*pl.* middlemen (-mĕn)], one who acts as agent between two people or groups of people; a broker; one who buys at wholesale and sells at retail.

mid-dling (mĭd'lĭng), *adj.* of moderate rank, size, or quality; neither good nor bad; mediocre: *n.pl.* a mixture of coarse wheat flour and fine bran.

mid-dy (mĭd'ĭ), *n.* [*pl.* middies (-ĭz)], a midshipman, or naval cadet. [Colloq.]

midge (mĭj), *n.* a very small fly; a very tiny gnat.

midg-et (mĭj'ĕt), *n.* a small dwarf; a little and active child.

mid-land (mĭd'lănd), *adj.* inland; in the central part of a country: *n.pl.* the interior of a country.

mid-night (mĭd'nīt"), *n.* the middle of the night; twelve o'clock at night.

mid-riff (mĭd'rĭf), *n.* the muscular partition separating the cavity of the chest from the abdomen.

mid-ship-man (mĭd'shĭp"măn), *n.* [*pl.* midshipmen (-mĕn)], a naval cadet, or youth in training for a naval officer's commission; one whose rank is next below that of ensign; a petty officer in the British navy.

midst (mĭdst), *n.* the middle; the central place; the situation of being beset.

mid-sum-mer (mĭd'sŭm"ẽr; mĭd"sŭm'ẽr), *n.* the period before and after June 21, or the longest day of summer: *adj.* in the middle of summer.

mid-way (mĭd'wā"; mĭd"wā'), *adj.* and *adv.* halfway between: *n.* (mĭd'wā"), the amusement section of an exposition or fair.

mid-wife (mĭd'wīf"), *n.* [*pl.* midwives (-wīvz)], a woman who assists at childbirth.

mid-wife-ry (mĭd'wīf"rĭ; mĭd'wĭf'rĭ), *n.* act, art, or practice, of assisting at childbirth.

mid-win-ter (mĭd'wĭn"tẽr; mĭd"wĭn'tẽr), *n.* the period before and after December 21, or the shortest day of winter: *adj.* in the middle of the winter.

mien (mēn), *n.* outward appearance; air; look; manner; aspect.

miff (mĭf), *v.t.* to cause to be vexed: *n.* a slight vexation. [Colloq.]

might (mīt), *p.t.* of *may*: *n.* power; force; strength.

might-y (mīt'ĭ), *adj.* [*comp.* mightier, *superl.* mightiest], powerful; strong; having influence; important; wonderful; huge: *adv.* colloquially, very or exceedingly.—*adv.* mightily.—*n.* mightiness.

mi-gnon-ette (mĭn"yŭn-ĕt'), *n.* a fragrant garden plant with greenish-white flowers.

mi-grant (mī'grănt), *adj.* moving from place to place; migratory.

mi-grate (mī'grāt), *v.i.* to move from one country to another for permanent residence; to go regularly from one climate or region to another at certain times of year, as many birds.

mi-gra-tion (mī-grā'shŭn), *n.* a moving from one place to another; a change of residence from one country to another.

mi-gra-to-ry (mī'grȧ-tō-rĭ), *adj.* removing or passing from one place to another; especially, moving constantly from one climate or region to another: as, *migratory* birds; roving.

Syn. strolling, wandering, journeying, vagrant.

Ant. (see settled).

mi-ka-do (mĭ-kä'dō), *n.* the popular title of the Emperor of Japan.

milch (mĭlch), *adj.* yielding milk; giving milk; as, a *milch* cow.

mild (mīld), *adj.* [*comp.* milder, *superl.* mildest], gentle in temper and disposition; kind; soft; calm; moderate; not sharp, sour, severe, or bitter.—*adv.* mildly.—*n.* mildness.

mil-dew (mĭl'dū), *n.* a very tiny, colorless growth, of the nature of a fungus, found on plants or other substances, by which it is nourished; a disease of plants produced by this growth; spots of mold on cloth, etc., caused by damp: *v.t.* to affect with mildew: *v.i.* to be affected with mildew.

mile (mīl), *n.* a measure of length varying in different countries; as, the English *mile*, in use in the United States, contains 1,760 yards; the geographical or nautical *mile*, 1-60th of a degree of latitude, or 2,029 yards.

mile-age (mīl'āj), *n.* an allowance for traveling expenses of so much per mile; length in miles; on railroads, a charge per mile; **mileage book**, a book of coupons bought for a certain sum and allowing the possessor to travel a given number of miles.

mile-post (mīl'pōst"), *n.* a signboard, usually at a crossroads, stating the distance in miles to certain points.

mile-stone (mīl'stōn"), *n.* a stone, usually set at intervals of a mile along a railroad track, to tell the distance in miles to a given point.

mil-i-tan-cy (mĭl'ĭ-tăn-sĭ), *n.* warfare; warlike or fighting spirit or policy.

mil-i-tant (mĭl'ĭ-tănt), *adj.* warlike; fighting; serving as a soldier: *n.* one who fights; one who uses warlike methods in aid of a cause, as woman's suffrage.

mil-i-ta-rism (mĭl'ĭ-tȧ-rĭzm), *n.* warlike or fighting spirit or policy; a government depending on the power of its armies for its strength; as, *militarism* in a country is liable to lead to war.

mil-i-ta-rist (mĭl'ĭ-tȧ-rĭst), *n.* one who believes in war and warlike policy; one who holds that a powerful army is the best source of power for a government.—*adj.* militaristic.

mil-i-ta-ry (mĭl'ĭ-tȧ-rĭ), *adj.* pertaining to soldiers or to arms; warlike;

n. soldiers collectively; army; troops: **military police**, a branch of the army, whose duty it is to preserve order, protect the inhabitants of an occupied or invaded district, care for prisoners of war, and arrest soldiers guilty of misconduct.

mil-i-tate (mĭl'ĭ-tāt), *v.i.* to be, or stand, opposed; operate: with *against;* to contend.

mi-li-tia (mĭ-lĭsh'ȧ), *n.* a body of citizens enrolled and trained for the defense of a state, or nation.

milk (mĭlk), *n.* a white fluid produced by the mammary glands of females among the higher animals for the nourishment of their young; especially, the milk of the cow: largely used as food; the white juice of certain plants: *v.t.* to draw milk from; supply with milk.—*n.* **milker.**

milk-sop (mĭlk'sŏp"), *n.* an effeminate, weak man.

milk tooth (mĭlk tōōth), one of the first set of teeth in the young of the higher animals.

milk-weed (mĭlk'wēd"), *n.* a wild plant whose juice is white like milk.

milk-y (mĭl'kĭ), *adj.* containing, or like, milk; giving milk; very mild.—*n.* **milkiness.**

Milk-y Way (mĭl'kĭ wā), a broad band of pale light across the heavens, visible at night, and consisting of countless stars.

mill (mĭl), *n.* a machine for grinding grain or other substances; a manufactory; one-tenth of a cent: *v.t.* to grind very fine in a machine; groove or stamp, as the edges of coins; full (cloth); roll into bars, as metal.

mill-board (mĭl'bōrd"), *n.* a kind of thick pasteboard.

mil-le-na-ri-an (mĭl"ē-nā'rĭ-ăn), *adj.* pertaining to, or consisting of, a thousand; pertaining to the millennium, or thousand years of peace, or to believers in it: *n.* a believer in the millennium.

mil-le-na-ry (mĭl'ē-nā-rĭ), *n.* a thousand years: *adj.* pertaining to a thousand.

mil-len-ni-al (mĭ-lĕn'ĭ-ăl), *adj.* of or pertaining to a period of a thousand years.

mil-len-ni-um (mĭ-lĕn'ĭ-ŭm), *n.* a period of a thousand years; the thousand years during which Satan will be bound and Christ will reign on earth—Rev. xx. 1–4; a period of great joy, prosperity, and righteousness.

mil-ler (mĭl'ẽr), *n.* one who keeps or works a flour mill; a kind of moth whose wings look as if powdered with flour.

mil-let (mĭl'ĕt), *n.* a grain-bearing grass, cultivated in Europe and Asia as a food for man and birds, and in the United States for hay; the seed of this grass.

mil-li-ard (mĭl'ĭ-ărd; mĭl'yărd), *n.* one thousand millions. [Fr.]

mil-lier (mē"yā'), *n.* a metric ton, equal to 1,000,000 grams, 1,000 kilograms, or 2,204.6 pounds, avoirdupois.

mil-li-gram (mĭl'ĭ-grăm), *n.* the thousandth part of a gram, equal to .01543 grain. Also, **milligramme.**

mil-li-li-ter (mĭl'ĭ-lē"tẽr), *n.* the thousandth part of a liter, or one cubic centimeter, equal to .06102 cubic inch, or .0338 fluid ounce. Also, **millilitre.**

mil-li-me-ter (mĭl'ĭ-mē"tẽr), *n.* in the metric system, the thousandth part of a meter, equal to .03937 inch. Also, **millimetre.**

mil-li-ner (mĭl'ĭ-nẽr), *n.* one who makes or trims women's bonnets, hats, headdresses, etc.

mil-li-ner-y (mĭl'ĭ-nẽr-ĭ), *n.* such articles as women's hats, bonnets, headdresses, etc.; the business or work of making, trimming, and selling hats.

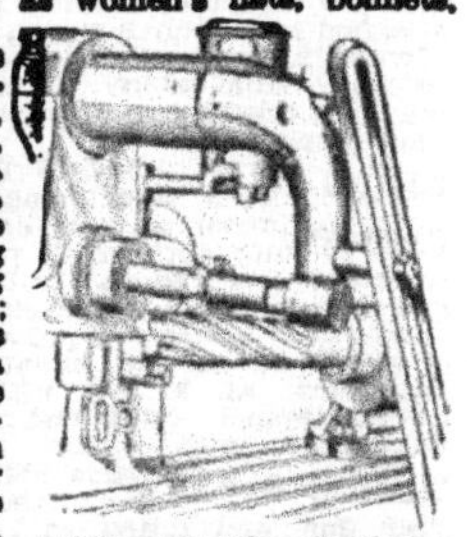

Milling Machine Cutting a Spiral Channel in a Drill

mill-ing (mĭl'ĭng), *n.* the act of grinding in or passing through a mill; the process of making a notched edge on a coin: **milling machine**, an apparatus for notching the edges of coins, cutting screw-heads, etc.

mil-lion (mĭl'yŭn), *n.* the number of ten hundred thousand; an indefinitely large number.

mil-lion-aire (mĭl"yŭn-âr'), *n.* a person who is worth ten hundred thousand, or a million, dollars; a very rich person. Also, **millionnaire.**

mil-lionth (mĭl'yŭnth), *n.* one of a million parts; the millionth unit or thing: *adj.* being one out of ten hundred thousand, or a million; coming last in a series of a million.

mill pond (mĭl pŏnd), a small body of water that supplies water for driving a mill.

mill race (mĭl rās), a stream or canal of water with a current that drives a mill.

mill-stone (mĭl'stōn"), *n.* one of two flat circular stones for grinding grain.

mill wheel (mĭl hwēl), a large wheel, moved by a current of water, which drives a mill.

milt (mĭlt), *n.* the spleen; the reproductive organ of a male fish: *v.t.* to make fertile (the egg, or roe, of a female fish).

mime (mīm), *n.* a kind of drama among the Greeks and Romans, in which real persons and events were represented in a laughable manner; an actor in such a drama.

mim-e-o-graph (mĭm'ē-ō-grăf"), *n.* an apparatus for making copies of written, or typewritten, matter by means of stencils and an ink roller: *v.t.* to copy by such an apparatus.

mi-met-ic (mĭ-mĕt'ĭk), *adj.* inclined to imitate; gifted as a mimic; pertaining to imitation.

mim-ic (mĭm'ĭk), *n.* one who imitates, especially to make fun of the person or thing imitated: *v.t.* to imitate, or ridicule by imitation; to make an imitation of; as, clouds *mimic* the land: *adj.* inclined to imitate; imitative; copying, usually in smaller form. Also, *n.*, **mimicker.**

Syn., *v.* ape, mock.

mim-ic-ry (mĭm'ĭk-rĭ), *n.* the practice of one who imitates; ridiculous imitation for sport or for the purpose of making fun of another; close outward likeness; as, certain insects are saved from destruction by their *mimicry* of the twigs or leaves on which they rest.

mi-mo-sa (mĭ-mō'sȧ; mĭ-mō'zȧ), *n.* a tropical shrub or tree with round heads of pink or white flowers.

min-a-ret (mĭn'ȧ-rĕt), *n.* a tall, slender tower attached to a Mohammedan place of worship, surrounded with several balconies from which the call to prayer is cried by an officer called the *muezzin.*

Minaret

min-a-to-ry (mĭn'ȧ-tō-rĭ), *adj.* threatening.

mince (mĭns), *v.t.* to cut or chop into very small pieces; to weaken; tell in part or by degrees; make less in importance; as, don't *mince* matters; to pronounce or speak with assumed elegance or daintiness: *v.i.* to talk with assumed elegance; walk with short steps or in a prim manner.

mince-meat (mĭns'mēt'), *n.* meat chopped very fine, and mixed with suet, raisins, lemon peel, etc.

minc-ing (mĭns'ĭng), *p.adj.* with assumed elegance; affected; walking primly.—*adv.* **mincingly.**

mind (mīnd), *n.* the mental or reasoning power in man; the understanding or intellect; soul; memory; intention; opinion: *v.t.* to attend to; as, to *mind* one's business; heed; obey; object to; as, I don't *mind* going: *v.i.* to obey; as, a child must learn to *mind;* to be troubled; as, never *mind* if you do fail.

mind-ed (mīn'dĕd), *p.adj.* having a mind; disposed or inclined; having the wish or purpose to.

mind-ful (mīnd'fo͝ol), *adj.* keeping in one's thought; attentive; regardful.—*adv.* **mindfully.**—*n.* **mindfulness.**
Syn. heedful, thoughtful.
Ant. (see heedless).

mine (mīn), *pron.* and *adj.* pertaining to me: *n.* an opening made in the earth, from which minerals, precious stones, etc., are taken; crude iron-stone; an abundant store; a rich source of wealth; a tunnel under an enemy's works to blow them up; a receptacle filled with explosives, moored beneath, or on, the water, the firing of which destroys or hinders an enemy: *v.i.* to carry on the work of digging for metals, etc.; to dig a mine; to burrow; practice secret methods; to lay explosives (in a harbor): *v.t.* to undermine or sap, as an enemy's works; to destroy slowly; to dig in for ore or metals; to make or get by digging underground; as, to *mine* a tunnel, or to *mine* coal.

min-er (mīn'ẽr), *n.* one engaged in digging for metals; a soldier who digs a way beneath the enemy's works to blow them up.

min-er-al (mĭn'ẽr-ăl), *n.* any substance not animal or vegetable; any chemical compound resulting naturally from inorganic processes; ore: *adj.* pertaining to, consisting of, or mingled with, a substance not animal or vegetable.

min-er-al-o-gist (mĭn'ẽr-ăl'ō-jĭst), *n.* one skilled in the knowledge of minerals, or substances neither animal nor vegetable.

min-er-al-o-gy (mĭn'ẽr-ăl'ō-jĭ), *n.* the science of minerals, or substances neither animal nor vegetable.

Min-er-va (mĭn-ẽr'vȧ), *n.* the Roman goddess of wisdom: identified with the Greek Athena.

mine sweep-er (mīn' swēp'ẽr), in the navy, a vessel used for dragging a body of water for submarine or floating mines and removing or exploding them.

min-gle (mĭŋ'gl), *v.t.* to combine by mixing; to associate; to blend: *v.i.* to be mixed or blended.

min-i-a-ture (mĭn'ĭ-ȧ-tūr), *n.* a very small painting, especially a portrait on ivory, etc.: *adj.* done on a very small scale; very tiny; minute.

Min-i-é ball (mĭn'ĭ-ā; popularly, mĭn'ĭ bôl), a conical rifle bullet, with a hollow base, and a plug driven in by the explosion, to expand the lead into the grooves of the rifle barrel.

min-im (mĭn'ĭm), *n.* the smallest liquid measure; a single drop; in music, a half note.

min-i-mize (mĭn'ĭ-mīz), *v.t.* to reduce to the smallest degree, part, or proportion: used often in a depreciatory or slighting sense; as, do not *minimize* the importance of being on time.

min-i-mum (mĭn'ĭ-mŭm), *n.* [*pl.* minima (-mȧ)], the least quantity; trifle: opposite to *maximum;* the lowest point reached or recorded, as of temperature; the least quantity allowable or admissible: *adj.* lowest; least possible or allowable.

min-ing (mīn'ĭng), *p.adj.* pertaining to openings in the earth where metals, ores, etc., are dug; burrowing in the earth: *n.* the act of making or working mines for digging metals, etc., or of laying military mines.

min-is-ter (mĭn'ĭs-tẽr), *n.* one intrusted by the head of a government with the direction of affairs of state; an ambassador sent to a foreign government; a clergyman or pastor of a church, authorized to preach and administer the sacraments: *v.t.* to serve; to act as an attendant or servant; to give aid by doing helpful things; to serve as pastor of a church.

min-is-te-ri-al (mĭn'ĭs-tē'rĭ-ăl), *adj.* pertaining to a high state official or ambassador, to a clergyman, or to the work of either; attendant.—*adv.* **ministerially.**

min-is-te-ri-al-ist (mĭn'ĭs-tē'rĭ-ăl-ĭst), *n.* a supporter of the officials in charge of a government, and hence of the party in power.

min-is-tra-tion (mĭn'ĭs-trā'shŭn), *n.* the act of serving (as a pastor, etc.); service.

min-is-try (mĭn'ĭs-trĭ), *n.* [*pl.* ministries (-trĭz)], the service of one who preaches a religion; the office or duties of an officer of state; clergy or officers of state collectively; term of service of an officer of state or of a clergyman.

min-i-ver (mĭn'ĭ-vẽr), *n.* any soft white fur; an ermine in its white winter fur. Also, **minever.**

mink (mĭŋk), *n.* an animal somewhat like the weasel; its valuable fur.

min-now (mĭn'ō), *n.* a small fresh-water fish of the carp family; any of several small fishes.

mi-nor (mī'nẽr), *n.* one of either sex who is under the age of twenty-one; a chord containing a minor third, in which the tones are a step and a half apart, etc.: *adj.* smaller; less; unimportant; as, a *minor* injury; in music, less by half a step than the corresponding major interval: indicating scales in which such intervals occur.

mi-nor-i-ty (mī-nŏr'ĭ-tĭ), *n.* [*pl.* minorities (-tĭz)], the smaller of two numbers: opposite to *majority;* the state of being under age.

min-ster (mĭn'stẽr), *n.* the church of a monastery; any church.

min-strel (mĭn'strĕl), *n.* originally, in the Middle Ages, a musical entertainer in the house of a lord; a poet; now, one of a company of performers who black their faces, and sing negro songs, crack jokes, etc.

min-strel-sy (mĭn'strĕl-sĭ), *n.* the art or occupation of those who play or sing ballads, songs, etc.; such performers collectively; ballads or lyrics collectively.

mint (mĭnt), *n.* the place where money is coined by government authority; source of unlimited supply; a fragrant plant yielding an oil of aromatic taste and odor: *v.t.* to coin or stamp (money); invent.

mint-age (mĭn'tāj), *n.* coinage; the cost of coining gold or silver; the stamp impressed upon a coin.

min-u-end (mĭn'ū-ĕnd), *n.* that number from which another number is to be subtracted.

min-u-et (mĭn'ū-ĕt'; mĭn'ū-ĕt), *n.* a slow graceful square dance; the music for such a dance.

mi-nus (mī'nŭs), *n.* the sign [—] indicating subtraction; less; lacking; decreased by.

min-ute (mĭn'ĭt), *n.* the sixtieth part of an hour or a degree; a moment; an official note; a memorandum; *pl.* the official record made of the proceedings of a meeting, etc.

mi-nute (mī-nūt'; mĭ-nūt'), *adj.* very small; precise; trifling; exact. —*adv.* minutely.—*n.* minuteness.
Ant. (see ample, huge).

min-ute hand (mĭn'ĭt hănd), the long hand of a timepiece which goes around the dial once an hour and marks the minutes.

min-ute-man (mĭn'ĭt-măn), *n.* [*pl.* minutemen (-mĕn)], in the American Revolution, a citizen ready to take arms at a minute's notice.

mi-nu-ti-æ (mĭ-nū'shĭ-ē), *n.pl.* smaller or less important details or particulars.

minx (mĭnks), *n.* a pert girl: used playfully.

mir (mēr), *n.* the village commune or civil community of the Russian peasants.

mir-a-cle (mĭr'ȧ-kl), *n.* an act or happening in the material or physical sphere that apparently departs from the laws of nature or goes beyond what is known concerning these laws; a wonder; a marvel.

mi-rac-u-lous (mĭ-răk'ū-lŭs), *adj.* wonderful; happening opposite to the laws of nature; able to perform, or performing, great wonders, or the supernatural.—*adv.* miraculously.—*n.* miraculousness.

mi-rage (mē-räzh'), *n.* a misleading effect presented to the eye on oceans, deserts, or plains, by which the inverted images of distant objects are seen, the objects so reflected being frequently quite out of sight.

mire (mīr), *n.* deep mud; wet earth; slush; dirt: *v.t.* and *v.i.* to soil with mud; to sink in mud.—*n.* miriness.

mir-ror (mĭr'ẽr), *n.* a looking-glass; any substance that reflects images; that which gives a true likeness, hence, a pattern: *v.t.* to reflect, as in a mirror.

mir-ror-scope (mĭr'ẽr-skōp), *n.* a kind of projector.

mirth (mûrth), *n.* noisy gaiety; social merriment; jollity.

mirth-ful (mûrth'fo͝ol), *adj.* merry; festive; jolly.—*adv.* mirthfully.—*n.* mirthfulness.

mirth-less (mûrth'lĕs), *adj.* without glee; without gladness or gaiety. —*adv.* mirthlessly.

mir-y (mīr'ĭ), *adj.* covered with deep mud; resembling mud; boggy; dirty.

mir-za (mēr'zä), *n.* a Persian title meaning prince.

mis- (mĭs-), a *prefix* meaning wrong, wrongly, ill; as, *mis*behave, *mis*call.

mis-ad-ven-ture (mĭs'ăd-vĕn'tūr), *n.* an unlucky accident; misfortune.

mis-al-li-ance (mĭs'ă-lī'ăns), *n.* an improper or undesirable union by marriage, especially with one of lower social standing. Also, mésalliance.

mis-an-thrope (mĭs'ăn-thrōp), *n.* a hater of mankind. Also, misanthropist.

mis-an-throp-ic (mĭs'ăn-thrŏp'ĭk), *adj.* hating mankind. Also, misanthropical.

mis-an-thro-py (mĭs-ăn'thrō-pĭ), *n.* hatred of mankind.

mis-ap-pre-hend (mĭs-ăp'rē-hĕnd'), *v.t.* to fail to understand.—*n.* misapprehension.

mis-ap-pro-pri-ate (mĭs'ă-prō'prĭ-āt), *v.t.* to apply to a wrong use or purpose, as money, etc.—*n.* misappropriation.

mis-be-have (mĭs'bē-hāv'), *v.i.* to act in a wrong or improper fashion.—*n.* misbehavior, misbehaviour.

mis-cal-cu-late (mĭs-kăl'kū-lāt), *v.t.* to make a mistake in; misjudge: *v.i.* to make an error in judgment or foresight.—*n.* miscalculation.

mis-car-riage (mĭs-kăr'ĭj), *n.* failure; mismanagement; a premature birth.

mis-car-ry (mĭs-kăr'ĭ), *v.i.* [*p.t.* and *p.p.* miscarried, *p.pr.* miscarrying], to go wrong; be unsuccessful.

mis-cel-la-ne-ous (mĭs'ĕ-lā'nē-ŭs), *adj.* consisting of several kinds mixed together; having many sides; consisting of various qualities.

mis-cel-la-ny (mĭs'ĕ-lā-nĭ), *n.* [*pl.* miscellanies (-nĭz)], a mixture of various kinds; a book containing a variety of literary compositions.

mis-chance (mĭs-chȧns'), *n.* misfortune; mishap.

mis-chief (mĭs'chĭf), *n.* harm; injury; hurt; damage; misfortune; vexation; tendency to vex or annoy; as, full of *mischief.*
Syn. evil, ill, annoyance.
Ant. (see benefit).

mis-chie-vous (mĭs'chĭ-vŭs), *adj.* producing injury or damage; hurtful; full of pranks; causing annoyance to others.—*adv.* mischievously.—*n.* mischievousness.

mis-con-ceive (mĭs'kŏn-sēv'), *v.t.* and *v.i.* judge wrongly; mistake; misunderstand.

mis-con-cep-tion (mĭs'kŏn-sĕp'shŭn), *n.* false opinion; misunderstanding.

mis-con-duct (mĭs-kŏn'dŭkt), *n.* improper or wrong behavior: *v.t.* (mĭs'kŏn-dŭkt'), to manage badly; to lead wrong.

mis-con-strue (mĭs-kŏn'strōō; mĭs'-kŏn-strōō'), *v.t.* to get the wrong meaning from; to misinterpret.—*n.* misconstruction.

mis-cre-ant (mĭs'krē-ănt), *n.* a villain; vile wretch: *adj.* unscrupulous.
Syn., n. caitiff, ruffian.

mis-deed (mĭs-dēd'), *n.* a wrong act; a crime; transgression.

mis-de-mean (mĭs'dē-mēn'), *v.t.* and *v.i.* to behave improperly; conduct (oneself) badly.

mis-de-mean-or (mĭs'dē-mēn'ẽr), *n.* ill conduct; a crime of only moderate seriousness.

mis-doubt (mĭs-dout'), *v.t.* and *v.i.* to suspect: *n.* suspicion.

mi-ser (mī'zẽr), *n.* a man who is interested in nothing except heaping up money; a covetous person.

mis-er-a-ble (mĭz'ẽr-ȧ-bl), *adj.* wretched; very unhappy; worthless; very mean or poor.—*adv.* miserably.
Syn. distressed, afflicted.
Ant. (see happy).

mi-ser-ly (mī'zẽr-lĭ), *adj.* of the disposition of, or like, one who hoards money; stingy; grasping; as, a *miserly* money lender; avaricious; saving.

mis-er-y (mĭz'ẽr-ĭ), *n.* extreme pain, distress, or misfortune; great unhappiness.
Syn. wretchedness, destitution, privation, beggary.
Ant. (see happiness).

mis-fit (mĭs-fĭt'), *n.* clothing which does not fit; sometimes, a person in a position for which he is unfitted.

mis-for-tune (mĭs-fôr'tūn), *n.* adversity; bad luck; a mishap; mischance.

mis-give (mĭs-gĭv') *v.t.* to cause to fail in confidence, courage, etc.; make fearful; as, my heart *misgives* me.

mis-giv-ing (mĭs-gĭv'ĭng), *n.* a feeling of doubt; a lack of confidence; as, I have many *misgivings* concerning his course of action.

mis-guid-ed (mĭs-gī'dĕd), *p.adj.* in error; under a wrong influence; wrong in opinion or act.

mis-hap (mĭs-hăp'), *n.* ill fortune; an unlucky accident.

mis-in-form (mĭs'ĭn-fôrm'), *v.t.* to tell news or facts wrongly to.—*n.* misinformation.

mis-in-ter-pret (mĭs'ĭn-tûr'prĕt), *v.t.* to misunderstand; to give a wrong explanation of.—*n.* misinterpretation.

mis-judge (mĭs-jŭj'), *v.t.* to form a wrong or unjust opinion of: *v.i.* to be mistaken in opinion.

mis-lay (mĭs-lā'), *v.t.* to lose temporarily; to put in the wrong place.

mis-lead (mĭs-lēd') *v.t.* to deceive; delude; misguide; to conduct in the wrong way.—*p.adj.* misleading.

mis-man-age (mĭs-măn'āj), *v.t.* and *v.i.* to direct badly.—*n.* mismanagement.

mis-no-mer (mĭs-nō'mẽr), *n.* a wrong naming or name.

mi-sog-y-nist (mī-sŏj'ĭ-nĭst), *n.* a woman hater.

mi-sog-y-ny (mī-sŏj'ĭ-nĭ), *n.* hatred of women.

mis-place (mĭs-plās'), *v.t.* to put in a wrong place; confer on an improper or undeserving object; as, to *misplace* one's affections.

mis-print (mĭs-prĭnt'), *v.t.* to print wrongly: *n.* a mistake in type.

mis-pri-sion (mĭs-prĭzh'ŭn), *n.* in law, a grave offense, not so serious as to be punishable by death, but bordering upon it; high misdemeanor.

mis-pri-sion of fel-o-ny (mĭs-prĭzh'-ŭn ŏv fĕl'ō-nĭ), the hiding of a crime by one who knows of it but has had nothing to do with it, directly or indirectly.

mis-pro-nounce (mĭs'prō-nouns'), *v.t.* and *v.i.* to speak with a wrong sound or accent.—*n.* mispronunciation.

mis-rep-re-sent (mĭs-rĕp'rē-zĕnt'), *v.t.* and *v.i.* to report incorrectly, either wilfully, or through carelessness.—*n.* misrepresentation.

mis-rule (mĭs-rōōl'), *v.t.* to govern badly: *n.* bad government; tumult.

miss (mĭs), *v.t.* to fail to hit, etc.; omit or pass by; do without; feel the want of: *v.i.* to fly wide of the mark: *n.* a young unmarried woman; failure to hit, reach, see, or obtain: **Miss**, a title used before the name of an unmarried woman.
Syn. v. omit, lose, fail, miscarry.

mis-sal (mĭs'ăl), *n.* the book containing the order of service for the Roman Catholic Mass; hence, loosely, a book of devotions.

mis-sile (mĭs'ĭl), *n.* a weapon or thing thrown, or made to be thrown, to injure another; a projectile.

miss-ing (mĭs'ĭng), *p.adj.* lost; wanting; absent.

mis-sion (mĭsh'ŭn), *n.* the act of sending, or state of being sent, with certain powers, to do some special service; a business or duty on which one is sent; a calling, especially to preach and spread a religion; a series of special religious services; an organization for doing religious and charitable work, especially one dependent on one or more churches; as, a rescue *mission*; a body of people sent to perform a special work, as envoys or delegates; a body of persons engaged in spreading a religion in a foreign land; also their organization and residence; *pl.* the organized work of spreading religion.

mis-sion-a-ry (mĭsh'ŭn-ā-rĭ), *n.* [*pl.* missionaries (-rĭz)], a person who is sent to spread the knowledge of religion and convert people to it, especially in foreign lands: *adj.* pertaining to organizations for doing religious work, or to those who do it; as, *missionary* services.

mis-sive (mĭs'ĭv), *n.* a letter or message: *adj.* sent specially.

mist (mĭst), *n.* visible watery vapor in the atmosphere, at or near the earth's surface; fog; anything that dims the sight: *v.i.* to rain in very fine drops.

mis-tak-a-ble (mĭs-tāk'ȧ-bl), *adj.* liable to be misunderstood.

mis-take (mĭs-tāk'), *v.t.* [*p.t.* mistook, *p.p.* mistaken, *p.pr.* mistaking], to misunderstand; to put wrongly in place of another person or thing; as, he *mistook* her for her sister: *v.i.* to err in judgment or opinion: *n.* an error in judgment; fault; misunderstanding.

mis-tak-en (mĭs-tāk'n), *p.adj.* incorrect; wrong; as, a *mistaken* idea; wrong in judgment; as, he is *mistaken;* misunderstood; as, a *mistaken* meaning.

Mis-ter (mĭs'tẽr), *n.* [*pl.* Messrs.], a title used before a man's name: abbreviated, *Mr.*

mis-tle-toe (mĭs'l-tō; mĭz'l-tō), *n.* an evergreen plant which grows and feeds on apple trees, oak trees, etc.

mis-tress (mĭs'trĕs), *n.* a woman who has authority or who governs; the female head of a family, school, etc.; a woman well skilled in anything; a woman courted and beloved; sweetheart: **Mistress,** a title used before the name of a married woman: abbreviated, *Mrs.*

mis-tri-al (mĭs-trī'ăl), *n.* a court trial which is worth nothing because of some error in the course of it.

mis-trust (mĭs-trŭst'), *n.* lack of confidence: *v.t.* and *v.i.* to doubt; suspect.—*adj.* **mistrustful.**

mist-y (mĭs'tĭ), *adj.* [*comp.* mistier, *superl.* mistiest], characterized by, or hidden by, watery vapor; dim; obscure; clouded.—*adv.* **mistily.**—*n.* **mistiness.**

mis-un-der-stand (mĭs"ŭn-dẽr-stănd'), *v.t.* and *v.i.* to take in a wrong sense; to get the wrong idea of; as, to be great is to be *misunderstood.*

mis-un-der-stand-ing (mĭs"ŭn-dẽr-stănd'ĭng), *n.* disagreement; a quarrel; a mistake as to meaning or motive.

mis-use (mĭs-ūs'), *n.* wrong use; abuse: *v.t.* (mĭs-ūz'), to use wrongly.

mite (mīt), *n.* a very tiny insect; a small coin used in former times; colloquially, a very small object or quantity.

mi-ter (mī'tẽr), *n.* a kind of crown, in two sections, worn by archbishops, bishops, and sometimes by abbots, on special occasions; the dignity or office of a bishop; a slanting junction at corners of moldings, laces, etc.: *v.t.* to place a bishop's crown on; hence, to raise to the office of a bishop; to adorn with such a crown; join (moldings, laces, etc.) on a slanting line at a corner: **miter square** an instrument having two blades, one at an angle (usually 45 degrees), with the other. Also, **mitre.**—*adj.* **mitral.**

Miter Square

mit-i-gate (mĭt'ĭ-gāt), *v.t.* to render less severe, hard, or painful; soften.—*adj.* **mitigative.**
Syn. relieve, diminish, abate.
Ant. (see aggravate).

mit-i-ga-tion (mĭt"ĭ-gā'shŭn), *n.* the act of making less severe, hard, or painful.

mit-i-ga-tor (mĭt'ĭ-gā"tẽr), *n.* one who, or that which, relieves, softens, or makes more bearable.

mi-tra-illeuse (mē"trȧ"yûz'), *n.* a machine gun. [Fr.]

mitt (mĭt), *n.* kind of glove, often of lace or net, without fingers or with half fingers.

mit-ten (mĭt'ẽn), *n.* a winter glove covering the four fingers together and the thumb separately. Also, **mitt.**

mit-ti-mus (mĭt'ĭ-mŭs), *n.* a warrant which commits to prison.

mix (mĭks), *v.t.* to unite or blend into one mass or compound; join: *v.i.* to become united in a compound; mingle: *n.* a confused mass of several elements; colloquially, a muddle.

mix-ture (mĭks'tūr), *n.* the state of being blended or mingled; a compound or mass formed by putting two or more things together.

miz-zen (mĭz'n), *n.* the hindmost of the sails which run the length of a three-masted vessel: **mizzenmast,** the hindmost of the masts of a three-masted vessel.

miz-zle (mĭz'l), *v.i.* to rain in very tiny drops: *n.* fine rain.

mne-mon-ic (nē-mŏn'ĭk), *adj.* assisting the memory: *n.pl.* the art or science of assisting the memory; a system of rules, etc., intended to aid the memory.

moan (mōn), *v.i.* to utter a low sound from, or as from, pain or sorrow: *v.t.* to utter in a low wail: *n.* a low, prolonged sound expressing sorrow or pain.

moat (mōt), *n.* a deep ditch around a fortress, etc., usually containing water: *v.t.* to surround with a moat.

mob (mŏb), *n.* the common people; a rude, disorderly crowd; rabble: *v.t.* to attack in a disorderly crowd; crowd about and annoy.

mo-bile (mō'bĭl; mō'bēl), *adj.* easily moved; easily changed in expression under the influence of the feelings.

mo-bil-i-ty (mō-bĭl'ĭ-tĭ), *n.* moveableness; ease of motion.

mo-bil-i-za-tion (mō"bĭ-lĭ-zā'shŭn; mŏb"ĭ-lĭ-zā'shŭn), *n.* the act of calling (troops) into active service.

mo-bil-ize (mō'bĭ-līz; mŏb'ĭ-līz), *v.t.* to call (troops) into active service: *v.i.* to gather, as troops, and prepare for active service.

moc-ca-sin (mŏk'ȧ-sĭn), *n.* a deerskin sandal or shoe worn by the North American Indians; a poisonous American snake; a kind of wild orchid.

Mo-cha (mō'kȧ), *n.* a kind of coffee from Mocha, a seaport of Arabia.

mock (mŏk), *v.t.* to ridicule; imitate in sport or contempt; to make fun of; disappoint the hopes of; tantalize: *n.* ridicule; a scornful jest; an object of ridicule: *adj.* false; counterfeit.—*n.* **mocker.**

mock-er-y (mŏk'ẽr-ĭ), *n.* the act of making fun of (a person or thing); ridicule; impertinent imitation; derision; an empty sham.

mock-ing (mŏk'ĭng), *p.adj.* scornful; mimicking.—*adv.* **mockingly.**

mock-ing bird (mŏk'ĭng bûrd), an American thrush noted for imitating exactly the calls of other birds.

mod-al (mōd'ăl), *adj.* pertaining to a manner or form; in grammar, pertaining to the manner in which a verb expresses action: that is, whether it expresses fact, possibility, command, etc.

mode (mōd), *n.* form; custom; fashion; manner; in grammar, a change in the form of a verb to denote the manner of its action or being: called also *mood.*

mod-el (mŏd'ĕl), *n.* a pattern of something to be made, copied, or imitated; standard copy; a small-sized representation of something to be made, as an engine, building, etc.; a person who poses for a painter or sculptor; a woman who tries on costumes so that customers may see their effect: *v.t.* to form after a pattern, especially in clay, etc.: *v.i.* to practice shaping objects out of clay; to make designs: *adj.* serving as a pattern; worthy of being imitated.
Syn., *n.* design, mold, standard.

mod-el-ing (mŏd'ĕl-ing), *n.* the act or art of making a pattern, especially of a work of art in clay or similar material.

mod-er-ate (mŏd'ĕr-āt), *v.t.* to keep within bounds; lessen; to make less violent, intense, or extreme; as, to *moderate* rage, heat, etc.: *v.i.* to become less violent or intense: *adj.* (mŏd'ĕr-āt), kept within bounds; not extreme nor excessive; restrained; frugal; calm; reasonable; mild. —*adv.* **moderately.**—*n.* **moderateness.**
Syn., adj. temperate, abstemious, sober.
Ant. (see immoderate).

mod-er-a-tion (mŏd"ĕr-ā'shŭn), *n.* the act of keeping within bounds; freedom from excess; calmness of mind, speech, or feeling.

mod-er-a-tor (mŏd'ĕr-ā"tẽr), *n.* one who, or that which, regulates or restrains; the presiding officer in a Presbyterian church meeting.

mod-ern (mŏd'ẽrn), *adj.* pertaining to the present time; recent: *n.* a person of recent and present times: usually in plural.—*n.* **modernist.**

mod-ern-ism (mŏd'ẽr-nizm), *n.* a thing of recent date, especially a usage, a method, or a characteristic of present times: **Modernism,** a school of theology based on modern scholarship.

mod-ern-ize (mŏd'ẽr-nīz), *v.t.* to make like present usage, taste, or speech.

mod-est (mŏd'ĕst), *adj.* held back by a sense of what is fit and proper; retiring, rather than pushing oneself forward; not excessive or extreme; chaste.—*adv.* **modestly.**
Syn. virtuous, bashful, reserved.
Ant. (see immodest).

mod-es-ty (mŏd'ĕs-tĭ), *n.* regard for what is proper in behavior or manner; purity in word and act; proper reserve concerning one's own powers, etc.; freedom from what is extreme; as, *modesty* in dress; moderation.

mod-i-cum (mŏd'ĭ-kŭm), *n.* a little; a small quantity.

mod-i-fi-ca-tion (mŏd"ĭ-fĭ-kā'shŭn), *n.* a slight reduction; a slight change in form.

mod-i-fy (mŏd'ĭ-fī), *v.t.* [*p.t.* and *p.p.* modified, *p.pr.* modifying], to change slightly in form; vary; limit; reduce.

mod-ish (mōd'ĭsh), *adj.* fashionable; according to the latest manner; full of style.—*adv.* **modishly.**—*n.* **modishness.**

mo-diste (mō"dēst'), *n.* a fashionable dressmaker. [Fr.]

mod-u-late (mŏd'ū-lāt), *v.t.* to vary the sound of; to tone down; in music, to change the key of: *v.i.* to pass from one musical key to another.—*n.* **modulator.**

mod-u-la-tion (mŏd"ū-lā'shŭn), *n.* the act of changing the sound of; the state of being changed in sound; a toning down.

mo-gul (mō-gŭl'), *n.* a great personage: **Mogul,** a person of the Mongolian race; especially, one of the Mongols who conquered India in the 16th century; the ruler of their empire, called the *Great Mogul;* any imposing personage: *adj.* pertaining to the Mongolians.

mo-hair (mō'hâr"), *n.* a woven material made from the hair of the Angora goat; an imitation of such a material.

Mo-ham-med-an (mō-hăm'ĕd-ăn), *n.* a believer in Mohammedanism, a religion which teaches that Mohammed was the only prophet of God: *adj.* pertaining to Mohammed, or to Mohammedanism. Also, **Mahometan, Mahomedan.**

Mo-ha-ve (mō-hä'vē), *n.* one of a tribe of American Indians formerly living in the region around the mouth of the Colorado River.

Mo-hawk (mō'hôk), *n.* one of a tribe of American Indians; one of certain ruffians who, during the 17th and 18th centuries, annoyed persons walking in the streets of London, especially at night. Also, **Mohock.**

Mo-hi-can (mō-hē'kăn), *n.* one of a tribe of American Indians formerly living in Connecticut and New York.

moi-e-ty (moi'ĕ-tĭ), *n.* a half; a small portion.

moil (moil), *n.* drudgery; a spot or defilement: *v.i.* to toil; drudge; to labor.

moire (mwär; mōr), *n.* a watered silk or mohair fabric. Also, **moiré.**

moi-ré (mwä"rā'; mō'rā), *adj.* watered; having a clouded finish, as silk: *v.t.* to give a watered appearance to. [Fr.]

moist (moist), *adj.* containing water or other liquid; damp.—*n.* **moistness.**
Syn. wet, dank, liquid.

mois-ten (mois'n), *v.t.* and *v.i.* to make, or become, damp or slightly wet.

mois-ture (mois'tūr), *n.* a moderate degree of dampness; slight wetness.

mo-lar (mō'lår), *n.* a double tooth or grinder: *adj.* used for, and capable of, grinding.

mo-las-ses (mō-lăs'ĕz), *n.* the dark-colored, sticky syrup left in sugar making.

mold (mōld), *n.* a fine, soft soil, rich in decayed matter; the substance of which anything is composed; a discoloration or tiny growth produced on damp or decaying animal or vegetable matter; the cavity or vessel in which anything is cast or shaped: nature; shape: *v.t.* to cover with a musty growth; cause to become spoiled by a musty growth; fashion in, or as in, a mold or form; to form into a particular shape or according to a particular pattern: *v.i.* to become spoiled by a musty growth. Also, **mould.**

mold-er (mōl'dẽr), *v.t.* to cause to crumble away: *v.i.* to crumble to dust by natural decay; waste away by degrees: *n.* one who shapes something, or makes a form in which something is to be shaped. Also, **moulder.**

mold-ing (mōl'dĭng), *n.* the act of shaping in a form; anything made in or by a mold or form; an ornamental strip used on a wall, picture frame, etc. Also, **moulding.**

mold-y (mōl'dĭ), *adj.* covered with, or containing, a musty growth; musty. Also, **mouldy.**—*n.* **moldiness, mouldiness.**

mole (mōl), *n.* a dark-colored mark or small lump on the skin; a small, soft-furred, burrowing animal with minute eyes, often covered with skin; a mound or heavy work formed of large stones, etc., laid in the sea before a port to defend it from the force of the waves.

mo-lec-u-lar (mō-lĕk'ū-lår), *adj.* pertaining to, consisting of, produced by, or existing between, molecules.—*n.* **molecularity.**

mol-e-cule (mŏl'ē-kūl; mō'lē-kūl), *n.* the smallest quantity of any substance which can exist separately; a group of atoms acting as a physical unit.

mole-hill (mōl'hĭl"), *n.* a little mound made by the burrowing of a mole; a small hindrance or difficulty.

mole-skin (mōl'skĭn"), *n.* a cloth with a soft surface like a mole's fur; the fur of the mole, a small burrowing animal.

mo-lest (mō-lĕst'), *v.t.* to interfere with; trouble; disturb maliciously.

mo-les-ta-tion (mō'lĕs-tā'shŭn; mŏl"-ĕs-tā'shŭn), *n.* the act of annoying, interfering with, or troubling; hostile interference.

mol-li-fy (mŏl'ĭ-fī) *v.t.* [*p.t.* and *p.p.* mollified, *p.pr.* mollifying], to calm; soften; to make less severe, violent, or hard.—*n.* **mollifier, mollification.**

mol-lusk (mŏl'ŭsk), *n.* one of the Mollusca, or animals with soft, fleshy bodies, covered usually with shells containing lime, as the oyster, snail, etc.

Mo-loch (mō'lŏk), *n.* the fire god of the ancient Phœnicians and Ammonites, to whom human sacrifices were offered. Also, **Molech.**

molt (mōlt), *v.i.* to cast the feathers, hair, skin, etc.: *v.t.* to shed, as the hair. Also, **moult.**

mol-ten (mōl'tn), *adj.* melted; made of melted metal.

mo-lyb-de-num (mō-lĭb'dē-nŭm; mŏl'ĭb-dē'nŭm), *n.* a leadlike metallic element of the chromium group.

mo-ment (mō'mĕnt), *n.* the smallest possible portion of time; the present time; an instant; importance; as, affairs of great *moment;* the measure of a force by its effect in causing motion around a central point, as in a wheel; momentum.

mo-men-ta-ry (mō'mĕn-tā-rĭ), *adj.* lasting only for, or done in, an instant; transitory.—*adv.* **momentarily.** —*n.* **momentariness.**

mo-men-tous (mō-mĕn'tŭs), *adj.* very important; as, a *momentous* decision or occasion.

mo-men-tum (mō-mĕn'tŭm), *n.* the power of overcoming resistance, because of motion; the quantity of motion in a moving body; as, a body gathers *momentum* as it moves; the product of the mass and velocity of a moving body.

mon-ad (mŏn'ăd; mō'năd), *n.* a unit of matter, etc.; a simple being; one of the smallest and simplest of living creatures, supporting life in the water; a simple organism or cell.

mon-arch (mŏn'ârk), *n.* a supreme ruler; sovereign; the chief of its class or kind: *adj.* supreme.—*adj.* **monarchal.**

mo-nar-chic (mō-när'kĭk), *adj.* pertaining to a king or emperor or the government of a king or emperor. Also, **monarchical.**

mon-arch-ism (mŏn'ẽr-kĭzm), *n.* the principles underlying government by a king, emperor, etc.; preference for such government.

mon-arch-ist (mŏn'ẽr-kĭst), *n.* one who believes in, or supports, a government whose power is possessed by a king, emperor, etc.

mon-arch-y (mŏn'ẽr-kĭ), *n.* [*pl.* monarchies (-kĭz)], government in which the supreme power is possessed by a king or emperor; kingdom; empire.

mon-as-ter-y (mŏn'ăs-tẽr-ĭ), *n.* [*pl.* monasteries (-ĭz)], a home to which men retire under vows to devote their lives to religion.

mo-nas-tic (mō-năs'tĭk), *adj.* pertaining to religious houses called monasteries, to monks, their rules, etc. Also, **monastical.**—*adv.* **monastically.**

mo-nas-ti-cism (mō-năs'tĭ-sĭzm), *n.* the life, system, rules, or conditions of monasteries, or religious houses for men; as, *monasticism* was an important feature of the life of the Middle Ages.

Mon-day (mŭn'dā), *n.* the second day of the week.

mon-e-ta-ry (mŏn'ē-tā-rĭ; mŭn'ē-tā-rĭ), *adj.* of or pertaining to money.

mon-e-tize (mŏn'ē-tīz), *v.t.* to convert into money; to give a standard value to as money; as, to *monetize* silver.—*n.* **monetization.**

mon-ey (mŭn'ĭ), *n.* [*pl.* moneys (-ĭz)], coin; gold, silver, or other metal stamped by legal authority, and used as a means of exchange; anything, as bank notes, checks, drafts, etc., used as a means of exchange; wealth: **money order**, an order, usually sold by a post office, requesting the payment of money to the holder.

Syn. coin, currency, bullion.

mon-eyed (mŭn'ĭd), *adj.* possessed of money; wealthy.

mon-ger (mŭṅ'gẽr), *n.* a dealer; a trader: used in combinations; as, a fish*monger;* scandal*monger.*

Mon-gol (mŏṅ'gŏl), *adj.* pertaining to Mongolia, in Asia, or to its people, or to the yellow race: *n.* a member of the yellow race. Also, **Mongolian.**

Mon-go-li-an (mŏṅ-gō'lĭ-ăn), *adj.* denoting one of the five great races of mankind, the yellow race of Asia, including the Chinese, Tatars, etc.; pertaining to Mongolia or its natives: *n.* one of the yellow race.

mon-goose (mŏṅ'gōōs), *n.* [*pl.* mongooses (-ĕz)], a mammal of India, of about the size of a ferret, which kills poisonous snakes.

mon-grel (mŭṅ'grĕl; mŏṅ'grĕl), *adj.* of a mixed breed or kind: *n.* anything of mixed breed or kind.

mo-ni-tion (mō-nĭsh'ŭn), *n.* warning; notice.

mon-i-tor (mŏn'ĭ-tẽr), *n.* one who warns or advises; a senior pupil selected to instruct or oversee the younger ones; an ironclad warship, having low sides and one or more turrets mounted with guns; a kind of large lizard.

mon-i-to-ri-al (mŏn"ĭ-tō'rĭ-ăl), *adj.* pertaining to, or performed by, an adviser or guide.—*adv.* **monitorially.**

mon-i-to-ry (mŏn'ĭ-tō-rĭ), *adj.* giving warning or advice.

mon-i-tress (mŏn'ĭ-trĕs), *n.* a female adviser or guide. Also, **monitrix.**

monk (mŭṅk), *n.* a man who devotes himself to a religious life and lives with others bound as he is by vows of purity, obedience, and poverty.

monk-er-y (mŭṅk'ẽr-ĭ), *n.* life, practices, vows, and customs of those who have bound themselves by vows to a religious life: used usually as a reproach.

mon-key (mŭṅ'kĭ), *n.* [*pl.* monkeys (-kĭz)], in the broadest sense, any one of the highest order of animals below man; in the narrower sense, one of the smaller, long-tailed forms differing from the larger, nearly tailless forms, called apes; a name for various mechanical contrivances; a name of pretended ridicule, especially for one who is mischievous.

mon-key jack-et (mŭṅ'kĭ jăk'ĕt), a short, closely fitting thick coat worn by sailors.

mon-key wrench (mŭṅ'kĭ rĕnch), a tool with a movable jaw for turning a nut, bolt, etc.

monk-ish (mŭṅ'kĭsh), *adj.* pertaining to, or like, one who has bound himself by vows to a religious life; monastic.

monks-hood (mŭṅks'hŏŏd''), *n.* a plant, so called from the shape of its flower; wolfsbane.

mon-o-chrome (mŏn'ō-krōm), *n.* a painting in one color or in different shades of the same color.

mon-o-cle (mŏn'ō-kl), *n.* an eyeglass for one eye.

mo-noc-u-lar (mō-nŏk'ū-lẽr; mŏn-ŏk'-ū-lẽr), *adj.* fitted for use in one eye; one-eyed.

mon-o-dy (mŏn'ō-dĭ), *n.* a mournful poem or song for one voice.

mo-nog-a-mous (mō-nŏg'ȧ-mŭs), *adj.* having only one wife; pairing with a single mate, as the dove or eagle. Also, monogamic.—*n.* monogamist.

mo-nog-a-my (mō-nŏg'ȧ-mĭ), *n.* marriage with one wife only; the habit of pairing with a single mate.

mon-o-gram (mŏn'ō-grăm), *n.* a character formed by the interweaving of two or more letters.

mon-o-graph (mŏn'ō-grȧf), *n.* a paper written on one particular subject or some branch of it.

mon-o-lith (mŏn'ō-lĭth), *n.* a pillar or column formed of a single stone; a building material which is both fireproof and waterproof, and is used especially for floors.—*adj.* monolithic.

mon-o-log (mŏn'ō-lŏg), *n.* a dramatic scene in which only one person speaks; a lengthy speech by one person. Also, monologue.

mon-o-ma-ni-a (mŏn''ō-mā'nĭ-ȧ), *n.* insanity in regard to one subject only; a craze.

mon-o-ma-ni-ac (mŏn''ō-mā'nĭ-ăk), *n.* one affected with insanity on one subject: *adj.* insane on one subject only; pertaining to such insanity.

mon-o-met-al-lism (mŏn''ō-mĕt'ăl-ĭzm), *n.* the use of one metal only as the standard of value of money.

mo-no-mi-al (mō-nō'mĭ-ăl), *adj.* in algebra consisting of a single term: *n.* an expression containing one term.

mon-o-plane (mŏn'ō-plān), *n.* a flying machine whose main supporting surface is a single wing on each side of the body.

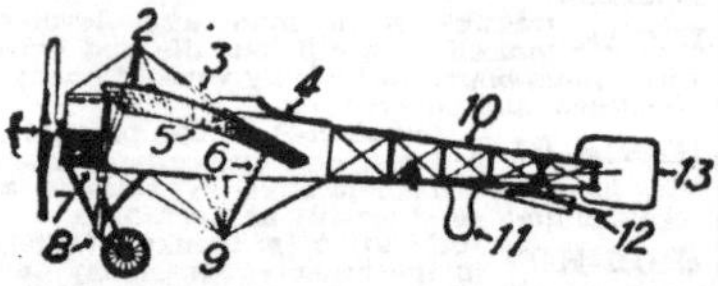

Two-seated Monoplane. 1, propeller; 2, guy post; 3, pilot's seat; 4, passenger seat; 5, wings; 6, warping stays; 7, revolving engine; 8, landing gear; 9, guy post; 10, fuselage; 11, tail skid; 12, elevator; 13, rudder.

mo-nop-o-list (mō-nŏp'ō-lĭst), *n.* one who, alone, or in connection with others, takes complete possession, or control of any interest, or any branch of trade, commerce, transportation, or production.

mo-nop-o-lize (mō-nŏp'ō-līz), *v.t.* to gain possession of so as to be the only producer or trader; to take the whole of; as, to *monopolize* the attention of another.—*n.* monopolization.

mo-nop-o-ly (mō-nŏp'ō-lĭ), *n.* a control of any industry; as, an oil company has a *monopoly* of the oil trade in the United States; a company that possesses such control; the sole possession of anything.

mon-o-rail (mŏn'ō-rāl''), *n.* in a railway system, a single rail on which cars are run: used also for a hanging car.

mon-o-syl-lab-ic (mŏn''ō-sĭ-lăb'ĭk), *adj.* not divided, as a word, in pronouncing; composed of one-syllabled words, or those that are not divided into parts in pronouncing.

mon-o-syl-la-ble (mŏn''ō-sĭl'ȧ-bl), *n.* a word of one syllable, or a word which is not divided into parts in pronouncing it.

mon-o-the-ism (mŏn'ō-thē-ĭzm), *n.* the doctrine of, or belief in, the existence of one God.—*n.* monotheist.

mon-o-tone (mŏn'ō-tōn), *n.* recitation on a single note or key; lack of variety in the style of a written composition: *v.t.* to recite (as prayers) on a single note; intone.

mo-not-o-nous (mō-nŏt'ō-nŭs), *adj.* continued in the same tone; wearisome; tedious; without variety.

mo-not-o-ny (mō-nŏt'ō-nĭ), *n.* dull sameness of tone; unvarying or tiresome sameness.

mon-o-type (mŏn'ō-tīp), *n.* a typesetting machine that sets single letters, instead of words and lines.

Mon-roe Doc-trine (mŭn-rō' dŏk'-trĭn), a principle announced by President Monroe and followed till 1917, by which the United States insisted upon mutual noninterference between Europe and the republics of America.

mon-sei-gneur (mŏṅ''sē''nyûr'') *n.* [*pl.* messeigneurs (mā''sē'-nyûr'')], formerly, a title in France given to persons of high birth or rank, especially to the heir to the throne: equivalent to *My lord*; a title of French bishops. [Fr.]

mon-sieur (mē''syû'; m'syû''), *n.* [*pl.* messieurs (mĕ''syû')], a French title of courtesy, equivalent to *Sir* or *Mr.*; formerly, the title of the eldest brother of the King of France: capitalized when used with a proper name. [Fr.]

mon-si-gnor (mŏn-sē'nyŏr; It. mŏn''sē-nyŏr''), *n.* [*pl.* monsignori (-rē)], a title conferred by the Pope on priests of the papal household: equivalent to *Lord*. [It.]

mon-soon (mŏn-sōōn''), *n.* a wind in the Indian Ocean blowing from the southwest from April to October, and from the northeast during the other part of the year; the rainy season that accompanies the former.

mon-ster (mŏn'stẽr), *n.* any animal or thing out of the usual course of nature; something very huge or remarkably deformed or hideous; a person remarkable for extreme wickedness, cruelty, etc.: *adj.* of unusual size.

mon-strance (mŏn′străns), *n.* one of the altar vessels in the Roman Catholic Church.

mon-stros-i-ty (mŏn-strŏs′ĭ-tĭ), *n.* [*pl.* monstrosities (-tĭz)], the state or quality of being deformed or hideous or extremely unusual; anything unnaturally huge, hideous, or deformed.

mon-strous (mŏn′strŭs), *adj.* out of the common course of nature; enormous; huge; horrible; hideous; causing disgust.—*adv.* monstrously.
Syn. shocking, dreadful, hateful, immense.

mon-te (mŏn′tā; mōn′tā), *n.* a Spanish gambling game played with dice or cards.

Mon-tes-so-ri meth-od (mŏn″tĕs-sō′rē mĕth′-ŭd), a system of training and instruction for small children, in which emphasis is placed upon freedom for physical activity, individual instruction, and the early development of various activities, as that of writing: developed by Doctor Maria Montessori.

month (mŭnth), *n.* one of the twelve parts into which the year is divided, each containing about four weeks, or 28 to 31 days.

month-ly (mŭnth′lĭ), *adj.* continued for a month; as, the *monthly* course of the moon around the earth: performed, happening, or published once a month; as, a *monthly* bill; a *monthly* magazine: *adv.* once each month; as, the magazine is issued *monthly*: *n.* a magazine or periodical published each month.

mon-u-ment (mŏn′ū-mĕnt), *n.* anything that keeps alive the memory of a person or event, as a pillar, a statue, an arch, a tomb, etc.
Syn. memorial, record, remembrancer, cenotaph.

mon-u-men-tal (mŏn″ū-mĕn′tăl), *adj.* serving, or fitted, to keep alive the memory of a person or event; of lasting greatness; as, Milton's *Paradise Lost* is a *monumental* work.—*adv.* monumentally.

moo (mōō), *n.* the lowing of a cow: *v.i.* to make the noise of a cow; low.

mood (mōōd), *n.* manner; temper of mind; change in the form of a verb to express the manner of action or being.
Syn. humor, disposition, vein.

mood-y (mōōd′ĭ), *adj.* [*comp.* moodier, *superl.* moodiest], absent-minded and thoughtful; out of temper; sad; gloomy; given to changes in the state of mind or temper.—*adv.* moodily.—*n.* moodiness.

moon (mōōn), *n.* the heavenly body that revolves round the earth; the heavenly body that revolves about any planet; a month; as, it is many *moons* since he went away: *v.i.* to wander and look about in an absent-minded and listless manner.—*adj.* moony.

moon-beam (mōōn′bēm″), *n.* a ray of light from the moon.

moon-light (mōōn′līt″), *n.* the light given by the moon: *adj.* lighted by the moon; occurring by moonlight; as, a *moonlight* flitting.

moon-sail (mōōn′sāl″), *n.* a light sail carried above the skysail: called also *moonraker*.

moon-shine (mōōn′shīn″), *n.* moonlight; empty show; colloquially, liquor smuggled or made against the law.

moon-shin-er (mōōn′shīn″ẽr), *n.* one who makes whisky without a government license; a smuggler of whisky. [COLLOQ.]

moon-stone (mōōn′stōn″), *n.* a stone of yellowish or yellow-white color, showing beautiful pearly reflections.

moon-struck (mōōn′strŭk″), *adj.* mentally deranged through the supposed influence of the moon.

moor (mōōr), *n.* in England, a broad tract of waste land covered with heather or certain kinds of shrubs, bushes, etc., sometimes marshy or peaty; a moorland: *v.t.* to fasten (a ship) in a particular place by a cable and anchor: *v.i.* to be secured by a cable and anchor.—**Moor**, *n.* a native of Morocco, in North Africa; in the Middle Ages, one of the Saracens who invaded and settled in Spain.

moor-age (mōōr′āj), *n.* a place for anchoring or fastening a vessel.

moor cock (mōōr kŏk), the male of the red grouse or partridge. Also, moor fowl.

moor-ing (mōōr′ĭng), *n.* the act of fastening a vessel to a particular place; the cables, anchors, etc. laid at the bottom of a harbor, to which a vessel is fastened: *pl.* the place where a vessel is anchored.

moor-ish (mōōr′ĭsh), *adj.* resembling, or growing on, a waste land or heath; marshy; as, *moorish* soil.—**Moorish**, pertaining to, or in the fashion of, the Moors of North Africa or, formerly, of Spain.

moor-land (mōōr′lănd), *n.* waste land covered with heath and shrubs.

moose (mōōs), *n.* a large North American deer resembling the European elk.

Moose

moot (mōōt), *v.t.* to propose for discussion; to discuss: *v.i.* to argue: *n.* discussion of a mock law-case for practice: *adj.* open to discussion or debate; as, a *moot* question.

mop (mŏp), *n.* an implement for washing floors, decks, etc., consisting of a bundle of cloth, rags, etc., fastened to the end of a long handle; a similar loose tangled bunch; as, a *mop* of hair: *v.t.* [*p.t.* and *p.p.* mopped, *p.pr.* mopping], to rub or dry with a mop.

mope (mōp), *n.* one who is dull or out of spirits: *v.i.* to be silent, dull, or out of spirits.

mo-quette (mō-kĕt′), *n.* a carpet with long, velvety fibers.

mo-raine (mō-rān′), *n.* a line of rocks and gravel at the edges and base of glaciers.

mor-al (mŏr′ăl), *n.* the lesson taught by, or the inner meaning of, a fable, event, etc.; *pl.* moral conduct or teachings; conduct of life; behavior: *adj.* pertaining to man's natural sense of what is right and proper; according to what is right and just; as, a *moral* life; capable of being governed by a sense of right and wrong; as, a lower animal is not a *moral* creature; virtuous; supported by reason; as, a *moral* certainty; serving to teach a lesson.—*adv.* morally.

mo-rale (mō-răl′), *n.* moral condition; that mental state which makes men capable of endurance and of showing courage in the presence of danger; as, the *morale* of an army.

mo-ral-i-ty (mô-răl'ĭ-tĭ), *n.* [*pl.* moralities (-tĭz)], the teaching or practice of the duties of life; virtue; formerly, a kind of play intended to teach a lesson, and representing such characters as Faith, Love, etc.

mor-al-ize (mŏr'ăl-īz), *v.t.* to apply or explain in a way that teaches a lesson; as, to *moralize* a story; make virtuous: *v.i.* to talk at length about right and wrong, duty, goodness, etc.—*n.* **moralizer, moralization.**

mor-al phi-los-o-phy (mŏr'ăl fĭ-lŏs'-ō-fĭ), the science and study of right and wrong.

mo-rass (mô-răs'), *n.* a swamp; a tract of wet ground.

mor-a-to-ri-um (mŏr-*ȧ*-tō'rĭ-ŭm'), *n.* a period established by law, during which a debtor may suspend payment of his obligations.

Mo-ra-vi-an (mô-rā'vĭ-ăn), *n.* a native of Moravia; a member of the sect of United Brethren: *adj.* pertaining to Moravia, in Austro-Hungary, or to its people; pertaining to a religious sect, the Moravians, or United Brethren.

mor-bid (môr'bĭd), *adj.* pertaining to, or caused by, disease; sickly; unhealthy; mentally gloomy or unwholesome. —*adv.* **morbidly.**—*n.* **morbidness.**

Syn. ailing, diseased, corrupt.
Ant. (see normal, sound).

mor-bid-i-ty (môr-bĭd'ĭ-tĭ), *n.* a sickly or unhealthy state of mind or body.

mor-dant (môr'dănt), *n.* a substance that serves to fix certain colors in dyeing; a substance to make gold leaf stick; a substance that eats into a surface: *adj.* having power to fix colors; sarcastic; biting.

more (mōr), *adj.* [*superl.* most], *comp.* of *many* and *much;* greater in number, quality, extent, etc.; additional; longer: *adv.* to a greater degree, etc.; again; besides: *n.* a greater quantity, number, etc.; something further or additional.

mo-reen (mô-rēn'), *n.* a stout woolen material, usually watered or figured.

more-o-ver (mōr-ō'vẽr), *adv.* besides; further; also.

Mo-resque (mô-rĕsk'), *n.* Moorish decoration or architecture: *adj.* decorated in the style of the Moors or Arabs; Moorish.

mor-ga-nat-ic (môr'g*ȧ*-năt'ĭk), *adj.* relating to the marriage of a man of royal or other high rank with a woman of lower degree, whose children cannot inherit their father's rank.

morgue (môrg), *n.* a place where the bodies of unknown persons found dead are left until recognized and claimed by friends or relatives.

mor-i-bund (mŏr'ĭ-bŭnd), *adj.* in a dying condition.

mo-ri-on (mō'rĭ-ŏn), *n.* an open helmet somewhat like a hat.

Mo-ris-co (mô-rĭs'kō), *n.* a Moor, usually a Christianized Moor, living in Spain after the Moorish power there was overthrown; the language of the Moriscos.

Mor-mon (môr'mŭn), *n.* a member of the sect, called also *Latter Day Saints*, founded in 1830 by Joseph Smith, who declared that he had found in the United States the Book of Mormon, which, it is claimed, is a sacred history of the ancient inhabitants of America: *adj.* of or pertaining to this sect.

Mor-mon-ism (môr'mŭn-ĭzm), *n.* the doctrines and practices of the Mormons.

morn-ing (môr'nĭng), *n.* the early part of the day; any early part; as, the *morning* of life: *adj.* pertaining to, occurring, or performed in, the early part of the day, or before noon.

morn-ing-glo-ry (môr'nĭng-glō'rĭ), *n.* a twining plant with heart-shaped leaves and funnel-shaped flowers, blue, pink, or white in color.

morn-ing watch (môr'nĭng wŏch), watch on shipboard from four A. M. to eight A. M.

Mo-ro (mō'rō), *n.* [*pl.* Moros (-rōz)], a native Mohammedan inhabitant of the southern Philippines; the language of the Moros.

mo-roc-co (mô-rŏk'ō), *n.* a fine kind of grained leather of goatskin: so called because first prepared in Morocco, Africa.

mor-on (mō'rŏn), *n.* a person whose mental development has been arrested at the point reached by the normal child of about twelve years.

mo-rone (mô-rōn'), *n.* a dark crimson color. Also, **maroon.**

mo-rose (mô-rōs'), *adj.* sullen; haughty; gloomy; as, a *morose* temper.—*adv.* **morosely.**—*n.* **moroseness.**

Syn. surly, fretful, crabbed.
Ant. (see joyous).

mor-phine (môr'fĭn; môr'fēn), *n.* a substance found in opium which has the power to deaden feeling and produce sleep. Also, **morphin, morphia.**

mor-phin-ism (môr'fĭn-ĭzm), *n.* a diseased state caused by the use of morphine, a drug obtained from opium.

mor-pho-log-i-cal (môr'fō-lŏj'ĭ-kăl), *adj.* pertaining to the science that treats of the form and structure of plants and animals. Also, **morphologic.**—*adv.* **morphologically.**

mor-phol-o-gy (môr-fŏl'ō-jĭ), *n.* that branch of science which deals with the form and structure of plants and animals.

mor-ris (mŏr'ĭs), *n.* a Moorish dance with tambourines, bells, etc., common in Old English parades and revels; an old game played with men and counters on squares. Also, **morrice.**

mor-row (mŏr'ō), *n.* the next day after any day specially mentioned; to-morrow; formerly, morning; as, good *morrow*, friend.

morse (môrs), *n.* a clasp for fastening a long circular garment worn on special occasions by a priest.

mor-sel (môr'sĕl), *n.* a bite; a mouthful; a small amount of anything; as, a *morsel* of bread; a *morsel* of comfort.

mort (môrt), *n.* a note or notes sounded on a hunting horn to announce that the game has been killed.

mor-tal (môr'tăl), *n.* a human being; man, as subject to death: *adj.* subject to death; as, *mortal* man; causing death; as, a *mortal* wound or illness; punishable with death; as, a *mortal* sin; filled with desire to kill; as, a *mortal* enemy; violent; extreme; as, *mortal* fear; pertaining to human beings.—*adv.* **mortally.**

Syn., adj. deadly, fatal, human.
Ant. (see immortal).

mor-tal-i-ty (mŏr-tăl′ĭ-tĭ), *n.* the condition of being subject to death; human nature; frequency or number of deaths in proportion to population.

mor-tar (môr′tẽr), *n.* a vessel in which substances are pounded with an implement called a pestle, chiefly used in making medicines; a short cannon used for throwing shells high upward, so as to drop from above on to the object aimed at; a building cement of lime, sand, and water: *v.t.* to plaster or secure with such building cement.

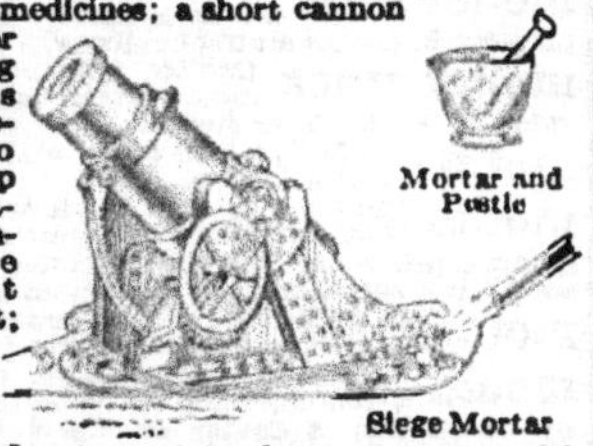

Mortar and Pestle

Siege Mortar

mor-tar board (môr′tẽr bōrd), a flat, square board supported by a handle, for holding mortar; a scholar's flat-topped cap.

mort-gage (môr′gāj), *n.* a giving over of property, as security for the payment of a debt, to become void when the debt is paid; as, a *mortgage* on a house; the legal paper making such a pledge of property: *v.t.* to make over property, etc., as security to one to whom a debt is owed; to pledge.

mort-ga-gee (môr″gā-jē′), *n.* the person to whom property is given as security.

mort-ga-gor (môr″gā-jôr′), *n.* the person who gives property as security. Also, **mortgageor, mortgager.**

mor-ti-fi-ca-tion (môr″tĭ-fĭ-kā′shŭn), *n.* the act of humbling or depressing; the death of one part of an animal body while the rest continues to live; a condition called gangrene; the subduing of the passions and appetites by self-denial; humiliation, or its cause; vexation.

mor-ti-fy (môr′tĭ-fī), *v.t.* [*p.t.* and *p.p.* mortified, *p.pr.* mortifying], to subdue by self-denial, etc.; as, to *mortify* the appetites; humble; humiliate; depress; cause (a part of the body) to decay, or undergo gangrene: *v.i.* to lose all living functions, as an injured part of the body; to be affected with gangrene.

mor-tise (môr′tĭs), *n.* a hole made in wood through which some corresponding part fits: *v.t.* to join, as timbers, by putting a projecting part into a hole made to fit. Also, **mortice.**

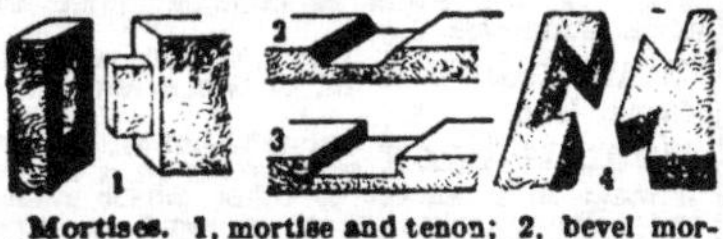

Mortises. 1, mortise and tenon; 2, bevel mortise; 3, right-angled mortise; 4, dovetail mortise.

mort-main (môrt′mān″), *n.* possession of lands or tenements by any organized body of persons.

mor-tu-a-ry (môr′tū-ā-rĭ), *n.* [*pl.* mortuaries (-rĭz)], a building for the dead awaiting burial: *adj.* pertaining to the burial of the dead.

mo-sa-ic (mô-zā′ĭk), *n.* a design, or form of artistic work, made by the union of very tiny pieces of glass, stone, etc., of various colors, inlaid in a ground of stucco or metal: *adj.* pertaining to, or consisting of, such work.—**Mosaic,** pertaining to Moses, to the laws, institutions, etc., given through him, or to his writings.

Mo-selle (mô-zĕl′), *n.* a mild white wine made in the valley of the Moselle.

Mo-ses (mō′zĕz), *n.* the great prophet and lawgiver of the Israelites who led them out of Egypt; hence, any great leader; a meek man.

Mos-lem (mŏz′lĕm; mŏs′lĕm), *n.* [*pl.* Moslems (-lĕmz)], a follower of the religion founded by Mohammed; a Mohammedan: *adj.* pertaining to Mohammedans, or a people who believe that Mohammed was the true prophet of God. Also, **Mussulman.**

mosque (mŏsk), *n.* a Mohammedan temple. Also, **mosk.**

mos-qui-to (mŏs-kē′tō), *n.* [*pl.* mosquitoes (-tōz)], an insect the females of which puncture the skin of men and animals, at times depositing disease germs.

moss (mŏs), *n.* a natural order of soft plants growing on the ground, rocks, trees, etc., and having simple narrow leaves; a lichen; a soft peaty swamp.

moss-y (mŏs′ĭ), *adj.* covered with, or like, moss, a tiny soft plant.—*n.* **mossiness.**

most (mōst), *adj.* superlative of *more;* greatest in number, quantity, or degree: *n.* the greatest number, part, quality, or value.

mot (mō), *n.* a witty saying; a bon mot; a bugle note. [Fr.]

mote (mōt), *n.* formerly, in England, an assembly for the discussion and management of public affairs; a very small particle; as, *motes* of dust in a sunbeam; a black spot in wool.

moth (mŏth), *n.* an insect which feeds upon cloth, fur, etc.; a four-winged insect somewhat like the butterfly, but flying chiefly at night.

moth-eat-en (mŏth′ēt″ĕn), *p.adj.* damaged by moths; having holes made by moths, as cloth.

moth-er (mŭ*th*′ẽr), *n.* a female parent, especially one of the human race; one who has given birth to anything; origin or source; as, necessity is the *mother* of invention; the female superior of a religious house; a thick, slimy substance or film in liquids: *v.t.* to act as a mother to, or to adopt, as a son or daughter: **Mother's Day,** a day appointed for the honoring of motherhood: instituted by Miss Anna Jarvis, of Philadelphia, who appointed the second Sunday in May, or for schools the second Friday, as the day, and designated the white carnation as the emblem: *adj.* native; as, one's *mother* tongue; producing others.

Moth-er Goose (mŭ*th*′ẽr gōōs), the pen name of the compiler of a collection of well-known, simple nursery rimes.

moth-er-hood (mŭ*th*′ẽr-hŏŏd), *n.* the state of being a mother; maternity.

moth-er-in-law (mŭ*th*′ẽr-ĭn-lô″), *n.* the mother of a husband or wife.

moth-er-less (mŭ*th*′ẽr-lĕs), *adj.* without a mother living.

moth-er-ly (mŭth'ẽr-lĭ), *adj.* tender and kind like a mother.

moth-er-of-pearl (mŭth'ẽr-ŏv-pûrl'), *n.* the hard, silvery inner layer of various kinds of shells.

moth-er wit (mŭth'ẽr wĭt), natural good sense; quick common sense or humor.

moth-y (mŏth'ĭ), *adj.* full of moths, or insects that feed on cloth, fur, etc.; moth-eaten.

mo-tif (mō'tēf'), *n.* the central and controlling idea of a work of art or literature. Also, **motive.** [Fr.]

mo-tion (mō'shŭn), *n.* the act, process, or state of changing place; the changing of position; a gesture; action, as opposed to rest; impulse or desire; a formal proposal made in a meeting of a society, etc.; as, a *motion* to adjourn is in order: *v.i.* to make a movement or gesture full of meaning; as, to *motion* to someone to come forward: *v.t.* to guide or invite by a gesture; as, to *motion* someone to come forward.—*adj.* **motionless.**

Syn., *n.* proposition, proposal, movement.

mo-tion pic-ture (mō'shŭn pĭk'tūr), a series of pictures of persons and things in action, taken by a special machine and thrown on a screen in such rapid succession as to form a continuous picture in which the action is reproduced. Also, **moving picture.**

mo-tive (mō'tĭv), *n.* that which urges to action; inducement; as, love of country is the *motive* that sends many men to war; reason; in art, a leading idea; in music, a passage which is repeated again and again in a composition: *adj.* causing action; as, steam is the *motive* power in the locomotive; able to change place or position.

mo-ti-vate (mō'tĭ-vāt), *v.t.* to act as an impulse or incentive for.

mo-tive pow-er (mō'tĭv pou'ẽr), any natural agent, as wind, water, steam, electricity, used to produce action in a machine.

mot-ley (mŏt'lĭ), *adj.* consisting of different colors; wearing party-colored clothing; as, "A *motley* fool"; composed of different kinds; as, a *motley* crew or crowd.

mo-tor (mō'tẽr), *n.* that which produces action or power; especially, a machine or engine which causes action; as, an electric *motor;* an automobile: *adj.* imparting action; as, *motor* nerves: *v.i.* to travel by automobile.

Electric Motor

mo-tor boat (mō'tẽr bōt), a boat moved by a gasoline or other small engine.

mo-tor bus (mō'tẽr bŭs), an automobile passenger car. Also, **motor-bus.**

mo-tor car (mō'tẽr kär), a vehicle with a small engine driven by means of oil, electricity, etc. Also, **motor-car.**

mo-tor cy-cle (mō'tẽr sī'kl), a bicycle moved by a small engine. Also, **motor-cycle.**

mo-tor-ize (mō'tẽr-īz), *v.t.* to put motor-driven vehicles in, in place of horses and horse-drawn vehicles, as in a city fire department.—*n.* **motorization.**

mo-tor lor-ry (mō'tẽr lŏr'ĭ; lŏr'ĭ), a long, low, motor-driven truck with a roomy platform somewhat overhanging the four wheels. Also, **motor lorrie.**

mo-tor-man (mō'tẽr-măn), *n.* one who drives a motor, especially an electric car on a street railway.

mo-tor truck (mō'tẽr trŭk), a heavy, motor-driven van for carrying bulky loads or freight.

mot-tle (mŏt'l), *v.t.* to mark with spots of various colors.

mot-to (mŏt'ō), *n.* [*pl.* mottoes (-ōz)], a brief sentence suggesting some guiding principle; as, "to be rather than to seem" is a suitable *motto* for a class in school.

mou-jik (mōō-zhĭk'), *n.* a Russian peasant. Also, **mushik.** [Russ.]

mould (mōld), *n.* a fine, soft, rich soil; a discoloration or growth caused by dampness; a cavity or vessel in which anything is shaped: *v.t.* to cover with a damp growth; to fashion or form into a particular shape: *v.i.* to become covered with a tiny growth caused by dampness. Also, **mold.**

mould-er (mōl'dẽr), *v.i.* to crumble into dust gradually: *v.t.* to cause to crumble away: *n.* one who shapes something, or makes a form for shaping something. Also, **molder.**

moult (mōlt), *v.i.* to shed or cast off the hair, feathers, or outer layer of skin: *v.t.* to shed and renew, as feathers: *n.* the act or season of shedding feathers, etc. Also, **molt.**

mound (mound), *n.* an artificial bank of earth or stone, originally for defensive purposes; a small hill; a small jeweled globe topped by a cross, which is a sign of empire: *v.t.* to furnish, or fortify, with a bank of earth, etc.; to heap up into a ridge or hillock.

mount (mount), *n.* a hill or mountain; a rocky mass or elevation rising above the level of the surrounding land; a horse suitable for riding; cardboard on which a drawing is fixed: *v.t.* to raise on high; climb; go up; bestride, as a horse; furnish with horses; prepare for use by fixing on, or in, something else; as, to *mount* a photograph on a card: *v.i.* to rise or increase; to tower; get on horseback; go up, as on a platform.

Syn., *v.* arise, soar, climb, scale.

moun-tain (moun'tĭn), *n.* a large mass of rock or earth rising above the level of the surrounding country, usually over two thousand feet; anything very large.

moun-tain-eer (moun'tĭ-nēr'), *n.* one who dwells among, or climbs, mountains, or great elevations of land; as, the Swiss *mountaineers:* *v.i.* to climb mountains.

moun-tain-ous (moun'tĭ-nŭs), *adj.* full of, or like, great elevations of land.

moun-te-bank (moun'tē-băṅk), *n.* one who stands on a bench or stage in a market or other public place, and sells remedies which pretend to cure diseases; a boastful pretender.

mount-ed (moun'tĕd), *p.adj.* seated or serving on horseback; as, *mounted* police; raised on a suitable support.

mount-ing (moun'tĭng), *n.* the act of rising or climbing or of getting on horseback; the act of placing on cardboard, decorating, or preparing for use; the preparation of specimens to be looked at under the microscope; the cardboard or other means by which anything is prepared for exhibition or use; the ornaments on harness, etc.

mourn (mōrn), *v.i.* to grieve or be sorrowful: *v.t.* to grieve for; to lament.
Syn. bemoan, bewail, sorrow, deplore.
Ant. (see rejoice).

mourn-er (mōrn'ẽr), *n.* one who grieves; one who attends a funeral.

mourn-ful (mōrn'fōōl), *adj.* causing, or expressing, sorrow; doleful. —*adv.* mournfully.—*n.* mournfulness.
Syn. sad, sorrowful, lugubrious, grievous, heavy.
Ant. (see happy).

mourn-ing (mōrn'ing), *n.* expression of grief; lamentation; a special garb, such as black clothes, worn as a sign of grief for one who has died.

mouse (mous), *n.* [*pl.* mice (mīs)], a small animal with teeth formed for gnawing, that infests houses, granaries, etc.: *v.i.* (mouz), to watch for or catch mice; watch for something in a sly manner; pry curiously: *v.t.* to tear, as a cat tears a mouse. —*n.* mouser.

mousse-line de laine (mōōs'lēn' dẽ lĕn'), [a very light woolen dress material. [Fr.]

mousse-line de soie (mōōs'lēn' dẽ swŏ), a very thin silk fabric, similar to chiffon. [Fr.]

mous-tache (mŭs-tȧsh'), *n.* the hair growing on the upper lip. Also, mustache.

mouth (mouth), *n.* the opening in the head of an animal through which it receives food and utters sounds; an opening through which to go in or out; as, the *mouth* of a cave; an opening for putting anything in or out; as, the *mouth* of a bottle; instrument of speaking; grimace: *v.t.* (mou*th*) to utter with a swelling or pompous voice; to seize in the mouth; as, a dog *mouths* a bone: *v.i.* to make faces.—*n.* mouther.

mouth-ful (mouth'fōōl), *n.* [*pl.* mouthfuls (-fōōlz)], as much as can be put into the mouth at one time; small quantity.

mouth-piece (mouth'pēs'), *n.* that part of an instrument which is held in, or applied to, the mouth; as, the *mouthpiece* of a cornet; one who speaks for others.

mov-a-ble (mōōv'ȧ-bl), *adj.* capable of being changed or carried from one place or position to another; changing from one time to another; as, Easter is a *movable* feast: *n.pl.* goods, wares, or furniture that can be carried from place to place. Also, moveable.—*adv.* movably.

mov-a-ble feasts (mōōv'ȧ-bl fēsts), certain church festivals, the dates of which are determined by Easter.

move (mōōv), *v.t.* to cause to change place or position in any way; set in action; rouse to action; influence; to stir the feelings of; propose formally, as in a meeting, etc.: *v.i.* to change place or position; go from place to place; change posture slightly; to begin to act; take action; change the place where one lives; in chess or checkers, to change the place of a piece: *n.* the act of changing place or position; change of position; in chess or checkers, the right or turn to change the place of a piece; an act in carrying out a plan; scheme.
Syn., *v.* actuate, induce, prompt, instigate, persuade, propel, push.

move-ment (mōōv'mĕnt), *n.* the act of changing place; any change of place or position; a series of acts and events which progress toward a desired end or aim; as, the temperance *movement*; the delicate wheelworks of a watch or clock; any single part in a musical composition; the act of throwing wastes from the body through the bowels.

mov-ie (mōōv'ĭ), *n.* popular name for a motion picture or a motion picture theater: usually in plural. [Colloq.]

mov-ing (mōōv'ing), *p.adj.* changing place or position; as, a *moving* shadow; causing action; stirring the feelings or affections; pathetic: *n.* movement; the act of changing one's residence.

mov-ing pic-ture (mōōv'ing pĭk'tūr), a series of pictures of persons and things in action, taken by a special machine and thrown on a screen in such rapid succession as to form a continuous picture in which the action is reproduced. Also, motion picture.

mow (mō), *v.t.* [*p.t.* mowed, *p.p.* mowed, mown, *p.pr.* mowing], to cut down with, or as with, a scythe or a machine: *v.i.* to cut grass, etc., with a scythe or a machine. —*n.* mower.

mow (mou), *n.* a heap of hay, etc., stowed in a barn; the compartment in a barn where hay, etc., are stowed: *v.t.* to stow in a special place in a barn.

mow-ing (mō'ing), *n.* the act of cutting grass with a scythe or a machine; meadow land.

mown (mōn), *p.adj.* cut down, as with a scythe or machine; as, new *mown* hay.

Mr. (mĭs'tẽr), the abbreviated form of the title Mister.

Mrs. (mĭs'ĭz), the abbreviated form of the title Mistress.

much (mŭch), *adj.* [*comp.* more, *superl.* most], great in quantity or amount; as, *much* wealth; long in duration; as, *much* time: *adv.* to a great degree or extent; as, to be *much* obliged; nearly: *n.* a great quantity; something considerable or unusual.

mu-ci-lage (mū'sĭ-lāj), *n.* a gummy fluid used to stick things together; a gum of certain plants.

mu-ci-lag-i-nous (mū'sĭ-lăj'ĭ-nŭs), *adj.* pertaining to, resembling, or producing, a gummy fluid; sticky.

muck (mŭk), *n.* moist manure; anything filthy or vile: *v.t.* to manure; to soil with filth.—*adj.* mucky.

muck-rake (mŭk'rāk'), *v.i.* to seek for and expose wrongdoing on the part of public men.—*n.* muckraker.

muck-worm (mŭk'wûrm'), *n.* a grub or worm bred in manure; a miser.

mu-cous (mū'kŭs), *adj.* pertaining to, resembling, or producing, mucus, a sticky fluid given off by the moist lining of the cavities and canals of the human body; sticky or slimy.

mu-cous mem-brane (mū'kŭs mĕm'-brān), the moist lining of the cavities and canals of the human body.

mu-cus (mū'kŭs), *n.* the ropy, sticky fluid given off by the moist lining of the cavities and canals of the human body; a gummy or slimy substance found in certain plants.

mud (mŭd), *n.* soft, wet earth; mire: *v.t.* to soil with soft, wet earth.

mud-dle (mŭd'l), *n.* a confused state; mental dulness or confusion: *v.t.* to make a mess of; to confuse, cloud, or stupefy; make partially drunk; spend recklessly: *v.i.* to act in a confused or stupid way.

mud-dy (mŭd'ĭ), *adj.* full of, or covered with, soft, wet earth; as, a *muddy* stream; *muddy* roads; clouded; confused; as, *muddy* ideas: *v.t.* to make dirty, befoul.—*adv.* **muddily.**—*n.* **muddiness.**

mud-sill (mŭd'sĭl"), *n.* the foundation timber of a building placed on the ground.

mu-ez-zin (mū-ĕz'ĭn), *n.* a Mohammedan public crier who, from the tower of a mosque, calls the people to prayer.

muff (mŭf), *n.* a warm soft cover of fur, etc., to keep the hands warm in cold weather; a stupid, spiritless fellow; in baseball, failure to hold a ball when catching it: *v.t.* to handle awkwardly; fail to hold (a ball) when catching.

muf-fin (mŭf'ĭn), *n.* a soft, light, spongy round cake, usually eaten hot with butter.

muf-fle (mŭf'l), *v.t.* to wrap up closely and warmly; to keep from seeing, hearing, or speaking by wrapping up the head; cover up so as to deaden the sound of; as, to *muffle* a bell; *v.i.* to speak indistinctly: *n.* anything used as a wrap or covering to deaden sound.

muf-fler (mŭf'lẽr), *n.* a scarf for the throat, or for wrapping around the head, throat, and ears.

muf-ti (mŭf'tĭ), *n.* in wartime, the dress of a civilian; ordinarily, civilian dress worn by a soldier. [Colloq.]

mug (mŭg), *n.* an earthenware or metallic drinking vessel with a handle; the quantity that it will contain.

mug-gi-ness (mŭg'ĭ-nĕs), *n.* the state of being warm, damp, and close: used especially of the atmosphere.

mug-gy (mŭg'ĭ), *adj.* warm, damp, and close; as, a *muggy* day; moldy, as hay.

mug-wump (mŭg'wŭmp"), *n.* a voter who belongs to one party, but who claims the right to vote with another, if he prefers the candidate of the latter.

mu-lat-to (mū-lăt'ō), *n.* [*pl.* mulattoes (-ōz)], the child of a negro and a white person; a person of mixed white and negro blood.

mul-ber-ry (mŭl'bĕr-ĭ), *n.* [*pl.* mulberries (-ĭz)], a tree bearing a dark, sweet berry; the fruit of such a tree; a dark purple color.

mulch (mŭlch; mŭlsh), *n.* half-rotten straw, etc., used to protect the roots of trees and plants: *v.t.* to cover, or protect, with half-rotten straw.

mulct (mŭlkt), *v.t.* to punish with a fine: *n.* a fine, especially for some misdeed.

mule (mūl), *n.* the offspring of a male ass and a mare; a machine for spinning cotton, etc.; colloquially, a very stubborn person: *v.i.* to whine; to whimper.

mu-le-teer (mū'lĕ-tēr'), *n.* a driver of a mule or mules.

mul-ish (mūl'ĭsh), *adj.* like a mule; stubborn.—*adv.* **mulishly.**—*n.* **mulishness.**

mull (mŭl), *n.* a snuffbox made of the end of a horn; a very thin, soft kind of muslin; a muddle or failure: *v.t.* to warm, spice, and sweeten (wine, ale, etc.): *v.i.* colloquially, to reflect or ponder: usually with *over.*

mul-lah (mŏŏl'*ȧ*; mŭl'*ȧ*), *n.* among the Mohammedans, a scholar and teacher of their religion.

mul-lein (mŭl'ĭn), *n.* a coarse plant having large leaves, and flowers in close spikes. Also, **mullen.**

mull-er (mŭl'ẽr), *n.* a flat-bottomed vessel used for grinding paints or drugs.

mul-let (mŭl'ĕt), *n.* a fish found in both fresh and salt water, and much valued for the table.

mul-lion (mŭl'yŭn), *n.* an upright bar or division between the panes of a window, screen, etc.: *v.t.* to furnish with, or divide by, upright bars.

mul-ti-fa-ri-ous (mŭl-tĭ-fā'rĭ-ŭs), *adj.* having much variety and diversity.—*adv.* **multifariously.**—*n.* **multifariousness.**

mul-ti-form (mŭl'tĭ-fôrm), *adj.* having many different shapes.

mul-ti-graph (mŭl'tĭ-grȧf), *n.* a machine that both sets type and prints; a rotary typesetting and printing machine.

mul-ti-plane (mŭl'tĭ-plān), *n.* an airplane with three or more planes.

mul-ti-ple (mŭl'tĭ-pl), *n.* a number or quantity which contains another an exact number of times without a remainder; as, 12 is a *multiple* of 4: *adj.* consisting of many parts; repeated many times.

mul-ti-plex (mŭl'tĭ-plĕks), *adj.* made up of many parts; repeated many times.

mul-ti-pli-cand (mŭl"tĭ-plĭ-kănd'; mŭl'tĭ-plĭ-kănd"), *n.* the number or quantity to be increased a given number of times.

mul-ti-pli-cate (mŭl'tĭ-plĭ-kāt), *adj.* consisting of many.

mul-ti-pli-ca-tion (mŭl"tĭ-plĭ-kā'shŭn), *n.* the act or process of increasing a given number of times; rule or operation by which any given number or quantity is increased a given number of times.

mul-ti-plic-i-ty (mŭl"tĭ-plĭs'ĭ-tĭ), *n.* a great number; as, a *multiplicity* of duties fill up a housekeeper's day.

mul-ti-pli-er (mŭl'tĭ-plī"ẽr), *n.* one who, or that which, increases; the number or quantity which shows how many times another is to be repeated or increased.

mul-ti-ply (mŭl'tĭ-plī), *v.t.* [*p.t.* and *p.p.* multiplied, *p.pr.* multiplying], to cause to increase in number; make more by natural production, or addition; repeat (any given number or quantity) a given number of times: *v.i.* to increase in number or extent; as, rabbits *multiply* very fast.

mul-ti-tude (mŭl'tĭ-tūd), *n.* a great number; crowd; assembly; people in general: with *the.*

Syn. throng, host, mob, swarm.

mul-ti-tu-di-nous (mŭl"tĭ-tū'dĭ-nŭs), *adj.* pertaining to, or consisting of, a great number; very numerous.—*adv.* **multitudinously.**—*n.* **multitudinousness.**

mul-tum in par-vo (mŭl'tŭm ĭn pär'vō), a phrase meaning much in a little space. [Lat.]

mum (mŭm), *adj.* silent: *interj.* be silent! *n.* a kind of strong ale: *v.i.* to wear a mask for sport.

mum-ble (mŭm'bl), *v.t.* and *v.i.* to mutter or speak indistinctly; chew gently with closed lips: *n.* a mutter.

mum-bo jum-bo (mŭm'bō jŭm'bō), a West African idol, or object of superstitious worship or dread; a vulgar bugbear.

mumm (mŭm), *v.i.* to mask or disguise oneself for sport. Also, **mum.**

mum-mer (mŭm'ẽr), *n.* one who makes sport in disguise; a masker; actor.

mum-mer-y (mŭm'ẽr-ĭ), *n.* masquerading; a frolic in disguise; ceremonies or performances regarded as ridiculous or insincere; as, the *mummery* of heathen religions.

mum-mi-fy (mŭm'ĭ-fī), *v.t.* to preserve (a corpse) by a drying process.

mum-my (mŭm'ĭ), *n.* [*pl.* mummies (-ĭz)]; a dead body embalmed by a drying process, after the manner of the ancient Egyptians; a rich brown color.

mump (mŭmp), *v.i.* to move the lips with the mouth nearly closed; to mutter; whine or sulk; play the beggar; cheat: *v.t.* to work, as food, with the mouth; utter indistinctly; impose upon.

mumps (mŭmps), *n.* a contagious disease marked by the swelling of the glands of the neck.

munch (mŭnch), *v.t.* and *v.i.* to chew with a crunching noise.

mun-dane (mŭn'dān), *adj.* pertaining to the world; as, this *mundane* sphere; worldly; as, *mundane* pleasures.—*adv.* **mundanely.**

mu-nic-i-pal (mū-nĭs'ĭ-păl), *adj.* pertaining to a city or town, or to its local self-government; as, *municipal* buildings; *municipal* courts.—*adv.* **municipally.**

mu-nic-i-pal-i-ty (mū-nĭs'ĭ-păl'ĭ-tĭ), *n.* [*pl.* municipalities (-tĭz)], a town or city having powers of local self-government.

mu-nif-i-cence (mū-nĭf'ĭ-sĕns), *n.* the quality or state of being bountiful; liberality.

mu-nif-i-cent (mū-nĭf'ĭ-sĕnt), *adj.* marked by great liberality in giving; bountiful; as, a *munificent* gift.—*adv.* **munificently.**

mu-ni-tion-ment (mū-nĭsh'ŭn-mĕnt), *n.* the supply of military stores possessed by an army.

mu-ni-tions (mū-nĭsh'ŭns), *n.pl.* military stores or material.

mu-ral (mū'răl), *adj.* pertaining to, being on, or resembling, a wall; as, *mural* paintings.

mur-der (mûr'dẽr), *n.* the offense of unlawfully killing a human being with definite purpose formed beforehand: *v.t.* to kill with deliberate malice; destroy; spoil.

Syn., *v.* kill, assassinate, slay, massacre, dispatch.

mur-der-er (mûr'dẽr-ẽr), *n.* [*fem.* murderess], one who is guilty of killing another unlawfully.

mur-der-ous (mûr'dẽr-ŭs), *adj.* pertaining to, guilty of, or causing, the unlawful killing of another; brutal; bloodthirsty.—*adv.* **murderously.**

mu-ri-at-ic (mū'rĭ-ăt'ĭk), *adj.* the popular name for hydrochloric: **muriatic acid**, hydrochloric acid, a colorless, corrosive compound of equal parts of hydrogen and chlorine, dissolved in water.

murk (mûrk), *n.* darkness; gloom; obscurity.

murk-i-ness (mûr'kĭ-nĕs), *n.* the state of being dark and gloomy; obscurity.

murk-y (mûr'kĭ), *adj.* dark; gloomy; obscure.—*adv.* **murkily.**

Mur-man (mûr'măn), *adj.* pertaining to the Arctic coast of Russian Lapland: the only ice-free coast of northern Russia.

mur-mur (mûr'mûr), *n.* a low, indistinct sound, as of a running stream; a complaint in a low, muttering tone; a grumble: *v.i.* to make a low, continued noise like the hum of bees; speak in a low voice; mutter in discontent; grumble: *v.t.* to utter complainingly or in a low voice; to grumble.

mur-rain (mûr'ĭn), *n.* an infectious and fatal disease among cattle.

mus-cat (mŭs'kăt), *n.* one of several kinds of musk-flavored European grapes; the wine made from them.

mus-ca-tel (mŭs'kȧ-tĕl'; mŭs'kȧ-tĕl"), *n.* a variety of rich wine; the grapes which produce it; a sweet, fragrant pear. Also, **muscadel, muscadine.**

mus-cle (mŭs'l), *n.* an organ of fiberlike tissue which is capable of being contracted and expanded, thus producing movement in an animal body; colloquially, the strength of such organs.

Mus-co-vite (mŭs'kō-vīt), *n.* a Russian: *adj.* Russian: from Muscovy, or Moscow, in Central Russia.

mus-cu-lar (mŭs'kū-lȧr), *adj.* pertaining to, consisting of, or performed by, muscles; strong; vigorous.

mus-cu-lar-i-ty (mŭs'kū-lăr'ĭ-tĭ), *n.* the quality or state of having strong, vigorous muscles; vigor or strength of muscular tissues; brawn.

muse (mūz), *v.i.* to study in silence; think deeply; be absent-minded: *v.t.* think deeply about: *n.* the inspiring power of poetry: **Muse**, any one of the nine Greek and Roman goddesses, each of whom presided over one of the arts and sciences, as poetry, music, dancing, history, etc.

Syn., *v.* contemplate, reflect, think, ponder.

mu-se-um (mū-zē'ŭm), *n.* a collection of natural, scientific, or literary curiosities, or of works of art; the building containing such a collection.

mush (mŭsh), *n.* boiled Indian corn meal; any mixture, soft and thick, like it.

mush-room (mŭsh'rōōm), *n.* an eatable fungus, or plant without stem, root, leaves, or flowers, shaped somewhat like an umbrella, and growing very quickly in a moist, dark place; anything like this fungus in quickness of growth; an upstart: *adj.* made from mushrooms; like them in quickness of growth; upstart.

Mushrooms

mush-y (mŭsh'ĭ), *adj.* mushlike; soft and yielding; weakly sentimental.

mu-sic (mū'zĭk), *n.* the art or science of the pleasing or harmonious expression of combinations of sound tones; harmony or melody; a musical composition; such a composition written or printed.

mu-si-cal (mū'zĭ-kăl), *adj.* pertaining to, producing, or full of, harmony or melody; melodious; as, the *musical* quality of a voice.—*adv.* **musically.**—*n.* **musicalness.**

Syn. tuneful, dulcet, sweet.

mu-si-cale (mū″zĭ-kăl′), *n.* a private social entertainment of singing and instrumental music.

mu-si-cal in-stru-ment (mū′zĭ-kăl ĭn′strōō-mĕnt), a mechanical apparatus for producing musical sounds.

mu-si-cian (mū-zĭsh′ăn), *n.* one skilled in the science of music; one who sings or who plays on a musical instrument, especially as a profession.

mus-ing (mūz′ĭng), *n.* deep thought: *adj.* engaged in deep thought; dreamful; meditative.—*adv.* **musingly.**

mus-ket-ry (mŭs′kĕt-rĭ), *n.* the fire of handguns, or the art of firing handguns; muskets collectively.

musk-mel-on (mŭsk′mĕl″ŭn), *n.* the gourdlike juicy fruit of a trailing vine.

musk ox (mŭsk ŏks), an Arctic, hoofed animal with curving horns.

musk-rat (mŭsk′răt″), *n.* a valuable fur-bearing animal of North America, having teeth formed for gnawing, and living in the water, through which it swims by means of its flat scaly tail and webbed hind feet: so called because of its musky odor.

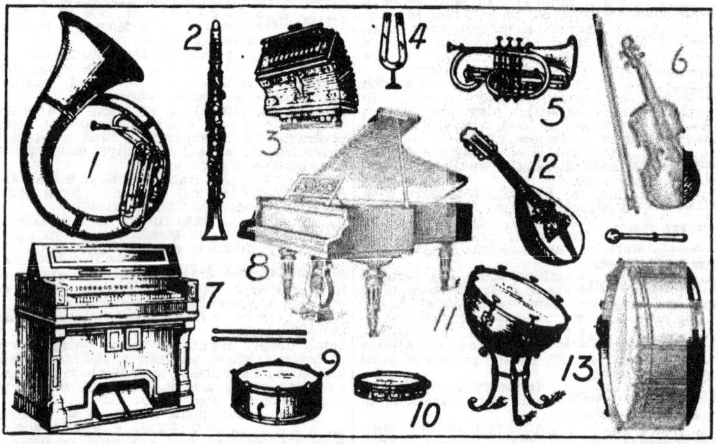

Musical Instruments. 1, helicon (horn); 2, clarinet; 3, accordeon; 4, tuning fork; 5, cornet; 6, violin; 7, organ; 8, grand piano; 9, snare drum; 10, tambourine; 11, kettle drum; 12, mandolin; 13, bass drum.

musk (mŭsk), *n.* a strong-scented substance obtained from the male musk deer: used in many perfumes; the odor of this substance.—*adj.* **musky.**

musk deer (mŭsk dēr), a small hornless deer of Central Asia, which yields a scented substance called musk.

Musk Deer

mus-kel-lunge (mŭs′kĕ-lŭnj; mŭs″kĕ-lŭnj′), *n.* a large fish of the pike variety found in the Great Lakes, and valued as food. Also, **muskallonge.**

mus-ket (mŭs′kĕt), *n.* a handgun formerly carried by infantry, or foot soldiers.

mus-ket-eer (mŭs″kĕt-ēr′), *n.* a foot soldier armed with a musket, or handgun. Also, **musqueteer.**

mus-lin (mŭz′lĭn), *n.* a cotton cloth, either fine and thin or stout and heavy in quality: *adj.* made of such cotton cloth.

muss (mŭs), *n.* confusion; disorder; mess: *v.t.* to disorder, as clothing; to wrinkle. [Colloq.]

mus-sel (mŭs′l), *n.* an eatable shellfish that lives in the sea.

Mus-sul-man (mŭs′ŭl-măn), *n.* [*pl.* Mussulmans (-mănz)], a Mohammedan, or believer in Mohammedanism, the religion which teaches that Mohammed, its founder, was the true prophet of God. Also, **Moslem.**

muss-y (mŭs′ĭ), *adj.* disordered; disarranged; soiled. [Colloq.]

must (mŭst), *n.* unfermented grape juice: *v.t.* and *v.i.* to make or become moldy and sour: *v.i.* to be obliged or compelled.

mus-tache (mŭs-tăsh′), *n.* hair worn on a man's upper lip. Also, **moustache.**

mus-tang (mŭs′tăng), *n.* the small, hardy, half-wild horse of the prairies of America.

mus-tard (mŭs′tẽrd), *n.* a plant, and its seed, from which a seasoning is made; the powdered seasoning made from the seed.—**mustard gas,** a deadly gas used in shells in the World War, producing severe burns when in contact with the body, and painful to the eyes: it is an organic compound containing chlorine and sulphur.

mus-ter (mŭs'tẽr), *n.* an assembly of troops for review or active service; list of troops assembled; assemblage; collection: *v.t.* to assemble, especially troops for review or active service; to collect and show; as, to *muster* one's courage: *v.i.* to meet in one place.

mus-ty (mŭs'tĭ), *adj.* [*comp.* mustier, *superl.* mustiest], spoiled with damp; moldy; spoiled by age; stale or sour.—*adv.* mustily.—*n.* mustiness.

mu-ta-bil-i-ty (mū"tȧ-bĭl'ĭ-tĭ), *n.* the quality of being subject to change; as, the *mutability* of human life.

mu-ta-ble (mū'tȧ-bl), *adj.* easily and frequently changed; fickle; unstable.—*adv.* mutably.

mu-ta-tion (mū-tā'shŭn), *n.* alteration; change; variation.

mute (mūt), *n.* one who cannot speak or who remains silent; a consonant which is not pronounced; a contrivance to deaden or soften the sound of a musical instrument: *adj.* silent; dumb; speechless; not pronounced or sounded.—*adv.* mutely.—*n.* muteness.

mu-ti-late (mū'tĭ-lāt), *v.t.* to cut off a limb or necessary part of; render incomplete or imperfect; maim.

Syn. cripple, disfigure.

mu-ti-la-tion (mū"tĭ-lā'shŭn), *n.* the act of depriving of any necessary part; as, the *mutilation* of a statue; disfigurement.

mu-ti-neer (mū-tĭ-nẽr'), *n.* one who is guilty of rebellion against authority: *v.i.* to rebel against authority.

mu-ti-nous (mū'tĭ-nŭs), *adj.* disposed to, or guilty of, active rebellion against authority.—*adv.* mutinously.—*n.* mutinousness.

Syn., adj. insurgent, tumultuous, turbulent, riotous.

Ant. (see obedient).

mu-ti-ny (mū'tĭ-nĭ), *n.* rebellion against, or forcible resistance to, authority, especially of soldiers or sailors against their officers: *v.i.* [*p.t.* and *p.p.* mutinied, *p.pr.* mutinying], to rise against established authority.

mut-ter (mŭt'ẽr), *n.* indistinct utterance; a murmur; a grumble: *v.t.* to utter words in a low voice with lips almost closed; murmur; to sound with low, rumbling noises, as thunder: *v.t.* to utter low and indistinctly.

mut-ton (mŭt'n), *n.* the flesh of sheep used as food.

mu-tu-al (mū'tū-ăl), *adj.* interchanged; given and received; joint; common; as, *mutual* affection; *mutual* interests.—*adv.* mutually.

Syn., correlative.

Ant. (see solitary).

mu-tu-al-i-ty (mū"tū-ăl'ĭ-tĭ), *n.* interchange; interdependence.

mu-zhik (mōō-zhĭk'; mōō'zhĭk), *n.* a Russian peasant. Also, moujik. [Russ.]

muz-zle (mŭz'l), *n.* the projecting mouth, lips, and nose of an animal; snout; the mouth of a gun, etc.; a fastening or cover for the mouth of a dog, etc., to prevent biting: *v.t.* to secure the mouth of with a fastening or cover; to prevent from talking.

my (mī), *poss. pron.* and *adj.* of or belonging to me.

Myn-heer (mīn-hâr'; mĭn-hâr'), *n.* Sir; Mister; a Dutchman. [Dutch]

my-o-pi-a (mī-ō'pĭ-ȧ), *n.* nearsightedness. Also, myopy.—*adj.* myopic.

myr-i-ad (mĭr'ĭ-ăd), *n.* the number of ten thousand; a very large number; as, the sky at night is covered with a *myriad* of stars: *adj.* innumerable.

myr-mi-don (mûr'mĭ-dŏn), *n.* a brutal or unprincipled subordinate officer who carries out all the orders of a superior without protest or pity: so called from the Myrmidons, warriors who unquestioningly followed Achilles in the Trojan War and carried out his orders.

myrrh (mûr), *n.* a yellowish-brown gummy substance with a spicy fragrance, and a bitter taste, obtained from a shrub growing in Arabia and Abyssinia.

myr-tle (mûr'tl), *n.* a fragrant evergreen shrub; also, the periwinkle.

my-self (mī-sĕlf'), *pron.* [*pl.* ourselves (our-sĕlvz')], I or me in person: an emphatic form.

mys-te-ri-ous (mĭs-tē'rĭ-ŭs), *adj.* not clear to the understanding; obscure; unexplained.—*adv.* mysteriously.—*n.* mysteriousness.

Syn. dark, hidden, secret, dim, mystic.

Ant. (see open).

mys-te-ry (mĭs'tẽr-ĭ), *n.* [*pl.* mysteries (-ĭz)], something secret, hidden, or unexplained; that which is beyond human understanding.—**mystery play**, a Biblical drama, or miracle play, of the Middle Ages: *pl.* among the ancients, sacred rites and ceremonies to which only certain persons were admitted.

mys-tic (mĭs'tĭk), *n.* a believer in direct communion with God: *adj.* beyond human understanding; involving some secret meaning; hidden; secret.—*adj.* mystical.—*adv.* mystically.

mys-ti-cism (mĭs'tĭ-sĭzm), *n.* the doctrine that man may have a more direct communion with God through the inward understanding of the mind than is gained by revelation; mysteriousness of thought or teaching.

mys-ti-fi-ca-tion (mĭs"tĭ-fĭ-kā'shŭn), *n.* the act of perplexing or puzzling; the state of being perplexed or puzzled.

mys-ti-fy (mĭs'tĭ-fī), *v.t.* [*p.t.* and *p.p.* mystified, *p.pr.* mystifying], to involve in secrecy; to obscure; bewilder; puzzle.

Syn. confuse, perplex.

Ant. (see clear).

myth (mĭth), *n.* a legend; a traditional story, often founded on some fact of nature, or on an event in the early existence of a people, and embodying some religious belief, idea of the world, of nature, or of the gods, etc., of that people; an imaginary person, thing, or event.

myth-i-cal (mĭth'ĭ-kăl), *adj.* pertaining to, or described in, a myth; imaginary; fictitious; false. Also, mythic.—*adv.* mythically.

myth-o-log-i-cal (mĭth"ō-lŏj'ĭ-kăl), *adj.* pertaining to the tales and legends in which are embodied the beliefs of a people as to their origin, gods, etc.

my-thol-o-gy (mĭ-thŏl'ō-jĭ), *n.* [*pl.* mythologies (-jĭz)], the collected body of the legends of a people, in which are recorded their beliefs concerning their origin, gods, heroes, etc.; the science of such legends; a book about them.

N

nab (năb), *v.t.* [*p.t.* and *p.p.* nabbed, *p.pr.* nabbing], to catch or seize unexpectedly. [COLLOQ.]

na-bob (nā'bŏb), *n.* a native governor of a province in India; any very rich man.

na-celle (nȧ'sĕl'), *n.* a boat-shaped body of an airplane; the car of a balloon or dirigible. [FR.]

na-cre (nā'kẽr), *n.* mother-of-pearl. Also, **nacker.**

na-dir (nā'dẽr), *n.* that part of the heavens directly beneath the place where one stands, or directly opposite to the zenith; the lowest point.

nag (năg), *n.* a small saddle horse: *v.t.* [*p.t.* and *p.p.* nagged, *p.pr.* nagging], to scold or find fault with continually; to keep constantly urging to something: *v.i.* to find fault constantly.

nag-gy (năg'ĭ), *adj.* disposed to scold or find fault; touchy.

Na-hum (nā'hŭm), *n.* a book of the Old Testament containing the message of the prophet Nahum.

na-iad (nā'yăd; nī'ăd), *n.* a water nymph, one of the imaginary beautiful maidens supposed to live in, and give life to, fountains, rivers, lakes, etc.

nail (nāl), *n.* the horny substance at the ends of the human fingers and toes; the claws of a bird or animal; a measure two and one-fourth inches long; a pointed piece of metal, furnished with a head, and used for driving into woodwork, etc.: *v.t.* to fasten with such a piece of metal; to secure or make certain; to hold down tightly; as, to *nail* an argument; to expose; as, to *nail* a lie.

nain-sook (nān'sŏŏk; năn'sŏŏk), *n.* a firm muslin, plain or striped.

na-ïve (nä-ēv'), *adj.* artless; frank; simple; as, *naïve* manners; a *naïve* person, etc.—*adv.* **naïvely.**

na-ïve-té (nä"ēv"tā'), *n.* natural, unaffected frankness or simplicity in speech or action. [FR.]

na-ked (nā'kĕd), *adj.* unclothed; bare; unarmed; defenseless; exposed to view; plain; without addition or ornament; without glasses; as, to see with the *naked* eye. —*adv.* **nakedly.**—*n.* **nakedness.**

Syn. nude, uncovered, rude, rough, simple.
Ant. (see covering).

nam-a-ble (nām'ȧ-bl), *adj.* able to be called by a special term or title; worthy of mention. Also, **nameable.**

nam-by-pam-by (năm'bĭ-păm"bĭ), *n.* that which is weakly sentimental, or affectedly pretty or nice: *adj.* weakly sentimental in writing or talk; affectedly nice.

name (nām), *n.* the term or title by which a person or thing is called or known; designation; character; reputation; fame; ownership; as, to hold property in one's own *name*: *v.t.* to give a special term or title to; nominate; specify; mention by a special term or title.

Syn., *n.* credit, repute: *v.* call, christen.

name-less (nām'lĕs), *adj.* without a special term or title; unknown; not fit to be mentioned.—*n.* **namelessness.**

name-ly (nām'lĭ), *adv.* that is to say; to wit; to state more particularly.

name-sake (nām'sāk"), *n.* one having the same name as another; one called after another.

nan-keen (năn-kēn'), *n.* a brownish-yellow cotton cloth, formerly brought from China. Also, **nankin.**

nap (năp), *n.* a short slumber; doze; the woolly substance on the surface of cloth; pile; downy covering of plants; colloquially, a card game, napoleon, or six-handed euchre: *v.i.* [*p.t.* and *p.p.* napped, *p.pr.* napping], to doze.

nape (nāp), *n.* the upper part of the back of the neck.

na-per-y (nā'pẽr-ĭ), *n.* table linen; any household linen.

naph-tha (năf'thȧ), *n.* a clear, easily evaporating, inflammable liquid obtained from petroleum, and classed between gasoline and benzine; rock oil.

nap-kin (năp'kĭn), *n.* a small cloth, usually of linen, used at table for wiping the fingers, etc.; a small towel.

na-po-le-on (nȧ-pō'lē-ŏn), *n.* a gold coin formerly used in France, of the value of twenty francs, or $3.86; a card game, six-handed euchre: often called *nap.*

nap-per (năp'ẽr), *n.* in English and World War slang, the head.

nar-cis-sus (när-sĭs'ŭs), *n.* a kind of ornamental plant of the daffodil family, with handsome fragrant flowers.

nar-cot-ic (när-kŏt'ĭk), *n.* a medicine which relieves pain and produces sleep, and sometimes, in excessive doses, causes death: *adj.* producing stupor or sleep.

nard (närd), *n.* a plant formerly used in medicine; spikenard, or a fragrant ointment prepared from it.

na-res (nā'rēz), *n.* openings from the nasal or nose passages; the nostrils.

nar-rate (nă-rāt'), *v.t.* to tell; recite; give an account of; write, as a story.

Syn. relate, detail, recount, describe, rehearse.

nar-ra-tion (nă-rā'shŭn), *n.* the act of telling of events in the order of their happening; an account or story, written or oral.

nar-ra-tive (năr'ȧ-tĭv), *n.* the art of story telling; recital of a story or event; a story or tale; *adj.* pertaining to, or of the nature of, story telling.

nar-ra-tor (nă-rā'tẽr), *n.* one who tells a story.

nar-row (năr'ō), *adj.* of little breadth or width; as, a *narrow* lane; a *narrow* space; limited; straitened; as, *narrow* circumstances; lacking breadth or broadness of view; as, a *narrow* mind; *narrow* opinions; close; near; as, a *narrow* escape; a *narrow* majority; *v.t.* to lessen the breadth or extent of; confine or contract; restrict; *v.i.* to become less broad; *n.pl.* a strait, or narrow passage between two seas.—*n.* **narrowness.**

nar-row-ly (năr'ō-lĭ), *adv.* by a slight margin; barely; with close scrutiny; carefully; with little breadth of view.

nar-row-mind-ed (năr'ō-mīn'dĕd), *adj.* without breadth of view or opinion; intolerant; prejudiced.

nar-whal (när'hwăl), *n.* a kind of whale with a large tusk; the sea unicorn. Also, **narwal, narwhale, narval.**

Narwhal

na-sal (nā'zăl), *adj.* pertaining to, affected by, or pronounced through, the nose: *n.* a letter pronounced through the nose, as *m, n, ng.*—*n.* **nasality.**

nas-cent (năs'ĕnt), *adj.* beginning to exist or to grow.

nas-tur-tium (năs-tûr'shŭm), *n.* a common garden plant having red and yellow flowers.

nas-ty (nȧs'tĭ), *adj.* [*comp.* nastier, *superl.* nastiest], dirty; filthy; disgusting to taste or smell; as, *nasty* medicine; stormy; as, *nasty* weather; troublesome; as, a *nasty* cut.—*adv.* **nastily.**—*n.* **nastiness.**

Syn. unclean, indecent, impure, gross, vile.

na-tal (nā'tăl), *adj.* pertaining to one's birth or birthday; as, one's *natal* day; native.

na-tant (nā'tănt), *adj.* swimming or floating on the surface: said of leaves of water plants.

na-ta-to-ri-al (nā"tȧ-tō'rĭ-ăl), *adj.* pertaining to swimming, or adapted for swimming; as, *natatorial* skill. Also, **natatory.**—*n.* **natatorium.**

na-tion (nā'shŭn), *n.* the people of one country united under the same government; a race of people having the same religion, language, history, etc.

Syn. people, realm, state.

na-tion-al (năsh'ŭn-ăl), *adj.* pertaining to, or peculiar to, a united people or country; as, *national* government; *national* characteristics; public; general: **National Army,** in the World War, that part of the American army secured by conscription: **national bank,** an institution, in the United States, for lending and caring for money, organized under a special act of Congress: **National Guard,** the organized militia of the several states of the United States.—*adv.* **nationally.**

na-tion-al-ism (năsh'ŭn-ăl-ĭzm), *n.* the state of being united as a people and country; devotion to the interests of one's country; an idiom or phrase peculiar to the language of the united people of a country; a trait or peculiarity of the united people of a country.—*n.* **nationalist.**

na-tion-al-i-ty (năsh"ŭn-ăl'ĭ-tĭ), *n.* the state of being, or belonging to, a united people or country; character or traits of the united people of a country; birth in a country; patriotism; a united people and country.

na-tion-al-ize (năsh'ŭn-ăl-īz), *v.t.* to make to belong to a united people and country; to make a united country of; to put under the control of the government of a country.—*n.* **nationalization.**

na-tive (nā'tĭv), *adj.* pertaining to one's birth or to the place of one's birth; as, one's *native* land; born or produced in, or belonging to, a country; as, the *native* population; *native* plants; peculiar to those born in a country; as, *native* customs; produced by nature; not artificial; as, *native* copper; inborn; not acquired; natural; as, *native* charm or grace of manner: *n.* one born in a certain country or place.—*adv.* **natively.**

na-tiv-ism (nā'tĭv-ĭzm), *n.* the practice of favoring the people born in the country rather than those who have come from foreign countries; the doctrine that the mind receives impressions from an internal rather than an external source.

na-tiv-i-ty (nȧ-tĭv'ĭ-tĭ), *n.* time, place, and manner of birth: **Nativity,** the birth of Christ.

nat-ty (năt'ĭ), *adj.* tidy, neat, smart, trim.—*adv.* **nattily.**—*n.* **nattiness.**

nat-u-ral (năt'yŏŏ-răl; năch'ŏŏ-răl), *adj.* pertaining to, produced by, or in the course of, nature; inborn; not artificial; as, *natural* ease; occurring in the ordinary course of things; as, a *natural* result; true to life; as, a *natural* likeness; unassumed; according to human nature; not spiritual; in music, according to the usual scale of C: *n.* in music, a sign used to correct the previous power of a sharp or flat; the tone or note so affected.—*adv.* **naturally.**—*n.* **naturalness.**

Syn., adj. original, regular, normal.

Ant. (see unnatural).

nat-u-ral his-to-ry (năt'yŏŏ-răl hĭs'tō-rĭ), the study of plants, minerals, and natural objects in general, especially, now, animals; account and classification of these plants, etc.

nat-u-ral-ism (năt'yŏŏ-răl-ĭzm), *n.* an uncivilized condition; in literature and art, a careful following or representation of things as they really are.

nat-u-ral-ist (năt'yŏŏ-răl-ĭst), *n.* one who has made a special study of natural objects, as plants, minerals, and, especially, animals.

nat-u-ral-is-tic (năt"yŏŏ-răl-ĭs'tĭk), *adj.* realistic.

nat-u-ral-i-za-tion (năt"yŏŏ-răl-ĭ-zā'shŭn), *n.* the act of legally granting a foreigner the rights and privileges of a citizen born in the country; a growing accustomed to new conditions.

nat-u-ral-ize (năt'yŏŏ-răl-īz), *v.t.* to make familiar by custom; accustom; grant to (a foreigner) the privileges of a citizen or subject born in the country.

nat-u-ral se-lec-tion (năt'yŏŏ-răl sē-lĕk'shŭn), the process of nature by which the strongest, best, or fittest plants and animals survive, thus improving their species.

na-ture (nāt'yŏŏr; nā'chŏŏr), *n.* that which is the source or essence of life; the forces that create; as, the laws of *nature;* the universe; original or essential qualities; kind; as, everything of this *nature;* usual or necessary order of things; constitution; personal character or disposition, as, a generous *nature;* normal affection; lack of culture; wildness; as, a state of *nature.*

naught (nôt), *n.* nothing; a cipher; the character [0]: *adj.* of no account; worthless.

naugh-ty (nô'tĭ), *adj.* [*comp.* naughtier, *superl.* naughtiest], bad; wayward; mischievous or disobedient.—*adv.* **naughtily.**—*n.* **naughtiness.**

nau-se-a (nô'shē-ȧ; nô'sē-ȧ), *n.* a strong feeling of sickness, with a desire to vomit; seasickness; loathing or disgust.

nau-se-ate (nô'shē-āt), *v.t.* to affect with a feeling of sickness or with strong disgust; be sickened by; loathe: *v.i.* to be inclined to vomit.

nau-seous (nô'shŭs; nô'shē-ŭs), *adj.* causing sickness of the stomach; loathsome; abhorrent.—*adv.* **nauseously.** —*n.* **nauseousness.**

nau-ti-cal (nô'tĭ-kăl), *adj.* pertaining to ships, sailors, or navigation; maritime. Also, **nautic.**—*adv.* **nautically.**
Syn. marine, naval, oceanic.

nau-ti-lus (nô'tĭ-lŭs), *n.* [*pl.* nautili (-lī)], a kind of shellfish of the South Pacific and Indian oceans; a kind of diving bell.

Nav-a-ho (năv'ȧ-hō), *n.* [*pl.* Navahos; Navahoes (-hōz)], one of a tribe of American Indians, originally inhabiting what is now New Mexico. Also, **Navajo.**

na-val (nā'văl), *adj.* pertaining to warships, or to the entire sea war force of a country; consisting of warships.

nave (nāv), *n.* the middle or body of a church, extending from the chancel to the main entrance; the center or hub of a wheel, in which the spokes are inserted.

na-vel (nā'vl), *n.* the depression in the center of the lower part of the abdomen or belly.

nav-i-ga-bil-i-ty (năv'ĭ-gȧ-bĭl'ĭ-tĭ), *n.* capability of being traveled over by a boat or ship; as, the *navigability* of a river.

nav-i-ga-ble (năv'ĭ-gȧ-bl), *adj.* capable of being traveled over by a boat or ship.—*n.* **navigableness.**

nav-i-gate (năv'ĭ-gāt), *v.i.* to travel on the water by ship or boat; to sail or direct a ship: *v.t.* to pass over in a ship or boat; steer or manage in sailing.

nav-i-ga-tion (năv'ĭ-gā'shŭn), *n.* the act of traveling on the water in ships; the science of managing ships.

nav-i-ga-tor (năv'ĭ-gā'tẽr), *n.* one who travels in ships; one skilled in the science of the management of ships.

nav-vy (năv'ĭ), *n.* [*pl.* navvies (-ĭz)], a laborer employed upon railways, canals, etc.

na-vy (nā'vĭ), *n.* the warships of a nation; the sea war force of a nation, including ships, shipyards, shops, officers, men, etc.

nay (nā), *adv.* no; not only so, but: *n.* a refusal or denial; a negative vote or voter.

Naz-a-rene (năz'ȧ-rēn'), *n.* a native of Nazareth: applied to Jesus Christ, his followers, and the early Christians as a term of contempt; in the Early Church, one of a sect of Jews.

Naz-a-rite (năz'ȧ-rīt), *n.* a Jew devoted by a religious vow to a life of purity.—Numbers vi.

neap (nēp), *adj.* low: applied to the tides which occur in the beginning of the second and fourth quarters of the moon: *n.* the lowest tide.

neaped (nēpt), *adj.* left aground by the tide: said of a ship.

Ne-a-pol-i-tan (nē'ȧ-pŏl'ĭ-tăn), *n.* one who is native to, or lives in, Naples, in Italy: *adj.* pertaining to Naples or to its people.

near (nēr), *adj.* [*comp.* nearer, *superl.* nearest], not far distant in time, place, or degree; close, intimate; dear; as, *near* to my heart; familiar; narrow; in riding or driving, on the left; as, the *near* horse; direct or quick; as, to go by the *near* way; mean or stingy: *adv.* at a little distance; almost; closely: *prep.* close to: *v.t.* to approach; come close to.—*adv.* **nearly.**—*n.* **nearness.**
Syn., adj. nigh, neighboring, adjacent.
Ant. (see distant).

near-sight-ed (nēr'sīt'ĕd), *adj.* seeing well at a short distance only; shortsighted.—*n.* **nearsightedness.**

neat (nēt), *adj.* tidy; trim and clean; as, a *neat* home; simple and elegant; clever; as, a *neat* reply: *n.* cattle, as oxen and cows.—*adv.* **neatly.**—*n.* **neatness.**

neat's-foot (nēts'fŏŏt), *n.* the foot of an ox or cow, from which neat's-foot oil is made.

neb (nĕb), *n.* the beak of a bird, etc.; a bill; a snout.

neb-u-la (nĕb'ū-lȧ), *n.* [*pl.* nebulæ (-lē)], a gaseous matter that looks like a faint, misty patch of light in the heavens, produced by groups of stars too distant to be seen clearly, or by masses of cloudlike matter.

neb-u-lar (nĕb'ū-lȧr), *adj.* pertaining to the faint, cloudlike matter or vapor near the stars; cloudy; hazy: **nebular hypothesis,** the theory that the planets of the solar system, and all the heavenly bodies, existed originally as cloudlike, gaseous masses, which formed into globes as they whirled in space.

neb-u-lous (nĕb'ū-lŭs), *adj.* pertaining to, or like, the faint, cloudlike haze or vapor near the stars; cloudy; hazy; perplexed.—*n.* **nebulosity.**

nec-es-sa-ry (nĕs'ĕ-sā-rĭ), *adj.* that cannot be otherwise; not to be done without; essential; indispensable; as, food is *necessary* to life; not to be avoided; as, the *necessary* result of an act: *n.* [*pl.* necessaries (-rĭz)], a thing which cannot be done without.—*adv.* **necessarily.**
Syn., adj. needful, expedient, requisite, inevitable.
Ant. (see useless).

ne-ces-si-tate (nē-sĕs'ĭ-tāt), *v.t.* to make unavoidable; compel; oblige.
Syn. force, require, constrain.

ne-ces-si-tous (nē-sĕs'ĭ-tŭs), *adv.* very poor; destitute; needy.

ne-ces-si-ty (nē-sĕs'ĭ-tĭ), *n.* the state or quality of being absolutely needed or indispensable; that which is unavoidable or which cannot be done without; compulsion; extreme poverty; *pl.* things which are needed for human life.
Syn. need, occasion, emergency, urgency.

neck (nĕk), *n.* that part of the body between the head and trunk; a long narrow stretch of land or water, as an isthmus or a strait; the long slender part of an object, especially if near one end; as, the *neck* of a bottle.

neck-er-chief (nĕk'ẽr-chĭf), *n.* a kerchief or cloth for the neck.

neck-lace (nĕk'lās), *n.* a chain of gold or other metal, or a string of beads, jewels, etc., worn around the neck.

neck-tie (nĕk'tī'), *n.* a narrow scarf or band worn round the neck and tied under the chin.

nec-rol-o-gy (nĕk-rŏl'ō-jĭ), *n.* a list of the dead; an obituary.

nec-ro-man-cer (nĕk'rō-măn'sẽr), *n.* one who claims to be able to foretell the future by communicating with the spirits of the dead; a conjurer.

nec-ro-man-cy (nĕk'rō-măn'sĭ), *n.* the pretended art of predicting future events by communication with the dead; hence, magic.

nec-rop-o-lis (nĕk-rŏp'ō-lĭs), *n.* a cemetery or graveyard.

nec-ro-sis (nĕk-rō'sĭs), *n.* mortification, or decay and death of part of the body, especially of a bone; a disease in plants, marked by small black spots that show decay.

nec-tar (nĕk'tȧr), *n.* in classic mythology, the wine of the gods; any delicious beverage; the honey of plants.

nec-tar-ine (nĕk'tȧr-ĭn; nĕk"tȧr-ēn'), *n.* a kind of peach with a smooth skin.

née (nā), *p.adj.* born: often placed before the maiden name of a married woman; as, Mrs. Smith, *née* Brown. [Fr.]

need (nēd), *n.* lack of anything desired or useful; necessity; urgent want; poverty; distress: *v.t.* to be in want of; to require; to have use for: *v.i.* to be in poverty or want.

need-ful (nēd'fo͝ol), *adj.* necessary; needy; required.—*adv.* **needfully.**—*n.* **needfulness.**

nee-dle (nē'dl), *n.* a small, sharp-pointed steel instrument furnished with an eye to hold thread; a thin, straight rod used in knitting or, when hooked at the end, for crocheting; anything sharply pointed like a needle; the magnetic needle.

nee-dle-ful (nē'dl-fo͝ol), *n.* the length of thread that can be used in a needle at one time.

nee-dle gun (nē'dl gŭn), a breech-loading small firearm, the cartridge of which is exploded by a blow from a spring-needle.

need-less (nēd'lĕs), *adj.* unnecessary; useless.—*adv.* **needlessly.**—*n.* **needlessness.**

nee-dle-wom-an (nē'dl-wo͝om"ȧn), *n.* [*pl.* needlewomen (-wĭm"ĕn)], a seamstress; a woman who does sewing.

nee-dle-work (nē'dl-wûrk"), *n.* hand sewing; embroidery done by hand; the occupation of sewing.

needs (nēdz), *n.pl.* necessities: *adv.* necessarily; of necessity; as, he *needs* must come.

need-y (nēd'ĭ), *adj.* very poor; poverty-stricken.—*n.* **neediness.**

ne'er (nâr; năr), *adv.* contraction of *never:* used chiefly in poetry.

ne-fa-ri-ous (nē-fâ'rĭ-ŭs), *adj.* extremely wicked; vile; infamous; as, *nefarious* conduct.—*adv.* **nefariously.**—*n.* **nefariousness.**

ne-ga-tion (nē-gā'shŭn), *n.* denial: opposite to *affirmation;* absence of positive qualities.

neg-a-tive (nĕg'ȧ-tĭv), *n.* a refusal or denial; the side of a question which denies what the opposite side affirms; as, to support the *negative* in a debate; a word expressing denial; as, to reply with a *negative;* right of veto; a picture in which right and left and light and shade are the reverse of those in the original: used to print a positive picture; in mathematics, a quantity less than zero or the symbol denoting such a quantity; in electricity, the plate in the cell which is not positive: *v.t.* to deny the truth of; to refuse assent to; dismiss or reject by vote: *adj.* implying refusal or denial; refusing assent; not positive; having the power of veto; in mathematics, noting a quantity to be subtracted; in photography, showing left and right, and dark and light reversed.—*adv.* **negatively.**

neg-lect (nĕg-lĕkt'), *n.* omission to do that which should be done; habitual lack of attention; disregard; carelessness: *v.t.* to omit to do, by carelessness or design; as, to *neglect* a duty; to slight; disregard.

neg-lect-ful (nĕg-lĕkt'fo͝ol), *adj.* indicating or showing disregard; careless; negligent.—*adv.* **neglectfully.**

neg-li-gee (nĕg"lĭ-zhā; nĕg"lĭ-zhā'), *n.* a loosely fitting dress or gown; easy and unceremonious dress in general: *adj.* carelessly attired.

neg-li-gence (nĕg'lĭ-jĕns), *n.* the habit of not doing that which should be done; carelessness; neglect; as, the accident was due to *negligence;* disregard of appearance, manner, or style.

neg-li-gent (nĕg'lĭ-jĕnt), *adv.* inclined to leave undone what should be done; careless; heedless; showing lack of attention.—*adv.* **negligently.**

neg-li-gi-ble (nĕg'lĭ-jĭ-bl), *adj.* that may be disregarded; of little account or value; as, the loss was *negligible.*

ne-go-ti-a-ble (nē-gō'shĭ-ȧ-bl), *adj.* capable of being transferred or exchanged; as, a *negotiable* note: **negotiable paper,** notes, bills, and drafts which may be transferred by indorsement or assignment.—*n.* **negotiability.**

ne-go-ti-ate (nē-gō'shĭ-āt), *v.t.* to sell, as commercial paper or securities; to conclude by treaty, bargain, or agreement; as, to *negotiate* peace; *v.i.* to treat with others in political or business affairs.—*n.* **negotiator.**

ne-go-ti-a-tion (nē-gō"shĭ-ā'shŭn), *n.* the act of transacting business, or of arranging some agreement; the discussion of a treaty.—*adj.* **negotiatory.**

ne-gress (nē'grĕs), *n.* a female of the black or Negro race.

Ne-gri-to (nē-grē'tō), *n.* one of a very small black, or negrolike, race of Africa and the Pacific Islands.

Ne-gro (nē'grō), *n.* [*pl.* Negroes (-grōz)], the African black race: *adj.* black or African: used of one of the great race divisions of mankind: **negro,** *n.* a black man: *adj.* pertaining to, or like, the black race or a member of it.

ne-groid (nē'groid), *adj.* resembling the Negro, or black, race.

ne-gus (nē'gŭs), *n.* a beverage or drink made of hot water and wine, sweetened and spiced.

Ne-he-mi-ah (nē"-hē-mī'ȧ), *n.* a book of the Old Testament; a Jewish leader.

neigh (nā), *n.* the cry of a horse; a whinny: *v.i.* to utter the cry, or whinny, of a horse.

neigh-bor (nā'bẽr), *n.* one who dwells near to another; one who is near by chance: *v.t.* to adjoin; to live or be near to: *v.i.* to be friendly. Also, **neighbour.**

neigh-bor-hood (nā'bẽr-ho͝od), *n.* the region near; vicinity; the state of being or of living near; all the people living near one another; a district with regard to its characteristics; as, a fashionable *neighborhood.* Also, **neighbourhood.**

Syn. environs, community, nearness.

neigh-bor-ing (nā'bẽr-ĭng), *adj.* living or being near; adjoining; adjacent. Also, **neighbouring.**

neigh-bor-ly (nā'bẽr-lĭ), *adj.* like, or appropriate to, those who live near each other; social; civil; friendly; *adv.* in a friendly, civil, or social manner. Also, **neighbourly.**—*n.* **neighborliness, neighbourliness.**

nei-ther (nē'thẽr; nī'thẽr), *pron.* not the one nor the other; as, I want *neither* of the books: *adj.* not either; as, *neither* book will do: *conj.* not either; not one or the other: often with *nor;* as, *neither* the book *nor* the paper.

Nem-e-sis (nĕm'ē-sis), *n.* in Greek mythology, the goddess of revenge: **nemesis**, the justice, especially the just punishment, that every man receives according to his deeds.

ne-o-lith-ic (nē'ō-lĭth'ĭk), *adj.* pertaining to, or like, the late stone age, when polished stone implements were used.

ne-ol-o-gism (nē-ŏl'ō-jĭzm), *n.* a new word or phrase introduced into a language; the use of such a word or phrase. Also, **neology.**

ne-ol-o-gist (nē-ŏl'ō-jĭst), *n.* one who introduces new words or phrases into a language. Also, **neologian.**

ne-o-phyte (nē'ō-fīt), *n.* a novice; a beginner; one recently baptized; a convert: *adj.* just beginning to learn.

ne-o-plasm (nē'ō-plăzm), *n.* a new growth of diseased tissue in the body, as a tumor.

Ne-o-zo-ic (nē'ō-zō'ĭk), *adj.* pertaining to the entire geologic period from the end of the Mesozoic to the present time.

nep (nĕp), *n.* catmint, a strong-scented herb liked by cats.

ne-pen-the (nē-pĕn'thē), *n.* a drug supposed by the ancient Greeks to cause forgetfulness of pain and sorrow.

neph-ew (nĕf'ū; nĕv'ū), *n.* the son of a brother or of a sister.

nep-o-tism (nĕp'ō-tĭzm), *n.* favoritism or partiality to nephews and other relatives; patronage or preference, especially in the case of those holding office, shown because of relationship.

Nep-tune (nĕp'tūn), *n.* in Roman mythology, the god of the sea, son of Saturn (Cronus) and Ops (Rhea); the planet of the solar system that is farthest from the sun.

ne-re-id (nē'rē-ĭd), *n.* a sea nymph, or imaginary maiden dwelling in the sea.

nerve (nûrv), *n.* one of the gray cordlike fibers which serve as a means of communication between the brain and all parts of the body; bodily or mental strength or control; coolness; the strong vein of a leaf: *v.t.* to fill with vigor, strength, or courage.

nerve-less (nûrv'lĕs), *adj.* having no strength or vigor; without force or courage; without nerves.—*adv.* **nervelessly.**

nerv-ine (nûr'vēn; nûr'vĭn), *n.* any tonic for the nerves: *adj.* affecting or quieting the nerves.

nerv-ous (nûr'vŭs), *adj.* pertaining to, or made of, nerves; having weak nerves; easily excited; timid; as, she is *nervous* in the dark; forceful; vigorous; as, a *nervous* literary style; restless or uneasy; as, the suspense made her *nervous.*—*adv.* **nervously.**—*n.* **nervousness.**

Syn. timorous, shaky.

nes-ci-ence (nĕsh'ĭ-ĕns; nĕsh'ĕns), *n.* ignorance; the state of not knowing.

nest (nĕst), *n.* the bed or dwelling made or chosen by a bird for the hatching of its eggs and the rearing of its young; a hatching place for insects, turtles, etc.; as, a hornets' *nest;* a cozy retreat or residence; the haunt of anything bad, or those who gather there; as, a *nest* of thieves; a number of boxes, one fitting inside another: *v.i.* to build and occupy a nest: *v.t.* to place in a nest.

nest egg (nĕst ĕg), an egg left in a nest to keep the hen from leaving it, and to cause her to lay more eggs in the same place; money laid by with intention of adding to it; as, the *nest egg* of a fortune.

nes-tle (nĕs'l), *v.i.* to make and use a nest; to lie close and snug; as, a child *nestles* in its mother's arms; to cuddle: *v.t.* to cherish or cuddle; to shelter.

nest-ling (nĕst'lĭng; nĕs'lĭng), *n.* a young bird recently hatched and not yet able to fly: *adj.* recently hatched.

net (nĕt), *n.* a fabric made of twine knotted into meshes or holes: used for catching birds, fish, etc.; any openwork fabric intended to confine something or protect from something; as, a *net* for the hair; a mosquito-*net;* any scheme to entrap; as, a *net* spread to capture a criminal; a snare: *v.t.* [*p.t.* and *p.p.* netted, *p.pr.* netting], to make into a net or network; catch in a net; to snare; produce as clear profit: *v.i.* to make nets or network: *adj.* clear of all charges and deductions; as, *net* gain: opposite to *gross;* as, *net* weight: **drag net,** a net intended to be drawn along the bottom of the water.—*n.* **netting.**

Drag Net

neth-er (nĕth'ẽr), *adj.* situated far below; lying beneath; lower; as, the *nether* regions: opposite to *upper.*

neth-er-most (nĕth'ẽr-mōst), *adj.* lowest; as, the *nethermost* depths of ocean.

net-tle (nĕt'l), *n.* any of various plants having prickles or stinging hairs: *v.t.* to provoke or irritate.

net-tle rash (nĕt'l răsh), an eruption on the skin resembling the effects of a nettle sting.

net-work (nĕt'wûrk'), *n.* meshwork; an openwork fabric made by interlacing threads of any material; any system of crossed or interlaced lines; as, a *network* of railroad tracks; the process of making any sort of meshwork.

neu-ral (nū'răl), *adj.* pertaining to the nerves or the nervous system.

neu-ral-gi-a (nū-răl'jĭ-ȧ), *n.* acute pain along the course of a nerve.

neu-ral-gic (nū-răl'jĭk), *adj.* pertaining to, or affected by, neuralgia, or severe pain in a nerve.

neu-ras-the-ni-a (nū'răs-thē'nĭ-ȧ; nū-răs'thē-nĭ'ȧ), *n.* nerve exhaustion or prostration.—*adj.* **neurasthenic.**

neu-ri-tis (nū-rī'tĭs), *n.* inflammation of a nerve or nerves.—*adj.* **neuritic.**

neu-rol-o-gy (nū-rŏl'ō-jĭ), *n.* the science of the nervous system.

neu-ron (nū'rŏn), *n.* a nerve cell with all its extensions.

neu-ro-path (nū'rō-păth), *n.* one who believes that the nervous system is largely responsible for disease.

neu-rop-a-thy (nū-rŏp'ȧ-thĭ), *n.* any disease or derangement of the nervous system.—*adj.* **neuropathic.**

neu-ro-sis (nū-rō'sĭs), *n.* a nervous disease, such as neuralgia and epilepsy.

neu-rot-ic (nū-rŏt'ĭk), *adj.* pertaining to, or affecting, the nerves; as, a *neurotic* disease or remedy; nervous: *n.* a drug affecting the nerves; a person whose nerves are disordered.

neu-ter (nū'tẽr), *adj.* in grammar, neither masculine nor feminine gender; neither active nor passive; intransitive; as, a *neuter* verb; in biology, having no sex; as, *neuter* bees: *n.* a plant or insect without sex.

neu-tral (nū'trăl), *adj.* unbiased; indifferent; taking no part on either side in a contest; as, a *neutral* nation; pertaining to a nation not taking sides; as, *neutral* ships; neither very good nor very bad; of no decided color; as, a *neutral* gray; a *neutral* tint; neither acid nor alkaline; said of chemical salts: *n.* one who, or that which, does not take sides in a dispute or conflict.—*adv.* **neutrally**.

neu-tral-i-ty (nū-trăl'ĭ-tĭ), *n.* the state of not taking sides; the state of being neither good nor bad; indifference.

neu-tral-ize (nū'trăl-īz), *v.t.* to make of no effect or to counteract; as, to *neutralize* the effects of a poison; render inactive; to declare by treaty to be free from taking sides; as, to *neutralize* small nations, such as Belgium.

nev-er (nĕv'ẽr), *adv.* not ever; not at any time; in no degree or way, under any condition: used for emphasis; as, *never* fear.

nev-er-more (nĕv"ẽr-mōr'), *adv.* not ever again; at no future time.

nev-er-the-less (nĕv"ẽr-*th*ē-lĕs'), *adv.* and *conj.* notwithstanding; in spite of that; yet; however; still.

new (nū), *adj.* recent in origin; modern; novel; lately made, produced, invented, or discovered; as, *new* wine; a *new* novel; a *new* motor; a *new* country; recently entered upon or commenced; as, *new* methods; not previously used; as, a *new* suit; beginning afresh; as, a *new* start in life; fresh.—*adv.* **newly**.—*n.* **newness**.

new-com-er (nū'kŭm"ẽr), *n.* one who has lately arrived.

new-el (nū'ĕl), *n.* in a winding staircase, the central upright pillar around which the steps turn; hence, the post at the foot of a stairway.

new-fan-gled (nū"făn'gld; nū'făn"gld), *adj.* new-fashioned; recently made; novel: usually said in disfavor of a thing; as, *newfangled* ideas or notions.

new-fash-ioned (nū"făsh'ŭnd; nū'făsh"ŭnd), *adj.* of a recent style; up to date in fashion.

New-found-land (nū-found'lănd; nū'fŭnd-lănd'), *n.* a large, black, shaggy breed of dog, originally from Newfoundland.

news (nūz), *n.* recent tidings; fresh information: plural in form, but used in singular.
Syn. intelligence.

news-boy (nūz'boi"), *n.* a boy who delivers or sells newspapers.

news-mon-ger (nūz'mŭn"gẽr), *n.* one who spreads news or gossip; a gossip.

news-pa-per (nūz'pā"pẽr), *n.* a paper published periodically, usually daily or weekly, containing the most recent news.

new style (nū stīl), the Gregorian or present style of reckoning the calendar: opposed to the former or Julian method, which made March the first month instead of January.

newt (nūt), *n.* a kind of water lizard; a salamander.

New Tes-ta-ment (nū tĕs'tá-mĕnt), the second of the two great divisions of the Bible, containing the Gospels and writings based upon them.

New Thought (nū thôt), a system of religious philosophy which affirms the creative power of spirit and the control of conditions by mental causes.

next (nĕkst), *adj.* [*superl.* of nigh], nearest in time, place, degree, or rank; as, the *next* day; the *next* street; the *next* quality; *next* in order: *adv.* immediately succeeding; in the nearest time, place, or order; as, you go *next*: **next of kin**, nearest relative.

Nez Per-cé (nā" pĕr"sā'), one of a tribe of American Indians, originally inhabiting Idaho, Oregon, and Washington.

nib (nĭb), *n.* a bird's beak or bill; the point of anything, especially of a pen.

nib-ble (nĭb'l), *n.* a small bite; a seizing to bite: *v.t.* and *v.i.* to bite a little at a time; continue to bite at gently and quickly; as, a fish *nibbles* bait, or *nibbles* at bait.

nib-lick (nĭb'lĭk), *n.* in golf, a small, narrow-headed, heavy iron club, used when the ball lies in bad places. Also, **niblic**.

nice (nīs), *adj.* precise; acute; as, *nice* judgment; fine; delicate; as, a *nice* discrimination; fastidious; overparticular; delicate; refined; as, to be *nice* in one's habits or dress; socially agreeable; pleasant; as, *nice* manners; *nice* people; pleasing to the taste; very exact; as, a *nice* piece of work.—*adv.* **nicely**.—*n.* **niceness**.
Syn. accurate, good, neat.
Ant. (see careless).

Ni-cene (nī'sēn; nī-sēn'), *adj.* pertaining to Nicæa, where was held the first great church council in the fourth century A. D.; denoting the creed adopted by that council.

ni-ce-ty (nī'sĕ-tĭ), *n.* a very small distinction, detail, or point; as, the *niceties* of a debate; delicate management; fastidious delicacy; subtlety; precision; as, *nicety* of decision; minute accuracy; as, *nicety* of measurement; a table delicacy.

niche (nĭch), *n.* a recess or hollow in a wall, as for a statue; a condition or position in life suitable to a person or thing: *v.t.* to put in a recess in a wall.

Niche

nick (nĭk), *n.* a notch; slit; a broken place in any edge or surface; as, a *nick* in the table; exact or critical point of time; as, he arrived in the *nick* of time; in old folk tales, an evil water sprite: *v.t.* to cut notches in; hit or grasp at the lucky moment.—**Nick**, the devil: usually, *Old Nick*.

nick-el (nĭk'l), *n.* a grayish-white metallic element or metal; a five-cent coin, made of nickel and copper.

nick-el-o-de-on (nĭk'l-ō'dē-ŭn), *n.* a five-cent moving-picture show.

nick-el sil-ver (nĭk'l sĭl'vẽr), an alloy of nickel, copper, and zinc, similar to German silver.

nick-nack (nĭk'năk'), *n.* a toy or bauble; a trinket. Also, **knickknack.**

nick-name (nĭk'nām'), *n.* a name given in sport or familiarity: *v.t.* to give a nickname to; call by a contemptuous name.

nic-o-tine (nĭk'ō-tĭn; nĭk'ō-tēn), *n.* a poison contained in tobacco. Also, **nicotin.**

niece (nēs), *n.* the daughter of one's brother or sister.

nig (nĭg), *v.t.* to cut off the edges of, as coin; to dress (stone) with a pointed hammer.

nig-gard (nĭg'ẽrd), *n.* a stingy and covetous person; a miser: *adj.* miserly; stingy.—*adv.* **niggardly.**

nig-gard-li-ness (nĭg'ẽrd-lĭ-nĕs), *n.* mean covetousness; stinginess; miserliness.

nig-gard-ly (nĭg'ẽrd-lĭ), *adj.* stingy; miserly; as, a *niggardly* person; scanty; as, a *niggardly* meal.

nig-ger (nĭg'ẽr), *n.* a vulgar or contemptuous term for a negro. [Colloq.]

nigh (nī), *adj.* [*comp.* nigher, *superl.* nighest or next], being near in time or place; as, the hour of his triumph is *nigh;* adjacent; closely related by blood or friendship; as, *nigh* relatives; on the left; as, the *nigh* horse: *adv.* near in time or place; as, they came *nigh* to us; close by; as, they live *nigh* here; almost; as, he was *nigh* starved: *prep.* near to; not remote or distant from; as, the well was *nigh* the house.—*n.* **nighness.**

night (nīt), *n.* the time from sunset to sunrise; period of darkness; the close of the day; figuratively, death; mental or moral darkness.

night-cap (nīt'kăp'), *n.* a head covering worn in bed; colloquially, a drink before going to bed.

night-dress (nīt'drĕs'), *n.* a garment worn in bed.

night-fall (nīt'fôl'), *n.* the coming of darkness at evening.

night-gown (nīt'goun'), *n.* a woman's or child's thin, loose garment worn in bed.

night-hawk (nīt'hôk'), *n.* a bird akin to the whippoorwill; a person who keeps late hours.

night-in-gale (nīt'ĭn-gāl), *n.* a small Old World bird which sings with a sweet note at night.

night let-ter (nīt lĕt'ẽr), a telegram sent at night, at reduced rates, to be delivered in the morning.

night-ly (nīt'lĭ), *adj.* pertaining to, or occurring at, night or every night: *adv.* night by night; every night.

night-mare (nīt'mâr'), *n.* a distressing dream accompanied with oppression in the chest and a feeling of helplessness; formerly, an evil spirit supposed to oppress people in their sleep; hence, any haunting or disturbing influence.

night-shade (nīt'shād'), *n.* a weedlike plant with white flowers, considered poisonous, but used in medicine.

night-shirt (nīt'shûrt'), *n.* a man's or boy's garment worn in bed.

night-walk-er (nīt'wôk'ẽr), *n.* a person who is abroad at night for an evil purpose.

ni-hil-ism (nī'hĭ-lĭzm), *n.* the doctrine that nothing can really be known, because nothing exists; nothingness: Nihilism, a socialist movement in Russia to destroy existing institutions and found a new order of things, with equal rights of land and property; violent revolutionism; anarchism.

ni-hil-ist (nī'hĭ-lĭst), *n.* a supporter of social and political revolution in Russia; an anarchist.—*adj.* **nihilistic.**

nil (nĭl), *n.* nothing; a thing of no account. Also, **nihil.**

nim-ble (nĭm'bl), *adj.* quick and active; alert; as, a *nimble* mind; lively; brisk; swift; as, *nimble* feet.—*adv.* **nimbly.** —*n.* **nimbleness.**

Syn. agile, prompt, smart.

Ant. (see awkward).

nim-bus (nĭm'bŭs), *n.* in art, the halo or cloud of light surrounding the heads of divinities, saints, and sovereigns; a rain cloud.

nine (nīn), *n.* eight and one; one less than ten; a symbol representing nine units, as 9 or ix.

nine-fold (nīn'fōld'), *adj.* nine times as many or as great: *adv.* so as to be nine times as many or as great.

nine-pins (nīn'pĭnz'), *n.pl.* a game in which nine pins or pegs of wood are stood up to be upset with wooden bowls or balls that are rolled up a wooden alley.

nine-teen (nīn-tēn'), *n.* eighteen and one; ten and nine; one less than twenty; a symbol representing nineteen units, as 19 or xix.

nine-teenth (nīn-tēnth'), *n.* one of nineteen equal parts; the quotient of a unit divided by nineteen: *adj.* ninth in order after the tenth; the ordinal of nineteen.

nine-ti-eth (nīn'tĭ-ĕth), *n.* one of ninety equal parts; the quotient of a unit divided by ninety: *adj.* tenth in order after the eightieth; the ordinal of ninety.

nine-ty (nīn'tĭ), *n.* nine times ten; eighty-nine and one; a symbol representing ninety units, as 90 or xc.

nin-ny (nĭn'ĭ), *n.* [*pl.* ninnies (-ĭz)], a foolish person; a simpleton; a dunce.

ninth (nīnth), *n.* one of nine equal parts; the quotient of a unit divided by nine: *adj.* next in order after the eighth; the ordinal of nine.—*adv.* **ninthly.**

nip (nĭp), *n.* a pinch, as with the nails or teeth; a blast or blight, as by cold; as, a *nip* of frost; a small drink of spirits; a small piece or bit: *v.t.* [*p.t.* and *p.p.* nipped, *p.pr.* nipping], to pinch; cut off the end of; check the growth or vigor of, especially by frost; blast or destroy.

nip-per (nĭp'ẽr), *n.* one who, or that which, pinches or cuts off: *pl.* a tool, such as pincers or tongs; the foreteeth of a horse; the large claws of a crab or lobster.

nip-ple (nĭp'l), *n.* that part of a female animal's breast through which milk is drawn; a teat; the mouthpiece of a nursing bottle.

Nir-va-na (nẽr-vä'nȧ; nẽr-vă'nȧ), *n.* in Buddhism, the highest religious state, when all desire of existence and worldly good is destroyed, and the soul becomes one with its creator.

nit (nĭt), *n.* the egg of any small insect, such as a louse.

ni-ter (nī'tẽr), *n.* nitrate of potash, or saltpeter; a drug; as, sweet spirits of *niter.* Also, **nitre.**

ni-trate (nī'trāt), *n.* a salt of nitric acid: **nitrate of silver**, a white crystalline salt, made by dissolving silver in nitric acid, and used in photography and for cauterizing, or burning the flesh; lunar caustic.

ni-tric (nī'trĭk), *adj.* pertaining to, or containing, nitrogen: **nitric acid**, a powerful acid which contains nitrogen, hydrogen, and oxygen, and which is used in chemistry, the arts, and medicine.

ni-trite (nī'trīt), *n.* a salt of nitrous acid, containing less oxygen than a nitrate.

ni-tro-ben-zene (nī"trō-bĕn'zēn; nī"-trō-bĕn-zēn'), *n.* a yellow, oily liquid formed by the action of nitric acid on benzene.

ni-tro-gen (nī'trō-jĕn), *n.* a colorless, odorless, tasteless gas which forms four-fifths of the volume of the atmosphere, and is the basis of nitric acid.

ni-trog-e-nous (nī-trŏj'ē-nŭs), *adj.* pertaining to, or containing, nitrogen, a gas which forms four-fifths of the atmosphere.

ni-tro-glyc-er-in (nī"trō-glĭs'ēr-ĭn), *n.* a highly explosive, oily liquid, prepared by the action of nitric and sulphuric acids upon glycerin. Also, **nitroglycerine, nitroleum.**

ni-trous (nī'trŭs), *adj.* resembling, obtained from, or soaked with, niter, or saltpeter: **nitrous acid**, the chemical base from which nitrites are formed: **nitrous oxide**, an anesthetic; laughing gas.

nix (nĭks), *n.* [*fem.* nixie], in Teutonic mythology, a water elf or fairy, similar to the kelpie in Scotch folklore.

no (nō), *adv.* nay; not so; as, *no*, I cannot go; opposite to *yes;* not any; not at all; as, he is *no* better, *no* worse: *adj.* not any; not one; as, he has *no* reason: *n.* a reply of denial or refusal; as, his answer was a decided *no;* he voted *no.*

No-ah (nō'*d*), *n.* in the Bible, the Hebrew patriarch who built the ark.—Genesis v. 28–x.

nob (nŏb), *n.* the head; a person of distinction; a nobleman. [SLANG.]

no-bil-i-ty (nō-bĭl'ĭ-tĭ), *n.* the state or quality of being lofty, excellent, worthy; high birth or rank as denoted by a title; dignity of character; greatness; the body of persons of rank and title above the common people; as, the *nobility* of Europe.

Syn. aristocracy, grandeur, peerage.

no-ble (nō'bl), *adj.* high in excellence or worth; as, a *noble* ambition; possessing dignity or greatness of mind; illustrious; as, a *noble* character; famous; great; as, *noble* deeds; high in rank; of ancient lineage or descent; as, *noble* birth; stately in appearance; grand; as, *noble* architecture: *n.* a peer or person of high rank and title; formerly, an English gold coin.—*adv.* **nobly.**—*n.* **nobleness.**

Syn., adj. elevated, lofty, magnanimous.

no-ble-man (nō'bl-măn), *n.* [*fem.* noblewoman], a man of rank above that of a commoner; a peer.

no-bod-y (nō'bŏd-ĭ), *n.* no one; a person of no importance or influence.

noc-turn (nŏk'tûrn), *n.* a Roman Catholic Church service held at daybreak.

noc-tur-nal (nŏk-tûr'năl), *adj.* pertaining to, done, or happening at night; as, a *nocturnal* visit: opposite to *diurnal;* seeking food or active at night; as, *nocturnal* insects or birds.—*adv.* **nocturnally.**

noc-turne (nŏk'tûrn; nŏk-tûrn'), *n.* a picture of a night scene; a dreamy, sentimental, musical composition appropriate to the night; a serenade.

nod (nŏd), *n.* a quick inclination of the head; a command: *v.t.* [*p.t.* and *p.p.* nodded, *p.pr.* nodding], to signify by a quick inclination of the head; incline or bend with a quick movement: *v.i.* to incline or bend the top with a quick, forward motion; as, flowers *nod* in the breeze; to bend the head in token of assent or as a salute; to be drowsy.

nod-dle (nŏd'l), *n.* the head: used in contempt. [COLLOQ.]

node (nōd), *n.* a knot; knob or swelling; a hard swelling on a tendon or bone; the points of the stem of a plant from which a leaf springs; one of the two points at which the orbit of a planet intersects the ecliptic.—*adj.* **nodose.**—*n.* **nodosity.**

nod-ule (nŏd'ūl), *n.* a little knot, or irregular, rounded lump.

No-el (nō'ĕl), *n.* Christmas day; a Christmas carol. [FR.]

nog-gin (nŏg'ĭn), *n.* a small cup or mug; a liquid measure equal to one gill.

noil (noil), *n.* short-staple wool combed from the long-staple and used for making yarn.

noise (noiz), *n.* sound, especially when confused or disagreeable; clamor; outcry; loud discussion: *v.t.* to spread by rumor; as, they *noise* their private affairs abroad.

Syn., n. cry, din, uproar, tumult.
Ant. (see silence).

noise-less (noiz'lĕs), *adj.* silent; making no sound.—*adv.* **noiselessly.**—*n.* **noiselessness.**

noi-some (noi'sŭm), *adj.* injurious to health; as, a *noisome* pestilence; harmful; as, *noisome* vapors; offensive; disgusting.—*adv.* **noisomely.**—*n.* **noisomeness.**

nois-y (noiz'ĭ), *adj.* full of loud, confused, disagreeable sounds; as, a *noisy* city; making or given to making an outcry or uproar; clamorous; as, a *noisy* crowd.—*adv.* **noisily.**—*n.* **noisiness.**

nom-ad (nŏm'ăd; nō'măd), *n.* one of an unsettled tribe of people who wander about in search of game, pasture, etc.: *adj.* wandering; roving.—*adj.* **nomadic.**

No Man's Land (nō mănz lănd), in the World War, a name given to the ground lying between the front line defenses of the opposing armies.

no-men-cla-ture (nō'mĕn-klā"tûr), *n.* the collection of words and terms, or the language, used in any art or science; as, the *nomenclature* of botany or chemistry.

nom-i-nal (nŏm'ĭ-năl), *adj.* pertaining to, or consisting of, a name or names; as, *nominal* differences; existing in name only; as, *nominal* authority or power.—*adv.* **nominally.**

nom-i-nate (nŏm'ĭ-nāt), *v.t.* to propose or name for an office; as, to *nominate* a candidate for election.

nom-i-na-tion (nŏm"ĭ-nā'shŭn), *n.* the act of naming for office; the state of being named for office.

nom-i-na-tive (nŏm'ĭ-nd-tĭv), *adj.* naming or being, in grammar, the case of the subject of a finite verb: *n.* the case of the subject of a finite verb.

nom·i·na·tor (nŏm'ĭ-nā'tẽr), *n.* one who names another for some office.

nom·i·nee (nŏm'ĭ-nē'), *n.* one who is named or proposed for an office or duty.

non- (nŏn-), a *prefix* meaning not: used before many words, which are self-explaining.

non·age (nŏn'āj), *n.* minority, or the period of life before one is legally old enough to look after one's own property.

non·a·ge·na·ri·an (nŏn'ȧ-jē-nā'rĭ-ăn), *n.* a person of from ninety to one hundred years old: *adj.* between the ages of ninety and one hundred years.

non·a·gon (nŏn'ȧ-gŏn), *n.* a plane figure with nine sides and nine angles.

nonce (nŏns), *n.* the present occasion or time; as, this will do for the *nonce.*

non·cha·lance (nŏn'shȧ-lăns), *n.* lack of interest; carelessness; indifference. [Fr.]

non·cha·lant (nŏn'shȧ-lănt), *adj.* being without interest or enthusiasm; cool; indifferent; careless; as, a *nonchalant* manner.—*n.* **nonchalantly.** [Fr.]

non·com·bat·ant (nŏn-kŏm'băt-ănt), *n.* one connected with an army or navy whose duties do not include fighting, as a surgeon, or nurse; one not in the army or navy.

non·com·mis·sioned (nŏn'kŏ-mĭsh'ŭnd), *adj.* not having a warrant or certificate to engage in a service: **noncommissioned officer,** an enlisted man who has risen to the rank of a sergeant or corporal; one who has not a certificate from a military academy.

non·com·mit·tal (nŏn'kŏ-mĭt'ăl), *adj.* not revealing one's opinion or purpose; as, his answer was wholly *noncommittal.*—*adv.* **noncommittally.**

non·con·duc·tor (nŏn'kŏn-dŭk'tẽr), *n.* any substance through which heat, light, electricity, etc., will not pass readily.

non·con·form·i·ty (nŏn'kŏn-fôr'mĭ-tĭ), *n.* failure or refusal to make one's conduct or opinion fit those prevailing generally: used especially of lack of agreement with established church beliefs or forms.—*n.* **nonconformist.**

non·de·script (nŏn'dē-skrĭpt), *n.* a person or thing that cannot be easily described or classed; as, a *nondescript* mineral: *adj.* not easily described; odd; of no particular character.

none (nŭn), *pron.* not any; not one; no one; as, *none* of them came: *adv.* in no respect; not at all; to no extent.

non·en·ti·ty (nŏn-ĕn'tĭ-tĭ), *n.* [*pl.* nonentities (-tĭz)], a thing not existing; a person of no importance or influence.

nones (nōnz), *n.pl.* in the Roman calendar, the ninth day before the ides (counting the ides, or the fifteenth day of March, May, July, and October, and the thirteenth of other months).

non·es·sen·tial (nŏn'ĕ-sĕn'shăl), *adj.* not necessary to life; as, *nonessential* industries: *n.* a thing not needed for life.

non·pa·reil (nŏn'pȧ-rĕl'), *adj.* without an equal; peerless: *n.* a person or thing of unequaled excellence; one of several kinds of birds, especially the finch; a small size of type.

non·plus (nŏn'plŭs), *v.t.* [*p.t.* and *p.p.* nonplussed, *p.pr.* nonplussing], to throw into complete perplexity; to puzzle: *n.* inability to say or do more.

non·res·i·dent (nŏn-rĕz'ĭ-dĕnt), *n.* one who does not live in a particular place: *adj.* not living in a particular place; always absent from one's office, estate, etc.—*n.* **nonresidence.**

non·re·sist·ant (nŏn'rē-zĭs'tănt), *adj.* not opposing attack; submissive: *n.* one who does not believe in using force to defend himself from attack.—*n.* **nonresistance.**

non·sense (nŏn'sĕns), *n.* language without meaning; anything absurd or trifling: *interj.* absurd!

non·sen·si·cal (nŏn-sĕn'sĭ-kăl), *adj.* absurd; unmeaning.—*adv.* **nonsensically.**—*n.* **nonsensicalness.**

non·suit (nŏn'sūt'), *n.* the withdrawal of a suit during trial, either voluntarily, or by judgment of the court, on discovery of error or defect in the case: *v.t.* to dismiss a case, usually for lack of sufficient cause or evidence.

non·un·ion (nŏn-ūn'yŭn), *adj.* not belonging to a trade-union; as, to employ *nonunion* labor; not favoring trade-unions; as, a *nonunion* factory.—*n.* **nonunionist.**

noo·dle (nōō'dl), *n.* a simpleton; a strip of dried dough, served in soup.

nook (nŏŏk), *n.* a small recess or secluded retreat; as, a shady *nook;* a corner.

noon (nōōn), *n.* the middle of the day; twelve o'clock; height or time of greatest brilliancy or power; as, the *noon* of life: *adj.* pertaining to midday; as, the *noon* hour.

noon·day (nōōn'dā'), *n.* the middle of the day; noon: *adj.* pertaining to midday; as, *noonday* heat. Also, **noontide.**

noose (nōōs), *n.* a slipknot which binds the closer the more tightly it is drawn; a snare: *v.t.* to catch or tie in a slipknot, as wild horses; ensnare.

nor (nôr), *conj.* and not; a negative connective used after the negatives *neither* and *not* to continue or complete their meaning: called a correlative of *neither* or *not.*

no·ri·a (nō'rĭ-ȧ), *n.* a device for raising water, used in Spain and other countries bordering on the Mediterranean.

Noria

norm (nôrm), *n.* a rule or standard; model; pattern; type.

nor·mal (nôr'măl), *adj.* according to rule; perpendicular; regular; natural; as, a *normal* heartbeat; serving as a standard or model.—*adv.* **normally.**

Syn. usual, ordinary.

nor-mal school (nôr'mȧl skōōl), a school whose methods serve as a model; a school for the training of teachers for elementary schools.

Nor-man (nôr'măn), *n.* a native or inhabitant of Normandy, in France; originally, a Northman, or Scandinavian: *adj.* pertaining to Normandy, the Normans, or to a style of architecture introduced into England by the Normans, and marked by the rounded arch and massive square towers.

Norse (nôrs), *adj.* pertaining to ancient Scandinavia, its language, and its people.

Norse-man (nôrs'măn), *n.* [*pl.* Norsemen (-mĕn)], a Northman; an ancient Scandinavian.

north (nôrth), *n.* one of the four points of the compass; the point opposite to the south, or to the left of a person facing the sunrise; a section of country lying north of another; as, the *north* of Europe: **North**, that part of the United States lying north of the southern boundary line of Pennsylvania: *adj.* pertaining to, situated in, or coming from, the north; as, a *north* wind: *adv.* to the north; as, walk *north* one block: **North Star**, the star toward which the northern end of the earth's axis points.

north-east (nôrth'ēst'), *n.* the point of the compass halfway between north and east; country lying in the direction of that point: *adj.* pertaining to, situated in, or coming from, the northeast: *adv.* toward the northeast.—*adj.* and *adv.* **northeasterly**.—*adj.* **northeastern**.—*adv.* **northeastward**.

north-east-er (nôrth'ēs'tẽr), *n.* a strong wind or a storm from the northeast.

north-er (nôr'*th*ẽr), *n.* a strong cold wind from the north, especially such a wind in Texas and the Gulf of Mexico.

north-er-ly (nôr'*th*ẽr-lĭ), *adj.* pertaining to, or situated in, or coming from, the north: *adv.* toward the north.

north-ern (nôr'*th*ẽrn), *adj.* in, from, or towards, the north; as, a *northern* course: **Northern**, pertaining to the United States north of the southern boundary of Pennsylvania.

north-ern-er (nôr'*th*ẽr-nẽr), *n.* a person living in, or coming from, the north: **Northerner**, a person living in, or coming from, the northern part of the United States.

north-ern lights (nôr'*th*ẽrn līts), the aurora borealis, or streams of light seen in the region of the north pole at night.

north-land (nôrth'lănd), *n.* the northern part of a country or continent.

North-man (nôrth'măn), *n.* [*pl.* Northmen (-mĕn)], an ancient Scandinavian; a Norseman.

north-ward (nôrth'wẽrd), *adj.* in, from, or towards, the north: *adv.* towards the north. Also, **northwardly**.—*adv.* **northwards**.

north-west (nôrth'wĕst'), *n.* the point of the compass halfway between north and west; country lying in the direction of that point: *adj.* pertaining to, situated in, or coming from, the northwest: *adv.* toward the northwest.—*adj.* and *adv.* **northwesterly**.—*adj.* **northwestern**.—*adv.* **northwestward**.

north-west-er (nôrth'wĕs'tẽr), *n.* a strong wind or storm from the northwest.

Nor-we-gian (nôr-wē'jăn; nôr-wē'jĭ-ăn), *n.* a native, or the language, of Norway: *adj.* pertaining to Norway, its language, or people.

nose (nōz), *n.* the organ of smell; scent; a snout; nozzle; a spout; anything like a nose: *v.t.* to smell or scent; to rub or push with the nose; as, horses *nose* each other; the boat *nosed* its way through the jam: *v.i.* to smell or scent; to pry curiously.

nose-cap (nōz'kăp'), *n.* a metal cap on a shell or gunstock.

nose dive (nōz dīv), an airplane maneuver, in which the pilot points his machine downward and dives rapidly.

nose-gay (nōz'gā'), *n.* a bouquet or bunch of flowers.

nos-tal-gi-a (nŏs-tăl'jĭ-ȧ), *n.* homesickness; especially the longing for home which causes intense mental depression.

nos-tril (nŏs'trĭl), *n.* one of the two external openings in the nose.

nos-trum (nŏs'trŭm), *n.* a quack medicine; a pet scheme or remedy for some evil condition.

not (nŏt), *adv.* a word expressive of denial or refusal.

no-ta-bil-i-ty (nō'tȧ-bĭl'ĭ-tĭ), *n.* [*pl.* notabilities (-tĭz)], a person of distinction or importance; the quality of being important or out of the ordinary.

no-ta-ble (nō'tȧ-bl), *adj.* worthy of attention; memorable; as, a *notable* event; notorious; as, a *notable* thief; remarkable; as, a *notable* achievement; industrious; thrifty: *n.* a person or thing of distinction.—*adv.* **notably**.—*n.* **notableness**.

Syn., *adj.* plain, evident, rare, signal, striking.

Ant. (see obscure).

no-ta-ri-al (nō-tā'rĭ-ăl), *adv.* pertaining to, or done by, a notary, or an official who has power to administer oaths, etc.

no-ta-ry (nō'tȧ-rĭ), *n.* [*pl.* notaries (-rĭz)], an official permitted by law to attest or certify deeds and contracts, administer oaths, etc. Also, **notary public**.

no-ta-tion (nō-tā'shŭn), *n.* the act or practice of recording by marks or symbols; a system of signs or symbols used in place of language, for brevity or clearness; especially, the system of numbers, letters, and signs used in arithmetic and algebra, and the signs used in writing or printing music.

notch (nŏch), *n.* a small nick or V-shaped cut, as in a stick; a narrow pass through mountains; *v.t.* to nick or cut into small hollows; to tally or record by nicks.

note (nōt), *n.* a memorandum; reputation; fame; as, a man of *note*; a brief explanation; as, the *notes* at the foot of the page make the text clear; short letter; a diplomatic communication; in music, a mark or sign representing a sound; the sound itself; a tone; as, a sad *note* in a voice; a call or cry; as, the *note* of a bird; a paper acknowledging a debt and promising payment; as, a promissory *note*; a bank note, or paper money issued by a bank: *pl.* a summary of a speech: *v.t.* to make a memorandum of; to mark; to observe; show respect or attention to; as, *note* what I say.

Syn., *n.* token, symbol, sign, indication, remark, comment.

not-ed (nōt'ĕd), *p.adj.* well known; celebrated; as, a *noted* musician;

remarkable; as, a *noted* achievement.—*adv.* **notedly.**—*n.* **notedness.**

note-wor-thy (nōt'wûr"*th*ĭ), *adj.* worthy of notice; distinguished; remarkable.

noth-ing (nŭth'ĭng), *n.* not anything; as, I have *nothing* to say; a thing of no value, use, or importance; as, the story is a mere *nothing;* a cipher; a nobody: *adv.* in no degree.

noth-ing-ness (nŭth'ĭng-nĕs), *n.* nonexistence; worthlessness; insignificance.

no-tice (nō'tĭs), *n.* a taking heed; attention; observation; as, to take *notice* of what passes before one; information; warning; as, he received *notice* to vacate the building; a printed announcement or sign; as, a *notice* of a death in a newspaper; the *notice* of sale on a building; press criticism: *v.t.* to see or observe; regard; attend to; make remarks upon.
Syn., *n.* notification, intelligence, information: *v.* observe, heed.

no-tice-a-ble (nō'tĭs-ȧ-bl), *adj.* worthy of observation or attention; likely to attract attention.—*adv.* **noticeably.**

no-ti-fi-ca-tion (nō"tĭ-fĭ-kā'shŭn), *n.* the act of giving warning or information; the warning or information given; the written or printed document by which information is sent, as an advertisement.

no-ti-fy (nō'tĭ-fī), *v.t.* [*p.t.* and *p.p.* notified, *p.pr.* notifying], to give warning or information to; to make known; to publish.
Syn. acquaint, inform, declare.

no-tion (nō'shŭn), *n.* an idea or theory; opinion; belief; inclination; as, to have a *notion* to do something; a clever contrivance: *pl.* small useful articles, such as pins, thread, etc.
Syn. sentiment, whim, caprice.

no-tion-al (nō'shŭn-ăl), *adj.* pertaining to, or conveying, an idea or fancy; ideal; imaginary; visionary; given to whims or fancies.
Syn. fanciful, whimsical.

no-to-ri-e-ty (nō"tō-rī'ē-tĭ), *n.* the state of being well known, especially in an undesirable sense.

no-to-ri-ous (nō-tō'rĭ-ŭs), *adj.* publicly known: usually in a bad sense; as, a *notorious* criminal.—*adv.* **notoriously.**—*n.* **notoriousness.**
Syn. conspicuous, ill-famed.

not-with-stand-ing (nŏt"wĭ*th*-stăn'dĭng), *prep.* in spite of: *conj.* yet; although: *adv.* nevertheless; however.

nou-gat (nōō'gȧ; nōō'gȧ'), *n.* a candy or sweetmeat of almonds, pistachio nuts, sugar, and flour.

nought (nôt), *n.* nothing; zero; naught; as, he gained *nought* and lost all.

noun (noun), *n.* the name of any person, place, thing, or quality.

nour-ish (nûr'ĭsh), *v.t.* to feed or bring up; as, to *nourish* a child; to supply with material for growth; as, food should *nourish* the tissues; support; maintain; foster; as, to *nourish* hatred or insurrection; educate: *v.i.* to promote growth; as, good food *nourishes.*
Syn. nurture, cherish.
Ant. (see starve).

nour-ish-ment (nûr'ĭsh-mĕnt), *n.* that which sustains or gives strength to the body, as food; that which assists growth of anything; the act of sustaining, or state of being sustained.
Syn. diet, sustenance.

nou-veau riche (nōō' vō' rēsh'), [*pl.* nouveaux riches (nōō'vō' rēsh')], a person who has lately become wealthy: *adj.* newly rich. [Fr.]

nov-el (nŏv'ĕl), *adj.* of recent origin or introduction; as, a *novel* plan; new, strange, or unusual; as, a *novel* machine: *n.* a long, fictitious story, in which the scenes, characters, and events are such as would be met with in real life.
Syn., *adj.* modern, fresh, unused, rare.
Ant. (see old).

nov-el-ette (nŏv"ĕl-ĕt'), *n.* a short fictitious story about people and events, which is true to everyday life; a short novel.

nov-el-ist (nŏv'ĕl-ĭst), *n.* a writer of long stories, in which the scenes, people, and events are true to everyday life.

nov-el-ty (nŏv'ĕl-tĭ), *n.* freshness; newness; as, the *novelty* of an idea or an experience; something new, or fresh, as an article of dress or of any kind.

No-vem-ber (nō-vĕm'bẽr), *n.* the eleventh month of the year, containing thirty days.

nov-ice (nŏv'ĭs), *n.* a beginner in any business, profession, or calling; in the Roman Catholic Church, one who has entered a religious house, but has not yet taken the vow.

no-vi-ti-ate (nō-vĭsh'ĭ-āt), *n.* the state of being a beginner; the time during which fitness for any position is being tested. Also, **noviciate.**

now (nou), *adv.* at the present time; as, the danger is *now* over; quite recently; as, he left just *now;* in the immediate future; at once; as, I am going *now;* under the circumstances; as, *now,* what will you do? *conj.* since; seeing that; now that; as, I need not stay, *now* you are here: *n.* the present time; as, *now* is the time to do it.

now-a-days (nou'ȧ-dāz"), *adv.* at the present time, or in the present age.

no-way (nō'wā"), *adv.* in no manner or degree; not at all; nowise.—Also, **noways.**

no-where (nō'hwâr"), *adv.* not in any place.

no-wise (nō'wīz"), *adv.* not in any manner or degree; noways.

nox-ious (nŏk'shŭs), *adj.* harmful; injurious; deadly; as, *noxious* gases.—*adv.* **noxiously.**—*n.* **noxiousness.**
Syn. hurtful, poisonous.
Ant. (see beneficial).

noz-zle (nŏz'l), *n.* a projecting mouthpiece or spout; as, the *nozzle* of a hose.

nub-bin (nŭb'ĭn), *n.* a small or imperfect ear of corn.

nu-cle-ate (nū'klē-āt), *adj.* having a center about which matter gathers: *v.t.* and *v.i.* (nū'klē-āt), to gather into or around a center.

nu-cle-o-lus (nū-klē'ō-lŭs), *n.* a minute body inside a nucleus, or starting point.

nu-cle-us (nū'klē-ŭs), *n.* the kernel; the central part about which matter collects; the central, bright part of a comet's head; the small, central mass of life-containing substance, called protoplasm, from which plants and animals grow.

.opr. 1911, J. C. W. Co. AMERICAN TREE LEAVES, FLOWERS AND FRUITS

1. White pine. 2. Shellbark hickory. 3. Red spruce. 4. Incense cedar. 5. Hemlock. 6. Black walnut. 7. Redwood. 8. Chestnut. 9. Cottonwood. 10. River birch.

nude (nūd), *adj.* bare; naked; in law, without consideration; void: *n.* in art, the undraped human form: with *the*.—*adv.* nudely.—*n.* nudeness.

nudge (nŭj), *v.t.* to touch or push gently, as with the elbow: *n.* a gentle touch or poke, as with the elbow.

nu-di-ty (nū'dĭ-tĭ), *n.* nakedness: *pl.* naked parts.

nu-ga-to-ry (nū'gȧ-tō-rĭ), *adj.* trifling; useless.

nug-get (nŭg'ĕt), *n.* a lump or mass, especially of gold or other precious metal.

nui-sance (nū'săns), *n.* anything offensive, injurious, vexatious, or annoying.

null (nŭl), *adj.* of no legal force; invalid; as, the law was *null* and void; of no value; having no existence.

nul-li-fi-ca-tion (nŭl'ĭ-fĭ-kā'shŭn), *n.* the act of rendering invalid or void.

nul-li-fy (nŭl'ĭ-fī), *v.t.* [*p.t.* and *p.p.* nullified, *p.pr.* nullifying], to deprive of legal force; to annul, or render void; as, to *nullify* a law; to make ineffective.

Syn. invalidate, repeal, quash, cancel.

nul-li-ty (nŭl'ĭ-tĭ), *n.* want of existence or force; insignificance; that which does not exist or which has no force.

numb (nŭm), *adj.* deprived of sensation or motion; torpid; dulled: *v.t.* to deprive of sensation; to benumb, as by cold.—*adv.* numbly.—*n.* numbness.

num-ber (nŭm'bẽr), *n.* a unit; one, or more than one; a total of units; multitude; one of a series; in grammar, quality of a word by which it refers to one (*singular number*), or to more than one (*plural number*); poetry, meter, or verse: usually in plural; as, he wrote in *numbers*: *pl.* the science of arithmetic: *v.t.* to count; mark with a number; amount to: Numbers, the fourth book of the Old Testament, recording the counting of the Hebrew tribes.

num-ber-less (nŭm'bẽr-lĕs), *adj.* having no number; countless.

nu-mer-al (nū'mẽr-ăl), *adj.* pertaining to, consisting of, or denoting, number: *n.* a sign or word expressing a number, as X for ten; 5 for five.—*adv.* numerically.

nu-mer-ate (nū'mẽr-āt), *v.t.* to count or number, as the census; to point off and read (several figures) as one number.

nu-mer-a-tion (nū'mẽr-ā'shŭn), *n.* the act of counting or numbering; the act or art of reading or naming numbers.

nu-mer-a-tor (nū'mẽr-ā'tẽr), *n.* one that counts or numbers; in fractions, the number above the line, which shows how many parts of a unit are taken.

nu-mer-i-cal (nū-mĕr'ĭ-kăl), *adj.* pertaining to numbers; expressed in numbers.—*adv.* numerically.

nu-mer-ous (nū'mẽr-ŭs), *adj.* consisting of a great number; many.—*adv.* numerously.—*n.* numerousness.

nu-mis-mat-ic (nū'mĭz-măt'ĭk; nū'mĭs-măt'ĭk), *adj.* pertaining to, or consisting of, coins or medals: *n.pl.* the science and study of coins and medals, with especial reference to their historic interest.—*n.* numismatology.

nu-mis-ma-tist (nū-mĭz'mȧ-tĭst; nū-mĭs'mȧ-tĭst), *n.* one who collects and studies coins and medals.

num-skull (nŭm'skŭl'), *n.* a blockhead; a dunce; a stupid fellow.

nun (nŭn), *n.* a woman living in a convent and devoted to a religious life under a vow of poverty and obedience to a superior; a variety of pigeon; the blue titmouse.

nun-ci-o (nŭn'shĭ-ō), *n.* an ambassador or agent of the Pope, especially at a foreign court; a messenger.

nun-ner-y (nŭn'ẽr-ĭ), *n.* [*pl.* nunneries (-ĭz)], a convent or religious house for women.

nup-tial (nŭp'shăl), *adj.* of or pertaining to marriage: *n.pl.* a marriage; marriage ceremony.

nurse (nûrs), *n.* a woman who has the care of the children of another person; one who tends the sick or infirm; one who, or that which, protects or fosters: *v.t.* to tend or suckle, as an infant; bring up; tend in sickness; promote growth or vigor in; encourage: *v.i.* to suckle; of an infant, to suck.

nurs-er-y (nûr'sẽr-ĭ), *n.* [*pl.* nurseries (-ĭz)], an apartment for young children; a place or garden for raising young plants; a trough in which young fish are reared.

nurs-er-y-man (nûr'sẽr-ĭ-măn), *n.* [*pl.* nurserymen (-mĕn)], one whose business is the starting and raising of young plants.

nurs-ling (nûrs'lĭng), *n.* an infant; a child; anything that is tenderly fostered.

nur-ture (nûr'tŭr), *n.* that which nourishes; the act or process of feeding or promoting growth; food; education; training: *v.t.* to bring up; educate; nourish.

nut (nŭt), *n.* the fruit of certain trees, consisting of a kernel inclosed in a hard shell; the kernel; a piece of metal with a threaded hole for screwing on to the end of a bolt; slang, a foolish person.

nut-crack-er (nŭt'krăk'ẽr), *n.* an implement for cracking nuts; a bird that feeds on nuts, seeds, etc.

nut-meg (nŭt'mĕg), *n.* the kernel of the fruit of an East Indian tree; also, the tree.

nu-tri-ent (nū'trĭ-ĕnt), *n.* anything, as an article of food, that nourishes or promotes growth: *adj.* nutritious or promoting growth.

nu-tri-ment (nū'trĭ-mĕnt), *n.* that which provides nourishment; food.

nu-tri-tion (nū-trĭsh'ŭn), *n.* the processes by which the body takes in and uses food, or is nourished and repaired; that which nourishes; food.

nu-tri-tious (nū-trĭsh'ŭs), *adj.* promoting growth and repair of the body; nourishing.—*adv.* nutritiously.

nu-tri-tive (nū'trĭ-tĭv), *adj.* having qualities that nourish and repair; nourishing; pertaining to the process of growth and repair in the body.—*adv.* nutritively.

nut-ty (nŭt'ĭ), *adj.* abounding in, or tasting like, nuts.

nux vom-i-ca (nŭks vŏm'ĭ-kȧ), the seed of an East Indian tree, which yields the deadly poison strychnine; also, the tree; the medicine made from this seed.

nymph (nĭmf), *n.* in classic mythology, a lesser goddess of nature living in the mountains, woods, streams, etc.; an attractive, handsome young woman.

O

O (ō), *interj.* an exclamation of wonder, pain, etc.; a term for calling or addressing a person.

oak (ōk), *n.* a tree of many species, found in all parts of the world, and noted for its peculiar fruit, the acorn; the wood of this tree; any of several plants resembling the oak in foliage.

oak ap-ple (ōk ăp'l), a spongy growth on the leaves or young branches of the oak.

oak-en (ōk'n), *adj.* made of, or consisting of, oak; as, an *oaken* bucket.

oa-kum (ō'kŭm), *n.* loose hemp-fiber obtained by untwisting old ropes: used for stopping leaks in boats, etc.

oar (ōr), *n.* a light pole with a broad, flat, or spoon-shaped blade at one end, used for rowing a boat; one who rows a boat; *v.i.* to row.

Spoon Oar

oar-lock (ōr'lŏk"), *n.* a U-shaped ring in which the oar rests in rowing a boat. Also, row'lock.

oars-man (ōrz'măn), *n.* [*pl.* oarsmen (-mĕn)], one who is skilled in rowing a boat.

o-a-sis (ō-ā'sis; ō'ȧ-sis), *n.* [*pl.* oases (-sēz)], a fertile, verdant place in a barren sandy desert.

oast (ōst), *n.* a kiln for drying hops or barley.

oat (ōt), *n.* a certain plant, or its grain, which is used as food: usually in plural; a musical instrument made of an oat stem.

oat-en (ōt'n), *adj.* made of oats, of oatmeal, or of the oat stem.

oath (ōth), *n.* a solemn declaration that one speaks the truth, with an appeal to God as witness; a profane use of the name of God or of any sacred thing.

oat-meal (ōt'mēl"), *n.* meal made from oats; porridge or pudding made from the meal.

O-ba-di-ah (ō"bȧ-dī'ȧ), *n.* a book of the Old Testament; the Hebrew prophet whose prophecy is recorded in the book.

ob-bli-ga-to (ŏb"blĭ-gä'tō), *n.* in music, an accompaniment which is important in itself, and is played by a single instrument. [It.]

ob-du-ra-cy (ŏb'dū-rȧ-sĭ), *n.* extreme hardness of heart; obstinacy.

ob-du-rate (ŏb'dū-rāt), *adj.* not to be moved by appeals to the feelings; hardened in heart or feelings, especially against moral influence; obstinate. —*adv.* obdurately.

Syn. hard, callous, unfeeling, insensible.
Ant. (see yielding).

o-be-di-ence (ō-bē'dĭ-ĕns), *n.* act or state of yielding willingly to the control of others; submission to authority; dutifulness.

o-be-di-ent (ō'bē'dĭ-ĕnt), *adj.* willing to do as one is bidden; submissive to authority; dutifully yielding.—*adv.* obediently.

Syn. compliant, respectful.
Ant. (see obstinate).

o-bei-sance (ō-bā'săns), *n.* a bow, or bend of the knee as an expression of obedience or respect; as, a subject makes *obeisance* to his king; an act of courtesy or reverence.

ob-e-lisk (ŏb'ĕ-lĭsk), *n.* a lofty, four-sided stone pillar shaped at the top like a pyramid; a reference mark [†]: called also a *dagger*.

Obelisk

ob-e-lus (ŏb'ĕ-lŭs), *n.* a mark [— or ÷ or †] used in old manuscripts to indicate a doubtful reading; in modern writing, a break [—].

o-bese (ō-bēs'), *adj.* very fat; corpulent; fleshy.—*n.* obeseness.

o-bes-i-ty (ō-bĕs'ĭ-tĭ), *n.* excessive corpulence or fatness, especially of an unhealthy kind.

o-bey (ō-bā'), *v.t.* [*p.t.* and *p.p.* obeyed, *p.pr.* obeying], to submit to the rule or authority of; as, to *obey* the commandments; comply with the orders or instructions of; as, to *obey* parents; to respond to direction or control of; as, a horse *obeys* the rein: *v.i.* to yield; do as bidden.

Syn. conform, mind.

ob-fus-cate (ŏb-fŭs'kāt), *v.t.* to bewilder; perplex; confuse the mind of.

o-bi (ō'bĭ), *n.* formerly, among the negroes of Africa, and later, among the West Indian natives, a system of secret sorcery or magical rites; a charm; a kind of sash worn by Japanese women.

Obi

o-bit-u-a-ry (ō-bĭt'ū-ā-rĭ), *n.* [*pl.* obituaries (-rĭz)], a notice of a death; a brief account of the life of a person just deceased: *adj.* pertaining to the death of a person, or recording deaths.

ob-ject (ŏb'jĕkt), *n.* anything that can be seen or touched; anything that can be known or understood by the mind; motive; end; aim; in grammar, a word, phrase, or clause that receives the action of the verb and completes the predicate: opposite to *subject*: *v.t.* (ŏb-jĕkt'), to urge as a reason against: *v.i.* to make opposition; usually with *to*; to disapprove.—*n.* objector.

Syn., n. purpose, design: *v.* oppose.
Ant. (see assent).

ob-ject glass (ŏb'jĕkt glȧs), the lens of a microscope or telescope nearest to the object to be observed and forming the image.

ob-jec-tion (ŏb-jĕk'shŭn), *n.* the act of opposing or of finding fault; reason against anything; opposition.

ob-jec-tion-a-ble (ŏb-jĕk'shŭn-ȧ-bl), *adj.* liable or open to opposition; calling for disapproval; offensive.—*adv.* objectionably.—*n.* objectionableness.

ob-jec-tive (ŏb-jĕk'tĭv), *n.* the point or purpose toward which any action is directed; an aim; in grammar, the case of a word governed by a transitive active verb or a preposition, or the word so governed; the lens of a microscope or telescope nearest to the object to be observed and forming the image: *adj.* belonging to a material thing; being outside of the mind: opposite to *subjective*, or existing only in the mind; in grammar, noting the case which follows, and is governed by, a transitive active verb or a preposition.—*adv.* **objectively.**—*n.* **objectiveness.**

ob-jec-tiv-i-ty (ŏb'jĕk-tĭv'ĭ-tĭ), *n.* the state or quality of being outside of the mind: opposite to *subjectivity*, or state of existing only in the mind.

ob-jur-gate (ŏb-jûr'gāt; ŏb'jûr-gāt), *v.t.* to chide, reprove, or rebuke —*n.* **objurgation.**

ob-jur-ga-to-ry (ŏb-jûr'gȧ-tō-rĭ), *adj.* expressing or implying reproof or rebuke.

ob-late (ŏb'lāt; ŏb-lāt'), *adj.* depressed or flattened at the poles, as the earth; orange-shaped; in the Roman Catholic Church, consecrated to sacred purposes.

ob-la-tion (ŏb-lā'shŭn), *n.* the act of making an offering or sacrifice to God or to the gods; anything presented as a religious sacrifice.

ob-li-gate (ŏb'lĭ-gāt), *v.t.* to bind legally or morally by promise or treaty, or by a sense of duty.

ob-li-ga-tion (ŏb'lĭ-gā'shŭn), *n.* the binding power of a vow, promise, contract, or sense of duty; any duty imposed by law, by propriety, etc.; the state of being bound to return a favor; a written deed or bond by which one binds himself under penalty to do a thing.

ob-li-ga-to-ry (ŏb'lĭ-gȧ-tō-rĭ; ŏb-lĭg'ȧ-tō-rĭ), *adj.* morally or legally binding; imposed by law, duty, etc.: often followed by *on* or *upon*.

o-blige (ō-blīj'), *v.t.* to compel by force, morally, legally, or physically; bind by some favor or kindness shown; render a favor to; gratify.—*n.* **obliger.**

o-blig-ing (ō-blīj'ĭng), *p.adj.* willing to do favors; civil or courteous; kindly; accommodating; as, an *obliging* neighbor.—*adv.* **obligingly.**—*n.* **obligingness.**

ob-lique (ŏb-lēk'; ŏb-līk'), *adj.* not horizontal nor perpendicular; not upright nor level; slanting; not direct or straightforward.—*adv.* **obliquely.**—*n.* **obliqueness.**

ob-lique an-gle (ŏb-lēk' ăn'g'l), an angle greater or less than a right angle.

ob-lique case (ŏb-lēk' kās), in grammar, any case except the nominative or the case indicating the person addressed

ob-liq-ui-ty (ŏb-lĭk'wĭ-tĭ), *n.* [*pl.* obliquities (-tĭz)], the quality possessed by lines which are neither parallel nor at right angles; moral error.

ob-lit-er-ate (ŏb-lĭt'ẽr-āt), *v.t.* to erase or blot out; as, to *obliterate* a mark; destroy by the effects of time or other means; remove all traces of.

ob-lit-er-a-tion (ŏb-lĭt'ẽr-ā'shŭn), *n.* the act of blotting out; effacement.

ob-liv-i-on (ŏb-lĭv'ĭ-ŭn), *n.* the state of being blotted out from memory; forgetfulness.

ob-liv-i-ous (ŏb-lĭv'ĭ-ŭs), *adj.* lost in thought; forgetful.

ob-long (ŏb'lŏng), *adj.* longer than broad; as, an *oblong* box: *n.* a geometric figure with sides longer in one direction than in the other, and usually with right angles.

ob-lo-quy (ŏb'lō-kwĭ), *n.* abusive or contemptuous language spoken to or about a person; state of being in disgrace; reproach; censure; slander; disgrace.

ob-nox-ious (ŏb-nŏk'shŭs), *adj.* hateful; offensive; unpopular.—*adv.* **obnoxiously.**—*n.* **obnoxiousness.**

Syn. annoying, unpleasant, odious, repugnant.

Ant. (see agreeable).

o-boe (ō'boi; ō'bō-ā), *n.* a musical wind instrument with a high, rich tone; an organ stop. Also, **hautboy.**

Oboe

ob-o-lus (ŏb'ō-lŭs), *n.* an ancient Greek coin worth about four cents; a weight of ancient Athens equal to one-sixth of a drachma; a small European coin of varying weight.

ob-o-vate (ŏb-ō'vāt), *adj.* having the broad end upward or toward the apex; as, *obovate* leaves.

ob-scene (ŏb-sēn'), *adj.* offensive to modesty; impure in language or action; indecent; filthy.—*adv.* **obscenely.**—*n.* **obsceneness.**

ob-scen-i-ty (ŏb-sĕn'ĭ-tĭ), *n.* quality of being indecent; indecency in action or expression.

ob-scur-ant (ŏb-skūr'ănt), *n.* one who, or that which, hinders the development of knowledge and education.—*n.* **obscurantism, obscurantist.**

ob-scure (ŏb-skūr'), *adj.* without clearness or distinctness; as, an *obscure* view; *obscure* objects; shadowy; dim; dark; as, an *obscure* room; not easily understood; as, an *obscure* meaning; illegible; as, faint or *obscure* writing; remote; unknown; as, he lived in an *obscure* little village, secluded; humble; as, he occupied an *obscure* position: *v.t.* to darken or hide from view; as, clouds *obscure* the sun; to disguise or render less intelligible; as, to *obscure* one's meaning.—*adv.* **obscurely.**—*n.* **obscureness.**

ob-scu-ri-ty (ŏb-skū'rĭ-tĭ), *n.* dimness or indistinctness of a place or object; lack of clearness of thought or expression; state or fact of being unknown.

ob-se-quies (ŏb'sē-kwĭz), *n.pl.* funeral rites or ceremonies.

ob-se-qui-ous (ŏb-sē'kwĭ-ŭs), *adj.* meanly submissive to the will of another; servile; fawning; as, an *obsequious* servant; humble to excess.—*adv.* **obsequiously.**—*n.* **obsequiousness.**

ob-serv-a-ble (ŏb-zûr'vȧ-b'l), *adj.* capable of being seen or noticed; worthy of, or attracting, attention; remarkable; noticeable; customary.—*adv.* **observably.**

ob-serv-ance (ŏb-zûr'văns), *n.* the act of keeping, or of paying attention to, laws or customs; as, the *observance* of the Sabbath; an act performed in token of worship or respect; occasionally, attention; heed.

ob-serv-ant (ŏb-zûr'vănt), *adj.* quick to notice; attentive; watchful; mindful of duties or authority.

ob-ser-va-tion (ŏb'zẽr-vā'shŭn), *n.* the act, power, or habit of taking notice; that which is noticed or learned; fact of being seen; as, he did not escape *observation;* a remark: **observation balloon** a captive balloon, behind the military line, used as a vantage point from which to watch the enemy: **observation post,** a position, usually near, or in advance of, the front line, where an artillery officer watches the result of gunfire.

ob-ser-va-tion-al (ŏb″zẽr-vā′shŭn-ăl), *adj.* consisting of, or containing, knowledge or results obtained by noticing carefully.

ob-serv-a-to-ry (ŏb-zûr′vȧ-tō-rĭ), *n.* [*pl.* observatories (-rĭz)], a building fitted up with telescopes, etc., for studying the heavens; a tower or other high place built to give an extensive view.

ob-serve (ŏb-zûrv′), *v.t.* to take notice of; to watch closely; to keep or celebrate; to remark: *v.i.* to take notice; to comment.—*n.* **observer.**

ob-serv-ing (ŏb-zûrv′ĭng), *p.adj.* giving particular attention to; sharp-sighted.

ob-sess (ŏb-sĕs′), *v.t.* to beset or rule; as, he is *obsessed* by one idea.

ob-ses-sion (ŏb-sĕsh′ŭn), *n.* the fact or state of being ruled by one idea; a fixed idea not to be driven from one's mind.

ob-sid-i-an (ŏb-sĭd′ĭ-ăn), *n.* lava of a glassy appearance from a volcano.

ob-so-les-cent (ŏb″sō-lĕs′ĕnt), *adj.* passing out of use; as, an *obsolescent* word.—*n.* **obsolescence.**

ob-so-lete (ŏb′sō-lēt), *adj.* gone out of use; as, *obsolete* firearms; no longer practiced or accepted; as, an *obsolete* custom; old.—*n.* **obsoleteness.**

ob-sta-cle (ŏb′stȧ-kl), *n.* that which hinders or stands in the way; an obstruction; an impediment; a hindrance.

ob-ste-tri-cian (ŏb″stē-trĭsh′ăn), *n.* a physician skilled in the knowledge of how to conduct childbirth.

ob-stet-rics (ŏb-stĕt′rĭks), *n.* that branch of medicine which has to do with the art of conducting childbirth.

ob-sti-na-cy (ŏb′stĭ-nȧ-sĭ), *n.* the state or quality of being unyielding or difficult to control; as, the *obstinacy* of a fever; stubborn and unreasonable determination to have one's own way; stubbornness.

ob-sti-nate (ŏb′stĭ-nāt), *adj.* not yielding to argument, persuasion, or entreaty; headstrong; as, an *obstinate* person; adhering to one's opinion or purpose; stubborn; not yielding to treatment, as a disease.—*adv.* **obstinately.**

Syn. obdurate, unyielding, unbending, inflexible.

Ant. (see yielding).

ob-strep-er-ous (ŏb-strĕp′ẽr-ŭs), *adj.* clamorous; noisy; as, an *obstreperous* person; turbulent.—*adv.* **obstreperously.**—*n.* **obstreperousness.**

ob-struct (ŏb-strŭkt′), *v.t.* to block up or close so as to prevent passage; as, a great pile of stones *obstructs* the road; to impede, or prevent from progress; as, to *obstruct* work; to *obstruct* travel; to be in the way of, or to cut off from sight; as, to *obstruct* the light; to *obstruct* the view.—*n.* **obstructer, obstructor.**

ob-struc-tion (ŏb-strŭk′shŭn), *n.* anything that stops, closes, or bars the way; that which prevents progress or hinders; an obstacle or barrier.

ob-struc-tion-ist (ŏb-strŭk′shŭn-ĭst), *n.* one who hinders progress; especially, a member of a legislative or lawmaking body who makes use of its rules to hinder the progress of public business.

ob-struc-tive (ŏb-strŭk′tĭv), *adj.* serving to stop or to hinder progress.

ob-tain (ŏb-tān′), *v.t.* to get possession of; gain; acquire; as, to *obtain* knowledge; win; procure: *v.i.* to be established in practice or use; to prevail or be in fashion; as, widely different customs *obtain* in different countries.—*adj.* **obtainable.**

ob-tain-ment (ŏb-tān′mĕnt), *n.* the act of gaining, acquiring, or procuring.

ob-trude (ŏb-trōōd′), *v.t.* to thrust into a place boldly or inconsiderately; urge or offer with unreasonable persistence: *v.i.* to force oneself upon the notice of others; to intrude.—*n.* **obtruder.**

ob-tru-sion (ŏb-trōō′zhŭn), *n.* the act of intruding, or of pushing into undue prominence.

ob-tru-sive (ŏb-trōō′sĭv), *adj.* inclined or apt to push oneself into undue prominence; intrusive.—*adv.* **obtrusively.**—*n.* **obtrusiveness.**

Obtuse Angle

ob-tuse (ŏb-tūs′), *adj.* not pointed or acute; as, an *obtuse* angle; greater than a right angle; blunt; dull; stupid; as, an *obtuse* person.—*adv.* **obtusely.**—*n.* **obtuseness.**

ob-verse (ŏb′vûrs), *n.* the front surface of anything; the side of a coin or medal having the principal design upon it: opposite to *reverse: adj.* (ŏb-vûrs′), facing the observer; narrower at the base than at the top: said of a leaf.—*adv.* **obversely.**

ob-vi-ate (ŏb′vĭ-āt), *v.t.* to remove, or clear away beforehand, as difficulties or objections.—*n.* **obviation.**

ob-vi-ous (ŏb′vĭ-ŭs), *adj.* evident; plain; as, the effect is *obvious.*

o-ca (ō′kȧ), *n.* a South American plant with a root like the potato.

oc-a-ri-na (ŏk″ȧ-rē′nȧ), *n.* a small musical instrument, giving soft pleasing sounds: usually made of terra-cotta, with a mouthpiece and finger holes.—[IT.]

Ocarina

oc-ca-sion (ŏ-kā′zhŭn), *n.* a particular event or celebration; as it was an unusual *occasion;* occurrence; as, on the *occasion* of her last visit; state or position of affairs leading to unexpected results; incidental cause; as, his carelessness was the *occasion* of the whole trouble; need; as, having *occasion* to buy food; chance or opportunity; as, he seized the *occasion* to speak his mind: *v.t.* to cause or influence directly or indirectly; give rise to.

oc-ca-sion-al (ŏ-kā′zhŭn-ăl), *adj.* incidental or casual; as, *occasional* remarks; happening now and then, but not regularly; as, an *occasional* visit; referring to some especial happening; as, an *occasional* poem.—*adv.* **occasionally.**

oc-ci-dent (ŏk′sĭ-dĕnt), *n.* the west; opposite to *orient,* or *east:* **Occident,** the west, or the countries west of Asia and the Turkish dominions.

Oc-ci-den-tal (ŏk″sĭ-dĕn′tăl), *adj.* of or pertaining to the Occident or the countries west of Asia: *n.* a native of the Occident or West: opposite to *Oriental.*

oc-cip-i-tal (ŏk-sĭp'ĭ-tăl), *adj.* pertaining to the occiput, or lower back part of the head: *n.* the bone of the lower back part of the head.

oc-ci-put (ŏk'sĭ-pŭt), *n.* the back part of the skull or head.

oc-clude (ŏ-klōōd'), *v.t.* to absorb, as gas by a metal; to close, as pores.—*n.* **occlusion.**

oc-cult (ŏ-kŭlt'), *adj.* hidden; secret; invisible; hence, supernatural, or full of mystery.—*adv.* **occultly.**

oc-cul-ta-tion (ŏk"ŭl-tā'shŭn), *n.* a concealment, especially a hiding from view of one heavenly body by another, as an eclipse of a planet or star by the moon.

oc-cult-ism (ŏ-kŭl'tĭzm), *n.* an inquiring into the mysterious or supernatural; a religious belief called theosophy, which claims to know through spiritual sight all that is hidden from material eyes.

oc-cu-pan-cy (ŏk'ū-păn-sĭ), *n.* the act of dwelling in, or of taking and holding in possession, as a house.

oc-cu-pant (ŏk'ū-pănt), *n.* one who dwells in, has possession, or holds in use.

oc-cu-pa-tion (ŏk"ū-pā'shŭn), *n.* the act or state of holding in possession or dwelling in; regular business, employment, or calling; state of being busy.

oc-cu-pi-er (ŏk'ū-pī"ẽr), *n.* one who has possession; an occupant.

oc-cu-py (ŏk'ū-pī), *v.t.* [*p.t.* and *p.p.* occupied, *p.pr.* occupying], to take possession of; have in possession or use; dwell in; as, to *occupy* a room; to fill or cover time or space; as, household duties *occupy* her day; the building *occupies* an entire block; to employ; to busy; as, to *occupy* oneself with work.

oc-cur (ŏ-kûr'), *v.i.* [*p.t.* and *p.p.* occurred, *p.pr.* occurring], to happen or take place; as, the same mistake must not *occur* again; come to the mind; as, did it *occur* to you to go?

oc-cur-rence (ŏ-kûr'ĕns), *n.* a happening; event; incident.

o-cean (ō'shăn), *n.* the vast body of salt water covering more than three-fifths of the globe; any one of its five chief divisions; as, the Atlantic *ocean;* an immense expanse or amount; as, the *ocean* of time.

o-ce-an-ic (ō"shē-ăn'ĭk), *adj.* pertaining to, occurring in, or produced by, the ocean.

Ocelot

o-ce-lot (ō'sē-lŏt), *n.* a leopardlike cat, yellowish- or reddish-gray with markings of black, found in both North and South America.

o-cher (ō'kẽr), *n.* a fine yellow- or brown-colored clay: used as a pigment, or color for painting. Also, **ochre.**

o'clock (ō-klŏk'), contraction for *of the clock*, or according to the clock.

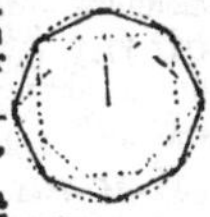

Octagon

oc-ta- (ŏk'tā-), a *prefix* meaning eight. Also, **oct-, octi-, octo-.**

oc-ta-gon (ŏk'tā-gŏn), *n.* a plane figure of eight sides and eight angles.

oc-tag-o-nal (ŏk-tăg'ō-năl), *adj.* having eight sides and eight angles.

oc-ta-he-dron (ŏk"tā-hē'drŏn), *n.* a solid figure having eight plane faces.—*adj.* **octahedral.**

Octahedron

oc-tan-gu-lar (ŏk-tăŋ'gū-lăr), *adj.* having eight angles.

oc-tave (ŏk'tāv), *n.* in music, an interval of twelve semitones or the eighth note in a scale; the eighth day after a church festival, the festival itself being included: *adj.* consisting of eight.

oc-ta-vo (ŏk-tā'vō; ŏk-tä'vō), *n.* a book in which the sheets of printing paper have been folded into eight leaves or sixteen pages: *adj.* having eight leaves or sixteen pages to the sheet. Also, **8vo.**

oc-tet (ŏk-tĕt'), *n.* a musical composition with eight parts for voices or instruments; the eight performers of such a composition.

oc-til-lion (ŏk-tĭl'yŭn), *n.* in French and American numeration, the number represented by one followed by twenty-seven ciphers; in English numeration, one followed by forty-eight ciphers.

Oc-to-ber (ŏk-tō'bẽr), *n.* the tenth month of the year, having thirty-one days.

oc-to-ge-na-ri-an (ŏk"tō-jē-nā'rĭ-ăn), *n.* one who is between eighty and ninety years old: *adj.* between eighty and ninety years old. Also, **octogenary.**

oc-to-pus (ŏk'tō-pŭs; ŏk-tō'pŭs), *n.* [*pl.* octopuses (-ĕz)], an eight-armed cuttlefish; hence, any powerful organization with many branches, reaching out to do injury.

Octopus

oc-to-roon (ŏk"tō-rōōn'), *n.* a person having seven-eighths white blood and one-eighth negro blood; the child of a white person and a quadroon, or person having one-fourth negro blood.

oc-u-lar (ŏk'ū-lăr), *adj.* pertaining to the eye or to eyesight; depending on, or seen by, the eye; known from actual sight; as, *ocular* evidence.

oc-u-list (ŏk'ū-lĭst), *n.* one who is skilled in the treatment of eye diseases.

o-da-lisque (ō'dā-lĭsk), *n.* a beautiful woman who is a slave in a Turkish harem. Also, **odalisk.**

odd (ŏd), *adj.* not paired or matched with another; as, an *odd* glove; not even; not exactly divisible by two; as, seven is an *odd* number; left over after equal division; extra; as, you may have the *odd* one; additional to an amount that is complete; as, if you have any *odd* dollars, give them to this cause; unusual; as, an *odd* occurrence; peculiar; eccentric; as, an *odd* person; occasional; as, he does *odd* jobs around the place.—*adv.* **oddly.**—*n.* **oddness.**

odd-i-ty (ŏd'ĭ-tĭ), *n.* a person, a thing, or a quality, that is peculiar; strangeness; singularity; eccentricity.

odds (ŏdz), *n.pl.* inequality; advantage; superiority; excess in favor of one as compared with another; as, the *odds* are in her favor; probability; a more than even wager; as, the *odds* are on a certain race horse; disagreement; quarrel; as, to be at *odds* with another person: **odds and ends**, remnants.

ode (ōd), *n.* a short song or poem expressing noble sentiments in a dignified style.

O-din (ō'dĭn), *n.* in Norse mythology, the chief of the gods: identified with the German Woden.

o-di-ous (ō'dĭ-ŭs), *adj.* deserving of, or calling forth, hatred or abhorrence; offensive; unpopular; as, his conduct was *odious*.—*adv.* **odiously**.—*n.* **odiousness**.

o-di-um (ō'dĭ-ŭm), *n.* hatred; state of being hated; abhorrence; the discredit or blame belonging to what is abhorrent or hateful.

o-dom-e-ter (ō-dŏm'ē-tẽr), *n.* an instrument for measuring the distance traveled by a vehicle.

o-don-tol-o-gy (ō"dŏn-tŏl'ō-jĭ), *n.* the science or study of the teeth.

o-dor (ō'dẽr) *n.* a scent; fragrance; smell, whether pleasant or offensive; estimation or repute.

o-dor-if-er-ous (ō"dẽr-ĭf'ẽr-ŭs), *adj.* diffusing or giving out fragrance; as, *odoriferous* spices.

o-dor-less (ō'dẽr-lĕs), *adj.* without smell, whether pleasant or offensive; scentless.

o-dor-ous (ō'dẽr-ŭs), *adj.* giving out an odor or scent; fragrant.—*adv.* **odorously**.—*n.* **odorousness**.

Od-ys-sey (ŏd'ĭ-sĭ), *n.* a Greek epic poem, by Homer, describing the ten years' wanderings of Odysseus (Ulysses) from Troy to Ithaca.

o'er (ōr), *prep.* and *adv.* over: used chiefly in poetry.

œ-soph-a-gus (ē-sŏf'ȧ-gŭs), *n.* the tube that leads from the pharynx to the stomach; the gullet. Also, **esophagus**.

of (ŏv), *prep.* from; as, to cure *of* a fever; rid *of* a nuisance; born *of* a line of kings; out of; as, he did it *of* necessity; about; concerning; as, talk *of* success; news *of* a thing; in; as, quick *of* speech; belonging to or connected with; as, the palace *of* the king; proceeding from; by; as, the plays *of* Shakespeare; showing kind, material, quality, measure, etc., as, a glass *of* milk; a woman *of* brains, a weight *of* ten pounds, etc.

off (ŏf), *adj.* most distant; on the opposite or farther side; as, the *off* horse of a team; noting the act of removing or separating; away; as, I must be *off*: *adv.* away; as, take *off* your hat; he stood afar *off*: *prep.* not on; away from; as, take the bowl *off* the shelf; not in condition; distant from; as, a mile *off* shore: *interj.* begone!

of-fal (ŏf'ăl), *n.* refuse or garbage; waste meat; as, the *offal* of a butchered animal; anything thrown away as worthless.

off-cast (ŏf'kȧst"), *p.adj.* thrown aside; cast off: *n.* one who is thrown aside or cast off.

off-col-or (ŏf'kŭl"ẽr), *adj.* not of a natural or satisfactory color; as, the jewel is *off-color*; colloquially, slightly improper or indecent; as, an *off-color* remark.

of-fence (ŏ-fĕns'), *n.* sin; wrong; crime; misdemeanor; that which injures, affronts, or angers; assault or attack. Also, **offense**.

of-fend (ŏ-fĕnd'), *v.t.* to displease or make angry; vex or annoy; pain or shock: *v.i.* to transgress; to sin; as, to *offend* against the law; do anything displeasing; as, in what way have I *offended*?

of-fense (ŏ-fĕns'), *n.* any cause of anger or displeasure; insult; injury; assault; any sin, wrong, or crime. Also, **offence**.—*adj.* **offenseless, offenceless**.

Syn. affront, misdeed, transgression, trespass.

of-fen-sive (ŏ-fĕn'sĭv), *adj.* causing displeasure; as, *offensive* actions; annoying; disagreeable; disgusting; as, an *offensive* odor; used in attack; as, *offensive* weapons: *n.* aggressive method or attitude.—*adv.* **offensively**.—*n.* **offensiveness**.

Syn., *adj.* insolent, abusive, obnoxious.

Ant. (see inoffensive).

of-fer (ŏf'ẽr), *n.* a proposal made; price bid; first advance; proffer: *v.t.* to present for acceptance or refusal; as, to *offer* money; proffer; as, to *offer* help or advice; propose; as, to *offer* a plan: present in worship or sacrifice; as, to *offer* a prayer; bid as a price or reward; as, how much am I *offered*? attempt to make or give; as, to *offer* resistance: *v.i.* to present itself or to appear; as, a favorable opportunity soon *offered*; express a willingness.

of-fer-ing (ŏf'ẽr-ĭng), *n.* the act of making a proffer or proposal; that which is proffered or given; a gift or contribution; a sacrifice.

of-fer-to-ry (ŏf'ẽr-tō-rĭ), *n.* that part of the Mass or church service at which the money offering is made; an anthem sung during the collection of alms; act of offering, or thing offered; hence, a collection of money taken at a religious service.

off-hand (ŏf'hănd"; ŏf"hănd'), *adj.* done without preparation; as, an *offhand* speech; informal; unceremonious; as, an *offhand* manner: *adv.* without preparation.

of-fice (ŏf'ĭs), *n.* position of trust or authority for a public purpose; as, the *office* of President; function; as, the *office* of the ears is to hear; a religious ceremony or rite; as, the *office* of marriage; a duty or service; as, an *office* of kindness; an apartment for the transaction of professional or clerical business; as, a doctor's *office*; an express *office*: *pl.* [ENG.] the outlying buildings of a mansion; the apartments of a house in which domestics discharge their duties.

of-fi-cer (ŏf'ĭ-sẽr), *n.* a person authorized to perform a certain public duty: *v.t.* to furnish with authorized leaders; to command as an authorized leader.

of-fi-cial (ŏ-fĭsh'ăl), *n.* one who holds a public position or performs duties of a public nature: *adj.* pertaining to an office or public duty; as, *official* business; derived from the proper authority; authorized; as, an *official* statement.—*adv.* **officially**.

of-fi-cial-ism (ŏ-fĭsh'ăl-ĭzm), *n.* government by established system; close observance of office order or routine; red-tapism.

of-fi-ci-ate (ŏ-fĭsh'ĭ-āt), *v.i.* to perform the duties of a divine service; to act in a public service or duty.

of-fi-cious (ŏ-fĭsh'ŭs), *adj.* too bold or insistent in offering services; meddling.—*adv.* **officiously**.—*n.* **officiousness**.

off-ing (ŏf'ĭng), *n.* the open visible sea that is remote from shore, beyond the anchoring ground.

off-ish (ŏf'ĭsh), *adj.* reserved; inclined to hold oneself aloof.

off-scour-ing (ŏf'skour"ĭng), *n.* refuse or cast-off filth.

off-set (ŏf'sĕt"), *n.* a young shoot or branch that takes root; a spur or branch from a chain of mountains; a thing, as a pipe, whose course is swerved to avoid an obstacle;

anything set off as an equivalent or compensation for something else; in surveying, a perpendicular let fall from the main line to an outlying point: *v.t.* (ŏf'sĕt"; ŏf"sĕt'), to balance; to compensate for.

off-shoot (ŏf'shōōt"), *n.* something branching off as a side issue; a branch of a family, race, stem, etc.

off-spring (ŏf'spring"), *n.* that which comes from, or grows out of, something; a child or children; a descendant or descendants; issue.

of-ten (ŏf'n), *adv.* many times; frequently. Also [POET.], oft.

of-ten-times (ŏf'n timz"), *adv.* often. Also [POET.], ofttimes.

o-gle (ō'gl), *v.t.* to look at with admiring or overfamiliar glances: *n.* an admiring or overfamiliar look; a side glance.

o-gre (ō'gẽr), *n.* [*fem.* ogress], an imaginary man-eating monster or giant; hence, a cruel or hideous person.—*adj.* ogreish.

oh (ō), *interj.* an exclamation of wonder, pain, or anxiety: *n.* one such exclamation; as, full of *oh's.* Also, O.

ohm (ōm), *n.* a unit of measurement in electrical science, used in calculating the resistance of a circuit.

oil (oil), *n.* an inflammable fatty liquid, insoluble in water, but soluble in ether, obtained from various animal and vegetable substances; a greenish-brown liquid found in rock or other mineral substance, and very inflammable: called also *petroleum: v.t.* to lubricate with oil: oil well, a well or boring for petroleum.—*n.* oiler, oiliness.

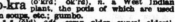

Oil Well

oil cake (oil kāk), the substance that remains after the oil has been extracted or taken out from a vegetable substance, as from flaxseed.

oil-cloth (oil'klŏth"), *n.* cloth coated with oil paint and used for garments, floor coverings, etc

oil col-or (oil kŭl'ẽr), a paint or pigment used by an artist and mixed in oil; a picture painted with such pigments: distinguished from *water color.*

oil-skin (oil'skin"), *n.* cloth made waterproof by having been treated with oil: *pl.* a waterproof suit.

oil-y (oil'ĭ), *adj.* containing, or like, oil; greasy; smooth in speech or manner; smooth-tongued; fawning; as, *oily* remarks or an *oily* tongue.—*adv.* oilily.—*n.* oiliness.

Okapi

oint-ment (oint'mĕnt), *n.* a fatty preparation of about the consistency of butter, containing medicinal qualities, and applied to wounds or injured parts.

o-ka-pi (ō-kä'pē), *n.* a giraffelike, cud-chewing animal of Central Africa.

o-kra (ō'krȧ; ŏk'rȧ), *n.* a West Indian plant, the pods of which are used in soups, etc.; gumbo.

old (ōld), *adj.* [*comp.* older, *superl.* oldest], having existed or lived many years; aged; as, an *old* oak; an *old* man; having an appearance of age; as, an *old* face; having reached a certain age; as, twenty-one years *old;* decayed by time; as, an *old* ruin; ancient; out of date; as, *old* customs; *old* coins; long used; not new; as, *old* shoes; long practiced; as, *old* habits; belonging to the past; as, one's *old* home; colloquially, familiar and dear; as, *Old* Glory; long experienced; as, he is an *old* hand at that work: *n.* former times; as, in days of *old.*—*n.* oldness.

Syn., adj. ancient, antique, antiquated, old-fashioned.

Ant. (see young).

old-en (ōl'dn), *adj.* ancient; bygone; as, in *olden* times.

Old Eng-lish (ōld ĭn'glĭsh), the language spoken in England until the 12th century, by the Anglo-Saxons.

old-fash-ioned (ōld"făsh'ŭnd), *adj.* having or adhering to old ideas or customs; as, an *old-fashioned* person; having the feelings or tastes of an older person; as, an *old-fashioned* child; out of style; as, an *old-fashioned* coat.

Old Glo-ry (ōld glō'rĭ), a familiar term applied to the flag of the United States.

old maid (ōld mād), a middle-aged or elderly unmarried woman; a crotchety person; a game of cards.

old-ster (ōld'stẽr), *n.* in the British navy, a midshipman who has served four years: distinguished from *youngster.*

old style (ōld stīl), the old mode of reckoning time according to the Julian calendar of a former style.

Old Tes-ta-ment (ōld tĕs'tȧ-mĕnt), the first of the two main divisions of the Bible.

Old World (ōld wûrld), the Eastern Hemisphere of the earth; Europe, Asia, and Africa.

o-le-ag-i-nous (ō-lē-ăj'ĭ-nŭs), *adj.* having greasy qualities; oily; sleek or smooth in appearance, voice, or manner; fawning.—*n.* oleaginousness.

o-le-an-der (ō"lē-ăn'dẽr), *n.* an evergreen shrub of a poisonous nature with handsome fragrant red or white flowers.

o-le-as-ter (ō"lē-ăs'tẽr), *n.* the wild olive; a shrub of southern Europe bearing yellow flowers and a bitter fruit resembling the olive.

o-le-o-graph (ō"lē-ō-grȧf), *n.* a print in oil colors in imitation of an oil painting.

o-le-o-mar-ga-rine (ō"lē-ō-mär'gȧ-rēn; ō"lē-ō-mär-gȧ-rin; often mispronounced ō"lē-ō-mär'jẽr-ēn), *n.* imitation butter made from animal fats. Abbreviated, oleo.

ol-fac-to-ry (ŏl-făk'tō-rĭ), *adj.* pertaining to, or used in, smelling; as, an *olfactory* nerve: *n.* organ or sense of smell: usually in plural.

ol-i-garch (ŏl'ĭ-gärk), *n.* one of the rulers in a government that is controlled by a few persons.

ol-i-gar-chy (ŏl'ĭ-gär"kĭ), *n.* [*pl.* oligarchies (-kĭz)], government in which the supreme power is in the hands of a few; a state so governed; the few who rule.—*adj.* oligarchic, oligarchical.

ol-ive (ŏl′ĭv), *n.* an evergreen tree cultivated for its oily fruit; the fruit of the tree; a dull brownish- or yellowish-green color: *adj.* pertaining to, or like, the olive; of a dull brownish- or yellowish-green color; tawny.

ol-ive branch (ŏl′ĭv brȧnch), a branch of the olive tree, considered as the emblem of peace.

O-lym-pi-ad (ȏ-lĭm′pĭ-ăd), *n.* in ancient Greece, the period of four years between two celebrations of the games held at Olympia in honor of the god Zeus: a standard used in reckoning time from the first Olympiad, which began 776 B. C.; a modern revival of the athletic games of ancient Greece, first held in 1906.

O-lym-pic (ȏ-lĭm′pĭk), *adj.* pertaining to Olympia in Elis, Greece, where games were celebrated every four years in honor of Zeus; in Greek mythology, pertaining to Mount Olympus, in Thessaly, the home of the gods: **Olympic games**, the athletic games and races of ancient Greece, celebrated every four years in honor of the god Zeus. Also, **Olympian.**

O-ma-ha (ō′mȧ-hô″), *n.* one of a tribe of American Indians living in Nebraska.

o-me-ga (ȏ-mē′gȧ; ō′mē-gȧ; ȏ-mĕg′ȧ), *n.* the last letter of the Greek alphabet; hence, the last; end.

om-e-let (ŏm′ĕ-lĕt; ŏm′lĕt), *n.* eggs and milk, with sometimes other ingredients, beaten together and fried.

o-men (ō′mĕn), *n.* a sign of some future event: *v.t.* to foreshow or foretell by signs; predict.

o-men-tum (ȏ-mĕn′tŭm), *n.* a free fold of the peritoneum, or membrane that lines the abdominal cavity.

om-i-nous (ŏm′ĭ-nŭs), *adj.* foreboding or foreshowing evil.—*adv.* **ominously.**—*n.* **ominousness.**

o-mis-sion (ȏ-mĭsh′ŭn), *n.* neglect or failure to do something required; something left out.

o-mit (ȏ-mĭt′), *v.t.* [*p.t.* and *p.p.* omitted, *p.pr.* omitting], to leave out; as, to *omit* the address; to leave undone; neglect; as, to *omit* a task; fail to mention.

om-ni-bus (ŏm′nĭ-bŭs), *n.* a public four-wheeled carriage for passenger traffic: *adj.* including many different objects or cases; as, in lawmaking, an *omnibus* bill.

om-ni-graph (ŏm′nĭ-grȧf), *n.* the trade name of an instrument designed for teaching telegraphy.

Omnigraph

om-nip-o-tence (ŏm-nĭp′ȏ-tĕns), *n.* unlimited power: **Omnipotence**, God, the all-powerful.

om-nip-o-tent (ŏm-nĭp′ȏ-tĕnt), *adj.* having unlimited power; as, the *omnipotent* God: **the Omnipotent**: *n.* God.—*adv.* **omnipotently.**

om-ni-pres-ence (ŏm″nĭ-prĕz′ĕns), *n.* universal presence, or the quality of being present everywhere at once.

om-ni-pres-ent (ŏm-nĭ-prĕz′ĕnt), *adj.* present everywhere at the same time.

om-nis-cience (ŏm-nĭsh′ĕns), *n.* unlimited knowledge: **Omniscience**, God, the all-knowing.

om-nis-cient (ŏm-nĭsh′ĕnt), *adj.* knowing all things; infinitely wise; as, the *omniscient* God.

om-niv-o-rous (ŏm-nĭv′ȏ-rŭs), *adj.* feeding upon both animal and vegetable food; as, *omnivorous* animals; all devouring; as, an *omnivorous* reader.—*adv.* **omnivorously.**—*n.* **omnivorousness.**

on (ŏn), *prep.* upon; as, to sit *on* a chair; in contact with the upper surface; as, we live *on* the earth; along or by; as, Paris is *on* the Seine; in the act or state of; as, *on* a journey; toward; as, he looked *on* her as his guide; in connection with; as, to go *on* business; showing the relation of following after; as, they are *on* his trail; in the direction of; as, the door opens *on* a lawn; about; as, an address *on* war; indicating time; as, *on* July first; resting against; as, a picture *on* the wall; supported by; as, *on* my honor: *adv.* forward; onward; along; as, to go *on*; so as to cover or be supported by; as, put *on* your coat; jump *on* before the train starts; in or into action or use; as, to turn *on* the gas; in progress; as, the fight is *on*.

once (wŭns), *adv.* at one time; formerly; as, *once* upon a time; this was *once* my home; one time only; as, read it over *once*; at any time; ever; as, if *once* they lose heart, their cause will be lost: *n.* one time: **at once**, together; immediately; as, do not all speak *at once;* do it *at once*.

one (wŭn), *n.* [*pl.* ones (wŭnz)], the first number used in counting by units; the sign representing it, as 1 or I; a single person or thing: *pron.* a certain person or thing considered indefinitely; anybody; as, *one* must take care: *adj.* single in number; united; as, they answered with *one* voice; individual; a certain; as, *one* Henry; the same.

O-nei-da (ȏ-nī′dȧ), *n.* one of a tribe of American Indians, originally inhabiting what is now Central New York.

one-ness (wŭn′nĕs), *n.* singleness; unity; the quality of being unique.

on-er-ous (ŏn′ẽr-ŭs), *adj.* burdensome; weighty; as, an *onerous* duty.—*adv.* **onerously.**—*n.* **onerousness.**

one-self (wŭn″sĕlf′), *pron.* an emphatic and reflexive form of the pronoun *one;* one's self.

one-step (wŭn′stĕp″), *n.* a modern dance of quick movement, in two-four time.

on-ion (ŭn′yŭn), *n.* a plant of the lily family having a strong-smelling eatable bulb; the bulb of the plant.—**onion shell**, a flaming, explosive shell, especially used against airplanes: so called from the odor it gives after exploding.

on-ly (ōn′lĭ), *adj.* sole; single; as, the *only* man there; one and no more: *adv.* singly, merely: *conj.* except.

on-o-mat-o-pœ-ia (ŏn″ȏ-măt″ȏ-pē′yȧ; ȏ-nŏm′ȧ-tȏ-pē′yȧ), *n.* the formation of words in imitation of natural sounds, as *rumble, hiss, buzz, splash;* the use of words so formed; such a word itself.

on-rush (ŏn′rŭsh″), *n.* an onset; a rushing on; an assault.

on-set (ŏn′sĕt″), *n.* an assault; attack; as, the *onset* was furious.

on-slaught (ŏn′slôt″), *n.* a furious attack or assault.

o-nus (ō′nŭs), *n.* a burden; duty; obligation; responsibility.

on-ward (ŏn′wẽrd), *adj.* advancing; forward; as, the *onward* march of troops: *adv.* in advance; toward the desired end; forward; as, to move *onward*. Also, **onwards.**

on-yx (ŏn′ĭks; ō′nĭks), *n.* a kind of quartz consisting of layers of various colors, such as brown, black, red, white.

oo-long (ōō′lŏng), *n.* a Chinese black tea, with a flavor like green tea.

ooze (ōōz), *n.* soft mud or slime; gentle flow, as of blood from a wound; a liquid used in tanning leather: *v.i.* to flow gently; leak out: *v.t.* to discharge or give out slowly; as, to *ooze* moisture.—*adj.* oozy.

o-pac-i-ty (ō-păs′ĭ-tĭ), *n.* quality of not allowing light to pass through; cloudiness; darkness; lack of transparency.

o-pal (ō′păl), *n.* a precious stone, opaque and lustrous, showing a play of various colors.

o-pal-es-cence (ō″păl-ĕs′ĕns), *n.* the quality of showing a play of various colors.

o-pal-es-cent (ō″păl-ĕs′ĕnt), *adj.* showing a play of delicate colors, like an opal.

o-pal-ine (ō′păl-ĭn; ō′păl-īn), *adj.* having a play of delicate colors; bluish-white, as the wings of certain insects.

o-paque (ō-pāk′), *adj.* not allowing light to pass through; shady; dark; not transparent; having no luster or brightness: said of some colors: *n.* that which will not admit light through.—*adv.* opaquely.—*n.* opaqueness.

ope (ōp), *v.* and *adj.* a poetical form of *open*; as, he could not *ope* his mouth.

o-pen (ō′pn), *adj.* not shut; not obstructed; as, an *open* path; unfastened; clear of trees; as, *open* country; unfolded or spread out; as, an *open* flower; ready to hear or receive; as, an *open* mind; ready to be affected by; as, *open* to suggestion, temptation, etc.; uncovered or exposed; as, an *open* secret; unsealed; as, the letter was *open;* not frozen nor frosty; as, an *open* winter; clear, unreserved; as, *open* criticism; public; as, an *open* meeting; generous; as, to give with *open* hand; frank; as, *open* confession; free for use, entrance, etc.; as, the competition is still *open;* uttered with the mouth and vocal organs comparatively unclosed: said of a vowel: *v.t.* to unclose, as a window; to spread out, as a fan; to begin; as, to *open* the discussion; to break the seal of or untie, as an envelope or package; to remove obstructions from; as, to *open* a road; to put in operation; as, to *open* a store: *v.i.* to unclose itself; commence; to lead into; as, the door *opens* into the hall: *n.* any wide space uninclosed and not covered with trees, rocks, etc.: with *the.* —*adv.* openly.—*n.* openness, opener.

Syn., *adj.* candid, unreserved, clear.
Ant. (see hidden).

o-pen ac-count (ō′pn ă-kount′), a running or unsettled account.

o-pen-eyed (ō′pn-īd″), *adj.* quick to observe; clear-sighted; intelligent; astonished.

o-pen-hand-ed (ō′pn-hăn″dĕd), *adj.* generous; liberal.

o-pen-heart-ed (ō′pn-här″tĕd), *adj.* frank; sincere; outspoken.

o-pen-ing (ō′pn-ĭng), *n.* an aperture, or a hole; as, an *opening* in a fence; a space in a woods where there are few trees and little undergrowth; the first steps; beginning; as, the *opening* of a trial; opportunity or chance: *adj.* first in order.

o-pen-mouthed (ō′pn-mouthd″), *adj.* gaping; greedy; amazed.

o-pen or-der (ō′pn ôr′dẽr), in tactics, an interval of about three yards between each rank; a formation in which ships are stationed 2,880 feet (4 cable lengths) apart.

o-pen ses-a-me (ō′pn sĕs′ȧ-mē), an unfailing means of entrance or access: from the magic words which opened the robbers' cave in the story of Ali Baba.

o-pen-work (ō′pn-wûrk″), *n.* carving, metal work, embroidery, etc., so made that it shows open spaces in its pattern.

op-er-a (ŏp′ẽr-ȧ), *n.* a musical drama, with scenery, acting, and the accompaniment of an orchestra.

op-er-a glass (ŏp′ẽr-ȧ glȧs), a small telescope made for both eyes and used in the theater, etc.

op-er-ate (ŏp′ẽr-āt), *v.i.* to work; produce a certain effect; perform a surgical action upon the body: *v.t.* to cause to perform certain work; as, to *operate* a machine.

op-er-at-ic (ŏp″ẽr-ăt′ĭk), *adj.* pertaining to, or suitable for, musical drama.

op-er-a-tion (ŏp″ẽr-ā′shŭn), *n.* working or way of working; regular action; as, the machine is in *operation;* agency; surgical action upon the body; a series of movements of an army or fleet; as, a naval *operation.*

Syn. action, force, execution.
Ant. (see inaction).

op-er-a-tive (ŏp′ẽr-ȧ-tĭv), *adj.* having the power of acting; having effect; as, an *operative* law; vigorous: *n.* an artisan or skilled workman; as, an *operative* in a spinning mill.

op-er-a-tor (ŏp′ẽr-ā″tẽr), *n.* one who, or that which, works or acts; one who is employed in a telephone exchange to make connections between lines; one who runs a machine in a factory, etc.; a broker, or one who acts for others; as, a coal *operator.*

op-er-et-ta (ŏp″ẽr-ĕt′ȧ), *n.* a short light, usually humorous, musical drama.

oph-thal-mi-a (ŏf-thăl′mĭ-ȧ), *n.* inflammation of the eye or eyeball. Also, **ophthalmitis.**

oph-thal-mic (ŏf-thăl′mĭk), *adj.* pertaining to the eye.

oph-thal-mol-o-gy (ŏf″thăl-mŏl′ō-jĭ), *n.* that branch of medical science which treats of the functions, structure, and diseases of the eye.

oph-thal-mo-scope (ŏf-thăl′mō-skōp), *n.* an instrument for examining the inside of the eye.

o-pi-ate (ō′pĭ-āt), *n.* a medicine containing or made from opium, that causes sleep, as laudanum; anything that soothes: *adj.* soothing; inducing sleep or quiet.

o-pine (ō-pīn′), *v.t.* to think; suppose; as, I *opine* that this is the case.

o-pin-ion (ō-pĭn′yŭn), *n.* belief; as, that is my *opinion;* what one thinks about any subject; judgment; the statement of the law bearing upon a case; as, an *opinion* handed down by a judge; estimation; as, I have a favorable *opinion* of the man.

Syn. notion, view, belief, sentiment.

o-pin-ion-at-ed (ō-pĭn′yŭn-āt″ĕd), *adj.* firm or obstinate in one's ideas or beliefs.

Syn. conceited, stubborn.
Ant. (see modest).

o-pi-um (ō'pĭ-ŭm), *n.* a powerful sleep-producing drug obtained from a certain species of the poppy.

o-pos-sum (ō-pŏs'ŭm), *n.* a small American animal which, when caught or threatened with danger, pretends to be dead; hence, the expression "to play *'possum*."

Opossum

op-po-nent (ŏ-pō'nĕnt), *n.* one who takes or supports the opposite side in argument or debate; an antagonist: *adj.* acting against each other; opposing; opposite.

op-por-tune (ŏp"ŏr-tūn'), *adj.* well-timed; seasonable; convenient; suitable; as, an *opportune* moment.—*adv.* **opportunely.**—*n.* **opportuneness.**

op-por-tu-nism (ŏp"ŏr-tū'nĭzm), *n* quickness to grasp favorable chances; a taking advantage of circumstances to gain one's ends regardless of consequences or principles, especially in politics.

op-por-tu-nist (ŏp"ŏr-tū'nĭst), *n.* one who takes advantage of circumstances to promote or push forward his own interest or the political interests of his party; one who waits for a suitable time before trying to force his beliefs upon others.

op-por-tu-ni-ty (ŏp'ŏr-tū'nĭ-tĭ), *n.* convenient time or occasion; chance.

op-pos-a-ble (ŏ-pōz'ȧ-bl), *adj.* that may be resisted; capable of being placed in front of, or over against, something else.

op-pose (ŏ-pōz'), *v.t.* to speak or act against; to contend or dispute with; resist; to set up as an obstacle; check; as, to *oppose* the enemy's progress.

Syn. withstand, thwart.

Ant. (see give way).

op-po-site (ŏp'ō-zĭt), *adj.* placed or standing in front of or over against; as, the *opposite* side of the street; the houses were *opposite* to each other; contrary; as, in an *opposite* direction; antagonistic; very different; as, *opposite* opinions: *n.* that which is contrary or in marked contrast.—*adv.* **oppositely.**—*n.* **oppositeness.**

op-po-si-tion (ŏp"ō-zĭsh'ŭn), *n.* the act of resisting or checking; the state of being resisted or checked; resistance; contradiction; the relation of two heavenly bodies to each other when their longitudes differ by 180°; the political party that does not support the party in power: with *the*.

op-po-si-tion-ist (ŏp"ō-zĭsh'ŭn-ĭst), *n.* a member of the political party that does not support an administration or government.

op-press (ŏ-prĕs'), *v.t.* to burden; crush by hardships or severity; as, to *oppress* the poor; weigh heavily upon; as, to be *oppressed* with anxiety; tyrannize over.

op-pres-sion (ŏ-prĕsh'ŭn), *n.* the act of burdening; state of being burdened; hardship; injustice; tyranny; dulness of spirits.

op-pres-sive (ŏ-prĕs'ĭv), *adj.* unreasonably burdensome; as, *oppressive* laws; unjustly severe; tyrannical; as, an *oppressive* ruler; overpowering; as, the *oppressive* air of a closed room; heavy; as, *oppressive* heat.—*adv.* **oppressively.**—*n.* **oppressiveness.**

op-pres-sor (ŏ-prĕs'ẽr), *n.* one who burdens or subjects others to cruelty or unjust hardship.

op-pro-bri-ous (ŏ-prō'brĭ-ŭs), *adj.* expressing disrespectful reproach or contemptuous abuse; as, *opprobrious* language; disgraceful; as, *opprobrious* conduct.—*adv.* **opprobriously.**—*n.* **opprobriousness.**

Syn. insulting, abusive, offensive, vulgar, vile.

op-pro-bri-um (ŏ-prō'brĭ-ŭm), *n.* abusive or insulting language; disgrace; shame.

op-ta-tive (ŏp'tȧ-tĭv), *adj.* expressing wish or desire.

op-tic (ŏp'tĭk), *adj.* pertaining to, or connected with, the eye or vision; as, the *optic* nerve: *n.* the eye: *pl.* the science that treats of light and vision.

op-ti-cal (ŏp'tĭ-kȧl), *adj.* pertaining to the science of light and vision; as, *optical* instruments; pertaining to the eyesight; as, an *optical* illusion.—*adv.* **optically.**

op-ti-cian (ŏp-tĭsh'ăn), *n.* one who makes or sells eyeglasses and instruments used in the study of light, vision, and sight.

op-ti-mism (ŏp'tĭ-mĭzm), *n.* the cheerful belief that everything in nature and history happens for the best; the inclination to look on the best side of things: opposite to *pessimism*.

op-ti-mist (ŏp'tĭ-mĭst), *n.* a person of hopeful disposition; one who looks on the bright side of things: opposite to *pessimist*.

op-ti-mis-tic (ŏp"tĭ-mĭs'tĭk), *adj.* hopeful; inclined always to look upon the best side of things; as, an *optimistic* person.—*adv.* **optimistically.**

op-tion (ŏp'shŭn), *n.* the right or power of choosing; as, you have the *option* of taking it or leaving it; act of choosing; choice; a right secured on property (generally securities, land, or staple commodities), giving one the privilege of buying it, at a specified price, within a specified time.

op-tion-al (ŏp'shŭn-ȧl), *adj.* left to one's wish or choice: *n.* a study which may be taken or not, as one chooses; an elective.—*adv.* **optionally.**

op-u-lence (ŏp'ū-lĕns), *n.* great riches; wealth; abundance. Also, **opulency.**

op-u-lent (ŏp'ū-lĕnt), *adj.* wealthy; rich; as, an *opulent* merchant; abundant; luxuriant.

o-pus (ō'pŭs), *n.* [*pl.* **opera** (ŏp'ẽr-ȧ)], a work; especially, a musical composition. [LAT.]

or (ôr), *conj.* otherwise; either; else; as, you may take this book *or* that one.

or-a-cle (ŏr'ȧ-kl), *n.* among the ancients, the reply of a deity or god, through an inspired priest, to some inquiry; the deity who gave the answer; the place where a deity might be consulted; the holy of holies in the Jewish temple; instruction given by God through his prophets; as, the divine *oracle*; a prophet or person of great wisdom.

o-rac-u-lar (ō-răk'ū-lȧr), *adj.* of the nature of a prophecy; having the quality of authority or solemnity; uttering wise sayings or prophecies; ambiguous, or having two possible meanings.—*adv.* **oracularly.**—*n.* **oracularness.**

o-ral (ō′răl), *adj.* uttered by the mouth; spoken; as, an *oral* statement; pertaining to, or situated near, the mouth; as, the *oral* cavity.—*adv.* **orally.**

or-ange (ŏr′ĕnj), *n.* an evergreen tree with fragrant white flowers and a deep golden-colored and juicy fruit; the fruit itself; the golden- or reddish-yellow color of such fruit: *adj.* pertaining to such fruit; of a deep golden- or reddish-yellow.

or-ange-ade (ŏr′ĕnj-ăd′), *n.* a drink made from orange juice.

Or-ange-man (ŏr′ĕnj-măn), *n.* [*pl.* orangemen (-mĕn)], a member of a secret society of Irish Protestants, named from William III, Prince of Orange and King of England, whose cause the Irish Protestants supported in 1688.

or-ange-ry (ŏr′ĕnj-rĭ), *n.* a sheltered place for growing oranges.

o-rang-u-tan (ō-răng′ōō-tăn″), *n.* a large manlike ape of Borneo and Sumatra. Also, **ourang-outang.**

o-ra-tion (ō-rā′shŭn), *n.* a formal and dignified public speech delivered on an occasion of special importance; as, a funeral *oration*.

or-a-tor (ŏr′ȧ-tẽr), *n.* one who makes an eloquent and dignified speech upon an occasion of special importance; a public speaker noted for skill and power.

or-a-tor-i-cal (ŏr″ȧ-tŏr′ĭ-kăl), *adj.* pertaining to, or suitable to, a skilful public speaker or to eloquent and dignified public speaking; as, *oratorical* gestures.—*adv.* **oratorically.**

or-a-to-ri-o (ŏr″ȧ-tō′rĭ-ō), *n.* a dramatic dialog in music, usually on a sacred theme, sung with an orchestra, but without action, scenery, or costume.

or-a-to-ry (ŏr′ȧ-tō-rĭ), *n.* the art of speaking well in public; eloquence or skill in public speaking: [*pl.* **oratories**], a small chapel, especially one for private devotion.

orb (ôrb), *n.* a globe; sphere; the eye or eyeball; that which is circular; as, the *orb* of the moon: *v.t.* to form into a circle; encircle; to shape into a globelike body.

orbed (ôrbd), *adj.* round; as, the *orbed* moon; encircled; as, *orbed* with light; having eyes: used in compounds; as, a bright-*orbed* maiden.

or-bit (ôr′bĭt), *n.* the bony cavity which contains the eye; the circular or nearly circular course followed by a heavenly body; as, the *orbit* of a planet.

or-chard (ôr′chẽrd), *n.* a garden of fruit trees; also, the trees collectively.

or-ches-tra (ôr′kĕs-trȧ), *n.* in the ancient Greek theater, the place where the chorus danced; in a modern theater, etc., the place occupied by the instrumental musicians; the body of musicians; the collection of instruments, principally of the viol class, on which they play; the forward part or all of the main floor of a theater.

or-ches-tral (ôr-kĕs′trăl; ôr′kĕs-trăl), *adj.* pertaining to, suited to, or performed by, a body of instrumental musicians; pertaining to certain instruments on which they play.

or-ches-tra-tion (ôr″kĕs-trā′shŭn), *n.* the arrangement of a musical score so that it can be played by a number of instruments.

or-chid (ôr′kĭd), *n.* a handsome showy flower, often oddly shaped.

or-dain (ôr-dān′), *v.t.* to appoint or set apart for some special work; as, to *ordain* a minister or priest; decree; establish; as, fate *ordains* our destiny; God *ordains* what we shall or shall not do.

or-de-al (ôr′dē-ăl; ôr′dēl), *n.* an ancient method of trial by fire, water, combat, etc., to determine the guilt or innocence of an accused person; hence, a severe trial or test.

or-der (ôr′dẽr), *n.* method or state of regular arrangement; as, to observe *order* in one's work; settled way of doing something; as, an *order* of worship; right working condition; as, the machine is in good *order;* rule; regulation; command; as, to issue or obey an *order;* class; as, an *order* of plants; rank; degree; as, the *order* of nobility or of the common people; *pl.* the clerical office; a religious fraternity; as, an *order* of monks; a group of persons set apart in some way, as by membership in a society, by honor conferred, or some other bond; public quiet or observance of law; as, *order* in the streets; a commission for something; as, an *order* for groceries: **holy orders,** the three orders (bishop, priest, deacon), of the Christian ministry: *v.t.* to regulate or manage; command; conduct; direct; to give a command for: *v.i.* to give a command or order.

or-der-ly (ôr′dẽr-lĭ), *adj.* regular; as, an *orderly* arrangement; methodical; systematic; as, an *orderly* worker; well conducted or regulated; as, an *orderly* meeting; performed carefully and methodically; as, the task was done in an *orderly* manner; peaceable; as, an *orderly* crowd; quiet; obedient; as, an *orderly* class; charged, on military duty, with the carrying of commands; as, an *orderly* officer: *adv.* properly: *n.* a soldier who attends upon an officer to carry his orders; as, the colonel's *orderly;* a man who acts as general attendant in a hospital: **orderly sergeant, orderly corporal,** non-commissioned officers who carry commands. —*n.* **orderliness.**

or-di-nal (ôr′dĭ-năl), *n.* a number showing succession in a series; as, first, second, third are *ordinals;* a book containing certain church forms and services: *adj.* noting succession in a series; as, the *ordinal* numbers are first, second, etc.; belonging to a class, as of plants, animals, etc.

or-di-nance (ôr′dĭ-năns), *n.* an established rule, rite, or law; as, a city *ordinance.*

or-di-na-ry (ôr′dĭ-nā-rĭ), *adj.* according to established custom or rule; usual; customary; commonplace; plain.—*adv.* **ordinarily.**

or-di-na-tion (ôr″dĭ-nā′shŭn), *n.* the act of admitting to the Christian ministry; as, the *ordination* of a minister; the state of being so appointed.

ord-nance (ôrd′năns), *n.* the general name for all kinds of weapons used in war; more strictly, the heavy guns; artillery; military supplies.

ore (ōr), *n.* a mineral substance containing one or more metals.

o-re-ad (ō′rē-ăd), *n.* in Greek and Roman mythology, a mountain nymph or fairy.

or-gan (ôr′găn), *n.* a part of an animal or vegetable, fitted to do some special duty; as, the *organ* of sight; a means of making known the opinions or official acts of a person or party, as a newspaper; a means by which an action is performed; as, courts are the *organs* of justice; a large musical wind instrument with pipes, sounded by compressed air from bellows, and played upon by keys; a smaller instrument of the same class, operated by pedals or a turning crank.

or-gan-die (ôr'găn-dĭ), *n.* a very fine muslin dress goods, often with delicately colored patterns. Also, **organdy.**

or-gan-ic (ôr-găn'ĭk), *adj.* pertaining to, of the nature of, or affecting, some organ of the body; as, an *organic* disease; pertaining to, or derived from, anything that has life in itself; as, fossils are remains of *organic* bodies; constitutional; inherent; as, an *organic* fault; containing carbon as an essential ingredient; as, an *organic* compound; systematized: **organic chemistry,** the chemistry of carbon compounds. Also, **organical.** —*adv.* **organically.**

or-gan-ism (ôr'găn-ĭzm), *n.* a member of the animal or vegetable kingdom; anything that has life in itself; a body composed of parts performing special duties that are dependent on each other; anything resembling such a body; as, the social *organism.*

or-gan-ist (ôr'găn-ĭst), *n.* a player on the musical wind instrument called an organ.

or-gan-i-za-tion (ôr"găn-ĭ-zā'shŭn), *n.* the set of parts of an animal or a plant, regarded as a whole, acting or working together; as, the *organization* of a fish; any body consisting of parts each of which performs a special duty; as, the educational *organization* of the country; a body of persons united for some end or work; as, a church *organization;* the act of forming a union to work together for a common end; as, the *organization* of a club.

or-gan-ize (ôr'găn-īz), *v.t.* to give life or being to; as, to *organize* a rebellion; to cause to unite and work together in orderly fashion; as, to *organize* forces for a campaign; to arrange for a given purpose; as, to *organize* a club.

or-gy (ôr'jĭ), *n.* [*pl.* orgies (-jĭz)], a wild, drunken revel: usually in plural.

o-ri-el (ō'rĭ-ĕl), *n.* a large bay window which rests on a bracket.

Oriel Window

o-ri-ent (ō'rĭ-ĕnt), *n.* the east: opposite to *occident,* or west: *adj.* pertaining to, or coming from, the East; like sunrise; bright; precious; as, *orient* pearls: *v.t.* to set facing the east; to find the position of, in relation to the east; to find the bearings of, as in surveying; to set right in relation to some fixed rule or principle: **Orient,** *n.* the East; the countries of Asia, or the Far East; the countries bordering the eastern Mediterranean, or the Near East.

O-ri-en-tal (ō"rĭ-ĕn'tăl), *adj.* pertaining to, or situated in, the East; proceeding from Asia or the East: *n.* a native of Asia or the East: **oriental,** *adj.* gorgeous or magnificent; of bright colors, like those seen in the East.—*adv.* **orientally.**

O-ri-en-tal-ism (ō"rĭ-ĕn'tăl-ĭzm), *n.* an expression or custom peculiar to the East; knowledge of Eastern languages and literature.

O-ri-en-tal-ist (ō"rĭ-ĕn'tăl-ĭst), *n.* one who knows well the history, language, and literature of the East.

o-ri-en-tate (ō'rĭ-ĕn-tāt"; ō"rĭ-ĕn'tāt), *v.t.* to place so as to face the east; to determine the position of, with reference to the points of the compass: *v.i.* to face the east in worship.

o-ri-en-ta-tion (ō"rĭ-ĕn-tā'shŭn), *n.* the finding of the east point so as to get one's bearings; eastward position; the placing of a church so that the altar shall be toward the east; the facing toward the east in worship; faculty or ability possessed by certain birds of finding their way home from distant places; ability to find and hold the right mental attitude toward a subject.

or-i-fice (ŏr'ĭ-fĭs), *n.* a mouth or opening into a cavity.

or-i-flamme (ŏr'ĭ-flăm), *n.* the ancient royal standard of France, a red flag split at one end and forming flame-shaped streamers; any symbol of glory. Also, **oriflamb, auriflamme.**

or-i-gin (ŏr'ĭ-jĭn), *n.* the beginning of anything; as, the *origin* of life; birth; parentage; source; cause; as, the *origin* of the trouble; derivation; as, the word is of Latin *origin.*

Syn. beginning, occasion, root, rise.

Ant. (see end, effect).

o-rig-i-nal (ō-rĭj'ĭ-năl), *adj.* of or pertaining to the beginning, or first state; as, *original* sin; an *original* edition of a book; not copied; as, an *original* painting; able to create or invent that which is new; as, an *original* writer; having new ideas: *n.* that from which anything is copied; the language in which a translated work was written; an unusual person.—*adv.* **originally.**

Syn. primitive, creative, novel.

o-rig-i-nal-i-ty (ō-rĭj"ĭ-năl'ĭ-tĭ), *n.* the ability to create or make something new; as, the *originality* of an inventor; the quality of being new or novel; as, the *originality* of an idea; oddity.

o-rig-i-nate (ō-rĭj'ĭ-nāt), *v.t.* to bring into existence; invent; create: *v.i.* to begin to exist; to rise or spring from a source.—*n.* **originator.**

o-rig-i-na-tion (ō-rĭj"ĭ-nā'shŭn), *n.* a beginning; creation; invention; the causing to begin.

o-ri-ole (ō'rĭ-ōl), *n.* any of various black and yellow birds which build hanging nests, especially the golden thrush or golden oriole of Europe; any of certain American birds which are colored black and orange, and which build hanging nests.

or-i-son (ŏr'ĭ-zŭn), *n.* a prayer of deep, earnest devotion, regularly offered.

or-mo-lu (ôr'mō-lōō), *n.* brass so finished as to appear like gold.

or-na-ment (ôr'nȧ-mĕnt), *n.* anything that adorns or beautifies: *v.t.* to adorn; bedeck; decorate.

or-na-men-tal (ôr'nȧ-mĕn'tăl), *adj.* serving to adorn.—*adv.* **ornamentally.**

or-na-men-ta-tion (ôr"nȧ-mĕn"tā'-shŭn), *n.* decoration; adornment.

or-nate (ôr-nāt'; ôr'nāt), *adj.* much adorned or decorated; very elegant or finished; as, an *ornate* style in writing. —*adv.* **ornately.**—*n.* **ornateness.**

or-ni-tho-log-i-cal (ôr"nĭ-thō-lŏj'ĭ-kăl), *adj.* pertaining to the study of birds.

or-ni-thol-o-gist (ôr"nĭ-thŏl'ō-jĭst), *n.* one who makes a special study of birds.

or-ni-thol-o-gy (ôr′nĭ-thŏl′ō-jĭ), *n.* the scientific study of birds, their form, structure, habits, etc.

o-rog-ra-phy (ō-rŏg′rȧ-fĭ), *n.* the science that treats of mountains, mountain systems, their height, etc. Also, **orology**.—*adj.* **orographic, orographical.**

o-ro-tund (ō′rō-tŭnd; ôr′ō-tŭnd), *adj.* having a full, clear, smooth quality; open, mellow, rich, and musical: said of the voice or manner of utterance.

Or-pheus (ôr′fūs; ôr′fē-ŭs), *n.* in mythology, a Thracian poet and musician, who, with his lyre, could draw to himself beasts, rocks, and trees.

or-ris (ŏr′ĭs), *n.* the iris, a plant, the dried roots of which are used as a perfume or sachet powder, called *orris root.* Also, **orrice.**

or-tho-dox (ôr′thō-dŏks), *adj.* holding what is regarded as the correct opinion, especially in regard to religion; approved; accepted: opposite to *heterodox.*

Ornithology. 1, flicker; 2, blue jay; 3, scarlet tanager; 4, Baltimore oriole; 5, bluebird; 6, brown thrasher; 7, red-winged blackbird; 8, bobolink.

or-phan (ôr′făn), *n.* a child who has lost one or, more commonly, both parents by death: *adj.* being without parents, because of their death: *v.t.* to deprive of a parent or parents.

or-phan-age (ôr′făn-āj), *n.* the state of being without parents; an institution for children whose parents are dead.

Or-phe-an (ôr-fē′ăn), *adj.* pertaining to Orpheus; hence, melodious, enchanting. Also, **Orphic.**

or-tho-dox-y (ôr′thō-dŏk′sĭ), *n.* a holding to, or a following of, the accepted or common belief or opinion of a church; soundness of belief or doctrine.

or-tho-ë-py (ôr′thō-ē-pĭ; ôr-thō′ē-pĭ), *n.* the art of correct pronunciation.—*n.* **orthoëpist.**—*adj.* **orthoëpic, orthoëpical.**

or-thog-ra-pher (ôr-thŏg′rȧ-fẽr), *n.* one who knows thoroughly the principles of spelling; one who spells correctly. Also, **orthographist.**

or-tho-graph-ic (ôr″thô-grăf′ĭk), *adj.* pertaining to correct spelling; correctly spelled; pertaining to right lines and angles. Also, **orthographical.**

or-thog-ra-phy (ôr-thŏg′rá-fĭ), *n.* the art of spelling words correctly; the way of grouping letters to form words.

or-tho-pe-dic (ôr″thô-pē′dĭk; ôr″thô-pĕd′ĭk), *adj.* having to do with the curing or preventing of deformities, especially in children; as, an *orthopedic* hospital.—*n.* **orthopedics.**

Ortolan

or-to-lan (ôr′tô-lăn), *n.* a member of the bunting family of birds, much prized for its flesh; in the United States, the bobolink.

o-ryx (ō′rĭks; ŏr′ĭks), *n.* an African oxlike animal of the antelope family.

O-sage (ō-sāj′; ō′sāj), *n.* one of a tribe of American Indians, originally inhabiting the region of the Arkansas and Osage rivers.

os-cil-late (ŏs′ĭ-lāt), *v.i.* to swing backwards and forwards, as the pendulum of a clock; vibrate: *v.t.* to cause to swing back and forth.

os-cil-la-tion (ŏs″ĭ-lā′shŭn), *n.* a swinging backwards and forwards, as a pendulum; vibration; a wavering, as of opinion.

os-cil-la-tor (ŏs′ĭ-lā″tẽr), *n.* one who, or that which, moves backward and forward like a pendulum; a device for producing electric waves of definite lengths from electric currents of definite frequency; a device for producing electric vibrations in a wireless telegraph system.

os-cil-la-to-ry (ŏs′ĭ-lá-tô-rĭ), *adj.* swinging back and forth; vibrating.

os-cu-late (ŏs′kū-lāt), *v.t.* to kiss: *v.i.* to kiss one another.

os-cu-la-tion (ŏs″kū-lā′shŭn), *n.* the act of kissing; a kiss.

os-cu-la-to-ry (ŏs′kū-lá-tô-rĭ), *n.* a tablet or board on which the picture of Christ or the Virgin Mary is painted for worshipers to kiss: *adj.* pertaining to kissing.

o-sier (ō′zhẽr), *n.* a willow, the twigs of which are used in basket making; a similar plant of another family, as the American dogwood: *adj.* made of, or consisting of, willow twigs.

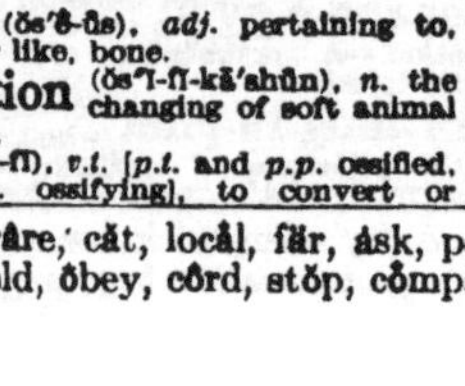
Osprey

os-prey (ŏs′prā), *n.* a large hawk that feeds on fish; the fish hawk. Also, **ossifrage.**

os-se-ous (ŏs′ē-ŭs), *adj.* pertaining to, consisting of, or like, bone.

os-si-fi-ca-tion (ŏs″ĭ-fĭ-kā′shŭn), *n.* the changing of soft animal tissue into bone.

os-si-fy (ŏs′ĭ-fī), *v.t.* [*p.t.* and *p.p.* ossified, *p.pr.* ossifying], to convert or change into bone or into a bonelike substance; harden: *v.i.* to become bone.

os-ten-si-ble (ŏs-tĕn′sĭ-bl), *adj.* seeming; professed; pretended; apparent; as, an *ostensible* reason or purpose. —*adv.* **ostensibly.**

os-ten-ta-tion (ŏs″tĕn-tā′shŭn), *n.* unnecessary show or parade; ambitious or vain display.
Syn. boast, pomp, flourish.
Ant. (see modesty).

os-ten-ta-tious (ŏs″tĕn-tā′shŭs), *adj.* fond of show; intended for vain display; showy; gaudy; as, *ostentatious* jewelry.—*adv.* **ostentatiously.**

os-te-ol-o-gist (ŏs″tē-ŏl′ō-jĭst), *n.* one who is skilled in the study of the bones of vertebrate animals, or those that have a backbone.

os-te-ol-o-gy (ŏs″tē-ŏl′ō-jĭ), *n.* the scientific study of the bones of vertebrate animals, or those that have a backbone.

os-te-o-path (ŏs′tē-ō-păth), *n.* one who treats disease by manipulating the bones, muscles, and nerves.

os-te-o-path-ic (ŏs″tē-ō-păth′ĭk), *adj.* pertaining to the system of treating disease by manipulating the bones, muscles, and nerves.

os-te-op-a-thist (ŏs″tē-ŏp′á-thĭst), *n.* one who is skilled in or who practices the treatment of disease by manipulating the bones, muscles, and nerves.

os-te-op-a-thy (ŏs″tē-ŏp′á-thĭ), *n.* a system of treating disease by manipulating the bones, muscles, and nerves.

ost-ler (ŏs′lẽr), *n.* a man who attends to horses at an inn; a stableman. Also, **hostler.**

os-tra-cism (ŏs′trá-sĭzm), *n.* banishment, or a driving out by popular vote: the ancient custom in Athens of banishing a citizen who was unpopular; exclusion from favor by general consent; as, his *ostracism* by society was the result of his own conduct.

os-tra-cize (ŏs′trá-sīz), *v.t.* to banish or drive out by popular vote; to put out of public or private favor; as, he was *ostracised* from good society.

Ostrich

os-trich (ŏs′trĭch), *n.* a very large and swift-footed African bird, the largest bird known, valued for its feathers.

oth-er (ŭth′ẽr), *adj.* not the same; different; as, I have *other* matters to attend to; additional; more; as, I have *other* sisters; opposite; as, the *other* side of the street; second; as, every *other* line: *adv.* otherwise; as, she could not do *other* than help him: *pron.* the opposite one of two; as, one or the *other* of you, a different person or thing: *conj.* or; either.

oth-er-wise (ŭth′ẽr-wīz″), *adv.* in a different way; differently; as, he could not do *otherwise*; in different conditions or respects; as, I know him professionally, but not *otherwise*: *conj.* else: *adj.* different.

ot-ter (ŏt′ẽr), *n.* a fish-eating animal of the weasel family living in the water, and valued for its fur.

Ot-to-man (ŏt'ô-măn), *adj.* pertaining to, or like, the Turks or their government: *n.* a Turk: **ottoman,** a cushioned seat, somewhat like those used in Turkey; a movable cushioned foot rest.

ou-bli-ette (ōō'blē-ĕt'), *n.* in ancient castles, a dungeon, commonly with an entrance only through the ceiling. [Fr.]

ought (ôt), *v.* to be under obligation; be fit, necessary, or proper: used chiefly as a helping verb: *n.* and *adv.* anything; aught.

ounce (ouns), *n.* a weight of one-sixteenth of a pound avoirdupois; one-twelfth of a pound troy; an Asiatic animal like the leopard.

our (our), *poss. pron.* and *adj.* of or pertaining to us; as, *our* school: when not followed by a noun, *ours;* as, this dear country of *ours.*

Ourebi

ou-re-bi (ōō'rē-bē), *n.* a South African antelope having lateral hoofs and tufts on the knees: it is yellowish with white below, and has straight, ringed horns.

our-selves (our-sĕlvz'), *pron. pl.* we or us, not others: an emphatic or reflexive form.

ou-sel (ōō'zl), *n.* the European blackbird. Also, **ouzel.**

oust (oust), *v.t.* to eject or turn out; as, to *oust* a person from a position.

out (out), *adv.* without; not within or at home; as, to live *out* at service; to let the secret *out;* abroad; forth; not in office, possession, or action; as, three players on our side are *out;* not in existence or continuance; as, put the light *out;* in error; as, your figures are *out;* without restraint or fully; loudly; as, to speak *out:* *interj.* begone! *n.* one who is not in office: **out-,** a prefix to many self-explaining compounds, in the sense of *more than* or *beyond;* as, *out*-balance.

out-and-out (out-ănd-out'), *adj.* thorough; complete: *adv.* completely; thoroughly.

out-break (out'brāk"), *n.* a bursting forth; as, an *outbreak* of fever.

out-build-ing (out'bĭl"dĭng), *n.* a structure apart from, but belonging to and used by, the main house, as a barn, shed, etc.

out-burst (out'bûrst"), *n.* a breaking forth; an outbreak.

out-cast (out'kȧst"), *n.* one who is turned or driven forth; one who is despised socially; a vagabond; exile: *adj.* driven forth; rejected; forlorn; degraded.

out-class (out-klȧs'), *v.t.* to surpass or excel in quality, skill, etc.

out-come (out'kŭm"), *n.* the result or consequence of an act.

out-crop (out'krŏp"), *n.* the coming out of strata or layers of rock, etc., to the surface of the ground: *v.i.* to come out to the surface of the ground.

out-cry (out'krī"), *n.* clamor; uproar; confused noise.

out-dis-tance (out-dĭs'tăns), *v.t.* to outstrip; to go faster than; excel in speed.

out-do (out-dōō'), *v.t.* to surpass; excel; as, he tried to *outdo* his opponents.

out-door (out'dōr"), *adj.* not inside the walls of a building; in the open air.—*adv.* and *n.* **outdoors.**

out-er (out'ẽr), *adj.* being on the outside: opposite to *inner.*

out-er-most (out'ẽr-mōst), *adv.* farthest on the outside.

out-face (out-fās'), *v.t.* to stare (one) out of countenance; to defy.

out-fall (out'fôl"), *n.* the mouth, or place of discharge, of a river, culvert, etc.

out-field (out'fēld"), *n.* the part of a baseball ground beyond the diamond; the players outside the diamond.—*n.* **outfielder.**

out-fit (out'fĭt), *n.* all the articles necessary for any undertaking; as, the *outfit* for a journey or expedition; a bride's *outfit:* *v.t.* and *v.i.* to furnish with everything necessary for an undertaking.—*n.* **outfitter.**

out-flank (out-flănk'), *v.t.* to go or pass around the sides of; to get the better of (an enemy) by passing or extending troops around the extreme right and left positions of his army.

out-gen-er-al (out-jĕn'ẽr-ăl), *v.t.* to excel in management; to surpass in military skill.

out-go (out'gō"), *n.* that which goes out; that which is paid out; outlay; as, the *outgo* was greater than the income: *v.t.* (out"gō'), to go beyond; surpass; excel.

out-go-ing (out'gō"ĭng), *adj.* leaving; departing; as, *outgoing* baggage: *n.* departure: *pl.* expenses.

out-growth (out'grōth"), *n.* anything that grows out of, or proceeds from, anything else; a result.

out-Her-od (out-hĕr'ŭd), *v.t.* to exceed the cruelty or violence of (Herod, the Great); hence, to exceed in any evil.

out-ing (out'ĭng), *n.* a short excursion or pleasure trip; an airing.

out-land-ish (out-lăn'dĭsh), *adj.* strange; unfamiliar; uncouth; as, *outlandish* conduct or dress; far away.—*adv.* **outlandishly.**—*n.* **outlandishness.**

out-law (out'lô"), *n.* one who is deprived of legal rights and protection; a disorderly person; one who flees from justice: *v.t.* to deprive of legal benefits and protection; to remove from legal control; as, to *outlaw* a claim.—*n.* **outlawry.**

out-lay (out'lā"), *n.* that which is spent, either money or effort, in any undertaking.

out-let (out'lĕt), *n.* a means of passing out; exit; vent.

out-line (out'līn"), *n.* the mark that shows the outer limits or shape of a figure; in drawing, a sketch which shows the shape of figures without light and shade; in writing or speaking, a first draft or sketch in words; as, an *outline* of a lecture: *v.t.* to draw the limiting mark or edge of; to state the plan of in words.

out-live (out-lĭv'), *v.t.* to be in existence longer than; to survive.

out-look (out'lōōk"), *n.* a view, as seen by one who looks from a window or other opening; present state or future prospect of things; as, a favorable *outlook;* foresight; a place where watch is kept; a watchtower; a lookout; a sentinel.

out-ly-ing (out'lī"ing), *adj.* being distant from the center, or main body: remote; detached.

out-most (out'mōst), *adv.* farthest outside; outermost.

out-num-ber (out-nŭm'bẽr), *v.t.* to be more than, in number.

out-port (out'pōrt"), *n.* a port or harbor at some distance from the chief port.

out-post (out'pōst"), *n.* a body of troops stationed at a distance from the main army to guard against surprise; the position occupied by them.

out-put (out'pŏŏt"), *n.* quantity produced, as from a mine or mill; the yield.

out-rage (out'rāj), *n.* gross insult or injury; a cruel or violent act: *v.t.* to treat with violence and abuse; to injure by rough treatment; to rape.

out-ra-geous (out-rā'jŭs), *adj.* violent; atrocious; excessive; without regard for decency; shocking; as, his conduct was *outrageous.*—*adv.* **outrageously.** —*n.* **outrageousness.**

ou-tré (ōō"trā'), *adj.* extremely odd; exaggerated. [FR.]

out-rid-er (out'rīd"ẽr), *n.* a servant on horseback who rides in advance of a carriage.

out-rig-ger (out'rĭg"ẽr), *n.* on a ship, a projecting spar or beam for extending sails or ropes; a boat with attachments at the sides to keep it from upsetting.

out-right (out'rīt"; out"rīt'), *adv.* completely; openly; at once; immediately: *adj.* (out'rīt"), downright; straightforward.

out-set (out'sĕt"), *n.* a start; the beginning of a business, journey, etc.

out-shine (out-shīn'), *v.t.* to be brighter or more splendid than: *v.i.* to shine forth.

out-side (out"sīd'; out'sīd"), *n.* the part of anything that is on the surface or that is seen; as, the *outside* of a house; the farthest limit; as, I shall return in a week, at the *outside*: *adj.* pertaining to, or situated upon, the surface or outside; external or exterior; reaching the limit; having no part in: *adv.* beyond the border; without: *prep.* beyond the limit of; out of; without.

out-sid-er (out"sīd'ẽr), *n.* one that does not belong to a given party, company, etc.

out-skirts (out'skûrts"), *n. pl.* the edges, as of a town; parts far from the center.

out-spo-ken (out"spō'kn; out'spō"kn), *adj.* candid; free or bold of speech; frank; as, he was very *outspoken.* —*adv.* **outspokenly.**—*n.* **outspokenness.**

out-stand-ing (out-stănd'ĭng), *adj.* uncollected; unpaid; as, *outstanding* debts.

out-strip (out-strĭp'), *v.t.* to go faster than; to leave behind; to excel.

out-ward (out'wẽrd), *adj.* pertaining to the exterior of an object; exterior; outside; external; outer; visible; as, *outward* appearance; moving out from within; as, the *outward* course of a ship: *adv.* away from an inner place; on the surface; externally; apparently. Also, *adv.* **outwards, outwardly.**

out-ward bound (out'wẽrd bound), sailing from a home port to foreign parts; as, *outward bound* vessels.

out-wear (out-wâr'), *v.t.* to last longer than; as, one pair of these shoes will *outwear* two pairs of those; to outlive; outgrow.

out-wit (out-wĭt'), *v.t.* to defeat, or get the better of, by superior skill or cunning; as, to *outwit* an enemy.

out-work (out'wûrk"), *n.* a defense or protection built beyond the main body of a fort, etc.

o-va (ō'vȧ), *n.pl.* of *ovum*: egg cells, or eggs, in the widest sense. [LAT.]

o-val (ō'văl), *adj.* shaped like an egg: *n.* anything egg-shaped.

o-va-ry (ō'vȧ-rĭ), *n.* [*pl.* ovaries (-rĭz)], the organ in a female animal in which the ova, or first germs of future life, are formed; the hollow seed-case of a plant.—*adj.* **ovarian.**

o-vate (ō'vāt), *adj.* shaped like the lengthwise section of an egg: used in botany, of a flat surface.

o-va-tion (ō-vā'shŭn), *n.* applause and admiration for a hero or favorite; a noisy demonstration of public esteem; as, Mr. Roosevelt received a tremendous *ovation.*

ov-en (ŭv'n), *n.* a place for baking, heating, or drying, usually connected with a stove or range.

o-ver (ō'vẽr), *prep.* in higher position, authority, dignity, excellence, or value than; above; as, the roof *over* one's head; upon; as, to carry a shawl *over* one's arm; across; as, to jump *over* a ditch; covering; as, to wear a cape *over* the shoulders; more than; as, he spent *over* ten dollars; throughout; as, to stay *over* the week-end; to travel *over* the plains: *adv.* from beginning to end; as, to talk the matter *over;* from one to another; as, to make *over* property; from one side to the other; as, to go *over* to the enemy; in excess; as, all that is left *over;* so as to bring the opposite side up; as, to turn a coin *over;* so as to be upright no longer; as, to topple *over;* from end to end; throughout; as, a landscape dotted *over* with trees; once again; as, I will do it *over;* across the brim; as, the kettle boiled *over;* at an end; as, it is all *over;* *adj.* higher; superior; as, an *over*-lord: *n.* in cricket, the time during which balls are delivered by one bowler: **over-**, a prefix to many self-explaining words, in the sense of *too much, too great, too long,* etc., as to *over*-act, etc.

o-ver-alls (ō'vẽr-ôlz"), *n.pl.* loose trousers worn over other trousers to protect them from soil, dirt, etc.

o-ver-bear (ō"vẽr-bâr'), *v.t.* to bear down, as by greater weight or force; overcome; to domineer over: *v.i.* to produce young or fruit too freely.

o-ver-bear-ing (ō"vẽr-bâr'ĭng), *adj.* domineering; as, an *overbearing* disposition or manner.

o-ver-board (ō'vẽr-bōrd"), *adv.* over the side of a ship; from a ship into the water.

o-ver-bur-den (ō"vẽr-bûr'dn), *v.t.* to load with too heavy a weight; to oppress with work, anxiety, etc.

o-ver-cap-i-tal-ize (ō"vẽr-kăp'ĭ-tăl-īz), *v.t.* to represent the capital value of as greater than it is.

o-ver-cast (ō"vẽr-kăst'), *v.t.* to cover over; to cloud; darken: (ō'vẽr-kăst"), sew over and over; take long, loose stitches over (the raw edges of a seam) to prevent raveling.

o-ver-charge (ō"vẽr-chärj'), *v.t.* to fill or load too heavily, as a gun; to ask too high a price from or for: *n.* (ō'vẽr-chärj"), too heavy a load; too high a price.

o-ver-coat (ō′vẽr-kōt′), *n.* an outside coat worn over the other garments.

o-ver-come (ō″vẽr-kŭm′), *v.t.* to get the better of; conquer; hence, to make helpless; *v.i.* to be victorious.

o-ver-do (ō″vẽr-dōō′), *v.t.* to go too far in doing; exaggerate; to weary by overwork; *v.i.* to go beyond one's strength; to exert oneself too much.

o-ver-draw (ō″vẽr-drô′), *v.t.* to exaggerate; in banking, to make drafts or checks in greater amounts than the money one has in bank.

o-ver-dress (ō″vẽr-drĕs′), *v.t.* to bedeck or array to excess; to put too many adornments on.

o-ver-due (ō′vẽr-dū″; ō″vẽr-dū′), *adj.* unpaid or not present at the proper time for payment or arrival.

o-ver-flow (ō′vẽr-flō″), *n.* the spreading of water or other liquid beyond its proper limits; that which goes beyond its proper limits; space allowed for something to spread or pour into: *v.t.* (ō″vẽr-flō′), to flood; to cover with liquid: *v.i.* to pass the limits; to be more than full.

o-ver-grown (ō′vẽr-grōn″; ō″vẽr-grōn′), *adj.* covered with too much herbage, etc.; as, a field *overgrown* with weeds; grown too large; too big for one's age, etc.

o-ver-hand (ō′vẽr-hănd″), *adj.* down from above; as, an *overhand* blow; grasping with the palm down, or in toward the body: *adv.* (ō′vẽr-hănd″; ō″vẽr-hănd′), so that the palm is down, or turned in toward the body; as, to catch a ball *overhand.*

o-ver-hang (ō″vẽr-hăng′), *v.t.* and *v.i.* to project beyond and above: *n.* (ō′vẽr-hăng), a projection or jutting out; the distance over which something projects.

o-ver-haul (ō″vẽr-hôl′), *v.t.* to examine thoroughly for the purpose of making repairs; overtake; gain upon.

o-ver-head (ō″vẽr-hĕd′), *adv.* above; on an upper floor; on high: *adj.* (ō′vẽr-hĕd″), situated above; passing through the air; pertaining to what is above or aloft; **overhead charges,** that part of the expense of a business which is not included in the actual purchase of materials, cost of production, etc., as rent, insurance, heating, advertising, etc.

o-ver-hear (ō″vẽr-hēr′), *v.t.* to hear (something) not said to one or intended for one to hear; to hear (some one) whose remarks are not spoken to one or intended for one to hear.

o-ver-land (ō′vẽr-lănd″), *adj.* and *adv.* across the land rather than the sea; as, *adj.*, an *overland* journey.

o-ver-lap (ō″vẽr-lăp′), *v.t.* and *v.i.* [*p.t.* and *p.p.* overlapped, *p.pr.* overlapping], to extend over the edge of something: *n.* (ō′vẽr-lăp″), the extension, and amount of extension, of one thing over the edge of another.

o-ver-lay (ō″vẽr-lā′), *v.t.* to spread above or across, as a cover or layer: *n.* a thin sheet of paper, used in printing, to make the impression heavier.

o-ver-look (ō″vẽr-lŏŏk′), *v.t.* to look down on from above; to inspect; to watch over; to fail to notice; to pass over without punishing, etc.

o-ver-match (ō″vẽr-măch′), *v.t.* to be more than equal to; to defeat; vanquish.

o-ver-much (ō′vẽr-mŭch″), *adj.* too great: *n.* too large an amount: *adv.* (ō″vẽr-mŭch′), too greatly.

o-ver-night (ō″vẽr-nīt′), *adj.* and *adv.* in the evening previous; for the time from evening till morning.

o-ver-plus (ō′vẽr-plŭs), *n.* excess; surplus; what remains.

o-ver-pow-er (ō″vẽr-pou′ẽr), *v.t.* to bear down or crush by superior force; vanquish or conquer; as, to *overpower* an enemy; to affect greatly.—*p.adj.* **overpowering.**

o-ver-pro-duc-tion (ō″vẽr-prō-dŭk′shŭn), *n.* a raising or making of more than is needed; supply in excess of demand; as, an *overproduction* of grain.

o-ver-rate (ō″vẽr-rāt′), *v.t.* to set too high a value upon.

o-ver-reach (ō″vẽr-rēch′), *v.t.* to reach above or beyond; to miss or overshoot by attempting too much; to defeat (oneself) by doing too much; to get the better of by trickery; cheat.

o-ver-ride (ō″vẽr-rīd′), *v.t.* to trample down; to set aside tyrannically; as, to *override* a decision; to disregard the right or wishes of.

o-ver-rule (ō″vẽr-rōōl′), *v.t.* to decide against; as, to *overrule* an objection; to cause to change an intention, decision, etc.: *v.i.* to control others by influence, character, etc.

o-ver-run (ō″vẽr-rŭn′), *v.t.* to grow or spread over in great quantity or numbers; invade; infest; in baseball, to go beyond, as a base; in printing, to carry over, as type, to another line; to change the arrangement of by a change of lines: *v.i.* to spread, flow, or extend over something or beyond the limits of something.

o-ver-seas (ō″vẽr-sēz′), *adj.* and *adv.* across the ocean. Also, **oversea.**

o-ver-see (ō″vẽr-sē′), *v.t.* to inspect; superintend.

o-ver-seer (ō″vẽr-sē′ẽr; ō′vẽr-sē″ẽr), *n.* the superintendent of some department of a business; one who looks over or inspects the work of laborers.

o-ver-shad-ow (ō″vẽr-shăd′ō), *v.t.* to throw a shade over; darken; to be more important than.

o-ver-shoe (ō′vẽr-shōō″), *n.* a waterproof shoe, worn over another.

o-ver-shot wheel (ō′vẽr-shŏt hwēl), a water wheel which is driven by water flowing over its top.

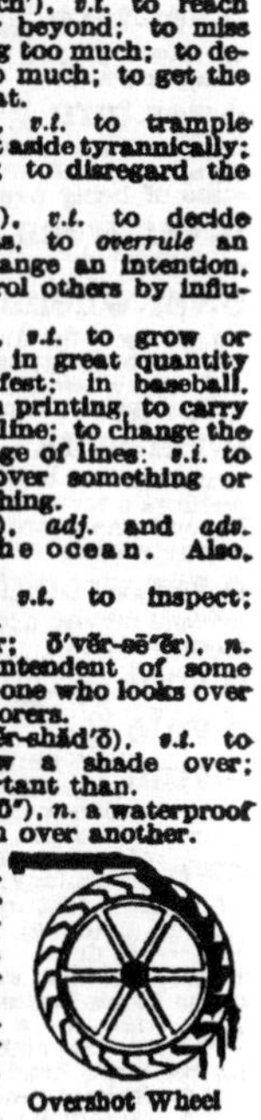

Overshot Wheel

o-ver-sight (ō′vẽr-sīt″), *n.* watchful care; management; failure to see or observe; something not seen or observed.

o-ver-state (ō″vẽr-stāt′), *v.t.* to put into too strong terms; to exaggerate; to express too forcefully.

o-ver-step (ō″vẽr-stĕp′), *v.t.* and *v.i.* to go too far; to go beyond one's right in speaking, acting, etc.; to transgress.

o-ver-sub-scribe (ō″vẽr-sŭb-skrīb′) *v.t.* to promise to buy a larger amount (of stock or bonds) than is offered for sale; as, the people *oversubscribed* the Liberty Loan.

o-vert (ō′vẽrt), *adj.* open to view; publicly seen or known; as, an *overt* act.—*adv.* **overtly.**

o-ver-take (ō″vẽr-tāk′), *v.t.* [*p.t.* and *p.p.* overtook, *p.pr.* overtaking], to catch up with; as, to *overtake* a runaway horse; take by surprise; as, to be *overtaken* by a storm.

o-ver the top (ō'vẽr *thē* tŏp), in the World War, the order to charge from the trenches: also applied to a successful effort to raise a sum of money or accomplish a desired end.

o-ver-throw (ō'vẽr-thrō'), *v.t.* to turn upside down; defeat; destroy: *n.* (ō'vẽr-thrō'), ruin; defeat.

o-ver-time (ō'vẽr-tīm'), *n.* hours of work beyond the regular hours: *adj.* and *adv.* after the regular hours.

o-ver-tone (ō'vẽr-tōn'), *n.* a harmonic, or partial tone heard with and above its fundamental, or lower, tone.

o-ver-ture (ō'vẽr-tūr), *n.* an offer or proposal; opening; a piece of music played before the commencement of an opera, etc.

o-ver-turn (ō'vẽr-tûrn'), *v.t.* to conquer; to cause to upset; to throw from a firm position: *v.i.* to upset: *n.* (ō'vẽr-tûrn), act of overthrowing or upsetting; state of being overthrown or upset.

o-ver-ween-ing (ō'vẽr-wēn'ing), *adj.* conceited; too self-confident.

o-ver-whelm (ō'vẽr-hwĕlm'), *v.t.* to flow over completely; swallow up, as by a flood; to crush utterly; oppress beyond bearing; as, *overwhelmed* by grief.—*adj.* overwhelming.—*adv.* overwhelmingly.

Syn. defeat, vanquish.

o-ver-work (ō'vẽr-wûrk'), *v.t.* to impose too much labor upon; demand results beyond one's capacity; as, to *overwork* a servant: *v.i.* to labor too hard or beyond one's strength: *n.* exertion beyond one's strength.

o-ver-wrought (ō'vẽr-rôt'), *p.adj.* greatly excited: as, *overwrought* nerves; done to excess; too elaborate, as embroidery.

o-void (ō'void), *n.* an egg-shaped body: *adj.* egg-shaped. Also, *adj.* ovoidal.

o-vule (ō'vūl), *n.* a little egg; an egg in an early stage of growth.

o-vum (ō'vŭm), *n.* [*pl.* ova (ō'vȧ)], an egg; a seed; in architecture, an egg-shaped ornament; an egg in an early stage of growth; an ovule.

owe (ō), *v.t.* to be obliged to pay; as, to *owe* an apology; be obliged or indebted for: *v.i.* to be in debt: often with *to*.

ow-ing (ō'ing), *p.pr.* and *adj.* due as a debt; ascribable to as a result: with *to*; as, his success was *owing* to his honesty.

owl (oul), *n.* a bird that flies at night, known for its large head and eyes and for its hoot.—*adj.* owlish.

Owl

owl-et (oul'ĕt), *n.* a young owl; a certain small owl of Europe.

own (ōn), *adj.* belonging to oneself or itself; peculiar or proper to: *v.t.* to possess or hold by right; admit or acknowledge, as a fault: *v.i.* to confess: followed by *to*.

own-er (ōn'ẽr), *n.* one who has or possesses; a proprietor.

own-er-ship (ōn'ẽr-ship), *n.* sole right of possession; proprietorship; as, the *ownership* of land.

ox (ŏks), *n.* [*pl.* oxen (ŏk'sn)], a domestic bovine, or animal of the cow family, used as a beast of burden.

ox-al-ic ac-id (ŏk-săl'ĭk ăs'ĭd), a poisonous compound obtained from many vegetable substances, and used in bleaching, removing stains, etc.

ox-eye (ŏks'ī), *n.* any of various plants of the aster family; as, the *oxeye* daisy; a name given to a number of birds, including the black-bellied plover.

Ox-ford (ŏks'fẽrd), *n.* a low, laced shoe, tying over the instep.

ox-i-da-tion (ŏk'sĭ-dā'shŭn), *n.* the operation of converting or changing into an oxide, or mixture of oxygen and another element.

ox-ide (ŏk'sīd; ŏk'sĭd), *n.* a mixture of oxygen and another element. Also, ox:d.

ox-i-dize (ŏk'sĭ-dīz), *v.t.* to convert into an oxide, or a compound of oxygen with another element; to give a dull finish to, as metal; as, *oxidized* silver: *v.i.* to be converted into an oxide. Also, oxidate.—*n.* oxidizer.

ox-lip (ŏks'lĭp), *n.* a variety of primrose, much like the cowslip.

ox-y-gen (ŏk'sĭ-jĕn), *n.* a colorless, odorless, tasteless gas, which forms one-fifth by volume of the atmosphere, and which when mixed with hydrogen forms water.

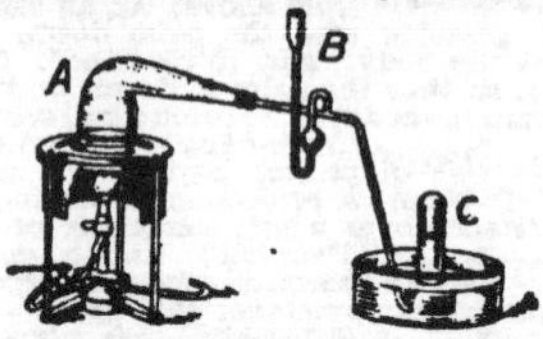

Apparatus for the preparation of Oxygen from Chlorate of Potassium. *A*, retort containing the chlorate; *B*, safety tube; *C*, test tube in which the gas is collected.

ox-y-gen-ate (ŏk'sĭ-jĕn-āt), *v.t.* to oxidize; to treat with oxygen.—*n.* oxygenation.

ox-y-hy-dro-gen (ŏk'sĭ-hī'drō-jĕn), *adj.* consisting of a mixture of oxygen and hydrogen: *n.* oxyhydrogen gas: oxyhydrogen blowpipe, an instrument by which an intense heat is produced by burning hydrogen in oxygen.

ox-y-tone (ŏk'sĭ-tōn), *n.* an acute sound: *adj.* having a sharp sound; having the last syllable accented.

o-yer (ō'yẽr; oi'yẽr), *n.* a hearing or trial of legal cases.

o-yer and ter-min-er (ō'yẽr ănd tûr'mĭ-nẽr), a higher criminal court.

o-yes (ō'yĕs'), *interj.* the introductory cry of an official or public crier demanding silence in a courtroom: usually repeated three times. Also, oyez.

oys-ter (ois'tẽr), *n.* an edible shellfish with a shell having two halves, found in salt water; the small piece of dark meat, found in the back of a fowl.

oys-ter plant (ois'tẽr plănt), a plant whose root when cooked has the flavor of oysters; salsify.

o-zone (ō'zōn), *n.* a colorless gas regarded as a form of oxygen, and found as an element in air.

P

pab-u-lum (păb'ū-lŭm), *n.* food; nourishment; that which feeds or nourishes anything; as, mental *pabulum.*

pace (pās), *n.* a step; the space covered by a step in walking; as, he went twenty *paces;* a measure of length, varying from thirty to sixty inches; gait, or manner of moving, such as a trot, gallop, etc.; a certain swaying gait of a horse; rate of speed; as, to keep up the *pace: v.t.* to measure by steps; to walk over with long, even steps; to train to go at a certain gait: *v.i.* to walk with long, regular steps; to go at a swaying gait, as a horse.

pac-er (pās'ẽr), *n.* one who moves with measured steps; a horse with a swaying gait called a pace, in which the legs on each side move together.

pa-cha (pȧ-shä'; păsh'ȧ), *n.* the title used in Turkey for officers of high rank. Also, **pasha.**

pach-y-derm (păk'ĭ-dûrm), *n.* formerly, one of a group of thick-skinned animals such as the elephant, rhinoceros, etc.; humorously, a person lacking sensitiveness.

pa-cif-ic (pȧ-sĭf'ĭk), *adj.* peacemaking; peaceable; mild; as, *pacific* words; peaceful; tranquil: **Pacific Ocean,** the ocean west of America and east of Asia and Australia: so called because of the calmness of its surface. Also, **pacifical.**—*adv.* **pacifically.**

pac-i-fi-ca-tion (păs'ĭ-fĭ-kā'shŭn; pȧ-sĭf'ĭ-kā'shŭn), *n.* the act of calming or of making peaceful; the state of being calmed.

pac-i-fism (păs'ĭ-fĭzm), *n.* the belief that war is wrong; the system of thought which seeks for peace between the nations.

pac-i-fist (păs'ĭ-fĭst), *n.* one who opposes war; one who believes in, and works for, peace between the nations; a peacemaker; an opponent of militarism.

pac-i-fy (păs'ĭ-fī), *v.t.* [*p.t.* and *p.p.* pacified, *p.pr.* pacifying], to calm or appease; as, to *pacify* an angry man; to free from war or violence; to restore to quiet.—*n.* **pacifier.**

pack (păk), *n.* a large bundle tied up for carrying, especially on the back; load; burden; a great number or quantity of things of the same kind; as, a *pack* of worries; a full set of things; as, a *pack* of playing cards; a number of dogs kept together for hunting, or a number of wild animals that keep together; as, a *pack* of wolves; gang; as, a *pack* of thieves; weight of wool equal to 240 pounds; a number of floating cakes of ice driven close together: *v.t.* to stow away, or to press into a bundle, as goods for carrying; to fill closely; as, to *pack* a trunk; to *pack* a car with people; to crowd together; as, to *pack* people in a room; to press into a hard mass; as, to *pack* earth; dismiss or discharge, as, to *pack* off a servant: *v.i.* to press into a hard mass; as, ice *packs* together; to stow things for safety or carrying; to admit of being stowed; as, these articles *pack* well; depart or remove in haste.—*n.* **packer.**

pack-age (păk'āj), *n.* a bundle or bale of goods; a parcel.

pack-et (păk'ĕt), *n.* a small bundle or parcel; a vessel sailing between two or more ports at regular periods, and carrying passengers, mails, and merchandise.

pack-ing (păk'ĭng), *p.pr.* of *pack: n.* the act of one who packs; straw, paper, or other material used in stowing goods for carrying.

pack-sad-dle (păk'săd'l), *n.* a saddle so constructed as to hold a load on a pack animal.

pack-thread (păk'thrĕd"), *n.* strong twine used in tying packages.

pact (păkt), *n.* an agreement or contract: usually not to be enforced by law.

pad (păd), *n.* a soft cushion; a cushionlike part of anything, especially the under part of the toes of some animals; a block of sheets of paper; the floating leaf of some water plants; a slow-paced horse: *v.t.* [*p.t.* and *p.p.* padded, *p.pr.* padding], to walk heavily and slowly: *v.t.* to stuff, or line thickly, as a coat; to fill with useless words; as, to *pad* a story.

pad-ding (păd'ĭng), *n.* a material used for stuffing; useless or unnecessary matter used for filling space, as in a newspaper or magazine article.

pad-dle (păd'l), *v.i.* to move a canoe or rowboat by means of a short oar without a rowlock; to row slowly; play or wade in the water: *v.t.* to propel or move with a short oar without a rowlock; to spank: *n.* a short oar with a broad blade at one or both ends, used without a rowlock; an oar blade; one of the broad boards of a water wheel or of the paddle wheel of a steamship.

pad-dle wheel (păd'l hwēl), a wheel for moving a steamboat, having broad boards arranged like spokes around its rim.

pad-dock (păd'ŭk), *n.* a small field for pasture, or an inclosure where horses are exercised, lying near to a stable; formerly, a large toad or frog.

pad-dy (păd'ĭ), *n.* rice in the husk; a North American duck.—**Paddy,** an Irishman: from the common Irish name Patrick.

pad-lock (păd'lŏk"), *n.* a portable lock with a jointed link to pass through a staple or eye: *v.t.* to fasten with such a lock.

pa-dre (pä'drā), *n.* the Spanish and Italian title for a priest or monk. [SPAN. and IT.]

pa-dro-ne (pȧ-drō'nā), *n.* a person, usually an Italian, who owns barrel organs, and lets them out for hire; in Italy, a master; a proprietor; a contractor for labor. [IT.]

pæ-an (pē'ăn), *n.* a loud and joyous song of praise or triumph. Also, **pean.**

pa-gan (pā'găn), *n.* a heathen; an idolater, or worshiper of idols or false gods: *adj.* heathen; idolatrous.

pa-gan-ism (pā'găn-ĭzm), *n.* heathenism; idolatry, or the worship of idols, or false gods.

page (pāj), *n.* formerly, a boy attending on a person of distinction; a serving boy in livery or uniform; a male attendant on a legislative, or lawmaking, body; one side of the leaf of a book; a record or writing; as, the *page* of history: *v.t.* to mark or number in pages.

pag-eant (păj'ĕnt; pā'jĕnt), *n.* a brilliant or stately display or procession; a series of scenes acted in costume, dramatic but without plot structure; anything merely showy.

pag-eant-ry (păj'ĕnt-rĭ; pā'jĕnt-rĭ), *n.* splendid display; pomp; show; parade.

pa-go-da (pȧ-gō'-dȧ), *n.* a Buddhist temple built like a tower with many stories; a Hindu idol temple of similar structure.

Pagoda

paid (pād), *p.t.* and *p.p.* of *pay*: *p.adj.* hired; as, a *paid* assistant; discharged; as, a *paid* bill; cashed; as, a *paid* check.

pail (pāl), *n.* an open vessel of wood or metal with a handle: used for carrying water, etc.

pail-lasse (păl'yăs'), *n.* a mattress of straw or some other cheap material. [Fr.]

pain (pān), *n.* distress of body or mind; penalty; as, on *pain* of death: *pl.* diligent effort; as, he took great *pains* with his work: *v.t.* to cause bodily suffering to; to hurt; to make uneasy; to grieve.
Syn., *n.* suffering, pang, agony, anguish.
Ant. (see pleasure).

pain-ful (pān'fōōl), *adj.* full of or causing distress of body or mind; distressing; as, a *painful* illness; a *painful* duty; difficult; as, a *painful* task.—*adv.* **painfully.**—*n.* **painfulness.**

pain-less (pān'lĕs), *adj.* free from distress or hurt; as, a *painless* operation.—*adv.* **painlessly.**—*n.* **painlessness.**

pains-tak-ing (pānz'tāk'ĭng), *adj.* using great effort; taking much trouble; careful; laborious.

paint (pānt), *v.t.* to represent or show by a colored picture; to describe in words; as, to *paint* the joys of heaven; coat or cover with color; as, to *paint* a house: *v.i.* to practice the art of making pictures with color; to use artificial color on the face: *n.* a coloring substance or pigment; rouge.

paint-er (pān'tẽr), *n.* one whose occupation is to cover surfaces with color; as, a house *painter;* one who makes pictures in color; a rope for fastening a boat; locally, in United States, the puma, or American panther.

paint-er's col-ic (pān'tẽrz kŏl'ĭk), a disease caused by poisoning resulting from the lead used in paint.

paint-ing (pānt'ĭng), *n.* the act, art, or occupation, of laying on colors with a brush; the art of showing objects on a surface by means of colors; a picture in colors; vivid, clear description in words.

pair (pâr), *n.* two things of a kind, similar in form and used together; as, a *pair* of shoes; a single thing composed of two like parts; as, a *pair* of spectacles; a married couple; a couple or brace; as, a *pair* of ducks: *v.t.* to join in couples; to mate: *v.i.* to come together in couples; as, to *pair* off in a dance; to match; suit or be adapted to each other.

pa-ja-mas (pȧ-jä'mȧz), *n.pl.* loose trousers of silk, etc., worn in Oriental countries; a garment consisting of a loose coat and trousers of silk, cotton, etc., for wear in the dressing room and during sleep. Also, **pyjamas.** [Hindu.]

pal (păl), *n.* an intimate friend; chum; mate. [Slang.]

pal-ace (păl'ās), *n.* the official residence of a king or other ruler, or of an archbishop or bishop; a magnificent house or building.

pal-a-din (păl'ȧ-dĭn), *n.* a knight, especially one of the knights of Charlemagne; hence, a notable champion.

pa-læ-o-lith-ic (pā'lē-ō-lĭth'ĭk), *adj.* pertaining to the Stone Age, or earliest period of human development.

pa-læ-on-tol-o-gist (pā'lē-ŏn-tŏl'ō-jĭst), *n.* one who is skilled in the science that treats of fossil remains. Also, **paleontologist.**

pa-læ-on-tol-o-gy (pā'lē-ŏn-tŏl'ō-jĭ), *n.* that branch of geology which treats of fossil or stonelike remains of animals and plants. Also, **paleontology.**

Pa-læ-o-zo-ic (pā'lē-ō-zō'ĭk), *adj.* in geology, pertaining to the earliest ages during which it is known that life existed, including the ages of fishes and of invertebrates: *n.* the geological division just before the Mesozoic, or age of reptiles. Also, **Paleozoic.**

pa-læs-tra (pȧ-lĕs'trȧ), *n.* in ancient Greece, a place for wrestling or gymnastic exercises. Also, **palestra.**

pal-an-quin (păl'ăn-kēn'), *n.* in India and China, a covered carriage for one passenger, carried on the shoulders of men. Also, **palankeen.**

pal-at-a-ble (păl'ăt-ȧ-bl), *adj.* agreeable to the taste; savory; acceptable; pleasing.—*adv.* **palatably.**

pal-ate (păl'āt), *n.* the roof of the mouth; sense of taste; relish.—*adj.* **palatal.**

pa-la-tial (pȧ-lā'shăl), *adj.* pertaining to, or suitable to, a palace; stately; magnificent.—*adv.* **palatially.**

pa-lat-i-nate (pȧ-lăt'ĭ-nāt), *n.* a province ruled over by an earl, count, etc., having certain royal privileges.

pal-a-tine (păl'ȧ-tĭn; păl'ȧ-tĭn), *adj.* clothed with or given certain royal privileges or rights; as, an elector *palatine:* *n.* a count, earl, etc. who is given such privileges.

pa-la-ver (pȧ-lä'vẽr; pȧ-lăv'ẽr), *n.* in Africa, a parley with natives; deceitful or idle talk; chatter: *v.i.* to talk in a deceitful way; to talk idly; to chatter.

pale (pāl), *adj.* wan; wanting in color; of a faint luster or brightness: *n.* a narrow board used in fencing; a pointed stake; space inclosed by rails; limit; district or territory; restricted locality: *v.i.* to turn white, or to lose color: *v.t.* to inclose with, or as with, pales or narrow upright boards.—*adv.* **palely.**—*n.* **paleness.**

pale-face (pāl'fās'), *n.* a white person: the American Indian's name for the white man.

pa-le-o-lith-ic (pā'lē-ō-lĭth'ĭk), *adj.* pertaining to the Stone Age, or earliest period of human development. Also, **palæolithic.**

pa-le-on-tol-o-gist (pā'lē-ŏn-tŏl'ō-jĭst), *n.* one who is skilled in paleontology, or the science that deals with fossil remains. Also, **palæontologist.**

pa-le-on-tol-o-gy (pā'lē-ŏn-tŏl'ō-jĭ), *n.* that branch of geology which treats of life in past geological periods, as shown by fossil or stonelike remains of animals and plants. Also, palaeontology.

Pa-le-o-zo-ic (pā'lē-ō-zō'ĭk), *adj.* in geology, pertaining to the earliest ages during which it is known that life existed, including the ages of invertebrates and fishes: *n.* the geological division just before the Mesozoic, or age of reptiles. Also, Palaeozoic.

pa-les-tra (pȧ-lĕs'trȧ), *n.* in ancient Greece, a place for wrestling or gymnastic exercises; any school for youth. Also, palaestra.

pal-ette (păl'ĕt), *n.* a thin, oval wood or porcelain plate with a hole for the thumb, used by artists for mixing and holding colors.

Palette

pal-frey (pôl'frĭ; păl'frĭ), *n.* a saddle horse, especially a small one for a lady's use; as, she rode a snowy *palfrey*.

pal-imp-sest (păl'ĭmp-sĕst), *n.* a parchment manuscript which, after the writing upon it has been partially erased, is used again, the former writing being more or less visible.

pal-ing (pāl'ĭng), *n.* a fence made of narrow upright boards, usually pointed at the top; strips of wood for making a fence.

pal-i-sade (păl'ĭ-sād'), *n.* a fence or fort formed of stakes driven into the ground and pointed at the top: *pl.* a long line of cliffs, usually along a river: *v.t.* to inclose or fortify with stakes.

pall (pôl), *n.* a black covering for a coffin, hearse, or tomb; hence, that which causes gloom or great sorrow: *v.i.* to become wearisome; lose strength: *v.t.* to become distasteful to.

Pal-la-di-um (pȧ-lā'dĭ-ŭm), *n.* any statue of Pallas Athena, especially the statue at Troy, said to have fallen from heaven, and believed to be necessary to the safety of the city: palladium, any safeguard of a liberty or privilege; a rare grayish metal similar to platinum.

pall-bear-er (pôl'bâr"ẽr), *n.* one of the persons who carry or attend a coffin at a funeral.

pal-let (păl'ĕt), *n.* a tongue or bolt that regulates the movement of a ratchet wheel; a small, rough bed, as of straw; a name for a wooden tool used in making pottery, etc.

pal-li-ate (păl'ĭ-āt), *v.t.* to excuse or cause to appear less wrong; as, to *palliate* a fault; lessen or abate the severity or painfulness of; as, to *palliate* disease.

Syn. cover, mitigate, screen.

pal-li-a-tion (păl'ĭ-ā'shŭn), *n.* the act of excusing or easing.

pal-li-a-tive (păl'ĭ-ȧ-tĭv), *adj.* tending to excuse or cover over; as, *palliative* circumstances; serving to relieve or remedy without curing: *n.* that which serves to excuse guilt or to lessen disease or pain.

pal-lid (păl'ĭd), *adj.* pale; wan; lacking in color; as, a *pallid* face.—*adv.* pallidly.—*n.* pallidness.

Ant. (see florid).

pall-mall (pĕl'mĕl'), *n.* a game formerly played with a ball which was driven through an iron ring by a mallet.—Pall Mall, a street in London famous for its clubs.

pal-lor (păl'ẽr), *n.* lack of color, as in the face; paleness.

palm (päm), *n.* the hollow inner part of the hand; a measure of length varying from three to four inches; a tropical tree of various species; a branch of the tree used as an emblem of victory or rejoicing: *v.t.* to conceal in the closed hand, as in the performance of a sleight-of-hand trick; impose by fraud: with *off;* as, to *palm* off inferior goods on a purchaser.

Palms. 1, Wax; 2, Kentia; 3, Chinese hemp.

pal-mate (păl'māt), *adj.* like a hand with fingers spread; as, a *palmate* leaf; having the toes united by a web; webfooted.—*adv.* palmately.

palm-er (päm'ẽr), *n.* a pilgrim to the Holy Land who carried a palm branch as a token or sign of his pilgrimage.

pal-met-to (păl-mĕt'ō), *n.* a kind of palm tree with fan-shaped leaves, growing in the West Indies and the southern part of the United States; the cabbage-palm.

palm-ist (päm'ĭst), *n.* one who claims to tell fortunes or read character from the lines inside the hand.

palm-is-try (päm'ĭs-trĭ; păl'mĭs-trĭ), *n.* the pretended art of reading character or foretelling the future by the lines and marks on the inside of a person's hand.

Palm Sun-day (päm sŭn'dā), the Sunday next before Easter: so called in commemoration of Christ's entry into Jerusalem when branches of palm were strewn before him.

palm-y (päm'ĭ), *adj.* abounding in palm trees; as, a *palmy* land; flourishing; prosperous; as, *palmy* days.

pal-pa-bil-i-ty (păl″pȧ-bĭl′ĭ-tĭ), *n.* the state or quality of being easily known by touch or feeling; as, the *palpability* of solid matter; obviousness.

pal-pa-ble (păl′pȧ-bl), *adj.* capable of being touched or felt; as, a *palpable* substance; easily seen; noticeable; plain; as, a *palpable* wrong.—*adv.* **palpably.**—*n.* **palpableness.**

pal-pi-tate (păl′pĭ-tāt), *v.i.* to beat or throb rapidly, as the heart; to flutter.

pal-pi-ta-tion (păl″pĭ-tā′shŭn), *n.* too rapid beating or throbbing of the heart; a fluttering movement; a quivering.

pal-sied (pôl′zĭd), *p.adj.* paralyzed; shaky; tottering.

pal-sy (pôl′zĭ), *n.* paralysis, or loss of motion or of feeling in any part of the body; loss of power to act: *v.t.* [*p.t.* and *p.p.* palsied, *p.pr.* palsying], to paralyze; to deprive of energy or of the power to act, as through fear.

pal-ter (pôl′tẽr), *v.i.* to act deceitfully; to play false; to use trickery; trifle.—*n.* **palterer.**

pal-try (pôl′trĭ), *adj.* worthless; contemptible; pitiful; small; as, a *paltry* gift to charity.—*adv.* **paltrily.**—*n.* **paltriness.**

pam-pas (păm′pȧz), *n.pl.* in South America, vast treeless plains covered with heavy pasture.

pam-per (păm′pẽr), *v.t.* to feed daintily so as to gratify the taste; as, to *pamper* the appetite; to treat with too much indulgence; as, to *pamper* a child.

pam-phlet (păm′flĕt), *n.* a small unbound book, of one or more sheets, usually with a paper cover.

pam-phlet-eer (păm″flĕt-ēr′), *n.* a writer of brief articles that are printed in unbound sheets or leaflets: often said in contempt: *v.i.* to write brief articles that are printed on unbound sheets.

pan (păn), *n.* a broad shallow vessel used in cooking, etc.; a vessel used for washing out gold, tin, etc., in mining: *v.t.* [*p.t.* and *p.p.* panned, *p.pr.* panning], to cook or wash in a shallow vessel; as, to *pan* oysters; to *pan* gravel for gold: *v.i.* colloquially, to yield a result; as, the trip did not *pan* out as expected; the gravel *panned* out an ounce of gold.

pan-a-ce-a (păn″ȧ-sē′ȧ), *n.* a remedy or medicine for all ills.

pan-a-ma (păn″ȧ-mä′), *n.* a hat of excellent quality made in South and Central America of the hand-plaited young leaves of the palm tree. Also, **Panama hat.**

Pan-A-mer-i-can (păn″ȧ-mĕr′ĭ-kăn), *adj.* pertaining to both North and South America or to all Americans.—*n.* **Pan-Americanism.**

pan-cake (păn′kāk″), *n.* a thin cake made of batter and baked on a griddle.

pan-cre-as (păn′krē-ăs; păn′krē-ăs), *n.* a large fleshy gland (the sweetbread) under and behind the stomach, producing a juice that helps digestion.

pan-cre-at-ic (păn″krē-ăt′ĭk), *adj.* pertaining to the pancreas, or large gland under and behind the stomach; as, *pancreatic* juice aids digestion.

Pan-de-an (păn-dē′ăn), *adj.* pertaining to Pan, the god of flocks and pastures and of the wild life of the forests: **Pandean pipes,** *n.pl.* a simple musical wind instrument made of hollow reeds.

Pan-de-mo-ni-um (păn″dē-mō′nĭ-ŭm), *n.* the abode of demons or the council chamber of the infernal regions: **pandemonium,** a place or abode of general disorder; wild uproar; as, *pandemonium* reigned when the lion escaped.

pane (pān), *n.* a square or oblong section or panel of a wall, door, etc., especially of glass in a window.

pan-e-gyr-ic (păn″ē-jĭr′ĭk), *n.* praise formally written or spoken in honor of some person or event; any high praise.—*adj.* **panegyrical.**—*n.* **panegyrist.**

pan-el (păn′ĕl), *n.* a division or section of a wall or ceiling; a piece of board, the edges of which are put in a frame; as, the *panel* of a door; a thin board on which a picture is painted; the picture itself; a strip of material of different kind or color put lengthwise in a skirt; a list of persons summoned to serve as jurors; the whole jury; the segment of an airplane wing: *v.t.* to form, fit, or decorate with strips or sections of different kind, color, or design.

pang (păng), *n.* a violent sudden pain, either mental or physical; as, the *pangs* of grief.

pan-ic (păn′ĭk), *n.* extreme and sudden fright, especially when without good cause; as, to create a *panic* in an audience; a kind of grass: *adj.* suddenly and violently alarming; as, *panic* fear.—*adj.* **panicky.**

pan-ic-strick-en (păn′ĭk-strĭk″n), *adj.* filled with overwhelming fear.—Also, **panic-struck.**

pan-nier (păn′yẽr; păn′ĭ-ẽr), *n.* a bread basket; one of two baskets suspended across the back of a horse for carrying market produce; a kind of framework to enlarge a woman's skirts at the hips; formerly, a basketwork shield to protect an archer during battle.

pan-o-plied (păn′ō-plĭd), *adj.* furnished with a complete set of armor.

pan-o-ply (păn′ō-plĭ), *n.* [*pl.* panoplies (-plĭz)], a complete suit of armor; anything covering completely and splendidly; as, the trees were covered with a *panoply* of blossoms.

pan-o-ra-ma (păn″ō-rä′mȧ), *n.* a picture giving a view in every direction seen from a central standpoint; a picture seen part at a time in several scenes unrolled and made to pass before the spectator; an entire, or complete, view of a region; as, the *panorama* viewed from a mountain top; a scene that moves constantly before one, as from the window of a moving train; a mental picture of events.

pan-o-ram-ic (păn″ō-răm′ĭk), *adj.* presenting a complete and extended view in all directions; passing before the eyes in a series of pictures. Also, **panoramical.**—*adv.* **panoramically.**

Pan-slav-ic (păn″släv′ĭk; păn″slăv′ĭk), *adj.* pertaining to all the Slavic races or to their union.

Pan-slav-ism (păn″släv′ĭzm; păn″slăv′-ĭzm), *n.* a Russian movement for the political union of all the Slavic races.

pan-sy (păn′zĭ), *n.* a kind of cultivated violet; heartsease.

pant (pȧnt; pănt), *v.i.* to breathe rapidly; as, to *pant* like a dog; gasp; desire earnestly or ardently: with *for* or *after*: *v.t.* to utter with a gasp; as, he *panted* forth the message he had brought: *n.* a short, rapid breath; a puff: *pl.* colloquially, trousers.

pan-ta-lettes (păn'tȧ-lĕts'), *n.pl.* long, frilled drawers formerly worn by women and children.

pan-ta-loon (păn'tȧ-lo͞on'), *n.* a buffoon or foolish character in a pantomime: *pl.* a pair of trousers.

pan-the-ism (păn'thē-ĭzm), *n.* the doctrine that God and nature are one.—*adj.* **pantheistic.**—*n.* **pantheist.**

pan-the-on (păn-thē'ŏn; păn'thē-ŏn), *n.* a temple dedicated to all the gods; a building where rest the famous dead of a nation: **Pantheon,** a building in ancient Rome dedicated to Mars and Jupiter.

Panther

pan-ther (păn'thẽr), *n.* [*fem.* **pantheress**], one of several wild, fierce species of the cat family; as, the leopard, the American puma, and the jaguar.

pan-tile (păn'tīl"), *n.* a curved roofing tile; a gutter tile.

pan-to-graph (păn'tō-grȧf), *n.* an instrument for copying drawings, designs, etc., on an enlarged or reduced scale. Also, **pantagraph.**

pan-to-mime (păn'tō-mīm), *n.* a series of actions that express meaning without spoken words; as, he replied in *pantomime:* a play in which there is no talking.—*adj.* **pantomimic, pantomimical.**

pan-try (păn'trĭ), *n.* a closet or room for bread and other food; a small room from which food is served for the table.

pap (păp), *n.* soft food for infants; a nipple; pulp of fruits.

pa-pa (pȧ-pä'; pä'pȧ), *n.* a child's word for father.

pa-pa-cy (pā'pȧ-sĭ), *n.* the office, dignity, or authority, of the Pope; the popes collectively; Roman Catholic system of church government.

pa-pal (pā'păl), *adj.* of or pertaining to the Pope, or to the Roman Catholic Church; as, *papal* authority; *papal* rites.

pa-paw (pȧ-pô'; pô'pô"), *n.* a tree of central and southern United States; the sweet, yellowish, pulpy fruit of the tree; the papaya. Also, **pawpaw.**

pa-pa-ya (pä-pä'yä), *n.* the edible fruit of a certain tropical American tree.

pa-per (pā'pẽr), *n.* a thin, easily bent or folded substance made of various materials, as, linen, straw, wood, rags, etc., used for writing or printing upon, or for wrapping; a piece or sheet of the substance; a packet wrapped in the substance; as, a *paper* of needles; a newspaper; an essay or other writing; a legal document; bank notes or bills of exchange; a covering for walls: *adj.* made of, or like, paper; thin: *v.t.* to cover with, or wrap in, paper.

pa-pier-mâ-ché (pȧ'pyā'mä"shā'; pȧ"pyā-mä'shā), *n.* a hard, strong material made of paper pulp mixed with glue, rosin, etc., and molded into various shapes, as buckets, etc. [Fr.]

pa-pil-la (pȧ-pĭl'ȧ), *n.* [*pl.* papillæ (-ē)], a very small projection like a nipple, especially those on the tongue.

pap-il-la-ry (păp'ĭ-lā-rĭ; pȧ-pĭl'ȧ-rĭ), *adj.* pertaining to, or like, a nipplelike projection, as on the tongue.

pa-pist (pā'pĭst), *n.* a term, often used scornfully, for one of the Roman Catholic faith.

Papyrus

pa-poose (pȧ-po͞os'), *n.* a young child of North American Indian parents.

pap-pus (păp'ŭs), *n.* [*pl.* pappi (-ī)], a downy tuft or appendage crowning the fruit in certain seed plants, as in thistles.

pa-pri-ka (pă'prē-kȧ; pȧ-prē'kȧ), *n.* the dried ripe fruit of various kinds of peppers; the red, pungent relish made from it.

pa-py-rus (pȧ-pī'rŭs), *n.* [*pl.* papyri (-rī)], a kind of Egyptian reed or plant from which the ancients made paper; a manuscript or writing on papyrus.

par (pär), *n.* full or normal value; as, the stock is below *par;* equality; as, the man is not on a *par* with his associates; in golf, the proper score estimated for each hole.

par-a-ble (păr'ȧ-bl), *n.* a short story to illustrate and enforce moral or religious truth.

pa-rab-o-la (pȧ-răb'ō-lȧ), *n.* one of the conic sections formed by the intersection of the cone with a plane parallel to a line drawn from its apex to the circumference of its base.

par-a-bol-ic (păr"ȧ-bŏl'ĭk), *adj.* pertaining to, or formed like, a parabola; allegorical, or of the nature of a short story that illustrates a moral or religious truth. Also, **parabolical.**

Parachute

par-a-chute (păr'ȧ-sho͞ot), *n.* an umbrella-shaped apparatus used in descending from a balloon; a device to decrease the speed of a descent through the air.

pa-rade (pȧ-rād'), *n.* pompous display or show; as, a *parade* of wealth; a military display, or review of troops; place of assembly for exercising and inspecting troops; a formal march or procession; as, a circus *parade:* *v.t.* to assemble and form in military order as for review; to march over or through; as, to *parade* the city; make a display of: *v.i.* to exhibit or walk about to show oneself; to take part in a formal march.

par-a-digm (păr'ȧ-dĭm; păr'ȧ-dīm), *n.* an example or model; an example of the declension or conjugation of a word to show all of its forms.

Par-a-dise (păr'ȧ-dīs), *n.* the garden of Eden; **paradise,** any place of happiness; a state of bliss.—*adj.* **paradisic, paradisiacal, paradisical.**

par-a-dos (păr'ȧ-dŏs), *n.* a parapet built behind a battery of guns to protect it from rear fire; in the World War, the rear wall of a trench.

par-a-dox (păr'ȧ-dŏks), *n.* something which seems absurd or unbelievable, yet may be true; a statement that appears contradictory.

par-a-dox-i-cal (păr"ȧ-dŏk'sĭ-kăl), *adj.* seemingly absurd or contradictory, but possibly true.—*adv.* **paradoxically.**—*n.* **paradoxicalness.**

par-af-fin (păr'ȧ-fĭn), *n.* a white, waxy, inflammable substance obtained from wood, coal, etc. Also, **paraffine.**

par-a-gon (păr'ȧ-gŏn), *n.* something of extraordinary excellence; model or pattern of perfection; as, a *paragon* of virtue.

par-a-graph (păr'ȧ-gråf), *n.* a small, definite section of a piece of writing; a short passage; a reference mark [¶]; an item in a newspaper, magazine, etc.: *v.t.* to arrange or divide into definite sections or passages of writing; to write a brief passage about.

par-al-lax (păr'ă-lăks), *n.* the apparent shifting of an object caused by change in the position of the observer, especially the difference between the apparent position of a heavenly body and its true place; in mathematics, the angle at any point subtended by any given line.

par-al-lel (păr'ȧ-lĕl), *adj.* lying side by side; extended in the same direction and equally distant from each other at all points; as, *parallel* lines; having the same course; similar; corresponding: *n.* a line equally distant at all points from another line; resemblance or likeness: *pl.* trenches dug by besiegers before, and parallel to, the defenses of a fort, etc.: *v.t.* to place or lay in the same direction, equally distant at all points; correspond to; equal.

par-al-lel-e-pi-ped (păr″ă-lĕl″ĕ-pī'pĕd; păr″ă-lĕl″ĕ-pĭp'ĕd; păr″ă-lĕl″ĕp'ĭ-pĕd), *n.* a regular solid figure bounded by six parallelograms of which the opposite pairs are equal and parallel. Also, **parallelepipedon.**

par-al-lel-ism (păr'ă-lĕl-ĭzm), *n.* the state or quality of being alike or equal; correspondence.

par-al-lel-o-gram (păr″ă-lĕl'ō-grăm), *n.* a plane four-sided figure whose opposite sides extend in the same direction and are equal in length.

pa-ral-y-sis (pȧ-răl'ĭ-sĭs), *n.* loss of the powers of feeling or motion in one or more parts of the body; palsy.

par-a-lyt-ic (păr″ȧ-lĭt'ĭk), *adj.* pertaining to, affected by, or inclined to, paralysis, or the loss of feeling or motion in any part of the body: *n.* one who is affected with loss of motion or feeling in any part of the body.

par-a-lyze (păr'ȧ-līz), *v.t.* [*p.t.* and *p.p.* paralyzed, *p.pr.* paralyzing], to strike or affect with loss of feeling or motion in any part of the body; unnerve; render useless or ineffective.

par-a-mount (păr'ȧ-mount), *adj.* above all others; as, of *paramount* importance; highest or chief.

par-a-mour (păr'ȧ-mōōr), *n.* one who unlawfully takes the place of a husband or wife.

par-a-noi-a (păr″ȧ-noi'ȧ), *n.* a form of insanity or mental unsoundness marked by fixed delusions, or false beliefs.—*adj.* and *n.* **paranoiac.**

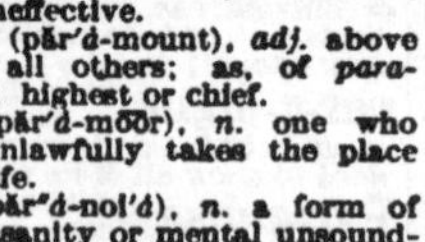

Bridge Parapets

par-a-pet (păr'ȧ-pĕt), *n.* a wall breast-high at the edge of a roof, platform, etc.; a wall to protect troops from the fire of an enemy; a rampart of earth, sandbags, etc., built along the top of the front wall of a trench.

par-a-pher-na-li-a (păr″ȧ-fẽr-nā'lĭ-ȧ), *n.pl.* personal belongings; ornaments of dress generally; articles of equipment; as, the *paraphernalia* of a show or circus.

par-a-phrase (păr'ȧ-frāz), *n.* a free translation or explanation of a text, etc., giving the meaning in another form; a hymn based on some Scriptural passage: *v.t.* to make a free translation of; explain in one's own words: *v.i.* to make a free translation; to put something into one's own words.

par-a-site (păr'ȧ-sīt), *n.* a hanger-on, or one who lives at another's expense; as, tramps and vagabonds are social *parasites;* a useless person, doing no work, but living in comfort at the expense of others; an animal or plant fed by another to which it attaches itself.

par-a-sit-ic (păr″ȧ-sĭt'ĭk), *adj.* of the nature of a hanger-on; living at the expense of another animal or plant. Also, **parasitical.**

par-a-sol (păr'ȧ-sŏl″; păr″ȧ-sŏl'), *n.* a lady's sunshade: *adj.* like a parasol: **parasol monoplane** or **biplane,** a flying machine in which the entire fuselage, motor, and propeller are suspended about two feet below the wings, so that the planes form a sort of umbrella.

par-boil (pär'boil″), *v.t.* to cook partially by pouring boiling water upon and allowing to stand; as, to *parboil* liver or sweetbreads.

par-cel (pär'sĕl), *n.* a small bundle or package; a small part; as, a *parcel* of land: *v.t.* [*p.t.* and *p.p.* parceled, *p.pr.* parceling], to divide into parts; as, to *parcel* out land into lots.

par-cel post (pär'sĕl pōst), a government system of carrying packages by mail and at postal rates.

parch (pärch), *v.t.* to scorch; burn slightly; as, to *parch* corn; to dry with heat; as, the sun *parches* the grass: *v.i.* to become dry and hot; as, the tongue *parches* for want of water.

parch-ment (pärch'mĕnt), *n.* the skin of a sheep, goat, etc., dressed and prepared for writing upon; a deed or document on such a prepared skin: *adj.* made of, or like, the dressed skin called parchment.

pard (pärd), *n.* a leopard; any spotted beast: used only in poetry.

par-don (pär'dŭn; pär'dn), *v.t.* to free from penalty; as, to *pardon* an offender; to forgive; as, to *pardon* an offense; overlook; excuse; as, *pardon* my mistake: *n.* forgiveness; release from punishment; an official act setting one free from penalty.—*n.* **pardoner.**

Syn., *n.* mercy, acquittal.
Ant. (see penalty).

par-don-a-ble (pär'dŭn-ȧ-bl), *adj.* that may be shown mercy; forgivable; excusable.

pare (pâr), *v.t.* to cut or shave off the outside or ends of; as, to *pare* an apple; to cut away little by little; as, to *pare* a corn; reduce or lessen; as, to *pare* one's profits.

par-e-gor-ic (păr″ĕ-gŏr'ĭk), *n.* a medicine obtained from opium and used to ease pain.

pa-ren-chy-ma (pȧ-rĕn'kĭ-mȧ), *n.* the tissue making up the substance of glandular and other organs, as the pith in plants or the pulp of fruits.

par-ent (pâr'ĕnt), *n.* a father or mother: the source of anything; that which causes; occasion.

par-ent-age (pâr'ĕn-tāj), *n.* fatherhood or motherhood; birth or descent; origin; state or fact of being the author or producer of.

pa-ren-tal (pȧ-rĕn'tăl), *adj.* of, pertaining to, or like, a father or mother; as, *parental* care or affection.—*adv.* **parentally.**

pa-ren-the-sis (pȧ-rĕn'thē-sĭs), *n.* [*pl.* parentheses (-sēz)], an explanatory word or clause put in a sentence which is grammatically complete without it; indicated by the marks ( ).

par-en-thet-ic (păr'ĕn-thĕt'ĭk), *adj.* introduced, or thrown in, by way of explanation; filled with, or given to, inserted explanations. Also, **parenthetical.** —*adv.* **parenthetically.**

par-e-sis (păr'ē-sĭs; pȧ-rē'sĭs), *n.* softening of the brain; partial paralysis, affecting only motion.

par ex-cel-lence (pär ĕk'sĕ'läɴs'), beyond comparison; superior. [Fr.]

par-he-li-on (pär-hē'lĭ-ŏn), *n.* a mock sun, or bright light, often seen near the sun and sometimes opposite to it.

pa-ri-ah (pä'rĭ-ȧ; păr'ĭ-ȧ; pȧ-rī'ȧ), *n.* one of the lowest class of Hindus; hence, an outcast or one despised by society.

par-ing (pâr'ĭng), *n.* a cutting off of the surface or edge; the part cut off: as, potato *parings.*

par-ish (păr'ĭsh), *n.* an ecclesiastical or church district under the particular charge of a priest, clergyman, or minister; in England, a civil district looking after its own poor, etc.; a congregation: *adj.* pertaining to, or maintained by, a church, congregation, or district; as, a *parish* school.

pa-rish-ion-er (pȧ-rĭsh'ŭn-ĕr), *n.* one who belongs to a church district in charge of a certain priest or minister; a member of a congregation.

Pa-ri-sian (pȧ-rĭzh'ăn; pȧ-rĭz'ĭ-ăn), *adj.* of or pertaining to Paris, in France: *n.* a native or inhabitant of Paris.

par-i-ty (păr'ĭ-tĭ), *n.* like state or degree; equality; likeness; equal value.

park (pärk), *n.* a large tract of ground used as a public place for recreation or pleasure; the train of artillery belonging to an army; an artillery encampment: *v.t.* to inclose in a ground for recreation or pleasure; to collect in a body; to station in orderly arrangement; as, to *park* automobiles.

par-lance (pär'lăns), *n.* conversation; talk; language.

par-ley (pär'lĭ), *n.* a conference, or a talk about a subject, especially with an enemy: *v.i.* [*p.t.* and *p.p.* parleyed, *p.pr.* parleying], to hold a conference, especially with an enemy with a view to peace; as, to *parley* with temptation.

par-lia-ment (pär'lĭ-mĕnt), *n.* a general council; **Parliament,** the supreme legislative assembly, or lawmaking body, of Great Britain and Ireland, consisting of the Sovereign, the House of Lords, and the House of Commons; a similar assembly existing in certain other countries.

par-lia-men-ta-ri-an (pär'lĭ-mĕn-tâ'rĭ-ăn), *n.* one who is versed in the laws and usages of supreme lawmaking bodies, such as the British Parliament.

par-lia-men-ta-ry (pär'lĭ-mĕn'tȧ-rĭ), *adj.* according to the rules and customs of public assemblies; as, *parliamentary* order.

par-lor (pär'lẽr), *n.* a room for conversation, reception of guests, etc.; family sitting room. Also, **parlour.**

Par-nas-si-an (pär-năs'ĭ-ăn), *adj.* of or pertaining to Mt. Parnassus, in Greece, the imaginary home of the Muses; hence, of or pertaining to poetry, art, music, etc., especially to a certain school of French poets.

pa-ro-chi-al (pȧ-rō'kĭ-ăl), *adj.* of or pertaining to a parish, or church district; narrow; local.—*n.* **parochialism.**

par-o-dist (păr'ō-dĭst), *n.* the writer of a ridiculous imitation.

par-o-dy (păr'ō-dĭ), *n.* [*pl.* parodies (-dĭz)], an imitation of a serious writing, as a poem or song, written in a ridiculous manner; a burlesque imitation: *v.t.* [*p.t.* and *p.p.* parodied, *p.pr.* parodying], to write a ridiculous imitation of; to burlesque.

pa-role (pȧ-rōl'), *n.* a word of honor; especially, a promise given by a prisoner that in return for conditional freedom he will not try to escape, or will return to prison on a certain day; a promise made by an officer, with no surety for the keeping of it but his sense of honor; a special password used by officers in a camp or garrison: *v.t.* to release (a prisoner) on his word of honor to observe certain conditions.

pa-rot-id (pȧ-rŏt'ĭd), *n.* a salivary gland below and in front of the ear: *adj.* pertaining to, or situated near, this salivary gland.

par-ox-ysm (păr'ŏk-sĭzm), *n.* a spasm, or fit of acute pain recurring at intervals; sudden outburst of emotion; a fit of any kind; as, a *paroxysm* of rage.

par-quet (pär-kā'; pär-kĕt'), *n.* wooden inlay for flooring; the floor space of a theater between the orchestra rail and the rail under the gallery line: called also the *orchestra:* **parquet circle,** the part of the lower floor of a theater that lies under the balcony. Also, **parquette.**

par-quet-ry (pär'kĕt-rĭ), *n.* wooden inlay or mosaic work for floors. Also, **parquet.**

parr (pär), *n.* a young salmon that has not yet left fresh water for the sea.

par-ra-keet (păr'ȧ-kēt), *n.* a small parrot, usually with a long, pointed tail. Also, **parakeet.**

par-ri-cide (păr'ĭ-sīd), *n.* the murder of a close relative, especially a father or mother; one who murders a father or mother, or other close relative.—*adj.* **parricidal.**

par-rot (păr'ŭt), *n.* a tropical bird with a hooked bill and brilliant feathers, able to imitate the human voice.

par-ry (păr'ĭ), *v.t.* [*p.t.* and *p.p.* parried, *p.pr.* parrying], to ward off, as a blow; to evade; as, to *parry* a question: *v.i.* to ward off or turn something aside; as, to thrust and *parry* with the sword: *n.* a warding off of a blow; evasion.

parse (pärs), *v.t.* to analyze, as a sentence, by the rules of grammar; to state the grammatical relations of, as a word.

Par-si (pär'sē; pär-sē'), *n.* a descendant of the old Persians, now living in India. Also, **Parsee.**

par-si-mo-ni-ous (pär'sĭ-mō'nĭ-ŭs), *adj.* close; stingy; miserly.

par-si-mo-ny (pär'sĭ-mō-nĭ), *n.* stinginess; extreme and unnecessary economy; closeness.

pars-ley (pärs'lĭ), *n.* a garden plant, the leaves of which are used to flavor soups, etc.

pars-nip (pärs'nĭp), *n.* a plant with an edible carrotlike root.

par-son (pär'sn), *n.* a clergyman of a parish; a minister or preacher.

par-son-age (pär'sn-āj), *n.* the residence of a clergyman in charge of a parish.

part (pärt), *n.* something less than the whole; as, *part* of an apple; piece or portion; share; as, to do one's *part;* member or organ; as, *parts* of the body; side or party; as, they took his *part;* concern or interest; as, he had no *part* in the business; any one of the characters of a play; as, the leading *part;* one of the melodies in a harmony; as, the soprano *part;* quarter; region; as, they live in these *parts;* ability or talent; as, a man of fine *parts:* *v.t.* to divide into two or more pieces or portions; distribute; disunite; separate: *v.i.* to be separated or divided; to go away; take leave; separate.
Syn., n. division, portion, share, fraction: *v.* divide, share, sunder.
Ant. (see whole).

par-take (pär-tāk'), *v.t.* [*p.t.* partook, *p.p.* partaken, *p.pr.* partaking], to have or receive a portion or share in common with others; as, to *partake* of food: *v.t.* to receive a share in.—*n.* **partaker.**

par-terre (pär-târ'), *n.* a series of flower beds arranged ornamentally, with spaces of gravel or turf between; a level space; part of the theater floor under the gallery.

Par-the-non (pär'thē-nŏn), *n.* the temple of Athene (Minerva) at Athens.

par-tial (pär'shăl), *adj.* inclined to favor one side or party; colloquially, having a liking (for); as, she is *partial* to candy; not entire; incomplete; as, a *partial* success.—*adv.* **partially.**

par-ti-al-i-ty (pär"shĭ-ăl'ĭ-tĭ), *n.* the state or quality of being biased or unfair; a strong liking; favoritism.

par-tic-i-pant (pär-tĭs'ĭ-pănt), *adj.* sharing: *n.* one who shares or takes part; as, he was a *participant* in the game.

par-tic-i-pate (pär-tĭs'ĭ-pāt), *v.i.* to have a share in common with others; to take part: *v.t.* to have a share of; take part in.—*n.* **participator.**

par-tic-i-pa-tion (pär-tĭs"ĭ-pā'shŭn), *n.* the act of sharing something with others; a taking part.

par-ti-cip-i-al (pär"tĭ-sĭp'ĭ-ăl), *adj.* having the nature of both a verb and an adjective.

par-ti-ci-ple (pär'tĭ-sĭ-pl), *n.* a part of a verb which does the work of an adjective.

par-ti-cle (pär'tĭ-kl), *n.* a very small piece; a bit; as, a *particle* of dust; the smallest possible amount of anything; as, not a *particle* of courage; in grammar, a word not used alone, as a conjunction or a preposition.
Syn. atom, grain, mite, scrap.
Ant. (see mass).

par-ti-col-ored (pär'tĭ-kŭl"ẽrd), *adj.* having many colors; as, a *party-colored* flower. Also, **parti-coloured, party-colored, party-coloured.**—*n.* **particolor, party-color, parti-colour, party-colour.**

-tic-u-lar (pär-tĭk'ū-lăr), *adj.* distinct fro[m] ... *ticular* person or thing; individual; or special; as, of *particular* im[portance] ... exact; as, *particular* in speech; minute.—*adv.* **particularly.**
Syn. singular, odd, strange.
Ant. (see general).

par-tic-u-lar-i-ty (pär-tĭk"ū-lăr'ĭ-tĭ), strict attention; ... actness; individuality; peculiarity.

par-tic-u-lar-ize (pär-tĭk'ū-lăr-īz), to give the details *v.i.* be attentive to single things or details

part-ing (pär'tĭng), *p.adj.* separa[ting]; dividing; as, a *parting* taking leave; hence, dying; as, a *parting* soul; given when taking leave; as, a *parting* gift: *n.* division; separation; a taking leave; as, the *parting* of friends.

par-ti-san (pär'tĭ-zăn), *n.* formerly, a long-handled weapon with a steel point; a pike or halberd; a devoted follower, especially of a political cause or faction: *adj.* pertaining to, or strongly in favor of, a person, cause, or faction, especially a political party or faction. Also, **partizan.** —*n.* **partisanship.**

par-ti-tion (pär-tĭsh'ŭn), *n.* the act of dividing or state of being divided; separation; distribution; a dividing wall; a section or division: *v.t.* to divide into shares; as, to *partition* an estate or a country; divide by walls.

par-ti-tive (pär'tĭ-tĭv), *adj.* serving to divide into parts; in grammar, denoting a part: *n.* a word that denotes a part or expresses partition or division.

part-ly (pärt'lĭ), *adv.* in part, not wholly; to some extent.

part-ner (pärt'nẽr), *n.* one who is associated with another, especially in a business, etc.; as, capital and labor should be *partners;* an associate; one who dances with another; a husband or wife.

part-ner-ship (pärt'nẽr-shĭp), *n.* the state of being associated for a common purpose; joint interest or ownership; relation between two or more persons who are in business together; union of two or more persons in the same business or profession.

par-took (pär-tŏŏk'), past tense of the verb *partake.*

par-tridge (pär'trĭj), *n.* a well-known game bird; in the United States, the ruffed grouse; the bobwhite.

par-tridge ber-ry (pär'trĭj bĕr'ĭ), an American trailing evergreen plant which bears a bright red berry.

par-tu-ri-ent (pär-tū'rĭ-ĕnt), *adj.* bringing forth young; pertaining to childbirth.

par-tu-ri-tion (pär"tū-rĭsh'ŭn), *n.* the act of bringing forth young; childbirth.

par-ty (pär'tĭ), *n.* [*pl.* parties (-tĭz)], a number of persons united for a particular purpose; as, a political *party;* faction; one of the sections into which any social group divides in opinion on a public question; one concerned in an affair, cause, or side; as, a *party* to a suit; a small body of troops sent to perform some special service; as, a scouting *party;* a social gathering assembled by invitation; a select company; as, a dinner *party.*

par-ty-col-ored (pär'tĭ-kŭl"ẽrd), *adj.* having many colors; as, a *party-colored* flower. Also, **parti-colored, party-coloured, parti-coloured.**—*n.* **party-color, parti-color, party-colour, parti-colour.**

par-ty wall (păr'tĭ wôl), a common wall separating two houses or properties.

par-ve-nu (păr'vē-nū"), *n.* one who has recently risen, because of his wealth, to a position above that in which he was born; an upstart.

pas (pä), *n.* a step or movement in a dance: occurring in names of dances. [Fr.]

pas-chal (păs'kăl), *adj.* of or pertaining to the feast of the Passover or Easter.

pa-sha (pá-shä'; păsh'ȧ), *n.* a Turkish title given to high officials. Also, **pacha.**

pas-quin-ade (păs"kwĭn-ād'), *n.* a sarcastic political squib posted in a public place.

pass (pás), *v.i.* to go or move from one place, state, or condition to another; to move along; as, the parade *passes* down the street; to be exchanged; as, money *passed* between them; to elapse or go by; as, the night *passed;* to make one's way; as, to *pass* through a crowd; to go unnoticed; as, his action *passed* without rebuke; to go from person to person; circulate; as, American money *passes* in Canada; to be enacted; as, the law finally *passed;* depart; die; as, he *passed* away: *v.t.* to go by, through, beyond, etc.; as, to *pass* the house; to *pass* an examination; to *pass* the age of twenty-one; to cause or allow to go; to hand; as, to *pass* the butter; to spend; as, to *pass* the day; to exceed; as, it *passes* belief; to give as a judgment; as, to *pass* sentence; utter or pronounce; as, to *pass* an opinion: *n.* a narrow passage, avenue, or entrance; defile; as, a *pass* in the mountains; license or permission; as, a railway *pass;* state of extremity; as, matters have come to a dreadful *pass;* a thrust, as in fencing.

pass-a-ble (pás'ȧ-bl), *adj.* that may be traveled or navigated; as, a *passable* road; not open to great objection; fairly good; as, a book in a *passable* condition; admissible; that may be circulated; as, American money is *passable* in Canada.—*adv.* **passably.**

pas-sage (păs'ĭj), *n.* the act of going from one place or condition to another; course or progress; as, the *passage* of time; a journey; a hall or corridor; an entrance or exit; right to go; as, to have free *passage;* legal enactment; as, *passage* of a law; a single clause or portion of a book; migratory habits; as, birds of *passage.*

pas-sage-way (păs'ăj-wā"), *n.* a hall, corridor, or alley.

pass book (pás bŏŏk), a customer's book in which a storekeeper enters the list of goods bought on credit; a bank book held by the depositor and containing the record of his deposits.

pas-sé (pă"sā'), *adj.* [*fem.* passée], past; worn out or faded. [Fr.]

passe-men-terie (pás-mĕn'trĭ), *n.* dress trimmings, as of braid, beads, jet, heavy lace, or silk embroidery.

pas-sen-ger (păs'ĕn-jĕr), *n.* one who travels in or on a conveyance, as a boat, train, etc.; formerly, a traveler or wayfarer.

passe par-tout (päs" pár"tōō'), a flat surface of cardboard, wood, etc., with a space cut out in its center so as to make a frame for a picture. [Fr.]

pass-er-by (pás'ĕr-bī'), *n.* [*pl.* passers-by], one who goes past.

pass-ing (pás'ĭng), *p.adj.* going by, beyond, or through; as, a *passing* car; departing; as, the *passing* hour; casual; as, a *passing* comment: *n.* the act of going by; departure; as, the *passing* of summer.

pas-sion (păsh'ŭn), *n.* a fit of violent anger; as, he flew into a *passion;* intense feeling or excitement; love; ardor; intense desire; as, a *passion* for music.—**Passion,** the sufferings of Christ in his last agonies.

pas-sion-ate (păsh'ŭn-āt), *adj.* capable of intense feeling; easily moved to anger; excitable; as, a *passionate* nature; ardent; as, a *passionate* desire.—*adv.* **passionately.**

pas-sion flow-er (păsh'ŭn flou'ĕr), a plant so named because its flower suggests the instruments or manner of Christ's death.

Pas-sion play (păsh'ŭn plā), a play showing scenes of the suffering and death of Christ, and given every ten years at Oberammergau, Bavaria.

pas-sive (păs'ĭv), *adj.* suffering without resisting; not acting but acted upon; as, a *passive* disposition; submissive; in grammar, indicating that form of the transitive verb which asserts that the subject is acted upon; not acting of itself; as, a *passive* balloon or airplane: **passive flight,** gliding or soaring without the use of motive power.—*n.* **passiveness, passivity.**

pass-key (pás'kē"), *n.* a master key, which will open all of a certain set of locks whose regular keys are not interchangeable; a key for opening more than one lock; a private key.

Pass-o-ver (pás'ō"vĕr), *n.* a Jewish feast commemorating the passing of the destroying angel over the houses of the Israelites when he slew the first-born of the Egyptians.—Exodus xii.

pass-port (pás'pōrt), *n.* an official paper giving one permission to travel in a foreign country.

pass-word (pás'wûrd"), *n.* a word by means of which friends are known from strangers or enemies and permitted to enter or pass; as, the *password* of a lodge; a watchword.

past (pást), *p.adj.* having formerly been; as, the *past* generation; gone by; last; as, the *past* hour; completed; in grammar, referring to time gone by; as, the *past* tense: *n.* the time gone by; as, memories of the *past;* previous life or history; as, we knew nothing of his *past:* *adv.* by; beyond; as, he just walked *past:* *prep.* beyond in time; after; as, it is *past* his time; he is *past* cure.

paste (pāst), *n.* a mixture of flour, etc., with water, used for joining or sticking things together; dough prepared for pies, etc.; a composition or mixture used for making artificial gems: *v.t.* to fasten with a sticky mixture; as, to *paste* together sheets of paper.

paste-board (pāste'bōrd"), *n.* thick, stiff material made by sticking together sheets of paper.

pas-tel (păs'tĕl; păs-tĕl'), *n.* a kind of crayon made by mixing ground paints with gum water; the mixture from which the crayon is made; a picture drawn with such crayon.

past-er (pās'tĕr), *n.* a strip of gummed paper, often with printed matter on it, to be pasted over something.

pas-tern (păs'tĕrn), *n.* that part of a horse's foot between the fetlock and coffin bone, or foot bone; a hobble for a horse's foot.

Pas-teur-ize (păs'tẽr-īz; pȧs-tûr'īz), *v.t.* to kill the germs in (a liquid) by applying heat; to sterilize, or make free from germs, by heating, as milk.

pas-til (păs'tĭl), *n.* a small mass of aromatic, or sweet-smelling, substances, burnt slowly to fumigate sick-rooms, etc. Also, **pastille.**

pas-time (pȧs'tīm"), *n.* diversion; sport; amusement; occupation that fills time agreeably.

pas-tor (pȧs'tẽr), *n.* a clergyman having charge of a church and congregation.

pas-tor-al (pȧs'tẽr-ăl), *adj.* pertaining to the care of a church; as, *pastoral* duties; pertaining to shepherds or to rural life or scenes: *n.* a poem showing happenings in country life; a picture showing rural life or scenes.—*adv.* **pastorally.**

pas-tor-ate (pȧs'tẽr-āt), *n.* the office or parish of a clergyman who holds a charge; the time during which a clergyman holds one charge; a body of pastors, or ministers.

pas-try (pās'trĭ), *n.* articles of food, as pies, etc., made of light, puffy dough.

pas-tur-age (pȧs'tûr-āj), *n.* feed for cattle, as grass; land used for feeding cattle; pasture.

pas-ture (pȧs'tûr), *n.* land or grass on which cattle feed: *v.t.* to supply with grass or pasture: *v.i.* to graze or eat grass.

past-y (pās'tĭ), *adj.* like, or covered with, paste, a mixture of flour, water, etc.: *n.* a pie, usually of meat, put in a crust and sometimes baked without a dish.

pat (păt), *n.* a light, quick blow with the hand; a small lump of butter shaped up; a light sound or tap: *adj.* apt; fitting: *adv.* aptly; readily: *v.t.* [*p.t.* and *p.p.* patted, *p.pr.* patting], to strike gently and quickly, as with the fingers or hand.

patch (păch), *n.* a piece of material, as cloth or metal, put on to cover a hole or rent or to strengthen; a small plot of ground; a small piece of black silk or court-plaster stuck on the face to increase its beauty: *v.t.* to mend or strengthen by putting on an extra piece of material; mend clumsily; piece together.—*n.* **patcher.**

patch-work (păch'wûrk"), *n.* a fabric made of pieces of cloth sewed together, especially pieces of various colors; hence, a jumble; work carelessly done.

pate (pāt), *n.* the head; crown of the head; as, a boy with an empty *pate.*

pa-tel-la (pȧ-tĕl'ȧ), *n.* the kneecap, or kneepan; the flat, movable bone forming the top of the knee joint.

pat-en (păt'ĕn), *n.* the plate used for the bread in the Communion service.

pat-ent (păt'ĕnt; pā'tĕnt), *adj.* apparent; evident; plain; as, the truth was *patent* to all; open to public view: said especially of an official paper which grants a privilege; as, letters *patent;* secured by government protection; as, a *patent* lock: *n.* a right or privilege granted by the government; as, the sole right to make, use, or sell an invention for a certain number of years; the official paper granting this right; the thing that is so protected: *v.t.* to grant or secure the sole right to.—*adj.* **patentable.**

pat-ent-ee (păt"ĕn-tē'; pā"tĕn-tē'), *n.* a person or inventor who has secured from the government the sole right to an invention.

pat-ent leath-er (păt'ĕnt lĕth'ẽr), a varnished leather with a smooth, glossy, usually black surface.

pa-ter-fa-mil-i-as (pā"tẽr-fȧ-mĭl'ĭ-ăs), *n.* the father of a family. [LAT.]

pa-ter-nal (pȧ-tûr'năl), *adj.* of, pertaining to, or like, a father; received from a father; related through the father; as, a *paternal* uncle.—*adv.* **paternally.**

pa-ter-nal-ism (pȧ-tûr'năl-ĭzm), *n.* a principle of government whereby the relationship between the government and the governed is like that between a father and his children.

pa-ter-ni-ty (pȧ-tûr'nĭ-tĭ), *n.* fatherhood; relation to a father; as, the *paternity* of a child; authorship.

pa-ter-nos-ter (pā'tẽr-nŏs"tẽr; păt'ẽr-nŏs"tẽr), *n.* the Lord's prayer; any formula used as a prayer; a rosary; every eleventh bead in a rosary, showing that the Lord's prayer must be said. [LAT.]

path (pȧth), *n.* a road; footway; track; course of conduct or action.

pa-thet-ic (pȧ-thĕt'ĭk), *adj.* arousing sorrow and pity; as, a *pathetic* condition or appearance; touching; as, her grief was *pathetic.* Also, **pathetical.**—*adv.* **pathetically.**

path-find-er (pȧth'fīn"dẽr), *n.* an explorer in an unknown country; a pioneer.

path-less (pȧth'lĕs), *adj.* without a beaten way; untrodden; trackless; as, the *pathless* forest.

path-o-log-i-cal (păth"ō-lŏj'ĭ-kăl), *adj.* pertaining to the science of diseases; due to disease; as, her depression is *pathological.* Also, **pathologic.**—*adv.* **pathologically.**

pa-thol-o-gist (pȧ-thŏl'ō-jĭst), *n.* one skilled in the science of diseases.

pa-thol-o-gy (pȧ-thŏl'ō-jĭ), *n.* the science that treats of diseases.

pa-thos (pā'thŏs), *n.* expression of deep feeling; that which excites sympathy and pity.

path-way (pȧth'wā"), *n.* a narrow footway; any course or road; as, one's *pathway* through life.

pa-tience (pā'shĕns), *n.* the quality of suffering without complaint; meekness; endurance and perseverance; forbearance; the power to wait calmly.

pa-tient (pā'shĕnt), *adj.* suffering pain, hardship, affliction, insult, etc., with meekness or calmness; forbearing; untiring in labor; persevering; as, a *patient* worker; waiting with calmness: *n.* one under the care of a doctor.—*adv.* **patiently.**

pa-tio (păt'yō), *n.* an open courtyard, around which a house is built: used in Spanish countries. [SPAN.]

pat-ness (păt'nĕs), *n.* fitness; appropriateness; as, the *patness* of a reply.

pa-tois (pȧ"twä'; păt'wä), *n.* language of uneducated people, used in a given locality; a dialect; as, the *patois* of the French Canadians is like neither French nor English. [FR.]

pa-tri-arch (pā'trĭ-ärk), *n.* the founder or head of a family or tribe; an aged and venerable man; in the Greek

Church, a bishop of the highest rank.—*adj.* patriarchal.

pa-tri-cian (pá-trĭsh'ăn), *n.* one of the senators or lawmakers of ancient Rome; a person of noble or high birth: *adj.* senatorial; noble; aristocratic.

pat-ri-cide (păt'rĭ-sīd), *n.* the killing of a father; one who murders a father.

pat-ri-mo-ni-al (păt"rĭ-mō'nĭ-ăl), *adj.* inherited from ancestors; as, a *patrimonial* estate.—*adv.* patrimonially.

pat-ri-mo-ny (păt'rĭ-mō-nĭ), *n.* an estate or property inherited from a father or other ancestor; property or estate settled on a church, etc., for its support.

pa-tri-ot (pā'trĭ-ŏt; păt'rĭ-ŏt), *n.* one who loves and supports his native country.

pa-tri-ot-ic (pā"trĭ-ŏt'ĭk), *adj.* characterized or influenced by love of one's country.—*adv.* patriotically.

pa-tri-ot-ism (pā'trĭ-ŏt-ĭzm), *n.* love of one's country.

pa-trol (pá-trōl'), *n.* a guard; a policeman; the act of going the rounds of a district in order to protect it; a small body of soldiers on guard duty; in the World War, a group of soldiers sent out at night to approach the enemy's trenches for information: *v.t.* [*p.t.* and *p.p.* patrolled, *p.pr.* patrolling], to go or walk round in order to protect; as, a policeman *patrols* his beat; to act as guard to (a camp or entrenchment): *v.i.* to go round a district in order to protect it.

pa-trol-man (pá-trōl'măn), *n.* a policeman whose duty is to go round a certain beat in order to protect it.

pa-tron (pā'trŭn), *n.* [*fem.* patroness], a guardian or protector; a defender or supporter; as, a *patron* of music; in business, a regular customer: *adj.* giving aid or acting as guardian; as, a *patron* saint.

pat-ron-age (păt'rŭn-āj; pā'trŭn-āj), *n.* special support; guardianship or protection; the act of buying goods regularly at one store.

pa-tron-ess (pā'trŭn-ĕs; păt'rŭn-ĕs), *n.* a woman who guarantees the disposal of tickets for an entertainment for charity.

pat-ron-ize (păt'rŭn-īz; pā'trŭn-īz), *v.t.* to act as guardian or benefactor towards; support or protect; to treat with condescension; favor; frequent as a customer; as, to *patronize* a store.—*adj.* patronizing.—*adv.* patronizingly.—*n.* patronizer.

pat-ro-nym-ic (păt"rō-nĭm'ĭk), *adj.* formed from the name of an ancestor: *n.* a name coming from an ancestor; the family name.

pa-troon (pá-trōōn'), *n.* one who received a large tract of land under the old Dutch government of New York.

pat-ten (păt'ĕn), *n.* a wooden shoe with a thick sole, or one with an iron ring under the sole to raise the foot from the ground, formerly worn by women as a protection against damp; a clog; the base of a column.

pat-ter (păt'ẽr), *v.i.* to strike with a quick succession of light sounds; as, the rain *patters* on the window; to move with light, quick steps; to mumble or mutter something over and over, especially the Lord's prayer: *v.t.* to mumble indistinctly; as, to *patter* one's prayers: *n.* a quick succession of slight sounds; colloquially, ignorant, idle talk or gossip.

pat-tern (păt'ẽrn), *n.* a model, sample, or specimen; anything cut out or formed into a shape to be copied; a design or figure; as, the *pattern* of a carpet; a piece of material sufficient for a garment; as, a dress *pattern;* *v.t.* to make in imitation of; to copy: with *after*, *from*, or *by;* as, to *pattern* a dress after a model: *v.i.* to form one thing like another; as, you would do well to *pattern* by him.

pat-ty (păt'ĭ), *n.* a small case made of pastry, holding meat, etc.; as, a chicken *patty.*

pau-ci-ty (pô'sĭ-tĭ), *n.* smallness of number or quantity; scarcity.

Paul (pôl), *n.* a Jew of Tarsus who became an apostle of Christ and whose epistles, or letters, to the Gentiles are contained in several books of the New Testament: originally known as *Saul.*

Paul-ine (pôl'īn; pôl'ĭn), *adj.* pertaining to the apostle Paul, or to his letters or teachings.

paunch (pänch; pônch), *n.* the abdomen; the belly and, sometimes, its contents.

pau-per (pô'pẽr), *n.* a very poor person; one who is supported by the public.

pau-per-ism (pô'pẽr-ĭzm), *n.* the state of being in need of charity, or of being supported by the public.

pau-per-ize (pô'pẽr-īz), *v.t.* to reduce to extreme poverty; to accustom to receive support from the public; as, too easy charity tends to *pauperise* the poor.

pause (pôz), *n.* a temporary stop or rest; a brief ceasing of action; interruption; hesitation; a break in speaking; a break in writing indicated by a punctuation mark; a mark in music over or under a note or rest to show that it is to be prolonged: *v.i.* to make a short stop; wait; hesitate: often with *on* or *upon.*

pave (pāv), *v.t.* to cover or lay with stones, bricks, etc.; as, to *pave* a street; to make smooth or easy; as, to *pave* the way for another.

pave-ment (pāv'mĕnt), *n.* a roadway or floor covered or laid with stone, brick, tile, etc.; a sidewalk; material used in covering a road, footway, or floor.

pa-vil-ion (pá-vĭl'yŭn), *n.* an ornamental dome-shaped building; as, a garden *pavilion;* a large tent; a temporary open building for shelter, entertainment, etc.; a part of a large building extending out from the main part, or rising above it.

paw (pô), *n.* the foot of a four-footed animal with claws: *v.t.* and *v.i.* to scrape with the forefoot; as, a horse *paws* the ground; a dog *paws* at his meat; to touch or caress with the forefoot; as, a dog *paws* his master's knee; colloquially, to handle awkwardly or fondly; as, to *paw* things over.

pawl (pôl), *n.* a short bar or bolt on a machine made to fall into notches in another part, as a wheel, of the machine, in order to prevent the movement from turning back.

pawn (pôn), *n.* something given or deposited as security for the payment of a debt or return of a loan; state of being so pledged; a common piece at chess: *v.t.* to give as security for a loan; as, to *pawn* a ring.

pawn-bro-ker (pôn'brō"kẽr), *n.* one whose business is to lend money on goods left with him.

Paw-nee (pô-nē'), *n.* one of a tribe of American Indians, originally inhabiting what is now the region of the Arkansas River in Nebraska and Kansas.

pawn-shop (pôn'shŏp"), *n.* a shop where money is lent on goods deposited.

paw-paw (pô'pô"), *n.* a tree of the custard-apple family, common in the southwestern United States. Also, papaw.

pax (păks), *n.* a small metal plate engraved with a crucifix or other sacred subject: formerly kissed by priest and worshipers.

pay (pā), *v.t.* [*p.t.* and *p.p.* paid, *p.pr.* paying], to satisfy the claims of; reward; recompense; as, to *pay* workmen; discharge, as a debt, by giving what is required; as, to *pay* taxes; to be profitable to; as, it will *pay* you to study; give without any sense of obligation; as, to *pay* a compliment: *v.i.* to make recompense; to discharge a debt; as, he always *pays* promptly; to make suitable return; be worth while; as, the business *pays* well; honesty always *pays*: *n.* money given for service done, for goods, etc.

pay-a-ble (pā'*d*-bl), *adj.* that may, can, or should be, paid; justly due; as, a note *payable* on demand.

pay-ee (pā-ē'), *n.* one to whom money is, or is to be, paid.

pay-mas-ter (pā'màs"tẽr), *n.* one who gives out money for wages; especially, an officer in the army or navy whose duty is to pay the officers and men.

pay-ment (pā'mĕnt), *n.* the act of giving money for wages, a debt, etc.; that which is given in discharge of a debt, duty, etc.; recompense.

pay-nim (pā'nĭm), *adj.* formerly, heathen; pagan: *n.* one of a false faith; an idol worshiper.

pea (pē), *n.* [*pl.* peas, or pease (pēz)], a pod-bearing vine of the bean family; its eatable seed.

peace (pēs), *n.* a state of rest or calm; freedom from war or disturbance; friendly relations; as, *peace* between nations.
Syn. quiet, tranquillity.

peace-a-ble (pēs'*d*-bl), *adj.* not quarrelsome; calm; quiet; tranquil; still.—*adv.* peaceably.—*n.* peaceableness.

peace-ful (pēs'fŏŏl), *adj.* free from war or commotion; mild; calm; undisturbed; quiet; as, a *peaceful* evening.—*adv.* peacefully.—*n.* peacefulness.

peace-mak-er (pēs'māk"ẽr), *n.* one who restores friendly feeling between two unfriendly parties.

peach (pēch), *n.* a well-known orchard tree; its fleshy, juicy fruit.

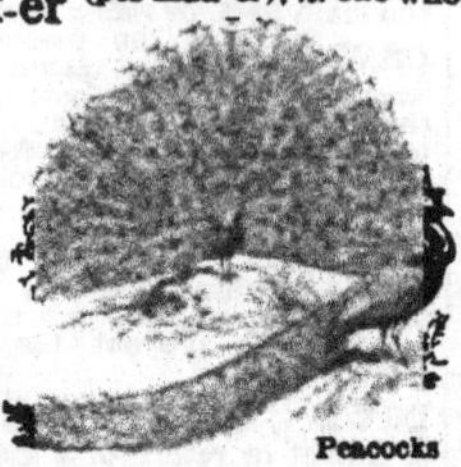
Peacocks

pea-cock (pē'kŏk"), *n.* [*fem.* peahen], the male bird of the peafowl, noted for its long, handsome tail coverts, commonly called tail-feathers, marked with eyelike spots.

pea-fowl (pē'foul"), *n.* a large domestic fowl, with vivid greenish-blue plumage.

pea-jack-et (pē'jăk"ĕt), *n.* a loose double-breasted coat of thick woolen cloth worn by sailors in bad weather.

peak (pēk), *n.* the sharp-pointed summit of a mountain or hill; a mountain standing alone; a pointed end of anything; as, the *peak* of a roof; the extended front of a cap; the upper outer corner of an extended sail; the narrow part, fore or aft, of a vessel's hull: *v.i.* to grow pale and wan.

peaked (pēkt; pēk'ĕd), *adj.* pointed; ridged; as, a *peaked* roof; colloquially, thin or sickly in appearance.

peal (pēl), *n.* a loud, long sound, as of thunder, bells, etc.; a set of bells, or the changes rung by them: *v.i.* to give forth loud sounds: *v.t.* to cause to sound loudly; as, to *peal* a bell.

pe-an (pē'ăn), *n.* a loud and joyous song of praise or triumph. Also, pæan.

pea-nut (pē'nŭt), *n.* the fruit of a trailing plant of the bean family: called also *groundnut*, because it ripens under ground.

pear (pâr), *n.* an orchard tree related to the apple; its juicy, fleshy, eatable fruit.

pearl (pûrl), *n.* a small round mass of lustrous substance, grayish-white or creamy in color, growing in the mother-of-pearl coating which lines the shell of the oyster, and used as a gem; anything like such a gem in form or value; a pale grayish-white color; a white speck in the eye; a small size of type: *adj.* consisting or made of pearl: *v.t.* to set or adorn with pearls.

pearl-ash (pûrl'ăsh"), *n.* crude potash with the impurities taken out.

pearl-y (pûr'lĭ), *adj.* having a soft grayish-white color or luster; round and lustrous; as, *pearly* tears.—*n.* pearliness.

peart (pērt), *adj.* in good spirits; sprightly; lively. [Colloq.]

peas-ant (pĕz'ănt), *n.* in Europe, a countryman, especially one who tills the soil and is of lowest rank: *adj.* rude; rustic; as, *peasant* manners.

peas-ant-ry (pĕz'ănt-rĭ), *n.* the whole class of rustics, or countrymen, of lowest rank.

pease (pēz), *n.pl.* peas in quantity or collectively.

peat (pēt), *n.* a substance formed of decayed vegetable matter, like moss or turf: used as fuel, especially in Ireland.

pea-vey (pē'vĭ), *n.* a lever, pointed with iron, with a movable iron hook near the end: used in lumbering. Also, peavy.

peb-ble (pĕb'l), *n.* a small roundish stone; transparent or clear rock crystal used for spectacles, etc.: *v.t.* to grain (leather) so as to produce an uneven surface.

peb-bly (pĕb'lĭ), *adj.* full of pebbles or small roundish stones; as, a *pebbly* shore.

pe-can (pē-kăn'; pē-kăn'), *n.* a kind of hickory tree of the southern United States; its thin-shelled nut.

pec-ca-dil-lo (pĕk"*d*-dĭl'ō), *n.* [*pl.* peccadillos, or -loes (-ōz)], a trifling fault or slight offense.

pec-ca-ry (pĕk'*d*-rĭ), *n.* [*pl.* peccaries (-rĭz)], a South American animal similar to the hog.

peck (pĕk), *n.* one-quarter of a bushel; eight quarts in dry measure; a quick, sharp stroke, as with the beak or with something pointed: *v.t.* to strike with the beak, as a bird: as, to *peck* the bark of a tree; to strike with a pointed instrument, as a pick; to make by striking with a pointed object; as, the chick *pecks* a hole in the shell; pick up with the beak; as, the hen *pecks* corn; eat daintily: as, she *pecks* her food: *v.i.* to make strokes with the beak, or with a sharp instrument; to pick up food with the beak.

peck-er (pĕk'ẽr), *n.* one that pecks, or picks; especially, a bird that picks holes in trees, such as the woodpecker; a pick, pickax, or other tool for making holes.

pec-to-ral (pĕk'tô-răl), *adj.* pertaining to, good for, or worn on, the chest; as, a *pectoral* muscle; a *pectoral* remedy; a *pectoral* ornament: *n.* an ornament worn on the breast, as the breastplate formerly worn by the Jewish high priest; a medicine for chest complaints.

pec-u-late (pĕk'ū-lāt), *v.i.* to take and use for oneself, money entrusted to one's care; to steal; to embezzle.—*n.* **peculator.**

pec-u-la-tion (pĕk'ū-lā'shŭn), *n.* the act of stealing, or of taking for one's own use, money intrusted to one's care; theft; embezzlement, as of a bank's funds.

pe-cul-iar (pē-kūl'yȧr), *adj.* one's own; as, my *peculiar* property; not like anything else; not owned in common; as, an idiom is an expression *peculiar* to one language; distinct; individual; as, her style of dress is *peculiar* to her; strange; queer; as, a person of *peculiar* appearance.—*adv.* **peculiarly.**

pe-cu-li-ar-i-ty (pē-kū'lĭ-ăr'ĭ-tĭ), *n.* [*pl.* peculiarities (-tĭz)], something which marks a person or thing as being different; the state or quality of being very different; an unusual or odd trait; queerness.

pe-cu-ni-a-ry (pē-kū'nĭ-ā-rĭ), *adj.* relating to, or consisting of, money; as, *pecuniary* difficulties.—*adv.* **pecuniarily.**

ped-a-gog (pĕd'ȧ-gŏg), *n.* a teacher of children; a schoolmaster, especially if conceited and narrow-minded. Also, **pedagogue.**

ped-a-gog-ic (pĕd'ȧ-gŏj'ĭk), *adj.* of or pertaining to a teacher or to the art of teaching: *n.pl.* the art or science of teaching. Also, *adj.* **pedagogical.**

ped-a-go-gy (pĕd'ȧ-gō'jĭ; pĕd'ȧ-gŏj'ĭ), *n.* the science or art of teaching; instruction and training.

ped-al (pĕd'ăl; pē'dăl), *adj.* pertaining to a foot or feet, or to a treadle, such as that of a bicycle; as, *pedal* digits, or toes; a *pedal* note in organ music: *n.* (pĕd'ăl), a lever attached to a musical instrument and moved by the foot, to lessen or swell the tone; a treadle.

ped-ant (pĕd'ănt), *n.* one who makes a needless display of his learning or who overvalues mere knowledge.

pe-dan-tic (pē-dăn'tĭk), *adj.* pertaining to, or marked by, a conceited and needless display of learning. Also, **pedantical.**—*adv.* **pedantically.**

ped-ant-ry (pĕd'ănt-rĭ), *n.* conceited and needless display of learning; the habit of mind that overvalues, and is vain of possessing, trifling details of learning.

ped-dle (pĕd'l), *v.t.* to travel about selling small wares; to do a small business; be busy about trifles: *v.t.* to sell in small quantities from house to house; to hawk; to deal out little by little.

ped-dler (pĕd'lẽr), *n.* one who travels about selling small articles; a hawker. Also, **pedlar, pedler.**

Pedestal. *B*, base; *C*, cornice; *D*, dado.

ped-es-tal (pĕd'ĕs-tăl), *n.* the base of a column, statue, vase, etc.

pe-des-tri-an (pē-dĕs'trĭ-ăn), *adj.* going on foot; walking: *n.* one who journeys on foot; a professional walker.

pe-des-tri-an-ism (pē-dĕs'trĭ-ăn-ĭzm), *n.* the art or practice of walking; the business of one who makes walking or running a specialty.

ped-i-cel (pĕd'ĭ-sĕl), *n.* any slender supporting stalk; a stock supporting various special organs; in seed plants, a flower stalk bearing one flower.

ped-i-cure (pĕd'ĭ-kūr), *n.* the care of the feet; a chiropodist, or one who doctors the feet.

ped-i-gree (pĕd'ĭ-grē), *n.* ancestry or line of descent; as, the *pedigree* of a horse; a family history.

ped-i-ment (pĕd'ĭ-mĕnt), *n.* originally, an ornamented triangular space, or low gable, over the front of a building; hence, any like decoration over a door, window, etc.

ped-ler (pĕd'lẽr), *n.* one who travels from place to place selling small articles; a hawker. Also, **peddler, pedlar.**

Pedometer

pe-dom-e-ter (pē-dŏm'ē-tẽr), *n.* a watch-shaped instrument for measuring the distance covered in walking.

pe-dun-cle (pē-dŭŋ'kl), *n.* a flower stalk: *adj.* **peduncular, pedunculate.**

peek (pēk), *v.i.* to look slyly through a crevice or crack; to peep: *n.* a peep; a glance.

peel (pēl), *v.t.* to strip the outer covering from, as bark, rind, husk, etc.; as, to *peel* an orange; to strip off; as, to *peel* the bark from a tree: *v.i.* to come off or strip; as, the bark of the tree *peels* easily: *n.* skin or rind; a baker's long, flat, wooden shovel; a contrivance for hanging up printed sheets to dry.

peep (pēp), *v.i.* to chirp or cry, as young birds; to look through a crack or from a hiding place; look slyly; begin to appear; as, the sun *peeps* over the horizon: *n.* the cry of a young chick, bird, etc.; a cheep; a sly look; a glimpse; first appearance; as, at *peep* of day.

peep-er (pēp'ẽr), *n.* one that peeps; especially, a young frog that makes a cheeping noise.

peer (pēr), *n.* one of the same rank; an equal; a nobleman; a member of the British House of Lords: *v.i.* to look narrowly or closely; as, to *peer* through the trees.

peer-age (pēr'āj), *n.* the rank or dignity of a nobleman; the whole body of noblemen; a book containing information about the nobility.

peer-ess (pēr'ĕs), *n.* the wife of a nobleman; a lady of noble rank.

peer-less (pēr'lĕs), *adj.* without an equal; matchless; as, a *peerless* diamond; *peerless* courage.—*adv.* **peerlessly.**—*n.* **peerlessness.**

pee-vish (pē'vĭsh), *adj.* childishly fretful; difficult to please; as, a *peevish* disposition; ill-tempered.—*adv.* **peevishly.**—*n.* **peevishness.**

peg (pĕg), *n.* a small pointed wooden pin; as, a shoe-*peg;* a piece of wood serving as a nail; as, to hang one's coat on a *peg:* *v.t.* [*p.t.* and *p.p.* pegged, *p.pr.* pegging], to fasten with small wooden pins; as, to *peg* shoes; to mark by driving in small stakes of wood; as, to *peg* out a mining claim: *v.i.* to work steadily; as, to *peg* away at one's lessons.

peg-ma-tite (pĕg'mȧ-tīt), *n.* a coarse-grained granite, often containing rare minerals.

pe-lag-ic (pē-lăj'ĭk), *adj.* pertaining to, or living in, the ocean far from land; as, *pelagic* fish.

pel-er-ine (pĕl'ĕr-ĭn; pĕl"ĕr-ēn'), *n.* a woman's cape, often of fur, longer in the back than in the front.

pelf (pĕlf), *n.* stolen property; money; wealth: used in a bad sense.

pel-i-can (pĕl'ĭ-kăn), *n.* a large water bird with a huge bill, and a large pouch on the throat for storing food (fish); a dentist's instrument for drawing teeth.

Pelicans

pe-lisse (pē-lēs'), *n.* a woman's long cloak, originally of fur, or fur-lined, now often of silk.

pel-lag-ra (pĕ-lăg'rȧ; pĕ-lā'grȧ), *n.* a skin disease, caused by a germ, which seriously disturbs the digestive and nervous systems and frequently results in insanity and death.

pel-let (pĕl'ĕt), *n.* a little ball, often of food or medicine, as a pill, etc.

pel-li-cle (pĕl'ĭ-kl), *n.* a very thin skin or film.

pell-mell (pĕl"mĕl'), *adv.* in a disorderly manner; in furious haste; as, they rushed *pell-mell* from the room. Also, **pellmell.**

pel-lu-cid (pĕ-lū'sĭd), *adj.* perfectly clear; transparent; as, a *pellucid* stream of water; *pellucid* thought.

pelt (pĕlt), *n.* a raw hide; the skin of a fur-bearing animal; a blow from something thrown: *v.t.* to strike by throwing something; as, to *pelt* a dog with stones: *v.i.* to fall heavily, as rain or hail.

pelt-ry (pĕl'trĭ), *n.* [*pl.* peltries (-trĭz)], skins or furs collectively: *pl.* kinds of skins or furs.

pel-vic (pĕl'vĭk), *adj.* pertaining to the pelvis, or bony cavity supporting the lower part of the body.

pel-vis (pĕl'vĭs), *n.* the bony cavity supporting the lower part of the abdomen, or body.

pem-mi-can (pĕm'ĭ-kăn), *n.* a foodstuff made of lean meat, with fat and, sometimes, fruit, dried, pounded, and pressed into cakes.

pen (pĕn), *n.* a small inclosure; as, a pigpen; a coop; an instrument for writing with ink, etc.: *v.t.* [*p.t.* and *p.p.* penned, *p.pr.* penning], to shut up or confine in a small inclosure; write, as to *pen* a letter.

pe-nal (pē'năl), *adj.* pertaining to, or liable to, punishment; as, the *penal* laws; a *penal* offense.

pe-nal-ize (pē'năl-īz), *v.t.* to inflict punishment upon; to make subject to punishment.

pen-al-ty (pĕn'ăl-tĭ), *n.* legal punishment either on the person or by a fine; fine or forfeit; suffering or punishment as the result of any wrongdoing.

pen-ance (pĕn'ăns), *n.* self-imposed suffering; an act showing sorrow for wrongdoing; in the Roman Catholic Church, the sacrament by which sins are pardoned after confession and reparation.

pe-na-tes (pē-nā'tēz), *n.pl.* the household gods of the ancient Romans. Also, **di penates.**

pence (pĕns), *n.* plural of *penny*, expressing total amount of money: distinct from *pennies*, which indicates separate coins.

pen-chant (päṅ"shäṅ'; pĕn'chănt), *n.* a strong leaning or taste; as, she has a *penchant* for music. [FR.]

pen-cil (pĕn'sĭl), *n.* a small fine brush used by artists; a pointed instrument of black lead, colored chalk, etc., often inclosed in wood, and used for writing, drawing, etc.: *v.t.* to write, sketch, paint, or mark with, or as with, a pencil.

pen-ciled (pĕn'sĭld), *p.adj.* written, drawn, or painted, with, or as with, a pencil; marked with fine lines.

pend-ant (pĕn'dănt), *n.* anything hanging for ornamentation; an earring or locket.

pend-ent (pĕn'dĕnt), *adj.* hanging; suspended; jutting over; as, a *pendent* rock; swinging; undetermined.

pend-ing (pĕnd'ĭng), *adj.* not yet finished or decided; as, a *pending* trial: *prep.* during the continuance of; awaiting.

pen-du-lous (pĕn'dū-lŭs), *adj.* hanging so as to swing; swaying.—*adv.* **pendulously.**—*n.* **pendulousness.**

pen-du-lum (pĕn'dū-lŭm), *n.* [*pl.* pendulums (-lŭmz)], a body suspended from a fixed point so that it may vibrate, or swing backwards and forwards; as, the *pendulum* of a clock.

pen-e-tra-bil-i-ty (pĕn"ē-trȧ-bĭl'ĭ-tĭ), *n.* capability of being entered or pierced by another body; as, the *penetrability* of steel by a bullet.

pen-e-tra-ble (pĕn'ē-trȧ-bl), *adj.* that may be entered or pierced by another body; capable of receiving an idea or impression.

pen-e-trate (pĕn'ē-trāt), *v.t.* to pierce; enter; as, light *penetrates* darkness; make a hole through or perforate; as, a bullet *penetrates* wood; make a way into; as, the idea at last *penetrated* his intelligence; affect deeply; reach the interior of; as, to *penetrate* a forest: *v.i.* to pass or pierce into something; to affect the feelings deeply; as, grief *penetrates* to the heart.

pen-e-trat-ing (pĕn'ē-trāt"ĭng), *p.adj.* piercing; sharp; discerning or knowing. Also, **penetrative.**

pen-e-tra-tion (pĕn"ē-trā'shŭn), *n.* the act of entering or piercing; mental acuteness or keenness.
Syn. sagacity, discernment.
Ant. (see dulness).

pen-guin (pĕn'gwĭn; pĕŋ'gwĭn), *n.* a large Antarctic sea fowl, unable to fly, but expert at swimming.

Penguins

pen-in-su-la (pĕn-ĭn'sū-lȧ), *n.* a piece of land extending from the mainland and almost surrounded by water.

pen-in-su-lar (pĕn-ĭn'sū-lẽr), *adj.* of, pertaining to, or shaped like, a peninsula, or body of land almost surrounded by water.

pen-i-tence (pĕn'ĭ-tĕns), *n.* sorrow for sin; state of being sorry.

pen-i-tent (pĕn'ĭ-tĕnt), *adj.* sorry; repentant: *n.* one who is repentant, or sorry for sin; one who is under the direction of a confessor.—*adv.* **penitently.**

pen-i-ten-tial (pĕn'ĭ-tĕn'shăl), *adj.* pertaining to, or expressing, sorrow for sins; of the nature of penance or punishment.

pen-i-ten-tia-ry (pĕn'ĭ-tĕn'shȧ-rĭ), *adj.* pertaining to penance or punishment for wrongdoing: *n.* a house of correction; a state prison in which convicted criminals are confined, usually at labor.

pen-knife (pĕn'nīf"), *n.* a small pocketknife, so called because used formerly for sharpening quill pens.

pen-man (pĕn'măn), *n.* a person considered with regard to his handwriting; as, a good *penman;* one who teaches handwriting.

pen-man-ship (pĕn'măn-shĭp), *n.* the art or style of handwriting; handwriting.

pen-nant (pĕn'ănt), *n.* a long narrow flag; as, a naval *pennant;* any small flag used for various purposes; as, a college *pennant.*

pen-nate (pĕn'āt), *adj.* having wings or feathers.

pen-ni-less (pĕn'ĭ-lĕs), *adj.* without money; very poor.

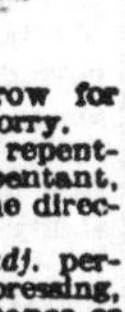
Pennon

pen-non (pĕn'ŭn), *n.* a small swallow-tailed flag or streamer, formerly borne by a knight on his lance; any flag or banner.

pen-ny (pĕn'ĭ), *n.* [*pl.* pennies (-ĭz), denoting number, pence (pĕns), denoting amount or value], an English bronze coin, equal to one-twelfth of a shilling, or to two cents of United States money; colloquially, in the United States, a cent.

pen-ny-roy-al (pĕn'ĭ-roi'ăl), *n.* a fragrant herb of the mint family.

pen-ny-weight (pĕn'ĭ-wāt"), *n.* a weight equal to twenty-four grains troy or to one-twentieth of an ounce.

pen-ny-wise (pĕn'ĭ-wīz"), *adj.* economical in small affairs; saving small sums while losing larger ones; as, "*penny-wise* and pound foolish." Also, **penny wise.**

pen-ny-worth (pĕn'ĭ-wûrth"), *n.* the amount that a penny will buy; a small amount.

pe-nol-o-gy (pē-nŏl'ō-jĭ), *n.* the scientific study of punishments for crime, prison management, etc.—*adj.* **penological.**

pen-sile (pĕn'sĭl), *adj.* hanging loosely; as, a *pensile* nest; having a hanging nest.

pen-sion (pĕn'shŭn), *n.* a certain sum paid regularly for past services; as, a *pension* paid by the government to ex-soldiers; a regular allowance paid to one through the good will of another; (Fr. päṅ"-syôṅ'), a boarding house or boarding school: *v.t.* to grant a regular allowance of money to.

pen-sion-a-ry (pĕn'shŭn-ā-rĭ), *adj.* depending for support upon an allowance made because of past services or through bounty: *n.* one who depends on such an allowance.

pen-sion-er (pĕn'shŭn-ẽr), *n.* one who receives a regular allowance because of past services or through the bounty of another.

pen-sive (pĕn'sĭv), *adj.* sadly thoughtful; musing; as, a *pensive* mood; expressing sad thoughtfulness; as, a *pensive* look.—*adv.* **pensively.**—*n.* **pensiveness.**

pen-stock (pĕn'stŏk"), *n.* a canal from a mill race to the gate of a water wheel; a sluice or floodgate; a pump barrel; a penholder.

pent (pĕnt), *p.adj.* shut up; closely confined; as, his *pent* anger broke forth at last.

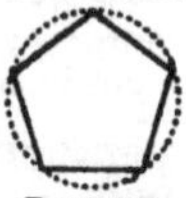
Pentagon

pen-ta-gon (pĕn'tȧ-gŏn), *n.* a plane figure of five sides and five angles.—*adj.* **pentagonal.**

pen-tam-e-ter (pĕn-tăm'ē-tẽr), *n.* a verse consisting of five feet: *adj.* having five metrical feet.

pen-ta-style (pĕn'tȧ-stīl), *n.* a building with five columns in front.

Pen-ta-teuch (pĕn'tȧ-tūk), *n.* the first five books of the Old Testament.

pen-tath-lon (pĕn-tăth'lŏn), *n.* in the modern Olympic games, a composite contest of five athletic events.

Pen-te-cost (pĕn'tē-kŏst), *n.* a Jewish festival kept the fiftieth day after the second day of the Passover; the Christian feast of Whitsunday, celebrating the descent of the Holy Ghost.—*adj.* **Pentecostal.**

pent-house (pĕnt'hous"), *n.* a shed with a slanting roof projecting from a main wall or building; a small, slanting roof over a doorstep.

pent-roof (pĕnt'rōōf"), *n.* a roof with a slant on one side only.

pe-nult (pē'nŭlt; pē-nŭlt'), *n.* the last syllable but one of a word. Also, **penultima.**

pe-nul-ti-mate (pē-nŭl'tĭ-māt), *adj.* last but one; as, a *penultimate* syllable: *n.* the penult, or the next to the last syllable of a word.

pe-num-bra (pē-nŭm'brȧ), *n.* a partial shadow on the outside of a complete shadow, as in an eclipse, or at the edge of a sun spot; in a picture, the space where shadow merges into light.—*adj.* **penumbral.**

pe-nu-ri-ous (pē-nū'rĭ-ŭs), *adj.* miserly; not liberal; scanty.—*adv.* **penuriously.**—*n.* **penuriousness.**

pen-u-ry (pĕn'ū-ri), *n.* want of the necessities of life: extreme poverty.

pe-on (pē'ŏn), *n.* a Mexican laborer, especially one who is forced to work for a creditor to pay a debt; in India, a native soldier or constable.

pe-on-age (pē'ŏn-āj), *n.* a system of contract labor, by which gangs of workmen are rented to employers: common in Mexico and in the southern United States.

pe-o-ny (pē'ō-ni), *n.* a plant of the crowfoot family with handsome flowers; the flower of the plant. Also, **paeony.**

peo-ple (pē'pl), *n.* [*pl.* people, peoples (-plz)], persons generally; as, many *people* on the streets; members of a community; inhabitants; as, the *people* of America; race; as, the different *peoples* of the world; kindred or family; as, my own *people;* the public as a whole; as, government should exist for the good of the *people;* commoners as distinct from nobles; as, Lloyd George was a man of the *people:* *v.t.* to fill with inhabitants; as, to *people* a country.
Syn., *n.* nation, persons, folks.

pep-per (pĕp'ẽr), *n.* a hot spice made of the ground seeds of various East Indian plants: *v.t.* to season with the hot spice called pepper; to season with spicy remarks; as, to *pepper* a speech with sarcasms; to shower objects upon; as, to *pepper* with stones.

pep-per-corn (pĕp'ẽr-kôrn"), *n.* the small berry of the pepper plant; hence, anything small or trifling.

pep-per-grass (pĕp'ẽr-gràs"), *n.* a kind of pungent cress.

pep-per-mint (pĕp'ẽr-mĭnt), *n.* a pungent herb; the oil prepared from it; a lozenge flavored with this oil.

pep-per-wort (pĕp'ẽr-wûrt"), *n.* a cress; a plant of the mustard family.

pep-per-y (pĕp'ẽr-ĭ), *adj.* fiery; pungent or sharp; as, a *peppery* dish; a *peppery* temper.

pep-sin (pĕp'sĭn), *n.* a ferment formed in the stomach; a preparation of this substance, sometimes obtained from the stomach of a pig, used in medicine to aid digestion. Also, **pepsine.**

pep-tic (pĕp'tĭk), *adj.* pertaining to or aiding digestion: *pl.* the science of digestion.

per- (pẽr-), a *prefix* meaning through; over the whole extent; by; very: *prep.* by; through; as, *per* diem, by the day. [LAT.]

per-ad-ven-ture (pẽr"ăd-vĕn'tûr; pûr"-ăd-vĕn'tûr), *adv.* and *conj.* perhaps; it may be; supposing; if: *n.* doubt; question; as, I shall prove it to you beyond any *peradventure.*

per-am-bu-late (pẽr-ăm'bū-lāt), *v.t.* to walk through or over, especially to inspect or oversee: *v.i.* to walk or stroll about.

per-am-bu-la-tion (pẽr-ăm"bū-lā'-shŭn), *n.* the act of walking or traveling through or over; an inspection of boundary lines to see that they still exist or are unchanged.

per-am-bu-la-tor (pẽr-ăm'bū-lā"tẽr), *n.* a baby carriage; an instrument for measuring distances traveled over.

per-cale (pẽr-kāl'; pẽr"kăl'), *n.* a cotton fabric with a linen finish, often printed.

per-ceiv-a-ble (pẽr-sēv'á-bl), *adj.* capable of being discerned, or known, by the senses or by the mind.

per-ceive (pẽr-sēv'), *v.t.* to obtain knowledge of by the senses; to see; hear, feel, taste, or smell; understand; as to *perceive* the point of an argument; discern.
Syn. note, observe, distinguish.

per cent (pẽr sĕnt), by the hundred; in the hundred; as, five *per cent* of the people means five people in every hundred: abbreviation of *per centum.* [LAT.]

per-cent-age (pẽr-sĕn'tāj), *n.* a certain part, amount or number of each hundred parts; the duty, interest, etc., on a hundred; that part of arithmetic which deals with computing interest, etc.

per-cept (pûr'sĕpt), *n.* an object as it appears to the senses; opposite to *concept,* a mental impression of an object.

per-cep-ti-bil-i-ty (pẽr-sĕp"tĭ-bĭl'ĭ-tĭ), *n.* the state or quality of being known through the senses.

per-cep-ti-ble (pẽr-sĕp'tĭ-bl), *adj.* that may be known by the senses or may be understood; evident.—*adv.* **perceptibly.**

per-cep-tion (pẽr-sĕp'shŭn), *n.* the act or state of receiving, or ability to receive, knowledge of outside things by means of the senses; idea, or notion.

per-cep-tive (pẽr-sĕp'tĭv), *adj.* having the ability or power to receive knowledge through the senses.—*adv.* **perceptively.**—*n.* **perceptiveness.**

perch (pûrch), *n.* a small, edible, fresh-water fish; a measure of length equal to five and one-half yards, or a surface measure equal to thirty and one-fourth square yards; anything, as a rod or pole, on which birds sit or roost; hence, any high seat: *v.i.* to sit on a high seat; to roost: *v.t.* to place on a roost or on a high seat or support.

per-chance (pẽr-chàns'), *adv.* perhaps; by chance; maybe.

per-cip-i-ent (pẽr-sĭp'ĭ-ĕnt), *adj.* having the power to know through the senses, or to understand.—*n.* **percipience.**

per-co-late (pûr'kō-lāt), *v.t.* to pass, as a liquid, through very small spaces; as, water *percolates* through sand: *v.t.* to cause, as a liquid, to pass through very small spaces; to strain.

per-co-la-tion (pûr"kō-lā'shŭn), *n.* the act of oozing or passing through very small spaces; filtration or straining.

per-co-la-tor (pûr'kō-lā"tẽr), *n.* a filtering or straining machine or vessel; a machine for making coffee by causing boiling water to filter through the ground coffee berries.

per-cus-sion (pẽr-kŭsh'ŭn), *n.* violent collision, or meeting; shock produced by the violent meeting of bodies; the striking of the hammer of a gun upon the cap containing powder; impression of sound on the ear; the medical examination of a part of the body by tapping it gently so as to determine its condition by the sound produced.—*adj.* **percussive.**

per-cus-sion cap (pẽr-kŭsh'ŭn kăp), in a rifle or revolver, a small copper cup attached to the cartridge and containing powder which, when the hammer strikes the cap, explodes and discharges the gun.

per-di-tion (pẽr-dĭsh'ŭn), *n.* total destruction; ruin; utter loss of the soul or of hopes of heaven.

per-e-gri-nate (pĕr'ē-grĭ-nāt), *v.t.* and *v.i.* to journey; to travel.—*n.* **peregrinator.**

per-e-gri-na-tion (pĕr"ē-grĭ-nā'shŭn), *n.* the act of traveling about; a wandering from place to place.

per-emp-to-ry (pĕr'ĕmp-tō-rĭ), *adj.* positive; final; decisive; allowing no discussion; as, a *peremptory* command; stubborn; dictatorial.—*adv.* **peremptorily.**—*n.* **peremptoriness.**

per-en-ni-al (pĕr-ĕn'ĭ-ăl), *adj.* lasting through the year; as, a *perennial* spring of water; lasting more than two years; as, *perennial* plants; enduring; unceasing; as, *perennial* youth: *n.* a plant that lives from year to year.—*adv.* **perennially.**

per-fect (pûr'fĕkt), *adj.* complete; without defect or blemish; as, a *perfect* day; blameless; pure; possessing every moral excellence; as, a *perfect* life; fully skilled or accomplished; as, a *perfect* workman; in grammar, denoting a tense that expresses completed action: *v.t.* (pûr'fĕkt; pĕr-fĕkt'), to make so as to be without fault or lack; complete or finish; as, to *perfect* an invention.—*adv.* **perfectly.**—*n.* **perfecter, perfectness.**

Syn., *adj.* correct, entire, sinless, complete: *v.* correct, finish.

per-fect-i-bil-i-ty (pĕr-fĕk"tĭ-bĭl'ĭ-tĭ), *n.* the ability to become faultless or complete.

per-fect-i-ble (pĕr-fĕk'tĭ-bl), *adj.* able to become faultless or complete.

per-fec-tion (pĕr-fĕk'shŭn), *n.* the state of being without fault or blemish, or of being complete; supreme excellence.

per-fid-i-ous (pĕr-fĭd'ĭ-ŭs), *adj.* false to trust; treacherous; faithless; disloyal; as, a *perfidious* friend.—*adv.* **perfidiously.**

per-fi-dy (pûr'fĭ-dĭ), *n.* treachery; breach of faith; disloyalty.

per-fo-rate (pûr'fō-rāt), *v.t.* to pierce or bore through; make a hole through; as, to *perforate* a wall with a bullet.—*n.* **perforator.**

per-fo-ra-tion (pûr"fō-rā'shŭn), *n.* the act of piercing or boring through; a hole bored through.

per-force (pĕr-fōrs'), *adv.* by force; violently; by necessity.

per-form (pĕr-fôrm'), *v.t.* to do or carry out; execute; achieve; as, to *perform* an operation; to discharge or fulfil; as, to *perform* a duty; to represent, render, or portray; as, to *perform* a part in a play: *v.i.* to act a part; as, to *perform* on the stage; to exhibit in public; as, to *perform* on the piano.—*n.* **performer.**

per-form-ance (pĕr-fôr'măns), *n.* the carrying out of something; as, the *performance* of an undertaking; completion; a thing done; deed or feat; a public exhibition, especially on the stage.

per-fume (pĕr-fūm'), *v.t.* to fill with a pleasant odor; scent: *n.* (pûr'fūm), a pleasing scent or odor, as of flowers, incense, etc.; fragrance; a fragrant mixture prepared to give out a pleasing odor.—*n.* **perfumer.**

per-fum-er-y (pĕr-fūm'ẽr-ĭ), *n.* fragrant mixtures, or sweet odors in general.

per-func-to-ry (pĕr-fŭnk'tō-rĭ), *adj.* done in a half-hearted or careless manner; without interest; done merely to get rid of a duty; careless.—*adv.* **perfunctorily.**—*n.* **perfunctoriness.**

per-go-la (pûr'gō-lȧ), *n.* a latticework covering a walk or veranda and used for climbing plants; an arbor.

per-haps (pĕr-hăps'), *adv.* possibly; perchance; maybe.

pe-ri (pē'rĭ), *n.* in Persian mythology, a fairy or elf, descended from the disobedient angels, and barred out of Paradise.

per-i-anth (pĕr'ĭ-ănth), *n.* the outside envelope of a flower; all the flower leaves taken together.

per-i-car-di-tis (pĕr"ĭ-kär-dī'tĭs), *n.* inflammation or soreness in the membrane that surrounds the heart.

per-i-car-di-um (pĕr"ĭ-kär'dĭ-ŭm), *n.* the membrane that surrounds the heart.—*adj.* **pericardiac, pericardial.**

per-i-cra-ni-um (pĕr"ĭ-krā'nĭ-ŭm), *n.* the tissue that covers the cranium, or skull.

per-i-gee (pĕr'ĭ-jē), *n.* that point in the orbit, or path, of the moon nearest the earth: opposite to *apogee.*

per-i-he-li-on (pĕr"ĭ-hē'lĭ-ŏn), *n.* [*pl.* perihelia (-ȧ)], that point in the orbit, or path, of a planet or comet nearest the sun: opposite to *aphelion.*

per-il (pĕr'ĭl), *n.* exposure to injury; danger; as, he was in great *peril;* risk: *v.t.* to expose to danger or risk.

per-il-ous (pĕr'ĭ-lŭs), *adj.* full of danger; dangerous; involving risk.—*adv.* **perilously.**—*n.* **perilousness.**

per-im-e-ter (pĕr-ĭm'ē-tẽr), *n.* the outer boundary of a plane surface, as the circumference of a circle.

pe-ri-od (pē'rĭ-ŏd), *n.* a definite portion of time the beginning and end of which are fixed; as, the *period* of summer; any space of time, or series of years; as, the *period* of the war; conclusion or end; as, the *period* of his rule was soon reached; a dot [.] to mark the end of a sentence; in rhetoric, a complete sentence.

pe-ri-od-ic (pē'rĭ-ŏd'ĭk), *adj.* pertaining to a definite round of time; happening again and again at definite intervals; occurring regularly, as day and night.

pe-ri-od-i-cal (pē"rĭ-ŏd'ĭ-kăl), *adj.* pertaining to a certain fixed length of time; occurring at regular intervals; as, *periodical* visits; published or appearing at regular stated times, but not daily; pertaining to such publications: *n.* a publication issued at stated times, but not daily, as a magazine.—*adv.* **periodically.**

pe-ri-o-dic-i-ty (pē"rĭ-ō-dĭs'ĭ-tĭ), *n.* the state or quality of occurring regularly.

per-i-os-te-um (pĕr"ĭ-ŏs'tē-ŭm), *n.* the membrane which covers the bones.—*adj.* **periosteal.**

per-i-pa-tet-ic (pĕr"ĭ-pȧ-tĕt'ĭk), *adj.* walking about; **Peripatetic**, pertaining to the philosophy of Aristotle, who taught his disciples while he walked about the Lyceum: *n.* a disciple of Aristotle.

pe-riph-er-y (pē-rĭf'ẽr-ĭ), *n.* [pl. peripheries (-ĭz)], the circumference of a circle, ellipse, or similar figure; the outside of a body; the surface.—*adj.* **peripheral.**

pe-riph-ra-sis (pē-rĭf'rȧ-sĭs), *n.* a roundabout way of speaking; the habit of saying little in many words. Also, **periphrase.**

per-i-phras-tic (pĕr'ĭ-frăs'tĭk), *adj.* roundabout; expressed in more words than are necessary. Also, **periphrastical.**—*adv.* **periphrastically.**

per-i-scope (pĕr'ĭ-skōp), *n.* an instrument consisting of a revolving prism capable of reflecting light from any quarter down an upright tube: used as an outlook over the water for guiding submarine boats when submerged; in the World War, a similar instrument projecting above the parapet of a trench and used as an outlook.

per-ish (pĕr'ĭsh), *v.i.* to lose life or vitality; decay or die; be destroyed or come to nothing.

per-ish-a-bil-i-ty (pĕr'ĭsh-ȧ-bĭl'ĭ-tĭ), *n.* the state of being liable to decay.

per-ish-a-ble (pĕr'ĭsh-ȧ-bl), *adj.* liable to decay; as, *perishable* food.—*adv.* **perishably.**—*n.* **perishableness.**

per-i-stal-tic (pĕr'ĭ-stăl'tĭk), *adj.* pertaining to the peculiar wormlike movement of the intestines by which their contents are forced onwards.

per-i-style (pĕr'ĭ-stīl), *n.* a row of columns surrounding a building or an open court and supporting a roof or cornice.

per-i-to-ne-um (pĕr'ĭ-tō-nē'ŭm), *n.* a thin membrane which lines the abdomen and covers the organs contained in it.—*adj.* **peritoneal.**

per-i-to-ni-tis (pĕr'ĭ-tō-nī'tĭs), *n.* inflammation of the peritoneum, or membrane which lines the abdomen.

per-i-wig (pĕr'ĭ-wĭg), *n.* a headdress of false hair, formerly worn by men as ornament or as a sign of rank.

per-i-win-kle (pĕr'ĭ-wĭn'kl), *n.* a creeping evergreen plant with blue, or sometimes white, flowers; a small shellfish.

per-jure (pûr'jŏŏr), *v.t.* to cause to swear falsely, or to break a vow; to make guilty of false swearing; as, to *perjure* oneself.—*n.* **perjurer.**

per-jur-y (pûr'jŏŏ-rĭ), *n.* the wilful breaking of an oath or solemn promise; the wilful giving, under oath, of false testimony.

perk (pûrk), *v.t.* to make trim or neat: *v.i.* to hold up the head in a saucy manner; to become brisk or jaunty: followed by *up.*

perk-y (pûr'kĭ), *adj.* jaunty; pert; smart; airy; lively.

per-ma-nence (pûr'mȧ-nĕns), *n.* the state or quality of being fixed or lasting.

per-ma-nen-cy (pûr'mȧ-nĕn-sĭ), *n.* quality or state of being fixed or lasting; a thing that is lasting or that cannot be destroyed.

per-ma-nent (pûr'mȧ-nĕnt), *adj.* lasting; fixed; durable; as, a *permanent* building; continuing in the same state.—*adv.* **permanently.**

per-me-a-bil-i-ty (pûr'mē-ȧ-bĭl'ĭ-tĭ), *n.* the state or quality of allowing the passage of fluids through or into; as, the *permeability* of sand to water.

per-me-a-ble (pûr'mē-ȧ-bl), *adj.* capable of allowing fluids to pass through or into; as, sand is *permeable* to water.

per-me-ate (pûr'mē-āt), *v.t.* to pass through the pores or crevices of; as, water *permeates* sand; to spread through or mingle with; pervade; as, the perfume of flowers *permeates* the air.

per-me-a-tion (pûr'mē-ā'shŭn), *n.* the act of passing or spreading through; the state of being pervaded, or filled.

per-mis-si-ble (pĕr-mĭs'ĭ-bl), *adj.* that may be allowed; allowable.—*adv.* **permissibly.**

per-mis-sion (pĕr-mĭsh'ŭn), *n.* the act of allowing; leave; as, he was given *permission* to speak; liberty or freedom given; consent.

per-mis-sive (pĕr-mĭs'ĭv), *adj.* giving consent; not forbidding; unopposed.

per-mit (pĕr-mĭt'), *v.t.* [*p.t.* and *p.p.* permitted, *p.pr.* permitting], to allow by not trying to prevent; to consent to; tolerate; as, to *permit* smoking: *v.i.* to give consent; to allow; as, if the weather *permits*, I shall go: *n.* (pûr'mĭt), a written warrant, or leave, to do something.

per-mu-ta-tion (pûr'mū-tā'shŭn), *n.* the exchange of one thing for another; any one of the ways in which a number of objects, letters, numbers, etc., may be arranged or combined.

per-ni-cious (pĕr-nĭsh'ŭs), *adj.* highly injurious or hurtful; destructive; as, foul air is *pernicious* to health. —*adv.* **perniciously.**—*n.* **perniciousness.**

per-nick-et-y (pĕr-nĭk'ĕt-ĭ), *adj.* trim; attentive to trifles; over-nice; fussily particular. [COLLOQ.]

per-o-ra-tion (pĕr'ō-rā'shŭn), *n.* the end or conclusion of a speech or oration.

per-ox-ide (pĕr-ŏk'sīd), *n.* the oxide, or compound of oxygen with another element, which contains a larger proportion of oxygen than another oxide of the same element. Also, **peroxid.**

per-pen-dic-u-lar (pûr'pĕn-dĭk'ū-lȧr), *adj.* at right angles to a given line or surface; perfectly upright: *n.* an upright line; a line at right angles with another.—*adv.* **perpendicularly.**—*n.* **perpendicularity.**

per-pe-trate (pûr'pē-trāt), *v.t.* to do or perform in a bad sense: as, to *perpetrate* a crime.—*n.* **perpetrator.**

per-pe-tra-tion (pûr'pē-trā'shŭn), *n.* the act of doing something unlawful, as a crime.

per-pet-u-al (pĕr-pĕt'ū-ăl), *adj.* neverceasing; continuous; endless; everlasting; as, *perpetual* motion.—*adv.* **perpetually.**

per-pet-u-ate (pĕr-pĕt'ū-āt), *v.t.* to make everlasting; as, to *perpetuate* the memory of a famous person.

per-pet-u-a-tion (pĕr-pĕt'ū-ā'shŭn), *n.* the act of preserving forever; a causing to last always; continuation.

per-pe-tu-i-ty (pûr'pē-tū'ĭ-tĭ), *n.* the state of being everlasting; endless time; something that lasts forever.

per-plex (pĕr-plĕks'), *v.t.* to make difficult to be understood; make anxious; puzzle; distract; embarrass; confuse.—*p.adj.* **perplexed.**

per-plex-i-ty (pĕr-plĕk'sĭ-tĭ), *n.* state of being anxious, confused, doubtful, or puzzled; embarrassment; that which puzzles or confuses.
Syn. confusion, bewilderment.

per-qui-site (pûr'kwĭ-zĭt), *n.* a gain or profit in addition to regular wages or salary.

per-se-cute (pûr'sē-kūt), *v.t.* to pursue in order to injure or afflict;

to harass or ill-treat, especially because of religious opinions; to annoy; vex.—*n.* **persecutor.**

per-se-cu-tion (pûr″sē-kū′shŭn), *n.* the act of ill-treating or of inflicting unjust pain or punishment; the state of being ill-treated or made to suffer unjustly; repeated injury of any kind.

per-se-ver-ance (pûr″sē-vēr′ăns), *n.* the act or state of persisting, or not giving up; steadfastness; constant effort.

per-se-vere (pûr″sē-vēr′), *v.i.* to persist in any enterprise or business undertaken; continue steadfastly.

Per-sian (pûr′shăn; pûr′zhăn), *adj.* of or pertaining to Persia, its people, or its language: *n.* a native of Persia; the language of Persia.

per-si-flage (pĕr″sē-flŏzh′; pûr′sĭ-flŏzh), *n.* a flippant or thoughtless style of talking or writing; banter.

per-sim-mon (pĕr-sĭm′ŭn), *n.* a tree with a plumlike fruit eatable only after frost; the fruit of the tree.

per-sist (pĕr-sĭst′), *v.i.* to continue steadily in any course commenced; persevere; to continue fixed; endure; as, certain features *persist* in certain races.

per-sist-ence (pĕr-sĭs′tĕns), *n.* perseverance; continuous effort; as, the inventor's *persistence* was crowned with success; obstinacy; lasting quality; endurance. Also, **persistency.**

per-sist-ent (pĕr-sĭs′tĕnt), *adj.* continuing; constant; persevering; as, a *persistent* worker; not falling off; as, a *persistent* rain.—*adv.* **persistently.**

per-son (pûr′sŭn; pûr′sn), *n.* a human being; an individual; one's actual self; the body of a human being; one's shape and looks; as, she is very dainty in *person;* in grammar, a characteristic by which nouns and pronouns indicate, and verbs express the action of, the one speaking (*first person*), spoken to (*second person*), or spoken of (*third person*).

per-son-a-ble (pûr′sŭn-*ȧ*-bl), *adj.* attractive in form and figure; handsome; graceful.

per-son-age (pûr′sŭn-āj), *n.* a man or woman, especially one of distinction.

per-son-al (pûr′sŭn-ăl), *adj.* relating or peculiar to an individual and his private affairs; as, *personal* business; pertaining to the outward appearance or looks; as, *personal* beauty; done by oneself; as, a *personal* greeting; relating to one's character or conduct; as, *personal* remarks; movable; as, *personal* property.—*adv.* **personally.**

per-son-al-i-ty (pûr″sŭn-ăl′ĭ-tĭ), *n.* the sum of one's qualities of body, mind, and character; that which makes one human being different from another; individuality; an offensive remark made about a person, his character, or condition.

per-son-al-ty (pûr′sŭn-ăl-tĭ), *n.* property other than land or buildings; all kinds of movable property, as stocks, bonds, clothing, furniture, etc.

per-son-ate (pûr′sŭn-āt), *v.t.* to act the part of; to imitate; represent falsely.—*n.* **personator.**

per-son-a-tion (pûr″sŭn-ā′shŭn), *n.* the assuming of the character of another; as, an actor's *personation* of a part; the pretending to be some one other than oneself.

per-son-i-fi-ca-tion (pĕr-sŏn″ĭ-fĭ-kā′shŭn), *n.* a striking example of some special quality; as, she is the *personification* of neatness; the act of regarding as a person; a figure of speech that gives to things the qualities of human beings.

per-son-i-fy (pĕr-sŏn′ĭ-fī), *v.t.* [*p.t.* and *p.p.* personified, *p.pr.* personifying], to treat or regard as a person; to give life to (things without life); to be a striking example of.

per-son-nel (pĕr″sŏ″nĕl′; pûr″sŏ-nĕl′), *n.* the persons, as distinguished from the arms, stores, etc., employed in any public service, especially the army and navy.

per-spec-tive (pĕr-spĕk′tĭv), *adj.* pertaining to, or in accordance with, the art of showing, on a surface, objects as they actually appear to the eye: *n.* a vista or distant view; the art of representing objects, on a plane surface, in three dimensions, as they appear to the eye; the effect of distance on the appearance of objects. —*adv.* **perspectively.**

per-spi-ca-cious (pûr″spĭ-kā′shŭs), *adj.* mentally acute or keen; mentally quick-sighted.—*adv.* **perspicaciously.**

per-spi-cac-i-ty (pûr″spĭ-kăs′ĭ-tĭ), *n.* keenness or quickness of sight and brain; mental clear-sightedness.

per-spi-cu-i-ty (pûr-spĭ-kū′ĭ-tĭ), *n.* clearness of thought or expression.

per-spic-u-ous (pĕr-spĭk′ū-ŭs), *adj.* clear to the understanding; plainly expressed; easily understood.—*adv.* **perspicuously.**—*n.* **perspicuousness.**

per-spi-ra-tion (pûr″spĭ-rā′shŭn), *n.* sweat, or the fluid secreted by the sweat glands of the skin.

per-spire (pĕr-spīr′), *v.t.* and *v.i.* to sweat; to throw off or pass off, as a fluid, through the pores of the skin.—*adj.* **perspiratory.**

per-suade (pĕr-swād′), *v.t.* to influence by argument, advice, entreaty, etc.; as, to *persuade* a person to believe or to do something; induce; prevail upon; convince.—*n.* **persuader.**

per-sua-si-ble (pĕr-swā′sĭ-bl), *adj.* capable of being influenced by advice or entreaty; open to conviction. Also, **persuadable.**

per-sua-si-bil-i-ty (pĕr-swā″sĭ-bĭl′ĭ-tĭ), *n.* the capability of being induced or influenced by advice, argument, or entreaty.

per-sua-sion (pĕr-swā′zhŭn), *n.* the act or art of influencing, or the state of being influenced, by argument or entreaty.

per-sua-sive (pĕr-swā′sĭv), *adj.* having power to convince or influence; as, a *persuasive* argument; influencing the will or passion: *n.* that which influences; inducement.—*adv.* **persuasively.** —*n.* **persuasiveness.**

pert (pûrt), *adj.* saucy; forward; bold; as, a *pert* child.—*adv.* **pertly.**—*n.* **pertness.**

per-tain (pĕr-tān′), *v.i.* to belong as a quality, duty, etc.; as, saltness *pertains* to the ocean; joy *pertains* to youth; to have relation to something; as, the telegram *pertains* to business.

per-ti-na-cious (pûr″tĭ-nā′shŭs), *adj.* unyielding; obstinate; resolute; holding stubbornly to any opinion or design; as, a *pertinacious* solicitor.—*adv.* **pertinaciously.**—*n.* **pertinaciousness.**

per-ti-nac-i-ty (pûr"tĭ-năs'ĭ-tĭ), *n.* the quality or state of holding stubbornly to a purpose; unyielding perseverance.

per-ti-nence (pûr'tĭ-nĕns), *n.* suitableness; fitness. Also, **pertinency.**

per-ti-nent (pûr'tĭ-nĕnt), *adj.* fitting or appropriate; to the point; belonging to; as, these remarks are *pertinent* to the subject.—*adv.* **pertinently.**

per-turb (pĕr-tûrb'), *v.t.* to agitate; disturb greatly; disquiet.

per-tur-ba-tion (pûr"tûr-bā'shŭn), *n.* mental disorder; great disquiet of mind; irregular or violent variation.

pe-ruke (pĕ-rōōk'), *n.* a wig, sometimes made to look like a natural head of hair; a periwig. Also, **perruque.**

pe-rus-al (pĕ-rōōz'ăl), *n.* the act of reading carefully; as, the *perusal* of a book.

pe-ruse (pĕ-rōōz'), *v.t.* to read with care and attention; as, to *peruse* a letter.

Pe-ru-vi-an (pĕ-rōō'vĭ-ăn), *adj.* of or pertaining to Peru; as, the *Peruvian* Mountains: *n.* one of the natives of Peru: **Peruvian bark,** a bitter bark, from various South American trees, from which quinine is made.

per-vade (pĕr-vād'), *v.t.* to pass or spread through every part of; as, a perfume *pervades* the air; to spread all over; as, a feeling of content *pervades* the country

per-va-sion (pĕr-vā'zhŭn), *n.* the act of going through or spreading all over.

per-va-sive (pĕr-vā'sĭv), *adj.* tending to pass through or fill every part of; as, a *pervasive* odor; a *pervasive* discontent.—*adv.* **pervasively.**—*n.* **pervasiveness.**

per-verse (pĕr-vûrs'), *adj.* wilfully wrong; set against doing right; obstinate; stubborn; wayward; as, a *perverse* child.—*adv.* **perversely.**—*n.* **perverseness.**

Syn. contrary, fractious.
Ant. (see compliant).

per-ver-sion (pĕr-vûr'shŭn), *n.* a turning from the true meaning or proper purpose; a using for wrong ends; a false form of something.

per-ver-si-ty (pĕr-vûr'sĭ-tĭ), *n.* the state or quality of being set against doing right; disposition to be contrary; stubbornness.

per-ver-sive (pĕr-vûr'sĭv), *adj.* tending to put to a wrong use; having a bad influence.

per-vert (pĕr-vûrt'), *v.t.* to turn from the true end or proper purpose; misapply; mislead; purposely give a wrong meaning to: *n.* (pûr'vĕrt), one who has turned from truth to error.—*p.adj.* **perverted.**—*adj.* **pervertible.**

per-vi-ous (pûr'vĭ-ŭs), *adj.* admitting passage of another substance, as a fluid; as, a *pervious* soil; that may be pierced or seen through.

pes-ky (pĕs'kĭ), *adj.* troublesome; annoying; as, a *pesky* fly. [Colloq.]

pe-so (pā'sō), *n.* the old Spanish dollar, or piece of eight; the Mexican dollar, worth about fifty cents; a Philippine silver coin worth fifty cents. [Span.]

pes-si-mism (pĕs'ĭ-mĭzm), *n.* belief that the world is bad rather than good; a habit of looking on the dark side or of expecting failure: opposite to *optimism.*

pes-si-mist (pĕs'ĭ-mĭst), *n.* one who looks on the worst side of things.

pes-si-mis-tic (pĕs"ĭ-mĭs'tĭk), *adj.* pertaining to, or marked by, the belief that the world is bad rather than good; gloomy.—*adv.* **pessimistically.**

pest (pĕst), *n.* a contagious disease that is widespread at any time, as smallpox; a plague; anything very mischievous, annoying, or injurious.

pes-ter (pĕs'tĕr), *v.t.* to annoy; bother; tease; irritate with little vexations.—*n.* **pesterer.**

pes-tif-er-ous (pĕs-tĭf'ĕr-ŭs), *adj.* carrying disease; mischievous; injurious.—*adv.* **pestiferously.**

pes-ti-lence (pĕs'tĭ-lĕns), *n.* an infectious or contagious disease that is widespread and fatal, as the bubonic plague.

pes-ti-lent (pĕs'tĭ-lĕnt), *adj.* poisonous; deadly; bad for health, morals, or society; making mischief; vexatious.—*adv.* **pestilently.**

pes-ti-len-tial (pĕs"tĭ-lĕn'shăl), *adj.* pertaining to, or causing, a contagious disease, like smallpox; wicked; destructive.

pes-tle (pĕs'l), *n.* a tool for pounding substances in a mortar, or druggist's mixing bowl.

pet (pĕt), *n.* any person or animal that is fondled or caressed; a sudden fit of peevishness or ill-humor: *adj.* favorite; accustomed to fondling and indulgence: *v.t.* [*p.t.* and *p.p.* petted, *p.pr.* petting], to fondle or indulge.

pet-al (pĕt'ăl), *n.* one of the leaves, usually bright-colored, of a blossom.—*adj.* **petaled, petalous.**

pe-tard (pĕ-tärd'), *n.* formerly, a bell-shaped explosive machine used for breaking through walls, bursting open gates, etc.

Pe-ter (pē'tĕr), *n.* in the Bible, one of the Twelve Apostles: called also *Simon* and *Simon Peter;* either of two books of the New Testament, containing his epistles, or letters, to the believers in Christ.—**peter,** *v.i.* to thin out or fail, as a vein or seam of coal; to diminish or lessen: usually with *out.*

pet-i-ole (pĕt'ĭ-ōl), *n.* the slender stem that bears the broad part of a leaf; a leafstalk; in zoölogy, a stalk, or slender part that joins two larger parts of a body, as in ants, wasps, etc.—*adj.* **petiolar, petiolate.**

pet-it (pĕt'ĭ), *adj.* small, insignificant, or inferior: used now only in law; as, *petit* larceny, or theft. Also, **petty.**

pe-tite (pĕ-tēt'), *adj.* having a small, trim figure: said of a woman or girl; little. [Fr.]

pe-ti-tion (pĕ-tĭsh'ŭn), *n.* an earnest request or prayer; a formal request from an inferior to a superior; a paper or document containing a written request: *v.t.* to solicit or ask for earnestly; entreat; pray.—*adj.* **petitionary.**—*n.* **petitioner.**

pet-it ju-ry (pĕt'ĭ jōō'rĭ), in law, a trial jury as distinguished from a grand jury. Also, **petty jury.**

pet-rel (pĕt'rĕl), *n.* a web-footed, strong-winged sea bird which flies far from the land.

pet-ri-fac-tion (pĕt″rĭ-făk′shŭn), *n.* the process of changing animal or vegetable substance into stone; an animal or vegetable body changed into stone; a fossil. Also, **petrification.**—*adj.* **petrifactive.**

pet-ri-fy (pĕt′rĭ-fī), *v.t.* [*p.t.* and *p.p.* petrified, *p.pr.* petrifying], to change into stone; fix in silent amazement or fear; as, to be *petrified* at the approach of danger: *v.i.* to become stone or of a stony hardness.

pet-rol (pĕt′rōl; pĕt′rŏl), *n.* gasoline: so called in Great Britain; a short term for petroleum.

pe-tro-le-um (pē-trō′lē-ŭm), *n.* an inflammable dark yellowish-brown liquid issuing from certain rocks or pumped from the earth; mineral oil.

pet-ti-coat (pĕt′ĭ-kōt), *n.* a loose underskirt worn by women and girls.

pet-ti-fog-ger (pĕt′ĭ-fŏg″ẽr), *n.* a lawyer who practices in small or mean cases, often using dishonest methods.

pet-tish (pĕt′ĭsh), *adj.* fretful; petulant; peevish.—*adv.* **pettishly.**—*n.* **pettishness.**

pet-ty (pĕt′ĭ), *adj.* having little worth; trifling; unimportant; as, a *petty* quarrel.—*adv.* **pettily.**—*n.* **pettiness.**

pet-u-lance (pĕt′ū-lăns), *n.* impatience; fretfulness; snappishness. Also, **petulancy.**

pet-u-lant (pĕt′ū-lănt), *adj.* fretful; peevish; impatient; as, a *petulant* answer.—*adv.* **petulantly.**

pe-tu-ni-a (pē-tū′nĭ-ȧ), *n.* a plant of the nightshade family, with beautiful funnel-shaped flowers.

Petunia

pew (pū), *n.* one of the long, fixed benches in a church.

pe-wee (pē′wē), *n.* a small olive-green bird; the phœbe: so called from its singing note.

pe-wit (pē′wĭt; pū′ĭt), *n.* the lapwing; the black-headed laughing gull; a phœbe, or pewee: so called from its cry.

pew-ter (pū′tẽr), *n.* a metal made of tin and lead, or of tin and some other metal, as copper, antimony, etc.: dishes or utensils made of this metal: *adj.* made of pewter.

pfen-nig (pfĕn′ĭg), *n.* a small copper coin of Germany equal to one-fourth of a cent.

pha-e-ton (fā′ē-tŏn), *n.* a light open four-wheeled carriage.

pha-lanx (fā′lăṅks; făl′ăṅks), *n.* [*pl.* phalanxes], among the ancient Greeks, a company of heavy-armed soldiers drawn up in close rank: hence, any compact body of persons, animals, or things: **phalanges,** (*fȧ*-lăn′jēz), *pl.* the small bones of the fingers and toes.

phan-tasm (făn′tăzm), *n.* a vision or specter; a ghost.—*adj.* **phantasmal.**

phan-tas-ma-go-ri-a (făn-tăz″mȧ-gō′rĭ-ȧ), *n.* a fantastic magic lantern show; a changing group of figures seen as if in a dream.

phan-ta-sy (făn′tȧ-sĭ), *n.* [*pl.* phantasies (-sĭz)], the power to create mental images; the mental image so created.

phan-tom (făn′tŭm), *n.* an apparition; spirit; illusion.

Pha-raoh (fā′rō; fā′rā-ō), *n.* a royal title in ancient Egypt; in the Bible, the name of many of the kings of Egypt.

Phar-i-sa-ic (făr″ĭ-sā′ĭk), *adj.* pertaining to, or like, the Pharisees, a sect of the ancient Jews: **pharisaic,** pretending to be religious without really being so; self-righteous; hypocritical. Also, **pharisaical.**

Phar-i-sa-ism (făr′ĭ-sā-ĭzm), *n.* the doctrines and practices of the Pharisees, a sect of the ancient Jews: **pharisaism,** pretense of religion; self-righteousness; hypocrisy.

Phar-i-see (făr′ĭ-sē), *n.* one of a religious sect among the ancient Jews who paid strict regard to outward forms: **pharisee,** one who observes the letter rather than the spirit of religion.

phar-ma-ceu-tics (făr″mȧ-sū′tĭks), *n.* the science of preparing drugs.—*adj.* **pharmaceutic, pharmaceutical.**

phar-ma-cist (făr′mȧ-sĭst), *n.* one skilled in drugs or in preparing medicines. Also, **pharmaceutist.**

phar-ma-co-pœ-ia (făr″mȧ-kō-pē′yȧ), *n.* an official book of directions for the preparation of medicines; a stock of drugs.

phar-ma-cy (făr′mȧ-sĭ), *n.* the art of preparing and mixing medicines; a drug store.

pha-ros (fā′rŏs), *n.* a lighthouse; a beacon; a watchtower.

phar-ynx (făr′ĭṅks), *n.* a cavity or passage behind the nose, mouth, and larynx, or upper part of the windpipe.—*adj.* **pharyngeal.**

phase (fāz), *n.* [*pl.* phases (fā′zĕz)], a particular aspect or appearance, as, a *phase* of the moon; any of the changing appearances that an object or thing may take; one side or view of a subject. Also, **phasis.**

Chinese Pheasant

pheas-ant (fĕz′ănt), *n.* a large gamebird with brilliant feathers, preserved for sport.

phe-nac-e-tin (fē-năs′ē-tĭn), *n.* a compound used in medicine as a remedy for fever.

Phe-nix (fē′nĭks), *n.* an imaginary bird, said to live five hundred years in the Arabian desert, and, after death by fire, to rise again from its own ashes; hence, the emblem of immortality. Also, **Phœnix.**

phe-nol (fē′nōl; fē′nŏl), *n.* carbolic acid, a substance obtained from coal tar.

phe-nom-e-na (fē-nŏm′ē-nȧ), *n.pl.* of *phenomenon.*

phe-nom-e-nal (fē-nŏm′ē-năl), *adj.* pertaining to, or of the nature of, an outward appearance or happening; remarkable; as, *phenomenal* speed.—*adv.* **phenomenally.**

phe-nom-e-non (fē-nŏm′ē-nŏn), *n.* [*pl.* phenomena (-nȧ)], any natural fact or event that can be seen; an appearance; as, sunrise is a natural *phenomenon;* something strange and uncommon; as, snow in summer or lightning in winter.

phi-al (fī′ăl), *n.* a small glass bottle or vessel; a vial.

phi-lan-der (fĭ-lăn′dẽr), *v.i.* to make light love; to flirt.—*n.* **philanderer.**

phil-an-throp-ic (fĭl″ăn-thrŏp′ĭk), *adj.* loving mankind; benevolent; kind; humane; as, *philanthropic* efforts for peace. Also, **philanthropical.**—*adv.* **philanthropically.**

phi-lan-thro-pist (fĭ-lăn′thrō-pĭst), *n.* one who loves and seeks to benefit mankind.

phi-lan-thro-py (fĭ-lăn′thrō-pĭ), *n.* love of mankind; desire to do good to men; benevolence; a benevolent act or agency.

phi-lat-e-list (fĭ-lăt′ĕ-lĭst), *n.* a collector of postage stamps.

Phi-le-mon (fĭ-lē′mŏn), *n.* a book of the New Testament, containing the epistle, or letter, of Paul, the apostle, to Philemon, a convert to the Christian faith.

phil-har-mon-ic (fĭl″här-mŏn′ĭk), *adj.* loving harmony; fond of music.

Phi-lip-pi-ans (fĭ-lĭp′ĭ-ănz), *n.* a book of the New Testament, containing the letter of Paul to the church at Philippi, in Macedonia.

phi-lip-pic (fĭ-lĭp′ĭk), *n.* an abusive or angry speech: so called from the three speeches of Demosthenes against Philip of Macedon.

Phil-ip-pine (fĭl′ĭ-pĭn; fĭl′ĭ-pēn), *adj.* of or pertaining to the Philippine Islands, in the Pacific Ocean.

Phi-lis-tine (fĭ-lĭs′tĭn; fĭl′ĭs-tĭn), *n.* an ancient inhabitant of the southwestern coast of Palestine; an uncultured person or one of narrow views; one who cares more for material than for intellectual interests: *adj.* pertaining to, or like, the Philistines; narrow-minded; uncultured. —*n.* **Philistinism.**

phil-o-log-i-cal (fĭl″ō-lŏj′ĭ-kăl), *adj.* pertaining to the scientific or historic study of language.

phi-lol-o-gist (fĭ-lŏl′ō-jĭst), *n.* one skilled in the scientific and historic study of language. Also, **philologer.**

phi-lol-o-gy (fĭ-lŏl′ō-jĭ), *n.* the scientific and historic study of language.

phil-o-mel (fĭl′ō-mĕl), *n.* a poetic name for the nightingale.

phil-o-pe-na (fĭl″ō-pē′nȧ), *n.* a social game in which the twin kernels of a nut are eaten; a forfeit, usually a gift, to be paid by one of the eaters on certain conditions; the gift made as a forfeit.

phil-o-pro-gen-i-tive-ness (fĭl″ō-prō-jĕn′ĭ-tĭv-nĕs), *n.* love of offspring or children.

phi-los-o-pher (fĭ-lŏs′ō-fẽr), *n.* a student of the principles that explain or govern facts and events; one noted for calm judgment and practical wisdom.

phil-o-soph-ic (fĭl″ō-sŏf′ĭk), *adj.* pertaining to the principles that govern or explain facts and events; wise; calm; thoughtful. Also, **philosophical.**—*adv.* **philosophically.**

phi-los-o-phize (fĭ-lŏs′ō-fīz), *v.i.* to reason about, or seek the causes or nature of, facts and events.—*n.* **philosophizer.**

phi-los-o-phy (fĭ-lŏs′ō-fĭ), *n.* the knowledge of the principles that cause, control, or explain facts and events; calmness of temper; practical wisdom.

phil-ter (fĭl′tẽr), *n.* a charm or potion supposed to have the power to excite love. Also, **philtre.**

phle-bot-o-my (flē-bŏt′ō-mĭ), *n.* the act or practice of opening a vein to let blood.

phlegm (flĕm), *n.* thick, stringy mucus discharged from the throat; heaviness of disposition; coldness; calmness.

phleg-mat-ic (flĕg-măt′ĭk), *adj.* sluggish; dull; not easily excited; cool; as, a *phlegmatic* temperament. Also, **phlegmatical.**—*adv.* **phlegmatically.**

phlox (flŏks), *n.* any of a variety of well-known bright-colored flowers.

phœ-be (fē′bē), *n.* a crested American fly-catcher; the pewee.

Phœ-bus (fē′bŭs), *n.* in Greek mythology, Apollo: so called as the sun god, and often combined: as, *Phœbus Apollo.*

Phœ-nix (fē′nĭks), *n.* an imaginary bird, said to live five hundred years in the desert of Arabia, and, after being consumed by fire, to rise again, fresh and beautiful, from its own ashes; hence, an emblem of immortality. Also, **Phenix.**

phone (fōn), *n.* and *v.* an abbreviation of *telephone.* [Colloq.]

pho-net-ic (fō-nĕt′ĭk), *adj.* pertaining to the voice or to speech sounds; representing the simple speech sounds; as, to write in a *phonetic* alphabet: *n.pl.* the science of sounds, especially of speech sounds, and of the symbols, or signs, that stand for them. Also, **phonetical.** —*adv.* **phonetically.**

phon-ic (fŏn′ĭk; fō′nĭk), *adj.* of the nature of sounds, usually speech sounds; phonetic; uttered with the voice: *n.pl.* the science of sounds, usually of speech sounds; phonetics.

Phonocinematograph

pho-no-cin-e-mat-o-graph (fō-nō-sĭn-ē-măt′ō-grȧf), *n.* an instrument which combines sight and sound in motion pictures. Also, **kinetophone.**

pho-no-gram (fō′nō-grăm), *n.* the record of sound produced by a phonograph; a written character representing a certain sound.

pho-no-graph (fō′nō-grȧf), *n.* a letter or character indicating a distinct spoken sound; an instrument to record or reproduce speech or sounds.

pho-no-graph-ic (fō″nō-grăf′ĭk), *adj.* pertaining to, or representing, sounds; pertaining to a system of shorthand writing. Also, **phonographical.**—*adv.* **phonographically.**

pho-nog-ra-phy (fō-nŏg′rȧ-fĭ), *n.* a description of sounds uttered by the human voice; a system of shorthand, by which every sound is represented by a separate character or mark. Also, **phonographer.**

pho-nol-o-gy (fō-nŏl′ō-jĭ), *n.* the science of speech sounds, together with their history and their changes.—*adj.* **phonologic, phonological.**—*n.* **phonologist.**

phos-gene (fŏs′jēn), *n.* a compound of carbon monoxide and chlorine:

a deadly gas, used in the World War in gas shells.

phos-phate (fŏs′fāt), *n.* a salt of phosphoric acid; any fertilizer valued for this acid.

phos-phite (fŏs′fīt), *n.* a salt of phosphorous acid.

Phos-phor (fŏs′fŏr), *n.* the morning star, especially the planet Venus; Lucifer.

phos-phor-esce (fŏs″fŏr-ĕs′), *v.i.* to give light without heat, or to shine in the dark.

phos-phor-es-cence (fŏs″fŏr-ĕs′ĕns), *n.* a faint light, given out without heat; the quality of shining in the dark; the act of giving out light without heat.

phos-phor-es-cent (fŏs″fŏr-ĕs′ĕnt), *adj.* shining in the dark; giving out light without heat.

phos-phor-ic (fŏs-fŏr′ĭk), *adj.* pertaining to, like, or obtained from, phosphorus; as, *phosphoric* acid. Also, **phosphorous.**

phos-phor-us (fŏs′fŏr-ŭs; fŏs-fō′rŭs), *n.* a yellowish, waxlike, inflammable substance which gives out light without heat.

phos-phu-ret-ted (fŏs′fū-rĕt″ĕd), *adj.* mixed with phosphorus.

pho-tik (fō′tĭk), *adj.* pertaining to light and the production of light.

pho-to (fō′tō), *n.* and *v.* an abbreviation for *photograph.* [COLLOQ.]

pho-toch-ro-my (fō-tŏk′rō-mĭ; fō″tō-krō′mĭ), *n.* the art or process of photographing in natural colors.

pho-to-en-grav-ing (fō′tō-ĕn-grāv′ĭng), *n.* a process of making reproductions of engraved pictures by photography; a picture so reprinted.

pho-to-graph (fō′tō-grȧf), *n.* a picture produced by exposing to the action of light a plate or film, sensitized, or coated with certain chemicals: *v.t.* to take a picture of, by exposing a sensitized plate or film to the action of the light.—*n.* **photographer.**

pho-to-graph-ic (fō″tō-grăf′ĭk), *adj.* pertaining to, or made by, the exposure of a sensitized plate or film to the action of light; reproducing life or nature in all its details; as, a *photographic* style of painting.—*adv.* **photographically.**

pho-tog-ra-phy (fō-tŏg′rȧ-fĭ), *n.* the art or process of making pictures by the action of light on plates or films coated with certain chemicals.

pho-to-gra-vure (fō″tō-grȧ-vūr′; fō″tō-grā′vūr), *n.* a process for printing pictures from an intaglio plate prepared photographically; a picture so printed.

pho-to-he-li-o-graph (fō″tō-hē′lĭ-ō-grȧf), *n.* an instrument for making pictures of the sun, as during an eclipse, etc.

pho-to-lith-o-graph (fō″tō-lĭth′ō-grȧf), *n.* a print made from a design put upon stone by means of photography.

pho-to-me-chan-i-cal (fō″tō-mē-kăn′ĭ-kăl), *adj.* pertaining to the mechanical printing of pictures from plates made photographically.

pho-tom-e-ter (fō-tŏm′ē-tẽr), *n.* an instrument by which the strength of light is measured.—*n.* **photometry.**—*adj.* **photometric.**

pho-to-phone (fō′tō-fōn), *n.* an instrument for communicating sounds by means of light.

pho-to-play (fō′tō-plā″), *n.* a moving-picture play; a play for exhibition by moving pictures.

pho-to-sphere (fō′tō-sfēr), *n.* the luminous, or shining, envelope of the sun.

pho-to-type (fō′tō-tīp), *n.* a block on whose surface a photograph is reproduced in such a way that from it engravings, etc., can be printed; the process of preparing such a block.

phrase (frāz), *n.* in grammar, a group of related words not containing a subject and a predicate; any brief pithy expression; style or manner of speech: *v.t.* to put into words, especially into suitable words.

phra-se-ol-o-gy (frā″zē-ŏl′ō-jĭ), *n.* style, manner, or peculiarity of expression.

phren-o-log-i-cal (frĕn″ō-lŏj′ĭ-kăl), *adj.* pertaining to the theory that qualities of mind and character are shown by the shape of the head.—*adv.* **phrenologically.**

phre-nol-o-gist (frē-nŏl′ō-jĭst), *n.* one who believes in the theory that the qualities of the mind and character are shown by the shape of the head; one who studies or practices the system of character reading based on this theory.

phre-nol-o-gy (frē-nŏl′ō-jĭ), *n.* a system of character reading based on the theory that the qualities of the mind and character are shown by the form of the skull.

phthis-ic (tĭz′ĭk), *n.* a wasting of the tissues, usually by tuberculosis or consumption. Also, **phthisis.**—*adj.* **phthisical.**

phthi-sis (thī′sĭs), *n.* tuberculosis of the lungs; a wasting of tissues; consumption. Also, **phthisic.**

phy-lac-ter-y (fĭ-lăk′tẽr-ĭ), *n.* [*pl.* phylacteries (-ĭz)], a small square box containing a thin strip of parchment upon which certain texts from the law are inscribed: worn, during prayer, by pious Jews upon the forehead and left wrist.

phys-ic (fĭz′ĭk), *n.* the science of medicine, or the art of healing; medicine in general; a cathartic: *v.t.* [*p.t.* and *p.p.* physicked, *p.pr.* physicking], to give medicine, especially a cathartic, to.

phys-i-cal (fĭz′ĭ-kăl), *adj.* relating to nature or natural science; material as opposed to moral or spiritual; pertaining to the body; as, *physical* weakness.

phy-si-cian (fĭ-zĭsh′ăn), *n.* one skilled in the art of healing and legally qualified to prescribe remedies for diseases; a doctor of medicine.

phys-i-cist (fĭz′ĭ-sĭst), *n.* a student or specialist in the science of matter and energy.

phys-ics (fĭz′ĭks), *n.pl.* the science which treats of matter and energy, including mechanics, heat, light, electricity, etc.

phys-i-og-no-mist (fĭz″ĭ-ŏg′nō-mĭst), *n.* one skilled in the study of character from the face.

phys-i-og-no-my (fĭz″ĭ-ŏg′nō-mĭ), *n.* the art of reading in the face the qualities of the mind; the face; outward appearance.

phys-i-og-ra-phy (fĭz″ĭ-ŏg′rά-fĭ), *n.* physical geography, especially that part which treats of the land.

phys-i-o-log-i-cal (fĭz″ĭ-ō-lŏj′ĭ-kăl), *adj.* pertaining to the science that treats of the life of animals and plants, especially of the human body. Also, **physiologic.**—*adv.* **physiologically.**

phys-i-ol-o-gist (fĭz″ĭ-ŏl′ō-jĭst), *n.* one who is skilled in the study of the life of plants and animals.

phys-i-ol-o-gy (fĭz″ĭ-ŏl′ō-jĭ), *n.* the science that treats of the life of plants and animals; the study of life processes, especially of the work of the organs and tissues in the human body.

phy-sique (fĭ-zēk′), *n.* formation of the body; constitution; appearance; as, a man of powerful *physique.*

pi (pī; pē), *n.* the number (3.1416+) by which the diameter of a circle must be multiplied in order to find the circumference: indicated by the Greek letter π.

pi (pī), *n.* jumbled printing type: *v.t.* to jumble, as type. Also, **pie.**

pi-a ma-ter (pī′ά mā′tẽr), a delicate membrane covering the brain and spinal cord.

pi-a-nis-si-mo (pē″ά-nĭs′ĭ-mō; pyä-nēs′-sē-mō), *adj.* and *adv.* very soft: a musical direction, abbreviated *pp.*

pi-an-ist (pĭ-ăn′ĭst; pē′ά-nĭst), *n.* a performer on the piano.

pi-an-o (pĭ-ăn′ō), *n.* a musical instrument whose tones come from steel wires struck by hammers operated from a keyboard; a pianoforte: *adj.* and *adv.* soft: a musical direction, abbreviated *p.*

pi-an-o-for-te (pĭ-ăn″ō-fôr′tā; pĭ-ăn″ō-fôrt′), *n.* a stringed musical instrument, played by means of keys; a piano.

pi-a-no-la (pĭ-ά-nō′lά), *n.* an apparatus attached to a piano, which plays tunes mechanically.

pi-as-ter (pĭ-ăs′tẽr), *n.* a coin current in Turkey, Egypt, Spain, etc., worth about five cents. Also, **piastre.**

pi-az-za (pĭ-ăz′ά; It. pyät′sä), *n.* in Italy, an open square surrounded by buildings or columns; a walk under a roof surrounded by pillars; in the United States, a veranda.

Pibroch

pi-broch (pē′brŏkh), *n.* the wild, warlike music of the Scottish bagpipes; a bagpipe.

pi-ca (pī′kά), *n.* a size of type (see *type*).

pic-a-dor (pĭk′ά-dōr′), *n.* a horseman who, in a bullfight, incites the bull by pricking it with a lance. [SPAN.]

pic-a-resque (pĭk″ά-rĕsk′), *adj.* pertaining to rascals or vagabonds; having a rogue as hero: said of a kind of fiction.

pic-a-roon (pĭk″ά-rōōn′), *n.* a robber, pirate, or rogue.

pic-a-yune (pĭk″ά-yōōn′), *n.* a small silver coin equal to 6¼ cents, formerly used in the United States; a trifle; a bit; as, it is not worth a *picayune.*

Pic-ca-dil-ly (pĭk″ά-dĭl′ĭ), *n.* a street in London famous for its clubs and shops.

pic-ca-lil-li (pĭk′ά-lĭl″ĭ), *n.* a pickle, or relish, made of finely chopped vegetables and hot spices.

pic-co-lo (pĭk′ō-lō), *n.* a small flute whose notes are an octave higher than the ordinary flute.

pick (pĭk), *n.* a heavy pointed iron tool with a wooden handle; a pickax; a wire or other sharp-pointed instrument; a blow with a pointed instrument; act of choosing; choice or selection; as, take your *pick;* the best of anything; as, the *pick* of the lot: *v.t.* to strike with a sharp instrument, or with the beak; pierce or peck; as, to *pick* a hole; open by an instrument; as, to *pick* a lock; lift: used with *up;* as, to *pick* up something fallen; pluck or gather; as, to *pick* berries; separate with the fingers; as, to *pick* rags; bring about intentionally; as, to *pick* a quarrel; choose or select; as, *pick* the best one; clean or clear of something, as, to *pick* a chicken; rob; as, to *pick* a pocket; pull or twitch the strings of; as, to *pick* a banjo: *v.i.* to eat slowly and daintily; pilfer; as, to *pick* and steal; to choose carefully; as, to *pick* one's way.

pick-a-back (pĭk′ά-băk″), *adv.* on the shoulders like a pack; as, to carry a child *pickaback.*

pick-a-nin-ny (pĭk′ά-nĭn″ĭ), *n.* [*pl.* pickaninnies (-ĭz)], a negro baby or child. Also, **piccaninny.**

pick-ax (pĭk′ăks″), *n.* a tool for digging, having a wooden handle and a heavy iron head pointed at the ends, or pointed at one end and broad at the other. Also, **pickaxe.**

picked (pĭkt), *p.adj.* chosen; carefully selected; as, a company of *picked* men; caused purposely; as, a *picked* quarrel.

Pickerel

pick-er-el (pĭk′ẽr-ĕl), *n.* an American fish of the pike family, smaller than the pike; sometimes, the pike.

pick-er-el weed (pĭk′ẽr-ĕl wēd), a plant with spikes and blue flowers that grows in shallow water.

pick-et (pĭk′ĕt), *n.* an upright pointed stake, used in making fences, for fastening a horse, etc.; a military guard, consisting of not more than half a company, stationed at a given place to prevent surprise by an enemy; one or more persons appointed by a trades-union to watch a factory, etc., where nonunion men are employed during a strike; hence, any person or persons appointed by an organization to watch at a given place for any purpose; as, the woman's suffrage *pickets* at the White House: *v.t.* to fence with pointed stakes; fasten to a stake; as, to *picket* a horse; to watch or guard; as, to *picket* a certain position; to place on guard; as, to *picket* men for duty: *v.i.* to serve as a picket.

pick-le (pĭk′l), *n.* brine, or a mixture of salt and water, used for preserving food; vinegar; vegetables, etc., preserved in brine or in vinegar; embarrassment or difficulty: *v.t.* to preserve in, or as in, brine, or strong salt water, or in vinegar.

pick-pock-et (pĭk′pŏk″ĕt), *n.* one who steals from the pocket of another.

pic-nic (pĭk′nĭk), *n.* a short trip into the country, etc., by a pleasure party carrying its own food: *v.i.* [*p.t.* and *p.p.* picnicked, *p.pr.* picnicking], to go on, or hold an outdoor pleasure party.—*n.* **picnicker.**

pic-ric ac-id (pĭk′rĭk ăs′ĭd), an intensely bitter, yellow acid formed by the action of nitric acid on phenol, etc., and used as a dye and in explosives; carbazotic acid.

pic-to-graph (pĭk′tō-grȧf), *n.* a drawing or crude figure which expresses an idea; a hieroglyphic; a specimen of the picture writing of certain ancient peoples.

pic-to-ri-al (pĭk-tō′rĭ-ăl), *adj.* pertaining to, of the nature of, shown by, or containing, pictures; as, a *pictorial* magazine; vividly described.—*adv.* **pictorially.**

pic-ture (pĭk′tûr), *n.* a painting, drawing, etc., of a person, object, scene, or incident; a likeness or image; as, she is the *picture* of her mother; a mental image; as, to have in one's mind a *picture* of future happiness; bodily representation; as, he was the *picture* of despair; vivid showing or description in words: *v.t.* to represent in a painting, drawing, etc.; to describe vividly in words; to form a mental image of.

Syn., *n.* engraving, print, representation, illustration.

pic-tur-esque (pĭk″tûr-ĕsk′), *adj.* giving a vivid impression, as a picture does; suitable to be drawn or painted as a picture; as, a *picturesque* cottage; graphic; as, *picturesque* language; having wild, rugged, or irregular beauty; romantic; as, *picturesque* scenery: *n.* that which has wild, rugged, or irregular beauty.—*adv.* **picturesquely.**—*n.* **picturesqueness.**

pidg-in Eng-lish (pĭj′ĭn ĭn′glĭsh), a corrupt form of English used by the Chinese in their commercial dealings with foreigners. Also, **pigeon English.**

pie (pī), *n.* an article of food made of meat, fruit, etc., baked between two pastry crusts or on one lower crust; the magpie; printer's type confusedly mixed; a jumble or mess.

pie-bald (pī′bôld″), *adj.* having patches of different colors, especially black and white or brown and white; as, a *piebald* horse; party-colored.

piece (pēs), *n.* a part of anything; a fragment; as, a *piece* of bread; a plot or division; as, a *piece* of land; a certain quantity; as, a *piece* of cloth; a single object of a group; as, each *piece* in the set; literary or artistic composition; as, a *piece* of music; a separate performance; as, a bad *piece* of business; coin; as, a *piece* of money; gun; as, a field *piece*, or cannon: *v.t.* to enlarge or mend by adding a patch or portion; as, to *piece* a breadth in a skirt; to make by joining sections together; as, to *piece* a quilt; patch: *v.i.* to fit or join.

piece-meal (pēs′mēl″), *adj.* made of small portions or parts; fragmentary: *adv.* in portions or parts; by degrees; gradually.

piece-work (pēs′wûrk″), *n.* work done by the piece or job: opposite to *timework*, or work paid for at so much per hour, day, etc.

pied (pīd), *adj.* many-colored or spotted; piebald.

pie-plant (pī′plănt″), *n.* the garden rhubarb.

pier (pēr), *n.* a mass of masonry supporting an arch, bridge, etc.; any other such support, as of iron or timbers, of a bridge or other building; a projecting part of a wall, such as a buttress; a mole, wharf, or dock for vessels; a landing place.

pierce (pērs), *v.t.* to run into or through, especially with a pointed instrument; affect deeply; as, to *pierce* the heart with sorrow; to force a way through; as, the bullet *pierced* his side; to *pierce* the lines of the enemy; to see through mentally; as, to *pierce* a mystery; dive into: *v.i.* to enter.

pierc-ing (pēr′sing), *adj.* cutting; penetrating; keen; as, a *piercing* look or cry.

pier glass (pēr glȧs), a large high mirror, especially one between windows.

pi-e-tism (pī′ĕ-tĭzm), *n.* a kind of religious thought which holds that devotional ardor should be sought by Christians rather than intellectual grasp of creeds, doctrines, etc.; affected religious devotion or goodness; a reform in the Lutheran Church in the latter part of the seventeenth century.

pi-e-ty (pī′ĕ-tĭ), *n.* the quality of being very religious; reverence for and duty towards God; honor and obedience to parents; as, filial *piety*.

pig (pĭg), *n.* a domestic animal of the hog kind, fattened for its meat; a swine, especially a young one; colloquially, a greedy or selfish person; an oblong mass of unforged metal, as of iron, formed by running into molds when melted: *v.i.* to bring forth, or to act like, swine.—*adj.* **piggish.**—*n.* **piggishness.**

pi-geon (pĭj′ŭn), *n.* a well-known bird with a stout body, short legs, and long wings; a dove.

pi-geon-hole (pĭj′ŭn-hōl″), *n.* a small, open, boxlike space in a desk, case, etc., for documents, letters, etc.: *v.t.* to place, as letters, in such a boxlike space; lay aside and forget; shelve.

pi-geon-toed (pĭj′ŭn-tōd″), *adj.* having the toes turned inwards.

pi-geon-wing (pĭj′ŭn-wĭng″), *n.* a dancing step in which the dancer jumps, striking his heels together.

pig-ger-y (pĭg′ĕr-ĭ), *n.* a place for keeping or raising pigs.

pig-head-ed (pĭg′hĕd″ĕd), *adj.* stupidly obstinate or stubborn.

pig-ment (pĭg′mĕnt), *n.* a coloring matter; any powder that mixed with a liquid makes paint; the coloring matter in animals and plants.—*adj.* **pigmentary.**

Pig-my (pĭg′mĭ), *n.* in classical antiquity, one of a race of dwarfs; one of a race of very small Africans: **pigmy,** a dwarf; any extremely small person or animal; a person of very small intelligence: *adj.* dwarfish; very small. Also, **Pygmy.**

pig-nut (pĭg′nŭt″), *n.* the sweetish-bitter nut of a species of hickory; the ground chestnut.

pig-skin (pĭg′skĭn″), *n.* leather made from the hide of a pig; the hide itself.

pig-sty (pĭg′stī″), *n.* a pen for pigs; a piggery.

pig-tail (pĭg′tāl″), *n.* hair twisted into the form of a long strand or plait, and hanging down from the back of the head; a long twist of tobacco.

pike (pīk), *n.* formerly, a weapon consisting of a long wooden shaft with a spearhead at one end; a spike, or sharp point, as in the center of a shield; a fresh-water fish with a narrow, long, pointed head; a road on which a charge is made for driving; a turnpike or toll road; any main road.

pike-staff (pīk′stȧf″), *n.* a pole or shaft with a spike at the end, carried by mountaineers, etc., to keep from slipping.

pi-las-ter (pĭ-lăs′tẽr), *n.* a square column or pillar, partly inserted in a wall.

Pi-late (pī′lăt), *n.* the surname, or last name, of Pontius Pilate, the Roman governor under whom Christ was crucified.

pil-chard (pĭl′chărd), *n.* a sea fish, resembling the herring, found chiefly on the coasts of Devon and Cornwall, England; the sardine.

pile (pīl), *n.* a large beam driven into the ground to make a firm foundation; a mass or heap; as, a *pile* of sand; colloquially, a great quantity; a collection; a large building; a series of metal plates arranged to produce an electric current; nap of cloth; slang, a fortune: *v.t.* to throw into a heap; as, to *pile* stone; to collect and arrange; as, to *pile* bricks; accumulate or collect; as, to *pile* up wealth; build; drive beams into: *v.i.* to form a mass or heap; collect.

pil-fer (pĭl′fẽr), *v.t.* and *v.i.* to steal in small amounts.—*n.* pilferer.

pil-grim (pĭl′grĭm), *n.* a traveler; one who travels from a distance to visit some sacred place or shrine: Pilgrims, the Puritans who settled in Massachusetts in 1620.

pil-grim-age (pĭl′grĭ-măj), *n.* a long journey, especially to some sacred place; man's life considered as a journey.

pill (pĭl), *n.* medicine prepared in the form of a small ball; a pellet; something disagreeable that must be accepted.

pil-lage (pĭl′āj), *n.* the act of plundering, or robbing openly, especially in war; spoil: *v.t.* to plunder, or rob openly; to spoil; lay waste.—*n.* pillager.

pil-lar (pĭl′ẽr), *n.* a column to support a structure or to serve as a monument; any firm, slender, upright support.

pill box (pĭl bŏks), a small fort for defensive warfare, constructed of concrete and steel, and containing small cannon and machine guns: first used by the Germans in the World War, and by them placed at irregular intervals between the first and second line trenches.

pil-lion (pĭl′yŭn), *n.* a pad put on the back of a horse behind a man's saddle so that a second person may ride: formerly much used for women.

pil-lo-ry (pĭl′ō-rĭ), *n.* [*pl.* pillories (-ĭz)], a wooden frame supported by an upright post, and having holes through which the head and hands of a person standing exposed to public disgrace may be passed and secured: *v.t.* to punish by putting in such a framework; expose to public disgrace or abuse.

pil-low (pĭl′ō), *n.* a case filled with feathers, etc., to support the head of a person lying down; any rest for the head: *v.t.* to place or lay on a head-rest.

Pillow Block

pil-low block (pĭl′ō blŏk), a support for a shaft which drives machinery.

pi-lot (pī′lŭt), *n.* one who steers a vessel; one licensed to conduct a vessel in or out of a port or in waters where sailing is difficult or dangerous; one qualified to fly a balloon, airship, or flying machine; the cowcatcher of a locomotive; a guide; a mechanical regulating device: *v.t.* to direct the course of, as a vessel or airship; to steer; to guide through difficulties.

pi-lot-age (pī′lŭt-āj), *n.* the act or business of conducting vessels in or out of a port or through dangerous waters; the fee paid for such service; the act of guiding or steering.

pi-lot bal-loon (pī′lŭt bă-lōōn′), a small balloon, launched unmanned ahead of a larger balloon, to show the direction and strength of the wind.

Pilot-fish

pi-lot-fish (pī′lŭt-fĭsh′), *n.* a fish which often accompanies sharks.

pi-lot light (pī′lŭt līt), a small, fixed, continuously burning gas flame used to ignite a larger gas flame.

pi-men-to (pĭ-mĕn′tō), *n.* allspice or the allspice tree; the Spanish sweet pepper. Also, pimiento.

pim-per-nel (pĭm′pẽr-nĕl), *n.* any one of various plants of the primrose family, with white, purple, or scarlet flowers.

pim-ple (pĭm′pl), *n.* a small swelling of the skin containing pus.

pim-pled (pĭm′pld), *adj.* having, or full of, small swellings of the skin. Also, pimply.

pin (pĭn), *n.* a short piece of wire with a sharp point at one end and a round head at the other, used for fastening together papers, clothing, etc.; a larger, pointed instrument of similar nature, used for holding the hair, the hat, etc.; as, a scarf *pin;* an ornament, badge, or jewel fitted with a pin and a clasp; as, a school *pin;* a bolt or peg; wooden roller; as, a rolling-*pin;* anything of small value: *v.t.* [*p.t.* and *p.p.* pinned, *p.pr.* pinning], to fasten with, or as with, a pin; inclose; seize and hold.

pin-a-fore (pĭn′á-fōr′), *n.* a loose sleeveless apron or covering to protect the clothing of a child or little girl.

pince-nez (păns′nā′), *n.* eyeglasses kept on the nose by a spring. [Fr.]

pin-cers (pĭn′sẽrz), *n.* an instrument with two handles and two jaws working on a pivot, used for gripping things; nippers. Also, pinchers.

pinch (pĭnch), *v.t.* to squeeze or nip between two hard edges; as, to *pinch* a finger; to press on so as to hurt; as, the shoe *pinches* my toe; oppress or distress; make thin or wan; as, to be *pinched* with hunger: *v.i.* to press hard; as, my shoe *pinches;* be mean or miserly: *n.* a squeeze or nip, as with the fingers and thumb; painful pressure; as, the *pinch* of poverty; a sudden difficulty or necessity; as, to do it at a *pinch;* as much as can be held between the thumb and finger; as, a *pinch* of salt.

pinch-beck (pĭnch′bĕk), *n.* a cheap imitation of gold made of copper, zinc, and tin: used in cheap jewelry; anything cheap or sham.

pinch-ers (pĭn′chẽrz), *n.* an instrument with two handles and two jaws, used for gripping things; nippers. Also, pincers.

pin-cush-ion (pĭn′kŏŏsh′ŭn), *n.* a small cushion used for holding pins.

pine (pīn), *n.* a cone-bearing tree with needlelike leaves; timber of the tree: *v.i.* to grow thin and weak from distress.

anxiety, etc.; as, to *pine* away and die: to long intensely; as, to *pine* for home, friends, etc.

pine-ap-ple (pīn'ăp'l), *n.* a tropical plant bearing a fruit that looks somewhat like a pine cone; the eatable juicy fruit of this plant.

pin-feath-er (pĭn'fĕth'ẽr), *n.* a feather just beginning to grow.

pin-foot-ed (pĭn'fo͝ot'ĕd), *adj.* having the toes or feet bordered by a very thin skin, or membrane, as those of a bird.

pin-head (pĭn'hĕd'), *n.* the head of a pin; hence, anything very small and trifling.

pin-hole (pĭn'hōl'), *n.* a very small hole made by, or as by, a pin.

Pinion and Gear

pin-ion (pĭn'yŭn), *n.* the last joint of a bird's wing; a wing; a feather; a small, toothed wheel acting with a larger wheel: *v.t.* to bind or cut the wings of; as, to *pinion* a bird; to bind or hold fast the arms of; confine or fetter.

pink (pĭnk), *n.* a very light-red color; a garden flower with sharp-pointed leaves and a sweet, spicy fragrance: in its most highly developed form called the *carnation;* a narrow-sterned vessel; anything of supreme excellence; as, her manners are the *pink* of perfection: *adj.* of a very light-red color: *v.t.* to stab; pierce or punch with small round holes; work in eyelet holes; scallop the edge of, as cloth, by cutting with an iron tool called a pinking iron; prick, as with a sword.

pink eye (pĭnk ī), a contagious inflammation of the eye, marked by redness of the eyeball; acute conjunctivitis.

pink-ing (pĭnk'ĭng), *n.* a method of ornamenting dress materials or leather by scalloping or cutting the edges into wavy lines: **pinking iron**, a small tool with a curved sharp edge at one end, used for cutting scallops on the edge of fabrics.

pin mon-ey (pĭn mŭn'ĭ), money allowed to a wife by her husband for her private expenses: originally, for buying pins.

pin-nace (pĭn'ās), *n.* a small, light, schooner-rigged vessel with oars; an eight-oared man-of-war's boat.

pin-na-cle (pĭn'ȧ-kl), *n.* a small tower or turret above the rest of a building; a high point like a spire; the highest point; as, the *pinnacle* of fame: *v.t.* to furnish with small towers or turrets.

pin-nate (pĭn'āt), *adj.* shaped like a feather: said of a leaf; divided into leaflets along a common stem. Also, **pinnated.**

pin-o-chle (pē'nŏ-kl; pĭn'ō-kl), *n.* a game of cards. Also, **pinocle.**

pint (pīnt), *n.* one-eighth of a gallon or one-half a quart, dry measure.

pin-tail (pĭn'tāl'), *n.* a duck with a pointed tail.

pin-tle (pĭn'tl), *n.* a pin upon which anything turns, as a hinge.

pin-to (pĭn'tō), *adj.* mottled; pied; as, a *pinto* horse: *n.* a mottled animal.

pi-o-neer (pī'ō-nēr'), *n.* one who goes before to prepare the way for another, as a settler in a frontier country; a soldier in an engineer corps whose special work is road building and repairing: *v.i.* to prepare a way; to open up a road: *v.t.* to take the lead in.

pi-ous (pī'ŭs), *adj.* showing reverence for God; religious; devout; as, *pious* people; done under pretense of religion; as, a *pious* fraud.—*adv.* **piously.**

pip (pĭp), *n.* the seed of certain fruit; as, an orange *pip;* a disease of chickens; a spot on a playing card: *v.i.* [*p.t.* and *p.p.* pipped, *p.pr.* pipping], to cry like a chicken or small bird.

pipe (pīp), *n.* any long hollow tube; as, iron *pipe;* a tube of clay, wood, etc., with a bowl at one end for smoking tobacco; as much tobacco as the bowl will hold; a wine measure equal to two hogsheads, or 105 imperial gallons, or 126 wine-gallons; a high-pitched voice; as, the *pipe* of a child; the note or call of a bird or insect; a musical wind instrument consisting of a hollow tube, as a flute: *pl.* the bagpipe: *v.t.* to play on a musical wind instrument; as, to *pipe* a tune; to utter in a high key; as, to *pipe* a song; to furnish with pipes, or tubes, as to *pipe* a house for water; to carry through a tube; as, to *pipe* water into a city: *v.i.* to play on the musical instrument called a pipe; to utter a shrill sound; to whistle.

pipe clay (pīp klā), grayish-white clay, used for making pipes and in various industrial processes.

pip-er (pīp'ẽr), *n.* one who plays on a musical wind instrument; especially, a Scottish bagpiper.

pi-pette (pĭ-pĕt'), *n.* a small tube of glass or metal, for removing small portions of fluid.

pip-ing (pīp'ĭng), *adj.* feeble, weak, shrill; playing upon a musical instrument called a pipe; hot, like boiling water; as, *piping* hot dishes; like the quiet music of wind instruments rather than the loud sounds of brass and drums; as, the *piping* times of peace: *n.* the music of a musical wind instrument called a pipe; the act of playing on it; a system of tubes for drainage, etc.; corded trimming for dresses.

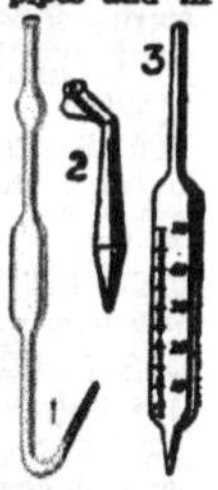

Pipettes. 1, cylindrical, bent; 2, taper; 3, graduated.

pip-it (pĭp'ĭt), *n.* a small bird, similar to the lark, which sings as it flies.

pip-kin (pĭp'kĭn), *n.* a small earthen jar or pot.

pip-pin (pĭp'ĭn), *n.* any one of several varieties of apple.

pip-sis-se-wa (pĭp-sĭs'ē-wȧ), *n.* an evergreen plant the leaves of which are used as a tonic.

pi-quan-cy (pē'kăn-sĭ), *n.* the state or quality of being sharp or pungent to the taste, or of arousing curiosity or interest.

pi-quant (pē'kănt), *adj.* agreeably sharp to the taste; exciting interest because of smartness or cleverness; lively; as, a *piquant* glance or smile; sharp or cutting to the feelings; severe; as, *piquant* criticism.—*adv.* **piquantly.**

pique (pēk), *n.* slight anger or resentment; wounded pride: *v.t.* to wound the pride of; irritate; displease; to pride or value (oneself); as, to *pique* oneself on doing something very well; to stir or prick; as, to *pique* the curiosity.

Syn., *n.* offense, resentment, grudge.

Ant. (see approval).

pi-qué (pē-kā'), *n.* a heavy ribbed or figured cotton cloth.

pi-quet (pē-kĕt'), *n.* a card game played by two persons.

pi-ra-cy (pī'rȧ-sĭ), *n.* robbery upon the sea; the using of another's literary work without permission.

pi-rate (pī'rāt), *n.* a robber on the high seas; one who uses another's literary work without permission and claims it as his own product; one who joins an army engaged in war, without regular standing in the ranks or as an officer, and who fights only off and on, returning home in the intervals: *v.t.* and *v.i.* to rob at sea; to take and publish without permission or payment.—*adj.* piratic, piratical.—*adv.* piratically.

pi-rogue (pĭ-rōg'), *n.* a canoe formed of a dugout log; any canoe.

pir-ou-ette (pĭr'ōō-ĕt'), *n.* a whirling or turning about on the toes; a turning of a horse on the same ground: *v.i.* to whirl or turn rapidly in one spot.

pis-ca-to-ry (pĭs'kȧ-tō-rĭ), *adj.* pertaining to fishes or fishing; living by fishing. Also, piscatorial.

Pis-ces (pĭs'ēz), *n.pl.* the twelfth sign of the zodiac, or the Fishes.

pis-ci-cul-ture (pĭs'ĭ-kŭl"tūr), *n.* the artificial breeding and rearing of fishes.—*adj.* piscicultural.

pish (pĭsh), *interj.* an exclamation of contempt or disgust: *v.i.* to express contempt.

pis-ta-chi-o (pĭs-tä'shĭ-ō), *n.* a nut the greenish almond-flavored kernel of which is used for flavoring; a small tree of Asia and southern Europe that bears the nut.

pis-til (pĭs'tĭl), *n.* the seed-bearing organ in the center of a flower.—*adj.* pistillate.

pis-tol (pĭs'tŭl), *n.* a small, short gun intended for use with one hand; a revolver.

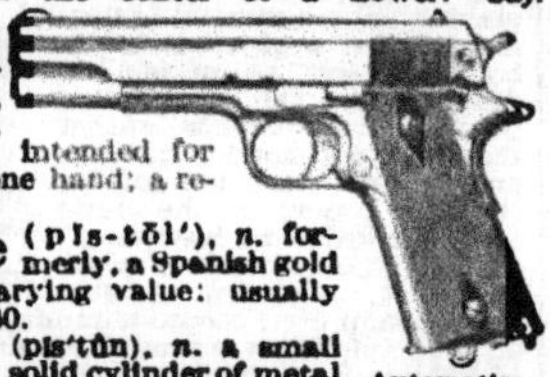

Automatic Pistol

pis-tole (pĭs-tōl'), *n.* formerly, a Spanish gold coin of varying value: usually about $3.60.

pis-ton (pĭs'tŭn), *n.* a small solid cylinder of metal or wood, fitting exactly and moving up and down in the barrel of a pump, or in the cylinder of a steam engine.

pis-ton rod (pĭs'tŭn rŏd), the rod which moves a sliding piece in a machine and connects it with the outside machinery; as, the *piston rod* of a locomotive.

pit (pĭt), *n.* a deep hole in the earth; an abyss; the shaft of a mine; a hole used for trapping wild animals; in England, the cheap part of the ground floor of a theater; an inclosed space in which animals are set to fight each other; as, a cock*pit*; in the United States, that part of a commercial exchange set aside for some special business; as, the wheat *pit*; a hollow part of the body; as, the arm*pit*; a small hole left, as by smallpox; Hades: with *the*; in the United States, the kernel of certain fruits, as the cherry or plum: *v.t.* [*p.t.* and *p.p.* pitted, *p.pr.* pitting], to mark with small hollows or holes; to match or set to fight against another; as, to *pit* one's strength against another; to *pit* one dog against another; place in a pit or hole.

pit-a-pat (pĭt'ȧ-păt"), *adv.* with quick beating; flutteringly; as, my heart went *pitapat*: *n.* a succession of light, quick sounds or taps; as, the *pitapat* of the rain.

pitch (pĭch), *n.* the solid black sticky substance obtained from boiled tar; a plunging forward or down; as, a headlong *pitch* from a rock; tossing motion, as of a ship in a storm; degree or rate; as, the highest *pitch* of excitement; slope; as, the *pitch* of a roof; the degree of a musical note, or the tone of a voice; distance between the centers of two gear teeth; at cricket, the distance between the wickets; the act or manner of throwing or tossing; a cast: *v.t.* to smear with boiled tar; throw or fling; cast headlong; set to a keynote; to fit, or set in order; fix in or on the ground; as, to *pitch* a tent: *v.i.* to settle; fall headlong; as, to *pitch* forward; encamp; rise and fall, as a ship; fix the choice: with *upon*.

pitch-blende (pĭch'blĕnd"), *n.* a lustrous black mineral, a chief source of radium, and used in coloring glass a pale sea-green.

pitch-er (pĭch'ẽr), *n.* one who throws or casts; a vessel for holding and pouring liquids, usually with a handle; in baseball, the player who throws the ball.

pitch-er plant (pĭch'ẽr plănt), a plant whose leaves are formed in the shape of a pitcher.

pitch-fork (pĭch'fôrk"), *n.* a pronged fork for tossing hay, straw, etc.: *v.t.* to lift or throw with, or as with, a pitchfork.

pitch pipe (pĭch pīp), a small pipe, sounded by the mouth, giving a standard musical note.

pitch wheel (pĭch hwēl), a toothed wheel that works in another.

pitch-y (pĭch'ĭ), *adj.* like, or smeared with, a tar substance called pitch; dark; black; dismal; as, a *pitchy* night.—*n.* pitchiness.

pit-e-ous (pĭt'ē-ŭs), *adj.* exciting sorrow or sympathy; mournful; sad.—*adv.* piteously.—*n.* piteousness.

Syn. doleful, woeful, rueful.

Ant. (see joyful).

pit-fall (pĭt'fôl"), *n.* a hole lightly covered, so that wild beasts may fall into it; a trap; a source of danger or temptation.

pith (pĭth), *n.* the soft spongy substance in the center of the stem of some plants; marrow; energy or force; vigor; as, he lacks *pith*; substance; as, the *pith* of his speech.

pith-y (pĭth'ĭ), *adj.* of the nature of, or full of, the soft spongy substance called pith; forcible; as, a *pithy* saying.—*adv.* pithily.—*n.* pithiness.

pit-i-a-ble (pĭt'ĭ-ȧ-bl), *adj.* deserving sympathy; as, he was in a *pitiable* condition; contemptible.—*adv.* pitiably.

pit-i-ful (pĭt'ĭ-fōōl), *adj.* miserable; sad; as, a *pitiful* sight; insignificant or small; as, a *pitiful* amount; paltry; contemptible; as, a *pitiful* ambition.—*adv.* pitifully.—*n.* pitifulness.

pit-i-less (pĭt'ĭ-lĕs), *adj.* without sympathy or mercy; as, war is *pitiless*; merciless.—*adv.* pitilessly.—*n.* pitilessness.

pit saw (pĭt sô), a two-handled saw. Also, pitsaw.

pit-tance (pĭt'ăns), *n.* a small allowance, especially of money.

pit-ted (pĭt'ĕd), *p.adj.* marked with holes or small hollows; as, *pitted* with smallpox.

pit-y (pĭt'ĭ), *n.* a feeling of sorrow for the suffering or distress of others; compassion; mercy; a reason for regret or grief: *v.t.* [*p.t.* and *p.p.* pitied, *p.pr.* pitying], to sympathize with; to feel sorry for: *v.i.* to be merciful or filled with compassion, as for the poor.

Syn., *n.* sympathy, commiseration.
Ant. (see cruelty).

piv-ot (pĭv'ŭt), *n.* a fixed pin or short shaft on which anything turns: *v.t.* to place on, or supply with, such a fixed pin or shaft: *v.i.* to turn on, or as on, such a fixed pin.

pix (pĭks), *n.* in the Roman Catholic Church, the box in which the Host, or consecrated wafer, is kept. Also, **pyx**.

pix-y (pĭk'sĭ), *n.* [*pl.* pixies (-ĭz)], in old folk tales, a fairy. Also, **pixie**.

pla-ca-bil-i-ty (plā'kȧ-bĭl'ĭ-tĭ), *n.* the state of being calmed, pacified, or willing to forgive; the quality of being yielding. Also, **placableness**.

pla-ca-ble (plā'kȧ-bl), *adj.* that may be calmed or pacified; willing to forgive; yielding.—*adv.* **placably**.

plac-ard (plăk'ärd; plȧ-kärd'), *n.* a printed bill or notice posted on a wall, etc., as an advertisement; a poster: *v.t.* (plȧ-kärd'; plăk'ärd), to advertise by a bill posted on a wall, etc.; to post bills on.

pla-cate (plā'kāt), *v.t.* to cause to change from anger to patience or kindness; to pacify; appease; make friendly.

place (plās), *n.* a special spot or locality; an open space or square in a city; a situation; as, a *place* as clerk; site; a building devoted to a special purpose; as, a *place* of business; a city, town, etc.; room; as, make *place* for him; duty; as, it is your *place* to do your best; passage in writing or in a book; as, I have lost my *place*; space belonging to a given body; as, to get out of *place*; a *place* in line; social position; as, keep your *place*: *v.t.* to put in a particular spot or position; settle; establish; to put in office; put out at interest; in baseball, cricket, tennis, etc., to bat or strike (the ball) to a point where it cannot be readily reached by the opposing players.

Syn., *n.* position, post, situation, station; *v.* post, station, dispose.

plac-er (plăs'ẽr), *n.* a deposit of earth, sand, etc., containing gold dust, etc.; a locality where gold is obtained by washing.

plac-id (plăs'ĭd), *adj.* calm; peaceful; mild; as, a *placid* disposition.—*adv.* **placidly**.—*n.* **placidity**.

plack-et (plăk'ĕt), *n.* an opening or slit in the upper part of a skirt or petticoat to make it easy to put on.

pla-gi-a-rism (plā'jĭ-ȧ-rĭzm; plā'jȧ-rĭzm), *n.* the act of stealing and using another's ideas, words, etc.; literary theft; the writing or other matter that is stolen and used. Also, **plagiary**.

pla-gi-a-rist (plā'jĭ-ȧ-rĭst; plā'jȧ-rĭst), *n.* one who steals and uses another's ideas, words, etc., as his own. Also, **plagiary**.

pla-gi-a-rize (plā'jĭ-ȧ-rīz; plā'jȧ-rīz), *v.t.* to steal and use another's ideas, words, etc., as one's own.

plague (plāg), *n.* a deadly disease; anything very troublesome or causing misery; a nuisance: *v.t.* to afflict with disease or evil; as, *plagued* with starvation; trouble or annoy greatly.—*adj.* **plaguy**.

plaid (plăd; plād), *n.* a cross-barred or checkered woolen cloth; originally, a garment made of such material worn by the Highlanders of Scotland: *adj.* having a pattern of stripes crossing at right angles.

plain (plān), *adj.* level; flat; even; smooth; clear; evident; as, in *plain* sight; easily understood; as, *plain* talk; unlearned; unpolished; simple in manners; as, a *plain* man; not luxurious; as, *plain* living; without ornament; as, *plain* furniture; without beauty; homely; as, a *plain* face: *adv.* clearly: *n.* level land; any flat expanse: *pl.* great tracts of level country without trees.—*adv.* **plainly**.—*n.* **plainness**.

plains-man (plānz'măn), *n.* [*pl.* plainsmen], a dweller in wide, open, level country.

plain song (plān sŏng), an ancient setting of the service of the church to a chant in unison.

plaint (plānt), *n.* the utterance of grief aloud; a complaint.

plain-tiff (plān'tĭf), *n.* one who begins a suit in a court of law.

plain-tive (plān'tĭv), *adj.* expressing grief or sorrow; mournful; sad.—*adv.* **plaintively**.—*n.* **plaintiveness**.

plait (plāt; plĕt; plăt), *n.* a part of material doubled over; a flat fold; a pleat; a braid, as of hair: *v.t.* to double over in narrow folds; braid or interweave.

plan (plăn), *n.* a drawing on a flat surface, showing the parts of anything; as, the *plan* of a building, etc.; scheme or project: *v.t.* [*p.t.* and *p.p.* planned, *p.pr.* planning], to make a sketch of; form in design; outline; arrange beforehand: *v.i.* to scheme; to arrange beforehand.—*n.* **planner**.

plan-chette (plăn-shĕt'; plăn-chĕt'), *n.* a heart-shaped board fitted with two wheels, and a pencil which traces marks as it moves over a paper when the hands of two persons rest lightly on the board.

plane (plān), *adj.* flat; level; even; without elevations or depressions: *n.* a flat or even surface; a grade or level of life; as, a person's social *plane*; a carpenter's tool for smoothing wood; abbreviation for *airplane*, etc.: *v.t.* to make level; make smooth or even with a tool: *v.i.* to rise partly out of the water while in motion, in a way similar to the start of a hydroplane's flight.

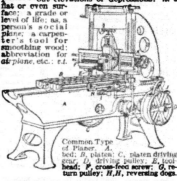

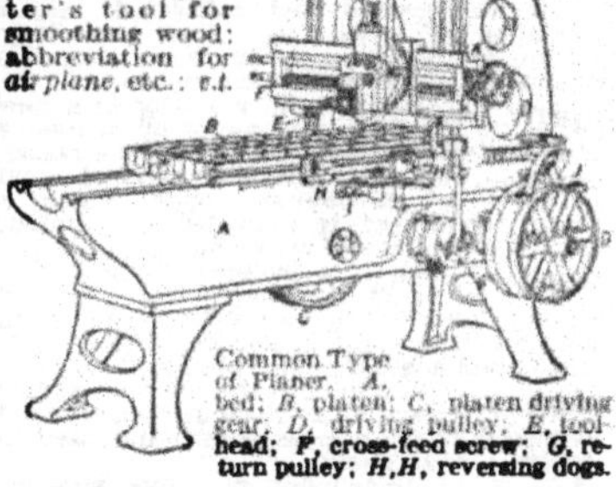
Common Type of Planer. *A*, bed; *B*, platen; *C*, platen driving gear; *D*, driving pulley; *E*, toolhead; *F*, cross-feed screw; *G*, return pulley; *H,H*, reversing dogs.

plan-er (plăn'ẽr), *n.* a machine for smoothing the surface of wood or metal.

plan-et (plăn'ĕt), *n.* a body revolving round the sun.

plane ta-ble (plān tā'bl), an instrument by which distances are computed, especially the distance covered by a shot in target practice or range shooting.

plan-e-ta-ri-um (plăn'ē-tā'rĭ-ŭm), *n.* a machine to show the planets, their motions round the sun, and their relative distances and size.

plan-et-a-ry (plăn'ĕt-ā-rĭ), *adj.* pertaining to, consisting of, or produced by, planets; erratic or wandering.

plan-et-oid (plăn'ĕt-oid), *n.* any one of the small planets revolving in the space between Mars and Venus; a minor planet.

plane tree (plān trē), a large tree with broad-spreading leaves; in America, the species called buttonwood or sycamore.

pla-nim-e-ter (plȧ-nĭm'ē-tĕr), *n.* an instrument by which the area of a plane surface, regular or irregular, may be measured.

plan-ish (plăn'ĭsh), *v.t.* in metal working, to polish or smooth by hammering; in woodworking, to make smooth.

plank (plăṅk), *n.* a long, broad piece of sawed timber thicker than a board; a support; an item in the platform of a political party: *v.t.* to cover with thick boards; colloquially, lay down as on a plank; hence, pay; as, to *plank* down money; to cook on a board; as, to *plank* shad.

plank-ing (plăṅk'ĭng), *n.* sawed timber suitable for floors, etc.; a bare, rough board floor or structure.

plant (plănt), *n.* any vegetable organism; a sprout or sapling; the tools, machinery, fixtures, and sometimes buildings, of any trade or business; as, a manufacturing *plant;* the equipment of an institution, as a college or hospital: *v.t.* to put into the ground for growth; as, to *plant* seed; to provide or prepare with seeds, roots, etc.; as, to *plant* a garden; fix in the mind; establish.

plan-tain (plăn'tān; plăn'tĭn), *n.* a tropical, broad-leaved tree yielding an eatable fruit like the banana; a common dooryard or roadside weed.

plan-ta-tion (plăn-tā'shŭn), *n.* a place where anything is sowed or set in the ground and cultivated; as, a *plantation* of trees; an oyster *plantation;* a large estate where cotton, sugar, etc., are cultivated; a new settlement or colony.

plant-er (plăn'tĕr), *n.* a settler in a new colony; the owner or cultivator of a farm where cotton, sugar, etc., are raised.

plaque (plȧk), *n.* a flat, thin piece of metal or earthenware upon which a picture or design is enameled or painted: used chiefly as a wall ornament.

plash (plăsh), *n.* a puddle; the sound of falling or splashing water: *v.t.* and *v.i.* to splash or dash with water; bend down and interweave the branches or twigs of; as, to *plash* a hedge.—*adj.* plashy.

plas-ma (plăz'mȧ), *n.* the colorless watery part of the blood in which the red corpuscles float; a grass-green stone used in jewelry. Also, plasm.

plas-mon (plăz'mŏn), *n.* a food product resembling flour, made from skim milk.

plas-ter (plȧs'tĕr), *n.* a mixture of lime, sand, and water for coating walls; a cloth coated with a sticky medical substance and applied to some part of the body as a remedy; as a porous *plaster:* plaster of Paris, a paste made of gypsum and water which soon hardens: used for casts, moldings, etc.: *adj.* made of such a pasty substance: *v.t.* to overlay or cover with, or as with, a mixture of lime, sand, and water; as, to *plaster* the wall. —*n.* plasterer.

plas-ter-ing (plȧs'tĕr-ĭng), *n.* act of putting on plaster or a plaster; a covering of lime, sand, and water for a wall, ceiling, etc.; sticky medicated cloth, collectively.

plas-tic (plăs'tĭk), *adj.* capable of being formed or molded; as, clay is *plastic;* giving form to matter; as, *plastic* art; quick to receive impressions; as, a *plastic* mind.—*adv.* plastically.—*n.* plasticity.

plat (plăt), *v.t.* to braid; plait; to make a map of; to lay out in plots: *n.* a small piece of ground; a plot.

plate (plāt), *n.* a thin piece or sheet of metal; as, armor *plate;* a shallow dish from which food is eaten; a piece of metal on which something is engraved; as, a door *plate;* a print made from an engraved metal surface; in photography, a thin sheet of glass treated with chemicals; household articles of gold or silver, as teapots, urns, etc.: *v.t.* to coat with metal; to cover with sheets of metal.

pla-teau (plȧ-tō'), *n.* [*pl.* plateaux (-tōz)], a broad, elevated tract of flat land; table-land; on a military map, a flat surface on top of a hill; a large ornamented center-dish.

plate glass (plāt glȧs), a fine kind of glass cast in thick plates: used for mirrors, etc.

plat-en (plăt'ĕn), *n.* the flat part of a printing press which presses the paper against the type; the cylinder, or roller, of a typewriter, around which the paper is placed, over against which the type strikes.

plat-form (plăt'fôrm'), *n.* a floor of wood, stone, etc., raised above the level of the ground or of the main floor; the place where guns are mounted on a fortress or battery; a political program or policy, of which each item is called a plank.

plat-ing (plāt'ĭng), *n.* the art of overlaying or covering anything with a thin sheet or coating of metal: a coating of metal or of thin metal sheets.

plat-i-num (plăt'ĭ-nŭm), *n.* a heavy, silver-white precious metal, hard to melt or resolve, but capable of being hammered or pressed thin. Also, platina.—*adj.* platinous.

plat-i-tude (plăt'ĭ-tūd), *n.* commonplaceness; dulness; flatness; a stupid and trite remark, especially one uttered as if it were novel or original.

Pla-ton-ic (plȧ-tŏn'ĭk), *adj.* pertaining to Plato, the ancient Greek philosopher, or to his philosophy: platonic, purely mental and spiritual; as, *platonic* love. —*n.* Platonism.

pla-toon (plȧ-tōōn'), *n.* a body of soldiers in command of a lieutenant: usually consisting of four squads of eight men, equal to one-fourth of a company.

plat-ter (plăt'ĕr), *n.* a large flat dish for serving meat, etc.

plau-dit (plô'dĭt), *n.* applause; praise given; the act of praising or applauding.

plau-si-bil-i-ty (plô'zĭ-bĭl'ĭ-tĭ), *n.* the state or quality of seeming to be true; anything that appears to be true without necessarily being so.

plau-si-ble (plô'zi-bl), *adj.* seeming to be true without necessarily being so; having the appearance of truth; as, a *plausible* excuse; likely to win a confidence not wholly deserved; as, a *plausible* speaker.—*adv.* plausibly.—*n.* plausibleness.

play (plā), *n.* any exercise or occupation for amusement; diversion; pastime; freedom or room to act; as, to give one's arm full *play* in throwing a ball; rapid and energetic action or motion; exercise of mental powers; as, a *play* of wit or fancy; a drama, as a tragedy, comedy, etc.; gambling; as, to lose money at *play;* one's turn to move a piece, lay down a card, etc., in a game; fun; jest; as, she did it in *play;* manner of dealing; as, fair *play:* *v.t.* [*p.t.* and *p.p.* played, *p.pr.* playing], to engage in (some pastime) for amusement; as, to *play* ball; to make believe; as, to *play* school; perform; as, to *play* a waltz on a piano; to perform music on; as, to *play* the violin; to act in the character of; as, to *play* Hamlet: *v.i.* to move back and forth; as, wind, fire, or lightning, *play;* to sport or frolic; to gamble; to perform on a musical instrument; to act on the stage.

play-bill (plā'bil"), *n.* a sheet on which is printed the program of a drama, with the names of the actors, etc.

play-day (plā'dā"), *n.* a day free from work; a holiday.

play-er (plā'ēr), *n.* one who takes part in a game; as, a baseball *player;* a musical performer; actor; gambler; idler.

play-fel-low (plā'fel"ō), *n.* one who engages in sport or games with another; a playmate.

play-ful (plā'fool), *adj.* sportive; lively; as, a *playful* kitten.—*adv.* playfully.—*n.* playfulness.

play-go-er (plā'gō"ēr), *n.* one who habitually goes to the theater.

play-house (plā'hous"), *n.* a theater; a small building for children to play in.

play-mate (plā'māt"), *n.* one who sports, or takes part in a game, with another; a playfellow.

play-thing (plā'thing"), *n.* a means of amusement; a toy.

play-wright (plā'rīt"), *n.* a writer of dramas.

pla-za (plä'zȧ), *n.* an open square or market place.

plea (plē), *n.* an excuse or apology; an entreaty; as, a *plea* for mercy; the defendant's answer to the charges in a lawsuit.

plead (plēd), *v.i.* to argue or reason in support of a cause against another; argue before a court of law; as, to *plead* for an acquittal; supplicate or beg earnestly; as, to *plead* for mercy: *v.t.* discuss or defend by arguments; as, to *plead* a case; offer as an excuse; as, to *plead* poverty.—*n.* pleader.

Syn. urge, beseech, beg, entreat, advocate.

plead-ings (plēd'ingz), *n.pl.* the written statements of the two parties in a lawsuit.

pleas-ant (plēz'ănt), *adj.* grateful to the mind or senses; as, a *pleasant* smell; delightful; as, *pleasant* weather; agreeable; as, a *pleasant* fellow; cheerful; lively; as, a *pleasant* time.—*adv.* pleasantly.—*n.* pleasantness.

pleas-ant-ry (plĕz'ănt-rĭ), *n.* merriment; lively talk; gaiety; a laughable speech or joke; a jest.

please (plēz), *v.t.* to gratify; give enjoyment to; gain approval from; as, to *please* one's parents: *v.i.* to afford satisfaction or enjoyment; as, we strive to *please;* like or choose; as, to do as you *please.*

pleased (plēzd), *p.adj.* satisfied; gratified; as, a *pleased* smile.

pleas-ing (plēz'ing), *p.adj.* giving satisfaction; agreeable.—*adv.* pleasingly.

pleas-ur-a-ble (plĕzh'ūr-ȧ-bl), *adj.* gratifying; delightful.—*adv.* pleasurably.

pleas-ure (plĕzh'ūr), *n.* delight; amusement; enjoyment; as, a day of *pleasure;* a delight; a joy; as, it is a *pleasure* to see you; choice; wish; as, what is your *pleasure?*

Syn. charm, comfort, happiness.

Ant. (see pain).

pleat (plēt), *n.* a fold, as of cloth, etc.: *v.t.* to fold, as cloth, etc. Also, plait.

plebe (plēb), *n.* a member of the lowest class in the military academy at West Point or the naval academy at Annapolis. [Colloq.]

ple-be-ian (plē-bē'yăn; plē-bē'ăn), *adj.* pertaining to the common people: from *plebs,* the common people of ancient Rome; hence, common or vulgar: *n.* one of the common people.

ple-be-ian-ism (plē-bē'yăn-izm; plē-bē'ăn-izm), *n.* the feelings and customs of the common people; vulgarity of conduct or manners.

pleb-i-scite (plĕb'ĭ-sĭt), *n.* a vote of all the people for or against a measure.

plec-trum (plĕk'trŭm), *n.* a small flat, usually oval, piece of horn, celluloid, etc., used by a player on certain stringed instruments, such as the mandolin, to strike the strings.

pledge (plĕj), *n.* anything placed as a security or guarantee; a pawn; a drinking of a health as an expression of good will or a promise; an agreement or promise to do or not to do something; a token of good will; as, a *pledge* of friendship: *v.t.* to give as security or guarantee; as, to pledge one's honor; put in pawn; to bind by a promise; as, to *pledge* oneself to secrecy; to stake; drink to the health of.

pledg-et (plĕj'ĕt), *n.* a flat piece of lint or cotton placed over a wound.

Ple-ia-des (plē'yȧ-dēz; plē'ȧ-dēz; plī'ȧ-dēz), *n.pl.* the cluster of seven stars in the constellation Taurus: named from the seven daughters of Atlas, changed after death into stars.

Plei-o-cene (plī'ō-sēn), *adj.* in geology, pertaining to the latest part of the Tertiary period, during which more than half of the modern species of life were developed: *n.* the geological period just before the Quaternary, or age of man. Also, Pliocene.

Pleis-to-cene (plīs'tō-sēn), *adj.* in geology, pertaining to the early part of the Quaternary period, or glacial age: *n.* the glacial age.

ple-na-ry (plē'nȧ-rĭ; plĕn'ȧ-rĭ), *adj.* full; complete; as, *plenary* authority.

plen-i-po-ten-ti-a-ry (plĕn"ĭ-pō-tĕn'shĭ-ā-rĭ; plĕn"ĭ-pō-tĕn'shȧ-rĭ), *adj.* having full power; unlimited: *n.* an ambassador or government agent to a foreign court given full powers.

plen-i-tude (plĕn'ĭ-tūd), *n.* fulness; abundance.

plen-te-ous (plĕn'tē-ŭs), *adj.* abundant; amply sufficient; yielding in abundance; fruitful.—*adv.* **plenteously.**—*n.* **plenteousness.**

plen-ti-ful (plĕn'tĭ-fŏŏl), *adj.* yielding abundance; as, a *plentiful* harvest; existing in great quantity.—*adv.* **plentifully.**

Syn. abundant, ample, full, lavish, bountiful, rich, overflowing.

Ant. (see scarce).

plen-ty (plĕn'tĭ), *n.* abundance; full supply.

ple-o-nasm (plē'ō-năzm), *n.* the use of more words than are necessary in writing or speaking; any instance of the use of too many words.

ple-o-nas-tic (plē'ō-năs'tĭk), *adj.* redundant; wordy.

pleth-o-ra (plĕth'ō-rȧ), *n.* state of being overfull; overabundance; excess, overfulness of blood.

ple-thor-ic (plē-thŏr'ĭk; plĕth'ō-rĭk), *adj.* having excess of blood; overfull; hence, bloated; bombastic.

pleu-ra (plōō'rȧ), *n.* [*pl.* pleuræ (-rē)], a delicate membrane covering the inside of the chest and the outside of each lung.

pleu-ral (plōō'răl), *adj.* pertaining to the pleura, or membrane covering the lungs and the inside of the chest.

pleu-ri-sy (plōō'rĭ-sĭ), *n.* inflammation of the pleura, or membrane of the chest and lungs.

pleu-ro-pneu-mo-ni-a (plōō'rō-nū-mō'nĭ-ȧ), *n.* inflammation of the pleura, or membrane of the chest and lungs, and of the lungs; pleurisy and pneumonia combined.

plex-us (plĕk'sŭs), *n.* a network, as of veins, nerves, etc.; as, the solar *plexus* is a mass of nerve fibers behind the stomach.

pli-a-bil-i-ty (plī'ȧ-bĭl'ĭ-tĭ), *n.* the quality of being easily bent.

pli-a-ble (plī'ȧ-bl), *adj.* easily bent; flexible; easily influenced; as, a *pliable* nature.—*adv.* **pliably.**—*n.* **pliableness.**

pli-an-cy (plī'ăn-sĭ), *n.* quality of being easily bent or influenced.

pli-ant (plī'ănt), *adj.* flexible; easily bent; limber; as, a *pliant* twig; easily influenced; yielding.

pli-cate (plī'kāt), *adj.* plaited; folded in the form of a fan. Also, **plicated.**

pli-ers (plī'ẽrz), *n.* a kind of small pinchers for bending wire, etc., or for holding small objects.

plight (plīt), *n.* a dangerous or distressed condition; predicament; pledge; promise: *v.t.* to promise earnestly; pledge, as one's faith.

plinth (plĭnth), *n.* the lowest, square-shaped part of the base of a column, pedestal, etc.; the projecting face at the bottom of a wall.

Pli-o-cene (plī'ō-sēn), *adj.* in geology, pertaining to the latest part of the Tertiary period: *n.* the geological period just before the Quaternary. Also, **Pleiocene.**

plod (plŏd), *v.i.* [*p.t.* and *p.p.* plodded, *p.pr.* plodding], to walk slowly and heavily; as, to *plod* along; drudge or toil; study laboriously: *v.t.* to walk over heavily and slowly; as, to *plod* one's way.—*n.* **plodder.**

plot (plŏt), *n.* a small area of ground; a ground plan; a diagram; a plat; a scheme, conspiracy, or plan; the plan or main story in a play, novel, etc.: *v.t.* [*p.t.* and *p.p.* plotted, *p.pr.* plotting], to lay plans for; scheme; as, to *plot* a crime; make a plan or map of; to locate or show on a map or chart: *v.i.* to scheme; form a plan; as, to *plot* against one's enemy.—*n.* **plotter.**

plov-er (plŭv'ẽr), *n.* a shore bird of various species.

plow (plou), *n.* a farming implement for turning up the soil; any implement that works in a similar way; as, a snow *plow*: *v.t.* to turn up with a plow; to till: *v.i.* to break or turn up soil with, or as with, a plow; to move onward by cutting a way through; as, the ship *plowed* on. Also, **plough.**

Gang Plow

plow-share (plou'shâr'), *n.* the iron part of a plow that cuts the soil. Also, **ploughshare.**

pluck (plŭk), *v.t.* to pull off, out, or up; as, to *pluck* weeds; pick or gather, as to *pluck* grapes; to pull or twitch; as, to *pluck* the strings of a banjo; to strip completely, as of feathers; as, to *pluck* a goose: *v.i.* to give a sudden pull; to tug; as, the child *plucked* at her mother's skirt: *n.* a pull; a snatch; a tug; the heart, liver, and lungs of an animal; colloquially, spirit or courage; as a man of *pluck.*

pluck-y (plŭk'ĭ), *adj.* [*comp.* pluckier, *superl.* pluckiest], full of spirit or courage.—*adv.* **pluckily.** [COLLOQ.]

plug (plŭg), *n.* a piece of wood, etc., used to fill or stop a hole; a piece of conducting material inserted between conductors to make an electrical connection; a cake of pressed tobacco: *v.t.* [*p.t.* and *p.p.* plugged, *p.pr.* plugging], to stop or make tight with a piece of wood, cork, etc.

plum (plŭm), *n.* a tree somewhat like the peach and cherry, or its well-known fruit; a raisin when used in cooking; something like the fruit in sweetness or shape; as, a sugar*plum;* the choice or best part of a thing.

plum-age (plōōm'āj), *n.* all of a bird's feathers; bright costume.

plumb (plŭm), *n.* a weight, usually of lead, fastened to a cord and dropped to indicate a vertical line; used for determining how nearly vertical is a piece of work done, as a wall, etc.; a similar weight used to find the depth of water: *adj.* perpendicular with the horizon; upright: *adv.* perpendicularly: *v.t.* to straighten; as, to *plumb* up a wall; make vertical or perpendicular; sound (the depth of water) by a plummet; test; get to the bottom of; as, to *plumb* a mystery.

plum-ba-go (plŭm-bā'gō), *n.* a mineral of carbon and iron, used for lead pencils; a form of carbon graphite.

plumb-er (plŭm'ẽr), *n.* one who works in tin, lead, zinc, etc.; especially one who supplies, repairs, or fits water-closets, water pipes, etc.

plumb-ing (plŭm'ĭng), *n.* the art or occupation of putting into buildings the pipes, traps, etc., for carrying water, gas, and sewage; pipes and other fittings used for carrying water, gas, and sewage.

plumb line (plŭm līn), a line attached to a weight of lead to show whether something, as a wall, is straight up and down; a perpendicular line, or a line straight up and down.

plume (plōōm), *n.* a long and beautiful feather or tuft of feathers; a feather worn as an ornament; crest; something like a feather in shape or lightness: *v.t.* to pick and adjust (the feathers); as, a bird *plumes* its feathers; adorn with feathers or with fine clothes; boast; feel proud of: used reflexively; as, to *plume* oneself on one's skill.—*adj.* **plumy.**

plum-met (plŭm'ĕt), *n.* a leaden weight attached to a string used for measuring depths, determining how nearly vertical is a wall, etc.; hence, a test.

plump (plŭmp), *adj.* well filled or rounded out; fat; as, a *plump* person; blunt; direct; as, a *plump* contradiction: *adv.* with a sudden or heavy drop; as, he fell *plump* into the water; bluntly: *v.i.* to fall or sink down heavily; as, to *plump* down into a chair; to grow round or full; as, her cheeks *plumped* out: *v.t.* to cause to fall heavily; to cause to fill out or become round.—*n.* **plumpness.**

plu-mule (plōō'mūl), *n.* the first bud of a young plant above the seed-leaves.

plun-der (plŭn'dẽr), *n.* booty; pillage; as, the *plunder* of thieves: *v.t.* to take from by open force; spoil; rob; as, to *plunder* a house; to seize or take by force; as, the enemy *plundered* all the food in the village: *v.i.* to commit robbery.—*n.* **plunderer.**

plunge (plŭnj), *v.t.* to put suddenly into water or any other liquid: *v.i.* to sink, fall, or rush, as into water; dive; throw the body forward; enter suddenly and quickly; as, to *plunge* into the woods: *n.* the act of suddenly and quickly jumping, falling, entering, etc.; a sudden fall.

plung-er (plŭn'jẽr), *n.* one who takes sudden action; a diver; the long solid cylinder or piston of a pump.

plu-per-fect (plōō'pûr"fĕkt; plōō"pûr'-fĕkt), *adj.* in grammar, noting an event or action completed before some other event or action that is also completed: *n.* the tense or verb form denoting such action.

plu-ral (plōō'răl), *adj.* consisting of more than one: *n.* that form of a word expressing more than one.—*adv.* **plurally.**

plu-ral-i-ty (plōō-răl'ĭ-tĭ), *n.* the majority; the greatest of three or more numbers; in politics, the excess of votes over those for any other candidate for an office.

plus (plŭs), *n.* a quantity to be added; the sign [+] used to denote addition: *adj.* more (by a certain amount); increased (by a certain addition); above zero.

plush (plŭsh), *n.* a kind of soft cloth with a pile or nap; woolen velvet.

Plu-to (plōō'tō), *n.* in Greek mythology, the god of the underworld.

plu-toc-ra-cy (plōō-tŏk'rȧ-sĭ), *n.* rule or government by the rich; the wealthy class.

plu-to-crat (plōō'tō-krăt), *n.* one who exercises power or influence because of his wealth.—*adj.* **plutocratic.**

Plu-to-ni-an (plōō-tō'nĭ-ăn), *adj.* pertaining to Pluto, the Greek god of the lower world, or to the lower regions of fire. Also, **Plutonic.**

plu-ton-ic rocks (plōō-tŏn'ĭk rŏks), rocks that have been formed by the action of fire.

plu-vi-al (plōō'vĭ-ăl), *adj.* in geology, resulting from the action of rain; as, a *pluvial* deposit.

plu-vi-om-e-ter (plōō"vĭ-ŏm'ē-tẽr), *n.* an instrument by which is ascertained the amount of rainfall in a given place and time.

ply (plī), *v.t.* [*p.t.* and *p.p.* plied, *p.pr.* plying], to work at steadily; as, to *ply* a trade; use diligently or earnestly; as, to *ply* an oar; to urge insistently; as, to *ply* one with questions: *v.i.* to run regularly between two ports, as a boat; work or be busy steadily: *n.* a web, or layer, as in a carpet, etc.

pneu-mat-ic (nū-măt'ĭk), *adj.* pertaining to, consisting of, containing, like, or moved by, air; as, *pneumatic* tires. Also, **pneumatical.**—*adv.* **pneumatically.**

pneu-mat-ic tire (nū-măt'ĭk tīr), a hollow rubber tubing filled with air, forming the cushionlike rim of a bicycle or automobile wheel: also used on carriage wheels.

pneu-mat-ics (nū-măt'ĭks), *n.pl.* the science that treats of air and other gases.

pneu-mo-ni-a (nū-mō'nĭ-ȧ), *n.* inflammation of the lungs.

pneu-mon-ic (nū-mŏn'ĭk), *adj.* pertaining to the lungs, or to pneumonia: **pneumonic plague,** an epidemic disease, known in its milder forms as influenza, from which pneumonia readily develops.

poach (pōch), *v.t.* to steal game from; plunder by stealth; cook (eggs) by breaking (them) into boiling water: *v.i.* to shoot or steal game upon forbidden land.—*n.* **poacher.**

pock (pŏk), *n.* a slight swelling on the skin filled with pus, as in smallpox; the spot left by such a swelling.

pock-et (pŏk'ĕt), *n.* a small bag inserted in a garment for carrying small articles; a small netted bag in a billiard table for catching the balls; a hole or opening in a mine; as, a gold *pocket*: *v.t.* to put in a pocket; as, to *pocket* money; to take unlawfully, as money; to receive (an insult), without showing any feeling.

pock-et-book (pŏk'ĕt-bŏŏk"), *n.* a small case for carrying money, papers, etc.

pock-et-knife (pŏk'ĕt-nīf"), *n.* a small knife with blades that close into the handle.

pock-et mon-ey (pŏk'ĕt mŭn'ĭ), an allowance of a small sum for everyday personal expenses; spending money.

pock-mark (pŏk'märk"), *n.* a scar or small hole left by smallpox.

pod (pŏd), *n.* the covering of the seed of certain plants, as the pea, etc.: *v.i.* [*p.t.* and *p.p.* podded, *p.pr.* podding], to swell or fill, as a pod; produce pods.

podg-y (pŏj'ĭ), *adj.* short and fat; dumpy; pudgy.

po-em (pō'ĕm), *n.* a composition in verse, marked by beauty of thought and language; a piece of poetry; any imaginative piece of writing in beautiful language; something like such a composition; as, a *poem* in stone.

po-e-sy (pō'ē-sĭ), *n.* the art of writing verses that express beautiful thoughts in beautiful words.

po-et (pō'ĕt), *n.* [*fem.* poetess], a writer of verse that has merit; one gifted in writing such verse; one who has a strong imagination.

po-et-as-ter (pō'ĕt-ăs"tẽr; pō"ĕt-ăs'tẽr), *n.* a writer of inferior verses.

po-et-ic (pō-ĕt'ĭk), *adj.* pertaining to, suitable to, or expressed in, beautiful verse: *n.pl.* the rules of the art of making verse. Also, **poetical.**—*adv.* **poetically.**

po-et-ize (pō'ĕt-īz), *v.i.* to make verses: *v.t.* to describe in verse.

po-et lau-re-ate (pō'ĕt lô'rē-āt), a court poet; one regularly appointed to write verses in celebration of great events or special occasions.

po-et-ry (pō'ĕt-rĭ), *n.* compositions in verse in which beautiful thought, feeling, or action is expressed in beautiful language; composition in verse as opposed to composition in prose.

po-grom (pō-grŏm'), *n.* an organized riot, or local disturbance, usually directed against the Jews, and instigated by officials. [Russ.]

poign-an-cy (poin'ăn-sĭ), *n.* the state or quality of being keen; sharpness; bitterness.

poign-ant (poin'ănt; poin'yănt), *adj.* severe; very painful; sharp and piercing; bitter.—*adv.* **poignantly.**

poi-lu (pwä'lü'), *n.* the name given to the French private soldier: used in the World War. [Fr.]

poin-set-ti-a (poin-sĕt'ĭ-ȧ), *n.* a Mexican plant with large, handsome, bright red leaves that resemble flowers.

point (point), *n.* the sharp end of a thing; as, the *point* of a pin; a tapering end of land; a cape; a speck or dot; a mark of punctuation; a particular spot; exact place; as, to reach a certain *point* on the road; a particular time or moment; as, the turning-*point* of a battle; a particular detail or item; as, an important *point* in a lesson; a particular aim or purpose; as, you missed the *point* of the story; to gain one's *point*; a step or stage; as, boiling *point*; one of the thirty-two divisions of a compass; lace made with the needle; a railway switch; a standard of measurement for printing type equal to one seventy-second of an inch, measured up and down: *v.t.* to sharpen; as, to *point* a pencil; to give force to; as, to *point* a moral; to show the direction of; as, to *point* the way; direct or aim; as, to *point* a gun; to punctuate; fill the joints of (masonry) with mortar and smooth with a trowel: *v.i.* to call attention by extending the finger; show clearly.

point-blank (point'blănk'), *adj.* horizontal; straight to the mark; as, a *point-blank* shot; direct; as, a *point-blank* refusal: *adv.* directly.

point-ed (poin'tĕd), *p.adj.* sharpened; having a sharp end, as a needle; direct; telling; personal; as, *pointed* remarks. —*adv.* **pointedly.**—*n.* **pointedness.**

point-er (poin'tẽr), *n.* one who, or that which, points, or shows the position of; the hand of a watch, etc.; a kind of dog trained to point, or to stop and show the place where game is hidden; colloquially, a timely hint; *pl.* two stars in the constellation of the Great Dipper, a line through which points to the North Star.

point-ing (poin'tĭng), *n.* punctuation; the act of showing the direction of; the act or operation of filling in the joints of masonry with mortar, or the finished work.

point-less (point'lĕs), *adj.* blunt; dull; having no real meaning; witless.—*adv.* **pointlessly.**

poise (poiz), *n.* balance; the manner of carrying the head and body; mental balance: *v.t.* to balance; weigh; to consider: *v.i.* to hang balanced or suspended.

poi-son (poi'zn), *n.* a substance which, if received into the body, destroys life or health; a destructive influence: *v.t.* to injure or kill by poison; to fill or taint with poison; as, to *poison* food; to corrupt; as, to *poison* one's mind.

poi-son i-vy (poi'zn ī'vĭ), a sumac with three-fingered leaves and white berries, poisonous to touch.

poi-son-ous (poi'zn-ŭs), *adj.* having qualities that injure or kill; deadly; injurious to health; morally corrupting.—*adv.* **poisonously.**

poke (pōk), *n.* a thrust or push; a bag or sack; an American herb with white flowers and purple berries; a bonnet with a very broad brim: *v.t.* to thrust or push against, especially with something pointed; to prod; to thrust in or out; as, to *poke* one's head out of the door: *v.i.* to thrust or push; as, to *poke* at the fire; go about idly; as, to *poke* over one's work; move lazily; grope or feel about in the dark; to pry.—*p.adj.* **poking.**

pok-er (pōk'ẽr), *n.* a metal rod for stirring fires; a gambling card game.

poke-weed (pōk'wēd'), *n.* a common American weed with white flowers and purple berries; poke.

pok-y (pōk'ĭ), *adj.* [*comp.* pokier, *superl.* pokiest], lacking spirit or interest; slow; stupid.

po-lar (pō'lẽr), *adj.* pertaining to, or situated near, either end of the axis of the earth, especially the northern end, or North Pole; as, the *polar* regions; pertaining to either of the opposite points of greatest force in a magnet.

po-lar-i-ty (pō-lăr'ĭ-tĭ), *n.* the quality possessed by magnets, electro-magnets, etc., of having two opposite poles, or centers of attraction, each of which exerts a force opposite to the other, one called *positive*, the other *negative*; as, the *polarity* of the earth; the property possessed by electrified or magnetized bodies, by which they exert directly opposite forces in opposite directions, the positive pole attracting and the negative pole repelling.—*n.* **polarization.**

po-lar-ize (pō'lẽr-īz), *v.t.* to give the quality of having two opposite poles, or polarity, to.

pole (pōl), *n.* a long staff; as, a flagpole; a measure equal to five and a half yards; a square measure equal to thirty and one-fourth square yards; a measuring instrument; one of the two ends of the axis of the earth; one of the two opposite points in a magnet; that on which anything revolves; the extreme opposite: *v.t.* to push with a long rod or staff; as, to *pole* a boat through the water.—**Pole,** a native of Poland.

pole-cat (pōl'kăt'), *n.* a small catlike animal akin to the weasel and ferret, which throws out a strong offensive odor: in the United States, a skunk.

po-lem-ic (pō-lĕm'ĭk), *n.* a paper written to support or dispute an opinion or argument; one who writes to support an opinion against another: *pl.* the science of disputation: *adj.* supporting or disputing an opinion or argument.—*adj.* **polemical.**

pole-star (pōl'stär'), *n.* the North Star (Polaris); a guide; an ideal for action.

po-lice (pō-lēs'), *n.* in a city, town, or district, that part of the government that enforces the laws and keeps order; an organized body of officers for keeping order: *v.t.* to protect and keep in order by regular officers.

po-lice-man (pō-lēs′măn), *n.* a member of a regular force of officers whose duty is to keep order and enforce the laws.

pol-i-cy (pŏl′ĭ-sĭ), *n.* [*pl.* policies (-sĭz)], the art or method of government; management of public affairs; line of action in relation to some special issue; as, the *policy* of watchful waiting; course of conduct; action based on worldly advantage rather than on a sense of right; as, honesty is the best *policy;* prudence; cunning; a document containing a contract of insurance; as, a life insurance *policy.*

pol-ish (pŏl′ĭsh), *v.t.* to make smooth or glossy by rubbing; as, to *polish* silverware; make polite or refined: *v.i.* to become smooth or glossy, or polite and refined: *n.* a smooth, glossy surface; as, the table has a high *polish;* a mixture for making a surface smooth and glossy; as, stove *polish;* elegance of manners.—*n.* polisher.

Pol-ish (pōl′ĭsh), *adj.* of or pertaining to Poland, its language, or its people: *n.* the language of the Poles.

po-lite (pō-līt′), *adj.* well-bred; refined in manner; courteous or obliging.—*adv.* politely.—*n.* politeness.

Syn. gracious, polished, courtly.

Ant. (see impolite).

pol-i-tic (pŏl′ĭ-tĭk), *adj.* prudent; shrewd; wise, especially in carrying out a plan; sometimes, crafty; cunning.

po-lit-i-cal (pō-lĭt′ĭ-kăl), *adj.* pertaining to, or treating of, the science of government; as, *political* writers; relating to, or having, a system of government; pertaining to, or connected with, a party advocating some special system or plan of government; as, a *political* club.—*adv.* politically.

po-lit-i-cal e-con-o-my (pō-lĭt′ĭ-kăl ē-kŏn′ō-mĭ), the science that treats of wealth, its nature, production, distribution, and consumption, and the laws which regulate and govern these.

pol-i-ti-cian (pŏl″ĭ-tĭsh′ăn), *n.* one who is skilled in the art of government; one who is occupied with the management of a system of government, or of the affairs of a special political party; one who acts for the interests of a single party.

pol-i-tics (pŏl′ĭ-tĭks), *n.* the art of government, or the management of public affairs; one's opinions as to government and party; party management or control.

pol-i-ty (pŏl′ĭ-tĭ), *n.* the form or constitution of the government of a state, church, etc.; any community living under an organized system of government.

pol-ka (pōl′kȧ), *n.* a dance of Bohemian origin, performed by two persons; music suitable for such a dance.

poll (pōl), *n.* the head, especially the back part of it; a list of persons, especially those entitled to vote at elections; an election; number of votes recorded at an election; place where votes are cast: usually *pl.:* *v.t.* to lop, clip, or shear; as, to *poll* trees or sheep; to enroll, as for voting; to examine or record the votes of; as, to *poll* a jury; receive votes; as, he *polled* a large majority; to cast or drop in a ballot box; as, to *poll* one's vote.

pol-lack (pŏl′ăk), *n.* a kind of codfish. Also, **pollock.**

pol-lard (pŏl′ẽrd), *n.* a tree cut off to the trunk so that it may put out shoots; an animal that has lost its horns: *v.t.* to cut off the branches or the horns of.

pol-len (pŏl′ĕn), *n.* a powder in the cells of the anthers of flowers necessary for producing more flowers.

pol-li-na-tion (pŏl″ĭ-nā′shŭn), *n.* the carrying of pollen, or dust-like powder, from the anther to the stigma of a flower, in order that seeds may be formed.

pol-li-wog (pŏl′ĭ-wŏg), *n.* the half developed young of the frog; a tadpole.

poll tax (pōl tăks), a tax on each person, or head.

pol-lute (pŏ-lūt′), *v.t.* to make unclean; as, to *pollute* water with filth; taint with guilt; corrupt.—*n.* polluter.

pol-lu-tion (pŏ-lū′shŭn), *n.* the act of making unclean; the state of being unclean; uncleanness; impurity.

Polo

po-lo (pō′lō), *n.* a ball game similar to hockey, played on horseback.

po-lo-naise (pō″lō-nāz′; pŏl″ō-nāz′), *n.* a garment consisting of a waist and overskirt made in one and worn over another skirt; a Polish dance, or the music for it.

pol-troon (pŏl-trōōn′), *n.* a mean-spirited coward.—*n.* poltroonery.

pol-y-an-dry (pŏl″ĭ-ăn′drĭ), *n.* the practice of having more than one husband at the same time: contrasted with *polygamy.*—*adj.* polyandrous.

pol-y-an-thus (pŏl″ĭ-ăn′thŭs), *n.* a plant of the daffodil family with small white or yellow flowers.

pol-y-chro-mat-ic (pŏl″ĭ-krō-măt′ĭk), *adj.* many-colored; showing a play of colors.

po-lyg-a-mist (pō-lĭg′ȧ-mĭst), *n.* one who practices or upholds the custom of having more than one wife at the same time.

po-lyg-a-mous (pō-lĭg′ȧ-mŭs), *adj.* pertaining to, or practicing, the custom of having more than one wife at the same time.—*adv.* polygamously.

po-lyg-a-my (pō-lĭg′ȧ-mĭ), *n.* the practice of having more than one wife at the same time.

pol-y-glot (pŏl′ĭ-glŏt), *adj.* containing or knowing many languages: *n.* a book, especially an edition of the Bible, in several languages; one who speaks or writes several languages.

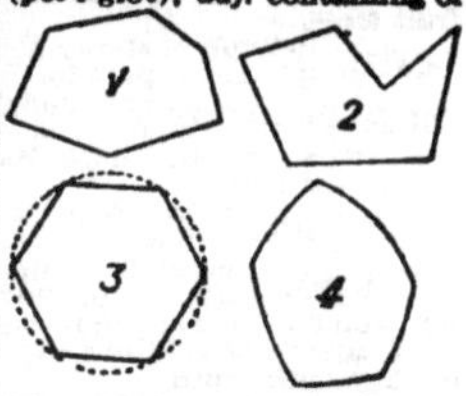

Polygons. 1, convex; 2, concave; 3, regular; 4, curvilineal.

pol-y-gon (pŏl′ĭ-gŏn), *n.* a figure having three or more angles and, hence, three or more sides.—*adj.* polygonal.

pol-y-he-dral (pŏl″ĭ-hē′drăl), *adj.* having many sides or faces. Also, polyhedrous, polyhedric.

pol-y-he-dron (pŏl'ĭ-hē'drŏn), *n.* a solid having many sides, or faces.

Pol-y-ne-sian (pŏl'ĭ-nē'zhăn), *adj.* pertaining to the Pacific islands called Oceania, or to their people: *n.* one of the people of Oceania; the language of Oceania.

pol-y-no-mi-al (pŏl'ĭ-nō'mĭ-ăl), *n.* an expression in algebra of two or more terms: *adj.* containing many terms.

pol-yp (pŏl'ĭp), *n.* a class of small invertebrate sea animals having a central mouth surrounded by tentacles; as, the coral *polyp.* Also, **polype.**

pol-y-pus (pŏl'ĭ-pŭs), *n.* [*pl.* **polypi** (-pī)], a kind of tumor or boil of the mucous membrane, as in the nose.

pol-y-syl-lab-ic (pŏl'ĭ-sĭ-lăb'ĭk), *adj.* pertaining to or having more than one syllable. Also, **polysyllabical.**

pol-y-syl-la-ble (pŏl'ĭ-sĭl'ȧ-bl), *n.* a word of more than one syllable.

pol-y-tech-nic (pŏl'ĭ-tĕk'nĭk), *adj.* pertaining to, including, or giving instruction in, many arts and sciences: *n.* a school for imparting instruction in the arts and sciences, especially various branches of engineering.

pol-y-the-ism (pŏl'ĭ-thē-ĭzm), *n.* the doctrine that there are many gods, each taking a part in the government of the world.

pol-y-the-ist (pŏl'ĭ-thē-ĭst), *n.* one who holds the belief that the world is governed by many gods.—*adj.* **polytheistic.**

pom-ace (pŭm'ās), *n.* crushed apples from a cider mill; anything crushed to a pulp.

po-made (pō-mäd'; pō'măd'), *n.* a perfumed ointment used for the hair. Also, **pomatum.**

pome (pōm), *n.* the typical fruit of trees of the apple family; an applelike fruit.

pome-gran-ate (pŏm-grăn'āt), *n.* a tree yielding an orangelike, eatable fruit with a thick rind and many seeds; the fruit of the tree.

pom-mel (pŭm'ĕl), *n.* the knob on a sword hilt; the high part of a saddlebow: *v.t.* to beat with anything thick or bulky; bruise.

pom-mel-ing (pŭm'ĕl-ĭng), *n.* a sound beating.

po-mol-o-gy (pō-mŏl'ō-jĭ), *n.* the science of cultivating fruit and fruit trees.

pomp (pŏmp), *n.* showy display; grandeur; splendor; parade.

pom-pa-dour (pŏm'pȧ-dōōr; pŏm'pȧ-dōr), *n.* a style of wearing the hair brushed back from the forehead, often over a roll.

pom-pom (pŏm'pŏm), *n.* a machine gun of large size.

pom-pon (pŏm'pŏn), *n.* an ornamental ball, as of feathers or ribbon, for women's wear; the round tuft or ball on a sailor's or soldier's cap, etc.; a variety of chrysanthemum.

pom-pos-i-ty (pŏm-pŏs'ĭ-tĭ), *n.* the state of being self-important. Also, **pompousness.**

pom-pous (pŏm'pŭs), *adj.* affectedly stately or grand; self-important; as, a *pompous* individual.—*adv.* **pompously.**

pon-cho (pŏn'chō), *n.* a blanket with a hole in the middle for the head: worn in Spanish America as a cloak.

pond (pŏnd), *n.* a small body of standing water.

pon-der (pŏn'dẽr), *v.t.* to consider carefully; think about: *v.i.* to reflect; to think deeply.—*n.* **ponderer.**

pon-der-a-ble (pŏn'dẽr-ȧ-bl), *adj.* capable of being weighed; having weight.

pon-der-ous (pŏn'dẽr-ŭs), *adj.* very heavy; weighty; labored; dull; as, a *ponderous* style.—*adv.* **ponderously.**—*n.* **ponderousness, ponderosity.**

pone (pōn), *n.* bread made of corn meal, milk, etc.

pon-gee (pŏn'jē; pŏn'jē'), *n.* a kind of undyed silk from China or India; also, a dyed silk fabric of like weave and texture.

Pons As-in-o-rum (pŏnz ăs'ĭn-ō'rŭm), a famous proposition in Euclid, so called because hard for stupid boys to learn.

pon-iard (pŏn'yărd), *n.* a kind of small dagger: *v.t.* to stab.

pon-tiff (pŏn'tĭf), *n.* a high priest; any bishop; the Pope. Also, **pontifex.**

pon-tif-i-cal (pŏn-tĭf'ĭ-kăl), *adj.* pertaining to a bishop, high priest, or pope; papal: *n.* a book containing church forms and ceremonies: *pl.* the full dress worn by a priest or bishop.—*adv.* **pontifically.**

pon-tif-i-cate (pŏn-tĭf'ĭ-kāt), *n.* the office or dignity of a high priest or pope; the reign of a pope.

Pon-ti-us Pi-late (pŏn'tĭ-ŭs pī'lāt), the Roman governor under whom Christ was crucified.

pon-toon (pŏn-tōōn'), *n.* a lighter or low flat boat; a boat often canvas-covered, or a hollow metal cylinder, used as one of the supports of a temporary or floating bridge; sometimes, the bridge so made: **pontoon bridge,** a temporary bridge, constructed for the use of an army, in which boats or floats are used as supports. Also, **ponton.**

po-ny (pō'nĭ), *n.* [*pl.* **ponies** (-nĭz)], a small horse of certain kinds; as, a Shetland *pony.*

poo-dle (pōō'dl), *n.* one of a breed of intelligent curly-haired dogs, black or white.

pooh (pōō; pōōh), *interj.* an exclamation of scorn or contempt; pshaw! nonsense!

pool (pōōl), *n.* a small body of water; a puddle; a kind of billiards; the money played for in certain gambling games or the place where it is kept; a common fund of money raised to speculate with, or the persons putting up the money: *v.t.* to put into a common fund in order to share the profits; as, to *pool* interests: *v.i.* to form a common fund.

Poop Deck

poop (pōōp), *n.* the stern or rear end of a ship; the raised deck in the stern of a vessel: *v.t.* to strike the stern of; break heavily over the stern of: said of waves: **poop deck,** the stern of a vessel.

poor (pŏŏr), *adj.* having little or no means; lacking riches; lacking in good qualities; without strength or vigor; as, *poor* health; without beauty or dignity; dejected; spiritless; humble; as, a *poor* sort of creature; lean; as, a *poor* horse; inferior; as, *poor* cloth or *poor* work; without fertility; as, *poor* soil; scanty; as, a *poor* harvest; calling forth tenderness, compassion, or disdain; as, *poor* child!—*adv.* **poorly.**—*n.* **poorness.**

poor-house (pŏŏr'hous"), *n.* a dwelling for paupers supported by the public; an almshouse.

poor-ly (pŏŏr'lĭ), *adj.* somewhat ill; delicate in health.—*n.* **poorliness.** [COLLOQ.]

pop (pŏp), *n.* a short, smart, quick sound; a bubbling, nonintoxicant drink: *v.t.* [*p.t.* and *p.p.* popped, *p.pr.* popping], to thrust suddenly; as, to *pop* one's head out of a door; to cause to burst open by heat; as, to *pop* corn: *v.i.* to make a short, smart, quick sound; as, we could hear the guns *pop;* move quickly; dart; come suddenly into view; as, he *popped* right out before us; to burst open with a sound; as, corn *pops* over the fire: *adv.* suddenly.

pop corn (pŏp kôrn), any variety of Indian corn, or maize, having small ears and small, hard grains which pop and expand when exposed to the heat of a fire.

pope (pōp), *n.* the bishop of Rome and head of the Roman Catholic Church; a title of priests of the Greek Church.

pope-dom (pōp'dŭm), *n.* the office or dignity of the Pope; papacy.

pop-er-y (pōp'ẽr-ĭ), *n.* a scornful term for the Roman Catholic system.

pop-gun (pŏp'gŭn"), *n.* a toy which shoots harmless bullets by the aid of air under pressure.

pop-in-jay (pŏp'ĭn-jā), *n.* formerly, a parrot; a fop or dude who chatters like a parrot.

pop-ish (pōp'ĭsh), *adj.* pertaining to the Roman Catholic Church; a scornful term.

pop-lar (pŏp'lẽr), *n.* a tree of rapid growth, with a light, soft wood.

pop-lin (pŏp'lĭn), *n.* a ribbed fabric of silk and worsted.

pop-py (pŏp'ĭ), *n.* a plant having bright, showy flowers, from one species of which opium is obtained.

pop-u-lace (pŏp'ū-lās), *n.* the common people.

pop-u-lar (pŏp'ū-lẽr), *adj.* pertaining to, suitable for, or pleasing to, the common people; easily understood; familiar; as, *popular* music; held in favor by large numbers of people; as, a *popular* writer; a *popular* girl.—*adv.* **popularly.**

pop-u-lar-i-ty (pŏp"ū-lăr'ĭ-tĭ), *n.* the state or quality of being pleasing to many people; general esteem.

pop-u-lar-ize (pŏp'ū-lẽr-īz), *v.t.* to make pleasing to many people; to make familiar to, or to adapt to the use of, the common people; as, to *popularize* methods of education.—*n.* **popularization.**

pop-u-late (pŏp'ū-lāt), *v.t.* to furnish with inhabitants or people; as, to *populate* a country; to inhabit.

pop-u-la-tion (pŏp"ū-lā'shŭn), *n.* the people of a country, place, town, etc.; the act of furnishing with inhabitants.

Pop-u-list (pŏp'ū-lĭst), *n.* a member of a political party in the United States known as the Populist or People's party. —*adj.* **Populistic.**

pop-u-lous (pŏp'ū-lŭs), *adj.* containing many inhabitants; full of people.—*adv.* **populously.**—*n.* **populousness.**

por-ce-lain (pôr'sē-lān; pōrs'lān), *n.* a fine, white, thin kind of earthenware: *adj.* made of such earthenware.

porch (pōrch), *n.* a covered entrance to a building, usually extending from the main wall, with a separate roof.

por-cine (pôr'sīn; pôr'sĭn), *adj.* pertaining to swine, or hogs.

por-cu-pine (pôr'kū-pīn), *n.* an animal akin to the squirrel, rat, and beaver, covered with spines or sharp quills which it is able to shoot out in self-defense.

pore (pōr), *n.* a minute hole in the skin through which sweat passes to the surface: *v.i.* to look with close and steady attention; as, to *pore* over a book.

por-gy (pôr'gĭ), *n.* a salt-water fish much esteemed for food.

pork (pōrk), *n.* the flesh of swine, or hogs, used for food.

pork-er (pōr'kẽr), *n.* a hog, especially when fattened.

po-ros-i-ty (pō-rŏs'ĭ-tĭ), *n.* the state or quality of being full of tiny holes through which fluids may pass; a pore.

po-rous (pō'rŭs), *adj.* having tiny holes through which a fluid may pass, as a sponge.—*n.* **porousness.**

por-phy-ry (pôr'fĭ-rĭ), *n.* a many-colored hard stone that takes a high polish: used in buildings for columns, decoration, etc.

por-poise (pôr'pŭs), *n.* a sea animal from five to eight feet long belonging to the class of the whale and dolphin; the sea hog.

por-ridge (pŏr'ĭj), *n.* a food made of oatmeal or other meal boiled slowly in water until it thickens; a broth or stew of vegetables, and sometimes meat.

por-rin-ger (pŏr'ĭn-jẽr), *n.* a small dish or bowl for broth.

port (pōrt), *n.* a place where vessels arrive and depart; a harbor; haven; as, the *port* of New York; the way in which one bears or carries himself; manner or bearing; the left side of a ship as one faces the bow; a round opening, or window, called a porthole, in the side of a ship; especially, such an opening used for a gun; a dark-colored sweet wine: *v.t.* to turn to the port, or left, side of a ship; as, to *port* the helm.

port-a-bil-i-ty (pōr"tȧ-bĭl'ĭ-tĭ), *n.* capability of being carried. Also, **portableness.**

port-a-ble (pōr'tȧ-bl), *adj.* that may be easily carried.

port-age (pōr'tāj), *n.* a break in a chain of waterways over which goods, boats, etc., have to be carried; the carrying of goods overland from one waterway to another; the cost of such carriage.

por-tal (pōr'tăl), *n.* a gate, door, or entrance, especially when large and stately.

port-cul-lis (pōrt-kŭl'ĭs), *n.* a strong grating hung over the gateway of a fortified place and capable of being let down to defend the gate.

Porte (pōrt), *n.* the Turkish government and court: so called from the gate of the Sultan's palace where justice was dispensed.

porte-co-chère (pōrt'kō"shâr"), *n.* a large gateway through which a carriage mây drive into a court; loosely, an extension of a porch roof over a driveway, where carriages stop. [Fr.]

porte-mon-naie (pôrt'mŏ'nĕ'), *n.* a small purse. [Fr.]

por-tend (pŏr-tĕnd'), *v.t.* to indicate in advance what is to happen; as, to *portend* a storm; forebode.

por-tent (pôr'tĕnt), *n.* an omen or sign, especially of ill.

por-ten-tous (pŏr-tĕn'tŭs), *adj.* foreshadowing evil; dreadful.—*adv.* **portentously.**—*n.* **portentousness.**

por-ter (pōr'tẽr), *n.* a doorkeeper or gatekeeper; one who carries luggage, etc., for hire; a dark-colored malt beer.

por-ter-age (pōr'tẽr-āj), *n.* the work or charge of one who carries burdens for hire.

port-fo-li-o (pôrt-fō'lĭ-ō; pôrt-fōl'yō), *n.* a case for loose papers, drawings, etc.; the office of a minister of state; as, he holds the *portfolio* of war.'

port-hole (pôrt'hōl"), *n.* a round opening, or window, in the side of a ship; an opening in the wall of a fort, blockhouse, etc.; especially, a hole through which to shoot.

Portico

por-ti-co (pōr'tĭ-kō), *n.* [*pl.* porticos (-kōz)], a walk covered by a roof supported on columns; a columned porch or covered entrance of a building.

por-tière (pōr"tyâr'), *n.* a door-curtain; a drapery in a doorway. [Fr.]

por-tion (pōr'shŭn), *n.* a piece or part of anything; a share, or a part given; part of an estate descending to an heir: *v.t.* to divide into shares; to give shares of; give part of an estate or fortune to.

Syn., *n.* lot, parcel: *v.* share.

port-li-ness (pōrt'lĭ-nĕs), *n.* the state of being stout, or of being dignified in bearing.

port-ly (pōrt'lĭ), *adj.* stately in appearance; dignified in bearing; corpulent or stout.

port-man-teau (pôrt-măn'tō), *n.* [*pl.* portmanteaux (-tōz)], a bag or trunk for carrying clothes or traveling necessities.

por-trait (pōr'trāt), *n.* a picture or representation of a person or face drawn from life; a likeness, especially one from life; a vivid or clear description of a person in words.

por-trai-ture (pōr'trā-tūr), *n.* the art, act, or practice, of drawing or painting pictures of persons; vivid or clear description of persons.

por-tray (pōr-trā'), *v.t.* [*p.t.* and *p.p.* portrayed, *p.pr.* portraying], to paint or draw the likeness of; describe in words.

por-tray-al (pōr-trā'ăl), *n.* the act of making a picture or representation by drawing, painting, or describing in words.

Por-tu-guese (pōr'tū-gēz; pōr"tū-gēz'; pōr'tū-gēs), *adj.* relating to Portugal or its people: *n.* a native, or natives, of Portugal; the language of Portugal.

pose (pōz), *n.* attitude or position; often, a manner put on for the sake of effect: *v.i.* to assume an attitude; to put on a certain manner for effect; as, she *poses* as very charitable: *v.t.* to place in an attitude; to puzzle or perplex.

pos-er (pōz'ẽr), *n.* a puzzling question; that which puzzles; one who assumes an attitude or does things for effect.

po-si-tion (pō-zĭsh'ŭn), *n.* the state of being set or placed; situation; as, the *position* of a house; office or employment; as, to lose one's *position;* posture; as, a graceful *position;* attitude toward any subject; as, to define one's *position;* principle laid down; social standing.

pos-i-tive (pŏz'ĭ-tĭv), *adj.* clearly expressed; leaving no doubt; actual; direct; as, *positive* proof; a *positive* promise; confident; as, I am *positive* that this is so; strongly or stubbornly assertive; as, a *positive* manner; not negative; as, a *positive* blessing; noting the simple form of an adjective; as, *positive* degree; in mathematics, reckoned as more than zero; as, a *positive* quantity; denoting that pole of a magnet which attracts; denoting one kind of electricity, or one end of an electric source: *n.* that which may be affirmed; reality; a word which affirms or asserts existence; a photograph with the natural lights and shades restored; in mathematics, electricity, etc., that which is opposite to a *negative.*—*adv.* **positively.**—*n.* **positiveness.**

Syn., *adj.* absolute, certain.

Ant. (see negative).

pos-se (pŏs'ē), *n.* a body of men called by the sheriff to assist in making an arrest: called in full, *posse comitatus.*

pos-sess (pŏ-zĕs'), *v.t.* to be the owner of; to have as a quality; hold in control; as, to *possess* one's soul in patience; to control mentally; as, anger *possessed* him; be master of; occupy; seize; as, to *possess* a city during war.—*n.* **possessor.**

pos-sessed (pŏ-zĕst'), *p. adj.* owned: mad; as, he raved as if *possessed.*

pos-ses-sion (pŏ-zĕsh'ŭn), *n.* ownership; occupancy; the thing owned: *pl.* property or estate.

pos-ses-sive (pŏ-zĕs'ĭv), *adj.* noting ownership or right; as, in grammar, the *possessive* case of nouns and pronouns: *n.* in grammar, the case of nouns and pronouns showing ownership.

pos-set (pŏs'ĕt), *n.* a drink made of hot milk curdled with wine, and often spiced.

pos-si-bil-i-ty (pŏs"ĭ-bĭl'ĭ-tĭ), *n.* the fact or state of taking place or happening; that which may take place, or that which may be done; something likely; likelihood.

pos-si-ble (pŏs'ĭ-bl), *adj.* that may be true or may become true; capable of happening or taking place.—*adv.* **possibly.**

pos-sum (pŏs'ŭm), *n.* a Southern colloquial expression for *opossum.*

post (pōst), *n.* a piece of timber, etc., set upright, usually to support something else; system of carrying and delivering letters; the mail; place, station, situation, or office; a size of paper double that of common notepaper; a military station: *v.t.* to fasten, as a notice, to a wall, etc.; to make known by means of notices fastened to a wall, etc.; to send by mail; in bookkeeping, to transfer an entry or item from journal or daybook to ledger; to inform fully: *v.i.* to travel with speed; as, to *post* o'er land and sea: *adv.* speedily: **post card**, a private card, as a picture, which can be sent through the mail by the affixing of a postage stamp.

post-age (pōs'tāj), *n.* the cost of sending letters by mail: **postage stamp**, an official stamp sold by the government to be pasted on mail matter as a sign that the postage has been paid.

post-al (pōs'tăl), *adj.* pertaining to the post office, or mail service: **postal card**, a card with a postage stamp officially printed on it; a post card.

post-date (pōst"dāt'), *v.t.* to date after the real time, or time of writing, as a check.

post-er (pōs'tẽr), *n.* a placard or bill put up in a public place, as on a wall, to advertise something; one who places bills on walls, etc.

pos-te-ri-or (pŏs-tē'rĭ-ẽr), *adj.* later; hinder: *n.pl.* the hinder parts of an animal.—*n.* **posteriority.**

pos-ter-i-ty (pŏs-tĕr'ĭ-tĭ), *n.* [*pl.* posterities (-tĭz)], future generations; descendants.

pos-tern (pōs'tẽrn), *n.* formerly, a back door or gate; private entrance: *adj.* behind; private; rear.

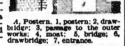

A, Postern. 1, postern; 2, drawbridge; 3, passage to the outer works; 4, moat; 5, bridge; 6, drawbridge; 7, entrance.

post ex-change (pōst ĕks-chānj'), a general store at a military station, licensed by the government.

post-grad-u-ate (pōst-grăd'ū-āt), *adj.* pertaining to studies pursued after having received a diploma from a school or college: *n.* one pursuing such studies.

post-haste (pōst"hāst'), *adj.* instant: *adv.* quickly; with great speed.

pos-thu-mous (pŏs'tū-mŭs; pŏst'hū-mŭs), *adj.* born after the death of the father; published after the death of an author; happening or continuing after one's death.—*adv.* **posthumously.**

pos-til-ion (pōs-tĭl'yŭn), *n.* one who rides the near, or left-hand horse in the team of a carriage; a guide. Also, **postillion.**

post-lude (pōst'lūd), *n.* organ music played at the end of a service in church.

post-man (pōst'măn), *n.* [*pl.* postmen (-mĕn)], one whose business it is to carry letters; a letter carrier.

post-mark (pōst'märk"), *n.* a mark stamped upon mail by post-office officials, showing the place and date of mailing or of receipt: *v.t.* to stamp, as mail, with such a mark.

post-mas-ter (pōst'măs"tẽr), *n.* [*fem.* postmistress], the superintendent of a mail office.

post-mas-ter-gen-er-al (pōst'măs-tẽr-jĕn'ẽr-ăl), *n.* the chief officer of the mail service department of a country.

post-me-rid-i-an (pōst"mē-rĭd'ĭ-ăn), *adj.* coming after the time when the sun is highest; of the afternoon: abbreviated *P. M.* or *p. m.*

post-mor-tem (pōst"môr'tĕm), *adj.* after death; made after death: referring especially to examination of organs of the dead body: *n.* an examination made of a body after death. [LAT.]

post-na-tal (pōst-nā'tăl), *adj.* happening after birth.

post of-fice (pōst ŏf'ĭs), the department of a government which receives and forwards mail; one of the offices under this department, where mail is received and distributed.

post-pone (pōst-pōn'), *v.t.* to delay; defer; put off to another time.

post-pone-ment (pōst-pōn'mĕnt), *n.* the act of putting off to a future time; brief delay.

post-pran-di-al (pōst-prăn'dĭ-ăl), *adj.* after-dinner; as, a *post-prandial* speaker.

post-script (pōst'skrĭpt), *n.* a paragraph added to a letter after the writer's signature; an addition to a book.

pos-tu-late (pŏs'tū-lāt), *v.t.* to assume without proof; use as an argument without proving; state as a fact to be taken for granted: *n.* a self-evident statement which may be taken for granted; a proposition accepted without proof; something that must be assumed in order to account for something else.

pos-ture (pŏs'tūr), *n.* attitude; placing or position of parts of the body; state: *v.t.* to place in a particular attitude or fixed position: *v.i.* to take a certain position.

po-sy (pō'zĭ), *n.* a flower or a bunch of flowers; originally, a motto or verse sent with a bouquet or inscribed in a ring.

pot (pŏt), *n.* a metal or earthenware vessel for holding or boiling liquids and other substances; the quantity such a vessel will hold; a vessel, usually of earthenware, for holding growing plants; a size of paper twelve and a half by fifteen inches; a large amount: *v.t.* [*p.t.* and *p.p.* potted, *p.pr.* potting], to preserve in, put into, or plant in, a vessel called a pot; to shoot (a bird or animal) for cooking; colloquially, to secure.

po-ta-ble (pō'tȧ-bl), *adj.* drinkable: *n.pl.* something drinkable.

pot-ash (pŏt'ăsh), *n.* a powerful white salt obtained from wood ashes and used in making soap, glass, etc.; potassium carbonate. Also, **potass, potassa.**

po-tas-si-um (pō-tăs'ĭ-ŭm), *n.* a soft, very light, bluish-white metal, occurring only in compounds: **potassium carbonate**, a white alkaline salt obtained from ashes of vegetable matter; potash.

po-ta-tion (pō-tā'shŭn), *n.* the act of drinking; a drink.

po-ta-to (pō-tā'tō), *n.* [*pl.* potatoes (-tōz)], a common plant having edible fleshy shoots, or tubers, growing from its roots underground; one of these tubers used as food; originally, the sweet potato.

pot-boil-er (pŏt'boil"ẽr), *n.* a piece of work, often inferior, done by an artist or writer merely for the money that will be paid for it.

pot-boy (pŏt'boi"), *n.* originally, a boy who carried pots of liquor in a tavern; hence, a servant in an inn or tavern.

po-ten-cy (pō'tĕn-sĭ), *n.* power, physical or mental. Also, **potence.**

po-tent (pō'tĕnt), *adj.* powerful; mighty; having great authority or influence.—*adv.* **potently.**

po-ten-tate (pō'tĕn-tāt), *n.* one who has great power; a monarch.

po-ten-tial (pō-tĕn'shăl), *adj.* capable of being, but not yet in being; possible, but not actual; in grammar, expressing power, possibility, liberty, or obligation: as, the *potential* mood: in physics, existing by reason of position; as, *potential* energy: *n.* a possibility; in electrical science, the electrical energy possessed by a body by virtue of the electric charge that it carries: **potential difference,** that condition in which an electric current tends to flow from a body containing a greater electric charge to a body containing a lesser electric charge: usually measured in volts.—*adv.* **potentially.**

po-ten-ti-al-i-ty (pō-tĕn"shĭ-ăl'ĭ-tĭ), *n.* possibility of development in some particular direction; possibility, but not actuality.

poth-er (pŏth'ẽr), *n.* confusion; bustle: *v.i.* to make a stir: *v.t.* to confuse; worry; bother.

pot-herb (pŏt'ûrb"; pŏt'hûrb"), *n.* any small plant the tops of which are boiled for eating.

pot-hook (pŏt'hŏŏk"), *n.* an iron hook shaped like an S, for hanging a pot over an open fire; a mark of similar shape, formerly used as an exercise in learning to write.

po-tion (pō'shŭn), *n.* a drink; dose, especially of liquid medicine.

pot-luck (pŏt'lŭk'), *n.* whatever may chance to be on hand to eat; a meal not prepared for guests.

pot-pour-ri (pō"pōō"rē'), *n.* a medley or mixture, as of musical airs; a dish made of various kinds of meats and vegetables; a mixture of dried fragrant flower petals used as perfume. [Fr.]

pot-sherd (pŏt'shûrd"), *n.* a piece of broken earthenware or crockery.

pot shot (pŏt shŏt), a hasty shot at an animal, bird, etc., by one who hunts not for sport but to secure food.

pot-tage (pŏt'āj), *n.* a stew or thick soup of meat or vegetables, or of both.

pot-ter (pŏt'ẽr), *n.* a maker of earthenware, stoneware, etc.: *v.i.* to work lazily or fussily.

pot-ter-y (pŏt'ẽr-ĭ), *n.* [*pl.* potteries (-ĭz)], ware of all kinds made from earth and clay; the place where it is manufactured; the art of making it.

pot-tle (pŏt'l), *n.* a liquid measure equal to four pints; a drinking vessel holding this amount, or the liquor contained in it.

pouch (pouch), *n.* a small bag; pocket; bag or sac of an animal, usually for carrying its young; cartridge box.

poul-ter-er (pōl'tẽr-ẽr), *n.* a dealer in chickens, etc., especially for the table.

poul-tice (pōl'tĭs), *n.* a soft mixture of bread, meal, etc., applied to a sore or inflamed part of the body: *v.t.* to apply such a mixture to.

poul-try (pōl'trĭ), *n.* domestic fowls, as chickens, turkeys, etc.

pounce (pouns), *n.* a fine powder formerly used for drying ink on paper, now chiefly used for sprinkling into holes in paper in pattern making; the talon or claw of a bird of prey; a sudden spring or swoop: *v.t.* to sprinkle with powder: *v.i.* to fall upon and seize with, or as with, the claws.

pound (pound), *n.* a standard weight equal to sixteen ounces avoirdupois, or twelve ounces troy; a British sum equal to twenty shillings, or about $4.86; a place for confining or keeping stray animals; as, a dog *pound:* *v.t.* to shut or confine in a place for stray animals; beat; pulverize, or make very fine: *v.i.* to walk heavily; to beat steadily; as, the noise *pounded* in my ears.

pour (pōr), *v.t.* to cause to flow in a stream; as, to *pour* a liquid in or out of a vessel; send forth freely; utter freely; rain very hard: *v.i.* to come or flow forth freely in a stream; as, the people *poured* out of the building; the rain *poured* down.

pour-par-ler (pōōr"pär'lā'), *n.* [*pl.* pourparlers (-lāz')], a diplomatic conference before a treaty is made. [Fr.]

pout (pout), *n.* a pushing out of the lips: *pl.* a fit of sullenness: *v.i.* to push out the lips in sullenness, contempt, or displeasure; look sulky: *v.t.* to push out; as, to *pout* the lips.

pout-er (pout'ẽr), *n.* one who pushes out the lips in ill humor; a kind of pigeon.

pov-er-ty (pŏv'ẽr-tĭ), *n.* the state of being poor; necessity; want; any lack of richness in quality; scarcity; need.

pow-der (pou'dẽr), *n.* any dry substance in fine particles; dust; an explosive mixture reduced to fine particles, called gunpowder; a fine, white, often perfumed, dustlike substance used for toilet purposes; a medicinal substance ground into fine particles: *v.t.* to reduce to, or sprinkle with, a dustlike substance: *v.i.* to be reduced to very small particles; to use a face preparation called powder.—*adj.* **powdery.**

pow-der flask (pou'dẽr flȧsk), a leather or metal holder for gunpowder.

pow-der mag-a-zine (pou'dẽr măg"ȧ-zēn'), a place for storing gunpowder, usually near the firing line but not exposed to fire.

pow-er (pou'ẽr), *n.* state of being able to do or perform something; as, physical or mental *power;* energy put forth; force; strength; as, the *power* of a man's arm; rule or authority; as, the *power* of government; legal authority; as, the *power* to veto a bill; a ruler or sovereign state or nation; as, the great *powers;* great effect or influence; as, the *power* of riches; the rate at which mechanical energy is put forth, as by an engine, electric motor, etc.; as, ten horse *power;* the result obtained by multiplying a number by itself; as, four is the second *power* of two.

pow-er-ful (pou'ẽr-fŏŏl), *adj.* having great influence; mighty; strong; as, a *powerful* nation.—*adv.* **powerfully.**

pow-er-less (pou'ẽr-lĕs), *adj.* weak; lacking strength; unable to bring about an effect; as, his efforts were *powerless.*—*adv.* **powerlessly.**—*n.* **powerlessness.**

pow-wow (pou'wou"), *n.* a North American Indian priest or medicine man; among the Indians, a ceremony in which magic rites are used to bring about things desired, as the cure of disease, success in war, etc.; in the United States, a colloquial term for a noisy political meeting.

pox (pŏks), *n.* any of various diseases marked by an eruption, or breaking out, on the skin; as, small*pox*.

prac-ti-ca-bil-i-ty (prăk"tĭ-kȧ-bĭl'ĭ-tĭ), *n.* capability of being done.

prac-ti-ca-ble (prăk'tĭ-kȧ-bl), *adj.* capable of being done or used.—*adv.* **practicably.**

prac-ti-cal (prăk'tĭ-kăl), *adj.* pertaining to, or obtained through, experience or use; as, *practical* knowledge; capable of being put to use; having useful ends in view; useful; tending to, or shown in, action; as, a *practical* education; inclined to useful action rather than thought; as, a *practical* disposition; applying knowledge to action; as, a *practical* chemist; capable of using knowledge gained from experience.

prac-ti-cal-ly (prăk'tĭ-kăl-ĭ), *adv.* in a useful way; through actual experience; really; in fact though not in name; as, he is *practically* the president.

prac-tice (prăk'tĭs), *n.* custom; habit; as, to make a *practice* of smoking; the putting to actual use of theoretic knowledge; as, he is skilled in theory but not in *practice*; exercise of any profession; as, the *practice* of medicine; regular exercise as a means to learning; as, *practice* in music; skill gained by such exercise: *v.t.* to do frequently; work at or pursue as a profession; as, to *practice* law; to perform often in order to learn; as, to *practice* a piece of music: *v.i.* to do something as a habit; to follow a profession; to do something often in order to learn. Also, *v.*, **practise.**

prac-ticed (prăk'tĭst), *p.adj.* skilled; proficient; experienced; as, a *practiced* hand.

prac-ti-tion-er (prăk-tĭsh'ŭn-ẽr), *n.* one who is engaged in any profession, especially medicine or law.

præ-no-men (prē-nō'mĕn), *n.* the first name, as John or Mary.

præ-tor (prē'tôr), *n.* a Roman magistrate ranking next to consul. Also, **pretor.**—*adj.* **prætorian, pretorian.**

prag-mat-ic (prăg-măt'ĭk), *adj.* practical; businesslike; pertaining to everyday matters; meddlesome; opinionated; in philosophy, dealing with, based on, or judging from, the actual working out of an idea rather than the theory back of it; as, a *pragmatic* conclusion; a *pragmatic* thinker. Also, **pragmatical.**—*adv.* **pragmatically.**—*n.* **pragmaticalness.**

prag-ma-tism (prăg'mȧ-tĭzm), *n.* a method of thought in which stress is laid upon practical results as standards in conduct.—*n.* **pragmatist.**

prai-rie (prā'rĭ; prâr'ĭ), *n.* a large treeless tract of level land covered with tall coarse grass, especially in the central United States.

prai-rie chick-en (prā'rĭ chĭk'ĕn), a grouse, or gamebird akin to the domestic fowls, found in the Mississippi Valley.

prai-rie dog (prā'rĭ dŏg), a small burrowing animal resembling the woodchuck and living on the plains.

praise (prāz), *n.* approval; fame; renown; applause; glorification of God: *v.t.* to bestow approval upon; honor; worship; glorify.

Syn., *v.* commend, extol, laud.

Ant. (see blame).

praise-wor-thy (prāz'wûr"thĭ), *adj.* deserving approval; commendable.—*adv.* **praiseworthily.**—*n.* **praiseworthiness.**

prance (prȧns), *n.* a springing or high-stepping movement: *v.i.* to spring or move with high steps, as a horse; strut about in a lively manner; caper.

pran-di-al (prăn'dĭ-ăl), *adj.* pertaining to a dinner or a meal.

prank (prăṅk), *n.* a frolic; a mischievous or playful trick: *v.t.* to dress up in a showy style; decorate: *v.i.* to make a great show.

prate (prāt), *v.i.* to prattle; talk idly: *v.t.* to utter without sense or meaning: *n.* trifling talk.—*n.* **prater.**

prat-tle (prăt'l), *n.* childish talk: *v.t.* and *v.i.* to talk much and lightly; chatter.—*n.* **prattler.**

prawn (prôn), *n.* a large, shrimplike, edible shellfish.

pray (prā), *v.t.* [*p.t.* and *p.p.* prayed, *p.pr.* praying], to ask earnestly; ask with humility and reverence; to speak to God, in request, confession, or praise: *v.t.* to request; to ask earnestly for.—*n.* **prayer.**

Syn. entreat, implore, petition, plead.

prayer (prâr), *n.* thanks and praise given to God, and requests made of him; a form of words suited to an appeal to God; a form of religious service for public worship.

Syn. petition, request, suit.

prayer book (prâr bŏŏk), a book of forms for public and private worship.

prayer-ful (prâr'fŏŏl), *adj.* given to devout appeal to God.—*adv.* **prayerfully.**—*n.* **prayerfulness.**

preach (prēch), *v.i.* to discourse or speak on a religious subject, especially from a text of Scripture; give advice on religious or moral subjects: *v.t.* to declare or teach by public discourse; to utter with moral or religious purpose, as a sermon.—*n.* **preacher.**

pre-ad-am-ite (prē-ăd'ăm-īt), *adj.* existing before Adam: *n.* something that preceded or came before Adam or man; a believer in the existence of men before Adam.

pre-am-ble (prē'ăm"bl), *n.* an introduction or preface; the opening clauses of a statute or law giving the reasons and object of the act: usually commencing with the word *whereas*.

preb-en-da-ry (prĕb'ĕn-dā-rĭ), *n.* [*pl.* prebendaries (-rĭz)], a clergyman receiving a salary as one of the body of clergy, called a chapter, attached to a cathedral.

pre-ca-ri-ous (prē-kā'rĭ-ŭs), *adj.* depending upon the will or pleasure of another, or upon a turn of circumstances; uncertain; insecure; as, a *precarious* position.—*adj.* **precariously.**—*n.* **precariousness.**

Syn. risky, dubious, perilous.

Ant. (see steady).

pre-cau-tion (prē-kô'shŭn), *n.* caution or care taken beforehand; care used to prevent mischief or secure good results.

pre-cau-tion-a-ry (prē-kô'shŭn-ā-rĭ), *adj.* pertaining to, or proceeding from, care taken beforehand; intended to prevent harm or loss.

pre-cede (prē-sēd'), *v.t.* and *v.i.* to go before in time, place, rank, or importance.

pre-ced-ence (prē-sēd'ĕns), *n.* the act or right of going before;

superiority in rank; a position in advance of others at a public ceremony. Also, **precedency.**

pre-ce-dent (prē-sē'dĕnt), *adj.* going before: *n.* (prĕs'ē-dĕnt), something previously said or done that may serve as a rule to be followed; a model.

pre-cen-tor (prē-sĕn'tŏr), *n.* the leader of a cathedral choir, etc.; a singer who leads an audience.

pre-cept (prē'sĕpt), *n.* a rule of action or of moral conduct; maxim: written order issued by a judge.

pre-cep-tor (prē-sĕp'tẽr), *n.* [*fem.* **preceptress**], an instructor or teacher.—*adj.* **preceptorial.**

pre-cep-to-ry (prē-sĕp'tō-rĭ), *adj.* giving, or containing, precepts, or rules of conduct: *n.* a college or religious house of the Knights Templars.

pre-ces-sion (prē-sĕsh'ŭn), *n.* act of going before others; a going forward: **precession of the equinoxes,** the slow westward movement of the equinoctial points on the earth's orbit, due to a slow change in the slant of the earth's axis. —*adj.* **precessional.**

pre-cinct (prē'sĭnkt), *n.* a place bounded, or marked off, by fixed lines; an outward limit or boundary; a district; as, a police *precinct*: *pl.* surrounding regions.

pre-cious (prĕsh'ŭs), *adj.* of great price or value; costly; very dear; highly esteemed.—*adv.* **preciously.**—*n.* **preciousness.**

prec-i-pice (prĕs'ĭ-pĭs), *n.* a steep descent; an abrupt declivity; an almost vertical cliff, or the edge of it; hence, a dangerous situation.

pre-cip-i-tance (prē-sĭp'ĭ-tăns), *n.* haste in resolving or carrying out a purpose; rashness. Also, **precipitancy.**

pre-cip-i-tant (prē-sĭp'ĭ-tănt), *adj.* falling headlong; too hasty or sudden; moving with rash haste: *n.* in chemistry, anything which causes the solid part of a solution to separate from the liquid and fall to the bottom of the vessel containing it.—*adv.* **precipitantly.**

pre-cip-i-tate (prē-sĭp'ĭ-tāt), *v.t.* to throw headlong; urge on violently; hurry on rashly, thoughtlessly, or unexpectedly; as, his act *precipitated* the disaster; to cause to change from vapor to liquid or solid and fall, as rain or snow; to cause to separate in solid form from a solution: *v.i.* to separate in solid form from a solution and fall to the bottom of a vessel: *n.* a solid substance separated from a solution by chemical action, or by heat or cold: *adj.* (prē-sĭp'ĭ-tāt), overhasty; rash; falling, flowing, or rushing headlong; descending steeply or vertically.—*adv.* **precipitately.**

pre-cip-i-ta-tion (prē-sĭp'ĭ-tā'shŭn), *n.* headlong fall; rashness; rash haste; a violent and swift descent; the process of causing the solid part of a solution to separate from the liquid and fall; the falling upon the earth's surface of dew, rain, snow, etc.

pre-cip-i-tous (prē-sĭp'ĭ-tŭs), *adj.* very steep, like a cliff; descending rapidly and violently.—*adv.* **precipitously.** —*n.* **precipitousness.**

pre-cise (prē-sīs'), *adj.* exact; strict; accurate; definite; keeping closely to rule.—*adv.* **precisely.**—*n.* **preciseness.**

pre-ci-sian (prē-sĭzh'ăn), *n.* one who is very careful to observe rules and forms.

pre-ci-sion (prē-sĭzh'ŭn), *n.* exactness; accuracy; definiteness.

pre-clude (prē-klōōd'), *v.t.* to shut out; hinder; stop; to keep from taking place; prevent; as, to *preclude* any necessity for doing a thing.

pre-clu-sion (prē-klōō'zhŭn), *n.* the act of preventing or of shutting out.

pre-clu-sive (prē-klōō'sĭv), *adj.* preventive.—*adv.* **preclusively.**

pre-co-cious (prē-kō'shŭs), *adj.* ripe before the natural time; forward in mental development; as, a *precocious* child; too forward.—*adv.* **precociously.** —*n.* **precociousness.**

pre-coc-i-ty (prē-kŏs'ĭ-tĭ), *n.* the state or quality of being ripe or developed before the usual time: too early growth; in a child, too early mental development.

pre-con-ceive (prē'kŏn-sēv'), *v.t.* to form an opinion of beforehand.—*n.* **preconception.**

pre-con-cert (prē'kŏn-sûrt'), *v.t.* to arrange together, or agree upon, beforehand.—*p.adj.* **preconcerted.**

pre-cur-sor (prē-kûr'sẽr), *n.* one who, or that which, precedes, or goes before, to show that a person or event is about to follow; forerunner.

pre-cur-so-ry (prē-kûr'sō-rĭ), *adj.* indicating something that is to happen or follow.

pre-da-cious (prē-dā'shŭs), *adj.* seizing and killing other animals as food; as, a *predacious* beast; living by plunder.

pred-a-to-ry (prĕd'ȧ-tō-rĭ), *adj.* plundering; robbing; as, a *predatory* war or tribe of people; living by preying on other animals; as, a *predatory* beast.

pred-e-ces-sor (prĕd'ē-sĕs'ẽr; prē'dē-sĕs'ẽr), *n.* one who has preceded or gone before another in the same office, business, position, etc.; an ancestor.

pre-des-ti-nate (prē-dĕs'tĭ-nāt), *v.t.* to decree or determine beforehand, or from the very beginning. Also, **predestine.**

pre-des-ti-na-tion (prē-dĕs'tĭ-nā'shŭn), *n.* the doctrine that God has from all eternity ordered whatever comes to pass; the decree that determines the happiness or misery of men; fate; destiny; foreknowledge.

pre-des-tine (prē-dĕs'tĭn), *v.t.* to decree or determine beforehand or from the beginning. Also, **predestinate.**

pre-de-ter-mine (prē'dē-tûr'mĭn), *v.t.* and *v.i.* to decide or resolve beforehand.—*n.* **predetermination.**

pred-i-ca-ble (prĕd'ĭ-kȧ-bl), *adj.* that may be affirmed or declared of something.

pre-dic-a-ment (prē-dĭk'ȧ-mĕnt) *n.* condition or situation; especially, a trying or unfortunate position; difficult situation.

pred-i-cate (prĕd'ĭ-kāt), *v.t.* to affirm as belonging to, or characteristic of, something; as, to *predicate* poverty as a result of ignorance; assert; declare: *v.i.* to affirm one thing of another; assert: *adj.* (prĕd'ĭ-kāt), in grammar, expressing that which is stated about the subject: *n.* in grammar, the part of a sentence which makes a statement about the subject.

pred-i-ca-tion (prĕd'ĭ-kā'shŭn), *n.* assertion; declaration.

pred-i-ca-tive (prĕd'ĭ-kā-tĭv), *adj.* affirmative or declarative.—*adv.* **predicatively.**

pre-dict (prē-dĭkt'), *v.t.* and *v.i.* to tell or make known beforehand; to foretell; prophesy.—*n.* **predictor.**

pre-dic-tion (prē-dĭk'shŭn), *n.* the foretelling of a future event; that which is foretold; prophecy.

pre-di-lec-tion (prē"dĭ-lĕk'shŭn; prĕd"ĭ-lĕk'shŭn), *n.* a previous liking; choice made beforehand; preference; partiality.

pre-dis-pose (prē"dĭs-pōz'), *v.t.* to incline beforehand; as, he was *predisposed* in her favor; fit or adapt beforehand; make liable to; as, *predisposed* to contagion.

pre-dis-po-si-tion (prē-dĭs"pō-zĭsh'ŭn), *n.* previous inclination; bias; tendency already existing.

pre-dom-i-nance (prē-dŏm'ĭ-năns), *n.* superiority in strength, power, authority, etc. Also, **predominancy.**

pre-dom-i-nant (prē-dŏm'ĭ-nănt), *adj.* having greater influence, etc.; superior; controlling.—*adv.* **predominantly.**

pre-dom-i-nate (prē-dŏm'ĭ-nāt), *v.i.* to be superior in strength, power, authority, etc.

pre-ëm-i-nence (prē-ĕm'ĭ-nĕns), *n.* superiority to all others in merit, rank, etc.

pre-ëm-i-nent (prē-ĕm'ĭ-nĕnt), *adj.* highly superior to others; above all others in merit or rank.—*adv.* **preëminently.**

pre-ëmpt (prē-ĕmpt'), *v.t.* establish a right or claim to before others: *v.i.* to take public land by virtue of the right to buy before others.—*n.* **preëmptor.**

pre-ëmp-tion (prē-ĕmp'shŭn), *n.* the act or right of purchasing before others.

preen (prēn), *v.t.* to cleanse, trim, and smooth with the beak, as a bird its plumage; to dress or fix (oneself) up.

pref-ace (prĕf'ās), *n.* the introduction to a book, speech, etc., separate from the body of the work: *v.t.* to introduce by some statement or remarks: *v.i.* to say, write, or do something, as an introduction.

pref-a-to-ry (prĕf'ȧ-tō-rĭ), *adj.* pertaining to, or of the nature of, an introduction; introductory.

pre-fect (prē'fĕkt), *n.* in ancient Rome, a civil magistrate or governor; commander; the civil governor of a department in France; as, the *prefect* of police.

pre-fec-ture (prē'fĕk-tûr), *n.* the office, authority, or official residence of a magistrate or governor called a prefect.

pre-fer (prē-fûr'), *v.t.* [*p.t.* and *p.p.* preferred, *p.pr.* preferring], to regard or esteem more than something else; present or offer for consideration; as, to *prefer* a petition; to choose instead of something else.

pref-er-a-ble (prĕf'ẽr-ȧ-bl), *adj.* more desirable than others; worthy to be chosen.—*adv.* **preferably.**—*n.* **preferableness.**

pref-er-ence (prĕf'ẽr-ĕns), *n.* choice of one thing more than another; that which is favored or chosen.

pref-er-en-tial (prĕf"ẽr-ĕn'shăl), *adj.* giving or having a choice; arising from favor or choice.

pre-fer-ment (prē-fûr'mĕnt), *n.* promotion to higher rank or office; a high post of honor, dignity, or profit, especially in the church.

pre-fig-ure (prē-fĭg'ūr), *v.t.* to show or declare beforehand by a type or symbol; to imagine to oneself beforehand.—*n.* **prefiguration.**

pre-fix (prē'fĭks), *n.* a letter, syllable, or group of syllables placed at the beginning of a word to change its meaning: *v.t.* (prē-fĭks'), to place before, or at the beginning of, anything.

preg-nan-cy (prĕg'năn-sĭ), *n.* fruitfulness; inventive power; the state of being with young; weight or significance.

preg-nant (prĕg'nănt), *adj.* being with young; fruitful; fertile; full of meaning; likely to have important consequences; weighty.

pre-hen-sile (prē-hĕn'sĭl), *adj.* adapted for seizing and holding.

pre-hen-sion (prē-hĕn'shŭn), *n.* a taking hold physically or mentally.

pre-his-tor-ic (prē"hĭs-tŏr'ĭk), *adj.* pertaining to a period before the time of which there is a written record.

prej-u-dice (prĕj'ōō-dĭs), *n.* judgment in advance, especially an unfavorable judgment; an opinion formed without due examination of the facts; injury or harm as a result of hasty or unfair judgment: *v.t.* to cause to form an opinion, usually unfavorable, before examination of the facts; hurt; harm or damage by some judgment or action.

Syn., *n.* unfairness, preconception.

Ant. (see reason).

prej-u-di-cial (prĕj"ōō-dĭsh'ăl), *adj.* injurious; hurtful; damaging.—*adv.* **prejudicially.**

prel-a-cy (prĕl'ȧ-sĭ), *n.* the office or position of a clergyman of high rank, as a bishop; bishops, collectively.

prel-ate (prĕl'āt), *n.* one of the higher order of clergy, as a bishop or archbishop.—*adj.* **prelatic, prelatical.**

pre-lim-i-na-ry (prē-lĭm'ĭ-nā-rĭ), *adj.* preceding the main discourse or business; introductory; as, *preliminary* remarks: *n.* an introduction; something preceding or going before.

prel-ude (prĕl'ūd; prē'lūd), *n.* a short piece of music played as an introduction to a longer piece; preface; something done to prepare the way for something more important: *v.t.* (prē-lūd'), to serve as an introduction to; precede: *v.i.* to be introductory.

pre-ma-ture (prē"mȧ-tūr'; prē'mȧ-tūr), *adj.* ripe before the proper time; arriving, occurring, or done, too soon, or before the proper time; as, a *premature* explosion.—*adv.* **prematurely.**—*n.* **prematureness.**

pre-med-i-tate (prē-mĕd'ĭ-tāt), *v.t.* to think carefully over or plan beforehand.

pre-med-i-ta-tion (prē-mĕd"ĭ-tā'shŭn), *n.* the act of thinking over and planning beforehand; forethought.

pre-mi-er (prē'mĭ-ẽr; prĕm'yẽr), *adj.* first in time, rank, or position; chief: *n.* a prime minister or chief officer.

pre-mi-er-ship (prē'mĭ-ẽr-shĭp"), *n.* the office or position of a prime minister or chief officer.

pre-mise (prē-mīz′), *v.t.* to state in advance, as an explanation or introduction: *v.i.* to make an explanation beforehand: *n.* (prĕm′ĭs), a statement accepted as true from which a conclusion is drawn: *pl.* foregoing statements; the property conveyed in a deed; real estate; a building or a piece of land; colloquially, a house and its surrounding property.

pre-mi-um (prē′mĭ-ŭm), *n.* a recompense or reward; prize or bounty; the rate paid for insurance; an extra price paid to obtain a loan; a sum above the par value or original value of anything; as, the stock sold at a *premium.*

pre-mo-ni-tion (prē″mō-nĭsh′ŭn), *n.* a warning in advance; foreboding.

pre-mon-i-to-ry (prē-mŏn′ĭ-tō-rĭ), *adj.* giving notice or warning beforehand.

pre-oc-cu-pa-tion (prē-ŏk″ū-pā′shŭn), *n.* state of being lost in thought, or of having the attention centered on one's own affairs; absent-mindedness.

pre-oc-cu-pied (prē-ŏk′ū-pīd), *adj.* lost in thought; taken up entirely with one's own affairs; absent-minded; absorbed.

prep-a-ra-tion (prĕp″*ȧ*-rā′shŭn), *n.* the act of making ready or fitting for a particular purpose; state of being ready; readiness; that which is ready or made ready, as a medicine, etc.

pre-par-a-tive (prē-păr′*ȧ*-tĭv), *adj.* tending to make ready or fit; preparatory: *n.* that which is ready; a making ready.—*adv.* **preparatively.**

pre-par-a-to-ry (prē-păr′*ȧ*-tō-rĭ), *adj.* serving to make ready or to fit for something further; being fitted or made ready, as by instruction.

pre-pare (prē-pâr′), *v.t.* to make ready, fit, or suitable; to provide, or fit out: *v.i.* to make or get things or oneself ready; as, to *prepare* for a journey; *prepare* to die; *prepare* for war.—*p.adj.* **prepared.**—*adv.* **preparedly.**

pre-par-ed-ness (prē-pâr′ĕd-nĕs), *n.* state of being ready; especially, national readiness for defense in case of war.

pre-pay (prē-pā′), *v.t.* to pay, or pay the cost of, in advance.—*n.* **prepayment.**

pre-pense (prē-pĕns′), *adj.* premeditated, or thought out beforehand; as, malice *prepense.*

pre-pon-der-ance (prē-pŏn′dẽr-ăns), *n.* state of being greater in weight, power, force, or influence.

pre-pon-der-ant (prē-pŏn′dẽr-ănt), *adj.* outweighing; being greater in weight, power, force or influence.

pre-pon-der-ate (prē-pŏn′dẽr-āt), *v.i.* to outweigh; exceed in power or influence.

prep-o-si-tion (prĕp″ō-zĭsh′ŭn), *n.* a word, followed by a noun or pronoun, as object, which shows the relation of the object to some other word; as, in the sentence, Mary went to the store, *to* is a *preposition* showing relation between *store* and *went.*

prep-o-si-tion-al (prĕp″ō-zĭsh′ŭn-ăl), *adj.* pertaining to a preposition, or word placed before a noun or pronoun to show relation to another word: **prepositional phrase,** a phrase, composed of a preposition and its object, and used as an adverb or adjective] modifier.—*adv.* **prepositionally.**

pre-pos-i-tive (prē-pŏs′ĭ-tĭv), *adj.* placed before: *n.* in grammar, a word or particle placed before another word.

pre-pos-sess (prē″pŏ-zĕs′), *v.t.* to occupy beforehand; as, to *prepossess* land; to fill (the mind) beforehand so as to shut out other thoughts; hence, to lead to a favorable opinion beforehand.

pre-pos-sess-ing (prē″pŏ-zĕs′ĭng), *p.adj.* tending to win or secure favor; attractive.

pre-pos-ses-sion (prē″pŏ-zĕsh′ŭn), *n.* an opinion, usually favorable, of a person or thing; formed in advance of actual knowledge, and shutting out other ideas from the mind; a preconceived liking; bias.

pre-pos-ter-ous (prē-pŏs′tẽr-ŭs), *adj.* contrary to nature or common sense; ridiculous; absurd; unreasonable; as a *preposterous* statement.—*adv.* **preposterously.**—*n.* **preposterousness.**

pre-req-ui-site (prē-rĕk′wĭ-zĭt), *adj.* necessary to secure an intended result: *n.* something necessary beforehand.

pre-rog-a-tive (prē-rŏg′*ȧ*-tĭv), *n.* a right or privilege that has always belonged to a person or class and that cannot be disputed: *adj.* pertaining to such a right or privilege.

pres-age (prĕs′āj; prē′sāj), *n.* a feeling that something is to happen; an omen or sign: *v.t.* (prē-sāj′), to foretell; predict: *v.i.* to foretell something to come.

pres-by-ter (prĕz′bĭ-tẽr; prĕs′bĭ-tẽr), *n.* a priest; an elder in the early church; in the Presbyterian Church, a minister or elder.—*adj.* **presbyterial.**

pres-by-te-ri-an (prĕz″bĭ-tē′rĭ-ăn; prĕs″bĭ-tē′rĭ-ăn), *adj.* pertaining to a presbyter, or to church government by presbyters: **Presbyterian,** *adj.* pertaining to church government by ministers and elders: *n.* a member or supporter of a church governed by ministers and elders.

Pres-by-te-ri-an-ism (prĕz″bĭ-tē′rĭ-ăn-ĭzm; prĕs″bĭ-tē′rĭ-ăn-ĭzm), *n.* the system of church government by ministers and elders, having no superior church officials such as bishops.

pres-by-ter-y (prĕz′bĭ-tẽr-ĭ; prĕs′bĭ-tẽr-ĭ), *n.* in the early church, a body of elders; in the Presbyterian Church, an organized body, having judicial power, composed of the ministers and ruling elders of the churches in a given district; the district so represented.

pre-sci-ence (prē′shĭ-ĕns; prĕsh′ĭ-ĕns), *n.* the knowing of events before they take place; foresight.

pre-sci-ent (prē′shĭ-ĕnt; prĕsh′ĭ-ĕnt), *adj.* foreseeing; foreknowing.

pre-scribe (prē-skrīb′), *v.t.* to order the use of as medicine; to set down as a guide or rule of action; give as a direction: *v.i.* to write medical directions; give laws or rules.—*n.* **prescriber.**

pre-scrip-tion (prē-skrĭp′shŭn), *n.* the giving of a direction or rule; the direction or rule given; a written direction for the preparation and use of a medicine.—*adj.* **prescriptive.**

pres-ence (prĕz′ĕns), *n.* the state or quality of being in a certain place; nearness; immediate neighborhood;

as, in the *presence* of danger; in the *presence* of a lady; one's appearance or bearing; as, a girl of pleasing *presence;* all the qualities that make a person what he is: **presence of mind,** quickness in thinking or deciding in time of danger or necessity.

pres-ent (prĕz'ĕnt), being in a certain place; being at hand or in sight; opposite to *absent;* existing at this time; not past or future; instant or immediate; in grammar, denoting time that now is: *n.* the time now here; a gift or donation: *v.t.* (prē-zĕnt'), to bring before someone, especially before a superior; to introduce; to bring to view or notice; to offer as a gift; to make a gift to; to lay before for consideration.—*n.* **presenter.**

pre-sent-a-ble (prē-zĕn'tȧ-bl), *adj.* suitable to be offered, given, or introduced; fit to be seen.—*n.* **presentability.**

pres-en-ta-tion (prĕz"ĕn-tā'shŭn), *n.* the act of introducing, offering, or bringing to consideration; that which is introduced, offered, or brought to consideration.

pre-sen-ti-ment (prē-sĕn'tĭ-mĕnt), *n.* a feeling of fear as to what will occur, usually of coming evil; a foreboding.

pres-ent-ly (prĕz'ĕnt-lĭ), *adv.* at once; soon; before long; in a little while.

pre-sent-ment (prē-zĕnt'mĕnt), *n.* the act of setting forth to view; the thing set forth to view; a representation or picture; a report or statement made by a grand jury concerning an offense of which they have personal knowledge, but which is not included in the list of cases before them.

pres-er-va-tion (prĕz"ĕr-vā'shŭn), *n.* the act of keeping from injury or decay; the state of being kept from injury or decay; as, the *preservation* of fruit.

pre-serv-a-tive (prē-zûr'vȧ-tĭv), *adj.* having the power to keep safe and sound: *n.* that which has power to keep safe and sound. Also, **preservatory.**

pre-serve (prē-zûrv'), *v.t.* to keep from injury; defend; uphold; save; as, to *preserve* life; keep in a sound state; put up with sugar, salt, etc., for keeping; as, to *preserve* fruit; keep up; maintain; as, to *preserve* peace: *n.* fruit, etc., put up and kept in sugar; a place set apart for keeping game, fish, etc.—*adj.* **preservable.**—*n.* **preserver.**

pre-side (prē-zīd'), *v.i.* to direct or control; act as head; as, to *preside* over one's household; to direct the proceedings of a meeting; as, the chairman *presided;* superintend.—*n.* **presider.**

pres-i-den-cy (prĕz'ĭ-dĕn-sĭ), *n.* the function, or duty, of one who directs a meeting, etc.; the office or term of office of a president: **Presidency,** the office of chief executive of the United States.

pres-i-dent (prĕz'ĭ-dĕnt), *n.* one who directs or acts as head of an organized body; the highest executive officer of a modern republic; the chief officer of a college, university, or society: **President,** the chief magistrate of the United States.

pres-i-den-tial (prĕz"ĭ-dĕn'shăl), *adj.* pertaining to a president, or chief magistrate, or to his office; as, a *presidential* election.

press (prĕs), *v.t.* to bear heavily down upon; squeeze or crush strongly; hug or embrace; urge; as, they *pressed* him to accept; compel; crowd upon; to force to hurry; make smooth, as cloth, etc.; formerly, to force for service into the navy: *v.i.* to bear heavily; move forward with steady force; as, to *press* on one's way; collect in throngs; crowd; to be urgent or insistent; as, time *presses:* *n.* an instrument or machine for condensing, crushing, or stamping anything; a printing machine; newspaper and magazine literature; as, the power of the *press;* literature generally; a crowd; a throng; act of crowding forward; pressure; hurry or urgency of affairs; as, the *press* of business; a closet with shelves.

press-ing (prĕs'ĭng), *p.adj.* urgent; as, a *pressing* engagement.

press-man (prĕs'măn), *n.* one who manages or operates a machine called a press, especially a printing press.

pres-sure (prĕsh'ŭr), *n.* a heavy bearing down or pushing against; a squeeze; force or weight acting against anything; a force which drives ahead; as, to work under *pressure;* burden; distress; urgent or insistent demand; as, the *pressure* of work.

pres-ti-dig-i-ta-tion (prĕs"tĭ-dĭj"ĭ-tā'shŭn), *n.* sleight of hand, especially that requiring skill with the fingers; juggling in general.—*n.* **prestidigitator.**

pres-tige (prĕs-tēzh'; prĕs'tĭj), *n.* authority, influence, or power, due to past reputation, achievements, etc.

pres-to (prĕs'tō), *adv.* quickly; suddenly; used as a musical direction, and as an exclamation by a worker of sleight of hand tricks.

pre-sum-a-ble (prē-zūm'ȧ-bl), *adj.* fair to suppose; reasonable.—*adv.* **presumably.**

pre-sume (prē-zūm'), *v.t.* to take for granted; suppose: *v.i.* to venture or risk without permission; as, to *presume* to offer advice; venture; behave with overconfidence or undue boldness; take liberties; as, to *presume* on one's good nature.—*n.* **presumer.**

pre-sump-tion (prē-zŭmp'shŭn), *n.* a going beyond due bounds; bold forwardness; acceptance and belief of something not fully proved; as, he acted on the *presumption* that the price would rise; that which is taken for granted.

pre-sump-tive (prē-zŭmp'tĭv), *adj.* affording reasonable ground for belief; probable.—*adv.* **presumptively.**

pre-sump-tu-ous (prē-zŭmp'tū-ŭs), *adj.* bold and overconfident; rash; foolhardy.—*adv.* **presumptuously.**—*n.* **presumptuousness.**

pre-sup-pose (prē"sŭ-pōz'), *v.t.* to take for granted; assume in advance.

pre-sup-po-si-tion (prē-sŭp"ō-zĭsh'ŭn), *n.* a belief previously formed; that which is taken for granted.

pre-tend (prē-tĕnd'), *v.t.* to put forward as an excuse or reason; make a false show of; as, to *pretend* friendship; to feign; to put forward a claim to; as, to *pretend* ownership: *v.i.* to put forward a claim, true or false; as, to *pretend* to a title; to make a false show; to play at make-believe.

pre-tend-ed (prē-tĕnd'ĕd), *p.adj.* feigned or imagined; false.—*adv.* **pretendedly.**

pre-tend-er (prē-tĕn'dẽr), *n.* one who lays claim to anything under the appearance of a right; one who makes a false show of anything.

pre-tense (prē-tĕns'), *n.* a putting on of a false appearance in order to hide what is real; deception; false show; sham; affectation; pretext; unfounded claim. Also, **pretence.**

pre-ten-sion (prē-tĕn'shŭn), *n.* a claim made, whether true or false; assumed right; outward show of importance or excellence beyond what the facts warrant.

pre-ten-tious (prē-tĕn'shŭs), *adj.* assuming an air of superiority; making a show.—*adv.* **pretentiously.**—*n.* **pretentiousness.**

pret-er-it (prĕt'ẽr-ĭt), *adj.* past; noting the tense which expresses past or completed time or action: *n.* the past tense. Also, **preterite.**

pre-ter-nat-u-ral (prē'tẽr-năt'ū-răl), *adj.* unlike ordinary occurrences; extraordinary; out of the common order; strange.—*adv.* **preternaturally.**

pre-text (prē'tĕkst; prē-tĕkst'), *n.* a pretense or excuse; false motive put forward to conceal the real one.

pre-tor (prē'tŏr), *n.* the Roman magistrate next below the consul. Also, **praetor.**—*adj.* **pretorian, praetorian.**

pret-ty (prĭt'ĭ), *adj.* [*comp.* prettier, *superl.* prettiest], pleasing because of grace and daintiness; pleasing to the eye; delicately pleasing; neatly arranged or ornamented; trim; moderately large or excellent; fine: *adv.* fairly; moderately; tolerably; as, *pretty* well.—*adv.* **prettily.**—*n.* **prettiness.**

pret-zel (prĕt'sĕl), *n.* a kind of salted biscuit made in the form of a knot.

pre-vail (prē-vāl'), *v.i.* to overcome; gain the advantage; obtain influence or superiority; continue in force; as, the custom *prevails* widely; persuade: with *on.* —*p.adj.* **prevailing.**

prev-a-lence (prĕv'ȧ-lĕns), *n.* the state of being widespread or in general use; frequency; superior strength or influence. Also, **prevalency.**

prev-a-lent (prĕv'ȧ-lĕnt), *adj.* powerful; victorious; most general; common; widespread; as, a *prevalent* belief. —*adv.* **prevalently.**

pre-var-i-cate (prē-văr'ĭ-kāt), *v.i.* to stray from the truth; quibble.

pre-var-i-ca-tion (prē-văr'ĭ-kā'shŭn), *n.* a quibbling to avoid the truth; a turning aside from truth or fair dealing.

pre-var-i-ca-tor (prē-văr'ĭ-kā'tẽr), *n.* one who strays from the truth.

pre-vent (prē-vĕnt'), *v.t.* to stop or keep from happening; to hinder, obstruct, or impede.—*adj.* **preventable, preventible.**—*n.* **preventer.**

pre-ven-tion (prē-vĕn'shŭn), *n.* the act of hindering or keeping from happening; hindrance or obstruction; that which hinders.

pre-ven-tive (prē-vĕn'tĭv), *adj.* tending to hinder: *n.* that which hinders; a medicine to keep disease from occurring.—*adv.* **preventively.**

pre-vi-ous (prē'vĭ-ŭs), *adj.* going before in time; prior; as, a *previous* action.—*adv.* **previously.**
Syn. former, preceding.
Ant. (see subsequent).

pre-vi-sion (prē-vĭzh'ŭn), *n.* foreknowledge; foresight.

prey (prā), *n.* any animal which may be or is seized by a wild beast for food; hence, anything taken by force or violence; plunder; booty: *v.i.* [*p.t.* and *p.p.* preyed, *p.pr.* preying], to take booty or plunder; to seize and devour an animal as food; to exert a destructive influence: with *on* or *upon;* as, his guilt *preyed* upon his mind.

price (prīs), *n.* worth; value; something of equal worth, usually money, given or asked in exchange for a thing; the cost of a commodity: *v.t.* to set a value on; ask the value of; as, to *price* goods.
Syn., n. expense, outlay, cost.

price-less (prīs'lĕs), *adj.* invaluable; of worth too great to be measured.

prick (prĭk), *n.* a puncture, dot, or point; a slender, pointed instrument; a sharp, stinging pain, usually caused by a pointed instrument; remorse; a thorn; footprint of a hare or deer: *v.t.* to pierce with, or as with, something pointed; mark out by puncturing; to pain or sting; as, his conscience *pricks* him; to erect or raise; as, a dog *pricks* up its ears; to spur; urge; as, to *prick* a horse on: *v.i.* to feel a sharp, stinging pain.

prick-er (prĭk'ẽr), *n.* a sharp point; usually, a tiny point on the stem or leaf of a plant, similar to, but differing from, a thorn or spine.

prick-le (prĭk'l), *n.* a sharp point growing from the bark of a plant; as, a thorn: *v.t.* to give a stinging sensation to the skin; to cover with small dots: *v.i.* to tingle.

prick-ly (prĭk'lĭ), *adj.* full of thorns or sharp points; stinging; as, a *prickly* sensation.—*n.* **prickliness.**

pride (prīd), *n.* undue self-esteem; conceit; haughtiness; disdain; sense of personal dignity; high and dignified self-respect; that of which one is proud; as, his daughter was his *pride;* the best or highest part of anything; as, he was in the *pride* of his manhood; loveliness; ornament; display: *v.t.* to indulge in self-esteem; as, to *pride* oneself.
Syn., n. vainglory, vanity.
Ant. (see humility, meekness).

priest (prēst), *n.* [*fem.* priestess], one devoted to the service of God or a god, with authority to perform religious rites; one ordained to the Christian ministry; a minister in the Roman Catholic Church.

priest-craft (prēst'krȧft'), *n.* a term, usually scornful, for the whole system and policy of the Roman Catholic Church.

priest-hood (prēst'hŏŏd), *n.* the entire order, office, or character of those ordained to serve God and perform religious rites.

priest-ly (prēst'lĭ), *adj.* of or pertaining to one ordained to serve God.—*n.* **priestliness.**

prig (prĭg), *n.* a conceited fellow who gives himself airs of wisdom: *v.t.* [*p.t.* and *p.p.* prigged, *p.pr.* prigging], to dress up; primp; prink.

prig-gish (prĭg'ĭsh), *adj.* conceited; affectedly nice.—*adv.* **priggishly.** —*n.* **priggishness.**

prim (prim), *adj.* precise; nice; formally neat: *v.t.* to dress or deck with nicety.—*adv.* **primly.**—*n.* **primness.**

pri-ma-cy (prī'ma-sĭ), *n.* the state of being first in rank or importance; the office or dignity of an archbishop.

pri-ma don-na (prē'mȧ dŏn'ȧ), the principal female singer in an opera; a woman concert singer of superior excellence. [It.]

pri-ma fa-ci-e (prī'mȧ fā'shĭ-ē), at first view; as far as at first appears; as, *prima facie* evidence. [Lat.]

pri-mal (prī'măl), *adj.* first; original; primary; chief.

pri-ma-ri-ly (prī'mȧ-rĭ-lĭ), *adv.* in the first place; originally; essentially.

pri-ma-ry (prī'mȧ-rĭ), *adj.* in the first order of time, place, or rank; original; chief; principal; first in order of development; hence, lowest; as, a *primary* school; preparatory: *n.* that which is first in rank, place, or importance; a meeting of voters to name candidates, etc., to be voted for in a coming election; one of the large flight-feathers in a bird's wing: **primary election,** a local meeting of the voters of a political party, at which the nominees, officials, or delegates of that party are chosen: **direct primary,** a primary election at which the nominees of a party are chosen directly by the voters of that party, without the intervention of a nominating convention.

pri-ma-ry col-ors (prī'mȧ-rĭ kŭl'ẽrz), red, yellow, blue: so called because from them all the other colors can be formed.

pri-mate (prī'māt), *n.* the highest church dignitary or official in a nation or province; archbishop.

prime (prīm), *adj.* first in order of rank, time, or importance; first in excellence; original; early; excellent; not to be divided by any number but itself and one; as, 13 is a *prime* number: *n.* the spring of life; the first or best part of anything; beginning of the day or year; the time of greatest vigor; height of perfection: *v.t.* to prepare for firing, as a gun; lay the first coat of paint on; to put into good working condition; to instruct as to what must be said; as, to *prime* a witness with evidence.—*adv.* **primely.**

prime num-ber (prīm nŭm'bẽr), a number not divisible without remainder by any number except itself and unity, as 5, 13, 23, etc.

prim-er (prĭm'ẽr), *n.* a small book from which children learn to read; a textbook containing the first principles of any subject; one of two sizes of type, *long primer* and *great primer.*

pri-me-val (prī-mē'văl), *adj.* pertaining to the earliest age or time; original.—*adv.* **primevally.**

Syn. old, ancient.

Ant. (see recent).

prim-ing (prīm'ĭng), *n.* act of one that primes something; the first coat of paint; the powder or other substance used to fire a charge from a gun.

prim-i-tive (prĭm'ĭ-tĭv), *adj.* pertaining to the beginning; original; simple or crude; old-fashioned: *n.* a word in its simplest form and not taken from another.—*adv.* **primitively.**—*n.* **primitiveness.**

pri-mo-gen-i-ture (prī'mō-jĕn'ĭ-tūr), *n.* state of being a first-born child; in law, the exclusive right of the eldest son to succeed to real estate.

pri-mor-di-al (prī-mŏr'dĭ-ăl), *adj.* existing from the beginning; first in order; original.

primp (primp), *v.t.* and *v.i.* to dress with exaggerated care or for show; as, to *primp* one's hair. [Colloq.]

prim-rose (prĭm'rōz"), *n.* an early spring flower of a pale yellow color, of several species: *adj.* pale yellow; flowery; gay.

prince (prĭns), *n.* a ruler or sovereign; the son of a king or emperor; a member of a royal family or of a high order of nobility; a chief or very distinguished member of a class of men; as, a merchant *prince.*

prince con-sort (prĭns kŏn'sôrt), the husband of a queen who reigns in her own right.

prince-ly (prĭns'lĭ), *adj.* like, or worthy of, one who is royal or of very high station; grand; noble; magnificent.—*n.* **princeliness.**

prin-cess (prĭn'sĕs), *n.* the daughter of a sovereign; the wife of a prince; a female member of a royal family.

prin-cess roy-al (prĭn'sĕs roi'ăl), the eldest daughter of a sovereign.

prin-ci-pal (prĭn'sĭ-păl), *adj.* first or highest in rank, value, character, degree, or importance; most important; main; chief: *n.* one who takes the lead; the chief in authority; head of a firm or school; a sum of money drawing interest.—*adv.* **principally.**

prin-ci-pal-i-ty (prĭn'sĭ-păl'ĭ-tĭ), *n.* the territory of a prince; the country from which he obtains his title; as, the *principality* of Wales; royal state; supreme power.

prin-ci-ple (prĭn'sĭ-pl), *n.* a source or cause from which a thing comes; a settled rule or law of action or conduct; a truth which is general and plain and upon which others are founded; as, the *principles* of government; reason; uprightness; as, a man of *principle.*

Syn. ground, motive, impulse, maxim, rule.

prink (prĭnk), *v.t.* to dress up, or deck out, in a showy fashion; arrange with nicety; primp: *v.i.* to dress or deck oneself for show.

print (prĭnt), *n.* a mark or character made by pressure; as, a foot*print;* a stamp or die for making an impression; as, a butter *print;* that which receives the impression; the letters used in type; an impression from type; as, large *print;* anything produced by type or from an engraved plate, as a newspaper, engraving, etc.; a picture reproduced by impression from a plate, as a photograph, photogravure, lithograph, etc.; stamped cotton cloth, especially calico: *v.t.* to make an impression on; as, their feet *print* the sand; fix or stamp in or on something; as, to *print* footsteps in the sand; to stamp with letters, patterns, etc.; as, to *print* calico; to reproduce from type, engraved plates, etc., as books, pictures, newspapers, etc.; to make in letters like those of type; as, a child *prints* a letter: *v.i.* to make impressions from type, plates, etc.; to publish books, etc.; to make letters like those used in type.

print-er (prĭn'tẽr), *n.* one whose trade is typesetting or making impressions from type; one whose business is publishing books, papers, magazines, etc.

print-ing (prĭnt'ĭng), *n.* the act, art, or business of putting matter for reading into type; the process of making books, newspapers, etc.

print-ing press (prĭn'tĭng prĕs''), a machine for making impressions from type, as in newspapers, books, etc.

pri-or (prī'ẽr), *adj.* going before in time or order; previous: *n.* [*fem.* prioress], the head of a convent or monastery, next in rank below an abbot.

pri-or-i-ty (prī-ŏr'ĭ-tĭ), *n.* the state of being first, or going before, in rank, time, or place; first claim.

pri-or-y (prī'ō-rĭ), *n.* [*pl.* priories (-rĭz)], a monastery or convent ruled by a prior, and next below an abbey.

prism (prĭzm), *n.* a solid whose bases are similar, equal, and parallel, and whose sides are parallelograms; such a solid, having triangular ends and made of glass or other transparent substance: used for separating the colors in the light ray.

pris-mat-ic (prĭz-măt'ĭk), *adj.* like, or pertaining to, a prism, especially a triangular glass prism; showing the colors formed by passing a ray of light through a prism; varied in color like the rainbow. Also, **prismatical.**

pris-mat-ic col-ors (prĭz-măt'ĭk kŭl'-ẽrz), the seven colors, called the spectrum, into which a ray of light breaks when passed through a refracting substance; the colors of the rainbow.

pris-mat-ic lens (prĭz-măt'ĭk lĕnz), an instrument of glass, or similar substance, used in various scientific apparatus; a peculiar form of eyeglass or spectacle. Also, prism **lens, prismatic glass,** prism **glass.**

Prism Lenses of a Lighthouse

pris-on (prĭz'n), *n.* a public building for the confinement of criminals, etc.; jail; any place of confinement or detention.

pris-on-er (prĭz'n-ẽr), *n.* one who is under arrest or on trial; one who is confined in a jail or prison; any one held against his will; a soldier who has been captured by the enemy in war; a captive.

pris-tine (prĭs'tĭn; prĭs'tīn), *adj.* pertaining to the earliest time or state; original; primitive.

prith-ee (prĭth'ē), *interj.* a short way of saying "I pray thee."

pri-va-cy (prī'vȧ-sĭ; prĭv'ȧ-sĭ), *n.* [*pl.* privacies (-sĭz)], the state of being away from public view; seclusion; place of seclusion or retirement; secrecy.

pri-vate (prī'vāt), *adj.* concerning or belonging to oneself alone; personal; not public; as, one's *private* affairs; away from public view; retired; secret; as, a *private* parlor; *private* information; not holding a public position; as, a *private* citizen: *n.* a common soldier.—*adv.* **privately.** —*n.* **privateness.**

pri-va-teer (prī'vȧ-tēr'), *n.* a vessel, not a government warship, licensed or permitted by the government to attack the ships of an enemy; the commander or one of the crew of such a vessel: *v.i.* to sail about in such a vessel in order to attack enemy ships.—*n.* **privateersman.**

pri-va-tion (prī-vā'shŭn), *n.* the state of being without, or of wanting, something; a lack of the necessaries of life; need; hardship; absence of a quality that an object should have.

priv-a-tive (prĭv'ȧ-tĭv), *adj.* causing want; having, or giving, a negative instead of a positive meaning; negative: *n.* a syllable attached to a word to change its positive meaning to a negative one.—*adv.* **privatively.**

priv-et (prĭv'ĕt), *n.* an ornamental shrub of the olive family much used for hedges.

priv-i-lege (prĭv'ĭ-lĕj), *n.* a special advantage, favor, or right, granted to or enjoyed by some to the exclusion of others; one of the rights granted to the people by a constitutional form of government; as, the *privilege* of free speech: *v.t.* to bestow some particular right or favor on; as, he is *privileged* to speak; exempt, or set free; as, his position *privileges* him not to be arrested.

Syn., *n.* advantage, favor, exemption, right, claim: *v.* favor, exempt.

priv-i-ty (prĭv'ĭ-tĭ), *n.* knowledge shared with another or others about something not publicly known; privacy; secrecy.

priv-y (prĭv'ĭ), *adj.* not public; retired; as, *privy* chambers; private; as, the *privy* purse; knowing secretly; as, he was *privy* to everything that went on.—*adv.* **privily.**

prize (prīz), *n.* a reward offered or won in a contest; that which is taken from an enemy in war, especially a captured vessel; anything of value obtained by chance, or worth striving for: *v.t.* to value highly, as a gift; esteem; to seize in war as a thing of value.

prob-a-bil-i-ty (prŏb'ȧ-bĭl'ĭ-tĭ), *n.* [*pl.* probabilities (-tĭz)], quality or state of being likely; likelihood; something likely: *pl.* a foretelling of the weather, especially by a government bureau.

prob-a-ble (prŏb'ȧ-bl), *adj.* upheld by evidence, but leaving some room for doubt; likely; most likely to be true, yet perhaps false.—*adv.* **probably.**

pro-bate (prō'bāt), *n.* official, legal proof, as of wills; the official copy of a will with the certificate of its having been proved.

pro-ba-tion (prō-bā'shŭn), *n.* act of proving; proof; any proceeding intended to put a person to a test as to character, ability, etc.; trial or test.

pro-ba-tion-a-ry (prō-bā'shŭn-ā-rĭ), *adj.* serving for a test or trial. Also, **probational.**

pro-ba-tion-er (prō-bā'shŭn-ẽr), *n.* one who is being subjected to a test or trial.

pro-ba-tion of-fic-er (prō-bā'shŭn ŏf'ĭ-sẽr), a person appointed by a juvenile court to have an oversight of child offenders who are serving a probation, or time of testing of good conduct.

probe (prōb), *n.* a slender surgical instrument for examining a wound or a cavity: *v.t.* to examine with a probe, or slender instrument; to inquire into, or look into closely.

prob-i-ty (prŏb'ĭ-tĭ; prō'bĭ-tĭ), *n.* virtue and honesty tested and proved.

Syn. uprightness, honesty, soundness.

Ant. (see dishonesty).

prob-lem (prŏb'lĕm), *n.* a doubtful question to be answered; a difficult matter to be settled; in mathematics, something to be worked out.

prob-lem-at-ic (prŏb'lĕm-ăt'ĭk), *adj.* questionable; doubtful. Also, **problematical.**—*adv.* **problematically.**
Syn. uncertain, disputable.
Ant. (see certain).

pro-bos-cis (prō-bŏs'ĭs), *n.* the trunk of an elephant; the snout, nose, or tube, of certain animals and insects.

pro-ce-dure (prō-sē'dūr), *n.* manner of carrying on a law case; process or manner of acting; a course of action or an act in a course of conduct.

pro-ceed (prō-sēd'), *v.i.* to go on or forward; continue; advance; as, *proceed* with your reading; *proceed* on your journey; to issue or come forth, as from a source; as, all good things *proceed* from God; to carry on an action in an orderly way; as, to *proceed* with good judgment; carry on a legal action: *n.pl.* (prō'sēdz), money resulting from a commercial transaction.

pro-ceed-ing (prō-sēd'ĭng), *n.* act of going on or forward; a transaction, as in business; course of conduct; a step in a law case: *pl.* course of action in a law case; as, legal *proceedings;* the records of the business of the meetings of a society, etc.

proc-ess (prŏs'ĕs; prō'sĕs), *n.* act of going on; advance; progress; a series of motions, actions, or events; an act which continues and progresses; an operation, or number of operations, leading to some result; any of the modern methods of producing illustrations by photo-engraving: often used as an adjective; as, a *process* cut, or illustration; proceedings in a legal action; an order of court issued as a part of a legal action; in anatomy, an outgrowth from, or projecting part of, the body, as an animal's horn.

pro-ces-sion (prō-sĕsh'ŭn), *n.* regular or orderly progress; that which moves forward, especially a train of persons in a formal march.

pro-ces-sion-al (prō-sĕsh'ŭn-ăl), *adj.* pertaining to a formal march or progress; *n.* a hymn sung at the beginning of a church service while clergy and choir are passing to their places; organ music played at the opening of a church service, or during a formal march down a church aisle.

pro-claim (prō-klām'), *v.t.* to make known publicly; announce officially; publish abroad.

proc-la-ma-tion (prŏk'lȧ-mā'shŭn), *n.* an official announcement to the public; the thing announced.

pro-cliv-i-ty (prō-klĭv'ĭ-tĭ), *n.* a natural inclination; tendency.

pro-con-sul (prō-kŏn'sŭl), *n.* a Roman official who performed the duties of a consul, or chief magistrate; a Roman governor of a province.—*adj.* **proconsular.**

pro-con-sul-ship (prō-kŏn'sŭl-shĭp), *n.* the office of a proconsul, or Roman official who governed a province. Also, **proconsulate.**

pro-cras-ti-nate (prō-krăs'tĭ-nāt), *v.t.* to put off from time to time; defer: *v.i.* to delay.

pro-cras-ti-na-tion (prō-krăs'tĭ-nā'shŭn), *n.* the act or habit of putting off from day to day; delay.

pro-cras-ti-na-tor (prō-krăs'tĭ-nā'tẽr), *n.* one who delays, or has the habit of putting off.

pro-cre-ate (prō'krē-āt), *v.t.* to produce, beget, or bring forth.—*n.* **procreator.**

pro-cre-a-tion (prō'krē-ā'shŭn), *n.* the bringing forth of young.

pro-cre-a-tive (prō'krē-ā'tĭv), *adj.* having power to beget or bring forth; reproductive.

proc-tor (prŏk'tẽr), *n.* one employed to manage the affairs of another; an attorney, or agent; an officer employed to enforce order in a school or university.—*adj.* **proctorial.**

pro-cur-a-ble (prō-kūr'ȧ-bl), *adj.* that may be obtained.

proc-u-ra-tion (prŏk'ū-rā'shŭn), *n.* the managing of affairs for another; authority to act for another, called a power of attorney.

proc-u-ra-tor (prŏk'ū-rā'tẽr), *n.* one who manages another's affairs, especially legal matters; an agent; a representative officer elected by the students of a university.

pro-cure (prō-kūr'), *v.t.* to get or obtain; cause or bring about; as, to *procure* a result.—*n.* **procurement.**

prod (prŏd), *n.* a pointed implement or instrument for pricking or puncturing, as a goad or pointed stick; a punch or prick: *v.t.* [*p.t.* and *p.p.* prodded, *p.pr.* prodding], to punch or poke with a pointed instrument; hence, to goad or urge.

prod-i-gal (prŏd'ĭ-găl), *adj.* reckless in spending money; lavish; wasteful: *n.* a spendthrift; one who is lavish or wasteful.—*adv.* **prodigally.**

prod-i-gal-i-ty (prŏd'ĭ-găl'ĭ-tĭ), *n.* the state or quality of being wasteful; extravagance; lavishness.

pro-di-gious (prō-dĭj'ŭs), *adj.* unusually great in size, extent, degree, or quantity; vast; immense; enormous.—*adv.* **prodigiously.**—*n.* **prodigiousness.**
Ant. (see insignificant).

prod-i-gy (prŏd'ĭ-jĭ), *n.* anything so out of the ordinary as to call forth wonder; a marvel.

pro-duce (prō-dūs'), *v.t.* to exhibit or bring to view; as, he *produced* the hidden money; yield or bring forth; as, the tree *produces* fruit; manufacture; as, a factory *produces* cloth; to lead to; as, wealth *produces* comfort: *n.* (prŏd'ūs), that which is yielded or brought forth; anything grown, made, or taken, by man's labor or skill; yield, especially farm products.

pro-duc-er (prō-dūs'ẽr), *n.* one who manufactures goods or raises crops; one who puts plays on the stage.

pro-duc-i-ble (prō-dūs'ĭ-bl), *adj.* capable of being grown, made, or brought forth.

prod-uct (prŏd'ŭkt), *n.* that which is yielded by nature, or made by labor, thought, etc.; result; the result obtained by multiplying two or more numbers together.

pro-duc-tion (prō-dŭk'shŭn), *n.* that which is yielded by nature or made by man's labor, thought, etc.; a theatrical exhibit; act of bringing forth or making; fruit.

pro-duc-tive (prō-dŭk'tĭv), *adj.* having the quality or power of yielding or bringing forth; fertile; leading to results; bringing forth in abundance.—*adv.* **productively.**—*n.* **productiveness.**

pro-em (prō'ĕm), *n.* a preface or introduction.

prof-a-na-tion (prŏf'ȧ-nā'shŭn), *n.* the act of treating sacred things with disrespect.

pro-fane (prō-fān'), *adj.* not sacred or holy; hence, having to do with this world; as, *profane* history; showing disrespect or irreverence toward God or sacred things; unholy; blasphemous; as, *profane* language: *v.t.* to treat (something sacred) with irreverence, contempt, or abuse; put to an improper or degrading use; debase.—*adv.* **profanely.**—*n.* **profaneness.**

pro-fan-i-ty (prō-făn'ĭ-tĭ), *n.* [*pl.* **profanities** (-tĭz)], contempt for holy things; blasphemy; swearing.

pro-fess (prō-fĕs'), *v.t.* to make an open or public statement of, as one's belief, intentions, etc.; avow or acknowledge; to pretend; as, to *profess* friendship; set up a claim of; as, to *profess* ignorance; to claim to be an authority in.

pro-fessed (prō-fĕst'), *p.adj.* openly declared; as, a *professed* enemy; pretended.—*adv.* **professedly.**

pro-fes-sion (prō-fĕsh'ŭn), *n.* the act of declaring; as, *profession* of faith or friendship; an open declaration or avowal; religious faith; a pretense; calling or vocation, especially one that requires learning; as, the *profession* of medicine; all the persons engaged in any one calling.
Syn. business, trade, occupation, employment.

pro-fes-sion-al (prō-fĕsh'ŭn-ăl), *adj.* pertaining to a calling or occupation requiring a superior education; following a calling as a means of livelihood; as, a *professional* baseball player: *n.* one who makes his living by an occupation, as distinguished from an amateur, or one who practices it occasionally or for pleasure; as, the singer has the air of a *professional.*—*adv.* **professionally.**—*n.* **professionalism.**

pro-fes-sor (prō-fĕs'ẽr), *n.* one who makes an open declaration of his feelings and opinions, especially concerning religion; one who teaches any branch of learning in a college, university, etc.

pro-fes-so-ri-al (prō'fĕ-sō'rĭ-ăl), *adj.* pertaining to a teacher in a college, university, etc.—*adv.* **professorially.**

pro-fes-sor-ship (prō-fĕs'ẽr-shĭp), *n.* the office, duties, or position, of a teacher in a college, university, etc.

prof-fer (prŏf'ẽr), *v.t.* to offer for acceptance; as, to *proffer* a gift or assistance: *n.* an offer.
Syn., *v.* volunteer, offer, propose.

pro-fi-cien-cy (prō-fĭsh'ĕn-sĭ), *n.* knowledge, skill, or expertness, in any branch of learning, science, art, or industry.

pro-fi-cient (prō-fĭsh'ĕnt), *adj.* thoroughly qualified or skilled in any work; expert: *n.* an expert; one thoroughly skilled.

pro-file (prō'fĭl; prō'fēl), *n.* outline or contour; a side view of a human head or face; a drawing in outline, especially of a building.

prof-it (prŏf'ĭt), *n.* money gain; amount by which income exceeds expense in a given time; benefit or advantage: *v.t.* to benefit; to be of service to: *v.i.* to receive benefit; gain; improve; to be of use; bring good.

prof-it-a-ble (prŏf'ĭt-ȧ-bl), *adj.* yielding or bringing gain or benefit; useful; paying; as, a *profitable* business.—*adv.* **profitably.**—*n.* **profitableness.**

prof-it-eer (prŏf'ĭ-tēr'), *n.* one who takes unfair advantage of an economic situation such as war brings about to make undue profits, as in steel, meat, wheat, sugar, cotton, munitions, or other necessities.

prof-it-less (prŏf'ĭt-lĕs), *adj.* without benefit or gain.—*adv.* **profitlessly.**

prof-li-ga-cy (prŏf'lĭ-gȧ-sĭ), *n.* an immoral or wicked course of life; state of being immoral, or given up to vice.

prof-li-gate (prŏf'lĭ-gāt), *adj.* given up to vice; wicked: *n.* a depraved or immoral person.—*adv.* **profligately.**—*n.* **profligateness.**
Syn., *adj.* abandoned, depraved, corrupt.
Ant. (see virtuous).

pro-found (prō-found'), *adj.* deep, as to space; as, the *profound* depths of ocean; deep, as to mental state; thorough; as, *profound* thought; *profound* learning; deep, as to feeling; intense; as, *profound* sorrow; bending low; as, a *profound* bow; coming from the depths; as, a *profound* sigh.—*adv.* **profoundly.**—*n.* **profoundness.**
Syn. fathomless, penetrating, solemn.
Ant. (see shallow).

pro-fun-di-ty (prō-fŭn'dĭ-tĭ), *n.* depth of place, thought, knowledge, feeling, etc.; that which is deep in any sense.

pro-fuse (prō-fūs'), *adj.* pouring forth freely; giving or given with great liberality; lavish; extravagant; produced or shown in great abundance.—*adv.* **profusely.**—*n.* **profuseness.**
Syn. prodigal, excessive, copious, bountiful.
Ant. (see succinct).

pro-fu-sion (prō-fū'shŭn), *n.* a very great plenty or supply; abundance; lavishness; excess; extreme liberality.

pro-gen-i-tor (prō-jĕn'ĭ-tẽr), *n.* an ancestor in a direct line; forefather.

prog-e-ny (prŏj'ē-nĭ), *n.* offspring; children; descendants.

prog-na-thous (prŏg'nȧ-thŭs), *adj.* having a lower jaw projecting forward; as, the *prognathous* skull of prehistoric man.

prog-no-sis (prŏg-nō'sĭs), *n.* a forecast of the probable result of a disease from its symptoms or signs; opinion so formed.

prog-nos-tic (prŏg-nŏs'tĭk), *adj.* showing something that is to come to pass; foreshadowing; foretelling: *n.* an omen or sign of what is to come.

prog-nos-ti-cate (prŏg-nŏs'tĭ-kāt), *v.t.* to tell beforehand by means of signs or symptoms; to foretell: *v.i.* to foretell the future by present signs.

prog-nos-ti-ca-tion (prŏg-nŏs'tĭ-kā'shŭn), *n.* the act of foretelling what is to come to pass; a sign of something about to happen; a prediction; a foretoken.

prog-nos-ti-ca-tor (prŏg-nŏs'tĭ-kā'tẽr), *n.* one who foretells what is going to happen.

pro-gram (prō'grăm), *n.* a brief outline giving in order the features that make up a public entertainment, ceremony, etc.; the features that make up the entertainment, etc.; a regular plan of action in any undertaking. Also, **programme.**

prog-ress (prŏg'rĕs; prō'grĕs), *n.* a moving or going forward; advancement; growth; improvement: *v.i.* (prô-grĕs'), to move forward; advance; grow; improve; increase in knowledge or skill.

pro-gres-sion (prô-grĕsh'ŭn), *n.* the act of going forward; advancement; course; passage; also, lapse of time.

pro-gres-sive (prô-grĕs'ĭv), *adj.* moving forward; making or favoring advancement or improvement; advancing; improving: *n.* one who believes in, and works for, changes and reforms, especially in political matters: **Progressive Party**, a political party of advanced Republicans which was formed in 1912 and which supported Theodore Roosevelt as presidential candidate.

pro-hib-it (prô-hĭb'ĭt), *v.t.* to forbid by law; as, to *prohibit* the sale of alcoholic liquors; hinder; prevent.

pro-hi-bi-tion (prō'hĭ-bĭsh'ŭn), *n.* a law forbidding some action; the act of forbidding by law; especially, the forbidding of the manufacture and sale of intoxicating drinks: **Prohibition Party**, a political party with the object of securing the prevention by law of the manufacture and sale of intoxicating drinks throughout the United States.

pro-hi-bi-tion-ist (prō'hĭ-bĭsh'ŭn-ĭst), *n.* one who is opposed to the manufacture and sale of intoxicating liquors.—*n.* **prohibitionism.**

pro-hib-i-tive (prô-hĭb'ĭ-tĭv), *adj.* tending to forbid, prevent, or hinder; as, *prohibitive* prices keep one from buying; prohibitory.

pro-hib-i-to-ry (prô-hĭb'ĭ-tô-rĭ), *adj.* serving to forbid; as, *prohibitory* laws.

proj-ect (prŏj'ĕkt), *n.* a design, scheme, or plan: *v.t.* (prô-jĕkt'), to throw, shoot, or cast forward; plan or scheme: *v.i.* to jut out; extend forward.

pro-ject-ile (prô-jĕk'tĭl), *n.* a body thrown or shot forward, especially through the air; a body intended to be hurled from a cannon by the force of an explosion, so as to strike and destroy a distant object: *adj.* forced or forcing forward; as, a *projectile* force.

pro-jec-tion (prô-jĕk'shŭn), *n.* the act or state of extending or jutting out; that which juts out; a plan; a scheming or planning.

pro-jec-tor (prô-jĕk'tẽr), *n.* one who makes schemes or plans; an optical instrument for throwing a picture upon a screen by a system of lenses.

pro-le-ta-ri-an (prō'lē-tā'rĭ-ăn; prŏl'ē-tā'rĭ-ăn), *adj.* pertaining to the common people: *n.* one of the lowest class of society; a wage-earner; day-laborer.

pro-le-ta-ri-at (prō'lē-tā'rĭ-ăt; prŏl'ē-tā'rĭ-ăt), *n.* the lowest class of society; the laboring people.

pro-lif-ic (prô-lĭf'ĭk), *adj.* producing young or fruit abundantly; as, a *prolific* vine; producing ideas or results abundantly; as, a *prolific* brain or writer; productive; fertile; fruitful.—*adv.* **prolifically.**

pro-lix (prō'lĭks; prô-lĭks'), *adj.* long drawn out; tedious; wordy; not concise; as, a *prolix* speaker or speech.

Syn. long, prolonged, tiresome, prosaic.
Ant. (see concise).

pro-lix-i-ty (prô-lĭk'sĭ-tĭ), *n.* quality of being long drawn out; tediousness; wordiness; much minute detail.

pro-log (prō'lŏg; prŏl'ŏg), *n.* an introduction or preface to a poem, drama, etc.; especially, verses spoken by an actor before the performance of a play by way of explanation, etc. Also, **prologue.**

pro-long (prô-lông'), *v.t.* to lengthen; draw out; extend; as, to *prolong* a line, a walk, a visit.

pro-lon-ga-tion (prō'lŏṅ-gā'shŭn), *n.* a lengthening in time or space; the part added by lengthening.

prom-e-nade (prŏm'ē-nȧd'), *n.* a walk for pleasure or exercise; a public place for walking: *v.i.* to walk for pleasure, etc.

prom-i-nence (prŏm'ĭ-nĕns), *n.* the state or quality of standing or jutting out beyond a regular line or surface; the quality of being distinguished or noticeable. Also, **prominency.**

prom-i-nent (prŏm'ĭ-nĕnt), *adj.* standing or jutting out beyond a regular line or surface; conspicuous, noticeable, or distinguished.—*adv.* **prominently.**

Syn. eminent, marked, important, leading.
Ant. (see obscure).

pro-mis-cu-ous (prô-mĭs'kū-ŭs), *adj.* confused; mingled; as, a *promiscuous* audience; not confined to any particular person or class.—*adv.* **promiscuously.**

Syn. mixed, disarranged.
Ant. (see select).

prom-ise (prŏm'ĭs), *n.* an engagement to do or not to do something; the thing to be done or left undone; a cause or ground for hope or expectation of good in the future: *v.t.* to assure, or engage to do, something; give reason for hope or expectation; as, the garden *promises* well: *v.i.* to engage to do or not to do for another; give reason to hope for or expect.—*n.* **promiser.**

prom-is-ing (prŏm'ĭs-ĭng), *p.adj.* giving reason to hope for or expect good; looking as if likely to turn out well; as, a *promising* youth.—*adv.* **promisingly.**

prom-i-sor (prŏm'ĭ-sôr), *n.* one who makes a legal agreement; a promiser.

prom-is-so-ry (prŏm'ĭ-sô-rĭ), *adj.* containing an agreement to do or not to do something.

prom-is-so-ry note (prŏm'ĭ-sô-rĭ nōt), a written agreement to pay a certain sum of money at a fixed date, or on demand, to a certain person or his order or bearer.

prom-on-to-ry (prŏm'ŭn-tô-rĭ), *n.* a high cape; a point of land jutting into the sea; a headland.

pro-mote (prô-mōt'), *v.t.* to help the growth or development of; advance; further; as, to *promote* one's interests; excite or stir up; encourage; as, to *promote* strife; raise to higher rank.

pro-mot-er (prô-mōt'ẽr), *n.* one who encourages or forwards any undertaking; especially, one who makes it his business to start new companies, etc.

pro-mo-tion (prô-mō'shŭn), *n.* the act of furthering or advancing any cause or course; state of being advanced; encouragement; as, *promotion* of industries; advancement to a better position or higher rank, as in school.

prompt (prŏmpt), *adj.* ready and quick to act as occasion demands; immediate; done without delay: *v.t.* to rouse to action; to suggest; remind (a speaker) when at a loss for words.—*adv.* **promptly.**—*n.* **promptness, prompter.**

Syn. punctual.

promp-ti-tude (prŏmp'tĭ-tūd), *n.* quickness of decision and action; readiness.

pro-mul-gate (prō-mŭl'gāt), *v.t.* to make known to the public formally and officially; to publish in any way.—*n.* **promulgator.**

pro-mul-ga-tion (prō'mŭl-gā'shŭn; prŏm'ŭl-gā'shŭn), *n.* an official declaration; publication.

prone (prōn), *adj.* lying with the face or front downwards; bending forward or downward; mentally disposed or inclined; apt; as, *prone* to mischief.—*n.* **proneness.**

prong (prŏng), *n.* a sharp point or sharp-pointed instrument; as, the *prongs* of a pitchfork.

prong-horn (prŏng'hôrn'), *n.* an antelope of the western plains of North America; also, the Rocky Mountain antelope.

pro-nom-i-nal (prō-nŏm'ĭ-năl), *adj.* pertaining to, or like, a pronoun, or word standing for a noun: **pronominal adjective,** a word, such as *this* or *that,* which occurs as an adjective but may also be used as a pronoun.—*adv.* **pronominally.**

pro-noun (prō'noun), *n.* a word which refers to, or is used in the place of, a noun or name; as, *he, she, you, it,* etc.

pro-nounce (prō-nouns'), *v.t.* to speak or utter the sound of; as, to *pronounce* words; to speak or utter with formal effect; as, to *pronounce* a eulogy; to speak or utter solemnly or formally; as, to *pronounce* a benediction; to declare positively; as, they *pronounced* him a failure: *v.i.* to utter words; to speak with confidence or authority.—*adj.* **pronounceable.**

pro-nounced (prō-nounst'), *p.adj.* strongly marked; decided; as, a *pronounced* change in the weather.

pro-nounce-ment (prō-nouns'mĕnt), *n.* a declaration; a formal announcement.

pro-nun-ci-a-tion (prō-nŭn'sĭ-ā'shŭn; prō-nŭn'shĭ-ā'shŭn), *n.* the act or manner of uttering the sounds of words.

proof (proōf), *n.* the means by which something is found to be true or correct; convincing evidence; a test or trial; in printing, an impression taken from type for correction; an early impression of an engraving: *adj.* capable of resisting; as, the cloth is *proof* against rain; capable of moral or physical resistance.

proof read-er (proōf rēd'ẽr), one whose trade is to find errors and mark corrections in printers' proofs, or sample impressions of type.

prop (prŏp), *n.* a support or stay: *v.t.* [*p.t.* and *p.p.* propped, *p.pr.* propping], to support by placing something under or against; sustain.

Syn., *v.* maintain, stay, hold.

prop-a-gan-da (prŏp'ȧ-găn'dȧ), *n.* any plan or method for spreading a certain opinion or belief; the opinion or belief thus spread.

prop-a-gan-dist (prŏp'ȧ-găn'dĭst), *n.* one who devotes himself to the spread of any system of principles, doctrines, opinions, etc.

prop-a-gate (prŏp'ȧ-gāt), *v.t.* to cause to increase or multiply by successive production; as to *propagate* plants; to spread from person to person; as, to *propagate* news; to cause to extend or spread in space; as, to *propagate* light: *v.i.* to be produced by generation or other means.—*n.* **propagator.**

Syn. circulate, breed, increase.

Ant. (see suppress).

prop-a-ga-tion (prŏp'ȧ-gā'shŭn), *n.* the act of producing or spreading.

pro-pel (prō-pĕl'), *v.t.* [*p.t.* and *p.p.* propelled, *p.pr.* propelling], to drive onward; urge forward by force; as, to *propel* a bicycle; push.

Ship's Propeller. 1, face; 2 profile.

pro-pel-ler (prō-pĕl'ẽr), *n.* one who, or that which, drives forward; as, the *propeller* of a ship; a screw-*propeller.*

pro-pen-si-ty (prō-pĕn'sĭ-tĭ), *n.* natural inclination or tendency.

prop-er (prŏp'ẽr), *adj.* fit or suitable; correct; as, *proper* language; appropriate; as, *proper* dress; relating to the nature of a certain person or thing; as, a *proper* noun opposite to *common;* peculiar; as, a *proper* instinct.—*adv.* **properly.**

Syn. right, just, fair, honest, fit, decent, becoming.

Ant. (see wrong).

prop-er-ty (prŏp'ẽr-tĭ), *n.* [*pl.* properties (-tĭz)], any quality or attribute that belongs to a thing, or one that especially marks it; as, sourness is a *property* of vinegar; ownership; the thing owned; estate; goods: *pl.* articles, including furniture, costumes, etc., required by actors on the stage.

proph-e-cy (prŏf'ē-sĭ), *n.* [*pl.* prophecies (-sĭz)], a foretelling of future events under divine influence; as, the Hebrew *prophecies* of the Old Testament; a book of the Bible containing such predictions; as, the *prophecy* of Isaiah; any foretelling of future happenings.—*n.* **prophesier.**

proph-e-sy (prŏf'ē-sī), *v.t.* [*p.t.* and *p.p.* prophesied, *p.pr.* prophesying], to foretell, especially under divine influence; predict: *v.i.* to foretell future events, especially under divine influence; to preach, or declare God's will to men.

proph-et (prŏf'ĕt), *n.* [*fem.* prophetess], one inspired by God to teach his will to men and to announce future events; one who declares what will happen in the future.

pro-phet-ic (prō-fĕt'ĭk), *adj.* pertaining to the foretelling of future events, or to one who foretells; as, a *prophetic* vision. Also, **prophetical.**—*adv.* **prophetically.**

pro-phy-lac-tic (prō'fĭ-lăk'tĭk; prŏf'ĭ-lăk'tĭk), *adj.* warding off, or preserving from, disease; as, a *prophylactic* medicine: *n.* a medicine that prevents disease.

pro-pin-qui-ty (prō-pĭn'kwĭ-tĭ), *n.* nearness in time, place, or blood relationship.

pro-pi-ti-ate (prō-pĭsh'ĭ-āt), *v.t.* to conciliate or appease; as, to *propitiate* another's anger; to remove displeasure from, or make favorable to: *v.i.* to atone for or make good a loss.

pro-pi-ti-a-tion (prō-pĭsh'ĭ-ā'shŭn), *n.* the act of appeasing, or removing displeasure.

pro-pi-ti-a-to-ry (prō-pĭsh'ĭ-ȧ-tō-rĭ), *adj.* having the power to appease or remove displeasure.

pro-pi-tious (prō-pĭsh'ŭs), *adj.* favorably inclined; gracious; favorable; fortunate; as, *propitious* weather or circumstances.—*adv.* **propitiously.**—*n.* **propitiousness.**

pro-por-tion (prō-pōr'shŭn), *n.* the relation in size, quantity, or degree of one to another; ratio or rate; a proper balance or relation of all the parts; equal or just share: *pl.* dimensions: *v.t.* to form symmetrically, or make the parts of suitable to each other; to cause to be in suitable relation; as, to *proportion* one's expenses to one's means.

pro-por-tion-al (prō-pōr'shŭn-ăl), *adj.* having, or being in, due or suitable relation; having a ratio or rate invariable under given conditions: *n.* a quantity or number having a certain ratio to another.—*adv.* **proportionally.**

pro-por-tion-ate (prō-pōr'shŭn-āt), *adj.* adjusted to something else according to a certain rate: *v.t.* (prō-pōr'shŭn-āt), to adjust according to a settled rate.—*adv.* **proportionately.**

pro-pos-al (prō-pōz'ăl), *n.* the act of offering something for acceptance, etc.; as, a *proposal* of marriage; that which is offered; an offer.

pro-pose (prō-pōz'), *v.t.* to bring forward or offer for consideration; as, to *propose* a candidate for election; to suggest; as, he *proposed* that I should go; to intend; purpose; as, I *propose* to stay at home: *v.i.* to make an offer of marriage.—*n.* **proposer.**

prop-o-si-tion (prŏp'ō-zĭsh'ŭn), *n.* that which is offered for consideration; an offer of terms; proposal; a complete sentence, or one that affirms or denies something; the formal statement of a topic to be discussed in a debate; in mathematics, a theorem or problem for solution.—*adj.* **propositional.**

pro-pound (prō-pound'), *v.t.* to offer for consideration; put or set forth, as a question.

pro-pri-e-ta-ry (prō-prī'ē-tā-rĭ), *adj.* pertaining to a proprietor, or owner: *n.* a possessor or owner in his own right; a body of owners.

pro-pri-e-tor (prō-prī'ē-tēr), *n.* [*fem.* proprietress; proprietrix], one who has a legal right to anything; owner.

pro-pri-e-ty (prō-prī'ē-tĭ), *n.* state of being proper; the following of established rule or custom; fitness; correctness.

pro-pul-sion (prō-pŭl'shŭn), *n.* the act of driving or pushing along.

pro-pul-sive (prō-pŭl'sĭv), *adj.* having power to drive or push along; urging. Also, **propulsory.**

pro ra-ta (prō rā'tȧ), in proportion; according to interest or share of each. [LAT.]

pro-ro-ga-tion (prō'rō-gā'shŭn), *n.* the act of ending a session of, as of parliament.

pro-rogue (prō-rōg'), *v.t.* to terminate or end a session of; to postpone, or put off.

pro-sa-ic (prō-zā'ĭk), *adj.* commonplace; dull; as, a *prosaic* person or speech. Also, **prosaical.**—*adv.* **prosaically.**—*n.* **prosaicalness.**

pro-sce-ni-um (prō-sē'nĭ-ŭm), *n.* the stage in front of the curtain or between the curtain and the orchestra.

pro-scribe (prō-skrīb'), *v.t.* to punish by declaring to be outside the protection of the law; banish; to condemn and reject; prohibit.

pro-scrip-tion (prō-skrĭp'shŭn), *n.* the act of outlawing, or of declaring outside the protection of the law; outlawry; the act of condemning and rejecting from favor; the state of being condemned and rejected.

pro-scrip-tive (prō-skrĭp'tĭv), *adj.* pertaining to, or consisting in, the punishment that outlaws or condemns and rejects.

prose (prōz), *n.* ordinary spoken or written language; language without meter: opposite to *verse*: *v.i.* and *v.t.* to write in a form not verse; to write or speak tediously or uninterestingly: *adj.* pertaining to composition that is not verse; dull; tedious; commonplace.

pros-e-cute (prŏs'ē-kūt), *v.t.* to follow up or pursue with the view to reach or accomplish; as, to *prosecute* an undertaking; to bring suit against or carry on a case against in a court of law: *v.i.* to carry on a lawsuit; to sue.—*n.* **prosecuter.**

pros-e-cu-tion (prŏs'ē-kū'shŭn), *n.* the act of following up a purpose to accomplish some result; the starting and carrying on of a lawsuit; the party starting the suit.

pros-e-cu-tor (prŏs'ē-kū'tēr), *n.* [*fem.* prosecutrix], one who carries on a lawsuit against another; one who pursues any purpose, etc.

pros-e-lyte (prŏs'ē-līt), *n.* a convert, or one won over, as to some religion or belief, or party: *v.t.* and *v.i.* to win over to a different opinion, belief, party, etc.; to obtain followers.

pros-e-ly-tism (prŏs'ē-lĭ-tĭzm), *n.* the act of converting or winning over, especially to some religion; the state of being won over.

pros-e-ly-tize (prŏs'ē-lĭ-tīz), *v.t.* and *v.i.* to make a convert of, or to make converts.

pros-o-dy (prŏs'ō-dĭ), *n.* that part of grammar that treats of quantity of syllables, accent, and the laws of verse making.

pros-pect (prŏs'pĕkt), *n.* a scene spread out before the sight; view; outlook; a looking forward; anticipation; expectation: *v.t.* and *v.i.* (prō-spĕkt'), to search or explore, especially for gold or valuable minerals.—*n.* **prospector.**

pro-spec-tive (prō-spĕk'tĭv), *adj.* looking forward; showing foresight; in anticipation; expected.—*adv.* **prospectively.**—*n.* **prospectiveness.**

pros-pec-tor (prŏs'pĕk-tēr), *n.* one who searches for valuable minerals, as gold, silver, etc.

pro-spec-tus (prō-spĕk'tŭs), *n.* an outline of a proposed undertaking; sketch or plan; yearly catalog, as of a school, hotel, etc.

pros-per (prŏs'pēr), *v.t.* to render successful; favor: *v.i.* to thrive; succeed.

Syn. flourish.

pros-per-i-ty (prŏs-pĕr'ĭ-tĭ), *n.* successful progress in any business or enterprise; good fortune.

Syn. well-being, welfare.

Ant. (see poverty).

pros-per-ous (prŏs'pĕr-ŭs), *adj.* favorable; successful; thriving; as, a *prosperous* business.—*adv.* **prosperously.**

pros-ti-tute (prŏs'tĭ-tūt), *v.t.* to use for a low and unworthy purpose for the sake of gaining money or advantage: *n.* a woman who leads a base and degraded life for pay.

pros-trate (prŏs'trāt), *adj.* lying at full length; extended on the ground; stretched out; lying at another's mercy: *v.t.* to lay flat; throw down from a standing position; destroy; ruin; bow in humble reverence; to cause to become weak.

pros-tra-tion (prŏs-trā'shŭn), *n.* the act of throwing down or state of being thrown down; a falling down in worship; great depression; as, *prostration* of mind; exhaustion of the vital powers under disease; as, nervous *prostration.*

pros-y (prōz'ĭ), *adj.* tedious; dull; commonplace; tiresome.—*adv.* **prosily.** —*n.* **prosiness.**

pro-tag-o-nist (prō-tăg'ō-nĭst), *n.* the central figure around whom the action of a drama turns; a dramatic hero.

prot-a-sis (prŏt'ȧ-sĭs), *n.* the *if*-clause in a conditional sentence.

pro-te-an (prō'tē-ăn; prō-tē'ăn), *adj.* readily taking on different shapes or forms: from Proteus, the sea god of classic mythology.

pro-tect (prō-tĕkt'), *v.t.* to keep in safety; guard; shield; shelter; to foster by a high tariff, as home industries.

pro-tec-tion (prō-tĕk'shŭn), *n.* the act of keeping in safety; the state of being kept in safety; that which keeps safe; defense; shelter; security; a passport; encouragement of home industry by duties on imported goods, etc.: opposite to *free trade.*

pro-tec-tion-ism (prō-tĕk'shŭn-ĭzm), *n.* the doctrine that certain home industries and produce should be encouraged by taxing imported goods.

pro-tec-tion-ist (prō-tĕk'shŭn-ĭst), *n.* one who believes in and supports protectionism, or the doctrine that all imported goods should be taxed to protect home industries; one who opposes free trade.

pro-tec-tive (prō-tĕk'tĭv), *adj.* serving to keep safe; defensive; serving to foster home industries; as, a *protective* tariff.—*adv.* **protectively.**

pro-tec-tor (prō-tĕk'tĕr), *n.* [*fem.* protectress], one who guards, especially from injury or oppression; a defender; guardian: **Protector,** the title of Oliver Cromwell as the head of the English Commonwealth, 1653-1659.

pro-tec-tor-ate (prō-tĕk'tŏr-ȧt), *n.* government by a regent, or one appointed to rule in place of a king; also, the rank and office of such a person; the relation of a great nation to a weak one which it defends and partly controls: the nation so defended and controlled; as, Great Britain held Egypt as a *protectorate.*

pro-té-gé (prō'tā'zhā'), *n.* [*fem.* protégée], one who is under the guardianship or care of another. [Fr.]

pro-te-id (prō'tē-ĭd), *n.* a foodstuff, such as albumen, that forms animal tissue.

pro-te-in (prō'tē-ĭn), *n.* an essential or necessary element in food; the muscle-making quality of food.

pro-test (prō-tĕst'), *v.i.* to make a solemn declaration against some public act or measure; remonstrate: *v.t.* to make a solemn declaration or affirmation of; assert, to declare formally to be insufficiently provided for by deposit or payment: said of a note, check, or bill of exchange: *n.* (prō'tĕst), a solemn declaration of opinion against something; a formal declaration by the holder of a note of its nonpayment or nonacceptance by the drawer.—*n.* **protester.**

prot-es-tant (prŏt'ĕs-tănt), *n.* one who declares an opinion in advance of, or opposing, those generally accepted: *adj.* declaring an opposing opinion: **Protestant,** a member of any of those bodies of Christians that deny the spiritual supremacy of the Church of Rome; originally, one of the party who adhered to Luther: *adj.* pertaining to Protestants or Protestantism.

Prot-es-tant-ism (prŏt'ĕs-tănt-ĭzm), *n.* the doctrines of religion of Protestants, or those who belong to other churches than the Church of Rome.

prot-es-ta-tion (prŏt'ĕs-tā'shŭn), *n.* the act of declaring solemnly; a formal declaration of disagreement; solemn affirmation.

pro-thon-o-ta-ry (prō-thŏn'ō-tȧ-rĭ), *n.* a chief clerk or notary; the principal clerk or registrar in certain courts; one of the chief secretaries of the Pope's court in Rome.

pro-to-col (prō'tō-kŏl), *n.* the rough draft of a treaty, government message, etc., often a basis for a final treaty or agreement.

pro-to-plasm (prō'tō-plăzm), *n.* the vital substance from which develop all forms of animal and plant life: resembling the white of an egg, and containing carbon, oxygen, nitrogen, and hydrogen, or the elements necessary to all animal and vegetable life.—*adj.* **protoplasmic.**

pro-to-type (prō'tō-tīp), *n.* the original from which others are copied; a pattern.

Pro-to-zo-a (prō'tō-zō'ȧ), *n.pl.* the first or lowest division of the animal kingdom, containing animals consisting of a single cell: **protozoan,** *n.* an animal consisting of a single cell: *adj.* pertaining to such an animal.

pro-tract (prō-trăkt'), *v.t.* to draw out or lengthen in time; prolong; as, to *protract* a meeting; to draw or map by means of a scale; in animals, to protrude or extend.

pro-trac-tion (prō-trăk'shŭn), *n.* the act of drawing out in time.

pro-trac-tor (prō-trăk'tĕr), *n.* an instrument for laying down and measuring angles on paper: used in surveying, etc.; a muscle that draws forward any part of the body.

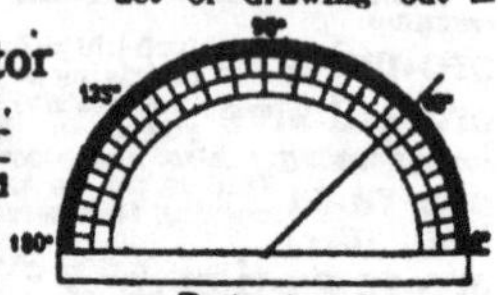

Protractor

pro-trude (prō-trōōd'), *v.t.* to thrust forward or push forward: *v.i.* to shoot forward; project.

pro-tru-sion (prō-trōō'shŭn), *n.* the act of thrusting out, as the tongue; the state of being thrust out.

pro-tru-sive (prō-trōō'sĭv), *adj.* thrusting or impelling forward.

pro-tu-ber-ance (prō-tū'bēr-ăns), *n.* a swelling; a knob; quality or state of swelling out.

pro-tu-ber-ant (prō-tū'bēr-ănt), *adj.* swelling out; prominent; bulging.

proud (proud), *adj.* having too great self-esteem; arrogant; haughty; having proper self-respect; as, too *proud* to beg; having a feeling of glad satisfaction; as, *proud* of a friend's success; gratified; spirited; grand.—*adv.* **proudly.**

prov-a-ble (prōōv'ȧ-bl), *adj.* that may be tested or shown to be true.

prove (prōōv), *v.t.* to test or try by an experiment; to make clear and certain by argument or other evidence; to cause to be accepted as genuine; as, to *prove* a will; to learn by experience; to try by suffering; show or demonstrate the accuracy of (a calculation): *v.i.* to turn out to be or be found to be.

Pro-ven-çal (prō-văn'săl; prō'vĕn-săl'; prō'vĕn-săl'), *adj.* pertaining to Provence, France, its language, or its people: *n.* the language of Provence; a native of Provence.

prov-en-der (prŏv'ĕn-dēr), *n.* dry food for domestic animals, as hay, etc.; feed.

prov-erb (prŏv'ērb), *n.* a short familiar saying, expressing some well-known truth or common fact of experience; adage: **Proverbs**, a book of the Old Testament containing wise sayings credited to Solomon.

pro-ver-bi-al (prō-vûr'bĭ-ăl), *adj.* pertaining to short, familiar, wise sayings; mentioned in, or like, a short, familiar, wise saying; being widely spoken or well-known; as, her kindness is *proverbial.*

pro-vide (prō-vīd'), *v.t.* to make ready beforehand; prepare; furnish or supply: followed by *with;* mention as a condition or requirement; as, the bill *provides* that taxes be raised: *v.i.* to procure supplies; make preparations: with *for* or *against.*—*n.* **provider.**

pro-vid-ed (prō-vīd'ĕd), *conj.* on condition; if: usually followed by *that.*

prov-i-dence (prŏv'ĭ-dĕns), *n.* timely care or preparation; economy; prudence; foresight and care of God for his creatures; an event directly caused by the power of God: **Providence**, God.

prov-i-dent (prŏv'ĭ-dĕnt), *adj.* careful for the future; prudent; economical; thrifty.—*adv.* **providently.**

prov-i-den-tial (prŏv'ĭ-dĕn'shăl), *adj.* effected by, resulting from, or showing, divine direction or foresight; fortunate.—*adv.* **providentially.**

prov-ince (prŏv'ĭns), *n.* a division of an empire or state; a country governed by a distant authority; an outlying district; proper sphere of action; as, this task is outside your *province;* department of knowledge, etc.: *pl.* the country districts.

pro-vin-cial (prō-vĭn'shăl), *adj.* pertaining to, or like, an outlying district or distant dependent country; countrified; crude and unfinished in appearance or manner; holding to the ideas and customs of one special region; hence, narrow: *n.* one who belongs to a distant dependent country or to an outlying district; countryman.

pro-vin-cial-ism (prō-vĭn'shăl-ĭzm), *n.* a word, expression, mannerism, or way of thinking, peculiar to an outlying district; devotion to the ideas and customs of one special region; hence, narrowness of view.

pro-vi-sion (prō-vĭzh'ŭn), *n.* the act of preparing beforehand; the things supplied, especially a stock of food; measures taken beforehand; as, to make *provision* for winter; a condition, requirement, etc.; as, a *provision* of a will: *pl.* food: *v.t.* to supply with food, etc.; as, to *provision* an army.

pro-vi-sion-al (prō-vĭzh'ŭn-ăl), *adj.* supplied for present use; temporary.—*adv.* **provisionally.**

pro-vi-so (prō-vī'zō), *n.* a conditional clause or stipulation, as in a deed.

pro-vi-so-ry (prō-vī'zō-rĭ), *adj.* conditional; provisional.

prov-o-ca-tion (prŏv'ō-kā'shŭn), *n.* that which excites to anger or resentment; act of exciting to anger; as, he was subjected to great *provocation.*

pro-voc-a-tive (prō-vŏk'ȧ-tĭv), *adj.* tending to rouse anger or resentment: *n.* anything that tends to excite.

pro-voke (prō-vōk'), *v.t.* to excite or stir up; as, to *provoke* criticism; to cause; as, to *provoke* a laugh; enrage or irritate; as, to *provoke* another to anger; offend.

prov-ost (prŏv'ŭst; prō'vō; prō-vō'), *n.* the head of a college; superintendent or president; chief officer of a cathedral; a Scotch chief magistrate of a city or town.

pro-vost guard (prō'vō gärd), one of the soldiers appointed to work together with the civil authorities to keep order in a large army post or camp.

pro-vost mar-shal (prō'vō mär'shăl), a military or naval officer who acts as chief of police, having charge of prisoners.

pro-vost ser-geant (prō'vō sär'jĕnt), in the army, a sergeant who has charge of prisoners and their work.

prow (prou), *n.* the bow or forward part of a ship.

prow-ess (prou'ĕs), *n.* daring bravery; valor; a brave act or feat.

prowl (proul), *v.i.* to wander stealthily, as for prey or plunder: *n.* a roving for prey or plunder.

prox-i-mate (prŏk'sĭ-māt), *adj.* immediately going before or following; nearest.—*adv.* **proximately.**

prox-im-i-ty (prŏk-sĭm'ĭ-tĭ), *n.* immediate nearness in place, time, or other relation.

prox-i-mo (prŏk'sĭ-mō), *adv.* in or of the next or coming month.

prox-y (prŏk'sĭ), *n.* [*pl.* proxies (-sĭz)], a person who is given authority to represent or act for another; the document by which one person is authorized to act or vote for another.

Syn. agent, representative, delegate, deputy.

prude (prōōd), *n.* a woman who affects great reserve, modesty, and virtue; a very proper person.

pru-dence (prōō'dĕns), *n.* the quality of being discreet, careful, or cautious; wisdom put into practice; economy.

Syn. carefulness, judgment, discretion, wisdom.

Ant. (see indiscretion).

pru-dent (prōō′dĕnt), *adj.* practically wise; careful of the result of measures or actions; wisely thoughtful; judicious; cautious; discreet.—*adv.* **prudently.**

pru-den-tial (prōō-dĕn′shăl), *adj.* proceeding from, or marked by, careful thought or wisdom; using sound judgment.—*adv.* **prudentially.**

prud-er-y (prōōd′ẽr-ĭ), *n.* affected niceness or modesty in conduct; extremely proper manners; primness.

pru-d'homme (prōō-dŏm′), *n.* in France, a member of a board to settle trade disputes; a trusted, wise man.

prud-ish (prōōd′ĭsh), *adj.* affectedly precise or nice.—*adv.* **prudishly.**—*n.* **prudishness.**

prune (prōōn), *n.* a dried plum: *v.t.* to cut unnecessary twigs or branches from (a vine, bush, or tree); trim; to cut out or clear away, as useless parts: *v.i.* to cut off useless branches, etc.

pru-nel-la (prōō-nĕl′*ȧ*), *n.* a smooth woolen stuff used for shoes and gaiters. Also, **prunello.**

prun-ing hook (prōōn′-ĭng hŏŏk), a knife with a curved blade for cutting vines, etc.

Pruning Hook

pru-ri-ence (prōō′rĭ-ĕns), *n.* the state or quality of being impure in thought or desire. Also, **pruriency.**

pru-ri-ent (prōō′rĭ-ĕnt), *adj.* impure in thought or desire; itching; lustful.—*adv.* **pruriently.**

Syn. craving, longing.

Prus-sian (prŭsh′ăn), *adj.* pertaining to Prussia, in Germany, or to its people: *n.* a native of Prussia.

Prus-sian blue (prŭsh′ăn blōō), a rich blue color obtained from iron.

prus-si-ate (prŭs′ĭ-āt), *n.* a salt of prussic acid.

prus-sic ac-id (prŭs′ĭk ăs′ĭd), a deadly poisonous acid, called also *hydrocyanic acid*, formed of hydrogen, carbon, and nitrogen.

pry (prī), *v.t.* [*p.t.* and *p.p.* pried, *p.pr.* prying], to inspect closely and inquisitively; as, to *pry* into another's affairs; peep; peer; *v.t.* to raise or work open with a lever: *n.* a bar used as a lever.

psalm (säm), *n.* a sacred song or poem: **Psalms**, a book of the Old Testament containing sacred songs and poems, many of which were formerly ascribed to David.

psalm-ist (säm′ĭst), *n.* a composer of psalms, or sacred hymns: **Psalmist**, any one of the authors of the sacred songs in the Bible; with *the*.

psalm-o-dist (säm′ō-dĭst; săl′mō-dĭst), *n.* one who composes or sings psalms, or sacred hymns.

psalm-o-dy (säm′ō-dĭ; săl′mō-dĭ), *n.* the art or practice of writing or singing psalms, or sacred hymns.

Psal-ter (sôl′tẽr), *n.* the Book of Psalms, especially as contained in the Book of Common Prayer.

psal-ter-y (sôl′tẽr-ĭ), *n.* [*pl.* psalteries (-ĭz)], a stringed musical instrument, used by the ancient Hebrews.

pseu-do (sū′dō), *adj.* false, counterfeit: **pseudo-**, a *prefix* meaning false.

pseu-do-nym (sū′dō-nĭm), *n.* a fictitious or false name: often used of the name taken by a writer; a pen name.—*adj.* **pseudonymous.**

pshaw (shô; pshô), *interj.* an expression of contempt, etc.

Psy-che (sī′kē; psī′kē), *n.* in Greek mythology, a beautiful maiden who represents the soul: **psyche**, the human soul.

psy-chic (sī′kĭk), *n.* a believer in a spiritual organism; a spiritual medium: *adj.* pertaining to, or connected with, the human soul, spirit, or mind; mental; spiritual: opposite to *physical*. Also, *adj.* **psychical.**—*adv.* **psychically.**

psy-cho-log-ic (sī″kō-lŏj′ĭk), *adj.* pertaining to the science of the mind. Also, **psychological.**—*adv.* **psychologically.**

psy-chol-o-gist (sī-kŏl′ō-jĭst), *n.* a student of, or one skilled in, the science of the mind.

psy-chol-o-gy (sī-kŏl′ō-jĭ), *n.* the science that treats of the mind.

psy-cho-phys-ics (sī″kō-fĭz′ĭks), *n.* the science which treats of the mind as affected by physical conditions.

psy-cho-ther-a-py (sī″kō-thĕr′*ȧ*-pĭ), *n.* the treatment of diseases by mental suggestion.

ptar-mi-gan (tär′mĭ-găn), *n.* a grouse found in the Arctic regions.

pter-o-dac-tyl (tĕr″ō-dăk′tĭl), *n.* a huge flying reptile, no longer existing.

Ptol-e-ma-ic sys-tem (tŏl″ē-mā′-ĭk sĭs′tĕm), the theory of astronomy held by Ptolemy, a scientist of the second century A.D., according to which sun and stars revolved about the earth as a center.

pto-ma-ines (tō′mȧ-ĭnz; tō′mā-ēns; tō′-mānz), *n.pl.* a substance found in decaying or dead matter, sometimes highly poisonous.

pu-ber-ty (pū′bẽr-tĭ), *n.* the earliest age at which persons can beget or bear children.

pu-bes-cence (pū-bĕs′ĕns), *n.* the state or age when a person is able to beget or bear children; a covering of soft, short, downy hair, as on certain plants.

pu-bes-cent (pū-bĕs′ĕnt), *adj.* arrived at the age when a person is able to bear or beget children; covered with soft, downy hairs, as some leaves.

pub-lic (pŭb′lĭk), *adj.* of or pertaining to the people at large; as, *public* property; open; generally known; common to all; open to general use: *n.* the people in general: **public house**, in Great Britain, an inn, tavern, or dramshop.

pub-li-can (pŭb′lĭ-kăn), *n.* in Great Britain, one who keeps an inn or public house; in ancient Rome, a collector of the taxes and public revenues; hence, a collector of tolls or tribute.

pub-li-ca-tion (pŭb″lĭ-kā′shŭn), *n.* the act of printing and placing on sale or of making generally known; that which is printed and placed on sale, as a book, magazine, etc.; that which is proclaimed or made generally known.

pub-li-cist (pŭb′lĭ-sĭst), *n.* one familiar with the laws of nations; also, a writer on politics.

pub-lic-i-ty (pŭb-lĭs′ĭ-tĭ), *n.* the state of being open to common knowledge; notoriety.

pub-lic-ly (pŭb′lĭk-lĭ), *adv.* without concealment; openly; in the interest, or with the consent, of the people.

pub-lic-spir-it-ed (pŭb′lĭk-spĭr′ĭt-ĕd), *adj.* having the interests of the community at heart; bent on the general welfare.

pub-lish (pŭb′lĭsh), *v.t.* to make known; announce or proclaim; print and offer for sale, especially a book, magazine, etc. —*n.* **publisher.**

puck (pŭk), *n.* in old folk tales, a fairy: **Puck**, a certain mischievous fairy or elf: called also *Robin Goodfellow.*

puck-er (pŭk′ẽr), *v.t.* and *v.i.* to gather into small folds; wrinkle: *n.* a small fold or wrinkle.

pud-ding (po͝od′ĭng), *n.* a soft kind of food, often a dessert, made of flour, milk, eggs, etc.; a piece of intestine stuffed with meat, etc.

pud-dle (pŭd′l), *n.* a small pool of dirty water; clay, sand, etc., worked together with water: *v.t.* to make muddy; to work water into (clay, etc.) so as to make a mixture through which water will not pass; to line with such clay in order to make watertight.—*n.* **puddler.**

pud-dling (pŭd′lĭng), *n.* the changing of pig iron into wrought iron by intense heat and frequent stirring.

pudg-y (pŭj′ĭ), *adj.* short and fat; dumpy. —*n.* **pudginess.**

pueb-lo (pwĕb′lō), *n.* [*pl.* pueblos (-lōz)], a building made of adobe or sundried brick by the Pueblo Indians of New Mexico, and serving as the dwelling of the entire village or tribe.

pu-er-ile (pū′ẽr-ĭl), *adj.* pertaining to childhood; trifling; silly.

pu-er-il-i-ty (pū′ẽr-ĭl′ĭ-tĭ), *n.* childishness; anything foolish or silly; a childish act or expression.

puff (pŭf), *n.* a short quick blast; a sudden breath forced out; a soft ball or pad used to apply powder to the skin or hair; a soft roll of hair; a very light cake or tart filled with cream, etc.; in dressmaking, a piece of material gathered on two sides so as to stand out in the center; colloquially, exaggerated praise printed in a newspaper, etc.: *v.i.* to send out air, smoke, breath, etc., with sudden force; breathe quick and hard, as a runner; swell with air; swell with importance: *v.t.* to blow, drive, etc., with whiffs or little blasts; swell, as with wind; praise in too high terms; arrange in puffs, as the hair, dress material, etc.

puff-ball (pŭf′bôl′), *n.* a bell-shaped fungus of several varieties that, when broken open, sends out a cloud of dustlike spores.

puff-y (pŭf′ĭ), *adj.* swollen with air or any soft matter; bloated; inflated; blowing in little gusts.—*n.* **puffiness.**

pug (pŭg), *n.* one of a breed of small pet dogs, with a short broad nose, wrinkled face, and tightly curled tail.

pug-ging (pŭg′ĭng), *n.* the act or operation of working up wet clay for pottery; clay or mortar used to deaden sound between spaces.

pu-gil-ism (pū′jĭ-lĭzm), *n.* the art or practice of boxing or fighting with the fists; prize fighting.

pu-gil-ist (pū′jĭ-lĭst), *n.* a prize fighter; boxer.

pu-gil-is-tic (pū′jĭ-lĭs′tĭk), *adj.* pertaining to boxing or prize fighting; having a disposition to fight.

pug-na-cious (pŭg-nā′shŭs), *adj.* inclined to fight; quarrelsome.—*adv.* **pugnaciously.**—*n.* **pugnaciousness.**

pug-nac-i-ty (pŭg-năs′ĭ-tĭ), *n.* inclination to fight; quarrelsomeness; combativeness.

pu-is-sance (pū′ĭ-săns; pū-ĭs′ăns), *n.* power; strength; force.

pu-is-sant (pū-ĭs′ănt), *adj.* powerful; strong; forceful.

pul-chri-tude (pŭl′krĭ-tūd), *n.* beauty; comeliness; loveliness.

pul-ing (pūl′ĭng), *adj.* whining; whimpering; crying plaintively.

pull (po͝ol), *v.t.* to draw towards one by exerting force; pluck; as, to *pull* grapes; rend or tear; as, to *pull* a dress to pieces; drag or haul; as, to *pull* a wagon; draw out; as, to *pull* a tooth; *v.i.* to draw forcibly; to tug: *n.* the act of using force to draw; a tug; colloquially, influence or advantage.

pul-let (po͝ol′ĕt), *n.* a young hen or one not fully grown.

pul-ley (po͝ol′ĭ), *n.* a small wheel turning about an axis and having a grooved rim in which a rope works: used in lifting weights, etc.

Pull-man (po͝ol′măn), *n.* a sleeping car fitted with berths and staterooms, or a day car fitted up with comfortable chairs: named from the inventor.

pul-mon-a-ry (pŭl′mō-nā-rĭ), *adj.* pertaining to, or affecting, the lungs; having lungs.

pul-mon-ic (pŭl-mŏn′ĭk), *adj.* affecting or useful for the lungs: *n.* a medicine for diseases of the lungs.

pul-mo-tor (pŭl′mō″tẽr), *n.* an instrument for producing artificial breathing by forcing oxygen into the lungs in case of suffocation, drowning, etc.

pulp (pŭlp), *n.* the soft, fleshy part of bodies, as of fruit; any soft, moist mass of matter.

pul-pit (po͝ol′pĭt), *n.* a raised stand or desk in a church, from which the sermon is delivered; preachers as a class, or preaching.

Pulpit

pulp-y (pŭl′pĭ), *adj.* consisting of, or like, a soft, moist mass of matter; soft; fleshy. —*n.* **pulpiness.**

pul-que (po͝ol′kā), *n.* a favorite Mexican drink made from the juice of the agave, or common century plant.

pul-sate (pŭl′sāt), *v.i.* to throb, as a pulse; to beat, as the heart.

pul-sa-tion (pŭl-sā′shŭn), *n.* a throb or beat, especially of the heart; act of throbbing.

pulse (pŭls), *n.* the throbbing or beating in the arteries due to the contractions of the heart; a stroke or beat occurring at regular intervals; as, the *pulse* of an engine; plants such as peas, beans, etc., and the seeds of them used for food: *v.i.* to beat or throb, as the blood in the veins.—*adj.* **pulseless.**

pul-som-e-ter (pŭl-sŏm'ē-tẽr), *n.* a pump for raising water by means of steam: called also a *vacuum pump.*

pul-ver-i-za-tion (pŭl"vẽr-ĭ-zā'shŭn), *n.* the act of reducing, or state of being reduced, to powder.

pul-ver-ize (pŭl'vẽr-īz), *v.t.* and *v.i.* to reduce or be reduced to powder by crushing, grinding, etc.—*n.* **pulverizer.**

pu-ma (pū'mȧ), *n.* a large catlike animal of America; the mountain lion; the cougar.

Puma

pum-ice (pŭm'ĭs), *n.* a hard, light, spongy, volcanic lava or rock. Also, **pumice-stone.**

pum-mel (pŭm'ĕl), *n.* the raised front part of a saddle; the knob on a sword handle: *v.t.* to beat or pound. Also, **pommel.**

pump (pŭmp), *n.* a machine for raising, compressing, etc., water or other fluids, by means of suction or pressure induced by the motion of a lever or crank; a plain low shoe or slipper: *v.t.* to raise or draw (water, etc.) by means of a pump; to draw water, etc., from; as, to *pump* a well dry; to draw out by artful questions; as, to *pump* a secret out of a friend: *v.i.* to raise water, etc., with a pump; to work a pump.

pump-kin (pŭmp'kĭn; pŭn'kĭn), *n.* a plant of the gourd family and its edible fruit.

pun (pŭn), *n.* a play on words: *v.i.* [*p.t.* and *p.p.* punned, *p.pr.* punning], to play on words similar in sound but having a different meaning.

punch (pŭnch), *n.* a tool for making dents or holes; a drink made of rum, whisky, etc., combined with water, lemon-juice, and sugar; a blow or thrust, especially with the fist: *v.t.* to perforate or make holes in with a punch; to strike with the fist.—**Punch**, a little hunchback with a hooked nose, the mock hero in a Punch and Judy show.

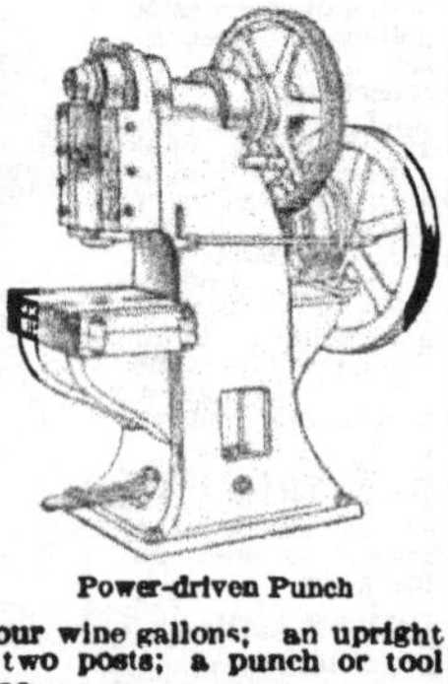

Power-driven Punch

punch-eon (pŭn'chŭn), *n.* a cask for liquor holding eighty-four wine gallons; an upright timber between two posts; a punch or tool for chipping stone.

punc-til-i-o (pŭnk-tĭl'ĭ-ō), *n.* a nice point in conduct or ceremony; formal exactness.

punc-til-i-ous (pŭnk-tĭl'ĭ-ŭs), *adj.* very nice or precise in conduct or ceremony; exact to excess.—*adv.* **punctiliously.**—*n.* **punctiliousness.**

punc-tu-al (pŭnk'tū-ăl), *adj.* observing, or done at, the exact time, prompt.—*adv.* **punctually.**
Syn. exact, timely.
Ant. (see dilatory).

punc-tu-al-i-ty (pŭnk"tū-ăl'ĭ-tĭ), *n.* the quality of being prompt, especially in keeping an appointment or engagement.

punc-tu-ate (pŭnk'tū-āt), *v.t.* to mark with points, such as the comma, semicolon, period, etc.; make clear by separating into parts with points such as the comma, etc.: *v.i.* to use marks of division in writing or printing; to mark something written or printed with commas, periods, etc.

punc-tu-a-tion (pŭnk"tū-ā'shŭn), *n.* the act or art of dividing sentences by points or stops; the marks used for such division.

punc-ture (pŭnk'tūr), *n.* a small hole or wound made by a pointed instrument: *v.t.* to make a hole in, or pierce, with a pointed instrument; to prick.

pun-dit (pŭn'dĭt), *n.* a learned Brahman, one versed in the Sanskrit language, the laws of India, the Hindu religion, etc. Also, **pandit.**

pun-gen-cy (pŭn'jĕn-sĭ), *n.* sharpness; tartness; biting quality.

pun-gent (pŭn'jĕnt), *adj.* stinging, pricking, or biting; as, a *pungent* acid; piercing; keen; sarcastic; caustic; as, *pungent* speech.—*adv.* **pungently.**

pun-ish (pŭn'ĭsh), *v.t.* to cause loss or pain to as a penalty for a crime or fault; correct; colloquially, to handle roughly.—*n.* **punisher.**

pun-ish-a-ble (pŭn'ĭsh-ȧ-bl), *adj.* deserving of, or liable to, a penalty of loss or pain.

pun-ish-ment (pŭn'ĭsh-mĕnt), *n.* pain, loss, or penalty, inflicted for a crime or fault; colloquially, rough treatment.

pu-ni-tive (pū'nĭ-tĭv), *adj.* pertaining to, involving, or inflicting penalty. Also, **punitory.**

punk (pŭnk), *n.* decayed or rotten wood; tinder; a substance that will hold fire without flame.

pun-kah (pŭn'kȧ), *n.* in British India, a hanging fan moved by a servant to cool a room. Also, **punka.**

pun-ster (pŭn'stẽr), *n.* one given to punning, or playing upon words.

punt (pŭnt), *n.* a flat-bottomed boat for fishing, usually driven along with a pole; in football, the act of kicking the ball: *v.t.* to propel, as a boat, by pushing with a pole; to kick (a football) before it touches the ground, when dropped by the hand: *v.i.* to propel a boat; to kick a football.—*n.* **punter.**

pu-ny (pū'nĭ), *adj.* [*comp.* punier, *superl.* puniest], small in strength or size; weak; feeble; as, a *puny* child.—*n.* **puniness.**

pup (pŭp), *n.* a young dog; a puppy; a young seal.

pu-pa (pū'pȧ), *n.* [*pl.* pupæ (-pē)], an insect in its cocoon or shell.—*adj.* **pupal.**

pu-pil (pū'pĭl), *n.* a young person who is under the care of a teacher; a scholar; a ward; in law, a boy or girl under the age of fourteen or twelve years respectively; the opening at the center of the eye through which rays of light pass to reach the retina.—*adj.* **pupillary.**—*n.* **pupilage.**

pup-pet (pŭp'ĕt), *n.* a small doll or image, especially one moved by wires in a mock drama; one who is under the influence and control of another.

pup-py (pŭp'ĭ), *n.* a young dog; a conceited young man; a silly fop.

pur-blind (pûr'blīnd'), *adj.* almost without sight; seeing dimly; mentally shortsighted or dull.

pur-chase (pûr'chās), *v.t.* to get by paying money or its equivalent; acquire; buy; obtain at the expense of some sacrifice, labor, etc.; move or raise by the application of some mechanical power: *n.* the act of buying; thing bought; a mechanical hold or advantage in raising heavy bodies; as, to get a *purchase* on a thing to be lifted or carried.—*n.* **purchaser.**

pure (pūr), *adj.* [*comp.* purer, *superl.* purest], genuine; real; clear; clean; innocent; honest; mere.—*adv.* **purely.**—*n.* **pureness.**

pu-rée (pü'rā'), *n.* a thick soup, as of boiled beans rubbed through a sieve. [Fr.]

pur-ga-tion (pûr-gā'shŭn), *n.* the act of cleansing; the act of clearing from guilt.

pur-ga-tive (pûr'gȧ-tĭv), *adj.* having the power of cleansing: *n.* a medicine for the purpose of cleansing the system of waste and impurities; a cathartic.

pur-ga-to-ri-al (pûr'gȧ-tō'rĭ-ăl), *adj.* pertaining to purgatory, or place of cleansing after death.

pur-ga-to-ry (pûr'gȧ-tō-rĭ), *n.* in the Roman Catholic creed, the state after death in which the souls of the faithful are purified from venial sins by suffering: *adj.* cleansing.

purge (pûrj), *v.t.* to cleanse or free from impurities; to clear of guilt; remove or wash away; as, to *purge* one's sins; to cleanse by the action of a cathartic medicine: *v.i.* to become pure or clean.—*n.* **purger.**

pu-ri-fi-ca-tion (pū'rĭ-fĭ-kā'shŭn), *n.* the act of cleansing; state of being cleansed; cleansing from guilt or uncleanness.

pu-ri-fy (pū'rĭ-fī), *v.t.* [*p.t.* and *p.p.* purified, *p.pr.* purifying], to make clean; free from guilt; free from impurities or corruptions: *v.i.* to become clean.—*n.* **purifier.**

Pu-rim (pū'rĭm), *n.* a Jewish feast (Feast of Lots) observed annually to commemorate the deliverance of the Jews in Persia from destruction by King Ahasuerus (Xerxes).—Esther ix.

pur-ism (pūr'ĭzm), *n.* great nicety as to the choice of words.

pur-ist (pūr'ĭst), *n.* one who is very precise in the choice of correct words.

pu-ri-tan (pū'rĭ-tăn), *n.* one who is very strict in his religious life: **Puritan,** one who in the 16th and 17th centuries insisted upon having simpler forms of faith and worship than those established by law: *adj.* pertaining to the Puritans or their doctrine or practice.

pu-ri-tan-ic (pū-rĭ-tăn'ĭk), *adj.* strict and precise in the matter of religious duties and conduct of life. Also, **puritanical.**—*adv.* **puritanically.**—*n.* **puritanicalness.**

Pu-ri-tan-ism (pū'rĭ-tăn-ĭzm), *n.* the doctrines and practices of the Puritans; great strictness in matters of religion and manner of living.

pu-ri-ty (pū'rĭ-tĭ), *n.* the state or quality of being clean; cleanness; freedom from foreign or adulterating matter; innocence.

purl (pûrl), *n.* a warm spiced ale or gin; an embroidered or puckered border; a reversed stitch in knitting; the continued murmuring sound of a shallow stream: *v.t.* to fringe or embroider with a waved edging; reverse (stitches) in knitting: *v.i.* to ripple or flow with a gentle murmur; to reverse knitting stitches.

pur-lieus (pûr'lūz), *n.pl.* adjacent districts or those lying near; environs; outskirts.

pur-lin (pûr'lĭn), *n.* a piece of timber lying horizontally to support the common rafters. Also, **purline.**

pur-loin (pûr-loin'), *v.t.* to steal: *v.i.* to be guilty of stealing.—*n.* **purloiner.**

pur-ple (pûr'pl), *adj.* of the color of blended blue and red; of the color of robes of state; hence, regal or royal; in poetry, dyed with blood: *n.* a color, resulting from a mixture of red and blue; the robe of this color formerly worn by royalty; hence, royal power or dignity; also, great wealth or high rank; as, born to the *purple:* *v.t.* to give a purple color to: *v.i.* to become purple.

pur-port (pûr'pōrt), *n.* meaning; design: *v.t.* (pûr-pōrt'), to mean or seem to intend.

pur-pose (pûr'pŭs), *n.* design; end or aim desired; settled intention; meaning: *v.t.* to intend or resolve; design: *v.i.* to have an intention.—*adj.* **purposeless.**—*adv.* **purposely.**

pur-pose-ful (pûr'pŭs-fōōl), *adj.* having an aim in view; not aimless; serving an end or aim.—*adv.* **purposefully.**

purr (pûr), *n.* the low murmuring of a cat when pleased: *v.t.* to show by making such a sound; as, she *purred* her contentment: *v.i.* utter a low murmuring sound. Also, **pur.**

purse (pûrs), *n.* a small bag or pouch for money; a sum of money collected for a purpose; as, they made up a *purse* for the widow; treasury; as, the public *purse:* *v.t.* to pucker or wrinkle; as, to *purse* the lips.

purs-er (pûr'sẽr), *n.* an officer having charge of the provisions, clothing, and money of a ship; paymaster.

purs-lane (pûrs'lān), *n.* a species of herb used as a salad or a potherb.

pur-su-ance (pûr-sū'ăns), *n.* the act of following out or state of being followed out; as, in *pursuance* of a plan or an order; prosecution.

pur-su-ant (pûr-sū'ănt), *adj.* done as a result (of anything); conformable: *adv.* in accordance; agreeably.

pur-sue (pûr-sū'), *v.t.* to follow with a view to overtake; chase; as, to *pursue* a thief; seek; as, to *pursue* pleasure; to go on with; continue; as, to *pursue* one's studies: *v.i.* to follow; to continue.—*n.* **pursuer.**

pur-suit (pûr-sūt'), *n.* the act of following or seeking; chase; as, the *pursuit* of a thief; a following up for a purpose; as, in *pursuit* of one's business; occupation; as, business *pursuits.*

pur-sui-vant (pûr'swĭ-vănt), *n.* an attendant or follower; state messenger.

pur-sy (pûr'sĭ), *adj.* fat, thick, and short-winded.—*n.* **pursiness.**

pu-ru-lent (pū'rōō-lĕnt), *adj.* consisting of, or containing, pus.—*n.* **purulence.**

pur-vey (pûr-vā'), *v.t.* to provide; procure, as provisions: *v.i.* to purchase provisions or food.

pur-vey-ance (pûr-vā'ăns), *n.* the act of providing; provisions supplied; the right formerly accorded to royalty of buying up provisions without the owner's consent.

pur-vey-or (pûr-vā'ẽr), *n.* one who supplies provisions or food.

pur-view (pûr'vū), *n.* extent or scope of anything; the body of a statute; range of vision; outlook.

pus (pŭs), *n.* the white or yellowish-white matter found in sores, etc.

push (po͝osh), *v.t.* to press against with force; urge forward or extend by effort; as, to *push* one's interests; drive by pressure; urge; as, to *push* a debtor: *v.i.* to make a steady forward effort; as, the army *pushed* on; press hard: *n.* a thrust; force applied; effort; assault; continued endeavor; an army's steady advance in the face of resistance.—*adj.* **pushing.**—*n.* **pusher.**

pu-sil-la-nim-i-ty (pū″sĭ-lȧ-nĭm'ĭ-tĭ), *n.* cowardice.

pu-sil-lan-i-mous (pū″sĭ-lăn'ĭ-mŭs), *adj.* cowardly; mean-spirited; faint-hearted.—*adv.* **pusillanimously.**

puss (po͝os), *n.* a pet name for a cat. Also, **pussy.**

pus-tu-lar (pŭs'tū-lȧr), *adj.* covered with pimples filled with pus.

pus-tule (pŭs'tūl), *n.* a small elevation of the skin, containing pus.

put (po͝ot'), *v.t.* [*p.t.* and *p.p.* put; *p.pr.* putting], to place; to lay; as, to *put* a book on the table; to cause to be in any state or condition; as, to *put* to shame; to *put* to flight; state; propose; as, to *put* a question; apply; as, to *put* one's mind on one's work; lay or deposit; as, to *put* money in a bank; throw in; state in words; as, to *put* one's thought into writing; shoot out or send forth; (pŭt), in golf, to drive into a hole with a short, careful stroke; to putt: *n.* a push; throw; thrust; (pŭt), in golf, a short, careful stroke for driving the ball into the hole; a putt.

pu-ta-tive (pū'tȧ-tĭv), *adj.* supposed; reputed.

pu-tre-fac-tion (pū″trē-făk'shŭn), *n.* the act or process of decaying; rottenness.

pu-tre-fac-tive (pū″trē-făk'tĭv), *adj.* pertaining to, or tending to, decay.

pu-tre-fy (pū'trē-fī), *v.t.* [*p.t.* and *p.p.* putrefied, *p.pr.* putrefying], to rot; corrupt: *v.i.* to decay or become rotten.
Syn. decompose, decay.

pu-tres-cent (pū-trĕs'ĕnt), *adj.* becoming rotten; decayed: *n.* **putrescence.**

pu-trid (pū'trĭd), *adj.* corrupt; rotten; stinking.—*n.* **putridity.**

putt (pŭt), *n.* in golf, a short, careful stroke to play a ball into a hole: *v.i.* to drive a ball into a hole with a short, careful stroke. Also, **put.**

put-tee (pŭt'ē), *n.* a gaiter made of cloth wrapped spirally from ankle to knee by officers, soldiers, or sportsmen; a stiff, heavy, leather legging. Also, **puttie, putty.**

put-ter (pŭt'ẽr), *n.* in golf, a short club, usually with a brass or iron head, used for playing a ball into a hole.

put-ting green (pŭt'ĭng grēn), in golf, the plot of smooth turf around a hole.

put-ty (pŭt'ĭ), *n.* a kind of gaiter wrapped around the leg; a puttee; a cement of whiting and linseed oil used for filling cracks, etc.: *v.t.* [*p.t.* and *p.p.* puttied, *p.pr.* puttying], to fill with such cement.

puz-zle (pŭz'l), *n.* something that perplexes or causes embarrassment; a toy made to tax skill in arranging its parts; a problem; a riddle: *v.t.* to think in perplexity; as, to *puzzle* over a mystery: *v.t.* to perplex; entangle; embarrass; to solve by clever thinking; as, to *puzzle* out a riddle.
Syn., v. confound, bewilder, confuse, mystify.
Ant. (see enlighten).

pyg-my (pĭg'mĭ), *adj.* very small; dwarfish; small of its kind: *n.* a dwarf; a very insignificant person. Also, **pigmy.**

py-ja-mas (pĭ-jä'mȧz; pĭ-jă'mȧz), *n.pl.* a suit of loose drawers and a jacket for wear during sleep. Also, **pajamas.**

py-lon (pī'lŏn), *n.* a gateway building in the form of a pyramid; a post or tower used as a marker to indicate the course over which an airplane is to fly.

py-lor-ic (pī-lŏr'ĭk), *adj.* pertaining to the pylorus, or the opening of the stomach leading to the small intestine.

py-lo-rus (pī-lō'rŭs; pĭ-lō'rŭs), *n.* the lower and right opening of the stomach leading to the small intestine.

Pyramids of Gizeh, Egypt

pyr-a-mid (pĭr'ȧ-mĭd), *n.* a solid body standing on a triangular, square, or polygonal base, having its triangular sides ending in a point at the apex or top: *pl.* tombs in Egypt of such shape; a game at billiards.

py-ram-i-dal (pĭ-răm'ĭ-dăl), *adj.* shaped like a pyramid. Also **pyramidic, pyramidical.**

pyre (pīr), *n.* a funeral pile; a pile of wood, etc., for burning a dead body.

py-rite (pī'rīt; pĭr'īt), *n.* a yellow mineral with a bright luster formed of iron and sulphur; iron pyrites.

py-ri-tes (pĭ-rī'tēz), *n.* a mixture of sulphur with iron, copper, etc., as pyrite.

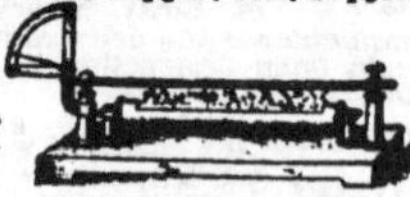
Pyrometer (dial)

py-rom-e-ter (pī-rŏm'ē-tẽr), *n.* an instrument for measuring very great heat.

py-ro-tech-nic (pī″rō-tĕk'nĭk; pĭr″ō-tĕk'nĭk), *adj.* pertaining to fireworks or the art of making them.

py-ro-tech-nics (pī″rō-tĕk'nĭks; pĭr″ō-tĕk'nĭks), *n.* fireworks or the art of making them; loud or prolonged speech. Also, **pyrotechny.**

py-ro-tech-nist (pī″rō-tĕk'nĭst; pĭr″ō-tĕk'nĭst), *n.* one skilled in the manufacture of fireworks.

py-thon (pī'thŏn), *n.* a large serpent closely resembling the boa.

pyx (pĭks), *n.* in the Roman Catholic Church, the box or container in which the consecrated wafer or Host is placed; the box in which coins are placed at the mint to be tested before being put into circulation.

Q

quack (kwăk), *n.* the cry of the duck, or a harsh sound like it: one who pretends to have medical skill or any skill that he does not possess; a pretender: *v.i.* to utter a harsh cry, as a duck; to pretend to be a doctor of medicine; to boast loudly: *adj.* pretending to know how to cure disease; as, a *quack* doctor.

quack-er-y (kwăk'ẽr-ĭ), *n.* the acts, arts, or ignorant practices of a pretender or impostor; humbug.

quad (kwŏd), *n.* in printing, an abbreviation for *quadrat*, a piece of type metal used to fill the spaces between words and to fill out blank lines; a slang abbreviation for the quandrangle, or court of a college, prison, etc.

Quad-ra-ges-i-ma (kwŏd″rȧ-jĕs'ĭ-mȧ), *n.* the first Sunday in Lent; Quadragesima Sunday.

quad-ra-ges-i-mal (kwŏd″rȧ-jĕs'ĭ-măl), *adj.* consisting of forty; pertaining to the forty days of Lent.

quad-ran-gle (kwŏd'răn″gl), *n.* a four-sided court or lawn, surrounded by buildings, especially on a college campus; a plane figure with four angles and four sides: a division of land, of varying size.

quad-ran-gu-lar (kwŏd-răn'gū-lȧr), *adj.* having the form of a plane figure with four angles and four sides.

Quadrant

quad-rant (kwŏd'rănt), *n.* one-fourth of a circle, or an arc of 90 degrees; an instrument for measuring heights; an instrument for raising a cannon to the height needed for the desired range.

quad-rat (kwŏd'răt), *n.* in printing, a piece of type metal used to space between words or to fill out blank lines.

quad-rat-ic (kwŏd-răt'ĭk), *n.* an equation in which the square, or second degree, is the highest power of an unknown quantity: *pl.* that part of algebra that treats of equations in which the square is the highest power: *adj.* in algebra, denoting the square, or second degree, as the highest power of an unknown quantity; square.

quad-ren-ni-al (kwŏd-rĕn'ĭ-ăl), *adj.* lasting through four years; happening once in four years.—*adv.* quadrennially.

Quadrilaterals. 1, square; 2, rectangle; 3, parallelogram; 4, losenge or diamond; 5, trapezoid.

quad-ri-lat-er-al (kwŏd″rĭ-lăt'ẽr-ăl), *n.* a plane figure with four sides and four angles: *adj.* having four sides and four angles.

qua-drille (kwȧ-drĭl'), *n.* a dance by four sets of couples; music for it; a game at cards played by four persons.

quad-ril-lion (kwŏd-rĭl'yŭn), *n.* in the French system of numbering, used in the United States, a thousand trillions, or one followed by fifteen ciphers; in the English system, the fourth power of a million, or one followed by twenty-four ciphers.

quad-roon (kwŏd-rōōn'), *n.* a person having one-fourth negro blood; the child of a mulatto and a white person.

quad-ru-ma-nous (kwŏd-rōō'mȧ-nŭs), *adj.* having all four feet like hands, as a monkey; four-handed.

quad-ru-ped (kwŏd'rōō-pĕd), *n.* a four-footed animal: *adj.* four-footed.

quad-ru-ple (kwŏd'rōō-pl), *adj.* fourfold: *n.* a sum or quantity four times as great as another: *v.t.* to multiply by four: *v.i.* to increase fourfold.

quad-ru-plex (kwŏd'rōō-plĕks), *adj.* fourfold: used especially to describe a system of telegraphing in which four messages, two in each direction, are sent at the same time over one wire.

quad-ru-pli-cate (kwŏd-rōō'plĭ-kāt), *v.t.* to multiply by four: *adj.* (kwŏd-rōō'plĭ-kăt), four times as great: *n.* one of four like things.

quaff (kwăf), *v.t.* to drink or swallow in large quantities: *v.i.* to drink deeply.

quag-ga (kwăg'ȧ), *n.* a South African four-footed animal of the zebra family: said to be no longer in existence.

quag-gy (kwăg'ĭ), *adj.* giving under the foot, as soft, wet ground; boggy.

quag-mire (kwăg'mīr″), *n.* soft, miry ground which yields under the feet; a bog.

qua-hog (kwô'hŏg; kwȧ-hŏg'), *n.* the hard-shell clam common in America. Also, quahaug.

quail (kwāl), *n.* a small game bird of the partridge family; the bobwhite: *v.i.* to shrink from facing pain or danger; lose heart or courage; cower.

quaint (kwānt), *adj.* pleasingly old-fashioned; curious and fanciful; not expressed or shown in the usual way; as, *quaint* speech; odd.—*adv.* quaintly.—*n.* quaintness.

quake (kwāk), *v.i.* to vibrate or shake; as, the earth *quakes;* to tremble or shake with fear, cold, etc.; quiver: *n.* a shaking or trembling; especially, an earthquake.—*p.adj.* quaking.—*adv.* quakingly.

Quak-er (kwāk'ẽr), *n.* [*fem.* Quakeress], one of a religious sect called by its members the Society of Friends.—*adj.* Quakerish.

Quak-er gun (kwāk'ẽr gŭn), a wooden gun or cannon mounted to deceive an enemy: so called because the Quakers do not believe in fighting an enemy.

qual-i-fi-ca-tion (kwŏl″ĭ-fĭ-kā'shŭn), *n.* the act of making, or state of being, fit; any trait or thing that fits a person for any place or occupation; fitness.

qual-i-fied (kwŏl'ĭ-fīd), *p.adj.* fitted; competent; as, she is well *quali-*

fied to fill the position; limited; restricted; as, *qualified* praise.

qual-i-fi-er (kwŏl'ĭ-fī"ēr), *n.* one that limits or modifies: used in grammar as a name for an adjective, adverb, etc.

qual-i-fy (kwŏl'ĭ-fī), *v.t.* [*p.t.* and *p.p.* qualified, *p.pr.* qualifying], to make fit for any office, occupation, etc.; to moderate; lessen; soften; as, to *qualify* censure; to limit; modify; alter slightly; as, to *qualify* a statement: *v.i.* to become competent or fit for any office or employment.

qual-i-ta-tive (kwŏl'ĭ-tā-tĭv), *adj.* pertaining to quality, or kind, as opposed to quantity, or amount; as, *qualitative* analysis.—*adv.* qualitatively.

qual-i-ty (kwŏl'ĭ-tĭ), *n.* [*pl.* qualities (-tĭz)], that which belongs to a thing and makes it what it is and different from other things; nature; kind; as, the *qualities* of cloth or iron; relative goodness; as, goods of high *quality;* trait or characteristic; as, generosity is one of his many fine *qualities;* special virtue; as, the healing *quality* of an ointment; rank; high birth; as, a lady of *quality;* distinctive tone; as, a voice of carrying *quality.*

qualm (kwäm), *n.* a feeling of sickness, especially of the stomach; a sudden misgiving or twinge of conscience.—*adj.* qualmish.

quan-da-ry (kwŏn'dȧ-rĭ), *n.* a state of hesitation or doubt; a puzzling difficulty; a dilemma.

quan-ti-ta-tive (kwŏn'tĭ-tā-tĭv), *adj.* of or pertaining to quantity, or amount, as opposed to quality, or kind; as, *quantitative* analysis.—*adv.* quantitatively.

quan-ti-ty (kwŏn'tĭ-tĭ), *n.* that property of anything that enables it to be increased or reduced; any uncertain bulk, weight, or number; a large portion, sum, or mass; the sound given to a syllable, as long or short; anything that can be increased, divided, or measured.

quar-an-tine (kwŏr'ăn-tēn), *n.* the time during which an incoming vessel suspected of carrying a dangerous disease is not allowed to communicate with the shore; the place where such vessels are held; the holding of them or the measures taken to hold them; any enforced restraint placed upon travel or intercourse on account of disease: *v.t.* to place under restraint because of disease.

quar-rel (kwŏr'ĕl), *n.* an arrow, especially one with a square head; an angry dispute; petty fight; a cause for dispute; a disagreement or falling out: *v.i.* to dispute violently; fall out; disagree; find fault; as, to *quarrel* with fortune.

quar-rel-some (kwŏr'ĕl-sŭm), *adj.* inclined to dispute, disagree, or find fault, or fight; easily provoked.—*adv.* quarrelsomely.—*n.* quarrelsomeness.

quar-ry (kwŏr'ĭ), *n.* a place from which stone is dug or cut out for building purposes, etc.; a beast or bird hunted with hawks or hounds: *v.t.* [*p.t.* and *p.p.* quarried, *p.pr.* quarrying], to dig or take from an excavation, or hole; as, to *quarry* stone.—*p.adj.* quarried.—*n.* quarryman.

quart (kwôrt), *n.* two pints; in liquid measure, one-fourth of a gallon; in dry measure, one-eighth of a peck.

quarte (kärt), *n.* a guard in fencing. Also, carte. [Fr.]

quar-ter (kwôr'tĕr), *n.* the fourth part of anything; twenty-five (often, twenty-eight) pounds, one-fourth of a hundredweight; one-fourth of a ton; in England, eight bushels; the fourth part of the moon's monthly revolution; three months, a fourth of a year; one-half of a term at school; fifteen minutes, a fourth of an hour; twenty-five cents, a fourth of a dollar; a silver coin of this value; one of the four points of the compass, as north, south, etc.; a part of the globe; a particular place or district; afterpart of a ship's side; one of the four limbs of an animal with the parts near it; as, a *quarter* of lamb; life granted to a captive or enemy; mercy; as, to give no *quarter;* the place or source from which anything comes; as, you may expect trouble from that *quarter:* *pl.* lodgings, especially for soldiers: *v.t.* to divide into four equal parts; furnish with lodgings, food, etc., as soldiers; station.—*p.adj.* quartered.

quar-ter day (kwôr'tĕr dā), one of the four days of the year on which rents, etc., paid every three months, are due.

quar-ter-deck (kwôr'tĕr-dĕk"), *n.* that part of a ship which is behind the mainmast.

quar-ter-foil (kwôr'tĕr-foil), *n.* a flower with four leaves, or a leaf with four leaflets; an ornament somewhat like a leaf and having four lobes. Also, quatrefoil.

quar-ter-ing (kwôr'tĕr-ĭng), *n.* assignment to lodgings, etc., as soldiers; the placing of more than one coat of arms on a shield to show the different families from whom a person is descended; any one of the coats of arms.

quar-ter-ly (kwôr'tĕr-lĭ), *n.* [*pl.* quarterlies (-lĭz)], a publication issued once in every three months: *adj.* consisting of, or containing, a fourth part; coming once in three months: *adv.* once in each fourth of the year.

quar-ter-mas-ter (kwôr'tĕr-mȧs"tĕr), *n.* in the army, an officer whose duty it is to assign lodgings and provide food, clothing, and other supplies, for soldiers; in the navy, a petty officer who attends to the steering, signals, stowage, etc., of ships.

quar-tern (kwôr'tĕrn), *n.* a quarter; a fourth, as a fourth of a pint, bushel, etc.; a gill.

quar-ter-staff (kwôr'tĕr-stȧf"), *n.* [*pl.* quarterstaves (-stāvz)], a stout stick about six and a half feet long and shod with iron, formerly used as a weapon of defense.

quar-tet (kwôr-tĕt'), *n.* a musical composition in four parts for four voices or instruments; the four performers of such a composition; anything made up of four. Also, quartette.

quar-to (kwôr'tō), *n.* [*pl.* quartos (-tōz)], a book having the sheet folded into four leaves and nearly square in size: *adj.* having four leaves in a sheet. Also, 4to.

Quartz Crystals

quartz (kwôrts), *n.* a hard mineral composed of pure silica: the most common of solid minerals, found in many kinds of rock, often in the form of crystals.

āte, senāte, râre, căt, locȧl, fär, ȧsk, pȧrade; scēne, ēvent, ĕdge, novĕl, refĕr; rīght, sĭn; cōld, ōbey, côrd, stŏp, cŏmpare; ūnit, ūnite, bûrn, cŭt, focŭs, menü;

quartz-ite (kwôrt'sīt), *n.* a compact rock composed of grains of quartz.

quash (kwŏsh), *v.t.* to put down or subdue; make an end of; as, to *quash* a rebellion; in law, to stop, as a suit; set aside; as, to *quash* an indictment.

qua-si- (kwā'sī-), a *prefix* meaning as if, as it were, apparently, nearly.

quas-si-a (kwŏsh'ĭ-ȧ), *n.* a very bitter drug from the wood of the bitter ash and several other trees of the West Indies and South America: used as a tonic.

qua-ter-na-ry (kwȧ-tûr'nȧ-rĭ), *adj.* consisting of four things; fourth in order: **Quaternary**, in geology, pertaining to the later period of the Cenozoic era, which extends to the present time: *n.* [*pl.* Quaternaries (-rĭz)], the latest geologic period; the age of man.

qua-ter-ni-on (kwȧ-tûr'nĭ-ŭn), *n.* the number four; a set or group of four persons or things; as, a *quaternion* of soldiers; a method of mathematical calculus.

quat-rain (kwŏt'rān), *n.* a stanza of four lines, of which the third usually rimes with the first, and the fourth with the second.

qua-ver (kwā'vēr), *n.* a shaking or trembling, as of the voice; a trill in singing or playing; in music, an eighth note: *v.i.* to shake or tremble; vibrate; have a tremulous sound, as a voice or musical instrument; trill: *v.t.* to utter or sing with trills or a tremulous sound.

quay (kē), *n.* a firmly built wharf for loading or unloading vessels.

quea-sy (kwē'zĭ), *adj.* affected with, or causing, nausea or vomiting; delicate; as, a *queasy* question.

queen (kwēn), *n.* a female sovereign, or woman who rules in her own right; the wife of a king; a gifted woman who is a natural leader; as, a social *queen;* the only perfect female of a swarm of bees (queen bee) or a colony of ants; a playing card on which is a picture of a queen; a piece in chess; the best or chief of her kind. *v.i.* to rule as, or play the part of, a sovereign or leader.

Vermont Marble Quarry

queen con-sort (kwēn kŏn'sôrt), the wife of a reigning king.

queen dow-a-ger (kwēn dou'ȧ-jēr), the widow of a king.

queen-ly (kwēn'lĭ), *adj.* like, becoming, or suitable to, a queen; stately: *adv.* in the manner of a queen; in a stately manner.—*n.* **queenliness.**

queen moth-er (kwēn mŭth'ēr), the widow of a king and mother of the reigning sovereign.

queen re-gent (kwēn rē'jĕnt), a queen reigning during the childhood, absence, etc., of the actual sovereign.

queen reg-nant (kwēn rĕg′nănt), a queen reigning in her own right.

queen's ware (kwēnz wâr), a cream-colored glazed pottery.

queer (kwēr), *adj.* odd; singular; droll; strange; mentally unsound; open to question.—*adv.* **queerly.**—*n.* **queerness.**

quell (kwĕl), *v.t.* to suppress or subdue; put an end to; as, to *quell* a riot; to calm; quiet; as, to *quell* rage.

quench (kwĕnch), *v.t.* to put out; as, to *quench* a fire; to cause to cease or stop; as, to *quench* thirst; cool suddenly; as, to *quench* hot iron in water.—*adj.* **quenchable, quenchless.**—*n.* **quencher.**

quer-u-lous (kwĕr′ŏŏ-lŭs), *adj.* complaining; discontented; faultfinding; as, a *querulous* old man; expressing complaint or fretfulness; as, a *querulous* voice.—*adv.* **querulously.**—*n.* **querulousness.**
Syn. repining, fretting.
Ant. (see patient).

que-ry (kwē′rĭ), *n.* a question; an inquiry; a question mark [?]: *v.t.* [*p.t.* and *p.p.* queried, *p.pr.* querying], to inquire into; ask; to express a doubt in regard to: *v.i.* to ask questions.

quest (kwĕst), *n.* search; as, an animal in *quest* of food; inquiry; adventure: *v.i.* to go forth seeking adventure; as, the knight *quested* forth.

ques-tion (kwĕs′chŭn), *n.* an inquiry; act of asking; that which is asked; interrogation; subject of dispute; subject under discussion; as, the *question* before the meeting; doubt; as, these beyond *question* are the facts; a matter to be decided; as, that is a *question* for you to settle: *v.t.* to ask or interrogate; examine by queries; treat as doubtful: *v.i.* to make inquiries.—*n.* **questioner.**

ques-tion-a-ble (kwĕs′chŭn-ȧ-bl), *adj.* that may be doubted or suspected; doubtful; suspicious; as, a *questionable* transaction.—*adv.* **questionably.**—*n.* **questionableness.**

ques-tion-naire (kwĕs-chŭn-âr′), *n.* a series of questions to be answered by a large number of people whose replies are to serve as a basis in investigation of a subject; especially, in the World War, a series of questions issued by the United States government to be answered by drafted men.

queue (kū), *n.* a pigtail, or the tail of a wig; a line of people waiting for tickets, rations, etc. Also, cue.

quib-ble (kwĭb′l), *n.* a turn or shift from the point in question; *v.i.* to avoid the truth by a skilful but trifling objection.—*n.* **quibbler.**
Syn., *v.* evade, shuffle.

quib-bling (kwĭb′lĭng), *n.* evasion or avoidance of the truth by means of a trifling objection.

quick (kwĭk), *adj.* rapid; swift; as, *quick* in action; nimble; as, *quick* on one's feet; alert; ready; as, a *quick* eye; *quick* wit; easily excited; hasty; as, a *quick* temper; sensitive; having life: *adv.* with haste; rapidly: *n.* the living flesh; as, the *quick* under the nail of a finger or toe; the feelings; as, she was hurt to the *quick*; a hedge of growing shrubs.—*adv.* **quickly.**—*n.* **quickness.**
Syn., *adj.* lively, brisk, swift, agile, active.
Ant. (see slow).

quick-en (kwĭk′n), *v.i.* to come to life; become alive; to act or move more rapidly: *v.t.* increase the speed of; hasten; as, to *quicken* one's steps; to bring to life; to make keen; give new life to; refresh; cheer.—*n.* **quickener.**

quick-lime (kwĭk′līm″), *n.* lime burnt but unslaked, or not mixed with water.

quick-sand (kwĭk′sănd″), *n.* sand soaked with water and yielding so easily that a person or thing will readily sink into it.

quick-set (kwĭk′sĕt″), *n.* a cutting from a living shrub, especially the hawthorn, set to grow, as for a hedge.

quick-sil-ver (kwĭk′sĭl″vẽr), *n.* mercury, a heavy silver white metallic element: used on the backs of mirrors, in thermometers, in amalgam fillings for the teeth, etc.

quick-step (kwĭk′stĕp), *n.* a lively march, written in quick time, frequently played by military bands.

quid (kwĭd), *n.* a piece to be chewed; as, a *quid* of tobacco; a cud; in British slang, a pound, or twenty shillings.

quid-di-ty (kwĭd′ĭ-tĭ), *n.* [*pl.* quiddities (-tĭz)], that which makes a thing what it is and different from other things; a trifling nicety.

quid-nunc (kwĭd′nŭngk″), *n.* one who is curious to know, or pretends to know, everything that goes on; a gossip.

qui-es-cence (kwī-ĕs′ĕns), *n.* repose or rest; mental calm. Also, **quiescency.**

qui-es-cent (kwī-ĕs′ĕnt), *adj.* reposing or resting; calm; silent; still.—*adv.* **quiescently.**

qui-et (kwī′ĕt), *adj.* free from motion, disturbance, or noise; as, a *quiet* river; *quiet* life; *quiet* children; still; calm; as, a *quiet* night; peaceable; gentle; as, a *quiet* disposition; secluded; as, a *quiet* woods; subdued and modest; as, *quiet* manners; not showy; as, *quiet* colors: *v.t.* to calm or make peaceful; bring to a state of rest: *v.i.* to become still or calm: *n.* freedom from motion, noise, or disturbance; rest; stillness; calm.—*adv.* **quietly.**—*n.* **quietness, quieter.**

qui-e-tude (kwī′ĕ-tūd), *n.* rest; repose; quietness.

qui-e-tus (kwī-ē′tŭs), *n.* rest; death; final settlement, as of an account; something which puts an end to action.

quill (kwĭl), *n.* the large strong feather of a bird's wing or tail; a pen made from such a feather; one of the long sharp spines of the porcupine: *v.t.* to plait or iron into small fluted ridges.

quill-ing (kwĭl′ĭng), *n.* a strip of material, as silk, net, etc., fluted into small ridges.

quilt (kwĭlt), *n.* a kind of coverlet or bed-cover: *v.t.* to stitch together, as two layers or pieces of cloth, etc., with a soft material between: *v.i.* to stitch material together with soft material between.—*n.* **quilter.**

quilt-ing (kwĭlt′ĭng), *n.* the act or process of stitching layers of material together with other soft material between; material for such work; the work when finished.

qui-na-ry (kwī′nȧ-rĭ), *n.* that which has five members: *adj.* consisting of, or arranged in, fives.

quince (kwĭns), *n.* the applelike fruit of a tree of the apple family, much used for preserves; also, the tree.

qui-nine (kwī'nīn; kwī-nēn'), *n.* a bitter drug obtained from the bark of the Cinchona tree. Also, **quinin, quinia, quinina.**

Quin-qua-ges-i-ma (kwĭn-kwȧ-jĕs'ĭ-mȧ), *n.* the Sunday next before Lent; Quinquagesima Sunday.

quin-quen-ni-al (kwĭn-kwĕn'ĭ-ăl), *adj.* occurring once in five years, or at the end of every five years, or lasting five years: *n.* such an event.

quin-sy (kwĭn'zĭ), *n.* inflammation of the tonsils.

quin-tal (kwĭn'tăl), *n.* a weight of one hundred or one hundred and twelve pounds.

quin-tan (kwĭn'tăn), *adj.* occurring every fifth day; as, a *quintan* fever.

quin-tes-sence (kwĭn-tĕs'ĕns), *n.* the pure essence, or most necessary part, of anything; hence, the summing up in concrete form of certain qualities in their greatest perfection; as, she is the *quintessence* of neatness.

quin-tet (kwĭn-tĕt'), *n.* a musical composition in five parts or for five voices or instruments; the five performers of such a composition; any set of five. Also, **quintette.**

quin-til-lion (kwĭn-tĭl'yŭn), *n.* in the system of numbering used in the United States and France, a thousand quadrillions, or one followed by eighteen ciphers; in the English system, a million raised to the fifth power, or one followed by thirty ciphers.

quin-tu-ple (kwĭn'tū-pl), *v.t.* and *v.i.* to make or become five times as much; *adj.* fivefold.

quip (kwĭp), *n.* a short sarcastic remark; a smart retort; jeer; quibble.

quire (kwīr), *n.* twenty-four sheets of paper of the same size and kind.

Quir-i-nal (kwĭr'ĭ-năl; kwĭ-rī'năl), *n.* at Rome, the royal palace of the King of Italy: so called because it stands on the hill of the same name.

quirk (kwûrk), *n.* a sudden twist, turn, or curve, as of the pen in writing; a flourish; an artful avoidance of the truth in speaking; a quibble; smart answer; a slang term for the pilot of an airplane.

quirt (kwûrt), *n.* a riding whip with a short handle and lash of braided rawhide.

quit (kwĭt), *v.t.* [*p.t.* and *p.p.* quit or quitted, *p.pr.* quitting], discharge, as an obligation or duty; stop; give up; as, to *quit* work; forsake; as, to *quit* the path of duty; to depart from; as, he *quit* the house forever; *adj.* freed from.

quit-claim (kwĭt'klām'), *n.* a full release, as from a demand, suit, etc.; a deed of release: *v.t.* to give up title to.

quite (kwīt), *adv.* wholly; completely; entirely; as, *quite* dead; *quite* certain; sometimes, very; considerably; as, *quite* cold; *quite* sick.

quits (kwĭts), *adj.* equal or even (with someone), as when returning or repaying something; as, now we are *quits*.

quit-tance (kwĭt'ăns), *n.* release from a debt, service, or obligation; repayment.

quiv-er (kwĭv'ẽr), *n.* a portable case or sheath for arrows; the act of trembling or shivering: *v.i.* to tremble, shake, or shiver; as, to *quiver* with anger.

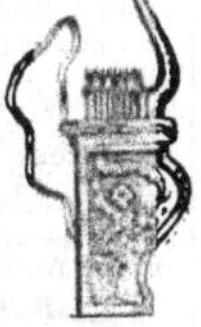

Ancient Quiver

qui vive (kē vēv'), the challenge of a sentinel in the French army, meaning, who goes there? **to be on the qui vive,** to be on the watch or the alert. [Fr.]

quix-ot-ic (kwĭk-sŏt'ĭk), *adj.* chivalrous or romantic to an absurd or extravagant degree: from *Don Quixote*, the hero of Cervantes' romance of that name.—*adv.* **quixotically.**—*n.* **quixotism.**

quiz (kwĭz), *n.* an absurd, jesting question, put in pretended seriousness; a joke; one who jests or asks absurd questions; colloquially, a questioning of a pupil, class, etc.: *v.t.* [*p.t.* and *p.p.* quizzed, *p.pr.* quizzing], to make game of by trying to puzzle; make fun of while pretending to be serious; chaff; examine narrowly with an air of mockery; colloquially, to examine (a pupil or class) by questions.—*n.* **quizzer.**

quiz-zi-cal (kwĭz'ĭ-kăl), *adj.* comical; humorously serious; queer; odd.—*adv.* **quizzically.**

quod (kwŏd), *n.* a quadrangle, as of a prison; a prison. [Slang.]

quoin (koin; kwoin), *n.* a large square stone at the corner of a wall; the outside angle of a building; a wedge of wood or metal to raise a gun; a wedge-shaped block to tighten the pages of type within a galley; a wedge-like piece used for any purpose.

quoit (kwoit; koit), *n.* a circular ring of iron to be pitched at a fixed object: *pl.* the game thus played.

quon-dam (kwŏn'dăm), *adj.* having been at some time; former; sometime; as, a *quondam* member of a society.

quo-rum (kwō'rŭm), *n.* the number of regularly assembled members of a body or corporation necessary, by law or constitution, to transact business.

quo-ta (kwō'tȧ), *n.* the part or share required from each to make up an amount or quantity.

quot-a-ble (kwōt'ȧ-bl), *adj.* that which may be, or deserves to be, repeated or cited.

quo-ta-tion (kwō-tā'shŭn), *n.* the act of repeating the words of another; the words repeated; a passage from a book, etc., repeated or referred to as illustration; the current price; a stating of the current price.

quo-ta-tion mark (kwō-tā'shŭn märk), one of the marks placed at the beginning and end of a cited or repeated passage or word: two inverted commas [“] at the beginning, and two apostrophes [”] at the end: of a quotation, each of the single marks used to show a quotation within a quotation; as, the witness replied, "He approached me and said, 'Good evening.'"

quote (kwōt), *v.t.* to repeat, as the words of some other person; repeat the words of, as an author or passage, as authority or illustration; name or cite, as an author or passage, as authority or illustration; give the present price of: *v.i.* to repeat the words of another.—*n.* **quoter.**

quoth (kwōth), *v.t.* said; spoke; uttered: used only in the first and third persons in the past tense, with the nominative always following the verb; as, *quoth* he.

quo-ti-di-an (kwō-tĭd'ĭ-ăn), *n.* an intermittent fever that returns every day: *adj.* daily.

quo-tient (kwō'shĕnt), *n.* the number resulting from the division of one number by another.

quo war-ran-to (kwō wŏ-răn'tō), a judicial writ or order commanding a person to show by what right, or authority, he exercises an office, or certain powers. [Lat.]

R

raad (rät), *n.* a legislative assembly, or lawmaking body, of South Africa.

rab-bet (răb'ĕt), *n.* a groove or cut, made in the edge of one plank, etc., so that another may fit into it: *v.t.* to join, as parts cut or grooved to fit together.

rab-bi (răb'ī; răb'ĭ), *n.* [*pl.* rabbis (-īz; -ĭz)]. a Jewish title for a doctor or interpreter of the law; a teacher; a pastor of a Jewish congregation, ordained to deal with questions of law and ritual. Also, **rabbin.**

rab-bin-ic (ră-bĭn'ĭk), *adj.* pertaining to Jewish doctors of the law, their doctrines, learning, and language. Also, **rabbinical.**

rab-bit (răb'ĭt), *n.* a well-known small animal of the hare family, esteemed for food and for its fur: *v.i.* to hunt and kill those animals.

rab-bit war-ren (răb'ĭt wŏr'ĕn), a place where rabbits make holes in the ground and breed.

rab-ble (răb'l), *n.* a noisy crowd or mob: **the rabble,** the lowest class of people: *adj.* noisy; coarse.

rab-id (răb'ĭd), *adj.* furious; raging; extremely unreasonable; excessively zealous; mad.—*adv.* **rabidly.**

ra-bi-es (rā'bĭ-ēz), *n.* dog madness; madness caused by the bite of a dog; hydrophobia.

ra-ca (rä'kȧ; rȧ-kä'), *adj.* worthless: used to express great contempt among the ancient Jews.

rac-coon (ră-kōōn'), *n.* a grayish-brown animal of North America with a bushy black-and-white ringed tail: valued for its fur. Also, **racoon.**

race (rās), *n.* a strong rapid current of water; also, its channel; as, a mill *race;* a contest of speed, as in running, swimming, etc.; length of life or career; as, my *race* is run; breed; a class of beings having similar qualities; as, the human *race;* a division of human beings; as, the white *race;* a nation; as, the English *race;* family line; as, the *race* of Stuart kings: *v.i.* to run swiftly; contend in running; to run, as an engine, too fast because of a lightened load: *v.t.* to cause to move swiftly in a contest of speed; to drive at great speed; as, to *race* a horse; to run with, in a speed contest.

ra-ceme (rȧ-sēm'; rā-sēm'), *n.* a flower cluster in which the flowers grow singly, at almost regular distances, along a stalk.—*adj.* **racemose.**

rac-er (rās'ẽr), *n.* one that engages in a speed contest; anything that has power to go at very great speed, as a race horse; a variety of snake, especially the American black snake.

race su-i-cide (rās sū'ĭ-sīd), the gradual dying out of a race because of the refusal of its members to have children enough to make up for the death rate.

race-way (rās'wā'), *n.* a water channel, as a mill race.

Ra-chel (rā'chĕl), *n.* in the Bible, the wife of Jacob and mother of Joseph and Benjamin.

ra-chi-tis (rȧ-kī'tĭs), *n.* a disease in which the head enlarges and the bones become misshapen, due to inflammation of the spine: called also *rickets.*

ra-cial (rā'shăl), *adj.* pertaining to a division or family of men.—*adv.* **racially.**

rack (răk), *n.* an instrument for torturing the body by stretching or straining the limbs: formerly used to force a confession; intense physical or mental suffering; as, pain or anxiety kept him on the *rack;* a framework on or in which articles are hung or arranged; a grating above a manger for holding hay; a straight bar having teeth which work with the teeth of a pinion or cogwheel; thin, broken, vapory clouds; wreck: used only in *rack and ruin;* a pacing gait of a horse: *v.t.* to stretch or strain on an instrument of torture; torture; torment; as, *racked* by remorse; strain; tear; as, *racked* by a cough; tax greatly; as, to *rack* one's brain: *v.i.* to go at a pacing gait, as a horse.
Syn., *v.* agonize, wring, distress.
Ant. (see soothe).

rack-et (răk'ĕt), *n.* a clattering noise; din; noisy talk or play; a network bat used in the game of tennis; a snowshoe: *v.i.* to make a loud noise; frolic: *v.t.* to strike with, or as with, a network bat.

rack rent (răk rĕnt), rent raised to the utmost rental value of the property. Also, **rackrent.**

ra-con-teur (rȧ"kôn"tûr'), *n.* a storyteller; one who relates anecdotes, etc., extremely well. [FR.]

ra-coon (ră-kōōn'), a grayish-brown North American animal having a bushy black-and-white ringed tail and a valuable fur. Also, **raccoon.**

rac-quet (răk'ĕt), *n.* a network bat for playing tennis, etc.: *v.t.* to strike with a network bat. Also, **racket.**

rac-y (rās'ĭ), *adj.* having a strong flavor; pungent; spicy; rich; fresh; as, a *racy* wine; mentally exciting; lively; spirited; smart; suggestive or immodest; as, a *racy* story.—*adv.* **racily.**—*n.* **raciness.**

ra-di-al (rā'dĭ-ăl), *adj.* pertaining to a ray, as of light, or to a radius, as of a circle; shooting out from a center; pertaining to the outer bone of the forearm.—*adv.* **radially.**

ra-di-an (rā'dĭ-ăn), *n.* a unit for the measurement of angles; the arc, or portion of a circle, whose length is equal to the radius.

ra-di-ance (rā'dĭ-ăns), *n.* brilliant brightness; splendor; as the *radiance* of the sun. Also, **radiancy.**
Syn. brilliancy, luster, glare.

ra-di-ant (rā'dĭ-ănt), *adj.* sending out rays of light or heat; as, the *radiant* sun; shining; brilliant; as, *radiant* beauty; beaming with kindness, joy, etc., as, a *radiant* smile; pouring out or issuing as in rays; as, *radiant* heat or *radiant* energy.—*adv.* **radiantly.**

ra-di-ate (rā'dĭ-āt), *v.t.* to send out in rays; as, the sun *radiates* light and heat: *v.i.* to issue forth in rays; as, heat and light *radiate* from the sun: *adj.* having rays.

ra-di-a-tion (rā"dĭ-ā'shŭn), *n.* the coming forth and spreading, as of rays, in all directions from a common center; as, the *radiation* of light or heat from a shining or heated body.

ra-di-a-tor (rā'dĭ-ā'tẽr), *n.* the body from which rays are sent out; a chamber, coil, drum, etc., in a building heated by steam, hot air, hot water, etc., for warming the building; an appliance used with a gasoline engine to cool the water which circulates around the engine.

rad-i-cal (răd′ĭ-kăl), *n.* a simple word, or root, from which other words are formed; the base of a chemical compound; a person who holds extreme views and takes extreme measures: *adj.* pertaining to the root or origin; original; extreme; as, a *radical* difference of opinion; in mathematics, showing or containing the root of a number; pertaining to a political party of advanced views: **Rad cal**, a member of a political party holding very advanced views, especially about social equality.—*adv.* **radically.**—*n.* **radicalness.**

rad-i-cel (răd′ĭ-sĕl), *n.* a little root. Also, **radicle.**

ra-di-o-ac-tive (rā″dĭ-ō-ăk′tĭv), *adj.* capable of sending forth invisible rays, such as X rays, composed of particles moving at high velocity.—*n.* **radioactivity.**

ra-di-o-graph (rā′dĭ-ō-grȧf), *n.* a picture obtained by means of invisible rays, as X rays, radium rays, etc.: *v.t.* to produce a likeness of, by means of invisible rays.—*n.* **radiographer.**

ra-di-og-ra-phy (rā″dĭ-ŏg′rȧ-fĭ), *n.* the art or process of producing pictures by the action of invisible rays upon a sensitive surface, like a photographic plate.

ra-di-om-e-ter (rā″dĭ-ŏm′ē-tẽr), *n.* an instrument by means of which radiant light or heat may be directly transformed into mechanical energy.

Radiometer

ra-di-o-te-leg-ra-phy (rā″dĭ-ō-tē-lĕg′rȧ-fĭ), *n.* the sending of messages through the air without the aid of wires; wireless telegraphy.—*adj.* **radiotelegraphic.**

ra-di-o-te-leph-o-ny (rā″dĭ-ō-tē-lĕf′ō-nĭ), *n.* the speaking of a message through the air without the aid of wires; wireless telephony.

rad-ish (răd′ĭsh), *n.* a plant with a pungent edible root, usually eaten raw; the root.

Radish

ra-di-um (rā′dĭ-ŭm), *n.* a chemical element, extracted from pitch-blende, which gives off invisible rays with extremely slow loss of power or weight.

ra-di-us (rā′dĭ-ŭs), *n.* [*pl.* radii (-ī); radiuses (-ĕz)], a straight line from the center of a circle or sphere to the circumference or surface; the thicker and shorter bone of the forearm; the ray of a flower.

raf-fi-a (răf′ĭ-ȧ), *n.* a kind of palm fiber, used in basket weaving, etc.

raf-fle (răf′l), *n.* a kind of lottery, or game of chance, in which each person pays a part of the value of a thing for a chance of winning it: *v.t.* to dispose of by selling chances on: *v.i.* to take part in the selling of a thing by chances.

raft (rȧft), *n.* a floating flat framework made of logs, boards, etc., fastened together: *v.t.* to carry on such a float.

raft-er (rȧf′tẽr), *n.* a sloping beam that helps to support the roof of a house: *v.t.* to form into, or furnish with, such beams.

rafts-man (rȧfts′măn), *n.* a man who works on or manages a raft, or float of logs, etc., on a river.

rag (răg), *n.* a worn or torn piece of cloth; shred; a mean dress; a piece of popular music in syncopated time; *pl.* tattered or worn-out garments: *v.i.* to play music in syncopated time; colloquially, to scold.

rag-a-muf-fin (răg′ȧ-mŭf″ĭn), *n.* a beggarly, usually disreputable, fellow who wears tattered clothing: *adj.* beggarly.

rage (rāj), *n.* uncontrolled anger; extreme violence; fury; enthusiasm; great eagerness; colloquially, anything eagerly sought because of fashion; as, high heels are the *rage:* *v.i.* to be furious with anger; storm; to act violently; have furious force or effect; as, a fever *rages;* be violently agitated; as, the sea *raged.*

rag-ged (răg′ĕd), *adj.* torn; having holes resulting from wear; as, a *ragged* coat; clothed in tattered garments; as, a *ragged* fellow; rough; jagged; as, a *ragged* stone.—*adv.* **raggedly.**—*n.* **raggedness.**

rag-ged rob-in (răg′ĕd rŏb′ĭn), a common garden flower, having small blossoms with jagged edges.

rag-lan (răg′lăn), *n.* a loose overcoat with large sleeves or a cape.

ra-gout (rȧ-gōō′), *n.* a stew of meat and vegetables highly seasoned.

rag-stone (răg′stōn″), *n.* any rough, coarse-grained rock.

rag-weed (răg′wēd″), *n.* a coarse weed with small greenish flowers and deeply cut or toothed leaves.

raid (rād), *n.* a hostile invasion; a sudden attack, especially to make arrests, seize property, or discover stolen goods; as, a police *raid.* In the World War, an attack by airships upon a region outside the fighting areas; a night excursion by a small party of soldiers to an enemy trench to secure prisoners, information, etc: *v.t.* to make a sudden attack upon; to invade.—*n.* **raider.**

rail (rāl), *n.* a bar of wood or metal placed in a horizontal position between two supports; a wooden or iron fence; especially that placed as a guard at the edge of the deck of a ship; one of two bars of iron or steel forming a track for the wheels of a vehicle; a wading bird of the crane family: *v.i.* to use bitter, scornful, or reproachful language; scoff: with *at* or *against:* *v.t.* to inclose with bars, etc.: with *in* or *off.*

Rails. 1, T-head; 2, double-head.

rail-ing (rāl′ĭng), *n.* material for rails; a fence or barrier made of bars upheld by posts: *adj.* insulting or reproaching; as, *railing* language.

rail-ler-y (răl′ẽr-ĭ; rāl′ẽr-ĭ), *n.* good-humored ridicule; merry jesting; banter.

rail-road (rāl′rōd″), *n.* a way or road laid with two parallel iron or steel rails, forming a track along which cars are drawn by steam power, electricity, etc.; such a road, with all the land, stations, cars, engines, etc., pertaining to it: *v.t.* colloquially, in the United States, to put through rapidly; rush; as, to *railroad* a bill through a legislature.

rail-way (rāl'wā"), *n.* in Great Britain, a railroad; in the United States, a railroad for light traffic; as, an electric *railway;* any track with rails for wheels.

rai-ment (rā'mĕnt), *n.* clothing; garments; wearing apparel.

rain (rān), *n.* water falling in drops from the clouds; the fall of such drops; a fall or shower of anything in such drops; as, a *rain* of bullets or compliments: *v.i.* to fall in drops of water from the clouds; fall like rain: *v.t.* to pour down like rain; shower; as, to *rain* favors on someone.—*n.* **rainless.**

rain-bow (rān'bō"), *n.* the bright-colored arc or bow formed in the heavens opposite the sun by the reflection of the sun's rays in drops of falling rain, or in spray, mist, etc.: *adj.* brilliant but passing quickly.

rain-coat (rān'kōt"), *n.* a coat or cloak made of waterproof material, intended to be worn in wet weather.

rain-fall (rān'fôl"), *n.* the amount of rain that falls during a definite period on any given area or space.

rain gage (rān gāj), an instrument to measure the fall of rain at a given place or during a given time. Also, **rain gauge.**

rain-y (rān'ĭ), *adj.* abounding with rain; showery; wet; as, *rainy* weather.—*n.* **raininess.**

raise (rāz), *v.t.* to cause to rise; lift up; elevate; as, to *raise* a flag; originate or produce; as, to *raise* wheat; to stir up; arouse; as, to *raise* the town; increase; as, to *raise* prices; construct; as, to *raise* a building; collect; as, to *raise* money; cause to appear; as, to *raise* a ghost; cause to swell; as, to *raise* a blister; to put an end to; as, to *raise* a siege; bring to notice; as, to *raise* a question.—*n.* **raiser, raising.**

rai-sin (rā'zn), *n.* a dried grape, containing much sugar and cured in the sun or in an oven.

ra-jah (rä'jȧ), *n.* a Hindu prince or chief. Also, **raja.**

Raj-put (räj'po͞ot; räj"po͞ot'), *n.* a Hindu of royal descent or of the higher military caste or rank. Also, **Rajpoot.**

rake (rāk), *n.* an implement with teeth or tines for gathering together loose matter, or for making soil loose and smooth; an immoral man; slant or slope: *v.t.* to gather, smooth, or loosen with a rake; as, to *rake* up leaves; *rake* a flower bed; to collect; to gather together by diligent effort; as, to *rake* together a few dollars; *rake* up evidence; to search through carefully; ransack; scour; as, they *raked* the records for proof; they *raked* the city in search of a suitable house; to fire upon, especially along the length of; as, to *rake* the deck of a ship, or a line of soldiers: *v.i.* to work with a rake; as, he *raked* in the garden; to make a close search; make careful collection; as, they *raked* and scraped to make both ends meet.—*n.* **raker.**

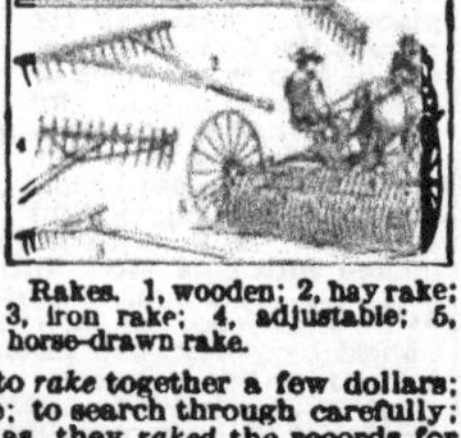

Rakes. 1, wooden; 2, hay rake; 3, iron rake; 4, adjustable; 5, horse-drawn rake.

rak-ish (rāk'ĭsh), *adj.* corrupt; intemperate; unrestrained; also, showy or dashing; as, a *rakish* appearance; nautically, showing speed by having the masts greatly inclined; as, a *rakish* yacht.—*adv.* **rakishly.**—*n.* **rakishness.**

ral-ly (răl'ĭ), *n.* the act of recovering order or of regaining strength; good-humored jesting; an assembling; as, the *rally* of the troops; colloquially, in the United States, a mass meeting; in tennis, the repeated return of the ball: *v.t.* [*p.t.* and *p.p.* rallied, *p.pr.* rallying], to gather and restore to order, as troops in flight; to call together for any purpose; as, to *rally* voters; revive; as, to *rally* a person's spirits; to joke with; banter: *v.i.* to return to order; as, the troops *rallied;* to come together for action; arouse to more vigorous action; as, *rally* round the flag; recover strength; as, to *rally* from an illness; in tennis, to send the ball rapidly back and forth over the net.

ram (răm), *n.* a male sheep; a military engine for battering, or crushing by heavy blows; a battering-ram; an engine for raising water; an ironclad war vessel with a steel beak designed to cut into an enemy ship: *v.t.* [*p.t.* and *p.p.* rammed, *p.pr.* ramming], to strike or butt against in order to crush; to press or force into something; stuff: *v.i.* to drive, pound, or batter.

ram-ble (răm'bl), *n.* an aimless roving or wandering from place to place; a leisurely stroll; as, a *ramble* in the woods: *v.i.* to wander or rove aimlessly about, as for pleasure; talk or write at length without aim; grow or spread at random.—*n.* **rambler.**

ram-e-kin (răm'ē-kĭn), *n.* a small, deep dish of pottery or metal, in which a food preparation is baked and served. Also, **ramequin.**

ram-i-fi-ca-tion (răm'ĭ-fĭ-kā'shŭn), *n.* a division or separation into branches; a division or part; manner of producing branches; a small branch or offshoot; as, a *ramification* of a tree, nerve, etc.

ram-i-fy (răm'ĭ-fī), *v.t.* [*p.t.* and *p.p.* ramified, *p.pr.* ramifying], to divide into branches, or divisions: *v.i.* to grow by dividing into branches; become divided or subdivided.

ram-mer (răm'ẽr), *n.* one that batters or drives.

ra-mose (rā'mōs; rȧ-mōs'), *adj.* pertaining to, like, or having, branches. Also, **ramous.**

ramp (rămp), *v.i.* to rear up and spring; as, a lion *ramps;* leap violently; to rush about wildly; romp: *n.* formerly, a leap or bound; a slope or incline, as of a road or corridor.

ramp-age (răm'pāj; răm"pāj'), *n.* a state of excitement or rage; angry or violent behavior; as, he is always on the *rampage* about something: *v.i.* to rush or romp about with high spirits; be furious; storm; rage.

ram-pa-geous (răm-pā'jŭs), *adj.* extremely noisy, violent, or unruly.

ram-pant (răm'pănt), *adj.* climbing or growing unchecked; as, *rampant* weeds; overleaping restraint or natural bounds; as, a *rampant* river; rearing; leaping; as, a *rampant* lion; unchecked or unrestrained; as, *rampant* ideas.—*adv.* **rampantly.**—*n.* **rampancy.**

ram-part (răm'pärt), *n.* a mound or wall surrounding a fortified place; any protection from assault or danger.

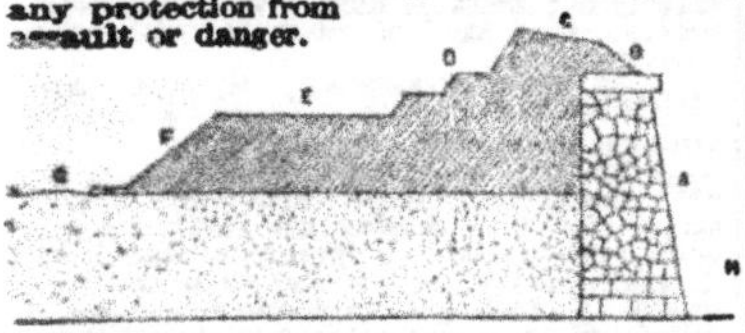

Rampart. *A*, wall; *B*, exterior slope; *C*, glacis; *D*, banquette; *E*, earth fill; *F*, interior slope; *G*, military road; *H*, ditch.

ram-rod (răm'rŏd'), *n.* a rod used for driving home, or pushing down, the charge of a muzzle-loading gun.

ram-shack-le (răm'shăk-l), *adj.* loose; out of repair; rickety; as, a *ramshackle* cottage.

ran (răn), past tense of the irregular verb *run*.

ranch (rănch), *n.* in the western United States, a farm for the grazing and rearing of cattle, horses, and sheep in large herds; a large farm.—*n.* **rancher**, **ranchman**.

ran-che-ro (rän-chā'rō), *n.* in Mexico, a herdsman or worker on a stock farm; sometimes, the owner or director; a rancher.

ran-cho (rän'chō), *n.* a hut or group of huts for workers on a Spanish American stock farm; a stock farm; ranch. [Sp. Am.]

ran-cid (răn'sĭd), *adj.* not fresh; having a rank, tainted smell or taste of spoiled oil; chemically sour.—*n.* **rancidness**.

ran-cid-i-ty (răn-sĭd'ĭ-tĭ), *n.* rank, sour, or tainted condition; as, the *rancidity* of butter.

ran-cor (răn'kẽr), *n.* deep spite or malice; a bitter, cherished grudge. Also, **rancour**.

Syn. hostility, ill will, resentment.
Ant. (see forgiveness).

ran-cor-ous (răn'kẽr-ŭs), *adj.* full of spite; bitterly malicious.

ran-dom (răn'dŭm), *n.* want of definite aim or method; chance: *adj.* done without definite aim or purpose; left to chance; as, a *random* shot; aimless: **at random**, without direction or method; aimlessly.

rang (răng), past tense of the irregular verb *ring*.

range (rānj), *n.* a line or row; a chain; as, a *range* of mountains; line of direction; as, the big tree in *range* with my window; entire space or time taken in or covered; as, the *range* of a view; the whole *range* of history; a great tract of land over which cattle graze; the entire region in which an animal or plant lives; as, the geographical *range* of certain birds; class or order; as, a *range* of animals; scope or extent; as, a *range* of ideas or subjects; carrying power, or reach; as, the *range* of a voice or a gun; distance to which a shot, etc., can be sent; place for shooting at a mark; a large cooking stove: *v.t.* to set or arrange in a row; to take sides with; as, to *range* oneself with a political party; place in proper order; classify; rove over, as, cattle *range* the plains: *v.i.* to wander; roam; to go over or through a place in order to explore it; to lie in the same direction; to go; as, the bullet *ranged* wide of the mark; to be classified or placed in order; as, they *range* in height from four to six feet.

range find-er (rānj fīn'dẽr), a telescopic instrument for determining the distance of an object from the instrument.

rang-er (rān'jẽr), *n.* in England, the keeper of a royal park or forest; a rover; one of a mounted armed band of men; in America, a forest guard; a kind of hunting dog.

rang-y (rān'jĭ), *adj.* built so as to be able to wander far and wide; hence, long in limb, lean, and muscular: used most of cattle and horses.

rank (răṅk), *n.* a row or line of objects; a line of soldiers drawn up side by side; high station or position; as, a man of *rank;* social or official class or grade; as a person of low *rank;* the *rank* of captain; degree of worth or eminence; as, a poet of the first *rank:* *pl.* the army as a whole; also, the body of common soldiers as distinguished from the officers: **rank and file**, the body of soldiers of an army: *v.t.* to draw up in line; include in a certain class, order, or division; to be of a higher grade than: *v.i.* to hold a certain grade or position: *adj.* very plentiful and coarse in growth; as, *rank* weeds; coarse; strong in taste or smell; as, *rank* butter; gross; extreme; as, *rank* treason or poison.—*adv.* **rankly**.—*n.* **rankness**.

Syn., *n.* order, degree, dignity, nobility.

ran-kle (răṅ'kl), *v.i.* to fester or to cause festering; to cause mental pain or irritation.

ran-sack (răn'săk), *v.t.* to search thoroughly; rummage; plunder; as, to *ransack* a house.

Syn. pillage, overhaul, explore.

ran-som (răn'sŭm), *n.* price paid for release from captivity, etc., or for return of goods captured by an enemy; release; redemption: *v.t.* to free from prison; slavery, or punishment, by a payment; redeem; deliver.—*adj.* **ransomless**.—*n.* **ransomer**.

rant (rănt), *n.* noisy, empty speech; bombast: *v.i.* to bluster or be noisily wordy; rave in extravagant or violent language.—*adj.* **ranting**.—*adv.* **rantingly**.

rant-er (răn'tẽr), *n.* a noisy, blustering speaker; a boisterous preacher.

rap (răp), *n.* a quick, sharp blow; something of no value; as, it is not worth a *rap:* *v.i.* [*p.t.* and *p.p.* rapped; *p.pr.* rapping], to strike a quick, sharp blow; knock: *v.t.* to strike sharply; to utter sharply; as, she *rapped* out the words.

ra-pa-cious (rȧ-pā'shŭs), *adj.* given to plunder; seizing by violence; greedy; grasping; as, a *rapacious* animal, appetite, or miser.—*adv.* **rapaciously**.—*n.* **rapaciousness**.

Syn. ravenous, voracious.
Ant. (see generous).

ra-pac-i-ty (rȧ-păs'ĭ-tĭ), *n.* the quality of being extremely greedy or grasping.

rape (rāp), *n.* a seizing and carrying away by force; robbery; violation by force; a plant of the cabbage family, from the seeds of which an oil (colza oil) is obtained.

rap-id (răp'ĭd), *adj.* very quick or swift; moving with speed; done quickly; as, a *rapid* decline in health: *n.pl.* a swift current in a river.—*adv.* **rapidly**.

rap-id fire (răp'ĭd fīr), the kind of fire used at a critical moment in battle, when about 200 yards from the enemy: **rapid fire gun**, a single-barreled gun discharging projectiles automatically in rapid succession.

ra-pid-i-ty (rȧ-pĭd'ĭ-tĭ), *n.* swiftness; quickness; speed.

ra-pi-er (rā'pĭ-ẽr), *n.* a long, thin sword, used for thrusting.

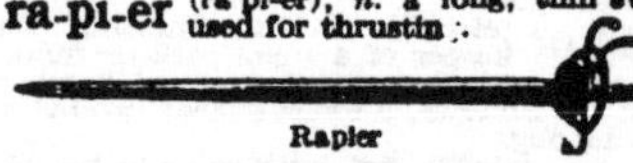

Rapier

rap-ine (răp'ĭn), *n.* the act of plundering or of seizing and carrying off property by force.

rap-port (rȧ'pôr'), *n.* a sympathetic relation; harmony; agreement. [Fr.]

rap-proche-ment (rȧ-prōsh'mäṅ'), *n.* the act of coming together; a state of harmony or agreement; an understanding. [Fr.]

rap-scal-lion (răp-skăl'yŭn), *n.* a rascal; scamp; vagabond.

rapt (răpt), *p.adj.* carried away with delight or pleasure, etc.; enraptured; deep in thought; as, *rapt* attention.

Syn. entranced, charmed.

Ant. (see distracted).

rap-ture (răp'tūr), *n.* the condition or state of being carried away with joy or delight; extreme pleasure; ecstasy; enthusiasm.

Syn. transport, delight, bliss.

Ant. (see dejection).

rap-tur-ous (răp'tūr-ŭs), *adj.* carried away with joy or delight; ecstatic.—*adv.* **rapturously.**

rare (râr), *adj.* [*comp.* rarer, *superl.* rarest], scarce; uncommon; as, a *rare* plant; seldom happening; unusual; as, a *rare* occasion; excellent; choice; precious; as *rare* old lace; thin; not dense; as, the *rare* air at the mountain top; not well cooked; almost raw; as, *rare* beefsteak.—*adv.* **rarely.**—*n.* **rareness.**

rare-bit (râr'bĭt), *n.* in cookery, a Welsh rabbit, or dish made of melted cheese; a dainty morsel of food.

rar-e-fac-tion (râr'ē-făk'shŭn; rǎr'ē-făk'shŭn), *n.* the act or process of making thin or less dense; state of being less dense.

rar-e-fy (râr'ē-fī; răr'ē-fī), *v.t.* [*p.t.* and *p.p.* rarefied, *p.pr.* rarefying], to make thin, or less dense; expand: *v.i.* to become thin, or less dense: opposite to *condense.*

rare-ripe (râr'rīp'), *n.* a fruit that ripens early, especially a peach: *adj.* ripe before the usual season.

rar-i-ty (râr'ĭ-tĭ; răr'ĭ-tĭ), *n.* the state or quality of being infrequent or uncommon; a choice or scarce article; unusual excellence; thinness; as, the *rarity* of the air at a height.

ras-cal (răs'kăl), *n.* a mean fellow; a scoundrel; one who is guilty of mean acts.

Syn. rogue, vagabond, scamp.

ras-cal-i-ty (răs-kăl'ĭ-tĭ), *n.* the character or quality of that which is knavish; villainy or dishonesty.

rash (răsh), *n.* a slight breaking out on the skin showing redness: *adj.* hasty; reckless; acting without caution or thought. —*adv.* **rashly.**—*n.* **rashness.**

Syn. foolhardy, heedless, careless.

Ant. (see deliberate).

rash-er (răsh'ẽr), *n.* a thin slice of ham or bacon.

rasp (råsp), *v.t.* to rub with, or as with, a file or rough instrument; to grate harshly on; irritate; as, her voice *rasps* one's nerves: *n.* a kind of rough file with points instead of lines.

rasp-ber-ry (răz'bĕr-ĭ), *n.* [*pl.* raspberries (-ĭz)], a garden bramble and its eatable fruit.

rat (răt), *n.* an animal somewhat like the mouse, but larger and more greedy; slang, one who deserts his party for base ends; colloquially, a workman who works during a strike, or for less than the usual wages; a small pad over which the hair is rolled: *pl.* an exclamation implying disbelief or derision: *v.i.* [*p.t.* and *p.p.* ratted, *p.pr.* ratting], slang, to desert one's party for base ends; colloquially, to work for less than union wages or to work during a strike; to catch rats.—*n.* **ratter.**

rat-a-ble (răt'ȧ-bl), *adj.* capable of being valued at a certain sum; liable to be taxed or to have a value placed upon; proportional. Also, **rateable.**—*adv.* **ratably, rateably.**

ra-tan (rȧ-tăn'), *n.* one of the long, smooth stems of several kinds of palms; a cane or switch, or a piece of wicker, made of such stems. Also, **rattan.**

ra-ta-plan (rȧ'tȧ-pläṅ'), *n.* the rattle or sound of a drum, or a musical composition imitating it. [Fr.]

ratch (răch), *n.* a notched wheel or bar, controlled by a tongue or tooth, called a *pawl*, so that it can move in only one direction.

ratch-et (răch'ĕt), *n.* a tooth or tongue, also called a *pawl* or a click, which fits into the notches of a toothed, or ratchet, wheel; the toothed wheel; the toothed wheel and the pawl, working together.

ratch-et wheel (răch'ĕt hwēl), a toothed wheel which is made to move in only one direction by a pawl, or tooth, which fits into its notches.

rate (rāt), *n.* amount, degree, speed, value, etc., estimated in proportion to a fixed standard; as, interest at a *rate* of five per cent; a *rate* of sixty miles an hour; price fixed or stated; as, theater *rates*; degree of value; as, goods bought at a low *rate*; in England, a tax or assessment; a grade or class; as, a first-*rate*, second-*rate*, etc.: *v.t.* to estimate; settle or fix the value, rank, or degree of; scold sharply: *v.i.* to be estimated; be placed in a certain class or rank.

Syn., *n.* value, grade: *v.* chide, abuse.

rath-er (råth'ẽr), *adv.* more willingly; as, I would *rather* read than write; better; on the contrary; instead; as, "go *rather* to them that sell"; more properly; as, they acted wisely, or *rather* their brother did for them; somewhat; to a certain extent; as, I *rather* like it.

rat-i-fi-ca-tion (răt'ĭ-fĭ-kā'shŭn), *n.* the act of confirming or approving; confirmation; sanction.

rat-i-fy (răt'ĭ-fī), *v.t.* [*p.t.* and *p.p.* ratified, *p.pr.* ratifying], to approve of formally; to give indorsement to; as, to *ratify* a contract or written agreement; settle or confirm; establish.—*n.* **ratifier.**

Syn. fix, authorize, sanction.

Ant. (see protest).

rat-ing (rāt'ĭng), *p.pr.* of *rate*: *n.* a placing in a class according to relative standing; rank; class; the grade of a man in the army or navy; a severe scolding.

ra-ti-o (rā'shĭ-ō; rā'shō), *n.* [*pl.* ratios (-ōz)], the relation of one number or quantity to another; the quotient of one quantity divided by another of like kind.

ra-ti-oc-i-na-tion (răsh'ĭ-ŏs'ĭ-nā'shŭn), *n.* reasoning; connected and exact thinking.

ra-ti-om-e-ter (rā-shĭ-ŏm'ē-tēr), *n.* an apparatus for calculating a series of numbers having the same relation to each other as a given series of numbers.

ra-tion (rā'shŭn; răsh'ŭn), *n.* an allowance or fixed share of food, etc., given daily to a soldier or a sailor: *pl.* fixed allowance of food, etc., given a man daily: *v.t.* to furnish with a fixed allowance of food, etc., as a regiment, or the civil population in time of war and scarcity: **emergency ration**, condensed or canned food provided for army use, on a march, or during a shortage of other food.

ra-tion-al (răsh'ŭn-ăl), *adj.* having the power to reason, or think connectedly; as, a *rational* being; agreeable to, or in accord with, reason; as, a *rational* way of considering things; neither extravagant nor foolish; as, *rational* conduct; wise; judicious.—*adv.* **rationally.**

Syn. reasonable, sensible, sound.

Ant. (see unreasonable).

ra-tion-a-le (răsh'ŭn-ā'lē), *n.* a series of reasons given for any opinion, action, etc.; the explanation of the principles of a science, opinion, etc.

ra-tion-al-ism (răsh'ŭn-ăl-ĭzm), *n.* a doctrine which makes reason the sole guide in matters of belief or conduct.—*n.* **rationalist.**

ra-tion-al-is-tic (răsh'ŭn-ăl-ĭs'tĭk), *adj.* pertaining to, leaning toward, rationalism, or the doctrine which makes reason the sole guide in matters of conduct or belief.

ra-tion-al-i-ty (răsh'ŭn-ăl'ĭ-tĭ), *n.* power of reasoning; reasonableness; mental sanity; intelligence.

ra-tion-al-ize (răsh'ŭn-ăl-īz), *v.t.* to explain according to reason; as, to *rationalize* a miracle; to make or show to be reasonable; to make to adopt reason as a guide: *v.i.* to rely solely on reason; to think as a philosopher.

Ratlins

rat-lins (răt'lĭnz), *n.pl.* small ropes forming a ladder in a ship's rigging. Also, **ratlines.**

rats-bane (răts'bān''), *n.* rat poison; especially, white arsenic.

rat-tan (ră-tăn'), *n.* one of the long, smooth, reedlike stems of several kinds of palms; a walking stick made of such a stem; any one of the palms. Also, **ratan.**

rat-tle (răt'l), *n.* a series of short, sharp, clattering sounds following each other quickly; noisy, rapid, empty talk; a child's toy for making a clattering sound: *v.i.* to produce short, sharp noises in quick succession; clatter; as, hail *rattles* on a roof; to talk in a noisy, rapid manner; as, she *rattled* on for an hour; to move with a clatter; as, the wagon *rattled* along the road: *v.t.* to cause to make a succession of rapid, sharp noises; as, the wind *rattles* the shutters; to utter in a rapid, noisy way; as, he *rattled* off his lesson; colloquially, to confuse or daze; as, he was completely *rattled.*

rat-tler (răt'lēr), *n.* a noisy, rapid talker; that which makes a clattering noise; a rattlesnake.

rat-tle-snake (răt'l-snāk''), *n.* a poisonous snake with hard bony rings or scales on the tail which make a clashing sound when the tail is in motion.

rat-tle-trap (răt'l-trăp''), *n.* an old, rickety, worn-out object, such as a wagon, etc.

rat-tling (răt'lĭng), *n.* noise made by the clattering together of small hard objects: *adj.* making a rapid succession of sharp, noisy sounds; colloquially, quick; as, they walked at a *rattling* pace: *adv.* colloquially, very; extremely; as, a *rattling* good story.

rau-cous (rô'kŭs), *adj.* hoarse; harsh; rough; as, a *raucous* voice.—*adv.* **raucously.**

rav-age (răv'āj), *n.* destruction by violence; ruin; waste; as, the *ravages* of intemperance: *v.t.* to lay waste; pillage; plunder or sack; as, the army *ravaged* the country.—*n.* **ravager.**

Syn., *v.* overrun, devastate, desolate, destroy.

rave (rāv), *v.t.* to say wildly, or in a frenzied manner; to affect by frenzied action; as, passion *raves* itself to rest: *v.i.* to act or talk wildly; rage, as a madman; as, it matters not, how wildly he may *rave;* to speak enthusiastically or with excitement.

rav-el (răv'l), *v.t.* to draw out the threads of, as of a woven or knitted fabric; unmesh; disentangle or make less difficult to understand: *v.i.* to become unwoven or unknit: often with *out;* as, a stocking *ravels* out; to become disentangled, or less difficult to understand.

rav-el-ings (răv'l-ĭngz), *n.pl.* threads drawn out of woven or twisted fabrics. Also, **ravellings.**

ra-ven (rā'vn), *n.* a large bird of the crow family, noted for its deep glossy black color: *adj.* jet black and shining.

rav-en (răv'n), *n.* the act of plundering; plunder; prey: *v.t.* to devour with greediness: *v.i.* to seize and devour prey with greediness.

rav-en-ing (răv'n-ĭng), *n.* eagerness for plunder: *adj.* seeking eagerly for prey; as, *ravening* wolves.

rav-en-ous (răv'n-ŭs), *adj.* furiously hungry; as, a *ravenous* beast; extremely greedy; as, a *ravenous* appetite.—*adv.* **ravenously.**—*n.* **ravenousness.**

ra-vine (rȧ-vēn'), *n.* a long, deep hollow, worn by the action of a stream or torrent; a mountain gorge; a gully.

rav-ing (rāv'ĭng), *n.* furious or wild talk; delirium: *p.adj.* talking furiously or wildly; delirious; frenzied.

rav-ish (răv'ĭsh), *v.t.* to seize and remove by force; to abduct or violate (a woman); carry away with delight or rapture.—*p.adj.* **ravishing.**—*adv.* **ravishingly.**—*n.* **ravisher.**

Syn. enrapture, enchant, delight.

rav-ish-ment (răv'ĭsh-mĕnt), *n.* violation; rapture or delight.

raw (rô), *adj.* uncooked; without whole skin; as, a *raw* spot; in the natural state; unprepared; as, *raw* silk; crude; inexperienced; unpracticed; as, *raw* judgment; *raw* troops; cold and damp; as, *raw* weather: *n.* a sore spot.—*adv.* **rawly.**—*n.* **rawness.**

raw-boned (rô'bōnd''), *adj.* with little flesh on the bones; gaunt; lean.

raw-hide (rô'hīd"), *n.* untanned skin, as of cattle: a whip made of a roll or braid of untanned leather.

ray (rā), *n.* a line of light streaming from a bright center or source; any line along which radiant energy, or streams of energy issuing from a central source, exerts its force; as, a *ray* of heat, or an X *ray;* one of a number of thin lines spreading from a center; a beam of mental light; as, a *ray* of intelligence; the petals of certain flowers, as of a daisy; one of the rods which support the fin of a fish; one of the radiating arms of a starfish, etc.; any one of various fishes having a flat body and thin tail: *v.t.* to send forth, as a beam of light: *v.i.* shine forth; send out lines of light, heat, etc.

Rays. 1, skate (top view); 2, same form below; 3, thorn-back.

raze (rāz), *v.t.* to level to the ground; as, to *raze* a building; formerly, blot out; efface; also, graze or shave.
Syn. demolish, destroy, overthrow, ruin, dismantle.

ra-zor (rā'zẽr), *n.* a sharp-edged cutting instrument used for shaving the face and head.

re (rā), *n.* in music, the second note of a scale: **re-** *prefix,* meaning back; backward; as, *re*call; *re*cline; again; as, *re*read; *re*write; anew; as, *re*birth; *re*number: used in these senses in a very large number of self-explaining words, only the most common or puzzling of which are here defined.

reach (rēch), *v.t.* to stretch out, as the hand; to touch or grasp, as with the extended hand; to pass or deliver to another; arrive at or come to; gain; to extend as far as; penetrate to; to influence; affect: *v.i.* to extend the hand, etc., so as to touch or seize something; endeavor to obtain something; to extend in time, space, amount, etc.: *n.* the act of stretching out, or the ability to stretch out, touch, grasp, etc.; distance within which one can touch, observe, etc.; limit of power or influence; an unbroken stretch, as of water or meadow land.
Syn., v. touch, stretch, strain.

re-act (rē-ăkt'), *v.i.* to produce effect in return for that received; to act in an opposite manner; to respond to an influence; to exert mutual chemical action.

re-ac-tion (rē-ăk'shŭn), *n.* return action or influence; response to influence or effort exerted; a return to a former or opposite state of things; contrary action following the effects of other action; the equal force that a body exerts on an opposing force; chemical change; a chemical process or its result.

re-ac-tion-a-ry (rē-ăk'shŭn-ā-rĭ), *n.* one who favors a return to an old or opposite system; one who seeks to undo political progress: *adj.* pertaining to, of the nature of, or causing, reverse or return action; favoring a return to an old or opposite system.

read (rēd), *v.t.* [*p.t.* and *p.p.* read (rĕd), *p.pr.* reading], to observe and understand the meaning of (something written, printed, or inscribed); peruse; as, to *read* a book; to utter aloud (something written or printed) as, he *reads* his sermons; discover or understand by observation; as, to *read* the stars; explain or make clear; as, it is easy to *read* his meaning; make a study of; as, to *read* law; learn, as from books, etc.; as, we *read* that the war has ended; impress upon or teach; as, he *read* them a lesson: *v.i.* to peruse written or printed matter; learn from written or printed matter; with *of* or *about;* utter aloud the words of a book, etc.; as, he *reads* well; make a careful study; as, to *read* up on history; to have a special form; as, the passage *reads* thus: *p.adj.* (rĕd), informed about, or acquainted with, by means of books; as, he is well *read* on most subjects.

read-a-ble (rēd'ā-bl), *adj.* easy and pleasant to read; interesting; legible, or plainly written.—*n.* **readableness.**

read-er (rēd'ẽr), *n.* one who reads; one who reads the lessons in church; one who criticizes manuscripts offered for publication; a university lecturer; a schoolbook for instruction and practice in reading; as, a fifth *reader.*

read-ing (rēd'ĭng), *n.* perusal of written or printed matter; utterance aloud of the words of books, etc.; study of books; scholarship; public recital; as, to give *readings* from the poets; version or form of a particular passage in a book; as, various *readings* of a passage in different editions of Shakespeare; written or printed matter to be perused; manner of interpreting, or showing, the hidden or real meaning of a thing; as, an actor's *reading* of his lines; that which is shown by a scientific instrument; as, the *reading* of a gas meter.

re-ad-just (rē"ă-jŭst'), *v.t.* to set in order again; to settle or regulate again.

read-y (rĕd'ĭ), *adj.* [*comp.* readier, *superl.* readiest], in condition to be used or to act immediately; quick; prompt; as, *ready* wit; *ready* payment; mentally fit or prepared; willing; as, *ready* to obey; about to do or be; likely; as, that tree is *ready* to fall; free to be used; easy to obtain; as, *ready* money.—*adv.* **readily.**—*n.* **readiness.**
Syn. ripe, apt, adroit, handy.

read-y-made (rĕd'ĭ-mād"), *adj.* not made to order; kept on hand; as, *ready-made* clothing; prepared beforehand; as, a *ready-made* speech.

re-a-gent (rē-ā'jĕnt), *n.* that which reacts; a chemical substance used to test the nature of another substance by observing the effect of one upon the other.

re-al (rē'ăl), *adj.* actually existing; not imaginary; genuine; true; pertaining to things fixed, as lands or tenements; of property, opposite to *personal;* as, *real* estate: *n.* (rā-äl') a Spanish coin equal to about five cents.
Syn., adj. actual, practical, positive, certain.

re-al es-tate (rē'ăl ĕs-tāt'), lands and all belonging to them, as trees, fences, permanent buildings, etc.

re-al-ism (rē'ăl-ĭzm), *n.* in art and literature, the practice of presenting people and scenes as they actually exist; the doctrine that the objects that can be seen, touched, etc., are actual existences.

re-al-ist (rē'ăl-ĭst), *n.* one who believes in being true to nature in art and literature; one who believes that objects that can be seen, touched, etc., actually exist.

re-al-is-tic (rē"ăl-ĭs'tĭk), *adj.* presenting people and scenes as they actually exist; true to fact; lifelike.—*adv.* **realistically.**

re-al-i-ty (rē-ăl'ĭ-tĭ), *n.* [*pl.* realities (-tĭz)], state or quality of being in existence, or of being actual; that which exists or is actual; fact; truth.

re-al-i-za-tion (rē"ăl-ĭ-zā'shŭn), *n.* the act of making, or causing to appear, actual or true to nature or fact; state of being present to the mind as actual or true to nature or fact; act of perceiving the true nature of, or of feeling fully and vividly; as, he had no *realisation* of his danger; the converting or changing of real estate into money.

re-al-ize (rē'ăl-īz), *v.t.* to bring into actual existence; hence, to accomplish; to cause to seem true to nature or fact; to perceive the true nature of; to feel fully and vividly; change, as real estate, into money; gain; as, he *realized* five thousand dollars from the sale: *v.i.* to sell property for ready money.—*adj.* **realizable.**

Syn. effect, get, acquire, comprehend.

re-al-ly (rē'ăl-ĭ), *adv.* actually; as a matter of fact; colloquially, certainly or indeed.

realm (rĕlm), *n.* a kingdom; an empire; hence, region, domain, or state; as, the *realm* of dreams.

re-al-ty (rē'ăl-tĭ), *n.* landed property or estate.

ream (rēm), *n.* twenty quires, or 480 sheets, of paper; also, 516 sheets (printers' ream): *v.t.* to enlarge or taper a hole, especially in metal: often with *out.*

ream-er (rēm'ẽr), *n.* a machinist's tool for enlarging or tapering holes; a quarryman's chisel, for use in blasting.

Reamer

re-an-i-mate (rē-ăn'ĭ-māt), *v.t.* to bring back to life; give new strength to; encourage.

reap (rēp), *v.t.* to cut down with a scythe, sickle, or machine; gather in; as, to *reap* grain; to go over and cut grain, etc. from; as, to *reap* a field; receive as a reward: *v.i.* to cut and gather grain; to receive the reward of one's actions.—*n.* **reaper.**

Syn. gain, get, acquire, obtain.

rear (rēr), *n.* the back or hinder part; as the *rear* of a building; place or position behind; as, the garden is at the *rear* of the house; background; that part of a fleet or army behind the rest: *v.t.* to raise or lift up; to elevate; as, to *rear* a telegraph pole; build up; erect; as, to *rear* a palace; bring up; educate; as, to *rear* children; breed or cause to grow; as, to *rear* cattle or plants: *v.i.* to rise up, especially on the hind legs: *adj.* pertaining to, or situated at, the back part: **rear guard,** the part of an army stationed behind the main body to guard it from the rear.

rear ad-mi-ral (rēr ăd'mĭ-răl), in the United States Navy, an officer ranking next below the admiral, or officer of highest rank; in other navies, an officer ranking next below a vice-admiral.

rear-ward (rēr'wôrd"), *adj.* and *adv.* at or toward the rear.

rea-son (rē'zn), *n.* the ability to form conclusions and know right from wrong; right judgment; intellect or thinking power; sanity or sane opinions; cause for opinion or act: *v.i.* to exercise the power of thinking logically or drawing conclusions; to argue: *v.t.* to persuade by argument; to prove or explain by means of the intellect; as, to *reason* out a solution.

Syn. *n.* motive, design, end, proof, cause, ground, purpose.

rea-son-a-ble (rē'zn-ȧ-bl), *adj.* having the power to think connectedly and reach conclusions; as, a *reasonable* being; governed by reason; just; as, a *reasonable* employer; moderate; fair; as, a *reasonable* price; sensible; as, a *reasonable* decision.—*adv.* **reasonably.**—*n.* **reasonableness.**

Syn. wise, just.

Ant. (see unreasonable).

rea-son-ing (rē'zn-ĭng), *n.* the act of one who reaches conclusions by careful and connected thinking; course of argument.

re-as-sure (rē"ȧ-shŏŏr'), *v.t.* to give back boldness, courage, or certainty to; give new confidence to; make certain.—*adv.* **reassuringly.**—*n.* **reassurance.**

re-bate (rē-bāt'; rē'bāt), *n.* a deduction from a usual sum; a discount, such as a return to shippers by railroad or express companies of part of freight charges: *v.t.* to make a deduction from; allow a discount to.

Rebec

re-bec (rē'bĕk), *n.* formerly, a musical instrument with strings, and played with a bow: the earliest form of violin. Also, **rebeck.**

Re-bec-ca (rē-bĕk'ȧ), *n.* in the Bible, the wife of Isaac, and mother of Esau and Jacob. Also, **Rebekah.**

reb-el (rĕb'ĕl), *n.* one who wars against his government or resists its laws; one who resists any authority or refuses to obey: *adj.* acting against government and law; unsubmissive: *v.i.* (rē-bĕl'), [*p.t.* and *p.p.* rebelled, *p.pr.* rebelling], to resist, and take up arms against, the law or government; revolt; rise against any authority.

re-bel-lion (rē-bĕl'yŭn), *n.* the act of taking up arms, or the state of being at war, against the government or its laws; resistance to, or defiance of, any authority; revolt.

re-bel-lious (rē-bĕl'yŭs), *adj.* opposing or resisting lawful authority; resisting control; as, *rebellious* locks; resisting treatment; as, a *rebellious* disease.—*adv.* **rebelliously.**—*n.* **rebelliousness.**

re-bound (rē-bound'), *v.i.* to spring or fly back from that which has been struck: *n.* the act of springing back; a flying back from that which has been struck.

re-buff (rē-bŭf'), *n.* a sudden check; defeat; a curt refusal; repulse: *v.t.* to repel curtly; refuse sharply; check suddenly.

re-buke (rē-būk'), *n.* a sharp reproof; chiding; reprimand: *v.t.* to censure; chide; reprove sharply.

re-bus (rē'bŭs), *n.* [*pl.* rebuses (-ĕz)], a puzzle in which words, phrases, and sentences are represented by pictures of objects whose names have the sounds of the words.

re-but (rē-bŭt'), *v.t.* [*p.t.* and *p.p.* rebutted, *p.pr.* rebutting], contradict or oppose by argument or proof; refute: *v.i.* to return an answer in contradiction to evidence already given by an opponent.

re-but-tal (rē-bŭt′ăl), *n.* the presenting of evidence in contradiction of testimony already given by the opposing side in a trial; act of refuting, or contradicting, in general; the answering of the arguments of one's opponent in a debate.

re-cal-ci-trant (rē-kăl′sĭ-trănt), *adj.* obstinately refusing to submit; refractory.—*n.* **recalcitrance.**

re-call (rē-kôl′), *n.* the power by which an unsatisfactory public official may be unseated, or put out of office, by vote of the people; the right of the citizens of a state to set aside by popular vote the decision of a court; a signal sounded on a drum, bugle, etc., to call back soldiers; a flag signal to a boat to return to a ship: *v.t.* to order or summon back; as, to *recall* an ambassador; remember; recollect; as, to *recall* a name; take back; as, to *recall* angry words; revoke; annul; as, to *recall* a decision.

re-cant (rē-kănt′), *v.t.* to withdraw or take back formally (one's opinion or belief); renounce: *v.i.* to renounce formally an opinion or religious belief previously held.

Syn. recall, revoke, abjure.

re-can-ta-tion (rē′kăn-tā′shŭn), *n.* the act of renouncing or withdrawing that which was previously believed or stated; the statement made in renouncing and withdrawing a former belief or declaration.

re-ca-pit-u-late (rē′kȧ-pĭt′ū-lāt), *v.t.* to go over or sum up the chief points of; restate briefly: *v.i.* to repeat briefly what has already been said at length. —*adj.* **recapitulatory.**

re-ca-pit-u-la-tion (rē′kȧ-pĭt′ū-lā′-shŭn), *n.* the act of restating briefly; a summing up.

re-cede (rē-sēd′), *v.i.* to fall back; retreat; retire; as, the tide *receded;* to withdraw a claim, support, proposal, etc.: *v.t.* to give back to a former owner.

re-ceipt (rē-sēt′), *n.* the act of getting, or state of having, anything that has been given, sent, etc.; as, the *receipt* of a letter; in *receipt* of news; a direction for making something by mixing certain things together, especially in cookery; a recipe; as, a *receipt* for cake; a written acknowledgment of anything, as money or goods, had from another; that which is taken, in distinction to that which is given out: usually in the *pl.* as, cash *receipts:* *v.t.* to sign in acknowledgment of payment; as, to *receipt* a bill: *v.i.* give a written acknowledgment of money paid.

re-ceiv-a-ble (rē-sēv′ȧ-bl), *adj.* capable of or requiring, acceptance when offered; of such sort that payment may be expected or demanded; as, bills *receivable.*

re-ceive (rē-sēv′), *v.t.* to take or accept, as a gift, message, payment, etc., from another; to get knowledge of; as, to *receive* news; admit to one's company; greet; entertain; as, to *receive* guests; to serve as a holder for; as, a channel to *receive* the overflow; to undergo; accept; as, they *received* the faith; get; as, to *receive* a shock; to have laid upon one; as, to *receive* a responsibility; to give lodging to, or to harbor; as, to *receive* stolen goods; in tennis, to strike (a served ball) in order to return (it): *v.i.* to obtain or be presented with something; to take what is given or paid; to welcome guests; in tennis, to strike a served ball in order to return it.

re-ceiv-er (rē-sēv′ẽr), *n.* one who, or that which, takes or obtains; the part of a telephone which takes the sound from the wire and imparts it to the ear; one who knowingly buys or obtains stolen goods; a person appointed by a court to hold and manage property which is the subject of a lawsuit, or property owned by a person or firm that is bankrupt.

re-cen-cy (rē′sĕn-sĭ), *n.* lateness of occurrence; newness.

re-cent (rē′sĕnt), *adj.* pertaining to time not long past; of origin or occurrence near the present; new; modern; fresh; newly arrived.—*adv.* **recently.**—*n.* **recentness.**

re-cep-ta-cle (rē-sĕp′tȧ-kl), *n.* anything, as a vessel, used to hold other things; a place where something is deposited.

re-cep-tion (rē-sĕp′shŭn), *n.* the act of taking or obtaining that which is offered, etc.; the state of being taken or obtained; as, the *reception* of news; admission; act or manner of welcoming; as, a cool *reception;* a social occasion for greeting guests; as, a wedding *reception;* the formal or official greeting of a person; a taking into membership in an organization; acceptance; as, the *reception* of new ideas.

re-cep-tive (rē-sĕp′tĭv), *adj.* having the quality or ability of taking in, or holding, especially mental impressions; as, a *receptive* mind.—*adv.* **receptively.**—*n.* **receptiveness.**

re-cep-tiv-i-ty (rē′sĕp-tĭv′ĭ-tĭ), *n.* power to take in and hold; especially, the quality of the mind by which it takes in impressions.

re-cess (rē-sĕs′; rē′sĕs), *n.* a place or space hollowed out in a wall, etc.; an alcove or niche; a quiet or secluded spot or nook; a brief time during which work ceases; an intermission; as, the court took a *recess;* school *recess.*

Syn. retreat, depth, vacation, intermission.

re-ces-sion (rē-sĕsh′ŭn), *n.* the act of going back or retiring; withdrawal; retirement: (rē-sĕsh′ŭn), the act of giving back.

re-ces-sion-al (rē-sĕsh′ŭn-ȧl), *n.* a hymn sung as the clergy and choir leave the chancel at the close of church service; organ music played at the close of a church service, or during the passing out of a procession, as at a wedding: *adj.* of or pertaining to withdrawal or retirement; pertaining to an intermission.

re-cher-ché (rē-shĕr′shā′), *adj.* uncommon; rare; exquisite; choice. [Fr.]

rec-i-pe (rĕs′ĭ-pē), *n.* a medical prescription; a formula, or prescribed form, for mixing anything; a receipt for cookery.

re-cip-i-ent (rē-sĭp′ĭ-ĕnt), *n.* one who receives; as, a *recipient* of high honors: *adj.* receiving or ready to receive.

re-cip-ro-cal (rē-sĭp′rō-kăl), *adj.* mutual; done, given, or offered by each to the other; as, *reciprocal* affection or benefits; alternating; offered in return for something done or given; able to be exchanged for one another; as, *reciprocal* conditions; in grammar, showing action of each upon the other, or relation of each to the other; as, *reciprocal* pronouns (each other, one another): *n.* that which is given or done by each to the other; the quotient obtained by dividing unity by a number.—*adv.* **reciprocally.**

re-cip-ro-cate (rē-sĭp′rō-kāt), *v.t.* to give and take from one another; as, they *reciprocate* each other's affection; to give something in return for; as, to *reciprocate* a favor; to cause to move to and fro; *v.i.* to move to and fro; interchange; to make an exchange with one another; to pay back an act or feeling.

re-cip-ro-ca-tion (rē-sĭp″rō-kā′shŭn), *n.* a giving and returning by each to the other; a moving to and fro; alternating motion.

rec-i-proc-i-ty (rĕs″ĭ-prŏs′ĭ-tĭ), *n.* free interchange of action or relation; commercial relationship between two nations by which each grants the other equal and similar advantages not enjoyed by nations outside such a relationship; equal mutual rights or benefits to be granted or enjoyed; as a treaty of *reciprocity* between the United States and Canada.

re-cit-al (rē-sīt′ăl), *n.* the act of telling of the particulars of an event; narration; the thing told; a story; rehearsal; a musical or dramatic entertainment by one performer.

rec-i-ta-tion (rĕs″ĭ-tā′shŭn), *n.* public rendering of prose or poetry committed to memory; the selection of prose or poetry so rendered; the repeating of a lesson by a pupil to a teacher; the conducting of a lesson by a teacher and a class.

rec-i-ta-tive (rĕs″ĭ-tȧ-tēv′), *n.* a kind of singing that imitates the accents of speech: used in opera and oratorio; the music for a passage to be sung in such a manner: *adj.* not conforming to strict musical rhythm; sung with the accents of speech.—*adv.* **recitatively.**

re-cite (rē-sīt′), *v.t.* and *v.i.* to repeat aloud from memory; rehearse; tell in detail; relate; repeat (a lesson) to a teacher; to take part in the progress of a lesson, as a pupil in a class.—*n.* **reciter.**

reck (rĕk), *v.t.* to care for; heed: *v.i.* to care; mind; as, he *recks* not of danger; to be of concern; matter; as, it *recks* not. [Poet.]

reck-less (rĕk′lĕs), *adj.* heedless of consequences or danger; rash; careless; thoughtless.—*adv.* **recklessly.**—*n.* **recklessness.**

reck-on (rĕk′n), *v.t.* to count or compute; number; as, to *reckon* the cost; look upon as being; consider; esteem; as, I *reckon* him among my foes; to think; suppose; as, I *reckon* it will rain: *v.i.* to depend or rely: with *on*; as, he *reckoned* on their friendship; to calculate; make up accounts; settle; suppose; guess.—*n.* **reckoner.**

reck-on-ing (rĕk′n-ĭng), *n.* the act of one who counts or computes; calculation; statement of accounts between debtor and creditor; bill or statement of money due at a hotel or other public house; settlement of debt, obligation, etc.; a making good; as, the day of *reckoning;* position of a ship estimated by its progress and course; calculation of such position; as, dead *reckoning.*

re-claim (rē-klām′), *v.t.* to demand the return of; as, to *reclaim* one's money; reform; as, to *reclaim* a drunkard; bring under cultivation; as, to *reclaim* land; tame; subdue; as, to *reclaim* a wild animal.—*adj.* **reclaimable.**—*n.* **reclaimer.**

rec-la-ma-tion (rĕk″lȧ-mā′shŭn), *n.* the act of recovering or restoring; restoration; the making of waste land habitable, as in the western United States.

re-cline (rē-klīn′), *v.t.* to cause to lean or lie back: *v.i.* to rest or repose; lie down.

re-cluse (rē-kloos′), *n.* one who lives alone; a hermit: *adj.* shut up from the world; solitary; secluded.—*n.* **reclusion.**

rec-og-ni-tion (rĕk″ŏg-nĭsh′ŭn), *n.* a perceiving or knowing a thing to be the same as, or similar to, something previously known; formal acknowledgment or commendation; as, *recognition* of a brave deed; friendly notice or attention.

re-cog-ni-zance (rē-kŏg′nĭ-zăns; rē-kŏn′ĭ-zăns), *n.* a legal agreement, entered into before, and recorded by, a magistrate or court, to do, or abstain from doing, some particular act; the sum of money to be forfeited if the obligation is not fulfilled.

rec-og-nize (rĕk′ŏg-nīz), *v.t.* to know the identity of; admit acquaintance with; salute; recall as having been previously known; as, to *recognise* an old friend; take formal notice of; acknowledge; as, to *recognize* the independence of a country; appreciate; as, to *recognize* merit; concede as true; as, to *recognize* the facts in the case.—*adv.* **recognizable.**—*n.* **recognizer.**

re-coil (rē-koil′), *n.* a shrinking back; a rebound; the sudden backward motion, or kick, of a gun after it is fired: *v.i.* to start back, as in dismay, fear, etc.; shrink; spring back because of some force; rebound; as, a gun *recoils;* retreat; as, she *recoiled* as the burglar approached.

rec-ol-lect (rĕk″ō-lĕkt′), *v.t.* to call back to the mind; remember; compose, or regain control of (oneself): (rē″kō-lĕkt′), to gather together again.

rec-ol-lec-tion (rĕk″ō-lĕk′shŭn), *n.* the recalling of ideas to the mind; memory; that which is remembered.

rec-om-mend (rĕk″ō-mĕnd′), *v.t.* to offer to the favor, attention, or use of another; speak in favor of; as, to *recommend* a servant; advise; as, I *recommend* you to change your ways; make attractive; as, her gentleness *recommends* her.—*n.* **recommender.**

rec-om-men-da-tion (rĕk″ō-mĕn-dā′shŭn), *n.* the act of offering a person or thing to favorable notice; that which procures favorable attention; as, good manners are a good *recommendation;* favorable introduction; as, a letter of *recommendation.*

rec-om-men-da-to-ry (rĕk″ō-mĕn′dȧ-tō-rĭ), *adj.* serving to procure favorable attention; advisory.

re-com-mit (rē″kō-mĭt′), *v.t.* [*p.t.* and *p.p.* recommitted, *p.pr.* recommitting], to send back; as, to *recommit* a person to prison; refer back to a committee.—*n.* **recommitment, recommittal.**

rec-om-pense (rĕk′ŏm-pĕns), *n.* something equal given in return for service, etc.; reward; compensation: *v.t.* to give something equal to; as, to *recompense* him for his devotion; to compensate; repay; as, to *recompense* a person for loss or service; repair; atone for; as, to *recompense* a loss.

rec-on-cil-a-ble (rĕk′ŏn-sīl″ȧ-bl), *adj.* capable of being made friendly or harmonious again; adjustable; consistent; capable of being made to agree or match; as, *reconcilable* statements.

rec-on-cile (rĕk′ŏn-sīl), *v.t.* to bring about peace or friendship between; as, to *reconcile* brothers who have quarreled; to adjust; settle; as, to *reconcile* their differences; to make content or quietly submissive; as, to *reconcile* a person to his losses; to make to agree or harmonize; as, to *reconcile* a man's words and actions.—*n.* **reconciler, reconcilement.**

rec-on-cil-i-a-tion (rĕk″ŏn-sĭl″ĭ-ā′-shŭn), *n.* renewal of friendship; the making up or settling of a quarrel; the act of making peace; the showing of agreement between things seemingly different.

rec-on-dite (rĕk′ŏn-dīt), *adj.* too deep or difficult for the ordinary mind to perceive or understand; obscure; profound; as, *recondite* studies.

re-con-nois-sance (rē-kŏn′ĭ-sāns), *n.* the act of examining or surveying; especially, an investigation or survey of a region made by soldiers to find out the enemy's position, strength, etc., before some action is taken. Also, **reconnaissance.** [Fr.]

rec-on-noi-ter (rĕk″ŏ-noi′tẽr), *v.t.* to explore and investigate with a view to action; make a survey of before taking some action, especially for military purposes: *v.i.* to make examination before taking action. Also, **reconnoitre.**

re-con-struct (rē″kŏn-strŭkt′), *v.t.* to rebuild; to put together again.

re-con-struc-tion (rē″kŏn-strŭk′shŭn), *n.* the act of rebuilding; state of being rebuilt: **Reconstruction,** in the United States, the process of restoring to the Southern States the rights and privileges of the Union after the Civil War.

re-con-struc-tive (rē″kŏn-strŭk′tĭv), *adj.* tending or able to rebuild or restore.

rec-ord (rĕk′ŏrd; rĕk′ŏrd), *n.* a written roll or register made for the purpose of keeping facts or events in memory; as, a school *record;* an official written or printed report of public acts; a copy of an official document; testimony; as, they bore *record* to this; in sports, the best performance so far achieved at any given time; as, he holds the *record* for the high jump; also, the register of performances; the cylinder or disk for reproducing sounds in phonographs, etc., the paper roll of an automatic piano player, etc.; the narrative of the successive events in the progress of anything; as, he left a good life *record; pl.* public documents: *v.t.* (rē-kôrd′), to write or enter a true account of; as, to *record* events; to put in writing; as, to *record* one's opinion; register; enroll; to fix in mind; to mark or indicate; as, the clock *records* time.

Syn., n. entry, account, history, catalog.

re-cord-er (rē-kôr′dẽr), *n.* a public officer whose duty is to register writings or transactions; as, a *recorder* of deeds; a judicial officer in a city or borough; a device that registers; as, a telegraph *recorder.*

re-count (rē-kount′), *v.t.* to tell or repeat in full the narrative of; recite; (rē-kount′), to count again: *n.* (rē-kount′; rē′kount), a counting again.

re-coup (rē-kōōp′), *v.t.* to make good; regain; as, to *recoup* a loss; indemnify; as, to *recoup* oneself for a loss; in law, to keep back (a part of something to be paid) in order to make good a counterclaim.

re-course (rē-kōrs′), *n.* an appeal for aid or protection; as, to have *recourse* to the law; the person or thing to which one turns for aid; as, his purse was a *recourse* for all the needy.

re-cov-er (rē-kŭv′ẽr), *v.t.* to get back the possession of; as, to *recover* one's health or lost property; obtain by judgment in a court of law; as, to *recover* damages; make good the loss or damage of; as, to *recover* lost time: *v.i.* to regain health, strength, or any former state; to succeed in a lawsuit; in boxing, fencing, etc., to regain one's position for a new movement.—*adj.* **recoverable.**

Syn. heal, restore.

Ant. (see fail).

re-cov-er-y (rē-kŭv′ẽr-ĭ), *n.* the act of regaining; restoration to health; the obtaining of one's right to something by judgment of a court.

rec-re-ant (rĕk′rē-ănt), *n.* a faithless person; a deserter; a coward: *adj.* cowardly; craven; unfaithful to a cause; false.—*n.* **recreancy.**

re-cre-ate (rē″krē-āt′), *v.t.* to make anew; remake.

rec-re-ate (rĕk′rē-āt), *v.t.* to refresh, especially after toil; divert; amuse: *v.i.* to take refreshment or amusement.

re-cre-a-tion (rē″krē-ā′shŭn), *n.* the act of making anew; something made anew.

rec-re-a-tion (rĕk″rē-ā′shŭn), *n.* refreshment of mind or body after toil, etc.; any exercise or occupation that diverts, or gives pleasure as a change from work.

Syn. sport, pastime, play, game, fun.

rec-re-a-tive (rĕk′rē-ā-tĭv), *adj.* refreshing; amusing.

re-crim-i-nate (rē-krĭm′ĭ-nāt), *v.t.* to return one accusation or charge with another: *v.i.* to accuse in return.

re-crim-i-na-tion (rē-krĭm″ĭ-nā′shŭn), *n.* the act of accusing in return; the accusation made.

re-crim-i-na-to-ry (rē-krĭm′ĭ-nȧ-tō-rĭ), *adj.* retorting or returning an accusation or charge. Also, **recriminative.**

re-cru-des-cence (rē″krōō-dĕs′ĕns), *n.* the state of becoming raw or sore again; a breaking out afresh.

re-cru-des-cent (rē″krōō-dĕs′ĕnt), *adj.* becoming raw or sore again; breaking out afresh; gaining new life and vigor.

re-cruit (rē-krōōt′), *n.* a man newly enlisted in an army; one who has just joined any cause: *v.t.* to add new soldiers to; as, to *recruit* an army; to fill up gaps or weak places in; hence, to build up; restore; as, to *recruit* health and strength: *v.i.* to obtain fresh supplies; recover health; enlist new men for an army.

re-cruit-ment (rē-krōōt′mĕnt), *n.* the business of enlisting new soldiers for the army, etc.

rec-tan-gle (rĕk′tăn″gl), *n.* a four-sided figure, with four right angles.

rec-tan-gu-lar (rĕk-tăn′gū-lȧr), *adj.* having four sides and four right angles.

rec-ti-fi-ca-tion (rĕk″tĭ-fĭ-kā′shŭn), *n.* the act of correcting or setting right; a refining or a making purer.

rec-ti-fy (rĕk′tĭ-fī), *v.t.* [*p.t.* and *p.p.* rectified, *p.pr.* rectifying], to correct the faults in; to remove mistakes from; to **set right**; to improve; refine or purify; as, to *rectify* whisky.—*n.* **rectifier.**

rec-ti-lin-e-ar (rĕk″tĭ-lĭn′ē-*ẽ*r), *adj.* straight; bounded by straight lines; right-lined or straight-lined. Also, **rectilineal.**

rec-ti-tude (rĕk′tĭ-tūd), *n.* rightness of intention and action; honesty; uprightness; freedom from error.

rec-tor (rĕk′tẽr), *n.* in the Episcopal Church, a clergyman in charge of a parish; in Scotland and, sometimes, in England, the headmaster of a public school, or the head of a university; the superior or head of a religious house.—*adj.* **rectorial.**—*n.* **rectorate, rectorship.**

rec-to-ry (rĕk′tō-rĭ), *n.* the house of a rector, or clergyman of the Episcopal Church.

rec-tum (rĕk′tŭm), *n.* the end of, and outlet from, the great intestine.

re-cum-ben-cy (rē-kŭm′bĕn-sĭ), *n.* the state of leaning or reclining; a reclining position. Also, **recumbence.**

re-cum-bent (rē-kŭm′bĕnt), *adj.* leaning; lying; reclining; as, a *recumbent* position.—*adv.* **recumbently.**

re-cu-per-ate (rē-kū′pẽr-āt), *v.t.* to bring back to health and strength; make to regain: *v.i.* to regain health and strength.

re-cu-per-a-tion (rē-kū″pẽr-ā′shŭn), *n.* recovery, especially of health and strength.

re-cu-per-a-tive (rē-kū′pẽr-ā-tĭv), *adj.* of, pertaining to, or tending to, recovery; as, *recuperative* powers. Also, **recuperatory.**

re-cur (rē-kûr′), *v.i.* [*p.t.* and *p.p.* recurred, *p.pr.* recurring], to come back or return; as, a thought *recurs* to the mind; to *recur* to a subject; happen again, or at stated intervals, as a fever.

re-cur-rence (rē-kûr′ĕns), *n.* the act or fact of returning; a return; as, the *recurrence* of a fever; recourse.

re-cur-rent (rē-kûr′ĕnt), *adj.* coming back at intervals, as a fever; running or turning back: said of nerves and arteries.

rec-u-san-cy (rĕk′ū-zăn-sĭ), *n.* refusal to obey or submit to authority; refusal to acknowledge the authority of a state church.

rec-u-sant (rĕk′ū-zănt), *n.* one who refuses to conform to a state church; a dissenter or nonconformist: *adj.* refusing to obey or submit to authority.

red (rĕd), *n.* one of the three original primary colors from which the others are made; the color of blood: *adj.* of the color of blood; of that color of the spectrum farthest from violet; anarchistic; as, a *red* republican.

re-dan (rē-dăn′), *n.* a fortification with two sides, or parapets, meeting in an angle in front and open in the rear; a form of ornamentation in architecture, cut in stone, and supposed to resemble teeth.

Redan

red-breast (rĕd′brĕst″), *n.* a common name for the robin.

red cross (rĕd krŏs), a red Greek cross on a white ground, adopted by the Geneva Convention, in 1864, as the sign of neutrality in war: **Red Cross,** a society for helping the sick and wounded in war, and for other benevolent purposes: the members wear a red cross on a white ground as a badge or sign that they do not belong to the fighting force.

red-den (rĕd′n), *v.t.* to make red: *v.i.* to become red; blush; flush.

red-dish (rĕd′ĭsh), *adj.* somewhat red.—*n.* **reddishness.**

re-deem (rē-dēm′), *v.t.* to buy back; to free from bondage or slavery by paying a ransom or price; rescue; ransom or free from sin and its consequences; make good; as, to *redeem* a promise; make up for; as, to *redeem* a fault; to pay what is due on, as a promissory note; to recover, as property given for security to a bank, loan office, etc.—*adj.* **redeemable.**

Syn. rescue, deliver, save, free.

re-deem-er (rē-dēm′ẽr), *n.* one who frees or buys back: **Redeemer,** Jesus Christ, the Savior.

re-demp-tion (rē-dĕmp′shŭn), *n.* the act of freeing or buying back; state of being freed or bought back; repurchase; release; ransom; salvation of mankind by Jesus Christ.

re-demp-tive (rē-dĕmp′tĭv), *adj.* ransoming or saving; as, *redemptive* work; serving or tending to fulfil, as a promise, or to buy back or recover, as property.

re-demp-to-ry (rē-dĕmp′tō-rĭ), *adj.* paid for ransom; serving to set free or buy back; serving to fulfil.

red-hot (rĕd′hŏt″), *adj.* heated to redness; greatly excited; furious; extreme.

re-din-te-grate (rē-dĭn′tē-grāt), *v.t.* to make complete or perfect again; put together again; restore.—*n.* **redintegration.**

red-let-ter day (rĕd′lĕt″ẽr dā), a happy or lucky day; so called from the Saints' days printed in red letters in the church calendars.

red-o-lence (rĕd′ō-lĕns), *n.* perfume; fragrance.

red-o-lent (rĕd′ō-lĕnt), *adj.* emitting an odor; fragrant; as, the air was *redolent* of roses.

re-doubt (rē-dout′), *n.* a fieldwork, or inclosed fortification, often temporary, for strengthening a military position. Also, **redout.**

re-doubt-a-ble (rē-dout′*ȧ*-bl), *adj.* causing fear or dread; formidable or valiant: often ironical.—*adv.* **redoubtably.**—*n.* **redoubtableness.**

re-dound (rē-dound′), *v.i.* to return in flowing abundance to the source or cause; to result; contribute; as, all of his acts *redound* to his glory.

red-poll (rĕd″pōl′), *n.* any of several small finches the males of which have a red crown.

re-dress (rē-drĕs″), *n.* the repairing, or making right, of wrong; correction; repayment for loss or injury; as, to get no *redress* for dishonest treatment: *v.t.* to make right, as a wrong; make amends for, as an injury; remedy; as, to *redress* grievances; give relief to; as, to *redress* those who suffer from wrongs.

Syn., n. remedy; *v.* repair.

red-skin (rĕd′skĭn″), *n.* a North American Indian.

red snow (rĕd snō), in arctic regions, snow colored by a certain red plant.

red-start (rĕd'stärt), *n.* a European bird of the nightingale family; an American warbler.

red tape (rĕd tāp), official conduct of business marked by formality and delay; so called from the custom of tying official papers with red tape: *adj.* pertaining to formality and delay in the conduct of official business. Also, **red-tape.**

re-duce (rē-dūs'), *v.t.* to make less in value, size, etc.; lessen; lower; as, to *reduce* the cost; *reduce* flesh; bring from a higher to a lower position; degrade; as, to *reduce* an officer to the ranks; subdue; conquer; as, to *reduce* an enemy to subjection; bring into classes or orders; as, to *reduce* mankind to races; bring into a particular form or condition; as, *reduce* sugar to a syrup; *reduce* one to despair; in arithmetic, change (numbers or quantities) from one name or form to another without changing their value; as, to *reduce* gallons to pints; *reduce* fractions to lowest terms; in chemistry, to take all nonmetallic elements out of (an ore); in surgery, to restore (a displaced part) to its right position; as, to *reduce* a fracture. —*adj.* **reducible.**—*n.* **reducer.**

Syn. decrease, shorten.

re-duc-tion (rē-dŭk'shŭn), *n.* the act of lessening, degrading, or changing the form of; the state of being lessened, degraded, or changed in form; conquest; as, the *reduction* of a fort.

re-dun-dan-cy (rē-dŭn'dăn-sĭ), *n.* the quality or state of being more than is required; excess; surplus; that which is more than enough; as, *redundancy* in writing is a burden to memory. Also, **redundance.**

re-dun-dant (rē-dŭn'dănt), *adj.* being more than is needed; superabundant; in writing or speaking, being too full, or too wordy; unnecessary to the sense; superfluous; more than enough.

re-du-pli-cate (rē-dū'plĭ-kāt), *v.t.* to double again; repeat; multiply: *adj.* (rē-dū'plĭ-kāt), repeated again and again; redoubled.—*adj.* **reduplicative.**

re-du-pli-ca-tion (rē-dū'plĭ-kā'shŭn), *n.* a doubling, redoubling, or repeating again and again.

red-wing (rĕd'wĭng"), *n.* in Europe, a red-winged thrush; in America, a red-winged blackbird.

red-wood (rĕd'wŏŏd"), *n.* any one of various trees having a reddish wood; especially, a very large California tree of the pine family; the wood of this tree.

reed (rēd), *n.* any of certain tall coarse grasses that grow in wet places; also, their jointed hollow stems; a mass of such grasses; a musical pipe made of a hollow stem or stalk of a plant; a thin elastic tongue at the opening of a pipe in a musical instrument; a musical instrument, as an oboe; in poetry, an arrow.—*adj.* **reedy.**—*n.* **reediness.**

reed-bird (rēd'bûrd"), *n.* in the United States, the bobolink: so called because the birds congregate among the reedlike rice fields in the autumn.

reef (rēf), *n.* that part of a sail which can be drawn in by small ropes running in eyelet holes, in order to lessen the size of the sail; a sand bar or shelf of rock lying level with, or just below, the surface of the water; as, a coral *reef:* *v.t.* to reduce (a sail) by rolling or folding up part of it.

reef-er (rēf'ẽr), *n.* familiarly, a midshipman; a short, rough, double-breasted jacket.

reek (rēk), *n.* vapor; steam; a disagreeable odor; in Scotland, smoke: *v.i.* to send out vapor, steam, or fumes, usually with a disagreeable odor; as, to *reek* with filth.—*adj.* **reeky.**

reel (rēl), *n.* a turning frame for winding yarn, rope, etc.; a bobbin; a device for winding up a fish line; a staggering movement; a lively country or folk dance; as, a Highland *reel;* the Virginia *reel;* the music for such a dance: *v.t.* to wind on a frame or bobbin; to draw in by winding; as, to *reel* fish in: *v.i.* to stagger or sway from side to side; as, to *reel* in walking; turn round and round; feel dizzy; as, his head *reeled;* to give way; waver; as, the whole line (of soldiers) *reeled.*

re-ën-force (rē"ĕn-fôrs'), *v.t.* to give new strength to; especially, to strengthen (an army) by bringing up new troops; add a strengthening part to; support.

re-ën-force-ment (rē"ĕn-fôrs'mĕnt), *n.* act of strengthening; state of being strengthened; that which strengthens: *pl.* more troops or ships sent to strengthen a position.

reeve (rēv), *n.* formerly, in England, a bailiff, steward, or overseer; the female of the ruff, or sandpiper: *v.t.* nautically, to pass the end of (a rope) through a hole, block, or ring.

re-fec-tion (rē-fĕk'shŭn), *n.* a light repast or lunch; refreshment.

re-fec-to-ry (rē-fĕk'tō-rĭ), *n.* originally, a dining room or hall in a convent; a room for refreshments.

re-fer (rē-fûr'), *v.t.* [*p.t.* and *p.p.* referred, *p.pr.* referring], to submit to another person or authority for information or decision; as, they *referred* the question to the president; to direct or send for information, etc.; as, to *refer* one to the dictionary; to place in a certain class, or explain as due to a certain cause: *v.i.* to direct attention; allude; as, he did not *refer* to the war; appeal; apply; as, he *referred* frequently to his notes; point by marks; as, that sign *refers* to a footnote; to direct one person to another for information; as, to *refer* to a former employer.

ref-er-a-ble (rĕf'ẽr-ȧ-bl), *adj.* capable of being considered as a result of, or related to, something; assignable. Also, **referrible.**

ref-er-ee (rĕf"ẽr-ē'), *n.* one to whom a matter is handed over for decision and settlement; an umpire; a person to whom a question in a case is sent by a court to be investigated and decided, or reported to the court.

ref-er-ence (rĕf'ẽr-ĕns), *n.* the act of submitting a matter to another to settle or of consulting an authority for information; a directing of attention to something; a passing allusion; a note, etc., in a book or writing directing attention to some other book or passage; also, the passage, etc., to which attention is directed; a person to whom inquiries may be directed regarding another person; a written statement of the ability of a person given by another; relation; respect; as, with *reference* to your request: *adj.* suitable to be used in securing information; as, a *reference* library.

ref-er-en-dum (rĕf"ẽr-ĕn'dŭm), *n.* the submission of a legislative act to the decision of a vote of the people; the right possessed by a people so to vote upon a legislative act.

re-fine (rē-fīn'), *v.t.* to make pure; as, to *refine* sugar; clear from dross or worthless matter; as, to *refine* gold; free from coarseness or rudeness; educate or improve; as, to *refine* manners or language: *v.i.* to become fine or pure; improve in quality; grow courteous.

re-fined (rē-find'), *p.adj.* made pure or fine; freed from coarseness; cultivated; polished.

re-fine-ment (rē-fin'mĕnt), *n.* the act of making pure or free from coarseness; state of being pure or free from coarseness; elegance; polish; purity of taste, mind, or morals.

re-fin-er-y (rē-fin'ēr-ĭ), *n.* [*pl.* refineries (-ĭz)], a place where anything, as metals, oil, sugar, etc., is made pure.

re-fit (rē-fit'), *v.t.* [*p.t.* and *p.p.* refitted, *p.pr.* refitting], to make ready for use again; equip or furnish anew; prepare afresh: *v.i.* to repair damages, especially damages of ships; to be made ready for use again; to be newly equipped.

re-flect (rē-flĕkt'), *v.t.* to throw back, as rays of light or heat which have struck on any substance; to give back an image of, as in a mirror; to give back as a result; as, his act *reflects* honor upon him; to show the effect of; as, her conduct *reflects* her mother's training: *v.i.* to throw back rays of light, etc.; to give back an image; to consider in the mind; think; cast reproach; cause shame or blame; as, bad behavior in school *reflects* upon home training.

Syn. consider, think, ponder, censure.

re-flec-tion (rē-flĕk'shŭn), *n.* the act of returning or throwing back; state of being returned or thrown back; as, the *reflection* of light or heat; that which is returned or thrown back, such as light or heat; an image given back; as, your *reflection* in a mirror; the turning of thought back upon past experiences or ideas; attentive consideration; thought; criticism; reproach; as, a *reflection* on one's character; the folding of a part back on itself.

re-flec-tive (rē-flĕk'tĭv), *adj.* throwing back light, images, etc., as a mirror; thoughtful; given to meditation; as, a *reflective* mind; in grammar, reflexive, or turning back to the subject.—*adv.* **reflectively**.—*n.* **reflectiveness**.

re-flec-tor (rē-flĕk'tēr), *n.* a polished, usually concave, surface that sends back rays of light or heat.

re-flex (rē'flĕks), *n.* a sending back of light or color; an image, as a reflection in a mirror; a picture or copy; light sent back from a bright surface to one in shade; an involuntary movement of some part of the body: *adj.* turned or thrown back from a surface, as light or color; caused by action in return; as, a *reflex* influence; of thought, tending to turn back to the past or within oneself; in physiology, of, pertaining to, or caused by, some impulse, independently of consciousness or will; in painting, represented as lighted by light sent off from another part of the same picture: *v.t.* (rē-flĕks'), to bend or turn back.—*adj.* **reflexed**.

re-flex ac-tion (rē'flĕks ăk'shŭn), action of the muscles caused by some impulse independently of consciousness or will.

re-flex-ive (rē-flĕk'sĭv), *adj.* in grammar, expressing an action that goes back to the subject; as, in the phrases "she helps herself" and "she behaves badly," *helps* and *behaves* are *reflexive* verbs; showing the same person or thing as the subject; as, in "she behaves herself," *herself* is a *reflexive* pronoun: *n.* a pronoun or verb that is the same as, or refers back to, the subject.—*adv.* **reflexively**.

re-flux (rē'flŭks), *n.* a flowing back; ebb: *adj.* flowing back; returning.

re-form (rē-fôrm'), *n.* change for the better; especially, a change from evil to upright character, or political correction of evils or abuses: *v.t.* to change from bad to good; bring back to a former good state; make better morally; free from evils and abuses; amend; correct: *v.i.* to give up evil for that which is good; become better.

Syn., *v.* better, restore, improve.

ref-or-ma-tion (rĕf'ŏr-mā'shŭn), *n.* the act of making or becoming better; state of being made or becoming better; change from worse to better: **Reformation**, the great religious movement, begun by Martin Luther, in the sixteenth century, resulting in the formation of the Protestant churches.

re-form-a-tive (rē-fôr'mȧ-tĭv), *adj.* forming again; tending to improve or make better.

re-form-a-to-ry (rē-fôr'mȧ-tō-rĭ), *n.* an institution or school for correcting and improving the habits and conduct, especially of young offenders: *adj.* tending to correct, or make better.

re-formed (rē-fôrmd'), *p.adj.* restored to a former good state: amended or changed: **Reformed Church**, that section of the Early Protestant Church which separated from the Lutherans and adopted the religious doctrines of Calvin, etc.

re-form-er (rē-fôr'mēr), *n.* one who carries out or urges a religious, moral, or political change for the better: **Reformer**, a leader of the great religious movement of the sixteenth century.

re-fract (rē-frăkt'), *v.t.* to break the natural course of, or bend from a straight line; as, to *refract* rays of light.—*adj.* **refractive**.—*n.* **refractor**.

re-frac-tion (rē-frăk'shŭn), *n.* the change of direction of a ray of light in passing obliquely from one medium to another of different density.

re-frac-to-ry (rē-frăk'tō-rĭ), *adj.* disobedient; unyielding; unmanageable; as, a *refractory* boy; difficult to fuse; as, *refractory* ore.—*adv.* **refractorily**.—*n.* **refractoriness**.

re-frain (rē-frān'), *n.* a phrase or strain repeated now and then throughout a poem or song; often, a verse or chorus of a song repeated at the end of each stanza: *v.i.* to hold back; do without; check oneself; as, to *refrain* from doing a thing.

re-fran-gi-bil-i-ty (rē-frăn'jĭ-bĭl'ĭ-tĭ), *n.* the capability of being bent from a straight line, as rays of light. Also, **refrangibleness**.

re-fran-gi-ble (rē-frăn'jĭ-bl), *adj.* capable of being bent from a straight line, as rays of light.

re-fresh (rē-frĕsh'), *v.t.* to make fresh again; revive after fatigue or exhaustion; restore; to renew; as, to *refresh* the memory.

re-fresh-ing (rē-frĕsh'ĭng), *adj.* reviving or making fresh again; cooling; as, a *refreshing* drink.—*adv.* **refreshingly**.

re-fresh-ment (rē-frĕsh'mĕnt), *n.* act of reviving; state of being revived; restoration of strength, liveliness, etc.; that which restores or revives, especially food, drink, or rest: *pl.* light, dainty food and drink served as a part of the entertainment of guests at a reception, dance, etc.

re-frig-er-ant (rē-frĭj'ēr-ănt), *n.* any medicine or material that lessens fever or reduces heat: *adj.* cooling; reducing fever or heat.

re-frig-er-ate (rē-frĭj'ēr-āt), *v.t.* to cool or freeze, as in a refrigerator, or ice box.—*adj.* **refrigerative, refrigeratory.**

re-frig-er-a-tion (rē-frĭj"ēr-ā'shŭn), *n.* act of cooling to a low point.

re-frig-er-a-tor (rē-frĭj'ēr-ā"tēr), *n.* an air-tight receptacle or chest, or a room, where food, etc., is kept cool by means of ice or cold air.

ref-uge (rĕf'ūj), *n.* a place of safety from trouble or danger; a shelter or secure retreat; one that protects or defends from danger or misfortune.
Syn. protection, harbor, retreat.

ref-u-gee (rĕf"ū-jē'), *n.* one who flees for protection, especially from political or religious persecution, to a foreign land; one who escapes from an invading army.

re-ful-gence (rē-fŭl'jĕns), *n.* brightness; flood of light; radiance; splendor. Also, **refulgency.**

re-ful-gent (rē-fŭl'jĕnt), *adj.* casting a bright light; very brilliant; splendid; shining.

re-fund (rē-fŭnd'), *v.t.* to give back or repay; replace by a new loan.

re-fus-al (rē-fūz'ăl), *n.* the act of rejecting or denying; rejection or denial of anything offered or asked; the right to refuse or take before others; as, to have the *refusal* of a ı office.

re-fuse (rē-fūz'), *v.t.* and *v.i.* to decline to take; be unwilling to receive; as, to *refuse* a gift; to decline to do or grant; deny; as, to *refuse* a demand or request; decline to have put upon one; as, to *refuse* a responsibility: *n.* (rĕf'ūs), waste or worthless matter; trash; rubbish: *adj.* rejected; worthless.
Syn., *v.* repudiate, decline, withhold: *n.* dregs, dross, scum.
Ant. (see accept).

re-fut-a-ble (rē-fūt'ȧ-bl), *adj.* capable of being conclusively answered or proved false; as, a *refutable* argument.—*adv.* **refutably.**

ref-u-ta-tion (rĕf"ū-tā'shŭn), *n.* the act of proving false; that which is proved false; the act of disproving; a conclusive answer to an argument.

re-fute (rē-fūt'), *v.t.* to prove to be false or wrong; to overthrow by argument or proof; disprove.

re-gain (rē-gān'), *v.t.* get back; as, to *regain* lost health; reach again; as, they at last *regained* the shore.

re-gal (rē'găl), *adj.* fit for, or like, a king; royal; hence, splendid or stately.

re-gale (rē-gāl'), *v.t.* to entertain with something that delights the senses; feast; delight: *v.i.* to feast.

re-ga-li-a (rē-gā'lĭ-ȧ), *n.pl.* the emblems of royalty, as the crown, etc.; decorations of an order or office, as of Masons, Odd Fellows, etc.

re-gal-i-ty (rē-găl'ĭ-tĭ), *n.* royalty; sovereign jurisdiction.

re-gard (rē-gärd'), *n.* affection; respect; consideration; care; close attention or notice; a look or gaze; reference: *pl.* good wishes: *v.t.* to observe closely; look upon; as, she *regarded* him with a frown; consider; as, I *regard* her as an enemy; heed; respect; as, *regard* my words; esteem; care for; as, I *regard* him highly; relate to; concern; as, the matter *regards* your happiness.
Syn., *v.* mind, heed, notice, view.

re-gard-ful (rē-gärd'fōōl), *adj.* taking notice; heedful; respectful.—*adv.* **regardfully.**—*n.* **regardfulness.**

re-gard-ing (rē-gärd'ĭng), *prep.* concerning; respecting.

re-gard-less (rē-gärd'lĕs), *adj.* heedless; careless; negligent.

re-gat-ta (rē-găt'ȧ), *n.* a race or races of sailboats and rowboats.

re-gen-cy (rē'jĕn-sĭ), *n.* the office of a ruler; authority; government; especially office, government, or authority of a ruler or body of rulers, acting for a time in the name and place of another; a body of rulers acting for another; period of government of a ruler who acts for another.

re-gen-er-a-cy (rē-jĕn'ēr-ȧ-sĭ), *n.* the state of being reformed, restored, or renewed.

re-gen-er-ate (rē-jĕn'ēr-āt), *v.t.* in theology, to renew spiritually, or cause to turn to the love of God; produce anew; fill with new life, or power: (rē-jĕn'ēr-āt), *adj.* having new life; renewed; reformed or made better; born again spiritually.

re-gen-er-a-tion (rē-jĕn"ēr-ā'shŭn), *n.* the act of renewing or reforming; the state of being renewed or reformed; in theology, the new birth of spiritual life; in biology, the forming of new tissue to supply that which has been lost.

re-gen-er-a-tor (rē-jĕn'ēr-ā"tēr), *n.* one who reforms or renews; a device, as in a furnace or a gas-burner, to save the waste heat of escaping gases; a furnace with this device.

re-gent (rē'jĕnt), *n.* one who governs during the youth, absence, or unfitness of the rightful ruler; any governor or ruler; a university officer; a member of a board of directors of colleges and schools in the state of New York: *adj.* ruling in place of another; as, prince *regent.*

reg-i-cid-al (rĕj'ĭ-sīd'ăl), *adj.* pertaining to the murder or murderer of a king.

reg-i-cide (rĕj'ĭ-sīd), *n.* the murder or murderer of a king.

ré-gime (rā'zhēm'), *n.* mode, system, or rule of government, social or political. Also, **regime.** [Fr.]

reg-i-men (rĕj'ĭ-mĕn), *n.* orderly government; control; especially, a systematic course of diet, etc.; the grammatical influencing of the form of one word by another.

reg-i-ment (rĕj'ĭ-mĕnt), *n.* an organized body of soldiers under the command of a colonel.

reg-i-men-tal (rĕj"ĭ-mĕn'tăl), *adj.* pertaining to a regiment, or body of troops under a colonel; as, *regimental* quarters: *n.pl.* the uniforms worn by the troops of a regiment.

re-gion (rē'jŭn), *n.* a large section of land; a country or district; a division or part of the body; as, in the *region* of the heart.

reg-is-ter (rĕj'ĭs-tēr), *n.* an official written record; a roll or list; as, a *register* of births; the book containing such record; as, a school *register;* that which records; as, a cash *register;* a device for admitting heated air to an apartment; an organ stop; musical compass or range of a voice or instrument: *v.t.* to enter in a list or record; enroll; record; as, to *register* one's name; to mark a record of; as, the thermometer *registers* 80 degrees; in motion pictures, to record or indicate vividly; show clearly; as, to *register* an emotion: *v.i.* to write one's name in a list or record.

reg-is-trar (rĕj'ĭs-trär), *n.* an official who keeps records; a secretary of an institution.

reg-is-tra-tion (rĕj"ĭs-trā'shŭn), *n.* the act of entering in a record; as, the *registration* of a mortgage; a list of names so entered; enrollment; as, a large *registration* of voters.

reg-is-try (rĕj'ĭs-trĭ), *n.* the act of entering on a record; the record of acts and facts; the place where an official written record is kept; as, the *registry* of vessels at a custom house.

reg-nant (rĕg'nănt), *adj.* reigning; exercising royal authority; as, a queen *regnant;* prevailing; as, a *regnant* fashion.

re-gress (rē'grĕs), *n.* passage back; return; as, the right of free egress and *regress;* power of returning; movement in a direction opposite to the usual direction, as of a star: *v.i.* (rē-grĕs'), to go back; return; of a heavenly body, to move or seem to move in a direction opposite to the usual direction of the stars, etc.—*adj.* **regressive.**

re-gres-sion (rē-grĕsh'ŭn), *n.* the act of passing back or returning; movement in a direction opposite to the usual direction, as of the stars, etc.

re-gret (rē-grĕt'), *n.* mental sorrow or concern for anything, as for past conduct or neglect, with a wish that it had not happened; *pl.* colloquially, polite expression of refusal to do something, accept an invitation, etc.: *v.t.* [*p.t.* and *p.p.* regretted, *p.pr.* regretting], to remember with distress; wish that (something) had not happened; feel sorry for the loss or want of; as, what we lose, we *regret.*

Syn., *n.* grief, sorrow, lamentation, repentance, remorse.

re-gret-ful (rē-grĕt'fo͝ol), *adj.* remembering with distress; feeling sorry for the loss or want of.—*adv.* **regretfully.**—*n.* **regretfulness.**

re-gret-ta-ble (rē-grĕt'ȧ-bl), *adj.* fit to cause distress or sorrow; as, a *regrettable* circumstance.—*adv.* **regrettably.**

reg-u-lar (rĕg'ū-lȧr), *adj.* according to rule, order, or established custom; as, *regular* habits; a *regular* meeting; directed by rule; orderly; following a certain law, plan, type, etc.; as, *regular* features; pertaining to the standing army; permanent; as *regular* troops; belonging to a religious order; as, *regular* clergy; colloquially, thorough or genuine; as, she is a *regular* bookworm; in grammar, following the usual form of declension or conjugation: **regular army,** the standing army of a nation, not including militia, volunteers, etc.: *n.* a soldier belonging to a standing army; one who belongs to a religious order.—*adv.* **regularly.**

Syn., *adj.* orderly, customary, ordinary.

Ant. (see irregular).

reg-u-lar-i-ty (rĕg"ū-lăr'ĭ-tĭ), *n.* the state or quality of being according to rule, order, or custom; conformity to a law, plan, or type.

reg-u-late (rĕg'ū-lāt), *v.t.* to put or keep in proper order; adapt to, or govern by, rule, method, or certain standard laws; as, to *regulate* one's conduct.—*adj.* **regulative.**

Syn. arrange, organize, govern, rule.

Ant. (see disorder).

reg-u-la-tion (rĕg"ū-lā'shŭn), *n.* the act of adjusting according to a rule, method, or law; a rule, direction, or law by which to govern or manage; as government *regulation* of the railroads.

reg-u-la-tor (rĕg'ū-lā"tẽr), *n.* one who, or that which, controls or governs in accordance with rules; a device for controlling motion; as, the *regulator* of a watch; a clock specially constructed to keep correct time, and used as a standard.

Clock Regulator

re-gur-gi-tate (rē-gûr'jĭ-tāt), *v.t.* and *v.i.* to pour, gush, or throw forth or out again, especially from the stomach; as, to *regurgitate* food.—*n.* **regurgitation.**

re-ha-bil-i-tate (rē"hȧ-bĭl'ĭ-tāt), *v.t.* to restore to a former state or rank; reinstate.—*n.* **rehabilitation.**

re-hash (rē-hăsh'; rē'hăsh), *n.* something made over into a new form; as, a *rehash* of an old story: *v.t.* (rē-hăsh'), to prepare or use again; work over into a new form; as, to *rehash* an old story.

re-hears-al (rē-hûr'săl), *n.* a recital or practice in private before a public performance; as, the *rehearsal* of a play; a telling over; as, a *rehearsal* of one's experiences.

re-hearse (rē-hûrs'), *v.t.* to repeat, as what has already been said or written; tell over; narrate; to practice in private before a public performance; as, to *rehearse* a play: *v.i.* to repeat or go over something for practice.

Reichs-rath (rīkhs'rät"), *n.* the legislature, or chief lawmaking body of the Austrian empire, excluding Hungary. [Ger.]

Reichs-tag (rīkhs'täkh"), *n.* the lower house of the German legislature: before the World War it corresponded roughly to the American House of Representatives, but had much less power. [Ger.]

reign (rān), *n.* supreme rule; royal power; time during which a ruler holds sway; prevailing control or influence; as, the *reign* of law: *v.i.* to exercise royal authority; rule; hold sway; hence, to prevail, as a plague, fear, etc: **Reign of Terror,** the fourth year of the French Revolution, characterized by wholesale slaughter of all opponents of the extreme revolutionary party.

re-im-burse (rē"ĭm-bûrs'), *v.t.* to refund or pay back; to cause to receive an amount equal to something spent; as, to *reimburse* him for his loss of time.

Syn. repay, satisfy, indemnify.

re-im-burse-ment (rē"ĭm-bûrs'mĕnt), *n.* a refunding or repaying.

rein (rān), *n.* a leather strap fastened to each side of the bit of a horse or other animal as a means of guiding and controlling it; any means of restraint or control; as, the *reins* of government: *v.t.* to hold in, direct, or cause to stop by means of reins; restrain; control.

re-in-car-nate (rē"ĭn-kär'nāt), *v.t.* to cause to take a new form or embodiment in flesh.—*n.* **reincarnation.**

rein-deer (rān'dēr'), *n.* any one of several kinds of large deer found in the northern parts of America, Europe, and Asia.

Reindeer

re-in-force (rē'in-fōrs'), *v.t.* to give new strength to; support. Also, reënforce.

re-in-forced con-crete (rē'in-fōrst' kŏn'krēt), concrete strengthened by rods of iron for building purposes.

re-in-force-ment (rē'in-fōrs'mĕnt), *n.* additional support. Also, reënforcement.

re-in-state (rē'in-stāt'), *v.t.* to restore to a former state, station, or authority.—*n.* reinstatement.

re-it-er-ate (rē-ĭt'ẽr-āt), *v.t.* to do or say again and again; repeat.

re-it-er-a-tion (rē-ĭt'ẽr-ā'shŭn), *n.* a repeating or repetition.

re-it-er-a-tive (rē-ĭt'ẽr-ā-tĭv), *n.* a word formed by repeating all or part of another word; as, *pell-mell;* a word expressing repeated action.

re-ject (rē-jĕkt'), *v.t.* to throw away as worthless; to discard; as, to *reject* waste matter; refuse to take; decline; as, to *reject* a gift; refuse to grant or agree to; as, to *reject* a suggestion.—*n.* rejecter, rejector.

re-jec-tion (rē-jĕk'shŭn), *n.* the act of refusing; state of being refused.

re-joice (rē-jois'), *v.i.* to feel or express joy or gladness; exult: *v.t.* to make joyful; gladden.

re-joic-ing (rē-jois'ĭng), *n.* a reason for joy or gladness; a feeling of joy or gladness, or its expression in words or actions.

re-join (rē-join'), *v.t.* to return to after separation; to answer: *v.i.* to answer to a reply.

re-join-der (rē-join'dẽr), *n.* an answer, especially to a reply; in law, the defendant's answer to the plaintiff's statements.

re-ju-ve-nate (rē-jōō'vē-nāt), *v.t.* to renew the youth of; to cause to feel young or full of vigor again.—*n.* rejuvenation.

re-ju-ve-nes-cence (rē-jōō-vē-nĕs'-ĕns), *n.* a state of feeling or seeming young again; renewal of youth.

re-ju-ve-nes-cent (rē-jōō-vē-nĕs'ĕnt), *adj.* tending to renew one's youth.

re-lapse (rē-lăps'), *n.* a falling into a former bad state; return of a disease after partial recovery: *v.i.* to fall back into illness after a state of partial recovery; return to a former bad state or habit.

re-late (rē-lāt'), *v.t.* to tell, as a story; recite; narrate; to bring about a connection between; as, to *relate* poetry and art; to have kinship with: *v.i.* to refer: with *to.*—*p.adj.* related.—*n.* relater.

re-la-tion (rē-lā'shŭn), *n.* the act of narrating or telling; the thing narrated or told; mutual connection between two or more things; basis of association in business or social matters; as, a pleasant *relation* between partners; strained *relations;* reference; respect; as, in *relation* to; proportion or ratio; connection by birth or marriage; a relative; kinsman or kinswoman.

re-la-tion-ship (rē-lā'shŭn-shĭp), *n.* the state of being connected by blood or otherwise.

rel-a-tive (rĕl'ȧ-tĭv), *n.* that which refers to, or is thought of in its connection with, something else; a person connected with another by blood or marriage; a kinsman; a word which refers to an antecedent; as, the pronouns *who, which, that,* are *relatives: adj.* having or expressing connection with, or reference to, something; as, their conversation was *relative* to business; comparative; as, the *relative* value of two things; having meaning only in connection with something else; as, *mother* and *daughter* are *relative* terms; in grammar, referring to an antecedent; as, a *relative* pronoun.—*adv.* relatively.—*n.* relativeness.

rel-a-tiv-i-ty (rĕl'ȧ-tĭv'ĭ-tĭ), *n.* the state or quality of being connected with, or of having reference to, something else.

re-la-tor (rē-lā'tẽr), *n.* [*fem.* relatrix], one who tells or recounts; a narrator. Also, relater.

re-lax (rē-lăks'), *v.t.* to slacken; make less tight or firm; as, to *relax* one's hold on a thing; render less strict, harsh, or severe; as, to *relax* punishment; relieve from strain; ease, as the mind; loosen, as the bowels: *v.i.* to becom less tight or firm; as, his hold *relaxed;* become less severe; as, to *relax* in discipline; to cease effort; unbend; lessen tension; rest; as, to *relax* after the day's labor.

re-lax-a-tion (rē'lăk-sā'shŭn; rĕl'ăk-sā'-shŭn), *n.* the act of loosening, easing, or making less severe; state of being loosened, eased, or less severe; lessening of tension or restraint; diversion or recreation; as, dreams appear to be the *relaxations* of the soul.

re-lay (rē-lā'), *v.t.* [*p.t.* and *p.p.* relaid, *p.pr.* relaying], to lay a second time; as, to *relay* a pavement: *n.* (rē'lā), a set of fresh men, horses, or dogs, etc., held ready to relieve a tired set, usually at a given time or place; a supply of anything arranged beforehand for affording relief from time to time; in military use, a small detachment of automobiles, or of men mounted on bicycles or motor cycles, who carry messages between widely separated points; an electrical device by which the opening or closing of a weak circuit opens or closes a stronger circuit: relay race, a race in which a series of runners succeed one another, each covering a part of the course.

re-lease (rē-lēs'), *n.* the act of setting free; state of being set free; deliverance from pain, anxiety, distress, etc.; a freeing from an obligation or penalty; as, *release* from debt: *v.t.* to set free; as, to *release* a man from prison; free from obligation or penalty; as, to *release* a person from debt; deliver from pain, care, trouble, etc.

rel-e-gate (rĕl'ē-gāt), *v.t.* to send away; to change to a worse or lower place or situation; as, to *relegate* furniture to the attic.

rel-e-ga-tion (rĕl'ē-gā'shŭn), *n.* the act of banishing or of removing to a worse position; state of being banished or removed; removal; banishment.

re-lent (rē-lĕnt'), *v.i.* to become less hard, severe, or cruel; become more gentle; feel pity; yield.

re-lent-less (rē-lĕnt'lĕs), *adj.* unmoved by sympathy; indifferent to the pain of others; pitiless.—*adv.* **relentlessly.**—*n.* **relentlessness.**

rel-e-vance (rĕl'ē-văns), *n.* the quality or state of bearing upon, or properly applying to, the case in hand. Also, **relevancy.**

rel-e-vant (rĕl'ē-vănt), *adj.* having to do with, or relating to, the case in hand; related.—*adv.* **relevantly.**
Syn. fit, proper, suitable, appropriate.
Ant. (see irrelevant).

re-li-a-bil-i-ty (rē-lī'ā-bĭl'ĭ-tĭ), *n.* the state or quality of being trustworthy or fit to be depended upon.

re-li-a-ble (rē-lī'ā-bl), *adj.* trustworthy; fit to be depended upon.—*adv.* **reliably.**—*n.* **reliableness.**

re-li-ance (rē-lī'ăns), *n.* act of trusting or depending; state of being confident or dependent; confidence; trust; dependence; that on which one depends; foundation for trust.
Syn. faith, belief.
Ant. (see suspicion).

re-li-ant (rē-lī'ănt), *adj.* trusting; having confidence; dependent.

rel-ic (rĕl'ĭk), *n.* that which is left after the loss or decay of the rest; memorial or souvenir; body or other memorial of a saint held in religious reverence.

rel-ict (rĕl'ĭkt), *n.* a widow or widower; especially, a widow.

re-lief (rē-lēf'), *n.* removal in whole or in part of pain, grief, want, etc.; the feeling caused by such removal; that which removes or lessens pain, grief, etc.; release from some post of duty; help given to the poor; fresh supplies of men, animals, food, etc., especially fresh troops, coming to take the place of those tired out or used up; the elevation of a sculptured design from a plane surface; as, the figures carved in *relief* on old furniture; in painting and drawing, the effect of standing out from the surface given to objects in the picture by shadows, etc.; hence, a vivid contrast between a figure and its background; in physical geography, the elevations and depressions of land surface.
Syn. succor, aid, help, redress.

re-lieve (rē-lēv'), *v.t.* to free from pain, suffering, grief, etc.; as, to *relieve* an anxious mind; give comfort or aid to; as, to *relieve* the needy; reduce in severity; lessen; as, to *relieve* anxiety; to free from a post of duty; as, to *relieve* a patrol; make less grave or gloomy; light up; as, a little pleasure *relieves* the monotony of work; a flash of light *relieved* the darkness; bring out by contrast; as, a touch of red will *relieve* the black.—*adj.* **relievable.**

re-li-gion (rē-lĭj'ŭn), *n.* the sense of man's relation to a divine or supernatural power to whom obedience and honor are due; the practice of life that grows out of the recognition of such relation; the life of God in the soul of man; the effort of man to attain the life of God; any system of faith and worship.

re-li-gious (rē-lĭj'ŭs), *adj.* feeling, and living in accordance with, a belief in a divine power to whom honor and obedience are due; striving to attain the life of God; pious; pertaining to, or set apart for, religion; holy; bound by monastic vows; strict; conscientious: *n.* one who is bound by monastic vows.

re-lin-quish (rē-lĭṅ'kwĭsh), *v.t.* to retire from; to give up using or having; leave; as, to *relinquish* one's position; to cease to demand; surrender; as, to *relinquish* a claim.
Syn. resign, forsake, forego.
Ant. (see retain).

re-lin-quish-ment (rē-lĭṅ'kwĭsh-mĕnt), *n.* the act of giving up or ceasing to demand.

rel-i-qua-ry (rĕl'ĭ-kwā-rĭ), *n.* [*pl.* reliquaries (-rĭz)], a casket or small chest for holding relics, usually of a religious nature.

rel-ish (rĕl'ĭsh), *n.* a taste or preference; a fondness; an eager appreciation; as, a *relish* for food or for adventure; flavor, especially when pleasing; as, that wine has a delightful *relish;* the quality that makes a thing pleasurable; as, novelty gave *relish* to the journey; something taken with food to give it flavor: *v.t.* to give flavor to; as, salt *relishes* meat; to like the taste of; enjoy; as, he *relishes* his dinner, or a good story: *v.i.* to have a pleasing taste.

re-luc-tance (rē-lŭk'tăns), *n.* unwillingness; disinclination. Also, **reluctancy.**

re-luc-tant (rē-lŭk'tănt), *adj.* unwilling; disinclined.—*adv.* **reluctantly.**

re-ly (rē-lī'), *v.i.* [*p.t.* and *p.p.* relied, *p.pr.* relying], to trust; have confidence in someone or something; to depend: with *on* or *upon.*

re-main (rē-mān'), *v.i.* to stay behind when others have gone; as, only he *remained* in the room; to stay alive; endure; last; as, the memory of that day *remains;* be left after a part has been used, taken away, lost, or destroyed; as, little of his wealth *remains;* to be left as a possibility or as something not included; as, that *remains* to be seen: *n.pl.* the portion left; a dead body; ruins; works published after an author's death; as, literary *remains.*

re-main-der (rē-mān'dẽr), *n.* the portion left after anything is taken away; remnant; residue.

re-mand (rē-mȧnd'), *v.t.* to order or send back; to recommit to custody; as, to *remand* an accused person to prison: *n.* the sending back of an accused person to custody after a hearing; the judicial order sending him back.

re-mark (rē-märk'), *n.* a brief, casual comment or statement; an observation; notice; as, his dress made him an object of *remark: pl.* conversational speech in general; as, his *remarks* were interesting: *v.t.* to take note of; observe; as, to *remark* an odd style of dress; to utter briefly and casually.

re-mark-a-ble (rē-mär'kā-bl), *adj.* worthy of observation or comment; noteworthy; unusual; uncommon.—*adv.* **remarkably.**—*n.* **remarkableness.**
Syn. strange, famous, extraordinary, wonderful.
Ant. (see ordinary).

re-me-di-a-ble (rē-mē'dĭ-ā-bl), *adj.* capable of being cured; as, a *remediable* disease.

re-me-di-al (rē-mē'dĭ-ăl), *adj.* affording, or intended to be used as, a cure; as, *remedial* treatment.

rem-e-di-less (rĕm'ē-dĭ-lĕs; rē-mĕd'ĭ-lĕs), *adj.* past cure or help; incurable; in a hopeless state.

rem-e-dy (rĕm'ē-dĭ), *n.* [*pl.* remedies (-dĭz)], that which cures or helps sickness; a helpful medicine; that which removes or corrects an evil; a relief: *v.t.* [*p.t.* and *p.p.* remedied, *p.pr.* remedying], to cure or heal; to repair or make right; to remove or correct.
Syn., *n.* help, relief, redress, cure.

re-mem-ber (rē-mĕm'bẽr), *v.t.* to retain or keep in the mind; recollect; as, an old man *remembers* the days of his youth; keep in mind carefully; give heed to; as, *remember* what I say; hold in mind with gratitude, regard, or reverence; as, to *remember* the soldiers on Memorial Day; remind someone of; as, *remember* me to her; do for out of kindness; give a present or fee to; as, *remember* the porter: *v.i.* to possess or use the faculty of memory.

re-mem-brance (rē-mĕm'brāns), *n.* the act or power of recalling to or keeping in the mind; state of being held in or recalled to mind; recollection; memory; length of time within which one has memories; as, the coldest winter in my *remembrance;* anything that recalls or keeps in mind a particular memory; a memento or keepsake; a gift; greetings showing regard; as, give her my *remembrances.*

re-mind (rē-mīnd'), *v.t.* to bring to the mind of; cause to recollect.

rem-i-nis-cence (rĕm"ĭ-nĭs'ĕns), *n.* the calling to mind and telling of past experiences; that which is recalled and told; memory.

rem-i-nis-cent (rĕm"ĭ-nĭs'ĕnt), *adj.* pertaining to, of the nature of, or having, memory of past experiences; recalling, or thinking much about, the past.

re-miss (rē-mĭs'), *adj.* careless in matters of duty, business, etc.; neglectful; hence, lacking energy and earnestness; not prompt.—*adv.* remissly.—*n.* remissness.

re-mis-sion (rē-mĭsh'ŭn), *n.* the canceling of a debt; discharge from a penalty; as, the *remission* of a fine; forgiveness; pardon; as, *remission* of sins.

re-mit (rē-mĭt'), *v.t.* [*p.t.* and *p.p.* remitted, *p.pr.* remitting], to forgive; pardon; as, to *remit* sins; send, as money, bills, etc.; refrain from demanding or insisting upon; as, to *remit* a fine; make less severe; relax; as, to *remit* one's watchfulness.—*n.* remitter.

re-mit-tal (rē-mĭt'ăl), *n.* a canceling; as, the *remittal* of a penalty; a discharge; remission.

re-mit-tance (rē-mĭt'āns), *n.* the sending of money, bills, etc., in payment; the sum so sent: **remittance man**, a person, usually a younger son of an aristocratic English family, who lives in the colonies on an allowance sent him from home.

re-mit-tent (rē-mĭt'ĕnt), *adj.* growing less temporarily, or at irregular intervals; abating; as, a *remittent* fever: *n.* a fever that abates irregularly.

rem-nant (rĕm'nānt), *n.* that which is left after a part has been removed; remainder; a short length of fabric left when most of the piece has been sold.

re-mod-el (rē-mŏd'ĕl), *v.t.* to put into new shape; rearrange.

re-mon-e-tize (rē-mŏn'ē-tīz), *v.t.* to restore to use as lawful money; as, to *remonetize* silver.

re-mon-strance (rē-mŏn'strāns), *n.* strong urging against something; protest; reproof.

re-mon-strant (rē-mŏn'strānt), *adj.* protesting or urging reasons against something: *n.* one that signs or presents a protest against something.

re-mon-strate (rē-mŏn'strāt), *v.i.* to urge or put forward strong reasons against some act or course complained of; as, to *remonstrate* against a wrong; to plead in protest.

re-morse (rē-môrs'), *n.* great pain or anguish of mind caused by the sense of guilt; keen self-reproach.

re-morse-ful (rē-môrs'fŏŏl), *adj.* full of sorrow or anguish caused by a sense of guilt; keenly self-reproachful.—*adv.* remorsefully.—*n.* remorsefulness.

re-morse-less (rē-môrs'lĕs), *adj.* cruel: merciless; pitiless; hardhearted.—*adv.* remorselessly.—*n.* remorselessness.
Syn. relentless, ruthless, barbarous.
Ant. (see merciful).

re-mote (rē-mōt'), *adj.* far off in time or space; as, *remote* centuries; *remote* peoples; distant; far removed from others; as, a *remote* village in the hills; having slight connection or relation; as, his remarks were *remote* from the subject; slight; not plainly seen; as, a *remote* likeness.—*adv.* remotely.—*n.* remoteness.
Syn. far, secluded, indirect.
Ant. (see near).

re-mount (rē-mount'), *v.t.* and *v.i.* to get or put on horseback again; to give a fresh horse to: *n.* a fresh horse to replace one killed or hurt.

re-mov-a-ble (rē-mōōv'ȧ-bl), *adj.* capable of being taken away, or of being transferred from one place to another.

re-mov-al (rē-mōōv'ăl), *n.* the act of taking away; change of place; dismissal; as, *removal* from office.

re-move (rē-mōōv'), *v.t.* to put from its place; transfer from one place to another; to take out of the way; as, to *remove* a hindrance; displace; as, to *remove* a man from office: *v.i.* to go from one place to another; change residence: *n.* a transfer from one place to another; a change of place; the space passed over in changing a thing from one place to another; a step or interval.—*n.* remover.

re-moved (rē-mōōvd'), *p.adj.* separated by degrees in relationship; as, a first cousin once *removed* is a cousin's child.

re-mu-ner-ate (rē-mū'nẽr-āt), *v.t.* to pay (someone) in return for service, for time spent, or for loss sustained on one's account; pay in return for; as, to *remunerate* a service; compensate; reward.

re-mu-ner-a-tion (rē-mū"nẽr-ā'shŭn), *n.* payment for loss sustained on one's account, or for service; compensation; wage or salary; reward.

re-mu-ner-a-tive (rē-mū'nẽr-ā-tĭv), *adj.* paying; profitable; as, a *remunerative* business.

ren-ais-sance (rĕn"ĕ-säns'; rē-nā'sāns; Fr. rē-nĕ"säns'), *n.* a new birth; a coming to life again, especially in art; the revival of anything that has been out of use a long time: **Renaissance**, the revival of learning and the arts in Europe during the fourteenth to sixteenth centuries; the style of art and architecture of that period. Also, **renascence.**

re-nal (rē'năl), *adj.* of or pertaining to the kidneys; as, *renal* colic.

re-nas-cence (rē-năs'ĕns), *n.* fact or state of being reborn; a coming into fresh life: **Renascence**, the revival of learning and the arts in Europe during the fourteenth to sixteenth centuries; the Renaissance.

re-nas-cent (rē-năs'ĕnt), *adj.* coming to life again; as, a *renascent* interest in art; being born again; reviving.

ren-coun-ter (rĕn-koun'tẽr), *n.* a sudden hostile meeting, as with an enemy; an unexpected meeting, as with a friend; a debate or argument between individuals. Also, **rencontre**.

rend (rĕnd), *v.t.* [*p.t.* and *p.p.* rent, *p.pr.* rending], to tear apart with violence; split; as, the wind did not *rend* the sail; to take away by force; as, to *rend* colonies from a mother country: *v.i.* to become torn; split apart.
Syn. break, sever, sunder.
Ant. (see mend).

ren-der (rĕn'dẽr), *v.t.* to give in answer; to pay back; as, to *render* gratitude; pay back as being owed; as, to *render* tribute; present; as, to *render* a bill or account; deliver; utter as final; as, to *render* a decision; yield; as, to *render* homage; furnish; give; as, to *render* aid; cause to be; as, to *render* anything fit for use; translate; as, to *render* French into English; to express or interpret; as, to *render* music; to clear or separate by melting; as, to *render* lard.

ren-dez-vous (rän'dĕ-vo͞o), *n.* appointed place of meeting, especially for warships or troops; a meeting by appointment: *v.t.* and *v.i.* [*p.t.* and *p.p.* rendezvoused (-vo͞od), *p.pr.* rendezvousing (-vo͞o-ing)], to meet or cause to meet at a certain place.

ren-di-tion (rĕn-dish'ŭn), *n.* a yielding or a surrender; a translation; form of narrating a story; style of performing, etc.; as, the *rendition* of a piece of music.

ren-e-gade (rĕn'ē-gād), *n.* one who denies or gives up his faith; traitor; a deserter from army or navy. Also, **renegado**.

re-nege (rē-nĕg'), *v.i.* in cards, to fail to follow suit when holding cards of the suit called for; to revoke.

re-new (rē-nū'), *v.t.* to cause to become new once more; bring back the youth and strength of; as, spring *renews* the earth; to begin again; as, to *renew* the fighting along a battle front; revive; reawaken: *v.i.* to become new; begin afresh; grow again.—*adj.* **renewable**.

re-new-al (rē-nū'ăl), *n.* the act of beginning again, or of making new; state of being begun again or made new.

ren-net (rĕn'ĕt), *n.* the lining membrane of the stomach of an unweaned calf, lamb, etc., used to curdle milk.

re-nounce (rē-nouns'), *v.t.* to disown; cast off; as, to *renounce* one's heir; to give up; as, to *renounce* a hope: *v.i.* in card playing, not to follow suit: *n.* failure to follow suit.—*n.* **renouncer**, **renouncement**.
Syn., *v.* abandon, discard.
Ant. (see advocate).

ren-o-vate (rĕn'ō-vāt), *v.t.* to make as good as new; restore to a former condition, or to a good state; repair.—*n.* **renovator**.

ren-o-va-tion (rĕn'ō-vā'shŭn), *n.* act of making, or state of being made, as good as new; a renewal; cleansing.

re-nown (rē-noun'), *n.* fame; the state of being widely known and well spoken of; widespread reputation; as the *renown* of a hero.

re-nowned (rē-nound'), *p.adj.* having a wide and honorable reputation; famous.

rent (rĕnt), *p.t.* and *p.p.* of *rend*: *n.* a tear; a hole or slit made by rending or tearing, especially in cloth; payment at stated times for the use of property: *v.t.* to hold in possession by paying for at stated times; hire; as, to *rent* a house from an owner; to give possession of, in return for regular stated payments; lease; as, to *rent* a house to a tenant; *v.i.* be leased or let; as, the house *rents* for $1,000.

rent-al (rĕn'tăl), *n.* amount of money paid at stated times for possession and use of property; entire income obtained from leased property.

re-nun-ci-a-tion (rē-nŭn'sĭ-ā'shŭn; rē-nŭn'shĭ-ā'shŭn), *n.* the act of disowning, casting off, or giving up; as, the *renunciation* of dower rights.
Syn. disavowal, abandonment, relinquishment.

re-or-gan-i-za-tion (rē-ôr'găn-ĭ-zā'shŭn; rē-ôr'găn-ī-zā'shŭn), *n.* the act of arranging or systematizing anew; state of being arranged or systematized anew.

re-or-gan-ize (rē-ôr'găn-īz), *v.t.* and *v.i.* to arrange or systematize anew; change to a more satisfactory form or system.

rep (rĕp), *n.* a silk, wool, or silk and wool, fabric having a fine, corded surface.

re-pair (rē-pâr'), *v.i.* to go; as, to *repair* to one's home; betake oneself: *v.t.* to put in good condition again after injury; mend; as, to *repair* a garment; remedy; make right; as, to *repair* a mistake; make amends for; as, to *repair* an unkindness: *n.* restoration after injury: usually plural; supply of loss; condition after use or restoration; as, the house is in good *repair*.—*adj.* **repairable**.—*n.* **repairer**.

rep-a-ra-ble (rĕp'ā-rā-bl), *adj.* capable of being mended or made good.

rep-a-ra-tion (rĕp'ā-rā'shŭn), *n.* the act of restoring to a good condition; state of being restored; act of making amends for a wrong, etc.; as, he made *reparation* for his neglect; that which is done by way of amends.
Syn. recompense, satisfaction, redress.

rep-ar-tee (rĕp'ăr-tē'), *n.* a quick-witted, bright reply; quick, clever replies in general; quick cleverness in making replies.

re-past (rē-påst'), *n.* a meal; a feast; food taken at one time

re-pa-tri-ate (rē-pā'trĭ-āt), *v.t.* and *v.i.* to give back citizenship to; to bring back to one's own country, as prisoners of war after peace is concluded.—*n.* **repatriation**.

re-pay (rē-pā'), *v.t.* to pay back; as, to *repay* borrowed money; to pay back to; as, to *repay* a creditor; to make a gift to or do a service for in return; as, to *repay* a friend for kindness; give a return for; as, to *repay* a favor.—*n.* **repayment**.

re-peal (rē-pēl'), *v.t.* to cancel, or make of no further effect, by recalling; as, to *repeal* a law: *n.* the recalling, with purpose to cancel, or make of no further effect; as, the *repeal* of a law.
Syn. annul, revoke, rescind.

re-peat (rē-pēt′), *v.t.* to do or speak a second time; say over from memory; recite: *v.i.* to say or do anything over or again: *n.* a sign in music, directing a part to be given again; anything said or done over or again.

re-peat-ed (rē-pēt′ĕd), *p.adj.* done or said again and again or over and over; frequent.—*adv.* **repeatedly.**

re-peat-er (rē-pēt′ẽr), *n.* one who, or that which, says or does a thing over; a revolver or rifle which fires several shots without being reloaded; a watch that strikes the hours, etc., when a spring is pressed; in the United States, one who votes more than once at an election; a kind of telegraph instrument.

re-pel (rē-pĕl′), *v.t.* [*p.t.* and *p.p.* repelled, *p.pr.* repelling], to drive back; check the advance of; keep at a distance; as, to *repel* an enemy; his manner *repels* everyone; in physics, to drive, or tend to drive, apart by mutual force acting across a distance. opposite to *attract:* *v.i.* to act with force against force; cause dislike.

re-pel-lent (rē-pĕl′ĕnt), *adj.* driving back; tending or able to keep at a distance; forbidding; as, a *repellent* manner.

re-pent (rē-pĕnt′), *v.i.* to feel pain or sorrow on account of something done or left undone; change from past evil: *v.t.* to feel regret or sorrow for; as, to *repent* a crime.—*n.* **repenter.**

re-pent-ance (rē-pĕn′tăns), *n.* act of regretting, or state of one who regrets, wrongdoing; sorrow for wrongdoing, with desire to undo the wrong.

Syn. regret, remorse, sorrow, contrition.

re-pent-ant (rē-pĕn′tănt), *adj.* feeling or showing sorrow because of wrongdoing; penitent.

re-per-cus-sion (rē″pẽr-kŭsh′ŭn), *n.* act of driving or throwing back; state of being forced or thrown back; reflection; rebound.—*adj.* **repercussive.**

rep-er-toire (rĕp′ẽr-twär), *n.* a list of plays, operas, songs, etc., which a performer or a company has ready to render; a repertory. Also, **répertoire.** [Fr.]

rep-er-to-ry (rĕp′ẽr-tō-rĭ), *n.* a place where things are stored; the things stored; collection; a list of dramas, operas, etc., ready for performance; a repertoire.

rep-e-ti-tion (rĕp″ē-tĭsh′ŭn), *n.* the doing, making, or saying of something more than once; that which is done, said, etc.; recital from memory.—*adj.* **repetitious.**

re-pine (rē-pīn′), *v.i.* to fret oneself; complain; feel discontent.—*n.* **repiner.**

re-place (rē-plās′), *v.t.* to put back in place; as, to *replace* a book on a shelf; take or fill the place of; as, a new house *replaces* the old one; restore; as, to *replace* goods which one has lost; repay; put in a new place.

re-place-ment (rē-plās′mĕnt), *n.* the putting of something back in place; the putting of something in place of another or in a new place: **replacement troops,** soldiers sent to the front as fast as they are sufficiently trained, to take the place of troops already there.

re-plen-ish (rē-plĕn′ĭsh), *v.t.* to fill up again; fill or stock in abundance; refill.—*n.* **replenisher.**

re-plen-ish-ment (rē-plĕn′ĭsh-mĕnt), *n.* the act of filling up again; state of being refilled.

re-plete (rē-plēt′), *adj.* completely filled; abundantly stocked; abounding.

re-ple-tion (rē-plē′shŭn), *n.* the state of being full to excess; surfeit.

re-plev-in (rē-plĕv′ĭn), *n.* the recovery by a person of goods claimed to have been wrongfully seized, on giving security to try the matter in court and accept the judgment; the writ or order issued by the court making such return: *v.t.* to take or get back by a writ, or order of court.

re-plev-y (rē-plĕv′ĭ), *v.t.* [*p.t.* and *p.p.* replevied, *p.pr.* replevying], to recover by a court order (goods wrongfully seized) on giving security to try the right to them at law.

rep-li-ca (rĕp′lĭ-kȧ), *n.* a copy of an original picture, or statue, especially one made by the artist or sculptor himself.

re-ply (rē-plī′), *n.* something spoken, written, or done in return for something that calls for it; an answer; a response: *v.t.* [*p.t.* and *p.p.* replied, *p.pr.* replying], to say or write something in answer; rejoin; to do something in return for something; respond: *v.i.* to say in answer.

re-port (rē-pōrt′), *n.* an official presentation of facts; as, a government *report;* a written or verbal statement telling of events, transactions, etc.; as, a *report* of a meeting; something widely talked of; hearsay; as, it is common *report;* fame; reputation; as, to win good *report;* a loud, sudden noise; as, the *report* of a pistol: *v.t.* to present an account of; as, to *report* the work of a committee; make a verbal or written statement about events; as, to *report* the news of the day; relate; tell; circulate publicly; take down (spoken words); as, to *report* a speech for a paper; make a formal statement of; as, to *report* a balance; make a charge against; as, to *report* a pupil for misconduct: *v.i.* to make or present a prepared statement, be in attendance at a given place; as, to *report* for duty.

Syn., n. recital, account, tale.

re-port-er (rē-pōr′tẽr), *n.* one who bears or gathers news; especially, one who gathers news and writes accounts of matters and events for a newspaper.

re-pose (rē-pōz′), *n.* sleep; rest; calmness; ease of manner: *v.t.* to place in a position to rest; refresh by rest; to cause to depend: with *in* or *on;* as, to *repose* confidence in God: *v.i.* to sleep; to lie at rest; to lie or rest on a support; to confide; to be calm or peaceful.

re-pos-i-to-ry (rē-pŏz′ĭ-tō-rĭ), *n.* [*pl.* repositories (-rĭz)], a place for the storing and safe-keeping of goods, as a bank, warehouse, etc.; a depository.

re-pous-sé (rē-pōō′sā′), *adj.* beaten or pressed up from the under side so as to show ornamental figures in relief; as, a *repoussé* ceiling of thin metal: *n.* a pattern formed in such relief; a surface adorned with a design so made. [Fr.]

rep-re-hend (rĕp″rē-hĕnd′), *v.t.* to blame; reprove sharply; charge with a fault; as, to *reprehend* a person; find fault with; censure; as, to *reprehend* conduct.

rep-re-hen-si-ble (rĕp″rē-hĕn′sĭ-bl), *adj.* blamable; deserving reproof.—*adv.* **reprehensibly.**—*n.* **reprehensibleness.**

rep-re-hen-sion (rĕp′rē-hĕn′shŭn), *n.* act of finding fault; blame; rebuke.

rep-re-hen-sive (rĕp′rē-hĕn′sĭv), *adj.* conveying or intended as reproof or blame; as, a *reprehensive* manner.—*adv.* **reprehensively.**

rep-re-hen-so-ry (rĕp-rē-hĕn′sō-rĭ), *adj.* given to fault-finding; censorious.

rep-re-sent (rĕp′rē-zĕnt′), *v.t.* to make clear to the mind; as, that story *represents* a great truth; to make or show a likeness of; as, the picture *represents* a moonlit sea; to make a statement about in order to influence opinion or to give a desired effect; as, he *represented* himself to be in want; act or speak in place of; as, he *represents* his father in the business; act the part of; as, he *represented* a clown in the play; stand for; as, letters *represent* sounds.

rep-re-sen-ta-tion (rĕp′rē-zĕn-tā′shŭn), *n.* the act of making statements in order to influence opinion; the statement, account, or assertion of fact so made; that which stands for or symbolizes something; as, Greek myths were *representations* of facts in nature; an image, model, or picture; a dramatic performance; a body of persons acting for others; as, the *representation* of a dis rict in the legislature; the acting for, or standing in the place of, another, or others; the state of having persons to speak or act in one's behalf; as, no taxation without *representation.*

rep-re-sen-ta-tive (rĕp′rē-zĕn′tȧ-tĭv), *n.* one who has power to act for another or others; deputy or delegate, especially one chosen by a body of electors; a member of the lower house in Congress, or of a State legislature; a member of any parliamentary body; one who, or that which, stands as a type, or shows the marked features of a group: *adj.* acting, or having power to act, for another or others; composed of those so acting; as, a *representative* assembly; having the marked features of a group; as, the gathering was *representative* of the best families; typical.

re-press (rē-prĕs′), *v.t.* to keep under control; check; as, to *repress* a wish; crush; overpower; subdue; as, to *repress* a rebellion.

re-pres-sion (rē-prĕsh′ŭn), *n.* the act of checking or keeping in control; state of being kept in control.

re-pres-sive (rē-prĕs′ĭv), *adj.* having power to control or check; as, a *repressive* law.

re-prieve (rē-prēv′), *n.* a temporary delay in carrying out the sentence of a judge; a temporary relief from pain or escape from ill: *v.t.* to grant a delay of punishment to; free for a time from pain or danger.

rep-ri-mand (rĕp′rĭ-mȧnd), *n.* a severe reproof or rebuke: *v.t.* to rebuke severely for a fault; reprove publicly and officially.

re-print (rē′prĭnt″; rē-prĭnt′), *n.* an exact copy of any printed work; a reproduction of printed matter: *v.t.* (rē-prĭnt′), to print again; print a new copy or edition of.

re-pris-al (rē-prīz′ăl), *n.* in war, something done to, or taken from, an enemy by way of satisfaction or payment for an injury or wrong suffered; as, the Allied airmen made *reprisals* for the Zeppelin raids by bombing German cities; any repayment of injury with injury.

re-proach (rē-prōch′), *n.* rebuke or blame with sorrow or anger; the cause or object of blame or scorn; condition of shame or disgrace: *v.t.* to charge with something wrong or disgraceful; rebuke or blame. *adj.* **reproachable.**—*n.* **reproacher.**

re-proach-ful (rē-prōch′fo͝ol), *adj.* containing or expressing rebuke or blame.—*adv.* **reproachfully.**

rep-ro-bate (rĕp′rō-bāt), *n.* a sinful or wicked person; a scoundrel: *v.t.* to disapprove of strongly; condemn; reject: *adj.* given up to sin; depraved.

rep-ro-ba-tion (rĕp′rō-bā′shŭn), *n.* the act of strongly disapproving or censuring; strong condemnation or blame.

re-pro-duce (rē′prō-dūs′), *v.t.* to bring forward or show again; repeat; as, to *reproduce* a play; to bear, yield, or bring forth; as, an animal *reproduces* its kind; to bring into being again; as, these colors *reproduce* the white light; to copy; to make an image of; as, to *reproduce* a person's features in marble.

re-pro-duc-tion (rē′prō-dŭk′shŭn), *n.* the act or power of bringing forward again, or of making an image of; the process by which animals and plants bring forth their own kind; the process of recalling to memory; revival of a drama, or copy of a work of art or literature.

re-pro-duc-tive (rē′prō-dŭk′tĭv), *adj.* of, pertaining to, or employed in, the process of bringing forth anew, physically or mentally.—*n.* **reproductiveness.**

re-proof (rē-pro͞of′), *n.* censure; blame; just and kindly rebuke.

re-prov-a-ble (rē-pro͞ov′ȧ-bl), *adj.* deserving of rebuke or blame.

re-prov-al (rē-pro͞ov′ăl), *n.* act of blaming or censuring; rebuke.

re-prove (rē-pro͞ov′), *v.t.* to rebuke with kindness and justice; to blame.—*adv.* **reprovingly.**—*n.* **reprover.**

rep-tile (rĕp′tĭl), *n.* a cold-blooded animal that creeps or crawls on its belly or on short legs; a mean, groveling person: *adj.* creeping; crawling; groveling or cringing; low; base.

rep-til-i-an (rĕp-tĭl′ĭ-ăn), *n.* any of a class of cold-blooded, air-breathing, vertebrate animals, as snakes, lizards, turtles, alligators, crocodiles: *adj.* pertaining to, or like, such animals. Also, *adj.* **reptilious.**

re-pub-lic (rē-pŭb′lĭk), *n.* a state or country in which the supreme power is held by the people, who elect their own representatives and executive officers; a commonwealth.

re-pub-lic-an (rē-pŭb′lĭ-kăn), *n.* one who favors government by the chosen representatives of the people: **Republican**, a member of the Republican party: **Republican party**, one of the two greater political parties in the United States: organized in 1854: *adj.* of, pertaining to, characteristic of, or believing in, government by chosen representatives of the people.

re-pub-lic-an-ism (rē-pŭb′lĭ-kăn-ĭzm), *n.* the system or principles of government by chosen representatives of the people; belief in such principles.

re-pub-li-ca-tion (rē-pŭb′lĭ-kā′shŭn), *n.* the act of reprinting, or issuing anew; as, the *republication* of a book; a reprint of a book, etc.; the act of declaring or making known again.

re-pub-lish (rē-pŭb′lĭsh), *v.t.* to put forth or issue anew, as a book; print a new edition of.

re-pu-di-ate (rē-pū′dĭ-āt), *v.t.* to divorce (a wife); to refuse to own; to cast off; as, to *repudiate* an old friend; to decline to be responsible or liable for; as, to *repudiate* a debt; refuse to admit the truth, justice, or authority of; as, to *repudiate* a statement.—*n.* **repudiator.**
Syn. discard, renounce.
Ant. (see acknowledge).

re-pu-di-a-tion (rē-pū″dĭ-ā′shŭn), *n.* the act of disowning or disclaiming; refusal to pay or acknowledge.

re-pug-nance (rē-pŭg′nāns), *n.* extreme dislike; disgust; a version. Also, **repugnancy.**

re-pug-nant (rē-pŭg′nānt), *adj.* highly distasteful or disagreeable; repulsive; as, a *repugnant* expression; contradictory; contrary; hostile; as, a *repugnant* attitude.—*adv.* **repugnantly.**
Syn. antagonistic, opposite, opposed.

re-pulse (rē-pŭls′), *v.t.* to drive back; beat off; as, to *repulse* the enemy; to drive away by coldness, etc.; refuse to accept or meet; as, to *repulse* the advances of a friend: *n.* the act of driving back; state of being driven back or beaten off; decided refusal; denial.

re-pul-sion (rē-pŭl′shŭn), *n.* the act of driving back; state of being driven back; a feeling of aversion; strong dislike; in physics, the action of two bodies upon each other which drives them apart: opposite to *attraction.*

re-pul-sive (rē-pŭl′sĭv), *adj.* able to drive back; as, a *repulsive* movement; cold; forbidding; as, a *repulsive* manner; offensive; disgusting; as, a *repulsive* sight.—*adv.* **repulsively.**—*n.* **repulsiveness.**
Syn. ugly, disagreeable, revolting.
Ant. (see attractive).

rep-u-ta-ble (rĕp′ū-tȧ-bl), *adj.* worthy of esteem; honorable; respectable; creditable.—*adv.* **reputably.**

rep-u-ta-tion (rĕp″ū-tā′shŭn), *n.* good name or standing; honor; credit; as, a citizen of *reputation;* the general opinion, good or bad, held of a person or thing; as, a *reputation* for meanness or generosity.

re-pute (rē-pūt′), *n.* reputation, or general opinion, good or bad, held of a person or thing; as, a man of good or evil *repute:* *v.t.* to hold in general opinion; consider: usually in a passive sense; as, he is *reputed* rich.

re-quest (rē-kwĕst′), *n.* act of asking for something; that which is asked for; expression of a wish; state of being asked for or in demand; as, he is in great *request* as a public speaker: *v.t.* to ask for with politeness; as, to *request* a favor; to ask (someone) for something; as, to *request* a person for a loan.

re-qui-em (rē′kwĭ-ĕm; rĕk′wĭ-ĕm), *n.* a Mass sung for the repose of the souls of the dead; the music for such a Mass; any hymn or solemn musical service in honor of the dead.

re-quire (rē-kwīr′), *v.t.* to claim as one's right; as, I *require* your attention; demand or insist upon; as, to *require* promptness at school; have need of; call for; as, a singular subject *requires* a singular verb; this will *require* haste.

re-quire-ment (rē-kwīr′mĕnt), *n.* the act of insisting upon or claiming as by right or authority; demand; necessity; that which is demanded or necessary: *pl.* conditions of entrance to a club, institution, etc.; as, college entrance *requirements.*

req-ui-site (rĕk′wĭ-zĭt), *n.* anything that cannot be done without; a necessity: *adj.* so needful that it cannot be done without; necessary; as, a *requisite* amount of food.

req-ui-si-tion (rĕk″wĭ-zĭsh′ŭn), *n.* a formal demand or claim made by right or authority; as, a *requisition* for troops or supplies; state of being demanded and put to use; as, horses were in *requisition:* *v.t.* to demand; to claim by authority; as, to *requisition* food for troops; to make a demand upon, especially upon a country invaded in war; as, to *requisition* a district for supplies.

re-quit-al (rē-kwīt′ăl), *n.* the act of repaying or making return for; just return for good or evil; reward or punishment.

re-quite (rē-kwīt′), *v.t.* to repay or return good or evil to; reward; punish; as, to *requite* one for a kindness; to repay or return good or evil for; as, to *requite* kindness with ingratitude.—*n.* **requiter.**

rere-dos (rēr′dŏs), *n.* an ornamental screen behind an altar.

re-scind (rē-sĭnd′), *v.t.* to recall; repeal, annul or cancel; as, to *rescind* a law.—*n.* **rescission.**

re-script (rē′skrĭpt), *n.* an edict or order, especially of an emperor or Pope in answer to some question officially submitted to him, and having the force of a law; hence, any official edict or order.

res-cue (rĕs′kū), *n.* deliverance from danger, imprisonment, or violence; forcible retaking of persons or goods held by legal authority: *v.t.* to set free from danger, imprisonment, or violence; liberate; save.—*n.* **rescuer.**

re-search (rē-sûrch′), *n.* careful inquiry or investigation; the effort to find fresh information in history, science, literature, etc., by a method of thorough investigation of sources; as, literary *research.* —*n.* **researcher.**

re-sem-blance (rē-zĕm′blāns), *n.* likeness; similarity of outward appearance.

re-sem-ble (rē-zĕm′bl), *v.t.* to be like to in appearance, character, etc.; as, the brothers *resemble* each other.

re-sent (rē-zĕnt′), *v.t.* to consider as an injury or insult; to be angry because of; be indignant at.

re-sent-ful (rē-zĕnt′fo͝ol), *adj.* disposed to consider oneself affronted; full of displeasure because of a wrong.—*adv.* **resentfully.**

re-sent-ment (rē-zĕnt′mĕnt), *n.* strong anger or displeasure because of a wrong; deep sense of injury with a feeling of ill will; indignant feeling.

res-er-va-tion (rĕz″ẽr-vā′shŭn), *n.* a holding back, or hiding; anything held back or concealed; a keeping back for oneself of a right or interest; as, the *reservation* of all rights in a published work; a withholding of full acceptance or agreement; as, to make a mental *reservation;* public land kept for some special use; as, an Indian *reservation.*

re-serve (rē-zûrv′), *n.* that which is kept in store for future use or for a particular purpose; a tract of land set apart for a special purpose; the act of suppressing or holding back; as, to state without *reserve;* that which is held back; restraint in speech and manner; the keeping of one's own counsel; funds kept on hand by a bank for emergencies: *pl.* troops not in action, but kept for the support of an army, or to meet any sudden need: *v.t.* to set aside and keep for future use; to keep as one's own; hold; as, to *reserve* all rights in a book; to except from something granted: **Federal Reserve Bank,** a bank with several branches, organized by the United States government, which issues money in the form of bank notes, and makes loans to other banks.

re-served (rē-zûrvd'), *p.adj.* keeping one's thoughts to oneself; showing little feeling; as, a *reserved* manner; kept back for future use; as, *reserved* seats.—*adv.* **reservedly.**—*n.* **reservedness.**

res-er-voir (rĕz'ĕr-vwôr), *n.* a place where anything, especially water, is collected and stored up for use; a reserve; a store.

re-side (rē-zīd'), *v.i.* to dwell for a length of time; live; to exist as an attribute or element.

res-i-dence (rĕz'ĭ-dĕns), *n.* the place where one lives; a settled or permanent home; state of living in a place more or less permanently.

res-i-dent (rĕz'ĭ-dĕnt), *n.* one who lives in a place; a government agent at a foreign court: *adj.* living in a place; as, a *resident* physician of a hospital.

res-i-den-tial (rĕz'ĭ-dĕn'shăl), *adj.* pertaining to, connected with, or fitted for, dwelling places; suitable for living or staying in; as, the *residential* parts of a city.

re-sid-u-al (rē-zĭd'ū-ăl), *adj.* remaining after a part has been taken away.

re-sid-u-a-ry (rē-zĭd'ū-ā-rĭ), *adj.* pertaining to, or consisting of, the remainder: **residuary legatee,** a person to whom is left the remainder of an estate, after deducting particular bequests, debts, and legal expenses.

res-i-due (rĕz'ĭ-dū), *n.* that which remains after a part has been removed; remainder; that part of an estate that remains after all debts, charges, and particular bequests have been paid.

re-sid-u-um (rē-zĭd'ū-ŭm), *n.* that which is left after any process of subtraction, purification, etc.

re-sign (rē-zīn'), *v.t.* to yield to another; surrender formally; give up; submit calmly; as, to *resign* oneself to a loss: *v.i.* to withdraw from a position or office.

res-ig-na-tion (rĕz'ĭg-nā'shŭn), *n.* the act of giving up or yielding; patient submission; a bowing to misfortune.

re-signed (rē-zīnd'), *p.adj.* submissive; yielding.—*adv.* **resignedly.**—*n.* **resignedness.**

re-sil-i-ence (rē-zĭl'ĭ-ĕns), *n.* the act or power of springing back to an original position; elasticity; as, the *resilience* of a rubber band. Also, **resiliency.**

re-sil-i-ent (rē-zĭl'ĭ-ĕnt), *adj.* springing back to a former position; elastic; having power of recovery; buoyant.

res-in (rĕz'ĭn), *n.* any of various oily, gummy substances obtained from certain trees, and dissolving in alcohol but not in water.—*adj.* **resinous.**

re-sist (rē-zĭst'), *v.t.* to oppose, try to conquer or ward off; set oneself against: *v.i.* to offer opposition; refuse to obey or agree.

re-sist-ance (rē-zĭs'tăns), *n.* the act of opposing; a striving against; any force that works against another to prevent motion or to make it slower; the amount of power possessed by a body to oppose the passage through it of an electric current.

re-sist-ant (rē-zĭs'tănt), *n.* one who, or that which, opposes or strives against: *adj.* opposing or acting against.

re-sist-i-ble (rē-zĭs'tĭ-bl), *adj.* capable of being opposed or withstood.

re-sist-less (rē-zĭst'lĕs), *adj.* having no power to oppose or withstand; powerless; not to be withstood; as, *resistless* energy.—*adv.* **resistlessly.**—*n.* **resistlessness.**

res-o-lute (rĕz'ō-lūt), *adj.* determined; having a fixed purpose; as, a *resolute* will; decided; not to be shaken.—*adv.* **resolutely.**—*n.* **resoluteness.**

res-o-lu-tion (rĕz'ō-lū'shŭn), *n.* the act of bringing something, as a chemical compound, into a simpler form or of dividing it into the parts of which it is made up; analysis; fixed determination; firmness of purpose; the purpose decided upon; a formal proposal or statement voted on and adopted in a legislative assembly or public meeting; as, the Senate passed a *resolution* to increase the army.

re-solve (rē-zŏlv'), *v.t.* to change in form by formal vote; as, the board *resolved* itself into a committee; reduce to simpler form; as, the matter *resolves* itself into a mere question of right and wrong; separate into the parts of which the whole is made up; as, to *resolve* a word into its elements; take to pieces; free from doubt or difficulty; explain; clear up; as, to *resolve* a mystery; work out or solve, as a problem; make up one's mind to; decide; determine; as, he *resolved* to do better; adopt by vote: *v.i.* to separate into elements or parts; be analyzed in any way; come to a determination; pass a formal resolution: *n.* fixed purpose; determination; that which has been determined on; a resolution.

re-solved (rē-zŏlvd'), *p.adj.* firm in purpose; determined.

re-sol-vent (rē-zŏl'vĕnt), *n.* in medicine, that which will reduce or scatter a swelling: *adj.* having power to cause separation into the parts of which the whole is made up.

res-o-nance (rĕz'ō-năns), *n.* the ability to send back or prolong sound; a round, full, vibrating quality of sound; as, the *resonance* of an organ; in physics, the lengthening or strengthening of a sound owing to sympathetic vibrations of a body set in motion by the waves of sound. Also, **resonancy.**

res-o-nant (rĕz'ō-nănt), *adj.* having the ability to return or prolong sound; echoing back; as, the *resonant* walls of a cave; round, full, and vibrant in sound; lengthened or strengthened in sound by sympathetic vibrations of another body.

re-sort (rē-zôrt'), *n.* act of visiting a place frequently; a place much visited; as, a summer *resort;* that to which, or a person to whom, one applies for aid; as, charity is his final *resort;* refuge; act of going for aid, advantage, etc.: *v.i.* to go often; betake oneself; to apply for assistance or for the gaining of an end; as, to *resort* to law.

re-sound (rē-zound'), *v.i.* to sound loudly; as, his voice *resounded* far; to be full of sound; as, the woods *resound* with song; be echoed; as, his shout *resounded* through the cave.

re-source (rē-sōrs'), *n.* that on which one depends for help or supply; knowledge of what to do in an emergency or difficulty; as, a man of *resource*: *pl.* money or means of raising money; means of any kind which can be made use of; as, a country's natural *resources*.

re-source-ful (rē-sōrs'fōōl), *adj.* full of the ability necessary to meet unusual demands or sudden needs.—*n.* **resourcefulness.**

re-spect (rē-spĕkt'), *n.* regard for worth; honor and esteem; as, the world's *respect* for a great man; thoughtful and attentive notice; as, have *respect* for my words; undue favor or bias; as, to show *respect* for wealth; courteous manner of treating others; a special point or particular; as, in certain *respects*; relation, reference, or regard; as, with *respect* to: *pl.* expression of good-will or regard; as, to pay one's *respects*: *v.t.* to honor or esteem; as, the world *respects* a good man; notice; heed; as, to *respect* the advice of parents; avoid intrusion upon; as, to *respect* private property; have relation to; as, the matter *respects* our welfare.

re-spect-a-bil-i-ty (rē-spĕk"tȧ-bĭl'ĭ-tĭ), *n.* the state or quality of being of good reputation, or good name; fair social standing.

re-spect-a-ble (rē-spĕk'tȧ-bl), *adj.* worthy of regard or esteem; being of good name, or repute; as, a *respectable* woman; of moderate excellence or size; as, a *respectable* performance; a *respectable* audience; fairly good.—*adv.* **respectably.**—*n.* **respectableness.**

re-spect-ful (rē-spĕkt'fōōl), *adj.* full of, or marked by, proper regard, esteem, or courtesy; as, a *respectful* manner.—*adv.* **respectfully.**—*n.* **respectfulness.**

re-spect-ing (rē-spĕk'tĭng), *prep.* concerning; with regard or relation to; as, *respecting* his conduct there is but one opinion.

re-spec-tive (rē-spĕk'tĭv), *adj.* relating to each of several persons or things; particular; as, their *respective* positions; the *respective* merits of two dogs.

re-spec-tive-ly (rē-spĕk'tĭv-lĭ), *adv.* as relating to each; as singly considered in the order named; as, the red, blue, and green ties are for James, George, and William, *respectively*.

re-spir-a-ble (rē-spīr'ȧ-bl; rĕs'pĭ-rȧ-bl), *adj.* that may be, or is fit to be, breathed; as, *respirable* air.

res-pi-ra-tion (rĕs"pĭ-rā'shŭn), *n.* the act or process of breathing.

res-pi-ra-tor (rĕs'pĭ-rā"tẽr), *n.* a helmet of cloth or other material, usually chemically treated, with glass eyeholes, worn in the World War as a protection against poison gas: used also in certain medical treatments.

re-spir-a-to-ry (rē-spīr'ȧ-tō-rĭ; rĕs'pĭ-rȧ-tō-rĭ), *adj.* pertaining to, serving for, or caused by, breathing.

re-spire (rē spīr'), *v.i.* to breathe: *v.t.* to breathe in and out, as air.

res-pite (rĕs'pĭt), *n.* a temporary putting off of the carrying out of a sentence; as, the murderer was granted a *respite*; postponement; delay; brief period of rest; as, a *respite* from labor: *v.t.* to grant a delay in the carrying out of a sentence upon; as, to *respite* a criminal; to relieve by a short period of rest.

Syn., *n.* forbearance, pause, interval, reprieve, stay.

re-splend-ence (rē-splĕn'dĕns), *n.* brilliant luster; intense light; splendor. Also, **resplendency.**

re-splend-ent (rē-splĕn'dĕnt), *adj.* shining brilliantly; lustrous; intensely bright; splendid.—*adv.* **resplendently.**

re-spond (rē-spŏnd'), *v.i.* to return an answer; make a reply; to act in answer or sympathy; as, the heart will *respond* to a friend's sorrow; be liable; as, the defendant is held to *respond* in damages: *v.t.* to answer or reply.

re-spond-ent (rē-spŏn'dĕnt), *n.* one who answers or replies; one who answers to a suit at law; a defendant: *adj.* giving, or given as, reply; answering.

re-sponse (rē-spŏns'), *n.* the act of answering; answer; reply; in a religious service, words said or sung by the congregation or choir in reply to the priest; an act or feeling called forth by something; as, a *response* to an appeal for the Red Cross.

re-spon-si-bil-i-ty (rē-spŏn"sĭ-bĭl'ĭ-tĭ), *n.* state of being answerable or accountable; a duty or obligation; ability to fulfil contracts.

re-spon-si-ble (rē-spŏn'sĭ-bl), *adj.* involving trust, duty, or obligation; as, a *responsible* position; answerable; liable to answer; as, a guardian is *responsible* to the law; able to answer for one's conduct; trustworthy.—*adv.* **responsibly.**—*n.* **responsibleness.**

re-spon-sive (rē-spŏn'sĭv), *adj.* answering; ready or inclined to answer; easily moved to action or feeling; as, a *responsive* audience.—*adv.* **responsively.**—*n.* **responsiveness.**

rest (rĕst), *n.* a ceasing from motion or labor; quiet; peace; repose; sleep; hence, death; place of quiet or repose; in music, a period of silence and its sign; a short pause in reading; that on which anything leans for support; **the rest**, a remainder; the others: *v.i.* to stop moving or acting; be quiet; to take repose; sleep; be dead; be free from excitement, annoyance, etc.; be at peace; to trust; be supported; stand; lean; to remain in one place: *v.t.* cause to cease from labor; cause to take repose; place on a support; lay; lean; to base or ground.

Syn., *n.* calm, ease, peace, quiet.

Ant. (see movement).

res-tau-rant (rĕs'tō-rȧnt), *n.* a house where meals or refreshments are served to the public.

res-tau-ra-teur (rĕs"tō"rȧ-tûr'), *n.* the keeper of a restaurant, or public eating house. [Fr.]

rest bil-let (rĕst bĭl'ĕt), a place of rest and shelter, as a house or barn, to which a soldier goes when relieved from active service in the trenches.

rest-ful (rĕst'fōōl), *adj.* full of, or giving, repose; as, *restful* sleep; being in repose; quiet.—*adv.* **restfully.**—*n.* **restfulness.**

res-ti-tu-tion (rĕs"tĭ-tū'shŭn), *n.* the act of giving back to the rightful owner that which has been taken

away or lost, or of making good any loss, injury, or damage.
Syn. return, restoration, compensation, amends.

res-tive (rĕs'tĭv), *adj.* unwilling to go forward; stubborn; uneasy; restless under control; as, a *restive* horse.—*adv.* **restively.**—*n.* **restiveness.**
Syn. fidgety, impatient, unruly.

rest-less (rĕst'lĕs), *adj.* without repose; uneasy; as, a *restless* manner; always active or in motion; never quiet; as, a *restless* child; *restless* waves; discontented; eager for change; as, a *restless* spirit; affording no repose; as, a *restless* night; sleepless.—*adv.* **restlessly.**—*n.* **restlessness.**

res-to-ra-tion (rĕs"tō-rā'shŭn), *n.* the act of bringing back a person or thing to a former state or place; state of being brought back to a former state or place; as, *restoration* to health; *restoration* to office; renewal; repair; return: **Restoration,** the return of Charles II to the throne of England in 1660.

re-stor-a-tive (rē-stŏr'ȧ-tĭv), *n.* that which has power to bring back to a former state; a medicine used to bring back health or strength; something that brings back consciousness after fainting: *adj.* having power to bring back to a former state.

re-store (rē-stōr'), *v.t.* to bring back to a former state; repair; rebuild; to bring back to the owner; to return.—*n.* **restorer.**
Syn. renew, replace, repay, revive, cure, heal.

re-strain (rē-strān'), *v.t.* to check; to hold back; as, to *restrain* one's feelings; to limit; set bounds to; as, to *restrain* a people's liberty.—*n.* **restrainer.**
Syn. bridle, confine, curb, hold.
Ant. (see free).

re-straint (rē-strānt'), *n.* the act of holding back or hindering from action of any kind; state of being held back or hindered; reserve; confinement.

re-strict (rē-strĭkt'), *v.t.* to keep within bounds; to confine or limit; as, to *restrict* a patient to a certain diet; to *restrict* the power of a government.—*p.adj.* **restricted.**—*adv.* **restrictedly.**

re-stric-tion (rē-strĭk'shŭn), *n.* the act of limiting; state of being limited; confinement within bounds; limitation; a rule preventing entire freedom; as, building *restrictions.*

re-stric-tive (rē-strĭk'tĭv), *adj.* serving or tending to limit; as, *restrictive* laws of trade.—*adv.* **restrictively.**

re-sult (rē-zŭlt'), *n.* conclusion or end to which any course or condition of things leads; consequence; effect; as, the *result* of overeating: *v.i.* to follow as a consequence or effect; as, much good will *result* from this law; be an outcome; end.

re-sult-ant (rē-zŭl'tănt), *n.* that which follows as a consequence: *adj.* following as a consequence.

ré-su-mé (rā"zü"mā'), *n.* a summary; as, a *résumé* of a book. [FR.]

re-sume (rē-zūm'), *v.t.* to take up again after interruption; begin again; as, to *resume* work; *resume* a conversation.

re-sump-tion (rē-zŭmp'shŭn), *n.* the act of taking up again after interruption, or of beginning again; as, the *resumption* of one's duties.

re-sur-gent (rē-sûr'jĕnt), *adj.* rising again, as from the grave: *n.* one who rises again, as from the dead.—*n.* **resurgence.**

res-ur-rect (rĕz"ŭ-rĕkt'), *v.t.* to raise from the dead; colloquially, to bring again to notice or use.

res-ur-rec-tion (rĕz"ŭ-rĕk'shŭn), *n.* a rising again; a springing into new life and freshness; especially, the rising again from the dead.

res-ur-rec-tion-ist (rĕz"ŭ-rĕk'shŭn-ĭst), *n.* one who steals dead bodies from their graves and sells them for dissection; a body-snatcher; one who revives.

re-sus-ci-tate (rē-sŭs'ĭ-tāt), *v.t.* to restore from apparent death; as, to *resuscitate* a drowned person: *v.i.* revive.

re-sus-ci-ta-tion (rē-sŭs"ĭ-tā'shŭn), *n.* the act of restoring to life; state of being restored to life.

re-sus-ci-ta-tive (rē-sŭs'ĭ-tā tĭv), *adj.* having power to bring back to life; restorative.

re-tail (rē'tāl), *n.* sale of goods in small quantities: opposite to *wholesale:* *adj.* pertaining to, or engaged in, the sale of goods in small quantities: *v.t.* (rē-tāl'; rē'tāl), to sell in small quantities, or directly to the consumer; to tell here and there; as, to *retail* gossip: *v.i.* to sell goods in small quantities.—*n.* **retailer.**

re-tain (rē-tān'), *v.t.* to hold or keep in possession; engage by a fee prepaid; hire; as, to *retain* a lawyer; keep in mind; remember.

re-tain-er (rē-tān'ẽr), *n.* one kept in the service of a person of high rank or position; an adherent; fee paid to a lawyer; also, the agreement made to employ a lawyer in a suit.

re-tain-ing wall (rē-tān'ĭng wôl), a wall to prevent a bank of earth from sliding; sometimes, a revetment. Also, **retain wall.**

re-tal-i-ate (rē-tăl'ĭ-āt), *v.t.* to return something of the same kind for; as, to *retaliate* a wrong: *v.i.* to give like for like, especially, evil for evil; as, to *retaliate* for a wrong.

re-tal-i-a-tion (rē-tăl"ĭ-ā'shŭn), *n.* the act of returning like for like, especially evil for evil; revenge.

re-tal-i-a-tive (rē-tăl'ĭ-ā-tĭv), *adj.* returning like for like, especially evil for evil; revengeful.

re-tal-i-a-to-ry (rē-tăl'ĭ-ȧ-tō-rĭ), *adj.* returning like for like, especially evil for evil.

re-tard (rē-tärd'), *v.t.* to cause to move more slowly; hinder; delay; defer; put off: *n.* delay.—*n.* **retarder.**

re-tar-da-tion (rē"tär-dā'shŭn), *n.* the act of holding back or hindering; a lessening of speed or progress; delay; hindrance; the amount of delay or hindrance.

retch (rĕch), *v.i.* to try to vomit; strain, as in vomiting.

re-ten-tion (rē-tĕn'shŭn), *n.* the act of keeping in one's power or possession; the state of being kept in possession; act of keeping, or power of keeping, things in the mind; memory.

re-ten-tive (rē-tĕn'tĭv), *adj.* tending, or having the power, to keep; as, a *retentive* memory.—*adv.* **retentively.**—*n.* **retentiveness.**

ret-i-cence (rĕt'ĭ-sĕns), *n.* the quality, act, or habit of keeping silence; reserve in speech. Also, **reticency.**

ret-i-cent (rĕt'ĭ-sĕnt), *adj.* disposed not to tell one's thoughts or feelings; silent; reserved in speech; as, a *reticent* man.—*adv.* **reticently.**

re-tic-u-lar (rē-tĭk′ū-lẽr), *adj.* like a network.

re-tic-u-late (rē-tĭk′ū-lāt), *v.t.* to make network of; to mark like a network: *v.i.* to form a network: *adj.* (rē-tĭk′ū-lāt), marked or veined like network; formed of fibers woven like network.—*n.* **reticulation.**

ret-i-cule (rĕt′ĭ-kūl), *n.* a small handbag or workbag, originally made of network, carried by women.

re-ti-form (rē′tĭ-fôrm), *adj.* arranged like a network.

ret-i-na (rĕt′ĭ-nȧ), *n.* the inner coat of the eye, containing the ends of the nerves of sight: that part of the eye which receives the images seen.

ret-i-nue (rĕt′ĭ-nū), *n.* the suite, or body of persons who attend a prince or person of distinction; train of attendants.

re-tire (rē-tīr′), *v.i.* to go to a place of privacy; withdraw; retreat; withdraw from business, official, or active life; to go to bed: *v.t.* to withdraw; as, to *retire* forces; to withdraw from circulation, or from the market; as, to *retire* stocks or currency; to cause to give up active service; as, to *retire* a policeman or naval officer.

re-tired (rē-tīrd′), *adj.* away or withdrawn from society; quiet; having given up business, etc.; private.

re-tire-ment (rē-tīr′mĕnt), *n.* the act of retreating or withdrawing; state of being withdrawn; privacy; solitude; a place removed from public notice.

re-tir-ing (rē-tīr′ĭng), *adj.* modest; not forward; quiet; shy; as, a *retiring* manner; of or pertaining to withdrawal from active service; as, a *retiring* board or pension.

re-tort (rē-tôrt′), *n.* the reply to an argument, charge, incivility, taunt, or witticism; a quick and witty or severe response; a vessel used in distilling or in decomposing by heat: *v.t.* to return, as an argument or accusation; as, to *retort* the charge of vanity; to say in sharp or spiteful reply: *v.i.* to make a quick, sharp answer; to return an argument or a charge.

re-touch (rē-tŭch′), *v.t.* to touch again; improve by going over; as, to *retouch* a work of art.

re-trace (rē-trās′), *v.t.* to follow back toward the place of beginning; to follow again from the beginning.

re-tract (rē-trăkt′), *v.t.* to draw back; to draw up or shorten; as, the cat can *retract* its claws; to recall or withdraw; as, to *retract* a charge of theft: *v.i.* to withdraw something said or written; to draw back or draw up; as, muscles *retract* after amputation.

re-trac-tile (rē-trăk′tĭl), *adj.* capable of being withdrawn, drawn up, or drawn in. Also, **retractable, retractible.**

re-trac-tion (rē-trăk′shŭn), *n.* act of taking back what has been said or written; act of drawing in or back; state of being withdrawn. Also, **retractation.**

re-trac-tor (rē-trăk′tẽr), *n.* one who, or that which, draws in or back; a muscle or an instrument for drawing back.

re-treat (rē-trēt′), *n.* the act of withdrawing or retiring; retirement or seclusion; place of privacy; shelter; asylum; the retiring of troops from the face of an enemy or from an advanced position; a bugle call which is a signal for retiring from an engagement, or to quarters: *v.i.* to go back or backward; withdraw to seclusion or to a place of safety; retire before an enemy.

re-trench (rē-trĕnch′), *v.t.* to reduce; lessen; to take away; as, to *retrench* certain rights: *v.i.* to cut down expenses.

Syn. abridge, decrease, diminish, economize.
Ant. (see expand, squander).

re-trench-ment (rē-trĕnch′mĕnt), *n.* act of reducing or lessening; reduction of expenses; a military work constructed inside another to resist an enemy should the outer line be taken.

re-tri-al (rē-trī′ăl), *n.* another trial; a second trial.

ret-ri-bu-tion (rĕt″rĭ-bū′shŭn), *n.* reward or punishment suitable to the action; especially, loss or evil inflicted as a just punishment.

re-trib-u-tive (rē-trĭb′ū-tĭv), *adj.* rewarding for good deeds and punishing for offenses; as, *retributive* justice.—*adv.* **retributively.**

re-trib-u-to-ry (rē-trĭb′ū-tō-rĭ), *adj.* serving as, or making, just reward or punishment.

re-triev-a-ble (rē-trēv′ȧ-bl), *adj.* capable of being recovered or restored; as, a *retrievable* loss.

re-triev-al (rē-trēv′ăl), *n.* the act of regaining or restoring; restoration from damage, failure, or loss.

re-trieve (rē-trēv′), *v.t.* to recover; regain; as, to *retrieve* a lost advantage; to restore; revive; as, to *retrieve* one's good name; to repair the harm done by; as, to *retrieve* a misfortune; to find and bring in (wounded or killed game), in hunting: *v.i.* to find and bring in game.

re-triev-er (rē-trēv′ẽr), *n.* a dog trained to find and bring in game.

re-tro-act (rē″trō-ăkt′; rĕt″rō-ăkt′), *v.i.* to act backward or in opposition; to affect by action that which has been done in the past; to alter the results of past action.—*adj.* **retroactive.**—*n.* **retroaction.**

re-tro-cede (rē″trō-sēd′; rĕt″rō-sēd′), *v.t.* to grant or give back; return: *v.i.* to go back; recede.

re-tro-ces-sion (rē″trō-sĕsh′ŭn; rĕt″-rō-sĕsh′ŭn), *n.* the act of going back; a retiring or retreating; the act of granting or giving back.

ret-ro-grade (rĕt′rō-grād; rē′trō-grād), *adj.* going or moving backward; reversed; retreating; going from a better to a worse state or character; as, a *retrograde* people, *retrograde* ideas: *v.i.* to go or appear to go backward or in an opposite direction; to go from better to worse.

re-tro-gres-sion (rē″trō-grĕsh′ŭn; (rĕt′rō-grĕsh′ŭn), *n.* the act of going or moving backward; retreat.

re-tro-gres-sive (rē″trō-grĕs′ĭv; rĕt″-rō-grĕs′ĭv), *adj.* going or moving backward; passing from a better to a worse state; retrograde.

ret-ro-spect (rĕt′rō-spĕkt; rē′trō-spĕkt), *n.* a looking back on things past; a review of the past.

ret-ro-spec-tion (rĕt″rō-spĕk′shŭn; rē″trō-spĕk′shŭn), *n.* the act of looking back on the past; meditation upon things past; a calling to remembrance.

ret-ro-spec-tive (rĕt″rō-spĕk′tĭv; rē″trō-spĕk′tĭv), *adj.* looking back, or given to looking back, on things past; referring to the past.—*adv.* **retrospectively.**

re-trous-sé (rẽ-trōō″sā′), *adj.* turned up; as, a *retroussé* nose. [Fr.]

re-tro-ver-sion (rē″trō-vûr′shŭn; rĕt″rō-vûr′shŭn), *n.* a turning or bending backward; the state of being turned or bent backward.

re-turn (rē-tûrn′), *n.* a coming or going back to or from a place, condition, etc.; as, one's *return* from a vacation; a *return* to health; a restoring or giving back; as, the *return* of a lost ring or borrowed book; repayment; that which is received from labor, investment, etc.; profit; advantage; a formal report or statement of results; as, election *returns;* a response or answer: *pl.* results; proceeds: *v.i.* to come or go back again to the same place or state; as, to *return* to one's home; to begin or appear again; as, spring *returns;* go back in thought, etc.; as, to *return* to the subject; to pass back into possession, as an estate; reply: *v.t.* to send, carry, or put back; restore; as, to *return* a borrowed book; to repay; as, to *return* a call; to produce or yield; as, the garden will *return* a large profit; to send in reply; as, to *return* an answer; report officially; render or give in, as to a superior; as, to *return* a report; elect; as, to *return* a man to office.

re-turn-a-ble (rē-tûrn′ȧ-bl), *adj.* capable of being given back; due, or required to be given back at a certain time and place; as, a book *returnable* within seven days.

re-un-ion (rē-ūn′yŭn), *n.* act of joining again; state of being joined again; a gathering of friends or of members of a family who have been separated.

re-u-nite (rē″ū-nīt′), *v.t.* to bring together or join again; reconcile after disagreement: *v.i.* to become joined again.

re-vamp (rē-vămp′), *v.t.* to supply (a shoe) with a new vamp, or upper: hence, to patch; make over; fit up anew.

re-veal (rē-vēl′), *v.t.* to make known; disclose; unveil; especially, to communicate, or make known, by divine or supernatural means.

re-veil-le (rē-vāl′yȧ; rĕv″ē-lē′; rĕv′ē-lē″), *n.* the early morning beat of a drum, or a bugle call, which turns the soldier or sailor out for his day's work.

rev-el (rĕv′ĕl), *n.* a noisy or riotous feast; wild merrymaking: *v.i.* to take part in wild merrymaking; to take great delight: with *in;* as, to *revel* in music or art.

rev-e-la-tion (rĕv″ē-lā′shŭn), *n.* the act of making known that which before was secret or private; state of being made known; that which is made known: **Revelation**, the last book of the New Testament, containing that which was made known to the apostle John concerning the Church of Christ; the Apocalypse.

rev-el-er (rĕv′ĕl-ẽr), *n.* one who takes part in wild merrymaking.

rev-el-ry (rĕv′ĕl-rĭ), *n.* noisy or boisterous merrymaking or festivity.

re-venge (rē-vĕnj′), *n.* the act of returning an injury; malicious injury in return for an injury or offense received; a feeling of desire to return evil for evil; an opportunity of getting satisfaction; as, to give a card player his *revenge:* *v.t.* to inflict pain or punishment in return for; avenge; as, to *revenge* an insult.—*n.* **revenger.**

Syn., *n.* vengeance, requital.

Ant. (see forgiveness).

re-venge-ful (rē-vĕnj′fŏŏl), *adj.* full of the desire to inflict harm or injury in return for i⁻jury received.—*adv.* **revengefully.**—*n.* **revengefulness.**

rev-e-nue (rĕv′ē-nū), *n.* that which returns, or comes back, from an investment; income from any property; the general income of a state, etc., from taxes, customs, etc.

Syn. produce, income, proceeds, fruits, wealth.

re-ver-ber-ant (rē-vûr′bẽr-ănt), *adj.* returning sound; resonant.

re-ver-ber-ate (rē-vûr′bẽr-āt), *v.t.* to send back; echo, as sound; reflect, as heat or light: *v.i.* to be driven back, or reflected, as heat or light; resound; reëcho, as sound.

re-ver-ber-a-tion (rē-vûr″bẽr-ā′shŭn), *n.* the act of reflecting light or heat, or reëchoing sound; reflection; echo.

re-ver-ber-a-tory (rē-vûr′bẽr-ȧ-tō-rĭ), *adj.* acting so as to send back or reflect flame or heat; as, a *reverberatory* furnace; reflecting; forced back, as flame.

re-vere (rē-vēr′), *v.t.* to regard with respect and affection mingled with awe or fear; to honor.

rev-er-ence (rĕv′ẽr-ĕns), *n.* deep respect mingled with awe and affection; veneration; a low bow to show respect; a title given to the clergy: with *his, your:* *v.t.* to regard with respect and affection mingled with awe or fear; to bow to with great respect.

Syn., *n.* deference, homage, worship.

rev-er-end (rĕv′ẽr-ĕnd), *adj.* worthy of reverence, or deep respect; of or pertaining to the clergy: **Reverend**, a title of respect given to clergymen.

rev-er-ent (rĕv′ẽr-ĕnt), *adj.* showing, or expressive of, respect and affection mingled with awe or fear; humble; submissive.—*adv.* **reverently.**

rev-er-en-tial (rĕv″ẽr-ĕn′shăl), *adj.* proceeding from or showing deep respect mingled with awe and affection; reverent.—*adv.* **reverentially.**

rev-er-ie (rĕv′ẽr-ĭ), *n.* deep musing; dreaminess; state of being lost in thought or dreams. Also, **revery.**

re-ver-sal (rē-vûr′săl), *n.* the causing to turn back or move in an opposite direction; as, the *reversal* of a rotating wheel; a causing to stand or lie upside down; a change to an opposite or to a former state; a setting aside or annulling; as, the *reversal* of a judgment.

re-verse (rē-vûrs′), *n.* the direct contrary or opposite; the back of a coin or medal: opposite to *obverse;* a change for the worse; misfortune; as, business *reverses;* check; defeat; as, the enemy met with a *reverse:* *v.t.* to turn back or upside down; to cause to move in an opposite direction; to put each in the place of the other; as, to *reverse* their positions; to set aside or annul; as, to *reverse* a judgment; revoke: *v.i.* to move in an opposite direction; change to a former state: *adj.* turned backward; opposite; causing an opposite motion; as the *reverse* gear in an automobile.—*adv.* **reversely.**

re-vers-i-ble (rē-vûr′sĭ-bl), *adj.* capable of being turned back or of being put each in the place of the other; that may be used on both sides; as, *reversible* cloth; that may be set aside, or annulled; as, a *reversible* judgment.

re-ver-sion (rē-vûr′shŭn), *n.* the returning of lands, etc., by law to the grantor or his heirs after the grant has terminated; right to future possession; as, the *reversion* of a title; return of an animal or plant to its original type or state.

re-ver-sion-a-ry (rē-vûr'shŭn-ā-rĭ), *adj.* pertaining to, of the nature of, or involving, the returning of an estate to the grantor or his heirs after the grant has terminated; pertaining to the right of future possession.

re-vert (rē-vûrt'), *v.i.* to return or go back; recur; return to the original owner or his heirs.

re-vert-i-ble (rē-vûr'tĭ-bl), *adj.* capable of being turned back; that may or must be returned to the original owner or his heirs; as, a *revertible* estate.

rev-er-y (rĕv'ĕr-ĭ), *n.* deep musing; state of being lost in thought. Also, **reverie.**

re-vest (rē-vĕst'), *v.t.* to clothe or vest again, as with rank or office; as, to *revest* a judge with authority.

re-vet-ment (rē-vĕt'mĕnt), *n.* a facing of stone or other materials for protecting a bank of earth, etc., as in fortifications; a retaining wall: **revetment hurdle,** a movable obstacle, usually constructed of barbed wire on metal posts, used to protect trenches or other military works. Also, **revetement.**

re-view (rē-vū'), *n.* a going over anything again; reëxamination by a higher court of the decision of a lower court; a lesson studied or recited again; survey of the past; a criticism, especially of a new publication; a magazine or newspaper with criticisms on new books, essays, etc.; inspection of troops under arms, by a higher officer, for the purpose of ascertaining the state of their discipline, equipment, etc.: *v.t.* to study or examine again; to go over in order to make corrections; revise; examine critically; inspect, as troops, etc.; write a critical notice of; look back on: *v.i.* to write criticisms of books, etc.—*n.* **reviewer.**

re-vile (rē-vīl'), *v.t.* to address with abusive or vile language; heap abuse upon.—*n.* **reviler.**

re-vise (rē-vīz'), *v.t.* to go over and examine for correction; to change and correct; as, to *revise* a manuscript: *n.* a review or revision.—*n.* **reviser, rev sor.**

Syn., *v.* review, reconsider.

re-vi-sion (rē-vĭzh'ŭn), *n.* the act of examining for correction; as, the *revision* of a manuscript; that which has been examined and corrected; a corrected form or edition.

re-viv-al (rē-vīv'ăl), *n.* renewed attention to, or interest in, something, as art, literature, religion, after a period of indifference; a meeting or series of meetings to arouse and stimulate interest in religion; recovery, as of spirits; restoration to life; renewed performance of; reproduction; as, the *revival* of an old play.

re-viv-al-ist (rē-vīv'ăl-ĭst), *n.* one who devotes his time to bringing about a religious awakening, and who conducts meetings or uses other means to arouse interest in religion.

re-vive (rē-vīv'), *v.i.* to come back to life; as, hope *revived* in him; return to vigor or activity, especially from a state of languor, neglect, etc.; as, learning *revived* in the fifteenth century; return to consciousness again; as, to *revive* after a fainting spell: *v.t.* to restore to life again; to give new vigor to; refresh; to bring back from a state of neglect; to recall to the mind.—*n.* **reviver.**

Syn. renew, animate, cheer.

re-viv-i-fy (rē-vĭv'ĭ-fī), *v.t.* [*p.t.* and *p.p.* revivified, *p.pr.* revivifying], to renew life or interest in; restore life to; quicken.—*n.* **revivification.**

rev-o-ca-ble (rĕv'ō-kȧ-bl), *adj.* that may be taken back, or recalled; that may be annulled or repealed.

rev-o-ca-tion (rĕv'ō-kā'shŭn), *n.* the act of annulling or repealing; reversal; repeal; as, the *revocation* of a law.

re-voke (rē-vōk'), *v.t.* to make of no effect by recalling; repeal; annul; as, to *revoke* a law or license; *v.i.* in card playing, to fail to follow suit when able, in violation of the rules: *n.* the act of thus failing to follow suit at cards.

re-volt (re-vōlt'; rē-vōlt'), *n.* an outbreak or uprising against authority; rebellion: *v.i.* to turn away in disgust; be shocked; to rebel: *v.t.* to cause to turn away or shrink with disgust or loathing; shock.

re-volt-ing (rē-vōl'tĭng; rē-vōl'tĭng), *p.adj.* disgusting; loathsome; as, *revolting* cruelty.

rev-o-lu-tion (rĕv'ō-lū'shŭn), *n.* the motion of a body, especially a heavenly body, in a closed curve around a fixed point, or the complete turn of the body made in such a course; as, the *revolution* of the earth in its orbit; the motion of a body in spinning, or rotating, on an axis; as, the *revolution* of a wheel; the space measured by the regular return of a turning body; a succession of changes or events happening in a cycle; the time occupied by such a cycle; circuit; a decided and sudden change; as, a *revolution* in ideas or character; a sudden change in the government of a country; the overthrow of one form of government and the setting up of another, by the people.

Syn. confusion, disorder, mutiny, rebellion, anarchy.

rev-o-lu-tion-a-ry (rĕv'ō-lū'shŭn-ā-rĭ), *adj.* of, pertaining to, or of the nature of a sudden and complete change, especially in the government of a country: *n.* one who takes part in such a change.

rev-o-lu-tion-ist (rĕv'ō-lū'shŭn-ĭst), *n.* one who favors or takes part in a sudden and complete change, especially in the government of a country.

rev-o-lu-tion-ize (rĕv'ō-lū'shŭn-īz), *v.t.* to cause an entire change in the government, affairs, or character of.

re-volve (rē-vŏlv'), *v.i.* to turn round, as on an axis or in a curving path; rotate; to move in cycles; occur again and again at regular intervals: *v.t.* to cause to turn or roll around; to turn over and over in the mind.—*adj.* **revolvable.**

re-volv-er (rē-vŏl'vĕr), *n.* that which turns around; a pistol having chambers in a cylinder that turns around, so that it may be fired several times without reloading.

re-volv-ing (rē-vŏl'vĭng), *adj.* turning round; arranged or constructed to be turned around; as, a *revolving* grate or chair.

re-vul-sion (rē-vŭl'shŭn), *n.* a sudden and violent change, especially of feeling; act of holding or drawing back from something; a strong reaction; a violent recoil.—*adj.* **revulsive.**

re-ward (rē-wôrd'), *n.* something given as a return for good or ill received, or in appreciation of praiseworthy conduct; money offered for service or for the return of something lost: *v.t.* to give in return for (good or ill received); to show appreciation of by giving something; to make a return to (somebody) or for (something); as, to *reward* the winner, or to *reward* success; requite; recompense.

Rey-nard (rā'nàrd; rĕn'ẽrd), *n.* the name given to the fox in tales, poetry, etc.: from the old fable of "Reynard the Fox": **reynard**, a fox, as representing cunning.

rhap-sod-ic (răp-sŏd'ĭk), *adj.* pertaining to, or of the nature of, extravagant, emotional, and disconnected composition; as, a book of *rhapsodic* verses; too enthusiastic; disconnected; confused. Also, **rhapsodical**.

rhap-so-dist (răp'sō-dĭst), *n.* among the ancient Greeks, one whose profession was to recite the Homeric or other epics; as, the brotherhood of *rhapsodists;* one who makes or recites verses; one who writes or speaks disconnectedly and with great show of feeling.

rhap-so-dize (răp'sō-dīz), *v.t.* and *v.i.* to write or speak in a rapturous, emotional, and disconnected way.

rhap-so-dy (răp'sō-dĭ), *n.* [*pl.* **rhapsodies** (-dĭz)], a disconnected or rambling composition, composed under the influence of excitement and marked by over-enthusiasm; rapturous utterance; that part of an epic poem suitable for recitation at one time; a musical composition.

rhe-a (rē'ȧ), *n.* the South American ostrich; the grass-cloth plant.—**Rhea**, in Greek mythology, the mother of the gods.

Rhen-ish (rĕn'ĭsh), *adj.* of or pertaining to the river Rhine, or to the country near it: *n.* Rhine wine.

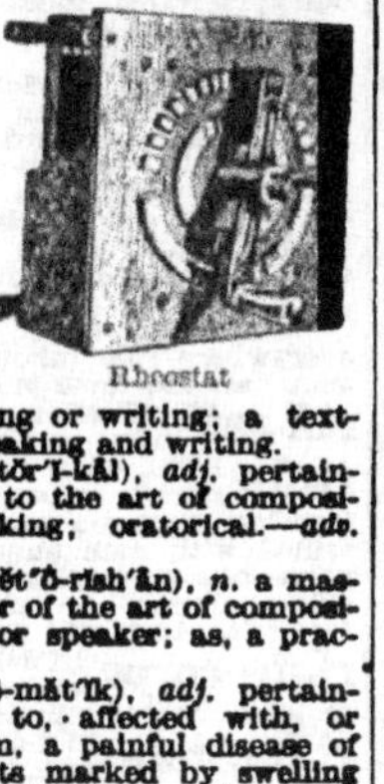

Rheostat

rhe-o-stat (rē'ō-stăt), *n.* an apparatus for regulating an electric current.

rhet-o-ric (rĕt'ō-rĭk), *n.* the art of speaking or writing with elegance and force; fine speaking without conviction or earnest feeling; the power of influencing by speaking or writing; a textbook on the art of speaking and writing.

rhe-tor-i-cal (rē-tŏr'ĭ-kăl), *adj.* pertaining to the art of composition or of fine speaking; oratorical.—*adv.* **rhetorically**.

rhet-o-ri-cian (rĕt'ō-rĭsh'ăn), *n.* a master of the art of composition; a showy writer or speaker; as, a practiced *rhetorician*.

rheu-mat-ic (ro͞o-măt'ĭk), *adj.* pertaining to, affected with, or caused by, rheumatism, a painful disease of the muscles and joints marked by swelling and stiffness; as, *rheumatic* inflammation. Also, **rheumatical**.

rheu-ma-tism (ro͞o'mȧ-tĭzm), *n.* a painful disease of the muscles and joints, often accompanied by swelling and stiffness.

rhine-stone (rīn'stōn'), *n.* a colorless stone, usually made of paste in imitation of a diamond, and used in cheap jewelry.

rhi-noc-er-os (rī-nŏs'ẽr-ŏs), *n.* a large, thick-skinned, herb-eating animal of tropical Asia and Africa, having one or two horns on the snout.

Rhinoceros. 1, African; 2, Asiatic.

rhi-zome (rī'zōm), *n.* a rootstock; a stem in the ground, which produces roots below and sends leaves above.

rho-di-um (rō'dĭ-ŭm), *n.* a whitish-gray metallic element, like platinum, rare and very hard.

rho-do-den-dron (rō'dō-dĕn'drŏn), *n.* a kind of evergreen shrub with large, handsome flowers of white, pink, or lavender.

rhom-boid (rŏm'boid), *n.* a four-sided figure of which the opposite sides are parallel and equal and the adjoining sides unequal, and whose angles not right angles: *adj.* shaped like such a figure. Also, *adj.* **rhomboidal**.

rhom-bus (rŏm'bŭs), *n.* a four-sided figure of which the sides are all equal and the opposite sides parallel, but which has two obtuse and two acute angles. Also, **rhomb**.—*adj.* **rhombic**.

rhu-barb (ro͞o'bärb), *n.* a plant whose fleshy, acid leafstalks are used for cooking purposes; pieplant; the medicinal roots of certain Oriental plants.

rhyme (rīm), *n.* the correspondence of final sounds in two or more words, especially at the ends of poetic lines; a verse or line in which the sound of the last word or syllable thus corresponds with that of another line; a word that sounds like another; verse, or poetry, in which the last words of some of the lines correspond in sound; a group of lines of verse in which some or all of the last words correspond in sound; as, a Mother Goose *rime:* *v.i.* to accord in sound; end in the same sound; make verses: *v.t.* to make to correspond in sound; to put into, or express in, lines the final words of which correspond in sound. Also, **rime**.

rhym-er (rīm'ẽr), *n.* one who composes verse: generally used in contempt; a poor poet. Also, **rimer, rimester, rhymester**.

rhythm (rĭthm; rĭthm), *n.* the regular recurrence in poetry, music, etc., of stress, accent, or quantity; movement marked by a regular, measured recurrence of beat, motion, etc., as, the *rhythm* of the pulse.

rhyth-mi-cal (rĭth'mĭ-kăl; rĭth'mĭ-kăl), *adj.* pertaining to, of the nature of, or marked by, regular recurring movement or accent; keeping time. Also, **rhythmic**.—*adv.* **rhythmically**.

rib (rĭb), *n.* one of the series of curved bony rods attached to the spine, and encircling the body cavity; anything like a rib, as a ridge, strip, or band; a piece of timber used to shape and strengthen the side of a ship; an element in the construction of an airplane wing;

a longitudinal, horizontal member of an airplane wing, to which the covering is attached, and by the shape of which the curve of the wing is determined; the main vein of a leaf: *v.t.* [*p.t.* and *p.p.* ribbed, *p.pr.* ribbing], to furnish, inclose, strengthen, or mark with rods or ridges.

rib-ald (rĭb'ăld), *adj.* indecent; low; filthy; as, a *ribald* song: *n.* a vulgar, foul-mouthed fellow.

rib-ald-ry (rĭb'ăld-rĭ), *n.* indecent conduct or language.

rib-bon (rĭb'ŭn), *n.* a fine fabric, usually of silk, satin, or velvet, woven in a narrow strip with two selvages; a strip or shred; as, a curtain torn to *ribbons*: *v.t.* to ornament with ribbons.

ric-co (rĭk'ō), *n.* a soldier's name for a ricochet bullet, or one that skips or skims along the ground, or rebounds after striking the ground.

rice (rīs), *n.* a valuable food grain produced extensively in hot countries; the grass bearing the grain or seed.

rice-bird (rīs'bûrd"), *n.* the bobolink: so called in the southern United States because it feeds on rice in the autumn.

rice pa-per (rīs pā'pẽr), a thin paper made from rice straw; a vegetable paper made in China and used for painting upon.

rich (rĭch), *adj.* having much money or many possessions; wealthy; expensive; valuable; as, *rich* clothing; great in amount; abundant; as, *rich* crops; fertile; as, *rich* soil or land; abounding in pleasing, desirable, or valuable qualities; as, *rich* perfumes, food, blood; vivid; as, *rich* colors; sweet and full in sound; as, *rich* tones: *n.* wealthy people collectively: with *the*: *pl.* wealth.—*adv.* **richly.**—*n.* **richness.**

Syn., *adj.* copious, bountiful, plentiful, affluent, opulent.

Ant. (see poor).

rick (rĭk), *n.* a stack, or rounded pile, as of hay or straw, in the open air: *v.t.* to pile or heap in a stack.

rick-ets (rĭk'ĕts), *n.* a child's disease marked by softness and curving of the bones.

rick-et-y (rĭk'ĕt-ĭ), *adj.* affected with rickets, a child's disease indicated by softness and curving of the bones; feeble in the joints; shaky; weak; as, a *rickety* chair.

ric-o-chet (rĭk"ō-shā'; rĭk"ō-shĕt'), *n.* the rebounding or skipping of a shot or shell, or of any missile, along the ground or over the surface of the water: *v.i.* [*p.t.* and *p.p.* ricocheted, *p.pr.* ricocheting], to rebound by touching the earth or the surface of water and glancing off, as a cannon ball; skip; skim: *v.t.* to cause to rebound or skip.

rid (rĭd), *v.t.* [*p.t.* and *p.p.* rid, *p.pr.* ridding], to free; deliver; clear; as, to *rid* one of a nuisance: **to be rid of** or **get rid of**, to be, or become, free from; as, to *get rid of* a cold.

rid-dance (rĭd'ăns), *n.* the act of freeing from something undesirable; state of being freed; as, his departure was a good *riddance*.

rid-den (rĭd'n), past participle of the verb *ride*.

rid-dle (rĭd'l), *n.* a puzzling or perplexing question; a person or thing that is difficult to understand; enigma; mystery; a coarse sieve: *v.t.* to explain; solve; to sift through a coarse sieve; to pierce with holes in many places; as, the side of the ship was *riddled* by shot and shell: *v.i.* to speak with doubtful meaning, as in riddles; to use a sieve.

Syn., *n.* problem, puzzle, conundrum.

Ant. (see answer).

ride (rīd), *n.* an excursion on horseback or in a vehicle; a road intended for horseback travel: *v.i.* [*p.t.* rode, *p.p.* ridden, *p.pr.* riding], to be carried along, as on horseback or in a vehicle; practice horsemanship; float or rest; as, the ship *rides* at anchor; to be borne along; as, to *ride* on the wave of success; support and carry one; as, the horse *rides* well: *v.t.* to sit on and be carried along by; as, to *ride* a horse; to float on and be borne along by; as, to *ride* the waves; to travel over on horseback or in any way; as, to *ride* one's rounds; to accomplish, as on horseback; as, to *ride* a race; to make ride; as, they *rode* the helpless baby on their backs; to domineer over.

rid-er (rīd'ẽr), *n.* a horseman; a section or clause added to a legislative bill.—*adj.* **riderless.**

ridge (rĭj), *n.* the back, or top of the back, of an animal; a range of hills or mountains; the horizontal angle or edge where the two slopes of a roof meet; a raised strip or line, as of earth, or in cloth, etc.: *v.t.* to cover with ridges, or raised lines: *v.i.* to become marked with ridges, or raised lines.

ridge-pole (rĭj'pōl"), *n.* the horizontal timber at the top of a roof, against which the upper ends of the rafters rest.

ridg-y (rĭj'ĭ), *adj.* having ridges, or raised lines or strips.

rid-i-cule (rĭd'ĭ-kūl), *n.* words, looks, or acts intended to cause the subject of them to be laughed at contemptuously; sarcasm; mockery; satire: *v.t.* to treat or address with mockery; make fun of; laugh at with contempt.

ri-dic-u-lous (rĭ-dĭk'ū-lŭs), *adj.* deserving or exciting mockery or contempt; absurd and laughable.—*adv.* **ridiculously.**—*n.* **ridiculousness.**

rid-ing (rīd'ĭng), *n.* a road cut through a wood or elsewhere for horsemen; formerly, one of the districts of Yorkshire and Lincolnshire, England.

rife (rīf), *adj.* prevalent; common; existing generally; as, the opinion was everywhere *rife*; abounding; full of: with *with*; as, the town is *rife* with tales of war.

riff-raff (rĭf'răf), *n.* refuse; the rabble; rubbish; as, the *riffraff* of society.

ri-fle (rī'fl), *n.* a firearm with the barrel spirally grooved for the purpose of insuring greater accuracy in fire: *pl.* troops armed with such guns: *v.t.* to groove (the barrel of a gun) spirally; pillage; rob; as, to *rifle* a church; to seize and bear away by force; as, they will *rifle* his goods.

ri-fle-corps (rī'fl-kōr), *n.* a body of soldiers armed with rifles, or guns having spirally grooved barrels.

ri-fle-man (rī'fl-măn), *n.* a man armed with, or skilled in using, the rifle, a firearm having a spirally grooved barrel; a sharpshooter.

ri-fle-pit (rī'fl-pĭt"), *n.* a short trench with a bank of earth in front, to protect riflemen.

ri-fler (rī'flẽr), *n.* one who seizes and carries away by force; a robber.

rift (rĭft), *n.* an opening made by splitting; cleft; as, a *rift* in a cloud: *v.i.* to cleave or split: *v.t.* to burst open.

rig (rĭg), *n.* the arrangement of sails, masts, etc., of a vessel; colloquially, a style of dress or odd costume; an outfit: *v.t.* [*p.t.* and *p.p.* rigged, *p.pr.* rigging], to furnish (a ship) with the necessary outfit of sails, etc., for service; to fit out; equip; colloquially, to dress: with *out* or *up;* as, to *rig* oneself out for a party.

rig-a-doon (rĭg'*ȧ*-dōōn'), *n.* an old-fashioned lively dance performed by one couple; the music for it.

rig-ger (rĭg'ẽr), *n.* one whose occupation is to fit the shrouds, stays, etc., of a ship to their masts and yards.

rig-ging (rĭg'ĭng), *n.* the cordage or ropes by which the masts of a vessel are supported and the sails extended or furled; gear; tackle.

right (rīt), *n.* that which is correct; that which accords with truth, justice, propriety, virtue, etc.: opposite to *wrong;* as, to fight for the *right;* that to which one has a moral or legal claim; as, to defend one's *rights;* the right-hand side: *v.t.* to restore to proper position; as, the cause *righted* itself; make straight; correct; do justice to; as, to *right* a person unfairly treated: *v.i.* to recover the natural position: *adj.* according to truth, justice, or law; correct; true; as, the answer is *right;* correct in opinion, etc.; not mistaken; as, he is always *right;* fit; suitable; as, the *right* man for the position; straight; direct; as, a *right* line; having one line or plane perpendicular to another; as, a *right* angle; pertaining to the stronger side, or the side opposite the left; well; healthy; as, to feel all *right;* made to be worn outward or placed in front; as, the *right* side of cloth; most convenient; as, that will be all *right;* well performed: *adv.* in a straight line; directly; as, he stood *right* in my way; justly; righteously; as, to act *right;* correctly; as, to get the facts *right;* suitably; properly; as, nothing has been done *right;* precisely; just; you are wrong *right* there; very; as, *right* honorable.—*n.* **rightness.**
Syn., *n.* claim, liberty, prerogative, privilege.
Ant. (see wrong).

right an-gle (rīt ăn'gl), an angle of ninety degrees, formed by one straight line standing perpendicular to another: *adj.* **right-angled.**

right-eous (rī'chŭs), *adj.* living according to, or ruled by, the law of God; blameless; virtuous; upright; as, a *righteous* man; becoming; fitting; as, *righteous* anger; just; as, a *righteous* cause.—*adv.* **righteously.**

right-eous-ness (rī'chŭs-nĕs), *n.* quality or state of being blameless or upright; quality of being just; uprightness; justice.

right-ful (rīt'fo͝ol), *adj.* having a just claim according to law; as, the *rightful* heir; just; as, a *rightful* claim.—*adv.* **rightfully.**—*n.* **rightfulness.**

right-hand (rīt'hănd"), *adj.* of, pertaining to, or situated on, the right side; chiefly depended upon; as, my *right-hand* man.

right-hand-ed (rīt'hănd"ĕd), *adj.* done with the right hand; able to use the right hand more easily than the left; hence, dexterous; skilful; rotating from left to right, as the hands of a clock.

right-ly (rīt'lĭ), *adv.* honestly; uprightly; as, duty *rightly* performed; properly; suitably; as, he is *rightly* called our benefactor; correctly; as, you are *rightly* informed.

rig-id (rĭj'ĭd), *adj.* unyielding; stiff; inflexible; strict; severe; as, *rigid* discipline.—*adv.* **rigidly.**—*n.* **rigidness.**

ri-gid-i-ty (rĭ-jĭd'ĭ-tĭ), *n.* stiffness; inflexibility; sternness; strictness in observing rules.

rig-ma-role (rĭg'm*ȧ*-rōl), *n.* foolish, disconnected talk; nonsense.

rig-or (rĭg'ẽr), *n.* the quality of being stiff or unyielding; strictness; sternness; state of being harsh or severe; as, the *rigors* of a northern winter: (rī'gôr; rĭg'ŏr), a violent chill or shivering caused by cold or nervous shock.

ri-gor mor-tis (rī'gôr, or rĭg'ŏr môr'tĭs), stiffness of the body caused by death.

rig-or-ous (rĭg'ẽr-ŭs), *adj.* marked by sternness or severity; as, *rigorous* discipline; exact; strict; as, *rigorous* honesty; harsh; bitter; as, a *rigorous* climate.—*adv.* **rigorously.**—*n.* **rigorousness.**

Rigs-dag (rĭgz'dăg), *n.* the Danish parliament, or chief lawmaking body.

rile (rīl), *v.t.* to vex; irritate; to make muddy by stirring; roil. [COLLOQ.]

rill (rĭl), *n.* a small stream or rivulet; a brooklet.

rim (rĭm), *n.* a border, edge, or margin of an object, especially when curving, or when raised: *v.t.* [*p.t.* and *p.p.* rimmed, *p.pr.* rimming], to furnish with a border or edge; be a border around.

rime (rīm), *n.* hoarfrost or white frost; the correspondence of sound in two or more words, especially at the end of poetic lines; a verse or line in which the sound of the last word or syllable thus corresponds with another; a word that sounds like another; verse, or poetry, in which the last words of some of the lines correspond in sound: *v.i.* to freeze into hoarfrost; to accord in sound; end in the same sound, as lines of verse: *v.t.* to cover with hoarfrost; to put into, or express in, verse some of whose lines end in the same sound; make to correspond in sound. Also, **rhyme.**

rim-er (rīm'ẽr), *n.* one who makes verses; an inferior poet. Also, **rhymer.**

rime-ster (rīm'stẽr), *n.* a maker of poor verses. Also, **rhymester.**

rim-y (rīm'ĭ), *adj.* frosty; covered with frost.

rind (rīnd), *n.* the outer skin or coat, as of fruit, trees, etc.

rin-der-pest (rĭn'dẽr-pĕst), *n.* a contagious disease in cattle; cattle plague.

ring (rĭng), *n.* the sound made by a bell or by metals made to vibrate; a circle; a hoop or circular band; a small hoop of gold, etc., worn as an ornament, usually on the finger or attached to the ear; a space set off for contests or displays; as, a circus *ring;* a race course; a combination of men, usually for a selfish aim or purpose; as, a political *ring:* *v.i.* [*p.t.* rang, *p.p.* rung, *p.pr.* ringing], to sound, as a bell when struck; to sound loudly and clearly; as, his voice *rang* out; have a sensation of buzzing sound; as, my ears *ring;* resound; as, the woods *ring* with song; to summon someone by sounding a bell; as, to *ring* for a maid; to be filled with report or talk; as, the whole town *rings* with his fame: *v.t.* to cause to sound, as metal when struck; to produce (a sound), as by striking a bell; as, *ring* the alarm; proclaim aloud or abroad; as, *ring* in the year; utter again; repeat; they *ring* his praises; to put a ring around; encircle;

hem in; to fit or decorate with a ring, or circlet.

ring-dove (ring'dŭv"), *n.* a European pigeon with a whitish patch on each side of the throat; the wood pigeon.

ring-ing (ring'ĭng), *p.adj.* sounding like a bell; resonant or resounding: *n.* the act of sounding, as a bell; sound produced by a bel., etc.

ring-lead-er (ring'lēd"ẽr), *n.* the head or leader of a number /of persons acting together in some unlawful enterprise, as, the *ringleader* of a gang of thieves.

ring-let (ring'lĕt), *n.* a little circle; a small ring; a curl of hair, especially a long one.

ring snake (ring snāk), a small, harmless, dark-colored snake, having a yellow collar.

ring-worm (ring'wûrm"), *n.* a skin disease marked by distinct circular patches.

rink (rĭnk), *n.* a long, clear space on the ice, marked off for the game of curling; an inclosed sheet of ice or a floor for skating.

rinse (rĭns), *v.t.* to wash lightly with clean water; cleanse with clean water after washing: *n.* the act of pouring clean water over or on something already washed. —*n.* **rinser.**

rins-ing (rĭns'ĭng), *n.* the liquid in which anything is rinsed; that which comes off in rinsing; dregs.

ri-ot (rī'ŭt), *n.* disorderly behavior; uproar; tumult; disturbance of the public peace by a number of persons; boisterous festivity; revelry; luxurious growth, as of shrubbery, undergrowth, or flowers: *v.i.* to raise an uproar; engage in a public disturbance; to eat and drink, etc., without restraint; revel; be in an excited state.—*n.* **rioter.**

ri-ot-ous (rī'ŭt-ŭs), *adj.* engaging in tumultuous disorder; indulging in revelry; wanton; seditious; boisterous; noisy.—*adv.* **riotously.**—*n.* **riotousness.**

rip (rĭp), *v.t.* [*p.t.* and *p.p.* ripped, *p.pr.* ripping], to divide by tearing or cutting; tear or cut out with violence; undo the seam of by cutting stitches; to saw (wood) with the grain; colloquially, to utter violently; as, to *rip* out an oath: *v.i.* to become torn apart: *n.* a rent made by the breaking of stitches; a tear.

ri-pa-ri-an (rĭ-pā'rĭ-ăn; rī-pā'rĭ-ăn), *adj.* of or pertaining to the banks of a river or other body of water; as, *riparian* rights; in botany, growing on the banks of streams.

ripe (rīp), *adj.* grown to maturity or perfection; ready for harvest; as, *ripe* grain or fruit; rosy; brought to a state most fit for use; mellow; advanced to a high degree; matured; as, *ripe* wisdom; ready to act; prepared; as, *ripe* for mischief.—*adv.* **ripely.** —*n.* **ripeness.**

rip-en (rīp'n), *v.t.* to make mature or bring into fit condition for use; bring to full growth or perfection: *v.i.* to become matured or fit for use; to come to perfection.

ri-post (rē-pōst'), *n.* a return thrust in fencing; a quick, clever reply: *v.i.* to make a quick, clever reply.

rip-per (rĭp'ẽr), *n.* one who, or that which, divides by cutting or tearing; a tool for such a purpose.

rip-ple (rĭp'l), *n.* a wavelet on the surface of water; any slight, curling wave; as, the *ripples* of her hair; the sound made by wavelets of water, or a sound like it; as, a *ripple* of laughter; a large comb for cleansing flax: *v.t.* to make small curling waves upon or in; as, the wind *ripples* the water; to *ripple* hair; to clean, as flax: *v.i.* to become fretted or slightly waved on the surface; to sound like water running over a rough surface. —*adj.* **ripply.**

rip-rap (rĭp'răp"), *n.* a foundation of broken stones loosely thrown together in deep water, on a soft bottom: also, stones so used.

rip-saw (rĭp'sô"), *n.* a special saw for cutting wood with the grain.

rise (rīz), *v.i.* [*p.t.* rose, *p.p.* risen, *p.pr.* rising], to move from a lower position to a higher; to ascend; get up from kneeling, sitting, or lying down; swell in quantity or extent; as, the river will *rise*; to increase in price, value, force, or intensity; as, his ire *rose*; grow or spring upward; become tall or lofty; appear above the horizon; come into view or into existence; originate; be promoted; thrive; revolt; rebel; as, they fear that the natives will *rise*; ascend from the grave: *n.* (rīz; rĭs), the act of going up; ascent; distance anything goes up; a place higher than the land around it; act of beginning to appear; origin; source; increase in price, value, force, intensity, etc.; advance in rank, power, or distinction.

ris-en (rĭz'n), past participle of the verb *rise*.

ris-er (rīz'ẽr), *n.* one who, or that which, gets up or ascends; the upright part of a step or stair.

ris-i-bil-i-ty (rĭz"ĭ-bĭl'ĭ-tĭ), *n.* inclination to laughter.

ris-i-ble (rĭz'ĭ-bl), *adj.* having the faculty or power of laughing; inclined to laugh; causing laughter; used in laughter; as, *risible* muscles.—*adv.* **risibly.**—*n.* **risibleness.**

ris-ing (rīz'ĭng), *n.* the act of one who, or that which, ascends, appears, rebels, etc.; as, the *rising* of the moon; a *rising* of the people: *adj.* increasing in wealth, ability, or influence; as, a *rising* young lawyer; appearing above the horizon; growing; as, the *rising* generation.

risk (rĭsk), *n.* possibility of loss or injury; peril; danger: *v.t.* to expose to danger or peril; as, to *risk* one's life; to take the chances on; as, to *risk* a battle.—*n.* **risker.**

risk-y (rĭs'kĭ), *adj.* dangerous; venturesome.

ris-sole (rē"sōl'; rĭs'ōl), *n.* a small ball of rich minced meat or fish, covered with a thin batter paste and fried.

rite (rīt), *n.* a formal act of religion or other solemn duty; any solemn ceremony; as, the *rite* of marriage; a prescribed form of religious service.

rit-u-al (rĭt'ū-ăl), *n.* a set form for the performance of divine service or other solemn ceremony; a book of ceremonial forms; body of ceremonies used in any church, Masonic order, etc.: *adj.* of or pertaining to formal, solemn ceremonies; as, the *ritual* law.—*adv.* **ritually.**

rit-u-al-ism (rĭt'ū-ăl-ĭzm), *n.* a system of prescribed forms of religion; strict observance of forms in church service.

rit-u-al-ist (rĭt'ū-ăl-ĭst), *n.* one who believes in, or is devoted to, the formal side of religious worship or ceremony.

rit-u-al-is-tic (rĭt"ū-ăl-ĭs'tĭk), *adj.* of or pertaining to formal church ceremonies, or to those who favor such ceremonies.

ri-val (rī'vål), *n.* one who tries to equal or excel another in the same object or pursuit; one striving to reach or obtain something which another is trying to reach or obtain, and which one only can possess: *v.t.* to strive to equal or excel; to stand or engage in competition with: *adj.* having the same claims; standing in competition with.
Syn., n. opponent, competitor.

ri-val-ry (rī'vål-rĭ), *n.* the act of trying to equal or excel; state of being in competition with; competition.

rive (rīv), *v.t.* [*p.t.* rived, *p.p.* riven, *p.pr.* riving], to split or tear apart; cleave: *v.i.* to be split or torn apart.

riv-en (rĭv'n), past participle of the verb *rive*.

riv-er (rĭv'ĕr), *n.* a large stream of water flowing into the sea, a lake, or another stream; any large flow; as, a *river* of blood, or a *river* of oil.

riv-er horse (rĭv'ĕr hôrs), the hippopotamus.

riv-et (rĭv'ĕt), *n.* a short metal bolt with a head on one end, used to fasten together two or more pieces of wood, metal, etc., by passing it through holes and forming a head on the plain end by hammering: *v.t.* to secure with, or as with, such a bolt; to clinch; make firm or secure; as, to *rivet* friendship.—*n.* **riveter.**

Rivets

riv-u-let (rĭv'ū-lĕt), *n.* a little stream or brook.

rix-dol-lar (rĭks'dŏl"ĕr), *n.* a British small silver coin of Cape Colony and Ceylon, worth about thirty-six cents; also, a silver coin of northern Europe of varied value.

roach (rōch), *n.* a fresh-water fish; a black, flat insect; a cockroach.

road (rōd), *n.* a public way for travel; highway; a way, course, or means by which anything is reached; as, the *road* to happiness: *pl.* a place where ships may ride safely at anchor; roadstead.
Syn. highway, route, course, anchorage.

road-bed (rōd'bĕd"), *n.* in railroads, the ground on which the ties, rails, etc., rest; in other roads, the materials laid in place and ready for use.

road rol-ler (rōd rōl"ĕr), a heavy cylinder or series of cylindrical rollers, usually driven by steam, for compressing and smoothing the surface of roads: often called *steam-roller*.

Steam Road Roller

road-stead (rōd'stĕd), *n.* a place off shore, not a harbor, where ships may safely anchor.

road-ster (rōd'stĕr), *n.* a horse suited for light driving rather than heavy drawing; a bicycle or other vehicle for use on ordinary roads; a two-seated, usually high-powered, automobile.

road-way (rōd'wā"), *n.* a road, especially the broad part along which vehicles, horses, etc., pass.

roam (rōm), *v.i.* to wander about without any definite object; ramble: *v.t.* to wander over.—*n.* **roamer.**
Syn. rove, stray, stroll.

roan (rōn), *adj.* of a bay, chestnut, brown, or black color, thickly mixed with gray or white; as, a *roan* horse: *n.* a grayish brown or black color; a horse of this color; grained sheepskin leather.

roar (rōr), *n.* the deep, full cry of a large animal; as, the *roar* of a lion; a cry, as of distress; any loud, confused noise; as, the *roar* of battle; loudly expressed mirth; as, a *roar* of laughter: *v.i.* to cry with a loud, full, deep sound, as, a lion *roars;* to cry loudly, as in pain, distress, or anger; to laugh loudly; to make a loud, confused noise, as wind, waves, passing vehicles, etc.: *v.t.* to utter boisterously, or with a full, prolonged sound.

roar-ing (rōr'ĭng), *n.* a loud, deep, prolonged sound, as, of a lion, the winds, etc.; a disease of horses marked by difficulty in breathing: *adj.* noisy; disorderly.

roast (rōst), *v.t.* to cook before a fire or in a closed oven, as meat; heat to excess; dry and parch under the action of heat; heat (broken ore) to free (it) from useless matter; slang, to banter or ridicule severely: *v.i.* to be cooked by heat, as before a fire or in an oven: *n.* a piece of meat cooked, or suitable to be cooked, before a fire or in an oven: *adj.* cooked before a fire or in an oven; roasted.—*n.* **roaster.**

rob (rŏb), *v.t.* [*p.t.* and *p.p.* robbed, *p.pr.* robbing], to carry away something from by secret theft or violence; to steal from; plunder; deprive unjustly; defraud: *v.i.* to commit theft.

rob-ber (rŏb'ĕr), *n.* one who takes what is not his; a thief.

rob-ber-y (rŏb'ĕr-ĭ), *n.* thievery; the unlawful and forcible taking away of the money and goods of another.

robe (rōb), *n.* a rich, loose, outer garment; state dress; an elegant gown: *pl.* costume; the dressed skin of an animal used for a carriage covering, etc.: *v.t.* to put on a robe or garment, especially a garment of state: *v.i.* to dress, especially in a garment of state.

rob-in (rŏb'ĭn), *n.* a small European bird of the thrush family; the robin redbreast; an American thrush somewhat like the English robin, but larger.

Rob-in Hood (rŏb'ĭn ho͝od), a courteous outlaw reputed in English legend to have lived in Sherwood forest, where he headed a band of chivalrous robbers.

ro-bust (rō-bŭst'), *adj.* hardy; strong; vigorous; muscular; as, *robust* health.
Syn. lusty, sturdy, stalwart.
Ant. (see puny).

roc (rŏk), *n.* an imaginary bird of Arabian and Persian legend, of enormous size and strength.

rock (rŏk), *n.* a large mass of stone or of stony matter; any mineral matter; a bed or mass of one mineral; that which resembles such a mass in firmness; a firm support; a defense; that on which one may be wrecked, or by which one may be ruined; the striped bass; a movement backward and forward: *v.t* to cause to move backward and forward; lull to sleep; cause to sway or reel: *v.i.* to move backward and forward; to sway or reel.—*n.* **rocker.**

rock-a-way (rŏk'ȧ-wā), *n.* a low, four-wheeled, two-seated pleasure carriage, with a standing top.

rock crys-tal (rŏk krĭs'tăl), transparent, or nearly transparent, quartz, or a piece of it.

rock drill (rŏk drĭl), an implement, driven by steam or compressed air, to bore or drill holes in rock, etc., for blasting.

rock-et (rŏk'ĕt), *n.* a firework which is made of a tube filled with saltpeter, sulphur, and charcoal, fastened to a stick, and which, when fired, is shot into the air and lets fall a shower of sparks.

rock-i-ness (rŏk'ĭ-nĕs), *n.* the state of being made up of stony mineral matter.

rock-ing-chair (rŏk'ĭng-châr"), *n.* a chair having the legs set on curving pieces on which the chair sways backward and forward.

rock oil (rŏk oil), petroleum, or mineral or natural oil.

rock-rose (rŏk'rōz"), *n.* any of a family of shrubs, having regular, often showy, flowers, resembling the wild rose.

rock ru-by (rŏk rōō'bĭ), a fine bluish-red garnet.

rock-wood (rŏk'wŏŏd"), *n.* a brown, compact kind of asbestos.

rock-y (rŏk'ĭ), *adj.* full of, or like, stony or mineral matter; stony; hard; inflexible; like a rock; without feeling.

ro-co-co (rō-kō'kō), *n.* a showy style of decoration, representing shells, leaves, scrolls, etc., massed together without meaning, popular in the seventeenth and eighteenth centuries; hence, anything odd or in bad taste in art or literature: *adj.* of or pertaining to this showy and overelaborate style; hence, showing bad taste in art or literature.

rod (rŏd), *n.* a straight and slender stick; any slender bar, especially one of metal; a fishing-pole; a switch used for inflicting punishment; hence, correction or discipline: with *the;* a scepter; hence, power; a measure of length containing five and a half yards.

rode (rōd), past tense of the transitive and intransitive verb *ride.*

ro-dent (rō'dĕnt), *n.* any of an order of gnawing animals, as rats, mice, squirrels, beavers, etc.: *adj.* gnawing; biting; like a gnawing animal.

rod-o-mon-tade (rŏd"ō-mŏn-tād'; rŏd"ō-mŏn-täd'), *n.* vain boasting; bluster; brag: from Rodomonte in Ariosto's *Orlando Furioso: v.i.* to bluster or brag.

roe (rō), *n.* a small deer of Europe and western Asia: called also the *roe deer;* the collected mass of eggs of fishes.

roe-buck (rō'bŭk"), *n.* the male of the roe, a small deer of Europe and western Asia.

Roent-gen rays (rûnt'gĕn rāz; rĕnt'gĕn rāz), rays having power to pass through objects which other light or heat rays cannot penetrate, and affecting sensitive photographic plates: called *X rays* by their discoverer, W. K. Roentgen. Also, **Röntgen rays.**

ro-ga-tion (rō-gā'shŭn), *n.* in the Episcopal and Roman Catholic churches, a litany or solemn supplication chanted on certain days: **Rogation Days,** the Monday, Tuesday, and Wednesday before Ascension Day.

rogue (rōg), *n.* a dishonest person; a cheat; a scoundrel; playfully, a mischievous, frolicsome person.

ro-guer-y (rō'gĕr-ĭ), *n.* dishonest practices; cheating; playfully mischievous conduct; as, the *roguery* of children.

ro-guish (rō'gĭsh), *adj.* dishonest; knavish; playfully mischievous.—*adv.* **roguishly.**—*n.* **roguishness.**

roil (roil), *v.t.* to render muddy by stirring; as, to *roil* a spring; vex or irritate; disturb, as the temper; colloquially, to rile. —*adj.* **roily.**

roist-er (rois'tẽr), *v.i.* to swagger; to act in a noisy or blustering way.

roist-er-er (rois'tẽr-ẽr), *n.* a bold, blustering, disorderly fellow.

rôle (rōl), *n.* a part or character taken by an actor in a play; hence, a part or character taken, or assumed, by any one.

roll (rōl), *v.i.* to move onward by turning over and over; as, a ball *rolls;* to run on wheels; as, the wagon *rolls* along; to toss from side to side; as, a ship *rolls;* to sweep along, as waves; give forth a long, deep sound; as, the thunder *rolls;* to take, through winding, the form of a cylinder; as, the cloth *rolls* easily: *v.t.* to cause to move onward by turning over and over; as to *roll* a ball; to move or push along on wheels; as, to *roll* a table across the room; to wrap round on itself or upon something else; as, to *roll* a rug; wrap up; as, to *roll* oneself in a blanket; to drive or sweep along; as, the waves *roll* the ship onward; to utter with a deep sound; as, the organ *rolls* forth majestic sounds; spread flat under a roller; as, to *roll* a road; to beat, as a drum: to pronounce with a prolonged trilling sound: *n.* the act of rolling; state of being rolled; that which rolls; a roller; anything wrapped upon itself in the form of a cylinder; a list or register; a kind of biscuit or bread; often doubled over; a cake spread with jelly and rolled up; as, a jelly *roll;* a long strip, as of cloth or carpet, wrapped upon itself; a continued, deep sound, as of a drum beaten, thunder, etc.; a twist of tobacco; a swell or unevenness on a surface: **roll of honor,** a list of names of persons who have distinguished themselves in some particular way; in the World War, the name given to the published casualty lists of the war.

roll call (rōl kôl"), the act or time of calling over a list of names of those belonging to an organization, soldiers, pupils in a school, etc., in order to find out those who are present, or to obtain responses from them.

roll-er (rōl'ẽr), *n.* that which turns round and round, or over and over; a cylinder used for grinding, smoothing, flattening, etc.; a small wheel; a long, heavy wave; a long, broad bandage; a tumbler pigeon.

roll-er coast-er (rōl'ẽr kōst'ẽr), a switchback railway, in which small cars are run on rollers or wheels.

roll-er skate (rōl'ẽr skāt), a skate with wheels instead of a runner.

rol-lic (rŏl'ĭk), *v.i.* [*p.t.* and *p.p.* rollicked, *p.pr.* rollicking], to move or act with a careless, swaggering air; to frolic. Also, rollick.

rol-lick-ing (rŏl'ĭk-ĭng), *adj.* moving with a joyous, careless, swaggering air or manner.

roll-ing (rōl'ĭng), *adj.* moving on by turning over and over; as, a *rolling* ball; moving on, or as on, wheels; as, a *rolling* chair; undulating; as, *rolling* country; turned back or down on itself; as, a *rolling* collar; used for smoothing, flattening, etc.: *n.* the act of one that rolls, or of one who uses a rolling tool; a deep, full, reverberating sound: **rolling stock,** the cars and other wheeled equipment of a railway.

roll-ing-pin (rōl′ĭng-pĭn″), *n.* a smooth implement, long and round, made of wood, glass, agate, etc., for rolling out dough.

ro-ly-po-ly (rō′lĭ-pō′lĭ), *n.* a game consisting of rolling a ball into a certain hole; a boiled or steamed pudding made of light dough spread with fruit and rolled up: *adj.* round; dumpy; as, a *roly-poly* little girl.

Ro-ma-ic (rō-mā′ĭk), *n.* modern Greek, especially the form spoken by uneducated Greeks: *adj.* of or relating to modern Greece, especially its language.

Ro-man (rō′măn), *n.* a native or citizen of ancient or modern Rome: **Romans**, a book of the New Testament, containing the Epistle, or letter, of the apostle Paul to the Christians at Rome: *adj.* pertaining or relating to ancient or modern Rome, or to the Romans; pertaining to, or connected with, the Church of Rome: **roman**, having the form of the ordinary type used in printing: distinguished from *italic*.

Ro-man Cath-o-lic (rō′măn kăth′ō-lĭk), of or pertaining to the Church of Rome, of which the Pope is the head: *n.* a member of the Church of Rome.

Ro-man Ca-thol-i-cism (rō′măn kȧ-thŏl′ĭ-sĭzm), the doctrines and practices of the Roman Catholic Church.

ro-mance (rō-măns′), *n.* a prose or poetical tale of adventure, chivalry, etc., such as the tales of King Arthur: so called because written originally in the Romance dialects; a form of prose fiction full of imagination and adventure; a series of acts or happenings that are strange and charming; a disposition to ignore what is real and to delight in what is fanciful or mysterious; as, a soul full of *romance;* falsehood; as, I fear she indulges in *romance:* *v.i.* to invent and tell fanciful or extravagant stories; to indulge in dreamy imaginings: **Romance**, *adj.* of or pertaining to the languages which developed from popular Latin, as Italian, Roumanian, French, Portuguese, and Spanish.—*n.* **romancer.**

Ro-man-esque (rō″măn-ĕsk′), *n.* that style of architecture and ornamentation developed from Roman principles during the period from the fifth to the twelfth century: *adj.* pertaining to, or designating, such a style of architecture.

Ro-man-ic (rō-măn′ĭk), *adj.* relating to the Romance languages, or those developed from popular Latin, as Italian, French, Spanish, etc.; related to the peoples that speak those languages.

ro-man-tic (rō-măn′tĭk), *adj.* pertaining to, or like, what is imaginary, sentimental, or extravagantly ideal; hence, fanciful; visionary; as, *romantic* ideas; pertaining to, or suggesting, what is strange and improbable; fantastic; of a disposition to ignore what is real and delight in what is fanciful and mysterious; as, a *romantic* girl; strangely wild and picturesque; as, *romantic* scenery; of or pertaining to the art and literature of the Middle Ages: opposite to *classical.*—*adv.* **romantically.**

ro-man-ti-cism (rō-măn′tĭ-sĭzm), *n.* the quality or characteristic of being imaginative, sentimental, or extravagantly ideal in literature, strangeness, and improbability; the movement in Germany and France at the beginning of the nineteenth century to restore to literature and art the spirit and style of the wonderful and fantastic: opposite to *classicism.*—*n.* **romanticist.**

romp (rŏmp), *n.* a girl who plays boisterously; rough, noisy play or frolic: *v.i.* to play in a rough, boisterous manner; to frisk about in play; to move rapidly, but with ease; in racing, to win easily.—*n.* **romping.**—*adj.* **rompish.**—*adv.* **rompishly.**

ron-deau (rŏn′dō; rŏn-dō′), *n.* [*pl.* rondeaux (-dōz)], a little poem of thirteen verses or lines, with but two rimes, and with a refrain after the eighth and thirteenth lines; in music, a light composition in which the first strain is repeated at intervals. Also, **rondel.**

ron-do (rŏn′dō), *n.* [*pl.* rondos (-dōz)], a musical composition for either voice or instrument, of a vivacious, ripply nature, characterized by many repetitions of the first melody; the musical setting for a rondeau.

Rönt-gen rays (rûnt′gĕn rāz; rĕnt′gĕn rāz), rays having power to pass through objects which other light or heat rays cannot penetrate and affecting sensitive photographic plates: called *X rays* by their discoverer, W. K. Roentgen. Also, **Roentgen rays.**

rood (rōōd), *n.* a cross or crucifix, especially a large crucifix, or representation of the cross with Christ hanging on it, over the altar screen of a church; a square measure equal to one-fourth of an acre, or forty square rods.

roof (rōōf), *n.* the top covering of a building; any similar top covering, as of a car or a cave: *v.t.* to cover with, or as with, a roof.—*n.* **roofing.**

roof-less (rōōf′lĕs), *adj.* having no top covering; having no shelter.

roof-tree (rōōf′trē″), *n.* the ridgepole, or highest horizontal timber of a roof, against which the rafters rest; hence, roof; figuratively, home.

rook (rŏŏk), *n.* a bird of the crow family with glossy black plumage; the castle in the game of chess.

rook-er-y (rŏŏk′ẽr-ĭ), *n.* [*pl.* rookeries (-ĭz)], a place where many rooks, or crowlike birds, gather and build their nests; a colony of rooks or crowlike birds; a place where other birds or animals, as seagulls or seals, gather and breed; a place of low resort; a low slum; a building falling to ruin through neglect, or a group of such buildings, occupied by many people of dubious character.

room (rōōm), *n.* free or unoccupied place or space; an apartment or chamber in a building; freedom to act; opportunity; a deep blue dye: *v.i.* colloquially, to lodge.

room-er (rōōm′ẽr), *n.* one who rents a room or chamber, especially temporarily; a lodger. [Colloq.]

room-ful (rōōm′fŏŏl), *n.* [*pl.* roomfuls (-fŏŏlz)], those in a room or chamber; as many as a room can contain.

room-mate (rōōm′māt″), *n.* a person with whom one shares a room.

room-y (rōōm′ĭ), *adj.* spacious; having plenty of room or space; not contracted.—*adv.* **roomily.**—*n.* **roominess.**

roor-back (rōōr′băk), *n.* a lie; an untrue report made for the purpose of influencing an election. [U. S.]

roost (rōōst), *n.* the pole, perch, etc., upon which a bird rests at night; a number of fowls resting together: *v.i.* to sit or sleep upon a perch, etc.; to rest.

roost-er (rōōs'tẽr), *n.* the domestic cock; male fowl.

root (rōōt), *n.* the underground part of a plant which fixes it in the earth and serves to absorb moisture and nourishment; an edible underground part of a plant, as a potato; anything like a root; an ancestor; the part of an organ that is most deeply embedded; as, the *root* of a hair or finger nail; that from which anything has its origin; cause; as, laziness is the *root* of his poverty; the lower part of a thing; foundation; as, the *roots* of the mountains; to strike at the *root* of an evil; a quantity which, multiplied by itself a given number of times, produces a given quantity; as, 2 is the second or square *root* of 4; the part of a word, without prefix or suffix, which expresses its primary or essential meaning: *v.t.* to plant and fix in the earth; implant deeply and firmly; to dig up or out with the snout: with *out* or *up;* to tear up or out; with *out* or *up;* eradicate; as, to *root* out an evil: *v.i.* to take root; to be firmly fixed or established; to turn up the earth with the snout.

root-let (rōōt'lĕt), *n.* a little root; a secondary root thrown out by climbing plants.

root-stock (rōōt'stŏk"), *n.* a rootlike stem of a plant running horizontally underground, and sending leaves upward and roots downward: called also *rhizome.*

rope (rōp), *n.* a thick, stout cord made of several strands of hemp, cotton, flax, etc., twisted together; a collection of things braided or twined together in a line or string; as, a *rope* of pearls; any glutinous or slimy thread formed in a liquid: *v.t.* to fasten, bind, or tie with a rope; to divide off, by means of a rope; as, to *rope* off a plot of ground; colloquially, to lasso, or draw in by means of a noosed rope, as a steer; slang, to deceive: with *in:* *v.i.* to become drawn out into threads; as, the jelly *ropes.*

rop-y (rōp'ĭ), *adj.* that may be drawn out into threads; stringy.—*n.* ropiness.

Roque-fort (rōk"fōr'; rŏk'fōrt), *n.* a kind of moldy cheese made in Roquefort, France, from the milk of ewes, or female sheep.

ro-quet (rō-kā'), *v.t.* in the game of croquet, to strike (a ball) with the player's ball: *n.* the act of so striking.

ror-qual (rôr'kwăl), *n.* a large whalebone whale with a fin on its back.

ro-sa-ceous (rō-zā'shŭs), *adj.* of or pertaining to the rose family.

ro-sa-ry (rō'zȧ-rĭ), *n.* [*pl.* rosaries (-rĭz)], a string of beads for counting a series of prayers to be said one after the other in a certain recurring order; the series of prayers thus recited on these beads; as, to tell her *rosaries;* a bed of roses or a place where roses grow; a garland of roses; hence, a collection of beautiful thoughts from various authors.

rose (rōz), *p.t.* of the verb *rise:* *n.* a well-known prickly shrub or its fragrant, beautiful flower; rose color, or crimson-pink; a fancy knot of ribbon or lace; a rosette: under the rose, secretly.

rose-bud (rōz'bŭd"), *n.* the bud of a rose; colloquially, a young girl approaching womanhood.

ro-se-ate (rō'zē-āt), *adj.* rose-colored; roselike; blooming.

rose-ma-ry (rōz'mā-rĭ), *n.* a sweet-smelling evergreen shrub with pungent leaves and blue flowers.

ro-sette (rō-zĕt'), *n.* a knot or bunch of ribbon or other fabric made in the shape of a rose; a painted or sculptured circular ornament, as leaves arranged in a circle around a bud.

rose win-dow (rōz wĭn'dō), a circular window with mullions, or divisions, branching from, or arranged around, its center.

Rose Window

rose-wood (rōz'-wŏŏd"), *n.* a valuable dark-red, hard wood, yielded by various tropical trees and used for furniture.

ros-in (rŏz'ĭn), *n.* the resin, or solid substance, that remains after distilling, or driving off, as by heat, the oil of turpentine from crude turpentine: *v.t.* to rub with rosin; as, to *rosin* the bow of a violin.

ross (rŏs), *n.* the rough, scaly surface of the bark of some trees; tan bark: *v.t.* to remove the outer scaly or rough surface of; as, to *ross* bark.

ros-ter (rŏs'tẽr), *n.* a list of officers and men enrolled for duty; a list showing the order in which officers, enlisted men, companies or regiments of soldiers are called on to serve; hence, any roll or list; as, the *roster* of a school or college class.

ros-trum (rŏs'trŭm), *n.* [*pl.* rostrums (-trŭmz), or rostra (-trȧ)], a pulpit, platform, or stage for public speaking; hence, public orators or lecturers collectively.

ros-y (rōz'ĭ), *adj.* like a rose; red; blooming; blushing; very favorable; bright; hopeful; as, *rosy* prospects.—*adv.* rosily.—*n.* rosiness.

rot (rŏt), *v.i.* [*p.t.* and *p.p.* rotted, *p.pr.* rotting], to become corrupt; decay: *v.t.* to cause to decay; as, to *rot* vegetable fiber: *n.* the process of decay; state of being decayed; that which is decayed; decay.

ro-ta-ry (rō'tȧ-rĭ), *adj.* turning around, as a wheel on an axis; as, a *rotary* motion; having parts that turn around; rotatory.

ro-tate (rō'tāt; rō-tāt'), *v.t.* to cause to turn on, or as on, an axis; cause to alternate or change about: *v.i.* to turn around its own center or axis; revolve; to alternate, or do any act, etc., in turn.

ro-ta-tion (rō-tā'shŭn), *n.* the act of turning round on an axis, like a wheel; regular succession; as, *rotation* in office; recurrence.

ro-ta-tive (rō'tȧ-tĭv), *adj.* connected with, or causing a movement on, or as on, an axis; rotating.

ro-ta-to-ry (rō'tȧ-tō-rĭ), *adj.* having, pertaining to, or causing movement on, or as on, an axis; following one after another.

rote (rōt), *n.* the repeating of words or sounds over and over in order to learn them, with little attention to their meaning; as, to learn rules by *rote;* a stringed instrument somewhat like a guitar: used in the Middle Ages.

ro-to-graph (rō'tō-grȧf), *n.* a photograph printed by a rapid automatic process.

ro-to-gra-vure (rō"tō-grȧ-vūr'), *n.* a process for the rapid printing of illustrations, from plates etched on copper cylinders; an illustration so printed.

rot-ten (rŏt'n), *adj.* decayed; putrid; as, *rotten* eggs; liable to break; not firm; as, a *rotten* plank; slang, corrupt or untrustworthy; as, *rotten* politics.—*n.* **rottenness.**

rot-ten-stone (rŏt'n-stōn"), *n.* a soft, easily crumbled, siliceous rock or limestone used as a polishing powder.

ro-tund (rō-tŭnd'), *adj.* round from plumpness; rounded out; as, a *rotund* figure; full toned; as, a *rotund* voice; having words that are full and round in sound.

ro-tun-da (rō-tŭn'dȧ), *n.* a circular building, especially one with a dome; a large round room; as, the *rotunda* of the Capitol at Washington.

ro-tun-di-ty (rō-tŭn'dĭ-tĭ), *n.* state of being round; roundness.

rou-ble (rōō'bl), *adj.* a Russian silver coin of varying value, averaging about 51.5 cents. Also, **rubl**e.

rou-é (rōō'ā'), *n.* an evil, dissipated man; a rake. [FR.]

rouge (rōōzh), *n.* a red substance used for coloring the cheeks and lips; a red powder used for polishing glass, metals, etc.: *v.i.* to color or paint the cheeks with rouge: *v.t.* to color with rouge, as the cheeks.

rough (rŭf), *adj.* having an uneven surface; rugged; not smooth or plain; as, a *rough* board; a *rough* road; *rough* cloth; uncut; unpolished; as, a *rough* diamond; harsh to the ear; as, a *rough* sound; uncivil; harsh; unfeeling; as, *rough* treatment; severe; violent; as, *rough* sports; boisterous; stormy; as, *rough* weather; rocky; said of roads; crude; unfinished; as, a *rough* sketch: *n.* a low, coarse fellow; a rowdy; a crude or unfinished condition; as, diamonds in the *rough;* in golf, long grass on the side of the course: *v.t.* to produce an uneven surface on; destroy the smoothness of; to shape or make imperfectly.—*adv.* **roughly.**—*n.* **roughness.**

rough-cast (rŭf'kȧst"), *n.* very coarse plaster for the outside of buildings; a rude model: *v.t.* to coat with coarse plaster, as a wall; make a rude plan or model of.

rough-en (rŭf'n), *v.t.* to produce an uneven surface on; to destroy the smoothness of: *v.i.* to become uneven or coarse on the surface.

rough-hew (rŭf'hū"), *v.t.* to cut (timber) roughly; to shape roughly.

rough-rid-er (rŭf'rĭd"ẽr), *n.* one who breaks horses to the saddle: **Roughrider,** colloquially, a soldier of the First United States Volunteer Cavalry in the Spanish-American War.

rou-lette (rōō-lĕt'), *n.* a French game of chance played with a revolving wheel and ball; an instrument used by draftsmen for making dotted lines.

round (round), *adj.* circular; spherical; cylindrical, as a gun barrel; having a curved outline or surface; as, a *round* arch; a *round* cheek; whole; complete; as, a *round* dozen; going from and returning to the same place; as, a *round* trip; liberal; large; as, a *round* sum; easy and energetic in motion; as, a *round* pace; full in sound; as, the *round* tones of a voice; well-balanced; as, a *round* sentence; bold; outspoken; as, a *round* rebuke; approximately, divisible by ten; as, *round* numbers: *n.* a circle, cylinder, or globe; a fixed course or route; a beat; as, a policeman's *round;* routine; as, the day's *round* of duties; a series of events, acts, etc.; as, a *round* of gaiety; a circular dance; a course of action in which a number of persons take part at one time; as, a *round* of cheers; one of a number of repeated actions; as, a *round* of whist; a song sung by several persons starting at successive intervals of time; a simultaneous discharge of shots by each soldier or gun in a company or detail; ammunition needed for such a discharge; the rung of a ladder; a crossbar connecting the legs of a chair: *v.t.* to give a curved form to; travel or pass around; as, in sailing, to *round* a cape; to bring to completion; finish; as, to *round* out a plan; *round* out a story; fill out smoothly or musically; as, to *round* out a sentence: *v.i.* to become curved, spherical, or circular in form; to wheel about; to grow full, complete, or perfect: *adv.* on all sides; so as to encircle; as, the people gathered *round;* with a rotating motion; as, the wheel turns *round;* from one side or party to another; as, he came *round* to their belief; from person to person or point to point; as, not food enough to go *round;* the summer comes *round* once more: *prep.* about; on every side of; past so as to encircle.—*adv.* **roundly.**—*n.* **roundness.**

round-a-bout (round'ȧ-bout"), *adj.* indirect; circuitous: *n.* a merry-go-round; a short coat or jacket.

roun-de-lay (roun'dē-lā), *n.* a song in which a simple melody or refrain is often repeated; a dance performed in a circle.

Round-head (round'hĕd"), *n.* a contemptuous name applied to the Puritans by the Cavaliers, from the close-cut hair of the former.

round-house (round'hous"), *n.* the cabin on the after part of a ship's quarter-deck; a circular building having stalls for locomotives, built around a turntable.

round-ish (round'ĭsh), *adj.* tending to be round; nearly round.

round rob-in (round rŏb'ĭn), a petition having the signatures written in a circle so as not to show who signed it first.

round-shoul-dered (round'shōl"-dẽrd), *adj.* not erect; having stooping shoulders.

rounds-man (roundz'măn), *n.* a police inspector who visits officers on their beats.

round-up (round'ŭp"), *n.* the gathering together of herds of cattle and driving them in; the herd so collected; the men and horses that collect them; the driving of animals together in hunting: *v.t.* to gather together and drive in, as cattle.

rouse (rouz), *v.t.* to awaken; stir to thought or action; drive (game) from a covert or hiding place: *v.i.* to start from sleep; show signs of activity; be stirred to action: *n.* a drinking bout.—*n.* **rouser.**

roust-a-bout (roust'ȧ-bout"), *n.* a wharf laborer; especially, a deck hand on a river steamboat.

rout (rout), *n.* total defeat and flight, as of an army; disorder resulting from such defeat; a noisy crowd; a rabble; mob; formerly, a large evening party: *v.t.* to defeat and put to disorderly flight; to root up, as with the snout; to scoop out; to bring to view; turn up; to turn out by force: *v.t.* to root about; rummage.

Syn., v. defeat, overthrow, scatter.

route (rōōt), *n.* way or road traveled; course; journey; march: *v.t.* to send or forward by a certain road or way.

Syn., n. path, journey, direction.

rou-tine (rōō-tēn'), *n.* course of business or official duties regularly pursued; regular habit or practice.

rove (rōv), *v.i.* to wander or ramble: *v.t.* to wander or ramble over; roam over; to draw out and join together, as fibers of wool or cotton, before spinning.

rov-er (rōv'ēr), *n.* a pirate; wanderer; fickle person.

row (rō), *n.* a series of things in a line; a file or rank; a trip in a rowboat; a turn at the oars: *v.i.* to labor with an oar in propelling a boat; be moved forward by oars: *v.t.* to propel, or move forward, by means of oars; as, to *row* a boat; to transport in a boat propelled by oars.

row (rou), *n.* a noisy disturbance; brawl; quarrel; fight. [COLLOQ.]

row-boat (rō'bōt"), *n.* a boat equipped with oars and oarlocks for rowing.

row-dy (rou'dĭ), *n.* a rough, riotous fellow: *adj.* rough and riotous; noisy and rude.—*adj.* **rowdyish.**—*n.* **rowdiness.**

row-dy-ism (rou'dĭ-ĭzm), *n.* rough, riotous conduct.

row-el (rou'ĕl), *n.* the small, sharp-pointed wheel of a spur: *v.t.* to prick with the wheel of a spur, as a horse.

row-en (rou'ĕn), *n.* a second crop, as of hay, on the same field during the same season.

row-lock (rō'lŏk), *n.* a notch in the gunwale of a boat, or a piece of metal with a U-shaped top, in which the oar rests in rowing: called also *oarlock*.

roy-al (roi'ăl), *adj.* pertaining to, or belonging to, a king; kingly; as, a *royal* household; pertaining to, or connected with, the government of a kingdom; as, the *royal* army; befitting, or like, a king; regal; specially patronized or founded by a king; as, the *Royal* Academy: *n.* a size of paper, twenty-five by twenty inches, for printing; the highest sail of a ship.—*adv.* **royally.**

roy-al-ism (roi'ăl-ĭzm), *n.* belief in, and support of, the principles or cause of government by a king; also, the principles of such government.—*n.* **royalist.**

roy-al-ty (roi'ăl-tĭ), *n.* [*pl.* royalties (-tĭz)], the state, station, birth, etc., of a king; person of a king or of one of sovereign rank; persons of sovereign rank collectively; kingly nature or quality; a tax paid to the crown, as a percentage of gold or silver mined, etc.; hence, a share of the product or profit (as of a mine, etc.) claimed by the owner for permitting another to use the property; a percentage paid to an inventor or author for the use of a patent or copyright; as, a *royalty* from the sale of a book.

rub (rŭb), *v.t.* [*p.t.* and *p.p.* rubbed, *p.pr.* rubbing], to move something with pressure over the surface of; as, to *rub* one's face with a towel; to pass over with a scraping or brushing movement; as, the wheel *rubbed* my dress; to cause to move over with pressure; as, to *rub* one's hand over one's arm; to clean or scour by moving something over with pressure; to polish; as, to *rub* up the silver; to remove by moving something over; erase; as, to *rub* out a black mark; renew one's knowledge of; as, to *rub* up one's history; to affect one's feelings disagreeably; as, to *rub* one the wrong way: *v.i.* to move along a surface with pressure; scrape; as, two things *rub* together; to get along with difficulty; as, to manage to *rub* along: *n.* a moving of something over with pressure; a rubbing; as, give the table a good *rub*; that which makes progress difficult; hindrance; something that is harsh to the feelings; a sarcasm.

rub-ber (rŭb'ēr), *n.* anything used for erasing, polishing, etc.; caoutchouc, or India rubber; an article made of it, as an elastic band, an overshoe, etc.; in card playing, the majority of several games, often two games out of three; also, the odd or winning game.

rub-bish (rŭb'ĭsh), *n.* mixed or waste fragments; ruins of buildings; anything of no value; trash.

rub-ble (rŭb'l), *n.* rough, irregular, broken stones or bricks, or masonry built of such fragments.

Ru-bi-con (rōō'bĭ-kŏn), *n.* the river dividing the province of Cæsar from that of Pompey, the crossing of which by Cæsar led to war: **to cross the Rubicon,** to perform any act that commits one irrevocably to some course or undertaking.

ru-bi-cund (rōō'bĭ-kŭnd), *adj.* inclined to redness; flushed; as, a *rubicund* face.

ru-ble (rōō'bl), *n.* a Russian silver coin of varying value, averaging about 51.5 cents. Also, **rouble.**

ru-bric (rōō'brĭk), *n.* the directions in prayer books, formerly printed in red; hence, any rule of conduct; the title of a law, formerly printed in red: *adj.* made prominent by being marked in red; red.

ru-bri-cate (rōō'brĭ-kāt), *v.t.* to mark or distinguish with red; as, to *rubricate* a book.

ru-by (rōō'bĭ), *n.* [*pl.* rubies (-bĭz)], a precious stone, usually a variety of corundum, varying in color from carmine-red to crimson; the color of the stone.

ruche (rōōsh), *n.* a frilled or plaited strip of lace, silk, etc., for edging dresses, especially at the neck or wrist, or for other trimming. Also, **rouche.**

ruch-ing (rōōsh'ĭng), *n.* material, such as lace, silk, etc., for making ruches, or plaited or frilled edgings; ruches collectively.

ruck (rŭk), *n.* colloquially, the multitude of common persons or things; throng; crowd.

rud-der (rŭd'ēr), *n.* a broad, flat piece of wood or metal hinged vertically to the stern of a vessel and used for steering; a hinged or pivoted part, used to steer an aircraft.—*adj.* **rudderless.**

Rudder

rud-dy (rŭd'ĭ), *adj.* red or approaching to redness; having a healthy glow; as, a *ruddy* complexion.—*adv.* **ruddily.**—*n.* **ruddiness.**

rude (rōōd), *adj.* [*comp.* ruder, *superl.* rudest], barbarous; uncultivated; ignorant; as, a *rude* people; impolite; uncivil; impudent; as, *rude* behavior; robust; strong; rugged; as, *rude* health; crude; unskilful; as, a *rude* carving; harsh; rough; severe; as, a *rude* awakening to the truth.—*adv.* **rudely.**—*n.* **rudeness.**

ru-di-ment (rōō'dĭ-mĕnt), *n.* the first or introductory principle of an art, science, etc.; as, the *rudiments* of composition; anything in its first or undeveloped state; a beginning.

ru-di-men-ta-ry (rōō"dĭ-mĕn'tȧ-rĭ), *adj.* pertaining to first principles; being in an early or undeveloped state. Also, **rudimental.**

rue (rōō), *n.* an herb of bitter taste and strong odor, formerly used as a medicine; regret: *v.t.* to lament or be sorry for; repent of.

rue-ful (rōō'fōōl), *adj.* showing sorrow or pity; mournful; sad; as, a *rueful* expression; causing sorrow or regret; pitiable; as, a *rueful* sight.—*adv.* **ruefully.**

ruff (rŭf), *n.* a large plaited or fluted collar; anything like such a collar; a growth of feathers around the neck of a bird or of hair around the neck of an animal; an Old World sandpiper: the female called *reeve;* also, a kind of pigeon; in card playing, the act of trumping: *v.t.* and *v.i.* in card playing, to trump when one has no card of the suit led.

ruf-fi-an (rŭf'ĭ-ăn; rŭf'yăn), *n.* a brutal, lawless fellow; one given to cruel deeds: *adj.* brutal; cruel.—*adj.* **ruffianly.** —*n.* **ruffianism.**

ruf-fle (rŭf'l), *n.* a plaited or gathered strip of material, used as a trimming; a slight vexation; a low, continuous beat of a drum: *v.t.* to draw into folds or gathers; to furnish or adorn with plaited or gathered strips; to make to stand up or out; as, a bird *ruffles* its feathers; to disturb slightly or make ripples upon; as, the wind *ruffles* the water; disarrange; as, to *ruffle* one's hair; annoy or vex; as, to *ruffle* one's temper: *v.i.* to be rumpled or disordered; flutter; to become vexed or annoyed.

ru-fous (rōō'fŭs), *adj.* yellowish-red or brownish-red.

rug (rŭg), *n.* heavy floor covering, usually made in one piece and of a size to cover only part of the floor; a mat made of animal skin with the hair or wool on; a coarse, warm woolen cloth, used as a coverlet or traveling wrap.

rug-ged (rŭg'ĕd), *adj.* having an uneven surface; rough; steep and rocky; as, *rugged* country; shaggy; disordered; unkempt; uncouth; unpolished; as, a *rugged* countryman; wrinkled; furrowed; as, a *rugged* brow; harsh; stern; as, a *rugged* character.—*adv.* **ruggedly.**—*n.* **ruggedness.**

ru-in (rōō'ĭn), *n.* overthrow; destruction; downfall; that which causes destruction or decay; that which remains of something destroyed or fallen into decay; the state of decay or desolation: *v.t.* to pull down, destroy, overthrow, or make poor: *v.i.* to decay; perish; be brought to poverty and misery.—*n.* **ruination.**

ru-ined (rōō'ĭnd), *adj.* demolished; destroyed; having suffered downfall and decay.

ru-in-ous (rōō'ĭ-nŭs), *adj.* fallen into decay; dilapidated; as, a house in a *ruinous* state; destructive; hurtful; as, *ruinous* conduct.—*adv.* **ruinously.**

rule (rōōl), *n.* a standard or principle of conduct; as, honesty should be the *rule* for all; regulation; as, a *rule* of the game; an established usage or law; government; authority; as, a democratic *rule;* usual course of action; as, I walk there as a *rule;* that which is true or may be expected in the majority of cases; as, among the people of some countries, ignorance is the *rule;* a straight strip for drawing lines; in printing, a strip of type-high metal for printing a line: *v.t.* to govern or control; settle, as by a rule; manage, control, influence, or restrain; establish by a decision; mark with lines with the aid of a straight strip: *v.i.* to decide a point; exercise superior authority.

Syn., *n.* sway, method, system, law, formula, test.

rul-er (rōōl'ẽr), *n.* one who governs; a strip of wood, metal, etc., used as a guide in drawing lines.

rul-ing (rōōl'ĭng), *p.adj.* governing or having control; predominant or in control: *n.* a decision laid down by a judge or court; the act of making lines, or the lines so made.

rum (rŭm), *n.* an alcoholic liquor made from molasses or the juice of the sugar cane; colloquially, any intoxicating drink.

rum-ble (rŭm'bl), *n.* a low, heavy, rolling sound; as, the *rumble* of thunder; a seat for servants behind a carriage; a seat for one behind the body of a motor vehicle: *v.i.* to make a low, heavy, continued sound: *v.t.* to cause to make a low, heavy, rolling sound.

ru-mi-nant (rōō'mĭ-nănt), *n.* a hoofed animal that chews the cud, as oxen, sheep, goats, deer, camels: *adj.* chewing the cud; hence, meditative; thoughtful.

ru-mi-nate (rōō'mĭ-nāt), *v.i.* to chew the cud; meditate or muse; reflect; as, to *ruminate* on the future: *v.t.* to chew again; to ponder.—*adj.* **ruminative.**

ru-mi-na-tion (rōō'mĭ-nā'shŭn), *n.* the act of chewing the cud; meditation or musing.

rum-mage (rŭm'āj), *n.* a thorough search made by turning things over in a disorderly way: *v.t.* to search thoroughly by turning over the contents of; ransack: *v.i.* to make a thorough but disorderly search.

ru-mor (rōō'mẽr), *n.* common talk; popular report; an unverified current story; as, a *rumor* of war: *v.t.* to spread by report.

rump (rŭmp), *n.* the hinder parts of an animal; buttocks; fag-end of anything.

rum-ple (rŭm'pl), *n.* a fold or plait: *v.t.* and *v.i.* to wrinkle; crumple; muss.

rum-pus (rŭm'pŭs), *n.* a disturbance; a row. [Colloq.]

run (rŭn), *v.i.* [*p.t.* ran, *p.p.* run, *p.pr.* running], to move or go on the feet at a swifter pace than a walk; to act in a way to suggest such motion; as, he *ran* away from home; travel; proceed; as, the express *runs* forty miles an hour; make a regular trip; as, the boat *runs* between Boston and New York; move on in a stream; flow; as, the river *runs* down hill; melt and flow; as, tallow *runs;* to be in action; as, the engine will not *run;* extend in space; as, the railroad *runs* through his land; continue in time; as, the play *ran* a year; pass into a different state or condition; as, to *run* into luck; *run* to seed; to *run* wild; engage in a contest; as, to *run* for office; pass or look through or over rapidly; as, to *run* through a book; follow a line of descent; as, laziness *runs* in the family; tend; incline; as, her taste does not *run* in that direction; of a wound or sore, discharge pus: *v.t.* to cause to move or act, as an engine, etc.; to thrust; stick; push; as, to *run* a pin into one's finger; to drive or force; as, to *run* one's head against a wall; perform or go through with; as, to *run* errands; to flow with; as, the earth *ran* blood; expose oneself to; as, to *run* a risk; to sew; as, to *run* up a seam: *n.* act of going at a swifter pace than a walk; a trip or journey; as, the boat made its usual *run;* act of flowing or that which flows; as, a *run* of maple sap; a course or succession; as, a *run* of ill luck; free use or enjoyment of; as, to have the *run* of a friend's house; sudden, continuous, pressing demand; as, a *run* on a bank; the kind usually met with; as, the ordinary *run* of people; a place passed over frequently, especially by animals; an inclosed place in which to confine and feed animals; a brook; a period of operation, or the work turned out during the period; in cricket or baseball, the act of running from one wicket or base to another and thus scoring a point.

run-a-bout (rŭn'ȧ-bout"), *n.* a kind of light automobile or uncovered carriage, ordinarily used for short trips.

run-a-gate (rŭn'ȧ-gāt"), *n.* a fugitive; wanderer; vagabond.

run-a-way (rŭn'ȧ-wā"), *n.* one who escapes or runs away; a fugitive; a horse of which the driver has lost control: *adj.* escaping from control; as, a *runaway* engine; brought about by running away; as, a *runaway* match.

rune (rōōn), *n.* one of the letters or characters of the alphabets of ancient nations of northern Europe; poetry expressed in such characters.

Runes (Alphabet)

rung (rŭng), *p.p.* of the verb *ring*: *n.* a crosspiece or round of a ladder or chair; a floor-timber in a ship.

ru-nic (rōō'nĭk), *adj.* pertaining to, or consisting of, runes, or the characters of the alphabets of the earliest Teutonic nations.

run-let (rŭn'lĕt), *n.* a little stream; a rivulet. Also, runnel.

run-ner (rŭn'ẽr), *n.* one who runs; a racer; a messenger; one of the pieces on which a sleigh, skate, or sled moves; a slender trailing branch that takes root at the end or joints; a soldier detailed or picked as an orderly for an officer while in the trenches; an officer's messenger.

run-ning (rŭn'ĭng), *p.adj.* moving swiftly; being in motion; successive; continuous; discharging pus; as, a *running* sore: *n.* the act of moving swiftly; that which runs or flows.

runt (rŭnt), *n.* a dwarf animal, as a small pig; a person of stunted growth.

run-way (rŭn'wā"), *n.* a beaten way or path over which something runs, as the bed of a stream followed by animals.

ru-pee (rōō-pē'), *n.* a coin of British India worth about 32.4 cents.

rup-ture (rŭp'tūr), *n.* the act of bursting or breaking; the state of being broken or violently burst apart; breach or interruption of friendly relations; hernia, or a coming out of a part of the intestines through the inner wall of the abdomen: *v.t.* to burst or break violently apart; to affect with hernia; to bring about a breach of; as, to *rupture* friendship: *v.i.* to suffer a breach or break.

ru-ral (rōō'răl), *adj.* pertaining to, or like, the country, or country life; as, *rural* free delivery; rustic.—*adv.* rurally.

ruse (rōōz), *n.* a trick; a stratagem; fraud or deceit.

rush (rŭsh), *n.* a driving forward with eagerness and haste; any of many plants growing on wet ground; anything worthless or of little value; colloquially, an extraordinary demand for activity and haste; as the Christmas *rush* in a store: *v.i.* to move or press forward with haste; enter or do with undue haste or eagerness: *v.t.* to cause to move with speed; hurry; as, to *rush* a man off to his work; to make an attack on and occupy; as, to *rush* a fortification.

rusk (rŭsk), *n.* a kind of light biscuit; sweetened bread.

rus-set (rŭs'ĕt), *n.* reddish-brown color; cloth or clothing of such a color, especially homespun; a kind of winter apple: *adj.* reddish-brown; homespun; coarse.—*adj.* russety.

Rus-sia leath-er (rŭsh'ȧ lĕth'ẽr), a strong, soft leather prepared from hides soaked in birch oil.

Rus-sian (rŭsh'ăn), *adj.* of or pertaining to Russia, its language, or its people: *n.* one of the people of Russia; the language of Russia.

rust (rŭst), *n.* the reddish matter formed by oxidation on iron and steel; a similar formation occurring on other metals; red oxide of iron; anything like rust; mildew on wheat, corn, etc.; loss of power through idleness: *v.i.* to form rust; to grow worthless because of idleness: *v.t.* to cause to contract rust; impair by time or inaction.—*adv.* rustily.—*n.* rustiness.

rus-tic (rŭs'tĭk), *n.* a countryman; a peasant: *adj.* pertaining to, or like, the country; rural; artless; unpolished; unadorned. Also, *adj.* rustical.—*adv.* rustically.

Syn., *adj.* rude, plain, uncouth.
Ant. (see polished).

rus-ti-cate (rŭs'tĭ-kāt), *v.i.* to reside in the country: *v.t.* to banish or discharge for a time from college.

rus-ti-ca-tion (rŭs"tĭ-kā'shŭn), *n.* residence in the country; temporary dismissal from a college.

rus-tic-i-ty (rŭs-tĭs'ĭ-tĭ), *n.* rural or countrylike manners or simplicity; rudeness.

rus-tle (rŭs'l), *n.* a soft, whispering sound such as that made by leaves: *v.i.* to make a soft, whispering sound, as the rubbing together of silk or dry leaves: *v.t.* to cause to make such a sound.—*n.* rustling.

rus-tler (rŭs'lẽr), *n.* one that rustles or hustles; an enterprising, successful man; a cattle thief. [SLANG.]

rust-y (rŭs'tĭ), *adj.* covered with rust; impaired or harmed by inactivity or idleness, as an engine; rust-colored.

rut (rŭt), *n.* the track of a wheel; a groove or hollow; *v.t.* to cut into grooves or hollows; to make wheel tracks.—*adj.* rutty.

ru-ta-ba-ga (rōō"tȧ-bā'gȧ), *n.* a kind of turnip larger than the common turnip and of a yellowish color.

ruth (rōōth), *n.* pity; compassion; tenderness; sorrow for the misery of another: **Ruth**, a book of the Old Testament, containing the story of the Jewish heroine of that name.—*adj.* ruthful.

ruth-less (rōōth'lĕs), *adj.* cruel; pitiless; savage; barbarous.—*adv.* ruthlessly.—*n.* ruthlessness.

rye (rī), *n.* a hardy plant closely related to wheat; also, its grain or seed; whisky made from rye grain.

S

Sab-ba-ta-ri-an (săb″ȧ-tā′rĭ-ăn), *adj.* pertaining to the Sabbath, or to the keeping of the Sabbath: *n.* a rigid observer of the Sabbath; one who keeps the Sabbath on the seventh day.

Sab-ba-ta-ri-an-ism (săb″ȧ-tā′rĭ-ăn-ĭzm), *n.* the rigid keeping of the Sabbath; the belief of the Sabbatarians or those who keep the Sabbath on the seventh day.

Sab-bath (săb′ȧth), *n.* the seventh day of the week, observed by the Jews as a day of rest, commencing at sunset on Friday and ending at sunset on Saturday; the Christian Sunday, or first day of the week, observed as a day of rest and worship.

sab-bat-i-cal (să-băt′ĭ-kăl), *adj.* pertaining to, or like, the Sabbath; as, *sabbatical* peace: **sabbatical year**, among the ancient Jews, every seventh year, in which the lands and vineyards of the Israelites were allowed to remain fallow or unsowed; every seventh year, allowed a college professor for study or rest.

Saber

sa-ber (sā′bẽr), *n.* a cavalry sword, having a curved blade: *v.t.* to cut, wound, or kill with, or as with, such a sword. Also, **sabre.**

Sa-bi-an-ism (sā′bĭ-ăn-ĭzm), *n.* the worship of the sun, moon, and stars as signs.

sa-ble (sā′bl), *n.* a kind of weasel valued for its handsome, dark, glossy fur; the fur of this animal; in heraldry or coats of arms, black: *pl.* mourning dress: *adj.* dark-colored; black.

Sabots. 1, wood; 2, leather.

sa-bot (sȧ′bō′), *n.* a wooden shoe worn by the peasantry or poor farmers; a kind of wooden-soled shoe. [Fr.]

sa-bo-tage (sȧ′bō-tȧzh′), *n.* the wilful injury or destruction of machinery or materials by workmen during labor troubles; similar methods used to interfere with government undertakings in time of war or emergency; destruction of property, as by poisoning wells or cutting down fruit trees, in order to injure an enemy in war. [Fr.]

sa-bre-tache (sā′bẽr-tăsh″), *n.* a leather pocket worn by a cavalry soldier, hung from his sword belt.

sac (săk), *n.* a baglike part of a plant or animal.

Sac (săk; sôk), *n.* one of a tribe of Algonquian Indians, who at one time lived along the upper Mississippi.

sac-cha-rin (săk′ȧ-rĭn), *n.* a product of coal tar, much sweeter than cane sugar.

sac-cha-rine (săk′ȧ-rĭn), *adj.* pertaining to, like, or producing, sugar; sweet.

sac-er-do-tal (săs″ẽr-dō′tăl), *adj.* pertaining to priests or to the priesthood; priestly.

sac-er-do-tal-ism (săs″ẽr-dō′tăl-ĭzm), *n.* priestly spirit or system; tendency to emphasize the priestly office or its sacred character.

sa-chem (sā′chĕm), *n.* a North American Indian chief.

sa-chet (sȧ′shā′), *n.* a small bag or cushion filled with a perfume in the form of powder.

sack (săk), *n.* a bag or pouch, especially a large coarse bag for holding grain, etc.; quantity contained by such a bag; a short, loose garment or cloak: also spelled *sacque*; a Spanish dry wine; plunder or pillage by soldiers of a town taken by storm: *v.t.* to plunder or pillage; ravage; put into bags.

sack-but (săk′bŭt), *n.* an ancient musical instrument of the lyre kind; in medieval times, a kind of trombone.

sack-cloth (săk′klôth″), *n.* coarse material of which sacks are made; coarse, rough cloth worn in ancient times as a token of mourning or repentance.

sack-ful (săk′fo͝ol), *n.* [*pl.* sackfuls (-fo͝olz)], the quantity a sack will hold.

sack-ing (săk′ĭng), *n.* coarse material used for making sacks or bags.

sacque (săk), *n.* a short loose garment or cloak. Also, **sack.**

sac-ra-ment (săk′rȧ-mĕnt), *n.* a holy or sacred ceremony, as baptism; the Eucharist; the Lord's Supper; a concrete symbol or form representing some sacred truth.—*adj.* **sacramental.**

Syn. service, rite, Communion.

sa-cred (sā′krĕd), *adj.* set apart for religious uses; as, a *sacred* edifice; pertaining to religion; as, *sacred* literature; consecrated; holy; not to be treated irreverently or put to unworthy use; as, he held his mother's memory *sacred.*—*adv.* **sacredly.** —*n.* **sacredness.**

Syn. hallowed, divine, dedicated, devoted.

Ant. (see profane).

sac-ri-fice (săk′rĭ-fīs; săk′rĭ-fīz), *n.* the act of offering to God, or to a deity, a victim on an altar; that which is offered; anything offered or consecrated to God; the destroying, losing, or giving up of one thing for another; the thing so destroyed or given up; goods sold at a loss: *v.t.* to offer to a god in worship; destroy or give up in order to gain some other object; as, to *sacrifice* health for riches; to kill; make a victim of; as, to *sacrifice* a child to his parents' interests; sell at a loss: *v.i.* to offer a victim on an altar. —*n.* **sacrificer.**

sac-ri-fi-cial (săk″rĭ-fĭsh′ăl), *adj.* pertaining to, consisting in, or offering, sacrifice.—*adv.* **sacrificially.**

sac-ri-lege (săk′rĭ-lĕj), *n.* the crime or sin of desecrating or profaning sacred things.

sac-ri-le-gious (săk″rĭ-lē′jŭs), *adj.* treating sacred things irreverently; profane.—*adv.* **sacrilegiously.**

sac-ris-tan (săk′rĭs-tăn), *n.* one who has the care of church vessels, vestments, etc., and of the church in general; a sexton.

sac-ris-ty (săk′rĭs-tĭ), *n.* an apartment in a church where the sacred vessels, minister's vestments or robes, etc., are kept; vestry.

sac-ro-sanct (săk'rô-săṅkt), *adj.* most sacred or holy; consecrated.

sa-crum (sā'krŭm), *n.* the lowest part of the backbone; in man, the five lowest vertebræ.

sad (săd), *adj.* [*comp.* sadder, *superl.* saddest], full of grief; mournful; sorrowful; causing mournfulness; dark: said of colors.—*adv.* **sadly.**—*n.* **sadness.**

sad-den (săd'n), *v.t.* to make mournful or sorrowful: *v.i.* to become depressed or cheerless.

sad-dle (săd'l), *n.* a seat for a rider on a horse's back, a bicycle, etc.; anything shaped like a saddle, as a certain cut of meat: *v.t.* to equip with a seat for a rider; burden or embarrass; as, to *saddle* a town with debt.

sad-dle-bag (săd'l-băg"), *n.* one of a pair of pouches attached to a saddle for carrying articles.

sad-dle-bow (săd'l-bō"), *n.* the pieces which form the pommel or arched front part of a saddle.

sad-dler (săd'lẽr), *n.* one who makes saddles and other harness and equipment for horses.

sad-dler-y (săd'lẽr-ĭ), *n.* the business of a saddler or harness maker; articles made by a harness maker; the materials for making saddles and harness.

sad-dle-tree (săd'l-trē"), *n.* the frame of a saddle.

Sad-du-cee (săd'ū-sē), *n.* one of an ancient aristocratic Jewish sect that clung to the letter of the law and denied the resurrection of the dead.

sad-i-ron (săd'ī"ŭrn), *n.* a flatiron, especially a hollow one, heated from within.

safe (sāf), *adj.* free from danger, risk, injury, or damage; secure; in secure keeping; as, the captive is *safe;* sound; unhurt; sure; *n.* a fireproof or burglar-proof iron or steel chest for valuables; cupboard; a holder for matches.—*adv.* **safely.**—*n.* **safeness.**
Syn., *adj.* harmless, trustworthy.
Ant. (see perilous).

safe-con-duct (sāf"kŏn'dŭkt), *n.* a guard or passport which guarantees a safe passage, especially through an enemy's country in war time.

safe-guard (sāf'gärd"), *n.* one who, or that which, guards or protects; a means of security; defense; safe-conduct; protective papers granted to a foreigner: *v.t.* to protect or watch over.

safe-keep-ing (sāf"kēp'ĭng), *n.* care; secure guardianship.

safe-ty (sāf'tĭ), *n.* freedom from danger, injury, or damage; safe-keeping.

safe-ty lamp (sāf'tĭ lămp), a lamp so constructed as to protect the flame; used in mines to prevent the explosion of gas.

safe-ty valve (sāf'tĭ vălv), an automatic valve in a boiler which opens when the steam exceeds a certain pressure; hence, a means of relief from worry or an outlet for strong feeling.

saf-fron (săf'rŭn), *n.* a kind of crocus with purple flowers whose pistils yield a deep yellow dye and are also used in medicine; a deep yellow color: *adj.* deep yellow.

sag (săg), *v.i.* [*p.t.* and *p.p.* sagged, *p.pr.* sagging], to sink or droop by weight, or under pressure; as, the rope *sags;* to lose firmness: *n.* the fact or the extent of sinking or drooping under weight; as, the *sag* of a skirt.

sa-ga (sä'gȧ; sā'gȧ), *n.* [*pl.* sagas (-gȧz)], a Scandinavian legend.

sa-ga-cious (sȧ-gā'shŭs), *adj.* shrewd; keen; having good judgment and practical common sense; wise; farsighted.—*adv.* **sagaciously.**—*n.* **sagaciousness.**

sa-gac-i-ty (sȧ-găs'ĭ-tĭ), *n.* readiness of understanding; keen practical judgment; shrewdness.

sag-a-more (săg'ȧ-mōr), *n.* an Indian chief among certain North American tribes.

sage (sāj), *adj.* wise; discerning; discriminating; of good judgment; shrewd; as, *sage* counsel: *n.* a man of profound wisdom and of venerable age; a spicy garden herb for flavoring meats, soups, etc.; the sagebrush.—*adv.* **sagely.**—*n.* **sageness.**

sage-brush (sāj'brŭsh"), *n.* any one of various low shrubs, grayish-green in color, found on the deserts of western America.

Sag-it-ta-ri-us (săj"ĭ-tā'rĭ-ŭs), *n.* the Archer, or the ninth sign of the zodiac; a southern constellation represented by a centaur shooting an arrow.

sag-it-tate (săj'ĭ-tāt), *adj.* of a shape resembling the pointed head of an arrow; as, a *sagittate* leaf.

Sago. *A*, fruit

sa-go (sā'gō), *n.* a kind of starch from the trunk of certain East Indian palms.

sa-hib (sä'ĭb), *n.* a term of address used by the natives of India when speaking to, or referring to, a European gentleman; master.

said (sĕd), *p.t.* and *p.p.* of the verb *say: p.adj.* already referred to; mentioned before: used chiefly in legal documents.

sail (sāl), *n.* a sheet of canvas by means of which the wind is made to drive a vessel forward in the water; a ship or vessel; vessels collectively; an excursion in a vessel moved by the wind; as, we went for a *sail:* *v.i.* to be moved by the action of the wind upon spread canvas; hence, to be moved through water by the force of steam, etc.; to go by water; as, we *sailed* from New York to Liverpool; to begin a voyage; as, the ship *sailed* at noon; glide like a boat, as an eagle through the air; pass smoothly along: *v.t.* to pass over in a ship; as, to *sail* the Spanish Main; to direct, steer, or manage the motion of; as, to *sail* a ship.

sail-boat (sāl'bōt"), *n.* a boat usually driven through the water by sails: generally applied to small craft.

sail-er (sāl'ẽr), *n.* a vessel moved by the wind, with special reference to its speed or manner of motion; as, a swift *sailer.*

sail-or (sāl'ẽr), *n.* one who makes a voyage in, or directs the motion of, a vessel moved by the wind; an enlisted man in a navy; a mariner; an ordinary seaman; a straw hat with a flat brim and top.—*adj.* **sailorly.**

saint (sānt), *n.* a holy or godly person; one noted for piety and virtue, especially one canonized, or declared a saint, by the

Roman Catholic Church; one dead and blessed in heaven: *v.t.* to canonize.—*adj.* **saintly.**—*n.* **saintliness.**

Saint Ber-nard (sānt bẽr-närd′), one of a breed of large dogs having unusual intelligence.

saint-ed (sān′tĕd), *p.adj.* canonized; pious; holy; gone to heaven.

Saint Nich-o-las (sānt nĭk′ō-lȧs), the patron saint of Russia, and of children, seafarers, and virgins; the legendary bringer of gifts to children on Christmas Eve, commonly known as *Santa Claus.*

sake (sāk), *n.* end; purpose; cause; account; regard; reason: used in for my *sake;* for his *sake,* etc.

sa-laam (sȧ-läm′), *n.* an Oriental form of salutation or respect: *v.i.* and *v.t.* to make, or to welcome or greet with, such a salutation.

sal-a-ble (sāl′ȧ-bl), *adj.* capable of being sold; fit to be sold; marketable.—*n.* **salability, salableness.**

sa-la-cious (sȧ-lā′shŭs), *adj.* impure; lustful.—*adv.* **salaciously.**—*n.* **salaciousness.**

sal-ad (săl′ȧd), *n.* a preparation of meat, fish, vegetables, or fruit, etc., usually served on lettuce and covered with a dressing, as of salt, pepper, vinegar, and oil; vegetables or herbs for salad.

sal-a-man-der (săl′ȧ-măn′dẽr), *n.* an animal resembling a lizard, able to live both on land and in water, and believed by the ancients to be able to live in fire.—*adj.* **salamandrine.**

sal-a-ry (săl′ȧ-rĭ), *n.* a regular payment for services rendered; recompense: *v.t.* to pay a regular recompense to.

sale (sāl), *n.* the act of selling; exchange of a commodity or goods for an agreed price; an offer by a store of goods of special quality for a specially low price; as, a bargain *sale;* a small fair for a charitable or public object; as, a cake *sale;* chance to dispose of goods or demand for them; as, a ready *sale* for meat; auction.

Syn. bargain, barter, deal, trade.

sal-e-ra-tus (săl′ē-rā′tŭs), *n.* commonly, sodium bicarbonate; cooking soda.

sales-man (sālz′măn), *n.* [*pl.* salesmen (-mĕn), *fem.* saleswoman], one whose business it is to sell goods.

sales-man-ship (sālz′măn-shĭp), *n.* the skill of one who sells goods; the art of selling.

Sal-ic (săl′ĭk), *adj.* pertaining to a certain tribe of the Franks: **Salic law,** the law of the Salic Franks excluding women from the succession to the French throne.

sal-i-cyl-ic (săl′ĭ-sĭl′ĭk), *adj.* pertaining to an acid much used in medicine: **salicylic acid,** a white crystalline substance, used as an antiseptic, and as a drug.

sa-li-ence (sā′lĭ-ĕns), *n.* the state of being conspicuous or prominent.

sa-li-ent (sā′lĭ-ĕnt), *adj.* leaping or bounding; outstanding; noticeable; as, *salient* traits or characteristics; projecting outward; as, a *salient* angle: *n.* a projecting angle; in trench warfare, a part of a trench system which projects farther than the rest into the enemy's territory, or an outward bending of the line of battle.—*adv.* **saliently.**

sa-line (sā′līn), *adj.* consisting of, containing, or like, salt; as, a *saline* substance; salty: *n.* a salt spring.—*n.* **salinity.**

sa-li-va (sȧ-lī′vȧ), *n.* the watery fluid or spittle secreted or formed in the mouth.

sal-i-va-ry (săl′ĭ-vā-rĭ), *adj.* of or pertaining to the fluid secreted in the mouth; as, the *salivary* glands.

sal-i-vate (săl′ĭ-vāt), *v.t.* to produce an abnormal flow of fluid in the mouth of, as with certain drugs.

sal-i-va-tion (săl′ĭ-vā′shŭn), *n.* the act of producing, or state of having, an abnormal flow of fluid in the mouth; the abnormally increased secretion of fluid.

sal-low (săl′ō), *adj.* of a pale, sickly, yellow color: *n.* a small tree of the willow kind.

sal-ly (săl′ĭ), *n.* [*pl.* sallies (-ĭz)], a sudden rushing forth of troops from a fortified place to attack a besieging enemy; sudden outburst of wit or fancy; excursion; wild gaiety: *v.i.* [*p.t.* and *p.p.* sallied, *p.pr.* sallying], to rush out, as troops from a besieged town; issue or rush forth suddenly.

sal-ma-gun-di (săl′mȧ-gŭn′dĭ), *n.* a dish made of chopped meats mixed with other ingredients; a mixed collection of things; medley.

salm-on (săm′ŭn), *n.* a sea fish, found in northern waters, which ascends rivers to lay its eggs; the yellowish-pink color of salmon flesh: *adj.* of the yellowish-pink color of salmon flesh.

Salmon

salm-on-ber-ry (săm′ŭn-bĕr′ĭ), *n.* [*pl.* salmonberries (-ĭz)], a large raspberry; its fruit.

sa-lon (sȧ-lôɴ′), *n.* a saloon or apartment for the reception of company; a fashionable assemblage; a fine art gallery; the paintings or sculpture exhibited there.

sa-loon (sȧ-lo͞on′), *n.* a hall or state apartment; large reception room; fine art gallery; a public room for special uses; as, a dancing *saloon;* especially, in the United States, a tavern or barroom.

sal-si-fy (săl′sĭ-fĭ), *n.* a European plant of the chicory family, the root of which, often called the *oyster plant,* is used for food.

salt (sôlt), *n.* chloride of sodium, used for seasoning, and for the preservation of meat, etc.: obtained from the earth or by the evaporation of sea water; a salt-cellar; anything like salt; in chemistry, the compound formed by the action of an acid on a metal or an oxide, replacing the hydrogen of the acid with a metal or a metallic element; wit; colloquially, a sailor: *pl.* any mineral salt used as a laxative or a cathartic: *v.t.* to sprinkle or season with salt: *adj.* flavored or seasoned with salt.—*n.* **saltness.**

sal-ta-to-ry (săl′tȧ-tō-rĭ), *adj.* pertaining to dancing; leaping or jumping.—*n.* **saltation.**—*adj.* **saltatorial.**

salt-cel-lar (sôlt′sĕl-ẽr), *n.* a little dish or shaker to hold salt at table.

salt-ish (sôl′tĭsh), *adj.* somewhat salt; salty.—*n.* **saltishness.**

salt-less (sôlt′lĕs), *adj.* without salt; flat of taste.

salt-pe-ter (sôlt′pē′tẽr), *n.* rock salt or stone salt; niter; used in explosives, matches, and as a food preservative. Also, **saltpetre.**

salt rheum (sôlt ro͞om), any of various eruptions on the skin.

salt-y (sôl'tĭ), *adj.* tasting of salt; somewhat salt.—*n.* **saltiness.**

sa-lu-bri-ous (sȧ-lū'brĭ-ŭs), *adj.* healthful; promoting health; as, a *salubrious* climate.—*n.* **salubriousness.**

sal-u-ta-ry (săl'ū-tā-rĭ), *adj.* healthful; as, *salutary* exercises; wholesome; resulting in benefit or advantage.

sal-u-ta-tion (săl"ū-tā'shŭn), *n.* act or manner of addressing or greeting; a greeting.

sa-lu-ta-to-ry (sȧ-lū'tȧ-tō-rĭ), *adj.* greeting; opening or introducing: applied to the opening oration at the commencement exercises of certain schools and colleges: *n.* the opening address at the commencement exercises in certain schools and colleges, usually made by the student second highest in rank; any address of welcome.—*n.* **salutatorian.**

sa-lute (sȧ-lūt'), *n.* in the army and navy, a mark of respect shown by taking a certain prescribed position; as, the officers exchanged *salutes* as they passed; in the army and navy, the discharge of cannon, the lowering of a flag, etc., as a mark of honor; a greeting; a bow; a kiss: *v.t.* to address with kind wishes; welcome; greet with a kiss or bow; honor by a discharge of guns, the lowering of a flag, etc.: *v.i.* in the army or navy, to make the prescribed gesture of respect.—*n.* **saluter.**

sal-vage (săl'vāj), *n.* the act of saving a ship or goods from the dangers of the sea, from a wreck, or from other grave danger; payment given to those who help to save property under such circumstances; the goods or vessel so saved.

sal-va-tion (săl-vā'shŭn), *n.* the act of saving; rescue; the setting free of the soul from sin and death; that which saves: **Salvation Army,** a religious body organized on a military basis for the purpose of relieving poverty and of bringing spiritual comfort to the needy and distressed.

salve (säv), *n.* a healing ointment; a healing application for sores or wounds consisting of a soft, greasy mixture of various drugs: *v.t.* to apply ointment to; to smooth over or palliate: *v.t.* and *v.i.* (sălv), to save, as a ship or property, from the dangers of the sea, a wreck, etc.

sal-ve (săl'vē), *interj.* Hail! a form of address or greeting. [LAT.]

sal-ver (săl'vẽr), *n.* a tray on which anything is presented; a waiter.

sal-vi-a (săl'vĭ-ȧ), *n.* any of various plants of the sage family.

sal-vo (săl'vō), *n.* the discharge all at once of a certain number of guns, intended as a salute; the cheers of a crowd.

sal vo-la-ti-le (săl vō-lăt'ĭ-lē), ammonium carbonate; an alcoholic solution of it, aromatic and stimulating.

Sa-mar-i-tan (sȧ-măr'ĭ-tăn), *adj.* pertaining to, or like, Samaria, or the Samaritans: *n.* a native of Samaria; a kind, charitable person.—Luke x. 30–37.

Sam Browne belt (săm broun bĕlt), a leather belt with a strap over the right shoulder, worn by army officers.

same (sām), *adj.* identical; as, this is the *same* picture; alike in kind or degree; equal; as, exactly the *same;* just mentioned.

same-ness (sām'nĕs), *n.* the state of being exactly alike; identity; lack of variety or difference; similarity.

sa-mite (sā'mīt), *n.* a rich silk generally interwoven with gold.

Sa-mo-an (sȧ-mō'ăn), *adj.* of or pertaining to the Samoa Islands, or their inhabitants: *n.* a native of the Samoa Islands; the language of the people of Samoa.

sam-o-var (săm'ō-vär), *n.* a metal vessel used to heat water for making tea: originally used in Russia.

samp (sămp), *n.* hulled Indian corn or coarse hominy.

sam-pan (săm'păn), *n.* a swift, flat-bottomed river boat, propelled by sails or oars, used in China and Java, sometimes as a house boat.

Sampan

sam-phire (săm'fīr), *n.* a salt-water plant of the parsley family, growing usually on cliffs, and formerly used as a pickle.

sam-ple (săm'pl), *n.* a specimen; model; pattern; part shown to prove the quality of the whole: *v.t.* to test a specimen of; as, to *sample* sugar or tea.

sam-pler (săm'plẽr), *n.* one who prepares specimens of goods for inspection; one who examines goods by means of specimens; as, a wool *sampler;* a piece of ornamental needlework made as an exhibition of skill.

Sam-son (săm'sŭn), *n.* in the Bible, one of the Israelites noted for his great strength.

Sam-u-el (săm'ū-ĕl), *n.* in the Bible, either of two books, called First and Second Samuel, in the Old Testament; a Hebrew judge and prophet.

Sa-mu-rai (sä'mōō-rī"), *n.* under the ancient feudal system of Japan, the noble military caste, or a member of it.

san-a-tive (săn'ȧ-tĭv), *adj.* healing; able to, or tending to, cure; health-giving.

san-a-to-ri-um (săn"ȧ-tō'rĭ-ŭm), *n.* a health resort; a locality conducive to the restoration of health; an institution for the care of invalids or the treatment of certain diseases; a sanitarium.

san-a-to-ry (săn'ȧ-tō-rĭ), *adj.* health-giving; tending to cure or to preserve health; healing.

sanc-ti-fi-ca-tion (săṅk"tĭ-fĭ-kā'shŭn), *n.* the act of making holy; state of being made holy; the act of setting apart for a sacred purpose.

sanc-ti-fied (săṅk'tĭ-fīd), *p.adj.* made holy; sometimes, insincerely, pious or devout.

sanc-ti-fy (săṅk'tĭ-fī), *v.t.* to make holy; to set apart for some sacred use; to hallow; to purify.—*n.* **sanctifier.**

sanc-ti-mo-ni-ous (săṅk"tĭ-mō'nĭ-ŭs), *adj.* having the appearance of, or making a show of, piety or holiness; hypocritical.—*adv.* **sanctimoniously.**—*n.* **sanctimoniousness.**

sanc-ti-mo-ny (săṅk'tĭ-mō-nĭ), *n.* pretended or assumed devoutness; show of piety.

sanc-tion (săṅk'shŭn), *n.* the act of giving authority to; authority; formal approval: *v.t.* to give indorsement to; to confirm; to approve; as, to *sanction* a marriage.

Syn. v. encourage, support, ratify, authorize.
Ant. (see disapprove).

sanc-ti-ty (săṅk'tĭ-tĭ), *n.* holiness; purity; sacredness; solemnity.

sanc-tu-a-ry (săṅk'tū-ā-rĭ), *n.* [*pl.* sanctuaries (-rĭz)], the most retired and sacred part of a temple; consecrated place; church or temple; the part of a Christian church nearest the altar; a place of shelter and protection; a place of refuge.

sanc-tum (săṅk'tŭm), *n.* a sacred or private place; as, an editor's *sanctum.*

sanc-tum sanc-to-rum (săṅk'tŭm săṅk-tō'rŭm), a most holy place; in the Jewish Temple, the Holy of Holies; a place of the utmost privacy; often used in jest. [Lat.]

Sanc-tus (săṅk'tŭs), *n.* a part of the Mass, or Communion service, which begins with the words, *Sanctus, sanctus, sanctus*, meaning Holy, holy, holy. [Lat.]

sand (sănd), *n.* dry soil composed of fine particles of crushed or worn rock: *pl.* a stretch of such soil; a beach; the sand in an hourglass; hence, hours or time; as, the *sands* are numbered that make my life: *v.t.* to sprinkle or mix with sand.

san-dal (săn'dăl), *n.* a kind of shoe consisting of a sole fastened by straps to the foot; a loose slipper; a kind of rubber overshoe.—*adj.* sandaled.

Roman Sandal

san-dal-wood (săn'-dăl-wŏŏd"), *n.* a fragrant wood from certain Oriental trees: used in cabinet-making. Also, sandal.

sand-bag (sănd'băg"), *n.* a bag filled with sand: used for ballast, trench parapets, etc.: *v.t.* to give a blow to, or stun with, such a bag.

sand-blast (sănd'blăst"), *n.* sand driven by a blast of air or steam: used to cut, polish, or decorate glass and other hard substances: also used to clean the outside walls of marble buildings.

sand-er-ling (săn'dẽr-lĭng), *n.* a small variety of sandpiper.

sand-glass (sănd'glăs"), *n.* an hourglass which measures time by the running of sand.

sand-pa-per (sănd'pā"pẽr), *n.* stout paper covered on one side with a coating of sand: used for smoothing and polishing: *v.t.* to smooth by rubbing with this paper.

sand-pip-er (sănd'pīp"ẽr), *n.* a kind of small shore bird with long legs and bill.

sand-stone (sănd'stōn"), *n.* a rock made of sand hardened into a solid mass.

sand-wich (sănd'wĭch), *n.* two thin slices of bread with ham, etc., between; anything like a sandwich: *v.t.* to place between two other persons or things.

sand-y (săn'dĭ), *adj.* composed of, abounding in, or covered with, sand; like sand; hence, shifting; not firm underfoot; of a yellowish-red color.—*n.* sandiness.

sane (sān), *adj.* mentally sound or healthy; rational; coming from a well-balanced mind; as, a *sane* suggestion.—*adv.* sanely.—*n.* saneness.

sang (săng), the past tense of the transitive and intransitive verb *sing.*

sang-froid (säṅ"frwä'), *n.* cool indifference or composure; coolness under trying circumstances. [Fr.]

san-gui-na-ry (săṅ'gwĭ-nā-rĭ), *adj.* attended with much bloodshed; as, a *sanguinary* battle; bloodthirsty; murderous; cruel.—*adv.* sanguinarily.—*n.* sanguinariness.

san-guine (săṅ'gwĭn), *adj.* having the color of blood; having an active circulation of blood; warm and ardent in temper; hopeful; confident; as, *sanguine* of success.—*adv.* sanguinely.—*n.* sanguineness.

San-he-drim (săn'hē-drĭm), *n.* the great council or court of the ancient Jews, composed of seventy-one priests, scribes, and elders, presided over by the high priest. Also, Sanhedrin.

san-i-ta-ri-um (săn"ĭ-tā'rĭ-ŭm), *n.* a health resort; a place for the care of invalids or the treatment of certain diseases; a sanatorium.

san-i-ta-ry (săn'ĭ-tā-rĭ), *adj.* pertaining to health; as, *sanitary* laws; producing or preserving health; hygienic.

san-i-ta-tion (săn"ĭ-tā'shŭn), *n.* the science of bringing about healthful conditions; the use of precautions to protect health; hygiene.

san-i-ty (săn'ĭ-tĭ), *n.* soundness or health of mind; the state of being in sound mind.

San Jo-sé scale (săn hō-sā' skāl), a scale insect very destructive to many varieties of fruit trees; first found in the United States at San José, California.

sank (săṅk), the past tense of the irregular verb *sink.*

sans (sănz; Fr. säṅ), *prep.* without; deprived of: not used in present-day English. [Fr.]

sans-cu-lotte (sănz"kū-lŏt'), *n.* a republican of the lower classes: a term of contempt applied to the French Revolutionists by the aristocrats; hence, a violent or extreme radical.

San-skrit (săn'skrĭt), *n.* the ancient language of the Hindus of India. Also, Sanscrit.—*adj.* Sanskritic.

sap (săp), *n.* the watery circulating juice of a plant; the layer of soft wood next the bark of a tree; vitality; vital fluid; in the military sense, a deep, narrow, concealed ditch run towards an enemy's works: *v.t.* [*p.t.* and *p.p.* sapped, *p.pr.* sapping], to deprive of vitality; undermine; as, to *sap* one's strength; to dig beneath: *v.i.* in the military sense, to approach the enemy's lines by digging a deep, narrow, concealed ditch at right angles to the front line.

sap-head (săp'hĕd"), *n.* a weak-minded or stupid fellow; a simpleton. [Colloq.]

sa-pi-ence (sā'pĭ-ĕns), *n.* knowledge; learning; wisdom: often used ironically.

sa-pi-ent (sā'pĭ-ĕnt), *adj.* wise; full of knowledge: often used ironically.—*adv.* sapiently.

sap-less (săp'lĕs), *adj.* without vitality; lacking in energy; without vigor.

sap-ling (săp'lĭng), *n.* a young tree; hence, a youth.

sa-pon-i-fy (sȧ-pŏn'ĭ-fī), *v.t.* and *v.i.* to make into soap.—*n.* saponification.

sap-o-na-ceous (săp"ō-nā'shŭs), *adj.* pertaining to, or like, soap; soapy.

sap-per (săp'ẽr), *n.* a soldier employed in digging hidden trenches running toward the enemy's lines.

Sap-phic (săf'ĭk), *adj.* of or pertaining to the Greek poetess named Sappho.

sap-phire (săf'īr), *n.* a precious stone of a bright blue color; the bright blue color of this gem.

sap-py (săp'ĭ), *adj.* full of juice, as a plant; immature; silly.—*n.* sappiness.

sap-suck-er (săp'sŭk"ẽr), *n.* one of several kinds of small American woodpeckers which feed in part on sap.

sap-wood (săp'wŏŏd"), *n.* the soft, living wood between the bark and the heartwood: called also *alburnum.*

sar-a-band (săr'ȧ-bănd), *n.* a slow Spanish dance; the music for this dance.

Sar-a-cen (săr'ȧ-sĕn), *n.* in ancient times, the name for an Arab; during the Middle Ages, the name for a Mohammedan.—*adj.* Saracenic.

Sa-rah (sā'rȧ), *n.* in the Bible, the wife of Abraham and mother of Isaac. Also, Sarai.

sar-casm (sär'kăzm), *n.* a bitter, cutting remark, usually ironical, expressing scorn or contempt; irony.

sar-cas-tic (sär-kăs'tĭk), *adj.* bitterly scornful or contemptuous; cutting; unkindly ironical; given to the use of bitter or scornful irony; as, a *sarcastic* teacher.—*adv.* sarcastically.

sar-co-ma (sär-kō'mȧ), *n.* a fleshy tumor, often of so serious a nature as to result fatally.

sar-coph-a-gus (sär-kŏf'ȧ-gŭs), *n.* a limestone used by the Greeks for coffins; a stone coffin or tomb.

Sarcophagus

sard (särd), *n.* a reddish-yellow or brownish-red stone of the quartz variety.

sar-dine (sär-dēn'; sär'dēn), *n.* a small fish of the herring family, good for food when preserved in oil or mustard.

sar-di-us (sär'dĭ-ŭs), *n.* a sard; one of the gems in the breastplate of the Jewish high priest.

sar-don-ic (sär-dŏn'ĭk), *adj.* forced, bitter, or heartless; sneering; as, a *sardonic* laugh or smile.—*adv.* sardonically.

sar-do-nyx (sär'dō-nĭks), *n.* a kind of onyx made up of alternating layers of chalcedony and sard.

sar-gas-so (sär-găs'ō), *n.* the floating seaweed or gulfweed of the South Atlantic. Also, sargassum.

sar-sa-pa-ril-la (sär"sȧ-pȧ-rĭl'ȧ), *n.* a kind of plant, the root of which is used as a medicine; a cooling drink made from this root.

sarse-net (särs'nĕt), *n.* a thin fine kind of woven silk, used for ribbons, linings, etc. Also, sarcenet.

sar-to-ri-al (sär-tō'rĭ-ăl), *adj.* pertaining to a tailor or to the work done by a tailor.

sash (săsh), *n.* a band, ribbon, or scarf, worn round the waist or over the shoulder; a frame in a door or window for holding panes of glass.—*adj.* sashless.

sas-sa-fras (săs'ȧ-frăs), *n.* a tree of the laurel family, whose root, wood, and flowers have a spicy smell and a pungent taste.

sat (săt), the past tense and past participle of the verb *sit.*

Sa-tan (sā'tăn), *n.* the chief of the fallen angels; the Devil, or Prince of Darkness: satan, a wicked person.

sa-tan-ic (sȧ-tăn'ĭk), *adj.* pertaining to, or like, Satan; devilish; infernal; wicked.—*adv.* satanically.

satch-el (săch'ĕl), *n.* a small bag in which to carry small personal belongings, papers, etc.; a handbag.

sate (sāt), *v.t.* to satisfy the appetites or desires of; to glut.

sa-teen (să-tēn'), *n.* a woolen or cotton fabric made in imitation of satin.

sat-el-lite (săt'ĕ-līt), *n.* a small planet revolving round a larger one; as, the moon is a *satellite* of the earth; an attentive follower; a fawning dependent.

sa-ti-a-ble (sā'shĭ-ȧ-bl), *adj.* capable of being gratified or filled: as, *satiable* desires.

sa-ti-ate (sā'shĭ-āt), *v.t.* to fill or gratify fully; surfeit; gratify beyond wish or appetite; as, to *satiate* one with sweets: *adj.* (sā'shĭ-ât), glutted; filled beyond need or natural requirement.

sa-ti-e-ty (sȧ-tī'ĕ-tĭ), *n.* state of being filled or satisfied beyond desire; repletion; surfeit.

sat-in (săt'ĭn), *n.* a closely woven glossy silk: *adj.* made of, or like, this silk.

sat-i-net (săt'ĭ-nĕt'), *n.* a kind of thin satin; a glossy cloth woven of wool and cotton made to resemble satin.

sat-in-wood (săt'ĭn-wŏŏd"), *n.* an East Indian tree; the yellowish wood of this tree, which has a satiny sheen.

sat-in-y (săt'ĭn-ĭ), *adj.* like satin; smooth; glossy.

sat-ire (săt'īr), *n.* a kind of literature, usually poetry, in which vice and folly are held up to ridicule; a single work of literature of this sort; sarcasm; ridicule.

sa-tir-ic (sȧ-tĭr'ĭk), *adj.* pertaining to, or containing, biting sarcasm or ridicule; given to the use of sarcasm or ridicule. Also, satirical.—*adv.* satirically.

sat-i-rize (săt'ĭ-rīz), *v.t.* to attack by ridiculing; to hold up to ridicule; to subject to the shafts of biting wit.—*n.* satirist.

sat-is-fac-tion (săt"ĭs-făk'shŭn), *n.* the act of filling a wish or of supplying enough of something; the act of paying off, compensating, contenting, etc.; the state of having one's wishes filled or of being gratified, paid off, contented, etc.; contentment; payment; redress; that which fills one's wishes, contents, or gratifies.

sat-is-fac-to-ry (săt"ĭs-făk'tō-rĭ), *adj.* sufficient; making redress; relieving the mind from doubt or uncertainty; filling the wishes.—*adv.* satisfactorily.—*n.* satisfactoriness.

sat-is-fy (săt'ĭs-fī), *v.t.* [*p.t.* and *p.p.* satisfied, *p.pr.* satisfying], to make content; to give enough to; to fill the wishes of; to gratify to the fullest degree; as, to *satisfy* hunger; free from doubt or uncertainty; to convince; as, to *satisfy* oneself of the truth of a report; pay in full; as, to *satisfy* a creditor or a claim: *v.i.* to give gratification; make atonement or payment.

Syn. satiate, surfeit, suffice, fill.

Ant. (see check, stint).

sa-trap (sā'trăp; săt'răp), *n.* the governor of a province in ancient Persia.

sa-trap-y (sā'trȧ-pĭ), *n.* the office or position of a satrap, or governor of a province in ancient Persia.

sat-u-rate (săt'ū-rāt), *v.t.* to cause to become soaked; to fill to the limit of the capacity for absorbing; as, to *saturate* a sponge with water; to *saturate* water with sugar.

sat-u-ra-tion (săt′ū-rā′shŭn), *n.* the act of soaking; the state of being soaked; condition of a substance when it has absorbed or soaked in as much as it can hold of another substance.

Sat-ur-day (săt′ûr-dā), *n.* the seventh day of the week.

Rings of Saturn

Sat-urn (săt′ûrn), *n.* the planet next smaller than Jupiter and next farther away from the sun; the ancient Roman god of seedtime and harvest; father of Jupiter.—*adj.* **Saturnian.**

Sat-ur-na-li-an (săt′ûr-nā′lĭ-ăn), *adj.* pertaining to, or like, the Saturnalia, an ancient Roman festival in honor of the god Saturn, which was a time of disorder and debauch; hence, dissolute; riotously mirthful.

Sat-ur-nine (săt′ûr-nīn), *adj.* born under, or under the influence of, the planet Saturn: saturnine, dull; gloomy; grave; heavy; as, a *saturnine* temper.

sat-yr (săt′ẽr; sā′tẽr), *n.* a forest or woodland Greek god who indulged in riotous merriment and lust: supposed to be part man and part goat, and represented as having long, pointed ears and short horns; a man inclined to free indulgence of base passions. Also, **Satyr.**—*adj.* **satyric, satyrical.**

sauce (sôs), *n.* a dressing or seasoning for food; any highly seasoned mixture of ingredients used as a relish; stewed or canned fruit; colloquially, pertness: *v.t.* to put seasoning into; to add flavor to; colloquially, treat with pertness or sauciness.

sauce-pan (sôs′păn″), *n.* a stewpan; a small vessel, usually of metal, having a handle, and used for stewing or boiling.

sau-cer (sô′sẽr), *n.* a shallow piece of china, etc., in which a cup is placed; anything like a saucer.

sau-cy (sô′sĭ), *adj.* [*comp.* saucier, *superl.* sauciest], pert; impudent; bold; uncivil.—*adv.* **saucily.**—*n.* **sauciness.**

Syn. impertinent, rude, insolent, flippant, forward.

Ant. (see modest).

sauer-kraut (sour′krout″), *n.* chopped cabbage which has fermented in a brine made of its own juice with salt.

Saul (sôl), *n.* in the Bible, the first king of Israel; the original name of the apostle Paul, who before his conversion was called *Saul* of Tarsus.

saun-ter (sän′tẽr; sôn′tẽr), *v.i.* to wander about idly; to stroll: *n.* a strolling gait; a leisurely manner of walking; an idle walk or ramble.

sau-ri-an (sô′rĭ-ăn), *n.* any animal of the lizard family: *adj.* pertaining to the lizards.

sau-sage (sô′sāj), *n.* meat, usually pork, ground fine and highly seasoned, inclosed in a skin or made into small cakes.

sau-té (sō′tā′), *adj.* fried quickly and lightly in a pan containing little grease: said of food, especially meat or fish. [Fr.]

sau-terne (sō″tẽrn′; sō-tûrn′), *n.* a French white wine.

sav-age (săv′āj), *adj.* uncivilized; wild; cruel; fierce; pitiless; uncultivated: *n.* a human being in a rude, uncivilized state; barbarian; a fierce, brutal person.—*adv.* **savagely.**—*n.* **savageness.**

sav-age-ry (săv′āj-rĭ), *n.* the state of being wild or uncivilized; barbarity; brutal roughness.

sa-van-na (să-văn′ȧ), *n.* an open plain or meadow having no trees.

sa-vant (sȧ′vän′), *n.* a learned man; a scholar. [Fr.]

save (sāv), *v.t.* to bring out of danger or preserve from evil; rescue; deliver from spiritual death; prevent; as, to *save* trouble; to prevent the waste of; as, to *save* time; lay by; as, to *save* money: *v.i.* to avoid unnecessary expense; to prevent waste; to lay by money, a little at a time: *prep.* except; not including.—*n.* **saver.**

sav-ing (sāv′ĭng), *p.adj.* preserving or redeeming; as, a *saving* grace; frugal; reserving or qualifying; as, a *saving* clause: *n.* economy; rescue; *pl.* money, etc., saved: *prep.* with the exception of; except.

sav-ings bank (sāv′ĭngz băṅk), a bank where small sums may be deposited at interest.

sav-ior (sāv′yẽr), *n.* one who brings out of danger or rescues: **Savior,** Jesus Christ, the Redeemer. Also, **saviour, Saviour.**

sa-vor (sā′vẽr), *n.* flavor; taste; relish; scent; essential quality; *v.i.* to have a certain flavor or smell: with *of;* to partake of the quality or nature of: with *of;* as, to *savor* of disobedience: *v.t.* to taste or smell with delight; to appreciate. Also, **savour.**—*adj.* **savorless, savourless.**

sa-vor-y (sā′vẽr-ĭ), *adj.* pleasing to taste or smell; reputable; in good repute: *n.* a fragrant herb, much used in cooking. Also, *adj.* **savoury.**—*n.* **savoriness, savouriness.**

sa-voy (să-voi′), *n.* a kind of winter cabbage with curled leaves.

saw (sô), *n.* a cutting tool with a thin, flat blade and a toothed edge; a proverb or wise saying: *v.t.* [*p.t.* sawed (sôd); *p.p.* sawed or sawn (sôn); *p.pr.* sawing], to cut with, or as with, a thin-bladed tool with a toothed edge; to form or fashion with such a tool; to make motions like those of such a tool in operation; as, he *sawed* the air with his hands and arms: *v.i.* to be cut with such a tool; to use such a tool: *p.t.* of *see.*—*n.* **sawer.**

saw-buck (sô′bŭk″), *n.* a rack on which sticks of wood are placed while being sawed. [U. S.]

saw-dust (sô′dŭst″), *n.* the small bits of wood or particles of dust which fly from wood when it is being cut by the saw.

saw-fish (sô′fĭsh″), *n.* a fish, similar to the shark, with a long, bony snout furnished with spines or teeth with which to tear open its prey.

saw-fly (sô′flī″), *n.* any of numerous insects, the female of which has a special sawlike organ for depositing eggs: by means of this organ she makes openings in plants or soft wood and deposits her eggs therein.

saw-horse (sô′hôrs″), *n.* a rack or frame on which sticks of wood are placed when being sawed.

saw-mill (sô′mĭl″), *n.* a mill where logs are sawed into lumber.

sawn (sôn), the past participle of the verb *saw*.

saw-yer (sô'yẽr), *n.* one who saws timber into planks, or wood for fuel.

sax-horn (săks'hôrn'), *n.* in music, a brass wind instrument, much used in military bands.

sax-i-frage (săk'sĭ-frāj), *n.* any of various plants, hardy and chiefly perennial, with white or yellow flowers.

Sax-on (săk'sŭn), *n.* a member of a Teutonic tribe, who, in the fifth and sixth centuries, together with the Angles and the Jutes, conquered and settled in England; an Anglo-Saxon; the language of the Saxons; an inhabitant of modern Saxony: *adj.* of or pertaining to the Saxons, or to their language; Anglo-Saxon.

Sax-o-ny (săk'sō-nĭ), *n.* a knitting yarn of fine, closely twisted wool.

sax-o-phone (săk'sō-fōn), *n.* in music, a keyed wind instrument consisting of a metal tube and a reed mouthpiece like that of a clarinet.

say (sā), *v.t.* [*p.t.* and *p.p.* said (sĕd), *p.pr.* saying], to utter in words; declare; speak; to state as a decision; as, I *say* he shall go; allege; suppose; as, he had, *say* ten thousand dollars a year; utter from memory; as, to *say* a poem: *v.i.* to express an opinion: *n.* something said, or what one has to say: used only in *to have one's say*, etc.; colloquially, one's turn or right to express an opinion.—*n.* **sayer.**

say-ing (sā'ĭng), *n.* a statement; that which is said; an adage or proverb.

says (sĕz), the third person singular present indicative of the verb *say*.

scab (skăb), *n.* a crust formed over a wound or sore; a disease of sheep; a disease of plants in which dark-colored spots of mold appear; cant, a workman who refuses to join a strike, or who takes the place abandoned by a striker.

scab-bard (skăb'ẽrd), *n.* the case in which the blade of a sword or bayonet is kept: *v.t.* to put into such a case.

scab-by (skăb'ĭ), *adj.* covered with or full of sores; affected with the disease called scab; mean.—*adv.* **scabbily.**—*n.* **scabbiness.**

sca-bi-es (skā'bĭ-ēz), *n.* the itch; the mange.

scaf-fold (skăf'ōld), *n.* a temporary timber stage or structure for supporting something; an elevated platform for the execution of a criminal: *v.t.* to furnish or support with such a frame or structure.

scaf-fold-ing (skăf'ōld-ĭng), *n.* a scaffold; materials for erecting scaffolds; temporary framework of ladders, platforms, etc., to hold workmen and materials employed on an unfinished building.

scal-a-wag (skăl'ȧ-wăg), *n.* colloquially, a scamp or rascal. Also, **scallawag.**

scald (skôld), *v.t.* to burn with hot liquid or steam; injure by contact with any hot fluid; expose to violent heat over a fire or hot liquid; to bring to a boil, as milk; to clean or peel by pouring boiling water in or upon: *n.* a burn or injury to the skin or flesh from hot liquid or steam; (skôld; skäld), one of the old Norse poets, who recited or sang heroic poems.

scale (skāl), *n.* one of the pans of a balance: often in the plural, a balance itself; an instrument or machine for weighing; one of the small bony or horny plates covering fish, and certain snakes and insects; one of the thick leaves which protect the bud of a plant in winter; any thin plate or layer like a scale; the thin crust which forms on the surface of iron forgings; the crust formed on the inside of a boiler; a graduated measure; especially, a series of marks designating proportionately greater distances; as, the *scale* of miles on a map; in music, a series of tones, regularly ascending or descending in an octave or more; a progressive series; as, a *scale* of taxation; proportion between a representation and what it represents; as, a drawing on the *scale* of an inch to a foot; basis for a system of numbering; as, the decimal *scale*; a scale-insect, or bark-louse, very destructive to fruit trees: **Scale**, the sign of the zodiac Libra: *v.t.* to strip of scales; weigh; measure; climb over, as by a ladder; clamber up; ascend by steps or by climbing: *v.i.* to separate and come off in thin layers; peel.—*adj.* **scaly.**—*n.* **scaliness.**

sca-lene (skā-lēn'), *adj.* having the sides and angles unequal: said of a triangle; oblique.

scal-ing lad-der (skāl'ĭng lăd'ẽr), a ladder used to mount the walls in taking a place by surprise.

scal-lion (skăl'yŭn), *n.* a kind of onion with a long thick stem and no bulb-shaped root; the shallot; the leek.

scal-lop (skŏl'ŭp), *n.* a marine shellfish having semicircular curves on the edge of its shell; a curve or one of a series of curves joined together to form an ornamental edge, as on lace, etc.: *v.t.* to cut the edge or border of in scallops or curves, as for ornament; to bake in scallop shells; to mix with bread or cracker crumbs, season, and bake, as oysters. Also, **scollop.**

scalp (skălp), *n.* the skin on the top of the head, from which the hair grows; the skin and hair of the head torn off by the North American Indians in token of victory: *v.t.* to deprive of the skin and hair of the head; colloquially, to buy and sell at a small, quick profit; colloquially, to buy and sell (railway tickets) at a reduced rate.—*n.* **scalper.**

scal-pel (skăl'pĕl), *n.* a small, keen-edged knife used by surgeons.

scamp (skămp), *n.* a rascal; a good-for-nothing fellow; rogue: *v.t.* to execute or perform in a careless manner and with bad material.

scam-per (skăm'pẽr), *v.i.* to run with haste; hasten away: *n.* a hasty flight.—*n.* **scamperer.**

scan (skăn), *v.t.* [*p.t.* and *p.p.* scanned, *p.pr.* scanning], to examine and divide, as a verse, into the metrical feet or syllables of which it is made up; to look closely at or into; examine carefully: *v.i.* to follow metrical rules: said of a verse.

scan-dal (skăn'dăl), *n.* careless or malicious gossip injurious to reputation; backbiting; repetition or spreading of evil reports; reproach caused by shameful actions; a cause of reproach; as, his conduct was a *scandal* to the community.

scan-dal-ize (skăn'dăl-īz), *v.t.* to offend or shock by some action considered immoral, unconventional, or improper; to disgrace or bring reproach upon. *Syn.* disgust, slander, defame.

scan-dal-ous (skăn'dăl-ŭs), *adj.* tending to harm the good name or reputation of someone; consisting of evil reports; disgraceful; defamatory.—*adv.* **scandalously.**—*n.* **scandalousness.**

Scan-di-na-vi-an (skăn'dĭ-nā'vĭ-ăn), *adj.* pertaining to Scandinavia (Sweden, Norway, and Denmark), its language, literature, or people: *n.* a native of Scandinavia.

scan-sion (skăn'shŭn), *n.* the act or art of dividing verses into the metrical feet of which they are composed; the scheme according to which any verse may be so divided.

scant (skănt), *adj.* [*comp.* scanter, *superl.* scantest], not full or abundant; having only a small amount: with *of*; as, *scant* of material; scarcely enough; as, a *scant* supply of food: *v.t.* to stint; limit the supply of; be stingy with.—*adv.* **scantly.**—*n.* **scantness.**

scant-ling (skănt'lĭng), *n.* a piece of timber of small dimensions, used for a joist or an upright in a lath-and-plaster partition; such timber taken collectively; prescribed size of a piece of building stone or timber.

scant-y (skăn'tĭ), *adj.* [*comp.* scantier, *superl.* scantiest], narrow; barely sufficient; not enough for necessity; meager; sparing; limited.—*adv.* **scantily.**—*n.* **scantiness.**

Syn. bare, pinched, insufficient.
Ant. (see ample).

scape (skāp), *n.* the shaft of a column; in botany, a long naked stalk rising directly from the ground or from underneath the ground; the shaft of a feather.

scape-goat (skāp'gōt'), *n.* among the ancient Jews, a goat selected by lot, over whose head the high priest confessed the sins of the people on the Day of Atonement, after which it was sent away into the wilderness; hence, one who bears the blame for others.

scape-grace (skāp'grās'), *n.* an unreliable, unprincipled fellow.

scap-u-la (skăp'ū-lȧ), *n.* [*pl.* scapulas (-lȧz)], the shoulder blade.

scap-u-lar (skăp'ū-lẽr), *adj.* pertaining to the scapula, or shoulder blade: *n.* in the Roman Catholic Church, a loose sleeveless garment worn by certain priests; two pieces of cloth worn over the shoulder, beneath the other garments, from motives of devotion.

scar (skär), *n.* a mark left on the skin after the healing of a wound or ulcer; a mark or blemish; a steep rock or bank: *v.t.* [*p.t.* and *p.p.* scarred, *p.pr.* scarring], to mark with, or as with, a scar: *v.i.* to form a scar.

scar-ab (skăr'ăb), *n.* a kind of beetle; a gem or seal cut in the form of a beetle and worn as a charm by the ancient Egyptians.

scarce (skârs), *adj.* not common; not plentiful; not equal to the demand; rare.

scarce-ly (skârs'lĭ), *adv.* seldom; rarely; not quite; hardly.

scar-ci-ty (skâr'sĭ-tĭ), *n.* lack; insufficiency; dearth; rareness.

scare (skâr), *v.t.* to strike with sudden terror, usually without real cause; frighten: *n.* colloquially, a sudden fright or panic.

scare-crow (skâr'krō'), *n.* a figure, usually a crude representation of a man, set up to frighten birds away from crops; that which terrifies or frightens without real cause; a person dressed in rags and tatters.

scarf (skärf), *n.* a light handkerchief or tie for the neck; a broad band of fabric worn loosely over the shoulders or about the neck, over the head, or around the waist; sash; in carpentry, a lapped joint; a groove formed by cutting: *v.t.* to unite (two pieces of timber) at the ends by a kind of dovetail; to cut a scarf or groove in, as for a joint.

scarf-skin (skärf'skĭn'), *n.* the cuticle or outer layer of skin.

scar-i-fy (skăr'ĭ-fī), *v.t.* [*p.t.* and *p.p.* scarified, *p.pr.* scarifying], to scratch or cut; in surgery, to make small cuts in by a lancet; as, to *scarify* the skin; to stir up on the surface; as, to *scarify* the soil.

scar-la-ti-na (skär'lȧ-tē'nȧ), *n.* a mild form of scarlet fever.

scar-let (skär'lĕt), *n.* a bright red color, tinged with orange; cloth of such a color: *adj.* of a bright red color: **scarlet fever,** *n.* a contagious disease marked by fever and a scarlet eruption, or rash, of the skin.

scarp (skärp), *n.* a steep slope or incline; in a fortress or line of defense, that slope of the protecting ditch which touches the wall or parapet: *v.t.* to cut straight up and down or nearly so; as, to *scarp* the face of a rock.

scathe (skāth), *v.t.* to injure or hurt; to blast or harm.

scathe-less (skāth'lĕs), *adj.* free from injury or harm.

scath-ing (skāth'ĭng), *adj.* injurious; hurtful; blasting; severe or bitter; as, *scathing* remarks.—*adv.* **scathingly.**

scat-ter (skăt'ẽr), *v.t.* to strew carelessly; to throw loosely about; disperse; drive in several directions; use wastefully; as, to *scatter* one's energies: *v.i.* to be dispersed or dissipated; to separate and go in different directions, as a crowd.—*n.* **scatterer.**

Syn. spread, dissipate, dispel.
Ant. (see collect).

scav-en-ger (skăv'ĕn-jẽr), *n.* a man employed to clean the streets; any animal that devours refuse or waste matter.

sce-na-ri-o (shā-nä'rĭ-ō), *n.* the sketch of a plot; an outline of the chief incidents to be represented in a moving-picture play.

scene (sēn), *n.* the time, place, or circumstance in which anything occurs, either in real life or in literature; as, the *scene* of his adventure, or the *scene* of a story; a division of a play; an episode; spectacle; exhibition; a landscape or part of a landscape; display of feeling or passion between two or more persons: *pl.* the decorations and fittings of a stage representing the place where the action of a play is supposed to take place.

scen-er-y (sēn'ẽr-ĭ), *n.* the appearance of anything presented to the vision; general character of a landscape; appearance of nature in a given locality; as, mountain *scenery;* a painted background on a stage.

sce-nic (sē'nĭk; sĕn'ĭk), *adj.* pertaining to the stage; dramatic; artistic; pertaining to a landscape or view of nature; offering fine views of nature.

scent (sĕnt), *n.* odor; sense of smell; the odor which an animal leaves as it moves; hence, a track followed by means of this odor; a perfume: *v.t.* smell; hence, to get a hint or intimation of; as, to *scent* trouble; perfume: *v.i.* to hunt animals by the sense of smell.

scep-ter (sĕp'tẽr), *n.* a staff borne by a sovereign or ruler as the emblem of authority; royal mace. Also, **sceptre.**

scep-tic (skĕp'tĭk), *n.* one who doubts: one who is unbelieving: *adj.* inclined to doubt; incredulous. Also, **skeptic.**

scep-ti-cal (skĕp'tĭ-kăl), *adj.* doubting; unbelieving; incredulous; pertaining to unbelief.

sched-ule (skĕd'ūl; shĕd'ūl), *n.* a written or printed paper containing a list or inventory; as, a railroad *schedule;* list or document attached to a more important paper, as a will, etc.; *v.t.* to place in such a list.

scheme (skēm), *n.* a carefully arranged and well-ordered plan; a plan or theory of action; a plot or device: *v.t.* to design or plan; plot: *v.i.* to form a plot or plan.

schism (sĭzm), *n.* a split or division, especially a permanent division or separation in the Christian church; sin of causing such a division; a body that has so separated in the church.

schis-mat-ic (sĭz-măt'ĭk), *adj.* pertaining to, or characteristic of, division in a church; as, *schismatic* opinions: *n.* one who causes or takes part in a division of a church.

schist (shĭst), *n.* a crystalline rock that readily splits into slates or slabs.—*adj.* **schistose, schistous.**

schol-ar (skŏl'ẽr), *n.* one who attends a school or learns of a teacher; a student; a learned man; one who holds a scholarship.
Syn. pupil, savant.
Ant. (see dunce).

schol-ar-ly (skŏl'ẽr-lĭ), *adj.* like, or characteristic of, a learned man; as, a *scholarly* book; learned; intellectual and highly cultivated; thorough and systematic in methods of study.

schol-ar-ship (skŏl'ẽr-shĭp), *n.* quality of work done by a student; as, his *scholarship* is satisfactory; quality of knowledge and attainment of a learned man; learning; financial support for a student, supplied by an educational institution or by an individual.

scho-las-tic (skō-lăs'tĭk), *adj.* pertaining to learned men, students, or institutions of learning; scholarlike: characteristic of the schoolmen of the Middle Ages; hence, pedantic, or devoted to mere book learning.

scho-las-ti-cism (skō-lăs'tĭ-sĭzm), *n.* the thoughts and beliefs of the schoolmen in the Middle Ages whose knowledge was based on books rather than on life; hence, pedantry or devotion to book learning; a point of view based on book learning rather than on knowledge of life.

school (skōōl), *n.* a place where instruction is given; the body of pupils and teachers in a place where instruction is given; a seminary or college in the Middle Ages for teaching theology, logic, etc.; the followers of the teachings or beliefs of a particular teacher or system; also, the system or beliefs of those so associated; figuratively, the channel through which knowledge is gained; as, the *school* of experience; a shoal or great number, as of fish: *v.t.* to train or instruct in a school; discipline: *adj.* pertaining to a school.

school-book (skōōl'bŏŏk''), *n.* a book for use in schools; a school text.

school-boy (skōōl'boi''), *n.* a boy who attends school.

school-fel-low (skōōl'fĕl''ō), *n.* a companion or associate at school.

school-girl (skōōl'gûrl''), *n.* a girl who attends school.

school-house (skōōl'hous''), *n.* the building where the sessions of school are held.

school-ing (skōōl'ĭng), *n.* instruction in school; education; the act of teaching; discipline; reproof; pay given for instruction.

school-man (skōōl'măn), *n.* [*pl.* **schoolmen** (-mĕn)], one of the divines or philosophers in the Middle Ages; one whose occupation is to teach school; one interested professionally in schools.

school-mas-ter (skōōl'màs''tẽr), *n.* a man who teaches a school; the head or principal of a school.

school-mis-tress (skōōl'mĭs''trĕs), *n.* a woman who teaches a school.

school-mate (skōōl'māt''), *n.* a companion or associate at school.

school-room (skōōl'rōōm''), *n.* a room in which sessions of school are held; a room in which pupils are instructed.

schoon-er (skōōn'ẽr), *n.* a vessel with two or more masts, rigged fore and aft; colloquially, a tall goblet or drinking glass.

Seven-masted Schooner

schot-tische (shŏt'ĭsh), *n.* a kind of dance, similar to the polka; also, the music for such a dance. Also, **schottish.**

sci-at-ic (sī-ăt'ĭk), *adj.* pertaining to, or affecting, the hip; as, sciatic rheumatism.

sci-at-i-ca (sī-ăt'ĭ-kȧ), *n.* neuralgia of the hip or thigh; a painful affection of the hip and adjoining parts.

sci-ence (sī'ĕns), *n.* knowledge, as of general truths or particular facts, obtained and shown to be correct by accurate observation and thinking; knowledge arranged or classified with reference to general truths or laws; especially, classified knowledge in reference to the physical world; expert ability to do, as a consequence of knowledge; systematized knowledge of some one subject.

sci-en-tif-ic (sī''ĕn-tĭf'ĭk), *adj.* pertaining to, or used in, the obtaining of knowledge by experiment and observation; as, *scientific* instruments; in accordance with, or following, the rules or method of systematized knowledge; as, *scientific* conclusions; systematic; exact; systematic in methods of study; versed in systematized knowledge; skilled in some branch of classified knowledge.—*adv.* **scientifically.**

Scimitar

sci-en-tist (sī'ĕn-tĭst), *n.* one learned in, or devoted to, systematized knowledge; especially that which deals with the physical world.

scim-i-tar (sĭm'ĭ-tẽr), *n.* an Oriental or Turkish sword with a curved blade. Also, **scimiter.**

scin-til-la (sin-til'ȧ), *n.* a spark; particle; as, there is not a *scintilla* of truth in his statement.

scin-til-late (sin'ti-lāt), *v.i.* to give forth sparks, fire, or firelike particles; twinkle; sparkle.

scin-til-la-tion (sin"ti-lā'shŭn), *n.* the act of twinkling or sparkling; a spark or flash; twinkle.

sci-on (sī'ŭn), *n.* the sprout or shoot of a plant, suitable for grafting; a descendant; as, the *scion* of a family.

scis-sion (sizh'ŭn; sish-ŭn), *n.* the act of cutting; a splitting; a division.

scis-sors (siz'ẽrz), *n.pl.* a cutting instrument smaller than shears, having two opposite sharp edges which meet when moved on a pivot: frequently, a *pair of scissors.*

scle-ro-sis (sklē-rō'sis), *n.* the hardening of a tissue of the body, caused by disease.

scle-rot-ic (sklē-rŏt'ĭk), *adj.* hard; denoting the firm white outermost membrane or skin of the eyeball.

scoff (skŏf), *n.* an expression of scorn or contempt; ridicule: *v.i.* to show scorn or contempt by mocking acts or language; followed by *at*; *v.t.* to mock at; to treat with scorn or contempt. — *adv.* **scoffingly.** — *n.* **scoffer.**

scold (skōld), *v.i.* to chide sharply or rudely; speak in a loud or violent manner: *v.t.* to find fault with; rebuke severely: *n.* one who habitually finds fault; especially, a rude, quarrelsome woman.

scol-lop (skŏl'ŭp), *n.* any of several mollusks having shells with wavy edges; one of a series of semicircular curves forming an ornamental edge on certain laces, etc.: *v.t.* to trim with, or make an edge on, of ornamental curves, or scallops; in cooking, to prepare, as oysters, with bread crumbs, seasoning, etc., and bake. Also, **scallop.**

sconce (skŏns), *n.* a small fort; protection; shelter; an ornamental bracket, fastened to a wall, holding one or more candlesticks; colloquially, the head: *v.t.* to shelter; to settle cosily; to protect.

scone (skōn), *n.* a thick batter cake of barley, oatmeal, or wheat, usually baked on a griddle. [Scot.]

scoop (skōōp), *n.* a large ladle; a deep shovel, as for dipping flour, etc.; any similar implement; a hollow; the act of making hollow or dipping out: *v.t.* to take out or up with a large ladle; to dip or ladle out; make hollow.

scoot (skōōt), *v.i.* to walk or run hastily; to dart: *n.* a scurrying. [Colloq.]

scope (skōp), *n.* extent or range of view or action; room for free action; liberty.

scor-bu-tic (skôr-bū'tĭk), *adj.* of or pertaining to scurvy; resembling scurvy; affected with scurvy.

scorch (skôrch), *v.t.* to burn slightly; parch; affect painfully with heat, as with that of the sun: *v.i.* to be burned slightly; colloquially, to go at high speed on a bicycle or in a motor car.—*adv.* **scorchingly.** —*n.* **scorcher.**

score (skōr), *n.* a notch or cut, especially one made for keeping tally or account; a tally or an account so kept; debt; bill; a grudge; as, to pay off old *scores*; a motive; the number of points, runs, etc., made in a game or contest; the number twenty; a line or groove; in music, the copy of a composition showing all the parts for all the instruments or voices: *v.t.* to notch or mark furrows in; keep record or account of; to win for oneself, as runs, points, etc., in a game; to remove by marking out; as, to *score* out certain paragraphs; to charge; as a debt; to blame or find fault with; in music, to adapt for an instrument: *v.i.* to keep the tally, in a game; to win a point or points, as in a game; to be winning or holding the advantages.—*n.* **scorer.**

sco-ri-a (skō'rĭ-ȧ), *n.* [*pl.*, Lat., scoriæ (-ē)], cinders from a volcano; refuse from the melting of metals or metallic ores; slag.—*adj.* **scoriaceous.**

scorn (skôrn), *n.* extreme contempt; haughty disdain; ridicule; an object of contempt: *v.t.* to hold in extreme contempt or disdain; reject with contempt; despise.—*n.* **scorner.**

scorn-ful (skôrn'fōōl), *adj.* expressing contempt; contemptuous; disdainful: often with *of*.—*adv.* **scornfully.**—*n.* **scornfulness.**

Scor-pi-o (skôr'pĭ-ō), *n.* the eighth sign of the zodiac, or the Scorpion; a southern constellation of the same name.

scor-pi-on (skôr'pĭ-ŭn), *n.* an insect akin to the spider, armed with a poisonous sting at the tip of the abdomen; a painful scourge: **Scorpion,** the eighth sign of the zodiac.

scot (skŏt), *n.* a tax; contribution; a reckoning; fine.

Scot (skŏt), *n.* a native or inhabitant of Scotland.

Scotch (skŏch), *adj.* pertaining to Scotland, its inhabitants, or its language; Scottish: *n.* the dialect or dialects of English spoken by the people of Scotland; the people of Scotland: used as a plural.

scotch (skŏch), *n.* a slight cut or incision; a notch: *v.t.* to cut or wound slightly; as, to *scotch*, but not kill, a snake.

Scotch-man (skŏch'măn), *n.* [*pl.* Scotchmen (-mĕn)], a native of Scotland, or a person of Scottish ancestry.

sco-ter (skō'tẽr), *n.* any of several kinds of sea ducks.

scot-free (skŏt'frē'), *adj.* untaxed; safe; unharmed.

Scots (skŏts), *adj.* pertaining to the Scottish people: *n.* the Scotch dialect.

Scots-man (skŏts'măn), *n.* [*pl.* Scotsmen (-mĕn)], a Scotchman.

Scot-ti-cism (skŏt'ĭ-sĭzm), *n.* a form or mode of expression peculiar to the Scotch.

Scot-tish (skŏt'ĭsh), *adj.* of or pertaining to the people of Scotland, their language, or country; Scotch.

scoun-drel (skoun'drĕl), *n.* a man without honor or virtue; a low, worthless rascal: *adj.* low; mean.—*adj.* **scoundrelly.**

scour (skour), *v.t.* to clean by rubbing; cleanse from grease or dirt, and make bright; to wash by flooding or flushing; to remove as if by rubbing; to purge; pass swiftly over; search thoroughly: *v.i.* to scrub anything with thoroughness; to become clean through rubbing; to move swiftly; scurry.

scourge (skûrj), *n.* a whip used to inflict pain or punishment; a means to inflict punishment or cause suffering; hence, severe punishment; a cause of affliction; hence, any disease that affects a large number of people; as, the *scourge* of Spanish influenza: *v.t.* to whip severely; grieve or torment greatly.

scour-ing rush (skour'ing rŭsh), the common horsetail plant used in scouring.

scout (skout), *n.* a person sent out to obtain and bring in information, especially of the movements, etc., of an enemy in war; in cricket, a fielder: *v.i.* to go in search of information, especially of the movements of an enemy; to explore; to mock: with *at:* *v.t.* to examine; to reconnoiter; to treat with contempt; to reject with scorn, as something ridiculous; as, to *scout* an opinion: **Boy Scout**, a member of an organization which, by a combination of moral and military training, seeks to develop a manly character in growing boys and to make them of service to the community: **scoutmaster**, the leader of one or more units of this organization.

scow (skou), *n.* a large flat-bottomed boat with square ends.

scowl (skoul), *v.i.* to wrinkle the brows in frowning or displeasure; look sullen or angry; to lower: *n.* the wrinkling of the brows in displeasure or anger; frown.

scrab-ble (skrăb'l), *v.i.* to scramble; to clamber: *v.t.* to gather hurriedly; scrape together: with *up, together,* etc.; as, he *scrabbled* his belongings together: *n.* a scramble; a hasty gathering in.

scrag (skrăg), *n.* anything thin, lean, or rough; the neck, especially the back of a sheep's neck.

scrag-gy (skrăg'ĭ), *adj.* lean, thin, and rough; rough, with uneven points; broken; jagged; lean and scrawny.—*adv.* **scraggily.**—*n.* **scragginess.**

scram-ble (skrăm'bl), *v.i.* to clamber or move on the hands and feet; to struggle in an undignified manner for something; as, to *scramble* for a place; to hunt for something with eagerness and roughness: *v.t.* to toss together at random; to prepare by stirring together while cooking; as, to *scramble* eggs: *n.* a rude, disorderly struggle; the act of so struggling.

scrap (skrăp), *n.* a small piece, cut or broken off; a fragment; a brief extract from something printed; in the plural, pieces of fat tissue left after trying out the fat; old iron or other metal: *adj.* in the form of fragments or pieces; as, *scrap* iron.

scrap-book (skrăp'bo͝ok"), *n.* a blank book in which newspaper clippings, etc., may be pasted.

scrape (skrāp'), *v.t.* to draw over harshly or gratingly; rub or scratch with something sharp; clean by rubbing with something sharp or rough; remove by, or as by, rasping or grating: followed by *out, from,* etc.; gather or accumulate in small amounts, with effort, as savings: *v.i.* to rub something gratingly; play awkwardly on the violin; to save money by being extremely economical; bow by awkwardly drawing back the foot: *n.* the act, noise, or effect of harsh rubbing or grating; a difficulty; a perplexity: **scraper**, any instrument or tool used for smoothing, grading, rubbing, or scratching.

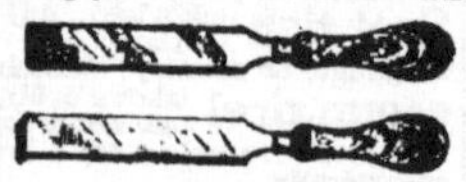

Scrapers for Metal

scrap-ple (skrăp'l), *n.* a food made by boiling together seasoned chopped meat, usually pork, and corn meal.

scrap-py (skrăp'ĭ), *adj.* made of fragments or small bits; consisting of scraps.

scratch (skrăch), *v.t.* to mark or tear the surface of with something pointed; wound slightly; tear or dig with the claws; cancel or erase; to scrape lightly with the finger nails to relieve itching: *v.i.* to use the nails or claws in rubbing, tearing, or digging; to cause irritation or pain by rubbing; as, the collar *scratches;* to save money by great effort: *n.* a mark or tear made by something pointed or rough; a slight wound; a disease of horses; the starting line in a race; formerly, a line across the prize ring, up to which boxers were brought when they began to fight; hence, a test of courage; as, he came up to the *scratch.*—*n.* **scratcher.**

scrawl (skrôl), *v.t.* and *v.i.* to write or draw irregularly or hastily, or in badly formed characters: *n.* careless or irregular writing; a scribble.—*n.* **scrawler.**

scraw-ny (skrô'nĭ), *adj.* lean; skinny; scraggy; as, a *scrawny* horse.—*n.* **scrawniness.** [Chiefly U. S.]

screak (skrēk), *v.i.* to utter a shrill sound or cry; screech; creak: *n.* a creaking.

scream (skrēm), *n.* a sharp, shrill cry, as of fear or pain: *v.i.* to utter such a cry: *v.t.* to utter in a loud, piercing voice.

scream-er (skrēm'ẽr), *n.* one who, or that which, cries out or screams; a South American wading bird.

scream-ing (skrēm'ing), *p.adj.* uttering cries or screams; resembling a scream; calling forth screams, as o[f] laughter; as, a *screaming* comedy.

screech (skrēch), *n.* a harsh, shrill cry as of fright or pain: *v.i.* to utt[er] a harsh, shrill cry: *v.t.* to cry out in a shri[ll] voice; to shriek.

screech owl (skrēch oul), any owl th[at] utters a shrill, screechi[ng] cry instead of hooting.

screed (skrēd), *n.* a long, noisy, ranti[ng] speech on any subject; an e[m]phatic piece of argumentative writing.

screen (skrēn), *n.* a light, movable par[ti]tion for protection; a shield; [...] a door *screen;* a curtain; anything in t[he] nature of a protection from observation, e[tc.;] a coarse sieve; a surface on which imag[es] are projected by a moving-picture machi[ne] or a magic lantern: *v.t.* to shut off from dang[er,] observation, etc.; to shelter or conce[al;] protect; pass through a coarse sieve; to p[ro]ject (a picture) upon a screen with a movi[ng-]picture machine or magic lantern.—*n.* **scree[ner].**

screw (skro͞o), *n.* a cylinder of metal [or] wood threaded in a forward-mov[ing] spiral on its external surface; also a ho[le] so threaded that such a cylinder fits [and] advances in it; anything containing [or] resembling such a device; as, a wood sc[rew;] a turn of, or as of, such a device; a mea[ns of] propelling steamships, etc.; a grasping per[son;] one who extorts money from others: *v.[t.]* press by means of, or fasten with, a sp[iral] threaded cylinder moving in a sim[ilarly] threaded hollow; twist; force; as, to [...] one's courage to the sticking point; to [...] as with a screw; to twist or distort; to ex[tort] with *out, of,* or *from:* *v.i.* to turn with a m[otion] like a screw.

screw driv-er (skro͞o drīv'ẽr), a [...] for driving screws [...] place. Also, **screwdriver.**

screw pro-pel-ler (skro͞o prō-pe[l'ẽr]) spiral-bladed [...] at the rear of a steam vessel for pro[pelling] it; the vessel thus propelled.

scrib-ble (skrib'l), *v.t.* to write hastily and carelessly: *v.i.* to scrawl: *n.* hasty, careless writing.—*n.* **scribbler**.

scribe (skrib), *n.* a writer; clerk; one who writes for another; a secretary; in ancient times, a teacher of the Jewish law.

scrim (skrim), *n.* a kind of fabric of cotton or linen for making curtains, etc.

scrim-mage (skrim'āj), *n.* a general quarrel or fight; a confused struggle.

scrimp (skrimp), *v.t.* to be sparing of; to be niggardly to; stint: *v.i.* to be sparing or niggardly: *adj.* short; narrow; scanty: *n.* colloquially, a miser.

scrimp-y (skrim'pi), *adj.* scanty; insufficient; stingy.—*n.* **scrimpiness**. [COLLOQ.]

scrip (skrip), *n.* formerly, a pouch or wallet; a written list, schedule, certificate, etc.; certificate of stock subscribed to a bank or other company.

script (skript), *n.* a piece of writing; style of writing; type in imitation of writing; in law, a writing, as a will.

Scrip-tur-al (skrip'tūr-ăl), *adj.* pertaining to, found in, or based upon, the Scriptures; Biblical.

Scrip-ture (skrip'tūr), *n.* the Bible: *pl.* the books of the Old and New Testaments, or of either of them: **scripture**, any sacred writing.

scrive-ner (skriv'nẽr; skriv'n-ẽr), *n.* one whose business is to write for others, by copying, etc.; one who draws up contracts, prepares writings, etc.

scrof-u-la (skrŏf'ū-lȧ), *n.* a disease marked by the enlargement and decay of the lymphatic glands, especially those of the neck.—*adj.* **scrofulous**.

scroll (skrōl), *n.* a roll of paper or parchment; in architecture, a spiral ornament; a flourish to a signature.

scroll saw (skrōl sô), a saw for sawing curved outlines.

scrub (skrŭb), *v.t.* [*p.t.* and *p.p.* scrubbed, *p.pr.* scrubbing], to wash by hard rubbing, as clothes; rub with a wet cloth or a wet brush, as a floor: *v.i.* to clean or scour something by hard rubbing: *n.* one who toils hard for a meager living; a drudge; brush; a thicket; as, an oak *scrub*: *adj.* mean or small; contemptible; dirty; in athletics, made up of players who are inexperienced or who have had no previous practice together: said of teams.

scrub-by (skrŭb'ĭ), *adj.* mean and small; stunted in growth; covered with brushwood.

scruff (skrŭf), *n.* the nape or back of the neck.

scrunch (skrŭnch), *v.t.* and *v.i.* to crunch; break with the teeth; squeeze: *n.* the act or sound of crunching.

scru-ple (skrōō'pl), *n.* in apothecaries' weight, a weight of one-third of a dram, or twenty grains; a very small quantity; hesitation, especially from difficulty in deciding what is right; unwillingness to do something because of a sense that it is wrong; conscientious *scruples* against an act: *v.i.* and *v.t.* to hesitate from conscientious motives.

scru-pu-los-i-ty (skrōō'pū-lŏs'ĭ-tĭ), *n.* the state or quality of being very conscientious or exact.

scru-pu-lous (skrōō'pū-lŭs), *adj.* inclined to be conscientious; exact; careful; strict.—*adv.* **scrupulously**.—*n.* **scrupulousness**.

scru-ti-nize (skrōō'tĭ-nīz), *v.t.* to inspect or examine closely.

scru-ti-ny (skrōō'tĭ-nĭ), *n.* close inspection or examination.

scud (skŭd), *v.i.* [*p.t.* and *p.p.* scudded, *p.pr.* scudding], to run or move swiftly; of a ship, to run before a gale of wind with little or no sail spread: *n.* the act of so moving or sailing; loose, vapory clouds driven by the wind.

scuff (skŭf), *v.i.* and *v.t.* to wear a rough place on the surface; shuffle; walk with a dragging movement of the feet.

scuf-fle (skŭf'l), *v.i.* to fight or struggle confusedly, especially hand to hand: *n.* a struggle for mastery with close grappling; confused conflict; fight.—*n.* **scuffler**.

scull (skŭl), *n.* a small rowboat; one of a pair of short oars; an oar used at the stern, or rear end, of a boat to push it forward: *v.t.* and *v.i.* to propel or move (a boat) with one or more short oars.—*n.* **sculler**.

Sculling

scul-ler-y (skŭl'ẽr-ĭ), *n.* [*pl.* sculleries (-ĭz)], a room where cooking utensils, etc., are kept and cleansed; a back kitchen for rough work.

scul-lion (skŭl'yŭn), *n.* a servant employed to clean cooking utensils and do rough work in the kitchen; a wretch.

scul-pin (skŭl'pĭn), *n.* any of certain spiny sea fish with large heads and broad mouths.

sculp-tor (skŭlp'tẽr), *n.* [*fem.* sculptress], one who practices the art of carving, cutting, or hewing stone, etc., into statues; one who models statues in clay or designs works of sculpture.

sculp-tur-al (skŭlp'tūr-ăl), *adj.* pertaining to sculpture, or the art of carving stone, etc., into statues.

sculp-ture (skŭlp'tūr), *n.* the art of carving, cutting, or hewing stone, etc., into figures of men, animals, etc.; a carved work or figure: *v.t.* to carve with the chisel, etc., on, in, or from wood, stone, etc.; to portray by carving; to ornament by carving; in physical geography, to change in form by gradually wearing away.

scum (skŭm), *n.* a layer of impurities formed on the surface of a liquid; the refuse or dross of metals in a melted state; anything worthless or vile; worthless people; as, the *scum* of the cities.

scup (skŭp), *n.* a common but valuable food fish, found on the coast of the eastern United States.

scup-per (skŭp'ẽr), *n.* a hole or tube in the side of a ship to carry off deck water.

scup-per-nong (skŭp'ẽr-nŏng), *n.* a kind of fox grape grown in the southeastern United States; wine made from this grape.

scurf (skûrf), *n.* white, flaky scales on the skin, especially on the scalp; dandruff; anything like flakes or scales sticking to a surface.—*adj.* **scurfy**.

scur-ril-i-ty (skŭ-rĭl'ĭ-tĭ), *n.* [*pl.* scurrilities (-tĭz)], vulgar, vile, or indecent joking or jesting; an indecent remark.

scur-ril-ous (skûr'ĭ-lûs), *adj.* using the low, indecent language of the vulgar; mean; foul-mouthed; vile; containing abuse.—*adv.* **scurrilously.**—*n.* **scurrilousness.**

scur-ry (skûr'ĭ), *v.i.* [*p.t.* and *p.p.* scurried, *p.pr.* scurrying], to hasten or move rapidly along: *n.* a hurried movement; a scampering.

scur-vy (skûr'vĭ), *n.* a disease of the blood caused by lack of vegetable food or lime juice, and marked by great weakness, thinness of the body, bleeding gums, etc.: *adj.* affected by scurvy, or a disease marked by weakness, bleeding gums, etc.; vile; contemptible; mean; paltry.—*adv.* **scurvily.**—*n.* **scurviness.**

scut (skŭt), *n.* the short, upright tail of an animal.

scu-tate (skū'tāt), *adj.* round in shape, like a large scale; shield-shaped; in zoölogy, covered with large, horny scales.

'scutch-eon (skŭch'ŭn), *n.* a shield bearing a coat of arms; a metal plate around a keyhole, etc. Also, **escutcheon.**

scu-ti-form (skū'tĭ-fôrm), *adj.* shaped like a shield.

scut-tle (skŭt'l), *v.i.* to hasten or hurry: *v.t.* to cut a hole or holes in (a ship) to sink it: *n.* a quick or short run; a hod for holding coal; lid or door closing or covering an opening in a roof, etc.; a hatchway or small opening in the deck of a ship.

scu-tum (skū'tŭm), *n.* [*pl.* scuta (-tȧ)], in ancient times, a Roman soldier's oblong leather shield; in zoölogy, a shieldlike plate.

Scyl-la (sĭl'ȧ), *n.* a dangerous rock on the Italian coast, represented in classic mythology as a monster with six fierce heads: closely opposite to Charybdis, a whirlpool on the coast of Sicily: **between Scylla and Charybdis,** between two evils, one of which must be accepted.

scythe (sīth), *n.* a curved cutting instrument used for mowing grass, etc., by hand.

Scyth-i-an (sĭth'ĭ-ăn), *adj.* of or pertaining to Scythia, its people, or language: *n.* one of an ancient, wandering, savage people who inhabited what is now southern Russia and the regions east of the Aral Sea; their language.

sea (sē), *n.* a body of salt water, smaller than an ocean; an inland body of water; the ocean; a billow or large wave; the swell of the ocean in a storm; as, there was a high *sea* after the storm; a large quantity; anything like the sea in vastness; as, a *sea* of glory: **at sea,** on a sea voyage; figuratively, bewildered; uncertain; lost.

sea a-nem-o-ne (sē ȧ-nĕm'ō-nē), any of several polyps, usually large, beautifully colored, and growing singly.

sea-board (sē'bōrd"), *n.* the seacoast: *adj.* near or on the border of the sea.

sea bread (sē brĕd), ship biscuit; hardtack; a kind of cracker.

sea calf (sē käf), the common seal, hunted for its fur, hide, and oil.

sea-coast (sē'kōst"), *n.* the coast of the sea.

sea cow (sē kou), one of several varieties of water animals, such as the manatee, dugong, walrus, etc.

sea dog (sē dŏg), the harbor seal; colloquially, an old sailor; in California, the California sea lion.

sea el-e-phant (sē ĕl'ē-fănt), a very large seal found in the Southern Hemisphere.

sea-far-er (sē'fâr"ẽr), *n.* a sailor; a mariner.

sea-far-ing (sē'fâr"ĭng), *adj.* following the life of a sailor; following the sea as a calling.

sea fowl (sē foul), a sea bird; sea birds collectively.

sea gage (sē gāj), an instrument for finding the depth of the sea.

sea-go-ing (sē'gō"ĭng), *adj.* seafaring: suitable or fitted for use on the open sea; as, a *seagoing* yacht.

sea-green (sē'grēn"), *adj.* of the greenish color of the sea.

sea gull (sē gŭl), any bird of the gull family that habitually stays near, or frequents, the sea.

sea hog (sē hŏg), the porpoise, a marine mammal from five to eight feet long.

sea horse (sē hôrs), an imaginary deep-sea animal, half horse and half fish; any of various small fish with head resembling that of a horse; the walrus; the hippopotamus.

sea king (sē kĭng), a viking; a pirate Norseman chief.

seal (sēl), *n.* a flesh-eating sea animal valuable for its skin and oil; a stamp or die engraved with some device, motto, or image, used for making an impression in wax; wax or other soft substance fixed upon a letter, document, etc. and marked with such a stamp; in law, any device given by statute law the effect of a seal; any act that approves or confirms; that which seals or fastens: *v.t.* to fasten with a device so that it cannot be tampered with, as, to *seal* a letter; set or affix a seal to, ratify or confirm; secure or give guaranty for; keep secure or secret; settle beyond question; as, to *seal* his fate: *v.i.* to hunt seals.

Seals

seal brown (sēl broun), the dark brown color of the fur of the seal after it has been dyed.

sea legs (sē lĕgz), legs able to walk on a ship's deck, when the vessel is pitching or rolling.

seal-er (sēl'ẽr), *n.* one who secures or gives guaranty; especially, an officer who inspects weights and measures, or who affixes seals on documents; a sailor or vessel that hunts seals.

sea let-tuce (sē lĕt'ĭs), a certain kind of seaweed, the green fronds of which are sometimes used as food.

sea lev-el (sē lĕv'ĕl), the level exactly continuous with that of the sea at mean tide.

seal-ing wax (sēl'ĭng wăks), a mixture, as of shellac and turpentine, that softens when heated and hardens quickly on cooling: used for sealing letters, documents, etc.

sea li-on (sē lī'ŭn), a name for several classes of large seals found in the Pacific Ocean.

seal-skin (sēl'skĭn"), *n.* the skin of a fur seal or a garment made from it.

seam (sēm), *n.* the line formed by the sewing of two pieces of material together; line of junction or union; narrow vein between two thicker layers of earth, etc.; as, a *seam* of coal; thin layer; a scar; a rent: *v.t.* to form a junction or union upon or of; join or sew together, as a garment; scar; line; knit with a certain kind of stitch: *v.i.* to crack open.

sea-man (sē′măn), *n.* [*pl.* seamen (-mĕn)], a sailor; a mariner; one who shares in the actual work of navigating a vessel.

sea-man-ship (sē′măn-shĭp), *n.* knowledge of the management of a vessel; the skill of an expert sailor.

seam-less (sēm′lĕs), *adj.* without seams; having no seams.

seam-stress (sēm′strĕs), *n.* a woman whose occupation is sewing; a needlewoman.

seam-y (sēm′ĭ), *adj.* showing, or having, seams; especially, roughly finished seams; hence, of low character; rough; hard and unpleasant; as, the *seamy* side of life.

sé-ance (sā′äns; sā″äns′), *n.* a meeting or session, especially a meeting of spiritualists to receive spirit messages.

sea-plane (sē′plān), *n.* an airplane so made that it can alight upon, and move along on, the water: called also a *hydroplane.*

sea-port (sē′pōrt″), *n.* a town, harbor, or port on the seashore, or at a point easy of access to seagoing vessels.

sea purse (sē pûrs), the horny envelope of the skate and certain sharks, in which they lay their eggs.

sear (sēr), *v.t.* to burn to dryness on the surface; brand; render callous or unfeeling; as, to *sear* one's conscience: *adj.* withered. Also, *adj.* **sere.**

search (sûrch), *v.t.* to seek for; look for; go over and examine; as, to *search* a house; explore; inspect; probe: *v.i.* seek; to make inquiry: *n.* the act of seeking or looking for something; investigation; examination; pursuit; quest.

search-ing (sûrch′ĭng), *p.adj.* penetrating; sharp; keen; as, a *searching* glance.—*adv.* **searchingly.**

search-light (sûrch′līt″), *n.* an electric light so arranged that by revolving it a powerful beam of light can be thrown in any direction.

search war-rant (sûrch wŏr′ănt), a warrant or written order giving a police officer authority to search a house, especially for stolen property.

seared (sērd), *adj.* hardened; callous; indifferent; unfeeling; as, a *seared* conscience.

sea room (sē rōōm), enough space for maneuvering or changing the position of a ship, as in war.

sea-scape (sē′skāp), *n.* a picture showing a scene at sea.

sea ser-pent (sē sûr′pĕnt), an imaginary snakelike animal of great size, said to live in the ocean.

sea-shore (sē′shōr″), *n.* the shore along the sea.

sea-sick-ness (sē′sĭk″nĕs), *n.* nausea caused by the motion of a ship.—*adj.* **seasick.**

sea-side (sē′sīd″), *n.* the shore along the sea.

sea-son (sē′zn), *n.* any particular time as distinguished from others; as, the holiday *season;* one of the four divisions of the year, as spring, summer, autumn, and winter; a suitable or convenient time; as, the *season* for shooting; a short time: *v.t.* to mature or make perfect; prepare by drying and hardening, or removing natural juices; as, to *season* timber; render eatable by adding salt, pepper, etc.; to moderate or temper: *v.i.* to become fit for use; to become used to the climate; to become cured.

sea-son-a-ble (sē′zn-ȧ-bl), *adj.* occurring or done in good or proper time; opportune; in keeping with the time of year; as, *seasonable* weather.—*adv.* **seasonably.**—*n.* **seasonableness.**

sea-son-al (sē′zn-ăl), *adj.* of, pertaining to, or changing with, the seasons; as, *seasonal* trades.

sea-son-ing (sē′zn-ĭng), *n.* that which is added to give relish to food; as, salt, pepper, etc.; the act or process of adding spice, etc., to give relish to food.

seat (sēt), *n.* that on which or in which one sits; chair; site; residence; mansion; regular or proper place of sitting; the right to sit; as, a *seat* in church; posture on horseback, etc.; the place where anything is settled or established; as, the *seat* of the trouble; place in Congress or other lawmaking body: *v.t.* to place on a chair, etc.; cause to sit down; establish; place in any site or position; to furnish with seats; to renew or restore the seat of.

sea ur-chin (sē ûr′chĭn), a globe-shaped sea animal, having a thin, prickly shell.

sea wall (sē wôl), an embankment for breaking the force of the waves of the sea.

sea-ward (sē′wērd), *adj.* going toward or situated in the direction of the sea: *adv.* in the direction of the sea. Also, **seawards.**

sea-way (sē′wā″), *n.* open sea; a rough sea: used in the expression *in a seaway.*

sea-weed (sē′wēd″), *n.* a plant growing in the sea, as kelp, sea lettuce, sea heather, etc.

sea-wor-thy (sē′wûr″thĭ), *adj.* fit for a voyage on the open sea: said of a vessel.—*n.* **seaworthiness.**

se-ba-ceous (sē-bā′shŭs), *adj.* pertaining to or resembling fat; containing or secreting fat; oily.

se-cant (sē′kănt), *adj.* cutting, especially into two parts: *n.* a line that cuts another, especially a straight line cutting a curve in two or more points; one of the trigonometric functions; in a right-angled triangle, the ratio of the hypotenuse to the side adjacent to an acute angle.

se-cede (sē-sēd′), *v.i.* to withdraw from fellowship, union, or association; especially, to withdraw from a political or religious body.—*n.* **seceder.**

se-ces-sion (sē-sĕsh′ŭn), *n.* the act of withdrawing; withdrawal or separation from the communion or association of others; withdrawal of a State from the Federal Union; as, the *secession* of the Southern States during the Civil War.—*n.* **secessionism.**

se-ces-sion-ist (sē-sĕsh′ŭn-ĭst), *n.* an upholder of secession, or the withdrawal of States from the Union; one who took the part of the Southern States in the Civil War of 1861.

se-clude (sē-klōōd′), *v.t.* to withdraw from others; to keep apart from the company or society of others; to place in solitude.

se-clud-ed (sē-klōōd'ĕd), *p.adj.* withdrawn from, or separated from, the society of others; retired; solitary. —*n.* **secludedness.**

se-clu-sion (sē-klōō'zhŭn), *n.* separation or withdrawal from the society of others; privacy; retirement.

se-clu-sive (sē-klōō'sĭv), *adj.* keeping or living apart from others.

sec-ond (sĕk'ŭnd), *adj.* immediately following the first; next to the first in order of place, or time; next to the first in value, excellence, merit, dignity, or importance; inferior; subordinate; as, a *second* lieutenant; being of the same kind as another that has gone before; as, a *second* Brutus; in music, lower in pitch; rendering a part that is lower in pitch than the main one: *n.* one who, or that which, is next to the first in place, rank, excellence, or power; one who attends a person who fights a duel; a backer; the one-sixtieth part of a minute of time or of a degree; an article of merchandise of a grade inferior to the best; in music, a part pitched below another, whether of instrument or voice: *v.t.* to follow; act as an assistant or supporter of; assist; in parliamentary practice, support, as a motion, etc., by giving formal approval to the proposal of the mover.

sec-ond-a-ry (sĕk'ŭn-dā-rĭ), *adj.* succeeding next in order to the first; of second place, origin, rank, etc.; subordinate; inferior; resultant; derived from something else as its source; as, *secondary* rocks; deriving information, etc., from another, or primary, source; as, a *secondary* authority; revolving round a primary planet; in electrical usage, of, pertaining to, or denoting, an induced current or its circuit: *n.* a delegate or deputy; a person or thing in an inferior position; a planet revolving around another planet; in zoölogy, any of the quill feathers that grow on the second joint of a bird's wing: **secondary school,** a high school, or any school of high school grade.—*adv.* **sec'ond-ar-i-ly.**

sec-ond-class (sĕk'ŭnd-klȧs"), *adj.* ranking in, or belonging to, the class next below the first, the highest, or the best; second-rate: *adv.* by a second-class conveyance; as, he traveled *second-class.*

sec-ond-er (sĕk'ŭn-dẽr), *n.* one who, in a meeting, formally approves what has been proposed by another.

sec-ond-hand (sĕk'ŭnd-hănd"), *adj.* not new; taken or bought from another; as, a *secondhand* car; dealing in goods that are not new; as, he keeps a *secondhand* store.

sec-ond lieu-ten-ant (sĕk'ŭnd lū-tĕn'ănt), the lowest commissioned officer in the United States army.

sec-ond-ly (sĕk'ŭnd-lĭ), *adj.* in the next place; in the second place.

sec-ond-rate (sĕk'ŭnd-rāt"), *adj.* not first-class; second in size, rank, quality, etc.

sec-ond-sight (sĕk'ŭnd-sīt"), *n.* the ability to foresee events; the power to see that which is not visible; clairvoyance.

se-cre-cy (sē'krē-sĭ), *n.* [*pl.* secrecies (-sĭz)], the state or quality of being hidden; concealment; retirement; solitude; the ability to keep things to oneself; closeness.

se-cret (sē'krĕt), *adj.* hidden or concealed; removed from sight; kept from the knowledge or view of all except those concerned; silent; mysterious; private: **secret service,** government detective service: *n.* that which is purposely concealed or left untold; something unknown; something unexplained; that which, when made known, makes something clear; as, the *secret* of his happiness.—*adv.* **se'cret-ly.**

Syn., adj. clandestine, sly, underhand.

Ant. (see open).

sec-re-ta-ry (sĕk'rē-tā-rĭ), *n.* [*pl.* secretaries (-rĭz)], one who does writing for another; one who attends to correspondence and business for a company or an individual; an executive who transacts the business of a government department; a writing desk.—*adj.* **secretarial.**

sec-re-ta-ry-ship (sĕk'rē-tā-rĭ-shĭp"), *n.* the office, or term of office, of a secretary.

se-crete (sē-krēt'), *v.t.* to hide or conceal; in physiology, to separate from the blood and make into a new substance; as, the liver *secretes* bile.

se-cre-tion (sē-krē'shŭn), *n.* in physiology, the act or process of separating from a circulating fluid materials out of which a new substance is made; any substance or fluid so separated, as saliva; the act of concealing or hiding.

se-cre-tive (sē-krē'tĭv), *adj.* given to reserve or concealment; inclined to be close-mouthed; in physiology, causing, or promoting, secretion; as, a *secretive* gland.—*n.* **secre'tiveness.**

se-cre-to-ry (sē-krē'tō-rĭ), *adj.* in physiology, causing, or tending to increase, secretion.

sect (sĕkt), *n.* a number of persons who, following a teacher or leader, hold certain opinions; a following; a party; especially, a religious denomination.

sec-ta-ri-an (sĕk-tā'rĭ-ăn), *adj.* pertaining to, or like, a certain denomination or party; devoted to a certain party or denomination, especially in religion; narrow-minded: *n.* a member of a denomination or party.

sec-ta-ri-an-ism (sĕk-tā'rĭ-ăn-ĭzm), *n.* the spirit, tendency, or principles of a party, especially a religious denomination; devotion to some particular religious denomination.

sec-ta-ry (sĕk'tȧ-rĭ), *n.* [*pl.* sectaries (-rĭz)], a member or supporter of a religious denomination or a party; one who separates from an established church.

sec-tile (sĕk'tĭl), *adj.* capable of being cut, especially smoothly.

sec-tion (sĕk'shŭn), *n.* the act of cutting, or separation by cutting; part or portion cut off; a representation of an object as if cut in two crosswise or lengthwise by a plane; as, a transverse *section* of a steam radiator; slice; division or subdivision of a chapter; a division of a law; distinct part of a country, people, community, or class; one of the portions of one square mile into which public lands in the United States are divided; in western United States, one thirty-sixth of a township; a division of a genus or class; a certain length of railway track for whose condition a certain gang of men is responsible; in a sleeping car, a compartment including an upper and a lower berth.

sec-tion-al (sĕk'shŭn-ăl), *adj.* of or pertaining to a certain district or part of a country; local; divisible or separable into parts; as, a *sectional* filing case.

sec-tion-al-ism (sĕk'shŭn-ăl-ĭzm), *n.* prejudice in favor of local interests; devotion to the affairs and interests of a certain district.

sec-tor (sĕk'tẽr), *n.* that part of a circle inclosed between two radii and the included arc; in solid geometry, the portion of a sphere generated by revolving such a figure about any diameter of the circle of which it is a part; in military use, one of the parts into which the fighting line is divided.

Sector of a Circle

sec-u-lar (sĕk'ū-lẽr), *adj.* pertaining to this present world, or to things not sacred; as, *secular* music; worldly; temporal; not bound by church vows; coming or observed once in an age or a century; as, a *secular* year; extending over, or occurring in, a long period of time.—*adv.* **secularly.**

sec-u-lar-ism (sĕk'ū-lẽr-ĭzm), *n.* the principles or beliefs of those who do not believe in religion; the quality or state of being devoted to worldly or temporal things.

sec-u-lar-ist (sĕk'ū-lẽr-ĭst), *n.* one who objects to religious teaching in schools or church control of schools or of state affairs; one who, throwing over the forms of religion, maintains that the duties and problems of this present life should be the principal objects of man's concern.

sec-u-lar-i-ty (sĕk"ū-lăr'ĭ-tĭ), *n.* devotion to the things of the present life; worldliness.

sec-u-lar-ize (sĕk'ū-lẽr-īz), *v.t.* to convert from sacred to secular or common use, as a building; render worldly.—*n.* **secularization.**

se-cure (sē-kūr'), *adj.* free from fear or danger; safe; protected; confident; careless; certain; assured: with *of*: *v.t.* to make safe; protect; guarantee; make fast; guard against, as the possibility of escape; gain possession of; put beyond chance of losing or not receiving; as, to *secure* oneself against loss; insure; obtain; get possession of.—*adv.* **securely.**

se-cu-ri-ty (sē-kū'rĭ-tĭ), *n.* [*pl.* securities (-tĭz)], the state or quality of being safe or protected; freedom from fear or danger; assurance; certainty; something given to guarantee the fulfilment of a contract, etc.; pledge; surety; backing; as, *security* for a loan; evidence of debt or ownership, as stocks, notes, bonds, etc.; one who becomes responsible for another.

Syn. bail, collateral, earnest.

se-dan (sē-dăn'), *n.* a portable covered chair, used as a vehicle for carrying one passenger, borne by two men by means of a pole on either side; an automobile with two seats, having the entire compartment for passengers inclosed with glass doors, etc. Also, **sedan-chair.**

se-date (sē-dāt'), *adj.* calm; composed; quiet; serious; habitually staid; unruffled.—*adv.* **sedately.**—*n.* **sedateness.**

sed-a-tive (sĕd'ȧ-tĭv), *adj.* tending to calm or soothe; quieting: *n.* medicine having a calming, soothing effect.

sed-en-ta-ry (sĕd'ĕn-tā-rĭ), *adj.* accustomed to pass much time in a sitting posture; marked by, or requiring, much sitting; as, *sedentary* work; a *sedentary* life; sluggish; inactive; remaining in one place; settled.—*adv.* **sedentarily.**—*n.* **sedentariness.**

sedge (sĕj), *n.* a coarse grass growing in wet places or swamps.—*adj.* **sedgy.**

sed-i-ment (sĕd'ĭ-mĕnt), *n.* the solid substance which settles at the bottom of a liquid; dregs; lees; settlings; in geology, matter deposited, as by water.

sed-i-men-ta-ry (sĕd"ĭ-mĕn'tȧ-rĭ), *adj.* pertaining to, or composed of, dregs or lees; in geology, denoting rocks, as sandstone, formed of material deposited by water, etc.

se-di-tion (sē-dĭsh'ŭn), *n.* any offense against the state not actually reaching the point of insurrection or treason; the stirring up of discontent or rebellious feeling against lawful authority.

se-di-tious (sē-dĭsh'ŭs), *adj.* pertaining to, like, or tending to excite, rebellion against lawful authority; as, *seditious* behavior; *seditious* words; guilty of rebellion, or of exciting rebellion, against lawful authority.—*adv.* **seditiously.**

se-duce (sē-dūs'), *v.t.* to draw away from the paths of right, duty, or virtue, by flattery, promises, etc.; to lead astray; especially, to persuade, as a woman, to give up her chastity.—*n.* **seducer.**

Syn. allure, decoy, abduct, deprave.

se-duc-tion (sē-dŭk'shŭn), *n.* the act of leading astray; the act or crime of persuading a woman to give up her chastity; that which leads astray or entices.

se-duc-tive (sē-dŭk'tĭv), *adj.* tending to lead astray; enticing; alluring; tempting.—*adv.* **seductively.**—*n.* **seductiveness.**

sed-u-lous (sĕd'ū-lŭs), *adj.* steadily industrious and persevering in business and endeavor; diligent; untiring.—*adv.* **sedulously.**—*n.* **sedulousness.**

see (sē), *v.t.* [*p.t.* saw, *p.p.* seen, *p.pr.* seeing], to perceive by the eye; to behold; to view; to perceive mentally; comprehend; as, I *see* what you mean; to escort or accompany; as, he *saw* Nelly home; to find out by experience; as, he wished to *see* what the result would be; to take care or make sure: with *that*; as, *see* that you address him properly; to visit or have a conference with; as, we went to *see* her; the reporter *saw* the great man; to admit to one's presence; receive; as, she refused to *see* us: *v.i.* to possess or use the power of sight; to comprehend or have mental perception; to find out something by inquiry; to consider; as, will you do it? I shall *see*; to take care; as, *see* to the dinner: *n.* the jurisdiction of a bishop or the Pope; the office of a bishop or the Pope; the territory included in such jurisdiction: **Holy See, See of Rome,** the Pope's jurisdiction or office.

seed (sēd), *n.* [*pl.* seed or seeds (sēdz)], that part of a plant, the ovule, that holds the embryo, or life-containing germ, of the future plant; any small, seedlike fruit; semen; first principle or source; that from which anything springs; offspring; descendants; race or birth: *v.i.* to sow, or shed, the seed; to go to seed: *v.t.* to sprinkle with seed, as a lawn; sow; to remove the seeds from, as raisins.—*n.* **seeder.**

seed bud (sēd bŭd), in botany, the ovule, or sac which contains the germ of the future plant; the plumule, or primary bud of a sprouting plant.

seed leaf (sēd lēf), the first leaf, or one of the first pair of leaves, developed in seed plants: called also the *cotyledon*.

seed-less (sēd'lĕs), *adj.* having no seeds; without seeds.

seed-ling (sēd'lĭng), *n.* a plant grown from a seed; a very small or young tree.

seeds-man (sēdz'măn), *n.* one who sows seeds; one whose business is to sell seed.

seed-time (sēd'tīm"), *n.* the proper season for sowing seed.

seed ves-sel (sēd vĕs'ĕl), any dry, hollow fruit, as a pod, which contains the seeds.

seed-y (sēd'ĭ), *adj.* full of seed; having run to seed; shabby; threadbare; worn-out; as, a *seedy* suit.—*n.* **seediness.**

see-ing (sē'ĭng), *n.* the act or power of sight; vision: *conj.* inasmuch as; considering; since.

seek (sēk), *v.t.* [*p.t.* and *p.p.* sought (sôt), *p.pr.* seeking], to go in search of; to aim at; look for; ask or appeal for; as, to *seek* aid; to try to come to or go to; as, he *sought* the theater; inquire for; to attempt or try; as, he *sought* to undo the harm: *v.i.* to make search or inquiry; to make effort to find someone or something.—*n.* **seeker.**

seem (sēm), *v.i.* to appear; look; have the semblance of truth or fact; to appear to one's own mind; as, I *seemed* to be floating in space.

seem-ing (sēm'ĭng), *p.adj.* apparent; often, having appearance without reality; as, *seeming* truth: *n.* appearance; show, especially false show.

seem-li-ness (sēm'lĭ-nĕs), *n.* the state or quality of being suitable; propriety; decency; fitness.

seem-ly (sēm'lĭ), *adj.* [*comp.* seemlier, *superl.* seemliest], fit or becoming; decent; proper; suited to the circumstances, character, or end desired; as, *seemly* behavior; a *seemly* answer.

seen (sēn), past participle of the irregular verb *see.*

se-er (sē'ēr; sēr), *n.* one who foresees future events; a prophet; one who sees.

seer-suck-er (sēr'sŭk"ēr), *n.* a thin, crinkly linen or cotton fabric.

see-saw (sē'sô"), *n.* motion to and fro, or up and down, as on a balanced plank; a plank balanced on some support, enabling those who sit at the ends to move up and down alternately: *v.i.* to move up and down or backward and forward.

seethe (sēth), *v.t.* to boil; to prepare, as food in a hot liquor; as, to *seethe* flesh: *v.i.* to be cooked in boiling water; to boil; as, a *seething* pot.

seg-ment (sĕg'mĕnt), *n.* a part divided from the rest of an object; a section; as, a *segment* of an orange; a part cut off from a geometrical figure, especially from a circle, by a line or plane: *v.t.* and *v.i.* to divide into sections.—*adj.* **segmental, segmentary.**

Segment of a Circle

seg-men-ta-tion (sĕg"mĕn-tā'shŭn), *n.* the act of dividing, or state of being divided, into sections.

seg-re-gate (sĕg'rē-gāt), *v.t.* to separate from others; cut off from the main body.

seg-re-ga-tion (sĕg"rē-gā'shŭn), *n.* the act of separating from others; state of being separated from others; as, the *segregation* of persons having leprosy.

Seid-litz (sĕd'lĭts), *n.* a sparkling mineral water: **Seidlitz powder,** a gentle laxative medicine.

seign-ior (sēn'yēr), *n.* an old-time title of honor; as, Othello spoke to the "grave and reverend *seigniors*"; a lord.

seign-ior-age (sēn'yēr-āj), *n.* something claimed or taken by royal right or authority; as, *seigniorage* is charged on metal brought by private persons to the royal mint to be coined; a share of the receipts of a business taken in payment for the use of a right, as a copyright or patent.

seign-io-ri-al (sēn-yō'rĭ-ăl), *adj.* pertaining to a lord or a gentleman; as, *seigniorial* rights belonged to the lord of the manor.—*n.* **seigniory.**

seine (sān; sēn), *n.* a large fishing net, equipped with sinkers and floats.

seis-mic (sīs'mĭk; sīz'mĭk), *adj.* pertaining to, or produced by, an earthquake. Also, **seismical, seismal.**

seis-mo-graph (sīs'mō-grăf; sīz'mō-grȧf), *n.* an instrument for recording the wavelike motions, duration, and direction, of an earthquake: with slight variations, known also as the *seismometer,* or the *seismoscope.*

seis-mol-o-gist (sīs-mŏl'ō-jĭst; sīz-mŏl'ō-jĭst), *n.* a student of the science of earthquakes.

seis-mol-o-gy (sīs-mŏl'ō-jĭ; sīz-mŏl'ō-jĭ), *n.* the scientific study of earthquakes.

seiz-a-ble (sēz'ȧ-bl), *adj.* capable of being taken or snatched by force.

seize (sēz), *v.t.* to take possession of forcibly or suddenly; grasp; snatch; take hold of; comprehend or understand; as, to *seize* an idea.

seiz-or (sēz'ēr), *n.* in law, one who takes possession.

sei-zure (sē'zhŭr), *n.* the act of taking possession of; sudden attack, as of a disease; as, a *seizure* of pneumonia.

se-lah (sē'lȧ), *n.* a Hebrew word found in the Psalms, indicating a pause or break in the recital as used in the ancient temple service.

sel-dom (sĕl'dŭm), *adv.* rarely; not often; at long intervals of time.

se-lect (sē-lĕkt'), *adj.* chosen or picked out as more valuable than others; hence, of great excellence; nicely chosen; exclusive, or made up of chosen persons; as, a *select* club: *v.t.* to take by choice from among others; choose.—*n.* **selector.**

se-lec-tion (sē-lĕk'shŭn), *n.* the act of choosing; thing or things chosen; state of being chosen.

se-lec-tive (sē-lĕk'tĭv), *adj.* pertaining to, or resulting from, choice.

se-lect-man (sē-lĕkt'măn), *n.* [*pl.* selectmen (-mĕn)], one of a board of town officials chosen annually in the New England States to transact the general public business of the town.

self (sĕlf), *n.* [*pl.* selves (sĕlvz)], one's own person or character; as, "to thine own *self* be true"; personality; personification; as, she was beauty's *self;* one's own private interest; as, a person who lives for *self* is unhappy: *adj.* same or very; used in composition, as in *self*same: *prefix,* denoting the agent or object of the act, or owner of the quality, implied in the word attached: used in many words which explain themselves, and of which only the most important or difficult are here given.

self-as-ser-tion (sĕlf″ă-sûr′shŭn), *n.* the setting up of one's own will or opinion; demand of one's own rights.—*adj.* **self-assertive.**

self-col-ored (sĕlf″kŭl′ẽrd), *adj.* all of one color. Also, **self-coloured.**

self-com-mand (sĕlf″kŏ-månd′), *n.* power to control oneself.

self-con-fi-dence (sĕlf″kŏn′fĭ-dĕns), *n.* a state of feeling sure that one's own ability is equal to the

self-es-teem (sĕlf″ĕs-tēm′), *n.* proper respect for oneself; often, an undeservedly high opinion of oneself.

self-ev-i-dent (sĕlf″ĕv′ĭ-dĕnt), *adj.* appearing clearly without need of proof.

self-gov-ern-ment (sĕlf″gŭv′ẽrn-mĕnt), *n.* state of being ruled by the action of the people of a nation rather than by a sovereign; a form of organization modeled on the national one, existing in smaller bodies, as in a school; democracy, or rule of the people.

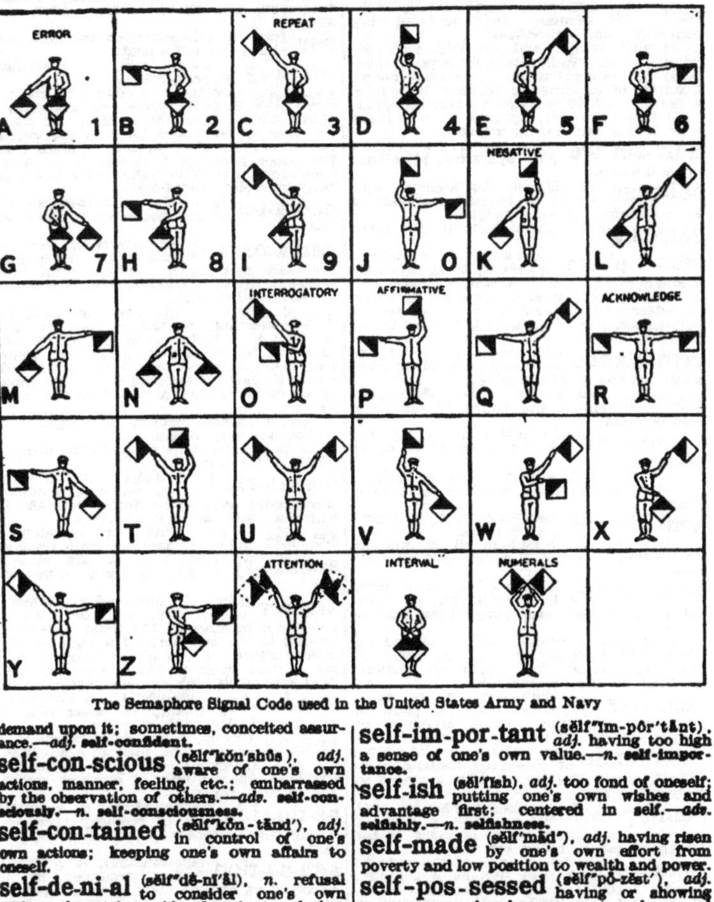

The Semaphore Signal Code used in the United States Army and Navy

demand upon it; sometimes, conceited assurance.—*adj.* **self-confident.**

self-con-scious (sĕlf″kŏn′shŭs), *adj.* aware of one's own actions, manner, feeling, etc.; embarrassed by the observation of others.—*adv.* **self-consciously.**—*n.* **self-consciousness.**

self-con-tained (sĕlf″kŏn-tānd′), *adj.* in control of one's own actions; keeping one's own affairs to oneself.

self-de-ni-al (sĕlf″dē-nī′ăl), *n.* refusal to consider one's own wishes; the setting aside of one's own desires for the sake of those of others.

self-im-por-tant (sĕlf″ĭm-pôr′tănt), *adj.* having too high a sense of one's own value.—*n.* **self-importance.**

self-ish (sĕl′fĭsh), *adj.* too fond of oneself; putting one's own wishes and advantage first; centered in self.—*adv.* **selfishly.**—*n.* **selfishness.**

self-made (sĕlf′măd″), *adj.* having risen by one's own effort from poverty and low position to wealth and power.

self-pos-sessed (sĕlf″pŏ-zĕst′), *adj.* having or showing composure and calmness; not embarrassed or confused.—*n.* **self-possession.**

self-re-spect (sĕlf'rē-spĕkt'), *n.* a proper sense of one's own value.—*adj.* **self-respecting.**

self-right-eous (sĕlf'rī'chŭs), *adj.* upright in one's own eyes. —*n.* **self-righteousness.**

self-start-er (sĕlf'stärt'ẽr), *n.* a mechanism for starting the engine of an automobile.

self-suf-fi-cient (sĕlf'sŭ-fĭsh'ĕnt), *adj.* needing no aid from another; often, haughtily satisfied with one's own character and acts.—*n.* **self-sufficiency.**

self-will (sĕlf'wĭl'), *n.* obstinacy; stubbornness; desire to have one's own way.—*adj.* **self-willed.**

sell (sĕl), *v.t.* [*p.t.* and *p.p.* sold, *p.pr.* selling], to give in return for a price, especially for money; to make, as one's honor, a matter of exchange or bargain; betray for a reward: *v.i.* to practice exchanging goods for a price; be sold; as, eggs *sell* at a lower price in summer than in winter.

Selt-zer wa-ter (sĕlt'sẽr wô'tẽr), a sparkling, alkaline, mineral water.

sel-vage (sĕl'vāj), *n.* the edge of cloth woven to prevent raveling; a woven border. Also, **selvedge.**

selves (sĕlvz), plural form of the noun *self.*

sem-a-phore (sĕm'ȧ-fōr), *n.* a railway apparatus for signaling by means of mechanical arms, lanterns, flags, etc.; in the army, a system of signaling in which the letters of the alphabet are represented by various positions of the arms in relation to the body.

sem-blance (sĕm'blȧns), *n.* likeness; resemblance; outside appearance; as, the *semblance* of truth.

se-men (sē'mĕn), *n.* a body-fluid containing the germs of life; the seed of plants.

se-mes-ter (sē-mĕs'tẽr), *n.* six months; one of the two terms of an academic year.

sem-i- (sĕm'ĭ-), a *prefix* meaning half, or partially; as, *semiannual*, or half-yearly.

sem-i-breve (sĕm'ĭ-brēv'), *n.* a whole note in music.

sem-i-cir-cle (sĕm'ĭ-sûr'kl), *n.* one half of a circle.—*adj.* **semicircular.**

sem-i-co-lon (sĕm'ĭ-kō'lŏn), *n.* a mark in punctuation [;], indicating the pause next longer than that of a comma.

sem-i-nal (sĕm'ĭ-nȧl), *adj.* pertaining to, containing, or consisting of, seed; as, *seminal* fluid; primary; radical; original; as, *seminal* principles.

sem-i-na-ry (sĕm'ĭ-nā-rĭ), *n.* [*pl.* seminaries (-rĭz)], a place of education; a higher school, academy, or college, especially a theological school.

Sem-i-nole (sĕm'ĭ-nōl), *n.* one of a tribe of American Indians originally living in Florida, but later removed to Indian Territory.

sem-i-pre-cious (sĕm'ĭ-prĕsh'ŭs), *adj.* denoting a gem of less than the highest degree of value, as the amethyst, garnet, topaz, etc.

Sem-ite (sĕm'īt), *n.* one of the race to which Jews, Syrians, Arabs, etc., belong; traditionally, a descendant of Shem.

Se-mit-ic (sē-mĭt'ĭk), *adj.* pertaining, or belonging, to that great division of the Caucasian race which includes Jews, Arabs, Syrians, Armenians, etc.; denoting the language of the Semites, represented in modern times by Hebrew and Arabic.

sem-i-tone (sĕm'ĭ-tōn'), *n.* half a tone in music, as the interval from C to C sharp.

sem-i-week-ly (sĕm'ĭ-wēk'lĭ), *adj.* occurring, coming, etc., twice a week: *n.* a periodical issued twice a week.

semp-stress (sĕmp'strĕs; sĕm'strĕs), *n.* a needlewoman; a woman who earns a living by sewing. Also, **seamstress.**

sen (sĕn), *n.* a Japanese copper coin worth about one-half a cent.

sen-a-ry (sĕn'ȧ-rĭ), *adj.* of, containing or pertaining to, six.

sen-ate (sĕn'āt), *n.* a council of state; in ancient Rome, an assembly of elders, chosen from the nobility, at first as an advisory body and later as the supreme council of state: **Senate**, in the United States, the upper house of Congress or of a state legislature; the upper house of the lawmaking body in various countries.

sen-a-tor (sĕn'ȧ-tẽr), *n.* a member of an upper house of a lawmaking body.

sen-a-to-ri-al (sĕn'ȧ-tō'rĭ-ȧl), *adj.* pertaining to, or befitting, a senator or a senate; as, *senatorial* duties; *senatorial* dignity; entitled to elect a senator, as, *senatorial* districts.

send (sĕnd), *v.t.* [*p.t.* and *p.p.* sent, *p.pr.* sending], to throw, cast, or drive; as, to *send* a ball; cause to go; dispatch; cause to be or happen; grant; as, Heaven *send* that no danger may befall you; inflict: *v.i.* to dispatch a messenger: *n.* the motion of a wave causing a vessel to be carried forward.

Syn., *v.* forward, project, discharge.
Ant. (see keep, retain).

sen-dal (sĕn'dȧl), *n.* a light, thin silk fabric.

sen-es-chal (sĕn'ĕ-shȧl), *n.* an official in the castle of a noble of the Middle Ages whose duties were those of a steward with military authority.

se-nile (sē'nīl; sē'nĭl), *adj.* pertaining to infirm old age; as, *senile* weakness.

se-nil-i-ty (sē-nĭl'ĭ-tĭ), *n.* the state or quality of being infirm with age.

sen-ior (sēn'yẽr), *adj.* before others in age, dignity, rank, or office; as, the *senior* member of the firm; elder; pertaining to the last year of a high school or college course: *n.* one who is before others in age, dignity, rank, or office; a student in the final year of his high school or college course.

sen-ior-i-ty (sēn-yŏr'ĭ-tĭ), *n.* the state or quality of being older, or ahead in dignity, rank, or office.

sen-na (sĕn'ȧ), *n.* the dried leaves of the cassia plant, used as a medicine.

se-ñor (sā-nyōr'), *n.* [*fem.* señora], a Spanish title of courtesy meaning *Mr.* or *Sir.* [SPAN.]

se-ño-ri-ta (sā'nyō-rē'tȧ), *n.* a Spanish title of courtesy given to a young lady, meaning *Miss;* a young lady. [SPAN.]

sen-sa-tion (sĕn-sā'shŭn), *n.* a state of feeling produced by the action of an outside force upon the body; a mental impression resulting from a bodily feeling; power to feel; as, anesthetics cause loss of *sensation;* state of excited feeling or interest, or its cause; as, a *sensation* was caused by the playing of the great violinist.

sen-sa-tion-al (sĕn-sā'shŭn ăl), *adj.* pertaining to, having, or causing, feeling; fitted to excite great interest; as, a *sensational* escape from prison; intended to work on the feelings; as, a *sensational* novel.

sen-sa-tion-al-ism (sĕn-sā'shŭn-ăl-ĭzm), *n.* writing or language intended to work on the feelings; the philosophical doctrine that our ideas are the outcome of sense perceptions, and consist of such perceptions transformed.

sen-sa-tion-al-ist (sĕn-sā'shŭn-ăl-ĭst), *n.* a believer in the philosophy of sense perceptions as the basis of knowledge; a writer or speaker who works on the feelings of his audience.

sense (sĕns), *n.* the power by which objects are seen or felt physically or mentally through certain bodily organs; also, the power to see or feel through one special organ; as, the *sense* of sight, of smell, etc.; mental perception or feeling; as, her *sense* of propriety; his *sense* of justice; good mental ability; correct judgment; that which is reasonable; meaning; as, the *sense* of a remark; moral perception; as, his high *sense* of honor: *v.t.* colloquially, to grasp the meaning of.

Syn., *n.* view, opinion, feeling, sensibility.

sense-less (sĕns'lĕs), *adj.* without feeling; unconscious; foolish; stupid; nonsensical; opposed to reason or sound judgment; as, a *senseless* argument.

sen-si-bil-i-ty (sĕn'sĭ-bĭl'ĭ-tĭ), *n.* [*pl.* sensibilities (-tĭz)], the state or quality of being quick to feel; fineness of feeling; capacity of emotion or feeling; as, *sensibility* to pleasure or pain.

sen-si-ble (sĕn'sĭ-bl), *adj.* capable of being seen or felt by the senses, or of making an impression on the mind through the bodily organs; as, *sensible* heat; capable of receiving impressions from external objects; as, the ear is *sensible* of sound; having some particular feeling; aware; as, *sensible* of being tired; marked by good judgment; reasonable; having moral perception or understanding.—*adv.* **sensibly.**

sen-si-tive (sĕn'sĭ-tĭv), *adj.* having keen power to feel; quickly and acutely alive to impressions from external objects; as, a nature *sensitive* to beauty; easily affected or changed by certain outside agents; as, a camera has a *sensitive* plate; quickly affected by kindness, cruelty, etc.—*adv.* **sensitively.**—*n.* **sensitiveness.**

sen-si-tize (sĕn'sĭ-tīz), *v.t.* to make alive to outside impressions; to cause to feel quickly and keenly; to make capable of being acted upon by rays of the sun, X-rays, etc., as a camera plate or film.

sen-so-ri-um (sĕn-sō'rĭ-ŭm), *n.* the seat of sensation; the nervous system, with the organs of sense; the gray matter of the brain.

sen-so-ry (sĕn'sō-rĭ), *adj.* pertaining to feeling: applied to the nerves which carry sense impressions to the brain. Also, **sensorial.**

sen-su-al (sĕn'shōō-ăl), *adj.* pertaining to, consisting in, or affecting, the senses; not spiritual or mental; basely material; gross; controlled by the passions or appetites.—*adv.* **sensually.**

sen-su-al-ism (sĕn'shōō-ăl-ĭzm), *n.* a state of being controlled by the passions and appetites instead of by mental or spiritual forces; the philosophy that all ideas have their origin in sensation.

sen-su-al-i-ty (sĕn'shōō-ăl'ĭ-tĭ), *n.* state or quality of being controlled by appetites and passions; grossness.

sen-su-ous (sĕn'shōō-ŭs), *adj.* of or pertaining to the senses; appealing to the senses; as, *sensuous* music; easily affected through the senses; quickly responsive to material impressions.—*adv.* **sensuously.**—*n.* **sensuousness.**

sent (sĕnt), past tense and past participle of the verb *send.*

sen-tence (sĕn'tĕns), *n.* judgment, opinion, or decision; judgment pronounced by a court; a series of words containing a subject and a predicate, and expressing a thought completely: *v.t.* to condemn by judgment of a court.

sen-ten-tious (sĕn-tĕn'shŭs), *adj.* short and energetic in expression; terse; expressing much meaning in few words; given to pithy sayings, wise maxims, etc.

sen-ti-ence (sĕn'shĭ-ĕns; sĕn'shĕns), *n.* power to feel or perceive.

sen-ti-ent (sĕn'shĭ-ĕnt; sĕn'shĕnt), *adj.* able to feel or to perceive; having sensation or feeling.

sen-ti-ment (sĕn'tĭ-mĕnt), *n.* an opinion or state of mind based on feeling rather than reason; refinement of feeling; quickness to feel; capacity for emotion; an emotional attitude toward some particular matter; as, the *sentiment* of America, even before engaging in the war, was strongly pro-Ally.

sen-ti-men-tal (sĕn'tĭ-mĕn'tăl), *adj.* having, expressing, or given to, feeling or emotion; appealing to, or based on, feeling rather than reason; artificially or affectedly tender; having an excessive capacity for feeling or emotion; weakly affectionate.—*adv.* **sentimentally.**

sen-ti-men-tal-ism (sĕn'tĭ-mĕn'tăl-ĭzm), *n.* an excessive display of overrefined feeling; control of action by feeling.

sen-ti-men-tal-ist (sĕn'tĭ-mĕn'tăl-ĭst), *n.* one who is guided by feeling rather than reason; one who shows excessive, often affected, refinement of feeling.

sen-ti-men-tal-i-ty (sĕn'tĭ-mĕn-tăl'ĭ-tĭ), *n.* state or quality of being guided by feeling rather than reason; weak emotionalism.

sen-ti-nel (sĕn'tĭ-nĕl), *n.* one who watches or guards, especially a soldier on guard at a camp or fort.

sen-try (sĕn'trĭ), *n.* [*pl.* sentries (-trĭz)], a sentinel, guard, or watch.

se-pal (sē'păl; sĕp'ăl), *n.* a leaf or section of the calyx of a flower.

sep-a-ra-bil-i-ty (sĕp'ȧ-rȧ-bĭl'ĭ-tĭ), *n.* the quality of being capable of being divided.

sep-a-ra-ble (sĕp'ȧ-rȧ-bl), *adj.* capable of being divided.—*adv.* **separably.**

sep-a-rate (sĕp'ȧ-rāt), *v.t.* [*p.t.* and *p.p.* separated, *p.pr.* separating], to part or divide; disunite; disconnect; set apart from a number for a particular purpose; withdraw: *v.i.* to part; be disunited; withdraw from each other: *adj.* (sĕp'ȧ-rāt), divided from the rest; disconnected; not united; distinct.—*adv.* **separately.**—*n.* **separateness.**

sep-a-ra-tion (sĕp'ȧ-rā'shŭn), *n.* the act of parting, dividing, or withdrawing; state of being divided or apart; disconnection; legal parting of married persons; the breaking of a union between two or more countries or states.

sep-a-ra-tist (sĕp'ȧ-rā-tĭst), *n.* one who divides himself from others; especially, one who withdraws from an established church.

sep-a-ra-tor (sĕp'ȧ-rā'tẽr), *n.* one who, or that which, divides; as, a cream *separator* divides the cream from the milk.

se-pi-a (sē'pĭ-ȧ), *n.* [*pl.* sepias (-ȧz)], the European cuttlefish; a dark-brown paint prepared from the black secretion or ink of the cuttlefish.

se-poy (sē'poi), *n.* [*pl.* sepoys (-poiz)], an Indian native employed as a soldier by a European government, especially by Great Britain.

sept- (sĕpt-), a *prefix* meaning seven; as, *sept*angular, having seven angles. Also, **septi-**.

Sep-tem-ber (sĕp-tĕm'bẽr), *n.* the ninth month of the year.

sep-te-na-ry (sĕp'tē-nā-rĭ), *adj.* consisting of, or relating to, the number seven; lasting seven years; occurring once in seven years.

sep-ten-ni-al (sĕp-tĕn'ĭ-ăl), *adj.* occurring once in seven years; lasting seven years.—*adv.* **septennially.**

sep-tet (sĕp-tĕt'), *n.* a set of seven persons or objects; a musical composition for seven voices. Also, **septette.**

sep-tic (sĕp'tĭk), *adj.* causing, or caused by, decay: *n.* a substance causing decay.

sep-ti-cæ-mi-a (sĕp'tĭ-sē'mĭ-ȧ), *n.* blood poisoning, caused by poisonous matter taken into the circulation. Also, **septicemia.**

sep-til-lion (sĕp-tĭl'yŭn), *n.* in the French system of numbering, followed in the United States, a number expressed by a unit followed by twenty-four ciphers; in the English system, a number expressed by a unit followed by forty-two ciphers.

sep-tu-a-ge-na-ri-an (sĕp'tū-ȧ-jē-nā'rĭ-ăn), *n.* a person between seventy and eighty years old.

sep-tu-ag-e-na-ry (sĕp'tū-ăj'ē-nā-rĭ), *adj.* consisting of seventy; seventy years old: *n.* [*pl.* septuagenaries (-rĭz)], a person between seventy and eighty years old.

sep-tu-a-ges-i-ma (sĕp'tū-ȧ-jĕs'ĭ-mȧ), *n.* seventy days: **Septuagesima Sunday**, the third Sunday before Lent.—*adj.* **septuagesimal.**

Sep-tu-a-gint (sĕp'tū-ȧ-jĭnt), *n.* a version of the Old Testament in Greek: so called because formerly considered the work of seventy translators.

sep-tum (sĕp'tŭm), *n.* a dividing wall or partition in a coral, seashell, or other organism.

sep-tu-ple (sĕp'tū-pl), *adj.* sevenfold; seven times repeated.

sep-ul-cher (sĕp'ŭl-kẽr), *n.* a grave or tomb; a place of burial: *v.t.* to bury; entomb. Also, **sepulchre.**

se-pul-chral (sē-pŭl'krăl), *adj.* pertaining to a tomb or to the burial of the dead; as, a *sepulchral* stone; gloomy or funereal; deep, grave, or hollow-toned; as, a *sepulchral* voice.

sep-ul-ture (sĕp'ŭl-tūr), *n.* the act of burying the dead.

se-quel (sē'kwĕl), *n.* a succeeding part; as, the *sequel* to a book; result; as, if you act in this way, the *sequel* will be ruin.

se-quence (sē'kwĕns), *n.* the state of following in orderly series; order of events in time; succession; result. *adj.* **sequential.**—*adv.* **sequentially.**

se-quent (sē'kwĕnt), *adj.* following; consequent: *n.* a result; something that follows another.

se-ques-ter (sē-kwĕs'tẽr), *v.t.* to separate from the owner for a time; take possession of (the property of another) until some claim is paid or established; cause to withdraw or retire; seclude: *v.i.* to renounce, as a widow may, any interest in the estate or property of a husband. Also, **sequestrate.**

se-ques-tered (sē-kwĕs'tẽrd), *adj.* secluded; retired; quiet and lonely.

se-ques-trate (sē-kwĕs'trāt), *v.t.* to seize; to hold as security for the claims of creditors; to seclude. Also, **sequester.**

se-ques-tra-tion (sē'kwĕs-trā'shŭn), *n.* the act of seizing as security; especially, the seizing of property by the state during dispute or for the benefit of creditors; retirement; seclusion.

se-ques-tra-tor (sē'kwĕs-trā'tẽr; sĕk'-wĕs-trā'tẽr), *n.* one who seizes property or takes possession of it for a time as security; one to whom the keeping of sequestered property is given.

se-quin (sē'kwĭn), *n.* a former gold coin of the republic of Venice, worth $2.25; a small spangle of jet, etc., used in dress trimmings.

se-quoi-a (sē-kwoi'ȧ), *n.* a California pine tree of two varieties, the redwood and the "big tree," both of which grow to immense size.

se-ragl-io (sē-răl'yō; sē-räl'yō), *n.* the palace of the sultan of Turkey, especially that part where the women are kept; a harem.

ser-aph (sĕr'ăf), *n.* [*pl.* seraphs (-ăfs), seraphim (-ĭm)], an angel of the highest order.

se-raph-ic (sē-răf'ĭk), *adj.* pertaining to, or like, a seraph, or angel of the highest rank; sublime; angelic.—*adv.* **seraphically.**

Serb (sûrb), *n.* a Slavic inhabitant of Serbia (Servia) or of the adjoining Slavonic territories, as Montenegro, Bosnia, Croatia, etc.; the language of Serbia and the adjoining Slavonic territories. Also, **Serbian, Servian.**

Ser-bo-Cro-a-tian (sûr'bō-krō-ā'-shăn), *n.* a Slavic native of Serbia, of Croatia in the southern part of Hungary, or of an adjoining Slavonic region, as Slavonia, Montenegro, Bosnia, etc.; the language spoken by these people, known as *West Slavic*: *adj.* pertaining to the Slavs of Serbia, Croatia, etc., or to their language. Also, **Serbo-Croat.**

sere (sēr), *adj.* dry; withered; as, a *sere* leaf. [POET.]

ser-e-nade (sĕr'ē-nād'), *n.* music sung or played by a lover under the window of a lady; a piece of music fitted to such an occasion: *v.t.* and *v.i.* to entertain by singing beneath a window.—*n.* **serenader.**

se-rene (sē-rēn'), *adj.* clear and calm; unclouded; placid; unruffled; as, a *serene* mind.—*adv.* **serenely.**—*n.* **sereneness.**

se-ren-i-ty (sē-rĕn′ĭ-tĭ), *n.* the state or quality of being placid or calm; balance of mind; evenness of temper; coolness; composure.

serf (sûrf), *n.* one of the lowest class of servants or slaves in the Middle Ages, who were attached to the land and sold with it: formerly, in Russia, one of the peasant class.

serge (sûrj), *n.* a ribbed fabric of wool or silk, used as a material for clothing.

ser-gean-cy (sär′jĕn-sĭ), *n.* the position of an army officer ranking next above a corporal. Also, **sergeantcy, serjeancy.**

ser-geant (sär′jĕnt), *n.* a noncommissioned army officer ranking next above a corporal, whose work is to train recruits, form the ranks, etc. Also, **serjeant.**

ser-geant ma-jor (sär′jĕnt mā′jĕr), the chief sergeant of a regiment, acting directly under the adjutant.

se-ri-al (sē′rĭ-ăl), *adj.* pertaining to, or consisting of, a succession of parts; occurring in regular succession; published in successive parts or numbers; as, a *serial* story: *n.* a tale, photoplay, etc., issued in successive parts.—*adv.* **serially.**

se-ri-a-tim (sē″rĭ-ā′tĭm), *adv.* in regular order. [LAT.]

se-ries (sē′rēz; sē′rĭ-ēz), *n.* a number of things or events succeeding one another in order, and similarly related to each other; a sequence.

se-ri-o-com-ic (sē″rĭ-ō-kŏm′ĭk), *adj.* having a mixture of gravity and humor.

se-ri-ous (sē′rĭ-ŭs), *adj.* grave in character or conduct; earnest; not trifling; thoughtful; solemn; important; weighty; disastrous; as, your carelessness may bring *serious* consequences.—*adv.* **seriously.**

ser-mon (sûr′mŭn), *n.* a formal talk or lecture on a moral or religious subject, often based on Scripture; a serious address.

ser-mon-ize (sûr′mŭn-īz), *v.i.* to compose or write a sermon; preach.

ser-pent (sûr′pĕnt), *n.* a snake, especially a large snake; a kind of firework; a sly, treacherous person; the devil.

ser-pen-tine (sûr′pĕn-tīn; sûr′pĕn-tĭn), *adj.* pertaining to, or like, a snake; moving or winding in coils or curves; sly and crafty: *n.* a kind of dull green rock, capable of being highly polished.

ser-rate (sĕr′āt), *adj.* having tooth-shaped projections on the edge like a saw; as, a *serrate* leaf. Also, **serrated.**

ser-ried (sĕr′ĭd), *p.adj.* crowded; pressed together; as, *serried* ranks.

se-rum (sē′rŭm), *n.* the watery portion of certain animal fluids, as blood, milk, etc.; the thin, yellowish, watery fluid filling certain cavities of the body.—*adj.* **serous.**

ser-val (sûr′văl), *n.* the African bush- or tiger-cat, having a valuable fur.

serv-ant (sûr′vănt), *n.* one who works for another, especially for wages; one who holds a menial position.

serve (sûrv), *v.t.* to work for; yield obedience to; worship; put on the table and distribute, as food; attend or wait on; as, the clerk *served* the customer courteously; be of use to: as, his wits will always *serve* him in an emergency; be enough for; as, this amount will *serve* my purpose; to treat; as, the Germans *served* their prisoners ill; to deliver, as a legal writ or summons; to undergo, as a term of apprenticeship, imprisonment, etc.; to supply; as, a farmer *serves* us with fresh eggs and vegetables; in tennis, to make the first stroke on (the ball): *v.i.* to be employed in labor for another; suit or be convenient; be in subjection; discharge the duties of an office or employment; be sufficient; with *for;* as, this will *serve* for an excuse.

serv-ice (sûr′vĭs), *n.* the condition or occupation of one who works for another in a menial position; duty required or performed in any office; employment; naval or military duty; a religious ceremony; as, a church *service;* manner of performing work, serving food, etc.; as, the hotel *service* is poor; a set of implements for some special purpose; as, a silver coffee *service;* the operation of some system which supplies a public need; as, the telephone *service;* the operation of some system of employment or public benefit under government control; as, the civil *service;* profession of respect; aid or kindness rendered to another.

serv-ice-a-ble (sûr′vĭs-ȧ-bl), *adj.* fit for work or use; useful; beneficial; helpful; having good wearing qualities.—*adv.* **serviceably.**—*n.* **serviceableness.**

serv-ice flag (sûr′vĭs flăg), a kind of flag used in the United States during the World War, consisting of a red border surrounding a white field, on which was one blue star for every man, from the house displaying the flag, who had entered the military or naval service of the United States, and one gold star for every man killed in the service of his country.

ser-vile (sûr′vĭl), *adj.* pertaining to, or like, a slave or menial; slavishly humble; cringing; fawning; as, *servile* fear; *servile* obedience.—*adv.* **servilely.**

ser-vil-i-ty (sẽr-vĭl′ĭ-tĭ), *n.* mean submission; baseness; slavishness; fawning humility.

ser-vi-tude (sûr′vĭ-tūd), *n.* the condition of a slave; state of slavish dependence; bondage; slavery; menial employment; subjection to a master; labor enforced as a punishment; as, penal *servitude.*

ses-sion (sĕsh′ŭn), *n.* the time during which any school, court, council, or lawmaking body holds its sittings; the sitting of such a body; the governing body of a single congregation in the Presbyterian Church.—*adj.* **sessional.**

ses-tet (sĕs-tĕt′; sĕs′tĕt), *n.* the last six lines of a sonnet; a musical composition for six performers; six players or singers rendering such a composition. Also, **sextet, sextette.**

set (sĕt), *v.t.* [*p.t.* and *p.p.* **set**, *p.pr.* **setting**], to place or put in any position; fix; plant; make secure; put on a nest of eggs; as, to *set* a hen; fit; as, to *set* a poem to music; render motionless; spread, as sails; make to agree with some standard; as, to *set* a clock; regulate; adjust; as, to *set* a broken limb; value; as, to *set* a person high in esteem; assign or prescribe; as, to *set* a time for a meeting; in printing, to arrange in words, lines, etc.; as, to *set* type: *v.i.* to sink below the horizon, as the sun; plant; be fixed closely or firmly; to harden; as, the jelly will *set* quickly; apply oneself; as, to *set* to work; flow or tend; as, the current *sets* to the north; start; as, to *set* out upon a journey; *adj.* fixed or established; regular; determined; firm; formal; as, a *set* speech; immovable; *n.* the descent of a heavenly body; flow or direction; a number of persons associated together; as, the younger *set* in society; a number of things of the same kind intended for use together; as, a *set* of tea things; a young plant ready to set out; a number of persons necessary to execute a quadrille; in lawn tennis, a series of as many games as will enable one side to win six.

set-off (sĕt'ôf"), *n.* a thing set off against another thing; discharge of a debt by setting against it a claim of the debtor; also, the claim itself; an ornament; the projecting part of a wall.

set-tee (sĕ-tē'), *n.* a long seat with a back; a vessel with a very long, sharp prow, used in the Mediterranean.

set-ter (sĕt'ẽr), *n.* one who, or that which, sets; as, a type*setter;* a kind of hunting dog trained to stand and point at game.

set-ting (sĕt'ĭng), *n.* the act of one who, or that which, sets; the direction of a current of wind; that in which something is fastened, as the mounting of a jewel; a background for a play or story.

set-tle (sĕt'l), *v.t.* to place in a fixed state; establish; as, the family were *settled* in a new home; free from doubt or uncertainty; as, to *settle* a difficult problem; to quiet; as, to *settle* one's nerves; to make up, as a quarrel; adjust the balance of, as an account; pay; as, to *settle* a bill; make pure or clear of dregs; as, to *settle* coffee; colonize; as, the Quakers *settled* Pennsylvania: *v.i.* to become fixed, or permanent; descend or stop; grow calm or clear; sink to the bottom, or by its own weight; adjust differences or accounts; marry and establish a home: *n.* a highbacked bench.

Syn., v. regulate, conclude, determine.

set-tle-ment (sĕt'l-mĕnt), *n.* the act of establishing, fixing, etc.; state of being established or fixed; establishment in life, business, or condition; a disposition of money for the benefit of someone; payment or adjustment of an account; dispute, etc.; a colony newly settled; legal residence.

set-tler (sĕt'lẽr), *n.* a colonist; something that finally decides a contest.

set-tlings (sĕt'lĭngz), *n.pl.* the matter which settles to the bottom of a liquid; dregs; lees; sediment.

set-to (sĕt'to͞o"), *n.* a contest in boxing; an argument; a fight. [Colloq.]

sev-en (sĕv'n), *n.* the sum of six and one; the sign representing seven units, as 7 or vii: *adj.* consisting of six and one.

sev-en-fold (sĕv'n-fōld"), *adv.* seven times as much: *adj.* multiplied seven times; having seven parts.

sev-en-teen (sĕv'n-tēn"; sĕv"n-tēn'), *adj.* one more than sixteen: *n.* the sum of seven and ten; the number next larger than sixteen; the sign representing seventeen units, as 17 or xvii.

sev-en-teenth (sĕv'n-tēnth"; sĕv"n-tēnth'), *adj.* next after the sixteenth: *n.* the ordinal of seventeen; one of seventeen equal parts.

sev-enth (sĕv'nth), *adj.* next in order after the sixth: *n.* the ordinal of seven; one of seven equal parts; in music, the space of five tones and a semitone, or the interval between any note and the sixth note above it, on the scale.

sev-en-ti-eth (sĕv'n-tĭ-ĕth), *adj.* next in order after the sixty-ninth: *n.* one of seventy equal parts; the ordinal of seventy.

sev-en-ty (sĕv'n-tĭ), *n.* [*pl.* seventies (-tĭz)], the sum of ten times seven; the sign representing seventy units, as 70 or lxx: *adj.* ten times seven; one more than sixty-nine.

sev-en-ty-five (sĕv'n-tĭ-fīv), *n.* in the World War, a French rapid-fire seventy-five millimeter field gun, firing thirty shells per minute.

sev-er (sĕv'ẽr), *v.t.* to divide or separate with violence; cut open or through; keep distinct or apart: *v.i.* to make a separation or distinction; be torn apart; part.

sev-er-al (sĕv'ẽr-ăl), *adj.* distinct; separate; as, two *several* items; consisting of more than two, but not many; different; various; numerous.—*adv.* seve ally.

Syn. sundry, divers, many.

sev-er-al-ty (sĕv'ẽr-ăl-tĭ), *n.* a state of separation from the rest, or from all others.

sev-er-ance (sĕv'ẽr-ăns), *n.* the act of separating, dividing, or cutting open or through; the state of being separated, divided, or cut open or through; separation; division.

se-vere (sē-vēr'), *adj.* strictly adhering to rule; grave in manner; forbidding in appearance; strict; harsh; as, *severe* methods of discipline; extremely plain; as, a gown of a *severe* style; extreme; sharp; distressing; as, *severe* pain; hard to bear or undergo; trying; as, a *severe* test.—*adv.* severely.

Syn. stern, stringent, unmitigated, rough, unyielding.

Ant. (see lenient).

se-ver-i-ty (sē-vĕr'ĭ-tĭ), *n.* [*pl.* severities (-tĭz)], the quality of being stern or strict; harshness; rigor; gravity; sharpness; strictness; lack of ornament, as in dress.

sew (sō), *v.t.* [*p.t.* sewed, *p.p.* sewed or sewn, *p.pr.* sewing], to join or fasten together with stitches: *v.i.* to make stitches: to work with needle and thread.

sew-age (sū'āj), *n.* contents of a sewer or drain; foul liquids or waste matter carried off by a sewer.

sew-er (sū'ẽr), *n.* an underground pipe or channel to carry off water, waste material, etc.

sew-er-age (sū'ẽr-āj), *n.* drainage by underground pipes; the system of drainage of a town, etc.; refuse matter carried off by a sewer.

sex (sĕks), *n.* the physical character that makes a human being, animal, or plant, distinctively male or female; one of the two divisions into which all living things are grouped, as being distinctly male or female: a *prefix* meaning six, as *sexenn*ial, occurring once in, or lasting, six years.

sex-a-ge-na-ri-an (sĕk"sȧ-jē-nā'rĭ-ăn), *n.* one who is between sixty and seventy years old: *adj.* between sixty and seventy years old.

sex-ag-e-na-ry (sĕk-săj'ē-nā-rĭ), *adj.* pertaining to the number sixty; sixty years old.

Sex-a-ges-i-ma (sĕk"sȧ-jĕs'ĭ-mȧ), *n.* the second Sunday before Lent.

sex-less (sĕks'lĕs), *adj.* having no sex; neither male nor female; neuter.

sex-tant (sĕks'tănt), *n.* the sixth part of a circle; an instrument for measuring angular distances, used especially at sea for determining latitude and longitude.

sex-tet (sĕks-tĕt'), *n.* a musical composition for six performers; six players or singers rendering such a composition. Also, **sextette.**

sex-til-lion (sĕks-tĭl'yŭn), *n.* in the French system of numbering, followed in the United States, a number expressed by 1 followed by twenty-one ciphers; in the English system, a number expressed by 1 followed by thirty-six ciphers.

sex-ton (sĕks'tŭn), *n.* an under-official, or janitor, of a church, whose duty is to take care of the church building, attend to burials, etc.

sex-tu-ple (sĕks'tū-pl), *adj.* sixfold; multiplied by six.

sex-u-al (sĕk'shū-ăl), *adj.* pertaining to sex or the sexes; in biology, having sex.

shab-by (shăb'ĭ), *adj.* [*comp.* shabbier, *superl.* shabbiest], threadbare or worn, as clothes; poorly dressed; mean, petty, or unworthy; as, *shabby* behavior.—*adv.* **shabbily.**—*n.* **shabbiness.**

shack (shăk), *n.* a shabby old house; hut; log cabin. [COLLOQ.]

shack-le (shăk'l), *n.* anything that confines the arms or legs so as to prevent free action, as a strap or chain; a fetter; a handcuff; the bar of a padlock; that which checks or prevents free action: *v.t.* to tie or confine so as to prevent free action; to fetter; embarrass or hinder; unite or fasten with a strap, chain, etc.

shad (shăd), *n.* a fish of the herring family, highly valued as food.

shade (shād), *n.* partial darkness caused by cutting off rays of light; darkness; dimness; a spot not exposed to the sun; something which cuts off or softens the rays of light; an adjustable screen or curtain fitting close to a window pane to keep out or admit light; special quality or degree of color; as, this peculiar *shade* of blue is difficult to match; a slight degree of difference in meaning, etc.; a ghost or phantom: *v.t.* to screen from light or heat; to darken or make dim; to mark or paint with varying degrees of light or color; to slightly lower (the price): *v.i.* to change by slight degrees; as, the sunset clouds *shade* from pale pink to deep purple.

shad-ow (shăd'ō), *n.* partial darkness within certain limits; a darkened portion of space, representing in its outline the form of the body which intercepts or cuts off from it the rays of light; the dark part of a picture; obscurity or darkness; protection or security; a reflected image; faint representation; a close companion; small degree; as, not the *shadow* of a doubt: *v.t.* to deprive of light; darken or cloud; mark with degrees of light or color; represent faintly; attend closely; follow and watch closely, as a detective.

shad-ow-y (shăd'ō-ĭ), *adj.* full of spots of darkness; obscure; sheltered from light or heat; dim; unreal; as, the *shadowy* past.—*n.* **shadowiness.**

shad-y (shād'ĭ), *adj.* [*comp.* shadier, *superl.* shadiest], dim; obscure; partially darkened; sheltered from the glare of light or heat; pertaining to darkness; hence, colloquially, unable to bear the light; questionable; of doubtful honesty; as, the deal was a *shady* transaction.—*adv.* **shadily.**—*n.* **shadiness.**

shaft (shăft), *n.* an arrow or its stem; anything shaped like an arrow; the long, narrow entrance to a mine; the pole of a wagon or carriage; stalk of a plant; stick or handle of a golf club; the narrow, vertical open space inside of a chimney; in an engine or machine, a bar to hold wheels or other rotating parts; a well-like space through which air and light reach the windows of a tenement or factory building; the body of a column between the base and the top; open vertical space in which an elevator runs.

shag (shăg), *n.* a kind of tobacco; rough, woolly hair; a kind of cloth having a long, coarse nap: *v.t.* and *v.i.* to make shaggy; roughen.

shag-bark (shăg'bärk'), *n.* a kind of hickory; the nut borne by this tree.

shag-gy (shăg'ĭ), *adj.* rough with long hair or wool; as, a *shaggy* dog; rugged; tangled.—*n.* **shagginess.**

sha-green (shȧ-grēn'), *n.* a kind of untanned, grained leather; the rough skin of sharks and dogfishes prepared as leather: *adj.* made of such leather.

shah (shä), *n.* the title of the ruler of Persia, and other Eastern countries.

shake (shāk), *v.t.* [*p.t.* shook, *p.p.* shaken, *p.pr.* shaking], to cause to shiver; move with a quick, short motion; to move from a firm position; as, to *shake* one's faith; in music, give a quivering note to: *v.i.* to tremble or quake.

Syn. shudder, quiver, quake.

Shak-er (shāk'ẽr), *n.* one of a religious sect living in community settlements: so called from the motions of a dance which forms part of their worship.

Shak-er-ism (shāk'ẽr-ĭzm), *n.* the doctrines or beliefs of the Shakers.

Shake-spear-e-an (shāk-spēr'ē-ăn), *adj.* pertaining to, or like, Shakespeare, or his works. Also, **Shaksperean.**

shak-o (shăk'ō), *n.* [*pl.* shakoes (-ōz)], a kind of high military cap.

shak-y (shāk'ĭ), *adj.* [*comp.* shakier, *superl.* shakiest], in an unsteady condition; easily made to tremble; feeble; unsound; colloquially, uncertain; embarrassed.—*adv.* **shakily.**—*n.* **shakiness.**

shale (shāl), *n.* a rock which is formed of clay and which is easily split.—*adj.* **shaly.**

shall (shăl), *v. auxiliary* [*p.t.* **should**], having no participles, imperative, or infinitive, and followed by the infinitive without *to;* used, together with *will,* to form the simple future tense: thus, to express simple futurity, singular, first person, I *shall;* second person, you *will;* third person, he *will;* plural, first person, we *shall;* second person, you *will;* third person, they *will;* used to express determination in an arrangement exactly the opposite: used in a question, according to the form expected in the answer; as, *shall* I? *will* you? etc.

shal-lop (shăl'ŭp), *n.* a small, light, open boat; any open boat.

shal-lot (shȧ-lŏt'), *n.* a kind of small onion. Also, **eschalot.**

shal-low (shăl'ō), *adj.* not deep; having no mental depth; as, a *shallow* mind; superficial: *n.* a place where the water is not deep; shoal.—*adv.* **shallowly.**—*n.* **shallowness.**

shalt (shălt), the second person singular, present tense, of the verb *shall.*

sham (shăm), *n.* that which deceives; a trick, fraud, or make-believe; a trimmed cover for the pillow of a bed, etc.: *adj.* feigned; false; unreal: *v.t.* [*p.t.* and *p.p.* shammed, *p.pr.* shamming], to make false pretenses: *v.i.* to make a pretense of in order to deceive; feign; as, to *sham* death.

sham-ble (shăm'bl), *v.i.* to walk awkwardly and unsteadily; shuffle: *n.* a shuffling gait: *pl.* a slaughterhouse.

shame (shām), *n.* a painful sensation caused by the consciousness of wrongdoing, immodesty, or dishonor; that which causes a sensation of guilt; reproach; sense of modesty or decency: *v.t.* to mortify; to disgrace, as one's family; cause to blush; cover with reproach; to make (a person) do a thing through the sense of shame or disgrace.

shame-faced (shām'fāst"), *adj.* bashful; easily confused or embarrassed; showing embarrassment.—*adv.* **shamefacedly.**—*n.* **shamefacedness.**

shame-ful (shām'fo͝ol), *adj.* causing disgrace; disgraceful; exciting a sense of guilt; indecent.—*adv.* **shamefully.** —*n.* **shamefulness.**

Syn. degrading, scandalous, outrageous.
Ant. (see honorable).

shame-less (shām'lĕs), *adj.* without decency; wanting modesty or self-respect; impudent; brazen.—*adv.* **shamelessly.**—*n.* **shamelessness.**

sham-my (shăm'ĭ), *n.* a kind of small, mountain antelope; soft, flexible leather made from the skin of this animal. Also, **chamois.**

sham-poo (shăm-po͞o'), *v.t.* [*p.t.* and *p.p.* shampooed, *p.pr.* shampooing], to cleanse and rub (the head) with soap, etc.: *n.* the act of washing the head.

sham-rock (shăm'rŏk), *n.* any one of several three-leaved plants accepted as the national emblem of Ireland.

shang-hai (shăng-hī'), *v.t.* to make insensible by drugs or liquor, and put aboard a ship as a sailor, usually for money.

shank (shăṅk), *n.* the leg from the knee to the ankle; that part of a tool, instrument, etc., connecting the cutting or acting part with the handle.

shan't (shänt; shȧnt), a contraction for *shall not.* [Colloq.]

shan-ty (shăn'tĭ), *n.* [*pl.* shanties (-tĭz)], a rude hut.

shape (shāp), *n.* the form or figure of a thing; external appearance; that which has form or figure; pattern; cast, embodiment, or definite form; as, he at last put his dream into *shape;* aspect; colloquially, state or condition: *v.t.* to make into a certain form; fashion; regulate; design: **shaper,** a machine for planing metals in which the work is stationary, and the tool moves: **pillar shaper,** such a machine mounted on a pedestal.

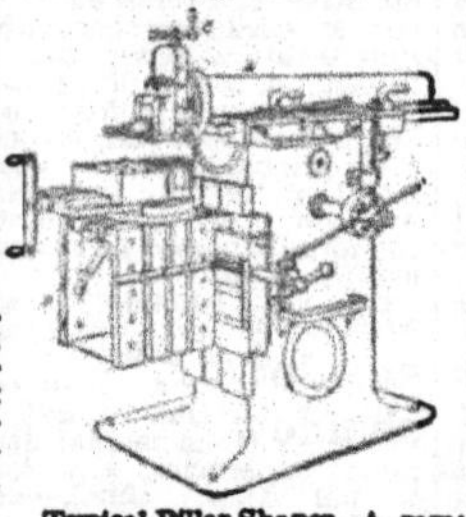

Typical Pillar Shaper. A, ram; B, work-table; C, vertical feed-handle.

shape-less (shāp'lĕs), *adj.* without definite contour; formless.—*n.* **shapelessness.**

shape-ly (shāp'lĭ), *adj.* well-formed; comely; symmetrical.—*n.* **shapeliness.**

shard (shärd), *n.* a piece or fragment of brittle material, as earthenware; any hard, thin covering, as an eggshell; a wing cover, as of a beetle. Also, **sherd.**

share (shâr), *n.* a portion or part; part given or belonging to one; any of a certain number of equal portions into which any property is divided; as, a *share* of stock; the blade of a plow; plowshare: *v.t.* to part among two or more; divide; take or possess in common; partake of or use with others: *v.i.* to have a part in something; to participate: often with *in.*—*n.* **sharer.**

Syn., n. portion, lot, division, quantity.

share-hold-er (shâr'hōl"dẽr), *n.* one who owns one or more parts, or shares, of a property, as a railway.

shark (shärk), *n.* a large, voracious fish with sharp teeth; often of a man-eating variety; colloquially, a dishonest, swindling fellow or a cheat.

sharp (shärp), *adj.* having a thin edge; as, a *sharp* knife; ending in a fine point; well-defined; distinct; keen; penetrating; as, a *sharp* eye; severe; as, a *sharp* pain; piercing; shrill; as, a *sharp* sound; acid, sour, or pungent; as, a *sharp* taste; sarcastic or bitter; as, a *sharp* reproof; intensely cold; attentive; as, a *sharp* lookout; violent; gritty; angular or abrupt; as, a *sharp* bend in the road; in music, above true pitch; raised a semitone in pitch: *adv.* piercingly; keenly; to an edge or point; colloquially, promptly or precisely; as, six o'clock *sharp:* *n.* in music, a tone or note raised a semitone in pitch; a character [#] on a degree of the staff indicating that the degree is a half step higher in pitch: *v.t.* to make higher in pitch by a semitone: *v.i.* to sing or play above the correct pitch.—*adv.* **sharply.**—*n.* **sharpness.**

sharp-en (shär'pn), *v.t.* to make sharp or sharper; give edge or point to; make more acute or eager: *v.i.* to become sharp.—*n.* **sharpener.**

sharp-er (shär'pẽr), *n.* a cheat; a swindler; a rogue.

sharp-shoot-er (shärp'sho͞ot"ẽr), *n.* one expert in shooting, especially with a rifle; a skilled marksman.

sharp-sight-ed (shärp'sīt"ĕd), *adj.* possessed of keen or acute sight.

sharp-wit-ted (shärp'wĭt"ĕd), *adj.* mentally alert; discerning; quick-witted.

shat-ter (shăt'ẽr), *v.t.* to break at once into many pieces; smash; to derange or disorder, as the mind; to destroy the health or power of, as the body; cause to disappear; as, to *shatter* hopes: *v.i.* to fly into splinters or pieces.

shave (shāv), *v.t.* [*p.t.* shaved, *p.p.* shaved or shaven, *p.pr.* shaving], to cut or pare off with a razor or other sharp-edged instrument; to remove as, hair from the face or head, with a razor; to remove the hair from: cut in thin slices; skim along the surface of: plunder or fleece: *v.i.* to use the razor to remove hair; hence, to practice cheating or to drive a hard bargain: *n.* a thin slice; the operation of removing hair with a razor; an instrument for shaving hoops, etc.; colloquially, a short time or distance, or a narrow escape; as, a close *shave.*

shave-ling (shāv′lĭng), *n.* a shaven person; a priest or monk: sometimes contemptuously.

shav-er (shāv′ẽr), *n.* one who, or that which, shaves; a barber; one who is close in bargains; a sharper; colloquially, a boy or lad.

shav-ing (shāv′ĭng), *n.* the act of one who pares, cuts off, etc.; a thin slice pared off, as from a plank or board.

shawl (shôl), *n.* a wrap or garment made of a square or oblong piece of cloth, used as a loose outer covering for the shoulders.

Shaw-nee (shô-nē′), *n.* one of a tribe of Algonquian Indians formerly living in what is now Georgia.

she (shē), *pron.* [*poss.* her or hers; *obj.* her; *pl. nom.* they; *poss.* they or theirs; *obj.* them], the feminine pronoun of the third person; this or that woman previously referred to.

sheaf (shēf), *n.* [*pl.* sheaves (shēvz)], a quantity of cut grain bound together; a bundle; enough arrows to fill a quiver: *v.t.* to gather or bind into bundles, as grain or straw.

shear (shēr), *v.t.* [*p.t.* sheared, *p.p.* sheared or shorn, *p.pr.* shearing], to cut or clip with a large cutting instrument like shears: *v.i.* to use a large cutting instrument for clipping, etc.: *n.* a machine for cutting metal: *pl.* a large cutting instrument working in a way similar to scissors, by the crossing of opposed cutting blades or edges; large scissors.

shear-wa-ter (shēr′wô″tẽr), *n.* a long-winged sea bird, related to the petrels.

sheath (shēth), *n.* a case for a sword or knife; a scabbard; any covering, as of a leaf, etc., resembling such a case in shape.

sheathe (shē*th*), *v.t.* to put into a case; to encase with a protecting covering; as, to *sheathe* a ship's hull with copper; to conceal, as in a case or sheath. Also, **sheath.**

sheath-ing (shē*th*′ĭng), *n.* that which forms an outside covering; material for covering; the act of one who covers or encases.

sheave (shēv), *n.* a grooved wheel in a block or pulley over which the rope runs: *v.t.* to gather and bind into bundles, as grain.

sheaves (shēvz), *n.* plural of *sheaf* and *sheave.*

shed (shĕd), *v.t.* [*p.t.* and *p.p.* shed, *p.pr.* shedding], to pour out or spread; cause to flow off without sinking in; as, oilskins *shed* water; to throw off; as, birds *shed* their feathers; to let fall or drop; as, trees *shed* leaves; to pour forth, as tears: *v.i.* to let fall seed; to throw off a covering, as scales, hair, etc.: *n.* a small building, often with the front or front and sides open, used for storing wood, farm implements, wagons, etc.; a cabin or hut.

sheen (shēn), *n.* brightness; splendor; luster.

sheep (shēp), *n., s.* and *pl.* a cud-chewing animal valued for its wool and edible flesh: a foolish, bashful fellow; leather made of sheepskin.

sheep-fold (shēp′fōld″), *n.* a pen or place where sheep are inclosed or kept.

sheep-ish (shēp′ĭsh), *adj.* abashed; shrinking; awkwardly bashful.—*adv.* **sheepishly.**—*n.* **sheepishness.**

sheep's eye (shēps ī), a sidelong glance; a quick, oblique look; an ardent or loving glance: usually in *pl.* Also, **sheep's-eye.**

sheeps-head (shēps′hĕd″), *n.* a valued food fish of the Atlantic coast of the United States.

sheep-skin (shēp′skĭn″), *n.* the skin of a sheep, or anything, as leather, made from it; cant, a graduation diploma; parchment.

sheer (shēr), *adj.* pure; downright; unmixed; utter; absolute; as, *sheer* folly; very thin or transparent: said of materials; as, a *sheer* fabric; straight up and down; vertical; steep; as, a *sheer* precipice: *adv.* perpendicularly; straight: *v.i.* to turn aside from the proper course; swerve.

sheet (shēt), *n.* a large, broad, thin piece of any substance; as paper, cloth, etc.; a broad piece of linen or cotton to cover a bed; a single piece of paper of differing size; a newspaper; a broad expanse or surface; as, a *sheet* of water; a rope attached to a sail to spread or move it.

sheet an-chor (shēt ăn′kẽr), a large, very heavy anchor, for use in emergency; figuratively, a sure reliance or refuge.

sheet-ing (shēt′ĭng), *n.* the act of spreading out or forming into sheets; material for making sheets for beds.

sheik (shēk; shāk), *n.* the head of an Arab family, tribe, or clan; the chief magistrate of an Arab village; title applied to a Mohammedan high priest. Also, **sheikh.**

shek-el (shĕk′l), *n.* an ancient Hebrew gold or silver coin.

She-ki-nah (shē-kī′nȧ), *n.* the Jewish name for the Divine Presence, shown by the pillar of cloud or fire which rested above the sacred Ark.

shel-drake (shĕl′drāk″), *n.* a goose-like duck of the Old World; a ducklike water bird: called also *merganser;* a canvasback duck.

shelf (shĕlf), *n.* [*pl.* shelves (shĕlvz)], a flat ledge or board, usually long and narrow and set horizontally into a wall, for holding things; as, a book*shelf;* a sandbank; a flat, projecting ledge of rock.

shell (shĕl), *n.* [*pl.* shells], a hard outside covering, as on a fruit, egg, tortoise, crab, etc.; a husk, as on corn, wheat, etc.; something like a shell; tortoise shell; a framework; as, after the fire only the *shell* of the house remained; a very light, long, narrow racing boat; a cartridge case to hold ammunition for breech-loading small arms; [*pl.* shell], a hollow metallic projectile for use in a cannon or mortar, filled with an explosive and so made that after it is fired it will burst at a certain point, forcibly scattering its contents: *v.t.* to take out of the outside covering, as peas from the pod, etc.; to separate from the cob, as corn; to bombard, as a stronghold: *v.i.* to cast or throw off the husk; to fall off, as a crust or shell.

Shotgun Shell

shel-lac (shĕ-lăk′; shĕl′ăk), *n.* a sticky, resinous substance used in varnishes: *v.t.* [*p.t.* and *p.p.* shellacked, *p.pr.* shellacking], to coat or treat with this substance, as a floor. Also, **shellack, shell lac.**

shell-bark (shĕl′bärk″), the shagbark; any of several kinds of rough-barked hickory.

shell-fish (shĕl'fĭsh″), *n.* an invertebrate water animal having a shell, as a clam, lobster, mollusk, etc.

shell shock (shĕl shŏk), mental disorder, often taking the form of loss of memory and sense of identity, caused by the violent sights and sounds of war.

shell-y (shĕl'ĭ), *adj.* of, pertaining to, or like, a shell; full of, abounding in, or consisting of, shells; as, a *shelly* beach.

shel-ter (shĕl'tẽr), *n.* that which protects or shields; that which covers, especially from the weather; a house; protection; refuge; defense; state of being protected or covered: *v.t.* to protect or shield from injury or violence; to cover or place in safety; conceal: *v.i.* to take refuge; to screen or cover oneself.—*adj.* **shelterless.**—*n.* **shelterer.**

Syn., *v.* defend, protect, screen: *n.* sanctuary, security.

shel-ter tent (shĕl'tẽr tĕnt), a small tent made of pieces of light cotton duck arranged to button together.

shelve (shĕlv), *v.t.* to place on a shelf; hence, to dismiss from service, or postpone indefinitely; as, to *shelve* an officer; to *shelve* a request; to furnish with shelves, as a room: *v.i.* to incline gradually; slope; as, the bottom *shelves* from the shore.

Shem (shĕm), *n.* in the Bible, Noah's eldest son.

Shem-ite (shĕm'īt), *n.* one of a race including the Jews, Arabs, ancient Assyrians, Babylonians, etc.—*adj.* **Shemitic.** Also, **Semite, Semitic.**

She-ol (shē'ōl), *n.* among the Hebrews, the place of departed spirits; Hades; the grave.

shep-herd (shĕp'ẽrd), *n.* [*fem.* shepherdess] one who tends sheep; a pastor: *v.t.* to tend as a herder tends sheep; guard; lead.

shep-herd's-purse (shĕp'ẽrdz-pûrs″), *n.* an annual weed akin to mustard and cress, bearing white flowers and sacklike pods.

sher-bet (shûr'bĕt), *n.* a cooling drink made of water and fruit juices sweetened and flavored; a water ice.

sherd (shûrd), *n.* a fragment or broken piece of pottery. Also, **shard.**

sher-iff (shĕr'ĭf), *n.* the chief executive officer of a county, whose duty consists in seeing that the law is carried out and that peace is preserved.

sher-ry (shĕr'ĭ), *n.* a dry amber-colored wine, made in Andalusia, Spain; any similar wine.

shew (shō), an ancient form of the verb *show.*

shew-bread (shō'brĕd″), *n.* in the ancient Jewish ritual, unleavened bread placed in the sanctuary. Also, **showbread.**

shib-bo-leth (shĭb'ō-lĕth), *n.* a Hebrew word which was made the test to distinguish the Ephraimites from the Gileadites, the former not being able to pronounce *sh.*—Judges xii; hence, the password of a secret society, or the test or watchword of a party; a party phrase; as, the *shibboleth* of the Democrats.

shied (shīd), past tense and past participle of the verb *shy.*

shield (shēld), *n.* one who, or anything which, defends or protects; a broad piece of armor, usually carried on the left arm to protect the body in fighting; a large buckler; in heraldry, the field upon which emblems or coats of arms are represented; a screen of steel protecting guns and the men who operate them; a defender; defense; shelter: *v.t.* to protect with, or as with, a protecting or sheltering screen; defend.

shift (shĭft), *n.* a turning from one thing to another; change; substitution; an expedient; as, to make one's way by *shifts;* hence, a trick, dodge, or evasion; the change of one set of workmen for another; turn of work; group of workers which takes turns with another group; as, the night *shift;* a woman's chemise: *v.t.* to change the place of; exchange; transfer; to move or remove: *v.i.* to change position; to contrive or manage; to practice evasions.—*n.* **shifter.**

shift-less (shĭft'lĕs), *adj.* lacking in energy; without resource; lazy; thriftless; taking no thought for the future; badly done.—*adv.* **shiftlessly.**—*n.* **shiftlessness.**

shift-y (shĭf'tĭ), *adj.* full of evasions; tricky; fickle; alert; capable of turning things or circumstances to good advantage.—*n.* **shiftiness.**

shil-la-lah (shĭ-lā'lȧ), *n.* an oaken cudgel or club. Also, **shillelah, shillelagh.** [Ir.]

shil-ling (shĭl'ĭng), *n.* a British silver coin, worth about twenty-four cents.

shil-ly-shal-ly (shĭl'ĭ shăl'ĭ), *adv.* in an undecided manner; irresolutely: *v.i.* to hesitate; to trifle; to be irresolute; to act with a lack of decision: *n.* trifling; weak indecision: *adj.* hesitating; irresolute.

shi-ly (shī'lĭ), *adv.* timidly; bashfully; watchfully. Also, **shyly.**

shim-mer (shĭm'ẽr), *v.i.* to shine unsteadily or tremulously; flicker: *n.* a tremulous gleam; flicker.

shin (shĭn), *n.* the front part of the leg between the ankle and knee; shank: *v.i.* to climb a tree by alternately gripping it with the arms and legs: usually with *up:* *v.t.* to climb, as a tree, with alternate movements of the arms and legs.

shin-dy (shĭn'dĭ), *n.* an uproar; spree; a row. [Slang.]

shine (shīn), *v.i.* [*p.t.* and *p.p.* shone, *p.pr.* shining], to emit or give out rays of light; beam; be bright; be noted or prominent: *v.t.* colloquially, to cause to glisten; polish: *n.* sunshine; bright weather; luster; sheen; illumination; colloquially, a polishing of the shoes; slang, a liking, or a caper.

Syn., *v.* glare, glitter, radiate.

shin-er (shīn'ẽr), *n.* one who, or that which, shows brightness; a kind of small fish.

shin-gle (shĭn'gl), *n.* a thin piece of wood used for roofing; humorously, a signboard, as for an office; coarse, round, water-worn gravel: *pl.* a serious, inflammatory skin disease of nervous origin: *v.t.* to cover, as a roof, with thin pieces of wood; to cut (the hair) short.—*n.* **shingler.**

shin-ing (shīn'ĭng), *adj.* giving light; radiant; distinguished: as, a *shining* instance of bravery.—*adv.* **shiningly.**

shin-ny (shĭn'ĭ), *n.* the game of hockey; the stick used to play hockey.

Shin-to-ism (shĭn'tō-ĭzm), *n.* the chief native religious belief in Japan, having as its important features sacrifice to dead heroes, and ancestor worship.

shin-y (shīn'ĭ), *adj.* [*comp.* shinier, *superl.* shiniest], diffusing or giving off light; bright; unclouded; polished; glossy.

ship (ship), *n.* any large seagoing vessel; of sailing vessels, especially one with three masts which are square-rigged; any masted vessel, large, and fitted for navigating deep water; something resembling a ship in shape or structure: *v.t.* [*p.t.* and *p.p.* shipped, *p.pr.* shipping], to place on board a vessel; carry or transport by water; to send through any regular channel of transportation, as by rail; put in the proper place or position, as oars; to hire for service on a ship, as sailors; to receive on the decks, etc., of a ship; as, to *ship* a sea; colloquially, to get rid of: *v.i.* to engage oneself for service on a vessel, as a sailor; to embark on a ship.

ship bis-cuit (ship bis'kit), hard-tack; hard biscuit made for use on shipboard.

ship-board (ship'bōrd"), *n.* the side of a ship; hence, a ship; as, on shipboard.

ship-mas-ter (ship'mȧs"tẽr), *n.* the master of a merchant ship, or a ship other than a war vessel.

ship-ment (ship'mĕnt), *n.* the act of sending goods for transportation; the consignment of goods.

ship-per (ship'ẽr), *n.* one who sends goods to be transported.

ship-ping (ship'ing), *n.* the act or business of one who sends goods to be transported; the business of one who transports goods, especially by water; ships of all kinds, collectively; tonnage.

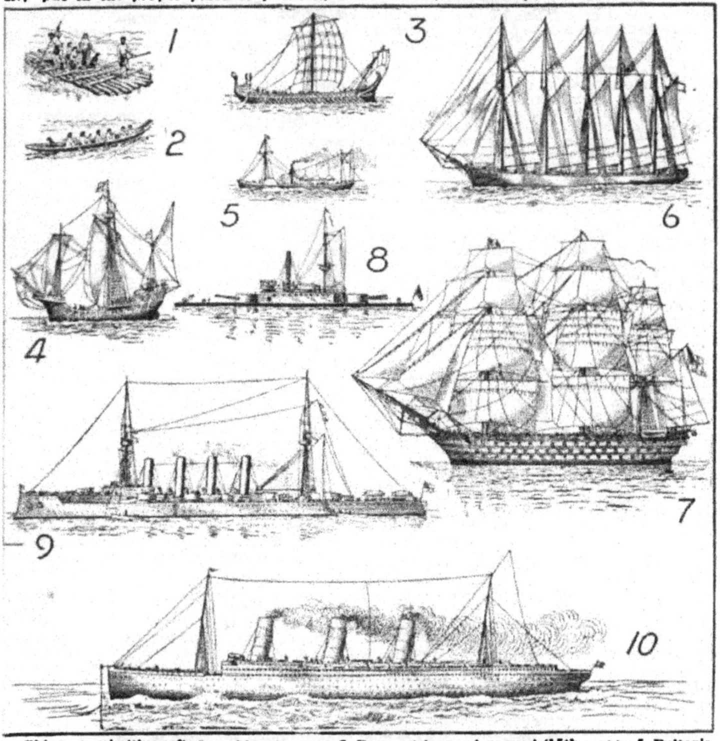

Ships. 1, primitive raft; 2, prehistoric canoe; 3, Roman trireme; 4, caravel (15th cent.); 5, Fulton's steamboat (1807); 6, five-masted schooner; 7, frigate with 120 guns in three tiers (1812); 8, Monitor (1890); 9, armored cruiser (1919); 10, passenger and freight steamship (1919).

ship-shape (ship'shāp"), *adj.* being in good order: *adv.* neatly.

ship-worm (ship'wûrm"), *n.* a wormlike mollusk that burrows by means of its shell into ship-bottoms, wharf-piles, etc.

ship-wreck (ship'rĕk"), *n.* the destruction of a ship by disaster at sea, or by grounding; a wrecked ship; utter ruin: *v.t.* to cause to suffer shipwreck; to bring ruin or destruction to.

ship-wright (ship'rīt"), *n.* a ship carpenter; a builder or repairer of vessels.

ship-yard (shĭp′yärd″), *n.* a place where ships are built or repaired.

shire (shīr; shĕr), *n.* a division of English territory for governmental purposes, usually the same as a county, but in some cases smaller.

shirk (shûrk), *v.t.* and *v.i.* to neglect purposely; to get out of the doing of; to avoid work: *n.* one who purposely neglects or evades work or obligation.

shirr (shûr), *n.* a puckering or fulling produced in a fabric by means of parallel gathering-threads: *v.t.* to draw up (cloth) by gathering on parallel gathering-threads; in cooking, to poach in cream, as eggs.

shirt (shûrt), *n.* a loose garment for the upper part of the body.

shirt-ing (shûrt′ĭng), *n.* cloth out of which shirts are made.

shiv-er (shĭv′ẽr), *v.t.* and *v.i.* to shake or tremble, as from cold or fright; to flutter in the wind, as a sail; to break suddenly into fragments or small pieces; shatter: *n.* the act of trembling or shaking from cold, etc.; a shaking or quivering; a fragment splintered off; a sliver; a small wedge or key.

shiv-er-y (shĭv′ẽr-ĭ), *adj.* tremulous; shaking; resembling a shiver; given to shivering; slightly cold or chilly.

shoal (shōl), *n.* a throng, as of fishes; a sand-bank or bar; a shallow: *adj.* shallow: *v.i.* to grow shallow; as, the color of the water shows where it *shoals;* to throng in schools, as fish.—*adj.* **shoaly.**

shoat (shōt), *n.* a young hog; a pig. Also, **shote.**

shock (shŏk), *v.t.* to cause to shake; to meet in violent encounter; to strike with surprise, horror, disgust, etc.; to subject (the body) to the passage of an electric current; to collect, as sheaves of grain, into stacks: *n.* a conical stack of sheaves of grain; a bushy mass, as of hair; a blow; a violent jar or shake; a rapid, forceful attack; an unexpected jarring of the feelings, mind, etc.; as, his death was a *shock* to me; colloquially, a stroke of paralysis; the effect of the passage of electric current through the body; the drop in vitality after a severe physical strain; as, *shock* following an operation; injury or destruction of certain of the faculties, as of speech, through violent strain; as, shell *shock:* **shock absorber,** in an automobile, a device to lessen the jar caused by rough places in the road; in aviation, a device to lessen the jar of an airplane when alighting: **shock troops,** troops especially trained to attack in mass.

shock-ing (shŏk′ĭng), *adj.* causing to shake or tremble as by a blow; causing disturbance of the feelings; as, *shocking* news; extremely offensive or disgusting; as, *shocking* language.—*adv.* **shockingly.**

shod (shŏd), past tense and past participle of the verb *shoe.*

shod-dy (shŏd′ĭ), *n.* the wool of old or refuse woolen or cotton fabrics torn to pieces and remade with a mixture of fresh wool into new cloth: *adj.* made of this material; hence, colloquially, not genuine; sham.

shoe (shōō), *n.* [*pl.* shoes (shōōz)], a covering for the foot, usually of leather; anything used for the protection of the foot, or the part touching the ground, as the metal plate protecting the hoof of an animal, the strip of steel fastened on a sled-runner, etc.; the outer covering of a rubber tire for automobiles: *v.t.* [*p.t.* and *p.p.* shod, *p.pr.* shoeing], to furnish with a shoe or shoes; as, to *shoe* a horse; to protect or strengthen by putting on a rim, plate, etc.

shoe-horn (shōō′hôrn″), *n.* a curved smooth piece of horn or other material to aid in putting on a shoe.

shoe-mak-er (shōō′māk″ẽr), *n.* one whose business it is to make shoes.

sho-er (shōō′ẽr), *n.* one who puts on shoes: as, a *shoer* of horses.

shone (shōn; shŏn), past tense and past participle of the verb *shine.*

shoo (shōō), *v.t.* and *v.i.* to scare away fowls; to drive by a cry of "shoo": *interj.* begone! be off! used in driving away fowls.

shook (shŏŏk), *p.t.* of the verb *shake:* *n.* a set of staves and headings sufficient for one cask, barrel, etc.; a set of boards ready to be assembled or nailed together to make some object, as a box, etc.

shoot (shōōt), *v.t.* [*p.t.* and *p.p.* shot, *p.pr.* shooting], to let fly, send out, or discharge with sudden force; strike, kill, or wound with a missile discharged from a gun; to fire off or discharge (a weapon); hurl; cause to grow forth; as, the trees *shot* forth their leaves; to stick out forcibly: usually with *out;* to pass rapidly through, over, or under; as, to *shoot* a rapid; to color in spots or patches: usually only in *p.p.;* as, *shot* with crimson: *v.i.* to protrude or project; be propelled forcibly, as a missile; rush or flash along swiftly; as, the star *shot* through the sky; sprout; grow or develop; feel a darting pain; to discharge a missile from a gun, etc.; to cause a gun, bow, etc., to discharge a missile: *n.* a young branch or growth; a passage or trough through which things are carried by gravity: also spelled *chute;* a shooting-match; a hunt.—*n.* **shooter.**

shoot-ing (shōōt′ĭng), *n.* the act of one who discharges a weapon; as, the *shooting* occurred just before dawn: *adj.* darting; as, *shooting* pains.

shoot-ing star (shōōt′ĭng stär), a small body of the solar system heated to incandescence by friction in passing through the earth's atmosphere; a meteor.

shop (shŏp), *n.* a building where goods are sold at retail; a store; place where mechanics carry on their trade; colloquially, one's own business as a subject of conversation; as, to talk *shop:* *v.i.* [*p.t.* and *p.p.* shopped, *p.pr.* shopping], to visit stores to look over or purchase goods.—*n.* **shopper.**

shop-keep-er (shŏp′kēp″ẽr), *n.* one who keeps a store; a tradesman.

shop-lift-ing (shŏp′lĭf″tĭng), *n.* the theft of goods from a shop or store under pretense of inspection or purchase.—*n.* **shoplifter.**

shop-worn (shŏp′wōrn″), *adj.* soiled or worn from having been kept a long time in stock in a shop.

shore (shōr), *n.* the coast or land bordering on the sea, etc.; a prop or support: *v.t.* to support by a prop: usually with *up.*

shore-less (shōr′lĕs), *adj.* having no shore; boundless.

shorn (shōrn), past participle of the verb *shear.*

short (shôrt), *adj.* [*comp.* shorter, *superl.* shortest], not long, either in space, distance, or time; not tall; brief; of limited duration; scant; deficient; not having enough of; as, *short* of cash; *short* of sugar;

not coming up to a measure, standard, requirement, etc.; as, the rule is too *short;* the sleeves are too *short;* those measurements are *short:* curt, abrupt, uncivil, or cross; as, she received a *short* answer; not retentive; as, a *short* memory; in financial usage, not possessing at the time of selling; as, to be *short* of copper; crisp or crumbly; as, *short* piecrust; brief in utterance, as a vowel or a syllable: opposite to *long:* *n.* the gist or pith of a matter; as, the long and *short* of it; something that is short; a sale, as of stocks, made by someone who does not at that time possess the stocks sold; the maker of such a sale: *pl.* milled grain somewhat finer than bran; fine bran mixed with coarse meal or flour: *adv.* abruptly; curtly; of selling, not in possession of the goods sold; as, to sell stocks *short.*—*n.* **shortness.**

short-age (shôr'tāj), *n.* the quantity needed to make up the whole amount; a deficit; as, his accounts at the end of each year showed a *shortage.*

short-cake (shôrt'kāk"), *n.* a cake resembling biscuit in texture, made crisp by butter or lard; such a cake split and served with fruit between the layers; as, strawberry *shortcake;* a sweetened layer or sponge cake served with fruit between the layers or over the cake.

short cir-cuit (shôrt sûr'kĭt), an electrical conductor of low resistance connecting two points electrically charged: **short-circuit** (shôrt'sûr"kĭt), *v.t.* to connect by an electrical conductor of low resistance: *v.i.* to connect two points electrically charged, by means of a conductor of low resistance.

short-com-ing (shôrt'kŭm"ĭng; shôrt"-kŭm'ĭng), *n.* a failing; failure or remissness in doing one's duty; negligence or carelessness in performing one's duty.

short-en (shôr'tn), *v.t.* to make short or shorter in time, extent, or measure; to reduce in amount; to lessen; to contract; to deprive: usually with *of;* to make crisp or brittle, as pastry, by using butter, lard, etc., to grow or become shorter or briefer.

short-en-ing (shôr'tn-ĭng; shôrt'nĭng), *n.* the act of making short or shorter; as, the *shortening* of the skirt took only a few minutes; that which makes pastry crisp and brittle, as lard, butter, cooking oils, etc.

short-hand (shôrt'hănd"), *n.* a system of rapid writing in which characters, symbols, etc. are used for letters, words, phrases, etc.; stenography.

short-lived (shôrt'lĭvd"), *adj.* of short duration; not of long life; not lasting long.

short-ly (shôrt'lĭ), *adv.* soon; quickly; curtly; in a few words.

short-sight-ed (shôrt'sīt"ĕd), *adj.* unable to see far; near-sighted; coming from, or marked by, lack of foresight.—*adv.* **shortsightedly.**—*n.* **shortsightedness.**

short-stop (shôrt'stŏp"), *n.* in baseball, an infielder stationed between the second and third bases.

short-wind-ed (shôrt'wĭn"dĕd), *adj.* affected with shortness of breath; liable to be so affected under the strain of exertion.

shot (shŏt), past tense and past participle of the verb *shoot:* *n.* [*pl.* shots or shot], the act of shooting; the discharge of a firearm, etc.; a missile, especially a solid bullet or ball: distinguished from *shell;* small balls or pellets of lead for killing game; the range of a missile; range in general; as, within gun*shot* or ear*shot;* in certain games, as croquet or billiards, a stroke or blow; a marksman; as, he is a good *shot.*

shote (shōt), *n.* a young hog; a pig. Also, **shoat.**

shot-gun (shŏt'gŭn"), *n.* a smoothbore gun, used for firing shot at short range.

should (shŏŏd), *p.t.* of the verb *shall;* used, first, in indirect discourse to express simple futurity or determination from the standpoint of past time according to the rule for the use of *shall* in direct discourse; as, expressing simple futurity, he said he *should* go; I said he *would* go; expressing determination, he said he *would* go; I said he *should* go; used, second, to express condition, supposition, etc.; as, if it *should* rain, do not go; used, third, to express obligation; as, you *should* try to do better.

shoul-der (shōl'dẽr), *n.* the projecting part of the human body between the neck and the place where the arm joins the trunk; in animals, the fore quarter; that which resembles a shoulder; a prominence; a support to keep something in place or to keep it from moving beyond a certain point: *v.t.* to take upon the shoulder; assume the responsibility of; as, to *shoulder* a burden; to push with, or as with, the shoulders; as, to *shoulder* one's way: *v.i.* to push or make one's way by using the shoulders.

shoul-der blade (shōl'dẽr blād), the flat bone of the shoulder; the scapula.

shoul-der strap (shōl'dẽr străp), a strap worn over the shoulders to support something; a narrow strap bearing certain insignia indicating rank, worn on the shoulder by commissioned officers of the army and navy.

shout (shout), *n.* a loud and sudden cry, as of joy, command, encouragement, etc.; a burst of voice or voices: *v.i.* to utter a loud and sudden cry: *v.t.* to utter with a loud, resonant voice: usually with *out;* as, he *shouted* out his orders and ran.

shove (shŭv), *n.* the act of pushing; a forcible push: *v.t.* to push along; drive before one: *v.i.* to move along; crowd against others; push something along.

shov-el (shŭv'l), *n.* a tool made of a broad flat scoop with a handle, for lifting and throwing coal, grain, etc., or for digging: *v.t.* to take and throw up with such a tool; gather up with, or as with, a shovel; toss as with a shovel; clear or clean by using this tool.

shov-el-board (shŭv'l-bōrd"), *n.* a game played with weights or metal disks shoved toward a certain line on a specially prepared board; the board. Also, **shuffleboard.**

shov-el-er (shŭv'l-ẽr), *n.* one who uses a shovel; a certain river duck.

show (shō), *v.t.* [*p.t.* showed, *p.p.* shown, *p.pr.* showing], to present to view; exhibit; display; to tell, reveal, or make known; make clear; make (a person) understand; prove by a process of reasoning; direct; as, to *show* one to his seat; bestow; as, to *show* favor: *v.i.* to present an appearance; to be visible or noticeable; as, the stain *shows;* to be known: *n.* the act of exhibiting or displaying; the exhibition or display; a public parade or spectacle; pomp;

deceitful appearance or pretense; as, a *show* of wealth; a *show* of wisdom; sign or promise, as of metal in a mine; colloquially, a fair opportunity.—*n.* **shower.**

show bill (shō bĭl), a large sheet containing advertisements.

show-bread (shō'brĕd"), *n.* in the ancient Jewish ritual, the unleavened bread placed in the sanctuary. Also, **shewbread.**

show case (shō kās), a glass case for displaying and protecting goods or wares in stores, articles or exhibits in museums, etc.

show-er (shou'ẽr), *n.* a brief fall of rain or hail; anything resembling a rainfall in its abundance; as, a *shower* of suggestions; an abundant supply of anything given, as to a bride; as, a kitchen *shower:* *v.t.* to water abundantly with rain; bestow liberally upon: *v.i.* to rain for a short time; to fall as in a shower.

show-er-y (shou'ẽr-ĭ), *adj.* raining for brief intervals or abounding in short rainy periods.—*n.* **showeriness.**

show-ing (shō'ĭng), *n.* a display; an exhibition of something; a presentation of a fact, etc.

show-man (shō'măn), *n.* [*pl.* showmen (-mĕn)], one who displays or exhibits; one who takes part in exhibiting a show.

shown (shōn), the past participle of the verb *show.*

show-room (shō'rōōm"), *n.* a room where goods to be sold are displayed.

show-y (shō'ĭ), *adj.* gaudy; gorgeous; sometimes, marked by pretentious parade; attracting attention; gay.—*adv.* **showily.**—*n.* **showiness.**

shrank (shrănk), the past tense of the verb *shrink.*

shrap-nel (shrăp'nĕl), *n.* a shell filled with bullets, pieces of iron, nails, etc., and exploded by means of a time-fuse which acts upon a charge of powder or high explosive.

shred (shrĕd), *n.* a long, narrow strip torn or cut off; piece; bit; fragment: *v.t.* [*p.t.* and *p.p.* shred or shredded, *p.pr.* shredding], to tear or cut into small pieces.

shrew (shrōō), *n.* a scolding, brawling woman; any of small mouselike animals that dig or burrow in the ground.

shrewd (shrōōd), *adj.* sharp-witted or clever in practical affairs; keen; as, a *shrewd* business man; cunning; as, a *shrewd* planner; biting; harsh.—*adv.* **shrewdly.** —*n.* **shrewdness.**

shrew-ish (shrōō'ĭsh), *adj.* scolding; sharp-tongued; peevish.—*adv.* **shrewishly.**—*n.* **shrewishness.**

shriek (shrēk), *v.t.* to cry out sharply; to utter with a sharp, shrill cry: *v.i.* to utter a sharp, shrill cry; to scream: *n.* a scream; a shrill outcry.

shriev-al-ty (shrēv'ăl-tĭ), *n.* the office, term, or authority of a sheriff.

shrift (shrĭft), *n.* confession to a priest and the resulting absolution; the act of hearing a confession and giving absolution.

shrike (shrīk), *n.* any of various birds which feed chiefly on insects, but which sometimes kill smaller birds, mice, etc.

shrill (shrĭl), *adj.* sharp and piercing in tone: *v.i.* to utter an acute, piercing sound: *v.t.* to utter in a sharp, piercing tone. —*adv.* **shrilly.**—*n.* **shrilliness.**

shrimp (shrĭmp), *n.* a small, edible shellfish of the lobster family; in contempt, a wizened or puny person, or anything very small of its kind.

shrine (shrīn), *n.* a case or box in which sacred relics are kept; the tomb of a saint; any sacred place or hallowed object; an altar: *v.t.* to cherish as sacred; to put in a sacred place, as a shrine.

shrink (shrĭnk), *v.i.* [*p.t.* shrank, *p.p.* shrunk, or, chiefly, as *p. adj.* shrunken, *p.pr.* shrinking], to contract; become smaller or shorter; to draw back from danger, etc.; to express fear, horror, or pain by contracting the body, or part of it: *v.t.* to cause to contract or grow smaller: *n.* a contraction; a withdrawal.

shrink-age (shrĭnk'āj), *n.* the act of contracting or making smaller; contraction; amount lost by contraction or shrinking; decrease in value.

shrive (shrīv), *v.t.* [*p.t.* shrived or shrove, *p.p.* shrived or shriven, *p.pr.* shriving], to hear or receive the confession of and give absolution to; *v.i.* to hear confession and give absolution; to make confession and receive absolution.

shriv-el (shrĭv'l), *v.i.* to be drawn into wrinkles; contract; shrink: often with *up:* *v.t.* to cause to contract into wrinkles; cause to shrink.

shroud (shroud), *n.* a winding sheet, dress, or covering for the dead: anything that covers or conceals, as a garment: *pl.* a set of ropes, usually in pairs, supporting the masts of a vessel: *v.t.* to hide or conceal with a covering; veil.

shrove (shrōv), the past tense of the verb *shrive.*

Shrove Sun-day (shrōv sŭn'dā), the Sunday before Shrove Tuesday; Quinquagesima Sunday.

Shrove-tide (shrōv'tīd"), *n.* a period of penitence and confession, covering sometimes only Shrove Tuesday, and sometimes including the three days preceding Ash Wednesday.

Shrove Tues-day (shrōv tūz'dā), the Tuesday before Ash Wednesday.

shrub (shrŭb), *n.* a woody perennial smaller than a tree; a bush; a drink made of raspberry or other acid fruit juice, with sugar, spirit, etc.

shrub-ber-y (shrŭb'ẽr-ĭ), *n.* [*pl.* shrubberies (-ĭz)], a collection of bushes or shrubs; a place where shrubs or bushes are planted or where they abound.

shrub-by (shrŭb'ĭ), *adj.* full of, or covered with, bushes or shrubs; of the nature of a bush or shrub; stunted.—*n.* **shrubbiness.**

shrug (shrŭg), *v.t.* [*p.t.* and *p.p.* shrugged, *p.pr.* shrugging], to contract or draw up (the shoulders) to express some emotion, as doubt, contempt, surprise, etc.: *v.i.* to raise the shoulders to express some emotion, as of displeasure, etc.: *n.* a raising or contracting of the shoulders to express some emotion.

shrunk-en (shrŭnk'n), *p.adj.* shriveled up; contracted.

shuck (shŭk), *n.* a shell; a husk or pod: *v.t.* to remove shells or husks from, as from peanuts or corn; husk.

shud-der (shŭd'ẽr), *n.* a convulsive trembling from fear or horror; a shiver of aversion or cold: *v.i.* to tremble or shake with fear or horror; quake; to shiver with cold.—*p.adj.* **shuddering.**—*adv.* **shudderingly.**

shuf-fle (shŭf'l), *v.t.* to shift from one to another; to rearrange, as cards in a pack; to move with a dragging motion, as the feet in walking or dancing; to put aside, sometimes carelessly; as, to *shuffle* off this mortal coil; to *shuffle* off a burden; to make with haste or fraud; as, to *shuffle* up a makeshift: *v.i.* to rearrange the cards in a pack; to shift one's ground; evade questions or issues; prevaricate; to do a task listlessly or awkwardly; as, she *shuffled* through the cleaning; to drag the feet in a slovenly manner; as, he *shuffled* along in his big slippers: *n.* the act of shifting, rearranging, etc.; a rearranging of cards in a pack; a trick or evasion; a dance characterized by a dragging motion of the feet.—*n.* **shuffler.**

shuf-fle-board (shŭf'l-bōrd"), *n.* a game played with counters or weights, by shoving or sliding them toward a line or goal, on a specially prepared board; the long, narrow board, often spread with a thin layer of sand, on which the game is played. Also, **shovelboard.**

shun (shŭn), *v.t.* [*p.t.* and *p.p.* shunned (shŭnd), *p.pr.* shunning], to avoid; keep clear of; as, to *shun* evil companions; escape from.

shunt (shŭnt), *v.t.* to turn off or switch, as a car or train; to supply another path for (an electric current); to put off upon someone else, as a task or duty: *v.i.* to turn aside or off: *n.* the act of turning off; a turning off, as of a car, to a side rail; the act of switching; a conductor joining two points of an electric circuit through which part of the current flows.

shut (shŭt), *v.t.* [*p.t.* and *p.p.* shut, *p.pr.* shutting], to close so as to prevent entrance or exit; to close, as a door; to bar; as, to *shut* the ports of a country because of submarine raids; exclude; close over; as, to *shut* the hand; to fold together, as an umbrella; to bring the parts of together, as a book; to imprison, confine, or hold within the parts of something: with *in, up, within,* etc.; as, to *shut* up a convict; to *shut* one's finger or garment in the door; to hide from sight: with *out;* as, to *shut* out the view: *v.i.* to close itself; become closed: **to shut down,** to stop work: said of machine shops, factories, etc.

shut-ter (shŭt'ẽr), *n.* one who, or that which, closes; a movable solid cover for a window; sometimes, a blind: a blind usually is made with slats, and a shutter is usually solid; in photography, a device for opening and shutting a lens; a cover; a lid: *v.t.* to close or supply with shutters; to separate or inclose with shutters.

shut-tle (shŭt'l), *n.* an instrument used in weaving to carry the thread of the weft, or woof, back and forth through the warp; the sliding holder inclosing the bobbin from which the thread unwinds in a sewing machine; any similar device, as one used in tatting.

shut-tle-cock (shŭt'l-kŏk"), *n.* a cork stuck with feathers and driven with a battledore, or bat; the game itself.

shy (shī), *adj.* [*comp.* shyer, *superl.* shyest], timid; bashful; coy; reserved; as, a *shy* girl; shunning approach, as, a *shy* animal; cautious; watchful through timidity; as, the draft dodger was *shy* of questions; suspicious: *v.i.* to start aside from fear: said of horses: *v.t.* to cause to start aside; to throw aside with a jerk; fling; as, to *shy* a stone: *n.* the act of starting aside from fear; a side throw.—*adv.* **shyly.**—*n.* **shyness.**

shy-ster (shī'stẽr), *n.* one who carries on business in a mean and tricky manner; especially, a rascally lawyer. [Colloq. U. S.]

si (sē), *n.* in music, the seventh note of the major diatonic scale.

Si-a-mese (sī'ȧ-mēz'; sī'ȧ-mēs), *adj.* of or pertaining to Siam, its natives, or its language: *n., sing.* and *pl.* one of the inhabitants of Siam; the language of the Siamese people.

Si-be-ri-an (sī-bē'rĭ-ăn), *adj.* of or pertaining to Siberia, or its people: one of the inhabitants of Siberia.

sib-i-lance (sĭb'ĭ-lăns), *n.* the state or quality of being uttered with a hissing sound.

sib-i-lant (sĭb'ĭ-lănt), *adj.* making, or uttering, a hissing sound; as, *s* has a *sibilant* sound: *n.* a sibilant sound or a symbol standing for such a sound; as, *s, sh, z,* and *zh* are *sibilants.*

sib-i-la-tion (sĭb'ĭ-lā'shŭn), *n.* utterance with a hissing sound

sib-yl (sĭb'ĭl), *n.* a woman supposed to have the power to foretell the future; a prophetess.

sib-yl-line (sĭb'ĭ-lĭn; sĭb'ĭ-līn), *adj.* pertaining to, uttered, or written by, a prophetess; hence, mysterious, prophetic.

sic (sĭk), *adj.* such [Scot.]: *adv.* thus: frequently inserted in a sentence or quotation, to indicate that an expression or misspelling, etc., is exactly as it is given. [Lat.]

sick (sĭk), *adj.* ill in health; indisposed; affected with nausea or vomiting; inclined to vomit; disgusted; surfeited; as, *sick* of flattery; longing or pining: with *for;* as, *sick* for recognition; used by, or set apart for the use of, a person who is ill; as a *sick* bed; a *sick* benefit: *n.* those who are ill: used collectively, with *the:* **sick leave,** a leave of absence granted to officers or privates because of illness or disability: **sick list,** a list, prepared each day from the army sick-report book, showing the names of the sick and incapacitated.

Syn. adj. diseased, sickly, unhealthy.
Ant. (see healthy).

sick-en (sĭk'n), *v.i.* to become ill; be filled with disgust; decay or languish; as, the flower *sickened* and died: *v.t.* to make ill; disgust.

sick-en-ing (sĭk'n-ĭng), *adj.* making sick; disgusting; repulsive; nauseating; as, a *sickening* odor.

sick-ish (sĭk'ĭsh), *adj.* somewhat ill; slightly nauseated; apt to nauseate one; as, *sickish* sweets.—*adv.* **sickishly.**—*n.* **sickishness.**

sick-le (sĭk'l), *n.* a reaping instrument consisting of a curved steel blade with a handle.

sick-ly (sĭk'lĭ), *adj.* ailing; weak; never well; characteristic of illness; as, a *sickly* look; apt to make one ill; as, *sickly* weather; weak-looking; marked by mawkishness; sickening; as, the letter was filled with *sickly* sentiments.—*n.* **sickliness.**

sick-ness (sĭk'nĕs), *n.* the state of being ill or in bad health; illness; diseased condition; a malady; nausea.

side (sīd), *n.* the edge or bounding line of a surface, especially one of the longer lines as distinguished from the ends;

one of the surfaces or faces that limit a solid; the right or left part of an object or of the body; a contrasted part or surface; as the upper *side;* the lower *side;* the in*side;* a party of men upholding a cause against another group; a faction; the cause that is upheld; as, truth is on our *side;* a view, considered in respect to its opposite; as, consider the other *side* of the question; a line of descent through a parent; as, a cousin on the mother's *side:* *adj.* lateral; laterally placed or situated; minor; incidental: *v.i.* to take the part of one against another; followed by *with;* as, he *sided* with the Unionists.

side arms (sīd ärmz), such weapons as are carried by the side and attached to the person, as bayonet, sword, and pistol.

side-board (sīd'bōrd"), *n.* a piece of dining-room furniture for holding articles used on the table.

side-ling (sīd'lĭng), *adj.* oblique; having a sidewise motion; directed toward the side: *adv.* laterally; obliquely.

side-long (sīd'lŏng"), *adv.* on the side; laterally; obliquely: *adj.* lateral; having an oblique direction; as, a *sidelong* glance.

si-de-re-al (sī-dē'rē-ăl), *adj.* pertaining to the stars; starry; astral; measured by the apparent motion of the stars, as, a *sidereal* hour.

sid-er-ite (sĭd'ẽr-īt), *n.* an iron ore, usually yellowish-brown in color.

side-sad-dle (sīd'săd"l), *n.* a woman's saddle having but one stirrup, so that both feet of the rider rest on the same side of the horse.

side-track (sīd'trăk"), *v.t.* to transfer (a car or train) from the main track to a siding; to lead away from the main subject or issue; to make inactive; as, we have successfully *sidetracked* our worst enemy: *v.i.* to run a train upon a siding: *n.* a siding.

side-walk (sīd'wôk"), *n.* a path beside a road or street for foot travel; a foot pavement.

side-way (sīd'wā"), *adj.* sidelong; indirect; lateral: *adv.* on or toward one side.

side-ways (sīd'wāz"), *adv.* toward or from the side; sidewise.

side-wheel (sīd'hwēl"), *n.* one of two paddle wheels at the side of a steamboat: *adj.* having sidewheels.

side-wise (sīd'wīz'), *adv.* toward or from the side; sideways.

sid-ing (sīd'ĭng), *n.* a railroad track by the side of the main track, on which cars may be switched; a short track connected with the main track; the act of favoring or espousing one side or another, as in a dispute; the boarding that forms the sides of a wooden house.

si-dle (sī'dl), *v.i.* to move sidewise, as from shyness or fear; as, he *sidled* up to us.

siege (sēj), *n.* the surrounding of a fortified place by an army to compel its surrender; continued attempt by force of arms to gain possession; investment.

siege gun (sēj gŭn), a heavy gun constructed to throw a solid projectile with the highest possible speed, in order to break through stone walls or revetments, and to lessen the curve of the projectile's flight, so as to increase its chances of hitting objects but slightly raised from the ground.

siege mor-tar (sēj môr'tẽr), a light cannon used to attack those portions of a work, by vertical fire, which are defended against the direct and ricochet fires of guns and howitzers, such as the ditch with its communications, the roofs of magazines, etc.

si-en-na (sĭ-ĕn'ȧ), *n.* a brownish-yellow clay pigment, or coloring matter; the color of this pigment; orange-yellow.

si-er-ra (sĭ-ĕr'ȧ), *n.* a mountain chain or range rising in irregular peaks.

si-es-ta (sĭ-ĕs'tȧ), *n.* a midday nap; an after-dinner nap.

sieve (sĭv), *n.* a utensil provided with meshes, as of wire, for separating the finer from the coarser parts of a substance.

sift (sĭft), *v.t.* to separate the fine parts of from the coarse with, or as with, a sieve; to pass through a sieve; to examine critically; to scrutinize; as, he *sifted* the facts carefully before forming an opinion.

sigh (sī), *v.i.* to breathe deeply and audibly as a result of fatigue, sorrow, etc.; lament; to make a sound like sighing; as, the winds *sigh;* to long; to yearn: with *for;* as, the nations *sighed* for peace: *v.t.* to express by sighs: *n.* a deep, audible, long-drawn respiration, expressing sorrow, anxiety, etc.

sight (sīt), *n.* the power of seeing; the act of seeing; a view; vision; that which is seen; a spectacle; something remarkable or worth seeing; the limit of the power of the eyesight; the visibility of something; as, in *sight;* out of *sight;* opinion, as, in his *sight,* she did well; insight; opportunity for study; as, to get a *sight* into the great man's methods; a small piece of metal, fixed or movable, on the muzzle, center, or trunnion of a firearm to guide the eye in aiming; the aim so taken: *v.t.* to see with the eye; to find by looking; as, to *sight* a distant object; to look at closely or critically; to direct by means of an aiming device; as, to *sight* a gun; to furnish with sights, or adjust the sights of, as an instrument or gun: *v.i.* to aim a gun by a sight.

sight-less (sīt'lĕs), *adj.* incapable of seeing; blind.—*n.* sightlessness.

sight-ly (sīt'lĭ), *adj.* pleasing to the eye; comely.—*n.* sightliness.

sight-see-ing (sīt'sē"ĭng), *adj.* engaged in visiting objects or places of interest: *n.* the act of visiting objects or places of interest.—*n.* sight-seer.

sign (sīn), *n.* a gesture or motion expressing command or wish; a symbol; a mark; token; an emblem; a symptom; a lettered board or plate used to point out a place of business, etc.; an event considered as indicating the will of God; a miracle; in astronomy, one of the twelve divisions of the zodiac; in mathematics, a mark or character used to indicate relation or operation; as the *signs* +, —, ×, etc.; any mark or character which has a certain fixed meaning: *v.t.* to affix a signature to; to transfer, as property, by affixing the signature; with *off* or *away;* to hire by getting the signature of: *v.i.* to write one's signature; in law, to assent to the terms of a writing by putting one's name to the document; to signal; as, he *signed* for them to approach.

sig-nal (sĭg'năl), *n.* a sign agreed upon, or intended to be understood, for giving notice, as of danger, especially at a distance; a token: *adj.* memorable; extraordinary; distinguished from the commonplace by some mark or sign; remarkable; as, a *signal* success; pertaining to signals; as, a *signal* flag: *v.t.* to communicate with by means of flags, lights, etc.; make signs to: *v.i.* to make signs: to communicate with someone by means of flags, lights, etc.—*adv.* **signally.**—*n.* **signaler.**

sig-nal code (sĭg'năl kōd), a list of signs used in signaling, each sign, or set of signs, having a fixed, definite meaning attached to it.

sig-nal corps (sĭg'năl kōr), in the United States army, the body of staff officers having charge of all methods of communication by balloons, airplanes, radio wireless, telegraph, telephones, and visual signaling.

sig-nal-ize (sĭg'năl-īz), *v.t.* to make especially conspicuous or prominent; to point out with care.

sig-nal serv-ice (sĭg'năl sûr'vĭs), in the United States, a government bureau under the War Department, organized to collect reports of atmospheric conditions and to issue predictions concerning the weather.

sig-nal sta-tion (sĭg'năl stā'shŭn), a place where a signal, or sign conveying a message, is displayed.

sig-nal tow-er (sĭg'năl tou'ẽr), a tower from which to display or send out signals, or signs that convey messages.

sig-na-to-ry (sĭg'nȧ-tō-rĭ), *adj.* having signed: *n.* one who signs or subscribes to a treaty, etc., for a state or power.

sig-na-ture (sĭg'nȧ-tûr), *n.* the name of a person written by himself; autograph; mark or stamp affixed in place of the written name; in music, flats or sharps placed after the clef to indicate the key; a sign placed after the key designation to indicate the time; all the signs at the beginning of the staff; in printing, a distinguishing mark at the bottom of the first page of each sheet of a book, etc., to guide the binder in assembling the sheets; the sheet so marked.

sig-net (sĭg'nĕt), *n.* a seal; the imprint, or stamp, made by, or as by, a seal.

sig-nif-i-cance (sĭg-nĭf'ĭ-kăns), *n.* meaning; often, the hidden or underlying meaning; import; consequence. Also, **significancy.**

sig-nif-i-cant (sĭg-nĭf'ĭ-kănt), *adj.* full of meaning; having meaning; expressive; as, a *significant* look; important; as, a *significant* event.—*adv.* **significantly.**

sig-ni-fi-ca-tion (sĭg'nĭ-fĭ-kā'shŭn), *n.* the act of expressing by signs, signals, etc.; a making known by signs; that which is suggested or expressed; the meaning of a sign, symbol, character, etc. —*adj.* **significative.**

sig-ni-fy (sĭg'nĭ-fī), *v.t.* [*p.t.* and *p.p.* signified, *p.pr.* signifying], to show by a sign, mark, or token; make known; to declare; as, to *signify* one's consent; to denote; to mean: *v.i.* to be of consequence or importance; to matter.

si-gnor (sē'nyōr), *n.* Mr.; sir: a title of address or respect among the Italians; an Italian gentleman of rank: English form, **signior.** [It.]

si-gno-re (sē-nyō'rā), *n.* [*pl.* signori (sē-nyō'rē)], a title of address or respect among the Italians corresponding to *Mr.* or *sir:* spelled, when used before a person's name, *signor;* a gentleman: **signora** (sē-nyō'-rā), a title of respectful address to an Italian lady, corresponding to *Mrs.* or *madam;* a lady: **signorina** (sē'nyō-rē'nä), a title of address to a young lady, corresponding to *Miss;* a young lady. [It.]

sign-post (sīn'pōst'), *n.* a guidepost; a pole to which signs are affixed.

si-lage (sī'lāj), *n.* finely cut fodder preserved by pressing it down, as in a silo, while green.

si-lence (sī'lĕns), *n.* the state of being still or mute; entire absence of sound or noise; general stillness; forbearance from, or absence of, mention; secrecy; oblivion: *v.t.* to cause to be still; to quiet; to put to rest; to take permission to speak away from; as, to *silence* the opposing forces; cause to cease firing, as hostile guns in an engagement.

Syn., n. speechlessness, dumbness, muteness.

Ant. (see noise).

si-lenc-er (sī'lĕn-sẽr), *n.* that which muffles or dulls, as the muffler of a gas engine: **Maxim silencer,** a device which may be attached to a rifle to reduce the sound when the gun is fired.

si-lent (sī'lĕnt), *adj.*, saying nothing; mute; not given to speech; as, a *silent* man; quiet; still; free from noise; as, a *silent* place; unexpressed; unspoken; as, a *silent* comment; calm; free from disturbance; as, a *silent* nook; having a share, not publicly acknowledged, in a business; as, a *silent* partner; not pronounced: said of a letter; as, the *b* in *doubt* is *silent.*—*adv.* **silently.**—*n.* **silentness.**

Syn. dumb, speechless.

Ant. (see talkative).

si-le-si-a (sī-lē'shĭ-ȧ; sī-lē'shȧ), *n.* a twilled cotton fabric, used for dress linings; a kind of linen cloth.

si-lex (sī'lĕks), *n.* in chemistry, silicon dioxide; quartz; opal.

sil-hou-ette (sĭl'ōō-ĕt'), *n.* the outline or profile filled in with a uniform color, usually black; the figure cast by a shadow, as on a wall or screen: *v.t.* to cause to appear in outline; to make a silhouette of.

sil-i-ca (sĭl'ĭ-kȧ), *n.* in chemistry, silicon dioxide; quartz; opal.

sil-i-cate (sĭl'ĭ-kāt), *n.* in chemistry, a salt or ester of silicic acid.

si-li-ceous (sĭ-lĭsh'ŭs), *adj.* pertaining to, containing, or of the nature of, silica.

si-lic-ic (sĭ-lĭs'ĭk), *adj.* in chemistry, pertaining to, containing, or like, silica or silicon.

sil-i-con (sĭl'ĭ-kŏn), *n.* a nonmetallic element or substance.

si-lique (sĭ-lēk'; sĭl'ĭk), *n.* a narrow pod or fruit containing many seeds and having two valves.

silk (sĭlk), *n.* a fine, soft, lustrous substance made from threads spun by various insect larvæ to form their cocoons; any similar thread, as that spun by a spider; fabric or garments made of silk; anything like silk; as, the *silk* on an ear of corn.

silk-en (sĭl'kn), *adj.* made of, or like, silk; soft; lustrous; smooth; dressed in silk; luxurious.

silk-worm (sĭlk'wûrm'), *n.* the larva of any of certain moths that makes a strong silk fiber in spinning its cocoon.

silk-y (sĭl'kĭ), *adj.* of, pertaining to, or like, silk; soft; smooth; lustrous.—*n.* **silkiness.**

sill (sĭl), *n.* a horizontal piece forming the foundation, or part of the foundation, of a structure; hence, a threshold; the bottom or lowest piece in a window frame.

sil-la-bub (sĭl'ȧ-bŭb), *n.* a dish made by mixing milk or cream with wine or cider, to form a soft curd; whipped cream, sweetened and flavored with wine. Also, **syllabub.**

sil-ly (sĭl'ĭ), *adj.* [*comp.* sillier, *superl.* silliest], weak in intellect; lacking good sense; foolish; simple; witless; stupid; absurd.—*adv.* **sillily.**—*n.* **silliness.**

si-lo (sī'lō), *n.* a pit or tower for preserving green fodder for winter use by excluding air and water.

silt (sĭlt), *n.* mud or fine earth carried in or deposited by water; a deposit of such mud or fine earth: *v.t.* to choke or block up by such a deposit: *v.i.* to become obstructed by such a deposit.—*adj.* **silty.**

sil-va (sĭl'vȧ), *n.* [*pl.* Eng. silvas; Lat. silvæ (sĭl'vē)], forest trees taken collectively. Also, **sylva.**

sil-van (sĭl'văn), *adj.* of or pertaining to forests, woods, or trees; rustic. Also, **sylvan.**

sil-ver (sĭl'vẽr), *n.* a precious, soft, white, ductile, metallic element; silverware, money, etc., made of this metal; anything like silver in luster or color: *adj.* pertaining to, or made of, silver; glistening white; like silver; soft and clear; as, the *silver* tones of her voice; gentle; calm: *v.t.* to cover or coat with silver or a substance resembling silver; to give a silverlike brightness to; to make white like silver: **silver nitrate,** a white compound obtained by dissolving silver in nitric acid and evaporating the solution: used in medicine and photography.

sil-ver-ing (sĭl'vẽr-ĭng), *n.* the act, art, or process of covering with silver, or with a substance resembling silver; the film or coating thus laid on.

sil-vern (sĭl'vẽrn), *adj.* a poetic form of *silvery.*

sil-ver-smith (sĭl'vẽr-smĭth"), *n.* a maker of silverware; a worker in silver.

sil-ver-ware (sĭl'vẽr-wâr"), *n.* silver plate; vessels, dishes, vases, table implements, etc., made of silver.

sil-ver-y (sĭl'vẽr-ĭ), *adj.* resembling silver; as the *silvery* hue of her hair; covered with, containing, or like, silver; soft and clear; as, a *silvery* voice; bright.

sim-i-an (sĭm'ĭ-ăn), *adj.* pertaining to, or like, an ape: *n.* an ape or monkey.

sim-i-lar (sĭm'ĭ-lȧr), *adj.* having a general likeness or correspondence; like, but not the same or exactly alike; of like nature, scope, etc.; in geometry, shaped alike, but not of the same size, etc.—*adv.* **similarly.**

sim-i-lar-i-ty (sĭm"ĭ-lăr'ĭ-tĭ), *n.* resemblance or likeness; the quality or state of bearing a strong resemblance to one another or to something else; the point or points of likeness.

sim-i-le (sĭm'ĭ-lē), *n.* [*pl.* similes (-lēz)], a figure of speech in which two different things having some accidental likeness are compared by the use of such words, as *like, so,* etc.; as, the girl is like a flower.

si-mil-i-tude (sĭ-mĭl'ĭ-tūd), *n.* similarity; likeness; a figure of speech expressing comparison; a facsimile.

sim-mer (sĭm'ẽr), *v.i.* and *v.t.* to boil gently; cook in liquid just at or below the boiling point: *n.* the state of boiling gently.

Si-mon (sī'mŏn), *n.* in the Bible, one of the Twelve Apostles, called also *Simon Peter* or *Peter:* the author of the Epistles of Peter.

sim-o-ny (sĭm'ō-nĭ), *n.* the act or crime of buying or selling church offices, or positions of honor; traffic in sacred things.

si-moom (sĭ-mōōm'), *n.* a hot, dry, suffocating, dust-laden wind which blows from the deserts of Arabia, etc. Also, **simoon.**

sim-per (sĭm'pẽr), *v.i.* to smile in an affected, silly, or self-conscious manner; to smirk: *n.* an affected smile; a smirk.

sim-ple (sĭm'pl), *adj.* [*comp.* simpler, *superl.* simplest], single, not complex; undivided; not mixed or compounded; mere; as, a *simple* fact; plain; not luxurious; unadorned; sincere; natural; artless; unaffected; direct; clear; as, *simple* language; having a taste for the plain, natural methods of living; humble; of low rank or degree; weak in intellect; resulting from feeblemindedness; as, a *simple* answer: *n.* an element; that which is unmixed; a plant from which medicine is extracted; the medicine so extracted: **simple fraction,** a fraction whose terms are whole numbers, as ¾: **simple interest,** interest paid only on the principal.—*n.* **simpleness.**

Syn., adj. innocent, guileless, straightforward.

Ant. (see complex).

sim-ple-ton (sĭm'pl-tŭn), *n.* one who is foolish or weak-minded.

sim-plex (sĭm'plĕks), *adj.* in telegraphy, naming, or pertaining to, a system by which only one message at a time can be sent over the wire.

sim-plic-i-ty (sĭm-plĭs'ĭ-tĭ), *n.* the state or quality of being clear, plain, unaffected, etc.; guilelessness; lack of cunning; lack of common sense; lack of average ability to think or judge.

sim-pli-fi-ca-tion (sĭm"plĭ-fĭ-kā'shŭn), *n.* the act of making something plainer or easier; the process of making something more easy to understand.

sim-pli-fy (sĭm'plĭ-fī), *v.t.* [*p.t.* and *p.p.* simplified, *p.pr.* simplifying], to make easier; render less hard; make plainer to the understanding.

sim-ply (sĭm'plĭ), *adv.* in a plain, unaffected manner; clearly; without addition; only; merely; artlessly; foolishly or weakly.

sim-u-late (sĭm'ū-lāt), *v.t.* to pretend or counterfeit; assume the character or semblance of; as, to *simulate* goodness: *adj.* (sĭm'ū-lāt), pretended; feigned; imitated.—*n.* **simulator.**

Syn., v. dissimulate, dissemble, feign.

sim-u-la-tion (sĭm"ū-lā'shŭn), *n.* the act of pretending that which is not true; feigning.

Syn. dissimulation, hypocrisy.

si-mul-ta-ne-ous (sī"mŭl-tā'nē-ŭs; sĭm"ŭl-tā'nē-ŭs), *adj.* happening, done, or existing, at the same time; as, *simultaneous* events.—*adv.* **simultaneously.**—*n.* **simultaneousness.**

sin (sĭn), *n.* wilful breaking of the divine law; violation of the laws of morality and religion, or of human rights; a special case or instance of such violation; the state of one who has thus transgressed; loosely, any fault: *v.i.* [*p.t.* and *p.p.* sinned, *p.pr.* sinning], to transgress, offend, or neglect the law of

God or any duty; to commit evil deeds; to violate human rights: *v.t.* to bring about by sin; as, he *sinned* his way to destruction; to commit (a sin).

since (sins), *adv.* from a certain past time until now; as, he left town six years ago and has not been heard from *since;* at some time before a certain past event and before now; as, he was then treasurer, but has *since* been elected president of the company; before this; as, we have long *since* dropped her acquaintance: *prep.* from the time of; during the time after; ever after; as, *since* that time, I have never visited the city: *conj.* from and after a certain time; as, I have never seen him *since* that unfortunate event happened; seeing that; because; as, *since* that is the case, I shall excuse you.

sin-cere (sin-sēr'), *adj.* true; honest; upright; genuine; frank.—*adv.* **sincerely.**—*n.* **sincereness.**
Syn. candid, hearty, straightforward.
Ant. (see insincere).

sin-cer-i-ty (sin-sĕr'ĭ-tĭ), *n.* the state or quality of being true or genuine; honesty of intention and appearance; uprightness.

sine (sīn), *n.* one of the trigonometric functions; in a right-angled triangle, the ratio of a side opposite to an acute angle, to the hypotenuse.

si-ne-cure (sī'nē-kūr), *n.* an office or position having a salary or fees but carrying with it little or no responsibility; the position of a clergyman who, though receiving a salary, has no spiritual duties.

si-ne di-e (sī'nē dī'ē), without day; without setting a day for reassembling: said of a meeting; as, Congress adjourned *sine die;* finally. [LAT.]

sin-ew (sin'ū), *n.* a tendon; strength; anything supplying strength; as, the *sinews* of war.—*adj.* **sinewless.**

sin-ew-y (sin'ū-ĭ), *adj.* pertaining to, or like, sinew; vigorous; tough; as, *sinewy* hands; nervous.

sin-ful (sin'fŏŏl), *adj.* full of wickedness; unholy; tainted with sin.—*adv.* **sinfully.**—*n.* **sinfulness.**

sing (sing), *v.i.* [*p.t.* sang, sung, *p.p.* sung, *p.pr.* singing], to lift the voice in song; to utter musical rhythmical sounds; make a shrill or humming noise; as, a flying arrow *sings;* celebrate some event in verse or poetry; as, he *sang* of the deeds of Æneas; to make pleasant, musical sounds; as, the brook *sings* merrily: *v.t.* to utter with musical inflections of the voice; to celebrate in song; chant; to lull by singing; as, to *sing* a child to sleep; to speak warmly of; as, he *sang* our praises.—*n.* **singer.**
Syn. carol, warble, hum.

singe (sinj), *v.t.* [*p.t.* and *p.p.* singed (sinjd), *p.pr.* singeing], to burn lightly or on the surface; to scorch; to burn so as to remove down, as a fowl: *n.* a slight burn; an outside, or surface, burn.—*n.* **singer.**

Sin-gha-lese (sing'gȧ-lēz'; sing'gȧ-lēs'), *adj.* naming, or pertaining to, the chief race of Ceylon, or their language: *n. sing.* and *pl.* a member of this race; their language. Also, **Sinhalese.**

sin-gle (sing'gl), *adj.* consisting of one only; separate; alone; unaided; unmarried; performed by one person; having only one on each side of a contest; as, *single* combat; straightforward; sincere; guileless; honest; having only one row of petals; as, a *single* tulip; having only one on a stem: opposite to *clustered:* said of flowers: *v.t.* to select (one person or thing) from others; separate; choose from others: with *out* or *from:* *n.* a unit; one.

sin-gle file (sing'gl fīl), a line of men walking one behind another; any such line.

sin-gle-foot (sing'gl-fŏŏt"), *n.* a horse's gait in which each foot strikes singly.

sin-gle-hand-ed (sing'gl-hănd'ĕd), *adj.* done without aid or assistance.

sin-gle-heart-ed (sing'gl-härt'ĕd), *adj.* sincere; inclined to be straightforward and free from deceitfulness.

sin-gle-mind-ed (sing'gl-mīnd'ĕd), *adj.* having a mind and heart free from guile or deceit; frank; single-hearted.

sin-gle-ness (sing'gl-nĕs), *n.* the state or quality of being separate or alone; freedom from selfish ends; sincerity; as, *singleness* of purpose.

sin-gle-stick (sing'gl-stĭk"), *n.* a back-sword or cudgel used for fencing or fighting; the game or sport of fencing with such sticks.

sin-gle-tree (sing'gl-trē"), *n.* the swinging bar to which the tugs of a harness are fastened; a whippletree.

sin-gly (sing'glĭ), *adv.* individually; one by one; particularly, single-handed.

sing-song (sing'sŏng"), *n.* singing or poetry marked by an unvaried, monotonous rhythm; a monotonous or drawling tone: *adj.* monotonous in rhythm.

sin-gu-lar (sing'gū-lȧr), *adj.* in grammar, denoting one person or thing; alone; uncommon; unparalleled; strange; extraordinary; exceptional; as, a woman of *singular* charm; peculiar; odd; unique: *n.* in grammar, the number denoting one person or thing; the form of a word denoting this number; a word in the form of this number.—*adv.* **singularly.**

sin-gu-lar-i-ty (sing"gū-lăr'ĭ-tĭ), *n.* [*pl.* singularities (-tĭz)], the state or quality of being uncommon, strange, or separated from others; state of being of the grammatical number denoting one, etc.; peculiarity; oddity; a person or thing that is uncommon, odd, etc.

sin-is-ter (sin'ĭs-tẽr), *adj.* on the left hand; observed from the left; hence, unlucky; ill-omened; evil; as, a *sinister* look; corrupt; dishonest; as, *sinister* intentions.—*adj.* **sinistral, sinistrous.**

sink (sĭnk), *v.i.* [*p.t.* sank, sunk, *p.p.* sunk, *p.pr.* sinking], to fall or go downward; fall to the bottom; descend lower and lower; decline gradually; become hollow: often said of the cheeks; enter deeply; as, to *sink* into the mind; subside; as, a flood soon *sinks:* *v.t.* to cause to go to the bottom; as, to *sink* ships; make by digging downward; as, to *sink* a well; place in the excavation made; lower in value or amount; reduce or extinguish by payment; as, to *sink* the national debt: *n.* a drain to carry off dirty or superfluous water; in geology, any slight depression of the land, especially one that has no water outlet, or an underground one.

sink-er (sink'ẽr), *n.* that which sinks or causes to sink; a weight attached to a fishing line.

sink-ing fund (sink'ing fŭnd), a sum of money set aside for investment, to be used, with its accumulated interest, to pay off a debt.

sin-ner (sĭn'ẽr), *n.* one who offends against the law of God; an offender; transgressor.

Sinn Fein (shĭn fān), literally, ourselves alone; an Irish Society organized in 1905 for the purpose of promoting home industries, and developing nationalism.

sin-ter (sĭn'tẽr), *n.* a geological deposit of porous flint or lime.

sin-u-ate (sĭn'ū-āt), *adj.* having a strongly indented margin; as, a *sinuate* leaf; wavy.

sin-u-os-i-ty (sĭn"ū-ŏs'ĭ-tĭ), *n.* a wavy line; the quality or state of that which curves or winds in and out.

sin-u-ous (sĭn'ū-ŭs), *adj.* curving in and out; winding; crooked; twisting.—*adv.* **sinuously.**—*n.* **sinuousness.**

si-nus (sī'nŭs), *n.* an opening; a hollow or depression; a curving arm of the sea, as a bay; in the human body, a cavity containing air, as within the substance of the skullbone.

Sioux (sōō), *n. sing.* and *pl.* one of an important and warlike tribe of American Indians.

sip (sĭp), *v.t.* [*p.t.* and *p.p.* sipped, *p.pr.* sipping], to drink by taking a small portion, as a teaspoonful, at a time; taste: *v.i.* to drink a liquid by taking a little at a time with the lips: *n.* the act of drinking a little at a time; a small taste.

si-phon (sī'fŏn), *n.* a bent pipe or tube having one end longer than the other, used for drawing off liquids from a higher to a lower level; a bottle fitted with such a tube: *v.t.* to draw off by such a tube. Also, **syphon.**

Sir (sûr), *n.* the title of respect prefixed to the Christian name of a baronet or knight: **sir,** a term of respect in addressing a man without using his name.

sir-dar (sẽr-där'), *n.* in India and other countries of the East, a leader, or person in authority; in Egypt, the commander-in-chief of the army, especially the one in command of the Anglo-Egyptian army.

sire (sīr), *n.* a title of respect used in addressing a sovereign or king; a father: often used in combination, as grand*sire;* the head of a family; the male progenitor of beasts: *v.t.* to procreate, or beget: used especially of beasts.

si-ren (sī'rĕn), *n.* one of certain imaginary nymphs on an island near the coast of Italy, said to have sung with such sweetness that sailors were lured to their destruction; hence, a woman dangerous because of her fascinating, enticing wiles; a foghorn; an instrument for producing musical tones: *adj.* pertaining to, or like, a siren; bewitching.

Sir-i-us (sĭr'ĭ-ŭs), *n.* the Dog Star, the most brilliant star in the sky.

sir-loin (sûr'loin"), *n.* a choice cut of beef, taken between the rib and the rump.

si-roc-co (sĭ-rŏk'ō), *n.* [*pl.* siroccos (-ōz)], a hot, dust-laden wind from the African deserts; a hot wind.

sir-rah (sĭr'ȧ), *n.* a term of address to a man or boy, implying inferiority and used in reproach or contempt.

sir-up (sĭr'ŭp), *n.* a thick liquid made of the juice of fruits boiled with sugar; any condensed solution of sugar. Also, **syrup.**—*adj.* **sirupy, syrupy.**

siss (sĭs), *n.* a hissing noise: *v.i.* to make a hissing noise.

sis-ter (sĭs'tẽr), *n.* a female born of the same parents as another person: a woman of the same religious society, order, or community; nun; one of the same kind or condition: **half sister,** a female having one parent in common with another person. —*adj.* **sisterly.**

sis-ter-hood (sĭs'tẽr-hŏŏd), *n.* the relationship between sisters; state of being a sister; sisters collectively; a number of women of the same religious society, etc.; the office or duty of a sister.

sis-ter-in-law (sĭs'tẽr-ĭn-lô"), *n.* [*pl.* sisters-in-law), a husband's or wife's sister; a brother's wife.

Sis-tine (sĭs'tēn; sĭs'tĭn), *adj.* of or pertaining to any of the Popes named Sixtus: the **Sistine Madonna,** a famous representation of the Madonna, painted by Raphael for the church of St. Sixtus at Piacenza, Italy, but now at Dresden.

sit (sĭt), *v.i.* [*p.t.* and *p.p.* sat, *p.pr.* sitting], to rest on the lower part of the trunk of the body; perch; rest or lie; repose on a seat; to fit; as, the dress *sits* well; press or weigh; occupy a seat officially; as, to *sit* in Parliament; hold a session; as, the court will *sit* in January; to cover and warm eggs for hatching, as a fowl; to pose; as, to *sit* for a portrait: *v.t.* to sit upon, as a horse; to seat.—*n.* **sitter.**

site (sīt), *n.* local position or situation; a place fitting or chosen for any certain permanent use or occupation; as, a *site* for a church.

sit-ting (sĭt'ĭng), *adj.* resting on the haunches; perching; pertaining to, or used for, sitting; *n.* the state, position, or act, of one who sits; a seat in a church, etc.; a session or meeting; time during which one sits; set of eggs for hatching.

sit-u-ate (sĭt'ū-āt), *adj.* placed; situated; located.

sit-u-at-ed (sĭt'ū-āt"ĕd), *adj.* having a position; placed with respect to any other object; located.

sit-u-a-tion (sĭt"ū-ā'shŭn), *n.* position; locality; circumstances; office; employment; the temporary state of affairs at any given moment.

Syn. condition, plight, predicament, state, station.

sitz bath (sĭts bȧth), a tub for bathing in a sitting posture; also, a bath so taken.

six (sĭks), *adj.* one more than five: *n.* the number greater by one than five; the sign representing six units, as 6 or vi.

six-fold (sĭks'fōld"), *adj.* six times as many or as much.

six-pence (sĭks'pĕns), *n.* a small British silver coin, value six pennies, or about twelve cents; this sum of money.

six-teen (sĭks'tēn"; sĭks"tēn'), *adj.* one more than fifteen: *n.* the number greater by one than fifteen; a symbol for sixteen units, as 16 or xvi.

six-teen-mo (sĭks-tēn'mō), *n.* [*pl.* sixteenmos (-mōz)], *adj.* having sixteen leaves to a sheet: *n.* a book made of sheets of which each is folded into sixteen leaves; the size of book so put together commonly written 16mo, or 16°.

six-teenth (sĭks'tēnth"; sĭks"tēnth'), *adj.* next in order after the fifteenth; being one of sixteen equal parts or units: *n.* in music, a note whose value is half that of an eighth; a sixteenth unit or object.

sixth (sĭksth), *adj.* first after the fifth, being one of six equal parts or units;

n. a sixth part or unit; in music, the sixth tone of a scale, counting upwards; the combination of two tones a sixth apart, according to the laws of harmony; an interval of six diatonic degrees; a tone at this interval.—*adv.* **sixthly.**

six-ti-eth (sĭks'tĭ-ĕth), *adj.* next in order after the fifty-ninth; being one of sixty equal parts or units: *n.* a sixtieth part or unit.

six-ty (sĭks'tĭ), *adj.* six times ten; three-score: *n.* [*pl.* sixties (-tĭz)], the sum of six times ten; sixty units or objects; a symbol for sixty units, as 60 or lx.

siz-a-ble (sīz'ȧ-bl), *adj.* of considerable or suitable size. Also, **sizeable.**—*n.* **sizableness.**—*adv.* **sizably.**

siz-ar (sīz'ẽr), *n.* in some British universities, a student who, having passed a certain examination, is excused from paying college fees. Also, **sizer.**

size (sīz), *n.* a kind of thin, weak glue for glazing plaster, etc.; magnitude or bulk; as, the *size* of a house, or of a load; extent of surface; as, the *size* of a piece of land; height; as, the *size* of a tree; a relative measure showing how large something is, as shoes, gloves, etc.: *v.t.* to prepare or cover with size, or thin glue; arrange in order of height, bulk, volume, or extent; colloquially, to form a conclusion about: with *up;* as, to *size* up a situation.

Syn., *n.* area, greatness, dimension.

sized (sīzd), *adj.* being of a particular size, bulk, volume, or dimension.

siz-ing (sīz'ĭng), *n.* the glutinous material used for glazing plaster, etc.

siz-zle (sĭz'l), *v.i.* to make a hissing sound; fry: *n.* a hissing sound. [COLLOQ.]

skat (skät), *n.* a certain three-handed card game.

skate (skāt), *n.* a kind of flat fish; a metallic runner with a frame shaped to fit the sole of a shoe: made to be fastened under the shoe, and used for gliding rapidly over ice; wheels or rollers on a frame which fits the sole of the shoe: used for gliding rapidly over any smooth surface: *v.i.* to move on skates.—*n.* **skater.**

skee (skē), *n.* a long, narrow strip of wood used as a snowshoe. Also, **ski.**

skein (skān), *n.* a quantity of thread, silk, etc., coiled together.

skel-e-ton (skĕl'ē-tŭn), *n.* the bony framework of an animal; framework of anything; outline.

skep-tic (skĕp'tĭk), *n.* one who is yet undecided as to what is true; one who doubts whether any fact or truth can be certainly known; one who doubts the truth of the religious belief of his associates. Also, **sceptic.**

Syn. doubter, infidel, unbeliever.

Ant. (see believer).

skep-ti-cal (skĕp'tĭ-kăl), *adj.* pertaining to, or like, a doubter, or skeptic; doubting everything; unbelieving; critically searching; disbelieving the religious belief of one's associates. Also, **sceptical.**—*adv.* **skeptically, sceptically.**

skep-ti-cism (skĕp'tĭ-sĭzm), *n.* an undecided, inquiring state of mind; uncertainty; doubt; the doctrine that no facts can be known with certainty beyond the range of experience; unbelief in the religious belief of one's associates. Also, **scepticism.**

sketch (skĕch), *n.* an outline; a simple, quickly made drawing from nature; as, a crayon *sketch;* first rough draft; preliminary study; a short, simple piece of literature; a short, simple, dramatic performance: *v.t.* to draw the outline or give the principal features of; make a draft of; outline the plan of: *v.i.* to make an outline or preliminary draft.

Syn., *n.* design, picture, plan.

sketch-book (skĕch'bo͝ok"), *n.* a book of drawings, or for drawings.

sketch-y (skĕch'ĭ), *adj.* suggestive of the whole; given in outline only; giving the main features in a rapid, incomplete fashion.—*adv.* **sketchily.**—*n.* **sketchiness.**

skew (skū), *adj.* twisted or turned to one side: *n.* a twisted movement; a distortion: *v.i.* to move in a sidelong fashion; to glance obliquely: *v.t.* to shape obliquely; to twist, or cause to be crooked.

skew-er (skū'ẽr), *n.* a pin of wood or metal for keeping meat, etc., in shape while roasting: *v.t.* to fasten with, or as with, a skewer or pin.

ski (skē), *n.* [*pl.* ski (skē) or skis (skēz)], one of a pair of long, narrow pieces of wood with the front end curved, fastened one on each foot, and used as snowshoes. Also, **skee.**

ski-a-graph (skī'ȧ-gráf), *n.* a shadow-picture produced by Roentgen rays, which pass through the object and fall upon a sensitive film. Also, **sciagraph.**

skid (skĭd), *n.* a wedge or drag to check the motion of a vehicle by pressure against the wheel; one of a pair or set of logs, rails, etc., used to form a track down which heavy objects may be rolled: *v.t.* [*p.t.* and *p.p.* skidded, *p.pr.* skidding], to cause to move on skids; protect or check with a drag or skid: *v.i.* to slip sideways on the road: said of an automobile; to slide without turning around: said of a locked wheel.

skiff (skĭf), *n.* a small, light boat for rowing.

skil-ful (skĭl'fo͝ol), *adj.* having or showing deftness or practical ability; expert in any art or science; clever; requiring expertness. Also, **skillful.**—*adv.* **skilfully, skillfully.**—*n.* **skilfulness, skillfulness.**

Syn. adroit, apt, deft.

Ant. (see awkward).

skill (skĭl), *n.* knowledge of any art or science, together with expert ability to put that knowledge to use; cleverness; dexterity; trained readiness in using knowledge.

skilled (skĭld), *adj.* having the knowledge and ability which come from experience; dexterous; clever; trained in some art, craft, or science; demanding practical efficiency; as, a *skilled* trade.

skil-let (skĭl'ĕt), *n.* a small metal vessel with a handle, used for cooking.

skim (skĭm), *v.t.* [*p.t.* and *p.p.* skimmed, *p.pr.* skimming], to remove the scum from; to remove something floating from the top of; as, to *skim* milk; to take off, as cream from milk, with a ladle or spoon; brush the surface of lightly; as, the boat *skims* the water; to glance over hurriedly or superficially: *v.i.* to pass lightly over a surface; read without thoroughness: *adj.* having the cream, etc., removed from the top; as, *skim* milk.

skim-mer (skĭm'ẽr), *n.* one who, or that which, takes off a floating substance from a surface, as a ladle or dipper for skimming cream from milk, etc.; a kind of sea bird.

skimp (skĭmp), *v.t.* to do badly or carelessly; to slight; to make insufficient allowance for: *v.i.* to save; to be miserly. [COLLOQ.]

skim-py (skĭm'pĭ), *adj.* [*comp.* skimpier, *superl.* skimpiest], stingy; miserly; narrow; as, a *skimpy* skirt. [COLLOQ.]

skin (skĭn), *n.* the membrane on the surface of the body of an animal which forms its outside covering; hide; pelt; bark, rind, or peel; as, the *skin* of an orange; anything like a skin; a vessel made of an animal's hide, for holding liquids: *v.t.* [*p.t.* and *p.p.* skinned, *p.pr.* skinning], to remove or strip the outer membrane from; flay; peel: *v.i.* to become covered over with skin.—*n.* **skinner.**

skin-flint (skĭn'flĭnt"), *n.* a miser; a niggardly person.

skin-ny (skĭn'ĭ), *adj.* like skin in appearance or texture; lean; emaciated.—*n.* **skinniness.**

skip (skĭp), *v.t.* [*p.t.* and *p.p.* skipped, *p.pr.* skipping], to leap lightly over; to pass over or omit; colloquially, to cause to rebound: *v.i.* to leap or bound lightly; to move with light trips and hops; caper; pass along rapidly; hurry along, omitting portions, as in reading, etc.: *n.* a light leap or bound; omission; a passing over.

skip-per (skĭp'ẽr), *n.* one who, or that which, moves with a light leaping or tripping gait; one who hurries along, as in reading, omitting portions; the cheese maggot or worm; a kind of small moth; the master of a merchant or fishing vessel.

skip-stop (skĭp'stŏp"), *n* a plan of operating street or electric railways, etc., by reducing the number of regular stopping places.

skir-mish (skûr'mĭsh), *n.* a brisk fight on a small scale in war, usually in connection with a greater conflict; contest: *v.i.* to fight in small parties; to take part in a brisk, short engagement.—*n.* **skirmisher.**

skirt (skûrt), *n.* the lower and loose part of a coat, dress, or other garment; an outer garment for women and girls, covering the body below the waist; a petticoat; margin or border; on a saddle, the side flaps: *v.t.* to border; run or pass along the edge of; as, to *skirt* a forest: *v.i.* to be on the border, or move along the edge.

skit (skĭt), *n.* a short literary composition, especially one that is simply constructed; in this sense, a sketch; a brief humorous or satirical writing.

skit-tish (skĭt'ĭsh), *adj.* shy; easily frightened; as, a *skittish* horse; lively; tricky; fickle.—*adv.* **skittishly.**—*n.* **skittishness.**

skit-tles (skĭt'-lz), *n. pl.* a game resembling ninepins.

skiv-er (skĭv'-ẽr), *n.* a leather made from the outside portion of a split sheepskin by tanning in sumac.

skulk (skŭlk), *v.i.* to hide or get out of the way in a sneaking or underhand manner: *n.* an idle, good-for-nothing fellow.—*n.* **skulker.**

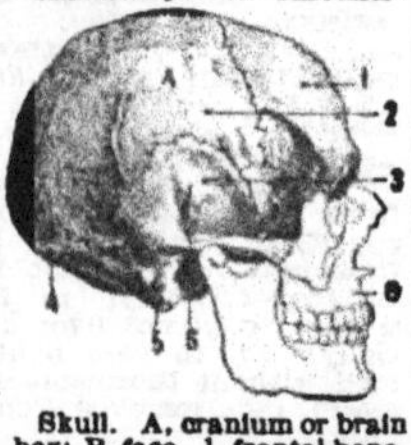

Skull. A, cranium or brain box; B, face. 1, frontal bone; 2, parietal; 3, temporal; 4, occipital; 5, mastoid process of temporal; 6, external auditory meatus.

skull (skŭl), *n.* the bony case inclosing the brain of an animal; the bones of the head and face.

skull-cap (skŭl'kăp"), *n.* a brimless cap for use indoors; a tight-fitting cap.

skunk (skŭnk), *n.* an American mammal of the weasel family, which, when pursued, casts forth an offensive liquid. called also, in the United States, a *polecat.*

sky (skī), *n.* [*pl.* skies (skīz)], the heavens or upper atmosphere; the region of clouds, storms, etc.; the climate or weather; heaven.

sky-lark (skī'lärk"), *n.* a kind of bird that mounts high in the air and sings as it soars; not found in America: *v.i.* to frolic or play boisterously.

sky-light (skī'līt"), *n.* a window in a roof, ceiling, etc., for letting in light from above.

sky pi-lot (skī pī'lŭt), a term used in lumber and mining camps, among ranchmen, etc., and in the army, for a clergyman, missionary preacher, or chaplain

sky-rock-et (skī'rŏk"ĕt), *n.* a kind of firework that ascends and explodes high in the air.

sky-sail (skī'sāl"; *naut.* skī'sl), *n.* the sail set at the top of a mast, above the royal.

sky-scrap-er (skī'skrāp"ẽr), *n.* a very tall building.

sky-ward (skī'wẽrd), *adj.* and *adv.* toward the sky. Also, *adv.* **skywards**

slab (slăb), *n.* a thick piece of anything, especially marble or stone, having flat surfaces; the outside piece, with or without the bark, removed from a log in sawing it into boards.

slack (slăk), *adj.* relaxed or loose; weak; slow; sluggish; as, *slack* water; not holding fast; not pressing; dull; as, business is *slack;* negligent: *n.* that part of anything, as a wire, etc., that hangs down loose.—*adv.* **slackly.**—*n.* **slackness.**

slack-en (slăk'n), *v.i.* to become less firm, tense, or rigid; be remiss or less diligent; languish; become slower; slake *v.t.* to loosen; to make less; as, to *slacken* speed. Also, **slack.**

slag (slăg), *n.* the dross or dregs of a melted metal; cinders; lava from a volcano.

slain (slān), past participle of the verb *slay.*

slake (slāk), *v.t.* to quench; as, to *slake* thirst; extinguish; mix with water, as, to *slake* lime: *v.i.* to become mixed with water.

slam (slăm), *v.t.* [*p.t.* and *p.p.* slammed, *p.pr.* slamming], to shut violently and with a loud noise; put down with force and loud noise: *v.i.* to bang; as, the door *slams:* *n.* a violent and noisy banging; the act of banging or shutting noisily; in some card games, as bridge, the case when the winner takes every trick.

slan-der (slăn'dẽr), *n.* a false or malicious report tending to injure the reputation of another; false tales of another *v.t.* to injure the reputation of by telling malicious falsehoods; to malign; libel; revile; calumniate.—*n.* **slanderer.**

slan-der-ous (slăn'dẽr-ŭs), *adj* uttering false reports about a person; of the nature of, or containing, malicious reports concerning the character of some one. —*adv.* **slanderously.**—*n.* **slanderousness.**

slang (slăng), *n.* vulgar language; a popular but unauthorized phrase, or mode of expression; an ordinary word that has acquired a certain meaning, perhaps quite apart from its usual one, and that is in popular, but inelegant, use; the language of some particular calling or class of people; as, the *slang* of the theater, of sailors, etc.

slang-y (slăng'ĭ), *adj.* of the nature of, or containing, words that are in common use, but are not considered strictly proper.—*adv.* **slangily.**—*n.* **slanginess.**

slant (slȧnt), *n.* an inclined plane; a slope: *v.t.* to give a sloping direction to: *v.i.* to slope; to incline from a certain line or level: *adj.* inclined from a straight line; oblique; sloping.

slant-ing (slȧnt'ĭng), *adj.* inclined or sloping; oblique.—*adv.* **slantingly.**

slant-wise (slȧnt'wīz″), *adv.* in a slanting direction; obliquely. Also, **slantly.**

slap (slăp), *n.* a blow, especially one given with the open hand; an insult; a repulse: *v.t.* [*p.t.* and *p.p.* slapped, *p.pr.* slapping], to strike with the open hand or with anything broad; colloquially, to throw down with careless force.

slap-dash (slăp'dăsh″), *adv.* in a bold, careless manner: *adj.* reckless; boldly careless of consequences. [Colloq.]

slap-jack (slăp'jăk″), *n.* a kind of flat batter cake. [U. S.]

slash (slăsh), *n.* a long cut; a stroke of a whip; random cut; slit; gash: *v.t.* to cut by striking violently and at random; cut into long slits; gash; cut with a whip: *v.i.* to strike violently and at random.—*n.* **slasher.**

slash-ing (slăsh'ĭng), *adj.* that cuts violently; hence, severe; as, *slashing* remarks: *n.* the act of cutting recklessly or at random.

slat (slăt), *n.* a thin, narrow strip of wood or metal; as, bed *slats.*

slate (slāt), *n.* a kind of rock that splits into thin plates; the dark gray color of this rock; a thin plate of this rock prepared for use in covering a roof, or as a tablet for writing upon; in the United States, a list of candidates, prepared for nomination or election: *v.t.* to cover with slate; in the United States, register for a political appointment; as, to *slate* Wilcox for governor.—*adj.* **slaty.**

slat-tern (slăt'ẽrn), *n.* a careless, slovenly woman; a woman who neglects her personal appearance; an untidy woman.—*adj.* and *adv.* **slatternly.**

slaugh-ter (slô'tẽr), *n.* the act of killing; wanton destruction of life; carnage; killing of cattle, etc., for human food: *v.t.* to slay or kill with violence; to massacre; to butcher (beasts) for the market.

Slav (slăv; slăv), *n.* a person belonging to that division of the Indo-European race, or parent race of Europe, which inhabits eastern Europe and includes Russians, Poles, Czechs, and natives of the Balkan states.

slave (slāv), *n.* a human being held in bondage; a bondsman; a serf; drudge; one under the power or influence of a habit or influence; as, a *slave* to drink: *v.i.* to work like a drudge; toil.

slave-hold-er (slāv'hōl″dẽr), *n.* one who owns or holds slaves.—*adj.* **slaveholding.**

slav-er (slăv'ẽr), *v.i.* to let saliva run from the mouth: *v.t.* to cover or dribble with saliva: *n.* saliva running from the mouth.

slav-er (slāv'ẽr), *n.* a vessel or trader engaged in the slave trade.

slav-er-y (slāv'ẽr-ĭ), *n.* [*pl.* slaveries (-ĭz)], the condition of a bondsman; the business of holding human beings in bondage; bondage; involuntary servitude; complete submission to the will of another, or to some influence or vice; drudgery.

Syn. thraldom, captivity, vassalage.

Ant. (see freedom).

Slav-ic (slăv'ĭk; slăv'ĭk), *adj.* pertaining to, or denoting, that one of the three great divisions of the Indo-European race, or parent stock of the races of Europe, which inhabits eastern Europe and includes Russians, Bulgarians, Serbians, etc.; denoting the language spoken by any one of these peoples: *n.* the language of any one of these peoples, or, in general, the language group to which they belong.

slav-ish (slāv'ĭsh), *adj.* pertaining to, or like, a bondservant or drudge.—*adv.* **slavishly.**—*n.* **slavishness.**

Sla-von-ic (slȧ-vŏn'ĭk), *adj.* pertaining to the Slavs of Serbia, Croatia, Slavonia, Montenegro, etc., known as the West Slavic peoples, or to the language spoken by them; pertaining to Slavonia, in South Hungary, a state of the Jugo-Slav group, or to its people. Also, **Slavonian.**

slaw (slô), *n.* sliced cabbage served, usually raw, as a salad.

slay (slā), *v.t.* [*p.t.* slew, *p.p.* slain, *p.pr.* slaying], to kill or put to death by violence; to destroy.—*n.* **slayer.**

sleave (slēv), *n.* the knotted or entangled part of silk or thread; floss.

slea-zy (slē'zĭ; slā'zĭ), *adj.* lacking firmness; thin; flimsy; as, *sleazy* silk or muslin.—*n.* **sleaziness.**

sled (slĕd), *n.* a conveyance made to glide rapidly over ice and snow on runners: used for sport; any similar conveyance, used for carrying loads; a sledge: *v.t.* [*p.t.* and *p.p.* sledded, *p.pr.* sledding], to carry on a sled or sledge.

sled-ding (slĕd'ĭng), *n.* the act of carrying or riding on a sled; the condition of the snow which admits of the gliding of sleds; as, the *sledding* is good.

sledge (slĕj), *n.* a strong vehicle with low runners, or one without runners, designed for carrying loads, especially on snow or ice; a sled; a large, heavy hammer, usually wielded with both hands: called also *sledge hammer.*

sleek (slēk), *adj.* smooth; glossy: *v.t.* to make smooth.—*adv.* **sleekly.**—*n.* **sleekness.**

sleep (slēp), *n.* a temporary, normal suspension of consciousness and will, occurring at regular intervals; slumber; rest; figuratively, death: *v.i.* [*p.t.* and *p.p.* slept, *p.pr.* sleeping], to take rest in sleep; be motionless or inactive; be dead: *v.t.* to make go away by sleep; as, he *slept* away his pain; to make pass through sleep; as, she *slept* the day away; to shake off through sleep; as, he *slept* off the evil effects of the poison.

Syn. doze, drowse, slumber.

sleep-er (slēp'ẽr), *n.* one who slumbers; a piece of timber laid at right angles to the rails of a railway track and supporting them: called also a *tie;* colloquially, a sleeping car.

sleep-ing car (slēp'ĭng kär), a car in use on railways, equipped with compartments and berths for sleeping.

sleep-less (slēp'lĕs), *adj.* having no rest; inclined not to sleep; wakeful.—*adv.* **sleeplessly.**—*n.* **sleeplessness.**

sleep-walk-ing (slēp'wôk″ĭng), *n.* the act or habit of walking in one's sleep.—*n.* **sleepwalker.**

sleep-y (slēp'ĭ), *adj.* [*comp.* sleepier, *superl.* sleepiest], inclined to, or overcome by, slumber; causing drowsiness or heaviness; as, a *sleepy* day; drowsy; sluggish.—*adv.* **sleepily.**—*n.* **sleepiness.**

sleet (slēt), *n.* driving rain mixed with snow or hail: *v.i.* to rain in driving snowy or icy sheets.

sleet-y (slēt'ĭ), *adj.* consisting of, or like, a driving snowy rain.—*n.* **sleetiness.**

sleeve (slēv), *n.* the part of a garment that covers the arm; in machinery, a part, usually shaped like a tube, to cover some other part: *v.t.* to furnish with sleeves.—*adj.* **sleeveless.**

sleigh (slā), *n.* a vehicle, equipped with runners, used for conveying loads over snow or ice.

sleigh-ing (slā'ĭng), *n.* the act of riding or traveling in a sleigh; the condition of the snow which permits this kind of traveling.

sleight (slīt), *n.* skill; expertness; scheme; artful trick; as, the juggler's *sleight:* **sleight of hand,** a trick or set of tricks requiring expert handling of the articles employed to produce the effect.

slen-der (slĕn'dẽr), *adj.* narrow in proportion to the length or height; slim; as, a *slender* figure; feeble; moderate; small; as, *slender* means of support; spare; as, a *slender* meal.—*adv.* **slenderly.**—*n.* **slenderness.**

slept (slĕpt), past tense and past participle of the verb *sleep.*

sleuth (slōōth), *n.* formerly, the track of a man or animal as known by the scent; colloquially, a detective.

sleuth-hound (slōōth'hound"), *n.* a dog that follows the scent of men or animals; a bloodhound.

slew (slōō), past tense of the verb *slay:* *n.* slang, a great number or amount.

slice (slīs), *n.* a thin, broad piece; a thin piece cut off; as, a *slice* of bread: *v.t.* to cut into thin pieces or layers; cut a layer or layers from; divide or cut off.—*n.* **slicer.**

slick (slĭk), *adj.* smooth-tongued or smooth-mannered; colloquially, sleek: *v.t.* to make sleek or smooth: *adv.* smoothly; smartly.

slick-er (slĭk'ẽr), *n.* an oilskin raincoat; a long, loose waterproof. [U. S.]

slid (slĭd), past tense and past participle of the verb *slide.*

slide (slīd), *v.i.* [*p.t.* slid, *p.p.* slidden, slid, *p.pr.* sliding], to pass smoothly over a surface without leaving it; glide; pass unobserved; to go away quietly or secretly: with *away;* slip: *v.t.* to push along; cause to slip into place; to put quietly, and so as to be unobserved: *n.* a smooth surface of ice for sliding upon; smooth incline; a glass plate containing a picture for projection on a screen or an object for examination through a microscope; fall of a mass of rock or snow down a mountain; that upon which anything moves by sliding; a cover, partition, etc., which moves by sliding.—*n.* **slider.**

slid-ing (slīd'ĭng), *adj.* varying; as, a *sliding* scale of wages; slipping along in a groove; as, a *sliding* door or panel; adjustable.

slight (slīt), *adj.* feeble; as, the enemy offered only *slight* resistance; frail; slender; as, a *slight* figure; unimportant; as, there may be a *slight* difference in color; not severe; as, a *slight* reproof; insignificant; as, the affair is too *slight* to be noticed: *n.* intentional neglect shown to a person; neglect or careless performance of tasks; deliberate, discourteous disregard; oversight: *v.t.* to treat with incivility; as, she *slighted* her guests; to neglect or perform carelessly; as, he habitually *slights* his work.—*n.* **slightness.**

slight-ing (slīt'ĭng), *p.adj.* containing or conveying the intention of discourtesy; detracting; characterized or marked by disregard.—*adv.* **slightingly.**

slight-ly (slīt'lĭ), *adv.* to a small or unimportant extent; partially.

slim (slĭm), *adj.* [*comp.* slimmer, *superl.* slimmest], of small diameter; slender; frail; slight; as, a *slim* person; weak or insufficient; as, a *slim* excuse; sparse; as, a *slim* audience.—*n.* **slimness.**

slime (slīm), *n.* soft, moist earth or clay; any moist, sticky substance, especially one that is dirty; sticky substance, such as the mucous secretion upon certain snails, plants, etc.—*adj.* **slimy.**—*n.* **sliminess.**

sling (slĭng), *n.* the act of hurling or flinging; an instrument for throwing stones; a throw; a device to suspend something, as a shoulder strap for a camera, etc.; the hanging bandage in which an injured arm is carried; a drink made of sweetened brandy, gin, etc.: *v.t.* [*p.t.* and *p.p.* slung, *p.pr.* slinging], to hurl with, or as with, an instrument for throwing; cast; fling; hang so as to swing; hang or suspend by a rope or tackle.—*n.* **slinger.**

slink (slĭnk), *v.i.* [*p.t.* and *p.p.* slunk, *p.pr.* slinking], to creep away as if ashamed; sneak off.

slip (slĭp), *v.i.* [*p.t.* and *p.p.* slipped, *p.pr.* slipping], to glide or slide; miss one's foothold; fall down; go or come unobserved; as, she *slipped* into the room; move, often unexpectedly, out of place; as, when the chair *slipped,* I fell; escape; as, the address has *slipped* from my mind: *v.t.* to put on or off with ease, as a ring or a garment; to cause to slide, as a door or panel; to let loose, as hounds; to get out of; as, to *slip* a bridle or collar; to carry secretly; to escape; as, the address has *slipped* my mind; to cut a part from (a plant) for planting; cut from a plant; *n.* the act of sliding or missing one's foothold; a sudden mischance; a fault; an error; a blunder; as, a *slip* of the tongue; a cutting from a plant; hence, an offshoot; a space between wharves for vessels; a dock; something that may be put on or off with ease, as a kind of underwaist, a pillowcase, etc.; a small piece of something, rather longer than wide; a strip; as, a *slip* of paper.

slip-knot (slĭp'nŏt"), *n.* a running knot; a knot which slips along the string, rope, or cord around which it was tied.

slip-per (slĭp'ẽr), *n.* one who, or that which, slips; a kind of low light shoe, easily put on or taken off.

slip-pered (slĭp'ẽrd), *adj.* wearing slippers; as, prettily *slippered* feet.

slip-per-y (slĭp'ẽr-ĭ), *adj.* so smooth as to allow people or things to slide about on; without firm hold or footing; causing bodies to slip; as, a *slippery* pavement; smooth; cunning; as, a *slippery* rascal.—*n.* **slipperiness.**

slip-per-y elm (slĭp'ẽr-ĭ ĕlm), a North American tree having a sticky inner bark; the bark, used to make a soothing medicine.

slip-shod (slĭp'shŏd"), *adj.* wearing shoes or slippers down at the heel;

hence, slovenly; careless and haphazard in the doing of tasks, etc.

slit (slĭt), *v.t.* [*p.t.* and *p.p.* slit or slitted, *p.pr.* slitting], to cut lengthwise or into long strips; to cut or tear a lengthwise opening in; split: *n.* a long cut; a lengthwise cut or tear; a narrow opening.—*n.* **slitter.**

sliv-er (slĭv'ẽr), *v.t.* and *v.i.* to divide into long, thin, or very small pieces; to cut or break off: *n.* a splinter; a sharp, thin, pointed piece, as of wood, etc.; a slim strand of fiber drawn together.

slob-ber (slŏb'ẽr), *v.i.* to let saliva dribble from the mouth: *v.t.* to wet by letting saliva run from the mouth.—*n.* **slobberer.**

sloe (slō), *n.* a small, bitter plum of the blackthorn tree; also, the tree.

slo-gan (slō'găn), *n.* the war cry or gathering cry of a Highland clan; hence, any rallying cry; as, the *slogan* of a political party, or of an idea, or movement, as "Food will win the war."

sloid (sloid), *n.* a system of elementary manual training, whereby a practical knowledge of tools and materials is acquired. Also, **sloyd.**

sloop (sloop), *n.* a one-masted vessel with a fore-and-aft rig.

slop (slŏp), *n.* water carelessly spilled; puddle; poor or weak liquid food: *pl.* dirty or refuse water; cheap ready-made clothes: *v.t.* [*p.t.* and *p.p.* slopped, *p.pr.* slopping], to soil by letting liquid fall upon; to spill: *v.i.* to be spilled.

slope (slōp), *n.* an inclined line; a slant; surface inclining downward; as, the *slope* of a hill; that part of the land that descends toward the ocean: *v.i.* and *v.t.* to incline; as, the ground *slopes;* to slant.—*adj.* **sloping.**

slop-py (slŏp'ĭ), *adj.* wet; unpleasant because wet; as, *sloppy* weather; wet enough to splash water up on one; as, *sloppy* streets; disordered and dirty; as, a *sloppy* kitchen; colloquially, slovenly; careless. —*adv.* **sloppily.**—*n.* **sloppiness.**

slop-shop (slŏp'shŏp"), *n.* a store or shop where cheap ready-made clothes are sold.

slop-work (slŏp'wûrk"), *n.* the manufacture of cheap clothing, or slops; clothing of such a sort.

slot (slŏt), *n.* a broad, flat wooden bar; bolt; narrow crack or groove; a small, narrow opening, big enough to insert a coin; a deer's track: *v.t.* [*p.t.* and *p.p.* slotted, *p.pr.* slotting], to groove; trace by a slot: **slot machine,** a vending, or selling, machine in which a coin may be inserted to purchase candy or peanuts, pay for a telephone call, or the like: **slotting machine, slotter,** a machine for cutting mortises, etc., in metals.

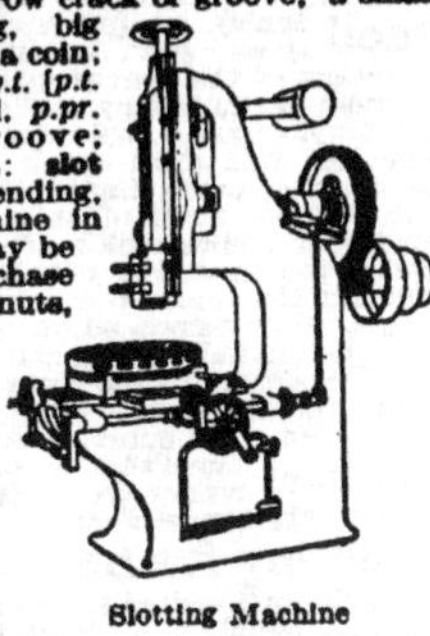

Slotting Machine

sloth (slōth; slŏth), idleness; laziness; indolence; a certain animal of South and Central America, so called from its slow movements.

sloth-ful (slōth'fōōl; slŏth'fōōl), *adj.* lazy; slow; idle; sluggish; indolent; as, a *slothful* youth.—*adv.* **slothfully.**—*n.* **slothfulness.**

slouch (slouch), *n.* a drooping, as of the head; a sidewise depression, as of a hat brim; an ungainly, clownish gait; as, to walk with a *slouch;* an awkward, dull fellow: *v.t.* to cause to droop; depress at the side: *v.i.* to walk in a clumsy, heavy, awkward manner: **slouch hat,** a soft hat, with a flexible brim.

slouch-y (slouch'ĭ), *adj.* awkward in manner or gait; ungainly; drooping.—*adv.* **slouchily.**—*n.* **slouchiness.**

slough (slou; slōō), *n.* a place full of deep mud; a bog; a very muddy place; a marsh; a muddy place caused by the emptying of a drain; hence, a place from which it is difficult to get out; as, a *slough* of despondency. —*adj.* **sloughy.**

slough (slŭf), *n.* the cast-off skin of a snake; the part that comes off from a festering sore; also used figuratively; as, to cast off the *slough* of ignorance: *v.i.* to come away in the form of dead matter from the sound flesh; come off or be shed, as the skin of an animal; to shed or cast the skin: *v.t.* to cast off.—*adj.* **sloughy.**

Slo-vak (slō-văk'; slō'văk), *n.* one of a race of Slavs living in northwestern Hungary, akin to the Czechs of Bohemia, with whom they form the Czecho-Slovak group; the language of these people.

slov-en (slŭv'n), *n.* one who is always untidy in his dress and personal habits; one who is careless of order and neatness; a lazy person.

Slo-vene (slō'vēn), *n.* one of a slavic people native to some of the states of southern Austria, especially Carniola, and included in the Jugo-Slav group: *adj.* pertaining to the Slavs of Carniola and adjoining territory. Also, **Slovenian.**

slov-en-ly (slŭv'n-lĭ), *adj.* untidy in appearance; careless; not neat. —*n.* **slovenliness.**

slow (slō), *adj.* not quick or rapid in motion; as, a *slow* step; not prompt; as, *slow* in arriving; occupying a long time; as, *slow* progress; not rash or hasty; as, *slow* to anger; dull or stupid; as, a *slow* pupil; not up to time; as, the clock is *slow: v.i.* to move with less speed; as, the train *slowed* down: *v.t.* to cause to move with less speed; to delay.—*adv.* **slowly.**—*n.* **slowness.**

slow match (slō măch), a slow-burning fuse for firing a blast, mine, or bomb.

slow-worm (slō'wûrm"), *n.* a small, harmless, burrowing lizard, like a snake in appearance; the blindworm.

sloyd (sloid), *n.* a system of manual training whereby a practical knowledge of tools and materials is acquired. Also, **sloid.**

sludge (slŭj), *n.* slush; mire; sticky mud; floating ice.—*adj.* **sludgy.**

slue (slōō), *v.t.* and *v.i.* to turn around; to slide around, as on a slippery surface. Also, **slew.**

slug (slŭg), *n.* a kind of land-snail without a shell; the creeping larva of a moth; a kind of rough, small bullet: *v.t.* [*p.t.* and *p.p.* slugged, *p.pr.* slugging], slang, to strike hard, especially with the fist or a club.

slug-gard (slŭg'ẽrd), *n.* one who is always lazy and idle.

slug-gish (slŭg'ĭsh), *adj.* always lazy and idle; dull; slothful; inactive; slow mentally.—*adv.* **sluggishly.**—*n.* **sluggishness.**

sluice (slōōs), *n.* a gate for regulating the flow of water in a canal, etc.; hence, an opening or channel through which anything flows; a stream of water issuing through a floodgate: *v.t.* to wash with water from, or as from, a sluice; as, to *sluice* gold: **sluice gate,** an apparatus for holding in or letting out water from a canal or other channel; a floodgate.

Sluice Gates

slum (slŭm), *n.* a low, dirty street or district of a city or town, inhabited by the very poor or criminal classes: *pl.* a neighborhood composed of such streets: *v.i.* [*p.t.* and *p.p.* slummed, *p.pr.* slumming], colloquially, to visit such neighborhoods as a fashionable amusement.—*n.* **slummer.**

slum-ber (slŭm'bẽr), *v.i.* to sleep, especially to sleep lightly; doze; be in a state of rest or inactivity: *n.* sleep; a doze.—*adj.* **slumberless.** —*n.* **slumberer.**

slum-ber-ous (slŭm'bẽr-ŭs), *adj.* bringing on, or inducing, a sleep or doze; heavy with sleepiness; drowsy. Also, **slumbrous.**

slump (slŭmp), *n.* colloquially, a sudden falling off; as, a *slump* in the price of eggs: *v.i.* to fall or sink suddenly; as, the price of wheat *slumped;* to experience such a fall.

slung (slŭng), past tense and past participle of the verb *sling.*

slung shot (slŭng shŏt), a weight attached to a cord, used by ruffians as a weapon.

slunk (slŭnk), past tense and past participle of the verb *slink.*

slur (slûr), *v.t.* [*p.t.* and *p.p.* slurred, *p.pr.* slurring], to soil; pass over in a slighting manner, sometimes with the effect of slipping important facts into the background; to speak slightingly of; pronounce indistinctly; in music, to sing or execute without breaks between two or more tones; to mark so as to indicate that the passage is to be sung or executed in this manner: *n.* a stain; slight reproach, or a remark implying reproach; stigma; in music, a mark (⌢ or ⌣), connecting notes that are to be sung or played without a break.

slush (slŭsh), *n.* half-melted snow; soft mud; a greasy mixture for oiling machinery.—*adj.* **slushy.**

slut (slŭt), *n.* a dirty, untidy woman; a female dog.

slut-tish (slŭt'ĭsh), *adj.* untidy and dirty. —*adv.* **sluttishly.**—*n.* **sluttishness.**

sly (slī), *adj.* [*comp.* slyer, *superl.* slyest], secretly mischievous; underhand and crafty; deceitful; playfully mischievous; roguish.—*adv.* **slyly, slily.**—*n.* **slyness.**

smack (smăk), *n.* a quick, resounding blow; loud kiss; a quick, sharp noise with the lips, as in eating; a slight taste or flavor; a smattering; a one-masted coasting or fishing vessel: *v.t.* to kiss with a quick, sharp noise; strike with a smart blow: *v.i.* to make a noise with the lips after tasting, in kissing, etc.; to have a flavor, tincture, or suggestion of anything: usually with *of;* as, this *smacks* of treason.

smack-ing (smăk'ĭng), *p.adj.* making a sharp noise; lively; brisk.

small (smôl), *adj.* [*comp.* smaller, *superl.* smallest], comparatively little in size, quantity, or degree: opposite to *large;* as, a *small* school; a *small* amount; unimportant or insignificant; as, his opinion is of *small* value; this is a *small* matter; not powerful: said of the voice; weak: said of diluted liquors, as beer; not long in duration; as, a *small* period of time; petty; not large-minded; narrow: *n.* a small part.—*n.* **smallness.**

small arms (smôl ärmz), firearms that can be carried on the person, such as muskets, rifles, pistols, etc.

small pi-ca (smôl pī'kȧ), a size of printing type, now called 11-point.

small-pox (smôl'pŏks'), *n.* a contagious disease marked by fever and a pimplelike eruption containing pus.

small talk (smôl tôk), light, unimportant conversation.

smart (smärt), *adj.* causing a stinging, sharp sensation; as, a *smart* punishment; brisk; fresh: said of a breeze; clever; pertly witty; shrewd; showy; fashionable; as, a *smart* gown: *n.* a quick, lively pain; keen grief: *v.i.* to feel a stinging sensation; to be the seat of a stinging sensation; to cause a stinging sensation; to suffer; to have one's feelings wounded.—*adv.* **smartly.**—*n.* **smartness.**

smart-en (smär'tn), *v.t.* to make stylish or spruce; as, to *smarten* up a gown. [Colloq.]

smash (smăsh), *v.t.* to break in pieces by violence; crush; shatter; to destroy utterly: *v.i.* to break into many pieces, as from pressure; to go into bankruptcy suddenly, as a business; to be thrown violently against something; as, the machine *smashed* against the wall: *n.* a breaking to pieces; utter destruction; colloquially, bankruptcy.—*n.* **smasher.**

smat-ter (smăt'ẽr), *n.* a slight knowledge of anything.

smat-ter-ing (smăt'ẽr-ĭng), *n.* a slight, superficial knowledge of anything.

smear (smēr), *v.t.* to overspread with anything oily or sticky; daub; to soil in any way: *n.* a blot or stain.

smell (smĕl), *v.t.* [*p.t.* and *p.p.* smelled or smelt, *p.pr.* smelling], to perceive by means of the nerves in the nose; obtain the scent of; to test by sniffing air; to seek or detect by, or as by, the odor: *v.i.* to have an odor; as, this room *smells* of sulphur; use the power of perceiving by the sense of smell: with *of;* as, *smell* of this flower: *n.* that quality of bodies which affects the sense of smell; the sensation felt by means of the nerves in the nose; odor.

Syn., *n.* fragrance, scent, perfume.

smelt (smĕlt), *n.* a small edible fish very similar to the trout: *v.t.* to melt, as an ore, for the purpose of separating the pure metal from other substances.

smelt-er (smĕl'tẽr), *n.* one who melts or refines ore; a furnace for reducing ore; the owner of such a furnace.

smelt-ing fur-nace (smĕlt'ĭng fûr'nās), a furnace in which ore is melted to obtain metal.

smew (smū), *n.* a diving bird of the duck family: found in northern Europe and Asia.

smi-lax (smī'lăks), *n.* a delicate, trailing foliage plant, much used for decoration.

smile (smīl), *v.i.* to show pleasure, joy, love, or kindness by an expression of the face; to show slight contempt by such an expression; to look gay, cheerful, or happy; look with favor; as, to *smile* on one's labors: *v.t.* to express by a look of pleasure, kindness, etc.: *n.* a change of expression, marked by an upward curve of the mouth, a sparkle of the eyes, etc., and indicating joy, pleasure, kindness, or happiness; an appearance of gladness. —*adv.* smilingly.

smile-age book (smīl'āj bŏŏk), a folder of coupon tickets, issued to soldiers in the United States National Army in the World War; each coupon being worth five cents and admitting the soldier to an entertainment at the camp theater.

smirch (smûrch) *v.t.* to smear; soil; make dirty; stain; to defame; as, to *smirch* one's reputation: *n.* a smear or stain.

smirk (smûrk), *v.i.* to smile affectedly or conceitedly: *n.* an affected smile.

smite (smīt), *v.t.* [*p.t.* smote, *p.p.* smitten, *p.pr.* smiting], to strike with, or as with, the hand or a weapon; destroy; overcome in battle; cast down; punish; trouble; touch with any strong feeling, as love, grief, fear, etc.: *v.i.* to affect something as would a heavy blow.

smith (smĭth), *n.* one who shapes metal with a hammer on a forge; a worker in metals.

smith-y (smĭth'ĭ), *n.* [*pl.* smithies (-ĭz)], the workshop of one who forges metal, especially of a blacksmith.

smock (smŏk), *n.* a chemise; a peasant's long, loose blouse, or smock frock; a woman's loose, unbelted blouse.

smock frock (smŏk frŏk), a coarse, long, loose blouse, worn over the rest of the garments by European peasants.

smock-ing (smŏk'ĭng), *n.* a kind of decorative needlework used for holding gathers in place in women's and children's dresses.

smoke (smōk), *n.* the visible, carbon-carrying gas that escapes when a substance is burned; vapor; the act of smoking a pipe or cigar; light, careless talk: *v.t.* to apply smoke to, as meat; to blacken by smoke; dry, scent, or medicate by the action of smoke; inhale and puff out the smoke of; force out by smoke; as, to *smoke* an animal from its hole; detect or search out: *v.i.* to emit or give out smoke; burn tobacco in a pipe, etc.; inhale and puff out smoke.

smoke con-sum-er (smōk kŏn-sūm'ẽr), a device used by coal-burning industries to do away with the black smoke from their chimneys.

smoke-less (smōk'lĕs), *adj.* burning without sending out visible gas; as, *smokeless* powder.

smoke-less pow-der (smōk'lĕs pou'dẽr), an explosive used in war, which burns without making smoke.

smok-er (smōk'ẽr), *n.* one given to the smoking of tobacco; colloquially, a railroad car for men smoking tobacco; also, a social gathering of men at which tobacco is smoked.

smoke-stack (smōk'stăk"), *n.* a chimney, especially of a factory, locomotive, etc.

smok-ing (smōk'ĭng), *p.adj.* giving out smoke; used for smoking tobacco; as, a *smoking* room.

smok-y (smōk'ĭ), *adj.* [*comp.* smokier, *superl.* smokiest], giving out, or filled with, smoke; as, a *smoky* stove; soiled with smoke; hazy in atmosphere; as, a *smoky* day; grayish-black in color, like smoke.—*adv.* smokily.—*n.* smokiness.

smol-der (smōl'dẽr), *v.i.* to burn slowly, giving forth smoke without flame; burn beneath the surface; exist in a stifled condition; as, their discontent *smolders*. Also, smoulder.

smolt (smōlt), *n.* a young salmon that has acquired its silver scales.

smooth (smōōth), *adj.* not rough; even in surface or texture; perfectly blended; gently flowing; as, a *smooth* river; glossy; unruffled; tending to calm or soothe ruffled feelings; flattering; as, to win by *smooth* words; easy and eloquent, as in speech or manner; steady in motion; without hair, especially on the face: *n.* the act of making even in surface, texture, motion, etc.; that part of anything that is not rough: *v.t.* to remove roughness from; to make even, steady, or calm; to soothe, as the feelings; to take away harshness from; to make light of; as, to *smooth* over an offense; to make pleasant by soft words; to remove, as difficulties or hindrances: with *away*.—*adv.* smoothly. —*n.* smoothness.

Syn., *adj.* level, polished, sleek.
Ant. (see rough).

smooth-bore (smōōth'bōr"), *adj.* having a tube, or bore, with a smooth inner surface: said of a gun. Also, smooth-bore.

smooth-faced (smōōth'fāst"), *adj.* without beard or mustache; calm in expression.

smote (smōt), past tense of the irregular verb *smite*.

smoth-er (smŭth'ẽr), *v.t.* to destroy the life of by depriving of air; stifle; suppress or conceal; as, to *smother* one's anger: *v.i.* to be suffocated or deprived of air: *n.* stifling smoke or thick dust.

smould-er (smōl'dẽr), *v.i.* to burn slowly without flame or beneath the surface. Also, smolder.

smudge (smŭj), *n.* a smear or stain; suffocating smoke; a smoldering fire of damp wood, etc., giving forth dense smoke to keep off insects: *v.t.* to smear or stain; blacken or stifle with smoke.—*adj.* smudgy.—*n.* smudginess.

smug (smŭg), *adj.* affectedly precise or prim; self-satisfied; spruce; neat.

smug-gle (smŭg'l), *v.t.* and *v.i.* to bring in or send out (goods) to or from a country, secretly, without paying customhouse duties or taxes; to carry or introduce secretly.—*n.* smuggler.

smut (smŭt), *n.* a spot or stain made by soot or dirt; a poor quality of soft coal; a disease affecting corn, wheat, etc.; foul language: *v.t.* [*p.t.* and *p.p.* smutted, *p.pr.* smutting], to soil or blacken with, or as with, soot: *v.i.* to become blackened, as by smut, as corn; to give off soot or dirt.

smutch (smŭch), *v.t.* to soil with smoke, soot, or coal: *n.* a dirty spot.

smut-ty (smŭt'ĭ), *adj.* [*comp.* smuttier, *superl.* smuttiest], soiled or stained with dirt or soot; indecent or foul in talk.—*adv.* smuttily.—*n.* smuttiness.

snack (snăk), *n.* a slight, hurried repast, or meal. [Colloq.]

snaf-fle (snăf'l), *n.* a horse's bit having a joint in the middle and no curb: *v.t.* to put such a bit in the mouth of.

snag (snăg), *n.* a rough branch broken off short; a jagged stump; a broken tree sticking up from the bottom of a river or lake and dangerous to boats; any sudden obstacle; a tooth projecting beyond the rest; a broken or decayed tooth: *v.t.* [*p.t.* and *p.p.* snagged, *p.pr.* snagging], to injure or destroy by contact with a broken, jagged stump.

snail (snāl), *n.* a slimy, slow-creeping little animal of the shellfish family, having a spiral shell; hence, any slow-moving person; a drone.

snake (snāk), *n.* a long, slim reptile without limbs, and often poisonous, having a winding motion; a serpent: *v.t.* slang, to draw out with a jerk.

snak-y (snāk'ĭ), *adj.* [*comp.* snakier, *superl.* snakiest], pertaining to, or like, a snake; infested with snakes; deceitful; sly; cunning.

snap (snăp), *v.i.* [*p.t.* and *p.p.* snapped, *p.pr.* snapping], to break off short; to snatch at something suddenly, especially with the teeth; to produce a sharp, sudden sound; speak crossly or angrily; miss fire: said of a gun; to flash; to crackle: *v.t.* to break off short; crack; seize suddenly and unexpectedly, as with the teeth; to speak to sharply and angrily: followed by *up;* cause to make a sudden, sharp sound; as, to *snap* the fingers: *n.* act of seizing or breaking suddenly; the sudden breaking of something stiff or tightly stretched; a sudden, sharp sound; as, the *snap* of a whip; a spring lock or catch; a sudden short period of severe weather; as, a cold *snap;* colloquially, energy or vim; a kind of small, thin, crisp cake: *adj.* colloquially, receiving or requiring little thought; as, a *snap* judgment; a *snap* course of study.

snap-drag-on (snăp'drăg"ŭn), *n.* a plant with a showy flower of curious shape; a game in which raisins are snatched from a bowl of burning brandy.

snap-per (snăp'ẽr), *n.* a flesh-eating, edible sea-fish, found in tropical waters.

snap-ping tur-tle (snăp'ĭng tûr'tl), a large freshwater turtle that seizes its prey by a snap of its jaws.

snap-pish (snăp'ĭsh), *adj.* likely to snatch with the jaws; eager to bite; as, a *snappish* dog; sharp in speech; peevish; easily irritated or made angry.—*adv.* snappishly.—*n.* snappishness.

snap-py (snăp'ĭ), *adj.* [*comp.* snappier, *superl.* snappiest], sharp and irritable in speech; full of energy; brisk. [COLLOQ.]

snap-shot (snăp'shŏt"), *n.* a photograph made without preparation by the subject. Also, snap shot.

snare (snâr), *n.* a running noose or loop of cord or wire, for catching an animal or bird; anything that entangles or entraps; a string stretched across the head of the drum called a *snare* drum: *v.t.* to catch or entangle with, or as with, a noose or net.

snare drum (snâr drŭm), a small double-headed drum, with catgut strings across one head to add to its resonance.

snarl (snärl), *v.i.* to make a growling noise, as an angry dog; speak in harsh, surly tones; to become tangled or knotted: *v.t.* to knot or entangle, as thread or hair; utter in a growl or a harsh, surly tone: *n.* the act of growling, or of speaking in surly tones; a growl; a surly tone; angry contention or quarrel; an entanglement or knot of thread, hair, etc.—*n.* snarler.

snarl-ing (snärl'ĭng), *n.* the decorating of hollow metal with raised work by hammering with a special tool on the inner surface.

snatch (snăch), *v.t.* to take or seize suddenly or rudely; to catch hurriedly; as, to *snatch* an hour of sleep: *v.i.* to attempt to seize anything suddenly: with *at:* *n.* a hasty catch or seizing; a small fragment; as, a *snatch* of music.—*adj.* snatchy.

snath (snăth), *n.* the handle of a scythe, or tool for cutting hay, grass, etc. Also, snathe.

sneak (snēk), *v.i.* to creep or steal away privately or meanly; slink; to act in cowardly fashion and with meanness; steal: *n.* a mean, cowardly fellow; a petty thief.—*adj.* sneaky, sneaking.

sneer (snēr), *v.i.* to show contempt by an expression of the face, as by curling the lips, etc.; to speak contemptuously or with ridicule: often followed by *at:* as, to *sneer* at religion: *v.t.* to utter in a scornful manner: *n.* contempt or scorn shown in speech or manner; a scornful or contemptuous smile.—*adv.* sneeringly.—*n.* sneerer.

sneeze (snēz), *n.* a sudden and brief spasm of the breathing organs, causing a violent and audible rush of air through the mouth and nostrils: *v.i.* to be seized with such a violent and brief spasm of the breathing organs.

snick-er (snĭk'ẽr), *n.* a half suppressed laugh; a giggle: *v.i.* to laugh slyly; giggle. Also, snigger.

sniff (snĭf), *v.i.* to draw in the breath audibly through the nose, often as an expression of contempt: *v.t.* to smell or scent; as, a dog will *sniff* an enemy; to *sniff* danger: *n.* the act of smelling; an audible, often scornful, drawing in of the breath through the nose.

snig-gle (snĭg'l), *v.i.* to fish for eels by pushing the baited hook into their hiding places.

snip (snĭp), *v.t.* [*p.t.* and *p.p.* snipped, *p.pr.* snipping], to cut into or clip off, as with scissors or shears; to nip: *n.* a single cut with scissors; a clip; colloquially, a small, unimportant person or thing.

snipe (snīp), *n.* a long-billed bird akin to the woodcock: usually found on the margin of water: *v.i.* and *v.t.* [*p.t.* and *p.p.* sniped, *p.pr.* sniping], to shoot from a safe position, especially to pick off individual soldiers of a hostile force.

snip-er (snī'pẽr), *n.* a person, often a soldier, who shoots from a safe position at individual men of a hostile force.

snip-py (snĭp'ĭ), *adj.* [*comp.* snippier, *superl.* snippiest], cut off short: colloquially, disagreeably self-assuming or conceited.—*adv.* snippily.—*n.* snippiness.

sniv-el (snĭv'l), *v.i.* to run at the nose; to cry or whine with running at the nose, as a child.—*n.* sniveler, sniveller.

snob (snŏb), *n.* a vulgar person who pretends to be better, richer, or more fashionable than he really is; one who respects position and wealth more than character.—*adj.* snobbish.—*n.* snobbery.

snob-bish-ness (snŏb'ĭsh-nĕs), *n.* vulgar show; false pride in one's own position or wealth; mean respect for wealth and position.

snood (snōōd), *n.* a little band for binding up the hair of a young woman; a short horsehair line to connect a fishing line with the hook.

snooze (snōōz), *v.i.* to take a nap; to doze: *n.* a nap. [Colloq.]

snore (snōr), *v.i.* to breathe audibly through the nose in sleep: *n.* a noisy breathing in sleep.

snort (snôrt), *v.i.* to force the air through the nose with a loud sound; to express feeling by such a sound; as, to *snort* with anger: *v.t.* to utter with such a sound: *n.* a loud, abrupt sound made through the nose.

snout (snout), *n.* the projecting nose of a beast, as of swine; the nozzle of a pipe, hose, etc.

snow (snō), *n.* frozen vapor in the form of white, feathery flakes, or crystals, falling through the air or lying upon the earth: *v.i.* to fall in frozen crystals: used impersonally; as, it *snows*: *v.t.* to pour out thickly, like falling snow; to obstruct or shut in with masses of snow: with *in* or *up*; as, the farm was *snowed* in for three days.

snow-bird (snō'bûrd"), *n.* a small American finch, common in time of heavy snow.

snow-blind (snō'blīnd"), *adj.* having the sight injured by the glare of snow in sunshine.

snow-bound (snō'bound"), *adj.* shut in or confined by masses of snow.

snow-drift (snō'drĭft"), *n.* a mass of snow heaped up by the wind.

snow-drop (snō'drŏp"), *n.* a plant with pretty white flowers, which blooms in very early spring.

snow-fall (snō'fôl"), *n.* the quantity of snow which falls during a given time or a single storm; a light snowstorm.

snow-flake (snō'flāk"), *n.* a white feathery crystal of frozen vapor.

snow line (snō līn), the lowest limit of perpetual snow; as, the *snow line* of a mountain.

snow-plow (snō'plou"), *n.* a machine or engine used to clear roads, tracks, etc., of heavy snow. Also, **snow-plough.**

snow-shed (snō'shĕd"), *n.* a roof or shelter to keep off snow, as from a railroad track in the mountains.

snow-shoe (snō'shōō"), *n.* a network of rawhide in a flat wooden frame, shaped like a short paddle, to be attached to the foot, to enable the wearer to walk on the top of the snow without sinking in.

snow-storm (snō'stôrm"), *n.* a heavy downfall of snow, usually with a strong wind.

snow-y (snō'ĭ), *adj.* [*comp.* snowier, *superl.* snowiest], white like fresh snow; as, *snowy* linen; covered with, or full of, snow; pure.—*adv.* **snowily.**—*n.* **snowiness.**

snub (snŭb), *v.t.* [*p.t.* and *p.p.* snubbed, *p.pr.* snubbing], to answer or interrupt with curt, rude, or scornful words; treat with scorn; ignore; slight intentionally: *n.* an intentional slight; a check.

snub-nosed (snŭb'nōzd"), *adj.* having a short, flat nose slightly turned up.

snuff (snŭf), *v.t.* to draw in through the nose; smell or scent; rid of the charred part of the wick; as, to *snuff* a candle: *v.i.* to snort or sniff: *n.* powdered tobacco to be inhaled through the nose; the burned part of the wick of a candle.

snuff-box (snŭf'bŏks"), *n.* a small, often ornamental, holder for snuff, or powdered tobacco.

snuff-er (snŭf'ẽr), *n.* one who snuffs: *pl.* a cutting instrument for removing the burned wick of a candle.

Candle Snuffers

snuf-fle (snŭf'l), *v.i.* to speak or breathe noisily through the nose when it is obstructed: *n.* a noisy breathing through the nose when it is obstructed; an affected nasal twang: *pl.* obstruction of the nostrils by mucus; colloquially, a cold in the head.

snuff-y (snŭf'ĭ), *adj.* soiled with snuff; of a dull brownish color.

snug (snŭg), *adj.* [*comp.* snugger, *superl.* snuggest], lying close and warm; compact and convenient; as, a *snug* house; sheltered; hidden; safe; cozy and comfortable: *v.i.* [*p.t.* and *p.p.* snugged, *p.pr.* snugging], to lie close and warm: with *up* or *together*.—*adv.* **snugly.**—*n.* **snugness.**

snug-ger-y (snŭg'ẽr-ĭ), *n.* [*pl.* snuggeries (-ĭz)], a warm, cosy place.

snug-gle (snŭg'l), *v.i.* to cuddle close for warmth and comfort: *v.t.* to hold close.

so (sō), *adv.* in a like manner or degree; as, she is not *so* tall as her sister; colloquially, very; in such a way, state, or amount as is indicated or known; as, he acted *so*; for this or that reason; therefore; more or less; as, get a dozen or *so*: *conj.* on condition that; if; therefore; as, it is raining, *so* we cannot go to town.

soak (sōk), *v.t.* to cause to absorb moisture; steep in a fluid; wet thoroughly; to draw in by the pores or openings; as, a sponge will *soak* up water: *v.i.* to become thoroughly wet; to be steeped in fluid; to enter by pores or small openings; as, water *soaks* into the earth.

soap (sōp), *n.* a substance for cleansing, made by mixing fats or oils with an alkali, such as potash or lye: *v.t.* to cover or wash with soap.

soap-bark (sōp'bärk"), *n.* a shrub with a bark of soapy quality; the bark of this shrub.

soap-stone (sōp'stōn"), *n.* a kind of soft mineral having a soapy or greasy feel.

soap-suds (sōp'sŭdz"), *n.pl.* water made frothy by mixture with soap.

soap-y (sōp'ĭ), *adj.* covered with, or like, soap; soft and smooth.—*n.* **soapiness.**

soar (sōr), *v.i.* to fly high in the air, as a bird; mount upwards with wings; rise high in thought or imagination: *n.* a lofty flight.

sob (sŏb), *v.i.* [*p.t.* and *p.p.* sobbed, *p.pr.* sobbing], to catch the breath convulsively; to weep with a convulsive heaving of the breast; to make a sound like a catch of the breath: *v.t.* to utter with a catch of the breath: *n.* a convulsive sigh; a sudden catching of the breath.

so-ber (sō'bẽr), *adj.* temperate by habit, especially in the use of intoxicating liquors; not under the influence of liquor; self-possessed; calm; steady; sedate; solemn; grave: *v.t.* and *v.i.* to recover from drunkenness; to make or become steady or calm.—*adv.* **soberly.**—*n.* **soberness.**

so-ber-mind-ed (sō'bẽr-mīn'dĕd), *adj.* grave and serious in disposition.

so-bri-e-ty (sō-brī'ē-tĭ), *n.* constant temperance; calmness; seriousness; gravity of manner.

so-bri-quet (sō'brē'kā'; sō'brĭ-kā), *n.* a nickname; a fanciful, or assumed name. [Fr.]

soc-age (sŏk'āj), *n.* a system of land holding in England in the Middle Ages by which the tenant paid a fixed amount of rent, or rendered a fixed amount of labor, and gave no military service to his lord.

so-called (sō'kōld'), *adj.* usually thus named, but not properly so.

soc-cer (sŏk'ẽr), *n.* a kind of football game.

so-cia-bil-i-ty (sō'shȧ-bĭl'ĭ-tĭ), *n.* the state or quality of being friendly and inclined to the company of others; disposition to associate and talk with others.

so-cia-ble (sō'shȧ-bl), *adj.* disposed to associate and talk with others; social; companionable; giving opportunity for friendly companionship; as, a *sociable* neighborhood: *n.* colloquially, in the United States, an informal party for friendly intercourse.—*adv.* **sociably.**—*n.* **sociableness.**

so-cial (sō'shăl), *adj.* pertaining to men as living in association with each other; relating to general conditions of human life; as, *social* welfare; *social* work; inclined to friendly relationship and conversation; as, a *social* disposition; pertaining to friendly association with others; as, she has fine *social* gifts; pertaining to the life of people of wealth and fashion; as, the *social* whirl; of plants, growing in groups; of insects, living in organized communities, as ants or bees.—*adv.* **socially.**

Syn. sociable, friendly, communicative.

Ant. (see unsocial).

so-cial-ism (sō'shăl-ĭzm), *n.* the economic doctrine that the welfare of society depends on government control of economic activities, and that economic opportunity should be equal for all; the political movement based on this doctrine; an organized system of government based on this doctrine.

so-cial-ist (sō'shăl-ĭst), *n.* one who believes in government control of industry and in equal economic opportunity for all.—*adj.* **socialistic.**

so-ci-al-i-ty (sō'shĭ-ăl'ĭ-tĭ), *n.* the state or quality of being inclined to friendly association with others.

so-cial-ize (sō'shăl-īz), *v.t.* to bring into friendly relations with others; to arouse to interest in the welfare of humanity in general; to put into control of a group rather than of an individual; as, to *socialize* a recitation; to organize, as a state, on the principle of government control of economic life.

so-ci-e-ty (sō-sī'ē-tĭ), *n.* [*pl.* societies (-tĭz)], an organized body of persons united by a common interest and purpose; people in general, considered as living in relationship with each other; as, to work for the uplift of *society;* companionship; people of culture and of good standing in any community: sometimes applied to people of wealth and fashion; as, all *society* was present at the wedding.

so-ci-o-log-i-cal (sō'shĭ-ō-lŏj'ĭ-kăl), *adj.* pertaining to, or like, the scientific study of human relationships and conditions.—*adv.* **sociologically.**

so-ci-ol-o-gist (sō'shĭ-ŏl'ō-jĭst), *n.* a student of the science of human relationships and conditions.

so-ci-ol-o-gy (sō'shĭ-ŏl'ō-jĭ), *n.* the science of human relationships and conditions; social science.

sock (sŏk), *n.* a light shoe worn by the ancient actors of comedy; a short-legged stocking.

sock-et (sŏk'ĕt), *n.* a hollow into which something is fitted; as, the socket of the eye.

So-crat-ic (sō-krăt'ĭk), *adj.* relating to Socrates, the Grecian philosopher, or to his method of teaching, or his belief.

sod (sŏd), *n.* that layer of the soil containing the roots of grass, etc.; turf; a piece of turf, usually cut square: *v.t.* [*p.t.* and *p.p.* sodded, *p.pr.* sodding], to cover with turf or pieces of turf.

so-da (sō'dȧ), *n.* a white substance formed of the alkali sodium in combination with carbonate, as *washing soda;* with bicarbonate, as *cooking soda;* or with hydrogen and oxygen, as *caustic soda* or sodium hydroxide.

so-dal-i-ty (sō-dăl'ĭ-tĭ), *n.* a brotherhood for religious or charitable purposes.

so-da wa-ter (sō'dȧ wô'tẽr), an effervescent solution of bicarbonate of soda with an acid; a popular drink composed of water charged with carbon dioxide gas and flavored.

sod-den (sŏd'n), *adj.* soaked; heavy with moisture; half cooked or baked, as cake; looking as if boiled or soaked; bloated.—*n.* **soddenness.**

so-di-um (sō'dĭ-ŭm), *n.* a waxy, white, alkaline metallic element, in nature always occurring in combination, as in common salt, alum, borax, etc.

so-fa (sō'fȧ), *n.* a long upholstered seat, usually having a back and arms.

soft (sŏft), *adj.* not hard; easily yielding to pressure; easily molded or shaped; as, *soft* wax; smooth to the touch; as, the *soft* fur of a cat; not glaring; as, a *soft* light; not loud; as, *soft* music; courteous; as, *soft* manners; mild or gentle; as, a *soft* answer; kind; as, *soft* treatment; having feelings easily moved; as, a *soft* heart; of the weather, moist or mild; colloquially, weak or foolish; colloquially, containing no alcohol; as, *soft* drinks: *adv.* softly; quietly: *interj.* gently! stop!—*adv.* **softly.**—*n.* **softness.**

Syn. meek, tender, susceptible, delicate.

soft-en (sŏf'n), *v.t.* and *v.i.* to make or become less hard, loud, glaring, etc.; tone down; make or become less rude, harsh, or severe; melt.

sog-gy (sŏg'ĭ), *adj.* [*comp.* soggier, *superl.* soggiest], soaked; wet; heavy with dampness.

soi-di-sant (swȧ'dē'zäṅ'), *adj.* self-styled; would-be; pretended. [Fr.]

soil (soil), *n.* the loose top layer of the earth's surface; land; the country; dirt or stain; manure: *v.t.* to make dirty; stain; as, to *soil* the hands; mar or sully: *v.i.* to become stained or dirty.

soi-rée (swȧ'rā'), *n.* an evening party, as a reception or ball. [Fr.]

so-journ (sō'jûrn; sō-jûrn'), *v.i.* to dwell for a time; to stay: *n.* a temporary dwelling place; a short stay.

Sol (sŏl), *n.* the sun: so called from the Roman god of the sun.

sol (sōl), *n.* the fifth note of the scale in music.

sol-ace (sŏl'ās), *n.* comfort in sorrow; lessening of pain or grief; consolation: *v.t.* to comfort in sorrow; to cheer: *v.i.* to be consoled or comforted.

so-lar (sō'lẽr), *adj.* pertaining to, measured by, or proceeding from, the sun; as, *solar* rays; *solar* light: **solar system**, the sun and the planets which circle around it: **solar year**, the period during which the earth makes one complete journey round the sun, or 365 days, 5 hours, 48 minutes, 52 seconds.

A, Solarium

so-la-ri-um (sō-lā'rĭ-ŭm), *n.* a sun parlor, usually for invalids or convalescents.

sold (sōld), past tense and past participle of the verb *sell*.

sold-er (sŏd'ẽr), *n.* a metal or metallic alloy used, when melted, to join metal surfaces, or to mend breaks in metal: *v.t.* to join with such an alloy; to patch.

sol-dier (sōl'jẽr), *n.* a man engaged in military service; a private as distinguished from a commissioned officer; a man of military experience: *v.i.* to serve in the army; colloquially (sō'jẽr), make a pretense of work.—*adj.* **soldierly.**

sol-dier-y (sōl'jẽr-ĭ), *n.* military forces collectively; an army or part of an army.

sole (sōl), *n.* the under side of the foot; the bottom of a boot, shoe, or slipper; any flat lower surface; a flat kind of fish: *v.t.* to furnish with a flat lower surface: *adj.* being or acting by oneself; only; single.—*adv.* **solely.**

sol-e-cism (sŏl'ē-sĭzm; sō'lē-sĭzm), *n.* a mistake in the use of words or in the structure of a sentence; a blunder in the use of forms peculiar to some special language; any rude or ridiculous breach of manners or taste.

sol-emn (sŏl'ĕm), *adj.* attended with sacred rites or ceremonies; as, a *solemn* feast-day; inspiring awe or fear; serious; devout; grave.—*adv.* **solemnly.**—*n.* **solemnness.**

so-lem-ni-ty (sō-lĕm'nĭ-tĭ), *n.* [*pl.* solemnities (-tĭz)], a sacred rite or ceremony; a formal and grave celebration; gravity; impressiveness; seriousness of manner or expression.

sol-em-ni-za-tion (sŏl"ĕm-nĭ-zā'shŭn), *n.* the act of performing according to ritual; as, the *solemnization* of a marriage.

sol-em-nize (sŏl'ĕm-nīz), *v.t.* to perform in a ceremonious or legally formal manner, or according to ritual.

sol-fa (sōl"fä'), *v.i.* [*p.t.* and *p.p.* sol-faed, *p.pr.* sol-faing], to sing the scale to the syllables *do, re, mi, fa*, etc.: *v.t.* to sing using these syllables.

so-lic-it (sō-lĭs'ĭt), *v.t.* to ask for with earnestness; as, to *solicit* a favor; entreat; invite or summon; endeavor to obtain; as, to *solicit* trade: *v.i.* to seek orders, support, votes, etc.

Syn. importune, urge.

so-lic-i-ta-tion (sō-lĭs"ĭ-tā'shŭn), *n.* earnest request; persistent asking; invitation.

so-lic-i-tor (sō-lĭs'ĭ-tẽr), *n.* one who seeks trade, votes, etc.; a person qualified and authorized to practice civil law; an attorney or lawyer; the civil law officer of a city, town, department, or government; as, the city *solicitor*.—*n.* **solicitorship.**

so-lic-it-ous (sō-lĭs'ĭ-tŭs), *adj.* eager; anxious; careful; concerned.—*adv.* **solicitously.**—*n.* **solicitousness.**

so-lic-i-tude (sō-lĭs'ĭ-tūd), *n.* the state of being anxious, especially regarding another person; concern; carefulness.

sol-id (sŏl'ĭd), *adj.* capable of withstanding pressure; opposite to *fluid;* compact; cubic; as, the *solid* contents of a mass; not hollow; dense; weighty; as, a *solid* argument; colloquially, continuous; as, a *solid* hour; unbroken; as, a *solid* line of defense; firm or reliable; as, a *solid* foundation: *n.* a body capable of resisting pressure; a substance not fluid; a body having length, breadth, and thickness.—*adv.* **solidly.**—*n.* **solidness.**

sol-i-dar-i-ty (sŏl"ĭ-dăr'ĭ-tĭ), *n.* a state of being united in opinion and effort; as, the *solidarity* of a nation; firmness; single-mindedness; as, *solidarity* of purpose.

so-lid-i-fi-ca-tion (sō-lĭd"ĭ-fĭ-kā'shŭn), *n.* the act of making hard or firm; the state of being hardened or made firm; the process of changing from a fluid to a solid state; a uniting or making compact.

so-lid-i-fy (sō-lĭd'ĭ-fī), *v.t.* and *v.i.* [*p.t.* and *p.p.* solidified, *p.pr.* solidifying], to make or become hard or firm; to change from a fluid to a solid state; to unite.

so-lid-i-ty (sō-lĭd'ĭ-tĭ), *n.* hardness; firmness; cubic contents of a body; volume; moral soundness.

sol-id shot (sŏl'ĭd shŏt), solid projectiles, used in guns and small-arms, which do not explode but wound by the force with which they strike a surface.

so-lil-o-quize (sō-lĭl'ō-kwīz), *v.i.* to talk to oneself; to think aloud in solitude.

so-lil-o-quy (sō-lĭl'ō-kwĭ), *n.* [*pl.* soliloquies (-kwĭz)], a discourse to oneself; an utterance in solitude of one's thoughts.

sol-i-taire (sŏl'ĭ-târ'), *n.* a game of cards played by one person; a precious stone set singly; as, her ring is a *solitaire;* a hermit.

sol-i-ta-ry (sŏl'ĭ-tā-rĭ), *adj.* living by oneself; lonely; single; done, passed, or suffered alone; as, *solitary* confinement; far removed; lonely; without inhabitants; as, the *solitary* desert; separate from others: *n.* a hermit.—*adv.* **solitarily.**—*n.* **solitariness.**

sol-i-tude (sŏl'ĭ-tūd), *n.* the state of being by oneself; loneliness; seclusion; a remote and lonely place.

so-lo (sō'lō), *n.* [*pl.* solos (-lōz)], the whole or part of a musical selection played or sung by one person.

so-lo-ist (sō'lō-ĭst), *n.* one who plays or sings a piece of music alone.

Sol-o-mon (sŏl'ō-mŭn), *n.* in the Bible, the son of David, who ruled Israel in the tenth century B. C., who was noted for his wisdom, and who built the first temple in Jerusalem.

sol-stice (sŏl'stĭs), *n.* that point in the sun's path at which the sun is farthest from the equator, north in summer, south in winter: **summer solstice**, June twenty-first or twenty-second, the longest day in the year: **winter solstice**, December twenty-first or twenty-second, the shortest day in the year.

sol-u-bil-i-ty (sŏl'ū-bĭl'ĭ-tĭ), *n.* capability of being dissolved in a fluid; as, the *solubility* of salt.

sol-u-ble (sŏl'ū-bl), *adj.* capable of being dissolved in a fluid; as, sugar is *soluble* in water; capable of being solved or explained; as a *soluble* problem; a *soluble* mystery.—*adv.* **solubly**.—*n.* **solubleness**.

so-lu-tion (sō-lū'shŭn), *n.* the division of a body into its component parts; a breaking up into parts; the state of being so divided; as, a substance in *solution;* the process of causing any substance to be absorbed into a liquid; also, the liquid which results from such a process; as, a salt *solution;* solving; explanation; as, the *solution* of a mystery; process of solving a problem or mystery; the answer to a problem.

solv-a-ble (sŏl'vȧ-bl), *adj.* capable of being dissolved; allowing explanation; capable of payment, as debts.—*n.* **solvability, solvableness**.

solve (sŏlv), *v.t.* to explain; reason out to a conclusion or result, as a problem; make clear, as a mystery.

sol-ven-cy (sŏl'vĕn-sĭ), *n.* capability of being dissolved; state of being able to pay just debts.

sol-vent (sŏl'vĕnt), *n.* any liquid in or by which a substance can be dissolved: *adj.* able to pay just claims or debts; having the power of dissolving.

som-ber (sŏm'bẽr), *adj.* dull; melancholy; dark; gloomy; as, *somber* thoughts. Also, **sombre**.—*adv.* **somberly, sombrely**.—*n.* **somberness, sombreness**.

som-bre-ro (sŏm-brā'rō), *n.* a kind of broad-brimmed hat, originally worn in Spain and in Spanish America, but now also in the southwestern United States.

some (sŭm), *adj.* a certain; as, *some* one whom I know; denoting a thing or person not definitely specified; as, *some* day I will come; more or less; as, she took *some* trouble: opposite to *other;* as, *some* people came, other people went: *pron.* one part, number, or amount, usually indefinite, in distinction from the rest; as, I will take *some*, but not all; any unspecified amount; as, give me *some* of your candy: opposite to *others;* as, *some* came, others went: *adv.* about; as, a distance of *some* four miles.

some-bod-y (sŭm'bŏd-ĭ), *n.* a person unknown or uncertain; a person of importance.

some-how (sŭm'hou'), *adv.* in one way or another; by means not yet decided upon.

som-er-sault (sŭm'ẽr-sôlt), *n.* an acrobatic feat in which one turns over by throwing the heels over the head. Also, **somerset**.

some-thing (sŭm'thĭng), *n.* a thing not definitely known, or not specified; a part or portion of greater or less size; an unknown amount or degree: *adv.* in an indefinite degree.

some-time (sŭm'tīm'), *adv.* at a past time unknown or not definitely stated; formerly; once; at a time not yet decided upon in the future: *adj.* former.

some-times (sŭm'tīmz'), *adv.* once in a while; now and then; on certain occasions.

some-what (sŭm'hwŏt'), *n.* an indefinite amount: *adv.* to an indefinite degree or extent; rather.

some-where (sŭm'hwâr'), *adv.* in one place or another; in a place not named or not known.

some-whith-er (sŭm'hwĭth'ẽr), *adv.* to some unknown place: to some place or other.

som-nam-bu-late (sŏm-năm'bū-lāt), *v.i.* to walk in one's sleep.—*n.* **somnambulation**.

som-nam-bu-lism (sŏm-năm'bū-lĭzm), *n.* a state in which a sleeping person walks, or otherwise acts, as if awake.

som-nam-bu-list (sŏm-năm'bū-lĭst), *n.* one who walks in his sleep; a sleepwalker.

som-nif-er-ous (sŏm-nĭf'ẽr-ŭs), *adj.* causing sleep.

som-no-lence (sŏm'nō-lĕns), *n.* sleepiness; drowsiness. Also, **somnolency**.

som-no-lent (sŏm'nō-lĕnt), *adj.* inclined to sleep; drowsy.

son (sŭn), *n.* a human male child; a boy or man spoken of in relation to his parent or parents; a male descendant; a native of a particular country; as, a *son* of England; a graduate of a certain college; as, *sons* of Harvard: **the Son, Jesus Christ, the Son of God**; the second person of the Trinity.

so-nant (sō'nănt), *adj.* of or pertaining to sound; having sound; vocal.

so-na-ta (sō-nä'tȧ), *n.* a musical composition in three or four related but varied movements, usually for one instrument, especially the piano.

song (sŏng), *n.* a rhythmic and tuneful musical sound uttered by the voice of a human being, bird, insect, etc.; a lyric or ballad; poetry; a poem which can be set to music; a musical composition to be rendered by the voice; a mere trifle; as, he sold it for a *song:* **Song of Solomon**, a poetical book of the Old Testament, consisting of a symbolic love poem: called also *Song of Songs*.

song-ster (sŏng'stẽr), *n.* [*fem.* **songstress**], one skilled in singing; a singing bird.

so-nif-er-ous (sō-nĭf'ẽr-ŭs), *adj.* producing, or carrying, sound.

son-in-law (sŭn'ĭn-lô'), *n.* [*pl.* **sons-in-law** (sŭnz-)], the husband of one's daughter.

son-net (sŏn'ĕt), *n.* a poem of fourteen lines, arranged according to one of several rime schemes.

son-net-eer (sŏn'ĕt-ẽr'), *n.* a composer of sonnets: *v.i.* to compose sonnets.

so-no-rous (sō-nō'rŭs), *adj.* giving sound when struck; resonant; giving a full or loud sound; deep-toned; as, a *sonorous* voice.—*adv.* **sonorously**.—*n.* **sonorousness**.

son-ship (sŭn'shĭp), *n.* the state or position of being a son.

soon (sōōn), *adv.* in a short time; quickly; in the near or immediate future; early; without delay; willingly; as, just as *soon* as not.

soot (sŏŏt; sōōt), *n.* the fine black powder, consisting chiefly of carbon, formed by burning substances and carried by the smoke from them.

soothe (sōōth), *v.t.* to make quiet or calm: to comfort or console; to make less painful; as, to *soothe* one's grief.

sooth-say-er (sōōth′sā′ẽr), *n.* one who claims to have power to foretell the future; a fortune teller.

soot-y (sŏŏt′ĭ; sōōt′ĭ), *adj.* [*comp.* sootier, *superl.* sootiest], pertaining to, causing, or covered with, the carbon from smoke; dusky; black.—*n.* sootiness.

sop (sŏp), *n.* anything steeped, dipped, or softened in a liquid, especially in broth; something given to calm or soothe the feelings: *v.t.* [*p.t.* and *p.p.* sopped, *p.pr.* sopping], to dip or soak in a liquid; to mop up.

soph-ism (sŏf′ĭzm), *n.* a plausible but unsound argument; any argument intended to make the worse appear the better cause.

Soph-ist (sŏf′ĭst), *n.* one of a body of philosophers and teachers in ancient Greece, famous for their clever, plausible, and unsound reasoning: **sophist,** one whose reasoning is clever but unsound.

so-phis-ti-cal (sō-fĭs′tĭ-kăl), *adj.* pertaining to, or like, an unsound reasoner or unsound reasoning; falsely clever; plausible but not sound; as, a *sophistical* argument. Also, **sophistic.**

so-phis-ti-cate (sō-fĭs′tĭ-kāt), *v.t.* to contrive with clever subtlety, as an argument; to deceive by false argument; to corrupt; to make knowing or worldly-wise.—*n.* sophistication.

soph-is-try (sŏf′ĭs-trĭ), *n.* [*pl.* sophistries (-trĭz)], plausible but unsound reasoning.

soph-o-more (sŏf′ō-mōr), *n.* a student in his second college year.

so-por (sō′pŏr), *n.* a deep sleep, occurring in illness, from which a patient is aroused with difficulty.

so-po-rif-ic (sō′pō-rĭf′ĭk), *adj.* causing, or tending to induce, sleep: *n.* a medicine, drug, plant, etc., that causes sleep.

sop-py (sŏp′ĭ), *adj.* soaked or saturated with a liquid; very wet.

so-pra-no (sō-prä′nō), *n.* [*pl.* sopranos (-nōz), soprani (-nē)], a woman's singing voice of high pitch; a singer with such a voice; a musical part intended for such a voice.

sor-cer-er (sôr′sẽr-ẽr), *n.* [*fem.* sorceress], a magician, wizard, or enchanter.

sor-cer-y (sôr′sẽr-ĭ), *n.* [*pl.* sorceries (-ĭz)], a foreseeing or foretelling of future events by the aid of evil spirits; witchcraft; magic; enchantment.

sor-did (sôr′dĭd), *adj.* mean; vile; base; as, a *sordid* purpose; without noble ideals; greedy of gain; miserly; as, a *sordid* wretch.—*adv.* sordidly.—*n.* sordidness.

sore (sōr), *adj.* tender or painful to the touch; inflamed; painful; sensitive; grieved; as, her heart was *sore;* severe; distressing; as, a *sore* disappointment; colloquially, resentful; as, he was *sore* at this unkind treatment: *adv.* grievously; severely; deeply: *n.* a painful or diseased spot in an animal body; ulcer; wound; a bruise or break in the skin; cause of annoyance.—*adv.* sorely.—*n.* soreness.

sor-ghum (sôr′gŭm), *n.* a canelike grass resembling broom corn, yielding sugar; molasses or sirup prepared from the juice of this grass.

so-ror-i-ty (sō-rŏr′ĭ-tĭ), *n.* a sisterhood; a women's or girls' club.

so-ro-sis (sō-rō′sĭs), *n.* a woman's club or association; a fleshy fruit, as a pineapple, growing from the union of many flowers.

sor-rel (sŏr′ĕl), *n.* a docklike plant; a reddish-brown color, or an animal of this color: *adj.* reddish-brown.

sor-row (sŏr′ō), *n.* mental pain or uneasiness caused by loss, regret, disappointment, etc.; grief; sadness; distress; unhappiness; affliction: *v.i.* to feel mental pain or uneasiness; grieve; lament; be sad.

sor-row-ful (sŏr′ō-fŏŏl), *adj.* full of, or showing, or causing, sadness or grief; unhappy; regretful; grievous.—*adv.* sorrowfully.—*n.* sorrowfulness.

sor-ry (sŏr′ĭ), *adj.* [*comp.* sorrier, *superl.* sorriest], feeling regret for loss, disappointment, etc.; pained; feeling pity; as, *sorry* for a cripple; repentant; as, *sorry* for sin; mournful; dismal; as, a *sorry* sight; mean; worthless; as, a *sorry* excuse.

Syn. grieved, poor, insignificant.

Ant. (see glad).

sort (sôrt), *n.* a kind or species; class, rank, or order; manner; nature: *v.t.* to separate and place in different divisions according to classes, kind, etc.; to classify: *v.i.* to join or associate; to agree.

sor-tie (sôr′tē), *n.* the issuing of a body of troops from a besieged place to attack the besiegers.

so-so (sō′sō′), *adj.* neither very good nor very bad; passable; tolerable.—*adv.* passably. Also, so-so. [Colloq.]

sot (sŏt), *n.* a person whose powers have become weakened by constant use of alcoholic liquors; a confirmed drunkard.

sot-tish (sŏt′ĭsh), *adj.* like a drunkard; stupid; drunken.—*adv.* sottishly.

sot-to vo-ce (sŏt′tō vō′chā), in an undertone, as if to oneself; with a moderate or low tone of voice. [It.]

sou (sōō), *n.* [*pl.* sous (sōōz; Fr. sōō)], an old French copper coin; the modern bronze five-centime piece, worth about one cent.

sou-brette (sōō-brĕt′), *n.* a theatrical term for an attractive, scheming lady's maid, or a lively young woman; the actress who plays such a part in a comedy.

souf-flé (sōō′flā′; sōō′flā), *adj.* beaten up light and puffy, as an omelet: *n.* a light, delicate baked dish of eggs, milk, cheese, etc., well beaten and baked. [Fr.]

sough (sŭf; sou), *n.* a hollow murmur or whistling, as of the wind: *v.i.* to murmur or sigh, as the wind.

sought (sôt), past tense and past participle of the verb *seek.*

soul (sōl), *n.* the spiritual and immortal part in man; the essential part of a person's identity; that part of man's nature where feelings, ideals, and morals center; the necessary or central part of anything; as, the *soul* of art; a person who leads and inspires; as, the *soul* of the company; any trait which indicates a noble nature, such as courage; a person; as, not a *soul* was there; a spirit separated from the body; as, the *souls* of the departed.

soul-ful (sōl′fŏŏl), *adj.* full of feeling; showing a noble nature.

soul-less (sōl′lĕs), *adj.* without a soul; lacking nobility of nature; spiritless; dull; mean.

sound (sound), *adj.* whole; as, safe and *sound;* entire; unbroken; as, a *sound* slumber; healthy; not decayed; as, a *sound* tooth; founded on truth or right; as, *sound* doctrine; morally good or honorable; firm; safe; strong; legal; valid; as, a *sound* title; laid on with force; as, a *sound* thrashing: *n.* the impression made on the ear by the vibrations of the air; noise; a straight, fairly wide passage of water; the air bladder of a fish; an instrument used by physicians for probing: *v.t.* to measure the depth of; cause to make a noise; order or announce by sound; as, to *sound* an alarm; play upon, as an instrument; examine or try; as, to *sound* one's opinions; probe: *v.i.* to make a noise or sound; be played upon, as an instrument; be spread or published audibly; to give a certain impression, when heard; as, her voice *sounds* sad.—*adv.* **soundly.**—*n.* **soundness, sounder.**

sound-ing (sound'ĭng), *n.* the act of measuring the depth of water; the result obtained by measuring the depth of water: *p.adj.* resounding; resonant or ringing.

sound-less (sound'lĕs), *adj.* silent; making no noise.

soup (sōōp), *n.* a liquid food made by boiling meat or vegetables, or both together, in water, with seasoning.

sour (sour), *adj.* having an acid or sharp, biting taste; turned or changed so as to become acid, rancid, or musty; disagreeable; cross: *v.t.* to cause to become acid; to turn; to make cross: *v.i.* become cross or disagreeable; to turn from sweet to acid.—*adv.* **sourly.**—*n.* **sourness.**

sour-crout (sour'krout"), *n.* cabbage cut fine and fermented in its own juice salted. Also, **sauerkraut.**

source (sōrs), *n.* that from which anything rises or originates; a spring or fountain; first cause; beginning.

souse (sous), *n.* brine, or salt pickle, for preserving food; anything soaked or preserved in pickle, especially pigs' feet; a drenching in water; a sudden swoop, as of a hawk: *v.t.* to steep in brine; plunge into water; attack with a sudden swoop: *v.i.* to make a sudden swoop.

south (south), *n.* that one of the principal points of the compass which is directly opposite the north; a region lying to the south of another: **the South**, the section of the United States lying below the southern boundary of Pennsylvania; the states that seceded in 1861: *adj.* lying in the direction of the point of the compass opposite the north; going to, or coming from, any point in that direction: *adv.* away from the north.—*adj.* and *adv.* **southerly, southward.**

south-east (south"ēst'), *n.* the point of the compass halfway between south and east; country lying in that direction: *adj.* lying in, going to, or coming from, the southeast: *adv.* to or from the southeast.—*adj.* **southeastern, southeasterly.**—*adv.* **southeasterly, southeastward.**

south-east-er (south"ēs'tẽr), *n.* a storm or gale coming from the southeast.

south-ern (sŭth'ẽrn), *adj.* pertaining to, situated in, or proceeding from or towards, the south.

south-ern-er (sŭth'ẽr-nẽr), *n.* a native of a southern land: **Southerner**, a native of the southern part of the United States; one of the Confederate army in the Civil War.

south-ern-most (sŭth'ẽrn-mōst), *adj.* lying farthest south.

south-west (south"wĕst'), *n.* the point of the compass halfway between south and west; country lying in that direction: *adj.* lying in, going to, or coming from, the southwest: *adv.* to or from the southwest.—*adj.* **southwestern, southwesterly.**—*adv.* **southwesterly, southwestward.**

south-west-er (south"wĕs'tẽr), *n.* a storm or gale from the southwest; a painted canvas or oilskin hat with a flap at the back, worn in bad weather by sailors and seafishers.

sou-ve-nir (sōō"vē-nẽr'; sōō'vē-nẽr), *n.* a thing by which to remember a person or event; a memento or keepsake.

sov-er-eign (sŏv'ẽr-ĭn; sŭv'ẽr-ĭn), *adj.* royal; supreme in power; possessing supreme dominion or authority; unrestricted; as, *sovereign* rights; effectual; as, a *sovereign* remedy: *n.* a ruler, as a king, emperor, or queen; a British gold coin equal to twenty shillings, or $4.8665: called also a *pound.*

sov-er-eign-ty (sŏv'ẽr-ĭn-tĭ; sŭv'ẽr-ĭn-tĭ), *n.* supreme power or dominion.

so-vi-et (sō-vĭ-ĕt'), *n.* a Russian unofficial political organization, or society, which came into great prominence after the revolution of 1917: any group of people, representing a trade, locality, etc., may form a soviet, which then may send delegates to a constituent assembly, and the soviet thus becomes the basis of a democratic or socialistic form of government. [Russ.]

sow (sou), *n.* the full-grown female of the swine species; feminine of *hog.*

sow (sō), *v.t.* [*p.t.* sowed, *p.p.* sown, *p.pr.* sowing], to strew, as seed, upon the earth; to plant by strewing; to scatter seed in, on, or over; as, to *sow* a field; to spread abroad; as, to *sow* discontent: *v.i.* to scatter seed for growth.—*n.* **sower.**

soy (soi), *n.* a kind of bean sauce used with fish in China and Japan.

spa (spä), *n.* a spring of mineral water; a resort or place containing such springs.

space (spās), *n.* that which has length, breadth, and height, and is unlimited in extension; the medium in which objects can exist and move; quality of unending extensiveness; room; distance between things; a length of time; a blank piece of type metal: *v.t.* in printing, to make distances between (lines or words) by separating them with thin pieces of type metal; to arrange with open places between.

spa-cious (spā'shŭs), *adj.* extending far and wide; roomy; as, a *spacious* house; great in expanse, as the *spacious* firmament.—*adv.* **spaciously.**—*n.* **spaciousness.**

spade (spād), *n.* a tool for digging, etc., consisting of a broad blade of iron with a handle; any tool of similar shape; one of a suit of cards having one or more figures resembling a spade: *v.t.* to dig or work with a spade.

spa-ghet-ti (spȧ-gĕt'ĭ), *n.* round dried sticks of flour paste, used, when cooked, for food; like macaroni, but solid and smaller. [It.]

spal-peen (spăl-pēn'; spăl'pēn), *n.* a scamp or rascal; an Irish term for a lazy and worthless fellow.

span (spăn), *n.* the distance from the end of the thumb to the tip of the little finger when extended; nine inches; a short space of time; an extent having two definite ends; horizontal distance between the two supports of an arch, or between any two supports of a bridge; a yoke of oxen; a pair of horses similar in color harnessed together: *v.t.* [*p.t.* and *p.p.* spanned, *p.pr.* spanning], to measure by the width of the extended fingers; to reach from one side to the other of.

span-gle (spăn'gl), *n.* a small disk, triangle, etc., of shining metallic substance; any glittering ornament, especially for a dress: *v.t.* to set or adorn with, or as with, small shining metal disks, or any bits of shining stuff; as, stars *spangle* the heavens.

Span-iard (spăn'yẽrd), *n.* a native or inhabitant of Spain.

span-iel (spăn'yĕl), *n.* a breed of dog with hanging ears and long, silky hair; a cringing, fawning person.

Spaniels

Span-ish (spăn'ĭsh), *adj.* pertaining to Spain, its language, or its people: *n.* the people or the language of Spain.

Span-ish fly (spăn'ĭsh flī), a bright green beetle of the southern part of Europe, used in making a medical preparation called *cantharides*.

Span-ish Main (spăn'ĭsh mān), the name originally applied to the northern coast of South America: later used of the southern part of the Caribbean Sea and the coasts of the West Indies.

spank (spănk), *v.t.* to strike or slap; to punish by striking the buttocks with the open hand: *n.* a slap.

spank-er (spănk'ẽr), *n.* one who, or that which, spanks; the after-sail of a ship.

spank-ing (spănk'ĭng), *adj.* moving with a quick, lively step; dashing; as, a *spanking* gray horse; fresh; brisk; as, a *spanking* breeze: *n.* a punishment given to a child, by striking him upon the buttocks with the open hand.

span-ner (spăn'ẽr), *n.* a wrench for tightening up or loosening the nuts on screws.

spar (spär), *n.* a mineral having a soft luster; a general name for a mast, yard, boom, etc.; a contest at boxing, or in words: *v.i.* [*p.t.* and *p.p.* sparred, *p.pr.* sparring], to box; contest in words.

spare (spâr), *v.t.* to use in a frugal or saving manner; use rarely; as, *spare* the rod; part with without inconvenience; refuse to punish; treat leniently; as, to *spare* the feelings: *v.i.* to live frugally or cheaply; forbear or forgive: *adj.* thin or lean; scanty; additional; held in reserve; as, a *spare* room; more than enough; as, *spare* cash.

spare-rib (spâr'rĭb'), *n.* ribs of pork having the meat closely trimmed.

spar-ing (spâr'ĭng), *p.adj.* frugal or saving; economical.—*adv.* **sparingly.**

spark (spärk), *n.* a tiny, burning particle thrown off by a body that is on fire; a bright, small flash of light; the first kindling of anything; as, the speech drew some *sparks* of enthusiasm; a small sign that indicates vitality; as, not a *spark* of life remained; a gay young fellow; a beau; *v.t.* and *v.i.* colloquially, to court or make love to.

spar-kle (spär'kl), *v.i.* to give off light in small flashes; glisten; flash; twinkle; gleam: *n.* a gleam of light; the quality of glistening or flashing.

spar-kling (spär'klĭng), *p.adj.* glittering; flashing; lively; brilliant in speech or manner.

spark plug (spärk plŭg), a device in an internal combustion engine, for igniting the charge, by means of an electric current.

spar-row (spăr'ō), *n.* a small gray and brown bird of the finch family, numerous in most parts of the world.

sparse (spärs), *adj.* thinly scattered; not dense or thick; few and thinly distributed; as, a *sparse* population; not abundant.—*adv.* **sparsely.**—*n.* **sparseness.**

Spar-ta-can (spär'tȧ-kăn), *adj.* denoting the most extreme group of radicals in Germany after the fall of the Hohenzollerns: so called from Spartacus, the gladiator who led the rebellion of slaves in Rome, 70 B. C.: *n.* a member of this group.

Spar-tan (spär'tăn), *adj.* pertaining to Sparta in ancient Greece, whose people were noted for their bravery and stern military discipline; hence, unflinching in courage and endurance.—*n.* **Spartanism.**

spasm (spăzm), *n.* a sudden, violent, involuntary contraction, or shortening, of the muscles; a sudden, violent effort or emotion that lasts but a short time; as, a *spasm* of anger.

spas-mod-ic (spăz-mŏd'ĭk), *adj.* pertaining to, or of the nature of, a spasm, or sudden, involuntary drawing up or shortening of muscles; convulsive; as a *spasmodic* cough; violent but short-lived; acting by fits and starts; as, *spasmodic* efforts. Also, **spasmodical, spasmatic.**—*adv.* **spasmodically.**

spat (spăt), *n.* the young of shellfish, especially the oyster; such young, collectively; a kind of short cloth gaiter; a soldier's legging, or spatterdash, reaching to the knee; colloquially, a slight blow with the open hand; a slap; a little quarrel: *v.i.* colloquially, to engage in a petty quarrel: *v.t.* colloquially, to slap.

spa-tial (spā'shăl), *adj.* of or pertaining to space.—*adv.* **spatially.**

spat-ter (spăt'ẽr), *v.t.* to splash a liquid upon; soil by splashing; as, to *spatter* a table cover with ink; to scatter in drops or by splashing; as, to *spatter* ink over a table cover; to injure by slander; as, to *spatter* a man's good name: *v.i.* to scatter or splash in drops: *n.* a small splash; sprinkling.

spat-ter-dash-es (spăt'ẽr-dăsh"ĕz), *n.pl.* leggings reaching to the knee, worn by soldiers as protection from mud.

spat-u-la (spăt'ū-lȧ), *n.* a broad, flat, thin knife for spreading plaster, paint, drugs, etc.—*adj.* **spatulate.**

spav-in (spăv'ĭn), *n.* a disease of horses, marked by a deposit of bony matter in the hock joint, near the knee, causing lameness.—*adj.* **spavined.**

spawn (spôn), *n.* the eggs of fishes, oysters, etc.; any offspring or product: *v.i.* to lay or produce eggs: used of fish, oysters, etc.; bring forth offspring: in contempt of human beings: *v.t.* to lay or produce (eggs or spawn), as fish; bring forth: in contempt.

speak (spēk), *v.i.* [*p.t.* spoke, *p.p.* spoken, *p.pr.* speaking], to utter words; as, to *speak* distinctly; talk; tell; mention; as, do not *speak* of this; make an address or speech; as, he *spoke* for an hour; convey ideas; as, our actions *speak* for us: *v.t.* to utter, as a word; pronounce; to tell in words; as, to *speak* the truth; to use, or be able to use, in conversation; as, he *speaks* four languages; to address; hail; as, ships *speak* each other in passing; cause to be known; show or reveal; as, his actions *speak* what he is.

speak-er (spēk'ẽr), *n.* one who utters words; one who delivers a speech or speeches in public; the presiding officer of the popular branch of a lawmaking body, as of Congress or a state legislature.

speak-ing (spēk'ĭng) *p. adj.* uttering speech; very expressive; vivid; lifelike; as, a *speaking* likeness: *n.* the act of uttering words; the making of addresses in public.—*adv.* **speakingly.**

spear (spēr), *n.* a weapon of war having a pointed iron or steel head at the end of a long shaft, and used for thrusting or throwing; a lance; an instrument with barbed prongs for catching fish; a shoot, as of grass: *v.t.* to pierce, or kill, with a long, pointed weapon: *v.i.* to shoot up into a long stem, as some plants.

spear grass (spēr grȧs), any one of various grasses, as the Kentucky blue grass; meadow grass.

spear-mint (spēr'mint"), *n.* a pungent, spicy herb similar to peppermint; the common garden mint.

spe-cial (spĕsh'ăl), *adj.* pertaining to, or forming, a species or sort; as, the *special* characteristics of man; designed for a particular purpose; as, a *special* course of study; hence, limited in range, extent, aim, or purpose; as, a *special* train; different from others; uncommon; particular; as, a *special* favor.—*adv.* **specially.**

Syn. individual, specific.

Ant. (see general).

spe-cial-ism (spĕsh'ăl-ĭzm), *n.* devotion to a particular and restricted line of study and work; as, medical *specialism.*

spe-cial-ist (spĕsh'ăl-ĭst), *n.* one who devotes himself to a particular branch of a profession, etc.; as, an eye *specialist.*

spe-ci-al-i-ty (spĕsh'ĭ-ăl'ĭ-tĭ), *n.* [*pl.* specialities (-tĭz)], the special or distinctive mark of a person or thing; as, the *speciality* of an author's style; an object possessing a distinctive quality that marks it off from others; as, the shop sold *specialities* of arts and crafts.

spe-cial-ize (spĕsh'ăl-īz), *v.t.* to apply to a particular use; as, *specialized* knowledge: *v.i.* to pursue a particular line of action or study; as, to *specialize* in science.—*n.* **specialization.**

spe-cial-ty (spĕsh'ăl-tĭ), *n.* [*pl.* specialties (-tĭz)], a study or work to which one is particularly devoted; as, his *specialty* is music; an article dealt in exclusively, or receiving particular attention; as, the *specialty* of the store was fruit; an article of particular character and use; as, we offer *specialties* in silver; a mark of particular or individual character of a person or thing; state or quality of being particular or individual.

spe-cie (spē'shĭ), *n.* coin; hard money, as of gold, silver, or copper.

spe-cies (spē'shēz; spē'shĭ-ēz), *n.* a group of animals or plants agreeing in common characteristics and called by a common name; a subdivision of a genus or class; kind; sort; variety.

spe-cif-ic (spē-sĭf'ĭk), *adj.* of or pertaining to a species, or group, of which the members have common characteristics and are called by a common name; definite or particular; precise; as, *specific* information; having some particular curing or healing quality; as, a *specific* medicine; peculiar; as, a *specific* form of a disease: *n.* a remedy for a particular disease; **specific duty,** a tax on goods, especially on imports, definitely fixed, and not calculated in proportion to the value of the goods: opposite to *ad valorem duty.* Also, *adj.* **specifical.**—*adv.* **specifically.**

spec-i-fi-ca-tion (spĕs'ĭ-fĭ-kā'shŭn), *n.* the act of particularizing, or naming in detail; a definite and full statement of particulars; as, the *specification* of a charge against an officer; one detail in such a statement: *pl.* a detailed statement of requirements for carrying out a contract; as, the *specifications* for a building.

spec-i-fy (spĕs'ĭ-fī), *v.t.* [*p.t.* and *p.p.* specified, *p.pr.* specifying], to mention or name particularly; state in full, so as to distinguish from other things; as, to *specify* the uses of a plant; to *specify* the contents of a trunk.

spec-i-men (spĕs'ĭ-mĕn), *n.* a sample; a part of something intended to show the quality, etc., of the whole; one of several things which represents all.

spe-cious (spē'shŭs), *adj.* appearing right at first sight but not really so; apparently, but not actually, fair, just, or right; as, a *specious* argument.—*adv.* **speciously.**—*n.* **speciousness.**

speck (spĕk), *n.* a spot; flaw; blemish; spot of decay, as in fruit; a very small thing; particle: *v.t.* to spot, or stain with small spots; speckle.

speck-le (spĕk'l), *n.* a small spot in anything, different in substance or color from the thing itself: *v.t.* to mark with spots of a color different from that of the thing itself.

spec-ta-cle (spĕk'tȧ-kl), *n.* something displayed to view, especially something unusual or worthy of notice; a pageant or parade; a grand exhibition: *pl.* a device for assisting the sight, consisting of two lenses mounted in a frame, with a bridge to fit over the nose and bows to pass over the ears.

spec-tac-u-lar (spĕk-tăk'ū-lȧr), *adj.* pertaining to a show or exhibition; marked by grand display; designed to excite wonder or admiration by scenic or dramatic effect; imposing.—*adv.* **spectacularly.**

spec-ta-tor (spĕk-tā'tẽr), *n.* one who looks on; a beholder.

spec-ter (spĕk'tẽr), *n.* a ghost or apparition. Also, **spectre.**

spec-tral (spĕk'trăl), *adj.* pertaining to, or like, a ghost; ghostly; produced by dividing a ray of light into its several colors; as, *spectral* tints; pertaining to a ray of light so divided; as, *spectral* analysis.—*adv.* **spectrally.**

spec-tro-scope (spĕk'trō-skōp), *n.* an optical instrument for dividing light into the rays of which it is composed, and for examining the image so produced.—*adj.* **spectroscopic, spectroscopical.**—*adv.* **spectroscopically.**

spec-tros-co-py (spĕk-trŏs'kō-pĭ; spĕk'-trō-skō"pĭ), *n.* the science of examining rays of light by means of an instrument called a spectroscope.

spec-trum (spĕk'trŭm), *n.* [*pl.* spectra (-trȧ)], an image formed by the dividing of a ray of light into parts arranged according to their different wavelengths, as in the rainbow or in the passing of light through a prism.

spec-u-lar (spĕk'ū-lȧr), *adj.* of or pertaining to a mirror or reflector.

spec-u-late (spĕk'ū-lāt), *v.i.* to consider a subject on all sides;

meditate upon a topic and form opinions upon it; purchase stock, land, goods, etc., at a risk, with the idea of selling them at a higher market value; to gamble in stocks, etc.—*n.* speculator.

spec-u-la-tion (spĕk″ū-lā′shŭn), *n.* mental examination or theorizing; reflective, inquiring consideration; the purchase of stock, goods, etc., at a risk, for future sale at a profit; any hazardous business venture, with a chance for large profits.

spec-u-la-tive (spĕk′ū-lā-tĭv), *adj.* pertaining to, or given to, contemplation, reflection, or theorizing.—*adv.* **speculatively.**—*n.* **speculativeness.**

spec-u-lum (spĕk′ū-lŭm), *n.* [*pl.* specula (-lȧ)], a mirror or reflector of polished metal, especially one used in an optical instrument; a surgical instrument used to examine certain passages of the body by expanding them and throwing light by reflection within them: **speculum metal,** an alloy of copper and tin, used for making reflectors in reflecting telescopes.

sped (spĕd), the past tense and past participle of the verb *speed.*

speech (spēch), *n.* the power of uttering articulate sounds or words; expression of thought in words; act of speaking; manner of speaking; as, his *speech* is indistinct; that which is spoken; conversation; a language or dialect; as, Italian is a musical *speech;* formal discourse in public, or the published report of it; as, to make a *speech;* oration.

Syn. *n.* talk, address, utterance.

Ant. (see silence).

speech-less (spēch′lĕs), *adj.* being without the power to speak; dumb; silent; not expressed in words; as, a *speechless* entreaty.—*adv.* **speechlessly.**—*n.* **speechlessness.**

speed (spēd), *n.* the act or state of moving rapidly; rate of motion, or velocity; swiftness; quickness; good fortune; as, he wished her good *speed:* *v.t.* [*p.t.* and *p.p.* sped, *p.pr.* speeding], to prosper; to make haste; move quickly; as, the bullet *sped* through the air: *v.t.* to prosper; send away with good wishes; as, to *speed* the parting guest; aid; as, God *speed* you on your way; to cause to move faster.

speed-ing (spēd′ĭng), *n.* the act of driving a motor vehicle at a greater speed than that permitted by law.

speed-om-e-ter (spēd-ŏm′ē-tẽr), *n.* an instrument for indicating speed, as, commonly in an automobile, miles per hour.

speed-way (spēd′wā″), *n.* a track or course where fast driving or racing, as of horses or automobiles, is permitted.

speed-y (spēd′ĭ), *adj.* [*comp.* speedier, *superl.* speediest], not slow; swift; prompt; quick; hasty.—*adv.* **speedily.**—*n.* **speediness.**

speiss (spīs), *n.* a poisonous, metallic chemical compound formed in the smelting of certain ores.

spell (spĕl), *n.* a charm; a spoken word or words supposed to act as a charm; fascination; a turn at work; as, a *spell* at the oars; time during which a person works; colloquially, any short period of time; as, mother visited us for a *spell;* a certain time marked by a definite characteristic; as, the hot *spell:* *v.i.* [*p.t.* and *p.p.* spelled (spĕld), or spelt; *p.pr.* spelling], to form words with letters, especially with the correct letters, either orally or in writing; as, he *spells* accurately: *v.t.* to write, repeat, or point out in order the proper letters of (a word); to make out with difficulty; as, to *spell* out a cipher; to indicate or mean; as, war *spells* hardship.

spell-bind (spĕl′bīnd″), *v.t.* [*p.t.* and *p.p.* spellbound, *p.pr.* spellbinding], to hold as by a spell; fascinate; especially, to interest others intensely by an oration.—*adj.* **spellbound.**—*n.* **spellbinder.**

spel-ler (spĕl′ẽr), *n.* one who spells; one apt in spelling; a book containing exercises and drills for training pupils in correct spelling.

spell-ing (spĕl′ĭng), *n.* the act or art of forming words by letters; orthography; the way in which a word is spelled; colloquially, a lesson or exercise in spelling: **spelling book,** a book containing exercises for training students to spell.

spelt (spĕlt), *p.t.* and *p.p.* of the verb *spell:* *n.* a kind of wheat.

spel-ter (spĕl′tẽr), *n.* zinc: used in commercial parlance only.

spen-cer (spĕn′sẽr), *n.* a kind of short jacket for women.

spend (spĕnd), *v.t.* [*p.t.* and *p.p.* spent, *p.pr.* spending], to lay out, as money; expend; squander; to exhaust by using; as, his violence soon *spent* itself; consume; to pass; as, to *spend* time: *v.i.* to incur expense; as, he *spends* unwisely; to waste away.

spend-thrift (spĕnd′thrĭft″), *adj.* wasteful; extravagant: *n.* one who spends foolishly or wastefully.

spent (spĕnt), *adj.* exhausted; worn out; without energy or force; as, *spent* steam: **spent ball,** a projectile which exhausts its force before striking, so that it neither passes through its object nor explodes.

sperm (spûrm), *n.* the fecundating or fertilizing fluid of male animals, which enables them to reproduce their kind: called also *semen;* a white, waxy solid, spermaceti, or an oil (sperm oil), found in the head of the sperm whale.

sper-ma-ce-ti (spûr′mȧ-sē″tĭ; spûr′mȧ-sĕt″ĭ), *n.* a white, waxy substance obtained from the head of the sperm whale, and used in making candles, etc.

sper-mat-ic (spẽr-măt′ĭk), *adj.* pertaining to, or containing, the fluid in male animals which enables them to reproduce their kind.

sperm whale (spûrm hwāl), a large whale found in warm seas, whose head yields sperm oil and a waxlike substance (spermaceti), used in making candles, etc.

spew (spū), *v.t.* and *v.i.* to vomit; cast forth; eject.

sphe-noid (sfē′noid), *adj.* wedge-shaped; as, a *sphenoid* crystal; pertaining to a certain wedge-shaped bone at the base of the skull.

Sphere

sphere (sfēr), *n.* a solid body bounded by a single surface, whose every point is equally distant from a point within called its center; the surface of such a solid; a globe or globelike body; a ball; the shape or extent of the heavens; a planet; extent or range of knowledge, influence, action, etc.; as, to seek a wider *sphere* for one's abilities; province; place of existence; social position.—*adj.* **spheral.**

spher-i-cal (sfĕr'ĭ-kăl), *adj.* pertaining to a sphere, or globe; globular or like a globe; round. Also, **spheric.**—*adv.* **spherically.**

sphe-ric-i-ty (sfē-rĭs'ĭ-tĭ), *n.* the state or fact of being a sphere, or globe; roundness.

sphe-roid (sfē'roid), *n.* a body having nearly the shape of a sphere, or globe; as, the earth is an oblate *spheroid.* —*adj.* **spheroidal.**

spher-ule (sfĕr'ōōl), *n.* a little sphere; a globule.

sphinc-ter (sfĭnk'tẽr), *n.* a muscle that surrounds an opening in the body, and can contract in order to close it.

sphinx (sfĭnks; *n.* [*pl.* sphinxes (-ĕz)], in Greek mythology, a winged monster having the head and bust of a woman and the body of a lioness, who proposed a riddle to passers-by, and destroyed them when they failed to guess it; a monument representing this creature, especially the famous one near Cairo, Egypt; a symbol of silence and mystery; one whose motives, intentions, opinions, etc., are not easily guessed.

Sphinx

spi-cate (spī'kāt), *adj.* having, or arranged in the form of, a spike or ear. Also, **spicated.**

spice (spīs), *n.* any of certain aromatic vegetable substances, sometimes ground or powdered, used for seasoning, as cinnamon, nutmeg, pepper; a relish; that which gives flavor or zest; as, a *spice* of mischief: *v.t.* to season or flavor, as with condiments or spice.

spick-and-span (spĭk'ănd-spăn'), *adj.* new; fresh; without blemish.

spic-ule (spĭk'ūl), *n.* a slender, sharp-pointed body.—*adj.* **spicular.**

spic-y (spīs'ĭ), *adj.* [*comp.* spicier, *superl.* spiciest], flavored with, containing, or having the qualities of, spice; fragrant; aromatic; full of life and point; as, a *spicy* discussion.—*adv.* **spicily.**—*n.* **spiciness.**

spi-der (spī'dẽr), *n.* an arachnid that spins webs of silken fibers to catch its prey; anything suggestive of a spider in form; a kind of frying pan.

spied (spīd), past tense and past participle of the verb *spy.*

spig-ot (spĭg'ŭt), *n.* a pointed piece of wood used to stop the opening in a cask; the plug of a faucet or cock; sometimes, the faucet or cock itself.

spike (spīk), *n.* a kind of large nail; any sharp, slender object; as, the *spikes* in a fence; anything like a spike, as, in botany, a certain kind of flower cluster; an ear of grain: *v.t.* to fasten or equip with large nails or sharp points; to run through with a sharp point; to close the mouth of by plugging: said of cannon.—*adj.* **spiky.**

spike-let (spīk'lĕt), *n.* in botany, a very slender, pointed, small flower cluster, as in grasses.

spike-nard (spīk'nẽrd), *n.* a fragrant oil or ointment used by the ancients.

spile (spīl), *n.* a large timber driven into the ground to give support to a building; a pile; a wooden pin used as a spigot; a spout driven into a sugar-maple tree to drain off the sap: *v.t.* to provide with a spigot; to drive piles into; to set up supporting timbers under.

spill (spĭl), *n.* a slender piece of anything, as a wooden pin, a small metal rod, etc.; a thin strip of paper or wood used for lighting a lamp, etc.; the act or state of overflowing, scattering, falling out, or running over; that which has overflowed or scattered, etc.: *v.t.* [*p.t.* and *p.p.* spilled, spilt, *p.pr.* spilling], to cause or permit to run over or fall out of a vessel; to cause to be scattered, wasted, lost, etc., through such action; to cause to pour forth, as blood: *v.i.* to run over, fall out, be scattered, etc.

spin (spĭn), *v.t.* [*p.t.* and *p.p.* spun, *p.pr.* spinning], to draw out and twist into threads; as, to *spin* cotton; draw out tediously; as, to *spin* a long story; form (a web or cocoon) by drawing out the threads of from a gland; cause to whirl rapidly, as a top; to make pass slowly by delays, as time: *v.i.* to draw out and twist fiber into threads, etc.; whirl; colloquially, move swiftly; as, to *spin* along the road on a bicycle; to make and expel a thread, as a spider: *n.* the act of drawing and twisting fiber into threads; the act of whirling; the state of being whirled; the making of threads, as by a spider.

spin-ach (spĭn'āj; spĭn'ĕch), *n.* a common potherb used as a vegetable. Also, **spinage.**

spi-nal (spī'năl), *adj.* pertaining to the backbone; as, *spinal* disease.

spin-dle (spĭn'dl), *n.* in a spinning wheel or machine, the long, thin rod used for twisting and winding the thread; in spinning by hand, a round stick tapering at each end, on which the thread is twisted and held; a slender rod or pin on which anything turns: *v.i.* to grow or shoot out into long, slim stalks.

spin-dle-leg-ged (spĭn'dl-lĕg"ĕd; spĭn'dl-lĕgd"), *adj.* having long, slender legs; as, a *spindle-legged* table.

spin-dle-shanks (spĭn'dl-shănks"), *n.* regarded as *singular,* a tall person with long, thin legs; regarded as *plural,* long, thin legs.—*adj.* **spindle-shanked.**

spin-dling (spĭn'dlĭng), *adj.* long and thin; especially, too thin in proportion to height.

spin-drift (spĭn'drĭft), *n.* foam or spray blown in from a stormy sea; spoondrift.

spine (spīn), *n.* the backbone; something like the backbone; a thorn-shaped or pointed stiff growth on a plant or animal.

spin-el (spĭn'ĕl; spĭ-nĕl'), *n.* a hard mineral occurring in several different colors.

spine-less (spīn'lĕs), *adj.* having no backbone; invertebrate; without courage; without the will to resist; without spines; as, the *spineless* cactus.

spin-et (spĭn'ĕt; spĭ-nĕt'), *n.* a keyed instrument like the harpsichord, but smaller: now no longer in use; an early form of piano.

spin-na-ker (spĭn'ȧ-kẽr), *n.* a large sail, triangular in shape, used when the vessel is running before the wind.

spin-ner-et (spĭn'ẽr-ĕt), *n.* an organ that spins silk, as in silkworms, or that produces the silk for the web, as in spiders.

spin-ney (spĭn'ĭ), *n.* a thicket; a small wood. [ENG.]

spin-ning jen-ny (spĭn'ĭng jĕn'ĭ), a machine having several spindles, so as to spin a number of threads at a time: named for the wife of the inventor.

spin-ning wheel (spĭn'ĭng hwēl), a machine with one wheel and one spindle, operated by hand and foot power, by which raw cotton, wool, etc., are spun into thread or yarn.

spi-nous (spī'nŭs), *adj.* full of, or covered with, sharp, pointed thorns or quills, as the porcupine; thorny. Also, **spinose.**

spin-ster (spĭn'stẽr), *n.* an unmarried woman, usually one no longer young and fair.

spin-y (spīn'ĭ), *adj.* full of, or covered with, thorny spines; thorny.

spin-y ant-eat-er (sp'n'ĭ ănt'ēt'ẽr), an egg-laying mammal of Australia, having a wormlike tongue, a tubular snout, and strong spines mixed with fur: a porcupinelike ant-eater.

Spiny Ant-eater

spir-a-cle (spĭr'-ȧ-kl), *n.* a hole through which many aquatic mammals, including whales, porpoises, etc., breathe.

spi-ræ-a (spī-rē'ȧ), *n.* any of several shrubs of the rose family, both cultivated and wild. Also, **spirea.**

spi-ral (spī'răl), *adj.* winding around a center and gradually receding from it; winding and going forward, like the thread of a screw; winding in a cone: *n.* a curve or curved line moving continually from or toward the center about which it revolves.

spi-rant (sp.'rănt), *n.* a consonant the sound of which may be continued by expelling the breath, as *f, s, sh, v.*

spire (spīr), *n.* a slender stalk or blade, as of grass; a body that tapers to a point; as, a church *spire;* steeple; pinnacle; a spiral, or single turn of a spiral; a twist: *v.i.* to shoot forth or point up, in, or as in, a spiral.

spir-it (spĭr'ĭt), *n.* the soul; immortal, nonphysical part of man; any supernatural being, as a ghost or fairy; a person, considered with reference to qualities of mind or temper; as, a noble *spirit;* courage, energy, and liveliness; as, the troops advanced with *spirit;* power of mind, moral or intellectual; as, "the *spirit* is willing"; condition of mind, temper, or disposition; as, the *spirit* of the army was loyal; enthusiasm for an object; as, school *spirit;* real meaning; as, the tone of the words contradicted their *spirit;* a strong distilled alcoholic liquor, as whisky, etc.; a solution in alcohol of certain drugs; as, *spirit* of ammonia; alcohol: *pl.* intoxicants, as brandy, etc.; liveliness; natural liveliness; as, high *spirits: v.t.* to carry away suddenly or secretly: often with *off* or *away:* **Spirit,** the third person of the Trinity; the Holy Spirit.

spir-it-ed (spĭr'ĭt-ĕd), *adj.* full of vigor or life; animated; lively; as, a *spirited* horse; courageous; showing a lofty temper; as, a *spirited* answer.—*adv.* **spiritedly.**—*n.* **spiritedness.**

spir-it-less (spĭr'ĭt-lĕs), *adj.* without vigor or animation; as, a *spiritless* address, or speaker; listless; dejected.—*adv.* **spiritlessly.**

spir-it rap-ping (spĭr'ĭt răp'ĭng), a supposed communication with the dead by means of rapping.

spir-it-u-al (spĭr'ĭt-ū-ăl), *adj.* not material; of or pertaining to the mind or soul, as distinguished from matter; opposite to *physical;* pertaining to the soul or higher nature of man; pure; holy; heavenly minded; pertaining to sacred or religious things; not lay or temporal; ecclesiastical.—*adv.* **spiritually.**

spir-it-u-al-ism (spĭr'ĭt-ū-ăl-ĭzm), *n.* the belief that nothing is real except soul, or spirit; the belief that the souls of the dead communicate with the living, especially through a sensitive person called a medium; the practice of such belief. Also, **spiritism.**

spir-it-u-al-ist (spĭr'ĭt-ū-ăl-ĭst), *n.* one who believes that the souls of the dead communicate with the living, especially through a medium.

spir-it-u-al-is-tic (spĭr"ĭt-ū-ăl-ĭs'tĭk), *adj.* of or pertaining to spiritualism, or the belief that the souls of the dead communicate with the living, especially through a medium.

spir-it-u-al-i-ty (spĭr"ĭt-ū-ăl'ĭ-tĭ), *n.* the state or quality of being neither physical nor material; soul as apart from matter; unworldliness; elevation of mind; the quality that springs from mental elevation; as, the *spirituality* of an author, or of a book; that which belongs to the church or to religion; as, the *spirituality* of a religion.

spir-it-u-al-ize (spĭr'ĭt-ū-ăl-īz), *v.t.* to free from the corrupting influence of the world; to take away material being from; to make lofty and pure in mind or soul; to animate; give a pure or religious meaning to.—*n.* **spiritualization.**

spi-ri-tu-el (spē'rē'tü"ĕl'), *adj.* [*fem.* spirituelle], having the higher and finer qualities of mind; having the appearance of grace, delicacy, etc.; refined; pure. [Fr.]

spir-it-u-ous (spĭr'ĭt-ū-ŭs), *adj.* containing, or of the nature of, alcohol; intoxicating; as, *spirituous* liquors.

spi-rom-e-ter (spī-rŏm'ē-tẽr), *n.* an instrument for measuring the capacity of the lungs in breathing.

spirt (spûrt), *n.* a sudden jet or gush of liquid; a sudden outbreak or effort: *v.i.* to gush forth in a sudden jet; to make a sudden, brief, extreme effort: *v.t.* to force out in a jet; squirt. Also, **spurt.**

spit (spĭt), *n.* a long, pointed rod on which meat is roasted; a small point of land or a long narrow shoal running into the sea; saliva; the act of ejecting saliva: *v.t.* [*p.t.* and *p.p.* spitted, *p.pr.* spitting], to push a pointed rod through; impale: [*p.t.* spit or spat], to eject from the mouth; hence, to eject or throw out from an opening; send forth in drops or flakes, as rain or snow: *v.i.* to throw out saliva from the mouth; come forth in drops or flakes, as rain or snow.

spite (spīt), *n.* ill will or hatred toward another, with the desire to irritate, annoy, or injure; petty malice; grudge: **in spite of, or spite of,** formerly, in contempt of; now, notwithstanding: *v.t.* to try to injure or baffle; annoy; thwart.

spite-ful (spīt'fo͝ol), *adj.* full of ill will; malicious; having a desire to annoy or injure.—*adv.* **spitefully.**—*n.* **spitefulness.**

spit-fire (spĭt'fīr"), *n.* a very quick-tempered person. [Colloq.]

spit-tle (spĭt'l), *n.* saliva, especially as ejected from the mouth; spit.

spit-toon (spĭ-to͞on'), *n.* a vessel for spittle, or spit; a cuspidor.

spitz dog (spĭts dŏg), a variety of Pomeranian dog, usually white, with a sharp muzzle, long, silky hair, and bushy tail.

splash (splăsh), *v.t.* to spatter or dash about; as, to *splash* water; to spatter or soil, with water, mud, etc.; as, the automobile *splashed* her dress: *v.i.* to dash or spatter about in drops; to fall or proceed with a dash or splatter; as, to *splash* into, or through, a puddle: *n.* a spot or daub made by a liquid thrown upon anything; a noise as from water dashed up, or by anything striking in or upon a liquid.—*adj.* **splashy.**—*n.* **splasher.**

splat-ter (splăt'ẽr), *v.t.* and *v.i.* to splash or spatter about; make a slight splashing sound.

splay (splā), *v.t.* [*p.t.* and *p.p.* splayed, *p.pr.* splaying], to dislocate, or throw out of joint, as the shoulder bone of a horse; to slope or slant, as a window opening: *n.* a sloped surface: *adj.* spread out; broad and flat; hence, clumsy: **splay foot,** unnatural flatness and turning out of the foot; a foot so deformed.

spleen (splēn), *n.* a glandlike organ near the stomach, supposed by the ancients to be the seat of anger, melancholy, or vexation; hence, ill-temper, melancholy, or spite.

splen-did (splĕn'dĭd), *adj.* magnificent; gorgeous; as, a *splendid* spectacle; very bright; brilliant; lustrous; as, *splendid* diamonds; heroic; grand; glorious; as, a *splendid* triumph; colloquially, very good; excellent; as, a *splendid* opportunity.—*adv.* **splendidly.**

splen-dor (splĕn'dẽr), *n.* great brightness; richness; magnificence; pomp. Also, **splendour.**

sple-net-ic (splē-nĕt'ĭk; splĕn'ē-tĭk), *adj.* fretful; peevish; melancholy.

splen-ic (splĕn'ĭk; splē'nĭk), *adj.* pertaining to the spleen, a glandlike organ near the stomach; as, the *splenic* artery.

splice (splīs), *v.t.* to unite without knots, as two ropes, by interweaving or joining the ends of; connect, as pieces of wood or metal, by overlapping parts and making them fast together: *n.* the union of ropes, etc., by interweaving or joining without knots.

splint (splĭnt), *n.* a small piece split off; a splinter; a thin piece of wood to keep a broken bone, etc., in position; a splint bone; a disease affecting the shankbone of a horse; a thin strip of wood for weaving baskets, etc.

splint bone (splĭnt bōn), in the leg of the horse and similar animals, one of the small, slender bones on either side of the cannon bone, or bone just above the fetlock.

splint coal (splĭnt kōl), a variety of coal with a slaty structure.

splin-ter (splĭn'tẽr), *n.* a thin piece of wood, etc., split or torn off lengthwise; fragment: *v.t.* to split or tear into long thin pieces; sliver: *v.i.* to be torn into slivers or fragments.—*adj.* **splintery.**

split (splĭt), *v.t.* [*p.t.* and *p.p.* split, *p.pr.* splitting], to divide lengthwise; rend or tear apart violently; to divide or break up into parts or sides, as a political party; divide between candidates; as, to *split* a ticket: *v.i.* to burst; to break apart; to divide lengthwise, or with the grain; to separate into parties or factions: *n.* a rent or crack; division or separation, as in a political party; rupture; a splint for weaving.

splotch (splŏch), *n.* a stain; daub; blotch; spot.—*adj.* **splotchy.**

splurge (splûrj), *n.* a showy display; a conceited personal demonstration: *v.i.* to show off offensively; to make a great display in any way. [COLLOQ.]

splut-ter (splŭt'ẽr), *v.t.* to utter hastily and confusedly: *v.i.* to speak or act hastily and confusedly: *n.* a confused noise; stir; bustle. [COLLOQ.]

spoil (spoil), *v.t.* [*p.t.* and *p.p.* spoiled, spoilt, *p.pr.* spoiling], to take away by force; plunder; corrupt; ruin; destroy; colloquially, to overindulge with harmful effects on character; as, to *spoil* a child: *v.i.* to practice plunder or robbery; to become corrupted; decay: *n.* that which is taken from another by force; pillage; plunder; booty.—*n.* **spoiler.**

spoils sys-tem (spoilz sĭs'tĕm), in the United States, the distribution of public official positions among the members of the party that has won at an election.

spoke (spōk), *p.t.* of *speak*: *n.* one of the bars of a wheel connecting the nave, or center, with the felly, or rim; a round of a ladder; a bar to keep a wheel from turning.

spo-ken (spō'kn), *p.p.* of *speak*: *adj.* uttered in speech; oral.

spoke-shave (spōk'shāv'), *n.* a kind of double-handled plane for dressing the spokes of wheels and other curved work.

spokes-man (spōks'măn), *n.* one who speaks for another; an agent or representative.

spo-li-ate (spō'lĭ-āt), *v.t.* to rob; to plunder; despoil.—*n.* **spoliator.**

spo-li-a-tion (spō'lĭ-ā'shŭn), *n.* the act of plundering or robbing, especially in time of war; injury done to a document.

spon-da-ic (spŏn-dā'ĭk), *adj.* pertaining to a spondee, or a poetic foot of two long syllables, both of which are accented.

spon-dee (spŏn'dē), *n.* a poetic foot of two syllables, both of which are accented.

sponge (spŭnj), *n.* the porous, elastic skeleton of certain salt-water animals; the animal producing it; any substance resembling sponge, as raised dough; a mop for cleansing a gun after its discharge; one who, or that which, sucks in anything as a sponge does water; hence, a parasite, or one who lives upon others: *v.i.* to suck in like a sponge; live upon others: *v.t.* to cleanse, wipe out, or dampen, with a sponge; obtain by mean methods without cost.—*n.* **sponger.**

Sponges. A, common; B, Hand of Neptune.

spon-gy (spŭn'jĭ), *adj.* full of small holes and easily compressed; having the quality of sucking in fluids.—*n.* **sponginess.**

spon-son (spŏn'sŭn), *n.* a part projecting from the side of a vessel, to protect some part; an air-filled compartment on either side of a canoe to keep it from upsetting.

spon-sor (spŏn'sẽr), *n.* one who binds himself to answer, or be responsible, for another; a godfather or godmother.—*adj.* **sponsorial.**—*n.* **sponsorship.**

spon-ta-ne-i-ty (spŏn'tȧ-nē'ĭ-tĭ), *n.* the quality or state of acting from quick, natural feeling or impulse; tendency in animal and vegetable organisms to undergo changes not produced by outside forces.

spon-ta-ne-ous (spŏn-tā'nē-ŭs), *adj.* done or acting from natural impulse, prompting, or desire; as, *spontaneous* applause; proceeding from internal impulse or natural law; not produced by outside force but resulting from forces within a thing; as, *spontaneous* combustion; produced without human labor; natural to the soil; as, weeds are a *spontaneous* growth.—*adv.* **spontaneously.**—*n.* **spontaneousness.**

Syn. free, impulsive, voluntary.

spook (spōōk), *n.* a ghost or spirit; an apparition: a humorous term.

spook-y (spōōk'ĭ), *adj.* ghostly; haunted. Also, **spookish.**

spool (spōōl), *n.* a hollow cylinder, usually of wood, with a ridge at each end, on which thread, etc., is wound; any part of a machine, etc., similarly shaped and used for winding: *v.t.* to wind on a spool.

spoon (spōōn), *n.* a small utensil having a round, or oval, shallow bowl and a handle, used in preparing, serving, and eating food; a club used in golf: *v.t.* to take up in, or as in, a spoon: *v.i.* slang, to act with foolish fondness.

spoon-bill (spōōn'bĭl''), *n.* a wading bird with a broad, flat bill, somewhat like a spoon.

spoon-ful (spōōn'fŏŏl), *n.* [*pl.* **spoonfuls** (-fŏŏlz)], as much as a spoon will hold; a small quantity.

spoon-y (spōōn'ĭ), *n.* a foolishly sentimental lover; a simpleton: *adj.* silly in lovemaking; acting with foolish fondness. [Colloq.]

spoor (spōōr), *n.* the track or trail of any wild animal: *v.t.* to follow by a track or footprints: *v.i.* to follow a track or trail.

spor-a-des (spŏr'ȧ-dēz), *n.pl.* formerly, stars not included in any constellation or group; scattered stars.

spo-rad-ic (spō-răd'ĭk), *adj.* occurring here and there, or apart from others of the same kind; separate; single; as, a *sporadic* case of disease. Also, **sporadical.**—*adv.* **sporadically.**

Syn. isolated, rare, uncommon.

Ant. (see general, prevalent).

spo-rad-ic dis-ease (spō-răd'ĭk dĭz-ēz'), a disease which attacks a few here and there, and does not spread.

spore (spōr), *n.* a very small grain in flowerless plants which performs the part of a seed.

spor-ran (spŏr'ăn), *n.* the furry pouch worn in the Highland costume in front of the kilt.

sport (spōrt), *n.* pastime; amusement; jest or pleasantry; as, he said it in *sport;* mockery or derision; as, they made *sport* of him; a toy or plaything; as, to be the *sport* of chance; outdoor play or recreation, as hunting, shooting, etc.; an athletic game or other game of skill for which prizes are given or money staked; an animal or plant, or a part of either, which exhibits a decided variation from the usual or normal type; colloquially, a gambler or a cheap, flashy person: *v.i.* to play or frolic; trifle; to practice field diversions, such as athletic contests: *v.t.* colloquially, to show off, or wear, in public; as, to *sport* a diamond ring.

sport-ful (spōrt'fŏŏl), *adj.* full of sport; indulging in mirth or play; merry; frolicsome.

sport-ing (spōr'tĭng), *adj.* pertaining to amusements, especially athletic games; as, a *sporting* goods store; inclined to make the best of defeat or difficulty; as, a *sporting* spirit.

spor-tive (spōr'tĭv), *adj.* frolicsome, merry.—*adv.* **sportively.**—*n.* **sportiveness.**

sports-man (spōrts'măn), *n.* one who patronizes or engages in field sports, as hunting, racing, fishing, etc.; one who is fair and honorable in sports; in a bad sense, one who games or gambles for money.

sports-man-ship (spōrts'măn-shĭp), *n.* skill or practice in field sports; fairness; generosity of spirit, shown especially in sports.

spot (spŏt), *n.* a blot or mark; discolored place or stain; blemish; disgrace or reproach; as, a *spot* on his reputation; locality; place; as, the exact *spot* where he fell; a small part of a surface, having a different color from the whole; a dark place on a bright disk or circle; as, a *spot* on the sun; mark on a billiard table where the red ball is placed: *v.t.* [*p.t.* and *p.p.* spotted, *p.pr.* spotting], to mark with spots; discolor; stain; disgrace or blemish; mark or note so as to recognize; as, to *spot* the guilty man; detect: *v.i.* to become marked or stained; as, this silk *spots* with water.—*adj.* **spotty.**—*n.* **spottiness.**

spot-less (spŏt'lĕs), *adj.* without a stain or flaw; faultless or blameless.—*adv.* **spotlessly.**—*n.* **spotlessness.**

spot stroke (spŏt strōk), a stroke in billiards that drives the object-ball from the spot into a pocket.

spot-ter (spŏt'ẽr), *n.* slang, one who keeps watch on suspicious persons; one who secretly keeps tally of the fares received and registered by conductors.

spouse (spouz), *n.* either one of a married couple considered in relation to the other.

spout (spout), *n.* the projecting mouth of a vessel; a pipe or tube for carrying off a liquid in a stream or jet: *v.t.* to throw out forcibly and in large amount in a jet or stream, as from a pipe; colloquially, to utter pompously; as, to *spout* poetry: *v.i.* to come forth with violence in a jet or stream, as from a pipe; to recite anything in a pompous manner.—*n.* **spouter.**

sprain (sprān), *n.* a severe twisting or straining of the muscles or ligaments around a joint; the condition resulting from such a twisting: *v.t.* to overstrain or twist, as the muscles or ligaments around a joint.

sprang (sprăng), past tense of the verb *spring.*

sprat (sprăt), *n.* a small fish, similar to the herring.

sprawl (sprôl), *v.i.* to lie with the body and limbs carelessly stretched out; stretch or toss out the limbs or move awkwardly; spread in an irregular manner, as a plant: *v.t.* to cause to lie or move with the limbs awkwardly stretched out: *n.* an awkward lying position, or movement.

spray (sprā), *n.* a small branch of a tree or plant, bearing shoots, leaves, or flowers; as, a *spray* of lilac; small particles of water driven or dashed in the air; a jet of liquid in fine drops, such as medicine, perfume, etc.; instrument for throwing such a jet or spray: *v.t.* [*p.t.* and *p.p.* sprayed, *p.pr.* spraying], to throw fine drops of liquid upon; to throw in small particles: *v.i.* be scattered in small particles.—*n.* **sprayer.**

spread (sprĕd), *v.t.* [*p.t.* and *p.p.* spread, *p.pr.* spreading], to scatter or extend over a surface; as, to *spread* new-cut hay; to *spread* butter on bread; to cover with a thin layer; as, to *spread* bread with butter; to publish or make widely known; as, to *spread* a report; unfold; open; as, a plant *spreads* its leaves; stretch out; as, a bird *spreads* its wings; diffuse; as, to *spread* a disease; display before the eye; as, to *spread* out goods; set or furnish with provisions; as, to *spread* the table; extend or scatter, as fire: *v.i.* to be extended or scattered: *n.* extension; extent; the distance between the tips of the wings of an airplane; a covering for a bed, table, etc.; colloquially, a table set with provisions; feast.—*n.* **spreader.**

Syn., *v.* disperse, diffuse, expand, scatter.

spread-ea-gle (sprĕd'ē'gl), *adj.* colloquially, pretentious or boastful; as, *spread-eagle* oratory: *n.* the figure of an eagle with its wings spread and its legs extended: the national emblem of the United States.

spree (sprē), *n.* a merry frolic; carousal; a drunken debauch: *v.i.* to carouse.

sprig (sprĭg), *n.* a small twig or shoot; a headless nail or brad; an ornament in the form of a spray; as, muslin with a pattern of *sprigs*: *v.t.* [*p.t.* and *p.p.* sprigged, *p.pr.* sprigging], to work or adorn with sprigs; drive brads into.

spright-ly (sprīt'lĭ), *adj.* [*comp.* sprightlier, *superl.* sprightliest], brisk; animated; airy; gay.—*n.* **sprightliness.**

spring (sprĭng), *v.i.* [*p.t.* sprang, *p.p.* sprung, *p.pr.* springing], to rise, as from a source; issue or proceed; as, great results often *spring* from small causes; originate; appear; shoot up; as, the grass *springs* up; leap; bound; as, to *spring* over a fence; dart, as a rabbit; start or rise up suddenly; as, a breeze *springs* up; fly back; as, the bent bow *springs* back; warp, as a board: *v.t.* to start or rouse; to do or disclose suddenly; as, to *spring* a surprise; explode; as, to *spring* a mine; crack; strain, as a mast or beam; cause to close suddenly; as, to *spring* a trap; leap over; cause to open; as, to *spring* a lock: *n.* a leap or bound; an elastic body that yields when pressed and returns to its original form when the pressure is removed; the elastic quality or force of a body; as, the *spring* of a bow; cause; origin; source; a fountain of water; the season of the year when plants begin to grow.

spring-board (sprĭng'bōrd″), *n.* an elastic board used by acrobats and others in leaping, or by swimmers in diving.

spring-bok (sprĭng'bŏk″), *n.* the South African gazelle, noted for its ability to spring lightly into the air. Also, **springbuck.**

springe (sprĭnj), *n.* a snare or noose fastened to a trap for small game.

spring-er (sprĭng'ẽr), *n.* one that leaps, etc.; the stone of an arch which rests upon its support.

spring-tide (sprĭng'tīd″), *n.* the high tide which happens at or near the new and full moon; any great flood of feeling, etc.; season of spring. Also, **springtime.**

spring-y (sprĭng'ĭ), *adj.* elastic; light; having springs of water; wet; spongy.—*n.* **springiness.**

sprin-kle (sprĭn'kl), *v.t.* to scatter in small drops or particles; to scatter on in small drops or particles; baptize with a few drops of water; cleanse or purify: *v.i.* to rain in small drops: *n.* a sprinkling.—*n.* **sprinkler.**

sprin-kling (sprĭn'klĭng), *n.* a small, scattered quantity or number; as, the hall contained a mere *sprinkling* of people.

sprint (sprĭnt), *n.* a run for a short distance at full speed: *v.i.* to run at full speed.—*n.* **sprinter.**

sprit (sprĭt), *n.* a small spar running from the bottom of the mast to the top outside corner of the sail of a boat.

sprite (sprīt), *n.* an elf, goblin, or fairy; a ghost or spirit.

sprock-et (sprŏk'ĕt), *n.* a tooth, as on a wheel, shaped so as to engage with the links of a chain; a wheel having such teeth on its rim.

sprout (sprout), *v.i.* to begin to grow; put forth shoots, as the seed of a plant: *v.t.* to cause to put forth shoots and begin to grow: *n.* a shoot; bud: *pl.* a vegetable, called in full *Brussels sprouts.*

spruce (sprōōs), *n.* a fir tree of the pine family, or its wood; a drink made from spruce leaves, etc.: *adj.* smart; trim; neat: *v.t.* and *v.i.* to dress smartly; to arrange in a neat and tidy manner: often followed by *up*.—*adv.* **sprucely.**—*n.* **spruceness.**

sprung (sprŭng), past participle of the verb *spring.*

spry (sprī), *adj.* [*comp.* sprier, *superl.* spriest], nimble; active; agile. [Colloq.]

spud (spŭd), *n.* a sharp, narrow spade, especially for digging up large-rooted weeds; colloquially, a potato.

spume (spūm), *n.* froth; foam; scum: *v.i.* to foam.

spu-mous (spū'mŭs), *adj.* frothy; foamy. Also, **spumy.**

spun (spŭn), past tense and past participle of the verb *spin.*

spunk (spŭnk), *n.* touchwood, or wood that instantly takes fire; punk; colloquially, mettle, spirit, or pluck; also, anger; *v.i.* to flame up; colloquially, to show spirit or quick temper.

spunk-y (spŭnk'ĭ), *adj.* mettlesome; plucky; touchy; obstinate; as, a *spunky*, disobedient child. [Colloq.]

spur (spûr), *n.* a small wheel with sharp points, worn on the heel of boots to urge on a horse; anything that urges to action; as, the challenge was a *spur* to his ambition; a projecting root of a tree; a mountain ridge running out to the side from a range of mountains; the stiff, sharp spine on a rooster's leg: *v.t.* [*p.t.* and *p.p.* spurred, *p.pr.* spurring], to prick with a spur; as, to *spur* a horse; excite to action; as, to *spur* one to greater effort; stimulate; urge: *v.i.* to travel with haste; as, to *spur* rapidly along the road; push on.—*adj.* **spurred.**

spu-ri-ous (spū'rĭ-ŭs), *adj.* not genuine; counterfeit; as, *spurious* coin; false.—*adv.* **spuriously.**—*n.* **spuriousness.**

spurn (spûrn), *v.t.* to drive away, as by kicking; reject with contempt; treat with disdain: *v.i.* to show contempt in declining anything.

spurt (spûrt), *n.* a sudden or forcible gushing forth of a liquid; a brief, sudden effort: *v.i.* to gush forth suddenly or violently in a stream or jet; make a sudden brief effort: *v.t.* to throw out in a stream or jet. Also, **spirt.**

sput-ter (spŭt'ẽr), *v.i.* to throw out small particles, as sparks from burning wood; to spit small, scattered drops, as in rapid or excited speech; hence, to speak rapidly and indistinctly: *v.t.* to throw out in small particles with a crackling or spluttering noise, as jets of steam, or as green wood burning; to utter in an excited or confused way: *n.* matter thrown out in small particles or drops: excited and indistinct talk.—*n.* **sputterer.**

spu-tum (spū'tŭm), *n.* saliva; spittle; spit.

spy (spī), *n.* a person who in time of war enters the enemy's camp to gain information; one who keeps watch on others; secret agent: *v.t.* [*p.t.* and *p.p.* spied, *p.pr.* spying], to discover, especially at a distance; gain sight of; discover by looking carefully; detect; examine or explore secretly: *v.i.* to examine narrowly; keep watch secretly: often with *on* or *upon.*

Syn., n. detective, scout.

spy-glass (spī'glȧs"), *n.* a small telescope for looking at distant objects on earth.

squab (skwŏb), *n.* a young pigeon, especially one still in the nest; a short, fat person; a cushioned sofa; a stuffed cushion: *adj.* short and fat; recently hatched.

squab-ble (skwŏb'l), *n.* a noisy quarrel; wrangle; dispute: *v.i.* to wrangle or dispute in a noisy manner.—*n.* **squabbler.**

squad (skwŏd), *n.* a small party of soldiers assembled for drill, inspection, etc.; the smallest of the organized groups into which a regiment is divided; any small group of persons engaged in a common effort.

squad-ron (skwŏd'rŭn), *n.* a division of a cavalry regiment containing two troops; a group of war vessels employed on some particular service.

squal-id (skwŏl'ĭd), *adj.* extremely dirty, through neglect; foul.—*adv.* **squalidly.**—*n.* **squalidness.**

squall (skwôl), *n.* a sudden and violent gust of wind, often accompanied with rain, sleet, etc.; a loud scream: *v.i.* to blow a sudden gust of wind, with rain or snow; to scream or cry violently.

squall-y (skwôl'ĭ), *adj.* gusty; stormy; blustering.

squal-or (skwŏl'ẽr; skwā'lôr), *n.* a wretched and filthy condition; foulness; dirt.

squan-der (skwŏn'dẽr), *v.t.* to spend lavishly or wastefully: *v.i.* to be very wasteful.—*n.* **squanderer.**

square (skwâr), *n.* a figure having four equal sides and four right angles; anything of such a figure, or nearly resembling it; the result reached by multiplying a number by itself; as, 4 is the *square* of 2; in a town or city, a four-sided space each of whose sides is a street; the distance along one of these sides; as, to walk three *squares;* an open space bounded by streets and used as a small park; as, Union *Square;* a body of troops drawn up in a four-sided array; a mathematical instrument for measuring right angles: *v.t.* to form with four equal sides and four right angles; to cause to make a right angle with another line; to balance; make even; as, to *square* accounts; multiply by itself; reduce to a given standard; adjust; regulate; as, to *square* our conduct by a certain rule: *v.i.* to accord or agree; with *with;* as, his story does not *square* with mine; fit; assume a boxing attitude: with *up* or *off:* *adj.* having four equal sides and four right angles; forming a right angle; as, a *square* corner; having a broad shape with straight outlines; as, *square* shoulders; true; upright; honest; just; as, a *square* deal; balanced; settled; as, our account is *square:* colloquially, full or satisfying; as, a *square* meal; changed from a unit of length to a unit of area bounded by four sides of the same length as the original unit of length; as, a *square* yard.—*adv.* **squarely.**—*n.* **squareness.**

square-rigged (skwâr'rĭgd"), *adj.* having the sails stretched on yards suspended horizontally by the middle.

square root (skwâr rōōt), that number or quantity which, multiplied by itself, produces the given number or quantity; as, 2 is the *square root* of 4.

squash (skwŏsh), *n.* something soft and easily crushed; a mashed object or mass; the sudden fall of a soft body; a plant of various kinds belonging to the cucumber family; also, its fruit: *v.t.* colloquially, to crush, especially into a flat mass or pulp: *v.i.* colloquially, to fall in a soft mass.

squash-y (skwŏsh'ĭ), *adj.* easily crushed; soft and wet.—*n.* **squashiness.**

squat (skwŏt), *v.i.* [*p.t.* and *p.p.* squatted, *p.pr.* squatting], to sit down on the heels, or with the knees drawn up; lie close to the ground, as an animal; crouch; to settle on public land with a view to gaining title to it; settle on the land of another without permission or right: *adj.* sitting on the heels, or with the knees drawn up; crouching; short and thick: *n.* the position of one who squats; a small vein of ore.

squat-ter (skwŏt'ẽr), *n.* one who settles on public or unimproved land without right or permission; in Australia and New Zealand, one who leases government land for pasturing sheep.

squat-ty (skwŏt'ĭ), *adj.* short and thick; dumpy.

squaw (skwô), *n.* a North American Indian woman or wife: **squaw man,** a white man who has married an Indian woman and who, therefore, has the rights of one of her tribe.

squawk (skwôk), *n.* a loud, harsh cry, as of a duck or hen: *v.i.* to utter a loud, harsh cry.

squeak (skwēk), *n.* a short, shrill, sharp cry, as of a mouse; a sharp, disagreeable noise; as the *squeak* of a door: *v.i.* to utter a short, shrill, sharp cry; make a sharp, disagreeable noise; slang, o break silence; betray a secret; confess.—*adj.* **squeaky.**—*adv.* **squeakily.**

squeal (skwēl), *n.* a shrill, prolonged cry, as of a pig: *v.i.* to utter a shrill, prolonged cry; slang, to betray a plot, or a companion in a crime or fault.—*n.* **squealer.**

squeam-ish (skwēm'ĭsh), *adj.* inclined to feel sick at the stomach; easily disgusted; nice to excess in taste; overly careful about trifles.—*adv.* **squeamishly.**—*n.* **squeamishness.**

squee-gee (skwē'jē), *n.* a hoe-shaped tool with a rubber edge or plate, for cleaning pavements, removing water from a vessel's deck, etc.; a similar smaller instrument used in photography, to press a film close to a mount. Also, **squeegee**.

squeeze (skwēz), *v.t.* to press between two bodies; compress; press out of shape; draw forth by pressure; extract; as, to *squeeze* juice out of a lemon; force into a place by pressure; as, to *squeeze* people into a car; to procure by force; as, to *squeeze* money from a person; to grasp closely, as the hand; to hug: *v.i.* to press; force one's way; push; as, to *squeeze* through a crowd: *n.* pressure; a crowding together; a hearty grasp, as of the hand; a hug.—*n.* **squeezer**.

squelch (skwĕlch), *v.t.* to crush; silence; disconcert. [COLLOQ.]

squib (skwĭb), *n.* a firecracker broken across; a paper roll or case filled with gunpowder; a kind of slow match or safety fuse; a brief, witty speech or writing.

squid (skwĭd), *n.* a name for various ten-armed cuttlefish; a kind of artificial fish-bait.

squill (skwĭl), *n.* a plant of the lily family, the bulb of which is used as a medicine; also, the bulb.

squint (skwĭnt), *n.* the act or habit of looking obliquely or cross-eyed; strabismus: *v.i.* to see or look obliquely; to look with eyes half closed; to be cross-eyed: *v.t.* to cause to look obliquely; to half close (the eyes): *adj.* looking obliquely; cross-eyed.

squire (skwīr), *n.* formerly, a shield bearer or armor-bearer of a knight; a male attendant on a great person; a devoted follower; a justice of the peace; a prominent citizen, as a title of respect; an English landholder of old standing: a shortened form of *esquire*.

squirm (skwûrm), *v.i.* to twist about like an eel or a snake; to wriggle; writhe.

squir-rel (skwûr'ĕl; skwĭr'ĕl), *n.* a small, active, gray or reddish-brown, gnawing animal with a long bushy tail.

squirt (skwûrt), *v.i.* to gush forth in a stream or jet from a small opening; to spurt: *v.t.* to force out in a quick jet: *n.* a small stream or jet; an instrument for squirting water, etc., as a syringe.

stab (stăb), *v.t.* [*p.t.* and *p.p.* stabbed, *p.pr.* stabbing], to pierce with, or as with, a pointed weapon; injure secretly, or by malicious falsehood or slander: *v.i.* to pierce; inflict a wound: *n.* a thrust with a sharp-pointed weapon; a wound so made; a sly, malicious injury.—*n.* **stabber**.

sta-bil-i-ty (stȧ-bĭl'ĭ-tĭ), *n.* the state or quality of being stable, or firm; firmness of character; strength of purpose or resolution; fixedness; the quality of an aircraft in flight that causes it to return to a state of equilibrium, or balance, when meeting a disturbance: sometimes called *dynamical stability*. Also, **stableness**.

stab-il-ize (stăb'ĭl-īz), *v.t.* to make stable, or firm.

stab-i-liz-er (stăb'ĭ-līz'ẽr), *n.* a device, variously constructed, for maintaining the equilibrium, or balance, of airplanes, or keeping them level.

sta-ble (stā'bl), *n.* a building for lodging horses, cows, etc.: *v.t.* to put or keep in such a building: *v.i.* to be lodged in such a building: *adj.* firm in purpose; steadfast; constant; as, a person of *stable* qualities; firmly established; fixed; as, a *stable* government; having permanence; durable; as, a *stable* position.—*adv.* **stably**.

stack (stăk), *n.* a large quantity of hay, corn, wood, etc., piled up in orderly fashion; a number of chimneys standing together; any chimney; one or more fixed frameworks containing shelves for books; colloquially, a large amount: *v.t.* to pile up: **to stack arms**, to set up rifles or muskets in a cone-shaped group with butts resting on the ground: **to stack cards**, to arrange playing cards secretly in order to cheat.

Stack of Arms

sta-di-um (stā'dĭ-ŭm), *n.* [*pl.* **stadia** (-ȧ)], a Greek linear, or line, measure equal to 606¾ feet; in ancient Greece, the course for foot races, surrounded by tiers of seats for spectators; in modern times, a similar structure, with its inclosed space, for athletic games, etc.

sta-dom-e-ter (stȧ-dŏm'ē-tẽr), *n.* a device for estimating distances: usually employed on the drill-ground, to save measuring.

staff (stȧf), *n.* [*pl.* staves (stāvz), **staffs** (stȧfs)], a stick carried for support in walking, or for defense; support; a prop; a building material composed principally of plaster, used instead of stone, especially for temporary structures; the five lines and four spaces on which music is written; a flag-pole; a body of officers attached to any department of an army, or to a commander, and having duties connected with the management of the army or any portion of it; a body of assistants serving to carry out the plans of a leader or manager; as, the *staff* of a newspaper.

stag (stăg), *n.* the full-grown male of various large deer.

stag bee-tle (stăg bē'tl), a beetle having, in the male, jaws like the horns of a stag.

stage (stāj), *n.* a raised platform, especially in a theater; a place on which an orator may speak, or a play may be presented; the theatrical profession; the drama; theater; a place of rest on a journey; a field of action; degree of progress in any business, process, etc.; a stagecoach: *v.t.* to put on the stage, as a play.

stag-er (stāj'ẽr), *n.* a horse for drawing a stagecoach; colloquially, one who has had long experience in anything; as, an old *stager*.

stag-ger (stăg'ẽr), *v.i.* to totter or reel; begin to doubt, weary, or give way; hesitate: *v.t.* to cause to totter or reel; shock; make less confident: *n.* a sudden reeling or tottering: *pl.* a disease of horses and cattle, marked by staggering and falling: often termed *blind staggers*.—*adv.* **staggeringly**.—*n.* **staggerer**.

stag-ing (stāj'ĭng), *n.* a temporary structure of boards and posts; scaffolding; the business of running and managing stagecoaches; the act of putting a play on the stage.

stag-nant (stăg'nănt), *adj.* not flowing; stale or foul from standing; not brisk or active; dull; sluggish.—*n.* **stagnancy**.

stag-nate (stăg'nāt), *v.i.* to cease to flow or run; be motionless; become inactive or dull; become impure or foul.

stag-na-tion (stăg-nā'shŭn), *n.* the state or quality of being inactive, dull, sluggish, or stale and foul from standing.

stag-y (stāj'ĭ), *adj.* theatrical.—*n.* **staginess.**

staid (stād), *p.t.* and *p.p.* of *stay*: *adj.* sober; sedate; regular; steady; not wild, flighty, or fanciful.—*adv.* **staidly.**—*n.* **staidness.**

stain (stān), *n.* a discoloration; spot or blot; a dye; taint of guilt or crime; cause of reproach: *v.t.* to blot; spot; mark with color; to dye; soil with guilt or crime: *v.i.* to take or make a stain.
Syn., *v.* soil, discolor, spot, sully.

stain-less (stān'lĕs), *adj.* free from taint or soil; incapable of being tainted or soiled; as, a *stainless* reputation or name.

stair (stâr), *n.* one of a set of steps for ascending or descending: *pl.* a set of steps.

stair-case (stâr'kās"), *n.* a flight of steps in a house, with railings, etc. Also, **stairway.**

stake (stāk), *n.* a post or strong stick sharpened at one end and fixed in the ground; formerly, a post to which a person condemned to be burnt was secured: hence, death by such burning; that which is pledged, wagered, or risked for loss or gain; the prize in any contest; small anvil: *v.t.* to fasten, support, or defend with stakes; mark out the limits of, with stakes; wager or pledge.

sta-lac-tite (stȧ-lăk'tīt), *n.* an iciclelike formation of carbonate of lime, hanging from the roof of caves, caverns, etc.

sta-lag-mite (stȧ-lăg'mīt), *n.* a cone of carbonate of lime, formed, by the dropping of water, on the floor of a cavern.

stale (stāl), *adj.* not fresh or new; tasteless; worn out by use or familiarity; trite; common; decayed: *v.t.* to make stale; destroy the freshness or charm of: *v.i.* to lose newness or freshness; wear out.—*n.* **staleness.**

stale-mate (stāl'māt"), *n.* the situation in chess when the king cannot move without being placed in check, and when no other move can be made: *v.t.* to put in the position of stalemate; bring to a standstill.

stalk (stôk), *n.* the stem or main axis of a plant; the support which attaches a flower or fruit to a plant or tree; anything like a stalk; a high, proud, stately step; the act of approaching game stealthily: *v.t.* to approach quietly and under cover so as to kill, as game: *v.i.* to walk with high and proud steps; to creep toward game stealthily.

stalk-ing-horse (stôk'ing-hôrs"), *n.* a horse, or figure of a horse, behind which a hunter conceals himself from his game; a mask.

stall (stôl), *n.* an inclosed space in a stable where a horse or cow is kept and fed; a bench or table where goods are exposed for sale; a small house or shed where business is carried on; a seat in the choir of a church; in Great Britain, a theater seat in the parquet or orchestra: *v.t.* to place or keep in a stall; to plunge into sand, mire, etc., so as not to be able to get on; as, to *stall* a cart; to stop by any obstruction, or by unskilful management; as, to *stall* an engine: *v.i.* to stick fast in mire, etc.; come to a standstill by any obstruction.

stall-age (stôl'āj), *n.* rent paid for a stall, or booth; right of erecting a stall, or booth, at a fair.

stal-lion (stăl'yŭn), *n.* a male horse kept for breeding.

stal-wart (stôl'wẽrt; stŏl'wẽrt), *adj.* sturdy; strong; tall and stout; brave; daring: *n.* a firm, loyal partisan.—*adv.* **stalwartly.**—*n.* **stalwartness.**

sta-men (stā'mĕn), *n.* that organ of a flower which furnishes the pollen, or male fertilizing element, and which consists of the filament and the anther.—*adj.* **staminal, staminate.**

stam-i-na (stăm'ĭ-nȧ), *n.pl.* that part of a body which supplies strength and firmness to the whole; backbone; power of endurance; as, the *stamina* of a nation.

stam-mer (stăm'ẽr), *v.i.* to hesitate or falter in speaking, especially from a defect in speech; stutter: *v.t.* to utter or pronounce with difficulty or hesitation: *n.* hesitating or faltering speech due to nervousness; any difficulty in pronouncing, or halting in speech; a stutter.—*n.* **stammerer.**

stamp (stămp), *n.* the act of making a mark or impress; a mark or design impressed upon a surface; as, the *stamp* on a coin; an implement or machine for making such a mark; a die; a small piece of paper, having a certain device and value printed on it, sold by the government, and fastened to a letter, document, etc., as payment of a fee or tax; as, a postage *stamp;* a revenue *stamp;* any special mark that denotes the ownership or quality of a thing; as, a *stamp* on a patent medicine; characteristic quality or nature; as, the picture bears the *stamp* of genius; sort; kind; as, avoid men of his *stamp;* act of striking downward with the foot; a heavy downward blow with the foot: *v.t.* to mark with a design by means of a die, etc.; as, to *stamp* a coin; impress a copy of on something; as, to *stamp* one's initials on note paper; put a stamp upon; as, to *stamp* a letter; to label; brand; as, our acts *stamp* our characters; fix deeply; as, to *stamp* a scene on the memory; to set (the foot) down heavily; crush by such a motion; as, to *stamp* anything under foot; crush or grind into powder: *v.i.* to strike or beat the foot forcibly downward.

stam-pede (stăm-pēd'), *n.* a sudden, wild running away of a herd of animals, caused by fear or panic; any sudden flight or rush, as of an army; any sudden, impulsive movement or action on the part of a crowd, etc.; as, a *stampede* in a political convention: *v.t.* to cause to take to sudden flight: *v.i.* to start off in a panic; to act together from a sudden impulse.

stanch (stånch; stänch), *v.t.* to stop the flow of; as, to *stanch* blood; stop the flow of blood from; as, to *stanch* a wound: *adj.* water-tight; sound; as, a *stanch* little craft; firm; constant; trustworthy; loyal; as a *stanch* friend. Also, **staunch.**—*adv.* **stanchly, staunchly.**—*n.* **stanchness, staunchness.**

stan-chion (stăn'shŭn), *n.* a support or post of iron or wood, as for a roof, an awning, etc.

stand (stănd), *v.i.* [*p.t.* and *p.p.* stood, *p.pr.* standing], to be stationary on the feet in an erect or upright position; hence, be upright or made to rest on end; cease to move; as, when they tired of walking, they *stood;* be at rest or lie stagnant; as, water *stands* in the pond; be placed or situated; as, the table *stands* in the corner; be a substitute; as, Esq. *stands* for esquire; become a candidate; as, to *stand* for office; remain firm; abide; as, I *stand* to what I have said; remain in existence, especially without injury or change; endure; last; as, the house still *stands;* take sides; as, to *stand* by one's friends; accord; agree; as, it *stands* to reason; continue in force; as, the rule *stands* good; hold a course at sea; as, to *stand* for the harbor: *v.i.* to set on the feet or on end in an upright position; place on a base; as, to *stand* a statue on a pedestal; put up with; endure; bear; as, to *stand* insult; pass through; as, to *stand* a test; colloquially, pay for; as, to *stand* treat: *n.* a stop or halt for the purpose of defense or resistance; interruption; station for the hire of vehicles; raised platform or series of raised seats for spectators; as, a grand *stand;* small table; any fixed station or position; as, to take one's *stand* at the window; firm or decided position; as, to make a *stand* for the right; state of perplexity or difficulty; as, to be at a *stand* what to do.

stand-ard (stăn'dẽrd), *n.* an ensign or flag under which men are united for some common purpose; especially, a national ensign, that which is established by authority as a fixed rule or measure; test; an upright support: *adj.* established by rule or model; as, a *standard* price; having a recognized value; as, a *standard* novel.

stand-ard-ize (stăn'dẽr-dīz), *v.t.* to regulate by, or make to conform to, an established rule, model, value, authority, etc.—*n.* **standardization.**

stand-ing (stănd'ĭng), *n.* the act of stopping or of being erect on the feet; station; maintenance of position; duration; as, a habit of long *standing;* reputation; rank; as, he is in good *standing:* *adj.* remaining erect, or upright; stagnant, or not flowing, as water; lasting; established or settled; fixed; as, a *standing* army or rule.

stand-pipe (stănd'pīp"), *n.* a very large upright pipe into which water is pumped from a reservoir, etc., so as to produce the necessary pressure in a water supply system; a water tower.

stand-point (stănd'point"), *n.* a position from which things are looked at, considered, and judged.

stand-still (stănd'stĭl"), *n.* a ceasing of action; a halt or stop; rest; as, business or traffic came to a *standstill.*

stan-hope (stăn'hōp; stăn'ŭp), *n.* a light two-wheeled, one-seated carriage without a top: given the name of the Englishman for whom the first one was built.

stan-za (stăn'zȧ), *n.* a group of lines, or verses, usually four or more, forming a section of a poem.

sta-pes (stā'pēz), *n.* the stirrup-shaped bone of the middle ear.

sta-ple (stā'pl), *n.* the chief product or industry of a country or district; settled market or place for wholesale traffic; principal element or chief item; unmanufactured or raw material; cotton, flax, or wool fiber; a loop of metal with two points to be driven into wood, etc., for holding a bolt, etc.: *adj.* chief; regularly produced; as, *staple* goods; established in commerce; as, *staple* trade: *v.t.* to sort according to the quality of its fiber; as, to *staple* cotton, etc.; to fasten by a staple.

sta-pler (stā'plẽr), *n.* one who deals in the regular products of a country; a sorter of wool, cotton, etc.

star (stär), *n.* any of the heavenly bodies that appear to be fixed points of light, or of others, called planets, that regularly change their position; anything like a star; a figure with five or more radiating points; a planet supposed to influence a person's life; a metal badge; as, a policeman's *star;* an asterisk [*]; a brilliant or prominent person, especially in the theatrical profession: *v.t.* [*p.t.* and *p.p.* starred, *p.pr.* starring], to set or adorn with stars; to mark with an asterisk: *v.i.* to shine as a star; be brilliant or prominent; to appear as principal actor in a play.

star-board (stär'bōrd; stär'bẽrd), *n.* the right-hand side of a vessel looking towards the bow, or front; opposite to *port:* *adj.* pertaining to, or lying on, the right side of a vessel: *v.t.* to put to the right, or starboard, side of a vessel.

starch (stärch), *n.* a well-known white vegetable substance; a paste made of this substance and used for laundry purposes, etc.; a stiff, formal manner; stiffness; courage; backbone: *v.t.* to stiffen with starch; make stiff.—*adj.* **starched.**

Star Cham-ber (stär chām'bẽr), the highest court of England under the Tudors and Stuarts, consisting of members of the Privy Council, who sat to try civil and criminal cases, severely and often unjustly: abolished during the reign of Charles I.

starch-y (stär'chĭ), *adj.* containing, or like, starch; as, *starchy* food; stiff; formal; precise.

stare (stâr), *n.* a fixed, steady look with wide-open eyes, as suggesting curiosity, wonder, boldness, etc.: *v.i.* to look with fixed eyes wide open; gaze fixedly in one direction; be very conspicuous or prominent: *v.t.* to gaze at.—*n.* **starer.**

star-fish (stär'fĭsh"), *n.* any of various marine animals, having a star-like body with five or more rays, or arms.

stark (stärk), *adj.* stiff; rigid; as, *stark* in death; hence, dead; utter; complete; as, *stark* nonsense: *adv.* wholly; completely; as, *stark* naked.—*adv.* **starkly.**

star-light (stär'līt"), *n.* the light given by the stars: *adj.* lighted by the stars only; starlit.

star-ling (stär'lĭng), *n.* a bird with brown or, in summer, greenish-black plumage and yellowish-white spots, and living about houses or towers; one of the upright piles or logs driven round the piers of a bridge for its protection.

starred (stärd), *p.adj.* decorated with stars; influenced by the stars: now, only in ill-*starred;* marked with an asterisk.

star-ry (stär'ĭ), *adj.* set with stars; as, a *starry* crown; lighted by stars; as, a *starry* night; shining like stars.

Stars and Stripes (stärz ănd strīps), a popular name for the flag of the United States.

star-shell (stär'shĕl"), *n.* a rocket, or thin iron shell, filled with an explosive that bursts into starlike lights; fired into the air from a light muzzle-loading gun, and intended to light up the enemy's position at night.

Star Span-gled Ban-ner (stär spăn'-gld băn'ẽr), the national anthem of the United States, the words of which were written by Francis Scott Key.

start (stärt), *v.i.* to move suddenly and quickly; spring; leap; bound; to make a startled movement or spring, as from surprise, etc.; set out; as, to *start* on a journey; begin a race, career, etc.; as, to *start* in business; become loosened: *v.t.*

to originate action in, or set going; as, to *start* a clock; rouse suddenly from concealment; as, to *start* a hare; originate or begin; as, to *start* a quarrel; to draw from a cask or draw the contents from: *n.* the act of beginning or setting in motion; a sudden motion or twitch, as of pain, joy, etc.; a quick spring; a going forth; as, an early *start;* outset; as, get it right at the *start;* a beginning; as, a *start* in business; lead; as, he had the *start* of them; a flashing forth; as, *starts* of fancy.—*n.* **starter.**

star-tle (stär'tl), *v.i.* to move suddenly, as in alarm: *v.t.* to excite or frighten suddenly; scare.

star-va-tion (stär-vā'shŭn), *n.* the act of suffering or dying from lack of food; state of being reduced to a condition of extreme hunger or killed by lack of food.

starve (stärv), *v.i.* to suffer extreme hunger; die of hunger; perish from lack of anything necessary: *v.t.* to cause to suffer extreme hunger; cause to die of hunger; subdue by famine; destroy by want of any kind.

starve-ling (stärv'lĭng), *n.* one who, or that which, pines from lack of food; a thin, weak animal or plant: *adj.* hungry; weak; lean.

sta-sis (stā'sĭs), *n.* a stopping of the circulation of blood in the small vessels.

state (stāt), *n.* mode or condition of existence; condition as to riches, social standing, etc.; rank; style of living; especially, ceremonious style or formal dignity; as, to receive in *state;* a body of people united under one government which they recognize and conform to as supreme; the civil powers and government of such a community; the territory occupied by it; one of several such communities forming a federation: *adj.* pertaining to the body politic; as, *state* papers; used upon formal or ceremonious occasions: *v.t.* to set forth clearly and formally; tell; as, to *state* the facts: **State,** one of the United States.

stat-ed (stāt'ĕd), *p.adj.* fixed; as, at a *stated* time; regular; as, *stated* business hours.

state-ly (stāt'lĭ), *adj.* [*comp.* statelier, *superl.* stateliest], having a grand or imposing appearance or manner; noble; majestic; dignified: *adv.* imposingly; majestically.—*n.* **stateliness.**

state-ment (stāt'mĕnt), *n.* the act of presenting clearly and formally; that which is presented; a recital.

state pris-on (stāt prĭz'n), a prison maintained by the government of a body politic: **State prison,** in the United States, a prison maintained by any one of the States for the punishment of felons, or those convicted of serious crimes. Also, **state's prison.**

State rights (stāt rīts), the rights and powers not given to the United States by the Constitution, but reserved to the people of the various States for their independent decision.

state-room (stāt'rōōm"), *n.* a private sleeping room on a vessel or railway car.

state's ev-i-dence (stāts ĕv'ĭ-dĕns), testimony presented by the government, or prosecution, in a criminal case; especially, testimony given by one who, having had part in the crime, confesses his own guilt and gives evidence against his accomplices; colloquially, one who so testifies; as, he turned *state's evidence.*

states-gen-er-al (stāts-jĕn'ẽr-ăl), *n.* a legislative assembly composed of representatives of the governing classes of citizens: **States General,** the Dutch parliament, or legislative body.

states-man (stāts'măn), *n.* [*pl.* **statesmen** (-mĕn)], one who is skilled in public affairs and the art of government; one who deals wisely with public matters.

states-man-ship (stāts'măn-shĭp), *n.* distinguished ability or skill in dealing with questions that arise in public affairs.

state tri-al (stāt trī'ăl), a trial for a political offense.

stat-ic (stăt'ĭk), *adj.* pertaining to bodies at rest, or motionless; acting by weight without motion; pertaining to passive forces, or those in equilibrium: opposite to *dynamic: n.pl.* that branch of mechanics which treats of pressure, weight, etc., of bodies at rest. Also, *adj.* **statical.**—*adv.* **statically.**

sta-tion (stā'shŭn), *n.* a place where a person or thing usually stands; as, a railroad flagman's *station;* headquarters for a body of persons, etc., ready for service; as, a police *station;* naval *station;* a stopping place on a railway for the use of passengers or for freight; position; situation; as, he took up his *station* on the hill; social condition; rank; standing: *v.t.* to place in a certain position; post; appoint or assign.

sta-tion-a-ry (stā'shŭn-ā-rĭ), *adj.* not moving, as machinery when at rest; fixed; not to be carried from one place to another; as *stationary* tubs; unchanging in state or condition; as, the size of the army remained *stationary.*

sta-tion-er (stā'shŭn-ẽr), *n.* one who sells paper, pens, pencils, and other writing materials.

sta-tion-er-y (stā'shŭn-ẽr-ĭ), *n.* paper, pens, ink, and other writing materials.

sta-tis-ti-cal (stȧ-tĭs'tĭ-kăl), *adj.* pertaining to statistics, or facts collected and arranged for general use. Also, **statistic.**—*adv.* **statistically.**

stat-is-ti-cian (stăt"ĭs-tĭsh'ăn), *n.* one skilled in collecting and arranging for general use facts about a given country, industry, etc.

sta-tis-tics (stȧ-tĭs'tĭks), *n.pl.* classified facts relating to a large body of people, as a nation or state, or to some special industry, interest, etc., especially such facts as can be stated in numbers: *sing.* art or science of collecting and arranging such facts; as, *statistics* is a profession requiring patience.

stat-o-scope (stăt'ō-skōp), *n.* an instrument to detect the distance of a small rate of ascent or descent: used in airship navigation.

stat-u-a-ry (stăt'ū-ā-rĭ), *n.* a sculptor; the art of carving the full form of a living being in marble, bronze, etc.; such carved forms, or statues, collectively.

stat-ue (stăt'ū), *n.* the full form of a living being sculptured or modeled out of solid material, as marble, bronze, etc.

stat-u-esque (stăt"ū-ĕsk'), *adj.* having the grace, quietude, or formal dignity of a statue, or modeled figure; as, a *statuesque* beauty.—*n.* **statuesquely.**

stat-u-ette (stăt"ū-ĕt'), *n.* a little statue, or modeled figure.

stat-ure (stăt'ūr), *n.* the natural height of an animal, especially man.

sta-tus (stā'tŭs), *n.* legal condition of a person; as, the *status* of a married woman; relative social standing or place; rank; position of affairs.

sta-tus quo (stā'tŭs kwō), a present condition or position; state in which a person or matter has been, is, or may be. [Lat.]

stat-ute (stăt'ūt), *n.* a law passed by a legislature, or lawmaking body; written law; an act of a corporation or company, or of its founders, designed to be a permanent rule; as, the *statutes* of a university.

stat-u-to-ry (stăt'ū-tō-rĭ), *adj.* enacted or imposed by statute, or law; depending on statute, or law, for its authority; as, a *statutory* provision.

stave (stāv), *n.* [*pl.* staves (stāvz)], one of the thin narrow strips of wood forming the sides of a cask or barrel; a pole or piece of wood of some length; in music, the five parallel lines on and between which the notes and rests are written; a staff: *v.t.* [*p.t.* and *p.p.* staved, stove, *p.pr.* staving], to break a hole in: with *in;* as, to *stave in* a boat; to make by breaking in the staves; as, to *stave* a hole in a boat; delay or put off; keep at a distance; drive away: with *off;* as, to *stave* off an illness or trouble.

stay (stā), *n.* a large, strong rope, usually of wire, which holds parts together or gives stiffness, as one which supports a mast; a prop or support; abode or continuance in a place; as, he made a long *stay* in Paris; a stand or stop; as, a *stay* of judgment: *pl.* pair of corsets; *v.t.* [*p.t.* and *p.p.* stayed, *p.pr.* staying], to hold up or support; prop; to sustain; to check; hold back; to put off for a time; postpone; to stiffen or steady, as a mast, by ropes; tack: *v.i.* to remain; as, to *stay* at home all day; abide for a time; as, to *stay* at a hotel; to stop; stand still; to wait; colloquially, hold out or last; as, a horse *stays* well.—*n.* stayer.

stay-sail (stā'sāl"; stā'sl), *n.* any sail extended on a stay, or rope which supports a mast.

stead (stĕd), *n.* the place which another had or might have; as, to go to war in another's *stead;* use; service; advantage; as, it will stand you in good *stead.*

stead-fast (stĕd'fȧst), *adj.* firmly fixed or settled; steady; constant; as, *steadfast* faith. Also, **stedfast.** —*adv.* **steadfastly, stedfastly.**—*n.* **steadfastness, stedfastness.**

stead-y (stĕd'ĭ), *adj.* [*comp.* steadier, *superl.* steadiest], firm in position or support; as, a *steady* foundation; constant in feeling or purpose; resolute; unwavering; as, *steady* devotion to a cause; regular; uniform; as, the *steady* beat of the pulse; sober; industrious; as, a *steady* young man; keeping nearly upright: said of a ship: *v.t.* [*p.t.* and *p.p.* steadied, *p.pr.* steadying], to make or keep steady or firm; make resolute: *v.i.* to become steady or firm. —*adv.* **steadily.**—*n.* **steadiness.**

steak (stāk), *n.* a slice of beef or other meat, for broiling etc.

steal (stēl), *v.t.* [*p.t.* stole, *p.p.* stolen, *p.pr.* stealing], to take by theft; take without leave or right; take or get by art or surprise; as, to *steal* a kiss; to move in a secret or stealthy manner; as, to *steal* a hand into a pocket; gain secretly and gradually; as, time *steals* away one's youth: *v.i.* to commit theft; slip in or out unnoticed; slip or creep along; as, to silently *steal* away: *n.* a theft. —*n.* **stealer.**

stealth (stĕlth), *n.* secret means used to accomplish an object; underhand action.

stealth-y (stĕl'thĭ), *adj.* [*comp.* stealthier, *superl.* stealthiest], acting or done slyly, or by stealth; secret; furtive; as, a *stealthy* tread.—*adv.* **stealthily.**—*n.* **stealthiness.**

steam (stēm), *n.* vapor into which water is changed when boiling; the visible mist of condensed water; vapor; colloquially, force; energy: *v.i.* to throw off steam; as, the soup *steams* in the kettle; rise or pass off in steam; as, moisture *steams* from the earth; move by steam; as, the vessel *steamed* out of the harbor: *v.t.* to treat or cook with steam; as, to *steam* a pudding. —*adj.* **steamy.**

steam-er (stēm'ẽr), *n.* a vessel or vehicle moved by steam; an apparatus for steaming food, etc.

steam-ship (stēm'shĭp"), *n.* a vessel moved by steam power.

steam tur-bine (stēm tûr'bĭn), a steam engine in which the steam acts upon a motor, or turbine, instead of on a piston.

ste-a-rin (stē'ȧ-rĭn), *n.* a white compound contained in many animal and vegetable fats, which raises the melting point of the fat.

ste-a-tite (stē'ȧ-tīt), *n.* an impure kind of talc, or soft mineral substance: called also *soapstone.*

steed (stēd), *n.* a horse, especially one which is spirited or high-strung.

steel (stēl), *n.* a variety of iron refined and combined with a small portion of carbon, very tough, hard, and elastic, and, for a given size, one of the strongest materials known; any instrument or weapon made of steel: *adj.* made of, or like, steel; hence, hard; unfeeling: *v.t.* to overlay, edge, or tip with steel; make hard, strong, or unfeeling; as, to *steel* one's heart.

steel bronze (stēl'brŏnz"), an alloy of tin and copper, so hardened as to render it as strong and durable as steel.

steel-y (stēl'ĭ), *adj.* made of, or like, steel; hard; unbending; colored like steel.

steel-yard (stēl'yärd; stĭl'yẽrd), *n.* a kind of balance, consisting of a horizontal bar or lever supported near one end, and marked in pounds and ounces, the article to be weighed being hung on the short arm, and a weight moved along the long arm.

steep (stēp), *adj.* having a sharp pitch or slope; being far from the horizontal; precipitous; as, a *steep* hill; colloquially, high; excessive; as, a *steep* price: *n.* a precipitous place; a cliff: *v.t.* to soak in a liquid, usually heated below boiling-point, so as to take out the essence or flavor of; as, to *steep* tea; to imbue with something; as, to *steep* oneself in learning.—*adv.* **steeply.**—*n.* **steepness.**

Syn., *adj.* high, abrupt, sharp.
Ant. (see flat, low).

stee-ple (stē'pl), *n.* a tower or turret tapering to a point; a spire.

stee-ple-chase (stē'pl-chās"), *n.* a cross-country horse race; hence, a race over a prescribed course in which obstructions have to be leaped.

stee-ple-jack (stē'pl-jăk"), *n.* a workman whose trade is to repair steeples, towers, or other high structures, and who is therefore an expert in climbing.

steer (stēr), *n.* a young castrated male of the ox kind: *v.t.* to guide the course of; as, to *steer* a ship; control; direct: *v.i.* to guide a ship in its course; to go in a given direction guided by the helm; as, the boat *steered* toward shore; obey the helm; as, the ship *steers* well; conduct oneself.

steer-age (stēr'āj), *n.* the act of steering, or guiding; the effect of the helm on a vessel; that part of a ship, usually on or below the main deck, set apart for those passengers who pay the lowest rates; in a warship, the part of the berth-deck used as the quarters of junior officers, etc.

steer-age-way (stēr'āj-wā"), *n.* rate of motion through the water sufficient to render a vessel governable by the helm.

stel-lar (stĕl'ẽr), *adj.* pertaining to stars; as, *stellar* rays; starry; as, *stellar* regions.

stel-late (stĕl'āt), *adj.* star-shaped or star-like; as, *stellate* leaves. Also, **stellated.**

stel-li-form (stĕl'ĭ-fôrm), *adj.* star-shaped.

stel-lu-lar (stĕl'ū-lẽr), *adj.* having the shape or appearance of little stars; as, the *stellular* fireflies; set or marked with spots like stars.

stem (stĕm), *n.* the principal stalk or trunk of a tree or plant; the slender stalk that bears the leaves, fruit, etc.; any slender support, handle, etc., resembling the stem of a plant; as, the *stem* of a goblet; a branch of a family; the part of a vessel's structure to which the sides are fastened at the bow; the prow; the part of an inflected word that does not change; in music, the perpendicular line joined to the head of a note: *v.t.* [*p.t.* and *p.p.* stemmed, *p.pr.* stemming], to stop or check; to make headway against; resist; as, a boat *stems* the tide; to remove the stems from: **stem-winder**, a watch wound by turning a head or knob on the end of the stem.

stench (stĕnch), *n.* a strong offensive odor; disgusting smell; stink: often used figuratively.

sten-cil (stĕn'sĭl), *n.* a thin sheet of metal, paper, etc., cut with an open pattern, so that when it is placed on a surface and color is laid on, a certain figure or design is made: *v.t.* [*p.t.* and *p.p.* stenciled, *p.pr.* stenciling], to mark or color with a stencil.

sten-o-graph (stĕn'ō-grȧf), *n.* a writing in shorthand: *v.t.* to write or report in shorthand.

ste-nog-ra-pher (stē-nŏg'rȧ-fẽr), *n.* a shorthand writer. Also, **stenographist.**

sten-o-graph-ic (stĕn"ō-grăf'ĭk), *adj.* pertaining to, or written in, shorthand, or stenography. Also, **stenographical.**—*adv.* **stenographically.**

ste-nog-ra-phy (stē-nŏg'rȧ-fĭ), *n.* the art of writing in shorthand, by using abbreviations or symbols for words, phrases, etc.; shorthand.

Sten-tor (stĕn'tôr), *n.* in the Trojan War, a Greek herald with a very loud voice: **stentor**, any person with a very loud and powerful voice.

sten-to-ri-an (stĕn-tō'rĭ-ȧn), *adj.* extremely loud or powerful; as, *stentorian* tones.

step (stĕp), *n.* a movement made by the foot in walking, running, etc.; a pace; the distance passed over by a single movement of the foot in walking or running; as, come a *step* nearer; any short distance; as, it is only a *step* to my house; footprint; manner of walking; gait; as, a steady *step;* the sound made by the placing of a foot in walking, etc.; a single tread in a flight of stairs; action; measure; as, the first *step* in an undertaking; grade; degree; as, to advance a *step* in a profession; an interval between two tones in a musical scale: *pl.* progress by walking: *v.i.* [*p.t.* and *p.p.* stepped, *p.pr.* stepping], to move the foot backward or forward, etc., and put it down, as in walking, dancing, etc.; to walk a short distance; as, to *step* around the corner; to walk slowly or with dignity: *v.t.* to set, as the foot; measure by steps; as, to *step* off the length of a room; fix the foot of in its frame or block, and so erect, as a mast.

step-broth-er (stĕp'brŭth"ẽr), *n.* the son of one's stepfather or stepmother by a marriage previous to the marriage with one's own mother or father.

step-child (stĕp'chīld"), *n.* the child of one's husband or wife by a marriage previous to marriage with oneself.

step-daugh-ter (stĕp'dô"tẽr), *n.* the daughter of one's husband or wife by a marriage previous to marriage with oneself.

step-fa-ther (stĕp'fä"thẽr), *n.* the husband of one's mother by a marriage subsequent to her marriage with one's own father.

step-lad-der (stĕp'lăd"ẽr), *n.* a portable set of steps, having a support attached to the back by hinges.

step-moth-er (stĕp'mŭth"ẽr), *n.* the wife of one's father by a marriage subsequent to his marriage with one's own mother.

steppe (stĕp), *n.* a vast level plain without forests, as in Russia.

step-ping-stone (stĕp'ĭng-stōn"), *n.* a stone that serves as a foothold, as in crossing a stream or a muddy road; hence, any means by which one may advance.

step-sis-ter (stĕp'sĭs"tẽr), *n.* a daughter of one's stepfather or stepmother by a marriage previous to marriage with one's own mother or father.

step-son (stĕp'sŭn"), *n.* a son of one's husband or wife by a marriage previous to marriage with oneself.

stere (stēr), *n.* in the metric system, a unit of cubic measurement equal to 35.31 cubic feet.

ster-e-om-e-ter (stẽr"ē-ŏm'ē-tẽr; stē"rē-ŏm'ē-tẽr), *n.* an instrument for measuring the solid contents of a body; an instrument for determining specific gravity.

ster-e-op-ti-con (stẽr"ē-ŏp'tĭ-kŏn; stē"rē-ŏp'tĭ-kŏn), *n.* a lantern for throwing pictures upon a screen by means of a powerful light.

ster-e-o-scope (stẽr'ē-ō-skōp"; stē'rē-ō-skōp), *n.* an instrument by means of which two pictures, taken from slightly different points of view, appear as one and stand out.—*adj.* **stereoscopic, stereoscopical.**—*adv.* **stereoscopically.**

ster-e-o-type (stẽr'ē-ō-tīp"; stē'rē-ō-tīp), *n.* a plate made by casting type metal into a mold taken in plaster, etc., from a printing surface: *v.t.* to make or cast such plates of; printing from such plates; fix into a permanent form.

ster-ile (stĕr'ĭl), *adj.* not fertile; unfruitful; producing little or nothing; as, *sterile* land; without power to reproduce;

barren; as, *sterile* seed; without ideas; as, a *sterile* mind.

ste-ril-i-ty (stē-rĭl'ĭ-tĭ), *n.* the state of being nonproductive; barrenness; unfruitfulness.

ster-i-li-za-tion (stĕr"ĭ-lĭ-zā'shŭn; stĕr"-ĭ-lĭ-zā'shŭn), *n.* the act or process of making fruitless or barren; state of being fruitless or barren.

ster-i-lize (stĕr'ĭ-līz), *v.t.* to make fruitless or barren; deprive of the power of reproduction; especially, to free from germs; as, to *sterilize* milk.—*n.* sterilizer.

ster-ling (stûr'lĭng), *adj.* pertaining to British money of standard value; as, pounds *sterling;* having full value; genuine; as, *sterling* silver; of high merit; as, a man of *sterling* character: *n.* the standard of purity of British money.

stern (stûrn), *adj.* severe or harsh in disposition or character; strict; unrelenting; as, a *stern* father; proceeding from such a nature; hard; as, a *stern* command or look; firm; rigid; unyielding; as, *stern* discipline; forbidding; as, a *stern*, rocky coast: *n.* the after or rear part of a vessel.—*adv.* sternly.—*n.* sternness.

ster-num (stûr'nŭm), *n.* the breastbone. —*adj.* sternal.

stern-way (stûrn'wā"), *n.* movement of a vessel backward.

ster-to-rous (stûr'tō-rŭs), *adj.* accompanied by a snoring sound; as, *stertorous* breathing.—*adv.* stertorously.—*n.* stertorousness.

stet (stĕt), *v.t.* a Latin word meaning *let it stand:* used in proof reading as a mark to indicate that something marked for omission is to remain. [Lat.]

ste-thom-e-ter (stē-thŏm'ē-tẽr), *n.* an apparatus for measuring the external movements of the walls of the chest during the process of breathing.

steth-o-scope (stĕth'ō-skōp), *n.* a kind of telephone for examining the chest or organs of the chest, by conveying to the ear of the examiner the sounds produced in the body; an instrument used in the trenches and elsewhere to detect the sounds of digging or other enemy operations.

ste-ve-dore (stē'vē-dōr"), *n.* one who loads or unloads a vessel in port, or stows cargo in a ship's hold or interior.

stew (stū), *v.t.* and *v.i.* to boil slowly or with a simmering heat; colloquially, to worry; *n.* a dish prepared by boiling slowly; colloquially, a state of nervous anxiety; worry.

stew-ard (stū'ẽrd), *n.* [*fem.* stewardess], one who manages the household affairs of a family or institution; the manager of a large estate or farm; a person employed at a hotel, club, or on board ship to superintend the buying and distribution of food; on board ship, a waiter or an attendant in staterooms; a fiscal agent; as, the *steward* of a church.

stew-ard-ship (stū'ẽrd-shĭp), *n.* the office or duties of a steward, or one who directs affairs for others; management of affairs for others.

stick (stĭk), *n.* a small branch or shoot cut off a tree; a long, thin piece of wood; something similar in shape to such a piece; as, a *stick* of candy; a rod or wand to be held in the hand, as a cane; a device used by printers in setting type by hand; a thrust or stab with a pointed instrument; colloquially, an ignorant or dull person: *v.t.* [*p.t.* and *p.p.* stuck, *p.pr.* sticking], to push or thrust so as to penetrate something; as, to *stick* a pin in a cushion; pierce with a pointed instrument; as, to *stick* a finger with a pin; stab; kill by thrusting a pointed instrument through; as, to *stick* pigs; to push or poke; as, to *stick* out one's foot; insert; fasten on carelessly; as, to *stick* a bow on one's hair; cause to adhere; as, to *stick* a stamp on a letter; compose or set up; as, to *stick* type: *v.i.* to be held or fixed by being thrust in; as, a pin *sticks* in a cushion; be pushed outward or forward; protrude; with *up, out, from, through;* to hold to a surface; adhere; as, dough *sticks* to the hands; cling closely; as, to *stick* to a cause; to be stopped from going farther; as, the cart *stuck* in the mud; be puzzled; hesitate; with *at;* as, he will *stick* at nothing to gain his ends.—*n.* sticker.

stick-i-ness (stĭk'ĭ-nĕs), *n.* the state or quality of being adhesive or gluey.

stick-le (stĭk'l), *v.i.* to wrangle or contend stubbornly, especially about something of little importance; to hesitate; to have scruples.—*n.* stickler.

stick-le-back (stĭk'l-băk"), *n.* a class of scaleless fish with spines, or thornlike projections, on their bodies.

stick-y (stĭk'ĭ), *adj.* [*comp.* stickier, *superl.* stickiest], adhesive; gluey.—*adv.* stickily.

stiff (stĭf), *adj.* not easily bent; rigid; firm; inflexible; as, *stiff* cardboard; not easily moved; not limber; as, a *stiff* neck; not liquid or fluid; as, a *stiff* paste; strong; violent; as, a *stiff* breeze; not natural or easy; formal; as, a *stiff* manner; not easily subdued; as, a *stiff* opponent; difficult; as, a *stiff* climb or examination; slang, high, dear; as, a *stiff* charge; slang, a dead body.—*adv.* stiffly.—*n.* stiffness.

stif-fen (stĭf'n), *v.t.* to make unbending or inflexible; make more thick; as, to *stiffen* paste; to make stubborn: *v.i.* to become less limber; grow rigid; become thicker; increase in force; as, the wind *stiffened;* grow more obstinate.

stiff-necked (stĭf'nĕkt"), *adj.* stubborn and obstinate; as, *stiff-necked* pride.

sti-fle (stī'fl), *v.t.* to suffocate or stop the breath of; smother; extinguish or put out; as, to *stifle* a fire; hide or conceal; as, to *stifle* a yawn: *v.i.* to be suffocated or smothered: *n.* the first joint above a horse's hock; corresponding to the knee in man.

sti-fling (stī'flĭng), *p.adj.* smothering; suffocating; as, the air is *stifling.*

stig-ma (stĭg'mȧ), *n.* [*pl.* stigmas (-mȧz), stigmata (-mȧ-tȧ)], a mark of disgrace or dishonor; a mark of taint, defect, blemish, etc.; a red speck on the skin; the upper part of the pistil of a flower, on which the pollen, or seedlike substance, falls.

stig-mat-ic (stĭg-măt'ĭk), *adj.* marked with a stigma, or red speck or spot.

stig-ma-tize (stĭg'mȧ-tīz), *v.t.* to mark with stigmata, or red specks or spots; hold up to disgrace, reproach, or dishonor; brand with infamy; denounce. Also, stigmatise.—*n.* stigmatization, stigmatisation.

stile (stīl), *n.* a set of steps to pass from one side of a fence or wall to the other; a pin set on the face of a sundial to cast a shadow; an upright piece in framing or paneling.

sti-let-to (stĭ-lĕt'tō), *n.* a small dagger with a thin, rounded, and pointed blade; a pointed instrument for making eyelet holes.

Still

still (stĭl), *adj.* being at rest or without motion; quiet; as, the boy is never *still;* calm; peaceful; as, a *still* lake; silent; hushed; subdued; as, a *still* night or voice; not sparkling, as wine: *adv.* to this time; nevertheless; always; after that; even more: *v.t.* to make calm; put at rest; as, to *still* the waves; *still* the passions; to make quiet; pacify; as, to *still* an infant: *n.* an apparatus for making alcoholic liquors, as whisky, etc.—*adj.* **stilly.**—*n.* **stillness.**

Syn., v. lull, subdue, allay, restrain.

stilt (stĭlt), *n.* a pole of wood with a rest for the foot: used in pairs in walking; a kind of wading shore bird having very long legs, three toes, and a straight slender bill: called also *stilt-bird:* *v.t.* to set or raise on stilts.

Stilt

stilt-ed (stĭlt'ĕd), *adj.* elevated or raised, as if on stilts; hence, pompous; stiffly formal; as, a *stilted* speech.—*n.* **stiltedness.**

Stil-ton (stĭl'tŭn), *n.* a kind of rich, white cheese.

stim-u-lant (stĭm'ū-lănt), *n.* that which excites or spurs on, or which produces a temporary increase of vitality or energy; a medicine or alcoholic drink having such an effect: *pl.* intoxicants: *adj.* serving to excite or spur on; producing greater vitality or energy; action.

stim-u-late (stĭm'ū-lāt), *v.t.* to excite or rouse to activity; animate; spur on; encourage; produce greater vitality in: *v.i.* to act as an agent producing temporary increase of vitality, or as a goad.—*n.* **stimulator.**

stim-u-la-tion (stĭm"ū-lā'shŭn), *n.* the act of exciting or spurring on, or of producing a temporary increase of vitality or energy in; state or condition of being so excited.

stim-u-la-tive (stĭm'ū-lā-tĭv), *adj.* having the power of exciting or spurring on: *n.* anything that excites or spurs on.

stim-u-lus (stĭm'ū-lŭs), *n.* [*pl.* stimuli (-lī)], something that rouses the mind or senses; anything that excites to action; that which produces a temporary increase of vitality or energy.

sti-my (stī'mĭ), *n.* the position of a ball in golf when it lies directly between the ball of an opponent and the hole for which he is playing: *v.t.* to put a ball thus in the way of.

sting (stĭng), *n.* the sharp-pointed, often poisonous, organ with which certain animals and insects are furnished; one of the stiff, sharp-pointed, hollow hairs of certain plants; the thrust of such an organ or hair; the wound made by it; a sharp, smarting mental or physical pain; that which goads to action; as, the *sting* of conscience: *v.t.* [*p.t.* and *p.p.* stung, *p.pr.* stinging], to pierce or wound with, or as with, a sting; cause a sharp, smarting pain to; as, cold *stings* the face; goad or drive, as by taunts or reproaches; cause to suffer keenly; as, remorse *stings* his soul: *v.i.* to inflict a sharp, smarting wound; as, the wasp *stings;* to be sharply painful.—*n.* **stinger.**

sting-ray (stĭng'rā), *n.* a fish with one or more sharp spines, or stingers, on the tail, capable of making a dangerous wound. Also, **sting ray, stingaree.**

stin-gy (stĭn'jĭ), *adj.* [*comp.* stingier, *superl.* stingiest], very saving of, and extremely eager to get, money; meanly ungenerous; miserly; scanty.—*adv.* **stingily.** —*n.* **stinginess.**

stink (stĭnk), *n.* an offensive odor; disgusting smell: *v.t.* [*p.t.* stank, stunk, *p.p.* stunk, *p.pr.* stinking], to throw off a strong, offensive odor: *v.t.* to cause to have an offensive smell: with *up:* **stinkpot,** a shell, often of earthenware, charged with matter that burns readily, which on bursting sends out a foul smell and suffocating smoke.

stint (stĭnt), *v.t.* to keep within certain limits; to limit to a scant allowance; as, to *stint* the food: *v.i.* to be sparing or frugal: *n.* a limit or bound; amount fixed or task assigned.

sti-pend (stī'pĕnd), *n.* settled pay or salary for services.

sti-pen-di-a-ry (stī-pĕn'dĭ-ā-rĭ), *adj.* receiving stipend, or salary: *n.* one who performs services for a salary.

stip-ple (stĭp''l), *v.t.* to draw or engrave by means of dots; to paint by means of small, short touches: *n.* a method or effect in oil or water-color painting obtained by means of dots instead of strokes. Also, *n.* **stippling.**

stip-u-late (stĭp'ū-lāt), *v.i.* to bargain or contract; to agree to do or not do a certain thing: *v.t.* to arrange or settle definitely; to specify, as a condition.

stip-u-la-tion (stĭp"ū-lā'shŭn), *n.* the act of stipulating, or agreeing; a contract, agreement, or bargain; a special condition in a contract.

stip-u-la-tor (stĭp'ū-lā"tẽr), *n.* one who makes an agreement or contract.

stip-ule (stĭp'ūl), *n.* a small leaflike appendage or stalk at the base of a leaf.

stir (stûr), *v.t.* [*p.t.* and *p.p.* stirred, *p.pr.* stirring], to put into motion; move; to change the relative position of the particles of, as a liquid; as, to *stir* soup; agitate; rouse; as, to *stir* men to devotion: *v.i.* to move or exert oneself; be in motion; change place; colloquially, rise in the morning: *n.* bustle; activity; agitation; tumult; noise; public interest; excitement.—*n.* **stirrer.**

stir-a-bout (stûr'ȧ-bout"), *n.* a thick soup or porridge made of oatmeal or corn meal boiled in water and stirred; a hasty pudding.

stir-ring (stûr'ĭng), *n.* the act of moving: *adj.* busy; bustling; exciting; stimulating; as, *stirring* events.

stir-rup (stĭr'ŭp), *n.* a kind of iron ring or hoop fastened to a saddle to support a rider's foot: **stirrup cup,** a cup of liquor drunk by a horseman about to depart; hence, a farewell cup.

stitch (stĭtch), *n.* a single pass of a needle and thread through anything, as in sewing; a link or loop of yarn in knitting; a particular arrangement of threads in needlework; a sudden, sharp pain; as, a *stitch* in the side; a furrow; colloquially, the least portion of clothing; as, he had not a clean *stitch*: *v.t.* to unite or trim by passing a needle and thread through; to form (land) into furrows: *v.i.* to practice stitching or sewing.

stith-y (stĭth'ĭ; stĭth'ĭ), *n.* a blacksmith's shop or forge; an anvil.

sti-ver (stī'vẽr), *n.* a Dutch coin worth about two cents; hence, anything of little value.

stoat (stōt), *n.* the European ermine or weasel, especially in its summer coat of reddish-brown; any ermine or weasel.

stock (stŏk), *n.* the trunk or stem of a tree or plant; a pillar, log, or post; a trunk or plant in which a graft is placed; race, line of descent, family, or relationship; domestic animals raised on a farm, etc.: called *live stock;* a garden flower with a woody stem; the wooden part of a firearm to which the barrel and lock are attached; as, a gun*stock;* a term used in ordnance for various things, such as the nave, or hub, of a wooden wheel, the handle of a tool, a part of a gun-carriage, etc.; foundation of soups, etc.; a fund due to persons for money loaned, or the securities for such a fund; the capital of a company or corporation; also, the shares of capital in a company; the capital or goods in a business; hence, any store or supply; a wide, close-fitting band of silk, etc., worn about the neck: *pl.* a wooden frame with holes in which to confine the legs, or hands and legs, of those found guilty of minor offenses; also, a frame on which a ship is built: *v.t.* to store up; fill; supply; as, to *stock* a warehouse: *v.i.* to take in or obtain supplies: *adj.* kept in stock, or on hand.

stock-ade (stŏk-ād'), *n.* a line of posts or trunks of trees set firmly in the earth and close together, often with loopholes, and used as a barrier for defense or an inclosure for cattle: *v.t.* to surround with, or defend by, such a barrier.

stock-bro-ker (stŏk'brō"kẽr), *n.* one who buys and sells shares in corporations, etc., for others.—*n.* **stockbroking.**

stock com-pa-ny (stŏk kŭm'pȧ-nĭ), a corporation, the capital of which is represented by shares that may be bought and sold.

stock ex-change (stŏk ĕks-chānj'), an association of dealers in shares of corporation who meet and conduct their business according to settled rules; a place where shares of corporations are bought and sold.

stock-fish (stŏk'fĭsh"), *n.* salted and dried fish.

stock-hold-er (stŏk'hōl"dẽr), *n.* one who holds shares in public funds or in a stock company or corporation.

stock-i-net (stŏk"ĭ-nĕt'), *n.* an elastic fabric used for making stockings, underwear, etc.

stock-ing (stŏk'ĭng), *n.* a close-fitting woven or knitted covering for the foot and leg, made of silk, wool, or cotton.

stock-job-ber (stŏk'jŏb"ẽr), *n.* one who deals or speculates in shares of corporations.—*n.* **stockjobbing.**

stock-man (stŏk'măn), *n.* one who has charge of live stock, as cattle; a ranchman.

stock-still (stŏk'stĭl"), *adj.* still as a post; motionless.

stock-y (stŏk'ĭ), *adj.* short and stout or thick.

stock-yard (stŏk'yärd"), *n.* a yard for live stock, as cattle, often with stables, pens, etc.

sto-gy (stō'gĭ), *n.* a long, coarse cigar; a coarse boot or shoe: *adj.* rough; coarse; heavy. [Colloq.]

Sto-ic (stō'ĭk), *n.* a follower of the Greek philosopher Zeno, who taught that a wise man should be governed by the reason, subdue all passions, and be indifferent to pleasure or pain: stoic, one indifferent to pleasure or pain: *adj.* pertaining to the Stoics; indifferent to pleasure or pain. Also, *adj.* **stoical.**—*adv.* **stoically.**—*n.* **stoicalness.**

sto-i-cism (stō'ĭ-sĭzm), *n.* the beliefs and teachings of the Stoics, or those who taught that one should be indifferent to pleasure or pain; uncomplaining endurance; grim courage.

stoke (stōk), *v.t.* to maintain and tend the fire in; as, to *stoke* a furnace: *v.i.* to tend a fire in a furnace, etc.

stok-er (stōk'ẽr), *n.* one who, or that which, supplies fuel to a furnace, as of a boiler; a fireman.

stole (stōl), *p.t.* of the verb *steal*: *n.* a long, narrow scarf fringed at the ends and worn over the shoulders by bishops and priests.

stol-id (stŏl'ĭd), *adj.* not easily aroused or excited; stupid; dull.—*adv.* **stolidly.**—*n.* **stolidness.**

sto-lid-i-ty (stō-lĭd'ĭ-tĭ), *n.* the state or quality of being slow and stupid; mental dulness.

stom-ach (stŭm'ŭk), *n.* the main organ of digestion in the body; desire for food; appetite; hence, inclination; liking; desire; as, he had no *stomach* for revenge: *v.t.* to put up with; bear without displeasure.

stom-ach-er (stŭm'ŭk-ẽr; stŭm'ȧ-chẽr), *n.* an ornamental breast covering, worn by women.

sto-mach-ic (stō-măk'ĭk), *adj.* pertaining to, exciting, or strengthening the stomach: *n.* a strengthening medicine for the stomach.

sto-mat-ic (stō-măt'ĭk), *adj.* of or pertaining to the mouth: *n.* a medicine for diseases of the mouth.

stone (stōn), *n.* a hard mass of earthy or mineral matter; rock as a material used for building, etc.; a small piece of rock; something made of such rock, as a monument to the dead; a gem; as, a precious *stone;* the hard covering of the kernel of certain fruits; as, a peach *stone;* in Great Britain, a weight of varying value, usually fourteen pounds avoirdupois; a stony substance sometimes found in the kidneys or bladder; as, gall*stones;* hardness: *v.t.* to pelt with pieces of rock; kill by hurling pieces of rock at; remove the stones, or pits, from; as, to *stone* cherries: *adj.* made of stone or earthenware; as, a *stone* jar: **stone age,** the period of civilization before the introduction of bronze, when stone weapons, tools, etc., were used.

stone-blind (stōn'blīnd"), *adj.* completely blind, physically or mentally.

stone bruise (stōn brōōz), a bruise made by a stone, as on the foot from walking barefoot on stones.

stone-cut-ting (stōn'kŭt"ĭng), *n.* the occupation of cutting or shaping stone, as for building, or of cutting gems.—*n.* **stonecutter.**

stone-ware (stōn′wâr″), *n.* a coarse kind of pottery, baked hard and glazed.

stone-wort (stōn′wûrt″), *n.* a kind of plant often covered with a stonelike substance.

ston-y (stōn′ĭ), *adj.* [*comp.* stonier, *superl.* stoniest], full of, or containing many, stones; as, a *stony* road; pertaining to, or like, stone; hard; cruel; pitiless; as, a *stony* heart.—*adv.* stonily.—*n.* stoniness.

stood (stŏŏd), past tense of the verb *stand*.

stool (stōōl), *n.* a seat without a back, often having three legs; a bench for the feet, or for the knees in kneeling; the seat used in emptying the bowels; an emptying of the bowels; a pole to which a bird, as a pigeon, is fastened to decoy, or entice, other birds within range: **stool pigeon**, a pigeon, used as a decoy; a person used to entice others into a snare; a police spy.

stoop (stōōp), *v.i.* to bend the body downward and forward; descend from rank or dignity; submit; yield; sweep down on prey: *v.t.* to bend (the body) downward and forward: *n.* a bending downward and forward; habitual forward bend of head and shoulders; descent from dignity; fall of a bird upon its prey; stairway, veranda, or porch with seats; a vessel of liquor; a stoup.

stop (stŏp), *v.t.* [*p.t.* and *p.p.* stopped, *p.pr.* stopping], to close, as a hole or opening, by filling, covering, etc.; close the opening of; hence, to stanch (a wound); to hinder, check, or impede; as, sobs *stopped* her utterance; make impassable; as, to *stop* a passage; to arrest the progress of; prevent from going on; as, to *stop* a car; to cause to cease; as, to *stop* a noise; desist from; regulate the sounds of: *v.i.* to cease from any motion or action; as, all work *stopped;* to come to an end; as, the noise *stopped;* colloquially, to tarry; stay: *n.* the act of stopping; state of being stopped; a hindrance or check; a pause or delay; a regulator for the motion of a machine; a device for regulating the pitch of a musical instrument; one of a series of organ pipes; mark used in punctuation.

stop-cock (stŏp′kŏk″), *n.* a faucet or tap with a stop or valve to cut off the flow of a fluid.

stop–gap (stŏp′găp″), *n.* that which closes or fills an opening or gap; hence, a temporary expedient or makeshift.

stop-page (stŏp′āj), *n.* the act of ceasing or of arresting motion or action; state of being stopped; as, the *stoppage* of circulation.

stop-per (stŏp′ẽr), *n.* one who, or that which, stops up or closes; a plug, as of glass, wood, or cork, that closes a vent or hole, as in a bottle, cask, etc.

stop-ple (stŏp′l), *n.* a cork or plug; a stopper; *v.t.* to close with a cork, etc.

stop watch (stŏp wŏch), a watch, the hands of which can be instantly stopped by pressing on a spring or catch: usually equipped with a large hand to indicate seconds or fractions of a second: used for timing races, etc.

stor-age (stōr′āj), *n.* the act of placing goods in a warehouse, etc.; safe keeping of goods in a warehouse, etc.; space for the safe keeping of goods; price for storage.

stor-age bat-ter-y (stōr′āj băt′ẽr-ĭ), an apparatus in which electric energy in the form of a current is transformed into chemical energy and stored up for future use, when it can be changed back into electric energy.

store (stōr), *n.* a great quantity; stock on hand or collected; a reserve fund; abundance or plenty; a warehouse; shop: *pl.* naval and military arms, ammunition, clothing, food, etc.: *v.t.* to furnish or supply; as, to *store* a building with coal; gather in quantities; accumulate or collect; hoard up; to put in a store or warehouse.

store-house (stōr′hous″), *n.* a building where goods, especially foodstuffs, are stored; a warehouse.

store-keep-er (stōr′kēp″ẽr), *n.* in the United States, one who keeps a shop.

store-room (stōr′rōōm″), *n.* a room in which things, especially supplies, are kept until needed.

sto-ried (stō′rĭd), *adj.* having floors or stories; as, a two-*storied* house: also spelled *storeyed;* told in, or associated with, story, legend, or history.

stork (stôrk), *n.* a large wading bird with long legs, long neck, and a large pointed bill.

storm (stôrm), *n.* a violent disturbance of the atmosphere, often with a heavy fall of rain, snow, or hail; an outburst of passion or excitement; a violent commotion; violent assault on a fortified place: *v.t.* to attack with violence or open force; as, to *storm* a fort: *v.i.* to blow violently, or to rain, hail, snow, etc.; to rage boisterously.

Syn., *n.* tempest, agitation, disturbance.
Ant. (see calm).

storm-ing (stôr′mĭng), *n.* the taking of a fortified place by a violent and open assault; *p.adj.* violently angry or raging: **storming party**, a body of troops detailed to storm a fortified place.

storm-y (stôr′mĭ), *adj.* [*comp.* stormier, *superl.* stormiest], marked by, or accompanied with, tempests or furious winds; boisterous; tempestuous; as, *stormy* weather; marked by passion or fury; turbulent; violent; as, a *stormy* life.—*adv.* stormily.—*n.* storminess.

Stor-thing (stôr′tĭng), *n.* the Norwegian parliament, or chief lawmaking body.

sto-ry (stō′rĭ), *n.* [*pl.* stories (-rĭz)], a narrative or recital of events either real or imagined; a short tale or romance; history; a report or statement; an anecdote; colloquially, a falsehood; a stage or floor of a building: also spelled *storey;* a set of rooms on a single floor; the space between two floors of a building: **story-teller**, one who relates tales or anecdotes.

Syn. account, legend, myth, incident, record.

stoup (stōōp), *n.* a small vessel or a cup for holding liquors; as, a *stoup* of wine; a basin for holy water at the entrance of a church. Also, **stoop**.

stout (stout), *adj.* bold; brave; resolute; as, a *stout* heart; firm; tough; strong; as, a *stout* vessel; large; bulky; strong; as, a *stout* horse: *n.* strong, dark porter; any strong ale or beer.—*adv.* stoutly.—*n.* stoutness.

sto-va-ine (stō′vā-ĭn), *n.* fluid that is injected into the spinal cord to produce insensibility during surgical operations.

stove (stōv), *n.* an apparatus for containing a fire for cooking or heating:

v.t. to heat or dry, as in a stove; to keep warm by artificial heat; as, to *stove* orange trees.

stow (stō), *v.t.* to fill by packing anything closely in; as, to *stow* the hold of a ship with goods; to put away compactly; pack; as, to *stow* cargo in a ship's hold.

stow-age (stō'āj), *n.* the act or manner of packing; state of being packed; room in which things may be packed; things packed away; money paid for packing things away.

stow-a-way (stō'ȧ-wā"), *n.* one who hides on a vessel or railway train in order to obtain a free passage.

stra-bis-mus (strȧ-bĭz'mŭs), *n.* cross-eye; squinting.—*adj.* **strabismic.**

stra-bot-o-my (strȧ-bŏt'ō-mĭ), *n.* a surgical operation for the cure of squinting, or cross-eye.

strad-dle (străd'l), *v.t.* to stand or sit astride of: *v.i.* to stand or walk with the legs wide apart: *n.* the act of standing, sitting, or walking with the legs wide apart; the space between the feet or legs when wide apart.

strafe (strä'fē), *v.t.* punish: the imperative form: often used as slang in the trenches, meaning to bombard heavily. [GER.]

strag-gle (străg'l), *v.i.* to wander out of the direct course or way; stray; ramble; roam idly about; spread apart irregularly; move irregularly and apart from others, or from each other; as, they *straggled* into the room.—*adj.* **straggly.**—*n.* **straggler.**

straight (strāt), *adj.* not crooked or curved; extending throughout in the same direction; as, a *straight* road; upright; as, to live a *straight* life; direct; not confused; as, *straight* reasoning; right; correct; as, *straight* accounts; slang, strong in support of a party; as, a *straight* Democrat: *adv.* in a direct course; directly; at once.—*adv.* **straightly.**—*n.* **straightness.**

straight-en (strāt'n), *v.t.* to make free of turns or curves; to put in order; to free from trouble: *v.i.* to become straight.

straight-for-ward (strāt"fôr'wẽrd), *adj.* proceeding in a direct course or manner; honest.—*adv.* **straightforwardly.**—*n.* **straightforwardness.**

straight-way (strāt'wā"), *adv.* at once; immediately.

strain (strān), *n.* stock; race; line of descent; inborn disposition; a trace or streak; as, a *strain* of madness; tune or melody; a poem or verse; tone or manner of speech or thought; as, to write or speak in a lofty *strain;* extreme stretching; as, a *strain* on a rope; a violent effort; injury due to overwork; as, nerve *strain;* a sprain: *v.t.* to draw out with force; stretch; as, to *strain* a rope; put to its utmost strength; as, to *strain* every muscle; injure by overtaxing; as, to *strain* one's back; make uneasy or unnatural; force; as, to *strain* a welcome; embrace; as, she *strained* the child to her breast; filter; as, to *strain* coffee: *v.i.* to make violent efforts; pass through tiny holes; be filtered.

strain-er (strān'ẽr), *n.* one who, or that which, stretches or exerts great tension; a device through which any liquid is passed to make it pure or to separate it from solid matter; as, a coffee *strainer.*

strait (strāt), *n.* a narrow passage of water connecting two larger bodies of water; perplexity; difficulty; as, to be in a financial *strait:* often plural: *adj.* narrow; not broad; as, the *strait* gate; confined; tight; as, a *strait*-jacket; restricted; hampered.—*adv.* **straitly.**—*n.* **straitness.**

strait-en (strāt'n), *v.t.* to make narrow; contract; confine; put into difficulties; embarrass.

strait-jack-et (strāt'jăk"ĕt), *n.* a strong, tight coat put on so as to confine the arms of violent prisoners or violently insane persons: called also a *strait-waistcoat.*

strait-laced (strāt'lāst"), *adj.* laced tightly, as corsets; very strict in manners or morals.

strake (strāk), *n.* a breadth of planking or plating forming a continuous strip on the bottom or sides of a vessel.

strand (strănd), *n.* the shore of a sea, ocean, or lake; one of the strings or twists of a rope; a single thread: *v.t.* to drive or force upon the seashore; run aground; as, to *strand* a ship; leave in a state of embarrassment or difficulty; as, to be *stranded* in a strange city; to break one of the strings or twists of (a rope); to make, as a rope, by twisting the parts of together: *v.i.* to be drawn ashore; be left helpless.

strange (strānj), *adj.* pertaining to another country; foreign; as, *strange* lands; of or belonging to others; not one's own; as, a *strange* cat; not before known or seen; unfamiliar; as, the writing is *strange* to me; odd; queer; unusual; as, *strange* jewelry; reserved; shy; timid; as, to feel *strange* in company; inexperienced; as, she is *strange* to that work.—*adv.* **strangely.**—*n.* **strangeness.**

stran-ger (strān'jẽr), *n.* a foreigner; a guest or visitor; one who is unknown or who is not an acquaintance; one who is unfamiliar with a certain thing; as, he is a *stranger* to every language but his own.

stran-gle (străn'gl), *v.t.* to choke; to stop the breath of by squeezing the throat; suppress or stifle; as, to *strangle* one's desires: *v.i.* to be choked or suffocated: *n.pl.* a disease of horses: called also *distemper.* —*n.* **strangler, strangulation.**

stran-gu-late (străn'gū-lāt), *v.t.* to obstruct or compress so as to stop circulation; a term used in medicine; as, to *strangulate* a blood vessel; to strangle.—*n.* **strangulation.**

strap (străp), *n.* a long, narrow strip, as of leather or cloth, used to fasten about objects; anything like such a strap; a narrow strip or band, as of metal; a razor strop: *v.t.* [*p.t.* and *p.p.* strapped, *p.pr.* strapping], to fasten or bind with a strap; beat with a strap; sharpen, as a razor, by rubbing on a strap.

strap-ping (străp'ĭng), *adj.* tall; strong; robust; as, a *strapping* fellow. [COLLOQ.]

stra-ta (strā'tȧ), *n.pl.* of *stratum,* layers, as of rock. [LAT.]

strat-a-gem (străt'ȧ-jĕm), *n.* a trick or scheme for deceiving or surprising an enemy, especially in war; any trick or plan for gaining some advantage.

stra-te-gic (stra-tē'jĭk; strȧ-tĕj'ĭk), *adj.* pertaining to, or effected by, clever trickery or scheming; suitable for, or important in, the carrying out of a diplomatic or military plan; as, a *strategic* position, or a *strategic* moment; pertaining to the science of military command, or the direction of military movements; as, a *strategic* position: *n.pl.* the science of military warfare the direction of a campaign. Also, *adj.* **strategical.**—*adv.* **strategically.**

strat-e-gist (străt'ē-jĭst), *n.* one skilled in the science of military command, and in the direction of military movements; a clever secret diplomatist; one skilled in clever trickery.

strat-e-gy (străt'ē-jĭ), *n.* the art or science of military command, or the direction of military movements of great importance, especially with troops not actually engaged in battle; a show of skill in carrying out some special design; clever trickery.

strat-i-fi-ca-tion (străt'ĭ-fĭ-kā'shŭn), *n.* the act or process of forming in layers; state of being arranged in layers.

strat-i-fied (străt'ĭ-fīd), *adj.* formed in layers; as, *stratified* rock.

strat-i-fy (străt'ĭ-fī), *v.t.* and *v.i.* [*p.t.* and *p.p.* stratified, *p.pr.* stratifying], to form or arrange in strata, or layers.

stra-tum (strā'tŭm), *n.* [*pl.* strata (-tȧ), stratums (-tŭmz)], a layer; as, a *stratum* of rock.

stra-tus (strā'tŭs), *n.* a cloud form in a horizontal layer at a low level.

straw (strô), *n.* the stalk of grain; such stalks when cut and threshed; anything practically worthless; as, he is not worth a *straw*; mere trifle: *adj.* made of, or stuffed with, straw; as, a *straw* bed.

straw bail (strô bāl), worthless or sham security given by a person who pretends that he will be responsible for the appearance of another person at a given time and place.

straw-ber-ry (strô'bĕr-ĭ), *n.* [*pl.* strawberries (-ĭz)], a small, slightly acid, fleshy red fruit, growing on a vine close to the ground; the vine itself.

straw bid (strô bĭd), a bid, as to do a piece of work for a certain sum, by one who is unable or does not intend to do the work.

straw-board (strô'bōrd"), *n.* pasteboard made of straw ground to a pulp: used for packing, etc.

straw vote (strô vōt), a vote taken at any gathering of people to test the chances of election of two persons who are running for office.

stray (strā), *v.i.* to wander from the path or beyond limits; to roam; to err: *adj.* gone from the right way or beyond limits; wandering; as, a *stray* dog; irregular; occasional; as, a *stray* remark: *n.* a domestic animal that has wandered beyond limits or is lost; a person who wanders aimlessly or who is lost.

streak (strēk), *n.* a line of color different from the ground color; a trait not strongly marked; trace; as, a *streak* of fancy; stripe: *v.t.* to form streaks in; mark with streaks; to stripe.

streak-y (strēk'ĭ), *adj.* marked with streaks, or irregular stripes.—*adv.* **streakily.**—*n.* **streakiness.**

stream (strēm), *n.* a current of water or other fluid; anything flowing out of a source; as, a *stream* of words; a continued current or course; as, the *stream* of life; drift or tendency; as, the *stream* of opinion: *v.i.* to issue or flow in a stream; run in a current; issue forth; as, the crowd *streamed* from the hall; float, or stretch out with a waving movement; as, banners *streamed* in the air; move with a trail of light: *v.t.* flow with; as, her eyes *streamed* tears; cause to stretch out.

stream-er (strēm'ẽr), *n.* that which floats out; a long, narrow flag; a column of light, as that of the aurora borealis, or northern lights.

stream-let (strēm'lĕt), *n.* a little stream; a rivulet; a rill.

street (strēt), *n.* a public way in a city or town, lined with houses on either side; that part of the way reserved for vehicles; colloquially, that street in which most of the financial business of a city is carried on, as Wall Street in New York: the body of bankers and brokers doing business there; as, the man on the *street.*

street Ar-ab (strēt ăr'ăb), a homeless child who lives in the streets; an outcast boy or girl.

street car (strēt kär), a car for passengers that runs through the public streets, usually on rails.

street rail-way (strēt rāl'wā"), a railway on the surface of the streets of a city, as apart from a railroad, elevated road, or subway road.

strength (strĕngth), *n.* the state or quality of being strong; power; muscular force; vigor; as, the *strength* of a man; power of resistance; toughness; as, the *strength* of a rope; power to withstand attack; as, the *strength* of a fort; numbers or amount of any body, as an army; boldness or vigor, as of style; intensity, as of light or color; legal or moral force; as, the *strength* of testimony; mental or moral power of endurance; as, *strength* of purpose; intensity or violence, as of indignation; one on whom one relies; support; as, God is our refuge and *strength.*

strength-en (strĕng'thn), *v.t.* to make stronger; increase the power or security of; encourage: *v.i.* to become stronger.—*n.* **strengthener.**

stren-u-ous (strĕn'ū-ŭs), *adj.* urgent or eagerly pressing; ardent; bold; earnest; as, a *strenuous* reformer; calling for strong effort or exertion; as, to lead a *strenuous* life.—*adv.* **strenuously.**—*n.* **strenuousness, strenuosity.**

stress (strĕs), *n.* strain; pressure; importance; significance; as, to lay *stress* on a particular fact; compulsion; as, the *stress* of circumstances; force of utterance; as, the *stress* falls on the last syllable; mechanical pressure of any kind, such as a force that changes the shape or size of a body: *v.t.* to accent; emphasize; subject to mechanical pressure.

stretch (strĕch), *v.t.* to draw out to a greater length or width; as, to *stretch* rubber; hence, to draw tight; as, to *stretch* a tent; extend or reach out; as, to *stretch* out the arm; extend between two points; as, to *stretch* a rope across a street; strain; as, to *stretch* every nerve; exaggerate; as, to *stretch* the truth: *v.i.* spread; reach; as, the rope *stretches* across the street; to admit of being extended; as, that cloth *stretches*; to extend or spread the body or limbs; sail by the wind under press of canvas: *n.* the act of straining or extending; state of being strained or extended; effort; extension; overstrain; a continuous line, space, or time.

stretch-er (strĕch'ẽr), *n.* one who, or that which, extends or draws out; a frame, usually covered with canvas, for carrying the sick, wounded, or dead, as from the field of battle; a footboard used in rowing: **stretcher bearers,** men whose special duty in war time is to carry the wounded from the field of battle to ambulances, wagons, or field-hospitals, usually on stretchers.

strew (strōō), *v.t.* to scatter, or let fall loosely; as, to *strew* flowers on a path; to cover by scattering something over; as, to *strew* a path with flowers; to lie loosely upon; as, flowers *strew* the path.

stri-a (strī'ȧ), *n.* [*pl.* striæ (-ē)], a very small groove or channel; a fine, threadlike line; as, *striæ* on a shell; a narrow stripe or band, as of color. [LAT.]

stri-ate (strī'āt), *adj.* marked with very small grooves or fine lines of color. Also, **striated.**

strick-en (strĭk'n), *p.p.* of the verb *strike*: *p.adj.* struck down; wounded; as, the *stricken* deer; worn out; as, he is *stricken* in years.

strict (strĭkt), *adj.* exacting; severe; as, *strict* laws; extremely careful and thorough; as, *strict* honesty; accurate; precise; as, the *strict* sense of a word; stretched tight; as, *strict* bandages.—*adv.* **strictly.**—*n.* **strictness.**

stric-ture (strĭk'tūr), *n.* a contraction or tightening of any passage of the body; severe censure or blame.

stride (strīd), *n.* a long step: *v.i.* [*p.t.* strode, *p.p.* stridden, *p.pr.* striding], to walk with long steps: *v.t.* to pass over with one step; to straddle.

stri-dent (strī'dĕnt), *adj.* harsh; shrill; grating; as, a *strident* voice.—*adv.* **stridently.**

strid-u-late (strĭd'ū-lāt), *v.i.* to make a shrill, creaking noise, as locusts, crickets, etc.—*n.* **stridulation.**

strid-u-lous (strĭd'ū-lŭs), *adj.* making a shrill, creaking noise, as locusts, crickets, etc.

strife (strīf), *n.* a contest to gain some advantage; contention for superiority; discord; conflict; quarrel; enmity; war.

strike (strīk), *v.t.* [*p.t.* struck, *p.p.* struck, stricken, *p.pr.* striking], to hit with force; inflict a blow upon; as, to *strike* a child; to give or deal; as, to *strike* a blow; dash against; collide with; as, the ship *struck* the rocks; lower or take down; as, the ship *struck* her colors; cause to sound; as, to *strike* a gong; produce, as by a blow or by friction; as, to *strike* a light or a match; coin or stamp with a die; to take down the tents or huts of, as a camp; affect suddenly and strongly; as, to be *struck* with pity; light upon; make, as a bargain: *v.i.* to deal a quick blow or thrust; make an attack; hit; collide; to run against a rock, etc., as a ship; sound as a result of a blow, as a clock; to lower a flag or sail, as a sign of respect or submission; cease from work in order to secure better conditions: *n.* a stopping of work in order to secure higher wages, shorter hours, etc.; an instrument for leveling a measure, as of grain; an unexpected or complete success; as, a lucky *strike* in mining; in baseball, an unsuccessful attempt by the batter to hit the ball, or a ball so pitched that the batter should have struck at it.

strike break-er (strīk brāk'ẽr), a workman who takes the place of one who has left his work in order to force his employer to agree to some demand; a person who supplies such workmen.

strik-er (strīk'ẽr), *n.* one who, or that which, strikes, especially one who stops work to gain better conditions.

strik-ing (strīk'ĭng), *adj.* very noticeable; as, a *striking* resemblance; remarkable; surprising; as, a *striking* fact.—*adv.* **strikingly.**—*n.* **strikingness.**

strik-ing dis-tance (strīk'ĭng dĭs'tăns), the distance at which a force is effective when directed against any target.

string (strĭng), *n.* a small cord or line; the cord of a musical instrument; as, a violin *string*; a cord on which things are strung or arranged; as, a *string* of beads; a series of things in, or as in, a line; as, a *string* of cars; a *string* of oaths: *v.t.* [*p.t.* and *p.p.* strung, *p.pr.* stringing], to furnish with slender cords or threads; as, to *string* a bow; make tight the cords of; hence, to make tense; as, to *string* one's nerves; thread on a cord; as, to *string* beads; extend in a line or series; as, to *string* out a speech; to hang: with *up*; take strings from, as beans: *v.i.* to form into cords or threads; stretch out into a line or series.—*adj.* **stringed.**

strin-gen-cy (strĭn'jĕn-sĭ), *n.* the state or quality of being severe or tight; strictness; as, the *stringency* of the law; closeness; as, the *stringency* of one's financial affairs.

strin-gent (strĭn'jĕnt), *adj.* making strict requirements; severe; rigid; as, *stringent* rules; tight; having little ready money; as, the money market is *stringent*.—*adv.* **stringently.**—*n.* **stringentness.**

string-er (strĭng'ẽr), *n.* one who strings: a heavy horizontal timber or plank supporting other parts of a structure.

string-halt (strĭng'hôlt"), *n.* a jerky affection of a horse's hind legs.

string-y (strĭng'ĭ), *adj.* consisting of, or like, fibers, or threads; as, *stringy* meat; gluey; ropy.—*n.* **stringiness.**

strip (strĭp), *v.t.* [*p.t.* and *p.p.* stripped, *p.pr.* stripping], to make naked; deprive of a covering; skin or peel, as an orange; to pull off; as, to *strip* bark from a tree; to deprive; rob; as, to *strip* a man of his riches; deprive of; plund to *strip* riches from a man; milk dry, as a cow: *v.i.* to undress: *n.* a long, piece; as, a *strip* of cloth or wood. er; as, narrow

stripe (strīp), *n.* a line upon, or a long, narrow division of, a surface, of a different color or finish from the ground; a strip of different color or material attached to anything; a discolored line or streak on the skin made by a blow of a whip; a blow made by a whip; particular sort; kind; as, they are persons of the same *stripe*: *pl.* a term sometimes applied to the chevron on the coat of a noncommissioned officer, or, after the World War, on the sleeve of any soldier who had seen service: *v.t.* to mark with lines or bands of different color, finish, or material.—*adj.* **striped.**

strip-ling (strĭp'lĭng), *n.* a mere youth; a lad.

strive (strīv), *v.i.* [*p.t.* strove, *p.p.* striven, *p.pr.* striving], to make efforts; labor hard or earnestly; as, to *strive* for success; struggle in opposition; to be a rival; to compete; as, to *strive* in a race.

strode (strōd), past tense of the verb *stride*.

stroke (strōk), *n.* the act of making a blow, or the blow made; as, the *stroke* of a hammer; a powerful or sudden action suggesting a blow; as, a *stroke* of lightning; a strong effort to bring about a result, or the result brought about; as, a *stroke* of business; ill effect caused by, or as if by, a blow; as, a sun *stroke*; a *stroke* of misfortune; a gently moving touch; as, a soft *stroke* of the hand; a movement with an instrument, as a pencil or pen, or the mark made; sound of a clock in marking the time, or the time marked; as, on the *stroke* of nine; one of a series of movements, or its extent or rate, as the length of the motion of a piston, or the sweep of an oar; the principal oarsman in a boat, who sets the time to the rowers: *v.t.* to rub gently with the hand; as, to *stroke* a cat.

stroll (strōl), *n.* a ramble; a wandering: *v.i.* to wander on foot; ramble or rove idly.—*n.* **stroller.**

strong (strông), *adj.* having bodily or muscular force; powerful; as, a *strong* arm; having power of endurance; robust; healthy; vigorous; as, a *strong* constitution; moving with force; violent; as, a *strong* wind; striking or convincing; as, a *strong* argument; very able or capable; as, a *strong* character; ardent; as, *strong* affections; deeply earnest; as, a *strong* partisan; deeply rooted; as, *strong* faith; keenly affecting the senses; as, a *strong* light or odor; firm; tough; as, a *strong* plank; having great resources; able to attack or resist; as, a *strong* fort, fleet, or bank; having great numbers, or a definite number; as, they marched five thousand *strong;* moving steadily upward; as, the market closed with prices *strong;* not mild or weak; as, *strong* coffee; containing much alcohol; as, *strong* drink; showing tense by changing the root vowel; as, *strong* verbs.

strong-hold (strông'hōld"), *n.* a fort or fortress; a place of security; a refuge.

strop (strŏp), *n.* a strip of leather for sharpening a razor: *v.t.* [*p.t.* and *p.p.* stropped, *p.pr.* stropping], to sharpen on a strop.

stro-phe (strō'fē), *n.* in the ancient Greek drama, a movement of the dance performed by the chorus in which they moved, while singing, to the right of the stage; hence, the part of the choral ode sung during this movement; sometimes, a stanza of modern verse.

strove (strōv), past tense of the verb *strive.*

struck (strŭk), past tense and past participle of the verb *strike.*

struc-tur-al (strŭk'tūr-ăl), *adj.* of or pertaining to the construction or formation of a thing, or to the special way in which a thing is made or put together.—*adv.* **structurally.**

struc-ture (strŭk'tūr), *n.* that which is built, as a bridge or building; construction; manner or form of building; arrangement of parts in a vegetable or animal substance; the special way in which a thing is put together; as, sentence *structure.*

strug-gle (strŭg'l), *n.* a violent effort or great endeavor; contest; strife; sometimes, war or battle: *v.i.* to put forth great effort; labor; contend; strive.—*n.* **struggler.**

strum (strŭm), *v.t.* and *v.i.* [*p.t.* and *p.p.* strummed, *p.pr.* strumming], to play badly and noisily on a stringed instrument; as, to *strum* a waltz, or to *strum* on a piano.

strum-pet (strŭm'pĕt), *n.* a woman of low moral character.

strung (strŭng), past tense and past participle of the verb *string.*

strut (strŭt), *n.* a proud or affected step or walk with the head erect; a brace or bar for keeping two parts of a framework from coming nearer together: *v.i.* [*p.t.* and *p.p.* strutted, *p.pr.* strutting], to walk with a pompous or conceited air, or with affected dignity: *v.t.* to brace or support.

strych-nine (strĭk'nĭn; strĭk'nēn), *n.* a very powerful poison obtained from certain plants and used in medicine to stimulate the nerves and the action of the heart. Also, **strychnin.**

stub (stŭb), *n.* the stump of a tree; the short, blunt part of anything after the larger part has been broken off or used up; as, the *stub* of a pencil; part of a leaf left in a check book after a check is torn out, and serving as a memorandum of the check; a pen with a short, blunt point: *v.t.* [*p.t.* and *p.p.* stubbed, *p.pr.* stubbing], to dig up, as roots; dig roots from; strike against some fixed object; as, to *stub* one's toe.

stub-bed (stŭb'ĕd; stŭbd), *adj.* cut off short, like a stump; full of stumps or roots; hardy; rugged.—*n.* **stubbedness.**

stub-ble (stŭb'l), *n.* short stalks or stumps of grain left in the ground after reaping.—*adj.* **stubbly.**

stub-born (stŭb'ẽrn), *adj.* very headstrong; determined to have one's own way; unreasonably obstinate in will or opinion; hard to deal with; not easily overcome; persistent.—*adv.* **stubbornly.**—*n.* **stubbornness.**

stub-by (stŭb'ĭ), *adj.* full of stumps or roots; as, a *stubby* field; short, stiff, and thick; as, a *stubby* beard; short and strong; as, a *stubby* pencil.

stub nail (stŭb nāl), a short, thick nail; an old horseshoe nail.

stuc-co (stŭk'ō), *n.* [*pl.* stuccoes (-ōz)], a fine plaster used as a coating for walls, or for inside decorations; work executed in such plaster: *v.t.* to overlay, or decorate, with stucco, or fine plaster.

stuck (stŭk), past tense and past participle of the verb *stick.*

stuck-up (stŭk'ŭp'), *adj.* colloquially, conceited.

stud (stŭd), *n.* an ornamental button; as, a shirt *stud;* a large-headed ornamental nail or knob; a post, or scantling, used in building, as in a partition; a collection of horses and mares for breeding; place where they are kept; a number of horses kept for racing, hunting, etc.: *v.t.* [*p.t.* and *p.p.* studded, *p.pr.* studding], to adorn with, or as with, studs or bright knobs; to be set thickly in or upon; as, stars *stud* the sky; to support with a post.

stud-ding (stŭd'ĭng), *n.* material for the studs, or joists, used to support the floors, etc., of a building; studs, or joists, collectively.

stud-ding sail (stŭd'ĭng sāl; stŭn'sl), a light sail set at the side of a square sail of a vessel to increase her speed.

stu-dent (stū'dĕnt), *n.* one who is engaged in study; one who attends school; one devoted to books or learning; a close observer; as, a *student* of human nature.

stud-horse (stŭd'hôrs"), *n.* a stallion, or horse kept for breeding.

stud-ied (stŭd'ĭd), *adj.* designed; planned; as, a *studied* compliment; made the subject of study; as, a *studied* speech.—*adv.* **studiedly.**—*n.* **studiedness.**

stu-di-o (stū'dĭ-ō), *n.* the workroom of an artist.

stu-di-ous (stū'dĭ-ŭs), *adj.* given to study, or to the gaining of knowledge; careful in using means; earnest and attentive; as, *studious* endeavor to please. —*adv.* studiously.—*n.* studiousness.

stud-y (stŭd'ĭ), *n.* the application of the mind to the gaining of knowledge; any particular form or case of mental work; any particular branch of learning; a particular product of study, as the sketched ideas of a painter, etc., to be referred to or finished later; a piece of music for special practice; a thoughtful state of mind; earnest desire or endeavor; a room set apart for mental work: *v.i.* [*p.t.* and *p.p.* studied, *p.pr.* studying], to devote oneself closely to books and learning, or to any subject of inquiry; to use thoughtful care in planning; to reflect: *v.t.* examine closely in order to learn thoroughly; to memorize; as, to *study* a speech; devote one's thoughts to; look at closely and thoughtfully.

stuff (stŭf), *n.* the material out of which anything may be made; the fundamental part or essence; as, the *stuff* of which brave men are made; raw material; woven fabrics or cloth; household goods; refuse or waste matter; nonsense: *v.t.* to fill by crowding something into; as, to *stuff* one's pockets; press or pack into a small space; fill with specially prepared material; as, to *stuff* a chicken; fill (the skin of a dead animal) so as to keep in its natural form; obstruct by filling up; put dishonest votes into; as, to *stuff* a ballot box: *v.i.* to eat more than enough; to cram.

stuff-y (stŭf'ĭ), *adj.* close or badly ventilated; as, a *stuffy* room.—*n.* stuffiness.

stul-ti-fi-ca-tion (stŭl"tĭ-fĭ-kā'shŭn), *n.* the act of making foolish; the state of being made foolish.

stul-ti-fy (stŭl'tĭ-fī), *v.t.* [*p.t.* and *p.p.* stultified, *p.pr.* stultifying], to make foolish; as, to *stultify* oneself by reversing a previous decision, or conduct.

stum-ble (stŭm'bl), *n.* a trip in walking or running; failure or blunder: *v.i.* to trip or fall in walking; to walk in an unsteady or clumsy manner; to fall into error or crime; to come upon something by chance: with *on*, *upon*, or *against*.—*adv.* stumblingly.—*n.* stumbler.

stum-bling-block (stŭm'bling-blŏk"), *n.* anything that hinders or prevents; something that may cause one to err or fall.

stump (stŭmp), *n.* that part of a tree which remains in the ground after the trunk is cut down; the part, as of an arm or leg, remaining after a portion has been cut off; an artist's soft pencil or rubber; one of three posts of the wicket at cricket; a place for political speaking: formerly, a tree stump; hence, political speaking: *v.t.* to lop; reduce to a stump; colloquially, to strike, as the toes, against a stone or something fixed; to travel over for the purpose of making political speeches: *v.i.* to walk heavily and stiffly.

stump or-a-tor (stŭmp ŏr'ȧ-tẽr), one who, from a stump or temporary stand, addresses people on some current question, usually political.

stump speech (stŭmp spēch), a political speech.

stump-y (stŭm'pĭ), *adj.* full of stumps; as, a *stumpy* field; colloquially, short and thick; as, *stumpy* fingers.

stun (stŭn), *v.t.* [*p.t.* and *p.p.* stunned, *p.pr.* stunning], to make senseless by, or as by, a blow; confuse or daze with noise; overpower with astonishment; astound: *n.* an overpowering blow or shock; condition of being so overpowered.

stung (stŭng), past tense and past participle of the verb *sting*.

stunk (stŭnk), past tense and past participle of the verb *stink*.

stun-ning (stŭn'ĭng), *adj.* overpowering the senses; as, a *stunning* blow; slang, handsome; as, a *stunning* dress.

stunt (stŭnt), *v.t.* to check the growth or development of; to dwarf: *n.* a check in growth; something of which the growth has been checked; colloquially, a feat or performance: slang, in aëronautics, any feat that is original and risky, such as looping-the-loop, nose diving, etc.

stupe (stūp), *n.* flax, flannel, etc., soaked in warm water or some healing liquid, and applied to a hurt or sore.

stu-pe-fac-tion (stū"pē-făk'shŭn), *n.* the act of dulling or deadening the senses of; state of being deadened or made dull; stupor.

stu-pe-fy (stū'pē-fī), *v.t.* [*p.t.* and *p.p.* stupefied, *p.pr.* stupefying], to dull the senses of; make stupid or torpid.—*n.* stupefier.

stu-pen-dous (stū-pĕn'dŭs), *adj.* overcoming the senses by enormous size or greatness; astonishing; wonderful; amazing.—*adv.* stupendously.—*n.* stupendousness.

stu-pid (stū'pĭd), *adj.* wanting in understanding; foolish; insensible, or incapable of feeling; showing lack of thought; senseless; dull.—*adv.* stupidly.—*n.* stupidness.

stu-pid-i-ty (stū-pĭd'ĭ-tĭ), *n.* great dullness of mind; slowness; foolishness.

stu-por (stū'pŏr), *n.* suspension or great lessening of the capacity for feeling; numbness, as from cold; mental insensibility.

stur-dy (stûr'dĭ), *adj.* hardy; robust; stout; strong; vigorous; as, a *sturdy* countryman; resolute; firm and unyielding; as, a man of *sturdy* faith.—*adv.* sturdily.—*n.* sturdiness.

stur-geon (stûr'jŭn), *n.* a large fish found in fresh and salt waters of the north temperate zone: the roes, or eggs, are made into caviar, the air-bladders into isinglass.

stut-ter (stŭt'ẽr), *n.* act of hesitating or stammering in speech; a stammer: *v.i.* to speak with hesitation or stammering: *v.t.* to utter with hesitation or stammering.—*n.* stutterer, stuttering.

sty (stī), *n.* a pen for swine, or hogs; a filthy or vile place; a small inflamed swelling on the eyelid.

Styg-i-an (stĭj'ĭ-ăn), *adj.* pertaining to the Styx, the river of Hades, in ancient mythology, over which the dead were ferried by the boatman Charon; hence, infernal or hellish.

style (stīl), *n.* a pointed instrument used by the ancients for writing upon wax tablets; a pen; an engraver's tool; a surgical instrument; the pin of a sundial; manner of writing or speaking with regard to the choice of words, etc.; mode of expression or execution in art; as, the Renaissance *style*; manner of conduct or action; as, a graceful *style* of dancing; fashion; as, the latest *style*; form of address; title; a method of reckoning time; as, according to the Old *Style* or New *Style* calendar: *v.t.* [*p.t.* and *p.p.* styled, *p.pr.* styling], to term, name, or call; as, he *styled* himself a prophet.

sty-let (stī'lĕt), *n.* any slender, pointed instrument.

styl-ish (stīl'ĭsh), *adj.* very fashionable; modish.—*adv.* **stylishly.**—*n.* **stylishness.**

styl-ist (stīl'ĭst), *n.* a master or a model of the art of speaking or writing; one who pays careful attention to form and to choice of words in writing and speaking.

sty-lo-graph (stī'lō-grăf), *n.* a stylographic pen, or pencil-like writing instrument with an ink barrel from which ink is fed to the pen point.

sty-lo-graph-ic (stī"lō-grăf'ĭk), *adj.* pertaining to stylography, or the art of writing with a style or with a stylographic pen: **stylographic pen,** a pencil-like writing instrument with an ink barrel from which ink is fed to the pen point.

sty-lus (stī'lŭs), *n.* a sharp-pointed instrument for making copies of writing by means of carbon paper; an ancient instrument for writing on wax tablets.

styp-tic (stĭp'tĭk), *adj.* able to stop bleeding; as, a *styptic* pencil used by barbers: *n.* a substance that stops bleeding.

sua-sion (swā'zhŭn), *n.* persuasion; as, moral *suasion.*

sua-sive (swā'sĭv), *adj.* having power to persuade; persuasive.

suave (swāv; swäv), *adj.* pleasant in manner; easy; gracious.—*adv.* **suavely.**

suav-i-ty (swăv'ĭ-tĭ; swä'vĭ-tĭ), *n.* agreeableness; pleasantness; blandness.

sub- (sŭb-), *prefix* meaning under, beneath, below, slightly: *n.* a familiar abbreviation used in the British army to signify a subaltern or any inferior officer.

sub-ac-id (sŭb-ăs'ĭd), *adj.* slightly sour, as fruit; slightly sharp, as temper: *n.* a mild acid.

sub-al-tern (sŭb-ôl'tērn), *n.* a military officer under the rank of captain: *adj.* of inferior, or lower, rank.

sub-a-que-ous (sŭb-ā'kwē-ŭs), *adj.* being or formed under water; intended for use under water.

sub-base (sŭb'bās"), *n.* the lowest part of a base when it is divided into layers.

sub-con-scious (sŭb-kŏn'shŭs), *adj.* being in the mind, but not present or uppermost in thought or attention.—*adv.* **subconsciously.**—*n.* **subconsciousness.**

sub-con-tract (sŭb"kŏn'trăkt), *n.* a contract, or formal agreement, subordinate to, or under, a previous contract.

sub-di-vide (sŭb"dĭ-vīd'), *v.t.* and *v.i.* to separate the parts of into parts; divide again.

sub-di-vi-sion (sŭb"dĭ-vĭzh'ŭn), *n.* the separation of the parts of into parts; a part of a larger part.

sub-due (sŭb-dū'), *v.t.* to overcome or conquer; vanquish; as, to *subdue* an enemy; reduce; lower; as, to *subdue* a fever; make gentle; tame; as, to *subdue* the passions; tone down; soften; as, a dark shade *subdues* the light.

sub-ja-cent (sŭb-jā'sĕnt), *adj.* lying directly under or below; situated lower, but not directly beneath; as, hills and *subjacent* valleys.

sub-ject (sŭb'jĕkt), *n.* one who is under the power or control of another; one who owes allegiance to a monarch; as, the rights of *subjects;* one who, or that which, is subjected to an operation or treatment, especially a dead body for the use of medical students; that which is treated in writing, speaking, etc., or concerning which anything is said or done; topic; the word or word group in a sentence, denoting that of which anything is affirmed: distinguished from *predicate,* the thing affirmed; a substance; the thinking agent or principal; the mind; in music, the theme of a movement: *adj.* being under the power or control of another; as, to be *subject* to a king; disposed; exposed; liable: with *to;* as, *subject* to temptation; *subject* to change: *v.t.* (sŭb-jĕkt'), to bring under power or control; to make subordinate or secondary; render liable; expose; as, to *subject* a person to unpleasantness; to cause to undergo; as, to *subject* a substance to heat.

sub-jec-tion (sŭb-jĕk'shŭn), *n.* the act of subduing or of bringing under the rule or power of another; state of being under the power or control of another or of some thing.

sub-jec-tive (sŭb-jĕk'tĭv), *adj.* pertaining to the subject as opposed to the object; relating to, or derived from, one's own consciousness or mind, as distinguished from outward or material things; based upon one's own feelings; as, a *subjective* view of life.—*adv.* **subjectively.**—*n.* **subjectiveness.**

sub-jec-tiv-i-ty (sŭb"jĕk-tĭv'ĭ-tĭ), *n.* the state or quality of being related to the mind.

sub-join (sŭb-join'), *v.t.* to add after something else has been said or written; to affix.

sub-ju-gate (sŭb'jōō-gāt), *v.t.* to conquer and bring under power, and rule by force; to subdue.

sub-ju-ga-tion (sŭb"jōō-gā'shŭn), *n.* the act of conquering and bringing under power and rule; state of being conquered.

sub-junc-tive (sŭb-jŭnk'tĭv), *adj.* noting a form of the verb expressing action or state not as a fact, but as a doubt, condition, or assumption: *n.* the subjunctive mood.

sub-let (sŭb-lĕt'), *v.t.* to give out to another (work that one has agreed to do); to lease to another (property that has been leased to oneself).

sub-lieu-ten-ant (sŭb"lū-tĕn'ănt), *n.* a subordinate, or second, lieutenant.

sub-li-mate (sŭb'lĭ-māt), *v.t.* to cause (a solid) to pass directly into vapor, and back again directly to the solid state; as, to *sublimate* sulphur; to refine and elevate: *adj.* having been changed by heat into vapor, and having again become solid; refined: *n.* (sŭb'lĭ-māt) a deposit of a substance obtained by sublimating.—*n.* **sublimation.**

sub-lime (sŭb-līm'), *adj.* causing a feeling of awe and reverence; filling the mind with a sense of greatness, power, or grandeur; as, a *sublime* sacrifice; *sublime* music; exalted in nature; noble; said of persons; elevated in style; very high in degree; as, *sublime* faith or trust in another: *n.* that which is grand or awe-inspiring in works of nature or art as distinguished from the merely beautiful: with *the:* *v.t.* to dignify or exalt; to make noble; to cause to pass from solid to vapor form and thence back to solid: *v.i.* to pass from a solid to vapor, and again change to solid form without showing a liquid form.—*adv.* **sublimely.**—*n.* **sublimeness.**

sub-lim-i-ty (sŭb-lĭm′ĭ-tĭ), *n.* state or quality of being exalted; loftiness or majesty of character; a feeling of awe aroused by that which is grand, lofty, or majestic; that which is exalted.

sub-lu-nar (sŭb-lū′nȧr), *adj.* situated beneath the moon; pertaining to this world. Also, **sublunary.**

sub-ma-rine (sŭb″mȧ-rēn′), *adj.* growing, done, or used under water in the sea; as, *submarine* plants or guns: *n.* a war vessel which can remain long under water, and which carries and fires torpedoes; an undersea plant or animal: **submarine gun,** a gun for firing a torpedo below the surface of the water: **submarine mine,** a mass of explosives sunk, as in a harbor, to destroy enemy vessels: **submarine diving bell,** a hollow chamber supplied with air, in which men may work under water without danger.

Submarine Diving Bell

sub-merge (sŭb-mûrj′), *v.t.* to put under water; cover with water; flood; overwhelm: *v.i.* to be, or lie, under water; be hidden, or lost to sight.

sub-merg-i-ble (sŭb-mûr′jĭ-bl), *adj.* capable of being put under water: *n.* a submarine boat capable of going completely under water.

sub-mers-i-ble (sŭb-mûr′sĭ-bl), *adj.* capable of being submerged, or put under water: *n.* a submarine boat capable of going partly under water.

sub-mer-sion (sŭb-mûr′shŭn), *n.* the act of submerging, or putting under water or other liquid, or of causing to be overflowed; the act of plunging under water; state of being put under water or other fluid, or of being overflowed. Also, **submergence.**

sub-mis-sion (sŭb-mĭsh′ŭn), *n.* the act of yielding to power or authority; obedience; humility or meekness.

sub-mis-sive (sŭb-mĭs′ĭv), *adj.* yielding to authority; obedient; as, a *submissive* child; humble.—*adv.* **submissively.**—*n.* **submissiveness.**

sub-mit (sŭb-mĭt′), *v.t.* [*p.t.* and *p.p.* submitted, *p.pr.* submitting], to yield to the authority or will of another; surrender; to present for, or refer to, the judgment of another; as, to *submit* a question to others; to offer as one's own opinion: *v.i.* to be obedient; yield or surrender.

sub-mul-ti-ple (sŭb-mŭl′tĭ-pl), *n.* a number or quantity which is contained in another an exact number of times; as, 4 is the *submultiple* of 28.

sub-or-di-nate (sŭb-ôr′dĭ-nāt), *adj.* lower in rank, value, power, or importance; subject to another; in grammar, denoting the less important clause of a complex sentence, or the conjunction which introduces it: *n.* one who is below another in rank, etc.; one who serves under another: *v.t.* (sŭb-ôr′dĭ-nāt), to place in a lower order; to make subject or obedient to.—*adv.* **subordinately.**—*n.* **subordinateness.**

sub-or-di-na-tion (sŭb-ôr″dĭ-nā′shŭn), *n.* the act of placing in a lower rank or of treating as inferior; state of being lower in rank, position, etc.; subjection to one of higher rank or position; obedience or submission.

sub-orn (sŭb-ôrn′), *v.t.* to induce (another) to take a false oath; as, to *suborn* a witness; to induce to do an evil act.—*n.* **suborner.**

sub-or-na-tion (sŭb″ôr-nā′shŭn), *n.* the act of inducing a person to take a false oath, as by persuasion or by payment of money, etc.

sub-pœ-na (sŭb-pē′nȧ), *n.* a written order commanding the attendance of a person in court as a witness, under a penalty for failure to obey: *v.t.* to serve or summon with such a written order. Also, **subpena.**

sub-scribe (sŭb-skrīb′), *v.t.* to write or put (one's name) to a paper or document; give or promise (a sum of money) for some object, by writing one's name; to give consent to, by writing one's name; to bear witness to, by signing one's name; as, to *subscribe* a will: *v.i.* to sign one's name to a letter or other document; to give consent; to set one's name to a paper in token of promise to give a certain sum, or to take and pay for something, as a book.—*n.* **subscriber.**

sub-scrip-tion (sŭb-skrĭp′shŭn), *n.* the act of putting one's name to by way of agreement; that which is agreed to; a signature; a formal agreement entered into by signing one's name; an order for a book or periodical; an amount pledged by the signing of one's name.

sub-se-quence (sŭb′sē-kwĕns), *n.* the condition or state of being after in time or order. Also, **subsequency.**

sub-se-quent (sŭb′sē-kwĕnt), *adj.* following, or coming after, in time or order; as, *subsequent* events; succeeding.—*adv.* **subsequently.**

sub-serve (sŭb-sûrv′), *v.t.* to be subject to; to advance or promote; as, to *subserve* another's interests.

sub-ser-vi-ence (sŭb-sûr′vĭ-ĕns), *n.* quality or state of being subordinate; fitness to promote some end; servility or obsequiousness.—*n.* **subserviency.**

sub-ser-vi-ent (sŭb-sûr′vĭ-ĕnt), *adj.* fitted to promote some end; being of service; servile; obsequious.

sub-side (sŭb-sīd′), *v.i.* to sink or fall to the bottom; settle; to sink to a lower level; as, the swollen river will *subside;* become quiet or calm; abate, as a storm.—*n.* **subsidence.**

sub-sid-i-a-ry (sŭb-sĭd′ĭ-ā-rĭ), *adj.* furnishing aid or help; assisting, especially in an inferior position; of the nature of a subsidy, or money granted by one nation to another, or by a government to an individual: *n.* one that gives aid or supplies; helper; an assistant.

sub-si-dize (sŭb′sĭ-dīz), *v.t.* to furnish with a subsidy, or financial help; to purchase the assistance of by the payment of money; to aid or promote, as a private enterprise, with public money.

sub-si-dy (sŭb'sĭ-dĭ), *n.* [*pl.* subsidies (-dĭz)], money granted by one government to another, especially for war expenses, or for coöperation or neutrality during war; a government grant of money to aid a private enterprise which serves to benefit the public.
Syn. aid, bonus, bounty, grant, tribute.

sub-sist (sŭb-sĭst'), *v.i.* to have existence; to remain in existence or keep a certain state; continue; to exist or be; to be supplied with food, etc.; to live: *v.t.* to provide with food, etc.; support.—*adj.* **subsistent.**

sub-sist-ence (sŭb-sĭs'tĕns), *n.* means of support, as food and clothing; maintenance; livelihood; act of existing; state of being existent.

sub-soil (sŭb'soil"), *n.* the bed or layer of earth just beneath the surface soil: *v.t.* to plow or turn up the under soil of.

sub-stance (sŭb'stăns), *n.* that which is real; matter or material of which anything is made; the main part expressed briefly; as, the *substance* of a speech; the vital part of anything; as, faith is the *substance* of religion; wealth or property; as, a man of *substance.*

sub-stan-tial (sŭb-stăn'shăl), *adj.* pertaining to that which is real or material; containing enough of the proper material; solid; strong; as, a *substantial* building; not imaginary; real; true; of real worth; valuable; as, a *substantial* gift to charity; having considerable wealth or property; as, a *substantial* business man; considerable; as, *substantial* gain: *n.* that which is real or material, or which is of value; the necessary part.—*adv.* **substantially.**—*n.* **substantialness.**

sub-stan-ti-al-i-ty (sŭb-stăn"shĭ-ăl'ĭ-tĭ), *n.* state or quality of being real or material, or of being strong or valuable.

sub-stan-ti-ate (sŭb-stăn'shĭ-āt), *v.t.* to make good; to establish the truth of by proof or reliable evidence; as, to *substantiate* a charge of theft.—*n.* **substantiation.**

sub-stan-tive (sŭb'stăn-tĭv), *adj.* expressing existence; as, the verb *to be* is the *substantive* verb; being used as a noun; as, a *substantive* phrase; essential or necessary; real; lasting: *n.* that part of speech which expresses the existence of anything; a noun, or a phrase, clause, etc., used as a noun.

sub-sti-tute (sŭb'stĭ-tūt), *n.* one who, or that which, is put in the place of another; a man who enlists in the army to take the place of a drafted man: *v.t.* to put in the place of someone or something else; exchange.

sub-sti-tu-tion (sŭb"stĭ-tū'shŭn), *n.* the act of putting in the place of another; state of being exchanged, or put in the place of another.

sub-stra-tum (sŭb-strā'tŭm), *n.* [*pl.* substrata (-tȧ); substratums (-tŭmz)], an under layer, as of soil or rock; hence, that which forms the groundwork. [LAT.]

sub-tend (sŭb-tĕnd'), *v.t.* to extend under, or be opposite to; as, the line of a triangle which *subtends* the right angle.

sub-ter-fuge (sŭb'tẽr-fūj), *n.* a trick, plan, etc., for escape or concealment; a false excuse.

sub-ter-ra-ne-an (sŭb"tĕr-ā'nē-ăn), *adj.* being below the surface of the earth; as, a *subterranean* cave; hence; hidden; secret. Also, **subterraneous.**

sub-tile (sŭb'tĭl; sŭt'l), *adj.* thin; finely formed, as a spider's web; delicate; refined, as a perfume; desc ibing qualities of concrete objects, as distinguished from *subtle,* which describes abstract qualities.—*adv.* **subtilely.**—*n.* **subtileness.**

sub-tle (sŭt'l), *adj.* artful; crafty; cunning; as, a *subtle* scheme; keen; nicely discriminating; as, a *subtle* mind; delicate; elusive; as, a *subtle* odor; not appearing on the surface; as, a *subtle* meaning; skilful, or done with skill; as, a *subtle* workman or work.—*adv.* **subtly.**

sub-tle-ty (sŭt'l-tĭ), *n.* keenness of mind; cunning; artifice; elusiveness; obscurity of meaning. Also, **sub'tleness.**

sub-tract (sŭb-trăkt'), *v.t.* to withdraw, or take away, as a part from a whole; as, to *subtract* five from ten; deduct.

sub-trac-tion (sŭb-trăk'shŭn), *n.* the act or process of taking away, as a part from a whole.

sub-trac-tive (sŭb-trăk'tĭv), *adj.* tending, or having power, to take away; negative.

sub-tra-hend (sŭb'trȧ-hĕnd"), *n.* the quantity or number to be taken from another.

sub-urb (sŭb'ûrb), *n.* an outlying district of a city or town; outer part; as, the *suburbs* of New York.

sub-ur-ban (sŭb-ûr'băn), *adj* pertaining to, in, or living within, the outlying districts of a city or town; as, *suburban* residents.

sub-ven-tion (sŭb-vĕn'shŭn), *n.* help or support; financial help from the government, as a grant or subsidy, especially for the advancement of art or learning.

sub-ver-sion (sŭb-vûr'shŭn), *n.* the act of overturning; overthrow; utter ruin; as, the *subversion* of a government.

sub-ver-sive (sŭb-vûr'sĭv), *adj.* tending to overthrow or ruin.

sub-vert (sŭb-vûrt'), *v.t.* to turn upside down; overthrow from the foundation; bring to ruin; as, to *subvert* a government; corrupt; as, to *subvert* a man's principles.—*adj.* **subvertible.**—*n.* **subverter.**

sub-way (sŭb'wā"), *n.* an underground passage, used for a railway or other purpose.

suc-ceed (sŭk-sēd'), *v.t.* to take the place of; follow: *v.i.* to follow in order; to come next in the possession of anything; with *to;* as, to *succeed* to a throne; accomplish something attempted; as, he *succeeded* in whatever he did; meet with success; prosper; as, all his plans *succeed.*

suc-cess (sŭk-sĕs'), *n.* favorable end or result of any undertaking; one who accomplishes that which is desired or intended; that which prospers.

suc-cess-ful (sŭk-sĕs'fo͝ol), *adj.* resulting or ending favorably; as, a *successful* business; obtaining what is desired or intended; as, a *successful* business man; prosperous; fortunate.—*adv.* **successfully.**—*n.* **successfulness.**

suc-ces-sion (sŭk-sĕsh'ŭn), *n.* the act of following in order; a series of persons or things that follow according to a fixed order; as, a *succession* of letters or kings; act of taking or right to take the place of another; as, *succession* to an office or an estate; rotation; as, a *succession* of crops.

suc-ces-sion-al (sŭk-sĕsh′ŭn-ăl), *adj.* pertaining to a following of things in order; existing in a regular order; consecutive, or following in order.—*adv.* **successionally.**

suc-ces-sive (sŭk-sĕs′ĭv), *adj.* following in a series, or in regular order; consecutive.—*adv.* **successively.**—*n.* **successiveness.**

suc-ces-sor (sŭk-sĕs′ẽr), *n.* one who follows, or takes the place of, another, as in office: correlative of *predecessor.*

suc-cinct (sŭk-sĭnkt′), *adj.* clearly expressed in a very few words; concise; brief.—*adv.* **succinctly.**—*n.* **succinctness.**

suc-cor (sŭk′ẽr), *v.t.* to help or relieve when in difficulty or distress; aid: *n.* relief; aid; help.

suc-co-tash (sŭk′ō-tăsh), *n.* a dish of green corn and beans boiled together.

suc-cu-lence (sŭk′ū-lĕns), *n.* juiciness; as, the *succulence* of an orange. Also, **succulency.**

suc-cu-lent (sŭk′ū-lĕnt), *adj.* juicy: said of plants.

suc-cumb (sŭ-kŭm′), *v.i.* to yield; submit; as, to *succumb* to a disease.

such (sŭch), *adj.* of that or the like kind; like; similar; as, never before was *such* a victory; having the particular quality or character named; as, be content to remain *such* as you are; the same that, or as referred to; as, *such* are his orders; indicating a certain person or thing; as, *such* a man should be avoided; being the same in quality: *pron.* such a person or thing, or, usually, such persons or things.

suck (sŭk), *v.t.* to draw in (a liquid) with the mouth; to draw a liquid from with the mouth; to drink in or absorb; as, a sponge *sucks* up water; draw in or engulf; as, a quicksand *sucks* anything in: *v.i.* to draw milk from the breast or udder: *n.* the act of drawing into the mouth, or of absorbing or engulfing; milk drawn from the breast.

suck-er (sŭk′ẽr), *n.* one that sucks, or draws in with the mouth, as a young pig or whale; a shoot or sprout of a plant from the lower part of the stem; any of certain fishes that suck in food, or have mouths shaped for that purpose.

suck-le (sŭk′l), *v.t.* and *v.i.* to nurse at the breast; to suck.

suck-ling (sŭk′lĭng), *n.* an unweaned child or animal.

suc-tion (sŭk′shŭn), *n.* the act or process of drawing a fluid into an empty space by removing the air; any like act or process of sucking, or drawing in.

su-da-to-ri-um (sū′dȧ-tō′rĭ-ŭm), *n.* a sweating bath.

su-da-to-ry (sū′dȧ-tō-rĭ), *adj.* exciting perspiration or sweat; sweating; perspiring; as, a *sudatory* bath: *n.* anything that causes sweating; a sweating bath.

sud-den (sŭd′n; sŭd′ĕn), *adj.* happening unexpectedly; without notice; as, a *sudden* death; quickly done; hasty; as, a *sudden* leave taking.—*adv.* **suddenly.**—*n.* **suddenness.**

su-dor-if-ic (sū′dŏr-ĭf′ĭk), *adj.* causing perspiration or sweating: *n.* a medicine producing such an effect.

suds (sŭdz), *n.pl.* soapy water, especially when in a frothy condition.

sue (sū), *v.t.* to seek after; to endeavor to win; to seek justice or right from, at law: *v.i.* to entreat, beg, or petition: with *for;* as, to *sue* for peace; pay court; as, to *sue* for her hand; to begin a lawsuit; as, to *sue* for damages.

suède (swād; swĕd), *n.* undressed kid, used for gloves, shoes, etc. [Fr.]

su-et (sū′ĕt), *n.* the hard fat around the kidneys and loins of sheep and oxen: used for cooking and for making tallow.

suf-fer (sŭf′ẽr), *v.t.* to feel with pain; undergo; bear; as, to *suffer* a wrong; to feel or endure; as, to *suffer* pain; be affected by; experience; as, to *suffer* a loss; *suffer* wrong; tolerate; as, they would no longer *suffer* his evil deeds: *v.i.* to feel pain or punishment; be in distress; endure loss or injury.—*n.* **sufferer.**

suf-fer-a-ble (sŭf′ẽr-ȧ-bl), *adj.* that may be allowed or tolerated; endurable.

suf-fer-ance (sŭf′ẽr-ăns), *n.* patience under pain; endurance; toleration; permission; leave.

suf-fer-ing (sŭf′ẽr-ĭng), *n.* the bearing of physical or mental pain; the pain borne; distress; loss or injury endured.

suf-fice (sŭ-fīs′; sŭ-fīz′), *v.i.* to be enough or sufficient: *v.t.* to satisfy.

suf-fi-cien-cy (sŭ-fĭsh′ĕn-sĭ), *n.* the state or quality of being sufficient or enough; skill or ability; enough substance or means; supply equal to wants; self-confidence; conceit.

suf-fi-cient (sŭ-fĭsh′ĕnt), *adj.* equal to any end or purpose; equal to the need; enough.—*adv.* **sufficiently.**

suf-fix (sŭf′ĭks), *n.* a letter or letters, syllable or syllables, added to the end of a word or root to alter the meaning; as, *-ant* is the *suffix* in defend*ant*: *v.t.* (sŭ-fĭks′), to add, as a letter or syllable, to the end of a word.

suf-fo-cate (sŭf′ō-kāt), *v.t.* to kill by stopping the breath; smother; stifle; to extinguish; as, to *suffocate* a fire: *v.i.* to become choked or stifled.

suf-fo-ca-tion (sŭf′ō-kā′shŭn), *n.* the act of choking, or stopping the breath; state of being choked or stifled; death due to smothering, etc.

suf-fra-gan (sŭf′rȧ-găn), *n.* an assistant bishop: *adj.* assisting; assistant; auxiliary.

suf-frage (sŭf′rāj), *n.* a vote; assent; the right or act of voting, especially in political matters.

suf-fra-gette (sŭf′rȧ-jĕt′), *n.* a woman who believes in, and works for, the right of women to vote in political matters. [Colloq.]

suf-fra-gist (sŭf′rȧ-jĭst), *n.* a voter; one who supports or pleads the cause of suffrage, or the right to vote; especially, one who favors voting by women.

suf-fuse (sŭ-fūz′), *v.t.* to spread over, as with a fluid or a color; as, tears *suffused* her eyes.

suf-fu-sion (sŭ-fū′zhŭn), *n.* the act of spreading over, as color in the cheeks; state of being spread over; that which spreads over.

sug-ar (shŏŏg′ẽr), *n.* a sweet crystalline substance obtained from sugar cane, sugar beets, etc.; any sweet substance like sugar, as glucose, or sugar of lead; flattering words: *adj.* like, made of, or yielding, sugar: *v.t.* to sprinkle or cover with sugar; sweeten; to make less disagreeable by flattery.

sug-ar-y (shŏŏg'ẽr-ĭ), *adj.* like, made of, or fond of, sugar; sweet; honeyed.

sug-gest (sŭg-jĕst'), *v.t.* to present or introduce indirectly to the mind or thoughts; hint: *v.i.* to give rise to thoughts. —*n.* **suggester.**

sug-ges-tion (sŭg-jĕs'chŭn), *n.* the act of presenting an idea indirectly to the mind; an idea introduced indirectly to the mind or thoughts; hint; insinuation.

sug-ges-tive (sŭg-jĕs'tĭv), *adj.* tending to excite thought; containing, or full of, thoughts; tending to bring into the mind what is improper.—*adv.* **suggestively.**—*n.* **suggestiveness.**

su-i-cid-al (sū'ĭ-sīd"ăl), *adj.* pertaining to, or of the nature of, suicide, or self-murder; fatal to one's own interests; as, *suicidal* plans.—*adv.* **suicidally.**

su-i-cide (sū'ĭ-sīd), *n.* the act of intentionally taking one's own life; self-murder; a person who kills himself intentionally; ruin of one's own interests.

suit (sūt), *n.* the act of seeking favor or justice; the process by which one tries to gain an end or an object; petition or prayer; courtship; an action or process at law for the recovery of a right or claim; a number of things used together; as, a *suit* of clothes; things that follow in a series or succession, making a set; as, a *suit* (or suite) of rooms; one of the four sets of a pack of cards: *v.t.* to fit, adapt; as, *suit* your words to the occasion; to be proper or suitable to; become; befit; as, your behavior does not *suit* your position; please; satisfy; as, I hope this will *suit* you: *v.i.* to correspond or accord; agree: with *with* or *to.*

suit-a-bil-i-ty (sūt'á-bĭl"ĭ-tĭ), *n.* the state or quality of being proper or fitting. Also, **suitableness.**

suit-a-ble (sūt'á-bl), *adj.* fitting; becoming; appropriate or proper. —*adv.* **suitably.**

suite (swēt), *n.* a company of attendants or servants; as, a king and his *suite;* a series or set; as, a *suite* of rooms, etc.; in music, a series of dance movements in the same key, written originally for one instrument, but now written also for an orchestra.

suit-or (sūt'ẽr), *n.* one who sues, petitions, or entreats; a lover; a party to a lawsuit.

sulk (sŭlk), *v.i.* to be sullen or silently obstinate: *n.* a sullen mood or humor: often plural.

sulk-y (sŭl'kĭ), *adj.* [*comp.* sulkier, *superl.* sulkiest], silently sullen, cross, or ill-humored: *n.* a light two-wheeled carriage, seating but one person.—*adv.* **sulkily.**—*n.* **sulkiness.**

Racing Sulky

sul-len (sŭl'ĕn), *adj.* inclined to be alone; gloomily ill-humored; as, a *sullen* disposition; dismal; heavy; gloomy; as, a *sullen* sky.—*adv.* **sullenly.**—*n.* **sullenness.**

sul-ly (sŭl'ĭ), *v.t.* [*p.t.* and *p.p.* sullied, *p.pr.* sullying], to tarnish or soil; to dirty or stain; as, to *sully* a mirror; figuratively, to lessen in purity or reputation; as, to *sully* one's fame: *v.i.* to become tarnished or soiled: *n.* soil; stain; tarnish.

sul-phate (sŭl'fāt), *n.* a salt of sulphuric acid, used in medicine and chemistry. Also, **sulfate.**

sul-phide (sŭl'fīd), *n.* a compound of sulphur with a metal or other element. Also, **sulfide, sulphid, sulfid.**

sul-phite (sŭl'fīt), *n.* a salt of sulphurous acid. Also, **sulfite.**

sul-phur (sŭl'fẽr), *n.* a pale-yellow nonmetallic substance which is used in making powder, matches, etc., and in bleaching cloth, etc., and which burns in air with a flame and suffocating odor; a yellow color. Also, **sulfur.**

sul-phur-ate (sŭl'fū-rāt), *v.t.* to combine with, or subject to, the action of sulphur, a pale-yellow nonmetallic substance: *adj.* composed of, or of the color of, sulphur. Also, **sulfurate.**—*n.* **sulphuret, sulfuret.**

sul-phu-re-ous (sŭl-fū'rē-ŭs), *adj.* made of, mixed with, or like, sulphur, a pale-yellow nonmetallic substance. Also, **sulfureous, sulphurous, sulfurous.**

sul-phu-ret (sŭl'fū-rĕt"), *v.t.* to combine with, or subject to, the action of sulphur, a pale-yellow nonmetallic substance. Also, **sulfuret, sulphurate, sulfurate.**

sul-phu-ric (sŭl-fū'rĭk), *adj.* of or pertaining to sulphur, a pale-yellow nonmetallic substance; obtained from or containing sulphur: **sulphuric acid,** a heavy, burning liquid, a compound of sulphur, oxygen, and water; oil of vitriol. Also, **sulfuric.**

sul-phur-ous (sŭl'fẽr-ŭs; sŭl-fū'rŭs), *adj.* of, pertaining to, or containing, sulphur, a pale-yellow nonmetallic substance; fiery; heated: **sulphurous acid,** an acid made of two parts of oxygen and two parts of sulphur. Also, **sulfurous.**

sul-phur-y (sŭl'fẽr-ĭ), *adj.* like sulphur, a pale-yellow nonmetallic substance. Also, **sulfury.**

sul-tan (sŭl'tăn; sŏŏl-tăn'), *n.* [*fem.* sultana], the title of a Mohammedan ruler: **Sultan,** the ruler of the Turkish Empire.

sul-tan-ate (sŭl'tăn-āt), *n.* the rule, authority, or territory of a sultan, or Mohammedan ruler.

sul-tan-ship (sŭl'tăn-shĭp), *n.* the office, rank, or authority of a sultan, or Mohammedan ruler.

sul-try (sŭl'trĭ), *adj.* [*comp.* sultrier, *superl.* sultriest], very hot, close, and oppressive; close and heavy, with a moist heat; as, a hot and *sultry* day.—*adv.* **sultrily.** —*n.* **sultriness.**

sum (sŭm), *n.* the total of two or more things; a quantity, as of money; the whole; all; substance; as, that is the *sum* of the evidence; utmost degree; highest point; as, the *sum* of happiness; in arithmetic, a problem: *v.t.* [*p.t.* and *p.p.* summed, *p.pr.* summing], to add into one amount; condense into few words; usually with *up;* as, to *sum* up a case: *v.i.* to make a brief restatement of all the facts: usually with *up;* as, and now, to *sum* up.

su-mac (sū'măk; shŏŏ'măk), *n.* any plant or shrub of the cashew family; the dried leaves and roots of certain kinds of the plant, used in tanning, dyeing, and in medicine: some kinds, as the poison sumac, produce a severe skin rash.

sum-ma-rize (sŭm'ȧ-rīz), *v.t.* to state briefly or concisely; sum up. Also, **summarise.**

sum-ma-ry (sŭm'ȧ-rĭ), *n.* a brief account containing the sum or substance of a fuller account; an abridgment; as, a *summary* of a law case: *adj.* giving the general idea; brief; concise; quickly performed; done without delay; as, the crime deserves *summary* punishment.—*adv.* **summarily.**—*n.* **summariness.**

sum-ma-tion (sŭm-ā'shŭn), *n.* the act of adding, or finding a total amount; that which is added up; a total.

sum-mer (sŭm'ẽr), *n.* the season of the year in any region in which the sun shines most directly; the warmest part of the year; that part of the year which composes the hottest months, June, July, and August, now estimated to extend from about June 21 to about September 22; a horizontal girder or timber which serves as a support; a stone to support an arch or arches: *v.i.* to pass the summer; as, to *summer* abroad: *v.t.* to feed or keep during the summer; as, to *summer* the cattle on a well-watered tract.—*adj.* **summery.**

sum-mer-house (sŭm'ẽr-hous"), *n.* a small rustic open building in a garden or park.

sum-mit (sŭm'ĭt), *n.* the top or highest point; as, the *summit* of a mountain; the *summit* of one's hopes, etc.

sum-mon (sŭm'ŭn), *v.t.* to call by authority; command to appear in court; to send for; call; bid; invite; rouse to exertion; as, to *summon* all one's strength: *n.pl.* an order or notice to appear in court on a certain day; a paper or document containing such a notice; an official call.—*n.* **summoner.**

sump-ter (sŭmp'tẽr), *n.* a burden-carrying animal; a pack horse or mule.

sump-tu-a-ry (sŭmp'tū-ā-rĭ), *adj.* pertaining to, or regulating, expenses, or the spending of money: **sumptuary laws,** laws to limit the amount of money spent on dress or other luxuries, and to regulate prices, wages, etc.

sump-tu-ous (sŭmp'tū-ŭs), *adj.* expensive; costly; luxurious; magnificent; as, a *sumptuous* feast.—*adv.* **sumptuously.**—*n.* **sumptuousness.**

sun (sŭn), *n.* the round, shining body around which the earth and other planets, etc., of the solar system revolve; the source of light and heat to the earth; any center of a system of worlds; anything like the sun in brightness or power; sunshine: *v.t.* [*p.t.* and *p.p.* sunned, *p.pr.* sunning], to expose to the sun's rays; as, to *sun* oneself; warm or dry in the sun.

sun-beam (sŭn'bēm"), *n.* a ray of sunlight: *pl.* sunlight.

sun-burn (sŭn'bûrn"), *n.* an inflammation of the skin caused by exposure to the sun: *v.t.* and *v.i.* to tan or discolor by the sun.

Sun-day (sŭn'dā), *n.* the first day of the week; the Christian Sabbath, or Lord's Day: *adj.* pertaining to, or happening on, Sunday.

sun-der (sŭn'dẽr), *v.t.* to divide or rend; break; separate: *v.i.* to become separated or broken apart: *n.* separation into parts.

sun-dew (sŭn'dū"), *n.* a plant whose leaves are covered with a dew-like sticky fluid.

sun-di-al (sŭn'-dī"ăl), *n.* a device to show the time of day by the shadow of a pin or triangular pointer, usually called a style or gnomon, on a dial.

Sundial

sun-dries (sŭn'-drĭz), *n.pl.* many different or small articles or matters.

sun-dry (sŭn'drĭ), *adj.* various; several; as, *sundry* reasons.

sun-fish (sŭn'fĭsh"), *n.* a large sea fish, peculiar in shape; an American fresh-water fish with brilliant coloring.

sun-flow-er (sŭn'flou"ẽr), *n.* a tall, straight plant of the aster family, with large yellow-rayed flowers and large leaves.

sung (sŭng), past participle of the verb *sing.*

sunk (sŭnk), past tense and past participle of the verb *sink.*

sunk-en (sŭnk'n), *adj.* lying on the bottom of the sea or other body of water; fallen or pressed down.

sun-less (sŭn'lĕs), *adj.* without light and heat from the sun; dark; cheerless.—*adv.* **sunlessly.**—*n.* **sunlessness.**

sunn (sŭn), *n.* an East Indian plant, the fiber of which is used as a substitute for hemp.

sun-ny (sŭn'ĭ), *adj.* pertaining to, or like, the sun; bright; warm; cheerful; as, a *sunny* disposition; filled with, or exposed to, the warmth and light of the sun; as, the *sunny* side of the street.—*adv.* **sunnily.**—*n.* **sunniness.**

sun-rise (sŭn rīz"), *n.* the appearance of the sun above the horizon in the early morning; the brightening of the sky at that time; the time at which the sun appears.

sun-set (sŭn'sĕt"), *n.* the disappearance of the sun below the horizon in the latter part of the day; the brightness of the sky at that time; the time at which the sun disappears.

sun-shade (sŭn'shād"), *n.* anything used to protect from the light or heat of the sun, as an awning; especially, a parasol or sun umbrella.

sun-shine (sŭn'shīn"), *n.* the light or rays of the sun, the space that they fill, or place where they fall; warmth; brightness.—*adj.* **sunshiny.**

sun-spot (sŭn'spŏt"), *n.* one of the dark, irregular spots appearing at certain periods on the surface of the sun.

sun-stroke (sŭn'strōk"), *n.* a prostration, often fatal, due to exposure to the sun or to other intense heat.

sup (sŭp), *v.t.* [*p.t.* and *p.p.* supped, *p.pr.* supping], to take into the mouth a little at a time, with the lips or in spoonfuls; sip: *v.i.* to take the evening meal, or supper: *n.* a small mouthful of liquid; sip.

su-per- (sū'pẽr-), a *prefix* meaning over, above, beyond, in excess.

su-per-a-bun-dance (sū"pẽr-ȧ-bŭn'-dăns), *n.* an amount much greater than is sufficient; excess.

su-per-a-bun-dant (sū"pẽr-ȧ-bŭn'-dănt), *adj.* being much more than is sufficient; excessive.

su-per-an-nu-ate (sū"pẽr-ăn'ū-āt), *v.t.* to impair, or render unfit, by age; to retire and give a pension to on account of old age or weakness, either mental or physical.

su-per-an-nu-a-tion (sū″pĕr-ăn″ū-ā′-shŭn), *n.* the state of being too old or too infirm for office or business; a becoming too old or too infirm.

su-perb (sū-pûrb′), *adj.* grand; proud; stately; as, a *superb* residence; rich; elegant; as, *superb* attire.—*adv.* **superbly.** —*n.* **superbness.**

su-per-car-go (sū″pĕr-kär′gō), *n.* an officer of a merchant ship who has charge of its cargo and business affairs during the voyage.

su-per-cil-i-ous (sū″pĕr-sĭl′ĭ-ŭs), *adj.* contemptuously haughty; proud; overbearing; as, a *supercilious* air or manner.—*adv.* **superciliously.**—*n.* **superciliousness.**

su-per-er-o-ga-tion (sū″pĕr-ĕr″ō-gā′-shŭn), *n.* the performance of more than is required by duty.

su-per-e-rog-a-to-ry (sū″pĕr-ē-rŏg′ȧ-tō-rĭ), *adj.* performed beyond what is required by duty; superfluous.

su-per-fi-cial (sū″pĕr-fĭsh′ăl), *adj.* pertaining to, or being on, the surface; not deep; shallow; reaching or understanding only what is apparent or on the surface; lacking depth of understanding or wisdom; as, a *superficial* mind.—*adv.* **superficially.**—*n.* **superficialness.**

su-per-fi-ci-al-i-ty (sū″pĕr-fĭsh″ĭ-ăl′ĭ-tĭ), *n.* the state or quality of being shallow, or on the surface only; shallowness; that which is shallow.

su-per-fine (sū′pĕr-fīn), *adj.* of the very choicest quality; very fine or good; very delicate; overnice.—*n.* **superfineness.**

su-per-flu-i-ty (sū″pĕr-flōō′ĭ-tĭ), *n.* [*pl.* superfluities (-tĭz)], state of being more than is needed or wanted; something beyond what is needed or wanted.

su-per-flu-ous (sū-pûr′flōō-ŭs), *adj.* being more than is needed or wanted; excessive; needless.—*adv.* **superfluously.**—*n.* **superfluousness.**

su-per-heat (sū″pĕr-hēt′), *v.t.* to heat to an extreme degree; heat (steam) until it resembles a perfect gas.

su-per-hu-man (sū″pĕr-hū′măn), *adj.* above or beyond what is human, or like the nature of man; as, *superhuman* skill or strength.

su-per-im-pose (sū″pĕr-ĭm-pōz′), *v.t.* to lay (something) on something else.

su-per-in-cum-bent (sū″pĕr-ĭn-kŭm′-bĕnt), *adj.* lying or resting on something else.

su-per-in-duce (sū″pĕr-ĭn-dūs′), *v.t.* to bring in, as an addition to something else; give rise to in addition to something else; superadd.

su-per-in-tend (sū″pĕr-ĭn-tĕnd′), *v.t.* to have, or exercise, the charge or oversight of; direct or control; as, to *superintend* a business or school.

su-per-in-tend-ence (sū″pĕr-ĭn-tĕn′-dĕns), *n.* act of managing or directing; supervision; oversight; control.

su-per-in-tend-en-cy (sū″pĕr-ĭn-tĕn′dĕn-sĭ), *n.* the office, or period of holding office, of a superintendent, or one who controls, directs, manages, etc.

su-per-in-tend-ent (sū″pĕr-ĭn-tĕn′-dĕnt), *n.* one who manages or controls; an overseer; director: *adj.* managing; directing; overseeing.

su-pe-ri-or (sū-pē′rĭ-ēr), *adj.* higher or above in place, position, rank, dignity, office, or excellence; finer; stronger; preferable; exceeding others; too fine or great to practice, or to feel the influence of: with *to:* as, *superior* to petty jealousies: *n.* one who surpasses another, as in rank or ability; one of higher rank or position; head of a religious house; as, a Mother *Superior.*—*adv.* **superiorly.**

su-pe-ri-or-i-ty (sū-pē″rĭ-ŏr′ĭ-tĭ), *n.* the state or quality of being finer or preferable, or above in ability, rank, dignity, or excellence.

su-per-la-tive (sū-pûr′lȧ-tĭv), *adj.* superior to all others; highest in degree; as, a man of *superlative* wisdom; in grammar, expressing the highest degree or amount: said of a form of adjectives and adverbs: *n.* the highest degree of excellence; the highest degree of comparison of an adjective or adverb; a word expressing the highest degree.—*adv.* **superlatively.**—*n.* **superlativeness.**

su-per-nal (sū-pûr′năl), *adj.* pertaining to, or situated in, a higher place or region; celestial or heavenly.

su-per-nat-u-ral (sū″pĕr-năt′ū-răl), *adj.* being outside, or exceeding, the forces or laws of nature; miraculous: *n.* that which exceeds or is outside the usual course of nature.—*adv.* **supernaturally.**

su-per-nu-mer-a-ry (sū″pĕr-nū′mĕr-ā-rĭ), *n.* [*pl.* supernumeraries (-rĭz)], a person or thing beyond the stated number, or beyond what is necessary or usual; especially, a person employed not for regular service, but merely to fill the place of another in case of need; as, a *supernumerary* in a ballroom scene of a play: *adj.* exceeding the number stated or required.

su-per-scribe (sū″pĕr-skrīb′), *v.t.* to write or engrave on the outside or top; to direct or address, as an envelope containing a letter.

su-per-scrip-tion (sū″pĕr-skrĭp′shŭn), *n.* the act of writing or engraving on the outside or top; that which is written or engraved on the outside; especially, the address on a letter or envelope.

su-per-sede (sū″pĕr-sēd′), *v.t.* to come into or take the place of, as by superior right or worth; to set aside and put another in place of; as, to *supersede* an officer; to replace; supplant.—*n.* **superseder, supersedure, supersession.**

su-per-sti-tion (sū″pĕr-stĭsh′ŭn), *n.* reverence for, and belief in, that which is unknown or mysterious; religious reverence for objects not worthy of worship; false worship or religion.

su-per-sti-tious (sū″pĕr-stĭsh′ŭs), *adj.* pertaining to, marked by, or disposed to, belief in that which is unknown or mysterious; as, a *superstitious* person.—*adv.* **superstitiously.**—*n.* **superstitiousness.**

su-per-struc-ture (sū″pĕr-strŭk′tûr), *n.* anything built or founded on something else; that which is raised on a foundation; a building above the basement.

su-per-vene (sū″pĕr-vēn′), *v.i.* to come as something additional; happen with reference or relation to something else; follow closely upon something.

su-per-vise (sū'pẽr-vīz'), *v.t.* to oversee or superintend.

su-per-vi-sion (sū'pẽr-vĭzh'ŭn), *n.* the act of inspecting with authority; the act of overseeing or superintending; superintendence.

su-per-vi-sor (sū'pẽr-vī'zẽr), *n.* an overseer or superintendent.

su-per-vi-so-ry (sū'pẽr-vī'zō-rĭ), *adj.* pertaining to, or exercising, general oversight.

su-pine (sū-pīn'; sū'pīn), *adj.* lying on the back; opposite to *prone;* careless; indifferent; listless: *n.* (sū'pīn), a Latin verbal noun, ending in *tum,* or *tu.*—*adv.* **supinely.**—*n.* **supineness.**

sup-per (sŭp'ẽr), *n.* the evening meal; the last meal of the day, sometimes following dinner, sometimes taking the place of it.

sup-plant (sŭ-plănt'), *v.t.* to displace and take the place of, as by craft or cunning.

sup-ple (sŭp'l), *adj.* easily bent; flexible; as, *supple* joints; submissive; yielding; as, a *supple* nature; meanly bending to the humor of others; flattering; *v.t.* to make soft and flexible; to make obedient and submissive: *v.i.* to grow soft and flexible.—*n.* **suppleness.**

sup-ple-ment (sŭp'lē-mĕnt), *n.* that which completes, or adds something to, something already made; especially, a part added to a book or paper to complete it, or to correct its mistakes: *v.t.* to complete by supplying what is lacking; to add something to.

sup-ple-men-tal (sŭp'lē-mĕn'tăl), *adj.* serving to provide what is lacking; additional; as, a *supplemental* clause in a document. Also, **supplementary.**

sup-pli-ance (sŭp'lĭ-ăns), *n.* the act of entreating, or asking, earnestly and humbly; state of being humbly entreating; humble entreaty.

sup-pli-ant (sŭp'lĭ-ănt), *n.* one who entreats, or asks, earnestly and humbly: *adj.* asking earnestly and humbly; beseeching; entreating; suing. Also, **supplicant.**

sup-pli-cant (sŭp'lĭ-kănt), *n.* one who entreats, or asks, earnestly and humbly: *adj.* asking humbly. Also, **suppliant.**

sup-pli-cate (sŭp'lĭ-kāt), *v.t.* to ask or beg for humbly and earnestly; address in prayer; beseech; implore: *v.i.* to pray or beseech humbly and earnestly.

sup-pli-ca-tion (sŭp'lĭ-kā'shŭn), *n.* the act of entreating, or asking, earnestly; humble and earnest prayer or entreaty.

sup-pli-ca-to-ry (sŭp'lĭ-kȧ-tō-rĭ), *adj.* expressing earnest and humble entreaty, or asking; as, a *supplicatory* letter.

sup-ply (sŭ-plī'), *v.t.* [*p.t.* and *p.p.* supplied, *p.pr.* supplying], to furnish with what is required; provide; as, to *supply* a people with food; to give; furnish; as, to *supply* food for a people; to fill temporarily; as, to *supply* a pulpit; make up for; as, to *supply* a loss: *n.* [*pl.* supplies (-plīz)], the act of providing or furnishing; that which is needed or furnished; amount of any article on hand to meet a demand; one who serves for another for a time, as in a pulpit: *pl.* reserve stores to be given out; as, the base of *supplies* for a fleet; **supply train,** in the army, a train including all vehicles, animals, and persons employed in transporting the divisional ration and grain reserve, or in bringing these provisions from the refilling point to the distributing point.

sup-port (sŭ-pōrt'), *v.t.* to bear the weight of; bear up; uphold; as, columns *support* the roof; endure; bear; suffer; as, to *support* pain; to keep from sinking; encourage; as, to *support* the spirits or courage; to act with; as, to *support* a star; to verify; make good; as, to *support* an accusation of theft; to aid, favor, or defend; as, to *support* a political party; carry on; as, to *support* a conversation; provide for; as, to *support* a family: *n.* the act of maintaining or upholding; that which maintains or upholds; maintenance; livelihood; aid; one who furnishes means of support, as to a family; one person or a company acting with a star.—*n.* **supporter.**

sup-port-a-ble (sŭ-pōr'tȧ-bl), *adj.* bearable; endurable; maintainable.—*adv.* **supportably.**

sup-pos-a-ble (sŭ-pōz'ȧ-bl), *adj.* capable of being assumed; not altogether unlikely.—*adv.* **supposably.**

sup-pose (sŭ-pōz'), *v.t.* to represent to oneself or another to be true or real; to imagine; believe; think; assume as true; to require to exist or be true: *v.i.* to think; imagine.

sup-posed (sŭ-pōzd'), *p.adj.* thought to be true; imagined: often with the idea of false belief.—*adv.* **supposedly.**

sup-po-si-tion (sŭp'ō-zĭsh'ŭn), *n.* the act of imagining, or of considering as true or existing, what is known to be not true, or what is not proved; opinion or belief without proof.—*adj.* **suppositional.** —*adv.* **suppositionally.**

sup-pos-i-ti-tious (sŭ-pŏz'ĭ-tĭsh'ŭs), *adj.* assumed or imagined; not genuine; counterfeit.—*adv.* **supposititiously.**

sup-pos-i-to-ry (sŭ-pŏz'ĭ-tō-rĭ), *n.* a conelike mass, containing medicine, for putting into some cavity or passage of the body, where it dissolves.

sup-press (sŭ-prĕs'), *v.t.* to subdue; crush; as, to *suppress* a rebellion; keep in; restrain; as, to *suppress* a smile; conceal; as, to *suppress* the facts in a case; stop the publication of; as, to *suppress* a magazine; cause to cease; check; as, to *suppress* a hemorrhage.—*n.* **suppresser, suppressor.**

sup-pres-sion (sŭ-prĕsh'ŭn), *n.* the act of crushing, checking, or concealing; state of being crushed, checked, or concealed; restraint; concealment; an omission, as of a letter or word.

sup-pres-sive (sŭ-prĕs'ĭv), *adj.* tending to crush, check, or conceal; subduing; concealing.

sup-pu-rate (sŭp'ū-rāt), *v.i.* to form pus; as, an abscess *suppurates.*

sup-pu-ra-tion (sŭp'ū-rā'shŭn), *n.* the act of forming pus, or foul matter; pus, or foul matter, formed in an abscess, etc.

sup-pu-ra-tive (sŭp'ū-rā-tĭv), *adj.* tending to produce, or produced by, pus, or foul matter: *n.* a medicine to promote suppuration, or the forming of pus.

su-prem-a-cy (sū-prĕm'ȧ-sĭ), *n.* the state of being supreme, or in the highest station of power; the supreme or highest authority.

su-preme (sū-prēm'), *adj.* highest in power or authority; as, a *supreme* ruler or court; highest in degree; greatest possible; utmost; as, *supreme* sacrifice.—*adv.* **supremely.**—*n.* **supremeness.**

sur- (sûr-), a *prefix* meaning over, beyond, above, upon.

su-rah (sōō'rȧ; sū'rȧ), *n.* a soft twilled silk material, for women's garments. Also, **surah silk.**

sur-cease (sûr-sēs'), *n.* final end; stop: *v.i.* to cease finally.

sur-charge (sûr-chärj'), *n.* an excessive charge, load, or burden; a charge beyond what is just and right; an additional or secondary printing on a stamp or document: *v.t.* to charge more than is due; overload; overburden.

sur-cin-gle (sûr'sĭn'gl), *n.* a girth, belt, or girdle for passing around the body of a horse or other animal to secure the saddle, blanket, etc.

sur-coat (sûr'kōt"), *n.* a coat worn over another coat or garment; especially, the long, loose garment of knights, worn over the armor.

surd (sûrd), *n.* a quantity that cannot be expressed by rational numbers, as the square root of 2; a consonant sound made without voice or tone, as *f, p, s*: *adj.* not capable of being expressed in rational numbers; |involving surds; uttered, as certain consonants, without voice or tone.

sure (shōōr), *adj.* certain; knowing and believing; confident beyond doubt; as, I am *sure* it is true; certain to find or retain; as, he is *sure* to succeed; fit to be depended upon; reliable; as, this is a *sure* investment; firmly fixed; not likely to change or fail; stable: *adv.* colloquially, certainly.

sure-foot-ed (shōōr'fōōt"ĕd), *adj.* not likely to fall or stumble.—*adv.* **sure-footedly.**—*n.* **sure-footedness.**

sure-ly (shōōr'lĭ), *adv.* certainly; without risk or doubt; firmly; securely.

sure-ness (shōōr'nĕs), *n.* the state or quality of being certain, firm, or secure; certainty.

sure-ty (shōōr'tĭ), *n.* [*pl.* sureties (-tĭz)], state of being certain; certainty; security or guaranty against loss or damage; security for the payment of a debt or for the performance of some act; bail; one who becomes bound, or agrees to be responsible, for another, as for payment of a debt.

sure-ty-ship (shōōr'tĭ-shĭp), *n.* the state of being answerable for another; the duty of one who is bound to answer for another.

surf (sûrf), *n.* the swell of the sea where it breaks and foams upon the shore or rocks.

sur-face (sûr'fās), *n.* the outside part of anything that has length, breadth, and thickness; a space-form that has only length and breadth; the upper face of a solid; outside; hence, outward appearance; as, all looks well, on the *surface.*

surf-boat (sûrf'bōt"), *n.* a strong, light boat for landing through the surf, or swell of the sea that breaks upon the shore.

sur-feit (sûr'fĭt), *n.* excess, especially in eating or drinking; fulness or sickness caused by such excess; indulgence in anything to excess: *v.t.* to feed to excess; cloy: *v.i.* to partake of food to excess; indulge in anything to excess.—*n.* **surfeiter.**

surge (sûrj), *n.* a large wave or billow; a great roll of water; swell; a great rolling motion; sweep; rush; as, the *surge* of a mob: *v.i.* to rise high and roll; swell.

sur-geon (sûr'jŭn), *n.* one who treats injuries, deformities, or diseases by manual operation, or the use of the knife; a staff officer of the Medical Department of an army: **surgeon-general,** the chief of the Medical Department in the United States army.

sur-ger-y (sûr'jẽr-ĭ), *n.* the act, art, or science of treating injuries, deformities, or diseases by manual operations, or the use of the knife; the place where a surgeon operates, or gives advice or treatment.

sur-gi-cal (sûr'jĭ-kăl), *adj.* pertaining to surgery, or the art of healing by the use of the knife, or to surgeons.—*adv.* **surgically.**

sur-loin (sûr'loin"), *n.* the upper portion of a loin of beef. Also, **sirloin.**

sur-ly (sûr'lĭ), *adj.* [*comp.* surlier, *superl.* surliest], gloomily ill-humored; morose; rough; uncivil; ill-natured; rudely abrupt.—*adv.* **surlily.**—*n.* **surliness.**

sur-mise (sûr-mīz'), *n.* a thought or supposition based upon little evidence; a guess: *v.t.* to imagine without certain knowledge; suppose; guess.

sur-mount (sûr-mount'), *v.t.* to rise above; overcome; conquer; vanquish; as, to *surmount* one's difficulties.—*adj.* **surmountable.**—*n.* **surmounter.**

sur-name (sûr'nām"), *n.* a name added to a baptismal or Christian name, and used as a family name; as, in the name John Smith, *Smith* is the *surname*: *v.t.* to give a family name to; call by a family name.

sur-pass (sûr-pȧs'), *v.t.* to exceed; excel; go beyond in excellence.—*adj.* **surpassable.**—*p.adj.* **surpassing.**

sur-plice (sûr'plĭs), *n.* the outer linen garment with wide sleeves, worn especially by the priests and choir members of the Roman Catholic and English Churches.

Surplice

sur-plus (sûr'plŭs), *n.* that which remains over and above what is required; excess: *adj.* exceeding what is used or needed; as, *surplus* supplies.—*n.* **surplusage.**

sur-prise (sûr-prīz'), *n.* the act of coming upon or attacking unexpectedly; state of being taken unawares; a feeling excited by what is sudden and strange; wonder; astonishment; a sudden or unexpected event or fact: *v.t.* to take unawares; to attack without notice; as, to *surprise* the enemy; to strike with wonder by something sudden or unexpected; astonish; to lead to do something suddenly and unexpectedly: with *into*; as, to *surprise* a thief into admitting his guilt.—*n.* **surprisal.**

sur-pris-ing (sûr-prīz'ĭng), *adj.* causing wonder or astonishment; unexpected; extraordinary; as, *surprising* news.—*adv.* **surprisingly.**

sur-ren-der (sŭ-rĕn'dẽr), *n.* the act of yielding, or giving up, oneself or a thing into the power or possession of another: *v.t.* to yield, under pressure, to the power of another; give up possession of on compulsion or demand; as, to *surrender* an army or arms; to resign possession of; give up; as, to *surrender* one's claim to property; to yield to any influence, emotion, or power; as, to *surrender* oneself to sorrow: *v.i.* to yield; give up oneself or a thing into the power of another.

sur-rep-ti-tious (sûr″ĕp-tĭsh′ŭs), *adj.* done by stealth or fraud, or without proper authority; as, a *surreptitious* departure.—*adv.* **surreptitiously.**

sur-rey (sûr′ĭ), *n.* a light four-wheeled pleasure carriage with two seats.

sur-ro-gate (sûr′ō-gāt), *n.* one appointed by a bishop to act in his place; a court officer who deals with the probating, or proving, of wills, and the settlement of estates.

sur-round (sŭ-round′), *v.t.* to inclose on all sides; to lie or to be on all sides of; to encircle.

sur-round-ings (sŭ-round′ĭngz), *n.* the things or conditions that make up an environment.

sur-tax (sûr′tăks″), *n.* an extra tax: *v.t.* (sûr-tăks′; sûr′tăks), to impose, or add, an extra tax on, as in railroad rates, etc.

sur-tout (sûr-tōōt′), *n.* a wide-skirted coat reaching below the knees; an overcoat, especially when long and tight fitting.

sur-veil-lance (sûr-vāl′yăns; sûr-vāl′-ăns), *n.* close watch; oversight; inspection; as, police *surveillance*.

sur-vey (sûr′vā; sûr-vā′), *n.* the act of examining carefully, or of determining the features of, as of land; a careful view or examination; a measured plan and description of any portion of country, etc.: *v.t.* (sûr-vā′), [*p.t.* and *p.p.* surveyed, *p.pr.* surveying], to inspect, or take a view of; as, to *survey* the landscape; to look at closely; as, she *surveyed* me coldly; examine closely; as, to *survey* a subject or a building; measure and determine the features of, as land.

sur-vey-ing (sûr-vā′ĭng), *n.* the science, art, or business, of measuring and determining the various features of land.

sur-vey-or (sûr-vā′ẽr), *n.* one whose business is to measure land; one who examines anything closely in order to find out its character, condition, etc.; an inspector of customs.

sur-viv-al (sûr-vīv′ăl), *n.* a living or continuing longer than, or beyond the life of, another person, thing, or event; any ancient use, custom, or belief continuing to the present day.

sur-vive (sûr-vīv′), *v.t.* to live longer than (another); to outlive; outlast; to live beyond or through (an event, state, etc.): *v.i.* to remain alive or in existence.—*p.adj.* **surviving.**

sur-viv-or (sûr-vīv′ẽr), *n.* one who outlives another person, or any time, event, or thing; as, a *survivor* of a wreck; the one of two persons having a common interest who outlives the other.

sus-cep-ti-bil-i-ty (sŭ-sĕp″tĭ-bĭl′ĭ-tĭ), *n.* the state or quality of receiving impressions, or of being easily affected; capacity for deep feeling or emotion; sensitiveness. Also, **susceptibleness.**

sus-cep-ti-ble (sŭ-sĕp′tĭ-bl), *adj.* capable of being changed, influenced, or easily affected, etc.: with *of* or *to;* tender; sensitive; easily acted upon. Also, **susceptive.**—*adv.* **susceptibly.**

sus-pect (sŭs-pĕkt′), *v.t.* to imagine to exist; to believe in the possible guilt of, without having proof; to doubt; mistrust: *v.i.* to imagine guilt, etc.; be suspicious: *n.* a person believed, but not proved, to be guilty of some crime.

sus-pend (sŭs-pĕnd′), *v.t.* to fasten to something above so as to hang down; to hang, or to hold as if by hanging, as particles of dust in the air; to delay; hold undecided; as, to *suspend* judgment; interrupt; to cause to cease for a time; as, to *suspend* a rule; debar, or keep out for a time; as, to *suspend* a pupil from school.

sus-pend-er (sŭs-pĕn′dẽr), *n.* one who, or that which, holds, holds back, or withholds: *pl.* braces to hold up clothing, especially trousers.

sus-pense (sŭs-pĕns′), *n.* a state of uncertainty, doubt, or anxiety; indecision; act of withholding, as judgment; pause; cessation.

sus-pen-sion (sŭs-pĕn′shŭn), *n.* the act of hanging from a support, or of stopping, delaying, or interrupting for a time; state of being hung, delayed, etc., especially, a brief stop, delay, or interruption; a stopping of payments in business; a floating, as of particles, in a fluid.

sus-pen-sion bridge (sŭs-pĕn′shŭn brĭj), a bridge of which the roadway is stretched, without support from below, from hanging cables.

sus-pen-so-ry (sŭs-pĕn′sō-rĭ), *adj.* fitting or serving to sustain or suspend; as, a *suspensory* muscle; serving to delay: *n.* that which holds up.

sus-pi-cion (sŭs-pĭsh′ŭn), *n.* the act of doubting, or of imagining on slight evidence; mistrust; imagination of something wrong, on slight or insufficient proof; colloquially, a very small quantity; hint; as, just a *suspicion* of humor.

sus-pi-cious (sŭs-pĭsh′ŭs), *adj.* apt to imagine without proof; full of, or inclined to, doubt or mistrust; open to, or exciting, mistrust; questionable.

sus-tain (sŭs-tān′), *v.t.* to hold up or support; as, to *sustain* a weight; maintain or keep up; as, to *sustain* an argument; support, or keep alive; as, food *sustains* life; undergo; as, to *sustain* a money loss; bear; endure without failing; as, to *sustain* a blow; keep up the courage or spirits of; as, his faith *sustained* him, prove; strengthen; as, to *sustain* a charge, at law; support or admit as just and true.

sus-tained (sŭs-tānd′), *adj.* held up to, or kept at, a certain pitch or level; uniform; as, *sustained* efforts.

sus-te-nance (sŭs′tē-năns), *n.* act of maintaining; that which supports life; food; maintenance or support.

sut-ler (sŭt′lẽr), *n.* a person who follows an army and sells food, liquor, etc., to the troops.

sut-tee (sŭ-tē′), *n.* a Hindu widow burned to death on the funeral pile of her husband; also, such an act.

su-ture (sū′tūr), *n.* the act of sewing; a seam or that which resembles a seam; the drawing together of the edges of a wound by stitches; the lines or seams where bones, as those of the skull, are united.

su-ze-rain (sū′zē-rān), *n.* a lord of the Middle Ages, who had authority over others and to whom loyalty and service were due; a state holding sovereign power over another state.

su-ze-rain-ty (sū′zē-rān-tĭ), *n.* the office, or dignity, of a suzerain, or lord of the Middle Ages who had authority over others; very high authority.

swab (swŏb), *n.* a mop for cleaning decks, floors, etc.; a sponge attached to a handle, for cleaning the barrel of a gun, etc.; a bit of sponge or cotton fastened to a handle to clean, or apply medicine to, the mouth, throat, etc.: *v.t.* [*p.t.* and *p.p.* swabbed, *p.pr.* swabbing], to rub or clean with a mop, sponge, etc.—*n.* **swabber.**

swad-dle (swŏd'l), *v.t.* to swathe, or wrap closely, with a bandage; as, to *swaddle* a baby: **swaddling band** or **swaddling cloth,** a bandage, or long strip of linen or cotton, wrapped around an infant, especially one newly born.

swag (swăg), *n.* property obtained by theft; booty; plunder. [SLANG.]

swage (swāj), *n.* a tool for shaping metal work, as wrought iron, by pounding with a hammer, or by pressure: *v.t.* to shape with a swage or swage block.

swag-ger (swăg'ẽr), *v.i.* to boast noisily; bluster; bully; to strut or walk with affected superiority: *n.* noisy boastfulness; an affected or insolent manner of walking: **swagger stick,** a light hand-stick carried by military men and others, when without arms or equipments, in order to occupy one or both hands.—*n.* **swaggerer.**

swain (swān), *n.* a young man living in the country; especially, a country gallant or lover.

swale (swāl), *n.* a piece of low, marshy ground, wet at certain seasons.

swal-low (swŏl'ō), *n.* a well-known bird noted for its swift and graceful flight; any of a class of swifts resembling the swallow; as, the chimney *swallow;* the gullet, or esophagus, or the passage between the mouth and the stomach; as much as can be taken through this passage at once; the act of taking through this passage: *v.t.* to take into the stomach through the esophagus, or gullet; to absorb or take in; cause to disappear; as, the crowd *swallowed* him up; to retract or take back; as, to *swallow* one's boasts; put up with; as, to *swallow* an insult: *v.i.* to perform the act of taking anything through the gullet.—*n.* **swallower.**

swal-low-tailed (swŏl'ō-tāld'), *adj.* being forked, like a swallow's tail; having tapering or forked skirts; as, a *swallow-tailed* coat.

swam (swăm), past tense of the irregular verb *swim.*

swamp (swŏmp), *n.* wet or spongy land; soft low land soaked with water; marshy land: *v.t.* to plunge, or sink, into spongy or marshy land; cause to fill, or to sink by filling, with water; as, to *swamp* a boat; to overwhelm; ruin, as with difficulties or numbers: *v.i.* to fill with water and sink; to stick or sink in spongy or marshy land; be overwhelmed or ruined by difficulties.

swamp-y (swŏm'pĭ), *adj.* soaked with water; spongy and marshy.

swan (swŏn), *n.* a web-footed bird of the goose family, with a very long neck, and noted for its grace in the water; a poet or singer.

Swan

swan's-down (swŏnz'doun'), *n.* the soft, fine feathers of the swan, often used as trimming, as on an evening cloak; a very soft, thick cloth of fine wool; cotton flannel.

swan-skin (swŏn'skĭn'), *n.* the skin of a swan with the down or feathers on it; a kind of soft cloth called canton flannel.

swan song (swŏn sŏng), the song that the swan is fabled to sing just before its death; hence, a last beautiful utterance or writing; as, a poet's *swan song.*

swap (swŏp) *v.t.* [*p.t.* and *p.p.* swapped, *p.pr.* swapping], to exchange or barter: *n.* an exchange. [COLLOQ.]

sward (swôrd), *n.* a stretch of land covered thickly with grass; turf.—*adj.* **swarded.**

sware (swâr), the old form of the past tense of the verb *swear.*

swarm (swôrm), *n.* a large number of insects in motion; as, a *swarm* of ants; a hive of bees, or a large number of them, with a queen, leaving one hive to find another; a crowd or multitude in motion; as, a *swarm* of people: *v.i.* to throng together in a crowd; move about in great numbers; as, people *swarmed* everywhere; to be crowded; as, the street *swarms* with people; to leave a hive in order to make a new colony, as bees; colloquially, to climb a tree, etc., by using the arms and legs: *v.t.* to throng or crowd; as, people *swarmed* the streets.

swart (swôrt), *adj.* of a dark or dusky hue or color; dark-skinned. Also, **swarthy.**

swarth-y (swôr'thĭ; swôr'*th*ĭ), *adj.* of a dark or dusky hue or color; dark-skinned. Also, **swart.**—*adv.* **swarthily.** —*n.* **swarthiness.**

swash (swŏsh), *n.* a dashing or splashing, as of water: *v.i.* to dash or wash with a splashing sound; dash or splash water about; hence, to bluster or brag: *v.t.* to dash or splash about, as water.

swash-buck-ler (swŏsh'bŭk'lẽr), *n.* a noisy, blustering bully or ruffian; a swaggerer.

swas-ti-ka (swăs'tĭ-kȧ), *n.* a certain symbol, or mark, signifying health, or good omen, and supposed to represent the sun in its daily course. Also, **swastica.**

Swastika

swath (swôth; swŏth), *n.* a line or row of grass or grain as cut down by the mower; the whole sweep or cut of a scythe in mowing; the space cut by a scythe or machine in one course.

swathe (swā*th*), *v.t.* to bind with a band or bandage; to wrap, as a bandage, about something: *n.* a band or bandage for wrapping about something.—*n.* **swather.**

sway (swā), *v.t.* [*p.t.* and *p.p.* swayed, *p.pr.* swaying], to cause to bend or to move backwards and forwards; as, the wind *sways* the trees; move with the hand; swing; as, to *sway* a sword; influence by power or moral force; direct; rule; as, to *sway* the lives of a people; cause to lean to one side; as, to *sway* opinion: *v.i.* to incline to one side; to move or swing from side to side: *n.* the act of leaning or swinging, or of turning from side to side; rule, dominion, or control; weight, influence, or authority that causes to lean to one side.

swear (swâr), *v.i.* [*p.t.* swore, *p.p.* sworn, *p.pr.* swearing], to make a solemn declaration, with an appeal to God for the truth of what is affirmed; to make a solemn vow or promise; to give evidence on oath; to use profane language: *v.t.* to utter or declare with an appeal to God; to vow or promise solemnly; cause to take, or bind by, an oath; as, to *swear* witnesses; to utter profanely.—*n.* **swearer.**

sweat (swĕt), *n.* the moisture which is given off through the pores of the skin; perspiration; moisture given off by any substance; act of giving off moisture; state of one who gives off moisture; toil; drudgery: *v.i.* to give off moisture through the pores of the skin; to perspire; to give off moisture, as plants; form moisture in drops on the outside, as a glass of water; to labor hard; drudge: *v.t.* to cause to perspire freely; to send forth through the pores; to wet with perspiration; to force the moisture out of by heat; force moisture out of by fermentation, as tobacco; colloquially, to employ at hard work for very low and unfair wages.—*adj.* sweaty.

sweat-er (swĕt′ẽr), *n.* a person who overworks and underpays those who work for him; a heavy outside jacket or jersey: in the army, an article of clothing that is part of a soldier's equipment.

sweat-shop (swĕt′shŏp″), *n.* a workroom where persons work very hard for very low wages.

sweat-ing sys-tem (swĕt′ĭng sĭs′tĕm), the system of labor by which people do piecework, sometimes at their own homes, for very low and unfair wages.

Swe-den-bor-gi-an (swē″dĕn-bôr′jĭ-ăn), *adj.* pertaining to the doctrines of Swedenborg (1688-1772), a Swedish philosopher, and founder of the New Jerusalem Church: *n.* a member of this church or a believer in its doctrines.—*n.* Swedenborgianism.

Swed-ish (swēd′ĭsh), *adj.* of or pertaining to Sweden, its people, or their language: *n.* the language of Sweden.

sweep (swēp), *v.t.* [*p.t.* and *p.p.* swept, *p.pr.* sweeping], to brush, pass over, or clean, with a broom, etc.; as, to *sweep* a carpet; remove or clean away with a broom, etc.; as to *sweep* up the dirt; drive, flow over, or carry along or off with force; as, waves *swept* the deck; the epidemic *swept* off people by thousands; the wind *swept* the house away; to brush against or over; as, to *sweep* the strings of a violin; to carry in a stately or proud fashion; as, she *swept* her skirts aside: *v.i.* to clean or clear away dirt with a brush, broom, etc.; to pass with speed or force; move with stateliness or dignity; to lie or extend for a long distance; as, the lawn *sweeps* away to the right: *n.* the act of sweeping; a clearing out or away; as, to make a clean *sweep;* range; extent; as, the *sweep* of a storm or an epidemic; a bend or curve; as, the *sweep* of a drive; rapid survey with the eye; extent of a stroke; as, the *sweep* of a scythe; one who makes a business of cleaning chimneys; as, a chimney *sweep;* a long oar.—*n.* sweeper.

sweep-ing (swēp′ĭng), *p.adj.* carrying off, or clearing away, as with a broom or by force; as, a *sweeping* wind; carrying all before it; as, a *sweeping* triumph; inclusive; comprehensive; as, a *sweeping* assertion: *n.pl.* a collection of dirt and particles swept up; refuse; as, street *sweepings.*

sweep-stakes (swēp′stāks″), *n.pl.* the whole sum of money or other prize put up to be won at a horse race or in gaming; a race for the whole sum staked.

sweet (swēt), *adj.* pleasing to the senses; tasting like sugar; not stale or sour; as, *sweet* butter or milk; fresh; not salt; as, *sweet* water; fragrant; as, *sweet* honeysuckle; pleasing in sound; soft; as, a *sweet* voice; fair; lovely; as, a *sweet* face; pleasing to the mind; attractive; mild; gentle; as, a *sweet* manner; containing sugar: *n.* quality of being sweet; something sweet; one dearly loved; darling: *pl.* confectionery or candy; homemade wines.—*adv.* sweetly.—*n.* sweetness.

sweet-bread (swēt′brĕd″), *n.* the pancreas, or gland lying behind the stomach, of a calf or a lamb, and used as food.

sweet-bri-ar (swēt′brī″ẽr), *n.* a thorny shrub of the rose family bearing single pink flowers.

sweet corn (swēt kôrn), a kind of maize, or corn, of a sweet taste, much used as a table food.

sweet-en (swēt′n), *v.t.* to make sweet; to make mild, kind, grateful, or pleasing; render less painful, difficult, or laborious; to make pure; as, to *sweeten* the air of a room: *v.i.* to become sweet.—*n.* sweetener.

sweet fern (swēt fûrn), a shrub about two feet high with long, fragrant, fernlike leaves.

sweet flag (swēt flăg), a fragrant plant with sword-shaped leaves.

sweet-heart (swēt′härt″), *n.* a lover; one who is the object of a lover's affection.

sweet-ish (swēt′ĭsh), *adj.* somewhat sweet.—*n.* sweetishness.

sweet-meat (swēt′mēt″), *n.* fruit or nuts preserved with sugar; candy.

sweet po-ta-to (swēt pō-tā′tō), a tropical plant of the morning glory family and its eatable root; a yam.

sweet Wil-liam (swēt wĭl′yŭm), a beautiful flowering plant of the pink family.

swell (swĕl), *v.i.* [*p.t.* swelled, *p.p.* swelled, swollen, *p.pr.* swelling], to expand or enlarge; increase in size, volume, or force; heave; be inflated, or bulge out; rise and increase by degrees; be puffed up; as, to *swell* with importance; grow louder and fuller; as, the music *swelled:* *v.t.* to cause to rise or increase; inflate or fill; puff up; make to grow louder and fuller; as, their voices *swelled* the chorus: *n.* act or state of swelling; increase in volume, force, value; gradual increase and decrease of sound; a long continuous wave or billow; gradual elevation of land; colloquially, a very fashionable person.

swell-ing (swĕl′ĭng), *n.* the act of expanding, or increasing in bulk, etc.; state of being so increased; a boil or any enlarged sore part of the body: *p.adj.* becoming inflated or filled; as, *swelling* sails.

swel-ter (swĕl′tẽr), *v.i.* to perspire, or sweat, very freely; to be faint from heat.—*p.adj.* sweltering.

swept (swĕpt), past tense and past participle of the verb *sweep.*

swerve (swûrv), *v.i.* to turn aside from any certain line, or any course or rule of duty: *v.t.* to turn aside: *n.* a turning aside suddenly.

swift (swĭft), *adj.* moving far in a short time; rapid; speedy; fleet; as, a *swift* train or horse; passing or coming suddenly or quickly; as, the *swift* hours; *swift* decision; acting quickly; prompt; as, *swift* to answer: *adv.* rapidly: *n.* a bird of the humming-bird family, but resembling the swallow; a kind of moth.—*adv.* swiftly.—*n.* swiftness.

swig (swig), *v.t.* and *v.i.* to drink in deep drafts; to gulp: *n.* a deep drink, as of liquor.

swill (swil), *v.t.* to drink or swallow greedily in large quantity; guzzle; to fill with drink: *n.* drink taken in large quantities; liquid food for animals, particularly the refuse or leavings of the kitchen, as given to swine.

swim (swim), *v.i.* [*p.t.* swam, swum, *p.p.* swum, *p.pr.* swimming], to float, as on water or other liquid; to propel or push oneself forward in the water with the hands and feet, or fins and tail; to be carried along by, or as by, a current; to glide smoothly; overflow; as, the eyes *swim* in tears; to have great abundance; as, to *swim* in luxury; be dizzy; as, the head *swims*: *v.t.* to cause to swim or float; to pass or move over, or through, by swimming; as, to *swim* a river: *n.* the act of swimming.—*n.* **swimmer.**

swin-dle (swin'dl), *v.t.* to cheat deliberately; to defraud: *n.* the act of cheating or defrauding; a fraud; a cheat.

swin-dler (swin'dlẽr), *n.* one who schemes to defraud; a cheat.

swin-dling (swin'dling), *n.* act of one who defrauds or deliberately cheats.

swine (swin), *n.* any animal of the hog family, with bristly skin and long snout: usually used collectively.

swine-herd (swin'hûrd″), *n.* a tender or keeper of swine, or hogs.

swing (swing), *v.i.* [*p.t.* and *p.p.* swung, *p.pr.* swinging], to move to and fro while hanging, as the pendulum of a clock; to turn on, or as on, a hinge, or axis; as, the gate *swings* open; to go along with a loose, free, swaying gait; as, the soldiers *swung* around the corner; to use a swing; to turn or wheel round, as a ship; colloquially, to be hanged; as, to *swing* on the gallows: *v.t.* to cause to move to and fro; as, to *swing* a pendulum; wave to and fro; brandish; as, to *swing* a cane; cause to turn or wheel about; as, to *swing* a ship about; put up so as to hang freely; as, to *swing* a hammock; hang on hinges; as, to *swing* a gate: *n.* the act of swinging; swaying motion from side to side; distance through which an object swings; loose, free gait; an apparatus, usually a rope bearing a seat, for swinging to and fro; full course or freedom; as, to give full *swing* to imagination.

swinge (swinj), *v.t.* to whip or thrash; to weld together.

swin-ish (swin'ish), *adj.* pertaining to, or like, swine, or hogs; beastly.—*adv.* **swinishly.**—*n.* **swinishness.**

swipe (swip), *n.* a vigorous blow, as with a bat or club: *v.t.* to give a strong blow to; hit with great force, as a ball in a ball game. [Colloq.]

swirl (swûrl), *v.i.* to rush along with a circular or wheeling motion: *v.t.* to cause to wheel, or whirl: *n.* a whirling or eddying motion; a curve or twist.

swish (swish), *v.t.* to cause to move with the rushing or whistling sound indicated by the word "swish": *n.* such a rustling or whistling sound, or the movement that makes it; as, the *swish* of her skirts; the *swish* of a cane.

Swiss (swis), *adj.* pertaining to Switzerland, its language, or its people: *n.* a native or inhabitant of Switzerland.

switch (swich), *n.* a small, thin, flexible rod; a movable section of rail for shifting cars from one track to another; a device for making, breaking, or shifting electric circuits; a tress of false hair, used by women in hair dressing: *v.t.* to whip or lash with a thin, flexible rod; to swing or jerk; as, to *switch* a cane; to shift to another track; as, to *switch* a train; shift to another circuit, or on or off a circuit; as, to *switch* off the electric light.

switch-back (swich'băk″), *n.* a railway for going up and down a steep incline by way of zigzag tracks; an amusement railway with steep ascents and descents.

switch-board (swich'bōrd″), *n.* a board with many switches for connecting, disconnecting, or combining electric currents.

switch-man (swich'măn), *n.* one who attends to shifting the movable rails or tracks of a railroad.

Swit-zer (swit'sẽr), *n.* a native or inhabitant of Switzerland; a Swiss.

swiv-el (swiv'l), *n.* anything that turns on a headed bolt or pin; as, the *swivel* of a watch chain; something fixed in another body so as to turn round in it; a twisting link in a chain: *v.t.* and *v.i.* [*p.t.* and *p.p.* swiveled, *p.pr.* swiveling], to turn on a swivel, or pivot: **swivel gun,** in artillery, a gun fixed on a swivel, or pivot, either on the back of an animal, such as a camel, or on a wall or other commanding position, so that it may be turned in any direction.

swol-len (swōl'n), past participle of the verb *swell.*

swoon (swōōn), *v.i.* to faint: *n.* the act of fainting; a faint.

swoop (swōōp), *v.t.* to fall upon and seize; as, the eagle *swoops* up its prey; to catch up: *v.i.* to sweep down swiftly and suddenly while on the wing; as, the eagle *swoops* down on its prey: *n.* a sudden sweeping down and seizing.

sword (sōrd), *n.* a long, keen-edged, sharp-pointed offensive weapon with one or two cutting edges, such as the small sword, rapier, saber, scimitar, etc.; hence, the symbol of military power, of justice, or vengeance; conflict or war; as, an appeal to the *sword*: **sword arm,** the right arm, as symbolic of strength: **sword belt,** a belt of suitable material worn over the right shoulder of an officer, and supporting his sword: **sword cane,** a cane which conceals the blade of a sword or dagger.

Swordfish

sword-fish (sōrd'fish″), *n.* a sea fish of the mackerel family, having the bones of the upper jaw formed into a swordlike beak.

sword-play (sōrd'plā″), *n.* fencing, or the art of attack and defense with the sword or foil.

swords-man (sōrdz'măn), *n.* one skilled in the use of the sword; a fencer.

swords-man-ship (sōrdz'măn-ship), *n.* the art or skill of one who is a master in the use of the sword.

swore (swōr), past tense of the verb *swear*.

sworn (swōrn), *p.p.* of *swear*: *p.adj.* bound by an oath; as, a *sworn* enemy.

Syb-a-rite (sĭb'*d*-rīt), *n.* a person devoted to luxury or pleasure: from the inhabitants of Sybaris, Italy, an ancient Greek city noted for its luxury and wealth. Also, **sybarite.**—*adj.* **Sybaritic, sybaritic.**

syc-a-more (sĭk'*d*-mōr), *n.* a tree of Syria, related to the fig; in England, a kind of maple; the American buttonwood.

syc-o-phan-cy (sĭk'ō-făn-sĭ), *n.* the character or practices of a servile flatterer; mean or servile flattery; fawning.

syc-o-phant (sĭk'ō-fănt), *n.* a mean or servile flatterer, especially of great men.

syc-o-phan-tic (sĭk-ō-făn'tĭk), *adj.* like a mean or servile flatterer; meanly flattering; cringing.

sy-e-nite (sī'ē-nīt), *n.* a rock of heat formation, much like granite, but containing very little quartz, and consisting chiefly of feldspar.

syl-lab-ic (sĭ-lăb'ĭk), *adj.* pertaining to, or consisting of, a syllable or syllables; as, *syllabic* shorthand.—*adv.* **syllabically.**

syl-lab-i-ca-tion (sĭ-lăb'ĭ-kā'shŭn), *n.* the act of forming or separating into syllables. Also, **syllabification.**

syl-la-ble (sĭl'*d*-bl), *n.* that part of a word which can be clearly spoken by a single effort of the voice; in writing and printing, such a part of a word separated from the rest of the word.

syl-la-bub (sĭl'*d*-bŭb), *n.* a dish made of milk or cream mixed with wine or cider, forming a curd and flavored. Also, **sillabub, sillibub.**

syl-la-bus (sĭl'*d*-bŭs), *n.* a brief statement of the main points of a subject, book, course of study, etc.

syl-lo-gism (sĭl'ō-jĭzm), *n.* an argument stated in a logical form, consisting of three propositions, the first two being called the premises, and the last the conclusion, which contains the matter to be proved.—*adj.* **syllogistic, syllogistical.**—*adv.* **syllogistically.**

sylph (sĭlf), *n.* an imaginary being living in the air; fairy; a slender, graceful young woman.

syl-van (sĭl'văn), *adj.* pertaining to woods or groves; rustic; woody; shady; as, a *sylvan* retreat. Also, **silvan.**

sym-bol (sĭm'bŏl), *n.* something, not a likeness, that stands for something else, and in some way brings it to mind, as by resemblance; an emblem, or sign of an idea, quality, or another thing; a type; a mark, character, or letter representing something; as, a *symbol* in mathematics.

sym-bol-ic (sĭm-bŏl'ĭk), *adj.* pertaining to a symbol, or sign, or to symbols; serving as a sign; expressing by signs: *n.pl.* the study of creeds, or religious beliefs. Also, *adj.* **symbolical.**—*adv.* **symbolically.**—*n.* **symbolicalness.**

sym-bol-ism (sĭm'bŏl-ĭzm), *n.* representation by symbols, or signs.—*n.* **symbolist.**

sym-bol-ize (sĭm'bŏl-īz), *v.t.* to represent or show by symbols, or signs; to be representative of; as, the lion *symbolizes* courage: *v.i.* to use symbols, or signs.—*n.* **symbolization.**

sym-met-ri-cal (sĭ-mĕt'rĭ-kăl), *adj.* regular or even; having harmonious parts; well-balanced; as, a *symmetrical* design. Also, **symmetric.**—*adv.* **symmetrically.**

sym-me-try (sĭm'ē-trĭ), *n.* harmony, balance, or right proportion of the several parts of a body; similarity of parts on two sides of a dividing line.

sym-pa-thet-ic (sĭm'p*d*-thĕt'ĭk), *adj.* resulting from, or expressive of, fellow-feeling or similar feelings; compassionate; as, *sympathetic* words; being in harmony with; congenial; as, *sympathetic* tastes. Also, **sympathetical.**—*adv.* **sympathetically.**

sym-pa-thize (sĭm'p*d*-thīz), *v.i.* to feel in consequence of what another feels; share the feelings or mental state of another; agree; harmonize; be affected or suffer because of another part; colloquially, to express one's feeling, as for another's sorrow.—*n.* **sympathizer.**

sym-pa-thy (sĭm'p*d*-thĭ), *n.* a feeling like that which another feels; harmony or agreement of affections or tastes, which makes persons pleasing to each other; fellow-feeling; kindness of feeling toward one who suffers; compassion or pity.

sym-phon-ic (sĭm-fŏn'ĭk), *adj.* agreeing in sound; harmonious; relating to, or in the manner of, a musical composition called a symphony.

sym-pho-ny (sĭm'fō-nĭ), *n.* [*pl.* symphonies (-nĭz)], harmony of sound; an agreeable blending of any kind; an elaborate musical composition, consisting of three or four movements, for a full orchestra; instrumental introduction or ending of a vocal composition.

sym-po-si-um (sĭm-pō'zĭ-ŭm), *n.* [*pl.* symposia (-*d*)], a drinking together, or a banquet at which there is brilliant and entertaining conversation; a collection of essays in which various writers express their views on some given topic.

symp-tom (sĭmp'tŭm), *n.* that which shows the existence of something else of which it is the effect; a token or sign; as, *symptoms* of unrest in a country; any noticeable change in the body or its functions, as indicating disease.

symp-tom-at-ic (sĭmp'tŭm-ăt'ĭk), *adj.* according to symptoms, or noticeable changes in the body; indicative, showing, or pointing out. Also, **symptomatical.**—*adv.* **symptomatically.**

syn-ær-e-sis (sĭn-ĕr'ē-sĭs), *n.* the drawing together into one syllable of two vowels that are ordinarily in two syllables, as *e'er* for *ever*. Also, **syneresis.**

syn-a-gogue (sĭn'*d*-gŏg), *n.* an assembly or gathering of Jews for worship; also, the place used for such worship.

syn-chro-nism (sĭn'krō-nĭzm), *n.* sameness in time of two or more events; arrangement in a table of historical events and personages, according to dates.

syn-chro-nize (sĭn'krō-nīz), *v.t.* to assign to the same date or period of time; to make to agree in time or speed: *v.i.* happen at the same time; agree in time.—*n.* **synchronizer.**

syn-chro-nous (sĭn'krō-nŭs), *adj.* happening at the same time or rate. Also, **synchronal**.—*adv.* **synchronously**.

syn-cli-nal (sĭn-klī'năl; sĭn'klĭ-năl), *adj.* sloping downward from opposite directions so as to meet; dipping downward on each side to a common line: said of strata.

syn-co-pate (sĭn'kō-pāt), *v.t.* to contract by omitting a letter or letters from the middle of (a word); in music, to begin (a tone) on an unaccented beat of a measure and end on an accented beat; as, a *syncopated* waltz.

syn-co-pa-tion (sĭn-kō-pā'shŭn), *n.* the beginning of a tone on an unaccented part of a measure, and ending it on an accented part; syncope, or the cutting out of a letter or letters from the middle of a word.

syn-co-pe (sĭn'kō-pē), *n.* the cutting out of a letter or letters from the middle of a word, as *e'er* for *ever;* fainting, or a fainting fit.

syn-dic (sĭn'dĭk), *n.* a government officer having varying powers in different countries; a business agent of a corporation or body of men.

syn-di-cal-ism (sĭn'dĭ-kăl-ĭzm), *n.* a plan or theory by which labor unions seek to gain control of the means and processes of production by the general strike, or even by violence.—*n.* **syndicalist**.

syn-di-cate (sĭn'dĭ-kāt), *n.* an association or company of persons who combine to carry out some special business project or plan, often requiring large capital; as, these *syndicates* fixed prices and crushed competition; the office of a syndic, or government office or agent; an association of persons for the purpose of buying manuscripts and selling them to numerous periodicals: *v.t.* (sĭn'dĭ-kāt), to form into, or manage by, a syndicate; to obtain for a syndicate; to sell or offer for sale (a literary work) to numerous periodicals; as, to *syndicate* a novel: *v.i.* to form a syndicate.

syn-ec-do-che (sĭ-nĕk'dō-kē), *n.* a figure of speech in which the whole is put for a part, or a part for the whole, as fifty *sail* for fifty *ships*.

syn-er-e-sis (sĭn-ĕr'ē-sĭs), *n.* the uniting into one syllable of two vowels that are ordinarily in two syllables, as *e'er* for *ever*. Also, **synaeresis**.

syn-od (sĭn'ŭd), *n.* a church council, or meeting to consult on religious matters; any assembly or council.

syn-od-ic (sĭ-nŏd'ĭk), *adj.* pertaining to, or transacted by, a synod, or church council. Also, **synodical**.—*adv.* **synodically**.

syn-o-nym (sĭn'ō-nĭm), *n.* a word having the same or nearly the same meaning as another, as *sharp* and *keen*. Also, **synonyme**.

syn-on-y-mous (sĭ-nŏn'ĭ-mŭs), *adj.* having the same or nearly the same meaning.—*adv.* **synonymously**.

syn-op-sis (sĭ-nŏp'sĭs), *n.* a general view, as of any subject; a summary or abstract; as, the *synopsis* of a book or play.

syn-op-tic (sĭ-nŏp'tĭk), *adj.* giving a general view of the whole, or of the principal parts of a thing; as, the *Synoptic* Gospels, Matthew, Mark, and Luke. Also, **synoptical**.—*adv.* **synoptically**.

syn-o-vi-a (sĭ-nō'vĭ-ȧ), *n.* the oily fluid in the joints of the body.—*adj.* **synovial**.

syn-tac-tic (sĭn-tăk'tĭk), *adj.* pertaining to, or arranged according to, the rules of syntax, or that part of grammar that treats of sentences. Also, **syntactical**.—*adv.* **syntactically**.

syn-tax (sĭn'tăks), *n.* that part of grammar which treats of the proper construction of sentences; sentence structure.

syn-the-sis (sĭn'thē-sĭs), *n.* [*pl.* syntheses (-sēz)], the putting of things together to form a whole; composition or combination: opposite to *analysis;* a process of reasoning from the whole to its parts.

syn-thet-ic (sĭn-thĕt'ĭk), *adj.* pertaining to, or of the nature of, synthesis, or the putting of things together to form a whole. Also, **synthetical**.—*adv.* **synthetically**.

syn-to-nize (sĭn'tō-nīz), *v.t.* to tune or turn (wireless telegraphic messages) in a certain direction.

syn-to-ny (sĭn'tō-nĭ), *n.* the electrical tuning of wireless transmitters and receivers to each other.

sy-phon (sī'fŏn), *n.* a bent pipe or tube having one end longer than the other, used for drawing off liquids from a higher to a lower level; a bottle fitted with such a tube; *v.t.* to draw off by such a tube. Also, **siphon**.

Syr-i-ac (sĭr'ĭ-ăk), *adj.* pertaining to Syria, or to its language: *n.* the language of Syria.

Syr-i-an (sĭr'ĭ-ăn), *adj.* pertaining to Syria, or to its people: *n.* a native of Syria, especially of the native Semitic race.

sy-rin-ga (sĭ-rĭn'gȧ), *n.* a class of garden shrubs of the olive family, including the lilac and the mock orange.

syr-inge (sĭr'ĭnj), *n.* an instrument for injecting a liquid in a jet or stream into the body; any of various devices for this purpose, as a bulb or a bag fitted with a tube and nozzle: *v.t.* to inject or cleanse by the use of a syringe.

syr-up (sĭr'ŭp), *n.* a thick, sticky liquid made from the juice of fruits, herbs, etc., boiled with sugar; a healing liquid containing medicine, sugar, and water. Also, **sirup**.

sys-tem (sĭs'tĕm), *n.* orderly combination of parts into a whole; a group or assemblage of objects forming a natural whole and arranged or acting according to some common law; as, the solar *system;* a school *system;* orderly collection of rules and principles; as, a *system* of laws; orderly grouping of facts and objects; as, a *system* of classification or of filing; regular method of transacting business; orderliness.

sys-tem-at-ic (sĭs"tĕm-ăt'ĭk), *adj.* of, or pertaining to, or of the nature of, a system, or orderly whole; acting according to a regular method or plan; methodical; as, *systematic* study. Also, **systematical**.—*adv.* **systematically**.

sys-tem-a-tize (sĭs'tĕm-ȧ-tīz), *v.t.* to reduce to a system, or regular method. Also, **systematise**, **systemize**.—*n.* **systematization**.

sys-to-le (sĭs'tō-lē), *n.* the shortening of a long syllable; the regular contraction of the heart that forces out the blood to circulate through the body.

syz-y-gy (sĭz'ĭ-jĭ), *n.* [*pl.* syzygies (-jĭz)], the point at which the moon or a planet is in conjunction with, or opposition to, the sun when seen from the earth; times of new and full moon.

T

tab (tăb), *n.* a small flap or tag attached to a garment, etc., usually to the edge, for use or ornament; a loop for pulling or lifting something; colloquially, account; as, to keep *tab* on someone's behavior.

tab-ard (tăb'ẽrd), *n.* formerly, a short, coarse outer coat worn by the poorer classes; a loose garment or mantle worn over armor; the coat of an ancient herald or messenger, often embroidered with the arms of his sovereign, etc.

ta-bas-co (tȧ-băs'kō), *n.* a very peppery Mexican sauce.

tab-by (tăb'ĭ), *n.* a taffeta silk or moreen, with a wavy marking: often called *watered silk;* a very hard substance, made by mixing equal parts of lime, water, and stone or shell; a gray and black striped cat; hence, any domestic cat; colloquially, an old maid or a gossip: *v.t.* [*p.t.* and *p.p.* tabbied, *p.pr.* tabbying], to put a wavy marking into: *adj.* having a wavy marking; brindled.

tab-er-na-cle (tăb'ẽr-nȧ-kl), *n.* a temporary dwelling; a movable residence, or tent; the human body as the temporary dwelling of the soul; the movable tent used as a place of worship by the Israelites in the wilderness.—Exodus xxvi; a Jewish church or temple; a place of worship, especially one erected temporarily for special services; a small box or cell for holding anything precious or holy.

Tabernacle

ta-bes (tā'bēz), *n.* a gradual wasting away of the body; a decline or wasting away.

ta-ble (tā'bl), *n.* a piece of furniture consisting of a flat, smooth top supported by legs; a flat surface or tablet suitable for an inscription; as, two *tables* of stone contained the ten commandments; persons sitting around a table; fare; as, the *table* at the hotel is good; supply of food; entertainment; index or summary; an arrangement of words, facts, figures, etc., in systematic order for reference; as, the multiplication *table;* a *table* of statistics: *v.t.* to catalog or index; to lay aside, as a report, for future consideration; to lay on a table, as a card or money.

tab-leau (tăb'lō; tȧ'blō'), *n.* [*pl.* tableaux (tăb'lōz; tȧ'blō'), or tableaus (tăb'lōz)], a striking and lifelike representation; a picture; a scene like a picture, showing persons properly dressed and grouped, and remaining silent and motionless.

tab-leau vi-vant (tȧ'blō' vē'väṅ'), a living picture; a picture represented by one or more silent and motionless performers suitably costumed and posed; a tableau. [Fr.]

ta-ble-cloth (tā'bl-klôth'), *n.* a cover, of linen, cotton, etc., spread upon a table, usually for the serving of a meal.

ta-ble d'hôte (tȧ'bl dōt'), a plan used by hotels, restaurants, etc., by which a meal consisting of certain fixed courses is served to all guests at a fixed price: opposite to *à la carte.* [Fr.]

ta-ble-land (tā'bl-lănd'), *n.* a plateau, or broad, elevated piece of land.

ta-ble-spoon (tā'bl-spōōn'), *n.* a large spoon for use in preparing and serving meals, holding four times as much as a teaspoon.

ta-ble-spoon-ful (tā'bl-spōōn'fōōl), *n.* [*pl.* tablespoonfuls (-fōōlz)], the amount of anything that a tablespoon will hold, equal to four times as much as a teaspoonful.

tab-let (tăb'lĕt), *n.* a small flat surface, especially one used for drawing, writing, etc.; a set of blank sheets of paper fastened together at one end and used for writing upon; a writing pad; in classic antiquity, one of a number of thin, flat pieces of ivory, wax, etc., fastened together and used for memoranda; a flat panel, often of stone, brass, bronze, etc., fastened in a wall and containing an inscription; medicine in the form of a small flat disk; a small flat cake, as of soap, candy, etc.

ta-boo (tȧ-bōō'), *n.* a religious system or practice, in use among the Polynesians and other savage races, by which certain acts and things were made sacred and therefore forbidden; ban; prohibition: *v.t.* [*p.t.* and *p.p.* tabooed, *p.pr.* tabooing], to forbid approach to, or use of: *adj.* set apart or sacred by religious custom; prohibited by social custom. Also, **tabu.**

ta-bor (tā'bẽr), *n.* a small drum, beaten with one stick. Also, **tabour.**

tab-o-ret (tăb'ō-rĕt), *n.* a small tabor, or drum; a small stand or stool. Also, **tabouret.**

tab-u-lar (tăb'ū-lẽr), *adj* arranged in the form of a table, or systematic outline; set down or arranged in schedules or columns; as, the report was in *tabular* form; reckoned or arrived at from sets of figures or facts arranged in systematic order; having a broad flat top, as a mountain.

tab-u-late (tăb'ū-lāt), *v.t.* to reduce to, or arrange in, a systematic outline, usually in columns; as, to *tabulate* election returns; shape with a flat surface.—*n.* **tabulation, tabulator.**

ta-chom-e-ter (tȧ-kŏm'ē-tẽr), *n.* a device for measuring velocity; a device for indicating the revolutions per minute of an engine: used to give engine speed in airplanes.

Tachometer

tac-it (tăs'ĭt), *adj.* given or existing in silence; implied, but not stated outright; as, *tacit* consent.—*adv.* **tacitly.**

tac-i-turn (tăs'ĭ-tûrn), *adj.* not apt to speak; habitually disinclined to talk.

Syn. mute, reticent, reserved, silent.

Ant. (see unreserved).

tac-i-tur-ni-ty (tăs'ĭ-tûr'nĭ-tĭ), *n.* habitual silence; reserve in speaking.

tack (tăk), *n.* a small broad-headed nail; a rope for holding down the lower corner of certain sails; the corner of the sail so held down; direction of a ship in regard to the trim, or position, of her sails; a change in a ship's direction; hence, any course or method of action: *v.t.* to fasten with small nails; as, to *tack* down matting; fasten slightly; attach; as, to *tack* a bow on a dress, or a sequel to a story; to change the course of (a vessel) by using the helm and shifting the sails: *v.i.* to change the course of a vessel by shifting the position of her sails.

tack-le (tăk'l), *n.* the ropes, pulleys, etc., of a vessel; an apparatus for raising or lowering heavy weights, consisting of pulleys and ropes; equipment; gear; as, hunting or fishing *tackle*: *v.t.* to harness; seize or lay hold of; in football, to meet and try to stop (an opposing player); colloquially, grasp or attack vigorously.

tact (tăkt), *n.* sympathetic understanding; delicate skill in saying and doing exactly what is best or most suitable in given circumstances; ability to manage others with consideration for their feelings.

tact-ful (tăkt'fo͝ol), *adj.* full of sympathetic understanding; wise and kind in managing others.—*adv.* **tactfully.**—*n.* **tactfulness.**

tac-ti-cal (tăk'tĭ-kăl), *adj.* having to do with military or naval science; marked by adroitness or clever management.

tac-ti-cian (tăk-tĭsh'ăn), *n.* one skilled in managing troops or ships in warfare; a skilful manager.

tac-tics (tăk'tĭks), *n.* the art or science of naval and military movements in actual warfare; hence, any clever means or method of accomplishing an aim.

tac-tile (tăk'tĭl), *adj.* pertaining to the sense of touch; capable of being touched.—*n.* **tactility.**

tact-less (tăkt'lĕs), *adj.* wanting in sympathetic understanding; not skilful in managing others; blundering.—*adv.* **tactlessly.**—*n.* **tactlessness.**

tac-tu-al (tăk'tū-ăl), *adj.* pertaining to touch or the organs of touch; giving the sensation of, or caused by, touch.

tad-pole (tăd'pōl"), *n.* the larva of certain animals, as the frog, which dwells in water and possesses external gills and a long tail.

tael (tāl), *n.* a Chinese silver coin worth about seventy-three cents; a Chinese weight of 1⅓ ounces.

taf-fe-ta (tăf'ē-tȧ), *n.* a fine, thin, glossy silken fabric or cloth. Also, **taffety.**

taff-rail (tăf'rāl), *n.* the rail round a ship's stern, or rear end. Also, **tafferel.**

taf-fy (tăf'ĭ), *n.* a well-known candy made of brown sugar or molasses boiled down, and often flavored with butter, nuts, etc.; colloquially, flattery.

tag (tăg), *n.* a card or label to be attached to a box, package, etc.; a loose end or rag, as of clothing; a metal binding at the end of a string or lace to make it stiff; a children's game in which one chases the others in order to touch, or "tag" them: *v.t.* [*p.t.* and *p.p.* tagged, *p.pr.* tagging], to fix a tag to; append or tack on; in the game of tag, to catch by touching; colloquially, to follow closely and persistently: *v.i.* colloquially, to follow another closely: with *after.*

tail (tāl), *n.* the end, or a prolongation of the end, of the backbone of an animal's body, usually hanging loose; the back, last, or lesser part of anything; as, the *tail*-end of a storm; anything hanging or apparently hanging; a plane or planes at the back of an airship to give it balance; in law, a limitation of ownership: *v.t.* to supply with a loose, hanging attachment; to follow close behind.

tail-board (tāl'bōrd"), *n.* the movable board at the rear of a cart or wagon.

tail-ing (tāl'ĭng), *n.* the part of a projecting stone or brick inserted in a wall: *pl.* refuse of stamped ore thrown behind the tail of the washing apparatus; chaff.

tai-lor (tā'lẽr), *n.* [*fem.* tailoress], one whose business it is to cut out and make outer garments for men and women.

tai-lor bird (tā'lẽr bûrd), an African and Asiatic bird, of the warbler family, which hides its nest by stitching leaves together.

tail-piece (tāl'pēs"), *n.* something added at the end; the piece to which the strings of certain instruments, as the violin, are attached; a decorative drawing or design at the bottom of a page of a book or magazine.

taint (tānt), *n.* corruption; infection; a trace, as of decay or corruption; a moral spot or stain; disgrace: *v.t.* to fill with something unpleasant or poisonous, as a disease; to infect or corrupt: *v.i.* to become spoiled, as meat.

take (tāk), *v.t.* [*p.t.* took, *p.p.* taken, *p.pr.* taking], to lay or seize hold of; as, to *take* the enemy's position; obtain; as, to *take* a prize; receive into one's hold or possession; as, to *take* six yards of silk; capture; engage or interest; as, to *take* the eye; choose; as, I shall *take* the smaller box; employ; assume; as, to *take* another name; quote; as, to *take* a passage from a Shakespearean play; subtract; transport; require or demand; as, it *takes* time to learn to swim; to contract by infection; as, to *take* a fever; to regard or look upon; as, to *take* a man for a detective; to observe; to gather; as, I *took* this meaning from what he said; to experience; as, he *took* much comfort in his home; to make or perform; as, to *take* a journey; to resort to; as, she has *taken* up music; to find out; as, to *take* his measure; to *take* the depth of the water; to accept; as, to *take* an oath; to *take* a woman in marriage; to *take* money from one who cannot afford to give; to carry; as, she *took* the package with her; to do; as, to *take* precautions, measures, etc.; to receive into the body; as, to *take* medicine; to make a photograph of: *v.i.* to have recourse; as, the man has *taken* to drink; colloquially, prove attractive; as, she will *take* in society; have the intended effect; as, the inoculation *took*: *n.* the amount or quantity received or caught, especially fish.—*n.* **taker.**

tak-ing (tāk'ĭng), *adj.* attractive; alluring; pleasing; as, *taking* manners: *n.* the act of gaining possession; seizure: *pl.* that which is accepted or received; receipts.

tal-bot (tôl'bŭt), *n.* an extinct breed of hunting dog with quick scent, from which the bloodhound is supposed to have descended.

talc (tălk), *n.* a soft mineral, appearing in the form of soapstone, French chalk, etc., and used in making soap, paper, toilet powders, etc.—*adj.* **talcose, talcous.**

tale (tāl), *n.* that which is told; a narrative or story; fable; anecdote; a false report or piece of gossip; a count or reckoning; as, the *tale* of bricks made by the Israelites in Egypt.

tale-bear-er (tāl′bâr′ẽr), *n.* one who carries false reports; one who delights in spreading gossip, scandal, etc.; a gossip.

tal-ent (tăl′ĕnt), *n.* among the ancients, a weight or a coin of varying value; as, the Hebrew *talent* of gold was worth $32,640; mental capacity or ability; skill; cleverness; a special gift, fitting one for a particular business, art, or profession; as, he has a *talent* for painting; collectively, persons with such gifts: with *the*.

tal-ent-ed (tăl′ĕnt-ĕd), *adj.* having superior ability; gifted; skilful along some special line.

ta-les (tā′lēz), *n.* (regarded as a singular), a writ, or court order, for summoning additional jurors for a session of court; (regarded as a plural), persons who are so summoned to fill vacant places in a jury.

tales-man (tālz′măn), *n.* [*pl.* talesmen (-mĕn)], a person summoned to fill up a jury when the regular panel, or group of persons from which the jury is chosen, is used up before the jury is complete.

tal-is-man (tăl′ĭs-măn; tăl′ĭz-măn), *n.* [*pl.* talismans (-mănz)], a figure cut in metal or stone supposed to possess magical powers in averting evil or bringing good luck; something that produces an extraordinary effect; a charm; an amulet.

tal-is-man-ic (tăl′ĭs-măn′ĭk; tăl′ĭz-măn′-ĭk), *adj.* having power to avert evil or bring good luck; magical. Also, **talismanical.**

talk (tôk), *v.i.* to utter words; speak familiarly; converse; express thoughts in speech; to confer; to consult; as, to *talk* with a teacher about one's progress; prattle: *v.t.* to utter; make a subject of conversation; as, to *talk* business; to discuss favorably; as, to *talk* socialism; to speak (a language) freely; as, to *talk* Fren[illegible]. to affect by talking; as, they *talked* him over to their side; to use or spend in talk[illegible]ith *away;* as, to *talk* away an evening: [illegible]act of expressing thoughts in words; [illegible] familiar conversation; as, an evening of fri[illegible]y *talk;* subject of discourse; as, the *talk* of the town; rumor; as, there is *talk* of a strike; a conference; as, *talk* about future plans; an informal address; as, a *talk* on food conservation.—*n.* **talker.**

talk-a-tive (tôk′ȧ-tĭv), *adj.* given to much speaking; loquacious. —*adv.* **talkatively.**—*n.* **talkativeness.**

Syn. communicative, voluble, fluent, glib, garrulous.

talk-ing (tôk′ĭng), *n.* conversation or speech: *adj.* given to speaking; able to speak: **talking machine,** any of various machines that reproduce voice and other sounds.

tall (tôl), *adj.* high in stature; of a certain height; as, six feet *tall;* lofty or high; as, a *tall* building.—*n.* **tallness.**

tal-low (tăl′ō), *n.* the melted fat of oxen and sheep; suet; fat or grease used for making candles: *v.t.* to cover with tallow; to fatten, as sheep.

tal-ly (tăl′ĭ), *n.* [*pl.* tallies (-ĭz)], originally, a stick notched as a means of keeping accounts; one of two books in which duplicate accounts are kept; any account or score kept by marks; a mark recording a score; a duplicate: *v.t.* to keep score of with marks, notches, etc.: *v.i.* to match; to correspond; as, make your account *tally* with mine; to keep score.

tal-ly board (tăl′ĭ bōrd), a board used to keep score upon, as with chalk-marks, etc.

tal-ly card (tăl′ĭ kärd), a card on which a score is kept in playing a game.

tal-ly-ho (tăl′ĭ-hō′), *interj.* the huntsman's cry to urge on his hounds: *n.* a four-in-hand coach.

tal-ly-man (tăl′ĭ-măn), *n.* [*pl.* tallymen (-mĕn)], one who keeps a shop where goods sold are paid for by instalments, accounts being kept in duplicate books.

tal-ly sheet (tăl′ĭ shēt), a sheet on which a score or account is kept.

tal-ly shop (tăl′ĭ shŏp), a shop where goods are sold on the tally system, or instalment plan, accounts being kept in duplicate books.

tal-ly sys-tem (tăl′ĭ sĭs′tĕm), the practice of selling goods on credit, to be paid for by instalments, buyer and seller each keeping an account in a duplicate book.

Tal-mud (tăl′mŭd), *n.* the book which contains the whole body of the Jewish civil and religious laws and traditions.

tal-on (tăl′ŭn), *n.* the claw of a bird of prey; as, the *talon* of an eagle; a kind of decorative molding or house decoration, usually called an *ogee molding,* whose curve is in the form of an S.

ta-lus (tā′lŭs), *n.* [*pl.* tali (-lī)], the ankle or ankle-bone; a sloping heap of broken rocks at the foot of a cliff or steep hill; the front slope of a fortification.

tam-a-ble (tām′ȧ-bl), *adj.* capable of being subdued, made gentle, or rescued from wildness or savagery. Also, **tameable.**

ta-ma-le (tȧ-mä′lē), *n.* a kind of dumpling made of chopped meat and corn meal, seasoned with red pepper, wrapped in corn husks, and boiled or steamed: of Mexican origin.

tam-a-rack (tăm′ȧ-răk), *n.* the American black larch of the pine tree family; the hackmatack.

tam-a-rin (tăm′ȧ-rĭn), *n.* a small South American marmoset, or kind of monkey, which runs about like a squirrel.

tam-a-rind (tăm′ȧ-rĭnd), *n.* a tall tropical tree having yellow flowers striped with red, and pods containing an acid pulp: used for food and drink, and to fix colors in dyeing.

tam-a-risk (tăm′ȧ-rĭsk), *n.* a tropical Asiatic tree or shrub with small pink or white flowers.

tam-bour (tăm′bōōr), *n.* a kind of small military drum; a drumlike embroidery frame, usually consisting of two closely fitting hoops, over which the material is stretched; embroidery made on such a frame: *v.t.* and *v.i.* to embroider with, or upon, such a frame.

tam-bou-rine (tăm′bōō-rēn′), *n.* a small hand-drum, having little metallic disks or jingles fastened in the hoop or rim, and played by striking, as with the knuckles; a lively old French dance.

tame (tām), *adj.* [*comp.* tamer, *superl.* tamest], altered from native wildness; made useful to man; subdued; harmless; gentle; lacking in spirit; dull: *v.t.* to bring from a wild to a gentle state; subdue; make harmless; as, to *tame* a wild animal; remove spirit or courage from; make quiet.—*adv.* **tamely.**—*n.* **tameness.**

tame-less (tām′lĕs), *adj.* wild; not capable of being subdued; high-spirited.

tam-o'-shan-ter (tăm″ō-shăn′tẽr), *n.* a Scottish cap with a tight fitting headband and a loose, round top: popularly called a *tam.*

tamp (tămp), *v.t.* to block up (the blast-hole in a rock) with clay or similar material, in order to direct the force of the explosion; drive in or down by repeated gentle strokes.

tam-per (tăm′pẽr), *v.i.* to meddle so as to injure or alter anything: followed by *with;* as, to *tamper* with a lock; to use unfair influence, especially to bribe; as, to *tamper* with a jury; to experiment foolishly; as, to *tamper* with stocks.

tam-pon (tăm′pŏn), *n.* a round stopper, made of cotton, used to cleanse a wound or to stop its bleeding.

tam-tam (tăm′tăm″), *n.* a drum used by jugglers, etc., in Turkey, Persia, India, etc. Also, tom-tom.

tan (tăn), *n.* oak bark, or other bark containing tannic acid, broken into small bits and used in making leather; a yellowish-brown color, like that of such bark; a brown color given to the skin by exposure to the sun; as, "barefoot boy, with cheek of *tan*": *v.t.* [*p.t.* and *p.p.* tanned, *p.pr.* tanning], to convert (a hide) into leather by soaking in bark water; to make brown by exposure to the sun: *v.i.* to become brown in the sun: *adj.* yellowish-brown.

tan-a-ger (tăn′ȧ-jẽr), *n.* a bird of the finch family, usually of brilliant color.

tan-bark (tăn′bärk″), *n.* oak or other bark containing tannic acid, used in making leather, and, when spent, for circus rings, etc.

tan-dem (tăn′dĕm), *adv.* one behind another: *adj.* arranged one behind another: *n.* a pair of horses harnessed one before the other; a bicycle or tricycle for two, with one seat placed before the other.

Tandem

tang (tăng), *n.* a strong taste or flavor; especially, a taste that is unusual or does not belong to the thing itself; as, the peas have a *tang* of the can; a sharp flavor or tinge; as, a *tang* of bitterness in a remark; that part of a knife, fork, tool, etc., which is inserted into the handle; a sharp, twanging sound: *v.t.* to cause to sound with a vibrant, ringing noise.

tan-gen-cy (tăn′jĕn-sĭ), *n.* act of touching; state of being in contact; especially, the touching of a curve by a straight line.

tan-gent (tăn′jĕnt), *adj.* touching; in geometry, meeting a curve only at one point, but not cutting it: *n.* a straight line that meets or touches a circle or curve, but does not cut it; any line or course leading abruptly away from the usual course; one of the trigonometric functions; in a right-angled triangle, the ratio between the side opposite and the side adjacent to an acute angle.

tan-gen-tial (tăn-jĕn′shăl), *adj.* pertaining to, or in the direction of, a tangent, or straight line that touches a circle or curve, but does not cut it.—*adv.* tangentially.

tan-ger-ine (tăn′jẽr-ēn; tăn″jẽr-ēn′), *n.* a kind of small, rather flat, red-skinned orange of high flavor.

tan-gi-bil-i-ty (tăn″jĭ-bĭl′ĭ-tĭ), *n.* the state or quality of being actual or real; capability of being touched.

tan-gi-ble (tăn′jĭ-bl), *adj.* capable of being touched; perceptible to the touch; capable of being possessed or realized; evident; real; as, *tangible* proof.—*adv.* tangibly.—*n.* tangibleness.

tan-gle (tăn′gl), *v.t.* to knot or snarl so as to make difficult to unravel; to involve or implicate; as, to *tangle* oneself in excuses: *v.i.* to be entangled or involved: *n.* a knot woven confusedly together; a snarl; perplexity; a confused and puzzling situation; as, his affairs were in a *tangle.*

tan-go (tăn′gō; tăn′gō), *n.* a dance in two-four time marked by a great variety of steps.

tank (tănk), *n.* a large cistern or basin built to hold water or other liquid; as, a swimming *tank;* a large, often circular, building for storing a fluid, as gas, gasoline, etc.; an armored motor truck, used as an engine of destruction, adapted from the caterpillar tractor and equipped with guns, remarkable for its power to go ahead over obstacles: first used by the British army in the World War.

Tank

tank-age (tănk′āj), *n.* the contents or capacity of a receptacle for liquid; the price for putting or storing liquid in a tank.

tank-ard (tănk′ẽrd), *n.* a large drinking vessel with a lid.

tank-drome (tănk′drōm″), *n.* a field for storing and repairing military tanks.

tank-er (tănk′ẽr), *n.* a naval or merchant ship which supplies other ships with oil.

tan-nate (tăn′āt), *n.* a salt of tannic acid, or tannin.

tan-ner (tăn′ẽr), *n.* one whose trade is to make leather from hides.

tan-ner-y (tăn′ẽr-ĭ), *n.* [*pl.* tanneries (-ĭz)], a place where hides are made into leather.

tan-nic (tăn′ĭk), *adj.* pertaining to, or obtained from, any bark, as oak, etc., which produces tan.

tan-nic ac-id (tăn′ĭk ăs′ĭd), a strong acid obtained from tea, sumac, gallnuts, etc., and used in tanning, dyeing, medicine, etc.: called also *tannin.*

tan-ning (tăn′ĭng), *p.pr.* of *tan:* *n.* the process of converting hides into leather; a browning of the skin by exposure to the sun or weather.

tan-sy (tăn′zĭ), *n.* a plant of the aster family, with a bitter taste, a sharp, spicy odor, and small yellow flowers.

tan-ta-li-za-tion (tăn″tȧ-lĭ-zā′shŭn), *n.* the act of teasing by exciting false hopes; the state of being so teased.

tan-ta-lize (tăn′tȧ-līz), *v.t.* to tease or torment by exciting hopes or fears which will not be realized; to provoke.

tan-ta-liz-ing (tăn′tȧ-līz″ĭng), *adj.* teasing or tormenting; provoking.—*adv.* tantalizingly.

tan-ta-mount (tăn′tȧ-mount″), *adj.* equivalent or equal to in value; as, your wish is *tantamount* to a command.

tan-trum (tăn'trŭm), *n.* a sudden outburst of temper or passion. [COLLOQ.]

tan-yard (tăn'yärd"), *n.* an inclosed space where hides are made into leather.

tap (tăp), *v.t.* [*p.t.* and *p.p.* tapped, *p.pr.* tapping], to strike or touch lightly; as, to *tap* one with the hand; to give a light stroke or touch with; as, to *tap* a pencil on the desk; put a new sole or heel on; as, to *tap* shoes; make an outlet from; as, to *tap* a barrel; bore into in order to draw something out; as, to *tap* a maple tree for its sap; hence, to draw out of; as, to *tap* a source of information: *v.i.* to strike a light blow: *n.* a gentle blow or touch; pat; place where liquor is drawn and retailed; pipe through which liquor is drawn from a cask; faucet for drawing water; a piece of leather nailed or sewed on the bottom of a boot or shoe in repairing; a tool for cutting screw threads on an inner surface, as in a nut: *pl.* in the army and navy, a signal given with drum or bugle to indicate the hour for retiring: **on tap,** ready for use, as beer in a cask.

Tap for Cutting Screw Threads

tape (tāp), *n.* a narrow woven band of linen or cotton; the narrow strip of paper used on a printing telegraph or stock ticker; the line held to mark the finish of a race; a narrow strip of steel marked with dimensions so as to be used for measuring length.

tape-line (tāp'līn"), *n.* a strip of fabric or of metal, marked with inches, feet, etc., and used for measuring.

ta-per (tā'pẽr), *n.* a small wax candle; a small light; a gradual lessening of thickness toward a point; as, the *taper* of a cone: *adj.* growing smaller towards the point, or from the bottom to the top: *v.i.* to become gradually more slender: *v.t.* to narrow to a point.

ta-per-ing (tā'pẽr-ĭng), *adj.* gradually growing smaller towards a point; as, *tapering* fingers.

tap-es-try (tăp'ĕs-trĭ), *n.* [*pl.* tapestries (-trĭz)], a fabric in which colored threads of wool or silk are so woven as to form a picture or design; originally woven by hand, later by machine, and used for hanging on walls, etc.: *v.t.* [*p.t.* and *p.p.* tapestried, *p.pr.* tapestrying], to hang, or adorn, with tapestry.

tap-es-try car-pet (tăp'ĕs-trĭ kär'pĕt), a kind of carpet somewhat resembling Brussels.

tape-worm (tāp'wûrm"), *n.* a long, flat, parasitic worm often found in the intestines of man and animals.

tap-i-o-ca (tăp'ĭ-ō'kȧ), *n.* a coarse, grainlike foodstuff made from cassava, a nutritious starch, and used in puddings, etc.

Tapir

ta-pir (tā'pẽr), *n.* a South American animal, of the rhinoceros family, having short hair, short legs, and a long snout.

ta-pis (tă'pĭs; tăp'ĭs; tȧ'pē'), *n.* tapestry, or similar material, used for wall hangings or floor covering: originally, the cover of a council table: **on the tapis,** on the table; up for, or under, consideration.

tap-pet (tăp'ĕt), *n.* in a machine, a small lever or projection, touching, or touched by, some other part of the machine, and used to regulate motion, as in the opening and closing of valves in steam pumps.

tap-room (tăp'rōōm"), *n.* a place where liquors are kept ready to be drawn and sold; a barroom.

tap-root (tăp'rōōt"), *n.* the main root of a plant, growing straight downward and sending off smaller roots.

tap-ster (tăp'stẽr), *n.* one whose business is to draw liquor from a cask or barrel; a bartender.

tar (tär), *n.* a thick, dark-brown, oily, sticky substance obtained from pine or fir trees, coal, etc.; a sailor or seaman: *v.t.* [*p.t.* and *p.p.* tarred, *p.pr.* tarring], to smear with, or as with, tar.

ta-ran-tel-la (tä'rän-tĕl'ȧ), *n.* a wild, rapid Italian dance; the music for such a dance.

ta-ran-tu-la (tȧ-răn'tū-lȧ), *n.* a large poisonous spider usually found in warm countries.

tar-dy (tär'dĭ), *adj.* [*comp.* tardier, *superl.* tardiest], moving with a slow pace or motion; not swift; not prompt; late.—*adv.* **tardily.**—*n.* **tardiness.**

tare (târ), *n.* an allowance of weight made to a purchaser by deducting the weight of a container; as, the *tare* of a barrel of sugar is the weight of the empty barrel; in the Bible, a kind of weed growing in grainfields, supposed to be the darnel.

tar-get (tär'gĕt), *n.* a small shield; a mark set up for archery, rifle, or artillery practice; one who, or that which, is made an object of criticism, remark, etc.; as, he was a *target* for their ridicule.

tar-iff (tăr'ĭf), *n.* a schedule or table of duties or taxes placed by a government on goods coming into, or going out of, the country; any schedule or system of rates, charges, etc.; a tax or duty levied or charged according to such a schedule.

tar-la-tan (tär'lȧ-tăn), *n.* a kind of thin, stiff, open-meshed dress-muslin.

tarn (tärn), *n.* a small lake or pool in the mountains or forests.

tar-nish (tär'nĭsh), *v.t.* to dull the brightness of; to sully or stain: *v.i.* to lose luster or brightness; become dull: *n.* dulness; lack of polish; stain.

tar-pau-lin (tär-pô'lĭn), *n.* stout waterproof canvas used for covering a ship's hatches, boats, etc.; a hat or coat of waterproof canvas.

tar-pon (tär'pŏn), *n.* a large sea fish found in West Indian waters.

tar-ry (tăr'ĭ), *v.i.* [*p.t.* and *p.p.* tarried, *p.pr.* tarrying], to live in a place for a time; stay; stay behind; delay; linger.

tar-ry (tär'ĭ), *adj.* covered with, or caused by, tar; like tar.

tar-sal (tär'săl), *adj.* pertaining to the ankle or its bone: *n.* an ankle bone.

tar-sus (tär'sŭs), *n.* [*pl.* tarsi (-sī)], the ankle; the ankle bones; the instep; the plate of tissue which stiffens the eyelids of man and many animals: called also the *tarsal plate.*

tart (tärt), *adj.* sharp to the taste; acid; severe; keen; as, a *tart* answer: *n.* a small open pie filled with custard, fruit, jelly, etc.

tar-tan (tär'tăn), *n.* woolen cloth, woven with a checkered or crossbarred pattern of narrow bands of various colors; such a pattern; any material, as gingham, of such a pattern: *adj.* made from, or in the pattern of, tartan; as, a *tartan* plaid.

tar-tar (tär'tẽr), *n.* a white substance often found encrusting the teeth; the salt of tartaric acid, found in grape juice and forming a reddish crust on the inside of wine casks.

Tar-tar (tär'tẽr), *n.* a resident of Tartary: better called *Tatar*: **tartar**, a person of irritable or savage temper; a person who is too strong for one who attacks him. Also, **Tatar.**

tar-tar e-met-ic (tär'tẽr ē-mĕt'ĭk), a poisonous white substance used to induce sweating or vomiting.

tar-tar-ic (tär-tăr'ĭk), *adj.* pertaining to, or derived from, the crystallized sediment of grape juice, or tartar.

tar-tar-ic ac-id (tär-tăr'ĭk ăs'ĭd), an acid found in the juice of grapes, mountain-ash berries, etc., and used in dyeing, calico printing, photography, medicine, etc.

Tar-ta-rus (tär'tȧ-rŭs), *n.* in mythology, the infernal regions; a place of punishment for wicked spirits; Hades.

task (tȧsk), *n.* labor, work, or study imposed by another: usually a certain amount; a lesson to be learned; duty; undertaking; work: *v.t.* to impose a certain amount of work upon; burden.

task-mas-ter (tȧsk'mȧs"tẽr), *n.* one who, or that which, sets a piece of work for another and oversees it.

task-work (tȧsk'wûrk"), *n.* a definite piece of work set to be done; piecework.

tas-sel (tăs''l), *n.* a hanging ornament consisting of a bunch of threads or cords of silk, wool, etc.; the hanging flower or head of certain plants; as, corn *tassels*: *v.t.* [*p.t.* and *p.p.* tasseled, *p.pr.* tasseling], to put forth hanging flowery heads: *v.t.* to trim with, or make into, tassels.

tas-seled (tăs''ld), *p.adj.* decorated with tassels, or hanging ornaments of silk, wool, etc.; as, a *tasseled* curtain; bearing hanging blossoms or heads.

taste (tāst), *v.t.* to perceive or know by the tongue and palate; to test by eating or drinking a little of; to find out the flavor of by eating or drinking a little; to participate in or experience; as, to *taste* remorse; to enjoy: *v.i.* to try food by the tongue or palate; to have a certain flavor; to eat or drink sparingly; to partake; to have experience or enjoyment: with *of*: *n.* the flavor of a substance as perceived by the tongue and palate; act of taking into the mouth to find out the quality or flavor; a little bit or piece; a small quantity tasted; the one of the five senses which perceives the flavor of substances by the tongue and palate; liking or inclination: with *for*; as, he had from his youth a *taste* for reading; ability to see and admire what is beautiful; critical judgment; habit or manner in relation to that which is refined or elegant; as, she dresses in good *taste*.—*n.* **taster.**

taste-ful (tāst'fo͝ol), *adj.* savory; marked by, or showing, refinement, good judgment, or sense of the beautiful; as, a *tasteful* arrangement of pictures on a wall.—*adv.* **tastefully.**—*n.* **tastefulness.**

Syn. dainty, delicate, tasty, nice, artistic.
Ant. (see distasteful).

taste-less (tāst'lĕs), *adj.* without flavor; flat; insipid, as food; lacking refinement and artistic appreciation; as, *tasteless* furnishings.—*n.* **tastelessness.**

tast-y (tās'tĭ), *adj.* savory; as, a *tasty* dish of food; colloquially, showing artistic refinement.—*adv.* **tastily.**—*n.* **tastiness.**

tat (tăt), *v.t.* and *v.i.* to make (trimming or lace) by looping and knotting thread wound on a shuttle. Also, **tatt.**

Ta-tar (tä'tẽr), *n.* a member of one of the tribes of Tatary (Tartary), or central and eastern Asia. Also, **Tartar.**

tat-ter (tăt'ẽr), *n.* a loose-hanging rag: *pl.* rags: *v.t.* to make ragged; to rend or tear: *v.i.* to become ragged.

tat-ter-de-mal-ion (tăt"ẽr-dē-măl'-yŭn), *n.* a ragged fellow; a ragamuffin.

tat-tered (tăt'ẽrd), *p.adj.* ragged; torn to pieces; raggedly dressed; hanging in shreds.

tat-ting (tăt'ĭng), *n.* a kind of narrow lace for edging, made with a small hand-shuttle; art of making such lace.

tat-tle (tăt''l), *v.i.* to chatter; to talk idly or triflingly; to tell tales or secrets: *n.* trifling or idle talk; gossip.—*n.* **tattler.**

tat-too (tă-to͞o'), *n.* a beat of drum, or other signal, especially for warning soldiers to retire to their quarters; marks or figures made by puncturing the skin with a needle and rubbing a stain or dye into the wounds: *v.t.* [*p.t.* and *p.p.* tattooed, *p.pr.* tattooing], to mark (the skin) permanently by puncturing (it) and staining the wounds.

tat-too-ing (tă-to͞o'ĭng), *n.* the operation or practice of puncturing the skin and rubbing a stain or dye into the wounds; the designs so made on skin.

tau-be (tô'bē), *n.* a German type of airplane having a single supporting plane; a monoplane.

taught (tôt), past tense and past participle of the verb *teach*.

taunt (tänt; tônt), *n.* a bitter or sarcastic reproach: *v.t.* to reproach with bitter, sarcastic, or insulting language; to revile or jeer at.—*adv.* **tauntingly.**—*n.* **taunter.**

Tau-rus (tô'rŭs), *n.* a constellation, or cluster of stars, containing the Pleiades; one of the signs of the zodiac called the Bull. [Lat.]

taut (tôt), *adj.* tight; stretched; as, a *taut* rope; snug; secure.

tau-to-log-i-cal (tô"tō-lŏj'ĭ-kăl), *adj.* full of needless repetition; tending without necessity to repeat the same idea in different words.—*adv.* **tautologically.**

tau-tol-o-gy (tô-tŏl'ō-jĭ), *n.* [*pl.* tautologies (-jĭz)], a useless repeating of the same idea in different words; needless repetition which adds nothing to the sense or sound; as, a panacea for all ills.

tav-ern (tăv'ẽrn), *n.* an inn or public house; a hotel; a house licensed to sell liquor in small quantities.

taw (tô), *v.t.* to soften and bleach (skins) ready for finishing: *n.* colloquially, a game of marbles; a marble to be played with.

taw-dry (tô'drĭ), *adj.* showy without elegance; cheap and gaudy; as, a *tawdry* dress.—*adv.* **tawdrily.**—*n.* **tawdriness.**

taw-ny (tô'nĭ), *adj.* of a yellowish-brown color; as, the *tawny* lion.

tax (tăks), *n.* a charge or duty on income or property, imposed by government for the use of the public; a heavy or oppressive burden; as, a *tax* on one's strength; *v.t.*

to impose a rate or duty upon for state or city purposes; as, to *tax* the use of luxuries; burden or oppress; as, to *tax* one's memory; accuse; as, to *tax* a man with crime or dishonor.

Syn., n. custom, duty, impost, excise, toll, assessment, rate.

tax-a-bil-i-ty (tăk'sȧ-bĭl'ĭ-tĭ), *n.* the state of being liable to have a duty levied upon.

tax-a-ble (tăk'sȧ-bl), *adj.* subject or liable to have a duty levied upon; as, *taxable* property.

tax-a-tion (tăk-sā'shŭn), *n.* the act of imposing a charge or duty on persons or property; rate or sum imposed; a system of raising money for public use; as, the business of *taxation*.

tax-i-cab (tăk'sĭ-kăb"), *n.* a motor cab having a mechanical device for registering time and distance traveled, the rate of fare being based on these.

tax-i-der-mist (tăk'sĭ-dûr"mĭst), *n.* one who is skilled in the art of preserving, stuffing, and mounting the skins of animals so as to show their natural appearance.

tax-i-der-my (tăk'sĭ-dûr"mĭ), *n.* the art of preserving, stuffing, and mounting the skins of animals so as to represent their natural appearance.

tax-im-e-ter (tăk-sĭm'ē-tẽr), *n.* an automatic device for measuring the distance traveled by a cab in order to show the fare due.

tax-ine (tăk'sĭn; tăk'sĭn), *n.* a narcotic drug obtained from the leaves and seeds of the yew tree.

tax-on-o-my (tăk-sŏn'ō-mĭ), *n.* the classification of animals and plants: a branch of biology.

tea (tē), *n.* a shrub or small tree cultivated in China, Japan, India, etc., for its leaves; the dried leaves of the tea plant; the drink obtained by pouring hot water on these leaves; in England, a late afternoon meal at which tea is served; in the United States, supper; an afternoon reception; a drink made of some other substance, as beef *tea*, etc.

teach (tēch), *v.t.* [*p.t.* and *p.p.* taught, *p.pr.* teaching], to make to know or understand; hence, to train in some line of activity; to give knowledge of; as, to *teach* Latin; give knowledge to; as, to *teach* a pupil; instruct; inform; cause to learn or acquire skill in: *v.i.* to give instruction.

Syn. drill, educate, train.

teach-a-ble (tēch'ȧ-bl), *adj.* open to instruction; able to learn; willing to receive knowledge.

teach-er (tēch'ẽr), *n.* an instructor; one who gives knowledge to others.

teach-ing (tēch'ĭng), *n.* the act or business of giving knowledge to others; instruction; that which is taught.

tea-cup (tē'kŭp"), *n.* a cup in which the beverage tea is served; a teacupful.

tea-cup-ful (tē'kŭp"fo͝ol), *n.* [*pl.* teacupfuls (-fo͝olz)], as much of any substance as can be contained in a teacup.

teak (tēk), *n.* a tall East Indian tree whose leaves yield a red dye; the hard, durable timber of this tree, used for shipbuilding, and yielding a medicinal oil.

tea-ket-tle (tē'kĕt"l), *n.* a kettle, of tin, copper, etc., with a handle and a spout, used for boiling water for tea, coffee, etc.

teal (tēl), *n.* a kind of small, wild, freshwater duck.

team (tēm), *n.* two or more horses or other beasts in one harness; the animals, with their harness and the vehicle that they draw; often, a single animal in harness and the vehicle; a group or brood of young, especially of ducks; a number of persons working or playing together, as to form a side in a game, to raise a sum of money, etc.

team-ster (tēm'stẽr), *n.* the driver of a team of horses or other animals; one whose business is hauling.

team-work (tēm'wûrk"), *n.* work done by a pair of animals in harness; efficient work done in harmony by a group of people for a common cause, no one seeking his own interest.

tea-pot (tē'pŏt"), *n.* a vessel with a spout, handle, and cover, in which tea is drawn, or made, and from which it is served.

tear (tēr), *n.* a small drop of the watery fluid secreted or given forth by a gland of the eye; any drop of a similar shape.

tear (târ), *n.* a rent; a hole made by pulling apart: *v.t.* [*p.t.* tore, *p.p.* torn, *p.pr.* tearing], to pull apart; to separate by violence or force; rend; scratch; as, the thorns will *tear* your hands; fill with distress; separate by disagreement; as, the state is *torn* by civil war: *v.i.* to part on being pulled or roughly handled; to move or act with force or agitated haste.

tear-ful (tēr'fo͝ol), *adj.* full of tears; given to weeping; causing tears.—*adv.* tearfully.—*n.* tearfulness.

tear-gas (tēr'găs"), *n.* in the World War, a gas released from a bomb or shell, which caused the eyes to water and thus brought on temporary blindness.

tear-less (tēr'lĕs), *adj.* not given to weeping; not able to weep; dry-eyed.

tease (tēz), *v.t.* to comb or unravel, as wool or flax; to separate the fibers of; to roughen, as cloth, with a teasel; annoy; to persist in making petty requests of or to; to vex by good-natured ridicule: *n.* colloquially, one who annoys by petty requests or by ridicule.

tea-sel (tē'zl), *n.* a prickly plant whose flower head is covered with hooked burrs; one of these flower heads dried and used to raise the nap of woolen cloth; a substitute for this head. Also, teazel.

tea-spoon (tē'spo͞on"), *n.* a spoon used for stirring tea; the spoon of ordinary size for table use.

tea-spoon-ful (tē'spo͞on"fo͝ol), *n.* [*pl.* teaspoonfuls (-fo͝olz)], as much of any substance as a teaspoon will hold.

teat (tēt), *n.* the nipple of the female breast, or the long nipples of the udder, or bag, of an animal, as a cow.

tech-nic (tĕk'nĭk), *adj.* pertaining to the mechanical arts; relating to art, science, or to a particular profession: *n.* manner of performance in an art: *pl.* those branches of learning which relate to the arts; doctrine of arts in general.

tech-ni-cal (tĕk'nĭ-kăl), *adj.* relating to the mechanical arts, or any art or science; having to do with the exact or mechanical part of any branch of learning. —*adv.* technically.

tech-ni-cal-i-ty (tĕk"nĭ-kăl'ĭ-tĭ), *n.* the state or quality of pertaining to the mechanical or exact side of any art or science; anything pertaining to the mechanical or exact side of any art or science; sometimes, a small point, well taken, but frequently of a trifling or quibbling nature; as, he was acquitted on the strength of a *technicality*.

tech-nique (tĕk'nēk'), *n.* the method of performance in any fine art.

tech-no-log-i-cal (tĕk'nō-lŏj'ĭ-kăl), *adj.* pertaining to technology, or the science of the industrial arts.

tech-nol-o-gist (tĕk-nŏl'ō-jĭst), *n.* one skilled in technology, or industrial science; one versed in the knowledge of industries, etc.

tech-nol-o-gy (tĕk-nŏl'ō-jĭ), *n.* the science of the industrial arts; the science which treats of industries and manufactures.

tech-y (tĕch'ĭ), *adj.* [*comp.* techier, *superl.* techiest], fretful; peevish; irritable; easily offended. Also, **tetchy.**

ted (tĕd), *v.t.* [*p.t.* and *p.p.* tedded, *p.pr.* tedding], to turn or spread for drying, as new-mown hay.

ted-der (tĕd'ẽr), *n.* a machine for spreading hay; one who spreads something for drying.

Te De-um (tē dē'ŭm), a hymn of praise or thanksgiving beginning, "We praise thee, O God"; music for this hymn. [Lat.]

te-di-ous (tē'dĭ-ŭs; tēd'yŭs), *adj.* wearisome; tiresome; as, *tedious* work or hours.—*adv.* **tediously.**—*n.* **tediousness.**

te-di-um (tē'dĭ-ŭm), *n.* wearisomeness; tiresomeness; monotony.

tee (tē), *n.* the mark aimed at in the games of quoits, curling, etc.; a little mound of earth from which the ball is struck in golf; a short piece of pipe shaped like the letter T: *v.t.* in golf, to place (the ball) on the mound of earth called the tee.

teem (tēm), *v.i.* to be very productive; be full; be stocked to overflowing; as, the river *teems* with fish.

teem-ing (tēm'ĭng), *p.adj.* producing freely, as young; fruitful; full; overflowing; as, a brook *teeming* with trout.

teens (tēnz), *n.pl.* years of one's age marked by numbers ending in *-teen;* as, a girl in her *teens*.

tee-pee (tē'pē), *n.* one of the cone-shaped tents or dwellings of the Indians.

tee-ter (tē'tẽr), *v.t.* and *v.i.* to seesaw: *n.* a seesaw.

teeth (tēth), *n.* plural of the noun *tooth;* as, clean *teeth* never decay.

teethe (tē*th*), *v.i.* [*p.t.* and *p.p.* teethed, *p.pr.* teething], to grow or cut the teeth.

teeth-ing (tē*th*'ĭng), *n.* the process of growing or cutting teeth.

tee-to-tal (tē-tō'tăl), *adj.* colloquially, entire or total; pertaining to those who do not drink intoxicating liquors.—*adv.* **teetotally.**

tee-to-tal-er (tē-tō'tăl-ẽr), *n.* a total abstainer, or one who does not drink intoxicating liquors. Also, **teetotaller.**

tee-to-tal-ism (tē-tō'tăl-ĭzm), *n.* the principle or practice of not drinking intoxicating liquors.

tee-to-tum (tē-tō'tŭm), *n.* a kind of top, often a flat circular plate with a peg through the center, spun by the fingers.

teg-u-ment (tĕg'ū-mĕnt), *n.* a natural covering or envelope; skin.

teil (tēl), *n.* the linden, or lime, tree of Europe; the terebinth.

tel-e-fer-i-ca (tĕl'ē-fĕr'ĭ-kȧ), *n.* a cableway built through the air, on the principle of an overhead ore tramway: used by the Italians in the World War to carry men and supplies to high mountain positions.

tel-e-gram (tĕl'ē-grăm), *n.* a written message sent, and received at a distance, by means of electric current passing over wires.

tel-e-graph (tĕl'ē-grăf), *n.* an instrument or system for sending and receiving written messages at a distance by means of electricity: *v.t.* to send by means of electricity passing through wires, as a message; to send such a message to; to signal: *v.i.* to send a message by means of electric current passing through wires.

te-leg-ra-pher (tē-lĕg'rȧ-fẽr; tĕl'ē-grăf'-ẽr), *n.* one who sends or receives messages sent by means of electric current passing through wires.

tel-e-graph-ic (tĕl'ē-grăf'ĭk), *adj.* of or pertaining to the instrument or system for sending and receiving written messages at a distance by means of electricity.—*adv.* **telegraphically.**

te-leg-ra-phist (tē-lĕg'rȧ-fĭst; tĕl'ē-grăf'ĭst), *n.* one skilled in the art of using the instrument for sending and receiving written messages sent at a distance by means of electricity; a telegrapher.

te-leg-ra-phone (tē-lĕg'rȧ-fōn), *n.* an instrument connected by a magnet with the receiver of a telephone, so that it records and reproduces the sound transmitted.

tel-e-graph-o-scope (tĕl'ē-grăf'ō-skōp), *n.* an instrument by which a picture may be transmitted and reproduced by the telegraph.

te-leg-ra-phy (tē-lĕg'rȧ-fĭ), *n.* the science, art, or process of making and using instruments that send or receive messages sent at a distance by means of electricity.

tel-e-lec-tric (tĕl'ē-lĕk'trĭk), *adj.* pertaining to the transmission of sound to a distance by electricity.

te-lem-e-ter (tē-lĕm'ē-tẽr), *n.* an instrument for measuring the distance of some point from the person observing, as the distance of a star from a telescope; an instrument to record measurements (as of a thermometer) at a distance.

tel-e-ol-o-gy (tĕl'ē-ŏl'ō-jĭ; tē'lē-ŏl'ō-jĭ), *n.* the idea or doctrine that the existence of everything in nature can be explained in terms of purpose; the philosophical study of evidence of a creator's design in nature.—*adj.* **teleological.**

te-lep-a-thy (tē-lĕp'ȧ-thĭ), *n.* the transference, or sending, of thought from one person to another, without words, consciously or unconsciously.—*adj.* **telepathic.**—*adv.* **telepathically.**

tel-e-phone (tĕl'ē-fōn), *n.* an instrument for sending and receiving speech or other sounds at a distance by means of electricity: *v.t.* and *v.i.* to communicate or talk by such an instrument.

tel-e-phon-ic (tĕl'ē-fŏn'ĭk), *adj.* pertaining to, or carried by, the instrument for sending and receiving speech or other sounds at a distance by means of electricity; as, a *telephonic* communication; carrying sound to a distance.

tel-e-phon-ist (tĕl'ē-fōn'ĭst), *n.* one who is skilled in using, or who operates, the instrument for sending and receiving speech or other sounds at a distance by means of electricity.

te-leph-o-ny (tē-lĕf'ō-nĭ; tĕl'ē-fō'nĭ), *n.* the science, art, or process of sending sounds to a distance, especially by electricity.

tel-e-pho-tog-ra-phy (tĕl'ē-fō-tŏg'rȧ-fĭ), *n.* the sending and reproducing of photographs at a distance by means of a method like that used in the electric telegraph; the taking of pictures at a distance by a camera which enlarges the objects so as to make them seem near by.

tel-e-post (tĕl'ē-pōst"), *n.* a system of telegraphing by aid of a punched tape, by which messages may be sent with extreme rapidity.

tel-e-scope (tĕl'ē-skōp), *n.* an optical instrument, made of a series of long tubes, provided with lenses: used for magnifying and making visible objects at a distance, especially the moon, stars, etc.; any article made of parts fitting within one another, as do the sections of some telescopes, so that it can be extended in size; as, a kind of extensible valise is called a *telescope:* *v.i.* to force a way endwise one within another, as cars in a railway collision.

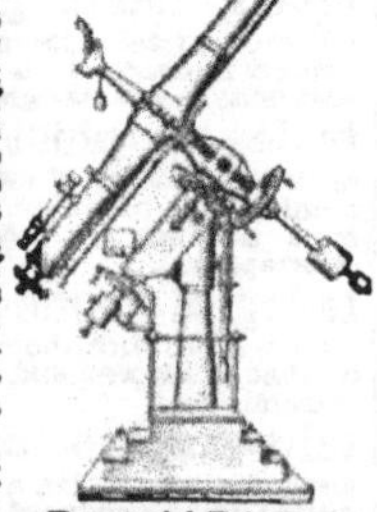

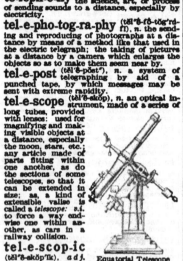

Equatorial Telescope

tel-e-scop-ic (tĕl'ē-skŏp'ĭk), *adj.* pertaining to, or to be seen by, an instrument for magnifying and making visible objects at a distance; as, *telescopic* study of the stars; farseeing; as, a *telescopic* eye; having the power to extend or close up, by sliding one part into another. Also, **telescopical.**—*adv.* **telescopically.**

te-les-co-pist (tē-lĕs'kō-pĭst), *n.* one who is skilled in using the instrument which magnifies and makes visible objects at a distance, or in making such instruments.

te-les-co-py (tē-lĕs'kō-pĭ), *n.* the art or science of making or using telescopes.

tell (tĕl), *v.t.* [*p.t.* and *p.p.* told, *p.pr.* telling], to count; to mention one by one; as, to *tell* one's beads; to disclose; to relate; to inform; to express or make known by words; narrate; explain; communicate; decide; as, I cannot *tell* what is best to do; order; as, I *told* the officer to report; confess; recognize; as, I cannot *tell* who she is at this distance: *v.i.* to give an account; report; play the informer; take effect; as, the continued attacks began to *tell* upon the enemy's defense.

tell-er (tĕl'ẽr), *n.* one who discloses, narrates, communicates, etc.; a bank clerk who receives and pays money over the counter; one who counts the votes in a legislative body, assembly, meeting, etc.

tell-ing (tĕl'ĭng), *n.* the act of relating or making known: *p.adj.* effective; as, his words had a *telling* effect.

tell-tale (tĕl'tāl"), *n.* a talebearer; an informer; one who betrays secrets or makes known private affairs; anything that gives information or warning; as, the snow is a great *telltale:* *adj.* betraying; giving information of what should be kept secret; as, a *telltale* blush.

tel-o-type (tĕl'ō-tīp), *n.* an electric telegraph that prints the message received.

te-mer-i-ty (tē-mĕr'ĭ-tĭ), *n.* foolhardiness; rashness; unwise willingness to take risks.
Syn. heedlessness, audacity, hastiness.
Ant. (see caution).

tem-per (tĕm'pẽr), *v.t.* to change or regulate; to soften; as, to *temper* a rebuke with a smile; make gentle; to mix to the proper degree of firmness or softness, as clay; bring to a proper degree of toughness or hardness; as, to *temper* steel: *n.* state of a metal as to its hardness or toughness; the degree of firmness or softness in a properly proportioned mixture, as of clay or mortar; mental disposition; as, a mild *temper;* mood; heat of mind or passion; readiness to anger; self-control; as, to keep one's *temper.*

tem-per-a-ment (tĕm'pẽr-ȧ-mĕnt), *n.* disposition; the natural mental and physical character or make-up of a person.

tem-per-a-men-tal (tĕm"pẽr-ȧ-mĕn'-tăl), *adj.* arising from, or pertaining to, the natural mental or physical make-up; as, a *temperamental* peculiarity; of changing temper; sensitive; easily irritated; as, she is so *temperamental* that she is hard to get along with.—*adv.* **temperamentally.**

tem-per-ance (tĕm'pẽr-ăns), *n.* moderation; habit of avoiding extremes; self-control, especially in the use of alcoholic liquors and of food; soberness.

tem-per-ate (tĕm'pẽr-āt), *adj.* moderate; not apt to go to extremes; not inclined to eat or drink to excess; calm; not liable to excess of heat or cold; mild in climate or temperature; as, the *temperate* zone.—*adv.* **temperately.**—*n.* **temperateness.**

tem-per-a-ture (tĕm'pẽr-ȧ-tūr), *n.* degree or amount of heat or cold; state as to heat or cold.

tem-pered (tĕm'pẽrd), *adj.* having some special kind of disposition; as, sweet-*tempered* or ill-*tempered;* hardened; as, *tempered* steel.

tem-pest (tĕm'pĕst), *n.* a very violent storm; wind rushing with great force, usually accompanied by rain, hail, etc.; a hurricane; any violent tumult or commotion.

tem-pes-tu-ous (tĕm-pĕs'tū-ŭs), *adj.* very stormy; pertaining to, or like, a furious storm; as, a *tempestuous* sea; violent.—*adv.* **tempestuously.**—*n.* **tempestuousness.**

Tem-plar (tĕm'plẽr), *n.* one of a religious and military order, the Knights Templars, first established in Jerusalem during the twelfth century for the protection of pilgrims and the Holy Sepulcher; a member of the order of Freemasonry, which claims to be descended from the ancient Templars.

tem-ple (tĕm'pl), *n.* a building for religious worship; the flat part of the head, at the side, above the cheek bone.

tem-po (tĕm'pō), *n.* in music, the time-rate in which a composition is rendered; time.

tem-po-ral (tĕm'pō-răl), *adj.* not eternal or everlasting; pertaining to the present life; secular; of the world; as, *temporal* affairs, such as business and pleasure; relating to civil or political matters, as distinct from religious; as, the popes used to have *temporal* power.—*n.* **temporality.**

tem-po-ra-ry (tĕm'pō-rā-rĭ), *adj.* transient, or passing; not permanent; existing or continuing for a limited time; as, *temporary* relief, or a *temporary* condition.—*adv.* **temporarily**.—*n.* **temporariness**.

tem-po-rize (tĕm'pō-rīz), *v.i.* to yield to current opinion or circumstances so as to gain time; delay; try to please both parties.—*n.* **temporizer**.

tempt (tĕmpt), *v.t.* to try to persuade; to lead, or try to lead, into evil ways; as, the serpent *tempted* Eve; entice; allure; defy: as, to *tempt* fate or fortune.

temp-ta-tion (tĕmp-tā'shŭn), *n.* the act of leading, or the state of being led, into evil; persuasion, especially to evil; enticement; that which allures.

tempt-er (tĕmp'tẽr), *n.* [*fem.* temptress], one who seeks to lead into evil, especially the devil.

tempt-ing (tĕmp'tĭng), *adj.* alluring; attractive; as, a *tempting* meal.—*adv.* **temptingly**.—*n.* **temptingness**.

ten (tĕn), *adj.* one more than nine; twice five: *n.* the sum of five and five; ten units; a sign for ten units, as 10 or x.

ten-a-bil-i-ty (tĕn'ȧ-bĭl'ĭ-tĭ), *n.* the state or quality of being capable of being defended or held.

ten-a-ble (tĕn'ȧ-bl), *adj.* capable of being held, maintained, or defended: as, a *tenable* argument or position.—*adv.* **tenably**.—*n.* **tenableness**.

te-na-cious (tē-nā'shŭs), *adj.* holding fast or firmly; as, the *tenacious* grip of a bulldog's jaw; *tenacious* of one's rights; sticky, as glue; tough, as steel; capable of holding or retaining; as, a *tenacious* memory.—*adv.* **tenaciously**.

te-nac-i-ty (tē-năs'ĭ-tĭ), *n.* the state or quality of being able or inclined to hold fast; as, *tenacity* of memory or purpose; stickiness; toughness, as of metal.

ten-an-cy (tĕn'ăn-sĭ), *n.* [*pl.* tenancies (-sĭz)], temporary holding of land or houses; the period of possession of one who rents property; in law, a holding of lands and houses by any title; ownership.

ten-ant (tĕn'ănt), *n.* one who holds possession of real estate by any sort of title or right; one who holds lands or houses from another; an occupant: *v.t.* to hold by rent from another.

ten-ant-ry (tĕn'ănt-rĭ), *n.* [*pl.* tenantries (-rĭz)], the entire group of tenants occupying land and houses on one estate.

tend (tĕnd), *v.t.* to care for; attend; watch over or protect: *v.i.* to attend or serve: with *on* or *upon*; move or go in a certain direction; as, the path *tends* downward; be directed, or be an influence, to any end or purpose; as, study *tends* to solitude.

ten-dance (tĕn'dăns), *n.* act of caring for or watching over; attention.

tend-en-cy (tĕn'dĕn-sĭ), *n.* [*pl.* tendencies (-sĭz)], inclination; as, he showed no *tendency* to study; aim; direction or course.

Syn. aptitude, drift, scope.

tend-er (tĕn'dẽr), *n.* one who takes care of or guards a person or thing; a vehicle containing coal and water attached to a locomotive; a smaller vessel attending and supplying a larger one; a rowboat used to land passengers from a ship; an offer or proposal for acceptance; offer of service, or of a sum due in money, under certain legal conditions; money offered in payment; as, legal *tender* is money which must legally be accepted in payment of a debt: *v.t.* to offer for acceptance; as, to *tender* one's services: *adj.* easily cut or chewed, as meat; soft; not hard; not tough; weak in body; easily hurt or injured; sensitive; easily touched by pain, grief, love, kindness, etc.; sympathetic; gentle; kind; immature; delicate: said of colors, sounds, etc.—*adv.* **tenderly**.—*n.* **tenderness**.

ten-der-foot (tĕn'dẽr-fo͝ot'), *n.* [*pl.* tenderfeet], one who is new to the life in a mining region or newly settled district. [Colloq.]

ten-der-heart-ed (tĕn'dẽr-härt'ĕd), *adj.* ready to be touched by the pain or grief of others; kind; sympathetic; of loving disposition.

ten-der-loin (tĕn'dẽr-loin'), *n.* the tenderest part of the loin of beef or other meat; a strip of tender meat under the short ribs, in beef, pork, etc.

ten-don (tĕn'dŭn), *n.* a tough cord or bundle of cords of fibrous tissue attaching a muscle to a bone, another muscle, or an organ of the body.

ten-dril (tĕn'drĭl), *n.* the slender, twining, leafless part of a plant which attaches itself to a support, thus enabling the plant to climb or to hold itself up.

ten-e-ment (tĕn'ē-mĕnt), *n.* a house, a shop, land, etc., rented by one person from another; a dwelling house; suite of rooms, or apartment; dwelling or abode.

ten-e-ment house (tĕn'ē-mĕnt hous), a large building containing suites of rooms, each occupied by a family as a dwelling: used commonly of such buildings in poor sections of large cities, occupied by many people of small means.

ten-et (tĕn'ĕt), *n.* a doctrine, dogma, opinion, or belief, maintained as true; as, the *tenets* of the Christian religion.

Syn. position, view, conviction, doctrine.

ten-fold (tĕn'fōld'), *adj.* and *adv.* ten times as much or as many.

ten-nis (tĕn'ĭs), *n.* a game played with rackets and balls, on a lawn or in an inclosed court of earth or gravel.

ten-on (tĕn'ŭn), *n.* a projection at the end of a timber cut so as to fit into a hole in another timber: *v.t.* to cut a projection at the end of (a timber); to fit such a projection into.

ten-or (tĕn'ẽr), *n.* usual manner; general tendency or drift; as, the *tenor* of his conversation; purport; the highest of adult male voices; a part written for this voice; one who sings the part written for the highest adult male voice, or the instrument that plays it: *adj.* pertaining to, or adapted for, the highest adult male voice; as, the *tenor* part in a choir.

ten-or clef (tĕn'ẽr klĕf), the C clef, when so placed as to govern the scale from D in the bass clef to E above middle C.

ten-pen-ny (tĕn'pĕn-ĭ), *adj.* worth ten pence; specifying a certain size of nail.

ten-pins (tĕn'pĭnz'), *n.* a bowling game played with ten pins set up at the farther end of a bowling alley.

tense (tĕns), *adj.* [*comp.* tenser, *superl.* tensest], drawn tightly; not lax; severely strained; rigid; as, a *tense* rope; *tense* nerves; a *tense* expression: *n.* a change in the form of a verb, showing the time of the action expressed; a verb form which indicates a certain distinction of time by changing its form or by the help of auxiliaries.—*adv.* **tensely**.—*n.* **tenseness**.

ten-sile (tĕn'sĭl), *adj.* of or pertaining to tightness or strain; capable of being stretched or strained; as, the *tensile* strength of wire.

ten-sion (tĕn'shŭn), *n.* the act of stretching or straining; the state of being stretched or strained; mental strain; strong excitement of feeling; strained relations; in machinery, a device to loosen or tighten the thread on a sewing machine; the condition or stress due to pulling.

ten-sor (tĕn'sŏr), *n.* a muscle that stretches a part of the body.

ten-strike (tĕn'strīk), *n.* in bowling, a knocking down of all the pins with one throw of the ball; colloquially, a successful performance.

tent (tĕnt), *n.* a shelter usually made of canvas, supported by poles and ropes: *v.i.* to camp out; pitch a tent. *v.t.* to cover with, or as with, a tent.

ten-ta-cle (tĕn'tȧ-kl), *n.* a threadlike sense organ of certain backboneless animals; a feeler; as, the *tentacles* of a spider or a devilfish; a feeler on the leaf of a plant.

ten-ta-tive (tĕn'tȧ-tĭv), *adj.* of or pertaining to an experiment or trial; used in experimenting; provisional; as, a *tentative* offer.—*adv.* **tentatively.**

tent-ed (tĕnt'ĕd), *p.adj.* covered with tents; as, the *tented* field; sheltered by a tent; like a tent.

ten-ter (tĕn'tĕr), *n.* a frame on which to stretch cloth by hooks to prevent shrinking in drying: *v.t.* to hang or stretch on such a frame.

ten-ter-hook (tĕn'tĕr-hŏŏk"), *n.* one of the sharp, hooked nails set on a tenter, or frame for stretching cloth: **on tenterhooks,** under a strain; in suspense.

tenth (tĕnth), *adj.* next in order after the ninth; being one of ten equal parts; the ordinal of ten.—*n.* one of ten equal parts. —*adv.* **tenthly.**

te-nu-i-ty (tē-nū'ĭ-tĭ), *n.* thinness; as, the *tenuity* of a leaf; slenderness; as, the *tenuity* of a hair; rareness; as, the *tenuity* of the air; rarity; lack of substance; as, the *tenuity* of the blood.

ten-u-ous (tĕn'ū-ŭs), *adj.* slender; thin; as, *tenuous* wire is very thin and fine; not dense or heavy; as, *tenuous* air or oil.

ten-ure (tĕn'ūr), *n.* the conditions under which a house or real estate is held; the right or manner of holding real estate; the period during which anything is held and enjoyed; as, the President's *tenure* of office is four years.

te-pee (tē'pē; tĕp'ē), *n.* an American Indian wigwam or tent. Also, **teepee.**

tep-e-fy (tĕp'ē-fī), *v.t.* [*p.t.* and *p.p.* tepefied, *p.pr.* tepefying], to make moderately warm: *v.i.* to become moderately warm.

tep-id (tĕp'ĭd), *adj.* moderately warm; lukewarm; as, *tepid* water.—*n.* **tepidness.**

te-pid-i-ty (tē-pĭd'ĭ-tĭ), *n.* moderate warmth; state of being lukewarm.

ter-cen-ten-a-ry (tûr-sĕn'tē-nȧ-rĭ), *adj.* comprising or including 300 years: *n.* anniversary of an event three centuries old; as, the *tercentenary* of the discovery of America.

te-re-do (tē-rē'dō), *n.* the shipworm, which bores into ship timbers.

term (tûrm), *n.* a limit or boundary; limited time; as, a *term* of five years; a division of a school year; the time of a court's session; a word or expression, especially one belonging particularly to one art, business, etc.; as, a legal *term*: *pl.* condition or arrangement; as, *terms* of a sale; relationship or condition; as, to be on good *terms* with a person; conditions or stipulations; as, the *terms* of an agreement: *v.t.* to name, point out, or call.

ter-ma-gant (tûr'mȧ-gănt), *n.* a noisy, violent woman: *adj.* noisy and quarrelsome; as, a *termagant* wife.

ter-mi-na-ble (tûr'mĭ-nȧ-bl), *adj.* capable of being limited or ended; certain to end at a given time.

ter-mi-nal (tûr'mĭ-năl), *adj.* pertaining to the end or boundary; forming the end; as, the Pennsylvania Railroad *terminal* station in New York; pertaining to a fixed length of time: *n.* a limit or boundary; an end; the limit or end of a railroad line, including the station, switches, etc.; either end of an electrical circuit.

ter-mi-nate (tûr'mĭ-nāt), *v.t.* to limit or bound; as, a wall *terminates* the garden; bring to an end; finish; as, to *terminate* a war: *v.i.* to be limited or bounded; as, his property *terminates* at the river; come to an end; as, his career *terminated* in disaster.

ter-mi-na-tion (tûr"mĭ-nā'shŭn), *n.* the act of limiting or ending; a bound or limit; end; conclusion or result; final syllable or letter of a word.

ter-mi-nol-o-gy (tûr"mĭ-nŏl'ō-jĭ), *n.* the special or technical expressions used in a science, art, business, etc.

ter-mi-nus (tûr'mĭ-nŭs), *n.* [*pl.* termini (-nī)], a limit or boundary; either end of a railway line; also the town, station, etc., at that place.

ter-mite (tûr'mīt), *n.* the tropical white ant, destructive to wood, furniture, etc.; any pale-colored, social insect.

tern (tûrn), *n.* a water bird belonging to the gull family and commonly known as the sea swallow.

ter-na-ry (tûr'nȧ-rĭ), *adj.* proceeding by, or consisting of, threes; as, a *ternary* compound is a mixture of three chemicals, etc.: *n.* the number three; three things together.

ter-nate (tûr'nāt), *adj.* arranged in threes, or consisting of threes; as, *ternate* leaves.

terp-si-cho-re-an (tûrp"sĭ-kō-rē'ăn), *adj.* of or pertaining to dancing; as, the *terpsichorean* art; from Terpsichore, the muse of dancing.

ter-race (tĕr'ās), *n.* a raised level space or platform of earth with sloping sides; a slanting bank of earth; the flat roof of an Oriental or Spanish house; a row of houses set along the top of a bank or slope; hence, often, any street or row of houses: *v.t.* to form or build in a terrace or terraces.

ter-ra cot-ta (tĕr'ȧ kŏt'ȧ), pottery of baked clay or earth, especially that of a reddish-brown color: *adj.* of the color of, or made of, terra cotta; as, a *terra cotta* vase.

ter-ra fir-ma (tĕr'ȧ fûr'mȧ), dry land; mainland; solid earth; land as opposed to water. [Lat.]

ter-rain (tē-rān'; tĕr'ān), *n.* a geological formation; ground considered for its fitness for military use, as for a battle, a line of trenches, a fortification, etc., or for other purposes. Also, **terrane.**

ter-ra-pin (tĕr'ȧ-pĭn), *n.* a kind of fresh-water tortoise or turtle used as food; its cooked flesh as a table dish.

ter-ra-que-ous (tĕr-ā'kwē-ŭs), *adj.* consisting of land and water; as, the earth is a *terraqueous* globe.

ter-res-tri-al (tĕ-rĕs'trĭ-ăl), *adj.* pertaining to, existing on, or consisting of, earth; belonging to the present world; not celestial or heavenly; living or growing on land, in distinction to water.—*adv.* **terrestrially.**

ter-ret (tĕr'ĕt), *n.* one of the rings on a harness pad, through which the driving reins pass.

ter-ri-ble (tĕr'ĭ-bl), *adj.* exciting or causing fear or awe; as, a *terrible* storm; dreadful; appalling.—*adv.* **terribly.** —*n.* **terribleness.**

ter-ri-er (tĕr'ĭ-ẽr), *n.* one of any of several breeds of small, intelligent dogs, used as pets and for hunting game, killing rats, etc.

ter-rif-ic (tĕ-rĭf'ĭk), *adj.* very alarming; causing fear; dreadful; as, a *terrific* explosion.—*adv.* **terrifically.**

ter-ri-fy (tĕr'ĭ-fī), *v.t.* [*p.t.* and *p.p.* terrified, *p.pr.* terrifying], to frighten or alarm exceedingly.

ter-ri-to-ri-al (tĕr"ĭ-tō'rĭ-ăl), *adj.* pertaining to a given region of land; as, *territorial* disputes; limited to a particular district; as, *territorial* laws: **Territorial,** pertaining to any one or all of the Territories of the United States: *n.* a soldier in the militia organization of Great Britain. —*adv.* **territorially.**

ter-ri-to-ry (tĕr'ĭ-tō-rĭ), *n.* [*pl.* territories (-rĭz)], a large tract of land; region; district; as, the unexplored *territory* in South America; entire extent of land and water under the control of one ruler or government; as, British or French *territory:* **Territory,** in the United States, a region, sometimes undeveloped, under a temporary government, that may become a State; as, Alaska *Territory.*

ter-ror (tĕr'ẽr), *n.* extreme fear; fright; one who, or that which, causes extreme fear.

ter-ror-ism (tĕr'ẽr-ĭzm), *n.* a system of government by methods which excite fear; a revolt against government, in which the methods used excite fear.

ter-ror-ist (tĕr'ẽr-ĭst), *n.* one who governs by impressing with fear, especially one of the revolutionary party during the Reign of Terror in France; one who seeks any end by arousing fear.

ter-ror-ize (tĕr'ẽr-īz), *v.t.* to intimidate, or make timid by fear; to put into a state of extreme fear.

ter-ry (tĕr'ĭ), *n.* a cloth of silk or wool, woven like velvet, but with the loops uncut.

terse (tûrs), *adj.* [*comp.* terser, *superl.* tersest], concise or brief; short; exactly to the point; as, a *terse* style of writing.—*adv.* **tersely.**—*n.* **terseness.**

ter-tian (tûr'shăn), *adj.* occurring every other day, as certain fevers: *n.* fever returning every other day.

Ter-ti-a-ry (tûr'shĭ-ā-rĭ; tûr'shȧ-rĭ), *adj.* in geology, pertaining to the earlier period of the Cenozoic era, between the Mesozoic era and the Quaternary period: *n.* the earlier period of the Cenozoic age.

tes-sel-late (tĕs'ĕ-lāt), *v.t.* to form into squares or checkers; as, a *tessellated* floor.—*n.* **tessellation.**

test (tĕst), *n.* proof; a close examination or a decisive trial; as, he stood the *test;* means of proving the strength or worth of a person's character; as, trouble is often a *test* of nobility; standard; in chemistry, an experiment for discovering the presence of any particular substance in a compound: *v.t.* to put to the proof; to try to find a particular substance in; as, to *test* rice for starch; to compare with a standard; to refine; as, to *test* gold or silver in a furnace.—*n.* **tester.**

tes-ta (tĕs'tȧ), *n.* [*pl.* testae (-tē)], the outer integument, or covering, of a seed; the shell-like covering of certain animals: called also a *test.*

tes-ta-ment (tĕs'tȧ-mĕnt), *n.* a written will; as, last will and *testament:* **Testament,** either of the two main parts of the Bible, as the *Old Testament* and the *New Testament.*

tes-ta-men-ta-ry (tĕs"tȧ-mĕn'tȧ-rĭ), *adj.* of or pertaining to a will, or the administration or settlement of a will; as, letters *testamentary.*

tes-tate (tĕs'tāt), *adj.* having left a will; as, he died *testate.*

tes-ta-tor (tĕs-tā'tẽr), *n.* [*fem.* testatrix], one who leaves a will at his death; one who makes a will.

tes-ter (tĕs'tẽr), *n.* a flat canopy or covering over a bed, supported by the bedposts; any flat canopy.

tes-ti-fy (tĕs'tĭ-fī), *v.i.* [*p.t.* and *p.p.* testified, *p.pr.* testifying], to bear witness; make a solemn declaration; give evidence; as, to *testify* at a court trial: *v.t.* to affirm or declare solemnly on oath; bear witness to.

tes-ti-mo-ni-al (tĕs"tĭ-mō'nĭ-ăl), *n.* a writing or certificate in favor of one's character, ability, etc.; a token of respect; as, they presented the retiring president with a gold watch as a *testimonial;* acknowledgment of services rendered: *adj.* pertaining to, or containing, recognition or acknowledgment of worth or services; as, a *testimonial* speech.

tes-ti-mo-ny (tĕs'tĭ-mō-nĭ), *n.* [*pl.* testimonies (-nĭz)], evidence; proof; a solemn statement made to establish or prove some fact; affirmation; the entire proof given in a case.

test-ing (tĕs'tĭng), *p.pr.* of *test: n.* the operation of refining gold and silver; proof; trial.

test pa-per (tĕst pā'pẽr), paper so prepared that it changes color when touched by certain chemicals, thus showing the nature of a given substance.

test tube (tĕst tūb), a narrow thin glass tube, used in making chemical tests.

tes-tu-do (tĕs-tū'dō), *n.* [*pl.* testudines (-dĭ-nēz)], a protective covering used by the ancient Roman soldiers in attacking a city, made by overlapping their shields; a screen to shelter miners in places likely to cave in; a kind of flat tumor under the scalp; a land tortoise.

tes-ty (tĕs'tĭ), *adj.* [*comp.* testier, *superl.* testiest], peevish; morose; easily irritated or angered.—*adv.* **testily.**—*n.* **testiness.**

tet-a-nus (tĕt'ȧ-nŭs), *n.* lockjaw; a disease causing muscular spasms, especially the setting of the lower jaw.

tetch-y (tĕch'ĭ), *adj.* fretful; peevish; irritable; cross. Also, **techy.**

tête-à-tête (tāt"ȧ-tāt'; tĕ"tȧ-tāt'), *n.* private conversation between two persons; a kind of settee or sofa for two persons: *adj.* face to face; confidential; private between two persons. [FR.]

teth-er (tĕth'ẽr), *n.* a rope to fasten an animal: *v.t.* to confine, as an animal, within certain limits bounded by the length of a rope.

tet-ra-chord (tĕt'rá-kôrd), *n.* in music, a series of four tones forming half of the octave, as the notes from C to F, inclusive, in the key of C major.

tet-ra-gon (tĕt'rá-gŏn), *n.* a plane figure with four sides and four angles.—*adj.* **tetragonal.**

tet-ra-he-dron (tĕt'rá-hē'drŏn), *n.* a solid figure bounded by four triangular plane surfaces.—*adj.* **tetrahedral.**

Tetrahedron

tet-ram-e-ter (tĕ-trăm'ē-tẽr), *n.* a verse, or line consisting of four measures.

te-trarch (tē'trärk; tĕt'rärk), *n.* a Roman governor whose authority extended over the fourth part of a province; an inferior prince or king; an inferior officer in the Greek army.—*n.* **tetrarchy.**

tet-ra-style (tĕt'rá-stīl), *n.* a building or portico with four columns or pillars in front: *adj.* having four columns.

tet-ter (tĕt'ẽr), *n.* a skin disease marked by itching and redness; herpes or eczema.

Teu-ton (tū'tŏn), *n.* a person belonging to that division of the Indo-European race, or parent race of Europe, which includes the ancient Franks, Goths, etc., and the modern Germans, Swedes, Danes, Norwegians, and Anglo-Saxons; loosely, a German.

Teu-ton-ic (tū-tŏn'ĭk), *adj.* denoting, or pertaining to, that one of the three great divisions of the Indo-European race, or parent stock of the races of Europe, which inhabits central and northern Europe and includes the ancient Franks, Goths, etc., and the modern Germans, Swedes, Danes, Norwegians, and Anglo-Saxons; denoting the language group to which these people belong: *n.* the language group to which these peoples belong.

Teu-ton-ism (tū-tŏn'ĭzm), *n.* a Germanism; an expression, act, or custom characteristic of the Germans; the state of being German.

tex-as (tĕk'sȧs), *n.* the pilot house, etc., on the hurricane deck of a steamer.

text (tĕkst), *n.* the printed or written words of a book, treatise, poem, play, etc., used as a basis for notes or critical discussion; as, to comment on the *text* of a play of Shakespeare; the original words of an author; a verse of Scripture forming the subject of a sermon; topic; argument; the main body of any piece of written or printed matter; the printed part of a book in distinction from the illustrations; black-letter or Old English type.

text-book (tĕkst'bo͝ok"), *n.* a standard book of instruction, used by a teacher and a class.

text-hand (tĕkst'hănd"), *n.* a large, clear style of handwriting.

tex-tile (tĕks'tĭl), *adj.* pertaining to weaving; as, *textile* machinery: formed by weaving or capable of being woven; as, *textile* fabrics: *n.* goods manufactured by weaving, such as cotton and woolen.

tex-tu-al (tĕks'tū-ăl), *adj.* serving for a text, or topic; pertaining to, or contained in, the printed or written words of a book or manuscript; as, *textual* criticism; a *textual* inaccuracy.

tex-ture (tĕks'tūr), *n.* manner of weaving; the arrangement or connection of threads, etc., that are woven together; as, a cloth of close *texture* or weave; a web; structure of any substance.

tha-ler (tä'lẽr), *n.* a German silver coin worth three marks, or about seventy-two cents. Also, **taler.**

than (thăn), *conj.* a particle used before the second member of a comparison.

thane (thān), *n.* a title of honor or dignity among the Anglo-Saxons, held by a free man attached to the service of a lord, and equivalent to knight or baron in later times. Also, **thegn.**

thane-ship (thān'shĭp), *n.* the dignity, state, or property of a thane, or minor nobleman, in early England.

thank (thăṅk), *v.t.* to express gratitude or obligation to.

thank-ful (thăṅk'fo͝ol), *adj.* feeling or expressing gratitude; grateful; feeling conscious of blessings received from God.—*adv.* **thankfully.**—*n.* **thankfulness.**

thank-less (thăṅk'lĕs), *adj.* ungrateful; not appreciative of favors; as, a *thankless* child; not gaining or deserving gratitude; as, a *thankless* task.—*adv.* **thanklessly.**—*n.* **thanklessness.**

Syn. ungracious, profitless, unthankful.

thanks (thăṅks), *n.pl.* an expression of gratitude or obligation.

thanks-giv-ing (thăṅks"gĭv'ĭng), *n.* the act of expressing gratitude for favors and mercies; a public celebration of divine goodness; a day set apart for such a celebration.

Thanks-giv-ing Day (thăṅks"gĭv'ĭng dā), in the United States, a day set apart each year, usually the last Thursday in November, for gratitude and praise to God for national mercies. Also, **Thanksgiving.**

that (thăt), *adj.* and *adj. pron.* [*pl.* those (thōz)], not this but the other, pointing to what is more or less distant; as, *that* house across the street; denoting something that has been spoken of or pointed out previously; as, *that* was what he meant: *rel. pron.* used for *who* or *which*: *conj.* introducing a noun clause; as, he said *that* he would come; introducing a clause of purpose or result; as, work hard, *that* you may succeed; act so *that* you need not be ashamed; introducing an exclamation; as, Oh, *that* you were here!

thatch (thăch), *n.* straw, reeds, etc., used for covering the roofs of cottages, straw stacks, etc.: *v.t.* to cover with, or as with, a roof of straw, etc.—*n.* **thatcher.**

thau-ma-tur-gy (thô'mȧ-tûr"jĭ), *n.* the act of performing so-called miracles; legerdemain; magic.

thaw (thô), *v.i.* to melt or become liquid, as ice or snow; to become warm enough to melt ice and snow; to become milder or more genial: *v.t.* to cause to melt or dissolve: *n.* the melting of ice or snow by temperature above freezing point; state of the weather when ice and snow are melting.

the (thē; thĕ; thē), definite article, denoting some particular object: *adv.* by so much; by that; as, *the* sooner, *the* better.

the-a-ter (thē'ȧ-tẽr), *n.* a public building where plays or dramatic performances are given; a place where events or things of importance take place; as, the *theater* of war. Also, **theatre.**

the-at-ri-cal (thē-ăt′rĭ-kăl), *adj.* of or pertaining to a theater or a dramatic performance; suitable in style or manner for the stage; affectedly emotional; hence, artificial or false: *n.pl.* dramatic performance, especially by amateurs. Also, *adj.* **theatric.**—*adv.* **theatrically.**

thee (thē), *pron.* the singular objective of the pronoun of the second person, grave form.

theft (thĕft), *n.* the act of stealing; robbery; the property stolen.

the-ine (thē′ĭn; thē′ēn), *n.* the bitter substance of tea, identical with caffeine in coffee. Also, **thein, theina.**

their (*th*âr), *pron.* of or belonging to them: the plural possessive of the pronoun of the third person.

theirs (*th*ârz), *pron.* the form of the possessive *their* used alone without a following noun.

the-ism (thē′ĭzm), *n.* the belief in the existence of a god or gods; belief in the personality and sovereignty of one righteous God: opposite to *atheism.*

the-ist (thē′ĭst), *n.* one who believes in the existence of a god or gods: the opposite to *atheist.*

the-is-tic (thē-ĭs′tĭk), *adj.* pertaining to those who believe in a god or gods or to their belief. Also, **theistical.**

them (*th*ĕm), *pron.* the objective plural of the pronoun of the third person.

theme (thēm), *n.* the subject or topic of a conversation, speech, essay, etc.; a short essay or composition on a given subject; in music, a series of notes forming the subject of a composition.

them-selves (*th*ĕm-sĕlvz′), *pron.* the plural form of *himself, herself,* and *itself;* the emphatic or reflexive form of *they* or *them.*

then (*th*ĕn), *conj.* in consequence; therefore; in that case: *adv.* next; at that, or at another, time; immediately after.

thence (*th*ĕns), *adj.* from that place or time; as, a week *thence.*

thence-forth (*th*ĕns′fōrth′; *th*ĕns′fōrth), from that time, or place, forward.

the-oc-ra-cy (thē-ŏk′rȧ-sĭ), *n.* [*pl.* theocracies (-sĭz)], the government of a state by the immediate direction of God; hence, government by an organized church; the state thus governed.

the-o-crat-ic (thē′ō-krăt′ĭk), *adj.* pertaining to a theocracy, or a government by direction of God; administered under the immediate direction of God; as, the *theocratic* government of the ancient Hebrews. Also, **theocratical.**

the-od-o-lite (thē-ŏd′ō-līt), *n.* a surveying instrument for measuring horizontal and vertical angles, and sometimes distances and heights.

Theodolite

the-og-o-ny (thē-ŏg′ō-nĭ), *n.* [*pl.* theogonies (-nĭz)], that branch of mythology which treats of the origin or descent of ancient gods; a poem treating of such histories.

the-o-lo-gi-an (thē′ō-lō′jĭ-ăn), *n.* one skilled in theology, or the science of religion; a professor of divinity or theology.

the-o-log-i-cal (thē′ō-lŏj′ĭ-kăl), *adj.* pertaining to theology, or the science of religion.—*adv.* **theologically.**

the-ol-o-gy (thē-ŏl′ō-jĭ), *n.* [*pl.* theologies (-jĭz)], the study of the existence, nature, and powers of God, especially of man's relations to God; divinity; the science of religion.

the-o-rem (thē′ō-rĕm), *n.* that which can be shown to be true, and has been established as a principle or law; in mathematics, a proposition which can be proved.

the-o-ret-i-cal (thē′ō-rĕt′ĭ-kăl), *adj.* pertaining to, or depending on, an abstract principle; based on ideas rather than on fact or experience; not practical; speculative or uncertain. Also, **theoretic.**—*adv.* **theoretically.**

the-o-rist (thē′ō-rĭst), *n.* one who draws conclusions from abstract principles, not from facts; an impractical person.

the-o-rize (thē′ō-rīz), *v.i.* to draw conclusions from abstract principles, not from facts; to speculate mentally; to form impractical ideas.—*n.* **theorizer.**

the-o-ry (thē′ō-rĭ), *n.* [*pl.* theories (-rĭz)], abstract or general principles of a science or art considered apart from practice; hypothesis; a general principle intended to explain observed facts; individual idea.

Syn. speculation, scheme, plea, conjecture.

the-os-o-phist (thē-ŏs′ō-fĭst), *n.* a believer in theosophy, a mystic philosophy similar to the religions of India.

the-os-o-phy (thē-ŏs′ō-fĭ), *n.* [*pl.* theosophies (-fĭz)], a philosophy which claims to put man into direct touch with God and the spiritual world by physical processes and extreme spiritual inspiration; a philosophy similar to the religions of India, whose chief feature is a belief in reincarnation, or the passing of the soul at death into another body.—*adj.* **theosophic, theosophical.**

ther-a-peu-tic (thĕr′ȧ-pū′tĭk), *adj.* pertaining to healing; curative: *n.pl.* the science of curing diseases: called also *therapy.*

there (*th*âr), *adv.* in that place; at that point or stage; in that matter or relation, etc.

there-a-bout (*th*âr′ȧ-bout″), *adv.* near that place, time, number, etc.; nearly. Also, **thereabouts.**

there-aft-er (*th*âr-ȧf′tẽr), *adv.* after that; afterward; accordingly.

there-at (*th*âr-ăt′), *adv.* at that place; as a result of that.

there

there

there

for that

respect.

there-of (*th*âr-ŏv′; *th*âr-ŏf′), *adv.* of or concerning that or this; from this cause.

there-on (*th*âr-ŏn′), *adv.* on that or this place, date, circumstance, etc.

there-to (*thâr*-tōō'), *adv.* to that or this time, place, etc.; in proof of this.

there-to-fore (*thâr*'tōō-fōr'), *adv.* up to that time; previously to a given date.

there-un-to (*thâr*"ŭn-tōō'), *adv.* thereto; to that or this.

there-up-on (*thâr*"ŭ-pŏn'), *adv.* therefore; thereon; upon that; by reason of that; immediately; without delay.

there-with (*thâr*-with'; *thâr*-with'), *adv.* with that or this; immediately; together with this.

there-with-al (*thâr*'with-ôl'), *adv.* over and above; besides; therewith; in addition.

ther-mal (thûr'măl), *adj.* of or pertaining to heat; as, *thermal* units; warm; hot; as, *thermal* baths. Also, **thermic.**

ther-mo-dy-nam-ics (thûr"mō-dī-năm'ĭks), *n.pl.* the science of the relations between heat and mechanical action.

ther-mo-e-lec-tric-i-ty (thûr"mō-ē-lĕk-trĭs'ĭ-tĭ), *n.* electricity generated, or produced, by the action of heat.

ther-mom-e-ter (thēr-mŏm'ē-tēr), *n.* an instrument for measuring changes of temperature; as, the Fahrenheit *thermometer*, in which the freezing point of water is 32 degrees and the boiling point 212 degrees; and the Centigrade *thermometer*, in which the corresponding points are 0 (zero) and 100.

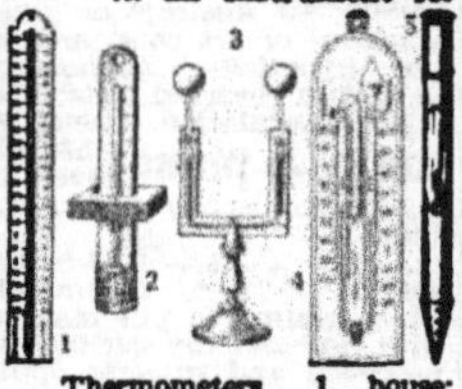

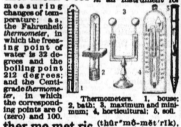

Thermometers. 1, house; 2, bath; 3, maximum and minimum; 4, horticultural; 5, soil.

ther-mo-met-ric (thûr"mō-mĕt'rĭk), *adj.* pertaining to, or found by, a thermometer. Also, **thermometrical.**—*adv.* **thermometrically.**

ther-mos bot-tle (thûr'mŏs bŏt'l), an air-tight receptacle for liquids, so prepared as to keep them at the same degree of heat or cold as when they are put into it.

ther-mo-scope (thûr'mō-skōp), *n.* an instrument for showing differences in temperature without exact measurement in degrees.

ther-mo-stat (thûr'mō-stăt), *n.* an automatic apparatus for regulating temperature.

ther-mot-ic (thûr-mŏt'ĭk), *adj.* pertaining to, or produced by, heat: *n.pl.* the science of heat.

the-sau-rus (thē-sô'rŭs), *n.* [*pl.* thesauri (-rī)], a storehouse or place where treasure is kept; a lexicon or dictionary; as, a *thesaurus* of the English language.

these (*thēz*), plural of the demonstrative pronoun and adjective *this:* opposite to *those.*

the-sis (thē'sĭs), *n.* [*pl.* theses (-sēz)], an essay or composition on some particular subject; a long essay, based on original research work, and offered by a candidate for an advanced degree; in logic, a statement which is to be maintained and proved by argument.

Thes-pi-an (thĕs'pĭ-ăn), *adj.* pertaining to Thespis, the founder of Greek drama; hence, dramatic.

Thes-sa-lo-ni-ans (thĕs"ă-lō'nĭ-ănz), *n.pl.* either of two books of the New Testament, consisting of epistles, or letters, written by the apostle Paul to the people of Thessalonica in Greece.

thews (thūz), *n.pl.* muscles; sinews; hence, muscular power or strength.

they (*thā*), *pron.* nominative plural of the pronoun of the third person.

thick (thĭk), *adj.* not thin; having considerable distance between two opposite surfaces; as, a *thick* book; not slender; as, a *thick* staff; closely set, as trees; dense; as, a *thick* cloud; crowded; not clear; as, the air was *thick;* misty; muddy; dull or stupid; as, *thick*-headed; colloquially, very intimate; as, friends who are constantly together are said to be very *thick;* indistinct; as, *thick* speech: *adv.* closely; as, *thick* and fast they came: *n.* the densest part; as, the *thick* of the fight.—*adv.* **thickly.**—*n.* **thickness.**
Syn., *adj.* close, solid, turbid, foggy.
Ant. (see thin).

thick-en (thĭk'n), *v.t.* to make less thin or slender; to make dense; as, to *thicken* gravy with flour; to set more closely; to make dark or obscure: *v.i.* become more dense or closer together, as trees; become dark; as, night *thickens;* lose thinness or slenderness.

thick-en-ing (thĭk'n-ĭng), *n.* something added to a liquid mass to make it more dense; as, flour or cornstarch is used as *thickening* for soups, sauces, etc.

thick-et (thĭk'ĕt), *n.* a dense wood or cluster of trees; a closely set tangle of bushes, etc.

thick-set (thĭk'sĕt"), *adj.* closely planted; as, a *thickset* hedge; having a short, stout body; as, a *thickset* man: *n.* a close, thick hedge; a dense growth of trees and bushes.

thick-skinned (thĭk'skĭnd"), *adj.* having thick skin; not sensitive; not affected by criticism.

thief (thēf), *n.* [*pl.* thieves (thēvz)], one who steals or robs by stealth.

thieve (thēv), *v.t.* and *v.i.* to steal; to rob by stealth; to practice stealing.

thiev-er-y (thēv'ēr-ĭ), *n.* [*pl.* thieveries (-ĭz)], act or habit of stealing; practice of robbing by stealth.

thiev-ish (thēv'ĭsh) *adj.* given to stealing; dishonest; resembling a theft.—*adv.* **thievishly.**—*n.* **thievishness.**

thigh (thī), *n.* the thick muscular part of the leg between the knee and the body.

thill (thĭl), *n.* one of the two shafts of a cart or carriage; the floor of a coal mine.

thim-ble (thĭm'bl), *n.* a metal cap to protect the finger in sewing; anything shaped like a thimble; an iron ring belonging to a sail, fitted to receive a rope.

thim-ble-ber-ry (thĭm'bl-bĕr"ĭ), *n.* [*pl.* thimbleberries (-ĭz)], an American raspberry whose fruit is shaped like a thimble.

thim-ble-rig (thĭm'bl-rĭg"), *n.* a sleight-of-hand trick in which a pea is supposed to be hidden under one of three thimbles: also known as *the shell game:* *v.t.*[*p.t.* and *p.p.* thimblerigged, *p.pr.* thimblerigging], to swindle by means of this trick; hence, to cheat by any trick.—*n.* **thimblerigger.**

thin (thĭn), *adj.* [*comp.* thinner, *superl.* thinnest], not thick; slim; slender; of little diameter; as, a *thin* tree trunk; not dense; as, *thin* smoke; not close or crowded; rare, as the air; slight; meager; not fully or well grown; flimsy, as cloth; wanting substance; shrill, as the voice: *adv.* not thickly: *v.t.* to make less thick: *v.i.* to grow less thick.—*adv.* **thinly.**—*n.* **thinness.**

Syn., adj. lean, scraggy.

thine (*th*īn), *pron.* of or belonging to thee: the possessive singular of the pronoun of the second person, grave form.

thing (thĭng), *n.* that which has a separate, individual existence; inanimate or lifeless matter, as a stone; any object of thought; as, to talk of many *things;* an event or act; as, great *things* are done by great men; a creature; as, poor *thing;* an indefinite object; as, a *thing* of beauty: *pl.* possessions, such as clothes, furniture, baggage, etc.

think (thĭngk), *v.i.* [*p.t.* and *p.p.* thought, *p.pr.* thinking], to occupy the mind with some subject; to work with the mind; to form an opinion; to meditate; to reason; believe; judge; intend or purpose; as, I *think* to start to-morrow; imagine; recollect; as, to *think* of the past; consider or reflect; presume: *v.t.* to imagine; to occupy the mind with; as, to *think* beautiful thoughts; to believe; as, I *think* it is not so; to suppose.

Syn. consider, ponder, conceive, fancy.

think-a-ble (thĭngk'ȧ-bl), *adj.* conceivable; imaginable; possible to be believed.

think-er (thĭngk'ẽr), *n.* one who uses his mind actively or seriously; a philosopher.

think-ing (thĭngk'ĭng), *adj.* having the power of thought; capable of a regular train of thought: *n.* meditation; judgment.

thin-skinned (thĭn'skĭnd"), *adj.* having thin skin; sensitive; easily hurt by criticism.

third (thûrd), *adj.* the next after the second; the ordinal of three; denoting one of three equal parts: *n.* one of three equal parts; a third part of anything; in music, an interval of three diatonic steps.

thirst (thûrst), *n.* great desire for drink; drought; eager wish; as, a *thirst* for knowledge: *v.i.* to desire to drink.

thirst-y (thûrs'tĭ), *adj.* [*comp.* thirstier, *superl.* thirstiest], feeling an eager desire for drink; without moisture; parched. —*adv.* **thirstily.**—*n.* **thirstiness.**

thir-teen (thûr'tēn"; thûr"tēn'), *adj.* ten and three: *n.* the sum of ten and three; a sign for thirteen units, as 13 or xiii.

thir-teenth (thûr'tēnth"; thûr"tēnth'), *adj.* next in order after twelfth; the ordinal of thirteen: *n.* one of thirteen equal parts; a thirteenth object or unit.

thir-ti-eth (thûr'tĭ-ĕth), *adj.* next in order after the twenty-ninth; the ordinal of thirty: *n.* a thirtieth part, or a thirtieth object or unit.

thir-ty (thûr'tĭ), *adj.* three times ten: *n.* the sum of three tens; a sign for thirty units, as 30 or xxx.

this (*th*ĭs), *pron.* and *adj.* [*pl.* these (*th*ēz)], a demonstrative word, pointing to that which is present, or near; as, *this* is my house; denoting that which is just now or last mentioned; as, *this* is what I mean: opposite to *that.*

this-tle (thĭs'l), *n.* any of various plants of the aster family with a prickly stem and leaves.

thith-er (*th*ĭ*th*'ẽr), *adv.* to that place or end; in that direction.

thith-er-ward (*th*ĭ*th*'ẽr-wẽrd), *adv.* in that direction; toward that end. Also, **thitherwards.**

thole (thōl), *n.* a pin used in a boat as a rowlock to keep the oar in place.

Thom-as (tŏm'ăs), *n.* the one of the twelve apostles who doubted the resurrection of Jesus until he had seen him, and who therefore is often called "doubting Thomas."—John xx. 24-29.

thong (thông), *n.* a thin leather strap or string for fastening something; the striking part of a whip.

Thor (thôr), *n.* in Norse mythology, the god of thunder, who always carried a hammer, and for whom Thursday is named.

tho-rac-ic (thō-răs'ĭk), *adj.* pertaining to the thorax, or part of the body above the abdomen.

tho-rax (thō'răks), *n.* in the human body, the chest, containing the heart, lungs, etc.; in insects, the middle of the three main sections of the body.

thorn (thôrn), *n.* a prickle, spine, or sharp point, as on a plant or an animal; a prickly tree or shrub; hence, anything that troubles or annoys; care.

thorn-y (thôr'nĭ), *adj.* full of sharp points or prickles; harassing; painful.

thor-ough (thŭr'ō), *adj.* going on to the end; perfect; finished; complete; not leaving work half-finished. Also, **thoro.**—*adv.* **thoroughly, thoroly.**—*n.* **thoroughness, thoroness.**

Syn. accurate, trustworthy, reliable.

Ant. (see superficial).

thor-ough bass (thŭr'ō bās"), loosely, the science of harmony; in particular, a method of indicating chords by means of figures placed below the bass staff.

thor-ough-bred (thŭr'ō-brĕd"), *adj.* of pure and unmixed breed; as, a *thoroughbred* horse; well brought up; accomplished; high-spirited: *n.* an animal of pure breed: used also of persons.

thor-ough-fare (thŭr'ō-fâr"), *n.* a passage through from one street to another; an open passageway for traffic. Also, **thorofare.**

thor-ough-go-ing (thŭr'ō-gō"ĭng), *adj.* going all lengths; complete; entire; extreme.

thorp (thôrp), *n.* a small cluster of houses; a hamlet or village. Also, **thorpe.**

those (*th*ōz), plural of the demonstrative pronoun and adjective *that:* opposite to *these.*

thou (*th*ou), *pron.* [*pl.* you], nominative singular of the pronoun of the second person, grave form.

though (*th*ō), *conj.* granting or supposing that; notwithstanding the fact that; if: used after *as;* and yet: *adv.* nevertheless; however. Also, **tho.**

thought (thôt), *p.t.* and *p.p.* of *think: n.* the act of using the mind; that with which the mind is occupied; meditation; mental activity; study; the intellect or understanding; care or anxiety.

Syn., n. idea, conception, consideration, opinion, reflection, deliberation.

thought-ful (thôt'fōōl), *adj.* full of mental activity; attentive; considerate for others; anxious or careful; as, the *thoughtful* boy always helps his mother.—*adv.* **thoughtfully.**—*n.* **thoughtfulness.**

Syn. reflective, cautious, heedful.

thought-less (thôt'lĕs), *adj.* unthinking; heedless; careless; inconsiderate.—*adv.* thoughtlessly.—*n.* thoughtlessness.

thought read-er (thôt rēd'ĕr), one who possesses the power to read another's thoughts.

thought read-ing (thôt rēd'ĭng), the act or art of learning what another person is thinking of; mind-reading.

thou-sand (thou'zănd), *adj.* consisting of ten times one hundred: *n.* ten hundreds; a sign for one thousand units, as 1000 or M; indefinitely, a large number.

thou-sandth (thou'zăndth), *adj.* the next in order after nine hundred and ninety-nine; the ordinal of one thousand: *n.* one of a thousand equal parts.

thral-dom (thrôl'dŭm), *n.* serfdom or slavery; a condition of bondage. Also, thralldom.

thrall (thrôl), *n.* a slave or serf; thraldom or bondage; as, held in *thrall*.

thrash (thrăsh), *v.t.* to beat out (grain) from the hull or husk; colloquially, to beat or flog soundly: *v.i.* to beat out grain; to move violently; often with *about*; as, the sleeper *thrashed*. Also, thresh.

thrash-er (thrăsh'ĕr), *n.* one who beats out grain; a kind of shark which kills with its great tail the small fish on which it feeds; a machine for beating out grain. Also, thresher.

thrash-ing (thrăsh'ĭng), *n.* the act of separating grain from the hull or husk; a sound flogging or whipping. Also, threshing.

thread (thrĕd), *n.* a very thin line or cord of flax, cotton, silk, or other fiberlike substance twisted and drawn out; a filament or fiber; something running through and connecting the parts of anything; as, the *thread* of a story; the spiral ridge of a screw: *v.t.* to pass something through the eye of; as, to *thread* a needle; to string, as beads; to pass or pierce through; as, to *thread* a narrow street; to make (one's way) with difficulty; as, to *thread* one's way through a forest.

thread-bare (thrĕd'bâr"), *adj.* worn to the threads; as, a *threadbare* garment; poverty-stricken; shabby; as, a *threadbare* appearance; hackneyed or worn-out; dull; as, a *threadbare* story.

threat (thrĕt), *n.* a menace; an announcement of coming evil or danger.

threat-en (thrĕt'n), *v.t.* to utter menaces; give notice of coming evil or danger: *v.t.* to utter evil intentions against; be dangerous to; menace; foretell (evil).

threat-en-ing (thrĕt'n-ĭng), *n.* the act of one who menaces; a menace: *p.adj.* indicating a menace or some approaching evil.—*adv.* threateningly.

three (thrē), *adj.* denoting the sum of two and one: *n.* the sum of two and one; the sign for three units, as 3 or iii.

three-fold (thrē'fōld"), *adj.* three times over; of three thicknesses; triple: *adv.* triply.

three-pence (thrĭp'ĕns; thrĕp'ĕns), *n.* a small British silver coin worth six cents.

three-pen-ny (thrĭp'ĕn-ĭ; thrĕp'ĕn-ĭ), *adj.* worth three pence; hence, of little value; worthless.

three-ply (thrē'plī"), *adj.* consisting of three parts, interwoven or otherwise made one.

three-score (thrē'skōr"), *adj.* twenty; sixty.

thren-o-dy (thrĕn'ō-dĭ), [*pl.* (-dīz)], a dirge or song; a lament in verse or music.

thresh (thrĕsh), *v.t.* to beat out grain from; to beat or flog soundly: *v.i.* to beat out grain. Also, thrash.

thresh-er (thrĕsh'ĕr), *n.* a shark of tropical seas, with a very long tail used as a weapon; one who beats out grain; a machine for beating out grain. Also, thrasher.

thresh-ing (thrĕsh'ĭng), *n.* the act of beating out grain; a beating or flogging. Also, thrashing.

thresh-old (thrĕsh'ōld), *n.* the stone, plank, or piece of timber under a door; a door-sill; entrance; door; place or point of entrance.

threw (thrōō), past tense of the irregular verb *throw*.

thrice (thrīs), *adv.* three times; in a threefold manner; hence, repeatedly.

thrift (thrĭft), *n.* frugality; a saving habit; economical or careful management; profit; a class of plants, including the sea-pink, and especially those bearing heads of pink or white flowers.

thrift-stamp (thrĭft'stămp"), *n.* a stamp sold by the United States government during the World War, to encourage the investment of small savings in loans to the government; exchangeable for war savings stamps, issued in larger denominations.

thrift-y (thrĭf'tĭ), *adj.* [*comp.* thriftier, *superl.* thriftiest], economical; frugal; saving; as, the *thrifty* housekeeper; prosperous through industry and economy; as, a *thrifty* village; growing quickly and vigorously; as, *thrifty* trees; thriving.—*adv.* thriftily.—*n.* thriftiness.

thrill (thrĭl), *v.t.* to fill with intense emotion; to stir deeply; cause to have a shivering, tingling sensation: *v.i.* to penetrate, as a keen emotion; to feel a sharp tingling or quivering sensation; to quiver: *n.* a tingling sensation; tremor; quivering excitement.

thrive (thrīv), *v.i.* [*p.t.* thrived, throve, *p.p.* thrived, thriven, *p.pr.* thriving], to prosper by industry, economy, and good management; to increase or prosper in business; grow rich; to grow vigorously; to increase or flourish.

thriv-ing (thrīv'ĭng), *p.adj.* increasing in wealth; prosperous or successful; growing.

throat (thrōt), *n.* the front part of the neck; the passage through it; a narrow entrance or passageway; as, the *throat* of a cannon.

throat-y (thrōt'ĭ), *adj.* harsh in sound; guttural; hoarse of voice.

throb (thrŏb), *v.i.* to beat, as the pulse, with more than usual force; to palpitate: *n.* a strong pulsation or beat.

throe (thrō), *n.* agony; extreme pain; the keenest kind of anguish.

throne (thrōn), *n.* the state chair of a king or bishop; sovereign or kingly power and dignity: *v.t.* to place in a position of kingly power; to exalt or elevate.

throng (thrŏng), *n.* a multitude, or great number; a crowd: *v.t.* to crowd or press together: *v.i.* to come in multitudes, or great numbers.

Syn. *n.* host, jam, concourse.

thros-tle (thrŏs'l), *n.* the song thrush; called also *throstil*; a machine for spinning wool and cotton.

throt-tle (thrŏt'l), *v.t.* to strangle or choke by pressure on the windpipe; to shut off, as steam from an engine; shut steam, etc., off from: *v.i.* to choke; strangle: *n.* the throat or windpipe; a valve to control the supply of steam, etc., to an engine.—*n.* **throttler.**

throt-tle valve (thrŏt'l vălv), a valve in the steam pipe of a boiler for controlling the flow of steam to the engine.

through (thrōō), *prep.* from end to end of; as, *through* life; between the sides of; into at one point and out at another point; as, to bore *through* a plank; in the midst of; as, to walk *through* the woods; by the agency of; as, I obtained the note *through* the influence of a friend; over all the steps of; as, *through* pleasant and *through* cloudy weather: *adv.* from end to end; as, to pierce a thing *through;* from the beginning to the end: *adj.* going from one place to another without change; as, a *through* train. Also, **thru.**

through-out (thrōō-out'), *adv.* everywhere in; in every part; as, the jewelry is gold *throughout: prep.* during; in every part of; as, *throughout* the year. Also, **thruout.**

throve (thrōv), past tense of the intransitive verb *thrive.*

throw (thrō), *v.t.* [*p.t.* threw, *p.p.* thrown, *p.pr.* throwing], to fling or hurl; cast to a distance; cast in any manner; as, to *throw* a ball; to *throw* dice; to unseat or upset; to lay flat, as in wrestling; put on hastily or carelessly, as clothing; to spin, as filaments of silk, into thread: *v.i.* to cast an object to a distance by force; fling: *n.* the act of flinging or hurling; a cast of dice; as, to stake one's fortune on a single *throw;* a venture; the distance an object can be hurled; as, within a stone's *throw;* stroke, as of a slide valve; a piece of drapery for the back of a chair, a couch, etc.

thrum (thrŭm), *n.* the end of a weaver's warp thread; the row of such threads on the loom after the web has been removed: *pl.* coarse yarn waste: *v.t.* [*p.t.* and *p.p.* thrummed, *p.pr.* thrumming], to fringe or put tufts on; to play on (a stringed instrument) idly and unskilfully: *v.i.* play idly or unskilfully on a stringed instrument with the fingers; as, to *thrum* on a piano; to strum; drum.

thrush (thrŭsh), *n.* a song bird; a mouth disease of infants; an affection of the feet in certain animals, as the horse.

thrust (thrŭst), *v.t.* [*p.t.* and *p.p.* thrust, *p.pr.* thrusting], to push or shove with force; as, to *thrust* a person off the sidewalk; drive or impel; pierce; as, their swords *thrust* him through: *v.i.* attack some one or something with a pointed weapon; as, to *thrust* with a dagger: *n.* a violent or sudden push; a stab; as, the *thrust* of a sword; a strain tending to push a part of a structure outward; as, the *thrust* of a roof.

thrust-ing (thrŭst'ĭng), *n.* a pushing with force or violence.

thud (thŭd), *n.* a dull sound produced by a body falling; a thump.

thug (thŭg), *n.* one of a band of religious robbers and assassins in India; hence, any assassin or ruffian.—*n.* **thuggery.**

Thu-le (thū'lē), *n.* the name given by the ancient geographers to the most northern part of the world as then known.

thumb (thŭm), *n.* the short, thick digit of the hand; the part of a glove which covers this digit: *v.t.* to play, as a musical instrument, awkwardly; soil with the thumb; as, to *thumb* the leaves of a book: *v.i.* to play a musical instrument awkwardly.

thumb-screw (thŭm'skrōō'), *n.* a screw made to turn by means of the forefinger and thumb; an instrument of torture for squeezing the thumb. Also, **thumbkin.**

thump (thŭmp), *n.* a hard, heavy blow; a heavy fall, or the sound of it: *v.t.* to pound; to strike or beat with dull, heavy blows: *v.i.* to pound or throb, as the heart.

thun-der (thŭn'dẽr), *n.* the noise following a flash of lightning; any similar loud noise; as, the *thunder* of the guns; a loud utterance: *v.i.* to produce thunder; send forth a similar sound; to utter violent threats: *v.t.* to utter with a loud and threatening voice.

thun-der-bolt (thŭn'dẽr-bōlt'), *n.* a shaft of lightning and the thunder accompanying the discharge; something resembling lightning and thunder in suddenness and terror.

thun-der-clap (thŭn'dẽr-klăp'), *n.* the quick, sharp, crashing noise accompanying a flash of lightning.

thun-der-cloud (thŭn'dẽr-kloud'), *n.* a storm cloud which produces thunder and lightning.

thun-der-ing (thŭn'dẽr-ĭng), *adj.* making, or producing, a great noise like thunder; very great: *n.* the report or sound following a discharge of lightning.

thun-der-ous (thŭn'dẽr-ŭs), *adj.* likely to produce thunder; exceedingly loud and heavy in sound.—*adv.* **thunderously.**

thun-der-storm (thŭn'dẽr-stôrm'), *n.* a storm, with lightning and thunder.

thun-der-struck (thŭn'dẽr-strŭk'), *p.adj.* astonished or struck dumb by sudden amazement, etc.

Thurs-day (thûrz'dā), *n.* the fifth day of the week: named for the god Thor.

thus (thŭs), *adv.* in this or that manner; as, write it *thus;* to this degree or extent; so; therefore.

thwack (thwăk), *v.t.* to strike with something flat and heavy; to thump: *n.* a heavy blow with something flat; a thump or bang.

thwart (thwôrt), *adj.* crosswise or sidewise: *adv.* across: *n.* a seat in a boat from side to side: *v.t.* to oppose or baffle; run counter to; hence, outwit or defeat; as, to *thwart* an enemy or his schemes.

thy (thī), *pron.* pertaining or belonging to thee: possessive singular of the pronoun of the second person, grave form.

thyme (tīm), *n.* a fragrant herb of the mint family used for seasoning.

thy-roid gland (thī'roid glănd), a large gland of the throat, an enlargement of which is known as goiter.

thy-self (thī-sĕlf'), *pron.* an emphasized form of the pronouns *thee* and *thou.*

ti-a-ra (tī-ā'rȧ; tē-ä'rȧ), *n.* the triple crown worn by the Pope; a form of headdress worn by the ancient Persians; a crownlike ornament for the head; a diadem or coronet; as, a *tiara* of diamonds.

Ti-bet-an (tĭ-bĕt'ăn; tĭb'ĕt-ăn), *adj.* of or pertaining to Tibet or the inhabitants of Tibet: *n.* one of the people of Tibet; the language of these people.

tib-i-a (tĭb'ĭ-ȧ), *n.* [*pl.* tibiæ (-ē)], the inner and larger of the two leg bones from knee to ankle; the shin bone.

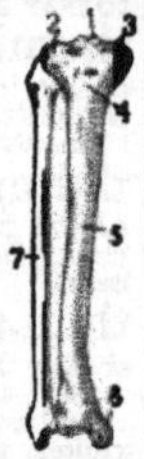

Human Tibia. 1, spine; 2, styloid process; 3, inner tuberosity; 4, tubercle; 5, tibia; 6, inner malleolas; 7, fibula.

tic (tĭk), *n.* a constant jerking or twitching of certain muscles of the face. [FR.]

tic dou-lou-reux (tĭk' dōō'-lōō-rōō'), neuralgia in the face, often with twitching and jerking of muscles. [FR.]

tick (tĭk), *n.* a small, bloodsucking insect; the case that holds the feathers, hair, etc., in a mattress or pillow; as, a bed*tick;* a small mark or check; a small, quick, clear sound, or beat: *v.i.* to make a small, quick, distinct sound; as, the clock *ticks:* *v.t.* to mark off by a tick or small check.

tick-er (tĭk'ẽr), *n.* a telegraphic instrument used to receive and print news on a paper strip, or "tape"; a similar instrument in a broker's office, which receives and prints reports of the stock market: so called because of the sound it makes.

tick-et (tĭk'ĕt), *n.* a marked label or card showing that its possessor has some special privilege, such as admission, a reserved seat, transportation by rail or boat, etc.; as, a theater *ticket;* a card or label stating price, etc., of goods; a printed list of candidates to be voted for; as, an election *ticket:* *v.t.* to distinguish or mark by a label; as, to *ticket* goods with prices, etc.

tick-ing (tĭk'ĭng), *n.* a strong, closely woven cloth, usually striped, used for mattress covers, etc.

tick-le (tĭk'l), *v.t.* [*p.t.* and *p.p.* tickled, *p.pr.* tickling], to touch lightly so as to produce a peculiar thrill or tingle; to please or amuse: *v.i.* to produce a peculiar thrill or tingle by a light touch: *n.* a peculiar thrill or tingle or the touch causing it.—*n.* tickler.

tick-lish (tĭck'lĭsh), *adj.* sensitive to slight touches; delicate to handle or achieve; as, a *ticklish* undertaking; risky; doubtful as to outcome.

tid-al (tīd'ăl), *adj.* pertaining to, or ebbing and flowing like, the rising and falling of the ocean; as, a *tidal* basin.

tid-al wave (tīd'ăl wāv), a wave which follows the sun and moon over the oceans, causing the tides; also, incorrectly, a great sea wave after an earthquake; a very high rise of the sea along a shore.

tide (tīd), *n.* time or season: rare except in Easter*tide*, Christmas*tide*, etc.; the regular rise and fall twice every day of the surface of the ocean and the waters connected with it; a stream or flood; the natural tendency of events: *v.t.* to be moved, as a ship, in or out of a river or harbor by drifting with the tide; to carry along; as, the money will *tide* him over his difficulties.

tide-wait-er (tīd'wāt"ẽr), *n.* an officer who watches the landing of goods from ships to secure the payment of duties or taxes.

tide-wa-ter (tīd'wô"tẽr), *n.* water affected by the rise and fall of the ocean; land bordered by such water.

ti-dings (tī'dĭngz), *n.pl.* news; as, I bring you glad *tidings* of great joy.

ti-dy (tī'dĭ), *adj.* [*comp.* tidier, *superl.* tidiest], trim; neat; orderly: *v.t.* and *v.i.* [*p.t.* and *p.p.* tidied, *p.pr.* tidying], to make neat; put in proper order; as, to *tidy* a room: *n.* an ornamental cover for the back of a chair, etc.—*adv.* tidily.—*n.* tidiness.

tie (tī), *n.* a knot or fastening; a knot of ribbon, silk, etc., used as a finish to the dress; a plank or rod for holding two parts together; as, railroad rails are held together by *ties;* equality in number of votes in an election, counts in a game, etc.; a bond or connection; as, *ties* of blood; in music, a curved line joining two notes of the same pitch; indicating that the note is to be sounded once, but held the length of both: *pl.* low, laced shoes: *v.t.* [*p.t.* and *p.p.* tied, *p.pr.* tying], to fasten by making the ends into a knot; draw together to form a knot; make (a knot) by drawing or weaving something together; bind; to knot a cord, string, etc., around; as, to *tie* a package; restrict; as, she was *tied* down by family cares; unite or connect firmly; in music, to unite, as notes; to make an equal score with, in a contest: *v.i.* to make a knot, equal score, etc.

tier (tēr), *n.* a row or rank; a series; as, a *tier* of seats.

tierce (tērs), *n.* a cask or barrel of forty-two gallons; a set of three playing cards in the same suit; as, a *tierce* of ace, king, and queen; in music, a third; in fencing, a certain thrust or position.

tie-up (tī'ŭp), *n.* a complete stoppage commonly used of obstruction of traffic or transportation. [COLLOQ.]

tiff (tĭf), *n.* a fit of anger; a slight quarrel: a disagreement.

ti-ger (tī'gẽr), *n.* a large, fierce beast of prey, of the cat family, having tawny yellow fur with black stripes; a servant-boy in livery; an added cheer after three cheers.

ti-ger cat (tī'gẽr kăt), any of various kinds of wild cat, similar to the tiger, but smaller and of different coloring.

ti-ger-ish (tī'gẽr-ĭsh), *adj.* savage; fierce; cruel; as, the *tigerish* cruelty of the Huns. Also, tigrish.

ti-ger lil-y (tī'gẽr lĭl'ĭ), a handsome lily having orange-colored flowers spotted with black.

ti-ger wood (tī'gẽr wŏŏd), a valuable wood from a tree of British Guiana.

tight (tīt), *adj.* not loose; fastened firmly together; close; as, a *tight* knot; closely built; as, a *tight* barrel; fitting close to the body; as, a *tight* shoe; not leaky; as, a water-*tight* ship; taut or stretched; as, a *tight* rope; not easily obtained: said of money; colloquially, stingy; as, he is *tight* with his money; slang, intoxicated: *n.pl.* closely fitting garments for the lower limbs, worn by actors, acrobats, dancers, etc. —*adv.* tightly.—*n.* tightness.

tight-en (tīt'n), *v.t.* and *v.i.* to make or become close or firm; to draw together; to stretch taut.

ti-gress (tī'grĕs), *n.* the female of the tiger, a beast of prey of the cat family.

tike (tīk), *n.* a dog or cur; colloquially, a mischievous child, or, playfully, any child.

til-bu-ry (tĭl'bẽr-ĭ), *n.* a two-wheeled carriage without a cover or top.

til-de (tĭl'dĕ), *n.* the diacritical mark used in señor, cañon, etc.

tile (tīl), *n.* a thin slab of baked clay, stone, etc., used for roofing, floors, wall decoration, etc.; colloquially, a stiff hat:

v.t. to cover with tiles; to drain by tiles; to guard (the door of a Masonic lodge).

til-er (til'ẽr), *n.* one who roofs houses, lays floors, etc., with tiles; the doorkeeper of a Masonic lodge: sometimes spelled *tyler.*

till (til), *n.* a money drawer in a desk or counter: *prep.* to the time of; as, wait *till* one o'clock: *conj.* until; to the time when; as, wait *till* I return: *v.t.* to prepare for seed, etc.; cultivate; as, to *till* the land: *v.i.* to cultivate the soil.

till-a-ble (til'á-bl), *adj.* capable of being cultivated.

till-age (til'āj), *n.* the art or business of improving land for raising crops etc.; husbandry; agriculture.

till-er (til'ẽr), *n.* one who cultivates land; a farmer; handle or lever for turning the rudder of a vessel; the shoot of a plant.

tilt (tilt), *n.* a tent; the cloth covering of a cart or wagon; cover for a boat; awning; a slanting incline; an ancient military contest with lances or spears; a tournament: *v.t.* to cover with an awning or tent; to point or thrust, as a lance; to forge or work (metal) with a machine called a tilt hammer; to raise on end; as, to *tilt* a stone; to lean or incline; as, to *tilt* a chair back: *v.i.* to lean or tip; to ride on horseback and thrust with a lance; to charge ahead.

tilth (tilth), *n.* cultivated land or land upon which good crops can be raised.

tilt ham-mer (tilt hăm'ẽr), a heavy hammer at the end of a lever, used in forging or working metal, and operated by steam or other power; a trip hammer.

tim-ber (tim'bẽr), *n.* the body or stem of a tree; wood suitable for carpentry, buildings, shipbuilding, etc.; a large piece of wood prepared for use in building or already in place; wooded land, as forests: *v.t.* to furnish or construct with wood suitable for building, etc.

tim-ber-land (tim'bẽr-lănd"), *n.* land covered with trees whose wood is suitable for use in carpentry and building.

tim-bre (tim'bẽr; Fr. tăn'br), *n.* quality, or tone-character of musical sound; as, the *timbre* of the voice, or the *timbre* of a violin.

tim-brel (tim'brĕl), *n.* a kind of small drum or tambourine.

time (tīm), *n.* measure of duration, whether past, present, or future; a certain period of duration; as, a long *time;* length of a person's life; a fixed hour for some event; period in which anything occurred or a person lived; present life or existence; season; age; date; era; as, the *time* of the Reformation; proper date; system of measurement by hours, days, weeks, etc.; system by which music is divided into measures of a given number of notes; colloquially, a term of imprisonment; as, he has done *time;* repetition: *pl.* a portion of time characterized by the occurrences within it; as, these are great *times* in which to live: *v.t.* to adapt to the occasion; as, I will *time* my visit to your convenience; do at a particular season; to regulate or measure; as, to *time* the speed of a machine: *v.i.* to keep or beat time.

time ball (tīm bôl), a ball on a pole, arranged to drop at a given time of day, usually noon.

time bar-gain (tīm bär'gin), a commercial agreement which is to be carried out at a certain time.

time bill (tīm bil), a bill payable at some future time, usually specified.

time clock (tīm klŏk), a clock at the entrance of a factory, office, etc., on which employees coming to work must indicate the time of their arrival.

time de-tec-tor (tīm dē-tĕk'tẽr), a clock which proves that a watchman has visited certain given places at certain regular times.

time draft (tīm drȧft), a draft payable in the future.

time fuse (tīm fūz), a fuse arranged so as to explode a charge a certain length of time after it is lighted.

time-hon-ored (tīm'ŏn"ẽrd), *adj.* respected, esteemed, or reverenced because of age or long continuance; as, a *time-honored* ceremony.

time-keep-er (tīm'kēp"ẽr), *n.* one who notes and records the time; one who gives a signal, as in a game, when a given time has passed.

time-li-ness (tīm'li-nĕs), *n.* seasonableness; suitableness to the occasion.

time-ly (tīm'lĭ), *adj.* [*comp.* timelier, *superl.* timeliest], seasonable; opportune; suitable to the moment or occasion.

time note (tīm nōt), a note payable at some specified future time.

time-piece (tīm'pēs"), *n.* a clock or watch; any instrument that records the time.

time-serv-er (tīm'sûr"vẽr), *n.* one who weakly or basely fits his action to suit the occasion or the wishes of influential persons.

time-serv-ing (tīm'sûr"vĭng), *adj.* weakly fitting one's action to suit the occasion or to please influential persons: *n.* such servile conduct.

time-ta-ble (tīm'tā"bl), *n.* a systematically arranged list of the dates and hours for events; especially, a list of trains with their time of leaving and arriving.

time-work (tīm'wûrk"), *n.* work paid for by the hour or day: opposite to *piecework.*

tim-id (tim'id), *adj.* shy; wanting in courage; faint-hearted; fearful.—*adv.* timidly.—*n.* timidness.

ti-mid-i-ty (ti-mid'ĭ-tĭ), *n.* want of courage; shyness.

tim-or-ous (tim'ẽr-ŭs), *adj.* fearful of danger; lacking in courage; timid; indicating fear or alarm; as, a *timorous* look.—*adv.* timorously.—*n.* timorousness.

Tim-o-thy (tim'ō-thĭ), *n.* in the Bible, a companion and follower of St. Paul; the person to whom were written the letters contained in the New Testament books, First and Second Timothy.

tim-o-thy (tim'ō-thĭ), *n.* a valuable grass with long round heads, used for hay. Also, timothy grass.

tin (tin), *n.* a silvery-white, soft metal from which many useful articles are made; as, boxes, cans, pans, etc.; thin plates of iron covered with this metal, or wares made of it: *v.t.* [*p.t.* and *p.p.* tinned, *p.pr.* tinning], to cover with tin, or with tinned iron; to put into tins, as food.—*n.* tinner.

tinc-ture (tĭnk'tūr), *n.* a tinge of color; a slight flavor; a solution of a drug: *v.t.* to color; tinge; imbue.

tin-der (tin'dẽr), *n.* any quick-burning material used to kindle a fire from a spark, as rotten wood or scorched linen.

tin-der box (tĭn'dẽr bŏks), a metal box for holding tinder, equipped with a flint and steel for lighting it; anything very easily set on fire.

tine (tīn), *n.* a tooth or spike; a prong; as, the *tine* of a fork.

tin foil (tĭn foil), tin beaten into thin leaf: used for wrapping cigarettes, chocolate bars, and many small articles.

ting (tĭng), *n.* a sharp, bell-like sound: *v.t.* and *v.i.* to sound or ring sharply.

tinge (tĭnj), *v.t.* [*p.t.* and *p.p.* tinged, *p.pr.* tingeing, tinging], to stain or color: to dye faintly; to give a slight flavor or touch of something else to: *n.* a slight degree of some color; a tint; touch; trace.

tin-gle (tĭṅ'gl), *v.i.* [*p.t.* and *p.p.* tingled, *p.pr.* tingling], to feel or have a stinging sensation or pricking pain; as, his fingers *tingled* with the cold: *n.* a stinging sensation or pain, as from cold or a sharp slap.

tink-er (tĭṅk'ẽr), *n.* a mender of metal pots, kettles, etc.: *v.t.* to mend in a bungling way; to patch up: *v.i.* to mend metal ware; to work at anything in a bungling or careless manner.

tin-kle (tĭṅ'kl), *n.* a small, quick, sharp, ringing sound; as, the *tinkle* of a cowbell: *v.i.* [*p.t.* and *p.p.* tinkled, *p.pr.* tinkling], to make such a sound: *v.t.* to cause to give out a sharp, ringing sound.

tinned (tĭnd), *adj.* covered with tin; packed or put up in tins; as, *tinned* vegetables.

tin-man (tĭn'măn), *n.* a worker in tin; a dealer in tinware; a tinsmith.

tin-ny (tĭn'ĭ), *adj.* pertaining to, or containing, tin; having a flat taste, as of tin; as, these canned peas taste *tinny*.

tin plate (tĭn plāt), thin sheet iron or steel coated with tin.

tin-sel (tĭn'sĕl), *n.* a kind of gauzy cloth covered or woven with gold and silver threads; thin, glittering, metallic material in strips or sheets, used for inexpensive but showy decoration, as of a Christmas tree; something showy but of little value; something cheap and gaudy; as, the *tinsel* of the stage: *adj.* showy to excess; superficial or cheap: *v.t.* to decorate with, or as with, cheap imitation gold or silver trimming; make outwardly gaudy.

tin-smith (tĭn'smĭth"), *n.* one who works with tin or tin plate; a tinman.

tint (tĭnt), *n.* a slight coloring; a tinge; a delicate hue or shade: *v.t.* to give a slight coloring to.

tin-tin-nab-u-la-tion (tĭn"tĭ-năb"ū-lā'shŭn), *n.* a tinkling sound, as of bells.

tin-type (tĭn'tīp"), *n.* a photograph taken on a thin iron plate. Also, **ferrotype.**

tin-ware (tĭn'wâr"), *n.* household articles made of tin, or tinned iron, as pans, cups, spoons, etc.

ti-ny (tī'nĭ), *adj.* [*comp.* tinier, *superl.* tiniest], very small; puny; wee; as, a *tiny* baby.

tip (tĭp), *n.* a point or end of anything small; as, the *tip* of a finger; nozzle; as, the *tip* of a gas burner; colloquially, a small fee or present; as, a *tip* to a waiter; colloquially, a private hint, especially in betting; as, a *tip* on the races: *v.t.* [*p.t.* and *p.p.* tipped, *p.pr.* tipping], to slant or tilt; as, to *tip* over a chair; to form a point to; cover the end of; strike lightly; colloquially, to give a private hint to; as, *tip* me off on the price of stocks; colloquially, give a small present to; as, to *tip* a waiter or servant: *v.i.* to lean, slant, or fall over; as, the boat *tipped* dangerously.

Syn., *v.* lean, dip, incline.

tip-pet (tĭp'ĕt), *n.* a neck scarf or small shoulder-cape made of fur, or other warm material; a muffler of wool or silk.

tip-ple (tĭp'l), *v.i.* to drink alcoholic liquors constantly in small amounts: *v.t.* to take (strong drink) in sips or almost continually: *n.* liquor in small amounts.—*n.* tippler.

tip-staff (tĭp'ståf"), *n.* [*pl.* tipstaves (-stāvz; -stăvz); tipstaffs (-ståfs)], a constable or police officer of a court; a staff with a metal top.

tip-ster (tĭp'stẽr), *n.* one who supplies private information about race horses, stock markets, etc. [COLLOQ.]

tip-sy (tĭp'sĭ), *adj.* [*comp.* tipsier, *superl.* tipsiest], intoxicated or drunk; weak or foolish from the effect of liquor.—*adv.* tipsily.—*n.* tipsiness.

tip-toe (tĭp'tō"), *n.* [*pl.* tiptoes (-tōz)], the end or point of a toe or the toes: *adj.* being on the ends of the toes; stretched to full height; stepping softly; hence, cautious: *adv.* on the ends of the toes; cautiously; eagerly: *v.i.* to walk or stand on the ends of the toes; to step softly; to strain upward; hence, to be on a strain or on the alert.

tip-top (tĭp'tŏp'), *n.* the highest point or degree; the best of anything: *adj.* fine; without equal. [COLLOQ.]

ti-rade (tĭ-rād'; tī'răd), *n.* a long, violent speech, especially of blame or abuse.

tire (tīr), *n.* a band or hoop of iron or rubber on the rim or tread of a wheel: *v.t.* to supply (a wheel) with a rim of iron or rubber; to make weary; exhaust or wear out the patience of: *v.i.* to become weary or exhausted.

Syn., *v.* harass, weary, fag.

Ant. (see refresh).

tired (tīrd), *adj.* weary; exhausted; fatigued; worn out.—*adv.* tiredly.—*n.* tiredness.

tire-less (tīr'lĕs), *adj.* unwearying; not to be wearied; having no tire: said of a wheel.—*adv.* tirelessly.

tire-some (tīr'sŭm), *adj.* wearisome; tedious; fatiguing; as, a *tiresome* journey; annoying; as, *tiresome* talk.—*adv.* tiresomely.—*n.* tiresomeness.

tire-wom-an (tīr'wo͝om"ăn), *n.* a woman who acts as an attendant in the dressing room of a theater; a lady's maid.

tir-ing-room (tīr'ĭng-ro͞om"), *n.* formerly, a dressing room in a theater.

tis-sue (tĭsh'ū), *n.* a woven fabric or cloth, especially thin, transparent silk used for veiling, formerly woven with gold or silver threads; that which forms the structure and substance of any organ or plant; as, muscular *tissue*; any thin or delicate texture or fabric; as, *tissue* paper; a closely woven network.

tis-sue pa-per (tĭsh'ū pā'pẽr), very thin, gauzelike paper used to wrap up delicate articles, protect engravings in books, etc.

tit (tĭt), *n.* a morsel or bit; a tap; a kind of small bird called the titmouse; the name for various other kinds of small singing birds.—**tit for tat,** a fair return; this in payment for that.

Ti-tan (tī'tăn), *n.* one of the fabled giants who fought against Jupiter; hence, a man of enormous strength.

Ti-tan-ic (tī-tăn'ĭk), *adj.* pertaining to, or like, the Titans: **titanic,** huge; of enormous strength.

ti-ta-ni-um (tī-tā'nĭ-ŭm), *n.* an extremely hard metallic substance, found in small amounts in clay and many minerals, and used, now and then, in alloys.

tit-bit (tĭt'bĭt"), *n.* a choice morsel or a tender piece, as of anything eatable: used figuratively, as of gossip.

tithe (tīth), *n.* the tenth part of anything, especially the tenth part of one's income given to the support of the church or to charity; small part: *v.t.* [*p.t.* and *p.p.* tithed, *p.pr.* tithing], to tax or levy a tenth of.

tith-ing (tīth'ĭng), *n.* the levying or taking of a tenth of one's income for the church or charity.

tit-il-late (tĭt'ĭ-lāt), *v.t.* to tickle; to rouse pleased excitement in: *v.i.* to tickle.—*n.* **titillation.**

tit-lark (tĭt'lärk"), *n.* a small singing bird of the lark family; the pipit.

ti-tle (tī'tl), *n.* the inscription or name of a book, poem, etc.; a heading; a name of dignity, rank, or distinction, as Your Honor, etc.; a claim or right; as, a *title* to respect; the legal right to property, especially real estate; as, a *title* to land; the paper giving such right: *v.t.* to entitle, or give a name to.

ti-tled (tī'tld), *p.adj.* having an honorary term attached to one's name; especially, belonging to the nobility.

ti-tle deed (tī'tl dēd), a document giving written evidence of right of ownership of property.

ti-tle rôle (tī'tl rōl), the part, or character, in a play for which it is named; as, the *title rôle* in "Hamlet."

ti-tle-page (tī'tl-pāj"), *n.* that page of a book giving its name, author, publisher, and date.

tit-mouse (tĭt'mous"), *n.* [*pl.* titmice (-mīs)], a small, active bird with gray, black, or white feathers.

tit-ter (tĭt'ẽr), *v.i.* to laugh or giggle, in an affected or hysterical fashion: *n.* a little laugh; a foolish, hysterical giggle.

tit-tle (tĭt'l), *n.* a small particle; an iota or jot; a mark over a letter to show pronunciation.

tit-tle-tat-tle (tĭt'l-tăt"l), *n.* trifling talk; senseless chatter; gossip: *v.i.* talk foolishly; gossip.

tit-u-lar (tĭt'ū-lẽr), *adj.* pertaining to, having, or resulting from, a title; existing in name or title only; nominal; as, a *titular* duke: *n.* one who holds the title of an office, but does not possess the power and authority belonging to it.—*adj.* **titulary.**

Ti-tus (tī'tŭs), *n.* a short book of the New Testament, consisting of the epistle, or letter, written by Paul to Titus; one of the Roman emperors, the conqueror of Jerusalem.

to (tōō), *prep.* in a direction toward; as, the sun moves from east *to* west; into a destination; into a certain place; as, he went *to* school; he went *to* church; the railroad runs from Albany *to* Buffalo; as far as; as, come *to* my office and wait; *to* occurs in many senses that are idiomatic; as, be true to yourself; keep your private affairs *to* yourself; he took a sudden liking *to* me; he went *to* court with the case; he took this woman *to* wife; he refused the advice, *to* his lasting regret; I played up *to* his lead; this family lived from hand *to* mouth; she was very dear *to* me; he showed the goods *to* me; the scenery did not appeal *to* me, etc.: denoting the infinitive verb; as, *to* know; *to* show.

toad (tōd), *n.* a tailless, leaping animal resembling the frog: it breeds in water, but in the later stages of its development lives for the most part on land; it eats worms, flies, etc.; one despised for currying favor by fawning, etc.

toad-eat-er (tōd'ēt"ẽr), *n.* a mean flatterer; one who curries favor.

toad-fish (tōd'fĭsh"), *n.* a salt-water fish with a large head and wide mouth.

toad-flax (tōd'flăks"), *n.* a weed akin to the cultivated snapdragon, with yellow and orange flowers: commonly called *butter-and-eggs.*

toad-stool (tōd'stōōl"), *n.* an umbrella-shaped poisonous mushroom.

toad-y (tōd'ĭ), *n.* [*pl.* toadies (-ĭz)], a mean flatterer; one who caters to the rich or powerful for the sake of gain or favor; a toadeater: *v.t.* and *v.i.* [*p.t.* and *p.p.* toadied, *p.pr.* toadying], to flatter for selfish reasons.

toad-y-ism (tōd'ĭ-ĭzm), *n.* selfish or mean flattery; the habit of currying favor with the rich or great.

toast (tōst), *n.* sliced bread browned by the heat of the fire; an after-dinner speech; one who is named when a health is drunk: *v.t.* to brown or heat at the fire; as, to *toast* bread; to show honor to in drinking; to name when a health is drunk.—*n.* **toaster.**

toast-mas-ter (tōst'mȧs"tẽr), *n.* one who presides over the drinking of healths after dinner, or who introduces after-dinner speakers.

to-bac-co (tō-băk'ō), *n.* [*pl.* tobaccos (-ōz)], an American plant of the nightshade family, the dried leaves of which are prepared and used for smoking and chewing, or as snuff.

to-bac-co bug (tō-băk'ō bŭg), a small insect which destroys the leaves of the tobacco plant by sucking the sap.

to-bac-co heart (tō-băk'ō härt), a disease marked by irregular action of the heart, caused by too constant use of tobacco.

to-bac-co-nist (tō-băk'ō-nĭst), *n.* a dealer in tobacco, cigars, etc.

to-bog-gan (tō-bŏg'ăn), *n.* a kind of long, flat sled, holding one or more persons, used for sliding down snow- or ice-covered hills: *v.i.* to slide downhill by means of such a sled; to slide rapidly as if coasting.

to-bog-gan slide (tō-bŏg'ăn slīd), a hill or inclined track prepared for coasting on a toboggan.

to-by (tō'bĭ), *n.* a small jug or mug in the form of an old man with a three-cornered hat.

toc-sin (tŏk'sĭn), *n.* an alarm bell or the sound made by it; any warning signal.

to-day (tōō-dā'), *n.* the present day; the present time: *adv.* on the present day; at the present time.

tod-dle (tŏd'l), *v.i.* [*p.t.* and *p.p.* toddled, *p.pr.* toddling], to walk with short, uncertain steps like a child: *n.* a walk marked by short, uncertain steps.

tod-dler (tŏd'lẽr), *n.* one who walks with short, unsteady steps; a young child.

tod-dy (tŏd'ĭ), *n.* a sweet juice obtained from certain palm trees of East India; a sweetened mixture of liquor and hot water.

to-do (tōō-dōō'), *n.* bustle; stir; fuss; as, to make a great *to-do* about nothing. [COLLOQ.]

toe (tō), *n.* one of the five digits of the foot; the front of the foot, or of a stocking or other foot covering: opposite to *heel*; the fore part of a horse's hoof; anything resembling a toe; a projection: *v.t.* [*p.t.* and *p.p.* toed, *p.pr.* toeing], to touch, reach, or strike with the tip of the foot; as, to *toe* the mark before starting a race; to attach the foot of (an upright timber) to a beam by nails driven slantwise.

toe-nail (tō'nāl"), *n.* the horny scale that protects the end of the toes on the human foot.

tof-fee (tŏf'ĭ), *n.* a sweetmeat; molasses taffy. Also, toffy.

tog (tŏg), *v.t.* and *v.i.* to dress up; as, he was all *togged* up. [SLANG.]

to-ga (tō'gȧ), *n.* [*pl.* togas (-gȧz), togæ (-jē)], the loose outer garment worn by the ancient Romans.

to-geth-er (tōō-gĕth'ẽr), *adv.* in company or association; as, to live *together* or walk *together*; mutually; as, to weep *together*; in union or concert; as, to mix things *together*; in succession; as, his troubles all came *together*.

tog-ger-y (tŏg'ẽr-ĭ), *n.* clothes; articles of dress or finery. [SLANG.]

tog-gle (tŏg'l), *n.* on shipboard, a small wooden pin or key to fasten a rope or a chain into a loop or ring; on clothing, a button or frog; in machinery, a device with an elbow-shaped joint.

tog-gle joint (tŏg'l joint), a joint in machinery like an elbow or knee joint.

togs (tŏgz), *n.pl.* toggery; clothes, especially new or showy ones. [SLANG.]

toil (toil), *n.* labor or work that tires, especially the body; exertion that tires the mind or body; *pl.* a snare or net: *v.i.* to labor or work with pain or fatigue; to be busy or work hard, usually with the body; to make slow and labored progress; as, he *toiled* up the hill.—*n.* toiler.

Syn., *n.* task, drudgery.

toi-let (toi'lĕt), *n.* a dressing table; the act of dressing, including bathing, etc.; style or manner of dressing; attire or dress; a room for dressing, bathing, etc.; a lavatory. Also, toilette.

toi-let wa-ter (toi'lĕt wô'tẽr), a fragrant liquid used in the bath; perfumed liquid.

toil-some (toil'sŭm), *adj.* laborious or tiresome; wearisome; wearied with labor; as, the *toilsome* and patient oxen. —*adv.* toilsomely.—*n.* toilsomeness.

To-kay (tō-kā'), *n.* a kind of large, sweet, white or purple grape; a rich wine, originally from Tokay, in Hungary.

to-ken (tō'kn), *n.* a mark or sign; a memorial or souvenir; as, a *token* of affection, respect, etc.; a symbol or sign of authority, right, pledge, etc.; a piece of money whose face value is more than its real value.

told (tōld), past tense and past participle of the verb *tell*.

To-le-do (tō-lē'dō), *n.* a sword or sword-blade of the finest temper, made originally at Toledo, Spain.

tol-er-a-ble (tŏl'ẽr-ȧ-bl), *adj.* capable of being borne or endured; as, his conduct was scarcely *tolerable*; endurable; supportable; fairly good; as, the work was *tolerable*.—*adv.* tolerably.

tol-er-ance (tŏl'ẽr-ăns), *n.* endurance; willingness to bear with others; as, a lack of *tolerance* is often the cause of religious disputes.

tol-er-ant (tŏl'ẽr-ănt), *adj.* willing to endure; willing to bear with others; forbearing; as, a *tolerant* attitude; able to take without harm large doses of dangerous drugs.—*adv.* tolerantly.

tol-er-ate (tŏl'ẽr-āt), *v.t.* to bear or endure; as, to *tolerate* a person one does not like; endure without harm, as a dose of a poisonous drug; permit; allow without hindering; as, to *tolerate* abuses.

tol-er-a-tion (tŏl"ẽr-ā'shŭn), *n.* the act of bearing or enduring; the allowing of that which is not wholly approved, especially of the right of private judgment in religious matters.

toll (tōl), *n.* the sound of a bell slowly and evenly repeated, as during funerals; a duty or tax on travelers or goods passing along a public road or bridge; a tax or duty paid for some privilege; pay taken for services; as, a miller takes *toll* for grinding grain: *v.i.* to sound or ring slowly, as a bell: *v.t.* to ring with slow, heavy strokes; announce by slow strokes; as, to *toll* the hour; to ring slow, even strokes for, as during a funeral; as, to *toll* a departed bishop; in hunting, to entice (game) by arousing curiosity.

to-lu (tō-lōō'), *n.* a fragrant medicinal balsam obtained from a South American tree.

tol-u-ol (tŏl'ū-ōl; tŏl'ū-ŏl), *n.* a chemical compound similar to benzene, obtained from balsam, coal tar, etc., and used in manufacturing dyes, explosives, etc.: called also *toluene*. Also, toluole.

Tom (tŏm), *n.* a shortened form of *Thomas*: tom, the male of certain animals, especially the cat.

tom-a-hawk (tŏm'ȧ-hôk), *n.* a hatchet used by the North American Indians in war and the chase: *v.t.* to strike, or kill, with such a hatchet.

to-ma-to (tō-mā'tō; tō-mä'tō), *n.* [*pl.* tomatoes (-tōz)], *n.* a garden plant of the nightshade family; the red or yellow edible fruit of this plant.

tomb (tōōm), *n.* a grave, or vault; a monument erected to the memory of the dead: *v.t.* to put in a grave or vault.

tom-boy (tŏm'boi"), *n.* a wild, romping girl with boyish ways; a hoyden.

tomb-stone (tōōm'stōn"), *n.* a stone marking a grave; a monument to the dead.

tom-cat (tŏm'kăt"), *n.* a full-grown domestic cat of the male sex.

tom-cod (tŏm'kŏd"), *n.* a small eatable fish of the cod family.

tome (tōm), *n.* a large book; a weighty volume; one volume of a work.

tom-fool (tŏm'fōōl"), *n.* a great fool; a silly trifler. [COLLOQ.]

tom-fool-er-y (tŏm"fōōl'ẽr-ĭ), *n.* nonsense; ridiculous trifling; silliness.

Tom-my At-kins (tŏm'ĭ ăt'kĭnz), a popular name for the British private soldier, frequently shortened to "Tommy."

Tom-my-waacs (tŏm'ĭ-wăks"), *n.pl.* in the World War, the popular name for the British "Women's Army Auxiliary Corps": a word spelled from the initials of the organization.

to-mor-row (tōō-mŏr'ō), *n.* the day after the present day; the

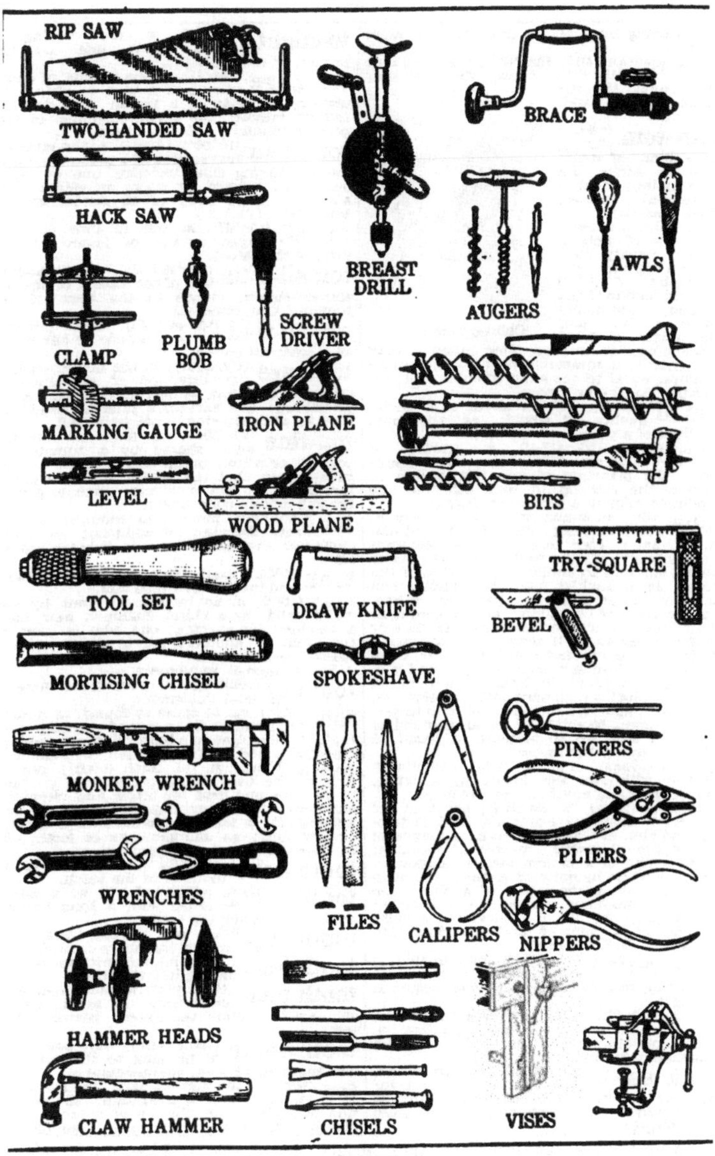
RIP SAW
TWO-HANDED SAW
BREAST DRILL
BRACE
HACK SAW
AUGERS
AWLS
CLAMP
PLUMB BOB
SCREW DRIVER
MARKING GAUGE
IRON PLANE
LEVEL
WOOD PLANE
BITS
TRY-SQUARE
TOOL SET
DRAW KNIFE
BEVEL
MORTISING CHISEL
SPOKESHAVE
PINCERS
MONKEY WRENCH
PLIERS
WRENCHES
FILES
CALIPERS
NIPPERS
HAMMER HEADS
CLAW HAMMER
CHISELS
VISES

TOOLS

next coming day: *adv.* on or for the day after to-day.

tom-tit (tŏm'tĭt"; tŏm"tĭt'), *n.* a small bird with either black, white, or gray feathers; the titmouse; in England, the wren.

tom-tom (tŏm'-tŏm"), *n.* a kind of drum used in Africa, the East Indies, and other Oriental countries. Also, **tam-tam.**

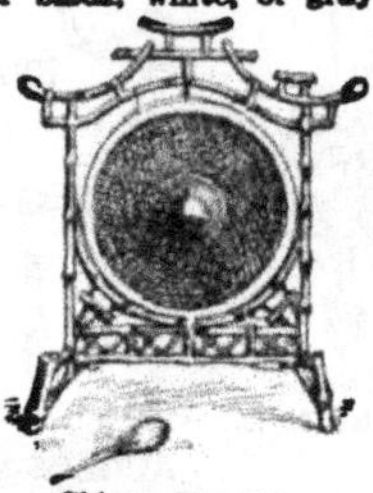

Chinese Tom-tom

ton (tŭn), *n.* a measure of weight, usually twenty hundredweight; the weight of 2,240 pounds, used in Great Britain, commonly called a *long ton;* the weight of 2,000 pounds, used in America, often called a *short ton;* a unit of measurement for cargo space in ships, equal to one hundred cubic feet; as, a ship of 6,000 *tons* burden.

ton-al (tōn'ăl), *adj.* pertaining to a special quality of sound; as, the *tonal* qualities of a piano.

to-nal-i-ty (tō-năl'ĭ-tĭ), *n.* quality of sound in a musical composition; the principle of key relationship in music; the relation to each other of the shades of color in a picture or design.

tone (tōn), *n.* sound, or quality of sound; note; accent; key; quality of the voice; as, a high *tone;* interval between two successive whole sound-steps in the major scale: opposite to *semitone;* condition of the body; as, a healthy *tone;* the quality and harmony of the colors of a painting; a hue, tint, or shade of color, etc.; as, a brown *tone;* the general character or tendency; as, the *tone* of the rebuke made it acceptable; the sound of the voice as expressive of feeling; as, there was contempt in her *tone:* *v.t.* [*p.t.* and *p.p.* toned, *p.pr.* toning], to bring to a required shade or color: *v.i.* to harmonize in color; as, the wall paper *tones* with the curtains.—**to tone down,** to soften or lessen in sound or color.—**to tone up,** to heighten in sound or color; to strengthen in health.

tongs (tôngz), *n.pl.* a metal instrument with two legs joined by a hinge, used for grasping anything; as, fire *tongs.*

tongue (tŭng), *n.* the fleshy organ in the mouth of mammals, used in tasting, and also, in man, for speech; a language; as, the French *tongue;* manner of speaking; as, he spoke in a broken *tongue;* discourse; the clapper or hammer of a bell; the strip of leather under the lacing of a shoe; the pole of a two-horse vehicle; as, the *tongue* of a wagon; the pin of a buckle; the point of a flame; a point of land extending into the water.—*adj.* **tongued.**

tongue-tied (tŭng'tīd"), *adj.* unable to speak clearly because the connecting membrane beneath the tongue is too short.

ton-ic (tŏn'ĭk), *adj.* pertaining to sounds; tending to strengthen; bracing: *n.* the keynote of a scale or composition in music; a strengthening medicine.

ton-ic sol-fa (tŏn'ĭk sōl"fä'), in music, a system of notation for the scale, in which the usual staff symbols are discarded for letters and the syllables *do, re, mi,* etc.

to-night (tōō-nīt'), *n.* the coming or present night: *adv.* on the present or coming night.

ton-nage (tŭn'āj), *n.* the weight of goods carried in a boat or ship; the carrying capacity of a vessel; the duty or toll on vessels; the entire shipping of any port or country. Also, **tunnage.**

ton-neau (tō"nō'; tŭn-ō'), *n.* the rounded rear section of a passenger automobile, having sides inclosing one or more seats, and entered by doors on either side; also, the entire body of an automobile of this kind. [FR.]

ton-sil (tŏn'sĭl), *n.* one of two almond-shaped masses of tissue at the sides of the throat.

ton-sil-li-tis (tŏn"sĭ-lī'tĭs), *n.* inflammation of the tonsils, or the two almond-shaped glands at the base of the tongue. Also, **tonsilitis.**

ton-so-ri-al (tŏn-sō'rĭ-ăl), *adj.* pertaining to a barber or his work; as, a *tonsorial* parlor.

ton-sure (tŏn'shŭr), *n.* the act of cutting the hair, or of shaving the crown, of the head, as by persons entering the priesthood; the part of a priest's head left bare by such shaving.—*adj.* **tonsured.**

ton-tine (tŏn'tēn; tŏn-tēn'), *n.* an annuity shared by a number of persons, or a loan raised on life annuities, on such a plan that the shares of those dying first go to the last survivors; such a policy; the subscribers collectively.

too (tōō), *adv.* more than enough; as, *too* long; likewise; in addition; as, he is going *too;* over and above; as, it is *too* heavy; also.

took (tŏŏk), past tense of the transitive and intransitive verb *take.*

tool (tōōl), *n.* an instrument used by the hand, as a chisel, hammer, saw, etc.; a machine for shaping; one who is used as the agent of another: *v.t.* to shape with a chisel, saw, file, etc.

Syn. n. utensil, implement.

tool-ing (tōōl'ĭng), *n.* work done with a hand implement.

toot (tōōt), *v.t.* to cause to sound, as a horn or flute: *v.i.* to sound shortly and rapidly: *n.* a blast on a horn; a short, sudden, repeated sound, as from a horn, whistle, etc.

tooth (tōōth), *n.* [*pl.* teeth (tēth)], one of the hard, bony projections growing in the jaws and used for biting and chewing; any projection resembling such a bone; as, a gear-*tooth;* a taste or fondness for a certain kind of food; as, she has a sweet *tooth:* *v.t.* to indent or form into jagged points.

tooth-ache (tōōth'āk"), *n.* pain in a tooth or in the teeth.

tooth-brush (tōōth'brŭsh"), *n.* a small brush with a long handle used for cleansing the teeth.

toothed (tōōtht), *adj.* having teeth of a given sort; as, sharp-*toothed.*

tooth-less (tōōth'lĕs), *adj.* without teeth; having lost the teeth.

tooth-pick (tōōth'pĭk"), *n.* a sharp-pointed instrument of wood, quill, etc., used to clear the spaces between the teeth.

tooth-some (tōōth'sŭm), *adj.* palatable or pleasing to the taste.—*adv.* **toothsomely.**—*n.* **toothsomeness.**

top (tŏp), *n.* the highest part; the summit; as, the *top* of a mountain; the upper side or surface; as, the *top* of a table; the highest person, place, or rank; the crown of the head; a small platform at the head of the lower mast of ships; a child's toy which can be made to spin upon its point: *v.t.* [*p.t.* and *p.p.* topped, *p.pr.* topping], to put a cover over; to rise to the highest point of; to surmount; to excel or surpass; cut off the upper part of, as a plant: *adj* pertaining to the highest part; highest; chief.

to-paz (tō'păz), *n.* a yellow, brown, or greenish semiprecious stone; the yellow sapphire.

top-boots (tŏp'bōōts"), *n.pl.* high boots having tops which are often light-colored, used for riding.

top-coat (tŏp'kōt"), *n.* a coat for outside wear; an overcoat.

top-er (tōp'ẽr), *n.* a drunkard; one who is habitually intoxicated.

top-gal-lant (tŏp"găl'ănt; tō-găl'ănt), *adj.* situated above the topmast of a vessel: as, a *topgallant* sail: *n.* such a mast or sail.

top-heav-y (tŏp'hĕv"ĭ), *adj.* heavier at the top than at the bottom.—*n.* **top-heaviness.**

To-phet (tō'fĕt), *n.* a place of uncertain location in the Holy Land, possibly in the Valley of Hinnom, where human sacrifices by fire are supposed to have been made in honor of a god called Moloch; hence, hell. Also, **Topheth.**

top-ic (tŏp'ĭk), *n.* a subject of discourse, conversation, or argument; also, the general or main subject of a conversation or composition.

Syn. theme, question, issue.

top-i-cal (tŏp'ĭ-kăl), *adj.* of or pertaining to a special subject; as, a *topical* recitation; relating to a place; local, not general.—*adv.* **topically.**

top-knot (tŏp'nŏt"), *n.* the crest or tuft of feathers on a bird's head; a knot of hair worn on the head, as by women.

top-mast (tŏp'măst), *n.* the second mast from the deck of a ship.

top-most (tŏp'mōst), *adj.* highest; at the summit.

to-pog-ra-pher (tō-pŏg'rá-fẽr), *n.* one who has scientific understanding of the geographical features of any region, or of the earth's surface in general.

top-o-graph-ic (tŏp"ō-grăf'ĭk), *adj.* descriptive of the geographical features of a particular place, or of the earth's surface. Also, **topographical.**—*adv.* **topographically.**

to-pog-ra-phy (tō-pŏg'rá-fĭ), *n.* the scientific description of a particular region or place; the geographical features of the earth's surface; the art of making a map on which are shown the physical characteristics of any place.

top-ping (tŏp'ĭng), *adj.* rising above or overlooking; as, *topping* mountains: *n.* the act of cutting off the highest part; as, the *topping* of plants.

top-ple (tŏp'l), *v.t.* [*p.t.* and *p.p.* toppled, *p.pr.* toppling], to overturn: *v.i.* to fall forward; tumble down; to project, as if about to fall.

top-sail (tŏp'sāl"; tŏp'sl), *n.* the second sail from the deck of a ship.

top-ser-geant (tŏp'sär"jĕnt), *n.* the sergeant of the highest rank in a company.

top-sy-tur-vy (tŏp'sĭ-tûr'vĭ), *adv.* upside down; in confusion: *adj.* being upset; disordered; confused.

toque (tōk), *n.* a kind of bonnet: a woman's close-fitting hat with no brim.

to-rah (tō'rä), *n.* in Jewish tradition, a precept or law; divine revelation: **Torah,** the Pentateuch or Law of Moses. Also, **thorah.**

torch (tôrch), *n.* a flaming light, made of wood, waxed tow, etc., and carried in the hand; a lamp on the end of a pole to be carried in a procession.

torch-light (tôrch'līt"), *n.* the illumination given by torches.

tor-chon lace (tôr'shŏn lās; Fr. tôr"-shôN'), a strong linen lace made in geometrical patterns.

tore (tōr), past tense of the transitive and intransitive verb *tear.*

to-re-a-dor (tō"rē-ā-dôr'; tôr"ē-á-dôr'), *n.* a bullfighter, especially one who rides a horse.

tor-ment (tôr'mĕnt), *n.* extreme pain; the infliction of torture; anguish; that which causes pain or anguish: *v.t.* (tôr-mĕnt') to put to extreme pain of mind or body; to torture; colloquially, to tease.—*n.* **tormentor.**

torn (tōrn), past participle of the transitive and intransitive verb *tear.*

tor-na-do (tôr-nā'dō), *n.* [*pl.* tornadoes (-dōz)], a violent and destructive whirlwind, in the form of a funnel-shaped cloud moving along a narrow path for long distances.

tor-pe-do (tôr-pē'dō), *n.* [*pl.* torpedoes (-dōz)], a cigar-shaped, self-moving, under-water projectile, carrying explosives, which blows up a ship on contact with it: usually fired from a submarine or torpedo boat; any shell or case filled with explosives, as an undersea mine, a signal cartridge on a railroad, etc.; a kind of firework which explodes when thrown against a hard surface, as a pavement; a kind of fish: *v.t.* to destroy or blow up by a torpedo; as, to *torpedo* a warship.

tor-pe-do boat (tôr-pē'dō bōt), a small, rapid war vessel for firing torpedoes, carrying light guns and torpedo tubes; a submarine.

tor-pe-do-boat de-stroy-er (tôr-pē'dō-bōt dē-stroi'ẽr), a large, very rapid torpedo boat equipped to pursue and destroy torpedo boats and submarines, as well as to fire torpedoes.

tor-pid (tôr'pĭd), *adj.* numb; sluggish; as, a *torpid* liver; inactive; as, a snake is *torpid* in winter; dull; stupid.—*adv.* **torpidly.**—*n.* **torpidness, torpidity.**

tor-por (tôr'pôr), *n.* loss of feeling or motion; dulness; numbness.

torque (tôrk), *n.* a twisted collar or necklace worn by certain early barbarians, such as the Gauls and Britons.

tor-rent (tŏr'ĕnt), *n.* a violent and rapid flow; as, a *torrent* of water; a *torrent* of abuse, etc.; heavy fall or downpour; as, a *torrent* of rain; a violent stream, rising suddenly and rushing rapidly along; as, the brook becomes a *torrent* after a heavy rain.—*adj.* **torrential.**

tor-rid (tŏr'ĭd), *adj.* dried with heat; extremely hot; as, a *torrid* desert; burning; parching; as, a *torrid* climate.

Syn. scorching, sultry.

tor-sion (tôr'shŭn), *n.* the act of turning or twisting; the wrenching or twisting of a body by lateral force, or side motion; the state of being twisted.—*adj.* **torsional.**

tor-so (tôr'sō), *n.* [*pl.* torsos (-sōz); torsi (-sē)], the trunk of a human body;

the trunk of a statue, especially one having the head or limbs broken off.

tort (tôrt), *n.* in law, any wrong, injury, or damage for which a civil suit can be brought.

tor-toise (tôr'tŭs; tôr'tĭs), *n.* a turtle, especially one that lives on land or in fresh water.

tor-toise shell (tôr'tŭs shĕl; tôr'tĭs shĕl), the horny outer covering of the turtles; this shell prepared for use in the manufacture of articles for ornament and use.

tor-tu-ous (tôr'tū-ŭs), *adj.* crooked; twisted; winding; as, a *tortuous* path; underhand; indirect; deceitful; as, a *tortuous* business policy.—*adv.* **tortuously.**—*n.* **tortuousness.**
Syn. roundabout, devious.
Ant. (see direct, straight).

tor-ture (tôr'tūr), *n.* agony of mind or body; extreme pain; infliction of pain as a punishment; as, the rack was an instrument of *torture*: *v.t.* [*p.t.* and *p.p.* tortured, *p.pr.* torturing], to punish with, or as with, torture; put to the rack.—*n.* **torturer.**
Syn., n. torment, anguish, agony.

To-ry (tō'rĭ), *n.* [*pl.* Tories (-rĭz)], formerly, in English politics, one who upheld the full rights of the crown; opposite to *Whig;* in the American Revolution, an American who favored yielding to Great Britain: hence, often used to designate those who are opposed to change.

To-ry-ism (tō'rĭ-ĭzm), *n.* the principles of the Tories, now called Conservatives, of England.

toss (tôs), *v.t.* to throw with the hand; to throw upward; to pitch; lift or throw up, as the head, quickly; put into violent motion; to cause to rise and fall; as, the waves *tossed* the vessel: *v.i.* to roll or tumble; be made to rise and fall: *n.* a throwing upward; a pitch; a fling; as, a *toss* of the head.

toss-ing (tôs'ĭng), *n.* the act of throwing upward, as a ball; a rolling or tumbling; as, the *tossing* of the waves.

tot (tŏt), *n.* anything very small, especially a little child.

to-tal (tō'tăl), *adj.* whole; not divided; as, the *total* amount; complete; utter; as, *total* darkness: *n.* the whole sum or amount: *v.t.* to find the sum of; add; as, to *total* a column of figures: *v.i.* to amount to a certain sum, number, etc.—*adv.* **totally.**

to-tal-i-ty (tō-tăl'ĭ-tĭ), *n.* the state or quality of being whole; the entire quantity, amount, or sum.

to-tem (tō'tĕm), *n.* an animal or object conceived among savages, as American Indians, as being closely related to a tribe or clan; a carved or painted representation of this relationship, as a *totem* pole.

tot-ter (tŏt'ĕr), *v.i.* to shake as if about to fall; as, a house will *totter* in a storm if its foundation is not firm; be unsteady on one's feet; lose strength and firmness, as a tree.

tot-ter-y (tŏt'ĕr-ĭ), *adj.* shaking as if about to fall; unsteady; as, the old man is very *tottery* on his feet.

tou-can (tōō-kän'; tōō'kăn), *n.* a tropical American fruit-eating bird with a large beak and bright-colored plumage.

touch (tŭch), *v.t.* to come in contact with; as, to *touch* something with the hand; to perceive or know by feeling; to handle slightly; to concern; to refer to in a light manner; as, in conversation, to *touch* a subject briefly; add a light stroke to; reach; affect the senses or feelings of; as, an act of kindness will *touch* a person; meddle with; disturb; injure or hurt; to affect to a slight extent; as, plants *touched* by frost: *v.i.* to be in contact; as, the two forms *touch;* to speak of a subject lightly: with *on* or *upon;* as, in the course of his talk, he *touched* upon the gravity of such an offense; to call at a port: with *at:* *n.* the act or state of coming or being in contact; contact; sense of feeling; sensation; the manner of action of the hand, as on a musical instrument; as, she has a light *touch;* the peculiar manner of execution, as of a painting, etc.; as, the *touch* of an expert; a single stroke on a painting, etc.; close understanding or sympathy; as, in close *touch* with a friend; a light attack of a disease; as, a *touch* of rheumatism.

touch-a-ble (tŭch'ȧ-bl), *adj.* capable of being felt or handled; fit for contact.

touch-down (tŭch'doun"), *n.* in football, the forcing of the ball through the opponents' goal.

touch-ing (tŭch'ĭng), *p.adj.* affecting; pathetic; as, a *touching* scene in a play: *n.* the act of coming in contact with: *prep.* with respect to; concerning; as, *touching* the matter referred to in your letter.

touch-me-not (tŭch'mē-nŏt"), *n.* a plant whose ripe seed containers burst open and scatter the seeds; the squirting cucumber; the balsam.

touch-stone (tŭch'stōn"), *n.* a kind of black stone used for testing the fineness of gold and silver by the streak left on the stone when rubbed by the metal; hence, a criterion or test.

touch-wood (tŭch'wŏŏd"), *n.* decayed wood which easily catches fire and burns slowly; tinder.

touch-y (tŭch'ĭ), *adj.* irritable; peevish; easily offended.—*n.* **touchiness.**

tough (tŭf), *adj.* standing great strain without breaking; not easily broken or separated; as, *tough* wood; *tough* meat; able to endure hardship or strain; strong; firm; sticky; as, *tough* pitch; colloquially, difficult; as, a *tough* problem; hard to influence; stubborn; colloquially, rough and bad: *n.* colloquially, a rough fellow; a rowdy.—*adv.* **toughly.**—*n.* **toughness.**

tough-en (tŭf'n), *v.t.* and *v.i.* to make or become hard to break or separate; make or become strong, stubborn, etc.

tou-pee (tōō-pē'), *n.* a small wig; a curled front of false hair.

tour (tōōr), *n.* a journey, especially one that begins and ends in the same place; an excursion or trip; a long journey; a circuit, for inspection, etc.; as, the watchman made his *tour* of the building: *v.i.* to make a journey: *v.t.* to make a circuit of or journey through; as, to *tour* the country by motor car.

tour-ing car (tōōr'ĭng kär), a large passenger automobile, suitable to be used for long trips.

tour-ist (tōōr'ĭst), *n.* one who makes a journey, usually for sightseeing; an excursionist; a traveler.

tour-ma-line (tōōr'mȧ-lĭn), *n.* a mineral that is usually black, but sometimes red, blue, green, or even without color; a semiprecious stone, of a very translucent pale lavender color. Also, **turmaline.**

tour-na-ment (tōōr'nȧ-mĕnt), *n.* in the Middle Ages, a contest, or series of contests, with blunt lances and swords, ɪy knights on horseback; a trial of skill in ports; as, a golf *tournament.* Also, **tourney.**

:our-ney (tōōr'nĭ; tûr'nĭ), *n.* a tournament or trial of skill: *v.i.* to take ɪart in a tournament, or knightly contest.

:our-ni-quet (tōōr'nĭ-kĕt), *n.* a device for stopping the flow of ɪlood when an artery in the arm or leg, etc., s cut.

:ou-sle (tou'zl), *v.t.* to pull about roughly; put in disorder; rumple; tumble. ɪlso, **touzle.** [Colloq.]

:out (tout; tōōt), *v.i.* to look out for customers; secretly to watch race ɪorses in training, in order to give private nformation to customers to guide them in ɪetting: *n.* one who looks out for customers; ɪne who gives tips on horses in a race. Colloq. and Cant.]

:out en-sem-ble (tōō"tăN" săN'bl), the general effect; all ɪarts of something together. [Fr.]

:ow (tō), *n.* the coarse part of flax or hemp; something dragged, as through water ɪy a rope; act of dragging; state of being ɪragged: *v.t.* to drag, as a vessel, through the ɪater by means of a rope.

:ow-age (tō'āj), *n.* the act of pulling through the water by a chain or ɪope; the price paid for towing, or pulling, ɪ boat, etc., through the water.

:o-ward (tō'ẽrd; tōrd), *prep.* in the direction of; with a tendency to; ɪpproaching to: *adj.* close in time; at hand; ɪs, great events were *toward;* ready to learn; ɪpt; as, a *toward* child. Also, *prep.* **towards.**

:ow-boat (tō'bōt"), *n.* a boat, especially a powerful steam vessel, used ɪor pulling other vessels; a tug.

:ow-el (tou'ĕl), *n.* a cloth for drying anything wet, as dishes.

:ow-el-ing (tou'ĕl-ĭng), *n.* material from which drying cloths are made.

:ow-er (tou'ẽr), *n.* a high structure, square or circular, rising above its surɪoundings, and either standing alone or atɪached to a building; ɪs, a watch*tower;* a church *tower;* a citadel or fortress: *v.i.* ɪo rise to a great ɪeight; to overtop ɪther objects; to ɪoar, as some birds.

Leaning Tower of Pisa

:ow-er-ing (tou'ẽr-ĭng), *p.adj.* very high; lofty; as, a *towering* tree or building; extreme or violent; as, he was in a *towering* rage.

:ow-head (tō'-hĕd"), ɪ. a person, usually child, having exɪremely pale yellow, ɪlmost white, hair.

:ow-line (tō'līn"), *n.* a line or rope used for pulling, ɪr towing, vessels.

:own (toun), *n.* any collection of houses, making a distinct place with a name, ɪarger than a village but not organized as a ɪity; the citizens or voters of such a place; ɪn New England, a unit of local government ɪf a certain definite character; in other states, ɪ unit of local government more or less simple ɪn character than that in New England; a closely populated place as contrasted with the country.

town clerk (toun klûrk), an official who acts as secretary for a town organization.

town hall (toun hôl), a public building belonging to a community, containing public offices and used for public meetings. Also, **townhouse.**

towns-folk (tounz'fōk"), *n.* the people of a town or community.

town-ship (toun'shĭp), *n.* a district, or unit of local government; a rural community organized as a unit of government; a division of land six miles square divided into thirty-six sections, of one square mile each; in Canada, a section of a county.

towns-man (tounz'măn), *n.* a citizen of a town; a fellow-citizen.

towns-peo-ple (tounz'pē"pl), *n.* the people of a town; townsfolk.

tow-path (tō'páth"), *n.* a path beside a canal or other stream along which men or animals walk in towing boats.

tox-e-mi-a (tŏk-sē'mĭ-ȧ), *n.* blood poisoning. Also, **toxæmia.**

tox-ic (tŏk'sĭk), *adj.* of or pertaining to poison; poisonous.

tox-i-col-o-gist (tŏk"sĭ-kŏl'ō-jĭst), *n.* one skilled in the science of poisons and their effects, etc.

tox-i-col-o-gy (tŏk"sĭ-kŏl'ō-jĭ), *n.* the science of poisons and their effects, etc.—*adj.* **toxicological.**

tox-in (tŏk'sĭn), *n.* a poison produced by secretion in animal or vegetable organisms. Also, **toxine.**

toy (toi), *n.* a child's plaything; something of no real value; a bauble: *v.i.* to trifle; as, to *toy* with another's affections; to play with something or handle something lovingly; as, she *toyed* with the child's curls.

trace (trās), *n.* a mark left by a past event, or by the passing of a person or thing; a footprint; a remainder; a small quantity; as, the food contained a *trace* of poison: *pl.* the straps by which a horse is attached to a vehicle: *v.t.* [*p.t.* and *p.p.* traced, *p.pr.* tracing], to form carefully, as letters; to delineate or show by marks; as, to *trace* a design on cloth; to follow and seek to find by tracks or indications; as, to *trace* a thief; to make out; find out the course or development of; follow exactly; copy, especially a drawing, by covering it with a transparent sheet upon which the drawing is reproduced; to follow out the course of; as, to *trace* the development of a nation.

Syn., *n.* track, token, sign, mark, vestige.

trace-a-ble (trās'ȧ-bl), *adj.* capable of being followed, copied, etc.

trac-er (trās'ẽr), *n.* a shell or bullet whose smoky course can be seen after firing; one whose business is to try to locate lost letters, packages, etc.

trac-er-y (trās'ẽr-ĭ), *n.* a fine, delicately executed design, as in carved stone.

tra-che-a (trā'kē-ȧ; trȧ-kē'ȧ), *n.* [*pl.* tracheæ (-ē)], the windpipe; the main air-tube leading to the lungs.

tra-cho-ma (trȧ-kō'mȧ), *n.* inflammation or soreness of the eyelids; granular conjunctivitis.

trac-ing (trās'ĭng), *n.* the act of one who follows up or copies; that which is traced, or marked out, as the copy of the lines of a drawing made by marking on thin paper over the original.

track (trăk), *n.* a mark or impression left by the foot; a trace; a beaten path; a road; a course or way; as, a race *track*; a pair of metal rails for cars or trains to run upon: *v.t.* to seek or follow by means of traces or signs left by someone; to traverse; to make footprints upon or with; as, to *track* mud into the house; to wear into a path or beaten road; as, constant passing has *tracked* a road through the woods.—*n.* **tracker.**

track-age (trăk'ăj), *n.* lines of railroad tracks; the right to use the tracks of another railroad.

track-less (trăk'lĕs), *adj.* pathless; without a road; without footprints; as, the *trackless* desert or forest.

tract (trăkt), *n.* a short pamphlet or leaflet, usually on some moral or religious subject; a large area of land; as, the desert is a vast *tract* of sand.

trac-ta-bil-i-ty (trăk"tȧ-bĭl'ĭ-tĭ), *n.* the quality of being easily managed or led.

trac-ta-ble (trăk'tȧ-bl), *adj.* docile; easily led or managed; as, a *tractable* child; easily handled or worked, as some metals.—*adv.* **tractably.**

tract-ate (trăk'tāt), *n.* a small book or treatise; a tract.

trac-tile (trăk'tĭl), *adj.* capable of being drawn out or lengthened; as, *tractile* metal.

trac-tion (trăk'shŭn), *n.* the act of drawing or pulling a body along a surface; as, electric *traction*.

trac-tion en-gine (trăk'shŭn ĕn'jĭn), a locomotive which runs on a road or field, not on a track.

trac-tion wheel (trăk'shŭn hwēl), a friction wheel which drives a locomotive or a machinery belt.

trac-tor (trăk'tŏr), *n.* that which draws, or is used in drawing; as, a farm *tractor* is a locomotive or gasoline engine used for drawing farm machinery; motor-driven containers used to draw loads about factories, stores, railway stations, etc.

trade (trād), *n.* an occupation; business; a particular means of livelihood learned and engaged in; buying and selling for money; commerce; traffic; as, the wheat *trade*, or the cotton *trade*; persons engaged in a particular business; as, the clothing *trade*: *pl.* the trade winds: *adj.* pertaining to, or carried on by, a special business or firm; commercial: *v.i.* to conduct a business; to buy and sell goods; to carry on commerce: followed by *with*: *v.t.* to exchange; as, to *trade* knives.

Syn., *n.* commerce, dealing, employment.

trade-mark (trād'märk"), *n.* a mark used by a merchant or manufacturer on his goods to distinguish them from the goods made or sold by other merchants or manufacturers.

trade name (trād nām), the commercial name of an article; the business name of a firm.

trad-er (trād'ĕr), *n.* one engaged in commerce; a merchant or storekeeper; a vessel engaged in commerce; one who barters or exchanges goods; as, a fur *trader* among the Indians.

trade school (trād skōōl), an institution, often public, where boys and girls, usually those who have been graduated from grammar schools, may learn trades.

trades-man (trādz'măn), *n.* [*pl.* tradesmen (-mĕn)], one who engages in buying and selling; a shopkeeper.

trades-peo-ple (trādz'pē"pl), *n.pl.* the employees in a store; people engaged in buying and selling commodities.

trade-un-ion (trād'ūn'yŭn), *n.* a society of workmen in any particular branch of industry, organized for the protection of their interests. Also, **trades-union.**

trade-un-ion-ism (trād'ūn"yŭn-ĭzm), *n.* the principles and practices of members of organized societies of workmen.

trade wind (trād wĭnd), a wind in or near the torrid zone which blows steadily in the same course, or *track*, toward the equator, from an easterly direction.

trad-ing (trād'ĭng), *adj.* pertaining to commerce or business; as, a *trading* company.

tra-di-tion (trȧ-dĭsh'ŭn), *n.* the oral handing down of information, opinions, doctrines, practices, etc., through successive generations, or from father to son; that which is so handed down; as, the *tradition* of King Arthur and the Round Table; an ancient custom or story; a story relating to historical characters but not itself based on fact; as, the *tradition* of George Washington and the cherry tree; any belief which owes its general acceptance to habit rather than to reason.

tra-di-tion-al (trȧ-dĭsh'ŭn-ăl), *adj.* of or pertaining to a custom, story, belief, etc., handed down from father to son; as, it is *traditional* to have fireworks on July 4th; not historically reliable; as, many of the Robin Hood stories are *traditional*, not actual. Also, **traditionary.**—*adv.* **traditionally.**

tra-duce (trȧ-dūs'), *v.t.* to defame or slander; to expose unjustly to shame.—*n.* **traducer.**

traf-fic (trăf'ĭk), *n.* business or trade; commerce; the business done by a railway, steamship line, etc., in carrying persons or goods; the congestion of passing of vehicles in a city street; as, it demands steady nerves to drive a car through the *traffic*: *v.i.* [*p.t.* and *p.p.* trafficked, *p.pr.* trafficking], to barter; to buy or sell goods: with *in*; to bargain; to do business in a mean spirit.—*n.* **trafficker.**

trag-a-canth (trăg'ȧ-kănth), *n.* a gum obtained from certain Asiatic or European trees, from which a thick mucilage is made.

tra-ge-di-an (trȧ-jē'dĭ-ăn), *n.* a writer of drama that presents the sad, solemn, or terrible aspects of life; an actor of such a play.

tra-gé-dienne (trȧ"zhā"dyĕn'; trȧ-jē"dĭ-ĕn'; trȧ-jē'dĭ-ĕn"), *n.* an actress of sad, solemn, or terrible drama. [Fr.]

trag-e-dy (trăj'ē-dĭ), *n.* [*pl.* tragedies (-dĭz)], a drama of which the outcome is bad, often fatal, for the hero or heroine; any work of literature of a similar character; a melancholy or fatal event; that quality which places grief or catastrophe on a plane which commands deep sympathy and respect.

trag-ic (trăj'ĭk), *adj.* pertaining to, or like, tragedy; as, a *tragic* play, or a *tragic* death; fatal; terrible. Also, **tragical.**—*adv.* **tragically.**

trag-i-com-e-dy (trăj"ĭ-kŏm'ē-dĭ), *n.* a play combining tragic and comic scenes and not having a fatal end.

trail (trāl), *v.t.* to draw or drag along the ground; to hunt or follow by tracking; as, to *trail* a rabbit: *v.i.* to fall or hang down or extend behind; as, her dress *trails* on the floor; to grow or climb at great length; as, the vine *trails* along the fence; to follow; as, the child *trails* after its mother; to go along in a leisurely fashion: *n.* a track left by a person or an animal; as, a bear's *trail*; a footpath or track through a wilderness; as, a blazed *trail* is made by chipping the bark of trees; anything drawn out in length or dragged on the ground.—*n.* **trailer.**

train (trān), *n.* a connected line of railroad cars; something drawn or dragged behind; as, the *train* of a dress; a retinue, or body of servants; a company or procession; the line of motor trucks, army wagons, etc., which carry supplies to an army; a series of connected things; as, a *train* of ideas; a course or process; a line of gunpowder laid to fire a charge; a heavy kind of Canadian sledge drawn by dogs: *v.t.* to instruct by practice; drill; discipline; educate; to aim or point at an object; as, to *train* a cannon upon the enemy; discipline or tame for use; as, to *train* a wild animal; to prepare for athletic contests or horse racing; to direct the growth of, as a plant: *v.i.* to prepare oneself for a contest of strength or skill; to drill.

train-er (trān'ẽr), *n.* an instructor, especially one who prepares men or horses for exercise of skill, races, etc.

train-ing (trān'ing), *n.* process of being drilled or prepared for an athletic contest, etc.; the state of being thus drilled; thorough instruction and ability along some special line; as, his *training* as an engineer was excellent.

train oil (trān oil), oil obtained from whales and other sea animals.

trait (trāt), *n.* a stroke or touch; a peculiar feature or characteristic; as, a *trait* of character.

trai-tor (trā'tẽr), *n.* [*fem.* traitress], one who is guilty of treason, or the betrayal of his country to an enemy; one who in time of war gives aid and comfort to the enemy; one who betrays a confidence or is false to a friend.

trai-tor-ous (trā'tẽr-ŭs), *adj.* capable or guilty of treason or of the betrayal of any trust or confidence; faithless; treacherous; false; characterized by treason. —*adv.* **traitorously.**

tra-jec-to-ry (trȧ-jĕk'tō-rĭ), *n.* [*pl.* trajectories (-rĭz)], the curve described by a body moving through space, as a ball or stone when thrown, or bullets, etc., discharged from guns.

tram (trăm), *n.* a kind of coal wagon used in mines; a railway; in England, a street railway car. Also, **tramcar.**

tram-mel (trăm'ĕl), *n.* a net used for catching birds, fish, etc.; a kind of shackle for controlling the motions of a horse; anything that hinders progress, action, or freedom, as a net or shackle: *v.t.* [*p.t.* and *p.p.* trammeled, trammelled, *p.pr.* trameling, trammelling], to hamper or hinder; to shackle or bind.

Syn., n. fetter, bond, chain, impediment.

tra-mon-tane (trȧ-mŏn'tān; trăm'ŏn-tān), *adj.* beyond the mountains; coming from the other side of the mountains; hence, foreign or savage: *n.* a foreigner or barbarian.

tramp (trămp), *v.t.* to step upon forcibly and repeatedly; colloquially, to travel over on foot; as, to *tramp* the highway: *v.i.* to wander on foot; to walk with a heavy step: *n.* a penniless foot traveler; a vagrant; a journey on foot; the sound of heavy footsteps; as, the *tramp* of soldiers.—*n.* **tramper.**

tram-ple (trăm'pl), *v.t.* to tread under the feet; to tread down, as dirt in a hole: *v.i.* to tread rapidly and repeatedly with the feet; to tread roughly, so as to hurt, crush, etc.; as, to *trample* upon a sore toe; to stamp: with *on* or *upon;* as, to *trample* on one's feelings.—*n.* **trampler.**

tram-road (trăm'rōd'), *n.* a roadway equipped with rails for wheeled vehicles; a railway in a mine.

tram-way (trăm'wā'), *n.* an English street railway; also, a metal track for cars, etc.

trance (trȧns), *n.* a state in which the soul appears to be absent from the body or to be rapt in visions; a deep, abnormal sleep while the heart and lungs continue to act; a swoon; a state of mental vacancy due to shock, etc.

tran-quil (trăn'kwĭl), *adj.* calm; quiet; as, a *tranquil* mind; undisturbed; not agitated; as, a *tranquil* lake in the mountains.—*adv.* **tranquilly.**

Syn. unruffled, peaceful, hushed.

Ant. (see noisy).

tran-quil-ize (trăn'kwĭl-īz), *v.t.* to make peaceful or calm.

tran-quil-li-ty (trăn-kwĭl'ĭ-tĭ; trăn-kwĭl'ĭ-tĭ), *n.* calmness; quiet; peace.

trans-act (trăns-ăkt'; trăn-zăkt'), *v.t.* to conduct or manage; as, to *transact* business; to carry through; to perform or do.—*n.* **transactor.**

trans-ac-tion (trăns-ăk'shŭn; trăn-zăk'shŭn), *n.* the management of any business or affair; that which is done or performed; a proceeding; affair; as, a dangerous *transaction: pl.* the report of the proceedings of a society, etc.

Syn. negotiation, occurrence.

trans-at-lan-tic (trăns'ăt-lăn'tĭk), *adj.* beyond the Atlantic; crossing the Atlantic; as, a *transatlantic* voyage.

tran-scend (trăn-sĕnd'), *v.t.* to rise above; to surpass; surmount; excel; exceed.

tran-scend-ence (trăn-sĕn'dĕns), *n.* the state or quality of being superior. Also, **transcendency.**

tran-scend-ent (trăn-sĕn'dĕnt), *adj.* surpassing others in excellence; superior or supreme; as, *transcendent* worth or ability—*adv.* **transcendently.**

tran-scen-den-tal (trăn'sĕn-dĕn'tăl), *adj.* pertaining to that which lies beyond the limits of human experience; vague; unknown; imaginary; fantastic; speculative; transcendent.—*adv.* **transcendentally.**

tran-scen-den-tal-ism (trăn'sĕn-dĕn'tăl-ĭzm), *n.* in philosophy, the going beyond human experience to find the main principles of knowledge; the theory that the spiritual side of human life rules over the actual facts of experience; impractical idealism.—*n.* **transcendentalist.**

tran-scribe (trăn-skrīb'), *v.t.* to copy or make a copy of; as, to *transcribe* shorthand notes on a typewriter.

tran-script (trăn'skrĭpt), *n.* a copy from an original; a copy; an imitation.

tran-scrip-tion (trăn-skrĭp'shŭn), *n.* a copy; the act of copying.

tran-sept (trăn'sĕpt), *n.* that part of a cruciform church crossing at right angles the main body of the building.

trans-fer (trăns-fûr'), *v.t.* [*p.t.* and *p.p.* transferred, *p.pr.* transferring], to convey or carry from one person or place to another; in law, to convey, as a right, title, etc.; as, to *transfer* a piece of land; to copy from one surface to another: *n.* (trăns'fûr), the conveyance or making over of a right, title, property, etc., from one person to another; the writing or deed by which such an exchange is made; a removal; the exchange of a soldier from one troop or company to another; a drawing or writing copied off from one surface to another.

trans-fer-a-ble (trăns-fûr'ȧ-bl), *adj.* capable of being carried to another place, or made over to another person; as, the ticket is *transferable.*

trans-fer-ence (trăns'fẽr-ĕns; trăns-fûr'ĕns), *n.* act of carrying, or state of being carried, from one place to another; a making over of property to another person.

trans-fig-u-ra-tion (trăns-fĭg"ŭ-rā'shŭn), *n.* a change of form or appearance: **Transfiguration**, the wonderful change in the personal appearance of Jesus Christ on the mount.—Matt. xvii. 1–9; the festival, August 6, celebrating this change.

trans-fig-ure (trăns-fĭg'ŭr), *v.t.* to change the outward form or appearance of; to change or transform to something high and glorious.

trans-fix (trăns-fĭks'), *v.t.* to pierce through with a pointed weapon; as, to *transfix* a body with a spear; to make stop as if pierced through; as, the sight that met his eyes *transfixed* him.

trans-form (trăns-fôrm'), *v.t.* to change the shape or appearance of; change the character of; as, to *transform* water into ice; to change the heart or mind of; to convert; as, to *transform* the nature of a child by kindness; change the form of (an algebraic equation) into another of different form without altering its value: *v.i.* to be or become changed.

trans-for-ma-tion (trăns"fôr-mā'shŭn), *n.* the act of changing the appearance of; the state of being changed in appearance; change of character, heart, etc.

trans-form-er (trăns-fôr'mẽr), *n.* a device for raising or lowering the potential of an alternating electrical current circuit.

trans-fuse (trăns-fūz'), *v.t.* [*p.t.* and *p.p.* transfused, *p.pr.* transfusing], to pour out of one vessel into another; to transfer, as blood, from the veins of one person or animal to those of another.

trans-fu-sion (trăns-fū'zhŭn), *n.* the act of transferring blood from the veins of one body to those of another; the transference of a liquid from one vessel to another; a mingling, as of liquids.

trans-gress (trăns-grĕs'), *v.t.* to break a law, rule, etc.: to sin: *v.t.* to break, sin against, or violate; as, to *transgress* a law.

trans-gres-sion (trăns-grĕsh'ŭn), *n.* the act of breaking any law or rule of moral duty; a fault; an offense; sin.

trans-gres-sor (trăns-grĕs'ẽr), *n.* one who breaks a rule or law; an offender; a sinner.

tran-sient (trăn'shĕnt), *adj.* fleeting; brief; passing; as, a *transient* view from the windows of a train; *transient* hopes; temporary; as, *transient* lodgers.—*n.* transience, transiency.

trans-it (trăn'sĭt), *n.* a passage through or over; as, the *transit* of goods through a state or country; conveyance; the passage of a heavenly body across the sun; an instrument used in surveying to measure angles: called in full a *transit theodolite.*

tran-si-tion (trăn-sĭzh'ŭn), *n.* the passage from one place, period, or state, to another; as, the *transition* from youth to old age; a change, as of a key in music, or of the subject of a speech or discourse.

tran-si-tion-al (trăn-sĭzh'ŭn-ăl), *adj.* of or pertaining to the passage from one state, time, or place, to another; as, the end of the 19th century was a *transitional* period.—*adv.* transitionally.

tran-si-tive (trăn'sĭ-tĭv), *adj.* able to make a passage across; in grammar, carrying action to a receiver; expressing action received: said of certain verbs.—*adv.* transitively.—*n.* transitiveness.

tran-si-to-ry (trăn'sĭ-tō-rĭ), *adj.* brief; continuing but a short time; fleeting; passing.—*adv.* transitorily.

trans-late (trăns-lāt'), *v.t.* to change from one language into another; as, to *translate* French into English; to interpret or make plain; as, to *translate* a cipher or code message; to remove suddenly to another place or position; remove to heaven without dying; as, Enoch was *translated*, that he should not see death.

trans-la-tion (trăns-lā'shŭn), *n.* the act of changing or removing; the act of changing from one language to another; a book, article, etc., changed from one language into another; a change or removal.

trans-la-tor (trăns-lā'tẽr), *n.* one who changes books, articles, etc., from one language into another; as, a *translator* of French into English.

trans-lu-cent (trăns-lū'sĕnt), *adj.* semi-transparent or capable of letting light through so as to allow objects to be indistinctly visible; as, *translucent* glass; allowing light to pass through.

trans-mi-gra-tion (trăns"mī-grā'shŭn), *n.* the going from one country, state, or condition, to another; especially, the passing of the soul at death from one body into that of another.

trans-mis-si-ble (trăns-mĭs'ĭ-bl), *adj.* capable of being passed from one to another, or through a body or substance.

trans-mis-sion (trăns-mĭsh'ŭn), *n.* the act of passing, or the state of being passed, through or over, as the *transmission* of telegrams, news, etc.; that part of the mechanism of an automobile which transfers the power from the engine to the driving shaft.

trans-mit (trăns-mĭt'), *v.t.* [*p.t.* and *p.p.* transmitted, *p.pr.* transmitting], to cause or allow to pass over or through; as, to *transmit* news by wire; conduct; as, to *transmit* heat; to send from one place or person to another; as, to *transmit* a package by post.—*n.* transmittal.

trans-mit-ter (trăns-mĭt'ẽr), *n.* one that sends over or through; especially, the mouthpiece of a telephone or the sending instrument of a telegraph.

rans-mut-a-ble (trăns-mūt'ȧ-bl), *adj.* capable of being hanged from one form or substance into nother.

rans-mu-ta-tion (trăns'mū-tā'shŭn), *n.* a change from one orm, nature, substance, or class, into another; s, the *transmutation* of metals.

rans-mute (trăns-mūt'), *v.t.* to change from one form, nature, substance, or class, into another; as, the chemist's ream is to *transmute* base metals into gold.

ran-som (trăn'sŭm), *n.* a crossbeam in a window or over a door; a rindow over a door, set on hinges so as to wing horizontally.

rans-par-en-cy (trăns-pâr'ĕn-sĭ), *n.* [*pl.* transparencies (-sĭz)], he state or quality of being easily seen hrough; that which is easily seen through, s a picture, placard, etc., shown by light hining through it from within; figuratively, implicity; as, the *transparency* of one's nature.

rans-par-ent (trăns-pâr'ĕnt), *adj.* having the property of allowng rays of light to pass through, or capable f being easily seen through; as, *transparent* auze; easy to understand; frank.

ran-spire (trăn-spīr'), *v.i.* to pass off as vapor; to breathe out; o become known or leak out: *v.t.* to throw ff, as vapor or moisture; to exhale or reathe out.

rans-plant (trăns-plănt'), *v.t.* to remove and fix or settle in another lace; as, to *transplant* trees; to remove and stablish; as, to *transplant* inhabitants or eople.

rans-plan-ta-tion (trăns'plăn-tā'shŭn), *n.* the act f removing and settling in another place; he state of being thus removed and settled.

rans-port (trăns-pōrt'), *v.t.* to carry across or from one place to nother; as, to *transport* goods or soldiers; n England, to banish to a penal colony cross the ocean; to carry away by violence f passion, or by pleasure; as, rage or joy *ansports* the soul: *n.* (trăns'pōrt), a coneyance for baggage or stores; a vessel mployed for carrying troops, stores, etc., rom one place to another; as, the *transports* rere accompanied by war vessels; a violent isplay of anger, passion, rapture, or any motion; as, the good news threw her into *transport* of joy.

rans-por-ta-tion (trăns'pōr-tā'shŭn), *n.* the act of carryng, or state of being carried, from one place o another; as, the *transportation* of goods, oldiers, etc.; the act of banishing, or sending o another place, for crime; as, the criminal as sentenced to *transportation;* means of onveyance; colloquially, a railway or steamhip ticket or pass, etc.

rans-pose (trăns-pōz'), *v.t.* to change the place or order of by puting one in the place of the other; as, to *anspose* letters or words; in music, to change ie key of; in algebra, to change (a term) om one side of an equation to the other y using the opposite sign.—*n.* transposal.

rans-po-si-tion (trăns'pō-zĭsh'ŭn), *n.* the act of changing ie place or order of; the state of being langed in order or place.

rans-ship (trăns-shĭp'), *v.t.* to move from one ship, car, etc., to nother for further conveyance. Also, anship.—*n.* transshipment, transhipment.

tran-sub-stan-ti-ate (trăn'sŭb-stăn'shĭ-āt), *v.t.* to change into another substance.

tran-sub-stan-ti-a-tion (trăn'sŭb-stăn'shĭ-ā'shŭn), *n.* a changing into another substance; a transformation; the doctrine held by the Roman Catholic Church that the bread and wine of the Eucharist, or Holy Communion, are changed into the body and blood of Christ by being consecrated.

trans-verse (trăns-vûrs'), *adj.* lying or being across or crosswise; as, *transverse* lines: *n.* anything that lies crosswise.—*adv.* transversely.

trap (trăp), *n.* a device, such as a snare or spring, to catch animals; as, the mouse*trap;* an ambush or snare; as, the soldiers were caught in a *trap;* a bend in a drain by which the liquid prevents the escape of sewer gas; colloquially, a light, twowheeled carriage; a machine for shooting into the air clay pigeons, balls, etc., to be shot at by sportsmen; a kind of rock: *pl.* colloquially, baggage; portable articles: *v.t.* [*p.t.* and *p.p.* trapped, *p.pr.* trapping], to catch in, or as in, a snare or spring; as, to *trap* a fox or rabbit, etc.; hence, to ambush or ensnare, as the enemy; to take by trick or stratagem; as, to *trap* a thief; to furnish with a trap, as a drain; colloquially, to dress up; adorn; *v.i.* to set snares, etc., for game.

trap-door (trăp'dōr'), *n.* a door which lifts up in a roof or floor to show an opening beneath.

tra-peze (trȧ-pēz'), *n.* a swinging horizontal bar suspended by a rope at each end and used by athletes in gymnasiums, etc.

tra-pe-zi-um (trȧ-pē'zĭ-ŭm), *n.* a plane figure bounded by four straight lines, of which no two are parallel; a bone of the wrist at the base of the thumb.

trap-e-zoid (trăp'ē-zoid), *n.* a plane figure with four sides, having two sides parallel to each other.

trap-per (trăp'ẽr), *n.* one who catches animals, especially to obtain their fur.

trap-pings (trăp'ĭngz), *n.pl.* ornamental harness of a horse, especially fancy saddle cloths, etc.; hence, ornaments or decorations in dress.

trash (trăsh), *n.* that which is worthless or useless; refuse or rubbish; injured parts cut or lopped off, as leaves, twigs, corn husks, etc.; also, a worthless person.

trash-y (trăsh'ĭ), *adj.* [*comp.* trashier, *superl.* trashiest], worthless; useless; as, a *trashy* novel.—*adv.* trashily.—*n.* trashiness.

trav-ail (trăv'āl), *n.* the suffering endured in childbirth; physical or mental agony or severe pain; as, a mind in *travail:* *v.i.* to suffer in childbirth.

trav-el (trăv'ĕl), *v.i.* [*p.t.* and *p.p.*, traveled, travelled; *p.pr.* traveling, travelling], to journey; to move or proceed: *v.t.* to journey over or through; as, to *travel* a hard road: *n.* the act of journeying; a journey; progress of any kind; number of persons, vehicles, etc., passing over a certain road; as, heavy *travel;* in mechanics, movement or stroke, as of a piston; *pl.* an account of things seen or experienced in journeying.

trav-eled (trăv'ĕld), *p.adj.* having made journeys; hence, experienced; as, a much-*traveled* man; much frequented, walked or ridden over; as, a much-*traveled* road. Also, travelled.

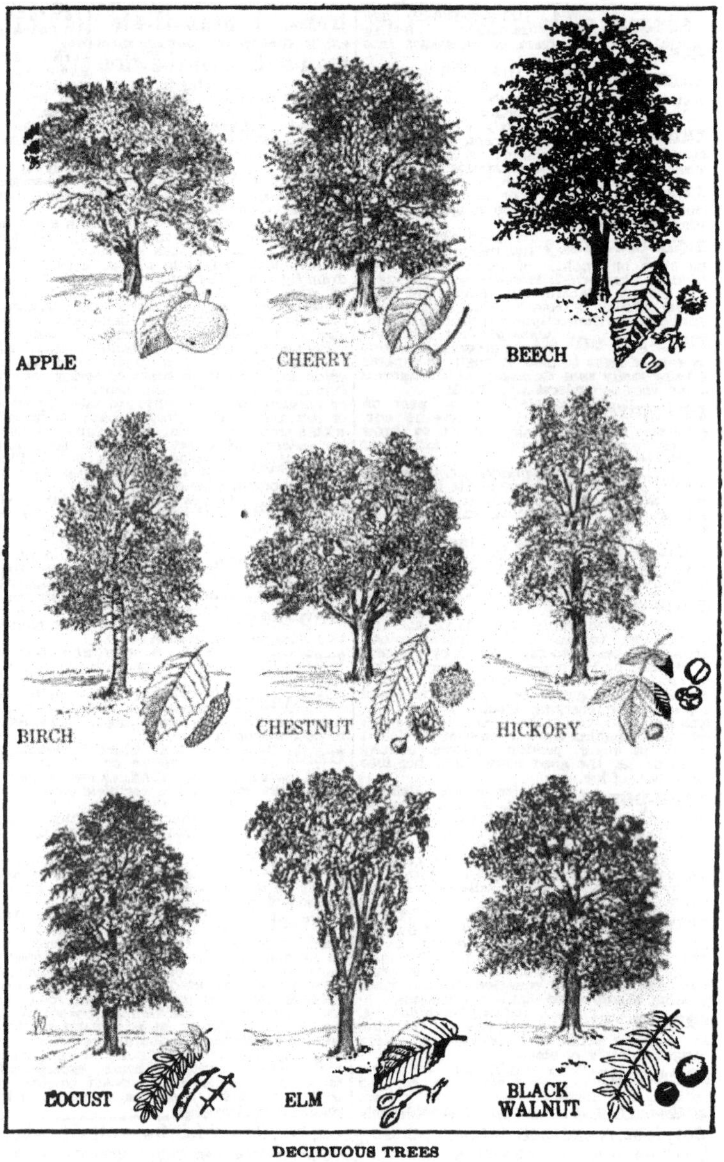

DECIDUOUS TREES

EVERGREEN TREES

trav-el-er (trăv'ĕl-ẽr), *n.* one who journeys; one who goes from place to place; as, a commercial *traveler.* Also, **traveller.**

trav-erse (trăv'ẽrs), *adj.* lying or being across: *adv.* (trăv'ẽrs; trȧ-vûrs'), athwart or crosswise: *n.* a crosspiece; something lying or placed across something else; a communication gallery or passage across a large building; in military use, a parapet across an exposed place, or a part of a trench at right angles to the main line: *v.t.* (trăv'-ẽrs), [*p.t.* and *p.p.* traversed, *p.pr.* traversing], to lay or place crosswise; to thwart or cross in opposition; to cross in traveling; to travel or pass over; as, to *traverse* Pennsylvania in going from New Jersey to Ohio: *v.i.* to turn, as on a pivot; to walk or move across.

trav-er-tine (trăv'ẽr-tĭn), *n.* a porous rock consisting of white calcium carbonate deposited from springs, streams, etc.

trav-es-ty (trăv'ĕs-tĭ), *n.* [*pl.* travesties (-tĭz)], a burlesque or parody; a burlesque translation or imitation of a literary work, etc.; also, any absurd or grotesque likeness: *v.t.* [*p.t.* and *p.p.* travestied, *p.pr.* travestying], to burlesque or parody; to represent or show so as to make ludicrous.

trawl (trôl), *n.* a large net of peculiar construction used in deep-sea fishing; a very long fishing line to which are attached many short lines with hooks: *v.i.* to fish with such a net or line.

trawl-er (trôl'ẽr), *n.* one who fishes on the ocean with a large net called a trawl; a fishing vessel used in deep-sea fishing with a net.

trawl-ing (trôl'ĭng), *n.* the act or process of fishing with a net which drags along the bottom of the sea.

tray (trā), *n.* a flat or shallow plate of wood, metal, porcelain, etc., with a raised edge or rim.

tray-ful (trā'fo͝ol), *n.* [*pl.* trayfuls (-fo͝olz)], as much as a tray will contain; as, a *trayful* of dishes.

treach-er-ous (trĕch'ẽr-ŭs), *adj.* betraying a trust or a pledge; apparently good, strong, sound, honest, etc., but in reality the opposite; as, a *treacherous* friend; a *treacherous* smile; [*treacherous* ice, etc.; faithless.—*adv.* **treacherously.**—*n.* **treacherousness.**

Syn. traitorous, disloyal, false-hearted.

treach-er-y (trĕch'ẽr-ĭ), *n.* [*pl.* treacheries (-ĭz)], treasonable or disloyal conduct; betrayal of faith or confidence; falseness to one's friends or country.

trea-cle (trē'kl), *n.* the English term for molasses; the syrup which drains from the sugar-refining molds.

tread (trĕd), *v.i.* [*p.t.* trod, *p.p.* trodden, *p.pr.* treading], to step or walk: *v.t.* to walk on; crush under the feet; subdue or overcome; dance: *n.* a walking or stepping; the upper horizontal part of a step; manner of stepping; as, a heavy *tread;* the part of a wheel or tire that touches the road.

trea-dle (trĕd'l), *n.* a flat leverlike device moved by the foot to operate a machine; as, the *treadle* of a sewing machine.

tread-mill (trĕd'mĭl"), *n.* a mill kept in motion by persons or animals walking on a wheel or endless belt.

trea-son (trē'zn), *n.* the crime of betraying or attacking the state or the government of the state to which the offender belongs; as, Benedict Arnold was guilty of *treason;* treachery; falseness to trust or pledge; in time of war, any act or utterance which gives aid and comfort to the enemy.

trea-son-a-ble (trē'zn-ȧ-bl), *adj.* tending to, or characterized by, falseness to pledges, friends, or country; as, *treasonable* speech or acts.—*adv.* **treasonably.**—*n.* **treasonableness.**

treas-ure (trĕzh'ûr), *n.* money, jewels, etc., hoarded up; abundance or wealth; something highly valued, or of great value: *v.t.* to lay up or collect for future use; hoard; value highly.

treas-ur-er (trĕzh'ûr-ẽr), *n.* one who has charge of receiving and expending public or collected funds.

treas-ur-er-ship (trĕzh'ûr-ẽr-shĭp), *n.* the office or position of a treasurer.

treas-ure-trove (trĕzh'ûr-trōv'), *n.* gold, silver, jewels, etc., found in a hiding place and not claimed by an owner.

treas-u-ry (trĕzh'ûr-ĭ), *n.* [*pl.* treasuries (-ĭz)], a place where wealth is stored; especially, a place where public funds are kept and paid out; that department of a government which has charge of the finances, or public funds; the officials of such a department.

treas-ur-y note (trĕzh'ûr-ĭ nōt), a note or bill issued by the United States treasury and used as money instead of gold, silver, etc.

treat (trēt), *v.t.* to handle, deal with, or manage; as, the speaker *treated* his subject cleverly; to behave towards; as, to *treat* others kindly; to cause to undergo a process for a special purpose; as, to *treat* a photograph with chemicals; to pay the cost of entertainment for; as, I will *treat* you to ice cream; to care for; as, a doctor *treats* his patients: *v.i.* to discuss a subject; to speak: to discuss or deal with a certain topic: with *of;* as, the paper *treats* of the ills of poor sanitation; negotiate or arrange; agree; give entertainment: *n.* an entertainment given as an expression of friendship or esteem; something which affords great pleasure; as, the opera is a great *treat.*—*n.* **treater.**

trea-tise (trē'tĭs), *n.* a rather long written discussion of some particular subject; a long and formal essay on a serious subject.

treat-ment (trēt'mĕnt), *n.* the act or manner of handling, or behaving toward; management; usage; as, the prisoner was given kind *treatment.*

trea-ty (trē'tĭ), *n.* [*pl.* treaties (-tĭz)], an agreement or contract between nations, either at the close of a war, or in time of peace, for the adjustment of differences or arrangement of commercial relations.

tre-ble (trĕb'l), *adj.* threefold or triple; belonging to the highest vocal or instrumental part of music; as, a *treble* violin: *n.* the highest vocal or instrumental part of music; as, she sings *treble;* a soprano: *v.t.* to make threefold: *v.i.* to become threefold.—*adv.* **trebly.**

tree (trē), *n.* any large perennial woody plant having a single trunk or stem, usually over ten feet high; anything shaped like a tree; a piece of timber or something usually made of timber; a cross: *v.t.* to drive up a tree; as, to *tree* a cat.

tree fern (trē fûrn), a large fern with a woody stem or trunk.

tree frog (trē frŏg), a creature shaped like a frog or toad and living in a tree: called also *tree toad.*

tree-less (trē'lĕs), *adj.* without trees; bare of woods or forests: as, a *treeless* plain.

tree-nail (trē'nāl"), *n.* a pin of dry wood which swells in its hole when wet, and is therefore a secure fastening for the planks of a ship. Also, **trenail.**

tre-foil (trē'foil), *n.* any three-leaved plant, such as the clover; an ornament used in architecture resembling a leaf with three divisions.

trek (trĕk), *v.i.* in South Africa, to travel by wagon, especially in search of a new settlement; to draw a load: in the World War, to transfer army equipment and supplies from one place to another.

trel-lis (trĕl'ĭs), *n.* a kind of wood or metal network or lattice, making a wall or roof for climbing vines: *v.t.* to provide with a lattice for vines; interlace.

trel-lis-work (trĕl'ĭs-wûrk"), *n.* small bars of wood or metal fastened together in a lattice; latticework.

trem-ble (trĕm'bl), *v.i.* [*p.t.* and *p.p.* trembled, *p.pr.* trembling], to shake, as with fear, cold, or weakness; to shudder; totter; shiver; quaver, as sound: *n.* an involuntary shaking; a shiver; a shudder.—*n.* **trembler.**

trem-bling (trĕm'blĭng), *p.adj.* shaking as with fear; quivering: *n.* condition of shaking; a fatal disease of sheep accompanied with a violent shaking of the muscles.

tre-men-dous (trē-mĕn'dŭs), *adj.* exciting fear or terror; dreadful; terrible; as, a *tremendous* blow or crash; arousing wonderment or awe; as, a *tremendous* battle; exceedingly great or large.—*adv.* **tremendously.**

trem-o-lo (trĕm'ō-lō), *n.* a trembling or quivering sound of a tone in vocal or instrumental music; a device in an organ by which such an effect is produced.

tre-mor (trē'mŏr; trĕm'ŏr), *n.* a trembling; a quivering; a quick vibration, or shaking; as, the *tremor* of a leaf.

trem-u-lous (trĕm'ū-lŭs), *adj.* trembling; quivering; shaking; showing fear or timidity; as, a *tremulous* voice; marked by unsteadiness; as, *tremulous* writing.—*adv.* **tremulously.**—*n.* **tremulousness.**

trench (trĕnch), *n.* a long, narrow cut or ditch in the earth; open ditch for draining; a deep ditch dug along the front line of battle and held as a defensive position or as a base from which to attack the enemy; as, American troops helped the French to hold the *trenches* before Rheims: **communication trench,** a zigzag ditch leading from the rear to the front-line trenches, through which troops, ammunition, and food are brought up: *v.t.* to cut a ditch in; to intrench, as an army: *v.i.* to encroach.

trench-an-cy (trĕn'chăn-sĭ), *n.* sharpness; keenness; biting directness.

trench-ant (trĕn'chănt), *adj.* sharp; keen; biting; cutting; as, a *trenchant* criticism.

trench-er (trĕn'chẽr), *n.* a large wooden tray or platter on which food was formerly served.

trench-er-man (trĕn'chẽr-măn), *n.* [*pl.* trenchermen (-mĕn)], a person fond of eating; a table companion.

trench fe-ver (trĕnch fē'vẽr), in the World War, an infectious fever induced by conditions of life in the trenches.

trench hel-met (trĕnch hĕl'mĕt), a steel hat, usually shaped like an inverted saucer, used for a protection from the head wounds frequent in trench warfare.

trench knife (trĕnch nīf), a broad-bladed knife, used for hand-to-hand fighting in a raid on an enemy's trench.

trend (trĕnd), *n.* inclination in a certain direction; as, the *trend* of public opinion; general tendency: *v.i.* to have a particular direction or course; as, the coast *trends* eastward; to tend or stretch.

tre-pan (trē-păn'), *n.* a surgeon's cylindrical saw for making a hole in the skull: *v.t.* [*p.t.* and *p.p.* trepanned, *p.pr.* trepanning], to perform the operation of making a hole in the skull with a trepan, or cylindrical saw: *v.t.* to perforate or make a hole in (the skull) with a trepan, or cylindrical saw.

tre-pan-ning (trē-păn'ĭng), *n.* a surgical operation on the skull to remove pressure on the brain.

tre-phine (trē-fīn'), *n.* the crown saw of a surgeon: *v.t.* to operate on (the skull) with such a saw.

trep-i-da-tion (trĕp"ĭ-dā'shŭn), *n.* trembling or vibration; state of nervous alarm; as, the news of war caused *trepidation* in many families; fear mingled with uncertainty.

tres-pass (trĕs'păs), *v.i.* to commit any offense; sin; enter unlawfully upon the property of another; intrude; as, the sign "do not *trespass*," means "keep out": *n.* the voluntary commission of an offense; any injury done to the person, rights, or property of another; transgression; sin.

tres-pass-er (trĕs'păs-ẽr), *n.* one who offends or sins; one who enters unlawfully upon the property of another.

tress (trĕs), *n.* a braid, curl, lock, or ringlet of human hair; as, her golden *tresses* were in confusion.

tres-tle (trĕs'l), *n.* a movable frame, or horse, made of a horizontal beam and several legs, for supporting anything; the frame supporting a table; a strong framework of timbers or steel over which a bridge is built across a ravine or gully.

tres-tle-board (trĕs'l-bōrd"), *n.* a draftsman's drawing or designing board.

tres-tle-tree (trĕs'l-trē"), *n.* one of two stout bars of timber fastened horizontally to a masthead to support the crosstrees.

tres-tle-work (trĕs'l-wûrk"), *n.* a series of trestles built to support a bridge, viaduct, etc.

tret (trĕt), *n.* an allowance to purchasers to cover waste in transporting goods.

trey (trā), *n.* a three at cards or dice; a card with three spots.

tri- (trī-), a *prefix* meaning three, threefold; as, *triangled*: *adj.* having three angles.

tri-ad (trī'ăd), *n.* a group or union of three; three united; as, a *triad* of virtues; three of a kind; in music, a chord of three tones; a tone together with its third and fifth.

tri-al (trī'ăl), *n.* the act of testing or proving; state of being tested; an attempt or endeavor; an experiment; an examination by test or experience; as, the man was engaged for a week on *trial;* hardship; suffering or temptation; that which puts to the test faith, mercy, patience, etc.; proof; a judicial examination; as, a *trial* in court.

tri-al bal-ance (trī'ăl băl'ăns), in double-entry bookkeeping, the statement of footings which tests whether the two sides of the ledger balance.

tri-al ju-ry (trī'ăl jōō'rĭ), a jury called to try a case in court: opposite to *grand jury*.

tri-an-gle (trī'ăṅ'gl), *n.* a plane figure bounded by three straight lines and having three angles; a musical instrument consisting of a steel rod bent in the form of a triangle, sounded by being struck.

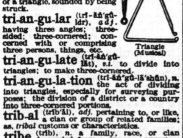

Triangle (Musical)

tri-an-gu-lar (trī-ăṅ'gū-lạ̈r), *adj.* having three angles; three-sided; three-cornered; concerned with or comprising three persons, things, etc.

tri-an-gu-late (trī-ăṅ'gū-lāt), *v.t.* to divide into triangles; to make three-cornered.

tri-an-gu-la-tion (trī-ăṅ'gū-lā'shŭn), *n.* the act of dividing into triangles, especially for surveying purposes; the division of a district or a country into three-cornered portions.

trib-al (trīb'ăl), *adj.* pertaining to, or like, a clan or group of related families; as, *tribal* customs or characteristics.

tribe (trīb), *n.* a family, race, or clan descended from a common ancestor; as, the *tribe* of Judah; a group of uncivilized people under one chief; as, a Tartar *tribe*; a group of people made akin to each other by some common trait.

tribes-man (trībz'măn), *n.* [*pl.* tribesmen (-mĕn)], a member of a clan or race-group.

trib-u-la-tion (trĭb'ū-lā'shŭn), *n.* severe affliction or distress; deep sorrow; acute trial.

tri-bu-nal (trī-bū'năl), *n.* the seat of a judge; a court of justice.

trib-une (trĭb'ūn), *n.* an ancient Roman magistrate elected by the people to protect their liberties; a raised stand or platform from which speeches were delivered during ancient Roman times.

trib-une-ship (trĭb'ūn-shĭp), *n.* the office or authority of a tribune, or ancient Roman magistrate; the period during which such a magistrate held office.

trib-u-ta-ry (trĭb'ū-tā-rĭ), *adj.* paying tribute or taxes to another; contributory; subordinate: *n.* [*pl.* tributaries (-rĭz)], a state or government which pays taxes to, or is under control of, a superior government; a stream or river flowing into a larger body of water.

trib-ute (trĭb'ūt), *n.* an annual or stated sum of money paid by one state or ruler to another for peace or protection, or on account of a treaty; an acknowledgment of worth, service rendered, etc.

trice (trīs), *n.* an instant: used only in the phrase, *in a trice*: *v.t.* to haul up and tie with a small rope, as a sail.

tri-cen-ni-al (trī-sĕn'ĭ-ăl), *adj.* pertaining to thirty years; occurring once in thirty years; as, a *tricennial* exposition or fair.

tri-cen-te-na-ry (trī-sĕn'tē-nā-rĭ), *adj.* including or relating to a period of 300 years: *n.* the 300th anniversary of any event. Also, **tercentenary.**

tri-ceps (trī'sĕps), *n.* the great extensor muscle having three heads, at the back of the upper arm.

tri-chi-na (trĭ-kī'nȧ), *n.* [*pl.* trichinæ (-nē)], a small, slender, parasitic worm which lives in the muscles of human beings, swine, and other animals.

trich-i-no-sis (trĭk'ĭ-nō'sĭs), *n.* the disease produced by the presence of trichinæ, or small parasitic worms, in the muscles and intestines. Also, **trichiniasis.**

trick (trĭk), *n.* an artifice or fraud; a crafty or deceitful device or action; as, a *trick* in trade; a puzzle, to amuse or annoy; a deception or imposition; a juggler's feat; a sleight-of-hand feat; a mischievous, sometimes annoying, prank; the entire number of cards falling to the winner in one round; a peculiarity of manner; as, she has a *trick* of lifting her eyebrows; a particular skill; as, he soon learned the *trick*: *v.t.* to cheat; impose upon; to deceive by cunning; to adorn fantastically.

trick-er-y (trĭk'ẽr-ĭ), *n.* [*pl.* trickeries (-ĭz)], the act or practice of deception; cheating; fraud; imposture.

trick-ish (trĭk'ĭsh), *adj.* full of craft, deceit, artifice, mischief, etc.

trick-le (trĭk'l), *v.i.* to flow gently down or in a small stream; to run down in drops; as, drops of water *trickle* through the walls of a cave: *n.* a small, gentle stream.

trick-ster (trĭk'stẽr), *n.* a cunning or crafty cheat or deceiver.

trick-sy (trĭk'sĭ), *adj.* full of mischief; prankish; playful.

trick-track (trĭk'trăk'), *n.* an old game resembling backgammon.

trick valve (trĭk vălv), a sliding valve in a steam engine.

trick-y (trĭk'ĭ), *adj.* [*comp.* trickier, *superl.* trickiest], given to deceit; knavish; shifty; artful; cunning; not to be trusted. —*adv.* trickily.—*n.* trickiness.

tri-col-or (trī'kŭl'ẽr), *n.* a flag of three colors arranged in equal strips; especially, the national flag of France, of blue, white, and red vertical strips. Also, **tricolour.**

tri-cot (trē'kō), *n.* material of wool, silk, or cotton resembling a knitted fabric; a soft, ribbed dress goods.

tri-cus-pid (trī-kŭs'pĭd), *adj.* having three cusps, or points, as certain teeth, or the *tricuspid* valve in the right side of the heart.

tri-cy-cle (trī'sĭ-kl), *n.* a light three-wheeled vehicle, with a single seat, made to go by pedals: usually of a size suitable for a child; a three-wheeled motor cycle: *v.i.* to ride in a three-wheeled vehicle.

tri-dent (trī'dĕnt), *n.* a spear with three prongs, especially that carried by the god of the sea, Neptune; hence, a three-pronged fish spear.

tri-den-tate (trī-dĕn'tāt), *adj.* having three points or teeth. Also, **tridentated.**

tried (trīd), *p.t.* and *p.p.* of the verb *try*: *p.adj.* proved; tested; trustworthy; faithful; as, a *tried* and true friend.

tri-en-ni-al (trī-ĕn'ĭ-ăl), *adj.* continuing three years; happening every three years; as, a *triennial* meeting: *n.* an event occurring every three years; the third anniversary of an event.—*adv.* triennially.

tri-er (trī'ẽr), *n.* one who makes experiments; a judge who hears a case in court.

tri-fle (trī'fl), *n.* anything of little value or importance; a dessert made of ponge cake covered with jam, cream, etc.: .i. [*p.t.* and *p.p.* trifled, *p.pr.* trifling], to act or talk without seriousness; to dally; as, she *rifled* with her necklace as she talked: *v.t.* to waste or fritter away; as, to *trifle* away one's ime or money: **a trifle,** a little; slightly.

ri-fler (trī'flẽr), *n.* one who makes light of serious things; one who talks or acts idly and uselessly; one who wastes his time.

ri-fling (trī'fling), *adj.* of small value or importance; as, a *trifling* matter; houghtless or shallow; as, a *trifling* character; nsignificant; as, a *trifling* sum.—*adv.* **triflingly.**

ri-fo-li-ate (trī-fō'lĭ-āt), *adj.* three-leaved, as clover; having a eaf divided into three parts.

rig (trĭg), *adj.* trim; neat: *v.t.* [*p.t.* and *p.p.* trigged, *p.pr.* trigging], to stop; as, to *rig* a wheel by putting a stone in the way; stop, as a drag or block.

rig-ger (trĭg'ẽr), *n.* a lever which, when pulled by the finger, releases the hammer of a gun; a catch doing similar work, as on a trap or other device.

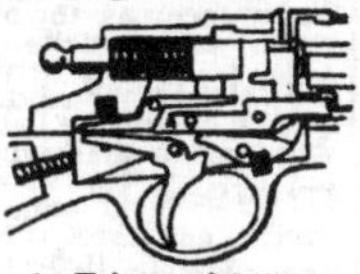
A, Trigger of Military Rifle

ri-gon (trī'gŏn), *n.* a triangle; a kind of three-cornered harp.

rig-o-nal (trĭg'ō-năl), *adj.* three-cornered or riangular.

rig-o-nom-e-try (trĭg"ō-nŏm'ē-trĭ), *n.* mathematics which reats of the relations between the sides and angles of triangles; a text treating of this cience.—*adj.* **trigonometric, trigonometrical.** —*adv.* **trigonometrically.**

ri-graph (trī'grăf), *n.* a group of three letters representing one sound; as, *eau* in beauty.

ri-he-dral (trī-hē'drăl), *adv.* having three sides or faces.

ri-he-dron (trī-hē'drŏn), *n.* a figure having three plane sides or aces.

ri-lat-er-al (trī-lăt'ẽr-ăl), *adj.* three-sided, or having three sides, as a triangle.—*adv.* **trilaterally.**

ri-lit-er-al (trī-lĭt'ẽr-ăl), *adj.* consisting of three letters, as a word or syllable: *n.* such a word or syllable.

rill (trĭl), *n.* a shake or vibration of the voice on a letter or musical tone; as, he *trill* of a bird; in music, a shake; any ound suggesting a trill: *v.t.* to utter with a ibration; as, to *trill* one's *r's*: *v.i.* to make he voice vibrate.

ril-lion (trĭl'yŭn), *n.* in the French system of numbering, followed in he United States, a unit followed by twelve iphers; in the English system, a unit followed by eighteen ciphers.—*adj.* **trillionth.**

ril-li-um (trĭl'ĭ-ŭm), *n.* a plant of several varieties, having three leaves with one large flower in the middle of them.

ri-lo-bate (trī-lō'bāt; trī'lō-bāt), *adj.* having three lobes, or rounded livisions.

ril-o-gy (trĭl'ō-jĭ), *n.* a series of three dramas, each complete in itself, but forming one connected whole; similarly, hree musical compositions, three novels, etc.

rim (trĭm), *adj.* [*comp.* trimmer, *superl.* trimmest], neat; compact; as, a *rim*, slender figure; being in good order; as, her hair was neat and *trim*: *v.t.* [*p.t.* and *p.p.* trimmed, *p.pr.* trimming], to decorate or adorn; as, to *trim* a dress; make neat; cut the edges of; adjust or balance; as, to *trim* a ship by making it sit even in the water; make ready for sailing; as, to *trim* the sails; make smooth; as, to *trim* lumber by planing it; clip, as a plant; colloquially, to lecture or reprove: *v.i.* to take a certain position in the water: said of a vessel; to try to please two sides or parties at the same time; to compromise: *n.* order; adjustment; dress; style; gear; fitness for sailing: said of a ship; suitable condition; as, they found everything in *trim* for the start.—*adv.* **trimly.**—*n.* **trimness.**

trim-e-ter (trĭm'ē-tẽr), *n.* a verse, or line of poetry, having three measures: *adj.* having three measures, as verse.

trim-mer (trĭm'ẽr), *n.* one who arranges, decorates, etc.; as, a hat *trimmer* or window *trimmer*, etc.; a machine for finishing lumber; one who tries to please two parties at once.

trim-ming (trĭm'ĭng), *n.* adornment, especially for articles of dress: *pl.* parts removed by cutting off the edges; as, the *trimmings* of a piece of meat.

Trin-i-ta-ri-an (trĭn'ĭ-tā'rĭ-ăn), *adj.* pertaining to the Trinity, or the doctrine of the Trinity: *n.* one who believes in the doctrine of the Trinity, or that the Father, Son, and Holy Ghost unite in one Godhead. Also, **trinitarian.**

Trin-i-ta-ri-an-ism (trĭn'ĭ-tā'rĭ-ăn-ĭzm), *n.* the doctrine or belief that there are three persons in the Godhead.

Trin-i-ty (trĭn'ĭ-tĭ), *n.* the union of the Father, the Son, and the Holy Ghost in one Godhead: **trinity,** any union of three in one; a trio.

Trin-i-ty Sun-day (trĭn'ĭ-tĭ sŭn'dā), the Sunday next after Pentecost or Whitsunday.

trin-ket (trĭn'kĕt), *n.* a small ornament or jewel; a trifle or a toy; something of little worth.

tri-no-mi-al (trī-nō'mĭ-ăl), *n.* a mathematical expression consisting of three terms, connected by the sign plus [+] or minus [—] or both.

tri-o (trē'ō; trī'ō), *n.* [*pl.* **trios** (-ōz)], a set of three; three united; in music, a composition for three voices or instruments.

trip (trĭp), *v.i.* [*p.t.* and *p.p.* tripped, *p.pr.* tripping], to run or step lightly or nimbly; take short, quick steps; to skip; to make a misstep; to stumble; as, to *trip* over a board; to make a mistake or error, mentally or morally; as, he *tripped* in giving his answer: *v.t.* to execute with light, agile steps, as a dance; to cause to stumble; as, the loose board *tripped* him so that he fell; to cause to halt by getting in the way of; to catch in a mistake or deception; as, the lawyer *tripped* the witness under cross-examination; in machinery, to set free, as by pulling a catch, trigger, etc.: *n.* a quick, short step; a misstep or false step; mistake; journey or excursion; in machinery, a device that unfastens, or releases.

tri-par-tite (trī-păr'tīt; trĭp'ár-tīt), *adj.* divided into three parts; made or concluded between three persons or groups of persons; as, a *tripartite* agreement.—*n.* **tripartition.**

tripe (trīp), *n.* the lining of the stomach of beef, prepared for use as food.

trip ham-mer (trĭp hăm'ẽr), a large hammer, consisting of a lever with a head, and moved by cams, or projections on a wheel; a heavy tilt hammer.

triph-thong (trĭf'thŏng), *n.* a combination of three separate and distinct vowels pronounced by one effort; as, *oya* in royal, *eau* in beau.

tri-plane (trī'plăn'), *n.* an airplane having three planes.

trip-le (trĭp'l), *adj.* threefold; consisting of three joined; as, a *triple* knot, a *triple* tie, etc.; three times repeated; as, a *triple* knock: *v.t.* and *v.i.* to increase threefold.—*adv.* **triply.**

Triplet

trip-let (trĭp'lĕt), *n.* a set of three of a kind or three united; in poetry, three lines riming together. In music, three notes sounded in the time of two or four; one of three children at one birth.

tri-plex (trī'plĕks; trĭp'lĕks), *adj.* having three parts; threefold: *n.* in music, triple time or measure.

trip-li-cate (trĭp'lĭ-kāt), *n.* something which matches two others of the same kind: *adj.* threefold: made in three copies; as, a *triplicate* agreement: *v.t.* (trĭp'lĭ-kāt), [*p.t.* and *p.p.* triplicated, *p.pr.* triplicating], to triple or treble; to increase threefold.—*n.* **triplication.**

tri-pod (trī'pŏd), *n.* a three-legged stand or support, as for a camera; a pot, kettle, etc., with three legs.

trip-ping (trĭp'ĭng), *p.adj.* stepping lightly or gracefully.—*adv.* **trippingly.**

tri-reme (trī'rēm), *n.* a galley, or ancient ship, with three banks of oars.

Trireme

tri-sect (trī-sĕkt'), *v.t.* to divide into three parts, especially, in geometry, into three equal parts; as, to *trisect* an angle.

tri-sec-tion (trī-sĕk'shŭn), *n.* the division of anything into three parts, especially the division of an angle into three equal parts.

tri-syl-la-ble (trĭ-sĭl'à-bl; trī-sĭl'à-bl), *n.* a word of three syllables.—*adj.* **trisyllabic.**

trite (trīt), *adj.* worn out; stale; commonplace; as, a *trite* remark.—*adv.* **tritely.** —*n.* **triteness.**

Syn. old, ordinary, hackneyed.
Ant. (see novel).

trit-u-rate (trĭt'ū-rāt), *v.t.* [*p.t.* and *p.p.* triturated, *p.pr.* triturating], to rub, grind, or bruise to a fine powder.—*n.* **trituration.**

tri-umph (trī'ŭmf), *n.* great joy for success; exultation; in ancient Rome, a grand parade in honor of a victorious general; conquest or victory; as, the *triumph* of knowledge: *v.i.* to rejoice over success; to obtain a victory; to be successful.

Syn., *n.* achievement, ovation.
Ant. (see defeat, failure).

tri-um-phal (trī-ŭm'făl), *adj.* of or pertaining to a victory or its celebration; as, a *triumphal* procession in honor of victory.

tri-um-phant (trī-ŭm'fănt), *adj.* rejoicing for victory; exultant; victorious; successful; as, a *triumphant* cause. —*adv.* **triumphantly.**

tri-um-vir (trī-ŭm'vĕr), *n.* [*pl.* triumviri (-vĭ-rī)], in ancient Rome, one of three men equally sharing authority and rule.

tri-um-vi-rate (trī-ŭm'vĭ-rāt), *n.* a government by three men having equal authority; a group of three.

tri-une (trī'ūn), *adj.* being three in one; as, the *triune* God.

triv-et (trĭv'ĕt), *n.* a three-legged stand for holding a kettle, etc., near the fire; anything supported by three legs: a tripod.

triv-i-al (trĭv'ĭ-ăl), *adj.* trifling; common; ordinary; of little worth or importance; as, the *trivial* affairs of everyday work.—*adv.* **trivially.**

triv-i-al-i-ty (trĭv'ĭ-ăl'ĭ-tĭ), *n.* [*pl.* trivialities (-tĭz)], the state or quality of being of little worth or importance: slightness or shallowness of character.

tri-week-ly (trī'wēk'lĭ), *adj.* coming three times a week or every three weeks: *adv.* three times a week.

tro-cha-ic (trō-kā'ĭk), *adj.* pertaining to, or consisting of, a metrical foot of two syllables, the first long and the second short, with the accent on the first.

tro-che (trō'kē), *n.* a tablet or small round cake containing medicine.

tro-chee (trō'kē), *n.* a metrical foot of two syllables, the first long and the second short, with the accent on the first.

trod (trŏd), past tense and past participle of the verb *tread.*

trod-den (trŏd'n), past participle of the verb *tread.*

trog-lo-dyte (trŏg'lō-dīt), *n.* a prehistoric caveman; an anthropoid, or manlike ape, such as the chimpanzee.

Tro-jan (trō'jăn), *adj.* of or pertaining to the ancient city of Troy, in Asia Minor, whose inhabitants fought bravely for ten years to defend their city from the Greeks: *n.* a brave and fearless person; as, he worked or fought like a *Trojan;* an inhabitant of Troy.

troll (trōl), *n.* in folk tales, a giant or dwarf of the caves or mountains; a round, or part song; a reel on a fishing rod: *v.t.* to sing the parts of in succession: to sing lustily; as, to *troll* a song; to fish for or in by dragging a line from a boat; as, to *troll* a lake: *v.i.* to share in a round, or part song; to be sung, as a song; to fish, as for pike, with a hook and line drawn along through the water.—*n.* **troller.**

trol-ley (trŏl'ĭ), *n.* in England, a small cart or truck; also, a kind of truck running on an overhead track and carrying a suspended load; as, the money-carrying *trolleys* in large stores; a grooved metal wheel traveling in contact with a live electric wire; as, the car stopped because the *trolley* was off the wire; in America, an electric car. Also, **trolly.**

trol-ley car (trŏl'ĭ kär), a car moved by means of a trolley and an electric motor; an electric car or a street car.

trol-ley line (trŏl'ĭ līn), a system of electric cars; a route taken by an electric car.

trol-ley pole (trŏl'ĭ pōl), the slanting pole attached to the roof of an electric car and having the trolley at its top, touching the wire.

trol-lop (trŏl'ŭp), *n.* a carelessly dressed woman; a woman of slovenly appearance; a prostitute.

trom-bone (trŏm'bōn), *n.* a large brass instrument of the trumpet kind, having a complete chromatic scale.

troop (trōōp), *n.* a collection of people; a company; a number; as, a *troop* of children going to school; a company of cavalry commanded by a captain; a company of actors: *pl.* armed forces; soldiers collectively: *v.i.* to march in a body; to collect or move in crowds.

Trombones. 1, slide; 2, key.

troop-er (trōōp'ẽr), *n.* a cavalryman; his horse, or charger.

troop-ship (trōōp'shĭp'), *n.* a vessel for carrying soldiers across the ocean; a military transport.

trope (trōp), *n.* a figure of speech, especially a metaphor; as, in the sentence, the wise man is a fox, the word fox is a *trope*.

tro-phy (trō'fĭ), *n.* [*pl.* trophies (-fĭz)], anything taken and preserved in memory of a victory; as, arms, flags, etc.; a memento or memorial; that which reminds one of deeds, achievements, etc.; as, a *trophy* of the hunt; in ancient Greece and Rome, a monument or other memorial raised in celebration of a victory; a prize in an athletic contest; as, a silver cup was the *trophy* won by the tennis champion.

trop-ic (trŏp'ĭk), *n.* one of the two small circles, running around the earth parallel to the equator, at a distance of 23½° on each side of it, between which as limits the sun moves in its yearly course.—**tropic of Cancer**, the circle to the north.—**tropic of Capricorn**, the circle to the south: *pl.* the region between these two circles, which has a very hot, damp climate.

trop-i-cal (trŏp'ĭ-kăl), *adj.* pertaining to, produced in, or situated within, the tropics; as, *tropical* fruit, *tropical* heat, etc.—*adv.* **tropically.**

trot (trŏt), *n.* that gait of a horse by which it moves faster than at a walk, and in which the right forefoot moves with the left hindfoot; a jogging pace; a brisk walk or run with short steps: *v.i.* [*p.t.* and *p.p.* trotted, *p.pr.* trotting], to move faster than at a walk; to run with a jogging pace: *v.t.* to cause to move faster than a walk.

troth (trōth; trŏth), *n.* faith or fidelity; truth to one's word; as, I pledge my *troth*; betrothal.

trot-ter (trŏt'ẽr), *n.* a trotting horse; the foot of an animal used for food; as, pigs' *trotters* or sheep's *trotters*.

trou-ba-dour (trōō'bȧ-dōōr), *n.* one of a class of French or Italian poets and singers of love songs, who flourished during the twelfth and thirteenth centuries.

trou-ble (trŭb'l), *n.* mental excitement, distress, or worry; that which causes such distress; inconvenience; exertion; pains; as, to take a great deal of *trouble*; annoyance or uneasiness; illness; as, stomach *trouble*: *v.t.* to excite, distress, or worry; to cause inconvenience to; to stir up, as water: *v.i.* to take pains.

trou-ble-some (trŭb'l-sŭm), *adj.* causing distress, annoyance, or worry; disturbing; as, a *troublesome* child; a *troublesome* cold in the head; tiresome.

troub-lous (trŭb'lŭs), *adj.* disturbed; full of distress or annoyance; as, *troublous* times followed the war.

trough (trôf), *n.* a long, shallow vessel for holding a liquid, food, etc., for the use of animals; anything hollowed out; any long channel; as, the *trough* between ocean waves.

trounce (trouns), *v.t.* [*p.t.* and *p.p.* trounced, *p.pr.* trouncing], to beat soundly; to whip or flog.

trounc-ing (troun'sĭng), *n.* a severe beating or whipping.

troupe (trōōp), *n.* a company of actors or theatrical performers.

trou-sers (trou'zẽrz), *n.pl.* an outer garment worn by men and boys, covering the body from the waist to the knee or ankle, and so divided as to cover each leg separately.

trous-seau (trōō'sō'), *n.* [*pl.* trousseaux (-sōz)], a bride's outfit, such as clothes, jewelry, etc.

trout (trout), *n.* a small fresh-water game fish of the salmon family.

tro-ver (trō'vẽr), *n.* an action at law to recover goods found and not delivered on demand.

trow (trō), *v.t.* and *v.i.* an ancient verb meaning to think; suppose.

trow-el (trou'ĕl), *n.* a flat implement or hand tool used for spreading mortar; a gardener's tool for digging up or setting out small plants.

Trowel

troy weight (troi wāt), a system of weights with twelve ounces to the pound, used for gold, silver, etc.

tru-an-cy (trōō'ăn-sĭ), *n.* the act or habit of staying away from business or any duty, especially of staying out of school without permission.

tru-ant (trōō'ănt), *n.* one who stays out of school without permission; one who remains away from any work or duty; a loafer: *adj.* pertaining to, or like, a truant; idle.

truce (trōōs), *n.* a temporary peace or stopping of war by agreement; an armistice; a brief cessation or pause; a temporary respite.

truck (trŭk), *n.* a wheeled vehicle for carrying heavy goods; a strong frame on wheels, used for baggage in railroad stations, etc.; a frame mounted on wheels to carry and guide one end of a locomotive, a railroad car, or a street car; a large motor vehicle used for the delivery and transportation of goods; as, the motor *truck* has taken the place of the army mule; a small wooden cap on the top of a flagpole, usually having holes for the ropes that control the flag; vegetables raised for the market; as, garden *truck*; system of paying wages in commodities, not in money; colloquially, useless articles or rubbish: *v.t.* to carry by means of such a vehicle; peddle or sell, as from door to door: *v.i.* to barter or exchange goods, etc.

truck-age (trŭk'āj), *n.* cost of transporting goods by truck; freight.

truck-le (trŭk'l), *n.* a small wheel or caster: *v.t.* to cause to move on rollers: *v.i.* to yield submissively to another's will; as, to *truckle* to a lord.—*n.* **truckler.**

truck-le-bed (trŭk'l-bĕd"), *n.* a bed with a very low frame mounted upon rollers, so that it may be rolled under a high bed. Also, **trundle-bed.**

truck-man (trŭk'măn), *n.* [*pl.* truckmen (-mĕn)], one who drives a truck; one who sells goods, especially vegetables, from door to door; one who barters.

truc-u-lence (trŭk'ū-lĕns; trōō'kū-lĕns), *n.* ferocity; cruelty or fierceness; quarrelsomeness. Also, **truculency.**

truc-u-lent (trŭk'ū-lĕnt; trōō'kū-lĕnt), *adj.* fierce, savage, or ferocious; cruel; barbarous.—*adv.* **truculently.**

trudge (trŭj), *v.i.* [*p.t.* and *p.p.* trudged, *p.pr.* trudging], to travel on foot, especially with labor or fatigue; as, he *trudged* along through the woods.

true (trōō), *adj.* [*comp.* truer, *superl.* truest], according to fact; as, a *true* statement; faithful or loyal; genuine; rightful; correct; certain.—*n.* **trueness.**
Syn. actual, sincere, honest, accurate.
Ant. (see false).

truf-fle (trŭf'l; trōōf'l; trōō'fl), *n.* a fleshlike kind of food that grows underground and is shaped somewhat like a potato.

tru-ism (trōō'ĭzm), *n.* an old and accepted truth; as, "Honesty is the best policy."

tru-ly (trōō'lĭ), *adv.* in agreement with truth or fact; precisely; sincerely; honestly; as, it was *truly* spoken; in fact; indeed.

trump (trŭmp), *n.* a horn or trumpet; slang, a genuine, good fellow; a winning card; any card of the suit which, for the time, can take any card of any other suit; *pl.* the suit itself: *v.t.* to take, as a trick, with such a card: *v.i.* to play such a card.—**to trump up,** to devise by unfair means.

trump-er-y (trŭm'pĕr-ĭ), *n.* worthless finery; rubbish: *adj.* having a showy appearance, but worthless; hence, deceiving or delusive.

trump-et (trŭm'pĕt), *n.* a metal wind instrument formed of a single curved tube with a flare at the end; a sound like that of this instrument; an organ stop producing such a sound: *v.t.* to publish by, or as by, the sound of such an instrument; noise abroad; praise extravagantly: *v.i.* to utter a sound like that of a trumpet.

trump-et-er (trŭm'pĕt-ẽr), *n.* one who sounds a trumpet; one who proclaims or noises abroad; a kind of pigeon; a wild swan of North America; a large South American bird.

trun-cate (trŭn̂'kāt), *adj.* appearing as if cut squarely off; having a top plane, as if cut evenly off: *v.t.* to lop or cut the top or end from.

trun-cat-ed (trŭn̂'kāt-ĕd), *adj.* cut off squarely; as, a *truncated* cone or pyramid is one whose top has been cut off.

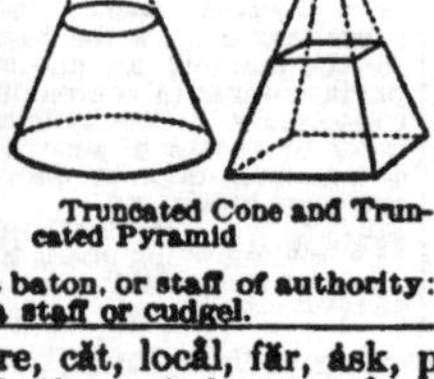
Truncated Cone and Truncated Pyramid

trun-cheon (trŭn'shŭn; trŭn'chŭn), *n.* a short staff or cudgel; a baton, or staff of authority: *v.t.* to beat with a staff or cudgel.

trun-dle (trŭn'dl), *v.t.* and *v.i.* to roll along; roll on small wheels: *n.* a kind of low-wheeled truck; a caster; a trundle-bed.

trun-dle-bed (trŭn'dl-bĕd"), *n.* a low bed that runs on casters or rollers, so that, when not in use, it may be rolled under a high bed. Also, **truckle-bed.**

trunk (trŭnk), *n.* the upright stem, body, or stock of a tree; the body of an animal, without the head and limbs; the central or most important part of anything which has branches or projections; an elephant's proboscis; a large traveling box or chest to hold personal belongings; *pl.* short, tight breeches; formerly, full breeches reaching about half way to the knee: called also *trunk hose:* *adj.* pertaining to a chief line; as, *trunk* lines of railroad.

trun-nion (trŭn'yŭn), *n.* one of the two pivots or axles that support a cannon, etc.

truss (trŭs), *n.* a bandage or support for rupture; a bundle or package; a measured mass of hay, straw, etc.; timbers or bars fastened together to form a framework for any structure: *v.t.* to bind or pack into a bundle; skewer; as, to *truss* a chicken with pointed sticks; make fast; tighten, as laces; to support by a brace, framework, etc.

trust (trŭst), *n.* confidence; faith; belief in someone's truth and goodness; hope; basis of confidence or belief; credit granted because of belief in one's honesty; as, he lent his friend the money on *trust*; a duty or responsibility; as, he committed to me the solemn *trust* of carrying out his wishes; a combination of business men or firms engaged in the production of some commodity or related group of commodities, designed to regulate the supply and price of their goods and to prosper by coöperation rather than by competition; often, such a combination formed to crush out smaller competitors and thus control an industry and raise prices; as, the Sherman anti-*trust* law was intended to do away with combination in restraint of trade; an estate left in someone's charge to be held and managed for another's benefit; the guardianship of such an estate; as, he left his property in *trust* for his grandchildren: *v.t.* to place confidence in; believe; rely upon; entrust to someone's care; risk; sell upon credit to: *v.i.* to have confidence; to hope: *adj.* held in charge for someone else; as, a *trust* fund.—*n.* **truster.**

trus-tee (trŭs-tē'), *n.* a person to whom property, or the management of property, is committed for the benefit of others.

trus-tee-ship (trŭs-tē'shĭp), *n.* the office or duties of one who takes charge of the property of others.

trust-ful (trŭst'fōōl), *adj.* full of hope and confidence; ready to believe in others.—*adv.* **trustfully.**—*n.* **trustfulness.**

trust-wor-thy (trŭst'wûr"thĭ), *adj.* reliable; meriting trust and confidence.—*adv.* **trustworthily.**—*n.* **trustworthiness.**

trust-y (trŭs'tĭ), *adj.* [*comp.* trustier, *superl.* trustiest], worthy to receive confidence; faithful; reliable; as, a *trusty* servant: *n.* a convict found worthy of special privileges.—*adv.* **trustily.**—*n.* **trustiness.**

truth (trōōth), *n.* [*pl.* truths (trōōthz; trōōths)], the quality of being according to fact; correctness; accuracy or exactness; something real and actual; a fact; a general statement of something proved to be always the case; as, that wastefulness brings poverty is a well-known *truth;* faithfulness; loyalty; sincerity; a moral, religious, or scientific principle.

truth-ful (trōōth'fōōl), *adj.* according to facts; as, a *truthful* statement; given to saying only what is the fact; reliable. —*adv.* **truthfully.**—*n.* **truthfulness.**

try (trī), *v.t.* [*p.t.* and *p.p.* tried, *p.pr.* trying], to prove by experiment; test; as, the bird *tried* its wings; prove; make a test of; as, to *try* an experiment; purify or refine, as metals; melt out, as fat; put through a trial or test; as, the times that *try* men's souls; examine judicially; as, the court will *try* the prisoner; subject to strain; as, the light *tries* the eyes; subject to trouble or affliction; as, a sadly *tried* people; test the strength or endurance of; as, to *try* the patience; decide, as by argument, contest, etc.; attempt to do; as, *try* to say it; use as an experiment; as, to *try* a new way; *v.i.* to endeavor; to make an effort; to try an experiment: *n.* [*pl.* tries], an attempt; an effort; a test.

try-ing (trī'ing), *p.adj.* annoying; hard to bear; difficult; severe.

try-sail (trī'sāl"; trī'sl), *n.* a fore-and-aft sail set on a gaff, or small boom, on the foremast or mainmast of a sailing vessel.

try-square (trī'skwâr"), *n.* a tool for laying off right angles and testing work for squareness, as in carpentry.

Try-square

tryst (trīst; trĭst), *n.* an engagement to meet at a certain place and time; a meeting; as, a lovers' *tryst;* a rendezvous, or place of meeting: called also *trysting place.*

tsar (tsär), *n.* a king; an emperor; formerly, the title of the ruler of Russia. Also, **czar, tzar.**

tsar-e-vitch (tsär'ĕ-vĭch), *n.* formerly, the crown prince of Russia, or eldest son of the emperor.

tsar-i-na (tsä-rē'nȧ), *n.* formerly, the wife of the emperor of Russia. Also, **czarina.**

tset-se (tsĕt'sē), *n.* an irritating African fly whose bite causes a disease in oxen and horses.

T square (tē skwâr), *n.* a T-shaped ruler used by draftsmen in making mechanical drawings.

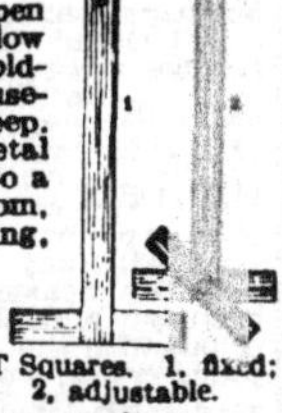
T Squares. 1, fixed; 2, adjustable.

tub (tŭb), *n.* a circular open wooden vessel, or low cask, used for washing, holding butter, and other household purposes; a large, deep, stationary receptacle, metal or porcelain lined, built into a laundry, kitchen, or bathroom, and used for washing, bathing, etc.; the amount of water held in such a receptacle: *v.t.* to place in a tub; to wash or bathe in a tub.

tu-ba (tū'bȧ), *n.* a large musical instrument similar to the trumpet or saxhorn.

tube (tūb), *n.* a hollow cylinder of glass, metal, etc., through which fluids may pass; an instrument having such a cylinder as an important part of it; a pipe; a subway or tunnel for an underground railway: *v.t.* [*p.t.* and *p.p.* tubed, *p.pr.* tubing], to furnish with a cylinder, tunnel, etc.; to put into a cylinder, tunnel, etc.

tu-ber (tū'bẽr), *n.* a thick, roundish, often edible, underground stem or root bearing small buds or "eyes," as the potato; an edible fungus, or truffle.

tu-ber-cle (tū'bẽr-kl), *n.* a small knob-like growth, especially on an animal or plant; a tiny unhealthy growth appearing in the tissues of the body; especially one found in the lungs and causing tuberculosis, or consumption.

tu-ber-cu-lar (tū-bûr'kū-lȧr), *adj.* full of, like, or pertaining to, the small growths called tubercles; affected with tuberculosis, or consumption.

tu-ber-cu-lin (tū-bûr'kū-lĭn), *n.* a liquid, free from disease-producing organisms, which is of such a nature that it can be used in testing cattle for tuberculosis.

tu-ber-cu-lo-sis (tū-bûr"kū-lō'sĭs), *n.* an infectious disease characterized by the growth of tubercles in the tissues of the body; especially, this disease affecting the lungs, called *consumption.*

tu-ber-cu-lous (tū-bûr'kū-lŭs), *adj.* affected with, or like, tuberculosis; full of tubercles, or small unhealthy growths.

tube-rose (tūb'rōz"; tū'bẽr-ōs"), *n.* a kind of plant that bears heavily fragrant white flowers growing on a spike.

tu-ber-ous (tū'bẽr-ŭs), *adj.* covered with knobs or swellings resembling warts; consisting of, producing, or like, a tuber, as the potato. Also, **tuberose.**

tub-ing (tūb'ĭng), *n.* material for tubes; a number of tubes; the act of making tubes.

tu-bu-lar (tū'bū-lȧr), *adj.* pertaining to, shaped like, or consisting of, a hollow cylinder or pipe.

tuck (tŭk), *n.* a sewed fold, as in a dress: *v.t.* to thrust or press into a small snug opening; to gather or turn up; fold under and sew; as, to *tuck* a dress; cover snugly; as, to *tuck* a child into bed.—**Tuck,** the friar of Robin Hood's band.

tuck-a-hoe (tŭk'ȧ-hō), *n.* an American plant whose root, when cooked, was formerly used by the Indians of Virginia as food.

tuck-er (tŭk'ẽr), *n.* a piece of lace, linen, or other thin material, folded across the front, or fastened into the neck, of a woman's dress; a machine for stitching folds into cloth.

Tu-dor (tū'dŏr), *adj.* pertaining to, or of the time of, one of the royal families of England, which occupied the throne from 1485 to 1603, and whose reigning members were Henry VII, Henry VIII, Edward VI, Mary, and Elizabeth: *n.* a member of this family.

Tues-day (tūz'dā), *n.* the third day of the week: named for the Norse god Tyr; the day after Monday.

tu-fa (tōō'fȧ), *n.* porous volcanic rock; soft or porous stone usually deposited from springs or streams.

tuft (tŭft), *n.* a knot or bunch made of long, slender parts; as, a *tuft* of grass; a cluster or clump; as, a *tuft* of plants: *v.t.* to divide into, or decorate with, such clusters.

tuft-hun-ter (tŭft'hŭn"tẽr), *n.* one who courts or invites the acquaintance of persons of rank; a toady.

tug (tŭg), *n.* a pull with great effort; a steam towing vessel; a rope or chain used for pulling; a trace of a harness: *v.t.*

[*p.t.* and *p.p.* tugged, *p.pr.* tugging], to pull or draw with great effort; tow: *v.i.* to use great effort in pulling, etc.—**tug of war**, a contest in which two equal groups pull on opposite ends of a rope; hence, any violent and evenly matched struggle.

tu-i-tion (tū-ĭsh'ŭn), *n.* instruction; teaching; charge for instruction.

tu-lip (tū'lĭp), *n.* a plant of the lily family, bearing brilliant flowers in spring; also, a bulb or flower of the plant.

tu-lip tree (tū'lĭp trē), an American tree of the magnolia family, having large red and yellow flowers resembling the tulip.

tulle (tōōl), *n.* a delicate silk open-meshed or netlike material, used for veils, etc.

tum-ble (tŭm'bl), *v.i.* [*p.t.* and *p.p.* tumbled, *p.pr.* tumbling], to fall suddenly and hard; as, to *tumble* downstairs; roll about; to execute gymnastic feats, such as springs, somersaults, etc.; move in a disorderly fashion; as, the children came *tumbling* into the room: *v.t.* to throw down; turn over; rumple; disorder: *n.* a fall; a rolling over.

tum-ble-bug (tŭm'bl-bŭg"), *n.* any of certain beetles which roll up balls of dung and use them as places in which to deposit their eggs.

tum-bler (tŭm'blẽr), *n.* one who performs feats of rolling, somersaulting, etc.; an acrobat; a cylindrical drinking glass without a stem; a kind of pigeon; one of the parts of a lock which must be moved to a certain position, as by a key, before the bolt can be moved; a child's toy weighted at the bottom so that it rolls about but will not fall over.

tum-ble-weed (tŭm'bl-wēd"), *n.* any of certain weeds, which, in the fall, become readily unfastened from their roots and are blown about by the wind.

tum-brel (tŭm'brĕl), *n.* a cart that may be tilted up; such a cart used in the French Revolution to take prisoners to the guillotine; a kind of two-wheeled covered cart for hauling tools, ammunition, etc., in an army. Also, **tumbril**.

tu-me-fac-tion (tū"mē-făk'shŭn), *n.* a swelling; a tumor.

tu-me-fy (tū'mē-fī), *v.t.* and *v.i.* to inflate; puff up; swell.

tu-mid (tū'mĭd), *adj.* bulging; swollen; full of high-sounding words: said of style.—*adv.* **tumidly**.—*n.* **tumidness**.

tu-mor (tū'mẽr), *n.* an abnormal swelling or growth within or upon the body. Also, **tumour**.

tu-mult (tū'mŭlt), *n.* the noise and confusion made by a number of excited people; a violent agitation or disturbance; great excitement; riot.

tu-mul-tu-ous (tū-mŭl'tū-ŭs), *adj.* marked by, or full of, noisy confusion; as, a *tumultuous* crowd of people; disorderly; agitated, as the feelings; rough; as, a *tumultuous* sea.—*adv.* **tumultuously**.—*n.* **tumultuousness**.

Syn. turbulent, riotous, disturbed, confused, unruly.

Ant. (see orderly).

tu-mu-lus (tū'mū-lŭs), *n.* [*pl.* tumuli (-lī)], a manmade hill or mound, as over a grave.—*adj.* **tumular**.

tun (tŭn), *n.* a large cask; a measure of wine formerly equal to 252 gallons.

tun-a-ble (tūn'à-bl), *adj.* capable of being made harmonious; as, the strings of a violin.

tun-dra (tōōn'drȧ), *n.* a stretch of mossy, marshy, flat land in northern Siberia or the Arctics. Also, **toondra**.

tune (tūn), *n.* a series of musical notes having rhythm and forming a connected theme; air; a melody; condition of giving forth tones of the proper pitch; as, the piano is out of *tune*; agreement of sounds; state of harmonious adjustment; fitting mood: *v.t.* [*p.t.* and *p.p.* tuned, *p.pr.* tuning], to cause to produce the proper sounds; to adjust, as a voice or instrument, to a certain musical pitch; as, to *tune* a piano.

tune-ful (tūn'fōōl), *adj.* full of music or melody; musical; harmonious.—*adv.* **tunefully**.—*n.* **tunefulness**.

tune-less (tūn'lĕs), *adj.* without harmony; without melody; hence, sometimes, monotonous; not producing music; silent; as, a *tuneless* lyre.—*adv.* **tunelessly**.—*n.* **tunelessness**.

tun-er (tūn'ẽr), *n.* one who adjusts musical instruments to their proper pitch; as, a piano *tuner*.

tung-sten (tŭng'stĕn), *n.* a rare, hard, brittle, grayish-white metallic element, much used in making steel and electric lamps.

tu-nic (tū'nĭk), *n.* an undergarment worn by both the men and women of the ancient Romans; a loose kind of frock worn by women and boys; a kind of military coat.

tun-ing fork (tūn'ĭng fôrk), a fork-shaped piece of steel with two equal prongs which, when struck, vibrate at a certain rate and give a certain fixed tone: used to test the pitch of musical tones and instruments.

Tuning Fork

tun-nel (tŭn'ĕl), *n.* an underground passage cut through a hill or under a river; as, a railroad *tunnel*; the shaft of a chimney: *v.t.* to form an underground passage through or under; as, to *tunnel* a rock, hill, or river: *v.i.* to make a tunnel.

tun-ny (tŭn'ĭ), *n.* [*pl.* tunnies (-ĭz)], a large salt-water fish of the mackerel family.

tu-pe-lo (tū'pē-lō), *n.* [*pl.* tupelos (-lōz)], a North American tree with red berries and a very hard wood.

tuque (tūk), *n.* a cap shaped like a long, round bag with one end tucked in: worn in Canada as part of a winter sport costume.

Tu-ra-ni-an (tū-rā'nĭ-ăn), *adj.* pertaining to, or denoting, those languages and peoples of Europe and Asia not included in the Aryan and Semitic families, as Chinese.

tur-ba (tûr'bȧ), *n.* in a passion play, the chorus which represents the crowd of Jewish common people.

tur-ban (tûr'băn), *n.* the men's headdress worn by Orientals, consisting of a cap around which a scarf or sash is wrapped; any similar headdress, as that worn by women of rank early in the 19th century; a small, close-fitting brimless hat, or one with the brim turned up close to the round crown, worn by women and children.

tur-beh (tûr'bĕ), *n.* a small building resembling a dome, built over the tomb of a Mohammedan saint or person of high rank.

tur-bid (tûr'bĭd), *adj.* having the sediment stirred up; hence, muddy; impure; thick; as, *turbid* waters; unsettled; confused.—*adv.* **turbidly**.—*n.* **turbidness**.

ur-bi-nal (tûr'bĭ-năl), *adj.* in zoölogy, shaped like a spiral; rolled in spiral-shaped coil.

ur-bine (tûr'bĭn; tûr'bĭn), . a rotary motor riven by water or team.

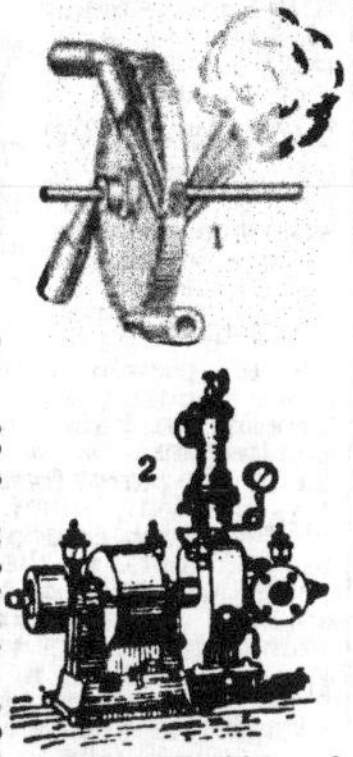

Steam Turbine. 1, view of wheel; 2, complete machine.

ur-bot (tûr'bŏt), *n.* a large flat sh found in European aters, used as food.

ur-bu-lence ûr'bū-lĕns), *n.* a state f disturbance; disrder; noisy agitation.

ur-bu-lent tûr'bū-lĕnt), *adj.* disrderly; uncontrollable s, a *turbulent* nature; gitated; wild; as, a *urbulent* stream; restss; noisy; riotous; isturbing; as, a *turulent* crowd of people.

u-reen (tū-rēn'), *n.* a deep essel for holding soup o be served at table.

urf (tûrf), *n.* the grassy surface of round; sod; peat: the turf, the race course: *.t.* to cover with grassy sod.

urf-y (tûr'fĭ), *adj.* having a grassy surface; well-sodded.—*n.* turfiness.

ur-gid (tûr'jĭd), *adj.* distended or swollen beyond the natural size; bloated; s, a *turgid* stream of water; turgid veins; nflated; bombastic; pompous; as, a *turgid* tyle in writing.—*adv.* turgidly.—*n.* turgidness.

ur-gid-i-ty (tûr-jĭd'ĭ-tĭ), *n.* the state of being swollen beyond the atural size.

Turk (tûrk), *n.* a native of Turkey; any member of the Turkish race.

Turkeys. A, domestic; B, wild.

ur-key (tûr'kĭ), *n.* [*pl.* turkeys (-kĭz)], a large wild or domestic American ird of the pheasant family, used as food.

ur-key buz-zard (tûr'kĭ bŭz'ẽrd), a large vulture of outh America and the southern United tates, that lives on the dead bodies of nimals.

Turk-ish (tûr'kĭsh), *adj.* of or pertaining to Turkey or the Turks; as, he *Turkish* empire; *Turkish* customs: *n.* the anguage of the Turks.

Turk-ish bath (tûr'kĭsh bȧth), a kind of bath, originally Orintal, in which the bather is made to erspire freely in an overheated room, and then bathed and rubbed down.

tur-mer-ic (tûr'mẽr-ĭk), *n.* an Australian tree and its aromatic root, used as a dye and as a condiment.

tur-moil (tûr'moil), *n.* wearisome or troublesome work; confused movement; disturbance; tumult or agitation.

turn (tûrn), *v.t.* to make to revolve or go round, as a wheel; to do by means of a revolving motion; as, to *turn* a handspring, a somersault, etc.; to change the direction or position of; as, to *turn* one's back; to *turn* an automobile; to change from one state to another; as, churning *turns* milk into butter; upset; as, success has *turned* her head; to cause to become; as, the shock *turned* her hair white; to nauseate; as, to *turn* the stomach; to guide or direct; as, he *turned* the horse toward home; to give into the hands of another: with *over;* as, *turn* the matter over to your lawyer; to bend or fold up, down, or over; as, to *turn* down the leaf of a book; to go around; as, to *turn* a corner; to shape in circular form, as by holding a revolving piece of wood against a sharp edge, or lathe; hence, to make or mold; as, he *turns* many a pretty compliment; to revolve in the mind; as, he *turned* the plan in every direction; to ponder; translate; as, he *turned* the Latin into English: *v.i.* to have a circular motion; revolve; become; as, her hair *turned* white; be changed; as, the syrup has *turned* to sugar; to start in another direction; as, the road *turns* sharply to the east; to change the behavior, especially to revolt; as, the people *turned* against their rulers; to depend; as, my action *turns* on yours; to incline to one side or the other: said of scales; hinge; to change from ebb to flow or from flow to ebb: said of the tide; to become spoiled, acid, or sour, as milk; to be nauseated, as the stomach; to become dizzy; as, my head *turns;* to result; as, the experiment *turned* out well: *n.* the act of revolving; circular motion, as of a wheel; a bend or curve; as, a *turn* of the road; change of direction; a good or evil act; as, to do a good *turn;* a single twist of a rope about a post; a critical change in the progress of a disease; colloquially, a startling surprise or shock; a short walk for air and exercise; as, to take a *turn* in the park; time for some act which one does in rotation with others; as, it is your *turn* to do the errand; special purpose; as, this will serve your *turn;* tendency; bent; a characteristic growing out of a particular cast of mind, thought, etc.; as, a man of his *turn* of mind; a short stage-piece or act.

turn-buck-le (tûrn'bŭk'l), *n.* a kind of catch to hold a window shutter, etc.; a metal loop which can be turned, by means of a swivel and a screw, so as to tighten a fastening of a rod, stay, etc.

turn-coat (tûrn'kōt'), *n.* one who forsakes his principles; one who goes over to an opposite party; a fickle person; a deserter.

turn-down (tûrn'doun'), *adj.* intended to have the upper part folded down; as, a *turndown* collar.

turn-er (tûr'nẽr), *n.* one who turns; one who shapes articles with a lathe; a utensil used to change the position of something; as, a cake-*turner;* a kind of tumbler pigeon.

turn-ing (tûr'nĭng), *n.* the act of one who, or that which, revolves, shapes, etc.; an angle or corner.

tur-nip (tûr'nĭp), *n.* the fleshy eatable root of either of two plants of the mustard family; also, either plant.

turn-key (tûrn'kē″), *n.* one who has charge of the keys of a prison or penitentiary; a warden or jailer.

turn-out (tûrn'out″), *n.* a coming forth; colloquially, a public gathering of persons, or attendance at a meeting; a labor strike; a railroad switch or siding; colloquially, a carriage and horses.

turn-o-ver (tûrn'ō″vẽr), *n.* the act or result of going round, upsetting, reversing the position of, etc.; an upset; a deal in the stock market; a pie or tart made by folding one-half of a circular crust over the other: *adj.* that can be bent over or under; made with a part folded over.

turn-pike (tûrn'pīk″), *n.* a gate or bar to stop wagons, carriages, etc., until toll is paid; a tollgate; a turnpike road.

turn-pike road (tûrn'pīk″ rōd), a public road that has, or once had, tollgates.

turn-sole (tûrn'sōl″), *n.* a plant whose flowers and stem seem to turn with the sun, as the sunflower.

turn-spit (tûrn'spĭt″), *n.* one who turns a spit, or slender, pointed rod for holding roasting meat; a kind of dog that used, by means of a treadmill, to turn a spit holding roasting meat.

turn-stile (tûrn'stīl″), *n.* formerly, a gate at the entrance of a path or passage, made of four arms pivoted on the top of a post and turning to let a person through; a similar but more complicated device, as at a doorway, to regulate or record the number of persons passing through.

turn-stone (tûrn'stōn″), *n.* a shore bird, similar to both the plover and the sandpiper.

turn-ta-ble (tûrn'tā″-bl), *n.* a platform that may be revolved or turned around, as for turning a locomotive or railroad engine.

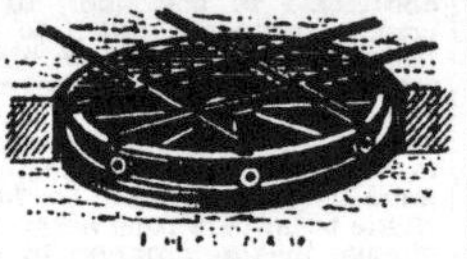

Turntable

tur-pen-tine (tûr'pĕn-tīn), *n.* a resin-like juice from pine and fir trees, used in mixing paints, varnishes, etc., and also in medicine; loosely, oil of turpentine.

tur-pi-tude (tûr'pĭ-tūd), *n.* baseness; downright, shameful wickedness; low badness.

tur-quoise (tûr-koiz'; tûr'kwoiz), *n.* a bright greenish-blue gem or precious stone; the birthstone for December. Also, turquois.

tur-ret (tŭr'ĕt), *n.* a small tower, usually at the corner of a building, sometimes merely decorative; a towerlike structure of thick steel, mounted on battleships or in fortifications and containing heavy guns that may be pointed in different directions by revolving the tower.

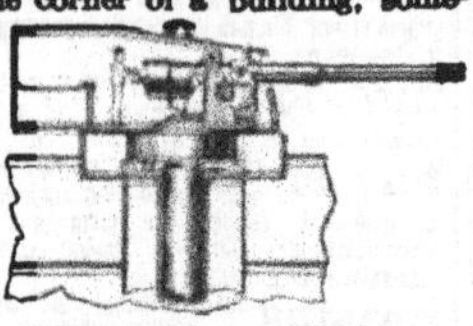

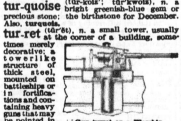

Gun-turret on a Warship

tur-ret-ed (tŭr'ĕt-ĕd), *adj.* furnished with, or shaped like, a small tower.

tur-tle (tûr'tl), *n.* a reptile whose body is inclosed in a bony shell covered with horny shields: used as food, especially in the form of soup; a tortoise.

Turtle

tur-tle-dove (tûr'tl-dŭv″), *n.* a kind of Old World wild dove, noted for its gentleness and its soft cooing.

Tus-can (tŭs'-kăn), *adj.* of, pertaining to, or belonging to, Tuscany, in Italy; naming a certain type of architecture: *n.* a native of Tuscany, in Italy; the purest form of the Italian language.

tush (tŭsh), *interj.* an expression of contempt, reproof, or restraint.

tusk (tŭsk), *n.* the long, pointed tooth on each side of the upper jaw of certain animals; as, the *tusk* of an elephant or a walrus; hence, any very long tooth.

tus-sle (tŭs'l), *n.* a scuffle; a contest of strength, usually in sport: *v.i.* to struggle; to wrestle.

tus-sock (tŭs'ŭk), *n.* a tuft or hummock of grass, twigs, etc.

tut (tŭt), *interj.* hush! be quiet! an expression of rebuke, impatience, etc.

tu-te-lage (tū'tē-lāj), *n.* the act of teaching and protecting; the state of being under a tutor or guardian; guardianship; protection.

tu-te-lar (tū'tē-lẽr), *adj.* having the guardianship of a person or thing; of or pertaining to a guardian or tutor; protecting. Also, tutelary.

tu-tor (tū'tẽr), *n.* one who instructs another; a private teacher; a guardian; a college instructor lower in rank than a professor: *v.t.* to instruct or teach privately: *v.i.* to do the work of a tutor; colloquially, to be taught privately.

tu-to-ri-al (tū-tō'rĭ-ăl), *adj.* pertaining to, or done by, a private instructor.

tu-tor-ship (tū'tẽr-shĭp), *n.* the office or position of a private teacher; guardianship; instruction of a tutor.

tut-ti-frut-ti (tōōt'tē-frōōt'tē), *n.* a candy or confection made of different kinds of preserved fruits: *adj.* made with, or flavored by, preserved fruits.

twad-dle (twŏd'l), *n.* silly talk: *v.t.* and *v.i.* to talk in a silly or foolish manner.—*n.* twaddler.

twain (twān), *n.* and *adj.* two; a pair. a poetic word.

twang (twăng), *n.* a sharp, quick, vibrating sound; a sharp nasal tone in speech; as, a Yankee *twang*: *v.t.* and *v.i.* to sound with a sharp, vibrating noise or nasal tone.

tweak (twēk), *v.t.* to pinch or pull with a jerk: *n.* a sudden, sharp pull or pinch; twitch; twist.

tweed (twēd), *n.* a soft, woolen fabric for men's wear.

tweez-ers (twēz'ẽrz), *n.pl.* small pincers for taking hold of, or pulling out, something tiny, as hairs; a tool used for grasping something; a set of surgeon's instruments.

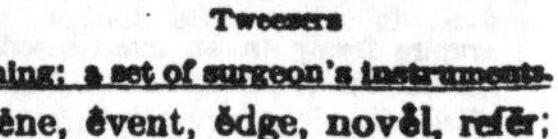

Tweezers

twelfth (twĕlfth), *adj.* next in order after the eleventh: *n.* one of twelve equal parts; the ordinal of twelve.

Twelfth-Night (twĕlfth'nīt''), *n.* the evening of the twelfth day after Christmas; Epiphany.

twelve (twĕlv), *adj.* one more than eleven; four times three: *n.* the number next after eleven; a dozen; a sign representing twelve units, as 12 or xii.

twelve-mo (twĕlv'mō), *n.* a book having the sheet folded into twelve leaves; a sheet so folded; duodecimo: also written *12mo:* *adj.* having twelve leaves to a sheet.

twelve-month (twĕlv'mŭnth''), *adj.* and *n.* a year.

twen-ti-eth (twĕn'tĭ-ĕth), *adj.* next in order after the nineteenth; being one of twenty equal parts: *n.* one of twenty equal parts; the ordinal of twenty.

twen-ty (twĕn'tĭ), *adj.* twice ten: *n.* the number next after nineteen; a score; a sign representing twenty units, as 20 or xx.

twen-ty-four-mo (twĕn'tĭ-fōr-mō''), *n.* a sheet folded into twenty-four leaves; a book of the size so made: also written *24mo:* *adj.* having twenty-four leaves to a sheet.

twi-bil (twī'bĭl), *n.* formerly, a double-bladed battle ax; also, an axlike garden tool.

twice (twīs), *adv.* two times; doubly; in twofold measure or degree.

twid-dle (twĭd''l), *v.t.* to twirl in a light manner; as, to *twiddle* one's thumbs: *v.i.* to play or trifle.

twig (twĭg), *n.* a small shoot or branch of a tree.

twi-light (twī'līt''), *n.* the faint light before sunrise and after sunset; partial light; dimness; obscurity: *adj.* of or pertaining to the time before sunrise or after sunset; dim; obscure.

twill (twĭl), *n.* a weave of cloth which shows diagonal lines or ribs on the surface; fabric woven with such ribs, as serge: *v.t.* to weave, as a fabric, with diagonal lines or ribs.

twin (twĭn), *adj.* double; as, *twin* towers, made of two separate, but equal, parts; closely resembling; born at the same birth with another; as, a *twin* brother: *n.* one of two born at one birth; a person or thing very like another.

twine (twīn), *v.t.* [*p.t.* and *p.p.* twined, *p.pr.* twining], to twist; wind round; embrace; make by twisting or coiling; as, to *twine* a garland: *v.i.* to twist; to wind or coil; as, the vine *twines* over the porch: *n.* a kind of strong cord made of twisted strands; an entwining.

twin-flow-er (twĭn'flou''ẽr), *n.* a hardy creeping evergreen plant that grows in damp, shady places.

twinge (twĭnj), *v.t.* [*p.t.* and *p.p.* twinged, *p.pr.* twinging], to feel a sudden, stinging pain: *v.t.* to cause to feel a sudden, stinging pain: *n.* a sudden, stinging pain.

twin-kle (twĭn'kl), *n.* a quick motion of the eye; a wink or gleam of the eye; a quick gleam; a flash that comes and goes, giving the effect of winking: *v.i.* [*p.t.* and *p.p.* twinkled, *p.pr.* twinkling], to open and shut rapidly; wink; sparkle; as, his eyes *twinkled;* shine with a gleam that comes and goes in flashes, as a star; to flash in and out rapidly: *v.t.* to cause to flash or sparkle; blink.

twin-kling (twĭn'klĭng), *n.* the time occupied by a wink or a brief flash; a moment; as, it happened in the *twinkling* of an eye; a wink or flash, as of light.

twirl (twûrl), *v.t.* to move or turn around rapidly; as, to *twirl* one's fingers; to whirl; as, to *twirl* a cane: *v.i.* to rotate rapidly: *n.* a quick, circular motion; a rapid whirling; a coil.

twist (twĭst), *v.t.* and *v.i.* to unite or form by winding two or more strands together; contort; distort; to wreathe; to twine or wind, as hair into a knot; to wrench or turn; as, to *twist* one's wrist; to turn from a direct line; as, the path down the cliff *twists* in and out: *n.* the act or manner of winding or twining; something made by winding strands together, as certain kinds of silk or cotton thread; as, buttonhole *twist;* a kind of roll tobacco; a twisted loaf of bread; a wrench or turn, as of a muscle.—*n.* twister.

twit (twĭt), *v.t.* [*p.t.* and *p.p.* twitted, *p.pr.* twitting], to annoy or tease by reminding of a mistake, weakness, etc.

twitch (twĭch), *v.t.* to pull with a sudden jerk: *v.i.* to move jerkily: *n.* a sudden jerk or pull; a short, jerky contraction of a muscle.

twite (twīt), *n.* the European mountain linnet or finch.

twit-ter (twĭt'ẽr), *v.i.* to utter in repetition small, sharp, broken sounds, as a bird; to feel a slight nervous excitement or tremor: *n.* a series of short, sharp, broken sounds; a nervous trembling.

'twixt (twĭkst), *prep.* between: an abbreviation of *betwixt*, used chiefly in poetical language.

two (tōō), *adj.* one added to one: *n.* the number next after one; a sign representing two units, as 2 or ii.

two-edged (tōō'ĕjd''; tōō'ĕj''ĕd), *adj.* having two edges, or one edge on each side; as, a *two-edged* saw.

two-fold (tōō'fōld''), *adj.* double; made of two folds, etc.: *adv.* in a double degree; doubly.

two-hand-ed (tōō'hănd''ĕd), *adj.* having two hands; used with two hands; able to use either hand with equal ease.

two-pence (tŭp'ĕns; tōō pĕns *only if two words*), *n.* the sum of two English pennies; a coin worth that amount.

two-pen-ny (tŭp'ĕn-ĭ), *adj.* of the value of two pence; hence, cheap, worthless, or commonplace.

two-ply (tōō'plī''), *adj.* having two thicknesses; woven double, as a carpet or other fabric.

two-some (tōō'sŭm), *adj.* performed or taken part in by two persons, as a game or dance; making a pair: *n.* a game, dance, etc., by two persons.

two-step (tōō'stĕp''), *n.* a kind of round dance in march or two-four time; the music for such a dance.

ty-coon (tī-kōōn'), *n.* the title given by foreigners to the shogun, or commander-in-chief of the Japanese army, who for over two centuries, till 1868, was the military governor, or actual ruler, of the nation.

ty-ing (tī'ĭng), the present participle and verbal noun of the verb *tie.*

tym-pan (tĭm'păn), *n.* in a printing press, a sheet of paper, parchment, etc., stretched between the sheets to be printed and the surface bearing the impression to be made.

tym-pan-ic (tĭm-păn'ĭk), *adj.* like a drum or drumhead; pertaining to the eardrum.

tym-pa-num (tĭm'pȧ-nŭm), *n.* [*pl.* tympanums (-nŭmz), tympana (-nȧ)], the middle ear; the eardrum; the diaphragm of a telephone.

type (tīp), *v.t.* [*p.t.* and *p.p.* typed, *p.pr.* typing], to make a copy of; to represent; to copy by means of a typewriter; to reproduce in letter-bearing metal blocks called type, or to make a plate impression of from such blocks: *n.* the mark or impression of something; an emblem; the first form of something, to be followed and copied; a model or pattern; an original design from which copies are to be made; a person who, or a thing which, stands as a foreshadowing of persons, things, or events which are to come later; a person in a story who represents an abstract quality; a person or thing representative of a group because of characteristics possessed in common with individuals of the group; a sample; in printing, a metal block bearing an impression of a letter, figure, etc., to be stamped in ink upon paper; such blocks taken collectively: formerly classified under names, as in the following table: now generally classified according to size, by a measure called a point, which equals 1-72 of an inch, each size corresponding to one of the names formerly used; as, 12-point type, formerly called pica, prints letters 1-6 of an inch high:

Size.		Former Name.	Sample of Type.
18	point	Great Primer.	abcdef
14	point	English.....	abcdef
12	point	Pica........	abcdefg
11	point	Small Pica...	abcdefgh
10	point	Long Primer.	abcdefghi
9	point	Bourgeois...	abcdefghijk
8	point	Brevier.....	abcdefghijk
7	point	Minion.....	abcdefghijkl
6	point	Nonpareil...	abcdefghijklm
5½	point	Agate.......	abcdefghijklm
5	point	Pearl.......	abcdefghijklm

type met-al (tīp mĕt'ăl), a kind of metal used for making blocks for printing.

type-set-ter (tīp'sĕt"ẽr), *n.* one who, or that which, sets type, or arranges it in the form of words as desired; a compositor or printer; a machine for setting type, such as a linotype.

type-set-ting (tīp'sĕt"ĭng), *n.* the act, process, or trade, of setting type.

typ-ewrite (tīp'rīt"), *v.t.* and *v.i.* to write with a machine; to type.

type-writ-er (tīp'rīt"ẽr), *n.* an instrument or machine for writing, by means of a keyboard, in letters similar to those used in print; one who operates such a machine; a typist.

type-writ-ing (tīp'rīt"ĭng), *n.* the act of using a machine which produces letters similar to those which are printed; the act or product of typing; manuscript made with such a machine.

ty-phoid (tī'foid), *adj.* pertaining to, or like, typhus, a contagious fever: typhoid fever, an infectious disease, contracted through the intestines, and due to impure water, poor food, etc., through which the bacillus is introduced into the system.

ty-phoon (tī-fōōn'), *n.* a violent tornado or whirlwind.

ty-phus (tī'fŭs), *n.* a dangerous contagious fever marked by great weakness, delirium, and a peculiar rash, or eruptions of red spots on the body.

typ-i-cal (tĭp'ĭ-kăl), *adj.* symbolic; representative of a class; showing the characteristics of its group; like others of its kind; as, a *typical* case, or a *typical* Yankee.—*adv.* typically.

typ-i-fy (tĭp'ĭ-fī), *v.t.* [*p.t.* and *p.p.* typified, *p.pr.* typifying], to represent or show by an image or emblem; to foreshadow; to show the qualities of (one's class or group).

typ-ing (tīp'ĭng), *n.* the act of using a typewriter; the manuscript so written; the act of reproducing from letter-bearing blocks called type, or of making impressions from such blocks; the impression so obtained.

typ-ist (tīp'ĭst), *n.* one who operates a typewriting machine; a typewriter.

ty-pog-ra-pher (tī-pŏg'rȧ-fẽr), *n.* a printer.

ty-po-graph-i-cal (tī"pō-grăf'ĭ-kăl), *adj.* of the nature of, or pertaining to, the art of printing; as, a *typographical* error. Also, typographic.—*adv.* typographically.

ty-pog-ra-phy (tī-pŏg'rȧ-fĭ), *n.* the art of printing with type.

ty-ran-ni-cal (tĭ-răn'ĭ-kăl), *adj.* pertaining to, or like, a tyrant; as, a *tyrannical* master; despotic; cruel; overbearing.—*adv.* tyrannically.

ty-ran-ni-cide (tĭ-răn'ĭ-sīd), *n.* one who kills a tyrant, or despot; the killing of a tyrant.

tyr-an-nize (tĭr'ă-nīz), *v.i.* to act like a despot; to rule severely and cruelly; *v.t.* to treat oppressively and unjustly.

tyr-an-nous (tĭr'ă-nŭs), *adj.* arbitrary; unjustly severe and oppressive; despotic.—*adv.* tyrannously.

tyr-an-ny (tĭr'ă-nĭ), *n.* the government or conduct of a despot, or cruel and unjust ruler or master; cruel or oppressive government; undue severity; as, the *tyranny* of the majority.

ty-rant (tī'rănt), *n.* an absolute monarch; a despot; a ruler or master who uses his great power to oppress those under him, as Nero of Rome.

Tyr-i-an (tĭr'ĭ-ăn), *adj.* pertaining to ancient Tyre; of a rich purple color: *n.* a native of Tyre.

ty-ro (tī'rō), *n.* [*pl.* tyros (-rōz)], a beginner; a novice or learner.

Tyr-o-lese (tĭr"ō-lēz'; tĭr"ō-lēs'), *adj.* pertaining to the Tyrol, an Austrian province, or to its natives: *n.* a native of the Tyrol.

ty-ro-ma (tī-rō'mȧ), *n.* a disease of the roots of the hair, causing patches of baldness without affecting the hair around the bald spots.

tzar (tsär), *n.* a king or an emperor; formerly, the title of the ruler of Russia. Also, tsar, czar.

tza-rin-a (tsä-rē'nȧ), *n.* formerly, the title of the wife of the emperor of Russia. Also, tsarina, czarina.

U

u-biq-ui-tous (ū-bĭk'wĭ-tŭs), *adj.* existing everywhere at one time; present everywhere at once.—*adv.* **ubiquitously.**—*n.* **ubiquitousness.**

u-biq-ui-ty (ū-bĭk'wĭ-tĭ), *n.* omnipresence, or existence everywhere at one time.

U-boat (ū'bōt"), *n.* a submarine boat: an abbreviation for the German *Unterseeboot*, undersea boat.

ud-der (ŭd'ẽr), *n.* the bag, or milk gland, of certain animals, as the cow.

ugh (ōō; ŭkh), *interj.* an exclamation of disgust or horror.

ug-ly (ŭg'lĭ), *adj.* [*comp.* uglier, *superl.* ugliest], displeasing to the eye; hideous; of a hateful or disagreeable temper; bad in character; as, an *ugly* report; ill-natured; quarrelsome.—*n.* **ugliness.**

Syn. unsightly, plain, homely, ill-favored, repulsive.

Ant. (see beautiful).

uh-lan (ōō'län; ōō-län'), *n.* a Prussian cavalryman. Also, **ulan.**

u-kase (ū-kās'), *n.* formerly, a decree of the Czar of Russia taking effect as law; hence, any official decree or proclamation.

u-ke-le-le (ū"kĕ-lā'lē), *n.* a stringed instrument, of Hawaiian origin, shaped like a small guitar, and popular for informal musical performances.

ul-cer (ŭl'sẽr), *n.* a surface sore, often discharging matter; hence, anything corrupt or festering.

ul-cer-ate (ŭl'sẽr-āt), *v.t.* [*p.t.* and *p.p.* ulcerated; *p.pr.* ulcerating], to affect with an ulcer, or surface sore: *v.i.* to be affected by an ulcer.

ul-cer-a-tion (ŭl"sẽr-ā'shŭn), *n.* the process of forming into an ulcer; state of being affected by an ulcer.

ul-cer-ous (ŭl'sẽr-ŭs), *adj.* having the character or appearance of a festering sore.

ul-na (ŭl'nȧ), *n.* [*pl.* ulnæ (-nē)], the inner of the two bones of the forearm.—*adj.* **ulnar.**

ul-ster (ŭl'stẽr), *n.* a long, loose overcoat of woolen cloth.

ul-te-ri-or (ŭl-tē'rĭ-ẽr), *adj.* lying beyond or on the farther side; more distant: beyond what is expressed or implied; as, an *ulterior* motive back of an act.—*adv.* **ulteriorly.**

ul-ti-ma (ŭl'tĭ-mȧ), *n.* the last syllable of a word.

ul-ti-mate (ŭl'tĭ-māt), *adj.* the last; as, an *ultimate* result; utmost; farthest off; as, an *ultimate* destination; extreme; final; not to be discussed further; as, an *ultimate* decision.—*adv.* **ultimately.**—*n.* **ultimateness.**

ul-ti-ma-tum (ŭl"tĭ-mā'tŭm), *n.* [*pl.* ultimata (-tȧ), ultimatums (-tŭmz)], the statement of a final proposition; a last offer of terms of agreement, not to accept which means a breaking off of friendly relations; as, Austria's *ultimatum* to Serbia.

ul-ti-mo (ŭl'tĭ-mō), *adv.* in the month before the present. [LAT.]

ul-tra (ŭl'trȧ), *adj.* extreme; extravagant; unreasonably advanced; more than others; as, an *ultra* conservative.

ul-tra-ma-rine (ŭl"trȧ-mȧ-rēn'), *n.* a beautiful blue coloring.

ul-tra-mon-tane (ŭl"trȧ-mŏn'tān), *adj.* on the other side of the mountains, especially the Alps: *n.* one who lives beyond the mountains; especially, one who lives south of the Alps.

ul-tra-vi-o-let (ŭl"trȧ-vī'ō-lĕt), *adj.* outside the visible spectrum at the violet end: said of certain rays capable of chemical action and of greater refraction than the violet rays.

U-lys-ses (ū-lĭs'ēz), *n.* the Roman name for Odysseus, king of Ithaca: the wisest and subtlest of the Greek chiefs in the Trojan War.

um-ber (ŭm'bẽr), *n.* a brown earth, used as coloring matter, containing iron and manganese: *adj.* of an olive-brown color; dark brown; dusky.

um-bra (ŭm'brȧ), *n.* [*pl.* umbræ (-brē)], a shade or shadow; especially, the dark cone of shadow cast by a planet or satellite on the side opposite to the sun, in whose limits the sun's disk is invisible; the dark central portion of a sunspot.

um-brage (ŭm'brāj), *n.* formerly, shade or obscurity; a sense of being put in the shade; hence, hurt pride; sense of injury; jealous suspicion; pique.

Syn. dissatisfaction, displeasure, offense.

um-bra-geous (ŭm-brā'jŭs), *adj.* shady; as, *umbrageous* trees.—*adv.* **umbrageously.**—*n.* **umbrageousness.**

um-brel-la (ŭm-brĕl'ȧ), *n.* a device for protection against rain, sun, etc., consisting of a collapsible metal frame, covered with silk, cotton, or other waterproof fabric, and carried in the hand: a small umbrella for protection against the sun is called a *sunshade* or *parasol.*

um-brel-la tree (ŭm-brĕl'ȧ trē), a low-growing, long-stemmed, wide-spreading tree, resembling an umbrella in shape.

u-mi-ak (ōō'mĭ-ăk), *n.* an Eskimo open boat, driven by paddles, and made of skins drawn over a framework of wood: often called *woman's boat.*

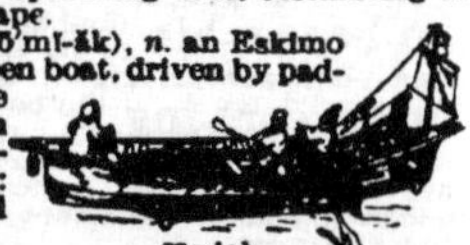

Umiak

um-laut (ōōm'lout), *n.* a modified vowel sound, especially in German; the sign [¨], used to indicate such modified vowel sound. [GER.]

um-pire (ŭm'pīr), *n.* a third party to whom a dispute is referred for settlement; one chosen in a game to see that its rules are observed and to decide disputes: *v.t.* and *v.i.* to settle, as a dispute; to decide as judge on the plays of a game; as, to *umpire* a game of baseball; to *umpire* in a game.

Syn., n. referee, arbitrator, judge.

un- (ŭn-), a *prefix* meaning not; also expressing reversal, or undoing, of the action or condition implied in the word: possible for use before almost any adjective, participle, or adverb, thus forming an unlimited number of words, of which only the most important or difficult are here included.

un-a-ble (ŭn-ā'bl), *adj.* incapable; without power enough; incompetent.

un-a-bridged (ŭn″ȧ-brĭjd'), *adj.* not shortened; having nothing omitted; as, an *unabridged* dictionary.

un-ac-cent-ed (ŭn″ăk-sĕnt'ĕd), *adj.* not stressed with the voice; as, an *unaccented* syllable.

un-ac-count-a-ble (ŭn″ă-koun'tȧ-bl), *adj.* not to be explained; without known reason; strange.—*adv.* **unaccountably.**—*n.* **unaccountableness.**

un-ac-cus-tomed (ŭn″ă-kŭs'tŭmd), *adj.* not usual; not familiar with: with *to;* as, she is *unaccustomed* to the work.

un-af-fect-ed (ŭn″ă-fĕk'tĕd), *adj.* without pretense; natural.—*adv.* **unaffectedly.**—*n.* **unaffectedness.**

un-al-loyed (ŭn″ă-loid'), *adj.* pure; without inferior part; unmixed; as, *unalloyed* pleasure.

u-na-nim-i-ty (ū″nȧ-nĭm'ĭ-tĭ), *n.* agreement in opinion; united consent.
Syn. accord, unity, concord.
Ant. (see discord).

u-nan-i-mous (ū-năn'ĭ-mŭs), *adj.* united in a single opinion; agreeing; showing that all agree; as, a *unanimous* vote.—*adv.* **unanimously.**—*n* **unanimousness.**

un-armed (ŭn-ärmd'), *adj.* without weapons; defenseless.

un-as-sum-ing (ŭn″ă-sūm'ĭng), *adj.* without self-conceit; retiring; modest.

un-a-void-a-ble (ŭn″ȧ-void'ȧ-bl), *adj.* not to be escaped; inevitable.—*adv.* **unavoidably.**

un-a-wares (ŭn″ȧ-wârz'), *adv.* in an unexpected manner; by surprise; as, they caught the enemy *unawares.* Also, **unaware.**

un-bal-anced (ŭn-băl'ănst), *adj.* of unequal weight; out of equilibrium; hence, mentally disordered; slightly insane.

un-bar (ŭn-bär'), *v.t.* to remove a bar from; to unlock.

un-bear-a-ble (ŭn-bâr'ȧ-bl), *adj.* not to be endured; intolerable.—*adv.* **unbearably.**—*n.* **unbearableness.**

un-be-com-ing (ŭn″bē-kŭm'ĭng), *adj.* not suitable or fit; improper; as, conduct *unbecoming* for a lady; not suited to one's appearance; as, an *unbecoming* hat.—*adv.* **unbecomingly.**—*n.* **unbecomingness.**
Syn. unseemly, indecorous, indecent, indelicate.

un-be-lief (ŭn″bē-lēf'), *n.* lack of faith; as, they could not enter in because of *unbelief;* skepticism; refusal to accept the teachings of revealed religion.
Syn. disbelief, incredulity.

un-be-liev-er (ŭn″bē-lēv'ẽr), *n.* one who doubts; one who lacks faith; one who refuses to accept as true the teachings of revealed religion.—*adj.* **unbelieving.**

un-bend (ŭn-bĕnd'), *v.t.* [*p.t.* and *p.p.* unbent, *p.pr.* unbending], to straighten; to relieve from a crooked position or a strain: *v.i.* to become straight; to relax; to become less stiff; hence, to become friendly in manner.

un-bend-ing (ŭn-bĕnd'ĭng), *adj.* straight and stiff; not relaxing; of determined and unyielding temper.—*adv.* **unbendingly.**

un-bi-ased (ŭn-bī'ăst), *adj.* not inclined to one side more than the other; impartial. Also, **unbiassed.**—*adv.* **unbiasedly, unbiassedly.**—*n.* **unbiasedness, unbiassedness.**

un-bid-den (ŭn-bĭd'n), *adj.* not ordered or commanded; not invited; as, an *unbidden* guest.

un-bind (ŭn-bīnd'), *v.t.* [*p.t.* and *p.p.* unbound, *p.pr.* unbinding], to make loose; untie.

un-blessed (ŭn-blĕst'), *adj.* without a blessing; miserable. Also, **unblest.**

un-bolt (ŭn-bōlt'), *v.t.* to draw back a bolt from; unfasten.—*p.adj.* **unbolted.**

un-born (ŭn-bôrn'), *adj.* not yet born; pertaining to the future.

un-bos-om (ŭn-bŏŏz'ŭm), *v.t.* to free oneself from, as a secret; disclose confidentially; relieve (oneself) by disclosing: *v.i.* to free one's mind by telling secret thoughts.

un-bound-ed (ŭn-boun'dĕd), *adj.* unlimited; unrestrained; as, *unbounded* goodness.—*adv.* **unboundedly.**—*n.* **unboundedness.**

un-bowed (ŭn-boud'), *adj.* not bent; not bowed or conquered, not beaten.

un-braid (ŭn-brād'), *v.t.* to take apart the strands of, as a plait of hair.

un-bri-dled (ŭn-brī'dld), *adj.* not fastened with a bridle; free; uncontrolled; as, an *unbridled* tongue.

un-bro-ken (ŭn-brō'kn), *adj.* whole; not interrupted; as, an *unbroken* silence; not tamed; as, an *unbroken* horse; continuous; as, an *unbroken* forest.—*adv.* **unbrokenly.**—*n.* **unbrokenness.**

un-called-for (ŭn-kôld'fôr″), *adj.* not needed; undemanded; out of place; superfluous.

un-can-ny (ŭn-kăn'ĭ), *adj.* weird; not to be explained reasonably; vaguely mysterious; unearthly.—*adv.* **uncannily.**—*n.* **uncanniness.**

un-ceas-ing (ŭn-sēs'ĭng), *adj.* never stopping; continuous; without interruption.—*adv.* **unceasingly.**

un-cer-tain (ŭn-sûr'tĭn), *adj.* not sure; doubtful; as, the result is *uncertain;* not positive; not steady; as, the shaky platform gave an *uncertain* support; not reliable.—*adv.* **uncertainly.**—*n.* **uncertainness.**

un-cer-tain-ty (ŭn-sûr'tĭn-tĭ), *n.* [*pl.* uncertainties (-tĭz)], state of being doubtful; lack of assurance; unreliability.

un-change-a-ble (ŭn-chān'jȧ-bl), *adj.* not to be altered, remaining always the same.—*adv.* **unchangeably.**—*n.* **unchangeableness.**

un-char-i-ta-ble (ŭn-chăr'ĭ-tȧ-bl), *adj.* not inclined to help the needy; not generous; unkind; harsh in judging others; as, she indulged in *uncharitable* criticism.—*adv.* **uncharitably.**—*n.* **uncharitableness.**

un-chris-tian (ŭn-krĭs'chăn), *adj.* heathen; not suitable for, or like, a Christian; as, *unchristian* conduct; not in accordance with the customs of the so-called Christian nations.

un-cir-cum-cised (ŭn-sûr'kŭm-sīzd), *adj.* not of the Israelites; hence, belonging to the Gentiles.

un-civ-il (ŭn-sĭv′ĭl), *adj.* rude; without courtesy; not civilized.

un-civ-i-lized (ŭn-sĭv′ĭ-līzd), *adj.* savage; barbarous.

un-clasp (ŭn-klȧsp′), *v.t.* to undo the clasp of, as a pin or buckle.

un-cle (ŭṅ′kl), *n.* the brother of one's father or mother; one's aunt's husband; colloquially, an old man, usually in an inferior position; **slang**, a pawnbroker.

Un-cle Sam (ŭṅ′kl săm′), a popular designation of the meaning of U. S.—United States.

un-clean (ŭn-klēn′), *adj.* physically or morally impure; soiled; foul. —*n.* **uncleanness.**

un-clean-ly (ŭn-klĕn′lĭ), *adj.* not inclined to purity, physical or moral; habitually dirty.—*n.* **uncleanliness.**

un-com-fort-a-ble (ŭn-kŭm′fẽr-tȧ-bl), *adj.* not at ease, physically or mentally; causing uneasiness.

un-com-mon (ŭn-kŏm′ŭn), *adj.* not usual; out of the ordinary; rare; scarce.

un-com-pro-mis-ing (ŭn-kŏm′prō-mīz′ĭng), *adj.* not willing to make concessions; not willing to yield; unbending; holding rigidly to opinions or beliefs.—*adv.* **uncompromisingly.**

un-con-cern (ŭn′kŏn-sûrn′), *n.* lack of interest or anxiety; indifference.

un-con-cerned (ŭn′kŏn-sûrnd′), *adj.* not disturbed or anxious; not interested.—*adv.* **unconcernedly.**

un-con-di-tion-al (ŭn′kŏn-dĭsh′ŭn-ăl), *adj.* not limited; without modifications; without special provisions; as, an *unconditional* surrender; absolute.—*adv.* **unconditionally.**

un-con-firmed (ŭn′kŏn-fûrmd′), *adj.* not based on official information; not authoritative; as, the report of the victory was *unconfirmed.*

un-con-scion-a-ble (ŭn-kŏn′shŭn-ȧ-bl), *adj.* unreasonable; unjust.—*adv.* **unconscionably.**

un-con-scious (ŭn-kŏn′shŭs), *adj.* not mentally awake; not in a state of ability to perceive by the senses; without apparent feeling or life; not aware: with *of.*—*adv.* **unconsciously.**—*n.* **unconsciousness.**

un-con-sti-tu-tion-al (ŭn-kŏn′stĭ-tū′shŭn-ăl), *adj.* not in accordance with the written framework of government of a country.—*n.* **unconstitutionality.**

un-couth (ŭn-kōōth′), *adj.* awkward; ungainly; odd; boorish.—*adv.* **uncouthly.**—*n.* **uncouthness.**

un-cov-er (ŭn-kŭv′ẽr), *v.t.* to remove a cover from; to take the hat or cap from; to cause to appear: *v.i.* to take off the hat or cap; as, *uncover* for the flag.

unc-tion (ŭṅk′shŭn), *n.* the act of anointing in sign of consecration; an ointment; anything soothing; as, lay this flattering *unction* to your soul; the gift of using words so as to arouse emotion, especially religious fervor.

unc-tu-ous (ŭṅk′tū-ŭs), *adj.* oily; smooth; extremely bland; fervid; especially, insincerely gushing; as, an *unctuous* and flattering speech.—*adv.* **unctuously.** —*n.* **unctuousness.**

Syn. suave, fulsome, smug.

un-curl (ŭn-kûrl′), *v.t.* and *v.i.* to straighten out, as hair, feathers, etc.

un-daunt-ed (ŭn-dăn′tĕd; ŭn-dôn′tĕd), *adj.* not dismayed; fearless.—*adv.* **undauntedly.**

un-dec-a-gon (ŭn-dĕk′ȧ-gŏn), *n.* a plane figure with eleven sides and eleven angles.

un-de-ceive (ŭn′dē-sēv′), *v.t.* to set free from error, mistake, or wrong idea; to correct in a wrong impression or belief.

un-de-ni-a-ble (ŭn′dē-nī′ȧ-bl), *adj.* not to be contradicted; compelling admission or acceptance; not to be disputed.—*adv.* **undeniably.**

un-der (ŭn′dẽr), *prep.* beneath or below; as, *under* a tree; oppressed or weighed down by; as, Belgium suffered *under* the German invasion; beneath, as acted upon by something; as, to be *under* treatment for a disease; inferior to; for less than; as, to sell goods *under* the market price: *adv.* below; in a lower state or position; as, the drowning boy went *under* for the third time: *adj.* lower in degree, rank, or position: usually in compound words, as *under*-officer, etc.

Syn., *prep.* below: *adj.* subordinate, inferior.

Ant. (see above).

un-der-bid (ŭn′dẽr-bĭd′), *v.t.* [*p.t.* underbid, *p.p.* underbidden, *p.pr.* underbidding], to offer to sell or do for a lower price than.

un-der-bred (ŭn′dẽr-brĕd′), *adj.* showing poor character and training; lacking good breeding.

un-der-brush (ŭn′dẽr-brŭsh′), *n.* bushes, shrubs, and small trees growing thickly beneath large trees in a forest.

un-der-clothes (ŭn′dẽr-klōthz′), *n.pl.* garments worn beneath other clothes. Also, **underclothing.**

un-der-cur-rent (ŭn′dẽr-kŭr′ĕnt), *n.* a current below the surface of air, water, etc.; a concealed tendency of thought or feeling.

un-der-done (ŭn′dẽr-dŭn′; ŭn′dẽr-dŭn′), *adj.* cooked too little; rare: said of meat.

un-der-foot (ŭn′dẽr-fŏŏt′), *adv.* beneath the feet; underneath.

un-der-go (ŭn′dẽr-gō′), *v.t.* [*p.t.* underwent, *p.p.* undergone, *p.pr.* undergoing], to pass through or experience; as, to *undergo* an operation; to suffer; as, to *undergo* great pain.

un-der-grad-u-ate (ŭn′dẽr-grăd′ū-āt), *n.* a student in a university or college who has not taken his first degree; a student in any school who has not received his diploma.

un-der-ground (ŭn′dẽr-ground′), *n.* a space or place beneath the earth's surface: *adj.* below the surface of the earth; colloquially, hidden.

un-der-growth (ŭn′dẽr-grōth′), *n.* underbrush; low shrubs and bushes growing beneath the trees of a forest.

un-der-hand (ŭn′dẽr-hănd′), *adj.* done by meanness or fraud; deceitful; sly; crookedly secretive; as, *underhand* methods of doing business; in baseball, thrown with the hand lower than the shoulder.

un-der-hand-ed (ŭn′dẽr-hăn′dĕd), *adj.* deceptive; secretive; dealing crookedly; sly.—*adv.* **underhandedly.**—*n.* **underhandedness.**

un-der-lay (ŭn″dẽr-lā′), *v.t.* [*p.t.* and *p.p.* underlaid, *p.pr.* underlaying], to put something beneath or spread something under: *n.* (ŭn′dẽr-lā″), a layer of paper or pasteboard put under type, etc., to raise it to the necessary level for printing.

un-der-lie (ŭn″dẽr-lī′), *v.t.* [*p.t.* underlay, *p.p.* underlain, *p.pr.* underlying], to lie or be beneath; to be at the bottom of, or to serve as the basis of; as, of an argument or theory; to be a support for.

un-der-line (ŭn″dẽr-līn′), *v.* to draw a line beneath, as in a manuscript to indicate italics.

un-der-ling (ŭn′dẽr-lĭng), *n.* a person occupying a low position; a person obeying the orders of another, as a servant.

un-der-mine (ŭn″dẽr-mīn′), *v.t.* [*p.t.* and *p.p.* undermined, *p.pr.* undermining], to dig beneath; to form a tunnel under; hence, to weaken; as, to *undermine* one's health; to seek to overthrow secretly or wickedly; as, to *undermine* someone's influence.

un-der-neath (ŭn″dẽr-nēth′; ŭn″dẽr-nēth′), *adv.* and *prep.* beneath; below; under.

un-der-pin (ŭn″dẽr-pĭn′), *v.t.* [*p.t.* and *p.p.* underpinned, *p.pr.* underpinning], to lay bricks, stones, etc., under, as for a foundation of a building to be erected; to support by a foundation; hence, to prop.

un-der-pin-ning (ŭn′dẽr-pĭn″ĭng), *n.* the foundation material of a building.

un-der-pro-duc-tion (ŭn″dẽr-prō-dŭk′shŭn), *n.* a condition of industry in which too little of some commodity or article is produced, with the result of raising the market price.

un-der-score (ŭn″dẽr-skōr′), *v.t.* [*p.t.* and *p.p.* underscored, *p.pr.* underscoring], to draw a line or mark under; as, to *underscore* a word in a manuscript: *n.* a line drawn beneath a word or phrase in a manuscript.

un-der-sea (ŭn′dẽr-sē″), *adj.* beneath the suface of the ocean; submarine: **undersea boat**, a submarine boat.

un-der-sell (ŭn″dẽr-sĕl′), *v.t.* to sell at a lower price than; as, to *undersell* a competitor in business.

un-der-shirt (ŭn′dẽr-shûrt″), *n.* a woven garment for the upper part of the body, worn next the skin.

un-der-shot (ŭn′dẽr-shŏt″), *adj.* having the lower front teeth more prominent than the upper ones: said of a bulldog; having a prominent lower jaw.

un-der-sign (ŭn″dẽr-sīn′), *v.t.* to write one's name below, as a petition.

un-der-skirt (ŭn′dẽr-skûrt″), *n.* a petticoat; a skirt worn beneath the dress.

un-der-slung (ŭn′dẽr-slŭng″), *adj.* of an automobile, being so constructed that the frame of the body of the car is beneath the axles.

un-der-stand (ŭn″dẽr-stănd′), *v.t.* [*p.t.* and *p.p.* understood, *p.pr.* understanding], to perceive or know by the mind; be informed of; know the meaning of; assume or infer; know by experience: *v.i.* to know what something means; to be informed; comprehend.

un-der-stand-ing (ŭn″dẽr-stănd′ĭng), *p.adj.* intelligent: *n.* the reasoning faculties; the mind; state of knowing, or power to know, the meaning of anything; comprehension; an agreement.—*adv.* **understandingly.**

Syn. knowledge, faculty, explanation.

un-der-state (ŭn″dẽr-stāt′), *v.t.* to tell less than the truth about; as, to *understate* the facts; to represent as less important than it really is.

un-der-strap-per (ŭn′dẽr-străp″ẽr), *n.* one who occupies an inferior position; an employee; a subordinate official.

un-der-stud-y (ŭn′dẽr-stŭd″ĭ), *v.t.* and *v.i.* to learn another actor's part in a play, in order to take his place, if necessary: *n.* an actor trained to serve as substitute for another; hence, a person who is able to imitate another.

un-der-take (ŭn″dẽr-tāk′), *v.t.* [*p.t.* undertook, *p.p.* undertaken, *p.pr.* undertaking], to take upon oneself; assume as a duty or responsibility; attempt or try; promise; as, I will *undertake* that the work shall be finished: *v.i.* to promise.

Syn. agree, begin.

un-der-tak-er (ŭn″dẽr-tāk′ẽr), *n.* one who assumes or attempts a task; (ŭn′dẽr-tāk″ẽr), one who makes the dead ready for burial and manages funerals.

un-der-tak-ing (ŭn″dẽr-tāk′ĭng), *n.* the taking upon oneself of a task or responsibility; especially, the business of managing funerals; an enterprise or project.

un-der-tone (ŭn′dẽr-tōn″), *n.* a low or subdued pitch of voice or sound; a dull or quiet color.

un-der-tow (ŭn′dẽr-tō″), *n.* a current below the surface of water, usually on the seashore, which moves in the opposite direction from the surface movement.

un-der-val-ue (ŭn″dẽr-văl′ū), *v.t.* [*p.t.* and *p.p.* undervalued, *p.pr.* undervaluing], to consider as of less worth than the real worth; to regard as unimportant or worth little; underestimate; depreciate.—*n.* **undervaluation.**

un-der-vest (ŭn′dẽr-vĕst″), *n.* an undershirt, usually sleeveless.

un-der-wa-ter (ŭn′dẽr-wô″tẽr), *adj.* and *adv.* below the surface of the water.

un-der-wear (ŭn′dẽr-wâr″), *n.* underclothing taken collectively.

un-der-world (ŭn′dẽr-wûrld″), *n.* Hades, or the place of the dead; the degraded and criminal classes.

un-der-write (ŭn″dẽr-rīt′), *v.t.* [*p.t.* underwrote, *p.p.* underwritten, *p.pr.* underwriting], to write underneath; to write one's name under, or sign (an insurance policy), in consideration of a premium paid, and thus become liable to make good a stated loss or damage; to sign an agreement to buy on a given date at a specified price (bonds or shares not yet issued); loosely, to subscribe to, as a project which requires capital: *v.i.* to carry on an insurance business.

un-der-writ-er (ŭn′dẽr-rīt″ẽr), *n.* one whose business is to underwrite insurance, issues of stock, etc.

un-dine (ŭn-dēn′; ŭn′dēn), *n.* a kind of water nymph said by legend to become human by marrying a mortal.

un-do (ŭn-dōō′), *v.t.* [*p.t.* undid, *p.p.* undone, *p.pr.* undoing], to make null and void; as, to overwork will *undo* all the ood you received from your vacation; to do way with the result of; to make of no ffect; to act upon in a way contrary to revious action; as, it was necessary to *ndo* all the work he had done; to destroy; o loosen; as, to *undo* a knot.

un-do-ing (ŭn-dōō'ĭng), *p.pr.* of *undo:* *n.* the act of making somehing of no effect; ruin; as, his family's exravagance proved to be his *undoing;* the ct of unfastening.

un-done (ŭn-dŭn'), *p.adj.* made of no effect; altered to an opposite ondition; ruined; as, alas! I am *undone;* unfastened; not accomplished; as, the task vas left *undone.*

un-doubt-ed (ŭn-dout'ĕd), *adj.* certain; not to be questioned; ure.—*adv.* **undoubtedly.**

un-dress (ŭn-drĕs'), *v.t.* to take clothes or decorations off from; to trip: *v.i.* to take off the clothes: *n.* (ŭn'drĕs; ŭn-drĕs'), informal, everyday costume: *adj.* (ŭn'drĕs), informal; as, an *undress* uniform: **undress parade,** a substitute for dress parade, ermissible in bad weather: the companies orming without arms, and the ceremony eing shortened.

un-due (ŭn-dū'; ŭn'dū), *adj.* not requiring payment as yet; as, the bill vas *undue;* wrong or illegal; more than roper or suitable; unreasonable; as, they aid *undue* attention to a small matter.—*dv.* **unduly.**

un-du-late (ŭn'dū-lāt), *v.t.* and *v.i.* [*p.t.* and *p.p.* undulated, *p.pr.* ndulating], to wave up and down or back nd forth; to move with a wavy motion.—*n.* **undulation.**

Syn. vibrate, fluctuate.

un-du-la-to-ry (ŭn'dū-lȧ-tō-rĭ), *adj.* wavelike; having a vavy motion: **undulatory theory,** the conecture that light is brought to the eye by vibrations, or wavelike motions, of the ether.

un-dy-ing (ŭn-dī'ĭng), *adj.* never ceasing; immortal; without end.—*adv.* **undyingly.**

un-earned in-cre-ment (ŭn-ûrnd' ĭn'krē-mĕnt), the natural increase in the value of and or property without labor on the part of the owner.

un-earth (ŭn-ûrth'), *v.t.* to take from the earth; to dig from underground; to uncover; hence, to bring to nowledge; to discover; as, to *unearth* a rime.

un-earth-ly (ŭn-ûrth'lĭ), *adj.* not belonging to earth; not according to nature; unlike anything natural; upernatural; hence, weird or uncanny; as, n *unearthly* sound.—*n.* **unearthliness.**

un-eas-y (ŭn-ēz'ĭ), *adj.* not at ease; restless; uncomfortable; anxous or worried; awkward in manner; contrained; causing discomfort.—*adv.* **uneasily.** —*n.* **uneasiness.**

un-e-qual (ŭn-ē'kwăl), *adj.* not of the same size, strength, amount, ability, weight, etc.; ill-balanced or illnatched; as, an *unequal* fight; not sufficiently arge, strong, etc.: with *to;* as, he was *nequal* to the task.—*adv.* **unequally.**

Syn. uneven, irregular.

Ant. (see even).

un-e-qualed (ŭn-ē'kwăld), *adj.* not matched; without a parallel or rival; so perfect as to admit no comarison. Also, **unequalled.**

un-e-quiv-o-cal (ŭn'ē-kwĭv'ō-kăl), *adj.* not doubtful or uncertain; unmistakable.

un-err-ing (ŭn-ûr'ĭng; ŭn-ĕr'ĭng), *adj.* not making mistakes; sure in judgment or action.—*adv.* **unerringly.**

un-e-ven (ŭn-ē'vn), *adj.* not regular; not smooth or flat; not equal: odd: used of a number not divisible by two without a remainder.—*adv.* **unevenly.**—*n.* **unevenness.**

un-ex-am-pled (ŭn"ĕg-zăm'pld; ŭn"ĕg-zȧm'pld), *adj.* being without a parallel; like nothing that has happened before.

un-ex-cep-tion-a-ble (ŭn"ĕk-sĕp'-shŭn-ȧ-bl), *adj.* not open to blame or criticism; irreproachable.—*adv.* **unexceptionably.**—*n.* **unexceptionableness.**

un-ex-pect-ed (ŭn"ĕks-pĕk'tĕd), *adj.* not looked for; sudden; coming as a surprise.—*adv.* **unexpectedly.**—*n.* **unexpectedness.**

un-fail-ing (ŭn-fāl'ĭng), *adj.* not liable to fall short; as, an *unfailing* supply; not growing less or weaker; reliable; as, a true friend is an *unfailing* help; continuous or unending.

un-fair (ŭn-fâr'), *adj.* not just; not honest.—*adv.* **unfairly.**—*n.* **unfairness.**

un-faith-ful (ŭn-fāth'fōōl), *adj.* not true; not loyal; not holding to duty, promise, vows, etc.—*adv.* **unfaithfully.** —*n.* **unfaithfulness.**

un-fas-ten (ŭn-fȧs'n), *v.t.* and *v.i.* to make or become loose.

un-fa-vor-a-ble (ŭn-fā'vĕr-ȧ-bl), *adj.* against the advantage; tending against; disapproving; as, an *unfavorable* opinion of an applicant; not contributing to success; as, the weather was *unfavorable* for the undertaking. Also, **unfavourable.**—*adv.* **unfavorably, unfavourably.**

un-feel-ing (ŭn-fēl'ĭng), *adj.* cruel; brutal; without human impulses or emotions; pitiless.—*adv.* **unfeelingly.**—*n.* **unfeelingness.**

un-feigned (ŭn-fānd'), *adj.* not put on; genuine; sincere; without pretense.

un-fin-ished (ŭn-fĭn'ĭsht), *adj.* not complete; not brought to a conclusion; not polished.

un-fit (ŭn-fĭt'), *v.t.* to make unsuitable for; to deprive of ability, appropriateness, etc.; to make unable: *adj.* not suitable. —*adv.* **unfitly.**—*n.* **unfitness.**

un-fledged (ŭn-flĕjd'), *adj.* without feathers: said of a young bird: hence, undeveloped; immature.

un-fold (ŭn-fōld'), *v.t.* to spread open; to reveal by degrees: *v.i.* to open, as a flower; to be revealed.

un-formed (ŭn-fôrmd'), *adj.* not developed; shapeless; not fully outlined or shaped.

un-for-tu-nate (ŭn-fôr'tū-nāt), *adj.* not lucky; not attended with success; not prosperous; regrettable; as, an *unfortunate* speech: *n.* an unlucky or unsuccessful person.—*adv.* **unfortunately.**

un-found-ed (ŭn-foun'dĕd), *adj.* without basis; hence, doubtful; as, an *unfounded* rumor; not established.

un-fre-quent-ed (ŭn"frē-kwĕn'tĕd), *adj.* not much visited; solitary; empty of people.

un-friend-ly (ŭn-frĕnd'lĭ), *adj.* hostile; not like a friend; lacking kindness or cordiality.—*n.* **unfriendliness.**

un-furl (ŭn-fûrl'), *v.t.* and *v.i.* to loose from fastenings and spread out, as a flag, a sail, etc.; to open.

un-gain-ly (ŭn-gān'lĭ), *adj.* awkward; rude or clumsy in appearance and manner.—*n.* **ungainliness.**

un-gen-er-ous (ŭn-jĕn'ẽr-ŭs), *adj.* stingy or mean; narrow in judgment of others; uncharitable.—*adv.* **ungenerously.**

un-god-ly (ŭn-gŏd'lĭ), *adj.* wicked; having no likeness to God.—*n.* **ungodliness.**

un-gov-ern-a-ble (ŭn-gŭv'ẽr-nȧ-bl), *adj.* not to be controlled; unruly.

un-gra-cious (ŭn-grā'shŭs), *adj.* unkind; discourteous; rude and abrupt.—*adv.* **ungraciously.**

un-grate-ful (ŭn-grāt'fo͝ol), *adj.* not thankful; not appreciating favors received.—*adv.* **ungratefully.**—*n.* **ungratefulness.**

un-guent (ŭŋ'gwĕnt), *n.* an oil or salve for burns, sores, etc.; an ointment.

un-hal-lowed (ŭn-hăl'ōd), *adj.* not made or kept sacred or holy.

un-hand (ŭn-hănd'), *v.t.* to let go of; to drop the hold of.

un-hand-y (ŭn-hăn'dĭ), *adj.* clumsy; awkward; inconvenient.

un-hap-py (ŭn-hăp'ĭ), *adj.* not fortunate; not glad; sorrowful; discontented; unlucky.—*adv.* **unhappily.**—*n.* **unhappiness.**

un-heard (ŭn-hûrd'), *adj.* not listened to; not treated with attention.

un-hinge (ŭn-hĭnj'), *v.t.* to remove from its hinges; to take from its place; to unsettle; as, his trouble *unhinged* his mind.

un-ho-ly (ŭn-hō'lĭ), *adj.* not sacred; unhallowed; profane; wicked.—*adv.* **unholily.**—*n.* **unholiness.**

un-horse (ŭn-hôrs'), *v.t.* to throw or drag from the back of a horse.

u-ni- (ū'nĭ-), a *prefix* meaning one; as, *unicellular*, having a single cell.

u-ni-corn (ū'nĭ-kôrn), *n.* a fabled animal, resembling the horse, but with one straight horn projecting from its forehead.

u-ni-fi-ca-tion (ū'nĭ-fĭ-kā'shŭn), *n.* the act of making two or more into one; the act of making, or state of being made, the same in form.

u-ni-form (ū'nĭ-fôrm), *adj.* not changing in form; the same as others in form, manner, or character; as, a *uniform* style of writing: *n.* an official or regulation dress belonging to a particular class or profession; as, a nurse's *uniform.*

Syn., adj. regular, even, equal, alike.

Ant. (see irregular).

u-ni-form-i-ty (ū'nĭ-fôr'mĭ-tĭ), *n.* the quality or state of having one unchanging form, or of being of the same form as others; resemblance.

u-ni-fy (ū'nĭ-fī), *v.t.* [*p.t.* and *p.p.* unified, *p.pr.* unifying], to form into one; make alike in form.

u-ni-lat-er-al (ū'nĭ-lăt'ẽr-ăl), *adj.* having one side or surface.

un-im-peach-a-ble (ŭn'ĭm-pēch'ȧ-bl), *adj.* not worthy of reproach or blame; unquestionably right.

un-im-proved (ŭn'ĭm-pro͞ovd'), *adj.* not made better; not used to good advantage.

un-in-formed (ŭn'ĭn-fôrmd'), *adj.* not acquainted with; not familiar with the facts.

un-ion (ūn'yŭn), *n.* the act of joining two or more things in one; the state of being so joined; a combination; agreement or concord; a whole made of parts joined together; as, a *union* of states; a device on a national flag, signifying the joining of the parts of the nation; an association of individuals or groups; a trade-union, or association of workers in a given trade or industry, for mutual benefit and defense of rights.

Syn. combination, alliance, league, concert.

Ant. (see disunion).

un-ion-ism (ūn'yŭn-ĭzm), *n.* belief in union; adherence to a union, as to that of the United States in the Civil War; belief that trade-unions are the solution of the labor problem.

un-ion-ist (ūn'yŭn-ĭst), *n.* one who believes in union; an adherent of a union; as, the people of the North in the Civil War were *unionists;* a member of a trade-union: **Unionist**, in Great Britain, a member of a party opposing Home Rule for Ireland.

un-ion jack (ūn'yŭn jăk), a flag consisting of the emblem of union of a nation; as, the *union jack* of the United States is a blue field with white stars the British military flag.

u-ni-ped (ū'nĭ-pĕd), *adj.* one-footed, or having but one foot.

u-nique (ū-nēk'), *adj.* without another of the same kind; unlike anything else; loosely, unusual; as, a *unique* design; alone of its sort; unequaled in excellence.—*adv.* **uniquely.**—*n.* **uniqueness.**

Syn. unequaled, uncommon, rare, choice, matchless.

Ant. (see common).

u-ni-son (ū'nĭ-sŭn; ū'nĭ-zŭn), *n.* oneness; agreement; concord; in music, sameness of pitch; the sounding at once of two tones an octave apart; the rendering of the same series of tones by all the voice parts at once: opposite to *harmony.*

u-nit (ū'nĭt), *n.* one person or thing of a number which make up a group; as, each citizen, though only a *unit* in the national body, is important; a single group in an association made up of groups; as, a local Red Cross Branch is made up of a number of *units,* or small societies; the least whole number; in mathematics, one undivided number or amount, as opposed to a fractional one; a fixed amount, quantity, distance, etc., taken as a standard of measurement; as, a pound is the *unit* of measurement for weight.

U-ni-ta-ri-an (ū'nĭ-tā'rĭ-ăn), *n.* one who does not believe in the doctrine of the Trinity; one who believes that God is only one person; a member of the Unitarian Church founded upon such a belief: *adj.* of or pertaining to Unitarians or their beliefs.

U-ni-ta-ri-an-ism (ū'nĭ-tā'rĭ-ăn-ĭzm), *n.* the system of doctrine of the Unitarians; the belief that God exists only in one person.

u-nite (ū-nīt'), *v.t.* [*p.t.* and *p.p.* united, *p.pr.* uniting], to join together; to put together so as to make one; to bind together legally or morally, as in marriage;

to bring into close relationship in thought, feeling, etc.; as, their common interests *united* them as friends: *v.i.* to be joined together; to grow into one; to act together; as, the great democratic nations *united* against Germany.

Syn. combine, add, attach, merge.

Ant. (see separate).

u-nit-ed (ū-nīt'ĕd), *p.adj.* joined together; in agreement.—*adv.* **unitedly.**

U-nit-ed Breth-ren (ū-nīt'ĕd brĕth'rĕn), the members of a church formed in Moravia, Austria, about 1450, and originally known as the Moravian Church.

u-ni-ty (ū'nĭ-tĭ), *n.* [*pl.* unities (-tĭz)], the state of being one; wholeness; agreement; as, dwelling together in *unity*; a whole made up of parts; in rhetoric, the quality of having all the parts of a speech or writing centered about one theme.

u-ni-ver-sal (ū'nĭ-vûr'săl), *adj.* pertaining to the whole system of created things; as, gravitation is a *universal* law; embracing or including the whole; general; prevailing everywhere; as, *universal* peace.—*adv.* **universally.**

Syn. all, entire, total, catholic.

Ant. (see sectional).

U-ni-ver-sal-ism (ū'nĭ-vûr'săl-ĭzm), *n.* the doctrine or belief that all men will finally be saved, or that there will be no eternal punishment.

U-ni-ver-sal-ist (ū'nĭ-vûr'săl-ĭst), *n.* a believer in the doctrine that all men will finally be saved.

u-ni-ver-sal-i-ty (ū'nĭ-vẽr-săl'ĭ-tĭ), *n.* the state or quality of being general; the state of prevailing everywhere, all-inclusiveness.

u-ni-verse (ū'nĭ-vûrs), *n.* the whole system of created things; creation; loosely, the world.

u-ni-ver-si-ty (ū'nĭ-vûr'sĭ-tĭ), *n.* [*pl.* universities (-tĭz)], an institution for education in the higher branches of learning, divided into various departments, as of the arts, medicine, law, engineering, etc., and having the right to confer degrees in each of these departments.

un-just (ŭn-jŭst'), *adj.* unfair; not righteous; not deserved; as, an *unjust* accusation; not in accordance with legal justice; as, the *unjust* decision of the magistrate.—*adv.* **unjustly.**—*n.* **unjustness.**

un-kempt (ŭn-kĕmpt'), *adj.* not combed; not neat; hence, rough; personally untidy.—*n.* **unkemptness.**

un-kind (ŭn-kīnd'), *adj.* not gentle, gracious, or sympathetic; harsh or severe in treatment of others; giving pain to the feelings of others; as, *unkind* words.—*adv.* **unkindly.**—*n.* **unkindness.**

un-lace (ŭn-lās'), *v.t.* to undo the lacing of, as a shoe.

un-law-ful (ŭn-lô'fōōl), *adj.* contrary to law; forbidden by authority; illegal.—*adv.* **unlawfully.**—*n.* **unlawfulness.**

un-learn-ed (ŭn-lûr'nĕd), *adj.* not educated; without schooling; (ŭn-lûrnd'), not acquired by study; as, his lessons were *unlearned.*

un-less (ŭn-lĕs'), *conj.* if not; in case not; on condition that not.

un-let-tered (ŭn-lĕt'ẽrd), *adj.* untaught; not educated; not able to read and write.

Syn. ignorant, untutored, illiterate.

un-like (ŭn-līk'), *adj.* different; not similar; without reservation.

un-like-ly (ŭn-līk'lĭ), *adj.* not probable; not destined to succeed; as, an *unlikely* plan.

un-lim-it-ed (ŭn-lĭm'ĭ-tĕd), *adj.* boundless; without restrictions; as, *unlimited* freedom; indefinite; as, a note which runs for an *unlimited* term.

un-load (ŭn-lōd'), *v.t.* to remove a burden from; as, to *unload* a wagon; to remove from a car, wagon, ship, etc.; as, to *unload* freight.

un-lock (ŭn-lŏk'), *v.t.* to unfasten by turning a key; hence, to make open or clear; as, to *unlock* a mystery.

un-looked-for (ŭn-lōōkt'fôr'), *adj.* not expected or foreseen.

un-love-ly (ŭn-lŭv'lĭ), *adj.* without charm; unattractive; disagreeable.

un-luck-y (ŭn-lŭk'ĭ), *adj.* not fortunate; as, an *unlucky* speech; tending to bring bad luck; as, an *unlucky* day.—*adv.* **unluckily.**—*n.* **unluckiness.**

un-man (ŭn-măn'), *v.t.* [*p.t.* and *p.p.* unmanned, *p.pr.* unmanning], to rob of courage and strength; to unnerve; to make weak.

un-man-ly (ŭn-măn'lĭ), *adj.* not brave; not chivalrous; cowardly; weak in courage.

un-man-ner-ly (ŭn-măn'ẽr-lĭ), *adj.* rude; without courtesy; impolite: *adv.* rudely.—*n.* **unmannerliness.**

un-mask (ŭn-màsk'), *v.t.* to remove a disguise from; show the true nature of: *v.i.* to take off a disguise.

un-mean-ing (ŭn-mēn'ĭng), *adj.* without sense or expression; signifying nothing.

un-mer-ci-ful (ŭn-mûr'sĭ-fōōl), *adj.* without kindness or pity; without human feeling; cruel.—*adv.* **unmercifully.**—*n.* **unmercifulness.**

un-mil-i-ta-ry (ŭn-mĭl'ĭ-tā-rĭ), *adj.* contrary to the rules of discipline, especially army discipline.

un-mis-tak-a-ble (ŭn'mĭs-tāk'ȧ-bl), *adj.* admitting no chance of error; certain; evident.—*adv.* **unmistakably.**

un-mor-al (ŭn-mŏr'ăl), *adj.* having no sense of, or not concerned with, right and wrong; in distinction from *immoral*, wrong or wicked.

un-nat-u-ral (ŭn-năt'ū-răl), *adj.* not normal or according to rule; not according to the laws of the physical world; unlike the usual ways of human beings; without the common impulses of humanity; as, it is an *unnatural* mother who does not care for her children.—*adv.* **unnaturally.**—*n.* **unnaturalness.**

un-nec-es-sa-ry (ŭn-nĕs'ĕ-sā-rĭ), *adj.* not needed; of no use.—*adv.* **unnecessarily.**

un-nerve (ŭn-nûrv'), *v.t.* to rob of nerve control; to weaken; to upset nervously; to disturb by a shock.

un-num-bered (ŭn-nŭm'bẽrd), *adj.* not counted; countless.

un-or-gan-ized (ŭn-ôr'găn-īzd), *adj.* not arranged in systematic form.

un-pack (ŭn-păk'), *v.t.* to take out from a receptacle, as a box, trunk, etc.; as, to *unpack* goods; to remove the contents of; as, to *unpack* a trunk.

un-par-al-leled (ŭn-păr'ă-lĕld), *adj.* not matched; without an equal; having nothing similar.

un-par-lia-men-ta-ry (ŭn-pär′lĭ-mĕn′tá-rĭ), *adj.* against the rules of parliamentary bodies.

un-pin (ŭn-pĭn′), *v.t.* to unfasten by taking out a pin or pins.

un-pleas-ant (ŭn-plĕz′ănt), *adj.* disagreeable; distasteful.—*adv.* **unpleasantly.**—*n.* **unpleasantness.**

un-prec-e-dent-ed (ŭn-prĕs′ē-dĕn-tĕd), *adj.* not authorized by previous custom; unexampled; new and unusual.—*adv.* **unprecedentedly.**

un-prej-u-diced (ŭn-prĕj′ŏŏ-dĭst), *adj.* not influenced by hastily formed or premature opinions; impartial; fair.

un-pre-med-i-tat-ed (ŭn′prē-mĕd′ĭ-tāt′ĕd), *adj.* not planned beforehand or in advance.—*adv.* **unpremeditatedly.**

un-prin-ci-pled (ŭn-prĭn′sĭ-pld), *adj.* without right moral ideals; careless of right and wrong.

un-ques-tion-a-ble (ŭn-kwĕs′chŭn-á-bl), *adj.* not to be doubted or disputed.—*adv.* **unquestionably.**

un-qui-et (ŭn-kwī′ĕt), *adj.* noisy; disturbed; not at peace.—*adv.* **unquietly.**

un-rav-el (ŭn-răv′l), *v.t.* [*p.t.* and *p.p.* unraveled, *p.pr.* unraveling], to pull apart the threads of; to pull out, as knitting: *v.i.* to be pulled apart or out.

un-read-y (ŭn-rĕd′ĭ), *adj.* not prepared; tardy or slow; not quick to act.—*adv.* **unreadily.**—*n.* **unreadiness.**

un-real (ŭn-rē′ăl), *adj.* not actual; imaginary; ideal.—*n.* **unreality.**

un-rea-son-a-ble (ŭn-rē′zn-á-bl), *adj.* not controlled by reason; demanding too much; as, an *unreasonable* demand; immoderate; as, *unreasonable* prices.—*adv.* **unreasonably.**—*n.* **unreasonableness.**

un-re-mit-ting (ŭn′rē-mĭt′ĭng), *adj.* never ceasing or relaxing; as, *unremitting* toil; persistent.

un-re-served (ŭn′rē-zûrvd′), *adj.* given without restriction; not held back; as, all the seats are *unreserved*; outspoken; keeping nothing secret; holding nothing back; as, *unreserved* confidence.—*adv.* **unreservedly.**—*n.* **unreservedness.**

un-rest (ŭn-rĕst′), *n.* lack of ease and quiet; anxiety; disturbance.

un-right-eous (ŭn-rī′chŭs), *adj.* not just; wicked.—*adv.* **unrighteously.**—*n.* **unrighteousness.**

un-ri-valed (ŭn-rī′văld), *adj.* unequaled; without comparison. Also, **unrivalled.**

un-roll (ŭn-rōl′), *v.t.* and *v.i.* to open by unwrapping, or by being unwrapped, on an axis.

un-rul-y (ŭn-rōōl′ĭ), *adj.* paying no attention to rules or commands; hard to manage; ungovernable.—*n.* **unruliness.**

un-sad-dle (ŭn-săd′l), *v.t.* to take off a saddle from, as a horse.

un-sa-vor-y (ŭn-sā′vẽr-ĭ), *adj.* lacking taste or seasoning; disagreeable to taste or smell; hence, morally offensive; as, an *unsavory* story. Also, **unsavoury.**

un-screw (ŭn-skrōō′), *v.t.* to loosen by taking out a screw or screws; as, to *unscrew* the handle of the drawer; to draw out or off by turning, as a screw, the top of a can, etc.

un-scru-pu-lous (ŭn-skrōō′pū-lŭs), *adj.* careless of right and wrong; as, *unscrupulous* business methods; without moral principles; not exact or particular.—*adv.* **unscrupulously.**—*n.* **unscrupulousness.**

un-seal (ŭn-sēl′), *v.t.* to open by breaking or removing a seal.

un-sea-son-a-ble (ŭn-sē′zn-á-bl), *adj.* not at a proper time; out of season; as, thunderstorms in winter are *unseasonable*.—*adv.* **unseasonably.**—*n.* **unseasonableness.**

un-seat (ŭn-sēt′), *v.t.* to remove from a seat; to take away a position or office from; as, he was *unseated* from his senatorial dignity.

un-seem-ly (ŭn-sēm′lĭ), *adj.* improper; not fitting; not suitable: *adv.* in an unsuitable manner.—*n.* **unseemliness.**

un-seen (ŭn-sēn′), *adj.* not perceived by the eye; beyond the range of vision.

un-set-tle (ŭn-sĕt′l), *v.t.* and *v.i.* [*p.t.* and *p.p.* unsettled, *p.pr.* unsettling], to loosen from a firm position; to disturb; to be disturbed.

un-sex (ŭn-sĕks′), *v.t.* to make unlike one's sex; as, some people believe that to vote will *unsex* a woman.

un-sheathe (ŭn-shēth′), *v.t.* to take from its scabbard, as a dagger.

un-sift-ed (ŭn-sĭf′tĕd), *adj.* not having passed through a sieve; not examined with care and thoroughness.

un-skil-ful (ŭn-skĭl′fŏŏl), *adj.* without expertness; inapt; not clever in performance of work, especially work with the hands. Also, **unskillful.**—*adv.* **unskilfully, unskillfully.**—*n.* **unskilfulness, unskillfulness.**

un-so-cia-ble (ŭn-sō′shá-bl), *adj.* not friendly; not disposed to seek the companionship of others; uncompanionable.—*adv.* **unsociably.**—*n.* **unsociability.**

un-so-phis-ti-cat-ed (ŭn′sō-fĭs′tĭ-kāt′ĕd), *adj.* not experienced in the ways of the world; free from artificiality of manner.—*n.* **unsophisticatedness.**

Syn. naive, simple, artless, innocent.

un-sound (ŭn-sound′), *adj.* not safe or reliable; not founded on truth; insecure; diseased.—*adv.* **unsoundly.**—*n.* **unsoundness.**

un-speak-a-ble (ŭn-spēk′á-bl), *adj.* not to be expressed in words; too bad to be talked of.—*adv.* **unspeakably.**—*n.* **unspeakableness.**

un-spot-ted (ŭn-spŏt′ĕd), *adj.* without stain; without sin or fault; pure.

un-sta-ble (ŭn-stā′bl), *adj.* not steady; easily thrown over or out of balance.

un-stop (ŭn-stŏp′), *v.t.* [*p.t.* and *p.p.* unstopped, *p.pr.* unstopping], to remove the cork or stopper from, as a bottle; to open by removing an obstruction.

un-strung (ŭn-strŭng′), *adj.* having a string or strings loosened or missing, as a harp or violin; nervously upset; unnerved; relaxed.

un-sub-stan-tial (ŭn′sŭb-stăn′shăl), *adj.* without material form or body; inconsiderable; fanciful or imaginary; not strong or solid.—*adv.* **unsubstantially.**

un-think-ing (ŭn-thĭnk'ĭng), *adj.* without thought; careless; inconsiderate.—*adv.* **unthinkingly.**

un-ti-dy (ŭn-tī'dĭ), *adj.* not neat; disorderly; slovenly.—*adv.* **untidily.** —*n.* **untidiness.**

un-tie (ŭn-tī'), *v.t.* [*p.t.* and *p.p.* untied, *p.pr.* untying], to unfasten by loosening a knot: *v.i.* to become unfastened.

un-til (ŭn-tĭl'), *prep.* to or up to: used in relation to time: *conj.* to the degree or place that; to the time when.

un-time-ly (ŭn-tīm'lĭ), *adj.* not at the right moment or on the right occasion; happening too soon: *adv.* inopportunely; too soon.

un-to (ŭn'tōō), *prep.* a formal or poetic word for *to.*

un-told (ŭn-tōld'), *adj.* not expressed or revealed; not counted; hence, very great.

un-to-ward (ŭn-tō'ẽrd; ŭn-tôrd'), *adj.* wayward and stubborn; unfortunate; as, *untoward* circumstances; inconvenient.—*adv.* **untowardly.**—*n.* **untowardness.**

un-tried (ŭn-trīd'), *adj.* not put to the test; inexperienced.

un-true (ŭn-trōō'), *adj.* false: opposite to *fact;* disloyal; faithless.

un-truth (ŭn-trōōth'), *n.* lack of adherence to fact; falseness; disloyalty; a falsehood or lie.
Syn. falsity, mendacity.

un-truth-ful (ŭn-trōōth'fŏŏl), *adj.* inclined to falseness in words; lying.—*adv.* **untruthfully.**—*n.* **untruthfulness.**

un-tu-tored (ŭn-tū'tẽrd), *adj.* not taught; having little learning; unadvised.

un-used (ŭn-ūzd'), *adj.* not accustomed; not in the habit of: with *to;* as, *unused* to hard labor.

un-u-su-al (ŭn-ū'zhŭ-ăl), *adj.* not customary; uncommon; rare; extraordinary.—*adv.* **unusually.**

un-ut-ter-a-ble (ŭn-ŭt'ẽr-ȧ-bl), *adj.* not to be spoken; inexpressible.—*adv.* **unutterably.**—*n.* **unutterability.**

un-val-ued (ŭn-văl'ūd), *adj.* not considered of much worth; unprized; having no price set on it.

un-var-nished (ŭn-vär'nĭsht), *adj.* not having a coating of varnish; not polished; in its original undecorated state; as, the *unvarnished* truth often hurts people's feelings by its unkindness.

un-veil (ŭn-vāl'), *v.t.* to disclose by taking off a veil or covering; to uncover; to reveal clearly: *v.i.* to take off a veil; to show one's own true nature.

un-war-rant-a-ble (ŭn-wŏr'ăn-tȧ-bl), *adj.* without authority; not to be justified, or proved right; as, he took an *unwarrantable* liberty with my property.—*adv.* **unwarrantably.**

un-wa-ry (ŭn-wâ'rĭ), *adj.* off one's guard; heedless; incautious.—*adv.* **unwarily.**—*n.* **unwariness.**

un-wea-ried (ŭn-wē'rĭd), *adj.* not tired; unresting; not ready to stop.

un-wield-y (ŭn-wēl'dĭ), *adj.* so large and heavy as to be hard to handle.—*n.* **unwieldiness.**

un-will-ing (ŭn-wĭl'ĭng), *adj.* reluctant; loath.—*adv.* **unwillingly.**—*n.* **unwillingness.**

un-wind (ŭn-wīnd'), *v.t.* [*p.t.* and *p.p.* unwound, *p.pr.* unwinding], to loosen by uncoiling: *v.i.* to uncoil.

un-wise (ŭn-wīz'), *adj.* not showing good judgment; rash; foolish.—*adv.* **unwisely.**

un-wit-ting (ŭn-wĭt'ĭng), *adj.* unconscious; unaware; not knowing.—*adv.* **unwittingly.**

un-wont-ed (ŭn-wŭn'tĕd), *adj.* not customary; unusual; not habitual; rare.—*adv.* **unwontedly.**—*n.* **unwontedness.**

un-wor-thy (ŭn-wûr'*th*ĭ), *adj.* lacking due merit, value, etc.; not deserving; not suitable or proper to: with *of;* as, such conduct is *unworthy* of your home training.—*adv.* **unworthily.**—*n.* **unworthiness.**

un-writ-ten (ŭn-rĭt'n), *adj.* not expressed or recorded in writing; verbal; due to custom rather than enactment; as, an *unwritten* law.

up (ŭp), *prep.* to a higher place on: as, *up* the hill; toward the source of: as, *up* the river: *adv.* higher in motion, direction, or position: opposite to *down;* into being or action; as, to start *up* an argument; into notice; as, to bring *up* a matter for discussion; completely or to a finished state; as, to hunt *up* a number, to write *up* a newspaper report, to bring *up* a child; not behind or worse than: with *to* or *with;* as, to live *up* to one's reputation, to keep *up* with the times; away or in safety; as, to store *up* wealth, to put *up* a car in a garage: *adj.* leading to a higher place; as, the train was on the *up* grade; well-trained; as, he is *up* in his subject; finished; as, the time is *up:* *n.pl.* fortunate occurrences: used only in the expression *ups and downs.*

u-pas (ū'pȧs), *n.* a tree, common in Java, with a poisonous juice used as arrow poison; also, the juice.

up-braid (ŭp-brād'), *v.t.* to reproach; to accuse of a wrong or shameful act; to chide or blame: *v.i.* to utter reproach.
Syn. censure, reprove, rebuke, scold, berate.

up-heav-al (ŭp-hēv'ăl), *n.* a lifting from below; especially, a lifting of some part of the earth's crust by an inside force; a political or social disturbance, as by a revolt against a government.

up-heave (ŭp-hēv'), *v.t.* to lift up by force exerted from beneath; as, to *upheave* mountain ridges: *v.i.* to rise by pressure from beneath or within.

up-hill (ŭp-hĭl'), *adv.* to a higher point on a hill or slope; on an upward incline: *adj.* sloping upward; ascending; hence, toilsome; as, study is *uphill* work for him.

up-hold (ŭp-hōld'), *v.t.* [*p.t.* and *p.p.* upheld, *p.pr.* upholding], to support; as, pillars *uphold* the roof; to prop up or keep standing; as, the tower was *upheld* by scaffolding so that it did not fall; to encourage or give aid to; as, the council *upheld* the mayor in his campaign for reform.—*n.* **upholder.**

up-hol-ster (ŭp-hōl'stẽr), *v.t.* to fit out with curtains, cushions, coverings, etc., as rooms or furniture.—*n.* **upholsterer.**

up-hol-ster-y (ŭp-hōl'stẽr-ĭ), *n.* [*pl.* upholsteries (-ĭz)], the business of one who fits out rooms and furniture with coverings, draperies, etc.; also, curtains, cushions, and other such interior fittings of a house.

up-keep (ŭp′kēp′), *n.* the maintaining of a house, store, etc., in which expense is involved; cost of maintenance.

up-land (ŭp′lănd), *n.* high ground; an elevated region bordering a low shore, valley, etc.: opposite to *lowland.*

up-on (ŭ-pŏn′), *prep.* on; resting on the top or surface of; as, *upon* the floor; touching; as, *upon* the wall; situated on; as, *upon* the coast; judging from; as, *upon* safe evidence; belonging to; as, *upon* the committee; in a state of; as, *upon* sale, *upon* the defensive; at the moment of; as, *upon* arrival; to or toward; as, we came *upon* them unexpectedly; relating to; as, a speech *upon* civic betterment.

up-per (ŭp′ẽr), *adj.* higher in place, rank, or degree; as, the *upper* story of a house; the *upper* classes; the part of a shoe above the sole.

up-per-most (ŭp′ẽr-mōst), *adj.* highest in place, rank, or authority.

up-pish (ŭp′ĭsh), *adj.* proud; airish; haughty.—*adv.* **uppishly.**—*n.* **uppishness.** [Colloq.]

up-right (ŭp′rīt′), *adj.* standing erect; as, an *upright* piano; just; honest; as, a man of *upright* character: *adv.* in an erect position: *n.* something standing straight up, as a timber supporting a rafter.—*adv.* **uprightly.**—*n.* **uprightness.**
Syn., adj. vertical, erect, true, honorable.
Ant. (see horizontal).

up-ris-ing (ŭp-rīz′ĭng), *n.* a rebellion or revolt against authority or government.

up-roar (ŭp′rōr′), *n.* noisy disturbance; confusion and clamor, especially of loud voices.

up-roar-i-ous (ŭp-rōr′ĭ-ŭs), *adj.* making great noise and disturbance; impolitely loud; as, *uproarious* laughter.—*adv.* **uproariously.**—*n.* **uproariousness.**

up-root (ŭp-rōōt′), *v.t.* to pull up by the roots; as, to *uproot* weeds; to remove thoroughly; as, to *uproot* a bad habit.

up-set (ŭp-sĕt′), *v.t.* [*p.t.* and *p.p.* upset, upsetted, *p.pr.* upsetting], to overthrow; overturn; as, to *upset* a glass of water; colloquially, to put out of normal mental or physical condition; as, to have one's nerves *upset:* *n.* (ŭp′sĕt), the act of overturning or disturbing; state of being overturned; colloquially, mental or physical disturbance.

up-shot (ŭp′shŏt′), *n.* final result; conclusion; summary.

up-side (ŭp′sīd′), *n.* the upper part: **upside down,** having the top part at the bottom; hence, in disorder.

up-stairs (ŭp-stârz′), *adv.* toward an upper floor: *adj.* (ŭp′stârz′), on an upper floor; as, an *upstairs* sitting room: *n.* the part above the first floor.

up-start (ŭp′stärt′), *n.* a vulgar and presuming person who has suddenly risen from a humble position to wealth or influence: *adj.* suddenly raised to a position of wealth and influence.

up-to-date (ŭp′tōō′dāt′), *adj.* in the latest style; as, an *up-to-date* hat. [Colloq.]

up-turn (ŭp-tûrn′), *v.t.* and *v.i.* to turn up; as, to *upturn* sod.

up-ward (ŭp′wẽrd), *adv.* in an ascending direction; from lower to higher; towards a higher rank or position; as, to climb *upward* on the social ladder; toward the beginning; as, they followed the river *upward* toward its source; indefinitely more; as, children of three years and *upward:* **upwards of,** more than; as, they collected *upwards* of a million dollars for the Red Cross: *adj.* directed from lower to higher; as, an *upward* slope. Also, **upwards.**

u-ræ-mi-a (ū-rē′mĭ-ȧ), *n.* a poisoned condition of the blood due to diseased kidneys. Also, **uremia.**—*adj.* **uræmic, uremic.**

u-ræ-us (ū-rē′ŭs), *n.* an Egyptian symbol of sovereignty: the emblem represents a serpent, and was worn as a headdress by divinities and kings.

Uræus

u-ra-ni-um (ū-rā′nĭ-ŭm), *n.* a hard nickel-white metallic element which possesses radioactive properties and is the probable basis of radium.

ur-ban (ûr′băn), *adj.* of or pertaining to a city or town; as, *urban* residents.

ur-bane (ûr-bān′), *adj.* courteous; polite; refined; suave.—*adv.* **urbanely.**

ur-ban-i-ty (ûr-băn′ĭ-tĭ), *n.* politeness; refinement; polish of manner; suavity.

ur-chin (ûr′chĭn), *n.* a small boy; especially, a pert or mischievous little fellow; a roguish elf; a sea urchin.

u-re-mi-a (ū-rē′mĭ-ȧ), *n.* a poisoned condition of the blood, due to diseased kidneys. Also, **uræmia.**—*adj.* **uremic, uræmic.**

urge (ûrj), *v.t.* [*p.t.* and *p.p.* urged, *p.pr.* urging], to persuade onward; to drive; to seek to influence the will of; as, to *urge* one to a course of action; to present insistently; as, to *urge* a point in an argument: *v.i.* to insist upon a statement, argument, etc.
Syn. push, drive, press, solicit, induce.

ur-gen-cy (ûr′jĕn-sĭ), *n.* pressure; insistence; need for immediate attention.

ur-gent (ûr′jĕnt), *adj.* pressing; calling for immediate attention; as, an *urgent* message; insistent or eager.—*adv.* **urgently.**
Syn. important, imperative, serious.
Ant. (see unimportant).

u-ric (ū′rĭk), *adj.* pertaining to, or derived from, urine: **uric acid,** a white, tasteless, almost insoluble compound, found in small quantities in human urine.

u-ri-nal (ū′rĭ-năl), *n.* a vessel for urine, or the fluid cast off by the kidneys.

u-ri-na-ry (ū′rĭ-nā-rĭ), *adj.* pertaining to urine, or to the organs that excrete and discharge it; as, a *urinary* disease.

u-rine (ū′rĭn), *n.* the fluid cast off as waste from the kidneys.

urn (ûrn), *n.* a vase, usually with a foot or pedestal.

Ur-sa Ma-jor (ûr′sȧ mā′jẽr), in astronomy, the Great Bear, or most noticeable of the northern groups of stars: called also *Big Dipper,* or *Charles's Wain,* and including two stars which point to the North Star. [Lat.]

Ur-sa Mi-nor (ûr′sȧ mī′nẽr), the *Little* Bear, or group of stars including the North Star: called also *Little Dipper.* [Lat.]

ur-sine (ûr′sīn; ûr′sĭn), *adj.* pertaining to, or like, a bear.

us (ŭs), *pron.* objective plural of I, the pronoun of the first person.

us-a-ble (ūz'ȧ bl), *adj.* fit to be employed or made use of.—*n.* **usableness.**

us-age (ūz'āj; ūs'āj), *n.* the act or mode of using; treatment; settled habit or custom; habitual employment by people at large; as, the *usage* of certain words differs in different localities.

Syn. custom, fashion, practice.

use (ūs), *n.* the act of employing something; state of being employed; application of anything to a particular purpose; as, the *use* of rags for making paper; employment; custom or practice; practical worth; as, it is of no *use;* treatment; reason for employing; as, we have no *use* for the goods you offer: *v.t.* (ūz), [*p.t.* and *p.p.* used, *p.pr.* using], to employ; as, to *use* a pen; to apply to a special purpose; avail oneself of; possess or enjoy for a time, as property; to make a habit of; as, to *use* economy; to treat; as, to *use* one's servants kindly; to make accustomed: chiefly in the passive voice and followed by *to;* as, the dog is *used* to kind treatment: *v.i.* to be accustomed: only in past; as, they *used* to go to the mountains every summer.

Syn., *n.* habit, advantage, utility: *v.* employ, exercise, occupy, accustom, inure.

Ant. (see disuse, abuse).

use-ful (ūs'fōōl), *adj.* full of practical worth, profit, or advantage; beneficial; as, *useful* work.—*adv.* **usefully.**—*n.* **usefulness.**

Syn. serviceable, available, helpful.

Ant. (see useless).

use-less (ūs'lĕs), *adj.* having, or being of, no practical worth or service; as, *useless* efforts; without results.—*adv.* **uselessly.**—*n.* **us lessness.**

Syn. unserviceable, fruitless, idle, profitless.

Ant. (see useful).

ush-er (ŭsh'ẽr), *n.* a doorkeeper; hence, one who escorts or directs persons to seats in a church, theater, etc.; in England, an assistant teacher in a boys' school: *v.t.* to announce; escort or accompany; show in.

u-su-al (ū'zhū-ăl), *adj.* common; ordinary; general.—*adv.* **usually.**—*n.* **usualness.**

Syn. customary, habitual.

Ant. (see unusual).

u-su-fruct (ū'zū-frŭkt), *n.* the temporary use and enjoyment of profits from lands and buildings belonging to another.

u-su-rer (ū'zhū-rẽr), *n.* one who lends money at a high and unlawful rate of interest; a loan shark.

u-su-ri-ous (ū-zū'rĭ-ŭs; ū-zhōō'rĭ-ŭs), *adj.* practicing usury, or lending money at an unlawful rate of interest.

u-surp (ū-zûrp'), *v.t.* to take possession of by force, or unjustly; as, to *usurp* the office, functions, powers, or rights of another, especially a king or ruler: *v.i.* to take possession of the office, functions, powers, or rights of another by force.—*n.* **usurper, usurpation.**

Syn. arrogate, seize, appropriate, assume.

u-su-ry (ū'zhū-rĭ), *n.* a high rate of interest, especially interest higher than a lawful rate; the practice of lending money at a high or unlawful rate of interest.

Ute (ūt; ū'tē), *n.* one of a western Indian tribe, formerly found in Colorado, Utah, New Mexico, and Arizona.

u-ten-sil (ū-tĕn'sĭl), *n.* an implement or vessel for use in practical work, especially one used in a kitchen; as, cooking *utensils.*

u-ter-us (ū'tẽr-ŭs), *n.* [*pl.* uteri (-ī)], the womb, or organ in mammals in which the young are carried and nourished before birth.—*adj.* **uterine.**

u-til-i-ta-ri-an (ū-tĭl'ĭ-tā'rĭ-ăn), *adj.* pertaining to, or consisting in, utility or usefulness; valuing things for their usefulness rather than their beauty, rarity, etc.: *n.* one who believes that only useful things are right or valuable.

u-til-i-ta-ri-an-ism (ū-tĭl'ĭ-tā'rĭ-ăn-ĭzm), *n.* the ethical doctrine that the greatest happiness of the greatest number should be the goal of all human efforts, and that all goodness is based on usefulness.

u-til-i-ty (ū-tĭl'ĭ-tĭ), *n.* [*pl.* utilities (-tĭz)], the quality or state of being suitable for use; general usefulness; something serviceable; as, the railroad is a great public *utility.*

u-ti-lize (ū'tĭ-līz), *v.t.* to make useful or profitable; to make use of.—*n.* **utilization.**

ut-most (ŭt'mōst), *adj.* greatest; most removed in space or time; farthest; extreme: *n.* the extreme limit; as, he can be trusted to the *utmost;* all that is possible; as, I will do my *utmost* to help you.

Syn., *adj.* remotest, uttermost.

U-to-pi-a (ū-tō'pĭ-ȧ), *n.* an imaginary island, described in Sir Thomas More's *Utopia* (1515–16), where a state of perfection existed in government, social life, etc.; any conception of an ideal state; a visionary plan for social reform.

U-to-pi-an (ū-tō'pĭ-ăn), *adj.* pertaining to the imaginary island, described in More's *Utopia*, where an ideally perfect system of laws and institutions existed; hence, ideal; visionary; impossible to be made actual; as, an ideal world is a *Utopian* dream: *n.* a dweller in Utopia; a person who dreams of ideal social perfection.

ut-ter (ŭt'ẽr), *adj.* entire; absolute; unqualified; as, *utter* denial; total: *v.t.* to speak; to make vocal; as, to *utter* a groan; to express in words; to put in circulation, as money, especially counterfeit notes or coins.—*adj.* **utterable.**

Syn., *adj.* extreme, sheer, pure: *v.* speak, express.

ut-ter-ance (ŭt'ẽr-ăns), *n.* expression by the voice; speech; style of speaking; as, his *utterance* was indistinct; something, usually of importance, expressed in words; as, the President's war speech was a memorable public *utterance.*

ut-ter-ly (ŭt'ẽr-lĭ), *adv.* fully; totally; altogether; as, *utterly* useless.

ut-ter-most (ŭt'ẽr-mōst), *adj.* extreme; utmost; in the furthest, greatest, or highest degree: *n.* the furthest extent or degree.

u-vu-la (ū'vū-lȧ), *n.* the fleshy, thimble-shaped body, attached to the soft palate, hanging above the back part of the tongue.—*adj.* **uvular.**

ux-o-ri-ous (ŭk'sō'rĭ-ŭs; ŭg-zō'rĭ-ŭs), *adj.* foolishly fond of a wife.—*adv.* **uxoriously.**—*n.* **uxoriousness.**

V

va-can-cy (vā'kăn-sĭ), *n.* [*pl.* vacancies (-sĭz)], state of being empty; emptiness of mind; idleness; lack of mental power; empty space; an office or position open to applicants; a room or rooms offered for rent.

va-cant (vā'kănt), *adj.* empty; lacking thought or reflection; as, a *vacant* stare; not occupied; as, a *vacant* building, or a *vacant* position; not made use of; as, *vacant* hours; free from care; as, Goldsmith wrote that country life gave the blessing of a *vacant* mind.
Syn. unfilled, thoughtless, void.
Ant. (see occupied).

va-cate (vā'kāt), *v.t.* [*p.t.* and *p.p.* vacated, *p.pr.* vacating], to make empty; give up the possession of; as, to *vacate* a house; to nullify or make void: *v.i.* to give up a house, office, etc.; colloquially, to go away.

va-ca-tion (vā-kā'shŭn), *n.* the act of making empty or leaving without an occupant; a making void; a short or long interruption in work or business; as, he took only a day's *vacation;* a period of leisure or rest; a holiday.

vac-ci-nate (văk'sĭ-nāt), *v.t.* [*p.t.* and *p.p.* vaccinated, *p.pr.* vaccinating], to inoculate, or give a mild form of a disease to, in order to prevent a severe attack; especially, to make immune from smallpox, by injecting into the body the virus, or poison, from the disease of cowpox.—*n.* **vaccinator.**

vac-ci-na-tion (văk"sĭ-nā'shŭn), *n.* act of inoculating, or making immune from smallpox, by injecting the virus of cowpox.

vac-cine (văk'sĭn; văk'sēn), *adj.* pertaining to, or obtained from, cows or cowpox: *n.* virus, or poison, obtained from cows affected with a disease called cowpox, or vaccinia, and used to prevent smallpox; loosely, any substance used for inoculation against disease.

vac-il-late (văs'ĭ-lāt), *v.i.* [*p.t.* and *p.p.* vacillated, *p.pr.* vacillating], to be changeable or uncertain in mind or opinion; to be unsteady; waver.

vac-il-la-tion (văs"ĭ-lā'shŭn), *n.* wavering of mind; unsteadiness; changeableness.

va-cu-i-ty (vă-kū'ĭ-tĭ), *n.* [*pl.* vacuities (-tĭz)], unfilled or unoccupied space; lack of intelligence in mind or expression.

vac-u-ous (văk'ū-ŭs), *adj.* empty; vacant; without expression.

vac-u-um (văk'ū-ŭm), *n.* a space entirely empty of matter; hence, a space, such as the inside of a bottle, emptied of air by artificial means.

vac-u-um clean-er (văk'ū-ŭm klēn'-ẽr), a machine for cleaning the interior of a house by means of suction which draws the dust into a vacuum, or empty bag, etc.

vac-u-um pump (văk'ū-ŭm pŭmp), a pump in which, by forming a partial vacuum, or empty space, water is forced through a pipe.

va-de me-cum (vā'dē mē'kŭm), an expression meaning, go with me; applied to something constantly carried with one, such as a handbook, manual, or book of reference. [LAT.]

vag-a-bond (văg'ă-bŏnd), *n.* one who roams about with no permanent abode; especially, an idle fellow without honest means of support; a vagrant or tramp; colloquially, a rascal or worthless fellow: *adj.* wandering about without fixed dwelling place; roaming; idle and vicious.—*n.* **vagabondage.**

va-ga-ry (vă-gā'rĭ), *n.* [*pl.* vagaries (-rĭz)], a mental extravagance; irresponsible dreaming; a freak of fancy; a whim.

va-gi-na (vă-jī'nă), *n.* in female mammals, the passage leading out from the uterus, or womb.

va-gran-cy (vā'grăn-sĭ), *n.* the state of one who wanders without a settled home; the habits and life of an idle wanderer or tramp.

va-grant (vā'grănt), *adj.* wandering from place to place without purpose and without a settled home: *n.* one who strolls from place to place without honest means of support; an idle wanderer; a tramp.
Syn., n. wanderer, beggar, vagabond, rogue.

vague (vāg), *adj.* [*comp.* vaguer, *superl.* vaguest], not clearly outlined, stated, or understood; hazy; as, a *vague* idea; not sure; doubtful; as, a *vague* rumor; not seeing or thinking clearly.—*adv.* **vaguely.** —*n.* **vagueness.**
Ant. (see definite).

vain (vān), *adj.* [*comp.* vainer, *superl.* vainest], valueless; empty; trifling; as, *vain* words; without force or effect; useless; as, *vain* efforts; proud of small accomplishments or of personal appearance; conceited; as, a *vain* person; showy; as, *vain* pomp: **in vain**, without success; to no purpose.—*adv.* **vainly.**
Syn. futile, worthless, unavailing, proud, conceited.
Ant. (see effectual, humble).

vain-glo-ri-ous (vān"glō'rĭ-ŭs), *adj.* boastful; full of excessive pride.—*adv.* **vaingloriously.**—*n.* **vaingloriousness.**

vain-glo-ry (vān"glō'rĭ), *n.* excessive vanity or pride over one's own accomplishments; satisfaction with all that pertains to oneself; vain pomp or show.

val-ance (văl'ăns), *n.* a kind of damask used for upholstering; also, a short, full curtain above a window, or around a bedstead from the mattress to the floor. Also, **valence.**

vale (vāl), *n.* a tract of low land between hills; a valley.

val-e-dic-tion (văl"ē-dĭk'shŭn), *n.* a farewell utterance; a saying farewell.

val-e-dic-to-ri-an (văl"ē-dĭk-tō'rĭ-ăn), *n.* a person who makes a farewell address; especially, a member of a graduating class in a school or college, usually that one with highest standing, who makes the farewell oration at commencement.

val-e-dic-to-ry (văl"ē-dĭk'tō-rĭ), *n.* [*pl.* valedictories (-rĭz)], a farewell speech, especially a farewell address at a school or college commencement: *adj.* pertaining to a farewell.

Va-len-ci-ennes (vȧ″lăṅ″syĕn′; vȧ-lĕn″sĭ-ĕnz′), *n.* a rich kind of lace made at Valenciennes, France: usually called *Val* lace.

val-en-tine (văl′ĕn-tīn), *n.* a sweetheart chosen on St. Valentine's Day; also, a love message, real, sentimental, or burlesque, sent on February 14th.

va-le-ri-an (vȧ-lē′rĭ-ăn), *n.* a drug with a strong, peculiar odor, obtained from the root of a plant, and used as a mild stimulant or tonic; the plant, or its root, from which this drug is obtained; any one of several other species of this plant.

val-et (văl′ĕt; văl′ā′), *n.* a manservant who personally attends a man, taking care of his apartment, clothes, etc.: called in full *valet de chambre*. [Fr.]

val-e-tu-di-na-ri-an (văl″ē-tū″dĭ-nā′rĭ-ăn), *n.* an invalid or sickly person; a person whose chief interest is health: *adj.* in poor health; seeking to recover health; overanxious about one's own health and that of others. Also, **valetudinary.**

Val-hal-la (văl-hăl′ȧ), *n.* in Scandinavian mythology, the palace of Odin, in which the souls of heroes slain in battle dwell.

val-iant (văl′yănt), *adj.* brave; courageous; as, *valiant* soldiers; done with bravery; heroic; as, *valiant* deeds.—*adv.* **valiantly.**—*n.* **valiantness.**

Syn. valorous, gallant.
Ant. (see cowardly).

val-id (văl′ĭd), *adj.* based on fact; sound; well-grounded; as, a *valid* argument; able to stand legally; not weak or defective; as, a *valid* agreement; not out of date.—*adv.* **validly.**—*n.* **validness.**

Syn. weighty, strong, powerful, efficient, binding.
Ant. (see invalid).

val-i-date (văl′ĭ-dāt), *v.t.* to make good or sound; justify or confirm; to give legal force to.

va-lid-i-ty (vȧ-lĭd′ĭ-tĭ), *n.* the state or quality of being founded on fact; soundness; justness; legality; as, the *validity* of a claim.

va-lise (vȧ-lēs′), *n.* a traveling bag of leather, wicker, etc.

val-la-tion (vă-lā′shŭn), *n.* a military defensive work, in the form of trenches or ramparts.

val-ley (văl′ĭ), *n.* [*pl.* valleys (-ĭz)], low land between hills or mountains.

val-or (văl′ẽr), *n.* strength of mind in facing danger; bravery; courage; prowess, especially in fighting.

Syn. gallantry, heroism.
Ant. (see cowardice).

val-or-ous (văl′ẽr-ŭs), *adj.* brave; courageous; as, a *valorous* foe. Also, **valourous.**—*adv.* **valorously, valourously.**

val-u-a-ble (văl′ū-ȧ-bl), *adj.* costly or worth a good price; as, a *valuable* ring; precious; of high worth; as, a *valuable* friend: *n.pl.* costly possessions, as jewels.

val-u-a-tion (văl″ū-ā′shŭn), *n.* the act of putting a price on; estimation; as, a *valuation* of property; estimated worth or price.

val-ue (văl′ū), *n.* worth; that which makes anything worth possessing; exact meaning; as, try to grasp the *value* of each word; estimated worth; as, to put a *value* on property; purchasing power; as, the *value* of money; market price; fair price: *v.t.* [*p.t.* and *p.p.* valued, *p.pr.* valuing], to estimate the worth of; put a price on; esteem highly; hold dear; as, to *value* a friend.—*n.* **valuer.**

Syn., *v.* assess, reckon, appreciate, estimate, prize, treasure.
Ant. (see despise).

val-ued (văl′ūd), *adj.* highly appreciated; dearly prized; as, a *valued* friend.

valv-ate (văl′vāt), *adj.* like, serving as, or having, a movable part which opens and closes a passage.

valve (vălv), *n.* a door; especially, one of a pair of folding doors; a mechanism for opening and closing a passage, and thus regulating or directing the movement through it of gas, liquid, etc.; as, a *valve* in a steam radiator; in the body, a structure which opens and shuts to allow a fluid to flow through the opening in one direction only; as, the *valves* of the heart; one of the halves, hinged together so as to open and shut, of the shell of a mollusk of the bivalve class, such as the oyster.

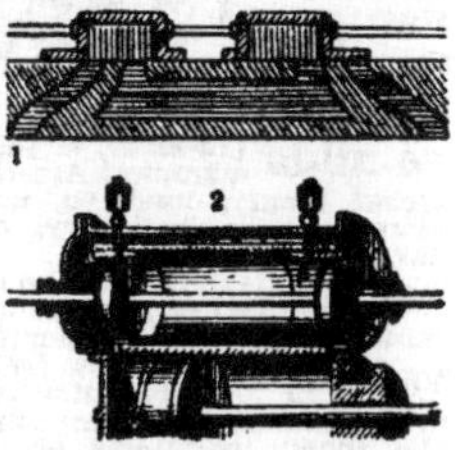

Valves of Steam Engine. 1, flat seat valve; 2, piston valve.

val-vu-lar (văl′vū-lȧr), *adj.* pertaining to valves, especially the valves of the heart; as, *valvular* disease of the heart.

vamp (vămp), *n.* the leather of a boot or shoe next above the sole and in front of the ankle seam; an upper; a piece added to something old to give it a new appearance: *v.t.* to furnish with an upper leather; to patch with new material: often with *up;* in music, to make up or improvise; as, to *vamp* an accompaniment or part.—*n.* **vamper.**

vam-pire (văm′pīr), *n.* in superstition, a ghost supposed to suck the blood of sleeping persons; one who preys on, or makes a living at the expense of, others, especially a woman of this sort; a kind of bat supposed to suck blood.

Vampire Bat

van (văn), *n.* front; the front of an army or fleet; as, the tanks moved forward in the *van;* the people who lead any movement; the place of those who so lead; as, he was in the *van* of all social reform; a large covered truck for moving household goods, circus animals, etc.

va-na-di-um (vȧ-nā′dĭ-ŭm), *n.* a grayish-white metallic powder obtained from a chemical element.

Van-dal (văn′dăl), *n.* one of a Teutonic race once inhabiting the south shores of the Baltic, noted for their fierceness and destructiveness, especially of works of art, when plundering Rome in the fifth century: **vandal,** one who wilfully destroys or injures anything beautiful, especially a work of art.

van-dal-ism (văn'dăl-ĭzm), *n.* deliberate destruction of what is beautiful, especially of works of art; as, the bombardment of Rheims cathedral was an act of *vandalism*.

Van-dyke (văn-dīk'), *adj.* in the style of Vandyke, the Dutch painter; as, a *Vandyke* beard is one cut in a point.

vane (vān), *n.* a movable device fastened to an elevated object to show which way the wind blows; a weathercock; a flat, fan-shaped arm projecting from an axis and moved around by the wind; as, the *vane* of a windmill; the web, or flat spreading part, of a feather.

van-guard (văn'gärd"), *n.* the first line or advance guard of an army; the troops who march in front; in trench warfare, those troops first arriving in the front lines of defense.

va-nil-la (vȧ-nĭl'ȧ), *n.* the pod or bean of a tropical American plant of the orchid family, used to make a flavoring extract for confectionery, cakes, etc.; the flavoring so obtained.

van-ish (văn'ĭsh), *v.i.* to disappear; fade; be lost from sight; to pass out of existence; be lost; as, hopes *vanish* away.

van-i-ty (văn'ĭ-tĭ), *n.* [*pl.* vanities (-tĭz)], love of admiration; shallow pride in appearance or accomplishments; conceit; idle show; emptiness of real worth; as, "*Vanity* of *vanities*, all is *vanity*"; lack of reality behind appearance; a frivolous trifle.

Syn. affectedness.

Van-i-ty Fair (văn'ĭ-tĭ fâr), in Bunyan's *Pilgrim's Progress*, a town fair where all the wares were vanities, and the buyers lovers of vanity; hence, worldly social life where the emphasis is placed on empty frivolities and idle show.

van-quish (văŋ'kwĭsh), *v.t.* to conquer; subdue; as, Cæsar *vanquished* Gaul; to get the better of; to defeat in an argument or debate.—*adj.* **vanquishable.**—*n.* **vanquisher.**

van-tage (vȧn'tȧj), *n.* a superior position or opportunity; in lawn tennis, the point in the game when either side has scored one point after deuce.

van-tage ground (vȧn'tȧj ground), a position which gives its holder a better opportunity than others have.

vap-id (văp'ĭd), *adj.* lacking life or spirit; flat; stale; tasteless; pointless; as, *vapid* talk.—*adv.* **vapidly.**—*n.* **vapidness, vapidity.**

va-por (vā'pẽr), *n.* the form taken by liquids and solids under the influence of heat, or reduction of pressure; gas; a cloudlike substance floating in the air and robbing it of clearness, as fog, smoke, etc.; anything impossible to seize and hold; something that vanishes like smoke or mist; as, life is but a *vapor*; *v.i.* to pass off in the form of gas, steam, etc.; to send out gas, steam, etc.; to indulge in idle talk. Also, **vapour.**—*n.* **vaporer, vapourer.**

va-por-i-za-tion (vā"pẽr-ĭ-zā'shŭn; văp"ō-rĭ-zā'shŭn), *n.* the act of changing, or state of being changed, into steam, gas, etc.

va-por-ize (vā'pẽr-īz), *v.t.* to change into gas, etc., by means of heat, or reduction of pressure.—*n.* **vapo izer.**

va-por-ous (vā'pẽr-ŭs), *adj.* full of, or like, vapor, or gas, etc.; unreal; without substance.—*adv.* **vaporously.**—*n.* **vaporousness.**

va-por-y (vā'pẽr-ĭ), *adj.* full of, or like, vapors or gas, etc.; peevish or melancholy.

va-que-ro (vä-kā'rō), *n.* [*pl.* vaqueros (-rōs)], in Spanish America, New Mexico, etc., a cattleman or cowboy. [SPAN.]

va-ri-a-bil-i-ty (vā"rĭ-ȧ-bĭl'ĭ-tĭ), *n.* the state or quality of being changeable; tendency to alter or differ.

va-ri-a-ble (vā'rĭ-ȧ-bl), *adj.* changeable: as, a *variable* wind; inconstant; fickle; as, *variable* love: *n.* that which is subject to change; in mathematics, a quantity that may be given many values.—*adv.* **variably.**—*n.* **variableness.**

Syn., adj. unsteady, shifting, wavering, fitful, restless.

Ant. (see constant).

va-ri-ance (vā'rĭ-ăns), *n.* the act of changing or differing; degree of alteration or change; a difference of opinion; a disagreement.

va-ri-ant (vā'rĭ-ănt), *adj.* differing in certain details from other objects in the same general class or kind: *n.* something different in details from others of its kind.

va-ri-a-tion (vā"rĭ-ā'shŭn), *n.* the act of altering or changing; a modification or change; a departure from a regular rule or course; extent to which a thing alters; as, there is little *variation* in the temperature; difference in details between two things of the same class; in music, the repeating of a single melody with changes and decorations in time, harmony, elaboration, etc.—*adj.* **variational.**

va-ri-col-ored (vā'rĭ-kŭl"ẽrd), *adj.* changeable in color; streaked, spotted, or marked with various colors; as, a *varicolored* rose.

var-i-cose (văr'ĭ-kōs), *p.adj.* swollen or enlarged; as, *varicose* veins.

va-ried (vā'rĭd), *p.adj.* altered; changed; of many different sorts.

va-ri-e-gate (vā'rĭ-ē-gāt), *v.t.* [*p.t.* and *p.p.* variegated; *p.pr.* variegating], to change the appearance of by marking with different colors.—*p.adj.* **variegated.**

va-ri-e-ga-tion (vā"rĭ-ē-gā'shŭn), *n.* the act of streaking or spotting, or state of being streaked or spotted, with different colors or tints; difference in color between two things.

va-ri-e-ty (vȧ-rī'ē-tĭ), *n.* [*pl.* varieties (-tĭz)], a collection of unlike objects; an individual differing in some details from others of the same general class or kind; a sort; as, one *variety* of palm bears dates, another coconuts; in biology, the group of next lower rank than a species; lack of monotony or sameness; as, *variety* is the spice of life.—*adj.* **varietal.**

Syn. diversity, change, mixture, medley.

Ant. (see sameness).

va-ri-o-la (vȧ-rī'ō-lȧ), *n.* smallpox, a contagious eruptive fever.

va-ri-o-loid (vā'rĭ-ō-loid; văr'ĭ-ō-loid), *n.* a mild form of smallpox, or variola.

va-ri-o-rum (vā"rĭ-ō'rŭm), *adj.* containing comments and explanations by different persons; said of an edition of a work of literature; as, a *variorum* edition of Shakespeare.

va-ri-ous (vā'rĭ-ŭs), *adj.* different; diverse; of several sorts; as, *various* plants; changeable; uncertain; differing in some details from one another; having several different characteristics or appearances; many-sided.—*adv.* **variously.**—*n.* **variousness.**

var-let (vär'lĕt), *n.* formerly, a servant, footman, or page; a scoundrel.

var-nish (vär'nĭsh), *n.* a liquid, oily preparation of resin used for giving gloss to the surface of wood or metal work; outside smoothness or gloss, as of politeness: *v.t.* to cover with such a liquid; give a gloss to; give a good outside appearance to; as, to *varnish* the defects in his character.—*n.* **varnisher.**

va-ry (vā'rĭ), *v.t.* [*p.t.* and *p.p.* varied, *p.pr.* varying], to alter or change in appearance, shape, substance, etc.; to make unlike one another; as, to *vary* the lessons in a course of study; in music, to adorn with variations; to relieve by changing; as, to *vary* the monotony: *v.i.* to alter or change; to undergo a change; to differ; to depart from a rule or course.

vat (văt), *n.* a large tank, tub, or vessel, for holding liquors, dyes, etc., in process of making.

Vat-i-can (văt'ĭ-kăn), *n.* the palace of the Pope at Rome, including library, museums, etc.; the papal authority, or the government of the Roman Catholic Church.

va-tic-i-nate (vȧ-tĭs'ĭ-nāt), *v.i.* and *v.t.* [*p.t.* and *p.p.* vaticinated, *p.pr.* vaticinating], to prophesy or foretell.—*n.* **vaticination.**

vaude-ville (vōd'vĭl; FR. vōd"vēl'), *n.* a kind of theatrical performance consisting of a series of songs, dances, acrobatic feats, short dramatic sketches, etc.; a variety show.

vault (vôlt), *n.* a leap over a high barrier using the hands for support; an arched roof or ceiling; storage space, usually in a cellar; a prison; a cavern; a tomb; a steel room in a bank, etc., for the safe-keeping of valuables, such as jewels or money; as,

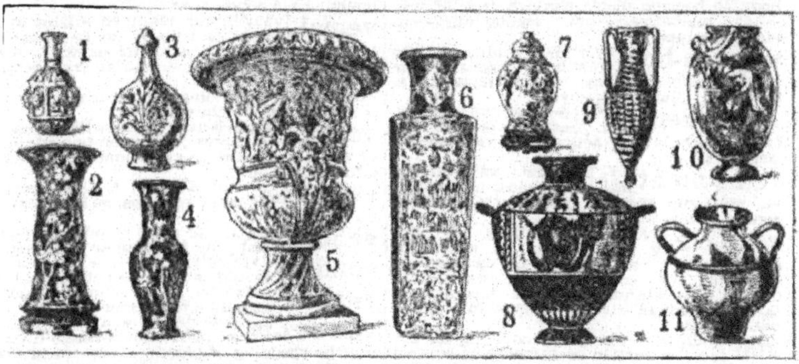

Vases. 1, glass vase from Jerusalem; 2, Chinese blue enamel; 3, Persian earthenware; 4, Chinese porcelain; 5, Grecian red earthenware, 6, Chinese green vase; 7, Chinese rose tea jar; 8, Grecian red earthenware; 9, Phœnician glass; 10, French flower jar in enamel; 11, brass jar (Flanders).

vas-cu-lar (văs'kū-lėr), *adj.* relating to the vessels of an animal or vegetable body which carry or convey fluids, as blood in animals and sap in plants.

vase (vās; văz, or BR. väz), *n.* a vessel, of glass, pottery, etc., usually circular in shape and of a height greater than its width, designed for ornament or use.

vas-e-line (văs'ē-lĭn; văs'ē-lēn), *n.* an oily, jellylike ointment or salve, obtained from coal oil or crude petroleum; petroleum jelly.

vas-sal (văs'ăl), *n.* in the feudal system, one who placed himself under the protection of another as his lord or master and in return rendered homage and service; a subject; a servant or bondsman; a slave: *adj.* under control of a superior power; as, a *vassal* state.

vas-sal-age (văs'ăl-āj), *n.* the state of one who renders service to a feudal lord in return for his protection; services so rendered; slavery or servitude; lands held under control of a superior state.

vast (vȧst), *adj.* far-stretching; very large; numerous; enormous; huge; immense.—*adv.* **vastly.**—*n.* **vastness.**

Syn. mighty, colossal, gigantic.

Ant. (see confined).

a safe deposit *vault;* the arch of heaven: *v.t.* to leap over; as, to *vault* a fence; to shape as a vault; to arch: *v.i.* to leap, over a high barrier, especially by aid of the hands or a pole; to show feats of leaping.

vault-ed (vôlt'ĕd), *adj.* arched and lofty; as, a *vaulted* roof.

vaunt (vänt; vônt), *v.i.* to brag: *v.t.* to boast of; display boastfully; as, to *vaunt* one's courage in public: *n.* a boast; a brag; vain display.—*adv.* **vauntingly.**—*n.* **vaunter.**

Syn., *v.* puff, hawk, advertise, flourish, parade.

veal (vēl), *n.* the flesh of the calf used as meat.

Ve-da (vā'dȧ; vē'dȧ), *n.* [*pl.* vedas (-dȧz)], one of the oldest sacred books of the Hindus, the basis of Brahmanism or the Hindu religion; one of the four groups in which these books are arranged.

ve-dette (vē-dĕt'), *n.* a mounted sentinel or soldier stationed in front of the regular pickets or guards of an army. Also, **vidette.**

veer (vēr), *v.t.* and *v.i.* to change in direction; to shift, as the wind.

veer-y (vēr'ĭ), *n.* [*pl.* veeries (-ĭz)], a variety of American thrush.

veg-e-ta-ble (vĕj'ē-tȧ-bl), *n.* a plant, especially a plant cultivated for food; the portion of such a plant gathered and prepared for market, or ready for the table: *adj.* of or pertaining to plants; as, *vegetable* fiber; having the nature of, or produced by, plants; composed of plants; as, *vegetable* life.

veg-e-ta-ri-an (vĕj"ē-tā'rĭ-ăn), *n.* one who lives on fruit, nuts, and vegetables; one who claims that plants, not animals, are the only proper source of food for man: *adj.* of or pertaining to those opposed to eating meat; consisting of vegetables; as, a *vegetarian* diet.

veg-e-ta-ri-an-ism (vĕj"ē-tā'rĭ-ăn-ĭzm), *n.* the theory and practice of eating only fruit, nuts, and vegetables.

veg-e-tate (vĕj'ē-tāt), *v.i.* [*p.t.* and *p.p.* vegetated, *p.pr.* vegetating], to grow with no more effort than a plant; to live a lazy, useless life; to allow mind and body to become feeble through lack of use. —*adj.* **vegetative.** —*adv.* **vegetatively.** —*n.* **vegetativeness.**

veg-e-ta-tion (vĕj"ē-tā'shŭn), *n.* the growth of vegetables or plants; plant life; as, tropical *vegetation* is luxuriant; plants in general.

ve-he-mence (vē'hē-mĕns; vē'ē-mĕns), *n.* passionate earnestness; force of words and action; violence; eagerness; urgency.

ve-he-ment (vē'hē-mĕnt; vē'ē-mĕnt), *adj.* very violent or forcible; as, *vehement* speech; passionate; ardent; earnest.—*adv.* **vehemently.**

ve-hi-cle (vē'hĭ-kl; vē'ĭ-kl), *n.* any kind of conveyance, as a wagon, carriage, etc.; any means of carrying or conveying or communicating something; hence, a substance in which medicine is taken, a form of literary composition, etc.—*adj.* **vehicular.**

veil (vāl), *n.* a thin, gauzy covering for the face; a curtain or covering to conceal something; a disguise: *v.t.* to cover with, or as with, a curtain; hide; conceal; as, to *veil* one's thoughts or intentions.—*adj.* **veiled.**

veiled (vāld), *adj.* covered by a curtain; disguised; wearing a covering over the face; having the real meaning hidden or disguised, as *veiled* speech.

veil-ing (vāl'ĭng), *n.* thin, gauzy material, as for veils.

vein (vān), *n.* one of the tubelike vessels which carry the blood to the heart; one of the branching ribs of a plant or of the wing of an insect; a crack or seam in rock filled by mineral matter; as, a *vein* of gold; a mineral bed; as, a *vein* of coal; a wave or streak in wood, marble, etc.; anything running through something else; as, a *vein* of humor ran through the serious address; a strain; as, he spoke in a solemn *vein*: *v.t.* to cover, fill, or form with veins.—*adj.* **veined.**—*n.* **veining.**

veldt (fĕlt; vĕlt), *n.* open or thinly wooded country in South Africa; grass country.

vel-lum (vĕl'ŭm), *n.* a fine parchment, made of the skin of an animal, intended for writing upon; also, a kind of paper or cotton cloth in imitation of such parchment or skin.

ve-loc-i-pede (vē-lŏs'ĭ-pēd), *n.* a light, two- or three-wheeled vehicle moved by the rider's feet: the form from which the bicycle and tricycle have developed.

ve-loc-i-ty (vē-lŏs'ĭ-tĭ), *n.* [*pl.* velocities (-tĭz)], rate of movement of a moving object; speed; swiftness; as, the *velocity* of a bullet.

ve-lours (vē-lōōr'), *n.* any of various woven fabrics having a pile, or raised surface, like that of velvet.

vel-ure (vĕl'ūr), *n.* velvet, or similar material; a linen or silk fabric with a velvety finish, used as drapery.

vel-vet (vĕl'vĕt), *n.* a silk material with a short, thick pile, or surface of upright cut threads; the soft skin on the horns of young deer; slang, money or funds secured without effort, as by speculation: *adj.* soft like velvet; velvety; as, a *velvet* touch.

vel-vet-een (vĕl"vē-tēn'), *n.* a cotton material resembling velvet: imitation velvet.

vel-vet-y (vĕl'vē-tĭ), *adj.* soft like velvet to the touch; soft and even in sound; as, a *velvety* tone.

ve-nal (vē'năl), *adj.* ready or willing to be bought or bribed; to be obtained by purchase or hire; as, *venal* services: used especially of a base or degrading transaction. —*adv.* **venally.**

Syn. salable, hireling, mercenary.

Ant. (see unpurchasable).

ve-nal-i-ty (vē-năl'ĭ-tĭ), *n.* willingness to lower or cheapen one's talents or services in order to gain money or reward; a mercenary spirit.

ve-na-tion (vē-nā'shŭn), *n.* the arrangement of veins, as in a leaf or an insect's wing.

vend (vĕnd), *v.t.* to sell; to offer for sale, especially by hawking or peddling.

vend-ee (vĕn-dē'), *n.* one to whom a thing is sold: a term used chiefly in law.

vend-er (vĕn'dĕr), *n.* a seller of goods, usually a hawker or peddler.

ven-det-ta (vĕn-dĕt'ȧ), *n.* a private feud or quarrel for revenge involving the shedding of blood: a custom in Corsica, Kentucky, etc.

vend-i-ble (vĕn'dĭ-bl), *adj.* marketable or salable: *n.* a marketable or salable article.

vend-or (vĕn'dôr), *n.* one who sells: opposite to *vendee*, and used chiefly in law.

ven-due (vĕn-dū'), *n.* a public sale by auction.

ve-neer (vē-nēr'), *v.t.* to overlay with a thin surface of more valuable material, as a piece of furniture with better wood; hence, to cover or conceal (something bad or common) with a surface polish; give a gloss to: *n.* a thin surface of fine wood overlaid above that of a poorer quality; outside show; pretense; surface elegance.—*n.* **veneering.**

ven-er-a-ble (vĕn'ĕr-ȧ-bl), *adj.* so old and wise as to be worthy of reverence; as, a *venerable* old man; sacred by reason of associations of a religious or historic nature; as, in the *venerable* cathedral at Rheims the kings of France were crowned.—*adv.* **venerably.**—*n.* **venerability.**

Syn. grave, sage, wise, old, reverend.

ven-er-ate (vĕn'ĕr-āt), *v.t.* [*p.t.* and *p.p.* venerated, *p.pr.* venerating], to regard as sacred; regard with the highest respect; revere because of age or wisdom.—*n.* **venerator.**

ven-er-a-tion (vĕn"ĕr-ā'shŭn), *n.* the highest degree of respect and reverence; respectful awe; worship.

ve-ne-re-al (vē-nē'rē-ăl), *adj.* due to immoral relations with an infected person: used of certain diseases usually contracted from immoral living, but also transmitted by infection from public drinking cups, towels, etc.

ven-er-y (věn'ẽr-ĭ), *n.* formerly, the art of hunting; the pleasures of the chase.

Ve-ne-tian (vē-nē'shăn), *adj.* of or pertaining to Venice, in Italy, or its people; as, *Venetian* lace: *n.* a native of Venice.

Ve-ne-tian blind (vē-nē'shăn blīnd), a window shade or blind made of long, thin, horizontal slats of wood, fastened together and drawn up and down by cords.

Ve-ne-tian door (vē-nē'shăn dōr), a door with long narrow side lights.

venge-ance (věn'jăns), *n.* revenge, usually just; righteous repayment of an injury or offense; retribution; as, "*Vengeance* is mine, saith the Lord."

venge-ful (věnj'fōōl), *adj.* revengeful; inclined to inflict stern punishment for an injury or offense; as, a *vengeful* spirit.—*adv.* **vengefully.**—*n.* **vengefulness.**

ve-ni-al (vē'nĭ-ăl), *adj.* not beyond forgiveness; pardonable; excusable; as, *venial* sins.—*adv.* **venially.**—*n.* **venialness, veniality.**

ve-ni-re (vē-nī'rē), *n.* a legal writ or judge's order for the summoning of a jury for a court trial: called in full *venire facias.*

ven-i-son (věn'ĭ-zn; *esp.* Br. **věn'zn**), *n.* deer's flesh used for meat.

ven-om (věn'ŭm), *n.* the poison of certain animals and insects, which makes their bite or sting injurious and often fatal; hence, anything which poisons or makes bitter; as, the *venom* of bitter speech; spite.
Syn. virus, malice, malignity.

ven-om-ous (věn'ŭm-ŭs), *adj.* full of poison; poisonous; as, a *venomous* sting; having poison glands; as, a *venomous* snake; baneful; spiteful; as, *venomous* speech.—*adv.* **venomously.**—*n.* **venomousness.**

ve-nous (vē'nŭs), *adj.* of or pertaining to veins; as, *venous* blood is that found in the veins, not in the arteries.

vent (věnt), *n.* a small opening for the escape of air, liquid, etc.; hence, an outlet; a passage; an utterance; as, to give *vent* to one's thoughts is a relief; the opening at the breech of a firearm, through which fire is communicated to the powder of the charge: *v.t.* to let out through a hole; to utter or express; as, to *vent* one's spite; to furnish with an outlet; to relieve by speech, etc.; as, to *vent* oneself in angry words.

ven-ti-late (věn'tĭ-lāt), *v.t.* [*p.t.* and *p.p.* ventilated, *p.pr.* ventilating], to supply with fresh air; as, to *ventilate* a room; to utter or express publicly.

ven-ti-la-tion (věn'tĭ-lā'shŭn), *n.* the act of supplying with fresh air; the state of being supplied with fresh air.

ven-ti-la-tor (věn'tĭ-lā'tẽr), *n.* a contrivance for admitting fresh air and letting out foul air.

ven-tral (věn'trăl), *adj.* of or pertaining to the abdomen, or belly, as of an animal or serpent; as, the *ventral* fins of a fish: opposite to *dorsal.*

ven-tri-cle (věn'trĭ-kl), *n.* either of the two lower chambers of the heart which deliver blood to the arteries; as, the right or left *ventricle.*—*adj.* **ventricular.**

ven-tril-o-quism (věn-trĭl'ō-kwĭzm), *n.* the act or art of speaking in such a manner that the voice seems to come from another person or place.

ven-tril-o-quist (věn-trĭl'ō-kwĭst), *n.* one who practices the art of speaking in such a way that the voice appears to come from another person or place.

ven-ture (věn'tūr), *n.* a dangerous or daring undertaking; an enterprise involving risk; as, a business *venture;* something risked; a hazard: *v.t.* [*p.t.* and *p.p.* ventured, *p.pr.* venturing], to risk; expose to danger; chance; as, to *venture* money in a business scheme; assume the risk of; undertake at a risk; dare; *v.i.* to dare; to take a chance; to run a risk.—*n.* **venturer.**
Syn., *n.* chance, peril, stake.

ven-ture-some (věn'tūr-sŭm), *adj.* daring; rash; willing to incur risks. Also, **adventuresome.**—*adv.* **venturesomely.**—*n.* **venturesomeness.**

ven-tur-ous (věn'tūr-ŭs), *adj.* rash; bold; daring. Also, **adventurous.** *adv.* **venturously.**—*n.* **venturousness.**

ven-ue (věn'ū), *n.* in a lawsuit, the locality where the events occurred that caused the suit; also, the place from which the jury is taken, and where the trial is held.

Ve-nus (vē'nŭs), *n.* a bright planet whose orbit is between those of Mercury and the earth, hence second from the sun: formerly called *Lucifer* when star of morning, and *Hesperus* when star of evening; in Roman mythology, the goddess of beauty and love, and the wife of Vulcan: identified with the Greek goddess Aphrodite.

ve-ra-cious (vē-rā'shŭs), *adj.* habitually telling the truth; truthful; as, a *veracious* person; marked by truth; true; as, a *veracious* report.—*adv.* **veraciously.**

ve-rac-i-ty (vē-răs'ĭ-tĭ), *n.* habitual regard for the truth; truthfulness; as, you can rely on his *veracity;* truth.
Syn. credibility, accuracy.
Ant. (see falsehood).

ve-ran-da (vē-răn'dȧ), *n.* an open balcony, attached to the outside of a house and having a roof supported by light pillars or posts; a porch; in the United States, a piazza. Also, **verandah.**

verb (vûrb), *n.* that part of speech which expresses action, existence, or condition.

ver-bal (vûr'băl), *adj.* of or pertaining to words; consisting merely of words; as, his sympathy was only *verbal;* concerned with words more than with the ideas which they contain; stated or expressed in words, especially spoken words; hence, spoken; not written; as, a *verbal* agreement; word for word; as, she gave a *verbal* recitation of her lesson without understanding it; in grammar, pertaining to, or derived from, a verb: **verbal noun,** a noun made from a verb by adding *-ing,* and meaning the act or process of doing what is indicated by the verb; as, in the sentence "Seeing is believing," *seeing* and *believing* are *verbal nouns.*—*adv.* **verbally.**

ver-bal-ism (vûr'băl-ĭzm), *n.* expression in words without attention to thought; as, the frequent repeating of a set form of words often becomes empty *verbalism.*

ver-ba-tim (vẽr-bā'tĭm), *adv.* word for word; as, to report a speech *verbatim.*

ver-be-na (vẽr-bē'nȧ), *n.* a garden plant of many varieties, with large flowers of various colors and spicy fragrance.

ver-bi-age (vûr'bĭ-āj), *n.* wordiness; the meaningless use of many words.

ver-bose (vẽr-bōs'), *adj.* wordy; full of words; using too many words.—*adv.* verbosely.—*n.* verboseness.

ver-bos-i-ty (vẽr-bŏs'ĭ-tĭ), *n.* the use of too many words; wordiness.

ver-dan-cy (vûr'dăn-sĭ), *n.* greenness; as, the *verdancy* of the foliage; inexperience; as, the *verdancy* of youth.

ver-dant (vûr'dănt), *adj.* covered with fresh green grass or foliage; as, the *verdant* landscape; having the freshness of spring; hence, fresh and untried in knowledge or judgment; inexperienced; as, *verdant* youth.

ver-dict (vûr'dĭkt), *n.* the decision of a jury on a case in court; as, the jury's *verdict* was "Not guilty"; the expression of any important decision.

ver-di-gris (vûr'dĭ-grēs), *n.* a green or bluish-green coloring matter and drug, produced by acetic acid acting on copper; colloquially, a greenish or bluish rust on copper, bronze, etc.

ver-dure (vûr'dūr), *n.* greenness or freshness, especially of grass and growing plants; also, green grass, growing plants, etc.; as the meadows were clad with *verdure*.

verge (vûrj), *n.* a rod or staff carried as a sign of authority; a limit or boundary; an extreme edge; as, the *verge* of a precipice: *v.i.* to be on the edge or border: with *on:* as, to *verge* on treason; to tend; to incline.

ver-ger (vûr'jẽr), *n.* an officer who carries a rod as a sign of authority; in the English Church, an attendant on a bishop, a dean, etc.; in the Protestant Episcopal Church, one who takes care of a church building or property; a sexton.

ver-i-fi-a-ble (vĕr'ĭ-fī'ȧ-bl), *adj.* capable of being proved true.

ver-i-fi-ca-tion (vĕr"ĭ-fĭ-kā'shŭn), *n.* the act of proving to be true; the state of being proved true.

ver-i-fy (vĕr'ĭ-fī), *v.t.* [*p.t.* and *p.p.* verified, *p.pr.* verifying], to prove to be true; to confirm or substantiate; as, to *verify* a statement.

ver-i-ly (vĕr'ĭ-lĭ), *adv.* in truth; in fact; certainly; really; truly; as, *verily* I believe.

ver-i-si-mil-i-tude (vĕr"ĭ-sĭ-mĭl'ĭ-tūd), *n.* the appearance of truth; probability; likelihood; likeness to the actual.

ver-i-ta-ble (vĕr'ĭ-tȧ-bl), *adj.* actual; genuine; true; as, the rain was a *veritable* godsend.—*adv.* veritably.

ver-i-ty (vĕr'ĭ-tĭ), *n.* [*pl.* verities (-tĭz)], that which is true; a truth; a fact; quality of being true or correct; truthfulness; reality; as, the *verity* of the Scripture narrative.

ver-mi-cel-li (vûr'mē-sĕl'ĭ; vûr'mē-chĕl'ĭ), *n.* a paste made of fine flour dried in slender, round sticks; a small, solid kind of macaroni.

ver-mi-form (vûr'mĭ-fôrm), *adj.* shaped like a worm: vermiform appendix, a small, useless, closed tube attached to the large intestine in the lower right-hand part of the abdomen: the seat of the disease appendicitis.

ver-mi-fuge (vûr'mĭ-fūj), *n.* a medicine that expels or forces parasitic worms from animal bodies.

ver-mil-ion (vẽr-mĭl'yŭn), *n.* a brilliant red coloring matter made from sulphide of mercury; a vivid red color.

ver-min (vûr'mĭn), *n.* [usually *pl.*], harmful and offensive small animals or insects, as bedbugs, flies, lice, fleas, mice, rats, etc.—*adj.* verminous.

ver-mor-el spray-er (vûr'môr-ĕl sprā'ẽr), a fruit tree and vineyard sprayer intended to rid the trees and vines of destroying worms; in the World War, the same device used to get rid of chlorine gas in the trenches after a gas attack: not effective for phosgene gas.

ver-muth (vûr'mōōth), *n.* a kind of spicy alcoholic cordial flavored with wormwood and other substances. Also, vermouth.

ver-nac-u-lar (vẽr-năk'ū-lȧr), *adj.* pertaining to one's native country: used of a language: *n.* one's mother tongue; the prevailing fashion of speech among the people in general in any locality; as, he could converse in the *vernacular* with his mountaineer friends; vocabulary peculiar to a business, profession, etc.; as, the *vernacular* of the motion picture studios.

ver-nal (vûr'năl), *adj.* pertaining to, or appearing in, the spring; as, the *vernal* equinox; springlike; hence, youthful; as, the *vernal* fires of enthusiasm.

ver-ni-er (vûr'nĭ-ẽr), *n.* a scale made to slide along the divisions of another scale in order to obtain accurate fractional parts of the subdivisions of the fixed scale.

ver-sa-tile (vûr'sȧ-tĭl), *adj.* turning easily from one action, style, subject, etc., to another; able to do many things well; as, a *versatile* writer.

ver-sa-til-i-ty (vûr"sȧ-tĭl'ĭ-tĭ), *n.* ability to change easily from one action, style, or subject to another; power to do many things well.

verse (vûrs), *n.* a line of poetry; a form of composition possessing rhythm; poetry; a short division of a chapter in the Bible: *pl.* a poem.

versed (vûrst), *adj.* thoroughly trained; taught by experience, practice, study, etc.; skilled; learned; informed.

ver-si-cle (vûr'sĭ-kl), *n.* a little verse, especially a short verse or sentence said or sung by a minister or priest, followed by a response from the congregation.

ver-si-fi-ca-tion (vûr"sĭ-fĭ-kā'shŭn), *n.* the art or practice of composing verses, as of poetry; the science of metrical construction.

ver-si-fy (vûr'sĭ-fī), *v.i.* [*p.t.* and *p.p.* versified, *p.pr.* versifying], to express thought or feeling in verse form; to make verses: *v.t.* to express in verse; to put into verse.—*n.* versifier.

ver-sion (vûr'shŭn), *n.* a translation from one language into another; as, the revised *version* of the Bible; an individual report of an occurrence which may differ from others according to the narrator's point of view; as, his *version* of the accident was not credited; a form taken by a story under particular circumstances of place and time; as, there is an Irish *version* of the story of Cinderella.

verst (vûrst), *n.* the Russian mile, equal to 3,500 English feet, or 0.6629 mile.

ver-sus (vûr'sŭs), *prep.* [abbrev. *vs.* or *v.*], against: used chiefly in legal or sporting language; as, the case of John Doe *versus* Richard Roe.

ver-te-bra (vûr'tē-brȧ), *n.* [*pl.* vertebræ (-brē)], a single bone of the spinal column, or backbone.—*adj.* **vertebral.**

ver-te-brate (vûr'tē-brāt), *adj.* having a backbone, or spinal column; as, a *vertebrate* animal: *n.* an animal with a spinal column.—*adj.* **vertebrated.**

ver-tex (vûr'tĕks), *n.* [*pl.* vertexes (-tĕk-sĕz), vertices (-tĭ-sēz)], the highest point; the apex; as, the *vertex* of a pyramid; the top.

ver-ti-cal (vûr'tĭ-kăl), *adj.* pertaining to, or situated at, the apex or top; leading toward the zenith; at right angles with the horizon; upright; in an up and down direction; as, draw a *vertical* line from top to bottom of the paper: *n.* a line, plane, or circle at right angles with the horizon.—*adv.* **vertically.**—*n.* **verticalness, verticality.**

ver-tig-i-nous (vẽr-tĭj'ĭ-nŭs), *adj.* affected with dizziness; giddy; making dizzy; turning around; whirling.

ver-ti-go (vûr'tĭ-gō), *n.* [*pl.* vertigoes (-gōz)], giddiness; extreme dizziness.

ver-tu (vûr'to͞o), *n.* artistic rarity; objects showing artistic or curious workmanship. Also, **virtu.**

verve (vûrv), *n.* the enthusiasm which inspires a poet or artist; quickness of imagination; energy; spirit.

ver-y (vĕr'ĭ), *adj.* [*comp.* verier, *superl.* veriest], absolute; complete; utter; as, that is the *very* truth; especial; as, his *very* own; the same; as, that is the *very* one; for emphasis, equivalent to *even the;* as, the *very* thought frightens me: *adv.* in a high degree; extremely; as, she does *very* good work: not used to modify verbs, or past participles in the predicate.

ves-i-cate (vĕs'ĭ-kāt), *v.t.* to cause the skin of to blister.—*n.* **vesication.**

ves-i-cle (vĕs'ĭ-kl), *n.* a small vessel, or sac, in the body, containing fluid; a blister; a cyst.

ves-per (vĕs'pẽr), *adj.* pertaining to the evening: *n.* evening; an evening hymn, prayer, etc.: **Vesper,** the evening star, or Hesper.

ves-pers (vĕs'pẽrz), *n.pl.* in the Protestant Episcopal Church, evening prayer; in Protestant churches generally, a late Sunday afternoon service, often musical.

ves-sel (vĕs'ĕl), *n.* a hollow receptacle or container, usually for liquids, as a barrel, bottle, cup, etc.; a tube or canal in the body through which a fluid passes or in which it is secreted; as, a blood *vessel,* etc.; a hollow, floating structure for conveyance of people and goods by water; any boat larger than a rowboat; a ship.

vest (vĕst), *n.* a waistcoat; a man's sleeveless body garment, worn beneath the coat; a woven or knitted undershirt; an ornamental insertion in the front of a woman's waist: *v.t.* to dress in, or as in, a garment; hence, to encircle or surround; to clothe, with authority or power: followed by *with:* to put into the care of another: with *in;* as, the control of the city is *vested* in its officials: *v.i.* to be fixed; to pass or take effect, as a title to property, etc.: with *in.*

ves-ta (vĕs'tȧ), *n.* a short wax match or taper; a short wooden match.

ves-tal (vĕs'tăl), *adj.* pertaining to, or sacred to, Vesta, the Roman goddess of the hearth and home, or to one of the virgins who served in her temple: *n.* in the Roman religion, a virgin vowed to the service of Vesta; a virgin; also, a nun: **Vestal Virgins,** the six virgin priestesses who tended the sacred fire on the altar of the temple of Vesta, at Rome.

vest-ed (vĕs'tĕd), *adj.* clothed, especially in priestly garments; fixed; having its rights established by law; as, *vested* interests.

ves-ti-bule (vĕs'tĭ-būl), *n.* a small, square inclosure between an outer and an inner door of a house; an inclosed porch or entrance hall outside the main door of a building; as, the *vestibule* of a church; an inclosed entrance to a railway passenger car.—*adj.* **vestibuled.**

ves-tige (vĕs'tĭj), *n.* a mark left in passing; a visible sign or trace of something that is gone or has disappeared or ceased; as, not a *vestige* of the house remained.

vest-ment (vĕst'mĕnt), *n.* a covering; a garment; an official dress or robe of ceremony: *pl.* garments or robes worn over the ordinary dress by priests, ministers, choir, etc., in the services of the church.

ves-try (vĕs'trĭ), *n.* [*pl.* vestries (-trĭz)], a room in a church where the clergy put on their vestments or robes; also, in some Protestant churches, a room or building attached to a church, and used as a chapel, Sunday-school room, etc.; in the Protestant Episcopal Church, a body of men who direct or govern the affairs of a parish.

ves-try-man (vĕs'trĭ-măn), *n.* [*pl.* vestrymen (-mĕn)], one of a group that directs or manages the affairs of a church and parish.

ves-ture (vĕs'tûr), *n.* clothing; garments taken collectively; a covering.

vetch (vĕch), *n.* a plant of the same family as the pea and bean, used for fodder.

vet-er-an (vĕt'ẽr-ăn), *adj.* possessing experience due to age; long trained or practiced, especially as a soldier: *n.* a person of age and experience; one grown old in service; a soldier of any age who has seen active service in war; as, though they were only boys, the first soldiers to return from the trenches in 1918 were called *veterans.*

vet-er-i-na-ri-an (vĕt″ẽr-ĭ-nā'rĭ-ăn), *n.* one who understands and practices the healing of diseases and injuries of domestic animals, especially horses, cattle, etc.

vet-er-i-na-ry (vĕt'ẽr-ĭ-nā-rĭ), *adj.* pertaining to the healing of diseases of domestic animals, especially horses, cattle, etc.; as, a *veterinary* surgeon: *n.* [*pl.* veterinaries (-rĭz)], one who treats the diseases of domestic animals.

ve-to (vē'tō), *n.* [*pl.* vetoes (-tōz)], the right to stop or prevent the enactment of a measure as law; a prohibition by one in authority; the refusal of a chief executive to agree to a legislative enactment: *v.t.* to refuse consent to; prohibit; forbid with authority; as, the President *vetoed* the measure.

vex (vĕks), *v.t.* to irritate by small annoyances; to harass; tease; make angry.

vex-a-tion (vĕk-sā'shŭn), *n.* the act of annoying; the state of being irritated or annoyed; annoyance; a cause of worry; displeasure.
Syn. chagrin, mortification.
Ant. (see pleasure).

vex-a-tious (vĕk-sā'shŭs), *adj.* causing irritation or annoyance; troublesome; harassing.—*adv.* **vexatiously.**

vexed (vĕkst), *adj.* much debated or contested, but not settled; as, a *vexed* question.

vi-a (vī'*d*), *prep.* by the way of; as, he traveled from New York to Chicago *via* Philadelphia. [LAT.]

vi-a-ble (vī'*d*-bl), *adj.* capable of living or maintaining life: used of a newborn infant.

vi-a-duct (vī'*d*-dŭkt), *n.* a bridge for carrying a roadway over a valley or ravine, etc.; built of masonry arches or of short steel spans mounted on high steel towers.

Viaduct

vi-al (vī'ăl), *n.* a small glass bottle; as, a *vial* for medicine. Also, **phial.**

vi-ands (vī'ăndz), *n.pl.* food or provisions; eatables.

vi-at-i-cum (vī-ăt'ĭ-kŭm), *n.* the Eucharist, or Communion, administered by a priest of the Roman Catholic Church to a dying person.

vi-brant (vī'brănt), *adj.* vibrating; thrilling; tremulous; resonant or resounding; as, a *vibrant* voice.

vi-brate (vī'brāt), *v.i.* [*p.t.* and *p.p.* vibrated, *p.pr.* vibrating], to move rapidly backward and forward, as a pendulum; to swing; shake; quiver; waver; to thrill or tremble, as a voice: *v.t.* to cause to move to and fro; cause to quiver, etc.

Syn. oscillate, sway, wave, undulate.

vi-bra-tion (vī-brā'shŭn), *n.* the act of swinging, quivering, or thrilling; as, the *vibration* of a piano string when it is struck; trembling or wavering motion or sound.—*adj.* **vibrational.**

vi-bra-tor (vī'brā-tẽr), *n.* one who, or that which, causes to move back and forth, to quiver, or to thrill: usually a mechanical or electrical device.

vi-bra-to-ry (vī'brȧ-tō-rĭ), *adj.* consisting of, or causing, a swinging, shaking, or quivering movement; pertaining to such a movement.

vic-ar (vĭk'ẽr), *n.* in the Roman Catholic Church, a member of the clergy representing one higher up; as, the Pope is said to be the *Vicar* of Christ, and is represented by a *vicar;* in England, the priest of a parish of which the tithes are owned by a layman; in the Protestant Episcopal Church, a minister who is the head of one chapel in a large parish; also, a bishop's representative in charge of a church or mission.

vic-ar-age (vĭk'ẽr-āj), *n.* in England, the office, position, or residence of a vicar, or minister of a parish controlled by a layman.

vic-ar-gen-er-al (vĭk'ẽr-jĕn'ẽr-ăl), *n.* in the Anglican Church, a legal officer who represents an archbishop in certain matters; in the Roman Catholic Church, a priest who represents and acts for a bishop in matters requiring the exercise of legal power or jurisdiction.

vi-ca-ri-ous (vī-kā'rĭ-ŭs), *adj.* acting for another; as, a *vicarious* agent; performed or suffered in place of another; as, *vicarious* suffering.—*adv.* **vicariously.**—*n.* **vicariousness.**

vice (vīs), *n.* a fault, defect, or blemish; an immoral practice or habit; abandonment to evil; immorality; an instrument used to hold things firmly in two jaws tightened by a screw: also spelled *vise.*

Syn. vileness, corruption, pollution, wickedness, guilt, iniquity.

Ant. (see virtue).

vice (vīs), *adj.* entitled to fill an office in the absence of its holder; as, *vice* president; denoting the office of one so entitled; second in rank; as, *vice* admiral.

vice-ge-rent (vīs-jē'rĕnt), *adj.* holding power from another; acting in the place of another: *n.* an officer authorized to exercise the powers of another: an agent or lieutenant.

vice-re-gal (vīs'rē'găl), *adj.* pertaining to a viceroy, or a governor of a province or colony ruling in the name and by the authority of a king or sovereign; as, *viceregal* authority.

vice-roy (vīs'roi), *n.* a ruler of a colony or province, acting with royal authority in the place of the king; as, the *viceroy* of India.

vice-roy-al-ty (vīs'roi'ăl-tĭ), *n.* the authority, office, or position of a viceroy, or royal governor of a colony or province.

vi-ce ver-sa (vī'sē vûr'sȧ), in reversed order; with relations made opposite; conversely. [LAT.]

vic-i-nage (vĭs'ĭ-nāj), *n.* neighborhood; vicinity; locality.

vi-cin-i-ty (vĭ-sĭn'ĭ-tĭ), *n.* [*pl.* vicinities (-tĭz)], nearness; closeness; a region about or near; neighborhood; as, he lives in our *vicinity.*

vi-cious (vĭsh'ŭs), *adj.* faulty; as, *vicious* reasoning; corrupt; depraved; wicked; as, he led a *vicious* life; unruly; spiteful; not well tamed or broken; as, a *vicious* horse; impure; as, *vicious* air.—*adv.* **viciously.**—*n.* **viciousness.**

Ant. (see gentle).

vi-cis-si-tude (vĭ-sĭs'ĭ-tūd), *n.* a complete, unexpected change; an unforeseen, usually disturbing, event; regular change.

vic-tim (vĭk'tĭm), *n.* a living being sacrificed in a religious rite or ceremony; a person or thing destroyed or hurt by another in the pursuit of some object, or injured by some accident, disease, etc.

Syn. sacrifice, prey, sufferer.

vic-tim-ize (vĭk'tĭm-īz), *v.t.* [*p.t.* and *p.p.* victimized, *p.pr.* victimizing], to injure, destroy, or sacrifice; to cheat or swindle.

vic-tor (vĭk'tẽr), *n.* conqueror; one who wins in a contest: *adj.* conquering.

vic-to-ri-a (vĭk-tō'rĭ-ȧ), *n.* a kind of low four-wheeled carriage with a op that may be lowered and a high coachman's eat; a very large South American water lily.

Vic-to-ri-a Cross (vĭk-tō'rĭ-ȧ krŏs), a decoration instituted at the close of the Crimean Campaign n 1856, and granted to a soldier of any rank and for a single act of valor: one of the highest nedals awarded in the British army.

Vic-to-ri-an (vĭk-tō'rĭ-ăn), *adj.* pertaining to the reign of Queen Victoria of England (1837–1901): *n.* a person living during that time, especially a writer; as, Dickens, Thackeray, Tennyson, and Carlyle were among the greatest *Victorians;* a person whose thoughts and habits are characteristic of the time of Queen Victoria's reign.

Vic-to-ri-a re-gi-a (vĭk-tō'rĭ-ȧ rē'jĭ-ȧ), the royal water lily, a plant of tropical South America, remarkable for its immense flowers, often one to two feet in diameter, and for its peculiar leaves.

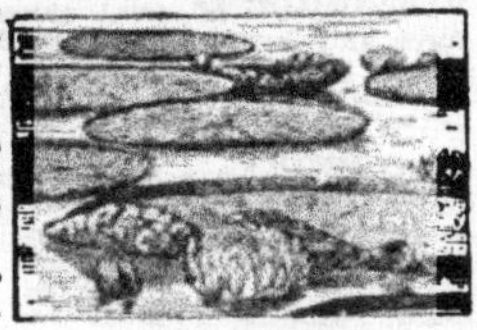

Victoria Regia

vic-to-ri-ous (vĭk-tō'-rĭ-ŭs), *adj.* having conquered in battle or contest; triumphant; as, a *victorious* army; marked by, or ending in, conquest or triumph; as, a *victorious* fight.—*adv.* **victoriously.**—*n.* **victoriousness.**

vic-to-ry (vĭk'tō-rĭ), *n.* [*pl.* victories (-rĭz)], the defeat of an enemy in battle, or an opponent in a contest; triumph; conquest.

vict-ual (vĭt'l), *v.t.* [*p.t.* and *p.p.* victualed, *p.pr.* victualing], to supply or stock with food: *n.pl.* food for human beings; especially, such food when ready for eating.

vict-ual-er (vĭt'l-ẽr; vĭt'lẽr), *n.* one who provides victuals, or food, especially a hotel keeper. Also, **victualler.**

vi-cu-ña (vĭ-kōōn'yȧ), *n.* an animal of the high Andes, belonging to the llama and alpaca family, and furnishing a fine, long, reddish wool; yarn or cloth made of the wool of this animal.

vi-de (vī'dē), a term meaning "See": used to direct attention: as, *vide supra* means see above. [Lat.]

vi-del-i-cet (vĭ-dĕl'ĭ-sĕt), *adv.* to wit or namely: often abbreviated *viz.* [Lat.]

vi-dette (vĭ-dĕt'), *n.* a mounted sentinel stationed in front of the regular pickets of an army. Also, **vedette.**

vie (vī), *v.i.* [*p.t.* and *p.p.* vied, *p.pr.* vying], to strive for superiority; to contend or endeavor, as in games, school, etc.

view (vū), *n.* the act of seeing; sight; a scene; objects, extent of landscape, etc., within sight; as, there is an extended view from the window; range of mental perception; as, a statesman must have great breadth of *view;* outlook, physical or mental; a picture of a scene or person looked at from a given direction; as, the *view* of him in the photograph does him justice; way of looking at anything mentally; opinion; as, he held advanced *views;* regard or consideration; as, make your plans with a *view* to real success: *v.t.* to see; gaze at; look upon; survey; consider closely and with care.—*n.* **viewer.**

view-point (vū'point"), *n.* the position or place from which one looks at something; mentally, a way of regarding or judging events, etc.; the attitude of mind lying at the basis of an opinion; as, our judgment of people's acts is dependent on our *viewpoint.*

vig-il (vĭj'ĭl), *n.* a keeping awake; wakefulness; a watch through the night; an evening religious service before a religious feast day: *pl.* devotional watching at night.

vig-i-lance (vĭj'ĭ-lăns), *n.* watchfulness; caution; alertness to avoid danger.

vig-i-lant (vĭj'ĭ-lănt), *adj.* keenly watchful to discover and avoid danger; alert; cautious.—*adv.* **vigilantly.**

Syn. wary, careful, attentive.

Ant. (see heedless).

vig-i-lan-te (vĭj'ĭ-lăn'tē), *n.* a member of a vigilance committee, or group of citizens who organize themselves, in United States communities, to deal severely and promptly with crimes for which ordinary legal action is not sufficient.

vi-gnette (vĭn-yĕt'), *n.* a small design decorating the blank space left at the beginning or end of a magazine article, a chapter in a book, etc.; any engraving, etc., which shades off gradually without definite border; a portrait of the head and shoulders only: *v.t.* to ornament with a vignette; make a vignette of.—*n.* **vignetter.**

vig-or (vĭg'ẽr), *n.* physical or mental strength and energy; force or power of mind or body. Also, **vigour.**

vig-or-ous (vĭg'ẽr-ŭs), *adj.* full of physical and mental strength and energy; full of life; powerful; energetic; strong; as, a *vigorous* constitution; a *vigorous* speech.—*adv.* **vigorously.**—*n.* **vigorousness.**

vi-king (vī'kĭng; vē'kĭng), *n.* one of the Scandinavian pirates, or Northmen, who plundered the coasts of Europe in the 8th to 10th centuries.

vile (vīl), *adj.* [*comp.* viler, *superl.* vilest], worthless; mean; ignoble; morally base or impure; as, *vile* language; foul or offensive.—*adv.* **vilely.**—*n.* **vileness.**

vil-i-fi-er (vĭl'ĭ-fī"ẽr), *n.* one who slanders or abuses another.

vil-i-fy (vĭl'ĭ-fī), *v.t.* [*p.t.* and *p.p.* vilified, *p.pr.* vilifying], to make low and base by report; to slander; as, to *vilify* a man's character; to abuse in words.—*n.* **vilification.**

vil-la (vĭl'ȧ), *n.* a residence in the country or suburbs.

vil-lage (vĭl'āj), *n.* a small collection of houses in a country district, too small to be organized as a town, but having a name, post office, etc.

vil-la-ger (vĭl'ā-jẽr), *n.* one who lives in a village.

vil-lain (vĭl'ĭn), *n.* one capable of great wickedness; a criminal; a rascal; under the feudal system, a serf; usually spelled *villein;* in drama, the evilly disposed person who makes trouble for the hero, as Iago in *Othello:* originally this word meant a village peasant.

vil-lain-ous (vĭl'ĭn-ŭs), *adj.* marked by extreme wickedness; as, a *villainous* character; evil; base. Also, **villanous.**—*adv.* **villainously, villanously.**

vil-lain-y (vĭl'ĭn-ĭ), *n.* [*pl.* villainies (-ĭz)], the quality or state of being very evil; great wickedness; a very wicked act; a crime.

vil-lein (vĭl'ĭn), *n.* under the feudal system, a serf. Also, **villain.**

vil-len-age (vĭl'ĕn-āj), *n.* under the feudal system, the position of a serf; the holding of land by a serf from his lord. Also, **villanage, villeinage.**

vil-lous (vĭl'ŭs), *adj.* covered with long, thin, soft hairs; downy; shaggy.

vim (vĭm), *n.* force; energy; spirit; vitality. [Colloq.]

vin-ai-grette (vĭn"ā-grĕt'), *n.* a small, usually ornamental, bottle for holding smelling salts.

vin-cu-lum (vĭn'kū-lŭm), *n.* a bond of union; a tie; a horizontal mark placed over two or more algebraic quantities to indicate that they are to be treated as one; as, $x + \overline{a - 1} = b$.

vin-di-cate (vĭn'dĭ-kāt), *v.t.* to defend successfully against accusation; to prove right or true against censure, blame, etc.; as, to *vindicate* one's conduct; to justify; to prove legally sound; as, to *vindicate* a claim.

vin-di-ca-tion (vĭn"dĭ-kā'shŭn), *n.* the act of proving something right or true against blame or accusation; the state of being so proved right; defense; support by proof.

vin-di-ca-tor (vĭn'dĭ-kā"tẽr), *n.* one who defends or supports by proof the rightness of something or someone accused.

vin-di-ca-to-ry (vĭn'dĭ-kȧ-tō-rĭ), *adj.* tending or serving to justify; having to do with, or inflicting, punishment.

vin-dic-tive (vĭn-dĭk'tĭv), *adj.* given to, or prompted by, revenge; inclined to hold a grudge; as, a *vindictive* person.—*adv.* **vindictively.**—*n.* **vindictiveness.**

vine (vīn), *n.* a grapevine; a climbing or trailing plant.

vin-e-gar (vĭn'ē-gẽr), *n.* a sour liquid obtained by fermentation from cider, wine, etc., and used to season or preserve food; hence, anything sour.—*adj.* **vinegary.**

vine-yard (vĭn'yȧrd), *n.* a plantation of grapevines. Also, **vinery.**

vin or-di-naire (văṅ"nôr"dē"nâr'), a cheap grade of claret; the common table wine of France. [Fr.]

vi-nous (vī'nŭs), *adj.* of, pertaining to, or like, wine; as, *vinous* spirits.

vin-tage (vĭn'tāj), *n.* the gathering of grapes; the season for gathering grapes and making wine; the process of wine making; the yearly produce of a vineyard, or of the vineyards of a country; the wine produced in a given season; as, the *vintage* of 1872.

vin-tag-er (vĭn'tā-jẽr), *n.* one who gathers a crop of grapes.

vint-ner (vĭnt'nẽr), *n.* a wine merchant, usually at wholesale.

vi-ol (vī'ŏl), *n.* a medieval four-stringed musical instrument from which the violin was developed, and one size of which survives as the *bass viol.*

vi-o-la (vē-ō'lȧ; vī-ō'lȧ), *n.* a stringed instrument of the violin class, between the violin and violoncello in size and range, and tuned below the violin.

vi-o-la-ble (vī'ō-lȧ-bl), *adj.* capable of being broken; as, a *violable* pledge or agreement.

vi-o-late (vī'ō-lāt), *v.t.* [*p.t.* and *p.p.* violated, *p.pr.* violating], to treat roughly or severely; to ill-use; to encroach or trespass upon; as, to *violate* another's rights or property; to profane or treat irreverently; as, to *violate* a tomb or grave; to transgress, as the law; to disregard, as a treaty; to break, as a promise; to outrage or dishonor.—*n.* **violator.**

vi-o-la-tion (vī"ō-lā'shŭn), *n.* an injury, trespass, or infringement; transgression; profanation; disregard; outrage.

vi-o-lence (vī'ō-lĕns), *n.* the forcible use of great strength or energy; force and fury; as, the *violence* of a storm; strong passion; as, the *violence* of grief; profanation; outrage; as, he did *violence* to his better nature; assault.

vi-o-lent (vī'ō-lĕnt), *adj.* urged or driven by extreme force; improperly forcible; passionate; as, *violent* language, or a *violent* temper; furious; severe; as, a *violent* storm, or *violent* pain; resulting from the use of force; as, he met a *violent* death.—*adv.* **violently.**

Syn. boisterous, vehement.
Ant. (see gentle).

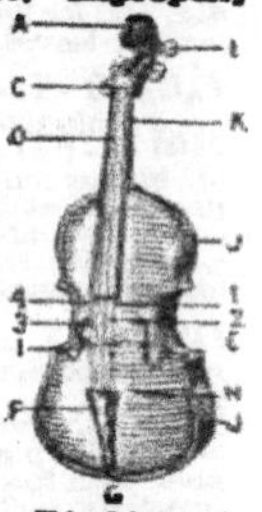

Violin. *A*, scroll; *B*, pegs; *C*, upper saddle; *D*, finger-board; *E*, bridge; *F*, tail piece; *G*, tail-piece button; *H*, front or belly; *I*, sound-holes; *J*, back; *K*, neck; 1, 2, 3, 4, first, second, third, and fourth strings.

vi-o-let (vī'ō-lĕt), *n.* a well-known low-growing plant with heart-shaped leaves, which in spring bears purple, white, or yellow blossoms; a color like that of the purple violet: *adj.* of a bluish-purple color.

vi-o-lin (vī"ō-lĭn'), *n.* the smallest and highest tuned of the group of four-stringed musical instruments, played with a bow; colloquially called *fiddle;* a violin player.

vi-o-lin-ist (vī"ō-lĭn'ĭst), *n.* a player or performer on the violin.

vi-o-lon-cel-list (vē"ō-lŏn-chĕl'ĭst; vī"ō-lŏn-sĕl'ĭst), *n.* a player on the violoncello: often shortened to *'cellist* or *cellist.*

vi-o-lon-cel-lo (vē"ō-lŏn-chĕl'ō; vī"ō-lŏn-sĕl'ō), *n.* a large four-stringed instrument of the violin class, tuned below the viola; a bass violin: often shortened to *'cello* or *cello.*

vi-per (vī'pẽr), *n.* a poisonous Asiatic and European snake of various kinds; an adder; hence, a harmful or evil person.—*adj.* **viperous, viperish.**

Viper

vi-rage (vĭ-rāj'), *n.* in aviation, a difficult sharp turn with the motor on.

vi-ra-go (vĭ-rā'gō; vī-rā'gō), *n.* [*pl.* viragoes (-gōz)], a bold, quarrelsome woman; a scold.

vir-e-o (vĭr'ē-ō), *n.* any of a class of small American song birds, olive-green or gray in color.

vir-gin (vûr'jĭn), *n.* a maid; a pure unmarried woman: **the Virgin**, Mary the mother of Jesus: *adj.* chaste; modest; as, *virgin* purity; pure; spotless; as, *virgin* snow; new; untouched; as, *virgin* gold.

vir-gin-al (vûr'jĭ-năl), *adj.* of, pertaining to, or like, a virgin; maidenly; chaste or pure: *n.* a 16th century musical instrument, in the shape of a small spinet without legs.

vir-gin-i-ty (vẽr-jĭn'ĭ-tĭ), *n.* maidenhood; virgin purity.

vir-ile (vĭr'ĭl; vī'rĭl), *adj.* characteristic of, or befitting, a man; manly; as, *virile* strength; masculine or manlike; forceful; masterful.

vir-il-i-ty (vĭ-rĭl'ĭ-tĭ; vī-rĭl'ĭ-tĭ), *n.* manhood or manliness; manly strength and energy.

vir-tu (vĭr-tōō'; vûr'tōō), *n.* artistic rarity and beauty; curiousness of workmanship; as, an article of *virtu*. Also, **vertu.**

vir-tu-al (vûr'tū-ăl), *adj.* in essence or effect, though not in fact; as, his words amounted to a *virtual* confession of guilt.—*adv.* **virtually.**

vir-tue (vûr'tū), *n.* strength or effectiveness; worth; goodness; morality; purity; excellence or merit; a specific kind of goodness, such as temperance or patience; as, the *virtues* of wisdom: opposite to *vice*.

vir-tu-o-so (vĭr"tōō-ō'sō; vûr"tōō-ō'sō), *n.* [*pl.* virtuosos (-sōz), virtuosi (-sē)], one who appreciates artistic quality; one with a taste for objects of art; a collector of articles of virtu; a musical performer having excellent technic.

vir-tu-ous (vûr'tū-ŭs), *adj.* full of, or showing, virtue; moral; chaste; pure; as, a *virtuous* life.—*adv.* **virtuously.**—*n.* **virtuousness.**

Syn. upright, honest, moral.

Ant. (see **profligate**).

vir-u-lence (vĭr'ōō-lĕns), *n.* the state or quality of being very poisonous; extreme bitterness; malignity. Also, **virulency.**

vir-u-lent (vĭr'ōō-lĕnt), *adj.* very poisonous or venomous; as, the *virulent* poison of a rattlesnake; bitter and malicious; as, a *virulent* speech.—*adv.* **virulently.**

vi-rus (vī'rŭs), *n.* poison; the poisonous matter produced by disease, containing the germs that cause the disease; hence, anything that poisons the mind or soul, as treachery.

vis-age (vĭz'āj), *n.* the face or countenance, especially of a human being; appearance, or aspect.—*adj.* **visaged.**

vis-à-vis (vē"zȧ-vē'), *adj.* and *adv.* face to face: *n.* one who is face to face with another; a settee with two seats so arranged that the occupants are face to face. [Fr.]

Vi-sa-yan (vē-sä'yăn), *n.* a Philippine islander, of the chief native race; the language of these natives.

vis-cer-a (vĭs'ẽr-*ȧ*), *n.pl.* the internal organs of a body; as, the heart, liver, intestines, etc.—*adj.* **visceral.**

vis-cid (vĭs'ĭd), *adj.* sticky or gluelike; as, *viscid* gum.—*n.* **viscidity.**

vis-count (vī'kount"), *n.* [*fem.* viscountess], in England, a nobleman next in rank below an earl or count and next above a baron.

vis-cous (vĭs'kŭs), *adj.* adhesive or sticky; as, a *viscous* liquid.—*n.* **viscosity.**

vise (vīs), *n.* a two-jawed instrument for holding objects firmly. Also, **vice.**

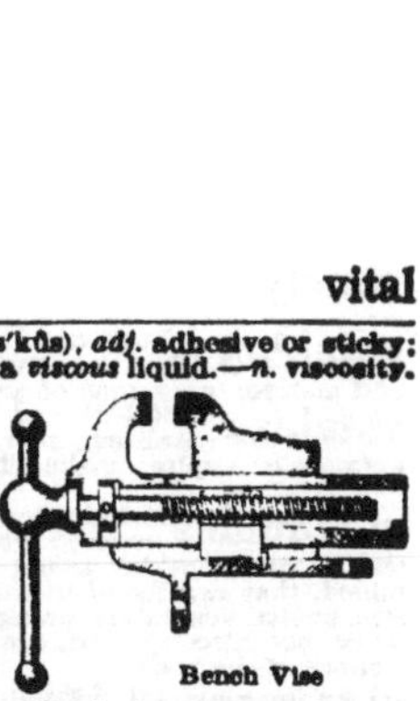

Bench Vise

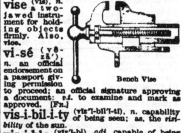

vi-sé (vē-zā'), *n.* an official endorsement on a passport giving permission to proceed; an official signature approving a document: *v.t.* to examine and mark as approved. [Fr.]

vis-i-bil-i-ty (vĭz"ĭ-bĭl'ĭ-tĭ), *n.* capability of being seen; as, the *visibility* of the sun.

vis-i-ble (vĭz'ĭ-bl), *adj.* capable of being seen; in sight; obvious; apparent; as, *visible* signs of grief.—*adv.* **visibly.**—*n.* **visibleness.**

vi-sion (vĭzh'ŭn), *n.* the act of seeing; sense of sight; extent of power to see, physically or mentally; as, a man of broad *vision*; something seen, especially with the mind's eye; a supernatural appearance; spiritual perception of the actually unseen.

Syn. ghost, phantom, specter.

vi-sion-a-ry (vĭzh'ŭn-ā-rĭ), *adj.* existing only in the imagination; fantastic; imaginative; dreamy; impracticable; as, a *visionary* undertaking: *n.* [*pl.* visionaries (-rĭz)], a person given to unreal imaginings; a dreamer; one to whom the unseen is real; an impractical person.

vis-it (vĭz'ĭt), *n.* the act of coming or going to see; a brief stay of friendship, courtesy, or business: *v.t.* to go or come to see; to come to with special marks of favor or disfavor; as, "*visit* us with thy salvation": *v.i.* to go or come to see someone; to be a guest.

vis-it-ant (vĭz'ĭ-tănt), *n.* one who comes to see someone with a special purpose or mission: *adj.* paying a visit.

vis-it-a-tion (vĭz"ĭ-tā'shŭn), *n.* the act of going or coming to see; a lengthy or tiresome visit; a special dealing out of divine punishment or reward; a formal inspection of church work by an official.

vis-i-tor (vĭz'ĭ-tẽr), *n.* one who goes or comes to see another. Also, **visiter.**

vis-or (vĭz'ẽr; vī'zẽr), *n.* the front piece of a helmet, especially the upper part, arranged so as to open or lift; the front piece of a cap. Also, **vizor.**

vis-ta (vĭs'tȧ), *n.* [*pl.* vistas (-t*ȧ*z)], a view through a narrow opening or down a long passage, such as an avenue of trees; the trees, buildings, etc., forming such a passage; hence, a far-reaching, but not widely extended, mental view; as, a *vista* of the past.

vis-u-al (vĭzh'ū-ăl), *adj.* of, pertaining to, or used in, sight; capable of being seen; visible.—*adv.* **visually.**

vis-u-al-ize (vĭzh'ū-ăl-īz), *v.t.* to make visible; especially, to make a picture of in the mind; to see in fancy.—*n.* **visualization.**

vi-tal (vī'tăl), *adj.* pertaining to, supporting, or necessary to, life; as, air and food are *vital* necessities; living; full of life; essential; as, things of *vital* importance: *n.pl.* parts of animal bodies necessary to life; as, the pain gnawed at his *vitals*.—*adv.* **vitally.**

vi-tal-i-ty (vī-tăl'ĭ-tĭ), *n.* living force; life; the power to keep alive and endure; as, a man of great *vitality*.

vi-tal-ize (vī'tăl-īz), *v.t.* [*p.t.* and *p.p.* vitalized, *p.pr.* vitalizing], to animate or inspire; make alive; fill with life. —*n.* **vitalizer.**

vi-ta-mines (vī'tȧ-mīnz), *n.* a newly discovered group of substances, the nature of which is not yet fully determined, that are found in carbon foods, as in rice, butter, vegetables, oranges, etc., and that, while not directly food, are essential to the welfare of the body.

vi-ta-scope (vī'tȧ-skōp), *n.* a machine for projecting, or throwing, moving pictures upon a canvas or screen; a cinematograph.

vi-ti-ate (vĭsh'ĭ-āt), *v.t.* [*p.t.* and *p.p.* vitiated, *p.pr.* vitiating], to corrupt or spoil; as, many affectations *vitiate* his style; to make impure; as, escaping gas will *vitiate* the air; to make worthless; as, to *vitiate* a contract.—*n.* **vitiation, vitiator.**

vit-i-cul-ture (vĭt'ĭ-kŭl"tūr), *n.* the act or business of cultivating or growing grapes.—*adj.* **viticultural.**—*n.* **viticulturist.**

vit-re-ous (vĭt'rē-ŭs), *adj.* glassy; consisting of, like, or obtained from, glass; as, *vitreous* rocks: **vitreous humor,** the jellylike substance filling the eyeball.—*n.* **vitreousness.**

vit-ric (vĭt'rĭk), *adj.* pertaining to glass: opposite to *ceramic*, pertaining to pottery.

vit-ri-fac-tion (vĭt"rĭ-făk'shŭn), *n.* the art or process of changing or converting into glass; state of being changed into glass. Also, **vitrification.**

vit-ri-fied (vĭt'rĭ-fīd), *p.adj.* changed into glass or into a substance like glass; given or having a glassy, or glazed, surface; as, *vitrified* brick.

vit-ri-form (vĭt'rĭ-fôrm), *n.* having the form or appearance of glass.

vit-ri-fy (vĭt'rĭ-fī), *v.t.* [*p.t.* and *p.p.* vitrified, *p.pr.* vitrifying], to change or convert by heat into glass: *v.i.* to be changed or converted into glass; to become glass, or like glass.—*adj.* **vitrifiable.**

vit-ri-ol (vĭt'rĭ-ŭl), *n.* a sulphate of copper, iron, or zinc, variously called *blue vitriol* (from copper), *green vitriol* (from iron), *white vitriol* (from zinc); sulphuric acid: commonly called *oil of vitriol*.

vit-ri-ol-ic (vĭt"rĭ-ŏl'ĭk), *adj.* pertaining to, or like, vitriol, or sulphuric acid; hence, bitter or sarcastic; as, a *vitriolic* tongue.

vi-tu-per-ate (vī-tū'pēr-āt), *v.t.* [*p.t.* and *p.p.* vituperated, *p.pr.* vituperating], to blame or censure abusively; to abuse in speech.

vi-tu-per-a-tion (vī-tū"pēr-ā'shŭn), *n.* the act of abusing in speech; wordy abuse; railing.

vi-tu-per-a-tive (vī-tū'pēr-ȧ-tĭv), *adj.* abusive; expressing blame noisily and bitterly.—*adv.* **vituperatively.**

vi-va (vē'vä), *interj.* long live! an expression of well wishing. [IT.]

vi-va-cious (vī-vā'shŭs; vĭ-vā'shŭs), *adj.* lively; gay; animated; full of spirits.—*adv.* **vivaciously.**—*n.* **vivaciousness.**

vi-vac-i-ty (vī-văs'ĭ-tĭ; vĭ-văs'ĭ-tĭ), *n.* liveliness; animation; high spirits.

vi-va-ri-um (vī-vā'rĭ-ŭm), *n.* a place for the keeping of animals in their natural state, as a zoölogical garden.

vi-va vo-ce (vī'vȧ vō'sē), by spoken word; orally; as, a *viva voce* vote. [LAT.]

vive (vēv), *interj.* long live! an expression of well wishing. [FR.]

viv-id (vĭv'ĭd), *adj.* brilliant; intense; as, a *vivid* color; active; lively; as, a *vivid* imagination; making a strong impression on, or producing lifelike images in, the mind; as, a *vivid* description.—*adv.* **vividly.**—*n.* **vividness.**

viv-i-fy (vĭv'ĭ-fī), *v.t.* [*p.t.* and *p.p.* vivified, *p.pr.* vivifying], to make alive; to animate; quicken.

vi-vip-a-rous (vī-vĭp'ȧ-rŭs), *adj.* producing young alive (instead of eggs): opposite to *oviparous*, or egg-producing.

viv-i-sect (vĭv"ĭ-sĕkt'; vĭv'ĭ-sĕkt), *v.t.* to dissect or divide (the living body of an animal); as, to *vivisect* a dog.—*n.* **vivisector.**

viv-i-sec-tion (vĭv"ĭ-sĕk'shŭn), *n.* the dissection, or cutting, of a living animal for scientific study.

viv-i-sec-tion-ist (vĭv"ĭ-sĕk'shŭn-ĭst), *n.* one who practices or upholds the dissection, or cutting, of living animals for scientific study.

vix-en (vĭk'sn), *n.* a female fox; a quarrelsome, ill-tempered woman.—*adj.* **vixenish.**

viz. (vĭz), *adv.* namely: abbreviation of *videlicet*.

vi-zier (vĭ-zēr'; vĭz'yēr), *n.* a high officer of various Mohammedan countries, especially of Turkey; a minister of state; a councilor. Also, **vizir.**

viz-or (vĭz'ēr; vī'zēr), *n.* the front piece of a helmet, especially the upper part, arranged so as to open or lift; the front piece of a cap. Also, **visor.**

vo-ca-ble (vō'kȧ-bl; vŏk'ȧ-bl), *n.* a word, thought of merely for the sounds which compose it.

vo-cab-u-la-ry (vō-kăb'ū-lā-rĭ), *n.* [*pl.* vocabularies (-rĭz)], a list or collection of words arranged alphabetically and explained; a dictionary or lexicon; the stock of words at command of a class of people, an individual, etc.; as, his *vocabulary* was limited.

vo-cal (vō'kăl), *adj.* of or pertaining to the voice; as, the *vocal* cords; uttered by the voice; oral; as, a *vocal* expression; produced by the voice; as, *vocal* music: *n.* a speech sound, as a vowel or diphthong.—*adv.* **vocally.**

vo-cal-ist (vō'kăl-ĭst), *n.* a singer; one who makes music with the voice.

vo-cal-ize (vō'kăl-īz), *v.t.* [*p.t.* and *p.p.* vocalized, *p.pr.* vocalizing], to utter with the voice; to give the quality of voice sound to; to use (a consonant) as a vowel; as, to *vocalize y*: *v.i.* to produce sound with the voice, as in singing.—*n.* **vocalization.**

vo-ca-tion (vō-kā'shŭn), *n.* regular employment; calling; occupation; trade; profession; as, his *vocation* is law.—*adj.* **vocational.**

voc-a-tive (vŏk'ȧ-tĭv), *adj.* relating to the act of calling or addressing by name; in grammar, pertaining to the case denoting a person or thing addressed: *n.* the vocative case.

vo-cif-er-ate (vō-sĭf'ēr-āt), *v.t.* [*p.t.* and *p.p.* vociferated, *p.pr.* vociferating], to clamor or cry out noisily; to bawl: *v.i.* to utter with a loud voice; to exclaim or assert noisily.

vo-cif-er-a-tion (vō-sĭf″ẽr-ā′shŭn), *n.* violent outcry; clamor; noisy assertion.

vo-cif-er-ous (vō-sĭf′ẽr-ŭs), *adj.* making a loud outcry; clamorous or noisy: as, *vociferous* applause.—*adv.* **vociferously.**—*n.* **vociferousness.**

vod-ka (vŏd′kȧ), *n.* a Russian intoxicating liquor distilled from rye.

vogue (vōg), *n.* a fashion prevailing during a given period; style in dress; temporary popularity; as, the author's works had a great *vogue* in his own time.

voice (vois), *n.* sound proceeding from the mouth; especially, human utterance in speech, cry, song, etc.; power to speak; as, my cold was so severe that I lost my *voice;* an expressed choice, wish, or opinion; as, let each member of the committee give his *voice* in the matter; the right to express a wish or choice; as, in an autocracy the people have no *voice* in public affairs; vote; as, he gave his *voice* for the popular candidate; a sound suggesting speech; as, the *voice* of the wind; teaching or instruction; as, the *voice* of conscience; in grammar, the form of the verb showing the relation of the subject of the verb to the action that the verb expresses: *v.t.* [*p.t.* and *p.p.* voiced, *p.pr.* voicing], to express in sound; as, to *voice* one's opinion, or to *voice* a cry of distress.—*adj.* **voiced, voiceless.**

voice-less (vois′lĕs), *adj.* being allowed no right to decide or vote; as, in some states women are *voiceless* in the government; soundless; silent; as, the *voiceless* desert; having no voice or tone.—*adv.* **voicelessly.**—*n.* **voicelessness.**

void (void), *adj.* empty; vacant; lacking: with *of;* without result; in vain; useless; as, all their efforts were *void;* unfilled, as an office; in law, having no force; null: *v.t.* to cause to be empty; to vacate; to send or throw out; to discharge; to annul or cancel, as a law: *n.* a vacuum; an empty space.—*adj.* **voidable.**

Vo-la-puk (vō″lȧ-pük′), *n.* a scheme for a universal language for business purposes, invented in Germany about 1879.

vol-a-tile (vŏl′ȧ-tĭl), *adj.* easily evaporating or changing into vapor; as, ether is a *volatile* liquid; hence, light-hearted; lively; quickly adaptable; also changeable; fickle.—*n.* **volatileness.**

vol-a-til-i-ty (vŏl″ȧ-tĭl′ĭ-tĭ), *n.* the state or quality of anything that evaporates, or changes into vapor; giddiness; fickleness.

vol-a-til-ize (vŏl′ȧ-tĭl-īz), *v.t.* and *v.i.* [*p.t.* and *p.p.* volatilized, *p.pr.* volatilizing], to make or become volatile; to evaporate, or change into vapor.—*n.* **volatilization.**

vol-can-ic (vŏl-kăn′ĭk), *adj.* of, pertaining to, or produced by, a volcano, or mountain which sends out fire, melted rock, etc.

vol-ca-no (vŏl-kā′nō), *n.* [*pl.* volcanoes (-nōz)], a conelike hill or mountain, with an opening at the top called a crater, from which melted rock, fire, and gas are often thrown out with great force.

vo-li-tion (vō-lĭsh′ŭn), *n.* the act or power of using the will to decide, choose, etc.; state of determination; decision; intention.

vo-li-tion-al (vō-lĭsh′ŭn-ăl), *adj.* pertaining to the power of willing; done of one's free will or choice.

vol-ley (vŏl′ĭ), *n.* [*pl.* volleys (-ĭz)], the throwing of many missiles at the same time; the missiles so thrown; a rapid discharge of a certain indicated number of rounds, by each gun of a battery or other unit, each gun firing, without regard to the others; hence, a sudden burst of any sort; as, a *volley* of words; a *volley* of thunder; the return of a ball at tennis before it reaches the ground: *v.t.* and *v.i.* [*p.t.* and *p.p.* volleyed, *p.pr.* volleying], to discharge, or be discharged, suddenly and all together; as, the cannon *volleyed* and thundered.

vol-plane (vŏl′plān″), *n.* a glide downward in an airplane, with the power shut off: *v.i.* to glide downward without power in an airplane or flying machine.

volt (vōlt), *n.* the standard unit for measuring electric force or pressure; as, a current of 110 *volts:* **voltmeter,** an instrument for making such measurements.

volt-age (vōl′tāj), *n.* amount of electric power in terms of volts.

vol-ta-ic (vŏl-tā′ĭk), *adj.* pertaining to current electricity; produced by chemical action: said of an electric current; galvanic: **voltaic battery,** an apparatus of one or more cells for producing current electricity.

vol-u-bil-i-ty (vŏl″ū-bĭl′ĭ-tĭ), *n.* unchecked flow of talk; too great ease in speech.

vol-u-ble (vŏl′ū-bl), *adj.* fluent; easy in speech; talkative, often to excess.—*adv.* **volubly.**—*n.* **volubleness.**

vol-ume (vŏl′ūm), *n.* number of printed sheets bound together; a book; one of several parts of a large work, each of which is bound separately; amount of space filled; as, measure the *volume* of water in this vessel; fulness of voice or tone; as, *volume* of sound.

vo-lu-mi-nous (vō-lū′mĭ-nŭs), *adj.* consisting of many books or volumes; as, a *voluminous* library; having produced many books; as, Balzac was a *voluminous* writer; filling much space; as, in old times ladies wore *voluminous* hoop skirts.—*adv.* **voluminously.**—*n.* **voluminousness.**

vol-un-ta-ry (vŏl′ŭn-tā-rĭ), *adj.* pertaining to the will; acting from choice or free will; intentional; as, the act of offense was *voluntary,* not accidental; not forced; as, his confession of guilt was *voluntary;* free; of one's own accord; controlled by one's own will or choice: *n.* an organ solo played before, during, or after, a church service; any organ prelude.—*adv.* **voluntarily.**—*n.* **voluntariness.**

vol-un-teer (vŏl″ŭn-tēr′), *n.* one who enters into any service of his own free will; one who offers himself for military service: *v.i.* to offer one's services freely; to enter of one's own accord into military service: *v.t.* to offer or bestow without constraint or compulsion: *adj.* pertaining to volunteers or to their work.

vo-lup-tu-a-ry (vō-lŭp′tū-ā-rĭ), *n.* [*pl.* voluptuaries (-rĭz)], one who is fond of pleasures that appeal to the senses: *adj.* devoted to luxury or pleasures of the senses.

Syn., n. epicure, sensualist.

vo-lup-tu-ous (vō-lŭp′tū-ŭs), *adj.* appealing, or giving pleasure, to the senses; enjoying pleasures that appeal to the senses.—*adv.* **voluptuously.**—*n.* **voluptuousness.**

vo-lute (vō-lūt′), *n.* a spiral, scroll-shaped architectural ornament or decoration such as appears in the Ionic capital.—*adj.* **voluted.**

vom-it (vŏm′ĭt), *v.i.* to throw up the contents of the stomach; come forth, or be sent out, with violence: *v.t.* to throw up from the stomach; to spew; to discharge with violence; to belch forth: *n.* matter thrown up by the stomach; an emetic.

voo-doo (vōō′dōō; vōō-dōō′), *n.* one who practices a form of sorcery or witchcraft among certain negroes, especially in Haiti; a negro sorcerer: *adj.* of or pertaining to voodooism or a voodoo; as, a *voodoo* doctor.

voo-doo-ism (vōō′dōō-ĭzm), *n.* a barbarous and ignorant superstition, or belief in sorcery, prevailing among certain negro populations, especially in Haiti.

vo-ra-cious (vō-rā′shŭs), *adj.* greedy in eating; ravenous; mad with hunger.—*adv.* **voraciously.**—*n.* **voraciousness.**

vo-rac-i-ty (vō-răs′ĭ-tĭ), *n.* the state of being mad with hunger; greediness in eating.

vor-tex (vôr′tĕks), *n.* [*pl.* vortices (-tĭ-sēz)], air or water with a circular current tending to suck bodies caught in it into a depression, or vacuum, at the center; an eddy or whirlpool.

vo-ta-ress (vō′tȧ-rĕs), *n.* a woman vowed to some service.

vo-ta-ry (vō′tȧ-rĭ), *adj.* promised; devoted: *n.* [*pl.* votaries (-rĭz)], one devoted by a vow or promise to some service; one devoted to any pursuit; as, a *votary* of pleasure or science.

vote (vōt), *n.* a formally stated choice, judgment, or wish, of one or more persons, as in an election; the right to express such a choice or wish; as, women have long worked to get the *vote;* a ballot; the entire number of ballots or expressions of opinion; as, a presidential *vote:* *v.t.* to put into effect by a formal expression of a wish; as to *vote* a reform; to grant; as, to *vote* money for repairs: *v.i.* to formally express a wish; to cast a ballot.

vot-er (vōt′ēr), *n.* an elector; one who has a right to vote; one who casts a ballot.

vo-tive (vō′tĭv), *adj.* given, consecrated, or promised by vow; as, a *votive* offering to the church.—*adv.* **votively.**—*n.* **votiveness.**

vouch (vouch), *v.i.* to bear witness; guarantee; stand surety: with *for:* as, to *vouch* for a man's honesty.

Syn. affirm, asseverate, assure.

vouch-er (vouch′ēr), *n.* one who bears witness; a book, paper, or the like, which confirms the truth of something; especially, a receipt showing pay; as, a canceled check is a *voucher.*

vouch-safe (vouch-sāf′), *v.t.* [*p.t.* and *p.p* vouchsafed, *p.pr.* vouchsafing], to condescend, or stoop, to grant; to concede or give; as, to *vouchsafe* an opinion.

vous-soir (vōō″swär′), *n.* one of the wedge-shaped sections of an arch.

vow (vou), *n.* a solemn promise or pledge, especially one made to God or before God; a pledge of love and faithfulness: *v.t.* to promise solemnly: *v.i.* to make a solemn promise.

vow-el (vou′ĕl), *n.* a simple vocal sound: opposite to *consonant;* a letter representing such a sound; as, *a, e, i, o, u,* and sometimes *w* and *y:* *adj.* of or pertaining to a vowel; as, a *vowel* sound.

voy-age (voi′āj), *n.* a journey by water from one country or place to another; as, a *voyage* to Europe: *v.i.* to make a journey by water.—*n.* **voyager.**

voy-a-geur (vwȧ″yȧ″zhûr), *n.* a Canadian boatman or fur trapper of the Northwest. [Fr.]

vrai-sem-blance (vrĕ″säṅ″bläṅs′), *n.* an appearance of truth. [Fr.]

vrille (vrĭl), *n.* in aviation, an acrobatic feat in which the airplane goes down with a spinning motion: *v.i.* to go down with such a motion.

Vul-can (vŭl′kăn), *n.* in Roman mythology, the god of fire and the working of metals: identified with the Greek god Hephæstus.

vul-can-ite (vŭl′kăn-īt), *n.* a hardened compound of India rubber: hard rubber, made by heating with sulphur or oxides, or by soaking in a sulphur chloride solution.

vul-can-ize (vŭl′kăn-īz), *v.t.* [*p.t.* and *p.p.* vulcanized, *p.pr.* vulcanizing], to harden (India rubber) by heating with sulphur, oxides, etc.—*n.* **vulcanization, vulcanizer.**

vul-gar (vŭl′gȧr), *adj.* of or pertaining to the common people; common; general; unrefined; in bad taste; as, *ain't* is a *vulgar* expression; low; mean; as, a *vulgar* fellow.—*adv.* **vulgarly.**

vul-gar frac-tions (vŭl′gȧr frăk′shŭnz), common fractions, expressed by placing the numerator above the denominator, with a horizontal or oblique line between.

vul-ga-ri-an (vŭl-gā′rĭ-ăn), *n.* a rich person with coarse or low ideas; an unrefined person.

vul-gar-ism (vŭl′gȧr-ĭzm), *n.* rudeness; lack of refinement; a phrase or expression not in use by cultivated speakers.

vul-gar-i-ty (vŭl-găr′ĭ-tĭ), *n.* [*pl.* vulgarities (-tĭz)], coarseness of manners or language.

vul-gar-ize (vŭl′gȧr-īz), *v.t.* and *v.i.* to make or become common, coarse, or low.—*n.* **vulgarization.**

Vul-gate (vŭl′gāt), *n.* an ancient Latin translation of the Bible in use in the Roman Catholic Church, made originally by St. Jerome: *adj.* pertaining to, or contained in, the Vulgate.

vul-ner-a-bil-i-ty (vŭl″nēr-ȧ-bĭl′ĭ-tĭ), *n.* liability to be wounded.

vul-ner-a-ble (vŭl′nēr-ȧ-bl), *adj.* capable of being wounded or hurt; liable to injury.—*n.* **vulnerableness.**

vul-ner-a-ry (vŭl′nēr-ā-rĭ), *adj.* used or tending to cure wounds. *n.* a remedy for healing wounds.

vul-pine (vŭl′pīn; vŭl′pĭn), *adj.* pertaining to, or like, a fox; cunning.

vul-ture (vŭl′tûr), *n.* a large bird of the eagle family, with weaker claws and naked head, which lives principally on carrion, or the bodies of dead animals.—*adj.* **vulturine.**

vy-ing (vī′ĭng), *p.pr.* of *vie:* *v.n.* a competing or contending, as in a race.

W

wab-ble (wŏb'l), *v.i.* [*p.t.* and *p.p.* wabbled, *p.pr.* wabbling], to shake unsteadily from side to side, or back and forth; hence, to sway or totter; to lack firmness: *n.* a rocking or swaying motion. Also, **wobble.** —*n.* **wabbler, wobbler.**

wab-bly (wŏb'lĭ), *adj.* rocking unsteadily from side to side; wavering; shaky; as, a *wabbly* chair. Also, **wobbly.**

wad (wŏd), *n.* a small mass of soft material; a soft bunch of cotton, wool, rope, etc., used to stop an opening, pad a garment, etc.; a soft plug to hold a charge of powder or shot in position; as, a gun *wad:* *v.t.* [*p.t.* and *p.p.* wadded, *p.pr.* wadding], to form into, close by, or stuff with, a small, soft mass or bunch.

wad-ding (wŏd'ĭng), *n.* soft material used for gun wads, plugs, or for stuffing or lining garments; cotton prepared in sheets for padding.

wad-dle (wŏd'l), *v.i.* [*p.t.* and *p.p.* waddled, *p.pr.* waddling], to sway from side to side in walking; to walk with short, clumsy steps, as a duck; to toddle: *n.* a clumsy, rocking gait; as, the *waddle* of a duck.—*n.* **waddler.**

wade (wād), *v.i.* [*p.t.* and *p.p.* waded, *p.pr.* wading], to walk through water, mud, snow, or other substance that hinders progress; hence, to proceed with difficulty or against hindrances; as, to *wade* through a tiresome lesson: *v.t.* to cross by passing through water, mud, etc.

wa-di (wä'dĭ), *n.* [*pl.* wadies (-dĭz)], in the Near East, the channel of a watercourse which is dry except in the rainy season. Also, **wady.**

wa-fer (wā'fẽr), *n.* a thin cake or biscuit; a thin cake of unleavened, or unraised, bread used in the Communion service in certain churches, especially the Roman Catholic Church; a small, colored disk of adhesive paper, paste, etc., for fastening letters, sealing documents, etc.

waf-fle (wŏf'l), *n.* a crisp kind of batter cake baked in an iron utensil whose two hinged parts close over each other.

waft (wȧft), *v.t.* to cause to float along through the air or on the water: *n.* the act of causing to float along; a current or wave; a gust or puff.

wag (wăg), *v.t.* [*p.t.* and *p.p.* wagged, *p.pr.* wagging], to sway or swing from side to side with a quick, jerky motion; as, a dog *wags* his tail; to sway or swing: *v.i.* to move jerkily one way and the other: *n.* the act of jerking to and fro; a person full of jests and humor; a witty person.

wage (wāj), *v.t.* [*p.t.* and *p.p.* waged, *p.pr.* waging], to engage in, or carry on, as war: *n.* usually *pl.*, payment for service; as, he earns good *wages:* used of payment by day or week for work with the hands.

wa-ger (wā'jẽr), *n.* a bet; something risked on an uncertainty: *v.t.* and *v.i.* to bet.

wag-ger-y (wăg'ẽr-ĭ), *n.* sport; jesting; humorous mischief; good-humored sarcasm.

wag-gish (wăg'ĭsh), *adj.* humorous; sportive; full of fun: said or done in sport.—*adv.* **waggishly.**—*n.* **waggishness.**

wag-gle (wăg'l), [*p.t.* and *p.p.* waggled, *p.pr.* waggling], *v.t.* and *v.i.* to move jerkily from side to side: *n.* a jerky movement from side to side.

wag-on (wăg'ŭn), *n.* a four-wheeled conveyance for goods or freight, drawn by horses, mules, etc. Also, **waggon.**

wag-on-er (wăg'ŭn-ẽr), *n.* the driver of a wagon, especially one whose business it is to drive a wagon. Also, **waggoner.**

wag-on-ette (wăg"ŭn-ĕt'), *n.* a light, open, four-wheeled pleasure carriage, with two side seats facing each other.

wag-on sol-dier (wăg'ŭn sōl'jẽr), in the World War, an artilleryman, riding on a gun or a gun carriage, or on horseback.

wag-on train (wăg'ŭn trān), army wagons used to convey ammunition, provisions, camp equipage, hospital supplies, the sick and wounded, etc.

wag-tail (wăg'tāl"), *n.* a small bird with a long tail which is habitually jerked up and down.

waif (wāf), *n.* anything found, or without an owner; a homeless wanderer; a foundling, or deserted child.

wail (wāl), *v.t.* and *v.i.* to mourn or lament aloud; to utter a loud cry: *n.* a lamentation or mournful cry; a sound like such a cry; as, the *wail* of the wind.

wain-scot (wān'skŏt; wăn'skŏt), *n.* a wooden facing around the walls of a room, hall, etc.: *v.t.* to face with boards or wooden panels.

wain-scot-ing (wān'skŏt-ĭng; wăn'skŏt-ĭng), *n.* the wooden facing or paneling surrounding the inner walls of a house; the material of which this paneling is made. Also, **wainscotting.**

wain-wright (wān'rīt"), *n.* a wagon maker.

waist (wāst), *n.* the narrowest part of the body, just below the ribs; the slender middle part of anything; a garment, or that section of a garment, which covers the body from shoulders to belt; the middle part of a vessel's deck, between the forecastle and quarter-deck.

waist-band (wāst'bănd"), *n.* the band, as of a skirt, which surrounds the middle of the body to hold up a garment.

waist-coat (wāst'kōt; Colloq. wĕs'kŭt), *n.* a short, sleeveless, usually ornamental man's garment, worn under the coat; a vest.

wait (wāt), *v.i.* to linger or tarry; to remain; to stay in a condition of watching or expecting: with *for;* as, we *waited* for her for an hour; to attend or serve; as, to *wait* upon a table: *v.t.* to expect or tarry for; to delay; as, to *wait* dinner: *n.* the act of staying in expectation; delay; length of time during which one stays in expectation; as, a long *wait:* *pl.* carol singers who sing in the streets at Christmas time.

wait-er (wāt'ẽr), *n.* one who stays expecting something; a manservant at table; a serving tray for dishes, etc.; a kind of small elevator; as, a dumb-*waiter.*

wait-ress (wāt'rĕs), *n.* a female servant at table.

waive (wāv), *v.t.* [*p.t.* and *p.p.* waived, *p.pr.* waiving], to give up a claim to; forego.—*n.* **waiver.**

wake (wāk), *v.i.* [*p.t.* and *p.p.* waked or woke, *p.pr.* waking], to be awake; be roused from sleep; cease to sleep; become alert and active: *v.t.* to rouse from sleep; to excite or make active; revive; watch: *n.* a vigil; the watching of a dead body prior to burial; a track or trail; as, the *wake* of a storm, or the *wake* of a vessel.

wake-ful (wāk′fo͝ol), *adj.* free from sleepiness; unable to sleep; watchful; as, a *wakeful* sentinel.—*adv.* **wakefully.**—*n.* **wakefulness.**
Syn. vigilant, heedful.
Ant. (see sleepy).

wak-en (wāk′n), *v.t.* and *v.i.* to rouse or be roused from sleep.—*n.* **wakener.**

wale (wāl), *n.* a ridge, as on the surface of cloth; a mark left by the stroke of a whip: *pl.* certain breadths of planks on the outside planking of a vessel: *v.t.* to mark with a wale; to whip.

walk (wôk), *v.i.* to go on foot; to move by steps; go at a moderate pace; to proceed; to behave: *v.t.* to traverse on foot; as, he *walked* the floor in anxiety; to cause to go on foot or at a moderate pace; as, *walk* your horses across the bridge: *n.* act or manner of going on foot; step or pace; gait; one of the four gaits of a horse; place for people on foot; as, the side*walk*; circle of life in which one moves; as, his *walk* in life was a humble one; conduct or deportment; as, let your *walk* and conversation be without reproach.—*n.* **walker.**

walk-out (wôk′out″), *n.* a labor strike in the United States. [Colloq.]

walk-o-ver (wôk′ō″vẽr), *n.* a success or victory easily won. [Colloq.]

wall (wôl), *n.* a solid fence of stone, brick, etc.; the outside structure which incloses a building; a partition forming the side of a room; a structure for defense; means of protection: *pl.* fortifications: *v.t.* to surround with, or as with, a structure for inclosure, security, or defense.

wal-let (wŏl′ĕt), *n.* a bag or knapsack for carrying about the person the necessaries for a march or journey; a folding pocketbook.

wall-eye (wôl′ī″), *n.* an eye, the iris of which is white, as of horses; a kind of fish with prominent eyes.

wall-eyed (wôl′īd″), *adj.* having a whitish, staring, or fierce eye.

wall-flow-er (wôl′flou″ẽr), *n.* a hardy plant of the cabbage family with sweet-scented yellow flowers; colloquially, one who, at a ball or party, remains by the wall watching the dance.

Wal-loon (wŏ-lo͞on′), *n.* one of the inhabitants of southern Belgium; the Belgian-French language of southern Belgium.

wal-lop (wŏl′ŭp), *v.t.* a Scotch term meaning to flog or beat soundly: *n.* a blow. [Colloq.]

wal-low (wŏl′ō), *v.i.* to roll about, as a hog in mire; tumble or roll in anything soft; to flounder; live in vice or filth; as, to *wallow* in dirt: *n.* a muddy place in which an animal rolls about; as, a *wallow* for pigs.

wall pa-per (wôl pā′pẽr), paper for covering the inner walls of houses.

Wall Street (wôl strēt), the narrow street in downtown New York, where the most important financial transactions of the country have their center; hence, high finance or the financier class.

wal-nut (wôl′nŭt), *n.* a well-known tree of the north temperate zone; also, its nut and its timber.

wal-rus (wôl′rŭs), *n.* a large, seal-like sea animal, found in the Arctic Ocean, and valuable for blubber, skin, and tusks.

waltz (wôltz), *n.* a kind of round dance; music for such a dance: *v.i.* to dance such a round dance.—*n.* **waltzer.**

wam-pee (wŏm-pē′), *n.* an Asiatic tree bearing a fruit with a hard rind.

wam-pum (wŏm′pŭm; wôm′pŭm), *n.* beads made of shells, used by the North American Indians as money and for ornament.

wan (wŏn), *adj.* pale; sickly; as, a wan child, or a *wan* smile.—*adv.* **wanly.**—*n.* **wanness.**

wand (wŏnd), *n.* a long, slender rod or stick; a staff of authority; in fairy lore, a staff with magic power; a conjurer's rod.

wan-der (wŏn′dẽr), *v.i.* to rove; to ramble; stroll; stray; be delirious or out of one's mind; digress or turn aside; as, the speaker *wandered* from his subject.—*n.* **wanderer.**
Syn. range, ramble, roam, rove.

wan-der-oo (wŏn″dẽr-o͞o′), *n.* a large, bearded monkey of southern India.

wane (wān), *v.i.* to grow less; decrease: said of the moon; to decline in power or importance; fail: *n.* the decrease of the visible bright part of the moon from full to new; decrease in power or importance, gradual failure.

want (wônt; wŏnt), *n.* lack; need; poverty: as, a family in *want;* desire; necessity: *v.t.* to be without; have need of; desire: *v.i.* to be deficient or lacking; come short; to be in poverty.
Syn., n. penury.
Ant. (see abundance).

want-ing (wônt′ĭng; wŏnt′ĭng), *adj.* lacking; missing; short of; not present.

wan-ton (wŏn′tŭn), *adj.* unrestrained; roving; sportive; trifling; as, *wanton* gambols with the wind; loose in morals; careless; reckless; malicious; as, *wanton* destruction of property: *n.* a man or woman of loose, immoral habits: *v.i.* to pass the time in reckless pleasure; revel: *v.t.* to spend or waste recklessly.—*adv.* **wantonly.**—*n.* **wantonness.**

wap-i-ti (wŏp′ĭ-tĭ; wăp′ĭ-tĭ), *n.* a variety of American deer, often called elk.

Wapiti

war (wôr), *n.* the state of armed attack or defense against another; a contest by force between states or nations; an armed conflict; opposition or contest; contention; as, a *war* of words; hostility or enmity: *v.i.* [*p.t.* and *p.p.* warred, *p.pr.*

warring], to engage in an armed conflict; fight.

war-ble (wôr'bl), *v.t.* and *v.i.* to trill; to sing melodiously; utter musically: *n.* a soft, sweet flow of melodious sounds; a carol.

war-bler (wôr'blẽr), *n.* one who carols; a singer; a small, bright-colored singing bird.

war bride (wôr brīd), during the World War, a term applied to the bride of a soldier, especially when the marriage was hastened because of the soldier's departure for camp or the front.

war cry (wôr krī), a party, or national, slogan in any contest.

ward (wôrd), *v.t.* to guard; to keep watch over; to defend from danger; turn aside: with *off;* as, to *ward* off an attack: *n.* a political division of a city or town; as, the fifth *ward;* the act of guarding or watching; a watch or guard; a person under guard or protection; as, the *ward* of a court or state; one section of a hospital; as, a surgical *ward.*

war dance (wôr dȧns), a dance of savage tribes before going to war.

ward-en (wôr'dn), *n.* a guardian; keeper; as, a prison *warden;* trustee; as, a church*warden;* chief officer of government in a college.—*n.* **wardenship.**

ward-er (wôr'dẽr), *n.* one who watches or keeps; a guard or keeper; as, the *warder* of an English prison.

ward-robe (wôrd'rōb″), *n.* a room or closet for clothes; one's stock of wearing apparel.

ward-room (wôrd'rōōm″), *n.* in a war vessel, the living quarters of the officers above the rank of ensign, not including the captain.

ward sur-geon (wôrd sûr'jŭn), a medical officer in the United States army, who is responsible for the professional care of the patients, for the condition of the wards, and for the proper performance of the duties devolving upon the nurses and attendants.

ware (wâr), *n.* an article of merchandise; articles of the same class; as, hard*ware: pl.* goods; commodities.

ware-house (wâr'hous″), *n.* a storehouse; a building for storing goods: *v.t.* to place in a building for storing: **warehouse receipt,** a receipt given to the owner of goods so stored.

war-fare (wôr'fâr″), *n.* a condition of armed conflict; contest; military operations between enemies; strife; struggle.

war horse (wôr hôrs), a horse used in war; a charger; a cavalry steed.

war-like (wôr'līk″), *adj.* fit for, or fond of, military life or fighting; as, a *warlike* nation; threatening conflict in arms; as, Germany made *warlike* preparations.

war-lock (wôr'lŏk), *n.* formerly, a wizard or witch; a magic spell.

warm (wôrm), *adj.* having heat in a moderate degree; not cold; giving out moderate heat; as, the October sun is pleasantly *warm;* preventing one from feeling cold; as, a *warm* coat; having little cold weather; as, a *warm* climate; earnest or eager; passionate; kindly; as, she has a *warm* heart; suggesting heat by color, as red or orange: *v.t.* to impart moderate heat to; to fill with interest or excitement: *v.i.* to become moderately heated; to become interested or excited; as, the audience *warmed* to the speaker.—*adv.* **warmly.**

warm-blood-ed (wôrm'blŭd″ĕd), *adj.* denoting animals whose temperature ranges from 98° to 112° Fahrenheit.

warmth (wôrmth), *n.* moderate heat; power to give heat; earnestness; zeal; ardor.

warn (wôrn), *v.t.* to put on guard; to make aware of possible danger; foretell a risk to; advise against something; to notify in advance or summon by authority.

warn-ing (wôrn'ĭng), *n.* caution against danger; previous notice; a summons; notice to quit.

warp (wôrp), *n.* lengthwise thread in weaving; the tow rope of a boat; a twist, as of a board: *v.t.* to turn or twist out of shape; to turn from the proper course; to tow (a vessel); to change the form of (an airship wing) by twisting, usually by changing the angle or inclination of the rear spar relative to the front spar: *v.i.* to swerve; to twist, as wood; to fly with a waving motion.

war paint (wôr pānt), paint put on the face and other parts of the body by savages, when about to go to war.

war-path (wôr'pȧth), *n.* the route taken by a party going on a warlike expedition; usually applied to hostile Indians.

war plane (wôr plān), an airplane specially designed and constructed for warfare.

war-rant (wŏr'ȧnt), *n.* an official paper giving authority; a writ or order for arresting a person; that which vouches for or guarantees anything; just ground; as, he acted without *warrant;* in the army, a certificate of rank or appointment issued to one of lower rank than a commissioned officer: *v.t.* to guarantee; give assurance to; authorize; declare as certain; make secure; give just ground for or to; as, the state of affairs *warrants* decided action.—*n.* **warranter, warrantor.**

war-rant-a-ble (wŏr'ȧn-tȧ-bl), *adj.* capable of being guaranteed or authorized; justifiable.—*adv.* **warrantably.**

war-rant of-fi-cer (wŏr'ȧnt ŏf'ĭ-sẽr), a noncommissioned officer in the army or navy.

war-ran-ty (wŏr'ȧn-tĭ), *n.* [*pl.* **warranties** (-tĭz)], authority; legal guarantee; security; as, a *warranty* that certain property is as it is represented.

war-ren (wŏr'ĕn), *n.* an inclosure for protecting game or breeding animals, especially rabbits; a place where rabbits live and breed.

war-rior (wŏr'yẽr), *n.* a soldier; a man in military life.

War Sav-ings Stamp (wôr sāv'ĭngs stămp), a small government security issued by the United States in 1918, and maturing in 1923.

wart (wôrt), *n.* a small, hard tumor or lump on the skin.—*adj.* **warty.**

wa-ry (wâ'rĭ), *adj.* [*comp.* warier, *superl.* wariest], careful or cautious of danger; as, a *wary* foe; marked by caution; as, a *wary* course of action.—*adv.* **warily.**—*n.* **wariness.**

Syn. shrewd, wily, careful.
Ant. (see foolhardy).

was (wŏz), the first and third persons singular, past tense, of the verb *be.*

wash (wŏsh), *v.t.* to cleanse with water; cover with water; flow against; as, the sea *washes* the rocks; to take away by the action of water; as, many houses were *washed* away in the flood; to overlay with thin metal; to cover with a thin coat of color: *v.i.* to become clean by the use of water; to cleanse something by rubbing it in water; to endure without harm by being rubbed in water; as, some kinds of silk *wash*; to move with a flowing, lapping sound: *n.* the act of becoming or making clean with water; a lot of clothing to be washed; the dash or sound of a body of water, as a wave; material deposited by water, as wreckage on a beach; a thin coat of water color; a liquid for cleansing, healing, or treating something; as, a *wash* for sunburn; the disturbed air behind an airplane when it is moving.—*adj.* **washable.**

Syn., *v.* clean, rinse, wet, moisten, tint.

wash-board (wŏsh'bōrd"), *n.* a board with a ribbed metal or glass surface on which clothes are rubbed in being washed.

wash-er (wŏsh'ẽr), *n.* one who, or that which, washes; a ring of metal, leather, or other material, used to secure the tightness of a joint, screw, etc.; a machine for washing clothes.

wash-er-wom-an (wŏsh'ẽr-wŏŏm"ăn), *n.* a woman who earns a living by washing clothes; a laundress.

wash-out (wŏsh'out"), *n.* the carrying away of earth, etc., as by a freshet or heavy rain; also, a place where earth has been so carried away.

wasp (wŏsp), *n.* a winged insect of the bee family with a sharp sting; hence, an irritable or peevish person.

wasp-ish (wŏsp'ĭsh), *adj.* irritable; sharp-tongued; peevish.

was-sail (wŏs'ĭl), *n.* an old form of merry-making accompanied with drinking, especially at Christmas time; liquor made of ale, spices, apples, and sugar; an ancient expression used in drinking a health. —*n.* **wassailer.**

wast-age (wās'tāj), *n.* loss through use, wear and tear, deterioration, evaporation, etc.

waste (wāst), *v.t.* to lay in ruins; to devastate or destroy; to wear away gradually; as, the fever *wasted* his strength; to spend or use recklessly; as, Americans had to learn not to *waste* food: *v.i.* to lose bulk, value, or strength; as, to *waste* away with disease: *adj.* lying unused; desolate; dreary; desert; unproductive; worthless; as, *waste* land: *n.* the act of spending carelessly; that which is discarded or unused; the state of being unused, squandered, etc.; something thrown aside in a manufacturing process; as, cotton *waste*; refuse; a desert or wilderness.

waste-ful (wāst'fŏŏl), *adj.* spending extravagantly or uselessly; inclined to use more than enough; as, she is *wasteful* in cooking; destructive.—*adv.* **wastefully.**—*n.* **wastefulness.**

watch (wŏch), *n.* close observation; vigilance; attendance without sleep; a watchman; a guard or sentry; division of the night; period, usually of four hours, during which a given part of a ship's crew are on duty on deck; a pocket timepiece: *v.i.* to be or keep awake; keep guard; act as an attendant: *v.t.* to tend; guard; keep in sight.—*n.* **watcher, watchmaker.**

watch-dog (wŏch'dŏg"), *n.* a dog quick to detect the approach of strangers, kept to protect property from burglars, etc.

watch-ful (wŏch'fŏŏl), *adj.* wide-awake; cautious; alert and attentive. —*adv.* **watchfully.**—*n.* **watchfulness.**

watch-man (wŏch'măn), *n.* [*pl.* watchmen (-mĕn)], a guard; especially, one who guards a locality or building at night.

watch-tow-er (wŏch'-tou"ẽr), *n.* an ancient or medieval tower, or high structure, upon which a sentinel was placed.

Watchtower

watch-word (wŏch'-wûrd"), *n.* a password; a secret word used as a countersign; a rallying cry; a motto or slogan.

wa-ter (wô'tẽr), *n.* a colorless fluid composed of two parts hydrogen and one part oxygen (H_2O); hence, rain; a sea, river, lake, etc.; the luster or brilliancy of a precious stone; as, a diamond of the first *water*; a kind of wavy, shiny pattern, as in silk: *v.t.* to moisten or sprinkle with water; as, to *water* plants; to allow or cause to drink; as, to *water* cattle; to lessen the quality or strength of by diluting; as, to *water* milk: *v.i.* to obtain, or take in, water; to fill with water or liquid matter; as, her eyes *watered.*

wa-ter-clos-et (wô'tẽr-klŏz"ĕt), *n.* a small room or compartment fitted with a hopper that can be flushed with water, to receive waste matter from the body; also, the hopper.

wa-ter col-or (wô'tẽr kŭl'ẽr), a kind of paint prepared for use by moistening with water; a picture made with paints of this kind, as distinguished from one painted with oil colors.

wa-ter-course (wô'tẽr-kōrs"), *n.* a stream of water; a channel for water; in map reading, the line defining the lowest part of a valley, whether occupied by a stream or not.

wa-ter cress (wô'tẽr krĕs), a plant with pungent leaves, growing in running water: used for salad, etc.

wa-tered (wô'tẽrd), *adj.* supplied with water; sprinkled; having a wavy appearance; as, *watered* silk.

wa-ter-fall (wô'tẽr-fôl"), *n.* a very steep descent, or fall, of the water of a stream or river; a cascade; a cataract.

wa-ter-fowl (wô'tẽr-foul"), *n.* a bird whose home is close to a river, a lake, the sea, etc., such as a wild duck, heron, gull, etc.

wa-ter gas (wô'tẽr găs), gas resulting from the passing of steam over heated carbon.

wa-ter glass (wô'tẽr glȧs), a substance made of silicates of sodium or potassium: often used as a preservative of eggs for winter use.

wa-ter-ing place (wô'tẽr-ĭng plās), a place for getting water; a fashionable resort for bathing, boating, etc.

wa-ter jack-et (wô'tẽr jăk'ĕt), a case for holding water, or through which water circulates, or moves, to cool the interior.

wa-ter lev-el (wô'tẽr lĕv'ĕl), the level of the surface of still water.

wa-ter lil-y (wô'tẽr lĭl'ĭ), a plant which grows in the water, bearing a fragrant, beautiful flower; the flower itself.

wa-ter-logged (wô'tẽr-lŏgd"), *adj.* soaked or filled with water, so as to be unmanageable or heavy like a log; as, a *water-logged* ship.

Wa-ter-loo (wô"tẽr-lōō'), *n.* a complete defeat or failure: so called from Napoleon's final defeat at Waterloo in Belgium.

wa-ter-mark (wô'tẽr-märk"), *n.* a mark showing the height of water; also a faint marking or lettering made in paper during its manufacture, as a trade-mark.

wa-ter-mel-on (wô'tẽr-mĕl"ŭn), *n.* the well-known large green fruit of a plant of the cucumber family; also, the plant.

wa-ter pow-er (wô'tẽr pou'ẽr), the force of water used to run machinery; a fall of water which may be used for such a purpose.

wa-ter-proof (wô'tẽr-prōōf"), *adj.* shedding moisture; not admitting water: *n.* anything which does not permit water to pass through, such as a raincoat made of rubber, etc.: *v.t.* to make secure against water, as a garment, roof, etc.

wa-ter-shed (wô'tẽr-shĕd"), *n.* a height of land lying between areas drained by two different river systems; the drainage area.

wa-ter-side (wô'tẽr-sīd"), *n.* the shore or edge of a body of water.

wa-ter-soaked (wô'tẽr-sōkt"), *p.adj.* having absorbed all the moisture possible; wet through.

wa-ter-spout (wô'tẽr-spout"), *n.* a column of water drawn up by a whirlwind at sea to meet a descending funnel-shaped cloud; a roof spout for the discharge of rainwater.

wa-ter-tight (wô'tẽr-tīt"), *adj.* permitting no water to enter.

wa-ter tow-er (wô'tẽr tou'ẽr), a tower serving as a reservoir or tank for holding water; a fire-fighting machine having a high pressure pipe which can be raised to various heights.

wa-ter-way (wô'tẽr-wā"), *n.* a channel for water; a body of water permitting navigation.

wa-ter wheel (wô'tẽr hwēl), a wheel turned by the direct action of water.

wa-ter-works (wô'tẽr-wûrks"), *n.* a pumping station; a system for supplying water to a city, town, etc.

wa-ter-y (wô'tẽr-ĭ), *adj.* pertaining to, or like, water; transparent or thin; tasteless; tearful; moist; soggy.

watt (wŏt), *n.* the electrical unit of power, or rate of work done by a current of one ampere with a potential of one volt.

wat-tle (wŏt'l), *n.* a twig; a rod easily bent; a hurdle of pliant rods; loose red flesh under the throat of a cock, etc.: *v.t.* to twist or interweave (twigs or rods) one with another; to fence with rods.

wat-tle-bird (wŏt'l-bûrd"), *n.* an Australian honey-eating bird.

watt-me-ter (wŏt'mē"tẽr), *n.* an instrument for measuring electric power by the unit called the watt.

wave (wāv), *n.* a swell on the surface of water; billow; vibrations by which sound, light, etc., are transmitted; a curving ridge on any surface; an up and down or back and forth motion: *v.i.* to be moved up and down or back and forth; to signal by such a motion; to have undulations, or curves; as, her hair *waves* beautifully: *v.t.* to swing; brandish; to cause to move to and fro; to signal by such a movement; to give an undulating, or curved, surface to.

wa-ver (wā'vẽr), *v.i.* to tremble to and fro or back and forth; to wave; hence, to reel or stagger; to hesitate or be undetermined; as, to *waver* in one's opinion.

wav-y (wāv'ĭ), *adj.* rising and swelling in waves; full of waves; as, *wavy* hair.—*n.* **waviness.**

wax (wăks), *n.* the secretion of bees from which they build their comb; any substance like beeswax, such as sealing *wax*, cobblers' *wax*, etc.: *v.t.* to smear or rub with beeswax; as, to *wax* a floor: *v.i.* to increase in size; to grow; as, to *wax* great in wealth.

wax-bill (wăks'bĭl"), *n.* a European bird of the weaver-bird family, having a conelike bill that resembles wax.

wax-en (wăk'sn), *adj.* made of, or like, wax; as, a *waxen* doll; soft or pliable.

wax-wing (wăks'wĭng"), *n.* a small brown bird with a showy crest and waxlike red tips on its wings.

wax-work (wăks'wûrk"), *n.* figures formed of wax in imitation of animals, flowers, people, etc.

wax-y (wăk'sĭ), *adj.* consisting of, or like, wax; adhesive or sticky; pliable. —*n.* **waxiness.**

way (wā), *n.* a road; route for passage; direction; as, turn this *way;* distance; as, he came a long *way*; method; as, let me show you the *way* to do it; habitual mode of life; as, the bachelor was set in his *ways;* detail or respect; as, in other *ways* the plan was good; will; as, she was determined to have her own *way;* room or space; as, make *way* for the procession: *pl.* timbers on which a ship is built, and down which it slides when launched.

Syn. method, system, means, fashion, course, route, habit, practice.

way-bill (wā'bĭl"), *n.* a document, or paper, describing, and containing shipping instructions for, goods carried by train or steamer.

way-far-er (wā'fâr"ẽr), *n.* a traveler, especially one who goes on foot.

way-lay (wā"lā'), *v.t.* [*p.t.* and *p.p.* waylaid, *p.pr.* waylaying], to lie in wait for; to beset by the road, in order to rob.

way-side (wā'sīd"), *n.* the edge of the road in the country.

way sta-tion (wā stā'shŭn), a small station between important places on a railroad.

way train (wā trān), a train which stops at all stations along the road.

way-ward (wā'wẽrd), *adj.* taking one's own way; perverse or disobedient; as, a *wayward* child.—*n.* **waywardness.**

way-worn (wā'wōrn"), *adj.* tired out by travel or by the happenings of life.

we (wē), nominative plural of the pronoun of the first person.

weak (wēk), *adj.* wanting strength, force, or power; as, a *weak* body; lacking mental or moral strength; simple; foolish; not effective; lacking power to endure; easily influenced; easily overcome; as, a *weak* defense or a *weak* argument; faint in sound; much diluted; as, *weak* tea.

Syn. infirm.

wea-ken (wē'k'n), *v.t.* to make less strong; reduce in quality or strength: *v.i.* to become less strong.
Syn. debilitate, enfeeble, enervate.

weak-fish (wēk'fĭsh"), *n.* any of several kinds of sea fish with very tender flesh.

weak-ling (wēk'lĭng), *n.* a person without strength, or feeble in body or character.

weak-ly (wēk'lĭ), *adj.* feeble; not strong: *adv.* in a faint manner; feebly.

weak-ness (wēk'nĕs), *n.* the state or quality of lacking strength; a fault or defect; as, a *weakness* of character.

weal (wēl), *n.* happiness; welfare; as, the law was made for the public *weal.*

weald (wēld), *n.* a region without woods; open country; a wold.

wealth (wĕlth), *n.* riches; affluence; great abundance.

wealth-y (wĕl'thĭ), *adj.* [*comp.* wealthier, *superl.* wealthiest], having riches; affluent; possessing great abundance.—*adv.* wealthily.

wean (wēn), *v.t.* to cease to feed (a child) by nursing; to alienate, or separate, the affections of, from any object or habit; to detach gradually.

weap-on (wĕp'ŭn), *n.* any instrument for fighting or for defense, as a gun or sword; any means of contest; as, his tongue was his best *weapon.*

wear (wâr), *v.t.* [*p.t.* wore, *p.p.* worn, *p.pr.* wearing], to carry on the body; as, to *wear* clothing; bear or show; as, to *wear* a careless manner; use up; make less in quantity or value; as, to *wear* out one's patience; to damage by continual friction; as, to *wear* the gloss off a surface; to make by use or friction; as, to *wear* a hole in cloth; to *wear* a path through the woods; to turn a ship: *v.i.* to be exhausted or damaged by use; as, your coat is *wearing* out; to last well under use; as, that cloth will *wear* for a long time: *n.* the state of being used; damage caused by use; as, his garments show signs of *wear;* garments worn; as, this shop sells ladies' *wear.*—*n.* wearer.

wea-ri-some (wē'rĭ-sŭm), *adj.* causing exhaustion or tiredness; tedious; irksome; as, a *wearisome* journey; fatiguing.—*adv.* wearisomely.—*n.* wearisomeness.

wea-ry (wē'rĭ), *adj.* [*comp.* wearier, *superl.* weariest], fatigued; tired; worn out physically or mentally; resulting from, or causing, exhaustion; irksome: *v.t.* [*p.t.* and *p.p.* wearied, *p.pr.* wearying], to wear out or make tired; to harass or worry by something irksome: *v.i.* to become tired or fatigued; become impatient.—*adv.* wearily.—*n.* weariness.
Syn., v. harass, jade, tire, fatigue.

wea-sel (wē'z'l), *n.* a small animal of the same family as the mink and ferret, having short legs and a long body, and destructive to poultry, rats, mice, etc.

weath-er (wĕth'ẽr), *n.* the state of the atmosphere as to cold, heat, wet, dryness, etc.: *v.t.* to expose to, or season by exposure to, the air; sail to the windward of; endure or resist bravely; as, to *weather* a gale at sea: *v.i.* to undergo change by the action of the air, sun, rain, etc.

weath-er-beat-en (wĕth'ẽr-bēt"n), *adj.* defaced or worn by the action of air, sun, rain, etc.; as, a *weather-beaten* house; toughened; as, a *weather-beaten* countenance.

weath-er-board (wĕth'ẽr-bōrd"), *n.* a board cut to form lapped joints with boards above and below, so as to make a waterproof outer wall for a house; clapboarding: *v.t.* to nail boards on (a building) so as to lap over one another.

Weath-er Bu-reau (wĕth'ẽr bū'rō), that part of the United States Department of Agriculture which keeps collected statistics of weather reports and foretells weather conditions.

weath-er-cock (wĕth'ẽr-kŏk"), *n.* a metal figure, often shaped like a cock, fastened to a high spire, roof, pole, etc., and turning with the wind to show which way it blows; a weather vane; especially, one shaped like a cock; a fickle person.

weath-er gage (wĕth'ẽr gāj), the situation of a vessel to the windward of another. Also, weather gauge.

weath-er-glass (wĕth'ẽr-glȧs"), *n.* an instrument to show the condition of the atmosphere, as a barometer.

weath-er vane (wĕth'ẽr vān), a thin strip of wood or metal, often shaped like a bird, fish, etc., and fastened to a high spire, roof, or pole, where it turns with the wind and shows which way it blows; a weathercock. Also, vane.

Weather Vanes

weath-er-wise (wĕth'ẽr-wīz"), *adj.* able to foretell the state of the weather.

weath-er-worn (wĕth'ẽr-wōrn"), *adj.* damaged or altered by exposure to sun, rain, wind, etc.

weave (wēv), *v.t.* to twist or interlace, as threads, together; form, as cloth, in a loom; compose or fabricate; as, to *weave* a thrilling story: *v.i.* to practice making cloth with a loom; to become twisted together or interlaced; to wind in and out: *n.* a special pattern made in a loom.

weav-er (wēv'ẽr), *n.* one whose trade is making cloth, etc., in a loom.

weav-er bird (wēv'ẽr bûrd), a bird of Asia and Africa that makes its nest by a complicated twisting together of twigs, grass, etc.

web (wĕb), *n.* anything woven; anything carefully contrived, as a plan or scheme; tissue or texture; a cobweb; the skin between the toes of many water birds, as a duck, etc.; a large roll of paper for printing: *v.t.* [*p.t.* and *p.p.* webbed, *p.pr.* webbing], to unite or surround with, or as with, a web; entangle.—*adj.* webbed.

web-bing (wĕb'ĭng), *n.* a heavy woven strip or tape of cotton or linen; the membrane joining the toes of a bird's foot.

web-foot (wĕb'fŏŏt"), *n.* a foot with the toes joined by a membrane; any animal with feet of this kind.—*adj.* web-footed.

wed (wĕd), *v.t.* [*p.t.* and *p.p.* wedded or wed, *p.pr.* wedding], to marry; to join in marriage; unite together firmly: *v.i.* to contract marriage.

wed-ding (wĕd'ĭng), *n.* a marriage; marriage ceremony or festivities;

a joining together; also, the celebration of a marriage anniversary; as, a golden *wedding*.

wedge (wĕj), *n.* a piece of wood or metal, thick at one end and thin at the other, used for splitting wood, rocks, etc.; anything of a similar shape: *v.t.* to cleave, force, drive, or fasten, with a wedge; press in closely.

Wedge

wed-lock (wĕd'lŏk), *n.* the state of being married; matrimony.

Wednes-day (wĕnz'dā), *n.* the fourth day of the week.

wee (wē), *adj.* very small; little; as, a *wee* bit of anything; a *wee* baby.

weed (wēd), *n.* any harmful, or useless plant; a wild plant which hinders the growth of cultivated ones; anything useless or troublesome: *pl.* a widow's mourning garments: *v.t.* to root out; to free from useless or wild plants; to rid of anything offensive, hurtful, or obstructive.

weed-y (wēd'ĭ), *adj.* pertaining to, consisting of, or abounding with, weeds; as, a *weedy* garden; ill-kept; not trim in shape.

week (wēk), *n.* a period of seven days, usually counted as beginning with Sunday.

week day (wēk dā), any day of the week except Sunday.

week-end (wēk'ĕnd'), *n.* the time from Friday night or Saturday noon to Monday morning, usually free from business.

week-ly (wēk'lĭ), *adj.* continuing for, produced within, or happening in, seven days; coming every seven days: *adv.* once a week: *n.* [*pl.* weeklies (-lĭz)], a paper or magazine issued once every seven days.

weep (wēp), *v.i.* to shed tears; to cry: *v.t.* to shed tears for; hence, to lament or mourn; bewail.—*n.* weeper.

weep-ing (wēp'ĭng), *n.* the act of shedding tears: *p.adj.* crying; having drooping branches; as, a *weeping* willow.

wee-vil (wē'vl), *n.* a small beetle, whose larvæ are injurious to fruit and grain.

weft (wĕft), *n.* in weaving, the threads that cross the warp, or lengthwise threads; woof; a web; a thing woven.

weigh (wā), *v.t.* to find the heaviness of; examine by a scale or balance; to ponder; reflect on carefully; to raise: used only in *to weigh anchor: v.i.* to have a given heaviness; to bear heavily; as, the burden of anxiety *weighs* on his mind; to be of importance; as, the common good should *weigh* heaviest in the decision.—*n.* weigher.

weight (wāt), *n.* the quality of being heavy; amount of heaviness; a mass of metal used as a balance in finding the heaviness of other bodies; a heavy mass; a load; something oppressive; as, a *weight* on the mind; pressure; power; importance: *v.t.* to load down; to make heavy.

Syn., *n.* heaviness, burden, load.
Ant. (see lightness).

weight-y (wāt'ĭ), *adj.* [*comp.* weightier, *superl.* weightiest], heavy; important; serious; as, a *weighty* matter.—*adv.* weightily.—*n.* weightiness.

weir (wēr), *n.* a dam in a stream to raise the water, send it to a mill, form a pond, etc.; also, a fence of brush or twigs set in a stream, channel, etc., for catching fish.

weird (wērd), *adj.* of or pertaining to fate or to witchcraft; hence, uncanny or unearthly; as, a *weird* sound; strange and mysterious.—*adv.* weirdly.—*n.* weirdness.

wel-come (wĕl'kŭm), *adj.* received with gladness or hospitality; as, a *welcome* guest; producing gladness; as, *welcome* news; permitted gladly; as, you are *welcome* to keep it: *n.* kind reception to a guest or newcomer: *v.t.* to salute with kindness; receive with hospitality.

weld (wĕld), *v.t.* to unite by heating and hammering; to press together, as two pieces of heated iron; to unite closely: *v.i.* to become melted, or firmly joined, together: *n.* state of being heated and pressed together; a joint made by heating and hammering.

weld-er (wĕl'dẽr), *n.* one who joins together, as metals by melting and pressing.

wel-fare (wĕl'fâr'), *n.* condition of health; prosperity; happiness.

wel-kin (wĕl'kĭn), *n.* the vault of heaven; the sky.

well (wĕl), *n.* a spring or fountain; a shaft sunk in the earth to reach a supply of water or other liquid, such as oil; something like a well in shape: *v.i.* to flow or pour forth as from a spring: *adv.* rightly; justly; suitably; as, the work was *well* done; favorably; fortunately; as, the experiment turned out *well;* sufficiently; fully; as, *well* under way: *adj.* in good condition or circumstances; fortunate; sound in body; healthy.

well-be-ing (wĕl'bē'ĭng), *n.* the state of general health and prosperity; welfare.

well-born (wĕl'bôrn'), *adj.* born of a good family.

well-bred (wĕl'brĕd'), *adj.* refined in manners; cultivated; of good breed, as an animal.

well-nigh (wĕl'nī'), *adv.* very nearly; almost; as, he was *well-nigh* exhausted.

well-spring (wĕl'sprĭng'), *n.* a source of never-failing supply; as, a *wellspring* of joy.

well-to-do (wĕl'tŏŏ-dōō'), *adj.* prosperous; fairly wealthy.

Wels-bach light (wĕlz'băk *or* wĕlz'băk lĭt), a gas burner for lighting purposes, in which a noncombustible mantle, suspended around the flame, becomes heated to incandescence and gives off a strong white light.

Welsh (wĕlsh), *adj.* pertaining to Wales, its people, or their language: *n.* the people of Wales; the language of Wales.

Welsh rab-bit (wĕlsh răb'ĭt), melted cheese, cooked with milk, etc., seasoned, and spread upon toasted bread.

welt (wĕlt), *n.* an edge or border fastened around something; a narrow strip of leather around a shoe between the upper leather and the sole; colloquially, a red, swollen mark raised on the skin by a blow: *v.t.* to put a welt upon; colloquially, to flog, or beat, so as to raise red, swollen marks.

wel-ter (wĕl'tẽr), *v.i.* to roll in mud or mire; to wallow, as a hog; to be in a state of moral corruption; to rise and fall with violent tossing, as waves; *n.* a rolling, as of waves, or a wallowing; a state of unrest and confusion; a wallow.

wen (wĕn), *n.* a painless tumor inclosed in a cyst, or closed sac.

wench (wĕnch), *n.* formerly, a young girl or maiden; a female servant.

wend (wĕnd), *v.i.* and *v.t.* to proceed on, or journey; as, to *wend* one's way homeward.

went (wĕnt), past tense of the irregular verb *go*.

wept (wĕpt), the past tense and past participle of the verb *weep*.

were (wûr), plural form of the past tense of the verb *be*.

were-wolf (wēr′wŏŏlf″; wûr′wŏŏlf″), *n.* in folklore, a person turned into a wolf in form, or one who could assume a wolf's form at certain periods. Also, **werwolf.**

wert (wûrt), second person singular past indicative and subjunctive, grave form, of *be*.

Wes-ley-an (wĕs′lĭ-ăn), *adj.* pertaining to John Wesley (1703-1791), or to Wesleyanism or Methodism, the religion which he founded: *n.* a Wesleyan Methodist.

west (wĕst), *n.* one of the four points of the compass, exactly opposite the east; the point where the sun appears to set; a region lying in the direction of the sunset: **the West**, the Western Hemisphere; the part of the United States between the Mississippi River and the Pacific Ocean: *adj.* pertaining to, situated in, proceeding toward, or coming from, the direction of the sunset; as, a *west* wind: *adv.* towards the sunset.

west-er-ly (wĕs′tĕr-lĭ), *adj.* and *adv.* toward the west; of winds, from the west.

west-ern (wĕs′tĕrn), *adj.* pertaining to, or of, the west; westerly: **Western**, of the Western Hemisphere; of the western part of the United States.

west-ern-er (wĕs′tĕr-nĕr), *n.* one who lives in, or comes from, a region toward the west: **Westerner**, a native of the western part of the United States.

west-ward (wĕst′wĕrd), *adj.* lying or facing towards the west: *adv.* towards the west. Also, **westwards.**—*adv.* **westwardly.**

wet (wĕt), *v.t.* [*p.t.* and *p.p.* wetted or wet, *p.pr.* wetting], to cover or soak with liquid; to soak or moisten with water or some other liquid: *n.* water; moisture; rainy or misty weather: *adj.* containing, consisting of, or soaked with, water or some other liquid; very damp; rainy or misty; as, *wet* weather.—*n.* **wetness.**

weth-er (wĕth′ĕr), *n.* a male sheep that has been made incapable of reproducing its kind.

whack (hwăk), *n.* a smart, resounding blow: *v.t.* to strike with a smart, resounding blow. [COLLOQ.]

whale (hwāl), *n.* a very large, warm-blooded, air-breathing sea mammal, shaped like a fish and valued for its oil and whalebone: **whale calf**, a young whale.

Whale and Calf

whale-back (hwāl′băk″), *n.* a freight steamer having a very convex, or curved, deck, like the back of a whale.

whale-boat (hwāl′bōt″), *n.* a long, narrow boat, sharp and slanting at both ends, first used by whale fishers.

whale-bone (hwāl′bōn″), *n.* a stiff, springy substance found in the upper jaw of whales.

whal-er (hwāl′ĕr), *n.* a vessel or person employed in hunting whales.

whang (hwăng), *v.t.* to flog: *n.* a blow: a whack. [COLLOQ.]

wharf (hwôrf), *n.* [*pl.* wharfs or wharves (hwôrvz)], a structure built at the water's edge, for loading or unloading ships; a pier or quay.

wharf-age (hwôr′fāj), *n.* the fee, or money, collected for use of a wharf; the entire wharf space at a port, etc.

wharf-in-ger (hwôr′fĭn-jĕr), *n.* the owner of a wharf.

what (hwŏt), *pron.* compound relative meaning that which; the thing that; as, have you found *what* you want? an interrogative; as, *what* are you doing? an indefinite; as, I do not know *what* happened: *adj.* interrogative; as, *what* trade does he follow? *adv.* how; how much; as, *what* does it profit? partly: followed by *with*; as, *what* with the cold and *what* with the darkness we could go no farther: *conj.* that; as, there is no doubt but *what* he will succeed; so far as; as well as.

what-ev-er (hwŏt-ĕv′ĕr), *pron.* all that; anything that; as, give *whatever* you can; no matter what; as, we must have sugar *whatever* its cost.

what-not (hwŏt′nŏt″), *n.* an article of furniture with shelves for books, ornaments, etc.

what-so-ev-er (hwŏt′sō-ĕv′ĕr), *pron.* and *adj.* emphatic form of *whatever*.

wheal (hwēl), *n.* a discolored swelling from the stroke of a whip; a weal.

wheat (hwēt), *n.* a well-known grain from which white flour is made; also, the grass that yields it.

wheat-ear (hwēt′ēr″), *n.* a small singing bird, with a white patch at the base of its tail.

wheat-en (hwēt′n), *adj.* made of wheat; as, a *wheaten* loaf.

whee-dle (hwē′d′l), *v.t.* to flatter; cajole; coax; as, she *wheedled* her father into consenting; to get by coaxing or flattery; as, she *wheedled* permission out of her father: *v.i.* to coax with flattery.

wheel (hwēl), *n.* a circular frame or body capable of turning on a central axis or axle; anything shaped like a wheel; a circular frame, with handles, for controlling the rudder of a ship; a bicycle; an old instrument of torture; a circular revolving firework; a complete turning around; that which makes active or which directs progress; as, he soon had the *wheels* of the business running smoothly; a maneuver in drill in which troops in line change direction without destroying their alignment: *v.t.* to move on wheels; to cause to turn: *v.i.* to turn on an axis or about a center; to revolve; to roll forward.—*adj.* **wheeled.**

wheel-bar-row (hwēl′băr″ō), *n.* a light vehicle with two handles and usually one wheel, used to carry small loads.

wheel-er (hwēl′ĕr), *n.* one who pushes, as a wheeled chair, barrow, etc.: the horse nearest to the wheels of a carriage.

wheel horse (hwēl hôrs), the horse nearest to the vehicle drawn, when there is a leader; hence, the person who bears the brunt of the hard work in an undertaking.

wheel-house (hwēl′hous″), *n.* a small structure on the forward deck of a ship, where the steering wheel is situated.

wheel-man (hwēl'măn), *n.* [*pl.* wheel-men (-mĕn)], one who rides a bicycle; the steersman of a boat.

wheel-wright (hwēl'rīt"), *n.* one who makes or repairs wheels and vehicles with wheels.

wheeze (hwēz), *v.i.* to breathe noisily with difficulty: to make a whistling noise; as, the pump *wheezes*: *n.* a whistling or gasping breath, as in asthma.

wheez-y (hwēz'ĭ), *adj.* affected with difficult breathing.

whelm (hwĕlm), *v.t.* to overpower, as with a mass of water; engulf.

whelp (hwĕlp), *n.* the young of a dog, lion, fox, etc.; a cub; a contemptuous term for a worthless youth: *v.t.* to give birth to (a whelp): *v.i.* to bring forth whelps, or cubs.

when (hwĕn), *adv.* at, or after, the time that; as, write *when* you can; at what time; as, *when* did it happen? as soon as; as, *when* the war is over.

whence (hwĕns), *adv.* from what place, source, or origin.

when-ev-er (hwĕn-ĕv'ẽr), *adv.* and *conj.* at whatever time.

where (hwâr), *adv.* at or in which place or places; to what or which place, places, or result; from what place or source; whither.

where-a-bouts (hwâr'ȧ-bouts"), *adv.* about where; near what or which place; about which or concerning which: *n. sing.* the place where a person or thing is. Also, **whereabout.**

where-as (hwâr-ăz'), *conj.* considering that; since; it being the case that; when in fact or truth; while on the contrary; the case being that.

where-at (hwâr-ăt'), *adv.* at which, or upon which; whereupon; at what: used in a question.

where-by (hwâr-bī'), *adv.* by which: used as a relative; by what; how: used in a question.

where-fore (hwâr'fōr), *adv.* for which reason; therefore; why: used in a question.

where-in (hwâr-ĭn'), *adv.* in which; in which time, place, respect, etc.: used as a relative; in what: used in a question; as, *wherein* am I mistaken?

where-of (hwâr-ŏv'), *adv.* of which; of whom: used as a relative; of what: used in a question.

where-on (hwâr-ŏn'), *adv.* on which: used as a relative; on what: used as a question.

where-so-ev-er (hwâr"sō-ĕv'ẽr), *adv.* in or to whatsoever place; wherever.

where-to (hwâr-tōō'), *adv.* to which: used as a relative; to what, or to what end or place: used in a question.

where-up-on (hwâr"ŭ-pŏn'), *adv.* upon which; as the result of, or after, which: used as a relative; whereon: used in a question.

wher-ev-er (hwâr-ĕv'ẽr), *adv.* at, from, to, or in, whatever place; wheresoever.

where-with (hwâr-wĭth'; hwâr-wĭth'), *adv.* with which: used as a relative; with what: used in a question.

where-with-al (hwâr"wĭth-ôl'), *adv.* with which: used as a relative; with what: used in a question: *n.* that with which anything can be bought or done. Also, **wherewith.**

wher-ry (hwĕr'ĭ), *n.* [*pl.* wherries (-ĭz)], a light, shallow rowboat; a light barge or fishing vessel.

whet (hwĕt), *v.t.* [*p.t.* and *p.p.* whetted, *p.pr.* whetting], to sharpen by rubbing, as a knife; to make keen or eager; as, sea air *whets* the appetite; stimulate.

wheth-er (hwĕth'ẽr), *pron.* which (of two) or which one (of two): *conj.* a particle introducing a following alternative, *or*, or *or whether*; as, I do not know *whether* this or that is the true reason.

whet-stone (hwĕt'stōn"), *n.* a stone for sharpening edge tools.

whew (hwū; hū), *interj.* an exclamation of surprise, disgust, or dismay; as, *whew!* how the wind blows.

whey (hwā), *n.* the thin, sweet, watery part of milk, separated from the curds, as in cheese making.—*adj.* **wheyey.**

which (hwĭch), *pron.* an interrogative; as, *which* is your house? a relative, meaning a particular one; the one that; as, point out *which* is yours: used of animals, ideas, or things: *adj.* interrogative; as, *which* house is yours?

which-ev-er (hwĭch-ĕv'ẽr), *pron.* whether one or the other; whether one or another. Also, **whichsoever.**

whiff (hwĭf), *n.* a sudden breath or blast, as of air or smoke; a light puff: *v.t.* and *v.i.* to puff or blow out in sudden breaths.

whif-fle (hwĭf'l), *v.i.* to blow unsteadily or in gusts, as the wind; hence, to be fickle or unsteady.—*n.* **whiffler.**

whif-fle-tree (hwĭf'l-trē"), *n.* a pivoted or swinging bar attached crosswise to the front of a carriage or wagon to hold the traces of the harness. Also, **whippletree.**

Whig (hwĭg), *n.* one of a former political party in the United States that favored a protective tariff, and was succeeded by the present Republican party; a supporter of the American Revolution; one of a liberal political party which originated in England in the 17th century, and developed into the Liberal party: *adj.* of or pertaining to Whigs.—*adj.* **Whiggish.**—*n.* **Whiggery.**

while (hwīl), *n.* a period of time; time or pains required to do something: used in the expressions, worth *while*, and worth one's *while*: *conj.* as long as; during the time that: *v.t.* to cause to pass; spend; as, to *while* away time.

whim (hwĭm), *n.* a fancy; freak; notion; a sudden, often unreasonable, wish.

whim-per (hwĭm'pẽr), *v.i.* to cry with a low, whining, broken voice: *n.* a low, broken complaint; a fretful whining.—*n.* **whimperer.**

whim-sey (hwĭm'zĭ), *n.* a caprice; a sudden freak; an unreasonable notion. Also, **whimsy.**

whim-si-cal (hwĭm'zĭ-kăl), *adj.* freakish; full of odd notions; capricious; queerly humorous.—*adv.* **whimsically.**

whin-chat (hwĭn'chăt"), *n.* a small European singing bird, brown and yellow in color.

whine (hwīn), *v.i.* to show distress by a plaintive, nasal cry; murmur in a mean or childish manner; to complain; to talk in a plaintive, nasal tone: *v.t.* to utter in a fretful or complaining way: *n.* a plaintive tone; the act or sound of weak, fretful complaining.

whin-ny (hwĭn'ĭ), *v.i.* to neigh: said of a horse: *n.* the usual call of a horse; a neigh.

whin-stone (hwĭn'stōn"), *n.* a miner's term for hard, resisting rock.

whip (hwĭp), *v.t.* [*p.t.* and *p.p.* whipped or whipt, *p.pr.* whipping], to strike or punish with a lash or rod; flog; to take, snatch, or jerk: with *out, off, from,* etc.; as, he *whipped* out his pistol and fired; colloquially, to defeat in a contest; conquer; as, the home team was badly *whipped;* beat into a froth; as, to *whip* cream; beat out; to overcast, as a seam; to bind the end of (a rope), to prevent it from fraying out; to wrap regularly, as a rope; fish in with a rod and artificial fly; as, to *whip* a stream for trout: *v.i.* to move nimbly; start suddenly and run: *n.* an instrument with a lash, used for driving horses or other animals or for correction; one who drives horses; a member of the British Parliament whose duty it is to keep the members of his party together.—*n.* whipper.

Whipped End of Rope

whip-cord (hwĭp'kôrd"), *n.* a kind of hard cord, often used for making whiplashes.

whip-lash (hwĭp'lăsh"), *n.* the lash, or cord, of a whip.

whip-per-in (hwĭp'ẽr-ĭn"), *n.* a huntsman who has charge of the hounds.

whip-per-snap-per (hwĭp'ẽr-snăp"ẽr), *n.* a small, insignificant person, who feels that he is important.

whip-pet (hwĭp'ĕt), *n.* in the World War, a small tank, or armored tractor, used by the British army.

whip-ple-tree (hwĭp'l-trē"), *n.* a swinging crosswise bar at the front of a vehicle, to which the traces of the harness are fastened. Also, whiffletree.

whip-poor-will (hwĭp'po͝or-wĭl"), *n.* a small American bird, named from its cry, which is heard only at night.

whip-saw (hwĭp'sô"), *n.* a long, narrow saw with coarse, hook teeth, used to cut wood with the grain.

whip-stock (hwĭp'stŏk"), *n.* the handle of a whip.

whir (hwûr), *v.i.* [*p.t.* and *p.p.* whirred, *p.pr.* whirring], to revolve or move quickly with a buzzing noise: *n.* a buzzing or whizzing noise caused by rapid motion; as, the *whir* of machinery.

whirl (hwûrl), *v.t.* to cause to turn round rapidly: *v.i.* to turn or move round with great speed; move along swiftly, especially on wheels: *n.* a turning round with great speed; rapid rotation or circular motion.

whirl-i-gig (hwûr'lĭ-gĭg"), *n.* a child's toy that spins or whirls round; a merry-go-round.

whirl-pool (hwûrl'po͞ol"), *n.* a current of water whirling round so as to make a hollow in the center into which objects may be drawn.

whirl-wind (hwûrl'wĭnd"), *n.* a violent wind moving with a circular current, or with a whirling, spiral motion; a tornado or cyclone; hence, a sudden, violent rush.

whisk (hwĭsk), *v.t.* to sweep or brush rapidly; move, or carry off, with a quick, sweeping motion: *v.i.* to move rapidly and nimbly; as, the squirrel *whisked* up the tree: *n.* the act of brushing with a quick motion; a quick, nimble movement; a small bunch or bundle of hair, grass, straw, etc., used as a brush; hence, a small-sized broom or brush.

whisk-ers (hwĭs'kẽrz), *n.pl.* the hair on the sides of a man's face, and on the chin; the bristly hairs around the mouth of a cat, etc.

whis-ky (hwĭs'kĭ), *n.* [*pl.* whiskies (-kĭz)], an alcoholic liquor distilled from grain or potatoes. Also, whiskey.

whis-per (hwĭs'pẽr), *v.i.* to speak in a low voice; to speak softly or under the breath; to make a hissing sound: *v.t.* to say under the breath; speak of privately: *n.* a low, soft tone of voice; speech under the breath without tone; a secret or private utterance; a hint or suggestion; a soft, rustling sound; as, the *whisper* of the trees.—*n.* whisperer.

whist (hwĭst), *n.* a card game: *interj.* hush! *adj.* hushed or quiet; as, the winds are *whist.*

whis-tle (hwĭs'l), *v.i.* to make a shrill sound by forcing the breath through the teeth or puckered lips; to utter or make a shrill sound by forcing air or steam through an opening; as, the engine *whistled* at the station; to go or pass with a sharp, shrill sound; as, the wind *whistled* through the woods: *v.t.* to utter by whistling; as, to *whistle* a tune; to call or signal by whistling; as, the hunter *whistled* his dog home: *n.* the shrill noise made by forcing the breath through the puckered lips; the sound of steam, or air forced through an opening; as, a factory or locomotive *whistle;* any like sound; an instrument, large or small, for producing such a sound.—*n.* whistler.

whit (hwĭt), *n.* the smallest particle; speck; jot.

white (hwīt), *adj.* of the color of clean snow: opposite to *black;* pure; innocent; having silvery hair; gray with age; having a fair skin; pale: *n.* the color formed by the combination of all the colors in the spectrum; the color of clean snow; a Caucasian, or white man; albumen of an egg; the part of the eyeball outside the iris: *v.t.* to make of the color of clean snow; whitewash; bleach.—*n.* whiteness.

white ant (hwīt ănt), a pale-colored, soft-bodied insect, living in an organized group which builds a very large hill: found largely in Africa, and very destructive to wooden structures, books, etc.

white-bait (hwīt'bāt"), *n.* the young of the herring, considered a delicacy in food.

white-cap (hwīt'kăp"), *n.* a wave crest breaking into foam.—White Cap, a member of a self-appointed law and order committee which punishes offenders by lynch law: so called from the white caps or hoods worn by such bodies in early days.

white feath-er (hwīt fĕth'ẽr), a symbol of cowardice.

white-fish (hwīt'fĭsh"), *n.* a fresh-water fish of the salmon family, good for food.

White Fri-ar (hwīt frī'ẽr), a Carmelite monk.

White House (hwīt hous), the official residence at Washington of the President of the United States: so called from its color.

white lead (hwīt lĕd), a heavy white substance composed of lead carbonate and used in the manufacture of paint.

white lie (hwīt lī), a trivial falsehood; a lie supposed to be harmless.

white-liv-ered (hwīt′lĭv″ẽrd), *adj.* of a pallid, feeble appearance; cowardly.

whit-en (hwīt′n), *v.t.* to make white; blanch: *v.i.* to become white.

white plague (hwīt plāg), tuberculosis, especially of the lungs.

white slave (hwīt slāv), a woman held against her will in a house of ill repute, where she is employed as a prostitute for the gain of the keeper of the house.

white-throat (hwīt′thrōt″), *n.* a small European singing bird of the warbler family.

white-wash (hwīt′wŏsh″), *n.* a white mixture of lime and water, for coating walls and ceilings, fences, etc.: *v.t.* to cover with a coat of lime and water; to gloss over in order to hide faults; to make appear better than fact.

white wings (hwīt wĭngz), a slang term applied to street cleaners wearing a white uniform.

white-wood (hwīt′wŏŏd″), *n.* a tree with light-colored wood; the wood of the tulip tree or of the cottonwood.

whith-er (hwĭth′ẽr), *adv.* to what place: used interrogatively and relatively; how far; to what end.

whith-er-so-ev-er (hwĭth″ẽr-sō-ĕv′ẽr), *adv.* to any place whatever.

whit-ing (hwīt′ĭng), *n.* powdered chalk used for polishing, as a coloring matter, etc.; a sea fish used for food.

whit-ish (hwīt′ĭsh), *adj.* somewhat white; pale.

whit-low (hwĭt′lō), *n.* a sore finger or toe; a felon; a foot disease in sheep.

Whit-sun (hwĭt′sŭn), *adj.* pertaining to, or observed at, Whitsuntide, or the season of Pentecost.

Whit-sun-day (hwĭt′sn-dā; hwĭt″sŭn′dā), *n.* the seventh Sunday after Easter, commemorating the day of Pentecost. Also, **Whit-Sunday.**

Whit-sun-tide (whĭt′sn-tīd″), *n.* the week after Whitsunday; the seventh week after Easter. Also, **Whitsun Tide.**

whit-tle (hwĭt′l), *v.t.* to cut, shape, or sharpen with a knife; as, to *whittle* a stick; to reduce bit by bit.

whiz (hwĭz), *v.i.* [*p.t.* and *p.p.* whizzed, *p.pr.* whizzing], to make a humming or hissing noise, as from rapid motion; to move rapidly with a humming or hissing sound: *n.* a humming noise accompanying rapid motion; as, the *whiz* of a bullet: **whiz bang,** a slang term for a shell of such high velocity that its *whiz* and its *bang* occur at almost the same instant.—Also, **whizz.**

who (hōō), *pron.* an interrogative; as, *who* comes here? a simple relative, used of persons; a compound relative, meaning the person or persons that; as, *who* crosses this line will suffer.

whoa (hwō), *interj.* stop! stand! hold! a call to a horse.

who-ev-er (hōō-ĕv′ẽr), *pron.* every one who; whatever person; he or she who.

whole (hōl), *adj.* containing all the parts; complete; entire; not defective or broken; hale and sound in body; intact; not fractional: said of a number: *n.* all the parts of something taken together; a total; the sum of all the parts.—*n.* **wholeness.**

whole-heart-ed (hōl′här″tĕd), *adj.* sincere; having one single purpose; energetic; done with earnestness.—*adv.* **whole-heartedly.**—*n.* **whole-heartedness.**

whole-sale (hōl′sāl″), *n.* sale of goods by the piece or in large quantity: opposite to *retail:* **by wholesale,** in large quantities; hence, incautiously or without distinction: *adj.* buying or selling in large quantities; widespread or indiscriminate.

whole-some (hōl′sŭm), *adj.* favorable to health; healthful; as, a *wholesome* diet; denoting health; as, she has a *wholesome* look; sound; mentally or morally beneficial; as, *wholesome* advice.—*adv.* **wholesomely.**—*n.* **wholesomeness.**

whol-ly (hōl′lĭ; hōl′ĭ), *adv.* in a complete manner; entirely; fully; altogether.

whom (hōōm), *pron.* objective case of the interrogative and relative *who.*

whom-so-ev-er (hōōm″sō-ĕv′ẽr), *pron.* the objective case of *whosoever.*

whoop (hōōp), *v.i.* to utter a loud, shrill, and prolonged cry; to shout; to halloo: *v.t.* to drive, call, or mock with loud cries or shouts: *n.* a loud shout, as of pursuit, attack, triumph, excitement, etc.; the hoot of an owl.

whoop-ing cough (hōōp′ĭng kôf), a violent cough, accompanied by a whooping sound: one of the infectious diseases of children.

whop (hwŏp), *v.t.* [*p.t.* and *p.p.* whopped, *p.pr.* whopping], to thrash or beat: *v.i.* to flop down suddenly. [Colloq.]

whop-per (hwŏp′ẽr), *n.* something unusually large; a lie; a daring untruth. [Colloq.]

whore (hōr), *n.* a prostitute; a woman who sells herself: not now used in polite speech.

whorl (hwûrl; hwôrl), *n.* a circular arrangement of leaves, petals, etc., around a common center; one of the turns of a spiral shell.—*adj.* **whorled.**

whor-tle-ber-ry (hwûr′tl-bĕr″ĭ), *n.* a small plant or shrub bearing a small, edible blue fruit; the huckleberry. Also, **hurtleberry.**

whose (hōōz), *pron.* possessive case of interrogative and relative *who* or *which.*

whose-so-ev-er (hōōz″sō-ĕv′ẽr), *pron.* possessive case of *whosoever.*

who-so (hōō′sō), *pron.* any person who; whoever.

who-so-ev-er (hōō″sō-ĕv′ẽr), *pron.* any person who; whoever.

why (hwī), *adv.* for what cause, reason, or purpose; on what account; wherefore; for which; on account of which: *n.* the reason or cause.

wick (wĭk), *n.* the cotton cord, tape, etc., through which oil in a lamp passes, and which is lighted at the top; the cord at the center of a tallow or wax candle, which is lighted at the top.

wick-ed (wĭk′ĕd), *adj.* evil; sinful; immoral; as, a *wicked* world, or a *wicked* heart; in a light or playful sense, mischievous; unrighteous.—*adv.* **wickedly.**—*n.* **wickedness.**

wick-er (wĭk′ẽr), *n.* a pliant twig; a kind of bending willow rod; baskets, etc., made from woven willow twigs: *adj.* made of plaited twigs or willow rods.

wick-er-work (wĭk'ẽr-wûrk"), *n.* plaited or woven baskets, etc., made of pliant willow twigs.

wick-et (wĭk'ĕt), *n.* a small gate or door, especially one in a larger gate or door; the three upright stumps in cricket at which the ball is bowled or pitched; an arch in a croquet set.

wide (wīd), *adj.* stretching for a given space in a direction at right angles to length; extended far each way; broad; vast; far across; containing plenty of space; inclusive of much; distended; far from the point aimed at; as, the arrow flew *wide* of the bull's-eye: *adv.* to a great distance; far apart; aside from the mark.—*adv.* **widely.** —*n.* **wideness.**

wid-en (wīd'n), *v.t.* to make broader; spread open: *v.i.* to become broader or larger; as, the river *widens* toward its mouth.

widg-eon (wĭj'ŭn), *n.* a kind of fresh-water duck.

wid-ow (wĭd'ō), *n.* a woman whose husband has died and who has not remarried: *v.t.* to bereave or deprive of a husband by death.

wid-ow-er (wĭd'ō-ẽr), *n.* a man whose wife has died, and who has not remarried.

wid-ow-hood (wĭd'ō-hŏŏd), *n.* the state of having lost a husband by death; the time during which a woman is a widow.

width (wĭdth), *n.* extent of a thing from side to side; breadth: opposite to *length.*

wield (wēld), *v.t.* to use or employ with the hand; as, to *wield* a hammer; have control of by influence or authority.

wife (wīf), *n.* [*pl.* wives (wīvz)], a woman joined to a man in marriage; a married woman.

wife-hood (wīf'hŏŏd), *n.* the state of being a married woman; the time during which a woman is married.

wife-ly (wīf'lĭ), *adj.* like, or becoming, a married woman; as, *wifely* devotion. Also, **wifelike.**

wig (wĭg), *n.* an artificial arrangement of hair for the head, worn to replace lost natural hair, to change one's appearance, etc.—*adj.* **wigged.**

wig-an (wĭg'ăn), *n.* a kind of cotton canvas, used for stiffening in garments, as coat lapels, etc.

wig-gle (wĭg'l), *v.i.* and *v.t.* to move to and fro, or back and forth, with a quick, jerky motion. [Colloq.]

wig-gler (wĭg'lẽr), *n.* one that moves to and fro, or back and forth, with a quick, jerky motion; the larva, or young, of the mosquito.

wight (wīt), *n.* a human being; as, he was a worthy *wight.*

wig-wag (wĭg'wăg"), *v.t.* and *v.i.* to move to and fro, or back and forth: especially, to signal by means of a flag, or a movable light, changed from one position to another, or flashed, according to a code, as in the army or navy.

wig-wam (wĭg'wŏm; wĭg'wôm), *n.* a cone-shaped hut made of poles covered with bark or skins of animals, used by the eastern American Indians.

wild (wīld), *adj.* living in its natural state; untamed; as, a *wild* animal; uncultivated; as, *wild* flowers; not civilized; savage; as, the *wild* men of Borneo; violent; as, the winds were *wild;* uncontrolled; passionate; as, *wild* youth or anger; unreasonable; as, a *wild* scheme; disorderly; reckless; as, he led a *wild* life; greatly excited; as, *wild* with joy; noisily gay; colloquially, eager; as, I am *wild* to see you: *n.* a desert or wilderness; as, the *wilds* of Africa.—*adv.* **wildly.**—*n.* **wildness.**

wild boar (wīld bōr), an untamed, savage European hog, from which the domestic hog has been developed.

wild cat (wīld kăt), a cat native to Europe and untamed, similar in color to the tame cat, but larger, stronger, and more savage, with a shorter, blunter tail: **wildcat,** *adj.* risky; unsafe; not to be depended on; running without order or control: said of a railroad train.

wilde-beest (wīld'bēst), *n.* a Dutch name for the African antelope or gnu.

wil-der-ness (wĭl'dẽr-nĕs), *n.* a region uncultivated and without human beings; a trackless forest; a desert or waste; also, an unarranged mass so great as to be confusing; as, a *wilderness* of flowers.

wild-fire (wīld'fīr"), *n.* any fire hard to quench or put out; Greek fire; a skin disease of sheep.

wild-goose chase (wīld'gōōs" chās), a chase after something which cannot be obtained; a useless pursuit or attempt.

wild-ing (wīl'dĭng), *n.* an uncultivated or wild plant and its fruit: *adj.* growing in a wild state; untamed or uncultivated.

wile (wīl), *n.* a sly trick; a charming use of craft or cunning; as, she used her feminine *wiles* to gain her end: *v.t.* to lead on by charm; to wheedle; to beguile; to make time pass pleasantly; used for *while.*

wil-ful (wĭl'fŏŏl), *adj.* governed by the will without regard to reason; bent on having one's own way; stubborn; obstinate; as, a *wilful* child; intentional; deliberate; as, *wilful* murder. Also, **willful.**—*adv.* **wilfully, willfully.**—*n.* **wilfulness, willfulness.**

will (wĭl), *n.* the power of the mind by which one chooses or determines; as, if you exert your *will,* you can do it; determination; choice; desire; as, he acted against his *will;* a determination by an authority; hence, a command; as, he did his master's *will;* a legal document disposing of one's property at death: *v. auxiliary* [*p.t.* and *p.p.* would], having no imperative or infinitive, and followed by the infinitive without *to:* used, together with *shall,* to form the simple future tense: thus, to express simple futurity, singular, first person, I *shall;* second person, you *will;* third person, he *will;* plural, first person, we *shall;* second person, you *will;* third person, they *will:* used to express determination in an arrangement exactly the opposite: used in all persons to express willingness: used in a question, in the second and third persons, according to the form expected in the answer; as, *shall* he? *will* you? etc.: often used in commands for the sake of courtesy; as, you *will* take this report to the colonel: *v.t.* [*p.t.* and *p.p.* willed, *p.pr.* willing], to wish or desire; to decide upon; to intend firmly; to determine; to choose; command; direct; bequeath or give at death; as, to *will* property to one's heirs; to influence by exerting the power of determining; as, she *willed* him to turn around; to influence by hypnotic power: *v.i.* to choose or decide; decree; to be willing; to wish.

Syn. n., wish, desire.

will-ing (wĭl'ĭng), *adj.* inclined to do or grant; as, *willing* to do your share; ready to act; prompt to do; as, *willing* hands; given or done freely.—*adv.* **willingly.**—*n.* **willingness.**

will-o'-the-wisp (wĭl'ō-*th*ē wĭsp'), *n.* a dull, glowing light seen in the air over marshy places at night; a corpse candle; a jack-o'-lantern; anything that misleads, or that escapes one's grasp in an attempt to catch it.

wil-low (wĭl'ō), *n.* a tree of several kinds, usually growing near water, having slender limbs and twigs which are easily bent and twisted; the wood of this tree.

wil-low-y (wĭl'ō-ĭ), *adj.* abounding or filled with willow trees; like a willow tree; hence, pliant or bending; flexible; swaying; as, a *willowy* walk; slender and graceful; as, a *willowy* figure.

wil-ly-nil-ly (wĭl'ĭ-nĭl'ĭ), *adv.* whether I will or not; by force of outside influence or authority.

wilt (wĭlt), *v.i.* to wither, as flowers; to droop; to lose strength: *v.t.* to cause to droop or fade; to deprive of strength; the second person singular, grave form, of *will.*

wil-y (wīl'ĭ), *adj.* cunning; crafty; as, the *wily* fox.—*adv.* **wilily.**—*n.* **wiliness.**

wim-ble (wĭm'bl), *n.* a gimlet; an auger; any tool for boring.

wim-ple (wĭm'pl), *n.* a covering of linen, silk, etc., for the neck, chin, and sides of the face, worn by nuns: *v.t.* to clothe or cover with such a covering; to plait; to cause to ripple: *v.i.* to lie in folds.

win (wĭn), *v.i.* [*p.t.* and *p.p.* won, *p.pr.* winning], to gain a victory; to prevail; as, to *win* in a battle; to succeed in reaching a certain place or state; as, to *win* to the other side of the stream: *v.t.* to get by labor; as, to *win* promotion; to obtain: to gain in a contest; as, he *won* the prize; to conquer or prevail in; as, food will *win* the war; to persuade; as, try to *win* him over to our side.—*n.* **winner.**

Syn. get, procure, effect, realize, accomplish, achieve.

Ant. (see lose).

wince (wĭns), *v.i.* to shrink, or draw back, as from a blow, or from pain; to flinch or hesitate: *n.* the act of drawing back from pain or danger.

winch (wĭnch), *n.* a crank with a handle used to start and keep in motion a machine, grindstone, etc.; any of various devices for turning something that requires force, as a kind of windlass. Also, wince.

Win-ches-ter (wĭn'chĕs-tẽr), *n.* a well-known make of repeating rifle of various models and calibers, used for both sporting and military purposes.

wind (wĭnd), *n.* air in motion; a natural current of air; breeze; breath; anything insignificant or light as air; idle words; air filled with a scent; as, the hound got *wind* of the fox; hence, news; as, to get *wind* of a plot; in an orchestra, the brass and wood instruments played with the breath; gas formed in the digestive organs of the body: *v.t.* to allow the air to blow upon; to scent, as hounds in a fox hunt; to put out of breath.

wind (wīnd), *v.t.* [*p.t.* and *p.p.* wound, *p.pr.* winding], to turn round something; as, the vine *winds* around the pillar; twist; to bend in a course; to go a roundabout way: *v.t.* to coil, twist, or twine; to set in motion by turning a crank or screw; as, to *wind* a clock; to entwine; as, to *wind* a garland; to turn, as about something fixed; as, to *wind* a bandage around a limb; to direct or introduce by artful means; as, he *winds* himself into favor; to blow (a horn): *n.* a bend, coil, or twist.

wind-age (wĭn'dāj), *n.* the space between the inside surface of the bore of a gun and the shot or shell loaded in it; the stir of the air caused by a moving shell or bullet; the force of the wind in turning aside a shell or bullet, or the distance it is turned aside; the surface of a ship exposed to the wind.

wind-break (wĭnd'brāk'), *n.* a shelter or protection from the wind.

wind-fall (wĭnd'fôl'), *n.* fruit blown down by the wind; unexpected good fortune.

wind-flow-er (wĭnd'flou'ẽr), *n.* any of various plants of the crowfoot family; the anemone.

wind gauge (wĭnd gāj), a graduated attachment on the rear sight of a rifle, by which allowance may be made in aiming for the effect of the wind upon the bullet, and for drift.

wind-ing sheet (wīn'dĭng shēt), a garment to cover the dead.

wind in-stru-ment (wĭnd ĭn'stro͞o-mĕnt), a musical instrument sounded by wind, especially by the breath, as a horn or mouth organ.

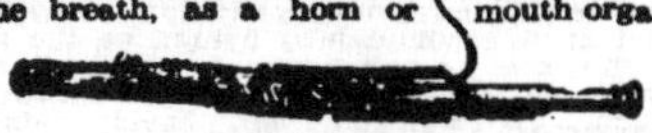

Wind Instrument

wind jam-mer (wĭnd jăm'ẽr), a sailing vessel: originally, a scornful term applied to sailing ships by sailors on newly invented steam vessels.

wind-lass (wĭnd'lăs), *n.* a machine consisting of a horizontal cylinder, or roller, moving on its axis, and used for hoisting weights, by means of a crank which winds up a rope to which the load is fastened.

Windlass

wind-mill (wĭnd'mĭl'), *n.* a mill operated by a wheel whose spokes are fan-shaped sails turned by the wind.

win-dow (wĭn'dō), *n.* an opening in the side of a building to let in light and air; the sash, shutter, or other framework which fills such a space.

wind-pipe (wĭnd'pīp'), *n.* the trachea, or breathing tube leading from the larnyx to the lungs.

wind-row (wĭnd'rō'), *n.* a row of hay raked up in a long ridge to dry before being made into piles; any row for drying, as of sheaves of wheat, etc., before being stacked; dry leaves, dust, etc., swept by the wind into a long ridge on the ground.

wind-up (wīnd'ŭp'), *n.* end of an affair; conclusion; as, the *wind-up* of a meeting; result; final outcome; closing-out; as, the *wind-up* of a business.

wind-ward (wĭnd'wẽrd), *n.* the direction from which the wind blows: opposite to *leeward: adj.* on the side toward the point from which the wind blows: *adv.* toward the wind.

wind-y (wĭn'dĭ), *adj.* [*comp.* windier, *superl.* windiest], pertaining to, like, or consisting of, air in motion; breezy; swept by the wind; stormy; exposed to the wind; colloquially, noisy or boastful.—*n.* windiness.

wine (win), *n.* the fermented juice of grapes; a drink made from the juice of other fruits or plants; as, currant *wine* or dandelion *wine*: *v.t.* and *v.i.* to furnish with wine, or to drink wine; as, to *wine* and dine one's friends or with one's friends.—*adj.* winy.

wine-bib-ber (win'bib"ĕr), *n.* one who is continually drinking wine.

wine-glass (win'glàs"), *n.* a small glass used for wine, or as a measure for medicine.

wine press (win prĕs), a large vessel in which grapes are trodden to press out the juice; a machine for pressing out the juice from grapes.

wine skin (win skin), the skin of an animal made into a bag and used in the Orient as a bottle for wine.

wing (wing), *n.* one of the two upper limbs of a bird, by which it flies; one of the thin appendages of membrane by which an insect flies; any part projecting from the main body of something; as, the *wing* of a house, or the right *wing* of an army; one of the main supporting surfaces of an airplane; passage by means of flying; as, he gave the bird *wing*: *v.t.* to furnish with, or as with, means of flying or moving swiftly; to carry by flying; to accomplish by flying; as, the airship *winged* its way eastward; wound in the wing; as, to *wing* a bird by a shot; *v.i.* to fly.

winged (wingd), *adj.* having wings; flying; swift.

wing-less (wing'lĕs), *adj.* without wings; unable to fly.

wing-tip (wing'tip"), *n.* the outer extremity of the wing of a monoplane, or any movable surface at the end of a wing.

wink (wink), *v.i.* to close and open the eyelid quickly; hint by the motion of the eyelid; to blink; to ignore or pass over; as, to *wink* at a wrong; to flicker or twinkle: *v.t.* to cause to open and shut the eyelids quickly; to accomplish by opening and shutting the eyelids quickly: *n.* the act of opening and shutting the eyelid, especially of one eye; a hint thus given; the time required for one such act; an instant; a gleam or sparkle.

wink-er (wink'ĕr), *n.* one that winks; a blinder for a horse; colloquially, an eyelash.

win-ning (win'ing), *adj.* attractive; charming; as, *winning* manners: *n.* the act of gaining or conquering: *pl.* that which one gains.

win-now (win'ō), *v.t.* to separate and drive the chaff from (grain) by the wind; to fan; to sift or separate; to scatter by wind: *v.i.* to separate chaff from grain by fanning.—*n.* winnower.

win-some (win'sŭm), *adj.* attractive; pretty; cheerful; gay; light-hearted; charming.—*adv.* winsomely.—*n.* winsomeness.

win-ter (win'tĕr), *n.* the cold season of the year when the sun is farthest from the zenith at noon; in the northern hemisphere, the months of December, January and February; cold weather; a period when vitality is low; as, old age is the *winter* of life: *v.i.* to pass the months of the cold season; as, snakes *winter* in the ground: *v.t.* to keep during the cold season: winter quarters, the quarters, or settled station, of an army during the winter.

win-ter-green (win'tĕr-grēn"), *n.* an evergreen plant of the heath family that bears red berries called *checkerberries*, and whose leaves produce oil of wintergreen.

win-ter-kill (win'tĕr-kil"), *v.t.* to kill by exposure to cold weather.

win-try (win'tri), *adj.* of or pertaining to the cold season. Also, wintery.

wipe (wip), *v.t.* to rub or dust the surface of with something soft; dry by rubbing; cleanse: *n.* act of cleansing by rubbing. —*n.* wiper.

Wi-pers (wi'pĕrz), *n.* in the World War, a slang term used by the British troops for Ypres.

wire (wir), *n.* a thread of metal; a telegraph wire or cable; colloquially, a telegram: *pl.* colloquially, unseen forces which can be used to gain an end; as, to pull *wires* to secure promotion: *v.t.* to bind with wire; stiffen with wire; thread on wire; colloquially, to send a message to by telegraph.

wire cut-ter (wir kŭt'ĕr), an implement used for cutting wire and barbed wire entanglements.

wire-draw (wir'drô"), *v.t.* to make into wire; to draw out very long and very fine; as, a *wiredrawn* argument.

wire glass (wir glàs), glass strengthened by a web of iron wire inclosed within it.

wire gauge (wir gāj), an instrument for measuring the diameter of wire, thickness of sheet metal, etc., generally consisting of a metal plate with a series of notches of various widths on its edge.

wire-less (wir'lĕs), *adj.* without the use of wires: used especially of a system of telegraphing, telephoning, etc., by means of electric waves in space without connecting wires.

wire-less te-leg-ra-phy (wir'lĕs tē-lĕg'rȧ-fi), any form of telegraphic communication effected by means of electric waves without the use of connecting wires: especially valuable in military operations, in the transmission of orders from the general commanding, and in sending aircraft information direct to headquarters.

wire-less te-leph-o-ny (wir'lĕs tē-lĕf'ō-ni), telephonic communication without the use of wires.

wire-pull-ing (wir'pōōl"ing), *n.* the act of using secret influence to gain one's ends, especially in politics. [Colloq.]

wire tap-ping (wir tăp'ing), in warfare, the act or plan of making connection with the service wires of the enemy, in order to obtain valuable information; the act of making a secret connection with any message-carrying wire in order to obtain information.

wir-y (wir'i), *adj.* made of, or like, wire; strong and flexible; lean and sinewy; as, a *wiry* horse; slight, but having much endurance.—*n.* wiriness.

wis-dom (wiz'dŭm), *n.* the quality of being wise; knowledge; the power of applying knowledge possessed; learning; skill in affairs; power to judge correctly what is best.

wis-dom tooth (wiz'dŭm tōōth), the name popularly given to the third molar, or extreme back tooth, on each side in each jaw, appearing between the ages of seventeen and twenty-five.

wise (wīz), *adj.* judging correctly from experience; having ability to decide rightly what is best to say or do; discreet; skilful; learned; based on good judgment; as, a *wise* plan: *n.* a way of acting or being; fashion; manner; as, in any *wise*, in no *wise*, etc.—*adv.* wisely.

wise-a-cre (wīz'ā-kẽr), *n.* a would-be wise person; a pretender to learning; hence, a simpleton or dunce.

wish (wĭsh), *v.i.* to have a strong desire: with *for* or an infinitive: *v.t.* to desire or long for; to crave; to express desire for; to desire for someone else; as, to *wish* one good fortune: *n.* strong or eager desire; the object or thing desired; a request.

wish-bone (wĭsh'bōn"), *n.* the forked bone in front of the breastbone in most birds.

wish-ful (wĭsh'fōōl), *adj.* having desire; full of longing; wistful.—*adv.* wishfully.—*n.* wishfulness.

wish-y-wash-y (wĭsh'ĭ-wŏsh"ĭ), *n.* thin and weak: said of liquids; feeble; spineless. [Colloq.]

wisp (wĭsp), *n.* a handful or small bundle, as of straw or hay.

wis-ta-ri-a (wĭs-tā'rĭ-ȧ), *n.* a climbing shrub of the bean family with purple flowers. Also, wisteria.

wist-ful (wĭst'fōōl), *adj.* earnestly thoughtful; pensive; longing; wishful; as, a *wistful* expression of the face.—*adv.* wistfully.—*n.* wistfulness.

wit (wĭt), *n.* mind; sense; knowledge; mental faculty or power; the power of combining ideas or words so as to produce a laughable effect; mental quickness; one who possesses power to make others laugh; a humorist or witty person.
Syn. humor, satire, fun.

witch (wĭch), *n.* a woman supposed to associate with evil spirits and to practice magic; a hag; colloquially, an attractive or fascinating young woman: *v.t.* to bewitch; enchant

witch-craft (wĭch'krăft"), *n.* the practice of magic; magical powers; sorcery; dealings with evil spirits.

witch-er-y (wĭch'ẽr-ĭ), *n.* fascination; compelling charm.

witch-ha-zel (wĭch'hā"zl), *n.* a shrub resembling the hazel and having small yellow flowers which appear after the leaves are dead; a medicinal extract from the bark of this shrub, used for bruises, sprains, etc.

witch-ing (wĭch'ĭng), *adj.* fascinating; weird; magical.

with (wĭth), *prep.* denoting nearness, association, or connection; as, they went *with* us; he had been *with* the firm for years; indicating the instrument of an action; as, he dug *with* a spade; indicating guardianship; as, the child was left *with* me; indicating agreement; as, he went *with* my permission; indicating opposition; as, to fight *with* a German; indicating result; as, he was left *with* no money.

with-al (wĭth-ôl'), *adv.* with the rest; in addition; likewise; moreover; at the same time.

with-draw (wĭth-drô'), *v.t.* to take away or back; to draw back; to recall or take back; as, to *withdraw* a charge in court: *v.i.* to retire; retreat; as, to *withdraw* from a room.

with-draw-al (wĭth-drô'ăl), *n.* the act of taking back; retirement; retreat.

withe (wĭth; wĭth), *n.* a tough, flexible twig, especially of willow, used as a fastening or for binding a fascine, or fagot used for filling ditches, raising batteries, etc.; a band made of twigs twisted together.

with-er (wĭth'ẽr), *v.t.* to cause to fade and become dry; to deprive of freshness; to cause to shrivel or wrinkle: *v.i.* to become sapless; to fade or shrivel.

with-ers (wĭth'ẽrz), *n.pl.* the part of the body lying between the shoulder-blades of the horse.

with-hold (wĭth-hōld'), *v.t.* to hold back or in; to restrain; to keep from action; to refuse to grant; as, to *withhold* consent or approval: *v.i.* to refrain or hold back.

with-in (wĭth-ĭn'), *adv.* in the inner part; inside; inwardly; in the house; indoors: *prep.* inside of; in the interior or inside part of; in the limits or space of; as, *within* an hour.

with-out (wĭth-out'), *adv.* outside; on or at the outside; outwardly; outdoors or out of doors; with the lack of a given thing; as, if you have no money left, you must go *without*: *prep.* outside of; at or on the outside of; beyond; as, *without* the pale; in the absence of; as, *without* companions; lacking; as, *without* hope.

with-stand (wĭth-stănd'), *v.t.* to stand against, especially successfully; to oppose or resist; as, to *withstand* temptation; to endure; as, to *withstand* a siege.

with-y (wĭth'ĭ; wĭth'ĭ), *n.* a kind of willow twig: *adj.* flexible and tough.

wit-less (wĭt'lĕs), *adj.* without understanding; foolish; unwise.

wit-ness (wĭt'nĕs), *n.* the act of declaring personal knowledge of the truth of a stated fact or event; testimony; evidence; one who has personal knowledge that a given thing has taken place; a person who tells in court under oath what he knows of a fact or event; one who puts his signature to a document to show that he has seen it signed: *v.t.* to look on at, so as to have personal knowledge; as, to *witness* a signature; to have direct knowledge of; to testify to; to give evidence of, as in court; to see; as, to *witness* a performance of a play: *v.i.* to testify.

wit-ti-cism (wĭt'ĭ-sĭzm), *n.* a witty remark; a clever saying.

wit-ting-ly (wĭt'ĭng-lĭ), *adv.* with knowledge; intentionally.

wit-ty (wĭt'ĭ), *adj.* [*comp.* wittier, *superl.* wittiest], having the faculty of arousing laughter by a bright or unusual way of expressing ideas; as, a *witty* person; marked by quickness and cleverness; as, *witty* remarks.—*adv.* wittily.—*n.* wittiness.

wiz-ard (wĭz'ẽrd), *n.* one supposed to possess magical powers, usually from the Evil One; a magician; conjurer; sorcerer; wonder worker.—*n.* wizardry.

wiz-en (wĭz'n), *adj.* dried up; shriveled: *v.i.* and *v.t.* to dry up or shrivel. —*adj.* wizened.

woad (wōd), *n.* a plant of the cabbage family yielding a blue dye; also, thedy estuff.

Wo-den (wō'dĕn), *n.* another name for Odin, the chief of the Teutonic gods, from whom Wednesday has its name. Also, Wodan.

woe (wō), *n.* deep sorrow; inconsolable grief; misery.

woe-be-gone (wō'bē-gŏn"), *adj.* overwhelmed with woe; full of sorrow; showing grief; as, a *woebegone* appearance. Also, **woebegone.**

woe-ful (wō'fōōl), *adj.* full of, or expressing, grief; sad; miserable. Also, **woful.**—*adv.* **woefully, wofully.**

wold (wōld), *n.* a plain or open country; a region without forests.

wolf (wōōlf), *n.* [*pl.* wolves (wōōlvz)], a fierce, flesh-eating wild animal of the dog family; hence, a person noted for cruelty.

wolf-hound (wōōlf'hound"), *n.* a large, long-haired dog of a breed formerly used for hunting wolves.

wolf-ish (wōōl'fish), *adj.* like a wolf; very hungry; savage.—*adv.* **wolfishly.**

wolf-ram (wōōl'frăm; wŏl'frăm), *n.* a hard, brittle, white or gray metal used for hardening steel and in the manufacture of electric lamps: called also *tungsten.*

wolfs-bane (wōōlfs'bān"), *n.* a purple-flowered plant of the crow-foot family, which yields a well-known drug called *aconite.*

wol-ver-ene (wōōl"vēr-ēn'), *n.* a small, shaggy mammal of the weasel or marten family: called also the *glutton.* Also, **wolverine.**

wom-an (wōōm'ăn), *n.* [*pl.* women (wĭm'-ĕn)], an adult female human being; womankind.

wom-an-hood (wōōm'ăn-hōōd), *n.* the state of being a woman; feminine character.

wom-an-ish (wōōm'ăn-ĭsh), *adj.* not manly; effeminate or weak; lacking force of character.

wom-an-kind (wōōm'ăn-kīnd"), *n.* adult female human beings collectively.

wom-an-like (wōōm'ăn-līk"), *adj.* womanly, or like a woman.

wom-an-ly (wōōm'ăn-lĭ), *adj.* suitable for a woman; having the noble qualities of feminine character: *adv.* in a manner suitable for a woman.—*n.* **womanliness.**

womb (wōōm), *n.* the uterus; the organ which holds the young of mammals before birth; a hidden place where anything is produced; as, coal comes from the *womb* of the earth.

wom-bat (wŏm'băt), *n.* a burrowing Australian animal resembling a small bear.

won (wŭn), past tense and past participle of the verb *win.*

won-der (wŭn'dẽr), *n.* the state of mind produced by anything new, strange, unexpected, or surprising; astonishment; cause of surprise; marvel; miracle; prodigy: *v.i.* to feel surprise; be astonished at; to feel doubt and curiosity: *v.t.* to be doubtful about; to wish to know.

Syn., *v.* admire, amaze, astonish.

won-der-ful (wŭn'dẽr-fōōl), *adj.* exciting surprise; strange; marvelous; as, a *wonderful* sight.—*adv.* **wonderfully.**

won-der-land (wŭn'dẽr-lănd"), *n.* a land full of strange and surprising things.

won-der-ment (wŭn'dẽr-mĕnt), *n.* surprise and astonishment.

won-drous (wŭn'drŭs), *adv.* wonderfully: *adj.* wonderful. Also, **wondrously.**—*n.* **wondrousness.**

wont (wŭnt), *adj.* used or accustomed; as, she is *wont* to give much to charity: *n.* habit or custom.

won't (wōnt; wŭnt), a contraction of *will not.*

wont-ed (wŭnt'ĕd), *adj.* accustomed; habitual; usual.

woo (wōō), *v.t.* to court; to make love to; to seek earnestly; as, to *woo* success: *v.i.* to go courting.

wood (wōōd), *n.* a thick growth of trees; a grove or forest; the hard part of a tree, beneath the bark; sticks for making a fire; lumber; timber; anything made of timber: *v.t.* to supply with wood; to cover with trees.—*adj.* **wooded.**

wood-bine (wōōd'bīn"), *n.* the common honeysuckle; the Virginia creeper; a climbing vine.

wood-chuck (wōōd'chŭk"), *n.* a coarse-furred, burrowing rodent found in America; a ground hog.

wood-cock (wōōd'kŏk"), *n.* a wild fowl akin to the snipe, plover, etc.

wood-craft (wōōd'krȧft"), *n.* knowledge of the woods, and how to live in them, especially if hunting, trapping, etc.

wood-cut (wōōd'kŭt"), *n.* an engraving on wood; also, a print or proof from such an engraving.

wood-en (wōōd''n), *adj.* made, or consisting, of wood; as, a *wooden* bucket; hence, stiff; awkward; expressionless; as, his face had a *wooden* look.

wood-land (wōōd'lănd; wōōd'lănd"), *n.* land covered with trees; a forest.

wood-man (wōōd'măn), *n.* a forest officer; one who cuts down trees; one who lives in a forest. Also, **woodsman.**

wood-note (wōōd'nōt"), *n.* the native call of a forest bird.

wood nymph (wōōd nĭmf), one of the maiden deities supposed to inhabit the trees; a dryad; a name given to a kind of moth.

wood-peck-er (wōōd'pĕk"ẽr), *n.* a bird that climbs the trunks of trees and taps them to find insects.

Woodpecker

wood pulp (wōōd pŭlp), pulp made from wood and used in making paper.

wood-ruff (wōōd'-rŭf"), *n.* a small sweet-scented herb of the madder family.

wood-screw (wōōd'-skrōō"), *n.* a metal screw for driving into wood.

woods-man (wōōdz'-măn), *n.* one who lives in the woods. Also, **woodman.**

wood wind (wōōd wĭnd), in an orchestra, the wind instruments made of wood, as the flute and oboe.

wood-work (wōōd'wûrk"), *n.* articles or finishings made of wood, as furniture, doors, etc.

wood-work-ing (wōōd'wûrk"ĭng), *adj.* working or shaping things in wood.

wood-y (wōōd'ĭ), *adj.* covered with, or full of, woods; consisting of, composed of, or like, wood.—*n.* **woodiness.**

woo-er (wōō'ẽr), *n.* one who courts or makes love; a suitor.

woof (wōōf), *n.* the weft, or cross-threads in weaving; texture.

wool (wŏŏl), *n.* the soft, fine, curly hair which covers sheep, goats, etc.; anything soft and downy like wool; thick, crispy, curly hair, as of a negro.

wool-en (wŏŏl'ĕn), *adj.* made of wool: *n.* cloth made of wool: *pl.* woolen goods. Also, **woollen.**

wool-gath-er-ing (wŏŏl'găth"ẽr-ĭng), *adj.* given to idle fancies; dreamy; inattentive: *n.* indulgence in idle dreaming.

wool-grow-er (wŏŏl'grō"ẽr), *n.* one who raises sheep for their wool.

wool-ly (wŏŏl'ĭ), *adj.* consisting of, like, or clothed with, wool; as, a *woolly* head.

wool-pack (wŏŏl'păk"), *n.* a bale of wool weighing 240 pounds; a cloth wrapper for such a bale; a rounded cloud seeming to rest on a flat base.

wool-sack (wŏŏl'săk"), *n.* a sack of wool; the Lord Chancellor's seat in the British House of Lords.

wool sta-pler (wŏŏl stā'plẽr), a dealer in, or a sorter of, wool.

word (wûrd), *n.* a group of letters representing one or more sounds and expressing an idea; that which is said or spoken, especially a brief expression; a statement; tidings; information; a message or communication; as, he received *word* to-day; a password; a command: *pl.* talk or discourse; a dispute; as, to have *words;* language; speech; conversation: *v.t.* to put into words; to group words so as to express an idea rightly.—**Word,** the second person of the Trinity; as, the *Word* was made flesh; the Holy Bible.

word-book (wûrd'bŏŏk"), *n.* a vocabulary or dictionary.

word build-ing (wûrd bĭl'dĭng), the formation or composition of words.

word-ing (wûr'dĭng), *n.* the manner in which anything is expressed in words; as, the *wording* of a letter.

word-y (wûr'dĭ), *adj.* full of words; verbose; as, a *wordy* argument.—*adv.* **wordily.**—*n.* **wordiness.**

wore (wōr), past tense of the irregular verb *wear.*

work (wûrk), *n.* physical or mental effort directed to some end or purpose; toil or labor; occupation or employment; a task or duty; something accomplished; as, a *work* of art; motion accomplished again t a force tending to resist it; in physics, the product of the force acting on a body and the distance the body is moved in line with the force: *pl.* structures in civil or mechanical engineering, as bridges, docks, forts, etc.; a shop, factory, etc., where industry is carried on; the moving parts of a machine; as, the *works* of a clock; *v.i.* [*p.t.* and *p.p* worked or wrought (rôt); *p.pr.* working], to put out mental or physical effort for some purpose; to toil or labor; to act or operate; to be occupied in some business or profession; to progress or move, etc., slowly and with difficulty; as, he *worked* up from poverty; to ferment, as wine: *v.t.* to make, fashion, or shape; as, to *work* a pattern in embroidery; to cause; as, to *work* confusion; to manage or operate; as, to *work* a machine; to set or keep in motion; to cause to labor; as, he *worked* his employees hard; to accomplish with effort; as, to *work* out a plan; to excite or provoke; to influence or control.—*n.* **worker.**

Syn., *n.* labor, task, toil.
Ant. (see play).

work-a-day (wûr'kȧ-dā"), *adj.* pertaining to working-days; every day; hence, prosaic or common.

work-bag (wûrk'băg"), *n.* a bag for holding tools or materials for work, especially a bag for needlework.

work-day (wûrk'dā"), *n.* a day for employment, as apart from Sunday, festivals, holidays, etc.

work-house (wûrk'hous"), *n.* a workshop; a poorhouse; a house of correction in which convicts are confined at labor; in England, a building where the able-bodied poor are supported by the public and made to work.

work-ing-day (wûr'kĭng-dā"), *n.* a day for work: *adj.* workaday.

work-ing-man (wûr'kĭng-măn), *n.* [*pl.* workingmen (-mĕn)], a man who works with his hands; an industrial worker; a laboring man; a common laborer.

work-man (wûrk'măn), *n.* [*pl.* workmen (-mĕn)], a man who is employed in productive effort or industry; often, a skilled laborer.

work-man-like (wûrk'măn-līk"), *adj.* and *adv.* befitting a trained or skilled laborer; showing skill in execution; careful and thorough.

work-man-ship (wûrk'măn-shĭp), *n.* manner of execution of work; style of, or skill in, work; the product of labor.

work-room (wûrk'rŏŏm"), *n.* a room in which work is done.

work-shop (wûrk'shŏp"), *n.* a room or building where manufacturing is carried on, or where laborers are employed at a trade.

work-wom-an (wûrk'wŏŏm"ăn), *n.* a woman who is employed at labor with her hands.

world (wûrld), *n.* the earth and its people; the whole system of natural objects; the universe; present or future state of existence; as, this *world* and the next; people generally; public life or society; as, to make your way in the *world;* life as concerned with secular, not religious, matters; as, the *world,* the flesh, and the devil; sphere or domain; a part or sphere of the earth, its people, or their activities; as, the social *world* or the *world* of industry; a planet; a large number or amount; as, it gave me a *world* of pleasure.

world-ling (wûrld'lĭng), *n.* one who is devoted to the pleasures and advantages of the present life.

world-ly (wûrld'lĭ), *adj.* pertaining to, or devoted to, this life and its enjoyment and advantages.—*n.* **worldliness.**

worm (wûrm), *n.* any small, creeping or crawling animal, usually having a soft, naked body; a spiral or wormlike thing, as a screw thread, etc.; any creature that is humble and abased; anything that gnaws or torments the mind; an implement used to take out the charge of a firearm: *pl.* a disease of the intestines, due to the presence of parasitic worms: *v.i.* to work slowly, secretly, and gradually: *v.t.* to accomplish by crooked, slow, and secret means; as, to *worm* one's way into confidence.

worm-eat-en (wûrm'ēt"n), *adj.* eaten, or bored into, by a worm or worms; as, a *worm-eaten* board.

worm-wheel (wûrm'hwēl"), *n.* a wheel used for elevating gears, having teeth formed to fit into the spiral spaces of a screw called a *work,* so that the wheel may be turned by a screw.

worm-wood (wûrm'wo͝od"), *n.* a bitter plant of the aster family, formerly used as a tonic; something bitter; a source of bitterness; as, remorse of conscience is *wormwood* to a man.

worm-y (wûr'mĭ), *adj.* full of worms; earthy; groveling, like a worm.

worn (wōrn), past participle of the irregular verb *wear.*

worn-out (wōrn'out"), *adj.* past repair; spoiled by constant use; exhausted or tired out from exertion.

wor-ried (wûr'ĭd), *p.adj.* harassed; upset in mind; anxious.

wor-ri-ment (wûr'ĭ-mĕnt), *n.* anxiety; trouble; disturbance of mind.

wor-ri-some (wûr'ĭ-sŭm), *adj.* causing anxiety; annoying; disposed to fret.

wor-ry (wûr'ĭ), *v.t.* [*p.t.* and *p.p.* worried, *p.pr.* worrying], to shake, tear, or mangle with the teeth; to trouble with anxiety or care; to vex or annoy; tease; harass: *v.i.* to feel or express undue anxiety; be fretful: *n.* trouble; anxiety; perplexity; disturbance of mind.—*n.* **worrier.**

worse (wûrs), *adj.* comparative of *bad;* bad or ill to a larger extent; more evil or corrupt; less good; more sick; as, the patient is *worse: adv.* in a less good manner or degree: *n.* that which is less good.

wor-ship (wûr'shĭp), *n.* the act of paying reverence, adoration, or homage to God, a god, or a sacred object; as, the *worship* of an idol; reverence; courtesy; excessive admiration; a title of honor used, especially in England, in addressing magistrates: *v.t.* to pay divine honors, or religious service, to; admire excessively; reverence with great respect: *v.i.* to perform acts of homage or adoration, such as religious services.

wor-ship-er (wûr'shĭp-ẽr), *n.* one who pays homage or reverence to a higher power. Also, **worshipper.**

wor-ship-ful (wûr'shĭp-fo͝ol), *adj.* claiming or worthy of respect or honor; esteemed or honorable; a term of respect.—*adv.* **worshipfully.**

worst (wûrst), *adj.* superlative of *bad;* bad or evil in the highest degree; most severe or dangerous: *adv.* in the most evil way possible: *n.* the most evil state; that which is most bad or evil: *v.t.* to get the advantage of in a contest; overthrow; defeat; as, to *worst* an enemy.

wor-sted (wo͝os'tĕd; wo͝or'stĕd), *n.* twisted yarn spun out of wool; also, the cloth made from such yarn; a soft woolen yarn, twisted or untwisted, used in knitting and embroidery: *adj.* made of woolen yarn: (wûrst'ĕd), defeated; beaten; as, *worsted* in a fight.

wort (wûrt), *n.* new ale or beer; a potherb or other plant: used in compounds.

worth (wûrth), *n.* that which makes a thing useful or valuable; hence, value or price; moral value; excellence or virtue; as, a man of sterling *worth: adj.* equal in value to; as, the goods are *worth* five dollars; having estate or wealth to the value of; as, he is *worth* a million; deserving of; meriting; as, these facts are *worth* attention.

worth-less (wûrth'lĕs), *adj.* having no value, virtue, or excellence; morally bad; contemptible; of no use.—*adv.* **worthlessly.**—*n.* **worthlessness.**
Syn. valueless, useless.
Ant. (see valuable).

wor-thy (wûr'thĭ), *adj.* [*comp.* worthier, *superl.* worthiest], having value or excellence; estimable; meriting; fit: *n.* a person of great importance.—*adv.* **worthily.**—*n.* **worthiness.**

would (wo͝od), *p.t.* of the auxiliary verb *will;* used, first, in indirect discourse to express simple futurity or determination from the standpoint of past time, according to the rule for the use of *will* in direct discourse; as, expressing simple futurity, I said he *would* go; he said he *should* go; expressing determination, he said he *would* go; I said he *should* go; used, second, to express a wish; as, I *would* I had acted differently; used, third, to express a usual or customary occurrence; as, last summer we *would* often take long walks; used, fourth, to express what is likely; as, that *would* make trouble.

would-be (wo͝od'bē"), *adj.* pretending, or desirous of being thought to be.

wound (wo͞ond; wound), *n.* a cut; an injury by which the skin is divided; a stab; a hurt; hence, injury or harm to feelings, reputation, etc.: *v.t.* to make a cut or hurt in; to hurt by violence; injure; hurt the feelings of: (wound), *p.t.* and *p.p.* of the verb *wind:* **wound chevron,** a gold chevron, of the same pattern as the war service chevron, worn on the lower half of the right sleeve of all uniform coats, except fatigue coats, by each officer and enlisted man who has received a wound in action with the enemy.

wove (wōv), past tense of the irregular verb *weave.*

wo-ven (wō'vn), past participle of the irregular verb *weave.*

wrack (răk), *n.* shipwreck; seaweed cast ashore; ruin; destruction; a thin, flying cloud; also spelled *rack.*

wraith (rāth), *n.* the ghost of a living person; apparition; spirit.

wran-gle (răṅ'gl), *v.i.* to argue or dispute angrily or noisily: *n.* an angry or noisy dispute; a noisy quarrel.

wran-gler (răṅ'glẽr), *n.* one who disputes or quarrels in a noisy manner; a name given to a man who wins certain mathematical honors at Cambridge University.

wrap (răp), *v.t.* [*p.t.* and *p.p.* wrapped (wrapt), *p.pr.* wrapping], to roll, fold, or wind together; cover by folding or winding; to infold; to do up in a package: *n.* an article of dress to be folded round the person, as a fur, cloak, shawl, etc.: *pl.* outside garments; as, lay off your *wraps.*

wrap-per (răp'ẽr), *n.* one who, or that which, folds or winds; that in which anything is inclosed or folded; a dressing gown.

wrath (răth; răth), *n.* deep, determined, and violent anger; indignation; extreme fury; as, the *wrath* of God.

wrath-ful (răth'fo͝ol; răth'fo͝ol), *adj.* very angry; furious; arising from or expressing great anger.—*adv.* **wrathfully.**

wreak (rēk), *v.t.* to execute, or do, in great anger or fury; to inflict; as, to *wreak* one's anger upon anyone.

wreath (rēth), *n.* [*pl.* wreaths (rēthz)], anything curled or twisted into circular shape; as, a *wreath* of flowers or leaves; a garland.

wreathe (rēth), *v.t.* and *v.i.* to twist into a garland; to entwine or enfold.

wreck (rĕk), *n.* the destruction of a ship which is driven ashore, or on a rock; the ruins of a ship; a railroad accident;

the remains of anything ruined; destruction; ruin; as, he became a *wreck* through drink: *v.t.* to destroy or cast away, as a ship, by violence; to ruin or destroy; as, to *wreck* one's life.

wreck-age (rĕk'ĭj), *n.* the remains of a destroyed ship, train, building, etc.; act of destroying or ruining; state of being destroyed or ruined.

wreck-er (rĕk'ẽr), *n.* one who causes wrecks; as, a train *wrecker;* one who rescues the cargo or passengers from a wrecked vessel; a ship used in such rescue work.

wren (rĕn), *n.* any of several kinds of small singing birds, having short wings, and a short tail that stands up.

wrench (rĕnch), *v.t.* to wring or pull with a twist; to strain or sprain; as, to *wrench* one's ankle: *n.* a violent twist; a sprain; a tool for turning nuts on bolts, etc.; as, a monkey *wrench.*

wrest (rĕst), *v.t.* to twist, wrench, or force by violence; as, they *wrested* victory from defeat; to turn from its natural meaning; pervert: *n.* twist; violence; the act of taking by force; a key used to tune a stringed musical instrument.

wres-tle (rĕs'l), *v.i.* to contend, by grappling with and trying to throw another; to grapple; to struggle; to strive earnestly; as, to *wrestle* with a problem: *n.* the act of one who grapples with and tries to throw another; a struggle.

wres-tler (rĕs'lẽr), *n.* one who, in a physical contest, grapples with and strives to throw an opponent.

wretch (rĕch), *n.* a worthless or miserable person; a degraded creature.

wretch-ed (rĕch'ĕd), *adj.* very miserable; unhappy; sunk in deep misery or woe; worthless; of miserable quality or character.—*adv.* **wretchedly.**—*n.* **wretchedness.**

wrig-gle (rĭg'l), *v.i.* to squirm or twist, like an eel; to be in uneasy motion: *n.* the act of twisting or squirming; a squirming motion.—*n.* **wriggler.**

wright (rīt), *n.* a workman, especially one who works in wood; as, a ship*wright;* wheel*wright,* etc.

wring (rĭng), *v.t.* [*p.t.* and *p.p.* wrung, *p.pr.* wringing], to twist; to turn and strain; compress; as, to *wring* clothes in washing; to extort or get by force; as, to *wring* a confession from a criminal; to give pain to as if by twisting; as, her sad story *wrings* my heart.

wring-er (rĭng'ẽr), *n.* one who, or that which, twists, strains, etc.; especially, a machine for pressing the water out of clothes after washing.

wrin-kle (rĭn'kl), *n.* a small ridge or furrow on a smooth surface; a crease; colloquially, a useful hint or idea or an innovation: *v.t.* to form or cause creases or furrows in or on: *v.i.* to become creased.

wrin-kly (rĭn'klĭ), *adj.* puckered, creased, or rumpled.

wrist (rĭst), *n.* the joint between the hand and the arm; the slender part of the arm nearest the hand.

wrist-band (rĭst'bănd; Colloq. rĭz'bănd), *n.* a band around the wrist, especially the band of a sleeve, as of a shirt.

wrist-let (rĭst'lĕt), *n.* a band worn around the wrist for a protection from cold.

writ (rĭt), *n.* anything written; a written document; an order of a court of justice: Writ, scripture; as, Holy *Writ.*

write (rīt), *v.t.* [*p.t.* wrote, *p.p.* written, *p.pr.* writing], to inscribe or set down with a pen or pencil; as, to *write* one's name; express in words on paper; engrave; produce as an author; as, to *write* a book: *v.i.* to form letters with the pen; to express in words on paper; compose.

writ-er (rīt'ẽr), *n.* one who, or that which, sets down words on paper; as, a type*writer;* a correspondent; an author; a journalist.

Syn. penman.

writhe (rīth), *v.t.* to twist with violence: *v.i.* to contort or change the form of the body; as, to *writhe* with pain.

writ-ing (rīt'ĭng), *n.* the act of forming letters with a pen or pencil, etc.; a composition, manuscript, or book.

wrong (rông), *adj.* amiss; out of order; as, at the *wrong* time; not morally right; false; unjust; not lawful; not according to truth or fact; as, his statement was *wrong;* not fit or suitable; not according to intention or purpose; *adv.* in a manner not right: *n.* that which is not right; an evil or injury: *v.t.* to do evil to; to harm; as, the untrue statements *wrong* the man.—*adv.* **wrongly.**

Syn., n. injustice, injury.

wrong-do-er (rông'dōō"ẽr; rông"dōō'ẽr), *n.* one who does evil; a lawbreaker.

wrong-do-ing (rông'dōō"ĭng), *n.* sin; wickedness; improper conduct.

wrong-ful (rông'fōōl), *adj.* full of evil, injury, or injustice; injurious; unjust; as, a *wrongful* accusation.—*adv.* **wrongfully.**

wrote (rōt), past tense of the irregular verb *write.*

wroth (rôth), *adj.* angry; full of wrath; furious.

wrought (rôt), past tense and past participle of the verb *work;* hence, worked.

wrought i-ron (rôt ī'ûrn), the purest form of iron, made directly from the ore or by purifying cast iron; iron which can be wrought or shaped while heated.

wrung (rŭng), past tense and past participle of the verb *wring.*

wry (rī), *adj.* twisted; turned to one side; as, to make a *wry* face; distorted or changed in meaning, perverted; as, a *wry* statement.—*adv.* **wryly.**—*n.* **wryness.**

wry-neck (rī'nĕk"), *n.* a bird of the woodpecker family, having the habit of writhing or twisting its head and neck; a stiff condition of the neck, due to the position of the body during sleep.

wych-elm (wĭch'ĕlm"), *n.* a kind of elm in northern Europe.

wynd (wīnd), *n.* a Scotch word meaning a lane; an alley, or a small court.

X

xan-the-in (zăn'thē-ĭn), *n.* the soluble yellow coloring matter of yellow flowers. Also, **xantheine.**

xan-thic (zăn'thĭk), *adj.* having, or inclined to, a yellow color.

xan-thin (zăn'thĭn), *n.* the insoluble yellow coloring matter in yellow flowers. Also, **xanthine.**

xan-thous (zăn'thŭs), *adj.* yellow: used of races having brown, flaxen, or red hair and blue eyes, as the Mongolian.

xy-lo-graph (zī'lō-grăf), *n.* an engraving on wood: an impression from such an engraving.

xy-log-ra-phy (zī-lŏg'rā-fĭ), *n.* the art or process of making prints from engraving on wood.—*adj.* **xylographic.**

xy-loid (zī'loid), *adj.* like wood; composed of woody tissue.

xy-loi-din (zī-loi'dĭn), *n.* an explosive compound produced by the action of nitric acid on starch.

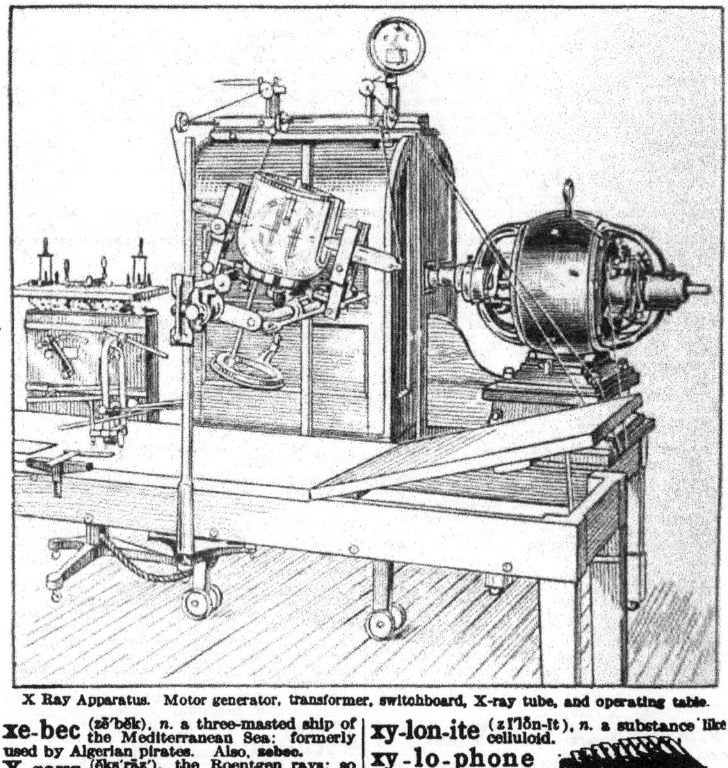

X Ray Apparatus. Motor generator, transformer, switchboard, X-ray tube, and operating table.

xe-bec (zē'bĕk), *n.* a three-masted ship of the Mediterranean Sea: formerly used by Algerian pirates. Also, **zebec.**

X rays (ĕks'rāz'), the Roentgen rays: so called because of their puzzling character, the letter X being used to indicate an unknown quantity.

xy-lene (zī'lēn), *n.* a colorless oily liquid in coal and wood tar.

xy-lo-gen (zī'lō-jĕn), *n.* lignin, the essential part of woody tissue.

xy-lon-ite (zī'lŏn-īt), *n.* a substance like celluloid.

xy-lo-phone (zī'lō-fōn), *n.* a musical instrument made of wooden bars, and played with small wooden hammers.

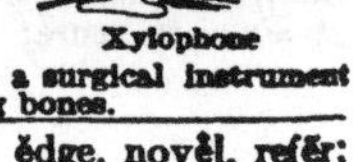

Xylophone

xys-ter (zĭs'tẽr), *n.* a surgical instrument for scraping bones.

Y

yac-ca-wood (yăk'ȧ-wo͝od), *n.* the wood of a tree of Jamaica, used in making furniture.

yacht (yŏt), *n.* a light and quick sailing or steam vessel, larger than a rowboat or motor boat, used for pleasure or racing: *v.i.* to sail or cruise about in a yacht.

Yachts. 1, sloop yacht; 2, steam yacht.

yacht-ing (yŏt'ĭng), *n.* the act of sailing for pleasure in a yacht.

yachts-man (yŏts'măn), *n.* [*pl.* yachtsmen (-mĕn)], one who owns or sails a yacht.

Ya-hoo (yä'ho͞o), *n.* a savage; a degraded, brutelike person: from the race of brutes in Swift's *Gulliver's Travels.*

Yah-weh (yä'wĕ), *n.* a modern translation of the Hebrew word translated *Jehovah* in the Bible. Also, **Jahveh.**

Yak

yak (yăk), *n.* a large, long-haired, wild or tame ox of central Asia.

yam (yăm), *n.* the eatable, potatolike root of a climbing plant of various kinds, used as a food; the sweet potato.

yank (yăṅk), *v.t.* to jerk or pull quickly: *n.* a jerk or twist. [Colloq.]

Yan-kee (yăṅ'kē), *n.* the popular name for New England Americans: used by foreigners for any citizens of the United States: *adj.* pertaining to, or like, citizens of the United States in general or New Englanders in particular. The word is probably a corrupted Indian form of *English.*

yard (yärd), *n.* a measure of length equal to three feet, thirty-six inches, or 0.9144 meter; a long piece of timber attached to the mast of a vessel to support a sail; an inclosed space before or about a house, barn, etc.; an inclosure where a special industry is carried on; as, a lumber *yard*, etc.

yard-arm (yärd'ärm"), *n.* either end of the spar which holds the sail of a square-rigged vessel.

yard-stick (yärd'stĭk"), *n.* a measuring stick three feet in length.

yarn (yärn), *n.* heavy thread spun out of wool; colloquially, an unlikely or exaggerated story, especially a tale of sea life: *v.i.* to tell an unlikely story.

yar-row (yăr'ō), *n.* a plant of the aster family, having a strong odor and bearing small white flowers.

yat-a-ghan (yăt'ȧ-găn), *n.* a curved Turkish dagger. Also, **yatagan.**

Yataghan

yaw (yô), *v.i.* and *v.t.* to steer wildly; to move from the right course: said of a ship or of an airplane: *n.* a changing from a straight course in steering a ship or guiding an airplane.

yawl (yôl), *n.* a ship's small boat; a single masted sailboat.

yawn (yôn), *n.* an involuntary or unintentional opening of the jaws, due to sleepiness; gape: *v.i.* to open the mouth wide involuntarily or unintentionally, through sleepiness; to gape in amazement; to open wide; as, the chasm *yawned* beneath him.

ye (yē), *pron.* grave form of plural of *thou*, second person of the personal pronoun.

yea (yā), *adv.* yes; indeed; truly; not only this, but: *n.* an affirmative vote.

yean-ling (yēn'lĭng), *n.* the young of the sheep or goat.

year (yēr), *n.* the period during which the earth makes one complete revolution or journey round the sun, a period of 365¼ days, or 365 days, 5 hours, 48 minutes, and 45.51 seconds; the calendar year, or a period of 365 days (in leap year 366 days) beginning January 1; colloquially, a very long time.

year-book (yēr'bo͝ok"), *n.* a book published once a year; an annual report or summary of figures.

year-ling (yēr'lĭng), *n.* an animal of one year old: *adj.* one year old.

year-ly (yēr'lĭ), *adj.* happening or coming once a year: *adv.* annually.

yearn (yûrn), *v.i.* to feel an earnest desire; wish with eager longing.
Syn. long, crave.

yeast (yēst), *n.* leaven for bread; an organic substance which causes liquor to ferment, dough to rise, etc.; ferment; froth or foam.

yeast-y (yēs'tĭ), *adj.* tending to ferment or rise; light; frothy.

yegg-man (yĕg'măn), *n.* a burglar, especially one who breaks open and robs safes.

yell (yĕl), *n.* a loud cry; a shriek; a cheer, consisting of rhythmic words or syllables, used by college students: *v.t.* to shout or utter noisily: *v.i.* to utter a sharp cry.
Syn. v. bellow, cry out.

yel-low (yĕl'ō), *adj.* of the color of gold, sulphur, etc.; slang, cowardly or dishonorable; as, the slacker showed his *yellow* streak; colloquially, sensational: said of some newspapers; as, *yellow* journals are not to be depended on: *n.* the third color of the rainbow, between orange and green; any dye or paint that colors things yellow; the yolk of an egg: *v.t.* and *v.i.* to make or become yellow.—*n.* **yellowness.**
Syn. adj. golden, saffronlike.

yel-low bird (yĕl'ō bûrd'), the American goldfinch; the yellow warbler; in England, the golden oriole.

yel-low fe-ver (yĕl'ō fē'vẽr), a dangerous, infectious fever of the tropics, marked by a yellow skin, vomiting, etc., and carried by mosquitoes.

yel-low-ham-mer (yĕl'ō-hăm'ẽr), *n.* a common European finch, the male of which is marked with bright yellow.

yel-low-ish (yĕl'ō-ĭsh), *adj.* somewhat yellow in color.

yel-low jack (yĕl'ō jăk), the yellow fever; the quarantine flag; a West Indian gold- and silver-colored fish, used for food.

yel-low jack-et (yĕl'ō jăk'ĕt), a kind of American wasp, whose body is partly bright yellow.

yelp (yĕlp), *v.i.* to utter a sharp bark, as a dog when hurt: *n.* a sharp, quick bark, as of a dog.—*n.* **yelper, yelping.**

yen (yĕn), *n.* the Japanese unit of coinage; a Japanese coin worth about fifty cents.

yeo-man (yō'măn), *n.* [*pl.* yeomen (-mĕn)], formerly, a retainer of a member of the English nobility; in England, a commoner; a small landowner; one of the farming class; in the navy, a petty officer who does clerical work: **yeoman of the guard,** one of the bodyguard of the English sovereign, consisting of one hundred yeomen, armed with partisans.—*adj.* **yeomanlike.**

yeo-man-ry (yō'măn-rĭ), *n.* yeomen collectively; the common people of England, especially the farming class.

yes (yĕs), *adv.* aye; yea; it is so: opposite to *no.*

yes-ter-day (yĕs'tẽr-dā), *n.* the day just past; recent time: *adv.* on the day last past.

yet (yĕt), *adv.* up until now; as, he has not come *yet;* still: in relation to time; as, I have your present *yet;* in addition or still; as, more important *yet;* finally; even though this is so; as, *yet* I cannot undertake it: *conj.* nevertheless; however; although; though.

yew (yōō), *n.* a large cone-bearing, evergreen tree with dark green foliage; also, its fine-grained wood.

Yid-dish (yĭd'ĭsh), *n.* a kind of mixed German and Hebrew language spoken by Jews.

yield (yēld), *v.t.* to produce; as, the land *yields* wheat; concede; as, I *yield* the point; surrender: *v.i.* to assent; comply; give way; submit; cease opposition; give a return, or produce; to give up a thing claimed; to surrender: *n.* amount returned for labor; product; return.—*n.* **yielder.**

Syn., v. bear, give, afford, relax, forego, waive, accede, succumb.

yield-ing (yēld'ĭng), *adj.* inclined to give way or comply; flexible; compliant; obedient; as, a *yielding* nature: *n.* the act of producing; submission; compliance.—*adv.* **yieldingly.**

Syn., adj. supple, pliant, unresisting.
Ant. (see obstinate).

yo-del (yō'dl), *v.t.* and *v.i.* to sing with sudden changes in the voice: *n.* a song so sung: a form of music common among Swiss shepherds. Also, **yodle.**—*n.* **yodeler, yodler, yodeller.**

yoke (yōk), *n.* a wooden frame to couple oxen together for work; a frame of wood fitted to a person's shoulders for carrying a bucket, etc., hanging from each end; a band or piece of cloth cut to fit the shoulders or hips to support a garment; that which binds or connects; a bond or tie; a mark or sign of slavery; hence, bondage; two animals yoked together; as, a *yoke* of oxen; also, a couple, or a pair that work together: *v.t.* to put a yoke on; as, to *yoke* oxen; to tie together; to couple; to place a yoke upon; hence, to enslave or confine.

Syn., v. couple, link, connect.

yoke-fel-low (yōk'fĕl'ō), *n.* a close companion; an associate in work.

yo-kel (yō'kl), *n.* a plowboy; a rustic; a country fellow.

yolk (yōk; yōlk), *n.* the yellow part of an egg; a greasy substance in sheep's wool.

yon-der (yŏn'dẽr), *adj.* being at a distance within view: *adv.* at that place; there. Also, **yon.**

yore (yōr), *adv.* in old time; long ago: used only in *of yore.*

you (yōō), *pron.* singular and plural, nominative and objective cases, of the pronoun of the second person.

young (yŭng), *adj.* being in the early part of life or growth; inexperienced; vigorous in body, or mind; fresh; strong; pertaining to youth; of youthful appearance: *n.* offspring of animals.—*adj.* **youngish.**

Syn., adj. juvenile, youthful.

young-ling (yŭng'lĭng), *n.* a person in early years; also, a young animal or plant.

young-ster (yŭng'stẽr), *n.* a person in early years; a child or youth; a lad; slang, a subaltern recently assigned to a regiment or corps.

your (yōōr), *pron.* possessive case of the pronoun of the second person. Also, **yours.**

your-self (yōōr-sĕlf'), *pron.* [*pl.* yourselves (-sĕlvz')], you in your own person; an emphasized form for *ye* and *you.*

youth (yōōth), *n.* [*pl.* youths (yōōths)], the state or quality of being in early life; a young person, especially a young man; young people; the part of life between childhood and maturity.

Syn. boy, lad, minority.
Ant. (see age).

youth-ful (yōōth'fōōl), *adj.* pertaining to the early part of life; fresh; vigorous; immature.—*adv.* **youthfully.**—*n.* **youthfulness.**

Syn. young, juvenile, boyish, girlish.
Ant. (see old).

yowl (youl), *n.* a howl: *v.i.* to howl or yell.

yuc-ca (yŭk'ȧ), *n.* a plant of the lily family, having long, pointed leaves, and bearing white blossoms.

Yucca

yule (yōōl), *n.* Christmas or Christmas time; the feast of midwinter, or the "turn" of the sun at the winter solstice.

yule log (yōōl lŏg), a huge log for the Christmas fire.

yule-tide (yōōl'tīd'), *n.* Christmas time; the holiday season.

Z

za-ny (zā'nĭ), *n.* a clown; a buffoon; a simpleton.

zeal (zēl), *n.* ardor in a cause, or in promoting some end; great earnestness; enthusiasm.

zeal-ot (zĕl'ŭt), *n.* an enthusiast; a fanatic; one who goes to extremes in his earnestness for a cause.—*n.* **zealotry.**

zeal-ous (zĕl'ŭs), *adj.* eager in the pursuit of an object; enthusiastic.—*adv.* **zealously.**—*n.* **zealousness.**

Syn. warm, fervent.

Ant. (see careless).

Zebra

ze-bec (zē'bĕk), *n.* a small three-masted ship, still seen in the Mediterranean: formerly used by Algerian pirates. Also, **zebec.**

ze-bra (zē'brȧ), *n.* an African wild animal of the horse family with black stripes on a white or tawny body.

ze-bu (zē'bū), *n.* the Indian ox or cow, with long ears, and a large hump on the shoulders.

Zebu

Zech-a-ri-ah (zĕk'ȧ-rī'ȧ), *n.* a book of the Old Testament containing the message of the Hebrew prophet Zechariah.

zed (zĕd), *n.* the English name for the last letter of the alphabet.

zem-stvo (zĕmst'fō), *n.* a local Russian elective body, managing the administration of local affairs, such as roads, schools, charity, etc.

ze-na-na (zē-nä'nȧ), *n.* in India, the part of the house set apart for the women; a harem. Also, **zanana.**

Zend-A-ves-ta (zĕnd'ȧ-vĕs'tȧ), *n.* the sacred writings of ancient Persia.

zen-dik (zĕn-dĭk'), *n.* in the East, a name for an unbeliever.

ze-nith (zē'nĭth), *n.* the point in the heavens directly overhead: opposite to *nadir;* greatest height; summit.

Zeph-a-ni-ah (zĕf'ȧ-nī'ȧ), a book of the Old Testament containing the teachings of the Hebrew prophet Zephaniah.

zeph-yr (zĕf'ẽr), *n.* the west wind; a soft, gentle breeze; a kind of soft, fine woolen yarn.

Zep-pe-lin (tsĕp'ĕ-lēn'), *n.* a cigar-shaped dirigible balloon, named after its inventor, Count von Zeppelin of Germany, and able to fly long distances and to carry a large weight: used by Germany in bombing raids over England and France during the World War.

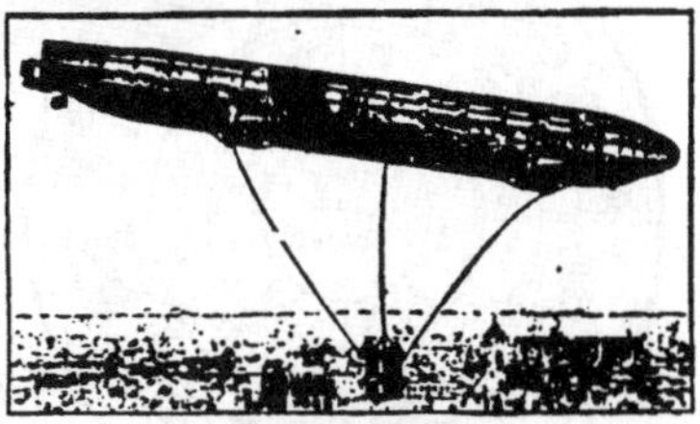

Zeppelin Airship

ze-ro (zē'rō), *n.* [*pl.* **zeros** or **zeroes** (-rōz)], a cipher; nothing; neutral point (°) on a scale, of temperature, etc., from which reckoning begins: **zero hour**, the hour fixed for beginning a military engagement, as an advance, or attack.

zest (zĕst), *n.* a spicy flavor; something that gives a pleasant taste or relish; keen enjoyment; eager enthusiasm; as, he went at his work with *zest.*

Syn. relish, gusto, flavor.

Ant. (see disgust).

zeug-ma (zūg'mȧ), *n.* a figure in grammar by which a verb or adjective agreeing with one noun is made to refer also to another.

Zeus (zūs), *n.* the Greek supreme god, corresponding to the Latin Jupiter.

Zif (zĭf), *n.* the second month of the Jewish church year (part of May-June), and eighth of the civil year.

zig-zag (zĭg'zăg'), *n.* one of a number of short, sharp angles or turns in a course; something with quick turns: *adj.* having short, sharp turns: *adv.* crookedly; with sharp turns.

zinc (zĭnk), *n.* a bluish-white metal, which can stand exposure to air and moisture: *v.t.* to coat or cover with such metal.—*adj.* **zincky, zinky, zincous.**

zin-cog-ra-phy (zĭn-kŏg'rȧ-fĭ), *n.* the art of drawing upon, or printing from, zinc plates.

zinc-oid (zĭnk'oid), *adj.* zinclike; derived from zinc, a bluish-white metal.

Zi-on (zī'ŏn), *n.* a hill in Jerusalem, the royal residence of King David and his successors and the seat of the temple; hence, the Church of God; the new Jerusalem, or heaven.

Zi-on-ism (zī'ŏn-ĭzm), *n.* a plan for the return of the Jews as a nation to Palestine; the belief that they will so return.

Zi-on-ist (zī'ŏn-ĭst), *n.* a member of a society of Jews which seeks to carry out the plan of colonizing their race in Palestine.

zith-er (zĭth'ẽr), *n.* a flat musical instrument with thirty to forty strings. Also, **zithern.**

zo-di-ac (zō'dĭ-ăk), *n.* an imaginary belt or zone in the heavens, containing the paths of the moon and the planets, with the sun's path in the middle, and divided into twelve parts, each represented by a symbol, as the Lion, the Crab, etc.

zo-di-a-cal (zō-dī'ȧ-kăl), *adj.* pertaining to, or situated within, the zodiac, or imaginary belt in the heavens: **zodiacal light**, a cloudy light in the sky, seen in the west after sunset and in the east before dawn

zo-ic (zō'ĭk), *adj.* pertaining to, or connected with, animal life; containing fossils or preserved animals or plants: said of rocks.

Zoll-ver-ein (tsōl'fĕr-īn"), *n.* the German customs union, formed in 1827 and gradually extended, with the aim of establishing uniform rates; any customs union.

zon-al (zōn'ăl), *adj.* pertaining to, or in the form of, a zone or zones.

zone (zōn), *n.* one of the five great belts into which the surface of the earth is divided with regard to climate: including the *torrid zone*, which extends 23° 28′ on each side of the equator; the two *temperate zones*, between the tropics and the polar circles, which are 23° 27′ from the poles; and the two *frigid zones*, between the polar circles and the poles; an area or region distinct from adjoining parts; as, during the World War, Germany established a danger *zone* for submarine warfare; in the United States parcel post system, one of the areas into which the country is divided with regard to rates of postage: **zone fire**, a gun fire whose purpose is to overwhelm a certain area with a storm of high explosive shells.—*adj.* **zoned.**

Zone of a Sphere

zoo (zōō), *n.* a park or other large inclosure in which live animals are kept for public exhibition; a zoölogical garden. [COLLOQ.]

zo-ö-ge-og-ra-phy (zō"ō-jē-ŏg'rȧ-fĭ), *n.* the study or description of the distribution of animals in different parts of the earth; animal geography.—*adj.* **zoögeographic, zoögeographical.**—*n.* **zoögeographer.**

zo-ög-ra-phy (zō-ŏg'rȧ-fĭ), *n.* the description of animals, their forms and habits.—*adj.* **zoögraphic, zoögraphical.**

zo-öl-a-try (zō-ŏl'ȧ-trĭ), *n.* animal worship, as the crocodile worship of Egypt.

zo-ö-log-i-cal (zō"ō-lŏj'ĭ-kăl), *adj.* pertaining to zoölogy, or the science of animal life.—*adv.* **zoölogically.**

zo-öl-o-gist (zō-ŏl'ō-jĭst), *n.* one skilled in the science of animal life.

zo-öl-o-gy (zō-ŏl'ō-jĭ), *n.* the science of animal life.

zoom (zōōm), *n.* the operation of an airplane, so that it flies up and down like a roller-coaster.

zo-ö-phyte (zō'ō-fīt), *n.* an invertebrate animal which has the appearance of a plant, as coral.

zo-öt-o-my (zō-ŏt'ō-mĭ), *n.* the dissection of animals, especially of animals other than man.

Zo-ro-as-tri-an (zō"rō-ăs'trĭ-ăn), *adj.* pertaining to Zoroaster, the reputed founder of the Persian religion, or to his doctrines.

Zo-ro-as-tri-an-ism (zō"rō-ăs'trĭ-ăn-ĭzm), *n.* the ancient religion of Persia, said to have been founded by Zoroaster, the lawmaker and prophet of ancient Persia.

Zou-ave (zōō-äv'), *n.* in the French army until 1914, an infantryman wearing a brightly colored uniform similar to Algerian dress; also, one of a body of soldiers adopting a similar dress and drill.

zounds (zoundz), *interj.* an exclamation expressing anger or wonder: God's wounds! an old oath.

Zu-lu (zōō'lōō), *n.* one of a warlike native tribe of Natal, South Africa.

Zulus

Zu-ñi (zōō'nyē), *n.* one of a tribe of Pueblo Indians of New Mexico.

zwie-back (tsvē'băk"), *n.* a kind of biscuit or roll first baked in a loaf and then cut and toasted.

zy-mol-o-gy (zī-mŏl'ō-jĭ), *n.* the science or study of the principles of fermentation.

zy-mo-sis (zī-mō'sĭs), *n.* a fermentation: any contagious or infectious disease caused by fermentation.

zy-mot-ic (zī-mŏt'ĭk), *adj.* producing fermentation; working through the body like a ferment: said of an infectious or contagious disease.

DICTIONARY OF MYTHOLOGICAL AND CLASSICAL NAMES.

A-cha-tes (ȧ-kā'tēz), the companion of Æneas in Vergil's *Æneid*. [Gr.]

Ach-er-on (ăk'ẽr-ŏn), the "river of woe," one of the five rivers of Hades. It was over this river (or the Styx) that the aged boatman, Charon, ferried the souls of the dead. [Gr.]

A-chil-les (ȧ-kĭl'ēz), the greatest Greek hero of the Trojan War; son of Peleus and Thetis; hero of Homer's *Iliad*; Greek type of youthful strength, beauty, and valor. In anger at Agamemnon for having taken Briseis, he withdrew from combat at the siege of Troy, but soon returned to avenge the death of his friend Patroclus. He was killed by Paris, who treacherously shot him in the heel, his one vulnerable spot.

Ac-tæ-on (ăk-tē'ŏn), a Greek hunter who came upon Artemis (Diana) bathing. In anger, she turned him into a stag. His own hounds killed him.

Ad-me-tus (ăd-mē'tŭs), king of Thessaly, saved from death by Alcestis, his wife, who offered to die in his stead. His old friend, Heracles (Hercules), however, restored her. [Gr.]

A-do-nis (ȧ-dō'nĭs), a beautiful youth beloved by Venus. He was killed by a wild boar. The tears which Venus shed at his death became anemones and his drops of blood became red roses. [Gr.]

Æ-a-cus (ē'ȧ-kŭs), a king of Ægina famous for his justice and piety; grandfather of Achilles. After his death, he was associated with Rhadamanthus and Minos, in judging the spirits of the dead. [Gr.]

Æ-ë-tes (ē-ē'tēz), father of Medea and king of Colchis, where the Golden Fleece was kept. [Gr.]

Æ-gir (ē'jĭr; ā'gĭr), the god of the sea. He entertained the gods every harvest-time and brewed ale for them. Also, **Æger, Egir.** [Teut.]

æ-gis (ē'jĭs), breastplate of Athena (Minerva), bordered with serpents and set with the Gorgon's head. Also, **egis.** [Gr.]

Æ-ne-as (ē-nē'ȧs), a Trojan prince, son of Anchises and the goddess Aphrodite (Venus); the hero of Vergil's poem, the *Æneid*.

Æ-ne-id (ē-nē'ĭd), Vergil's Latin epic poem, of which Æneas is the hero.

Æ-o-lus (ē'ō-lŭs), the Greek god and king of the winds.

Æs-cu-la-pi-us (ĕs'kū-lā'pĭ-ŭs), the Roman god of medicine, and the son of Apollo, killed by Jupiter with a thunderbolt on account of his skill, and particularly for having restored Hippolytus to life: identical with the Greek god Asclepius.

Æ-sir (ē'sĭr; ā'sĭr), the chief Teutonic gods, including: Odin or Woden, Thor or Donar, Tyr or Tiu, Balder, Forseti, Heimdall, Loki, and others. Loki later became leader of the forces of Hel, in conflict with whom most of the Æsir were to be destroyed on the last day (Ragnarok). Associated with these gods were eighteen goddesses (Asynjur). Also, **Asas.**

Æ-son (ē'sŏn), the father of Jason, the Argonaut; restored to youth by Medea, the enchantress. [Gr.]

Ag-a-mem-non (ăg'ȧ-mĕm'nŏn), king of Mycenæ, brother of Menelaus, and commander-in-chief of the Greeks at the siege of Troy.

A-gla-ia (ȧ-glā'yȧ), brilliance, one of the three Graces. [Gr.]

Ag-ni (ăg'nē), the Vedic god of fire: similar to the Greek god Hephæstus (Vulcan). [Hind.]

A-jax (ā'jăks), the son of Telamon, and next to Achilles, the bravest of all the Greeks in the Trojan War.

Al-bi-on (ăl'bĭ-ŏn), a son of Poseidon (Neptune), founder of a kingdom in Britain, slain by Heracles (Hercules). [Gr.]

Al-ces-tis (ăl-sĕs'tĭs), wife of Admetus, king of Thessaly: permitted by the Fates to die in his place, but later restored to life by Hercules. [Gr.]

Al-ci-des (ăl-sī'dēz), Hercules (Heracles): so called because Alcæus was the father of his mother's husband. [Gr.]

A-lec-to (ȧ-lĕk'tō), one of the three Furies (Erinyes). [Gr.]

Al-phe-us (ăl-fē'ŭs), a Greek river god who loved and pursued the wood nymph Arethusa until Artemis (Diana) changed her into a stream; then their waters united in the fountain of Arethusa on the island of Ortygia in Sicily.

Am-a-zons (ăm'ȧ-zŏnz), a warlike race of women from Asia Minor, who helped the Trojans in the Trojan War.

am-bro-si-a (ăm-brō'zhĭ-ȧ; -zĭ-ȧ), the substance which with nectar formed the food and drink of the Greek gods

A-mon (ā'mŏn), the supreme Theban god: identified by the Romans with Jupiter in Jupiter-Amon (Zeus Amon). Also, **Ammon, Amen.** [Egypt.]

Am-phi-on (ăm-fī'ŏn), the son of Zeus (Jupiter) and Antiope; husband of Niobe. He built the walls of Thebes by charming each stone into position with a lyre given him by Hermes (Mercury). [Gr.]

Am-phi-tri-te (ăm'fĭ-trī'tē), a Nereid; the wife of Poseidon (Neptune), and the goddess of the sea. [Gr.]

An-chi-ses (ăn-kī'sēz), the father of Æneas, whom Æneas carried on his shoulders from the burning city of Troy. [Gr.]

An-drom-a-che (ăn-drŏm'ȧ-kē), the loving and beloved wife of Hector. At his death she was carried off and married by Neoptolemus, son of Achilles. Later she became the wife of Helenus, a brother of Hector. [Gr.]

An-drom-e-da (ăn-drŏm'ē-dȧ), a daughter of Cepheus and Cassiopeia, rulers of Ethiopia in Africa; exposed to a sea monster that she might save her country from destruction; rescued and married by Perseus. [Gr.]

An-dva-ri (än'dwä-rē), the dwarf whom Loki robbed of his treasure and of his cursed magic ring. [Teut.]

An-tæ-us (ăn-tē'ŭs), a Libyan giant, invincible as long as he touched the earth, his mother. Heracles (Hercules) lifted him from the ground and then choked him to death. Also, **Antaios.**

An-tig-o-ne (ăn-tĭg'ō-nē), a faithful daughter of Œdipus and Jocasta of Thebes. In defiance of her uncle, Creon, she performed the funeral rites over the body of her brother, Polynices. [Gr.]

An-ti-o-pe (ăn-tī'ō-pē), a Theban princess, who narrowly escaped death at the hands of her own sons, Amphion and Zethus. They fortunately discovered her identity in time, and fastened in her place Dirce, her persecutor, to the horns of the wild bull. [Gr.]

A-nu-bis (ȧ-nū'bĭs), a jackal god of Egypt, who conducted the spirits of the dead to the judgment hall.

Aph-ro-di-te (ăf'rō-dī'tē), the Greek goddess of love: identified with the Roman Venus.

A-pis (ā'pĭs), the sacred white bull of the Egyptians, supposed to embody the god Ptah. He was treated like a god both in life and in death.

A-pol-lo (ȧ-pŏl'ō), the son of Zeus (Jupiter) and Leto (Latona); the god of the sun, music, poetry, eloquence, medicine, and the fine arts. Also, **Helios.** [Gr.]

A-rach-ne (ȧ-răk'nē), a Lydian maiden, turned into a spider for competing with Athena (Minerva) at weaving.

A-res (ā'rēz), the Greek god of war; son of Zeus and Hera: identified by the Romans with Mars.

Ar-e-thu-sa (ăr'ē-thū'sȧ), a Greek wood nymph, beloved of the river god Alpheus. To escape him, she was changed by Artemis (Diana) into a stream and emerged as a fountain in Sicily; here Alpheus joined her.

Ar-go (är'gō), the ship which carried the Argonauts in search of the Golden Fleece. [Gr.]

Ar-go-nauts (är'gō-nôts), the Greek heroes who sailed with Jason in the *Argo*.

Ar-gus (är'gŭs), the hundred-eyed son of Zeus (Jupiter) and Niobe; founder of Argos. After his murder by Hermes (Mercury), Hera (Juno) placed his eyes in the tail of the peacock. [Gr.]

Ar-i-ad-ne (ăr'ĭ-ăd'nē), the daughter of King Minos of Crete. She loved Theseus and gave him the thread to guide him out of the Labyrinth. Later she was deserted by Theseus and married to Dionysus (Bacchus). [Gr.]

A-ri-on (ȧ-rī'ŏn), a Greek poet and musician from Lesbos, who was once robbed by sailors and thrown overboard. He was immediately saved and carried to shore by a dolphin, which his music had drawn to the ship.

Ar-te-mis (är'tē-mĭs), the Greek virgin goddess of wild nature, the moon, maidenhood; twin sister of Apollo: identified by the Romans with Diana.

A-sas (ā'säs), the twelve gods who with Odin lived in Asgard. They were distinguished from the Vans (Vanir). [Teut.]

As-ca-ni-us (ăs-kā'nĭ-ŭs), the son and companion of Æneas on his wanderings after the fall of Troy; founder of Alba Longa and supposed ancestor of Julius Cæsar. Also, **Iulus.** [Gr.]

As-gard (ăs'gärd), the residence of the Teutonic gods (Æsir, Asas). Also, **Asgardhr.**

Ask (ăsk), the first man, created by Odin, Hœnir, and Loki from an ash tree. Also, **Askr.** [Teut.]

As-ty-a-nax (ăs-tī'ȧ-năks), the infant son of Hector, dashed by the Greeks from the walls of Troy. [Gr.]

At-a-lan-ta (ăt'ȧ-lăn'tȧ), a beautiful Greek heroine, beloved of Meleager, who took part in the Calydonian boar hunt and in the Argonautic Expedition. In another legend she challenged her suitors to a race, offering death to the vanquished, her hand to the victor. All lost save Hippomenes, who threw down on the course three golden apples, which Atalanta stooped to pick up.

A-the-na (ȧ-thē'nȧ), the Greek goddess of wisdom: identified by the Romans with Minerva. Also, **Athene, Pallas Athena.**

At-las (ăt'lăs), in Homer, a deity in charge of the pillars of heaven; later a Titan who supported the heavens on his shoulders, or a king changed to a mountain. [Gr.]

At-li (ăt'lē), king of Hunland. He treacherously slew his wife Gudrun's brothers to get the treasure left them by Sigurd. In revenge, Gudrun slew her own and Atli's children. [Teut.]

At-ro-pos (ăt'rō-pŏs), one of the three Fates; she cut off the thread of life after Clotho had spun it, and Lachesis had measured it off. [Gr.]

Au-dhum-la (ou'thŏŏm-lä), the cow whose milk fed the giant Ymir. [Teut.]

Au-ge-an (ô-jē'ăn), of Augeas, king of Elis, whose enormous stables containing 3,000 oxen remained uncleaned for thirty years. Hercules cleaned them in a day by turning two rivers, the Alpheus and the Peneus, through them. [Gr.]

Au-ro-ra (ô-rō'rȧ), the Greek goddess of the morning: identified by the Greeks with Eos. Also, **Mater Matuta.**

A-ver-nus (ȧ-vûr'nŭs), a lake in Italy, through which one entered the infernal regions.

bac-chante (bȧ-kănt'; băk'ănt; bȧ-kăn'tē), a woman follower of Dionysus (Bacchus). [Gr.]

Bac-chus (băk'ŭs), the son of Jupiter (Zeus) and Semele, and the god of wine and drunkards: identified by the Greeks with Dionysus. Also, **Liber.**

Bal-der (bôl'dēr), the god of the summer sunlight, peace, of the good, beautiful, eloquent, and wise; the son of Odin and Frigg. He was slain by Hödr (Hoder) who was instigated by Loki. His dwelling was Breidablik. [Teut.]

Bast (băst), a lion- or cat-headed Egyptian goddess; the "lady of life." Also, **Pacht, Pakht, Pasht.**

Bau-cis (bô'sĭs), an aged Phrygian woman who with her devoted husband Philemon entertained Zeus (Jupiter) and Hermes (Mercury) unawares. As a reward, when their inhospitable country was destroyed by a flood, their house was changed into a temple; here they served as priest and priestess. At death, they were changed at the same moment into trees. [Gr.]

Bel-ler-o-phon (bē-lĕr'ō-fŏn), a Greek hero, who killed the monster Chimera with the aid of his winged horse Pegasus.

Bel-lo-na (bē-lō'nȧ), the Roman goddess of war, closely associated with Mars (Ares).

Principal Mythological Characters. 1, Achilles; 2, Ammon; 3, Amphitrite; 4, Anubis; 5, Apollo (Belvidere); 6, Arion; 7, Atlantis; 8, Atropos; 9, Bacchus; 10, Castor and Pollux; 11, Clio; 12, Euterpe; 13, Ganymede; 14, Hercules; 15, Hermes; 16, Horus; 17, Iris; 18, Jupiter; 19, Laocoön; 20, Mars and Venus; 21, Minerva; 22, Minotaur; 23, Neptune; 24, Nereid; 25, Proserpine.

Be-lus (bē'lŭs), the son of Poseidon (Neptune) and Libya; an early king of Babylon or Assyria; ancestor of many Greek heroes.

Bif-rost (bĭf'rŏst), the rainbow bridge between Asgard, the home of the Teutonic gods, and the world below.

Bo-re-as (bō'rē-ăs), the North Wind; son of Æolus and Eos (Aurora); brother of Hesperus, Zephyrus, and Notus. [Gr.]

Bra-gi (brä'gē), the Teutonic god of poetry and eloquence. Also, **Brage.**

Bri-a-re-us (brī-ā'rē-ŭs), a Greek hundred-handed giant.

Bri-se-is (brī-sē'ĭs), a beautiful girl, captured by Achilles in the Trojan War, whom Agamemnon took to replace Chryseis. [Gr.]

Bryn-hild (brün'hĭlt), a Valkyrie, whom Sigurd found asleep in an enchanted castle and waked. When he became untrue and married Gudrun, Brynhild procured his murder and killed herself. [Teut.]

Bu-ri (bōō'rē), a being licked out of salty frost stones by the cow Audhumla; the ancestor of the Teutonic gods.

Bu-si-ris (bū-sī'rĭs), an Egyptian king, who sacrificed strangers to end a famine; killed by Heracles (Hercules).

Bu-to (bū'tō), the Egyptian goddess of the North; nurse of Horus and Bast; identified by the Greeks with Leto (Latona).

Ca-cus (kā'kŭs), a crafty Italian giant, slain by Hercules (Heracles) for stealing the cattle of Geryon. [Rom.]

Cad-mus (kăd'mŭs), son of Agenor, king of Phœnicia, who killed a dragon and sowed its teeth. From these grew soldiers, who fought together until only five were left. These helped Cadmus to found Thebes.

ca-du-ce-us (kȧ-dū'sē-ŭs), the winged staff of Hermes (Mercury), entwined with two serpents. [Gr.]

Cal-chas (kăl'kăs), the wisest prophet among the Greeks at Troy, surpassed only by Mopsus at Claros.

Cal-li-o-pe (kȧ-lī'ō-pē), the Muse of eloquence and epic poetry. [Gr.]

Cal-lis-to (kȧ-lĭs'tō), an Arcadian nymph, attendant of Artemis (Diana), beloved of Zeus (Jupiter); therefore changed into a bear by Hera (Juno). She narrowly escaped being hunted to death by her own son, but was then, with him, placed in the sky as the Great and Little Bear.

Cal-y-do-ni-an Hunt (kăl'ĭ-dō'nĭ-ăn hŭnt), the pursuit of a destructive wild boar sent by Artemis (Diana) to punish King Œneus for neglected sacrifices. The boar was killed by the hero Meleager, who gave the spoils to Atalanta. [Gr.]

Ca-lyp-so (kȧ-lĭp'sō), a sea nymph, who kept Odysseus (Ulysses) seven years on her island of Ogygia. [Gr.]

Ca-mil-la (kȧ-mĭl'ȧ), the swift-footed maiden queen of the Volsci, an Italian tribe, who opposed Æneas on his landing in Italy. [Rom.]

Cap-a-neus (kăp'ȧ-nūs; kȧ-pā'nē-ŭs), one of the seven Greek heroes who marched against Thebes to help Polynices gain the throne. As he was scaling the walls, he was struck by lightning and killed.

Cas-san-dra (kȧ-săn'drȧ), a daughter of Priam and Hecuba of Troy; inspired by Apollo to prophesy, but later condemned never to be believed. [Gr.]

Cas-tor (kăs'tẽr), a son of Zeus (Jupiter) and Leda; champion horse-tamer. At his death in the Argonautic Expedition, his immortal twin brother Pollux also asked for death. His father decreed that the brothers should live in the upper and lower world on alternate days. Later, they were placed in the sky as the constellation Gemini. [Gr.]

Ce-crops (sē'krŏps), a Greek hero, represented as half snake; first king of Attica; founder of Athens.

cen-taurs (sĕn'tôrz), a mythical Thessalian tribe, half man and half horse. [Gr.]

Ceph-a-lus (sĕf'ȧ-lŭs), a Greek hunter, whose devotion to his wife Procris (Procne) was so determined, that Eos (Aurora), who sought his love, caused him accidentally to kill Procris with his unerring javelin.

Cer-ber-us (sûr'bẽr-ŭs), the three-headed dog of Hades, which guarded the gates to the lower world; carried away by Heracles (Hercules). [Gr.]

Ce-res (sē'rēz), daughter of Saturn (Cronos) and Ops (Rhea); Roman goddess of the growing vegetation; later of corn, harvest, and flowers; identified with the Greek goddess Demeter.

Cha-ron (kā'rŏn), the boatman who ferried souls across the Acheron (or the Styx) in the lower world. A coin for his fare was always placed in the mouth of a dead man. [Gr.]

Char-i-tes (kăr'ĭ-tēz), the three Greek Graces, goddesses of grace and beauty.

Cha-ryb-dis (kȧ-rĭb'dĭs), a very dangerous whirlpool on the Sicilian coast opposite Scylla, a rock on the Italian shore.

chi-me-ra (kĭ-mē'rȧ; kī-mē'rȧ), a fire-breathing monster with the head of a lion, the body of a goat, the tail of a dragon; killed by Bellerophon. Also, **chimæra.** [Gr.]

Chi-ron (kī'rŏn), a Greek centaur, son of Cronos (Saturn) and Philyra; teacher of Achilles, Asclepius (Æsculapius), and Heracles (Hercules).

Chry-se-is (krī-sē'ĭs), a beautiful captive in the Trojan War, whom Agamemnon was forced to restore to her father, Chryses; to replace her, he took Briseis from Achilles. [Gr.]

Cir-ce (sûr'sē), the noted enchantress of Ææa, who changed some of the companions of Odysseus (Ulysses) into animals. Odysseus, protected by an herb, the gift of Hermes (Mercury), secured their restoration. [Gr.]

Cli-o (klī'ō), the Muse who presided over history. [Gr.]

Clo-tho (klō'thō), the youngest of the three Fates, who spun the thread of life. [Gr.]

Cly-tem-nes-tra (klī'tĕm-nĕs'trȧ), the faithless wife of Agamemnon, who murdered him upon his return from the Trojan War; killed for her crime by her son Orestes. Also, **Clytæmnestra.** [Gr.]

Co-cy-tus (kō-sī'tŭs), the "river of wailing"; one of the five rivers of Hades. [Gr.]

Col-chis (kŏl'kĭs), the country east of the Black Sea, where the Golden Fleece was kept; the home of Medea. [Gr.]

Co-mus (kō'mŭs), the youthful Roman god of revelry, feasting, and jollity.

Cor-y-ban-tes (kŏr'ĭ-băn'tēz), attendants and priests of Cybele in Phrygia: often identified with the Curetes, Dactyli, and Telchines. Also, **Corybants.** [Gr.]

Cre-u-sa (krē-ū'sȧ), a daughter of Priam; first wife of Æneas; separated from her husband and lost during the flight from Troy on the night of its capture.

Cro-cus (krō'kŭs), the beloved friend of the nymph Smilax; changed into the crocus flower. [Gr.]

Crœ-sus (krē'sŭs), a very wealthy king of Lydia in Asia Minor of the sixth century B. C.

Cro-nus (krō'nŭs), a Greek Titan; father of Zeus (Jupiter), Poseidon (Neptune), and Hades (Pluto).

Cu-mæ (kū'mē), an ancient Italian city near Naples; the home of the Sibyl who helped Æneas and sold the Sibylline Books to King Tarquin of Rome.

Cu-pid (kū'pĭd), the Roman god of love: identified with the Greek god Eros. Also, **Amor.**

Cyb-e-le (sĭb'ē-lē), a nature goddess introduced into the West from Asia Minor: identified with the Greek goddess Rhea and with the Roman goddess Ops. Also, **Mater Turrita.**

Cy-clo-pes (sī-klō'pēz), one-eyed Sicilian shepherd giants, who may also have worked at the forges of Hephæstus (Vulcan) under Mt. Etna.

Cyn-thi-a (sĭn'thĭ-ȧ), a name given to the hunting goddess Artemis (Diana), because she was born on Mt. Cynthus, on the island Delos. [Gr.]

Cyth-er-e-a (sĭth'ẽr-ē'ȧ), a name given to Aphrodite (Venus), because she rose from the sea-foam on the island of Cythera. [Gr.]

Dæd-a-lus (dĕd'ȧ-lŭs; dē'dȧ-lŭs), an Athenian artist, artificer, and architect; inventor of the saw, ax, gimlet; exiled for murder to Crete, where he built the Labyrinth. Later, he and his son Icarus were forced to escape by flight on wings. Dædalus reached Sicily; the son flew too near the sun, the wax melted and he was drowned in the sea named Icarian for him.

Da-na-e (dăn'ȧ-ē), a Greek princess of Argos; mother of Perseus by Zeus (Jupiter), who visited her in the form of a golden shower.

Da-na-i-des (dȧ-nā'ĭ-dēz), the fifty daughters of King Danaüs of Argos, all of whom, except Hypermnestra, killed their husbands on their wedding night. They were doomed in Tartarus to pour water into a broken cistern, or, as some say, to draw it with a sieve. [Gr.]

Daph-ne (dăf'nē), the lovely daughter of the river god Peneus, beloved by Apollo; to escape him, she was changed into a laurel tree. [Gr.]

De-ia-ni-ra (dē'yȧ-nī'rȧ), the deserted wife of Heracles (Hercules), whose death she unwittingly caused by a poisoned magic shirt, the gift of Nessus; in despair she killed herself. [Gr.]

Del-phi (dĕl'fī), a sacred city of Greece, famous for a cleft in the rock, out of which came poisonous vapors. These overpowered a priestess of Apollo seated there on a golden tripod, so that she uttered wild words, interpreted as the will of Apollo.

De-me-ter (dē-mē'tẽr), the Greek goddess of agriculture and fruitfulness: identified with the Roman goddess Ceres.

Deu-ca-li-on (dū-kā'lĭ-ŏn), the son of Prometheus; like Noah, he with his wife Pyrrha was saved from the great flood. They repeopled the world by throwing stones behind them, as directed by the oracle. [Gr.]

Di-an-a (dī-ăn'ȧ; dī-ā'nȧ), the daughter of Jupiter (Zeus) and Latona (Leto); the Roman goddess of the moon and chase: identified with the Greek goddess Artemis. Also, **Cynthia, Phœbe, Selene.**

Di-do (dī'dō), a Tyrian princess, founder and queen of Carthage in Africa; a cordial hostess of Æneas on his wanderings from Troy. After his desertion of her by divine command, she killed herself.

Di-o-med (dī'ō-mĕd), a brave Greek warrior in the Trojan War. The opponent of Hector and Æneas; joined Odysseus (Ulysses) in carrying off the horses of Rhesus and the Palladium. Also, **Diomedes.**

Di-o-ny-sus (dī'ō-nī'sŭs), the Greek god of vegetation and wine; known commonly among the Romans as Bacchus (Liber).

Di-os-cu-ri (dī'ŏs-kū'rī), the twin sons of Zeus (Jupiter): Castor and Pollux; patrons of warriors and travelers; in Rome, of the order of knights and of chariot races. Also, **Dioscuroi.**

Dir-ce (dûr'sē), a wicked queen of Thebes, whom the sons of unfortunate Antiope fastened to a wild bull. [Gr.]

Dis-cor-di-a (dĭs-kôr'dĭ-ȧ), the Roman goddess of strife and disagreement: identified with the Greek goddess Eris.

Do-do-na (dō-dō'nȧ), an ancient Greek oracle of Zeus (Jupiter), where priests interpreted the rustling of the oak leaves.

dry-a-des (drī'ȧ-dēz), [*sing.* dryad], Greek nymphs who lived and died with the trees which were their abode.

Dyaus (dyous), in Vedic mythology, Heaven, the father of the gods. [Hind.]

Ech-o (ĕk'ō), a Greek nymph, who pined away for unrequited love of Narcissus, until only her voice was left.

Ed-das (ĕd'ȧz), two old Norse books: (*a*) The Elder Edda, a collection of thirty-three mythological songs from the 10th to 13th centuries. (*b*) The Younger Edda, a prose mythology from about 1200.

E-lec-tra (ē-lĕk'trȧ), a daughter of Agamemnon, who induced her brother Orestes to avenge their father's murder by their mother. [Gr.]

elves (ĕlvz), [*sing.* elf], fairies of light and of darkness. The god Frey was the king of the light fairies; Alfheim, their home. [Teut.]

E-ly-si-um (ē-lĭzh'ĭ-ŭm; ē-lĭz'ĭ-ŭm), the eternal dwelling place of the happy souls after death. Also, **Elysian Fields.** [Gr.]

Em-bla (ĕm'blȧ), the first woman, created by Odin, Hoenir, and Loki from an elm. [Teut.]

En-cel-a-dus (ĕn-sĕl'ȧ-dŭs), a Greek hundred-armed giant buried under Mt. Etna.

En-dym-i-on (ĕn-dĭm'ĭ-ŏn), a beautiful youth beloved by the moon goddess Selene (Diana), who caressed him nightly with her moonbeams. [GR.]

E-os (ē'ŏs), the Greek goddess of dawn: identified with the Roman goddess Aurora.

E-pe-us (ē-pē'ŭs), the Greek who built the wooden horse left as a decoy outside the walls of Troy.

Ep-i-me-theus (ĕp''ĭ-mē'thūs; ĕp''ĭ-mē'thē-ŭs), brother of Prometheus and husband of Pandora, the first woman. [GR.]

Er-a-to (ĕr'ȧ-tō), the Muse of lyric and love poetry. [GR.]

Er-e-bus (ĕr'ē-bŭs), the dark space through which spirits pass into Hades. [GR.]

E-rin-y-es (ē-rĭn'ĭ-ēz), the Greek Furies: Alecto, Tisiphone, and Megæra, who relentlessly pursued with secret stings unpunished criminals: called by the Romans *Diræ, Furiæ*. Also, **Semnæ, Eumenides, Erinnyes.**

E-ris (ē'rĭs; ĕr'ĭs), the Greek goddess of discord. At the wedding of Peleus and Thetis, she threw among the guests a golden apple, inscribed "For the fairest." The decision was left to Paris, the shepherd son of Priam of Troy. To gain his favor, Hera (Juno) offered him power and riches; Athena (Minerva), martial glory; but when Aphrodite (Venus) promised the most beautiful woman in the world, Paris awarded her the prize. The elopement of Paris and Helen was the result. Identified with the Roman goddess Discordia.

E-ros (ē'rŏs), the Greek god of love; son of Aphrodite (Venus): identified with the Roman god Cupid.

Er-y-man-thus (ĕr''ĭ-măn'thŭs), a mountain in Arcadia, where the devastating boar killed by Heracles (Hercules) lived. [GR.]

E-te-o-cles (ē-tē'ō-klēz), a king of Thebes, son of Œdipus and Jocasta. He and his brother Polynices were to reign in alternate years, but Eteocles broke the agreement and provoked the expedition of the Seven against Thebes; here the brothers killed each other. [GR.]

Eu-men-i-des (ū-mĕn'ĭ-dēz), the "gracious goddesses," a flattering name for the avenging Furies. [GR.]

Eu-phros-y-ne (ū-frŏs'ĭ-nē), joy, one of the three Greek Graces.

Eu-ro-pa (ū-rō'pȧ), a Phœnician princess, loved by Zeus (Jupiter) in the form of a white bull. On his back she rode to Crete, where she became the mother of Minos, Rhadamanthus, and Sarpedon.

Eu-ryd-i-ce (ū-rĭd'ĭ-sē), beloved wife of Orpheus, the Greek poet and musician. Killed by a poisonous snake bite, she was in Hades only until Orpheus could by his persuasive strains gain permission to lead her out. When almost in the upper world, Orpheus looked back at her, against the divine command, and Eurydice vanished forever.

Eu-ter-pe (ū-tûr'pē), the Muse of music. [GR.]

Faf-nir (fäv'nĕr), a Teutonic giant who, in the form of a dragon, guarded a golden treasure, until killed by Sigurd.

Fa-ma (fā'mȧ), the Roman goddess of rumor and slander.

Fates (fāts), the three Greek goddesses who determined the course of each life. Clotho held the distaff, Lachesis measured the thread of life, Atropos cut it off: identified by the Romans with the Parcæ. Also, **Mœræ.**

fau-ni (fô'nī), [*sing.* faun], rural deities with the legs, feet, and ears of a goat. [GR.]

Fen-rir (fĕn'rĕr), a monster wolf, son of Loki; bound by the Æsir and thrown into Niflheim; at Ragnarok, to be loosed for the final combat. Also, **Fenris-wolf.** [TEUT.]

Flo-ra (flō'rȧ), the Roman goddess of flowers and gardens.

For-set-i (fŏr-sĕt'ē), the Teutonic god of justice; son of Balder and Nanna.

Frey (frā), the Teutonic god of rain, sunshine, and fruits. Also, **Freyr.**

Frey-a (frā'ȧ), the Teutonic goddess of love and beauty, presiding also over the regions of the dead; daughter of Njorth; wife of Odur. Also, **Freyja.**

Frigg (frĭg), queen of the Teutonic gods; wife of Odin; mother of Balder and other gods. With Odin her court was in Hlithskjalf. Similar to the Greek Hera and the Roman Juno. Also, **Frigga.**

Fu-ries (fū'rĭz), the three Greek goddesses of vengeance: Alecto, Tisiphone, Megæra: identified with the Roman Furiæ, Diræ. Also, **Erinyes, Erinnyes, Semnæ, Eumenides.**

Gæ-a (jē'ȧ), the Greek goddess Earth: identified by the Romans with Terra, Tellus. Also, **Gaia, Ge.**

Gal-a-te-a (găl''ȧ-tē'ȧ), a sea nymph beloved by Polyphemus, a Cyclops, the jealous murderer of her preferred lover Acis. An ivory statue of a maiden, the work of Pygmalion, a king of Cyprus. In answer to his prayer, Aphrodite (Venus) made her to live that he might make her his wife. [GR.]

Gan-y-mede (găn'ĭ-mēd), a handsome Trojan lad carried off by Zeus (Jupiter) in the form of an eagle, to be his cupbearer.

Gerth (gĕrth), a beautiful young Teutonic giantess, whose union with Frey probably symbolized the new life of spring. Also, **Gerthr, Gerd, Gerdh.**

giants (jī'ănts), mythical beings of great size and strength. In classic myth they were the enemies of the gods and were defeated by them. In Teutonic myth there was less hostility, for some of the Teutonic giants represented kindly natural forces.

Gin-nun-ga-gap (gĭn'nŏŏn-gä-găp''; yĭn'nŏŏn-gä-găp''), the formless void before creation. [TEUT.]

Glaths-heim (glăths'hām), Odin's dwelling in Asgard, containing the thrones of the Æsir. Also, **Glathsheimr.** [TEUT.]

Glau-cus (glô'kŭs), a Greek fisherman, lover of Scylla; changed into a sea deity by eating magic grass.

Gold-en Fleece (gōld'n flēs), the wool of gold covering the ram that bore Phrixus through the air to Colchis; here it was hung up in a sacred grove by King Æetes and guarded by a dragon until it was carried off by Jason. [GR.]

Gor-di-us (gôr'dĭ-ŭs), king of Phrygia: author of a most intricate knot. Alexander the Great was told that, according to an oracle, the master of the knot should be master of Asia; he straightway cut the knot with his sword.

Gor-gons (gôr'gŏnz), three hideous monsters, sisters, with snaky locks, which turned the beholder to stone: Stheno, Euryale, Medusa. [Gr.]

Gra-ces (grā'sēz), three beautiful sister goddesses: Aglaia (Brilliance), Euphrosyne (Joy), and Thalia (Bloom); attendants on Eros (Cupid), Aphrodite (Venus), and Dionysus (Bacchus): called *Gratiæ* by the Romans, *Charites* by the Greeks.

Græ-æ (grē'ē), three sisters, hoary, misshapen, and hideous from birth, with but one eye and one tooth between them; watchers for the Gorgons. Also, **Graiæ.** [Gr.]

Gud-run (gōōd'rōōn), wife of Sigurd, whom she won from Brynhild by a magic drink; later, wife of the Hun king Atli. [Teut.]

Ha-des (hā'dēz), the god of the lower world: also called *Pluto;* the lower world itself. [Gr.]

ham-a-dry-ads (hăm'ȧ-drī'ădz), Greek tree nymphs. Also, **hamadryades.**

Har-mo-ni-a (här-mō'nĭ-ȧ), the wife of the Greek king Cadmus; famous for her wedding gift from Hephæstus (Vulcan) of an ill-omened necklace.

Har-pies (här'pĭz), [*sing.* Harpy], rapacious, defiling monsters having the head and body of a maiden, the wings and claws of a bird. [Gr.]

Ha-thor (hä'thŏr), the Egyptian goddess of love, represented with a cow's head: similar to the Greek goddess Aphrodite (Venus).

He-be (hē'bē), the Greek goddess of youth; cupbearer to the gods before Ganymede; later, the wife of the deified Heracles (Hercules), with the power of restoring youth.

Hec-a-te (hĕk'ȧ-tē), an ancient Greek goddess of the moon, earth, and lower world, and especially of magic: often merged with Artemis and Selene. Also, **Hekate.**

Hec-tor (hĕk'tẽr), son of Priam and Hecuba of Troy; husband of Andromache; bravest of Trojan warriors in the Trojan War; slain by Achilles to avenge the death of Patroclus.

Hec-u-ba (hĕk'ū-bȧ), the wife of Priam, king of Troy; mother of Hector, Paris, Helenus, and many other heroes.

Heim-dall (hām'däl), the vigilant watchman of Asgard. His horn Gjallarhorn was to summon the gods on the last day (Ragnarok). Also, **Heimdallr, Heimdal.** [Teut.]

Hel (hĕl), daughter of Loki; queen of Hel, the lower world: similar to the Greek goddess Persephone (Proserpina). Also, **Hela.** [Teut.]

Hel-en (hĕl'ĕn), the daughter of Zeus (Jupiter) and Leda; wife of Menelaus, king of Sparta; the most beautiful woman in the world. Her elopement with Paris to Troy caused the Trojan War. [Gr.]

Hel-e-nus (hĕl'ē-nŭs), a son of Priam and Hecuba of Troy; spared by the Greeks for his prophetic gift; later, husband of Andromache and ruler of Epirus.

He-li-os (hē'lĭ-ŏs), the Greek sun god, who drove his four-horse chariot through the sky.

Hel-le (hĕl'ē), the sister of Phrixus, with whom she was fleeing, when she fell from the ram with the golden fleece into the sea named for her the Hellespont (Sea of Helle). [Gr.]

He-phæs-tus (hē-fĕs'tŭs), the Greek god of fire and master of the forge; identified with the Roman god Vulcan. Also, **Hephaistos.**

He-ra (hē'rȧ), the queen of the Greek gods; sister and wife of Zeus (Jupiter); goddess of women and marriage: identified with the Roman goddess Juno. Also, **Here, Parthenos,** etc.

Her-cu-les (hûr'kū-lēz), a famous Greek hero, son of Zeus (Jupiter) and Alcmene. His remarkable physical strength was shown in the achievement of twelve great "labors": the killing of the Nemean lion; the killing of the Lernean hydra; the capture of the Cerynean hind; the capture of the Erymanthian boar; the cleaning of the Augean stables; the capture of the mad Cretan bull; the taking of the man-eating mares of Diomed; the procuring of Hippolyte's girdle; the slaughter of the Stymphalian birds; the capture of the red cattle of Geryon; the securing of the golden apples of the Hesperides; the bringing up of Cerberus from Hades. Also, **Heracles, Herakles.**

Her-mes (hûr'mēz), the son of Zeus (Jupiter) and Maia; messenger of the gods; god of eloquence, commerce, and travelers; conductor of the dead to the lower world: identified with the Roman god Mercury. [Gr.]

Her-mi-o-ne (hẽr-mī'ō-nē), the daughter of Menelaus and Helen; wife of Neoptolemus (Pyrrhus), and later, of Orestes. [Gr.]

He-ro (hē'rō), a beautiful priestess of Aphrodite (Venus) at Sestos in Thrace; loved by Leander, who swam the Hellespont (Dardanelles) nightly to see her. Leander was finally drowned and Hero threw herself into the sea. [Gr.]

He-si-o-ne (hē-sī'ō-nē), the daughter of Laomedon, king of Troy; exposed on a rock to a sea monster to avert disaster from her country, but soon rescued by Heracles (Hercules), who slew the monster. [Gr.]

Hes-per-i-des (hĕs-pĕr'ĭ-dēz), three nymphs, daughters of Hesperus, the evening star; with the help of a dragon, they guarded the golden apples which Hera (Juno) received as a wedding gift from Gæa (Terra). [Gr.]

Hes-ti-a (hĕs'tĭ-ȧ), the Greek goddess of the hearth and of intimate family relations; daughter of Cronus (Saturn) and Rhea (Ops): identified with the Roman goddess Vesta.

Hip-po-da-mi-a (hĭp'ō-dȧ-mī'ȧ), a Greek princess, daughter of Œnomaus of Elis; won by Pelops with the aid of winged horses from Neptune. The wife of Pirithous, friend of Theseus; the cause of the battle of the Centaurs and Lapithæ.

Hip-pol-y-te (hĭ-pŏl'ĭ-tē), a queen of the Amazons; wife of Theseus; possessor of a famous girdle. [Gr.]

Hip-pol-y-tus (hĭ-pŏl'ĭ-tŭs), the noble son of Theseus and Hippolyte; falsely accused and killed through the efforts of his young stepmother, Phædra, whose love for him was not returned. [Gr.]

Hip-pom-e-nes (hĭ-pŏm'ē-nēz), the Greek hero who outran Atalanta and so won her for his bride.

Hlith-skjalf (hlĭth'skyälf"), the seat of Odin, above Asgard, from which he looked out over all the worlds. Also, **Hlidhskjalf.** [Teut.]

Hœ-nir (hû-nẽr), the Teutonic god, strong but dull, who helped create Ask and Embla, the first mortals; one of the few survivors of the last day (Ragnarok).

Ho-rus (hō'rŭs), the hawk-headed Egyptian god of day; similar to the Greek god Apollo. Also, **Harpocrates.**

Hö-thr (hû'*th*r), the blind god who unwittingly slew Balder. Also, **Hoder, Hodur.** [Teut.]

Hy-a-cin-thus (hī'ȧ-sĭn'thŭs), a beautiful Greek youth beloved by Apollo; killed from jealousy by Zephyrus, the west wind; or perhaps, unwittingly by Apollo, who caused the hyacinth to grow from his blood.

Hy-dra (hī'drȧ), a many-headed monster in the swamp of Lerna; killed by Heracles (Hercules). [Gr.]

Hy-las (hī'lăs), a handsome Greek lad beloved by Heracles (Hercules). While drawing water at a spring for his master, he was drawn in by the amorous nymphs.

Hy-men (hī'mĕn), the Greek god of marriage.

Hy-mir (hü'mẽr), a Teutonic giant personifying the unfriendly sea. Also, **Hymer.**

Hy-per-bo-re-ans (hī"pẽr-bō'rē-ănz), a mythical people dwelling beyond the north wind (Boreas) in everlasting bliss, free from disease and old age. [Gr.]

Hy-perm-nes-tra (hī"pẽrm-nĕs'trȧ), the only one of the fifty daughters of Danaüs who did not kill her husband. Her descendants ruled in Argos. [Gr.]

Ic-a-rus (ĭk'ȧ-rŭs), the young son of Dædalus, who tried to fly with his father from Crete, but rose too near the sun, melted the wax in his wings and fell into the sea named Icarian for him. [Gr.]

Il-i-ad (ĭl'ĭ-ăd), a Greek epic poem in twenty-four books by Homer, giving the events of part of the last year of the Trojan War, from the quarrel of Achilles and Agamemnon to the burial of Hector.

Il-i-um (ĭl'ĭ-ŭm), a poetical name for Troy in Asia Minor.

In-dra (ĭn'drȧ), greatest of the Vedic gods; wielder of the thunderbolt, dispenser of rain. [Hind.]

I-o (ī'ō), daughter of the river god Inachus; beloved by Zeus (Jupiter), who changed her into a heifer to escape the wrath of Hera (Juno). Then Io, tormented with a stinging gadfly sent by Hera, swam through the sea, named Ionian for her, to Egypt, where she regained her form and freedom. [Gr.]

Iph-i-ge-ni-a (ĭf"ĭ-jē-nī'ȧ), a daughter of Agamemnon; sacrificed to secure favorable winds for the Greeks in the expedition against Troy. At the fatal moment, Artemis (Diana) rescued her and made her a priestess in Tauris, where Orestes found her. [Gr.]

I-ris (ī'rĭs), the Greek goddess of the rainbow; messenger of Zeus (Jupiter) and Hera (Juno).

I-sis (ī'sĭs), the Egyptian goddess of fruitfulness; wife of Osiris. Also, **Hes.**

Is-me-ne (ĭs-mē'nē), the timid, practical sister of Antigone; daughter of Œdipus and Jocasta. [Gr.]

Ith-a-ca (ĭth'ȧ-kȧ), the island home of Odysseus (Ulysses), off the west coast of Greece.

I-thunn (ē'*th*ŏŏn), the wife of Bragi and goddess of early spring; possessed of the golden apples of youth, which kept the gods young. Also, **Ithun, Idun.** [Teut.]

I-u-lus (ī-ū'lŭs), son of Æneas and Creusa; reputed ancestor of Julius Cæsar, the Roman emperor. Also, **Ascanius.**

Ix-i-on (ĭk-sī'ŏn), father of the centaurs; for wickedly aspiring to the love of Hera (Juno), he was bound in Tartarus to a perpetually revolving wheel. [Gr.]

Ja-nus (jā'nŭs), the ancient Roman god of all beginnings; his temple in the Roman Forum was closed only in times of peace: January is named for him.

Ja-son (jā'sŭn), the leader of the Greek Argonauts in the successful expedition to Colchis for the Golden Fleece.

Jo-tunn (yō'tŏŏn), a Teutonic giant. Also, **Jotun, Jötunn.**

Jo-tunn-heim (yō'tŏŏn-hām), the home of the Teutonic giants on the outermost edge of the world. Also, **Jotunnheimr, Jötunnheim, Jötunnheimr.**

Jove (jōv), Jupiter, the greatest Roman god: identified with the Greek Zeus.

Ju-no (jōō'nō), the daughter of Saturn (Cronus) and Ops (Rhea); sister and wife of Jupiter (Zeus); the queen of the Roman gods; goddess of marriage and births: identified with the Greek goddess Hera.

Ju-pi-ter (jōō'pĭ-tẽr), an ancient Italian god of the heavens, supreme ruler over all things; son of Saturn (Cronus) and Ops (Rhea): identified with the Greek god Zeus.

Ko-re (kō'rē), the name under which Persephone (Proserpina), the queen of the lower world, was worshiped. Also, **Cora.**

Lab-y-rinth (lăb'ĭ-rĭnth), the maze constructed for King Minos of Crete by Dædalus, to hold the Minotaur.

Lach-e-sis (lăk'ē-sĭs), the one of the three Greek Fates who measured off the thread of life.

Laksh-mi (lŭksh'mē), the Hindu goddess of fortune and beauty; wife of Vishnu. Also, **Sri.**

La-oc-o-on (lā-ŏk'ō-ŏn), a faithful priest of Apollo at Troy, who mistrusted and condemned the wooden horse left in the shore by the Greeks. The Greek gods then sent two serpents out of the sea to kill him and his two sons.

La-od-a-mi-a (lā-ŏd"ȧ-mī'ȧ), the wife of Protesilaus, a Greek hero killed before Troy. In answer to her prayer, Protesilaus was restored to her for three hours; then she went to the lower world with him.

La-om-e-don (lā-ŏm'ē-dŏn), a king of Troy; father of Priam and Hesione; killed by Heracles (Hercules) for denying him Hesione to wife, after he had rescued her from a sea monster.

la-res (lā'rēz), Roman tutelary spirits of the house, fields, and, especially, of the ancestors of the family.

La-ti-nus (lȧ-tī'nŭs), king of Latium when Æneas came to Italy; father of Lavinia, the second wife of that Trojan hero.

La-to-na (lȧ-tō'nȧ), mother of Apollo and Diana (Artemis): called *Leto* by the Greeks. [Rom.]

La-vin-i-a (lȧ-vĭn'ĭ-ȧ), daughter of King Latinus of Latium; engaged to Turnus, but finally married to Æneas.

Le-an-der (lē-ăn'dẽr), lover of Hero of Sestos, for whom he swam the Hellespont (Dardanelles) nightly, until drowned in a storm. [Gr.]

Le-da (lē'dȧ), beloved by Zeus (Jupiter) in the form of a swan; mother of Castor, Pollux, and Helen. [Gr.]

Le-the (lē'thē), the "river of forgetfulness" in Hades. [Gr.]

Le-to (lē'tō), a beautiful maiden beloved by Zeus (Jupiter); persecuted by Hera (Juno) in her wanderings to the island Delos in the Ægean Sea, where Apollo and Artemis (Diana) were born: called *Latona* by the Romans. [Gr.]

Lo-ki (lō'kē), the evil Teutonic god, contriver of constant discord and mischief, even to the death of Balder; father of Sleipnir and the Midgard serpent; finally bound by Thor and placed by Skathi beneath a venom-dripping serpent; deserted by all save his wife Signy. On the last day (Ragnarok) Loki was to lead forth the forces of Hel. Also, **Loke.**

mæn-a-des (mĕn'ȧ-dēz), [*sing.* mænad], women devotees of Dionysus (Bacchus). Also, **mænads, Bacchæ, bacchantes.** [Gr.]

Ma-ia (mā'yȧ; mī'ȧ), eldest and most beautiful of the Pleiades; mother of Hermes (Mercury). [Gr.]

ma-nes (mā'nēz), the spirits of the ancestors of the Romans, worshiped as gods. Also, **Manes.**

Mars (märz), the Roman god of war: identified with the Greek god Ares.

Mar-sy-as (mär'sĭ-ăs), originally a god of nature from Asia Minor, punished, for competing with Apollo on the lute, by being flayed alive.

Me-de-a (mē-dē'ȧ), a sorceress, daughter of King Æetes of Colchis. For love of Jason she helped him win the Golden Fleece and then sailed away with him.

Me-du-sa (mē-dū'sȧ), originally a maiden, whose pride in her glorious hair caused it to be changed into snakes: one of the three Gorgons; slain by the Greek hero **Perseus.**

Mel-e-a-ger (mĕl'ē-ā'jẽr), son of Althæa, queen of Calydon. At his birth it was foretold that his life would be only as long as that of the brand then burning on the hearth. His mother quenched it and hid it. Years later, after his success in the Calydonian boar hunt, Althæa decided to avenge the death of her brothers at Meleager's hands; she threw the fatal brand on the fire; Meleager soon died. In remorse, his mother killed herself.

Mel-pom-e-ne (mĕl-pŏm'ē-nē), the Muse of tragedy. [Gr.]

Men-e-la-us (mĕn'ē-lā'ŭs), king of Sparta, husband of Helen.

Men-tor (mĕn'tŏr), the faithful friend of Odysseus (Ulysses); the guide and teacher of Telemachus. [Gr.]

Mer-cu-ry (mûr'kū-rĭ), the son of Jupiter (Zeus) and Maia; messenger of the gods; Roman god of eloquence, commerce, and travelers: identified with the Greek god Hermes.

Mi-das (mī'dȧs), a king of Phrygia, in answer to whose prayer, Dionysus (Bacchus) turned everything he touched to gold. When even his food became gold, he prayed for help and was freed of the curse by bathing in the river Pactolus. King Midas had ass's ears, inflicted on him for giving the preference in a musical contest to Pan, rather than to Apollo.

Mid-gard (mĭd'gärd), the earth. The Midgard serpent was a horrible sea monster, offspring of Loki; to be slain by Thor, whom it was destined to kill on the last day (Ragnarok). Also, **Midgarth, Mithgarthr.** [Teut.]

Mi-mir (mē'mẽr), the Teutonic god of wisdom and knowledge.

Mi-ner-va (mĭ-nûr'vȧ), the Roman goddess of wisdom, thought, and invention: identified with the Greek goddess Athena.

Mi-nos (mī'nŏs), king and lawgiver of Crete; after death, a judge in the lower world. His grandson, also a king of Crete, was the husband of Pasiphaë; the father of Ariadne; the owner of the Labyrinth; the oppressor of Athens.

Min-o-taur (mĭn'ō-tŏr), a monster, half man and half bull, which fed on Athenian maidens and lads, until slain by Theseus in its lair, the Labyrinth in Crete.

Mne-mos-y-ne (nē-mŏs'ĭ-nē), the Greek goddess of memory and mother of the Muses.

Mœræ (mē'rē), the Greek goddesses of destiny: identified with the Roman Parcæ. Also, the **Fates.**

Mor-pheus (mŏr'fūs; mŏr'fē-ŭs), the Greek god of dreams.

Mors (mŏrz), the Roman personification of death: called *Thanatos* by the Greeks.

Mu-ses (mū'zĕz), the nine Greek goddesses who presided over the arts and sciences: Calliope, Clio, Erato, Euterpe, Melpomene, Polymnia or Polyhymnia, Terpsichore, Thalia, and Urania.

Mus-pells-heim (mōōs'pĕls-hām'), one of the Teutonic Nine Worlds; the region of warmth and sunlight south of Ginnungagap. Also, **Muspel.**

Mut (mōōt), the Theban goddess of womanhood: similar to the Greek goddess Demeter. [Egypt.]

na-iads (nā'yădz; nī'ădz), the nymphs who lived in springs, rivers, lakes, and fountains. [Gr.]

Nan-na (năn'nȧ), the devoted wife of Balder, at whose loss she grieved to death. [Teut.]

Nar-cis-sus (när-sĭs'ŭs), a handsome Greek youth, for vain love of whom Echo pined away. Narcissus was punished, for he fell in love with his own reflection and also pined away, until he was changed into the flower narcissus.

Na-strond (nä'strŏnd), the place of punishment in Niflheim: similar to the Greek Tartarus. Also, **Naströnd.** [Teut.]

Nau-sic-a-a (nô-sĭk'ā-ȧ; nou-sĭk'ā-ȧ), the Phæacian princess who found Odysseus (Ulysses) after his shipwreck and brought him to the court of her father, Alcinous. [Gr.]

nec-tar (nĕk'tȧr), the substance which with ambrosia formed the food and drink of the Greek gods.

Ne-ith (nā'ĭth), the Theban goddess of the upper heaven, of wisdom and the arts of peace and war. Likened by the Greeks to Athena. [Egypt.]

Nem-e-sis (nĕm'ē-sĭs), the Greek goddess of righteous vengeance.

Ne-op-tol-e-mus (nē″ŏp-tŏl′ē-mŭs), son of Achilles; a Greek hero in the Trojan War; at the fall of Troy, he cruelly killed the aged Priam and hurled the infant son of Hector from the walls. Later, he married Hermione, daughter of Menelaus and Helen. Also, **Pyrrhus.**

Neph-thys (nĕf′thĭs), an Egyptian goddess of the dead.

Nep-tune (nĕp′tūn), the son of Saturn (Cronus) and Ops (Rhea); Roman god of the sea; represented with a trident in his hand: identified with the Greek Poseidon.

Ne-re-ids (nē′rē-ĭdz), Greek sea nymphs, daughters of Nereus and Doris; att n ants of Pos.idon (Neptune).

Ne-reus (nē′rūs), a Greek sea god, father of the Nereids.

Nes-sus (nĕs′ŭs), a centaur shot with a poisoned arrow by Heracles (Hercules) for trying to carry off his wife Deianira. Nessus bequeathed his blood-stained shirt to Deianira, but when she used it to regain the love of her husband, it fatally poisoned him. [Gr.]

Nes-tor (nĕs′tŏr), a Greek king of Pylus, who fought in his old age with the Greeks in the Trojan War.

Nif-l-heim (nĕv′l-hām), the northern region of cold and mist; the underworld (Hel), or even the place of punishment (Nifhel). Also, **Niflheimr.** [Teut.]

Nine Worlds (nīn wûrldz), the Teutonic divisions of the universe. Five are certain: Asgard, Midgard, Jotunnheim, Muspellsheim, Niflheim.

Ni-o-be (nī′ō-bē), the daughter of Tantalus and Amphion; bereft of her fourteen children by Apollo and Artemis (Diana), because she dared to compare herself with their mother Leto (Latona), who had but the two. Niobe herself was changed to stone by Zeus (Jupiter). [Gr.]

Njorth (nyŏrth), a Teutonic god of the sea and winds; protector of sailors; the hostage given by the Vanir to the Æsir to insure peace; he lived in Noatun (Noatunn). Also, **Njörthr, Njord.**

Norns (nŏrnz), the Teutonic Fates; three sisters: Urth (Past), Verthandi (Present), Skuld (Future); possessed of absolute power over the lives of gods and men: similar to the Greek Fates.

Nox (nŏks), the Roman goddess of night: identified with the Greek goddess Nyx.

Nut (nōōt), the Heavens: similar to the Greek goddess Rhea. [Egypt.]

nymphs (nĭmfs), lesser Greek divinities of nature in the form of beautiful maidens, dwelling in streams, mountains, trees, sea, or ocean.

O-ce-a-nids (ō-sē′ȧ-nĭdz), Greek ocean nymphs.

O-ce-a-nus (ō-sē′ȧ-nŭs), a Greek Titan; the first sea god, succeeded by Poseidon (Neptune).

O-din (ō′dĭn), the chief of the Teutonic gods; husband of Frigg. With Vili and Ve, he constructed the world out of Ymir's body; with Hœnir and Loki, he created the first man and woman; he was the progenitor of kings, the lord of battle; his throne was Hlithskjalf. Also, **Woden.**

O-dys-seus (ō-dĭs′ūs; ō-dĭs′ē-ŭs), a famous king of Ithaca; the wisest, shrewdest, and most eloquent of the Greek chiefs who fought against Troy; the hero of Homer's *Odyssey*: called by the Romans *Ulixes, Ulysses.*

Od-ys-sey (ŏd′ĭ-sĭ), Homer's Greek epic poem describing the ten years' wanderings of Odysseus (Ulysses) from Troy to Ithaca.

Œd-i-pus (ĕd′ĭ-pŭs; ē′dĭ-pŭs), the unfortunate son of Laius and Jocasta of Thebes in Greece. At his birth an oracle foretold that he would kill his father and marry his mother. He was exposed, but rescued, and adopted by the king of Corinth. Later, while on a journey, he unwittingly did kill his own father Laius. Then at Thebes he answered the riddle of the Sphinx, was made king of Thebes and given the hand of his mother Jocasta. Trouble and persecution followed the fulfillment of the oracle. At the revelation of his identity, he even blinded himself. Of four children: Eteocles, Polynices, Antigone, and Ismene, Antigone alone remained with him until his sad death in exile.

Œ-no-ne (ē-nō′nē), a nymph of Mt. Ida in Asia Minor; the loving, but deserted, wife of Paris.

O-lym-pi-an games (ō-lĭm′pĭ-ăn gāmz), a great Panhellenic festival held in northwest Greece every fourth summer, beginning 776 B. C.

O-lym-pus (ō-lĭm′pŭs), a mountain in Thessaly, where the Greek gods lived.

Ops (ŏps), the Roman goddess of the harvest: identified with the Greek goddess Rhea.

o-re-ads (ō′rē-ădz), Greek mountain nymphs.

O-res-tes (ō-rĕs′tēz), the son of Agamemnon and Clytemnestra of Argos in Greece; in obedience to Apollo, he avenged the murder of his father by slaying his mother and Ægisthus. Terrible persecution by the Furies followed this crime until his purification by bringing from Tauris, with the help of his friend Pylades, his sister Iphigenia and the Tauric cult of Artemis (Diana).

O-ri-on (ō-rī′ŏn), a Greek hunter beloved by Artemis (Diana), who accidentally killed him. In sorrow she placed him and his dog Sirius in the sky as a constellation.

Or-pheus (ŏr′fŭs; ŏr′fē-ŭs), a Thracian poet and musician, son of Apollo and Calliope, who, with his lyre, could draw to himself beasts, rocks, and trees. He descended into Hades and so charmed Pluto with his music that he was permitted to bring his dead wife Eurydice back to earth, if only he should not look back at her. He did look back and she vanished. [Gr.]

O-si-ris (ō-sī′rĭs), once a good, wise Egyptian king, treacherously slain by his brother Set; afterward, the great god of the lower world and judge of the dead. He has many characteristics of the Greek gods Apollo and Dionysus (Bacchus).

Os-sa (ŏs′ȧ), a mountain in Greece. In a vain attempt to climb to heaven, the Titans piled Ossa on Pelion, and Pelion on Olympus.

Pal-i-nu-rus (păl″ĭ-nū′rŭs), the pilot of Æneas. While asleep at the helm, he fell overboard and was murdered by natives on the shore of Italy.

Pal-la-di-um (pȧ-lā′dĭ-ŭm), a famous statue of Athena (Minerva), which fell from heaven to Troy; on its preservation depended the safety of 'roy, which fell only after the Palladium ıad been stolen by the Greeks Odysseus Ulysses) and Diomed.

?al-las (păl'ȧs), an epithet of Athena (Minerva). [Gr.]

?an (păn), the son of Hermes (Mercury): the Greek god of flocks and herds: dentified with the Roman Faunus and nuus.

?an-do-ra (păn-dō'rȧ), a beautiful woman whom the gods created ınd inflicted upon Epimetheus, to punish nortals for having received the gift of fire. Ier sinful curiosity led her to open a certain ox and let out into the world all the mortal lls and diseases. Hope alone remained. [Gr.]

?ar-cæ (pär'sē), the Roman Fates: identified with the Mœræ.

?ar-is (păr'is), the handsome son of Priam of Troy; judge in the famous eauty contest between Hera (Juno), Athena Minerva), and Aphrodite (Venus). Bribed y her promise of the fairest woman in the vorld, Paris awarded the prize to Aphrodite. This woman was Helen, whom Paris soon tole from her husband Menelaus of Sparta. The Trojan War followed to regain Helen. 'aris was fatally shot by Philoctetes with one f the arrows of Hercules.

?ar-nas-sus (pär-năs'ŭs), a mountain in Greece sacred to Apollo ınd the Muses.

?a-siph-a-e (pȧ-sĭf'ȧ-ē), wife of King Minos of Crete; mother of Ariadne, Phædra; also of the Minotaur.

?a-tro-clus (pȧ-trō'klŭs), a Greek hero of the Trojan War; devoted riend of Achilles, who lent him his armor and vho later avenged his death.

Peg-a-sus (pĕg'ȧ-sŭs), a winged horse belonging to Apollo and the Muses. [Gr.]

?e-leus (pē'lūs), king of the Myrmidons; father by Thetis of Achilles. Gr.]

?e-li-as (pē'lĭ-ăs; pĕl'ĭ-ăs), a Greek king for whom Jason secured the Golden Fleece. In vain hope of restoring ıis youth, as Medea had done that of her ather-in-law, his own daughters killed and oiled him.

?e-li-on (pē'lĭ-ŏn), a mountain in Greece, which the Titans vainly tried o place on Olympus in an endeavor to scale ıeaven.

?e-na-tes (pē-nā'tēz), the Roman household gods of family and city.

?e-nel-o-pe (pē-nĕl'ō-pē), the wife of Odysseus (Ulysses) of Ithaca; oted for her persistent faithfulness to him uring his long absence in the Trojan War.

?en-the-si-le-a (pĕn"thē-sĭ-lē'ȧ), the brave queen of the Amazons; slain before Troy by Achilles.

?er-seph-o-ne (pēr-sĕf'ō-nē), the daughter of Zeus (Jupiter) and Demeter (Ceres); wife of Hades Pluto) and queen of the lower world: called y the Romans *Persephone*, *Proserpina*, *Proserpine*. Also, **Kore**, **Cora**. [Gr.]

?er-seus (pûr'sūs; pûr'sē-ŭs), the Greek hero who slew the Gorgon Medusa, giving her head to Athena (Minerva), nd who delivered Andromeda.

?hæ-dra (fē'drȧ), the daughter of King Minos of Crete; wife of Theseus; a suicide for unrequited love of Hippolitus, her stepson.

?ha-e-thon (fā'ē-thŏn), the son of Apollo, the sun god. Attempting to drive the sun chariot one day, he lost control of the horses; the earth was parched and he was struck down by a thunderbolt of Zeus (Jupiter). [Gr.]

Phi-le-mon (fĭ-lē'mŏn), a hospitable old Phrygian, who helped Baucis, his wife, entertain Zeus (Jupiter) and Hermes (Mercury) unawares; the couple were rewarded by being installed as priest and priestess in a temple, and changed at death into two trees.

Phil-o-me-la (fĭl"ō-mē'lȧ), the daughter of Pandion of Athens; sister of Procne; changed into a nightingale (or swallow). [Gr.]

Phleg-e-thon (flĕg'ē-thŏn; flē'-), the "river of fire" in the lower world. [Gr.]

Phœ-be (fē'bē), another name for Artemis (Diana), the Greek goddess of the chase.

Phœ-bus (fē'bŭs), another name for Apollo, the Greek sun god.

Ple-ia-des (plē'yȧ-dēz; plē'ȧ-dēz; plī'ȧ-dēz), seven beautiful nymphs of Artemis (Diana), beloved and pursued by Orion; changed by Zeus (Jupiter), in answer to prayer, into pigeons and then into stars. Six are still visible; one left her place that she might not behold the fall of Troy. [Gr.]

Plu-to (ploo'tō), the son of Cronus (Saturn) and Rhea (Ops); Greek god of the lower world: usually called *Dis* by the Romans. Also, **Hades**.

Plu-tus (ploo'tŭs), the blind god of riches. [Gr.]

Pol-lux (pŏl'ŭks), champion boxer; son of Zeus (Jupiter); immortal twin brother of the mortal Castor, with whom he was allowed to share alternate life and death; later they were both placed in the sky as the constellation Gemini. Also, **Polydeuces**. [Gr.]

Pol-y-hym-ni-a (pŏl'ĭ-hĭm'nĭ-ȧ), the Muse of oratory and sacred poetry. Also, **Polymnia**. [Gr.]

Pol-y-phe-mus (pŏl'ĭ-fē'mŭs), a Cyclops who, confining Odysseus (Ulysses) and his companions in his cave, devoured two daily, until Odysseus bored out his one eye, as he lay in drunken sleep. The Greeks escaped by clinging to the stomachs of the sheep as they passed out of the cave to pasture. [Gr.]

Pol-y-ni-ces (pŏl'ĭ-nī'sēz), a son of Œdipus slain in the expedition of the Seven against Thebes by his brother Eteocles, from whom he sought to gain the throne. Also, **Polyneices**.

Po-lyx-e-na (pō-lĭk'sē-nȧ), a daughter of Priam and Hecuba of Troy; the affianced wife of Achilles. After his tragic death, she killed herself at his tomb (or was sacrificed to his shade).

Po-mo-na (pō-mō'nȧ), the ancient Italian goddess of gardens and fruit trees.

Po-sei-don (pō-sī'dŏn), the Greek god of the sea, horses, and chivalry: identified with the Roman god Neptune.

Pri-am (prī'ăm), the king of Troy during the Trojan War; father of Hector and Paris.

Proc-ris (prŏk'rĭs; prō'krĭs), the jealous wife of Cephalus, who accidentally slew her. Also, **Procne**. [Gr.]

Pro-crus-tes (prō-krŭs'tēz), a notorious Greek robber, who laid his victims on an iron bed, stretching them out or cutting them off to make them fit; killed by Theseus.

Pro-me-theus (prō-mē'thūs; prō-mē'-thē-ūs), a Greek Titan who created the human race and founded civilization; in punishment for his theft of fire from heaven for men, he passed many years chained to Mt. Caucasus, with a vulture gnawing at his liver.

Pro-ser-pi-na (prō-sûr'pĭ-nȧ), daughter of Jupiter (Zeus) and Ceres (Demeter); carried off to the lower world by Dis (Hades) and made his queen: called *Kore, Cora, Persephone* by the Greeks. Also, **Proserpine.** [Rom.]

Pro-tes-i-la-us (prō-tĕs'ĭ-lā'ŭs), the first Greek hero to meet death in the Trojan War, in the assurance of thus securing an ultimate Greek victory; his faithful wife was Laodamia.

Pro-teus (prō'tūs; prō'tē-ūs), a Greek sea god and prophet, who could change himself into any form at will.

Psy-che (sī'kē; psī'kē), a lovely Greek maiden personifying the human soul; wooed and won by Eros (Cupid).

Ptah (ptä), the chief god of Memphis in Egypt; father of gods and men. Also, **Ptha.**

Pyg-ma-li-on (pĭg-mā'lĭ-ŏn), a king and sculptor of Cyprus, who fell in love with an ivory statue of Galatea, a beautiful maiden. In answer to his ardent prayer, Aphrodite (Venus) gave the statue life and she became his wife.

Pyl-a-des (pĭl'ȧ-dēz), cousin and friend of the Greek hero Orestes.

Pyr-a-mus (pĭr'ȧ-mŭs), a secret lover of Thisbe in ancient Babylon. When he arrived one day at their tryst outside the walls, he saw only her blood-stained veil, which she had left behind in her flight from a lion. Pyramus supposed that she was dead, however, and killed himself. Thisbe presently returned, saw that she had lost him forever and then killed herself.

Pyr-rha (pĭr'ȧ), wife of Deucalion, the Greek Noah.

Pyr-rhus (pĭr'ŭs), a Greek hero of the Trojan War; son of Achilles. Also, **Neoptolemus.**

Py-thon (pī'thŏn), an enormous serpent which crept forth after the flood subsided; killed by Apollo. [Gr.]

Qui-ri-nus (kwĭ-rī'nŭs), the deified Romulus; Roman god of armed peace.

Ra (rä), the great Egyptian god of the sun, life, and right, from whom most of the Pharaohs claimed descent: similar to the Greek god Helios. Also, **Re.**

Rag-na-rok (räg'nȧ-rŏk'), the last day for gods and men. Also, **Ragnarök.** [Teut.]

Ran (rän), the Teutonic goddess of the sea; wife of Ægir.

Re-ginn (rā'yĭn), the treacherous dwarf who taught Sigurd and forged his sword. Also, **Regin.** [Teut.]

Re-mus (rē'mŭs), the twin brother of Romulus, the founder of Rome; slain for ridiculing the walls of the new city.

Rhad-a-man-thus (răd'ȧ-măn'thŭs), son of Zeus (Jupiter) and Europa. Because of his justice in life he became one of the three judges of the lower world. Also, **Rhadamanthys.** [Gr.]

Rhe-a (rē'ȧ), wife of Cronus (Saturn); "Mother of the Gods": identified with Cybele and the Roman Ops. [Gr.]

Rom-u-lus (rŏm'ū-lŭs), the son of Mars and Ilia; thrown into the Tiber with his twin brother Remus, but rescued and adopted by a shepherd; later, the founder and first king of Rome.

Sa-ga (sä'gȧ; sä'gä), the Teutonic goddess of history; her home was Sokkvabekk.

Sat-urn (săt'ûrn), the ancient Roman god of the seed-sowing; son of Uranus; father of Jupiter (Zeus): identified with the Greek god Cronus.

sat-yrs (săt'ērz; sā'tērz), Greek sylvan deities, represented as youths with the ears, horns, and legs of goats.

Sav-i-tar (säv'ĭ-tȧr), the Vedic golden-handed sun in his daily course; the shining wanderer. [Hind.]

Scyl-la (sĭl'ȧ), a Greek sea nymph beloved by Glaucus; changed into a ravenous monster by the jealous Circe. From a cliff on the Italian coast, opposite the whirlpool of Charybdis on the Sicilian coast, she thrust forth her long neck and seized sailors as they passed.

Seb (sĕb), the Egyptian god of earth and its vegetation: similar to the Greek god Cronus.

Se-le-ne (sē-lē'nē), the Greek goddess of the moon; often identified with Artemis (Diana) and Hecate. Also, **Selena.**

Sem-e-le (sĕm'ē-lē), mother of Dionysus (Bacchus) by Zeus (Jupiter); consumed by lightning, when Zeus appeared to her, at her request, in all his glory. [Gr.]

Se-ra-pis (sē-rā'pĭs), an Egyptian deity representing Osiris in the lower world.

Set (sĕt), the Egyptian personification of evil.

Sev-en a-gainst Thebes (thēbz), the expedition against the Greek city of Thebes of seven heroes: Adrastus, Amphiaraüs, Capaneus, Hippomedon or Eteoclus, Polynices, Parthenopæus and Tydeus, in an unsuccessful effort to wrest the throne for Polynices from his brother Eteocles. All save Adrastus were killed.

Sev-en Won-ders of the World Seven noted objects of antiquity, usually: the pyramids of Egypt, the temple of Diana (Artemis) at Ephesus, the hanging gardens of Babylon, the Colossus of Rhodes, the mausoleum built by Artemisia at Halicarnassus, the statue of Zeus (Jupiter) by Phidias at Olympia, the Pharos (lighthouse) of Alexandria in Egypt.

Sib-yl (sĭb'ĭl), a prophetess, especially the one who lived in a cave at Cumæ near Naples and guided Æneas through Hades; the authoress of the inspired Sibylline Books.

Sif (sēf), wife of Thor; the Teutonic goddess of the sanctity of the family and wedlock.

Sig-mund (sĭg'mŭnd; zēkh'mōōnt), the Volsung hero, father of Sigurd. [Teut.]

Si-gurd (zē'gōōrt), the hero of the Volsunga Saga, who delivered Brynhild, but deserted her for Gunnar's sister Gudrun; he was treacherously slain, through the instigation of Brynhild, by Gunnar's brother. [Teut.]

Si-gyn (sē'gün), the faithful wife of Loki, who went with him to his place of punishment and tried to keep the ever-dripping venom of the serpent from falling on his face. [TEUT.]

Si-le-nus (sī-lē'nŭs), a Greek woodland god, tutor of Dionysus (Bacchus). Also, **Seilenos.**

Si-non (sī'nŏn), a wily Greek of the Trojan War, whose false tale persuaded the Trojans to take the wooden horse into the city, that he might free the Greek warriors concealed within.

si-rens (sī'rĕnz), nymphs on an island near Italy, where they sang so sweetly that they lured many sailors to their destruction.

Sir-i-us (sĭr'ĭ-ŭs), the faithful hunting dog of Orion, with whom he was translated to the skies as a constellation. [GR.]

Sis-y-phus (sĭs'ĭ-fŭs), a greedy king of Corinth in Greece; condemned in Tararus to roll uphill a large stone, which constantly fell back again.

Ska-thi (skä'*th*ē), the Teutonic goddess of winter; wife of Njorth. Her home was Thrymheim. Also, **Skadhi, Skadi.**

Sleip-nir (slāp'nẽr), Odin's eight-footed horse. Also, **Sleipner.** [TEUT.]

Som-nus (sŏm'nŭs), the Roman god of sleep: identified with the Greek god Hypnos

Sten-tor (stĕn'tŏr), a Greek herald, whose voice had the strength of fifty men.

Styx (stĭks), the river in Hades by which the gods swore their most irrevocable oaths. [GR.]

Tan-ta-lus (tăn'tȧ-lŭs), a wicked Greek king punished in Tartarus by being placed in water up to his neck, with fruit hanging just above his head. If he stooped to drink, the water receded; if he reached for food, the wind snatched it away.

Tar-ta-rus (tär'tȧ-rŭs), the place of punishment in the lower world. [GR.]

Te-lem-a-chus (tē-lĕm'ȧ-kŭs), son of Odysseus (Ulysses) and Penelope; he tried unsuccessfully to find his father after the Trojan War, but returned in time to greet him and help him avenge Penelope. [GR.]

Terp-sich-o-re (tûrp-sĭk'ō-rē), the Muse of dancing. [GR.]

Tha-li-a (thȧ-lī'ȧ), the Muse of comedy; one of the three Graces. [GR.]

Than-a-tos (thăn'ȧ-tŏs), death personified: identified with the Roman Mors. [GR.]

The-mis (thē'mĭs), a Greek Titaness of justice.

The-seus (thē'sūs; thē'sē-ŭs), the great Attic hero, king of Athens. He killed Procrustes; slew the Minotaur and eloped with Ariadne; conquered the Amazons, carrying off their queen, Hippolyte (or Antiope); went on the Argonautic expedition; hunted the Calydonian boar; tried to help Pirithoüs abduct Persephone (Proserpina).

The-tis (thē'tĭs), a Nereid, wife of Peleus; mother of Achilles.

This-be (thĭz'bē), a beautiful maiden of ancient Babylon, who killed herself, when she found that her lover Pyramus had killed himself in despair at her supposed death.

Thor (thôr), son of Odin; Teutonic god of thunder and might; keeper of the hammer; defender of the earth, the heavens, and the gods. Also, **Thorr.**

Thy-es-tes (thī-ĕs'tēz), a wicked Greek hero, to whom his brother Atreus, father of Agamemnon and Menelaus, served at dinner the bodies of his three sons, and who then cursed the house of Atreus forever.

Ti-tans (tī'tănz), Greek giants who warred unsuccessfully against the gods of Olympus.

Ti-tho-nus (tĭ-thō'nŭs), son of Laomedon, king of Troy; beloved by Eos (Aurora), who secured immortality for him, but forgot to ask for immortal youth. Tithonus grew old and feeble, and was finally changed into a grasshopper.

Tit-y-us (tĭt'ĭ-ŭs), a Greek giant so large that he covered nine acres in Tartarus, where two vultures continually gnawed his liver.

Tri-mur-ti (trē-mŏŏr'tē), the Hindu trinity, consisting of Brahma (the Creator), Vishnu (the Preserver), and Siva (the Destroyer).

Tri-ton (trī'tŏn), a Greek sea demigod, provided with a conch shell trumpet to raise or calm the waves.

Tro-jan (trō'jăn), an inhabitant of the city of Troy in Asia Minor.

Troy (troi), an ancient city of Asia Minor, famous for its ten years' siege and final destruction by the Greeks. This was to regain Helen, whom Paris, a Trojan prince, had stolen from her husband Menelaus of Sparta. Also, **Ilium, Ilion.**

Tur-nus (tûr'nŭs), the chief of the Rutuli, an Italian tribe; the unsuccessful rival of Æneas for the hand of Lavinia; slain by Æneas.

Tyr (tẽr), the ancient Teutonic god of war and the sky; son of Odin. Also, **Tyrr.**

Ull (ŏŏl), the Teutonic god of the chase; skilful with the bow and ski. Also, **Ullr.**

U-lys-ses (ū-lĭs'ēz), the Roman name for Odysseus, king of Ithaca; the wisest, shrewdest, and subtlest of the Greek chiefs in the Trojan War.

U-ra-ni-a (ū-rā'nĭ-ȧ), the Muse of astronomy. [GR.]

U-ra-nus (ū'rȧ-nŭs), heaven personified. [GR.]

U-shas (ŏŏ'shȧs; ŏŏ-shäs'), the Vedic goddess of dawn: similar to the Greek Eos, or the Roman Aurora. [HIND.]

Val-hal-la (văl-hăl'ȧ), the hall of the slain, where fallen warriors were entertained. [TEUT.]

Va-li (vä'lē), Odin's precocious son, who, as soon as born, avenged the death of Balder. He was to rule with Vidar after Ragnarok. Also, **Vale.** [TEUT.]

Val-kyr-ie (văl-kĭr'ĭ; văl-kī'rĭ), one of a troop of Teutonic goddesses, handmaids of Odin. Hovering over the field of battle, they woke up heroes with a kiss, and led away their souls to Valhalla, there to fight and to drink ale, as of old. Also, **Valkyria.**

Va-nir (vä'nẽr; wä'nẽr), Njorth, Frey, and Freya, gods of trade and commerce, who lived in Vanaheim; at first enemies, later allies of the Æsir in Asgard.

Va-yu (vä'yŏŏ; wä'yŏŏ), the Hindu god of the winds: similar to the Greek god Æolus.

Ve (vā), brother of Odin and Vili, whom he helped slay the giant Ymir. [TEUT.]

Ve-nus (vē'nŭs), the Roman goddess of beauty and love; wife of Vulcan: identified with the Greek goddess Aphrodite.

Ves-ta (vĕs'tȧ), the Roman goddess of virginity, fire, and the domestic hearth; similar to the Greek goddess Hestia.

Vi-li (vē'lē), brother of Odin and Ve, whom he helped slay the giant Ymir. [TEUT.]

Vi-tharr (vē'*thär*), son of Odin and the giantess Grid; destined to be the slayer of Fenrir at Ragnarok and then to rule with Vali. [TEUT.]

Vul-can (vŭl'kăn), the Roman god of fire and the working of metals: identified with the Greek god Hephæstus.

Wo-den (wō'dĕn), another name for Odin, the chief of the Teutonic gods. Also, **Wodan.**

Ya-ma (yä'mȧ), the first man; after death he and Yami, the first woman, became king and queen of the other world: similar to Hades (Pluto) and Persephone (Proserpina). [HIND.]

Ygg-dra-sill (ĭg'drȧ-sĭl), the ash tree which embraces and supports the world. [TEUT.]

Y-mir (ü'mēr; ē'mĭr), the ancestor of the Teutonic giants; formed of the frost and fire in Ginnungagap; from his body the present world was created. His flesh became earth; his blood, the sea; his bones, the mountains; his teeth, the cliffs; his skull, the heavens, wherein his brains float in the form of clouds.

Zeph-y-rus (zĕf'ĭ-rŭs), the West Wind, mildest and gentlest of all Greek sylvan deities.

Zeus (zūs), the supreme deity of the Greeks; god of nature, giver of victory, god of law and order, of social virtues; the beginning and end of all things; identified by the Romans with Jupiter (Jove).

FOREIGN WORDS AND PHRASES

Frequently Occurring in English Literature, Including Proverbs, Colloquial Expressions, Mottoes of States and Nations, Current War Expressions.

Note for Pronunciation of Latin Expressions.

There are in use two methods of pronouncing Latin: one, the so-called English method, follows in general the principles of English pronunciation; the other, the so-called Roman method, follows more or less closely the pronunciation of the ancient Romans themselves. The English pronunciation is still generally used for Latin scientific terms, for names, phrases, and quotations in English context. The proper accentuation and syllabification according to the Roman method is here indicated for all Latin words and phrases. Then the pronunciation of the word or phrase according to the English method follows in parentheses; as, di'ri-go (dĭr'ĭ-gō). A Latin grammar should be consulted for further details of the Roman pronunciation.

à bas (ȧ bä'), down with (in disapproval). [Fr.]

ab-bé (ȧ"bā'), a French secular ecclesiastic without a benefice. [Fr.]

ab ex'tra (ăb ĕk'strȧ), from without. [Lat.]

ab in-i'ti-o (ăb ĭn-ĭsh'ĭ-ō), from the beginning; originally. [Lat.]

ab in'tra (ăb ĭn'trȧ), from within. [Lat.]

à bon mar-ché (ȧ bôṅ" mȧr"shā'), at a bargain; cheap. [Fr.]

ab o-ri'gi-ne (ăb ō-rĭj'ĭ-nē), from the beginning. [Lat.]

ab o'vo us'que ad ma'la (ăb ō'vō ŭs'kwē ăd mā'lȧ), from the egg to the apples: said of a dinner; from beginning to end. [Lat.]

a-bri (ȧ"brē'), a shelter, dugout. [Fr.]

ab'sit in-vi'di-a (ăb'sĭt ĭn-vĭd'ĭ-ȧ), let there be no ill will. [Lat.]

ab u'no di'sce om'nes (ăb ū'nō dĭs'ē ŏm'nēz), from one learn all. [Lat.]

ab ur'be con'di-ta (ăb ûr'bē kŏn'dĭ-tȧ), from the founding of the city (Rome)—about 753 B. C. [Lat.]

à che-val (ȧ shē-vȧl'), lit., on horseback; on both sides. [Fr.]

à compte (ȧ kôṅt'), on account; in part payment. [Fr.]

ad ar-bi'tri-um (ăd är-bĭt'rĭ-ŭm), at will. [Lat.]

ad a'stra per a'spe-ra (ăd ăs'trȧ pĕr ăs'pē-rȧ), to the stars through difficulties: motto of Kansas. [Lat.]

ad cap-tan'dum vul'gus (ăd kăp-tăn'dŭm vŭl'gŭs), to catch the crowd. [Lat.]

à de-mi (ȧ dē-mē'), half; incompletely. [Fr.]

ad fi'nem (ăd fī'nĕm), to the end. [Lat.]

ad hoc (ăd hŏk), with respect to this. [Lat.]

ad in"fi-ni'tum (ăd ĭn"fĭ-nī'tŭm), to infinity; without limit. [Lat.]

ad in'te-rim (ăd ĭn'tẽr-ĭm), meanwhile, temporary. [Lat.]

a-dios (ä"dyōs'), adieu. [Span.]

ad ka-len'das Græ'cas (ăd kȧ-lĕn'dăs grē'kăs), lit., at the Greek calends; *i. e.*, never—the Greeks had no calends. [Lat.]

ad lib'i-tum (ăd lĭb'ĭ-tŭm), at pleasure. [Lat.]

ad nau'se-am (ăd nô'shē-ăm), to (the point of) disgust. [Lat.]

ad pa'tres (ăd pā'trēz), (gathered) to his fathers; dead. [Lat.]

ad quem (ăd kwĕm), at, or to, which: opposite to *a quo*. [Lat.]

à droite (ȧ drwät'), to the right; on the right. [Fr.]

ad va-lo'rem (ăd vȧ-lō'rĕm), according to the value. [Lat.]

ad vivum (ăd vī'vŭm), to the life. [Lat.]

æ'quo a'ni-mo (ē'kwō ăn'ĭ-mō), lit., with equal mind; calmly. [Lat.]

af-faire d'a-mour (ȧ"fâr' dȧ"mōōr'), a love affair. [Fr.]

af-faire d'hon-neur (ȧ"fâr' dō"nûr'), an affair of honor; a duel. [Fr.]

af-faire du cœur (ȧ"fâr' dü kûr'), an affair of the heart. [Fr.]

à fond (ȧ fôṅ'), to the bottom; thoroughly. [Fr.]

a for"ti-o'ri (ā fôr"shĭ-ō'rī; fôr"-), with the greater force: said of an argument. [Lat.]

à gauche (ȧ gōsh'), to the left; on the left. [Fr.]

a-gen'da (ȧ-jĕn'dȧ), things to be done [Lat.]

à grands frais (ȧ gräṅ" frē'), at great expense. [Fr.]

à haute voix (ȧ ōt" vwȧ'), aloud. [Fr.]

à la carte (ȧ lȧ kärt'), according to the bill of fare; with a price given for each dish: opposite to *table d'hôte*. [Fr.]

à la fran-çaise (ȧ lȧ fräṅ"sâz'), in the French fashion. [Fr.]

à la mode (ȧ lȧ mōd'), in fashion. [Fr.]

à l'an-glaise (ȧ läṅ"glâz'), in the English fashion. [Fr.]

a'lis vo'lat pro'pri-is (ā'lĭs vō'lăt prō'prĭ-ĭs), she flies with her own wings: motto of Oregon. [Lat.]

al-le-gret-to (äl"lā-grĕt'tō), rather quick. [It.]

al-le-gro (äl-lā'grō), quick. [It.]

Al'ma Ma'ter (ăl'mȧ mā'tẽr), lit., fostering mother; a school in which one has been educated. [Lat.]

al'ter e'go (ăl'tẽr ē'gō), lit., a second I; a bosom friend. [Lat.]

a-mende ho-no-ra-ble (ȧ"mäṅd' ō"nō"rȧ'bl), a reparation publicly made to the injured party. [Fr.]

bōōt, fŏŏt; found; boil; function; chase; good; joy; *th*en, thick; hw = wh as in when; zh = z as in azure; kh = ch as in loch. See pronunciation key, pages xix to xxii.

a'mor pa'tri-æ (ă'môr păt'rĭ-ē), love of one's country. [LAT.]
a-mour pro-pre (ȧ"mōōr' prô'pr), self-love. [FR.]
an-ci-en ré-gime (äṅ"syăṅ' rā"zhēm'), the ancient order of things. [FR.]
an-dan-te (ăn-dăn'tā; ăn-dăn'tē), moderately slow. [IT.]
an'guis in her'ba (ăṅ'gwĭs ĭn hûr'bȧ), a snake in the grass. [LAT.]
a'ni-mis o"pi-bus'que pa-ra'ti (ăn'ĭ-mĭs ŏp"ĭ-bŭs'kwē pȧ-rā'tī), prepared in minds and resources: one of the mottoes of South Carolina. [LAT.]
an'no æ-ta'tis su'æ (ăn'ō ē-tā'tĭs sū'ē), in the year of his, or her, age. [LAT.]
an'no Do'mi-ni (ăn'ō dŏm'ĭ-nī), in the (given) year of (our) Lord. [LAT.]
an'no ur'bis con'di-tæ (ăn'ō ûr'bĭs kŏn'dĭ-tē), in the year of the founded city (Rome, founded about 753 B. C.). [LAT.]
an'nus mi-ra'bi-lis (ăn'ŭs mĭ-răb'ĭ-lĭs), wonderful year. [LAT.]
an'te bel'lum (ăn'tē bĕl'ŭm), before the war (especially the American Civil War). [LAT.]
an'te me-ri'di-em (ăn'tē mē-rĭd'ĭ-ĕm), before noon. [LAT.]
à outrance (ȧ ōō"träṅs'), to the bitter end; to the utmost. [FR.]
à peu près (ȧ pû"prĕ'), nearly. [FR.]
à plomb (ȧ plôṅ'), perpendicularly. [FR.]
a po-ste"ri-o'ri (ā pŏs-tē"rĭ-ō'rī), from that which follows; from effect to cause: opposite to *a priori*. [LAT.]
ap-pli-qué (ȧ"plē"kā'), put on: as patterns on textiles. [FR.]
a-près moi le dé-luge! (ȧ"prĕ mwȧ' lē dā"lüzh'), after me the deluge! [FR.]
a pri-o'ri (ā prī-ō'rī; ä prĭ-ō'rē), from that which precedes; from cause to effect: opposite to *a posteriori*. [LAT.]
à pro-pos de rien (ȧ prō"pō'dē ryăṅ'), apropos of nothing; irrelevant. [FR.]
a quo (ā kwō), from which: opposite to *ad quem*. [LAT.]
ar'bi-ter e"le-gan'ti-æ (är'bĭ-tēr ĕl"ē-găn'shĭ-ē), judge of elegance. Also, **ar'bi-ter e"le-gan"ti-a'rum.** [LAT.]
ar"gu-men'tum ad ho'mi-nem (är"gū-mĕn'tŭm ăd hŏm'ĭ-nĕm), an argument to the man (*i. e.*, to his interests). [LAT.]
a ri-ve-der-ci (ȧ rē"vā-dâr'chē), lit., to seeing one another again; au revoir. [IT.]
ar-peg-gio (är-pĕd'jō), a chord played in rapid succession. [IT.]
ar-rec'tis au'ri-bus (ȧ-rĕk'tĭs ô'rĭ-bŭs), with ears pricked up. [LAT.]
ar-ron-disse-ment (ȧ"rôṅ"dēs"mäṅ'), the largest division of a French department, serving as a "congressional district." [FR.]
ars est ce-la're ar'tem (ärz ĕst sē-lā'rē är'tĕm), it is (true) art to conceal art. [LAT.]
ars lon'ga, vi'ta bre'vis (ärz lŏṅ'gȧ vī'tȧ brĕv'ĭs), art is long, life is short. [LAT.]
a-te-lier (ȧ"tē-lyā'), a studio. [FR.]
a tem'po (ä tĕm'pō), in time. [IT.]
au con-traire (ō kôṅ"trâr'), on the contrary. [FR.]
au cou-rant (ō kōō"räṅ'), lit., with the current; up-to-date. [FR.]
au fait (ō"fĕ'), expert. [FR.]
au fond (ō"fôṅ'), at bottom; fundamentally. [FR.]
auf wie-der-seh-en (ouf"vē'dēr-zā"ĕn), till we meet again; good-by. [GER.]
au grand sérieux (ō"gräṅ sĕr"yû'), in all seriousness. [FR.]
au reste (ō"rĕst'), for the rest; besides; as for what is left. [FR.]
au re-voir (ō"rē-vwȧr'), till we meet again; good-by. [FR.]
au'ri sa'cra fa'mes (ô'rī sā'krȧ fā'mēz), accursed greed of gold. [LAT.]
au-tres temps, au-tres mœurs (ō"tr täṅ', ō"tr mûrs'), other times, other ways or customs. [FR.]
aut vin'ce-re, aut mo'ri (ôt vĭn'sē-rē, ôt mō'rī), either to conquer or to die. [LAT.]
aux armes! (ō-zȧrm'), to arms! [FR.]
a-vec per-mis-sion (ȧ"vĕk' pĕr"mē"syôṅ'), with permission. [FR.]
a-vec plai-sir (ȧ"vĕk" plā"zēr'), with pleasure. [FR.]
a ver'bis ad ver'be-ra (ā vûr'bĭs ăd vûr'bē-rȧ), from words to blows. [LAT.]
a vin'cu-lo ma"tri-mo'ni-i (ā vĭṅ'kū-lō măt"rĭ-mō'nĭ-ī), from the bond of marriage. [LAT.]
à vo-tre san-té (ȧ vō'tr säṅ"tā'), to your health. [FR.]
ba-di-nage (bȧ"dē"nŏzh'), banter. [FR.]
bar-rage (bȧ"rŏzh'), curtain of fire, or of fire and smoke. [FR.]
bas bleu (bä"blû'), a bluestocking. [FR.]
be-a'tæ me-mo'ri-æ (bē-ā'tē mē-mō'rĭ-ē), of blessed memory. [LAT.]
beau monde (bō"môṅd'), the fashionable world. [FR.]
bel—es-prit (bĕl'ĕs-prē'), a genius; man of wit. [FR.]
belles—let-tres (bĕl" lĕt'r), literature. [FR.]
ben tro-va'to (bĕn trō-vä'tō), well invented. [IT.]
bête noire (bât" nwär'), black beast; object of abhorrence. [FR.]
bil-let—doux (bĭl'ē-dōō'; bē"yē"dōō'), a love letter. [FR.]
bis dat qui ci'to dat (bĭs dăt kwī sī'tō dăt), he gives twice who gives quickly. [LAT.]
bla-sé (blȧ"zā'), surfeited. [FR.]
bles-sé (blĕ"sā'), a wounded soldier. [FR.]
bligh-ty (blī'tĭ), over the seas; home. [EAST INDIAN.]
Boche (bôsh), a German soldier. Also, **boche.** [FR.]
bo'na fi'de (bō'nȧ fī'dē), in good faith; without deceit. [LAT.]
bon gré, mal gré (bôṅ' grā", mȧl' grā"), with good grace (or) with bad grace; willy-nilly. [FR.]
bon jour (bôṅ" zhōōr'), good day; good morning. [FR.]
bon mot (bôṅ"mō'), lit., good word; a witty, adroit expression. [FR.]
bonne (bôn), a maid servant. [FR.]
bonne foi (bôn" fwä'), good faith. [FR.]
bon soir (bôṅ" swȧr'), good evening. [FR.]
bon ton (bôṅ" tôṅ'), high society. [FR.]
bon vi-vant (bôṅ"vē"väṅ'), a lover of good living. [FR.]
bon vo-yage! (bôṅ"vwȧ"yŏzh'), a good journey! as a farewell. [FR.]
bru'tum ful'men (brōō'tŭm fŭl'mĕn), a thunderbolt striking blindly; an ineffectual display of force. [LAT.]
ca-mou-flage (kȧ"mōō"flŏzh'), disguising (as by coloration, etc.); to disguise. [FR.]
ca'put mor'tu-um (kā'pŭt môr'tū-ŭm; kăp'ŭt), lit., skull; worthless remains. [LAT.]
car'pe di'em (kär'pē dī'ĕm), enjoy the day; make the most of the present. [LAT.]
carte blanche (kärt" bläṅsh'), lit., white paper; unconditional power. [FR.]
ca'sus bel'li (kā'sŭs bĕl'ī), an event of war (*i. e.*, a cause, or an alleged justification of war). [LAT.]
cau'sa si'ne qua non (kô'zȧ sī'nē kwā nŏn), lit., cause without which not; an indispensable condition. [LAT.]

cau-se-rie (kōz″rē′; kōz′rē), informal discussion. [Fr.]
ca′ve-at emp′tor (kā′vē-ăt ĕmp′tŏr), lit., let the buyer beware; sold without guarantee. [Lat.]
ca′ve ca′nem (kā′vē kā′nĕm), beware of the dog. [Lat.]
ce′dant ar′ma to′gæ (sē′dănt är′mȧ tō′jē), lit., let arms yield to the civilian costume: *i. e.*, military, to civil power. [Lat.]
c′est-à-dire (sĕ″-tȧ″dēr′), that is to say; namely. [Fr.]
c′est se-lon (sĕ″s-lôṅ′), that depends. [Fr.]
ce′te-ra de′sunt (sĕt′ē-rȧ dē′sŭnt), the rest are wanting. [Lat.]
ce′te-ris pa′ri-bus (sĕt′ē-rĭs păr′ĭ-bŭs), other things being equal. [Lat.]
cha-cun à son goût (shȧ″kŭṅ′-nȧ″ sôṅ″gōō′), everyone to his taste. [Fr.]
Champs É-ly-sées (shäṅ″-zā″lē″zā′), Elysian Fields; name of an avenue in Paris. [Fr.]
cha-peau bas (shȧ″pō″bä′), hats off! [Fr.]
chas-seur (shȧ″sûr′), one of a body of light cavalry or infantry. [Fr.]
châ-teau en E-spagne (shä″tō′äṅ-nĕs″păṅ′yĕ), a castle in Spain; a castle in the air. [Fr.]
chef de cui-sine (shĕf″ dĕ kwē″zēn′), head cook. [Fr.]
che-min de fer (shĕ″măṅ′dĕ fâr′), lit., iron road; railroad. [Fr.]
cher a-mi (shâr″ ȧ″mē′), dear friend (masc.). [Fr.]
cher-chez la femme (shĕr″shā′ lȧ fȧm′), look for the woman. [Fr.]
chère a-mie (shâr″ ȧ″mē′), dear friend (fem.). [Fr.]
che sa-rà′sa-rà′ (kā sä-rä′ sä-rä′), what will be, will be. [It.]
che-va-lier d′in-dus-trie (shĕ-vȧl″yā′ dăṅ″dŭs″trē′), a swindler. [Fr.]
chia-ro-scu-ro (kyä″rō-skōō′rō), pictorial art employing only light and shade. Also, **chia-ro—o-scu-ro.** [It.]
ci-ce-ro-ne (chē″chā-rō′nā; sĭs″ē-rō′nē), a local guide. [It.]
cir′ca (sûr′kȧ), about. Also, **circiter.** [Lat.]
comme il faut (kō″mēl″fō′; kō″mē″fō′), as it should be; proper. [Fr.]
com-mu-ni-qué (kō″mü″nē″kā′), official report. [Fr.]
compte ren-du (kôṅt″ räṅ″dü′), an account given; a report. [Fr.]
con a-mo-re (kōn ä-mō′rā), with love; earnestly. [It.]
con-cours (kôṅ″kōōr′), a competition. [Fr.]
con do-lo-re (kōn dō-lō′rā), with grief; sadly. [It.]
con-fet-ti (kōn-fĕt′tē), bonbons; tiny, bright-colored scraps of paper thrown at weddings. [It.]
con-gé (kôṅ″zhā′), leave of absence. [Fr.]
con′tra bo′nos mo′res (kŏn′trȧ bō′nōs mō′rēz), against good morals or manners. [Lat.]
con-tre-temps (kôṅ″tr-täṅ′), an untoward accident. [Fr.]
co-pain (kō″păṅ′), comrade. [Fr.]
co′ram po′pu-lo (kō′răm pŏp′ū-lō), publicly. [Lat.]
cor′pus de-lic′ti (kôr′pŭs dē-lĭk′tī), the body of a crime; the essential fact of a crime. [Lat.]
cor″ri-gen′da (kŏr″ĭ-jĕn′dȧ), things to be corrected. [Lat.]
cor-tège (kôr″tĕzh′), a procession. Also, **cor-tege.** [Fr.]
coup de grâce (kōō″ dĕ gräs′), lit., a stroke of mercy; a finishing stroke. [Fr.]
coup de main (kōō″ dĕ măṅ′), a sudden movement. [Fr.]
coup de maî-tre (kōō″ dĕ mâ′tr), a master stroke. [Fr.]
coup de so-leil (kōō″ dĕ sō″lā′yĕ), a sunstroke. [Fr.]
coup d′é-tat (kōō″ dā″tȧ′), a stroke of policy. [Fr.]
coûte que coûte (kōōt″ kĕ kōōt′), let it cost what it may. [Fr.]
crème (krâm). Cream. [Fr.]
cre′sci-te et mul″ti-pli-ca′mi-ni (krĕs′ĭ-tē ĕt mŭl″tĭ-plĭ-kăm′ĭ-nī), increase and multiply: motto of Maryland. [Lat.]
cre′scit e-un′do (krĕs′ĭt ē-ŭn′dō), it grows by going (or as it goes): motto of New Mexico. [Lat.]
Croix de Guerre (krwä′ dĕ gâr′), War Cross. [Fr.]
Croix Rouge (krwä′ rōōzh′), Red Cross. [Fr.]
cui bo′no? (kī bō′nō), lit., to whom (is it) for a benefit? to whose advantage? [Lat.]
cui-sine (kwē″zēn′), the kitchen; style of cooking. [Fr.]
cul de sac (kü″ d-sȧk′; kŭl″dĕ sȧk′), a blind alley. [Fr.]
cum gra′no sa′lis (kŭm grā′nō sā′lĭs), with a grain of salt; with some allowance. [Lat.]
cu-ré (kü″rā′), a parish priest. [Fr.]
cur-ren′te ca′la-mo (kŭ-rĕn′tē kăl′ȧ-mō), with a running (or ready) pen. [Lat.]
d′ac-cord (dȧ″kôr′), in accord. [Fr.]
dame d′hon-neur (dȧm″ dō″nûr′), a maid of honor. [Fr.]
de bonne grâce (dĕ bōn″ gräs′), with good grace; willingly. [Fr.]
dé-col-le-té (dā″kō″l-tā′), leaving the neck and shoulders uncovered. [Fr.]
de fac′to (dē făk′tō), in fact; actually; in reality. [Lat.]
de gus′ti-bus non est dis″pu-tan′dum (dē gŭs′tĭ-bŭs nŏn ĕst dĭs″pū-tăn′dŭm), there is no disputing about tastes. [Lat.]
De′i gra′ti-a (dē′ī grā′shĭ-ȧ), by the grace of God. [Lat.]
de ju′re (dē jōō′rē), by right. [Lat.]
de-len′da est Car-tha′go (dē-lĕn′dȧ ĕst kär-thā′gō), Carthage must be destroyed. [Lat.]
de luxe (dĕ lüks′), sumptuous. [Fr.]
de-mi—tasse (dē-mē′ täs′; dĕm′ĭ-tăs), a small cup of black coffee. [Fr.]
de mor′tu-is nil ni′si bonum (dē môr′tū-ĭs nĭl nī′sī bō′nŭm), of the dead (say) nothing but good. [Lat.]
de ni′hi-lo ni′hil (dē nī′hĭ-lō nī′hĭl), from nothing nothing (can come). [Lat.]
dé-noue-ment (dā-nōō′mäṅ; dā″nōō″mäṅ′), the outcome (of a plot or mystery). [Fr.]
de no′vo (dē nō′vō), anew; afresh. [Lat.]
De′o fa-ven′te (dē′ō fȧ-vĕn′tē), with God′s favor. [Lat.]
De′o gra′ti-as (dē′ō grā′shĭ-ăs), thanks to God. [Lat.]
De′o vo-len′te (dē′ō vō-lĕn′tē), God willing. [Lat.]
de pro-fun′dis (dē prō-fŭn′dĭs), out of the depths. [Lat.]
der-nier res-sort (dĕr″nyā′ rĕ-sôr′), a last resource. [Fr.]
de trop (dĕ trō′), too much; in the way. [Fr.]
de′us ex ma′chi-na (dē′ŭs ĕks măk′ĭ-nȧ), a god (let down) from a machine (as in ancient theaters); an unexpected occurrence. [Lat.]
di′es fau′stus (dī′ēz fôs′tŭs), a lucky day. [Lat.]
di′es i′ræ (dī′ēz ī′rē), day of wrath. [Lat.]

Dieu dé-fend le droit (dyû' dā"fäń' le drwä'), God defends the right. [Fr.]

Dieu et mon droit (dyû' ā môń drwä'), God and my right: motto in British royal arms. [Fr.]

Dios y fe-de-ra-ción (dyōs' ē fā"dā-rä-thyōn'). God and federation: motto of Venezuela. [Span.]

di'ri-go (dĭr'ĭ-gō), I direct or lead: motto of Maine. [Lat.]

dis a'li-ter vi'sum (dēs ăl'ĭ-tĕr vī'sŭm), to the gods it has seemed otherwise. [Lat.]

dis-jec'ta mem'bra (dĭs-jĕk'tȧ mĕm'brȧ), scattered parts. [Lat.]

dis-tin-gué (dēs-tăń'gā), distinguished; of splendid bearing. [Fr.]

di'tat De'us (dī'tăt dē'ŭs), God enriches: motto of Arizona. [Lat.]

di'vi-de et im'pe-ra (dĭv'ĭ-dē ĕt ĭm'pē-rȧ), divide and rule. [Lat.]

do-cen'do dis'ci-mus (dō-sĕn'dō dĭs'ĭ-mŭs), we learn by teaching. [Lat.]

dol-ce far nien-te (dōl'chā fär nyĕn'tā), charming idleness. [It.]

Do'mi-ne, di'ri-ge nos (dŏm'ĭ-nē, dĭr'ĭ-jē nōs), Lord, direct us: motto of the city of London. [Lat.]

Do'mi-nus vo-bis'cum (dŏm'ĭ-nŭs vō-bĭs'kŭm), the Lord (be) with you. [Lat.]

dou-ble—en-ten-dre (dōō'bl -äń"täń'dr), a word or expression admitting of two interpretations, one often improper. [Fr.]

dra'ma-tis per-so'nae (drăm'ȧ-tĭs pĕr-sō'nē), the characters in a play. [Lat.]

Drei-bund (drī'bōōnt), a triple alliance; especially, that between Germany, Austria, and Italy before the World War. [Ger.]

du'cit a'mor pa'tri-ae (dū'sĭt ā'mōr păt'rĭ-ē), love of country leads. [Lat.]

dul'ce et de-co'rum est pro pa'tri-a mo'ri (dŭl'sē ĕt dē-kō'rŭm ĕst prō păt'rĭ-ȧ mō'rī), it is sweet and fitting to die for one's country. [Lat.]

dum spi'ro, spe'ro (dŭm spī'rō, spē'rō), while I breathe, I hope: one of the mottoes of South Carolina. [Lat.]

dum vi'vi-mus, vi-va'mus (dŭm vĭv'ĭ-mŭs, vī-vā'mŭs), while we live, let us live; let us make the most of life. [Lat.]

du-o (dōō'ō), duet. [It.]

eau de vie (ō' dē vē'). Water of life; brandy. [Fr.]

ec'ce sig'num (ĕk'sē sĭg'nŭm), behold the sign; look at the proof. [Lat.]

e con-tra'ri-o (ē kŏn-trā'rĭ-ō), on the contrary. [Lat.]

e-di'ti-o prin'ceps (ē-dĭsh'ĭ-ō prĭn'sĕps), the first edition. [Lat.]

é-ga-li-té (ā"gȧ"lē"tā'), equality. [Fr.]

em-bon-point (äń"bôń"pwăń'), stoutness. [Fr.]

em-bus-qué (äń"büs"kā'), a soldier who has taken a post free from danger: more severe than slacker. [Fr.]

en a-mi (äń"nȧ"mē'), like a friend. [Fr.]

en ar-rière (äń" -nȧ"ryâr'), in the rear; in arrears. [Fr.]

en a-vant (äń" -nȧ"väń'), forward; into the future. [Fr.]

en dés-ha-bil-lé (äń" dā"zȧ"bē"yā'), in undress. [Fr.]

en ef-fet (äń"-nā"fē'), in effect; in deed. [Fr.]

en fa-mille (äń"fȧ"mē'yē), in (or with) the family; at home. [Fr.]

en-fants per-dus (äń"fäń' pĕr"dü'), lit., lost children; a forlorn hope. [Fr.]

en-fant ter-ri-ble (äń"fäń' tĕ"rē'bl), a terrible child; a child whose loquaciousness embarrasses his elders. [Fr.]

en fin (äń"făń'), at last. [Fr.]

en masse (äń"mȧs'), in a body. [Fr.]

en pas-sant (äń"pȧ"säń'), in passing. [Fr.]

en rap-port (äń"rȧ"pōr'), in sympathetic relation. [Fr.]

en rè-gle (äń"rĕ'gl), according to rule; right. [Fr.]

en route (äń"rōōt'), on the way. [Fr.]

en'se pe'tit pla'ci-dam sub li'ber-ta'te qui-e'tem (ĕn'sē pĕt'ĭt plăs'ĭ-dăm sŭb lĭb"ĕr-tā'tē kwī-ē'tĕm), with the sword she seeks calm repose under liberty: motto of Massachusetts. [Lat.]

en suite (äń"swēt'), in a series or set. [Fr.]

En-tente (äń"täńt'), understanding; England, France, Russia as arrayed against the Dreibund at the outbreak of the World War. [Fr.]

en-tou-rage (äń"tōō"räzh'), surroundings; esp. body of associates. [Fr.]

en-tre nous (äń'tr nōō'), between ourselves. [Fr.]

e plu'ri-bus u'num (ē plōō'rĭ-bŭs ū'nŭm), one out of many: motto of the United States of America. [Lat.]

er-ra're hu-ma'num est (ĕ-rā'rē hū-mā'nŭm ĕst), to err is human. [Lat.]

es-ca-drille (ĕs"kȧ"drē'yē), an airplane unit in the army. [Fr.]

es-prit de corps (ĕs"prē' dē kōr'), the spirit of enthusiasm and loyalty pervading a body of persons. [Fr.]

es'se quam vi-de'ri (ĕs'ē kwăm vĭ-dē'rī), to be rather than to seem: motto of North Carolina. [Lat.]

est mo'dus in re'bus (ĕst mō'dŭs ĭn rē'bŭs), there is a limit in things. [Lat.]

es'to per-pe'tu-a (ĕs'tō pĕr-pĕt'ū-ȧ), may she last forever; motto of Idaho. [Lat.]

é-tat des pertes (ā"tȧ' dā pârt'), casualty list. [Fr.]

et tu, Bru'te! (ĕt tū, brōō'tē), and thou, Brutus! the cry of Julius Cæsar when he saw his friend among his assassins. [Lat.]

eu-re'ka! (ū-rē'kȧ), I have found (it)! exclamation of triumph: the motto of California. [Gr.]

ex a'ni-mo (ĕks ăn'ĭ-mō), from the heart; sincerely.

ex ca-the'dra (ĕks kȧ-thē'drȧ; -kăth'ē-drȧ), lit., from the chair; with authority. [Lat.]

ex-cel'si-or (ĕk-sĕl'sĭ-ŏr), higher; ever upward: motto of New York State. [Lat.]

ex-cep'ti-o pro'bat re'gu-lam (ĕk-sĕp'shĭ-ō prō'băt rĕg'ū-lăm), the exception proves the rule. [Lat.]

ex-em'pli gra'ti-a (ĕg-zĕm'plī grā'shĭ-ȧ), for the sake of example. [Lat.]

ex'e-unt om'nes (ĕk'sē-ŭnt ŏm'nēz), all go out. [Lat.]

ex li'bris (ĕks lī'brĭs), from the books (of): an inscription used with the owner's name in a book. [Lat.]

ex ne-ces"si-ta'te re'i (ĕks nē-sĕs'ĭ-tā'tē rē'ī), from the necessity of the case. [Lat.]

ex ni'hi-lo ni'hil fit (ĕks nī'hĭ-lō nī'hĭl fĭt), from nothing nothing is made. [Lat.]

ex of-fi'ci-o (ĕks ō-fĭsh'ĭ-ō), from office; by virtue of an office. [Lat.]

ex par'te (ĕks pär'tē), upon, from, or in the interest of, one side only. [Lat.]

ex-per'to cre'di-te (ĕks-pûr'tō krĕd'ĭ-tē), believe one who speaks from experience. [Lat.]

ex-po-sé (ĕks"pō"zā'), an exposure of something discreditable. [Fr.]

ex post fac'to (ĕks pōst făk'tō), from what is done afterward; retrospective. [Lat.]

ex u'no di'sce om'nes (ĕks ū'nō dĭs'ē ŏm'nēz), from one learn all. [Lat.]

fa'ci-le prin'ceps (făs'ĭ-lē prĭn'sĕps), easily chief. [Lat.]
fa'ci-lis de-scen'sus A-ver'ni (făs'ĭ-lĭs dē-sĕn'sŭs ȧ-vĕr'nī), the descent of Avernus is easy; the road to evil is easy. [Lat.]
faire sui-vre (fâr" swē'vr), lit., to make to follow; please forward. [Fr.]
fait ac-com-pli (fĕ"-tȧ"kôṅ"plē'), an accomplished fact. [Fr.]
Fa'ta ob'stant (fā'tȧ ŏb'stănt), the Fates oppose. [Lat.]
fat-ti ma-schi-i, pa-ro-le fe-mi-ne (făt'tē mä'skē-ē pȧ-rō'lā fĕm'ē-nā), deeds (are) males, words females: motto of Maryland. [It.]
fau-teuil (fō"tû'yĕ), an armchair. [Fr.]
faux pas (fō" pä'), a false step; especially, an offense against social convention. [Fr.]
femme de cham-bre (fȧm dē shäṅ'br), a lady's maid; chambermaid. [Fr.]
fe'ræ na-tu'ræ (fē'rē nȧ-tū'rē), of a wild nature. [Lat.]
fer'vet o'pus (fûr'vĕt ō'pŭs), the work boils; there is great activity. [Lat.]
fe-sti'na len'te (fĕ-stī'nȧ lĕn'tē), make haste slowly. [Lat.]
fête cham-pê-tre (fāt shäṅ"pâ'tr), a rural or open air festival. [Fr.]
feu de joie (fû"dē zhwä'), a bonfire; a firing of guns in token of joy. [Fr.]
fi'at jus-ti'ti-a, ru'at cæ'lum (fī'ăt jŭs-tĭsh'ĭ-ȧ, rōō'ăt sē'lŭm), let justice be done, though the heavens fall. [Lat.]
fi'at lux' (fī'ăt lŭks'), let there be light: the command of God at Creation. [Lat.]
fi'de-i de-fen'sor (fī'dē-ī dē-fĕn'sēr; -sôr), defender of the faith: a title of the sovereigns of England. [Lat.]
fi'des Pu'ni-ca (fī'dēz pū'nĭ-kȧ), Punic faith; treachery. [Lat.]
fi'dus A-cha'tes (fī'dŭs ȧ-kā'tēz), faithful Achates; a trusty friend. [Lat.]
fies-ta (fyĕs'tä), a holiday. [Span.]
fi'nis co-ro'nat o'pus (fī'nĭs kō-rō'năt ō'pŭs), the end crowns the work. [Lat.]
fla-gran'te bel'lo (flȧ-grăn'tē bĕl'ō), while the war is blazing; during actual war. [Lat.]
fla-gran'te de-lic'to (flȧ-grăn'tē dē-lĭk'tō), while the crime is blazing; in the very act. [Lat.]
for'tes for-tu'na ju'vat (fôr'tēz fôr-tū'nȧ jōō'văt), fortune favors the brave. [Lat.]
for'ti-ter in re, sua'vi-ter in mo'do (fôr'tĭ-tĕr ĭn rē, swăv'ĭ-tĕr ĭn mō'dō), strongly in deed, gently in manner. [Lat.]
four-ra-gère (fōō"rȧ"zhâr'), a decoration granted to an entire body of troops for distinguished bravery in action, consisting of a braided cord of a designated color, to be worn about the left shoulder seam of the coat by every man of the unit so decorated. [Fr.]
fran-co (frăn'kō), postage free. [It.]
frap-pé (frȧ"pā'), frozen; a frozen mixture, as a water ice. [Fr.]
Fritz (frĭts), a German soldier. [Ger.]
fu'git ho'ra (fū'jĭt hō'rȧ), the hour flies; time flies. [Lat.]
fu'it I'li-um (fū'ĭt ĭl'ĭ-ŭm), Troy has been (*i. e.*, exists no longer). [Lat.]
func'tus of-fi'ci-o (fŭnk'tŭs ō-fĭsh'ĭ-ō), having fulfilled his office; hence, out of office. [Lat.]
fu'ror po-e'ti-cus (fū'rôr pō-ĕt'ĭ-kŭs), poetic frenzy. [Lat.]
fu'ror scri-ben'di (fū'rôr skrī-bĕn'dī), a rage for writing. [Lat.]
Gal'li-ce (găl'ĭ-sē), in French; after the French manner. [Lat.]
gar-çon (gȧr"sôṅ'), a boy; a waiter. [Fr.]
garde du corps (gȧrd" dü kôr'), a bodyguard. [Fr.]
gauche (gōsh), left-handed; clumsy. [Fr.]
ge'ni-us lo'ci (jē'nĭ-ŭs lō'sī), the spirit of the place. [Lat.]
gen-re (zhäṅ'r), a species; a style, especially of painting, dealing realistically with everyday life. [Fr.]
Ger-ma'ni-ce (jẽr-măn'ĭ-sē), in German; after the German manner. [New Lat.]
gla-cé (glȧ"sā'), smooth and glossy; iced. [Fr.]
gno-thi se-au-ton (gnō'thī sē-ou-tŏn'), know thyself. [Gr.]
Gott mit uns (gŏt mĭt ōōns), God with us: motto of the Order of the Crown, Prussia. [Ger.]
gour-met (gōōr"mē'), a glutton. [Fr.]
grande pas-sion (gräṅd" pȧ"syôṅ'), great passion; love. [Fr.]
grand monde (gräṅ" môṅd'), great world; high society. [Fr.]
guerre à ou-trance (gâr" ȧ ōō"träṅs'), war to the uttermost. [Fr.]
han-gar (häṅ'gär"; äṅ"gär'), a shed for aircraft. [Fr.]
haut goût (ō"gōō'; hō"gōō'), high flavor; a slight taint. [Fr.]
hic et u-bi'que (hĭk ĕt ū-bī'kwē), here and everywhere. [Lat.]
hic ja'cet (hĭk jā'sĕt), here lies: used in epitaphs. [Lat.]
hinc il'læ la'cri-mæ (hĭnk ĭl'ē lăk'rĭ-mē), hence those tears. [Lat.]
hoc o'pus, hic la'bor est (hŏk ō'pŭs, hĭk lā'bẽr ĕst), this (is) the work, this is the labor. [Lat.]
hoc tem'po-re (hŏk tĕm'pō-rē), at this time. [Lat.]
hoi pol-loi (hoi pŏ-loi'), the many; the populace. [Gr.]
ho'mi-nis est er-ra're (hŏm'ĭ-nĭs ĕst ĕ-rā'rē), to err is human. [Lat.]
homme d'af-faires (ŏm" dȧ"fâr'), an agent, one who does business for another. [Fr.]
homme d'es-prit (ŏm" dĕs"prē'), a man of wit. [Fr.]
ho-ni soit qui mal y pense (ō'nē swȧ kē mȧl ē päṅs'), shamed be he who thinks evil of it: the motto of the Order of the Garter. [Fr.]
hon-neur et pa-trie (ō"nûr' ā pȧ"trē'), honor and fatherland: motto of the French Legion of Honor. [Fr.]
ho'ra fu'git (hō'rȧ fū'jĭt), the hour flies; time flies. [Lat.]
hor-ri'bi-le dic'tu (hŏ-rĭb'ĭ-lē dĭk'tū), horrible to relate. [Lat.]
hors de com-bat (hôr dē kôṅ"bȧ'; ôr), out of the fight; disabled. [Fr.]
hors d'oeuvre (hôr dû'vr; ôr), a side dish; a relish. [Fr.]
hô-tel de ville (ō"tĕl' dē vēl'), the town hall. [Fr.]
hu-ma'num est er-ra're (hū-mā'nŭm ĕst ĕ-rā'rē), to err is human. [Lat.]
i-bi'dem (ĭ-bī'dĕm), in the same place; abbrev., *ib.*, *ibid.* [Lat.]
ich dien (ĭkh dēn'), I serve: motto of the Prince of Wales. [Ger.]
ich und Gott (ĭkh ōōnt gŏt), I and God: phrase ascribed to William II. [Ger.]
i-ci on parle fran-çais (ē"sē' ôṅ pȧrl fräṅ"sĕ'), French is spoken here. [Fr.]
id est (ĭd ĕst), that is; abbrev., *i. e.* (*v*) [Lat.]
id ge'nus om'ne (ĭd jē'nŭs ŏm'nē), all of that sort. [Lat.]
il pen-se-ro-so (ēl pĕn"sē-rō'sō), the pensive (man): opposite to *l'allegro*. [Old It.]

ils ne pas-se-ront pas (ēl nē pȧ"sē"rôṅ'pä), they shall not pass. [Fr.]

im-me"di-ca'bi-le vul'nus (ĭ-mĕd"ĭ-kăb'ĭ-lē vŭl'nŭs), an incurable wound. [Lat.]

im-pe'ri-um in im-pe'ri-o (ĭm-pē'rĭ-ŭm ĭn ĭm-pē'rĭ-ō), a government within a government. [Lat.]

im-pri'mis (ĭm-prī'mĭs), in the first place; first in order. [Lat.]

in æ-ter'num (ĭn ē-tûr'nŭm), forever, always. [Lat.]

in ar-ti'cu-lo mor'tis (ĭn är-tĭk'ū-lō môr'tĭs), at point of death. [Lat.]

in es'se (ĭn ĕs'ē), in existence. [Lat.]

in ex-ten'so (ĭn ĕks-tĕn'sō), at full length; in full. [Lat.]

in ex-tre'mis (ĭn ĕks-trē'mĭs), at point of death. [Lat.]

in'fra dig"ni-ta'tem (ĭn'frȧ dĭg"nĭ-tā'tĕm), beneath one's dignity. [Lat.]

in hoc sig'no vin'ces (ĭn hŏk sĭg'nō vĭn'sēz), in (or by) this sign, (the Cross), thou shalt conquer: motto of Constantine the Great. [Lat.]

in li'mi-ne (ĭn lĭm'ĭ-nē), on the threshold; at the beginning. [Lat.]

in lo'co (ĭn lō'kō), in the (proper) place; in position. [Lat.]

in lo'co pa-ren'tis (ĭn lō'kō pȧ-rĕn'tĭs), in the place of a parent. [Lat.]

in me'di-as res (ĭn mē'dĭ-ăs rēz), into the midst of things. [Lat.]

in me-mo'ri-am (ĭn mē-mō'rĭ-ăm), in memory. [Lat.]

in om'ni-a pa-ra'tus (ĭn ŏm'nĭ-ȧ pȧ-rā'tŭs), ready for all things. [Lat.]

in per-pe'tu-um (ĭn pĕr-pĕt'ū-ŭm), forever. [Lat.]

in pos'se (ĭn pŏs'ē), potentially; in possibility. [Late Lat.]

in pro'pri-a per-so'na (ĭn prō'prĭ-ȧ pĕr-sō'nȧ), in one's own person. [Lat.]

in pu'ris na"tu-ra'li-bus (ĭn pū'rĭs năt"ū-răl'ĭ-bŭs), stark naked. [Lat.]

in re (ĭn rē), in the matter of; concerning; in fact. [Lat.]

in sæ'cu-la sæ"cu-lo'rum (ĭn sĕk'ū-lȧ sĕk"ū-lō'rŭm), for ages of ages; forever. [Lat.]

in-sculp'sit (ĭn-skŭlp'sĭt), he, or she, engraved it; the sculptor is. [Lat.]

in si'tu (ĭn sī'tū), in its original position; in place. [Lat.]

in sta'tu quo' (ĭn stā'tū kwō'), in the state in which (it is or was). [Lat.]

in'ter a'li-a (ĭn'tẽr ā'lĭ-ȧ), among other things. [Lat.]

in'ter a'li-os (ĭn'tẽr ā'lĭ-ōs), among other persons. [Lat.]

in'ter nos (ĭn'tẽr nōs), between ourselves; secret; secretly. [Lat.]

in ter-ro'rem (ĭn tĕ-rō'rĕm), as a warning; to inspire fear. [Lat.]

in'ter se (ĭn'tẽr sē'), among themselves; between themselves. [Lat.]

in to'to (ĭn tō'tō), in the whole; in general; in the entirety. [Lat.]

in u-trum'que pa-ra'tus (ĭn ū-trŭm'kwē pȧ-rā'tŭs), prepared for either (event); ready for anything. [Lat.]

in va'cu-o (ĭn văk'ū-ō), in a vacuum. [Lat.]

ip'se dix-it (ĭp'sē dĭk'sĭt), he himself has said (it); hence a dictum. [Lat.]

ip-sis'si-ma ver'ba (ĭp-sĭs'ĭ-mȧ vûr'bȧ), the very words. [Lat.]

ip'so fac'to (ĭp'sō făk'tō), by the act itself; as a result of the mere act. [Lat.]

ip'so ju're (ĭp'sō jōō'rē), by the law itself. [Lat.]

I-tal'ia ir-re-den'ta (ē-täl'yä ĭr"rā-dĕn'tä), unredeemed Italy: the districts adjoining Italy, inhabited by men of Italian stock and speech. [It.]

jac'ta est a'le-a (jăk'tȧ ĕst ā'lē-ȧ), the die is cast. [Lat.]

je main-tien-drai (zhẽ măṅ"tyăṅ"drā'), I will maintain: motto of Holland. [Fr.]

je ne sais quoi (zhẽ nē sā kwȧ'), I know not what. [Fr.]

jeu de mots (zhû' dē mō'), a play on words; a pun. [Fr.]

Jo-an'nes est no'men e'jus (jō-ăn'ēz ĕst nō'mĕn ē'jŭs), his name is John: motto of Porto Rico. [Lat.]

ju"bi-la'te De'o (jōō"bĭ-lā'tē dē'ō), rejoice in the Lord. [Lat.]

ju-lienne (zhü"lyĕn'; jōō"lĭ-ĕn'), a clear soup containing thin strips of carrots, onions, etc. [Fr.]

Ju'pi-ter To'nans (jōō'pĭ-tẽr tō'năns), Jupiter the thunderer. [Lat.]

jus ci-vi'le (jŭs sĭ-vī'lē), civil law. [Lat.]

jus di-vi'num (jŭs dĭ-vī'nŭm), divine law. [Lat.]

jus gen'ti-um (jŭs jĕn'shĭ-ŭm), the law of nations; international law. [Lat.]

juste-mi-lieu (zhüst"mē"lyû'), the golden mean. [Fr.]

jus-ti'ci-a om'ni-bus (jŭs-tĭsh'ĭ-ȧ ŏm'nĭ-bŭs), ustice for all: motto of the District of Columbia. [Lat.]

Ka-me-rad (kä-mĕ-rät'), comrade. [Ger.]

Kul-tur (kōōl-tōōr'), civilization. [Ger.]

la"bo-ra're est o-ra're (lăb"ō-rā'rē ĕst ō-rā'rē), to work is to pray. [Lat.]

la'bor ip'se vo-lup'tas (lā'bẽr ĭp'sē vō-lŭp'tăs), work itself (is) a pleasure. [Lat.]

la'bor om'ni-a vin'cit (lā'bẽr ŏm'nĭ-ȧ vĭn'sĭt), work conquers all things: motto of Oklahoma. [Lat.]

læ'sa ma-jes'tas (lē'sȧ mȧ-jĕs'tăs), a crime against the sovereign. [Lat.]

lais-sez faire (lĕ-sā' fâr'), let (people) do (what they choose); hence, noninterference in industry by the government. [Fr.]

l' al-le-gro (läl-lā'grō), the cheerful (man); opposite to *il penseroso*. [It.]

Land-sturm (länt'shtōōrm"), the final reserve military force of all able-bodied males between 17 and 45, not otherwise in the service: for use only in times of great emergency. [Ger.]

Land-tag (länt'täkh"), the Prussian legislature. [Ger.]

Land-wehr (länt'vār"), the Territorial Reserve, composed of men between 27 and 39, who have completed the required military training, but are liable for duty in war. [Ger.]

la'pis (lā'pĭs; lăp'ĭs), a stone. [Lat.]

lap'sus ca'la-mi (lăp'sŭs kăl'ȧ-mī), a slip of the pen. [Lat.]

lap'sus lin'guæ (lăp'sŭs lĭṅ'gwē), a slip of the tongue. [Lat.]

la'res et pe-na'tes (lā'rēz ĕt pē-nā'tēz), household gods. [Lat.]

lau-da'tor tem'po-ris ac'ti (lô-dā'tôr tĕm'pō-rĭs ăk'tī), a praiser of time past. [Lat.]

laus De'o (lôs dē'ō), praise (be) to God. [Lat.]

leb' wohl (lāp vōl'), good-by. [Ger.]

le grand Mo-narque (lẽ grăṅ mō"närk'), the Great Monarch (Louis XIV). [Fr.]

le pas (lẽ pä'), lit., the step; precedence; superiority. [Fr.]

le roi le veut (lẽ rwä" lẽ vû'), the king wills it. [Fr.]

l'é-toile du nord (lā twȧl' dü nôr'), the star of the north: motto of Minnesota. [Fr.]

le tout en-sem-ble (lĕ tōō″-tăṅ-säṅ′bl), the whole (taken) together. [Fr.]
let-tre de ca-chet (lĕt′r dĕ kȧ″shĕ′), a sealed letter, especially one from a sovereign. [Fr.]
lex lo′ci (lĕks lō′sī), the law of the place. [Lat.]
lex non scrip′ta (lĕks nŏn skrĭp′tȧ), unwritten law; common law. [Lat.]
lex scrip′ta (lĕks skrĭp′tȧ), written law; statute law. [Lat.]
l'homme pro-pose, et Dieu dis-pose (lôm prō″pōz′, ā dyû dēs″pōz′), man proposes and God disposes. [Fr.]
li-ai-son′ (lē″ā″zôṅ′), an improper intimacy between a man and a woman; coöperation between military forces. [Fr.]
li-ber-tad y or-den (lē″bĕr-täth ē ôr′dān), liberty and order: motto of Colombia. [Span.]
li-cen′ti-a va′tum (lī-sĕn′shĭ-ȧ vā′tŭm), the license of poets; poetic license. [Lat.]
lit″e-ra′ti (lĭt″ē-rā′tī), men of letters. [Lat.]
lit″e-ra′tim (lĭt″ē-rā′tĭm), letter for letter. [Late Lat.]
lit′te-ra scrip′ta ma′net (lĭt′ē-rȧ skrĭp′tȧ mā′nĕt), the written letter remains. [Lat.]
lo′co ci-ta′to (lō′kō sī-tā′tō), in the place quoted; abbrev., *loc. cit.* [Lat.]
lo′cum te′nens (lō′kŭm tē′nĕnz), a substitute. [Lat.]
lo′cus si-gil′li (lō′kŭs sī-jĭl′ī), the place of the seal; abbrev., *L. S.* [Lat.]
lon′go in″ter-val′lo (lŏṅ′gō ĭn″tĕr-văl′ō), by a long interval. [Lat.]
lu′cus a non lu-cen′do (lū′kŭs ā nŏn lū-kĕn′dō), anything illogical. [Lat.]
l' u-nion fait la force (lü″nyôṅ′ fĕ″ lȧ fôrs′), union makes strength: motto of Belgium. [Fr.]
lu′sus na-tu′rae (lū′sŭs nȧ-tū′rē), a freak of nature. [Lat.]
ma chère (mȧ″ shâr′), my dear (fem.). [Fr].
mac′te vir-tu′te (măk′tē vûr-tū′tē), go on in virtue. [Lat.]
ma-de-moi-selle (mȧd″mwȧ″zĕl′), Miss; an unmarried lady. [Fr.]
ma foi! (mȧ fwä′), my faith! for goodness' sake! [Fr.]
mag′na est ve′ri-tas, et prae″va-le′bit (măg′nȧ ĕst vĕr′ĭ-tăs, ĕt prĕv″ȧ-lē′bĭt), great is truth, and it will prevail. [Lat.]
mag′num o′pus (măg′nŭm ō′pŭs), the chief work (of an author). [Lat.]
maî-tre d'hô-tel (mâ′tr dō″tĕl′), a butler; hotel landlord. [Fr.]
ma′la fi′de (mā′lȧ fī′dē), in bad faith. [Lat.]
mal de mer (mȧl″ dē mâr′), seasickness. [Fr.]
ma-ña-na (mä-nyä′nä), to-morrow. [Span.]
ma′re clau′sum (mā′rē klô′sŭm), a closed sea. [Lat.]
ma-riage de con-ve-nance (mȧ″ryȯzh′ dē kôṅ″v-näṅs), a marriage of convenience. [Fr.]
mar-mite (mȧr″mēt′), a stewpot; a large shell. [Fr.]
mau-vais goût (mō″vē′gōō′), bad taste. [Fr.]
mehr Licht (mār lĭkht), more light. [Ger.]
me ju′di-ce (mē jōō′dĭ-sē), I being judge; in my judgment. [Lat.].
me-men′to mo′ri (mē-mĕn′tō mō′rī), remember that you must die. [Lat.]
mens sa′na in cor′po-re sa′no (mĕnz sā′nȧ ĭn kôr′pō-rē sā′nō), a sound mind in a sound body. [Lat.]
mé-sal-liance (mā″zȧl″yäṅs′) a marriage with one who is of inferior social standing. [Fr.]
mé-tier (mā″tyā′), calling; profession; trade. [Fr.]
mez-zo (mĕd′zō), middling. [It.]
mi-ra′bi-le dic′tu (mĭ-răb′ĭ-lē dĭk′tū) wonderful to relate. [Lat.]
mi-ra′bi-le vi-su (mĭ-răb′ĭ-lē vī′sū), wonderful to see. [Lat.]
mi″ra-bi′li-a (mĭr″ȧ-bĭl′ĭ-ȧ), miracles. [Lat.]
mi-tra-illeuse (mē″trȧ″yûz′), a machine gun. [Fr.]
mo-diste (mō″dēst′), one who makes, or deals in, articles of fashion; a dressmaker or milliner. [Fr.]
mo′dus o″pe-ran′di (mō′dŭs ŏp″ē-răn′dī), manner of operating. [Lat.]
mon cher (môṅ shâr′), my dear (masc.). [Fr.]
monde (môṅd), world; society. [Fr.]
mon-ta′ni sem′per li′be-ri (mŏn-tā′nī sĕm′pĕr lĭb′ē-rī), mountaineers (are) always free (men): motto of West Virginia. [Lat.]
mo′re ma-jo′rum (mō′rē mȧ-jō′rŭm), after the manner of one's ancestors. [Lat.]
mo″ri-tu′ri te sa″lu-ta′mus (mŏr″ĭ-tū′rī tē săl″ū-tā′mŭs), we (who are) about to die salute thee: cry of Roman gladiators to the emperor. [Lat.]
mo-tif (mō″tēf′), the theme. [Fr.]
mul′tum in par′vo (mŭl′tŭm ĭn pär′vō), much in little. [Lat.]
mu-ta′tis mu-tan′dis (mū-tā′tĭs mū-tăn′dĭs), necessary changes being made; with necessary changes. [Lat.]
mu-ta′to no′mi-ne (mū-tā′tō nŏm′ĭ-nē), the name being changed. [Lat.]
na-ïve-té (nȧ″ēv″tā′), artlessness. [Fr.]
na-tu′ra ab-hor′ret a va′cu-o (nȧ-tū′rȧ ăb-hŏr′ĕt ā văk′ū-ō), nature abhors a vacuum. [Lat.]
née (nā), born; to introduce a married woman's maiden family name. [Fr.]
ne′mi-ne con″tra-di-cen′te (nĕm′ĭ-nē kŏn″trȧ-dī-sĕn′tē), no one contradicting; unanimously. [Lat.]
ne′mo me im-pu′ne la-ces′sit (nē′mō mē ĭm-pū′nē lȧ-sĕs′ĭt), no one attacks me with impunity: motto of Scotland. [Lat.]
ne plus ul′tra (nē plŭs ŭl′trȧ), the summit of achievement. [Lat.]
ne quid ni′mis (nē kwĭd nĭm′ĭs), not anything too much; *i. e.*, avoid excess. [Lat.]
n'est-ce pas? (nĕs-pä′), isn't that so? [Fr.]
nil ad″mi-ra′ri (nĭl ăd″mĭ-rā′rī), to wonder at nothing. [Lat.]
nil de″spe-ran′dum (nĭl dĕs″pē-răn′dŭm), nothing must be despaired of. [Lat.]
nil si′ne nu′mi-ne (nĭl sī′nē nū′mĭ-nē), nothing without the divine will: motto of Colorado. [Lat.]
n'im-porte (năṅ″pôrt′), it's no matter; it does not matter. [Fr.]
no-blesse o-blige (nō″blĕs′ ō″blēzh′), rank imposes obligation. [Fr.]
no′lens vo′lens (nō′lĕnz vō′lĕnz), unwilling (or) willing. [Lat.]
no′li me tan′ge-re (nō′lī mē tăn′jē-rē), touch me not. [Lat.]
nol′le pro′se-qui (nŏl′ē prŏs′ē-kwī), to be unwilling to proceed. [Lat.]
nom de plume (nôṅ dē plüm′), a name assumed by an author as a signature. [Fr.]
non com′pos men′tis (nŏn kŏm′pŏs mĕn′tĭs), not of sound mind. [Lat.]
non om′ni-a pos′su-mus om′nes (nŏn ŏm′nĭ-ȧ pŏs′ū-mŭs ŏm′nēz), we cannot all (do) everything. [Lat.]

non om'nis mo'ri-ar (nŏn ŏm'nĭs mō'rĭ-är), I shall not wholly die. [Lat.]

non pas'si-bus æ'quis (nŏn păs'ĭ-bŭs ē'kwĭs), not with equal steps. [Lat.]

non pos'su-mus (nŏn pŏs'ū-mŭs), we cannot; we have not the ability. [Lat.]

non sans droict (nôn"sänz"droit'), not without right: motto on Shakespeare's coat of arms. [Old Fr.]

non si'bi sed pa'tri-æ (nŏn sĭb'ī sĕd păt'rĭ-ē), not for himself, but for his country. [Lat.]

no'sce te ip'sum (nŏs'ē tē ĭp'sŭm), know thyself. [Lat.]

no'ta be'ne (nō'tȧ bē'nē), note well; abbrev., *N. B.* [Lat.]

nous ver-rons (nōō"vĕ"rôn'), we shall see. [Fr.]

no'vus ho'mo (nō'vŭs hō'mō), a new man; an upstart. [Lat.]

nu-ance (nü"äns'), a slight variation (of color, tone). [Fr.]

nunc aut nun'quam (nŭngk ôt nŭn'kwăm), now or never. [Lat.]

nunc di-mit'tis (nungk dĭ-mĭt'ĭs), lit., now thou lettest depart; departure. [Lat.]

o'bi-it (ō'bĭ-ĭt), he, or she, died. [Lat.]

ob'i-ter dic'tum (ŏb'ĭ-tẽr dĭk'tŭm), said by the way; a passing remark. [Lat.]

ob-jet d'art (ōb"zhĕ' där'), an object of artistic worth. [Fr.]

o-keh (ō-kā'), it is so; all right. [Choctaw Indian.]

om'ne bo'num de'su-per (ŏm'nē bō'nŭm dē'sū-pẽr), all good (is) from above. [Lat.]

om'ni-a mu-tan'tur (ŏm'nĭ-ȧ mū-tăn'tŭr), all things change. [Lat.]

om'ni-a vin'cit a'mor (ŏm'nĭ-ȧ vĭn'sĭt ā'mŏr), love conquers all things. [Lat.]

on dit (ôn dē'), they say; it is said. [Fr.]

on les au-ra (ôn"lā"-zō"-rȧ'), we'll get them. [Fr.]

o'nus pro-ban'di (ō'nŭs prō-băn'dī), the burden of proof. [Lat.]

o'pus (ō'pŭs), a work, especially a musical composition. [Lat.]

o-ra e sem-pre (ō'rä ā sĕm'prā), now and always. [It.]

o'ra et la-bo'ra (ō'rȧ et lȧ-bō'rȧ), pray and work. [Lat.]

o'ra pro no'bis (ō'rȧ prō nō'bĭs), pray for us. [Lat.]

o're ro-tun'do (ō'rē rō-tŭn'dō), with round mouth; with well turned speech. [Lat.]

o-ro y pla-ta (ō'rō ē plä'tä), gold and silver: motto of Montana. [Span.]

O tem'po-ra! O mo'res! (ō tĕm'pō-rȧ ō mō'rēz), Oh the times! Oh the manners: in depreciation of the present. Lat.]

o'ti-um cum dig" ni-ta'te (ō'shĭ-ŭm kŭm dĭg" nĭ-tā'tē), leisure with dignity. [Lat.]

oui-dire (wē"dēr'), hearsay. [Fr.]

pal'li-da Mors (păl'ĭ-dȧ môrz), pale death. [Lat.]

pal'mam qui me'ru-it fe'rat (păl'măm kwī mĕr'ū-ĭt fē'răt), let him bear the palm who has deserved (it). [Lat.]

par ex-cel-lence (pär ĕk"sĕ"läns'), preëminently. [Fr.]

par ex-em-ple (pär ĕg"zän'pl), for example. [Fr.]

par o'ne-ri (pär ō'nē-rī), equal to the burden. [Lat.]

par'ti-ceps cri'mi-nis (pär'tĭ-sĕps krĭm'ĭ-nĭs), an accomplice. [Lat.]

pa'ter-nos'ter (pā'tẽr-nŏs"tẽr), our father: the Lord's prayer. [Lat.]

pa'ter pa'tri-æ (pā'tẽr păt'rĭ-ē), father of his country. [Lat.]

pa-tio (pät'yō), a courtyard. [Span.]

pa-trie (pȧ"trē'), fatherland. [Fr.]

pax vo-bis'cum (păks vō-bĭs'kŭm), peace be with you. [Lat.]

pen-chant (päṅ"shäṅ'; pĕn'chănt), a strong inclination. [Fr.]

pen-den'te li'te (pĕn-dĕn'tē lī'tē), pending the suit. [Lat.]

per an'num (pẽr ăn'ŭm), by the year. [Lat.]

per ca'pi-ta (pẽr kăp'ĭ-tȧ), lit., by heads; for each individual. [Lat.]

per di'em (pẽr dī'ĕm), by the day. [Lat.]

per men'sem (pẽr mĕn'sĕm), by the month. [Lat.]

per-mis-sion (pĕr"mē"syôn'), leave. [Fr.]

per se (pẽr sē), by itself; intrinsically. [Lat.]

per-so'na non gra'ta (pẽr-sō'nȧ nŏn grā'tȧ), an unacceptable person. [Lat.]

pe-tite (pē-tēt'), small. [Fr.]

peu à peu (pû"ȧ pû'), little by little. [Fr.]

peu de chose (pû"dē shōz'), a trifle. [Fr.]

pièce de ré-sis-tance (pyĕs'dē rā"zēs"täns'), Lit., piece of resistance; the chief article of any collection. [Fr.]

pince-nez (päns"nā'), eyeglasses. [Fr.]

pinx'it (pĭnk'sĭt), he, or she, painted it: the painter is. [Lat.]

pis al-ler (pē"-zȧ"lā'), lit., to go worst; a last resource. [Fr.]

po-co a po-co (pō'kō ä pō'kō), little by little. [It.]

po-e'ta nas'ci-tur, non fit (pō-ē'tȧ năs'ĭ-tŭr, nŏn fĭt), a poet is born, not made. [Lat.]

Poi-lu (pwȧ"lü'), a French private soldier. Also, **poilu.** [Fr.]

pol'li-ce ver'so (pŏl'ĭ-sē vûr'so), with thumb turned; the sign by which spectators condemned a defeated gladiator to death. [Lat.]

po-sa-da (pō-sä'*th*ä), inn. [Span.]

post me-ri'di-em (pōst mē-rĭd'ĭ-ĕm), afternoon; abbrev., *P. M.* or *p. m.* [Lat.]

post mor'tem (pōst môr'tĕm), after death. [Lat.]

pour faire vi-site (pōōr" fâr" vē"zēt'), to pay a visit. [Fr.]

pour le mé-rite (pōōr" lē mā"rēt'), for merit. [Fr.]

pou sto (pōō stō; pou stō), lit., where I may stand; a place to stand on. [Gr.]

pre-mière (prē-myâr', first, chief; a first performance. [Fr.]

pri'ma fa'ci-e (prī'mȧ fā'shĭ-ē), a first view. [Lat.]

pri'mus in'ter pa'res (prī'mŭs ĭn'tẽr pā'rēz), first among his peers. [Lat.]

prin-ci'pi-is ob'sta (prĭn-sĭp'ĭ-ĭs ŏb'stȧ), resist the beginnings. [Lat.]

pro a'ris et fo'cis (prō ā'rĭs ĕt fō'sĭs), for altars and firesides. [Lat.]

pro bo'no pu'bli-co (prō bō'nō pŭb'lĭ-kō), for the public good. [Lat.]

pro-fa'num vul'gus (prō-fā'nŭm vŭl'gŭs), the unhallowed multitude. [Lat.]

pro me-mo'ri-a (prō mē-mō'rĭ-ȧ), for a memorial. [Lat.]

pro pa'tri-a (prō păt'rĭ-ȧ), for native land. [Lat.]

pro ra'ta (prō rā'tȧ), in proportion. [Lat.]

pro tem'po-re (prō tĕm'pō-rē), temporarily; for the time. [Lat.]

prox'i-mo (prŏk'sĭ-mō), in the next (month after the present); abbrev., *prox.* [Lat.]

punc-ta'tim (pŭngk-tā'tĭm), point for point. [Lat.]

quan'tum li'bet (kwŏn'tŭm lĭ'bĕt), as much as you please. [Lat.]

quan'tum suf'fi-cit (kwŏn'tŭm sŭf'ĭ-sĭt), as much as is sufficient. [Lat.]

quan′tum vis (kwŏn′tŭm vĭs), as much as you will. [Lat.]
qui do′cet, dis′cit (kwī dō′sĕt, dĭs′ĭt), he who teaches, learns. [Lat.]
quid pro quo (kwĭd prō kwō), one thing for another; an equivalent. [Lat.]
quién sa′be? (kyĕn″ sä′bā), who knows? [Span.]
qui s'ex-cuse, s'ac-cuse (kē sĕks″küz′, sȧ″-küz′), who excuses himself, accuses himself. [Fr.]
qui trans′tu-lit, sus′ti-net (kwī trăns′tū-lĭt, sŭs′tĭ-nĕt), he who transplanted, sustains: motto of Connecticut. [Lat.]
qui va là? (kē vȧ lȧ′), who goes there? [Fr.]
quo′ad hoc (kwō′ăd hŏk), as to this. [Lat.]
quod e′rat de″mon-stran′dum (kwŏd ĕ′răt dĕm″ŏn-străn′dŭm), which was to be demonstrated. [Lat.]
quod vi′de (kwŏd vī′dē), which see. [Lat.]
quo ju′re? (kwō jōō′rē), by what right? [Lat.]
quot ho′mi-nes, tot sen-ten′ti-æ (kwŏt hŏm′ĭ-nēz, tŏt sĕn-tĕn′shĭ-ē), as many opinions as men. [Lat.]
rai-son-né (rĕ″zō″nā′), logical. [Fr.]
rai-son d'ê-tre (rĕ″zôṅ′ dā′tr), reason for existence. [Fr.]
ra′ra a′vis (rā′rȧ ā′vĭs), a rare bird; a rarity. [Lat.]
re-cher-ché (rĕ-shĕr″shā′), choice. [Fr.]
re-duc′ti-o ad ab-sur′dum (rē-dŭk′shĭ-ō ăd ăb-sûr′dŭm), reduction to absurdity; proof of a statement by showing the falsity of its opposite. [Lat.]
ré-gime (rā″zhēm′), a system of government; a social order. [Fr.]
reg′nat po′pu-lus (rĕg′năt pŏp′ū-lŭs), the people rule: motto of Arkansas. [Lat.]
ré-pon-dez, s'il vous plaît (rā″pôṅ″dā′ sēl vōō plĕ′), reply if you please; abbrev., *R. S. V. P.* [Fr.]
re-pos (rē″pō′), rest. [Fr.]
re-pous-sé (rē-pōō″sā′), formed in relief; adorned with designs in relief. [Fr.]
re″qui-es′cat in pa′ce (rĕk″wĭ-ĕs′kăt ĭn pā′sē), may he or she rest in peace; abbrev., *R. I. P.* [Lat.]
res an-gus′ta do′mi (rēz ăn-gŭs′tȧ dō′mī), pinching conditions at home; financial need. [Lat.]
res ges′tæ (rēz jĕs′tē), things done; deeds. [Lat.]
re′spi-ce fi′nem (rĕs′pĭ-sē fī′nĕm), regard the end. [Lat.]
ré-su-mé (rā″zü″mā′), a summary. [Fr.]
re-sur′gam (rē-sûr′găm), I shall rise again. [Lat.]
re-ve-nons à nos mou-tons (rē-v-nôṅ′-zȧ nō″mōō″tôṅ′), let us return to our sheep; let us return to our subject. [Fr.]
ris-qué (rēs″kā′), improper. [Fr.]
robe-de-cham-bre (rōb″ dē-shäṅ′br), a dressing gown. [Fr.]
roo-ti (rōō′tĭ), bread. [East Indian.]
ruse de guerre (rüz″ dē gâr′), a stratagem of war. [Fr.]
rus in ur′be (rŭs ĭn ûr′bē), the country in the city. [Lat.]
sa-bot (sȧ″bō′), a kind of wooden shoe. [Fr.]
sa-bo-tage (sȧ″bō″tȧzh′), malicious damage done to an employer's property by employees during labor troubles. [Fr.]
salle à man-ger (sȧl″ ȧ mäṅ″zhā′), dining room. [Fr.]
sa′lus po′pu-li su-pre′ma lex es′to (sā′lŭs pŏp′ū-lī sū-prē′mȧ lĕks ĕs′tō), let the welfare of the people be the supreme law: motto of Missouri. [Lat.]
sal′ve (săl′vē). Hail. [Lat.]
sanc′tum sanc-to′rum (săṅk′tŭm săṅk-tō′-rŭm), holy of holies. [Lat.]
sang-froid (säṅ″frwä′), composure. [Fr.
sans gêne (säṅ zhân′), without constraint. [Fr.]
sans peur et sans re-proche (säṅ pûr″ ā säṅ rē-prōsh′), without fear and without reproach. [Fr.]
sans sou-ci (säṅ sōō″sē′), without care. [Fr.]
sar′tor re-sar′tus (sär′tŏr rē-sär′tŭs), the tailor retailored. [Lat.]
sa′tis ver-bo′rum (sā′tĭs vĕr-bō′rŭm), enough of words. [Lat.]
sauve qui peut (sōv″ kē pû′), save (himself) who can. [Fr.]
sa-vant′ (sȧ″väṅ′), a man of learning. [Fr.]
sa-voir—faire (sȧ″vwȧr′fâr′), lit., a knowing how to do; ability. [Fr.]
sa-voir—vi-vre (sȧ″vwȧr′vē′vr), lit., a knowing how to live; good breeding. [Fr.]
sculp′sit (skŭlp′sĭt), he, or she, carved or engraved (it); the sculptor is. [Lat.]
scu′to bo′næ vo″lun-ta′tis tu′æ co″ro-nas′-sti nos (skū′tō bō′nē vŏl″ŭn-tā′tĭs tū′ē kŏr″ō-năs′tī nōs), with the shield of thy good will thou hast encompassed us: motto of Maryland. [Lat.]
se-cun′dum ar′tem (sē-kŭn′dŭm är′tĕm), according to art. [Lat.]
sem′per e′a-dem (sĕm′pĕr ē′ȧ-dĕm), always the same (fem.): motto of Queen Elizabeth. [Lat.]
sem′per fi-de′lis (sĕm′pĕr fī-dē′lĭs), always faithful. [Lat.]
sem′per i′dem (sĕm′pĕr ī′dĕm), always the same (masculine and neuter). [Lat.]
se-ñor (sā-nyŏr′), Mr. [Span.]
se-ño-ra (sā-nyō′rä), Mrs. [Span.]
se-ño-ri-ta (sā″nyō-rē′tä), Miss. [Span.]
ses″qui-pe-da′li-a ver′ba (sĕs″kwĭ-pē-dā′lĭ-ȧ vûr′bȧ), words a foot and a half long. [Lat.]
sic i′tur ad a′stra (sĭk ī′tŭr ăd ăs′trȧ), thus one goes to the stars; such is the way to immortality. [Lat.]
sic pas′sim (sĭk păs′ĭm), so everywhere. [Lat.]
sic sem′per ty-ran′nis (sĭk sĕm′pĕr tĭ-răn′ĭs), ever thus to tyrants: motto of Virginia. [Lat.]
sic tran′sit glo′ri-a′ mun′di (sĭk trăn′sĭt glō′rĭ-ȧ mŭn′dī), so passes away the glory of the world. [Lat.]
sic′ut pa′tri-bus, sit De′us no′bis (sĭk′ŭt păt′rĭ-bŭs, sĭt dē′ŭs nō′bĭs), as with our fathers, may God be with us: motto of Boston. [Lat.]
si-gnor (sē′nyŏr), a lord or gentleman; Mr. [It.]
si-gno′ra (sē-nyō′rä), Mrs. [It.]
si-gno-ri-na (sē″nyō-rē′nä), Miss. [It.]
s'il vous plaît (sēl″ vōō plĕ′), if you please. [Fr.]
si-mi′li-a si-mi′li-bus cu-ran′tur (sĭ-mĭl′ĭ-ȧ sĭ-mĭl′ĭ-bŭs kū-răn′tŭr), likes are cured by likes. [Lat.]
si′ne cu′ra (sī′nē kū′rȧ) without care. [Lat.]
si′ne di′e (sī′nē dī′ē), without day; finally. [Lat.]
si′ne qua non (sī′nē kwā nŏn), an indispensable condition. [Lat.]
si quæ′ris pen-in′su-lam a-mœ′nam, cir-cum′spi-ce (sī kwē′rĭs pĕn-ĭn′sū-lăm ȧ-mē′-năm, sĕr-kŭm′spĭ-sē), if thou seekest a beautiful peninsula, look around: motto of Michigan. [Lat.]
sis′te vi-a′tor (sĭs′tē vī-ā′tŏr), stop, traveler. [Lat.]

sit ti'bi ter'ra le'vis (sĭt tĭb'ī tĕr'ȧ lĕv'ĭs), may the earth lie lightly upon thee. [LAT.]

so-bri-quet (sō"brē"kā'; sō'brē-kā), a nickname. [FR.]

splen'di-de men'dax (splĕn'dī-dē mĕn'dăks), nobly mendacious. [LAT.]

spur-los ver-senkt (shpōōr'lōs fĕr-zĕṅkt'), sunken without a trace. [GER.]

sta'tus quo (stā'tŭs kwō), the state in which (it is); the existing condition. [LAT.]

stet (stĕt), let it stand. [LAT.]

stra-fe (shträ'fē), punish. [GER.]

sua'vi-ter in mo'do, for'ti-ter in re (swăv'ī tĕr ĭn mō'dō, fôr'tī-tĕr ĭn rē), gently in manner, strongly in deed. [LAT.]

sub ju'di-ce (sŭb jōō'dī-sē), before the judge. [LAT.]

sub ro'sa (sŭb rō'zȧ), under the rose; secretly. [LAT.]

sub vo'ce (sŭb vō'sē), under the word; abbrev., *s. v.* [LAT.]

su'i ge'ne-ris (sū'ī jĕn'ē-rĭs), of its own kind; unique. [LAT.]

sum'mum bo'num (sŭm'ŭm bō'nŭm), the supreme good. [LAT.]

ta-ble d'hôte (tȧ'bl dōt'), a meal served at a fixed price. [FR.]

ta'bu-la ra'sa (tăb'ū-lȧ rā'zȧ), a blank tablet. [LAT.]

tæ'di-um vi'tæ (tē'dĭ-ŭm vī'tē), weariness of life. [LAT.]

tant mieux (tăṅ"myû'), so much the better. [FR.]

tant pis (tăṅ pē'), so much the worse. [FR.]

Tau-be (tou'bē), a kind of airplane. [GER.]

Te De'um (tē' dē'ŭm), (we praise) thee, O God. [LAT.]

tem'po-ra mu-tan'tur, et nos mu-ta'mur in il'lis (tĕm'pō-rȧ mū-tăn'tŭr, ĕt nōs mū-tā'mŭr ĭn ĭl'ĭs), the times are changed and we are changed with them. [LAT.]

tem'pus e'dax re'rum (tĕm'pŭs ē'dăks rē'-rŭm), time devouring (all) things. [LAT.]

tem'pus fu'git (tĕm'pŭs fū'jĭt), time flies. [LAT.]

ter'ræ fil'i-us (tĕr'ē fĭl'ĭ-ŭs), a son of the earth; a man of humble birth. [LAT.]

ter'ra fir'ma (tĕr'ȧ fûr'mȧ), solid earth. [LAT.]

ter'ra in-cog'ni-ta (tĕr'ȧ ĭn-kŏg'nĭ-tȧ), an unknown land. [LAT.]

ter'ti-um quid (tûr'shĭ-ŭm kwĭd), a third something; something intermediate. [LAT.]

tête à tête (tāt" ȧ tāt'; tĕ"-tȧ-tāt'), privately: said of two persons. [FR.]

tiers é-tat (tyâr"-zā"tȧ'), the third estate (or commonalty, in France). [FR.]

ti'me-o Da'na-os et do'na fe-ren'tes (tĭm'-ē-ō dăn'ā-ŏs, ĕt dō'nȧ fē-rĕn'tēz), I fear the Greeks even (when they are) bringing gifts. [LAT.]

ti-rail-leur (tē"rȧ"yûr'), an infantry skirmisher. [FR.]

tor-tue (tôr"tü'), grenade. [FR.]

to'ti-dem ver'bis (tŏ'tĭ-dĕm vûr'bĭs), in so many words. [LAT.]

tour de force (tōōr" dē fôrs'), a feat of strength. [FR.]

tout à fait (tōō"-tȧ fĕ'), entirely; quite. [FR.]

tout à vous (tōō"-tȧ vōō'), wholly yours. [FR.]

tout en-sem-ble (tōō"-täṅ säṅ'bl), all together. [FR.]

tu'um est (tū'ŭm ĕst), it is thine. [LAT.]

u'bi su'pra (ū'bī sū'prȧ), where above (mentioned). [LAT.]

ul'ti-ma ra'ti-o re'gum (ŭl'tĭ-mȧ rā'shĭ-ō rē'gŭm), the final argument of kings; war. [LAT.]

ul'ti-ma Thu'le (ŭl'tĭ-mȧ thū'lē), lit., most distant Thule; utmost limit. [LAT.]

ul'ti-mo (ŭl'tĭ-mō), in the (month) preceding the present; abbrev., *ult.* [LAT.]

u'na vo'ce (ū'nȧ vō'sē), with one voice; unanimously. [LAT.]

und so wei-ter (ōōnt zō vī'tĕr), and so forth. [GER.]

Un-ter-see-boot (ōōn"tĕr-zā'bōt), a submarine boat. [GER.]

u'ti-le dul'ci (ū'tĭ-lē dŭl'sī), the useful with the agreeable. [LAT.]

ut su'pra (ŭt sū'prȧ), as above. [LAT.]

va'de in pa'ce (vā'dē ĭn pā'sē), go in peace. [LAT.]

va'de me'cum (vā'dē mē'kŭm), lit., go with me; a manual. [LAT.]

væ vic'tis (vē vĭk'tĭs), woe to the vanquished. [LAT.]

va'le (vā'lē), farewell. [LAT.]

va-let de cham-bre (vȧ"lĕ' dē shäṅ'br), a body servant. [FR.]

va'ri-æ lec"ti-o'nes (vā'rĭ-ē lĕk"shĭ-ō'nēz), variant readings. [LAT.]

va"ri-o'rum no'tæ (vā"rĭ-ō'rŭm nō'tē), notes of various commentators. [LAT.]

ve'ni, vi'di, vi'ci (vē'nī, vī'dī, vī'sī), I came, I saw, I conquered. [LAT.]

ver-ba'tim et lit"e-ra'tim (vĕr-bā'tĭm ĕt lĭt"ē-rā'tĭm), word for word and letter for letter. [LAT.]

ver'bum sat sa"pi-en'ti (vûr'bŭm săt săp"ĭ-ĕn'tī), a word to the wise is sufficient. [LAT.]

vi'a me'di-a (vī'ȧ mē'dĭ-ȧ), a middle way; the golden mean. [LAT.]

vi'ce ver'sa (vī'sē vûr'sȧ), conversely. [LAT.]

vi-de'li-cet (vĭ-dĕl'ĭ-sĕt), namely; abbrev., *viz.* [LAT.]

vi'de ut su'pra (vī'dē ŭt sū'prȧ), see what is stated above. [LAT.]

vi et ar'mis (vī ĕt är'mĭs), by force and arms; by main force. [LAT.]

vin (văṅ), wine. [FR.]

vin'cet a'mor pa'tri-æ (vĭn'sĕt ā'môr păt'rĭ-ē), love of country will prevail. [LAT.]

vin'cit om'ni-a ve'ri-tas (vĭn'sĭt ŏm'nĭ-ȧ vĕr'ĭ-tăs), truth conquers all things. [LAT.]

vin'cu-lum ma"tri-mo'ni-i (vĭṅ'kū-lŭm măt"rĭ-mō'nĭ-ī), the bond of matrimony. [LAT.]

vir-gi'ni-bus pu"e-ris'que (vĕr-jĭn'ĭ-bŭs pū"-ĕr-ĭs'kwē), for girls and boys. [LAT.]

vis a ter'go (vĭs ā tûr'gō), force from behind. [LAT.]

vis-à-vis (vē" zȧ-vē'), opposite. [FR.]

vis vi'tæ (vĭs vī'tē), vital force. [LAT.]

vi'ta bre'vis, ars lon'ga (vī'tȧ brĕv'ĭs, ärz lŏṅ'gȧ), life (is) short, art (is) long. [LAT.]

vi'vat rex (vī'văt rĕks), (long) live the king. [LAT.]

vi'va vo'ce (vī'vȧ vō'sē), orally. [LAT.]

vive la ré-pu-blique (vēv" lȧ rā"pü"blēk'), (long) live the republic. [FR.]

vive le roi (vēv" lē rwȧ'), (long) live the king. [FR.]

voi-là tout (vwȧ" lȧ' tōō'), that is all. [FR.]

vox, et præ-te're-a ni'hil (vŏks, ĕt prē-tē'-rē-ȧ nī'hĭl), a voice and nothing more. [LAT.]

vox po'pu-li vox De'i (vŏks pŏp'ū-lī, vŏks dē'ī), the voice of the people (is) the voice of God. [LAT.]

vul'go (vŭl'gō), commonly. [LAT.]

Wan-der-lust (väṅ'dĕr-lōōst"), passion for traveling or tramping. [GER.]

Welt-krieg (vĕlt'krēkh"), world war. [GER.]

Zeit-geist (tsīt'gīst"), the spirit of the time. [GER.]

NAMES AND PLACES.

Giving the spelling and pronunciation of the names of prominent people, together with a brief biography.

Also the spelling, pronunciation, location, size, and other items of interest of the important towns, cities, states, countries, etc., of the various nations, with populations of same in accordance with the latest census reports. For towns in the United States, the figures are those of the 1910 census, except in a few instances where later statistics are available.

Populations given in units of nearest thousands.
Examples: 50 = 50,000; 500 = 500,000; 5,000 = 5,000,000.
Special abbreviations used. See also general list of abbreviations, page 803.

abp. archbishop.
act. actor, actress.
adj. adjutant.
admin. administrator.
adven. adventurer.
anat. anatomist.
anc. ancient.
art. artist.
astron. astronomer.
b. born.
bet. between.
bor. borough.
bp. bishop.
cap. capital.
cen. center, central.
clergy. clergyman.
co. county.
coll. college.
com. commissioner.
comm. commune.
Confed. Confederate.
depend. dependency.
dept. department.
disc. discoverer.
dist. district.
dipl. diplomat.
dram. dramatist.
ecclesias. ecclesiastical.
ed. editor.
educ. educator.
emp. emperor, empress.
essay. essayist.
est. estuary.
estab. established.
explor. explorer.
extrem. extremity.
fr. from.
gen. general.
geol. geologist.
geomet. geometrician.
govt. government.
hist. historian.
illus. illustrator.
indepen. independent.
isl. island.
jour. journalist.
law. lawyer.
legis. legislator.
m. miles.
manufac. manufacturer.
math. mathematician.
mgr. manager.
mission. missionary.
mt. mountain.
natur. naturalist.
nav. naval.
navig. navigator.
novel. novelist.
oc. ocean.
off. officer.
p. population.
pen. peninsula.
penin. peninsula.
Phil. Philippines.
philan. philanthropist.
philos. philosopher.
polit. politician.
protec. protectorate.
prov. province.
repub. republic.
Rev. Revolution, Revolutionary.
riv. river.
sculp. sculptor.
secy. secretary.
sen. senator.
sp. seaport.
sq. m. square miles.
stsm. statesman.
str. strait.
tech. technology.
ter. territory.
theatr. theatrical.
theolog. theologian.
trib. tributary.
vil. village.
vol. volcano, volcanic.

Abbey (ăb'ĭ), Edwin Austin. Am. painter & illus. (1852–1911).
Abbott (ăb'ŏt), Lyman. Am. clergy. & ed. (1835–).
Abd-ul-Hamid (ăb"dōōl-hȧ-mēd'). Sultans of Turkey. **I** (1725–89). **II** (1842–1918).
A **Becket** (*ȧ* bĕk'ĕt), Thomas. Eng. prelate (1118–1170).
Abélard (ăb'ē-lärd; Fr. ȧ'bā'lȧr'), Pierre. Fr. scholastic philos. & theolog. (1079–1142).
Abercromby (ăb"ēr-krŭm'bĭ), James. Br. gen. in Am. (1706–81).
Aberdeen (ăb"ēr-dēn'), co. Scot., p. 312.—cap. of co., p. 165.—George Hamilton Gordon, 4th Earl of. Br. stato. (1784–1860).
Abruzzi (ȧ-brōōt'sē), Prince Luigi Amedoo of Savoy-Aosta. It. traveler & Arctic explorer (1873–).
Abyssinia (ăb"ĭs-sin'ĭ-*ȧ*), country, E. Africa, 350,000 sq. m., p. 7,000; cap. Adis Ababa.
Achin (ȧ-chēn'), Dutch depen., Sumatra, p. 580.
Adams (ăd'*ȧ*mz), Charles Francis. Am. dipl. & stsm. (1807–86).—Frank Dawson, Can. geol. (1859–).—John, 2d pres. U. S., 1797–1801 (1735–1826).—John [Alexander Smith], founder of Pitcairn Isl. govt. (1760–1829).—John Quincy, 6th pres. U. S., 1825–29 (1767–1848).—Maudo K., Am. act. (1872–).—Samuel, a leader in Am. Rev. (1722–1803).—William, Anglo-Jap. pioneer (1575–1620).
Addams (ăd'*ȧ*mz), Jane. Am. social worker (1860–).
Addison (ăd'ĭ-sŏn), Joseph. Eng. essay. (1672–1719).
Adelaide (ăd'ē-lād), cap. of S. Australia, p. 190.
Aden (ä'dĕn or ā'dĕn), pen. & town, Arabia, p. 46.—**Gulf of**, bet. Arabia & Africa.
Adirondacks (ăd"ĭ-rŏn'dăks), group of mts. in N. N. Y.; Mt. Marcy, 5,344 ft.; Mt. McIntyre, 5,112 ft.
Adler (ăd'lēr), Felix. Am. educ.; founder Ethical Culture Society (1851–).
Adrian, name of 6 popes, notably **IV.** Nicholas Brakspere, Pope 1154–59.
Adrianople (ā"drĭ-*ȧ*n-ō'pl), vilayet, European Turkey, p. 610.—city, cap. of vilayet, p. 81.
Adriatic Sea (ā"drĭ-ăt'ĭk), arm of Medit., 500 m. long, 130 m. broad.
Ægean Sea (ē-jē'ăn), between Asia Minor & Greece, 400 m. long.
Æschylus (ĕs'kĭ-lōōs). Gr. poet (525–456 B. C.).
Æsop (ē'sŏp). Gr. fabulist of 7th century.
Afghanistan (ăf-găn"ĭ-stăn'), country in Cen. Asia, 245,000 sq. m., p. 5,000; cap. Kabul.
Africa (ăf'rĭ-k*ȧ*), continent, 11,500,000 sq. m., p. 180,000.

Agassiz (ăg'ȧ-sē), Jean Louis Rodolphe. Swiss-Am. natur. (1807–73).

Aguinaldo (ä"gē-näl'dō), Emilio. Filipino leader (1870–).

Ahmadabad (ä'mȧ-dȧ-bäd'), city, presidency Bombay, India, p. 216.

Ainsworth (ānz'wûrth), William Harrison. Eng. novel. (1805–82).

Aisne (ān), riv., N. France; trib. of Oise; battles, 1914–18.—dept. France, cap. Laon, p. 530.

Aix-la-Chapelle (āks"lȧ-shȧ"pĕl'), city, Rhine prov., Prussia, p. 156. Also, **Aachen**.

Ajaccio (ȧ-yät'chō), sp. town, cap. Corsica; Napoleon's birthplace, p. 19.

A Kempis (ȧ kĕm'pĭs), Thomas. Ger. theolog. (1380–1471).

Akron (ăk'rŏn), city, Summit co., Ohio, p. 70.

Alabama (ăl"ȧ-bä'mȧ), state of U. S., 52,000 sq. m., p. 2,138; cap. Montgomery.—riv., Ala., 320 m. to Mobile riv.

Alaska (ȧ-lăs'kȧ), ter. U. S., 590,844 sq. m., p. 64; cap. Juneau.

Albani (äl-bä'nē), Emma. Canadian soprano (1852–).

Albania (ăl-bā'nĭ-ȧ), state in Europe, Balkan pen., 12,000 sq. m., p. 2,000; cap. Scutari.

Albany (ôl'bȧ-nĭ), city, cap. N. Y. State, p. 100.

Albert (ăl'bĕrt; Fr. ȯl"bâr'), formerly Ancre, town, dept. of Somme, Fr., p. 10; battles, 1915–18.

Albert I, king of Belgians fr. 1909 (1875–).—Albert (ăl'bĕrt), Prince of Saxe-Coburg Gotha, husband of Queen Victoria (1819–61).

Alberta (ăl-bûr'tȧ), prov. Can., 255,285 sq. m., p. 375.

Albert Nyanza (nĭ-ăn'zȧ), lake E. cen. Africa, 110 m. long, 25 m. broad.

Albertus Magnus (ăl-bûr'tŭs măg'nŭs) [Albert the Great]. Swabian philos. (1453–1515).

Alcibiades (ăl-sĭ-bī'ȧ-dēz). Athenian gen. (450–404 B. C.).

Alcott (ôl'kŭt), Louisa May. Am. novel. (1832–88).

Alexander (ăl'ĕg-zăn'dẽr), name of 8 popes, notably **VI,** Roderico L. Borgia, fr. 1492 (1431–1503).—**I,** king of Scotland [the Fierce] (1078–1124).—**I,** Prince & ruler of Bulgaria (1857–93).—**I,** king of Serbia (1876–1903).—**I,** emp. of Russia (1777–1825).—**II,** emp. of Russia (1818–81).—**III,** emp. of Russia (1845–94).

Alexander the Great, king of Macedonia & conqueror of eastern world (365–323 B. C.).

Alexandria (ăl"ĕg-zăn'drĭ-ȧ), sp. city Egypt, on Medit., p. 400.

Alfieri (äl-fyâ'rē), Vittorio, Count. It. poet (1749–1803).

Alfonso XIII (ăl-fŏn'sō), king of Spain fr. 1902 (1886–).

Alfred (ăl'frĕd), **the Great,** king of Wessex fr. 871 (848–900).

Alger (ăl'jẽr), Horatio 2d. Am. juvenile writer (1832–99).

Algeria (ăl-jē'rĭ-ȧ), Fr. colony, N. Africa, 200,000 sq. m., p. 5,600; cap. Algiers, p. 160.

Ali Pasha (ä'lē pȧ-shä'), ruler of Albania [The Lion of Janina] (1741–1822).

Allahabad (äl-lȧ-hȧ-bäd'), division N. W. Provs., India, p. 5,757.—city, India, p. 172.

Allegheny (ăl'ē-gā-nĭ), mts., Appalachian system of Pa., Md., Va. & W. Va.—riv. of Pa., about 350 m. long; branch of Ohio riv.

Allen (ăl'ĕn), Ethan. Am. soldier (1737–89).—Grant. Can.-Eng. author (1848–99).—Ira. Am. soldier & legis. ["Father of Univ. of Vermont"] (1751–1814).—James Lane. Am. novel. (1849–).—Jerome. Am. educ. & essayist; dean, N. Y. School of Pedagogy (1830–94).

Allenby (ăl'ĕn-bĭ), Sir Edmund Henry Hynman. Br. gen. (1861–).

Allentown (toun), city, Lehigh co., Pa., p. 52.

Allston (ôl'stŏn), Washington. Am. painter & author (1779–1843).

Alma-Tadema (ăl'mȧ tăd'ē-mȧ), Sir Laurence. Eng. painter of Dutch origin (1836–1912).

Alost (ȧ'lōst), town, E. Flanders, Belgium, on Dender riv., p. 30.

Alps (ălps), mt. system, S. cen. Europe, Mont Blanc the highest, 15,781 ft.

Alsace-Lorraine (ăl-säs lō-răn'), Fr. provinces, annexed in 1870 by Germany, recovered by Fr. 1918; 5,601 sq. m., p. 1,872.

Altai (äl-tī'), mts., N. cen. Asia, 12,000 ft.

Altoona (ăl-tōō'nȧ), city, Blair co., Pa., p. 52.

Alva (äl'vȧ), or **Alba,** Fernando Alvarez de Toledo, Duke of. Span. gen. & statesm. (1508–82).

Alvarado (äl-vȧ-rä'thō), Pedro de. Span. adv. Conqueror of Guatemala (1486–1541).

Amato (ȧ-mä'tō), Pasquale. It. baritone (1878–).

Amazon (ăm'ȧ-zŏn), largest riv. in world, 4,000 m. long, Peruvian Andes, to Atlantic oc.

Ambrose (ăm'brōz). Latin Church Father (340–397).

America (ȧ-mĕr'ĭ-kȧ), the western continent: N. Am., 8,300,000 sq. m.; S. Am., 7,700,000; p. 180,000.

Amerigo Vespucci (ä"mā-rē'gō vĕs-pōōt'chē). It. navig. (1452–1512).

Amherst (ăm'hẽrst), Jeffrey, Baron. Eng. soldier; conqueror of Canada (1717–97).

Amiel (ȧ"myĕl'), Henri Frédéric. Swiss author (1821–81).

Amiens (ȧ"myăn'), city on Somme riv., Fr., p. 90.

Ampere (ăn"pâr'), André Marie. Fr. physicist & natur. (1775–1836).

Amsterdam (ăm'stẽr-dăm), city, Netherlands, on Zuider Zee, p. 616.

Amu (ȧ-mōō'), riv. in Turkestan, cen. Asia, 1,280 m. to Aral sea.

Amundsen (ä'mŭn-sĕn), Roald. Norweg. explorer (1872–).

Amur (ȧ-mōōr'), riv. E. Asia, 2,500 m. to N. Pacific.

Anastasius (ăn'ăs-tā'shĭ-ŭs). **I,** pope fr. 398 to 402.—**II,** pope fr. 496–498.—**III,** pope fr. 911 to 913.—**IV,** pope fr. 1153 to 1154.

Anaxagoras (ăn-ăk-săg'ō-răs). Ionian philos. & geomet. (500–428 B. C.).

Andersen (ăn'dẽr-sĕn), Hans Christian. Dan. writer of fairy tales (1805–75).

Anderson (ăn'dẽr-sŭn), Alexander. Pioneer of wood engraving in U. S. (1775–1870).

Andes (ăn'dēz), mt. system, 4,500 m. long; Cape Horn to Panama, S. Am.; Aconcagua, 23,080 ft.

André (ăn'drā), John. Eng. soldier in Am. Rev., executed at Tappan, N. Y. (1751–80).

Andros (ăn'drŏs), Sir Edmund. Colonial gov. in Am. (1637–1714).

Androscoggin (ăn"drŏs-kŏg'gĭn), riv., 175 m. long, flows to Kennebec riv., near Bath, Me.

Angelico (ăn-jĕl'ĭ-kō), Fra. Florentine painter (1387–1455).

Ann, Cape (ăn), E. extremity of Essex co., Mass.

Annapolis (ă-năp'ō-lĭs), sp. city, cap. of Md., p. 9; U. S. Naval Academy.

Anne (ăn), **of Austria**, wife of Louis XIII of Fr. & Queen Regent for Louis XIV (1606–66).—**of Denmark**, queen of Scot. & Eng., wife of James VI of Scot., James I of Eng. (1574–1619).—**of England**, queen of Gr. B. & Ire., last Br. sovereign of the house of Stuart (1665–1714).—**Boleyn**, 2d wife of Henry VIII of Eng. (1507–36).
Annunzio (dän-nōōn′dzē-ō), Gabrielle d′. It poet, novelist & patriot (1864–).
Anselm (ăn′sĕlm), Saint. Abp. of Canterbury fr. 1093 (1033–1109).
Antarctic Ocean (ănt-ärk′tĭk), around S. pole, within Antarctic Circle.
Anthony (ăn′thō-nĭ), Susan Brownell. Am. woman suffrage leader (1820–1906).
Antietam (ăn-tē′tăm), creek, Pa. & Md. to Potomac; battle in Md. 1862.
Antigonus (ăn-tĭg′ō-nŭs). Macedonian gen. under Alexander (380–301 B. C.).
Antilles (ăn-tĭl′lēz), two group isls., Greater & Lesser Antilles, W. Indies.
Antoninus Pius (ăn-tō-nī′nŭs pī′ŭs). Rom. emp. fr. 138 (86–161).
Antonius (ăn-tō′nĭ-ŭs), Marcus [Mark Antony]. Rom. triumvar (83–30 B. C.).
Antony (ăn′tō-nĭ), Saint, of Thebes; father of Monastic asceticism (251–356).
Antrim (ăn′trĭm), co. of Ulster, Ireland, p. 570; cap. Belfast.
Antwerp (ănt′wĕrp; Fr. **Anvers**), cap. of Bel., on Scheldt riv., p. 392.
Appalachians (ăp″ȧ-lă′chĭ-ănz), mt. range in N. A., fr. Newfoundland to cen. Ala.
Appomattox Court House (ăp-pō-măt′-tŏks), vil., Va. Here General Lee surrendered, 1865.
Aquinas (ȧ-kwī′nȧs). Thomas. It. theolog. (1225–74).
Arabia (ȧ-rā′bĭ-ȧ), country, S. W. Asia, 1,200,000 sq. m., p. 5,000.
Aral Sea (ăr′ăl), inland sea, Asiatic Russia, 26,166 sq. m.
Ararat (ăr′ȧ-răt), Mt. Armenia; highest peaks about 17,000 ft.
Arc, Jeanne d′ (zhăn därk), [Joan of Arc]. Fr. national heroine (1412–31).
Archangel (ärk-ān′jĕl), sp. town, near Arctic ocean, N. Russia, p. 18.
Archimides (är-kĭ-mē′dēz). Greek geomet. & math. (287–212 B. C.).
Arctic Ocean (ärk′tĭk), around North pole, 5,541,600 sq. m., greatest depth 13,200 ft.
Argentina (är″jĕn-tē′nȧ), repub. S. Am. 1,131,849 sq. m., p. 7,250; cap. Buenos Aires.
Argonne (är″gŏn′), forest, border of Lorraine & Champagne, France; battles, 1792, 1870 & 1914–18.
Argyll (är-gīl′), 9th Duke of. Eng. stsm. & author; gov. gen. of Canada 1878–83; as Marquis of Lorne (1845–1914).
Ariosto (ä-rē-yŏs′tō), Ludovico. It. poet (1474–1533).
Aristides (ăr-ĭs-tī′dēz), **the Just**. Athenian stsm. (550–467 B. C.).
Aristophanes (ăr-ĭs-tŏf′ȧ-nēz). Gr. comedy playwright (445–385 B. C.).
Aristotle (ăr′ĭs-tŏtl). Gr. philos. (384–322 B. C.).
Arizona (ăr-ĭ-zō′nȧ), state U. S. A., 113,020 sq. m., p. 204; cap. Phoenix.
Arkansas (är′kȧn-sô), state U. S. A., 53,850 sq. m., p. 1,574; cap. Little Rock.—riv., 2,000 m. long, rises Rocky mts., Colo., flows to Mississippi riv.
Arkwright (ärk′rīt), Sir Richard. Eng. inventor of cotton-spinning machinery (1732–92).
Armagh (är-mä′), co. of Ulster, Ire., p. 120.
Armenia (är-mē′nĭ-ȧ), country in W. Asia, S. W of Caucasus mts.
Armentières (är″măṅ″tyâr′), town, N. Fr., on Lys riv., p. 29.
Arminius (är-mĭn′ĭ-ŭs), Jacobus H. Dutch theolog.; founder of Arminianism (1560–1609).
Arnold (är′nŏld), Benedict. Soldier of Am. Rev., known as "the Traitor" (1741–1801). —Sir Edwin. Eng. poet & journalist (1832–1904).—Matthew. Eng. poet (1822–88).
Aroostook (ȧ-rōōs′tŏŏk), riv., over 100 m. long, Me.; flows to St. John riv.
Arras (är″räs′), city, dept. of Pas-de-Calais, Fr., p. 26; battles, 1917–18.
Artaxerxes (är″tăks-ẽrks′ēz). Name of 3 kings of Persia, fr. 465 to 338 B. C.
Arthur (är′thŭr). King of Eng., 6th century, according to legend.—Chester Alan, 21st pres. U. S. (1830–86).
Ashanti (ȧ-shăn′tē), country in W. Africa; cap. Kumassi, p. 3,000.
Asia (ā′shȧ), continent, 17,000,000 sq. m., p. 910,000.
Asia Minor, pen. forming W. extremity of Asia, part Turkish, p. 9,500.
Asquith (ăsk′wĭth), Herbert Henry. Eng. stsm. (1852–).
Assam (ăs″săm′), prov. Br. India, 53,000 sq. m., p. 6,700.
Assyria (ăs-sĭr′ĭ-ȧ), anc. empire W. Asia; its cap. was Nineveh.
Athabasca (ăth″ȧ-băs′kȧ), lake N. W. Can., 195 m. long.—riv. N. W. Can., 800 m.
Athens (ăth′ĕnz), city, cap. of Greece, p. 167.
Atlanta (ăt-lăn′tȧ), city, cap. of Ga., p. 155.
Atlantic City (ăt-lăn′tĭk), city & seaside resort N. J. on Absecon beach; p. 50; summer, p. 350.
Atlantic Ocean, bet. Am. & Europe & Africa; 31,530,000 sq. m.; average breadth 3,000 m.; greatest depth 31,366 ft.
Atlas (ăt′lȧs), mts. N. Africa, 1,500 m.
Atterbury (ăt′tẽr-bẽr″ĭ), William Wallace. Am. railway official; director U. S. military railways in Fr., 1917–18, during war (1866–).
Attila (ăt′ĭ-lȧ). King of the Huns (406–53).
Auber (ō″bâr′), Daniel François. Fr. composer (1782–1871).
Auckland (ôk′lănd), city & prov. New Zealand, p. city, 102; prov. 260.
Audran (ō′drăṅ), Edmond. Fr. composer (1842–1901).
Audubon (ô′dū-bŏn), John James. Am. natur. (1780–1851).
Augustine (ô-gŭs′tĭn), Saint. One of the Latin Fathers (354–430).
Augustus (ô-gŭs′tŭs), Octavius. 1st Rom. emp. (63 B. C.–14 A. D.).
Aurelian (ô-rē′lĭ-ȧn), Lucius Domitius. Rom. emp. (212–275).
Aurelius (ô-rē′lĭ-ŭs), Marcus [Antoninus]. Rom. emp. (121–180).
Austen (ôs′tĕn), Jane. Eng. novelist (1775–1817).
Austerlitz (ous′tẽr-lĭts), town, Moravia on the Littawa; battle, 1805, p. 4.
Austin, Alfred. Eng. poet laureate (1835–1913).—John. Eng. writer on jurisprudence (1790–1859).
Australasia (ôs″trăl-ā′shȧ), term applied to Australia & New Zealand; sometimes to all isls. of S. Pacific.
Australia (ôs-trā′lĭ-ȧ), commonwealth within Br. Empire; island continent bounded E. by Pacific, W. & S. by Indian oceans; 3,063,041 sq. m., p. 5,000; cap. Canberra.
Austria (ôs′trĭ-ȧ), empire, W. part of Austria-Hungary, 134,634 sq. m., p. 29,000; cap. Vienna.

Austria-Hungary (hŭn'gȧ-rĭ), monarchy cen. Europe; 241,513 sq. m., p. 45,000.
Avlona. See Valona.
Ayr (âr), co. of Scot., p. 269.
Azores (ȧ-zōrz'), Portuguese isls., N. Atl. ocean, 1,005 sq. m., p. 243; cap. Ponta Delgada.
Azov (ȧ-zŏf'), **Sea of,** 14,520 sq. m., S. Russia, arm of Black sea.

B

Bab el Mandeb (băb'ĕl măn'dĕb), strait bet. Red sea & Indian ocean.
Babylon (băb'ĭ-lŭn), anc. city on Euphrates riv., 55 m. S. of Bagdad.
Bach (băkh), Johann Sebastian. Ger. composer (1685–1750).
Bacon (bā'kn), Francis, Baron Verulam, Viscount St. Albans. Eng. essayist (1561–1626).
Baden (bä'dĕn), grand duchy, Ger. empire, 5,823 sq. m., p. 2,100; cap. Karlsruhe.
Baffin (băf'ĭn), William. Eng. navig. (1584–1622).—**Bay,** W. of Greenland, N. America, 800 m. long.—**Land,** Br. isl. W. of Greenland; part of Can., 236,000 sq. m.
Bagdad (băg'dăd), city, Mesopotamia; captured by Br., March 11, 1917, p. 150.
Bagehot (băj'ŭt), Walter. Eng. author (1826–77).
Bahama islands, (bȧ-hā'mȧ), Br. isls. W. Indies, p. 56; cap. Nassau.
Bahia (bä-ē'ä), state of Brazil, p. 2,000.
Baikal (bī'käl'), lake S. Siberia, 13,000 sq. m.
Bainbridge (bān'brĭj), William. Am. naval officer (1774–1833).
Baker (bā'kẽr), Newton Diehl. Am. lawyer & cabinet officer; Secy. of War during Great War (1871–).
Baku (bä-kōō'), cap. of Baku govt., Transcaucasia, p. 206.
Balboa (băl-bō'ȧ), Vasco Nuñez de. Sp. explorer (1475–1517).
Balfe (bălf), Michael. Irish composer (1808–70).
Balfour (băl'fōōr), Arthur J. Br. stsm. (1848–).
Balkan (bôl'kȧn), mt. range S. E. Europe—peninsula, bounded by Adriatic, Black & Ægean seas, comprising Bulgaria, Serbia, Bosnia, Herzegovina, Albania, Roumania, Greece, Montenegro & Turkey in Europe.
Baltic Provinces (bôl'tĭk), countries bordering Baltic sea: Esthonia, Livonia, Courland, p. 2,688.
Baltic Sea, in N. Europe, inclosed by Denmark, Sweden, Russia & Prussia, 158,000 sq. m.
Baltimore (bôl'tĭ-mōr), city on Patapsco riv., Md., p. 580.
Baluchistan (bȧ-lōō'chēs-tăn'), country in Asia N. of Arabian sea, 141,600 sq. m., p. 847; cap. Khelat.
Balzac (băl'zăk'), Honoré de. Fr. novelist (1799–1850).
Bancroft (băn'krŏft), George. Am. historian (1800–91).
Bangkok (băng-kŏk'), cap. of Siam, on Menam riv., p. 630.
Bapaume (bȧ'pōm'), town, dept. Pas-de-Calais, Fr., battles, 1871 & 1914–18, p. 3.
Barbados (bä -bā'dōz), Br. isl., W. Indies; 166 sq. m., p. 172; cap. Bridgetown.
Barbary (bär'bȧ-rĭ), region, N. Africa, from Egypt to Atlantic oc.
Barcelona (bär'sĕ-lō'nȧ; Span. bär'thä-), city, Spain, on Medit. sea, p. 560.
Barfrush (băr-frōōsh'), town, Persia, near Caspian sea, p. 50.
Bar-le-duc (bär'lē-dōōk'), town, dept. Meuse, France, p. 18.
Barnard (bär'nȧrd), George Grey. Am. sculptor (1863–).—Henry. Am. educ. (1811–1900).
Barnum (bär'nŭm), Phineas Taylor. Am. showman (1810–91).
Barrie (băr'ĭ), Sir J. M. Scot. novelist (1860–).
Barrow, Cape, Br. Am., Coronation gulf.—**Point Barrow,** headland, N. extremity Alaska.
Bartholdi (bär'tŏl'dē'), Frédéric Auguste. Fr. sculptor (1834–1904).
Bartolommeo (bär'tō-lŏm-mā'ō), Fra. It. painter (1472–1517).
Bartram (bär'trăm), John. Am. botanist (1699–1777).
Basel (bä'zĕl), city on Rhine riv., Switzerland, p. 129.
Basil the Great (bă'zĭl), one of the fathers of the Greek church (329–379).
Bass Strait (băs), 80–150 m. wide; bet. Australia & Tasmania.
Basutoland (bȧ-sōō'tō), Br. colony S. Africa, 10,300 sq. m., p. 350.
Batavia (bȧ-tā'vĭ-ȧ), city & cap., Java, Dutch East Indies, p. 138.
Batum (bȧ-tōōm'), Russ. town, S. E. shore Black sea, p. 30.
Baudelaire (bōd'lâr'), Charles. Fr. decadent poet (1821–67).
Bavaria (bȧ-vā'rĭ-ȧ), state of Ger., 29,291 sq. m., p. 6,876; cap. Munich.
Bayard (bä'yär'), Pierre du Terrail. Fr. knight, famous chevalier (1476–1524).
Bayard (bī'ẽrd), Thomas Francis. Am. stsm. & dipl. (1828–98).
Bayonne (bā-yŏn'), city, Hudson co., N. J., p. 56.
Beaconsfield (bē'kŭns-fēld), Earl [Benjamin Disraeli]. Br. stsm. & novelist (1804–81).
Beatty (bē'tĭ), Sir David. Br. admiral (1871–).
Beauharnais (bō'är'nā'), Hortense Eugénie de. Daughter of Josephine; queen of Holland (1783–1837).
Beaumarchais (bō'mär'shā'), de [Pierre Augustin Caron]. Fr. dramatist (1732–99).
Beaumont (bō'mŏnt), Francis. Eng. dramatist (1584–1616).
Beauregard (bō'rē-gärd'), Pierre G. Toutant. Am. Confed. gen. (1818–93).
Beauvais (bō-vā'), cap., dept. of Oise, France, p. 20.
Bede (bēd), **The Venerable.** Eng. monk & writer (673–735).
Bedford (bĕd'fẽrd), city & co., Eng., p. city, 40; county, 145.—John Plantagenet, Duke of, Regent of Fr. (1389–1435).
Beecher (bē'chẽr), Henry Ward. Am. clergy. (1813–87).
Beethoven (bā-tō'vĕn), Ludwig von. Ger. composer (1770–1827).
Beirut (bā-rōōt'), chief sp. Syria, p. 120.
Belfast (bĕl'făst), city, sp., Ulster, Ire., p. 390.
Belfort (bĕl'fōr'), cap. of territory of Belfort, France; battle, 1871; p. comm., 40; ter. 101.
Belgium (bĕl'jĭ-ŭm or bĕl'jŭm), kingdom of Europe, 11,372 sq. m.; many battles, notably 1815 & 1914–18, p. 7,500; cap. Brussels.
Belgrade (bĕl-grăd'), cap. Serbia; battles 1688, 1717, 1789 & 1914–18, p. 90.
Bell, Alexander Graham. Scot.-Am. inventor (1847–).
Belle Isle, Strait of, bet. Labrador & Newfoundland, 10–15 m. wide, 80 m. long.

Bellini (běl-lē'nē), Venetian painters: Jacopo (1400–70); Gentile (1429–1507); Giovanni (1430–1516).—**Vicenzo.** Sicilian composer (1801–35).

Benares (bě-nä'rēz), holy city of Hindus, Agra prov., on Ganges riv., India, p. 204. —division of India, 10,430 sq. m., p. 4,809.

Benedict (běn'ē-dĭkt), name of many popes; notably **XIV,** Prospero Lambertini, pope fr. 1740 to 1758, & **XV,** Giacomo della Chiesa, pope fr. 1915 (1854–).—**Saint Benedict,** It. abbot, founder of Western monachism (480–543).

Bengal (běn-gôl'), prov. of India, 70,000 sq. m., p. 42,000.—**Bay of,** part of Indian ocean, bet. India and E. India.

Benjamin (běn'jā-mĭn), Judah Philip. Am. lawyer & stsm.; Confed. leader (1811–84).

Bennett (běn'ĕt), Arnold. Eng. novelist (1867–).—James Gordon. Am. journalist (1795–1872).—James Gordon, son of former. Am. journalist (1841–1918).

Bennington (běn'ĭng-tŭn), township of Vt., home of Ethan Allen; battle, 1777, p. 9.

Benson (běn'sŭn), Edward Frederick. Eng. novelist (1867–).

Bentham (běn'thăm), Jeremy. Eng. philos. & jurist (1748–1832).

Bentley (běnt'lĭ), Richard. Eng. scholar & critic (1662–1742).

Benton (běn'tŭn), Thomas Hart. Am. stsm. (1782–1858).

Berditchev (bĕr-dyē'chĕf), cap. of dist. in govt. of Kiev, Russia, p. 77.

Beresford (bĕr'ĕs-fērd), Lord Charles W. de la Poer. Br. admiral (1846–).

Bergerac (bĕr'zhā-răk'), Cyrano de. Fr. novel. & dram. (1619–55).

Bergh (bĕrg), Henry. Am. humanitarian, founder of S. P. C. C. & S. P. C. A.

Bergson (bĕrg'sôn'), Henri Louis. Fr. philos. (1859–).

Bering (bā'rĭng), or **Behring,** Vitus. Dan. navigator (1680–1741).—**Sea,** bet. Aleutian isls. & Bering strait, latter separating Asia & America; 878,000 sq. m.

Berkeley (bûrk'lĭ), George. Irish bishop & philos. (1685–1753).—Sir William. Colonial gov. of Va. (1610–77).

Berks (bûrks), co. of Eng., p. 281.

Berlin (bĕr-lĭn'), cap. Prussia, on Spree riv., p. 2,080.

Berlioz (bĕr'lē'ōs'), Hector. Fr. composer (1803–69).

Bermuda (bĕr-mū'dā), Br. isls., W. Atl. oc.; 20 sq. m., p. 19; cap. Hamilton.

Bern (bĕrn), city, canton & Federal cap. Switz., p. of city, 85; of canton, 647.

Bernard (bĕr'nārd or bĕr-närd'; Fr. bĕr'-när'), Saint [de Clairvaux]. Fr. priest, mystic, Crusader (1091–1153).

Bernhardt (bĕrn'härt), Sara [Rosa]. Fr. actress of Fr. & Dutch parentage (1845–).

Berry-au-Bac (bā'rē'ō'bäk'), town, dept. of Aisne, Fr.; battles, 1914–18; p. 3.

Berzelius (bĕr-zē'lĭ-ŭs; Swed. bĕr-tsā'lĭ-ŭs), Johan Jacob, Baron. Swed. chemist; originator of chemical symbols (1779–1848).

Besant (bē-zănt'), Sir Walter. Eng. novelist (1836–1901).

Bessarabia (bĕs'ā-rā'bĭ-ā), govt. S. W. Russia; cap. Kishinev, p. 2,500.

Bessemer (bĕs'ē-mēr), Sir Henry. Eng. engineer & inv. (1813–98).

Bethlehem (bĕth'lē-hĕm), town in Palestine, 6 m. S. of Jerusalem; birthplace of David and Jesus; modern Beit-Lahm.

Bethmann-Hollweg- (bāt'män-hŏl'vākh), Theobald von. Ger. stsm.; chancellor at outbreak of war of 1914–18. (1856–).

Bethune (bā'tōōn'), town, dept. of Pas-de-Calais, Fr., p. 15.

Bienville (byăn'vēl'), Jean Baptiste. Colonial gov. of La. (1680–1768).

Bigelow (bĭg'ē-lō), John. Am. author & dipl. (1817–1911).—Poultney, son of former. Am. historian & traveler (1855–).

Birkenhead (bĭr'kĕn-hĕd), sp. city, Cheshire, Eng., p. 140.

Birmingham (bĭr'mĭng-ăm), city, Warwick, Eng., p. 868.—city, Jefferson co., Ala., p. 160.

Biscay, Bay of (bĭs'kā), part of Atlantic oc.; Ushant isl., Fr. to Cape Ortegal, Sp.

Bismarck-Schönhausen (bĭs'märk shĕn'hou-zĕn), Otto Leopold, Prince. Ger. stsm. (1815–98).

Bizet (bē-zā'), Alexandre Cesar Leopold [Georges]. Fr. composer (1838–75).

Bjornsen (byûrn'sŭn), Bjornstjerne. Norw. dram. & novel. (1832–1910).

Black, Jeremiah Sullivan. Am. jurist (1810–83).—William. Scot. novel. (1841–98).

Black Forest, Baden & Württemberg, Ger.

Black Hawk, Am. Indian chief (1767–1838).

Black Sea, sea S. of Russia, bet. Europe & Asia.

Blackstone, Sir William. Eng. jurist & law writer (1723–80).

Blaine (blān), James Gillespie. Am. stsm. (1830–93).

Blake (blāk), Robert. Eng. admiral (1599–1657).—William. Eng. engraver & poet (1757–1827).—William Hume. Canadian jurist (1809–70).

Blanc, Mont (môn blän), highest mt. of Alps, on frontier of Fr. & Italy; alt. 15,780 ft.

Blennerhassett (blĕn'ĕr-hăs'ĕt), Harman. Eng. co-conspirator with Aaron Burr in Am. (1764–1831).

Bliss (blĭs), Tasker Howard. Am. gen. (1853–).

Bloemfontein (blōōm'fŏn-tīn), city, cap. Orange Free State; stronghold in Boer War, 1900, p. 27.

Blücher (blü'kh'ĕr), Gebhard Leberecht von. Prussian field marshal (1742–1819).

Blue Ridge, the S. E. range of the Appalachians in Va. & N. C.

Boadicea (bō'ā-dĭ-sē'ā). Br. queen during Rom. occupation (?–62 A. D.).

Boccaccio (bōk-kät'chō), Giovanni. It. novel. (1313–75).

Boccherini (bōk-kā-rē'nē), Luigi. It. composer (1743–1805).

Bogota (bō'gō-tä'), cap. of Colombia, p. 120.

Bohemia (bō-hē'mĭ-ā), former kingdom of Europe, now crownland in Austro-Hungarian monarchy, 20,000 sq. m., p. 6,770.

Bokhara (bō-kā-rä'), depend. of Russia in cen. Asia, p. 1,250.

Bolingbroke (bŏl'ĭng-brŏŏk), Henry St. John, Viscount. Eng. premier (1678–1751).

Bolivar (bŏl-ē-vär), Simon ["The Liberator"]. Venezuelan gen. & stsm. (1783–1830).

Bolivia (bō-lē'vyā), S. Am. repub., 570,000 sq. m., p. 2,200; cap. La Paz.

Bologna (bō-lō'nyā), city, cap. of prov., Italy, p. 173.

Bolton (bōl'tŭn), city, Lancashire, Eng., p. 185.

Bombay (bŏm-bā'), sp. city & presidency India, p. city, 980; presidency, 19,672.

Bonaparte (bō'nā-pärt), or **Buonaparte** (bwō'nä'pär'tē), Corsican family: **Napoleon I,** emp. of Fr. fr. 1804 to 1815 & fr. March, 1815 to June, 1815 (1769–1821).—his brothers, **Jerome,** king of Westphalia

(1784–1860); **Joseph,** king of Naples & Spain (1768–1844); **Louis,** king of Holland (1778–1846); **Lucien,** prince of Canino (1775–1840).—his son, **Charles Joseph, Napoleon II,** duke of Reichstadt [L'Aiglon] (1811–32).—**Charles Louis, Napoleon III,** son of Louis, emp. of Fr. (1808–73).

Bonheur (bô″nûr′), Rosa [Marie Rosalie]. Fr. painter of animals (1822–99).

Boniface (bŏn′ĭ-făs), name of 9 popes, notably **Boniface VIII** [Cajetan], pope fr. 1294 to 1303 (1228–1303).—**Saint** ["the Apostle of Germany"]. (680–755).

Boone (bōōn), Daniel. Am. pioneer in Ky. (1735–1820).

Booth (bōōth), Edwin Thomas. Am. actor (1833–93).—John Wilkes. Am. actor, assassin of Pres. Lincoln (1839–65).—William ["General"]. Eng. clergy., founder of Salvation Army (1829–1912).

Bordeaux (bôr″dō′), sp. city, cap. dept. of Gironde, Fr., p. 262.

Borden (bôr′dĕn), Sir Robert Laird. Can. stsm. (1854–).

Borgia (bôr′jä), Cesare, son of pope Alexander VI, cardinal & soldier (1476–1507).—Lucrezia, his sister, duchess of Ferrara (1480–1519).

Boris (bō-rēs′), king of Bulgaria for one month; succeeded his father, Ferdinand I, Oct. 3d; abdicated Nov. 2, 1918 (1894–).

Borneo (bôr′nē-ō), isl. East Indies, Br. & Dutch; 290,000 sq. m., p. 1,731.

Bosnia (bŏz′nĭ-ȧ), country in S. E. Europe, annexed with Herzegovina by Austria-Hungary, 1908; p. with Herzegovina, 1,900.

Bosporus (bŏs′pō-rŭs), strait, 18 m. long; bet. Black & Marmora seas.

Boston (bŏs′tŭn), sp. city, cap. of Mass., p. 756.

Boswell (bŏz′wĕl), James. Scot. lawyer; biographer of Samuel Johnson (1740–95).

Botha (bō′tä), Louis. Boer gen. & stsm.; premier of Union of S. Africa (1862–).

Botticelli (bŏt″tĭ-chĕl′lĭ), Sandro, originally Alessandro Filipepi. It. painter (1447–1510).

Boucicault (bōō′sē-kō), Dion. Irish-Am. playwright & actor (1822–90).

Bougainville (bōō″găn″vēl′), Louis Antoine de. Fr. navigator (1729–1811).

Boulanger (bōō″läṅ″zhā′), Georges Ernest Jean Marie. Fr. gen. (1837–91).

Boulogne (bōō-lōn′; Fr. bōō″lō′ny), sp. city, dept. of Pas-de-Calais, Fr., p. 53.—town, dept. of Seine, Fr., suburb of Paris, p. 57.

Bourget (bōōr″zhā′), Paul. Fr. novel. & essay. (1852–).

Bowen (bō′ĕn), Francis. Am. writer on philosophy & political economy (1811–90).

Boyne (boin), riv. in E. Ireland; battle, 1690.

Braddock (brăd′ŏk), Edward. Br. gen. in Am. (1695–1755).

Bradford (brăd′fẽrd), city, Yorkshire, Eng., p. 288.—William. Second gov. of Plymouth Colony (1589–1657).

Bradstreet (brăd′strēt), Simon. Colonial gov. of Mass. (1603–97).

Braga (brä′gȧ), Theophile. Port. author & pres. of repub. (1843–).

Bragg (brăg), Braxton. Am. Confed. gen. (1817–76).

Brahe (brä′hē), Tycho. Dan. astronomer (1546–1601).

Brahmaputra (brä″mȧ-pōō′trȧ), riv. Tibet & India, 1,680 m. long.

Brahms (bräms), Johannes. Ger. composer (1833–97).

Brandeis (brăn′dīs), Louis Dembitz. Am. jurist (1856–).

Brandenburg (brăn′dĕn-bōōrkh′), prov. of cen. Prussia, p. 4,093.

Brant (brănt), Joseph. Mohawk Indian chief (1742–1807).

Brazil (brȧ-zĭl′), **United States of,** repub. S. Am., 3,300,000 sq. m., p. 23,600; cap. Rio de Janeiro.

Brazos (brä′zōs), riv. of Texas, 900 m. to Gulf of Mexico.

Bremen (brā′mĕn), state of Ger. empire, 99 sq. m., p. 300.—cap. of state, p. 247.

Bremerhaven (brā′mẽr-hä′fĕn), sp. city, Weser riv., Ger., p. 24.

Breslau (brĕs′lou), cap. of Silesia prov., Prussia, p. 512.

Brest-Litovsk (brĕst″lyē-tōfsk′), fortress & cap. of dist. Grodno, Russia, p. 47.

Brewster (brōō′stẽr), William. Pilgrim Father (1560–1644).

Briand (brē″äṅ′), Aristide. Fr. premier (1862–).

Bridgeport (brĭj′pōrt), city, Fairfield co., Conn., p. 102.

Bright (brīt), John. Eng. stsm. (1811–89).

Brighton (brīt′ŭn), city, S. England, p. 133.

Brisbane (brĭz′băn), sp. city, cap. of Queensland, Australia, p. 140.

Bristol (brĭs′tŭl), city, on Avon riv., Eng., p. 363.

British Columbia, prov., Canada on Pacific. 353,000 sq. m.; cap. Victoria, p. 393.

British Empire. See **Great Britain, India, Canada, Newfoundland, Australia, New Zealand, Union of South Africa.**

Brockton (brŏk′tŭn), Mass., p. 57.

Bronte (brŏn′tē), Charlotte. Eng. author (1816–55).

Bronx (brŏṅks), bor. of New York City, p. 600.

Brooke (brōōk), Rupert. Eng. poet (1887–1915).

Brooklyn (brōōk-lĭn), bor. of New York City, p. 1,976.

Brougham (brōō′ȧm), Henry Peter, Baron. Eng. jurist (1778–1868).

Brown (broun), John. Am. abolitionist (1800–59).

Browning (broun′ĭng), Elizabeth Barrett. Eng. poet (1806–61).—Robert. Husband of former. Eng. poet (1812–89).

Bruce (brōōs), Robert. King of Scot. fr 1306 (1274–1329).

Bruges (brōōzh), city, cap. of W. Flanders, Belgium, p. 53.

Brummell (brŭm′ĕl), George Bryan [Beau Brummell]. Eng. exquisite (1778–1840).

Brunelleschi (brōō″nĕl-lĕs′kē), Filippo. Florentine architect (1377–1446).

Brussels (brŭs′ĕls), city, cap. of Belgium, p. comm. 720.

Brutus (brōō′tŭs), Marcus Junius. Rom. polit.; conspirator against Cæsar (85–42 B. C.).

Bryan (brī′ȧn), William Jennings. Am. stsm. & lecturer (1860–).

Bryant (brī′ȧnt), William Cullen. Am. poet (1794–1878).

Bryce (brīs), James, Viscount. Br. stsm. dipl. & author (1838–).

Bryn Mawr (brĭn mär), town near Philadelphia, Pa., famous for its college for women.

Buchanan (bŭ-kăn′ȧn), James. 15th pres. of U. S. (1791–1868).—Robert. Eng. poet (1841–1901).

Bucharest (bōō-kȧ-rĕst′), city, cap. of Roumania, p. 338.

Buckingham (bŭk′ĭng-ȧm), or **Bucks,** co. of Eng., p. 220.

Buckner (bŭk'nẽr), Simon Bolivar. Am. Confed. soldier (1823–1914).

Budapest (bōō'dȧ-pĕst), cap. of kingdom of Hungary, p. 880.

Buddha (bōōd'dhȧ), Gautama, Indian mystic, founder of Buddhism in 6th century B. C.

Buell (bū'ĕl), Don Carlos. Am. gen. (1818–98).

Buenos Aires (bwā'nōs ī'rās; bō'nŭs ā'rīz), prov. of Argentina, p. 1,597.—city, cap. of Argentina, on La Plata, p. 1,232.

Buffalo (bŭf'ȧ-lō), city, N. Y., on Lake Erie, p. 423.

Buffon (bü'fôṅ'), George Louis Leclerc, Count de. Fr. natur. (1707–1788).

Bug (bōōg), riv. Russia, Volhynia to Black sea, 500 m.—riv. Galicia, to Vistula, 450 m.

Bukowina (bōō-kō-vē'nȧ), crownland of Austria, S. E. of Galicia, 4,031 sq. m., p. 800; cap. Czernowitz.

Bulgaria (bŏŏl-gā'rĭ-ȧ), kingdom in Balkans, 42,000 sq. m., p. 5,500; cap. Sofia.

Bull, Ole Bornemann. Norwegian violinist (1810–80)

Bullard (bŏŏl'ărd), Robert Lee. Am. soldier in command 2d Army in Fr., 1917-18 (1861–).

Bull Run, stream in N. E. Va.; battles, 1861–62.

Bulwer-Lytton (-lĭt'ŭn), Edward George Earle, 1st Lord Lytton. Eng. novel. (1803–73).—Edward Robert, 1st Earl of Lytton [Owen Meredith]. Eng. poet (1831–91).

Bunker Hill (bŭṅk'ẽr), Charlestown, Mass., battle, June 17, 1775.

Bunyan (bŭn'yȧn), John. Eng. author *Pilgrim's Progress* (1628–88).

Burbank (bûr'băṅk), Luther. Am. horticulturist (1849–).

Burgoyne (bûr-goin'), John. Eng. gen. in Am. Rev. (1722–92).

Burke (bûrk), Edmund. Br. stsm. (1729–97).

Burma (bûr'mȧ), prov. of Br. India, on Bay of Bengal, 231,000 sq. m., p. 12,115.

Burne-Jones (bûrn-jōnz), Sir Edward. Br. painter (1833–98).

Burns (bûrnz), John. Eng. labor leader & cabinet officer (1858–).—Robert. Scot. poet (1759–96).

Burnside (bûrn'sīd), Ambrose Everett. Am. soldier (1824–81).

Burr (bûr), Aaron. Am. polit.; vice-pres. of U. S. (1756–1836).

Burroughs (bûr'ōz), George. Am. clergy., executed for witchcraft (1650–92).—John. Am. natur. (1837–).

Bushnell (bŏŏsh'nĕl), Horace. Am. clergy. & author (1802–76).

Butler (bŭt'lẽr), Benjamin Franklin. Am. gen. & polit. (1818–93).—Joseph. Eng. theolog. (1692–1752).—Nicholas Murray. Am. educ. & publicist (1862–).—Samuel. Eng. satirist (1612–80).—William Orlando. Am. gen. & polit. (1791–1880).

Buzzard's Bay, on S. coast of Mass., 30 m. long.

By (bī), John. Can. engineer, founder of Bytown, now Ottawa, Can. (1781–1836).

Byng (bĭng), Sir Julian Hedworth George. Br. gen. (1862–).

Byron (bī'rŭn), George Gordon, 6th Lord. Eng. poet (1788–1824).

C

Cable (kā'bl), George Washington. Am. novel. (1844–).

Cabot (kă'bŏt), John. Italian navig. (1450–98).—Sebastian. Eng. navig. (1475–1557).

Cadiz (kā'dĭz), sp. city of Spain, p. 67.

Cadorna (kȧ-dōr'nȧ), Count Luigi. It. gen. (1850–).

Cædmon (kăd mŏn), Anglo-Saxon poet of 7th century.

Cæsar (sē'zȧr), Gaius Julius. Rom. gen., stsm. & hist. (102–44 B. C.).

Caine (kān), Sir Thomas Hall. Eng. novel. (1853–).

Cairo (kī'rō), city on the Nile; cap. of Egypt, p. 654.

Calais (kȧ-lā'), sp. town, dept. of Pas-de-Calais, Fr., on Str. of Dover, p. 72.

Calcutta (kăl-kŭt'ȧ), cap. of presidency of Bengal, India, on Hooghly riv., p. 1,222.

Calgary (kăl'gȧ-rĭ), city, Alberta, Can., p. 90.

Calhoun (kăl-hōōn'), John Caldwell. Am. stsm. & orator (1782–1850).

California (kă"lĭ-fôr'nĭ-ȧ), state in U. S., 158,297 sq. m., p. 2,378; cap., Sacramento. —**Gulf of**, on W. coast of N. Am. in Mex. —**Lower**, territory of Mex., 61,562 sq. m., p. 52.

Caligula (kȧ-lĭg'ū-lȧ), Gaius Cæsar Augustus [Germanicus]. Emp. of Rome fr. 37 A. D. (12–41 A. D.).

Calixtus (kȧ-lĭks'tŭs), name of 3 popes: 219–223; 1119–24; 1455–58.

Callao (kȧl-yä'ō), sp. town of Peru, p. 48.

Calvé (kȧl"vā'), Emma. Fr. soprano (1866–).

Calvin (kăl'vĭn), John. Fr.-Swiss reformer & theolog. (1509–64).

Cambon (käṅ"bôṅ'), Jules. Fr. dipl. (1845–).

Cambrai (käṅ"brā'), city on Scheldt riv., Fr., p. 22.

Cambridge (kām'brĭj), city on Charles riv., opposite Boston, Mass., p. 105; Harvard Univ. & Mass. Inst. of Tech.—town on Cam riv., Eng., p. 40; Cambridge Univ., p. 41.—co. of Eng., p. 200.

Camden (kăm'dĕn), city, Camden co., N. J., on Delaware riv.; home of Walt Whitman, p. 95.

Cameroon (kăm'ẽr-ōōn), or **Kameruns**, dist. on W. coast of Africa; Ger. colony prior to 1914, 293,800 sq. m., p. 2,542.

Camoens (kăm'ō-ĕns), Luis de. Port. poet (1524–80).

Campbell (kăm'ĕl; kăm'bl), Alexander. Irish-Am. theolog., founder of Disciples of Christ (1788–1866).—Sir Colin, Lord Clyde. Br. field marshal (1792–1863).—Thomas. Scot. poet (1774–1844).

Campbell-Bannerman (-băn'ẽr-măn), Sir Henry. Br. stsm. (1836–1908).

Campeche (kȧm-pā'chē), state of Mex., 18,087 sq. m., p. 87.

Canada (kăn'ȧ-dȧ), **Dominion of**, country in N. Am. within Br. empire; 3,729,920 sq. m., p. 8,075.

Canal Zone (kȧn-ăl' zōn), ter. surrounding Panama canal, owned by U. S.; 47 m. long, 10 m. wide.

Canberra (kăn-bẽr'ȧ), new cap. of Australia.

Canby (kăn'bĭ), Edward R. S. Am. gen. (1818–73).

Cannon (kăn'ŭn), Joseph Gurney. Am. polit. (1836–).

Canova (kȧn-ō'vȧ). It. sculptor (1757–1822).

Canterbury (kăn'tẽr-bẽr"ĭ), cathedral city, Eng., p. 25.—dist. South Isl., N. Z., p. 173.

Cantigny (käṅ"tē'ńē"), vil., dept. Seine et Marne, Fr.; 1st Am. battle in Great War, May, 1918.

Canton (kăn'tŏn'), city, S. China, p. 1,250.

Canute (kȧ-nūt), or **Cnut**, king of Eng. & Den. (995–1036).

Cape Cod (kŏd), pen., Barnstable co., Mass., 65 m. long.—**Canal,** ship canal, 8 m., across cape.

Cape Colony. See Cape Province.

Cape Hatteras (hăt'ĕr-ăs), coast of N. C.

Cape Horn, most southerly point of S. Am.

Cape May, at S. end of N. J., 5 m. long.

Cape of Good Hope, at S. end of Africa in Cape Colony.

Cape Province, formerly Cape Colony, prov. of Union of S. Africa, 277,000 sq. m., p. 2,565.

Cape St. Vincent (vĭn'sĕnt), S. W. point of Portugal.

Cape Town, city, cap. of Cape Province, Union of S. Africa, p. 263.

Cape Verde (vûrd), extreme W. point of Africa; disc. by Fernandez, 1445.—**Islands,** in Atlantic, 320 m. W. of Cape Verde; owned by Port.; p. 148.

Capri (kä'prē), famous It. isl. in Bay of Naples, 5 m. long, 2 broad.

Cardiff (kär'dĭf), sp. town, cap. of Glamorgan, Wales, p. 188.

Caribbean Sea (kăr-ĭ-bē'ăn), arm of Atlantic bet. Central & S. Am. & W. Indies.

Carlos (kär'lōs), Don. Infant of Sp.; son of Philip II (1545–68).—name of several pretenders to Sp. crown. Present Carlist pretender, Don Jaime de Borbon (1870–).

Carlyle (kär-līl'), Thomas. Scot. essayist & hist. (1795–1881).

Carmarthen (kär-mär'thĕn), co. of S. Wales, p. 160.

Carnarvon (kär-när'vŭn), co. of N. Wales, p. 125.

Carnegie (kär-nĕg'ĕ), Andrew. Scot.-Am. ironmaster & philan. (1835–).

Carnot (kär"nō'), Lazare Nicolas Marguerite ["Organizer of Victory"]. Fr. strategist & math. (1753–1823).—Lazare Hippolyte, son of former. Fr. polit. & author (1801–88).—Marie François Sadi. Pres. of Fr., 1887–94 (1837–94).

Caroline (kăr'ō-līn). Br. queen, wife of George IV (1768–1821).

Carolines. N. Pacific isls., bet. Philippines & Marshall isls.; owned by Ger. prior to 1914.

Carpathians (kär-pā'thĭ-ănz), mts. in cen. Europe on boundary of Hungary, E. of Danube.

Carracci (kär-rät'chē). It. painters: Ludovico (1555–1619).—Agostino (1557–1602).—Annibale (1560–1609).

Carranza (kȧ-rän'zȧ), Venustiano. Pres. of Mex., inaugurated May 1, 1917.

Carrel (kȧr"rĕl'), Alexis. Fr.-Am. biologist; Nobel prize 1912 (1873–).

Carson (kär'sŭn), Christopher [Kit Carson]. Am. trapper & guide (1809–68).—Sir Edward. Anglo-Irish stsm. (1854–).

Cartagena (kär'tȧ-hā'nȧ), sp. town of Sp., p. 103.

Cartier (kär'tyā'), Sir George Etienne. Can. stsm. (1814–73).—Jacques. Fr. navig. (1494–1557).

Cartwright (kärt'rīt), Edmund. Eng. inven. of power loom (1743–1823).

Caruso (kȧ-rōō'sō), Enrico. It. tenor (1873–).

Carver (kär'vẽr), John. 1st gov. of Plymouth colony (1575–1621).

Cary (kā'rĭ), name of two Am. poets: Alice (1820–71).—Phoebe (1824–71).

Cascade Range (kăs-kād'), mts. in N. Am., near Pacific coast, fr. N. Cal. to Br. Columbia.

Casco Bay (kăs'kō), in Maine, 20 m. wide, contains 300 small isls.

Casimir (kăs'ĭ-mẽr), **the Great.** King of Poland (1300–70).

Casimir-Perier (kȧ"zē"mẽr'pā"ryā), Jean Paul Pierre. Fr. pres. (1847–1907).

Caspian Sea (kăs'pĭ-ăn), bet. Europe & Asia, 730 m. long; 115 to 280 broad.

Cassius (kăsh'ĕ-ŭs), Gaius C. Longinus. Rom. stsm.; one of assassins of Julius Cæsar (?–42 B. C.).

Castro (kä'strō), Cipriano. Venezuelan insurgent; pres. 1904–08 (1861–).

Catherine (kăth'ẽr-ĭn). **I,** emp. of Russia (1684–1727).—**II,** emp. of Russia (1729–96).—**of Aragon,** queen of Eng., 1st wife of Henry VIII (1485–1536).—**de Medici,** queen of Fr. (1519–89).—**Parr,** 6th & last wife of Henry VIII (1512–48).

Catiline (kăt'ĭ-līn), Lucius Sergius. Rom. conspirator (108–62 B. C.).

Cato (kā'tō), Marcus Porcius [The Censor]. Rom. stsm. (234–149 B. C.).—Marcus Porcius [of Utica], his great grandson. Rom. soldier & stsm. (95–46 B. C.).

Catskills (kăts'kĭlz), mts. in N. Y., west of Hudson; highest, 4,205 ft.

Catullus (kȧ-tŭl'ŭs). Rom. poet (94–54 B. C.).

Caucasus (kô'kȧ-sŭs), mts. S. E. Russia, separating Black sea fr. Caspian; 18,000 ft.—region in S. E. Russia; p. 12,000.

Cavour (kȧ-vōōr'), Count Camillo Benso di.

& engraver (1500–71).

Central America, section of Am. continent fr. Mex. to Colombia, 180,000 sq. m.

Cervantes Saavedra (sẽr-văn'tez sä'ȧ-vā'drȧ). Miguel de. Sp. writer, author *Don Quixote* (1547–1616).

Ceylon (sĭ-lŏn'), Br. isl. in Indian ocean, 60 m. S. E. of India, 25,000 sq. m., p. 4,110.

Châlons-sur-Marne (shä"lon'sōōr-märn'), city, dept. of Marne, Fr., on Marne riv.; battles, 1870, 1914–18; p. comm. 31.

Chamberlain (chām'bẽr-lĭn), Joseph. Br. stsm. (1836–1908).—Joseph Austen, his son. Br. stsm. (1863–).

Chamonix (shȧ"mō"nē'), vil. in Alps, dept. of Haute-Savoie, Fr.

Champagne (shäṅ"pȧ'ny), anc. prov. of Fr., now comprising depts. of Aube, Haute-Marne, Marne, & Ardennes.

Champlain (shăm-plān'), a lake in U. S. bet. Vt. & N. Y., 110 m. long; naval battle, 1814.—Samuel de. Fr. explorer; founder of Quebec (1567–1635).

Channel Islands, in English Channel, near Fr., owned by Gr. Br.; comprise Jersey, Guernsey, & dependencies; 75 sq. m.; p. 97.

Channing (chăn'ĭng), William Ellery. Am. Unit. clergy. & author (1780–1842).

Chantilly (shäṅ"tē"yē'), town, dept. of Oise, Fr., p. 6; battles, 1914–18.

Charlemagne (shär'lē-mān). King of the Franks [Charles the Great], (742–814).

Charleroi (shärl″rwä′), town, prov. of Hainaut, Belgium, p. 27.

Charles, name of 10 kings of Fr.: **I**, the Bald (823–877); **II**, the Fat (832–888); **III**, the Simple (879–929); **IV**, the Fair (1294–1328); **V**, the Wise (1337–80); **VI** (1368–1422); **VII** (1403–61); **VIII** (1470–98); **IX** (1550–74); **X** (1757–1836). —kings of Gr. Br. & Ire.: **I** (1600–49); **II** (1630–85).—**Charles Edward Stuart**, the Pretender (1720–88).—**I**, king of Port. (1863–1908).—**I**, king of Roumania (1839–1914).—**XII**, king of Sweden (1682–1718).—**XIII**, king of Sweden (1763–1818).—**XIV**, **Bernadotte**, king of Sweden (1763–1844).—**I**, **Carl** or **Karl**, emp. of Austria & king of Hungary, succeeded Francis Joseph 1916 (1887–).

Charleston (chärlz′tŏn), sp. city, S. C., p. 58.

Charlestown (chärlz′toun), city, Middlesex co., Mass., now part of Boston; Bunker Hill battle, 1775.

Charlotte Amalie (shär-lŏt′ á-mä′lē-ĕ), town on isl. of St. Thomas, Virgin Isls., U. S., p. 12.

Charlottesville (shär′lŏts-vĭl), city, co. seat of Albemarle co., Va.; seat of Univ. of Va., p. 7.

Chateaubriand (shá″tō″brē-äṅ′), Francois Auguste, Vicomte de. Fr. author & polit. (1768–1848).

Château-Thierry (shá″tō′tyâ″rē′), town, dept. Aisne, Fr., on Marne; battle, 1918, p. 8.

Châtillon (shá″tē″yôṅ′), town on Seine, Fr.; battles, 1870, 1918.

Chattanooga (chăt″ȧ-nōō′gȧ), city, co. seat of Hamilton co., Tenn., p. 100.

Chatterton (chăt′ẽr-tŏn), Thomas [The Marvelous Boy]. Eng. poet (1752–70).

Chaucer (chô′sẽr), Geoffrey. Father of Eng. poetry (1340–1400).

Chauny (shō′nē′), town on Oise, dept. of Aisne, Fr., p. 10.

Chautauqua (chȧ-tô′kwȧ), lake in N. Y., 18 m.

Chemnitz (kĕm′nĭts), town in Saxony, p. 287.

Cheops (kē′ŏps), Egypt, king of 4th dyn. (about 2900 B. C.).

Cherbourg (shär″bōōr′), sp. town, dept. La Manche, Fr., p. comm. 44.

Cherubini (kā-rōō-bē′nē), Maria Luigi. It. composer (1760–1842).

Chesapeake Bay (chĕs′ȧ-pēk), in Md. & Va., 200 m. long.

Cheshire (chĕsh′ĭr), co. of Eng., p. 955.

Chesterfield (chĕs′tẽr-fēld), Philip Dormer Stanhope, Earl of. Eng. stsm., author of *Letters* (1694–1773).

Chesterton (chĕs′tẽr-tŭn), Gilbert Keith. Eng. author (1874–).

Chiapas (chē′ä-päs), state in Mex., 27,222 sq. m., p. 439.

Chicago (shē-kä′gō), city on Lake Michigan, Ill., p. 2,498.

Chickamauga (chĭk-ȧ-mô′gȧ), trib. of Tennessee riv., in Tenn.; battle, 1863.

Chihuahua (chē-wä′wä″), state in Mex., 90,000 sq. m., p. 405.

Chile (chē′lā; chĭl′ĭ), rep. in S. Am., 295,000 sq. m., p. 3,500; cap. Santiago.

Chili (chē′lē′), formerly Pechili, prov. of China, 115,800 sq. m., p. 20,000.

China (chī′nȧ), rep. in Asia, 4,300,000 sq. m.; total p. including Manchuria, 400,000; cap. Peking.

Choate (chōt), Joseph Hodges. Am. law. & dipl. (1832–1917).—Rufus. Am. law. (1799–1858).

Choisy-le-Roi (shwä″zē′l′rwä′), town on Seine riv., Fr., 7 m. fr. Paris, p. 12.

Chopin (shō″păṅ′), Frédéric François. Polish pianist & composer (1810–49).

Christian, name of 10 Danish kings: **II**, king of Den., Nor. & Swe. (1480–1559); **IV**, king of Den. & Nor. (1577–1648); **IX**, king of Den. (1818–1906); **X**, king of Nor. fr. 1912 (1870–).

Christiania (krĭs-tĭ-ä′nĭ-ȧ), sp. city, cap. of Nor., p. 242.

Christophe (krēs″tŏf′), Henri, king of Haiti (1767–1820).

Christopher (krĭs′tō-fẽr), Saint, martyr of early church (about 250).

Chrysostom (krĭs′ŏs-tŏm), John, Saint, the Golden-Mouthed. Gr. father of church (344–407).

Churchill (church′ĭl), Randolph, Lord. Br. stsm. (1849–95).—Winston. Am. author (1871–).—Winston Leonard Spencer, son of Randolph. Br. stsm. (1874–).

Cicero (sĭs′ē-rō), Marcus Tullius. Rom. orator & philos. (106–43 B. C.).

Cienfuegos (thē″ĕn-fō-ā′gōs), sp. town, Cuba, p. 30.

Cimon (sī′mŏn). Ath. gen. & stsm. (500–44 B. C.).

Cincinnati (sĭn-sĭn-ä′tĭ), city on Ohio riv., O., p. 402.

Cincinnatus (sĭn-sĭn-ā′tŭs), Lucius Quinctius. Rom. patrician (519 B. C.–?).

Clare (klâr), co. of Munster, Ire., p. 104.

Clark (klärk), Champ. Am. polit. (1850–).—George Rogers. Am. soldier & frontiersman (1752–1818).

Claudius (klô′dĭ-ŭs), Tiberius C. Nero Drusus Germanicus. Rom. emp. (10 B. C.–54 A. D.).

Clay (klā), Henry. Am. stsm. (1777–1852).

Clayton (klā′tŭn), John Middleton. Am. jurist & stsm. (1796–1856).

Clemenceau (klā″mäṅ″sō′), Georges Benjamin Eugene. Fr. jour. & premier (1841–).

Clemens (klĕm′ĕnz), Samuel Langhorne [Mark Twain]. Am. novel. & humorist (1835–1910).

Clement (klĕ′mĕnt), name of 14 popes, notably **Clement VII**, Giulio de Medici, pope fr. 1523 to 1534.

Cleopatra (klē-ō-pā′trȧ). Gr. queen of Egypt (69–30 B. C.).

Cleveland (klēv′lȧnd), city, on Lake Erie, O., p. 674.—(Stephen) Grover. 22d & 24th pres. of U. S. (1837–1908).

Clinton (klĭn′tŭn), De Witt. Am. law. stsm. (1769–1828).—Sir Henry. Br. gen. in Am. (1738–95).

Clive (klīv), Robert, Lord. Eng. gen. & stsm. (1725–74).

Clyde (klīd), riv. of Scot., in Lanark, Renfrew & Dumbarton, 75 m.

Clymer (klī′mẽr), George. Am. patriot (1739–1813).

Coahuila (kō-ä-wē′lä), state in Mex., 63,745 sq. m., p. 368.

Coast Range, mts. along Pacific coast of U. S., 11,000 ft.

Cobbett (kŏb′ĕt), William. Eng. publicist (1762–1835).

Cobden (kŏb′dĕn), Richard. Eng. polit., apostle of free trade (1804–65).

Cochin China (kō′chĭn), country S. E. Asia, owned by Fr., p. 3,050.

Cody (kō′dĭ), William Frederick [Buffalo Bill]. Am. scout & showman (1845–1917).

Coghlan (kŏg′lăn), Rose. Am. act. (1853–).

Coleridge (kōl′rĭj), Samuel Taylor. Eng. poet (1772–1834).

Coleridge-Taylor (-tā'lẽr), Samuel. Eng. composer (1875–1912).

Collingwood (kŏl'ing-wŏŏd), Cuthbert, Lord. Eng. naval com. (1750–1810).

Collins (kŏl'inz), Wilkie. Eng. novel. (1824–89).

Collyer (kŏl'yẽr), Robert. Am. Unit. clergy. & author (1823–1912).

Cologne (kō-lōn'), or **Cöln**, city on Rhine, Rhenish Prussia, p. 517.

Colombia (kō-lōm'bī-ȧ), rep. in S. Am., 461,000 sq. m., p. 5,475; cap. Bogotá.

Colombo (kō-lōm'bō), sp. town, cap. of Ceylon, p. 214.

Colon (kō-lōn'), sp. town Panama, on Manzanillo isl., p. 20.

Colorado (kŏl-ō-rä'dō), state in U. S., 103,948 sq. m., p. 800; cap. Denver.—riv. in S. W. U. S., 2,000 m.—riv. in Texas, 900 m.—riv. in Argentina, 620 m.

Columbia (kō-lŭm'bĭ-ȧ), poetical name for U. S.

Columbia River, or **Oregon**, riv. of Br. Columbia, 1,400 m. to Pacific.

Columbus (kō-lŭm'bŭs), city, cap. of Ohio, p. 182.—Christopher. Genoese discoverer of Am. (1451–1506).

Como (kō'mō), prov. in N. It., 1,049 sq. m., p. 576.—**Lake**, in N. It., foot of Alps, 2½ m. wide.

Commodus (kŏ-mō'dŭs), Lucius Ælius Aurelius. Rom. emp., 180–192 (161–192).

Compiègne (kôṅ'pyā'ny'), town on Oise; dept. of Oise, Fr., p. 14.

Comte (kôṅt), Isidore Auguste. Fr. philos. (1798–1857).

Concord (kŏṅ'kōrd), town, Middlesex co., Mass.; home of Emerson, Hawthorne, Thoreau; p. 7.—city, cap. of New Hampshire, p. 22.

Condé (kŏṅ"dā'), Louis de Bourbon, Prince of. Fr. gen. (1621–87).

Confucius (kŏn-fū'shĭ-ŭs), [Chinese, **Kung-fu-tze**, Kung, the Teacher]. Chinese sage (551–478 B. C.).

Congo (kŏṅ'gō), or **Kongo**, state in S. cen. Africa, owned by Belgium, 920,000 sq. m., p. 15,000.—riv., Africa, 3,000 m. to Atlantic.

Connaught (kŏn'nôt), W. prov. of Ire., 6,571 sq. m., p. 595.—Arthur William, Duke of. Br. prince, gov.-gen. of Canada 1911–14 (1850–).

Connecticut (kŏn-nĕt'ĭ-kŭt), state in U. S., 4,990 sq. m., p. 1,115; cap. Hartford.

Conrad (kŏn'răd), Joseph. Polish-Br. novel. (1857–).

Constable (kŭn'stȧ-bl), John. Eng. landscape painter (1776–1837).

Constance (kŏn'stȧns), lake in cen. Europe, bordering Switzerland & Austria; 300 ft. above sea level; 208 sq. m.

Constant (kŏṅ"stäṅ'), Benjamin. Fr. painter (1845–1902).

Constantine (kŏn'stăn-tīn), Gaius Flavius, the Great. Rom. emp. (274–337).—**I**, king of Greece, 1913–17 (1868–).

Constantinople (kŏn"stăn-tĭ-nō'pl), or **Stamboul**, city on Sea of Marmora & Bosporus, p. 1,000.

Conwell (kŏn'wĕl), Russell H. Am. Bap. clergy.; founder Temple Univ., Phila., Pa. (1843–).

Cooch-Behar (kōōch-bē-här'), state in India, 1,307 sq. m., p. 567.

Cook, James. Br. navig. (1728–79).

Cooper (kōōp'ẽr), James Fenimore. Am. novel. (1789–1851).—Peter. Am. inven. & philan. (1791–1883).

Copenhagen (kō"pĕn-hā'gĕn), city on Sound; cap. Den., p. 605.

Copernicus (kō-pẽr'nĭ-kŭs), Nicholas. Pol. astron. (1473–1543).

Coppée (kŏ"pā'), François Edouard Joachim. Fr. poet & dram. (1842–1908).

Coquelin (kŏk"läṅ'), Benoit Constant. Fr. act. (1841–1909).

Corday d'Armans (kôr"dā"dȧr"mäṅ'), Marie Charlotte [Charlotte Corday]. Fr. patriot; assassin of Marat (1768–93).

Cordova (kôr-dō'vȧ), or **Cordoba**, prov. & city of Sp., p. of prov. 500, of city 66.—city & prov. Argentina, p. of prov. 500, of city 75.

Corelli (kō-rĕl'ē), Marie. Eng. novel.; b. Italy (1864–).

Corfu (kôr'fōō), Gr. isl. in Medit., 227 sq. m., p. 19.

Cork (kôrk), co. of Munster, Ire., p. 392.—cap. of co., p. 76.

Corneille (kôr"nā'y'), Pierre. Father of Fr. tragedy & classical comedy (1606–84).

Cornell (kôr-nĕl'), Ezra. Am. inven.; founder Cornell Univ., Utica (1807–74).

Cornwall (kôrn'wȧl), co. of Eng., p. 328.

Cornwallis (kôrn-wăl'ĭs), Charles, Marquis of. Eng. gen. in Am; defeated Yorktown, 1781 (1738–1806).

Corot (kō"rō'), Jean Baptiste Camille. Fr. painter (1796–1875).

Correggio (kō-rĕj'ō), Antonio Allegri. It. painter (1494–1534).

Corrientes (kōr"rē-ān'tās), prov. Argentina, p. 300.

Corsica (kôr'sĭ-kȧ), Fr. isl. in Medit.; birthplace Napoleon, 3,377 sq. m., p. 291.

Cort (kôrt), Henry. Eng. inven. (1740–1800).

Cortés (kōr"tās'), Hernando. Sp. conqueror of Mex. (1485–1547).

Corunna (kō-rŭn'ȧ), prov. in Sp., 3,051 sq. m., p. 653.

Corwin (kôr'wĭn), Thomas. Am. stsm. (1794–1865).

Cossacks (kŏs'ăks), tribes of S. Russ. on steppes of Don, Cis-Caucasia & S. end of Ural mts., p. 3,000.

Costa Rica (kŏs'tȧ rē'kȧ), rep. Cen. Am., 23,000 sq. m., p. 427; cap. San José.

Côte-d'or (kōt"dōr'), dept. of Fr., p. 358; cap. Dijon.—chain of hills in E. Fr.

Cotopaxi (kō"tō-păks'ĭ), volcanic mt. of Andes, Ecuador, 19,500 ft.

Courland (kōōr'lănd), one of Baltic prov., 10,535 sq. m., p. 714.

Courtrai (kōōr"trā'), town on Lys riv., Bel.; battles, 1302, 1914–18, p. 35.

Coventry (kŭv'ĕn-trĭ), city, Warwick, Eng., p. 119.

Covington (kŭv'ing-tŭn), city, Ohio riv., Ky., p. 53.

Cowper (kou'pẽr, or kōō'pẽr), William. Eng. poet (1731–1800).

Cracow (krā'kō), city, Vistula riv., Galicia, anc. cap. of Poland, p. 150.

Crane (krān), Stephen. Am. novel. (1870–1900).—Walter. Eng. art. (1845–1915).

Cranmer (krăn'mẽr), Thomas. Eng. martyr; abp. of Canterbury (1489–1556).

Crassus (krăs'ŭs), Marcus Licinius. Rom. triumvir (115–53 B. C.).

Crawford (krô'fẽrd), Francis Marion. Eng. novel. (1854–1909).—Thomas. Am. sculp. (1814–57).—William Harris. Am. stsm. (1772–1834).

Cremona (krē-mōn'ȧ), prov. of It., 695 sq. m., p. 328.

Crete (krēt), Gr. isl. in Med., p. 344.

Crichton (krī'tŭn), James ["The Admirable"]. Scot. scholar & swordsman (1560–85).

Crimea (krī-mē'ȧ), penin. of S. Russ., on Black sea; battles, 1854–56; 10,000 sq. m., p. 450.

Croatia (krō-ā'shĭ-ȧ), with Slavonia, prov. of Hungary, 16,773 sq. m., p. 2,417.

Crockett (krŏk'ĕt), David. Am. frontiersman (1786–1836).—Samuel Rutherford. Scot. novel. (1859–1914).

Cromer (krō'mẽr), Evelyn Baring, 1st Earl. Eng. dipl. & admin. (1841–).

Crœsus (krē'sŭs), last king of Lydia fr. 560 B. C. (? –546 B. C.).

Cromwell (krŏm'wĕl), Oliver. Lord-protector of Commonwealth of Eng. fr. 1653 (1599–1658).

Crookes (krōōks), Sir William. Eng. physicist (1832–).

Crosby (krŏs'bĭ), Frances Jane [Fanny]. Am. hymnist (1820–1915).

Croydon (kroi'dŭn), city, Surrey, Eng., p. 181.

Cruikshank (krōōk'shănk), George. Eng. satirical art. (1792–1878).

Cuba (kū'bȧ), isl. repub., W. India isls., 44,178 sq. m., p. 2,150; cap. Havana.

Cumberland (kŭm'bẽr-lănd), co. N. W. Eng., p. 266.—mts. in Tenn., in Appalachian system, 2,000 ft.

Curaçao (kōō-rȧ-sä'ō), isl. of Dutch W. Indies, p. 30; with dependencies 50.

Curie (kü'rē'), Pierre. Fr. physicist & chemist (1859–1906).—Marie, wife of former, discoverer of radium (1867–).

Curzon (kûr'zŭn), George Nathaniel, Earl, of Kedleston. Eng. stsm. (1859–).

Cushman (kōōsh'măn), Charlotte. Am. act. (1816–76).

Custer (kŭs'tẽr), George Armstrong. Am. soldier (1839–76).

Cuvier (kōō'vyā'), Georges Léopold, Baron. Fr. natur. (1769–1832).

Cuyp (koip), Albert. Dutch painter (1620–91).

Cyprus (sī'prŭs), Br. isl. S. of Asia Minor in Medit., 3,584 sq. m., p. 275.

Czecho-Slovak (chĕkh'ō-slō-văk'), races inhabiting Bohemia, Moravia & sections of Austria & Hungary, formed into separate govt. in 1918 during war; p. 8,500.

Czernowitz (chĕr-nō-vits'), cap. of Bukowina, p. 70.

D

Daguerre (dȧ'gâr'), Louis Jacques. Fr. scene-painter; early photographer (1789–1851).

Dahlgren (dăl'grĕn), John Adolf. Am. admiral & inv. (1809–70).

Dahomey (dȧ'ho-mē'), Fr. colony, W. Africa, 41,000 sq. m., p. 902.

Dale (dāl), Sir Thomas. Colonial gov. of Va. (? –1619).

Dallas (dăl'ȧs), city on Trinity riv., Tex., p. 131.

Dalmatia (dăl-mā'shĭ-ȧ), prov. of Austria on Adriatic sea, 4,940 sq. m., p. 592.

Damascus (dȧ-măs'kŭs), anc. city of Syria, p. 300.

Dana (dā'nȧ), Charles Anderson. Am. ed. (1819–97).—Francis. Am. stsm. (1743–1811).—James Dwight. Am. geol. (1813–95).

Daniels (dăn'yĕls), Josephus. Am. cabinet officer, Secy. of Navy during Great War (1862–).

D'Annunzio (dán-nūn'zē-ō), Gabriele. It. poet, novel. & patriot (1864–).

Dante (dán'tā), Alighieri. It. poet (1265–1321).

Danton (däN'tôN'), George Jacques. Leader in Fr. revolution (1759–94).

Dantzig (dánt'zĭkh), town & port of Prussia, on Vistula riv., p. 170.

Danube (dăn'ūb), riv. of Europe; Baden to Black sea, 1,725 m.

Dardanelles (där'dȧ-nĕlz'; anc. **Hellespont**), channel bet. Marmora & Ægean seas, 40 m. long; naval battles, 1915.

Darien (dā-rĭ'ĕn), **Gulf of**, gulf of Caribbean sea, at N. end of S. Am.—**Isthmus of**, bet. Gulf of Darien & Pacific.

Darjeeling (där-jē'lĭng), dist. of Bengal, India, 1,234 sq. m., p. 249.

Darling (där'lĭng), Grace. Eng. heroine (1815–42).

Darmstadt (därm'stät), cap. of Hesse, Ger., on Rhine, p. 90.

Darnley (därn'lĭ), Henry Stuart, Lord. Husband of Mary, Queen of Scots (1541–67).

Darwin (där'wĭn), Charles Robert. Eng. natur.; published *Origin of Species* in 1859 (1809–82).

Daubigny (dō'bēn'yē'), Charles François. Fr. painter (1817–78).

Daudet (dō'dā'), Alphonse. Fr. novel. (1840–97).

Davenport (dăv'ĕn-pōrt), city, Scott co., Iowa, p. 58.

David (dā'vĭd), king of Israel about 1085 B. C.—**I**, king of Scot. fr. 1124 (1080–1153).—**II**, king of Scot. fr. 1329 (1322–70).—Jacques Louis. Fr. painter (1738–1825).

Davis (dā'vĭs), Jefferson. Am. soldier, stsm. & pres. of Confederate States (1808–89).—Richard Harding. Am. novel. (1864–1916).

Davis Strait, narrow sea bet. Greenland & Baffin Land.

Davy (dā'vĭ), Sir Humphry. Eng. chem.; inv. of lamp for miners (1778–1829).

Davys (dā'vĭs), or **Davis**, John. Eng. navigator (1550–1605).

Dawson (dô'sŭn), Sir John William. Can. geol. (1820–99).—William James. Eng. clergy. & author (1854–).

Day (dā), William Rufus. Am. stsm. & jurist (1849–).

Dayton (dā'tŭn), cap. Montgomery co., Ohio, p. 117.

Dead Sea, lake in Palestine, 1,312 ft. below level of Medit., 46 m. long, 9 wide.

Debussy (dē-bōō'sē'), Claude Achille. Fr. composer (1862–).

Decatur (dē-kā'tẽr), Stephen. Am. naval commander (1779–1820).

Defoe (dē-fō'), David. Eng. novel.; published *Robinson Crusoe* in 1719 (1661–1731).

De Kalb (dē kălb), John. Ger. soldier in Am. (1721–80).

Delaroche (dē-lȧ-rōsh'), Fr. painter (1797–1856).

Delaware (dĕl'ȧ-wâr), state of U. S., 2,050 sq. m., p. 203; cap. Dover.—riv. of U. S.; Catskill mts., N. Y., to Delaware bay, 400 m.—bay bet. Del. & N. J., 60 m. long.

Delcassé (dĕl'kȧ'sā'), Theophile. Fr. stsm. (1852–).

Delhi (dĕl'ē), cap. of Delhi prov. & of Br. India; Ind. mutiny 1857; p. 233.

De Mille (dē mĭl'), James. Can. novel. (1837–80).

Democritus (dē-mŏk'rĭ-tŭs). Gr. philos. (470–370 B. C.).

De Morgan (dē môr'gȧn), William Frend. Eng. novel. (1839–1917).

Demosthenes (dē-mŏs'thē-nēz). Gr. orator (382–322 B. C.).

Denain (dē'nän'), town, dept. Nord, Fr., p. 23.
Denbigh (dĕn'bĭ), co. of Wales, p. 145.
Denmark (dĕn'märk), kingdom N. Europe, 15,500 sq. m., p. 2,800; cap. Copenhagen.
Denver (dĕn'vẽr), cap. of Colorado, on S. Platte riv., Colo., p. 240.
Depew (dē-pū'), Chauncey Mitchell. Am. orator & stsm. (1834–).
De Quincey (dē quĭn'sĭ), Thomas. Eng. author (1785–1859).
Derby (dẽr'bĭ; där'bĭ), co. of Eng., p. 560.—cap. of co., p. 126.
Descartes (dā'kärt'), René. Fr. philos. (1596–1650).
Des Moines (dē moin), cap. of Iowa, on Des Moines riv., Ia., p. 105.
Desmoulins (dā'mōō'lăn'), Benoit Camille. Fr. revolutionist (1760–94).
De Soto (dē sō'tō), Hernando. Sp. explor.; disc. of Mississippi, 1539 (1496–1542).
Detroit (dē-troit'), city on Detroit riv., Mich., p. 580.—riv. 28 m. long, fr. Lake St. Clair to Lake Erie.
Devon (dĕv'ŭn), co. of S. W. Eng., p. 700.
Dewey (dōō'ā), George. Am. admiral (1837–1917).
Diaz (dē-äz'), Bartolommeo. Port. navig. (1450–1500).—Porfirio. Pres. of Mex. 1877–80 & 1884–1911 (1830–1915).—Armando. It. gen. (1870–).
Dickens (dĭk'ĕns), Charles. Eng. novel. (1812–70).
Dillon (dĭl'ŭn), John. Irish stsm. (1851–).
Dinant (dē'nän'), town in prov. of Namur, Bel., p. 8.
Diocletian (dī-ō-klē'shē-ȧn), G. Valerius. Rom. emp. (284–305).
Diogenes (dī-ŏj'ē-nēz). Gr. cynic (412–323 B. C.).
Dionysius (dī-ō-nĭsh'ē-ŭs), Tyrant of Syracuse (431–367 B. C.).
Disraeli (dĭz'rā-ē-lĭ), Benjamin, Lord Beaconsfield. Br. stsm. & novel. (1804–81).
District of Columbia, ter. of U. S., 70 sq. m., seat of cap. of U. S., p. 400.
Dix (dĭks), John Adams. Am. stsm. (1798–1879).
Dnieper (nē'pẽr), riv. of Russ., flows to Black sea, 1,230 m.
Dniester (nēs'tẽr), riv. of Europe, rises Carpathian mts., Galicia, flows to Black sea, 750 m.
Dobrudja (dō-brŭd'jȧ), part of Roumania, bounded by Danube riv., Bulgaria & Black sea, 9,500 sq. m., p. 500.
Dobson (dŏb'sŭn), Henry Austin. Eng. poet (1840–).
Dodgson (dŏdj'sŭn), Charles Lutwidge [Lewis Carroll]. Eng. author (1832–98).
Dominic (dŏm'ĭ-nĭk), Saint. Sp. Friar, founder of Dominican Order (1170–1221).
Dominican Republic (dō-mĭn'ĭ-kȧn), or **Santo Domingo**, repub. of Haiti, 19,300 sq. m., p. 708; cap. Santo Domingo.
Domitian (dō-mĭsh'ē-ăn), Titus Flavius Augustus. Rom. emp. (51–96 A. D.).
Donatello (dŏn-ȧ-tĕl'ō). Florentine sculpt. (1386–1466).
Donegal (dŏn'-ē-gôl), co. of Ulster, Ire., p. 169.
Donizetti (dŏn-ē-zĕt'tē), Gaetano. It. composer (1797–1848).
Doré (dō-rā'), Paul Gustave. Fr. painter (1833–83).
Dorset (dôr'sĕt), co. of S. Eng., p. 223.
Dostoyevsky (dôs'tō-yĕv'skē), Fiodor Michailovitch. Russ. novel. (1821–81).
Douai (dōō'ā'), town in dept. of Nord, Fr., p. 36.
Douglas (dŭg'lȧs), Sir James. Can. admin., founder of British Columbia (1803–77).—Stephen Arnold. Am. stsm. (1813–61).
Dover (dō'vẽr), bor. of Kent co., Eng., p. 44. —**Strait of**, bet. Eng. & Fr., 20–27 m. wide.
Down (doun), co. of Ulster, Ire., p. 204.
Doyle (doil), Arthur Conan. Br. novel. (1859–).
Drake (drāk), Sir Francis. Eng. navig. (1545–96).
Dresden (drĕs'dĕn), cap. of Saxony, on Elbe riv., p. 547.
Dreyfus (drā'fōōs'), Alfred. Jewish off. in Fr. army (1859–).
Drummond (drŭm'mŭnd), Henry. Scot. theolog. (1851–97).—William Henry. Can. poet (1854–1907).
Dryden (drī'dĕn), John. Eng. poet (1631–1700).
Du Barry (dōō bär'ĭ), Marie Jeanne, Comtesse. Mistress of Louis XV (1743–93).
Dublin (dŭb'lĭn), co. of Leinster, Ire., p. 477. —city, cap. of Ire., on Liffey riv., p. 305.
Dudevant (dŭd'vän'), Madame [George Sand]. Fr. novel. (1804–76).
Dudley (dŭd'lĭ), John, Duke of Northumberland. Eng. stsm. (1502–53).—Joseph. Colonial gov. of Mass. (1647–1720).—Thomas. Colonial gov. of Mass. (1576–1653).
Duluth (dū-lōōth'), city & lake port, St. Louis co., Minn., on Lake Superior, p. 90.
Dumas (dū'mä'), Alexandre. Fr. novel. (1802–70).—Alexandre, son of former. Fr. novel. & dram. (1824–95).—Matthieu. Fr. gen. & military writer (1753–1837).
Du Maurier (dū'mō'rĭ-ā'), George Louis. Fr.-Eng. artist & novel. (1834–96).
Dumbarton (dŭm-bär'tŏn), co. of Scot., 267 sq. m., p. 140.
Dumouriez (dū'mō'rĭ'ā'), Charles François. Fr. gen. & polit. (1739–1823).
Düna (dü'nȧ), or **Southern Dwina**, riv. of Russ., flows bet. Livonia & Courland to Gulf of Riga, 650 m.
Dunbar (dŭn'bȧr), Paul Laurence. Am. poet of African race (1872–1906).
Dundee (dŭn-dē') city and sp. in Forfar co., Scot., on Firth of Tay, p. 176.
Dunkirk (dŭn'kẽrk'), sp. of Fr. on Strait of Dover, p. 39.
Durango (dū-rän'gō), state of Mex., 38,000 sq. m., p. 483.
Durazzo (dōō-rät'sō), sp. of Albania, on Adriatic, p. 5.
Durham (dŭr'ȧm), co. of N. E. Eng., p. 1,370.
Duse (dōō'zā'), Eleonora. It. act. (1861–).
Dusseldorf (düs'sĕl-dôrf), city, Rhenish Prussia, p. 358.
Dutch East Indies, isls. in Malay Archipelago owned by Netherlands, 739,559 sq. m., p. 37,980; cap. Batavia.
Dvorak (dvôr'zhäk), Antonin. Bohemian composer (1841–1904).
Dwina (dwē'nȧ), or **Dvina**, riv. of N. Russ., flows to White sea, 1,100 m.

E

Eads (ēdz), James Buchanan. Am. engineer (1820–87).
Eames (āmz), Emma. Am. soprano (1867–).
Early (ẽr'lĭ), Jubal Anderson. Am. Confed. soldier (1816–94).
East Indies, S. E. part of Asia: India, Indo-China & Malay Archipelago.
East River, strait connecting Long Island Sound with New York Bay, 15 m. long.
East St. Louis, city on Mississippi riv., Ill., p. 69.

Ecuador (ĕk'wȧ-dôr), rep. of S. Am., 116,530 sq. m., p. 1,500; cap. Quito.
Eddy (ĕd'dĭ), Mary Baker. Am. metaphysician, founder of Christian Science (1821–1910).
Eden (ē'dĕn), Sir Robert. Last proprietary gov. of Md. (1741–84).
Edinburgh (ĕd'ĕn-bŭr'ŭ), city, Midlothian; cap. of Scot., p. 320.
Edison (ĕd'ĭ-sŭn), Thomas Alva. Am. inven. (1847–).
Edmonton (ĕd'mŭn-tŭn), city, Alberta, Can., p. 67.
Edmund (ĕd'mŭnd), **I**, king of Eng. (922–946).—**II**, Ironside, king of Eng. (981–1016).
Edward (ĕd'wẽrd), name of several kings of Eng.: **I** (1239–1307); **II** (1248–1327); **III** (1312–77); **IV** (1442–83); **V** (1470–83); **VI** (1537–53); **VII**, king of Gr. Br. & Ir., 1901–10 (1841–1910).—**The Confessor**, king of the Eng. (1004–66).—**The Black Prince**, son of Edward **III** (1330–76).
Edwards (ĕd'wẽrdz), Jonathan. Am. theolog. (1703–58).—Jonathan, son of former. Am. theolog. (1745–1801).
Eggleston (ĕg'lĕs-tŭn), Edward. Am. novel. (1837–1902).
Egypt (ē'jĭpt), country in N. E. corner of Africa, Br. protectorate, 400,000 sq. m., p. 12,000; cap. Cairo.
Eiffel (ā'fĕl'), Alexandre Gustave. Fr. engineer, builder of Eiffel Tower (1832–).
Ekaterinoslav (yā-kä'tā-rē'nō-slăf), town of S. Russ., on Dnieper riv., p. 196.—govt. in S. Russ., 24,500 sq. m., p. 3,138.
Elba (ĕl'bȧ), It. isl. in Medit., 86 sq. m., p. 30.
Elbe (ĕlb), riv. of cen. Europe, Bohemia to North sea, 725 m.
Elgar (ĕl'gȧr), Sir Edward William. Eng. composer (1857–).
Eliot (ĕl'ĭ-ŭt), Charles William. Am. educ. (1834–).—George [Mary Ann Evans]. Eng. novel. (1819–80).—John. Am. "Apostle to the Indians" (1604–90).—Sir John. Eng. patriot & stsm. (1592–1632).
Elizabeth (ē-lĭz'ȧ-bĕth), queen of Eng. fr. 1558 (1533–1603).—Pauline Ottilie Louise, queen of Roumania [Carmen Sylva], (1843–1916).—city, cap. of Union co., N. J., p. 74.
Emerson (ĕm'ẽr-sŏn), Ralph Waldo. Am. essayist, philos. & poet (1803–82).
Emmet (ĕm'ĕt), Robert. Irish patriot (1778–1803).
Endicott (ĕn'dĭ-kŏt), John. Colonial gov. of Mass. (1588–1665).
England (ĭng'lȧnd), div. of Gr. Br., 50,851 sq. m., p. 34,045.
Epaminondas (ē-pă"mĭ-nŏn'dȧs). Gr. stsm. & gen. (418–362 B. C.).
Epictetus (ĕp"ĭk-tē'tŭs). Gr. Stoic philos. (50 A. D.–?).
Epicurus (ĕp"ĭ-kū'rŭs). Gr. philos. (342–270 B. C.).
Erasmus (ē-răz'mŭs), Desiderius. Dutch scholar (1466–1536).
Ericsson (ĕr'ĭks-sŏn), John. Swed. engineer (1803–89).
Erie (ē'rĭ), one of great lakes drained by St. Lawrence, bet. U. S. & Can., 250 m. long; battle, 1813.—city on Lake Erie, p. 72.—**Canal**, waterway fr. Buffalo to Troy, connecting Great Lakes with Hudson riv., 340 m.
Erin (ĕr'ĭn), anc. & poetic name for Ireland.
Erzerum (ĕr'zĕ-rŏm), vilayet of Armenia, 27,000 sq. m., p. 583.
Essen (ĕs'en), city S. W. Prussia, p. 295; Krupp gun works.
Essex (ĕs'ĕks), co. of S. E. Eng., p. 1,352.—Robert Devereux, Earl of. Favorite of Queen Elizabeth (1567–1601).
Esthonia (ĕs"thō'nĭ-ȧ), one of Baltic prov., 7,818 sq. m., p. 414; cap. Reval.
Etna (ĕt'nȧ), volcanic mt. in Sicily, 10,874 ft.
Eucken (oik'ĕn), Rudolph. Ger. philos. (1846–).
Euclid (ū'klĭd). Gr. geomet. (lived about 300 B. C.).
Eugénie (ū"zhā̃n'ē"), Marie de Guzman, ex-emp. of the Fr.; wife of Napoleon III (1826–).
Euphrates (ū-frā'tēz), riv. of Asia; Armenia to Persian Gulf, 1,750 m.
Euripides (ū-rĭp'ĭ-dēz). Gr. tragic poet (480–406 B. C.).
Europe (ū'rŏp), continent, 3,750,000 sq. m., p. 400,000.
Eusebius (ū-sē'bĭ-ŭs). Ecclesias. hist. (260–340).
Evans (ĕ'vȧnz), Robert Dunglison ["Fighting Bob"]. Am. naval off. (1846–1912).
Evansville (ĕv'ȧnz-vĭl), cap. of Vanderburg co., Ind., p. 70.
Everest (ĕv'ẽr-ĕst), highest mt. in world; Himalayas; 29,002 ft.
Everett (ĕv'ẽr-ĕt), Edward. Am. stsm. (1794–1865).
Eyck, Van (văn-īk'), Hubert. Flemish painter (1366–1426).—Jan. Flemish painter (1385–1441).

F

Fabius (fā'bĭ-ŭs), Maximus [Cunctator, "the Delayer"]. Rom. gen. (?–203 B. C.).
Fabre (fȧ'br), Jean Henri. Fr. entomologist (1823–1915).
Fairbanks (fâr'bănks), Charles Warren. Vice-pres. U. S., 1904–08 (1852–1918).
Falkland (fôk'lȧnd), Br. isls. in S. Atlantic 300 m. E. of Magellan, 6,500 sq. m., p. 3.
Fallières (fȧ"lyâr'), Clement Armand. Pres. of Fr., 1906–13 (1841–).
Fall River, city, Bristol co., Mass., p. 126.
Farley (fär'lĭ), John Murphy. Am. cardinal (1842–1918).
Farnese (fär-nā'sā), famous It. family: Pietro, Florentine gen. (died 1363).—Alessandro, became Pope as Paul III in 1534.—Alessandro, Prince of Parma, famous gen. (1547–92).
Faroe (fā'rō), Dan. isls. bet. Iceland & Shetlands, 530 sq. m., p. 18.
Farragut (făr'ȧ-gŭt), David Glasgow. Am. admiral (1801–70).
Faure (fōr), François Felix. Pres. of Fr. fr. 1895 (1841–99).
Fawkes (fôks), Guy. Eng. conspirator; gunpowder plot, Nov. 5, 1605 (1570–1606).
Felix (fē'lĭks), name of 4 popes: **I**, Pope 269–274; **II**, 355–358; **III**, 483–492; **IV**, 526–530.—**Antonius**. Rom. procurator of Judæa under emp. Claudius (52 A. D.?)
Fénelon (fā̃n"lôṅ'), François de Salignac du la Mothe. Fr. prelate & author (1651–1715).
Ferdinand (fẽr'dĭ-nănd), **I**, The Just, king of Aragon (1379–1416).—**V**, The Catholic, king of Spain (1452–1516).—**VI**, king of Spain (1784–1833).—**I**, king of Bulgaria fr. 1908; abdicated in favor of Boris 1918 (1861–).—**I**, king of Roumania fr. 1914 (1865–).
Fernandez (fẽr-năn'dĕz; Sp. fĕr-năn'dāth), Juan. Sp. navig. (1536–1602).
Ferrara (fĕr-rä'rȧ), prov. of N. It., 1,100 sq. m., p. 326.—cap. of prov., p. 95.

Ferrero (fĕr-rā'rō), Guglielmo. It. hist. & lecturer (1872–).

Fessenden (fĕs'ĕn-dĕn), William Pitt. Am. stsm. (1806–69).

Fez, one of the capitals of Morocco, p. 100.

Field, Cyrus West. Am. telegraphic promoter (1819–92).—Eugene. Am. poet & journ. (1850–95).

Fielding (fēld'ĭng), Henry. Eng. novel. (1707–54).

Fife (fīf), co. of Scot., p. 268; cap. Cupar.

Fiji (fē'jē), Br. isls. in S. Pacific, 7,435 sq. m., p. 140.

Fillmore (fĭl'mōr), Millard. 13th pres. of U. S. (1800–74).

Finland (fĭn'lănd), former grand-duchy of Russ., E. of Gulf of Bothnia; indepen. state 1918; 134,829 sq. m., p. 3,154; cap. Helsingfors.—**Gulf of,** arm of Baltic, 250 m. long.

Fionn Maccumhail (fĭn"măk-kōōl'), Irish epic hero of 3d century.

Fish, Hamilton. Am. stsm. (1808–93).

Fisher, John Arbuthnot, Baron. Br. admiral (1841–).

Fiske (fĭsk), John. Am. philos. (1842–1901).

Fitch (fĭch), John. Am. inven. (1743–98).—Clyde. Am. playwright (1865–1909).

Fitzgerald (fĭtz-jĕr'ăld), Edward. Eng. poet, translator *Rubaiyat* (1809–83).

Fiume (fyōō'mē), port of Croatia, on Quarnero bay, Adriatic, p. 50.

Flammarion (flȧ"mä'rē"ŏn'), Camille. Fr. astron. (1842–).

Flanders (flăn'dĕrz), two Belgian prov.: **East,** 1,172 sq. m., p. 1,134; cap. Ghent.—**West,** 1,249 sq. m., p. 885; cap. Bruges.

Flaubert (flō"bâr'), Gustave. Fr. novel. (1821–80).

Fletcher (flĕch'ĕr), Frank Friday. Am. admiral (1855–).—John. Eng. author with Beaumont (1579–1625).

Fleury (flû"rē'), André Hercule de. Fr. cardinal & stsm. (1653–1743).—Claude. Fr. hist. (1640–1723).

Florence (flŏr'ĕns; It. **Firenze**), city of It., on the Arno, p. 233.—prov. of It., 2,262 sq. m., p. 938.

Florida (flŏr'ĭ-dȧ), state of U. S., 58,666 sq. m., p. 753; cap. Tallahassee.

Flotow (flō'tō), Friedrich von. Ger. composer (1812–83).

Foch (fōsh), Ferdinand. Marshal of France; generalissimo of Allied armies, 1918 (1851–).

Fontainebleau (fōn"tăn"blō'), town, dept. of Seine-et-Marne, Fr., p. 15.

Foochow (fū'chou'), city S. E. China on Min riv., p. 700.

Foote (fōōt), Andrew Hull. Am. naval off. (1806–63).—Henry Stuart. Am. polit. (1800–80).

Foraker (fŏr'ȧ-kĕr), Joseph Benson. Am. polit. (1846–1917).

Forbes-Robertson (fŏrbz-rŏ'bĕrt-sŭn), Sir Johnston. Eng. act. (1853–).

Ford (fōrd), Henry. Am. auto. manufac. & polit. (1863–).—Paul Leicester. Am. novel. (1865–1902).

Forfar (fŏr'fȧr), co. on E. coast of Scot., p. 284.

Formosa (fŏr-mō'sȧ), or **Taiwan,** isl. in China sea, ceded to Jap. 1895; 13,500 sq. m., p. 3,341.

Forrest (fŏr'ĕst), Edwin. Am. act. (1806–72).—Nathan Bedford. Am. Confed. soldier (1821–77).

Forth (fōrth), riv. of cen. Scot.—**Bridge,** viaduct across Firth of Forth, Scot., 8,295 ft.

Fort Wayne (wān), city of Allen co., Ind., p. 79.

Fort Worth, city of Tarrant co., Tex., p. 73.

Fourier (fōō"ryā'), François Charles. Fr. Socialist (1772–1837).—Jean Baptiste. Fr. math. (1768–1830).

Fox (fŏks), Charles James. Eng. stsm. (1749–1806).—George. Eng. founder of Society of Friends, or Quakers (1624–91).

France (frȧns; anc. **Gallia**), repub. in W. Europe, 207,100 sq. m., p. 40,000; cap. Paris.—Anatole [Jacques Thibault]. Fr. novel. & critic (1844–).

Francis (frȧn'sĭs). **I,** king of Fr. (1494–1547).—**II,** king of Fr. (1544–60).—**of Assisi.** It. Friar, founder of Franciscans (1182–1226).—**of Paula,** founder of Order of Minims (1416–1507).—**Xavier,** Jesuit mission (1506–52).—**Ferdinand,** archduke of Austria, assassinated June 28, 1914 (1863–1914).—**Joseph, I,** emp. of Austria & king of Hung. (1830–1916).

Frankfort (frănk'fōōrt), city of Prussia on Main riv., p. 415.

Franklin (frănk'lĭn), Benjamin. Am. writer & stsm. (1706–90).—Sir John. Eng. Arctic explor. (1786–1847).—William Buel. Am. soldier (1823–1903).

Fraser (frā'zĕr), riv. in British Columbia. 500 m.

Frederick (frĕd'ĕr-ĭk). **I, Barbarossa,** Ger. emp. (1121–90).—**II,** Ger. emp. (1194–1250).—**I,** king of Prussia (1657–1713).—**II, The Great,** king of Prussia (1712–86).—**III,** emp. of Ger. (1831–88).—**VIII,** king of Den. (1843–1912).—**William,** of Prussia, the **Great Elector** (1620–88).—**William I,** king of Prussia (1688–1740).

Fremont (frē-mŏnt'), John Charles. Am. explor. & soldier (1813–90).

Fremstad (frĕm'stăd), Olive. Am. soprano (1870–).

French (frĕnsh), Daniel Chester. Am. sculptor (1850–).—John Denton Pinkstone, Viscount. Br. field-marshal (1852–).

French Congo, Fr. colony in W. cen. Africa, 560,000 sq. m., p. 9,800.

French Guinea, Fr. colony in W. Africa, 92,000 sq. m., p. 1,927.

French Indo-China, Fr. colonies in S. E. Asia, 256,200 sq. m., p. 18,000.

Friendly Islands. See **Tonga Islands.**

Frohman (frō'mȧn), Charles. Am. theatr. mgr. (1860–1915).

Froissart (frwä"sär'), Jean. Fr. poet & hist. (1338–1410).

Frontenac (frōnt"nȧk'), Louis de Buade, Comte. Fr. gov. in Can. (1620–98).

Froude (frōōd), James Anthony. Eng. hist. (1818–94).

Fujiyama (fōō'jē-yä'mȧ), or **Fuji-San,** volcanic mt. of Japan, 12,400 ft.

Fulton (fōōl'tŭn), Robert. Am. engineer; steamboat inv. (1765–1815).

Fundy (fŭn'dĭ), **Bay of.** An inlet of Atlantic, bet. Nova Scotia & New Brunswick, 180 m. long.

Funston (fŭn'stŭn), Frederick. Am. soldier (1865–1917).

G

Gaboriau (gȧ-bō"ryō'), Emile. Fr. novel. (1835–73).

Gainsborough (gānz'bŭr-ō), Thomas. Eng. painter (1727–88).

Galba (găl'bȧ), Servius Sulpicius. Rom. emp. (3 B. C.–69 A. D.).

Galicia (găl-ĭsh'ĭ-ȧ), crownland of Austria, 30,311 sq. m., p. 8,026, mostly Poles & Ruthenians; battles, 1914–17.

Galilee (găl'ĭ-lē), anc. prov. of Palestine, now in vilayet of Syria.—**Sea of,** lake in cen. Palestine, 13 m. long.
Galileo (găl"ĭ-lē'ō). It. astron. (1564–1642).
Gallieni (găl"yĕ"nē'), Joseph Simon. Fr. gen. (1849–1916).
Gallinger (găl'ĭn-gẽr), Jacob H. Am. polit. (1837–1918).
Gallipoli (găl-lē'pō-lē), penin. bet. Dardanelles & Gulf of Saros, 55 m. long; battles, 1915.
Galsworthy (gȯlz'wûr-thĭ), John. Br. playwright & essayist (1867–).
Galvani (gȧl-vä'nē), Luigi. It. physicist (1737–98).
Galveston (găl'vĕs-tŭn), city, S. E. Texas, p. 51.
Galway (gôl'wā), co. of Connaught, Ire., p. 182.
Gambetta (gäṅ"bĕt"ȧ'), Leon Michel. Fr. stsm. (1838–82).
Ganges (găn'jēz), riv. of N. India, 1,500 m. to Bay of Bengal.
Garfield (gär'fēld), James Abram. 20th pres. of U. S. (1831–81).—his sons, Harry A., coll. pres. & National Fuel Administrator (1863–); James Rudolph, cabinet officer (1865–).
Garibaldi (gä"rĭ-băl'dĭ), Giuseppe. It. patriot (1807–82).
Garonne (gȧ"rŏn'), riv. S. W. France, 355 m.
Garrick (găr'ĭk), David. Eng. act. (1716–79).
Garrison (găr'ĭ-sŭn), William Lloyd. Am. abolitionist & internationalist (1805–79).
Gatun (gȧ-toon'), town Canal Zone, p. 7.—**Dam,** part of Panama Canal, 8,000 ft. long.
Gautier (gō"tyā'), Theophile. Fr. poet & novel. (1811–72).
Gaynor (gā'nẽr), William J. Am. jurist, mayor N. Y. 1909 (1851–1913).
Geddes (gĕd'ĕs), Sir Eric Campbell. Br. R. R. expert, first lord of admiralty (1875–).
Geneva (jē-nē'vȧ), canton of Switz., 108 sq. m., p. 154.—cap. of canton, p. 126.—**Lake of,** largest lake in Switz.
Genghis Khan (jĕn'gis kän). Mongol conqueror (1160–1227).
Genoa (jĕn'ō-ȧ), prov. of Italy, 1,580 sq. m., p. 1,050.—city, sp. of Italy, p. 272.
George (jôrj), name of 5 kings of Gr. Br. & Ir.: **I** (1660–1727); **II** (1683–1760); **III** (1738–1820); **IV** (1762–1830); **V,** king fr. 1910 (1865–).—**I,** king of Greece (1845–1913).—**Saint,** patron saint of Eng., martyred April 23, 303.—lake, in N. Y., 33 m. long.
Georgia (jôr'jĭ-ȧ), state of U. S., 59,475 sq. m., p. 2,609; cap. Atlanta.
German East Africa, ter. owned by Ger., prior to 1914, on E. coast Africa, 384,170 sq. m., p. 7,660.
German Empire, cen. Europe, 208,780 sq. m., p. 65,000; cap. Berlin.
Germanicus (jẽr-măn'ĭ-kŭs), Cæsar. Rom. gen. (15 B. C.–19 A. D.).
German Southwest Africa, ter. owned by Ger., prior to 1914, on W. coast Africa, 322,000 sq. m., p. 84.
Germantown, N. part of Philadelphia, Pa.; battle, Oct. 4, 1777.
Gerry (gĕr'ĭ), El ridge. Am. stsm.; vice-pres. of U. S. (1744–1814).
Gettysburg (gĕt'tĭs-bûrg), city of Adams co., Pa., p. 4; battle, July 1–3, 1863.
Ghent (gĕnt), cap. of E. Flanders, Belgium, p. 162.
Ghiberti (gē"bĕr'tē), Lorenzo. It. sculpt. (1378–1455).
Gibbon (gĭb'ŭn), Edward. Eng. hist. (1737–94).
Gibbons (gĭb'ŭnz), James. Am. cardinal (1834–).
Gibraltar (jĭ-brôl'tẽr), town & strongly ft. rock, S. Spain, annexed by Gr. Br. 1704, p. 25.
Gibson (gĭb'sŭn), Charles Dana. Am. illus. (1867–).
Gilbert (gĭl'bẽrt), Sir Humphrey. Eng. navig. (1539–83).—**Sir William Schwenck.** Eng. librettist with Sullivan (1836–1911).
Gioberti (jō-bâr'tē), Vincenzo. It. stsm. & philos. (1801–52).
Giotto (jŏt'tō), Bondone. Florentine painter (1276–1336).
Girard (jĭ-rärd'), Stephen. Am. merchant & philan. (1769–1831).
Gironde (zhē"rônd'), dept. of Fr., on Bay of Biscay, 3,160 sq. m., p. 824.
Gladden (glăd'ĕn), Washington. Am. clergy. & author (1836–1918).
Gladstone (glăd'stŭn), William Ewart. Br. stsm. (1809–98).
Glamorgan (glă-môr'gȧn), co. of S. Wales, p. 1,120.
Glasgow (glăs'gō), city, on Clyde riv., Scot., p. 1,095.
Gloucester (glŏs'tẽr), co. of Eng., p. 736.
Gluck (glük), Alma. Am. soprano (1886–).—Christopher Willibald Ritter von. Ger. composer (1714–87).
Goethals (gō'thălz), George Washington. Am. military eng. (1858–).
Goethe (geu'tē), Johann Wolfgang von. Ger. poet, novel. & dram. (1749–1831).
Goldsmith (gōld'smĭth), Oliver. Irish poet (1728–74).
Gomez (gōm'ĕz), Maximo. Cuban patriot (1826–1905).
Gompers (gŏm'pẽrz), Samuel. Am. labor leader, b. London, Eng. (1850–).
Gordon (gôr'dŏn), Charles George. Br. gen. (1833–85).—Charles William [Ralph Connor]. Can. clergy. & author (1860–).—John Brown. Am. Confed. soldier (1832–1904).
Gorky (gôr'kĭ), Maxim [A. M. Pyeshkov]. Russ. novel. (1868–).
Goritz (geu"rĭts'), or **Görz,** town on Isonzo, 35 m. N. W. of Trieste, p. 26.
Gothard (gŏth'ȧrd), mt. group of Switz.; 10,600 ft.—tunnel through Alps, 9½ m.
Gottenburg (gŏt'ĕn-bûrg), sp. town in Swe., p. 177.
Gough (gŏf), John B. Am. temperance orator (1817–86).
Gounod (gōō"nō'), Charles François. Fr. composer (1817–93).
Gracchus (grăk'ŭs), famous Rom. family: Tiberius Sempronius (169–133 B. C.).—Gaius (159–121 B. C.).
Granada (grä-nä'dȧ), prov. of Sp., 4,928 sq. m., p. 493.—cap. of prov., p. 76.
Grand Cañon (kăn'yŭn), gorge of the Colorado riv. in Ariz., 217 m. long.
Grand Rapids, city of Kent co., Mich., p. 113.
Grant, Ulysses Simpson. Am. gen. & 18th pres. of the U. S. (1822–85).—Frederick Dent, son of former. Am. soldier & dipl. (1850–1912).—James. Br. novel. (1822–87).
Grattan (grăt'ȧn), Henry. Irish stsm. & orator (1746–1820).
Gray (grā), Asa. Am. bot. (1810–88).—Thomas. Eng. poet (1716–71).
Great Barrier Reef, natural breakwater coast of Queensland, Australia, 1,000 m.
Great Britain (brĭt'ȧn), isl., part of United Kingdom, 88,603 sq. m., p. 41,000.

Great Salt Lake, in Utah, 4,000 ft. above sea, 75 m. long, 50 wide.
Great Slave Lake, in N. W. Territories, Can., 300 m. long, 60 wide.
Greece (grēs), kingdom of S. E. Europe, 43,522 sq. m., p. 5,000; cap. Athens.
Greeley (grē'lĭ), Horace. Am. ed. & publicist (1811–72).
Greene (grēn), Nathaniel. Am. gen. (1742–86).
Greenland, Dan. isl. N. E. of N. Am., 827,300 sq. m., p. 12.
Green Mountains, in New England, 4,400 ft.
Greenough (grēn'ō), Horatio. Am. sculpt. (1805–52).
Greenwich (grĕn'ĭj), bor. of Kent co., Eng., p. 96; observatory.
Gregory (grĕg'ŏr-ĭ), name of 16 popes: I, The Great (540–604).—XIII, who reformed the calendar (1502–85).
Greuze (grüz), Jean Baptiste. Fr. painter (1725–1805).
Grévy (grā'vē'), François Paul Jules. Pres. of Fr. repub. (1807–91).
Grey (grā), Earl. Eng. stsm. (1764–1845).—Lady Jane. Heir to Eng. throne (1537–54).—Viscount, of Fallodon. Br. stsm.; foreign secretary at opening of Great War, 1914 (1862–).
Grieg (grēg), Edvard. Norweg. composer (1843–1907).
Grimm (grĭm), Wilhelm Karl. Writer of fairy tales (1786–1859).
Grodno (grŏd'no), city, W. Russia, p. 67.
Grouchy (grōō'shē), Emmanuel de, Marquis. Fr. gen. (1766–1847).
Guadalquivir (gwä'dăl-kwĭv'ĕr), riv. of Spain, 360 m. to Cadiz gulf.
Guadiana (gwä'dĭ-än'ȧ), riv. of Spain & Portugal, 515 m. to Atlantic oc.
Guam (gwăm), Am. isl., Ladrone group, Pacific oc., 200 sq. m., p. 12.
Guatemala (gwä'tĕ-mä'lȧ), repub. Cen. Am., 47,500 sq. m., p. 2,000.—city, cap. of repub., p. 90.
Guiana (gē-ä'nȧ), section of S. Am., owned by Br., Fr., & Dutch, p. 440.
Guinea (gĭn'ĭ), **Gulf of,** on W. coast of Africa.
Guizot (gē'zō'), François Pierre Guillaume. Fr. hist. & stsm. (1787–1874).

H

Haakon VII (hä'kōn), Prince Charles of Denmark, king of Nor. fr. 1905 (1872–).
Habana. See **Havana.**
Hadrian (hā'drĭ-ăn), Publius Aelius. Rom. emp. (76–138).
Hague (hāg), **The,** cap. of Netherlands, p. 295; Hague Tribunal estab. 1899.
Hahnemann (hä'nĕ-măn), Samuel Christian Friedrich. Ger. physician, founder of homeopathy (1755–1843).
Haig (hāg), Sir Douglas. Br. field marshal (1861–).
Hainaut (ā'nō'), prov. of Bel.; cap. Mons; p. 1,147.
Haiti (hā'tĭ), isl. in W. Indies, 28,200 sq. m., p. 2,500.—**Republic of,** part of W. Haiti & isls., 10,200 sq. m.; cap. Port-au-Prince.
Hakodate (hä'kō-dä'tĕ), city on isl. of Yesso, Japan, p. 78.
Hale (hāl), Edward Everett. Am. clergy. & author (1822–1909).—Nathan. Am. patriot (1755–76).
Halifax (hăl'ĭ-făx), city, Yorkshire, Eng., p. 102.—cap. Nova Scotia, p. 47.
Hallam (hăl'ăm), Henry. Eng. hist. (1777–1859).
Halleck (hăl'ĕk), Fitz Greene. Am. poet (1790–1867).—Henry Wager. Am. gen. (1815–72).
Halley (hăl'ĭ), Edmund. Eng. astron.; disc. of comet 1682 (1656–1742).
Hals (häls), Franz. Dutch painter, founder of school (1580–1666).
Hamburg (hăm'bŭrkh), city on Elbe riv., Ger., p. 953.
Hamilcar (hăm'ĭl-kär), name of several Carthaginian generals.
Hamilton (hăm'ĭl-tŭn), city, Ontario, Can., p. 101.—Alexander. Am. soldier & stsm. (1757–1804).
Hampden (hămp'dĕn), John. Br. anti-royalist (1594–1643).
Hampshire (hămp'shĭr), or **Hants,** co. of S. Eng., p. 951.
Hancock (hăn'kŏk), John. Am. Rev. patriot, 1st governor of Mass. (1737–93).—Winfield Scott. Am. gen. (1824–86).
Handel (hăn'dĕl), George Frederick. Ger.-Eng. composer (1685–1759).
Hang-Chow (hăng'chou'), cap. of Chekiang, China, p. 594.
Hankow (hăn'kou'), city & port, Hupeh, China, p. 900.
Hannibal (hăn'nĭ-bȧl). Carthaginian gen. (247–183 B. C.).
Hanover (hăn-o'vĕr), prov. Prussia, p. 2,760.—city, cap. of prov., p. 303.
Hardie (här'dĭ), James Keir. Br. labor leader (1856–1915).
Hardy (här'dĭ), Thomas. Eng. novel. (1840–).
Harlem (här'lĕm), upper section of Manhattan isl., part of N. Y. City.—**River,** connects East riv. with Hudson, N. Y.
Harper (här'pĕr), William Rainey. Am. educ. (1856–1906).
Harper's Ferry, town, on Potomac riv., W. Va. Scene of notable events in Civil War.
Harriman (hăr'ĭ-măn), Edward Henry. Am. railroad financier (1847–1909).
Harris (hăr'ĭs), Joel Chandler. Am. novel. (1848–1908).
Harrisburg, cap. of Pa., on Susquehanna riv., p. 64.
Harrison, Benjamin. 23d pres. of U. S. (1833–1901).—Frederick. Eng. essayist (1831–).—William Henry. Am. soldier, 9th pres. of U. S. 1840 (1773–1841).
Harte (härt), Francis Bret. Am. story writer & poet. (1837–1902).
Hartford (härt'fĕrd), cap. of Conn., on Connecticut riv., p. 99.
Harun-al-Rashid (hä-rōōn'ăl-rä'shēd), or **Haroun-al-Raschid.** Caliph of Bagdad (766–809).
Harvey (här'vĭ), William. Eng. anat. (1578–1657).
Hasdrubal (hăs'drōō-bȧl), name of several Carthaginian generals.
Hastings (hās'tĭngz), Warren. Eng. gov. gen. of India (1732–1818).
Hauptmann (houpt'män), Gerhart. Ger. dram. (1862–).
Havelock (hăv'lŏk), Sir Henry. Br. gen. (1795–1857).
Havre (hä'vĕr), sp. city, France, p. 136.
Hawaii (hä-wī'ĭ), isl. ter. of U. S. in Pacific, p. 192; cap. Honolulu.
Hawthorne (hô'thôrn), Nathaniel. Am. novel. (1804–64).
Hay (hā), John. Am. stsm. & author (1838–1905).
Haydn (hī'dn), Joseph. Aus. composer (1732–1809).
Hayes (hāz), Rutherford Birchard. 19th pres. of U. S. (1822–93).

Hazlitt (hăz'lĭt), William. Eng. critic (1778–1830).
Hearn (hĕrn), Lafcadio. Br.-Jap. author (1850–1904).
Hebrides (hĕb'rĭ-dēz), isls. W. of Scot., 3,000 sq. m., p. 100.
Hegel (hā'gĕl), Georg Wilhelm Friedrich. Ger. philos. (1770–1831).
Heine (hī'nē), Heinrich. Ger. poet (1797–1856).
Helsingfors (hĕl'sĭng-fôrs), sp. town, cap. Finland, p. 112.
Hemans (hĕ'mănz), Felicia. Eng. poet (1793–1835).
Hendricks (hĕn'drĭks), Thomas Andrews. Vice-Pres. of U. S. (1819–85).
Henley (hĕn'lĭ), William Ernest. Eng. poet (1849–1903).
Henry, name of 8 kings of Eng., notably: **V** (1387–1422); **VIII** (1491–1547).—name of 4 kings of Fr. and 7 Ger. kings & Rom. emps.—also **IV, of Navarre** (1553–1610).—Patrick. Am. patriot (1736–99).
Heraclitus (hĕr-ă-klī'tŭs), Gr. philos. (500 B.C.)
Hereford (hĕr'ē-fŏrd), co. of Eng., p. 114.
Herkimer (hĕr'kĭ-mĕr), Nicholas. Am. gen. (1715–77).
Herod (hĕr'ŭd), **the Great**, king of the Jews (62–4 B. C.).
Herodotus (hē-rŏd'ō-tŭs). Gr. hist. (484–425 B. C.).
Herrick (hĕr'ĭk), Robert. Eng. poet (1591–1674).
Herschel (hĕr'shĕl), Sir John. Eng. astron. (1792–1871).
Hertford (härt'fĕrd), co. of Eng., p. 311.
Herzegovina (hĕr"tsĕ-gō-vē'nă), country in Balkans, with Bosnia annexed by Austria-Hungary 1908.
Hesiod (hē'sĭ-ŏd). Gr. poet (about 776 B. C.).
Hewlett (hū'lĕt), Maurice. Eng. novel. (1861–).
Hill (hĭl), Ambrose Powell. Am. Confed. gen. (1825–65).—James Jerome. Am. R. R. builder (1838–1916).
Himalaya (hĭ-mä'lă-yă, or hĭ-mă-lā'yă), mt. system, 1,600 m. long, bet. India & Tibet; Mt. Everest, 29,000 ft.
Hindenburg (hĭn'dĕn-bŏŏrkh), Paul von. Ger. field marshal (1847–).
Hindu Kush (hĭn'dōō kōōsh), mt. range of Afghanistan, 20,000 ft.
Hindustan (hĭn-dōō-stän'), Persian name of India.
Hippocrates (hĭ-pŏk'ră-tēz). Gr. physician (460–359 B. C.).
Hoar (hōr), George Frisbie. Am. sen. (1826–1904).
Hobart (hō'bărt), Garret Augustus. Vice-Pres. of U. S. (1844–99).—city, cap. of Tasmania, p. 25.
Hoboken (hō-bō'kĕn), sp. city, Hudson co., N. J., p. 70.
Hobson (hŏb'sŭn), Richmond Pearson. Am. naval off. (1870–).
Hofmann (hŏf'măn), Josef. Pol.-Am. pianist (1876–).
Hogarth (hō'gärth), William. Eng. satirical painter (1697–1764).
Hokkaido (hŏk-kī'dō), isl. of Japan, 36,500 sq. m., p. 1,460.
Holbein (hŏl'bīn), Hans. Ger. painter (1460–1524).—Hans, son of former. Painter (1497–1543).
Holland (hŏl'ănd). See **Netherlands**.
Holman-Hunt (hŏl'măn-hŭnt'), William. Eng. painter (1827–1910).
Holmes (hōmz), Oliver Wendell. Am. author & physician (1809–94).
Holyoke (hōl'yōk), city, Hampden co., Mass., p. 58.
Homer (hō'mĕr). Gr. poet of 9th century.—Winslow. Am. painter (1836–1910).
Hondo (hŏn'dō), or **Honshu**, largest isl. of Japan, 87,483 sq. m., p. 35,000.
Honduras (hŏn-dōō'răs), repub. of Cen. Am., 44,275 sq. m., p. 560; cap. Tegucigalpa.
Hongkong (hŏng'kŏng'), Br. isl., mouth of Canton riv., China, p. 400.
Honolulu (hō"nō-lōō'lōō), cap. of Hawaii ter., p. 52.
Honshu (hŏn'shōō). See **Hondo**.
Hood (hŏŏd), Thomas. Eng. poet (1799–1845).—**Mount**, peak of Cascades, Ore., 11,225 ft.
Hoover (hōō'vĕr), Herbert Clark. Am. eng., com. of Belgian relief during Great War, 1914–18; U. S. food admin. (1874–).
Hopkins (hŏp'kĭnz), Edward. Colonial gov. of Conn. (1600–57).—Mark. Am. educ. (1802–87).—Stephen. Am. patriot (1707–85).
Horace (hŏr'ās), Quintus Flaccus. Latin poet (65–8 B. C.).
Horn, Cape, S. extrem. S. Am., on Tierra del Fuego isls.
Hortense (ŏr"täns'), Eugénie. Wife of Louis Bonaparte (1783–1837).
Houston (hūs'tŭn), city, Harris co., Tex., p. 79.—Sam. Am. gen.; pres. of Texas (1793–1863).
Howard (hou'ărd), Oliver Otis. Am. gen. (1830–1909).
Howe (hou), William, Viscount. Br. gen. in Am. (1729–1814).
Howells (hou'ĕlz), William Dean. Am. novel. (1837–).
Hudson (hŭd'sŭn), Henry. Eng. navig. in Dutch service (1576–1611).—**Bay**, 900 m. long, N. E. Can.: opens into Arctic oc.; disc. 1610.—**River**, in N. Y., 300 m. to
Hugo (hū'gō), Victor Marie, Viscount. Fr. novel. (1802–85).
Hull (hŭl), Isaac. Am. commodore (1773–1843).—city, Yorks., Eng., p. 291.
Humbert (hŭm'bĕrt), **I.** King of Italy (1844–1900).
Hume (hūm), David. Scot. hist. (1711–76).
Humperdinck (hŏŏm'pĕr-dĭnk), Engelbert. Ger. composer (1854–).
Hungary (hŭn'gă-rĭ), kingdom, cen. Europe, 125,400 sq. m., p. 21,000; cap. Budapest.
Hunt (hŭnt), Leigh. Eng. poet (1784–1859).
Hunyadi Janos (hŏŏn'yŏd-ĭ yä'nŏsh). Hungarian gen. (?–1456).
Huron, Lake (hū'rŭn), one of 5 great lakes of N. Am., 23,800 sq. m.
Huss (hŭs), John. Bohemian reformer (1369–1415).
Huxley (hŭks'lĭ), Thomas Henry. Eng. biologist (1825–95).
Hwang-Ho (hwăng-hō), riv. in China, 2,600 m. to Yellow sea.
Hyderabad (hī"dĕr-ä-băd'), state, Deccan, India, 82,690 sq. m., p. 13,375.—cap. of state, p. 500.

I

Ibsen (ĭb'sĕn), Henrik. Norweg. dram. (1828–1906).
Iceland (īs'lănd), Dan. isl. N. Atlantic oc., 40,000 sq. m., p. 85; cap. Reykjavik.
Idaho (ī'dă-hō), state of U. S., 84,800 sq. m., p. 437; cap. Boise.

Illinois (ĭl-ĭ-noi′; or -noiz′), state of U. S., 56,650 sq. m., p. 5,639; cap. Springfield.—**River**, 350 m. long, flows to Mississippi riv.

India (ĭn′dĭ-ȧ), country, mostly under Br. rule, S. Asia, S. of Himalaya mts., 1,944,700 sq. m., p. 300,000.

Indiana (ĭn-dĭ-ăn′ȧ), state of U. S., 36,350 sq. m., p. 2,701; cap. Indianapolis.

Indianapolis (ĭn″dĭ-ăn-ăp′ō-lĭs), cap. of Indiana, p. 234.

Indian Ocean, one of the 5 great oceans, S. of Asia & E. of Africa, to Antarctic circle, 28,350,000 sq. m., greatest depth, 22,968 ft.

Indo-China (ĭn-dō-chī′nȧ), or **Farther India,** the S. E. pen. of Asia.

Indus (ĭn′dŭs), riv. S. Asia, Tibet to Arabian sea, 1,700 m.

Ingelow (ĭn′jĕ-lō), Jean. Eng. poet & novel. (1820–97).

Inness (ĭn′ĕs), George. Am. painter (1825–94).

Innocent, name of 13 popes, notably: **III** (1161–1216).

Ionian Islands (ī-ō′nĭ-ȧn), group, Medit. sea, 1,117 sq. m., p. 226.

Ionian Sea, part of Medit., bet. Greece & S. Italy.

Iowa (ī′ō-wȧ), state of U. S., 56,025 sq. m., p. 2,225; cap. Des Moines.

Ireland (īr′lănd), isl., part of United Kingdom, 32,600 sq. m., p. 4,390; cap. Dublin.

Irrawaddy (ĭr-ȧ-wăd′ĭ), riv. of Burmah, 1,500 m. to Bay of Bengal.

Irving (ûr′vĭng), Sir Henry [John Henry Brodribb]. Eng. act. (1838–1905).—Washington. Am. essayist & hist. (1783–1859).

Isabella (ĭz″ȧ-bĕl′ȧ), **I.** Queen of Castile & Leon (1451–1504).

Isocrates (ī-sŏk′rȧ-tēz). Athenian orator (436–338 B. C.).

Isonzo (ē-zôn′tsō), riv. in Goritz, 75 m. to Gulf of Trieste.

Israels (ēs″rä-ĕls′), Joseph. Dutch painter (1824–1911).

Italy (ĭt′ȧ-lĭ; IT. **Italia**), kingdom S. Europe, 110,623 sq. m., p. 35,000; cap. Rome.

Ivan (ē-vän′), **the Great.** Founder of Russ. Empire (1440–1505).—**the Terrible.** Czar of Russ. (1529–84).

Ivangorod (-gō-rŏt), town, Russ. Poland.

J

Jackson (jăk′sŭn), Andrew. Am. soldier; 7th pres. of U. S. (1767–1845).—Thomas Jonathan ["Stonewall Jackson"]. Am. Confed. gen. (1824–63).

Jacksonville (-vĭl), city, Duval co., Fla., on St. Johns riv., p. 58.

Jamaica (jȧ-mā′kȧ), Br. isl. W. Indies, 4,193 sq. m., p. 850; cap. Kingston.

James (jāmz), name of 5 kings of Scot.: **I** (1394–1437); **II** (1430–60); **III** (1451–88); **IV** (1473–1513); **V** (1512–42).—**I** of Eng. & **VI** of Scot. (1566–1625).—**II** of Eng. & **VII** of Scot. (1633–1701).—Henry. Am. novel. (1843–1916).—William. Am. psychologist (1842–1910).—riv. in Va., 325 m. to Chesapeake bay.

Japan (jȧ-păn′), an isl. empire off E. coast of Asia, 140,200 sq. m., p. 65,100; cap. Tokyo.—**Sea,** bet. Japan & Korea, 405,000 sq. m.

Jassy (yäs′sē), city, former cap. of Moldavia, Roumania, p. 78.

Jaurès (zhō″rĕs′), Jean Léon. Fr. Socialist & author (1859–1914).

Java (jä′vȧ), isl. Dutch East Indies, 48,400 sq. m., p., with Madura, 30,000.

Jay (jā), John. Am. jurist & stsm. (1745–1829).

Jefferson (jĕf′ĕr-sŭn), Joseph. Am. actor (1829–1905).—Thomas. 3d pres. of U. S. (1743–1826).

Jena (yā′nä), town, Saxe-Weimar, Ger., p. 39; battle, 1806.

Jerome (jĕr-ōm′), Saint. Latin father (340–420).

Jersey (jĕr′zĭ), one of Channel isls., 45 sq. m., p. 53; cap. St. Helier.—**City,** city, Hudson co., N. J., on Hudson riv., p. 268.

Jerusalem (jē-rōō′sȧ-lĕm), cap. of Palestine; captured by British 1917; p. 51.

Joan of Arc. Fr. heroine (1412–31). See **Arc, Jeanne d'.**

Joffre (zhō′fr), Joseph Jacques Césaire. Fr. commander-in-chief. Marshal of Fr. (1852–).

Johannesburg (yō-hăn′nĕs-bŭrg), town, Transvaal, Union of S. Africa, p. 220.

John, name of several kings: **Of Eng.** (1167–1216).—**Of France** (1319–64).—**III, of Poland** [Sobieski] (1624–96).—**Of Bohemia** (1296–1346).—**Of Hungary** [Zapolya] (1487–1540).

Johnson (jŏn′sŭn), Andrew. 17th pres. of U. S. (1808–75).—Samuel. Eng. author (1709–84).—Sir William. Br. soldier & admin. in Am., founder of Johnstown, N. Y. (1715–74).

Johnston (jŏnz′tŏn), Albert Sidney. Am. Confed. soldier (1803–62).—Joseph Eggleston. Am. Confed. soldier (1807–91).—Mary. Am. novel. (1870–).

Johnstown (jŏnz′toun), city, Fulton co., N. Y., p. 11.—city, Cambria co., Pa., p. 65.

Jones (jōns), John Paul. Am. naval commander (1747–92).

Jonson (jŏn′sŭn), Ben. Eng. poet & dram. (1574–1637).

Jordan (jôr′dȧn), riv. of Palestine, 200 m.—David Starr. Am. natur. (1851–).

Josephine (zhō′zĕ-fēn). Empress of the French 1804–09 (1763–1814).

Josephus (jō-sē′fŭs), Flavius. Jewish hist. (37 A. D.–?).

Juarez (hŭ-ä′rĕth), Benito Pablo. Pres. of Mex. fr. 1861 (1806–72).

Jugo-Slav (yōō′gō-släf), the South Slavs of cen. Europe.

Julian (jōō′lĭ-ăn), Flavius Claudius. Rom. emp. (331–?).

Julius (jōō′lĭ-ŭs), **I,** pope 337–352.—**II,** pope 1503–13.—**III,** pope 1550–55.

Julius Cæsar. See **Cæsar.**

Jungfrau (yōōng′frou; "Maiden"), mt. of Switz., Bernese Alps, 13,670 ft.

Junius (jōō′nĭ-ŭs). Eng. anonymous writer of "Letters," fr. 1769 to 1812.

Justinian (jŭs-tĭn′ĭ-ăn), I, Flavius Anicius, the Great. Byzantine emp. (483–565).

Justin Martyr (jŭs′tĭn mär′tĕr), early church father (100–165).

Jutland (jŭt′lănd), penin. of Den., 9,755 sq. m., p. 1,062; naval battle, 1916.

Juvenal (jōō′vē-năl), Decimus Junius. Latin satirist (42 A. D.– ?).

K

Kamchatka (kăm-chăt′kȧ), Russ. prov. N. E. Asia, 502,424 sq. m., p. 37.

Kansas (kăn′zȧs), state in U. S., 82,158 sq. m., p. 1,690; cap. Topeka.—**City,** in Mo., on Missouri riv., p. 282.—**City,** in Kans., on Missouri riv., p. 94.

Kant (känt), Immanuel. Ger. philos. (1724–1804).

Karlsruhe (kärls′rōō-ē), cap. of Baden, p. 134.

Kashmir (kăsh′mēr), native state N. W. India, p. 2,898.
Kean (kēn), Charles John. Eng. act. (1811–68).—Edmund, his father. Eng. act. (1789–1833).
Keats (kēts), John. Eng. poet (1795–1821).
Keble (kē′bl), John. Eng. clergy. & poet (1792–1866).
Keller (kĕl′ēr), Helen Adams. Am. blind & deaf author (1880–).
Kelvin (kĕl′vin), William Thomson, Baron. Br. math. (1824–1907).
Kemble (kĕm′bl), Charles. Eng. act. (1775–1854).—Frances Anne [Fanny]. Eng. act. (1811–93).—John Philip. Eng. act. (1757–1823).
Kennebec (kĕn′ē-bĕk), riv. in Me., 150 m.
Kent (kĕnt), co. of Eng., p. 1,046.
Kentucky (kĕn-tŭk′ĭ), state in U. S., 40,598 sq. m., p. 2,290; cap. Frankfort.
Kepler (kĕp′lēr), Johann. Ger. math. & astron. (1571–1630).
Kerry (kĕr′ĭ), co. of Munster, Ire., p. 160.
Key (kē), Francis Scott. Am. poet; author national hymn (1780–1843).
Khartum (kär-tōōm′), town in E. Sudan on Blue Nile, p. 69; battle, 1885.
Kiao-chau (kyä′ō-chou′), bay & section of Shantung, China, 213 sq. m., p. 165; leased by Ger. 1898; seized by Japan 1915.
Kidd (kĭd), William ["Captain Kidd"]. Br. shipmaster & pirate (about 1696).
Kiel (kēl), town in Schleswig-Holstein, on bay of Baltic, p. 211.—**Canal**, connects Kiel with Elbe riv., 61 m. long; completed in 1914; haven of Ger. navy in Great War, 1914–18.
Kiev (kē′yĕf), or **Kieff**, govt. S. W. Russia, 19,691 sq. m., p. 4,206.—city, on Dnieper riv., p. 505.
Kilkenny (kĭl-kĕn′nĭ), co. in prov. of Leinster, Ire., p. 79.—city, on Nore riv., Ire., p. 10.
Killarney (kĭl-lär′nĭ), **Lakes of**, in Kerry co., Ire.; largest 5 m. long.
Kilmer (kĭl′mēr), Joyce. Am. poet (1886–1918).
Kimberley (kĭm′bēr-lĭ), dist. of W. Australia; goldfields.—city, cap. of Griqualand West, Cape Prov., cen. of S. Africa diamond fields; p. 50.
Kingsley (kĭngz′lĭ), Charles. Eng. clergy. & novel. (1819–75).
Kioto (kē-ō′tō), **Kyoto**, or **Saikio**, city on isl. of Hondo, Japan, p. 442.
Kipling (kĭp′lĭng), Rudyard. Anglo-Indian novel. & poet (1865–).
Kitchener of Khartum (kĭch′ĕn-ēr), Horatio Herbert, Baron. Br. gen. (1850–1916).
Klondike (klŏn′dīk), section of Yukon ter., Can.; gold fields; about 800 sq. m.; cap. Dawson.
Knox (nŏks), John. Scot. clergy. & reformer (1505–72).—Philander Chase. Am. stam. (1853–).
Koch (kōkh), Robert. Ger. bacteriologist (1843–1910).
Kola (kō′la), pen. of N. Russ., occupied by Br. & Am. troops, 1918.
Komura (kō′mōō′rä), Jutaro, Baron. Jap. stam. (1858–1911).
Kongo. See **Congo.**
Königsberg (kē′nĭkhs-bĕrkh), sp. town in E. Prussia, p. 246.
Korea (kō-rē′ȧ), or **Cho-sen**, kingdom of Asia, annexed by Japan 1910, 84,100 sq. m., p. 14,056; cap. Seoul.
Kosciusko (kŏs-ĭ-ŭs′kō), Thaddeus. Polish patriot (1746–1817).
Kossuth (kŏs′sŭth), Louis. Hungarian patriot (1802–94).
Kreisler (krīs′lēr), Fritz. Austrian violinist (1875–).
Kronstadt (krōn′shtät), town, Transylvania, Hungary, p. 41.
Kruger (krü′gēr), Stephen J. Paul [Oom Paul]. Pres. of former S. African Republic (1825–1904).
Kurdistan (kōōr-dĭ-stän′), ter. in W. Asia, govts. of Persia & Turkey, p. 1,800.
Kut-el-Amara (kōōt′ĕl-ä-mä′rȧ), town on Tigris riv., Mesopotamia, p. 6.
Kuyp (koip), or **Cuyp**, Albert. Dutch painter (1605–91).

L

Labouchère (läb′ōō-shâr), Henry. Br. polit. & writer (1831–1912).
Labrador (lăb′rȧ-dôr″), depend. of Newfoundland, most easterly part of Br. N. Am., p. 5.
Ladd (lăd), George Trumbull. Am. psycho. (1843–).
Ladoga (lä′dō-gȧ), lake, N. W. Russ., largest in Europe, 7,000 sq. m.
La Farge (lȧ färzh′), John. Am. painter (1835–1910).
Lafayette (lä″fä-yĕt′), Marquis de. Fr. gen., aided Am. in Rev. War (1757–1834).
La Fère (lä fâr′), town on Oise riv., France; battles, 1914–18.
Lafontaine (lä-fôn″tān′), Jean de. Fr. story writer (1621–95).
Lagrange (lä″gränzh′), Joseph Louis, Comte. Fr. math. (1736–1813).
Lahore (lȧ-hōr′), cap. of Punjab, India, p. 229
Lamartine (lä″mär″tēn′), Alphonse. Fr. poet & stam. (1790–1869).
Lamb, Charles. Eng. essayist (1755–1834).
Lanark (lăn′ärk), co. of Scot., 879 sq. m., p. 1,447.
Lancashire (lăn′kȧ-shēr), or **Lancs**, co. in N. W. Eng., p. 4,768.
Landor (lăn′dŭr), Walter Savage. Eng. poet & prose writer (1775–1864).
Landseer (lănd′sēr), Sir Edwin. Eng. animal painter (1802–73).
Lang, Andrew. Br. miscellaneous writer (1844–1912).
Lanier (lȧ′nĭ-ēr), Sidney. Am. poet (1842–81)
Lansing (lăn′sĭng), Robert. Am. stam. (1864–).
Laon (län), town in dept. Aisne, Fr.; battles, 1814, 1914–18; p. 10.
Lao-tze (lä′ō-tsē′). Chinese sage, founder of Taoism (600 B. C.–?).
La Paz (lä päs), dept. of Bolivia, 53,777 sq. m., p. 446.—cap. of dept., p. 79.
Laplace (lä″pläs′), Pierre Simon, Marquise de. Fr. math. & astron. (1749–1827).
Lapland (lăp′lănd), country in N. Europe fr. Norway to White sea, 130,000 sq. m., owned by Swed., Nor., & Russ., p. 27.
La Plata (lä plä′tä), city, cap. Buenos Aires prov., Argentina, p. 106.—**Rio de**, estuary of Parana & Uruguay rivs.
La Rochefoucauld (lä rōsh″fōō″kō′), François de, Duc. Fr. essay. (1613–80).
La Salle (lȧ säl), Robert Cavalier de. Fr. explorer (1643–87).
Las Casas (läs kä′säs), Bartolomé de. Sp. prelate in Cuba (1474–1556).
Lassa (läs′sä), or **Lhassa**, cap. of Tibet, cen. of Buddhism, p. 10.
Latimer (lăt′ĭ-mēr), Hugh. Eng. prelate & reformer (1490–1555).
Laurentians (lō-rĕn′shĭ-ănz), mts. in Can., fr. Labrador to Arctic, 4,000 ft.

Laurier (lō″rĭ″ā′), Sir Wilfrid. Can. premier 1896–1911 (1841–).
Lavoisier (lȧ″vwȯ″sĭ-ā′), Antoine Laurent. Fr. chemist (1743–94).
Lawrence (lô′rĕns), city in Mass. on Merrimac riv., p. 85.
Le Brun (lē brŭṅ′), Charles. Fr. painter (1609–90).
Lecky (lĕk′ĭ), William Edward Hartpole. Ir. hist. (1838–1903).
Lee, Fitzhugh. Am. Confed. gen. (1835–1905).—Henry ["Light-Horse Harry"]. Am. Rev. gen. (1756–1818).—Richard Henry. Va. delegate to 1st Am. Congress at Phila., Pa., 1774 (1732–94).—Robert Edward. Commander of Confed. army, son of Henry (1807–70).
Leech, John. Eng. humorous artist (1817–64).
Leeds (lēds), city, Yorkshire, Eng., p. 459.
Leeward Islands, Br. isls. in W. Indies.
Le Gallienne (lē găl′ĭ-ĕn″), Richard. Anglo-Am. essay. (1866–).
Leicester (lĕs′tĕr), co. in Eng., p. 476.—city on Soar riv., Eng., p. 232.
Leighton (lā′tŭn), Frederick, Baron. Eng. painter (1830–96).
Leinster (lĭn′stĕr), E. prov. of Ireland, 7,620 sq. m., p. 1,150.
Leipzig (līp′zĭkh), or **Leipsic,** city, kingdom of Saxony; battle of nations 1813; p. 586.
Lemberg (lĕm-bĕrg), cap. of Galicia, on Peltew riv., p. 206; battles, 1914–15.
Lena (lē′nȧ), riv. Siberia, 3,000 m. to Arctic oc.
Lenine (lĕ-nēn′), Nikolai. Russ. Socialist; Bolsheviki leader (1870–).
Lens (läṅs), town, dept. of Pas-de-Calais, Fr., p. 32; battles, 1914–18.
Leo (lē′ō), name of 13 popes, notably **I,** Saint, the Great, pope 440–461.—**III,** pope 795–816.—**X,** Giovanni de Medici, pope 1513–21.—**XIII,** pope 1878–1903.
Leon (lā′ōn), prov. of Sp., 5,986 sq. m., p. 386.
Leoncavallo (lā″ōn-kä-väl′lō), Ruggiero. It. composer (1858–).
Leopold (lē′ō-pōld), **I.** King of Belgians (1790–1865).—**II,** king of Belgians (1835–1909).
Lesseps (lā″sĕp′), Ferdinand, Vicomte de. Fr. dipl. & eng., builder of Suez canal (1805–94).
Lever (lē′vĕr), Charles James. Irish novel. (1806–72).
Lewis (lōō′ĭs), Merriwether. Am. explorer of west, with George R. Clark (1770–1809).
Lexington (lĕks′ĭng-tŭn), city in Fayette co., Ky., p. 40.—town in Mass.; first battle of Rev. War, April 19, 1775, p. 5.
Libau (lē′bou), sp. town in Courland, Baltic prov., p. 90.
Liberia (lī-bē′rĭ-ȧ), negro rep. of W. Africa, 40,000 sq. m., under supervision U. S., p. 2,000; cap. Monrovia.
Liechtenstein (lĭkh′tĕn-shtīn), independ. state of Europe; bet. Austria & Switz.; 61 sq. m., p. 11.
Liége (lē″ĕzh′), cap. of Liége prov. Belgium, p. 243; first battle Great War, 1914.
Liggett (lĭg′ĕt), Hunter. Am. army off., in command of First Army in Fr., 1917-18 (1857-).
Li Hung Chang (lē hŭng chăng). Chinese stsm. (1823–1901).
Liliuokalani (lĭl″ĭ-ū-ō′kä-lä′nĭ). Queen of Hawaii 1891–92 (1838–1917).
Lille (lēl), cap., dept. of Nord, Fr., p. comm., 218; battles, 1914–18.
Lima (lē′ma), cap. of Peru, p. 143.
Limerick (lĭm′ĕr-ĭk), co. of Munster, Ire., p. 143.
Lincoln (lĭng′kŭn), co. of Eng., p. 564.
Lincoln, Abraham. 16th pres. U. S. (1809–65).—Benjamin. Am. Rev. soldier (1733–1810).
Lind (lĭnd), Jenny. Swed. soprano (1820–87).
Linnaeus (lĭ-nē′ŭs), Carolus Karl von Linne. Swed. botanist (1707–78).
Lippi (lĭp′pē), Fra Filippo. It. painter (1412–69).—Filippino, son of former. It. painter (1457–1504).
Lisbon (lĭz′bŭn), cap. of Portugal, on the Tagus, p. 435.
Lister (lĭs′tĕr), Sir Joseph. Eng. surgeon (1827–1912).
Lithuania (lĭth″ū-ā′nĭ-ȧ), former grand duchy in E. Europe, then part of Poland, then part of Russia, independence declared 1918.
Liverpool (lĭv′ĕr-pōōl), sp. city, Lancs., Eng., p. 768.
Livingston (lĭv′ĭng-stŭn), Edward. Am. stsm. (1764–1836).—Robert R., brother of Edward. Am. jurist & stsm.; negotiated purchase of Louisiana (1746–1813).—William. Am. lawyer, soldier & gov. of N. J. 1776–90 (1723–90).
Livingstone (lĭv′ĭng-stŭn), David. Br. missionary & African explorer (1813–73).
Livonia (lĭ-vō′nĭ-ȧ), one of Baltic prov., 17,000 sq. m., p. 1,480.
Livy (lĭv′ĭ), Titus Livius. Rom. historian (59 B. C.–17 A. D.).
Lloyd George (loid jôrj), David. Br. stsm., premier during war, fr. 1916 (1863–).
Locke (lŏk), John. Eng. philos. (1632–1704). —William John. Br. novel. (1863–).
Lockyer (lŏk′yĕr), Norman. Eng. astron. (1836–).
Lodge (lŏj), Henry Cabot. Am. polit. & writer (1850–).—Sir Oliver. Eng. scien. (1851–).
Lodz (lōdz), town in govt. of Piotrokow, Russian Poland, p. 450; battles, 1914–15.
Logan (lō′gȧn), Benjamin. Am. scout & Indian fighter (1752–1802).—George. Am. agricul. & scien. (1753–1821).—James. Am. Colonial stsm.; secy. to William Penn.
Loire (lwär), riv. Fr., 543 m., to Bay of Biscay.
Lombardy (lŏm′bär-dĭ), div. of Italy, 9,300 sq. m., p. 4,790.
Lombroso (lŏm-brō′zō), Cesare. It. criminologist (1836–1909).
Lomond (lō′mŏnd), Loch, lake in Scot., 23 m. long.
London (lŭn′dŭn), city on Thames riv., Eng., cap. of United Kingdom, p. 7,419.—co. of Eng., p. 4,522.
Londonderry (-dĕr′ĭ), co. of Ulster, Ire., 816 sq. m., p. 140.—cap. of co., p. 40; siege, 1689.
Longfellow (lŏng′fĕl-ō), Henry Wadsworth. Am. poet (1807–82).
Long Island, isl., N. Y., 118½ m. long, in Atlantic oc.—**Sound,** bet. Connecticut & Long Island, 110 m.
Longstreet (lŏng′strēt), James. Am. Confed. gen. (1821–1904).
Longwy (lōṅ″vē′), town, Meurthe-et-Moselle. Fr., first Fr. town attacked by Ger. in 1914. p. 9.
Lorraine (lō″răṅ′), prov. of Fr., annexed with Alsace by Ger. 1871; recovered by Fr. 1918. See **Alsace-Lorraine.**
Los Angeles (lōs ăn′jĕl-ĕs), city, S. Cal., p. 400.
Loti (lō″tē′), Pierre [Louis Viaud]. Fr. novel. (1850–).
Loubet (lōō″bā′), Emile. Pres. of Fr., 1899–1906 (1838–).
Louis (lōō′ĭs; Fr. lōō′ĭ), name of several

... **Fr.: IX, Saint Louis** (1214–70); ... (1601–43); **XIV**, the Great (1638– ...; **XV** (1710–74); **XVI** (1754–93); ... (1785–95); **XVIII** (1755–1824).

Lou... (lōō″ē-zē-ă′nȧ), state of U. S., 48,506 sq. m., p. 1,773; cap. Baton Rouge.

Louisville (lōō′ĭ-vĭl), city, Jefferson co., Ky., p. 224.

Louvain (lōō″văṅ′), city, Brabant, Belgium, p. 42; destroyed by Ger. 1914.

Lovejoy (lŭv′joi), Elijah Parish. Am. abolitionist (1802–37).

Lover (lŭv′ẽr), Samuel. Eng. novel. (1797–1868).

Lowell (lō′ĕl), James Russell. Am. poet, essay. & dipl. (1819–91).—city, Middlesex co., Mass., p. 106.

Loyola (lō-yo′lä), Ignatius. Sp. founder of Jesuits (1491–1556).

Lubbock (lŭb′ŏk), Sir John. Eng. scien. (1834–1913).

Lublin (lyōō′blyĕn), govt. of Russ. Poland, 6,500 sq. m., p. 1,575.—cap. of govt., p. 66.

Lucerne (lōō-sẽrn′), canton Switz., 580 sq. m., p. 167.—**Lake of**, cen. Switz.

Lucknow (lŭk′nou), city, India, p. 264; mutiny 1857.

Lunéville (lü″nā″vēl′), town, dept. of Meurthe-et-Moselle, Fr., p. 26.

Luther (lōō′thẽr), Martin. Leader of Ger. reformation (1483–1546).

Luxemburg (lŭks′ĕm-bûrg), grand duchy, E. of Belgium, 1,000 sq. m.; p. 260.—cap. of duchy, p. 21.

Luzon (lōō-thōn′; lōō-zŏn′), chief isl. Phil. isls., 41,000 sq. m., p. 3,798.

Lyell (lī′ĕl), Sir Charles. Scot. geol. (1797–1875).

Lynn (lĭn), city, Essex co., Mass., p. 90.

Lyons (lī′ŭnz; Fr. **Lyon**), city, dept. of Rhone, p. 524.

Lys (lēs), riv. France & Belgium, 100 m. to Scheldt riv.

Lytton (lĭt′ŭn), Edward George Earle Bulwer-. See **Bulwer-Lytton**.—Edward Robert. Earl of, Owen Meredith. Eng. poet (1831–91).

M

Mabie (mā′bē), Hamilton Wright. Am. essay. & ed. (1846–).

McAdoo (măk′ȧ-dōō), William Gibbs. Am. lawyer, secy. of treasury, director-gen. of railroads during Great War (1863–).

MacArthur (măk-är′thŭr), Arthur. Am. soldier (1845–1912).

Macaulay (mȧ-kô′lĭ), Thomas Babington, Lord. Eng. hist. & stsm. (1800–59).

McCarthy (mȧ-kär′thĭ), Justin. Eng. hist. (1830–1912).—Justin Huntley. Eng. dram. (1860–).

McClellan (mȧ-klĕl′ȧn), George Brinton. Am. gen. (1826–85).

Macdonald (măk-dŏn′ăld), George. Scot. novel. (1824–1905).

MacDowell (măk-dou′ĕl), Edward Alexander. Am. composer (1861–1908).

Machiavelli (mä″kyä-vĕl′lē), Niccolo. It. politician (1469–1527).

Mackensen (măk′ĕn-zĕn), August von. Ger. gen. (1849–).

Mackenzie (mȧ-kĕn′zĭ), Sir Morrell. Eng. laryngologist (1837–92).—William Lyon. Leader of rebellion in Upper Can., 1837–38 (1795–1861).—**River**, N. W. Ter., Can., 2,300 m. to Arctic oc.

McKinley (mȧ-kĭn′lĭ), William. 25th pres. of U. S. (1843–1901).—**Mount**, highest peak of N. Am.; in Alaska, 20,464 ft.

Maclaren (mȧ-klăr′ĕn), Ian [John Watson]. Scot. writer (1850–1907).

MacMonnies (măk-mŏn′ēz), Frederick William. Am. sculpt. (1863–).

Macready (măk-rē′dĭ), William Charles. Eng. act. (1793–1873).

Madagascar (măd″ȧ-găs′kȧr), Fr. isl., Indian oc., off E. Africa, 228,000 sq. m., p. 3,000.

Madeira (mȧ-dē′rȧ), isls. in Atlantic oc., W. of Morocco; Portuguese; 315 sq. m., p. 150.

Madero (mä-dā′rō), Francisco. Mex. pres. fr. 1911 (1873–1913).

Madison (măd′ĭ-sŭn), James. 4th pres. of U. S., 1809–17 (1751–1836).

Madras (mȧ-drăs′), presidency of India, 141,726 sq. m., p. 45,882.—city, India, p. 562.

Madrid (mȧ-drĭd′), cap. of Sp., on Manzanares riv., p. 600.

Mæcenas (mē-sē′năs), Gaius Cilnius. Rom. stsm. (73 B. C.–?).

Maeterlinck (mä′tẽr-lĭṅk), Maurice. Bel. dram. (1862–).

Magdalena (măg″dä-lē′nȧ), **Bay**, on Pacific coast, Lower Cal., Mex., 40 m. long.

Magellan (mȧ-jĕl′ăn), Fernando. Portuguese navig. (1480–1521).—**Strait of**, bet. S. Am. & Tierra del Fuego, 370 m.

Mahan (mȧ-hăn′), Alfred Thayer. Am. naval off. & author (1840–1914).

Maine (mān), state of U. S., 33,040 sq. m., p. 742; cap. Augusta.

Maintenon (măṅ″t-nôṅ′), Marquise de. Wife of Louis XIV (1635–1719).

Majorca (mȧ-jôr′kȧ), Sp. isl. Medit. sea, p. 249.

Malacca (mȧ-lăk′ȧ), Br. ter. Straits Settlement, p. 141.

Malay Archipelago (mȧ-lā′), isl. groups S. E. of Asia in Pacific & Indian ocs.

Malta (môl′tȧ), Br. isl. Medit. sea, p. 184.

Man, Isle of, isl. Irish sea, 220 sq. m., p. 52; cap. Douglas.

Manchester (măn′chĕs-tẽr), city, N. H., p. 70.—city, Lancs., Eng., p. 716.

Manchuria (măn-chōō′rĭ-ȧ), div. Chinese empire, 363,600 sq. m., p. 21,000.

Mandalay (măn′dȧ-lā), cap. Upper Burmah, p. 184.

Manhattan (măn-hăt′ȧn), isl., mouth of Hudson riv., N. Y., 13 m. long, 2½ wide; bor. of N. Y. city, p. 2,683.

Manila (mȧ-nĭl′ȧ), city, Luzon, cap. of Phil. isls., p. 220.—**Bay**, inlet of China sea, Luzon; battle, 1898.

Manitoba (măn″ĭ-tō′bȧ), prov. Can., 251,832 sq. m., p. 554.

Mann (măn), Horace. Am. educ. (1796–1859).

Mannheim (măn′hīm), city on Rhine riv., N. Baden, p. 193.

Mansfield (măns′fēld), Richard. Am. act. (1857–1907).

Marat (mȧ″rä′), Jean Paul. Leader of Fr. Rev. (1744–93).

March, Peyton Conway. Am. gen. (1864–).

Marconi (mär-kō′nĭ), Guglielmo. It. electrician; wireless (1874–).

Mare Island, in San Pablo bay, Cal., U. S. navy yard.

Margaret. Queen of Den., Nor., & Swe. (1353–1412).—**of Anjou**, wife of Henry VI, of Eng. (1430–82).—**of Valois**, wife of Henry of Navarre (1553–1615).

Maria Louisa. 2d wife of Napoleon I (1791–1847).

Maria Theresa. Queen of Hungary & Bohemia, archduchess of Austria, & Emp. of Ger. (1717–80).

Marie Antoinette. Queen of Fr.; consort of Louis XVI (1755–93).

Marius (mā'rĭ-ŭs), Gaius. Rom. gen. (156–86 B. C.).

Markham (märk'ám), Edwin. Am. poet (1852–).—William. Am. Colonial gov. (1635–1704).

Marlowe (mär'lō), Christopher. Eng. poet & dram. (1564–93).—Julia. Am. act. (1870–).

Marmora (mär'mō-rá), **Sea of,** bet. Black sea & Ægean, 140 m. long, 50 m. wide.

Marne (märn), riv. France, 306 m. long; battles, 1914–18.—dept. France, cap. Châlons, p. 436.

Marquesas (mär-kā'sás), **Islands,** group in S. Pacific, annexed by France, p. 3.

Marryat (măr'ĭ-ăt), Frederick. Br. novel. & naval commander (1792–1848).

Marseilles (mär"sālz'), sp. S. France, p. 550.

Marshall (mär'shăl), John. Am. jurist (1755–1835).—Thomas Riley. Vice-Pres. of U. S., 1912; re-elected 1916 (1854–).

Martha's Vineyard, isl. off Mass., 20 m. long, 10 m. wide, p. 4.

Martineau (mär'tĭ-nō), James. Eng. Unit. clergy. (1805–1900).

Martinique (mär'tē-nēk'), isl. in W. Indies; Fr. colony; cap. Fort de France, p. 184.

Marx (märks), Karl. Ger. economist; founder of Socialism (1818–83).

Mary I, Tudor ["Bloody Mary"], queen of Eng. fr. 1553 (1516–58).—**II,** wife of William III, queen of Gr. Br. (1662-94). —**Stuart,** queen of Scot. (1542–87).

Maryland (mĕr'ĭ-lánd), state in the U. S. A., 12,210 sq. m., p. 1,341; cap. Annapolis.

Mascagni (mȧ-skä'nyē), Pietro. It. composer (1863–).

Masefield (mās'fēld), John. Eng. poet (1875–).

Mashonaland (mȧ-shō'nȧ-lănd), prov. of S. Rhodesia, p. 512.

Mason (mā'sŏn), James Murray. Am. lawyer & Confed. stsm. (1798–1871).

Massachusetts (măs'ȧ-chōō'sĕts), state in the U. S. A., 8,266 sq. m., p. 3,366; cap. Boston.

Massenet (mȧs'nā'), Jules Emile **Frédéric.** Fr. composer (1842–1912).

Matanzas (mȧ-tȧn'zȧs), prov. of Cuba, 3,700 sq. m., p. 266; cap. Matanzas.

Mathew (măth'ū), Theobald ["Father Mathew"]. Irish priest & temperance orator (1790–1856).

Matisse (mȧ-tēs'), Henri. Fr. painter & sculptor, Impressionist School (1869–).

Matterhorn (măt'ĕr-hôrn), mt., Alps, Switz. & Italy; 14,661 ft. high.

Maubeuge (mō"bĕzh'), town, dept. of Nord, Fr., on Sambre riv., siege 1914, p. 23.

Maude (môd), Sir Frederick Stanley. Br. gen. (1864–1917).

Maupassant (mō"pȧ-sän'), Guy de. Fr. novel. (1850–93).

Mauritius (mô-rĭsh'ŭs), Br. isl., Indian oc., 720 sq. m., p. 377.

Mayo (mā'yō), Henry Thomas. Am. admiral (1856–).—co. of Connaught, Ire., p. 192.

Mazzini (mȧt-sē'nē), Giuseppe. It. patriot (1805–72).

Meade (mēd), George Gordon. Am. gen. (1815–72).

Meaux (mō), town, dept. Seine-et-Marne, Fr., p. 13; battles, 1914–18.

Mecca (mĕk'kȧ), holy city of Mohammedans, cap. of Hejas, Arabia; p. 60.

Medici (mĕd'ĭ-chĭ), famous Florentine family: Catherine (1519–89); Lorenzo (1448–92).

Mediterranean (mĕd'ĭ-tĕr-rā'nē-ȧn), inland sea, bet. Europe & Africa, 2,320 m.; 1,145,000 sq. m.

Meissonier (mā"sō"nyā'), Jean Louis Ernest. Fr. painter (1815–91).

Melba (mĕl'bȧ), Nellie [Mitchell]. Australian soprano (1865–).

Melbourne (mĕl'bûrn), cap. of Victoria, Australia, p. 680.

Memphis (mĕm'fĭs), city & port of entry, Shelby co., Tenn., p. 132.

Mencius (mĕn'shĭŭs). Chinese sage (371–287 B. C.).

Mendelssohn-Bartholdy (mĕn'dĕls-sōn-bär-tŏl'dĭ), Felix. Ger. composer (1809–47).

Menéndez de Avilés (mā-nān'dāth dā ä"vē-lās'), Pedro. Sp. founder of St. Augustine, Fla. (1519–74).

Menin (mē-năn'), town, W. Flanders, Belgium, p. 18; battle, 1914.

Mercator (mĕr-kā'tŭr), Gerard. Flem. geog. (1512–94).

Mercier (mâr"syā'), Desiré Joseph. Belgian cardinal & patriot (1851–).

Meredith (mĕr'ĕ-dĭth), George. Eng. novel. (1828–1909).

Mérimée (mā"rē"mā'), Prosper. Fr. novel. (1803–70).

Merritt (mĕr'ĭt), Wesley. Am. soldier (1836–1910).

Mesopotamia (mĕs"ō-pō-tā'mĭ-ȧ), country bet. Tigris & Euphrates, Asia.

Messina (mĕs-sē'nȧ), cap. of Messina prov., Sicily, p. 127; earthquake, 1908.—**Strait of,** bet. Sicily & It., 24 m. long.

Metchnikoff (mĕch'nĭ-kŏf). Russ. biologist (1841–1916).

Metz (mĕts), cap. of Lorraine, on Moselle riv.; p. 68.

Meunier (mē"nyā'), Constantin. Bel. scupl. (1831–1905).

Meuse (mûz), riv. Fr., Bel. & Hol., 498 m. to North sea.—dept. of Fr., 2,404 sq. m., p. 280; cap. Bar-le-Duc.

Mexico (mĕks'ĭ-kō; Mex. **Méjico**), repub. of N. Am., on Pacific oc., 769,000 sq. m., p. 16,000.—city, cap. of Mex., p. 470.

Meyerbeer (mī'ĕr-bâr), Giacomo. Ger. composer (1791–1864).

Michelangelo (mē"kĕl-ăn'jā-lō), Buonarroti. Florentine sculpt., painter, poet, architect (1475–1564).

Michelet (mēsh"lā'), Jules. Fr. hist. (1798–1874).

Michigan (mĭsh'ĭ-gȧn), state of U. S., 57,980 sq. m., p. 2,810; cap. Lansing.—**Lake,** one of great lakes of N. Am., wholly within U. S., 320 m. long.

Middlesex (mĭd'l-sĕks), co. of Eng., p. 1,126.

Milan (mĭl'ăn; It. **Milano**), city N. It., p. 663.

Miles (mīlz), Nelson Appleton. Am. soldier (1839–).

Mill (mĭl), John Stuart. Eng. philos. (1806–73).

Millais (mĭl-lā'), Sir John Everett. Eng. painter (1829–96).

Miller (mĭl'ĕr), Joaquin [Cincinnatus Heine]. Am. poet (1841–1913).—Henry. Am. act. (1860–).—Hugh. Scot. geol. (1802–56).

Millet (mē"lā'), Jean François. Fr. painter (1814–75).

Milton (mĭl'tŭn), John. Eng. poet (1608–74).

Milwaukee (mĭl-wô'kē), city & port, Wis., on Lake Michigan, p. 401.

Milyukov (mĭl"yōō-kŏf'), Paul Nikolaevitch. Russ. stsm. (1859–).

Mindanao (mĭn"dȧ-nä'ō), one of Phil. Isls., 37,000 sq. m., p. 499.

Minneapolis (mĭn"nē-ăp'ō-lĭs), city on Mississippi riv., Minn., p. 324.

Minnesota (mĭn″nē-sō′tȧ), state of U. S., 84,682 sq. m., p. 2,076; cap. St. Paul.

Minsk (mĭnsk), govt. of Lithuania, 35,283 sq. m., p. 2,964.—cap. of govt., p. 106.

Minuit (mĭn′ū-ĭt), Peter. Dutch gov. New Netherland (1580–1641).

Mirabeau (mē″rȧ″bō′), Gabriel Honoré Riquetti, Compte de. Fr. stsm. (1749–91).

Mississippi (mĭs″ĭs-sĭp′pĭ), state of U. S., 46,865 sq. m., p. 1,797; cap. Jackson.—riv. of U. S., 3,160 m., Minn. to Gulf of Mex.

Missouri (mĭz-zōō′rĭ), state of U. S., 69,420 sq. m., p. 3,294; cap. Jefferson City.—riv. of U. S., trib. of Mississippi; 3,000 m.

Mitchel (mĭ′chĕl), John. Irish polit. (1815–75).—John Purroy. Am. public official & soldier (1879–1918).

Mitchell (mĭ′chĕl), John. Am. labor leader (1870–).

Mobile (mō-bēl′), city on Mobile riv., Ala., p. 52.—**Bay**, est. of Gulf of Mex.; battle, 1864.

Modjeska (mō-jĕs′kȧ), Helena. Polish act. (1844–1909).

Mohammed (mō-hăm′ĕd), **Mahomet**, or **Muhammed**. Founder of Islamism, b. Mecca (570–632).—name of 5 sultans of Turkey: **V**, succeeded Abdul Hamid II 1909 (1844–).

Molière (mō″lyâr′), [Jean Baptiste Poquelin]. Fr. dram. (1622–73).

Monaco (mŏn-ȧ-kō), smallest independent state of Europe, bet. Fr. & Medit., 8 sq. m., p. 22; chief town, Monte Carlo, gambling casino.

Monastir (mŏn″ȧs-tēr′), city, S. Serbia; taken fr. Turkey, 1912; p. 60.

Mongolia (mŏn-gō′lĭ-ȧ), Chinese ter. N. E. Asia, 1,400,000 sq. m., p. 5,000.

Monmouth (mŏn′mŭth), co. of Eng., p. 396.—co. of N. J.; battle, 1778.—James, Duke of. Claimant to Eng. throne (1649–85).

Monroe (mŏn-rō′), James. 5th pres. of U. S. (1758–1831).

Mons (môɴs), city, Hainault, Bel., p. 28; captured by Germans 1914; recovered by Canadians 1918.

Montaigne (mŏn″tān′), Michel Eyquem de. Fr. essay. (1533–92).

Montana (mŏn-tä′nȧ), state of U. S., 146,572 sq. m., p. 376; cap. Helena.

Mont Blanc (môɴ″bläɴ′), highest mt. Europe, W. Alps, 15,781 ft.

Montcalm (môɴ″käm′), Louis Joseph St. Veran, Marquis de. Fr. gen. in Can. (1712–59).

Montenegro (mŏn″tā-nā′grō), kingdom, Balkan pen., 5,800 sq. m., p. 500; cap. Cettinje.

Montevideo (mŏn″tē-vĭd′ē-ō), cap. Uruguay, p. 268.

Montezuma (mŏn″tē-zōō′mȧ), Aztec emp. of Mex. (1390–1469).

Montreal (mŏn″trē-ôl′), city on St. Lawrence riv., Quebec prov., Can., p. 640.

Moore (mōōr), Sir John. Br. gen. (1761–1809).—Thomas. Irish national poet (1779–1852).

Moravia (mō-rā′vĭ-ȧ), prov. of Austria-Hungary, 8,578 sq. m., p. 2,435.

Moresnet (môr″nā′), repub. of Europe, bet. Bel. & Prussia, 1½ sq. m., p. 3.

Morley (môr′lĭ), of Blackburn, John, 1st Viscount. Br. author & stsm. (1838–).

Morocco (mō-rŏk′kō), Fr. protec., N. W. Africa, 193,000 sq. m., p. 7,000; cap. Fez.—part controlled by Sp., 10,000 sq. m., p. 404.—neutral zone, 140 sq. m.

Morris (mŏr′rĭs), Charles. Am. commodore (1784–1856).—Sir Edward. Newfoundland stsm. (1859–).—Gouverneur. Am. stsm. & dipl. (1752–1816).—Robert. Am. financier (1734–1806).—William. Eng. poet (1834–96).

Morse (môrs), Samuel Finley Breese. Am. inv. (1791–1872).

Moscow (mŏs′kō), 2d cap. of Russia, p. 1,818. Also, **Moskva**.

Moselle (mō″zĕl′), riv. Fr., Vosges mts. to Rhine, 314 m.

Motley (mŏt′lĭ), John Lothrop. Am. hist. (1814–77).

Moultrie (mōl′trĭ), William. Am. gen. (1731–1805).

Mozambique (mō′zȧm-bēk′), channel bet. Africa & Madagascar, 1,000 m. long.—prov. in Port. E. Africa, p. 3,000.

Mozart (mō″zärt′; Ger. mō′tsärt), Wolfgang Amadeus. Aus. composer (1756–91).

Mulhouse (mül′hous), city, Alsace-Lorraine, p. 95; recovered fr. Ger. 1918. Also, **Mulhausen**.

Munich (mū′nĭk), cap. of Bavaria, p. 600. Also, **München**.

Munster (mŭn′stẽr), S. prov. of Ire., 9,480 sq. m., p. 1,035.

Murat (mü″rä′), Joachim. Marshal of Fr. (1771–1815).

Murillo (mū-rĭl′yō), Bartolomeo Esteban. Sp. painter (1618–82).

Murray (mŭr′rĭ), Lindley. Am. grammarian (1745–1826).

Musset (mü″sā′), Alfred de. Fr. poet, novel. & dram. (1810–57).

Mutsuhito (mōōt″sū-hē′tō), emp. of Japan (1852–79).

Mysore (mī-sōr′), state of S. India, 27,936 sq. m., p. 5,540.

N

Nagasaki (nä″gȧ-sä′kē), city & port, Kiushu isl., Jap., p. 161.

Namur (nä″mür′), prov. of Bel., 1,413 sq. m., p. 363.—cap. of prov., on Sambre & Meuse rivs., p. 32; battles, 1692, 1792, 1914. Also, **Namen**.

Nancy (näɴ″sē′), cap., dept. of Meurthe-et-Moselle, Fr., p. 120.

Nanking (năn″kĭng′), cap. Kiangsu prov., China, p. 267.

Nansen (năn′sĕn), Fridtjof. Arctic explorer, b. Norway (1861–).

Nantes (näɴt), city on Loire, Fr., p. 171.

Naples (nā′plz), city S. It., p. 698.—**Bay of**, W. coast It., in Medit., 20 m. wide. Also, It., **Napoli**.

Napoleon. See **Bonaparte**.

Nashville (năsh′vĭl), cap. of Tenn., p. 140; battle, 1864.

Natal (nȧ-täl′), state in Union of S. Africa, 34,600 sq. m., p. 1,207.

Nebraska (nē-brăs′kȧ), state of U. S., 77,530 sq. m., p. 1,250; cap. Lincoln.

Negros (nā′grōs), one of Phil. isls., 4,880 sq. m., p. 460.

Nelson (nĕl′sŭn), Horatio, Viscount. Br. admiral (1758–1805).—**River**, riv. of Manitoba, Can., 350 m., to Hudson bay.

Nero (nē′rō). Rom. emp. (37–68 A. D.).

Netherlands (nĕth′ẽr-lȧndz), or **Holland**, kingdom, N. W. Europe, 12,761 sq. m., p. 6,000; cap. the Hague.

Neva (nē′vȧ), riv. of Russ., 40 m. to Gulf of Finland.

Nevada (nē-vä′dȧ), state of U. S., 110,690 sq. m., p. 109; cap. Carson City.

Nevin (nĕv′ĭn), Ethelbert. Am. composer (1862–1901).—Arthur Finley. Am. composer (1871–).

Newark (nū'ărk), city, N. J., on Passaic riv., p. 400.

New Bedford (bĕd'fẽrd), city, Mass., on Acushnet riv., p. 110.

New Britain (brĭt'n), city, Conn., p. 56.

New Brunswick (brŭnz'wĭk), prov. of Can., 27,985 sq. m., p. 352.

New Caledonia (kăl-ē-dō'nĭ-ȧ), Fr. isl. in Pacific, p. 50.

Newcastle (kȧs'l), city, New S. Wales, on Hunter riv., p. 60.—city, on Tyne riv., Eng., p. 274.

New England, N. E. U. S., comprising Me., N. H., Vt., Mass., R. I., & Conn.

Newfoundland (nū'fŭnd-lănd), Br. colony in N. Am., 40,200 sq. m.; with Labrador, 162,750 sq. m.; p. 250; cap. St. John's.

New Guinea (gĭn'ē), isl. Australasia; divisions prior to 1914: Dutch, 151,789 sq. m., p. 200; Ger. 70,135 sq. m., p. 531; Br. 87,786, p. 252.

New Hampshire (hămp'shĭr), state of U. S., 9,341 sq. m., p. 431; cap. Concord.

New Haven (hā'vn), sp. town, Conn., p. 150; Yale univ.

New Hebrides (hĕb'rĭ-dēz), Br.-Fr. isls. in Pacific, p. 70.

New Jersey (jẽr'zĭ), state of U. S., 8,224 sq. m., p. 2,538; cap. Trenton.

Newman (nū'mȧn), John Henry. Eng. cardinal & author (1801–90).

New Mexico (nū mĕks'ĭ-kō), state of U. S., 122,634 sq. m., p. 384; cap. Santa Fé.

New Orleans (ôr'lē-ȧnz), city & port, La., p. 362.

New Rochelle (rō-shĕl'), city, Westchester co., N. Y., founded by Huguenots 1687; p. 32.

New South Wales (wālz), state of Australia, 310,372 sq. m., p. 1,650.

Newton (nū'tŭn), Sir Isaac. Eng. math. (1642–1727).

New York (nū-yôrk'), state of U. S., 49,204 sq. m., p. 9,688; cap. Albany.—city, on Hudson riv., commercial cap. of U. S., p. of Greater New York, 7,300.

New Zealand (zē'lănd), Br. isls. in S. Pacific, 105,000 sq. m., p. 1,100.

Ney (nā), Michel. One of Napoleon's marshals (1769–1815).

Niagara (nī-ăg'ȧ-rȧ), riv. of N. Am., 33 m. fr. Lake Erie to Lake Ontario.

Nicaragua (nĭ-kȧ-rä'gwȧ), repub. Cen. Am., 51,700 sq. m., p. 600; cap. Managua.

Nice (nēs), city, S. Fr., on Medit., p. comm. 143.

Nicholas I, Czar of Russ. (1796–1855).—**II,** Czar of Russ., 1894–1917 (1868–1918).—**Saint,** patron of youth (about 326).—name of 5 popes, notably Nicholas V, pope fr. 1447 to 1455.

Nietzsche (nēt'shē), Friedrich Wilhelm. Ger. philos. (1844–1900).

Nieuport (ne'ōō-pōr''), town, W. Flanders, Bel.; battles, 1488–89, 1600 & 1914–18.

Niger (nī'jẽr), riv. W. Africa, 3,000 m. to Gulf of Guinea.

Nigeria (nī-jē'rĭ-ȧ), Br. ter. in Africa, 335,580 sq. m., p. 17,124.

Nile (nīl), riv. of Africa, 3,600 m. fr. Tanganyika to Medit.

Nineveh (nĭn'ē-vē), ancient cap. of Assyria, opposite Mosul on Tigris riv.

Nish (nēsh), or **Nissa,** city, Serbia, on Nishava riv.; temp. cap. of Serbia, 1914–18; p. 25.

Nobel (nō-bĕl'), Alfred. Swed. inventor (1833–96).

Norfolk (nôr'fŏk), city & port, Va., p. 85.—co. of Eng., p. 499.

Northampton (nôrth-ămp'tŭn), co. of Eng., 998 sq. m., p. 348.—cap. of co., p. 100.

North Carolina (kă'rō-lī'nȧ), state of U. S., 52,426 sq. m., p. 2,208; cap. Raleigh.

Northcliffe (nôrth'klĭf), Alfred Charles Harmsworth, Baron. Br. pub. (1865–).

North Dakota (dȧ-kō'tȧ), state of U. S., 70,837 sq. m., p. 637; cap. Bismarck.

North Island, isl., of New Zealand, 44,500 sq. m.

North Pole, reached by Peary, 1909.

North Sea, branch of Atlantic oc., bet. Gr. Br. & the continent of Europe, 221,000 sq. m.

Northumberland (nôr-thŭm'bẽr-lănd), co. of Eng., p. 697.

Norway (nôr'wā), kingdom N. Europe, 124,400 sq. m., p. 2,400.

Norwich (nŏr'ĭch), city, Norfolk, Eng., p. 124.

Nottingham (nŏt'ĭng-ȧm), co. of Eng., p. 604.—cap. of co., p. 260.

Nova Scotia (nō'vȧ-skō'shĭ-ȧ), prov. of Can., 21,428 sq. m., p. 493; cap. Halifax.

Nova Zembla (zĕm'blȧ), Russ. isls. Arctic oc., 30,900 sq. m.

Noyon (ṅwä''yôṅ'), town in dept. of Oise, Fr., p. 7; battles, 1914–18.

Nubia (nū'bĭ-ȧ), region of N. Africa bet. Egypt & Kordofan; annexed by Gr. Br., 1915.

Nuremberg (nū'rĕm-bẽrg), town, Bavaria, p. 333.

O

Oakland (ōk'lănd), city on San Francisco bay, Cal., p. 184.

Obi (ō'bē), riv. Siberia, 2,700 m. to Arctic oc.

Oceania (ō'shē-ăn'ĭ-ȧ), or **Oceanica,** isls. of Pacific & Malay Archipelago; formerly included Australia.

O'Connell (ō-kŏn'ĕl), Daniel. Ir. patriot (1775–1847).

Offenbach (ŏf'ĕn-băkh). Fr. composer (1819–80).

Ohio (ō-hī'ō), state of U. S., 41,060 sq. m., p. 5,090; cap. Columbus.—riv. of U. S., 1,280 m., affluent of Mississippi.

Oise (wäz), riv. Bel. & Fr., 180 m. to Seine.—dept. of Fr., 2,261 sq. m., p. 410.

Okhotsk (ō-kŏtsk'), **Sea of,** inlet of Pacific; E. Siberia, 582,000 sq. m.

Oklahoma (ōk''lȧ-hō'mȧ), state of U. S., 70,057 sq. m., p. 2,115.—cap. of state, p. 83.

Oku (ō'kōō'), Yasukata, Count. Jap. soldier (1846–).

Okuma (ō'kōō'mȧ), Shigenobu, Count. Jap. stsm. (1838–).

Oldenburg (ōl'dĕn-bŭrkh), grand duchy Ger. empire, 2,480 sq. m., p. 484.

Oldham (ōld'ăm), city, Lancs., Eng., p. 147.

Oliphant (ŏl'ĭ-fănt), Margaret. Br. novel. (1820–97).

Omaha (ō'mȧ-hô), city, Neb., on Missouri, p. 210.

Omar (ō'mȧr), 2d caliph of Mussulmans (582–644).—**Khayyam** (kī-yäm'), Persian poet (?–1123).

Ontario (ŏn-tā'rĭ-ō), prov. of Can., 365,888 sq. m. of land, 41,382 sq. m. of water; p. 2,523.—**Lake,** one of great lakes of N. Am., 5,400 sq. m.

Orange Free State, prov. of U. of S. Africa, 50,400 sq. m., p. 527.

Orange River, principal riv. of S. Africa, 1,300 m. to Atlantic.

Oregon (ŏr'ē-gŏn), state of U. S., 96,700 sq. m., p. 810; cap. Salem.

Orkney (ôrk'nē), isls. off N. Scot., 375 sq. m., p. 29.

Osaka (ō-sä'kȧ), city, sp., W. Hondo, Japan, p. 1,460.

Oscar (ŏs'kär), **I**, king of Swe. & Nor. (1799–1857).—**II**, king of Swe. & Nor. (1829–1907).
Osler (ŏs'lẽr), Sir William. Canadian physician (1849–).
Ostend (ŏs-tĕnd'), sp. town of Bel., on North sea, p. 43; occupied by Germans 1914; evacuated 1918.
Otis (ō'tĭs), Elwell Stephen. Am. soldier (1838–1909).—James. Am. patriot (1725–83).
Ottawa (ŏt'ȧ-wȧ), city, Ontario, Can., on Ottawa riv., p. 134.
Ovid (ŏv'ĭd), Publius Naso. Rom. poet (43 B. C.–18 A. D.).
Owen (ō'ĕn), Sir Richard. Eng. anatomist (1804–92).—Robert. Br. social theorist (1771–1858).
Oxford (ŏks'fẽrd), co. of Eng., p. 190.—cap. of co., p. 53; univ.
Ozark (ō'zärk), mts. in Ark. & Mo., 1,400 ft.

P

Pacific Ocean (pȧ-sĭf'ĭk), bet. America & Asia-Australia, 63,986,000 sq. m.; greatest length 9,000 m., greatest breadth 10,300 m.
Paderewski (pä"dĕ-rĕf'skĭ), Ignace Jan. Pol. pianist, composer, & stsm. (1860–).
Padua (păd'ū-ȧ), city, cap. of prov., Italy, p. 96.
Paganini (pä"gä-nē'nē), Niccolo. Genoese violinist (1784–1840).
Page (pāj), Thomas Nelson. Am. novel. (1853–).—Walter Hines. Am. dipl. & ed. (1855–).
Paine (pān), Thomas. Am. political & deistical writer, one of the founders of Am. independence (1737–1809).
Palermo (pȧ-lẽr'mō), prov. Sicily, 1,963 sq. m., p. 785.—cap. of prov., p. 341.
Palestine (păl'ĕs-tīn), Canaan or the Holy Land, country S. W. Syria, 10,000 sq. m., p. 650; part of Turkey fr. 1516 to 1917.
Palestrina (pä-lĕs-trē'nȧ), Giovanni Pierluigi da. It. composer (1524–94).
Paley (pā'lĭ), William. Eng. theolog. (1743–1805).
Palisades (păl'ĭ-sādz), cliffs on W. shore Hudson riv., N. Y., 30 m.
Palissy (păl'ĭ-sĭ), Bernard. Fr. potter (1510–90).
Palmer (pä'mẽr), A. Mitchell. Am. polit., Alien Property Custodian (1872–).
Palmerston (pä'mẽr-stŭn), Henry John Temple, Viscount. Eng. stsm. (1784–1865).
Panama (păn-ȧ-mä'), repub. Cen. Am., 33,000 sq. m., p. 337, exclusive of Canal Zone.—**Canal**, across Isthmus of Panama, 40½ m.—**Isthmus**, connects N. & S. Am., 32,280 sq. m.
Paraguay (pä'rȧ-gwī), repub. S. Am., 97,700 sq. m., p. 800.—riv. Brazil, 1,500 m. to Paraná riv.
Parana (pä'rȧ-nä'), riv. Brazil, 2,950 m. to Plata riv.
Paris (pă'rĭs; Fr. pȧ"rē'), cap. of Fr., on Seine, p. 2,888.
Park, Mungo. Scot. traveler in Africa (1771–1806).
Parker, Alton B. Am. jurist & polit. (1852–).—Sir Gilbert. Br. novel. (1862–).—Horatio. Am. composer (1863–).—Joseph. Eng. clergy. (1830–1902).—Theodore. Am. clergy. (1810–60).
Parnell (pär'nĕl), Charles Stewart. Irish stsm. (1846–91).
Parrish (păr'ĭsh), Maxfield. Am. painter (1870–).
Parry (păr'rĭ), Sir William Edward. Br. Arctic explorer (1790–1855).
Pascal (päs'kȧl), Blaise. Fr. philos. (1623–62).
Passaic (păs-sā'ĭk), city, N. J., p. 61.—riv., N. N. J., 100 m. to Newark bay.
Pasteur (päs"tẽr'), Louis. Fr. biolg. chem. (1822–95).
Patagonia (pă"tȧ-gō'nĭ-ȧ), former name of S. portion of S. Am.
Pater (pā'tẽr), Walter Horatio. Eng. essay. (1839–94).
Paterson (păt'ẽr-sŭn), city, N. J., on Passaic riv., p. 134.
Patmos (păt'mŏs), It. isl. Ægean sea, 15 sq. m., where St. John was exiled.
Patrick (păt'rĭk), Saint. The apostle of Ireland, b. in Roman Britain (389–463).
Patti (păt'ī), Adelina. It.-Span. soprano (1843–).
Pau (pō), Paul. Fr. gen. (1848–).
Paul (pôl), name of 5 popes, notably, Camillo Borghese, pope 1605–21.
Pauncefote (pôns'fŏŏt), Julian, 1st Baron. Br. dipl. (1828–1902).
Pawtucket (pō-tŭk'ĕt), city, Providence co., R. I., p. 57.
Payne (pān), John Howard. Am. act., author "Home, Sweet Home" (1791–1852).
Peabody (pē'bŏ-dĭ), George. Am. philan. (1795–1869).
Peace River, rises in Br. Columbia, 1,000 m. to Athabasca lake.
Peary (pē'rĭ), Robert Edwin. Am. Arctic explor., disc. of N. Pole 1909 (1856–).
Pechili. See **Chili**.
Peel (pēl), Sir Robert. Br. stsm. (1788–1850).
Peking (pē-kĭng'), cap. of China, in prov. of Chili (Pechili), p. 1,000.
Pelee (pĕ"lā'), **Mont**, volcano on Martinique isl., W. Indies, 5,200 ft.; eruption 1902.
Peloponnesus (pĕl"ō-pŏn-nē'sŭs), anc. name of pen. S. Greece, now called Morea.
Penang (pē-năng'), or **Betel-Nut Island**, div. of Br. Straits Settlements, 571 sq. m., p. 287.
Penn (pĕn), William. Eng. Quaker, founder of Pa. (1644–1718).
Pennsylvania (pĕn"sĭl-vā'nĭ-ȧ), state of U. S., 45,126 sq. m., p. 8,383; cap. Harrisburg.
Penobscot (pē-nŏb'skŏt), riv. of Me., 300 m. to Atlantic.—**Bay**, in Me., inlet of Atlantic, 28 m. long.
Peoria (pē-ō'rĭ-ȧ), city, Ill., on Illinois riv., p. 70.
Pepys (pĕps), Samuel. Eng. diarist (1633–1703).
Pericles (pĕr'ĭ-klēs), stsm. of anc. Gr. (?–429 B. C.).
Pernambuco (pĕr"nȧm-bōō'kō), state of Brazil, 50,000 sq. m., p. 1,375.—cap. of state, p. 250.
Peronne (pā"rŏn'), town, dept. of Somme, Fr., p. 5, battles 1915–18.
Perry (pĕr'ĭ), Matthew Galbraith. Am. naval off.; treaty with Jap. 1854 (1794–1858).—Oliver Hazard, brother of former. Am. naval off. (1785–1819).
Persia (pẽr'zhȧ), native state under Br. & Russ. influence, S. W. Asia, 628,000 sq. m., p. 9,500.
Pershing (pẽr'shĭng), John Joseph. Am. gen.; command of Am. forces in Fr., 1917–18 (1860–).
Persian Gulf, arm of Arabian sea, 520 m. long.
Perth (pẽrth), co. of Scot., p. 124.
Peru (pē-rōō'), repub. of S. Am., 680,026 sq. m., p. 3,530.

Pétain (pĕ″tăn′), Henri Philippe. Fr. gen., Marshal of Fr. (1856–).

Peter (pē′tĕr), **I,** the Great, emp. of Russ. (1672–1725).—**II,** emp. of Russ. (1715–30).—**III,** emp. of Russ. (1728–62).—**I,** Karageorgevitch, king of Serbia (1846–).

Petrograd (pyĕ′trō-grăt), cap. of Russ., on Neva riv., p. 2,318. Formerly St. Petersburg.

Philadelphia (fĭl″ȧ-dĕl′fĭ-ȧ), city of Pa., p. 1,750.

Philippines (fĭl′ĭ-pēnz), isls. in Pacific, off coast of China, annexed by U. S., 1898; p. 7,635; cap. Manila.

Phillips (fĭl′ĭps), Wendell. Am. abolitionist (1811–84).

Phocion (fō′shĭ-ŭn). Athenian gen. (? – 317 B. C.).

Pickett (pĭk′ĕt), George. Am. Confed. gen. (1825–75).

Piedmont (pēd′mŏnt), prov. of Italy, p. 3,070; cap. Turin.

Pierce (pērc), Franklin. 14th pres. of U. S. (1804–69).

Pike, Zebulon Montgomery. Am. gen. & explorer (1779–1813).

Pike's Peak, mt. in Colo., 14,000 ft. high.

Pinckney (pĭnk′nĭ), Charles Cotesworth. Am. soldier (1746–1825).

Pindar (pĭn′dăr). Gr. poet (522–443 B. C.).

Pinero (pĭn-ĕr′ō), Sir Arthur Wing. Br. dram. (1855–).

Pisistratus (pĭ-sĭs′trȧ-tŭs). Athenian stsm. (?–527 B. C.).

Pitman (pĭt′măn), Sir Isaac. Eng. inventor of shorthand known as phonography (1813–97).

Pitt (pĭt), William, Earl of Chatham. Eng. stsm. (1708–78).

Pittsburgh (pĭts′bûrg), city, Pa., p. 590.

Pius (pī′ŭs), name of several popes: **X,** Giuseppe Sarto, pope fr. 1903 (1835–1914).

Pizarro (pĭ-zăr′ō), Francisco. Sp. conqueror of Peru (1475–1541).

Plato (plā′tō). Gr. philos. (427–347 B. C.).

Plautus (plô′tŭs). Rom. dram. (254–184 B. C.).

Pliny (plĭ′nĭ), **the Elder** [Gaius P. Secundus]. Rom. natur. (23–79).—**the Younger** [Gaius P. Cæcilius Secundus]. Rom. author & orator (62–110).

Plutarch (plōō′tärk). Gr. biographer (46–120).

Plymouth (plĭ′mŭth), town, S. E. Mass., where Pilgrim Fathers landed, p. 12.—naval station, Devon, Eng., p. 124.

Pocahontas (pō″cȧ-hŏn′tȧs), daughter of Powhattan, Indian chief (1595–1617).

Po (pō), riv. N. It., 418 m. to Adriatic.

Poe (pō), Edgar Allan. Am. poet, essay. & story writer (1809–49).

Poincaré (pwăṅ″kȧ″rā′), Raymond. Pres. Fr. repub. fr. 1913 (1860–).

Poland (pō′lănd), former kingdom of Europe; about 375,000 sq. m., distributed bet. Russia, Germany, & Austria-Hungary; reconstructed as separate state 1918.

Polk (pōk), James Knox. 11th pres. of U. S. (1795–1849).—Leonidas. Am. clergy. Confed. gen. (1806–64).

Polo (pō′lō), Marco. Venetian traveler & author (1254–1324).

Polycarp (pŏ′lĭ-cärp), Saint. Apostolic father (about 69–166).

Polynesia (pŏl″ĭ-nē′zĭ-ȧ), isls. of cen. Pacific; New Zealand & Hawaiian isls. the largest.

Pompadour (pŏm′pȧ-dōr), Marquise de. Mistress of Louis XV (1721–64).

Pompeii (pŏm-pā′yē), anc. city of It., near Naples; buried by volcano 79 A. D.

Pompey (pŏm′pĭ), **the Great.** Rom. gen. & triumvar (106–48 B. C.).

Ponce de Leon (pōn′thā dā lā′on), Juan. Sp. explorer of Florida (1460–1521).

Poniatowski (pō″nĭ′ȧ-tŏv′skĭ), Joseph Antony. Pol. nationalist, marshal of Fr. (1762–1813).—Stanislaus. Pol. prince & soldier (1677–1762.—king of Poland (1732–98).

Pontiac (pŏn′tĭ-ăk). Ottawa Indian chief (?–1769).

Pope (pōp), Alexander. Eng. poet (1688–1744).

Porter (pōr′tĕr), David Dixon. Am. admiral (1813–91).

Portland (pōrt′lănd), city, Me., on Casco bay, p. 65.—city, Ore., on Willamette riv., p. 265.

Porto Rico (pōr′tō rē′kō; Sp. **Puerto Rico**), Am. isl. W. Indies, 3,596 sq. m., p. 1,118.

Port Said (pōrt sä-ēd′), town, Egypt, on Medit., Suez Canal, p. 50.

Portsmouth (pōrts′mŭth), city, Hampshire, Eng., on Eng. Channel; naval station; p. 245.

Portugal (pôr′tū-gȧl), repub. S. W. Europe, on Atlantic oc., 35,490 sq. m., p. 5,500.

Portuguese East Africa, on E. coast Africa, 301,000 sq. m., p. 3,120.

Portuguese Guinea, on W. African coast, p. 300.

Portuguese India, on W. coast India, comprising Goa, Daman, and Diu, p. 605.

Posen (pō′zĕn), city, Prussian Poland; cap. of anc. Poland, p. 157.

Potomac (pō-tō′mȧk), riv. bet. Md. & Va., 400 m. to Chesapeake bay.

Potsdam (pŏts′dȧm), cap. of Brandenburg, Prussia, p. 62.

Potter (pŏt′ĕr), Henry Codman. Bishop of New York (1835–1908).—Paul. Dutch painter (1625–54).

Powhatan (pou″hȧ-tăn′), Am. Indian Sachem (1550–1618).

Prague (prăg), cap. of Bohemia, p. 237.

Praxiteles (prăks-ĭt′ĕ-lēz). Gr. sculp. (about 364 B. C.).

Prescott (prĕs′kŭt), William Hickling. Am. hist. (1796–1859).

Preston (prĕs′tŭn), bor. Lancs., Eng., p. 119.

Prince Edward Island, prov. of Can., isl. in Gulf St. Lawrence, 2,134 sq. m., p. 93,728; cap. Charlottetown.

Princeton (prĭns′tŭn), town, Mercer co., N. J., p. 6; univ.

Prior (prī′ĕr), Matthew. Eng. poet (1664–1721).

Proudhon (prōō″dôṅ′), Pierre Joseph. Fr. publicist (1809–65).

Providence (prŏv′ĭ-dĕns), cap. R. I., p. 225.

Prussia (prŭsh′ȧ), state of Ger. empire, 136,488 sq. m., p. 34,473; cap. Berlin.

Przemysl (pshĕ′mĕshl), town, Galicia, p. 60; battles, 1915.

Ptolemy (tŏl′ē-mĭ), name of several Græco-Egyptian kings fr. 329 B. C. to 30 B. C.

Puccini (pōōt-chēn′ē), Giacomo. It. composer (1858–).

Puebla (pwāb′lȧ), state of Mex., 12,042 sq. m., p. 1,021; cap. of state, p. 95.

Puget Sound (pū′jĕt), arm of Pacific, N. W. coast Wash.

Pulaski (pōō-lăs′kĭ), Casimir, Count. Pol. patriot & Am. soldier (1747–79).

Pulitzer (pū′lĭt-zĕr), Joseph. Am. ed. & publisher (1847–1911).

Punjab (pŭn-jäb′), prov. India, 133,741 sq. m., p. 29,179.

Putnam (pŭt′nȧm), Israel. Am. soldier (1718–90).

Pyrenees (pĭr'ē-nēz), mt. range bet. Fr. & Sp., 280 m., 11,424 ft. high.

Pythagoras (pĭ-thăg'ō-răs). Gr. philos. (586–506 B. C.).

Q

Quatre-Bras (kă'tr-brä'), town, S. Brabant, Bel.: battle, 1815.

Quebec (kwē-bĕk'), prov. of Can., 703,653 sq. m., p. 2,003; cap. of prov., p. 79.

Queensland (kwēnz'lănd), state of Australia, 670,500 sq. m., p. 700.—sp. city, Ire., on Atlantic oc., p. 8.

Quiller-Couch (kwĭl'ēr-kōōch), Sir Arthur Thomas. Eng. novel. (1863–).

Quintilian (kwĭn-tĭl'ĭ-ăn), Marcus Fabius. Rom. rhetorician (35–118).

R

Rabelais (răb'lā'). François. Fr. satirical & humorous writer (1495–1553).

Racine (rá'sēn'), Jean Baptiste. Fr. dram. (1639–99).

Rainier (rā'nĭr), **Mount,** Cascade range, Wash., 14,444 ft.

Raleigh (rô'lĭ), Sir Walter. Eng. navig. & soldier (1552–1618).

Rameses (răm'e-sīz), name of several Egyptian monarchs.

Ramsey (răm'zĭ), Sir William. Br. chemist (1852–1916).

Rangoon (răń'gōōn'), cap. Lower Burmah, p. 293.

Rankin (răńg'kĭn), Jeannette. First woman member U. S. Congress (1882–).

Raphael (ră'fā-ĕl), Sanzio. It. painter (1483–1520).

Ravenna (ră-ven'nă), prov. of It., 715 sq. m., p. 236.—cap. of prov., p. 74.

Reading (rĕd'ĭng), Rufus Daniel Isaacs, first Earl of. Br. jurist & dipl. (1860–). —city, Pa., on Schuylkill riv., p. 110.—city, Berks co., Eng., p. 76.

Redmond (rĕd'mŭnd), John Edward. Ir. stsm. (1851–1918).

Red River, trib. of Mississippi riv., rises N. Texas, 1,550 m.

Red Sea, branch of Indian oc., bet. Arabia & Egypt, 178,000 sq. m.

Reed (rēd), Thomas Brackett. Am. stsm. (1839–1902).

Reid (rēd), Whitelaw. Am. ed. & dipl. (1837–1912).

Rembrandt (rĕm'brănt), Hermansz Van Ryn. Dutch painter (1606–69).

Renan (rē-nań'), Joseph Ernest. Fr. hist. & essayist (1823–92).

Renfrew (rĕn'frōō), co. of Scot., 240 sq. m., p. 315.

Reval (rē-väl'), cap. of Esthonia, on Gulf Finland, p. 100.

Revere (rē-vēr'), Paul. Am. patriot (1735–1818).

Reynolds (rĕn'ŭldz), Sir Joshua. Br. painter (1723–92).

Rheims (rańs; Eng. rēmz), city, dept. of Marne, p. 116; battles 1914–18.

Rhine (rīn), riv. of Europe, rises in Switz., 800 m. to North Sea

Rhode Island (rōd), state of U. S., 1,248 sq. m., p. 543; cap. Providence.

Rhodes (rōdz), Cecil John. Eng. admin. in S. Africa (1853–1902).

Rhodesia (rō-dē'zĭ-ă), div. of S. Africa: Northern, 291,000 sq. m., p. 876; Southern, 149,000 sq. m., p. 769.

Rhone (rōn), riv. of Europe, rises Switz., 500 m. to Gulf of Lyons.—dept. of Fr., 1,077 sq. m., p. 860; cap. Lyons.

Richard, name of 3 kings of Eng.: **I,** Cœur de Lion (1157–99); **II** (1366–1400); **III,** last of Plantagenets (1450–85).

Richardson, Samuel. Eng. novel. (1689–1761).

Richelieu (rēsh'lyōō'), Armand Jean du Plessis, Cardinal, Duc de. Fr. stsm. (1585–1642).

Richmond (rĭch'mŭnd), cap. of Va., on James riv., p. 128; Confed. cap., surrendered 1865.

Richter (rĭkh'tĕr), Jean Paul. Ger. author (1763–1825).

Rienzi (rē-ĕn'zē), Cola di. It. reformer (1312–54).

Riga (rē'gá), cap. of Livonia, Baltic province, p. 370.—**Gulf of,** arm of Baltic.

Riis (rēs), Jacob August. Am. social worker (1849–1914).

Riley (rī'lĭ), James Whitcomb. Am. poet (1849–1916).

Rio de Janeiro (rē'ō dā zhá-nā'rō), state of Brazil, 26,634 sq. m., p. 1,130.—cap. of Brazil, p. 1,000.

Rio Grande (rē'ō grän'dā), riv. of U. S.; S. W. Colo., 2,000 m. to Gulf of Mex.

Rittenhouse (rĭt'ĕn-hous), David. Am. astron. (1732–96).

Robert, name of several kings of Scot., notably **I, Bruce** (1274–1329).

Robespierre (rōb'ĕs-pĭ-âr), François Maximilien. Fr. revolutionist (1758–94).

Rob Roy (rŏb roi) ["Robert the Red"]. Scot. freebooter (1660–1743).

Rochambeau (rō'shăń'bō'), Jean Baptiste, Count de. Marshal of Fr. (1725–1807).

Rochester (rŏch'ĕs-tĕr), city, N. Y., on Genesee riv., p. 240.

Rockefeller (rŏk'ē-fĕl-ēr), John Davidson. Am. financier (1839–).

Rock River, riv. of U. S., 330 m., Wis. to Mississippi.

Rocky Mountains, western range of N. Am. 4,000 m. fr. N. to S., highest peak, 14,341.

Rodin (rō'dăń'), Auguste. Fr. sculp. (1840–1917).

Roebling (rōb'lĭng), Washington Augustus. Am. eng. (1837–1917).

Roentgen (rûnt'gĕn), Wilhelm Konrad. Ger. physicist; disc. of Roentgen rays. (1845–).

Rome (rōm), city on Tiber riv., cap. of It., p. 542.

Roosevelt (rō'zĕ-vĕlt), Theodore. 26th pres. of U. S. (1858–1919).—his youngest son, Quentin, b. 1896; killed in battle in France, 1918.

Root, Elihu. Am. stsm. (1845–).

Rosecrans (rō'zē-krănz), William Starke. Am. soldier (1819–98).

Rossetti (rō-sĕt'ĭ), Christina. Eng. poet (1830–94).—her brother, Dante Gabriel, Eng. poet (1828–82).

Rossini (rōs-sē'nĭ), Gioacchino Antonio. It. composer (1792–1868).

Rostand (rō'stăń'), Edmond. Fr. dram. (1868–1918).

Rotterdam (rŏt'ēr-dăm), sp. city of Netherlands, p. 447.

Rouen (rōō'äń'), city, Fr.; anc. cap. of Normandy, p. 125.

Roumania (rōō-mā'nĭ-ă), or **Rumania,** kingdom of Europe, p. 7,230; cap. Bucharest. Overrun by Teutonic Allies in 1916.

Rousseau (rōō'sō'), Jean Jacques. Fr. essay. (1712–79).

Roye (rwä'y'), town, dept. of Somme, Fr., on Avre riv., p. 5; battles, 1914–18.

Rubens (rōō'bĕnz), Peter Paul. Flem. painter (1577–1640).

Rubinstein (rōō'bin-stīn), Anton Grigory-evitch. Russ. composer (1829–94).

Rumania. See Roumania.

Runnimede (rŭn'nĭ-mēd), meadow on bank of Thames riv., Eng.; Magna Charta signed 1215.

Rush (rŭsh), Benjamin. Am. physician (1745–1813).—Richard. Am. stsm. (1780–1859).

Ruskin (rŭs'kĭn), John. Eng. essay. (1819–1900).

Russell (rŭs'ĕl), John, Earl. Eng. stsm. (1792–1878).—John Scott. Scot. eng. & naval architect (1808–82).—William Clark. Eng. novel. (1844–1911).

Russia (rŭsh'ȧ), repub. of Europe & Asia; area (1914) 8,417,118 sq. m., p. 171,060.

Ruthenia (rōō-thē'nĭ-ȧ), section of Europe included in Austria & Hungary.

S

Sacramento (săk"rȧ-mĕn'tō), cap. of Cal., p. 75.—riv., Cal., 500 m. to San Francisco bay.

Saginaw (săg'ĭ-nô), city, Mich., p. 67.

Saguenay (săg'ĕ-nā), riv., Quebec, 100 m. to St. Lawrence.

Sahara (sȧ-hä'rȧ), desert, N. Africa, 2,000,000 sq. m.; Fr. possession.

St. Gaudens (gô'dĕnz), Augustus. Am. sculp. (1848–1907).

St.-Gobain (gō"băn'), forest in Fr., whence Germans shelled Paris, 60 miles distant, with long-range gun, 1918.

St. Helena (hē-lē'nȧ), Br. isl., Atlantic oc.; Napoleon exiled.

St. Joseph, city, Mo., on Missouri riv., p. 84.

St. Lawrence, riv. of Can., 775 m., Lake Ontario to Gulf of St. Lawrence.—**Gulf of,** inlet of N. Atlantic.

St. Louis (lōō'ĭ; lōō'ĭs), city, Mo., on Mississippi, p. 757.

St.-Mihiel (săṅ"mē"yĕl'), town in N. E. France; captured by Americans, 1918.

St. Paul, cap. of Minn., on Mississippi riv., p. 255.

St. Petersburg. Former name of Petrograd, cap. of Russ.

St.-Quentin (săṅ"kăṅ"tăṅ'), town N. E. Fr., p. 56; battles, 1914–18.

Saint Saens (săṅ"säṅs'), Charles Camille. Fr. composer (1835–).

Saint Simon (săṅ"sē"môn'), Claude Henry, Comte de. Fr. religious-socialist (1760–1825).

Sakhalin (sä"kȧ-lyēn'), or **Saghalien,** isl. off E.Siberia; Russ. & Jap.; 29,100 sq. m., p. 56.

Salamanca (săl"ȧ-măṅ'kȧ), prov. of Sp., 4,829 sq. m., p. 321.—cap. of prov., p. 26.

Salem (sā'lĕm), sp. city, Mass., p. 50; birthplace of Hawthorne.

Salford (säl'fẽrd), city, Lancs., Eng., p. 235.

Salisbury (sôls'brĭ), Robert Cecil, Marquis of. Br. stsm. (1830–1903).—**Plain,** tract of country Wiltshire, Eng., 20 m. by 14 m.; military camp, 1914–18.

Sallust (săl'ŭst). Rom. hist. (86–34 B. C.).

Saloniki (sä"lō-nē'kĭ) [anc. Thessalonica], sp. city in Balkans, on Ægean sea; Gr. since 1913; p. 160.

Salt Lake City, cap. of Utah, p. 120; metropolis of Mormons.

Salvador (säl"vȧ-dōr'), repub. of Cen. Am., 7,212 sq. m., p. 1,116; cap. San Salvador.

Samaria (sȧ-mā'rĭ-ȧ), anc. town of Palestine, former cap. Israel, 36 m. N. N. W. of Jerusalem; now village of Sebustieh.

Sambre (säṅ'br), riv. of N. Fr.; battles, 1914–18.

Samoa (sä-mō'ä), U. S. & Br. isls. in S. Pacific, 1,700 sq. m., p. 40.

Sampson (sămp'sŭn), William Thomas. Am. naval off. (1840–1902).

San Antonio (săn ăn-tō'nĭ-ō), city, Texas, p. 125.

Sand (sănd), George [Amantine Dudevant]. Fr. novel. (1804–76).

San Francisco (săn frăn-sĭs'kō), sp. city, Cal., p. 417.

San Salvador (săl'vȧ-dôr), cap. of Salvador, Cen. Am., p. 60.

Santiago (săn"tē ä'gō), cap. of Chile, p. 378.—sp. town, Cuba, p. 62; battle, 1898.

Santo Domingo (săn'tō dō-mĭṅ'gō), repub. Haiti, 19,300 sq. m., p. 708. Also, **Dominican Republic.**

San Francisco (souṅ frăṅ-sēs'kō), riv. E. Brazil, 1,800 m. to Atlantic.

Sappho (săf'ō). Gr. poet (about 600 B. C.).

Sarajevo (sẽr-ä-jē-vō), town in Bosnia, where occurred assassination of Austrian archduke, starting the War of 1914–18.

Sardinia (sär-dĭn'ĭ-ȧ), It. isl. in Medit., 9,350 sq. m., p. 792.

Sardou (sär"dōō'), Victorien. Fr. dram. (1831–1908).

Sargent (sär'gĕnt), John Singer. Am. painter in Eng. (1856–).

Sarto (sär'tō), Andrea del. Florentine painter (1486–1531).

Saskatchewan (săs-kăch'ĕ-wŏn), prov. of Can., 250,650 sq. m., p. 493.—riv. of Can. Rocky mts., 1,300 m. to Lake Winnepeg.

Savannah (sȧ-văn'ȧ), city, Ga., on Savannah riv., p. 65.—riv. Ga., 400 m. to Atlantic oc.

Savonarola (sä"vō-nȧ-rō'lȧ), Girolamo. It. monk (1452–98).

Saxony (săks'ŭn-ĭ), kingdom of Ger. empire, 5,786 sq. m., p. 4,800; cap. Dresden.

Scanderbeg (skăn'dẽr-bĕg). Prince of Albania (1404–67).

Scandinavia (skăn"dĭ-nā'vĭ-ȧ), anc. name of Den., Swe., & Nor.; more recently of Swe. & Nor. alone.

Schiller (shĭl'ẽr), Johann Friedrich Christoph von. Ger. poet (1759–1805).

Schleswig-Holstein (shlĕs'vĭkh-hōl'shtīn), former prov. of Den.; annexed by Ger. 1864.

Schley (shlī), Winfield Scott. Am. naval off. (1839–1911).

Schofield (skō'fēld), John McAllister. Am. soldier (1831–1906).

Schomberg (shŏm'bẽrg), Frederick Hermann, Duke of. Ger.-Eng. soldier in Ire. (1619–90).

Schopenhauer (shō'pĕn-hou"ẽr), Arthur. Ger. philos. (1788–1860).

Schubert (shōō'bẽrt), Franz. Austrian composer (1797–1828).

Schumann (shōō'män). Saxon composer (1810–56).

Schumann-Heink (hīngk). Bohemian contralto (1861–).

Schurz (shŭrz), Carl. Ger.-Am. soldier (1829–1906).

Schuyler (skī'lẽr), Philip. Am. soldier (1733–1804).

Schuylkill (skōōl'kĭl), riv. of Pa., 120 m. to Delaware riv.

Scipio (sĭp'ĭ-ō), **the Elder.** Rom. gen. (235–183 B. C.).—**the Younger.** Rom. gen. (187–129 B. C.).

Scotland (skŏt'lănd), N. div. of Gr. Br., 30,400 sq. m., p. 4,800.

Scott (skŏt), Winfield. Am. gen. (1786–1866).

Scranton (skrăn'tŭn), city, Pa., on Lackawanna riv., p. 136.
Seattle (sē-ăt''l), sp. city, Wash., p. 237.
Sebastopol (sē-băs'tō-pōl), Russ. town, Black sea, p. 77; naval station.
Sedan (sē'dăṅ'), town, dept. of Ardennes, Fr., p. 16; surrender Napoleon III, 1870; occupied by Americans November, 1918.
Seine (sāṅ), riv. of Fr., 480 m. to Eng. channel.—dept. of Fr., 185 sq. m., p. 3,848.
Selkirk (sĕl'kirk), Alexander. Scot. buccaneer (1676–1723).
Seneca (sĕn'ē-kȧ), Lucius Annæus. Rom. philos. (3–66).—lake, W. N. Y., 37 m. long.
Serbia (sẽr'bĭ-ȧ), kingdom of Europe; occupied by Central Powers 1915–18; area (1914) 33,900 sq. m., p. 4,594; cap. Belgrade.
Servetus (sẽr-vē'tŭs), Miguel. Sp. theolog. & anat. (1509–53).
Seton (sē'tŭn), Ernest Thompson. Can. novel. & nature lover (1860–).
Severn (sĕv'ẽrn), riv., Eng., 210 m. to Bristol channel.
Severus (sē-vē'rŭs). Rom. emp. (146–211).
Seville (sē-vĭl'), city, Sp., on Guadalquivir, p. 555.
Seward (sōō'ẽrd), William Henry. Am. stsm. (1801–77).
Shackleton (shăk''l-tŭn), Sir Ernest Henry. Br. Antarctic explorer (1869–).
Shafter (shăf'tẽr), William Ryfus. Am. soldier (1833–1906).
Shaftesbury (shăfts'bŭr-ĭ), Anthony, Earl of. Eng. monarchist (1621–83).
Shakespeare (shāks'pẽr), William. Eng. dram. & poet (1564–1616).
Shanghai (shăng'hī), sp. city, China, p. 639.
Shantung (shăn-tŭng'), prov. of China, 65,000 sq. m., p. 37,500; cap. Tse-nan-foo.
Shaw (shô), Anna Howard. Am. suffragist (1847–).—George Bernard. Irish dram., wit & publicist (1856–).
Sheffield (shĕf'fēld), bor. Yorkshire, Eng., p. 477.
Shelley (shĕl'ĭ), Percy Bysshe. Eng. poct (1792–1821).
Sheridan (shĕr'ĭ-dȧn), Philip Henry. Am. gen. (1831–88).—Richard Brinsley. Br. dram. (1751–1816).
Sherman (shẽr'mȧn), James Schoolcraft. Vice-Pres. U. S. (1855–1912).—John. Am. stsm. (1823–1900).—William Tecumseh. Am. gen. (1820–91).—Roger. Am. polit. (1721–93).
Shropshire (shrŏp'shẽr), co. of Eng., p. 246.
Siam (sī-ăm'), kingdom of Asia, 195,000 sq. m., p. 8,118; cap. Bangkok.
Siberia (sī-bē'rĭ-ȧ), section of Asiatic Russ., 4,832,000 sq. m., p. 10,378.
Sicily (sĭs'ĭ-lĭ), isl. Medit. sea, part of Italy, 10,000 sq. m., p. 3,672; cap. Palermo.
Sickles (sĭk''lz), Daniel Edgar. Am. soldier (1825–1914).
Siddons (sĭd'ŭnz), Sarah. Br. act. (1755–1831).
Sidney (sĭd'nĭ), Algernon. Eng. antiroyalist (1622–83).—Sir Philip. Eng. soldier & stsm. (1554–86).
Sienkiewicz (shĕn-kyā'vĭch), Henry. Pol. novel. (1845–1916).
Sierra Leone (sĭ-ĕr'rȧ lē-ō'nē), Br. colony & protectorate, W. Africa, 31,000 sq. m., p. 1,480.
Sierra Nevada (sĭ-ĕr'rȧ nē-vä'dȧ), mt. range, Cal., 400 m.; Mt. Whitney, 14,898 ft.
Sigsbee (sĭgz'bē), Charles Dwight. Am. naval off. (1845–).
Silesia (sĭ-lē'shĭ-ȧ), ter. of cen. Europe, annexed by Austria 1675; greater part ceded to Prussia 1763; 1,987 sq. m., p. 757.
Sims (sĭmz), William Sowden. Am. naval off. (1858–).
Singapore (sĭṅ'gȧ-pōr'), cap. of Straits Settlements; commercial cen. S. E. Asia, p. 359.
Sixtus V (sĭks'tŭs), Felix Peretti. Pope & stsm. (1521–90).
Skager Rack (skä'gẽr-răk'), arm of N. sea; bet. Nor. & Den.; 130 m. long, 80 broad.
Slave Lake, in N. W. Can., 300 m. by 60.
Sligo (slī'gō), co. of Ire., 707 sq. m., p. 84.
Slocum (slō'kŭm), Henry Warner. Am. soldier (1827–94).
Smiles (smīlz), Samuel. Eng. essay. (1845–1904).
Smith, Adam. Br. author (1723–90).—Francis Hopkinson. Am. author & artist (1838–1915).—Goldwin. Can. hist. (1823–1910).—John. One of the founders of Va. colony (1580–1631).
Smolensk (smȯ-lyĕnsk'), govt. in Russia, W. of Moscow, 21,632 sq. m., p. 1,763.
Smolett (smŏl'ĕt), Tobias George. Br. novel. (1721–71).
Smyrna (smẽr'nȧ), sp. city, Asia Minor, p. 375.
Socinus (sō-sī'nŭs), Lælius (1525–62); & Faustus (1539–1604). It. theologs.
Socrates (sŏk'rȧ-tēz). Gr. philos. (469–399 B. C.).
Solomon Islands (sŏl'o-mŏn), group, Pacific oc., 17,000 sq. m., p. 200.
Somaliland (sō-mä'lē-lănd), section E. Africa; Br., 68,000 sq. m., p. 300; Fr., 40,000 sq. m.; It., 140,000 sq. m.
Somerset (sŭm'ẽr-sĕt), co. S. W. Eng., p. 458.
Somerville (sŭm'ẽr-vĭl), city, Mass., on Mystic riv., p. 77.
Somme (sôm), riv. N. Fr., 150 m. to Eng. channel.—dept. Fr., 2,443 sq. m., p. 520.
Sophocles (sŏf'ō-klēz). Athenian dram. (496–406 B. C.).
Sousa (sōō'zȧ), John Philip. Am. bandmaster & composer (1854–).
South Africa. See **Union of South Africa.**
South America. See **America.**
Southampton (south-ămp'tŏn), bor. Hampshire, Eng., p. 120.
South Australia, state in Commonwealth of Australia, 380,000 sq. m., p. 409; cap. Adelaide.
South Bend, city, Ill., on St. Joseph riv., p. 54.
South Carolina, state of U. S., 30,495 sq. m., p. 1,516; cap. Columbia.
South Dakota (dȧ-kō'tȧ), state of U. S., 77,615 sq. m., p. 584; cap. Pierre.
Southey (south'ĭ), Robert. Eng. poet (1774–1843).
South Island, largest isl. of New Zealand, 58,500 sq. m.
South Pole, reached by Amundsen, 1911.
Spain (spān), kingdom of Europe, on Atl. & Bay of Biscay, 194,783 sq. m., p. 20,000; cap. Madrid.
Sparta (spär'tȧ), anc. capital of Laconia, Peloponnesus.
Spencer (spĕn'sẽr), Herbert. Eng. philos. (1820–1903).
Spenser (spĕn'sẽr), Edmund. Eng. poet (1552–99).
Spinoza (spē-nō'zȧ), Baruch. Dutch-Jewish philos. (1632–77).
Spitzbergen (spĭts-bẽr'gĕn), Arctic archipelago.
Spokane (spō-kăn'), city, Wash., on Spokane riv., p. 105.
Springfield (spring'fēld), city, Mass., on Connecticut riv., p. 89.

Spring-Rice, Sir Cecil Arthur. Br. dipl. (1859–1918).
Stafford (stăf'ẽrd), co. of Eng., p. 1,280.
Stainer (stān'ẽr), Sir John. Eng. composer (1840–1901).
Stanislas (stăn'ĭs-läs), **I** king of Poland 1704–09 & 1733 (1677–1766).—**II,** king of Poland 1764–95 (1732–98).
Stanley (stăn'lĭ), Sir Henry Morton. Br. explor. in Africa (1841–1904).
Stanton (stăn'tŭn), Edwin McMasters. Am. stsm. (1814–69).—Elizabeth Cady. Am. suffragist (1815–1902).
Staten Island (stăt'ĕn), isl. N. Y. bay, constituting bor. of N. Y., 70 sq. m.
Stead (stĕd), William Thomas. Eng. journ. (1849–1912).
Steele (stēl), Sir Richard. Eng. essay. (1672–1729).
Stefansson (stă'fdns-sŏn), Vilhjalmur. Can. explor. in Arctic (1879–).
Stephen, name of 9 popes.
Stephens (stē'vĕnz), Alexander Hamilton. Am. stsm. (1812–83).
Stephenson (stē'vn-sŭn), George. Eng. eng. & inv. (1781–1848).
Sterne (stẽrn), Laurence. Br. humor. (1713–68).
Steuben (stū'bĕn), Friedrich Wilhelm von, Baron. Ger.-Am. soldier (1730–94).
Stevens (stē'vĕns), Edwin Augustus. Am. R. R. organizer, founder Stevens Inst. of Tech., Hoboken, N. J. (1795–1868).
Stevenson (stē'vĕn-sŭn), Robert Louis Balfour. Scot. novel., essay. & poet (1850–94).—Adlai E. Vice-Pres. U. S. (1835–1914).
Stirling (stẽr'lĭng), co. of Scot., 451 sq. m., p. 161.
Stockholm (stŏk'hŏlm), cap. of Swe., p. 343.
Stockton (stŏk'tŭn), Frank R. Am. novel. (1834–1902).—Robert Field. Am. naval off. (1795–1866).
Stoke-on-Trent, city, Staffordshire, Eng., p. 242.
Stone (stōn), William Joel. Am. stsm. (1848–1918).
Story, Joseph. Am. jurist (1779–1845).—William Wetmore. Am. sculp. (1819–95).
Stowe (stō), Harriet Beecher. Am. novel. & abolitionist (1811–96); pub. *Uncle Tom's Cabin*, 1852.
Stradivari (strä"dē-vä'rī), Antonio. Cremona violin maker (1644–1737).
Strafford (străf'ŭrd), Thomas Wentworth, Earl of. Eng. stsm. (1593–1641).
Straits Settlements, Br. colony S. Malay pen. & isls., 1,600 sq. m., p. 722.
Strasbourg (sträs'bōōr; GER. shträs'bŭrkh), former Fr. city, dept. of Bas-Rhin, annexed by Ger. 1871 & made cap. of Alsace-Lorraine, p. 170.
Stratford-on-Avon (ā'vŏn), bor. & town, Warwickshire, Eng., p. 8; Shakespeare's birthplace.
Strathcona and Mount Royal, Donald Alexander Smith, Baron. Can. R. R. builder (1820–1914).
Strauss (strous), Johann (1804–49).—Johann, son of former (1825–99). Austrian composers.—Richard. Ger. composer (1864–).
Stuart (stū'drt), Scot. & Eng. royal family.—Gilbert. Am. painter (1755–1828).—James Ewell Brown. Am. Confed. soldier (1833–64).
Stuyvesant (stī'vē-sdnt), Peter. Dutch colonial governor of New Netherland (1592–1672).
Suckling (sŭk'lĭng), Sir John. Eng. poet (1609–42).
Sudan (sōō-dän'), region of N. Africa, bet. Red sea & Atl. oc.; Anglo-Egyptian Sudan, 984,520 sq. m., p. 3,000.
Suez (sōō-ĕz'), **Isthmus of,** connects Medit. with Red sea, 100 m. long; **Canal,** built by Fr., now controlled by Gr. Br.
Suffolk (sŭf'ŏk), co. of Eng., p. 394.
Sulla (sŭl'd), Lucius Cornelius. Rom. gen. & stsm. (138–78 B. C.).
Sullivan (sŭl'ĭ-vdn), Sir Arthur Seymour. Eng. composer (1842–1900).—John. Am. soldier (1740–95).—John L. Am. pugilist & temperance lecturer (1858–1918).—Robert Baldwin. Can. stsm. (1802–53).
Sully (sŭl'ĭ), Maximilien de Bethune, Duc de. Marshal of Fr., minister of Henry IV (1560–1641).—Thomas. Am. painter (1783–1872).
Sulu (sōō-lōō'), U. S. isl. group of Philippine isls., 1,561 sq. m., p. 75.
Sumatra (sōō-mä'trd), one of Sunda isls., Dutch East Indies, 160,000 sq. m., p. 4,000.
Sumner (sŭm'nẽr), Charles. Am. stsm. (1811–74).—Edwin Vose. Am. soldier (1797–1863).
Sumter (sŭm'tẽr), Thomas. Am. soldier (1734–1832).
Sunda Islands (sŭn'dd), isls. of Malay archipelago.
Sunday, William Ashley, known as "Billy Sunday." Am. evangelist (1863–).
Sunderland (sŭn-dẽr-lănd), sp. city, Durham, Eng., p. 152.
Superior (sū-pē'rĭ-ŭr), **Lake,** largest of the great lakes of N. Am., bet. U. S. & Can., 412 m. long.
Surrey (sŭr'ĭ), co. of Eng., p. 846.
Susquehanna (sŭs"kwē-hăn'nd), riv. of Pa., rises Otsego Lake, N. Y., 500 m. to Chesapeake bay.
Sussex (sŭs'ĕks), co. of Eng., p. 663.
Sutlej (sŭt'lĕj), riv. of N. Hindustan; 900 m. fr. Tibet to Indus riv.
Swansea (swŏn'sĭ), sp. city, Glamorgan, S. Wales, p. 121.
Swaziland (swä'zē-lănd), Br. protectorate, S. Africa, 6,536 sq. m., p. 107.
Sweden (swē'dĕn), kingdom N. Europe, 172,900 sq. m., p. 5,500.
Swedenborg (bôrg), Emanuel. Swedish scientist & theolog. (1688–1772).
Swift, Jonathan [Dean Swift]. Eng. satirist (1667–1745); b. Dublin.
Swinburne (swĭn'bŭrn), Algernon Charles. Eng. poet (1837–1909).
Switzerland (swĭt'zŭr-lănd), repub. cen. Europe, 15,950 sq. m., p. 3,800.
Sydney (sĭd'nĭ), cap. of New South Wales, p. 636.
Sylvester (sĭl'vĕs-tẽr), name of 2 popes: **I,** pope 314–335; **II,** pope 999–1003.—James Joseph. Eng. math. (1814–97).
Synge (sĭng), John Millington. Irish dram. (1871–1909).
Syracuse (sĭr'd-kūs), city, N. Y., on Erie canal, p. 138.—anc. city of Sicily.
Syria (sĭr'ĭ-d), region of Asia bet. Euphrates riv. & Medit. sea, consisting of East Syria (see **Mesopotamia**), Syrian Desert, and Syria proper, including former Turkish provs. of Jerusalem, Beirut, Aleppo, Lebanon, Syria & Zor.

T

Tabriz (tȧ-brēz'), town of Persia, cap. of Azerbaijan prov., p. 200.
Tacitus (tăs'ĭ-tŭs), Marcus Claudius. Rom. emp. (200–276).—Publius Cornelius. Rom. hist. (55–117).
Tacoma (tȧ-kō'md), city, Wash., p. 84.

Taft (tăft), William Howard. 27th pres. of U. S. 1909–13 (1857–).
Tagliamento (tăl-yä-mĕn'tō), riv. N. E. It., Venetian Alps, 100 m. to Gulf of Venice.
Tagore (tȧ-gōr'), Sir Rabindranath. Hindu poet (1860–).
Tagus (tā'gŭs; Sp. **Tajo**), riv. Sp. & Port., 565 m. to Atlantic oc.
Tahiti (tä'hē-tē), one of Society isls., S. Pacific, 600 sq. m., p. 11.
Taine (tān), Hippolyte Adolphe. Fr. hist. (1828–93).
Talleyrand (tȧ'lā'räṅ'), Charles Maurice [Perigord], Duc de. Fr. stsm. (1754–1838).
Talmage (tăl'māj), Thomas DeWitt. Am. clergy. (1832–1902).
Tamerlane, Mongol conqueror (1336–1405). Also, **Timur**.
Tandy (tăn'dĭ), James Napper. Irish agitator (1740–1803).
Taney (tô'nĭ), Roger Brooke. Am. jurist (1777–1864).
Tanganyika (tăn'găn-yē'kȧ), lake, cen. Africa, 400 m. long.
Tangier (tăn-jēr'), chief sp. of Morocco, p. 40.
Tarleton (tärl'tŏn), Sir Banastre. Eng. soldier in Am. (1754–1833).
Tasmania (tăs-mā'nĭ-ȧ), isl. & state of Australia, 26,215 sq. m., p. 191; cap. Hobart.
Tasso (tä'sō), Torquato. It. poet (1544–95).
Taylor (tā'lẽr), Bayard. Am. poet & travel writer (1825–78).—Henry Clay. Am. naval off. (1842–1904).—Jeremy. Eng. prelate (1613–67).—Zachary. 12th pres. of U. S. (1784–1850).
Tchaikovsky (chī-kŏf'skĭ), Peter Ilyitch. Russ. composer (1840–93).
Tecumseh (tē-kŭm'sē). Indian chief (1775–1813).
Teheran (tĕ-hē-rän'), cap. of Persia, p. 250.
Tehuantepec (tā-wän'tā-pĕk'), isth. of S. Mex., 130 m.
Teneriffe (tĕn'ẽr-ĭf'), one of Canary isls., 782 sq. m., p. 180.
Teniers (tĕ'nyā'), David. Flemish painter (1610–90).
Tennessee (ten'nĕs-sē'), state of U. S., 42,000 sq. m., p. 2,185; cap. Nashville.—riv., S. W. Va., 1,200 m. to Ohio riv.
Tenniel (tĕn-nēl'), Sir John. Eng. painter (1820–).
Tennyson (tĕn'ĭ-sŏn), Alfred, Baron. Eng. poet (1809–92).
Terence (tĕr'ĕns), Publius Afer. Rom. writer of comedies (185–159 B. C.).
Terre Haute (tĕr-rē-hōt'), city, Ind., p. 58.
Terry (tĕr'ĭ), Ellen Alicia. Eng. act. (1848–).
Tertullian (tẽr-tŭl'lĭ-ȧn), Quintus Septimus Florens. Latin father (about 200).
Tesla (tĕs'lȧ), Nikola. Am. electrician (1857–).
Texas (tĕks'ȧs), state of U. S., 265,780 sq. m., p. 3,897; cap. Austin.
Thackeray (thăk'ẽr-ĭ), William Makepeace. Eng. novel. (1811–63).
Thames (tĕmz), riv., Eng., 250 m. to North sea; traverses London.—riv., Ontario, Can., 160 m. to Lake St. Clair.
Thebes (thēbz), city of anc. Egypt, on Nile riv.—city of Bœotia, anc. Gr.
Themistocles (thē-mĭs'tŏk-lēz). Athenian gen. (514–449 B. C.).
Theocritus (thē-ŏk'rĭ-tŭs). Gr. bucolic poet (310–245 B. C.).
Theodoric (thē-ŏd'ō-rĭk), **the Great**. Founder of Ostrogothic kingdom in Italy (454–526).
Theodosius (thē'ō-dō'shĭ-ŭs). Rom. emp. (346–395).
Theophrastus (thē'ō-frăs'tŭs). Gr. philos. (?–287 B. C.).
Thiers (tē'âr'), Adolph. Fr. stsm. & hist. (1797–1877).
Thomas (tŏm'ȧs), George Henry. Am. soldier (1816–70).—Theodore. Am. orchestra leader (1835–1905).
Thoreau (thō'rō), Henry David. Am. naturalist & essay. (1817–62).
Thorwaldsen (tôr'väld-zĕn), Bertel. Dan. sculp. (1770–1844).
Thucydides (thū-sĭd'ĭ-dēz). Gr. hist. (?–399 B. C.).
Tiber (tī'bẽr), riv. of Italy, 245 m. to Tyrrhenian sea.
Tiberius (tī-bē'rĭ-ŭs). Rom. emp. (42 B. C.–37 A. D.).
Tibet (tĭb'ĕt), or **Thibet**, prov. of Cen. Asia, suzerainty of China, 463,000 sq. m., p. 3,500.
Tien-tsin (tyĕn'tsĭn'), city & treaty port, Chih-li, China, p. 850.
Tiepolo (tē-ā'pō-lō), Giovanni Battista. Venetian painter (1696–1770).
Tierra del Fuego (tē-ĕr'rȧ dĕl fwā'gō), isls. S. end S. Am.; main isl., 18,500 sq. m.; Chile & Argentina.
Tigris (tī'grĭs), riv., Mesopotamia, 950 m. to Euphrates, to Persian Gulf.
Tilden (tĭl'dĕn), Samuel Jones. Am. stsm. (1814–86).
Tillman (tĭl'măn), Benjamin Ryan. Am. polit. (1847–1918).
Tilsit (tĭl'sĭt), town, E. Prussia, on Niemen riv., p. 35.
Timur (tē-mōōr'), or **Tamerlane**, Mongol conqueror (1336–1405).
Tintoretto (tĭn'tôr-ĕt'ō), Il [Giacomo Robusti]. Venetian painter (1518–94).
Tissot (tēs'sō'), James Joseph Jacques. Fr. painter (1836–1902).
Tisza (tĭs'sȯ), Istvan, Count. Hungarian premier, 1903–05 & 1913–17 (1861–1918).
Titian (tĭsh'ȧn). Venetian painter (1477–1576).
Titus (tī'tŭs), Flavius Sabinus Vespasianus. Rom. emp. (40–81 A. D.).
Tocqueville (tŏk'vēl'), Alexis Charles Henri de. Fr. stsm. & writer (1805–59).
Togoland, ter. on Gulf of Guinea, W. Africa, 33,700 sq. m., p. 1,000; Ger. colony prior to 1914.
Tokyo (tō'kĭ-ō), formerly Yedo, cap. of Japan, p. 2,225.
Toledo (tō-lē'dō), city, Lucas co., O., p. 168.—(tō-lā'thō), city of Sp., on Tagus riv., p. 25.
Tolstoy (tŏl-stoi'), Leo. Russ. novel. & social reformer (1828–1910).
Tombigbee (tŏm-bĭg'bē), riv. of Ala., 450 m. to Mobile bay.
Tonga (tŏṅ'gȧ), isls. in Pacific oc., Polynesia, p. 24; Br. protec.—district of Zululand, S. E. Africa, included in Natal.
Tongking (tŏn'kĕn'), Fr. protectorate in Indo-China, 46,000 sq. m., p. 6,118.
Toronto (tō-rŏn'tō), cap. of Ontario, Can., on Lake Ontario, p. 376.
Torquemada (tôr'kȧ-mä'thä), Tomas de. Sp. Inquisitor gen. (1420–98).
Toul (tōōl), town, dept. of Meurthe-et-Moselle, Fr., p. 14.
Toulon (tōō'lôṅ'), city of Fr. on Medit. sea, p. 105.
Tourcoing (tōōr'kwăṅ'), city, dept. of Nord, Fr., p. 82.
Toussaint (tōō'săṅ'), François Dominique [L'Ouverture]. Haitian soldier & stsm. (1743–1803).
Townshend (toun'shĕnd), Charles Vere Ferrers. Br. soldier in Mesopotamia 1914–18 (1861–).

Trafalgar (trá-făl'gár), **Cape.** S. Spain, at entrance Gibraltar Strait; naval battle, 1805.

Trajan (trā'ján), Marcus Ulpius. Rom. emp. (51–117).

Transcaucasia (trăns"kô-kā'shĭ-á), section of Russ., S. Caucasus, 95,405 sq. m., p. 7,000.

Transvaal (trăns-väl'), state in Union of S. Africa, 110,400 sq. m., p. 1,686.

Transylvania (tran"sĭl-vē'nĭ-á), Hungarian crownland, 21,518 sq. m., p. 2,678.

Travancore (trăv"ăn-kōr'), native state Br. India, prov. of Madras, 7,000 sq. m., p. 3,430.

Trebizond (trĕb'ĭ-zŏnd), city, Asiatic Turkey, on Black sea, p. 55.

Tree, Sir Herbert Beerbohm. Eng. act. (1853–1917).

Treitschke (trītsh'kĕ), Heinrich. Ger. militarist writer (1834–96).

Trent (trĕnt; It. **Trento**), town of It. Tirol, Austria, on Adige riv., p. 30.

Trenton (trĕn'tŭn), cap. of N. J., on Delaware riv., p. 97.

Triest (trē-ĕst'), sp. of Austria, on Adriatic, p. 161.

Trinidad (trĭn"ĭ-dăd'), Br. isl., W. Indies, 1,754 sq. m., p., with Tobago, 330.

Tripoli (trĭp'ō-lĭ), country, N. Africa, under It. sovereignty since 1911, p. 523.

Trollope (trŏl'ŭp), Anthony. Eng. novel. (1815–82).

Troy (troi), city, N. Y., on Hudson riv., p. 77.

Troyon (trwä"yôn'), Constant. Fr. painter (1810–65).

Trumbull (trŭm'bŏŏl), James Hammond. Am. philol. (1821–97).—John. Am. painter (1756–1843).

Truxtun (trŭks'tŭn), Thomas. Am. naval off. (1755–1822).

Tryon (trī'ŭn), Sir George. Br. admiral (1832–93).

Tsarskoye Selo (tsär'skō-yĕ syĕ'lō; "the czar's village"), town in govt. of Petrograd, Russ., p. 31.

Tsing-tau (tsing-tou'), city of China, annexed with Kiaochow by Japan 1914.

Tulane (tū-lān'), Paul. Am. philan.; founder Tulane Univ., New Orleans (1801–87).

Tunis (tū'nĭs), Fr. protectorate in N. Africa, 50,000 sq. m., p. 1,930.

Tupper (tŭp'ĕr), Sir Charles. Can. stsm. (1821–1915).

Turenne (tü"rĕn'), Henri de Latour, Vicomte de. Marshal of Fr. (1611–75).

Turgenev (tŏŏr-gĕn'yĕf), Ivan Sergeyevitch. Russ. novel. (1818–83).

Turin (tū'rĭn; It. **Torino**), city on Po riv., It., p. comm. 428.

Turkestan (tûr'kĕ-stän), region Cen. Asia.—Russ., 420,807 sq. m., p. 6,417.—Chinese, p. 2,000.

Turkey (tûr'kĭ), empire, Europe & Asia, 695,000 sq. m., p. 20,000. (Revised figures of 1919 following Great War not yet available.)

Turner (tûr'nĕr), Joseph Mallord William. Eng. painter (1775–1851).

Tutuila (tōō"tōō-ē'lā), isl., Am. Samoa, 40 sq. m., p. 7.

Twain, Mark. See **Clemens, Samuel L.**

Tweed, riv. of Scot., 97 m. to North sea.

Tyler (tī'lĕr), John. 10th pres. of U. S. (1790–1862).—Wat. Eng. revolutionist (?–1381).

Tyndall (tĭn'dál), John. Br. physicist (1820–93).

Tyne (tīn), riv., N. Eng., 80 m. to North sea.

Tyrconnel (tĕr-kŏn'ĕl), Richard Talbot, Earl. Irish Jacobite (1639–91).

Tyrone (tĭ-rōn'), co. of Ulster, Ire., p. 143.

Tzi-Hi (tsē-hē'). Empress dowager of China (1834–1908).

U

Uganda (ū-găn'dá), Br. protectorate in Africa, 109,120 sq. m., p. 2,888.

Ukraine (yū'krān), section of S. W. Russ.; separated in 1917, during Great War.

Ulster (ŭl'stĕr), N. prov. of Ire., 8,567 sq. m., p. 1,581.

Union of South Africa, commonwealth within Br. empire, comprising Cape Province, Transvaal, Natal, & Orange.

United Kingdom, or **British Isles,** comprising Gr. Britain & Ire.

United States, federal repub. of N. Am., 3,026,789 sq. m.; including possessions 3,743,306 sq. m., p. 110,000; cap. Washington.

Ural (yū'rál), mts. in Russ., bet. Europe & Asia, 5,000 ft. high.

Urban (ûr'bán), name of 8 popes.

Uruguay (yū'rū-gwā), repub. of S. Am., 72,153 sq. m., p. 1,346; cap. Montevideo.—riv. of S. Am., 900 m. to Plata.

Utah (yū'tä), state of U. S., 84,990 sq. m., p. 439; cap. Salt Lake City.

Utica (yū'tĭ-ká), city, N. Y., p. 74.—anc. city of N. Africa.

Utrecht (yū'trĕkt), city of Netherlands, p. 130.

V

Valentinian (văl"ĕn-tĭn'ĭ-án), **I,** Rom. emp. (321–375).—**II,** Rom. emp. (371–392).—**III,** Rom. emp. (419–455).

Valerian (vá-lē'rĭ-án), Publius Licinius. Rom. emp. (?–260).

Valona (vä-lō'nä), sp. city of Albania, on Adriatic.

Valparaiso (văl"pá-rī'sō), sp. city of Chile, p. 191.

Van Buren (văn bū'rĕn), Martin. 8th pres. of U. S. (1782–1862).

Vancouver (văn-kōō'vĕr), city, Br. Columbia, p. 100.—**Island,** part of Br. Columbia, 20,000 sq. m.

Van Dorn (văn dôrn'), Earl. Am. Confed. gen. (1820–63).

Van Dyck (văn dīk'), Sir Anthony. Dutch painter; Eng. school (1599–1641).

Van Dyke (văn dīk'), Henry. Am. author & dipl. (1852–).

Vane (vān), Sir Harry. Eng. stsm. (1613–62).

Velasquez (vā-läs'kāth), Diego Rodriguez. Sp. painter (1599–1660).

Venezuela (vĕn"ĭ-zwē'lá), repub. of S. Am., 398,594 sq. m., p. 2,817; cap. Caracas.

Venice (vĕn'ĭs; It. **Venetia**), sp. city, Italy, p. 168.

Venizelos (vĕn"ē-zā'lōs), Eleutherios. Gr. stsm. (1864–).

Vera Cruz (vĕ'rá krōōs), sp. city, Mex., p. 50.

Verdi (vâr'dē), Giuseppe. It. composer (1813–1901).

Verdun (vĕr"dŭn'), town & fortress, N. E. Fr., battles, 1916–18.

Vereshchagin (vyĕ'rĕsh-chä'gĭn), Vasili Vasilevich. Russ. painter (1842–1904).

Vergil (vĕr'jĭl). Rom. poet (70–19 B. C.). Also, **Virgil.**

Vermont (vĕr-mŏnt'), state of U. S., 9,564 sq. m., p. 365; cap. Montpelier.

Verne (vĕrn), Jules. Fr. novel. (1828–1905).

Veronese (vā"rō-nā'sā), Paul [Cagliari]. It. painter (1528–88).

Vespasian (vĕs-pā'zĭ-ăn). Rom. emp. (9–79).
Vespucci (vĕs-pōō'chē), Amerigo. It. navig. for whom America was named (1451–1512).
Vesuvius (vē-sōō'vĭ-ŭs), volcano, bay of Naples; 4,000 ft. high.
Viaud (vē-yō'), Louis [Pierre Loti]. Fr. novel. (1850–).
Victor Emmanuel, III, king of It. fr. 1900 (1869–).
Victoria. Queen of Gr. Br. & Ire. (1819–1901).—state of Australia, p. 1,316; cap. Melbourne.—**Nyanza,** Lake, E. Africa; 32,000 sq. m.
Vienna (vē-ĕn'ȧ; Ger. **Wien**), cap. of Austria, on Danube riv., p. 2,150.
Vieuxtemps (vyû"tăń'), Henri. Belgian composer (1820–81).
Villiers (vĭl'ĕrs), George, Duke of Buckingham. Eng. stam. (1627–87).
Villon (vē"yôń'), François [Montcorbier]. Fr. poet (1431–?).
Vinci (dä vēn'chē), Leonardo da. It. sculp. & painter (1452–1519).
Virgil (vĭr'jĭl). Rom. poet (70–19 B. C.). Also, Ve gil.
Virginia (vĭr-jĭn'ĭ-ȧ), state of U. S., 42,620 sq. m., p. 2,203; cap. Richmond.
Virgin Islands, Am. isls., formerly Dan. W. Indies: St. Thomas, St. John, & St. Croix.
Vistula (vĭs'tū-lȧ), riv. of Europe, 650 m. to Baltic sea.
Vladivostok (vlăd"ĭ-vŏs-tŏk'), sp. of Asiatic Russ., p. 92.
Volga (vŏl'gȧ), riv. of Russ., 2,400 m. to Caspian sea.
Voltaire (vŏl"târ'), Aronet. Fr. philos. & poet (1694–1778).
Vosges (vōzh), mt. chain bet. Fr. & Ger.

W

Wabash (wô'băsh), riv. Ohio & Ind., 517 m. to Ohio riv.
Wagner (väkh'nĕr), Wilhelm Richard. Ger. composer (1813–83).
Wales (wālz), part of United Kingdom, 7,470 sq. m., p. 1,713.
Wallace (wŏl'ŭs), Alfred Russel. Eng. naturalist (1823–1913).—Sir William. Scot. soldier; national hero (1270–1305).
Walpole (wôl'pōl), Horace. Eng. author (1717–97).—Sir Robert. Eng. stam. (1676–1745).
Ward (wôrd), Artemus [Chas. Farrar Browne]. Am. humorist (1834–67).
Warsaw (wôr'sô), cap. of Poland, on Vistula riv., p. 909; captured by Ger., 1915.
Warwick (wăr'ĭk), co. of Eng., p. 1,247.—Earl of. Eng. stsm. & soldier (1428–71).
Washington (wŏsh'ĭng-tŭn), Booker Taliaferro. Am. negro educ. (1856–1915).—George. Am. soldier; 1st pres. of U. S. (1732–99).—state of U. S., 69,127 sq. m., p. 1,566; cap. Olympia.—city, D. C., cap. of U. S., p. 365.
Waterbury (wô'tĕr-bĕr"ĭ), city, Conn., p. 100.
Waterloo (wô"tĕr-lōō'), vil. Belgium; battle, 1815.
Watt (wŏt), James. Scot. inv. of steam engine (1736–1819).
Watteau (wŏt"ō'), Antoine. Fr. painter (1684–1721).
Watts (wŏts), George Frederick. Eng. painter & sculp. • (1817–1904).—Isaac. Eng. theolog. & hymnist (1674–1748).
Wayne (wān), Anthony. Am. gen. ["Mad Anthony"] (1745–96).
Weber (vē'bĕr), Baron von. Ger. composer (1786–1826).
Webster (wĕb'stĕr), Daniel. Am. stsm. (1782–1852).—Noah. Am. lexicog. (1758–1843).
Weihaiwei (wā'hī'wā'), Br. ter., N. Shantung, China, 300 sq. m., p. 160.
Wellesley (wĕlz'lĭ), town, Mass., p. 5; coll. for women.
Wellington (wĕl'ĭng-tŭn), Duke of. Br. gen. (1769–1852).
Wells (wĕlz), Herbert George. Eng. novel. (1866–).
Wesley (wĕs'lĭ), Charles. Eng. hymnist (1707–88).—John. Eng. clergy.; founder of Methodism (1703–91).
West, Benjamin. Am. painter (1738–1820).
Western Australia, state of Australian Commonwealth, 975,920 sq. m., p. 310.
West Indies (ĭn'dĭz), isl. group, E. of Cen. Am.
West Point, vil. in Orange co., N. Y., on Hudson riv.; U. S. Military Academy.
West Virginia, state of U. S., 24,780 sq. m., p. 1,393; cap. Charleston.
Wexford (wĕks'fĕrd), co. of Leinster, Ire., p. 102.
Wheeler (hwē'lĕr), Joseph. Am. Confed. & U. S. gen. (1836–1906).
Whistler (hwĭs'lĕr), James Abbott McNeill. Am. painter (1834–1903).
White, Edward Douglass. Am. jurist (1845–).
Whitefield (hwĭt'fēld), George. Eng. clergy. (1714–70).
Whitman (hwĭt'măn), Walt. Am. poet (1819–92).
Whitney (hwĭt'nĭ), Eli. Am. inv. of cotton gin (1765–1825).—**Mount,** peak in Sierra Nevada range, Cal., 14,500 ft.
Whittier (hwĭt'ĭ-ĕr), John Greenleaf. Am. poet (1807–92).
Wichita (wĭch'ĭ-tȧ), city, Kans., p. 71.
Wight (wīt), **Isle of,** isl. off S. Eng., p. 88.
Wilberforce (wĭl'bĕr-fōrs), William. Eng. abolitionist (1759–1833).
Wilhelmina (wĭl"hĕl-mī'nȧ). Queen of Netherlands (1880–).
Wilkes-Barre (wĭlks'-băr-ĭ), city, Pa., p. 76.
Willard (wĭl'ărd), Frances E. Am. social reformer & philan. (1839–98).
William (wĭl'yăm), **I,** the Conqueror. King of Eng. (1027–87).—**III,** Prince of Orange & king of Eng. (1650–1702).—**I,** emp. of Ger. (1797–1888).—**II,** emp. of Ger. fr. 1888; abdicated November, 1918 (1859–).
Williams (wĭl'yămz), Roger. Eng. theolog., founder of Rhode Island (1599–1683).
Wilmington (wĭl'mĭng-tŭn), city, Del., p. 106.
Wilson (wĭl'sŭn), Woodrow. 28th pres. of U. S.; attended peace conference in Fr., at conclusion of war of 1914–18; first pres. to visit Europe while holding office. 1856–).
Wiltshire (wĭlt'shĭr), co. of Eng., p. 287.
Windsor (wĭnd'zĕr), name of royal house of Eng.
Windward Islands (wĭnd'wĕrd), group of Br. isls. in W. Indies, p. 164.
Winnipeg (wĭn'ĭ-pĕg), cap. of Manitoba, Can., p. 136.—lake in Can., 260 m. long.
Winslow (wĭnz'lō), Edward. Gov. of Plymouth colony (1595–1655).—John. Am. admiral (1811–73).
Winthrop (wĭn'thrŏp), John. Gov. of Mass. colony (1588–1649).—John. Gov. of Conn. colony (1606–76).
Wisconsin (wĭs-kŏn'sĭn), state of U. S., 55,066 sq. m., p. 2,514; cap. Madison.

Wolfe (wŭlf), James. Eng. gen. (1727–59).
Wolseley (wŭlz-lĭ), Sir Garnet. Br. gen. (1833–1913).
Wolsey (wŭl'zĭ), Thomas. Eng. cardinal (1475–1530).
Woolsey (wŏŏl'sĭ), Theodore Dwight. Am. educ. (1801–89).
Woolwich (wŏŏl'ĭch), bor. of Eng., p. 121; arsenal.
Worcester (wŏŏs'tẽr), co. of Eng., p. 287.—cap. of co., p. 50.—Joseph Emerson. Am. lexicog. (1784–1865).
Wordsworth (wûrdz'wẽrth), William. Eng. poet (1770–1850).
Worth (wûrth), William Jenkins. Am. gen. (1794–1849).
Wren (rĕn), Sir Christopher. Br. architect (1632–1723).
Wright (rīt), Orville (1871–), & his brother, Wilbur (1867–1912). Am. aviators.
Württemberg (vür'tĕm-bĕrkh), kingdom of Ger., 7,536 sq. m., p. 2,438.
Wycliffe (wĭ'klĭf), John. Eng. reformer (?–1384).
Wyoming (wī-ō'mĭng), state of U. S., 97,914 sq. m., p. 182; cap. Cheyenne.

X

Xantippe (zăn-tĭp'ĭ), wife of Socrates.
Xavier (zăv'ĭ-ẽr), Francis. Span. Jesuit missionary (1506–52).
Xenocrates (zē-nŏk'ra-tēz). Gr. phil. (396–314 B. C.).
Xenophon (zĕn'ō-fŏn). Gr. soldier & author (435–355 B. C.).
Xerxes (zẽrks'ēz), king of Persia (?–465 B. C.).

Y

Yangtze-kiang (yăng'tsĕ'kyăng'), riv., China, 3,400 m., Tibet to Pacific oc.
Yeats (yāts), William Butler. Irish author (1865–).
Yellowstone (yĕl'ō-stōn), riv., Wyo. & Mon., 1,000 m. to Missouri riv.—**National Park**, in Wyo., Mon. & Idaho, 3,300 sq. m.
Yenisei (yĕn'ē-sā'ē), riv., Siberia, 3,300 m. to Arctic sea.
Yokohama (yō'kō-hä'mä), sp. city, Japan, p. 394.
Yonkers (yŏṅ'kẽrz), city, N. Y., on Hudson riv., p. 95.
York (yôrk), city, Pa., p. 55.
Yorktown, town, Va.; Cornwallis surrendered 1781.
Yosemite (yō-sĕm'ĭ-tĭ), national park in Cal., 720,000 acres.
Youngstown (yŭngz'toun), city, O., p. 125.
Ypres (ē'pr), town in Belgium; battles, 1914–18.
Yuan-Shi-Kai (yü-än'shē-kī). Pres. of Chinese repub. (1846–1916).
Yukon (yōō'kŏn), ter. of Can., p. 8.—riv., Yukon ter., Can., 2,300 m. to Bering sea.

Z

Zambesi (zäm-bā'zē), riv., Africa, 1,600 m. to Mozambique Channel.
Zangwill (zăng'wĭl), Israel. Eng. novel. (1864–).
Zanzibar (zăn'zĭ-bär), Br. isl. off E. Africa, p. 114.
Zeno (zē'nō). Gr. philos., founder of Stoics (336–264 B. C.).
Zeppelin (zĕp'ĕ-lĭn), Count Ferdinand von. Ger. airship inv. (1838–1917).
Ziska (zĭs'ka), John. Bohemian leader of Hussites (1378–1424).
Zola (zō'lä'), Emile. Fr. novel. (1840–1902).
Zuider Zee (zoi'dẽr zā), arm of North sea in Netherlands.
Zwingli (tsvĭng'lē), Ulrich. Protestant reformer in Switz. (1484–1531).

GLOSSARY OF BUSINESS TERMS.

A 1, a registry mark given to ships in first-class condition; also used to imply excellence: hence, prime; first-class; first-rate. Also, **A number 1.**

acceptance, an agreement by a person on whom a bill of exchange, or draft, is drawn to pay it when due according to the terms of the acceptance: usually made by writing the word *accepted* across the face of the bill, or draft.

accepter, one who agrees to pay a bill of exchange, or draft.

accommodation, a loan of money or credit made as a favor.

accommodation paper, a promissory note made, or indorsed by one person for another without consideration, to enable the other to raise money or obtain credit thereby: as distinguished from a note given for value received.

account, a systematized record of business dealings, or debits and credits; a reckoning of money transactions; as, to keep one's *account* with a bank.

accountant, an expert in keeping or adjusting financial records; a person who has charge of such records in a business, or public office.

account current, an open or running account showing what is due.

account sales, a statement sent by one person to another giving details, as to sales made by the sender on the other's behalf: it usually shows the amount and rate of sales, expenses of freight, commission, and other charges.

acknowledgment, an admission, avowal, or confession of a fact to give it legal force; specifically, such an admission, avowal, or confession made before a duly qualified public officer; the formal certificate issued by an officer before whom an acknowledgment has been made.

actuary, a person engaged in the work of calculating insurance risks and premiums: the statistician of an insurance company.

adjustment, the settlement of a business transaction by the apportionment among the various parties in it of a liability, claim, loss, or payment.

administer, to manage; to carry out; specifically, to settle the estate of one who dies without having made a will.

administrator, one who manages and settles the estate of a person who has died without having made a will.

ad valorem, literally, in proportion to value: used to designate a duty or tax laid upon goods at a certain per cent of their value.

ad valorem duty, a tax, duty, or charge levied upon goods at a certain rate per cent upon their value as stated in their invoice; as distinguished from a specific charge upon a given quantity or number.

advance, an increase in the price, or a rise in price or value; something furnished before an equivalent is received; payment beforehand; the money thus furnished; to pay before due; to increase the price; to raise the market value.

affidavit, a sworn statement; especially, a written declaration, made upon oath, before an authorized public officer.

agent, a person authorized to act for, or in the place of, another, by authority from him; one intrusted with the business of another; a substitute.

agreement, an exchange of promises; a mutual understanding in reference to something that shall be done or omitted.

allowance, a sum granted as a reimbursement or repayment; a deduction from the gross weight or value of goods.

amount gross, the total sum or aggregate.

amount net, the total sum less proper deduction for expenses, discounts, or charges.

annuity, an amount, allowance, or income, especially of money, payable yearly.

appraise, to set a value on; to estimate the worth of; as, to *appraise* goods.

appraisement, setting a value on, or estimating the worth of goods, especially by persons appointed for the purpose.

appraiser, one who sets a value on goods, or estimates their worth.

appreciation, a rise in value, an increase in the market price: opposite to *depreciation.*

appropriation, funds set apart for a specific purpose; especially, a grant of money by a government.

appurtenance, something incidental to another, particularly, property.

arbitrage, the buying and selling of stocks, bills of exchange, etc., for the profit arising from the difference of value of the same thing in different markets at the same time.

arbitration, the hearing and determination of a matter of dispute by a person or persons chosen by the parties concerned.

arbitration of exchange, the process of calculating and determining the difference in money values or rates of exchange among three or more countries, currencies, or markets, for the purpose of a transaction between two through the other.

arbitrator, a person chosen by parties who have a controversy to settle their differences.

article, a single piece of goods; a division of a document, agreement, or contract.

articles of partnership, a written agreement setting forth the purposes and conditions of the association of a number of persons for the carrying on of a joint enterprise; especially, such a written agreement duly carried out according to law and filed so as to have the force of a charter.

assessment, a levy of tax or share of expenses.

assets, the entire property of a person, association, or corporation, applicable to the payment of his or its debts: opposite to *liabilities.*

assignee, a person designated by another to do some act, or enjoy some right, privilege, or property; a person to whom an assignment is made.

assignment, a transfer of title or interest by writing; as, of a note, bond, or lease; especially, a transfer of property in trust or for the benefit of creditors.

assignor, a person who makes an assignment.

association, a body of persons organized for

the prosecution of a business undertaking, usually without a charter, but having the general form and mode of procedure of a corporation; as, a stock company; a society.

assortment, a quantity of goods varying in form, color, style, size, and price.

assurance, an agreement to pay on a contingency or event sure to occur: otherwise used in a sense nearly synonymous with *insurance*.

attachment, taking property into custody by legal process to compel compliance with a judicial decision of a controversy.

attest, to certify; to bear witness to; as, to *attest* the truth of a document, a copy of a record, etc.

attorney, an agent; a counselor; specifically, a legal agent empowered to act for suitors in legal and judicial proceedings.

attorney, power of, written authority for one person to act for another.

auction, a public sale of property to the highest bidder; especially, such a sale by a person licensed and authorized for the purpose.

audit, a formal examination and authentication of accounts, with witnesses and vouchers, etc.; an official settling of accounts; the final statement of account.

auditor, a person authorized to examine accounts, compare charges with vouchers, examine parties and witnesses, allow or reject charges, and state the balance.

average, the mean value; medium quality; a fair sample.

avoid, to defeat, evade; to invalidate.

B

bail, to turn over something in trust under an agreement that the purpose of the delivery shall be faithfully carried out.

bailee, the person to whom goods are committed in trust, and who has a conditional possession of them.

bailment, a delivery of goods by one person to another in trust for some special purpose.

balance, the difference between the debits and credits of an account; to adjust and settle such a difference.

balance sheet, a written statement giving a summary and the balances of a set of accounts.

bale, a large, closely pressed, bound package of merchandise; a large bundle or package of goods for storage or transportation.

bank, an establishment for the custody, loan, exchange, or issue of money, and for facilitating the settlement of business transactions by the transmission and collection of funds.

bankable, receivable as good at a bank.

bank book, the depositor's book in which a bank enters his deposits, or his deposit, and withdrawals. Also, **pass book**.

banker, a person or a corporation engaged in the business of banking.

bank discount, a deduction equal to the interest at a given rate on the principal of a note or bill of exchange from the time of discounting until it becomes due.

bank draft, a bill of exchange drawn by one bank on another bank.

bankrupt, one unable to meet his business liabilities.

bargain, a favorable business transaction; an agreement of sale.

barrel, the quantity constituting a full barrel: in the United States, a barrel, liquid measure, is usually 31½ gallons; but a barrel of flour is 196 lbs., of beef or pork, 200 lbs., of fish 200 lbs.

barrel bulk, in freight measurement, five cubic feet.

bear, a speculator who sells stocks, bonds, or other securities for future delivery in expectation of a fall in the market price.

bearer, one who holds and presents for payment a note, bill of exchange, check, or draft.

bearer, payable to, a phrase making notes, bills of exchange, checks, or drafts, payable to holder with or without indorsement.

bill, a general term for all negotiable paper; specifically, a statement of account of goods sold, or services rendered, with price or charge.

bill book, a book in which a person keeps a record of his notes and drafts, thus showing all he issues and receives.

billhead, a printed form of bills or statements of account with business address at the top.

bill of exchange, a written order or request from one person to another to pay to some designated person at a future time a specified sum of money.

bill, domestic or inland, a bill of exchange, or draft, payable in the country where drawn.

bill, foreign, a bill of exchange payable in a foreign country.

bill of lading, a receipt given by a transportation agency to a shipper for goods shipped.

bill of sale, a contract under seal for the sale of goods.

bills payable, bills of exchange, drafts, and notes issued in favor of others.

bills receivable, bills of exchange, drafts, and notes made by others and payable to ourselves.

board of trade, an association of business men to regulate matters of trade and promote their interests.

bolt, a roll of cloth, as of canvas or silk, generally containing about forty yards.

bond, a promise in writing under seal made by a person or corporation to pay a certain sum or do something under penalty of paying a fixed sum on or before a future day; specifically, formal obligation issued by a government or corporation as an evidence of debt, generally for the purpose of borrowing money.

bonded goods, goods on which import duties or taxes have been met by bonds instead of cash.

bonded warehouse, warehouses owned by persons approved by the Treasury Department, and under bond or guarantee for the strict observance of the revenue laws; utilized for storing goods or merchandise until duties are paid or the goods are reshipped without entry into the country.

bondholder, a creditor whose debt is secured by a bond.

bondsman, one who undertakes an obligation to assure payment of money, performance of an act, or integrity of another.

bonus, a special allowance beyond what is due; extra profits; as, the employees were given a *bonus* for their hard work.

book debts, debts or accounts charged on the books.

bounty, a special payment, premium, or additional allowance given to encourage trade or manufacture.

brand, a particular kind of goods; a mark of designation; a trade-mark, device, or name.

breach of trust, violation of a legal duty by one holding goods or property in trust.

breadstuffs, any kind of grain, corn, or meal.

breakage, allowance made by a shipper for loss due to injury or destruction.
breaking bulk, opening package of goods or merchandise in transit or in process of transportation.
broker, an agent in buying and selling; a middleman paid by commission.
building and loan association, an association organized to afford a safe investment for savings, and to aid its members in buying, building, or improving houses and other real property.
bull, a speculator who buys stocks, bonds, or other securities in expectation of a rise in the price, or in order to bring about such a rise.
bullion, ld and silver, considered merely as so much metal; specifically, uncoined silver and gold in the shape of bars or ingots.
bushel, a dry measure containing four pecks or thirty-two quarts.
by-laws, rules or regulations adopted by an association or a corporation for its own government.

C

call, a formal demand for the payment of money due; a notice to a stockholder to pay in an instalment of his subscription; a right to demand an amount of stock or goods, at a definite price, within a certain time; specifically, in stock speculation such a transaction in stock dealing closed by payment of the difference in price in favor of the holder of the call.
capital, accumulated wealth; specifically, the amount of property owned by an individual or corporation; the amount of such property used for business purposes.
capitalist, one who has capital invested, or capital for investment; generally, a person of large property which is or may be employed in business.
carat, a unit of weight for precious stones and, sometimes, precious metals, varying somewhat in different countries: in international trade, a carat is about 3 1/6 grains troy or about 205 milligrams.
cargo, a general term for all goods, merchandise, or whatever is conveyed in a vessel or boat; load; freight.
carrier, a person or agency engaged in the business of carrying goods for others.
cartage, transporting in a cart, dray, or truck; the price paid for carting.
carte blanche, unlimited authority; full power to exercise liberty of judgment.
case, a box or covering of any kind, or its contents; the quantity contained in a box or covering.
cash, money; strictly, coin, but also paper money, bank notes, bills of exchange, drafts, notes, checks, and other commercial paper easily convertible into money.
cash book, a book in which is kept a record of money received and paid out.
cashier, an officer who has charge of cash payments and receipts of a bank or mercantile establishment.
cashier's check, a check drawn by a bank upon its own funds, signed by the cashier.
cash sale, a sale of goods for cash; in mercantile transactions such a sale usually permits payment in ten or thirty days.
certificate of deposit, a written acknowledgment of a bank that a person has on deposit with it a specified sum.
certified check, a check guaranteed to be good by the bank upon which it is drawn: usually marked by the signature of the cashier or the paying teller with the word, *good* or its equivalent, across its face.
chamber of commerce, an association of merchants or traders having as its purpose the protection of the interests of its members; a term used distinctly by some to designate a body intrusted with the protection of general commercial interests, especially in connection with foreign trade.
charter, a formal instrument in writing from a state creating and defining the form, rights, and privileges of an association or corporation.
charter party, a mercantile lease of a vessel.
check, a written order on a bank to pay money on demand; a mark placed against an item in an account, etc., to indicate that it has been given proper attention.
check book, a book containing blank checks upon a bank.
circular, a communication, usually printed, copies of which are sent to various persons.
clearance, passage of checks, bills of exchange, drafts, and other similar negotiable paper, through the clearing house; settlement of debts or claims; act of clearing a ship or vessel at the customhouse.
clearance papers, papers or certificates issued by a customhouse giving permission for the departure of a ship or vessel, and showing that all formalities have been observed and duties met.
clearing, a method adopted by banks and other business agencies, for making settlement of claims against each other.
clearing house, an institution or establishment, especially in the business of banking, for making settlement of daily balances.
c. o. d., collect on delivery: a call for immediate payment of goods or merchandise at time of delivery.
collateral, a pledge of personal property for assuring the fulfilment of an obligation; commonly stocks and bonds.
collateral security, an additional pledge given, to guarantee the performance of a duty or promise, or the settlement of a debt.
collector, one authorized to receive money for another; chief officer of a customhouse.
commerce, the buying and selling of merchandise, or commodities; particularly, the exchange of merchandise on a large scale between different places, or countries.
commercial paper, bills of exchange, drafts, promissory notes, or other negotiable paper, given and passed in due course of business.
commission, the percentage or allowance made to an agent for transacting business for another; an act to be done as agent for another.
commission broker, one who buys or sells on commission.
common carrier, one who carries on the business of transporting goods or persons for compensation and for all persons impartially.
company, an association of persons for carrying on a commercial or industrial enterprise.
compound interest, interest on both the original principal and accrued interest from the time it was due.
consideration, compensation; recompense; anything given for something else; value in a contract.
consign, to send to an agent in another place to be cared for or sold.
consignee, one to whom something is consigned or sent.

consignment, that which is consigned; act of one who consigns anything.
consigner, one who consigns something.
consul, an agent appointed by a government to represent it in a foreign country, to care for the commercial interests of its citizens, and to protect its seamen.
contraband, goods or merchandise not lawfully subject to import or export; smuggled goods.
contract, an agreement legally enforceable between two or more persons to carry out some purpose; a bargain; a compact.
contracter, one who agrees by contract to do anything for another; specifically, one who contracts to do work, or supply goods or merchandise on a large scale, at a certain price, or rate.
conveyance, act by which the title to property, especially real estate, is transferred; the written instrument by which title to property is transferred.
cooper, one who makes or repairs barrels, hogsheads, casks, etc.
cooperage, work done by a cooper, or the pay for it.
copying press, a machine for making by pressure copies of letters, etc., written in copying ink.
copyright, an exclusive right granted by the government for the multiplication and sale of a literary or artistic work.
corner, a control of the supply of a commodity, stock issue, etc., to such an extent as to enable the one in control to fix the marketing price.
corporation, an association of persons formed and authorized by law to act as a single body, and endowed by law with the capacity of succession or providing for its continued existence.
coupon, a certificate of interest due, attached to a transferable bond.
credit, financial faith and confidence existing between two persons; business reputation entitling one to be trusted; the extent of a person's ability to get goods or money on trust; specifically, an amount turned over to a person's use by a bank or other business establishment; the balance due a person as shown by an account; entering payment or an item of settlement in an account; the right-hand side of an account on which are entered all items reckoned as values given or produced.
creditor, one to whom money is due; one who extends credit in a business transaction.
curb, the general market for stocks and bonds, or commodities, as distinguished from an established exchange or market place.
currency, the accepted medium of exchange: coin, paper money, and bank notes.
customhouse, the government office where customs and duties are paid, and, if a seaport, where vessels are entered or cleared.
customhouse broker, an agent who acts for an importer or an exporter in handling the business arising from entering and clearing goods and vessels in foreign commerce.
customs, duties, taxes, or imposts, levied by the government of a country on commodities imported or exported.

D

damages, estimated money reparation for an injury suffered; compensation regarded as an equivalent reparation for a wrong or injury caused by a violation of a legal right.
date, the time at which a transaction or event takes place, or is appointed to take place.
day book, a book record in which transactions are entered consecutively at the time they occur.
debit, an entry of an item in an account showing something charged or due, or the sum of several items so entered; the left-hand side of an account on which such entries are made.
debtor, one who owes a debt or is indebted.
deed, an instrument in writing under seal duly carried out and delivered according to law conveying or transferring title to land or other real property.
deficit, a shortage in resources, income, or amount.
demurrage, the detention of a vessel or freight car by one for whom freight has been transported, beyond the time allowed for loading or unloading; payment made for such detention.
deposit, funds and money turned over to a bank subject to withdrawal by order or request; anything handed over as a pledge or security.
deposit slip, a statement which a depositor leaves with a deposit, as a memorandum and evidence that the money, checks, or other funds, have been deposited.
depot, a railroad station; a building for the accommodation and protection, and sometimes for the sale, of goods.
depreciation, a decline in value or market price.
directors, a body of persons selected to manage the affairs of a company or corporation.
discount, a deduction made as an interest charge in lending money upon a bill of exchange, draft, or promissory note not due; a deduction from the gross amount; an allowance upon a debt, or price asked, usually made to bring about prompt or cash payment.
dividend, a share of profits distributed among stockholders.
dividend warrant, a formal order, by which a stockholder receives his dividend.
dock, a waterway, between two piers, for the reception of ships to come or go into dock.
dockage, a payment exacted for the use of a dock; docking facilities.
double name paper, a note, draft, bill of exchange, or trade acceptance, final payment of which is additionally assured by the indorsement of some one approved by the bank that accepts or discounts it.
draft, an order from one person or party to another directing the payment of money; a drawing upon a fund or stock.
draw, to obtain by use of a draft; to take away from a place of deposit.
drawback, an amount of money paid back after having been collected; especially, duties or customs remitted by the government.
drawee, the person on whom an order, draft, or bill of exchange is drawn.
drawer, one who draws a bill of exchange, draft, or order for payment.
drayage, the charge or sum paid for hauling or for the use of a dray or truck.
dry goods, textile fabrics.
due bill, an informal written acknowledgment of a debt, nonnegotiable in form.
dun, to ask persistently for payment.
duty, a tax levied by a government on the importation, exportation, or use and consumption of goods.

E

effects, movables; personal property; sometimes loosely used to designate real as well as personal property.

ejectment, a legal action for the recovery of possession of real property, and, usually, to secure damages for wrongful withholding; the official authorization, or writ, by which this action is begun.

embargo, an order of the government prohibiting the departure or entry of ships at ports, or traffic in commodities, within its dominions.

embark, to go on board a vessel for a voyage; to engage in a business enterprise.

entry, act of reporting at a customhouse the arrival of a ship and procuring permission to land its cargo; act of taking formal possession of lands and other property; putting on record in proper form and order.

equity of redemption, the time allowed a mortgagor, or other pledgor, to reclaim property by paying an obligation secured by it.

estate, the nature and extent of ownership in property.

excess profits, profits above average; specifically, under the United States war emergency taxation system of 1917, profits exceeding the average business gain of the three years preceding the outbreak of war with Germany and Austria-Hungary.

exchange, the process involved in carrying on trade and commerce; specifically, a place where merchants and traders meet to carry on particular business transactions; the process of settling accounts between parties located at a distance from each other by the use of bills of exchange and drafts, or by a transfer of credits; the amount paid for the collection of a bill of exchange, draft, check, or other negotiable instrument; conversion of the money of one country into that of another, with an allowance for difference in value.

exchange broker, one who deals in foreign bills of exchange and money.

excise, a duty or tax levied upon the manufacture, sale, use or consumption of goods within a country; also, a tax upon the pursuit or following of certain trades or occupations.

executed, performed; carried out; specifically, carried out and performed according to law.

executor, a person appointed by another to execute his will, or to see its provisions carried into effect after the latter's death.

exhibit, an object, or a collection of objects, displayed to public view; an object or a document shown in court and held for future use as evidence.

exporter, one who exports; a person who sends goods or commodities to a foreign country in the way of commerce.

exports, commodities sent from one country to another.

express business, a system of rapid transportation of goods or merchandise, generally managed by express companies, providing special care, security, and quickness of delivery.

express company, an association or corporation engaged as a common carrier in the express business.

express money order, an order for the payment of money issued by one office of an express company and payable at another.

extension, an allowance of additional time by a creditor to a debtor for the payment of a debt.

F

face, the principal amount of a note or other financial obligation.

facsimile, a copy of anything, so made as to give every part and detail of the original.

failure, suspension of payment; a state of insolvency or bankruptcy.

fair, average; middling; free from marked merit or defect; of reasonably good kind or quality.

fall, a decline in value or price; to suffer a decline in value or price.

false pretense, a false representation of facts made with the purpose of defrauding another.

federal reserve bank, a bank established under the laws of the United States to act as an agent in the maintenance of money reserves, to issue bank currency, and to rediscount commercial paper accepted and discounted in the business of banking.

fee, a charge fixed by law for the services of a public officer; sometimes, pay; wages; salary.

file, an orderly collection of papers, arranged and classified for reference and preservation, usually with title and date indorsed; any device to keep letters and papers in order, such as a hook or a drawer; to insert in its proper place in a file.

finance, the science and practice of handling monetary affairs, especially those involving large sums or having especial relation to investments.

financier, one skilled in the problems of finance, or occupied with them.

firm, a partnership of two or more persons; the name under which a partnership or company transacts business; steady; not declining in value or price.

fixture, anything annexed to houses and lands so as legally to constitute a part thereof.

flat, without additional charge or interest.

f. o. b., free on board, delivered free of charge to a vessel or train.

footing, the act of adding up a column of figures; the amount or sum total of such a column.

forced sale, sale of goods under compulsion or foreclosure.

foreclose, to take away the right of redeeming.

foreclosure, a legal proceeding which cancels a mortgagor's right of redeeming a mortgaged property.

foreign bill, a bill of exchange, or draft, payable in a foreign country.

forwarder, one who accepts goods for transportation and delivery to another carrier.

franchise, a special privilege granted by law to an individual or corporation, which does not pertain to persons of common right.

franking privilege, the right of sending letters, packages, telegrams, etc., without charge, for postage carriage.

fraud, an intentional misrepresentation of the truth for the purpose of inducing another to make a contract to his detriment.

free list, the schedule of goods or merchandise admitted to a country free of duty; a list of persons entitled to something without payment.

free trade, commerce and trade not subjected to duties or tariff regulations.

freight, the compensation paid by any one for the transportation of goods by rail or water; the cargo.

funds, money and negotiable paper immediately or readily convertible into cash; available financial resources.

G

goods, merchandise; wares.
good will, the custom or patronage of any trade or business.
great gross, twelve gross; *i. e.*, 1,728 articles.
gross, whole; entire; total; without any deduction; also, twelve dozen.
gross amount, the total sum or aggregate.
gross ton, 2,240 pounds avoirdupois; a unit of internal capacity of ships—100 cubic feet.
gross weight, total weight of goods or merchandise, without deduction for tare or waste.
guarantee, to become responsible for the fulfilment of an obligation of another; to be surety for.
guarantor, a person who gives a guaranty or surety.
guaranty, an agreement to pay a debt, or perform a duty, of another, in case of the failure of the other to fulfil the obligation.
gunny sack, a bag of coarse material, usually jute or hemp, for packing loose commodities for shipment.

H

harbor, a port or place of shelter for ships; a protected waterway equipped with docking facilities.
harbor master, a government officer charged with the duty of carrying out the regulations governing the use of a harbor.
hogshead, a large cask or barrel; especially, one containing two barrels or sixty-three gallons.
holder, a person in possession of, and legally entitled to payment of, a bill of exchange or note.
honor, to accept and pay when due.
hypothecate, to pledge as security without giving title or ownership.

I

immovable, fixed; permanent in place; *pl.* sometimes used in referring to real estate.
import, to bring in goods or merchandise from a foreign country.
importer, one who imports; especially, a merchant who brings goods or merchandise into a country from abroad.
imports, goods or merchandise imported, or brought into a country from abroad.
impost, a tax or duty laid by a government on goods imported into a country.
income, the return, from labor, business, or property. The total receipts from any branch of business are called the *gross income;* that portion which remains after paying costs and expenses is known as the *net income*.
income tax, a tax on income or on an excess of income over a certain amount.
indemnify, to secure against loss or damage; to reimburse in case of loss or damage.
indemnification, indemnifying or reimbursing in case of loss, damage, or penalty.
indemnity, compensation for loss or damage sustained.
indorse, to order a negotiable instrument paid to another by writing one's name on the back of the instrument; to guarantee payment.
indorsee, the person to whom a negotiable instrument is indorsed.
indorsement, act of indorsing; that which is written in indorsing.
indorser, the person who indorses.
inland bill, a bill of exchange, or draft, payable in the country where drawn: generally called a *domestic bill*.
insolvent, not having sufficient assets to meet all debts.
instalment, a part of a debt which is divided into portions that are made payable at different times.
instalment plan, the system of making sales for a sum made payable in portions at stated intervals.
instant, present; current: used with a date to indicate the current month.
insurable interest, such an interest in the subject of insurance as carries with it legal damage in the event of the loss insured against.
insurance, a contract whereby one party, for a stipulated consideration, called a *premium*, undertakes to indemnify or guarantee another against loss of a specific kind, known as a *risk*.
insurance broker, a broker who handles or places insurance.
insurance policy, a written contract of insurance.
insure, to secure against loss, or damage.
interest, a rate per cent of money paid for the use of funds; a share in property or profits.
internal revenue, a revenue or income derived by a government from licenses, duties, and special taxes levied on personal property or the production and use of domestic goods.
intestate, a person who dies without having made a will.
in transit, on the road; not brought to an end or destination.
inventory, a list of goods or merchandise on hand; an enumeration of articles; a schedule.
invest, to apply capital, money, or funds to the purchase of property for income or profit.
investment, the capital, money, or funds invested; that in which capital, money, or funds is invested.
invoice, a written account or itemized statement of merchandise shipped or sent to a purchaser or consignee, setting forth the quantity, value or prices, and charges; the lot of goods or merchandise as shipped or received.
invoice book, a book for recording or entering copies of invoices.
involved, embarrassed by debts or liabilities; confused.

J

jobber, one who buys from importers or manufacturers and sells to retailers: a middleman.
job lot, goods or merchandise left over; an odd assortment.
joint note, a promissory note signed by several persons, each of whom is liable for a proportional part of the amount.
joint and several note, a promissory note signed by two or more persons, each of whom agrees to hold himself liable for the full amount in case the others are unable to pay.
joint stock, stock or capital held and used in a joint enterprise.
joint stock company, an association consisting of a number of persons organized to conduct a business with a joint capital.
journal, a book of accounts in which is recorded a condensed statement of daily

business transactions arranged according to debit and credit.

judgment, the final order of a court in civil or criminal proceedings; an obligation created by an order or decree of a court; the official certificate evidencing such an obligation.

judgment note, a promissory note, containing in addition to its usual contents, a power of attorney authorizing a confession of judgment against the maker or signer upon default of payment.

L

leakage, an allowance or deduction made for waste by leaking of casks or barrels.

lease, a contract by which one person conveys to another person the use of lands, buildings, or other real property, usually for a specified rent or compensation and length of time; the act and instrument by which such conveyance is made, or the term for which it is made.

ledger, the final book of record in business transactions, in which all debits and credits from other books of original entry are brought together, classified, and summarized under appropriate heads.

legal tender, coin or currency which a government has declared shall be received in payment of debts; a formal proffer of money to pay a debt.

lessee, one to whom a lease is given, or who takes property under a contract of lease; a tenant under a lease.

lessor, one who gives a lease; one who leases.

letter copying book, a book in which copies are made of letters.

letter of advice, a written report from an agent to a principal or from a consignor to a consignee transmitting special information; a letter by which the drawer of a bill of exchange, or draft, notifies the drawee that the bill has been drawn.

letter of credit, a letter addressed by a bank to one or more of its correspondents certifying that the holder is entitled to draw upon it for funds up to a certain sum; such a letter addressed to several correspondents is sometimes called a *circular letter of credit*.

letters of administration, an official instrument issued by a court by which an administrator is granted authority to manage and settle the business affairs and estate of a person who has died.

liability, a debt; that which one is under obligation to pay.

license, the formal permission from the proper authorities to perform certain acts.

lien, a legal claim upon real or personal property for the satisfaction of some debt or duty.

lighterage, compensation paid for unloading into a lighter for conveyance to or from shore.

liquidate, to apportion the assets of a business in settlement of indebtedness.

liquidation, the settling of the liabilities of a business.

Lloyd's, a marine insurance association with its central offices located in London, having for its main objects the carrying on of marine insurance.

loan, act of lending; that which one lends or borrows; especially, a sum of money lent at interest.

long, a term used to describe a purchase of goods or stocks in expectation of a rise in price: opposite to *short*.

M

manifest, an invoice of a ship's cargo, to be shown at the customhouse.

manifold, to make many or several copies of a letter, statement, or document.

margin, an amount of time or money which is allowed or reserved in addition to what is directly needed or used; the percentage paid in money to a broker to secure him against loss on contracts entered into by him on behalf of his principal.

mark, to put a price or sign on articles, goods or merchandise; to affix a significant identifying mark.

market, opportunity for selling or buying of commodities, or the rate or price offered for them; a meeting of people at a stated time and place for the purpose of buying and selling; a place where provisions are sold.

maturity, termination of the period of time a note or other obligation has to run.

mercantile agency, an organization which collects information as to the credit and reputation of merchants or others doing business, and furnishes this to others for compensation; a commercial agency.

mercantile paper, negotiable paper, given by merchants for goods bought or received.

merchant, one who buys and sells on a large scale.

merchantable, fit for market; such as is usually sold in the market, or such as will bring the ordinary price.

merchant marine, shipping under the control of a country employed in the carriage of goods and passengers between several countries.

mint, a place where money is coined by public authority.

mixed fabrics, a textile fabric composed of two or more kinds of fiber.

money, coined metal or printed certificates issued or authorized by a government as a medium of exchange or a means of payment; wealth considered in terms of money; capital reckoned as a cash asset.

money market, the opportunities for loanable wealth or capital; the whole body of agencies, which regulate and direct financial operations and equalize the supply of and demand for capital.

money order, an order for the payment of money.

mortgage, a conditional conveyance or transfer of property, as security for the payment of a debt, which is to become void upon fulfilment of the obligation and stipulated terms.

mortgagee, the person to whom property is mortgaged.

mortgagor, one who gives a mortgage.

movable, in general, wares or goods; now only an article of furniture.

N

negotiable, capable of being transferred in the ordinary course of business by delivery, with or without indorsement.

negotiable paper, bills of exchange, drafts, promissory notes, checks, or other similar instruments, that are payable to bearer or order; also, under some laws, other business instruments, such as bonds, forms of stock, and bills of lading.

net, free from all charges, deductions, and allowances; as, *net* profits, *net* proceeds, *net* income, or *net* weight.

nominal, merely named or stated or given without reference to reality; existing in reference only; as, *nominal* value.

notary public, a public officer authorized to take acknowledgments, and to attest or certify deeds and other business instruments, usually under his official seal, to make them authentic; and to take affidavits, and protests of negotiable paper.

note, a short term for promissory note; a written instrument acknowledging a debt, and promising payment.

O

obligation, a formal acknowledgment of a liability or agreement to pay a certain sum or do a certain thing; sometimes coupled with a condition and a penalty for nonfulfilment.

open account, an account not settled or adjusted.

open policy, an insurance policy in which the value is to be proved by the insured, in case of loss.

option, a privilege, allowed in a time contract, of buying or selling at a specified price within a specified time.

order, an instruction to buy, sell, or supply, goods or merchandise; a written instruction to admit to a building; an indorsement by which the holder of negotiable paper directs to whom payment shall be made.

outstanding accounts, accounts showing debts due, but unsettled and unpaid.

overdraw, to draw more than the amount standing to the credit of the drawer.

overdue, unpaid beyond the stipulated time.

P

package, an article, or a collection of articles packed together.

panic, a widespread alarm and distrust in financial affairs, causing depreciation in values.

paper, a short term for negotiable paper.

par, the face or established value; the equality of the value or price of securities at which they are issued and at which they are sold.

partner, one of two or more members of a partnership for carrying on a business.

partnership, an association of two or more persons who have placed their resources, labor, and skill, at the disposal of a lawful business undertaking.

pass book, the depositor's book in which an account of deposits and withdrawals is kept; especially, of a bank account.

passport, an official permission to enter or leave a port, or to pass into or through a country.

payable, justly due; that which should be paid.

payee, the person to whom a sum of money is to be made payable.

payer, the person who is to pay a financial obligation

permit, an authorization for an act or the conduct of a business.

petty cash, money paid out or received in small amounts.

petty cash book, book in which a record is kept of petty cash receipts and payments.

plaintiff, one who sues another or brings an action in court.

policy, a contract of insurance; a definite or settled course of action adopted and followed by a government, individual, or business enterprise.

post, to transfer an entry or entries from a book of original record to one of final classification and summary; as, from a journal to a ledger.

postdate, to date after the real time.

power of attorney, written authority from one person to another to act for him.

premium, the amount paid for a contract of insurance; an amount in addition to the face value of anything.

price, the value of a commodity expressed in terms of money.

price list, a list of prevailing prices.

prime, of first quality.

principal, one who employs another to act for him; one primarily liable on an obligation; a capital sum placed at interest.

proceeds, the financial return that is derived from some possession or transaction; especially, the amount realized from a sale of property.

produce, that which is yielded; especially, in agriculture.

profit, the excess of returns over costs and expenses; gain in a business undertaking.

promissory note, a written promise to pay a sum of money at a future time to, or to the order of, a specified person or to bearer.

property, anything of value that may be owned; the legal right to a thing; generally classified as *personal property*, when movable; and *real property*, when immovable.

pro rata, in proportion; a proportional distribution.

protest, a formal declaration and notification that payment of a negotiable instrument has been refused; to make such a formal declaration and notification.

Q

quitclaim deed, an instrument transferring ownership of real estate without warranty of title.

quitrent, a fixed rent paid by a tenant, discharging him from other duties or obligations.

quotation, current prices of merchandise or other commodities.

R

real estate, land, houses, and fixtures; all immovable property.

rebate, a deduction or allowance; a giving back of part of a sum already paid.

receipt, a written acknowledgment of payment.

receipt book, a book of printed receipt forms or one in which receipts are filed.

receiver, an officer appointed by a court to hold in trust and manage the property and funds involved in a suit at law, or to wind up the affairs of a bankrupt or insolvent business enterprise.

recoup, to counterbalance losses by gains.

register and recorder, a public officer charged with recording certain business transactions and dealings; as, registry of deeds, mortgages, and judgments.

re-insurance, transfer of part of the contract of insurance from one insurer to another.

release, a conveyance by which the releasor gives up his right or estate to a person who already has some estate or possession in property.

remittance, payment on account; transfer of funds from one party to another.

renewal, extension of time; giving a new note for an old one.

rent, compensation for the use of real property.

retail, to sell in small quantities.

returns, profit on an investment, or gains accruing from labor or business enterprise.

S

safe-deposit box, a steel box generally, fitted into the wall of a vault, provided by banks or safe-deposit companies, for containing and safe-guarding securities and other valuables.
sale, transfer of property for money.
sample, a small quantity or portion of goods or merchandise shown as an example of quality.
savings bank, a bank employed in the business of receiving small deposits, chiefly savings, investing them, and paying interest thereon.
security, something given as a pledge to assure the fulfilment of an obligation or the payment of a debt; a person who becomes responsible as a surety for the performance of another's obligation or the payment of his debts; any document or evidence of debt or of property, such as a bond or a share of stock.
sell, to make a sale; to transfer for a consideration.
set-off, an opposing claim arising from a matter different from the one in question.
share, unit division of a capital stock issue; interest owned by one of a number.
shipment, quantity of goods sent or consigned.
shipper, one who sends or consigns goods by vessel, railroad, or other transportation agency.
shipping clerk, one who oversees the forwarding and shipping of goods and merchandise.
short, a term used to denote a sale of goods, stocks, etc., at a fixed price, for future delivery, of what one does not possess, in expectation of a fall in price.
shrinkage, decrease in bulk or measurement.
sight, the term used to designate when a bill of exchange, or draft, is presented to the drawee.
sight draft, a draft payable at sight, *i. e.,* when presented for payment.
sinking fund, a fund set apart from income to pay a debt; particularly, a bond issue.
smuggling, taking goods into a country without paying the import duties or taxes.
solvent, able to meet all debts; excess of assets over liabilities.
specie, any kind of coined money: generally, gold and silver.
specification, a written description and enumeration of particulars accompanying a contract.
specific duty, a fixed tax levied on an article of a certain kind or quantity without regard to its value or market price.
speculation, a risky investment for large profit; a business undertaking out of the ordinary run of affairs.
staple, the principal commodity of a country or district.
stock, shares in the capital of a corporation or stock company; goods on hand.
stock broker, one who buys and sells stocks on commission.
stock exchange, an association of stock brokers who meet to buy and sell stocks and bonds; the place where such brokers meet.
stockholder, one who holds or owns shares of stock.
storage, price paid for storing and safeguarding goods.
storekeeper, officer in charge of a bonded warehouse; one in charge of stores.
street, a short term used in a general way to designate the financial district of a city.
sundries, unclassified articles.
surety, one who makes himself liable to pay money in case another fails to pay, to fill a contract, or to serve with integrity.
surtax, a supplementary or extra tax, levied in addition to the ordinary rate, as in the custom duties, or in the income tax.
suspend, to stop business; to stop payment; to fail.

T

tally, keeping account by checking off.
tare, deduction, allowance in weight or quantity on account of case, cask, bag, or covering.
tariff, a schedule of duties; a price list.
teller, officer of a bank who receives or pays out money.
tenant, one who leases or rents real property.
tender, an offer of money or other thing in settlement of a debt or claim.
testator, one who has died leaving a will.
textile fabrics, all woven goods.
title, the right to exclusive possession of property; also, the legal evidence of one's right of property.
tonnage, the weight of a ship; the weight a ship will carry; capacity of a vessel.
tort, an injury or detriment for which damages may be obtained.
trade, buying and selling; traffic; commerce.
trade acceptance, a draft drawn by the seller on the purchaser of goods, and accepted by the purchaser for payment at a definite time.
trade discount, an allowance made to dealers in the same line of business.
trade-mark, letters, figures, or devices legally registered, used on goods and labels by a manufacturer or merchant to designate his goods.
trade price, the price allowed by wholesalers to retailers.
traffic, business carried on; especially, by a railroad.
transportation, conveying goods or merchandise from one place to another.
transshipment, removing goods or merchandise from one ship or means of transportation to another.
trust, faith and confidence; that which is turned over to one in faith and confidence.
trust company, a corporation engaged in the business of acting as a trustee, and carrying on banking to a greater or less extent.
trust deed, a kind of mortgage granted a trustee to secure a body of creditors, with power to foreclose on all its mortgaged property in the event of nonfulfilment of the debtor's obligation.
trustee, one legally holding property in trust; one intrusted with property for another.

U

under seal, a term used to show lawful consideration for the promise or agreement made in a contract, and commonly evidenced by the use of the letters "*L. S.*" or the word "*seal*" in addition to the signatures of the parties in the contract.
undersell, to sell below the trade price.
unsound, in bad financial condition; of doubtful solvency.
usury, interest greater than the lawful rate.

V

valid, good in law; binding; of force.
value, the estimated worth of a commodity, expressed in money; market price.

value received, phrases used in notes and bills to express a lawful consideration.

valued policy, an insurance policy in which the value is inserted in the nature of liquidated damages.

void, not enforceable by law.

voucher, a receipt, entry, or document which establishes the truth or authenticity of a business transaction or record.

W

waiver, a voluntary surrender of a legal right or privilege.

warehouse, a storehouse for storing and safe-guarding goods or merchandise.

warehouse receipt, a receipt, sometimes negotiable, given at a warehouse for goods in storage.

warranty, a guarantee of the accurate representation of goods or of title.

warranty deed, a deed carrying with it the assurance of the one who grants it that his title to the property is as represented.

wastage, the loss due to handling of commodities.

way bill, list or statement of goods given to a carrier.

wharfage, charges paid for the use of a wharf.

wholesale, trade in large quantities; selling to retailers rather than consumers.

will, the legal document by which a person makes provision for the settlement or distribution of his estate after his death.

without recourse, restrictive words added to an indorsement of a note or bill of exchange to prevent the indorser from liability.

PREFIXES AND SUFFIXES.

PREFIXES.

a-, on, in, at, to; as *a*shore, *on* shore; *a*bed, *in* bed; *a*far, *at* a distance; *a*field, *to* the field. [AS.]

a-, without, un-, not; as *a*pathy, *without* feeling; *a*sexual, *not* sexual, sexless. Also, **an-**; as *an*archy. [GR.]

ab-, from, away; as *ab*duct, to lead *away* or *from*. Also, **a-**, **abs-**; as *a*vert, *abs*tain. [LAT.]

ad-, to, at, toward, in addition to; as *ad*here, to stick *to*; *ad*mire, to wonder *at*; *ad*duct, to draw *toward* the axis; *ad*join, to join *in addition to*. Also, **a-**, **ac-**, **af-**, **ag-**, **al-**, **an-**, **ap-**, **ar-**, **as-**, **at-**; as *a*scend, *ac*cept, *af*fect, *ag*gravate, *al*lot, *an*nounce, *ap*pear, *ar*rest, *as*sent, *at*tend. [LAT.]

amb-, around; as *amb*ient, going *around*. Also, **am-**; as *am*putate. [LAT.]

amphi-, both, round about; as *amphi*bious, living *both* on land and in water. [GR.]

ana-, up; as *ana*tomy, a cutting *up*. [GR.]

ante-, before; as *ante*cedent, going *before* in time, prior; *ante*date, to date *before*. Also, **anti-**, **anci-**, **ant-**, **an-**; as *anti*cipate, *anci*ent, *ant*ique, *an*cestor. [LAT.]

anti-, opposite of, against; as *anti*climax, the *opposite of* climax; *anti*pathy, a feeling *against* a person. Also, **ant-**; as *ant*agonist. [GR.]

apo-, from; as *apo*stasy, desertion *from* one's faith. [GR.]

arch-, chief; as *arch*angel, *chief* angel. Also, **archi-**, **arche-**; as *archi*tect, *arche*type. [GR.]

auto-, self; as *auto*mobile, *self*-moving; *auto*biography, a biography by one*self*. [GR.]

be-, thoroughly, completely; as *be*daub, to smear *thoroughly*; to affect with; as *be*witch, *to affect with* witchcraft; to deprive of; as *be*head, *to deprive of* a head, to decapitate. [AS.]

bis-, twice; as *bis*cuit, bread originally baked *twice*. Also, **bi-**, **bin-**; as *bi*ennial, *bin*ocular. [LAT.]

by-, near, out of the way, secondary; as *by*stander, one *near*; *by*path, a path *out of the way*; *by*-name, *secondary* or nickname. [AS.]

cata-, down; as *cata*ract, that which strikes *down*, a waterfall. Also, **cat-**, **cath-**; as *cat*echism, *cath*olic. [GR.]

circum-, around, roundabout; as *circum*navigate, to sail *around*; *circum*locution, *roundabout* language. Also, **circu-**; as *circu*it. [LAT.]

cis-, on this side; as *cis*alpine, *on this side* of the Alps. [LAT.]

com-, together, with; as *com*pose, to place *together*; *com*pete, to contend *with*. Also, **co-**, **col-**, **con-**, **cor-**, **coun-**; as *co*here, *col*lect, *con*nect, *cor*rect, *coun*cil. [LAT.]

contra-, contrary, against; as *contra*diction, an assertion of the *contrary*; *contra*position, a placing over *against*. Also, **contro-**; as *contro*vert. [LAT.]

counter-, in opposition to, against; as *counter*act, to act *in opposition to*; *counter*balance, to balance *against*. [FR.]

de-, down, away, to deprive of; as *de*jected, cast *down*; *de*ter, to frighten *away*; *de*nature, *to deprive of* its original nature, completely; as *de*nude, to strip *completely*; reversal of; as *de*mobilize, to do the *reversal of* mobilizing. [LAT.]

demi-, half; less than usual; inferior; as *demi*god, an *inferior* deity. [FR.]

dia-, through, trans-; as *dia*phanous, showing *through*, *transparent*. [GR.]

dis-, in verbs: away, apart; as *dis*pel, to drive *away*; *dis*sect, to cut *apart*; to destroy, to deprive, to undo; as *dis*able, *to destroy* the power of; *dis*arm, *to deprive of* arms; *dis*join, *to separate* that which has been united; in nouns and adjectives: absence of, opposite to, not; as *dis*composure, *absence of* or *opposite to* calmness; *dis*obedient, *not* obedient; completely; as *dis*annul, to annul *completely*. Also, **dif-**, **di-**, **s-**; as *dif*fuse, *di*vert, *s*pend. [LAT.]

dis-, two, twice; as *dis*syllable, a word of *two* syllables. Also, **di-**; as *di*lemma. [GR.]

dys-, difficult; as *dys*pepsia, *difficult* digestion. [GR.]

ec-, out of; as *ec*centric, *out of* the center, peculiar. [GR.]

en-, in, on, to make; as *en*snare, to catch *in* a snare; *en*grave, to carve *on*; *en*feeble, *to make* feeble. Also, **em-**, **im-**; as *em*bark, *im*merge. [GR., LAT.]

epi-, to, upon; as *epi*stle, a writing sent *to* a person; *epi*taph, writing *upon* a tomb; beside, among; as *epi*sode, an occurrence *beside* the main issue; *epi*demic, a disease *among* the people; on the outside, above, over; as *epi*dermis, the skin *on the outside*; *epi*glottis, the plate of cartilage *above* or *over* the glottis. Also, **ep-**, **eph-**; as *ep*och, *eph*emeral. [GR.]

eso-, within; as *eso*teric, for those *within*, private. [GR.]

eu-, well; as *eu*phony, a sounding *well*. Also, **ev-**; as *ev*angelist. [GR.]

ex-, out; as *ex*tract, to draw *out*; from; as *ex*clude, to shut *from*; beyond; as *ex*cessive, *beyond* the limits; thoroughly; as *ex*asperate, to irritate *thoroughly*; formerly, but not now; as *ex*-Kaiser, *formerly* Emperor, *but not now*. Also, **e-**, **ef-**, **s-**; as *e*vade, *ef*fect, *s*ample [LAT.]; out of; as *ex*odus, a going *out of*. [GR.]

exo-, without; as *exo*tic, from *without*. [GR.]

extra-, beyond; as *extra*ordinary, *beyond* the ordinary. [LAT.]

for-, from, away; as *for*bid, to warn *from*; *for*give, to give *away* resentment, pardon. [AS.]

fore-, before; as *fore*tell, to tell *before*. [AS.]

hemi-, half; as *hemi*sphere, *half* a sphere. [GR.]

hetero-, other; as *hetero*dox, an opinion *other* (than the standard one). [GR.]

hydro-, water; as *hydro*plane, an airship that can float on the *water*. [GR.]

hyper-, over, excessively; as *hyper*critical, *over*critical; *hyper*acid, *excessively* acid. GR.]

hypo-, under; as *hypo*dermic, *under* the skin. Also, **hyph-**, **hyp-**; as *hyph*en, *hyp*allage. [GR.]

in-, in, into, upon, within; as *in*flux, *in*flow; *in*ject, to force *into;* *in*scribe, to write *upon;* *in*side, the side *within*. Also, **il-**, **im-**, **ir-**; as *il*lumine, *im*pend, *ir*rigate. [LAT.]

in-, not; as *in*accurate, *not* accurate. Also, **i-**, **il-**, **im-**, **ir-**; as *i*gnoble, *il*legal, *im*mobilize; *ir*regular. [LAT.]

inter-, between, among, mutual; as *inter*pose, to place *between;* *inter*sperse, to scatter *among;* *inter*change, *mutual* exchange. [LAT.]

intra-, within, inside; as *intra*mural, *within* or *inside* the walls. [LAT.]

intro-, into, within; as *intro*spect, to look *into* or *within*. [LAT.]

juxta-, near; as *juxta*position, a position *near*. [LAT.]

male-, badly, evil; as *male*volent, *badly*, ill-disposed; *male*factor, *evil*doer. Also, **mal-**, **mau-**; as *mal*ady, *mau*ger. [LAT.]

mega-, great; as *mega*phone, a device to make sound *great*, to magnify it; a million; as *mega*farad, a *million* farads. Also, **megalo-**, **meg-**; as *megalo*mania, *meg*ampere. [GR.]

meta-, change; as *meta*morphose, to *change* in form; after; as *meta*physics, the science *after* physics. Also, **meth-**, **met-**; as *meth*od, *met*eor. [GR.]

micro-, small; as *micro*be, a *small* organism. [GR.]

mis-, wrong, wrongly; as *mis*deed, a *wrong* deed; *mis*take, to take *wrongly*. [AS.]

mono-, one, single; as *mono*theism, belief in *one* God; *mono*syllable, a word of a *single* syllable. Also, **mon-**; as *mon*k. [GR.]

multi-, many; as *multi*form, of *many* forms. [LAT.]

neg-, not; as *neg*ative, *not* positive. [LAT.]

non-, not; as *non*sense, *not* sense. [LAT.]

ob-, to, before, against, upon; as *ob*ey, to give ear *to;* *ob*struct, to build up *before;* *ob*stacle, that which stands *against*, in the way; *ob*trude, to thrust *upon;* completely, reversely; as *ob*durate, *completely* hardened; *ob*ovate, *reversely* ovate. Also, **o-**, **oc-**, **of-**, **op-**, **os-**; as *o*mit, *oc*cur, *of*fer, *op*pose, *os*tensible. [LAT.]

out-, out, beyond; as *out*flow, a flowing *out;* *out*run, to run *beyond*. [AS.]

over-, above, beyond, overmuch, excessively; as *over*top, to tower *above;* *over*flow, to flow *beyond;* *over*eat, to eat *overmuch;* *over*curious, *excessively* curious. [AS.]

pan-, all; as *pan*acea, a cure-*all*. Also, **panto-**; as *panto*mime. [GR.]

para-, alongside, contrary; as *para*ble, a throwing *alongside*, a comparison; *para*dox, a *contrary* opinion. Also, **par-**, **pa-**; as *par*ody, *pa*lsy. [GR.]

pen-, almost; as *pen*insula, *almost* an island. [LAT.]

per-, through, throughout, completely; as *per*vade, to spread *through;* *per*petual, lasting *throughout;* *per*form, to finish *completely*. Also, **par-**, **pel-**, **pil-**; as *par*son, *pel*lucid, *pil*grim. [LAT.]

peri-, around, about, inclosing, circum-; as *peri*scope, a submarine instrument to look *around;* *peri*style, a system of columns *about* a building; *peri*cardium, the membrane *inclosing* the heart; *peri*phrasis, *circum*locution. [GR.]

phono-, sound; as *phono*graph, an instrument that writes *sounds*. [GR.]

photo-, light, photographic; as *photo*graph, to draw, or make a likeness, by *light;* *photo*-engraving, a *photographic* engraving. [GR.]

poly-, many; as *poly*syllabic, having *many* syllables. [GR.]

post-, after, afterwards; as *post*pone, to put *after*, off; *post*script, a writing made *afterwards*. [LAT.]

pre-, before, fore-, most; as *pre*cede, to go *before;* *pre*dict, to *fore*tell; *pre*dominant, *most* dominant. [LAT.]

preter-, beyond; as *preter*natural, *beyond* the natural. [LAT.]

pro-, in front, forth, forward, in place of, for, favoring, beforehand; as *pro*tect, to cover *in front;* *pro*fuse, pouring *forth;* *pro*ceed, to go *forward;* *pro*noun, a word standing *in place of* a noun; *pro*phesy, to speak *for* God; *pro*-German, *favoring* the Germans; *pro*gnostic, knowing *beforehand*. [LAT., GR.]

proto-, first; as *proto*col, the *first* memorandum of a treaty. Also, **prot-**; as *prot*agonist. [GR.]

pseudo-, false, pretended; as *pseudo*clergy, *false, pretended* clergy. Also, **pseud-**; as *pseud*onym. [GR.]

re-, back, again; as *re*cede, to go *back;* *re*patriate, to bring *again* to one's native land. Also, **red-**, **ren-**; as *red*eem, *ren*der. [LAT.]

retro-, backward; as *retro*spect, a *backward* look. [LAT.]

se-, aside, apart, without; as *se*cede, to go *aside* in rebellion; *se*clude, to shut *apart;* *se*cure, *without* care. Also, **sed-**; as *sed*ition. [LAT.]

semi-, half, partly; as *semi*circle, *half* a circle; *semi*transparent, *partly* transparent. [LAT.]

sine-, without; as *sine*cure, *without* care. Also, **sim-**, **sin-**; as *sim*ple, *sin*cere. [LAT.]

sub-, under, somewhat, subordinate; as *sub*marine, *under* the sea; *sub*angular, *somewhat* angular; *sub*divide, to divide into *subordinate* classes. Also, **s-**, **so-**, **su-**, **suc-**, **suf-**, **sug-**, **sum-**, **sup-**, **sur-**, **sus-**; as *s*omber, *so*journ, *su*spect, *suc*ceed, *suf*fuse, *sug*gest, *sum*mon, *sup*pose, *sur*reptitious, *sus*tain. [LAT.]

subter-, under; as *subter*fuge, a fleeing *under*, an evasion. [LAT.]

super-, above, beyond, over, very; as *super*natural, *above* or *beyond* the natural; *super*abundant, *over*abundant; *super*fine, *very* fine. [LAT.]

supra-, above, beyond; as *supra*mundane, *above* or *beyond* the world. [LAT.]

sur-, above, beyond, over; as *sur*mount, to rise *above;* *sur*pass, to pass *beyond;* *sur*charge, *over*charge. [FR.]

syn-, with, together; as *syn*agogue, a bringing *with* or *together*, an assembly. Also, **sy-**, **syl-**, **sym-**; as *sy*stem, *syl*logism, *sym*pathy. [GR.]

trans-, across, through, over, beyond; as *trans*atlantic, *across* the Atlantic; *trans*it, passage *through* or *over;* *trans*port, to carry *beyond*, from one place to another. Also, **tran-**, **tra-**, **tres-**, **tre-**; as *tran*scend, *tra*duce, *tres*pass, *tre*ason. [LAT.]

ultra-, beyond, excessively; as *ultra*marine, *beyond* the sea; *ultra*radical, *excessively* radical. [LAT.]

un-, not, to undo, to deprive of; as *un*conditional, *not* conditional; *un*bolt, *to undo* the bolt of; *un*crown, *to deprive of* the crown; completely; as *un*loose, to loose *completely*. [AS.]

under-, below, insufficiently, subordinate; as *under*ground, *below* ground; *under*fed, *insufficiently* fed; *under*officer, a *subordinate* officer. [AS.]

uni-, one; as *uni*corn, an animal with *one* horn. Also, **un-**; as *un*animous. [LAT.]

with-, against, back; as *with*stand, to stand *against;* *with*draw, to draw *back*. [AS.]

SUFFIXES.

-able, capable of being; fit to be; able to; inclined to; as port*able*, *capable of being* carried; lov*able*, *fit to be* loved; dur*able*, *able to* last; peace*able*, *inclined to* peace. Also, **-ible**, **-ble.** [LAT.]

-ac, pertaining to; as elegi*ac*, *pertaining to* an elegy. [GR.]

-acy, quality, state, or office of; as adequ*acy*, *quality of* being equal to; accur*acy*, *state of* being accurate; magistr*acy*, *office of* a magistrate. Also, **-ancy**, **-ency**, **-mancy.** [LAT.]

-age, collection, sum; as foli*age*, *collection* of leaves; mile*age*, the *sum* of miles; act, process; as pass*age*, the *act* or *process* of passing. [LAT.]

-al, pertaining to; as crimin*al*, *pertaining to* a crime. [LAT.]

-an, belonging or pertaining to, one who; as Americ*an*, *belonging* or *pertaining to* America, or *one who* is a native of America. Also, **-ane;** as hum*ane*. [LAT.]

-ance, state, act, quality of; as radi*ance*, *state, act*, or *quality of* radiating; that which is; as contriv*ance*: *that which is* contrived. Also, **-ancy;** as radi*ancy*. [LAT.]

-ant, -ing; one who; as pleas*ant*, pleas*ing*; assist*ant*, *one who* assists. Also, **-ent.** [LAT.]

-ar, pertaining to; one who; as insul*ar*, *pertaining to* an island; begg*ar*, *one who* begs. [LAT.]

-ard, one who does something to excess; as drunk*ard*, *one who* drinks *to excess*. [AS.]

-ary, one who; as mission*ary*, *one who* is sent; place where; as gran*ary*, *place where* grain is kept. [LAT.]

-ate, to make; as liber*ate*, *to make* free; one who; as potent*ate*, *one who* has power; office; as consul*ate*, *office* of consul; having; as anim*ate*, *having* breath. [LAT.]

-ation, act, state, or quality of; as form*ation*, *act of* forming; rel*ation*, *state* or *quality of* being related; that which; as ornament*ation*, *that which* ornaments; that which is; as cre*ation*, *that which is* created. Also, **-tion**, **-sion.** [LAT.]

-cle, little; as parti*cle*, a very *little* portion. Also, **-ule**, **-cule;** as glob*ule*, animal*cule*. [LAT.]

-cracy, government; as demo*cracy*, *government* by the people. [GR.]

-crat, one who has power; as pluto*crat*, *one who has power* because of his wealth. [GR.]

-cy, quality, state, or office of; as secre*cy*, *quality of* being secret; bankrupt*cy*, *state of* being bankrupt; captain*cy*, *office of* captain. Also, **-acy**, **-ancy**, **-ency**, **-mancy.** [LAT.]

-dom, dignity; jurisdiction; as duke*dom*, *dignity* or *jurisdiction* of a duke; state of being; as free*dom*, *state of being* free; those having the office of; as official*dom*, *those having the office of* officials. [AS.]

-ed, the ending of the preterit and past participle of regular or weak verbs; as ask*ed*; possessed of; as money*ed*, *possessed of* money. [ENG.]

-ee, one who; one to whom; as absent*ee*, *one who* is absent; assign*ee*, *one to whom* an assignment is made. [FR.]

-eer, one who; as engin*eer*, *one who* drives an engine. Also, **-ier.** [FR.]

-en, made of; wood*en*, *made of* wood; to make; as dark*en*, *to make* dark. [AS.]

-ence, state, act, or quality of; as emerg*ence*, *state, act*, or *quality of* emerging; that which is; as emin*ence*, *that which is* eminent. Also, **-ency;** as clem*ency*. [LAT.]

-ent, -ing; one who; as ard*ent*, burn*ing*; presid*ent*, *one who* presides. Also, **-ant.** [LAT.]

-er, one who; that which; as sing*er*, *one who* sings; New York*er*, *one who* is a native or inhabitant of New York; bind*er*, *one who*, or *that which*, binds; more; as warm*er*, *more* warm. [AS.]

-erly, in the direction of; south*erly*, *in the direction of* south. Also, **-ern;** as south*ern*. [AS.]

-ery, qualities of; as prud*ery*, *qualities of* a prude; art, trade, or occupation of; as potter*y*, *art, trade*, or *occupation of* a potter; place where; as pigg*ery*, *place where* pigs are kept; products of; as potter*y*, *products of* a potter; state of; as slave*ry*, *state of* a slave. Also, **-ry**, as foundr*y*. [FR.]

-escence, state of growing or becoming; as qui*escence*, *state of growing or becoming* quiet. [LAT.]

-escent, growing, becoming; one who is growing; as conval*escent*, *growing* or *becoming* well, one who is growing well. [LAT.]

-ese, belonging to; as Japan*ese*, *belonging to* Japan; having the style of; as Kipling*ese*, *having the style of* Kipling; a native or inhabitant of; as Japan*ese*, *a native or inhabitant of* Japan. [LAT.]

-esque, like; as pictur*esque*, *like* a picture. [FR.]

-ess, a female; as lion*ess*, a *female* lion. [LAT.]

-est, most; as simpl*est*, *most* simple. [AS.]

-et, little; as flower*et*, a *little* flower. [FR.]

-ette, little; as statu*ette*, a *little* statue. [FR.]

-ey, having, bearing, full of; as clay*ey*, *having*, *bearing*, or *full of* clay. Also, **-y.** [AS.]

-ferous, bearing; as odori*ferous*; *bearing* an odor. [LAT.]

-fold, times; as four*fold*, four *times*. [AS.]

-form, shaped; as cruci*form*, cross-*shaped*. [LAT.]

-ful, full of; as joy*ful*, *full of* joy. [AS.]

-fy, to make; as puri*fy*, *to make* pure. [LAT.]

-gram, something drawn or written; a record; as cable*gram*, a *record* made by the cable. [GR.]

-graph, writing, writer; as radio*graph*, *writing* produced by radiation; phono*graph*, a sound *writer*. [GR.]

-graphy, art of writing; description; as geo*graphy*, *art of writing* about the earth, a *description* of the earth. [GR.]

-hood, state, quality, or character of being; as man*hood*, *state* or *quality of* being a man; priest*hood*, *character of* being a priest; body of; as man*hood*, the *body of* men. Also, **-head**, as God*head*. [AS.]

-ible, capable of being, fit to be, able to be, inclined to; as flex*ible*, *capable of being* bent; ed*ible*, *fit to be* eaten; aud*ible*, *able to be* heard; irasc*ible*, *inclined to* anger. Also, **-able**, **-ble.** [LAT.]

-ic, pertaining to; like; as angel*ic*, *pertaining to*, or *like*, angels; that which, one who; as class*ic*, *that which* is of the first class; mechan*ic*, *one who* works in the mechanic arts. Also, **-ical**, as naut*ical*. [GR., LAT.]

-ics, science of; as mathemat*ics*, the *science of* mathematical knowledge. Also, **-ic;** as mus*ic*. [GR.]

-ie, little, dear little; as dogg*ie*, *little* dog; girl*ie*, *dear little* girl. [ENG.]

-ier, one who; as cash*ier*, *one who* has charge of money. Also, **-eer.** [FR.]

-ile, pertaining to; as juven*ile*, *pertaining to* youth; capable of; as doc*ile*, *capable of* being taught. Also, **-il;** as civ*il*. [LAT.]

-ine, belonging to; pertaining to; as mar*ine*, *belonging* or *pertaining to* the sea. [LAT.]

-ing, performing the act of; being; as drink*ing*, *performing the act of* taking a drink; liv*ing*, *being* alive; act or fact of; as writ*ing*, *act or fact of* one who writes; that which results from, or is used for; as sweep*ings*, *that which results from* one who sweeps; roofing, *that which is used for* a roof. [AS.]

-ish, belonging to, like, like in weaknesses; as girl*ish*, *belonging to* or *like* a girl; woman*ish*, *like* a woman *in* her *weaknesses*. [AS.]

-ism, act of, state or quality of being, diseased condition due to too much; as baptism, *act of* baptizing; fanaticism, *state or quality of being* a fanatic; alcoholism, *diseased condition due to too much* alcohol; peculiar to; doctrine of; as colloquialism, an expression *peculiar to* common speech; Methodism, *doctrine of* the Methodists. Also, **-asm,** as pleonasm. [Gr.]

-ist, one who; as suffragist, *one who* advocates suffrage. Also, **-ast;** as gymnast. [Gr.]

-ite, one who, especially a descendant, follower, or native of; as Israelite, *a descendant of* Israel; Hussite, *a follower of* John Huss; Jerseyite, *a native of* Jersey. [Gr.]

-itis, inflammation of; as appendicitis, *inflammation of* the appendix. [Gr.]

-ity, quality, state, or condition of being; as brevity, *quality, state, or condition of being* short. Also, **-ty.** [Lat.]

-ive, relating to, involving; as persuasive, *relating to* persuasion; appreciative, *involving* appreciation. [Lat.]

-ize, to subject to; as baptize, *to subject to* baptism; to make; as legalize, *to make* legal; to treat with, as oxidize, *to treat with* oxygen; to practice; as botanize, *to practice* botany. Also, **-ise,** as advertise. [Gr.]

-kin, little; as lamb*kin*, a *little* lamb. [AS.]

-lent, full of; as fraudulent, *full of* fraud. [Lat.]

-less, without; as worthless, *without* worth; unable to; as ceaseless, *unable to* cease. [AS.]

-let, little; as eaglet, a *little* eagle. [Fr.]

-like, like; as godlike, *like* a god. [AS.]

-ling, one who is; as hireling, *one who is* hired; little; as duckling, a *little* duck. [AS.]

-logy, discourse on, science of; as geology, *discourse on*, or *science of* the structure of the earth. [Gr.]

-ly, like; as manly, *like* a man; every; as weekly, *every* week; in a direction, manner, or degree; as westerly, *in a* western *direction;* quickly, *in a* quick *manner;* greatly, *in a* great *degree.* [AS.]

-mancy, divination; as necromancy, *divination* by communication with the dead. [Lat.]

-ment, act of, state of being; as government, *act of* governing; excitement, *state of being* excited; that which; as adornment, *that which* adorns; abridgment, *that which* is abridged. [Lat.]

-meter, an instrument for measuring; as thermometer, *an instrument for measuring* heat; measure; as hexameter, a verse of six *measures*. [Gr.]

-mony, state or quality of being; as acrimony, *state or quality of being* sharp; that which; as testimony, *that which* is offered by a witness. [Lat.]

-most, in the highest degree; as foremost, advanced *in the highest degree*. [AS.]

-ness, state, condition, or quality of being; as kindness, *state or quality of being* kind; blindness, *condition of being* blind; an act, or thing, that is; as kindness, *an act that is* kind. [AS.]

-ock, little; as hillock, a *little* hill. [AS.]

-or, act, state, or quality of; as favor, the *act of* favoring; splendor, *state or quality of* shining; one who, that which; as imitator, *one who* imitates; elevator, *that which* elevates. [Lat.]

-ory, pertaining to; place where; as prefatory, *pertaining to* the preface; dormitory, *place where* one sleeps. [Lat.]

-ose, full of, like; as verbose, *full of* words; globose, *like* a globe. [Lat.]

-ous, full of, like; as lustrous, *full of* luster; bulbous, bulb*like*. [Lat.]

-scope, an instrument for seeing; as periscope, *an instrument* on a submarine *for seeing* around. [Gr.]

-ship, state, condition, or quality of being; as friendship, *state* or *quality of being* a friend; office, or profession, of; art, or skill, of; as clerkship, *office of* clerk; horsemanship, *art*, or *skill*, *of* a horseman. [AS.]

-sion, act, state, or quality of; as cession, *act, state, or quality of* yielding; that which; as fusion, *that which* has been melted. Also, **-ation, -tion.** [Lat.]

-ster, one who; as teamster, *one who* drives a team. [AS.]

-tion, act, state, or quality of; as invention, *act of* inventing; dejection, *state or quality of* being dejected; that which; as production, *that which* is produced. Also, **-ation, -sion.** [Lat.]

-tomy, a cutting; as appendectomy, *a cutti g* away of the appendix. [Gr.]

-tude, state of being, -ness; as servitude, *state of being* a servant; gratitude, thankful*ness*. [Lat.]

-ty, quality, state, or condition of; as poverty, *quality, state,* or *condition of* being poor. [Lat.]

-ule, little; as globule, a *little* globe. Also, **-cle.** [Lat.]

-ure, act of, state of being, that which; as rupture, the *act of* breaking; verdure, the *state of being* green or *that which* is green, vegetation. [Lat.]

-ward, in the direction of; as homeward, *in the direction of* home. Also, **-wards;** as home*wards*. [AS.]

-ways, in a way, manner, or fashion; as noways, *in* no *way, manner, or fashion.* Also, **-wise;** as like*wise*. [AS.]

-y, having, bearing, or full of; as stony *having, bearing,* or *full of* stones; pertaining to; as earthy, *pertaining to* the earth. [AS.]

ABBREVIATIONS USED IN WRITING AND PRINTING.

a., about; acre; active; adjective; afternoon; alto; are (metric system); at.
A., Academician; Academy; America; American; Artillery; Augustus.
@, at.
A. A., Anti-aircraft Artillery.
A. A. A., Amateur Athletic Association.
A. A. G., Assistant Adjutant General.
A. A. of A., Automobile Association of America.
A. A. S. S. (Americanæ Antiquarianæ Societatis Socius), Fellow of the American Antiquarian Society. [LAT.]
ab., about.
a. b., able-bodied (seaman). Also, **A. B.**
A. B. (Artium Baccalaureus), Bachelor of Arts. [LAT.]
abbr., abbreviated; abbreviation. Also, **abbrev.**
A. B. C. F. M., American Board of Commissioners for Foreign Missions.
abd., abdicated.
A. B. F. M., American Board of Foreign Missions.
abl., ablative.
Abp., Archbishop.
abr., abridged; abridgment.
abs., absolutely; abstract.
A. B. S., American Bible Society.
abs. re (absente reo), in the absence of the defendant. [LAT.]
a/c, account.
A. C. (ante Christum), before Christ [LAT.]; Ambulance Corps; Army Corps.
Acad., Academy.
acc., acceptance; account; accusative.
accel. (accelerando), more quickly. [IT.]
acct., account.
A. C. G., Assistant Commissary General.
A. C. of S., Assistant Chief of Staff.
a. d. (ante diem), before the day [LAT.]; after date.
A. D. (anno Domini), in the year of our Lord. [LAT.]
ad. (*pl.* **ads.**), advertisement.
A. D. C., Aid-de-camp; Aide-de-camp.
ad fin. (ad finem), at the end. [LAT.]
ad inf. (ad infinitum), to infinity. [LAT.]
ad init. (ad initium), at the beginning. [LAT.]
ad int. (ad interim), in the meantime. [LAT.]
adj., adjective.
Adj., Adjutant. Also, **Adjt.**
Adj. Gen., Adjutant General.
ad lib. (ad libitum), at pleasure. [LAT.]
ad loc. (ad locum), at the place. [LAT.]
Adm., Admiral; Admiralty.
admin., administrator; administration.
admr., administrator.
admx., administratrix. Also, **admix.**
ads. (ad sectam), at the suit of [LAT.]; advertisements.
A. D. S., American Druggists' Syndicate.
adv. (ad valorem), according to the value; (adversus), against [LAT.]; adverb; advocate.
Adv., Advent.
adven., adventurer.
Adv. Gd., Advance Guard. Also, **A. G.**
æ. (ætatis), of age, aged. Also, **æt., ætat.** [LAT.]
A. E. F., American Expeditionary Forces.
Aero Sq., Aero Squadron.
A.-F., Anglo-French.
A. F. A. M., Ancient Free and Accepted Masons.
aff., affectionate; affirmative; affirming.
afft., affidavit.
A. F. L., American Federation of Labor. Also, **A. F. of L.**
Afr., Africa; African.
Ag (argentum), silver. [LAT.]
A. G., Advance Guard; Adjutant General; Attorney General.
A. G. O., Adjutant General's Office.
agr., agriculture; agricultural. Also, **agric.**
agt., agent.
A. H. (anno hegiræ), in the year of the hegira. [LAT.]
A. H. C., Army Hospital Corps.
A. I., American Institute.
Al, aluminum.
Ala., Alabama (official).
A. L. A., American Library Association; Automobile Legal Association.
Alas., Alaska.
ald., alderman. Also, **aldm.**
Alex., Alexander.
alg., algebra.
Alg., Algernon; Algiers.
alt., alternate; altitude; alto.
Alta., Alberta (Canada).
am., ammunition.
Am., America; American.
a. m. (ante meridiem), before noon. [LAT.]
A. M. (ante meridiem), before noon; (Artium Magister), Master of Arts; (Ave Maria), Hail, Mary; (anno mundi), in the year of the world. [LAT.]
Amb. Co., Ambulance Company.
Amb. Col., Ambulance Column.
A. M. D., Army Medical Department.
A. M. S., Army Medical Staff.
A.-N., Anglo-Norman.
anal., analogous; analogy; analysis; analytic.
anat., anatomy; anatomist.
anc., ancient; anciently.
A. N. C., Army Nurse Corps.
Angl., Anglican.
ans., answer.
ant., antonym; antiquarian.
Ant., Anthony; Antigua.
anthrop., anthropology; anthropological.
antiq., antiquities; antiquarian.
A. N. Z. A. C., Australian and New Zealand Army Corps.
A. O. C., Army Ordnance Corps.
A. O. D., Army Ordnance Department.
A. O. F., Ancient Order of Foresters.
A. O. H., Ancient Order of Hibernians.
aor., aorist.
A. P. A., American Philological Association; American Protective Association.
A. P. C., Army Pay Corps.

A. P. D., Army Pay Department.
Apoc., Apocalypse; Apocrypha; Apocryphal.
app., appendix; appointed.
approx., approximately.
Apr., April.
aq. (aqua), water. Also, **Aq.** [Lat.]
A. Q. M. G., Assistant Quartermaster General.
Ar., Arabian; Arabic. Also, **Arab.**
A. R. (anno regni), in the year of the reign. [Lat.]
A. R., Aërial Reconnoiterer; Army Regulations.
A. R. A., Associate of the Royal Academy (of Arts, London).
Arab., Arabian; Arabic.
Aram., Aramaic.
arch., archaic; archaism; archery; archipelago; architect; architecture.
Arch., Archibald.
archæol., archæology.
Archd., Archdeacon; Archduke.
arg., argent.
arith., arithmetic.
Ariz., Arizona (official).
Ark., Arkansas (official).
Arm., Armenian.
arr., arranged; arrived; arrivals.
A. R. R. (anno regni Regis, or Reginæ), in the year of the King's, or Queen's, reign. [Lat.]
art., article; artificial; artillery; artist.
A.-S., Anglo-Saxon. Also, **A-S.**
A. S. A., American Statistical Association.
A. S. C., Army Service Corps.
A. S. C. E., American Society of Civil Engineers.
A. S. M. E., American Society of Mechanical Engineers.
assn., association.
assoc., associate; association.
asst., assistant.
A. S. S. U., American Sunday School Union.
astr., astronomer; astronomy. Also, **astron.**
astrol., astrologer; astrology.
Atl., Atlantic.
A. T. S. Q. M. C., Army Transport Service Quartermaster Corps.
att., attorney. Also, **atty.**
attrib., attributive.
Atty. Gen., Attorney General.
at. wt., atomic weight.
Au (aurum), gold. [Lat.]
A. U. C. (ab urbe condita), from the founding of the city (Rome, about 753 B. C.). [Lat.]
Aug., August.
Aus., Austria; Austrian. Also, **Aust.**
Aust. Hung., Austria-Hungary.
Austral., Australasia; Australia.
Auth. Ver., Authorized Version.
auxil., auxiliary.
av., avenue; average.
a. v. (annos vixit), he, or she, lived (so many) years. [Lat.]
A. V., Authorized Version; Artillery Volunteers.
A. V. C., Army Veterinary Corps.
A. V. D., Army Veterinary Department.
avdp., avoirdupois.
ave., avenue. Also, **av.**
Av. Sec., Aviation Section.
Av. Sec. S. R. C., Aviation Section, Signal Reserve Corps.
a. w. l., absent with leave.
a. w. o. l., absent without leave.
ax., axiom.
B, boron.
b., base; bass; bay; book; born; brother.
Ba, barium.
B. A., Bachelor of Arts; British Academy; British America.
B. Agr., Bachelor of Agriculture.
bal., balance.
bap., baptized.
Bapt., Baptist.
bar., barometer; barometric; barrel.
Barb., Barbados.
barr., barrister.
Bart., Baronet.
Bat., Battalion. Also, **Batt.**, **Bn.**
Batt., Battery. Also, **B.**
bbl. (*pl.* **bbls.**), barrel. Also, **bl.**
B. C., before Christ; British Columbia; Battery Commander.
B. C. L., Bachelor of Civil Law.
bd., board; bond; bound.
B. D., Bachelor of Divinity.
bdl. (*pl.* **bdls.**), bundle.
bds., bound in boards.
Be, beryllium.
b. e., bill of exchange.
B. E. F., British Expeditionary Forces.
Belg., Belgian; Belgium. Also, **Bel.**
Benj., Benjamin.
B. ès L. (Bachelier ès Lettres), Bachelor of Letters. [Fr.]
bet., between.
bg. (*pl.* **bgs.**), bag.
b. h. p., brake horse power.
Bi, bismuth.
B. I., British India.
Bib., Bible; Biblical.
biog., biographer; biography.
biol., biologist; biology.
bk., bank; book.
bkg., banking.
bkt. (*pl.* **bkts.**), basket.
bl. (*pl.* **bls.**), bale; barrel.
b. l., bill of lading; breech-loading.
B. L., Bachelor of Laws.
B. L., breech-loader.
bldg. (*pl.* **bldgs.**), building.
B. L. E., Brotherhood of Locomotive Engineers.
B. Litt., Bachelor of Literature, or of Letters.
B. L. R., breech-loading rifle.
b. m., board measure.
B. M., Bachelor of Medicine; Brigade Major.
B. Mus., Bachelor of Music.
b. . branch office; buyer's option.
., Bohemia; Bohemian.
. Bolivia.
o. borough.
Bot., botanical; botanist; botany.
Bp., Bishop.
b. p., below proof; bill of parcels; bills payable.
B. Ph., Bachelor of Philosophy.
bpl., birthplace.
B. P. O. E., Benevolent and Protective Order of Elks.
Br, bromine.
br., brig; brother; brown.
Br., Britain; British.
Br. Am., British America.
Braz., Brazil, Brazilian.
b. rec., bills receivable.
Brig., Brigade; Brigadier.
Brig. Gen., Brigadier General.
Brit., Britain; British.
Brit. Mus., British Museum.
bro. (*pl.* **bros.**), brother.
b. s., balance sheet; bill of sale.
B. S., Bachelor of Surgery.
B. Sc., Bachelor of Science.
B. T. U., British thermal unit.
bu., bushel; bushels. Also, **bus.**
bul., bulletin.
Bulg., Bulgaria; Bulgarian.
B. V. (Beata Virgo), Blessed Virgin. [Lat.]
B. V. M. (Beata Virgo Maria), Blessed Virgin Mary. [Lat.]
Bvt., Brevet; Breveted.
bx., box.
C, carbon.

c. (circa), about [LAT.]; carton; cathode; cent; centime; centimeter; century; chapter; child; cost; cubic; current.
C., Cape; Catholic; Centigrade (thermometer); Chancellor; Chancery; Congress; Conservative; Consul; Corps; Court.
Ca, calcium.
C. A., Chief Accountant; Court of Appeal.
C. A. C., Coast Artillery Corps.
cal., calendar; calends; calorie.
Cal., California (official). Also, **Calif.**
Can., Canada; Canadian.
Cant., Canterbury; Canticles.
Cantab. (Cantabrigiensis), of Cambridge. [LAT.]
Cantuar. (Cantuaria), Canterbury; (Cantuariensis), of Canterbury. [LAT.]
cap. (capitulum), chapter [LAT.]; capital; capitalize; captain.
Capt., Captain.
car., caret; carpentry.
C. A. R. C., Coast Artillery Reserve Corps.
Card., Cardinal.
cash., cashier.
cat., catalog; catechism.
cath., cathedral.
Cath., Catherine; Catholic.
caus., causation; causative.
Cav., Cavalry.
Cb, columbium.
C. B., Cape Breton; Cavalry Brigade; Common Bench; Companion of the Bath; Confined to Barracks.
cc., cubic centimeter; cubic centimeters.
c.c. (compte courant), account current [FR.] cubic centimeter; cubic centimeters.
C. C., Caius College (Cambridge, England); Circuit Court; City Councillor; Civil Court; Common Councilman; County Clerk; County Commissioner.
C. C. A., Circuit Court of Appeals.
C. C. D., Commander of Coast Defenses.
c. e. (caveat emptor), at buyer's risk. [LAT.]
C. E., Civil Engineer; Church of England; Corps of Engineers.
Celt., Celtic.
cen., central; century.
Cen. Am., Central America.
cent., centigrade; central; century; centum.
cert., certificate; certify.
certif., certificate; certificated.
cf. (confer), compare. Also, **cp., comp.** [LAT.]
C. F. A., Chief of Field Artillery.
c. f. & i., cost, freight, and insurance.
cg., centigram.
C. G., Captain General; Captain of the Guard; Coast Guard; Commanding General; Commissary General; Consul General.
C. G. S., Centimeter, Gram, Second (system of units); Commissary General of Subsistence; Chief of General Staff in the Field.
ch., chapter; chief; child; church.
Ch., Chancery; Charles; China; Church.
C. H., Captain of the Horse; Courthouse; Customhouse.
chanc., chancellor; chancery.
chap., chaplain; chapter.
Chas., Charles.
chem., chemical; chemist; chemistry.
Chin., China; Chinese.
Ch. J., Chief Justice.
Chr., Christ; Christian; Christopher.
chron., chronological; chronology.
Chron., Chronicles.
C. I. E., Companion of the (Order of the) Indian Empire.
c. i. f., cost, insurance, and freight.
circ. (circa, circiter, circum), about. [LAT.]
cit., citation; cited; citizen.
civ., civil; civilian.
Cl, chlorine.
cl., centiliter; class; clause; clergyman; cloth.
class., classic; classical; classification.
cld., cleared; colored.
clk., clerk.
C. L. S. C., Chautauqua Literary and Scientific Circle.
clergy., clergyman. Also, **cl.**
cm., centimeter.
C. M., common meter; Corresponding Member; Court Martial.
C. M. G., Companion of St. Michael and St. George.
cml., commercial.
Co, cobalt.
Co., Company; County.
c. o., care of; carried over.
C. O., Commanding Officer.
coch. (cochleare), spoonful. Also, **cochl.** [LAT.]
coad., coadjutor.
C. O. D., cash, or collect, on delivery.
C. of O., Chief of Ordnance.
C. of S., Chief of Staff.
cog., cognate.
col., college; collegiate; colonial; colony; colored; column.
Col., Colonel; Colorado; Colossians; Column.
coll., colleague; collection; collector; college.
collat., collateral; collaterally.
colloq., colloquial; colloquially.
Colo., Colorado (official). Also, **Col.**
Col. Serg., Color Sergeant.
com., comedy; commentary; commerce; common; commonly; commune; communication.
Com., Commander; Commission; Commissioner; Committee; Commodore.
Comdg., Commanding.
Comdr., Commander. Also, **Com.**
Comdt., Commandant.
comm., commune.
Com. Off., Commissioned Officer.
comp., compare; comparative; composer; compositor; compound; comprising.
Com. Serg., Commissary Sergeant.
Com. Ver., Common Version.
con. (contra), against. [LAT.]
Confed., Confederate.
Cong., Congregational; Congregationalist; Congress; Congressional.
conj., conjunction.
Conn., Connecticut (official).
cont., containing; contents; continent; continue; continued.
contemp., contemporary.
contr., contracted; contraction; contrary.
cor., corner; cornet; corrected; correction; correlative; correspondent; corresponding.
Cor., Corinthians; Coroner.
coroll., corollary.
Corp., Corporal.
cos, cosine.
cosec, cosecant.
cot, cotangent.
cp., compare. Also, **comp., cf.**
c. p., candle power; chemically pure.
C. P., Common Pleas; Common Prayer; Court of Probate.
C. P. A., Certified Public Accountant. Also, **c. p. a.**
c. p. o., chief petty officer.
cr., created; credit; creditor; crown.
cresc. (crescendo), with a constantly increasing volume. [IT.]
crim. con., criminal conversation.
Cs, cæsium.
C. S. A., Confederate States Army; Confederate States of America.

C. S. C., Conspicuous Service Cross.
C. S. I., Companion of the Star of India.
C. S. N., Confederate States Navy.
C. S. O., Chief Surgeon's Office; Chief Signal Officer.
ct., cent; count.
Ct., Connecticut; Count; Court.
C. T. A. U., Catholic Total Abstinence Union.
cts., cents; centimes.
Cu (cuprum), copper. [LAT.]
cu., cubic. Also, **cub.**
cur., currency; current.
curt., current, the present month.
C. V., Common Version.
c. w. o., cash with order.
cwt. (centum [LAT.], weight), hundredweight; hundredweights.
cyc., cyclopedia; cyclopedic. Also, **cyclo.**
C. Z., Canal Zone.
D. (Deus), God [LAT.]; (Dominus), Lord [LAT.]; Democrat; Department; Duke; Dutch.
d. (denarius, denarii), penny, pence [LAT.]; date; daughter; day; dead; degree; deputy; died; dime; dollar; dose.
Dan., Daniel; Danish.
D. A. R., Daughters of the American Revolution.
dat., dative.
dau., daughter. Also, **d.**
d. b., daybook.
dbk., drawback.
D. C. (da capo), from the beginning [IT.]; Dental Corps; District Court; District of Columbia.
D. C. L., Doctor of Civil Law.
D. C. M., Distinguished Conduct Medal.
D. Cn. L., Doctor of Canon Law.
d. d., days after date.
D. D., Doctor of Divinity.
D. D. S., Doctor of Dental Surgery.
Dea., Deacon.
deb., debenture.
dec., declension; declination; decorative.
Dec., December.
def., defendant; definition.
deft., defendant.
deg., degree.
del. (delineavit), he, or she, drew it [LAT.]; delegate.
Del., Delaware (official).
Dem., Democrat; Democratic.
Den., Denmark.
dep., department; departs; deponent; deputy.
depend., dependency.
dept., department; deponent. Also, **dep.**
der., derivation; derivative; derived.
Det., Detachment.
Deut., Deuteronomy.
D. F. (Defensor Fidei), Defender of the Faith [LAT.]; Dean of the Faculty.
dft., defendant; draft.
dg., decigram.
D. G. (Dei gratia), by the grace of God; (Deo gratias), thanks to God [LAT.]; Director General.
D. H., Deadhead.
Di, didymium.
dial., dialect; dialectic.
diam., diameter.
dict., dictator; dictionary.
dim. (diminuendo), with gradually diminishing volume [IT.]; diminutive. Also, **dimin.**
disc., discount; discovered; discoverer.
dist., distant; distinguished; district.
div., divide; divided; dividend; divine; division; divisor.
dl., deciliter.
D. Lit., Doctor of Literature.
D. L. O., Dead Letter Office.
dm., decimeter.
D. M. S., Director of Medical Service.
do., ditto.
D. O., Doctor of Osteopathy.
D. of Ry., Director of Railways.
dol., dollar; dollars.
dols., dollars.
dom., domestic; dominion.
D. O. M. (Deo Optimo Maximo), to God, the Best, the Greatest. [LAT.]
D. O. R. C., Dental Officers' Reserve Corps.
dow., dowager.
doz., dozen; dozens.
D. Pd., Doctor of Pedagogy.
dpl., diplomat.
dpt., deponent; department.
dr., dram; drawer.
Dr., debtor; Doctor.
D. R., Drill Regulations.
dram., dramatist.
dram. pers. (dramatis personæ), the characters or actors in a drama. [LAT.]
d. s. (dal segno), from the sign: musical direction [IT.]; days after sight.
D. S., Director of Supplies; Dental Surgeon; Detached Service.
D. Sc., Doctor of Science.
D. S. C., Distinguished Service Cross.
D. S. O., Distinguished Service Order (British Army and Navy).
d. s. p. (decessit sine prole), died without issue. [LAT.]
D. T.'s, delirium tremens. [COLLOQ.]
Du., Dutch.
D. V. (Deo volente), God willing. [LAT.]
D. V. M., Doctor of Veterinary Medicine.
d. v. p. (decessit vita patris), died during the lifetime of his, or her, father. [LAT.]
dwt. (denarius [LAT.], weight), pennyweight; pennyweights.
Dy. dysprosium.
E., Earl; Earth; East; Eastern; Engineer; English.
ea., each.
E. & O. E., errors and omissions excepted.
Ebor. (Eboracensis), of York. [LAT.]
E. C., Established Church.
eccl., ecclesiastical. Also, **eccles**, **ecclesias.**
Eccl., Ecclesiastes. Also, **Eccles.**
Ecclus., Ecclesiasticus.
Ecua., Ecuador.
E. D., Eastern Department; **Extra Duty.**
ed., edition; editor.
Edin., Edinburgh.
edit., edition. Also, **ed.**
educ., educator.
Edw., Edward.
E. E., Early English; Electrical Engineer; errors excepted.
E. E. & M. P., Envoy Extraordinary and Minister Plenipotentiary.
E. F., Expeditionary Forces.
Eg., Egypt; Egyptian.
e. g. (exempli gratia), for example. [LAT.]
E. I., East India; East Indies.
elec., electrical; electrician; electricity.
Eliz., Elizabeth; Elizabethan.
E. long., East longitude.
Em., Emmanuel; Emily; Emma.
E. M., Earl Marshall.
E. M. F., electromotive force.
Emp., Emperor; Empress.
ency., encyclopedia. Also, **encyc.**
E. N. E., East-northeast.
eng., engineer; engraving.
Eng., England; English; Engineers.
engin., engineer; engineering.
Ens., Ensign.
entom., entomology.
E. O., Engineer Officer.
Eph., Ephesians; Ephraim.
Epiph., Epiphany.
Epis., Episcopal. Also, **Episc.**

eq., equal; equivalent.
Er, erbium.
E. S. E., East-southeast.
esp., especially. Also, **espec.**
Esq., Esquire.
essay., essayist.
est., estuary.
estab., established. Also, **est.**
Esth., Esther.
E. T., electric telegraph; English translation. Also, **e. t.**
et al. (et alibi), and elsewhere; (et alii), and others. [LAT.]
etc. (et cetera), and others, and so forth. [LAT.]
et seq. (et sequens), and the following. [LAT.]
et sequ. (et sequentes, et sequentia), and the following. [LAT.]
etym., etymology. Also, **etymol.**
ex., examined; example; exception; exchange; excursion; executed; executive; export; extract.
Ex., Exodus. Also, **Exod.**
ex div., ex, or without, dividend.
exp., export; express.
explor., explorer.
exr., executor.
exrx., executrix.
ext., external; extinct; extra; extract.
extrem., extremity.
Ezek., Ezekiel.
F, fluorine.
f., farthing; fathom; feminine; flower; foot; (forte), loud [IT.]; franc.
F., Fahrenheit; French.
F. A., Field Artillery.
f. a. a., free of all average.
fac., facsimile.
Fahr., Fahrenheit. Also, **F.**
F. A. I. A., Fellow of the American Institute of Architects.
fam., familiar; family.
F. A. M., Free and Accepted Masons. Also, **F. and A. M.**
F. Amb., Field Ambulance.
F. A. S., Fellow of the Antiquarian Society.
F. B., Fenian Brotherhood.
F. B. A., Fellow of the British Academy.
F. B. S., Fellow of the Botanical Society.
fcap., foolscap.
F. C. C., First-class Certificate.
F. D. (Fidei Defensor), Defender of the Faith. [LAT.]
Fe (ferrum), iron. [LAT.]
Feb., February.
fec. (fecit), he, or she, made it. [LAT.]
fem., feminine. Also, **f.**
ff. (fecerunt), they made it [LAT.]; folios; following (pages); (fortissimo), very loudly [IT.].
f. g. a., free of general average.
F. G. S., Fellow of the Geological Society.
F. Hosp., Field Hospital.
f. i., for instance.
F. I. A., Fellow of the Institute of Actuaries.
fict., fiction.
fig., figurative; figuratively; figure.
Fin., Finland; Finnish.
fl., florin; flourished; fluid.
Fl., Flanders; Flemish.
Fla., Florida (official).
Flem., Flemish.
fm., fathom.
F. M., Field Marshal; Foreign Mission.
fo., folio.
F. O., Field Officer; Foreign Office; Field Order.
f. o. b., free on board.
fol., folio; following.
for., foreign.
fort., fortification; fortified.
f. p. a., free of particular average.
fr., fragment; franc; from.
Fr., Father; France; Frau; French; Friar; Friday.
F. R. A. M., Fellow of the Royal Academy of Music (London).
F. R. A. S., Fellow of the Royal Astronomical Society; Fellow of the Royal Asiatic Society.
F. R. C. P., Fellow of the Royal College of Physicians (London).
F. R. C. S., Fellow of the Royal College of Surgeons (London).
Fred., Frederick.
freq., frequent; frequentative.
F. R. G. S., Fellow of the Royal Geographical Society.
Fri., Friday.
F. R. S., Fellow of the Royal Society (scientific, London).
frs., francs.
F. R. S. E., Fellow of the Royal Society of Edinburgh.
F. S., Field Service.
F. S. R., Field Service Regulations
ft., feet; foot; fort; fortified
fur., furlong; further.
fut., future.
F. Z. S., Fellow of the Zoölogical Society (London).
g., gauge; genitive; gram; guide; guinea; guineas; gulf.
G., German. Also, **Ger.**
Ga, gallium.
Ga., Georgia (official). Also, **Geo.**
G. A., General Assembly.
gal. (*pl.* **gals.**), gallon.
Gal., Galatians.
galv., galvanic; galvanism.
G. A. R., Grand Army of the Republic.
gaz., gazette; gazetteer.
G. B., Great Britain.
G. B. & I., Great Britain and Ireland.
G. C., Gun Captain; Grand Chancellor; Grand Chaplain; Grand Chapter; Grand Council.
G. C. B., Grand Commander of the Bath; Grand Cross of the Bath.
g. c. d., greatest common divisor.
g. c. m., greatest common measure.
G. C. M., General Court Martial.
G. C. M. G., Grand Cross of St. Michael and St. George.
gen., gender; general; generic; genitive; genus.
Gen., General; Genesis.
gent., gentleman.
Geo., George; Georgia.
geog., geographer; geographic; geographical; geography.
geol., geologic; geological; geologist; geology.
geom., geometry; geometrician. Also, **geomet.**
ger., gerund.
Ger., German; Germany.
g. gr., great gross, or 144 dozen.
G. H. Q., General Headquarters.
gi., gill; gills.
G. L., Grand Lodge.
Gl, glucinum.
gm., gram.
G. M., Grand Master.
G. O., General Orders.
G. O. C., General Officer Commanding.
G. O. P., Grand Old Party (the U. S. Republican Party).
gov., government; governor.
Gov. Gen., Governor General.
govt., government. Also, **gov.**
G. P. (Gloria Patri), Glory to the Father [LAT.]; Graduate in Pharmacy.
G. P. O., General Post Office.
gr., grain; grand; great; gross.
Gr., Greece; Greek; Grecian.

gram., grammar.
Gr. Br., Great Britain. Also, **Gr. Brit.**
G. S., General Secretary; Grand Scribe; Grand Secretary; General Service; General Staff.
gt. (gutta; *pl.* **gtt.** guttæ), drop. [LAT.]
H., Headquarters. Also, **Hqrs., Hq.**
H, hydrogen.
h., harbor; hard; hardness; height; high; hour; husband.
ha., hectare.
H. A., Horse Artillery.
Hab., Habakkuk.
Hag., Haggai.
H. B. M., His, or Her, Britannic Majesty.
H. C., Heralds' College; House of Commons.
h. c. f., highest common factor.
H. D., Headquarters Detachment; Hawaiian Department.
hdkf., handkerchief.
He, helium.
H. E., Horizontal Equivalent; High Explosive.
H. E., His Eminence; His Excellency.
h. e. (hoc est), this. [LAT.]
Heb., Hebrew; Hebrews.
hectol., hectoliter.
hectom., hectometer.
her., heraldry.
H. F. A., Heavy Field Artillery.
hg., hectogram; heliogram.
Hg (hydrargyrum), mercury. [LAT.]
H. G., His, or Her, Grace; High German.
H. H., His, or Her, Highness; His Holiness (the Pope).
hhd., hogshead; hogsheads.
H. I., Hawaiian Islands.
H. I. H., His, or Her, Imperial Highness.
H. I. M., His, or Her, Imperial Majesty.
Hind., Hindu; Hindustan; Hindustani.
hist., historian; historical; history.
H. J. (hic jacet), here lies. [LAT.]
hl., hectoliter.
H. L., House of Lords.
hm., hectometer.
H. M., His, or Her, Majesty.
H. M. S., His, or Her, Majesty's Service, or Ship.
ho., house.
Holl., Holland.
Hon., Honorable; Honorary.
hor., horizon; horology.
hort., horticulture.
Hos., Hosea.
Hosp., Hospital.
H. P., half pay; high pressure; horse power. Also, **h. p.**
hr. (*pl.* **hrs.**), hour.
H. R., Home Rule; House of Representatives.
H. R. H., His, or Her, Royal Highness.
H. S. (hic sepultus), here is buried; (hic situs), here lies [LAT.]; High School.
H. S. H., His, or Her, Serene Highness.
ht., height.
Hung., Hungarian; Hungary. Also, **Hun.**
Hv. A., Heavy Artillery.
H. W. M., high-water mark.
Hy., Henry.
hyd., hydrostatics.
hyp., hypothesis; hypothetical.
I, iodine.
I. (Imperator), Emperor [LAT.]; Idaho; Island.
Ia., Iowa (official).
ib. (ibidem), in the same place. Also, **ibid.** [LAT.]
I. C. (Iesus Christus), Jesus Christ [LAT.]; inspected, condemned.
Ice., Iceland; Icelandic. Also, **Icel.**
I. C. S. A., Intercollegiate Community Service Association.
id. (idem), the same. [LAT.]
I. D., Intelligence Department.
Ida., Idaho. Also, **I., Id.**
I. D. R., Infantry Drill Regulations.
i. e. (id est), that is. [LAT.]
I. G., Inspector General.
ign. (ignotus), unknown. [LAT.]
i. h. p., indicated horse power.
I H S, three letters of the Greek for Jesus.
ill., illustrated; illustration; illustrator. Also, **illus., illust.**
Ills., Illinois (official). Also, **Ill.**
illus., illustrator.
imp. (imprimatur), let it be printed [LAT.]; imperative; imperfect; imperial; impersonal; imported; importer.
In, indium.
in. (*pl.* **ins.**), inch.
inc., including; inclusive; incorporated; increase.
inch., inchoative. Also, **incho.**
incl., including; inclusive. Also, **inc.**
incog., incognito.
incor., incorporated.
ind., independent; indicative; indigo.
Ind., India; Indian; Indiana (official).
indepen., independent. Also, **ind.**
inf., infinitive.
Inf., Infantry.
in f. (in fine), at the end. [LAT.]
in lim. (in limine), at the outset. [LAT.]
in loc. cit. (in loco citato), the place cited. [LAT.]
I. N. R. I. (Iesus Nazarenus, Rex Iudæorum), Jesus of Nazareth, King of the Jews. [LAT.]
ins., inches; inscribed; inspector; insurance.
insp., inspector.
inst., instant; institute; institution.
int., interest; interior; interjection; internal; international; interpreter; intransitive.
interj., interjection. Also, **int.**
intrans., intransitive. Also, **int.**
in trans. (in transitu), on the way. [LAT.]
introd., introduction; introductory.
inv. (invenit), he, or she, designed it [LAT.]; inventor; invoice.
Io., Iowa. Also, **Ia.** (official).
I. O. F., Independent Order of Foresters.
Ion., Ionic.
I. O. O. F., Independent Order of Odd Fellows.
I. O. R., Independent Order of Rechabites.
I. O. R. M., Improved Order of Red Men.
I O U, I owe you.
i. q. (idem quod), the same as. [LAT.]
Ir, iridium
Ir., Ireland; Irish.
I. R., Internal Revenue.
Ire., Ireland. Also, **Ir.**
is., island; isle.
Is., Isaiah. Also, **Isa.**
isl. (*pl.* **isls.**), island; isle.
It., Italian; Italy. Also, **Ital.**
ital., italic; italics.
J., Judge; Justice.
J. A., Judge Advocate.
J. A. G., Judge Advocate General.
Jam., Jamaica.
Jan., January.
Jap., Japan; Japanese.
Jas., James.
J. C., Jesus Christ; Julius Cæsar; jurisconsult.
J. C. D. (Juris Civilis Doctor), Doctor of Civil Law. [LAT.]
J. D. (Jurum Doctor), Doctor of Laws. [LAT.]
Jer., Jeremiah.
JJ., Justices.
Jno., John.
Jon., Jonathan. Also, **Jona.**

Jos., Joseph.
Josh., Joshua.
jour., journal; journalist; journeyman.
J. P., Justice of the Peace.
Jr., Junior. Also, **Jun.**, **Junr.**
J. U. D. (Juris Utriusque Doctor), Doctor of Both (Canon and Civil) Laws. [LAT.]
Judg., Judges.
Jun., Junior. Also, **Jun.**
Junc., Junction.
Jus., justice. Also, **just.**, **Jus.**, **Just.**
K, kalium.
K., King; Kings; Knight.
K. A., Knight of St. Andrew (Russia).
Kans., Kansas (official). Also, **Kan.**, **Kas.**
K. B., Knight of Bath.
K. C., Knights of Columbus. Also, **K. of C.**
K. C. B., Knight Commander of the Bath.
K. C. I. E., Knight Commander of the Indian Empire.
K. C. M. G., Knight Commander of St. Michael and St. George.
K. C. S. I., Knight Commander of the Star of India.
K. C. V. O., Knight Commander of the Royal Victorian Order.
Ken., Kentucky. Also, **Ky.** (official).
kg., kilogram.
K. G., Knight of the Garter.
K. G. F., Knight of the Golden Fleece.
Kl., Kings.
kilom., kilometer.
K. K. K., Ku-Klux Klan.
kl., kiloliter.
K. L. H., Knight of the Legion of Honor (France).
km., kilometer; kingdom.
K. M., Knight of Malta.
knt., knight.
K. P., Kitchen Police; Knight of Pythias; Knight of St. Patrick.
Kr, krypton.
K. T., Knight of the Thistle; Knight Templar.
Ky., Kentucky (official). Also, **Ken.**
l. (libra), a pound [LAT.]; lake; land; latitude; leaf; league; left; length; line; link; liter.
L. (Liber), Book [LAT.]; Lady; Latin; Law; Liberal; Low.
La, lanthanum.
La., Louisiana (official).
Lab., Labrador.
Lam., Lamentations.
lat., latitude.
Lat., Latin. Also, **L.**
law., lawyer.
lb. (libra; *pl.* **lbs.**, libræ), pound. [LAT.]
l. c. (loco citato), in the place cited [LAT.]; letter of credit; lower case.
L/c, Letter of Credit.
L. C. J., Lord Chief Justice.
l. c. m., least common multiple.
Ld., Lord. Also, **ld.**
Ldp., Lordship.
lea., league.
leg., legal; legate; legato; legislative; legislature.
legis., legislator.
Lev., Leviticus.
L. F. M., Lieutenant Field Marshal.
L G., Low German. Also, **L. G.**
L. G., Life Guards.
l. h., left hand.
L. H., Light Horse.
L. H. A., Lord High Admiral.
Li, lithium.
L. I., Light Infantry; Long Island.
lib. (liber), book [LAT.]; librarian; library.
Lieut., Lieutenant. Also, **Lt.**
Lieut. Gen., Lieutenant General.
lin., lineal; linear.
liq., liquid; liquor.
lit., liter; literal; literally; literary; literature.
Lit. D. (Literarum Doctor), Doctor of Letters. [LAT.]
Lith., Lithuanian.
Litt. D. (Litterarum Doctor), Doctor of Letters. [LAT.]
LL., Late Latin; Low Latin.
l. l. (loco laudato), in the place quoted. [LAT.]
L. L., Late Latin; Lord Lieutenant; Low Latin.
LL. B. (Legum Baccalaureus), Bachelor of Laws. [LAT.]
LL. D. (Legum Doctor), Doctor of Laws. [LAT.]
L. L. I., Lord Lieutenant of Ireland.
L. M., long meter.
loc. cit. (loco citato), in the place cited. [LAT.]
L. of C., Line of Communication.
log., logarithm.
lon., longitude. Also, **long.**
loq. (loquitur), he, or she, speaks. [LAT.]
l. s., left side.
L. S. (loco sigilli), place of the seal. [LAT.]
L. S. D. (libræ, solidi, denarii), pounds, shillings, pence. Also, **£ s. d.**, **l. s. d.** [LAT.]
L. S. S., Life Saving Station.
Lt., Lieutenant. Also, **Lieut.**
l. t., long ton.
ltd., limited.
LXX, Septuagint. Also, **Sep.**, **Sept.**
m., male; manual; married; masculine; measure; medicine; medium; meridian; meter; middle; mile; mill; minute; month; moon; morning; mountain.
M., Majesty; Manitoba; Marshal; Marquis; Master; Member; Militia; Monday; Monsieur.
M. A. (Magister Artium), Master of Arts [LAT.]; Military Academy; Mountain Artillery.
Mac., Maccabees.
Maced., Macedonia; Macedonian.
mach., machinery.
Mad., Madam.
mag., magazine; magnitude.
Maj., Major.
Maj. Gen., Major General.
Mal., Malachi; Malayan.
man., manual.
Manit., Manitoba. Also, **M.**
manuf., manufactory; manufacture; manufacturer. Also, **manufac.**
mar., maritime.
Mar., March.
March., Marchioness.
Marq., Marquis.
mas., masculine. Also, **masc.**
Mass., Massachusetts (official).
math., mathematician; mathematics.
Matt., Matthew.
max., maximum.
M. C., Master Commandant; Master of Ceremonies; Member of Congress; Member of Council.
M. C., Medical Corps.
Md., Maryland (official).
M. D. (Medicinæ Doctor), Doctor of Medicine. [LAT.]
M/D, months' date (i. e., months after date).
mdse., merchandise.
Me., Maine (official).
ME., Middle English.
M. E., Mechanical, Military, or Mining, Engineer; Methodist Episcopal; Middle English; Most Excellent.
meas., measure.
mech., mechanics; mechanical.

med., medical; medicine; medieval; medium.
Medit., Mediterranean.
mem., memento; memoir; memorandum; memorial.
mer., meridian; meridional.
Messrs., Messieurs; Misters.
metal., metallurgy.
meteor., meteorology.
Meth., Methodist.
Mex., Mexican; Mexico.
Mf. (mezzo forte), moderately loud. Also, **mf.** [It.]
mfg., manufacturing.
M. F. H., Master of Foxhounds.
mfr. (*pl.* **mfrs.**), manufacturer.
Mg, magnesium.
mg., milligram.
M. G., Machine Gun; Machine Gun Unit.
M. G. C., Machine Gun Company.
mgr., manager.
Mgr., Monseigneur; Monsignor.
M. H. G., Middle High German. Also, **M H G.**
M. H. R., Member of the House of Representatives.
M. H. S., Massachusetts Historical Society.
Mic., Micah.
Mich., Michaelmas; Michigan (official).
mid., middle; midshipman.
mil., military; militia.
min., minim; minimum; mining; minister; minor; minute.
Minn., Minnesota (official).
Min. Plen., Minister Plenipotentiary.
misc., miscellaneous.
Miss., Mississippi.
mission., missionary.
ml., mail; milliliter.
M. L. A., Modern Language Association.
Mlle. (*pl.* **Mlles.**), Mademoiselle.
mm., millimeter.
M M., Their Majesties; Messieurs.
M. M., Motor Mechanics.
Mme. (*pl.* **Mmes.**), Madame.
Mn, manganese.
M. N. A. S., Member of the National Academy of Sciences.
Mo, molybdenum.
mo. (*pl.* **mos.**), month.
Mo., Missouri (official).
M. O., money order.
mod. (moderato), moderately [It.]; moderate; modern.
Moham., Mohammedan.
mol. wt., molecular weight.
Mon., Monastery; Monday.
Monsig., Monseigneur; Monsignor.
Mont., Montana (official).
Mor., Morocco.
M. O. R. C., Medical Officers' Reserve Corps.
M. P., Member of Parliament; Methodist Protestant; Military Police.
M. P. C., Member of Parliament, Canada.
m. p. h., miles per hour.
Mr., Mister.
Mrs., Mistress; Madame.
MS. (*pl.* **M S S.**), manuscript. Also, **ms.**
M. S. (memoriæ sacrum), sacred to the memory [Lat.]; Master of Science; Master of Surgery; Mess Sergeant.
m. s. l., mean sea level.
MSS., manuscripts. Also, **mss.**
mt. (*pl.* **mts.**), mount; mountain.
mun., municipal.
mus., museum; music; musician.
Mus. B., Bachelor of Music.
Mus. D., Doctor of Music.
M. W., Most Worshipful; Most Worthy.
M. W. V., Mexican War Veterans.
myg., myriagram.
myl., myrialiter.
mym., myriameter.
myth., mythology.
N, nitrogen.
n. (natus), born [Lat.]; nephew; neuter; new; nominative; note; noun; number.
N., name; Navy; Noon; Norse; North; Northern.
N. A., National Academy; National Army; North America; North American.
N. A. A., National Automobile Association.
N. A. D., National Academy of Design.
Nah., Nahum.
N. A. S., National Academy of Sciences.
nat., national; native; natural.
Nath., Nathanael; Nathaniel.
natur., naturalist.
naut., nautical.
nav., naval; navigable; navigation.
navig., navigation; navigator. Also, **nav.**
Nb, niobium.
N. B. (nota bene), note well, or take notice [Lat.]; New Brunswick.
N. C., North Carolina (official).
N. C. O., Noncommissioned Officer.
Nd, neodymium.
n. d., no date.
N. Dak., North Dakota (official). Also, **N. D.**
N. E., New England.
N. E. A., National Education Association.
Nebr., Nebraska (official). Also, **Neb.**
neg., negative.
Neh., Nehemiah.
nem. con. (nemine contradicente), no one contradicting, unanimously. [Lat.]
Neth., Netherlands.
neut., neuter.
Nev., Nevada (official).
NF, Norman French. Also, **N. F.**
N. F., Norman French; Newfoundland.
Ng., Norwegian.
N. G., National Guard; New Granada; slang, no good.
N. H., New Hampshire (official).
Nicar., Nicaragua.
N. J., New Jersey (official).
N. L., New Latin. Also, **N L.**
N. Lat., North latitude.
N. Mex., New Mexico (official). Also, **N. M.**
N. N. E., North-northeast.
N. N. W., North-northwest.
No. (numero; *pl.* **Nos.**), by number. Also, **no.** [Lat.]
nol. pros. (nolle prosequi), to be unwilling to prosecute. [Lat.]
nom., nominative.
non obst. (non obstante), notwithstanding. [Lat.]
non pros. (non prosequitur), he does not prosecute. [Lat.]
non seq. (non sequitur), it does not follow. [Lat.]
n. o. p., not otherwise provided for.
Nor., Norman; North.
Norw., Norway; Norwegian. Also, **Nor.**
Norweg., Norwegian. Also, **Nor.**, **Norw.**
nos., numbers.
nov., novelist.
Nov., November.
N. P., New Providence; Notary Public.
nr., near.
N. R. A., National Rifle Association.
N. S., National Society; New Series; New Style; Nova Scotia.
N/S, not sufficient (funds).
N. S. W., New South Wales.
N. T., New Testament.
n. u., name unknown.
Num., Numbers.
N. W., Northwest; Northwestern.
N. W. S. A., National Woman's Suffrage Association.

N. W. T., Northwest Territories.
N. Y., New York (official).
N. Z., New Zealand.
O, oxygen.
O., (octarius), pint [LAT.]; October; Ohio; Old; Ontario; Order.
o/a, on account (of).
ob., (obiit), he, or she, died. [LAT.]
Obad., Obadiah.
obdt., obedient.
O. B. E., Order of the British Empire.
obj., object; objection; objective.
obl., oblique; oblong.
obs., observation; observatory; obsolete.
oc., ocean.
O. C., Officer Commanding.
Oct., October.
O. D., Ordnance Datum; Olive Drab.
O. E., Old English. Also, **O E.**
O. E., omissions excepted.
O. E. D., Oxford English Dictionary.
O. F., Old French. Also, **O F.**
off., offered; officer; official.
O. G., Outside Guard; Officer of the Guard.
O. H. G., Old High German. Also, **O H G.**
O. H. M. S., On His, or Her, Majesty's Service.
O. K. (Okeh), it is so, all right. Also, **O K.** [CHOCTAW INDIAN.]
Okla., Oklahoma (official).
ol. (oleum), oil. [LAT.]
Ol., Olympiad.
O. M., Old Measurement; Order of Merit.
Ont., Ontario.
o/o, per cent.
O. O., Ordnance Officer.
op., opera; opposite; opus.
opp., opposed; opposite.
opt., optative; optics.
Or., Oriental.
O. R. C., Order of the Red Cross.
ord., ordained; order; ordinance; ordinary; ordnance.
Ore., Oregon (official) Also, **Oreg.**, **Or.**
O. S., Old School; Old Series; Old Style; ordinary seaman.
O. T., Old Testament.
O. T. C., Officers' Training Camp.
oz., ounce; ounces.
Oxon. (Oxonia), Oxford; (Oxoniensis), of Oxford. [LAT.]
P, phosphorus.
p. (piano), softly [IT.]; page; part; participle; past; penny; pint; pipe; pole; population; professional.
P. (pater), father [LAT.]; (père), father [FR.]; pastor; post; president; priest; prince.
P., Philippine Scouts. Also, **P. S.**
Pa., Pennsylvania (official). Also, **Penn.**, **Penna.**
p. a. (per annum), by the year [LAT.]; participial adjective.
P/A, power of attorney; private account.
P. A., Post Adjutant.
Pac., Pacific.
p. adj., participial adjective.
Pan., Panama.
par., paragraph; parallel; parenthesis; parish.
Para., Paraguay.
parl., parliament; parliamentary.
part., participle. Also, **p.**, **ptc.**
pass., passive.
Pat. Off., Patent Office.
Paym., Paymaster.
payt., payment.
Pb. (plumbum), lead. [LAT.]
P. B., Prayer Book.
P. C., Police Constable; Principal Chaplain; Privy Council; Privy Councilor.
p. c., per cent; postal card; postcard.
P. C. D., Panama Canal Department.
Pd., palladium.
pd., paid.
Pd. D. (Pædagogiæ Doctor), Doctor of Pedagogy. [LAT.]
pen., peninsula.
Penn., Pennsylvania. Also, **Pa.** (official), **Penna.**
Pent., Pentecost.
per an. (per annum), by the year. [LAT.]
per ct. (per centum), per cent. Also, **p. c.** [LAT.]
perf., perfect.
perh., perhaps.
per pro. (per procurationem), by proxy. [LAT.]
pers., person; personal.
Pers., Persia; Persian.
pert., pertaining.
Pet., Peter.
pf., preferred.
Pg., Portugal; Portuguese.
P. G. M., Past Grand Master.
Phar., pharmacy; Pharmacopœia.
Pharm., pharmaceutical; pharmacy.
Ph. B. (Philosophiæ Baccalaureus), Bachelor of Philosophy. [LAT.]
Ph. D. (Philosophiæ Doctor), Doctor of Philosophy. [LAT.]
Ph. G., Graduate in Pharmacy.
Phil., Philemon; Philip; Philippians; Philippine; Philippines.
Phila., Philadelphia.
philan., philanthropist.
Philem., Philemon.
philol., philology; philologist.
philos., philosopher; philosophical; philosophy.
Phil. Soc., Philological Society.
physiol., physiologist; physiology.
P. I., Philippine Islands.
pinx. (pinxit), he, or she, painted it. Also, **pxt.** [LAT.]
P. J., presiding judge; probate judge.
pk. (*pl.* **pks.**), peck.
pkg. (*pl.* **pkgs.**), package.
pl., place; plural. Also, **plur.**
P. L., Poet Laureate.
plup., pluperfect. Also, **plupf.**
P. M. (post meridiem), afternoon; (post mortem), after death. Also, **p.m.** [LAT.]
P. M., Past Master; Postmaster; Provost Marshal.
P. M. G., Postmaster-general.
pnxt. (pinxit), he, or she, painted it. [LAT.]
P. O., Post Office; Province of Ontario.
P. O. B., post-office box.
P. O. D., pay on delivery; Post Office Department.
Pol., Poland; Polish.
pol., political. Also, **polit.**
pol. econ., political economy.
P. O. O., post-office order.
pop., popular; population.
Port., Portugal; Portuguese.
pos., positive; possessor.
poss., possession; possessive.
pp., pages; past participle; (pianissimo), very softly [IT.].
p. p., past participle; postpaid.
P. P., parish priest.
P. P. C. (pour prendre congé), to take leave. Also, **p. p. c.** [FR.]
pph., pamphlet.
p. pr., present participle.
P. Q., previous question; Province of Quebec.
Pr, praseodymium.
pr., pair; present; price; priest; prince.
Pr., preferred (stock).
P. R., Porto Rico.
pref., preface; preferred; prefix.
prep., preparatory; preposition.
pres., president; presidency. Also, **Pres.**

Presb., Presbyterian. Also, **Presby.**
pret., preterit.
prin., principal.
P. R. N. (pro re nata), according to the occasion, as needed. [Lat.]
prob., probably; problem.
Prof., Professor.
prom., promontory.
pron., pronominal; pronoun; pronounced; pronunciation.
P. R. R., Porto Rico Regiment.
pros., prosody.
Prot., Protestant.
protec., protectorate
pro tem. (pro tempore), temporarily. [Lat.]
prov., provident; province; provisional.
Prov., Provençal; Proverbs; Provost.
prox. (proximo), next, of the next month. [Lat.]
prs., pairs.
Prus., Prussia; Prussian.
Ps., Psalms.
P. S. (post scriptum), postscript. [Lat.]
pseud., pseudonym.
P. S. R., Public Service Reserve.
psychol., psychologist; psychology.
Pt. platinum.
pt. (*pl.* **pts.**), part; payment; pint; point; port.
p. t., post town.
p. t. o., please turn over.
p. v., post village.
Pvt., Private.
pwt., pennyweight; pennyweights.
q. (quadrans), a farthing [Lat.]; quart; queen; quintal; quire.
q. d. (quasi dicat), as if he should say. [Lat.]
Q. E. D. (quod erat demonstrandum), which was to be demonstrated. [Lat.]
Q. E. F. (quod erat faciendum), which was to be done. [Lat.]
ql., quintal.
q. l. (quantum libet), as much as you please. [Lat.]
Q. M., Quartermaster.
Q. M. C., Quartermaster Corps.
Q. M. G., Quartermaster General.
q. p. (quantum placet), as much as you please. [Lat.]
qr. (*pl.* **qrs.**), quarter; quire; (quadrans), a farthing [Lat.].
q. s. (quantum sufficit), a sufficient quantity. Also, **quant. suff.** [Lat.]
qt., quantity; (*pl.* **qts.**), quart.
qu., quart; quarterly; queen; query; question.
Que., Quebec. Also, **Q.**
q. v. (quantum vis), as much as you will; (quod vide), which see. [Lat.]
qy., query.
r. (regina), queen; (rex), king [Lat.]; railroad; railway; rare; received; rector; resides; retired; right; river; rises; road; rod; royal.
R., rabbi; Radical; Réaumur; Republican; response.
R. (recipe), take. [Lat.]
R. A., Rear Admiral; Royal Academy; Rear Artillery; Regular Army, Royal Artillery.
rad., radical; radix.
ral. (rallentando), slackening. [It.]
R. A. M., Royal Academy of Music; Royal Arch Mason.
R. A. M. C., Royal Army Medical Corps.
Rb., rubidium.
R. C., Red Cross; Roman Catholic.
R. C. A., Reformed Church in America.
R. C. P., Royal College of Physicians (London).
R. C. S., Royal College of Surgeons (London).
R. D., Royal Dragoons.
rs., rupee.
R. E., Reformed Episcopal; Right Excellent; Royal Engineers.
Réaum., Réaumur.
rec., receipt; recipe; record; recorded; recorder.
recd., received.
rec. sec., recording secretary.
rect., receipt; rector; rectory.
ref., referee; reference; referred; reformation; reformed.
Ref. Ch., Reformed Church.
reg., regent; region; register; registered; registry; regular.
Reg. (Regina), queen. [Lat.]
Reg. Prof., Regius Professor.
Regt., Regiment.
rel., relating; relative; relatively; religion; religious.
rep., repeat; report; reporter; representative; republic.
Rep., Republican. Also, **Repub.**
repub., republic.
retd., returned.
rev., revenue; reverse; revolution; revolutionary; review; revise; revises; revision.
Rev., Revelation; Reverend.
Rev. Ver., Revised Version.
r. f., rapid-fire.
R. F. A., Royal Field Artillery.
R. F. C., Royal Flying Corps.
R. F. D., Rural Free Delivery.
R. G. S., Royal Geographical Society.
Rh. rhodium.
r. h., right hand.
R. H., Royal Highlanders; Royal Highness.
R. H. A., Royal Horse Artillery.
rhet., rhetoric; rhetorical.
R. H. S., Royal Historical Society.
R. I., Rhode Island (official).
R. I. P. (requiescat in pace), may he rest in peace. [Lat.]
rit. (ritardando), retarding. Also, **ritard.** [It.]
riten. (ritenuto), abruptly slackened. [It.]
riv., river.
R. M., Resident Magistrate; Royal Mail; Royal Marines.
R. M. A., Royal Military Academy; Royal Military Asylum; Royal Marine Artillery.
R. M. S., Royal Mail Steamer.
R. N., Royal Navy.
R. N. A. S., Royal Naval Air Service.
R. N. W. M. P., Royal Northwest Mounted Police.
ro., rood.
Robt., Robert.
Rom., Roman; Romance; Romans.
Rom. Cath., Roman Catholic.
R. O. T. C., Reserve Officers' Training Camp (or Corps).
R. P., Regius Professor; Reformed Presbyterian.
R. P. D. (Rerum Politicarum Doctor), Doctor of Political Science. [Lat.]
R. P. E., Reformed Protestant Episcopal.
r. p. m., revolutions per minute.
R. P. O., Railroad Post Office.
rpt., report.
R. R., railroad.
Rs., rupees.
R. S., Recruiting Service.
R. S., Recording Secretary; Revised Statutes.
R. S. M., Regimental Sergeant Major.
R. S. V. P. (répondez s'il vous plaît), reply, if you please. [Fr.]
Rt. Hon., Right Honorable.
Rt. Rev., Right Reverend.
Russ., Russia; Russian. Also, **Rus.**
R. V., Revised Version.
R. V. O., Royal Victorian Order.
R. W., Right Worshipful; Right Worthy.

Ry., railway.
S, sulphur.
S., Saint; Saturday; Saxon; school; senate; September; Socialist; Society; (Socius), Fellow [LAT.]; South; Southern; Sunday.
s., section; see; series; shilling; signed; singular; son; soprano; stem; sun; surplus. Also, **S.**
S. A., Salvation Army; South Africa; South America; South Australia.
S. A., Small-arms.
Sab., Sabbath.
S. Afr., South Africa; South African.
Salv., Salvador.
Sam., Samaritan; Samuel.
S. Amer., South America; South American. Also, **S. Am.**
San. C., Sanitary Corps.
Sans., Sanskrit. Also, **Skr.**, **Skrt.**, **Skt.**
S. A. R., Sons of the American Revolution; South African Republic.
Sar., Sardinia; Sardinian.
Sask., Saskatchewan.
Sat., Saturday.
S. A. T. C., Students' Army Training Corps.
Sax., Saxon; Saxony.
Sb (stibium), antimony. [LAT.]
S. B., Bachelor of Science.
Sc, scandium.
sc. (scilicet), namely; (sculpsit), he, or she, carved it [LAT.]; scene; science; scruple.
Sc., Scotch; Scottish.
s. c., small capitals. Also, **s. caps.**
S. C., South Carolina; Staff Corps; Supreme Court; Signal Corps.
Scand., Scandinavia; Scandinavian.
S. C. A. S., Signal Corps Aviation School.
sch., scholium; schooner.
sci., science; scientific.
scil. (scilicet), namely. Also, **sc.** [LAT.]
S. C. M., Summary Court-Martial.
Scot., Scotch; Scotland; Scottish.
scr., scruple.
Script., Scripture.
sculp. (sculpsit), he, or she, carved it [LAT.]; sculptor.
s. d. (sine die), indefinitely. [LAT.]
S. Dak., South Dakota (official). Also, **S. D.**
Se, selenium.
S. E., Southeast.
sec. (secundum), according to [LAT.]; secant; second; secretary; section.
Sec. Leg., Secretary of Legation.
sect., section.
secy., secretary.
sem., semicolon.
Sem., Seminary; Semitic.
Sen., Senate; Senator; Senior.
Sen. Doc., Senate Document.
Sep., September; Septuagint. Also, **Sept.**
ser., series; sermon.
Serg., Sergeant. Also, **Sergt.**, **Sgt.**
serv., servant.
sfz. (sforzando), forced. Also, **sf.** [IT.]
s. g., specific gravity.
S. G., Solicitor-general.
Sgt. Maj., Sergeant Major. Also, **S. M.**
Sh., share; shilling; shillings. Also, **sh.**
Si, silicon.
S. I., Sandwich Island; Staten Island.
Sib., Siberia; Siberian.
Sic., Sicilian; Sicily.
sin., sine.
sing., singular.
S. J., Society of Jesus.
S. J. C., Supreme Judicial Court.
Skrt., Sanskrit. Also, **Skt.**, **Sans.**, **Skr.**
S. Lat., South latitude.
Slav., Slavic; Slavonic.
sld., sailed.
sm. c., small capitals. Also, **sm. caps.**
Sm, samarium.
S. M., short meter.
S. M. E. (Sancta Mater Ecclesia), Holy Mother Church. [LAT.]
Sn (stannum), tin. [LAT.]
Sn. Col., Sanitary Column.
S. O., seller's option. Also, **s. o.**
S. O., Staff Officer; Signal Officer; Special Order.
S. O. C., Society of Organized Charity.
Soc. Isl., Society Islands.
S. of Sol., Song of Solomon.
sop., soprano.
S. O. S., send out succor. Also, **S O S.** Service of Supplies.
sov., sovereign.
sp., species; specimen; spelling; spirit; seaport.
Sp., Spain; Spaniard; Spanish.
s. p. (sine prole), without issue. [LAT.]
Span., Spanish.
S. P. C. A., Society for Prevention of Cruelty to Animals.
S. P. C. C., Society to Protect Children from Cruelty.
specif., specifically.
sp. gr., specific gravity.
S. P. Q. R. (Senatus Populusque Romanus), the Senate and People of Rome. [LAT.]
spt., seaport. Also, **sp.**
Sq., Squadron.
sq. (sequens), the following one [LAT.]; square.
sq. in., square inch.
sq. m., square mile.
sqq. (sequentes, sequentia), the following ones. [LAT.]
Sr, strontium.
Sr., Sir; Senior.
S. R. C., Signal Reserve Corps.
ss. (scilicet), namely; (semis), half. [LAT.]
S. S., Steamship; Sunday School.
S. S. D. (Sanctissimus Dominus), Most Holy Lord. [LAT.]
S. S. E., South-southeast.
S. S. W., South-southwest.
st. (stet), let it stand [LAT.]; stanza; stone; street.
St., Saint; Saturday; Strait; Street.
stat., statuary; statue; statutes.
S. T. D. (Sacræ Theologiæ Doctor), Doctor of Sacred Theology. [LAT.]
Ste. (Sainte), Saint. [FR.]
ster., sterling. Also, **stg.**
S. T. P. (Sacræ Theologiæ Professor), Professor of Sacred Theology. [LAT.]
str., strait; steamer.
stsm., statesman.
Sub., Subaltern.
subj., subject; subjunctive.
subst., substantive; substitute.
suff., suffix.
Sun., Sunday. Also, **Sund.**
sup. (supra), above [LAT.]; superior; superlative; supine; supplement.
Sup. C., Supreme Court.
Sup. Col., Supply Column.
Sup. O., Supply Officer.
supp., supplement.
Supt., Superintendent.
surg., surgeon; surgery.
Surg. Gen., Surgeon General. Also, **S. G.**
surv., surveying; surveyor.
s. v. (sub verbo), under the word; (sub voce), under the title. [LAT.]
S. V. (Sancta Virgo), Holy Virgin. [LAT.]
S. W., Southwest.
Sw., Sweden; Swedish. Also, **Swed.**
Switz., Switzerland.
syn., synonym; synonymous.
Syr., Syria; Syriac.
t., temperature; tenor; time; tome; ton; town; township; transitive.

T., Territory; **Testament; Tuesday; Turkish.**
Ta, **tantalum.**
tan., tangent.
Tb., terbium.
T. B., tuberculosis. [Colloq.]
T. C. N. A., Tank Corps, National **Army.**
T. E., Topographical Engineers.
tech., technology.
tel., telegram; telegraph; telephone.
Tenn., Tennessee (official).
ter., terrace; **territory.**
Test., Testament.
Tetryl, tetranitromethylaniline.
Teut., Teuton; Teutonic.
Tex., **Texas (official).**
Th, thorium.
Th., Thomas; Thursday.
theatr., **theatrical.**
Theo., Theodore; Theodosia.
theol., theological; theology.
theolog., theologian.
Theoph., Theophilus.
Thess., Thessalonians.
Tho., Thomas. Also, **Thos.**
Thurs., Thursday. Also, **Th.**
Ti, titanium.
t. i. d. (ter in die), **three times a day.** [Lat.]
Tim., Timothy.
Tit., Titus.
Tl, thallium.
T. M., **True Mean.**
T. M. U., **Trench Mortar Unit.**
T. N. T., trinitrotoluine or trinitrotoluol. Also, **TNT.**
t. o., **turn over.** Also, **T. O.**
T. O., Telegraph Office; Transport Officer.
tp., township. Also, **twp.**
tr., translated; translation; translator; transpose; treasurer; trustee.
trav., travel; traveler.
treas., treasurer; treasury.
trib., tributary.
trig., trigonometric; trigonometrical; trigonometry.
Trin., Trinity.
trop., tropic; tropical.
T. S., Transport and Supply.
T. T., telegraphic transfer.
T. U., Trade Union.
Tu, thulium.
Tues., Tuesday. Also, **Tu.**, **T.**
Turk., Turkey; Turkish.
typ., typographer; typographical; typography.
U, uranium.
U., uncle, upper.
U. K., United Kingdom.
ult. (ultimo), of the preceding month [Lat.]; ultimately.
Unit., Unitarian.
univ., universally, university.
Univ., Universalist.
U. of S. A., Union of South Africa.
U. P. C., United Presbyterian Church.
U. R., Uniform Regulations.
Uru., Uruguay.
U. S., Uncle Sam; United States.
U. S. A., United States Army; United States of America.
U. S. C., United States of Colombia.
U. S. C. G., United States Coast Guard.
U. S. M., United States Mail. United States Marine.
U. S. M. A., United States Military Academy.
U. S. N., United States Navy.
U. S. N. A., United States Naval Academy.
U. S. N. G., United States National Guard.
U. S. P., United States Pharmacopœia. Also, **U. S. Pharm.**
U. S. R., United States Reserves.
U. S. S., United States Senate. United States Ship (or Steamer).
U. S. S. B. E. F. C., United States **Shipping** Board Emergency **Fleet Corporation.**
usu., usual; usually.
U. S. V., United **States Volunteers.**
Ut., Utah.
ut dict. (ut dictum), **as said.** [Lat.]
ux. (uxor), **wife.** [Lat.]
V, vanadium.
v. (verte), turn over [Lat.]; (vide), **see** [Lat.]; (von), of [Ger.]; **valve; verb; verse; version;** versus; **very; vicar; vice-; village;** violin; **vocative; volt; volts; volume.**
V., Victoria; **Venerable; Viscount; Volunteers.**
Va., Virginia (official).
v. a., **verb active.**
V. A., **Vicar Apostolic; Vice Admiral; Royal Order of Victoria and Albert.**
var., **variant; variation; variety; various.**
var. lect. **(varia lectio), different reading.** [Lat.]
Vat., **Vatican.**
V. C., **Veterinary Corps; Victoria Cross.**
V. D. M. **(Verbi Dei Minister), Minister of the Word of God.** [Lat.]
Ven., Venerable; **Venice.**
Venez., **Venezuela.**
ver., verse; **verses.**
Vet., **Veterinary.**
V. G., **Vicar General.**
v. i., **verb intransitive.**
Vic., **Victoria.**
vid. (vide), **see.** [Lat.]
vil., **village.**
Visc., **Viscount.**
viz. (videlicet), **namely.** [Lat.]
V. M. D., **Doctor of Veterinary Medicine.**
v. n., **verb neuter.**
voc., vocative.
vocab., vocabulary.
vol. (*pl.* **vols.**), volume; volunteer.
vol., volcano; volcanic.
V. P., Vice-President.
v. r., **verb reflexive.**
V. Rev., **Very Reverend.**
vs., versus.
v. s. **(vide supra), see above.** [Lat.]
V. S., **Veterinary Surgeon.**
Vt., **Vermont (official).**
v. t., **verb transitive.**
Vul., **Vulgate.**
vv., **verses.**
V. V., **vice versa.**
w., **wanting; week; wide; wife; with.**
W., Wales; **Washington; Wednesday; Welsh;** West; **Western.**
W. A., **West Africa; Western Australia.**
W. A. A. C., **Women's Army Auxiliary Corps (British Army).**
Wash., **Washington (official).**
w. b., **warehouse book; water ballast; water board; waybill.**
w. c., **water-closet; without charge.**
W. C. T. U., **Woman's Christian Temperance** Union.
W. D., **War Department. Also, War D.**
Wed., Wednesday. **Also, We., W.**
w. f., **wrong font.**
w. g., **wire gauge.**
W. G. C., **Worthy Grand Chaplain.**
W. G. M., **Worthy Grand Master.**
W. I., West Indies; **West Indians. Also, W. Ind.**
W. I. R., **West Indian Regiment.**
Wis., Wisconsin **(official). Also, Wisc.**
wk., **week.**
W. long., **West longitude.**
Wm., **William.**
W. M., **Worshipful Master.**
W. N. W., **West-northwest.**
W. O., **Warrant Officer; War Office.**
wp., **worship.**
W. P., **Worthy Patriarch.**

W. S. W., West-southwest.
wt., weight.
W. Va., West Virginia (official).
Wyo., Wyoming (official). Also, **Wy.**
X, the first letter, in the Greek, of Christos (Christ).
X., Xavier. Christian.
Xmas., Christmas.
Xn., Christian. Also, **X.**
Xnty., Christianity. Also, **Xty.**
y., yard; year.
yd. (*pl.* **yds.**), yard.
Y. M. C. A., Young Men's Christian Association.
Y. M. Cath. A., Young Men's Catholic Association.
Y. M. C. U., Young Men's Christian Union.
Y. M. H. A., Young Men's Hebrew Association.
Y. P. S. C. E., Young People's Society of Christian Endeavor.
yr. (*pl.* **yrs.**), year; younger; your.
Y. W. C. A., Young Women's Christian Association.
Y. W. C. T. U., Young Women's Christian Temperance Union.
Zach., Zacharias; Zachary.
Zeb., Zebadiah; Zebedee.
Zech., Zechariah.
Zeph., Zephaniah.
Zoo, Zoölogical Gardens.
zoöl., zoölogical; zoölogist; zoölogy.

SYMBOLS USED IN WRITING AND PRINTING.

ASTRONOMICAL.

☉ the Sun. Also ☉.
● the Moon; Monday. Also ☾ ☽.
● New Moon.
☽ First Quarter. Also ☽.
○ Full Moon. Also ○.
☾ Last Quarter. Also ☾.
☿ Mercury; Wednesday.
♀ Venus; Friday.
⊕ the Earth. Also ⊖ ♁.
♂ Mars; Tuesday.
♃ Jupiter; Thursday.
♄ Saturn; Saturday.
♅ Uranus. Also ♅
♆ Neptune.
☄ Comet.
✱ Fixed Star. Also ✳.

FINANCIAL.

$ dollar; dollars; as $1; $5.
¢ cent; cents; as 1¢; 12¢.
/ shilling; shillings; as 1/6=1s. 6d.
£ pound, pounds (sterling); as £1; £5.
℔ pound, pounds (in weight); as 1 ℔; 2 ℔.
@ at; as gingham @ $.50 per yd.
℘ per; as horses $100 ℘ head.
% per cent; as interest 3%.
℅ account; as Wm. Jones ℅ with J. Brown.

MATHEMATICAL.

Relations of Quantities.

+ plus, and, more; as 3+2=5.
− minus, less; as 6−3=3.
± plus or minus; as the square root of 4 is±2.
× multiplied by; as 6×2=12.
÷ divided by; as 6÷2=3.
> is greater than; as 6>5.
< is less than; as 5<6.
: is to; as 6:3∷8:4.
∷ as; as 6:3∷8:4.
∠ angle; as ∠ ABC= ∠CEF.
√ the square root; as √9=3.
° degrees; as 30°.
′ minutes of arc; as 30′.
″ seconds of arc; as 30″.

MEDICAL.

℞ take.
S mark: preceding directions for taking medicine.
℔ pound.
℥ ounce.
ʒ dram.
℈ scruple.
♏ minim.

MISCELLANEOUS.

& and; as Smith & Co.
&c. and the rest; and so forth.
℟ response: used in church service books.
X cross: made in lieu of a signature by persons unable to write. Also +.
4to. quarto; four leaves to a sheet. Also 4°.
8vo. octavo; eight leaves to a sheet. Also 8°.
12mo. duodecimo; twelve leaves to sheet. Also 12°.
< derived from: in giving etymologies.
> whence is derived: in giving etymologies.
B/L bill of lading.
c/o care of.
L/c letter of credit.
′ foot; feet; as a room 12′ long.
″ inch; inches; as a 3″ pipe.
x by; as a room 12′x15′.
number; numbered; as room #5.

TYPOGRAPHICAL.

, comma.
; semicolon.
: colon.
. period.
— dash.
? interrogation.
! exclamation.
( ) parentheses.
[ ] brackets.
' apostrophe.
- hyphen; as pseudo-Kaiser.
´ acute accent; as naïveté.
` grave accent; as à la mode.
^ broad, circumflex accent; as maître.
~ circumflex, tilde. Also ⌢; as cañon.
¯ long accent; macron; as date (dāt).
˘ short; breve; as pet (pĕt).
¨ diæresis; as naïveté.
¸ cedilla; as garçon.
‸ caret; as m‸n. (a)
" " quotation marks; as "blessed."
{ } brace.
* * * ellipsis; as John * * * book.
. . . ellipsis; as John . . . book.
—— ellipsis; as John —— book.
* asterisk: a mark of reference.
† dagger, obelisk: a mark of reference.
‡ double dagger: a mark of reference.
§ section.
‖ parallel.
¶ paragraph.
☞ index.
⁂ asterism: to direct attention to a particular passage. Also ⁂.

TABLES OF WEIGHTS, MEASURES, AND MONEY.

The Meter, unit of length, is nearly the ten-millionth part of a quadrant of a meridian, or the distance between Equator and Pole. The International Standard Meter is, practically, a length defined by the distance between two lines on a platinum-iridium bar at 0° Centigrade, deposited at the International Bureau of Weights and Measures, Paris, France.

The Liter, unit of capacity, is derived from the weight of one kilogram pure water at greatest density, a cube whose edge is one-tenth of a meter and, therefore, the one-thousandth part of a metric ton.

The Gram, unit of weight, is a cube of pure water at greatest density, whose edge is one-hundredth of a meter, and, therefore, the one-thousandth part of a kilogram, and the one-millionth part of a metric ton.

The Metric System was legalized in the United States on July 28, 1866.

MEASURES OF LENGTH.

Metric Denominations and Values.			Equivalents.
1 myriameter	=	10,000 meters.....	6.2137 miles.
1 kilometer	=	1,000 meters.....	0.62137 mile, or 3,280 feet 10 inches.
1 hectometer	=	100 meters.....	328 feet 1 inch.
1 decameter	=	10 meters.....	393.7 inches.
1 meter	=	1 meter	39.37 inches.
1 decimeter	=	1-10 of a meter	3.937 inches.
1 centimeter	=	1-100 of a meter	0.3937 inch.
1 millimeter	=	1-1000 of a meter	0.0394 inch.

MEASURES OF SURFACE.

Metric Denominations and Values.			Equivalents.
1 hectare	=	10,000 square meters......	2.471 acres.
1 are	=	100 square meters......	119.6 square yards.
1 centare	=	1 square meter	1,550 square inches.

MEASURES OF CAPACITY.

Metric Denominations and Values.		Equivalents.	
Liters.	Cubic Measure.	Dry Measure.	Liquid Measure.
1 hectostere = 100,000	100 cubic meters....	130.8 cubic yards...	26417 gallons.
1 kiloliter or stere = 1,000	1 cubic meter.....	1.308 cubic yards..	264.17 gallons.
1 hectoliter = 100	1-10 of a cubic meter.	2 bushels, 3.35 pecks............	26.417 gallons.
1 dekaliter = 10	10 cubic decimeters.	9.08 quarts......	2.6417 gallons.
1 liter = 1	1 cubic decimeter..	0.908 quart.......	1.0567 quarts.
1 deciliter = 1-10 liter	1-10 cubic decimeter..	6.1022 cubic inches.	0.845 gill.
1 centiliter = 1-100 "	10 cubic centimeters	0.6102 cubic inch...	0.338 fluid ounce.
1 milliliter = 1-1000 "	1 cubic centimeter.	0.061 cubic inch....	0.27 fluid dram

WEIGHTS.

Metric Denominations and Values.			Equivalents.	
		Grams.	Quantity of Water at Maximum Density.	Avoirdupois Weight.
1 millier or tonneau	=	1,000,000	1 cubic meter	2204.6 pounds.
1 quintal	=	100,000	1 hectoliter	220.46 pounds.
1 myriagram	=	10,000	10 liters	22.046 pounds.
1 kilogram or kilo	=	1,000	1 liter	2.2046 pounds.
1 hectogram	=	100	1 deciliter	3.5274 ounces.
1 decagram	=	10	10 cubic centimeters	0.3527 ounce.
1 gram	=	1	1 cubic centimeter	15.432 grains.
1 decigram	=	1-10 gram	1-10 of a cubic centimeter	1.5432 grains.
1 centigram	=	1-100 "	10 cubic millimeters	0.1543 grain.
1 milligram	=	1-1000 "	1 cubic millimeter	0.0154 grain.

METRIC EQUIVALENTS.

Measures of Length.

1 inch =	2.54 centimeters.	1 yard =	0.9144 yard.
1 foot =	0.3048 meter.	1 mile =	1609.35 meters.

Measures of Surface.

1 square inch =	6.452 square centimeters.	1 acre =	4.047 square meters.
1 square foot =	.093 square meter.	1 acre =	40.47 ares.
1 square yard =	.836 square meter.	1 square mile =	259.004 hectares.

Measures of Volume and Capacity.

1 cubic inch =	16.39 cubic centimeters.	1 fluid dram =	3.69 cubic centimeters.
1 cubic inch =	.0164 liter.	1 fluid ounce =	29.57 cubic centimeters.
1 cubic foot =	28.339 liters.	1 fluid ounce =	.0296 liter.
1 cubic yard =	765.16 liters.	1 gill =	.1183 liter.
1 quart, dry measure =	1.1011 liters.	1 quart, liquid measure =	.9463 liter.
1 peck (U. S.) =	8.81 liters.	1 gallon (231 cubic inches) =	3.785 liters.
1 bushel (U. S.) =	35.24 liters.		

Weights.

1 grain =	6.479 centigrams.	1 pound =	.4536 kilogram.
1 ounce, avoirdupois =	28.3495 grams.	1 ton (2000 pounds) =	907.2 kilograms.
1 ounce, troy =	31.103 grams.	1 ton (2000 pounds) =	.9072 metric ton.
1 pound =	453.59 grams.	1 ton (2240 pounds) =	1.016 metric tons.

THE METRIC SYSTEM SIMPLIFIED.

The following tables of the metric system of weights and measures have been simplified as much as possible by omitting such denominations as are not in practical, everyday use in the countries where the system is used exclusively.

TABLES OF THE SYSTEM.

Length.

The denominations in practical use are millimeters (mm.), centimeters (cm.), meters (m.), and kilometers (km.).

10 millimeters = 1 centimeter. 100 centimeters = 1 meter.
10 centimeters = 1 decimeter. 1,000 meters = 1 kilometer.

Weight.

The denominations in use are gram (g.), kilogram (kg.), and ton (metric ton).

1,000 grams = 1 kilogram. 1,000 kilograms = 1 metric ton.

Capacity.

The denominations in use are cubic centimeter (c.c.) and liter (l.).

1,000 cubic centimeters = 1 liter. 100 liters = 1 hectoliter.

Relation of capacity and weight to length: a cubic decimeter is a liter, and a liter of water weighs one kilogram.

APPROXIMATE EQUIVALENTS.

A meter is about a yard.
A kilogram is about two pounds.
A liter is about a quart.
A centimeter is about one-half inch.
A metric ton is about the same as a ton.
A kilometer is about two-thirds of a mile.
A cubic centimeter is about a thimbleful.
A nickel weighs about five grams.

DOMESTIC WEIGHTS AND MEASURES.

Apothecaries' Weight.

20 grains	= 1 scruple.
3 scruples	= 1 dram.
8 drams	= 1 ounce.
12 ounces	= 1 pound.

Avoirdupois Weight.

27 11-32 grains	= 1 dram.
16 drams	= 1 ounce.
16 ounces	= 1 pound.
25 pounds	= 1 quarter.
4 quarters	= 1 hundredweight.
20 hundredweight	= 1 short ton.
2240 pounds	= 1 long ton.

Troy Weight.

24 grains	= 1 pennyweight.
20 pennyweights	= 1 ounce.
12 ounces	= 1 pound.

Circular Measure.

60 seconds	= 1 minute.
60 minutes	= 1 degree.
30 degrees	= 1 sign.
360 degrees	= 1 circle or circumference.

Cubic Measure.

1,728 cubic inches	= 1 cubic foot.
27 cubic feet	= 1 cubic yard.

Dry Measure.

2 pints	= 1 quart.
8 quarts	= 1 peck.
4 pecks	= 1 bushel.

Liquid Measure.

4 gills	= 1 pint.
2 pints	= 1 quart.
4 quarts	= 1 gallon.
31½ gallons	= 1 barrel.
2 barrels	= 1 hogshead.

Long Measure.

12 inches	= 1 foot.
3 feet	= 1 yard.
5½ yards	= 1 rod or pole.
40 rods	= 1 furlong.
8 furlongs	= 1 statute mile (1,760 yards or 5,280 feet).
3 miles	= 1 league.

Square Measure.

144 square inches	= 1 square foot.
9 square feet	= 1 square yard.
30¼ square yards	= 1 square rod or perch.
40 square rods	= 1 rood.
4 roods	= 1 acre.
640 acres	= 1 square mile.

Mariner's Measure.

6 feet	= 1 fathom.
120 fathoms	= 1 cable length.
7½ cable lengths	= 1 mile.
5,280 feet	= 1 statute mile.
6,085 feet	= 1 nautical mile.

Paper Measure.

24 sheets	= 1 quire.
20 quires	= 1 ream (480 sheets).
2 reams	= 1 bundle.
5 bundles	= 1 bale.

Time Measure.

60 seconds	= 1 minute.
60 minutes	= 1 hour.
24 hours	= 1 day.
7 days	= 1 week.
28 to 31 days	= 1 month.
365 days	= 1 year.
366 days	= 1 leap year.

FOREIGN CURRENCY.

Austria-Hungary.

100 heller	= 1 krone.
100 kreutzer	= 1 florin.
2 krone	= 1 florin.

Belgium.

100 centimes = 1 franc.

Bulgaria.

100 stotinki = 1 lev.

Canada.

100 cents = 1 dollar.

Denmark.

100 öre = 1 krone.

France.

100 centimes = 1 franc.

Germany.

100 pfennig = 1 mark.

Great Britain.

4 farthings	= 1 penny.
12 pence	= 1 shilling.
20 shillings	= 1 pound.
21 shillings	= 1 guinea.
4 shillings	= 1 crown.

Greece.

100 lepta = 1 drachma.

FOREIGN CURRENCY (Continued).

India.

3 pies = 1 pice.
4 pice = 1 anna.
16 annas = 1 rupee.
15 rupees = 1 pound sterling.
100,000 rupees = 1 lac.
10,000,000 rupees = 1 crore.

Italy.

100 centesimi = 1 lira.

Netherlands.

100 cents = 1 florin.

Norway.

100 öre = 1 krone.

Russia.

100 kopecks = 1 ruble.

Servia.

100 paras = 1 dinar.

Spain.

100 centimos = 1 peseta.

Sweden.

100 öre = 1 krona.

VALUE OF FOREIGN COINS IN UNITED STATES MONEY.

Country.	Monetary Unit.	Value in U. S. Gold Dollars.
Argentina	peso	$0.9648
Austria-Hungary	krone	.2026
Belgium	franc	.1930
Bolivia	boliviano	.3893
Brazil	milreis	.5462
Bulgaria	lev	.1930
Canada	dollar	1.0000
Chile	peso	.3650
Colombia	dollar	1.0000
Cuba	peso	1.0000
Denmark	krone	.2680
Ecuador	sucre	.4867
France	franc	.1930
Germany	mark	.2382
Great Britain	pound sterling	4.8665
Greece	drachma	.1930
India	rupee	.3244
Italy	lira	.1930
Japan	yen	$0.4985
Mexico	peso	.4985
Netherlands	florin	.4020
Newfoundland	dollar	1.0139
Norway	krone	.2680
Panama	balboa	1.0000
Paraguay	peso	[illegible]
Persia	kran	.1790
Peru	libra	4.8665
Philippine Islands	peso	.5000
Portugal	escudo	1.0805
Roumania	lei	.1930
Russia	ruble	.5146
Serbia	dinar	.1930
Spain	peseta	.1930
Sweden	krona	.2680
Switzerland	franc	.1930
Turkey	piaster	.0440
Uruguay	peso	1.0342
Venezuela	bolivar	.1930

The values given above are the equivalent gold values of the coins of the several countries named as proclaimed by the Secretary of the Treasury of the United States. The exchange value often varies widely from these figures, and is subject to constant fluctuation.